New World Translation

of the

Holy Scriptures

Rendered from the Original Languages
by the

NEW WORLD BIBLE TRANSLATION COMMITTEE

—Revised 1970 C.E.—

"THIS IS WHAT THE LORD JEHOVAH [יהוה, YHWH]
HAS SAID: '. . . HERE I AM CREATING NEW HEAVENS
AND A NEW EARTH; AND THE FORMER THINGS
WILL NOT BE CALLED TO MIND, NEITHER
WILL THEY COME UP INTO THE HEART.'"
—ISAIAH 65:13, 17; also see 2 Peter 3:13.

PUBLISHERS
WATCHTOWER BIBLE AND TRACT SOCIETY
OF NEW YORK, INC.
International Bible Students Association
Brooklyn, New York, U.S.A.

Made in the United States of America

FOREWORD

IT IS a very responsible thing to translate the Holy Scriptures from their original languages, Hebrew, Aramaic and Greek, into modern speech. Translating the Holy Scriptures means a rendering into another language the thoughts and sayings of the heavenly Author of this sacred library of sixty-six books, Jehovah God, which holy men of long ago put down in writing under inspiration for our benefit today.

That is a sobering thought. The translators who have a fear and love of the divine Author of the Holy Scriptures feel especially a responsibility toward Him to transmit his thoughts and declarations as accurately as possible. They also feel a responsibility toward the searching readers of the modern translation who depend upon the inspired Word of the Most High God for their everlasting salvation.

It was with such a sense of solemn responsibility that the committee of dedicated men have produced the New World Translation of the Holy Scriptures, over the course of many years. As soon as each part of the translation became available for publication it was turned over to the publishers for printing, all together in six volumes. The New World Translation of the Christian Greek Scriptures, containing the twenty-seven books from Matthew through The Revelation, first appeared in 1950. In due order the volumes of the New World Translation of the Hebrew-Aramaic Scriptures appeared, the first volume in 1953, the second in 1955, the third in 1957, the fourth in 1958, and the fifth in 1960.

From the start of the work it was the desire of the translators to have all these contemplated volumes brought together in the form of one book, inasmuch as the Holy Scriptures are in fact one book by the One Author. To this end, as soon as the final volume of the series had been issued in 1960, the committee set to work to prepare the entire translation for publication

5

under one cover. The committee was then able to take under survey the translation as a whole, and to discern where improvements could be made.

An effort was put forth to bring about even greater consistency in the renderings of the related parts of the Holy Scriptures, such as in harmonizing with the original Hebrew readings the reading of quotations made in the Christian Greek Scriptures. Since the one-volume edition of the Holy Scriptures was to contain no footnotes, many footnote readings that had appeared in the earlier translation in six distinct volumes were lifted and put in the main text of the one-volume edition. This does not mean that the earlier rendering that was now replaced was rejected. Rather, the purpose was to attain to closer conformity to the literal reading in the original languages. All this process has resulted in revisions in the main text of the translation.

The now completed one-volume edition may therefore be properly called a revised edition of the New World Translation of the Holy Scriptures. In releasing it for publication we do so with a deep sense of gratitude to the Divine Author of the Holy Scriptures, who has thus privileged us and in whose spirit we have trusted to co-operate with us in this worthy work. We hope for His blessing upon the published translation in behalf of all who read and use it in learning his holy will.

New World Bible Translation Committee.

January 17, 1961, New York, N.Y.
FIRST REVISION 1961; SECOND REVISION 1970

"YOU" AND VERBS IN THE PLURAL NUMBER

"You" printed in all capital letters means that the pronoun is in the plural number. Also, where the plural number of a verb is not certainly apparent to the reader, its plurality is indicated by printing it capitalized.

[ ] Brackets enclose words inserted to complete the sense in the English text; [[ ]] suggest interpolations in original text.

NAMES AND ORDER OF THE BOOKS:

of the Hebrew-Aramaic Scriptures

of the Christian Greek Scriptures

Alphabetical Order, Abbreviations and Pages
of the Books of the Holy Scriptures

GENESIS

1 In [the] beginning God created the heavens and the earth.

2 Now the earth proved to be formless and waste and there was darkness upon the surface of [the] watery deep; and God's active force was moving to and fro over the surface of the waters.

3 And God proceeded to say: "Let light come to be." Then there came to be light. 4 After that God saw that the light was good, and God brought about a division between the light and the darkness. 5 And God began calling the light Day, but the darkness he called Night. And there came to be evening and there came to be morning, a first day.

6 And God went on to say: "Let an expanse come to be in between the waters and let a dividing occur between the waters and the waters." 7 Then God proceeded to make the expanse and to make a division between the waters that should be beneath the expanse and the waters that should be above the expanse. And it came to be so. 8 And God began to call the expanse Heaven. And there came to be evening and there came to be morning, a second day.

9 And God went on to say: "Let the waters under the heavens be brought together into one place and let the dry land appear." And it came to be so. 10 And God began calling the dry land Earth, but the bringing together of the waters he called Seas. Further, God saw that [it was] good. 11 And God went on to say: "Let the earth cause grass to shoot forth, vegetation bearing seed, fruit trees yielding fruit according to their kinds, the seed of which is in it, upon the earth." And it came to be so. 12 And the earth began to put forth grass, vegetation bearing seed according to its kind and trees yielding fruit, the seed of which is in it according to its kind. Then God saw that [it was] good.

13 And there came to be evening and there came to be morning, a third day.

14 And God went on to say: "Let luminaries come to be in the expanse of the heavens to make a division between the day and the night; and they must serve as signs and for seasons and for days and years. 15 And they must serve as luminaries in the expanse of the heavens to shine upon the earth." And it came to be so. 16 And God proceeded to make the two great luminaries, the greater luminary for dominating the day and the lesser luminary for dominating the night, and also the stars. 17 Thus God put them in the expanse of the heavens to shine upon the earth, 18 and to dominate by day and by night and to make a division between the light and the darkness. Then God saw that [it was] good. 19 And there came to be evening and there came to be morning, a fourth day.

20 And God went on to say: "Let the waters swarm forth a swarm of living souls and let flying creatures fly over the earth upon the face of the expanse of the heavens." 21 And God proceeded to create the great sea monsters and every living soul that moves about, which the waters swarmed forth according to their kinds, and every winged flying creature according to its kind. And God got to see that [it was] good. 22 With that God blessed them, saying: "Be fruitful and become many and fill the waters in the sea basins, and let the flying creatures become many in the earth." 23 And there came to be evening and there came to be morning, a fifth day.

24 And God went on to say: "Let the earth put forth living souls according to their kinds, domestic animal and moving animal and wild beast of the earth according to its kind." And it came to be so.

25 And God proceeded to make the wild beast of the earth according to its kind and the domestic animal according to its kind and every moving animal of the ground according to its kind. And God got to see that [it was] good.

26 And God went on to say: "Let us make man in our image, according to our likeness, and let them have in subjection the fish of the sea and the flying creatures of the heavens and the domestic animals and all the earth and every moving animal that is moving upon the earth." 27 And God proceeded to create the man in his image, in God's image he created him; male and female he created them. 28 Further, God blessed them and God said to them: "Be fruitful and become many and fill the earth and subdue it, and have in subjection the fish of the sea and the flying creatures of the heavens and every living creature that is moving upon the earth."

29 And God went on to say: "Here I have given to you all vegetation bearing seed which is on the surface of the whole earth and every tree on which there is the fruit of a tree bearing seed. To you let it serve as food. 30 And to every wild beast of the earth and to every flying creature of the heavens and to everything moving upon the earth in which there is life as a soul I have given all green vegetation for food." And it came to be so.

31 After that God saw everything he had made and, look! [it was] very good. And there came to be evening and there came to be morning, a sixth day.

2 Thus the heavens and the earth and all their army came to their completion. 2 And by the seventh day God came to the completion of his work that he had made, and he proceeded to rest on the seventh day from all his work that he had made. 3 And God proceeded to bless the seventh day and make it sacred, because on it he has been resting from all his work that God

has created for the purpose of making.

4 This is a history of the heavens and the earth in the time of their being created, in the day that Jehovah God made earth and heaven.

5 Now there was as yet no bush of the field found in the earth and no vegetation of the field was as yet sprouting, because Jehovah God had not made it rain upon the earth and there was no man to cultivate the ground. 6 But a mist would go up from the earth and it watered the entire surface of the ground.

7 And Jehovah God proceeded to form the man out of dust from the ground and to blow into his nostrils the breath of life, and the man came to be a living soul. 8 Further, Jehovah God planted a garden in Eden, toward the east, and there he put the man whom he had formed. 9 Thus Jehovah God made to grow out of the ground every tree desirable to one's sight and good for food and also the tree of life in the middle of the garden and the tree of the knowledge of good and bad.

10 Now there was a river issuing out of Eden to water the garden, and from there it began to be parted and it became, as it were, four heads. 11 The first one's name is Pi'shon; it is the one encircling the entire land of Hav'i·lah, where there is gold. 12 And the gold of that land is good. There also are the bdellium gum and the onyx stone. 13 And the name of the second river is Gi'hon; it is the one encircling the entire land of Cush. 14 And the name of the third river is Hid'de·kel; it is the one going to the east of As·syr'i·a. And the fourth river is the Eu·phra'tes.

15 And Jehovah God proceeded to take the man and settle him in the garden of Eden to cultivate it and to take care of it. 16 And Jehovah God also laid this command upon the man: "From every tree of the garden you may eat to satisfaction. 17 But as for the tree

of the knowledge of good and bad you must not eat from it, for in the day you eat from it you will positively die."

18 And Jehovah God went on to say: "It is not good for the man to continue by himself. I am going to make a helper for him, as a complement of him." 19 Now Jehovah God was forming from the ground every wild beast of the field and every flying creature of the heavens, and he began bringing them to the man to see what he would call each one; and whatever the man would call it, each living soul, that was its name. 20 So the man was calling the names of all the domestic animals and of the flying creatures of the heavens and of every wild beast of the field, but for man there was found no helper as a complement of him. 21 Hence Jehovah God had a deep sleep fall upon the man and, while he was sleeping, he took one of his ribs and then closed up the flesh over its place. 22 And Jehovah God proceeded to build the rib that he had taken from the man into a woman and to bring her to the man.

23 Then the man said:

"This is at last bone of my bones
    And flesh of my flesh.
This one will be called Woman,
    Because from man this one
        was taken."

24 That is why a man will leave his father and his mother and he must stick to his wife and they must become one flesh. 25 And both of them continued to be naked, the man and his wife, and yet they did not become ashamed.

3 Now the serpent proved to be the most cautious of all the wild beasts of the field that Jehovah God had made. So it began to say to the woman: "Is it really so that God said you must not eat from every tree of the garden?" 2 At this the woman said to the serpent: "Of the fruit of the trees of the garden we may eat. 3 But as for [eating] of the fruit of the tree that is in the middle of the garden, God

has said, 'You must not eat from it, no, you must not touch it that you do not die.'" 4 At this the serpent said to the woman: "You positively will not die. 5 For God knows that in the very day of your eating from it your eyes are bound to be opened and you are bound to be like God, KNOWING good and bad."

6 Consequently the woman saw that the tree was good for food and that it was something to be longed for to the eyes, yes, the tree was desirable to look upon. So she began taking of its fruit and eating it. Afterward she gave some also to her husband when with her and he began eating it. 7 Then the eyes of both of them became opened and they began to realize that they were naked. Hence they sewed fig leaves together and made loin coverings for themselves.

8 Later they heard the voice of Jehovah God walking in the garden about the breezy part of the day, and the man and his wife went into hiding from the face of Jehovah God in between the trees of the garden. 9 And Jehovah God kept calling to the man and saying to him: "Where are you?" 10 Finally he said: "Your voice I heard in the garden, but I was afraid because I was naked and so I hid myself." 11 At that he said: "Who told you that you were naked? From the tree from which I commanded you not to eat have you eaten?" 12 And the man went on to say: "The woman whom you gave to be with me, she gave me [fruit] from the tree and so I ate." 13 With that Jehovah God said to the woman: "What is this you have done?" To this the woman replied: "The serpent—it deceived me and so I ate."

14 And Jehovah God proceeded to say to the serpent: "Because you have done this thing, you are the cursed one out of all the domestic animals and out of all the wild beasts of the field. Upon your belly you will go and dust is what you will eat all the days of your life. 15 And I shall put enmity between

you and the woman and between your seed and her seed. He will bruise you in the head and you will bruise him in the heel."

16 To the woman he said: "I shall greatly increase the pain of your pregnancy; in birth pangs you will bring forth children, and your craving will be for your husband, and he will dominate you."

17 And to Adam he said: "Because you listened to your wife's voice and took to eating from the tree concerning which I gave you this command, 'You must not eat from it,' cursed is the ground on your account. In pain you will eat its produce all the days of your life. 18 And thorns and thistles it will grow for you, and you must eat the vegetation of the field. 19 In the sweat of your face you will eat bread until you return to the ground, for out of it you were taken. For dust you are and to dust you will return."

20 After this Adam called his wife's name Eve, because she had to become the mother of everyone living. 21 And Jehovah God proceeded to make long garments of skin for Adam and for his wife and to clothe them. 22 And Jehovah God went on to say: "Here the man has become like one of us in knowing good and bad, and now in order that he may not put his hand out and actually take [fruit] also from the tree of life and eat and live to time indefinite,—" 23 With that Jehovah God put him out of the garden of Eden to cultivate the ground from which he had been taken. 24 And so he drove the man out and posted at the east of the garden of Eden the cherubs and the flaming blade of a sword that was turning itself continually to guard the way to the tree of life.

4 Now Adam had intercourse with Eve his wife and she became pregnant. In time she gave birth to Cain and said: "I have produced a man with the aid of Jehovah." 2 Later she again gave birth, to his brother Abel.

And Abel came to be a herder of sheep, but Cain became a cultivator of the ground. 3 And it came about at the expiration of some time that Cain proceeded to bring some fruits of the ground as an offering to Jehovah. 4 But as for Abel, he too brought some firstlings of his flock, even their fatty pieces. Now while Jehovah was looking with favor upon Abel and his offering, 5 he did not look with any favor upon Cain and upon his offering. And Cain grew hot with great anger, and his countenance began to fall. 6 At this Jehovah said to Cain: "Why are you hot with anger and why has your countenance fallen? 7 If you turn to doing good, will there not be an exaltation? But if you do not turn to doing good, there is sin crouching at the entrance, and for you is its craving; and will you, for your part, get the mastery over it?"

8 After that Cain said to Abel his brother: ["Let us go over into the field."] So it came about that while they were in the field Cain proceeded to assault Abel his brother and kill him. 9 Later on Jehovah said to Cain: "Where is Abel your brother?" and he said: "I do not know. Am I my brother's guardian?" 10 At this he said: "What have you done? Listen! Your brother's blood is crying out to me from the ground. 11 And now you are cursed in banishment from the ground, which has opened its mouth to receive your brother's blood at your hand. 12 When you cultivate the ground, it will not give you back its power. A wanderer and a fugitive you will become in the earth." 13 At this Cain said to Jehovah: "My punishment for error is too great to carry. 14 Here you are actually driving me this day from off the surface of the ground, and from your face I shall be concealed; and I must become a wanderer and fugitive on the earth, and it is certain that anyone finding me will kill me." 15 At this Jehovah said to him: "For that reason anyone killing Cain must suffer vengeance seven times."

And so Jehovah set up a sign for Cain in order that no one finding him should strike him. 16 With that Cain went away from the face of Jehovah and took up residence in the land of Fugitiveness to the east of Eden.

17 Afterward Cain had intercourse with his wife and she became pregnant and gave birth to E'noch. Then he engaged in building a city and called the city's name by the name of his son E'noch. 18 Later there was born to E'noch I'rad. And I'rad became father to Me·hu'ja·el, and Me·hu'ja·el became father to Me·thu'sha·el, and Me·thu'sha·el became father to La'mech.

19 And La'mech proceeded to take two wives for himself. The name of the first was A'dah and the name of the second was Zil'lah. 20 In time A'dah gave birth to Ja'bal. He proved to be the founder of those who dwell in tents and have livestock. 21 And the name of his brother was Ju'bal. He proved to be the founder of all those who handle the harp and the pipe. 22 As for Zil'lah, she too gave birth to Tu'bal-cain, the forger of every sort of tool of copper and iron. And the sister of Tu'bal-cain was Na'a·mah. 23 Consequently La'mech composed these words for his wives A'dah and Zil'lah:

"Hear my voice, you wives of La'mech;
Give ear to my saying:
A man I have killed for wounding me,
Yes, a young man for giving me a blow.
24 If seven times Cain is to be avenged,
Then La'mech seventy times and seven."

25 And Adam proceeded to have intercourse again with his wife and so she gave birth to a son and called his name Seth, because, as she said: "God has appointed another seed in place of Abel, because Cain killed him." 26 And to Seth also there was born a son and he proceeded to call his name E'nosh. At that time a start was made of calling on the name of Jehovah.

5 This is the book of Adam's history. In the day of God's creating Adam he made him in the likeness of God. 2 Male and female he created them. After that he blessed them and called their name Man in the day of their being created.

3 And Adam lived on for a hundred and thirty years. Then he became father to a son in his likeness, in his image, and called his name Seth. 4 And the days of Adam after his fathering Seth came to be eight hundred years. Meanwhile he became father to sons and daughters. 5 So all the days of Adam that he lived amounted to nine hundred and thirty years and he died.

6 And Seth lived on for a hundred and five years. Then he became father to E'nosh. 7 And after his fathering E'nosh Seth continued to live eight hundred and seven years. Meanwhile he became father to sons and daughters. 8 So all the days of Seth amounted to nine hundred and twelve years and he died.

9 And E'nosh lived on for ninety years. Then he became father to Ke'nan. 10 And after his fathering Ke'nan E'nosh continued to live eight hundred and fifteen years. Meanwhile he became father to sons and daughters. 11 So all the days of E'nosh amounted to nine hundred and five years and he died.

12 And Ke'nan lived on for seventy years. Then he became father to Ma·hal'a·lel. 13 And after his fathering Ma·hal'a·lel Ke'nan continued to live eight hundred and forty years. Meanwhile he became father to sons and daughters. 14 So all the days of Ke'nan amounted to nine hundred and ten years and he died.

15 And Ma·hal'a·lel lived on for sixty-five years. Then he became father to Ja'red. 16 And after his fathering Ja'red Ma·hal'a·lel continued to live eight hundred and thirty years. Meanwhile he became father to sons and daughters. 17 So all the days of Ma·hal'a·lel

amounted to eight hundred and ninety-five years and he died.

18 And Ja′red lived on for a hundred and sixty-two years. Then he became father to E′noch. 19 And after his fathering Ja′red continued to live eight hundred years. Meanwhile he became father to sons and daughters. 20 So all the days of Ja′red amounted to nine hundred and sixty-two years and he died.

21 And E′noch lived on for sixty-five years. Then he became father to Me·thu′se·lah. 22 And after his fathering Me·thu′se·lah E′noch went on walking with the [true] God three hundred years. Meanwhile he became father to sons and daughters. 23 So all the days of E′noch amounted to three hundred and sixty-five years. 24 And E′noch kept walking with the [true] God. Then he was no more, for God took him.

25 And Me·thu′se·lah lived on for a hundred and eighty-seven years. Then he became father to La′mech. 26 And after his fathering La′mech Me·thu′se·lah continued to live seven hundred and eighty-two years. Meanwhile he became father to sons and daughters. 27 So all the days of Me·thu′se·lah amounted to nine hundred and sixty-nine years and he died.

28 And La′mech lived on for a hundred and eighty-two years. Then he became father to a son. 29 And he proceeded to call his name Noah, saying: "This one will bring us comfort from our work and from the pain of our hands resulting from the ground which Jehovah has cursed." 30 And after his fathering Noah La′mech continued to live five hundred and ninety-five years. Meanwhile he became father to sons and daughters. 31 So all the days of La′mech amounted to seven hundred and seventy-seven years and he died.

32 And Noah got to be five hundred years old. After that Noah became father to Shem, Ham and Ja′pheth.

6 Now it came about that when men started to grow in numbers on the surface of the ground and daughters were born to them, 2 then the sons of the [true] God began to notice the daughters of men, that they were good-looking; and they went taking wives for themselves, namely, all whom they chose. 3 After that Jehovah said: "My spirit shall not act toward man indefinitely in that he is also flesh. Accordingly his days shall amount to a hundred and twenty years."

4 The Neph′i·lim proved to be in the earth in those days, and also after that, when the sons of the [true] God continued to have relations with the daughters of men and they bore sons to them, they were the mighty ones who were of old, the men of fame.

5 Consequently Jehovah saw that the badness of man was abundant in the earth and every inclination of the thoughts of his heart was only bad all the time. 6 And Jehovah felt regrets that he had made men in the earth, and he felt hurt at his heart. 7 So Jehovah said: "I am going to wipe men whom I have created off the surface of the ground, from man to domestic animal, to moving animal and to flying creature of the heavens, because I do regret that I have made them." 8 But Noah found favor in the eyes of Jehovah.

9 This is the history of Noah.

Noah was a righteous man. He proved himself faultless among his contemporaries. Noah walked with the [true] God. 10 In time Noah became father to three sons, Shem, Ham and Ja′pheth. 11 And the earth came to be ruined in the sight of the [true] God and the earth became filled with violence. 12 So God saw the earth and, look! it was ruined, because all flesh had ruined its way on the earth.

13 After that God said to Noah: "The end of all flesh has come before me, because the earth is full of violence as a result of them; and here I am bringing them to ruin

together with the earth. **14** Make for yourself an ark out of wood of a resinous tree. You will make compartments in the ark, and you must cover it inside and outside with tar. **15** And this is how you will make it: three hundred cubits the length of the ark, fifty cubits its width, and thirty cubits its height. **16** You will make a *tso'har* [roof; or, window] for the ark, and you will complete it to the extent of a cubit upward, and the entrance of the ark you will put in its side; you will make it with a lower story, a second story and a third story.

17 "And as for me, here I am bringing the deluge of waters upon the earth to bring to ruin all flesh in which the force of life is active from under the heavens. Everything that is in the earth will expire. **18** And I do establish my covenant with you; and you must go into the ark, you and your sons and your wife and your sons' wives with you. **19** And of every living creature of every sort of flesh, two of each, you will bring into the ark to preserve them alive with you. Male and female they will be. **20** Of the flying creatures according to their kinds and of the domestic animals according to their kinds, of all moving animals of the ground according to their kinds, two of each will go in there to you to preserve them alive. **21** And as for you, take for yourself every sort of food that is eaten; and you must gather it to yourself, and it must serve as food for you and for them."

22 And Noah proceeded to do according to all that God had commanded him. He did just so.

7 After that Jehovah said to Noah: "Go, you and all your household, into the ark, because you are the one I have seen to be righteous before me among this generation. **2** Of every clean beast you must take to yourself by sevens, the sire and its mate; and of every beast that is not clean just two, the sire and its mate; **3** also of the flying creatures of the heavens by sevens, male and female, to preserve offspring alive on the surface of the

entire earth. **4** For in just seven days more I am making it rain upon the earth forty days and forty nights; and I will wipe every existing thing that I have made off the surface of the ground." **5** And Noah proceeded to do according to all that Jehovah had commanded him.

6 And Noah was six hundred years old when the deluge of waters occurred on the earth. **7** So Noah went in, and his sons and his wife and his sons' wives with him, into the ark ahead of the waters of the deluge. **8** Of every clean beast and of every beast that is not clean and of the flying creatures and everything that moves on the ground, **9** they went in by twos to Noah inside the ark, male and female, just as God had commanded Noah. **10** And seven days later it turned out that the waters of the deluge came upon the earth.

11 In the six hundredth year of Noah's life, in the second month, on the seventeenth day of the month, on this day all the springs of the vast watery deep were broken open and the floodgates of the heavens were opened. **12** And the downpour upon the earth went on for forty days and forty nights. **13** On this very day Noah went in, and Shem and Ham and Ja'pheth, Noah's sons, and the wife of Noah and the three wives of his sons with him, into the ark; **14** they and every wild beast according to its kind, and every domestic animal according to its kind, and every moving animal that moves on the earth according to its kind, and every flying creature of the heavens according to its kind, every bird, every winged creature. **15** And they kept going to Noah inside the ark, two by two, of every sort of flesh in which the force of life was active. **16** And those going in, male and female of every sort of flesh, went in, just as God had commanded him. After that Jehovah shut the door behind him.

17 And the deluge went on for forty days upon the earth, and the waters kept increasing and began carrying the ark and it was floating high above the earth. **18** And the waters became overwhelming and kept increasing greatly upon the earth, but the ark kept going on the surface of the waters. **19** And the waters overwhelmed the earth so greatly that all the tall mountains that were under the whole heavens came to be covered. **20** Up to fifteen cubits the waters overwhelmed them and the mountains became covered.

21 So all flesh that was moving upon the earth expired, among the flying creatures and among the domestic animals and among the wild beasts and among all the swarms that were swarming upon the earth, and all mankind. **22** Everything in which the breath of the force of life was active in its nostrils, namely, all that were on the dry ground, died. **23** Thus he wiped out every existing thing that was on the surface of the ground, from man to beast, to moving animal and to flying creature of the heavens, and they were wiped off the earth; and only Noah and those who were with him in the ark kept on surviving. **24** And the waters continued overwhelming the earth a hundred and fifty days.

8 After that God remembered Noah and every wild beast and every domestic animal that was with him in the ark, and God caused a wind to pass over the earth, and the waters began to subside. **2** And the springs of the watery deep and the floodgates of the heavens became stopped up, and so the downpour from the heavens was restrained. **3** And the waters began receding from off the earth, progressively receding; and at the end of a hundred and fifty days the waters were lacking. **4** And in the seventh month, on the seventeenth day of the month, the ark came to rest on the mountains of Ar'a·rat. **5** And the waters kept on progressively lessening until the tenth month. In the tenth month, on the first of the month, the tops of the mountains appeared.

6 So it occurred that at the end of forty days Noah proceeded to open the window of the ark that he had made. **7** After that he sent out a raven, and it continued flying outdoors, going and returning, until the waters dried off the earth.

8 Later he sent out from him a dove to see whether the waters had abated from the surface of the ground. **9** And the dove did not find any resting place for the sole of its foot, and so it returned to him into the ark because the waters were yet upon the surface of the whole earth. At that he put his hand out and took it and brought it to himself inside the ark. **10** And he went on waiting still another seven days, and once again he sent out the dove from the ark. **11** Later on the dove came to him about the time of evening and, look! there was an olive leaf freshly plucked in its bill, and so Noah got to know that the waters had abated from the earth. **12** And he went on waiting still another seven days. Then he sent out the dove, but it did not come back again to him any more.

13 Now in the six hundred and first year, in the first month, on the first day of the month, it came about that the waters had drained from off the earth; and Noah proceeded to remove the covering of the ark and to look, and here the surface of the ground had drained dry. **14** And in the second month, on the twenty-seventh day of the month, the earth had dried off.

15 God now spoke to Noah, saying: **16** "Go out of the ark, you and your wife and your sons and your sons' wives with you. **17** Every living creature that is with you of every sort of flesh, among the flying creatures and among the beasts and among all the moving animals that move upon the earth, bring out with you, as they must swarm in the earth and be fruitful and become many upon the earth."

18 At that Noah went out, and also his sons and his wife and his sons' wives with him. **19** Every living creature, every moving animal and every flying creature, everything that moves on the earth, according to their families they went out of the ark. 20 And Noah began to build an altar to Jehovah and to take some of all the clean beasts and of all the clean flying creatures and to offer burnt offerings upon the altar. 21 And Jehovah began to smell a restful odor, and so Jehovah said in his heart: "Never again shall I call down evil upon the ground on man's account, because the inclination of the heart of man is bad from its youth up; and never again shall I deal every living thing a blow just as I have done. 22 For all the days the earth continues, seed sowing and harvest, and cold and heat, and summer and winter, and day and night, will never cease."

9 And God went on to bless Noah and his sons and to say to them: "Be fruitful and become many and fill the earth. 2 And a fear of you and a terror of you will continue upon every living creature of the earth and upon every flying creature of the heavens, upon everything that goes moving on the ground, and upon all the fishes of the sea. Into your hand they are now given. 3 Every moving animal that is alive may serve as food for you. As in the case of green vegetation, I do give it all to you. 4 Only flesh with its soul—its blood —you must not eat. 5 And, besides that, your blood of your souls shall I ask back. From the hand of every living creature shall I ask it back; and from the hand of man, from the hand of each one who is his brother, shall I ask back the soul of man. 6 Anyone shedding man's blood, by man will his own blood be shed, for in God's image he made man. 7 And as for you men, be fruitful and become many, make the earth swarm with you and become many in it."

8 And God went on to say to Noah and to his sons with him: 9 "And as for me, here I am establishing my covenant with you men and with your offspring after you, 10 and with every living soul that is with you, among fowls, among beasts and among all living creatures of the earth with you, from all those going out of the ark to every living creature of the earth. 11 Yes, I do establish my covenant with you: No more will all flesh be cut off by waters of a deluge, and no more will there occur a deluge to bring the earth to ruin."

12 And God added: "This is the sign of the covenant that I am giving between me and you and every living soul that is with you, for the generations to time indefinite. 13 My rainbow I do give in the cloud, and it must serve as a sign of the covenant between me and the earth. 14 And it shall occur that when I bring a cloud over the earth, then the rainbow will certainly appear in the cloud. 15 And I shall certainly remember my covenant which is between me and you and every living soul among all flesh; and no more will the waters become a deluge to bring all flesh to ruin. 16 And the rainbow must occur in the cloud, and I shall certainly see it to remember the covenant to time indefinite between God and every living soul among all flesh that is upon the earth."

17 And God repeated to Noah: "This is the sign of the covenant that I do establish between me and all flesh that is upon the earth."

18 And Noah's sons who came out of the ark were Shem and Ham and Ja'pheth. Later Ham was the father of Ca'naan. 19 These three were Noah's sons, and from these was all the earth's population spread abroad.

20 Now Noah started off as a farmer and proceeded to plant a vineyard. 21 And he began drinking of the wine and became intoxicated, and so he uncovered himself in the midst of his tent. 22 Later Ham the father of Ca'naan saw his father's nakedness and went telling it to his two brothers outside. 23 At that Shem and Ja'pheth took a mantle and put it upon both their shoulders and walked in back-

wards. Thus they covered their father's nakedness, while their faces were turned away, and they did not see their father's nakedness.

24 Finally Noah awoke from his wine and got to know what his youngest son had done to him. 25 At this he said:

"Cursed be Ca'naan.
Let him become the lowest slave to his brothers."

26 And he added:

"Blessed be Jehovah, Shem's God,
And let Ca'naan become a slave to him.

27 Let God grant ample space to Ja'pheth,
And let him reside in the tents of Shem.
Let Ca'naan become a slave to him also."

28 And Noah continued to live three hundred and fifty years after the deluge. 29 So all the days of Noah amounted to nine hundred and fifty years and he died.

10 And this is the history of Noah's sons, Shem, Ham and Ja'pheth.

Now sons began to be born to them after the deluge. 2 The sons of Ja'pheth were Go'mer and Ma'gog and Ma'da·i and Ja'van and Tu'bal and Me'shech and Ti'ras.

3 And the sons of Go'mer were Ash'ke·naz and Ri'phath and To'gar'mah.

4 And the sons of Ja'van were E·li'shah and Tar'shish, Kit'tim and Do'da·nim.

5 From these the population of the isles of the nations was spread about in their lands, each according to its tongue, according to their families, by their nations.

6 And the sons of Ham were Cush and Miz'ra·im and Put and Ca'naan.

7 And the sons of Cush were Se'ba and Hav'i·lah and Sab'tah and Ra'a·mah and Sab'te·ca.

And the sons of Ra'a·mah were She'ba and De'dan.

8 And Cush became father to Nim'rod. He made the start in becoming a mighty one in the earth. 9 He displayed himself a mighty hunter in opposition to Jehovah.

That is why there is a saying: "Just like Nim'rod a mighty hunter in opposition to Jehovah." 10 And the beginning of his kingdom came to be Ba'bel and E'rech and Ac'cad and Cal'neh, in the land of Shi'nar. 11 Out of that land he went forth into As·syr'i·a and set himself to building Nin'e·veh and Re·ho'both-Ir and Ca'lah 12 and Re'sen between Nin'e·veh and Ca'lah: this is the great city.

13 And Miz'ra·im became father to Lu'dim and An'a·mim and Le·ha'bim and Naph·tu'him 14 and Path·ru'sim and Cas·lu'him (from among whom the Phi·lis'tines went forth) and Caph'to·rim.

15 And Ca'naan became father to Si'don his first-born and Heth 16 and the Jeb'u·site and the Am'or·ite and the Gir'ga·shite 17 and the Hi'vite and the Ark'ite and the Si'nite 18 and the Ar'vad·ite and the Zem'a·rite and the Ha'math·ite; and afterward the families of the Ca'naan·ite were scattered. 19 So the boundary of the Ca'naan·ite came to be from Si'don as far as Ge'rar, near Ga'za, as far as Sod'om and Go·mor'rah and Ad'mah and Ze·boi'im, near La'sha. 20 These were the sons of Ham according to their families, according to their tongues, in their lands, by their nations.

21 And to Shem, the forefather of all the sons of E'ber, the brother of Ja'pheth the oldest, there was also progeny born. 22 The sons of Shem were E'lam and As'shur and Ar·pach'shad and Lud and A'ram.

23 And the sons of A'ram were Uz and Hul and Ge'ther and Mash.

24 And Ar·pach'shad became father to She'lah, and She'lah became father to E'ber.

25 And to E'ber there were two sons born. The name of the one was Pe'leg, because in his days the earth was divided; and the name of his brother was Jok'tan.

26 And Jok'tan became father to Al·mo'dad and She'leph and Ha·zar·ma'veth and Je'rah 27 and Ha·do'ram and U'zal

and Dik'lah 28 and O'bal and A·bim'a·el and She'ba 29 and O'phir and Hav'i·lah and Jo'-bab; all these were the sons of Jok'tan.

30 And their place of dwelling came to extend from Me'sha as far as Se'phar, the mountainous region of the East.

31 These were the sons of Shem according to their families, according to their tongues, in their lands, according to their nations.

32 These were the families of the sons of Noah according to their family descents, by their nations, and from these the nations were spread about in the earth after the deluge.

11 Now all the earth continued to be of one language and of one set of words. 2 And it came about that in their journeying eastward they eventually discovered a valley plain in the land of Shi'nar, and they took up dwelling there. 3 And they began to say, each one to the other: "Come on! Let us make bricks and bake them with a burning process." So brick served as stone for them, but bitumen served as mortar for them. 4 They now said: "Come on! Let us build ourselves a city and also a tower with its top in the heavens, and let us make a celebrated name for ourselves, for fear we may be scattered over all the surface of the earth."

5 And Jehovah proceeded to go down to see the city and the tower that the sons of men had built. 6 After that Jehovah said: "Look! They are one people and there is one language for them all, and this is what they start to do. Why, now there is nothing that they may have in mind to do that will be unattainable for them. 7 Come now! Let us go down and there confuse their language that they may not listen to one another's language." 8 Accordingly Jehovah scattered them from there over all the surface of the earth, and they gradually left off building the city. 9 That is why its name was called Ba'bel, because there Jehovah had confused the language of all the earth, and Jehovah had scattered them from there over all the surface of the earth.

10 This is the history of Shem.

Shem was a hundred years old when he became father to Ar·pach'-shad two years after the deluge. 11 And after his fathering Ar-pach'shad Shem continued to live five hundred years. Meanwhile he became father to sons and daughters.

12 And Ar·pach'shad lived thirty-five years. Then he became father to She'lah. 13 And after his fathering She'lah Ar·pach'shad continued to live four hundred and three years. Meanwhile he became father to sons and daughters.

14 And She'lah lived thirty years. Then he became father to E'ber. 15 And after his fathering E'ber She'lah continued to live four hundred and three years. Meanwhile he became father to sons and daughters.

16 And E'ber lived on for thirty-four years. Then he became father to Pe'leg. 17 And after his fathering Pe'leg E'ber continued to live four hundred and thirty years. Meanwhile he became father to sons and daughters.

18 And Pe'leg lived on for thirty years Then he became father to Re'u. 19 And after his fathering Re'u Pe'leg continued to live two hundred and nine years. Meanwhile he became father to sons and daughters.

20 And Re'u lived on for thirty-two years. Then he became father to Se'rug. 21 And after his fathering Se'rug Re'u continued to live two hundred and seven years. Meanwhile he became father to sons and daughters.

22 And Se'rug lived on for thirty years. Then he became father to Na'hor. 23 And after his fathering Na'hor Se'rug continued to live two hundred years. Meanwhile he became father to sons and daughters.

24 And Na'hor lived on for twenty-nine years. Then he became father to Te'rah. 25 And after his fathering Te'rah Na'hor continued

to live a hundred and nineteen years. Meanwhile he became father to sons and daughters.

26 And Te'rah lived on for seventy years, after which he became father to A'bram, Na'hor and Ha'ran.

27 And this is the history of Te'rah.

Te'rah became father to A'bram, Na'hor and Ha'ran; and Ha'ran became father to Lot. 28 Later Ha'ran died while in company with Te'rah his father in the land of his birth, in Ur of the Chal·de'ans. 29 And A'bram and Na'hor proceeded to take wives for themselves. The name of A'bram's wife was Sar'ai, while the name of Na'hor's wife was Mil'cah, the daughter of Ha'ran, the father of Mil'cah and father of Is'cah. 30 But Sar'ai continued to be barren; she had no child.

31 After that Te'rah took A'bram his son and Lot, the son of Ha'ran, his grandson, and Sar'ai his daughter-in-law, the wife of A'bram his son, and they went with him out of Ur of the Chal·de'ans to go to the land of Ca'naan. In time they came to Ha'ran and took up dwelling there. 32 And the days of Te'rah came to be two hundred and five years. Then Te'rah died in Ha'ran.

12 And Jehovah proceeded to say to A'bram: "Go your way out of your country and from your relatives and from the house of your father to the country that I shall show you; 2 and I shall make a great nation out of you and I shall bless you and I will make your name great; and prove yourself a blessing. 3 And I will bless those who bless you, and him that calls down evil upon you I shall curse, and all the families of the ground will certainly bless themselves by means of you."

4 At that A'bram went just as Jehovah had spoken to him, and Lot went with him. And A'bram was seventy-five years old when he went out from Ha'ran. 5 So A'bram took Sar'ai his wife and Lot the son of his brother and all the goods that they had accumulated and the souls whom they had acquired in Ha'ran, and they got on their way out to go to the land of Ca'naan. Finally they came to the land of Ca'naan. 6 And A'bram went on through the land as far as the site of She'chem, near the big trees of Mo'reh; and at that time the Ca'naan·ite was in the land. 7 Jehovah now appeared to A'bram and said: "To your seed I am going to give this land." After that he built an altar there to Jehovah, who had appeared to him. 8 Later he moved from there to the mountainous region to the east of Beth'el and pitched his tent with Beth'el on the west and A'i on the east. Then he built an altar there to Jehovah and began to call on the name of Jehovah. 9 Afterward A'bram broke camp, going then from encampment to encampment toward the Neg'eb.

10 Now a famine arose in the land and A'bram made his way down toward Egypt to reside there as an alien, because the famine was severe in the land. 11 And it came about that as soon as he got near to entering Egypt, then he said to Sar'ai his wife: "Please, now! I well know you are a woman beautiful in appearance. 12 So it is bound to happen that the Egyptians will see you and will say, 'This is his wife.' And they will certainly kill me, but you they will preserve alive. 13 Please say you are my sister, in order that it may go well with me on your account, and my soul will be certain to live due to you."

14 So it happened that, as soon as A'bram entered Egypt, the Egyptians got to see the woman, that she was very beautiful. 15 And the princes of Phar'aoh also got to see her and they began praising her to Phar'aoh, so that the woman was taken to the house of Phar'aoh. 16 And he treated A'bram well on her account, and he came to have sheep and cattle and asses and menservants and maidservants and she-asses and camels. 17 Then Jehovah touched Phar'aoh and his

household with great plagues because of Sar′ai, A′bram's wife. 18 With that Phar′aoh called A′bram and said: "What is this you have done to me? Why did you not tell me that she was your wife? 19 Why did you say, 'She is my sister,' so that I was about to take her as my wife? And now here is your wife. Take her and go!" 20 And Phar′aoh issued commands to men concerning him, and they went escorting him and his wife and all that he had.

13 Following that A′bram went up out of Egypt, he and his wife and all that he had, and Lot with him, to the Neg′eb. 2 And A′bram was heavily stocked with herds and silver and gold. 3 And he made his way from encampment to encampment out of the Neg′eb and to Beth′el, to the place where his tent had been at first between Beth′el and A′i, 4 to the place of the altar that he had made there originally; and A′bram proceeded to call there on the name of Jehovah. 5 Now Lot, who was going along with A′bram, also owned sheep and cattle and tents. 6 So the land did not allow for them to dwell all together, because their goods had become many and they were not able to dwell all together. 7 And a quarrel arose between the herders of A′bram's livestock and the herders of Lot's livestock; and at that time the Ca′naan·ite and the Per′iz·zite were dwelling in the land. 8 Hence A′bram said to Lot: "Please, do not let any quarreling continue between me and you and between my herdsmen and your herdsmen, for we men are brothers. 9 Is not the whole land available to you? Please, separate from me. If you go to the left, then I will go to the right; but if you go to the right, then I will go to the left." 10 So Lot raised his eyes and saw the whole District of the Jordan, that all of it was a well-watered region before Jehovah brought Sod′om and Go·mor′rah to ruin, like the garden of Jehovah, like the land of Egypt as far as Zo′ar. 11 Then Lot chose for him-

self the whole District of the Jordan, and Lot moved his camp to the east. So they separated the one from the other. 12 A′bram dwelt in the land of Ca′naan, but Lot dwelt among the cities of the District. Finally he pitched tent near Sod′om. 13 And the men of Sod′om were bad and were gross sinners against Jehovah.

14 And Jehovah said to A′bram after Lot had separated from him: "Raise your eyes, please, and look from the place where you are, northward and southward and eastward and westward, 15 because all the land at which you are looking, to you and to your seed I am going to give it until time indefinite. 16 And I will constitute your seed like the dust particles of the earth, so that, if a man could be able to count the dust particles of the earth, then your seed could be numbered. 17 Get up, go about in the land through its length and through its breadth, because to you I am going to give it." 18 So A′bram continued to live in tents. Later on he came and dwelt among the big trees of Mam′re, which are in He′bron; and there he proceeded to build an altar to Jehovah.

14 Now it came about in the days of Am′ra·phel king of Shi′nar, Ar′i·och king of El·la′sar, Ched·or·la·o′mer king of E′lam, and Ti′dal king of Goi′im, 2 that these made war with Be′ra king of Sod′om, and with Bir′sha king of Go·mor′rah, Shi′nab king of Ad′mah, and Shem·e′ber king of Ze·boi′im, and the king of Be′la (that is to say, Zo′ar). 3 All these marched as allies to the Low Plain of Sid′dim, that is, the Salt Sea. 4 Twelve years they had served Ched·or·la·o′mer, but the thirteenth year they rebelled. 5 And in the fourteenth year Ched·or·la·o′mer came, and also the kings who were with him, and they inflicted defeats on the Reph′a·im in Ash′te·roth·kar·na′im, and the Zu′zim in Ham, and the E′mim in Sha′veh-kir·i·a·tha′im, 6 and the Ho′rites in their mountain of Se′ir, down to El-pa′ran, which is at the wilderness. 7 Then they turned about and came to En·mish'pat, that is, Ka'desh, and defeated the whole field of the A·mal'ek·ites and also the Am'or·ites who were dwelling in Haz'a·zon-ta'mar.

8 At this point the king of Sod'om went on the march, and also the king of Go·mor'rah and the king of Ad'mah and the king of Ze·boi'im and the king of Be'la (that is to say, Zo'ar), and they drew up in battle order against them in the Low Plain of Sid'dim, 9 against Ched·or·la·o'mer king of E'lam and Ti'dal king of Goi'im and Am'ra·phel king of Shi'nar and Ar'i·och king of El·la'sar; four kings against the five. 10 Now the Low Plain of Sid'dim was pits upon pits of bitumen; and the kings of Sod'om and Go·mor'rah took to flight and went falling into them, and those who remained fled to the mountainous region. 11 Then the victors took all the goods of Sod'om and Go·mor'rah and all their food and went on their way. 12 They also took Lot the son of A'bram's brother and his goods and continued on their way. He was then dwelling in Sod'om.

13 After that a man who had escaped came and told A'bram the Hebrew. He was then tabernacling among the big trees of Mam're the Am'or·ite, the brother of Esh'col and brother of A'ner; and they were confederates of A'bram. 14 Thus A'bram got to hear that his brother had been taken captive. With that he mustered his trained men, three hundred and eighteen slaves born in his household, and went in pursuit up to Dan. 15 And by night he resorted to dividing his forces, he and his slaves, against them, and thus he defeated them and kept in pursuit of them up to Ho'bah, which is north of Damascus. 16 And he proceeded to recover all the goods, and he recovered also Lot his brother and his goods and also the women and the people.

17 Then the king of Sod'om went out to meet him after he returned from defeating Ched·or·la·o'mer and the kings that were with him, to the Low Plain of Sha'veh, that is, the king's Low Plain. 18 And Mel·chiz'e·dek king of Sa'lem brought out bread and wine, and he was priest of the Most High God. 19 Then he blessed him and said:

"Blessed be A'bram of the Most High God,
   Producer of heaven and earth;
20 And blessed be the Most High God,
   who has delivered your oppressors into your hand!"

At that A'bram gave him a tenth of everything.

21 After that the king of Sod'om said to A'bram: "Give me the souls, but take the goods for yourself." 22 At this A'bram said to the king of Sod'om: "I do lift up my hand [in an oath] to Jehovah the Most High God, Producer of heaven and earth, 23 that, from a thread to a sandal lace, no, I shall take nothing from anything that is yours, in order that you may not say, 'It was I who made A'bram rich.' 24 Nothing for me! Only what the young men have already eaten, and the share of the men who went with me, A'ner, Esh'col and Mam're—let them take their share."

15 After these things the word of Jehovah came to A'bram in a vision, saying: "Do not fear, A'bram. I am a shield for you. Your reward will be very great." 2 At this A'bram said: "Lord Jehovah, what will you give me, seeing that I am going childless and the one who will possess my house is a man of Damascus, E·li·e'zer?" 3 And A'bram added: "Look! You have given me no seed, and, look! a son of my household is succeeding me as heir." 4 But, look! the word of Jehovah to him was in these words: "This man will not succeed you as heir, but one who will come out of your own inward parts will succeed you as heir."

5 He now brought him outside and said: "Look up, please, to the heavens and count the stars, if you

are possibly able to count them." And he went on to say to him: "So your seed will become." 6 And he put faith in Jehovah; and he proceeded to count it to him as righteousness. 7 Then he added to him: "I am Jehovah, who brought you out of Ur of the Chal·de′ans to give you this land to take it in possession." 8 To this he said: "Lord Jehovah, by what shall I know that I shall take it in possession?" 9 In turn he said to him: "Take for me a three-year-old heifer and a three-year-old she-goat and a three-year-old ram and a turtledove and a young pigeon." 10 So he took all these to himself and cut them in two and put each part of them so as to match the other, but the young birds he did not cut in pieces. 11 And the birds of prey began to descend upon the carcasses, but A′bram kept driving them away.

12 After a while the sun was about to set, and a deep sleep fell upon A′bram, and, look! a frightfully great darkness was falling upon him. 13 And he began to say to A′bram: "You may know for sure that your seed will become an alien resident in a land not theirs, and they will have to serve them, and these will certainly afflict them for four hundred years. 14 But the nation that they will serve I am judging, and after that they will go out with many goods. 15 As for you, you will go to your forefathers in peace; you will be buried at a good old age. 16 But in the fourth generation they will return here, because the error of the Am′or·ites has not yet come to completion."

17 The sun was now setting and a dense darkness came and, look! a smoking furnace and a fiery torch that passed in between these pieces. 18 On that day Jehovah concluded with A′bram a covenant, saying: "To your seed I will give this land, from the river of Egypt to the great river, the river Eu·phra′tes: 19 the Ken′ites and the Ken′iz·zites and the Kad′mon·ites 20 and the Hit′tites and the Per′iz·zites and the Reph′a·im 21 and the Am′orites and the Ca′naan·ites and the Gir′ga·shites and the Jeb′u·sites."

16 Now Sar′ai, A′bram's wife, had borne him no children; but she had an Egyptian maidservant and her name was Ha′gar. 2 Hence Sar′ai said to A′bram: "Please now! Jehovah has shut me off from bearing children. Please, have relations with my maidservant. Perhaps I may get children from her." So A′bram listened to the voice of Sar′ai. 3 Then Sar′ai, A′bram's wife, took Ha′gar, her Egyptian maidservant, at the end of ten years of A′bram's dwelling in the land of Ca′naan, and gave her to A′bram her husband as his wife. 4 Accordingly he had relations with Ha′gar, and she became pregnant. When she became aware that she was pregnant, then her mistress began to be despised in her eyes.

5 At this Sar′ai said to A′bram: "The violence done me be upon you. I myself gave my maidservant over to your bosom, and she became aware that she was pregnant, and I began to be despised in her eyes. May Jehovah judge between me and you." 6 So A′bram said to Sar′ai: "Look! Your maidservant is at your disposal. Do to her what is good in your eyes." Then Sar′ai began to humiliate her so that she ran away from her.

7 Later Jehovah's angel found her at a fountain of waters in the wilderness, at the fountain on the way to Shur. 8 And he began to say: "Ha′gar, maidservant of Sar′ai, just where have you come from and where are you going?" To this she said: "Why, from Sar′ai my mistress I am running away." 9 And Jehovah's angel went on to say to her: "Return to your mistress and humble yourself under her hand." 10 Then Jehovah's angel said to her: "I shall greatly multiply your seed, so that it will not be numbered for multitude." 11 Further Jehovah's angel added to her: "Here you are pregnant, and you shall give birth to a son and must call his name Ish′ma·el; for Jehovah has heard your afflic-

tion. 12 As for him, he will become a zebra of a man. His hand will be against everyone, and the hand of everyone will be against him; and before the face of all his brothers he will tabernacle."

13 Then she began to call the name of Jehovah, who was speaking to her: "You are a God of sight," for she said: "Have I here actually looked upon him who sees me?" 14 That is why the well was called Be·er-la′hai-roi. Here it is between Ka′desh and Be′red. 15 Later on Ha′gar bore to A′bram a son and A′bram called the name of his son whom Ha′gar bore Ish′ma·el. 16 And A′bram was eighty-six years old at Ha′gar's bearing Ish′ma·el to A′bram.

17 When A′bram got to be ninety-nine years old, then Jehovah appeared to A′bram and said to him: "I am God Almighty. Walk before me and prove yourself faultless. 2 And I will give my covenant between me and you, that I may multiply you very, very much."

3 At this A′bram fell upon his face, and God continued to speak with him, saying: 4 "As for me, look! my covenant is with you, and you will certainly become a father of a crowd of nations. 5 And your name will not be called A′bram any more, and your name must become Abraham, because a father of a crowd of nations I will make you. 6 And I will make you very, very fruitful and will make you become nations, and kings will come out of you.

7 "And I will carry out my covenant between me and you and your seed after you according to their generations for a covenant to time indefinite, to prove myself God to you and to your seed after you. 8 And I will give to you and to your seed after you the land of your alien residences, even the entire land of Ca′naan, for a possession to time indefinite; and I will prove myself God to them."

9 And God said further to Abraham: "As for you, you are to keep my covenant, you and your seed after you according to their genera-

tions. 10 This is my covenant that YOU men will keep, between me and YOU men, even YOUR seed after you: Every male of YOURS must get circumcised. 11 And YOU must get circumcised in the flesh of YOUR foreskins, and it must serve as a sign of the covenant between me and YOU. 12 And every male of YOURS eight days old must be circumcised, according to your generations, anyone born in the house and anyone purchased with money from any foreigner who is not from your seed. 13 Every man born in your house and every man purchased with money of yours must without fail get circumcised; and my covenant in the flesh of YOU men must serve as a covenant to time indefinite. 14 And an uncircumcised male who will not get the flesh of his foreskin circumcised, even that soul must be cut off from his people. He has broken my covenant."

15 And God went on to say to Abraham: "As for Sar′ai your wife, you must not call her name Sar′ai, because Sarah is her name. 16 And I will bless her and also give you a son from her; and I will bless her and she shall become nations; kings of peoples will come from her." 17 At this Abraham fell upon his face and began to laugh and to say in his heart: "Will a man a hundred years old have a child born, and will Sarah, yes, will a woman ninety years old give birth?"

18 After that Abraham said to the [true] God: "O that Ish′ma·el might live before you!" 19 To this God said: "Sarah your wife is indeed bearing you a son, and you must call his name Isaac. And I will establish my covenant with him for a covenant to time indefinite to his seed after him. 20 But as regards Ish′ma·el I have heard you. Look! I will bless him and will make him fruitful and will multiply him very, very much. He will certainly produce twelve chieftains, and I will make him become a great nation. 21 However, my covenant I shall establish with Isaac,

whom Sarah will bear to you at this appointed time next year."

22 With that God finished speaking with him and went up from Abraham. 23 Abraham then proceeded to take Ish′ma·el his son and all the men born in his house and everyone purchased with money of his, every male among the men of the household of Abraham, and he went to circumcising the flesh of their foreskins in this very day, just as God had spoken with him. 24 And Abraham was ninety-nine years old when he had the flesh of his foreskin circumcised. 25 And Ish′ma·el his son was thirteen years old when he had the flesh of his foreskin circumcised. 26 In this very day Abraham got circumcised, and also Ish′ma·el his son. 27 And all the men of his household, anyone born in the house and anyone purchased with money from a foreigner, got circumcised with him.

18 Afterward Jehovah appeared to him among the big trees of Mam′re, while he was sitting at the entrance of the tent about the heat of the day. 2 When he raised his eyes, then he looked and there three men were standing some distance from him. When he caught sight of them he began running to meet them from the entrance of the tent and proceeded to bow down to the earth. 3 Then he said: "Jehovah, if, now, I have found favor in your eyes, please do not pass by your servant. 4 Let a little water be taken, please, and YOU must have YOUR feet washed. Then recline under the tree. 5 And let me get a piece of bread, and refresh YOUR hearts. Following that, YOU can pass on, because that is why YOU have passed this way to YOUR servant." At this they said: "All right. You may do just as you have spoken."

6 So Abraham went hurrying to the tent to Sarah and said:"Hurry! Get three seah measures of fine flour, knead the dough and make round cakes." 7 Next Abraham ran to the herd and proceeded to get a tender and good young bull

and to give it to the attendant, and he went hurrying to get it ready. 8 He then took butter and milk and the young bull that he had got ready and set it before them. Then he himself kept standing by them under the tree as they were eating.

9 They now said to him: "Where is Sarah your wife?" To this he said: "Here in the tent!" 10 So he continued: "I am surely going to return to you next year at this time, and, look! Sarah your wife will have a son." Now Sarah was listening at the tent entrance, and it was behind the man. 11 And Abraham and Sarah were old, being advanced in years. Sarah had stopped having menstruation. 12 Hence Sarah began to laugh inside herself, saying: "After I am worn out, shall I really have pleasure, my lord being old besides?" 13 Then Jehovah said to Abraham: "Why was it that Sarah laughed, saying, 'Shall I really and truly give birth although I have become old?' 14 Is anything too extraordinary for Jehovah? At the appointed time I shall return to you, next year at this time, and Sarah will have a son." 15 But Sarah began to deny it, saying: "I did not laugh!" For she was afraid. At this he said: "No! but you did laugh."

16 Later the men got up from there and looked down toward Sod′om, and Abraham was walking with them to escort them. 17 And Jehovah said: "Am I keeping covered from Abraham what I am doing? 18 Why, Abraham is surely going to become a nation great and mighty, and all the nations of the earth must bless themselves by means of him. 19 For I have become acquainted with him in order that he may command his sons and his household after him so that they shall keep Jehovah's way to do righteousness and judgment; in order that Jehovah may certainly bring upon Abraham what he has spoken about him."

20 Consequently Jehovah said: "The cry of complaint about Sod′om and Go·mor′rah, yes, it is loud,

and their sin, yes, it is very heavy. 21 I am quite determined to go down that I may see whether they act altogether according to the outcry over it that has come to me, and, if not, I can get to know it."

22 At this point the men turned from there and got on their way to Sod'om; but as for Jehovah, he was still standing before Abraham. 23 Then Abraham approached and began to say: "Will you really sweep away the righteous with the wicked? 24 Suppose there are fifty righteous men in the midst of the city. Will you, then, sweep them away and not pardon the place for the sake of the fifty righteous who are inside it? 25 It is unthinkable of you that you are acting in this manner to put to death the righteous man with the wicked one so that it has to occur with the righteous man as it does with the wicked! It is unthinkable of you. Is the Judge of all the earth not going to do what is right?" 26 Then Jehovah said: "If I shall find in Sod'om fifty righteous men in the midst of the city I will pardon the whole place on their account." 27 But Abraham went on to answer and say: "Please, here I have taken upon myself to speak to Jehovah, whereas I am dust and ashes. 28 Suppose the fifty righteous should be lacking five. Will you for the five bring the whole city to ruin?" To this he said: "I shall not bring it to ruin if I find there forty-five."

29 But yet again he spoke further to him and said: "Suppose forty are found there." In turn he said: "I shall not do it on account of the forty." 30 But he continued: "May Jehovah, please, not grow hot with anger, but let me go on speaking: Suppose thirty are found there." In turn he said: "I shall not do it if I find thirty there." 31 But he continued on: "Please, here I have taken upon myself to speak to Jehovah: Suppose twenty are found there." In turn he said: "I shall not bring it to ruin on account of the twenty." 32 Finally he said: "May Jehovah,

please, not grow hot with anger, but let me speak just this once: Suppose ten are found there." In turn he said: "I shall not bring it to ruin on account of the ten." 33 Then Jehovah went his way when he had finished speaking to Abraham, and Abraham returned to his place.

19 Now the two angels arrived at Sod'om by evening, and Lot was sitting in the gate of Sod'om. When Lot caught sight of them, then he got up to meet them and bowed down with his face to the earth. 2 And he proceeded to say: "Please, now, my lords, turn aside, please, into the house of YOUR servant and stay overnight and have YOUR feet washed. Then YOU must get up early and travel on YOUR way." To this they said: "No, but in the public square is where we shall stay overnight." 3 But he was very insistent with them, so that they turned aside to him and came into his house. Then he made a feast for them, and he baked unfermented cakes, and they went to eating.

4 Before they could lie down, the men of the city, the men of Sod'om, surrounded the house, from boy to old man, all the people in one mob. 5 And they kept calling out to Lot and saying to him: "Where are the men who came in to you tonight? Bring them out to us that we may have intercourse with them."

6 Finally Lot went out to them to the entrance, but he shut the door behind him. 7 Then he said: "Please, my brothers, do not act badly. 8 Please, here I have two daughters who have never had intercourse with a man. Please, let me bring them out to YOU. Then do to them as is good in YOUR eyes. Only to these men do not do a thing, because that is why they have come under the shadow of my roof." 9 At this they said: "Stand back there!" And they added: "This lone man came here to reside as an alien and yet he would actually play the judge. Now we are going to do worse to you than to them." And they came pressing

heavily in on the man, on Lot, and were getting near to break in the door. 10 So the men thrust out their hands and brought Lot in to them, into the house, and they shut the door. 11 But they struck with blindness the men who were at the entrance of the house, from the least to the greatest, so that they were wearing themselves out trying to find the entrance.

12 Then the men said to Lot: "Do you have anyone else here? Son-in-law and your sons and your daughters and all who are yours in the city, bring out of the place! 13 For we are bringing this place to ruin, because the outcry against them has grown loud before Jehovah, so that Jehovah sent us to bring the city to ruin." 14 Hence Lot went on out and began to speak to his sons-in-law who were to take his daughters, and he kept on saying: "Get up! Get out of this place, because Jehovah is bringing the city to ruin!" But in the eyes of his sons-in-law he seemed like a man who was joking.

15 However, when the dawn ascended, then the angels became urgent with Lot, saying: "Get up! Take your wife and your two daughters who are found here, for fear you may be swept away in the error of the city!" 16 When he kept lingering, then in the compassion of Jehovah upon him, the men seized hold of his hand and of the hand of his wife and of the hands of his two daughters and they proceeded to bring him out and to station him outside the city. 17 And it came about that, as soon as they had brought them forth to the outskirts, he began to say: "Escape for your soul! Do not look behind you and do not stand still in all the District! Escape to the mountainous region for fear you may be swept away!"

18 Then Lot said to them: "Not that, please, Jehovah! 19 Please, now, your servant has found favor in your eyes so that you are magnifying your loving-kindness, which you have exercised with me to preserve my soul alive, but I—I am not able to escape to the mountainous region for fear calamity may keep close to me and I certainly die. 20 Please, now, this city is nearby to flee there and it is a small thing. May I, please, escape there—is it not a small thing?—and my soul will live on." 21 So he said to him: "Here I do show you consideration to this extent also, by my not overthrowing the city of which you have spoken. 22 Hurry! Escape there, because I am not able to do a thing until your arriving there!" That is why he called the name of the city Zo'ar.

23 The sun had gone forth over the land when Lot arrived at Zo'ar. 24 Then Jehovah made it rain sulphur and fire from Jehovah, from the heavens, upon Sod'om and upon Go·mor'rah. 25 So he went ahead overthrowing these cities, even the entire District and all the inhabitants of the cities and the plants of the ground. 26 And his wife began to look around from behind him, and she became a pillar of salt.

27 Now Abraham made his way early in the morning to the place where he had stood before Jehovah. 28 Then he looked down toward Sod'om and Go·mor'rah and toward all the land of the District and saw a sight. Why, here thick smoke ascended from the land like the thick smoke of a kiln! 29 And it came about that when God brought the cities of the District to ruin God kept Abraham in mind in that he took steps to send Lot out of the midst of the overthrow when overthrowing the cities among which Lot had been dwelling.

30 Later Lot went up from Zo'ar and began dwelling in the mountainous region, and his two daughters along with him, because he got afraid of dwelling in Zo'ar. So he began dwelling in a cave, he and his two daughters. 31 And the first-born proceeded to say to the younger woman: "Our father is old and there is not a man in the land to have relations with us according to the way of the whole earth. 32 Come, let us give our father

wine to drink and let us lie down with him and preserve offspring from our father."

33 So they kept giving their father wine to drink during that night; then the first-born went in and lay down with her father, but he did not know when she lay down and when she got up. 34 And it came about on the next day that the first-born then said to the younger: "Here I lay down with my father last night. Let us give him wine to drink tonight also. Then you go in, lie down with him, and let us preserve offspring from our father." 35 So they repeatedly gave their father wine to drink during that night also; then the younger got up and lay down with him, but he did not know when she lay down and when she got up. 36 And both the daughters of Lot became pregnant from their father. 37 In time the first-born became mother to a son and called his name Mo'ab. He is the father of Mo'ab, to this day. 38 As for the younger, she too gave birth to a son and then called his name Ben-am'mi. He is the father of the sons of Am'mon, to this day.

20 Now Abraham moved camp from there to the land of the Neg'eb and took up dwelling between Ka'desh and Shur and residing as an alien at Ge'rar. 2 And Abraham repeated concerning Sarah his wife: "She is my sister." With that A·bim'e·lech king of Ge'rar sent and took Sarah. 3 Afterward God came to A·bim'e·lech in a dream by night and said to him: "Here you are as good as dead because of the woman whom you have taken, since she is owned by another owner as his wife." 4 However, A·bim'e·lech had not gone near her. Hence he said: "Jehovah, will you kill a nation that is really righteous? 5 Did not he say to me, 'She is my sister'? and she—did not she too say, 'He is my brother'? In the honesty of my heart and with innocency of my hands I have done this." 6 At that the [true] God said to him in the dream: "I too have known that

in the honesty of your heart you have done this, and I was also holding you back from sinning against me. That is why I did not allow you to touch her. 7 But now return the man's wife, for he is a prophet, and he will make supplication for you. So keep living. But if you are not returning her, know that you will positively die, you and all who are yours."

8 So A·bim'e·lech got up early in the morning and proceeded to call all his servants and to speak of all these things in their ears. And the men got very much afraid. 9 Then A·bim'e·lech called Abraham and said to him: "What have you done to us, and what sin have I committed against you, in that you have brought upon me and my kingdom a great sin? Deeds that should not have been done you have done in connection with me." 10 And A·bim'e·lech went on to say to Abraham: "What did you have in view in that you have done this thing?" 11 To this Abraham said: "It was because I said to myself, 'Doubtless there is no fear of God in this place, and they will certainly kill me because of my wife.' 12 And, besides, she is truly my sister, the daughter of my father, only not the daughter of my mother; and she became my wife. 13 And it came about that, when God caused me to wander from the house of my father, then I said to her, 'This is your loving-kindness which you may exercise toward me: At every place where we shall come say of me: "He is my brother." ' "

14 Following that A·bim'e·lech took sheep and cattle and menservants and maidservants and gave them to Abraham and returned to him Sarah his wife. 15 Further A·bim'e·lech said: "Here my land is available to you. Dwell where it is good in your eyes." 16 And to Sarah he said: "Here I do give a thousand silver pieces of money to your brother. Here it is for you a covering of the eyes to all who are with you, and before everybody, and you are cleared of reproach." 17 And Abraham began to make

supplication to the [true] God; and God proceeded to heal A·bim′e·lech and his wife and his slave girls, and they began bearing children. 18 For Jehovah had tightly shut up every womb of the house of A·bim′e·lech because of Sarah, Abraham's wife.

21 And Jehovah turned his attention to Sarah just as he had said, and Jehovah now did to Sarah just as he had spoken. 2 And Sarah became pregnant and then bore a son to Abraham in his old age at the appointed time of which God had spoken to him. 3 Accordingly Abraham called the name of his son who had been born to him, whom Sarah had borne to him, Isaac. 4 And Abraham proceeded to circumcise Isaac his son when eight days old, just as God had commanded him. 5 And Abraham was a hundred years old when Isaac his son was born to him. 6 Then Sarah said: "God has prepared laughter for me: everybody hearing of it will laugh at me." 7 And she added: "Who would have uttered to Abraham, 'Sarah will certainly suckle children,' whereas I have given birth to a son in his old age?"

8 Now the child kept growing and came to be weaned; and Abraham then prepared a big feast on the day of Isaac's being weaned. 9 And Sarah kept noticing the son of Ha′gar the Egyptian, whom she had borne to Abraham, poking fun. 10 So she began to say to Abraham: "Drive out this slave girl and her son, for the son of this slave girl is not going to be an heir with my son, with Isaac!" 11 But the thing proved to be very displeasing to Abraham as regards his son. 12 Then God said to Abraham: "Do not let anything that Sarah keeps saying to you be displeasing to you about the boy and about your slave girl. Listen to her voice, because it is by means of Isaac that what will be called your seed will be. 13 And as for the son of the slave girl, I shall also constitute him a nation, because he is your offspring."

14 So Abraham got up early in the morning and took bread and a skin water bottle and gave it to Ha′gar, setting it upon her shoulder, and the child, and then dismissed her. And she went her way and wandered about in the wilderness of Be′er-she′ba. 15 Finally the water became exhausted in the skin bottle and she threw the child under one of the bushes. 16 Then she went on and sat down by herself, about the distance of a bowshot away, because she said: "Let me not see it when the child dies." So she sat down at a distance and began to raise her voice and weep.

17 At that God heard the voice of the boy, and God's angel called to Ha′gar out of the heavens and said to her: "What is the matter with you, Ha′gar? Do not be afraid, because God has listened to the voice of the boy there where he is. 18 Get up, lift up the boy and take hold of him with your hand, because I shall constitute him a great nation." 19 Then God opened her eyes so that she caught sight of a well of water; and she went and began to fill the skin bottle with water and to give the boy a drink. 20 And God continued to be with the boy, and he kept growing and dwelling in the wilderness; and he became an archer. 21 And he took up dwelling in the wilderness of Pa′ran, and his mother proceeded to take a wife for him from the land of Egypt.

22 Now it came about at that time that A·bim′e·lech together with Phi′col the chief of his army said to Abraham: "God is with you in everything you are doing. 23 So now swear to me here by God that you will not prove false to me and to my offspring and to my posterity; that, according to the loyal love with which I have dealt with you, you will deal with me and with the land in which you have been residing as an alien." 24 So Abraham said: "I shall swear."

25 When Abraham criticized A·bim′e·lech severely as regards the well of water that the servants of

A·bim′e·lech had seized by violence, 26 then A·bim′e·lech said: "I do not know who did this thing, neither did you yourself tell it to me, and I myself have also not heard of it except today." 27 With that Abraham took sheep and cattle and gave them to A·bim′e·lech, and both of them proceeded to conclude a covenant. 28 When Abraham set seven female lambs of the flock by themselves, 29 A·bim′e·lech went on to say to Abraham: "What is the meaning here of these seven female lambs that you have set by themselves?" 30 Then he said: "You are to accept the seven female lambs at my hand, that it may serve as a witness for me that I have dug this well." 31 That is why he called that place Be′er-she′ba, because there both of them had taken an oath. 32 So they concluded a covenant at Be′er-she′ba, after which A·bim′e·lech got up together with Phi′col the chief of his army and they returned to the land of the Phi·lis′tines. 33 After that he planted a tamarisk tree at Be′er-she′ba and called there upon the name of Jehovah the indefinitely lasting God. 34 And Abraham extended his residence as an alien in the land of the Philis′tines many days.

22 Now after these things it came about that the [true] God put Abraham to the test. Accordingly he said to him: "Abraham!" to which he said: "Here I am!" 2 And he went on to say: "Take, please, your son, your only son whom you so love, Isaac, and make a trip to the land of Mo·ri′ah and there offer him up as a burnt offering on one of the mountains that I shall designate to you."

3 So Abraham got up early in the morning and saddled his ass and took two of his attendants with him and Isaac his son; and he split the wood for the burnt offering. Then he rose and went on the trip to the place that the [true] God designated to him. 4 It was first on the third day that Abraham raised his eyes and began to see the place from a distance.

5 Abraham now said to his attendants: "You stay here with the ass, but I and the boy want to go on over there and worship and return to you."

6 After that Abraham took the wood of the burnt offering and put it upon Isaac his son and took in his hands the fire and the slaughtering knife, and both of them went on together. 7 And Isaac began to say to Abraham his father: "My father!" In turn he said: "Here I am, my son!" So he continued: "Here are the fire and the wood, but where is the sheep for the burnt offering?" 8 To this Abraham said: "God will provide himself the sheep for the burnt offering, my son." And both of them walked on together.

9 Finally they reached the place that the [true] God had designated to him, and Abraham built an altar there and set the wood in order and bound Isaac his son hand and foot and put him upon the altar on top of the wood. 10 Then Abraham put out his hand and took the slaughtering knife to kill his son. 11 But Jehovah's angel began calling to him out of the heavens and saying: "Abraham, Abraham!" to which he answered: "Here I am!" 12 And he went on to say: "Do not put out your hand against the boy and do not do anything at all to him, for now I do know that you are Godfearing in that you have not withheld your son, your only one, from me." 13 At that Abraham raised his eyes and looked and there, deep in the foreground, there was a ram caught by its horns in a thicket. So Abraham went and took the ram and offered it up for a burnt offering in place of his son. 14 And Abraham began to call the name of that place Je·ho′vah-ji′reh. This is why it is customarily said today: "In the mountain of Jehovah it will be provided."

15 And Jehovah's angel proceeded to call to Abraham the second time out of the heavens 16 and to say: " 'By myself I do swear,' is the utterance of Jehovah,

Abraham had Abraham gave gifts. Then he sent them away from Isaac his son, while he was still alive, eastward, to the land of the East. 7 And these are the days of the years of Abraham's life which he lived, a hundred and seventy-five years. 8 Then Abraham expired and died in a good old age, old and satisfied, and was gathered to his people. 9 So Isaac and Ish'ma·el his sons buried him in the cave of Mach·pe'lah in the field of E'phron the son of Zo'har the Hit'tite that is in front of Mam're, 10 the field that Abraham had purchased from the sons of Heth. There Abraham was buried, and also Sarah his wife. 11 And it developed that after Abraham's death God continued to bless Isaac his son, and Isaac was dwelling close by Be·er-la'hai-roi.

12 And this is the history of Ish'ma·el the son of Abraham whom Ha'gar the Egyptian the maidservant of Sarah bore to Abraham.

13 Now these are the names of the sons of Ish'ma·el, by their names, according to their family origins: Ish'ma·el's first-born Ne-ba'ioth and Ke'dar and Ad'be·el and Mib'sam 14 and Mish'ma and Du'mah and Mas'sa, 15 Ha'dad and Te'ma, Je'tur, Na'phish and Ked'e·mah. 16 These are the sons of Ish'ma·el, and these are their names by their courtyards and by their walled camps: twelve chieftains according to their clans. 17 And these are the years of Ish'ma·el's life, a hundred and thirty-seven years. Then he expired and died and was gathered to his people. 18 And they took up tab-ernacling from Hav'i·lah near Shur, which is in front of Egypt, as far as As·syr'i·a. In front of all his brothers he settled down.

19 And this is the history of Isaac the son of Abraham.

Abraham became father to Isaac. 20 And Isaac happened to be forty years old at his taking Re·bek'ah the daughter of Be·thu'el the Syrian of Pad'dan-a'ram, the sister of La'ban the Syrian, as his wife.

21 And Isaac kept on entreating Jehovah especially for his wife, because she was barren; so Jehovah let himself be entreated for him, and Re·bek'ah his wife became pregnant. 22 And the sons within her began to struggle with each other, so that she said: "If this is the way it is, just why am I alive?" With that she went to inquire of Jehovah. 23 And Jehovah proceeded to say to her: "Two nations are in your belly, and two national groups will be separated from your inward parts; and the one national group will be stronger than the other national group, and the older will serve the younger."

24 Gradually her days came to the full for giving birth, and, look! twins were in her belly. 25 Then the first came out red all over like an official garment of hair; so they called his name E'sau. 26 And after that his brother came out and his hand was holding onto the heel of E'sau; so he called his name Jacob. And Isaac was sixty years old at her giving them birth.

27 And the boys got bigger, and E'sau became a man knowing how to hunt, a man of the field, but Jacob a blameless man, dwelling in tents. 28 And Isaac had love for E'sau, because it meant game in his mouth, whereas Re·bek'ah was a lover of Jacob. 29 Once Jacob was boiling up some stew, when E'sau came along from the field and he was tired. 30 So E'sau said to Jacob: "Quick, please, give me a swallow of the red—the red there, for I am tired!" That is why his name was called E'dom. 31 To this Jacob said: "Sell me, first of all, your right as first-born!" 32 And E'sau continued: "Here I am simply going to die, and of what benefit to me is a birthright?" 33 And Jacob added: "Swear to me first of all!" And he proceeded to swear to him and to sell his right as first-born to Jacob. 34 And Jacob gave E'sau bread and lentil stew, and he went to eating and drinking. Then he got up and went his way. So E'sau despised the birthright.

26 Now there arose a famine in the land, besides the first famine that occurred in the days of Abraham, so that Isaac directed himself to A·bim′e·lech, king of the Phi·lis′tines, to Ge′rar. 2 Then Jehovah appeared to him and said: "Do not go down to Egypt. Tabernacle in the land that I designated to you. 3 Reside as an alien in this land, and I shall continue with you and bless you, because to you and to your seed I shall give all these lands, and I will carry out the sworn statement that I swore to Abraham your father, 4 'And I will multiply your seed like the stars of the heavens and I will give to your seed all these lands; and by means of your seed all nations of the earth will certainly bless themselves,' 5 due to the fact that Abraham listened to my voice and continued to keep his obligations to me, my commands, my statutes, and my laws." 6 So Isaac went on dwelling at Ge′rar.

7 Well, the men of the place kept asking with respect to his wife, and he would say: "She is my sister." For he was afraid to say "My wife" for fear that, to quote him, "the men of the place should kill me because of Re·bek′ah," because she was attractive in appearance. 8 So it came about that as his days there extended themselves A·bim′e·lech, king of the Phi·lis′tines, was looking out of the window and taking in the sight, and there was Isaac having a good time with Re·bek′ah his wife. 9 At once A·bim′e·lech called Isaac and said: "Why, she is no other than your wife! So how is it that you said, 'She is my sister'?" At this Isaac said to him: "I said it for fear I should die on her account." 10 But A·bim′e·lech continued: "What is this you have done to us? A little more and certainly one of the people would have lain down with your wife, and you would have brought guilt upon us!" 11 Then A·bim′e·lech commanded all the people, saying: "Anybody touching this man and his wife will surely be put to death!"

12 Afterward Isaac began to sow seed in that land, and in that year he was getting up to a hundred measures to one, as Jehovah was blessing him. 13 Consequently the man became great and went on advancing more and more and growing great until he got very great. 14 And he came to have flocks of sheep and herds of cattle and a large body of servants, so that the Phi·lis′tines began to envy him.

15 As for all the wells that the servants of his father had dug in the days of Abraham his father, these the Phi·lis′tines stopped up and they would fill them with dry earth. 16 Finally A·bim′e·lech said to Isaac: "Move from our neighborhood, because you have grown far stronger than we are." 17 So Isaac moved from there and encamped in the torrent valley of Ge′rar and took up dwelling there. 18 And Isaac proceeded to dig again the wells of water that they had dug in the days of Abraham his father but which the Phi·lis′tines went stopping up after Abraham's death; and he resumed calling their names by the names that his father had called them.

19 And the servants of Isaac went on digging in the torrent valley and so they found there a well of fresh water. 20 And the shepherds of Ge′rar fell to quarreling with the shepherds of Isaac, saying: "The water is ours!" Hence he called the name of the well E′sek, because they had contended with him. 21 And they went digging another well, and they fell to quarreling over it also. Hence he called its name Sit′nah. 22 Later he moved away from there and dug another well, but they did not quarrel over it. Hence he called its name Re·ho′both and said: "It is because now Jehovah has given us ample room and has made us fruitful in the earth."

23 Then he went up from there to Be′er-she′ba. 24 And Jehovah proceeded to appear to him during that night and to say: "I am the God of Abraham your father. Do

not be afraid, because I am with you, and I will bless you and multiply your seed on account of Abraham my servant." 25 Accordingly he built an altar there and called on the name of Jehovah and pitched his tent there, and the servants of Isaac went excavating a well there.

26 Later on A·bim′e·lech came to him from Ge′rar with A·huz′zath his confidential friend and Phi′col the chief of his army. 27 At this Isaac said to them: "Why have YOU come to me, seeing that YOU yourselves hated me and so sent me away from YOUR neighborhood?" 28 To this they said: "We have unmistakably seen that Jehovah has proved to be with you. Hence we said, 'Let, please, an oath of obligation occur between us, between us and you, and let us conclude a covenant with you, 29 that you will do nothing bad toward us just as we have not touched you and just as we have done only good toward you in that we sent you away in peace. You now are the blessed of Jehovah.'" 30 Then he made a feast for them and they ate and drank. 31 Next morning they were early in rising and they made sworn statements one to the other. After that Isaac sent them away and they went from him in peace.

32 Now on that day it occurred that the servants of Isaac proceeded to come and report to him regarding the well that they had dug, and to say to him: "We have found water!" 33 Hence he called its name Shi′bah. That is why the name of the city is Be′er-she′ba, down to this day.

34 And E′sau grew to be forty years old. Then he took as wife Ju′dith the daughter of Be·e′ri the Hit′tite and also Bas′e·math the daughter of E′lon the Hit′tite. 35 And they were a source of bitterness of spirit to Isaac and Re·bek′ah.

27 Now it came about that when Isaac was old and his eyes were too dim to see he then called E′sau his older son and said to him: "My son!" at which he said to him: "Here I am!" 2 And he went on to say: "Here, now, I have become old. I do not know the day of my death. 3 So at this time take, please, your implements, your quiver and your bow, and go out to the field and hunt some venison for me. 4 Then make me a tasty dish such as I am fond of and bring it to me and, ah, let me eat, in order that my soul may bless you before I die."

5 However, Re·bek′ah was listening while Isaac spoke to E′sau his son. And E′sau went on out into the field to hunt game and to bring it in. 6 And Re·bek′ah said to Jacob her son: "Here I just heard your father speaking to E′sau your brother, saying, 7 'Bring me some game and make me a tasty dish and, ah, let me eat, that I may bless you before Jehovah before my death.' 8 And now, my son, listen to my voice in what I am commanding you. 9 Go, please, to the herd and get me from there two kids of the goats, good ones, that I may make them up into a tasty dish for your father such as he is fond of. 10 Then you must bring it to your father and he must eat it, in order that he may bless you before his death."

11 And Jacob proceeded to say to Re·bek′ah his mother: "But E′sau my brother is a hairy man and I am a smooth man. 12 What if my father feels me? Then I shall certainly become in his eyes like one making a mockery, and I shall certainly bring upon myself a malediction and not a blessing." 13 At this his mother said to him: "Upon me be the malediction meant for you, my son. Only listen to my voice and go, get them for me." 14 Accordingly he went and got them and brought them to his mother, and his mother made a tasty dish such as his father was fond of. 15 After that Re·bek′ah took garments of E′sau her older son, the most desirable ones which were with her in the house, and put them on Jacob her younger

son. 16 And the skins of the kids of the goats she put upon his hands and upon the hairless part of his neck. 17 Then she gave the tasty dish and the bread that she had made into the hand of Jacob her son.

18 So he went on in to his father and said: "My father!" to which he said: "Here I am! Who are you, my son?" 19 And Jacob went on to say to his father: "I am E′sau your first-born. I have done just as you have spoken to me. Raise yourself up, please. Sit down and eat some of my game, in order that your soul may bless me." 20 At that Isaac said to his son: "How is it that you have been so quick in finding it, my son?" In turn he said: "Because Jehovah your God caused it to meet up with me." 21 Then Isaac said to Jacob: "Come near, please, that I may feel you, my son, to know whether you are really my son E′sau or not." 22 So Jacob came near to Isaac his father, and he went feeling him, after which he said: "The voice is the voice of Jacob, but the hands are the hands of E′sau." 23 And he did not recognize him, because his hands proved to be hairy like the hands of E′sau his brother. Hence he blessed him.

24 After that he said: "You are really my son E′sau?" to which he said: "I am." 25 Then he said: "Bring it near to me that I may eat some of the game of my son, to the end that my soul may bless you." With that he brought it near to him and he began to eat, and he brought him wine and he began to drink. 26 Then Isaac his father said to him: "Come near, please, and kiss me, my son." 27 So he came near and kissed him, and he could smell the scent of his garments. And he proceeded to bless him and to say:

"See, the scent of my son is like the scent of the field which Jehovah has blessed. 28 And may the [true] God give you the dews of the heavens and the fertile soils of the earth and an abundance of grain and new wine. 29 Let peoples serve you and let national groups bow low to you. Become master over your brothers, and let the sons of your mother bow low to you. Cursed be each one of those cursing you, and blessed be each one of those blessing you."

30 Now it came about as soon as Isaac had finished blessing Jacob, yes, it indeed came about when Jacob had barely come out from before the face of Isaac his father, that E′sau his brother came back from his hunting. 31 And he too went about making a tasty dish. Then he brought it to his father and said to his father: "Let my father get up and eat some of his son's game, in order that your soul may bless me." 32 At this Isaac his father said to him: "Who are you?" to which he said: "I am your son, your first-born, E′sau." 33 And Isaac began to shake with a great trembling in extreme measure, and so he said: "Who, then, was it that hunted for game and came bringing it to me, so that I ate of everything before you could come in and I blessed him? Blessed too he will become!"

34 On hearing his father's words E′sau began to cry out in an extremely loud and bitter manner and to say to his father: "Bless me, even me too, my father!" 35 But he went on to say: "Your brother came with deception that he might get the blessing meant for you." 36 At this he said: "Is that not why his name is called Jacob, in that he should supplant me these two times? My birthright he has already taken, and here at this time he has taken my blessing!" Then he added: "Have you not reserved a blessing for me?" 37 But in answer to E′sau Isaac continued: "Here I have appointed him master over you, and all his brothers I have given to him as servants, and grain and new wine I have bestowed for his support, and where is there anything I can do for you, my son?"

38 Then E′sau said to his father: "Is there just one blessing that you have, my father? Bless me, even

me too, my father!" With that E'sau raised his voice and burst into tears. 39 So in answer Isaac his father said to him:

"Behold, away from the fertile soils of the earth your dwelling will be found, and away from the dew of the heavens above. 40 And by your sword you will live, and your brother you will serve. But it will certainly occur that, when you grow restless, you will indeed break his yoke off your neck."

41 However, E'sau harbored animosity for Jacob on account of the blessing with which his father had blessed him, and E'sau kept saying in his heart: "The days of the period of mourning for my father are getting closer. After that I am going to kill Jacob my brother." 42 When the words of E'sau her older son were told to Re·bek'ah, she at once sent and called Jacob her younger son and said to him: "Look! E'sau your brother is comforting himself in regard to you—to kill you. 43 Now, then, my son, listen to my voice and get up, run away to La'ban my brother at Ha'ran. 44 And you must dwell with him for some days until the rage of your brother calms down, 45 until the anger of your brother turns away from you and he has forgotten what you have done to him. And I shall certainly send and get you from there. Why should I be bereaved also of both of you in one day?"

46 After that Re·bek'ah kept saying to Isaac: "I have come to abhor this life of mine because of the daughters of Heth. If Jacob ever takes a wife from the daughters of Heth like these from the daughters of the land, of what good is life to me?"

28 Consequently Isaac called Jacob and blessed him and commanded him and said to him: "You must not take a wife from the daughters of Ca'naan. 2 Get up, go to Pad'dan-a'ram to the house of Be·thu'el the father of your mother and from there take yourself a wife from the daughters of La'ban the brother of your

mother. 3 And God Almighty will bless you and make you fruitful and multiply you, and you will certainly become a congregation of peoples. 4 And he will give to you the blessing of Abraham, to you and to your seed with you, that you may take possession of the land of your alien residences, which God has given to Abraham."

5 So Isaac sent Jacob away, and he struck out for Pad'dan-a'ram, for La'ban the son of Be·thu'el the Syrian, the brother of Re·bek'ah, mother of Jacob and E'sau.

6 When E'sau saw that Isaac had blessed Jacob and had sent him away to Pad'dan-a'ram to take from there a wife for himself, and that when he blessed him he laid the command upon him, saying: "Do not take a wife from the daughters of Ca'naan"; 7 and that Jacob was obeying his father and his mother and was on his way to Pad'dan-a'ram; 8 then E'sau saw that the daughters of Ca'naan were displeasing in the eyes of Isaac his father. 9 Hence E'sau went to Ish'ma·el and took as wife Ma'halath the daughter of Ish'ma·el the son of Abraham, the sister of Ne·ba'ioth, besides his other wives.

10 And Jacob continued on his way out from Be'er-she'ba and kept going to Ha'ran. 11 In time he came across a place and set about spending the night there because the sun had set. So he took one of the stones of the place and set it as his head supporter and lay down in that place. 12 And he began to dream, and, look! there was a ladder stationed upon the earth and its top reaching up to the heavens; and, look! there were God's angels ascending and descending on it. 13 And, look! there was Jehovah stationed above it, and he proceeded to say:

"I am Jehovah the God of Abraham your father and the God of Isaac. The land upon which you are lying, to you I am going to give it and to your seed. 14 And your seed will certainly become like the dust particles of the earth, and you will certainly spread abroad to the west and to the east and to the north and to the south, and by means of you and by means of your seed all the families of the ground will certainly bless themselves. 15 And here I am with you and I will keep you in all the way you are going and I will return you to this ground, because I am not going to leave you until I have actually done what I have spoken to you."

16 Then Jacob awoke from his sleep and said: "Truly Jehovah is in this place and I myself did not know it." 17 And he grew fearful and added: "How fear-inspiring this place is! This is nothing else but the house of God and this is the gate of the heavens." 18 So Jacob got up early in the morning and took the stone that was there as his head supporter and he set it up as a pillar and poured oil on the top of it. 19 Further, he called the name of that place Beth′el; but the fact is, Luz was the city's name formerly.

20 And Jacob went on to vow a vow, saying: "If God will continue with me and will certainly keep me on this way on which I am going and will certainly give me bread to eat and garments to wear 21 and I shall certainly return in peace to the house of my father, then Jehovah will have proved to be my God. 22 And this stone that I have set up as a pillar will become a house of God, and as for everything that you will give me I shall without fail give the tenth of it to you."

29 After that Jacob set his feet in motion and traveled on to the land of the Orientals. 2 Now he looked, and here there was a well in the field and here three droves of sheep were lying down there by it, because from that well they were accustomed to water the droves; and there was a great stone over the mouth of the well. 3 When all the droves had been gathered there, they rolled away the stone from off the mouth of the well, and they watered the flocks, after which they returned

the stone over the mouth of the well to its place.

4 So Jacob said to them: "My brothers, from what place are YOU?" to which they said: "We are from Ha′ran." 5 Then he said to them: "Do YOU know La′ban the grandson of Na′hor?" to which they said: "We know him." 6 At this he said to them: "Is it all right with him?" In turn they said: "It is all right. And here is Rachel his daughter coming with the sheep!" 7 And he went on to say: "Why, it is yet full day. It is not the time for gathering the herds. WATER the sheep, then go feed them." 8 To this they said: "We are not allowed to do so until all the droves are gathered and they actually roll away the stone from off the mouth of the well. Then we must water the sheep."

9 While he was yet speaking with them, Rachel came with the sheep that belonged to her father, for she was a shepherdess. 10 And it came about that when Jacob saw Rachel the daughter of La′ban his mother's brother and the sheep of La′ban his mother's brother, Jacob immediately approached and rolled away the stone from off the mouth of the well and watered the sheep of La′ban his mother's brother. 11 Then Jacob kissed Rachel and raised his voice and burst into tears. 12 And Jacob began to tell Rachel that he was the brother of her father and that he was the son of Re·bek′ah. And she went running and telling her father.

13 Now it came about that as soon as La′ban heard the report about Jacob the son of his sister, he went running to meet him. Then he embraced him and kissed him and brought him on into his house. And he began to relate to La′ban all these things. 14 After that La′ban said to him: "You are indeed my bone and my flesh." So he dwelt with him a full month.

15 After that La′ban said to Jacob: "Are you my brother, and must you serve me for nothing? Tell me, What are your wages to be?" 16 As it was, La′ban had

two daughters. The name of the older was Le'ah and the name of the younger Rachel. 17 But the eyes of Le'ah had no luster, whereas Rachel had become beautiful in form and beautiful of countenance. 18 And Jacob was in love with Rachel. So he said: "I am willing to serve you seven years for Rachel your younger daughter." 19 To this La'ban said: "It is better for me to give her to you than for me to give her to another man. Keep dwelling with me." 20 And Jacob proceeded to serve seven years for Rachel, but in his eyes they proved to be like some few days because of his love for her.

21 Then Jacob said to La'ban: "Give over my wife, because my days are up, and let me have relations with her." 22 With that La'ban gathered all the men of the place and made a feast. 23 But it turned out that during the evening he resorted to taking Le'ah his daughter and bringing her to him that he might have relations with her. 24 Moreover, La'ban gave to her Zil'pah his maidservant, even to Le'ah his daughter, as a maidservant. 25 So it followed in the morning that here it was Le'ah! Consequently he said to La'ban: "What is this you have done to me? Was it not for Rachel that I served with you? So why have you tricked me?" 26 To this La'ban said: "It is not customary to do this way in our place, to give the younger woman before the first-born. 27 Celebrate to the full the week of this woman. After that there shall be given to you also this other woman for the service that you can serve with me for seven years more." 28 Accordingly Jacob did so and celebrated fully the week of this woman, after which he gave him Rachel his daughter as his wife. 29 Besides, La'ban gave Bil'hah his maidservant to Rachel his daughter as her maidservant.

30 Then he had relations also with Rachel and also expressed more love for Rachel than for Le'ah, and he went serving with him for yet seven years more. 31 When Jehovah came to see that Le'ah was hated, he then opened her womb, but Rachel was barren. 32 And Le'ah became pregnant and brought a son to birth and then called his name Reu'ben, for she said: "It is because Jehovah has looked upon my wretchedness, in that now my husband will begin to love me." 33 And she became pregnant again and brought a son to birth and then said: "It is because Jehovah has listened, in that I was hated and so he gave me also this one." Hence she called his name Sim'e·on. 34 And she became pregnant yet again and brought a son to birth and then said: "Now this time my husband will join himself to me, because I have borne him three sons." His name was therefore called Le'vi. 35 And she became pregnant once more and brought a son to birth and then said: "This time I shall laud Jehovah." She therefore called his name Judah. After that she left off giving birth.

30 When Rachel came to see that she had borne nothing to Jacob, Rachel got jealous of her sister and began to say to Jacob: "Give me children or otherwise I shall be a dead woman." 2 At this Jacob's anger burned against Rachel and he said: "Am I in the place of God, who has held back the fruit of the belly from you?" 3 So she said: "Here is my slave girl Bil'hah. Have relations with her, that she may give birth upon my knees and that I, even I, may get children from her." 4 With that she gave him Bil'hah her maidservant as wife, and Jacob had relations with her. 5 And Bil'hah became pregnant and in time bore Jacob a son. 6 Then Rachel said: "God has acted as my judge and has also listened to my voice, so that he gave me a son." That is why she called his name Dan. 7 And Bil'hah, Rachel's maidservant, became pregnant once more and in time bore a second son to Jacob. 8 Then Rachel said: "With strenuous wrestlings I have wrestled

with my sister. I have also come off winner!" So she called his name Naph'ta·li.

9 When Le'ah came to see that she had left off giving birth, she proceeded to take Zil'pah her maidservant and to give her to Jacob as wife. 10 In time Zil'pah, Le'ah's maidservant, bore a son to Jacob. 11 Then Le'ah said: "With good fortune!" So she called his name Gad. 12 After that Zil'pah, Le'ah's maidservant, bore a second son to Jacob. 13 Then Le'ah said: "With my happiness! For the daughters will certainly pronounce me happy." So she called his name Ash'er.

14 Now Reu'ben went walking in the days of the wheat harvest and got to find mandrakes in the field. So he brought them to Le'ah his mother. Then Rachel said to Le'ah: "Give me, please, some of your son's mandrakes." 15 At this she said to her: "Is this a little thing, your having taken my husband, with your now taking also my son's mandrakes?" So Rachel said: "For that reason he is going to lie down with you tonight in exchange for your son's mandrakes."

16 When Jacob was coming from the field in the evening, Le'ah went on out to meet him and then said: "It is with me you are going to have relations, because I have hired you outright with my son's mandrakes." Accordingly he lay down with her that night. 17 And God heard and answered Le'ah and she became pregnant and in time bore to Jacob a fifth son. 18 Then Le'ah said: "God has given me a hireling's wages, because I have given my maidservant to my husband." So she called his name Is'-sa·char. 19 And Le'ah became pregnant once more and in time bore a sixth son to Jacob. 20 Then Le'ah said: "God has endowed me, yes, me, with a good endowment. At last my husband will tolerate me, because I have borne him six sons." So she called his name Zeb'-u·lun. 21 And afterward she bore a daughter and then called her name Di'nah.

22 Finally God remembered Rachel, and God heard and answered her in that he opened her womb. 23 And she became pregnant and brought a son to birth. Then she said: "God has taken away my reproach!" 24 So she called his name Joseph, saying: "Jehovah is adding another son to me."

25 And it followed that when Rachel had given birth to Joseph, Jacob immediately said to La'ban: "Send me away that I may go to my place and to my country. 26 Give over my wives and my children, for whom I have served with you, that I may go; for you yourself must know my service which I have rendered you." 27 Then La'ban said to him: "If, now, I have found favor in your eyes,—I have taken the omens to the effect that Jehovah is blessing me due to you." 28 And he added: "Stipulate your wages to me and I shall give them." 29 So he said to him: "You yourself must know how I have served you and how your herd has fared with me; 30 that it was little that you actually had before my coming, and it went expanding to a multitude, in that Jehovah blessed you since I stepped in. So now when am I to do something also for my own house?"

31 Then he said: "What shall I give you?" And Jacob went on to say: "You will give me nothing whatsoever! If you will do this thing for me, I shall resume shepherding your flock. I shall continue guarding it. 32 I will pass among your whole flock today. You set aside from there every sheep speckled and with color patches, and every dark-brown sheep among the young rams and any color-patched and speckled one among the she-goats. Hereafter such must be my wages. 33 And my right-doing must answer for me on whatever future day you may come to look over my wages; every one that is not speckled and color-patched among the she-goats and dark brown among the young rams is something stolen if it is with me."

34 To this La'ban said: "Why,

that is fine! Let it be according to your word." 35 Then he set aside on that day the he-goats striped and color-patched and all the she-goats speckled and color-patched, every one in which there was any white and every one dark brown among the young rams, but he gave them over into the hands of his sons. 36 After that he set a distance of three days' journey between himself and Jacob, and Jacob was shepherding the flocks of La′-ban that remained over.

37 Then Jacob took for his use staffs still moist of the storax tree and of the almond tree and of the plane tree and peeled in them white peeled spots by laying bare white places which were upon the staffs. 38 Finally the staffs that he had peeled he placed in front of the flock, in the gutters, in the water drinking troughs, where the flocks would come to drink, that they might get into a heat before them when they came to drink.

39 Consequently the flocks would get in heat before the staffs, and the flocks would produce striped, speckled and color-patched ones. 40 And Jacob separated the young rams and then turned the faces of the flocks to the striped ones and all the dark-brown ones among the flocks of La′ban. Then he set his own droves by themselves and did not set them by the flocks of La′-ban. 41 And it always occurred that whenever the robust flocks would get in heat, Jacob would locate the staffs in the gutters before the eyes of the flocks, that they might get in heat by the staffs. 42 But when the flocks showed feebleness he would not locate them there. So the feeble ones always came to be La′ban's, but the robust ones Jacob's.

43 And the man went on increasing more and more, and great flocks and maidservants and menservants and camels and asses came to be his.

31 In time he got to hear the words of the sons of La′ban, saying: "Jacob has taken everything that belonged to our father;

and from what belonged to our father he has amassed all this wealth." 2 When Jacob would look at the face of La′ban, here it was not with him as formerly. 3 Finally Jehovah said to Jacob: "Return to the land of your fathers and to your relatives, and I shall continue with you." 4 Then Jacob sent and called Rachel and Le′ah out to the field to his flock, 5 and he said to them:

"I am seeing the face of YOUR father, that he is not the same toward me as formerly; but the God of my father has proved to be with me. 6 And YOU yourselves certainly know that with all my power I have served YOUR father. 7 And YOUR father has trifled with me and he has changed my wages ten times, but God has not allowed him to do me harm. 8 If on the one hand he would say, 'The speckled ones will become your wages,' then the whole flock produced speckled ones; but if on the other hand he would say, 'The striped ones will become your wages,' then the whole flock produced striped ones. 9 So God kept taking the herd of YOUR father away and giving it to me. 10 At last it came about at the time when the flock got in heat that I raised my eyes and saw a sight in a dream and here the he-goats springing upon the flock were striped, speckled and spotty. 11 Then the angel of the [true] God said to me in the dream, 'Jacob!' to which I said, 'Here I am.' 12 And he continued, 'Raise your eyes, please, and see all the he-goats springing upon the flock are striped, speckled and spotty, for I have seen all that La′ban is doing to you. 13 I am the [true] God of Beth′el, where you anointed a pillar and where you vowed a vow to me. Now get up, go out of this land and return to the land of your birth.'"

14 At this Rachel and Le′ah answered and said to him: "Is there a share of inheritance for us any more in the house of our father? 15 Are we not really considered as foreigners to him since he has sold

us, so that he keeps eating continually even from the money given for us? 16 For all the riches that God has taken away from our father are ours and our children's. So now everything God has said to you do."

17 Then Jacob got up and lifted his children and his wives onto the camels; 18 and he began driving all his herd and all the goods that he had accumulated, the herd of his acquisition that he had accumulated in Pad'dan-a'ram, in order to go to Isaac his father to the land of Ca'naan.

19 Now La'ban had gone to shear his sheep. Meantime Rachel stole the teraphim that belonged to her father. 20 So Jacob outwitted La'-ban the Syrian, because he had not told him that he was running away. 21 And he proceeded to run away and to get up and cross the River, he and all he had. After that he directed his face to the mountainous region of Gil'e·ad. 22 Later, on the third day, it was told to La'ban that Jacob had run away. 23 With that he took his brothers with him and went chasing after him for a distance of seven days' journey and caught up with him in the mountainous region of Gil'e·ad. 24 Then God came to La'ban the Syrian in a dream by night and said to him: "Watch yourself that you do not go speaking either good or bad with Jacob."

25 So La'ban approached Jacob, as Jacob had pitched his tent in the mountain and La'ban had encamped his brothers in the mountainous region of Gil'e·ad. 26 Then La'ban said to Jacob: "What have you done, in that you resorted to outwitting me and driving my daughters off like captives taken by the sword? 27 Why did you have to run away secretly and outwit me and not tell me, that I might send you away with rejoicing and with songs, with tambourine and with harp? 28 And you did not give me a chance to kiss my children and my daughters. Now you have acted foolishly. 29 It is in

the power of my hand to do harm to YOU people, but the God of YOUR father talked to me last night, saying, 'Watch yourself against speaking either good or bad with Jacob.' 30 While you have actually gone now because you have been yearning intensely for the house of your father, why, though, have you stolen my gods?"

31 In answer Jacob proceeded to say to La'ban: "It was because I was afraid. For I said to myself, 'You might tear your daughters away from me.' 32 Whoever it is with whom you may find your gods, let him not live. Before our brothers, examine for yourself what is with me and take them for yourself." But Jacob did not know that Rachel had stolen them. 33 So La'ban went on into the tent of Jacob and into the tent of Le'ah and into the tent of the two slave girls, but did not find them. Finally he went out of Le'ah's tent and went on into Rachel's tent. 34 Now Rachel had taken the teraphim, and she resorted to putting them in the woman's saddle basket of the camel, and she kept sitting upon them. So La'ban went feeling through the whole tent, but did not find them. 35 Then she said to her father: "Do not let anger gleam in the eyes of my lord, because I am not able to get up before you, for the customary thing with women is upon me." So he searched on carefully, but did not find the teraphim.

36 And Jacob became angry and began to quarrel with La'ban, and in answer Jacob went on to say to La'ban: "What is the revolt on my part, what the sin of mine, as a reason why you have hotly pursued after me? 37 Now that you have felt through all my goods, what of all the goods of your house have you found? Put it here in front of my brothers and your brothers, and let them decide between us two. 38 These twenty years I have been with you. Your female sheep and your she-goats did not suffer abortions, and the rams of your flock I never ate.

39 Any animal torn to pieces I did not bring to you. I myself would stand the loss of it. Whether one was stolen by day or was stolen by night, you would put in a claim for it from my hand. **40** It has been my experience that by day the heat consumed me and the cold by night, and my sleep would flee from my eyes. **41** This makes twenty years for me in your house. I have served you fourteen years for your two daughters and six years for your flock, and you kept changing my wages ten times. **42** If the God of my father, the God of Abraham and the Dread of Isaac, had not proved on my side, you would now have sent me away empty-handed. My wretchedness and the toil of my hands God has seen, and so he reproved you last night."

43 Then La′ban in answer said to Jacob: "The daughters are my daughters and the children my children and the flock my flock, and everything you are looking at is mine and my daughters'. What can I do against these today or against their children whom they have borne? **44** And now, come, let us conclude a covenant, I and you, and it must serve as a witness between me and you." **45** Accordingly Jacob took a stone and set it up as a pillar. **46** Then Jacob said to his brothers: "Pick up stones!" And they went taking stones and making a heap. After that they ate there on the heap. **47** And La′ban began calling it Je′gar-sa·ha·du′tha, but Jacob called it Gal′e·ed.

48 And La′ban proceeded to say: "This heap is a witness between me and you today." That is why he called its name Gal′e·ed, **49** and The Watchtower, because he said: "Let Jehovah keep watch between me and you when we are situated unseen the one from the other. **50** If you go to afflicting my daughters and if you go to taking wives in addition to my daughters, there is no man with us. See! God is a witness between me and you." **51** And La′ban went on to say to

Jacob: "Here is this heap and here is the pillar that I have erected between me and you. **52** This heap is a witness, and the pillar is something that bears witness, that I will not pass this heap against you and that you will not pass this heap and this pillar against me for harm. **53** Let the god of Abraham and the god of Na′hor judge between us, the god of their father." But Jacob swore by the Dread of his father Isaac.

54 After that Jacob sacrificed a sacrifice in the mountain and invited his brothers to eat bread. Accordingly they ate bread and passed the night in the mountain. **55** However, La′ban got up early in the morning and kissed his children and his daughters and blessed them. Then La′ban got on his way that he might return to his own place.

32 And as for Jacob, he got on his way, and the angels of God now met up with him. **2** Immediately Jacob said, when he saw them: "The camp of God this is!" Hence he called the name of that place Ma·ha·na′im.

3 Then Jacob sent messengers ahead of him to E′sau his brother to the land of Se′ir, the field of E′dom, **4** and he commanded them, saying: "This is what you will say to my lord, to E′sau, 'This is what your servant Jacob has said: "With La′ban I have resided as an alien and I have stayed for a long time till now. **5** And I have come to have bulls and asses, sheep, and menservants and maidservants, and I would like to send to notify my lord, that I may find favor in your eyes." ' "

6 In time the messengers returned to Jacob, saying: "We got to your brother E′sau, and he is also on his way to meet you, and four hundred men with him." **7** And Jacob became very much afraid and grew anxious. So he divided the people who were with him, and the flocks and the cattle and the camels into two camps, **8** and he said: "If E′sau should come to the one camp and assault it, then there is certain to be a camp remaining to make an escape."

9 After that Jacob said: "O God of my father Abraham and God of my father Isaac, O Jehovah, you who are saying to me, 'Return to your land and to your relatives and I will deal well with you,' 10 I am unworthy of all the loving-kindnesses and of all the faithfulness that you have exercised toward your servant, for with but my staff I crossed this Jordan and now I have become two camps. 11 Deliver me, I pray you, from my brother's hand, from E'sau's hand, because I am afraid of him that he may come and certainly assault me, mother together with children. 12 And you, you have said, 'Unquestionably I shall deal well with you and I will constitute your seed like the grains of sand of the sea, which cannot be numbered for multitude.' "

13 And he kept lodging there on that night. And from what came to his hand he proceeded to take a gift for E'sau his brother: 14 two hundred she-goats and twenty he-goats, two hundred female sheep and twenty rams, 15 thirty camels giving suck and their young ones, forty cows and ten bulls, twenty she-asses and ten full-grown asses.

16 Then he handed over to his servants one drove after another by itself and repeatedly said to his servants: "Cross over ahead of me, and you are to set an interval between drove and drove." 17 Further he commanded the first one, saying: "In case that E'sau my brother should meet you and ask you, saying, 'To whom do you belong, and where are you going and to whom do these ahead of you belong?' 18 then you must say, 'To your servant, to Jacob. A gift it is, sent to my lord, to E'sau, and look! he himself is also behind us.' " 19 And he went on to command also the second, also the third, also all those following the droves, saying: "According to this word you are to speak to E'sau on your en-

countering him. 20 And you must say also, 'Here is your servant Jacob behind us.' " For he said to himself: "I may appease him by the gift going ahead of me, and afterward I shall see his face. Perhaps he will give a kindly reception." 21 So the gift went crossing over ahead of him, but he himself lodged that night in the camp.

22 Later during that night he rose and took his two wives and his two maidservants and his eleven young sons and crossed over the ford of Jab'bok. 23 So he took them and brought them over the torrent valley, and he brought over what he had.

24 Finally Jacob was left by himself. Then a man began to grapple with him until the dawn ascended. 25 When he got to see that he had not prevailed over him, then he touched the socket of his thigh joint; and the socket of Jacob's thigh joint got out of place during his grappling with him. 26 After that he said: "Let me go, for the dawn has ascended." To this he said: "I am not going to let you go until you first bless me." 27 So he said to him: "What is your name?" to which he said: "Jacob." 28 Then he said: "Your name will no longer be called Jacob but Israel, for you have contended with God and with men so that you at last prevailed." 29 In turn Jacob inquired and said: "Tell me, please, your name." However, he said: "Why is it that you inquire for my name?" With that he blessed him there. 30 Hence Jacob called the name of the place Pe·ni'el, because, to quote him, "I have seen God face to face and yet my soul was delivered."

31 And the sun began to flash upon him as soon as he passed by Pe·nu'el, but he was limping upon his thigh. 32 That is why the sons of Israel are not accustomed to eat the sinew of the thigh nerve, which is on the socket of the thigh joint, down to this day, because he touched the socket of Jacob's thigh joint by the sinew of the thigh nerve.

33 In time Jacob raised his eyes and looked, and here E'sau was coming and with him four hundred men. Consequently he divided off the children to Le'ah and to Rachel and to the two maidservants, 2 and he put the maidservants and their children foremost and Le'ah and her children after them and Rachel and Joseph to the rear of them. 3 And he himself passed on ahead of them and proceeded to bow down to the earth seven times until he got near to his brother.

4 And E'sau went running to meet him, and he began to embrace him and fall upon his neck and kiss him, and they burst into tears. 5 Then he raised his eyes and saw the women and the children and said: "Who are these with you?" to which he said: "The children with whom God has favored your servant." 6 At that the maidservants came forward, they and their children, and bowed down; 7 and Le'ah too came forward, and her children, and they bowed down, and afterward Joseph came forward, and Rachel, and they bowed down.

8 He now said: "What do you mean by all this camp of travelers that I have met?" To this he said: "In order to find favor in the eyes of my lord." 9 Then E'sau said: "I have a great many, my brother. Let continue yours what is yours." 10 However, Jacob said: "No, please, if, now, I have found favor in your eyes, then you must take my gift at my hand, because in harmony with its purpose I have seen your face as though seeing God's face in that you received me with pleasure. 11 Take, please, the gift conveying my blessing which was brought to you, because God has favored me and because I have everything." And he continued to urge him, so that he took it.

12 Later on he said: "Let us pull out and go, and let me go in advance of you." 13 But he said to him: "My lord is aware that the children are delicate and sheep and cattle that are giving suck are in my charge, and should they drive them too quickly for one day, then the whole flock will certainly die. 14 Let my lord, please, pass on ahead of his servant, but may I myself continue the journey at my leisure according to the pace of the livestock that is before me and according to the pace of the children until I shall come to my lord at Se'ir." 15 Then E'sau said: "Let me, please, put at your disposal some of the people who are with me." To this he said: "Why this? Let me find favor in the eyes of my lord." 16 So on that day E'sau turned back on his way to Se'ir.

17 And Jacob pulled out for Suc'coth, and he proceeded to build himself a house and for his herd he made booths. That was why he called the name of the place Suc'coth.

18 In time Jacob came safe and sound to the city of She'chem, which is in the land of Ca'naan, while he was coming from Pad'dan-a'ram; and he pitched camp in front of the city. 19 Then he acquired a tract of the field where he pitched his tent at the hand of the sons of Ha'mor the father of She'chem, for a hundred pieces of money. 20 After that he set up there an altar and called it God the God of Israel.

34 Now Di'nah the daughter of Le'ah, whom she had borne to Jacob, used to go out to see the daughters of the land. 2 And She'chem the son of Ha'mor the Hi'vite, a chieftain of the land, got to see her and then took her and lay down with her and violated her. 3 And his soul began clinging to Di'nah the daughter of Jacob, and he fell in love with the young woman and kept speaking persuasively to the young woman. 4 Finally She'chem said to Ha'mor his father: "Get me this young lady as a wife."

5 And Jacob heard that he had defiled Di'nah his daughter. And his sons happened to be with his herd in the field; and Jacob kept silent until they should come in. 6 Later Ha'mor, She'chem's father,

went out to Jacob to speak with him. 7 And the sons of Jacob came in from the field as soon as they heard of it; and the men became hurt in their feelings and they grew very angry, because he had committed a disgraceful folly against Israel in lying down with Jacob's daughter, whereas nothing like that ought to be done.

8 And Ha'mor proceeded to speak with them, saying: "As for She'chem my son, his soul is attached to YOUR daughter. Give her, please, to him as a wife, 9 and form marriage alliances with us. YOUR daughters YOU are to give to us, and our daughters YOU are to take for yourselves. 10 And with us YOU may dwell, and the land will become available for YOU. Dwell and carry on business in it and get settled in it." 11 Then She'chem said to her father and to her brothers: "Let me find favor in YOUR eyes, and whatever YOU will say to me I shall give it. 12 Raise very high the marriage money and gift imposed upon me, and I stand willing to give according to what YOU may say to me; only give me the young woman as a wife."

13 And Jacob's sons began to answer She'chem and Ha'mor his father with deceit and to speak so because he had defiled Di'nah their sister. 14 And they went on to say to them: "We cannot possibly do such a thing, to give our sister to a man who has a foreskin, because that is a reproach to us. 15 Only on this condition can we give consent to YOU, that YOU become like us, by every male of YOURS getting circumcised. 16 Then we shall certainly give our daughters to YOU, and YOUR daughters we shall take for ourselves, and we shall certainly dwell with YOU and become one people. 17 But if YOU do not listen to us to get circumcised, then we will take our daughter and go."

18 And their words seemed good in the eyes of Ha'mor and in the eyes of She'chem, Ha'mor's son, 19 and the young man did not delay to perform the condition, be-

cause he did find delight in Jacob's daughter and he was the most honorable of the whole house of his father.

20 So Ha'mor and She'chem his son went to the gate of their city and began to speak to the men of their city, saying: 21 "These men are peace-loving toward us. Hence let them dwell in the land and carry on business in it, as the land is quite wide before them. Their daughters we can take as wives for ourselves and our own daughters we can give to them. 22 Only on this condition will the men give us their consent to dwell with us so as to become one people, that every male of ours gets circumcised just the way they are circumcised. 23 Then their possessions and their wealth and all their livestock, will they not be ours? Only let us give them our consent that they may dwell with us." 24 Then all those going out by the gate of his city listened to Ha'mor and to She'chem his son, and all the males got circumcised, all those going out by the gate of his city.

25 However, it came about that on the third day, when they got to be aching, the two sons of Jacob, Sim'e·on and Le'vi, brothers of Di'nah, proceeded to take each one his sword and to go unsuspectedly to the city and to kill every male. 26 And Ha'mor and She'chem his son they killed with the edge of the sword. Then they took Di'nah from She'chem's house and went on out. 27 The other sons of Jacob attacked the fatally wounded men and went plundering the city, because they had defiled their sister. 28 Their flocks and their herds and their asses and what was in the city and what was in the field they took. 29 And all their means of maintenance and all their little children and their wives they carried off captive, so that they plundered all that was in the houses.

30 At this Jacob said to Sim'e·on and to Le'vi: "You have brought ostracism upon me in making me a stench to the inhabitants of the land, with the Ca'naan·ites and the

Per'iz·zites; whereas I am few in number, and they will certainly gather together against me and assault me and I must be annihilated, I and my house." 31 In turn they said: "Ought anyone to treat our sister like a prostitute?"

35 After that God said to Jacob: "Rise, go up to Beth'el and dwell there, and make an altar there to the [true] God who appeared to you when you were running away from E'sau your brother."

2 Then Jacob said to his household and to all who were with him: "Put away the foreign gods that are in the midst of YOU and cleanse yourselves and change YOUR mantles, 3 and let us rise and go up to Beth'el. And there I shall make an altar to the [true] God who answered me in the day of my distress in that he proved to be with me in the way that I have gone." 4 So they gave Jacob all the foreign gods that were in their hands and the earrings that were in their ears, and Jacob hid them under the big tree that was close by She'chem.

5 After that he pulled away, and the terror of God came to be upon the cities that were round about them, so that they did not chase after the sons of Jacob. 6 Eventually Jacob came to Luz, which is in the land of Ca'naan, that is to say, Beth'el, he and all the people who were with him. 7 Then he built an altar there and began to call the place El-beth'el, because there the [true] God had revealed himself to him at the time of his running away from his brother. 8 Later Deb'o·rah the nursing woman of Re·bek'ah died and was buried at the foot of Beth'el under a massive tree. Hence he called its name Al'lon-bac'uth.

9 God now appeared to Jacob once again during his coming from Pad'dan-a'ram and blessed him. 10 And God went on to say to him: "Your name is Jacob. No longer is your name to be called Jacob, but Israel will your name become." And he began to call his name Israel. 11 And God said further to him:

"I am God Almighty. Be fruitful and become many. Nations and a congregation of nations will proceed out of you, and kings will come out of your loins. 12 As for the land that I have given to Abraham and to Isaac, to you I shall give it, and to your seed after you I shall give the land." 13 After that God went up from above him at the place where he had spoken with him.

14 Consequently Jacob stationed a pillar in the place where he had spoken with him, a pillar of stone, and he poured a drink offering upon it and poured oil upon it. 15 And Jacob continued to call the name of the place where God had spoken with him Beth'el.

16 Then he pulled away from Beth'el. And while there was yet a good stretch of land before coming to Eph'rath, Rachel proceeded to give birth, and it was going hard with her in making the delivery. 17 But so it was that while she had difficulty in making the delivery the midwife said to her: "Do not be afraid, for you will have this son also." 18 And the result was that as her soul was going out (because she died) she called his name Ben-o'ni; but his father called him Benjamin. 19 Thus Rachel died and was buried on the way to Eph'rath, that is to say, Beth'le·hem. 20 Hence Jacob stationed a pillar over her grave. This is the pillar of Rachel's grave down to this day.

21 After that Israel pulled away and pitched his tent a distance beyond the tower of E'der. 22 And it came about while Israel was tabernacling in that land that once Reu'ben went and lay down with Bil'hah his father's concubine, and Israel got to hear of it.

So there came to be twelve sons of Jacob. 23 The sons by Le'ah were Jacob's first-born Reu'ben and Sim'e·on and Le'vi and Judah and Is'sa·char and Zeb'u·lun. 24 The sons by Rachel were Joseph and Benjamin. 25 And the sons by Bil'hah, Rachel's maidservant, were Dan and Naph'ta·li. 26 And the sons by Zil'pah, Le'ah's maidservant, were Gad and Ash'er. These are Jacob's sons who were born to him in Pad'dan-a'ram.

27 At length Jacob came to Isaac his father to Mam're, to Kir'i·ath-ar'ba, that is to say, He'bron, where Abraham and also Isaac had resided as aliens. 28 And the days of Isaac came to be a hundred and eighty years. 29 After that Isaac expired and died and was gathered to his people, old and satisfied with days, and E'sau and Jacob his sons buried him.

36 And this is the history of E'sau, that is to say, E'dom.

2 E'sau took his wives from the daughters of Ca'naan: A'dah the daughter of E'lon the Hit'tite and O·hol·i·ba'mah the daughter of A'nah, the granddaughter of Zib'-e·on the Hi'vite, 3 and Bas'e-math, Ish'ma·el's daughter, the sister of Ne·ba'ioth.

4 And A'dah proceeded to bear El'i·phaz to E'sau, and Bas'e·math bore Reu'el.

5 and O·hol·i·ba'mah bore Je'-ush and Ja'lam and Ko'rah.

These are the sons of E'sau who were born to him in the land of Ca'naan. 6 After that E'sau took his wives and his sons and his daughters and all the souls of his house and his herd and all his other beasts and all his wealth, which he had accumulated in the land of Ca'naan, and went to a land away from Jacob his brother, 7 because their goods had become too great for them to dwell together and the land of their alien residences was not able to sustain them as a result of their herds. 8 So E'sau took up dwelling in the mountainous region of Se'ir. E'sau is E'dom.

9 And this is the history of E'sau the father of E'dom in the mountainous region of Se'ir.

10 These are the names of the sons of E'sau: El'i·phaz the son of A'dah, E'sau's wife; Reu'el the son of Bas'e·math, E'sau's wife.

11 And the sons of El'i·phaz came to be Te'man, O'mar, Ze'pho and Ga'tam and Ke'naz. 12 And Tim'na became the concubine of El'i·phaz, E'sau's son. In time she bore to El'i·phaz Am'a·lek. These are the sons of A'dah, E'sau's wife.

13 These are the sons of Reu'el: Na'hath and Ze'rah, Sham'mah and Miz'zah. These came to be the sons of Bas'e·math, E'sau's wife.

14 And these came to be the sons of O·hol·i·ba'mah the daughter of A'nah, the granddaughter of Zib'e·on, E'sau's wife, in that she bore to E'sau Je'ush and Ja'-lam and Ko'rah.

15 These are the sheiks of the sons of E'sau: The sons of El'i-phaz, E'sau's first-born: Sheik Te'-man, sheik O'mar, sheik Ze'pho, sheik Ke'naz, 16 sheik Ko'rah, sheik Ga'tam, sheik Am'a·lek. These are the sheiks of El'i·phaz in the land of E'dom. These are the sons by A'dah.

17 These are the sons of Reu'el, E'sau's son: Sheik Na'hath, sheik Ze'rah, sheik Sham'mah, sheik Miz'zah. These are the sheiks of Reu'el in the land of E'dom. These are the sons by Bas'e·math, E'sau's wife.

18 Finally these are the sons of O·hol·i·ba'mah, E'sau's wife: Sheik Je'ush, sheik Ja'lam, sheik Ko'rah. These are the sheiks of O·hol·i-ba'mah the daughter of A'nah, E'sau's wife.

19 These are the sons of E'sau, and these are their sheiks. He is E'dom.

20 These are the sons of Se'ir the Ho'rite, the inhabitants of the land: Lo'tan and Sho'bal and Zib'-e·on and A'nah 21 and Di'shon and E'zer and Di'shan. These are the sheiks of the Ho'rite, the sons of Se'ir, in the land of E'dom.

22 And the sons of Lo'tan came to be Ho'ri and He'mam; and Lo'-tan's sister was Tim'na.

23 And these are the sons of Sho'bal: Al'van and Man'a·hath and E'bal, She'pho and O'nam.

24 And these are the sons of Zib'e·on: A'iah and A'nah. This is the A'nah who found the hot springs in the wilderness while he was tending the asses for Zib'e·on his father.

25 And these are the children of A'nah: Di'shon and O·hol·i·ba'mah the daughter of A'nah.

26 And these are the sons of Di'shon: Hem'dan and Esh'ban and Ith'ran and Che'ran.

27 These are the sons of E'zer: Bil'han and Za'a·van and A'kan.

28 These are the sons of Di'shan: Uz and A'ran.

29 These are the sheiks of the Ho'rite: Sheik Lo'tan, sheik Sho'bal, sheik Zib'e·on, sheik A'nah, 30 sheik Di'shon, sheik E'zer, sheik Di'shan. These are the sheiks of the Ho'rite according to their sheiks in the land of Se'ir.

31 Now these are the kings who reigned in the land of E'dom before any king reigned over the sons of Israel. 32 And Be'la son of Be'or proceeded to reign in E'dom, and the name of his city was Din'habah. 33 And Be'la died, Jo'bab son of Ze'rah from Boz'rah began to reign instead of him. 34 When Jo'bab died, Hu'sham from the land of the Te'man·ites began to reign instead of him. 35 When Hu'sham died, Ha'dad son of Be'dad, who defeated the Mid'i·an·ites in the field of Mo'ab, began to reign instead of him, and the name of his city was A'vith. 36 When Ha'dad died, Sam'lah from Mas·re'kah began to reign instead of him. 37 When Sam'lah died, Sha'ul from Re·ho'both by the River began to reign instead of him. 38 When Sha'ul died, Ba'al-ha'nan son of Ach'bor began to reign instead of him. 39 When Ba'al-ha'nan son of Ach'bor died, Ha'dar began to reign instead of him; and the name of his city was Pa'u, and the name of his wife was Me·het'a·bel the daughter of Ma'tred the daughter of Me'za·hab.

40 So these are the names of the sheiks of E'sau according to their families, according to their places, by their names: Sheik Tim'na, sheik Al'vah, sheik Je'theth, 41 sheik O·hol·i·ba'mah, sheik E'lah, sheik Pi'non, 42 sheik Ke'naz, sheik Te'man, sheik Mib'zar, 43 sheik Mag'di·el, sheik I'ram. These are the sheiks of E'dom according to

their dwellings in the land of their possession. This is E'sau the father of E'dom.

37 And Jacob continued to dwell in the land of the alien residences of his father, in the land of Ca'naan.

2 This is the history of Jacob.

Joseph, when seventeen years old, happened to be tending sheep with his brothers among the flock, and, being but a boy, he was with the sons of Bil'hah and the sons of Zil'pah, the wives of his father. So Joseph brought a bad report about them to their father. 3 And Israel loved Joseph more than all his other sons, because he was the son of his old age; and he had a long, striped shirtlike garment made for him. 4 When his brothers came to see that their father loved him more than all his brothers, they began to hate him, and they were not able to speak peacefully to him.

5 Later on Joseph had a dream and told it to his brothers, and they found further reason to hate him. 6 And he went on to say to them: "Listen, please, to this dream that I have dreamed. 7 Well, here we were binding sheaves in the middle of the field when here my sheaf got up and also stood erect and here your sheaves proceeded to encircle and bow down to my sheaf." 8 And his brothers began to say to him: "Are you going to be king over us for certain? or, Are you going to dominate over us for certain?" So they found fresh reason to hate him over his dreams and over his words.

9 After that he had still another dream, and he related it to his brothers and said: "Here I have had a dream once more, and here the sun and the moon and eleven stars were bowing down to me." 10 Then he related it to his father as well as his brothers, and his father began to rebuke him and say to him: "What does this dream that you have dreamed mean? Am I and also your mother and your brothers for certain going to come and bow down to the earth to you?" 11 And his brothers grew

jealous of him, but his father observed the saying.

12 His brothers now went to feed the flock of their father close by She'chem. 13 After a while Israel said to Joseph: "Your brothers are tending flocks close by She'chem, are they not? Come, and let me send you to them." At this he said to him: "Here I am!" 14 So he said to him: "Go, please. See whether your brothers are safe and sound and whether the flock is safe and sound, and bring me back word." With that he sent him away from the low plain of He'bron, and he went on toward She'chem. 15 Later a man found him and here he was wandering in a field. Then the man inquired of him, saying: "What are you looking for?" 16 To this he said: "It is my brothers I am looking for. Tell me, please, Where are they tending flocks?" 17 And the man continued: "They have pulled away from here, because I heard them saying, 'Let us go to Do'than.'" So Joseph kept on after his brothers and found them at Do'than.

18 Well, they caught sight of him from a distance, and before he could get close by them they began plotting cunningly against him to put him to death. 19 So they said to one another: "Look! Here comes that dreamer. 20 And now come and let us kill him and pitch him into one of the waterpits; and we must say a vicious wild beast devoured him. Then let us see what will become of his dreams." 21 When Reu'ben heard this he tried to deliver him out of their hand. So he said: "Let us not strike his soul fatally." 22 And Reu'ben went on to say to them: "Do not spill blood. Pitch him into this waterpit which is in the wilderness and do not lay a violent hand upon him." His purpose was to deliver him out of their hand in order to return him to his father.

23 So it came about that as soon as Joseph came to his brothers, they went stripping Joseph of his long garment, even the long striped garment that was upon him;

24 after which they took him and pitched him into the waterpit. At the time the pit was empty; there was no water in it.

25 Then they sat down to eat bread. When they raised their eyes and took a look, why, here was a caravan of Ish'ma·el·ites that was coming from Gil'e·ad, and their camels were carrying labdanum and balsam and resinous bark, on their way to take it down to Egypt. 26 At this Judah said to his brothers: "What profit would there be in case we killed our brother and did cover over his blood? 27 Come and let us sell him to the Ish'ma·el·ites, and do not let our hand be upon him. After all, he is our brother, our flesh." So they listened to their brother. 28 Now men, Mid'i·an·ite merchants, went passing by. Hence they drew and lifted up Joseph out of the waterpit and then sold Joseph to the Ish'ma·el·ites for twenty silver pieces. Eventually these brought Joseph into Egypt.

29 Later Reu'ben returned to the waterpit and here Joseph was not in the waterpit. Consequently he ripped his garments apart. 30 When he returned to his other brothers he exclaimed: "The child is gone! And I—where am I really to go?"

31 However, they took Joseph's long garment and slaughtered a male goat and repeatedly dipped the long garment in the blood. 32 After that they sent the long striped garment and had it brought to their father and said: "This is what we found. Examine, please, whether it is your son's long garment or not." 33 And he went examining it and exclaimed: "It is my son's long garment! A vicious wild beast must have devoured him! Joseph is surely torn to pieces!" 34 With that Jacob ripped his mantles apart and put sackcloth upon his hips and carried on mourning over his son for many days. 35 And all his sons and all his daughters kept rising up to comfort him, but he kept refusing to take comfort and saying: "For

I shall go down mourning to my son into She'ol!" And his father continued weeping for him. 36 However, the Mid'i·an·ites sold him into Egypt to Pot'i·phar a court official of Phar'aoh, the chief of the bodyguard.

38 Now in the meantime it came about that when Judah went down from his brothers he pitched his tent near a man, an A·dul'lam·ite, and his name was Hi'rah. 2 And there Judah got to see a daughter of a certain Ca'naan·ite, and his name was Shu'a. So he took her and had relations with her. 3 And she became pregnant. Later she bore a son and he called his name Er. 4 Again she became pregnant. In time she bore a son and called his name O'nan. 5 Yet another time she went on to bear a son and then called his name She'lah. Now he happened to be in Ach'zib at the time she bore him.

6 In time Judah took a wife for Er his first-born, and her name was Ta'mar. 7 But Er, Judah's first-born, proved to be bad in the eyes of Jehovah; hence Jehovah put him to death. 8 In view of that Judah said to O'nan: "Have relations with your brother's wife and perform brother-in-law marriage with her and raise up offspring for your brother." 9 But O'nan knew that the offspring would not become his; and it occurred that when he did have relations with his brother's wife he wasted his semen on the earth so as not to give offspring to his brother. 10 Now what he did was bad in the eyes of Jehovah; hence he put him also to death. 11 So Judah said to Ta'mar his daughter-in-law: "Dwell as a widow in the house of your father until She'lah my son grows up." For he said to himself: "He too may die like his brothers." Accordingly Ta'mar went and continued to dwell at her own father's house.

12 Thus the days became many and the daughter of Shu'a, Judah's wife, died; and Judah kept the period of mourning. After that he went up to the shearers of his sheep, he and Hi'rah his companion the A·dul'lam·ite, to Tim'nah. 13 Then it was told to Ta'mar: "Here your father-in-law is going up to Tim'nah to shear his sheep." 14 With that she removed the garments of her widowhood from her and covered herself with a shawl and veiled herself and sat down at the entrance of E·na'im, which is along the road to Tim'nah. For she saw that She'lah had grown up and yet she had not been given as a wife to him.

15 When Judah caught sight of her, he at once took her for a harlot, because she had covered her face. 16 So he turned aside to her by the road and said: "Allow me, please, to have relations with you." For he did not know that she was his daughter-in-law. However, she said: "What will you give me that you may have relations with me?" 17 To this he said: "I myself shall send a kid of the goats from the herd." But she said: "Will you give a security until you send it?" 18 And he continued: "What is the security that I shall give you?" to which she said: "Your seal ring and your cord and your rod that is in your hand." Then he gave them to her and had relations with her, so that she became pregnant by him. 19 After that she got up and went and removed her shawl off her and clothed herself with the garments of her widowhood.

20 And Judah proceeded to send the kid of the goats by the hand of his companion the A·dul'lam·ite in order to get back the security from the hand of the woman, but he never found her. 21 And he went inquiring of the men of her place, saying: "Where is that temple prostitute in E·na'im along the road?" But they kept saying: "No temple prostitute has ever been in this place." 22 Finally he returned to Judah and said: "I never found her and, besides, the men of the place said, 'No temple prostitute has ever been in this place.'" 23 So Judah said: "Let her take them for herself, in order that we

may not fall into contempt. At any rate, I have sent this kid, but you—you never found her."

24 However, about three months later it happened that it was told to Judah: "Ta′mar your daughter-in-law has played the harlot, and here she is also pregnant by her harlotry." At that Judah said: "BRING her out and let her be burned." 25 As she was being brought out she herself sent to her father-in-law, saying: "By the man to whom these belong I am pregnant." And she added: "Examine, please, to whom these belong, the seal ring and the cord and the rod." 26 Then Judah examined them and said: "She is more righteous than I am, for the reason that I did not give her to She′lah my son." And he had no further intercourse with her after that.

27 Now it developed that in the time of her giving birth, why, here there were twins in her belly. 28 Further, it turned out that when she was giving birth one extended his hand, and the midwife at once took and tied a scarlet piece about his hand, saying: "This one came out first." 29 Finally it developed that as soon as he drew back his hand, why, here his brother came out, so that she exclaimed: "What do you mean by this, that you have produced a perineal rupture for yourself?" Hence his name was called Pe′rez. 30 And afterward his brother upon whose hand the scarlet piece was came out and his name came to be called Ze′rah.

39 As for Joseph, he was brought down to Egypt, and Pot′i·phar, a court official of Phar′aoh, the chief of the bodyguard, an Egyptian, got to buy him from the hand of the Ish′ma·el·ites who had brought him down there. 2 But Jehovah proved to be with Joseph, so that he turned out a successful man and came to be over the house of his master, the Egyptian. 3 And his master got to see that Jehovah was with him and that everything he was doing Jehovah was making turn out successful in his hand.

4 And Joseph kept finding favor in his eyes and waited upon him continually, so that he appointed him over his house, and all that was his he gave into his hand. 5 And it followed that from the time he appointed him over his house and in charge of all that was his Jehovah kept blessing the house of the Egyptian due to Joseph, and Jehovah's blessing came to be upon all that he had in the house and in the field. 6 Finally he left everything that was his in Joseph's hand; and he did not know what was with him at all except the bread he was eating. Moreover, Joseph grew to be beautiful in form and beautiful in appearance.

7 Now after these things it came about that the wife of his master began to raise her eyes toward Joseph and say: "Lie down with me." 8 But he would refuse and would say to his master's wife: "Here my master does not know what is with me in the house, and everything he has he has given into my hand. 9 There is no one greater in this house than I am, and he has not withheld from me anything at all except you, because you are his wife. So how could I commit this great badness and actually sin against God?"

10 So it turned out that as she spoke to Joseph day after day he never listened to her to lie alongside her, to continue with her. 11 But it happened that on this day as other days he went into the house to do his business, and there was none of the men of the house there in the house. 12 Then she grabbed hold of him by his garment, saying: "Lie down with me!" But he left his garment in her hand and took to flight and went on outside. 13 So it occurred that as soon as she saw that he had left his garment in her hand that he might flee outside, 14 she began to cry out to the men of her house and to say to them: "Look! He brought to us a man, a Hebrew, to make us a laughingstock. He came to me to lie down with me, but I began to cry out at the top of my voice. 15 And it followed that

as soon as he heard that I raised my voice and began crying out, he then left his garment beside me and took to flight and went on outside." 16 After that she kept his garment laid up beside her until his master came to his house.

17 Then she spoke to him according to these words, saying: "The Hebrew servant whom you brought to us came to me to make me a laughingstock. 18 But it followed that as soon as I raised my voice and began to cry out, he then left his garment beside me and went fleeing outside." 19 The result was that as soon as his master heard the words of his wife which she spoke to him, saying: "Like this and this your servant did to me," his anger blazed. 20 So Joseph's master took him and gave him over to the prison house, the place where the prisoners of the king were kept under arrest, and he continued there in the prison house.

21 However, Jehovah continued with Joseph and kept extending loving-kindness to him and granting him to find favor in the eyes of the chief officer of the prison house. 22 So the chief officer of the prison house gave over into Joseph's hand all the prisoners who were in the prison house; and everything that they were doing there he proved to be the one having it done. 23 The chief officer of the prison house was looking after absolutely nothing that was in his hand, because Jehovah was with Joseph and what he was doing Jehovah was making it turn out successful.

40 Now after these things it came about that the cupbearer of the king of Egypt and the baker sinned against their lord the king of Egypt. 2 And Phar'aoh grew indignant at his two officers, at the chief of the cupbearers and at the chief of the bakers. 3 So he committed them to the jail of the house of the chief of the bodyguard, to the prison house, the place where Joseph was a prisoner. 4 Then the chief of the bodyguard assigned Joseph to be with them that he might wait upon them; and they continued in jail for some days.

5 And both of them proceeded to dream a dream, each one his own dream in the one night, each one his dream with its own interpretation, the cupbearer and the baker who belonged to the king of Egypt who were prisoners in the prison house. 6 When Joseph came in to them in the morning and saw them, why, here they were looking dejected. 7 And he began to inquire of the officers of Phar'aoh who were with him in the jail of his master's house, saying: "For what reason are YOUR faces gloomy today?" 8 At this they said to him: "We have dreamed a dream, and there is no interpreter with us." So Joseph said to them: "Do not interpretations belong to God? Relate it to me, please."

9 And the chief of the cupbearers went on to relate his dream to Joseph and to say to him: "In my dream, why, here there was a vine before me. 10 And on the vine there were three twigs, and it was apparently sprouting shoots. Its blossoms pushed forth. Its clusters ripened their grapes. 11 And Phar'aoh's cup was in my hand, and I proceeded to take the grapes and squeeze them out into Phar'aoh's cup. After that I gave the cup into Phar'aoh's hand." 12 Then Joseph said to him: "This is its interpretation: The three twigs are three days. 13 In three days from now Phar'aoh will lift up your head and he will certainly return you to your office; and you will certainly give Phar'aoh's cup into his hand, according to the former custom when you acted as his cupbearer. 14 Nevertheless, you must keep me in your remembrance as soon as it goes well with you, and you must, please, perform loving-kindness with me and mention me to Phar'aoh, and you must get me out of this house. 15 For I was in fact kidnaped from the land of the Hebrews; and here also I have done nothing at all for which they should put me in the prison hole."

16 When the chief of the bakers saw that he had interpreted something good, he, in turn, said to Joseph: "I too was in my dream, and here there were three baskets of white bread upon my head, 17 and in the topmost basket there were all sorts of eatables for Phar'-aoh, the product of a baker, and there were fowls eating them out of the basket on top of my head." 18 Then Joseph answered and said: "This is its interpretation: The three baskets are three days. 19 In three days from now Phar'aoh will lift up your head from off you and will certainly hang you upon a stake; and the fowls will certainly eat your flesh from off you."

20 Now on the third day it turned out to be Phar'aoh's birthday, and he proceeded to make a feast for all his servants and to lift up the head of the chief of the cupbearers and the head of the chief of the bakers in the midst of his servants. 21 Accordingly he returned the chief of the cupbearers to his post of cupbearer, and he continued to give the cup into Phar'aoh's hand. 22 But the chief of the bakers he hung up, just as Joseph had given them the interpretation. 23 However, the chief of the cupbearers did not remember Joseph and went on forgetting him.

41 And it came about at the end of two full years that Phar'aoh was dreaming and here he was standing by the river Nile. 2 And here ascending out of the river Nile were seven cows beautiful in appearance and fat-fleshed, and they went feeding among the Nile grass. 3 And here there were seven other cows ascending after them out of the river Nile, ugly in appearance and thin-fleshed, and they took their stand alongside the cows by the bank of the river Nile. 4 Then the cows that were ugly in appearance and thin-fleshed began to eat up the seven cows that were beautiful in appearance and fat. At this Phar'aoh woke up.

5 However, he went back to sleep and dreamed a second time. And here there were seven ears of grain coming up on one stalk, fat and good. 6 And here there were seven ears of grain, thin and scorched by the east wind, growing up after them. 7 And the thin ears of grain began to swallow up the seven fat and full ears of grain. At this Phar'aoh woke up and here it was a dream.

8 And it developed in the morning that his spirit became agitated. So he sent and called all the magic-practicing priests of Egypt and all her wise men, and Phar'-aoh went on to relate his dreams to them. But there was no interpreter of them for Phar'aoh.

9 Then the chief of the cupbearers spoke with Phar'aoh, saying: "My sins I am mentioning today. 10 Phar'aoh was indignant at his servants. So he committed me to the jail of the house of the chief of the bodyguard, both me and the chief of the bakers. 11 After that we both dreamed a dream in the one night, both I and he. We dreamed each one his dream with its own interpretation. 12 And there was with us there a young man, a Hebrew, a servant of the chief of the bodyguard. When we related them to him, he proceeded to interpret our dreams to us. He interpreted to each according to his dream. 13 And it turned out that just as he had interpreted to us so it happened. Me he returned to my office, but him he hanged."

14 And Phar'aoh proceeded to send and to call Joseph, that they might bring him quickly from the prison hole. Hence he shaved and changed his mantles and went in to Phar'aoh. 15 Then Phar'aoh said to Joseph: "I have dreamed a dream, but there is no interpreter of it. Now I myself have heard it said about you that you can hear a dream and interpret it." 16 At this Joseph answered Phar'aoh, saying: "I need not be considered! God will announce welfare for Phar'aoh."

17 And Phar'aoh went on to speak to Joseph: "In my dream

here I was standing on the bank of the river Nile. 18 And here ascending out of the river Nile were seven cows fat-fleshed and beautiful in form, and they began to feed among the Nile grass. 19 And here there were seven other cows ascending after them, poor and very bad in form and thin-fleshed. For badness I have not seen the like of them in all the land of Egypt. 20 And the skinny and bad cows began to eat up the first seven fat cows. 21 So these came into their bellies, and yet it could not be known that they had come into their bellies, as their appearance was bad just as at the start. At that I woke up.

22 "After that I saw in my dream and here there were seven ears of grain coming up on one stalk, full and good. 23 And here there were seven ears of grain shriveled, thin, scorched by the east wind, growing up after them. 24 And the thin ears of grain began to swallow up the seven good ears of grain. So I stated it to the magic-practicing priests, but there was none telling me."

25 Then Joseph said to Phar'aoh: "The dream of Phar'aoh is but one. What the [true] God is doing he has told to Phar'aoh. 26 The seven good cows are seven years. Likewise the seven good ears of grain are seven years. The dream is but one. 27 And the seven skinny and bad cows that came up after them are seven years; and the seven empty ears of grain, scorched by the east wind, will prove to be seven years of famine. 28 This is the thing that I have spoken to Phar'aoh: What the [true] God is doing he has caused Phar'aoh to see.

29 "Here there are seven years coming with great plenty in all the land of Egypt. 30 But seven years of famine will certainly arise after them, and all the plenty in the land of Egypt will certainly be forgotten and the famine will simply consume the land. 31 And the plenty once in the land will not be known as a result of that famine afterward, because it will certainly be very severe. 32 And the fact that the dream was repeated to Phar'aoh twice means that the thing is firmly established on the part of the [true] God, and the [true] God is speeding to do it.

33 "So now let Phar'aoh look for a man discreet and wise and set him over the land of Egypt. 34 Let Phar'aoh act and appoint overseers over the land, and he must take up one fifth of the land of Egypt during the seven years of plenty. 35 And let them collect all the foodstuffs of these coming good years, and let them pile up grain under Phar'aoh's hand as foodstuffs in the cities, and they must safeguard it. 36 And the foodstuffs must serve as a supply for the land for the seven famine years, which will develop in the land of Egypt, in order that the land may not be cut off by the famine."

37 Well, the thing proved to be good in the eyes of Phar'aoh and of all his servants. 38 So Phar'aoh said to his servants: "Can another man be found like this one in whom the spirit of God is?" 39 After that Phar'aoh said to Joseph: "Since God has caused you to know all this, there is no one as discreet and wise as you are. 40 You will personally be over my house, and all my people will obey you implicitly. Only as to the throne shall I be greater than you." 41 And Phar'aoh added to Joseph: "See, I do place you over all the land of Egypt." 42 With that Phar'aoh removed his signet ring from his own hand and put it upon Joseph's hand and clothed him with garments of fine linen and placed a necklace of gold about his neck. 43 Moreover, he had him ride in the second chariot of honor that he had, so that they should call out ahead of him, "*A·vrékh!*" thus putting him over all the land of Egypt.

44 And Phar'aoh further said to Joseph: "I am Phar'aoh, but without your authorization no man may

lift up his hand or his foot in all the land of Egypt." 45 After that Phar'aoh called Joseph's name Zaph'e·nath-pa·ne'ah and gave him As'e·nath the daughter of Pot·i'phe·ra the priest of On as a wife. And Joseph began to go out over the land of Egypt. 46 And Joseph was thirty years old when he stood before Phar'aoh the king of Egypt.

Then Joseph went out from before Phar'aoh and toured about in all the land of Egypt. 47 And during the seven years of plenty the land went on producing by the handfuls. 48 And he kept collecting all the foodstuffs of the seven years that came upon the land of Egypt and he would put the foodstuffs in the cities. The foodstuffs of the field that was round about a city he put in the midst of it. 49 And Joseph continued piling up grain in very great quantity, like the sand of the sea, until finally they gave up counting it, because it was without number.

50 And before the year of the famine arrived there were born to Joseph two sons, whom As'e·nath the daughter of Pot·i'phe·ra the priest of On bore to him. 51 So Joseph called the name of the first-born Ma·nas'seh, because, to quote him, "God has made me forget all my trouble and all the house of my father." 52 And the name of the second he called E'phra·im, because, to quote him, "God has made me fruitful in the land of my wretchedness."

53 And the seven years of the plenty that had obtained in the land of Egypt gradually ended, 54 and, in turn, the seven years of the famine started to come, just as Joseph had said. And the famine developed in all the lands, but in all the land of Egypt there was found bread. 55 Finally all the land of Egypt became famished and the people began to cry to Phar'aoh for bread. Then Phar'aoh said to all the Egyptians: "Go to Joseph. Whatever he says to you, you are to do." 56 And the famine obtained over all the surface of the earth. Then Joseph began to open up all the grain depositories that were among them and to sell to the Egyptians, as the famine got a strong grip on the land of Egypt. 57 Moreover, people of all the earth came to Egypt to buy from Joseph, because the famine had a strong grip on all the earth.

42 Eventually Jacob got to see that there were cereals in Egypt. Then Jacob said to his sons: "Why do you keep looking at one another?" 2 And he added: "Here I have heard that there are cereals in Egypt. Go down there and buy for us from there, that we may keep alive and not die off." 3 Accordingly ten brothers of Joseph went down to buy grain from Egypt. 4 But Jacob did not send Benjamin, Joseph's brother, with his other brothers, because he said: "Otherwise a fatal accident may befall him."

5 So Israel's sons came along with the others who were coming to buy, because the famine existed in the land of Ca'naan. 6 And Joseph was the man in power over the land. He was the one that did the selling to all people of the earth. Consequently Joseph's brothers came and bowed low to him with their faces to the earth. 7 When Joseph got to see his brothers, he at once recognized them, but he made himself unrecognizable to them. So he spoke harshly with them and said to them: "Where have you come from?" to which they said: "From the land of Ca'naan to buy foodstuffs."

8 Thus Joseph recognized his brothers, but they themselves did not recognize him. 9 Immediately Joseph remembered the dreams that he had dreamed respecting them, and he went on to say to them: "You are spies! You have come to see the exposed condition of the land!" 10 Then they said to him: "No, my lord, but your servants have come to buy foodstuffs. 11 We are all of us sons of but one man. We are upright men. Your servants do not act as

spies." 12 But he said to them: "Not so! Because you have come to see the exposed condition of the land!" 13 At this they said: "Your servants are twelve brothers. We are the sons of but one man in the land of Ca'naan; and here the youngest is with our father today, whereas the other one is no more."

14 However, Joseph said to them: "It is what I have spoken to you, saying, 'You are spies!' 15 By this you will be tested out. As Phar'aoh lives, you will not go out of here except when your youngest brother comes here. 16 Send one of you that he may get your brother while you have been bound, that your words may be tested out as the truth in your case. And if not, then, as Phar'aoh lives, you are spies." 17 With that he put them together in custody for three days.

18 After that Joseph said to them on the third day: "Do this and keep alive. I fear the [true] God. 19 If you are upright, let one of your brothers be kept bound in your house of custody, but the rest of you go, take cereals for the famine in your houses. 20 Then you will bring your youngest brother to me, that your words may be found trustworthy; and you will not die." And they proceeded to do so.

21 And they began to say one to the other: "Unquestionably we are guilty with regard to our brother, because we saw the distress of his soul when he implored compassion on our part, but we did not listen. That is why this distress has come upon us." 22 Then Reu'ben answered them, saying: "Did not I say to you, 'Do not sin against the child,' but you did not listen? And now his blood, here it is certainly asked back." 23 As for them, they did not know that Joseph was listening, because there was an interpreter between them. Consequently he turned away from them and began to weep. Then he returned to them and spoke to them and took Sim'e·on from them and bound him before their eyes. 25 After that Joseph gave the

command, and they went filling up their receptacles with grain. Also, they were to return the money of the men to each one's individual sack and to give them provisions for the journey. Accordingly it was done so to them.

26 So they loaded their cereals upon their asses and got on their way from there. 27 When one opened his sack to give fodder to his ass at the lodging place, he got to see his money, and here it was in the mouth of his bag. 28 At that he said to his brothers: "My money has been returned and now here it is in my bag!" Then their hearts sank, so that they turned trembling to one another, saying: "What is this God has done to us?"

29 At length they came to Jacob their father to the land of Ca'naan and told him all the things that had befallen them, saying: 30 "The man who is the lord of the country spoke harshly with us, since he took us for men spying on the country. 31 But we said to him, 'We are upright men. We do not act as spies. 32 We are twelve brothers, the sons of our father. One is no more, and the youngest is today with our father in the land of Ca'naan.' 33 But the man who is the lord of the country said to us, 'By this I am going to know you are upright: Have one brother of yours stay with me. Then you take something for the famine in your houses and go. 34 And bring your youngest brother to me, that I may know that you are no spies but you are upright. Your brother I shall give back to you, and you may carry on business in the land.'"

35 And it came about that when they were emptying their sacks here was each one's bundle of money in his sack. And they as well as their father got to see their bundles of money, and they became afraid. 36 Then Jacob their father exclaimed to them: "It is I you have bereaved! Joseph is no more and Sim'e·on is no more, and Benjamin you are going to take! It is upon me that all these

things have come!" 37 But Reu'-ben said to his father: "My own two sons you may put to death if I do not bring him back to you. Give him over to my care, and I shall be the one to return him to you." 38 However, he said: "My son will not go down with you men, because his brother is dead and he has been left by himself. If a fatal accident should befall him on the way on which you would go, then you would certainly bring down my gray hairs with grief to She'ol."

43 And the famine was severe in the land. 2 And it came about that as soon as they had finished eating up the cereals they had brought from Egypt, their father proceeded to say to them: "Return, buy a little food for us." 3 Then Judah said to him: "The man unmistakably bore witness to us, saying, 'You must not see my face again unless your brother is with you.' 4 If you are sending our brother with us, we are willing to go down and buy food for you. 5 But if you are not sending him, we shall not go down, because the man did say to us, 'You must not see my face again unless your brother is with you.'" 6 And Israel exclaimed: "Why did you have to do harm to me by telling the man you had another brother?" 7 At this they said: "The man directly inquired concerning us and our relatives, saying, 'Is your father yet alive? Do you have another brother?' and we went on to tell him according to these facts. How could we know for certain that he would say, 'Bring your brother down'?"

8 Finally Judah said to Israel his father: "Send the boy with me, that we may get up and go and that we may keep alive and not die off, both we and you and our little children. 9 I shall be the one to be surety for him. Out of my hand you may exact the penalty for him. If I fail to bring him to you and present him to you, then I shall have sinned against you for all time. 10 But if we had not lin-

gered around, we should by now have been there and back these two times."

11 So Israel their father said to them: "If, then, that is the case, do this: Take the finest products of the land in your receptacles and carry them down to the man as a gift: a little balsam, and a little honey, labdanum and resinous bark, pistachio nuts and almonds. 12 Also, take double the money in your hand; and the money that was returned in the mouth of your bags you will take back in your hand. Maybe it was a mistake. 13 And take your brother and get up, return to the man. 14 And may God Almighty give you pity before the man, that he may certainly release to you your other brother and Benjamin. But I, in case I must be bereaved, I shall certainly be bereaved!"

15 Accordingly the men took this gift, and they took double the money in their hand and Benjamin. Then they rose and went their way down to Egypt and got to stand before Joseph. 16 When Joseph saw Benjamin with them, he at once said to the man who was over his house: "Take the men to the house and slaughter animals and make preparation, because the men are to eat with me at noon." 17 Immediately the man did just as Joseph had said. So the man took the men to Joseph's house. 18 But the men got afraid because they had been taken to Joseph's house, and they began to say: "It is because of the money that went back with us in our bags at the start that we are being brought here for them to fall upon us and attack us and to take us for slaves and also our asses!"

19 Hence they approached the man who was over Joseph's house and spoke to him at the entrance of the house, 20 and they said: "Excuse us, my lord! We surely did come down at the start to buy food. 21 But what occurred was that when we came to the lodging place and began opening our bags, why, here was the money of each

one in the mouth of his bag, our money in full weight. So we would like to return it with our own hands. 22 And more money we have brought down in our hands to buy food. We certainly do not know who placed our money in our bags." 23 Then he said: "It is all right with you. Do not be afraid. YOUR God and the God of YOUR father gave YOU treasure in YOUR bags. YOUR money came first to me." After that he brought out Sim′e·on to them.

24 Then the man brought the men into Joseph's house and gave water that they might have their feet washed, and he gave fodder for their asses. 25 And they proceeded to get the gift ready for Joseph's coming at noon, because they had heard that it was there they were going to eat bread. 26 When Joseph went on into the house, then they brought the gift that was in their hand to him into the house, and prostrated themselves to him to the earth. 27 After this he inquired whether they were getting along well and said: "Is YOUR father, the aged man of whom YOU have spoken, getting along well? Is he still alive?" 28 To this they said: "Your servant our father is getting along well. He is still alive." Then they bowed down and prostrated themselves.

29 When he raised his eyes and saw Benjamin his brother, the son of his mother, he went on to say: "Is this YOUR brother, the youngest one of whom YOU have spoken to me?" And he added: "May God show you his favor, my son." 30 Joseph was now in a hurry, because his inward emotions were excited toward his brother, so that he looked for a place to weep and he went into an interior room and gave way to tears there. 31 After that he washed his face and went out and kept control of himself and said: "SET on the meal." 32 And they proceeded to set it on for him by himself and for them by themselves and for the Egyptians who were eating with him by themselves; for the Egyptians were

not able to eat a meal with the Hebrews, because that is a detestable thing to the Egyptians. 33 And they were seated before him, the first-born according to his right as first-born and the youngest according to his youngness; and the men kept looking at one another in amazement. 34 And he kept having portions carried from before him to them, but he would increase Benjamin's portion five times the size of the portions of all the others. So they continued banqueting and drinking with him to the full.

44 Later on he commanded the man who was over his house, saying: "Fill the bags of the men with food to the extent they are able to carry it and place the money of each one in the mouth of his bag. 2 But you must place my cup, the silver cup, in the mouth of the bag of the youngest and the money for his cereals." So he did according to the word of Joseph which he had spoken.

3 The morning had become light when the men were sent away, both they and their asses. 4 They went out of the city. They had not gone far when Joseph said to the man who was over his house: "Get up! Chase after the men and be certain to overtake them and to say to them, 'Why have YOU repaid bad for good? 5 Is not this the thing that my master drinks from and by means of which he expertly reads omens? It is a bad deed YOU have committed.'"

6 Eventually he overtook them and spoke these words to them. 7 But they said to him: "Why does my lord speak with such words as these? It is unthinkable that your servants should do anything like this. 8 Why, the money that we found in the mouth of our bags we brought back to you from the land of Ca′naan. How, then, could we steal silver or gold from the house of your master? 9 Let the one of your slaves with whom it may be found die and let us ourselves also become slaves to my master." 10 So he said: "Let it be now

exactly according to YOUR words. Thus the one with whom it may be found will become a slave to me, but YOU yourselves will be proved innocent." 11 With that they quickly let down each one his bag to the earth and they opened each one his own bag. 12 And he went searching carefully. He started with the oldest and finished with the youngest. At last the cup was found in Benjamin's bag.

13 Then they ripped their mantles apart and lifted each one his load back onto his ass and returned to the city. 14 And Judah and his brothers went on into Joseph's house, and he was still there; and they proceeded to fall upon their faces to the earth. 15 Joseph now said to them: "What sort of deed is this that YOU have done? Did YOU not know that such a man as I am can expertly read omens?" 16 At this Judah exclaimed: "What can we say to my master? What can we speak? And how can we prove ourselves righteous? The [true] God has found out the error of your slaves. Here we are slaves to my master, both we and the one in whose hand the cup was found!" 17 However, he said: "It is unthinkable for me to do this! The man in whose hand the cup was found is the one who will become a slave to me. As for the rest of YOU, go up in peace to YOUR father."

18 Judah now came near to him and said: "I pray you, my master, please let your slave speak a word in the hearing of my master, and do not let your anger grow hot against your slave, because it is the same with you as with Phar´aoh. 19 My master asked his slaves, saying, 'Do YOU have a father or a brother?' 20 So we said to my master, 'We do have an aged father and a child of his old age, the youngest. But his brother is dead so that he alone is left of his mother, and his father does love him.' 21 After that you said to your slaves, 'Bring him down to me that I may set my eye upon him.' 22 But we said to my mas-

ter, 'The boy is not able to leave his father. If he did leave his father, he would certainly die.' 23 Then you said to your slaves, 'Unless YOUR youngest brother comes down with YOU, YOU may not see my face any more.'

24 "And it came about that we went up to your slave my father and then told him the words of my master. 25 Later our father said, 'Return, buy a little food for us.' 26 But we said, 'We are not able to go down. If our youngest brother is with us we will go down, because we are not able to see the man's face in case our youngest brother is not with us.' 27 Then your slave my father said to us, 'YOU yourselves well know that my wife bore but two sons to me. 28 Later the one went out from my company and I exclaimed: "Ah, he must surely be torn to pieces!" and I have not seen him till now. 29 If YOU were to take this one also out of my sight and a fatal accident were to befall him, YOU would certainly bring down my gray hairs with calamity to She´ol.'

30 "And now, as soon as I should come to your slave my father without the boy along with us, when that one's soul is bound up with this one's soul, 31 then it is certain to occur that as soon as he sees that the boy is not there he will simply die, and your slaves will indeed bring down the gray hairs of your slave our father with grief to She´ol. 32 For your slave became surety for the boy when away from his father, saying, 'If I fail to bring him back to you, then I shall have sinned against my father forever.' 33 So now, please, let your slave stay instead of the boy as a slave to my master, that the boy may go up with his brothers.' 34 For how can I go up to my father without the boy along with me, for fear that then I may look upon the calamity that will find out my father?"

45 At this Joseph was no longer able to control himself before all those who were stationed by him. So he cried out: "HAVE everybody go out from me!" And no one else stood with him while Joseph made himself known to his brothers.

2 And he began to raise his voice in weeping, so that the Egyptians got to hear it and Phar'aoh's house got to hear it. 3 Finally Joseph said to his brothers: "I am Joseph. Is my father still alive?" But his brothers were unable to answer him at all, because they were disturbed by reason of him. 4 So Joseph said to his brothers: "Come close to me, please." With that they came close to him.

Then he said: "I am Joseph YOUR brother, whom YOU sold into Egypt. 5 But now do not feel hurt and do not be angry with yourselves because YOU sold me here; because for the preservation of life God has sent me ahead of YOU. 6 For this is the second year of the famine in the midst of the earth, and there are yet five years in which there will be no plowing time or harvest. 7 Consequently God sent me ahead of YOU in order to place a remnant for YOU men in the earth and to keep YOU alive by a great escape. 8 So now it was not YOU who sent me here, but it was the [true] God, that he might appoint me a father to Phar'aoh and a lord for all his house and as one dominating over all the land of Egypt.

9 "Go up quickly to my father, and YOU must say to him, 'This is what your son Joseph has said: "God has appointed me lord for all Egypt. Come down to me. Do not delay. 10 And you must dwell in the land of Go'shen, and you must continue near me, you and your sons and the sons of your sons and your flocks and your herds and everything you have. 11 And I will supply you with food there, for there are yet five years of famine; for fear you and your house and everything you have may come to poverty."' 12 And here YOUR eyes and the eyes of my brother Benjamin are seeing that it is my mouth that is speaking to YOU. 13 So YOU must tell my father about all my glory in Egypt and everything YOU have seen; and YOU must hurry and bring my father down here."

14 Then he fell upon the neck of Benjamin his brother and gave way to weeping, and Benjamin wept upon his neck. 15 And he proceeded to kiss all his brothers and to weep over them, and after that his brothers spoke with him.

16 And the news was heard at the house of Phar'aoh, saying: "Joseph's brothers have come!" And it proved to be good in the eyes of Phar'aoh and of his servants. 17 Accordingly Phar'aoh said to Joseph: "Say to your brothers, 'Do this: Load YOUR beasts of burden and go enter the land of Ca'naan, 18 and take YOUR father and YOUR households and come here to me, that I may give YOU the good of the land of Egypt; and eat the fat part of the land. 19 And you yourself are commanded: "Do this: TAKE for yourselves wagons from the land of Egypt for YOUR little ones and YOUR wives, and YOU must lift YOUR father on one and come here. 20 And do not let YOUR eye feel sorry over YOUR equipment, because the good of all the land of Egypt is YOURS."'"

21 Following that the sons of Israel did so, and Joseph gave them wagons according to Phar'aoh's orders and gave them provisions for the way. 22 To each of them he gave individual changes of mantles, but to Benjamin he gave three hundred silver pieces and five changes of mantles. 23 And to his father he sent as follows: ten asses carrying good things of Egypt and ten she-asses carrying grain and bread and sustenance for his father for the way. 24 Thus he sent his brothers off, and they proceeded to go. However, he said to them: "Do not get exasperated at one another on the way."

25 And they began going up out of Egypt and at length came into the land of Ca'naan to Jacob their father. 26 Then they reported to him, saying: "Joseph is still alive, and he is the one dominating over all the land of Egypt!" But his

heart grew numb, because he did not believe them. 27 When they went on speaking to him all of Joseph's words that he had spoken to them and he got to see the wagons that Joseph had sent to carry him, the spirit of Jacob their father began to revive. 28 Then Israel exclaimed: "It is enough! Joseph my son is still alive! Ah, let me go and see him before I die!"

46 Accordingly Israel and all who were his pulled out and came to Be'er-she'ba, and he proceeded to sacrifice sacrifices to the God of his father Isaac. 2 Then God talked to Israel in visions of the night and said: "Jacob, Jacob!" to which he said: "Here I am!" 3 And he went on to say: "I am the [true] God, the God of your father. Do not be afraid to go down to Egypt, for I shall constitute you there into a great nation. 4 I myself shall go down with you to Egypt and I myself shall surely bring you up also; and Joseph will lay his hand upon your eyes."

5 After that Jacob got up out of Be'er-she'ba, and the sons of Israel continued transporting Jacob their father and their little ones and their wives in the wagons that Phar'aoh had sent to transport him. 6 Further, they took along their herds and their goods, which they had accumulated in the land of Ca'naan. Eventually they came into Egypt, Jacob and all his offspring with him. 7 He brought his sons and his sons' sons with him, his daughters and his sons' daughters, even all his offspring, with him into Egypt.

8 Now these are the names of Israel's sons who came into Egypt: Jacob and his sons: Jacob's first-born was Reu'ben.

9 And the sons of Reu'ben were Ha'noch and Pal'lu and Hez'ron and Car'mi.

10 And the sons of Sim'e·on were Jem·u'el and Ja'min and O'had and Ja'chin and Zo'har and Sha'ul the son of a Ca'naan·ite woman.

11 And the sons of Le'vi were Ger'shon, Ko'hath and Me·rar'i.

12 And the sons of Judah were Er and O'nan and She'lah and Pe'rez and Ze'rah. However, Er and O'nan died in the land of Ca'naan.

And the sons of Pe'rez came to be Hez'ron and Ha'mul.

13 And the sons of Is'sa·char were To'la and Pu'vah and Iob and Shim'ron.

14 And the sons of Zeb'u·lun were Se'red and E'lon and Jah'-le·el.

15 These are the sons of Le'ah, whom she bore to Jacob in Pad'dan-a'ram, together with his daughter Di'nah. All the souls of his sons and of his daughters were thirty-three.

16 And the sons of Gad were Ziph'i·on and Hag'gi, Shu'ni and Ez'bon, E'ri and Ar·o'di and A·re'li.

17 And the sons of Ash'er were Im'nah and Ish'vah and Ish'vi and Be·ri'ah, and there was Se'rah their sister.

And the sons of Be·ri'ah were He'ber and Mal'chi·el.

18 These are the sons of Zil'pah, whom La'ban gave to his daughter Le'ah. In time she bore these to Jacob: sixteen souls.

19 The sons of Rachel, Jacob's wife, were Joseph and Benjamin.

20 And there came to be born to Joseph in the land of Egypt Manas'seh and E'phra·im, whom As'e·nath the daughter of Pot·i'phe-ra the priest of On bore to him.

21 And the sons of Benjamin were Be'la and Be'cher and Ash'-bel, Ge'ra and Na'a·man, E'hi and Rosh, Mup'pim and Hup'pim and Ard.

22 These are the sons of Rachel who were born to Jacob. All the souls were fourteen.

23 And the sons of Dan were Hu'shim.

24 And the sons of Naph'ta·li were Jah'ze·el and Gu'ni and Je'zer and Shil'lem.

25 These are the sons of Bil'hah, whom La'ban gave to his daughter Rachel. In time she bore these to Jacob; all the souls were seven.

26 All the souls who came to Jacob into Egypt were those who

issued out of his upper thigh, aside from the wives of Jacob's sons. All the souls were sixty-six. 27 And Joseph's sons who were born to him in Egypt were two souls. All the souls of the house of Jacob who came into Egypt were seventy.

28 And he sent Judah in advance of him to Joseph to impart information ahead of him to Go'shen. After that they came into the land of Go'shen. 29 Then Joseph had his chariot made ready and went up to meet Israel his father at Go'shen. When he appeared to him he at once fell upon his neck and gave way to tears upon his neck again and again. 30 Finally Israel said to Joseph: "This time I am willing to die, now that I have seen your face, since you are still alive."

31 Then Joseph said to his brothers and to his father's household: "Let me go up and report to Phar'aoh and say to him, 'My brothers and my father's household who were in the land of Ca'naan have come here to me. 32 And the men are shepherds, because they became stock raisers; and their flocks and their herds and all they have they have brought here.' 33 And what must occur is that when Phar'aoh will call YOU and actually say, 'What is YOUR occupation?' 34 YOU must say, 'Your servants have continued to be stock raisers from our youth until now, both we and our forefathers,' in order that YOU may dwell in the land of Go'shen, because every herder of sheep is a detestable thing to Egypt."

47 Accordingly Joseph came and reported to Phar'aoh and said: "My father and my brothers and their flocks and their herds and all they have have come from the land of Ca'naan, and here they are in the land of Go'shen." 2 And from the whole number of his brothers he took five men, that he might present them to Phar'aoh. 3 Then Phar'aoh said to his brothers: "What is YOUR occupation?" So they said to Phar'aoh: "Your servants are herders of sheep, both we and our forefathers."

4 After that they said to Phar'aoh: "We have come to reside as aliens in the land, because there is no pasturage for the flock that your servants have, for the famine is severe in the land of Ca'naan. And now let your servants dwell, please, in the land of Go'shen." 5 At that Phar'aoh said to Joseph: "Your father and your brothers have come here to you. 6 The land of Egypt is at your disposal. Have your father and your brothers dwell in the very best of the land. Let them dwell in the land of Go'shen, and if you know that there are among them courageous men, you must appoint them cattle chiefs over what is mine."

7 Then Joseph brought in Jacob his father and introduced him to Phar'aoh, and Jacob proceeded to bless Phar'aoh. 8 Phar'aoh now said to Jacob: "How many are the days of the years of your life?" 9 So Jacob said to Phar'aoh: "The days of the years of my alien residences are a hundred and thirty years. Few and distressing the days of the years of my life have proved, and they have not reached the days of the years of the lives of my fathers in the days of their alien residences." 10 After that Jacob blessed Phar'aoh and went out from before Phar'aoh.

11 Thus Joseph had his father and his brothers dwell and he gave them a possession in the land of Egypt, in the very best of the land, in the land of Ram'e·ses, just as Phar'aoh had commanded. 12 And Joseph kept supplying his father and his brothers and the entire household of his father with bread, according to the number of the little ones.

13 Now there was no bread in all the land, because the famine was very severe; and the land of Egypt and the land of Ca'naan became exhausted as a result of the famine. 14 And Joseph went on picking up all the money that was to be found in the land of Egypt and in the land of Ca'naan for the cereals which people were buy-

ing; and Joseph kept bringing the money into Phar'aoh's house. 15 In time the money from the land of Egypt and the land of Ca'naan was spent, and all the Egyptians began coming to Joseph, saying: "Give us bread! And why should we die in front of you because money has run out?" 16 Then Joseph said: "Hand over YOUR livestock and I shall give YOU bread in exchange for YOUR livestock, if money has run out." 17 And they began bringing their livestock to Joseph; and Joseph kept giving them bread in exchange for their horses and the livestock of the flock and the livestock of the herd and the asses, and he kept providing them with bread in exchange for all their livestock during that year.

18 Gradually that year came to its close, and they began coming to him in the next year and saying to him: "We shall not hide it from my lord but the money and the stock of domestic animals have been spent to my lord. There remains nothing before my lord but our bodies and our land. 19 Why should we die before your eyes, both we and our land? Buy us and our land for bread, and we together with our land will become slaves to Phar'aoh; and give us seed that we may live and not die and our land not be laid desolate." 20 So Joseph bought all the land of the Egyptians for Phar'aoh, because the Egyptians sold each one his field, for the famine had got a strong grip on them; and the land came to be Phar'aoh's.

21 As for the people, he removed them into cities from one end of the territory of Egypt to its other end. 22 Only the land of the priests he did not buy, because the rations for the priests were from Phar'aoh and they ate their rations that Phar'aoh gave them. That is why they did not sell their land. 23 Then Joseph said to the people: "See, I have today bought YOU and YOUR land for Phar'aoh. Here is seed for YOU, and YOU must sow the land with it. 24 When it has

resulted in produce, then YOU must give a fifth to Phar'aoh, but four parts will become YOURS as seed for the field and as food for YOU and for those who are in YOUR houses and for YOUR little ones to eat." 25 Consequently they said: "You have preserved our lives. Let us find favor in the eyes of my lord, and we will become slaves to Phar'aoh." 26 And Joseph proceeded to make it a decree down to this day over the landed estate of Egypt for Phar'aoh to have to the amount of a fifth. Only the land of the priests as a distinct group did not become Phar'aoh's.

27 And Israel continued to dwell in the land of Egypt, in the land of Go'shen; and they became settled in it and were fruitful and grew to be very many. 28 And Jacob lived on in the land of Egypt for seventeen years, so that Jacob's days, the years of his life, came to be a hundred and forty-seven years.

29 Gradually the days approached for Israel to die. So he called his son Joseph and said to him: "If, now, I have found favor in your eyes, place your hand, please, under my thigh, and you must exercise loving-kindness and trustworthiness toward me. (Please, do not bury me in Egypt.) 30 And I must lie with my fathers, and you must carry me out of Egypt and bury me in their grave." Accordingly he said: "I myself shall do in keeping with your word." 31 Then he said: "Swear to me." So he swore to him. At that Israel prostrated himself over the head of the couch.

48 And it came about after these things that it was said to Joseph: "Look, your father is becoming weak." At that he took with him his two sons Ma·nas'seh and E'phra·im. 2 Then it was reported to Jacob and said: "Here your son Joseph has come to you." So Israel exerted his strength and sat up on his couch. 3 And Jacob proceeded to say to Joseph:

"God Almighty appeared to me at Luz in the land of Ca'naan that he might bless me. 4 And he went on to say to me, 'Here I am making you fruitful, and I will make you many and I will transform you into a congregation of peoples and I will give this land to your seed after you for a possession to time indefinite.' 5 And now your two sons who were born to you in the land of Egypt before I came here to you into Egypt, they are mine. E'phra·im and Ma·nas'seh will become mine like Reu'ben and Sim'e·on. 6 But your progeny to which you shall become father after them will become yours. Together with the name of their brothers they will be called in their inheritance. 7 And as for me, when I was coming from Pad'dan, Rachel died alongside me in the land of Ca'naan on the way while there was yet a good stretch of land before coming to Eph'rath, so that I buried her there on the way to Eph'rath, that is to say, Beth'le·hem."

8 Then Israel saw Joseph's sons and said: "Who are these?" 9 So Joseph said to his father: "They are my sons whom God has given me in this place." At this he said: "Bring them, please, to me that I may bless them." 10 Now the eyes of Israel were dull from old age. He was unable to see. Accordingly he brought them close to him, and he then kissed them and embraced them. 11 And Israel went on to say to Joseph: "I had no idea of seeing your face, but here God has let me see also your offspring." 12 After that Joseph brought them out away from his knees, and he bowed down with his face to the earth.

13 Joseph now took the two of them, E'phra·im by his right hand to Israel's left, and Ma·nas'seh by his left hand to Israel's right, and brought them close to him. 14 However, Israel put out his right hand and placed it on E'phra·im's head, although he was the younger, and his left hand upon Ma·nas'seh's head. He purposely laid his hands so, since Ma·nas'seh was the first-born. 15 And he proceeded to bless Joseph and to say:

"The [true] God before whom my fathers Abraham and Isaac walked,
The [true] God who has been shepherding me during all my existence until this day,
16 The angel who has been recovering me from all calamity, bless the boys.
And let my name be called upon them and the name of my fathers, Abraham and Isaac,
And let them increase to a multitude in the midst of the earth."

17 When Joseph saw that his father kept his right hand placed on E'phra·im's head, it was displeasing to him, and he tried to take hold of his father's hand to remove it from E'phra·im's head to Ma·nas'seh's head. 18 Hence Joseph said to his father: "Not so, my father, because this is the first-born. Put your right hand on his head." 19 But his father kept refusing and said: "I know it, my son, I know it. He too will become a people and he too will become great. But, just the same, his younger brother will become greater than he will, and his offspring will become the full equivalent of nations." 20 And he continued to bless them on that day, saying:

"By means of you let Israel repeatedly pronounce blessing, saying,
'May God constitute you like E'phra·im and like Ma·nas'seh.'"
Thus he kept putting E'phra·im before Ma·nas'seh.

21 After that Israel said to Joseph: "Look, I am dying, but God will certainly continue with you people and return you to the land of your forefathers. 22 As for me, I do give you one shoulder [of land] more than to your brothers, which I took from the hand of the Am'or·ites by my sword and by my bow."

49 Later on Jacob called his sons and said: "Gather yourselves together that I may tell you what will happen to you in the final part of the days. 2 Assemble yourselves and listen, YOU sons of Jacob, yes, listen to Israel YOUR father.

3 "Reu'ben, you are my firstborn, my vigor and the beginning of my generative power, the excellence of dignity and the excellence of strength. 4 With reckless license like waters, do not you excel, because you have gone up to your father's bed. At that time you profaned my lounge. He went up to it!

5 "Sim'e·on and Le'vi are brothers. Instruments of violence are their slaughter weapons. 6 Into their intimate group do not come, O my soul. With their congregation do not become united, O my disposition, because in their anger they killed men, and in their arbitrariness they hamstrung bulls. 7 Cursed be their anger, because it is cruel, and their fury, because it acts harshly. Let me parcel them out in Jacob and let me scatter them in Israel.

8 "As for you, Judah, your brothers will laud you. Your hand will be on the back of the neck of your enemies. The sons of your father will prostrate themselves to you. 9 A lion cub Judah is. From the prey, my son, you will certainly go up. He bowed down, he stretched himself out like a lion and, like a lion, who dares rouse him? 10 The scepter will not turn aside from Judah, neither the commander's staff from between his feet, until Shi'loh comes; and to him the obedience of the peoples will belong. 11 Tying his full-grown ass to a vine and the descendant of his own she-ass to a choice vine, he will certainly wash his clothing in wine and his garment in the blood of grapes. 12 Dark red are his eyes from wine, and the whiteness of his teeth is from milk.

13 "Zeb'u·lun will reside by the seashore, and he will be by the shore where the ships lie anchored; and his remote side will be toward Si'don.

14 "Is'sa·char is a strong-boned ass, lying down between the two saddlebags. 15 And he will see that the resting place is good and that the land is pleasant; and he will bend down his shoulder to bear burdens and he will become subject to slavish forced labor.

16 "Dan will judge his people as one of the tribes of Israel. 17 Let Dan prove to be a serpent by the roadside, a horned snake at the wayside, that bites the heels of the horse so that its rider falls backward. 18 I shall indeed wait for salvation from you, O Jehovah.

19 "As for Gad, a marauder band will raid him, but he will raid the extreme rear.

20 "Out of Ash'er his bread will be fat, and he will give the dainties of a king.

21 "Naph'ta·li is a slender hind. He is giving words of elegance.

22 "Offshoot of a fruit-bearing tree, Joseph is the offshoot of a fruit-bearing tree by the fountain, that propels its branches up over a wall. 23 But the archers kept harassing him and shot at him and kept harboring animosity against him. 24 And yet his bow was dwelling in a permanent place, and the strength of his hands was supple. From the hands of the powerful one of Jacob, from there is the shepherd, the stone of Israel. 25 He is from the God of your father, and he will help you; and he is with the Almighty, and he will bless you with the blessings of the heavens above, with the blessings of the watery deep lying down below, with the blessings of the breasts and womb. 26 The blessings of your father will indeed be superior to the blessings of the eternal mountains, to the ornament of the indefinitely lasting hills. They will continue upon the head of Joseph, even upon the crown of the head of the one singled out from his brothers.

27 "Benjamin will keep on tearing like a wolf. In the morning he will eat the animal seized and at evening he will divide spoil."

28 All these are the twelve tribes of Israel, and this is what their

father spoke to them when he was blessing them. He blessed them each one according to his own blessing.

29 After that he commanded them and said to them: "I am being gathered to my people. Bury me with my fathers in the cave that is in the field of E′phron the Hit′tite, 30 in the cave that is in the field of Mach·pe′lah that is in front of Mam′re in the land of Ca′naan, the field that Abraham purchased from E′phron the Hit′tite for the possession of a burial place. 31 There they buried Abraham and Sarah his wife. There they buried Isaac and Re·bek′ah his wife, and there I buried Le′ah. 32 The field purchased and the cave that is in it were from the sons of Heth."

33 Thus Jacob finished giving commands to his sons. Then he gathered his feet up onto the couch and expired and was gathered to his people.

50 Then Joseph fell upon the face of his father and burst into tears over him and kissed him. 2 After that Joseph commanded his servants, the physicians, to embalm his father. So the physicians embalmed Israel, 3 and they took fully forty days for him, for this many days they customarily take for the embalming, and the Egyptians continued to shed tears for him seventy days.

4 Finally the days of weeping for him passed, and Joseph spoke to Phar′aoh's household, saying: "If, now, I have found favor in YOUR eyes, speak, please, in the hearing of Phar′aoh, saying, 5 'My father made me swear, saying: "Look! I am dying. In my burial place which I have excavated for myself in the land of Ca′naan is where you are to bury me." And now, please, let me go up and bury my father, after which I am willing to return.' " 6 Accordingly Phar′aoh said: "Go up and bury your father just as he made you swear."

7 So Joseph went up to bury his father, and there went up with him all of Phar′aoh's servants, the older men of his household and all the older men of the land of Egypt, 8 and all of Joseph's household and his brothers and the household of his father. Only their little children and their flocks and their herds they left in the land of Go′shen. 9 There also went up with him both chariots and horsemen, and the camp came to be very numerous. 10 Then they came to the threshing floor of A′tad, which is in the region of the Jordan, and there they carried on a very great and heavy wailing and kept up the mourning rites for his father seven days. 11 And the inhabitants of the land, the Ca′naan·ites, got to see the mourning rites in the threshing floor of A′tad, and they exclaimed: "This is a heavy mourning for the Egyptians!" That is why its name was called A′bel-miz′ra·im, which is in the region of the Jordan.

12 And his sons proceeded to do for him exactly as he had commanded them. 13 So his sons carried him into the land of Ca′naan and buried him in the cave of the field of Mach·pe′lah, the field that Abraham had purchased for the possession of a burial place from E′phron the Hit′tite in front of Mam′re. 14 Afterward Joseph returned to Egypt, he and his brothers and all those who went up with him to bury his father, after he had buried his father.

15 When the brothers of Joseph saw that their father was dead, they began to say: "It may be that Joseph is harboring animosity against us and he will be sure to repay us for all the evil that we have rendered him." 16 So they expressed a command to Joseph in these words: "Your father gave the command before his death, saying, 17 'This is what YOU are to say to Joseph: "I beseech you, pardon, please, the revolt of your brothers and their sin in that they have rendered evil to you." ' And now pardon, please, the revolt of the servants of your father's God." And Joseph burst into tears

when they spoke to him. 18 Following that his brothers also came and fell down before him and said: "Here we are as slaves to you!" 19 Then Joseph said to them: "Do not be afraid, for am I in the place of God? 20 As for YOU, YOU had evil in mind against me. God had it in mind for good for the purpose of acting as at this day to preserve many people alive. 21 So now do not be afraid. I myself shall keep supplying YOU and YOUR little children with food." Thus he comforted them and spoke reassuringly to them.

22 And Joseph continued to dwell in Egypt, he and the house of his father; and Joseph lived for a hundred and ten years. 23 And Joseph got to see E′phra·im's sons of the third generation, also the sons of Ma′chir, Ma·nas′seh's son. They were born upon Joseph's knees. 24 At length Joseph said to his brothers: "I am dying; but God will without fail turn his attention to YOU, and he will certainly bring YOU up out of this land to the land about which he swore to Abraham, to Isaac and to Jacob." 25 Hence Joseph made the sons of Israel swear, saying: "God will without fail turn his attention to YOU. Accordingly YOU must take my bones up out of here." 26 After that Joseph died at the age of a hundred and ten years; and they had him embalmed, and he was put in a coffin in Egypt.

EXODUS

1 Now these are the names of Israel's sons who came into Egypt with Jacob; each man and his household came: 2 Reu′ben, Sim′e·on, Le′vi and Judah, 3 Is′sa·char, Zeb′u·lun and Benjamin, 4 Dan and Naph′ta·li, Gad and Ash′er. 5 And all the souls who issued out of Jacob's upper thigh came to be seventy souls, but Joseph was already in Egypt. 6 Eventually Joseph died, and also all his brothers and all that generation. 7 And the sons of Israel became fruitful and began to swarm; and they kept on multiplying and growing mightier at a very extraordinary rate, so that the land got to be filled with them.

8 In time there arose over Egypt a new king who did not know Joseph. 9 And he proceeded to say to his people: "Look! The people of the sons of Israel are more numerous and mightier than we are. 10 Come on! Let us deal shrewdly with them, for fear they may multiply, and it must turn out that, in case war should befall us, then they certainly will also be added to those who hate us and will fight against us and go up out of the country."

11 So they set over them chiefs of forced labor for the purpose of oppressing them in their burden-bearing; and they went building cities as storage places for Pharaoh, namely, Pi′thom and Ra·am′ses. 12 But the more they would oppress them, the more they would multiply and the more they kept spreading abroad, so that they felt a sickening dread as a result of the sons of Israel. 13 Consequently the Egyptians made the sons of Israel slave under tyranny. 14 And they kept making their life bitter with hard slavery at clay mortar and bricks and with every form of slavery in the field, yes, every form of slavery of theirs in which they used them as slaves under tyranny.

15 Later on the king of Egypt said to the Hebrew midwives, the name of one of whom was Shiph′rah and the name of the other Pu′ah, 16 yes, he went so far as

to say: "When you help the Hebrew women to give birth and you do see them on the stool for childbirth, if it is a son, you must also put it to death; but if it is a daughter, it must also live." 17 However, the midwives feared the [true] God, and they did not do as the king of Egypt had spoken to them, but they would preserve the male children alive. 18 In time the king of Egypt called the midwives and said to them: "Why is it you have done this thing, in that you preserved the male children alive?" 19 In turn the midwives said to Phar'aoh: "Because the Hebrew women are not like the Egyptian women. Because they are lively, they have already given birth before the midwife can come in to them."

20 So God dealt well with the midwives; and the people kept growing more numerous and becoming very mighty. 21 And it came about that because the midwives had feared the [true] God he later presented them with families. 22 Finally Phar'aoh commanded all his people, saying: "Every new-born son you are to throw into the river Nile, but every daughter you are to preserve alive."

2 Meantime, a certain man of the house of Le'vi went ahead and took a daughter of Le'vi. 2 And the woman became pregnant and brought a son to birth. When she saw how good-looking he was, she kept him concealed for three lunar months. 3 When she was no longer able to conceal him, she then took for him an ark of papyrus and coated it with bitumen and pitch and put the child in it and put it among the reeds by the bank of the river Nile. 4 Further, his sister stationed herself at a distance to find out what would be done with him.

5 After a while Phar'aoh's daughter came down to bathe in the Nile River, and her female attendants were walking by the side of the Nile River. And she caught sight of the ark in the middle of the reeds. Immediately she sent her slave girl that she might get it. 6 When she opened it she got to see the child, and here the boy was weeping. At that she felt compassion for him, although she said: "This is one of the children of the Hebrews." 7 Then his sister said to Phar'aoh's daughter: "Shall I go and specially call for you a nursing woman from the Hebrew women that she may nurse the child for you?" 8 So Phar'aoh's daughter said to her: "Go!" At once the maiden went and called the child's mother. 9 Phar'aoh's daughter then said to her: "Take this child with you and nurse him for me, and I myself shall give you your wages." Accordingly the woman took the child and nursed him. 10 And the child grew up. Then she brought him to Phar'aoh's daughter, so that he became a son to her; and she proceeded to call his name Moses and to say: "It is because I have drawn him out of the water."

11 Now it came about in those days, as Moses was becoming strong, that he went out to his brothers that he might look at the burdens they were bearing; and he caught sight of a certain Egyptian striking a certain Hebrew of his brothers. 12 So he turned this way and that and saw there was nobody in sight. Then he struck the Egyptian down and hid him in the sand.

13 However, he went out on the following day and here there were two Hebrew men struggling with each other. So he said to the one in the wrong: "Why should you strike your companion?" 14 At this he said: "Who appointed you as a prince and judge over us? Are you intending to kill me just as you killed the Egyptian?" Moses now got afraid and said: "Surely the thing has become known!"

15 Subsequently Phar'aoh got to hear of this thing, and he attempted to kill Moses; but Moses ran away from Phar'aoh that he might dwell in the land of Mid'i·an; and he took a seat by a well. 16 Now the priest of Mid'i·an had seven daughters, and as usual they

came and drew water and filled the gutters to water their father's flock. 17 And as usual the shepherds came and drove them away. At this Moses got up and helped the women out and watered their flock. 18 So when they came home to Reu'el their father he exclaimed: "How is it you have come home so quickly today?" 19 To this they said: "A certain Egyptian delivered us out of the hand of the shepherds and, besides, he actually drew water for us that he might water the flock." 20 Then he said to his daughters: "But where is he? Why is it that you have left the man behind? Call him, that he may eat bread." 21 After that Moses showed willingness to dwell with the man, and he gave Zip·po'rah his daughter to Moses. 22 Later she bore a son and he called his name Ger'shom, because, he said: "An alien resident I have come to be in a foreign land."

23 And it came about during those many days that the king of Egypt finally died, but the sons of Israel continued to sigh because of the slavery and to cry out in complaint, and their cry for help kept going up to the [true] God because of the slavery. 24 In time God heard their groaning and God remembered his covenant with Abraham, Isaac and Jacob. 25 So God looked on the sons of Israel and God took notice.

3 And Moses became a shepherd of the flock of Jeth'ro, the priest of Mid'i·an, whose son-in-law he was. While he was driving the flock to the west side of the wilderness, he came at length to the mountain of the [true] God, to Ho'reb. 2 Then Jehovah's angel appeared to him in a flame of fire in the midst of a thornbush. As he kept looking, why, here the thornbush was burning with the fire and yet the thornbush was not consumed. 3 At this Moses said: "Let me just turn aside that I may inspect this great phenomenon, as to why the thornbush is not burnt up." 4 When Jehovah saw that he turned aside to inspect, God at

once called to him out of the midst of the thornbush and said: "Moses! Moses!" to which he said: "Here I am." 5 Then he said: "Do not come near here. Draw your sandals from off your feet, because the place where you are standing is holy ground."

6 And he went on to say: "I am the God of your father, the God of Abraham, the God of Isaac and the God of Jacob." Then Moses concealed his face, because he was afraid to look at the [true] God. 7 And Jehovah added: "Unquestionably I have seen the affliction of my people who are in Egypt, and I have heard their outcry as a result of those who drive them to work; because I well know the pains they suffer. 8 And I am proceeding to go down to deliver them out of the hand of the Egyptians and to bring them up out of that land to a land good and spacious, to a land flowing with milk and honey, to the locality of the Ca'naan·ites and the Hit'tites and the Am'or·ites and the Per'iz·zites and the Hi'vites and the Jeb'u·sites. 9 And now, look! the outcry of the sons of Israel has come to me, and I have seen also the oppression with which the Egyptians are oppressing them. 10 And now come and let me send you to Phar'aoh, and you bring my people the sons of Israel out of Egypt."

11 However, Moses said to the [true] God: "Who am I that I should go to Phar'aoh and that I have to bring the sons of Israel out of Egypt?" 12 To this he said: "Because I shall prove to be with you, and this is the sign for you that it is I who have sent you: After you have brought the people out of Egypt, you people will serve the [true] God on this mountain."

13 Nevertheless, Moses said to the [true] God: "Suppose I am now come to the sons of Israel and I do say to them, 'The God of your forefathers has sent me to you,' and they do say to me, 'What is his name?' What shall I say to them?" 14 At this God said to Moses: "I SHALL PROVE TO BE WHAT

I SHALL PROVE TO BE." And he added: "This is what you are to say to the sons of Israel, 'I SHALL PROVE TO BE has sent me to you.'" 15 Then God said once more to Moses:

"This is what you are to say to the sons of Israel, 'Jehovah the God of YOUR forefathers, the God of Abraham, the God of Isaac and the God of Jacob, has sent me to YOU.' This is my name to time indefinite, and this is the memorial of me to generation after generation. 16 You go, and you must gather the older men of Israel, and you must say to them, 'Jehovah the God of YOUR forefathers has appeared to me, the God of Abraham, Isaac and Jacob, saying: "I will without fail give attention to YOU and to what is being done to YOU in Egypt. 17 And so I say, I shall bring YOU up out of affliction by the Egyptians to the land of the Ca′naan·ites and the Hit′tites and the Am′or·ites and the Per′iz·zites and the Hi′vites and the Jeb′u·sites, to a land flowing with milk and honey."'

18 "And they will certainly listen to your voice, and you must come, you and the older men of Israel, to the king of Egypt, and YOU men must say to him, 'Jehovah the God of the Hebrews has come in touch with us, and now we want to go, please, a journey of three days into the wilderness, and we want to sacrifice to Jehovah our God.' 19 And I, even I, well know that the king of Egypt will not give YOU permission to go except by a strong hand. 20 And I shall have to stretch out my hand and strike Egypt with all my wonderful acts that I shall do in the midst of it; and after that he will send YOU out. 21 And I will give this people favor in the eyes of the Egyptians; and it will certainly occur that when YOU go, YOU will not go empty-handed. 22 And each woman must ask from her neighbor and from the woman residing as an alien in her house articles of silver and articles of gold and mantles, and YOU must put them upon YOUR

sons and YOUR daughters; and YOU must strip the Egyptians."

4 However, Moses in answering said: "But suppose they do not believe me and do not listen to my voice, because they are going to say, 'Jehovah did not appear to you.'" 2 Then Jehovah said to him: "What is that in your hand?" to which he said: "A rod." 3 Next he said: "Throw it on the earth." So he threw it on the earth, and it became a serpent; and Moses began to flee from it. 4 Jehovah now said to Moses: "Thrust your hand out and grab hold of it by the tail." So he thrust his hand out and grabbed hold of it, and it became a rod in his palm. 5 "In order that," to quote him, "they may believe that Jehovah the God of their forefathers, the God of Abraham, the God of Isaac and the God of Jacob, has appeared to you."

6 Then Jehovah said to him once more: "Stick your hand, please, into the upper fold of your garment." So he stuck his hand into the upper fold of his garment. When he drew it out, why, here his hand was stricken with leprosy like snow! 7 After that he said: "Return your hand into the upper fold of your garment." So he returned his hand into the upper fold of his garment. When he drew it out of the upper fold of his garment, why, here it was restored like the rest of his flesh! 8 "And it must occur that," to quote him, "if they will not believe you and will not listen to the voice of the first sign, then they will certainly believe the voice of the later sign. 9 Still, it must occur that, if they will not believe even these two signs and will not listen to your voice, then you will have to take some water from the Nile River and pour it out on the dry land; and the water that you will take from the Nile River will certainly become, yes, it will indeed become blood on the dry land."

10 Moses now said to Jehovah: "Excuse me, Jehovah, but I am not a fluent speaker, neither since yesterday nor since before that nor

since your speaking to your servant, for I am slow of mouth and slow of tongue." 11 At that Jehovah said to him: "Who appointed a mouth for man or who appoints the speechless or the deaf or the clear-sighted or the blind? Is it not I, Jehovah? 12 So now go, and I myself shall prove to be with your mouth and I will teach you what you ought to say." 13 But he said: "Excuse me, Jehovah, but send, please, by the hand of the one whom you are going to send." 14 Then Jehovah's anger grew hot against Moses and he said: "Is not Aaron the Levite your brother? I do know that he can really speak. And, besides, here he is on his way out to meet you. When he does see you, he will certainly rejoice in his heart. 15 And you must speak to him and put the words in his mouth; and I myself shall prove to be with your mouth and his mouth, and I will teach you men what you are to do. 16 And he must speak for you to the people; and it must occur that he will serve as a mouth to you, and you will serve as God to him. 17 And this rod you will take in your hand that you may perform the signs with it."

18 Accordingly Moses went and returned to Jeth'ro his father-in-law and said to him: "I want to go, please, and return to my brothers who are in Egypt that I may see whether they are still alive." So Jeth'ro said to Moses: "Go in peace." 19 After that Jehovah said to Moses in Mid'i·an: "Go, return to Egypt, because all the men who were hunting for your soul are dead."

20 Then Moses took his wife and his sons and made them ride on an ass, and he proceeded to return to the land of Egypt. Moreover, Moses took the rod of the [true] God in his hand. 21 And Jehovah went on to say to Moses: "After you have gone and returned to Egypt see that you men actually perform all the miracles that I have put in your hand before Phar'aoh. As for me, I shall let his heart become obstinate; and he

will not send the people away. 22 And you must say to Phar'aoh, 'This is what Jehovah has said: "Israel is my son, my first-born. 23 And I say to you: Send my son away that he may serve me. But should you refuse to send him away, here I am killing your son, your first-born." ' "

24 Now it came about on the road at the lodging place that Jehovah got to meet him and kept looking for a way to put him to death. 25 Finally Zip·po'rah took a flint and cut off her son's foreskin and caused it to touch his feet and said: "It is because you are a bridegroom of blood to me." 26 Consequently he let go of him. At that time she said: "A bridegroom of blood," because of the circumcision.

27 Then Jehovah said to Aaron: "Go to meet Moses into the wilderness." With that he went and met him in the mountain of the [true] God and kissed him. 28 And Moses proceeded to tell Aaron all the words of Jehovah, who had sent him, and all the signs that he had commanded him to do. 29 After that Moses and Aaron went and gathered all the older men of the sons of Israel. 30 Then Aaron spoke all the words that Jehovah had spoken to Moses, and he performed the signs under the eyes of the people. 31 At this the people believed. When they heard that Jehovah had turned his attention to the sons of Israel and that he had seen their affliction, then they bowed down and prostrated themselves.

5 And afterward Moses and Aaron went in and proceeded to say to Phar'aoh: "This is what Jehovah the God of Israel has said, 'Send my people away that they may celebrate a festival to me in the wilderness.' " 2 But Phar'aoh said: "Who is Jehovah, so that I should obey his voice to send Israel away? I do not know Jehovah at all and, what is more, I am not going to send Israel away." 3 However, they went on to say: "The God of the Hebrews has

come in touch with us. We want to go, please, a journey of three days into the wilderness and sacrifice to Jehovah our God; otherwise he may strike us as with pestilence or with sword." 4 At this the king of Egypt said to them: "Why is it, Moses and Aaron, that you cause the people to leave off from their works? Go bearing your burdens!" 5 And Phar'aoh continued: "Look! The people of the land are now many, and you indeed make them desist from their bearing of burdens."

6 Immediately on that day Phar'aoh commanded those who drove the people to work and their officers, saying: 7 "You must not gather straw to give to the people to make bricks as formerly. Let them themselves go and gather straw for themselves. 8 Moreover, the required amount of bricks that they were making formerly, you will further impose upon them. You must not make any reduction for them, because they are relaxing. That is why they are crying out, saying, 'We want to go, we want to sacrifice to our God!' 9 Let the service be heavy upon the men and let them work at it, and let them not pay attention to false words."

10 So those who drove the people to work and their officers went out and said to the people: "Here is what Phar'aoh has said, 'I am giving you no more straw. 11 You yourselves go, get straw for yourselves wherever you may find it, because there is to be no reducing of your services one bit.'" 12 Consequently the people scattered about over all the land of Egypt to gather stubble for straw. 13 And those who drove them to work kept urging them, saying: "Finish your works, each one his work, day for day, just as when straw was available." 14 Later on the officers of the sons of Israel, whom Phar'aoh's taskmasters had set over them, were beaten, these saying: "Why is it you did not finish your prescribed task in making bricks as formerly, both yesterday and today?"

15 Consequently the officers of the sons of Israel went in and began to cry out to Phar'aoh, saying: "Why do you deal this way with your servants? 16 There is no straw given to your servants and yet they are saying to us, 'Make bricks!' and here your servants are beaten, whereas your own people are at fault." 17 But he said: "You are relaxing, you are relaxing! That is why you are saying, 'We want to go, we want to sacrifice to Jehovah.' 18 And now go, serve! Though no straw will be given to you, yet you are to give the fixed amount of bricks."

19 Then the officers of the sons of Israel saw themselves in an evil plight at the saying: "You must not deduct from your bricks one bit of anyone's daily rate." 20 After that they encountered Moses and Aaron, who were standing there to meet them as they came out from Phar'aoh. 21 At once they said to them: "May Jehovah look upon you and judge, since you have made us smell offensive before Phar'aoh and before his servants so as to put a sword in their hand to kill us." 22 Then Moses turned to Jehovah and said: "Jehovah, why have you caused evil to this people? Why is it that you have sent me? 23 For from the time that I went in before Phar'aoh to speak in your name, he has done evil to this people, and you have by no means delivered your people."

6 So Jehovah said to Moses: "Now you will see what I shall do to Phar'aoh, because on account of a strong hand he will send them away and on account of a strong hand he will drive them out of his land."

2 And God went on to speak to Moses and to say to him: "I am Jehovah. 3 And I used to appear to Abraham, Isaac and Jacob as God Almighty, but as respects my name Jehovah I did not make myself known to them. 4 And I also established my covenant with them to give them the land of Ca'naan, the land of their alien residences in which they resided as aliens. 5 And I, even I, have heard the

groaning of the sons of Israel, whom the Egyptians are enslaving, and I remember my covenant.

6 "Therefore say to the sons of Israel, 'I am Jehovah, and I shall certainly bring YOU out from under the burdens of the Egyptians and deliver YOU from their slavery, and I shall indeed reclaim YOU with an outstretched arm and with great judgments. 7 And I shall certainly take YOU to me as a people, and I shall indeed prove to be God to YOU; and YOU will certainly know that I am Jehovah YOUR God who is bringing YOU out from under the burdens of Egypt. 8 And I shall certainly bring YOU into the land that I raised my hand in oath to give to Abraham, Isaac and Jacob; and I shall indeed give it to YOU as something to possess. I am Jehovah.'"

9 Afterward Moses spoke to this effect to the sons of Israel, but they did not listen to Moses out of discouragement and for the hard slavery.

10 Then Jehovah spoke to Moses, saying: 11 "Go in, speak to Phar'-aoh, Egypt's king, that he should send the sons of Israel away out of his land." 12 However, Moses spoke before Jehovah, saying: "Look! The sons of Israel have not listened to me; and how will Phar'-aoh ever listen to me, as I am un-circumcised in lips?" 13 But Jehovah continued to speak to Moses and Aaron and to issue the command by them to the sons of Israel and to Phar'aoh, Egypt's king, in order to bring the sons of Israel out from the land of Egypt.

14 These are the heads of the house of their fathers: The sons of Reu'ben, Israel's first-born, were Ha'noch and Pal'lu, Hez'ron and Car'mi. These are the families of Reu'ben.

15 And the sons of Sim'e·on were Jem'u·el and Ja'min and O'had and Ja'chin and Zo'har and Sha'ul the son of a Ca'naan·ite woman. These are the families of Sim'e·on.

16 And these are the names of the sons of Le'vi, according to their family descents: Ger'shon and Ko'hath and Me·rar'i. And the years of Le'vi's life were a hundred and thirty-seven years.

17 The sons of Ger'shon were Lib'ni and Shim'e·i, according to their families.

18 And the sons of Ko'hath were Am'ram and Iz'har and He'-bron and Uz'zi·el. And the years of Ko'hath's life were a hundred and thirty-three years.

19 And the sons of Me·rar'i were Mah'li and Mu'shi.

These were the families of the Levites, according to their family descents.

20 Now Am'ram took Joch'e·bed his father's sister as his wife. Later she bore him Aaron and Moses. And the years of Am'ram's life were a hundred and thirty-seven years.

21 And the sons of Iz'har were Ko'rah and Ne'pheg and Zich'ri.

22 And the sons of Uz'zi·el were Mi'sha·el and El·za'phan and Sith'ri.

23 Now Aaron took E·li'she·ba, Am·min'a·dab's daughter, the sister of Nah'shon, as his wife. Later she bore him Na'dab and A·bi'hu, E·le-a'zar and Ith'a·mar.

24 And the sons of Ko'rah were As'sir and El·ka'nah and A·bi'a-saph. These were the families of the Ko'rah·ites.

25 And E·le·a'zar, Aaron's son, took for himself one of the daughters of Pu'ti·el as his wife. Later she bore him Phin'e·has.

These are the heads of the fathers of the Levites, according to their families.

26 This is the Aaron and Moses to whom Jehovah said: "BRING the sons of Israel out from the land of Egypt according to their armies." 27 They were the ones speaking to Phar'aoh, Egypt's king, to bring the sons of Israel out from Egypt. This is the Moses and Aaron.

28 And it came about on the day that Jehovah spoke to Moses in the land of Egypt, 29 that Jehovah went on to speak to Moses, saying: "I am Jehovah. Speak to Phar'aoh king of Egypt everything I am

speaking to you." 30 Then Moses said before Jehovah: "Look! I am uncircumcised in lips, so how will Phar'aoh ever listen to me?"

7 Consequently Jehovah said to Moses: "See, I have made you God to Phar'aoh, and Aaron your own brother will become your prophet. 2 You—you will speak all that I shall command you; and Aaron your brother will do the speaking to Phar'aoh, and he must send the sons of Israel away from his land. 3 As for me, I shall let Phar'aoh's heart become obstinate, and I shall certainly multiply my signs and my miracles in the land of Egypt. 4 And Phar'aoh will not listen to you men; and I shall have to lay my hand upon Egypt and bring my armies, my people, the sons of Israel, out from the land of Egypt with great judgments. 5 And the Egyptians will certainly know that I am Jehovah when I stretch out my hand against Egypt, and I shall indeed bring the sons of Israel out from their midst." 6 And Moses and Aaron went ahead doing as Jehovah had commanded them. They did just so. 7 And Moses was eighty years old and Aaron was eighty-three years old at the time of their speaking to Phar'aoh.

8 Jehovah now said to Moses and Aaron: 9 "In case that Phar'aoh speaks to you, saying, 'Produce a miracle for yourselves,' then you must say to Aaron, 'Take your rod and throw it down before Phar'aoh.' It will become a big snake." 10 So Moses and Aaron went on in to Phar'aoh and did exactly as Jehovah had commanded. Accordingly Aaron threw his rod down before Phar'aoh and his servants and it became a big snake. 11 However, Phar'aoh also called for the wise men and the sorcerers; and the magic-practicing priests of Egypt themselves also proceeded to do the same thing with their magic arts. 12 So they threw down each one his rod, and they became big snakes; but Aaron's rod swallowed up their rods. 13 Still, Phar'aoh's heart became obstinate, and he did

not listen to them, just as Jehovah had spoken.

14 Then Jehovah said to Moses: "Phar'aoh's heart is unresponsive. He has refused to send the people away. 15 Go to Phar'aoh in the morning. Look! He is going out to the water! And you must put yourself in position to meet him by the edge of the Nile River, and the rod that turned into a serpent you are to take in your hand. 16 And you must say to him, 'Jehovah the God of the Hebrews has sent me to you, saying: "Send my people away that they may serve me in the wilderness," but here you have not obeyed until now. 17 This is what Jehovah has said: "By this you will know that I am Jehovah. Here I am striking with the rod that is in my hand upon the water that is in the Nile River, and it will certainly turn into blood. 18 And the fish that are in the Nile River will die, and the Nile River will actually stink, and the Egyptians will simply have no stomach for drinking water from the Nile River." ' "

19 Subsequently Jehovah said to Moses: "Say to Aaron, 'Take your rod and stretch your hand out over the waters of Egypt, over their rivers, over their Nile canals and over their reedy pools and over all their impounded waters, that they may become blood.' And there will certainly be blood in all the land of Egypt and in the wooden vessels and in the stone vessels." 20 Immediately Moses and Aaron did so, just as Jehovah had commanded, and he lifted up the rod and struck the water that was in the Nile River under the eyes of Phar'aoh and his servants, and all the water that was in the Nile River was turned into blood. 21 And the fish that were in the Nile River died, and the Nile River began to stink; and the Egyptians were unable to drink water from the Nile River; and the blood came to be in all the land of Egypt.

22 Nevertheless, the magic-practicing priests of Egypt proceeded to do the same thing with

their secret arts; so that Phar'aoh's heart continued to be obstinate, and he did not listen to them, just as Jehovah had spoken. 23 Hence Phar'aoh turned and went into his house, and he did not set his heart to have any regard for this either. 24 And all the Egyptians went digging round about the Nile River for water to drink, because they were unable to drink any water of the Nile River. 25 And seven days came to be fulfilled after Jehovah's striking the Nile River.

8 Then Jehovah said to Moses: "Go in to Phar'aoh, and you must say to him, 'This is what Jehovah has said: "Send my people away that they may serve me. 2 And if you keep refusing to send them away, here I am plaguing all your territory with frogs. 3 And the Nile River will fairly teem with frogs, and they will certainly come up and enter into your house and your inner bedroom and upon your couch and into the house of your servants and on your people and into your ovens and into your kneading troughs. 4 And on you and on your people and on all your servants the frogs will come up."'"

5 Later on Jehovah said to Moses: "Say to Aaron, 'Stretch your hand with your rod out over the rivers, the Nile canals and the reedy pools and make the frogs come up over the land of Egypt.'" 6 At that Aaron stretched his hand out over the waters of Egypt, and the frogs began to come up and to cover the land of Egypt. 7 However, the magic-practicing priests did the same thing by their secret arts and made the frogs come up over the land of Egypt. 8 In time Phar'aoh called Moses and Aaron and said: "Entreat Jehovah that he may remove the frogs from me and my people, as I want to send the people away that they may sacrifice to Jehovah." 9 Then Moses said to Phar'aoh: "You take the glory over me to say when I shall make entreaty for you and your servants and your people in order to cut the frogs off from you and your houses. Only in the Nile River will they be left." 10 To this he said: "Tomorrow." So he said: "It will be according to your word, in order that you may know that there is no one else like Jehovah our God, 11 in that the frogs will certainly turn away from you and your houses and your servants and your people. Only in the Nile River will they be left."

12 Accordingly Moses and Aaron went out from Phar'aoh, and Moses cried out to Jehovah because of the frogs that He had put upon Phar'aoh. 13 Then Jehovah did according to Moses' word, and the frogs began to die off from the houses, the courtyards and the fields. 14 And they went piling them up, heaps upon heaps, and the land began to stink. 15 When Phar'aoh got to see that relief had taken place, he made his heart unresponsive; and he did not listen to them, just as Jehovah had spoken.

16 Jehovah now said to Moses: "Say to Aaron, 'Stretch your rod out and strike the dust of the earth, and it must become gnats in all the land of Egypt.'" 17 And they proceeded to do this. So Aaron stretched out his hand with his rod and struck the dust of the earth, and the gnats came to be on man and beast. All the dust of the earth became gnats in all the land of Egypt. 18 And the magic-practicing priests tried to do the same by their secret arts, in order to bring forth gnats, but they were unable. And the gnats came to be on man and beast. 19 Hence the magic-practicing priests said to Phar'aoh: "It is the finger of God!" But Phar'aoh's heart continued to be obstinate, and he did not listen to them, just as Jehovah had spoken.

20 Then Jehovah said to Moses: "Get up early in the morning and take a position in front of Phar'aoh. Look! He is coming out to the water! And you must say to him, 'This is what Jehovah has said: "Send my people away that they may serve me. 21 But if you are not sending my people away, here I am sending upon you and your

servants and your people and into your houses the gadfly; and the houses of Egypt will simply be full of the gadfly, and also the ground upon which they are. 22 And on that day I shall certainly make the land of Go′shen upon which my people are standing distinct, that no gadfly may exist there; in order that you may know that I am Jehovah in the midst of the earth. 23 And I shall indeed set a demarcation between my people and your people. Tomorrow this sign will take place.″ ′ ″

24 And Jehovah proceeded to do so; and heavy swarms of gadflies began to invade the house of Phar′aoh and the houses of his servants and all the land of Egypt. The land came to ruin as a result of the gadflies. 25 Finally Phar′aoh called Moses and Aaron and said: "Go, sacrifice to YOUR God in the land." 26 But Moses said: "It is not admissible to do so, because we would sacrifice to Jehovah our God a thing detestable to the Egyptians. Suppose we would sacrifice a thing detestable to the Egyptians before their eyes; would they not stone us? 27 We shall go a journey of three days into the wilderness and we shall definitely sacrifice to Jehovah our God just as he has said to us."

28 Phar′aoh now said: "I—I shall send YOU away, and YOU will indeed sacrifice to Jehovah YOUR God in the wilderness. Only do not make it quite so far away that YOU are going. Make entreaty in my behalf." 29 Then Moses said: "Here I am going forth from you, and I shall indeed make entreaty to Jehovah, and the gadflies will certainly turn away from Phar′aoh, his servants and his people tomorrow. Only let not Phar′aoh trifle again in not sending the people away to sacrifice to Jehovah." 30 After that Moses went out from Phar′aoh and made entreaty to Jehovah. 31 So Jehovah did according to Moses' word, and the gadflies turned away from Phar′aoh, his servants and his people. Not one was left. 32 However, Phar′-

aoh made his heart unresponsive this time also and did not send the people away.

9 Consequently Jehovah said to Moses: "Go in to Phar′aoh and you must state to him, 'This is what Jehovah the God of the Hebrews has said: "Send my people away that they may serve me. 2 But if you continue refusing to send them away and you are still keeping hold of them, 3 look! Jehovah's hand is coming upon your livestock that is in the field. On the horses, the asses, the camels, the herd and the flock there will be a very heavy pestilence. 4 And Jehovah will certainly make a distinction between the livestock of Israel and the livestock of Egypt, and not a thing of all that belongs to the sons of Israel will die." ' " 5 Moreover, Jehovah set an appointed time, saying: "Tomorrow Jehovah will do this thing in the land."

6 Accordingly Jehovah did this thing on the next day, and all sorts of livestock of Egypt began to die; but not one of the livestock of the sons of Israel died. 7 Then Phar′aoh sent, and, look! not so much as one of Israel's livestock had died. Nevertheless, Phar′aoh's heart continued to be unresponsive, and he did not send the people away.

8 After that Jehovah said to Moses and Aaron: "Take for yourselves both hands full of soot from a kiln, and Moses must toss it toward the heavens in Phar′aoh's sight. 9 And it must become a powder upon all the land of Egypt, and it must become boils breaking out with blisters upon man and beast in all the land of Egypt."

10 So they took the soot of a kiln and stood before Phar′aoh, and Moses tossed it toward the heavens, and it became boils with blisters, breaking out on man and beast. 11 And the magic-practicing priests were unable to stand before Moses as a result of the boils, because the boils had developed on the magic-practicing priests and on all the Egyptians. 12 But Jehovah let Phar′aoh's heart become obstinate,

and he did not listen to them, just as Jehovah had stated to Moses.

13 Then Jehovah said to Moses: "Get up early in the morning and take a position in front of Phar'aoh, and you must say to him, 'This is what Jehovah the God of the Hebrews has said: "Send my people away that they may serve me. 14 For at this time I am sending all my blows against your heart and upon your servants and your people, to the end that you may know that there is none like me in all the earth. 15 For by now I could have thrust my hand out that I might strike you and your people with pestilence and that you might be effaced from the earth. 16 But, in fact, for this cause I have kept you in existence, for the sake of showing you my power and in order to have my name declared in all the earth. 17 Are you still behaving haughtily against my people in not sending them away? 18 Here I am causing it to rain down tomorrow about this time a very heavy hail, the like of which has never occurred in Egypt from the day it was founded until now. 19 And now send, bring all your livestock and all that is yours in the field under shelter. As for any man or beast that will be found in the field and not gathered into the house, the hail will have to come down upon them, and they will have to die." '"

20 Anyone who feared Jehovah's word among Phar'aoh's servants caused his own servants and his livestock to flee into the houses, 21 but whoever did not set his heart to have any regard for Jehovah's word left his servants and his livestock in the field.

22 Jehovah now said to Moses: "Stretch out your hand toward the heavens, that hail may come on all the land of Egypt, upon man and beast and all vegetation of the field in the land of Egypt." 23 So Moses stretched out his rod toward the heavens; and Jehovah gave thunders and hail, and fire would run down to the earth, and Jehovah kept making it rain down hail upon the land of Egypt. 24 Thus there came hail, and fire quivering in among the hail. It was very heavy, so that there had not occurred any like it in all the land of Egypt from the time it became a nation. 25 And the hail went striking at all the land of Egypt. The hail struck everything that was in the field, from man to beast, and all sorts of vegetation of the field; and it shattered all sorts of trees of the field. 26 Only in the land of Go'shen, where the sons of Israel were, there occurred no hail.

27 Eventually Phar'aoh sent and called Moses and Aaron and said to them: "I have sinned this time. Jehovah is righteous, and I and my people are in the wrong. 28 Entreat Jehovah that this may be enough of the occurring of God's thunders and hail. Then I am willing to send YOU away, and YOU will not stay any longer." 29 So Moses said to him: "As soon as I go out of the city I shall spread my hands up to Jehovah. The thunders will stop and the hail will not continue any longer, in order that you may know that the earth belongs to Jehovah. 30 As for you and your servants, I know already that YOU will not even then show fear because of Jehovah God."

31 As it was, the flax and the barley had been struck, because the barley was in the ear and the flax had flower buds. 32 But the wheat and the spelt had not been struck, because they were seasonally late. 33 Moses now went out of the city from Phar'aoh and spread his hands up to Jehovah, and the thunders and the hail began to stop and rain did not pour down on the earth. 34 When Phar'aoh got to see that the rain and the hail and the thunders had stopped, he went sinning again and making his heart unresponsive, he as well as his servants. 35 And Phar'aoh's heart continued obstinate, and he did not send the sons of Israel away, just as Jehovah had stated by means of Moses.

10 Then Jehovah said to Moses: "Go in to Phar'aoh, because I—I have let his heart and the hearts of his servants become unresponsive, in order that I may set these signs of mine right before him, 2 and in order that you may declare in the ears of your son and your son's son how severely I have dealt with Egypt and my signs that I have established among them; and YOU will certainly know that I am Jehovah."

3 So Moses and Aaron went in to Phar'aoh and said to him: "This is what Jehovah the God of the Hebrews has said, 'How long must you refuse to submit yourself to me? Send my people away that they may serve me. 4 For if you continue refusing to send my people away, here I am bringing locusts within your boundaries tomorrow. 5 And they will actually cover the visible surface of the earth and it will not be possible to see the earth; and they will simply eat up the rest of what has escaped, what has been left to YOU people by the hail, and they will certainly eat every sprouting tree of YOURS out of the field. 6 And your houses and the houses of all your servants and the houses of all Egypt will be filled to an extent that your fathers and your fathers' fathers have not seen it from the day of their existing upon the ground until this day.'" With that he turned and went out from Phar'aoh.

7 After that Phar'aoh's servants said to him: "How long will this man prove to be as a snare to us? Send the men away that they may serve Jehovah their God. Do you not yet know that Egypt has perished?" 8 So Moses and Aaron were brought back to Phar'aoh, and he said to them: "Go, serve Jehovah YOUR God. Who in particular are the ones going?" 9 Then Moses said: "With our young people and our old people we shall go. With our sons and our daughters, with our sheep and our cattle we shall go, for we have a festival to Jehovah." 10 In turn he said to them: "Let it prove to be so, that Jehovah is with YOU when I shall send YOU and YOUR little ones away! See, on the contrary, something evil is YOUR aim. 11 Not so! Go, please, YOU who are able-bodied men, and serve Jehovah, because that is what YOU are seeking to secure." With that they were driven out from before Phar'aoh.

12 Jehovah now said to Moses: "Stretch your hand out over the land of Egypt for the locusts, that they may come up over the land of Egypt and eat up all the vegetation of the land, everything that the hail has let remain." 13 At once Moses stretched his rod out over the land of Egypt, and Jehovah caused an east wind to blow upon the land all that day and all night. The morning came and the east wind carried the locusts. 14 And the locusts began to come up over all the land of Egypt and to settle down upon all the territory of Egypt. They were very burdensome. Before them there had never turned up in this way locusts like them, and there will never turn up any in this way after them. 15 And they went covering the visible surface of the entire land, and the land grew dark; and they went on eating up all the vegetation of the land and all the fruit of the trees that the hail had left; and there was left nothing green on the trees or on the vegetation of the field in all the land of Egypt.

16 So Phar'aoh hurriedly called Moses and Aaron and said: "I have sinned against Jehovah YOUR God and against YOU. 17 And now pardon, please, my sin just this once and ENTREAT Jehovah YOUR God that he may turn away just this deadly plague from upon me." 18 So he went out from Phar'aoh and made entreaty to Jehovah. 19 Then Jehovah made a shift to a very stiff west wind, and it carried the locusts away and drove them into the Red Sea. Not a single locust was let remain in all the territory of Egypt. 20 However, Jehovah let Phar'aoh's heart be-

come obstinate, and he did not send the sons of Israel away.

21 Jehovah then said to Moses: "Stretch your hand out toward the heavens, that darkness may occur over the land of Egypt and the darkness may be felt." 22 Moses immediately stretched his hand out toward the heavens, and a gloomy darkness began to occur in all the land of Egypt for three days. 23 They did not see one another, and none of them got up from his own place three days; but for all the sons of Israel there proved to be light in their dwellings. 24 After that Phar'aoh called Moses and said: "Go, SERVE Jehovah. Only YOUR sheep and YOUR cattle will be detained. YOUR little ones also may go with YOU." 25 But Moses said: "You yourself will also give into our hands sacrifices and burnt offerings, as we must render them to Jehovah our God. 26 And our livestock will also go with us. Not a hoof will be allowed to remain, because it is from them that we shall take some to worship Jehovah our God, and we ourselves do not know what we shall render in worship to Jehovah until our arriving there." 27 At this Jehovah let Phar'aoh's heart become obstinate, and he did not consent to send them away. 28 So Phar'aoh said to him: "Get out from me! Watch yourself! Do not try to see my face again, because on the day of your seeing my face you will die." 29 To this Moses said: "That is the way you have spoken. I shall not try to see your face any more."

11 And Jehovah proceeded to say to Moses: "One plague more I am going to bring upon Phar'aoh and Egypt. After that he will send YOU away from here. At the time he sends YOU away altogether, he will literally drive YOU out from here. 2 Speak, now, in the ears of the people, that they should ask every man of his companion and every woman of her companion articles of silver and articles of gold." 3 Accordingly Jehovah gave the people favor in the eyes of the Egyptians. The man Moses too was very great in the land of Egypt, in the eyes of Phar'aoh's servants and in the eyes of the people.

4 And Moses went on to say: "This is what Jehovah has said, 'About midnight I am going out into the midst of Egypt, 5 and every first-born in the land of Egypt must die, from the first-born of Phar'aoh who is sitting on his throne to the first-born of the maidservant who is at the hand mill and every first-born of beast. 6 And there will certainly occur a great outcry in all the land of Egypt, the like of which has never yet occurred, and the like of which will never be brought about again. 7 But against any of the sons of Israel will no dog move eagerly its tongue, from man to beast; in order that YOU people may know that Jehovah can make a distinction between the Egyptians and the sons of Israel.' 8 And all these servants of yours will certainly come down to me and prostrate themselves to me, saying, 'Go, you and all the people who follow your steps.' And after that I shall go out." With that he went out from Phar'aoh in the heat of anger.

9 Then Jehovah said to Moses: "Phar'aoh will not listen to YOU men, in order for my miracles to be increased in the land of Egypt." 10 And Moses and Aaron performed all these miracles before Phar'aoh; but Jehovah would let Phar'aoh's heart become obstinate, so that he did not send the sons of Israel away from his land.

12 Jehovah now said to Moses and Aaron in the land of Egypt: 2 "This month will be the start of the months for YOU. It will be the first of the months of the year for YOU. 3 Speak to the entire assembly of Israel, saying, 'On the tenth day of this month they are to take for themselves each one a sheep for the ancestral house, a sheep to a house. 4 But if the household proves to be too small for the sheep, then he and his neighbor close by must take it into his house according to the number of souls; YOU should compute each

one proportionate to his eating as regards the sheep. 5 The sheep should prove to be sound, a male, a year old, for you. You may pick from the young rams or from the goats. 6 And it must continue under safeguard by you until the fourteenth day of this month, and the whole congregation of the assembly of Israel must slaughter it between the two evenings. 7 And they must take some of the blood and splash it upon the two doorposts and the upper part of the doorway belonging to the houses in which they will eat it.

8 "'And they must eat the flesh on this night. They should eat it roasted with fire and with unfermented cakes along with bitter greens. 9 Do not eat any of it raw or boiled, cooked in water, but roast with fire, its head together with its shanks and its interior parts. 10 And you must not leave any of it over till morning, but what is left over of it till morning you should burn with fire. 11 And in this way you should eat it, with your hips girded, sandals on your feet and your staff in your hand; and you must eat it in haste. It is Jehovah's passover. 12 And I must pass through the land of Egypt on this night and strike every first-born in the land of Egypt, from man to beast; and on all the gods of Egypt I shall execute judgments. I am Jehovah. 13 And the blood must serve as your sign upon the houses where you are; and I must see the blood and pass over you, and the plague will not come on you as a ruination when I strike at the land of Egypt.

14 "'And this day must serve as a memorial for you, and you must celebrate it as a festival to Jehovah throughout your generations. As a statute to time indefinite you should celebrate it. 15 Seven days you are to eat unfermented cakes only. On the first day you are to take away sour dough from your houses, because anyone eating what is leavened, from the first day down to the seventh, that soul must be cut off from Israel. 16 And on the first day there is to take place for you a holy convention, and on the seventh day a holy convention. No work is to be done on them. Only what every soul needs to eat, that alone may be done for you.

17 "'And you must keep the festival of unfermented cakes, because on this very day I must bring your armies out from the land of Egypt. And you must keep this day throughout your generations as a statute to time indefinite. 18 In the first month, on the fourteenth day of the month, in the evening you are to eat unfermented cakes down till the twenty-first day of the month in the evening. 19 Seven days no sour dough is to be found in your houses, because anyone tasting what is leavened, whether he is an alien resident or a native of the land, that soul must be cut off from the assembly of Israel. 20 Nothing leavened are you to eat. In all your dwellings you are to eat unfermented cakes.'"

21 Promptly Moses called all the older men of Israel and said to them: "Draw out and take for yourselves small cattle according to your families, and slaughter the passover victim. 22 And you must take a bunch of hyssop and dip it into the blood in a basin and strike upon the upper part of the doorway and upon the two doorposts some of the blood that is in the basin; and none of you should go out of the entrance of his house until morning. 23 Then when Jehovah does pass through to plague the Egyptians and does see the blood upon the upper part of the doorway and upon the two doorposts, Jehovah will certainly pass over the entrance, and he will not allow the ruination to enter into your houses to plague you.

24 "And you must keep this thing as a regulation for you and your sons to time indefinite. 25 And it must occur that when you come into the land that Jehovah will give you, just as he has stated, then you must keep this service. 26 And it must occur that when your sons say to you, 'What

does this service mean to you?' 27 then you must say, 'It is the sacrifice of the passover to Jehovah, who passed over the houses of the sons of Israel in Egypt when he plagued the Egyptians, but he delivered our houses.'"

Then the people bowed low and prostrated themselves. 28 Subsequently the sons of Israel went and did just as Jehovah had commanded Moses and Aaron. They did just so.

29 And it came about that at midnight Jehovah struck every first-born in the land of Egypt, from the first-born of Phar'aoh sitting on his throne to the first-born of the captive who was in the prison hole, and every first-born of beast. 30 Then Phar'aoh got up at night, he and all his servants and all other Egyptians; and there began arising a great outcry among the Egyptians, because there was not a house where there was not one dead. 31 At once he called Moses and Aaron by night and said: "Get up, get out from the midst of my people, both you and the [other] sons of Israel, and go, serve Jehovah, just as you have stated. 32 Take both your flocks and your herds, just as you have stated, and go. Also, you must bless me besides."

33 And the Egyptians began to urge the people in order to send them away quickly out of the land, "because," they said, "we are all as good as dead!" 34 Consequently the people carried their flour dough before it was leavened, with their kneading troughs wrapped up in their mantles upon their shoulder. 35 And the sons of Israel did according to the word of Moses in that they went asking from the Egyptians articles of silver and articles of gold and mantles. 36 And Jehovah gave the people favor in the eyes of the Egyptians, so that these granted what was asked; and they stripped the Egyptians.

37 And the sons of Israel proceeded to depart from Ram'e·ses for Suc'coth, to the number of six hundred thousand able-bodied men on foot, besides little ones. 38 And a vast mixed company also went up with them, as well as flocks and herds, a very numerous stock of animals. 39 And they began to bake the flour dough that they had brought out from Egypt into round cakes, unfermented cakes, because it had not leavened, for they had been driven out of Egypt and had not been able to linger and too they had not prepared any provisions for themselves.

40 And the dwelling of the sons of Israel, who had dwelt in Egypt, was four hundred and thirty years. 41 And it came about at the end of the four hundred and thirty years, it even came about on this very day that all the armies of Jehovah went out of the land of Egypt. 42 It is a night for observance with regard to Jehovah for bringing them out of the land of Egypt. With regard to Jehovah this night is one for observance on the part of all the sons of Israel throughout their generations.

43 And Jehovah went on to say to Moses and Aaron: "This is the statute of the passover: No foreigner may eat of it. 44 But where there is any slave man purchased with money, you must circumcise him. Then first he may share in eating it. 45 A settler and a hired laborer may not eat of it. 46 In one house it is to be eaten. You must not take any of the flesh out of the house to some place outside. And you must not break a bone in it. 47 All the assembly of Israel are to celebrate it. 48 And in case an alien resident resides as an alien with you and he will actually celebrate the passover to Jehovah, let there be a circumcising of every male of his. First then he may come near to celebrate it; and he must become like a native of the land. But no uncircumcised man may eat of it. 49 One law is to exist for the native and for the alien resident who is residing as an alien in your midst."

50 So all the sons of Israel did just as Jehovah had commanded

Moses and Aaron. They did just so. 51 And it came about on this very day that Jehovah brought the sons of Israel together with their armies out of the land of Egypt.

13 And Jehovah spoke further to Moses, saying: 2 "Sanctify to me every male first-born that opens each womb among the sons of Israel, among men and beasts. It is mine."

3 And Moses went on to say to the people: "Let there be a remembering of this day on which you went out of Egypt, from the house of slaves, because by strength of hand Jehovah brought you out from here. So nothing leavened may be eaten. 4 Today you are going out in the month of A'bib. 5 And it must occur that when Jehovah will have brought you into the land of the Ca'naan·ites and the Hit'tites and the Am'or·ites and the Hi'vites and the Jeb'usites, which he swore to your forefathers to give you, a land flowing with milk and honey, then you must render this service in this month. 6 Seven days you are to eat unfermented cakes, and on the seventh day is a festival to Jehovah. 7 Unfermented cakes are to be eaten for the seven days; and nothing leavened is to be seen with you, and no sour dough is to be seen with you within all your boundaries. 8 And you must tell your son on that day, saying, 'It is because of that which Jehovah has done to me when I came out of Egypt.' 9 And it must serve for you as a sign upon your hand and as a memorial between your eyes, in order that Jehovah's law may prove to be in your mouth; because by a strong hand Jehovah brought you out of Egypt. 10 And you must keep this statute at its appointed time from year to year.

11 "And it must occur that when Jehovah brings you into the land of the Ca'naan·ites, just as he has sworn to you and to your forefathers, and when he does give it to you, 12 then you must devote everyone that opens the womb to Jehovah, and every firstling, the young of a beast, which will come to be yours. The males belong to Jehovah. 13 And every firstling ass you are to redeem with a sheep, and if you will not redeem it, then you must break its neck. And every first-born of man among your sons you are to redeem.

14 "And it must occur that in case your son should inquire of you later on, saying, 'What does this mean?' then you must say to him, 'By strength of hand Jehovah brought me out of Egypt, from the house of slaves. 15 And it came about that Phar'aoh showed obstinacy toward sending us away, and Jehovah proceeded to kill every first-born in the land of Egypt, from the first-born of man to the first-born of beast. That is why I am sacrificing to Jehovah all the males that open the womb, and every first-born of my sons I redeem.' 16 And it must serve as a sign upon your hand and as a frontlet band between your eyes, because by strength of hand Jehovah brought us out of Egypt."

17 And it came about at the time of Phar'aoh's sending the people away that God did not lead them by the way of the land of the Phi·lis'tines just because it was near, for God said: "It might be the people will feel regret when they see war and will certainly return to Egypt." 18 Hence God made the people go round about by the way of the wilderness of the Red Sea. But it was in battle formation that the sons of Israel went up out of the land of Egypt. 19 And Moses was taking Joseph's bones with him, because he had made the sons of Israel solemnly swear, saying: "God will without fail turn his attention to you, and you must take my bones up out of here with you." 20 And they proceeded to depart from Suc'coth and to encamp at E'tham at the edge of the wilderness.

21 And Jehovah was going ahead of them in the daytime in a pillar of cloud to lead them by the way, and in the nighttime in a pillar of fire to give them light to go in the

daytime and nighttime. 22 The pillar of cloud would not move away from before the people in the daytime nor the pillar of fire in the nighttime.

14 Jehovah now spoke to Moses, saying: 2 "Speak to the sons of Israel, that they should turn back and encamp before Pi·ha·hi'roth between Mig'dol and the sea in view of Ba'al-ze'phon. In front of it you are to encamp by the sea. 3 Then Phar'aoh will certainly say respecting the sons of Israel, 'They are wandering in confusion in the land. The wilderness has closed in upon them.' 4 So I shall indeed let Phar'aoh's heart become obstinate, and he will certainly chase after them and I shall get glory for myself by means of Phar'aoh and all his military forces; and the Egyptians will certainly know that I am Jehovah." Accordingly they did just that.

5 Later it was reported to the king of Egypt that the people had run away. Immediately the heart of Phar'aoh as well as his servants was changed regarding the people, so that they said: "What is this that we have done, in that we have sent Israel away from slaving for us?" 6 So he proceeded to make his war chariots ready, and he took his people with him. 7 And he proceeded to take six hundred chosen chariots and all the other chariots of Egypt and warriors upon every one of them. 8 Thus Jehovah let the heart of Phar'aoh the king of Egypt become obstinate, and he went chasing after the sons of Israel, while the sons of Israel were going out with uplifted hand. 9 And the Egyptians went chasing after them, and all the chariot horses of Phar'aoh and his cavalrymen and his military forces were overtaking them while camping by the sea, by Pi·ha·hi'roth in view of Ba'al-ze'phon.

10 When Phar'aoh got close by, the sons of Israel began to raise their eyes and here the Egyptians were marching after them; and the sons of Israel got quite afraid and began to cry out to Jehovah.

11 And they proceeded to say to Moses: "Is it because there are no burial places at all in Egypt that you have taken us here to die in the wilderness? What is this that you have done to us in leading us out of Egypt? 12 Is this not the word we spoke to you in Egypt, saying, 'Let us alone, that we may serve the Egyptians'? For it is better for us to serve the Egyptians than for us to die in the wilderness." 13 Then Moses said to the people: "Do not be afraid. Stand firm and see the salvation of Jehovah, which he will perform for you today. For the Egyptians whom you do see today you will not see again, no, never again. 14 Jehovah will himself fight for you, and you yourselves will be silent."

15 Jehovah now said to Moses: "Why do you keep crying out to me? Speak to the sons of Israel that they should break camp. 16 As for you, lift up your rod and stretch your hand out over the sea and split it apart, that the sons of Israel may go through the midst of the sea on dry land. 17 As for me, here I am letting the hearts of the Egyptians become obstinate, that they may go in after them and that I may get glory for myself by means of Phar'aoh and all his military forces, his war chariots and his cavalrymen. 18 And the Egyptians will certainly know that I am Jehovah when I get glory for myself by means of Phar'aoh, his war chariots and his cavalrymen."

19 Then the angel of the [true] God who was going ahead of the camp of Israel departed and went to their rear, and the pillar of cloud departed from their van and stood in the rear of them. 20 So it came in between the camp of the Egyptians and the camp of Israel. On the one hand it proved to be a cloud together with darkness. On the other hand it kept lighting up the night. And this group did not come near that group all night long.

21 Moses now stretched his hand out over the sea; and Jehovah began making the sea go back by a strong east wind all night long and

converting the sea basin into dry ground, and the waters were being split apart. 22 At length the sons of Israel went through the midst of the sea on dry land, while the waters were a wall to them on their right hand and on their left. 23 And the Egyptians took up the pursuit, and all the horses of Phar'aoh, his war chariots and his cavalrymen began going in after them, into the midst of the sea. 24 And it came about during the morning watch that Jehovah began to look out upon the camp of the Egyptians from within the pillar of fire and cloud, and he went throwing the camp of the Egyptians into confusion. 25 And he kept taking wheels off their chariots so that they were driving them with difficulty; and the Egyptians began to say: "Let us flee from any contact with Israel, because Jehovah certainly fights for them against the Egyptians."

26 Finally Jehovah said to Moses: "Stretch your hand out over the sea, that the waters may come back over the Egyptians, their war chariots and their cavalrymen." 27 Moses at once stretched his hand out over the sea, and the sea began to come back to its normal condition at the approaching of morning. All the while the Egyptians were fleeing from encountering it, but Jehovah shook the Egyptians off into the midst of the sea. 28 And the waters kept coming back. Finally they covered the war chariots and the cavalrymen belonging to all of Phar'aoh's military forces and who had gone into the sea after them. Not so much as one among them was let remain.

29 As for the sons of Israel, they walked on dry land in the midst of the seabed, and the waters were for them a wall on their right hand and on their left. 30 Thus on that day Jehovah saved Israel from the hand of the Egyptians, and Israel got to see the Egyptians dead on the seashore. 31 Israel also got to see the great hand that Jehovah put in action against the Egyptians; and the people began to fear Jehovah and to put faith in Jehovah and in Moses his servant.

15 At that time Moses and the sons of Israel proceeded to sing this song to Jehovah and to say the following:

"Let me sing to Jehovah, for he has become highly exalted. The horse and its rider he has pitched into the sea.

2 My strength and my might is Jah, since he serves for my salvation.

This is my God, and I shall laud him; my father's God, and I shall raise him on high.

3 Jehovah is a manly person of war. Jehovah is his name.

4 Phar'aoh's chariots and his military forces he has cast into the sea,

And the choice of his warriors have been sunk in the Red Sea.

5 The surging waters proceeded to cover them; down they went into the depths like a stone.

6 Your right hand, O Jehovah, is proving itself powerful in ability,

Your right hand, O Jehovah, can shatter an enemy.

7 And in the abundance of your superiority you can throw down those who rise up against you;

You send out your burning anger, it eats them up like stubble.

8 And by a breath from your nostrils waters were heaped up;

They stood still like a dam of floods;

The surging waters were congealed in the heart of the sea.

9 The enemy said, 'I shall pursue! I shall overtake!

I shall divide spoil! My soul will be filled with them!

I shall draw my sword! My hand will drive them away!'

10 You blew with your breath, the sea covered them;

They sank like lead in majestic waters.

11 Who among the gods is like you,
  O Jehovah?
  Who is like you, proving your-
    self mighty in holiness?
  The One to be feared with
    songs of praise, the One
    doing marvels.
12 You stretched out your right
    hand, the earth proceeded
    to swallow them up.
13 You in your loving-kindness
    have led the people whom
    you have recovered;
  You in your strength will cer-
    tainly conduct them to your
    holy abiding place.
14 Peoples must hear, they will be
    agitated;
  Birth pangs must take hold
    on the inhabitants of Phi-
    lis'ti·a.
15 At that time the sheiks of E'dom
    will indeed be disturbed;
  As for the despots of Mo'ab,
    trembling will take hold on
    them.
  All the inhabitants of Ca'naan
    will indeed be disheartened.
16 Fright and dread will fall upon
    them.
  Because of the greatness of
    your arm they will be mo-
    tionless like a stone,
  Until your people pass by, O
    Jehovah,
  Until the people whom you
    have produced pass by.
17 You will bring them and plant
    them in the mountain of
    your inheritance,
  An established place that you
    have made ready for you to
    inhabit, O Jehovah,
  A sanctuary, O Jehovah, that
    your hands have established.
18 Jehovah will rule as king to time
    indefinite, even forever."

19 When Phar'aoh's horses with
his war chariots and his cavalrymen went into the sea, then Jehovah brought back the waters of
the sea upon them, while the sons
of Israel walked on dry land
through the midst of the sea.
20 And Mir'i·am the prophetess,
Aaron's sister, proceeded to take a
tambourine in her hand; and all
the women began going out with
her with tambourines and in
dances. 21 And Mir'i·am kept responding to the men:

  "Sing to Jehovah, for he has
    become highly exalted.
  The horse and its rider he has
    pitched into the sea."

22 Later Moses caused Israel to
depart from the Red Sea and they
went out to the wilderness of Shur
and marched on for three days in
the wilderness, but they did not
find water. 23 In time they came
to Ma'rah, but they were not able
to drink the water from Ma'rah
because it was bitter. That is why
he called its name Ma'rah. 24 And
the people began to murmur against
Moses, saying: "What are we to
drink?" 25 Then he cried out to
Jehovah. So Jehovah directed him
to a tree, and he threw it into the
water and the water became sweet.
There He established for them a
regulation and a case for judgment
and there he put them to the test.
26 And he went on to say: "If you
will strictly listen to the voice of
Jehovah your God and will do what
is right in his eyes and will indeed
give ear to his commandments and
keep all his regulations, I shall put
none of the maladies upon you that
I put upon the Egyptians; because
I am Jehovah who is healing you."
27 After that they came to E'lim,
where there were twelve springs of
water and seventy palm trees. So
they went camping there by the
water.

16 Later they departed from
E'lim, and the entire assembly
of the sons of Israel finally came
to the wilderness of Sin, which is
between E'lim and Si'nai, on the
fifteenth day of the second month
after their coming out of the land
of Egypt.
2 And the entire assembly of the
sons of Israel began to murmur
against Moses and Aaron in the wilderness. 3 And the sons of Israel
kept saying to them: "If only we
had died by Jehovah's hand in the
land of Egypt while we were sitting

by the pots of meat, while we were eating bread to satisfaction, because YOU have brought us out into this wilderness to put this whole congregation to death by famine."

4 Then Jehovah said to Moses: "Here I am raining down bread for YOU from the heavens; and the people must go out and pick up each his amount day for day, in order that I may put them to the test as to whether they will walk in my law or not. 5 And it must occur on the sixth day that they must prepare what they will bring in, and it must prove double what they keep picking up day by day."

6 So Moses and Aaron said to all the sons of Israel: "At evening YOU will certainly know that it is Jehovah who has brought YOU out from the land of Egypt. 7 And in the morning YOU will indeed see Jehovah's glory, because he has heard YOUR murmurings against Jehovah. And what are we that YOU should murmur against us?" 8 And Moses continued: "It will be when Jehovah gives YOU in the evening meat to eat and in the morning bread to satisfaction, because Jehovah has heard YOUR murmurings that YOU are murmuring against him. And what are we? YOUR murmurings are not against us, but against Jehovah."

9 And Moses went on to say to Aaron: "Say to the entire assembly of the sons of Israel, 'Come near before Jehovah, because he has heard YOUR murmurings.'" 10 Then it occurred that as soon as Aaron had spoken to the entire assembly of the sons of Israel, they turned and faced toward the wilderness, and, look! Jehovah's glory appeared in the cloud.

11 And Jehovah spoke further to Moses, saying: 12 "I have heard the murmurings of the sons of Israel. Speak to them, saying, 'Between the two evenings YOU will eat meat and in the morning YOU will be satisfied with bread; and YOU will certainly know that I am Jehovah YOUR God.'"

13 Accordingly it occurred that in the evening the quails began to come up and cover the camp, and in the morning there had developed a layer of dew round about the camp. 14 In time the layer of dew evaporated and here upon the surface of the wilderness there was a fine flaky thing, fine like hoarfrost upon the earth. 15 When the sons of Israel got to see it, they began to say to one another: "What is it?" For they did not know what it was. Hence Moses said to them: "It is the bread that Jehovah has given YOU for food. 16 This is the word that Jehovah has commanded, 'Pick up some of it, each one in proportion to his eating. YOU are to take an omer measure for each individual according to the number of the souls that each of YOU has in his tent.'" 17 And the sons of Israel began to do so; and they went picking it up, some gathering much and some gathering little. 18 When they would measure it by the omer, he that had gathered much had no surplus and he that had gathered little had no shortage. They picked it up each one in proportion to his eating.

19 Then Moses said to them: "Let nobody leave any of it until the morning." 20 But they did not listen to Moses. When some men would leave some of it until the morning, it would breed worms and stink; so that Moses became indignant at them. 21 And they would pick it up morning by morning, each one in proportion to his eating. When the sun got hot, it melted.

22 And it came about on the sixth day that they picked up twice as much bread, two omer measures for one person. So all the chieftains of the assembly came and reported it to Moses. 23 At that he said to them: "It is what Jehovah has spoken. Tomorrow there will be a sabbath observance of a holy sabbath to Jehovah. What YOU can bake, bake, and what YOU can boil, boil, and all the surplus that there is save it up for YOU as something to be kept until the morning." 24 Accordingly they saved it up until the

morning, just as Moses had commanded; and it did not stink nor did maggots develop in it. 25 Then Moses said: "Eat it today, because today is a sabbath to Jehovah. Today YOU will not find it in the field. 26 Six days YOU will pick it up, but on the seventh day is a sabbath. On it none will form." 27 However, it came about on the seventh day that some of the people did go out to pick [it] up, but they found none.

28 Consequently Jehovah said to Moses: "How long must YOU people refuse to keep my commandments and my laws? 29 Mark the fact that Jehovah has given YOU the sabbath. That is why he is giving YOU on the sixth day the bread of two days. Keep sitting each one in his own place. Let nobody go out from his locality on the seventh day." 30 And the people proceeded to observe the sabbath on the seventh day.

31 And the house of Israel began to call its name "manna." And it was white like coriander seed, and its taste was like that of flat cakes with honey. 32 Then Moses said: "This is the word that Jehovah has commanded, 'Fill an omer measure of it as something to be kept throughout YOUR generations, in order that they may see the bread that I made YOU eat in the wilderness when I was bringing YOU out of the land of Egypt.' " 33 So Moses said to Aaron: "Take a jar and put in it an omerful of manna and deposit it before Jehovah as something to be kept throughout YOUR generations." 34 Just as Jehovah had commanded Moses, Aaron proceeded to deposit it before the Testimony as something to be kept. 35 And the sons of Israel ate the manna forty years, until their coming to a land inhabited. The manna was what they ate until their coming to the frontier of the land of Ca'naan. 36 Now an omer is a tenth of an e'phah measure.

17 And the entire assembly of the sons of Israel proceeded to depart from the wilderness of Sin by stages, which they took according to the order of Jehovah, and went camping at Reph'i·dim. But there was no water for the people to drink.

2 And the people fell to quarreling with Moses and saying: "Give us water that we may drink." But Moses said to them: "Why are YOU quarreling with me? Why do YOU keep putting Jehovah to the test?" 3 And the people went on thirsting there for water, and the people kept murmuring against Moses and saying: "Why is it that you have brought us up out of Egypt to put us and our sons and our livestock to death by thirst?" 4 Finally Moses cried out to Jehovah, saying: "What shall I do with this people? A little longer and they will stone me!"

5 Then Jehovah said to Moses: "Pass in front of the people and take with you some of the older men of Israel and your rod with which you struck the Nile River. Take it in your hand and you must walk on. 6 Look! I am standing before you there on the rock in Ho'reb. And you must strike on the rock, and water must come out of it, and the people must drink it." Subsequently Moses did so under the eyes of the older men of Israel. 7 So he called the name of the place Mas'sah and Mer'i·bah, because of the quarreling of the sons of Israel and because of their putting Jehovah to the test, saying: "Is Jehovah in our midst or not?"

8 And the A·mal'ek·ites proceeded to come and fight against Israel in Reph'i·dim. 9 At this Moses said to Joshua: "Choose men for us and go out, fight against the A·mal'ek·ites. Tomorrow I am stationing myself upon the top of the hill, with the rod of the [true] God in my hand." 10 Then Joshua did just as Moses had said to him, in order to fight against the A·mal'ek·ites; and Moses, Aaron and Hur went up to the top of the hill.

11 And it occurred that as soon as Moses would lift his hand up, the Israelites proved superior; but

as soon as he would let down his hand, the A·mal′ek·ites proved superior. 12 When the hands of Moses were heavy, then they took a stone and put it under him, and he sat upon it; and Aaron and Hur supported his hands, one on this side and the other on that side, so that his hands held steady until the sun set. 13 Hence Joshua vanquished Am′a·lek and his people with the edge of the sword.

14 Jehovah now said to Moses: "Write this as a memorial in the book and propound it in Joshua's ears, 'I shall completely wipe out the remembrance of Am′a·lek from under the heavens.'" 15 And Moses proceeded to build an altar and to call its name Je·ho′vah-nis′si, 16 saying: "Because a hand is against the throne of Jah, Jehovah will have war with Am′a·lek from generation to generation."

18 Now Jeth′ro the priest of Mid′i·an, Moses' father-in-law, got to hear about all that God had done for Moses and for Israel his people, how Jehovah had brought Israel out of Egypt. 2 So Jeth′ro, Moses' father-in-law, took Zip·po′rah, Moses' wife, after the sending of her away, 3 and her two sons, the name of one of whom was Ger′shom, "because," he said, "an alien resident I have come to be in a foreign land"; 4 and the name of the other was E·li·e′zer, "because," to quote him, "the God of my father is my helper in that he delivered me from Phar′aoh's sword."

5 So Jeth′ro, Moses' father-in-law, and his sons and his wife came to Moses into the wilderness where he was camping, at the mountain of the [true] God. 6 Then he sent word to Moses: "I, your father-in-law, Jeth′ro, am come to you, and also your wife and her two sons with her." 7 At once Moses went on out to meet his father-in-law, and he proceeded to prostrate himself and to kiss him; and they each one began asking how the other was getting along. After that they went into the tent.

8 And Moses went to relating to his father-in-law all that Jehovah had done to Phar′aoh and Egypt on account of Israel, and all the hardship that had befallen them in the way, and yet Jehovah was delivering them. 9 Then Jeth′ro felt glad over all the good that Jehovah had done for Israel in that he had delivered them from the hand of Egypt. 10 Consequently Jeth′ro said: "Blessed be Jehovah, who has delivered you from the hand of Egypt and from the hand of Phar′aoh, and who has delivered the people from under the hand of Egypt. 11 Now I do know that Jehovah is greater than all the other gods by reason of this affair in which they acted presumptuously against them." 12 Then Jeth′ro, Moses' father-in-law, took a burnt offering and sacrifices for God; and Aaron and all the older men of Israel came to eat bread with Moses' father-in-law, before the [true] God.

13 And it came about on the next day that Moses sat down as usual to serve as judge for the people, and the people kept standing before Moses from the morning till the evening. 14 And Moses' father-in-law got to see all that he was doing for the people. So he said: "What kind of business is this that you are doing for the people? Why do you alone continue sitting and all the people continue taking their stand before you from morning till evening?" 15 Then Moses said to his father-in-law: "Because the people keep coming to me to inquire of God. 16 In the event that they have a case arise, it must come to me and I must judge between the one party and the other, and I must make known the decisions of the [true] God and his laws."

17 At this Moses' father-in-law said to him: "It is not good the way you are doing. 18 You will surely wear out, both you and this people who are with you, because this business is too big a load for you. You are unable to do it by yourself. 19 Now listen to my

voice. I shall advise you, and God will prove to be with you. You yourself serve as representative for the people before the [true] God, and you yourself must bring the cases to the [true] God. 20 And you must warn them of what the regulations and the laws are, and you must make known to them the way in which they should walk and the work that they should do. 21 But you yourself should select out of all the people capable men, fearing God, trustworthy men, hating unjust profit; and you must set these over them as chiefs over thousands, chiefs over hundreds, chiefs over fifties and chiefs over tens. 22 And they must judge the people on every proper occasion; and it must occur that every big case they will bring to you, but every small case they themselves will handle as judges. So make it lighter for yourself, and they must carry the load with you. 23 If you do this very thing, and God has commanded you, you will then certainly be able to stand it and, besides, this people will all come to their own place in peace."

24 Immediately Moses listened to the voice of his father-in-law and did all that he had said. 25 And Moses proceeded to choose capable men out of all Israel and to give them positions as heads over the people, as chiefs of thousands, chiefs of hundreds, chiefs of fifties and chiefs of tens. 26 And they judged the people on every proper occasion. A hard case they would bring to Moses, but every small case they themselves would handle as judges. 27 After that Moses saw his father-in-law off, and he went his way to his land.

19 In the third month after the sons of Israel came out of the land of Egypt, on the same day, they came into the wilderness of Si'nai. 2 And they proceeded to pull away from Reph'i·dim and to come into the wilderness of Si'nai and to encamp in the wilderness; and Israel went camping there in front of the mountain.

3 And Moses went up to the [true] God, and Jehovah began to call to him out of the mountain, saying: "This is what you are to say to the house of Jacob and to tell the sons of Israel, 4 'You yourselves have seen what I did to the Egyptians, that I might carry YOU on wings of eagles and bring YOU to myself. 5 And now if YOU will strictly obey my voice and will indeed keep my covenant, then YOU will certainly become my special property out of all [other] peoples, because the whole earth belongs to me. 6 And YOU yourselves will become to me a kingdom of priests and a holy nation.' These are the words that you are to say to the sons of Israel."

7 So Moses came and called the older men of the people and set before them all these words that Jehovah had commanded him. 8 After that all the people answered unanimously and said: "All that Jehovah has spoken we are willing to do." Immediately Moses took back the words of the people to Jehovah. 9 At this Jehovah said to Moses: "Look! I am coming to you in a dark cloud, in order that the people may hear when I speak with you, and that in you also they may put faith to time indefinite." Then Moses reported the words of the people to Jehovah.

10 And Jehovah went on to say to Moses: "Go to the people, and you must sanctify them today and tomorrow, and they must wash their mantles. 11 And they must prove ready for the third day, because on the third day Jehovah will come down before the eyes of all the people upon Mount Si'nai. 12 And you must set bounds for the people round about, saying, 'Guard yourselves against going up into the mountain, and do not touch the edge of it. Anybody touching the mountain will positively be put to death. 13 No hand is to touch him, because he will positively be stoned or will positively be shot through. Whether beast or man, he will not live.' At

the blowing of the ram's horn they themselves may come up to the mountain."

14 Then Moses went down from the mountain to the people, and he set about sanctifying the people; and they engaged in washing their mantles. 15 Accordingly he said to the people: "Get ready during the three days. Do not you men come near a woman."

16 And on the third day when it became morning it came about that thunders and lightnings began occurring, and a heavy cloud upon the mountain and a very loud sound of a horn, so that all the people who were in the camp began to tremble. 17 Moses now brought the people out of the camp to meet the [true] God, and they went taking their stand at the base of the mountain. 18 And Mount Si′nai smoked all over, due to the fact that Jehovah came down upon it in fire; and its smoke kept ascending like the smoke of a kiln, and the whole mountain was trembling very much. 19 When the sound of the horn became continually louder and louder, Moses began to speak, and the [true] God began to answer him with a voice.

20 So Jehovah came down upon Mount Si′nai to the top of the mountain. Then Jehovah called Moses to the top of the mountain, and Moses went on up. 21 Jehovah now said to Moses: "Go down, warn the people, that they do not try to break through to Jehovah to take a look and many of them have to fall. 22 And let the priests also who regularly come near to Jehovah sanctify themselves, that Jehovah may not break out upon them." 23 At this Moses said to Jehovah: "The people are not able to come up to Mount Si′nai, because you yourself already warned us, saying, 'Set bounds for the mountain and make it sacred.'" 24 However, Jehovah said to him: "Go, descend, and you must come up, you and Aaron with you; but let not the priests and the people break through to come up to Jehovah, that he may not break out upon them."

25 Accordingly Moses descended to the people and told them.

20 And God proceeded to speak all these words, saying:

2 "I am Jehovah your God, who have brought you out of the land of Egypt, out of the house of slaves. 3 You must not have any other gods against my face.

4 "You must not make for yourself a carved image or a form like anything that is in the heavens above or that is on the earth underneath or that is in the waters under the earth. 5 You must not bow down to them nor be induced to serve them, because I Jehovah your God am a God exacting exclusive devotion, bringing punishment for the error of fathers upon sons, upon the third generation and upon the fourth generation, in the case of those who hate me; 6 but exercising loving-kindness toward the thousandth generation in the case of those who love me and keep my commandments.

7 "You must not take up the name of Jehovah your God in a worthless way, for Jehovah will not leave the one unpunished who takes up his name in a worthless way.

8 "Remembering the sabbath day to hold it sacred, 9 you are to render service and you must do all your work six days. 10 But the seventh day is a sabbath to Jehovah your God. You must not do any work, you nor your son nor your daughter, your slave man nor your slave girl nor your domestic animal nor your alien resident who is inside your gates. 11 For in six days Jehovah made the heavens and the earth, the sea and everything that is in them, and he proceeded to rest on the seventh day. That is why Jehovah blessed the sabbath day and proceeded to make it sacred.

12 "Honor your father and your mother in order that your days may prove long upon the ground that Jehovah your God is giving you.

13 "You must not murder.

14 "You must not commit adultery.

15 "You must not steal.

16 "You must not testify falsely as a witness against your fellow man.

17 "You must not desire your fellow man's house. You must not desire your fellow man's wife, nor his slave man nor his slave girl nor his bull nor his ass nor anything that belongs to your fellow man."

18 Now all the people were seeing the thunders and the lightning flashes and the sound of the horn and the mountain smoking. When the people got to see it, then they quivered and stood at a distance. 19 And they began to say to Moses: "You speak with us, and let us listen; but let not God speak with us for fear we may die." 20 So Moses said to the people: "Do not be afraid, because for the sake of putting YOU to the test the [true] God has come, and in order that the fear of him may continue before YOUR faces that YOU may not sin." 21 And the people kept standing at a distance, but Moses went near to the dark cloud mass where the [true] God was.

22 And Jehovah went on to say to Moses: "This is what you are to say to the sons of Israel, 'YOU yourselves have seen that it was from the heavens I spoke with YOU. 23 YOU must not make along with me gods of silver, and YOU must not make gods of gold for yourselves. 24 An altar of ground you are to make for me, and you must sacrifice upon it your burnt offerings and your communion sacrifices, your flock and your herd. In every place where I shall cause my name to be remembered I shall come to you and shall certainly bless you. 25 And if you should make an altar of stones for me, you must not build them as hewn stones. In the event that you do wield your chisel upon it, then you will profane it. 26 And you must not go up by steps to my altar, that your private parts may not be exposed upon it.'

21 "And these are the judicial decisions that you are to set before them:

2 "In case you should buy a Hebrew slave, he will be a slave six years, but in the seventh he will go out as one set free without charge. 3 If he should come in by himself, by himself he will go out. If he is the owner of a wife, then his wife must go out with him. 4 If his master should give him a wife and she does bear him sons or daughters, the wife and her children will become her master's and he will go out by himself. 5 But if the slave should insistently say, 'I really love my master, my wife and my sons; I do not want to go out as one set free,' 6 then his master must bring him near to the [true] God and must bring him up against the door or the doorpost; and his master must pierce his ear through with an awl, and he must be his slave to time indefinite.

7 "And in case a man should sell his daughter as a slave girl, she will not go out in the way that the slave men do out. 8 If she is displeasing in the eyes of her master so that he does not designate her as a concubine but causes her to be redeemed, he will not be entitled to sell her to a foreign people in his treacherously dealing with her. 9 And if it should be to his son that he designates her, he is to do to her according to the due right of daughters. 10 If he should take another wife for himself, her sustenance, her clothing and her marriage due are not to be diminished. 11 If he will not render these three things to her, then she must go out for nothing, without money.

12 "One who strikes a man so that he actually dies is to be put to death without fail. 13 But where one does not lie in wait and the [true] God lets it occur at his hand, then I must fix for you a place where he can flee. 14 And in case a man becomes heated against his fellow to the point of killing him with craftiness, you are to take him even from being at my altar to die. 15 And one who

strikes his father and his mother is to be put to death without fail.

16 "And one who kidnaps a man and who actually sells him or in whose hand he has been found is to be put to death without fail.

17 "And one who calls down evil upon his father and his mother is to be put to death without fail.

18 "And in case men should get into a quarrel and one does strike his fellow with a stone or a hoe and he does not die but must keep to his bed; 19 if he gets up and does walk about out of doors upon some support of his, then the one who struck him must be free from punishment; he will make compensation only for the time lost from that one's work until he gets him completely healed.

20 "And in case a man strikes his slave man or his slave girl with a stick and that one actually dies under his hand, that one is to be avenged without fail. 21 However, if he lingers for a day or two days, he is not to be avenged, because he is his money.

22 "And in case men should struggle with each other and they really hurt a pregnant woman and her children do come out but no fatal accident occurs, he is to have damages imposed upon him without fail according to what the owner of the woman may lay upon him; and he must give it through the justices. 23 But if a fatal accident should occur, then you must give soul for soul, 24 eye for eye, tooth for tooth, hand for hand, foot for foot, 25 branding for branding, wound for wound, blow for blow.

26 "And in case a man should strike the eye of his slave man or the eye of his slave girl and he really ruins it, he is to send him away as one set free in compensation for his eye. 27 And if it should be the tooth of his slave man or the tooth of his slave girl that he knocks out, he is to send him away as one set free in compensation for his tooth.

28 "And in case a bull should gore a man or a woman and that one actually dies, the bull is to be stoned without fail, but its flesh is not to be eaten; and the owner of the bull is free from punishment. 29 But if a bull was formerly in the habit of goring and warning was served on its owner but he would not keep it under guard, and it did put a man or a woman to death, the bull is to be stoned and also its owner is to be put to death. 30 If a ransom should be imposed upon him, then he must give the redemption price for his soul according to all that may be imposed upon him. 31 Whether it gored a son or gored a daughter, it is to be done to him according to this judicial decision. 32 If it was a slave man or a slave girl that the bull gored, he will give the price of thirty shekels to that one's master, and the bull will be stoned.

33 "And in case a man should open a pit, or in case a man should excavate a pit and should not cover it, and a bull or an ass does fall into it, 34 the owner of the pit is to make compensation. The price he is to return to its owner, and the dead animal will become his own. 35 And in case a man's bull should hurt another's bull and it does die, then they must sell the live bull and divide the price paid for it; and also the dead one they should divide. 36 Or if it was known that a bull was in the habit of goring formerly but its owner would not keep it under guard, he should without fail make compensation with bull for bull, and the dead one will become his own.

22 "In case a man should steal a bull or a sheep and he does slaughter it or sell it, he is to compensate with five of the herd for the bull and four of the flock for the sheep.

2 ("If a thief should be found in the act of breaking in and he does get struck and die, there is no bloodguilt for him. 3 If the sun has shone forth upon him, there is bloodguilt for him.)

"He is to make compensation without fail. If he has nothing, then he must be sold for the things he stole. 4 If there should be unmistakably found in his hand what was stolen, from bull to ass and to sheep, alive, he is to make double compensation.

5 "If a man causes a field or a vineyard to be grazed over and he does send out his beasts of burden and cause a consuming in another field, he is to make compensation with the best of his own field or with the best of his own vineyard.

6 "In case a fire should spread out and it does catch thorns, and sheaves or standing grain or a field gets consumed, the one who started the fire is to make compensation without fail for what was burned.

7 "In case a man should give his fellow money or articles to keep, and it gets stolen from the man's house, if the thief should be found, he is to make double compensation. 8 If the thief should not be found, then the owner of the house must be brought near to the [true] God to see whether he did not put his hand upon the goods of his fellow. 9 As regards any case of transgression, concerning a bull, an ass, a sheep, a garment, anything lost of which he may say, 'This is it!' the case of them both is to come to the [true] God. The one whom God will pronounce wicked is to make double compensation to his fellow.

10 "In case a man should give his fellow an ass or bull or sheep or any domestic animal to keep, and it does die or get maimed or gets led off while nobody is looking, 11 an oath by Jehovah is to take place between them both that he did not put his hand on the goods of his fellow; and their owner must accept it, and the other is not to make compensation. 12 But if they should for a fact be stolen from him, he is to make compensation to their owner. 13 If it should for a fact be torn by a wild beast, he is to bring it as evidence. For something torn by a wild beast he is not to make compensation.

14 "But in case anybody should ask for something of his fellow, and it does get maimed or die

while its owner is not with it, he is to make compensation without fail. 15 If its owner is with it, he is not to make compensation. If it is hired, it must come in its hire.

16 "Now in case a man seduces a virgin who is not engaged, and he actually lies down with her, he is to obtain her without fail as his wife for the purchase price. 17 If her father flatly refuses to give her to him, he is to pay over the money at the rate of purchase money for virgins.

18 "You must not preserve a sorceress alive.

19 "Anyone lying down with a beast is positively to be put to death.

20 "One who sacrifices to any gods but Jehovah alone is to be devoted to destruction.

21 "And you must not maltreat an alien resident or oppress him, for you people became alien residents in the land of Egypt.

22 "You people must not afflict any widow or fatherless boy. 23 If you should afflict him at all, then if he cries out to me at all, I shall unfailingly hear his outcry; 24 and my anger will indeed blaze, and I shall certainly kill you with the sword, and your wives must become widows and your sons fatherless boys.

25 "If you should lend money to my people, to the afflicted alongside you, you must not become like a usurer to him. You must not lay interest upon him.

26 "If you should at all seize the garment of your fellow as a pledge, you are to return it to him at the setting of the sun. 27 For it is his only covering. It is his mantle for his skin. In what will he lie down? And it must occur that he will cry out to me, and I shall certainly hear, because I am gracious.

28 "You must not call down evil upon God nor curse a chieftain among your people.

29 "Your full produce and the overflow of your press you must not give hesitantly. The first-born of your sons you are to give to me.

30 The way you are to do with your bull and your sheep is this: Seven days it will continue with its mother. On the eighth day you are to give it to me.

31 "And you should prove yourselves holy men to me; and you must not eat flesh in the field that is something torn by a wild beast. You should throw it to the dogs.

23 "You must not take up an untrue report. Do not co-operate with a wicked one by becoming a witness who schemes violence. 2 You must not follow after the crowd for evil ends; and you must not testify over a controversy so as to turn aside with the crowd in order to pervert justice. 3 As for the lowly one, you must not show preference in a controversy of his.

4 "Should you come upon your enemy's bull or his ass going astray, you are to return it without fail to him. 5 Should you see the ass of someone who hates you lying down under its load, then you must refrain from leaving him. With him you are without fail to get it loose.

6 "You are not to pervert the judicial decision of your poor man in his controversy.

7 "You are to keep far from a false word. And do not kill the innocent and the righteous, for I shall not declare the wicked one righteous.

8 "You are not to accept a bribe, for the bribe blinds clear-sighted men and can distort the words of righteous men.

9 "And you must not oppress an alien resident, as you yourselves have known the soul of the alien resident, because you became alien residents in the land of Egypt.

10 "And for six years you are to sow your land with seed and you must gather its produce. 11 But the seventh year you are to leave it uncultivated and you must let it lie fallow, and the poor ones of your people must eat of it; and what is left over by them the wild beasts of the field are to eat. That is the way you are to do

with your vineyard and your olive grove.

12 "Six days you are to do your work; but on the seventh day you are to desist, in order that your bull and your ass may rest and the son of your slave girl and the alien resident may refresh themselves.

13 "And you are to be on your guard respecting all that I have said to you; and you must not mention the name of other gods. It should not be heard upon your mouth.

14 "Three times in the year you are to celebrate a festival to me. 15 You will keep the festival of unfermented cakes. You will eat unfermented cakes seven days, just as I have commanded you, at the appointed time in the month of A′bib, because in it you came out of Egypt. And they must not appear before me empty-handed. 16 Also, the festival of harvest of the first ripe fruits of your labors, of what you sow in the field; and the festival of ingathering at the outgoing of the year, when you gather in your labors from the field. 17 On three occasions in the year every male of yours will appear before the face of the [true] Lord, Jehovah.

18 "You must not sacrifice along with what is leavened the blood of my sacrifice. And the fat of my festival should not stay overnight until morning.

19 "The best of the first ripe fruits of your ground you are to bring to the house of Jehovah your God.

"You must not boil a kid in its mother's milk.

20 "Here I am sending an angel ahead of you to keep you on the road and to bring you into the place that I have prepared. 21 Watch yourself because of him and obey his voice. Do not behave rebelliously against him, for he will not pardon your transgression; because my name is within him. 22 However, if you strictly obey his voice and really do all that I shall speak, then I shall certainly

be hostile to your enemies and harass those who harass you. 23 For my angel will go ahead of you and will indeed bring you to the Am'or·ites and the Hit'tites and the Per'iz·zites and the Ca'-naan·ites, the Hi'vites and the Jeb'-u·sites, and I shall certainly efface them. 24 You must not bow down to their gods or be induced to serve them, and you must not make anything like their works, but you will without fail throw them down and you will without fail break down their sacred pillars. 25 And you must serve Jehovah your God, and he will certainly bless your bread and your water; and I shall indeed turn malady away from your midst. 26 Neither a woman suffering an abortion nor a barren woman will exist in your land. I shall make the number of your days full.

27 "And I shall send the fright of me ahead of you, and I shall certainly throw into confusion all the people among whom you come, and I shall indeed give the back of the neck of all your enemies to you. 28 And I will send the feeling of dejection ahead of you, and it will simply drive the Hi'vites, the Ca'naan·ites and the Hit'tites out from before you. 29 I shall not drive them out from before you in one year, that the land may not become a desolate waste and the wild beasts of the field really multiply against you. 30 Little by little I shall drive them out from before you, until you become fruitful and really take possession of the land.

31 "And I will fix your boundary from the Red Sea to the sea of the Phi·lis'tines and from the wilderness to the River; because I shall give into your hand the inhabitants of the land, and you will certainly drive them out from before yourself. 32 You are not to conclude a covenant with them or their gods. 33 They should not dwell in your land, that they may not cause you to sin against me. In case you should serve their gods, it would become a snare to you."

24 And to Moses he said: "Go up to Jehovah, you and Aaron, Na'dab and A·bi'hu and seventy of the older men of Israel, and you must bow down from a distance. 2 And Moses by himself must approach Jehovah; but they should not approach, and the people should not go up with him."

3 Then Moses came and related to the people all the words of Jehovah and all the judicial decisions, and all the people answered with one voice and said: "All the words that Jehovah has spoken we are willing to do." 4 Accordingly Moses wrote down all the words of Jehovah. Then he got up early in the morning and built at the foot of the mountain an altar and twelve pillars corresponding with the twelve tribes of Israel. 5 After that he sent young men of the sons of Israel and they offered up burnt offerings and sacrificed bulls as sacrifices, as communion sacrifices to Jehovah. 6 Then Moses took half the blood and put it in bowls, and half the blood he sprinkled upon the altar. 7 Finally he took the book of the covenant and read it in the ears of the people. Then they said: "All that Jehovah has spoken we are willing to do and be obedient." 8 So Moses took the blood and sprinkled it upon the people and said: "Here is the blood of the covenant that Jehovah has concluded with you as respects all these words."

9 And Moses and Aaron, Na'dab and A·bi'hu and seventy of the older men of Israel proceeded to go up, 10 and they got to see the God of Israel. And under his feet there was what seemed like a work of sapphire flagstones and like the very heavens for purity. 11 And he did not put out his hand against the distinguished men of the sons of Israel, but they got a vision of the [true] God and ate and drank.

12 Jehovah now said to Moses: "Come up to me in the mountain and stay there, as I want to give you the stone tablets and the law and the commandment that I must

write in order to teach them." 13 So Moses and Joshua his minister got up and Moses went up into the mountain of the [true] God. 14 But to the older men he had said: "You wait for us in this place until we return to you. And, look! Aaron and Hur are with you. Whoever has a case at law, let him approach them." 15 Thus Moses went up into the mountain while the cloud was covering the mountain.

16 And Jehovah's glory continued to reside upon Mount Si'nai, and the cloud continued to cover it for six days. At length on the seventh day he called to Moses from the midst of the cloud. 17 And to the eyes of the sons of Israel the sight of Jehovah's glory was like a devouring fire on the mountaintop. 18 Then Moses entered into the midst of the cloud and went on up the mountain. And Moses continued in the mountain forty days and forty nights.

25 And Jehovah proceeded to speak to Moses, saying: 2 "Speak to the sons of Israel, that they may take up a contribution for me: From every man whose heart incites him you people are to take up the contribution of mine. 3 And this is the contribution that you are to take up from them: gold and silver and copper, 4 and blue thread, and wool dyed reddish purple, and coccus scarlet material, and fine linen, and goat's hair, 5 and ram skins dyed red, and sealskins, and acacia wood; 6 oil for the luminary, balsam oil for the anointing oil and for perfumed incense; 7 and onyx stones and setting stones for the eph'od and for the breastpiece. 8 And they must make a sanctuary for me, as I must tabernacle in the midst of them. 9 According to all that I am showing you as the pattern of the tabernacle and pattern of all its furnishings, that is the way you are to make it.

10 "And they must make an Ark of acacia wood, two and a half cubits its length and a cubit and a half its width and a cubit and a

half its height. 11 And you must overlay it with pure gold. Inside and outside you are to overlay it, and you must make a border of gold round about upon it. 12 And you must cast four rings of gold for it and put them above its four feet, with two rings upon the one side of it and two rings upon its other side. 13 And you must make poles of acacia wood and overlay them with gold. 14 And you must put the poles through the rings upon the sides of the Ark in order to carry the Ark with them. 15 In the rings of the Ark the poles are to stay. They are not to be removed from it. 16 And you must place in the Ark the testimony that I shall give you.

17 "And you must make a cover of pure gold, two and a half cubits its length and a cubit and a half its width. 18 And you must make two cherubs of gold. Of hammered work you are to make them on both ends of the cover. 19 And make one cherub on this end and one cherub on that end. On the cover you are to make the cherubs at its two ends. 20 And the cherubs must be spreading out their two wings upward, screening over the cover with their wings, with their faces one toward the other. Toward the cover the faces of the cherubs should be. 21 And you must place the cover above upon the Ark, and in the Ark you will place the testimony that I shall give you. 22 And I will present myself to you there and speak with you from above the cover, from between the two cherubs that are upon the ark of the testimony, even all that I shall command you for the sons of Israel.

23 "And you must make a table of acacia wood, two cubits its length and a cubit its width and a cubit and a half its height. 24 And you must overlay it with pure gold, and you must make for it a border of gold round about. 25 And you must make for it a rim of a handbreadth round about, and you must make the border of gold for its rim round about. 26 And you

must make for it four rings of gold and place the rings on the four corners that are for the four feet. 27 The rings should be close by the rim as supports for the poles to carry the table. 28 And you must make the poles of acacia wood and overlay them with gold, and they must carry the table with them.

29 "And you must make its dishes and its cups and its pitchers and its bowls with which they will pour libations. You are to make them out of pure gold. 30 And you must put the showbread upon the table before me constantly.

31 "And you must make a lampstand of pure gold. Of hammered work the lampstand is to be made. Its base, its branches, its cups, its knobs and its blossoms are to proceed out from it. 32 And six branches are running out from its sides, three branches of the lampstand from its one side and three branches of the lampstand from its other side. 33 Three cups shaped like flowers of almond are on the one set of branches, with knobs and blossoms alternating, and three cups shaped like flowers of almond on the other set of branches, with knobs and blossoms alternating. This is the way it is with the six branches running out from the lampstand. 34 And on the lampstand are four cups shaped like flowers of almond, with its knobs and its blossoms alternating. 35 And the knob under two branches is out of it and the knob under the two other branches is out of it and the knob under two more branches is out of it, for the six branches running out from the lampstand. 36 Their knobs and their branches are to proceed out from it. All of it is one piece of hammered work, of pure gold. 37 And you must make seven lamps for it; and the lamps must be lit up, and they must shine upon the area in front of it. 38 And its snuffers and its fire holders are of pure gold. 39 Of a talent of pure gold he should make it with all these utensils of it. 40 And see that you make them after their

pattern that was shown to you in the mountain.

26 "And the tabernacle you are to make of ten tent cloths, of fine twisted linen and blue thread and wool dyed reddish purple and coccus scarlet material. With cherubs, the work of an embroiderer, you will make them. 2 The length of each tent cloth is twenty-eight cubits and the width of each tent cloth is four cubits. There is one measure for all the tent cloths. 3 Five tent cloths are to form a series with the one joined to the other, and five tent cloths a series with the one joined to the other. 4 And you must make loops of blue thread upon the edge of the one tent cloth at the end of the series; and you are to do the same upon the edge of the outermost tent cloth at the other place of junction. 5 You will make fifty loops on the one tent cloth, and fifty loops you will make on the extremity of the tent cloth that is at the other place of junction, the loops being opposite one to the other. 6 And you must make fifty hooks of gold and join the tent cloths one to the other by means of the hooks, and it must become one tabernacle.

7 "And you must make cloths of goat's hair for the tent upon the tabernacle. You will make eleven tent cloths. 8 The length of each tent cloth is thirty cubits, and the width of each tent cloth is four cubits. There is one measure for the eleven tent cloths. 9 And you must join five tent cloths by themselves and six tent cloths by themselves, and you must fold double the sixth tent cloth at the forefront of the tent. 10 And you must make fifty loops upon the edge of the one tent cloth, the outermost one in the series, and fifty loops upon the edge of the tent cloth at the other place of junction. 11 And you must make fifty hooks of copper and put the hooks in the loops and join the tent together, and it must become one. 12 And what remains over of the cloths of the tent is an over-

hanging. Half of the tent cloth that remains over is to hang over the back of the tabernacle. 13 And the cubit on this side and the cubit on that side in what remains over in the length of the cloths of the tent will serve as an overhanging on the sides of the tabernacle, to cover it on this side and on that.

14 "And you must make a covering for the tent of ram skins dyed red and a covering of sealskins up on top.

15 "And you must make the panel frames for the tabernacle of acacia wood, standing on end. 16 Ten cubits is the length of a panel frame, and a cubit and a half is the width of each panel frame. 17 Each panel frame has two tenons joined one to the other. That is the way you will do with all the panel frames of the tabernacle. 18 And you must make the panel frames for the tabernacle, twenty panel frames for the side toward the Neg′eb, to the south.

19 "And you will make forty socket pedestals of silver under the twenty panel frames; two socket pedestals under the one panel frame with its two tenons, and two socket pedestals under the other panel frame with its two tenons. 20 And for the other side of the tabernacle, the northern side, twenty panel frames, 21 and their forty socket pedestals of silver, two socket pedestals under the one panel frame and two socket pedestals under the other panel frame. 22 And for the rear sections of the tabernacle to the west you will make six panel frames. 23 And you will make two panel frames as corner posts of the tabernacle on its two rear sections. 24 And they should be duplicates at the bottom, and together they should be duplicates up to the top of each one at the first ring. That is the way it should be for the two of them. They will serve as two corner posts. 25 And there must be eight panel frames and their socket pedestals of silver, sixteen pedestals, two socket pedestals under the one

panel frame and two socket pedestals under the other panel frame.

26 "And you must make bars of acacia wood, five for the panel frames of the one side of the tabernacle, 27 and five bars for the panel frames of the other side of the tabernacle and five bars for the panel frames of the side of the tabernacle for the two rear sections to the west. 28 And the middle bar at the center of the panel frames is running through from end to end.

29 "And you will overlay the panel frames with gold, and their rings you will make of gold as supports for the bars; and you must overlay the bars with gold. 30 And you must set up the tabernacle according to the plan of it that you have been shown in the mountain.

31 "And you must make a curtain of blue thread and wool dyed reddish purple and coccus scarlet material and fine twisted linen. He will make it with cherubs, the work of an embroiderer. 32 And you must put it upon four pillars of acacia overlaid with gold. Their pegs are of gold. They are upon four socket pedestals of silver. 33 And you must put the curtain under the hooks and bring the ark of the testimony there within the curtain; and the curtain must make a division for you between the Holy and the Most Holy. 34 And you must put the cover upon the ark of the testimony in the Most Holy.

35 "And you must set the table outside the curtain, and the lampstand opposite the table on the side of the tabernacle toward the south; and the table you will put on the north side. 36 And you must make a screen for the entrance of the tent of blue thread and wool dyed reddish purple and coccus scarlet material and fine twisted linen, the work of a weaver. 37 And you must make for the screen five pillars of acacia and overlay them with gold. Their pegs are of gold. And you must cast for them five socket pedestals of copper.

27 "And you must make the altar of acacia wood, five cubits its length and five cubits its width.

The altar should be foursquare, and its height three cubits. 2 And you must make its horns upon its four corners. Its horns will proceed out of it, and you must overlay it with copper. 3 And you must make its cans for clearing away its fatty ashes, and its shovels, and its bowls, and its forks, and its fire holders; and you will make all its utensils of copper. 4 And you must make a grating for it, a network of copper; and you must make upon the net four rings of copper at its four extremities. 5 And you must put it under the altar's rim down within, and the net must be toward the center of the altar. 6 And you must make poles for the altar, its poles being of acacia wood, and you must overlay them with copper. 7 And its poles must be put into the rings, and the poles must be upon the two sides of the altar when carrying it. 8 A hollow chest of planks you will make it. Just as he showed you in the mountain, so they will make it.

9 "And you must make the courtyard of the tabernacle. For the side toward the Neg′eb, to the south, the courtyard has hangings of fine twisted linen, a hundred cubits being the length for the one side. 10 And its twenty pillars and their twenty socket pedestals are of copper. The pegs of the pillars and their joints are of silver. 11 So, too, it is for the north side in length, the hangings being for a hundred cubits of length, and its twenty pillars and their twenty socket pedestals being of copper, the pegs of the pillars and their joints being of silver. 12 As for the width of the courtyard, on the west side the hangings are of fifty cubits, their pillars being ten and their socket pedestals ten. 13 And the width of the courtyard on the east side toward the sunrising is fifty cubits. 14 And there are fifteen cubits of hangings to one side, their pillars being three and their socket pedestals three. 15 And for the other side there are fifteen cubits of hangings, their pillars being

three and their socket pedestals three.

16 "And for the gate of the courtyard there is a screen twenty cubits long, of blue thread and wool dyed reddish purple and coccus scarlet material and fine twisted linen, the work of a weaver, their pillars being four and their socket pedestals four. 17 All the pillars of the courtyard round about have fastenings of silver, and their pegs are of silver but their socket pedestals of copper. 18 The length of the courtyard is a hundred cubits, and the width fifty cubits, and the height five cubits, of fine twisted linen, and their socket pedestals being of copper. 19 And all the utensils of the tabernacle in all its service, and all its tent pins, and all the pins of the courtyard are of copper.

20 "As for you, you are to command the sons of Israel that they get for you pure, beaten olive oil for the luminary, in order to light up the lamps constantly. 21 In the tent of meeting, outside the curtain that is by the Testimony, Aaron and his sons will set it in order from evening till morning before Jehovah. It is a statute to time indefinite for their generations, to be performed by the sons of Israel.

28 "And as for you, bring near to yourself Aaron your brother and his sons with him from the midst of the sons of Israel that he may act as priest to me, Aaron, Na′dab and A·bi′hu, E·le·a′zar and Ith′a·mar, the sons of Aaron. 2 And you must make holy garments for Aaron your brother, for glory and beauty. 3 And you yourself are to speak to all the ones wise with a heart that I have filled with the spirit of wisdom, and they must make Aaron's garments for sanctifying him, that he may act as priest to me.

4 "And these are the garments that they will make: a breastpiece, and an eph′od and a sleeveless coat and a robe of checker work, a turban and a sash; and they must make the holy garments for Aaron your brother and his sons,

that he may act as priest to me. 5 And they themselves will take the gold and the blue thread and the wool dyed reddish purple and coccus scarlet material and the fine linen.

6 "And they must make the eph'od of gold, blue thread and wool dyed reddish purple, coccus scarlet material and fine twisted linen, the work of an embroiderer. 7 And it is to have two shoulder pieces to be joined at its two extremities, and it must be joined. 8 And the girdle, which is upon it for tying it close, according to its workmanship should be of its materials, of gold, blue thread and wool dyed reddish purple and coccus scarlet material and fine twisted linen.

9 "And you must take two onyx stones and engrave upon them the names of the sons of Israel, 10 six of their names upon the one stone and the names of the six remaining ones upon the other stone in the order of their births. 11 With the work of a craftsman in stones, with the engravings of a seal, you are to engrave the two stones with the names of the sons of Israel. Set in settings of gold is how you will make them. 12 And you must put the two stones upon the shoulder pieces of the eph'od as memorial stones for the sons of Israel; and Aaron must carry their names before Jehovah upon his two shoulder pieces as a memorial. 13 And you must make settings of gold, 14 and two chains of pure gold. As cords you will make them, with the workmanship of a rope; and you must attach the ropelike chains to the settings.

15 "And you must make the breastpiece of judgment with the workmanship of an embroiderer. Like the workmanship of the eph'od you will make it. Of gold, blue thread and wool dyed reddish purple and coccus scarlet material and fine twisted linen you will make it. 16 It should be foursquare when doubled, a span of the hand being its length and a span of the hand its width. 17 And you must fill it with a filling of stones, there being

four rows of stones. A row of ruby, topaz and emerald is the first row. 18 And the second row is turquoise, sapphire and jasper. 19 And the third row is lesh'em stone, agate and amethyst. 20 And the fourth row is chrys'o·lite and onyx and jade. Sockets of gold should be in their fillings. 21 And the stones should be according to the names of the sons of Israel, the twelve according to their names. With the engravings of a seal they should be, each one according to its name, for the twelve tribes.

22 "And you must make upon the breastpiece wreathed chains, in rope work, of pure gold. 23 And you must make upon the breastpiece two rings of gold, and you must put the two rings upon the two extremities of the breastpiece. 24 And you must put the two ropes of gold through the two rings at the extremities of the breastpiece. 25 And you will put the two ends of the two ropes through the two settings, and you must put them upon the shoulder pieces of the eph'od, at the forefront of it. 26 And you must make two rings of gold and set them at the two extremities of the breastpiece upon its edge that is on the side toward the eph'od inward. 27 And you must make two rings of gold and put them upon the two shoulder pieces of the eph'od from below, on its forefront, near its place of joining, above the girdle of the eph'od. 28 And they will bind the breastpiece by its rings to the rings of the eph'od with a blue string, that it may continue above the girdle of the eph'od and the breastpiece may not get displaced from on top the eph'od.

29 "And Aaron must carry the names of the sons of Israel on the breastpiece of judgment over his heart when he comes into the Holy as a memorial before Jehovah constantly. 30 And you must put the U'rim and the Thum'mim into the breastpiece of judgment, and they must prove to be over Aaron's heart when he comes in before Jehovah; and Aaron must carry the judg-

ments of the sons of Israel over his heart before Jehovah constantly.

31 "And you must make the sleeveless coat of the eph'od completely of blue thread. 32 And there must be an opening at its top in the middle of it. Its opening should have a border round about, the product of a loom worker. Like the opening of a coat of mail it should be for it, that it may not be torn. 33 And you must make upon the hem of it pomegranates of blue thread and wool dyed reddish purple and coccus scarlet material, upon its hem round about, and bells of gold in between them round about; 34 a bell of gold and a pomegranate, a bell of gold and a pomegranate upon the hem of the sleeveless coat round about. 35 And it must be upon Aaron that he may minister, and the sound from him must be heard when he goes into the sanctuary before Jehovah and when he comes out, that he may not die.

36 "And you must make a shining plate of pure gold and engrave upon it with the engravings of a seal, 'Holiness belongs to Jehovah.' 37 And you must fasten it with a blue string, and it must come to be upon the turban. On the forefront of the turban it should come to be. 38 And it must come to be upon Aaron's forehead, and Aaron must answer for the error committed against the holy objects, which the sons of Israel will sanctify, that is to say, all their holy gifts; and it must stay upon his forehead constantly, to gain approval for them before Jehovah.

39 "And you must weave in checker work the robe of fine linen and make a turban of fine linen, and you will make a sash, the work of a weaver.

40 "And for Aaron's sons you will make robes, and you must make sashes for them, and you will make headgears for them for glory and beauty. 41 And with them you must clothe Aaron your brother and his sons with him, and you must anoint them and fill their hand with power and sanctify

them, and they must act as priests to me. 42 And make drawers of linen for them to cover the naked flesh. From the hips and to the thighs they are to extend. 43 And they must be upon Aaron and his sons when they come into the tent of meeting or when they go near to the altar to minister in the holy place, that they may not incur error and certainly die. It is a statute to time indefinite for him and his offspring after him.

29 "And this is the thing that you are to do to them to sanctify them for acting as priests to me: Take a young bull, and two rams, sound ones, 2 and unfermented bread and unfermented ring-shaped cakes moistened with oil and unfermented wafers smeared with oil. Out of fine wheat flour you will make them. 3 And you must put them upon a basket and present them in the basket, and also the bull and the two rams.

4 "And you will present Aaron and his sons at the entrance of the tent of meeting, and you must wash them with water. 5 Then you must take the garments and clothe Aaron with the robe and the sleeveless coat of the eph'od and with the eph'od and the breastpiece, and you must tie it closely to him with the girdle of the eph'od. 6 And you must set the turban upon his head and put the holy sign of dedication upon the turban. 7 And you must take the anointing oil and pour it upon his head and anoint him.

8 "Then you will bring his sons near and you must clothe them with the robes. 9 And you must gird them with the sashes, Aaron as well as his sons, and you must wrap the headgear upon them; and the priesthood must become theirs as a statute to time indefinite. So you must fill the hand of Aaron and the hand of his sons with power.

10 "You must now present the bull before the tent of meeting, and Aaron and his sons must lay their hands upon the bull's head. 11 And you must slaughter the bull

before Jehovah, at the entrance of the tent of meeting. 12 And you must take some of the bull's blood and put it with your finger upon the horns of the altar, and all the rest of the blood you will pour out at the base of the altar. 13 And you must take all the fat that covers the intestines, and the appendage upon the liver, and the two kidneys and the fat that is upon them, and you must make them smoke upon the altar. 14 But the bull's flesh and its skin and its dung you will burn with fire outside the camp. It is a sin offering.

15 "Then you will take the one ram, and Aaron and his sons must lay their hands upon the ram's head. 16 And you must slaughter the ram and take its blood and sprinkle it round about upon the altar. 17 And you will cut up the ram into its pieces, and you must wash its intestines and its shanks and put its pieces to one another and up to its head. 18 And you must make the entire ram smoke upon the altar. It is a burnt offering to Jehovah, a restful odor. It is an offering made by fire to Jehovah.

19 "Next you must take the other ram, and Aaron and his sons must lay their hands upon the ram's head. 20 And you must slaughter the ram and take some of its blood and put it upon the lobe of Aaron's right ear and upon the lobe of his sons' right ear and upon the thumb of their right hand and the big toe of their right foot, and you must sprinkle the blood round about upon the altar. 21 And you must take some of the blood that is upon the altar and some of the anointing oil, and you must spatter it upon Aaron and his garments and upon his sons and the garments of his sons with him, that he and his garments and his sons and the garments of his sons with him may indeed be holy.

22 "And you must take from the ram the fat and the fat tail and the fat that covers the intestines, and the appendage of the liver, and

the two kidneys and the fat that is upon them, and the right leg, for it is a ram of installation; 23 also a round loaf of bread and a ring-shaped cake of oiled bread and a wafer out of the basket of unfermented cakes that is before Jehovah. 24 And you must place them all upon the palms of Aaron and upon the palms of his sons, and you must wave them to and fro as a wave offering before Jehovah. 25 And you must take them off their hands and make them smoke upon the altar upon the burnt offering as a restful odor before Jehovah. It is an offering made by fire to Jehovah.

26 "And you must take the breast of the ram of installation, which is for Aaron, and wave it to and fro as a wave offering before Jehovah, and it must become your portion. 27 And you must sanctify the breast of the wave offering and the leg of the sacred portion that was waved and that was contributed from the ram of installation, from what was for Aaron and from what was for his sons. 28 And it must become Aaron's and his sons' by a regulation to time indefinite to be performed by the sons of Israel, because it is a sacred portion; and it will become a sacred portion to be rendered by the sons of Israel. From their communion sacrifices it is their sacred portion for Jehovah.

29 "And the holy garments that are Aaron's will serve for his sons after him to anoint them in them and to fill their hand with power in them. 30 Seven days the priest who succeeds him from among his sons and who comes into the tent of meeting to minister in the holy place will wear them.

31 "And you will take the ram of installation, and you must boil its flesh in a holy place. 32 And Aaron and his sons must eat the flesh of the ram and the bread that is in the basket at the entrance of the tent of meeting. 33 And they must eat the things with which atonement has been made to fill their hand with power, in order to

sanctify them. But a stranger may not eat them, because they are something holy. 34 And if any of the flesh of the installation sacrifice and of the bread should be left over until the morning, then you must burn what is left over with fire. It must not be eaten, because it is something holy.

35 "And you must do this way to Aaron and his sons according to all that I have commanded you. You will take seven days to fill their hand with power. 36 And you will offer the bull of the sin offering daily for an atonement, and you must purify the altar from sin by your making atonement over it, and you must anoint it to sanctify it. 37 You will take seven days to make atonement over the altar, and you must sanctify it that it may indeed become a most holy altar. Anyone who touches the altar is to be holy.

38 "And this is what you will offer upon the altar: young rams each a year old, two a day constantly. 39 And you will offer the one young ram in the morning, and you will offer the other young ram between the two evenings. 40 And a tenth part of an e'phah measure of fine flour moistened with the fourth of a hin of beaten oil, and a drink offering of the fourth of a hin of wine, will go for the first young ram. 41 And you will offer the second young ram between the two evenings. With a grain offering like that of the morning and with a drink offering like its, you will render it as a restful odor, an offering made by fire to Jehovah. 42 It is a constant burnt offering throughout YOUR generations at the entrance of the tent of meeting before Jehovah, where I shall present myself to YOU people to speak to you there.

43 "And I will present myself there to the sons of Israel, and it will certainly be sanctified by my glory. 44 And I will sanctify the tent of meeting and the altar; and I shall sanctify Aaron and his sons for them to act as priests to me. 45 And I will tabernacle in the midst of the sons of Israel, and I will prove to be their God. 46 And they will certainly know that I am Jehovah their God, who brought them out of the land of Egypt that I may tabernacle in the midst of them. I am Jehovah their God.

30 "And you must make an altar as a place for burning incense; out of acacia wood you will make it. 2 A cubit in length and a cubit in width, it should be foursquare, and its height two cubits. Its horns extend out of it. 3 And you must overlay it with pure gold, its top surface and its sides round about and its horns; and you must make a border of gold round about for it. 4 You will also make for it two rings of gold. Down below its border upon two of its sides you will make them, upon two opposite sides of it, as they must serve as supports for the poles with which to carry it. 5 And you must make the poles of acacia wood and overlay them with gold. 6 And you must put it before the curtain that is near the ark of the testimony, before the cover that is over the Testimony, where I shall present myself to you.

7 "And Aaron must make perfumed incense smoke upon it. Morning by morning, when he dresses the lamps, he will make it smoke. 8 And when Aaron lights up the lamps between the two evenings, he will make it smoke. It is an incense constantly before Jehovah during YOUR generations. 9 You must not offer upon it illegitimate incense or a burnt offering or a grain offering; and YOU must not pour a drink offering upon it. 10 And Aaron must make atonement upon its horns once a year. With some of the blood of the sin offering of the atonement he will make atonement for it once a year during YOUR generations. It is most holy to Jehovah."

11 And Jehovah went on to speak to Moses, saying: 12 "Whenever you take the sum of the sons of Israel as a census of them, then they must each give a ransom for his soul to Jehovah when taking a cen-

sus of them, that there may come to be no plague upon them when taking a census of them. 13 This is what all those will give who pass over to those numbered: a half shekel by the shekel of the holy place. Twenty ge'rahs equal a shekel. A half shekel is the contribution to Jehovah. 14 Everyone passing over to those registered from twenty years old and upward will give Jehovah's contribution. 15 The rich should not give more, and the lowly must not give less than the half shekel, in order to give Jehovah's contribution so as to make atonement for YOUR souls. 16 And you must take the silver money of the atonement from the sons of Israel and give it in behalf of the service of the tent of meeting, that it may indeed serve as a memorial before Jehovah for the sons of Israel, to make atonement for YOUR souls."

17 And Jehovah spoke further to Moses, saying: 18 "You must make a basin of copper and its stand of copper for washing, and you must put it between the tent of meeting and the altar and put water into it. 19 And Aaron and his sons must wash their hands and their feet at it. 20 When they go into the tent of meeting they will wash with water that they may not die, or when they go near the altar to minister in order to make an offering made by fire smoke to Jehovah. 21 And they must wash their hands and their feet that they may not die, and it must serve as a regulation to time indefinite for them, for him and his offspring throughout their generations."

22 And Jehovah continued to speak to Moses, saying: 23 "As for you, take to yourself the choicest perfumes: myrrh in congealed drops five hundred units, and sweet cinnamon in half that amount, two hundred and fifty units, and sweet calamus two hundred and fifty units, 24 and cassia five hundred units by the shekel of the holy place, and olive oil a hin. 25 Then you must make out of it a holy anointing oil, an

ointment, a mixture that is the work of an ointment maker. It is to be a holy anointing oil.

26 "And you must anoint with it the tent of meeting and the ark of the testimony, 27 and the table and all its utensils and the lampstand and its utensils and the altar of incense, 28 and the altar of burnt offering and all its utensils and the basin and its stand. 29 And you must sanctify them that they may indeed become most holy. Anyone touching them is to be holy. 30 And you will anoint Aaron and his sons, and you must sanctify them for acting as priests to me.

31 "And you will speak to the sons of Israel, saying, 'This is to continue as a holy anointing oil to me during YOUR generations. 32 It is not to be rubbed in the flesh of mankind, and with its composition YOU must not make any like it. It is something holy. It is to continue as something holy for YOU. 33 Anyone who makes an ointment like it and who puts some of it upon a stranger must be cut off from his people.'"

34 And Jehovah went on to say to Moses: "Take to yourself perfumes: stacte drops and onycha and perfumed galbanum and pure frankincense. There should be the same portion of each. 35 And you must make it into an incense, a spice mixture, the work of an ointment maker, salted, pure, something holy. 36 And you must pound some of it into fine powder and put some of it before the Testimony in the tent of meeting, where I shall present myself to you. It should be most holy to YOU people. 37 And the incense that you will make with this composition, YOU must not make for yourselves. For you it is to continue as something holy to Jehovah. 38 Whoever makes any like it to enjoy its smell must be cut off from his people."

31 And Jehovah continued to speak to Moses, saying: 2 "See, I do call by name Bez'al·el the son of U'ri the son of Hur of

the tribe of Judah. 3 And I shall fill him with the spirit of God in wisdom and in understanding and in knowledge and in every kind of craftsmanship, 4 for designing devices, for working in gold and silver and copper, 5 and in working of stones to set them and in working of wood to make products of every kind. 6 As for me, look! I do put with him O·ho′li·ab the son of A·hi′sa·mach of the tribe of Dan, and in the heart of everyone wise of heart I do put wisdom, that they may indeed make everything I have commanded you: 7 the tent of meeting and the Ark for the testimony and the cover that is upon it, and all the utensils of the tent, 8 and the table and its utensils, and the lampstand of pure gold and all its utensils, and the altar of incense, 9 and the altar of burnt offering and all its utensils, and the basin and its stand, 10 and the garments of knitted work and the holy garments for Aaron the priest and the garments of his sons for acting as priests; 11 and the anointing oil and the perfumed incense for the sanctuary. According to everything I have commanded you they will do."

12 And Jehovah said further to Moses: 13 "As for you, speak to the sons of Israel, saying, 'Especially my sabbaths you are to keep, for it is a sign between me and you during your generations that you may know that I Jehovah am sanctifying you. 14 And you must keep the sabbath, for it is something holy to you. A profaner of it will positively be put to death. In case there is anyone doing work on it, then that soul must be cut off from the midst of his people. 15 Six days may work be done, but on the seventh day is a sabbath of complete rest. It is something holy to Jehovah. Anyone doing work on the sabbath day will positively be put to death. 16 And the sons of Israel must keep the sabbath, so as to carry out the sabbath during their generations. It is a covenant to time indefinite. 17 Between me and the sons of Israel it is a sign

to time indefinite, because in six days Jehovah made the heavens and the earth and on the seventh day he rested and proceeded to refresh himself.'"

18 Now as soon as he had finished speaking with him on Mount Si′nai he proceeded to give Moses two tablets of the Testimony, tablets of stone written on by God's finger.

32 Meanwhile the people got to see that Moses was taking a long time about coming down from the mountain. So the people congregated themselves about Aaron and said to him: "Get up, make for us a god who will go ahead of us, because as regards this Moses, the man who led us up out of the land of Egypt, we certainly do not know what has happened to him." 2 At this Aaron said to them: "Tear off the gold earrings that are in the ears of your wives, of your sons and of your daughters and bring them to me." 3 And all the people began tearing off the gold earrings that were in their ears and bringing them to Aaron. 4 Then he took the gold from their hands, and he formed it with a graving tool and proceeded to make it into a molten statue of a calf. And they began to say: "This is your God, O Israel, who led you up out of the land of Egypt."

5 When Aaron got to see this, he went to building an altar before it. Finally Aaron called out and said: "There is a festival to Jehovah tomorrow." 6 So on the next day they were early in rising, and they began offering up burnt offerings and presenting communion sacrifices. After that the people sat down to eat and drink. Then they got up to have a good time.

7 Jehovah now said to Moses: "Go, descend, because your people whom you led up out of the land of Egypt have acted ruinously. 8 They have turned aside in a hurry from the way I have commanded them to go. They have made a molten statue of a calf for themselves and keep bowing down to it and sacrificing to it and saying, 'This is your God, O Israel,

who led you up out of the land of Egypt.'" 9 And Jehovah went on to say to Moses: "I have looked at this people and here it is a stiff-necked people. 10 So now let me be, that my anger may blaze against them and I may exterminate them, and let me make you into a great nation."

11 And Moses proceeded to soften the face of Jehovah his God and to say: "Why, O Jehovah, should your anger blaze against your people whom you brought out of the land of Egypt with great power and with a strong hand? 12 Why should the Egyptians say, 'With evil intent he brought them out in order to kill them among the mountains and to exterminate them from the surface of the ground'? Turn from your burning anger and feel regret over the evil against your people. 13 Remember Abraham, Isaac and Israel your servants, to whom you swore by yourself, in that you said to them, 'I shall multiply YOUR seed like the stars of the heavens, and all this land that I have designated I shall give to YOUR seed, that they may indeed take possession of it to time indefinite.'"

14 And Jehovah began to feel regret over the evil that he had spoken of doing to his people.

15 After that Moses turned and went down from the mountain with the two tablets of the Testimony in his hand, tablets written upon on both their sides. On this side and on that they were written upon. 16 And the tablets were the workmanship of God, and the writing was the writing of God engraved upon the tablets. 17 And Joshua began to hear the noise of the people because of their shouting, and he proceeded to say to Moses: "There is a noise of battle in the camp." 18 But he said:

"It is not the sound of the singing
      over mighty performance,
And it is not the sound of the
      singing of defeat;
It is the sound of other singing
      that I am hearing."

19 So it came about that as soon as he got near the camp and could see the calf and the dances, Moses' anger began to blaze, and he at once threw the tablets from his hands and shattered them at the foot of the mountain. 20 Then he took the calf that they had made and he burnt it with fire and crushed it till it was fine, after which he scattered it upon the surface of the waters and made the sons of Israel drink it. 21 After that Moses said to Aaron: "What did this people do to you that you have brought a great sin upon it?" 22 To this Aaron said: "Do not let the anger of my lord blaze. You yourself well know the people, that they are evil-inclined. 23 So they said to me, 'Make for us a god who will go ahead of us, because as regards this Moses, the man who led us up out of the land of Egypt, we certainly do not know what has happened to him.' 24 Hence I said to them, 'Who have any gold? They must tear it off themselves that they may give it to me.' And I proceeded to throw it into the fire and this calf came on out."

25 And Moses got to see that the people went unrestrained, because Aaron had let them go unrestrained for a disgrace among their opposers. 26 Then Moses took his stand in the gate of the camp and said: "Who is on Jehovah's side? To me!" And all the sons of Le'vi began gathering themselves to him. 27 He now said to them: "This is what Jehovah the God of Israel has said, 'Put each one of YOU his sword on his side. Pass through and return from gate to gate in the camp and kill each one his brother and each one his fellow and each one his intimate acquaintance.'" 28 And the sons of Le'vi proceeded to do as Moses had said, so that there fell of the people on that day about three thousand men. 29 And Moses went on to say: "Fill YOUR hand today with power for Jehovah, because each one of YOU is against his own son and his own brother, and that he may confer a blessing upon YOU today."

30 And it came about on the very next day that Moses proceeded to say to the people: "You—you have sinned with a great sin, and now I shall go up to Jehovah. Perhaps I can make amends for your sin." 31 So Moses returned to Jehovah and said: "Ah, but this people has sinned with a great sin, in that they made a god of gold for themselves! 32 But now if you will pardon their sin,—and if not, wipe me out, please, from your book that you have written." 33 However, Jehovah said to Moses: "Whoever has sinned against me, I shall wipe him out of my book. 34 And now, come, lead the people to where I have spoken to you of. Look! My angel will go ahead of you, and on the day of my bringing punishment I shall certainly bring punishment upon them for their sin." 35 And Jehovah began plaguing the people because they had made the calf, which Aaron had made.

33 And Jehovah said further to Moses: "Go, move up from here, you and the people whom you led up out of the land of Egypt, to the land about which I swore to Abraham, Isaac and Jacob, saying, 'To your seed I shall give it.' 2 And I will send an angel ahead of you and drive out the Ca'naan·ites, the Am'or·ites, and the Hit'tites and the Per'iz·zites, the Hi'vites and the Jeb'u·sites; 3 to a land flowing with milk and honey, for I shall not go up in the midst of you, because you are a stiff-necked people, that I may not exterminate you on the way."

4 When the people got to hear this evil word, they began to mourn; and none of them put his ornaments on himself. 5 And Jehovah went on to say to Moses: "Say to the sons of Israel, 'You are a stiff-necked people. In one moment I could go up into the midst of you and certainly exterminate you. So now put down your ornaments off yourself, as I want to know what I am going to do to you.'" 6 And the sons of Israel went stripping their ornaments

off themselves from Mount Ho'reb onward.

7 As for Moses, he proceeded to take his tent away and he pitched it outside the camp, far away from the camp; and he called it a tent of meeting. And it occurred that everyone inquiring of Jehovah would go out to the tent of meeting, which was outside the camp. 8 And it occurred that as soon as Moses went out to the tent, all the people would rise, and they stationed themselves each one at the entrance of his own tent, and they gazed after Moses until he went into the tent. 9 It also occurred that as soon as Moses had gone into the tent, the pillar of cloud would come down, and it stood at the entrance of the tent and he spoke with Moses. 10 And all the people saw the pillar of cloud standing at the entrance of the tent, and all the people rose and bowed down each one at the entrance of his own tent. 11 And Jehovah spoke to Moses face to face, just as a man would speak to his fellow. When he returned to the camp, his minister Joshua, the son of Nun, as attendant, would not withdraw from the midst of the tent.

12 Now Moses said to Jehovah: "See, you are saying to me, 'Lead this people up,' but you yourself have not let me know whom you will send with me. Moreover, you yourself have said, 'I do know you by name and, besides, you have found favor in my eyes.' 13 And now, if, please, I have found favor in your eyes, make me know, please, your ways, that I may know you, in order that I may find favor in your eyes. And consider that this nation is your people." 14 So he said: "My own person will go along and I shall certainly give you rest." 15 At this he said to him: "If your own person is not going along, do not lead us up from here. 16 And by what, now, will it be known that I have found favor in your eyes, I and your people? Is it not by your going along with us, in that I and your people have been

made distinct from all the other people who are upon the surface of the ground?"

17 And Jehovah went on to say to Moses: "This thing, too, of which you have spoken, I shall do, because you have found favor in my eyes and I know you by name." 18 At this he said: "Cause me to see, please, your glory." 19 But he said: "I myself shall cause all my goodness to pass before your face, and I will declare the name of Jehovah before you; and I will favor the one whom I may favor, and I will show mercy to the one to whom I may show mercy." 20 And he added: "You are not able to see my face, because no man may see me and yet live." 21 And Jehovah said further: "Here is a place with me, and you must station yourself upon the rock. 22 And it has to occur that while my glory is passing by I must place you in a hole in the rock, and I must put my palm over you as a screen until I have passed by. 23 After that I must take my palm away, and you will indeed see my back. But my face may not be seen."

34 Then Jehovah said to Moses: "Carve out for yourself two tablets of stone like the first ones, and I must write upon the tablets the words that appeared on the first tablets, which you shattered. 2 And get ready for the morning, as you must go up in the morning into Mount Si'nai and station yourself by me there on the top of the mountain. 3 But nobody may go up with you and, too, let nobody else be seen in all the mountain. What is more, no flock or herd should be pasturing in front of that mountain."

4 Accordingly Moses carved out two tablets of stone like the first ones and got up early in the morning and went on up into Mount Si'nai, just as Jehovah had commanded him, and he was taking the two tablets of stone in his hand. 5 And Jehovah proceeded to come down in the cloud and station himself with him there and declare

the name of Jehovah. 6 And Jehovah went passing by before his face and declaring: "Jehovah, Jehovah, a God merciful and gracious, slow to anger and abundant in loving-kindness and truth, 7 preserving loving-kindness for thousands, pardoning error and transgression and sin, but by no means will he give exemption from punishment, bringing punishment for the error of fathers upon sons and upon grandsons, upon the third generation and upon the fourth generation."

8 Moses at once hurried to bow low to the earth and prostrate himself. 9 Then he said: "If, now, I have found favor in your eyes, O Jehovah, let Jehovah, please, go along in the midst of us, because it is a stiff-necked people, and you have to forgive our error and our sin, and you must take us as your possession." 10 In turn he said: "Here I am concluding a covenant: Before all your people I shall do wonderful things that have never been created in all the earth or among all the nations; and all the people in the midst of whom you are will indeed see the work of Jehovah, because it is a fear-inspiring thing that I am doing with you.

11 "For your part keep what I am commanding you today. Here I am driving out from before you the Am'or·ites and the Ca'naan·ites and the Hit'tites and the Per'iz·zites and the Hi'vites and the Jeb'-u·sites. 12 Watch yourself that you do not conclude a covenant with the inhabitants of the land to which you are going, for fear it may prove itself a snare in your midst. 13 But their altars YOU people are to pull down, and their sacred pillars YOU are to shatter, and their sacred poles YOU are to cut down. 14 For you must not prostrate yourself to another god, because Jehovah, whose name is Jealous, he is a jealous God; 15 for fear that you may conclude a covenant with the inhabitants of the land, as they will certainly have immoral intercourse with their gods

and sacrifice to their gods, and someone will be certain to invite you, and you will certainly eat some of his sacrifice. 16 Then you will have to take some of their daughters for your sons, and their daughters will be certain to have immoral intercourse with their gods and make your sons have immoral intercourse with their gods.

17 "You must not make molten idol gods for yourself.

18 "The festival of unfermented cakes you are to keep. You will eat unfermented cakes, just as I have commanded you, seven days at the appointed time in the month of A'bib, because it was in the month of A'bib that you came out of Egypt.

19 "Everything that first opens the womb is mine, and, as regards all your livestock, the male firstling of bull and of sheep. 20 And the firstling of an ass you are to redeem with a sheep. But if you will not redeem it, then you must break its neck. Every first-born of your sons you are to redeem. And they must not appear before me empty-handed.

21 "Six days you are to labor, but on the seventh day you will keep sabbath. In plowing time and in harvest you will keep sabbath.

22 "And you will carry on your festival of weeks with the first ripe fruits of the wheat harvest, and the festival of ingathering at the turn of the year.

23 "Three times in the year every male of yours is to appear before the [true] Lord, Jehovah, the God of Israel. 24 For I shall drive the nations away from before you, and I will make your territory spacious; and nobody will desire your land while you are going up to see the face of Jehovah your God three times in the year.

25 "You must not slaughter along with what is leavened the blood of my sacrifice. And the sacrifice of the festival of the passover should not stay overnight until the morning.

26 "The best of the first ripe fruits of your soil you are to bring to the house of Jehovah your God.

"You must not boil a kid in its mother's milk."

27 And Jehovah went on to say to Moses: "Write down for yourself these words, because it is in accordance with these words that I do conclude a covenant with you and Israel." 28 And he continued there with Jehovah forty days and forty nights. He ate no bread and he drank no water. And he proceeded to write upon the tablets the words of the covenant, the Ten Words.

29 Now it came about when Moses came down from Mount Si'nai that the two tablets of the Testimony were in the hand of Moses when he came down from the mountain, and Moses did not know that the skin of his face emitted rays because of his having spoken with him. 30 When Aaron and all the sons of Israel got to see Moses, why, look! the skin of his face emitted rays and they grew afraid of coming near to him.

31 And Moses proceeded to call them. So Aaron and all the chieftains among the assembly came back to him, and Moses began to speak to them. 32 First after that all the sons of Israel came near to him, and he began commanding them all that Jehovah had spoken with him on Mount Si'nai. 33 When Moses would finish speaking with them, he would put a veil over his face. 34 But when Moses would go in before Jehovah to speak with him, he would take away the veil until his going out. And he went out and spoke to the sons of Israel what he would be commanded. 35 And the sons of Israel saw Moses' face, that the skin of Moses' face emitted rays; and Moses put the veil back over his face until he went in to speak with him.

35 Later Moses called the entire assembly of the sons of Israel together and said to them: "These are the words that Jehovah has commanded, to do them: 2 Six days may work be done, but on the seventh day it will become something holy to YOU, a sabbath of complete rest to Jehovah. Anybody doing work on it will be put to death. 3 YOU must not light a fire in any of YOUR dwelling places on the sabbath day."

4 And Moses went on to say to the entire assembly of the sons of Israel: "This is the word that Jehovah has commanded, saying, 5 'From among yourselves take up a contribution for Jehovah. Let every willing-hearted one bring it as Jehovah's contribution, namely, gold and silver and copper 6 and blue thread and wool dyed reddish purple and coccus scarlet material and fine linen and goat's hair 7 and ram skins dyed red and sealskins and acacia wood 8 and oil for the luminary and balsam oil for the anointing oil and for the perfumed incense 9 and onyx stones and setting stones for the eph'od and for the breastpiece.

10 "'And let all the wise-hearted ones among YOU come and make all that Jehovah has commanded, 11 namely, the tabernacle with its tent and its covering, its hooks and its panel frames, its bars, its pillars and its socket pedestals; 12 the Ark and its poles, the cover and the curtain of the screen; 13 the table and its poles and all its utensils and the showbread; 14 and the lampstand of illumination and its utensils and its lamps and the oil for illumination; 15 and the altar of incense and its poles; and the anointing oil and the perfumed incense; and the screen of the entrance for the tabernacle's entrance; 16 the altar of burnt offering and the copper grating that is for it, its poles and all its utensils; the basin and its stand; 17 the hangings of the courtyard, its pillars and its socket pedestals; and the screen of the gate of the courtyard; 18 the tent pins of the tabernacle and the tent pins of the courtyard and their cords; 19 the garments of knitted work for ministering in the sanctuary, the holy garments for Aaron the priest and the garments of his sons for acting as priests.'"

20 Accordingly all the assembly of the sons of Israel went out from before Moses. 21 Then they came, everyone whose heart impelled him, and they brought, everyone whose spirit incited him, Jehovah's contribution for the work of the tent of meeting and for all its service and for the holy garments. 22 And they kept coming, the men along with the women, every willing-hearted one. They brought brooches and earrings and rings and female ornaments, all sorts of articles of gold, that is, everyone who presented the wave offering of gold to Jehovah. 23 And all those with whom there were found blue thread and wool dyed reddish purple and coccus scarlet material and fine linen and goat's hair and ram skins dyed red and sealskins, brought them. 24 All those contributing the contribution of silver and copper brought Jehovah's contribution, and all those with whom there was found acacia wood for all the work of the service brought it.

25 And all the women who were wise of heart spun with their hands, and they kept bringing as yarn the blue thread and the wool dyed reddish purple, the coccus scarlet material and the fine linen. 26 And all the women whose hearts impelled them with wisdom spun the goat's hair.

27 And the chieftains brought onyx stones and setting stones for the eph'od and the breastpiece, 28 and the balsam oil and the oil for illumination and for the anointing oil and for the perfumed incense. 29 Every man and woman whose hearts incited them to bring something for all the work that Jehovah had commanded to make by means of Moses did so; the sons of Israel brought a voluntary offering to Jehovah.

30 Then Moses said to the sons of Israel: "See, Jehovah has called by name Bez'al·el the son of U'ri the son of Hur of the tribe of Judah. 31 And he proceeded to fill him with the spirit of God in wisdom, in understanding and in

knowledge and in every sort of craftsmanship 32 and for designing devices, for working in gold and silver and copper, 33 and in working of stones to set them and in working of wood to make ingenious products of every sort. 34 And he has put it into his heart that he should teach, he and O·ho′li·ab the son of A·his′a·mach of the tribe of Dan. 35 He has filled them with wisdom of heart to do all the work of a craftsman and an embroiderer and of a weaver in blue thread and wool dyed reddish purple, in coccus scarlet material and fine linen, and of a loom worker, men doing every sort of work and designing devices.

36 "And Bez′al·el must work, also O·ho′li·ab and every wise-hearted man to whom Jehovah has given wisdom and understanding in these things in order to know how to do all the work of the holy service according to all that Jehovah has commanded."

2 And Moses proceeded to call Bez′al·el and O·ho′li·ab and every wise-hearted man into whose heart Jehovah had put wisdom, everyone whose heart impelled him to approach the work in order to do it. 3 Then they took from before Moses all the contribution that the sons of Israel had brought for the work of the holy service so as to do it, and, as for the latter, they still brought to him a voluntary offering morning after morning.

4 And all the wise ones who were doing all the holy work began to come, one man after another, from their work that they were doing, 5 and to say to Moses: "The people are bringing much more than what the service needs for the work that Jehovah has commanded to be done." 6 So Moses commanded that they should cause an announcement to pass through the camp, saying: "Men and women, do not produce any more stuff for the holy contribution." With that the people were restrained from bringing it in. 7 And the stuff proved to be enough for all the work to be done, and more than enough.

8 And all the wise-hearted among those doing the work went making the tabernacle, the ten tent cloths of fine twisted linen and blue thread and wool dyed reddish purple and coccus scarlet material; with cherubs, the work of an embroiderer, he made them. 9 The length of each tent cloth was twenty-eight cubits, and the width of each tent cloth four cubits. There was one measure for all the tent cloths. 10 Then he joined five tent cloths one to another, and the five other tent cloths he joined one to another. 11 After that he made loops of blue thread upon the edge of the one tent cloth at the junction end. He did the same on the edge of the outermost tent cloth at the other place of junction. 12 He made fifty loops on the one tent cloth, and he made fifty loops on the extremity of the tent cloth that was at the other place of junction, the loops being opposite one another. 13 Finally he made fifty hooks of gold and joined the tent cloths to one another by the hooks, so that it became one tabernacle.

14 And he went on to make tent cloths of goat's hair for the tent upon the tabernacle. Eleven tent cloths were what he made. 15 The length of each tent cloth was thirty cubits, and the width of each tent cloth four cubits. There was one measure for the eleven tent cloths. 16 Then he joined five tent cloths together by themselves and the six other tent cloths by themselves. 17 Next he made fifty loops upon the edge of the outermost tent cloth at the place of junction, and he made fifty loops upon the edge of the other tent cloth that joined with it. 18 After that he made fifty hooks of copper for joining the tent together to become one piece. 19 And he proceeded to make a covering for the tent out of ram skins dyed red and a covering out of sealskins up on top.

20 Then he made the panel frames for the tabernacle out of acacia wood, standing on end. 21 Ten cubits was the length of a

panel frame, and one cubit and a half the width of each panel frame. 22 Each panel frame had two tenons fitted one to the other. That is the way he did to all the panel frames of the tabernacle. 23 So he made the panel frames for the tabernacle, twenty panel frames for the side toward the Neg′eb, to the south. 24 And he made forty socket pedestals of silver for beneath the twenty panel frames, two socket pedestals beneath the one panel frame with its two tenons and two socket pedestals beneath the other panel frame with its two tenons. 25 And for the other side of the tabernacle, the northern side, he made twenty panel frames 26 and their forty socket pedestals of silver, two socket pedestals beneath the one panel frame and two socket pedestals beneath the other panel frame.

27 And for the rear sections of the tabernacle to the west he made six panel frames. 28 And he made two panel frames as corner posts of the tabernacle on its two rear sections. 29 And they proved to be duplicates at the bottom and together they came to be twins to the top of each one at the first ring. That is what he did to them both, to the two corner posts. 30 So they amounted to eight panel frames and their socket pedestals of silver to sixteen, two socket pedestals next to two socket pedestals beneath each panel frame.

31 And he went on to make bars of acacia wood, five for the panel frames of the one side of the tabernacle 32 and five bars for the panel frames of the other side of the tabernacle and five bars for the panel frames of the tabernacle for the two rear sections to the west. 33 Then he made the middle bar to run through at the middle of the panel frames from one end to the other. 34 And he overlaid the panel frames with gold, and he made their rings of gold as supports for the bars, and he went on to overlay the bars with gold.

35 And he proceeded to make a curtain of blue thread and wool dyed reddish purple and coccus scarlet material and fine twisted linen. With the work of an embroiderer he made it with cherubs. 36 Then he made for it four acacia pillars and overlaid them with gold, their pegs being of gold, and cast four socket pedestals of silver for them. 37 And he went on to make a screen for the entrance of the tent out of blue thread and wool dyed reddish purple and coccus scarlet material and fine twisted linen, the work of a weaver, 38 and its five pillars and their pegs. And he overlaid their tops and their joints with gold, but their five socket pedestals were of copper.

37 Bez′al·el now made the Ark of acacia wood. Two cubits and a half was its length, and a cubit and a half its width, and a cubit and a half its height. 2 Then he overlaid it with pure gold inside and outside and made a border of gold round about for it. 3 After that he cast four rings of gold for it, for above its four feet, with two rings on its one side and two rings on its other side. 4 He next made poles of acacia wood and overlaid them with gold. 5 Then he put the poles through the rings on the sides of the Ark for carrying the Ark.

6 And he went on to make the cover of pure gold. Two cubits and a half was its length, and a cubit and a half its width. 7 He further made two cherubs of gold. Of hammered work he made them on both ends of the cover. 8 One cherub was on the end over there, and the other cherub on the end over here. He made the cherubs on the cover on both of its ends. 9 And they came to be cherubs spreading out two wings upward, screening over the cover with their wings, and their faces were one to the other. The faces of the cherubs proved to be toward the cover.

10 And he proceeded to make the table of acacia wood. Two cubits was its length, and a cubit and a cubit and a half its width, and a cubit and a half its height. 11 Then he overlaid it

with pure gold and made a border of gold round about for it. 12 Next he made for it a rim of a handbreadth round about and made a border of gold for its rim round about. 13 Further, he cast four rings of gold for it and put the rings upon the four corners that were for the four feet. 14 The rings proved to be near the rim, as supports for the poles for carrying the table. 15 Then he made the poles of acacia wood and overlaid them with gold for carrying the table. 16 After that he made the utensils that are upon the table, its dishes and its cups and its bowls and its pitchers with which libations would be poured, out of pure gold.

17 Then he made the lampstand of pure gold. Of hammered work he made the lampstand. Its sides and its branches, its cups, its knobs and its blossoms proceeded out of it. 18 And six branches were running out from its sides, three branches of the lampstand out from its one side and three branches of the lampstand out from its other side. 19 Three cups shaped like flowers of almond were on the one set of branches, with knobs and blossoms alternating; and three cups shaped like flowers of almond were on the other set of branches, with knobs and blossoms alternating. That is the way it was for the six branches running out from the lampstand. 20 And on the lampstand there were four cups shaped like flowers of almond, with its knobs and its blossoms alternating. 21 And the knob under two branches was out of it, and the knob under two other branches was out of it, and the knob under two more branches was out of it, for the six branches running out from the lampstand. 22 Their knobs and their branches proceeded out from it. All of it was one piece of hammered work of pure gold. 23 Then he made its seven lamps and its snuffers and its fire holders out of pure gold. 24 Of a talent of pure gold he made it and all its utensils.

25 He now made the altar of incense out of acacia wood. A cubit was its length and a cubit its width, it being foursquare, and two cubits was its height. Its horns proceeded out of it. 26 Then he overlaid it with pure gold, its top surface and its sides round about and its horns, and he made a border of gold round about for it. 27 And he made for it two rings of gold down below its border upon two of its sides, upon two opposite sides of it, as supports for the poles with which to carry it. 28 After that he made the poles of acacia wood and overlaid them with gold. 29 He made additionally the holy anointing oil and the pure, perfumed incense, the work of an ointment maker.

38 And he went on to make the altar of burnt offering out of acacia wood. Five cubits was its length, and five cubits its width, it being foursquare, and three cubits was its height. 2 Then he made its horns upon its four corners. Its horns proceeded out of it. Next he overlaid it with copper. 3 After that he made all the utensils of the altar, the cans and the shovels and the bowls, the forks and the fire holders. All its utensils he made of copper. 4 He further made for the altar a grating, a network of copper, under its rim, down toward its center. 5 Then he cast four rings on the four extremities near the grating of copper, as supports for the poles. 6 After that he made the poles of acacia wood and overlaid them with copper. 7 Then he put the poles into the rings on the sides of the altar for carrying it with them. He made it a hollow chest of planks.

8 Then he made the basin of copper and its stand of copper, by the use of the mirrors of the women servants who did organized service at the entrance of the tent of meeting.

9 And he proceeded to make the courtyard. For the side toward the Neg'eb, to the south, the hangings of the courtyard were of fine twisted linen, for a hundred cubits. 10 Their twenty pillars and their

twenty socket pedestals were of copper. The pegs of the pillars and their joints were of silver. 11 Also, for the north side there were a hundred cubits. Their twenty pillars and their twenty socket pedestals were of copper. The pegs of the pillars and their joints were of silver. 12 But for the west side the hangings were for fifty cubits. Their pillars were ten and their socket pedestals ten. The pegs of the pillars and their joints were of silver. 13 And for the east side toward the sunrising there were fifty cubits. 14 The hangings were for fifteen cubits to the one wing. Their pillars were three and their socket pedestals three. 15 And for the other wing, on this as well as that side, of the gate of the courtyard, the hangings were for fifteen cubits. Their pillars were three and their socket pedestals three. 16 All the hangings of the courtyard round about were of fine twisted linen. 17 And the socket pedestals for the pillars were of copper. The pegs of the pillars and their joints were of silver and the overlaying of their tops was of silver, and there were silver joinings for all the pillars of the courtyard.

18 And the screen of the gate of the courtyard was the work of a weaver, of blue thread and wool dyed reddish purple and coccus scarlet material and fine twisted linen, and twenty cubits was the length, and the height throughout its extent was five cubits equally with the hangings of the courtyard. 19 And their four pillars and their four socket pedestals were of copper. Their pegs were of silver and the overlaying of their heads and their joints were of silver. 20 And all the tent pins for the tabernacle and for the courtyard round about were of copper.

21 The following are the things inventoried of the tabernacle, the tabernacle of the Testimony, which was inventoried at the command of Moses, as the service of the Levites under the guidance of Ith'a·mar the son of Aaron the priest.

22 And Bez'al·el the son of U'ri the son of Hur of the tribe of Judah did all that Jehovah had commanded Moses. 23 And with him was O·ho'li·ab the son of A·his'a·mach of the tribe of Dan, a craftsman and embroiderer and weaver in the blue thread and the wool dyed reddish purple and coccus scarlet material and fine linen.

24 All the gold that was used for the work in all the work of the holy place came to the amount of the gold of the wave offering, twenty-nine talents and seven hundred and thirty shekels by the shekel of the holy place. 25 And the silver of the ones registered of the assembly was a hundred talents and one thousand seven hundred and seventy-five shekels by the shekel of the holy place. 26 The half shekel for an individual was the half of a shekel by the shekel of the holy place, for every man who was passing over to those who were registered from twenty years of age and upward, amounting to six hundred and three thousand five hundred and fifty.

27 And a hundred talents of silver went into the casting of the socket pedestals of the holy place and the socket pedestals of the curtain. A hundred socket pedestals equaled a hundred talents, a talent to a socket pedestal. 28 And out of the thousand seven hundred and seventy-five shekels he made pegs for the pillars and overlaid their tops and joined them together.

29 And the copper of the wave offering was seventy talents and two thousand four hundred shekels. 30 And with this he proceeded to make the socket pedestals of the entrance of the tent of meeting and the copper altar and the copper grating that belonged to it, and all the utensils of the altar, 31 and the socket pedestals of the courtyard round about, and the socket pedestals of the gate of the courtyard, and all the tent pins of the tabernacle and all the tent pins of the courtyard round about.

39 And out of the blue thread and wool dyed reddish purple and coccus scarlet material they made garments of knitted work for ministering in the holy place. So they made the holy garments that were for Aaron, just as Jehovah had commanded Moses.

2 Accordingly he made the eph′od of gold, blue thread and wool dyed reddish purple and coccus scarlet material and fine twisted linen. 3 Then they beat plates of gold to thin sheets, and he cut out threads to work in among the blue thread and the wool dyed reddish purple and the coccus scarlet material and the fine linen, as the work of an embroiderer. 4 They made shoulder pieces for it that were joined. It was joined at its two extremities. 5 And the girdle, which was upon it for tying it close, was of the same material according to its workmanship, of gold, blue thread, and wool dyed reddish purple and coccus scarlet material and fine twisted linen, just as Jehovah had commanded Moses.

6 Then they made the onyx stones set with settings of gold, engraved with the engravings of a seal according to the names of the sons of Israel. 7 So he placed them upon the shoulder pieces of the eph′od as memorial stones for the sons of Israel, just as Jehovah had commanded Moses. 8 Then he made the breastpiece with the workmanship of an embroiderer, like the workmanship of the eph′od, out of gold, blue thread and wool dyed reddish purple and coccus scarlet material and fine twisted linen. 9 It proved to be foursquare when doubled. They made the breastpiece, when doubled, a span of the hand in its length and a span in its width. 10 Then they filled it with four rows of stones. A row of ruby, topaz and emerald was the first row. 11 And the second row was turquoise, sapphire and jasper. 12 And the third row was lesh′em stone, agate and amethyst. 13 And the fourth row was chrys′o·lite and onyx and jade. They were set with settings of gold in their fillings. 14 And the stones were according to the names of the sons of Israel. They were twelve according to their names, with the engravings of a seal, each according to its name for the twelve tribes.

15 And they proceeded to make upon the breastpiece wreathed chains, in rope work, of pure gold. 16 Then they made two settings of gold and two rings of gold and put the two rings upon the two extremities of the breastpiece. 17 After that they put the two ropes of gold through the two rings at the extremities of the breastpiece. 18 And they put the two ends of the two ropes through the two settings. Then they put them upon the shoulder pieces of the eph′od, at the forefront of it. 19 Next they made two rings of gold and set them at the two extremities of the breastpiece upon its edge that is on the side toward the eph′od inward. 20 Then they made two rings of gold and put them upon the two shoulder pieces of the eph′od from below, on its forefront, near its place of joining, above the girdle of the eph′od. 21 Finally they bound the breastpiece by its rings to the rings of the eph′od with a blue string, that it might continue above the girdle of the eph′od and the breastpiece might not get displaced from on top the eph′od, just as Jehovah had commanded Moses.

22 Then he made the sleeveless coat of the eph′od, the workmanship of a loom worker, all of blue thread. 23 And the opening of the sleeveless coat was in the middle of it, like the opening of a coat of mail. Its opening had a border round about that it might not be torn. 24 Then they made upon the hem of the sleeveless coat pomegranates of blue thread and wool dyed reddish purple and coccus scarlet material, twisted together. 25 Further, they made bells of pure gold and put the bells in between the pomegranates upon the hem of the sleeveless coat round about, in between the pomegranates; 26 a bell and a pome-

granate, a bell and a pomegranate upon the hem of the sleeveless coat round about, for ministering, just as Jehovah had commanded Moses.

27 Next they made the robes of fine linen, the workmanship of a loom worker, for Aaron and his sons, 28 and the turban of fine linen and the ornamental headgears of fine linen and the linen drawers of fine twisted linen, 29 and the sash of fine twisted linen and blue thread and wool dyed reddish purple and coccus scarlet material, the work of a weaver, just as Jehovah had commanded Moses.

30 Finally they made the shining plate, the holy sign of dedication, out of pure gold and inscribed upon it an inscription with the engravings of a seal: "Holiness belongs to Jehovah." 31 Then they put a string of blue thread to it in order to put it upon the turban up above, just as Jehovah had commanded Moses.

32 So the work for the tabernacle of the tent of meeting all came to its completion, in that the sons of Israel kept doing according to all that Jehovah had commanded Moses. They did just so.

33 And they proceeded to bring the tabernacle to Moses, the tent and all its utensils, its hooks, its panel frames, its bars and its pillars and its socket pedestals, 34 and its covering of ram skins dyed red and its covering of sealskins and the curtain of the screen, 35 and the ark of the testimony and its poles and the cover, 36 the table, all its utensils and the showbread, 37 the lampstand of pure gold, its lamps, the row of lamps, and all its utensils and the oil of illumination, 38 and the altar of gold and the anointing oil and the perfumed incense and the screen for the entrance of the tent, 39 the altar of copper and the grating of copper that belonged to it, its poles and all its utensils, the basin and its stand, 40 the hangings of the courtyard, its pillars and its socket pedestals and the screen for the gate of the court-

yard, its tent cords and its tent pins and all the utensils for the service of the tabernacle, for the tent of meeting, 41 the garments of knitted work for ministering in the sanctuary, the holy garments for Aaron the priest and the garments of his sons for acting as priests.

42 According to all that Jehovah had commanded Moses, that was the way the sons of Israel did all the service. 43 And Moses got to see all the work, and, look! they had done it just as Jehovah had commanded. That was the way they had done. Consequently Moses blessed them.

40 Then Jehovah spoke to Moses, saying: 2 "On the day of the first month, on the first of the month, you are to set up the tabernacle of the tent of meeting. 3 And you must place the ark of the testimony in it and shut off approach to the Ark with the curtain. 4 And you must bring the table in and set its arrangement in order, and you must bring in the lampstand and light up its lamps. 5 And you must put the golden altar for incense before the ark of the testimony and put the screen of the entrance for the tabernacle in place.

6 "And you must put the altar of burnt offering before the entrance of the tabernacle of the tent of meeting, 7 and you must put the basin between the tent of meeting and the altar and put water in it. 8 And you must place the courtyard round about and put up the screen of the gate of the courtyard. 9 And you must take the anointing oil and anoint the tabernacle and all that is in it, and you must sanctify it and all its utensils, and so it must become something holy. 10 And you must anoint the altar of burnt offering and all its utensils and sanctify the altar, and so it must become a most holy altar. 11 And you must anoint the basin and its stand and sanctify it.

12 "Then you must bring Aaron and his sons near to the entrance

of the tent of meeting and wash them with water. 13 And you must clothe Aaron with the holy garments and anoint him and sanctify him, and so he must act as priest to me. 14 After that you will bring his sons near and you must clothe them with robes. 15 And you must anoint them just as you anointed their father, and so they must act as priests to me, and their anointing must serve continually for them as a priesthood to time indefinite during their generations."

16 And Moses proceeded to do according to all that Jehovah had commanded him. He did just so.

17 Accordingly it came about that in the first month, in the second year, on the first day of the month, the tabernacle was set up. 18 When Moses proceeded to set up the tabernacle, he went putting its socket pedestals down and placing its panel frames and putting its bars in and setting up its pillars. 19 Then he spread out the tent over the tabernacle and placed the covering of the tent above upon it, just as Jehovah had commanded Moses.

20 After that he took the Testimony and put it into the Ark and placed the poles on the Ark and put the cover above upon the Ark. 21 Then he brought the Ark into the tabernacle and put the curtain of the screen in place and shut off approach to the ark of the testimony, just as Jehovah had commanded Moses.

22 Next he put the table in the tent of meeting on the side of the tabernacle to the north outside the curtain, 23 and he arranged the row of bread upon it before Jehovah, just as Jehovah had commanded Moses.

24 Then he placed the lampstand in the tent of meeting in front of the table, on the side of the tabernacle to the south. 25 He then lit up the lamps before Jeho-

vah, just as Jehovah had commanded Moses.

26 He next placed the golden altar in the tent of meeting before the curtain, 27 that he might make perfumed incense smoke upon it, just as Jehovah had commanded Moses.

28 Finally he put the screen of the entrance of the tabernacle in place.

29 And he placed the altar of burnt offering at the entrance of the tabernacle of the tent of meeting, that he might offer up the burnt offering and the grain offering upon it, just as Jehovah had commanded Moses.

30 Then he placed the basin between the tent of meeting and the altar and put water in it for washing. 31 And Moses and Aaron and his sons washed their hands and their feet at it. 32 When they went into the tent of meeting and when they went near to the altar they would wash, just as Jehovah had commanded Moses.

33 Finally he set up the courtyard round about the tabernacle and the altar and put up the screen of the gate of the courtyard.

So Moses finished the work. 34 And the cloud began to cover the tent of meeting, and Jehovah's glory filled the tabernacle. 35 And Moses was not able to go into the tent of meeting, because the cloud resided over it and Jehovah's glory filled the tabernacle.

36 And when the cloud lifted itself up from over the tabernacle the sons of Israel would break camp during all their stages of journey. 37 However, if the cloud did not lift itself up, then they would not break camp until the day when it lifted itself up. 38 For Jehovah's cloud was over the tabernacle by day, and a fire continued upon it by night in the sight of all the house of Israel during all their stages of journey.

LEVITICUS

1 And Jehovah proceeded to call Moses and speak to him out of the tent of meeting, saying: 2 "Speak to the sons of Israel, and you must say to them, 'In case some man of YOU would present an offering to Jehovah from the domestic animals, YOU should present YOUR offering from the herd and from the flock.

3 "'If his offering is a burnt offering from the herd, a male, a sound one, is what he should present. At the entrance of the tent of meeting he should present it of his own free will before Jehovah. 4 And he must lay his hand upon the head of the burnt offering, and it must be graciously accepted for him to make atonement for him.

5 "'Then the young bull must be slaughtered before Jehovah; and the sons of Aaron, the priests, must present the blood and sprinkle the blood round about upon the altar, which is at the entrance of the tent of meeting. 6 And the burnt offering must be skinned and cut up into its parts. 7 And the sons of Aaron, the priests, must put fire on the altar and set wood in order on the fire. 8 And the sons of Aaron, the priests, must set the pieces in order with the head and the suet over the wood that is on the fire that is on the altar. 9 And its intestines and its shanks will be washed with water; and the priest must make all of it smoke on the altar as a burnt offering, an offering made by fire of a restful odor to Jehovah.

10 "'And if his offering for a burnt offering is from the flock, from the young rams or the goats, a male, a sound one, is what he will present. 11 And it must be slaughtered at the side of the altar to the north before Jehovah, and the sons of Aaron, the priests, must sprinkle its blood round about upon the altar. 12 And he must cut it up into its parts and its head

and its suet, and the priest must set them in order over the wood that is on the fire that is on the altar. 13 And he will wash the intestines and the shanks with water; and the priest must present all of it and make it smoke on the altar. It is a burnt offering, an offering made by fire of a restful odor to Jehovah.

14 "'However, if his offering as a burnt offering to Jehovah is from the fowls, then he must present his offering from the turtledoves or the male pigeons. 15 And the priest must present it at the altar and nip off its head and make it smoke upon the altar, but its blood must be drained out upon the side of the altar. 16 And he must remove its crop with its feathers and throw it beside the altar, to the east, to the place for the fatty ashes. 17 And he must cleave it at its wings. He must not divide it. Then the priest must make it smoke on the altar over the wood that is on the fire. It is a burnt offering, an offering made by fire of a restful odor to Jehovah.

2 "'Now in case some soul would present as an offering a grain offering to Jehovah, his offering should prove to be fine flour; and he must pour oil over it and put frankincense upon it. 2 And he must bring it to the sons of Aaron, the priests, and the priest must grasp from it his handful of its fine flour and its oil along with all its frankincense; and he must make it smoke as a remembrancer of it upon the altar, as an offering made by fire of a restful odor to Jehovah. 3 And what is left of the grain offering belongs to Aaron and his sons, as something most holy from Jehovah's offerings made by fire.

4 "'And in case you would present as an offering a grain offering in the way of something baked in the oven, it should be of fine flour, unfermented ring-shaped

cakes moistened with oil or un-fermented wafers smeared with oil. 5 "'And if your offering is a grain offering from off the grid-dle, it should prove to be of fine flour moistened with oil, unfer-mented. 6 There should be a breaking of it up into pieces, and you must pour oil upon it. It is a grain offering.

7 "'And if your offering is a grain offering out of the deep-fat kettle, it should be made of fine flour with oil. 8 And you must bring the grain offering that was made of these to Jehovah; and it must be presented to the priest and he must bring it near to the altar. 9 And the priest must lift off some of the grain offering as a remem-brancer of it and must make it smoke on the altar, as an offering made by fire of a restful odor to Jehovah. 10 And what is left of the grain offering belongs to Aaron and his sons, as something most holy of Jehovah's offerings by fire.

11 "'No grain offering that you will present to Jehovah should be made a leavened thing, because you must make no sour dough and no honey at all smoke as an offer-ing made by fire to Jehovah.

12 "'As an offering of the first fruits, you will present them to Jehovah, and they must not come up onto the altar for a restful odor.

13 "'And every offering of your grain offering you will season with salt; and you must not allow the salt of the covenant of your God to be missing upon your grain of-fering. Along with every offering of yours you will present salt.

14 "'And if you would present the grain offering of the first ripe fruits to Jehovah, you should pre-sent green ears roasted with fire, the grits of new grain, as the grain offering of your first ripe fruits. 15 And you must put oil upon it and place frankincense upon it. It is a grain offering. 16 And the priest must make the remembranc-er of it smoke, that is, some of its grits and oil, along with all its frankincense, as an offering made by fire to Jehovah.

3 "'And if his offering is a com-munion sacrifice, if he is pre-senting it from the herd, whether a male or a female, a sound one is what he will present before Jeho-vah. 2 And he must lay his hand upon the head of his offering, and it must be slaughtered at the en-trance of the tent of meeting; and Aaron's sons, the priests, must sprinkle the blood round about up-on the altar. 3 And he must pre-sent some of the communion sac-rifice as an offering made by fire to Jehovah, namely, the fat that covers the intestines, even all the fat that is over the intestines, 4 and the two kidneys and the fat that is upon them, the same as that upon the loins. And as for the ap-pendage upon the liver, he will re-move it along with the kidneys. 5 And Aaron's sons must make it smoke on the altar, upon the burnt offering that is over the wood that is on the fire, as an offering made by fire of a restful odor to Jehovah.

6 "'And if his offering is from the flock for a communion sacrifice to Jehovah, a male or a female, a sound one is what he will present. 7 If he is presenting a young ram as his offering, then he must pre-sent it before Jehovah. 8 And he must lay his hand upon the head of his offering, and it must be slaughtered before the tent of meet-ing; and Aaron's sons must sprin-kle its blood round about upon the altar. 9 And from the commun-ion sacrifice he must present its fat as an offering made by fire to Jehovah. The entire fatty tail is what he will remove near the back-bone, and the fat that covers the intestines, even all the fat that is upon the intestines, 10 and the two kidneys and the fat that is upon them, the same as that upon the loins. And as for the appendage upon the liver, he will remove it along with the kidneys. 11 And the priest must make it smoke on the altar as food, an offering made by fire to Jehovah.

12 "'And if his offering is a goat, then he must present it be-

fore Jehovah. 13 And he must lay his hand upon its head, and it must be slaughtered before the tent of meeting; and Aaron's sons must sprinkle its blood round about upon the altar. 14 And from it he must present as his offering, as an offering made by fire to Jehovah, the fat that covers the intestines, even all the fat that is upon the intestines, 15 and the two kidneys and the fat that is upon them, the same as that upon the loins. And as for the appendage upon the liver, he will remove it along with the kidneys. 16 And the priest must make them smoke upon the altar as food, an offering made by fire for a restful odor. All the fat belongs to Jehovah.

17 " 'It is a statute to time indefinite for YOUR generations, in all YOUR dwelling places: YOU must not eat any fat or any blood at all.' "

4 And Jehovah went on to speak to Moses, saying: 2 "Speak to the sons of Israel, saying, 'In case a soul sins by mistake in any of the things that Jehovah commands should not be done, and he actually does one of them:

3 " 'If the priest, the anointed one, sins so as to bring guiltiness upon the people, then he must present for his sin that he has committed a sound young bull to Jehovah as a sin offering. 4 And he must bring the bull to the entrance of the tent of meeting before Jehovah and must lay his hand upon the bull's head, and he must slaughter the bull before Jehovah. 5 And the priest, the anointed one, must take some of the bull's blood and bring it into the tent of meeting; 6 and the priest must dip his finger in the blood and spatter some of the blood seven times before Jehovah in front of the curtain of the holy place. 7 And the priest must put some of the blood upon the horns of the altar of perfumed incense before Jehovah, which is in the tent of meeting, and all the rest of the bull's blood he will pour at the base of the altar of burnt offering, which is

at the entrance of the tent of meeting.

8 " 'As to all the fat of the bull of the sin offering, he will lift up from it the fat that covers over the intestines, even all the fat that is over the intestines, 9 and the two kidneys and the fat that is upon them, the same as that upon the loins. And as for the appendage upon the liver, he will remove it along with the kidneys. 10 It will be the same as what is lifted up of a bull of the communion sacrifice. And the priest must make them smoke upon the altar of burnt offering.

11 " 'But as for the skin of the bull and all its flesh along with its head and its shanks and its intestines and its dung, 12 he must have the entire bull taken out to the outskirts of the camp to a clean place where the fatty ashes are poured out, and he must burn it upon wood in the fire. Where the fatty ashes are poured out it should be burned.

13 " 'Now if the entire assembly of Israel makes a mistake and the matter has been hidden from the eyes of the congregation in that they have done one of all the things that Jehovah commands should not be done and so have become guilty, 14 and the sin that they have committed against it has become known, then the congregation must present a young bull for a sin offering and must bring it before the tent of meeting. 15 And the older men of the assembly must lay their hands upon the bull's head before Jehovah, and the bull must be slaughtered before Jehovah.

16 " 'Then the priest, the anointed one, must bring some of the bull's blood into the tent of meeting. 17 And the priest must dip his finger into some of the blood and spatter it seven times before Jehovah in front of the curtain. 18 And he will put some of the blood upon the horns of the altar that is before Jehovah, which is in the tent of meeting; and all the rest of the blood he will pour at

the base of the altar of burnt offering, which is at the entrance of the tent of meeting. 19 And he will lift up all its fat from it, and he must make it smoke on the altar. 20 And he must do to the bull just as he did to the other bull of the sin offering. That is the way he will do to it; and the priest must make an atonement for them, and so it must be forgiven them. 21 And he must have the bull taken out to the outskirts of the camp and must burn it, just as he burned the first bull. It is a sin offering for the congregation.

22 "'When a chieftain sins and he does commit unintentionally one of all the things that Jehovah his God commands should not be done, and so has become guilty, 23 or his sin that he has committed against the commandment has been made known to him, then he must bring as his offering a male kid of the goats, a sound one. 24 And he must lay his hand upon the head of the young goat and slaughter it in the place where the burnt offering is regularly slaughtered before Jehovah. It is a sin offering. 25 And the priest must take some of the blood of the sin offering with his finger and put it upon the horns of the altar of burnt offering, and he will pour the rest of its blood at the base of the altar of burnt offering. 26 And he will make all its fat smoke on the altar like the fat of the communion sacrifice; and the priest must make an atonement for him for his sin, and so it must be forgiven him.

27 "'And if any soul of the people of the land sins unintentionally by his doing one of the things that Jehovah commands should not be done and he does become guilty, 28 or his sin that he has committed has been made known to him, then he must bring as his offering a female kid of the goats, a sound one, for his sin that he has committed. 29 And he must lay his hand upon the head of the sin offering and slaughter the sin offering in the same place as the

burnt offering. 30 And the priest must take some of its blood with his finger and put it upon the horns of the altar of burnt offering, and he will pour all the rest of its blood at the base of the altar. 31 And he will remove all its fat, just as the fat was removed from off the communion sacrifice; and the priest must make it smoke on the altar as a restful odor to Jehovah; and the priest must make an atonement for him, and so it must be forgiven him.

32 "'But if he would bring a lamb as his offering for a sin offering, a sound female lamb is what he should bring. 33 And he must lay his hand upon the head of the sin offering and slaughter it as a sin offering in the place where the burnt offering is regularly slaughtered. 34 And the priest must take some of the blood of the sin offering with his finger and put it upon the horns of the altar of burnt offering, and he will pour all the rest of its blood at the base of the altar. 35 And he will remove all its fat the same as the fat of the young ram of the communion sacrifice is regularly removed, and the priest must make them smoke on the altar upon Jehovah's offerings made by fire; and the priest must make an atonement for him for his sin that he has committed, and so it must be forgiven him.

5 "'Now in case a soul sins in that he has heard public cursing and he is a witness or he has seen it or has come to know of it, if he does not report it, then he must answer for his error.

2 "'Or when a soul touches some unclean thing, whether the dead body of an unclean wild beast or the dead body of an unclean domestic animal or the dead body of an unclean swarming creature, although it has been hidden from him, still he is unclean and has become guilty. 3 Or in case he touches the uncleanness of a man as respects any uncleanness of his with which he may become unclean, although it had been hidden from him, and yet he him-

self has come to know it, then he has become guilty.

4 " 'Or in case a soul swears to the extent of speaking thoughtlessly with his lips to do evil or to do good as respects anything at all that the man might speak thoughtlessly in a sworn statement, although it had been hidden from him, and yet he himself has come to know it, then he has become guilty as respects one of these things.

5 " 'And it must occur that in case he becomes guilty as respects one of these things, then he must confess in what way he has sinned. 6 And he must bring his guilt offering to Jehovah for his sin that he has committed, namely, a female from the flock, a female lamb or a female kid of the goats, for a sin offering; and the priest must make an atonement for him for his sin.

7 " 'If, though, he cannot afford enough for a sheep, then he must bring as his guilt offering for the sin that he has committed two turtledoves or two male pigeons to Jehovah, one for a sin offering and one for a burnt offering. 8 And he must bring them to the priest, who must present first the one for the sin offering and nip off its head at the front of its neck, but he should not sever it. 9 And he must spatter some of the blood of the sin offering upon the side of the altar, but the remainder of the blood will be drained out at the base of the altar. It is a sin offering. 10 And the other one he will handle as a burnt offering according to the regular procedure; and the priest must make an atonement for him for his sin that he has committed, and so it must be forgiven him.

11 " 'Now if he does not have the means for two turtledoves or two male pigeons, then he must bring as his offering for the sin he has committed the tenth of an e'phah of fine flour for a sin offering. He must not put oil upon it and he must not place frankincense upon it, for it is a sin offering.

12 And he must bring it to the priest, and the priest must grasp from it his handful as a remembrancer of it and must make it smoke on the altar upon Jehovah's offerings made by fire. It is a sin offering. 13 And the priest must make an atonement for him for his sin that he has committed, any one of these sins, and so it must be forgiven him; and it must become the priest's the same as a grain offering.' "

14 And Jehovah continued to speak to Moses, saying: 15 "In case a soul behaves unfaithfully in that he actually sins by mistake against the holy things of Jehovah, then he must bring as his guilt offering to Jehovah a sound ram from the flock, according to the estimated value in silver shekels, by the shekel of the holy place, as a guilt offering. 16 And he will make compensation for the sin he has committed against the holy place and he will add to it a fifth of it, and he must give it to the priest, that the priest may make an atonement for him with the ram of the guilt offering, and so it must be forgiven him.

17 "And if a soul sins in that he does do one of all the things that Jehovah commands should not be done, although he did not know it, yet he has become guilty and must answer for his error. 18 And he must bring a sound ram from the flock according to the estimated value, for a guilt offering, to the priest; and the priest must make an atonement for him for his mistake that he committed unintentionally, although he himself did not know it, and so it must be forgiven him. 19 It is a guilt offering. He has positively become guilty against Jehovah."

6 And Jehovah went on to speak to Moses, saying: 2 "In case a soul sins in that he does behave unfaithfully toward Jehovah and does deceive his associate about something in his charge or a deposit in hand or a robbery or he does defraud his associate, 3 or he does find something lost and is ac-

tually deceptive about it and does swear falsely over any of all the things that the man might do to sin by them; 4 then it must occur that in case he sins and indeed becomes guilty, he must return the robbed thing which he has robbed or the extorted thing which he has taken by fraud or the thing in his charge which was put in his charge or the thing lost that he has found, 5 or anything at all over which he might swear falsely, and he must make compensation for it in its full amount, and he will add to it a fifth of it. To the one whose it is he will give it on the day his guilt is proved. 6 And as his guilt offering he will bring to Jehovah a sound ram from the flock according to the estimated value, for a guilt offering, to the priest. 7 And the priest must make an atonement for him before Jehovah, and so it must be forgiven him regarding any of all the things that he might do resulting in guiltiness by it."

8 And Jehovah continued to speak to Moses, saying: 9 "Command Aaron and his sons, saying, 'This is the law of the burnt offering: The burnt offering will be on the hearth upon the altar all night long until the morning, and the fire of the altar will be kindled in it. 10 And the priest must clothe himself with his official dress of linen, and he will put the linen drawers on over his flesh. Then he must lift up the fatty ashes of the burnt offering that the fire regularly consumes upon the altar, and he must place them beside the altar. 11 And he must strip off his garments and put on other garments, and he must take the fatty ashes out to a clean place outside the camp. 12 And the fire on the altar will be kept burning on it. It must not go out. And the priest must burn wood on it morning by morning and set the burnt offering in order over it, and he must make the fatty pieces of the communion sacrifices smoke over it. 13 Fire will be kept constantly burning on the altar. It must not go out.

14 "'Now this is the law of the grain offering: You sons of Aaron, present it before Jehovah in front of the altar. 15 And one of them must lift up by his handful some of the fine flour of the grain offering and some of its oil and all the frankincense that is upon the grain offering, and he must make it smoke upon the altar as a restful odor for a remembrancer of it to Jehovah. 16 And what is left of it Aaron and his sons will eat. It will be eaten as unfermented cakes in a holy place. They will eat it in the courtyard of the tent of meeting. 17 It should not be baked with anything leavened. I have given it as their share out of my offerings made by fire. It is something most holy, like the sin offering and like the guilt offering. 18 Every male among the sons of Aaron will eat it. It is an allowance to time indefinite throughout your generations from Jehovah's offerings made by fire. Everything that may touch them will become holy.'"

19 And Jehovah went on speaking to Moses, saying: 20 "This is the offering of Aaron and his sons that they will present to Jehovah on the day of his being anointed: the tenth of an e'phah of fine flour as a grain offering constantly, half of it in the morning and half of it in the evening. 21 It will be made with oil upon a griddle. You will bring it well mixed. You will present the pastries of the grain offering in pieces as a restful odor to Jehovah. 22 And the priest, the one anointed in place of him from among his sons, will make it. It is a regulation to time indefinite: As a whole offering it will be made. 23 And every grain offering of a priest should prove to be a whole offering. It must not be eaten."

24 And Jehovah spoke further to Moses, saying: 25 "Speak to Aaron and his sons, saying, 'This is the law of the sin offering: In the place where the burnt offering is regularly slaughtered the sin offering will be slaughtered before Jehovah. It is a most holy thing.

26 The priest who offers it for sin will eat it. In a holy place it will be eaten in the courtyard of the tent of meeting.

27 "Everything that may touch its flesh will become holy, and when anyone spatters some of its blood upon the garment, you will wash what he spatters blood upon in a holy place. 28 And the earthenware vessel in which it may be boiled is to be shattered. But if it was boiled in a copper vessel, then it must be scoured and rinsed with water.

29 "Every male among the priests will eat it. It is something most holy. 30 However, no sin offering of which some of the blood will be brought into the tent of meeting to make atonement in the holy place must be eaten. It is to be burned with fire.

7 "And this is the law of the guilt offering: It is something most holy. 2 In the place where they regularly slaughter the burnt offering they will slaughter the guilt offering, and its blood one will sprinkle round about upon the altar. 3 As for all its fat, he will present of it the fatty tail and the fat that covers the intestines, 4 and the two kidneys and the fat that is upon them the same as that upon the loins. And as for the appendage upon the liver, he will remove it along with the kidneys. 5 And the priest must make them smoke on the altar as an offering made by fire to Jehovah. It is a guilt offering. 6 Every male among the priests will eat it. In a holy place it will be eaten. It is something most holy. 7 Like the sin offering, so is the guilt offering. There is one law for them. The priest who will make atonement with it, his it will become.

8 "As for the priest who presents the burnt offering of any man, the skin of the burnt offering that he has presented to the priest will become his.

9 "And every grain offering that may be baked in the oven and every one made in the deep-fat kettle and upon the griddle be-longs to the priest who presents it. It will become his. 10 But every grain offering that is moistened with oil or dry will come to be for all of Aaron's sons, for the one the same as for the other.

11 "Now this is the law of the communion sacrifice that anyone will present to Jehovah: 12 If he would present it in expression of thanksgiving, then he must present along with the sacrifice of thanksgiving unfermented ring-shaped cakes moistened with oil and unfermented wafers smeared with oil and well-mixed fine flour as ring-shaped cakes moistened with oil. 13 Along with ring-shaped cakes of leavened bread he will present his offering together with the thanksgiving sacrifice of his communion sacrifices. 14 And out of it he must present one of each offering as a sacred portion to Jehovah; as for the priest who sprinkles the blood of the communion sacrifices, it will become his. 15 And the flesh of the thanksgiving sacrifice of his communion sacrifices is to be eaten on the day of his offering. He must not save up any of it until morning.

16 "And if the sacrifice of his offering is a vow or a voluntary offering, it is to be eaten on the day of his presenting his sacrifice, and on the next day what is left of it also may be eaten. 17 But what is left of the flesh of the sacrifice on the third day is to be burned with fire. 18 However, if any of the flesh of his communion sacrifice should at all be eaten on the third day, the one presenting it will not be accepted with approval. It will not be put to his account. It will become a foul thing, and the soul that eats some of it will answer for his error. 19 And the flesh that may touch anything unclean is not to be eaten. It is to be burned with fire. As for the flesh, everybody clean may eat the flesh.

20 "And the soul who eats the flesh of the communion sacrifice, which is for Jehovah, while his uncleanness is upon him, that soul

must be cut off from his people. 21 And in case a soul touches anything unclean, the uncleanness of a man or an unclean beast or any unclean loathsome thing, and actually eats some of the flesh of the communion sacrifice, which is for Jehovah, that soul must be cut off from his people.' "

22 And Jehovah continued to speak to Moses, saying: 23 "Speak to the sons of Israel, saying, 'You must not eat any fat of a bull or a young ram or a goat. 24 Now the fat of a body [already] dead and the fat of an animal torn to pieces may be used for anything else conceivable, but you must not eat it at all. 25 For anyone eating fat from the beast from which he presents it as an offering made by fire to Jehovah, the soul that eats must be cut off from his people.

26 " 'And you must not eat any blood in any places where you dwell, whether that of fowl or that of beast. 27 Any soul who eats any blood, that soul must be cut off from his people.' "

28 And Jehovah went on to speak to Moses, saying: 29 "Speak to the sons of Israel, saying, 'He who presents his communion sacrifice to Jehovah will bring his offering to Jehovah from his communion sacrifice. 30 His hands will bring as Jehovah's offerings made by fire the fat upon the breast. He will bring it with the breast to wave it to and fro as a wave offering before Jehovah. 31 And the priest must make the fat smoke upon the altar, but the breast must become Aaron's and his sons'.

32 " 'And you will give the right leg as a sacred portion to the priest from your communion sacrifices. 33 That one of Aaron's sons who presents the blood of the communion sacrifices and the fat, the right leg will become his as a portion. 34 For the breast of the wave offering and the leg of the sacred portion I do take from the sons of Israel from their communion sacrifices, and I shall give them to Aaron the priest and his sons, as a regulation to time indefinite, from the sons of Israel.

35 " 'This was the priestly share of Aaron and the priestly share of his sons from Jehovah's offerings made by fire, on the day that he presented them to act as priests to Jehovah, 36 just as Jehovah had commanded to give it to them on the day of his anointing them from among the sons of Israel. It is a statute to time indefinite for their generations.' "

37 This is the law concerning the burnt offering, the grain offering and the sin offering and the guilt offering and the installation sacrifice and the communion sacrifice, 38 just as Jehovah had commanded Moses in Mount Si'nai in the day of his commanding the sons of Israel to present their offerings to Jehovah in the wilderness of Si'nai.

8 And Jehovah proceeded to speak to Moses, saying: 2 "Take Aaron and his sons with him and the garments and the anointing oil and the bull of the sin offering and the two rams and the basket of unfermented cakes, 3 and make all the assembly congregate at the entrance of the tent of meeting."

4 Then Moses did just as Jehovah had commanded him, and the assembly congregated at the entrance of the tent of meeting. 5 Moses now said to the assembly: "This is the thing that Jehovah has given command to do." 6 So Moses brought Aaron and his sons near and washed them with water. 7 After that he put the robe upon him and girded him with the sash and clothed him with the sleeveless coat and put the eph'od upon him and girded him with the girdle of the eph'od and bound it closely to him with it. 8 Next he placed the breastpiece upon him and put in the breastpiece the U'rim and the Thum'mim. 9 Then he placed the turban upon his head and placed upon the turban at the forefront of it the shining plate of gold, the holy sign of dedication, just as Jehovah had commanded Moses.

10 Moses now took the anointing oil and anointed the tabernacle and all that was in it and sanctified them. 11 After that he spattered some of it seven times upon the altar and anointed the altar and all its utensils and the basin and its stand so as to sanctify them. 12 Finally he poured some of the anointing oil upon Aaron's head and anointed him so as to sanctify him.

13 Moses then brought Aaron's sons near and clothed them with robes and girded them with sashes and wrapped the headgear upon them, just as Jehovah had commanded Moses.

14 Then he led up the bull of the sin offering and Aaron and his sons laid their hands upon the head of the bull of the sin offering. 15 And Moses proceeded to slaughter it and take the blood and put it with his finger upon the horns of the altar round about and purify the altar from sin, but the rest of the blood he poured at the base of the altar, that he might sanctify it to make atonement upon it. 16 After that he took all the fat that was upon the intestines, and the appendage of the liver and the two kidneys and their fat and Moses made them smoke upon the altar. 17 And he had the bull and its skin and its flesh and its dung burned with fire outside the camp, just as Jehovah had commanded Moses.

18 He now brought the ram of the burnt offering near, and Aaron and his sons then laid their hands upon the head of the ram. 19 After that Moses slaughtered it and sprinkled the blood round about upon the altar. 20 And he cut up the ram into its pieces, and Moses proceeded to make the head and the pieces and the suet smoke. 21 And the intestines and the shanks he washed with water, and Moses then made the entire ram smoke upon the altar. It was a burnt offering for a restful odor. It was an offering made by fire to Jehovah, just as Jehovah had commanded Moses.

22 Then he brought the second ram, the ram of the installation, near, and Aaron and his sons laid their hands upon the ram's head. 23 After that Moses slaughtered it and took some of its blood and put it upon the lobe of Aaron's right ear and upon the thumb of his right hand and upon the big toe of his right foot. 24 Next Moses brought Aaron's sons near and put some of the blood upon the lobe of their right ear and upon the thumb of their right hand and upon the big toe of their right foot; but Moses sprinkled the rest of the blood round about upon the altar.

25 Then he took the fat and the fat tail and all the fat that was upon the intestines, and the appendage of the liver and the two kidneys and their fat and the right leg. 26 And out of the basket of unfermented cakes that was before Jehovah he took one unfermented ring-shaped cake and one ring-shaped cake of oiled bread and one wafer. He then placed them upon the fatty pieces and the right leg. 27 After that he put all of them upon the palms of Aaron and the palms of his sons and began to wave them to and fro as a wave offering before Jehovah. 28 Then Moses took them off their palms and made them smoke upon the altar on top of the burnt offering. They were an installation sacrifice for a restful odor. It was an offering made by fire to Jehovah.

29 And Moses proceeded to take the breast and to wave it to and fro as a wave offering before Jehovah. From the installation ram it became the portion for Moses, just as Jehovah had commanded Moses.

30 After that Moses took some of the anointing oil and some of the blood that was upon the altar and spattered it upon Aaron and his garments and upon his sons and the garments of his sons with him. Thus he sanctified Aaron and his garments and his sons and the garments of his sons with him.

31 Then Moses said to Aaron and

his sons: "Boil the flesh at the entrance of the tent of meeting, and there is where you will eat it and the bread that is in the installation basket, just as I was given the command, saying, 'Aaron and his sons will eat it.' 32 And what is left over of the flesh and the bread you will burn with fire. 33 And you must not go out from the entrance of the tent of meeting for seven days, until the day of fulfilling the days of your installation, because it will take seven days to fill your hand with power. 34 Just as it has been done this day, Jehovah has commanded to be done so as to make atonement for you. 35 And you will stay at the entrance of the tent of meeting day and night for seven days, and you must keep the obligatory watch of Jehovah, that you may not die; for so I have been commanded."

36 And Aaron and his sons proceeded to do all the things that Jehovah had commanded by means of Moses.

9 And it came about on the eighth day that Moses called Aaron and his sons and the older men of Israel. 2 Then he said to Aaron: "Take for yourself a young calf for a sin offering and a ram for a burnt offering, sound ones, and present them before Jehovah. 3 But to the sons of Israel you will speak, saying, 'Take a male goat for a sin offering and a calf and a young ram, each a year old, sound ones, for a burnt offering, 4 and a bull and a ram for communion sacrifices to sacrifice them before Jehovah, and a grain offering moistened with oil, because today is when Jehovah will certainly appear to you.'"

5 Accordingly they took what Moses had commanded before the tent of meeting. Then the whole assembly came near and stood before Jehovah. 6 And Moses went on to say: "This is the thing that Jehovah has commanded you should do, that the glory of Jehovah may appear to you." 7 Then Moses said to Aaron: "Go near to the altar and render up your sin offering and your burnt offering, and make atonement in your own behalf and in behalf of your house; and render up the offering of the people and make atonement in their behalf, just as Jehovah has commanded."

8 Aaron immediately went near to the altar and slaughtered the calf of the sin offering that was for him. 9 Then Aaron's sons presented the blood to him and he dipped his finger in the blood and put it upon the horns of the altar, and the rest of the blood he poured at the base of the altar. 10 And he made the fat and the kidneys and the appendage of the liver from the sin offering smoke upon the altar, just as Jehovah had commanded Moses. 11 And he burned the flesh and the skin with fire outside the camp.

12 Then he slaughtered the burnt offering and Aaron's sons handed him the blood and he sprinkled it round about upon the altar. 13 And they handed him the burnt offering in its pieces and the head, and he proceeded to make them smoke upon the altar. 14 Further, he washed the intestines and the shanks and made them smoke upon the burnt offering on the altar.

15 He now went presenting the offering of the people and took the goat of the sin offering that was for the people and slaughtered it and made an offering for sin with it as with the first. 16 Then he presented the burnt offering and handled it according to the regular procedure.

17 He next presented the grain offering and filled his hand with some of it and made it smoke upon the altar, apart from the burnt offering of the morning.

18 After that he slaughtered the bull and the ram of the communion sacrifice that was for the people. Then Aaron's sons handed him the blood and he sprinkled it round about upon the altar. 19 As for the fatty pieces of the bull and the fat tail of the ram and the fat covering and the kidneys and the appendage of the liver, 20 they

now placed the fatty pieces upon the breasts, after which he made the fatty pieces smoke upon the altar. 21 But the breasts and the right leg Aaron waved to and fro as a wave offering before Jehovah, just as Moses had commanded.

22 Then Aaron raised his hands toward the people and blessed them and came down from rendering the sin offering and the burnt offering and the communion sacrifices. 23 Finally Moses and Aaron went into the tent of meeting and came out and blessed the people.

Then Jehovah's glory appeared to all the people, 24 and fire came out from before Jehovah and began consuming the burnt offering and the fatty pieces upon the altar. When all the people got to see it, they broke out into shouting and went falling upon their faces.

10 Later on Aaron's sons Na'dab and A·bi'hu took up and brought each one his fire holder and put fire in them and placed incense upon it, and they began offering before Jehovah illegitimate fire, which he had not prescribed for them. 2 At this a fire came out from before Jehovah and consumed them, so that they died before Jehovah. 3 Then Moses said to Aaron: "This is what Jehovah has spoken, saying, 'Among those near to me let me be sanctified, and before the face of all the people let me be glorified.'" And Aaron kept silent.

4 So Moses called Mish'a·el and El'za'phan, the sons of Uz'zi·el, Aaron's uncle, and said to them: "Come near, carry YOUR brothers from in front of the holy place to outside the camp." 5 They accordingly came near and carried them in their robes to outside the camp, just as Moses had spoken.

6 Subsequently Moses said to Aaron and to E·le·a'zar and Ith'a·mar his [other] sons: "Do not let YOUR heads go ungroomed, and YOU must not tear YOUR garments, that YOU may not die and that he may not become indignant against all the assembly; but YOUR brothers of

the whole house of Israel will do the weeping over the burning, which Jehovah has made burn. 7 And from the entrance of the tent of meeting YOU must not go out for fear YOU may die, because Jehovah's anointing oil is upon YOU." So they did according to Moses' word.

8 And Jehovah proceeded to speak to Aaron, saying: 9 "Do not drink wine or intoxicating liquor, you and your sons with you, when YOU come into the tent of meeting, that YOU may not die. It is a statute to time indefinite for YOUR generations, 10 both in order to make a distinction between the holy thing and the profane and between the unclean thing and the clean, 11 and in order to teach the sons of Israel all the regulations that Jehovah has spoken to them by means of Moses."

12 Then Moses spoke to Aaron and to E·le·a'zar and Ith'a·mar, his sons that were left: "Take the grain offering that was left over from Jehovah's offerings made by fire and eat it unfermented near the altar, because it is something most holy. 13 And YOU must eat it in a holy place, because it is your allowance and the allowance of your sons from Jehovah's offerings made by fire; for so I have been commanded. 14 And YOU will eat the breast of the wave offering and the leg of the sacred portion in a clean place, you and your sons and your daughters with you, because they have been given as your allowance and the allowance of your sons from the communion sacrifices of the sons of Israel. 15 They will bring the leg of the sacred portion and the breast of the wave offering along with the offerings made by fire, of the fatty pieces, in order to wave the wave offering to and fro before Jehovah; and it must serve as an allowance to time indefinite for you and your sons with you, just as Jehovah has commanded."

16 And Moses searched thoroughly for the goat of the sin offering, and, look! it had been burned up.

So he grew indignant at E·le·a′zar and Ith′a·mar, Aaron's sons that were left, saying: 17 "Why did you not eat the sin offering in the place that is holy, since it is something most holy and he has given it to you that you may answer for the error of the assembly so as to make atonement for them before Jehovah? 18 Look! Its blood has not been brought into the holy place within. You should have eaten it without fail in the holy place, just as I had been commanded." 19 At this Aaron spoke to Moses: "Look! Today they have presented their sin offering and their burnt offering before Jehovah, while such things as these began to befall me; and had I eaten the sin offering today, would it prove satisfactory in Jehovah's eyes?" 20 When Moses got to hear that, then it proved satisfactory in his eyes.

11 And Jehovah proceeded to speak to Moses and Aaron, saying to them: 2 "Speak to the sons of Israel, saying, 'This is the living creature that you may eat of all the beasts that are upon the earth: 3 Every creature that splits the hoof and forms a cleft in the hoofs and chews the cud among the beasts, that is what you may eat.

4 "'Only this is what you must not eat among the chewers of the cud and the splitters of the hoof: the camel, because it is a chewer of the cud but is no splitter of the hoof. It is unclean for you. 5 Also the rock badger, because it is a chewer of the cud but does not split the hoof. It is unclean for you. 6 Also the hare, because it is a chewer of the cud but it does not have the hoof split. It is unclean for you. 7 Also the pig, because it is a splitter of the hoof and a former of a cleft in the hoof, but it itself does not chew the cud. It is unclean for you. 8 You must not eat any of their flesh, and you must not touch their dead body. They are unclean for you.

9 "'This is what you may eat of everything that is in the waters: Everything that has fins and scales in the waters, in the seas and in the torrents, those you may eat. 10 And everything in the seas and the torrents that has no fins and scales, out of every swarming creature of the waters and out of every living soul that is in the waters, they are a loathsome thing for you. 11 Yes, they will become a loathsome thing to you. You must not eat any of their flesh, and you are to loathe their dead body. 12 Everything in the waters that has no fins and scales is a loathsome thing to you.

13 "'And these are what you will loathe among the flying creatures. They should not be eaten. They are a loathsome thing: the eagle and the osprey and the black vulture, 14 and the red kite and the black kite according to its kind, 15 and every raven according to its kind, 16 and the ostrich and the owl and the gull and the falcon according to its kind, 17 and the little owl and the cormorant and the long-eared owl, 18 and the swan and the pelican and the vulture, 19 and the stork, the heron according to its kind, and the hoopoe and the bat. 20 Every winged swarming creature that goes on all fours is a loathsome thing to you.

21 "'Only this is what you may eat of all the winged swarming creatures that go upon all fours, those that have leaper legs above their feet with which to leap upon the earth. 22 These are the ones of them you may eat of: the migratory locust according to its kind, and the edible locust after its kind, and the cricket according to its kind, and the grasshopper according to its kind. 23 And every other winged swarming creature that does have four legs is a loathsome thing to you. 24 So by these you would make yourselves unclean. Everyone touching their dead bodies will be unclean until the evening. 25 And everyone carrying any of their dead bodies will wash his garments, and he must be unclean until the evening.

26 "'As for any beast that is a splitter of the hoof but is not a former of a cleft and is not a chewer of the cud, they are unclean for YOU. Everyone touching them will be unclean. 27 As for every creature going upon its paws among all the living creatures that go on all fours, they are unclean to YOU. Everyone touching their dead bodies will be unclean until the evening. 28 And he who carries their dead bodies will wash his garments, and he must be unclean until the evening. They are unclean to YOU.

29 "'And this is what is unclean to YOU among the swarming creatures that swarm upon the earth: the mole rat and the jerboa and the lizard according to its kind, 30 and the gecko fanfoot and the large lizard and the newt and the sand lizard and the chameleon. 31 These are unclean to YOU among all the swarming creatures. Everyone touching them in their death state will be unclean until the evening.

32 "'Now anything upon which any of them should fall in its death state will be unclean, whether it be some wooden vessel or a garment or a skin or sackcloth. Any vessel of which some use is made will be put in water, and it must be unclean until the evening and then be clean. 33 As for any earthenware vessel into which any of them should fall, anything that is within it will be unclean, and YOU will smash it. 34 Any sort of food that may be eaten upon which water may come from it will be unclean, and any drink that may be drunk in any vessel will be unclean. 35 And everything upon which any of their dead bodies may fall will be unclean. Whether oven or jar stand, it is to be broken down. They are unclean, and they will become unclean to YOU. 36 Only a spring and a pit of impounded waters will continue clean, but anyone touching their dead bodies will be unclean. 37 And should any of their dead bodies fall upon any seed of a plant that is to be sown, it is clean. 38 But in case

water should be put upon seed and something of their dead bodies had fallen upon it, it is unclean to YOU. 39 "'Now in case any beast that is YOURS for food should die, he who touches its dead body will be unclean until the evening. 40 And he who eats any of its dead body will wash his garments, and he must be unclean until the evening; and he who carries off its dead body will wash his garments, and he must be unclean until the evening. 41 And every swarming creature that swarms upon the earth is a loathsome thing. It must not be eaten. 42 As for any creature that goes upon the belly and any creature that goes on all fours or any great number of feet of all the swarming creatures that swarm upon the earth, YOU must not eat them, because they are a loathsome thing. 43 Do not make YOUR souls loathsome with any swarming creature that swarms, and YOU must not make yourselves unclean by them and actually get unclean by them. 44 For I am Jehovah YOUR God; and YOU must sanctify yourselves and YOU must prove yourselves holy, because I am holy. So YOU must not make YOUR souls unclean by any swarming creature that moves upon the earth. 45 For I am Jehovah who is leading YOU up out of the land of Egypt to prove myself God to YOU; and YOU must prove yourselves holy, because I am holy.

46 "'This is the law about the beast and the flying creature and every living soul that moves about in the waters and concerning every soul that swarms upon the earth, 47 in order to make a distinction between the unclean and the clean and between the living creature that is eatable and the living creature that may not be eaten.'"

12 And Jehovah went on to speak to Moses, saying: 2 "Speak to the sons of Israel, saying, 'In case a woman conceives seed and does bear a male, she must be unclean seven days; as in the days of the impurity when she is menstruating she will be unclean. 3 And

on the eighth day the flesh of his foreskin will be circumcised. 4 For thirty-three days more she will stay in the blood of purification. She should not touch any holy thing, and she should not come into the holy place until the fulfilling of the days of her purification.

5 "'Now if she should bear a female, she must then be unclean fourteen days, as during her menstruation. For sixty-six days more she will stay with the blood of purification. 6 Then at the fulfilling of the days of her purification for a son or for a daughter she will bring a young ram in its first year for a burnt offering and a male pigeon or a turtledove for a sin offering to the entrance of the tent of meeting to the priest. 7 And he must present it before Jehovah and make atonement for her, and she must be clean from the source of her blood. This is the law about her who bears either a male or a female. 8 But if she cannot afford enough for a sheep, she must then take two turtledoves or two male pigeons, one for a burnt offering and one for a sin offering, and the priest must make atonement for her, and she must be clean.'"

13 And Jehovah proceeded to speak to Moses and Aaron, saying: 2 "In case a man develops in the skin of his flesh an eruption or a scab or a blotch and it does develop in the skin of his flesh into the plague of leprosy, he must then be brought to Aaron the priest or to one of his sons the priests. 3 And the priest must look at the plague in the skin of the flesh. When the hair in the plague has turned white and the appearance of the plague is deeper than the skin of his flesh, it is the plague of leprosy. And the priest must look at it, and he must declare him unclean. 4 But if the blotch is white in the skin of his flesh and its appearance is not deeper than the skin and its hair has not turned white, the priest must then quarantine the plague

seven days. 5 And the priest must look at him on the seventh day, and if in the way it looks the plague has stopped, the plague has not spread in the skin, the priest must also quarantine him another seven days.

6 "And the priest must look at him on the seventh day the second time, and if the plague has grown dull and the plague has not spread in the skin, the priest must also pronounce him clean. It was a scab. And he must wash his garments and be clean. 7 But if the scab has unquestionably spread in the skin after his appearing before the priest for the establishment of his purification, he must then appear the second time before the priest, 8 and the priest must take a look; and if the scab has spread in the skin, the priest must then declare him unclean. It is leprosy.

9 "In case the plague of leprosy develops in a man, he must then be brought to the priest. 10 And the priest must take a look; and if there is a white eruption in the skin and it has turned the hair white and the raw of the living flesh is in the eruption, 11 it is chronic leprosy in the skin of his flesh; and the priest must declare him unclean. He should not quarantine him, for he is unclean. 12 Now if the leprosy unquestionably breaks out in the skin, and the leprosy does cover all the skin of the one with the plague from his head to his feet to the full sight of the priest's eyes; 13 and the priest has looked and there the leprosy has covered all his flesh, he must then pronounce the plague clean. All of it has turned white. He is clean. 14 But on the day the living flesh appears in it, he will be unclean. 15 And the priest must see the living flesh, and he must declare him unclean. The living flesh is unclean. It is leprosy. 16 Or in case the living flesh goes back and it does change to white, he must then come to the priest. 17 And the priest must look at him, and if the plague has been changed to white, the priest must

then pronounce the plague clean. He is clean.

18 "As for the flesh, in case a boil develops in its skin and it does get healed, 19 and in the place of the boil a white eruption has developed or a reddish-white blotch, he must then show himself to the priest. 20 And the priest must look, and if its appearance is lower than the skin and its hair has turned white, the priest must then declare him unclean. It is the plague of leprosy. It has broken out in the boil. 21 But if the priest looks at it, and, there now, there is no white hair in it and it is not deeper than the skin and it is dull, the priest must then quarantine him seven days. 22 And if it unmistakably spreads in the skin, the priest must then declare him unclean. It is a plague. 23 But if in its place the blotch should stand, it has not spread, it is the inflammation of the boil; and the priest must pronounce him clean.

24 "Or in case there comes to be a scar in the skin of the flesh from the fire, and the raw flesh of the scar does become a reddish-white blotch or a white one, 25 the priest must then look at it; and if the hair has been changed white in the blotch and its appearance is deeper than the skin, it is leprosy. It has broken out in the scar, and the priest must declare him unclean. It is the plague of leprosy. 26 But if the priest looks at it, and, there now, there is no white hair in the blotch and it is not lower than the skin and it is dull, the priest must then quarantine him seven days. 27 And the priest must look at him on the seventh day. If it unmistakably spreads in the skin, the priest must then declare him unclean. It is the plague of leprosy. 28 But if the blotch stands in its place, it has not spread in the skin and it is dull, it is an eruption of the scar; and the priest must pronounce him clean, because it is an inflammation of the scar.

29 "As for a man or a woman, in case a plague develops in such one on the head or on the chin, 30 the priest must then see the plague; and if its appearance is deeper than the skin, and the hair is yellow and scarce in it, the priest must then declare such one unclean. It is an abnormal falling off of hair. It is leprosy of the head or of the chin. 31 But in case the priest sees the plague of abnormal falling off of hair, and, look! its appearance is not deeper than the skin and there is no black hair in it, the priest must then quarantine the plague of abnormal falling off of hair seven days. 32 And the priest must look at the plague on the seventh day; and if the abnormal falling off of hair has not spread, and no yellow hair has developed in it and the appearance of the abnormal falling off of hair is not deeper than the skin, 33 he must then have himself shaved, but he will not have the abnormal falling off of hair shaved; and the priest must quarantine the abnormal falling off of hair seven days again.

34 "And the priest must look at the abnormal falling off of hair on the seventh day; and if the abnormal falling off of hair has not spread in the skin, and its appearance is not deeper than the skin, the priest must then pronounce him clean, and he must wash his garments and be clean. 35 But if the abnormal falling off of hair unmistakably spreads in the skin after the establishment of his purification, 36 the priest must then see him; and if the abnormal falling off of hair has spread in the skin, the priest need not make examination for yellow hair; he is unclean. 37 But if in its look the abnormal falling off of hair has stood and black hair has grown in it, the abnormal falling off of hair has been healed. He is clean, and the priest must pronounce him clean.

38 "As for a man or a woman, in case blotches develop in the skin of their flesh, white blotches, 39 the priest must then take a look; and if the blotches in the skin of their flesh are dull white, it is a harm-

less eruption. It has broken out in the skin. He is clean.

40 "As for a man, in case his head grows bald, it is baldness. He is clean. 41 And if his head grows bald up in front, it is forehead baldness. He is clean. 42 But in case a reddish-white plague develops in the baldness of the crown or of the forehead, it is leprosy breaking out in the baldness of his crown or of his forehead. 43 And the priest must look at him; and if there is an eruption of the reddish-white plague in the baldness of his crown or of his forehead like the appearance of leprosy in the skin of the flesh, 44 he is a leper. He is unclean. Unclean is what the priest should declare him. His plague is on his head. 45 As for the leprous one in whom the plague is, his garments should be torn, and his head should become ungroomed, and he should cover over the mustache and call out, 'Unclean, unclean!' 46 All the days that the plague is in him he will be unclean. He is unclean. He should dwell isolated. Outside the camp is his dwelling place.

47 "As for a garment, in case the plague of leprosy develops in it, whether in a woolen garment or in a linen garment, 48 or in the warp or in the woof of the linen and of the wool, or in a skin or in anything made of skin, 49 and the yellowish-green or reddish plague does develop in the garment or in the skin or in the warp or in the woof or in any article of skin, it is the plague of leprosy, and it must be shown to the priest. 50 And the priest must see the plague, and he must quarantine the plague seven days. 51 When he has seen the plague on the seventh day, that the plague has spread in the garment or in the warp or in the woof or in the skin for any use for which the skin may be made, the plague is malignant leprosy. It is unclean. 52 And he must burn the garment or the warp or the woof in the wool or in the linen, or any article of skin in which the plague may develop, because it is

malignant leprosy. It should be burned in the fire.

53 "But if the priest takes a look, and, there now, the plague has not spread in the garment or in the warp or in the woof or in any article of skin, 54 the priest must also command that they should wash that in which the plague is, and he must quarantine it a second seven days. 55 And the priest must look at the plague after it has been washed out, and if the plague has not changed its look and yet the plague has not spread, it is unclean. You should burn it in the fire. It is a low spot in a threadbare patch on either its underside or its outside.

56 "But if the priest has taken a look, and, there now, the plague is dull after it has been washed out, he must then tear it out of the garment or the skin or the warp or the woof. 57 However, if it still appears in the garment or in the warp or in the woof or in any article of skin, it is breaking out. You should burn in the fire whatever it is in which the plague is. 58 As for the garment or the warp or the woof or any article of skin that you may wash, when the plague has disappeared from them, it must then be washed a second time; and it must be clean.

59 "This is the law of the plague of leprosy in a garment of wool or of linen, or in the warp or in the woof, or in any article of skin, in order to pronounce it clean or to declare it unclean."

14 And Jehovah continued to speak to Moses, saying: 2 "This will become the law of the leper in the day for establishing his purification, when he must be brought to the priest. 3 And the priest must go forth outside the camp, and the priest must look; and if the plague of leprosy has been cured in the leprous one, 4 the priest must then give command; and he must take for cleansing himself two live clean birds and cedar wood and coccus scarlet material and hyssop. 5 And the priest must give command, and the one

bird must be killed in an earthenware vessel over running water. 6 As for the living bird, he should take it and the cedar wood and the coccus scarlet material and the hyssop, and he must dip them and the living bird in the blood of the bird that was killed over the running water. 7 Then he must spatter it seven times upon the one cleansing himself from the leprosy and he must pronounce him clean, and he must send away the living bird over the open field.

8 "And the one cleansing himself must wash his garments and shave off all his hair and bathe in water and must be clean, and afterward he may come into the camp. And he must dwell outside his tent seven days. 9 And it must occur on the seventh day that he should shave off all his hair on his head and his chin and his eyebrows. Yes, he should shave off all his hair, and he must wash his garments and bathe his flesh in water; and he must be clean.

10 "And on the eighth day he will take two sound young rams and one sound female lamb, in its first year, and three tenths of an e'phah of fine flour as a grain offering moistened with oil and one log measure of oil; 11 and the priest who pronounces him clean must present the man who is cleansing himself, and the things, before Jehovah at the entrance of the tent of meeting. 12 And the priest must take the one young ram and offer it for a guilt offering together with the log measure of oil and must wave them to and fro as a wave offering before Jehovah. 13 And he must slaughter the young ram in the place where the sin offering and the burnt offering are regularly slaughtered, in a holy place, because, like the sin offering, the guilt offering belongs to the priest. It is something most holy.

14 "And the priest must take some of the blood of the guilt offering, and the priest must put it upon the lobe of the right ear of the one cleansing himself and upon

the thumb of his right hand and upon the big toe of his right foot. 15 And the priest must take some of the log measure of oil and pour it upon the priest's left palm. 16 And the priest must dip his right finger into the oil that is upon his left palm and must spatter some of the oil with his finger seven times before Jehovah. 17 And of the rest of the oil that is upon his palm the priest will put some upon the lobe of the right ear of the one cleansing himself and upon the thumb of his right hand and upon the big toe of his right foot over the blood of the guilt offering. 18 And what is left over of the oil that is upon the priest's palm he will put upon the head of the one cleansing himself, and the priest must make atonement for him before Jehovah.

19 "And the priest must render up the sin offering and make atonement for the one cleansing himself from his impurity, and afterward he will slaughter the burnt offering. 20 And the priest must offer up the burnt offering and the grain offering upon the altar, and the priest must make atonement for him; and he must be clean.

21 "However, if he is lowly and does not have enough means, he must then take one young ram as a guilt offering for a wave offering in order to make atonement for him and one tenth of an e'phah of fine flour moistened with oil as a grain offering and a log measure of oil, 22 and two turtledoves or two male pigeons, according as he may have the means, and the one must serve as a sin offering and the other as a burnt offering. 23 And on the eighth day he must bring them for establishing his purification to the priest at the entrance of the tent of meeting before Jehovah.

24 "And the priest must take the young ram of the guilt offering and the log measure of oil, and the priest must wave them to and fro as a wave offering before Jehovah. 25 And he must slaughter the young ram of the guilt offering, and the priest must take some of the blood

of the guilt offering and put it upon the lobe of the right ear of the one cleansing himself and upon the thumb of his right hand and upon the big toe of his right foot. 26 And the priest will pour some of the oil upon the priest's left palm. 27 And the priest must spatter with his right finger some of the oil that is upon his left palm seven times before Jehovah. 28 And the priest must put some of the oil that is on his palm upon the lobe of the right ear of the one cleansing himself and upon the thumb of his right hand and upon the big toe of his right foot over the place of the blood of the guilt offering. 29 And what is left over of the oil that is on the priest's palm he will put upon the head of the one cleansing himself in order to make atonement for him before Jehovah.

30 "And he must render up the one of the turtledoves or of the male pigeons for which he may have the means, 31 the one of them for which he may have the means as a sin offering and the other as a burnt offering along with the grain offering; and the priest must make atonement for the one cleansing himself before Jehovah.

32 "This is the law for the one in whom the plague of leprosy was who may not have the means when establishing his purification."

33 And Jehovah proceeded to speak to Moses and Aaron, saying: 34 "When YOU come into the land of Ca′naan, which I am giving YOU as a possession, and I do put the plague of leprosy in a house of the land of YOUR possession, 35 the one to whom the house belongs must then come and tell the priest, saying, 'Something like a plague has appeared to me in the house.' 36 And the priest must give orders, and they must clear out the house before the priest may come in to see the plague, that he may not declare unclean everything that is in the house; and after that the priest will come in to see the house. 37 When he has seen the plague, then if the plague is in the walls

of the house, with yellowish-green or reddish depressions, and their appearance is lower than the wall surface, 38 the priest must then go out of the house to the entrance of the house and he must quarantine the house seven days.

39 "And the priest must return on the seventh day and must take a look; and if the plague has spread in the walls of the house, 40 the priest must then give orders, and they must tear out the stones in which the plague is, and they must throw them outside the city into an unclean place. 41 And he will have the house scraped off all around inside, and they must pour the clay mortar that they cut off outside the city into an unclean place. 42 And they must take other stones and insert them in the place of the former stones; and he will have different clay mortar taken, and he must have the house plastered.

43 "If, though, the plague returns and it does break out in the house after having torn out the stones and after having cut off the house and plastered it, 44 the priest must then come in and take a look; and if the plague has spread in the house, it is malignant leprosy in the house. It is unclean. 45 And he must have the house pulled down with its stones and its timbers and all the clay mortar of the house and must have it carried forth outside the city to an unclean place. 46 But whoever comes into the house any of the days of quarantining it will be unclean until the evening; 47 and whoever lies down in the house should wash his garments, and whoever eats in the house should wash his garments.

48 "However, if the priest comes at all and he does take a look, and, there now, the plague has not spread in the house after having plastered the house, the priest must then pronounce the house clean, because the plague has been healed. 49 And to purify the house from sin he must take two birds and cedar wood and coccus scarlet material and hyssop. 50 And he must

kill the one bird in an earthenware vessel over running water. 51 And he must take the cedar wood and the hyssop and the coccus scarlet material and the live bird and dip them in the blood of the bird that was killed and in the running water, and he must spatter it toward the house seven times. 52 And he must purify the house from sin with the blood of the bird and the running water and the live bird and the cedar wood and the hyssop and the coccus scarlet material. 53 And he must send the live bird away outside the city into the open field and must make atonement for the house; and it must be clean.

54 "This is the law respecting any plague of leprosy and respecting the abnormal falling off of hair 55 and respecting the leprosy of the garment and in the house, 56 and respecting the eruption and the scab and the blotch, 57 in order to give instructions when something is unclean and when something is clean. This is the law about leprosy."

15 And Jehovah continued to speak to Moses and Aaron, saying: 2 "Speak to the sons of Israel, and YOU must say to them, 'In case any man has a running discharge occur from his genital organ, his discharge is unclean. 3 And this will become his uncleanness by his discharge: Whether his genital organ has flowed with a running discharge or his genital organ is obstructed from his running discharge, it is his uncleanness.

4 "'Any bed upon which the one having a running discharge may lie down will be unclean, and any article upon which he may sit will be unclean. 5 And a man who may touch his bed should wash his garments, and he must bathe in water and be unclean until the evening. 6 And whoever sits upon the article upon which the one having a running discharge was sitting should wash his garments, and he must bathe in water and be unclean until the evening. 7 And whoever touches the flesh of the one having a running discharge should wash his garments, and he must bathe in water and be unclean until the evening. 8 And in the case of the one who has a running discharge spitting upon someone clean, he must in that case wash his garments and bathe in water and be unclean until the evening. 9 And any saddle upon which the one having a running discharge was riding will be unclean. 10 And anyone touching anything that happens to be under him will be unclean until the evening; and he who carries them will wash his garments, and he must bathe in water and be unclean until the evening. 11 And anyone whom the one having a running discharge might touch when he has not rinsed his hands in water must then wash his garments and bathe in water and be unclean until the evening. 12 And an earthenware vessel that the one having a running discharge might touch should be smashed; and any wooden vessel should be rinsed with water.

13 "'Now in case the one having a running discharge would become clean from his running discharge, he must then count for himself seven days for his purification, and he must wash his garments and bathe his flesh in running water; and he must be clean. 14 And on the eighth day he should take for himself two turtledoves or two male pigeons, and he must come before Jehovah to the entrance of the tent of meeting and give them to the priest. 15 And the priest must offer them, the one as a sin offering and the other as a burnt offering; and the priest must make atonement for him before Jehovah concerning his running discharge.

16 "'Now in case a man has an emission of semen go out from him, he must then bathe all his flesh in water and be unclean until the evening. 17 And any garment and any skin upon which the emission of semen gets to be must be washed with water and be unclean until the evening.

18 " 'As for a woman with whom a man may lie down with an emission of semen, they must bathe in water and be unclean until the evening.

19 " 'And in case a woman is having a running discharge, and her running discharge in her flesh proves to be blood, she should continue seven days in her menstrual impurity, and anyone touching her will be unclean until the evening. 20 And anything upon which she may lie down in her menstrual impurity will be unclean, and everything upon which she may sit will be unclean. 21 And anyone touching her bed should wash his garments, and he must bathe in water and be unclean until the evening. 22 And anyone touching any article upon which she was sitting should wash his garments, and he must bathe in water and be unclean until the evening. 23 And if it was upon the bed or upon another article that she was sitting, by his touching it he will be unclean until the evening. 24 And if a man lies down with her at all and her menstrual impurity comes to be upon him, he must then be unclean seven days, and any bed upon which he might lie down will be unclean.

25 " 'As for a woman, in case the running discharge of her blood should be flowing many days when it is not the regular time of her menstrual impurity, or in case she should have a flow longer than her menstrual impurity, all the days of her unclean running discharge will prove as in the days of her menstrual impurity. She is unclean. 26 Any bed upon which she may lie any of the days of her running discharge will become for her as the bed of her menstrual impurity, and any article upon which she may sit will become unclean like the uncleanness of her menstrual impurity. 27 And anyone touching them will be unclean, and he must wash his garments and bathe in water and be unclean until the evening.

28 " 'However, if she has become clean from her running discharge, she must also count for herself seven days, and afterward she will be clean. 29 And on the eighth day she should take for herself two turtledoves or two male pigeons, and she must bring them to the priest at the entrance of the tent of meeting. 30 And the priest must make the one a sin offering and the other a burnt offering; and the priest must make atonement for her before Jehovah concerning her unclean running discharge.

31 " 'And YOU must keep the sons of Israel separate from their uncleanness, that they may not die in their uncleanness for their defiling of my tabernacle, which is in their midst.

32 " 'This is the law about the man having a running discharge and the man from whom an emission of semen may go out so that he becomes unclean by it; 33 and the menstruating woman in her uncleanness, and anyone who has a flow of his running discharge, whether a male or a female, and whether a man who lies down with an unclean woman.' "

16 And Jehovah proceeded to speak to Moses after the death of Aaron's two sons for their approaching before Jehovah so that they died. 2 And Jehovah proceeded to say to Moses: "Speak to Aaron your brother, that he should not at all times come into the holy place inside the curtain, in front of the cover which is upon the Ark, that he may not die; because in a cloud I shall appear over the cover.

3 "With the following Aaron should come into the holy place: with a young bull for a sin offering and a ram for a burnt offering. 4 He should put on the holy linen robe, and the linen drawers should come upon his flesh, and he should gird himself with the linen sash and wrap himself with the linen turban. They are holy garments. And he must bathe his flesh in water and put them on.

5 "And from the assembly of the sons of Israel he should take two male kids of the goats for a sin

offering and one ram for a burnt offering.

6 "And Aaron must present the bull of the sin offering, which is for himself, and he must make atonement in behalf of himself and his house.

7 "And he must take the two goats and make them stand before Jehovah at the entrance of the tent of meeting. 8 And Aaron must draw lots over the two goats, the one lot for Jehovah and the other lot for A·za′zel. 9 And Aaron must present the goat over which the lot came up for Jehovah, and he must make it a sin offering. 10 But the goat over which the lot came up for A·za′zel should be stood alive before Jehovah to make atonement for it, so as to send it away for A·za′zel into the wilderness.

11 "And Aaron must present the bull of the sin offering, which is for himself, and make an atonement in behalf of himself and his house; and he must slaughter the bull of the sin offering, which is for himself.

12 "And he must take the fire holder full of burning coals of fire from off the altar before Jehovah, and the hollows of both his hands full of fine perfumed incense, and he must bring them inside the curtain. 13 He must also put the incense upon the fire before Jehovah, and the cloud of the incense must overspread the Ark cover, which is upon the Testimony, that he may not die.

14 "And he must take some of the bull's blood and spatter it with his finger in front of the cover on the east side, and he will spatter some of the blood with his finger seven times before the cover.

15 "And he must slaughter the goat of the sin offering, which is for the people, and he must bring its blood inside the curtain and do with its blood the same as he did with the bull's blood; and he must spatter it toward the cover and before the cover.

16 "And he must make atonement for the holy place concerning the uncleannesses of the sons of Israel and concerning their revolts in all their sins; and that is the way he should do for the tent of meeting, which is residing with them in the midst of their uncleannesses.

17 "And no other man should happen to be in the tent of meeting from when he goes in to make atonement in the holy place until he comes out; and he must make atonement in behalf of himself and in behalf of his house and in behalf of the entire congregation of Israel.

18 "And he must come out to the altar, which is before Jehovah, and make atonement for it, and he must take some of the bull's blood and some of the goat's blood and put it upon the horns of the altar round about. 19 He must also spatter some of the blood upon it with his finger seven times and cleanse it and sanctify it from the uncleannesses of the sons of Israel.

20 "When he has finished making atonement for the holy place and the tent of meeting and the altar, he must also present the live goat. 21 And Aaron must lay both his hands upon the head of the live goat and confess over it all the errors of the sons of Israel and all their revolts in all their sins, and he must put them upon the head of the goat and send it away by the hand of a ready man into the wilderness. 22 And the goat must carry upon itself all their errors into a desert land, and he must send the goat away into the wilderness.

23 "And Aaron must come into the tent of meeting and strip off the linen garments that he put on when he went into the holy place, and he must lay them down there. 24 And he must bathe his flesh in water in a holy place and put on his garments and come out and render up his burnt offering and the people's burnt offering and make atonement in his own behalf and in behalf of the people. 25 And he will make the fat of the sin offering smoke upon the altar.

26 "As for the one who sent the

goat away for A·za′zel, he should wash his garments, and he must bathe his flesh in water, and after that he may come into the camp. 27 "However, he will have the bull of the sin offering and the goat of the sin offering, the blood of both of which was brought in to make atonement in the holy place, taken forth outside the camp; and they must burn their skins and their flesh and their dung in the fire. 28 And the one who burned them should wash his garments, and he must bathe his flesh in water, and after that he may come into the camp.

29 "And it must serve as a statute to time indefinite for YOU people: In the seventh month on the tenth of the month YOU should afflict YOUR souls, and YOU must not do any work, either the native or the alien resident who is residing as an alien in YOUR midst. 30 For on this day atonement will be made for YOU to pronounce YOU clean. YOU will be clean from all YOUR sins before Jehovah. 31 It is a sabbath of complete rest for YOU, and YOU must afflict YOUR souls. It is a statute to time indefinite.

32 "And the priest who will be anointed and whose hand will be filled with power to act as priest as successor of his father must make an atonement and must put on the linen garments. They are holy garments. 33 And he must make atonement for the holy sanctuary, and for the tent of meeting and for the altar he will make atonement; and for the priests and for all the people of the congregation he will make atonement. 34 And this must serve as a statute to time indefinite for YOU, in order to make atonement for the sons of Israel concerning all their sins once in the year."

Accordingly he did just as Jehovah had commanded Moses.

17 And Jehovah went on to speak to Moses, saying: 2 "Speak to Aaron and his sons and all the sons of Israel, and you must say to them, 'This is the thing that Jehovah has commanded, saying:

3 " ' "As for any man of the house of Israel who slaughters a bull or a young ram or a goat in the camp or who slaughters it outside the camp 4 and does not actually bring it to the entrance of the tent of meeting to present it as an offering to Jehovah before the tabernacle of Jehovah, bloodguilt will be counted to that man. He has shed blood, and that man must be cut off from among his people, 5 in order that the sons of Israel may bring their sacrifices, which they are sacrificing in the open field, and they must bring them to Jehovah to the entrance of the tent of meeting to the priest, and they must sacrifice these as communion sacrifices to Jehovah. 6 And the priest must sprinkle the blood upon Jehovah's altar at the entrance of the tent of meeting, and he must make the fat smoke as a restful odor to Jehovah. 7 So they should no longer sacrifice their sacrifices to the goat-shaped demons with which they are having immoral intercourse. This will serve as a statute to time indefinite for YOU, throughout YOUR generations." '

8 "And you should say to them, 'As for any man of the house of Israel or some alien resident who may be residing as an alien in YOUR midst who offers up a burnt offering or a sacrifice 9 and does not bring it to the entrance of the tent of meeting to render it to Jehovah, that man must be cut off from his people.

10 " 'As for any man of the house of Israel or some alien resident who is residing as an alien in their midst who eats any sort of blood, I shall certainly set my face against the soul that is eating the blood, and I shall indeed cut him off from among his people. 11 For the soul of the flesh is in the blood, and I myself have put it upon the altar for YOU to make atonement for YOUR souls, because it is the blood that makes atonement by the soul in it. 12 That is why I have said to the sons of Israel: "No soul of YOU must eat blood and no alien

resident who is residing as an alien in YOUR midst should eat blood."

13 "'As for any man of the sons of Israel or some alien resident who is residing as an alien in YOUR midst who in hunting catches a wild beast or a fowl that may be eaten, he must in that case pour its blood out and cover it with dust. 14 For the soul of every sort of flesh is its blood by the soul in it. Consequently I said to the sons of Israel: "YOU must not eat the blood of any sort of flesh, because the soul of every sort of flesh is its blood. Anyone eating it will be cut off." 15 As for any soul that eats a body [already] dead or something torn by a wild beast, whether a native or an alien resident, he must in that case wash his garments and bathe in water and be unclean until the evening; and he must be clean. 16 But if he will not wash them and will not bathe his flesh, he must then answer for his error.'"

18 And Jehovah continued to speak to Moses, saying: 2 "Speak to the sons of Israel, and you must say to them, 'I am Jehovah YOUR God. 3 The way the land of Egypt does, in which YOU dwelt, YOU must not do; and the way the land of Ca'naan does, into which I am bringing YOU, YOU must not do; and in their statutes YOU must not walk. 4 My judicial decisions YOU should carry out, and my statutes YOU should keep so as to walk in them. I am Jehovah YOUR God. 5 And YOU must keep my statutes and my judicial decisions, which if a man will do, he must also live by means of them. I am Jehovah.

6 "'YOU people must not come near, any man of YOU, to any close fleshly relative of his to lay bare nakedness. I am Jehovah. 7 The nakedness of your father and the nakedness of your mother YOU must not lay bare. She is your mother. You must not lay bare her nakedness.

8 "The nakedness of your father's wife you must not lay bare. It is your father's nakedness.

9 "'As for the nakedness of your sister, the daughter of your father or the daughter of your mother, whether born in the same household or born outside it, you must not lay bare their nakedness.

10 "'As for the nakedness of the daughter of your son or the daughter of your daughter, you must not lay bare their nakedness, because they are your nakedness.

11 "'As for the nakedness of the daughter of your father's wife, the offspring of your father, she being your sister, you must not lay bare her nakedness.

12 "The nakedness of your father's sister you must not lay bare. She is the blood relation of your father.

13 "The nakedness of your mother's sister you must not lay bare, because she is a blood relation of your mother.

14 "The nakedness of your father's brother you must not lay bare. You must not come near his wife. She is your aunt.

15 "The nakedness of your daughter-in-law you must not lay bare. She is your son's wife. You must not lay her nakedness bare.

16 "The nakedness of your brother's wife you must not lay bare. It is your brother's nakedness.

17 "The nakedness of a woman and her daughter you must not lay bare. The daughter of her son and the daughter of her daughter you must not take in order to lay her nakedness bare. They are cases of blood relationship. It is loose conduct.

18 "'And you must not take a woman in addition to her sister as a rival to uncover her nakedness, that is, besides her during her lifetime.

19 "'And you must not come near a woman during the menstruation of her impurity to lay her nakedness bare.

20 "'And you must not give your emission as semen to the wife of your associate to become unclean by it.

21 "'And you must not allow the devoting of any of your offspring

to Mo'lech. You must not profane the name of your God that way. I am Jehovah.

22 "'And you must not lie down with a male the same as you lie down with a woman. It is a detestable thing.

23 "'And you must not give your emission to any beast to become unclean by it, and a woman should not stand before a beast to have connection with it. It is a violation of what is natural.

24 "'Do not make yourselves unclean by any of these things, because by all these things the nations whom I am sending out from before YOU have made themselves unclean. 25 Consequently the land is unclean, and I shall bring punishment for its error upon it, and the land will vomit its inhabitants out. 26 And YOU yourselves must keep my statutes and my judicial decisions, and YOU must not do any of all these detestable things, whether a native or an alien resident who is residing as an alien in YOUR midst. 27 For all these detestable things the men of the land who were before YOU have done, so that the land is unclean. 28 Then the land will not vomit YOU out for YOUR defiling it the same way as it will certainly vomit the nations out who were before YOU. 29 In case anyone does any of all these detestable things, then the souls doing them must be cut off from among their people. 30 And YOU must keep YOUR obligation to me not to carry on any of the detestable customs that have been carried on before YOU, that YOU may not make yourselves unclean by them. I am Jehovah YOUR God.'"

19 And Jehovah spoke further to Moses, saying: 2 "Speak to the entire assembly of the sons of Israel, and you must say to them, 'YOU should prove yourselves holy, because I Jehovah YOUR God am holy.

3 "'YOU should fear each one his mother and his father, and my sabbaths YOU should keep. I am Jehovah YOUR God. 4 Do not turn yourselves to valueless gods, and

YOU must not make molten gods for yourselves. I am Jehovah YOUR God.

5 "'Now in case YOU should sacrifice a communion sacrifice to Jehovah, YOU should sacrifice it to gain approval for yourselves. 6 On the day of YOUR sacrifice and directly the next day it should be eaten, but what is left over till the third day should be burned in the fire. 7 If, though, it should at all be eaten on the third day, it is a foul thing. It will not be accepted with approval. 8 And the one eating it will answer for his error, because he has profaned a holy thing of Jehovah; and that soul must be cut off from his people.

9 "'And when YOU people reap the harvest of YOUR land, you must not reap the edge of your field completely, and the gleaning of your harvest you must not pick up. 10 Also, you must not gather the leftovers of your vineyard, and you must not pick up the scattered grapes of your vineyard. For the afflicted one and the alien resident you should leave them. I am Jehovah YOUR God.

11 "'YOU people must not steal, and YOU must not deceive, and YOU must not deal falsely any one with his associate. 12 And YOU must not swear in my name to a lie, so that you do profane the name of your God. I am Jehovah. 13 You must not defraud your fellow, and you must not rob. The wages of a hired laborer should not stay all night with you until morning.

14 "'You must not call down evil upon a deaf man, and before a blind man you must not put an obstacle; and you must be in fear of your God. I am Jehovah.

15 "'YOU people must not do injustice in the judgment. You must not treat the lowly with partiality, and you must not prefer the person of a great one. With justice you should judge your associate.

16 "'You must not go around among your people for the sake of slandering. You must not stand up against your fellow's blood. I am Jehovah.

17 " 'You must not hate your brother in your heart. You should by all means reprove your associate, that you may not bear sin along with him.

18 " 'You must not take vengeance nor have a grudge against the sons of your people; and you must love your fellow as yourself. I am Jehovah.

19 " 'You people should keep my statutes: You must not interbreed your domestic animals of two sorts. You must not sow your field with seeds of two sorts, and you must not put upon yourself a garment of two sorts of thread, mixed together.

20 " 'Now in case a man lies down with a woman and has an emission of semen, when she is a maidservant designated for another man, and she has not in any way been redeemed nor has freedom been given her, punishment should take place. They should not be put to death, because she was not set free. 21 And he must bring his guilt offering to Jehovah to the entrance of the tent of meeting, a ram of guilt offering. 22 And the priest must make atonement for him with the ram of the guilt offering before Jehovah for his sin that he committed; and his sin that he committed must be forgiven him.

23 " 'And in case you people come into the land, and you must plant any tree for food, you must also consider its fruitage impure as its "foreskin." For three years it will continue uncircumcised for you. It should not be eaten. 24 But in the fourth year all its fruit will become a holy thing of festal exultation to Jehovah. 25 And in the fifth year you may eat its fruit in order to add its produce to yourselves. I am Jehovah your God.

26 " 'You must eat nothing along with blood.

" 'You must not look for omens, and you must not practice magic.

27 " 'You must not cut your side locks short around, and you must not destroy the extremity of your beard.

28 " 'And you must not make cuts in your flesh for a deceased soul, and you must not make tattoo marking upon yourselves. I am Jehovah.

29 " 'Do not profane your daughter by making her a prostitute, in order that the land may not commit prostitution and the land actually be filled with loose morals.

30 " 'My sabbaths you should keep, and you should stand in awe of my sanctuary. I am Jehovah.

31 " 'Do not turn yourselves to the spirit mediums, and do not consult professional foretellers of events, so as to become unclean by them. I am Jehovah your God.

32 " 'Before gray hair you should rise up, and you must show consideration for the person of an old man, and you must be in fear of your God. I am Jehovah.

33 " 'And in case an alien resident resides with you as an alien in your land, you must not mistreat him. 34 The alien resident who resides as an alien with you should become to you like a native of yours; and you must love him as yourself, for you became alien residents in the land of Egypt. I am Jehovah your God.

35 " 'You must not commit injustice in judging, in measuring, in weighing or in measuring liquids. 36 You should prove to have accurate scales, accurate weights, an accurate e'phah and an accurate hin. Jehovah your God I am, who have brought you out of the land of Egypt. 37 So you must keep all my statutes and all my judicial decisions, and you must do them. I am Jehovah.' "

20 And Jehovah went on speaking to Moses, saying: 2 "You are to say to the sons of Israel, 'Any man of the sons of Israel, and any alien resident who resides as an alien in Israel, who gives any of his offspring to Mo'lech, should be put to death without fail. The people of the land should pelt him to death with stones. 3 And as for me, I shall set my face against that man, and I will cut him off from among his people, because he has given some of his offspring to Mo'lech for the purpose of defiling my holy place and to profane my holy name. 4 And if the people of the land should deliberately hide their eyes from that man when he gives any of his offspring to Mo'lech by not putting him to death, 5 then I, for my part, shall certainly fix my face against that man and his family, and I shall indeed cut him and all those who have immoral intercourse along with him in having immoral intercourse with Mo'lech off from among their people.

6 "'As for the soul who turns himself to the spirit mediums and the professional foretellers of events so as to have immoral intercourse with them, I shall certainly set my face against that soul and cut him off from among his people.

7 "'And you must sanctify yourselves and prove yourselves holy, because I am Jehovah your God. 8 And you must keep my statutes and do them. I am Jehovah who is sanctifying you.

9 "'In case there should be any man who calls down evil upon his father and his mother, he should be put to death without fail. It is his father and his mother upon whom he has called down evil. His own blood is upon him.

10 "'Now a man who commits adultery with another man's wife is one who commits adultery with the wife of his fellow man. He should be put to death without fail, the adulterer and the adulteress as well. 11 And a man who lies down with his father's wife has laid bare the nakedness of his father. Both of them should be put to death without fail. Their own blood is upon them. 12 And where a man lies down with his daughter-in-law, both of them should be put to death without fail. They have committed a violation of what is natural. Their own blood is upon them.

13 "'And when a man lies down with a male the same as one lies down with a woman, both of them have done a detestable thing. They should be put to death without fail. Their own blood is upon them.

14 "'And where a man takes a woman and her mother, it is loose conduct. They should burn him and them in the fire, in order that loose conduct may not continue in your midst.

15 "'And where a man gives his seminal emission to a beast, he should be put to death without fail, and you should kill the beast. 16 And where a woman approaches any beast to have a connection with it, you must kill the woman and the beast. They should be put to death without fail. Their own blood is upon them.

17 "'And where a man takes his sister, the daughter of his father or the daughter of his mother, and he does see her nakedness, and she herself sees his nakedness, it is shame. So they must be cut off before the eyes of the sons of their people. It is the nakedness of his sister that he has laid bare. He should answer for his error.

18 "'And where a man lies down with a menstruating woman and does lay bare her nakedness, he has exposed her source, and she herself has laid bare the source of her blood. So both of them must be cut off from among their people.

19 "'And the nakedness of your mother's sister and of your father's sister you must not lay bare, because it is his blood relation that one has exposed. They should answer for their error. 20 And a man who lies down with his uncle's wife has laid bare the nakedness of his uncle. They should answer for their sin. They should die childless. 21 And where a man takes his brother's wife, it is something abhorrent. It is the nakedness of his brother that he has laid bare. They should become childless.

22 "'And you people must keep all my statutes and all my judicial decisions and do them, that the land to which I am bringing you to dwell in it may not vomit you out. 23 And you must not walk in the statutes of the nations whom I am sending out from before you, because they have done all these things and I abhor them. 24 Hence I said to you: "You,

for YOUR part, will take possession of their ground, and I, for my part, shall give it to YOU to take possession of it, a land flowing with milk and honey. Jehovah YOUR God I am, who have divided YOU off from the peoples." 25 And YOU must make a distinction between the clean beast and the unclean and between the unclean fowl and the clean; and YOU must not make YOUR souls loathsome with the beast and the fowl and anything that moves on the ground that I have divided off for YOU in declaring them unclean. 26 And YOU must prove yourselves holy to me, because I Jehovah am holy; and I am proceeding to divide YOU off from the peoples to become mine. 27 "'And as for a man or woman in whom there proves to be a mediumistic spirit or spirit of prediction, they should be put to death without fail. They should pelt them to death with stones. Their own blood is upon them.'"

21 And Jehovah went on to say to Moses: "Talk to the priests, Aaron's sons, and you must say to them, 'For a deceased soul no one may defile himself among his people. 2 But for a blood relation of his who is close to him, for his mother and for his father and for his son and for his daughter and for his brother 3 and for his sister, a virgin who is close to him, who has not become a man's, for her he may defile himself. 4 He may not defile himself for a woman possessed by an owner among his people so as to make himself profane. 5 They should not produce baldness upon their heads, and the extremity of their beard they should not shave, and on their flesh they should not make an incision. 6 They should prove themselves holy to their God, and they should not profane the name of their God, because they are those presenting Jehovah's offerings made by fire, the bread of their God; and they must prove themselves holy. 7 A prostitute or a violated woman they should not take; and a woman divorced from her husband they should not take, because he is holy to his God. 8 So you must sanctify him, because he is one presenting the bread of your God. He should prove to be holy to you, because I Jehovah, who am sanctifying YOU, am holy.

9 "'Now in case the daughter of a priest should make herself profane by committing prostitution, it is her father that she is profaning. She should be burned in the fire.

10 "'And as for the high priest of his brothers upon whose head the anointing oil would be poured and whose hand was filled with power to wear the garments, he should not let his head go ungroomed, and he should not tear his garments. 11 And he should not come to any dead soul. For his father and his mother he may not defile himself. 12 He should also not go out from the sanctuary and not profane the sanctuary of his God, because the sign of dedication, the anointing oil of his God, is upon him. I am Jehovah.

13 "'And for his part, he should take a woman in her virginity. 14 As for a widow or a divorced woman and one violated, a prostitute, none of these may he take, but he should take a virgin from his people as a wife. 15 And he should not profane his seed among his people, because I am Jehovah who is sanctifying him.'"

16 And Jehovah continued to speak to Moses, saying: 17 "Speak to Aaron, saying, 'No man of your seed throughout their generations in whom there proves to be a defect may come near to present the bread of his God. 18 In case there is any man in whom there is a defect, he may not come near: a man blind or lame or with his nose slit or with one member too long, 19 or a man in whom there proves to be a fracture of the foot or a fracture of the hand, 20 or hunchback or thin or diseased in his eyes or scabby or having ringworms or having his testicles broken. 21 Any man of the seed of Aaron the priest in whom there is a defect may not approach to pre-

sent Jehovah's offerings made by fire. There is a defect in him. He may not approach to present the bread of his God. 22 He may eat the bread of his God from the most holy things and from the holy things. 23 However, he may not come in near the curtain, and he may not approach the altar, because there is a defect in him; and he should not profane my sanctuary, for I am Jehovah who is sanctifying them.'"

24 Accordingly Moses spoke to Aaron and his sons and all the sons of Israel.

22 And Jehovah spoke further to Moses, saying: 2 "Speak to Aaron and his sons, that they may keep themselves separate from the holy things of the sons of Israel and not profane my holy name in the things they are sanctifying to me. I am Jehovah. 3 Say to them, 'Throughout YOUR generations any man of all YOUR offspring who comes near to the holy things, which the sons of Israel will sanctify to Jehovah, while his uncleanness is upon him, that soul must be cut off from before me. I am Jehovah. 4 No man of Aaron's offspring when he is leprous or has a running discharge may eat of the holy things until he becomes clean, neither he who touches anyone unclean by a deceased soul or a man from whom there goes out a seminal emission, 5 nor a man who touches any swarming thing that is unclean for him or touches a man who is unclean for him as respects any uncleanness of his. 6 The soul who touches any such must be unclean until the evening and may not eat any of the holy things, but he must bathe his flesh in water. 7 When the sun has set, he must also be clean, and afterward he may eat some of the holy things, because it is his bread. 8 He should also not eat any body [already] dead or anything torn by wild beasts so as to become unclean by it. I am Jehovah.

9 "'And they must keep their obligation to me, that they may not carry sin because of it and have

to die for it because they were profaning it. I am Jehovah who is sanctifying them.

10 "'And no stranger at all may eat anything holy. No settler with a priest nor a hired laborer may eat anything holy. 11 But in case a priest should purchase a soul, as a purchase with his money, he as such may share in eating it. As for slaves born in his house, they as such may share in eating his bread. 12 And in case the daughter of a priest should become a man's who is a stranger, she as such may not eat of the contribution of the holy things. 13 But in case the daughter of a priest should become a widow or divorced when she has no offspring, and she must return to her father's house as in her youth, she may eat some of her father's bread; but no stranger at all may feed on it.

14 "'Now in case a man eats a holy thing by mistake, he must then add the fifth of it to it and must give the holy thing to the priest. 15 So they should not profane the holy things of the sons of Israel, which they may contribute to Jehovah, 16 and actually cause them to bear the punishment of guiltiness because of their eating their holy things; for I am Jehovah who is sanctifying them.'"

17 And Jehovah continued to speak to Moses, saying: 18 "Speak to Aaron and his sons and all the sons of Israel, and you must say to them, 'As for any man of the house of Israel or some alien resident in Israel who presents his offering, for any of their vows or for any of their voluntary offerings, which they may present to Jehovah for a burnt offering, 19 to gain approval for YOU it must be sound, a male among the herd, among the young rams or among the goats. 20 Anything in which there is a defect YOU must not present, because it will not serve to gain approval for YOU.

21 "'And in case a man should present a communion sacrifice to Jehovah in order to pay a vow or as a voluntary offering, it should

prove to be a sound one among the herd or the flock, in order to gain approval. No defect at all should prove to be in it. 22 No case of blindness or fracture or having a cut or wart or scabbiness or ring-worm, none of these must you present to Jehovah, and no offering made by fire from them must you put upon the altar for Jehovah. 23 As for a bull or a sheep having a member too long or too short, you may make it a voluntary offer-ing; but for a vow it will not be accepted with approval. 24 But one having the testicles squeezed or crushed or pulled off or cut off you must not present to Jehovah, and in your land you should not render them up. 25 And any of all these from the hand of a foreigner you must not present as the bread of your God, because their corruption is in them. There is a defect in them. They will not be accepted with approval of you.' "

26 And Jehovah spoke further to Moses, saying: 27 "Should a bull or a young ram or a goat be born, then it must continue under its mother seven days, but from the eighth day and forward it will be accepted with approval as an offer-ing, an offering made by fire to Jehovah. 28 As for a bull and a sheep, you must not slaughter it and its young one on the one day. 29 "And in case you should sac-rifice a thanksgiving sacrifice to Jehovah, you should sacrifice it to gain approval for you. 30 On that day it should be eaten. You must not leave any of it until morning. I am Jehovah.

31 "And you must keep my com-mandments and do them. I am Je-hovah. 32 And you must not pro-fane my holy name, and I must be sanctified in the midst of the sons of Israel. I am Jehovah who is sanctifying you, 33 the One bring-ing you out of the land of Egypt to prove myself God to you. I am Jehovah."

23 And Jehovah went on speaking to Moses, saying: 2 "Speak to the sons of Israel, and you must say to them, 'The seasonal festivals of Jehovah that you should pro-claim are holy conventions. These are my seasonal festivals:

3 "'Six days may work be done, but on the seventh day is a sab-bath of complete rest, a holy con-vention. You may do no sort of work. It is a sabbath to Jehovah in all places where you dwell.

4 "'These are the seasonal fes-tivals of Jehovah, holy conventions, which you should proclaim at their appointed times: 5 In the first month, on the fourteenth day of the month, between the two eve-nings is the passover to Jehovah.

6 "'And on the fifteenth day of this month is the festival of un-fermented cakes to Jehovah. Seven days you should eat unfermented cakes. 7 On the first day you will have a holy convention occur. No sort of laborious work may you do. 8 But you must present an offering made by fire to Jehovah seven days. On the seventh day there will be a holy convention. No sort of laborious work may you do.' "

9 And Jehovah continued to speak to Moses, saying: 10 "Speak to the sons of Israel, and you must say to them, 'When you eventually come into the land that I am giving you, and you have reaped its har-vest, you must also bring a sheaf of the first fruits of your harvest to the priest. 11 And he must wave the sheaf to and fro before Jehovah to gain approval for you. Directly the day after the sabbath the priest should wave it to and fro. 12 And on the day of your having the sheaf waved to and fro you must render up a sound young ram, in its first year, for a burnt offering to Jehovah; 13 and as its grain offering two tenths of an e'phah of fine flour moistened with oil, as an offering made by fire to Jehovah, a restful odor; and as its drink offering a fourth of a hin of wine. 14 And you must eat no bread nor roasted grain nor new grain until this very day, until your bringing the offering of your God. It is a statute to time indefi-nite for your generations in all places where you dwell.

15 " 'And you must count for yourselves from the day after the sabbath, from the day of your bringing the sheaf of the wave offering, seven sabbaths. They should prove to be complete. 16 To the day after the seventh sabbath you should count, fifty days, and you must present a new grain offering to Jehovah. 17 Out of your dwelling places you should bring two loaves as a wave offering. Of two tenths of an e'phah of fine flour they should prove to be. They should be baked leavened, as first ripe fruits to Jehovah. 18 And you must present along with the loaves seven sound male lambs, each a year old, and one young bull and two rams. They should serve as a burnt offering to Jehovah along with their grain offering and their drink offerings as an offering made by fire, of a restful odor to Jehovah. 19 And you must render up one kid of the goats as a sin offering and two male lambs, each a year old, as a communion sacrifice. 20 And the priest must wave them to and fro along with the loaves of the first ripe fruits, as a wave offering before Jehovah, along with the two male lambs. They should serve as something holy to Jehovah for the priest. 21 And you must proclaim on this very day Jehovah's holy convention for yourselves. No sort of laborious work may you do. It is a statute to time indefinite in all your dwelling places for your generations.

22 " 'And when you people reap the harvest of your land, you must not do completely the edge of your field when you are reaping, and the gleaning of your harvest you must not pick up. You should leave them for the afflicted one and the alien resident. I am Jehovah your God.' "

23 And Jehovah went on speaking to Moses, saying: 24 "Speak to the sons of Israel, saying, 'In the seventh month, on the first of the month, there should occur for you a complete rest, a memorial by the trumpet blast, a holy convention. 25 No sort of laborious work may

you do, and you must present an offering made by fire to Jehovah.' "

26 And Jehovah spoke further to Moses, saying: 27 "However, on the tenth of this seventh month is the day of atonement. A holy convention should take place for you, and you must afflict your souls and present an offering made by fire to Jehovah. 28 And you must do no sort of work on this very day, because it is a day of atonement to make atonement for you before Jehovah your God; 29 because every soul that will not be afflicted on this very day must be cut off from his people. 30 As for any soul that will do any sort of work on this very day, I must destroy that soul from among his people. 31 You must do no sort of work. It is a statute to time indefinite for your generations in all places where you dwell. 32 It is a sabbath of complete rest for you, and you must afflict your souls on the ninth of the month in the evening. From evening to evening you should observe your sabbath."

33 And Jehovah continued to speak to Moses, saying: 34 "Speak to the sons of Israel, saying, 'On the fifteenth day of this seventh month is the festival of booths for seven days to Jehovah. 35 On the first day is a holy convention. No sort of laborious work may you do. 36 Seven days you should present an offering made by fire to Jehovah. On the eighth day there should occur a holy convention for you, and you must present an offering made by fire to Jehovah. It is a solemn assembly. No sort of laborious work may you do.

37 " 'These are the seasonal festivals of Jehovah that you should proclaim as holy conventions, for presenting an offering made by fire to Jehovah: the burnt offering and the grain offering of the sacrifice and the drink offerings according to the daily schedule, 38 besides the sabbaths of Jehovah and besides your gifts and besides all your vow offerings and besides all your voluntary offerings, which you should give to Jehovah.

39 However, on the fifteenth day of the seventh month, when you have gathered the produce of the land, you should celebrate the festival of Jehovah seven days. On the first day is a complete rest and on the eighth day is a complete rest. 40 And you must take for yourselves on the first day the fruit of splendid trees, the fronds of palm trees and the boughs of branchy trees and poplars of the torrent valley, and you must rejoice before Jehovah your God seven days. 41 And you must celebrate it as a festival to Jehovah seven days in the year. As a statute to time indefinite during your generations, you should celebrate it in the seventh month. 42 It is in the booths you should dwell seven days. All the natives in Israel should dwell in the booths, 43 in order that your generations may know that it was in the booths that I made the sons of Israel to dwell when I was bringing them out of the land of Egypt. I am Jehovah your God.'"

44 Accordingly Moses spoke of the seasonal festivals of Jehovah to the sons of Israel.

24 And Jehovah proceeded to speak to Moses, saying: 2 "Command the sons of Israel that they get for you pure, beaten olive oil for the luminary, to light up the lamp constantly. 3 Outside the curtain of the Testimony in the tent of meeting Aaron should set it in order from evening to morning before Jehovah constantly. It is a statute to time indefinite during your generations. 4 Upon the lampstand of pure gold he should set the lamps in order before Jehovah constantly.

5 "And you must take fine flour and bake it up into twelve ring-shaped cakes. Two tenths of an e'phah should go to each ring-shaped cake. 6 And you must place them in two sets of layers, six to the layer set, upon the table of pure gold before Jehovah. 7 And you must put pure frankincense upon each layer set, and it must serve as the bread for a remembrancer, an offering made by fire to Jehovah. 8 On one sabbath day after another he should set it in order before Jehovah constantly. It is a covenant to time indefinite with the sons of Israel. 9 And it must become Aaron's and his sons', and they must eat it in a holy place, because it is something most holy for him from Jehovah's offerings made by fire, as a regulation to time indefinite."

10 Now a son of an Israelite woman, who, however, was the son of an Egyptian man, went out into the midst of the sons of Israel, and the son of the Israelitess and an Israelite man began to struggle with each other in the camp. 11 And the son of the Israelite woman began to abuse the Name and to call down evil upon it. So they brought him to Moses. Incidentally, his mother's name was She·lo'mith, the daughter of Dib'ri of the tribe of Dan. 12 Then they committed him into custody till there should be a distinct declaration to them according to the saying of Jehovah.

13 And Jehovah proceeded to speak to Moses, saying: 14 "Bring forth the one who called down evil to the outside of the camp; and all those who heard him must lay their hands upon his head, and the entire assembly must pelt him [with stones]. 15 And you should speak to the sons of Israel, saying, 'In case any man calls down evil upon his God, he must then answer for his sin. 16 So the abuser of Jehovah's name should be put to death without fail. The entire assembly should without fail pelt him with stones. The alien resident the same as the native should be put to death for his abusing the Name.

17 "'And in case a man strikes any soul of mankind fatally, he should be put to death without fail. 18 And the fatal striker of the soul of a domestic animal should make compensation for it, soul for soul. 19 And in case a man should cause a defect in his associate, then just as he has done, so it should be done to him. 20 Fracture for fracture, eye for

eye, tooth for tooth; the same sort of defect he may cause in the man, that is what should be caused in him. 21 And the fatal striker of a beast should make compensation for it, but the fatal striker of a man should be put to death.

22 " 'One judicial decision should hold good for you. The alien resident should prove to be the same as the native, because I am Jehovah your God.' "

23 After that Moses spoke to the sons of Israel, and they brought forth the one who had called down evil to the outside of the camp, and they pelted him with stones. Thus the sons of Israel did just as Jehovah had commanded Moses.

25 And Jehovah spoke further to Moses in Mount Si′nai, saying: 2 "Speak to the sons of Israel, and you must say to them, 'When you eventually come into the land that I am giving you, then the land must observe a sabbath to Jehovah. 3 Six years you should sow your field with seed, and six years you should prune your vineyard, and you must gather the land's produce. 4 But in the seventh year there should occur a sabbath of complete rest for the land, a sabbath to Jehovah. Your field you must not sow with seed, and your vineyard you must not prune. 5 The growth from spilled kernels of your harvest you must not reap, and the grapes of your unpruned vine you must not gather. There should occur a sabbath of complete rest for the land. 6 And the sabbath of the land must serve you people for food, for you and your slave man and your slave girl and your hired laborer and the settler with you, those who are residing as aliens with you, 7 and for your domestic animal and for the wild beast that is in your land. All its produce should serve for eating.

8 " 'And you must count for yourself seven sabbaths of years, seven times seven years, and the days of the seven sabbaths of years must amount to forty-nine years for you. 9 And you must cause the horn of loud tone to sound in the seventh month on the tenth of the month; on the day of atonement you people should cause the horn to sound in all your land. 10 And you must sanctify the fiftieth year and proclaim liberty in the land to all its inhabitants. It will become a Jubilee for you, and you must return each one to his possession and you should return each one to his family. 11 A Jubilee is what that fiftieth year will become for you. You must not sow seed nor reap the land's growth from spilled kernels nor gather the grapes of its unpruned vines. 12 For it is a Jubilee. It should become something holy to you. From the field you may eat what the land produces.

13 " 'In this year of the Jubilee you should return each one to his possession. 14 Now in case you should sell merchandise to your associate or be buying from your associate's hand, do not you wrong one another. 15 By the number of the years after the Jubilee you should buy from your associate; by the number of the years of the crops he should sell to you. 16 In proportion to the great number of years he should increase its purchase value, and in proportion to the fewness of years he should reduce its purchase value, because the number of the crops is what he is selling to you. 17 And you must not wrong anyone his associate, and you must be in fear of your God, because I am Jehovah your God. 18 So you must carry out my statutes and you should keep my judicial decisions and you must carry them out. Then you will certainly dwell on the land in security. 19 And the land will indeed give its fruitage, and you will certainly eat to satisfaction and dwell in security on it.

20 " 'But in case you should say: "What are we going to eat in the seventh year seeing that we may not sow seed or gather our crops?" 21 in that case I shall certainly command my blessing for you in the sixth year, and it must yield

its crop for three years. 22 And
YOU must sow seed the eighth year
and YOU must eat from the old
crop until the ninth year. Until the
coming of its crop YOU will eat the
old.

23 "'So the land should not be
sold in perpetuity, because the land
is mine. For YOU are alien residents
and settlers from my standpoint.
24 And in all the land of YOUR
possession YOU should grant to the
land the right of buying back.

25 "'In case your brother grows
poor and has to sell some of his
possession, a repurchaser closely related to him must also come and
buy back what his brother sold.
26 And in case anyone proves to
have no repurchaser and his own
hand does make gain and he does
find enough for its repurchase,
27 he must also calculate the years
from when he sold it and he must
return what money remains over to
the man to whom he made the
sale, and he must return to his
possession.

28 "'But if his hand does not
find enough to give back to him,
what he sold must also continue in
the hand of its purchaser until
the Jubilee year; and it must go
out in the Jubilee, and he must
return to his possession.

29 "'Now in case a man should
sell a dwelling house in a walled
city, his right of repurchase must
also continue till the year from the
time of his sale finishes out; his
right of repurchase should continue
a whole year. 30 But if it should
not be bought back before the complete year has come to the full for
him, the house that is in the city
that has a wall must also stand in
perpetuity as the property of its
purchaser during his generations.
It should not go out in the Jubilee.
31 However, the houses of settlements that have no wall about
them should be accounted as part
of the field of the country. Right
of repurchase should continue for
it, and in the Jubilee it should go
out.

32 "'As for cities of the Levites
with the houses of the cities of

their possession, the right of repurchase should continue to time indefinite for the Levites. 33 And
where property of the Levites is
not bought back, the house sold in
the city of his possession must also
go out in the Jubilee; because the
houses of the cities of the Levites
are their possession in the midst
of the sons of Israel. 34 Moreover, the field of pasture ground
of their cities may not be sold, because it is a possession to time indefinite for them.

35 "'And in case your brother
grows poor and so he is financially
weak alongside you, you must also
sustain him. As an alien resident
and a settler, he must keep alive
with you. 36 Do not take interest
and usury from him, but you must
be in fear of your God; and your
brother must keep alive with you.
37 You must not give him your
money on interest, and you must
not give your food out on usury.
38 I am Jehovah YOUR God, who
brought YOU out of the land of
Egypt to give YOU the land of Ca'-
naan, to prove myself YOUR God.

39 "'And in case your brother
grows poor alongside you and he
has to sell himself to you, you must
not use him as a worker in slavish
service. 40 He should prove to be
with you like a hired laborer, like
a settler. He should serve with you
till the Jubilee year. 41 And he
must go out from you, he and his
sons with him, and he must return
to his family, and he should return to the possession of his forefathers. 42 For they are my slaves
whom I brought out of the land of
Egypt. They must not sell themselves the way a slave is sold.
43 You must not tread down upon
him with tyranny, and you must be
in fear of your God. 44 As for
your slave man and your slave
girl who become yours from the
nations that are round about YOU
people, from them YOU may buy a
slave man and a slave girl. 45 And
also from the sons of the settlers
who are residing as aliens with
YOU, from them YOU may buy, and
from their families that are with

YOU whom they had born to them in YOUR land; and they must become YOUR possession. 46 And YOU must pass them on as an inheritance to YOUR sons after YOU to inherit as a possession to time indefinite. You may use them as workers, but upon YOUR brothers the sons of Israel, you must not tread, the one upon the other, with tyranny.

47 "'But in case the hand of the alien resident or the settler with you becomes wealthy, and your brother has become poor alongside him and must sell himself to the alien resident or the settler with you, or to a member of the family of the alien resident, 48 after he has sold himself, the right of repurchase will continue in his case. One of his brothers may buy him back. 49 Or his uncle or the son of his uncle may buy him back, or any blood relative of his flesh, one of his family, may buy him back.

"'Or if his own hand has become wealthy, he must also buy himself back. 50 And he must reckon with his purchaser from the year he sold himself to him till the Jubilee year, and the money of his sale must correspond with the number of years. The way workdays of a hired laborer are reckoned he should continue with him. 51 If there are yet many years, he should in proportion to them pay his repurchase price over from the money of his purchase. 52 But if only a few remain of the years until the Jubilee year, he must then make a calculation for himself. In proportion to the years of his he should pay over his repurchase price. 53 He should continue with him like a hired laborer from year to year. He may not tread him down with tyranny before your eyes. 54 However, if he cannot buy himself back on these terms, he must then go out in the year of Jubilee, he and his sons with him.

55 "'For to me the sons of Israel are slaves. They are my slaves whom I brought out of the land of Egypt. I am Jehovah YOUR God.

26 "'You must not make valueless gods for yourselves, and YOU must not set up a carved image or a sacred pillar for yourselves, and YOU must not put a stone as a showpiece in YOUR land in order to bow down toward it; for I am Jehovah YOUR God. 2 You should keep my sabbaths and stand in awe of my sanctuary. I am Jehovah.

3 "'If YOU continue walking in my statutes and keeping my commandments and YOU do carry them out, 4 I shall also certainly give YOUR showers of rain at their proper time, and the land will indeed give its yield, and the tree of the field will give its fruit. 5 And YOUR threshing will certainly reach to YOUR grape gathering, and the grape gathering will reach to the sowing of seed; and YOU will indeed eat YOUR bread to satisfaction and dwell in security in YOUR land. 6 And I will put peace in the land, and YOU will indeed lie down, with no one making [YOU] tremble; and I will make the injurious wild beast cease out of the land, and a sword will not pass through YOUR land. 7 And YOU will certainly chase YOUR enemies, and they will indeed fall before YOU by the sword. 8 And five of YOU will certainly chase a hundred, and a hundred of YOU will chase ten thousand, and YOUR enemies will indeed fall before YOU by the sword.

9 "'And I will turn myself to YOU and make YOU fruitful and multiply YOU, and I will carry out my covenant with YOU. 10 And YOU will certainly eat the old of the preceding year, and YOU will bring out the old ahead of the new. 11 And I shall certainly put my tabernacle in the midst of YOU, and my soul will not abhor YOU. 12 And I shall indeed walk in the midst of YOU and prove myself YOUR God, and YOU, on YOUR part, will prove yourselves my people. 13 I am Jehovah YOUR God, who brought YOU out of the land of Egypt from acting as slaves to them, and I proceeded to break the bars of YOUR yoke and make YOU walk erect.

14 " 'However, if YOU will not listen to me nor do all these commandments, **15** and if YOU will reject my statutes, and if YOUR souls will abhor my judicial decisions so as not to do all my commandments, to the extent of YOUR violating my covenant, **16** then I, for my part, shall do the following to YOU, and in punishment I shall certainly bring upon YOU disturbance with tuberculosis and burning fever, causing the eyes to fail and making the soul pine away. And YOU will simply sow YOUR seed for nothing, as YOUR enemies will certainly eat it up. **17** And I shall indeed set my face against YOU, and YOU will certainly be defeated before YOUR enemies; and those who hate YOU will just tread down upon YOU, and YOU will actually flee when no one is pursuing YOU.

18 " 'If, though, despite these things, YOU will not listen to me, I shall then have to chastise YOU seven times as much for YOUR sins. **19** And I shall have to break the pride of YOUR strength and make YOUR heavens like iron and YOUR earth like copper. **20** And YOUR power will simply be expended for nothing, as YOUR earth will not give its yield, and the tree of the earth will not give its fruit.

21 " 'But if YOU keep walking in opposition to me and not wishing to listen to me, I shall then have to inflict seven times more blows upon YOU according to YOUR sins. **22** And I will send the wild beasts of the field among YOU, and they will certainly bereave YOU of children and cut off YOUR domestic animals and reduce the number of YOU, and YOUR roads will actually be desolated.

23 " 'Nevertheless, if with these things YOU do not let yourselves be corrected by me and YOU just have to walk in opposition to me, **24** I, yes, I, shall then have to walk in opposition to YOU; and I, even I, shall have to strike YOU seven times for YOUR sins. **25** And I shall certainly bring upon YOU a sword wreaking vengeance for the covenant; and YOU will indeed gather yourselves into YOUR cities, and I shall certainly send pestilence into the midst of YOU, and YOU must be given into the hand of an enemy. **26** When I have broken for YOU the rods around which ring-shaped loaves are suspended, ten women will then actually bake YOUR bread in but one oven and give back YOUR bread by weight; and YOU must eat but YOU will not be satisfied.

27 " 'If, however, with this YOU will not listen to me and YOU just must walk in opposition to me, **28** I shall then have to walk in heated opposition to YOU, and I, yes, I, shall have to chastise YOU seven times for YOUR sins. **29** So YOU will have to eat the flesh of YOUR sons, and YOU will eat the flesh of YOUR daughters. **30** And I shall certainly annihilate YOUR sacred high places and cut off YOUR own incense stands and lay YOUR own carcasses upon the carcasses of YOUR dungy idols; and my soul will simply abhor YOU. **31** And I shall indeed give YOUR cities to the sword and lay YOUR sanctuaries desolate, and I shall not smell YOUR restful odors. **32** And I, for my part, will lay the land desolate, and YOUR enemies who are dwelling in it will simply stare in amazement over it. **33** And YOU I shall scatter among the nations, and I will unsheathe a sword after YOU; and YOUR land must become a desolation, and YOUR cities will become a desolate ruin.

34 " 'At that time the land will pay off its sabbaths all the days of its lying desolated, while YOU are in the land of YOUR enemies. At that time the land will keep sabbath, as it must repay its sabbaths. **35** All the days of its lying desolated it will keep sabbath, for the reason that it did not keep sabbath during YOUR sabbaths when YOU were dwelling upon it.

36 " 'As for those remaining among YOU, I shall certainly bring timidity into their hearts in the lands of their enemies; and the sound of a leaf driven about will indeed chase them away, and they will actually flee as in flight from a sword and fall without anyone chasing. 37 And they will certainly stumble against one another as if from before a sword without anyone chasing, and for YOU there will prove to be no ability to stand [in resistance] before YOUR enemies. 38 And YOU must perish among the nations, and the land of YOUR enemies must eat YOU up. 39 As for those remaining among YOU, they will rot away because of their error in the lands of YOUR enemies. Yes, even because of the errors of their fathers with them they will rot away. 40 And they will certainly confess their own error and the error of their fathers in their unfaithfulness when they behaved unfaithfully toward me, yes, even when they walked in opposition to me. 41 Yet I, for my part, proceeded to walk in opposition to them, and I had to bring them into the land of their enemies.

" 'Perhaps at that time their uncircumcised heart will be humbled, and at that time they will pay off their error. 42 And I shall indeed remember my covenant with Jacob; and even my covenant with Isaac and even my covenant with Abraham I shall remember, and the land I shall remember. 43 All the while the land was left abandoned by them and was paying off its sabbaths while it was lying desolated without them and they themselves were paying for their error, because, even because, they had rejected my judicial decisions, and their souls had abhorred my statutes. 44 And yet for all this, while they continue in the land of their enemies, I shall certainly not reject them nor abhor them so as to exterminate them, to violate my covenant with them; for I am Jehovah their God. 45 And I will remember in their behalf the covenant of the ancestors whom I brought forth out of the land of Egypt under the eyes of the nations, in order to prove myself their God. I am Jehovah.' "

46 These are the regulations and the judicial decisions and the laws that Jehovah set between himself and the sons of Israel in Mount Si'nai by means of Moses.

27 And Jehovah continued to speak to Moses, saying: 2 "Speak to the sons of Israel, and you must say to them, 'In case a man makes a special vow offering of souls to Jehovah according to the estimated value, 3 and the estimated value has to be of a male from twenty years old up to sixty years old, the estimated value must then become fifty shekels of silver by the shekel of the holy place. 4 But if it is a female, the estimated value must then become thirty shekels. 5 And if the age is from five years old up to twenty years old, the estimated value of the male must then become twenty shekels and for the female ten shekels. 6 And if the age is from a month old up to five years old, the estimated value of the male must then become five shekels of silver and for the female the estimated value must be three shekels of silver.

7 " 'Now if the age is from sixty years old upward, if it is a male, the estimated value must then become fifteen shekels and for the female ten shekels. 8 But if he has become too poor for the estimated value, he must then stand the person before the priest, and the priest must put a valuation upon him. According to what the vower can afford, the priest will put a valuation upon him.

9 " 'And if it is a beast such as one presents in offering to Jehovah, everything of what he may give to Jehovah will become something holy. 10 He may not replace it, and he may not exchange it with good for bad or with bad for good. But if he should exchange it at all with beast for beast, it itself must then become and what is exchanged for it should become something holy. 11 And if it is any unclean beast such as one may not present in offering to Jehovah, he must then stand the beast before the priest. 12 And the priest must put a valuation upon it whether it is good or bad. According to the

value estimated by the priest, so it should become. 13 But if he wants to buy it back at all, he must then give a fifth of it in addition to the estimated value.

14 " 'Now in case a man should sanctify his house as something holy to Jehovah, the priest must then make a valuation of it whether it is good or bad. According to what valuation the priest makes of it, so much it should cost. 15 But if the sanctifier wants to buy his house back, he must then give a fifth of the money of the estimated value in addition to it; and it must become his.

16 " 'And if it is some of the field of his possession that a man would sanctify to Jehovah, the value must then be estimated in proportion to its seed: if a ho'mer of barley seed, then at fifty shekels of silver. 17 If he should sanctify his field from the year of Jubilee on, it should cost according to the estimated value. 18 And if it is after the Jubilee that he sanctifies his field, the priest must then calculate for him the price in proportion to the years that are left over until the next year of Jubilee, and a deduction should be made from the estimated value. 19 But if the sanctifier of it would at all buy the field back, he must then give a fifth of the money of the estimated value in addition to it, and it must stand fast as his. 20 Now if he should not buy the field back but if the field is sold to another man, it may not be bought back again. 21 And the field when it goes out in the Jubilee must become something holy to Jehovah, as a field that is devoted. The possession of it will become the priest's.

22 " 'And if he sanctifies to Jehovah a field purchased by him that is no part of the field of his possession, 23 the priest must then calculate for him the amount of the valuation up till the year of Jubilee, and he must give the estimated value on that day. It is something holy to Jehovah. 24 In the year of Jubilee the field will return to the one from whom he bought it, to the one to whom the possession of the land belongs.

25 " 'Now every value should be estimated in the shekel of the holy place. The shekel should amount to twenty ge'rahs.

26 " 'Only the first-born among beasts, which is born as the first-born for Jehovah, no man should sanctify it. Whether bull or sheep, it belongs to Jehovah. 27 And if it is among the unclean beasts and he must redeem it according to the estimated value, he must then give a fifth of it in addition to it. But if it should not be bought back, it must then be sold according to the estimated value.

28 " 'Only no sort of devoted thing that a man might devote to Jehovah for destruction out of all that is his, whether from mankind or beasts or from the field of his possession, may be sold, and no sort of devoted thing may be bought back. It is something most holy to Jehovah. 29 No devoted person who might be devoted to destruction from among mankind may be redeemed. He should be put to death without fail.

30 " 'And every tenth part of the land, out of the seed of the land and the fruit of the tree, belongs to Jehovah. It is something holy to Jehovah. 31 And if a man wants to buy any of his tenth part back at all, he should give a fifth of it in addition to it. 32 As for every tenth part of the herd and flock, everything that passes under the crook, the tenth head should become something holy to Jehovah. 33 He should not examine whether it is good or bad, neither should he exchange it. But if he would exchange it at all, it itself must then become and what is exchanged for it should become something holy. It may not be bought back.' "

34 These are the commandments that Jehovah gave Moses as commands to the sons of Israel in Mount Si'nai.

NUMBERS

1 And Jehovah proceeded to speak to Moses in the wilderness of Si′nai, in the tent of meeting, on the first day of the second month in the second year of their coming out of the land of Egypt, and he said: 2 "Take the sum of the whole assembly of the sons of Israel according to their families, according to the house of their fathers, by the number of names, all the males, head by head of them, 3 from twenty years old upward, everyone going out to the army in Israel. You should register them according to their armies, you and Aaron.

4 "And some men should be with you, one man to a tribe; each is a head to the house of his fathers. 5 And these are the names of the men who will stand with you: Of Reu′ben, E·li′zur the son of Shed′e·ur; 6 of Sim′e·on, She·lu′mi·el the son of Zu·ri·shad′dai; 7 of Judah, Nah′shon the son of Am·min′a·dab; 8 of Is′sa·char, Ne·than′el the son of Zu′ar; 9 of Zeb′u·lun, E·li′ab the son of He′lon; 10 of the sons of Joseph: of E′phra·im, E·lish′a·ma the son of Am·mi′hud; of Ma·nas′seh, Ga·ma′li·el the son of Pe·dah′zur; 11 of Benjamin, Ab′i·dan the son of Gid·e·o′ni; 12 of Dan, A·hi·e′zer the son of Am·mi·shad′dai; 13 of Ash′er, Pa′gi·el the son of Och′ran; 14 of Gad, E·li′a·saph the son of Deu′el; 15 of Naph′ta·li, A·hi′ra the son of E′nan. 16 These are the ones called of the assembly, the chieftains of the tribes of their fathers. They are the heads of the thousands of Israel."

17 So Moses and Aaron took these men who had been designated by names. 18 And they congregated all the assembly on the first day of the second month, that they might have their descent acknowledged as regards their families in the house of their fathers, by the number of the names, from twenty years old upward, head by head of them, 19 just as Jehovah had commanded Moses; and he proceeded to register them in the wilderness of Si′nai.

20 And the sons of Reu′ben, Israel's first-born, their births according to their families in the house of their fathers, came to be by the number of names, head by head of them, all the males from twenty years old upward, everyone going out to the army, 21 those registered of them of the tribe of Reu′ben, forty-six thousand five hundred.

22 Of the sons of Sim′e·on, their births according to their families in the house of their fathers, those registered ones of his by the number of names, head by head of them, all the males from twenty years old upward, everyone going out to the army, 23 those registered of them of the tribe of Sim′e·on were fifty-nine thousand three hundred.

24 Of the sons of Gad, their births according to their families in the house of their fathers by the number of names from twenty years old upward, everyone going out to the army, 25 those registered of them of the tribe of Gad were forty-five thousand six hundred and fifty.

26 Of the sons of Judah, their births according to their families in the house of their fathers by the number of names from twenty years old upward, everyone going out to the army, 27 those registered of them of the tribe of Judah were seventy-four thousand six hundred.

28 Of the sons of Is′sa·char, their births according to their families in the house of their fathers by the number of names from twenty years old upward, everyone going out to the army, 29 those registered of them of the tribe of

Is'sa·char were fifty-four thousand four hundred.

30 Of the sons of Zeb'u·lun, their births according to their families in the house of their fathers by the number of names from twenty years old upward, everyone going out to the army, 31 those registered of them of the tribe of Zeb'u·lun were fifty-seven thousand four hundred.

32 Of the sons of Joseph: of the sons of E'phra·im, their births according to their families in the house of their fathers by the number of names from twenty years old upward, everyone going out to the army, 33 those registered of them of the tribe of E'phra·im were forty thousand five hundred.

34 Of the sons of Ma·nas'seh, their births according to their families in the house of their fathers by the number of names from twenty years old upward, everyone going out to the army, 35 those registered of them of the tribe of Ma·nas'seh were thirty-two thousand two hundred.

36 Of the sons of Benjamin, their births according to their families in the house of their fathers by the number of names from twenty years old upward, everyone going out to the army, 37 those registered of them of the tribe of Benjamin were thirty-five thousand four hundred.

38 Of the sons of Dan, their births according to their families in the house of their fathers by the number of names from twenty years old upward, everyone going out to the army, 39 those registered of them of the tribe of Dan were sixty-two thousand seven hundred.

40 Of the sons of Ash'er, their births according to their families in the house of their fathers by the number of names from twenty years old upward, everyone going out to the army, 41 those registered of them of the tribe of Ash'er were forty-one thousand five hundred.

42 Of the sons of Naph'ta·li, their births according to their families in the house of their fathers by the number of names from twenty years old upward, everyone going out to the army, 43 those registered of them of the tribe of Naph'ta·li were fifty-three thousand four hundred.

44 These are the ones registered, whom Moses registered, together with Aaron and the chieftains of Israel, twelve men. They represented one each the house of his fathers. 45 And all those registered of the sons of Israel according to the house of their fathers from twenty years old upward, everyone going out to the army in Israel, came to be, 46 yes, all those registered came to be six hundred and three thousand five hundred and fifty.

47 However, the Levites according to the tribe of their fathers did not get registered in among them. 48 Accordingly Jehovah spoke to Moses, saying: 49 "Only the tribe of Le'vi you must not register, and the sum of them you must not take in among the sons of Israel. 50 And you yourself appoint the Levites over the tabernacle of the Testimony and over all its utensils and over everything that belongs to it. They themselves will carry the tabernacle and all its utensils, and they themselves will minister at it; and around the tabernacle they are to camp. 51 And whenever the tabernacle is setting out, the Levites should take it down; and when the tabernacle encamps, the Levites should set it up; and any stranger coming near should be put to death.

52 "And the sons of Israel must encamp each with reference to his camp, and each man by his [three-tribe] division by their armies. 53 And the Levites should encamp around the tabernacle of the Testimony, that no indignation may arise against the assembly of the sons of Israel; and the Levites must keep the service due to the tabernacle of the Testimony."

54 And the sons of Israel proceeded to do according to all that Jehovah had commanded Moses. They did just so.

2 Jehovah now spoke to Moses and Aaron, saying: 2 "The sons of Israel should encamp, each man by his [three-tribe] division, by the signs for the house of their fathers. Round about in front of the tent of meeting they should encamp.

3 "And those camping eastward toward the sunrising will be the [three-tribe] division of the camp of Judah in their armies, and the chieftain for the sons of Judah is Nah′shon the son of Am·min′a·dab. 4 And his army and the ones registered of them are seventy-four thousand six hundred. 5 And those camping alongside him will be the tribe of Is′sa·char, and the chieftain for the sons of Is′sa·char is Ne·than′el the son of Zu′ar. 6 And his army and his registered ones are fifty-four thousand four hundred. 7 And the tribe of Zeb′u·lun; and the chieftain for the sons of Zeb′u·lun is E·li′ab the son of He′lon. 8 And his army and his registered ones are fifty-seven thousand four hundred.

9 "All the registered ones of the camp of Judah are one hundred eighty-six thousand four hundred in their armies. They should set out first.

10 "The [three-tribe] division of the camp of Reu′ben will be toward the south in their armies, and the chieftain for the sons of Reu′ben is E·li′zur the son of Shed′e·ur. 11 And his army and his registered ones are forty-six thousand five hundred. 12 And those camping alongside him will be the tribe of Sim′e·on, and the chieftain for the sons of Sim′e·on is She·lu′mi·el the son of Zu·ri·shad′dai. 13 And his army and the ones registered of them are fifty-nine thousand three hundred. 14 And the tribe of Gad; and the chieftain for the sons of Gad is E·li′a·saph the son of Reu′el. 15 And his army and the ones registered of them are forty-five thousand six hundred and fifty.

16 "All the registered ones of the camp of Reu′ben are one hundred and fifty-one thousand four hun-

dred and fifty in their armies, and they should set out second.

17 "When the tent of meeting must set out, the camp of the Levites will be in the middle of the camps.

"Just as they should encamp, so they should set out, each one at his place, according to their [three-tribe] divisions.

18 "The [three-tribe] division of the camp of E′phra·im in their armies will be toward the west, and the chieftain for the sons of E′phra·im is E·lish′a·ma the son of Am·mi′hud. 19 And his army and the ones registered of them are forty thousand five hundred. 20 And alongside him will be the tribe of Ma·nas′seh, and the chieftain for the sons of Ma·nas′seh is Ga·ma′li·el the son of Pe·dah′zur. 21 And his army and the ones registered of them are thirty-two thousand two hundred. 22 And the tribe of Benjamin; and the chieftain for the sons of Benjamin is Ab′i·dan the son of Gid·e·o′ni. 23 And his army and the ones registered of them are thirty-five thousand four hundred.

24 "All the registered ones of the camp of E′phra·im are one hundred and eight thousand one hundred in their armies, and they should set out third.

25 "The [three-tribe] division of the camp of Dan will be toward the north in their armies, and the chieftain for the sons of Dan is A·hi·e′zer the son of Am·mi·shad′dai. 26 And his army and the ones registered of them are sixty-two thousand seven hundred. 27 And the ones camping alongside him will be the tribe of Ash′er, and the chieftain for the sons of Ash′er is Pa′gi·el the son of Och′ran. 28 And his army and the ones registered of them are forty-one thousand five hundred. 29 And the tribe of Naph′ta·li; and the chieftain for the sons of Naph′ta·li is A·hi′ra the son of E′nan. 30 And his army and the ones registered of them are fifty-three thousand four hundred.

31 "All the registered ones of the

camp of Dan are one hundred fifty-seven thousand six hundred. They should set out last—according to their [three-tribe] divisions."

32 These were the registered ones of the sons of Israel according to the house of their fathers; all the registered ones of the camps in their armies were six hundred and three thousand five hundred and fifty. 33 But the Levites did not get registered in among the sons of Israel, just as Jehovah had commanded Moses. 34 And the sons of Israel proceeded to do according to all that Jehovah had commanded Moses. That is the way they encamped in their [three-tribe] divisions, and that is the way they set out, each one in his families with regard to the house of his fathers.

3 Now these were the generations of Aaron and Moses in the day that Jehovah spoke with Moses in Mount Si'nai. 2 And these were the names of Aaron's sons: the first-born Na'dab and A·bi'hu, E·le·a'zar and Ith'a·mar. 3 These were the names of Aaron's sons, the anointed priests whose hands had been filled with power to act as priests. 4 However, Na'dab and A·bi'hu died before Jehovah when they offered illegitimate fire before Jehovah in the wilderness of Si'nai; and they did not come to have any sons. But E·le·a'zar and Ith'a·mar continued to act as priests along with Aaron their father.

5 And Jehovah proceeded to speak to Moses, saying: 6 "Bring the tribe of Le'vi near, and you must stand them before Aaron the priest, and they must minister to him. 7 And they must keep their obligation to him and their obligation to all the assembly before the tent of meeting in discharging the service of the tabernacle. 8 And they must take care of all the utensils of the tent of meeting, even the obligation of the sons of Israel in discharging the service of the tabernacle. 9 And you must give the Levites to Aaron and his sons. They are given ones, given to him from the sons of Israel. 10 And

you should appoint Aaron and his sons, and they must take care of their priesthood; and any stranger coming near should be put to death."

11 And Jehovah continued to speak to Moses, saying: 12 "As for me, look! I do take the Levites from among the sons of Israel in place of all the first-born opening the womb of the sons of Israel; and the Levites must become mine. 13 For every first-born is mine. In the day that I struck every first-born in the land of Egypt I sanctified to myself every first-born in Israel from man to beast. They should become mine. I am Jehovah."

14 And Jehovah spoke further to Moses in the wilderness of Si'nai, saying: 15 "Register the sons of Le'vi according to the house of their fathers by their families. Every male from a month old upward you should register." 16 And Moses began to register them at the order of Jehovah, just as he had been commanded. 17 And there came to be the sons of Le'vi by their names: Ger'shon and Ko'hath and Me·rar'i.

18 Now these were the names of the sons of Ger'shon by their families: Lib'ni and Shim'e·i.

19 And the sons of Ko'hath by their families were Am'ram and Iz'har, He'bron and Uz'zi·el.

20 And the sons of Me·rar'i by their families were Mah'li and Mu'shi.

These were the families of the Levites according to the house of their fathers.

21 Of Ger'shon there were the family of the Lib'nites and the family of the Shim'e·ites. These were the families of the Ger'shon·ites. 22 Their registered ones were by number of all males from a month old upward. Their registered ones were seven thousand five hundred. 23 The families of the Ger'shon·ites were behind the tabernacle. They were encamped to the west. 24 And the chieftain of the paternal house for the Ger'shon·ites was E·li'a·saph the son of La'el.

25 And the obligation of the sons of Ger'shon in the tent of meeting was the tabernacle and the tent, its covering and the screen of the entrance of the tent of meeting, 26 and the hangings of the courtyard and the screen of the entrance of the courtyard that is round about the tabernacle and the altar, and its tent cords, for all its service.

27 And of Ko'hath there were the family of the Am'ram·ites and the family of the Iz'har·ites and the family of the He'bron·ites and the family of the Uz·zi'el·ites. These were the families of the Ko'hathites. 28 Among the number of all the males from a month old upward there were eight thousand six hundred, taking care of the obligation to the holy place. 29 The families of the sons of Ko'hath were encamped on the side of the tabernacle to the south. 30 And the chieftain of the paternal house for the families of the Ko'hath·ites was E·li·za'phan the son of Uz'zi·el. 31 And their obligation was the Ark and the table and the lampstand and the altars and the utensils of the holy place with which they would minister and the screen, and all its service.

32 And the chieftain of the chieftains of the Levites was E·le·a'zar the son of Aaron the priest, who had the oversight of those taking care of the obligation to the holy place.

33 Of Me·rar'i there were the family of the Mah'lites and the family of the Mu'shites. These were the families of Me·rar'i. 34 And their registered ones by the number of all the males from a month old upward were six thousand two hundred. 35 And the chieftain of the paternal house for the families of Me·rar'i was Zu'ri·el the son of Ab·i·ha'il. They were encamped on the side of the tabernacle toward the north. 36 And the oversight for which the sons of Me·rar'i were obligated was over the panel frames of the tabernacle and its bars and its pillars and its socket pedestals and all its utensils and all its service, 37 and the pillars of the courtyard round about and their socket pedestals and their tent pins and their tent cords.

38 And those camping before the tabernacle toward the east, before the tent of meeting toward the sunrising, were Moses and Aaron and his sons, those taking care of the obligation to the sanctuary, as the obligation for the sons of Israel. And any stranger coming near would be put to death.

39 All the registered ones of the Levites whom Moses and Aaron registered at the order of Jehovah by their families, all the males from a month old upward, were twenty-two thousand.

40 Then Jehovah said to Moses: "Register all the first-born males of the sons of Israel from a month old upward, and take the number of their names. 41 And you must take the Levites for me—I am Jehovah—in place of all the first-born among the sons of Israel, and the domestic animals of the Levites in place of all the first-born among the domestic animals of the sons of Israel." 42 And Moses proceeded, just as Jehovah had commanded him, to register all the first-born among the sons of Israel. 43 And all the first-born males by the number of the names from a month old upward of their registered ones came to be twenty-two thousand two hundred and seventy-three.

44 And Jehovah continued to speak to Moses, saying: 45 "Take the Levites in place of all the first-born among the sons of Israel, and the domestic animals of the Levites in place of their domestic animals; and the Levites must become mine. I am Jehovah. 46 And as the ransom price of the two hundred and seventy-three from the first-born of the sons of Israel, who are in excess of the Levites, 47 you must take five shekels for each individual. In the shekel of the holy place you should take it. A shekel is twenty ge'rahs. 48 And you must give the money to Aaron and his sons as the ransom price of those who are in excess of them."

49 So Moses took the money of the redemption price from those who were in excess of the ransom price of the Levites. **50** From the first-born of the sons of Israel he took the money, a thousand three hundred and sixty-five shekels, in the shekel of the holy place. **51** Then Moses gave the money of the ransom price to Aaron and his sons according to the order of Jehovah, just as Jehovah had commanded Moses.

4 Jehovah now spoke to Moses and Aaron, saying: **2** "There will be a taking of the sum of the sons of Ko'hath from among the sons of Le'vi, according to their families in the house of their fathers, **3** from thirty years old upward to fifty years old, all those going into the service group to do the work in the tent of meeting. **4** "This is the service of the sons of Ko'hath in the tent of meeting. It is something most holy: **5** And Aaron and his sons must come in when the camp is departing, and they must take down the screening curtain and must cover the ark of the testimony with it. **6** And they must put a covering of seal-skins over it and spread out an entire cloth of blue on top and put in its poles.

7 "And they will spread out a cloth of blue over the table of showbread, and they must put upon it the dishes and the cups and the bowls and the pitchers of the drink offering; and the constant bread should continue on it. **8** And they must spread out a cloth of coccus scarlet over them, and they must cover it with a covering of sealskins and put in its poles. **9** And they must take a cloth of blue and cover the lampstand of the luminary and its lamps and its snuffers and its fire holders and all its vessels for oil with which they regularly minister to it. **10** And they must put it and all its utensils into a covering of sealskins and put it upon a bar. **11** And over the golden altar they will spread out a cloth of blue, and they must cover it with a covering of sealskins and put in

its poles. **12** And they must take all the utensils of the ministry with which they regularly minister in the holy place, and they must put them in a cloth of blue and cover them with a covering of sealskins and put them upon a bar.

13 "And they must clear away the fatty ashes of the altar and spread out a cloth of wool dyed reddish purple over it. **14** And they must put upon it all its utensils with which they regularly minister at it, the fire holders, the forks and the shovels and the bowls, all the utensils of the altar; and they must spread out over it a covering of sealskins and put in its poles.

15 "And Aaron and his sons must finish covering the holy place and all the utensils of the holy place when the camp is departing, and after that the sons of Ko'hath will come in to carry them, but they must not touch the holy place so that they have to die. These things are the load of the sons of Ko'hath in the tent of meeting.

16 "And the oversight of E·le·a'-zar the son of Aaron the priest is over the oil of the luminary and the perfumed incense and the constant grain offering and the anointing oil, the oversight of all the tabernacle and all that is in it, namely, the holy place and its utensils."

17 And Jehovah spoke further to Moses and Aaron, saying: **18** "Do not let the tribe of the families of the Ko'hath·ites be cut off from among the Levites. **19** But do this for them that they may indeed keep alive and may not die for their approaching the most holy things. Aaron and his sons will come in, and they must assign them each one to his service and to his load. **20** And they must not come in to see the holy things for the least moment of time, and so they have to die."

21 Then Jehovah spoke to Moses, saying: **22** "There will be a taking of the sum of the sons of Ger'shon, yes, them by the house of their fathers according to their families.

23 From thirty years old upward to fifty years you will register them, all who come to enter into the service group to render service in the tent of meeting. **24** This is the service of the families of the Ger'shon·ites as to serving and as to carrying. **25** And they must carry the tent cloths of the tabernacle and the tent of meeting, its covering and the sealskin covering that is on top over it, and the screen of the entrance of the tent of meeting, **26** and the hangings of the courtyard and the entrance screen of the gate of the courtyard that is round about the tabernacle and the altar, and their tent cords and all their service utensils, and all things with which work is regularly done. Thus they must serve. **27** At the order of Aaron and his sons all the service of the sons of the Ger'shon·ites should take place as regards all their loads and all their service, and you must assign all their loads to them by obligation. **28** This is the service of the families of the sons of the Ger'shon·ites in the tent of meeting, and their obligatory service is under the hand of Ith'a·mar the son of Aaron the priest.

29 "As for the sons of Me·rar'i, you will register them by their families in the house of their fathers. **30** From thirty years old upward to fifty years you will register them, all who enter into the service group to render the service of the tent of meeting. **31** And this is their obligation, their load, according to all their service in the tent of meeting: the panel frames of the tabernacle and its bars and its pillars and its socket pedestals, **32** and the pillars of the courtyard round about and their socket pedestals and their tent pins and their tent cords together with all their equipment and all their service. And by their names you will assign the equipment for which they are obligated, as their load. **33** This is the service of the families of the sons of Me·rar'i according to all their service in the tent of meeting, under the hand of Ith'a·mar the son of Aaron the priest."

34 And Moses and Aaron and the chieftains of the assembly proceeded to register the sons of the Ko'hath·ites by their families and by the house of their fathers, **35** from thirty years old upward to fifty years, all who entered into the service group for the service in the tent of meeting. **36** And the ones registered of them by their families came to be two thousand seven hundred and fifty. **37** These are the registered ones of the families of the Ko'hath·ites, all those serving in the tent of meeting, whom Moses and Aaron registered at the order of Jehovah by means of Moses.

38 As for the registered ones of the sons of Ger'shon by their families and by the house of their fathers, **39** from thirty years old upward to fifty years, all who entered into the service group for the service in the tent of meeting, **40** the ones registered of them by their families, by the house of their fathers, came to be two thousand six hundred and thirty. **41** These were the registered ones of the families of the sons of Ger'shon, all those serving in the tent of meeting, whom Moses and Aaron registered at the order of Jehovah.

42 As for the registered ones of the families of the sons of Me·rar'i by their families by the house of their fathers, **43** from thirty years old upward to fifty years old, all those entering into the service group for the service in the tent of meeting, **44** the ones registered of them by their families came to be three thousand two hundred. **45** These were the registered ones of the families of the sons of Me·rar'i, whom Moses and Aaron registered at the order of Jehovah by means of Moses.

46 All the registered ones whom Moses and Aaron and the chieftains of Israel registered as Levites by their families and by the house of their fathers, **47** from thirty years old upward to fifty years old, all those coming to render the laborious service and the service of carrying loads in the tent of meeting, **48** their registered ones came to be eight thousand five hundred and eighty. **49** At the order of Jehovah they were registered by means of Moses, each one according to his service and his load; and they were registered just as Jehovah had commanded Moses.

5 And Jehovah spoke further to Moses, saying: **2** "Command the sons of Israel that they send out of the camp every leprous person and everyone having a running discharge and everyone unclean by a deceased soul. **3** Whether a male or a female YOU should send them out. YOU should send them outside the camp, that they may not contaminate the camps of those in the midst of whom I am tabernacling." **4** And the sons of Israel proceeded to do so, even to send them outside the camp. Just as Jehovah had spoken to Moses, so the sons of Israel did.

5 And Jehovah continued speaking to Moses, saying: **6** "Speak to the sons of Israel, 'As for a man or a woman, in case they do any of all the sins of mankind in committing an act of unfaithfulness against Jehovah, that soul has also become guilty. **7** And they must confess their sin that they have done, and he must return the amount of his guilt in its principal, also adding a fifth of it to it, and he must give it to the one against whom he did wrong. **8** But if the latter has no near relative to whom to return the amount of the guilt, the amount of the guilt that is being returned to Jehovah belongs to the priest, except the ram of atonement with which he will make atonement for him. **9** "'And every contribution of all the holy things of the sons of Israel, which they will present to the priest, should become his. **10** And the holy things of each one will remain his own. Whatever each one may give to the priest, that will become his.'"

11 And Jehovah went on to speak to Moses, saying: **12** "Speak

to the sons of Israel, and you must say to them, 'In case any man's wife turns aside in that she does commit an act of unfaithfulness against him, **13** and another man actually lies down with her and has an emission of semen, and it has been hidden from the eyes of her husband and has remained undiscovered, and she, on her part, has defiled herself but there is no witness against her, and she herself has not been caught; **14** and the spirit of jealousy has passed upon him, and he has become suspicious of his wife's faithfulness, and she in fact has defiled herself, or the spirit of jealousy has passed upon him, and he has become suspicious of his wife's faithfulness, but she in fact has not defiled herself; **15** then the man must bring his wife to the priest and bring her offering along with her, a tenth of an e′phah of barley flour. He must not pour oil upon it nor put frankincense upon it, because it is a grain offering of jealousy, a memorial grain offering bringing error to remembrance.

16 "'And the priest must bring her forward and make her stand before Jehovah. **17** And the priest must take holy water in an earthenware vessel, and the priest will take some of the dust that happens to be on the floor of the tabernacle, and he must put it in the water. **18** And the priest must make the woman stand before Jehovah and loosen the hair of the woman's head and put upon her palms the memorial grain offering, that is, the grain offering of jealousy, and in the hand of the priest there should be the bitter water that brings a curse. **19** "'And the priest must make her swear, and he must say to the woman: "If no man has lain down with you and if while under your husband you have not turned aside in any uncleanness, be free of the effect of this bitter water that brings a curse. **20** But you, in case you have turned aside while under your husband and in case you have defiled yourself and some man has put in you his seminal emission, besides your husband,—" 21 The priest must now make the woman swear with an oath involving cursing, and the priest must say to the woman: "May Jehovah set you for a cursing and an oath in the midst of your people by Jehovah's letting your thigh fall away, and your belly swell. 22 And this water that brings a curse must enter into your intestines to cause your belly to swell and the thigh to fall away." To this the woman must say: "Amen! Amen!"

23 "'And the priest must write these cursings in the book and must wipe them out into the bitter water. 24 And he must make the woman drink the bitter water that brings a curse, and the water that brings a curse must enter into her as something bitter. 25 And the priest must take the grain offering of jealousy from the woman's hand and wave the grain offering to and fro before Jehovah, and he must bring it near the altar. 26 And the priest must grasp some of the grain offering as a remembrancer of it and must make it smoke upon the altar, and afterward he will make the woman drink the water. 27 When he has made her drink the water, it must also occur that if she has defiled herself in that she committed an act of unfaithfulness toward her husband, the water that brings a curse must then enter into her as something bitter, and her belly must swell, and her thigh must fall away, and the woman must become a cursing in among her people. 28 However, if the woman has not defiled herself but she is clean, she must then be free from such punishment; and she must be made pregnant with semen.

29 "'This is the law about jealousy, where a woman may turn aside while under her husband, and she does defile herself, 30 or in the case of a man where the spirit of jealousy may pass upon him, and he does suspect his wife of unfaithfulness; and he must make the wife stand before Jehovah, and the priest must carry out toward her all this law. 31 And the man must be innocent of error, but that wife will answer for her error.'"

6 And Jehovah spoke further to Moses, saying: 2 "Speak to the sons of Israel and you must say to them, 'In case a man or a woman takes a special vow to live as a Naz'i·rite to Jehovah, 3 he should keep away from wine and intoxicating liquor. He should not drink the vinegar of wine or the vinegar of intoxicating liquor, nor drink any liquid made from grapes, nor eat grapes either fresh or dried. 4 All the days of his Naziriteship he should not eat anything at all that is made from the wine vine, from the unripe grapes to the skins.

5 "'All the days of the vow of his Naziriteship no razor should pass over his head; until the days that he should be separated to Jehovah come to the full, he should prove holy by letting the locks of the hair of his head grow. 6 All the days of his keeping separate to Jehovah he may not come toward any dead soul. 7 Not even for his father or his mother or his brother or his sister may he defile himself when they die, because the sign of his Naziriteship to his God is upon his head.

8 "'All the days of his Naziriteship he is holy to Jehovah. 9 But in case anyone dying should die quite suddenly alongside him so that he has defiled the head of his Naziriteship, he must then shave his head in the day of establishing his purification. On the seventh day he should shave it. 10 And on the eighth day he should bring two turtledoves or two male pigeons to the priest to the entrance of the tent of meeting. 11 And the priest must handle one as a sin offering and the other as a burnt offering and make atonement for him, since he has sinned because of the [dead] soul. Then he must sanctify his head on that day. 12 And he must live as a Naz'i·rite to Jehovah for the days of his Naziriteship, and he must bring a young ram in its first year as a guilt offering;

and the former days will go un-
counted because he defiled his
Naziriteship.

13 "'Now this is the law about
the Naz'i·rite: On the day that the
days of his Naziriteship come to
the full, he will be brought to the
entrance of the tent of meeting.
14 And he must present as his offering to Jehovah one sound young
ram in its first year as a burnt offering and one sound female lamb
in its first year as a sin offering
and one sound ram as a communion sacrifice, 15 and a basket of
unfermented ring-shaped cakes of
fine flour, moistened with oil, and
unfermented wafers smeared with
oil, and their grain offering and
their drink offerings. 16 And the
priest must present them before Jehovah and render up his sin offering and his burnt offering. 17 And
he will render up the ram as a
communion sacrifice to Jehovah
along with the basket of unfermented cakes; and the priest must
render up its grain offering and its
drink offering.

18 "'And the Naz'i·rite must
shave the head of his Naziriteship
at the entrance of the tent of
meeting, and he must take the hair
of the head of his Naziriteship and
put it upon the fire that is under
the communion sacrifice. 19 And
the priest must take a boiled shoulder from the ram and one unfermented ring-shaped cake out of the
basket, and one unfermented wafer,
and put them upon the palms of
the Naz'i·rite after he has had the
sign of his Naziriteship shaved off.
20 And the priest must wave them
to and fro as a wave offering before Jehovah. It is something holy
for the priest, along with the breast
of the wave offering and the leg
of the contribution. And afterward
the Naz'i·rite may drink wine.

21 "'This is the law about the
Naz'i·rite who vows—his offering to
Jehovah over his Naziriteship, besides that which he can afford.
According to his vow that he may
make, so he should do because of
the law of his Naziriteship.'"

22 Then Jehovah spoke to Moses,
saying: 23 "Speak to Aaron and
his sons, saying, 'This is the way
you should bless the sons of Israel,
saying to them:
24 "May Jehovah bless you and
    keep you.
25 May Jehovah make his face
    shine toward you, and may
    he favor you.
26 May Jehovah lift up his face
    toward you and assign
    peace to you."'
27 And they must place my name
upon the sons of Israel, that I
myself may bless them."

7 Now it came about on the day
that Moses finished setting up
the tabernacle that he proceeded to
anoint it and to sanctify it and all
its furnishings and the altar and
all its utensils. Thus he anointed
them and sanctified them. 2 Then
the chieftains of Israel, the heads
of the house of their fathers, made
a presentation, they being the chieftains of the tribes and standing
over the ones registered, 3 and
they brought their offering before
Jehovah, six covered wagons and
twelve cattle, a wagon for two
chieftains and a bull for each one;
and they presented them before the
tabernacle. 4 At this Jehovah said
to Moses: 5 "Accept them from
them, as they must serve for
carrying on the service of the tent
of meeting, and you must give
them to the Levites, each one in
proportion to his own service."

6 So Moses accepted the wagons
and the cattle and gave them to
the Levites. 7 Two wagons and
four cattle he gave to the sons of
Ger'shon in proportion to their
service, 8 and four wagons and
eight cattle he gave to the sons of
Me·rar'i in proportion to their
service, under the hand of Ith'a-
mar the son of Aaron the priest.
9 But to the sons of Ko'hath he
gave none, because the service of
the holy place was upon them.
They did their carrying on the
shoulder.

10 Now the chieftains made their
presentation at the inauguration of
the altar on the day of its being
anointed, and the chieftains pro-

ceeded with presenting their offering before the altar. 11 So Jehovah said to Moses: "One chieftain on one day and another chieftain on another day is the way they will present their offering for the inauguration of the altar."

12 Now the one presenting his offering on the first day proved to be Nah'shon the son of Am·min'a·dab of the tribe of Judah. 13 And his offering was one silver dish, its weight being a hundred and thirty shekels, one silver bowl of seventy shekels by the shekel of the holy place, both of them full of fine flour moistened with oil for a grain offering; 14 one gold cup of ten shekels, full of incense; 15 one young bull, one ram, one male lamb in its first year, for a burnt offering; 16 one kid of the goats for a sin offering; 17 and for a communion sacrifice two cattle, five rams, five he-goats, five male lambs each a year old. This was the offering of Nah'shon the son of Am·min'a·dab.

18 On the second day Ne·than'el the son of Zu'ar, the chieftain of Is'sa·char, made a presentation. 19 He presented as his offering one silver dish, its weight being a hundred and thirty shekels, one silver bowl of seventy shekels by the shekel of the holy place, both of them full of fine flour moistened with oil for a grain offering; 20 one gold cup of ten shekels, full of incense; 21 one young bull, one ram, one male lamb in its first year, for a burnt offering; 22 one kid of the goats for a sin offering; 23 and for a communion sacrifice two cattle, five rams, five he-goats, five male lambs each a year old. This was the offering of Ne·than'el the son of Zu'ar.

24 On the third day there was the chieftain for the sons of Zeb'u·lun, E·li'ab the son of He'lon. 25 His offering was one silver dish, its weight being a hundred and thirty shekels, one silver bowl of seventy shekels by the shekel of the holy place, both of them full of fine flour moistened with oil for a grain offering; 26 one gold cup

of ten shekels, full of incense; 27 one young bull, one ram, one male lamb in its first year, for a burnt offering; 28 one kid of the goats for a sin offering; 29 and for a communion sacrifice two cattle, five rams, five he-goats, five male lambs each a year old. This was the offering of E·li'ab the son of He'lon.

30 On the fourth day there was the chieftain for the sons of Reu'ben, E·li'zur the son of Shed'e·ur. 31 His offering was one silver dish, its weight being a hundred and thirty shekels, one silver bowl of seventy shekels by the shekel of the holy place, both of them full of fine flour moistened with oil for a grain offering; 32 one gold cup of ten shekels, full of incense; 33 one young bull, one ram, one male lamb in its first year, for a burnt offering; 34 one kid of the goats for a sin offering; 35 and for a communion sacrifice two cattle, five rams, five he-goats, five male lambs each a year old. This was the offering of E·li'zur the son of Shed'e·ur.

36 On the fifth day there was the chieftain for the sons of Sim'e·on, She·lu'mi·el the son of Zu·ri·shad'dai. 37 His offering was one silver dish, its weight being a hundred and thirty shekels, one silver bowl of seventy shekels by the shekel of the holy place, both of them full of fine flour moistened with oil for a grain offering; 38 one gold cup of ten shekels, full of incense; 39 one young bull, one ram, one male lamb in its first year, for a burnt offering; 40 one kid of the goats for a sin offering; 41 and for a communion sacrifice two cattle, five rams, five he-goats, five male lambs each a year old. This was the offering of She·lu'mi·el the son of Zu·ri·shad'dai.

42 On the sixth day there was the chieftain for the sons of Gad, E·li'a·saph the son of Deu'el. 43 His offering was one silver dish, its weight being a hundred and thirty shekels, one silver bowl of seventy shekels by the shekel of the holy place, both of them full of fine flour moistened with oil for a grain

offering; 44 one gold cup of ten shekels, full of incense; 45 one young bull, one ram, one male lamb in its first year, for a burnt offering; 46 one kid of the goats for a sin offering; 47 and for a communion sacrifice two cattle, five rams, five he-goats, five male lambs each a year old. This was the offering of E·li′a·saph the son of Deu′el.

48 On the seventh day there was the chieftain for the sons of E′phra·im, E·lish′a·ma the son of Am·mi′hud. 49 His offering was one silver dish, its weight being a hundred and thirty shekels, one silver bowl of seventy shekels by the shekel of the holy place, both of them full of fine flour moistened with oil for a grain offering; 50 one gold cup of ten shekels, full of incense; 51 one young bull, one ram, one male lamb in its first year, for a burnt offering; 52 one kid of the goats for a sin offering; 53 and for a communion sacrifice two cattle, five rams, five he-goats, five male lambs each a year old. This was the offering of E·lish′a·ma the son of Am·mi′hud.

54 On the eighth day there was the chieftain for the sons of Ma·nas′seh, Ga·ma′li·el the son of Pe·dah′zur. 55 His offering was one silver dish, its weight being a hundred and thirty shekels, one silver bowl of seventy shekels by the shekel of the holy place, both of them full of fine flour moistened with oil for a grain offering; 56 one gold cup of ten shekels, full of incense; 57 one young bull, one ram, one male lamb in its first year, for a burnt offering; 58 one kid of the goats for a sin offering; 59 and for a communion sacrifice two cattle, five rams, five he-goats, five male lambs each a year old. This was the offering of Ga·ma′li·el the son of Pe·dah′zur.

60 On the ninth day there was the chieftain for the sons of Benjamin, Ab′i·dan the son of Gid·e·o′ni. 61 His offering was one silver dish, its weight being a hundred and thirty shekels, one silver bowl of seventy shekels by the shekel of

the holy place, both of them full of fine flour moistened with oil for a grain offering; 62 one gold cup of ten shekels, full of incense; 63 one young bull, one ram, one male lamb in its first year, for a burnt offering; 64 one kid of the goats for a sin offering; 65 and for a communion sacrifice two cattle, five rams, five he-goats, five male lambs each a year old. This was the offering of Ab′i·dan the son of Gid·e·o′ni.

66 On the tenth day there was the chieftain for the sons of Dan, A·hi·e′zer the son of Am·mi·shad′dai. 67 His offering was one silver dish, its weight being a hundred and thirty shekels, one silver bowl of seventy shekels by the shekel of the holy place, both of them full of fine flour moistened with oil for a grain offering; 68 one gold cup of ten shekels, full of incense; 69 one young bull, one ram, one male lamb in its first year, for a burnt offering; 70 one kid of the goats for a sin offering; 71 and for a communion sacrifice two cattle, five rams, five he-goats, five male lambs each a year old. This was the offering of A·hi·e′zer the son of Am·mi·shad′dai.

72 On the eleventh day there was the chieftain for the sons of Ash′er, Pa′gi·el the son of Och′ran. 73 His offering was one silver dish, its weight being a hundred and thirty shekels, one silver bowl of seventy shekels by the shekel of the holy place, both of them full of fine flour moistened with oil for a grain offering; 74 one gold cup of ten shekels, full of incense; 75 one young bull, one ram, one male lamb in its first year, for a burnt offering; 76 one kid of the goats for a sin offering; 77 and for a communion sacrifice two cattle, five rams, five he-goats, five male lambs each a year old. This was the offering of Pa′gi·el the son of Och′ran.

78 On the twelfth day there was the chieftain for the sons of Naph′ta·li, A·hi′ra the son of E′nan. 79 His offering was one silver dish, its weight being a hundred and thirty shekels, one silver bowl of

seventy shekels by the shekel of the holy place, both of them full of fine flour moistened with oil for a grain offering; 80 one gold cup of ten shekels, full of incense; 81 one young bull, one ram, one male lamb in its first year, for a burnt offering; 82 one kid of the goats for a sin offering; 83 and for a communion sacrifice two cattle, five rams, five he-goats, five male lambs each a year old. This was the offering of A·hi′ra the son of E′nan.

84 This was the inauguration offering of the altar on the day of its being anointed, on the part of the chieftains of Israel: twelve silver dishes, twelve silver bowls, twelve gold cups; 85 a hundred and thirty shekels to each silver dish, and seventy to each bowl, all the silver of the vessels being two thousand four hundred shekels by the shekel of the holy place; 86 the twelve gold cups full of incense being ten shekels respectively to a cup by the shekel of the holy place, all the gold of the cups being a hundred and twenty shekels; 87 all the cattle for the burnt offering being twelve bulls, twelve rams, twelve male lambs each a year old and their grain offerings, and twelve kids of the goats for a sin offering; 88 and all the cattle of the communion sacrifice being twenty-four bulls, sixty rams, sixty he-goats, sixty male lambs each a year old. This was the inauguration offering of the altar after its being anointed.

89 Now whenever Moses went into the tent of meeting to speak with him, then he would hear the voice conversing with him from above the cover that was upon the ark of the testimony, from between the two cherubs; and he would speak to him.

8 And Jehovah proceeded to speak to Moses, saying: 2 "Speak to Aaron, and you must say to him, 'Whenever you light up the lamps, the seven lamps should shine on the area in front of the lampstand.'" 3 And Aaron began to do so. He lit up its lamps for the area in front of the lampstand,

just as Jehovah had commanded Moses. 4 Now this was the workmanship of the lampstand. It was hammered work of gold. Up to its sides and up to its blossoms it was hammered work. According to the vision that Jehovah had shown Moses, so he had made the lampstand.

5 And Jehovah spoke further to Moses, saying: 6 "Take the Levites from among the sons of Israel, and you must cleanse them. 7 And this is what you should do to them to cleanse them: Spatter sin-cleansing water upon them, and they must have a razor pass over all their flesh and must wash their garments and cleanse themselves. 8 Then they must take a young bull and its grain offering of fine flour moistened with oil, and you will take another young bull for a sin offering. 9 And you must present the Levites before the tent of meeting and congregate all the assembly of the sons of Israel. 10 And you must present the Levites before Jehovah, and the sons of Israel must lay their hands upon the Levites. 11 And Aaron must cause the Levites to move to and fro before Jehovah as a wave offering from the sons of Israel, and they must serve for carrying on the service of Jehovah.

12 "Then the Levites will lay their hands upon the heads of the bulls. After that, render up the one as a sin offering and the other as a burnt offering to Jehovah to make atonement for the Levites. 13 And you must have the Levites stand before Aaron and his sons and must cause them to move to and fro as a wave offering to Jehovah. 14 And you must separate the Levites from among the sons of Israel, and the Levites must become mine. 15 And afterward the Levites will come in to serve at the tent of meeting. So you must cleanse them and cause them to move to and fro as a wave offering. 16 For they are given ones, given to me from among the sons of Israel. In place of those opening all wombs, all the first-born of the

sons of Israel, you must take them for me. 17 For every first-born among the sons of Israel is mine, among man and among beast. On the day of my striking every first-born in the land of Egypt I sanctified them to myself. 18 And I shall take the Levites in place of all the first-born among the sons of Israel. 19 And I shall give the Levites as given ones to Aaron and his sons from among the sons of Israel, to carry on the service of the sons of Israel in the tent of meeting and to make atonement for the sons of Israel, that no plague may occur among the sons of Israel because the sons of Israel approach the holy place."

20 And Moses and Aaron and all the assembly of the sons of Israel proceeded to do so to the Levites. In accord with all that Jehovah had commanded Moses as regards the Levites, that is the way the sons of Israel did to them. 21 So the Levites purified themselves and washed their garments, after which Aaron caused them to move to and fro as a wave offering before Jehovah. Then Aaron made an atonement for them to cleanse them. 22 First after that the Levites came in to carry on their service in the tent of meeting before Aaron and his sons. Just as Jehovah had commanded Moses respecting the Levites, so they did to them.

23 Jehovah now spoke to Moses, saying: 24 "This is what applies to the Levites: From twenty-five years old upward he will come to enter into the company in the service of the tent of meeting. 25 But after the age of fifty years he will retire from the service company and serve no longer. 26 And he must minister to his brothers in the tent of meeting in taking care of the obligation, but he must render no service. In accord with this you will do to the Levites in their obligations."

9 And Jehovah proceeded to speak to Moses in the wilderness of Si′nai in the second year of their coming out of the land of Egypt, in the first month, saying: 2 "Now

the sons of Israel should prepare the passover sacrifice at its appointed time. 3 On the fourteenth day in this month between the two evenings YOU should prepare it at its appointed time. According to all its statutes and all its regular procedures YOU should prepare it.'

4 So Moses spoke to the sons of Israel to prepare the passover sacrifice. 5 Then they prepared the passover sacrifice in the first month, on the fourteenth day of the month between the two evenings, in the wilderness of Si′nai. According to all that Jehovah had commanded Moses, so the sons of Israel did.

6 Now there happened to be men who had become unclean by a human soul so that they were not able to prepare the passover sacrifice on that day. Hence they presented themselves before Moses and Aaron on that day. 7 Then those men said to him: "We are unclean by a human soul. Why should we be restrained from presenting the offering to Jehovah at its appointed time in the midst of the sons of Israel?" 8 At this Moses said to them: "Stand there, and let me hear what Jehovah may command regarding YOU."

9 Then Jehovah spoke to Moses, saying: 10 "Speak to the sons of Israel, saying, 'Although any man of YOU or of YOUR generations should happen to be unclean by a soul or off on a distant journey, he too must prepare the passover sacrifice to Jehovah. 11 In the second month, on the fourteenth day between the two evenings, they should prepare it. Together with unfermented cakes and bitter greens they should eat it. 12 They must not let any of it remain until morning, and they should break no bone in it. According to the whole statute of the passover they should prepare it. 13 But when the man was clean or did not happen to be off on a journey and neglected to prepare the passover sacrifice, that soul must then be cut off from his people, because the offering of Jehovah he did not pre-

sent at its appointed time. For his sin that man will answer.

14 " 'And in case an alien resident should be residing with YOU as an alien, he also must prepare the passover sacrifice to Jehovah. According to the statute of the passover and according to its regular procedure is the way he should do. There should exist one statute for YOU people, both for the alien resident and for the native of the land.' "

15 Now on the day of setting up the tabernacle the cloud covered the tabernacle of the tent of the Testimony, but in the evening what appeared to be fire continued over the tabernacle until morning. 16 That is the way it went on constantly: The cloud would cover it by day, and the appearance of fire by night. 17 And whenever the cloud would go up from over the tent, the sons of Israel would pull away right afterward, and in the place where the cloud would reside, there is where the sons of Israel would encamp. 18 At the order of Jehovah the sons of Israel would pull away, and at the order of Jehovah they would encamp. All the days that the cloud would reside over the tabernacle, they would remain encamped. 19 And when the cloud prolonged its stay over the tabernacle many days, the sons of Israel also kept their obligation to Jehovah that they should not pull away. 20 And sometimes the cloud would continue a few days over the tabernacle. At the order of Jehovah they would remain encamped, and at the order of Jehovah they would pull away. 21 And sometimes the cloud would continue from evening to morning; and the cloud lifted itself in the morning, and they pulled away. Whether it was by day or by night that the cloud lifted itself, they also pulled away. 22 Whether it was two days or a month or more days during which the cloud prolonged its stay over the tabernacle by residing over it, the sons of Israel remained encamped and would not pull away, but when it

lifted itself they would pull away. 23 At the order of Jehovah they would encamp, and at the order of Jehovah they would pull away. They kept their obligation to Jehovah at the order of Jehovah by means of Moses.

10 And Jehovah proceeded to speak to Moses, saying: 2 "Make for yourself two trumpets of silver. You will make them of hammered work, and they must be at your service for convening the assembly and for breaking up the camps. 3 And they must blow on them both, and the whole assembly must keep their appointment with you at the entrance of the tent of meeting. 4 And if they should blow on just one, the chieftains as heads of the thousands of Israel must also keep their appointment with you.

5 "And YOU men must blow a fluctuating blast, and the camps of those camping to the east must pull away. 6 And YOU must blow a fluctuating blast a second time, and the camps of those camping to the south must pull away. They should blow a fluctuating blast for each time one of them pulls away. 7 "Now when calling the congregation together, YOU should blow, but YOU must not sound a fluctuating blast. 8 And Aaron's sons, the priests, should blow on the trumpets, and the use of them must serve as a statute for YOU men to time indefinite during YOUR generations.

9 "And in case YOU should enter into war in YOUR land against the oppressor who is harassing YOU, YOU must also sound a war call on the trumpets, and YOU will certainly be remembered before Jehovah YOUR God and be saved from YOUR enemies.

10 "And in the day of YOUR rejoicing and in YOUR festal seasons and at the commencements of YOUR months, YOU must blow on the trumpets over YOUR burnt offerings and YOUR communion sacrifices; and their use must serve as a memorial for YOU before YOUR God. I am Jehovah YOUR God."

11 Now it came about that in the second year, in the second month, on the twentieth day in the month, the cloud lifted itself from over the tabernacle of the Testimony. 12 And the sons of Israel began to pull away in the manner of their departures from the wilderness of Si'nai, and the cloud proceeded to reside in the wilderness of Pa'ran. 13 And they began pulling away for the first time, according to the order of Jehovah by means of Moses.

14 So the [three-tribe] division of the camp of the sons of Judah pulled away first of all in their armies, and Nah'shon the son of Am·min'a·dab was over its army. 15 And over the army of the tribe of the sons of Is'sa·char there was Ne·than'el the son of Zu'ar. 16 And over the army of the tribe of the sons of Zeb'u·lun there was E·li'ab the son of He'lon.

17 And the tabernacle was taken down, and the sons of Ger'shon and the sons of Me·rar'i as carriers of the tabernacle pulled away.

18 And the [three-tribe] division of the camp of Reu'ben pulled away in their armies, and E·li'zur the son of Shed'e·ur was over its army. 19 And over the army of the tribe of the sons of Sim'e·on there was She·lu'mi·el the son of Zu·ri·shad'dai. 20 And over the army of the tribe of the sons of Gad there was E·li'a·saph the son of Deu'el.

21 And the Ko'hath·ites as carriers of the sanctuary pulled away, as they will have set up the tabernacle by the time of their coming. 22 And the [three-tribe] division of the camp of the sons of E'phra·im pulled away in their armies, and E·lish'a·ma the son of Am·mi'hud was over its army. 23 And over the army of the tribe of the sons of Ma·nas'seh there was Ga·ma'li·el the son of Pe·dah'zur. 24 And over the army of the tribe of the sons of Benjamin there was Ab'i·dan the son of Gid·e·o'ni.

25 And the [three-tribe] division of the camp of the sons of Dan pulled away as forming the rear guard for all the camps in their armies, and A·hi·e'zer the son of Am·mi·shad'dai was over its army. 26 And over the army of the tribe of the sons of Ash'er there was Pa'gi·el the son of Och'ran. 27 And over the army of the tribe of the sons of Naph'ta·li there was A·hi'ra the son of E'nan. 28 In this manner were the departures of the sons of Israel in their armies when they would pull away.

29 Then Moses said to Ho'bab the son of Reu'el the Mid'i·an·ite, the father-in-law of Moses: "We are pulling away for the place about which Jehovah said, 'I shall give it to you.' Do come with us, and we shall certainly do good to you, because Jehovah has spoken good concerning Israel." 30 But he said to him: "I shall not go along, but I shall go to my own country and to my relatives." 31 At this he said: "Please, do not leave us, because, for the reason that you well know where we may encamp in the wilderness, you must serve as eyes for us. 32 And it must occur that in case you should come with us, yes, it must occur that with what goodness Jehovah will do good with us, we, in turn, will do good to you."

33 So they went marching from the mountain of Jehovah for a journey of three days, and the ark of Jehovah's covenant was marching before them for a journey of three days to search out a resting place for them. 34 And Jehovah's cloud was over them by day at their marching out from the encampment.

35 And it would occur that when the Ark would set out, Moses would say: "Do arise, O Jehovah, and let your enemies be scattered; and let those who intensely hate you flee from before you." 36 And when it would rest, he would say: "Do return, O Jehovah, to the myriads of thousands of Israel."

11 Now the people became as men having something evil to complain about in the ears of Jehovah. When Jehovah got to hear it, then his anger grew hot, and a fire of Jehovah began to blaze against them and to consume some in the

extremity of the camp. 2 When the people began to cry out to Moses, then he made supplication to Jehovah, and the fire sank down. 3 And the name of that place got to be called Tab′e·rah, because a fire of Jehovah had blazed against them.

4 And the mixed crowd that was in the midst of them expressed selfish longing, and the sons of Israel too began to weep again and say: "Who will give us meat to eat? 5 How we remember the fish that we used to eat in Egypt for nothing, the cucumbers and the watermelons and the leeks and the onions and the garlic! 6 But now our soul is dried away. Our eyes are on nothing at all except the manna."

7 Incidentally, the manna was like coriander seed, and its look was like the look of bdellium gum. 8 The people spread out and picked it up and ground it in hand mills or pounded it in a mortar, and they boiled it in cooking pots or made it into round cakes, and its taste proved to be like the taste of an oiled sweet cake. 9 And when the dew descended upon the camp by night, the manna would descend upon it.

10 And Moses got to hear the people weeping in their families, each man at the entrance of his tent. And Jehovah's anger began growing very hot, and in the eyes of Moses it was bad. 11 Then Moses said to Jehovah: "Why have you caused evil to your servant, and why have I not found favor in your eyes, in placing the load of all this people upon me? 12 Have I myself conceived all this people? Is it I who have given them birth, so that you should say to me, 'Carry them in your bosom, just as the male nurse carries the suckling,' to the soil about which you swore to their forefathers? 13 From where do I have meat to give to all this people? For they keep weeping toward me, saying, 'Do give us meat, and let us eat!' 14 I am not able, I by myself, to carry all this people, because they

are too heavy for me. 15 So if this is the way you are doing to me, please kill me off altogether, if I have found favor in your eyes, and let me not look upon my calamity."

16 In turn Jehovah said to Moses: "Gather for me seventy men of the older men of Israel, whom you do know that they are older men of the people and officers of theirs, and you must take them to the tent of meeting, and they must station themselves there with you. 17 And I shall have to come down and speak with you there; and I shall have to take away some of the spirit that is upon you and place it upon them, and they will have to help you in carrying the load of the people that you may not carry it, just you alone. 18 And to the people you should say, 'Sanctify yourselves for tomorrow, as YOU will certainly eat meat, because YOU have wept in the ears of Jehovah, saying: "Who will give us meat to eat, for it was well with us in Egypt?" And Jehovah will certainly give YOU meat, and YOU will indeed eat. 19 YOU will eat, not one day nor two days nor five days nor ten days nor twenty days, 20 but up to a month of days, until it comes out of YOUR nostrils and it has become a loathing to YOU, just because YOU rejected Jehovah, who is in YOUR midst, and YOU went weeping before him, saying: "Why is it that we have come out of Egypt?" '"

21 Then Moses said: "The people in the midst of whom I am are six hundred thousand men on foot, and yet you—you have said, 'Meat I shall give them, and they will certainly eat for a month of days'! 22 Will flocks and herds be slaughtered for them, for it to be adequate for them? Or will all the fish of the sea be caught for them, for it to be adequate for them?"

23 At this Jehovah said to Moses: "The hand of Jehovah is cut short, is it? Now you will see whether what I say befalls you or not."

24 After that Moses went out and spoke to the people the words of Jehovah. And he went gathering

seventy men from the older men of the people and proceeded to have them stand round about the tent. 25 Then Jehovah came down in a cloud and spoke to him and took away some of the spirit that was upon him and put it upon each of the seventy older men. And it came about that as soon as the spirit settled down upon them, then they proceeded to act as prophets; but they did not do it again.

26 Now there were two of the men remaining in the camp. The name of the one was El′dad, and the name of the other was Me′dad. And the spirit began to settle down upon them, as they were among those written down, but they had not gone out to the tent. So they proceeded to act as prophets in the camp. 27 And a young man went running and reporting to Moses and saying: "El′dad and Me′dad are acting as prophets in the camp!" 28 Then Joshua the son of Nun, the minister of Moses from his young manhood on, responded and said: "My lord Moses, restrain them!" 29 However, Moses said to him: "Are you feeling jealous for me? No, I wish that all of Jehovah's people were prophets, because Jehovah would put his spirit upon them!" 30 Later Moses withdrew to the camp, he and the older men of Israel.

31 And a wind burst forth from Jehovah and began driving quails from the sea and letting them fall above the camp about a day's journey this way and about a day's journey that way, all around the camp, and about two cubits above the surface of the earth. 32 Then the people got up all that day and all night and all the next day and kept gathering the quail. The one collecting least gathered ten homers, and they kept spreading them extensively all around the camp for themselves. 33 The meat was yet between their teeth, before it could be chewed, when Jehovah's anger blazed against the people, and Jehovah began striking at the people with a very great slaughter.

34 The name of that place came to be called Kib′roth-hat·ta′a·vah, because there they buried the people who showed selfish craving. 35 From Kib′roth-hat·ta′a·vah the people pulled away for Ha·ze′roth, and they continued in Ha·ze′roth.

12 Now Mir′i·am and Aaron began to speak against Moses on account of the Cush′ite wife whom he had taken, because it was a Cush′ite wife he had taken. 2 And they kept saying: "Is it just by Moses alone that Jehovah has spoken? Is it not by us also that he has spoken?" And Jehovah was listening. 3 And the man Moses was by far the meekest of all the men who were upon the surface of the ground.

4 Then Jehovah suddenly said to Moses and Aaron and Mir′i·am: "Go out, the three of you, to the tent of meeting." So the three of them went out. 5 After that Jehovah came down in the pillar of cloud and stood at the entrance of the tent and called Aaron and Mir′i·am. At this both of them went out. 6 And he went on to say: "Hear my words, please. If there came to be a prophet of yours for Jehovah, it would be in a vision I would make myself known to him. In a dream I would speak to him. 7 Not so my servant Moses! He is being entrusted with all my house. 8 Mouth to mouth I speak to him, thus showing him, and not by riddles; and the appearance of Jehovah is what he beholds. Why, then, did you not fear to speak against my servant, against Moses?"

9 And Jehovah's anger got to be hot against them, and he went his way. 10 And the cloud turned away from over the tent, and, look! Mir′i·am was struck with leprosy as white as snow. Then Aaron turned toward Mir′i·am, and, look! she was struck with leprosy. 11 Immediately Aaron said to Moses: "Excuse me, my lord! Do not, please, attribute to us the sin in which we have acted foolishly and which we have committed! 12 Please, do not let her continue like someone dead, whose flesh at

the time of his coming out of his mother's womb is half eaten off!" 13 And Moses began to cry out to Jehovah, saying: "O God, please! Heal her, please!"

14 Then Jehovah said to Moses: "Were her father to spit directly in her face, would she not be humiliated seven days? Let her be quarantined seven days outside the camp, and afterward let her be received in." 15 Accordingly Mir′i-am was quarantined outside the camp seven days, and the people did not pull away until Mir′i-am was received in. 16 And afterward the people pulled away from Ha-ze′roth and took up camping in the wilderness of Pa′ran.

13 Jehovah now spoke to Moses, saying: 2 "Send out for yourself men that they may spy out the land of Ca′naan, which I am giving to the sons of Israel. You will send out one man for each tribe of his fathers, each one a chieftain among them."

3 So Moses sent them out from the wilderness of Pa′ran at the order of Jehovah. All the men were heads of the sons of Israel. 4 And these are their names: Of the tribe of Reu′ben, Sham·mu′a the son of Zac′cur; 5 of the tribe of Sim′e·on, Sha′phat the son of Ho′ri; 6 of the tribe of Judah, Ca′leb the son of Je·phun′neh; 7 of the tribe of Is′sa·char, I′gal the son of Joseph; 8 of the tribe of E′phra·im, Ho·she′a the son of Nun; 9 of the tribe of Benjamin, Pal′ti the son of Ra′phu; 10 of the tribe of Zeb′u·lun, Gad′-di·el the son of So′di; 11 of the tribe of Joseph, for the tribe of Ma·nas′seh, Gad′di the son of Su′-si; 12 of the tribe of Dan, Am′mi-el the son of Ge·mal′li; 13 of the tribe of Ash′er, Se′thur the son of Mi′cha·el; 14 of the tribe of Naph′ta·li, Nah′bi the son of Voph′-si; 15 of the tribe of Gad, Geu′el the son of Ma′chi. 16 These are the names of the men whom Moses sent to spy out the land. And Moses continued to call Ho·she′a the son of Nun Je·hosh′u·a.

17 When Moses was sending them to spy out the land of Ca′naan, he proceeded to say to them: "Go up here into the Neg′eb, and you must go up into the mountainous region. 18 And you must see what the land is and the people who are dwelling on it, whether they are strong or weak, whether they are few or many; 19 and what the land is in which they are dwelling, whether it is good or bad, and what the cities are in which they are dwelling, whether it is in encampments or in fortifications; 20 and what the land is, whether it is fat or lean, whether there are trees in it or not. And you must show yourselves courageous and take some of the fruitage of the land." Now the days were the days of the first ripe fruits of the grapes.

21 So they went up and spied out the land from the wilderness of Zin to Re′hob to the entering in of Ha′math. 22 When they went up into the Neg′eb, they then came to He′bron. Now A·hi′man, She′shai and Tal′mai, those born of A′nak, were there. Incidentally, He′bron had been built seven years before Zo′an of Egypt. 23 When they came to the torrent valley of Esh′-col, they then proceeded to cut down from there a shoot with one cluster of grapes. And they went carrying it with a bar on two of the men, and also some of the pomegranates and some of the figs. 24 They called that place the torrent valley of Esh′col, on account of the cluster that the sons of Israel cut down from there.

25 Finally at the end of forty days they returned from spying out the land. 26 So they walked and came to Moses and Aaron and all the assembly of the sons of Israel in the wilderness of Pa′ran, at Ka′-desh. And they came bringing back word to them and all the assembly and showing them the fruitage of the land. 27 And they went on to report to him and say: "We entered into the land to which you sent us out, and it is indeed flowing with milk and honey, and this is its fruitage. 28 Nevertheless, the facts are that the people who dwell

in the land are strong, and the fortified cities are very great; and, too, those born of A'nak we saw there. 29 The A·mal'ek·ites are dwelling in the land of the Neg'eb, and the Hit'tites and the Jeb'u·sites and the Am'or·ites are dwelling in the mountainous region, and the Ca'naan·ites are dwelling by the sea and by the side of the Jordan."

30 Then Ca'leb tried to still the people toward Moses and went on to say: "Let us go up directly, and we are bound to take possession of it, because we can surely prevail over it." 31 But the men who went up with him said: "We are not able to go up against the people, because they are stronger than we are." 32 And they kept on bringing forth to the sons of Israel a bad report of the land that they had spied out, saying: "The land, which we passed through to spy it out, is a land that eats up its inhabitants; and all the people whom we saw in the midst of it are men of extraordinary size. 33 And there we saw the Neph'i·lim, the sons of A'nak, who are from the Neph'i·lim; so that we became in our own eyes like grasshoppers, and the same way we became in their eyes."

14 Then all the assembly raised their voice, and the people continued giving vent to their voice and weeping all through that night. 2 And all the sons of Israel began to murmur against Moses and Aaron, and all the assembly began to say against them: "If only we had died in the land of Egypt, or if only we had died in this wilderness! 3 And why is Jehovah bringing us to this land to fall by the sword? Our wives and our little ones will become plunder. Is it not better for us to return to Egypt?" 4 They even went to saying to one another: "Let us appoint a head, and let us return to Egypt!"

5 At this Moses and Aaron fell upon their faces before all the congregation of the assembly of the sons of Israel. 6 And Joshua the son of Nun and Ca'leb the son of Je·phun'neh, who were of those who spied out the land, ripped their garments apart, 7 and they proceeded to say this to all the assembly of the sons of Israel: "The land that we passed through to spy it out is a very, very good land. 8 If Jehovah has found delight in us, then he will certainly bring us into this land and give it to us, a land that is flowing with milk and honey. 9 Only against Jehovah do not rebel; and you, do not you fear the people of the land, for they are bread to us. Their shelter has turned away from over them, and Jehovah is with us. Do not fear them."

10 However, all the assembly talked of pelting them with stones. And Jehovah's glory appeared on the tent of meeting to all the sons of Israel.

11 Finally Jehovah said to Moses: "How long will this people treat me without respect, and how long will they not put faith in me for all the signs that I performed in among them? 12 Let me strike them with pestilence and drive them away, and let me make you a nation greater and mightier than they are."

13 But Moses said to Jehovah: "Then the Egyptians will be bound to hear that you by your power have led this people up out of their midst. 14 And they will be bound to tell it to the inhabitants of this land. They have heard that you are Jehovah in among this people, who has appeared face to face. You are Jehovah, and your cloud is standing over them, and you are going before them in the pillar of cloud by day and in the pillar of fire by night. 15 Were you to put this people to death as one man, then the nations who have heard of your fame would certainly say this, 16 'Because of Jehovah's not being able to bring this people into the land about which he swore to them he proceeded to slaughter them in the wilderness.' 17 And now, please, let your power become great, O Jehovah, just as you have spoken, saying, 18 'Jehovah, slow to anger and abundant in loving-

kindness, pardoning error and transgression, but by no means will he give exemption from punishment, bringing punishment for the error of the fathers upon sons, upon the third generation and upon the fourth generation.' 19 Forgive, please, the error of this people according to the greatness of your loving-kindness, and just as you have pardoned this people from Egypt onward until now."

20 Then Jehovah said: "I do forgive according to your word. 21 And, on the other hand, as I live, all the earth will be filled with the glory of Jehovah. 22 But all the men who have been seeing my glory and my signs that I have performed in Egypt and in the wilderness and yet kept testing me these ten times, and have not listened to my voice, 23 will never see the land about which I swore to their fathers, yes, all those treating me without respect will not see it. 24 As for my servant Ca′leb, because a different spirit has proved to be with him and he kept following wholly after me, I shall certainly bring him into the land where he has gone, and his offspring will take possession of it. 25 While the A·mal′ek·ites and the Ca′naan·ites are dwelling in the low plain, you people make a turn tomorrow and pull away to march to the wilderness by way of the Red Sea."

26 And Jehovah went on to speak to Moses and Aaron, saying: 27 "How long will this evil assembly have this murmuring that they are carrying on against me? I have heard the murmurings of the sons of Israel that they are murmuring against me. 28 Say to them, ' "As I live," is the utterance of Jehovah, "if I shall not do to you just that way as you have spoken in my ears! 29 In this wilderness your carcasses will fall, yes, all your registered ones of all your number from twenty years old upward, you who have murmured against me. 30 As for you, you will not enter into the land in which I lifted up my hand [in oath] to reside with you, except

Ca′leb the son of Je·phun′neh and Joshua the son of Nun.

31 "'"And your little ones who you said would become plunder, these also I shall certainly bring in, and they will indeed know the land that you have rejected. 32 But the carcasses of you yourselves will fall in this wilderness. 33 And your sons will become shepherds in the wilderness forty years, and they will have to answer for your acts of fornication, until your carcasses come to their end in the wilderness. 34 By the number of the days that you spied out the land, forty days, a day for a year, a day for a year, you will answer for your errors forty years, as you must know what my being estranged means.

35 "'"I Jehovah have spoken if this is not what I shall do to all this evil assembly, those who have gathered together against me: In this wilderness they will come to their end, and there they will die. 36 And the men whom Moses sent to spy out the land and who, when they returned, began making the whole assembly murmur against him, by bringing forth a bad report against the land, 37 yes, the men bringing forth the bad report about the land will die by the scourge before Jehovah. 38 But Joshua the son of Nun and Ca′leb the son of Je·phun′neh will certainly live on, of those men who went to spy out the land."'"

39 When Moses proceeded to speak these words to all the sons of Israel, then the people began to mourn a great deal. 40 Moreover, they got up early in the morning and tried to go up to the top of the mountain, saying: "Here we are, and we have to go up to the place that Jehovah mentioned. For we have sinned." 41 But Moses said: "Why is it that you are passing beyond the order of Jehovah? But that will not succeed. 42 Do not go up, because Jehovah is not in your midst, that you may not be defeated before your enemies. 43 For the A·mal′ek·ites and the Ca′naan·ites are there before you;

and you are certain to fall by the sword, because, for the reason that you turned back from following Jehovah, Jehovah will not continue with you."

44 However, they presumed to go up to the top of the mountain, but the ark of Jehovah's covenant and Moses did not move away from the midst of the camp. 45 Then the A·mal′ek·ites and the Ca′naan·ites who were dwelling in that mountain came on down and began striking them and went scattering them as far as Hor′mah.

15 And Jehovah spoke further to Moses, saying: 2 "Speak to the sons of Israel, and you must say to them, 'When you eventually come into the land of your dwelling places, which I am giving you, 3 and you must render up an offering made by fire to Jehovah, a burnt offering or a sacrifice to perform a special vow or voluntarily or during your seasonal festivals, in order to make a restful odor to Jehovah, from the herd or from the flock; 4 the one presenting his offering must also present to Jehovah a grain offering of fine flour, a tenth of an e′phah, moistened with a fourth of a hin of oil. 5 And you should render up wine as a drink offering, the fourth of a hin, together with the burnt offering or for the sacrifice of each male lamb. 6 Or for a ram you should render up a grain offering of two tenths of fine flour, moistened with a third of a hin of oil. 7 And you should present wine as a drink offering, a third of a hin, as a restful odor to Jehovah.

8 "'But in case you should render up a male of the herd as a burnt offering or a sacrifice to perform a special vow or communion sacrifices to Jehovah, 9 one must also present together with the male of the herd a grain offering of three tenths of fine flour, moistened with half a hin of oil. 10 And you should present wine as a drink offering, half a hin, as an offering made by fire, of a restful odor to Jehovah. 11 This is the way it should be done for each bull or for each ram or for one head among the male lambs or among the goats. 12 Whatever may be the number that you may render up, that is the way you should do for each one according to the number of them. 13 Every native should render up these in this way in presenting an offering made by fire, of a restful odor to Jehovah.

14 "'And in case there should be residing as an alien with you an alien resident or one who is in your midst for generations of you, and he must render up an offering made by fire, of a restful odor to Jehovah, just as you should do, so he should do. 15 You who are of the congregation and the alien resident who is residing as an alien will have one statute. It will be a statute to time indefinite for your generations. The alien resident should prove to be the same as you before Jehovah. 16 There should prove to be one law and one judicial decision for you and for the alien resident who is residing as an alien with you.'"

17 And Jehovah went on to speak to Moses, saying: 18 "Speak to the sons of Israel, and you must say to them, 'On your coming into the land where I am bringing you, 19 it must also occur that when you eat any of the bread of the land, you should make a contribution to Jehovah. 20 You should make a contribution of the first fruits of your coarse meal as ring-shaped cakes. Like the contribution of a threshing floor is the way you should contribute it. 21 Some of the first fruits of your coarse meal you should give as a contribution to Jehovah throughout your generations.

22 "'Now in case you should make a mistake and not do all these commandments, which Jehovah has spoken to Moses, 23 all that Jehovah has commanded you by means of Moses from the day that Jehovah commanded and onward for your generations, 24 it must then occur that if it has been done far from the eyes of the assembly by mistake, the whole as-

sembly must then render up one young bull as a burnt offering for a restful odor to Jehovah, and its grain offering and its drink offering according to the regular procedure, and one kid of the goats as a sin offering. 25 And the priest must make atonement for the whole assembly of the sons of Israel, and it must be forgiven them; because it was a mistake, and they, for their part, brought as their offering an offering made by fire to Jehovah and their sin offering before Jehovah for their mistake. 26 And it must be forgiven the whole assembly of the sons of Israel and the alien resident who is residing as an alien in their midst, because it was by mistake on the part of all the people.

27 "'And if any soul should sin by mistake, then he must present a female goat in its first year for a sin offering. 28 And the priest must make atonement for the soul who made a mistake by a sin unintentionally before Jehovah, so as to make atonement for it, and it must be forgiven him. 29 As to the native among the sons of Israel and the alien resident who is residing as an alien in their midst, there should prove to be one law for YOU as respects doing something unintentionally.

30 "'But the soul that does something deliberately, whether he is a native or an alien resident, he speaking abusively of Jehovah, in that case that soul must be cut off from among his people. 31 Because it is Jehovah's word that he has despised and his commandment that he has broken, that soul should be cut off without fail. His own error is upon him.'"

32 While the sons of Israel were continuing in the wilderness, they once found a man collecting pieces of wood on the sabbath day. 33 Then those who found him collecting pieces of wood brought him up to Moses and Aaron and the whole assembly. 34 So they committed him into custody, because it had not been distinctly stated what should be done to him.

35 In time Jehovah said to Moses: "Without fail the man should be put to death, the whole assembly pelting him with stones outside the camp." 36 Accordingly the whole assembly brought him forth outside the camp and pelted him with stones so that he died, just as Jehovah had commanded Moses.

37 And Jehovah went on to say this to Moses: 38 "Speak to the sons of Israel, and you must say to them that they must make for themselves fringed edges upon the skirts of their garments throughout their generations, and they must put a blue string above the fringed edge of the skirt, 39 'And it must serve as a fringed edge for YOU, and YOU must see it and remember all the commandments of Jehovah and do them, and YOU must not go about following YOUR hearts and YOUR eyes, which YOU are following in immoral intercourse. 40 The purpose is that YOU may remember and may certainly do all my commandments and indeed prove to be holy to YOUR God. 41 I am Jehovah YOUR God, who have brought YOU out of the land of Egypt in order to prove myself YOUR God. I am Jehovah YOUR God.'"

16 And Ko'rah the son of Iz'har, the son of Ko'hath, the son of Le'vi, proceeded to get up, together with Da'than and A·bi'ram the sons of E·li'ab, and On the son of Pe'leth, the sons of Reu'ben. 2 And they proceeded to rise up before Moses, they and two hundred and fifty men of the sons of Israel, chieftains of the assembly, summoned ones of the meeting, men of fame. 3 So they congregated themselves against Moses and Aaron and said to them: "That is enough of YOU, because the whole assembly are all of them holy and Jehovah is in their midst. Why, then, should YOU lift yourselves up above the congregation of Jehovah?"

4 When Moses got to hear it he at once fell upon his face. 5 Then he spoke to Ko'rah and to his entire assembly, saying: "In the

morning Jehovah will make known who belongs to him and who is holy and who must come near to him, and whoever he may choose will come near to him. 6 Do this: Take fire holders for yourselves, Ko'rah and his entire assembly, 7 and put fire in them and place incense upon them before Jehovah tomorrow, and it must occur that the man whom Jehovah will choose, he is the holy one. That is enough of YOU, YOU sons of Le'vi!"

8 And Moses went on to say to Ko'rah: "Listen, please, YOU sons of Le'vi. 9 Is it such a little thing for YOU men that the God of Israel has separated YOU men from the assembly of Israel to present YOU to himself to carry on the service of Jehovah's tabernacle and to stand before the assembly to minister to them, 10 and that he should bring you and all your brothers the sons of Le'vi with you near? So must YOU men also try to secure the priesthood? 11 For that reason you and all your assembly who are gathering together are against Jehovah. As for Aaron, what is he that YOU men should murmur against him?"

12 Later Moses sent to call Da'than and A·bi'ram the sons of E·li'ab, but they said: "We are not going to come up! 13 Is it so little a thing that you have brought us up out of a land flowing with milk and honey to put us to death in the wilderness, that you should also try to play the prince over us to the limit? 14 As it is, you have not brought us into any land flowing with milk and honey, that you may give us an inheritance of field and vineyard. Is it the eyes of those men that you want to bore out? We are not going to come up!"

15 At this Moses became very angry and said to Jehovah: "Do not turn to look at their grain offering. Not one male ass have I taken away from them, nor have I harmed one of them."

16 Then Moses said to Ko'rah: "You and all your assembly, be present before Jehovah, you and they and Aaron, tomorrow. 17 And

take each one his fire holder, and YOU men must put incense upon them and present each one his fire holder before Jehovah, two hundred and fifty fire holders, and you and Aaron each his fire holder." 18 So they took each one his fire holder and put fire upon them and placed incense upon them and stood at the entrance of the tent of meeting together with Moses and Aaron. 19 When Ko'rah got all the assembly together against them at the entrance of the tent of meeting, then Jehovah's glory appeared to all the assembly.

20 Jehovah now spoke to Moses and Aaron, saying: 21 "Separate yourselves from the midst of this assembly, that I may exterminate them in an instant." 22 At this they fell upon their faces and said: "O God, the God of the spirits of every sort of flesh, will just one man sin and you become indignant against the entire assembly?"

23 In turn Jehovah spoke to Moses, saying: 24 "Speak to the assembly, saying, 'Get away from around the tabernacles of Ko'rah, Da'than and A·bi'ram!'"

25 After that Moses got up and went to Da'than and A·bi'ram, and the older men of Israel went with him. 26 Then he spoke to the assembly, saying: "Turn aside, please, from before the tents of these wicked men and do not touch anything that belongs to them, that YOU may not be swept away in all their sin." 27 Immediately they got away from before the tabernacle of Ko'rah, Da'than and A·bi'ram, from every side, and Da'than and A·bi'ram came out, taking their stand at the entrance of their tents, together with their wives, and their sons and their little ones.

28 Then Moses said: "By this YOU will know that Jehovah has sent me to do all these deeds, that it is not of my own heart: 29 If it is according to the death of all mankind that these people will die and with the punishment of all mankind that punishment will be brought upon them, then it is not

Jehovah that has sent me. 30 But if it is something created that Jehovah will create, and the ground has to open its mouth and swallow up them and everything that belongs to them and they have to go down alive into She′ol, you will then know for certain that these men have treated Jehovah disrespectfully."

31 And it came about that as soon as he had finished speaking all these words, the ground that was under them began to be split apart. 32 And the earth proceeded to open its mouth and to swallow up them and their households and all humankind that belonged to Ko′rah and all the goods. 33 So down they went, and all who belonged to them, alive into She′ol, and the earth went covering them over, so that they perished from the midst of the congregation. 34 And all the Israelites who were round about them fled at the screaming of them, for they began to say: "We are afraid that the earth may swallow us up!" 35 And a fire came out from Jehovah and proceeded to consume the two hundred and fifty men offering the incense.

36 Jehovah now spoke to Moses, saying: 37 "Say to E·le·a′zar the son of Aaron the priest that he should take up the fire holders from within the conflagration, 'And you scatter the fire over there; for they are holy, 38 even the fire holders of these men who sinned against their own souls. And they must make them into thin metal plates as an overlaying for the altar, because they presented them before Jehovah, so that they became holy; and they should serve as a sign to the sons of Israel.' " 39 Accordingly E·le·a′zar the priest took the copper fire holders, which those who had been burned up had presented, and they proceeded to beat them out into an overlaying for the altar, 40 as a memorial for the sons of Israel, to the end that no strange man who is not of the offspring of Aaron should come near to make incense smoke

before Jehovah, and no one might become like Ko′rah and his assembly, just as Jehovah had spoken to him by means of Moses.

41 And directly the next day the whole assembly of the sons of Israel began to murmur against Moses and Aaron, saying: "You men, you have put Jehovah's people to death." 42 And it came about that when the assembly had congregated themselves together against Moses and Aaron, they then turned toward the tent of meeting; and, look! the cloud covered it, and Jehovah's glory began to appear.

43 And Moses and Aaron proceeded to come before the tent of meeting. 44 Then Jehovah spoke to Moses, saying: 45 "You men, rise up from the midst of this assembly, that I may exterminate them in an instant." At this they fell upon their faces. 46 After that Moses said to Aaron: "Take the fire holder and put fire from upon the altar in it and put on incense and go to the assembly in a hurry and make atonement for them, because the indignation has gone out from the face of Jehovah. The plague has started!" 47 Aaron at once took it, just as Moses had spoken, and went running into the midst of the congregation; and, look! the plague had started among the people. So he put the incense on and began making atonement for the people. 48 And he kept standing between the dead and the living. Eventually the scourge was stopped. 49 And those dead from the scourge amounted to fourteen thousand seven hundred, aside from those dead on account of Ko′rah. 50 When at last Aaron returned to Moses at the entrance of the tent of meeting, the scourge had been stopped.

17 Jehovah now spoke to Moses, saying: 2 "Speak to the sons of Israel and take from them one rod for each paternal house from all their chieftains, by the house of their fathers, twelve rods. You will write the name of each one upon his rod. 3 And Aaron's name you will write upon Le′vi's rod, because there is one rod for the head of the house of their fathers. 4 And you must deposit them in the tent of meeting before the Testimony, where I regularly present myself to you. 5 And what must occur is that the man whom I shall choose, his rod will bud, and I shall certainly make subside from against me the murmurings of the sons of Israel, which they are murmuring against you."

6 So Moses spoke to the sons of Israel, and all their chieftains went giving him a rod for each chieftain, a rod for each chieftain, by the house of their fathers, twelve rods; and Aaron's rod was in among their rods. 7 Then Moses deposited the rods before Jehovah in the tent of the Testimony.

8 And it came about the next day that when Moses went into the tent of the Testimony, look! Aaron's rod for the house of Le'vi had budded, and it was bringing forth buds and blossoming flowers and was bearing ripe almonds. 9 Moses then brought out all the rods from before Jehovah to all the sons of Israel, and they went looking and taking each man his own rod.

10 Subsequently Jehovah said to Moses: "Put Aaron's rod back before the Testimony as something to be kept for a sign to the sons of rebelliousness, that their murmurings may cease from against me, that they may not die." 11 At once Moses did just as Jehovah had commanded him. He did just so.

12 And the sons of Israel began to say this to Moses: "Now we are bound to expire, we are bound to perish, we are all of us bound to perish. 13 Anyone approaching, coming near to Jehovah's tabernacle, will die! Must we end up in expiring that way?"

18 And Jehovah proceeded to say to Aaron: "You and your sons and the house of your father with you will answer for error against the sanctuary, and you and your sons with you will answer for error against your priesthood. 2 And bring near, also, your brothers of the tribe of Le'vi, the clan of your father, with you, that they may be joined to you and may minister to you, to both you and your sons with you, before the tent of the Testimony. 3 And they must keep their obligation to you and their obligation to the entire tent. Only to the utensils of the holy place and to the altar they must not come near that they may not die, neither they nor you men. 4 And they must be joined to you and must keep their obligation to the tent of meeting as respects all the service of the tent, and no stranger may come near to you men. 5 And you must keep your obligation to the holy place and your obligation to the altar, that no further indignation may occur against the sons of Israel. 6 And I, look! I have taken your brothers, the Levites, from among the sons of Israel, as a gift for you, as those given to Jehovah to carry on the service of the tent of meeting. 7 And you and your sons with you should safeguard your priesthood as regards every concern of the altar and as regards what is inside the curtain; and you men must render service. As a service of gift I shall give your priesthood, and the stranger drawing near should be put to death."

8 And Jehovah spoke further to Aaron: "As for me, look! I have given you the custody of the contributions made to me. Of all the holy things of the sons of Israel I have given them to you and to your sons as a portion, as an allowance to time indefinite. 9 This should become yours out of the most holy things, out of the offering made by fire, every offering of theirs together with every grain offering of theirs and every sin offering of theirs and every guilt offering of theirs, which they will return to me. It is something most holy for you and for your sons. 10 In a most holy place you should eat it. Every male should eat it. It should become something holy to you. 11 And this belongs to you: the contribution of their gift together with all the wave offerings of the

sons of Israel. I have given them to you and your sons and your daughters with you, as an allowance to time indefinite. Everyone clean in your house may eat it.

12 "All the best of the oil and all the best of the new wine and the grain, their first fruits, which they will give to Jehovah, I have given them to you. 13 The first ripe fruits of all that is on their land, which they will bring to Jehovah, yours it should become. Everyone clean in your house may eat it.

14 "Every devoted thing in Israel should become yours.

15 "Everything opening the womb, of every sort of flesh, which they will present to Jehovah, among man and among beast, should become yours. However, you should without fail redeem the first-born of mankind; and the first-born of the unclean beast you should redeem. 16 And with a redemption price for it from a month old onward you should redeem it, by the estimated value, five silver shekels by the shekel of the holy place. It is twenty ge'rahs. 17 Only the first-born bull or first-born male lamb or first-born goat you should not redeem. They are something holy. Their blood you should sprinkle upon the altar, and their fat you should make smoke as an offering made by fire for a restful odor to Jehovah. 18 And their flesh should become yours. Like the breast of the wave offering and like the right leg, it should become yours. 19 All the holy contributions, which the sons of Israel will contribute to Jehovah, I have given to you and your sons and your daughters with you, as an allowance to time indefinite. It is a covenant of salt before Jehovah for you and your offspring with you."

20 And Jehovah went on to say to Aaron: "In their land you will not have an inheritance, and no share will become yours in their midst. I am your share and your inheritance in the midst of the sons of Israel.

21 "And to the sons of Le'vi, look! I have given every tenth part in Israel as an inheritance in return for their service that they are carrying on, the service of the tent of meeting. 22 And the sons of Israel should no more come near to the tent of meeting to incur sin so as to die. 23 And the Levites themselves must carry on the service of the tent of meeting, and they are the ones who should answer for their error. It is a statute to time indefinite during YOUR generations that in the midst of the sons of Israel they should not get possession of an inheritance. 24 For the tenth part of the sons of Israel, which they will contribute to Jehovah as a contribution, I have given to the Levites as an inheritance. That is why I have said to them, 'In the midst of the sons of Israel they should not get possession of an inheritance.'"

25 Then Jehovah spoke to Moses, saying: 26 "And you should speak to the Levites, and you must say to them, 'You will receive from the sons of Israel the tenth part that I have given to YOU from them for YOUR inheritance, and YOU must contribute from it as a contribution to Jehovah a tenth part of the tenth part. 27 And it must be reckoned to YOU as YOUR contribution, like the grain of the threshing floor and like the full produce of the wine or oil press. 28 In this way YOU yourselves also will contribute a contribution to Jehovah from all YOUR tenth parts that YOU will receive from the sons of Israel, and from them YOU must give the contribution to Jehovah to Aaron the priest. 29 From all the gifts to YOU, YOU will contribute every sort of contribution to Jehovah, of the very best of it, as some holy thing from them.'

30 "And you must say to them, 'When YOU contribute the best of them, then it will certainly be reckoned to the Levites as the produce of the threshing floor and as the produce of the wine or oil press. 31 And YOU must eat it in every place, YOU and YOUR household, because it is YOUR wages in return

for YOUR service in the tent of meeting. 32 And YOU must not incur sin for it when YOU contribute the best from them, and YOU must not profane the holy things of the sons of Israel, that YOU may not die.'"

19 And Jehovah proceeded to speak to Moses and Aaron, saying: 2 "This is a statute of the law that Jehovah has commanded, saying, 'Speak to the sons of Israel that they should take for you a sound red cow in which there is no defect and upon which no yoke has come. 3 And YOU must give it to E·le·a′zar the priest, and he must lead it forth outside the camp, and it must be slaughtered before him. 4 Then E·le·a′zar the priest must take some of its blood with his finger and spatter some of its blood straight toward the front of the tent of meeting seven times. 5 And the cow must be burned under his eyes. Its skin and its flesh and its blood together with its dung must be burned. 6 And the priest must take cedar wood and hyssop and coccus scarlet material and throw it into the midst of the burning of the cow. 7 And the priest must wash his garments and bathe his flesh in water, and afterward he may come into the camp; but the priest must be unclean until the evening.

8 "'And the one who burned it will wash his garments in water and must bathe his flesh in water, and he must be unclean until the evening.

9 "'And a clean man must gather up the ashes of the cow and deposit them outside the camp in a clean place; and they must serve the assembly of the sons of Israel as something to be kept for the water for cleansing. It is a sin offering. 10 And the one gathering the ashes of the cow must wash his garments and be unclean until the evening.

"'And it must serve the sons of Israel and the alien resident who is residing as an alien in their midst as a statute to time indefinite. 11 Anyone touching the corpse of any human soul must also be unclean seven days. 12 Such one should purify himself with it on the third day, and on the seventh day he will be clean. But if he will not purify himself on the third day, then on the seventh day he will not be clean. 13 Everyone touching a corpse, the soul of whatever man may die, and who will not purify himself, has defiled Jehovah's tabernacle, and that soul must be cut off from Israel. Because the water for cleansing has not been sprinkled upon him, he continues unclean. His uncleanness is still upon him.

14 "'This is the law in case a man should die in a tent: Everyone coming into the tent, and everyone who is in the tent, will be unclean seven days. 15 And every opened vessel upon which there is no lid tied down is unclean. 16 And everyone who on the open field may touch someone slain with the sword or a corpse or a bone of a man or a burial place will be unclean seven days. 17 And they must take for the unclean one some of the dust of the burning of the sin offering and put running water upon it in a vessel. 18 Then a clean man must take hyssop and dip it into the water and spatter it upon the tent and all the vessels and the souls that happened to be there and upon the one who touched the bone or the slain one or the corpse or the burial place. 19 And the clean person must spatter it upon the unclean one on the third day and on the seventh day and must purify him from sin on the seventh day; and he must wash his garments and bathe in water, and he must be clean in the evening.

20 "'But the man who may be unclean and who will not purify himself, well, that soul must be cut off from the midst of the congregation, because it is Jehovah's sanctuary that he has defiled. The water for cleansing was not sprinkled upon him. He is unclean.

21 "'And it must serve as a statute to time indefinite for them, that the one spattering the water

for cleansing should wash his garments, also the one touching the water for cleansing. He will be unclean until the evening. 22 And anything the unclean one may touch will be unclean, and the soul who touches it will be unclean until the evening.'"

20 And the sons of Israel, the entire assembly, proceeded to come into the wilderness of Zin in the first month, and the people took up dwelling in Ka'desh. It was there that Mir'i·am died and there that she was buried.

2 Now there proved to be no water for the assembly, and they began to congregate themselves against Moses and Aaron. 3 And the people went quarreling with Moses and saying: "If only we had expired when our brothers expired before Jehovah! 4 And why have YOU men brought Jehovah's congregation into this wilderness for us and our beasts of burden to die there? 5 And why have you conducted us up out of Egypt to bring us into this evil place? It is no place of seed and figs and vines and pomegranates, and there is no water to drink." 6 Then Moses and Aaron came from before the congregation to the entrance of the tent of meeting and fell upon their faces, and Jehovah's glory began to appear to them.

7 Then Jehovah spoke to Moses, saying: 8 "Take the rod and call the assembly together, you and Aaron your brother, and YOU must speak to the crag before their eyes that it may indeed give its water; and you must bring out water for them from the crag and give the assembly and their beasts of burden drink."

9 So Moses took the rod from before Jehovah, just as he had commanded him. 10 After that Moses and Aaron called the congregation together before the crag, and he proceeded to say to them: "Hear, now, YOU rebels! Is it from this crag that we shall bring out water for YOU?" 11 With that Moses lifted his hand up and struck the crag with his rod twice; and much

water began to come out, and the assembly and their beasts of burden began to drink.

12 Later Jehovah said to Moses and Aaron: "Because YOU did not show faith in me to sanctify me before the eyes of the sons of Israel, therefore YOU will not bring this congregation into the land that I shall certainly give them." 13 These are the waters of Mer'i·bah, because the sons of Israel quarreled with Jehovah, so that he was sanctified among them.

14 Subsequently Moses sent messengers from Ka'desh to the king of E'dom: "This is what your brother Israel has said, 'You yourself well know all the hardship that has overtaken us. 15 And our fathers proceeded to go down to Egypt, and we continued to dwell in Egypt many days; and the Egyptians began doing harm to us and our fathers. 16 Finally we cried out to Jehovah and he heard our voice and sent an angel and brought us out of Egypt; and here we are in Ka'desh, a city at the extremity of your territory. 17 Let us pass, please, through your land. We shall not pass through a field or a vineyard, and we shall not drink the water of a well. On the king's road we shall march. We shall not bend toward the right or the left, until we shall pass through your territory.'"

18 However, E'dom said to him: "You must not pass through me, for fear I may come out with the sword to meet you." 19 In turn the sons of Israel said to him: "By the highway we shall go up; and if I and my livestock should drink your water, I shall also certainly give the value of it. I want nothing more than to pass through on my feet." 20 Still he said: "You must not pass through." With that E'dom came on out to encounter him with a great many people and a strong hand. 21 So E'dom refused to grant Israel to pass through his territory. Hence Israel turned away from him.

22 And the sons of Israel, the entire assembly, proceeded to pull away from Ka'desh and come to

Mount Hor. 23 Then Jehovah said this to Moses and Aaron in Mount Hor by the border of the land of E'dom: 24 "Aaron will be gathered to his people, for he will not enter into the land that I shall certainly give to the sons of Israel, on the ground that YOU men rebelled against my order respecting the waters of Mer'i·bah. 25 Take Aaron and E·le·a'zar his son and bring them up into Mount Hor. 26 And strip Aaron of his garments, and you must clothe with them E·le·a'zar his son; and Aaron will be gathered and must die there."

27 So Moses did just as Jehovah had commanded; and before the eyes of all the assembly they went climbing Mount Hor. 28 Then Moses stripped Aaron of his garments and clothed E·le·a'zar his son with them, after which Aaron died there on the top of the mountain. And Moses and E·le·a'zar came on down from the mountain. 29 And all the assembly got to see that Aaron had expired, and all the house of Israel continued weeping for Aaron thirty days.

21 Now the Ca'naan·ite the king of A'rad, who dwelt in the Neg'eb, got to hear that Israel had come by the way of Ath'a·rim, and he began to fight with Israel and carry away some of them as captives. 2 Consequently Israel made a vow to Jehovah and said: "If you will without fail give this people into my hand, I shall also certainly devote their cities to destruction." 3 So Jehovah listened to Israel's voice and gave the Ca'naan·ites over; and they devoted them and their cities to destruction. Hence they called the name of the place Hor'mah.

4 While they continued trekking from Mount Hor by the way of the Red Sea to go around the land of E'dom, the soul of the people began tiring out because of the way. 5 And the people kept speaking against God and Moses: "Why have YOU brought us up out of Egypt to die in the wilderness? For there is no bread and no water, and our soul has come to abhor the contemptible bread." 6 So Jehovah sent poisonous serpents among the people, and they kept biting the people, so that many people of Israel died.

7 Finally the people came to Moses and said: "We have sinned, because we have spoken against Jehovah and against you. Intercede with Jehovah that he may remove the serpents from upon us." And Moses went interceding in behalf of the people. 8 Then Jehovah said to Moses: "Make for yourself a fiery snake and place it upon a signal pole. And it must occur that when anyone has been bitten, he then has to look at it and so must keep alive." 9 Moses at once made a serpent of copper and placed it upon the signal pole; and it did occur that if a serpent had bitten a man and he gazed at the copper serpent, he then kept alive.

10 After that the sons of Israel pulled away and encamped in O'both. 11 Then they pulled away from O'both and encamped in I'ye-ab'a·rim, in the wilderness that is toward the front of Mo'ab, toward the rising of the sun. 12 From there they pulled away and took up camping by the torrent valley of Ze'red. 13 From there they pulled away and went camping in the region of the Ar'non, which is in the wilderness that extends from the border of the Am'or·ites; for the Ar'non is the boundary of Mo'ab, between Mo'ab and the Am'or·ites. 14 That is why it is said in the book of the Wars of Jehovah:

"Va'heb in Su'phah and the torrent valleys of Ar'non, 15 and the mouth of the torrent valleys, which has bent itself toward the seat of Ar and has leaned against the border of Mo'ab."

16 Next from there on to Be'er. This is the well about which Jehovah said to Moses: "Gather the people, and let me give them water."

17 At that time Israel proceeded to sing this song:

"Spring up, O well! Respond to it, YOU people!

18 A well, princes dug it. The
nobles of the people excavated it,
With a commander's staff, with
their own staffs."

Then from the wilderness on to
Mat'ta·nah. 19 And from Mat'ta-
nah on to Na·hal'i·el, and from
Na·hal'i·el on to Ba'moth. 20 And
from Ba'moth on to the valley that
is in the field of Mo'ab, at the head
of Pis'gah, and it projects over
toward the face of Jesh'i·mon.

21 Israel now sent messengers to
Si'hon the king of the Am'or·ites,
saying: 22 "Let me pass through
your land. We shall not turn off
into a field or a vineyard. We shall
drink water of no well. On the
king's road we shall march until
we pass through your territory."
23 And Si'hon did not allow Israel
to pass through his territory, but
Si'hon gathered all his people and
went out to meet Israel in the wilderness, and came to Ja'haz and
began fighting with Israel. 24 At
that Israel struck him with the
edge of the sword and took possession of his land from the Ar'non to
the Jab'bok, near the sons of Am'-
mon; because Ja'zer is the border
of the sons of Am'mon.

25 So Israel took all these cities,
and Israel began dwelling in all the
cities of the Am'or·ites, in Hesh'-
bon and all its dependent towns.
26 For Hesh'bon was the city of
Si'hon. He was the king of the
Am'or·ites, and it was he who
fought with the king of Mo'ab formerly and went taking all his land
out of his hand as far as the
Ar'non. 27 That is why the sayers
of mock verses would say:

"Come to Hesh'bon.
Let the city of Si'hon be built
and be proved firmly set up.
28 For a fire has come out of
Hesh'bon, a flame from the
town of Si'hon.
It has consumed Ar of Mo'ab,
the owners of the high
places of the Ar'non.
29 Woe to you, Mo'ab! You will
certainly perish, O people of
Che'mosh!

He will certainly give his sons
as escaped ones and his
daughters in the captivity
to the king of the Am'or-
ites, Si'hon.
30 So let us shoot at them.
Hesh'bon will certainly perish
up to Di'bon,
And the women up to No'phah,
the men up to Med'e·ba."
31 And Israel began to dwell
in the land of the Am'or·ites.
32 Then Moses sent some to spy on
Ja'zer. So they captured its dependent towns and dispossessed the
Am'or·ites who were there. 33 After that they turned and went up
by the way of Ba'shan. At this Og
the king of Ba'shan came out to
meet them, he and all his people, to
the battle of Ed're·i. 34 Jehovah
now said to Moses: "Do not be
afraid of him, for into your hand
I shall certainly give him and all
his people and his land; and you
must do to him just as you did to
Si'hon, the king of the Am'or·ites,
who used to dwell in Hesh'bon."
35 So they went striking him and
his sons and all his people, until
there was no survivor remaining to
him; and they went taking possession of his land.

22 Then the sons of Israel pulled
away and encamped on the
desert plains of Mo'ab across the
Jordan from Jer'i·cho. 2 And Ba'-
lak the son of Zip'por got to see
all that Israel had done to the
Am'or·ites. 3 And Mo'ab became
very frightened at the people, because they were many; and Mo'ab
began to feel a sickening dread of
the sons of Israel. 4 And Mo'ab
proceeded to say to the older men
of Mid'i·an: "Now this congregation will lick up all our surroundings like the bull licking up the
green growth of the field."

And Ba'lak the son of Zip'por
was king of Mo'ab at that particular time. 5 He now sent messengers to Ba'laam the son of Be'or
at Pe'thor, which is by the River of
the land of the sons of his people,
to call him, saying: "Look! A people has come out of Egypt. Look!
They have covered the earth as far

as one can see, and they are dwelling right in front of me. 6 And now do come, please; do curse this people for me, for they are mightier than I am. Perhaps I may be able to strike them and I may drive them out of the land; for I well know that the one whom you bless is a blessed one and the one whom you curse is cursed."

7 So the older men of Mo'ab and the older men of Mid'i·an traveled with the payments for divination in their hands and went to Ba'laam and spoke to him Ba'lak's words. 8 At that he said to them: "Lodge here tonight, and I shall certainly return YOU word just as Jehovah may speak to me." Accordingly the princes of Mo'ab stayed with Ba'laam.

9 Then God came to Ba'laam and said: "Who are these men with you?" 10 So Ba'laam said to the [true] God: "Ba'lak the son of Zip'por, the king of Mo'ab, has sent to me, saying, 11 'Look! The people who are coming out of Egypt, and they go covering the earth as far as the eye can see. Now do come, do execrate them for me. Perhaps I may be able to fight against them and I shall actually drive them out.'" 12 But God said to Ba'laam: "You must not go with them. You must not curse the people, for they are blessed."

13 After that Ba'laam got up in the morning and said to the princes of Ba'lak: "Go to YOUR country, because Jehovah has refused to let me go with YOU." 14 So the princes of Mo'ab got up and came to Ba'lak and said: "Ba'laam has refused to come with us."

15 However, Ba'lak sent again other princes in greater number and more honorable than the former. 16 In turn they came to Ba'laam and said to him: "This is what Ba'lak the son of Zip'por has said, 'Do not be detained, please, from coming to me. 17 For I shall without fail honor you greatly, and everything you may say to me I shall do. So do come, please. Do execrate this people for me.'" 18 But Ba'laam answered and said to the servants of Ba'lak: "If Ba'lak were to give me his house full of silver and gold, I should not be able to pass beyond the order of Jehovah my God, so as to do something small or great. 19 And now YOU men also stay here, please, tonight that I may know what further Jehovah will speak with me."

20 Then God came to Ba'laam by night and said to him: "If it is to call you that the men have come, get up, go with them. But only the word that I shall speak to you is what you may speak." 21 After that Ba'laam got up in the morning and saddled his she-ass and went with the princes of Mo'ab.

22 And the anger of God began to blaze because he was going; and Jehovah's angel proceeded to station himself in the road to resist him. And he was riding upon his she-ass, and two attendants of his were with him. 23 And the ass got to see Jehovah's angel stationed in the road with his drawn sword in his hand; and the ass tried to turn aside from the road that she might go into the field, but Ba'laam began to strike the ass in order to turn her aside to the road. 24 And Jehovah's angel kept standing in the narrow way between the vineyards, with a stone wall on this side and a stone wall on that side. 25 And the she-ass kept seeing Jehovah's angel and began to squeeze herself against the wall and so to squeeze Ba'laam's foot against the wall; and he went beating her some more.

26 Jehovah's angel now passed by again and stood in a narrow place, where there was no way to turn aside to the right or the left. 27 When the ass got to see Jehovah's angel she now lay down under Ba'laam; so that Ba'laam's anger blazed, and he kept beating the ass with his staff. 28 Finally Jehovah opened the mouth of the ass and she said to Ba'laam: "What have I done to you so that you have beaten me these three times?" 29 At this Ba'laam said to the ass: "It is because you have dealt ruthlessly with me. If only there were a sword in my hand, for

now I should have killed you!" 30 Then the she-ass said to Ba'-laam: "Am I not your she-ass that you have ridden upon all your life long until this day? Have I ever been used to do to you this way?" To which he said: "No!" 31 And Jehovah proceeded to uncover Ba'-laam's eyes, so that he saw Jehovah's angel stationed in the road with his drawn sword in his hand. At once he bowed low and prostrated himself on his face.

32 Then Jehovah's angel said to him: "Why have you beaten your she-ass these three times? Look! I—I have come out to offer resistance, because your way has been headlong against my will. 33 And the she-ass got to see me and tried to turn aside before me these three times. Supposing she had not turned aside from before me! For by now even you I should have killed, but her I should have preserved alive." 34 At this Ba'laam said to Jehovah's angel: "I have sinned, because I did not know that it was you stationed in the road to meet me. And now, if it is bad in your eyes, let me go my way back." 35 But Jehovah's angel said to Ba'-laam: "Go with the men; and nothing but the word that I shall speak to you is what you may speak." And Ba'laam continued going with the princes of Ba'lak.

36 When Ba'lak got to hear that Ba'laam had come, he at once went out to meet him at the city of Mo'ab, which is on the bank of the Ar'non, which is on the extremity of the territory. 37 Then Ba'lak said to Ba'laam: "Have I not for a fact sent to you to call you? Why did you not come to me? Am I not really and truly able to honor you?" 38 At this Ba'laam said to Ba'lak: "Here I have come to you now. Shall I be able at all to speak something? The word that God will place in my mouth is what I shall speak."

39 So Ba'laam went with Ba'lak and they came to Kir'i·ath-hu'zoth. 40 And Ba'lak proceeded to sacrifice cattle and sheep and to send some to Ba'laam and the princes who were with him. 41 And it came about in the morning that Ba'lak went taking Ba'laam and bringing him up to Ba'moth-ba'al, that he might see from there the whole of the people.

23 Then Ba'laam said to Ba'lak: "Build for me on this spot seven altars and make ready for me on this spot seven bulls and seven rams." 2 Ba'lak immediately did just as Ba'laam had spoken. After that Ba'lak and Ba'laam offered up a bull and a ram on each altar. 3 And Ba'laam went on to say to Ba'lak: "Station yourself by your burnt offering, and let me go. Perhaps Jehovah will get in touch and meet with me. In that case whatever he will show me, I shall certainly tell you." So he went to a bare hill.

4 When God got in touch with Ba'laam, he then said to Him: "I set the seven altars in rows, and I proceeded to offer up a bull and a ram on each altar." 5 Accordingly Jehovah put a word in the mouth of Ba'laam and said: "Return to Ba'lak, and this is what you will speak." 6 So he returned to him, and, look! he and all the princes of Mo'ab were stationed by his burnt offering. 7 Then he took up his proverbial utterance and said:

"From A'ram Ba'lak the king of
    Mo'ab tried to conduct me,
From the mountains of the
    east:
'Do come, do curse Jacob for me.
    Yes, do come, do denounce
    Israel.'
8 How could I execrate those
    whom God has not exe-
    crated?
    And how could I denounce
     those whom Jehovah has
     not denounced?
9 For from the top of the rocks
    I see them,
    And from the hills I behold
     them.
There as a people they keep
    tabernacling isolated,
    And among the nations they
     do not reckon themselves.

10 Who has numbered the dust
	particles of Jacob,
	And who has counted the
		fourth part of Israel?
	Let my soul die the death of
		the upright ones,
	And let my end turn out
		afterward like theirs."
11 At this Ba′lak said to Ba′-
laam: "What have you done to me?
It was in order to execrate my
enemies that I took you, and here
you have blessed them to the
limit." 12 In turn he answered and
said: "Is it not whatever Jehovah
may put in my mouth that I should
take care to speak?"
13 Then Ba′lak said to him: "Do
come, please, with me to another
place from which you can see
them. Only the extremity of them
you will see, and you will not see
all of them. And execrate them for
me from there." 14 So he took
him to the field of Zo′phim, to the
top of Pis′gah, and proceeded to
build seven altars and to offer up a
bull and a ram on each altar.
15 After that he said to Ba′lak:
"Station yourself here by your
burnt offering, and, as for me, let
me get in touch with him there."
16 Subsequently Jehovah got in
touch with Ba′laam and put a
word in his mouth and said: "Return to Ba′lak, and this is what
you will speak." 17 So he came to
him, and, look! he was stationed
by his burnt offering, and the
princes of Mo′ab with him. Then
Ba′lak said to him: "What has Jehovah spoken?" 18 At this he
took up his proverbial utterance
and said:

"Get up, Ba′lak, and listen.
	Do give ear to me, O son of
		Zip′por.
19 God is not a man that he should
		tell lies,
	Neither a son of mankind
		that he should feel regret.
	Has he himself said it and will
		he not do it,
	And has he spoken and will
		he not carry it out?
20 Look! I have been taken to bless,
	And He has blessed, and I
		shall not reverse it.

21 He has not looked upon any un-
		canny power against Jacob,
	And no trouble has he seen
		against Israel.
	Jehovah his God is with him,
	And the loud hailing of a
		king is in his midst.
22 God is bringing them out of
		Egypt.
	The swift course like that of
		a wild bull is his.
23 For there is no unlucky spell
		against Jacob,
	Nor any divination against
		Israel.
	At this time it may be said re-
		specting Jacob and Israel,
	'What has God worked out!'
24 Behold, a people will get up like
		a lion,
	And like the lion it will lift
		itself up.
	It will not lie down until it may
		eat prey,
	And the blood of slain ones it
		will drink."

25 At this Ba′lak said to Ba′-
laam: "If, on the one hand, you
cannot execrate him at all, then,
on the other hand, you should not
bless him at all." 26 In turn Ba′-
laam answered and said to Ba′lak:
"Did I not speak to you, saying,
'All that Jehovah will speak is what
I shall do'?"
27 Then Ba′lak said to Ba′laam:
"O come, please. Let me take you
to still another place. Perhaps it
will be right in the eyes of the
[true] God so that you will certainly execrate him for me from
there." 28 With that Ba′lak took
Ba′laam to the top of Pe′or, which
looks toward Jesh′i·mon. 29 Then
Ba′laam said to Ba′lak: "Build for
me on this spot seven altars and
make ready for me on this spot
seven bulls and seven rams." 30 So
Ba′lak did just as Ba′laam had
said, and he went offering up a
bull and a ram on each altar.

24 When Ba′laam got to see that
it was good in the eyes of Jehovah to bless Israel, he did not go
away as at the other times to come
upon any unlucky omens, but he
directed his face to the wilderness.
2 When Ba′laam raised his eyes

and saw Israel tabernacling by his tribes, then the spirit of God came to be upon him. 3 Hence he took up his proverbial utterance and said:

"The utterance of Ba′laam the son of Be′or,
    And the utterance of the able-bodied man with the eye unsealed,
4 The utterance of the one hearing the sayings of God,
    Who got to see a vision of the Almighty
    While falling down with the eyes uncovered:
5 How good-looking are your tents, O Jacob, your tabernacles, O Israel!
6 Like torrent valleys they have extended a long way,
    Like gardens by the river.
    Like aloe plants that Jehovah has planted,
    Like cedars by the waters.
7 Water keeps trickling from his two leather buckets,
    And his seed is by many waters.
    His king also will be higher than A′gag,
    And his kingdom will be lifted up.
8 God is bringing him out of Egypt;
    The swift course of a wild bull is his.
    He will consume the nations, his oppressors,
    And their bones he will gnaw, and he will break them to pieces with his arrows.
9 He bowed down, he lay down like the lion,
    And, like a lion, who dares rouse him?
    Those blessing you are the ones blessed,
    And those cursing you are the ones cursed."

10 At that Ba′lak's anger blazed against Ba′laam and he clapped his hands, and Ba′lak went on to say to Ba′laam: "It was to execrate my enemies that I called you, and, look! you have blessed them to the limit these three times. 11 And now run your way off to your place. I had said to myself I

was without fail going to honor you, but, look! Jehovah has held you back from honor."

12 In turn Ba′laam said to Ba′lak: "Was it not also to your messengers whom you sent to me that I spoke, saying, 13 'If Ba′lak were to give me his house full of silver and gold, I should not be able to pass beyond the order of Jehovah so as to do something good or bad out of my own heart. Whatever Jehovah may speak is what I shall speak'? 14 And now here I am going away to my people. Do come, let me advise you what this people will do to your people afterward in the end of the days." 15 So he took up his proverbial utterance and said:

"The utterance of Ba′laam the son of Be′or,
    And the utterance of the man with the eye unsealed,
16 The utterance of the one hearing the sayings of God,
    And the one knowing the knowledge of the Most High—
    A vision of the Almighty he got to see
    While falling down with the eyes uncovered:
17 I shall see him, but not now;
    I shall behold him, but not near.
    A star will certainly step forth out of Jacob,
    And a scepter will indeed rise out of Israel.
    And he will certainly break apart the temples of Mo′ab's [head]
    And the cranium of all the sons of tumult of war.
18 And E′dom must become a possession,
    Yes, Se′ir must become the possession of his enemies,
    While Israel is displaying his courage.
19 And out of Jacob one will go subduing,
    And he must destroy any survivor from the city."

20 When he got to see Am′a·lek, he carried further his proverbial utterance and went on to say:

"Am'a·lek was the first one of
the nations,
But his end afterward will be
even his perishing."
21 When he got to see the Ken'-
ites, he carried further his proverbial utterance and went on to say:
"Durable is your dwelling, and
set on the crag is your abode.
22 But there will come to be one
to burn Ka'in down.
How long will it be till As-
syr'i·a will carry you away
captive?"
23 And he carried further his
proverbial utterance and went on
to say:
"Woe! Who will survive when
God causes it?
24 And there will be ships from
the coast of Kit'tim,
And they will certainly afflict
As·syr'i·a,
And they will indeed afflict
E'ber.
But he too will eventually
perish."
25 After that Ba'laam got up and
went and returned to his place.
And Ba'lak also went his own way.

25 Now Israel was dwelling in
Shit'tim. Then the people
started to have immoral relations
with the daughters of Mo'ab.
2 And the women came calling the
people to the sacrifices of their
gods, and the people began to eat
and to bow down to their gods.
3 So Israel attached itself to the
Ba'al of Pe'or; and the anger of
Jehovah began to blaze against Israel. 4 Hence Jehovah said to
Moses: "Take all the head ones of
the people and expose them to Jehovah toward the sun, that the
burning anger of Jehovah may turn
back from Israel." 5 Then Moses
said to the judges of Israel: "Each
one of you kill his men who have
an attachment with the Ba'al of
Pe'or."
6 But, look! a man of the sons
of Israel came, and he was bringing
near to his brothers a Mid'i·an·ite
woman before Moses' eyes and before the eyes of all the assembly of
the sons of Israel, while they were
weeping at the entrance of the tent

of meeting. 7 When Phin'e·has
the son of E·le·a'zar the son of
Aaron the priest caught sight of
it, he at once got up from the midst
of the assembly and took a lance
in his hand. 8 Then he went after
the man of Israel into the vaulted
tent and pierced both of them
through, the man of Israel and the
woman through her genital parts.
At that the scourge was halted
from upon the sons of Israel.
9 And those who died from the
scourge amounted to twenty-four
thousand.
10 Then Jehovah spoke to Moses, saying: 11 "Phin'e·has the
son of E·le·a'zar the son of Aaron
the priest has turned back my
wrath from upon the sons of Israel
by his tolerating no rivalry at all
toward me in the midst of them,
so that I have not exterminated the
sons of Israel in my insistence on
exclusive devotion. 12 For that
reason say, 'Here I am giving him
my covenant of peace. 13 And it
must serve as the covenant of a
priesthood to time indefinite for
him and his offspring after him,
due to the fact that he tolerated no
rivalry toward his God and proceeded to make atonement for the
sons of Israel.' "
14 Incidentally the name of the
fatally struck Israelite man who
was fatally struck with the Mid'i-
an·i·tess was Zim'ri the son of
Sa'lu, a chieftain of a paternal
house of the Sim'e·on·ites. 15 And
the name of the Mid'i·an·ite woman fatally struck was Coz'bi the
daughter of Zur; he was a head one
of the clans of a paternal house
in Mid'i·an.
16 Later Jehovah spoke to Moses,
saying: 17 "Let there be a harassing of the Mid'i·an·ites, and
you men must strike them, 18 because they are harassing you with
their deeds of cunning that they
committed against you cunningly
in the affair of Pe'or and in the
affair of Coz'bi the daughter of a
chieftain of Mid'i·an, their sister
who was fatally struck in the day
of the scourge over the affair of
Pe'or."

26 And it came about after the scourge, that Jehovah went on to say this to Moses and E·le·a′zar the son of Aaron the priest: 2 "TAKE the sum of the whole assembly of the sons of Israel from twenty years of age and upward, according to the house of their fathers, all those going out to the army in Israel." 3 And Moses and E·le·a′zar the priest proceeded to speak with them in the desert plains of Mo′ab by the Jordan at Jer′i·cho, saying: 4 "[Take the sum of them] from the age of twenty years and upward, just as Jehovah had commanded Moses."

Now the sons of Israel who went out of the land of Egypt were: 5 Reu′ben, Israel's first-born; Reu′ben's sons: Of Ha′noch the family of the Ha′noch·ites; of Pal′lu the family of the Pal′lu·ites; 6 of Hez′ron the family of the Hez′ron·ites; of Car′mi the family of the Car′mites. 7 These were the families of the Reu′ben·ites, and their registered ones amounted to forty-three thousand seven hundred and thirty.

8 And the son of Pal′lu was E·li′ab. 9 And the sons of E·li′ab: Nem′u·el and Da′than and A·bi′ram. This Da′than and A·bi′ram were summoned ones of the assembly, who engaged in a struggle against Moses and Aaron in the assembly of Ko′rah, when they engaged in a struggle against Jehovah. 10 Then the earth opened its mouth and swallowed them up. As for Ko′rah, [he died] at the death of the assembly when the fire consumed two hundred and fifty men. And they came to be a symbol. 11 However, the sons of Ko′rah did not die.

12 The sons of Sim′e·on by their families: Of Nem′u·el the family of the Nem′u·el·ites; of Ja′min the family of the Ja′min·ites; of Ja′chin the family of the Ja′chin·ites; 13 of Ze′rah the family of the Ze′rah·ites; of Sha′ul the family of the Sha·u′lites. 14 These were the families of the Sim′e·on·ites: twenty-two thousand two hundred.

15 The sons of Gad by their families: Of Ze′phon the family of the Ze′phon·ites; of Hag′gi the family of the Hag′gites; of Shu′ni the family of the Shu′nites; 16 of Oz′ni the family of the Oz′nites; of E′ri the family of the E′rites; 17 of Ar′od the family of the Ar′od·ites; of A·re′li the family of the A·re′lites. 18 These were the families of the sons of Gad, of their registered ones: forty thousand five hundred.

19 The sons of Judah were Er and O′nan. However, Er and O′nan died in the land of Ca′naan. 20 And the sons of Judah came to be, by their families: Of She′lah the family of the She·la′nites; of Pe′rez the family of the Per′e·zites; of Ze′rah the family of the Ze′rah·ites. 21 And the sons of Pe′rez came to be: Of Hez′ron the family of the Hez′ron·ites; of Ha′mul the family of the Ha·mu′lites. 22 These were the families of Judah, of their registered ones: seventy-six thousand five hundred.

23 The sons of Is′sa·char by their families were: Of To′la the family of the To′la·ites; of Pu′vah the family of the Pu′nites; 24 of Ja′shub the family of the Jash′u·bites; of Shim′ron the family of the Shim′ron·ites. 25 These were the families of Is′sa·char, of their registered ones: sixty-four thousand three hundred.

26 The sons of Zeb′u·lun by their families were: Of Se′red the family of the Ser′e·dites; of E′lon the family of the E′lon·ites; of Jah′le·el the family of the Jah′le·el·ites. 27 These were the families of the Ze·bu′lu·nites, of their registered ones: sixty thousand five hundred.

28 The sons of Joseph by their families were Ma·nas′seh and E′phra·im. 29 The sons of Ma·nas′seh were: Of Ma′chir the family of the Ma′chir·ites. And Ma′chir became father to Gil′e·ad. Of Gil′e·ad the family of the Gil′e·ad·ites. 30 These were the sons of Gil′e·ad: Of Ie′zer the family of the Ie′zer·ites; of He′lek the family of the He′lek·ites; 31 of As′ri·el the family of the As′ri·el·ites; of She′chem the family of the She′chem·ites; 32 of She·mi′da the family of the

She·mi'da·ites; of He'pher the family of the He'pher·ites. 33 Now Ze·lo'phe·had the son of He'pher proved to have no sons, but daughters, and the names of the daughters of Ze·lo'phe·had were Mah'lah and No'ah, Hog'lah, Mil'cah and Tir'zah. 34 These were the families of Ma·nas'seh, and their registered ones were fifty-two thousand seven hundred.

35 These were the sons of E'phra·im by their families: Of Shu'the·lah the family of the Shu'thel·a'·hites; of Be'cher the family of the Be'cher·ites; of Ta'han the family of the Ta'han·ites. 36 And these were the sons of Shu'the·lah: Of E'ran the family of the E'ran·ites. 37 These were the families of the sons of E'phra·im, of their registered ones: thirty-two thousand five hundred. These were the sons of Joseph by their families.

38 The sons of Benjamin by their families were: Of Be'la the family of the Be'la·ites; of Ash'bel the family of the Ash'bel·ites; of A·hi'ram the family of the A·hi'ram·ites; 39 of She·phu'pham the family of the Shu'pham·ites; of Hu'pham the family of the Hu'pham·ites. 40 The sons of Be'la came to be Ard and Na'a·man: [Of Ard] the family of the Ard'·ites; of Na'a·man the family of the Na'a·mites. 41 These were the sons of Benjamin by their families, and their registered ones were forty-five thousand six hundred.

42 These were the sons of Dan by their families: Of Shu'ham the family of the Shu'ham·ites. These were the families of Dan by their families. 43 All the families of the Shu'ham·ites, of their registered ones, were sixty-four thousand four hundred.

44 The sons of Ash'er by their families were: Of Im'nah the family of the Im'nites; of Ish'vi the family of the Ish'vites; of Be·ri'ah the family of the Be·ri'ites; 45 of the sons of Be·ri'ah: Of He'ber the family of the He'ber·ites; of Mal'chi·el the family of the Mal'chi·el·ites. 46 And the name of Ash'er's daughter was Se'rah. 47 These

were the families of the sons of Ash'er, of their registered ones: fifty-three thousand four hundred.

48 The sons of Naph'ta·li by their families were: Of Jah'ze·el the family of the Jah'ze·el·ites; of Gu'ni the family of the Gu'nites; 49 of Je'zer the family of the Je'zer·ites; of Shil'lem the family of the Shil'lem·ites. 50 These were the families of Naph'ta·li by their families, and their registered ones were forty-five thousand four hundred.

51 These were the registered ones of the sons of Israel: six hundred and one thousand seven hundred and thirty.

52 After that Jehovah spoke to Moses, saying: 53 "To these the land should be apportioned for an inheritance by the number of the names. 54 According to the great number you should increase one's inheritance, and according to the fewness you should reduce one's inheritance. Each one's inheritance should be given in proportion to his registered ones. 55 Only by the lot should the land be apportioned. According to the names of the tribes of their fathers they should get an inheritance. 56 By the determination of the lot one's inheritance should be apportioned between the many and the few."

57 Now these were the registered ones of the Levites by their families: Of Ger'shon the family of the Ger'shon·ites; of Ko'hath the family of the Ko'hath·ites; of Me·rar'i the family of the Me·rar'ites. 58 These were the families of the Levites: the family of the Lib'nites, the family of the He'bron·ites, the family of the Mah'lites, the family of the Mu'shites, the family of the Ko'rah·ites.

And Ko'hath became father to Am'ram. 59 And the name of Am'ram's wife was Joch'e·bed, Le'vi's daughter, whom his wife bore to Le'vi in Egypt. In time she bore to Am'ram Aaron and Moses and Mir'i·am their sister. 60 Then there were born to Aaron Na'dab and A·bi'hu, E·le·a'zar and Ith'a·mar. 61 But Na'dab and A·bi'hu died for their presenting illegitimate fire before Jehovah.

62 And their registered ones amounted to twenty-three thousand, all males from a month old and upward. For they did not get registered in among the sons of Israel, because no inheritance was to be given to them in among the sons of Israel.

63 These were the ones registered by Moses and E·le·a′zar the priest when they registered the sons of Israel in the desert plains of Mo′ab by the Jordan at Jer′i·cho. 64 But among these there did not prove to be a man of those registered by Moses and Aaron the priest when they registered the sons of Israel in the wilderness of Si′nai. 65 For Jehovah had said concerning them: "They will die without fail in the wilderness." So there was not left of them a man except Ca′leb the son of Je·phun′neh and Joshua the son of Nun.

27 Then the daughters of Ze·lo′phe·had the son of He′pher the son of Gil′e·ad the son of Ma′chir the son of Ma·nas′seh, of the families of Ma·nas′seh the son of Joseph, came near. And these were the names of his daughters: Mah′lah, No′ah and Hog′lah and Mil′cah and Tir′zah. 2 And they proceeded to stand before Moses and before E·le·a′zar the priest and before the chieftains and all the assembly at the entrance of the tent of meeting, saying: 3 "Our father has died in the wilderness, and yet he did not prove to be in among the assembly, that is, those who ranged themselves against Jehovah in the assembly of Ko′rah, but for his own sin he has died; and he did not get to have any sons. 4 Why should the name of our father be taken away from the midst of his family because he had no son? O give us a possession in the midst of our father's brothers." 5 At that Moses presented their case before Jehovah.

6 Jehovah then said this to Moses: 7 "The daughters of Ze·lo′phe·had are speaking right. By all means you should give them the possession of an inheritance in the midst of their father's brothers, and you must cause their father's inheritance to pass to them. 8 And to the sons of Israel you should speak, saying, 'In case any man should die without his having a son, you must then cause his inheritance to pass to his daughter. 9 And if he has no daughter, you must then give his inheritance to his brothers. 10 And if he has no brothers, you must then give his inheritance to his father's brothers. 11 And if his father has no brothers, you must then give his inheritance to his blood relation who is closest to him of his family, and he must take possession of it. And it must serve as a statute by judicial decision for the sons of Israel, just as Jehovah has commanded Moses.'"

12 Subsequently Jehovah said to Moses: "Go up into this mountain of Ab′a·rim and see the land that I shall certainly give the sons of Israel. 13 When you have seen it, then you must be gathered to your people, yes, you, just as Aaron your brother was gathered, 14 inasmuch as you men rebelled against my order in the wilderness of Zin at the quarreling of the assembly, in relation to sanctifying me by the waters before their eyes. These are the waters of Mer′i·bah at Ka′desh in the wilderness of Zin."

15 Then Moses spoke to Jehovah, saying: 16 "Let Jehovah the God of the spirits of all sorts of flesh appoint over the assembly a man 17 who will go out before them and who will come in before them and who will bring them out and who will bring them in, that Jehovah's assembly may not become like sheep that have no shepherd." 18 So Jehovah said to Moses: "Take for yourself Joshua the son of Nun, a man in whom there is spirit, and you must lay your hand upon him; 19 and you must stand him before E·le·a′zar the priest and before all the assembly, and you must commission him before their eyes. 20 And you must put some of your dignity upon him, in order that all

the assembly of the sons of Israel may listen to him. 21 And it is before E·le·a′zar the priest that he will stand, and he must inquire in his behalf by the judgment of the U′rim before Jehovah. At his order they will go out and at his order they will come in, he and all the sons of Israel with him and all the assembly."

22 And Moses proceeded to do just as Jehovah had commanded him. Accordingly he took Joshua and stood him before E·le·a′zar the priest and before all the assembly 23 and laid his hands upon him and commissioned him, just as Jehovah had spoken by means of Moses.

28 And Jehovah spoke further to Moses, saying: 2 "Command the sons of Israel, and you must say to them, 'YOU should take care to present to me my offering, my bread, for my offerings made by fire as a restful odor to me, at their appointed times.'

3 "And you must say to them, 'This is the offering made by fire that YOU will present to Jehovah: two sound year-old male lambs a day as a burnt offering constantly. 4 The one male lamb you will render up in the morning, and the other male lamb you will render up between the two evenings, 5 together with the tenth of an e′phah of fine flour as a grain offering moistened with the fourth of a hin of beaten oil; 6 the constant burnt offering, which was rendered up at Mount Si′nai as a restful odor, an offering made by fire to Jehovah, 7 along with its drink offering, the fourth of a hin to each male lamb. Pour out in the holy place the drink offering of intoxicating liquor to Jehovah. 8 And you will render up the other male lamb between the two evenings. With the same grain offering as of the morning and with its same drink offering you will render it up as an offering made by fire, of a restful odor to Jehovah.

9 "However, on the sabbath day there will be two sound year-old male lambs and two tenth measures of fine flour as a grain offering moistened with oil, together with its drink offering, 10 as a sabbath burnt offering on its sabbath, along with the constant burnt offering and its drink offering.

11 "'And at the commencements of YOUR months YOU people will present as a burnt offering to Jehovah two young bulls and one ram, seven sound male lambs each a year old, 12 and three tenth measures of fine flour as a grain offering moistened with oil for each bull and two tenth measures of fine flour as a grain offering moistened with oil for the one ram, 13 and a tenth measure of fine flour respectively as a grain offering moistened with oil for each male lamb, as a burnt offering, a restful odor, an offering made by fire to Jehovah. 14 And as their drink offerings there should go half a hin of wine for a bull and a third of a hin for the ram and a fourth of a hin for a male lamb. This is the monthly burnt offering in its month for the months of the year. 15 Also, one kid of the goats should be rendered up as a sin offering to Jehovah in addition to the constant burnt offering together with its drink offering.

16 "'And in the first month, on the fourteenth day of the month, will be Jehovah's passover. 17 And on the fifteenth day of this month will be a festival. Seven days unfermented cakes will be eaten. 18 On the first day there will be a holy convention. No sort of laborious work must YOU do. 19 And YOU must present as an offering made by fire, a burnt offering to Jehovah, two young bulls and one ram and seven male lambs each a year old. They should prove to be sound ones for YOU. 20 And as their grain offerings of fine flour moistened with oil YOU will render up three tenth measures for a bull and two tenth measures for the ram. 21 You will render up a tenth measure respectively for each male lamb of the seven male lambs; 22 and one goat of sin offering to make atonement for YOU.

23 Aside from the morning burnt offering, which is for the constant burnt offering, YOU will render these up. 24 The same as these YOU will render up daily for the seven days as bread, an offering made by fire, of a restful odor to Jehovah. Along with the constant burnt offering it should be rendered, and its drink offering. 25 And on the seventh day YOU should hold a holy convention. No sort of laborious work must YOU do.

26 " 'And on the day of the first ripe fruits, when YOU present a new grain offering to Jehovah, in YOUR feast of weeks YOU should hold a holy convention. No sort of laborious work must YOU do. 27 And YOU must present as a burnt offering for a restful odor to Jehovah two young bulls, one ram, seven male lambs each a year old; 28 and as their grain offering of fine flour moistened with oil three tenth measures for each bull, two tenth measures for the one ram, 29 a tenth measure respectively for each male lamb of the seven male lambs; 30 one kid of the goats to make atonement for YOU. 31 Aside from the constant burnt offering and its grain offering YOU will render them up. They should prove to be sound ones for YOU, together with their drink offerings.

29 " 'And in the seventh month, on the first of the month, YOU should hold a holy convention. No sort of laborious work must YOU do. It should prove to be a day of the trumpet blast for YOU. 2 And YOU must render up as a burnt offering for a restful odor to Jehovah one young bull, one ram, seven male lambs each a year old, sound ones; 3 and their grain offering of fine flour moistened with oil, three tenth measures for the bull, two tenth measures for the ram, 4 and one tenth measure for each male lamb of the seven male lambs; 5 and one male kid of the goats as a sin offering to make atonement for YOU; 6 aside from the monthly burnt offering and its grain offering and the constant burnt offering and its grain offer-

ing, together with their drink offerings, according to the regular procedure for them, as a restful odor, an offering made by fire to Jehovah.

7 " 'And on the tenth of this seventh month YOU should hold a holy convention, and YOU must afflict YOUR souls. No sort of work must YOU do. 8 And YOU must present as a burnt offering to Jehovah, as a restful odor, one young bull, one ram, seven male lambs each a year old. They should prove to be sound ones for YOU. 9 And as their grain offering of fine flour moistened with oil three tenth measures for the bull, two tenth measures for the one ram, 10 a tenth measure respectively for each male lamb of the seven male lambs; 11 one kid of the goats as a sin offering, aside from the sin offering of atonement and the constant burnt offering and its grain offering, together with their drink offerings.

12 " 'And on the fifteenth day of the seventh month YOU should hold a holy convention. No sort of laborious work must YOU do, and YOU must celebrate a festival to Jehovah seven days. 13 And YOU must present as a burnt offering, an offering made by fire, of a restful odor to Jehovah, thirteen young bulls, two rams, fourteen male lambs each a year old. They should prove to be sound ones. 14 And as their grain offering of fine flour moistened with oil three tenth measures for each bull of the thirteen bulls, two tenth measures for each ram of the two rams, 15 and a tenth measure for each male lamb of the fourteen male lambs; 16 and one kid of the goats as a sin offering, aside from the constant burnt offering, its grain offering and its drink offering.

17 " 'And on the second day twelve young bulls, two rams, fourteen male lambs each a year old, sound ones; 18 and their grain offering and their drink offerings for the bulls, the rams and the male lambs by their number according to the regular procedure; 19 and one kid of the goats as a

sin offering, aside from the constant burnt offering and its grain offering, together with their drink offerings.

20 "'And on the third day eleven bulls, two rams, fourteen male lambs each a year old, sound ones; 21 and their grain offering and their drink offerings for the bulls, the rams and the male lambs by their number according to the regular procedure; 22 and one goat as a sin offering, aside from the constant burnt offering and its grain offering and its drink offering.

23 "'And on the fourth day ten bulls, two rams, fourteen male lambs each a year old, sound ones; 24 their grain offering and their drink offerings for the bulls, the rams and the male lambs by their number according to the regular procedure; 25 and one kid of the goats as a sin offering, aside from the constant burnt offering, its grain offering and its drink offering.

26 "'And on the fifth day nine bulls, two rams, fourteen male lambs each a year old, sound ones; 27 and their grain offering and their drink offerings for the bulls, the rams and the male lambs by their number according to the regular procedure; 28 and one goat as a sin offering, aside from the constant burnt offering and its grain offering and its drink offering.

29 "'And on the sixth day eight bulls, two rams, fourteen male lambs each a year old, sound ones; 30 and their grain offering and their drink offerings for the bulls, the rams and the male lambs by their number according to the regular procedure; 31 and one goat as a sin offering, aside from the constant burnt offering, its grain offering and its drink offerings.

32 "'And on the seventh day seven bulls, two rams, fourteen male lambs each a year old, sound ones; 33 and their grain offering and their drink offerings for the bulls, the rams and the male lambs by their number according to the regular procedure for them; 34 and one goat as a sin offering, aside from the constant burnt offering, its grain offering and its drink offering.

35 "'And on the eighth day you should hold a solemn assembly. No sort of laborious work must you do. 36 And you must present as a burnt offering, an offering made by fire, of a restful odor to Jehovah, one bull, one ram, seven male lambs each a year old, sound ones; 37 and their grain offering and their drink offerings for the bull, the ram and the male lambs by their number according to the regular procedure; 38 and one goat as a sin offering, aside from the constant burnt offering and its grain offering and its drink offering.

39 "'These you will render up to Jehovah at your seasonal festivals, besides your vow offerings and your voluntary offerings as your burnt offerings and your grain offerings and your drink offerings and your communion sacrifices.'"

40 And Moses proceeded to talk to the sons of Israel according to everything that Jehovah had commanded Moses.

30 Then Moses spoke to the heads of the tribes of the sons of Israel, saying: "This is the word that Jehovah has commanded: 2 In case a man makes a vow to Jehovah or swears an oath to bind a vow of abstinence upon his soul, he must not violate his word. According to all that has gone out of his mouth he should do.

3 "And in case a woman makes a vow to Jehovah or she does bind herself with a vow of abstinence in the house of her father in her youth, 4 and her father actually hears her vow or her abstinence vow that she has bound upon her soul and her father does keep silent toward her, all her vows must also stand, and every abstinence vow that she has bound upon her soul will stand. 5 But if her father has forbidden her on the day of his hearing all her vows or her abstinence vows that she has bound upon her soul, it will not stand, but Jehovah will forgive her, because her father forbade her.

6 "However, if she at all happens to belong to a husband, and her vow is upon her or the thoughtless promise of her lips that she has bound upon her soul, 7 and her husband actually hears it and keeps silent toward her on the day of his hearing it, her vows must also stand or her abstinence vows that she has bound upon her soul will stand. 8 But if her husband on the day of hearing it forbids her, he has also annulled her vow that was upon her or the thoughtless promise of her lips that she bound upon her soul, and Jehovah will forgive her.

9 "In the case of the vow of a widow or a divorced woman, everything that she has bound upon her soul will stand against her.

10 "However, if it is in the house of her husband that she has vowed or has bound an abstinence vow upon her soul by an oath, 11 and her husband has heard it and has kept silent toward her, he has not forbidden her; and all her vows must stand or any abstinence vow that she has bound upon her soul will stand. 12 But if her husband has totally annulled them on the day of his hearing any expression of her lips as her vows or as an abstinence vow of her soul, they will not stand. Her husband has annulled them, and Jehovah will forgive her. 13 Any vow or any oath of an abstinence vow to afflict the soul, her husband should establish it or her husband should annul it. 14 But if her husband absolutely keeps silent toward her from day to day, he has also established all her vows or all her abstinence vows that are upon her. He has established them because he kept silent toward her on the day of his hearing them. 15 And if he totally annuls them after his hearing them, he also actually bears her error.

16 "These are the regulations that Jehovah commanded Moses as between a husband and his wife, as between a father and his daughter in her youth in the house of her father."

31 Jehovah then spoke to Moses, saying: 2 "Take vengeance for the sons of Israel upon the Mid′i·an·ites. Afterward you will be gathered to your people."

3 So Moses spoke to the people, saying: "Equip men from among you for the army, that they may serve against Mid′i·an to execute Jehovah's vengeance upon Mid′i·an. 4 A thousand of each tribe of all the tribes of Israel you will send into the army." 5 Accordingly from the thousands of Israel a thousand were assigned of a tribe, twelve thousand equipped for the army.

6 Then Moses sent them out, a thousand of each tribe, to the army, them and Phin′e·has the son of E·le·a′zar the priest to the army, and the holy utensils and the trumpets for blowing calls were in his hand. 7 And they went waging war against Mid′i·an, just as Jehovah had commanded Moses, and they proceeded to kill every male. 8 And they killed the kings of Mid′i·an along with the others slain, namely, E′vi and Re′kem and Zur and Hur and Re′ba, the five kings of Mid′i·an; and they killed Ba′laam the son of Be′or with the sword. 9 But the sons of Israel carried off the women of Mid′i·an and their little ones captive; and all their domestic animals and all their livestock and all their means of maintenance they plundered. 10 And all their cities in which they had settled and all their walled camps they burned with fire. 11 And they went taking all the spoil and all the booty in the way of humans and domestic animals. 12 And they came bringing to Moses and E·le·a′zar the priest and to the assembly of the sons of Israel the captives and the booty and the spoil, to the camp, to the desert plains of Mo′ab, which are by the Jordan at Jer′i·cho.

13 Then Moses and E·le·a′zar the priest and all the chieftains of the assembly went out to meet them outside the camp. 14 And Moses grew indignant at the appointed men of the combat forces,

the chiefs of the thousands and the chiefs of the hundreds who were coming in from the military expedition. 15 So Moses said to them: "Have YOU preserved alive every female? 16 Look! They are the ones who, by Ba′laam's word, served to induce the sons of Israel to commit unfaithfulness toward Jehovah over the affair of Pe′or, so that the scourge came upon the assembly of Jehovah. 17 And now kill every male among the little ones, and kill every woman who has had intercourse with man by lying with a male. 18 And preserve alive for yourselves all the little ones among the women who have not known the act of lying with a male. 19 As for YOU yourselves, camp outside the camp seven days. Everyone who has killed a soul and everyone who has touched someone slain, YOU should purify yourselves on the third day and on the seventh day, YOU and YOUR captives. 20 And every garment and every article of skin and everything made of goat's hair and every article of wood YOU should purify for yourselves from sin."

21 E·le·a′zar the priest then said to the men of the army who had gone into the battle: "This is the statute of the law that Jehovah commanded Moses, 22 'Only the gold and the silver, the copper, the iron, the tin and the lead, 23 everything that is processed with fire, YOU should pass through the fire, and it must be clean. Only it should be purified by the water for cleansing. And everything that is not processed with fire YOU should pass through the water. 24 And YOU must wash YOUR garments on the seventh day and be clean, and afterward YOU may come into the camp.' "

25 And Jehovah proceeded to say this to Moses: 26 "Take the sum of the booty, the captives both of humankind and of domestic animals, you and E·le·a′zar the priest and the heads of the fathers of the assembly. 27 And you must divide the booty in two between those taking part in the battle who went out on the expedition and all the rest of the assembly. 28 And as a tax for Jehovah you must take away from the men of war who went out on the expedition one soul out of five hundred, of humankind and of the herd and of the asses and of the flock. 29 From their half YOU should take it and you must give it to E·le·a′zar the priest as Jehovah's contribution. 30 And from the half of the sons of Israel you should take one out of fifty, of humankind, of the herd, of the asses and of the flock, of every sort of domestic animal, and you must give them to the Levites, the keepers of the obligation of Jehovah's tabernacle."

31 And Moses and E·le·a′zar the priest went doing just as Jehovah had commanded Moses. 32 And the booty, the rest of the plunder that the people of the expedition had taken as plunder, amounted to six hundred and seventy-five thousand of the flock, 33 and seventy-two thousand of the herd, 34 and sixty-one thousand asses. 35 As for human souls from the women who had not known the act of lying with a male, all the souls were thirty-two thousand. 36 And the half that was the share of those who went out on the expedition amounted in number to three hundred and thirty-seven thousand five hundred of the flock. 37 And the tax for Jehovah from the flock amounted to six hundred and seventy-five. 38 And of the herd there were thirty-six thousand, and the tax on them for Jehovah was seventy-two. 39 And the asses were thirty thousand five hundred, and the tax on them for Jehovah was sixty-one. 40 And the human souls were sixteen thousand, and the tax on them for Jehovah was thirty-two souls. 41 Then Moses gave the tax as Jehovah's contribution to E·le·a′zar the priest, just as Jehovah had commanded Moses.

42 And from the half belonging to the sons of Israel, which Moses divided from that belonging to the men who waged war: 43 Now the half of the assembly from the flock

amounted to three hundred and thirty-seven thousand five hundred, 44 and of the herd, thirty-six thousand, 45 and the asses, thirty thousand five hundred, 46 and human souls, sixteen thousand. 47 Then Moses took from the half belonging to the sons of Israel the one to be taken out of fifty, of humankind and of domestic animals, and gave them to the Levites, the keepers of the obligation of Jehovah's tabernacle, just as Jehovah had commanded Moses.

48 And the appointed men who were of the thousands of the army, the chiefs of the thousands and the chiefs of the hundreds, proceeded to approach Moses, 49 and to say to Moses: "Your servants have taken the sum of the men of war who are in our charge and not one has been reported missing from us. 50 So let us present each one what he has found as Jehovah's offering, articles of gold, ankle chainlets, and bracelets, signet rings, earrings, and female ornaments, in order to make atonement for our souls before Jehovah."

51 Accordingly Moses and E·le·a'zar the priest accepted the gold from them, all the jewelry. 52 And all the gold of the contribution that they contributed to Jehovah amounted to sixteen thousand seven hundred and fifty shekels, from the chiefs of the thousands and the chiefs of the hundreds. 53 The men of the army had taken plunder each for himself. 54 So Moses and E·le·a'zar the priest accepted the gold from the chiefs of the thousands and of the hundreds and brought it into the tent of meeting as a memorial for the sons of Israel before Jehovah.

32 Now the sons of Reu'ben and the sons of Gad had come to have numerous livestock, very many, in fact. And they began to see the land of Ja'zer and the land of Gil'e·ad, and, look! the place was a place for livestock. 2 Hence the sons of Gad and the sons of Reu'ben came and said this to Moses and E·le·a'zar the priest and to the chieftains of the assembly:

3 "At'a·roth and Di'bon and Ja'zer and Nim'rah and Hesh'bon and E·le·a'leh and Se'bam and Ne'bo and Be'on, 4 the land that Jehovah defeated before the assembly of Israel, is a land for livestock, and your servants have livestock." 5 And they went on to say: "If we have found favor in your eyes, let this land be given to your servants as a possession. Do not make us cross the Jordan."

6 Then Moses said to the sons of Gad and the sons of Reu'ben: "Are YOUR brothers to go to war while YOU yourselves keep dwelling here? 7 And why should YOU dishearten the sons of Israel from crossing into the land that Jehovah will certainly give them? 8 That is the way YOUR fathers did when I sent them from Ka'desh-bar'ne·a to see the land. 9 When they went up to the torrent valley of Esh'col and saw the land, then they disheartened the sons of Israel, so as not to go into the land that Jehovah was certain to give them. 10 Consequently Jehovah's anger blazed on that day so that he swore, saying, 11 'The men who came up out of Egypt from twenty years old upward will not see the soil of which I have sworn to Abraham, Isaac and Jacob, because they have not followed me wholly, 12 except Ca'leb the son of Je·phun'neh the Ken'iz·zite and Joshua the son of Nun, because they have followed Jehovah wholly.' 13 So Jehovah's anger blazed against Israel and he made them wander about in the wilderness forty years, until all the generation that was doing evil in the eyes of Jehovah came to their end. 14 And here YOU have risen in the place of YOUR fathers as the brood of sinful men in order to add further to the burning anger of Jehovah against Israel. 15 In case YOU should turn back from following him, he also would certainly once again let them stay longer in the wilderness, and YOU would have acted ruinously toward all this people."

16 Later they approached him and said: "Let us build here stone

flock pens for our livestock and cities for our little ones. 17 But we ourselves shall go equipped in battle formation before the sons of Israel until whenever we have brought them to their place, while our little ones must dwell in the cities with fortifications away from the face of the inhabitants of the land. 18 We shall not return to our houses until the sons of Israel have provided themselves with landed property, each with his own inheritance. 19 For we shall not get an inheritance with them from the side of the Jordan and beyond, because our inheritance has come to us from the side of the Jordan toward the sunrising."

20 At this Moses said to them: "If you will do this thing, if you will equip yourselves before Jehovah for the war, 21 and every equipped one of yours will actually pass over the Jordan before Jehovah, until he drives away his enemies from before him, 22 and the land is actually subdued before Jehovah, and afterward you return, you also will indeed prove yourselves free from guilt against Jehovah and against Israel; and this land must become yours as a possession before Jehovah. 23 But if you will not do this way, you will also certainly sin against Jehovah. In that case know that your sin will catch up with you. 24 Build for yourselves cities for your little ones and stone pens for your flocks, and what has gone forth from your mouth you should do."

25 Then the sons of Gad and the sons of Reu'ben said this to Moses: "Your servants will do just as my lord is commanding. 26 Our little ones, our wives, our livestock and all our domestic animals will stay there in the cities of Gil'e·ad, 27 but your servants will pass over, everyone equipped for the army, before Jehovah for the war, just as my lord is speaking."

28 Accordingly Moses gave a command respecting them to E·le·a'zar the priest and to Joshua the son of Nun and to the heads of the fathers of the tribes of the sons of Israel. 29 So Moses said to them: "If the sons of Gad and the sons of Reu'ben pass with you over the Jordan, everyone equipped for the war, before Jehovah, and the land is actually subdued before you, you must then give them the land of Gil'e·ad as a possession. 30 But if they do not pass over equipped with you, they must then be settled in your midst in the land of Ca'naan."

31 To this the sons of Gad and the sons of Reu'ben answered, saying: "What Jehovah has spoken to your servants is the way we shall do. 32 We ourselves will pass over equipped before Jehovah to the land of Ca'naan, and the possession of our inheritance will be with us on this side of the Jordan." 33 At this Moses gave to them, that is, to the sons of Gad and to the sons of Reu'ben and to half the tribe of Ma·nas'seh the son of Joseph, the kingdom of Si'hon the king of the Am'or·ites and the kingdom of Og the king of Ba'shan, the land belonging to its cities in the territories, and the cities of the land round about.

34 And the sons of Gad proceeded to build Di'bon and At'a·roth and A·ro'er, 35 and At'roth-sho'phan and Ja'zer and Jog'be·hah, 36 and Beth-nim'rah and Beth-ha'ran, cities with fortifications, and stone flock pens. 37 And the sons of Reu'ben built Hesh'bon and E·le·a'leh and Kir·i·a·tha'im, 38 and Ne'bo and Ba'al-me'on—their names being changed—and Sib'mah; and they began to call by their own names the names of the cities that they built.

39 And the sons of Ma'chir the son of Ma·nas'seh proceeded to march to Gil'e·ad and to capture it and to drive away the Am'or·ites who were in it. 40 So Moses gave Gil'e·ad to Ma'chir the son of Ma·nas'seh, and he took up dwelling in it. 41 And Ja'ir the son of Ma·nas'seh marched and went capturing their tent villages, and he began to call them Hav'voth-ja'ir. 42 And No'bah marched and went capturing Ke'nath and its depend-

ent towns; and he began to call it No'bah by his own name.

33 These were the stages of the sons of Israel who went out of the land of Egypt in their armies by the hand of Moses and Aaron. 2 And Moses kept recording the departure places by their stages at the order of Jehovah; and these were their stages from one departure place to another: 3 And they proceeded to pull away from Ram'e·ses in the first month, on the fifteenth day of the first month. Directly the day after the passover the sons of Israel went out with uplifted hand before the eyes of all the Egyptians. 4 All the while the Egyptians were burying those whom Jehovah had struck among them, that is, all the first-born; and upon their gods Jehovah had executed judgments.

5 So the sons of Israel pulled away from Ram'e·ses and went camping in Suc'coth. 6 Then they pulled away from Suc'coth and went camping in E'tham, which is on the edge of the wilderness. 7 Next they pulled away from E'tham and turned back toward Pi·ha·hi'roth, which is in view of Ba'al-ze'phon; and they went camping before Mig'dol. 8 After that they pulled away from Pi·ha·hi'roth and went passing through the midst of the sea to the wilderness and kept marching a three-day journey in the wilderness of E'tham and took up camping at Ma'rah.

9 Then they pulled away from Ma'rah and came to E'lim. Now in E'lim there were twelve springs of water and seventy palm trees. So they camped there. 10 Next they pulled away from E'lim and went camping by the Red Sea. 11 After that they pulled away from the Red Sea and took up camping in the wilderness of Sin. 12 Then they pulled away from the wilderness of Sin and went camping at Doph'kah. 13 Later they pulled away from Doph'kah and went camping at A'lush. 14 They next pulled away from A'lush and went camping in Reph'i·dim. And there proved to be no water there for the people to drink. 15 After that they pulled away from Reph'i·dim and went camping in the wilderness of Si'nai.

16 Subsequently they pulled away from the wilderness of Si'nai and went camping at Kib'roth-hat·ta'a·vah. 17 Then they pulled away from Kib'roth-hat·ta'a·vah and went camping in Ha·ze'roth. 18 After that they pulled away from Ha·ze'roth and went camping in Rith'mah. 19 Next they pulled away from Rith'mah and took up camping in Rim'mon-pe'rez. 20 Then they pulled away from Rim'mon-pe'rez and went camping in Lib'nah. 21 Later they pulled away from Lib'nah and went camping in Ris'sah. 22 Next they pulled away from Ris'sah and went camping in Ke·he·la'thah. 23 Then they pulled away from Ke·he·la'thah and went camping in Mount She'pher.

24 After that they pulled away from Mount She'pher and went camping in Har·a'dah. 25 Then they pulled away from Har·a'dah and went camping in Mak·he'loth. 26 Next they pulled away from Mak·he'loth and went camping in Ta'hath. 27 After that they pulled away from Ta'hath and went camping in Te'rah. 28 Then they pulled away from Te'rah and went camping in Mith'kah. 29 Later they pulled away from Mith'kah and went camping in Hash·mo'nah. 30 Next they pulled away from Hash·mo'nah and went camping in Mo·se'roth. 31 Then they pulled away from Mo·se'roth and went camping in Ben'e-ja'a·kan. 32 After that they pulled away from Ben'e-ja'a·kan and went camping in Hor-hag·gid'gad. 33 Next they pulled away from Hor-hag·gid'gad and went camping in Jot'ba·thah. 34 Later they pulled away from Jot'ba·thah and went camping in A·bro'nah. 35 Then they pulled away from A·bro'nah and went camping in E'zi·on-ge'ber. 36 After that they pulled away from E'zi·on-ge'ber and went camping in the wilderness of Zin, that is to say, Ka'desh.

37 Later they pulled away from Ka'desh and went camping in Mount Hor, on the frontier of the land of E'dom. 38 And Aaron the priest proceeded to go up into Mount Hor at the order of Jehovah and to die there in the fortieth year of the going out of the sons of Israel from the land of Egypt, in the fifth month, on the first of the month. 39 And Aaron was a hundred and twenty-three years old at his death on Mount Hor.

40 Now the Ca'naan·ite, the king of A'rad, as he was dwelling in the Neg'eb, in the land of Ca'naan, got to hear about the coming of the sons of Israel.

41 In time they pulled away from Mount Hor and went camping in Zal·mo'nah. 42 After that they pulled away from Zal·mo'nah and went camping in Pu'non. 43 Next they pulled away from Pu'non and went camping in O'both. 44 Then they pulled away from O'both and went camping in I'ye-ab'a·rim on the border of Mo'ab. 45 Later they pulled away from I'yim and went camping in Di'bon-gad. 46 After that they pulled away from Di'bon-gad and went camping in Al'mon-dib·la·tha'im. 47 Then they pulled away from Al'mon-dib·la·tha'im and went camping in the mountains of Ab'a·rim before Ne'bo. 48 Finally they pulled away from the mountains of Ab'a·rim and took up camping on the desert plains of Mo'ab by the Jordan at Jer'i·cho. 49 And they continued camping by the Jordan from Beth-jesh'i·moth to A'bel-shit'tim on the desert plains of Mo'ab.

50 And Jehovah proceeded to speak to Moses on the desert plains of Mo'ab by the Jordan at Jer'i·cho, saying: 51 "Speak to the sons of Israel, and you must say to them, 'You are crossing the Jordan into the land of Ca'naan. 52 And you must drive away all the inhabitants of the land from before you and destroy all their stone figures, and all their images of molten metal you should destroy, and all their sacred high places you should annihilate. 53 And you must take possession of the land and dwell in it, because to you I shall certainly give the land to take possession of it. 54 And you must apportion the land to yourselves as a possession by lot according to your families. To the populous one you should increase his inheritance, and to the sparse one you should reduce his inheritance. To where the lot will come out for him, there it will become his. By the tribes of your fathers you should provide yourselves with landed property.

55 "'If, though, you will not drive the inhabitants of the land away from before you, then those whom you leave of them will certainly become as pricks in your eyes and as thorns in your sides, and they will indeed harass you on the land in which you will be dwelling. 56 And it must occur that just as I had figured doing to them I shall do to you.'"

34 And Jehovah spoke further to Moses, saying: 2 "Command the sons of Israel, and you must say to them, 'You are going into the land of Ca'naan. This is the land that will fall to you by inheritance, the land of Ca'naan according to its boundaries.

3 "'And your south side must prove to be from the wilderness of Zin alongside E'dom, and your south boundary must prove to be from the extremity of the Salt Sea on the east. 4 And your boundary must change direction from the south of the ascent of A·krab'bim and cross over to Zin, and its termination must prove to be on the south of Ka'desh-bar'ne·a; and it must go out to Ha'zar-ad'dar and pass over to Az'mon. 5 And the boundary must change direction at Az'mon to the torrent valley of Egypt, and its termination must prove to be at the Sea.

6 "'As for a west boundary, it must prove to be for you the Great Sea and the shoreline. This will become your west boundary.

7 "'Now this will become your north boundary: From the Great Sea you will mark out to Mount

Hor as a boundary for yourselves. 8 From Mount Hor you will mark out the boundary to the entering in of Ha′math, and the termination of the boundary must prove to be at Ze′dad. 9 And the boundary must go out to Ziph′ron, and its termination must prove to be Ha′zar-e′nan. This will become your north boundary.

10 " 'Then you must mark for yourselves as your boundary on the east from Ha′zar-e′nan to She′pham. 11 And the boundary must go down from She′pham to Rib′lah on the east of A′in, and the border must go down and strike upon the eastern slope of the sea of Chin′nereth. 12 And the border must go down to the Jordan, and its termination must prove to be the Salt Sea. This will become your land according to its boundaries all around.' "

13 So Moses commanded the sons of Israel, saying: "This is the land that you will apportion to yourselves as a possession by lot, just as Jehovah has commanded to give to the nine and a half tribes. 14 For the tribe of the sons of the Reu′ben·ites by the house of their fathers and the tribe of the sons of the Gad′ites by the house of their fathers have already taken, and the half tribe of Ma·nas′seh have already taken their inheritance. 15 The two and a half tribes have already taken their inheritance from the region of the Jordan by Jer′i·cho eastward toward the sunrising."

16 And Jehovah spoke further to Moses, saying: 17 "These are the names of the men who will divide the land to you people for a possession, E·le·a′zar the priest and Joshua the son of Nun. 18 And you will take one chieftain out of each tribe to divide the land for a possession. 19 And these are the names of the men: Of the tribe of Judah, Ca′leb the son of Je·phun′neh; 20 and of the tribe of the sons of Sim′e·on, She·mu′el the son of Am·mi′hud; 21 of the tribe of Benjamin, E·li′dad the son of Chis′lon; 22 and of the tribe of

the sons of Dan a chieftain, Buk′ki the son of Jog′li; 23 of the sons of Joseph, of the tribe of the sons of Ma·nas′seh a chieftain, Han′niel the son of E′phod; 24 and of the tribe of the sons of E′phra·im a chieftain, Ke·mu′el the son of Shiph′tan; 25 and of the tribe of the sons of Zeb′u·lun a chieftain, E·li·za′phan the son of Par′nach; 26 and of the tribe of the sons of Is′sa·char a chieftain, Pal′ti·el the son of Az′zan; 27 and of the tribe of the sons of Ash′er a chieftain, A·hi′hud the son of She·lo′mi; 28 and of the tribe of the sons of Naph′ta·li a chieftain, Ped·ah′el the son of Am·mi′hud." 29 These are the ones whom Jehovah commanded to make the sons of Israel landholders in the land of Ca′naan.

35 And Jehovah went on to speak to Moses on the desert plains of Mo′ab by the Jordan at Jer′icho, saying: 2 "Give the sons of Israel the command that they must give the Levites cities to inhabit out of the inheritance of their possession, and they should give the Levites the pasture ground of the cities all around them. 3 And the cities must serve for them to inhabit, while their pasture grounds will serve for their domestic animals and their goods and for all their wild beasts. 4 And the pasture grounds of the cities, which you will give the Levites, will be from the wall of the city and out for a thousand cubits all around. 5 And you must measure outside the city on the east side two thousand cubits and on the south side two thousand cubits and on the west side two thousand cubits and on the north side two thousand cubits, with the city in the middle. This will serve them as pasture grounds of the cities.

6 "These are the cities that you will give to the Levites: six cities of refuge, which you will give for the manslayer to flee there, and besides them you will give forty-two other cities. 7 All the cities that you will give to the Levites will be forty-eight cities, they together with their pasture grounds. 8 The

cities that YOU will give will be from the possession of the sons of Israel. From the many YOU will take many, and from the few YOU will take few. Each one, in proportion to his inheritance that he will take as a possession, will give some of his cities to the Levites."

9 And Jehovah continued to speak to Moses, saying: 10 "Speak to the sons of Israel, and you must say to them, 'YOU are crossing the Jordan to the land of Ca′naan. 11 And YOU must choose cities convenient for yourselves. As cities of refuge they will serve for YOU, and the manslayer must flee there who fatally strikes a soul unintentionally. 12 And the cities must serve YOU as a refuge from the blood avenger, that the manslayer may not die until he stands before the assembly for judgment. 13 And the cities that YOU will give, the six cities of refuge, will be at YOUR service. 14 Three cities YOU will give on this side of the Jordan, and three cities YOU will give in the land of Ca′naan. As cities of refuge they will serve. 15 For the sons of Israel and for the alien resident and for the settler in the midst of them these six cities will serve as a refuge, for anyone to flee there that fatally strikes a soul unintentionally.

16 "'Now if it was with an instrument of iron that he has struck him so that he dies, he is a murderer. Without fail the murderer should be put to death. 17 And if it was with a small stone by which he could die that he has struck him so that he dies, he is a murderer. Without fail the murderer should be put to death. 18 And if it was with a small instrument of wood by which he could die that he has struck him so that he dies, he is a murderer. Without fail the murderer should be put to death.

19 "'The avenger of blood is the one who will put the murderer to death. When he chances upon him he himself will put him to death. 20 And if in hatred he was pushing him or he has thrown at him

while lying in wait that he might die, 21 or in enmity he has struck him with his hand that he might die, without fail the striker should be put to death. He is a murderer. The avenger of blood will put the murderer to death when he chances upon him.

22 "'But if it was unexpectedly without enmity that he has pushed him or has thrown any article toward him without lying in wait, 23 or any stone by which he could die without seeing him or he should cause it to fall upon him, so that he died, while he was not at enmity with him and was not seeking his injury, 24 the assembly must then judge between the striker and the avenger of blood according to these judgments. 25 And the assembly must deliver the manslayer out of the hand of the avenger of blood, and the assembly must return him to his city of refuge to which he had fled, and he must dwell in it until the death of the high priest who was anointed with the holy oil.

26 "'But if the manslayer without fail goes out of the boundary of his city of refuge to which he may flee, 27 and the avenger of blood does find him outside the boundary of his city of refuge, and the avenger of blood does slay the manslayer, he has no bloodguilt. 28 For he ought to dwell in his city of refuge until the high priest's death, and after the high priest's death the manslayer may return to the land of his possession. 29 And these must serve as a statute of judgment for YOU throughout YOUR generations in all YOUR dwelling places.

30 "'Every fatal striker of a soul should be slain as a murderer at the mouth of witnesses, and one witness may not testify against a soul for him to die. 31 And YOU must take no ransom for the soul of a murderer who is deserving to die, for without fail he should be put to death. 32 And YOU must not take a ransom for one who has fled to his city of refuge, to resume

dwelling in the land before the death of the high priest.

33 " 'And you must not pollute the land in which you are; because it is blood that pollutes the land, and for the land there may be no atonement respecting the blood that has been spilled upon it except by the blood of the one spilling it. 34 And you must not defile the land in which you are dwelling, in the midst of which I am residing; for I Jehovah am residing in the midst of the sons of Israel.' "

36 And the heads of the fathers of the family of the sons of Gil'e·ad the son of Ma'chir the son of Ma·nas'seh of the families of the sons of Joseph proceeded to come near and speak before Moses and the chieftains, the heads of the fathers of the sons of Israel, 2 and say: "Jehovah commanded my lord to give the land in inheritance by lot to the sons of Israel; and my lord was commanded by Jehovah to give the inheritance of Ze·lo'phe·had our brother to his daughters. 3 If any of the sons of the other tribes of the sons of Israel happened to get them as wives, the women's inheritance must also be withdrawn from the inheritance of our fathers and must be added to the inheritance of the tribe to which they may come to belong, so that it would be withdrawn from the lot of our inheritance. 4 Now if the Jubilee takes place for the sons of Israel, the women's inheritance must also be added to the inheritance of the tribe to which they may come to belong; so that their inheritance would be withdrawn from the inheritance of the tribe of our fathers."

5 Then Moses commanded the sons of Israel at the order of Je-

hovah, saying: "The tribe of the sons of Joseph is speaking right. 6 This is the word that Jehovah has commanded for the daughters of Ze·lo'phe·had, saying, 'To whom it is good in their eyes they may become wives. Only it is to the family of the tribe of their fathers that they should become wives. 7 And no inheritance of the sons of Israel should circulate from tribe to tribe, because the sons of Israel should cleave each one to the inheritance of the tribe of his forefathers. 8 And every daughter getting possession of an inheritance out of the tribes of the sons of Israel, to one of the family of the tribe of her father she should become a wife, in order that the sons of Israel may get possession each one of the inheritance of his forefathers. 9 And no inheritance should circulate from one tribe to another tribe, because the tribes of the sons of Israel should cleave each to its own inheritance.' "

10 Just as Jehovah had commanded Moses, that is the way the daughters of Ze·lo'phe·had did. 11 Accordingly Mah'lah, Tir'zah and Hog'lah and Mil'cah and No'ah, the daughters of Ze·lo'phe-had, became the wives of the sons of their father's brothers. 12 To some of the families of the sons of Ma·nas'seh the son of Joseph they became wives, that their inheritance might continue together with the tribe of the family of their father.

13 These are the commandments and the judicial decisions that Jehovah commanded by means of Moses to the sons of Israel on the desert plains of Mo'ab by the Jordan at Jer'i·cho.

DEUTERONOMY

1 These are the words that Moses spoke to all Israel in the region of the Jordan in the wilderness, on the desert plains in front of Suph, between Pa′ran and To′phel and La′ban and Ha·ze′roth and Di′za-hab, 2 it being eleven days from Ho′reb by the way of Mount Se′ir to Ka′desh-bar′ne·a. 3 And it came about that in the fortieth year, in the eleventh month, on the first of the month, Moses spoke to the sons of Israel according to all that Jehovah had commanded him for them, 4 after his defeating Si′hon the king of the Am′or·ites, who was dwelling in Hesh′bon, and Og the king of Ba′-shan, who was dwelling in Ash′ta-roth, in Ed′re·i. 5 In the region of the Jordan in the land of Mo′ab Moses undertook to explain this law, saying:

6 "Jehovah our God spoke to us in Ho′reb, saying, 'You have dwelt long enough in this mountainous region. 7 Turn and set out on YOUR way and go into the mountainous region of the Am′or·ites and to all their neighbors in the Ar′a·bah, the mountainous region and the She·phe′lah and the Neg′-eb and the seacoast, the land of the Ca′naan·ites, and Leb′a·non, up to the great river, the river Eu·phra′tes. 8 See, I do put the land before YOU people. Go in and take possession of the land about which Jehovah swore to YOUR fathers, to Abraham, Isaac and Jacob, to give it to them and their seed after them.'

9 "And I proceeded to say this to YOU at that particular time, 'I am not able by myself to carry YOU. 10 Jehovah YOUR God has multiplied YOU, and here YOU are today like the stars of the heavens for multitude. 11 May Jehovah the God of YOUR forefathers increase YOU a thousand times as many as YOU are, and may he bless YOU just as he has promised YOU.

12 How can I carry by myself the burden of YOU and the load of YOU and YOUR quarreling? 13 Get wise and discreet and experienced men of YOUR tribes, that I may set them as heads over YOU.' 14 At that YOU answered me and said, 'The thing you have spoken for us to do is good.' 15 So I took the heads of YOUR tribes, men wise and experienced, and put them as heads over YOU, chiefs of thousands and chiefs of hundreds and chiefs of fifties and chiefs of tens and officers of YOUR tribes.

16 "And I went on to command YOUR judges at that particular time, saying, 'When having a hearing between YOUR brothers, YOU must judge with righteousness between a man and his brother or his alien resident. 17 YOU must not be partial in judgment. YOU should hear the little one the same as the great one. YOU must not become frightened because of a man, for the judgment belongs to God; and the case that is too hard for YOU, YOU should present to me, and I must hear it.' 18 And I proceeded to command YOU at that particular time all the things that YOU should do.

19 "Then we pulled away from Ho′reb and went marching through all that great and fear-inspiring wilderness, which YOU have seen, by the way of the mountainous region of the Am′or·ites, just as Jehovah our God had commanded us; and we eventually came to Ka′desh-bar′ne·a. 20 I now said to YOU, 'YOU have come to the mountainous region of the Am′or·ites, which Jehovah our God is giving to us. 21 See, Jehovah your God has abandoned the land to you. Go up, take possession, just as Jehovah the God of your forefathers has spoken to you. Do not be afraid, nor be terrified.'

22 "However, all of YOU came near to me and said, 'Do let

us send men ahead of us that they may search out the land for us and bring us back word concerning the way by which we should go up and the cities to which we will come.' 23 Well, the thing proved to be good in my eyes, so that I took twelve men of YOURS, one for each tribe. 24 Then they turned and went up into the mountainous region and got as far as the torrent valley of Esh'col and went spying on it. 25 And they proceeded to take some of the fruitage of the land in their hand and to bring it down to us, and they came bringing us back word and saying, 'The land that Jehovah our God is giving us is good.' 26 But YOU did not wish to go up, and YOU began to behave rebelliously against the order of Jehovah YOUR God. 27 And YOU kept grumbling in YOUR tents and saying, 'It was because Jehovah hated us that he brought us out of the land of Egypt to give us into the hand of the Am'or·ites, to annihilate us. 28 Where are we going up? Our brothers have caused our heart to melt, saying: "A people greater and taller than we are, cities great and fortified to the heavens and also the sons of the An'a·kim we saw there." '

29 "So I said to YOU, 'YOU must not suffer a shock or be afraid because of them. 30 Jehovah YOUR God is the one going before YOU. He will fight for YOU according to all that he did with YOU in Egypt under YOUR own eyes, 31 and in the wilderness, where you saw how Jehovah your God carried you just as a man carries his son, in all the way that YOU walked until YOUR coming to this place.' 32 But despite this word YOU were not putting faith in Jehovah YOUR God, 33 who was going before YOU in the way to spy out for YOU a place for YOU to camp, by fire at night for YOU to see by what way YOU should walk and by a cloud in daytime.

34 "All the while Jehovah heard the voice of YOUR words. So he became indignant and swore, saying, 35 'Not one among these men of this evil generation will see the good land that I swore to give to YOUR fathers, 36 except Ca'leb the son of Je·phun'neh. He will see it, and to him and to his sons I shall give the land upon which he trod, by reason of the fact that he has followed Jehovah fully. 37 (Even against me Jehovah got incensed on YOUR account, saying, 'You too will not go in there. 38 Joshua the son of Nun, who is standing before you, is the one who will go in there.' Him he has made strong, because he will cause Israel to inherit it.) 39 As for YOUR little ones of whom you said: "Plunder they will become!" and YOUR sons who today do not know good or bad, these will go in there, and to them I shall give it, and they will take possession of it. 40 As for YOU yourselves, change YOUR direction and pull away for the wilderness by the way of the Red Sea.'

41 "At this YOU answered and said to me, 'We have sinned against Jehovah. We—we shall go up and fight in accord with all that Jehovah our God has commanded us!' So YOU girded on, each one, his weapons of war and regarded it as easy to go up into the mountain. 42 But Jehovah said to me, 'Say to them: "YOU must not go up and fight, because I am not in YOUR midst; that YOU may not be defeated before YOUR enemies." ' 43 So I spoke to YOU, and YOU did not listen but began to behave rebelliously against Jehovah's order and to get all heated up, and you tried to go up into the mountain. 44 Then the Am'or·ites who were dwelling in that mountain came out to meet YOU and went chasing YOU, just as bees do, and scattering YOU in Se'ir as far as Hor'mah. 45 After that YOU returned and began to weep before Jehovah, but Jehovah did not listen to YOUR voice, neither did he give ear to YOU. 46 So YOU kept dwelling in Ka'desh many days, as many days as YOU did dwell there.

2 "Then we turned and pulled away for the wilderness by the way of the Red Sea, just as Jehovah had spoken to me; and we were many days in going around Mount Se′ir. 2 Finally Jehovah said this to me, 3 'YOU have gone around this mountain long enough. Change YOUR direction to the north. 4 And command the people, saying: "YOU are passing along by the border of YOUR brothers, the sons of E′sau, who are dwelling in Se′ir; and they will be afraid because of YOU, and YOU must be very careful. 5 Do not engage in strife with them, because I shall not give YOU of their land so much as the width of the sole of the foot; because I have given Mount Se′ir to E′sau as a holding. 6 What food YOU may buy from them for money, YOU must eat; and also what water YOU may purchase from them for money, YOU must drink. 7 For Jehovah your God has blessed you in every deed of your hand. He well knows of your walking through this great wilderness. These forty years Jehovah your God has been with you. You have not lacked a thing."' 8 So we passed on away from our brothers, the sons of E′sau, who are dwelling in Se′ir, from the way of the Ar′a·bah, from E′lath and from E′zi·on-ge′ber.

"Next we turned and passed on by the way of the wilderness of Mo′ab. 9 Jehovah then said to me, 'Do not molest Mo′ab or engage in war with them, because I shall not give you any of his land as a holding, for to the sons of Lot I have given Ar as a holding. 10 (The E′mim dwelt in it in former times, a people great and numerous and tall like the An′a·kim. 11 As for the Reph′a·im, they also were considered like the An′a·kim, and the Mo′ab·ites used to call them E′mim. 12 And the Hor′ites dwelt in Se′ir in former times, and the sons of E′sau proceeded to dispossess them and to annihilate them from before them and to dwell in their place, just the same as Israel must do to the land that is his holding, which Jehovah will certainly give to them.) 13 At this time rise and make YOUR way across the torrent valley of Ze′red.' Accordingly we went crossing the torrent valley of Ze′red. 14 And the days that we walked from Ka′desh-bar′ne·a until we crossed the torrent valley of Ze′red were thirty-eight years, until all the generation of the men of war had come to their end from the midst of the camp, just as Jehovah had sworn to them. 15 And the hand of Jehovah also proved to be upon them to disquiet them out of the midst of the camp, until they came to their end.

16 "And it came about that as soon as all the men of war had finished dying off from the midst of the people, 17 Jehovah spoke further to me, saying, 18 'You are passing today by the territory of Mo′ab, that is, Ar, 19 and you must get close in front of the sons of Am′mon. Do not molest them or engage in strife with them, because I shall not give you any of the land of the sons of Am′mon as a holding, for it is to the sons of Lot that I have given it as a holding. 20 As the land of the Reph′a·im it also used to be considered. (The Reph′a·im dwelt in it in former times, and the Am′mon·ites used to call them Zam·zum′mim. 21 They were a great and numerous and tall people like the An′a·kim; and Jehovah went annihilating them from before them, that they might dispossess them and dwell in their place; 22 just the same as he did for the sons of E′sau, who are dwelling in Se′ir, when he annihilated the Hor′ites from before them, that they might dispossess them and dwell in their place until this day. 23 As for the Av′vim, who were dwelling in settlements as far as Ga′za, the Caph′to·rim, who came out from Caph′tor, annihilated them, that they might dwell in their place.)

24 " 'GET up, pull away and cross the torrent valley of Ar′non. See, I have given into your hand Si′hon the king of Hesh′bon, the Am′or·ite. So start to take possession of

his land, and engage in war with him. 25 This day I shall start to put the dread of you and the fear of you before the peoples beneath all the heavens, who will hear the report about you; and they will indeed be agitated and have pains like those of childbirth because of you.'

26 "Then I sent messengers from the wilderness of Ked'e·moth to Si'hon the king of Hesh'bon with words of peace, saying, 27 'Let me pass through your land. Only on the road I shall walk. I shall not turn to the right or to the left. 28 What food you will sell me for money, I must eat; and what water you will give me for money, I must drink. Only let me pass through on my feet, 29 just the same as the sons of E'sau dwelling in Se'ir and the Mo'ab·ites dwelling in Ar did to me, until I shall pass over the Jordan into the land that Je-hovah our God is giving to us.' 30 And Si'hon the king of Hesh'-bon did not let us pass through him, because Jehovah your God had let his spirit become obstinate and his heart become hard, in order to give him into your hand just as at this day.

31 "At this Jehovah said to me, 'See, I have started to abandon Si'hon and his land to you. Start to take possession of his land.' 32 When Si'hon came on out, he and all his people, to meet us in battle at Ja'haz, 33 then Jehovah our God abandoned him to us, so that we defeated him and his sons and all his people. 34 And we went capturing all his cities at that particular time and devoting every city to destruction, men and women and little children. We left no sur-vivor. 35 Only the domestic ani-mals did we take as plunder for ourselves, together with the spoil of the cities that we had captured. 36 From A·ro'er, which is by the bank of the torrent valley of Ar'-non, and the city that is in the torrent valley, as far as Gil'e·ad, there proved to be no town that was too high up for us. Jehovah our God abandoned them all to us.

37 Only you did not go near the land of the sons of Am'mon, the whole bank of the torrent valley of Jab'bok, nor the cities of the mountainous region, nor anything about which Jehovah our God had given command.

3 "Then we turned and went up by the way of Ba'shan. At this Og the king of Ba'shan came on out, he and all his people, to meet us in battle at Ed're·i. 2 So Je-hovah said to me, 'Do not be afraid of him, for I shall certainly give him and all his people and his land into your hand; and you must do to him just as you did to Si'hon the king of the Am'or·ites, who was dwelling in Hesh'bon.' 3 Ac-cordingly Jehovah our God gave into our hand also Og the king of Ba'shan and all his people, and we kept striking him until he had no survivor remaining. 4 And we went capturing all his cities at that particular time. There proved to be no town that we did not take from them, sixty cities, all the re-gion of Ar'gob, the kingdom of Og in Ba'shan. 5 All these were cities fortified with a high wall, doors and bar, aside from very many rural towns. 6 However, we de-voted them to destruction, just as we had done to Si'hon the king of Hesh'bon, in devoting every city to destruction, men, women and little children. 7 And all the domestic animals and the spoil of the cities we took as plunder for ourselves.

8 "And we proceeded to take at that particular time the land from the hand of the two kings of the Am'or·ites who were in the region of the Jordan, from the torrent valley of Ar'non as far as Mount Her'mon; 9 (the Si·do'ni·ans used to call Her'mon Sir'i·on, and the Am'or·ites used to call it Se'nir,) 10 all the cities of the tableland and all Gil'e·ad and all Ba'shan as far as Sal'e·cah and Ed're·i, the cities of the kingdom of Og in Ba'shan. 11 For only Og the king of Ba'shan remained of what was left of the Reph'a·im. Look! His bier was a bier of iron. Is it not in Rab'bah of the sons of Am'mon?

Nine cubits is its length, and four cubits its width, by the cubit of a man. 12 And we took possession of this land at that particular time; from A·ro'er, which is by the torrent valley of Ar'non, and half of the mountainous region of Gil'e·ad, and its cities I have given to the Reu'ben·ites and the Gad'ites. 13 And the rest of Gil'e·ad and all Ba'shan of the kingdom of Og I have given to the half tribe of Ma·nas'seh. All the region of Ar'gob of all Ba'shan, is it not called the land of the Reph'a·im?

14 "Ja'ir the son of Ma·nas'seh took all the region of Ar'gob as far as the boundary of the Gesh'ur·ites and the Ma·ac'a·thites, and he proceeded to call those villages of Ba'shan by his own name, Hav'voth-ja'ir, to this day. 15 And to Ma'chir I have given Gil'e·ad. 16 And to the Reu'ben·ites and the Gad'ites I have given from Gil'e·ad to the torrent valley of Ar'non, the middle of the torrent valley being a boundary, and as far as Jab'bok, the torrent valley that is the boundary of the sons of Am'mon; 17 and the Ar'a·bah and the Jordan and the border, from Chin'ne·reth to the sea of the Ar'a·bah, the Salt Sea, at the base of the slopes of Pis'gah toward the sunrising.

18 "So I commanded YOU men at that particular time, saying, 'Jehovah YOUR God has given YOU this land to take possession of it. YOU will pass over, equipped, before YOUR brothers, the sons of Israel, all the valiant men. 19 Only YOUR wives and YOUR little ones and YOUR livestock (I well know that YOU have a great deal of livestock) will continue dwelling in YOUR cities that I have given YOU, 20 until Jehovah gives YOUR brothers rest, as well as YOU, and they also have taken possession of the land that Jehovah YOUR God is giving them across the Jordan; after which YOU must come back, each one to his holding that I have given YOU.'

21 "And I commanded Joshua at that particular time, saying, 'Your

eyes are seeing all that Jehovah YOUR God has done to these two kings. The same way Jehovah will do to all the kingdoms to which you are passing over there. 22 YOU men must not be afraid of them, for Jehovah YOUR God is the One fighting for YOU.'

23 "And I proceeded to implore favor from Jehovah at that particular time, saying, 24 'O Lord Jehovah, you yourself have started to make your servant see your greatness and your strong arm, for who is a god in the heavens or on the earth that does deeds like yours and mighty performances like yours? 25 Let me pass over, please, and see the good land that is across the Jordan, this good mountainous region and Leb'a·non.' 26 And Jehovah continued to be furious against me on YOUR account and did not listen to me; but Jehovah said to me, 'That is enough of you! Never speak to me further on this matter. 27 Go up to the top of Pis'gah and raise your eyes to the west and north and south and east and see with your eyes, for you will not pass over this Jordan. 28 And commission Joshua and encourage him and strengthen him, because he is the one to pass over before this people and he is the one to cause them to inherit the land that you will see.' 29 All this while we were dwelling in the valley in front of Beth-pe'or.

4 "And now, O Israel, listen to the regulations and the judicial decisions that I am teaching YOU to do, in order that YOU may live and may indeed go in and take possession of the land that Jehovah the God of YOUR forefathers is giving YOU. 2 YOU must not add to the word that I am commanding YOU, neither must YOU take away from it, so as to keep the commandments of Jehovah YOUR God that I am commanding YOU.

3 "YOUR own eyes are the ones that saw what Jehovah did in the case of the Ba'al of Pe'or, that every man who walked after the Ba'al of Pe'or was the one whom

Jehovah your God annihilated from your midst. 4 But YOU who are cleaving to Jehovah YOUR God are all of YOU alive today. 5 See, I have taught YOU regulations and judicial decisions, just as Jehovah my God has commanded me, for YOU to do that way in the midst of the land to which YOU are going to take possession of it. 6 And YOU must keep and do them, because this is wisdom on YOUR part and understanding on YOUR part before the eyes of the peoples who will hear of all these regulations, and they will certainly say, 'This great nation is undoubtedly a wise and understanding people.' 7 For what great nation is there that has gods near to it the way Jehovah our God is in all our calling upon him? 8 And what great nation is there that has righteous regulations and judicial decisions like all this law that I am putting before YOU today?

9 "Only watch out for yourself and take good care of your soul, that you may not forget the things that your eyes have seen and that they may not depart from your heart all the days of your life; and you must make them known to your sons and to your grandsons, 10 the day that you stood before Jehovah your God in Ho'reb, when Jehovah said to me, 'Congregate the people together to me that I may let them hear my words, that they may learn to fear me all the days that they are alive on the soil and that they may teach their sons.'

11 "So YOU people came near and stood at the base of the mountain, and the mountain was burning with fire up to midheaven; there was darkness, cloud and thick gloom. 12 And Jehovah began to speak to YOU out of the middle of the fire. The sound of words was what YOU were hearing, but no form were YOU seeing—nothing but a voice. 13 And he proceeded to state to YOU his covenant, which he commanded YOU to perform—the Ten Words, after which he wrote them upon two tablets of stone. 14 And it was I whom Jehovah commanded at that particular time to teach YOU regulations and judicial decisions, for YOU to do them in the land to which YOU are passing over to take possession of it.

15 "And YOU must take good care of YOUR souls, because YOU did not see any form on the day of Jehovah's speaking to YOU in Ho'reb out of the middle of the fire, 16 that YOU may not act ruinously and may not really make for yourselves a carved image, the form of any symbol, the representation of male or female, 17 the representation of any beast that is in the earth, the representation of any winged bird that flies in the heavens, 18 the representation of anything moving on the ground, the representation of any fish that is in the waters under the earth; 19 and that you may not raise your eyes to the heavens and indeed see the sun and the moon and the stars, all the army of the heavens, and actually get seduced and bow down to them and serve them, which Jehovah your God has apportioned to all the peoples under the whole heavens. 20 But YOU are the ones Jehovah took that he might bring YOU out of the iron furnace, out of Egypt, to become a people of private ownership to him as at this day.

21 "And Jehovah got incensed at me on YOUR account, so that he swore that I should not cross the Jordan or go into the good land that Jehovah your God is giving you as an inheritance. 22 For I am dying in this land. I am not crossing the Jordan, but YOU are crossing, and YOU must take possession of this good land. 23 Watch out for yourselves that YOU may not forget the covenant of Jehovah YOUR God that he concluded with YOU and that YOU do not make for yourselves a carved image, the form of anything about which Jehovah your God has commanded you. 24 For Jehovah your God is a consuming fire, a God exacting exclusive devotion.

25 "In case you become father

to sons and grandsons and you have resided a long time in the land and do act ruinously and do make a carved image, a form of anything, and do commit evil in the eyes of Jehovah your God so as to offend him, 26 I do take as witnesses against you today the heavens and the earth, that you will positively perish in a hurry from off the land to which you are crossing the Jordan to take possession of it. You will not lengthen your days on it, because you will positively be annihilated. 27 And Jehovah will certainly scatter you among the peoples, and you will indeed be let remain few in number among the nations to which Jehovah will drive you away. 28 And there you will have to serve gods, the product of the hands of man, wood and stone, which cannot see or hear or eat or smell.

29 "If you do look for Jehovah your God from there, you will also certainly find him, because you will inquire for him with all your heart and with all your soul. 30 When you are in sore straits and all these words have found you out at the close of the days, then you will have to return to Jehovah your God and to listen to his voice. 31 For Jehovah your God is a merciful God. He will not desert you or bring you to ruin or forget the covenant of your forefathers that he swore to them.

32 "Now ask, please, concerning the former days that occurred before you, from the day that God created man on the earth and from one end of the heavens clear to the other end of the heavens, Was any great thing brought about like this or was anything heard like it? 33 Has any other people heard the voice of God speaking out of the middle of the fire the way you yourself have heard it, and kept on living? 34 Or did God attempt to come to take a nation to himself out of the midst of another nation with provings, with signs and with miracles and with war and with a strong hand and with an outstretched arm and with great fearsomeness like all that Jehovah your God has done for you in Egypt before your eyes? 35 You —you have been shown, so as to know that Jehovah is the [true] God; there is no other besides him. 36 Out of the heavens he made you hear his voice so as to correct you; and upon the earth he made you see his great fire, and his words you heard from the middle of the fire.

37 "And yet you continue to live, because he loved your forefathers so that he chose their seed after them and brought you out of Egypt in his sight with his great power, 38 to drive away nations greater and mightier than you from before you, so as to bring you in, to give you their land as an inheritance as at this day. 39 And you well know today, and you must call back to your heart that Jehovah is the [true] God in the heavens above and on the earth beneath. There is no other. 40 And you must keep his regulations and his commandments that I am commanding you today, that it may go well with you and your sons after you, and in order that you may lengthen your days on the soil that Jehovah your God is giving you, always."

41 At that time Moses proceeded to set apart three cities on the side of the Jordan toward the rising of the sun, 42 for the manslayer to flee there who slays his fellow without knowing it, while he was not hating him formerly; and he must flee to one of these cities and live, 43 namely, Be'zer in the wilderness on the tableland for the Reu'ben·ites, and Ra'moth in Gil'e·ad for the Gad'ites, and Go'lan in Ba'shan for the Ma·nas'sites.

44 Now this is the law that Moses set before the sons of Israel. 45 These are the testimonies and the regulations and the judicial decisions that Moses spoke to the sons of Israel on their coming out of Egypt, 46 in the region of the Jordan in the valley in front of Beth-pe'or, in the land of Si'hon the king of the Am'or·ites, who was dwelling in Hesh'bon, whom Moses

and the sons of Israel defeated on their coming out of Egypt. 47 And they went taking possession of his land and of the land of Og the king of Ba′shan, the two kings of the Am′or·ites who were in the region of the Jordan toward the rising of the sun, 48 from A·ro′er, which is on the bank of the torrent valley of Ar′non, up to Mount Si′on, that is to say, Her′mon, 49 and all the Ar′a·bah in the region of the Jordan toward the east, and as far as the sea of the Ar′a-bah at the base of the slopes of Pis′gah.

5 And Moses proceeded to call all Israel and to say to them: "Hear, O Israel, the regulations and the judicial decisions that I am speaking in YOUR ears today, and YOU must learn them and be careful to do them. 2 Jehovah our God concluded a covenant with us in Ho′reb. 3 It was not with our forefathers that Jehovah concluded this covenant, but with us, all those of us alive here today. 4 Face to face Jehovah spoke with YOU in the mountain out of the middle of the fire. 5 I was standing between Jehovah and YOU at that particular time to tell YOU the word of Jehovah, (for YOU were afraid because of the fire and did not go up into the mountain,) saying,

6 " 'I am Jehovah your God, who brought you out of the land of Egypt, out of the house of slaves. 7 You must never have any other gods against my face.

8 " 'You must not make for yourself a carved image, any form like anything that is in the heavens above or that is on the earth underneath or that is in the waters under the earth. 9 You must not bow down to them or be led to serve them, because I Jehovah your God am a God exacting exclusive devotion, bringing punishment for the error of fathers upon sons and upon the third generation and upon the fourth generation, in the case of those who hate me; 10 but exercising loving-kindness toward the thousandth generation in the case of those who love me and keep my commandments.

11 " 'You must not take up the name of Jehovah your God in a worthless way, for Jehovah will not leave anyone unpunished who takes up his name in a worthless way.

12 " 'Keeping the sabbath day to hold it sacred, just as Jehovah your God commanded you, 13 you are to render service, and you must do all your work six days. 14 But the seventh day is a sabbath to Jehovah your God. You must not do any work, you nor your son nor your daughter nor your slave man nor your slave girl nor your bull nor your ass nor any domestic animal of yours nor your alien resident who is inside your gates, in order that your slave man and your slave girl may rest the same as you. 15 And you must remember that you became a slave in the land of Egypt and Jehovah your God proceeded to bring you out from there with a strong hand and an outstretched arm. That is why Jehovah your God commanded you to carry on the sabbath day.

16 " 'Honor your father and your mother, just as Jehovah your God has commanded you; in order that your days may prove long and it may go well with you on the ground that Jehovah your God is giving you.

17 " 'You must not murder.

18 " 'Neither must you commit adultery.

19 " 'Neither must you steal.

20 " 'Neither must you testify to a falsehood against your fellow man.

21 " 'Neither must you desire your fellow man's wife. Neither must you selfishly crave your fellow man's house, his field or his slave man or his slave girl, his bull or his ass or anything that belongs to your fellow man.'

22 "These Words Jehovah spoke to all YOUR congregation in the mountain out of the middle of the fire, the cloud and the thick gloom, with a loud voice, and he added nothing; after which he wrote

them upon two tablets of stone and gave me them.

23 "And it came about that as soon as YOU had heard the voice out of the middle of the darkness, while the mountain was burning with fire, YOU proceeded to come near to me, all the heads of YOUR tribes and YOUR older men. 24 Then YOU said, 'Here Jehovah our God has shown us his glory and his greatness, and we have heard his voice out of the middle of the fire. This day we have seen that God may speak with man and he may actually keep living. 25 And now why should we die, for this great fire may consume us? If we are again hearing the voice of Jehovah our God any further, we are also certain to die. 26 For who is there of all flesh that has heard the voice of the living God speaking out of the middle of the fire as we did and yet goes on living? 27 You yourself go near and hear all that Jehovah our God will say; and you will be the one to speak to us all that Jehovah our God will speak to you, and we shall certainly listen and do.'

28 "So Jehovah heard the voice of YOUR words when YOU spoke to me, and Jehovah went on to say to me, 'I have heard the voice of the words of this people, which they have spoken to you. They have done well in all they have spoken. 29 If only they would develop this heart of theirs to fear me and to keep all my commandments always, in order that it might go well with them and their sons to time indefinite! 30 Go say to them: "Return home to YOUR tents." 31 And you stand here with me, and let me speak to you all the commandment and the regulations and the judicial decisions that you should teach to them and that they must do in the land that I am giving them to take possession of it.' 32 And YOU people must take care to do just as Jehovah YOUR God has commanded YOU. You must not turn to the right or to the left. 33 In all the way that

Jehovah YOUR God has commanded YOU, YOU should walk, in order that YOU may live and it may be well with YOU and YOU may indeed lengthen YOUR days in the land of which YOU will take possession.

6 "Now these are the commandment, the regulations and the judicial decisions that Jehovah YOUR God has commanded to teach YOU, so as to do them in the land to which YOU are passing over there to take possession of it; 2 in order that you may fear Jehovah your God so as to keep all his statutes and his commandments that I am commanding you, you and your son and your grandson, all the days of your life, and in order that your days may prove long. 3 And you must listen, O Israel, and take care to do [them], that it may go well with you and that YOU may become very many, just as Jehovah the God of your forefathers has promised you, as respects the land flowing with milk and honey.

4 "Listen, O Israel: Jehovah our God is one Jehovah. 5 And you must love Jehovah your God with all your heart and all your soul and all your vital force. 6 And these words that I am commanding you today must prove to be on your heart; 7 and you must inculcate them in your son and speak of them when you sit in your house and when you walk on the road and when you lie down and when you get up. 8 And you must tie them as a sign upon your hand, and they must serve as a frontlet band between your eyes; 9 and you must write them upon the doorposts of your house and on your gates.

10 "And it must occur that when Jehovah your God will bring you into the land that he swore to your forefathers Abraham, Isaac and Jacob to give you, great and good-looking cities that you did not build, 11 and houses full of all good things and that you did not fill, and cisterns hewn out that you did not hew out, vineyards and olive trees that you did not plant,

and you shall have eaten and become satisfied, 12 watch out for yourself that you may not forget Jehovah, who brought you out of the land of Egypt, out of the house of slaves. 13 Jehovah your God you should fear, and him you should serve, and by his name you should swear. 14 You must not walk after other gods, any gods of the peoples who are all around you, 15 (for Jehovah your God in your midst is a God exacting exclusive devotion,) for fear the anger of Jehovah your God may blaze against you and he must annihilate you from off the surface of the ground.

16 "You must not put Jehovah your God to the test, the way you put him to the test at Mas'sah. 17 You should by all means keep the commandments of Jehovah your God and his testimonies and his regulations that he has commanded you. 18 And you must do what is right and good in Jehovah's eyes, in order that it may go well with you and you may indeed enter and take possession of the good land about which Jehovah has sworn to your forefathers, 19 by pushing away all your enemies from before you, just as Jehovah has promised.

20 "In case your son should ask you in a future day, saying, 'What do the testimonies and the regulations and the judicial decisions mean that Jehovah our God has commanded you?' 21 then you must say to your son, 'We became slaves to Phar'aoh in Egypt, but Jehovah proceeded to bring us out of Egypt with a strong hand. 22 So Jehovah kept putting signs and miracles, great and calamitous, upon Egypt, upon Phar'aoh and upon all his household before our eyes. 23 And he brought us out from there in order that he might bring us here to give us the land about which he had sworn to our forefathers. 24 Hence Jehovah commanded us to carry out all these regulations, to fear Jehovah our God for our good always, that we might keep alive as at this day. 25 And it will mean righteousness for us, that we take care to do all this commandment before Jehovah our God, just as he has commanded us.'

7 "When Jehovah your God at last brings you into the land to which you are going so as to take possession of it, he must also clear away populous nations from before you, the Hit'tites and the Gir'ga·shites and the Am'or·ites and the Ca'naan·ites and the Per'iz·zites and the Hi'vites and the Jeb'u·sites, seven nations more populous and mighty than you are. 2 And Jehovah your God will certainly abandon them to you, and you must defeat them. You should without fail devote them to destruction. You must conclude no covenant with them nor show them any favor. 3 And you must form no marriage alliance with them. Your daughter you must not give to his son, and his daughter you must not take for your son. 4 For he will turn your son from following me, and they will certainly serve other gods; and Jehovah's anger will indeed blaze against you, and he will certainly annihilate you in a hurry.

5 "On the other hand, this is what you should do to them: Their altars you should pull down, and their sacred pillars you should break down, and their sacred poles you should cut down, and their graven images you should burn with fire. 6 For you are a holy people to Jehovah your God. It is you Jehovah your God has chosen to become his people, a special property, out of all the peoples that are on the surface of the ground.

7 "It was not because of your being the most populous of all the peoples that Jehovah showed affection for you so that he chose you, for you were the least of all the peoples. 8 But it was because of Jehovah's loving you, and because of his keeping the sworn statement that he had sworn to your forefathers, that Jehovah brought you out with a strong hand, that he might redeem you

from the house of slaves, from the hand of Phar'aoh the king of Egypt. 9 And you well know that Jehovah your God is the [true] God, the faithful God, keeping covenant and loving-kindness in the case of those who love him and those who keep his commandments to a thousand generations, 10 but repaying to his face the one who hates him by destroying him. He will not hesitate toward the one who hates him; he will repay him to his face. 11 And you must keep the commandment and the regulations and the judicial decisions that I am commanding you today by doing them.

12 "And it must occur that, because you continue listening to these judicial decisions and you do keep them and do carry them out, Jehovah your God must keep toward you the covenant and the loving-kindness about which he swore to your forefathers. 13 And he will certainly love you and bless you and multiply you and bless the fruit of your belly and the fruit of your soil, your grain and your new wine and your oil, the young of your cows and the progeny of your flock, on the soil that he swore to your forefathers to give to you. 14 The most blessed of all the peoples you will become. There will not prove to be in you a male or a female without offspring, nor among your domestic animals. 15 And Jehovah will certainly remove from you every sickness; and as for all the evil diseases of Egypt that you have known, he will not place them upon you, and he will indeed put them upon all those who hate you. 16 And you must consume all the peoples whom Jehovah your God is giving to you. Your eye must not feel sorry for them; and you must not serve their gods, because that will be a snare to you.

17 "In case you say in your heart, 'These nations are too populous for me. How shall I be able to drive them away?' 18 you must not be afraid of them. You should by all means remember what Jehovah your God did to Phar'aoh and all Egypt, 19 the great provings that your eyes saw, and the signs and the miracles and the strong hand and the outstretched arm with which Jehovah your God brought you out. That is the way Jehovah your God will do to all the peoples before whom you are afraid. 20 And Jehovah your God will also send the feeling of dejection upon them, until those perish who were let remain and who were concealing themselves from before you. 21 You must not suffer a shock because of them, for Jehovah your God is in your midst, a great and fear-inspiring God.

22 "And Jehovah your God will certainly push these nations away from before you little by little. You will not be allowed to finish them off quickly, for fear the wild beasts of the field may multiply against you. 23 And Jehovah your God will indeed abandon them to you and rout them with a great rout, until they are annihilated. 24 And he will certainly give their kings into your hand, and you must destroy their names from under the heavens. Nobody will take a firm stand against you, until you have exterminated them. 25 The graven images of their gods you should burn in the fire. You must not desire the silver and the gold upon them, nor indeed take it for yourself, for fear you may be ensnared by it; for it is a thing detestable to Jehovah your God. 26 And you must not bring a detestable thing into your house and actually become a thing devoted to destruction like it. You should thoroughly loathe it and absolutely detest it, because it is something devoted to destruction.

8 "Every commandment that I am commanding you today you should be careful to keep, in order that you may continue living and indeed multiply and go in and take possession of the land about which Jehovah swore to your forefathers. 2 And you must remember all the way that Jehovah your God made you walk these forty years in the

wilderness, in order to humble you, to put you to the test so as to know what was in your heart, as to whether you would keep his commandments or not. 3 So he humbled you and let you go hungry and fed you with the manna, which neither you had known nor your fathers had known; in order to make you know that not by bread alone does man live but by every expression of Jehovah's mouth does man live. 4 Your mantle did not wear out upon you, nor did your foot become swollen these forty years. 5 And you well know with your own heart that just as a man corrects his son, Jehovah your God was correcting you.

6 "And you must keep the commandments of Jehovah your God by walking in his ways and by fearing him. 7 For Jehovah your God is bringing you into a good land, a land of torrent valleys of water, springs and watery deeps issuing forth in the valley plain and in the mountainous region, 8 a land of wheat and barley and vines and figs and pomegranates, a land of oil olives and honey, 9 a land in which you will not eat bread with scarcity, in which you will lack nothing, a land the stones of which are iron and out of the mountains of which you will mine copper.

10 "When you have eaten and satisfied yourself, you must also bless Jehovah your God for the good land that he has given you. 11 Watch out for yourself that you may not forget Jehovah your God so as not to keep his commandments and his judicial decisions and his statutes that I am commanding you today; 12 for fear that you may eat and indeed satisfy yourself, and you may build good houses and indeed dwell in them, 13 and your herd and your flock may increase, and silver and gold may increase for you, and all that is yours may increase; 14 and your heart may indeed be lifted up and you may indeed forget Jehovah your God, who brought you out of the land of Egypt, out of the house of slaves; 15 who caused you to walk through the great and fear-inspiring wilderness, with poisonous serpents and scorpions and with thirsty ground that has no water; who brought forth water for you out of the flinty rock; 16 who fed you with manna in the wilderness, which your fathers had not known, in order to humble you and in order to put you to the test so as to do you good in your afterdays; 17 and you do say in your heart, 'My own power and the full might of my own hand have made this wealth for me.' 18 And you must remember Jehovah your God, because he is the giver of power to you to make wealth; in order to carry out his covenant that he swore to your forefathers, as at this day.

19 "And it must occur that if you should at all forget Jehovah your God and you should actually walk after other gods and serve them and bow down to them, I do bear witness against you today that you people will absolutely perish. 20 Like the nations that Jehovah is destroying from before you, that is the way you will perish, because you will not listen to the voice of Jehovah your God.

9 "Hear, O Israel, you are today crossing the Jordan to go in and dispossess nations greater and mightier than you, cities great and fortified to the heavens, 2 a people great and tall, the sons of An'a·kim, about whom you yourself have known and you yourself have heard it said, 'Who can make a firm stand before the sons of A'nak?' 3 And you well know today that Jehovah your God is crossing before you. A consuming fire he is. He will annihilate them, and he himself will subdue them before you; and you must dispossess them and destroy them speedily, just as Jehovah has spoken to you.

4 "Do not say in your heart when Jehovah your God pushes them away from before you this, 'It was for my own righteousness that Jehovah has brought me in to take possession of this land,'

whereas it is for the wickedness of these nations that Jehovah is driving them away from before you. 5 It is not for your righteousness or for the uprightness of your heart that you are going in to take possession of their land; in fact, it is for the wickedness of these nations that Jehovah your God is driving them away from before you, and in order to carry out the word that Jehovah swore to your forefathers, Abraham, Isaac and Jacob. 6 And you must know that it is not for your righteousness that Jehovah your God is giving you this good land to take possession of it; for you are a stiff-necked people.

7 "Remember: Do not forget how you have provoked Jehovah your God in the wilderness. From the day that you went out of the land of Egypt until YOUR coming to this place YOU people have proved rebellious in YOUR behavior with Jehovah. 8 Even in Ho'reb YOU provoked Jehovah to anger so that Jehovah got incensed at YOU to the point of annihilating YOU. 9 When I went up the mountain to receive the stone tablets, the tablets of the covenant that Jehovah had concluded with YOU, and I kept dwelling in the mountain forty days and forty nights, (I neither ate bread nor drank water,) 10 then Jehovah gave me the two tablets of stone written upon with God's finger; and upon them were all the words that Jehovah had spoken with YOU in the mountain out of the middle of the fire in the day of the congregation. 11 And it came about that at the end of the forty days and forty nights Jehovah gave me the two tablets of stone, the tablets of the covenant; 12 and Jehovah proceeded to say to me, 'Get up, go down quickly from here, because your people whom you brought out of Egypt have acted ruinously. They have turned aside quickly from the way about which I commanded them. They have made themselves a molten image.' 13 And Jehovah went on to say this to me, 'I have seen this

people, and, look! it is a stiff-necked people. 14 Let me alone that I may annihilate them and wipe out their name from under the heavens, and let me make you a nation mightier and more populous than they are.'

15 "After that I turned and went down from the mountain, while the mountain was burning with fire; and the two tablets of the covenant were in both my hands. 16 Then I looked, and there YOU had sinned against Jehovah YOUR God! YOU had made yourselves a molten calf. YOU had turned aside quickly from the way about which Jehovah had commanded YOU. 17 At that I took hold of the two tablets and flung them down from both my hands and shattered them before YOUR eyes. 18 And I proceeded to prostrate myself before Jehovah, as at first, forty days and forty nights. I neither ate bread nor drank water, because of all YOUR sin that YOU had committed in doing evil in the eyes of Jehovah so as to offend him. 19 For I was scared because of the hot anger with which Jehovah had got indignant at YOU to the point of annihilating YOU. However, Jehovah listened to me also that time.

20 "At Aaron, too, Jehovah got very incensed to the point of annihilating him; but I made supplication also in behalf of Aaron at that particular time. 21 And YOUR sin that YOU had made, the calf, I took, and I proceeded to burn it in the fire and to crush it, grinding it thoroughly until it had become fine like dust; after which I threw its dust into the torrent that was descending from the mountain.

22 "Further, at Tab'e·rah and at Mas'sah and at Kib'roth-hat·ta'a·vah YOU proved yourselves provokers of Jehovah to anger. 23 And when Jehovah sent YOU out of Ka'desh-bar'ne·a, saying, 'Go up and take possession of the land that I shall certainly give YOU!' then YOU behaved rebelliously against the order of Jehovah YOUR God, and YOU did not exercise

faith toward him and did not listen to his voice. 24 You have proved yourselves rebellious in behavior with Jehovah from the day of my knowing you.

25 "So I kept prostrating myself before Jehovah forty days and forty nights, for I prostrated myself thus because Jehovah talked of annihilating you. 26 And I began to make supplication to Jehovah and to say, 'O Lord Jehovah, do not bring to ruin your people, even your private property, whom you redeemed with your greatness, whom you brought out of Egypt with a strong hand. 27 Remember your servants Abraham, Isaac and Jacob. Do not turn your face to the hardness of this people and their wickedness and their sin, 28 for fear the land out of which you brought them may say: "Because Jehovah was unable to bring them into the land that he had promised them, and because he hated them he brought them out to put them to death in the wilderness." 29 They are, too, your people and your private property whom you brought out with your great power and your outstretched arm.'

10 "At that particular time Jehovah said to me, 'Carve for yourself two tablets of stone like the first ones, and come up to me into the mountain, and you must make an ark of wood for yourself. 2 And I shall write upon the tablets the words that appeared on the first tablets, which you shattered, and you must place them in the ark.' 3 So I made an ark of acacia wood and carved two tablets of stone like the first ones and went up into the mountain, and the two tablets were in my hand. 4 Then he wrote upon the tablets the same writing as the first, the Ten Words, which Jehovah had spoken to you in the mountain out of the middle of the fire in the day of the congregation; after which Jehovah gave them to me. 5 Then I turned and went down from the mountain and placed the tablets in the ark that I had made, that they might

continue there, just as Jehovah had commanded me.

6 "And the sons of Israel pulled away from Be·er′oth Ben′e-ja′a·kan for Mo·se′rah. There Aaron died, and he got to be buried there; and E·le·a′zar his son began to act as priest instead of him. 7 From there they pulled away for Gud′go-dah, and from Gud′go·dah for Jot′-ba·thah, a land of torrent valleys running with water.

8 "At that particular time Jehovah separated the tribe of Le′vi to carry the ark of Jehovah's covenant, to stand before Jehovah for ministering to him and to bless in his name until this day. 9 That is why Le′vi has come to have no share and inheritance with his brothers. Jehovah is his inheritance, just as Jehovah your God had said to him. 10 And I—I stayed in the mountain the same as the first days, forty days and forty nights, and Jehovah proceeded to listen to me also on that occasion. Jehovah did not want to bring you to ruin. 11 Then Jehovah said to me, 'Get up, go before the people for a pulling away, that they may go in and take possession of the land that I have sworn to their forefathers to give to them.'

12 "And now, O Israel, what is Jehovah your God asking of you but to fear Jehovah your God, so as to walk in all his ways and to love him and to serve Jehovah your God with all your heart and all your soul; 13 to keep the commandments of Jehovah and his statutes that I am commanding you today, for your good? 14 Behold, to Jehovah your God belong the heavens, even the heavens of the heavens, the earth and all that is in it. 15 Only to your forefathers did Jehovah get attached so as to love them, so that he chose their offspring after them, even you, out of all the peoples, as at this day. 16 And you must circumcise the foreskin of your hearts and not harden your necks any longer. 17 For Jehovah your God is the God of gods and the Lord of lords, the God great, mighty and fear-

inspiring, who treats none with partiality nor accepts a bribe, 18 executing judgment for the fatherless boy and the widow and loving the alien resident so as to give him bread and a mantle. 19 You too must love the alien resident, for you became alien residents in the land of Egypt.

20 "Jehovah your God you should fear. Him you should serve, and to him you should cling, and by his name you should make sworn statements. 21 He is the One for you to praise, and he is your God, who has done with you these great and fear-inspiring things that your eyes have seen. 22 With seventy souls your forefathers went down into Egypt, and now Jehovah your God has constituted you like the stars of the heavens for multitude.

11 "And you must love Jehovah your God and keep your obligation to him and his statutes and his judicial decisions and his commandments always. 2 And you well know today (for I do not address your sons who have not known and who have not seen the discipline of Jehovah your God, his greatness, his strong hand and his outstretched arm, 3 nor his signs and his deeds that he did in the midst of Egypt to Phar'aoh the king of Egypt and to all his land; 4 nor what he did to the military forces of Egypt, to his horses and his war chariots against the faces of which he made the waters of the Red Sea overflow when they were chasing after them, and Jehovah proceeded to destroy them till this day; 5 nor what he has done to you in the wilderness until your coming to this place; 6 nor what he did to Da'than and A·bi'-ram the sons of E·li'ab the son of Reu'ben, when the earth opened its mouth and proceeded to swallow them up and their households and their tents and every existing thing that stepped after them in the midst of all Israel); 7 for your eyes were the ones seeing all the great deeds of Jehovah that he did.

8 "And you must keep the whole commandment that I am com-manding you today, in order that you may grow strong and may indeed enter in and take possession of the land to which you are crossing to take possession of it, 9 and in order that you may lengthen your days on the soil that Jehovah swore to your forefathers to give to them and their seed, a land flowing with milk and honey.

10 "For the land to which you are going to take possession of it is not like the land of Egypt out of which you came, where you used to sow your seed and you had to do irrigating with your foot, like a garden of vegetables. 11 But the land to which you are crossing to take possession of it is a land of mountains and valley plains. Of the rain of the heavens it drinks water; 12 a land that Jehovah your God is caring for. The eyes of Jehovah your God are constantly upon it, from the beginning of the year to the close of the year.

13 "And it must occur that if you will without fail obey my commandments that I am commanding you today so as to love Jehovah your God and to serve him with all your heart and all your soul, 14 I also shall certainly give rain for your land at its appointed time, autumn rain and spring rain, and you will indeed gather your grain and your sweet wine and your oil. 15 And I shall certainly give vegetation in your field for your domestic animals, and you will indeed eat and be satisfied. 16 Watch out for yourselves for fear your heart may be enticed, and you do turn aside and worship other gods and bow down to them, 17 and Jehovah's anger does blaze against you, and he does shut up the heavens so that no rain will occur and the ground will not give its produce and you have to perish speedily from off the good land that Jehovah is giving you.

18 "And you must apply these words of mine to your heart and your soul and bind them as a sign upon your hand, and they must serve as a frontlet band between your eyes. 19 You must

also teach them to YOUR sons, so as to speak of them when you sit in your house and when you walk on the road and when you lie down and when you get up. 20 And you must write them upon the doorposts of your house and on your gates, 21 in order that YOUR days and the days of YOUR sons may be many on the soil that Jehovah swore to YOUR forefathers to give to them, as the days of the heavens over the earth.

22 "For if YOU strictly keep all this commandment that I am commanding YOU so as to do it, to love Jehovah YOUR God, to walk in all his ways and to cling to him, 23 Jehovah also must drive away all these nations on account of YOU, and YOU will certainly dispossess nations greater and more numerous than YOU are. 24 Every place on which the sole of YOUR foot will tread will become YOURS. From the wilderness up to Leb′a-non, from the River, the river Eu-phra′tes, to the western sea YOUR boundary will become. 25 No man will make a firm stand against YOU. The dread of YOU and the fear of YOU Jehovah YOUR God will put before the face of all the land on which YOU will tread, just as he has promised YOU.

26 "See, I am putting before YOU today blessing and malediction: 27 the blessing, provided YOU will obey the commandments of Jehovah YOUR God that I am commanding YOU today; 28 and the malediction, if YOU will not obey the commandments of Jehovah YOUR God and YOU do turn aside from the way about which I am commanding YOU today, so as to walk after other gods whom YOU have not known.

29 "And it must occur that when Jehovah your God brings you into the land to which you are going to take possession of it, you must also give the blessing upon Mount Ger′i-zim and the malediction upon Mount E′bal. 30 Are they not on the side of the Jordan toward the direction of the sunset, in the land of the Ca′naan·ites dwelling in the

Ar′a·bah, in front of Gil′gal, beside the big trees of Mo′reh? 31 For YOU are crossing the Jordan to go in and take possession of the land that Jehovah YOUR God is giving YOU, and YOU must take possession of it and dwell in it. 32 And YOU must be careful to carry out all the regulations and the judicial decisions that I am putting before YOU today.

12 "These are the regulations and the judicial decisions that YOU should be careful to carry out in the land that Jehovah the God of your forefathers will certainly allow you to take possession of, all the days that YOU are alive on the soil. 2 You should absolutely destroy all the places where the nations whom YOU are dispossessing have served their gods, on the tall mountains and the hills and under every luxuriant tree. 3 And YOU must pull down their altars and shatter their sacred pillars, and YOU should burn their sacred poles in the fire and cut down the graven images of their gods, and YOU must destroy their names from that place.

4 "YOU must not do that way to Jehovah YOUR God, 5 but to the place that Jehovah YOUR God will choose out of all YOUR tribes to place his name there, to have it reside, YOU will seek, and there you must come. 6 And there YOU must bring YOUR burnt offerings and YOUR sacrifices and YOUR tenth parts and the contribution of YOUR hand and YOUR vow offerings and YOUR voluntary offerings and the first-born ones of YOUR herd and of YOUR flock. 7 And there YOU must eat before Jehovah YOUR God and rejoice in every undertaking of YOURS, YOU, and YOUR households, because Jehovah your God has blessed you.

8 "YOU must not do according to all that we are doing here today, each one whatever is right in his own eyes, 9 because YOU have not yet come into the resting place and the inheritance that Jehovah your God is giving you. 10 And YOU must cross the Jordan and dwell

in the land that Jehovah YOUR God is giving YOU as a possession, and he will certainly give YOU rest from all YOUR enemies round about, and YOU will indeed dwell in security. 11 And it must occur that the place that Jehovah YOUR God will choose to have his name reside there, is where YOU will bring all about which I am commanding YOU, YOUR burnt offerings and YOUR sacrifices, YOUR tenth parts and the contribution of YOUR hand and every choice of YOUR vow offerings that YOU will vow to Jehovah. 12 And YOU must rejoice before Jehovah YOUR God, YOU and YOUR sons and YOUR daughters and YOUR man slaves and YOUR slave girls and the Levite who is inside YOUR gates, because he has no share or inheritance with YOU. 13 Watch out for yourself for fear you may offer up your burnt offerings in any other place you may see. 14 But in the place that Jehovah will choose in one of your tribes is where you should offer up your burnt offerings, and there you should do all that I am commanding you.

15 "Only whenever your soul craves it you may slaughter, and you must eat meat according to the blessing of Jehovah your God that he has given you, inside all your gates. The unclean one and the clean one may eat it, like the gazelle and like the stag. 16 Only the blood YOU must not eat. On the earth you should pour it out as water. 17 You will not be allowed to eat inside your gates the tenth part of your grain or of your new wine or of your oil or the first-born ones of your herd and of your flock or any of your vow offerings that you will vow or your voluntary offerings or the contribution of your hand. 18 But before Jehovah your God you will eat it, in the place that Jehovah your God will choose, you and your son and your daughter and your man slave and your slave girl and the Levite who is inside your gates; and you must rejoice before Jehovah your God in every undertaking of yours. 19 Watch out for yourself that you

may not abandon the Levite all your days on your soil.

20 "When Jehovah your God will widen out your territory, just as he has promised you, and you will be certain to say, 'Let me eat meat,' because your soul craves to eat meat, whenever your soul craves it you may eat meat. 21 In case the place that Jehovah your God will choose to put his name there should be far away from you, you must then slaughter some of your herd or some of your flock that Jehovah has given you, just as I have commanded you, and you must eat inside your gates whenever your soul craves it. 22 Only in the way that the gazelle and the stag may be eaten, so you may eat it: the unclean one and the clean one together may eat it. 23 Simply be firmly resolved not to eat the blood, because the blood is the soul and you must not eat the soul with the flesh. 24 You must not eat it. You should pour it out upon the ground as water. 25 You must not eat it, in order that it may go well with you and your sons after you, because you will do what is right in Jehovah's eyes. 26 Merely your holy things that will become yours, and your vow offerings you should carry, and you must come to the place that Jehovah will choose. 27 And you must render up your burnt offerings, the flesh and the blood, upon the altar of Jehovah your God; and the blood of your sacrifices should be poured out against the altar of Jehovah your God, but the flesh you may eat.

28 "Watch, and you must obey all these words that I am commanding you, in order that it may go well with you and your sons after you to time indefinite, because you will do what is good and right in the eyes of Jehovah your God.

29 "When Jehovah your God will cut off from before you the nations to whom you are going to dispossess them, you must also dispossess them and dwell in their land. 30 Watch out for yourself for fear you may

be entrapped after them, after they have been annihilated from before you, and for fear you may inquire respecting their gods, saying, 'How was it these nations used to serve their gods? And I, yes, I, will do the same way.' 31 You must not do that way to Jehovah your God, for everything detestable to Jehovah that he does hate they have done to their gods, for even their sons and their daughters they regularly burn in the fire to their gods. 32 Every word that I am commanding you is what you should be careful to do. You must not add to it nor take away from it.

13 "In case a prophet or a dreamer of a dream arises in your midst and does give you a sign or a portent, 2 and the sign or the portent does come true of which he spoke to you, saying, 'Let us walk after other gods, whom you have not known, and let us serve them,' 3 you must not listen to the words of that prophet or to the dreamer of that dream, because Jehovah your God is testing you to know whether you are loving Jehovah your God with all your heart and all your soul. 4 After Jehovah your God you should walk, and him you should fear, and his commandments you should keep, and to his voice you should listen, and him you should serve, and to him you should cling. 5 And that prophet or that dreamer of the dream should be put to death, because he has spoken of revolt against Jehovah your God, who has brought you out of the land of Egypt and has redeemed you from the house of slaves, to turn you from the way in which Jehovah your God has commanded you to walk; and you must clear out what is evil from your midst.

6 "In case your brother, the son of your mother, or your son or your daughter or your cherished wife or your companion who is like your own soul, should try to allure you in secrecy, saying, 'Let us go and serve other gods,' whom you have not known, neither you nor your forefathers, 7 some of the gods of the peoples who are all around you, the ones near you or those far away from you, from one end of the land to the other end of the land, 8 you must not accede to his wish or listen to him, nor should your eye feel sorry for him, nor must you feel compassion, nor cover him [protectively]; 9 but you should kill him without fail. Your hand first of all should come upon him to put him to death, and the hand of all the people afterward. 10 And you must stone him with stones, and he must die, because he has sought to turn you away from Jehovah your God, who has brought you out of the land of Egypt, out of the house of slaves. 11 Then all Israel will hear and become afraid, and they will not do anything like this bad thing again in your midst.

12 "In case you hear it said in one of your cities, which Jehovah your God is giving you to dwell there, 13 'Good-for-nothing men have gone out from your midst that they may try to turn away the inhabitants of their city, saying: "Let us go and serve other gods," whom you have not known,' 14 you must also search and investigate and inquire thoroughly; and if the thing is established as the truth, this detestable thing has been done in your midst, 15 you should without fail strike the inhabitants of that city with the edge of the sword. Devote it and everything that is in it, and its domestic animals, to destruction at the edge of the sword. 16 And all its spoil you should collect into the middle of its public square, and you must burn in the fire the city and all its spoil as a whole offering to Jehovah your God, and it must become a heap of ruins to time indefinite. It should never be rebuilt. 17 And nothing at all should stick to your hand of the thing made sacred by ban, in order that Jehovah may turn from his burning anger and may indeed give you mercy and he may certainly show you mercy and multiply you, just as he has sworn to your forefathers.

18 For you should listen to the voice of Jehovah your God by keeping all his commandments that I am commanding you today, so as to do what is right in the eyes of Jehovah your God.

14 "Sons YOU are of Jehovah YOUR God. YOU must not make cuttings upon yourselves or impose baldness on YOUR foreheads for a dead person. **2** For you are a holy people to Jehovah your God, and Jehovah has chosen you to become his people, a special property, out of all the peoples who are on the surface of the ground. **3** "You must eat no detestable thing of any sort. **4** This is the sort of beast that YOU may eat: the bull, the sheep and the goat, **5** the stag and gazelle and roebuck and wild goat and antelope and wild sheep and chamois; **6** and every beast that splits the hoof and that forms a cleft into two hoofs, chewing the cud among the beasts. It YOU may eat. **7** Only this sort YOU must not eat out of those that chew the cud or that split the hoof, cloven: the camel and the hare and the rock badger, because they are chewers of the cud but do not split the hoof. They are unclean for YOU. **8** The pig also, because it is a splitter of the hoof but there is no cud. It is unclean for YOU. None of their flesh must YOU eat, and their carcasses YOU must not touch.

9 "This sort out of everything that is in the waters YOU may eat: Everything that has fins and scales YOU may eat. **10** And everything that has no fins and scales YOU must not eat. It is unclean for YOU.

11 "Any clean bird YOU may eat. **12** But these are the ones of which YOU must not eat: the eagle and the osprey and the black vulture, **13** and the red kite and the black kite and the glede according to its kind; **14** and every raven according to its kind; **15** and the ostrich and the owl and the gull and the falcon according to its kind; **16** the little owl and the long-eared owl and the swan, **17** and the pelican and the vulture and the cormorant, **18** and the stork and the heron according to its kind, and the hoopoe and the bat. **19** And every winged swarming creature is unclean for YOU. They should not be eaten. **20** Any clean flying creature YOU may eat.

21 "YOU must not eat any body [already] dead. To the alien resident who is inside your gates you may give it, and he must eat it; or there may be a selling of it to a foreigner, because you are a holy people to Jehovah your God.

"You must not boil a kid in its mother's milk.

22 "Without fail you should give a tenth of all the produce of your seed, that which comes forth of the field year by year. **23** And before Jehovah your God, in the place that he will choose to have his name reside there, you must eat the tenth part of your grain, your new wine and your oil and the first-born ones of your herd and of your flock; in order that you may learn to fear Jehovah your God always.

24 "Now in case the journey should be too long for you, because you will not be able to carry it, since the place that Jehovah your God will choose to place his name there will be too far away for you, (because Jehovah your God will bless you,) **25** you must then turn it into money, and you must wrap the money up in your hand and travel to the place that Jehovah your God will choose. **26** You must also give the money for whatever your soul may crave in the way of cattle and sheep and goats and wine and intoxicating liquor and anything that your soul may ask of you; and you must eat there before Jehovah your God and rejoice, you and your household. **27** And the Levite who is inside your gates, you must not abandon him, for he has no share or inheritance with you.

28 "At the end of three years you will bring out the entire tenth part of your produce in that year, and you must deposit it inside your gates. **29** And the Levite, because he has no share or inheritance with you, and the alien resident and the fatherless boy and the widow, who are inside your gates, must come, and they must eat and satisfy themselves; in order that Jehovah your God may bless you in every deed of your hand that you will do.

15 "At the end of every seven years you should make a release. 2 And this is the manner of the release: there will be a releasing by every creditor of the debt that he may let his fellow incur. He should not press his fellow or his brother for payment, because a release to Jehovah must be called. 3 The foreigner you may press for payment; but whatever of yours may prove to be with your brother let your hand release. 4 However, no one should come to be poor among you, because Jehovah will without fail bless you in the land that Jehovah your God is giving you as an inheritance to take possession of it, 5 only if you will without fail listen to the voice of Jehovah your God so as to be careful to do all this commandment that I am commanding you today. 6 For Jehovah your God will indeed bless you just as he has promised you, and you will certainly lend on pledge to many nations, whereas you yourself will not borrow; and you must dominate over many nations, whereas over you they will not dominate.

7 "In case some one of your brothers becomes poor among you in one of your cities, in your land that Jehovah your God is giving you, you must not harden your heart or be closefisted toward your poor brother. 8 For you should generously open your hand to him and by all means lend him on pledge as much as he needs, which he is in want of. 9 Watch out for yourself for fear a base word should come to be in your heart, saying, 'The seventh year, the year of the release, has come close,' and your eye should indeed become ungenerous toward your poor brother, and you should give him nothing, and he has to call out to Jehovah against you, and it has become a sin on your part. 10 You should by all means give to him, and your heart should not be stingy in your giving to him, because on this account Jehovah your God will bless you in every deed of yours and in every undertaking of yours. 11 For someone poor will never cease to be in the midst of the land. That is why I am commanding you, saying, 'You should generously open up your hand to your afflicted and poor brother in your land.'

12 "In case there should be sold to you your brother, a Hebrew or a Hebrewess, and he has served you six years, then in the seventh year you should send him out from you as one set free. 13 And in case you should send him out from you as one set free, you must not send him out empty-handed. 14 You should surely equip him with something from your flock and your threshing floor and your oil and wine press. Just as Jehovah your God has blessed you, you should give to him. 15 And you must remember that you became a slave in the land of Egypt and Jehovah your God proceeded to redeem you. That is why I am commanding you this thing today.

16 "And it must occur that in case he says to you, 'I shall not go out from your company!' because he does love you and your household, since it was well with him while with you, 17 you must also take an awl and put it through his ear and to the door, and he must become your slave to time indefinite. And to your slave girl you should also do this way. 18 It should not be something hard in your eyes when you send him out from your company as one set free; because for double the value of a hired laborer he served you six years, and Jehovah your God has blessed you in everything that you would do.

19 "Every male first-born that will be born in your herd and in your flock you should sanctify to Jehovah your God. You must do no service with the first-born of

your bull, nor shear the first-born of your flock. 20 Before Jehovah your God you should eat it year by year in the place that Jehovah will choose, you and your household. 21 And in case there should prove to be in it a defect, being lame or blind, any bad defect, you must not sacrifice it to Jehovah your God. 22 Inside your gates you should eat it, the unclean one and the clean one together, like the gazelle and like the stag. 23 Only its blood you must not eat. Upon the earth you should pour it out as water.

16 "Let there be an observing of the month of A'bib, and you must celebrate the passover to Jehovah your God, because in the month of A'bib Jehovah your God brought you out of Egypt by night. 2 And you must sacrifice the passover to Jehovah your God, of the flock and of the herd, in the place that Jehovah will choose to have his name reside there. 3 You must eat nothing leavened along with it for seven days. You should eat along with it unfermented cakes, the bread of affliction, because it was in haste that you came out of the land of Egypt, that you may remember the day of your coming out of the land of Egypt all the days of your life. 4 And no sour dough should be seen with you in all your territory seven days, neither should any of the flesh, which you will sacrifice in the evening on the first day, stay all night until the morning. 5 You will not be allowed to sacrifice the passover in any one of your cities that Jehovah your God is giving you. 6 But at the place that Jehovah your God will choose to have his name reside there, you should sacrifice the passover in the evening as soon as the sun sets, at the appointed time of your coming out of Egypt. 7 And you must do the boiling and the eating in the place that Jehovah your God will choose, and in the morning you must turn around and go to your own tents. 8 Six days you should eat unfermented cakes; and on the seventh day there will

be a solemn assembly to Jehovah your God. You must do no work.

9 "Seven weeks you should count for yourself. From when the sickle is first put to the standing grain you will start to count seven weeks. 10 Then you must celebrate the festival of weeks to Jehovah your God, according to the voluntary offering of your hand that you will give, just as Jehovah your God may bless you. 11 And you must rejoice before Jehovah your God, you and your son and your daughter and your man slave and your slave girl and the Levite who is inside your gates and the alien resident and the fatherless boy and the widow, who are in your midst, in the place that Jehovah your God will choose to have his name reside there. 12 And you must remember that you became a slave in Egypt, and you must observe and carry out these regulations.

13 "The festival of booths you should celebrate for yourself seven days when you make an ingathering from your threshing floor and your oil and wine press. 14 And you must rejoice during your festival, you and your son and your daughter and your man slave and your slave girl and the Levite and the alien resident and the fatherless boy and the widow, who are inside your gates. 15 Seven days you will celebrate the festival to Jehovah your God in the place that Jehovah will choose, because Jehovah your God will bless you in all your produce and in every deed of your hand, and you must become nothing but joyful.

16 "Three times in the year every male of yours should appear before Jehovah your God in the place that he will choose: in the festival of the unfermented cakes and the festival of weeks and the festival of booths, and none should appear before Jehovah empty-handed. 17 The gift of each one's hand should be in proportion to the blessing of Jehovah your God that he has given you.

18 "You should set judges and officers for yourself inside all your

gates that Jehovah your God is giving you by your tribes, and they must judge the people with righteous judgment. 19 You must not pervert judgment. You must not be partial or accept a bribe, for the bribe blinds the eyes of wise ones and distorts the words of righteous ones. 20 Justice— justice you should pursue, in order that you may keep alive and may indeed take possession of the land that Jehovah your God is giving you.

21 "You must not plant for yourself any sort of tree as a sacred pole near the altar of Jehovah your God that you will make for yourself.

22 "Neither should you set up for yourself a sacred pillar, a thing Jehovah your God hates indeed.

17 "You must not sacrifice to Jehovah your God a bull or a sheep in which there proves to be a defect, anything bad; because it is a thing detestable to Jehovah your God.

2 "In case there should be found in your midst in one of your cities that Jehovah your God is giving you a man or a woman who should practice what is bad in the eyes of Jehovah your God so as to overstep his covenant, 3 and he should go and worship other gods and bow down to them or to the sun or the moon or all the army of the heavens, a thing that I have not commanded, 4 and it has been told you and you have heard it and have searched thoroughly, and, look! the thing is established as the truth, this detestable thing has been done in Israel! 5 you must also bring that man or that woman who has done this bad thing out to your gates, yes, the man or the woman, and you must stone such one with stones, and such one must die. 6 At the mouth of two witnesses or of three witnesses the one dying should be put to death. He will not be put to death at the mouth of one witness. 7 The hand of the witnesses first of all should come upon him to put him to death, and the hand of all the peo-

ple afterward; and you must clear out what is bad from your midst.

8 "In case a matter for judicial decision should be too extraordinary for you, one in which blood has been shed, in which a legal claim has been raised, or a violent deed has been committed, matters of dispute, inside your gates, you must also rise and go up to the place that Jehovah your God will choose, 9 and you must go to the priests, the Levites, and to the judge who will be acting in those days, and you must make inquiry, and they must hand down to you the word of the judicial decision. 10 Then you must do in accordance with the word that they will hand down to you from that place which Jehovah will choose; and you must be careful to do according to all that they instruct you. 11 In accordance with the law that they will point out to you, and according to the judicial decision that they will say to you, you should do. You must not turn aside from the word that they will hand down to you, to the right or to the left. 12 And the man who will behave with presumptuousness in not listening to the priest who is standing to minister there to Jehovah your God or to the judge, that man must die; and you must clear out what is bad from Israel. 13 And all the people will hear and become afraid, and they will not act presumptuously any more.

14 "When you eventually come into the land that Jehovah your God is giving you, and you have taken possession of it and have dwelt in it, and you have said, 'Let me set a king over myself like all the nations who are round about me'; 15 you should without fail set over yourself a king whom Jehovah your God will choose. From among your brothers you should set a king over yourself. You will not be allowed to put over yourself a foreigner who is not your brother. 16 Only he should not increase horses for himself, nor make the people go back to Egypt in order to increase horses; whereas Jeho-

vah has said to you, 'You must never go back again by this way.' 17 He should also not multiply wives for himself, that his heart may not turn aside; nor should he increase silver and gold for himself very much. 18 And it must occur that when he takes his seat on the throne of his kingdom, he must write in a book for himself a copy of this law from that which is in the charge of the priests, the Levites.

19 "And it must continue with him, and he must read in it all the days of his life, in order that he may learn to fear Jehovah his God so as to keep all the words of this law and these regulations by doing them; 20 that his heart may not exalt itself above his brothers and that he may not turn aside from the commandment to the right or to the left, in order that he may lengthen his days upon his kingdom, he and his sons in the midst of Israel.

18 "No share or inheritance with Israel should come to belong to the priests, the Levites, the entire tribe of Le'vi. The offerings made by fire of Jehovah, even his inheritance, they should eat. 2 So no inheritance should come to belong to him in the midst of his brothers. Jehovah is his inheritance, just as he has spoken to him.

3 "Now this should continue as the due right of the priests from the people, from the ones who sacrifice a victim, whether a bull or a sheep: One must give to the priest the shoulder blade and the jaws and the stomach. 4 The first of your grain, your new wine and your oil and the first of the shorn wool of your flock you should give him. 5 For he is the one whom Jehovah your God has chosen out of all your tribes to stand to minister in the name of Jehovah, he and his sons, always.

6 "And in case the Levite goes out of one of your cities of all Israel, where he had resided for a while, and he does come because of any craving of his soul to the place that Jehovah will choose, 7 he must also minister in the name of Jehovah his God the same as all his brothers, the Levites, who are standing there before Jehovah. 8 An equal share he should eat, besides what he gets from things he sells of his ancestral goods.

9 "When you are entered into the land that Jehovah your God is giving you, you must not learn to do according to the detestable things of those nations. 10 There should not be found in you anyone who makes his son or his daughter pass through the fire, anyone who employs divination, a practicer of magic or anyone who looks for omens or a sorcerer, 11 or one who binds others with a spell or anyone who consults a spirit medium or a professional foreteller of events or anyone who inquires of the dead. 12 For everybody doing these things is something detestable to Jehovah, and on account of these detestable things Jehovah your God is driving them away from before you. 13 You should prove yourself faultless with Jehovah your God.

14 "For these nations whom you are dispossessing used to listen to those practicing magic and to those who divine; but as for you, Jehovah your God has not given you anything like this. 15 A prophet from your own midst, from your brothers, like me, is what Jehovah your God will raise up for you—to him you people should listen— 16 in response to all that you asked of Jehovah your God in Ho'reb on the day of the congregation, saying, 'Do not let me hear again the voice of Jehovah my God, and this great fire do not let me see any more, that I may not die.' 17 At that Jehovah said to me, 'They have done well in speaking what they did. 18 A prophet I shall raise up for them from the midst of their brothers, like you; and I shall indeed put my words in his mouth, and he will certainly speak to them all that I shall command him. 19 And it must occur that the man who will not listen to my words that he will speak in

my name, I shall myself require an account from him.

20 " 'However, the prophet who presumes to speak in my name a word that I have not commanded him to speak or who speaks in the name of other gods, that prophet must die. 21 And in case you should say in your heart: "How shall we know the word that Jehovah has not spoken?" 22 when the prophet speaks in the name of Jehovah and the word does not occur or come true, that is the word that Jehovah did not speak. With presumptuousness the prophet spoke it. You must not get frightened at him.'

19 "When Jehovah your God cuts off the nations whose land Jehovah your God is giving you, and you have dispossessed them and have dwelt in their cities and their houses, 2 you will set apart three cities for yourself in the midst of your land that Jehovah your God is giving you to take possession of it. 3 You will prepare for yourself the way, and you must divide up the territory of your land that Jehovah your God proceeded to give you as a possession into three parts, and it must be for any manslayer to flee there.

4 "Now this is the case of the manslayer who may flee there and has to live: When he strikes his fellow man without knowing it and he was no hater of him formerly; 5 or when he goes with his fellow man into the woods to gather wood, and his hand has been raised to strike with the ax to cut the tree, and the iron has slipped off from the wooden handle, and it has hit his fellow man and he has died, he himself should flee to one of these cities and must live. 6 Otherwise, the avenger of blood may, because his heart is hot, chase after the manslayer and actually overtake him, since the way is great; and he may indeed strike his soul fatally, whereas there is no sentence of death for him, because he was no hater of him formerly. 7 That is why I am commanding you, saying, 'Three cities you will set apart for yourself.'

8 "And if Jehovah your God widens out your territory according to what he swore to your forefathers, and he has given you all the land that he promised to give to your forefathers, 9 because you will keep all this commandment that I am commanding you today by doing it, to love Jehovah your God and to walk in his ways always, you must then add three other cities for yourself to these three, 10 that no innocent blood may be spilled in the midst of your land that Jehovah your God is giving you as an inheritance, and no bloodguilt has to be upon you.

11 "But in case there should happen to be a man hating his fellow man, and he has lain in wait for him and has risen up against him and struck his soul fatally and he has died, and the man has fled to one of these cities, 12 the older men of his city must then send and take him from there, and they must deliver him into the hand of the avenger of blood, and he must die. 13 Your eye should not feel sorry for him, and you must clear away the guilt of innocent blood out of Israel, that you may have good.

14 "You must not move back the boundary marks of your fellow man, when the ancestors will have set the boundaries in your inheritance that you will inherit in the land that Jehovah your God is giving you to take possession of it.

15 "No single witness should rise up against a man respecting any error or any sin, in the case of any sin that he may commit. At the mouth of two witnesses or at the mouth of three witnesses the matter should stand good. 16 In case a witness scheming violence should rise up against a man to bring a charge of revolt against him, 17 the two men who have the dispute must also stand before Jehovah, before the priests and the judges who will be acting in those days. 18 And the judges must search thoroughly, and if the wit-

ness is a false witness and has brought a false charge against his brother, 19 you must also do to him just as he had schemed to do to his brother, and you must clear away what is bad from your midst. 20 So those who remain will hear and be afraid, and they will never again do anything bad like this in your midst. 21 And your eye should not feel sorry: soul will be for soul, eye for eye, tooth for tooth, hand for hand, foot for foot.

20 "In case you go out to the battle against your enemies and you actually see horses and war chariots, a people more numerous than you, you must not be afraid of them; for Jehovah your God is with you, who brought you up out of the land of Egypt. 2 And it must occur that when you have drawn near to the battle, the priest must also approach and speak to the people. 3 And he must say to them, 'Hear, O Israel, you are drawing near today to the battle against your enemies. Do not let your hearts be timid. Do not be afraid and run in panic or shudder because of them, 4 for Jehovah your God is marching with you to fight for you against your enemies so as to save you.'

5 "The officers too must speak to the people, saying, 'Who is the man that has built a new house and has not inaugurated it? Let him go and return to his house, for fear he may die in the battle and another man should inaugurate it. 6 And who is the man that has planted a vineyard and not begun to use it? Let him go and return to his house, for fear he may die in the battle and another man should begin to use it. 7 And who is the man that has become engaged to a woman and has not taken her? Let him go and return to his house, for fear he may die in the battle and another man should take her.' 8 And the officers must speak further to the people and say, 'Who is the man that is fearful and faint-hearted? Let him go and return to his house, that he may not cause the hearts of his brothers to melt

as his own heart.' 9 And it must occur that when the officers have finished speaking to the people, they must also appoint chiefs of the armies at the head of the people.

10 "In case you draw near to a city to fight against it, you must also announce to it terms of peace. 11 And it must occur that if it gives a peaceful answer to you and it has opened up to you, it must even occur that all the people found in it should become yours for forced labor, and they must serve you. 12 But if it does not make peace with you, and it actually makes war with you and you have to besiege it, 13 Jehovah your God also will certainly give it into your hand, and you must strike every male in it with the edge of the sword. 14 Only the women and the little children and the domestic animals and everything that happens to be in the city, all its spoil you will plunder for yourself; and you must eat the spoil of your enemies, whom Jehovah your God has given to you.

15 "That is the way you will do to all the cities very far away from you that are not of the cities of these nations. 16 It is only of the cities of these peoples that Jehovah your God is giving you as an inheritance that you must not preserve any breathing thing alive, 17 because you should without fail devote them to destruction, the Hit'tites and the Am'or·ites, the Ca'naan·ites and the Per'iz·zites, the Hi'vites and the Jeb'u·sites, just as Jehovah your God has commanded you; 18 in order that they may not teach you to do according to all their detestable things, which they have done to their gods, and you may indeed sin against Jehovah your God.

19 "In case you lay siege to a city many days by fighting against it so as to capture it, you must not ruin its trees by wielding an ax against them; for you should eat from them, and you must not cut them down, for is the tree of the field a man to be besieged by you? 20 Only a tree that you know is

not a tree for food, it is the one you should ruin, and you must cut it down and build siegeworks against the city that is making war with you, until it falls.

21 "In case someone is found slain on the ground that Jehovah your God is giving you to take possession of it, fallen on the field, and it has not become known who struck him fatally, 2 your older men and your judges must also go out and measure to the cities that are all around the slain one; 3 and it must prove to be the city nearest to the slain one. And the older men of that city must take a young cow of the herd that has not been worked with, that has not pulled in a yoke; 4 and the older men of that city must lead the young cow down to a torrent valley running with water in which there was customarily no tilling or sowing of seed, and they must break the neck of the young cow there in the torrent valley.

5 "And the priests the sons of Le′vi must approach, because they are the ones Jehovah your God has chosen to minister to him and to bless in the name of Jehovah and at whose mouth every dispute over every violent deed should be disposed of. 6 Then all the older men of that city who are nearest to the slain one should wash their hands over the young cow, the neck of which was broken in the torrent valley; 7 and they must answer and say, 'Our hands did not shed this blood, neither did our eyes see it shed. 8 Do not set it to the account of your people Israel, whom you redeemed, O Jehovah, and do not put the guilt of innocent blood in the midst of your people Israel.' And the bloodguilt must not be set to their account. 9 And you—you will clear away the guilt of innocent blood from your midst, because you will do what is right in Jehovah's eyes.

10 "In case you go out to the battle against your enemies and Jehovah your God has given them into your hand and you have carried them away captive; 11 and

you have seen among the captives a woman beautiful in form, and you have got attached to her and taken her for your wife, 12 you must then bring her into the midst of your house. She must now shave her head and attend to her nails, 13 and remove the mantle of her captivity from off her and dwell in your house and weep for her father and her mother a whole lunar month; and after that you should have relations with her, and you must take possession of her as your bride, and she must become your wife. 14 And it must occur that if you have found no delight in her, you must then send her away, agreeably to her own soul; but you must by no means sell her for money. You must not deal tyrannically with her after you have humiliated her.

15 "In case a man comes to have two wives, the one loved and the other hated, and they, the loved one and the hated one, have borne sons to him, and the first-born son has come to be of the hated one, 16 it must also occur that in the day that he gives as an inheritance to his sons what he happens to have, he will not be allowed to constitute the son of the loved one his first-born at the expense of the hated one's son, the first-born. 17 For he should recognize as the first-born the hated one's son by giving him two parts in everything he is found to have, because that one is the beginning of his generative power. The right of the first-born's position belongs to him.

18 "In case a man happens to have a son who is stubborn and rebellious, he not listening to the voice of his father or the voice of his mother, and they have corrected him but he will not listen to them, 19 his father and his mother must also take hold of him and bring him out to the older men of his city and to the gate of his place, 20 and they must say to the older men of his city, 'This son of ours is stubborn and rebellious; he is not listening to our voice, being a glutton and a drunkard.' 21 Then all

the men of his city must pelt him with stones, and he must die. So you must clear away what is bad from your midst, and all Israel will hear and indeed become afraid.

22 "And in case there comes to be in a man a sin deserving the sentence of death, and he has been put to death, and you have hung him upon a stake, 23 his dead body should not stay all night on the stake; but you should by all means bury him on that day, because something accursed of God is the one hung up; and you must not defile your soil, which Jehovah your God is giving you as an inheritance.

22 "You must not see the bull of your brother or his sheep straying about and deliberately withdraw from them. You should by all means lead them back to your brother. 2 And if your brother is not near you and you have not got to know him, you must also bring it home into the midst of your house, and it must continue with you until your brother has searched for it. And you must return it to him. 3 That is the way too that you will do with his ass, and that is the way you will do with his mantle, and that is the way you will do with anything lost of your brother's, which gets lost from him and which you have found. You will not be allowed to withdraw yourself.

4 "You must not see the ass of your brother or his bull fall down on the road and deliberately withdraw from them. You should by all means help him raise them up.

5 "No garb of an able-bodied man should be put upon a woman, neither should an able-bodied man wear the mantle of a woman; for anybody doing these things is something detestable to Jehovah your God.

6 "In case a bird's nest happens to be before you in the way, in any tree or on the earth with young ones or eggs, and the mother is sitting upon the young ones or the eggs, you must not take the mother along with the offspring. 7 You should by all means send the mother away, but you may take the offspring for yourself; in order that it may go well with you, and you may indeed lengthen your days.

8 "In case you build a new house, you must also make a parapet for your roof, that you may not place bloodguilt upon your house because someone falling might fall from it.

9 "You must not sow your vineyard with two sorts of seed, for fear that the full produce of the seed that you might sow and the product of the vineyard may be forfeited to the sanctuary.

10 "You must not plow with a bull and an ass together.

11 "You must not wear mixed stuff of wool and linen together.

12 "You should make tassels for yourself on the four extremities of your clothing with which you cover yourself.

13 "In case a man takes a wife and actually has relations with her and has come to hate her, 14 and he has charged her with notorious deeds and brought forth a bad name upon her and has said, 'This is the woman I have taken, and I proceeded to go near her, and I did not find evidence of virginity in her'; 15 the father of the girl and her mother must also take and bring forth the evidence of the girl's virginity to the older men of the city at the gate of it; 16 and the girl's father must say to the older men, 'I gave my daughter to this man as a wife, and he went hating her. 17 And here he is charging her with notorious deeds, saying: "I have found your daughter does not have evidence of virginity." Now this is the evidence of my daughter's virginity.' And they must spread out the mantle before the older men of the city. 18 And the older men of that city must take the man and discipline him. 19 And they must fine him a hundred silver shekels and give them to the girl's father, because he brought forth a bad name upon a virgin of Israel; and she will continue to be his wife. He will not be allowed to divorce her all his days.

20 "If, though, this thing has

proved to be the truth, evidence of virginity was not found in the girl, 21 they must also bring the girl out to the entrance of her father's house, and the men of her city must pelt her with stones, and she must die, because she has committed a disgraceful folly in Israel by committing prostitution in the house of her father. So you must clear away what is bad from your midst.

22 "In case a man is found lying down with a woman owned by an owner, both of them must then die together, the man lying down with the woman and the woman. So you must clear away what is bad out of Israel.

23 "In case there happened to be a virgin girl engaged to a man, and a man actually found her in the city and lay down with her, 24 you must also bring them both out to the gate of that city and pelt them with stones, and they must die, the girl for the reason that she did not scream in the city, and the man for the reason that he humiliated the wife of his fellow man. So you must clear away what is evil from your midst.

25 "If, however, it is in the field that the man found the girl who was engaged, and the man grabbed hold of her and lay down with her, the man who lay down with her must also die by himself, 26 and to the girl you must do nothing. The girl has no sin deserving of death, because just as when a man rises up against his fellow man and indeed murders him, even a soul, so it is with this case. 27 For it was in the field that he found her. The girl who was engaged screamed, but there was no one to rescue her.

28 "In case a man finds a girl, a virgin who has not been engaged, and he actually seizes her and lies down with her, and they have been found out, 29 the man who lay down with her must also give the girl's father fifty silver shekels, and she will become his wife due to the fact that he humiliated her.

He will not be allowed to divorce her all his days.

30 "No man should take his father's wife, that he may not uncover the skirt of his father.

23 "No man castrated by crushing the testicles or having his male member cut off may come into the congregation of Jehovah.

2 "No illegitimate son may come into the congregation of Jehovah. Even to the tenth generation none of his may come into the congregation of Jehovah.

3 "No Am'mon·ite or Mo'ab·ite may come into the congregation of Jehovah. Even to the tenth generation none of theirs may come into the congregation of Jehovah to time indefinite, 4 for the reason that they did not come to YOUR aid with bread and water in the way when YOU were going out of Egypt, and because they hired against you Ba'laam the son of Be'or from Pe'thor of Mes·o·po·ta'mi·a to call down evil upon you. 5 And Jehovah your God did not want to listen to Ba'laam; but Jehovah your God in your behalf changed the malediction into a blessing, because Jehovah your God loved you. 6 You must not work for their peace and their prosperity all your days to time indefinite.

7 "You must not detest an E'dom·ite, for he is your brother.

"You must not detest an Egyptian, for you became an alien resident in his country. 8 The sons that may be born to them as the third generation may come for themselves into the congregation of Jehovah.

9 "In case you go out into camp against your enemies, you must also keep yourself from every bad thing. 10 In case there happens to be in you a man who does not continue clean, because of a pollution that occurs at night, he must also go outside the camp. He may not come into the midst of the camp. 11 And it must occur that at the falling of evening he should wash with water, and at the setting of the sun he may come into the midst of the camp. 12 And a pri-

vate place should be at your service outside the camp, and you must go out there. 13 And a peg should be at your service along with your implements, and it must occur that when you squat outside, you must also dig a hole with it and turn and cover your excrement. 14 For Jehovah your God is walking about within your camp to deliver you and to abandon your enemies to you; and your camp must prove to be holy, that he may see nothing indecent in you and certainly turn away from accompanying you.

15 "You must not hand over a slave to his master when he escapes from his master to you. 16 With you he will keep on dwelling in among you in whatever place he may choose in one of your cities, wherever he likes. You must not maltreat him.

17 "None of the daughters of Israel may become a temple prostitute, neither may anyone of the sons of Israel become a temple prostitute. 18 You must not bring the hire of a harlot or the price of a dog into the house of Jehovah your God for any vow, because they are something detestable to Jehovah your God, even both of them.

19 "You must not make your brother pay interest, interest on money, interest on food, interest on anything on which one may claim interest. 20 You may make a foreigner pay interest, but your brother you must not make pay interest; in order that Jehovah your God may bless you in every undertaking of yours on the land to which you are going so as to take possession of it.

21 "In case you vow a vow to Jehovah your God, you must not be slow about paying it, because Jehovah your God will without fail require it of you, and it would indeed become a sin on your part. 22 But in case you omit making a vow, it will not become a sin on your part. 23 The utterance of your lips you should keep, and you must do just as you have vowed to Jehovah your God as a voluntary offering that you spoke of with your mouth.

24 "In case you go into the vineyard of your fellow man, you must eat only enough grapes for you to satisfy your soul, but you must not put any into a receptacle of yours.

25 "In case you go into the standing grain of your fellow man, you must pluck off only the ripe ears with your hand, but the sickle you must not swing to and fro upon the standing grain of your fellow man.

24 "In case a man takes a woman and does make her his possession as a wife, it must also occur that if she should find no favor in his eyes because he has found something indecent on her part, he must also write out a certificate of divorce for her and put it in her hand and dismiss her from his house. 2 And she must go out of his house and go and become another man's. 3 If the latter man has come to hate her and has written out a certificate of divorce for her and put it in her hand and dismissed her from his house, or in case the latter man who took her as his wife should die, 4 the first owner of her who dismissed her will not be allowed to take her back again to become his wife after she has been defiled; for that is something detestable before Jehovah, and you must not lead the land that Jehovah your God is giving you as an inheritance into sin.

5 "In case a man takes a new wife, he should not go out into the army, nor should anything else be imposed onto him. He should continue exempt at his house for one year, and he must make his wife whom he has taken rejoice.

6 "No one should seize a hand mill or its upper grindstone as a pledge, because it is a soul that he is seizing as a pledge.

7 "In case a man is found kidnaping a soul of his brothers of the sons of Israel, and he has dealt tyrannically with him and sold him, that kidnaper must also die.

And you must clear away what is bad from your midst.

8 "Be on your guard in the plague of leprosy to take good care and do according to all that the priests, the Levites, will instruct you. Just as I have commanded them, you should be careful to do. 9 There should be a remembering of what Jehovah your God did to Mir′i·am in the way when you were coming out of Egypt.

10 "In case you lend your fellow man a loan of any sort, you must not enter into his house to take from him what he has pledged. 11 You should stand on the outside, and the man to whom you are making a loan should bring the pledge outside to you. 12 And if the man is in trouble, you must not go to bed with his pledge. 13 You should by all means return the pledge to him as soon as the sun sets, and he must go to bed in his garment, and he must bless you; and it will mean righteousness for you before Jehovah your God.

14 "You must not defraud a hired laborer who is in trouble and poor, whether of your brothers or of your alien residents who are in your land, within your gates. 15 In his day you should give him his wages, and the sun should not set upon them, because he is in trouble and is lifting up his soul to his wages; that he may not cry out to Jeho-vah against you, and it must become sin on your part.

16 "Fathers should not be put to death on account of children, and children should not be put to death on account of fathers. Each one should be put to death for his own sin.

17 "You must not pervert the judgment of the alien resident or of the fatherless boy, and you must not seize the garment of a widow as a pledge. 18 And you must re-member that you became a slave in Egypt, and Jehovah your God proceeded to redeem you from there. That is why I am commanding you to do this thing.

19 "In case you reap your har-vest in your field, and you have forgotten a sheaf in the field, you must not go back to get it. It should stay for the alien resident, for the fatherless boy and for the widow; in order that Jehovah your God may bless you in every deed of your hand.

20 "In case you beat your olive tree, you must not go over its boughs following up yourself. It should stay for the alien resident, for the fatherless boy and for the widow.

21 "In case you gather the grapes of your vineyard, you must not gather the leftovers following up yourself. They should stay for the alien resident, for the fatherless boy and for the widow. 22 And you must remember that you be-came a slave in the land of Egypt. That is why I am commanding you to do this thing.

25 "In case a dispute arises be-tween men, and they have presented themselves for the judg-ment, they must also judge them and pronounce the righteous one righteous and pronounce the wick-ed one wicked. 2 And it must occur that if the wicked one de-serves to be beaten, the judge must also have him laid prostrate and given strokes before him by num-ber to correspond with his wicked deed. 3 With forty strokes he may beat him. He should add none, for fear he should continue to beat him with many strokes in addition to these and your brother is actually disgraced in your eyes.

4 "You must not muzzle a bull while it is threshing.

5 "In case brothers dwell to-gether and one of them has died without his having a son, the wife of the dead one should not be-come a strange man's outside. Her brother-in-law should go to her, and he must take her as his wife and perform brother-in-law marriage with her. 6 And it must occur that the first-born whom she will bear should succeed to the name of his dead brother, that his name may not be wiped out of Israel.

7 "Now if the man finds no de-light in taking his brother's widow,

his brother's widow must then go up to the gate to the older men and say, 'My husband's brother has refused to preserve his brother's name in Israel. He has not consented to perform brother-in-law marriage with me.' 8 And the older men of his city must call him and speak to him, and he must stand and say, 'I have found no delight in taking her.' 9 At that his brother's widow must approach him before the eyes of the older men and draw his sandal off his foot and spit in his face and answer and say, 'That is the way it should be done to the man who will not build up his brother's household.' 10 And his name must be called in Israel 'The house of the one who had his sandal drawn off.'

11 "In case men struggle together with one another, and the wife of the one has come near to deliver her husband out of the hand of the one striking him, and she has thrust out her hand and grabbed hold of him by his privates, 12 you must then amputate her hand. Your eye must feel no sorrow.

13 "You must not come to have in your bag two sorts of weights, a great one and a small one. 14 You must not come to have in your house two sorts of e'phahs, a great one and a small one. 15 A weight accurate and just you should continue to have. An e'phah accurate and just you should continue to have, in order that your days may become long on the soil that Jehovah your God is giving you. 16 For everyone doing these things, every doer of injustice, is something detestable to Jehovah your God.

17 "There should be a remembering of what Am'a·lek did to you in the way when you were coming out of Egypt, 18 how he met you in the way and proceeded to strike in the rear of you all those straggling after you, while you were exhausted and weary; and he did not fear God. 19 And it must occur that when Jehovah your God has given you rest from all your enemies round about in the land that Jehovah your God is giving

you as an inheritance to take possession of it, you should wipe out the mention of Am'a·lek from under the heavens. You must not forget.

26 "And it must occur that when at last you enter into the land that Jehovah your God is giving you as an inheritance, and you have taken possession of it and dwelt in it, 2 you must also take some of the first fruits of all the fruitage of the soil, which you will bring in from the land of yours that Jehovah your God is giving you, and you must put them in a basket and go to the place that Jehovah your God will choose to have his name reside there. 3 And you must come to the priest who will be acting in those days and say to him, 'I must report today to Jehovah your God that I have come into the land that Jehovah swore to our forefathers to give to us.'

4 "And the priest must take the basket out of your hand and deposit it before the altar of Jehovah your God. 5 And you must answer and say before Jehovah your God, 'My father was a perishing Syrian; and he proceeded to go down to Egypt and to reside there as an alien with very few in number; but there he became a great nation, mighty and numerous. 6 And the Egyptians went treating us badly and afflicting us and putting hard slavery upon us. 7 And we began to cry out to Jehovah the God of our forefathers, and Jehovah proceeded to hear our voice and to look on our affliction and our trouble and our oppression. 8 Finally Jehovah brought us out of Egypt with a strong hand and an outstretched arm and with great fearsomeness and with signs and miracles. 9 Then he brought us to this place and gave us this land, a land flowing with milk and honey. 10 And now here I have brought the first fruits of the fruitage of the ground that Jehovah has given me.'

"You must also deposit it before Jehovah your God and bow down before Jehovah your God. 11 And you must rejoice over all the good that Jehovah your God has given you and your household, you and the Levite and the alien resident who is in your midst.

12 "When you finish with tithing the entire tenth of your produce in the third year, the year of the tenth, you must also give it to the Levite, the alien resident, the fatherless boy and the widow, and they must eat it within your gates and satisfy themselves. 13 And you must say before Jehovah your God, 'I have cleared away what is holy from the house and I have also given it to the Levite and the alien resident, the fatherless boy and the widow, in accord with all your commandment that you have commanded me. I have not overstepped your commandments, nor have I forgotten. 14 I have not eaten of it during my mourning, nor have I removed any of it while unclean, nor have I given any of it for anyone dead. I have listened to the voice of Jehovah my God. I have done in accord with all that you have commanded me. 15 Do look down from your holy dwelling, the heavens, and bless your people Israel and the soil that you have given us, just as you swore to our forefathers, the land flowing with milk and honey.'

16 "This day Jehovah your God is commanding you to carry out these regulations and judicial decisions; and you must observe and carry them out with all your heart and all your soul. 17 Jehovah you have induced to say today that he will become your God while you walk in his ways and observe his regulations and his commandments and his judicial decisions and listen to his voice. 18 As for Jehovah, he has induced you to say today that you will become his people, a special property, just as he has promised you, and that you will observe all his commandments, 19 and that he will put you high above all the other nations that he has made, resulting in praise and reputation and beauty, while you prove yourself a people holy to Jehovah your God, just as he has promised."

27 And Moses together with the older men of Israel went on to command the people, saying: "There should be an observing of every commandment that I am commanding you today. 2 And it must occur that in the day when you will cross the Jordan into the land that Jehovah your God is giving you, you must also set up for yourself great stones and whitewash them with lime. 3 And you must write upon them all the words of this law when you have crossed, in order that you may enter into the land that Jehovah your God is giving you, a land flowing with milk and honey, according to what Jehovah the God of your forefathers has spoken to you. 4 And it must occur that when you have crossed the Jordan, you should set up these stones, just as I am commanding you today, in Mount E'bal, and you must whitewash them with lime. 5 You must also build an altar there to Jehovah your God, an altar of stones. You must not wield an iron tool upon them. 6 With whole stones you should build the altar of Jehovah your God, and you must offer burnt offerings to Jehovah your God on it. 7 And you must sacrifice communion sacrifices and eat them there, and you must rejoice before Jehovah your God. 8 And you must write on the stones all the words of this law, making them quite clear."

9 Then Moses and the priests, the Levites, spoke to all Israel, saying: "Keep silent and listen, O Israel. This day you have become the people of Jehovah your God. 10 And you must listen to the voice of Jehovah your God and carry out his commandments and his regulations, which I am commanding you today."

11 And Moses went on to command the people on that day, saying: 12 "The following are the ones who will stand to bless the people on Mount Ger'i·zim when you have crossed the Jordan: Sim'e·on and Le'vi and Judah and Is'-

sa·char and Joseph and Benjamin. 13 And the following are the ones who will stand for the malediction on Mount E'bal: Reu'ben, Gad and Ash'er and Zeb'u·lun, Dan and Naph'ta·li. 14 And the Levites must answer and say with raised voice to every man of Israel:

15 " 'Cursed is the man who makes a carved image or a molten statue, a thing detestable to Jehovah, the manufacture of the hands of a wood-and-metal worker, and who has put it in a hiding place.' (And all the people must answer and say, 'Amen!')

16 " 'Cursed is the one who treats his father or his mother with contempt.' (And all the people must say, 'Amen!')

17 " 'Cursed is the one who moves back the boundary mark of his fellow man.' (And all the people must say, 'Amen!')

18 " 'Cursed is the one who causes the blind to go astray in the way.' (And all the people must say, 'Amen!')

19 " 'Cursed is the one who perverts the judgment of an alien resident, a fatherless boy and a widow.' (And all the people must say, 'Amen!')

20 " 'Cursed is the one who lies down with his father's wife, because he has uncovered the skirt of his father.' (And all the people must say, 'Amen!')

21 " 'Cursed is the one who lies down with any beast.' (And all the people must say, 'Amen!')

22 " 'Cursed is the one who lies down with his sister, the daughter of his father or the daughter of his mother.' (And all the people must say, 'Amen!')

23 " 'Cursed is the one who lies down with his mother-in-law.' (And all the people must say, 'Amen!')

24 " 'Cursed is the one who fatally strikes his fellow man from a hiding place.' (And all the people must say, 'Amen!')

25 " 'Cursed is the one who accepts a bribe to strike a soul fatally, when it is innocent blood.' (And all the people must say, 'Amen!')

26 " 'Cursed is the one who will not put the words of this law in force by doing them.' (And all the people must say, 'Amen!')

28 "And it must occur that if you will without fail listen to the voice of Jehovah your God by being careful to do all his commandments that I am commanding you today, Jehovah your God also will certainly put you high above all other nations of the earth. 2 And all these blessings must come upon you and overtake you, because you keep listening to the voice of Jehovah your God:

3 "Blessed will you be in the city, and blessed will you be in the field.

4 "Blessed will be the fruit of your belly and the fruit of your ground and the fruit of your domestic beast, the young of your cattle and the progeny of your flock.

5 "Blessed will be your basket and your kneading trough.

6 "Blessed will you be when you come in, and blessed will you be when you go out.

7 "Jehovah will cause your enemies who rise up against you to be defeated before you. By one way they will come out against you, but by seven ways they will flee before you. 8 Jehovah will decree for you the blessing on your stores of supply and every undertaking of yours, and he will certainly bless you in the land that Jehovah your God is giving you. 9 Jehovah will establish you as a holy people to himself, just as he swore to you, because you continue to keep the commandments of Jehovah your God, and you have walked in his ways. 10 And all the peoples of the earth will have to see that Jehovah's name has been called upon you, and they will indeed be afraid of you.

11 "Jehovah will also make you overflow indeed with prosperity in the fruit of your belly and the fruit of your domestic animals and the fruitage of your ground, on the ground that Jehovah swore to your forefathers to give you. 12 Jehovah will open up to you his good storehouse, the heavens, to give the rain on your land in its season and

to bless every deed of your hand; and you will certainly lend to many nations, while you yourself will not borrow. 13 And Jehovah will indeed put you at the head and not at the tail; and you must come to be only on top, and you will not come to be on the bottom, because you keep obeying the commandments of Jehovah your God, which I am commanding you today to observe and to do. 14 And you must not turn aside from all the words that I am commanding you today, to the right or to the left, to walk after other gods to serve them.

15 "And it must occur that if you will not listen to the voice of Jehovah your God by taking care to do all his commandments and his statutes that I am commanding you today, all these maledictions must also come upon you and overtake you:

16 "Cursed will you be in the city, and cursed will you be in the field.

17 "Cursed will be your basket and your kneading trough.

18 "Cursed will be the fruit of your belly and the fruitage of your ground, the young of your cattle and the progeny of your flock.

19 "Cursed will you be when you come in, and cursed will you be when you go out.

20 "Jehovah will send upon you the curse, confusion and rebuke in every undertaking of yours that you try to carry out, until you have been annihilated and have perished in a hurry, because of the badness of your practices in that you have forsaken me. 21 Jehovah will cause the pestilence to cling to you until he has exterminated you from off the ground to which you are going to take possession of it. 22 Jehovah will strike you with tuberculosis and burning fever and inflammation and feverish heat and the sword and scorching and mildew, and they will certainly pursue you until you have perished. 23 Your skies that are over your head must also become copper, and the earth that is beneath you iron.

24 Jehovah will give powder and dust as the rain of your land. From the heavens it will come down upon you until you have been annihilated. 25 Jehovah will cause you to be defeated before your enemies. By one way you will go out against them, but by seven ways you will flee before them; and you must become a frightful object to all the earth's kingdoms. 26 And your dead body must become food for every flying creature of the heavens and to the beast of the field, with no one to make [them] tremble.

27 "Jehovah will strike you with the boil of Egypt and piles and eczema and skin eruption, from which you will not be able to be healed. 28 Jehovah will strike you with madness and loss of sight and bewilderment of heart. 29 And you will indeed become one who gropes about at midday, just as a blind man gropes about in the gloom, and you will not make your ways successful; and you must become only one who is always defrauded and robbed, with no one to save you. 30 You will become engaged to a woman, but another man will rape her. You will build a house, but you will not dwell in it. You will plant a vineyard, but you will not begin to use it. 31 Your bull slaughtered there before your eyes—but you will not eat any of it. Your ass taken in robbery from before your face—but it will not return to you. Your sheep given to your enemies—but you will have no savior. 32 Your sons and your daughters given to another people and your eyes looking on and yearning for them always—but your hands will be without power. 33 The fruitage of your ground and all your production a people will eat whom you have not known; and you must become one who is only defrauded and crushed always. 34 And you will certainly become maddened at the sight of your eyes that you will see.

35 "Jehovah will strike you with a malignant boil upon both knees and both legs, from which you will

not be able to be healed, from the sole of your foot to the crown of your head. 36 Jehovah will march you and your king whom you will set up over you to a nation whom you have not known, neither you nor your forefathers; and there you will have to serve other gods, of wood and of stone. 37 And you must become an object of astonishment, a proverbial saying and a taunt among all the peoples to whom Jehovah will lead you away.

38 "A lot of seed you will take out to the field, but little will you gather, because the locust will devour it. 39 Vineyards you will plant and certainly cultivate, but you will drink no wine and gather nothing in, because the worm will eat it up. 40 You will come to have olive trees in all your territory, but you will rub yourself with no oil, because your olives will drop off. 41 Sons and daughters you will bring forth, but they will not continue yours, because they will go off into captivity. 42 All your trees and the fruitage of your ground whirring insects will take in possession. 43 The alien resident who is in your midst will keep ascending higher and higher above you, while you—you will keep descending lower and lower. 44 He will be the one to lend to you, while you—you will not lend to him. He will become the head, while you—you will become the tail.

45 "And all these maledictions will certainly come upon you and pursue you and overtake you until you have been annihilated, because you did not listen to the voice of Jehovah your God by keeping his commandments and his statutes that he commanded you. 46 And they must continue on you and your offspring as a sign and a portent to time indefinite, 47 due to the fact that you did not serve Jehovah your God with rejoicing and joy of heart for the abundance of everything. 48 And you will have to serve your enemies whom Jehovah will send against you with hunger and thirst and nakedness and the want of everything; and

he will certainly put an iron yoke upon your neck until he has annihilated you.

49 "Jehovah will raise up against you a nation far away, from the end of the earth, just as an eagle pounces, a nation whose tongue you will not understand, 50 a nation fierce in countenance, who will not be partial to an old man or show favor to a young man. 51 And they will certainly eat the fruit of your domestic animals and the fruitage of your ground until you have been annihilated, and they will let no grain, new wine or oil, no young of your cattle or progeny of your flock, remain for you until they have destroyed you. 52 And they will indeed besiege you within all your gates until your high and fortified walls in which you are trusting fall in all your land, yes, they will certainly besiege you within all your gates in all your land, which Jehovah your God has given you. 53 Then you will have to eat the fruit of your belly, the flesh of your sons and your daughters, whom Jehovah your God has given you, because of the tightness and stress with which your enemy will hem you in.

54 "As for the very delicate and dainty man among you, his eye will be evil-inclined toward his brother and his cherished wife and the remainder of his sons whom he has remaining, 55 so as not to give one of them any of the flesh of his sons that he will eat, because he has nothing at all remaining to him because of the tightness and stress with which your enemy will hem you in within all your gates. 56 As for the delicate and dainty woman among you who never attempted to set the sole of her foot upon the earth for being of dainty habit and for delicateness, her eye will be evil-inclined toward her cherished husband and her son and her daughter, 57 even toward her afterbirth that comes out from between her legs and toward her sons whom she proceeded to bear, because she will eat them in secrecy for the want of everything

because of the tightness and stress with which your enemy will hem you in within your gates.

58 "If you will not take care to carry out all the words of this law that are written in this book so as to fear this glorious and fear-inspiring name, even Jehovah, your God, 59 Jehovah also will certainly make your plagues and the plagues of your offspring especially severe, great and long-lasting plagues, and malignant and long-lasting sicknesses. 60 And he will indeed bring back upon you all the diseases of Egypt before which you got scared, and they will certainly hang onto you. 61 Also, any sickness and any plague that is not written in the book of this law, Jehovah will bring them upon you until you have been annihilated. 62 And you will indeed be left with very few in number, although you have become like the stars of the heavens for multitude, because you did not listen to the voice of Jehovah your God.

63 "And it must occur that just as Jehovah exulted over you to do you good and to multiply you, so Jehovah will exult over you to destroy you and to annihilate you; and you will simply be torn away from off the soil to which you are going to take possession of it.

64 "And Jehovah will certainly scatter you among all the peoples from the one end of the earth to the other end of the earth, and there you will have to serve other gods whom you have not known, neither you nor your forefathers, wood and stone. 65 And among those nations you will have no ease, nor will there prove to be any resting place for the sole of your foot; and Jehovah will indeed give you there a trembling heart and a failing of the eyes and despair of soul. 66 And you will certainly be in the greatest peril for your life and be in dread night and day, and you will not be sure of your life. 67 In the morning you will say, 'If it only were evening!' and in the evening you will say, 'If it only were morning!' because of the dread of your heart with which you will be in dread and because of the sight of your eyes that you will see. 68 And Jehovah will certainly bring you back to Egypt by ships by the way about which I have said to you, 'You will never see it again,' and you will have to sell yourselves there to your enemies as slave men and maidservants, but there will be no buyer."

29 These are the words of the covenant that Jehovah commanded Moses to conclude with the sons of Israel in the land of Mo'ab aside from the covenant that he had concluded with them in Ho'reb.

2 And Moses proceeded to call all Israel and to say to them: "You were the ones seeing all that Jehovah did before your eyes in the land of Egypt to Phar'aoh and all his servants and all his land, 3 the great provings that your eyes saw, those great signs and miracles. 4 And yet Jehovah has not given you a heart to know and eyes to see and ears to hear down to this day. 5 'While I kept guiding you forty years in the wilderness, your garments did not wear out upon you, and your sandal did not wear out upon your foot. 6 Bread you did not eat, and wine and intoxicating liquor you did not drink, in order that you might know that I am Jehovah your God.' 7 Eventually you came to this place, and Si'hon the king of Hesh'bon and Og the king of Ba'shan proceeded to come out to meet us in battle, but we defeated them. 8 After that we took their land and gave it as an inheritance to the Reu'ben·ites and the Gad'ites and half the tribe of the Ma·nas'sites. 9 So you must keep the words of this covenant and do them, in order that you may make everything you will do turn out well.

10 "You are all of you stationed today before Jehovah your God, the heads of your tribes, your older men and your officers, every man of Israel, 11 your little ones, your wives, and your alien resident who is in the midst of your camp, from the gatherer of your wood to

the drawer of your water, **12** in order for you to enter into the covenant of Jehovah your God and his oath, which Jehovah your God is concluding with you today; **13** for the purpose of establishing you today as his people and that he may prove himself your God, just as he has promised you and just as he has sworn to your forefathers Abraham, Isaac and Jacob.

14 "Now it is not with you alone that I am concluding this covenant and this oath, **15** but it is with him who is here standing with us today before Jehovah our God and with those who are not here with us today; **16** (for you yourselves well know how we dwelt in the land of Egypt and how we passed through the midst of the nations through whom you passed. **17** And you used to see their disgusting things and their dungy idols, wood and stone, silver and gold, that were with them;) **18** that there may not be among you a man or a woman or a family or a tribe whose heart is turning today away from Jehovah our God to go and serve the gods of those nations; that there may not be among you a root bearing the fruit of a poisonous plant and wormwood.

19 "And it must occur that when someone has heard the words of this oath, and he has blessed himself in his heart, saying, 'I shall come to have peace, although I shall walk in the stubbornness of my heart,' with the intention of sweeping away the well-watered one along with the thirsty ones, **20** Jehovah will not want to forgive him, but then Jehovah's anger and his ardor will smoke against that man, and all the oath written in this book will certainly settle down on him, and Jehovah will indeed wipe out his name from under the heavens. **21** So Jehovah will have to separate him for calamity from all the tribes of Israel in accord with all the oath of the covenant that is written in this book of the law.

22 "And the future generation, your sons who will rise up after you, will be bound to say, also the foreigner who will come from a distant land, even [when] they have seen the plagues of that land and its maladies with which Jehovah has sickened it, **23** sulphur and salt and burning, so that its whole land will not be sown, nor sprout, nor will any vegetation spring up in it, like the overthrow of Sod'om and Go·mor'rah, Ad'mah and Ze·boi'im, which Jehovah overthrew in his anger and in his wrath; **24** yes, all the nations will be bound to say, 'Why did Jehovah do like this to this land? Why the heat of this great anger?' **25** Then they will have to say, 'It was because they abandoned the covenant of Jehovah the God of their forefathers, which he concluded with them when he brought them out of the land of Egypt. **26** And they proceeded to go and serve other gods and to bow down to them, gods that they had not known and he had not apportioned to them. **27** Then Jehovah's anger blazed against that land by bringing upon it the whole malediction written in this book. **28** Hence Jehovah uprooted them from off their soil in anger and rage and great indignation and threw them into another land as at this day.'

29 "The things concealed belong to Jehovah our God, but the things revealed belong to us and to our sons to time indefinite, that we may carry out all the words of this law.

30 "And it must occur that when all these words will come upon you, the blessing and the malediction, which I have put before you, and you have brought them back to your heart among all the nations where Jehovah your God has dispersed you, **2** and you have returned to Jehovah your God and listened to his voice according to all that I am commanding you today, you and your sons, with all your heart and all your soul, **3** Jehovah your God must also bring back your captives and show you mercy and collect you again from all the peoples where Jehovah your God has scattered you. 4 If your dispersed people should be at the end of the heavens, from there Jehovah your God will collect you and from there he will take you. 5 Jehovah your God will indeed bring you into the land of which your fathers took possession, and you will certainly take possession of it; and he will indeed do you good and multiply you more than your fathers. 6 And Jehovah your God will have to circumcise your heart and the heart of your offspring, that you may love Jehovah your God with all your heart and all your soul for the sake of your life. 7 And Jehovah your God will certainly put all these oaths upon your enemies and those who hate you, who have persecuted you.

8 "As for you, you will turn and certainly listen to the voice of Jehovah and do all his commandments that I am commanding you today. 9 And Jehovah your God will indeed make you have more than enough in every work of your hand, in the fruit of your belly and the fruit of your domestic animals and the fruitage of your soil, resulting in prosperity; because Jehovah will again exult over you for good, just as he exulted over your forefathers; 10 for you will listen to the voice of Jehovah your God so as to keep his commandments and his statutes written in this book of the law, because you will return to Jehovah your God with all your heart and all your soul.

11 "For this commandment that I am commanding you today is not too difficult for you, nor is it far away. 12 It is not in the heavens, so as to result in saying, 'Who will ascend for us into the heavens and get it for us, that he may let us hear it that we may do it?' 13 Neither is it on the other side of the sea, so as to result in saying, 'Who will pass over for us to the other side of the sea and get it for us, that he may let us hear it that we may do it?' 14 For the word is very near you, in your own mouth and in your own heart, that you may do it.

15 "See, I do put before you today life and good, and death and bad. 16 If you will listen to the commandments of Jehovah your God, which I am commanding you today, so as to love Jehovah your God, to walk in his ways and to keep his commandments and his statutes and his judicial decisions, then you will be bound to keep alive and to multiply, and Jehovah your God must bless you in the land to which you are going to take possession of it.

17 "But if your heart turns away and you do not listen, and you are actually seduced and bow down to other gods and serve them, 18 I do tell YOU today that YOU will positively perish. YOU will not lengthen YOUR days on the ground to which you are crossing the Jordan to go to take possession of it. 19 I do take the heavens and the earth as witnesses against YOU today, that I have put life and death before you, the blessing and the malediction; and you must choose life in order that you may keep alive, you and your offspring, 20 by loving Jehovah your God, by listening to his voice and by sticking to him; for he is your life and the length of your days, that you may dwell upon the ground that Jehovah swore to your forefathers Abraham, Isaac and Jacob to give to them."

31 Then Moses went and spoke these words to all Israel 2 and said to them: "A hundred and twenty years old I am today. I shall no more be allowed to go out and come in, as Jehovah has said to me, 'You will not cross this Jordan.' 3 Jehovah your God is the one crossing before you. He himself will annihilate these nations from before you, and you must drive them away. Joshua is the one crossing before you, just as Jehovah has spoken. 4 And Jehovah will certainly do to them just as he has done to Si'hon and to Og, the kings of the Am'or·ites, and to their land, when he annihilated

them. 5 And Jehovah has abandoned them to you, and you must do to them according to all the commandment that I have commanded you. 6 BE courageous and strong. Do not be afraid or suffer a shock before them, because Jehovah your God is the one marching with you. He will neither desert you nor leave you entirely."

7 And Moses proceeded to call Joshua and say to him before the eyes of all Israel: "Be courageous and strong, because you—you will bring this people into the land that Jehovah swore to their forefathers to give to them, and you yourself will give it to them as an inheritance. 8 And Jehovah is the one marching before you. He himself will continue with you. He will neither desert you nor leave you entirely. Do not be afraid or be terrified."

9 Then Moses wrote this law and gave it to the priests the sons of Le'vi, the carriers of the ark of Jehovah's covenant, and to all the older men of Israel. 10 And Moses went on to command them, saying: "At the end of every seven years, in the appointed time of the year of the release, in the festival of booths, 11 when all Israel comes to see the face of Jehovah your God in the place that he will choose, you will read this law in front of all Israel in their hearing. 12 Congregate the people, the men and the women and the little ones and your alien resident who is within your gates, in order that they may listen and in order that they may learn, as they must fear Jehovah your God and take care to carry out all the words of this law. 13 And their sons who have not known should listen, and they must learn to fear Jehovah your God all the days that you are living upon the soil to which you are crossing the Jordan to take possession of it."

14 After that Jehovah said to Moses: "Look! The days have drawn near for you to die. Call Joshua, and station yourselves in the tent of meeting, that I may commission him." So Moses and Joshua went and stationed themselves in the tent of meeting. 15 Then Jehovah appeared at the tent in the pillar of cloud, and the pillar of cloud began to stand by the entrance of the tent.

16 Jehovah now said to Moses: "Look! You are lying down with your forefathers; and this people will certainly get up and have immoral intercourse with foreign gods of the land to which they are going, in their very midst, and they will certainly forsake me and break my covenant that I have concluded with them. 17 At that my anger will indeed blaze against them in that day, and I shall certainly forsake them and conceal my face from them, and they must become something to be consumed; and many calamities and distresses must come upon them, and they will be bound to say in that day, 'Is it not because our God is not in our midst that these calamities have come upon us?' 18 As for me, I shall absolutely conceal my face in that day because of all the badness that they have done, because they have turned to other gods.

19 "And now WRITE for yourselves this song and teach it to the sons of Israel. Place it in their mouths in order that this song may serve as my witness against the sons of Israel. 20 For I shall bring them to the ground that I have sworn about to their forefathers, which flows with milk and honey, and they will certainly eat and be satisfied and grow fat and turn to other gods, and they will indeed serve them and treat me with disrespect and break my covenant. 21 And it must occur that when many calamities and distresses will come upon them, this song must also answer before them as a witness, because it should not be forgotten out of the mouth of their offspring, for I well know their inclination that they are developing today before I bring them into the land about which I have sworn."

22 So Moses wrote this song in that day, that he might teach it to the sons of Israel.

23 And he proceeded to commission Joshua the son of Nun and to say: "Be courageous and strong, because you—you will bring the sons of Israel into the land about which I have sworn to them, and I myself shall continue with you."

24 And it came about that as soon as Moses had finished writing the words of this law in a book until their completion, 25 Moses began to command the Levites, the carriers of the ark of Jehovah's covenant, saying: 26 "Taking this book of the law, YOU must place it at the side of the ark of the covenant of Jehovah YOUR God, and it must serve as a witness there against you. 27 For I—I well know your rebelliousness and your stiff neck. If while I am yet alive with YOU today, YOU have proved rebellious in behavior toward Jehovah, then how much more so after my death! 28 Congregate to me all the older men of YOUR tribes and YOUR officers, and let me speak in their hearing these words, and let me take the heavens and the earth as witnesses against them. 29 For I well know that after my death YOU will without fail act ruinously, and YOU will certainly turn aside from the way about which I have commanded YOU; and calamity will be bound to befall YOU at the close of the days, because YOU will do what is bad in the eyes of Jehovah so as to offend him by the works of YOUR hands."

30 And Moses proceeded to speak in the hearing of all the congregation of Israel the words of this song until their completion:

32 "Give ear, O heavens, and let me speak;
    And let the earth hear the sayings of my mouth.
2 My instruction will drip as the rain,
    My saying will trickle as the dew,
    As gentle rains upon grass
        And as copious showers upon vegetation.
3 For I shall declare the name of Jehovah.

    Do YOU attribute greatness to our God!
4 The Rock, perfect is his activity,
    For all his ways are justice.
    A God of faithfulness, with whom there is no injustice;
    Righteous and upright is he.
5 They have acted ruinously on their own part;
    They are not his children, the defect is their own.
    A generation crooked and twisted!
6 Is it to Jehovah that YOU keep doing this way,
    O people stupid and not wise?
    Is he not your Father who has produced you,
    He who made you and proceeded to give you stability?
7 Remember the days of old,
    CONSIDER the years back from generation to generation;
    Ask your father, and he can tell you;
    Your old men, and they can say it to you.
8 When the Most High gave the nations an inheritance,
    When he parted the sons of Adam from one another,
    He proceeded to fix the boundary of the peoples
    With regard for the number of the sons of Israel.
9 For Jehovah's share is his people;
    Jacob is the allotment that he inherits.
10 He came to find him in a wilderness land,
    And in an empty, howling desert.
    He began to encircle him, to take care of him,
    To safeguard him as the pupil of his eye.
11 Just as an eagle stirs up its nest,
    Hovers over its fledglings,
    Spreads out its wings, takes them,
    Carries them on its pinions,
12 Jehovah alone kept leading him,
    And there was no foreign god along with him.
13 He kept making him ride upon earth's high places,

So that he ate the produce of the field.
And he kept making him suck honey out of a crag,
And oil out of a flinty rock;
14 Butter of the herd and milk of the flock
Together with the fat of rams,
And male sheep, the breed of Ba'shan, and he-goats
Together with the kidney fat of wheat;
And the blood of the grape you kept drinking as wine.
15 When Jesh'u·run began to grow fat, then he kicked.
You have grown fat, you have become thick, you have become gorged.
So he forsook God, who made him,
And despised the Rock of his salvation.
16 They began inciting him to jealousy with strange gods;
With detestable things they kept offending him.
17 They went sacrificing to demons, not to God,
Gods whom they had not known,
New ones who recently came in,
With whom your forefathers were not acquainted.
18 The Rock who fathered you, you proceeded to forget,
And you began to leave God out of memory, the One bringing you forth with childbirth pains.
19 When Jehovah saw it, then he came to disrespect them,
Because of the vexation his sons and his daughters gave.
20 So he said, 'Let me conceal my face from them,
Let me see what their end will be afterward.
For they are a generation of perverseness,
Sons in whom there is no faithfulness.
21 They, for their part, have incited me to jealousy with what is no god;
They have vexed me with their vain idols;

And I, for my part, shall incite them to jealousy with what is no people;
With a stupid nation I shall offend them.
22 For a fire has been ignited in my anger
And it will burn down to She'ol, the lowest place,
And it will consume the earth and its produce
And will set ablaze the foundations of mountains.
23 I shall increase calamities upon them;
My arrows I shall spend upon them.
24 Exhausted from hunger they will be and eaten up by burning fever
And bitter destruction.
And the teeth of beasts I shall send upon them,
With the venom of reptiles of the dust.
25 Outdoors a sword will bereave them,
And indoors fright,
Of both young man and virgin,
Suckling together with gray-haired man.
26 I should have said: "I shall disperse them,
I will make the mention of them cease from mortal men,"
27 Were it not that I was afraid of vexation from the enemy,
That their adversaries might misconstrue it,
That they might say: "Our hand has proved superior,
And it was not Jehovah who worked all this out."
28 For they are a nation on whom counsel perishes,
And among them there is no understanding.
29 O that they were wise! Then they would ponder over this.
They would consider their end afterward.
30 How could one pursue a thousand,
And two put ten thousand to flight?
Not unless their Rock had sold them

And Jehovah had surrendered them.

31 For their rock is not like our Rock,
Even our enemies being the ones to decide.
32 For their vine is from the vine of Sod′om
And from the terraces of Gomor′rah.
Their grapes are grapes of poison,
Their clusters are bitter.
33 Their wine is the venom of big snakes
And the cruel poison of cobras.
34 Is it not laid up with me,
With a seal affixed to it in my storehouse?
35 Vengeance is mine, and retribution.
At the appointed time their foot will move unsteadily,
For the day of their disaster is near,
And the events in readiness for them do make haste.'
36 For Jehovah will judge his people
And he will feel regret over his servants,
Because he will see that support has disappeared
And there is only a helpless and worthless one.
37 And he will certainly say, 'Where are their gods,
The rock in whom they sought refuge,
38 Who used to eat the fat of their sacrifices,
To drink the wine of their drink offerings?
Let them get up and help you.
Let them become a concealment place for you.
39 See now that I—I am he
And there are no gods together with me.
I put to death, and I make alive.
I have severely wounded, and I—I will heal,
And there is no one snatching out of my hand.
40 For I raise my hand to heaven [in an oath],
And I do say: "As I am alive to time indefinite,"

41 If I do indeed sharpen my glittering sword,
And my hand takes hold on judgment,
I will pay back vengeance to my adversaries
And render retribution to those who intensely hate me.
42 I shall intoxicate my arrows with blood,
While my sword will eat flesh,
With the blood of the slain and the captives,
With the heads of the leaders of the enemy.'
43 Be glad, you nations, with his people,
For he will avenge the blood of his servants,
And he will pay back vengeance to his adversaries
And will indeed make atonement for the ground of his people."

44 Thus Moses came and spoke all the words of this song in the hearing of the people, he and Ho·she′a the son of Nun. 45 After Moses finished speaking all these words to all Israel, 46 he went on to say to them: "Apply your hearts to all the words that I am speaking in warning to you today, that you may command your sons to take care to do all the words of this law. 47 For it is no valueless word for you, but it means your life, and by this word you may lengthen your days upon the soil to which you are crossing the Jordan to take possession of it."

48 And Jehovah proceeded to speak to Moses on this same day, saying: 49 "Go up into this mountain of Ab′a·rim, Mount Ne′bo, which is in the land of Mo′ab, which fronts toward Jer′i·cho, and see the land of Ca′naan, which I am giving to the sons of Israel as a possession. 50 Then die on the mountain into which you are going up, and be gathered to your people, just as Aaron your brother died on Mount Hor and got to be gathered to his people; 51 for the reason that you men acted undutifully toward me in the middle of the sons of Israel at the waters of

Mer′i·bah of Ka′desh in the wilderness of Zin; for the reason that you men did not sanctify me in the middle of the sons of Israel. 52 For from a distance you will see the land, but you will not go there into the land that I am giving to the sons of Israel."

33 Now this is the blessing with which Moses the man of the [true] God blessed the sons of Israel before his death. 2 And he proceeded to say:

"Jehovah—from Si′nai he came,
And he flashed forth from Se′ir upon them.
He beamed forth from the mountainous region of Pa′ran,
And with him were holy myriads,
At his right hand warriors belonging to them.
3 He was also cherishing his people;
All their holy ones are in your hand.
And they—they reclined at your feet;
They began to receive some of your words.
4 (Moses laid as a command upon us a law,
A possession of the congregation of Jacob.)
5 And he came to be king in Jesh′u·run,
When the heads of the people gathered themselves,
The entire number of the tribes of Israel.
6 Let Reu′ben live and not die off,
And let his men [not] become few."
7 And this was Judah's blessing, as he went on to say:
"Hear, O Jehovah, the voice of Judah,
And may you bring him to his people.
His arms have contended for what is his;
And may you prove yourself a helper from his adversaries."
8 And as to Le′vi he said:
"Your Thum′mim and your U′rim belong to the man loyal to you,

Whom you put to the test at Mas′sah.
You began to contend with him by the waters of Mer′i·bah,
9 The man who said to his father and his mother, 'I have not seen him.'
Even his brothers he did not acknowledge,
And his sons he did not know.
For they kept your saying,
And your covenant they continued to observe.
10 Let them instruct Jacob in your judicial decisions
And Israel in your law.
Let them render up incense before your nostrils
And a whole offering on your altar.
11 Bless, O Jehovah, his vital energy,
And may you show pleasure in the activity of his hands.
Wound severely in their hips those who rise up against him,
And those who intensely hate him, that they may not rise up."
12 As to Benjamin he said:
"Let the beloved one of Jehovah reside in security by him,
While he shelters him the whole day,
And he must reside between his shoulders."
13 And as to Joseph he said:
"May his land be continually blessed from Jehovah
With the choice things of heaven, with dew,
And with the watery deep lying down below,
14 And with the choice things, the products of the sun,
And with the choice things, the yield of the lunar months,
15 And with the choicest from the mountains of the east,
And with the choice things of the indefinitely lasting hills,
16 And with the choice things of the earth and its fullness,

And with the approval of the
One residing in the thornbush.
May they come upon the head
of Joseph
And upon the crown of the
head of the one singled out
from his brothers.
17 As the first-born of a bull his
splendor is,
And his horns are the horns
of a wild bull.
With them he will push peoples
All together to the ends of the
earth,
And they are the tens of thousands of E'phra·im,
And they are the thousands of
Ma·nas'seh."
18 And as to Zeb'u·lun he said:
"Rejoice, O Zeb'u·lun, in your
going out,
And, Is'sa·char, in your tents.
19 Peoples to the mountain they
will call.
There they will sacrifice the
sacrifices of righteousness.
For they will suck the abounding wealth of the seas
And the hidden hoards of the
sand."
20 And as to Gad he said:
"Blessed is the one widening the
borders of Gad.
As a lion he must reside,
And he must tear the arm,
yes, the crown of the head.
21 And he will pick out the first
part for himself,
For there the allotment of a
statute-giver is reserved.
And the heads of the people will
gather themselves together.
The righteousness of Jehovah
will he certainly execute
And his judicial decisions with
Israel."
22 And as to Dan he said:
"Dan is a lion cub.
He will leap out from Ba'-
shan."
23 And as to Naph'ta·li he said:
"Naph'ta·li is satisfied with the
approval
And full of the blessing of
Jehovah.
Do take possession of the west
and south."

24 And as to Ash'er he said:
"Blessed with sons is Ash'er.
Let him become one approved
by his brothers,
And one dipping his foot in oil.
25 Iron and copper are your gate
locks,
And in proportion to your
days is your leisurely walk.
26 There is none like the [true]
God of Jesh'u·run,
Who rides upon heaven in
help of you
And upon cloudy skies in his
eminence.
27 A hiding place is the God of
ancient time,
And underneath are the indefinitely lasting arms.
And he will drive away from
before you the enemy,
And he will say, 'Annihilate
[them]!'
28 And Israel will reside in security,
The fountain of Jacob by itself,
Upon a land of grain and new
wine.
Yes, his heavens will let the
dew drip down.
29 Happy you are, O Israel!
Who is there like you,
A people enjoying salvation in
Jehovah,
The shield of your help,
And the One who is your
eminent sword?
So your enemies will cringe before you,
And you—upon their high
places you will tread."

34 Then Moses proceeded to go
up from the desert plains of
Mo'ab into Mount Ne'bo, to the top
of Pis'gah, which fronts toward
Jer'i·cho. And Jehovah went showing him all the land, Gil'e·ad as
far as Dan, 2 and all Naph'ta·li
and the land of E'phra·im and Ma-
nas'seh and all the land of Judah
as far as the western sea, 3 and
the Neg'eb and the District, the
valley plain of Jer'i·cho, the city
of the palm trees, as far as Zo'ar.
4 And Jehovah went on to say
to him: "This is the land about

which I have sworn to Abraham, Isaac and Jacob, saying, 'To your seed I shall give it.' I have caused you to see it with your own eyes, as you will not cross over there."

5 After that Moses the servant of Jehovah died there in the land of Mo'ab at the order of Jehovah. 6 And he proceeded to bury him in the valley in the land of Mo'ab in front of Beth-pe'or, and nobody has come to know his grave down to this day. 7 And Moses was a hundred and twenty years old at his death. His eye had not grown dim, and his vital strength had not fled. 8 And the sons of Israel proceeded to weep for Moses on the desert plains of Mo'ab thirty days. At length the days of weeping of the mourning period for Moses were completed.

9 And Joshua the son of Nun was full of the spirit of wisdom, for Moses had laid his hand upon him; and the sons of Israel began to listen to him and they went doing just as Jehovah had commanded Moses. 10 But there has never yet risen up a prophet in Israel like Moses, whom Jehovah knew face to face, 11 as respects all the signs and the miracles that Jehovah sent him to do in the land of Egypt to Phar'aoh and all his servants and all his land, 12 and as regards all the strong hand and all the great awesomeness that Moses exercised before the eyes of all Israel.

JOSHUA

1 And it came about after the death of Moses the servant of Jehovah that Jehovah proceeded to say to Joshua the son of Nun, the minister of Moses: 2 "Moses my servant is dead; and now get up, cross this Jordan, you and all this people, into the land that I am giving to them, to the sons of Israel. 3 Every place upon which the sole of YOUR foot will tread, to YOU people I shall certainly give it, just as I promised to Moses. 4 From the wilderness and this Leb'a·non to the great river, the river Eu·phra'tes, that is, all the land of the Hit'tites, and to the Great Sea toward the setting of the sun YOUR territory will prove to be. 5 Nobody will take a firm stand before you all the days of your life. Just as I proved to be with Moses I shall prove to be with you. I shall neither desert you nor leave you entirely. 6 Be courageous and strong, for you are the one who will cause this people to inherit the land that I swore to their forefathers to give to them.

7 "Only be courageous and very strong to take care to do according to all the law that Moses my servant commanded you. Do not turn aside from it to the right or to the left, in order that you may act wisely everywhere you go. 8 This book of the law should not depart from your mouth, and you must in an undertone read in it day and night, in order that you may take care to do according to all that is written in it; for then you will make your way successful and then you will act wisely. 9 Have I not commanded you? Be courageous and strong. Do not suffer shock or be terrified, for Jehovah your God is with you wherever you go."

10 And Joshua proceeded to command the officers of the people, saying: 11 "Pass through the midst of the camp and command the people, saying, 'Get provisions ready for yourselves, because three days from now YOU are crossing this Jordan to go in and take possession of the land that Jehovah YOUR God is giving YOU to take possession of it.'"

12 And to the Reu'ben·ites and the Gad'ites and the half tribe of Ma·nas'seh Joshua said: **13** "Let there be a remembering of the word that Moses the servant of Jehovah commanded YOU, saying, 'Jehovah YOUR God is giving YOU rest and has given YOU this land. **14** YOUR wives, YOUR little ones and YOUR livestock will dwell in the land that Moses has given YOU on this side of the Jordan; but YOU men will pass over in battle formation before YOUR brothers, all the valiant mighty men, and YOU must help them. **15** First when Jehovah gives rest to YOUR brothers the same as to YOU and they also have taken possession of the land that Jehovah YOUR God is giving them, YOU must also return to the land of YOUR holding and take possession of it, the one that Moses the servant of Jehovah has given YOU on the side of the Jordan toward the rising of the sun.' "

16 Accordingly they answered Joshua, saying: "All that you have commanded us we shall do, and wherever you may send us we shall go. **17** As we listened to Moses in everything, so we shall listen to you. Only may Jehovah your God prove to be with you just as he proved to be with Moses. **18** Any man that behaves rebelliously against your order and does not listen to your words in all that you may command us will be put to death. Only be courageous and strong."

2 Then Joshua the son of Nun sent two men out secretly from Shit'tim as spies, saying: "Go, take a look at the land and Jer'i·cho." So they went and came to the house of a prostitute woman whose name was Ra'hab, and they took up lodging there. **2** In time it was said to the king of Jer'i·cho: "Look! Men from the sons of Israel have come in here tonight to search out the land." **3** At that the king of Jer'i·cho sent to Ra'hab, saying: "Bring out the men that came to you, that have come into your house, for it is to search

out all the land that they have come."

4 Meantime the woman took the two men and concealed them. And she proceeded to say: "Yes, the men did come to me, and I did not know from where they were. **5** And it came about at the closing of the gate by dark that the men went out. I just do not know where the men have gone. Chase after them quickly, for YOU will overtake them." **6** (She, though, had taken them up to the roof, and she kept them out of sight among stalks of flax laid in rows for her upon the roof.) **7** And the men chased after them in the direction of the Jordan at the fords, and they shut the gate immediately after those chasing after them had gone out.

8 As for these, before they could lie down, she herself came up to them on the roof. **9** And she went on to say to the men: "I do know that Jehovah will certainly give YOU the land, and that the fright of YOU has fallen upon us, and that all the inhabitants of the land have become disheartened because of YOU. **10** For we have heard how Jehovah dried up the waters of the Red Sea from before YOU when YOU came out of Egypt, and what YOU did to the two kings of the Am'or·ites who were on the other side of the Jordan, namely, Si'hon and Og, whom YOU devoted to destruction. **11** When we got to hear it, then our hearts began to melt, and no spirit has arisen yet in anybody because of YOU, for Jehovah YOUR God is God in the heavens above and on the earth beneath. **12** And now, please, swear to me by Jehovah that, because I have exercised loving-kindness toward YOU, YOU also will certainly exercise loving-kindness toward the household of my father, and YOU must give me a trustworthy sign. **13** And YOU must preserve alive my father and my mother and my brothers and my sisters and all who belong to them, and YOU must deliver our souls from death."

14 At that the men said to her: "Our souls are to die instead of

camp. That was the way they did for six days.

15 And it came about on the seventh day that they proceeded to get up early, as soon as the dawn ascended, and they went marching round the city in this manner seven times. Just on that day they marched round the city seven times. 16 And it came about on the seventh time that the priests blew the horns, and Joshua proceeded to say to the people: "Shout; for Jehovah has given YOU the city. 17 And the city must become a thing devoted to destruction; it with everything that is in it belongs to Jehovah. Only Ra'hab the prostitute may keep on living, she and all who are with her in the house, because she hid the messengers whom we sent out. 18 As for YOU people, only keep away from the thing devoted to destruction, for fear YOU may get a desire and YOU do take some of the thing devoted to destruction and do constitute the camp of Israel a thing devoted to destruction and bring ostracism upon it. 19 But all the silver and the gold and the articles of copper and iron are something holy to Jehovah. Into the treasure of Jehovah it should go."

20 Then the people shouted, when they proceeded to blow the horns. And it came about that as soon as the people heard the sound of the horn and the people began to shout a great war cry, then the wall began to fall down flat. After that the people went up into the city, each one straight before him, and captured the city. 21 And they went devoting all that was in the city, from man to woman, from young man to old man and to bull and sheep and ass, to destruction by the edge of the sword.

22 And to the two men who had done the spying on the land, Joshua said: "Go into the house of the woman, the prostitute, and bring out of there the woman and all who belong to her, just as YOU have sworn to her." 23 So the young men who had done the spy-

ing went in and brought out Ra'hab and her father and her mother and her brothers and all who belonged to her, yes, all her family relationship they brought out; and they proceeded to set them down outside the camp of Israel.

24 And they burned the city with fire and everything that was in it. Only the silver and the gold and the articles of copper and iron they gave to the treasure of Jehovah's house. 25 And Ra'hab the prostitute and the household of her father and all who belonged to her, Joshua preserved alive; and she dwells in the midst of Israel down to this day, because she hid the messengers whom Joshua sent out to spy on Jer'i·cho.

26 Then Joshua had an oath pronounced at that particular time, saying: "Cursed may the man be before Jehovah who gets up and does build this city, even Jer'i·cho. At the forfeit of his first-born let him lay the foundation of it, and at the forfeit of his youngest let him put up its doors."

27 So Jehovah proved to be with Joshua, and his fame came to be in all the earth.

7 And the sons of Israel went committing an act of unfaithfulness respecting the thing devoted to destruction in that A'chan the son of Car'mi, the son of Zab'di, the son of Ze'rah, of the tribe of Judah, took some of the thing devoted to destruction. At this Jehovah's anger grew hot against the sons of Israel.

2 Then Joshua sent men out from Jer'i·cho to A'i, which is close by Beth-a'ven, to the east of Beth'el, and said to them: "Go up and spy on the land." Accordingly the men went up and spied on A'i. 3 After that they returned to Joshua and said to him: "Let not all the people go up. Let about two thousand men or about three thousand men go up and strike A'i. Do not weary all the people with going there, for they are few."

4 So about three thousand men of the people went up there, but

they took to flight before the men of A'i. 5 And the men of A'i got to strike down about thirty-six men of them, and they went pursuing them from before the gate as far as Sheb'a·rim and continued striking them down on the descent. Consequently the heart of the people began to melt and became as water.

6 At this Joshua ripped his mantles and fell upon his face to the earth before the ark of Jehovah until the evening, he and the older men of Israel, and they kept putting dust upon their heads. 7 And Joshua went on to say: "Alas, Lord Jehovah, why did you bring this people all the way across the Jordan, just to give us into the hand of the Am'or·ites for them to destroy us? And if only we had taken it upon ourselves and continued dwelling on the other side of the Jordan! 8 Excuse me, O Jehovah, but what can I say after Israel has turned his back before his enemies? 9 And the Ca'naan-ites and all the inhabitants of the land will hear of it, and they will certainly surround us and cut our name off from the earth; and what will you do for your great name?"

10 In turn Jehovah said to Joshua: "Get up, you! Why is it that you are falling upon your face? 11 Israel has sinned, and they have also overstepped my covenant that I laid as a command upon them; and they have also taken some of the thing devoted to destruction and have also stolen and also kept it secret and have also put it among their own articles. 12 And the sons of Israel will not be able to rise up against their enemies. The back is what they will turn before their enemies, because they have become a thing devoted to destruction. I shall not prove to be with you again unless you annihilate the thing devoted to destruction out of your midst. 13 Get up! Sanctify the people, and you must say, 'Sanctify yourselves tomorrow, for this is what Jehovah the God of Israel has said: "A thing devoted

to destruction is in your midst, O Israel. You will not be able to rise up against your enemies until you people have removed the thing devoted to destruction from your midst. 14 And you must present yourselves in the morning, tribe by tribe, and it must occur that the tribe that Jehovah will pick will come near, family by family, and the family that Jehovah will pick will come near, household by household, and the household that Jehovah will pick will come near, able-bodied man by able-bodied man. 15 And it must occur that the one picked with the thing devoted to destruction will be burned with fire, he and all that belongs to him, because he has overstepped the covenant of Jehovah and because he has committed a disgraceful folly in Israel." ' "

16 Then Joshua rose early in the morning and had Israel come near, tribe by tribe of it, and the tribe of Judah got to be picked. 17 Next he had the families of Judah come near and picked the family of the Ze'rah·ites, after which he had the family of the Ze'rah·ites come near, able-bodied man by able-bodied man, and Zab'di got to be picked. 18 Finally he had his household come near, able-bodied man by able-bodied man, and A'chan the son of Car'mi, the son of Zab'di, the son of Ze'rah, of the tribe of Judah, got to be picked. 19 Then Joshua said to A'chan: "My son, render, please, glory to Jehovah the God of Israel and make confession to him, and tell me, please, What have you done? Do not hide it from me."

20 At this A'chan answered Joshua and said: "For a fact I—I have sinned against Jehovah the God of Israel, and this way and that way I have done. 21 When I got to see among the spoil an official garment from Shi'nar, a good-looking one, and two hundred shekels of silver and one gold bar, fifty shekels being its weight, then I wanted them, and I took them; and, look! they are hidden in the

earth in the midst of my tent with the money underneath it."

22 At once Joshua sent messengers, and they went running to the tent, and, look! it was hidden in his tent with the money underneath it. 23 So they took them from the midst of the tent and brought them to Joshua and all the sons of Israel and poured them out before Jehovah. 24 Joshua, and all Israel with him, now took A'chan the son of Ze'rah and the silver and the official garment and the bar of gold and his sons and his daughters and his bull and his ass and his flock and his tent and everything that was his and they brought them up to the low plain of A'chor. 25 Then Joshua said: "Why have you brought ostracism upon us? Jehovah will bring ostracism upon you on this day." With that all Israel went pelting him with stones, after which they burned them with fire. Thus they stoned them with stones. 26 And they proceeded to raise up over him a big pile of stones, down to this day. At this Jehovah turned away from his hot anger. That is why the name of that place has been called Low Plain of A'chor, down to this day.

8 Then Jehovah said to Joshua: "Do not be afraid or be terrified. Take with you all the people of war and get up, go up to A'i. See, I have given into your hand the king of A'i and his people and his city and his land. 2 And you must do to A'i and to its king just as you did to Jer'i·cho and its king. Only you people may plunder its spoil and its domestic animals for yourselves. Set an ambush of yours against the city at its rear."

3 Accordingly Joshua and all the people of war rose to go up to A'i, and Joshua proceeded to choose thirty thousand men, valiant mighty ones, and to send them off by night. 4 And he went on to command them, saying: "See, you are lying in ambush against the city to the rear of the city. Do not go very far away from the city, and you must all of you hold

yourselves in readiness. 5 As for me and all the people who are with me, we shall go close to the city. And it must occur that, in case they should come out to meet us just as at the first, we must then flee before them. 6 And they must come out after us until we have drawn them away from the city, for they will say, 'They are fleeing before us just as at the first.' And we must flee before them. 7 Then you—you will rise up from the ambush, and you must take possession of the city; and Jehovah your God will certainly give it into your hands. 8 And it must occur that as soon as you have seized the city, you should set the city on fire. According to Jehovah's word you should do. See, I have commanded you."

9 After that Joshua sent them out and they marched to the place of ambush and took up quarters between Beth'el and A'i to the west of A'i, while Joshua kept lodging on that night in the midst of the people.

10 Then Joshua rose up early in the morning and reviewed the people and went up, he and the older men of Israel, before the people to A'i. 11 And all the people of war who were with him went up, that they might approach and get in front of the city, and they proceeded to camp to the north of A'i, with the valley between them and A'i. 12 In the meantime he took about five thousand men and set them as an ambush between Beth'el and A'i, to the west of the city. 13 So the people set the main camp that was to the north of the city and the extreme rear of it that was to the west of the city, and Joshua proceeded to go during that night into the middle of the low plain.

14 And it came about that, as soon as the king of A'i saw it, then the men of the city got in a hurry and rose up early and went out to meet Israel in battle, he and all his people, at the appointed time, before the desert plain. As for him,

he did not know that there was an ambush against him to the rear of the city. 15 When Joshua and all Israel suffered a blow before them, then they took to flight by the way of the wilderness. 16 At that all the people who were in the city were called out to chase after them, and they went chasing after Joshua and got to be drawn away from the city. 17 And there was not a man remaining in A'i and Beth'el that did not go out after Israel, so that they left the city wide open and went chasing after Israel.

18 Jehovah now said to Joshua: "Stretch out the javelin that is in your hand toward A'i, for into your hand I shall give it." Accordingly Joshua stretched out the javelin that was in his hand toward the city. 19 And the ambush rose up quickly from its place, and they began to run at the instant that he stretched out his hand, and they proceeded to enter the city and capture it. Then they hurried and set the city on fire.

20 And the men of A'i began to turn back and look, and there the smoke of the city ascended to the heavens, and there proved to be no ability in them to flee this way or that. And the people that were fleeing to the wilderness turned upon the pursuers. 21 And Joshua and all Israel saw that the ambush had captured the city, and that the smoke of the city ascended, and so they turned around and went striking the men of A'i down. 22 And these others came out of the city to meet them, so that they got to be in between Israel, these on this side and those on that, and they went striking them down until there did not remain of them either a survivor or an escapee. 23 And the king of A'i they caught alive and proceeded to bring him near to Joshua.

24 And it came about that while Israel was finishing the killing of all the inhabitants of A'i in the field, in the wilderness in which they had pursued them, they kept falling, all of them, by the edge of the sword until they came to their end. After that all Israel returned to A'i and struck it with the edge of the sword. 25 And all those who fell on that day, from man to woman, amounted to twelve thousand, all the people of A'i. 26 And Joshua did not draw back his hand with which he stretched out the javelin until he had devoted all the inhabitants of A'i to destruction. 27 Only the domestic animals and the spoil of that city Israel plundered for themselves, according to Jehovah's word that he had laid in command upon Joshua.

28 Then Joshua burned A'i and reduced it to an indefinitely lasting mound, as a desolation down to this day. 29 And he hanged the king of A'i upon a stake until the evening time; and as the sun was about to set Joshua gave the command, and then they took his dead body down from the stake and pitched it at the entrance of the gate of the city and raised up a great pile of stones over him, down to this day.

30 It was then that Joshua proceeded to build an altar to Jehovah the God of Israel, in Mount E'bal, 31 just as Moses the servant of Jehovah had commanded the sons of Israel, as it is written in the book of the law of Moses: "An altar of whole stones, upon which no iron tool has been wielded"; and they went offering up burnt offerings upon it to Jehovah and sacrificing communion sacrifices.

32 Then he wrote there upon the stones a copy of the law of Moses that he had written before the sons of Israel. 33 And all Israel and their older men and the officers and their judges were standing on this side and on that side of the Ark in front of the priests, the Levites, carrying the ark of the covenant of Jehovah, the alien resident as well as the native, one half of them in front of Mount Ger'i·zim and the other half of them in front of Mount E'bal, (just as Moses the servant of Je-

hovah had commanded,) to bless the people of Israel first of all. 34 And after this he read aloud all the words of the law, the blessing and the malediction, according to all that is written in the book of the law. 35 There proved to be not a word of all that Moses had commanded that Joshua did not read aloud in front of all the congregation of Israel, together with the women and the little ones and the alien residents who walked in their midst.

9 And it came about that as soon as all the kings who were on the side of the Jordan in the mountainous region and in the She·phe'lah and along the whole coast of the Great Sea and in front of Leb'a·non, the Hit'tites and the Am'or·ites, the Ca'naan·ites, the Per'iz·zites, the Hi'vites and the Jeb'u·sites, heard of it, 2 they began to assemble themselves all together to make war against Joshua and Israel unanimously.

3 And the inhabitants of Gib'e·on heard what Joshua had done to Jer'i·cho and A'i. 4 So they, even of their own accord, acted with shrewdness and went and stocked themselves with provisions and took worn-out sacks for their asses, and wine skin-bottles worn out and burst and tied up, 5 and worn-out and patched sandals on their feet, and worn-out garments upon themselves, and all the bread of their provisions proved to be dry and crumby. 6 Then they went to Joshua at the camp at Gil'gal and said to him and the men of Israel: "It is from a distant land that we have come. And now CONCLUDE a covenant with us." 7 At this the men of Israel said to the Hi'vites: "Perhaps it is in our vicinity that you are dwelling. So how could we conclude a covenant with you?" 8 In turn they said to Joshua: "We are your servants."

Then Joshua said to them: "Who are YOU, and where do YOU come from?" 9 At this they said to him: "It is from a very distant land that your servants have come

in regard to the name of Jehovah your God, because we have heard of his fame and of all that he did in Egypt, 10 and of all that he did to the two kings of the Am'or·ites who were on the other side of the Jordan, namely, Si'hon the king of Hesh'bon and Og the king of Ba'shan, who was in Ash'ta·roth. 11 Hence our older men and all the inhabitants of our land said this to us, 'Take provisions in YOUR hands for the journey and go to meet them, and YOU must say to them: "We are YOUR servants. And now conclude a covenant with us."' 12 This bread of ours, it was hot when we took it as our provisions out of our houses on the day of our going out to come here to YOU, and now, look! it is dry and has become crumby. 13 And these are the wine skin-bottles that we filled new, and, look! they have burst, and these garments and sandals of ours, they have worn out because of the great length of the journey."

14 Upon that the men took some of their provisions, and at the mouth of Jehovah they did not inquire. 15 And Joshua went making peace with them and concluding a covenant with them to let them live, and so the chieftains of the assembly swore to them.

16 And it came about that at the end of three days, after they had concluded a covenant with them, they got to hear that they were near to them and it was in their vicinity they were dwelling. 17 Then the sons of Israel pulled out and came to their cities on the third day, and their cities were Gib'e·on and Che·phi'rah and Be·er'oth and Kir'i·ath-je'a·rim. 18 And the sons of Israel did not strike them, because the chieftains of the assembly had sworn to them by Jehovah the God of Israel. And all the assembly began to murmur against the chieftains. 19 At this all the chieftains said to all the assembly: "We, for our part, have sworn to them by Jehovah the God of Israel, and now we are not al-

lowed to hurt them. 20 This is what we shall do to them while letting them live, that no indignation may come upon us over the oath that we have sworn to them." 21 So the chieftains said to them: "Let them live and let them become gatherers of wood and drawers of water for all the assembly, just as the chieftains have promised them."

22 Joshua now called them and spoke to them, saying: "Why did YOU trick us, saying, 'We are very far away from YOU,' whereas YOU are dwelling in our very midst? 23 And now YOU are cursed people, and a slave's position and being gatherers of wood and drawers of water for the house of my God will never be cut off from YOU." 24 Then they answered Joshua and said: "It was because your servants were plainly told that Jehovah your God had commanded Moses his servant to give YOU all the land and to annihilate all the inhabitants of the land from before YOU, and we became very much afraid for our souls because of YOU. So we did this thing. 25 And now here we are, in your hand. Just as it is good and right in your eyes to do to us, do." 26 And he proceeded to do so to them and to deliver them from the hand of the sons of Israel, and they did not kill them. 27 Accordingly Joshua constituted them on that day gatherers of wood and drawers of water for the assembly and for Jehovah's altar, down to this day, at the place that he should choose.

10 And it came about that as soon as A·do′ni-ze′dek the king of Jerusalem heard that Joshua had captured A′i and then devoted it to destruction, that just as he had done to Jer′i·cho and its king, so he had done to A′i and its king, and that the inhabitants of Gib′e·on had made peace with Israel and were continuing in their midst, 2 he became very much afraid, because Gib′e·on was a great city, like one of the royal

cities, and because it was greater than A′i, and all its men were mighty ones. 3 Consequently A·do′ni-ze′dek the king of Jerusalem sent to Ho′ham the king of He′bron and to Pi′ram the king of Jar′muth and to Ja·phi′a the king of La′chish and to De′bir the king of Eg′lon, saying, 4 "Come up to me and help me and let us strike Gib′e·on, because it has made peace with Joshua and the sons of Israel." 5 At this they gathered together and went on up, five kings of the Am′or·ites, the king of Jerusalem, the king of He′bron, the king of Jar′muth, the king of La′chish, the king of Eg′lon, these and all their camps, and they proceeded to camp against Gib′e·on and to war against it.

6 Upon that the men of Gib′e·on sent to Joshua at the camp at Gil′gal, saying: "Do not let your hand relax from your slaves. Come up to us quickly and do save us and help us, for all the kings of the Am′or·ites inhabiting the mountainous region have collected together against us." 7 So Joshua went on up from Gil′gal, he and all the people of war with him and all the valiant mighty men.

8 Then Jehovah said to Joshua: "Do not be afraid of them, for into your hand I have given them. Not a man of them will stand against you." 9 And Joshua proceeded to come against them by surprise. All night long he had gone up from Gil′gal. 10 And Jehovah went throwing them into confusion before Israel, and they began to slay them with a great slaughter at Gib′e·on and went pursuing them by way of the ascent of Beth-ho′ron and slaying them as far as A·ze′kah and Mak′ke′dah. 11 And it came about that while they were fleeing from before Israel and were on the descent of Beth-ho′ron, Jehovah hurled great stones from the heavens upon them as far as A·ze′kah, so that they died. There were more who died from the hailstones than those whom the sons of Israel killed with the sword.

12 It was then that Joshua proceeded to speak to Jehovah on the day of Jehovah's abandoning the Am'or·ites to the sons of Israel, and he went on to say before the eyes of Israel:

"Sun, be motionless over Gib'-
　　e·on,
　And, moon, over the low plain
　　of Ai'ja·lon."

13 Accordingly the sun kept motionless, and the moon did stand still, until the nation could take vengeance on its enemies. Is it not written in the book of Ja'shar? And the sun kept standing still in the middle of the heavens and did not hasten to set for about a whole day. **14** And no day has proved to be like that one, either before it or after it, in that Jehovah listened to the voice of a man, for Jehovah himself was fighting for Israel.

15 After that Joshua and all Israel with him returned to the camp at Gil'gal.

16 Meantime these five kings fled and went hiding themselves in the cave at Mak·ke'dah. **17** Then the report was made to Joshua, saying: "The five kings have been found hidden in the cave at Mak·ke'dah." **18** At that Joshua said: "ROLL great stones up to the mouth of the cave and assign men over it to guard them. **19** As for YOU men, do not stand still. Chase after YOUR enemies, and YOU must strike them in the rear. Do not allow them to enter into their cities, for Jehovah YOUR God has given them into YOUR hands."

20 And it came about that as soon as Joshua and the sons of Israel had finished slaying them with a very great slaughter, until these came to their end, and those who did survive of them escaped and went entering into the fortified cities, **21** all the people then began to return to the camp, to Joshua, at Mak·ke'dah in peace. Not a man moved his tongue eagerly against the sons of Israel. **22** Then Joshua said: "OPEN the mouth of the cave and bring out these

five kings from the cave to me." **23** At that they did so and brought out to him from the cave these five kings, the king of Jerusalem, the king of He'bron, the king of Jar'muth, the king of La'chish, the king of Eg'lon. **24** And it came about that as soon as they had brought out these kings to Joshua, Joshua proceeded to call all the men of Israel and to say to the commanders of the men of war that had gone with him: "Come forward. Place YOUR feet on the back of the necks of these kings." So they came forward and placed their feet on the back of their necks. **25** And Joshua went on to say to them: "Do not be afraid or be terrified. Be courageous and strong, for it is like this that Jehovah will do to all YOUR enemies against whom YOU are warring."

26 And after that Joshua proceeded to strike them and put them to death and hang them upon five stakes, and they continued hanging upon the stakes until the evening. **27** And it came about that at the time of the setting of the sun Joshua commanded, and they went taking them down off the stakes and throwing them into the cave where they had hid themselves. Then they placed big stones at the mouth of the cave—until this very day.

28 And Joshua captured Mak·ke'dah on that day and went striking it with the edge of the sword. As for its king, he devoted him and every soul that was in it to destruction. He let no survivor remain. So he did to the king of Mak·ke'dah just as he had done to the king of Jer'i·cho.

29 Then Joshua and all Israel with him passed on from Mak·ke'-dah to Lib'nah and warred against Lib'nah. **30** Accordingly Jehovah gave it also and its king into Israel's hand, and they went striking it and every soul that was in it with the edge of the sword. They did not let a survivor remain in it. So they did to its king just as they had done to the king of Jer'-i·cho.

31 Next Joshua and all Israel with him passed on from Lib'nah to La'chish and went camping against it and warring upon it. 32 Accordingly Jehovah gave La'-chish into Israel's hand so that they captured it on the second day, and they went striking it and every soul that was in it with the edge of the sword, according to all that they had done to Lib'nah.

33 It was then that Ho'ram the king of Ge'zer went up to help La'chish. So Joshua struck him and his people until he had let not a survivor of his remain.

34 Then Joshua and all Israel with him passed on from La'chish to Eg'lon and went camping against it and warring against it. 35 And they got to capture it on that day and began to smite it with the edge of the sword, and they devoted every soul that was in it to destruction on that day, according to all that they had done to La'-chish.

36 Then Joshua and all Israel with him went up from Eg'lon to He'bron and began to war against it. 37 And they got to capture it and went striking it and its king and all its towns and every soul that was in it with the edge of the sword. He did not let a survivor remain, according to all that he had done to Eg'lon. So he devoted it and every soul that was in it to destruction.

38 Finally Joshua and all Israel with him came back to De'bir and began to war against it. 39 And he got to capture it and its king and all its towns, and they went striking them with the edge of the sword and devoting every soul that was in it to destruction. He did not let a survivor remain. Just as he had done to He'bron, so he did to De'bir and its king, and just as he had done to Lib'nah and its king.

40 And Joshua proceeded to strike all the land of the mountain-ous region and the Neg'eb and the She·phe'lah and the slopes and all their kings. He did not let a sur-vivor remain, and everything that breathed he devoted to destruction, just as Jehovah the God of Israel had commanded. 41 And Joshua went striking them from Ka'desh-bar'ne·a to Ga'za and all the land of Go'shen and up to Gib'e·on. 42 And Joshua captured all these kings and their land at one time, because it was Jehovah the God of Israel who was fighting for Is-rael. 43 After that Joshua and all Israel with him returned to the camp at Gil'gal.

11 And it came about that as soon as Ja'bin the king of Ha'zor heard of it, he went sending to Jo'bab the king of Ma'don and to the king of Shim'ron and the king of Ach'shaph, 2 and to the kings that were to the north in the mountainous region and in the desert plains south of Chin'ne·reth and in the She·phe'lah and on the mountain ridges of Dor to the west, 3 the Ca'naan·ites to the east and the west, and the Am'or·ites and the Hit'tites and the Per'iz·zites and the Jeb'u·sites in the moun-tainous region and the Hi'vites at the base of Her'mon in the land of Miz'pah. 4 So they went out, they and all their camps with them, a people as numerous as the grains of sand that are on the sea-shore for multitude, and very many horses and war chariots. 5 Then all these kings met together by appointment and came and en-camped together at the waters of Mer'om to fight against Israel.

6 At this Jehovah said to Josh-ua: "Do not be afraid because of them, for tomorrow about this time I am abandoning all of them slain to Israel. Their horses you will hamstring, and their chariots you will burn in the fire." 7 And Joshua and all the people of war with him proceeded to come against them along the waters of Mer'om by surprise and to fall upon them. 8 Then Jehovah gave them into Is-rael's hand, and they went striking them and pursuing them as far as populous Si'don and Mis're·photh-

ma'im and the valley plain of Miz'peh to the east; and they kept striking them until they had not let a survivor of theirs remain. 9 After that Joshua did to them just as Jehovah had said to him: their horses he hamstrung, and their chariots he burned in the fire.

10 More than that, Joshua turned about at that time and captured Ha'zor; and its king he struck down with the sword, because Ha'zor was before that the head of all these kingdoms. 11 And they went striking every soul that was in it with the edge of the sword, devoting them to destruction. No breathing thing at all was left over, and he burned Ha'zor in the fire. 12 And all the cities of these kings and all their kings Joshua captured and went striking them with the edge of the sword. He devoted them to destruction, just as Moses the servant of Jehovah had commanded. 13 It was only all the cities standing on their own mounds that Israel did not burn, except that Joshua did burn Ha'zor by itself. 14 And all the spoil of these cities and the domestic animals the sons of Israel plundered for themselves. It was only all humankind that they struck with the edge of the sword until they had annihilated them. They did not let anyone that breathed remain. 15 Just as Jehovah had commanded Moses his servant, so Moses commanded Joshua, and so Joshua did. He did not remove a word from all that Jehovah had commanded Moses.

16 And Joshua proceeded to take all this land, the mountainous region and all the Neg'eb and all the land of Go'shen and the She-phe'lah and the Ar'a·bah and the mountainous region of Israel and its She·phe'lah, 17 from Mount Ha'lak, which goes up to Se'ir, and as far as Ba'al-gad in the valley plain of Leb'a·non at the base of Mount Her'mon, and he captured all their kings and went striking them and putting them to death. 18 Many days it was that Joshua

waged war with all these kings. 19 There proved to be no city that made peace with the sons of Israel but the Hi'vites inhabiting Gib'-e·on. All the others they took by war. 20 For it proved to be Jehovah's course to let their hearts become stubborn so as to declare war against Israel, in order that he might devote them to destruction, that they might come to have no favorable consideration, but in order that he might annihilate them, just as Jehovah had commanded Moses.

21 Furthermore, at that particular time Joshua went and cut off the An'a·kim from the mountainous region, from He'bron, from De'bir, from A'nab and from all the mountainous region of Judah and from all the mountainous region of Israel. Along with their cities Joshua devoted them to destruction. 22 No An'a·kim were left in the land of the sons of Israel. It was only in Ga'za, in Gath and in Ash'dod that they remained. 23 So Joshua took all the land, according to all that Jehovah had promised Moses, and Joshua then gave it as an inheritance to Israel by their shares, according to their tribes. And the land had no disturbance from war.

12 Now these are the kings of the land whom the sons of Israel defeated and whose land they then took possession of on the side of the Jordan toward the rising of the sun, from the torrent valley of Ar'non up to Mount Her'-mon and all the Ar'a·bah toward the sunrise: 2 Si'hon the king of the Am'or·ites, who dwelt in Hesh'-bon, ruling from A·ro'er, which was on the bank of the torrent valley of Ar'non, and the middle of the torrent valley, and half of Gil'e·ad as far as Jab'bok the torrent valley, the boundary of the sons of Am'mon, 3 and the Ar'a-bah as far as the sea of Chin'ne-reth toward the east and as far as the sea of the Ar'a·bah, the Salt Sea, to the east in the direction of

Beth-jesh'i-moth, and toward the south under the slopes of Pis'gah.

4 And the territory of Og the king of Ba'shan, of what was left over of the Reph'a-im, who dwelt in Ash'ta-roth and Ed're-i, 5 and who ruled in Mount Her'mon and in Sal'e-cah and in all Ba'shan, as far as the boundary of the Gesh'ur-ites and the Ma-ac'a-thites, and half of Gil'e-ad, to the territory of Si'hon the king of Hesh'bon.

6 It was Moses the servant of Jehovah and the sons of Israel who defeated them, after which Moses the servant of Jehovah gave it as a holding to the Reu'ben-ites and the Gad'ites and half of the tribe of Ma-nas'seh.

7 And these are the kings of the land whom Joshua and the sons of Israel defeated on the side of the Jordan toward the west, from Ba'al-gad in the valley plain of Leb'a-non and as far as Mount Ha'lak, which goes up to Se'ir, after which Joshua gave it to the tribes of Israel as a holding by their shares, 8 in the mountainous region and in the She-phe'lah and in the Ar'a-bah and on the slopes and in the wilderness and in the Neg'eb—the Hit'tites, the Am'or-ites and the Ca'naan-ites, the Per'iz-zites, the Hi'vites and the Jeb'u-sites:

9 The king of Jer'i-cho, one; the king of A'i, which was beside Beth'el, one;

10 the king of Jerusalem, one; the king of He'bron, one;

11 the king of Jar'muth, one; the king of La'chish, one;

12 the king of Eg'lon, one; the king of Ge'zer, one;

13 the king of De'bir, one; the king of Ge'der, one;

14 the king of Hor'mah, one; the king of A'rad, one;

15 the king of Lib'nah, one; the king of A-dul'lam, one;

16 the king of Mak-ke'dah, one; the king of Beth'el, one;

17 the king of Tap'pu-ah, one; the king of He'pher, one;

18 the king of A'phek, one; the king of Las-shar'on, one;

19 the king of Ma'don, one; the king of Ha'zor, one;

20 the king of Shim'ron-me'ron, one; the king of Ach'shaph, one;

21 the king of Ta'a-nach, one; the king of Me-gid'do, one;

22 the king of Ke'desh, one; the king of Jok'ne-am in Car'mel, one;

23 the king of Dor on the mountain ridge of Dor, one; the king of Goi'im in Gil'gal, one;

24 the king of Tir'zah, one; all the kings being thirty-one.

13 Now Joshua was old, being advanced in years. So Jehovah said to him: "You yourself have grown old and have advanced in years, and to a very great extent the land yet remains to be taken in possession. 2 This is the land yet remaining: all the regions of the Phi-lis'tines and all the Gesh'ur-ites 3 (from the branch of the Nile that is in front of Egypt and up to the border of Ek'ron to the north, it used to be reckoned as belonging to the Ca'naan-ites) ; five axis lords of the Phi-lis'tines, the Ga'zites and the Ash'dod-ites, the Ash'ke-lon-ites, the Git'tites and the Ek'ron-ites; and the Av'vim. 4 To the south all the land of the Ca'naan-ites; and Me-ar'ah, which belongs to the Si-do'ni-ans, as far as A'phek, as far as the border of the Am'or-ites; 5 and the land of the Ge'bal-ites and all of Leb'a-non toward the rising of the sun, from Ba'al-gad at the base of Mount Her'mon as far as to the entering in of Ha'math; 6 all the inhabitants of the mountainous region, from Leb'a-non to Mis're-photh-ma'im, all the Si-do'ni-ans; I myself shall dispossess them from before the sons of Israel. Only make it fall to Israel as an inheritance, just as I have commanded you. 7 And now apportion this land as an inheritance to the nine tribes and the half tribe of Ma-nas'seh."

8 With the other half tribe the Reu'ben·ites and the Gad'ites took their inheritance that Moses gave them on the side of the Jordan toward the east, just as Moses the servant of Jehovah had given them, 9 from A·ro'er, which is on the bank of the torrent valley of Ar'non, and the city that is in the middle of the torrent valley, and all the tableland of Med'e·ba as far as Di'bon; 10 and all the cities of Si'hon the king of the Am'or·ites, who reigned in Hesh'bon, up to the border of the sons of Am'mon; 11 and Gil'e·ad and the territory of the Gesh'ur·ites and the Ma·ac'a·thites and all of Mount Her'mon and all Ba'shan as far as Sal'e·cah; 12 all the royal realm of Og in Ba'shan, who reigned in Ash'ta·roth and in Ed're·i—he it was who remained of what was left of the Reph'a·im—and Moses went striking them and dispossessing them. 13 And the sons of Israel did not dispossess the Gesh'ur·ites and the Ma·ac'a·thites, but Gesh'ur and Ma·a'cath keep dwelling in the midst of Israel down to this day.

14 It was only to the tribe of the Levites that he did not give an inheritance. The offerings made by fire of Jehovah the God of Israel are their inheritance, just as he has promised them.

15 Then Moses made a gift to the tribe of the sons of Reu'ben by their families, 16 and the territory came to be theirs from A·ro'er, which is on the bank of the torrent valley of Ar'non, and the city that is in the middle of the torrent valley, and all the tableland by Med'e·ba; 17 Hesh'bon and all its towns that are on the tableland, Di'bon and Ba'moth-ba'al and Beth-ba'al-me'on, 18 and Ja'haz and Ked'e·moth and Meph'a·ath, 19 and Kir'i·a·tha'im and Sib'mah and Ze'reth-sha'har in the mountain of the low plain, 20 and Beth-pe'or and the slopes of Pis'gah and Beth-jesh'i·moth, 21 and all the cities of the tableland and all the royal realm of Si'hon the king of the Am'or·ites, who reigned in Hesh'bon, and whom Moses struck, together with the chieftains of Mid'i·an, E'vi and Re'kem and Zur and Hur and Re'ba, the dukes of Si'hon, who were dwelling in the land. 22 And Ba'laam the son of Be'or, the diviner, was one whom the sons of Israel killed with the sword along with their slain ones. 23 And the boundary of the sons of Reu'ben came to be the Jordan; and this as a territory was the inheritance of the sons of Reu'ben by their families, with the cities and their settlements.

24 Furthermore, Moses made a gift to the tribe of Gad, the sons of Gad by their families, 25 and their territory came to be Ja'zer and all the cities of Gil'e·ad and half of the land of the sons of Am'mon as far as A·ro'er, which is in front of Rab'bah; 26 and from Hesh'bon to Ra'math-miz'peh and Bet'o·nim and from Ma·ha·na'im to the border of De'bir; 27 and in the low plain Beth-ha'ram and Beth-nim'rah and Suc'coth and Za'phon, the rest of the royal realm of Si'hon the king of Hesh'bon, the Jordan being the border as far as the extremity of the sea of Chin'ne·reth on the side of Jordan toward the east. 28 This was the inheritance of the sons of Gad by their families, with the cities and their settlements.

29 Further, Moses made a gift to the half tribe of Ma·nas'seh. and it came to be that of the half tribe of the sons of Ma·nas'seh by their families. 30 And their territory came to be from Ma·ha·na'im all of Ba'shan, all the royal realm of Og the king of Ba'shan, and all the tent villages of Ja'ir that are in Ba'shan, sixty towns. 31 And half of Gil'e·ad, and Ash'ta·roth and Ed're·i, the cities of the royal realm of Og in Ba'shan, went to the sons of Ma'chir the son of Ma·nas'seh, to half of the sons of Ma'chir by their families.

32 These were what Moses caused [them] to inherit, on the desert plains of Mo'ab on the side

of the Jordan, at Jer′i·cho, toward the east.

33 And to the tribe of the Levites Moses did not give an inheritance. Jehovah the God of Israel is their inheritance, just as he has promised them.

14 Now this is what the sons of Israel took as a hereditary possession in the land of Ca′naan, which E·le·a′zar the priest and Joshua the son of Nun and the heads of the fathers of the tribes of the sons of Israel caused them to inherit. 2 Their inheritance was by lot, just as Jehovah had commanded by means of Moses for the nine tribes and the half tribe. 3 For Moses had given the inheritance of the two other tribes and the other half tribe on the other side of the Jordan; and to the Levites he did not give an inheritance in their midst. 4 For the sons of Joseph had become two tribes, Ma·nas′seh and E′phra·im; and they had not given a share in the land to the Levites, except cities to dwell in and their pasture grounds for their livestock and their property. 5 Just as Jehovah had commanded Moses, so the sons of Israel did; and they proceeded to apportion the land.

6 Then the sons of Judah approached Joshua in Gil′gal, and Ca′leb the son of Je·phun′neh the Ken′iz·zite said to him: "You yourself well know the word that Jehovah spoke to Moses the man of the [true] God with regard to me and with regard to you at Ka′desh-bar′ne·a. 7 Forty years old I was when Moses the servant of Jehovah sent me out of Ka′desh-bar′ne·a to spy out the land, and I came bringing him back word just as it was in my heart. 8 And my brothers who went up with me caused the heart of the people to melt; but as for me, I followed Jehovah my God fully. 9 Consequently Moses swore on that day, saying, 'The land upon which your foot has trod will become yours and your sons' as an inheritance to time indefinite, because you have

followed Jehovah my God fully.' 10 And now here Jehovah has preserved me alive, just as he promised, these forty-five years since Jehovah made this promise to Moses when Israel walked in the wilderness, and now here I am today eighty-five years old. 11 Yet I am today as strong as on the day of Moses' sending me out. As my power was then, so my power is now for the war, both to go out and to come in. 12 And now do give me this mountainous region that Jehovah promised on that day, for you yourself heard on that day that there were An′a·kim there and great fortified cities. Likely Jehovah will be with me, and I shall certainly dispossess them, just as Jehovah promised."

13 At that Joshua blessed him and gave He′bron to Ca′leb the son of Je·phun′neh as an inheritance. 14 That is why He′bron has come to belong to Ca′leb the son of Je·phun′neh the Ken′iz·zite as an inheritance down to this day, for the reason that he followed Jehovah the God of Israel fully. 15 The name of He′bron before that was Kir′i·ath-ar′ba (said Ar′ba was the great man among the An′a·kim). And the land had no disturbance from war.

15 And the lot of the tribe of the sons of Judah by their families came to be to the boundary of E′dom, the wilderness of Zin, to the Neg′eb at its southern end. 2 And their southern boundary came to be from the extremity of the Salt Sea, from the bay that faces southward. 3 And it went out southward to the ascent of A·krab′bim and passed over to Zin and went up from the south to Ka′desh-bar′ne·a and passed over to Hez′ron and went up to Ad′dar and went around to Kar′ka. 4 And it passed on to Az′mon and went out to the torrent valley of Egypt; and the boundary's termination proved to be at the sea. This came to be their southern boundary.

5 And the eastern boundary was the Salt Sea up to the end of the

Jordan, and the boundary at the northern corner was at the bay of the sea, at the end of the Jordan. 6 And the boundary went up to Beth-hog'lah and passed over at the north of Beth-ar'a·bah, and the boundary went up to the stone of Bo'han the son of Reu'ben. 7 And the boundary went up to De'bir at the low plain of A'chor and turning northward to Gil'gal, which is in front of the ascent of A·dum'mim, which is south of the torrent valley; and the boundary passed over to the waters of En-she'mesh, and its termination proved to be En-ro'gel. 8 And the boundary went up to the valley of the son of Hin'nom to the slope of the Jeb'u·site at the south, that is to say, Jerusalem; and the boundary went up to the top of the mountain that faces the valley of Hin'nom to the west, which is at the extremity of the low plain of Reph'a·im to the north. 9 And the boundary was marked out from the top of the mountain to the spring of the waters of Neph·to'ah, and went out to the cities of Mount E'phron; and the boundary was marked out to Ba'al·ah, that is to say, Kir'i·ath-je'a·rim. 10 And the boundary went around from Ba'-al·ah westward to Mount Se'ir and passed over to the slope of Mount Je'ar·im at the north, that is to say, Ches'a·lon; and it went down to Beth-she'mesh and passed over to Tim'nah. 11 And the boundary went out to the slope of Ek'ron to the north, and the boundary was marked out to Shik'ke·ron and passed over to Mount Ba'al·ah and went out to Jab'ne·el; and the boundary's termination proved to be at the sea.

12 And the western boundary was at the Great Sea and its shoreland. This was the boundary all around, of the sons of Judah by their families.

13 And to Ca'leb the son of Je·phun'neh he gave a share in the midst of the sons of Judah at the order of Jehovah to Joshua, namely, Kir'i·ath-ar'ba (said Ar'ba

being the father of A'nak), that is to say, He'bron. 14 So Ca'leb drove away from there the three sons of A'nak, namely, She'shai and A·hi'man and Tal'mai, those born of A'nak. 15 Then he went up from there to the inhabitants of De'bir. (Now the name of De'bir before that was Kir'i·ath-se'pher.) 16 And Ca'leb proceeded to say: "Whoever strikes Kir'i·ath-se'pher and does capture it, I shall certainly give him Ach'sah my daughter as a wife." 17 At that Oth'ni·el the son of Ke'naz, Ca'leb's brother, captured it. Accordingly he gave him Ach'sah his daughter as a wife. 18 And it came about that when she was going home, she kept inciting him to ask a field from her father. Then she clapped her hands while upon the ass. At this Ca'leb said to her: "What do you want?" 19 So she said: "Do give me a blessing, for it is a piece of land to the south you have given me, and you must give me Gul'loth-ma'im." Accordingly he gave her Upper Gul'loth and Lower Gul'loth.

20 This was the inheritance of the tribe of the sons of Judah by their families.

21 And the cities at the extremity of the tribe of the sons of Judah toward the boundary of E'dom in the south came to be Kab'ze·el and E'der and Ja'gur, 22 and Ki'nah and Di·mo'nah and A·da'dah, 23 and Ke'desh and Ha'zor and Ith'nan, 24 Ziph and Te'lem and Be·a'loth, 25 and Ha'zor-ha·dat'-tah and Ke'ri·oth-hez'ron, that is to say, Ha'zor, 26 A'mam and She'ma and Mo·la'dah, 27 and Ha'zar-gad'dah and Hesh'mon and Beth-pel'et, 28 and Ha'zar-shu'al and Be'er-she'ba and Biz·i·o·thi'ah, 29 Ba'al·ah and I'im and E'zem, 30 and El·to'lad and Che'sil and Hor'mah, 31 and Zik'lag and Mad·man'nah and San·san'nah, 32 and Le·ba'oth and Shil'him and A'in and Rim'mon; all the cities being twenty-nine, together with their settlements.

33 In the She·phe'lah there were Esh'ta·ol and Zo'rah and Ash'nah,

34 and Za·no'ah and En-gan'nim, Tap'pu·ah and E'nam, 35 Jar'-muth and A·dul'lam, So'coh and A·ze'kah, 36 and Sha'a·ra'im and Ad·i·tha'im and Ge·de'rah and Ged·e·ro·tha'im; fourteen cities and their settlements.

37 Ze'nan and Ha·dash'ah and Mig'dal-gad, 38 and Di'le·an and Miz'peh and Jok'the·el, 39 La'-chish and Boz'kath and Eg'lon, 40 and Cab'bon and Lah'mam and Chit'lish, 41 and Ge·de'roth, Beth-da'gon and Na'a·mah and Mak·ke'dah; sixteen cities and their settlements.

42 Lib'nah and E'ther and A'shan, 43 and Iph'tah and Ash'-nah and Ne'zib, 44 and Kei'lah and Ach'zib and Ma·re'shah; nine cities and their settlements.

45 Ek'ron and its dependent towns and its settlements. 46 From Ek'ron westward all that is alongside Ash'dod and their settlements.

47 Ash'dod, its dependent towns and its settlements; Ga'za, its dependent towns and its settlements, down to the torrent valley of Egypt, and the Great Sea and the adjacent region.

48 And in the mountainous region Sha'mir and Jat'tir and So'-coh, 49 and Dan'nah and Kir'-i·ath-san'nah, that is to say, De'bir, 50 and A'nab and Esh'te·moh and A'nim, 51 and Go'shen and Ho'-lon and Gi'loh; eleven cities and their settlements.

52 A'rab and Du'mah and E'shan, 53 and Ja'nim and Beth-tap'pu·ah and A·phe'kah, 54 and Hum'tah and Kir'i·ath-ar'ba, that is to say, He'bron, and Zi'or; nine cities and their settlements.

55 Ma'on, Car'mel and Ziph and Jut'tah, 56 and Jez're·el and Jok'-de·am and Za·no'ah, 57 Ka'in, Gib'e·ah and Tim'nah; ten cities and their settlements.

58 Hal'hul, Beth-zur and Ge'dor, 59 and Ma'a·rath and Beth-a'noth and El'te·kon; six cities and their settlements.

60 Kir'i·ath-ba'al, that is to say, Kir'i·ath-je'a·rim, and Rab'bah; two cities and their settlements.

61 In the wilderness Beth-ar'a-bah, Mid'din and Se·ca'cah, 62 and Nib'shan and the City of Salt and En-ge'di; six cities and their settlements.

63 As for the Jeb'u·sites who were dwelling in Jerusalem, the sons of Judah were not able to drive them away; and the Jeb'u-sites continue dwelling with the sons of Judah in Jerusalem down to this day.

16 And the lot came out for the sons of Joseph from the Jordan at Jer'i·cho to the waters of Jer'i·cho eastward, the wilderness going up from Jer'i·cho into the mountainous region of Beth'el. 2 And it went out from Beth'el belonging to Luz and passed over to the boundary of the Ar'chites at At'a·roth, 3 and it went down westward to the boundary of the Japh'le·tites as far as the boundary of Lower Beth-ho'ron and Ge'zer, and its termination proved to be at the sea.

4 And the sons of Joseph, Ma-nas'seh and E'phra·im, proceeded to take possession of land. 5 And the boundary of the sons of E'phra-im by their families came to be, yes, the boundary of their inheritance toward the east came to be At'a·roth-ad'dar, as far as Upper Beth-ho'ron; 6 and the boundary went out to the sea. Mich·me'thath was on the north, and the boundary went around eastward to Ta'a-nath-shi'loh, and passed over eastward to Ja·no'ah. 7 And it went down from Ja·no'ah to At'a·roth and Na'a·rah and reached to Jer'-i·cho and went out to the Jordan. 8 From Tap'pu·ah the boundary moved on westward to the torrent valley of Ka'nah, and its termination proved to be at the sea. This is the inheritance of the tribe of the sons of E'phra·im by their families. 9 And the sons of E'phra·im had enclave cities in the midst of the inheritance of the sons of Ma·nas'seh, all the cities and their settlements.

10 And they did not drive away the Ca'naan·ites who were dwelling

in Ge'zer, and the Ca'naan·ites continue dwelling in among E'phra·im down to this day and came to be subject to slavish forced labor.

17 And the lot came to be for the tribe of Ma·nas'seh, because he was Joseph's first-born, for Ma'chir the first-born of Ma·nas'seh, the father of Gil'e·ad, because he was one who proved to be a man of war; and Gil'e·ad and Ba'shan came to belong to him. 2 And there came to be a lot for the sons of Ma·nas'seh who were left over according to their families, for the sons of A'bi·e'zer and the sons of He'lek and the sons of As'ri·el and the sons of She'chem and the sons of He'pher and the sons of She·mi'da. These were the sons of Ma·nas'seh the son of Joseph, the males according to their families. 3 As for Ze·lo'phe·had the son of He'pher, the son of Gil'e·ad, the son of Ma'chir, the son of Ma·nas'seh, he proved to have, not sons, but daughters, and these were the names of his daughters: Mah'lah and No'ah, Hog'lah, Mil'cah and Tir'zah. 4 So they presented themselves before E·le·a'zar the priest and Joshua the son of Nun and the chieftains, saying: "Jehovah it was who commanded Moses to give us an inheritance in the midst of our brothers." Accordingly he gave them, at the order of Jehovah, an inheritance in the midst of the brothers of their father.

5 And there were ten allotments falling to Ma·nas'seh apart from the land of Gil'e·ad and Ba'shan, which were on the other side of the Jordan; 6 for the daughters of Ma·nas'seh came into an inheritance in the midst of his sons; and the land of Gil'e·ad became the property of the sons of Ma·nas'seh who were left over.

7 And the boundary of Ma·nas'seh came to be from Ash'er to Mich·me'thath, which is in front of She'chem, and the boundary moved to the right to the inhabitants of En-Tap'pu·ah. 8 The land of Tap'pu·ah became Ma·nas'seh's,

but Tap'pu·ah at the boundary of Ma·nas'seh belonged to the sons of E'phra·im. 9 And the boundary went down to the torrent valley of Ka'nah, southward to the torrent valley of these cities of E'phra·im in the midst of the cities of Ma·nas'seh, and the boundary of Ma·nas'seh was on the north of the torrent valley, and its termination came to be at the sea. 10 To the south it was E'phra·im's and to the north, Ma·nas'seh's, and the sea came to be his boundary; and on the north they reach to Ash'er and on the east, to Is'sa·char.

11 And there came to belong to Ma·nas'seh in Is'sa·char and in Ash'er Beth-she'an and its dependent towns and Ib'le·am and its dependent towns and the inhabitants of Dor and its dependent towns and the inhabitants of En-dor and its dependent towns and the inhabitants of Ta'a·nach and its dependent towns and the inhabitants of Me·gid'do and its dependent towns, three of the heights.

12 And the sons of Ma·nas'seh did not prove able to take possession of these cities, but the Ca'naan·ites persisted in dwelling in this land. 13 And it turned out that when the sons of Israel had grown strong, they went putting the Ca'naan·ites at forced labor, and they did not dispossess them entirely.

14 And the sons of Joseph proceeded to speak with Joshua, saying: "Why is it that you have given me as an inheritance one lot and one allotment, whereas I am a numerous people for the reason that Jehovah has blessed me until now?" 15 At this Joshua said to them: "If you are a numerous people, go your way up to the forest, and you must cut it down for yourself there in the land of the Per'iz·zites and the Reph'a·im, because the mountainous region of E'phra·im has become too narrow for you." 16 Then the sons of Joseph said: "The mountainous region is not enough for us, and there are war chariots with iron

scythes among all the Ca'naan·ites dwelling in the land of the low plain, both those who are in Beth-she'an and its dependent towns and those who are in the low plain of Jez're·el." 17 So Joshua said this to the house of Joseph, to E'phra·im and Ma·nas'seh: "A numerous people you are, and great power is yours. You ought not to get one lot, 18 but the mountainous region should become yours. Because it is a forest, you must cut it down, and it must become the termination point for you. For you should drive away the Ca'naanites, although they have war chariots with iron scythes and they are strong."

18 Then all the assembly of the sons of Israel were congregated at Shi'loh, and they proceeded to locate the tent of meeting there, as the land was now subdued before them. 2 But there were still left among the sons of Israel those whose inheritance they had not apportioned out, namely, seven tribes. 3 So Joshua said to the sons of Israel: "How long are you going to be delinquent about going in to take possession of the land that Jehovah the God of your forefathers has given you? 4 Furnish for yourselves three men of each tribe and let me send them out, that they may get up and walk about in the land and map it out in accord with their inheritance, and let them come to me. 5 And they must apportion it among themselves into seven shares. Judah will keep standing on his territory to the south, and the house of Joseph will keep standing on their territory to the north. 6 As for you people, you will map out the land into seven shares, and you must bring them here to me, and I must cast lots here for you before Jehovah our God. 7 For the Levites have no share in among you, because the priesthood of Jehovah is their inheritance; and Gad and Reu'ben and the half tribe of Ma·nas'seh have taken their inheritance on the side of

the Jordan toward the east, which Moses the servant of Jehovah has given them."

8 So the men got up that they might go, and Joshua proceeded to command those who were going to map out the land, saying: "Go and walk about in the land and map it out and return to me, and here is where I shall draw lots for you before Jehovah in Shi'loh." 9 With that the men went and passed through the land and mapped it out by cities into seven shares, in a book. After that they came to Joshua at the camp in Shi'loh, 10 and Joshua went drawing lots for them in Shi'loh before Jehovah. Thus Joshua there apportioned the land to the sons of Israel in their shares.

11 Then the lot came up of the tribe of the sons of Benjamin by their families, and the territory of their lot went out between the sons of Judah and the sons of Joseph. 12 And their boundary came to be at the northern corner from the Jordan, and the boundary went up to the slope of Jer'i·cho on the north and went up on the mountain westward, and its termination proved to be at the wilderness of Beth-a'ven. 13 And the boundary passed over from there to Luz, at the southern slope of Luz, that is to say, Beth'el; and the boundary went down to At'a·roth-ad'dar upon the mountain that is on the south of Lower Beth-ho'ron. 14 And the boundary was marked out and went around at the western side to the south from the mountain that faces Beth-ho'ron to the south; and its termination proved to be at Kir'i·ath-ba'al, that is to say, Kir'i·ath-je'a·rim, a city of the sons of Judah. This is the western side.

15 And the side to the south was from the extremity of Kir'i·ath-je'a·rim, and the boundary went out westward and went out to the spring of the waters of Neph·to'ah. 16 And the boundary went down to the extremity of the mountain that faces the valley of

the son of Hin'nom, which is in the low plain of Reph'a·im to the north, and it went down to the valley of Hin'nom, to the slope of the Jeb'u·site on the south, and went down to En-ro'gel. 17 And it was marked out northward and went out to En-she'mesh and went out to Gel·i'loth, which is in front of the ascent of A·dum'mim; and it went down to the stone of Bo'han the son of Reu'ben. 18 And it passed over to the northern slope in front of the Ar'a·bah and went down to the Ar'a·bah. 19 And the boundary passed over to the northern slope of Beth-hog'lah, and the termination of it (the border) proved to be at the northern bay of the Salt Sea at the southern end of the Jordan. This was the southern boundary. 20 And the Jordan served as its boundary on the eastern side. This was the inheritance of the sons of Benjamin by their families, by its boundaries all around.

21 And the cities of the tribe of the sons of Benjamin by their families proved to be Jer'i·cho and Beth-hog'lah and E'mek-ke'ziz, 22 and Beth-ar'a·bah and Zam·a·ra'im and Beth'el, 23 and Av'vim and Pa'rah and Oph'rah, 24 and Che'phar-am'mo·ni and Oph'ni and Ge'ba; twelve cities and their settlements.

25 Gib'e·on and Ra'mah and Be·er'oth, 26 and Miz'peh and Che·phi'rah and Mo'zah, 27 and Re'kem and Ir'pe·el and Tar'a·lah, 28 and Ze'lah, Ha-e'leph and Je·bu'si, that is to say, Jerusalem, Gib'e·ah and Kir'i·ath; fourteen cities and their settlements.

This was the inheritance of the sons of Benjamin by their families.

19 Then the second lot came out for Sim'e·on, for the tribe of the sons of Sim'e·on by their families. And their inheritance came to be in the midst of the inheritance of the sons of Judah. 2 And they came to have in their inheritance Be'er-she'ba with She'ba, and Mo·la'dah, 3 and Ha'zar-shu'al and Ba'lah and E'zem,

4 and El·to'lad and Be'thul and Hor'mah, 5 and Zik'lag and Beth-mar'ca·both and Ha'zar-su'sah, 6 and Beth-le·ba'oth and Sha·ru'hen; thirteen cities and their settlements. 7 A'in, Rim'mon and E'ther and A'shan; four cities and their settlements, 8 and all the settlements that were all around these cities as far as Ba'al-ath-be'er, Ra'mah of the south. This was the inheritance of the tribe of the sons of Sim'e·on by their families. 9 The inheritance of the sons of Sim'e·on was out of the allotment of the sons of Judah, because the share of the sons of Judah proved to be too large for them. So the sons of Sim'e·on got a possession in the midst of their inheritance.

10 Next the third lot came up for the sons of Zeb'u·lun by their families, and the boundary of their inheritance came to be as far as Sa'rid. 11 And their boundary went up westward also to Mar'e·al and reached to Dab'be·sheth and reached to the torrent valley that is in front of Jok'ne·am. 12 And it went back from Sa'rid eastward toward the rising of the sun to the border of Chis'loth-ta'bor and went out to Dab'e·rath and went up to Ja·phi'a. 13 And from there it passed over eastward toward the sunrise to Gath-he'pher, to Eth-ka'zin, and went out to Rim'mon and was marked out to Ne'ah. 14 And the boundary went around it on the north to Han'na·thon, and its terminations proved to be at the valley of Iph'tah-el, 15 and Kat'tath and Na·hal'al and Shim'-ron and I'da·lah and Beth'le·hem; twelve cities and their settlements. 16 This was the inheritance of the sons of Zeb'u·lun by their families. These were the cities and their settlements.

17 It was for Is'sa·char that the fourth lot came out, for the sons of Is'sa·char by their families. 18 And their boundary came to be to Jez're·el and Che·sul'loth and Shu'nem, 19 and Haph'a·ra'im and Shi'on and An·a·ha'rath,

20 and Rab'bith and Kish'i·on and E'bez, 21 and Re'meth and En-gan'nim and En-had'dah and Beth-paz'zez. 22 And the boundary reached to Ta'bor and Sha·ha-zu'mah and Beth-she'mesh, and the terminations of their border proved to be at the Jordan; sixteen cities and their settlements. 23 This was the inheritance of the tribe of the sons of Is'sa·char by their families, the cities and their settlements.

24 Then the fifth lot came out for the tribe of the sons of Ash'er by their families. 25 And their boundary came to be Hel'kath and Ha'li and Be'ten and Ach'shaph, 26 and Al·lam'me·lech and A'mad and Mi'shal. And it reached westward to Car'mel and to Shi'hor-lib'nath, 27 and it went back toward the rising of the sun to Beth-da'gon and reached to Zeb'u-lun and the valley of Iph'tah-el to the north, to Beth-e'mek and Ne-i'el, and it went out to Ca'bul on the left, 28 and to E'bron and Re'hob and Ham'mon and Ka'nah as far as populous Si'don. 29 And the boundary went back to Ra'mah and as far as the fortified city of Tyre. And the boundary went back to Ho'sah, and its terminations came to be at the sea in the region of Ach'zib, 30 and Um'mah and A'phek and Re'hob; twenty-two cities and their settlements. 31 This was the inheritance of the tribe of the sons of Ash'er by their families. These were the cities and their settlements.

32 It was for the sons of Naph'-ta·li that the sixth lot came out, for the sons of Naph'ta·li by their families. 33 And their boundary came to be from He'leph, from the big tree in Za·a·nan'nim, and Ad'a-mi-ne'keb and Jab'ne·el as far as Lak'kum; and its terminations came to be at the Jordan. 34 And the boundary went back westward to Az'noth-ta'bor and went out from there to Huk'kok and reached to Zeb'u·lun on the south, and to Ash'er it reached on the west and to Judah at the Jordan toward the

rising of the sun. 35 And the fortified cities were Zid'dim, Zer and Ham'math, Rak'kath and Chin'ne·reth, 36 and Ad'a·mah and Ra'mah and Ha'zor, 37 and Ke'desh and Ed're·i and En-ha'zor, 38 and Yi'ron and Mig'dal-el, Ho'-rem and Beth-a'nath and Beth-she'mesh; nineteen cities and their settlements. 39 This was the inheritance of the tribe of the sons of Naph'ta·li by their families, the cities and their settlements.

40 It was for the tribe of the sons of Dan by their families that the seventh lot came out. 41 And the border of their inheritance came to be Zo'rah and Esh'ta·ol and Ir-she'mesh, 42 and Sha·al-ab'bin and Ai'ja·lon and Ith'lah, 43 and E'lon and Tim'nah and Ek'-ron, 44 and El'te·keh and Gib'-be·thon and Ba'al·ath, 45 and Je'hud and Ben'e-be'rak and Gath-rim'mon, 46 and Me-jar'kon and Rak'kon, with the border in front of Jop'pa. 47 And the territory of the sons of Dan was too cramped for them. And the sons of Dan proceeded to go up and war against Le'shem and to capture it and strike it with the edge of the sword. Then they took possession of it and went dwelling in it, and they began to call Le'shem Dan, according to the name of Dan their forefather. 48 This was the inheritance of the tribe of the sons of Dan by their families. These were the cities and their settlements.

49 Thus they finished dividing the land for a possession by its territories. Then the sons of Israel gave an inheritance to Joshua the son of Nun in their midst. 50 At the order of Jehovah they gave him the city for which he asked, namely, Tim'nath-se'rah, in the mountainous region of E'phra·im; and he began to build up the city and dwell in it.

51 These were the inheritances that E·le·a'zar the priest and Joshua the son of Nun and the heads of the fathers of the tribes of the sons of Israel distributed as a pos-

session by lot in Shi'loh before Jehovah, at the entrance of the tent of meeting. So they left off from apportioning the land.

20 Then Jehovah spoke to Joshua, saying: 2 "Speak to the sons of Israel, saying, 'Give for yourselves the cities of refuge of which I spoke to YOU by means of Moses, 3 for the manslayer who fatally strikes a soul unintentionally without knowing it to flee there; and they must serve YOU as a refuge from the avenger of blood. 4 And he must flee to one of these cities and stand at the entrance of the gate of the city and speak his words in the hearing of the older men of that city; and they must receive him into the city to themselves and give him a place and he must dwell with them. 5 And in case the avenger of blood chases after him, then they should not surrender the manslayer into his hand; for it was without knowing it that he struck his fellow man fatally, and he was not hating him formerly. 6 And he must dwell in that city until his standing before the assembly for judgment, until the death of the high priest who happens to be in those days. It is then that the manslayer may return, and he must enter into his city and into his house, into the city from which he had fled.'"

7 Accordingly they gave a sacred status to Ke'desh in Gal'i·lee in the mountainous region of Naph'ta·li, and She'chem in the mountainous region of E'phra·im, and Kir'i·ath-ar'ba, that is to say, He'bron, in the mountainous region of Judah. 8 And in the region of the Jordan, at Jer'i·cho, toward the east they gave Be'zer in the wilderness on the tableland out of the tribe of Reu'ben, and Ra'moth in Gil'e·ad out of the tribe of Gad, and Go'lan in Ba'shan out of the tribe of Ma·nas'seh.

9 These became the cities appointed for all the sons of Israel and for the alien resident who resides as an alien in their midst, for anyone to flee there who fatally strikes a soul unintentionally, that he may not die by the hand of the avenger of blood until his standing before the assembly.

21 The heads of the fathers of the Levites now approached E·le·a'zar the priest and Joshua the son of Nun and the heads of the fathers of the tribes of the sons of Israel, 2 and they proceeded to speak to them in Shi'loh in the land of Ca'naan, saying: "Jehovah by means of Moses commanded cities to be given us in which to dwell, together with their pasture grounds for our domestic animals." 3 So the sons of Israel gave the Levites, at the order of Jehovah, these cities and their pasture grounds out of their inheritance.

4 Then the lot came out for the families of the Ko'hath·ites, and thirteen cities came to belong to the sons of Aaron the priest, of the Levites, by lot, out of the tribe of Judah and out of the tribe of the Sim'e·on·ites and out of the tribe of Benjamin.

5 And for the sons of Ko'hath that were left over there were by lot ten cities out of the families of the tribe of E'phra·im and out of the tribe of Dan and out of the half tribe of Ma·nas'seh.

6 And for the sons of Ger'shon there were by lot thirteen cities out of the families of the tribe of Is'sa·char and out of the tribe of Ash'er and out of the tribe of Naph'ta·li and out of the half tribe of Ma·nas'seh in Ba'shan.

7 For the sons of Me·rar'i by their families there were twelve cities out of the tribe of Reu'ben and out of the tribe of Gad and out of the tribe of Zeb'u·lun.

8 Thus the sons of Israel gave the Levites these cities and their pasture grounds by lot, just as Jehovah had commanded by means of Moses.

9 So out of the tribe of the sons of Judah and out of the tribe of the sons of Sim'e·on they gave these cities that were called by name, 10 and they came to belong to the sons of Aaron out of

the families of the Ko'hath·ites of the sons of Le'vi, because the first lot became theirs. 11 Thus they gave them Kir'i·ath-ar'ba (said Ar'ba being the father of A'nak), that is to say, He'bron, in the mountainous region of Judah, and its pasture ground all around it; 12 and the field of the city and its settlements they gave to Ca'leb the son of Je·phun'neh as his possession.

13 And to the sons of Aaron the priest they gave the city of refuge for the manslayer, namely, He'bron, and its pasture ground, also Lib'nah and its pasture ground, 14 and Jat'tir and its pasture ground, and Esh·te·mo'a and its pasture ground, 15 and Ho'lon and its pasture ground, and De'bir and its pasture ground, 16 and A'in and its pasture ground, and Jut'tah and its pasture ground, Beth-she'mesh and its pasture ground; nine cities out of these two tribes.

17 And out of the tribe of Benjamin, Gib'e·on and its pasture ground, Ge'ba and its pasture ground, 18 An'a·thoth and its pasture ground, and Al'mon and its pasture ground; four cities.

19 All the cities of the sons of Aaron, the priests, were thirteen cities and their pasture grounds.

20 And for the families of the sons of Ko'hath, the Levites who were left out of the sons of Ko'hath, there came to be by their lot cities out of the tribe of E'phra·im. 21 Accordingly they gave them the city of refuge for the manslayer, namely, She'chem, and its pasture ground in the mountainous region of E'phra·im, and Ge'zer and its pasture ground, 22 and Kib'za·im and its pasture ground, and Beth-ho'ron and its pasture ground; four cities.

23 And from the tribe of Dan, El'te·ke and its pasture ground, Gib'be·thon and its pasture ground, 24 Ai'ja·lon and its pasture ground, Gath-rim'mon and its pasture ground; four cities.

25 And from the half tribe of Ma·nas'seh, Ta'a·nach and its pasture ground, and Gath-rim'mon and its pasture ground; two cities.

26 All the cities together with their pasture grounds that the families of the sons of Ko'hath who were left out had were ten.

27 And for the sons of Ger'shon, of the families of the Levites, there was out of the half tribe of Ma·nas'seh the city of refuge for the manslayer, namely, Go'lan, in Ba'shan, and its pasture ground, and Be·esh'te·rah and its pasture ground; two cities.

28 And out of the tribe of Is'sachar, Kish'i·on and its pasture ground, Dab'e·rath and its pasture ground, 29 Jar'muth and its pasture ground, En-gan'nim and its pasture ground; four cities.

30 And out of the tribe of Ash'er, Mi'shal and its pasture ground, Ab'don and its pasture ground, 31 Hel'kath and its pasture ground, and Re'hob and its pasture ground; four cities.

32 And out of the tribe of Naph'ta·li, the city of refuge for the manslayer, namely, Ke'desh in Gal'i·lee, and its pasture ground, and Ham'moth-dor and its pasture ground, and Kar'tan and its pasture ground; three cities.

33 All the cities of the Ger'shonites by their families were thirteen cities and their pasture grounds.

34 And the families of the sons of Me·rar'i, the Levites who were left out, had out of the tribe of Zeb'u·lun Jok'ne·am and its pasture ground, Kar'tah and its pasture ground, 35 Dim'nah and its pasture ground, Na'ha·lal and its pasture ground; four cities.

36 And out of the tribe of Reu'ben, Be'zer and its pasture ground, and Ja'haz and its pasture ground, 37 Ked'e·moth and its pasture ground, and Meph'a·ath and its pasture ground; four cities.

38 And out of the tribe of Gad, the city of refuge for the manslayer, namely, Ra'moth in Gil'e·ad, and its pasture ground, and Ma·ha·na'im and its pasture ground, 39 Hesh'bon and its pas-

ture ground, Ja'zer and its pasture ground; all the cities being four.

40 All the cities that came to belong to the sons of Me·rar'i by their families, who were left out from the families of the Levites, were, as their lot, twelve cities.

41 All the cities of the Levites in the midst of the possession of the sons of Israel were forty-eight cities together with their pasture grounds. 42 These cities came to be each a city together with its pasture ground all around it—thus as to all these cities.

43 So Jehovah gave Israel all the land that he had sworn to give to their forefathers, and they proceeded to take possession of it and to dwell in it. 44 Furthermore, Jehovah gave them rest all around, according to everything that he had sworn to their forefathers, and not one of all their enemies stood before them. All their enemies Jehovah gave into their hand. 45 Not a promise failed out of all the good promise that Jehovah had made to the house of Israel; it all came true.

22 At that time Joshua proceeded to call the Reu'benites and the Gad'ites and the half tribe of Ma·nas'seh 2 and to say to them: "For YOUR part, YOU have kept all that Moses the servant of Jehovah commanded YOU, and YOU were obedient to my voice in all that I have commanded YOU. 3 YOU have not left YOUR brothers these many days down to this day, and YOU have kept the obligation of the commandment of Jehovah YOUR God. 4 And now Jehovah YOUR God has given YOUR brothers rest, just as he promised them. So now turn and go YOUR way to YOUR tents in the land of YOUR possession, which Moses the servant of Jehovah gave YOU on the other side of the Jordan. 5 Only be very careful to carry out the commandment and the law that Moses the servant of Jehovah commanded YOU by loving Jehovah YOUR God and by walking in all his ways and by keeping his commandments and

by cleaving to him and by serving him with all YOUR heart and with all YOUR soul."

6 With that Joshua blessed them and sent them away that they might go to their tents. 7 And to the half tribe of Ma·nas'seh Moses had made a gift in Ba'shan, and to the other half of it Joshua made a gift with their brothers on the side of the Jordan to the west. So, too, when Joshua sent them away to their tents, he proceeded to bless them. 8 And he went on to say to them: "Return to YOUR tents with many riches and with very much livestock, with silver and gold and copper and iron and garments in very great quantity. Take YOUR share of the spoil of YOUR enemies together with YOUR brothers."

9 After that the sons of Reu'ben and the sons of Gad and the half tribe of Ma·nas'seh returned and went away from the other sons of Israel, from Shi'loh, which is in the land of Ca'naan, so as to go to the land of Gil'e·ad, to the land of their possession in which they had been settled at the order of Jehovah by means of Moses. 10 When they came to the regions of the Jordan that were in the land of Ca'naan, then the sons of Reu'ben and the sons of Gad and the half tribe of Ma·nas'seh built there an altar by the Jordan, an altar great in conspicuousness. 11 Later on the other sons of Israel heard it said: "Look! The sons of Reu'ben and the sons of Gad and the half tribe of Ma·nas'seh have built an altar on the frontier of the land of Ca'naan in the regions of the Jordan on the side belonging to the sons of Israel." 12 When the sons of Israel got to hear of it, the whole assembly of the sons of Israel were then congregated at Shi'loh to go up for military action against them.

13 Then the sons of Israel sent to the sons of Reu'ben and the sons of Gad and the half tribe of Ma·nas'seh in the land of Gil'e·ad Phin'e·has the son of E·le·a'zar

the priest, 14 and ten chieftains with him, one chieftain of each paternal house of all the tribes of Israel, and they were each a head of the house of their fathers of the thousands of Israel. 15 In time they came to the sons of Reu'ben and the sons of Gad and the half tribe of Ma·nas'seh in the land of Gil'e·ad and began to speak with them, saying:

16 "This is what all the assembly of Jehovah have said, 'What is this act of unfaithfulness that YOU have perpetrated against the God of Israel in turning back today from following Jehovah by YOUR building for yourselves an altar, that YOU may rebel today against Jehovah? 17 Was the error of Pe'or too small for us, from which we have not cleansed ourselves down to this day, although the plague came to be upon the assembly of Jehovah? 18 And YOU —YOU would turn back today from following Jehovah; and it must occur that should YOU, for YOUR part, rebel today against Jehovah, then tomorrow it will be against the entire assembly of Israel that he will be indignant. 19 Now if it is indeed that the land of YOUR possession is unclean, make YOUR way across to the land of Jehovah's possession where the tabernacle of Jehovah has resided, and get settled in our midst; and against Jehovah do not YOU rebel and do not make us the ones to rebel by YOUR building for yourselves an altar in addition to the altar of Jehovah our God. 20 Was it not A'chan the son of Ze'rah that perpetrated an act of unfaithfulness in the thing devoted to destruction, and was it not against all the assembly of Israel that there came indignation? And he was not the only man to expire in his error.'"

21 At this the sons of Reu'ben and the sons of Gad and the half tribe of Ma·nas'seh answered and spoke with the heads of the thousands of Israel: 22 "Divine One, God, Jehovah, Divine One, God, Jehovah, he is knowing, and Israel,

he too will know. If it is in rebellion and if it is in unfaithfulness against Jehovah, do not save us this day. 23 If it was to build for ourselves an altar so as to turn back from following Jehovah, and if it was to offer up burnt offerings and grain offerings on it, and if it was to render up communion sacrifices on it, Jehovah himself will search out; 24 or if it was not rather out of anxious care for something else that we did this, saying, 'In a future day YOUR sons will say to our sons: "What do YOU have to do with Jehovah the God of Israel? 25 And there is a boundary that Jehovah has put between us and YOU, the sons of Reu'ben and the sons of Gad, namely, the Jordan. YOU have no share in Jehovah." And YOUR sons will certainly make our sons desist from fearing Jehovah.'

26 "Hence we said, 'Let us take action in our behalf, please, by building the altar, not for burnt offering nor for sacrifice, 27 but that it may be a witness between us and YOU and our generations after us that we shall render the service of Jehovah before him with our burnt offerings and our sacrifices and our communion sacrifices, that YOUR sons may not say in a future day to our sons: "YOU have no share in Jehovah."' 28 So we said, 'And it must occur that in case they should say that to us and to our generations in a future day, we must also say: "See the representation of Jehovah's altar that our fathers made, not for burnt offering nor for sacrifice, but it is a witness between us and YOU."' 29 It is unthinkable, on our part, to rebel of our own accord against Jehovah and to turn back today from following Jehovah by building an altar for burnt offering, grain offering and sacrifice besides the altar of Jehovah our God that is before his tabernacle!"

30 Now when Phin'e·has the priest and the chieftains of the assembly and the heads of the thousands of Israel who were with

him heard the words that the sons of Reu'ben and the sons of Gad and the sons of Ma·nas'seh spoke, it came to be good in their eyes. 31 So Phin'e·has the son of E·le·a'zar the priest said to the sons of Reu'ben and the sons of Gad and the sons of Ma·nas'seh: "Today we do know that Jehovah is in our midst, because you have not perpetrated against Jehovah this act of unfaithfulness. Now you have delivered the sons of Israel out of the hand of Jehovah."

32 With that Phin'e·has the son of E·le·a'zar the priest and the chieftains returned from the sons of Reu'ben and the sons of Gad in the land of Gil'e·ad to the land of Ca'naan to the other sons of Israel and brought back word to them. 33 And the word came to be good in the eyes of the sons of Israel; and the sons of Israel proceeded to bless God, and they did not talk of going up for army service against them to ruin the land in which the sons of Reu'ben and the sons of Gad were dwelling.

34 And the sons of Reu'ben and the sons of Gad began to name the altar, because "it is a witness between us that Jehovah is the [true] God."

23 And it came about many days after Jehovah had given Israel rest from all their enemies all around, when Joshua was old and advanced in days, 2 that Joshua proceeded to call all Israel, its older men and its heads and its judges and its officers, and to say to them: "As for me, I have grown old, I have advanced in days. 3 And as for you, you have seen all that Jehovah your God did to all these nations on your account, because Jehovah your God was the one who was fighting for you. 4 See, I assigned to you by lot these nations that remain as an inheritance for your tribes, and all the nations that I cut off, from the Jordan to the Great Sea at the setting of the sun. 5 And Jehovah your God was the one who kept pushing them away from before you,

and he dispossessed them on your account, and you took possession of their land, just as Jehovah your God had promised you.

6 "And you must be very courageous to keep and to do all that is written in the book of the law of Moses by never turning away from it to the right or to the left, 7 by never going in among these nations, these that remain with you. And you must not mention the names of their gods nor swear by them, neither must you serve them nor bow down to them. 8 But it is to Jehovah your God that you should cleave, just as you have done down to this day. 9 And Jehovah will drive away great and mighty nations from before you. (As for you, not a man has stood before you down to this day.) 10 Just one man of you will chase a thousand, because Jehovah your God is the one who is fighting for you, just as he has promised you. 11 And you must be on constant guard for your souls by loving Jehovah your God.

12 "But if you should turn back at all and you do cleave to what is left of these nations, these that remain with you, and you do form marriage alliances with them and go in among them, and they among you, 13 you should positively know that Jehovah your God will not continue to dispossess these nations on your account; and they must become to you as a trap and as a snare and as a scourge on your flanks and as thorns in your eyes until you have perished off this good ground that Jehovah your God has given you.

14 "Now, look! I am going today in the way of all the earth, and you well know with all your hearts and with all your souls that not one word out of all the good words that Jehovah your God has spoken to you has failed. They have all come true for you. Not one word of them has failed. 15 And it must occur that, just as all the good word that Jehovah your God has spoken to you has come upon you,

so Jehovah will bring upon you all the evil word until he has annihilated you from off this good ground that Jehovah your God has given you, 16 because of your overstepping the covenant of Jehovah your God that he commanded you, and because you have gone and served other gods and bowed down to them. And Jehovah's anger will certainly blaze against you, and you will certainly perish in a hurry from off the good land that he has given you."

24 And Joshua proceeded to assemble all the tribes of Israel together at She'chem and to call the older men of Israel and its heads and its judges and its officers, and they went taking their stand before the [true] God. 2 And Joshua went on to say to all the people: "This is what Jehovah the God of Israel has said, 'It was on the other side of the River that your forefathers dwelt a long time ago, Te'rah the father of Abraham and the father of Na'hor, and they used to serve other gods.

3 "'In time I took your forefather Abraham from the other side of the River and had him walk through all the land of Ca'naan and made his seed many. So I gave him Isaac. 4 Then to Isaac I gave Jacob and E'sau. Later to E'sau I gave Mount Se'ir to take possession of it; and Jacob and his sons went down to Egypt. 5 Later on I sent Moses and Aaron, and I went plaguing Egypt with what I did in its midst; and afterward I brought you out. 6 When I was bringing your fathers out of Egypt and you came to the sea, then the Egyptians went chasing after your fathers with war chariots and cavalrymen to the Red Sea. 7 And they began to cry out to Jehovah. So he placed a darkness between you and the Egyptians and brought the sea upon them and covered them, and your eyes got to see what I did in Egypt; and you took up dwelling in the wilderness many days.

8 "'Eventually I brought you to the land of the Am'or·ites who were dwelling on the other side of the Jordan, and they went fighting against you. At that I gave them into your hand that you might take possession of their land, and I annihilated them from before you. 9 Then Ba'lak the son of Zip'por, the king of Mo'ab, got up and went fighting against Israel. So he sent and summoned Ba'laam the son of Be'or to call down evil upon you. 10 And I did not want to listen to Ba'laam. Consequently he blessed you repeatedly. Thus I delivered you out of his hand.

11 "'Then you went crossing the Jordan and came to Jer'i·cho. And the landowners of Jer'i·cho, the Am'or·ites and the Per'iz·zites and the Ca'naan·ites and the Hit'tites and the Gir'ga·shites, the Hi'vites and the Jeb'u·sites began fighting against you; but I gave them into your hand. 12 So I sent the feeling of dejection ahead of you, and it gradually drove them out before you—two kings of the Am'or·ites —not with your sword and not with your bow. 13 Thus I gave you a land for which you had not toiled and cities that you had not built, and you took up dwelling in them. Vineyards and olive groves that you did not plant are what you are eating.'

14 "And now fear Jehovah and serve him in faultlessness and in truth, and remove the gods that your forefathers served on the other side of the River and in Egypt, and serve Jehovah. 15 Now if it is bad in your eyes to serve Jehovah, choose for yourselves today whom you will serve, whether the gods that your forefathers who were on the other side of the River served or the gods of the Am'or·ites in whose land you are dwelling. But as for me and my household, we shall serve Jehovah."

16 At this the people answered and said: "It is unthinkable, on our part, to leave Jehovah so as to serve other gods. 17 For it is Jehovah our God who brought us and our

fathers up out of the land of Egypt, out of the house of slaves, and who performed these great signs before our eyes and who kept guarding us in all the way in which we walked and among all the peoples through the midst of whom we passed. 18 And Jehovah proceeded to drive out all the peoples, even the Am′or-ites, dwelling in the land from before us. As for us, too, we shall serve Jehovah, because he is our God."

19 Then Joshua said to the people: "You are not able to serve Jehovah, for he is a holy God; he is a God exacting exclusive devotion. He will not pardon your revolting and your sins. 20 In case you should leave Jehovah and you do serve foreign gods, he also will certainly turn back and do you injury and exterminate you after he has done you good."

21 In turn the people said to Joshua: "No, but Jehovah we shall serve!" 22 At this Joshua said to the people: "You are witnesses against yourselves that you of your own accord have chosen Jehovah for yourselves, to serve him." To this they said: "We are witnesses."

23 "And now remove the foreign gods that are among you, and incline your hearts to Jehovah the God of Israel." 24 In turn the people said to Joshua: "Jehovah our God we shall serve, and to his voice we shall listen!"

25 And Joshua proceeded to conclude a covenant with the people on that day and to constitute for them a regulation and judicial decision in She′chem. 26 Then Joshua wrote these words in the book of God's law and took a great stone and set it up there under the massive tree that is by the sanctuary of Jehovah.

27 And Joshua went on to say to all the people: "Look! This stone is what will serve as a witness against us, because it has itself heard all the sayings of Jehovah that he has spoken with us, and it must serve as a witness against you, that you may not deny your God." 28 With that Joshua sent the people away, each one to his inheritance.

29 And it came about that after these things Joshua the son of Nun, the servant of Jehovah, gradually died at the age of a hundred and ten years. 30 So they buried him in the territory of his inheritance in Tim′nath-se′rah, which is in the mountainous region of E′phra·im, north of Mount Ga′ash. 31 And Israel continued to serve Jehovah all the days of Joshua and all the days of the older men who extended their days after Joshua and who had known all the work of Jehovah that he did for Israel.

32 And Joseph's bones, which the sons of Israel had brought up out of Egypt, they buried in She′-chem in the tract of the field that Jacob had acquired from the sons of Ha′mor, She′chem's father, for a hundred pieces of money; and it came to belong to the sons of Jo-seph as an inheritance.

33 Also, E·le·a′zar the son of Aaron died. So they buried him in the Hill of Phin′e·has his son, which he had given him in the mountainous region of E′phra·im.

JUDGES

1 And after the death of Joshua it came about that the sons of Israel proceeded to inquire of Jehovah, saying: "Who of us will go up first to the Ca'naan·ites to fight against them?" 2 To this Jehovah said: "Judah will go up. Look! I shall certainly give the land into his hand." 3 Then Judah said to Sim'e·on his brother: "Come up with me into my lot and let us fight against the Ca'naan-ites, and I myself in turn will go with you into your lot." Accordingly Sim'e·on went with him.

4 With that Judah went on up and Jehovah gave the Ca'naan·ites and the Per'iz·zites into their hands, so that they defeated them in Be'zek, ten thousand men. 5 When they found A·do'ni-be'zek in Be'zek, then they fought against him and defeated the Ca'naan·ites and the Per'iz·zites. 6 When A·do'ni-be'zek took to flight, then they went chasing after him and got hold of him and cut off the thumbs of his hands and the great toes of his feet. 7 At this A·do'ni-be'zek said: "There have been seventy kings with the thumbs of their hands and the great toes of their feet cut off picking up food under my table. Just the way I have done, so God has repaid me." After that they brought him to Jerusalem and he died there.

8 Furthermore, the sons of Judah carried on war against Jerusalem and got to capture it, and they went striking it with the edge of the sword, and the city they consigned to the fire. 9 And afterward the sons of Judah went down to fight against the Ca'naan·ites inhabiting the mountainous region and the Neg'eb and the She·phe'lah. 10 So Judah marched against the Ca'naan·ites who were dwelling in He'bron (now the name of He'bron before that was Kir'i·ath-ar'ba), and they went striking down She'shai and A·hi'man and Tal'mai.

11 And they marched on from there against the inhabitants of De'bir. (Now the name of De'bir before that was Kir'i·ath-se'pher.) 12 Then Ca'leb said: "Whoever strikes Kir'i·ath-se'pher and does capture it, why, I will give him Ach'sah my daughter as a wife." 13 And Oth'ni·el the son of Ke'naz, Ca'leb's younger brother, got to capture it. For that he gave him Ach'sah his daughter as a wife. 14 And it came about that while she was going home, she kept inciting him to ask a field from her father. Then she clapped her hands while upon the ass. At this Ca'leb said to her: "What do you want?" 15 So she said to him: "Do grant me a blessing, for it is a southern piece of land you have given me, and you must give me Gul'loth-ma'im." Accordingly Ca'leb gave her Upper Gul'loth and Lower Gul'loth.

16 And the sons of the Ken'ite, whose son-in-law Moses was, came up out of the city of palm trees with the sons of Judah to the wilderness of Judah, which is to the south of A'rad. Then they went and took up dwelling with the people. 17 But Judah marched on with Sim'e·on his brother, and they proceeded to strike the Ca'naan-ites inhabiting Ze'phath and to devote it to destruction. Hence the name of the city was called Hor'mah. 18 After that Judah captured Ga'za and its territory and Ash'ke·lon and its territory and Ek'ron and its territory. 19 And Jehovah continued with Judah, so that he took possession of the mountainous region, but he could not dispossess the inhabitants of the low plain, because they had war chariots with iron scythes. 20 When they gave Ca'leb He'bron, just as Moses had promised, then

he drove out from there the three sons of A'nak.

21 And the sons of Benjamin did not drive out the Jeb'u·sites inhabiting Jerusalem; but the Jeb'u·sites keep on dwelling with the sons of Benjamin in Jerusalem down to this day.

22 Meantime the house of Joseph itself also went up against Beth'el, and Jehovah was with them. 23 And the house of Joseph began to spy on Beth'el (incidentally, the name of the city before that was Luz), 24 and the watchers got to see a man going out of the city. So they said to him: "Show us, please, the way to get into the city, and we shall certainly exercise kindness toward you." 25 Accordingly the man showed them the way to get into the city; and they went striking the city with the edge of the sword, but the man and all his family they let go. 26 Upon that the man went to the land of the Hit'tites and built a city and called its name Luz. That is its name down to this day.

27 And Ma·nas'seh did not take possession of Beth-she'an and its dependent towns and Ta'a·nach and its dependent towns and the inhabitants of Dor and its dependent towns and the inhabitants of Ib'le·am and its dependent towns and the inhabitants of Me·gid'do and its dependent towns, but the Ca'naan·ites persisted in dwelling in this land. 28 And it came about that Israel grew strong and proceeded to set the Ca'naan·ites to forced labor, and they did not drive them out completely.

29 Neither did E'phra·im drive out the Ca'naan·ites who were dwelling in Ge'zer, but the Ca'naan·ites continued to dwell in among them in Ge'zer.

30 Zeb'u·lun did not drive out the inhabitants of Kit'ron and the inhabitants of Na'ha·lol, but the Ca'naan·ites continued to dwell in among them and came to be subject to forced labor.

31 Ash'er did not drive out the inhabitants of Ac'co and the in-

habitants of Si'don and Ah'lab and Ach'zib and Hel'bah and A'phik and Re'hob. 32 And the Ash'er-ites continued to dwell in among the Ca'naan·ites inhabiting the land, because they did not drive them out.

33 Naph'ta·li did not drive out the inhabitants of Beth-she'mesh and the inhabitants of Beth-a'nath, but they continued to dwell in among the Ca'naan·ites inhabiting the land; and the inhabitants of Beth-she'mesh and of Beth-a'nath became theirs for forced labor.

34 And the Am'or·ites kept pressing the sons of Dan into the mountainous region, for they did not allow them to come down into the low plain. 35 So the Am'or-ites persisted in dwelling in Mount He'res and in Ai'ja·lon and Sha-al'bim. But the hand of the house of Joseph got to be so heavy that they were forced into task work. 36 And the territory of the Am'-or·ites was from the ascent of A·krab'bim, from Se'la upward.

2 Then Jehovah's angel went up from Gil'gal to Bo'chim and said: "I proceeded to bring you up out of Egypt and to bring you into the land about which I swore to your forefathers. Furthermore, I said, 'Never shall I break my covenant with you. 2 And for your part, you must not conclude a covenant with the inhabitants of this land. Their altars you should pull down.' But you have not listened to my voice. Why have you done this? 3 So I, in turn, have said, 'I shall not drive them away from before you, and they must become snares to you, and their gods will serve as a lure to you.'"

4 And it came about that as soon as Jehovah's angel had spoken these words to all the sons of Israel, the people began to raise their voices and weep. 5 Hence they called the name of that place Bo'chim. And they proceeded to sacrifice there to Jehovah.

6 When Joshua sent the people away, then the sons of Israel went

their way, each to his inheritance, to take possession of the land. 7 And the people continued to serve Jehovah all the days of Joshua and all the days of the older men who extended their days after Joshua and who had seen all of Jehovah's great work that he did for Israel. 8 Then Joshua the son of Nun, the servant of Jehovah, died at the age of a hundred and ten years. 9 So they buried him in the territory of his inheritance in Tim′nath-he′res in the mountainous region of E′phra·im, on the north of Mount Ga′ash. 10 And all that generation too were gathered to their fathers, and another generation began to rise after them that did not know Jehovah or the work that he had done for Israel.

11 And the sons of Israel fell to doing what was bad in the eyes of Jehovah and serving the Ba′als. 12 Thus they abandoned Jehovah the God of their fathers who had brought them out of the land of Egypt and went following other gods from among the gods of the peoples who were all around them and they began bowing down to them, so that they offended Jehovah. 13 Thus they abandoned Jehovah and took up serving Ba′al and the Ash′to·reth images. 14 At this Jehovah's anger blazed against Israel, so that he gave them into the hands of the pillagers, and they began to pillage them; and he proceeded to sell them into the hand of their enemies round about, and they were no longer able to stand before their enemies. 15 Everywhere that they went out, the hand of Jehovah proved to be against them for calamity, just as Jehovah had spoken and just as Jehovah had sworn to them; and they got to be in very sore straits. 16 So Jehovah would raise up judges, and they would save them out of the hand of their pillagers.

17 And even to their judges they did not listen, but they had immoral intercourse with other gods and went bowing down to them. They quickly turned aside from the

way in which their forefathers had walked by obeying the commandments of Jehovah. They did not do like that. 18 And when Jehovah did raise up judges for them, Jehovah proved to be with the judge, and he saved them out of the hand of their enemies all the days of the judge; for Jehovah would feel regret over their groaning because of their oppressors and those who were shoving them around.

19 And it occurred that when the judge died they would turn around and act more ruinously than their fathers by walking after other gods to serve them and bow down to them. They did not refrain from their practices and their stubborn behavior. 20 Finally Jehovah's anger blazed against Israel and he said: "For the reason that this nation have overstepped my covenant that I commanded their forefathers and have not listened to my voice, 21 I too, for my part, shall not drive out again from before them a single one of the nations that Joshua left behind when he died, 22 in order by them to test Israel, whether they will be keepers of Jehovah's way by walking in it just as their fathers kept it, or not." 23 Accordingly Jehovah let these nations stay by not driving them out quickly, and he did not give them into Joshua's hand.

3 Now these are the nations that Jehovah let stay so as by them to test Israel, that is, all those who had not experienced any of the wars of Ca′naan; 2 it was only in order for the generations of the sons of Israel to have the experience, so as to teach them war, that is, only those who before that had not experienced such things: 3 The five axis lords of the Phi-lis′tines, and all the Ca′naan·ites, even the Si·do′ni·ans and the Hi′-vites inhabiting Mount Leb′a·non from Mount Ba′al-her′mon as far as to the entering in of Ha′math. 4 And they kept serving as agents to test Israel so as to know wheth-

er they would obey Jehovah's commandments that he had commanded their fathers by means of Moses. 5 And the sons of Israel dwelt in among the Ca'naan·ites, the Hit'-tites and the Am'or·ites and the Per'iz·zites and the Hi'vites and the Jeb'u·sites. 6 And they proceeded to take their daughters as wives for themselves, and their own daughters they gave to their sons, and they took up serving their gods.

7 So the sons of Israel did what was bad in Jehovah's eyes, and they were forgetful of Jehovah their God and went serving the Ba'als and the sacred poles. 8 At this Jehovah's anger blazed against Israel, so that he sold them into the hand of Cu'shan-rish·a·tha'im the king of Mes·o·po·ta'mi·a; and the sons of Israel continued to serve Cu'shan-rish·a·tha'im eight years. 9 And the sons of Israel began to call to Jehovah for aid. Then Jehovah raised a savior up for the sons of Israel that he might save them, Oth'ni·el the son of Ke'naz, the younger brother of Ca'leb. 10 The spirit of Jehovah now came upon him, and he became the judge of Israel. When he went out to battle, then Jehovah gave Cu'shan-rish·a·tha'im the king of Syria into his hand so that his hand overpowered Cu'shan-rish·a·tha'im. 11 After that the land had no disturbance for forty years. Eventually Oth'ni·el the son of Ke'naz died.

12 And once again the sons of Israel went doing what was bad in Jehovah's eyes. At that Jehovah let Eg'lon the king of Mo'ab grow strong against Israel, because they did what was bad in Jehovah's eyes. 13 Furthermore, he gathered against them the sons of Am'-mon and Am'a·lek. Then they went and struck Israel and took possession of the city of palm trees. 14 And the sons of Israel continued to serve Eg'lon the king of Mo'ab eighteen years. 15 And the sons of Israel began to call to Jehovah for aid. So Jehovah raised up for

them a savior, E'hud the son of Ge'ra, a Ben'ja·mite, a left-handed man. In time the sons of Israel sent tribute by his hand to Eg'lon the king of Mo'ab. 16 Meanwhile E'hud made a sword for himself, and it had two edges, its length being a cubit. Then he girded it underneath his garment upon his right thigh. 17 And he proceeded to present the tribute to Eg'lon the king of Mo'ab. Now Eg'lon was a very fat man.

18 And it came about that when he had finished presenting the tribute, he at once sent the people away, the bearers of the tribute. 19 And he himself turned back at the quarries that were at Gil'gal, and he proceeded to say: "I have a secret word for you, O king." So he said: "Keep silence!" With that all those who were standing by him went on out from him. 20 And E'hud came to him as he was sitting in his cool roof chamber that he had to himself. And E'hud went on to say: "A word of God I have for you." At that he rose up from his throne. 21 Then E'hud thrust in his left hand and took the sword off his right thigh and plunged it into his belly. 22 And the handle kept going in also after the blade so that the fat closed in over the blade, for he did not draw the sword out of his belly, and the fecal matter began to come out. 23 And E'hud proceeded to go out through the airhole, but he closed the doors of the roof chamber behind him and locked them. 24 And he himself went out.

And his servants came and began looking, and there the doors of the roof chamber were locked. So they said: "He is just easing nature in the cool interior room." 25 And they kept waiting until they were ashamed, and, look! there was no one opening the doors of the roof chamber. At this they took the key and opened them, and, look! their lord was fallen to the earth dead!

26 As for E'hud, he escaped while they were lingering, and he

himself passed by the quarries and made his escape to Se·i′rah. 27 And it came about that when he got there he began blowing the horn in the mountainous region of E′phra·im; and the sons of Israel began going down with him out of the mountainous region, he being at their head. 28 Then he said to them: "Follow me, because Jehovah has given YOUR enemies, the Mo′ab·ites, into YOUR hand." And they went following him and got to capture the fords of the Jordan against the Mo′ab·ites, and they did not allow anybody to pass over. 29 And at that time they went striking down Mo′ab, about ten thousand men, every one robust and every one a valiant man; and not a single one escaped. 30 And Mo′ab came to be subdued on that day under Israel's hand; and the land had no further disturbance for eighty years.

31 And after him there proved to be Sham′gar the son of A′nath, and he went striking down the Phi·lis′tines, six hundred men, with a cattle goad; and he too got to save Israel.

4 Then the sons of Israel again began to do what was bad in Jehovah's eyes now that E′hud was dead. 2 So Jehovah sold them into the hand of Ja′bin the king of Ca′naan, who reigned in Ha′zor; and the chief of his army was Sis′e·ra, and he was dwelling in Ha·ro′sheth of the nations. 3 And the sons of Israel began to cry out to Jehovah, because he had nine hundred war chariots with iron scythes, and he himself oppressed the sons of Israel with harshness twenty years.

4 Now Deb′o·rah, a prophetess, the wife of Lap′pi·doth, was judging Israel at that particular time. 5 And she was dwelling under Deb′o·rah's palm tree between Ra′mah and Beth′el in the mountainous region of E′phra·im; and the sons of Israel would go up to her for judgment. 6 And she proceeded to send and call Ba′rak the son of A·bin′o·am out of Ke′desh-

naph′ta·li and to say to him: "Has not Jehovah the God of Israel given the command? 'Go and you must spread yourself out on Mount Ta′bor, and you must take with you ten thousand men out of the sons of Naph′ta·li and out of the sons of Zeb′u·lun. 7 And I shall certainly draw to you at the torrent valley of Ki′shon Sis′e·ra, the chief of Ja′bin's army and his war chariots and his crowd, and I shall indeed give him into your hand.' "

8 At this Ba′rak said to her: "If you will go with me, I also shall certainly go; but if you will not go with me, I shall not go." 9 To this she said: "Without fail I shall go with you. Just the same, the beautifying thing will not become yours on the way that you are going, for it will be into the hand of a woman that Jehovah will sell Sis′e·ra." With that Deb′o·rah got up and went with Ba′rak to Ke′desh. 10 And Ba′rak began to call Zeb′u·lun and Naph′ta·li together to Ke′desh, and ten thousand men went on up following his steps; and Deb′o·rah went on up with him.

11 Incidentally He′ber the Ken′ite had separated from the Ken′ites, the sons of Ho′bab, whose son-in-law Moses was, and he had his tent pitched near the big tree in Za·a-nan′nim, which is at Ke′desh.

12 Then they reported to Sis′e·ra that Ba′rak the son of A·bin′o·am had gone up to Mount Ta′bor. 13 At once Sis′e·ra called together all his war chariots, the nine hundred war chariots with iron scythes, and all the people that were with him, out of Ha·ro′sheth of the nations to the torrent valley of Ki′shon. 14 Deb′o·rah now said to Ba′rak: "Get up, for this is the day that Jehovah will certainly give Sis′e·ra into your hand. Is it not Jehovah that has gone out before you?" And Ba′rak went descending from Mount Ta′bor with ten thousand men behind him. 15 And Jehovah began to throw Sis′e·ra and all his war chariots and all the camp into confusion

by the edge of the sword before Ba′rak. Finally Sis′e·ra got down off the chariot and took to flight on foot. 16 And Ba′rak chased after the war chariots and the camp as far as Ha·ro′sheth of the nations, so that all the camp of Sis′e·ra fell by the edge of the sword. Not as much as one remained.

17 As for Sis′e·ra, he fled on foot to the tent of Ja′el the wife of He′ber the Ken′ite, for there was peace between Ja′bin the king of Ha′zor and the household of He′ber the Ken′ite. 18 Then Ja′el came on out to meet Sis′e·ra and said to him: "Turn this way, my lord, turn this way to me. Do not be afraid." So he turned aside to her into the tent. Later she covered him with a blanket. 19 In time he said to her: "Give me, please, a little water to drink, for I am thirsty." Accordingly she opened a skin bottle of milk and gave him a drink, after which she covered him. 20 And he went on to say to her: "Stand at the entrance of the tent, and it must occur that if anybody comes and does ask you and says, 'Is there a man here?' you must then say, 'No!' "

21 And Ja′el the wife of He′ber proceeded to take a pin of the tent and to put the hammer into her hand. Then she went to him stealthily and drove the pin into his temples and beat it into the earth, while he was fast asleep and weary. So he died.

22 And, look! there was Ba′rak pursuing Sis′e·ra. Ja′el now came on out to meet him and said to him: "Come and I shall show you the man you are looking for." So in he went to her, and, look! there was Sis′e·ra fallen dead, with the pin in his temples.

23 Thus God subdued Ja′bin the king of Ca′naan before the sons of Israel on that day. 24 And the hand of the sons of Israel went on getting harder and harder against Ja′bin the king of Ca′naan, until they had cut off Ja′bin the king of Ca′naan.

5 And on that day Deb′o·rah along with Ba′rak the son of A·bin′o·am broke out in song, saying:

2 "For letting the hair hang loose in Israel for war,
For the people's volunteering,
BLESS Jehovah.
3 Listen, YOU kings; give ear, YOU high officials:
I to Jehovah, yes, I, will sing.
I shall make melody to Jehovah, Israel's God.
4 Jehovah, at your going forth from Se′ir,
At your marching out of the field of E′dom,
Earth rocked, heavens also dripped,
Clouds also dripped with water.
5 Mountains flowed away from the face of Jehovah,
This Si′nai away from the face of Jehovah, Israel's God.
6 In the days of Sham′gar the son of A′nath,
In the days of Ja′el, pathways had no traffic,
And the travelers of roadways would travel by roundabout pathways.
7 The dwellers in open country ceased, in Israel they ceased,
Until I, Deb′o·rah, rose up,
Until I rose up as a mother in Israel.
8 They proceeded to choose new gods.
It was then there was war in the gates.
A shield could not be seen, nor a lance,
Among forty thousand in Israel.
9 My heart is for the commanders of Israel,
Who were volunteers among the people.
BLESS Jehovah.
10 YOU riders on yellowish-red she-asses,
YOU who sit on rich carpets,
And YOU who walk on the road, Consider!
11 Some of the voices of the water distributors among the places of drawing water,

There they began to recount the righteous acts of Je-hovah,
The righteous acts of his dwell-ers in open country in Israel.
It was then Jehovah's people made their way down to the gates.

12 Awake, awake, O Deb'o·rah;
Awake, awake, utter a song!
Rise up, Ba'rak, and lead your captives away, you son of A·bin'o·am!

13 It was then the survivors came down to the majestic ones;
Jehovah's people came down to me against the mighty ones.

14 Out of E'phra·im was their origin in the low plain,
With you, O Benjamin, among your peoples.
Out of Ma'chir the commanders went down,
And out of Zeb'u·lun those handling the equipment of a scribe.

15 And the princes in Is'sa·char were with Deb'o·rah,
And as Is'sa·char, so was Ba'rak.
Into the low plain he was sent on foot.
Among the divisions of Reu'-ben great were the search-ings of the heart.

16 Why did you sit down between the two saddle bags,
To listen to the pipings for the flocks?
For the divisions of Reu'ben there were great searchings of the heart.

17 Gil'e·ad kept to his residence on the other side of the Jordan;
And Dan, why did he con-tinue to dwell for the time in ships?
Ash'er sat idle at the seashore,
And by his landing places he kept residing.

18 Zeb'u·lun was a people that scorned their souls to the point of death;
Naph'ta·li also, on the heights of the field.

19 Kings came, they fought;
It was then that the kings of Ca'naan fought

In Ta'a·nach by the waters of Me·gid'do,
No gain of silver did they take.

20 From heaven did the stars fight,
From their orbits they fought against Sis'e·ra.

21 The torrent of Ki'shon washed them away,
The torrent of ancient days, the torrent of Ki'shon.
You went treading down strength, O my soul.

22 It was then that the hoofs of horses pawed
Because of dashings upon dashings of his stallions.

23 'Curse Me'roz,' said the angel of Jehovah,
'Curse its inhabitants inces-santly,
For they did not come to the assistance of Jehovah,
To the assistance of Jehovah with the mighty ones.'

24 Ja'el the wife of He'ber the Ken'ite will be most blessed among women,
Among women in the tent she will be most blessed.

25 Water he asked, milk she gave;
In the large banquet bowl of majestic ones she presented curdled milk.

26 Her hand to the tent pin she then thrust out,
And her right hand to the mallet of hard workers.
And she hammered Sis'e·ra, she pierced his head through,
And she broke apart and cut up his temples.

27 Between her feet he collapsed, he fell, he lay down;
Between her feet he collapsed, he fell;
Where he collapsed, there he fell overcome.

28 From the window a woman looked out and kept watch-ing for him,
The mother of Sis'e·ra from the lattice,
'Why has his war chariot delayed in coming?
Why must the hoofbeats of his chariots be so late?'

29 The wise ones of her noble ladies would answer her,

Yes, she too would talk back to herself with her own sayings,

30 'Ought they not to find, ought they not to distribute spoil,
A womb—two wombs to every able-bodied man,
Spoil of dyed stuffs for Sis'e·ra, spoil of dyed stuffs,
An embroidered garment, dyed stuff, two embroidered garments
For the necks of [men of] spoil?'

31 Thus let all your enemies perish, O Jehovah,
And let your lovers be as when the sun goes forth in its mightiness."

And the land had no further disturbance for forty years.

6 Then the sons of Israel began to do what was bad in the eyes of Jehovah. So Jehovah gave them into the hand of Mid'i·an for seven years. 2 And the hand of Mid'i·an came to prevail over Israel. Due to Mid'i·an the sons of Israel made for themselves the underground store places that were in the mountains, and the caves and the places difficult to approach. 3 And it occurred that, if Israel sowed seed, Mid'i·an and Am'a·lek and the Easterners came up, yes, they came up against them. 4 And they would camp against them and would ruin the yield of the earth all the way to Ga'za, and they would not let any sustenance or sheep or bull or ass remain in Israel. 5 For they and their livestock would come up with their tents. They would come as numerous as the locusts, and they and their camels were without number; and they would come into the land to ruin it. 6 And Israel became greatly impoverished due to Mid'i·an; and the sons of Israel began to call to Jehovah for aid.

7 And it came about that because the sons of Israel called to Jehovah for aid on account of Mid'i·an, 8 Jehovah proceeded to send a man, a prophet, to the sons of Israel and to say to them: "This is what Jehovah the God of Israel has said, 'It was I who brought YOU up from Egypt and thus brought YOU out of the house of slaves. 9 So I delivered YOU out of the hand of Egypt and out of the hand of all YOUR oppressors, and drove them out from before YOU and gave YOU their land. 10 Furthermore, I said to YOU: "I am Jehovah YOUR God. YOU must not fear the gods of the Am'or·ites in whose land YOU are dwelling." And YOU did not listen to my voice.'"

11 Later Jehovah's angel came and sat under the big tree that was in Oph'rah, which belonged to Jo'ash the A'bi·ez'rite, while Gid'e·on his son was beating out wheat in the wine press so as to get it quickly out of the sight of Mid'i·an. 12 Then Jehovah's angel appeared to him and said to him: "Jehovah is with you, you valiant, mighty one." 13 At this Gid'e·on said to him: "Excuse me, my lord, but if Jehovah is with us, then why has all this come upon us, and where are all his wonderful acts that our fathers related to us, saying, 'Was it not out of Egypt that Jehovah brought us up?' And now Jehovah has deserted us, and he gives us into the palm of Mid'i·an." 14 Upon that Jehovah faced him and said: "Go in this power of yours, and you will certainly save Israel out of Mid'i·an's palm. Do I not send you?" 15 In turn he said to him: "Excuse me, Jehovah. With what shall I save Israel? Look! My thousand is the least in Ma·nas'seh, and I am the smallest in my father's house." 16 But Jehovah said to him: "Because I shall prove to be with you, and you will certainly strike down Mid'i·an as if one man."

17 At this he said to him: "If, now, I have found favor in your eyes, you must also perform a sign for me that you are the one speaking with me. 18 Do not, please, move away from here until I come to you and I have brought out my gift and set it before you." Accord-

ingly he said: "I, for my part, shall keep sitting here until you return." 19 And Gid′e·on went in and proceeded to make ready a kid of the goats and an e′phah of flour as unfermented cakes. The meat he put in the basket, and the broth he put in the cooking pot, after which he brought it out to him under the big tree and served it.

20 The angel of the [true] God now said to him: "Take the meat and the unfermented cakes and set them on the big rock there, and pour out the broth." At that he did so. 21 Then Jehovah's angel thrust out the tip of the staff that was in his hand and touched the meat and the unfermented cakes, and fire began to ascend out of the rock and to consume the meat and the unfermented cakes. As for Jehovah's angel, he vanished from his sight. 22 Consequently Gid′e·on realized that it was Jehovah's angel.

At once Gid′e·on said: "Alas, Lord Jehovah, for the reason that I have seen Jehovah's angel face to face!" 23 But Jehovah said to him: "Peace be yours. Do not fear. You will not die." 24 So Gid′e·on built an altar there to Jehovah, and it continues to be called Jehovah-sha′lom down to this day. It is yet in Oph′rah of the A′bi-ez′rites.

25 And it came about during that night that Jehovah went on to say to him: "Take the young bull, the bull that belongs to your father, that is, the second young bull of seven years, and you must tear down the altar of Ba′al that is your father's, and the sacred pole that is by it you should cut down. 26 And you must build an altar to Jehovah your God at the head of this stronghold, with the row of stones, and you must take the second young bull and offer it up as a burnt offering on the pieces of wood of the sacred pole that you will cut down." 27 Accordingly Gid′e·on took ten men of his servants and went doing just as Jehovah had spoken to him; but it

came about that, as he feared the household of his father and the men of the city too much to do it by day, he went doing it by night.

28 When the men of the city got up early in the morning as usual, why, look! the altar of Ba′al had been pulled down and the sacred pole that was beside it had been cut down, and the second young bull had been offered up on the altar that had been built. 29 And they began to say one to another: "Who has done this thing?" And they went inquiring and seeking. Finally they said: "Gid′e·on the son of Jo′ash is the one that has done this thing." 30 So the men of the city said to Jo′ash: "Bring your son out that he may die, because he has pulled down the altar of Ba′al, and because he has cut down the sacred pole that was by it." 31 At this Jo′ash said to all those who stood against him: "Will you be the ones to make a legal defense for Ba′al to see whether you yourselves may save him? Whoever makes a legal defense for him ought to be put to death even this morning. If he is God, let him make a legal defense for himself, because someone has pulled down his altar." 32 And he began to call him Jer·ub·ba′al on that day, saying: "Let Ba′al make a legal defense in his own behalf, because someone has pulled down his altar."

33 And all Mid′i·an and Am′a·lek and the Easterners gathered together as one and proceeded to cross over and camp in the low plain of Jez′re·el. 34 And Jehovah's spirit enveloped Gid′e·on so that he went blowing the horn, and the A′bi-ez′rites got to be called together after him. 35 And he sent out messengers through all of Ma·nas′seh, and they too got to be called together after him. He also sent out messengers through Ash′er and Zeb′u·lun and Naph′ta·li, and they came on up to meet him.

36 Then Gid′e·on said to the [true] God: "If you are saving Israel by means of me, just as you

have promised, 37 here I am keeping a fleece of wool exposed on the threshing floor. If dew comes to be on the fleece alone but on all the earth there is dryness, then I must know that you will save Israel by means of me, just as you have promised." 38 And it turned out to be that way. When he rose up early the next day and wrung the fleece, he got to drain off enough dew from the fleece to fill a large banquet bowl with water. 39 However, Gid'e·on said to the [true] God: "Do not let your anger blaze against me, but let me speak just once more. Let me, please, make a test only once more with the fleece. Let, please, dryness occur to the fleece alone, and upon all the earth let there come to be dew." 40 So God did that way on that night; and dryness came to be on the fleece alone, and upon all the earth dew occurred.

7 Then Jer·ub·ba'al, that is to say, Gid'e·on, and all the people who were with him, rose early and took up camping at the well of Ha'rod; and the camp of Mid'i·an happened to be on the north of him, at the hill of Mo'reh, in the low plain. 2 Jehovah now said to Gid'e·on: "The people who are with you are too many for me to give Mid'i·an into their hand. Perhaps Israel would brag about itself against me, saying, 'My hand it was that saved me.' 3 And now call out, please, in the hearing of the people, saying, 'Who is there afraid and trembling? Let him retire.'" So Gid'e·on put them to the proof. With that, twenty-two thousand of the people retired, and there were ten thousand that remained.

4 Still Jehovah said to Gid'e·on: "There are yet too many people. Have them go down to the water that I may put them to the proof for you there. And it must occur that of whomever I say to you, 'This one will go with you,' he is one that will go with you, but every one of whom I say to you, 'This one will not go along with you,' he

is one that will not go along." 5 So he had the people go down to the water.

Then Jehovah said to Gid'e·on: "Every one that laps up some of the water with his tongue just as a dog laps, you will set him by himself, also every one that bends down upon his knees to drink." 6 And the number of those lapping with their hand to their mouth turned out to be three hundred men. As for all the rest of the people, they bent down upon their knees to drink water.

7 Jehovah now said to Gid'e·on: "By the three hundred men who did the lapping I shall save you people, and I will give Mid'i·an into your hand. As for all the other people, let them go each one to his place." 8 So they took the provisions of the people in their hand, and their horns, and all the men of Israel he sent away each one to his home; and he kept hold of the three hundred men. As for the camp of Mid'i·an, it happened to be down below him in the low plain.

9 And it came about during that night that Jehovah proceeded to say to him: "Rise up, descend upon the camp, for I have given it into your hand. 10 But if you are afraid to descend, descend, you with Pu'rah your attendant, to the camp. 11 And you must listen to what they will speak, and afterward your hands will certainly grow strong, and you will be certain to descend upon the camp." At that he and Pu'rah his attendant made their descent to the edge of those in battle formation who were in the camp.

12 Now Mid'i·an and Am'a·lek and all the Easterners were plumped in the low plain as numerous as locusts; and their camels were without number, as numerous as the grains of sand that are on the seashore. 13 Gid'e·on now came, and, look! there was a man relating a dream to his companion, and he went on to say: "Here is a dream that I have dreamed. And, look!

there was a round cake of barley bread turning over and over into the camp of Mid′i·an. Then it came to a tent and struck it so that it fell, and it went turning it upside down, and the tent fell flat." 14 At this his companion answered and said: "This is nothing else but the sword of Gid′e·on the son of Jo′ash, a man of Israel. The [true] God has given Mid′i·an and all the camp into his hand."

15 And it came about that as soon as Gid′e·on heard the relating of the dream and its explanation, he began to worship. After that he returned to the camp of Israel and said: "Get up, for Jehovah has given the camp of Mid′i·an into YOUR hand." 16 Then he divided the three hundred men up into three bands and put horns in the hands of all of them and large empty jars, and torches inside the large jars. 17 And he went on to say to them: "YOU should learn from watching me, and that is how YOU should do. And when I am come to the edge of the camp, it must also occur that just as I shall do, so YOU will do. 18 When I have blown the horn, I and all who are with me, YOU also must blow the horns, YOU too, round about all the camp, and YOU must say, 'Jehovah's and Gid′e·on's!'"

19 In time Gid′e·on came with the hundred men who were with him to the edge of the camp at the start of the middle night watch. They had just got through posting the sentries. And they proceeded to blow the horns, and there was a dashing to pieces of the large water jars that were in their hands. 20 At that the three bands blew the horns and shattered the large jars and took fresh hold on the torches with their left hand and with their right hand on the horns to blow them, and they began calling out: "Jehovah's sword and Gid′e·on's!" 21 All the while they kept standing each one in his place all around the camp, and the whole camp got on the run and broke out into shouting and went fleeing.

22 And the three hundred continued to blow the horns, and Jehovah proceeded to set the sword of each one against the other in all the camp; and the camp kept up their flight as far as Beth-shit′tah, on to Zer′e·rah, as far as the outskirts of A′bel-me·ho′lah by Tab′bath.

23 Meantime the men of Israel were called together from Naph′ta·li and Ash′er and all of Ma·nas′seh, and they went chasing after Mid′i·an. 24 And Gid′e·on sent messengers into all the mountainous region of E′phra·im, saying: "Go down to meet Mid′i·an and capture ahead of them the waters as far as Beth-bar′ah and the Jordan." So all the men of E′phra·im were called together, and they got to capture the waters as far as Beth-bar′ah and the Jordan. 25 They also got to capture the two princes of Mid′i·an, namely, O′reb and Ze′eb; and they proceeded to kill O′reb on the rock of O′reb, and they killed Ze′eb at the wine vat of Ze′eb. And they kept on pursuing Mid′i·an, and they brought the head of O′reb and that of Ze′eb to Gid′e·on in the region of the Jordan.

8 Then the men of E′phra·im said to him: "What sort of thing is this that you have done to us in not calling us when you went to fight against Mid′i·an?" And they vehemently tried to pick a quarrel with him. 2 Finally he said to them: "What now have I done in comparison with YOU? Are not the gleanings of E′phra·im better than the grape gathering of A′bi-e′zer? 3 It was into YOUR hand that God gave Mid′i·an's princes O′reb and Ze′eb, and what have I been able to do in comparison with YOU?" It was then that their spirit calmed down toward him when he spoke this word.

4 Eventually Gid′e·on came to the Jordan, crossing it, he and the three hundred men that were with him, tired but keeping up the pursuit. 5 Later he said to the men of Suc′coth: "Please give round loaves of bread to the people that

are following my steps, for they are tired and I am chasing after Ze'bah and Zal·mun'na, the kings of Mid'i·an." 6 But the princes of Suc'coth said: "Are the palms of Ze'bah and of Zal·mun'na already in your hand so that bread has to be given to your army?" 7 At this Gid'e·on said: "That is why when Jehovah gives Ze'bah and Zal·mun'na into my hand, I shall certainly give YOUR flesh a threshing with the thorns of the wilderness and the briers." 8 And he continued on his way up from there to Pe·nu'el and went speaking to them in this same manner, but the men of Pe·nu'el answered him just as the men of Suc'coth had answered. 9 Hence he said also to the men of Pe·nu'el: "When I return in peace, I shall pull down this tower."

10 Now Ze'bah and Zal·mun'na were in Kar'kor, and their camps with them, about fifteen thousand being all who were left over out of the entire camp of the Easterners; and those already fallen were a hundred and twenty thousand men who used to draw the sword. 11 And Gid'e·on continued on up by the way of those residing in tents to the east of No'bah and Jog'be·hah and began to strike the camp while the camp happened to be off guard. 12 When Ze'bah and Zal·mun'na took to flight, he at once went in pursuit of them and got to capture Mid'i·an's two kings, Ze'bah and Zal·mun'na; and he drove all the camp into trembling.

13 And Gid'e·on the son of Jo'ash began his return from the war by the pass that goes up to He'res. 14 En route he captured a young man of the men of Suc'coth and made inquiries of him. So he wrote out for him the names of the princes of Suc'coth and its older men, seventy-seven men. 15 With that he went to the men of Suc'coth and said: "Here are Ze'bah and Zal·mun'na respecting whom YOU taunted me, saying, 'Are the palms of Ze'bah and of Zal·mun'na al-

ready in your hand so that bread has to be given to your tired-out men?'" 16 Then he took the older men of the city and thorns of the wilderness and briers, and with them he put the men of Suc'coth through an experience. 17 And the tower of Pe·nu'el he pulled down, and he proceeded to kill the men of the city.

18 He now said to Ze'bah and Zal·mun'na: "What sort of men were they whom YOU killed in Ta'bor?" To this they said: "As you are, so were they, each one, like the sons of a king in form." 19 At that he said: "They were my brothers, the sons of my mother. As Jehovah lives, if YOU had preserved them alive, I would not have to kill YOU." 20 Then he said to Je'ther his first-born: "Get up, kill them." And the young man did not draw his sword, because he was afraid, for he was yet a young man. 21 So Ze'bah and Zal·mun'na said: "Get up yourself and assault us, for as a man is, so is his mightiness." Accordingly Gid'e·on got up and killed Ze'bah and Zal·mun'na and took the moon-shaped ornaments that were on the necks of their camels.

22 Later the men of Israel said to Gid'e·on: "Rule over us, you and your son and your grandson as well, for you have saved us out of the hand of Mid'i·an." 23 But Gid'e·on said to them: "I myself shall not rule over YOU, nor will my son rule over YOU. Jehovah is the one who will rule over YOU." 24 And Gid'e·on went on to say to them: "Let me make a request of YOU: Give me, each one of YOU, the nose ring of his booty." (For they had nose rings of gold, because they were Ish'ma·el·ites.) 25 Then they said: "We shall surely give them." With that they spread out a mantle and went throwing each one the nose ring of his spoil into it. 26 And the weight of the nose rings of gold that he had requested amounted to one thousand seven hundred gold shekels, besides the moon-

shaped ornaments and the ear-drops and the garments of wool dyed reddish purple that were upon the kings of Mid'i·an and besides the necklaces that were on the necks of the camels.

27 And Gid'e·on proceeded to make it into an eph'od and to exhibit it in his city Oph'rah; and all Israel began to have immoral intercourse with it there, so that it served as a snare to Gid'e·on and to his household.

28 Thus Mid'i·an was subdued before the sons of Israel, and they did not lift up their head any more; and the land had no further disturbance for forty years in the days of Gid'e·on.

29 And Jer·ub·ba'al the son of Jo'ash went his way and continued to dwell in his house.

30 And Gid'e·on came to have seventy sons that issued out of his upper thigh, for he came to have many wives. 31 As for the concubine of his that was in She'-chem, she too bore him a son. So he named him A·bim'e·lech. 32 Eventually Gid'e·on the son of Jo'ash died at a good old age and was buried in the burial place of Jo'ash his father in Oph'rah of the A'bi·ez'rites.

33 And it came about that as soon as Gid'e·on had died the sons of Israel again took up having immoral intercourse with the Ba'als, so that they appointed Ba'al-be'-rith as their god. 34 And the sons of Israel did not remember Jehovah their God, who had delivered them out of the hand of all their enemies round about; 35 and they did not exercise loving-kindness toward the household of Jer·ub·ba'al, Gid'e·on, in return for all the goodness that he had exercised toward Israel.

9 In time A·bim'e·lech the son of Jer·ub·ba'al went to She'chem to the brothers of his mother and began speaking to them and to all the family of the house of his mother's father, saying: 2 "Speak, please, in the hearing of all the landowners of She'chem, 'Which is better for you, for seventy men,

all the sons of Jer·ub·ba'al, to rule over you or for one man to rule over you? And you must remember that your bone and your flesh I am.' "

3 So the brothers of his mother began speaking all these words about him in the hearing of all the landowners of She'chem so that their heart inclined toward A·bim'-e·lech, for they said: "He is our own brother." 4 Then they gave him seventy pieces of silver from the house of Ba'al-be'rith, and with them A·bim'e·lech proceeded to hire idle and insolent men, that they might accompany him. 5 After that he went to the house of his father at Oph'rah and killed his brothers, the sons of Jer·ub·ba'al, seventy men, upon one stone, but Jo'tham the youngest son of Jer·ub·ba'al was left over, because he had hid.

6 Subsequently all the landowners of She'chem and all the house of Mil'lo gathered together and went and made A·bim'e·lech reign as king, close by the big tree, the pillar that was in She'chem.

7 When they reported it to Jo'-tham he at once went and stood on the top of Mount Ger'i·zim and raised his voice and called out and said to them: "Listen to me, you landowners of She'chem, and let God listen to you:

8 "Once upon a time the trees went to anoint a king over them. So they said to the olive tree, 'Do be king over us.' 9 But the olive tree said to them, 'Must I give up my fatness with which they glorify God and men, and must I go to wave over the other trees?' 10 Then the trees said to the fig tree, 'You come, be queen over us.' 11 But the fig tree said to them, 'Must I give up my sweetness and my good produce, and must I go to wave over the other trees?' 12 Next the trees said to the vine, 'You come, be queen over us.' 13 In turn the vine said to them, 'Must I give up my new wine that makes God and men rejoice, and must I go to wave over the trees?' 14 Finally

all the other trees said to the bramble, 'You come, be king over us.' 15 At this the bramble said to the trees, 'If it is in truth that YOU are anointing me as king over YOU, come, seek refuge under my shadow. But if not, let fire come out of the bramble and consume the cedars of Leb'a·non.'

16 "And now if it is in truth and in faultlessness that YOU have acted and that YOU went making A·bim'-e·lech king, and if it is goodness that YOU have exercised toward Jer·ub·ba'al and his household, and if YOU have done to him as the doing of his hands deserved, 17 when my father fought for YOU and went risking his soul that he might deliver YOU out of Mid'i·an's hand; 18 and YOU, for YOUR part, have risen up against the household of my father today that YOU might kill his sons, seventy men, upon one stone, and that YOU might make A·bim'e·lech, the son of his slave girl, king over the landowners of She'chem just because he is YOUR own brother; 19 yes, if it is in truth and in faultlessness that YOU have acted toward Jer·ub·ba'al and his household this day, rejoice over A·bim'e·lech and let him too rejoice over YOU. 20 But if not, let fire come out of A·bim'-e·lech and consume the landowners of She'chem and the house of Mil'lo, and let fire come out of the landowners of She'chem and the house of Mil'lo and consume A·bim'e·lech."

21 Then Jo'tham took to flight and went running off and made his way to Be'er, and he took up dwelling there because of A·bim'-e·lech his brother.

22 And A·bim'e·lech kept playing the prince over Israel three years. 23 Then God let develop a bad spirit between A·bim'e·lech and the landowners of She'chem, and the landowners of She'chem proceeded to deal treacherously with A·bim'e·lech, 24 that the violence done to the seventy sons of Jer·ub·ba'al might come and that he might put their blood upon A·bim'e·lech their brother because he killed them, and upon the landowners of She'chem because they strengthened his hands to kill his brothers. 25 So the landowners of She'chem set ambush men for him upon the tops of the mountains, and they would rob everyone that would pass by them on the road. In time it was reported to A·bim'e·lech.

26 Then Ga'al the son of E'bed and his brothers came and crossed over into She'chem, and the landowners of She'chem began to trust in him. 27 And they went out as usual into the field and engaged in gathering the grapes of their vineyards and in treading them and in carrying on a festal exultation, after which they went into the house of their god and ate and drank and called down evil upon A·bim'e·lech. 28 And Ga'al the son of E'bed went on to say: "Who is A·bim'e·lech, and who is She'-chem that we should serve him? Is he not the son of Jer·ub·ba'al, and is not Ze'bul a commissioner of his? Serve the men of Ha'mor, She'chem's father, YOU others, but why should we ourselves serve him? 29 And if only this people were in my hand! Then I would remove A·bim'e·lech." And he went on to say to A·bim'e·lech: "Make your army numerous and come on out."

30 And Ze'bul the prince of the city got to hear the words of Ga'al the son of E'bed. Then his anger blazed. 31 So he sent messengers by subterfuge to A·bim'e·lech, saying: "Look! Ga'al the son of E'bed and his brothers are now come to She'chem, and here they are massing the city against you. 32 And now rise up by night, you and the people that are with you, and lie in wait in the field. 33 And it must occur in the morning that as soon as the sun shines forth you should get up early, and you must make a dash against the city; and when he and the people that are with him are going out against you, you must also do to him just as your hand finds it possible."

34 Accordingly A·bim'e·lech and

all the people that were with him rose up by night, and they began to lie in wait against She'chem in four bands. 35 Later Ga'al the son of E'bed went out and stood at the entrance of the city gate. Then A·bim'e·lech and the people that were with him rose up from the place of ambush. 36 When Ga'al caught sight of the people, he at once said to Ze'bul: "Look! People coming down from the tops of the mountains." But Ze'bul said to him: "The shadows of the mountains are what you are seeing as though they were men."

37 Later Ga'al spoke once more and said: "Look! People coming down out of the center of the land, and one band is coming by the way of the big tree of Me·on'e·nim." 38 At this Ze'bul said to him: "Where now is that saying of yours that you mouthed, 'Who is A·bim'-e·lech that we should serve him?' Is not this the people whom you rejected? Go out now, please, and fight against them."

39 So Ga'al went on out at the head of the landowners of She'-chem and took up the fight against A·bim'e·lech. 40 And A·bim'e·lech set out after him, and he went fleeing before him; and the slain kept falling in numbers as far as the entrance of the gate.

41 And A·bim'e·lech continued to dwell in A·ru'mah, and Ze'bul proceeded to drive Ga'al and his brothers out from dwelling in She'-chem. 42 And it came about on the next day that the people began to go out into the field. So they told A·bim'e·lech. 43 Hence he took the people and divided them up into three bands and began to lie in wait in the field. Then he looked, and there the people were going out of the city. He now rose up against them and struck them down. 44 And A·bim'e·lech and the bands that were with him made a dash that they might stand at the entrance of the city gate, while two bands made a dash against all who were in the field, and they went striking them down. 45 And

A·bim'e·lech fought against the city all that day and got to capture the city; and he killed the people that were in it, after which he pulled the city down and sowed it with salt.

46 When all the landowners of the tower of She'chem heard of it, they immediately went to the vault of the house of El-be'rith. 47 Then it was reported to A·bim'e·lech that all the landowners of the tower of She'chem had collected together. 48 At that A·bim'e·lech went up Mount Zal'mon, he and all the people that were with him. A·bim'e·lech now took an ax in his hand and cut down a branch of the trees and lifted it up and put it on his shoulder and said to the people that were with him: "What you have seen me do—hurry up, do like me!" 49 So all the people cut down also each one a branch for himself and went following A·bim'e·lech. Then they put them against the vault, and over them they set the vault on fire, so that all the men of the tower of She'-chem died too, about a thousand men and women.

50 And A·bim'e·lech proceeded to go to The'bez and to camp against The'bez and capture it. 51 As a strong tower happened to be in the middle of the city, there was where all the men and women and all the landowners of the city went fleeing, after which they shut it behind them and climbed onto the roof of the tower. 52 And A·bim'e·lech made his way to the tower and began fighting against it, and he went on up close to the entrance of the tower to burn it with fire. 53 Then a certain woman pitched an upper millstone upon A·bim'e·lech's head and broke his skull in pieces. 54 So he quickly called the attendant bearing his weapons and said to him: "Draw your sword and put me to death, for fear they should say about me, 'It was a woman that killed him.'" Immediately his attendant ran him through, so that he died.

55 When the men of Israel got to see that A·bim′e·lech had died, they now went each one to his place. 56 Thus God made the evil of A·bim′e·lech that he had done to his father by killing his seventy brothers come back. 57 And all the evil of the men of She′chem God made come back upon their own heads, that the malediction of Jo′tham the son of Jer·ub·ba′al might come upon them.

10 Now after A·bim′e·lech there rose up to save Israel To′la the son of Pu′ah, the son of Do′do, a man of Is′sa·char, and he was dwelling in Sha′mir in the mountainous region of E′phra·im. 2 And he continued to judge Israel for twenty-three years, after which he died and was buried in Sha′mir.

3 Then after him Ja′ir the Gil′e·ad·ite rose up, and he continued to judge Israel for twenty-two years. 4 And he came to have thirty sons who rode on thirty full-grown asses, and they had thirty cities. These they continue to call Hav′voth-ja′ir down to this day; they are in the land of Gil′e·ad. 5 After that Ja′ir died and was buried in Ka′mon.

6 And the sons of Israel again proceeded to do what was bad in the eyes of Jehovah, and they began to serve the Ba′als and the Ash′to·reth images and the gods of Syria and the gods of Si′don and the gods of Mo′ab and the gods of the sons of Am′mon and the gods of the Phi·lis′tines. So they left Jehovah and did not serve him. 7 At this Jehovah′s anger blazed against Israel, so that he sold them into the hand of the Phi·lis′tines and into the hand of the sons of Am′mon. 8 Hence they shattered and heavily oppressed the sons of Israel in that year—for eighteen years all the sons of Israel that were on the side of the Jordan in the land of the Am′or·ites that was in Gil′e·ad. 9 And the sons of Am′mon would cross the Jordan to fight even against Judah and Benjamin and the house of E′phra·im; and Israel was greatly distressed.

10 And the sons of Israel began to call to Jehovah for aid, saying: "We have sinned against you, because we have left our God and we serve the Ba′als."

11 Then Jehovah said to the sons of Israel: "Was it not from Egypt and from the Am′or·ites and from the sons of Am′mon and from the Phi·lis′tines 12 and the Si·do′ni·ans and Am′a·lek and Mid′i·an, when they oppressed you and you went crying out to me, that I proceeded to save you out of their hand? 13 As for you, you abandoned me and took up serving other gods. That is why I shall not save you again. 14 Go and call for aid to the gods whom you have chosen. Let them be the ones to save you in the time of your distress." 15 But the sons of Israel said to Jehovah: "We have sinned. You yourself do to us according to anything that is good in your eyes. Only deliver us, please, this day." 16 And they began to remove the foreign gods from their midst and to serve Jehovah, so that his soul became impatient because of the trouble of Israel.

17 In time the sons of Am′mon were called together and pitched camp in Gil′e·ad. So the sons of Israel gathered themselves together and pitched camp in Miz′pah. 18 And the people and the princes of Gil′e·ad began to say to one another: "Who is the man that will take the lead in fighting against the sons of Am′mon? Let him become the head of all the inhabitants of Gil′e·ad."

11 Now Jeph′thah the Gil′e·ad·ite had become a mighty, valiant man, and he was the son of a prostitute woman, and Gil′e·ad came to be the father of Jeph′thah. 2 And Gil′e·ad′s wife kept bearing sons to him. When the sons of the wife got big, they proceeded to drive Jeph′thah out and to say to him: "You must have no inheritance in the household of our father, for you are the son of another woman." 3 So Jeph′thah ran away because of his brothers and took up dwell-

ing in the land of Tob. And idle men kept bringing themselves together to Jeph'thah, and they would go out with him.

4 And it came about after a while that the sons of Am'mon began to fight against Israel. 5 And it came about that when the sons of Am'mon did fight against Israel, the older men of Gil'e·ad immediately went to take Jeph'thah out of the land of Tob. 6 Then they said to Jeph'thah: "Do come and serve as our commander, and let us fight against the sons of Am'mon." 7 But Jeph'thah said to the older men of Gil'e·ad: "Was it not YOU that hated me so that YOU drove me out of my father's house? And why is it that YOU have come to me now just when YOU are in distress?" 8 At this the older men of Gil'e·ad said to Jeph'thah: "That is why now we have returned to you, and you must go with us and fight against the sons of Am'mon, and you must become for us the head of all the inhabitants of Gil'e·ad." 9 So Jeph'thah said to the older men of Gil'e·ad: "If YOU are bringing me back to fight against the sons of Am'mon, and Jehovah does abandon them to me, I, for my part, shall become YOUR head!" 10 In turn the older men of Gil'e·ad said to Jeph'thah: "Let Jehovah prove to be the listener between us if the way we shall do is not according to your word." 11 Consequently Jeph'thah went with the older men of Gil'e·ad and the people set him over them as head and commander. And Jeph'thah proceeded to speak all his words before Jehovah in Miz'pah.

12 Then Jeph'thah sent messengers to the king of the sons of Am'mon, saying: "What do I have to do with you, seeing that you have come against me to fight in my land?" 13 So the king of the sons of Am'mon said to the messengers of Jeph'thah: "It is because Israel took my land when they came up out of Egypt, from the Ar'non as far as the Jab'bok

and as far as the Jordan. And now do return it peacefully." 14 But Jeph'thah sent once more messengers to the king of the sons of Am'mon 15 and said to him:

"This is what Jeph'thah has said, 'Israel did not take the land of Mo'ab and the land of the sons of Am'mon. 16 For when they came up out of Egypt Israel went walking through the wilderness as far as the Red Sea and got to come to Ka'desh. 17 Then Israel sent messengers to the king of E'dom, saying: "Let me pass, please, through your land," and the king of E'dom did not listen. And also to the king of Mo'ab they sent, and he did not consent. And Israel kept dwelling in Ka'desh. 18 When they walked on through the wilderness, they went their way around the land of E'dom and the land of Mo'ab, so that they went toward the rising of the sun as respects the land of Mo'ab and took up camping in the region of the Ar'non; and they did not come within the boundary of Mo'ab, because Ar'non was the boundary of Moab.

19 "'After that Israel sent messengers to Si'hon the king of the Am'or·ites, the king of Hesh'bon, and Israel said to him: "Let us pass, please, through your land to my own place." 20 And Si'hon did not feel sure about Israel's crossing through his territory, and Si'hon went gathering all his people together and camping in Ja'haz and fighting against Israel. 21 At this Jehovah the God of Israel gave Si'hon and all his people into Israel's hand, so that they struck them and Israel took possession of all the land of the Am'or·ites inhabiting that land. 22 Thus they took possession of all the territory of the Am'or·ites from the Ar'non as far as the Jab'bok and from the wilderness as far as the Jordan.

23 "'And now Jehovah the God of Israel it was that dispossessed the Am'or·ites from before his people Israel, and you, for your part, would dispossess them. 24 Is it not whomever Che'mosh your god

causes you to dispossess that you will dispossess? And every one whom Jehovah our God has dispossessed from before us is the one we shall dispossess. 25 And now are you any better than Ba'lak the son of Zip'por, the king of Mo'ab? Did he ever contend with Israel, or did he ever fight against them? 26 While Israel was dwelling in Hesh'bon and its dependent towns and in A·ro'er and its dependent towns and in all the cities that are by the banks of Ar'non for three hundred years, why, then, did you never snatch them away during that time? 27 As for me, I have not sinned against you, but you are dealing wrong with me by fighting against me. Let Jehovah the Judge judge today between the sons of Israel and the sons of Am'mon.'"

28 And the king of the sons of Am'mon did not listen to the words of Jeph'thah that he had sent to him.

29 Jehovah's spirit now came upon Jeph'thah, and he proceeded to pass through Gil'e·ad and Ma·nas'seh and to pass through Miz'peh of Gil'e·ad, and from Miz'peh of Gil'e·ad he passed along to the sons of Am'mon.

30 Then Jeph'thah made a vow to Jehovah and said: "If you without fail give the sons of Am'mon into my hand, 31 it must also occur that the one coming out, who comes out of the doors of my house to meet me when I return in peace from the sons of Am'mon, must also become Jehovah's, and I must offer that one up as a burnt offering."

32 So Jeph'thah passed along to the sons of Am'mon to fight against them, and Jehovah proceeded to give them into his hand. 33 And he went striking them from A·ro'er all the way to Min'nith—twenty cities—and as far as A'bel-ker'a·mim with a very great slaughter. Thus the sons of Am'mon were subdued before the sons of Israel.

34 Finally Jeph'thah came to Miz'pah to his home, and, look!

his daughter coming out to meet him with tambourine playing and dancing! Now she was absolutely the only child. Besides her he had neither son nor daughter. 35 And it came about that when he caught sight of her, he began to rip his garments and to say: "Alas, my daughter! You have indeed made me bend down, and you yourself have become the one I was ostracizing. And I—I have opened my mouth to Jehovah, and I am unable to turn back."

36 But she said to him: "My father, if you have opened your mouth to Jehovah, do to me according to what has gone forth from your mouth, since Jehovah has executed acts of vengeance for you upon your enemies, the sons of Am'mon." 37 And she went on to say to her father: "Let this thing be done to me: Let me alone for two months, and let me go, and I will descend upon the mountains, and let me weep over my virginity, I and my girl companions."

38 At this he said: "Go!" So he sent her away for two months; and she kept going, she with her girl companions, and weeping over her virginity upon the mountains. 39 And it came about at the end of two months that she made her return to her father, after which he carried out his vow that he had made toward her. As for her, she never had relations with a man. And it came to be a regulation in Israel: 40 From year to year the daughters of Israel would go to give commendation to the daughter of Jeph'thah the Gil'e·ad·ite, four days in the year.

12 Then the men of E'phra·im were called together and crossed over northward and said to Jeph'thah: "Why is it that you crossed over to fight against the sons of Am'mon, and to us you did not issue a call to go with you? Your very house we shall burn over you with fire." 2 But Jeph'thah said to them: "I became a special contender, I and my people, with the sons of Am'mon. And I proceeded to call to YOU for aid, and YOU did not save me out of their hand. 3 When I got to see that YOU were no savior, then I determined to put my soul in my own palm and go over against the sons of Am'mon. At that Jehovah gave them into my hand. So why have YOU come up against me this day to fight against me?"

4 Immediately Jeph'thah collected all the men of Gil'e·ad together and fought E'phra·im; and the men of Gil'e·ad went striking E'phra·im down, for they had said: "Men escaped from E'phra·im is what YOU are, O Gil'e·ad, inside of E'phra·im, inside of Ma·nas'seh." 5 And Gil'e·ad got to capture the fords of the Jordan ahead of E'phra·im; and it occurred that when the escaping men of E'phra·im would say: "Let me pass over," then the men of Gil'e·ad would say to each one: "Are you an E'phra·im·ite?" When he would say: "No!" 6 then they would say to him: "Please say Shib'bo·leth," And he would say: "Sib'bo·leth," as he was unable to say the word correctly. And they would lay hold of him and slay him at the fords of the Jordan. So there fell at that time forty-two thousand out of E'phra·im.

7 And Jeph'thah continued to judge Israel for six years, after which Jeph'thah the Gil'e·ad·ite died and was buried in his city in Gil'e·ad.

8 And Ib'zan from Beth'le·hem began to judge Israel after him. 9 And he came to have thirty sons and thirty daughters. He sent outside and brought in thirty daughters for his sons from outside. And he continued to judge Israel for seven years. 10 Then Ib'zan died and was buried in Beth'le·hem.

11 And after him E'lon the Zeb'u·lun·ite began to judge Israel. And he continued to judge Israel ten years. 12 Then E'lon the Zeb'u·lun·ite died and was buried in Ai'ja·lon in the land of Zeb'u·lun.

13 And after him Ab'don the son of Hil'lel the Pir'a·thon·ite began to judge Israel. 14 And he came to have forty sons and thirty grandsons who rode on seventy full-grown asses. And he continued to judge Israel eight years. 15 Then Ab'don the son of Hil'lel the Pir'a·thon·ite died and was buried in Pir'a·thon in the land of E'phra·im in the mountain of the A·mal'ek·ite.

13 And the sons of Israel engaged again in doing what was bad in Jehovah's eyes, so that Jehovah gave them into the hand of the Phi·lis'tines for forty years.

2 Meanwhile there happened to be a certain man of Zo'rah of the family of the Dan'ites, and his name was Ma·no'ah. And his wife was barren and had borne no child. 3 In time Jehovah's angel appeared to the woman and said to her: "Look, now, you are barren and have borne no child. And you will certainly become pregnant and give birth to a son. 4 And now watch yourself, please, and do not drink wine or intoxicating liquor, and do not eat anything unclean. 5 For, look! you will be pregnant, and you will certainly give birth to a son, and no razor should come upon his head, because a Naz'i·rite of God is what the child will become on leaving the belly; and he it is who will take the lead in saving Israel out of the hand of the Phi·lis'tines."

6 Then the woman went and said to her husband: "There was a man of the [true] God that came to me, and his appearance was like the appearance of the angel of the [true] God, very fear-inspiring. And I did not ask him from just where he was, neither did he tell me his name. 7 But he said to me, 'Look! You will be pregnant, and you will certainly give birth to a son. And now do not drink wine or intoxicating liquor, and do not eat any unclean thing, because a Naz'i·rite of God is what the child will become on leaving the belly until the day of his death.'"

8 And Ma·no'ah began to entreat

Jehovah and say: "Excuse me, Jehovah. The man of the [true] God that you just sent, let him, please, come again to us and instruct us as to what we ought to do to the child that will be born." 9 Accordingly the [true] God listened to the voice of Ma·no'ah, and the angel of the [true] God came again to the woman while she was sitting in the field, and Ma·no'ah her husband was not with her. 10 Immediately the woman hurried and ran and told her husband and said to him: "Look! The man that came the other day to me has appeared to me."

11 At that Ma·no'ah got up and accompanied his wife and came to the man and said to him: "Are you the man that spoke to the woman?" to which he said: "I am." 12 Then Ma·no'ah said: "Now let your words come true. What will become the child's mode of life and his work?" 13 So Jehovah's angel said to Ma·no'ah: "From everything that I mentioned to the woman she should keep herself. 14 Nothing at all that comes forth from the wine vine should she eat, and no wine or intoxicating liquor let her drink, and no unclean thing of any sort let her eat. Everything that I have commanded her let her keep."

15 Ma·no'ah now said to Jehovah's angel: "Let us, please, detain you and fix up a kid of the goats before you." 16 But Jehovah's angel said to Ma·no'ah: "If you detain me, I shall not feed myself on your bread; but if you will render up a burnt offering to Jehovah, you may offer it up." For Ma·no'ah did not know that he was Jehovah's angel. 17 Then Ma·no'ah said to Jehovah's angel: "What is your name, that when your word comes true we shall certainly do you honor?" 18 However, Jehovah's angel said to him: "Just why should you ask about my name, when it is a wonderful one?"

19 And Ma·no'ah proceeded to take the kid of the goats and the grain offering and to offer it upon the rock to Jehovah. And He was doing something in a wonderful way while Ma·no'ah and his wife were looking on. 20 So it came about that, as the flame ascended from off the altar heavenward, then Jehovah's angel ascended in the flame of the altar while Ma·no'ah and his wife were looking on. At once they fell upon their faces to the earth. 21 And Jehovah's angel did not repeat appearing to Ma·no'ah and his wife any more. Then it was that Ma·no'ah knew that he had been Jehovah's angel. 22 Consequently Ma·no'ah said to his wife: "We shall positively die, because it is God that we have seen." 23 But his wife said to him: "If Jehovah had been delighted only to put us to death, he would not have accepted a burnt offering and grain offering from our hand, and he would not have shown us all these things, and he would not as now have let us hear anything like this."

24 Later the woman gave birth to a son and called his name Samson; and the boy kept getting bigger, and Jehovah continued to bless him. 25 In time Jehovah's spirit started to impel him in Ma'ha·neh-dan between Zo'rah and Esh'ta·ol.

14 Then Samson went down to Tim'nah and saw a woman in Tim'nah of the daughters of the Phi·lis'tines. 2 So he went up and told his father and his mother and said: "There is a woman that I have seen in Tim'nah of the daughters of the Phi·lis'tines, and now get her for me as a wife." 3 But his father and his mother said to him: "Is there not among the daughters of your brothers and among all my people a woman, so that you are going to take a wife from the uncircumcised Phi·lis'tines?" Still Samson said to his father: "Get just her for me, because she is the one just right in my eyes." 4 As for his father and his mother, they did not know that that was from Jehovah, that he was looking for an opportunity against the Phi·lis'tines, as at that particular time the Phi·lis'tines were ruling over Israel.

5 Accordingly Samson went on down with his father and his mother to Tim'nah. When he got as far as the vineyards of Tim'nah, why, look! a maned young lion roaring upon meeting him. 6 Then Jehovah's spirit became operative upon him, so that he tore it in two, just as someone tears a male kid in two, and there was nothing at all in his hand. And he did not tell his father or his mother what he had done. 7 And he continued on his way down and began to speak to the woman; and she was still right in Samson's eyes.

8 Now after a while he went on back to take her home. Meantime he turned aside to look at the carcass of the lion, and there there was a swarm of bees in the lion's corpse, and honey. 9 So he scraped it out into his palms and walked on, eating as he walked. When he rejoined his father and his mother, he at once gave them some, and they began to eat. And he did not tell them that it was out of the corpse of the lion that he had scraped the honey.

10 And his father continued on his way down to the woman, and Samson proceeded to hold a banquet there; for that was the way the young fellows used to do. 11 And it came about that, on their seeing him, they immediately took thirty groomsmen, that these should keep with him. 12 Then Samson said to them: "Let me, please, propound a riddle to you. If you will without fail tell it to me during the seven days of the banquet and you do solve it, I shall in that case have to give you thirty undergarments and thirty outfits of clothing. 13 But if you are unable to tell it to me, you yourselves also must give me thirty undergarments and thirty outfits of clothing." At this they said to him: "Do propound your riddle, and let us hear it." 14 So he said to them:

"Out of the eater something to eat came forth,

And out of the strong something sweet came forth."

And they proved unable to tell the riddle for three days. 15 And it came about on the fourth day that they began to say to Samson's wife: "Fool your husband that he may tell us the riddle. Otherwise we shall burn you and the house of your father with fire. Was it to take our possessions that you people invited us here?" 16 Consequently Samson's wife began to weep over him and to say: "You only hate me, you do, and you do not love me. There was a riddle that you propounded to the sons of my people, but to me you have not told it." At this he said to her: "Why, to my own father and my own mother I have not told it, and ought I to tell it to you?" 17 But she kept weeping over him the seven days that the banquet continued for them, and it came about on the seventh day that finally he told her, because she had pressured him. Then she told the riddle to the sons of her people. 18 So the men of the city said to him on the seventh day before ever he could go into the interior room:

"What is sweeter than honey,
And what is stronger than a lion?"

In turn he said to them:

"If you had not plowed with my young cow,
You would not have solved my riddle."

19 And Jehovah's spirit became operative upon him, so that he went down to Ash'ke·lon and struck down thirty men of theirs and took what he stripped off them and gave the outfits to the tellers of the riddle. And his anger continued hot, and he went his way up to his father's house.

20 And Samson's wife came to belong to a groomsman of his who had associated with him.

15 And it came about after a while, in the days of wheat harvest, that Samson went visiting his wife with a kid of the goats. So he said: "I will go in to my

wife in the interior room." And her father did not allow him to go in. 2 But her father said: "I really said to myself, 'You must unquestionably hate her.' Hence I gave her to your groomsman. Is not her younger sister better than she is? Let her, please, become yours instead of the other." 3 However, Samson said to them: "This time I must be free of guilt against the Phi·lis′tines in case I am dealing with them to their injury."

4 And Samson went his way and proceeded to catch three hundred foxes and to take torches and turn tail to tail and put one torch between two tails, right in the middle. 5 With that he set fire to the torches and sent them out into the fields of standing grain of the Phi·lis′tines. Thus he set on fire everything from sheaf to standing grain and the vineyards and the olive groves.

6 And the Phi·lis′tines began to say: "Who did this?" Then they said: "It was Samson the son-in-law of the Tim′nite, because he took his wife and then gave her to his groomsman." At that the Phi·lis′tines went up and burned her and her father with fire. 7 In turn Samson said to them: "If you do like this, there is nothing but for me to avenge myself upon you, and afterward I shall quit." 8 And he went smiting them, piling legs upon thighs with a great slaughter, after which he went down and began to dwell in a cleft of the crag E′tam.

9 Later the Phi·lis′tines came up and camped in Judah and went tramping about in Le′hi. 10 Then the men of Judah said: "Why have you come up against us?" to which they said: "It is to tie Samson that we have come up, to do to him just as he has done to us." 11 So three thousand men of Judah went down to the cleft of the crag E′tam and said to Samson: "Do you not know that the Phi·lis′tines are ruling over us? So what does this mean that you have done to us?" Then he said to them:

"Just as they did to me is the way I have done to them." 12 But they said to him: "It is to tie you that we have come down, to give you into the hand of the Phi·lis′tines." At that Samson said to them: "Swear to me that you yourselves will not assault me." 13 And they went on to say to him: "No, but we shall merely tie you, and we will give you into their hand; but we shall by no means put you to death."

Accordingly they bound him with two new ropes and brought him up out of the crag. 14 He, for his part, came as far as Le′hi, and the Phi·lis′tines, for their part, shouted exultantly at meeting him. And Jehovah's spirit became operative upon him, and the ropes that were upon his arms came to be like linen threads that have been scorched with fire, so that his fetters melted off his hands. 15 He now found a moist jawbone of a male ass and thrust his hand out and took it and went striking down a thousand men with it. 16 Then Samson said:

"With the jawbone of a male ass
  —one heap, two heaps!
With the jawbone of a male
  ass I have struck down a
  thousand men."

17 And it came about that when he finished speaking, he immediately threw the jawbone out of his hand and called that place Ra′math-le′hi. 18 Now he became very thirsty, and he began to call on Jehovah and say: "It was you that gave this great salvation into the hand of your servant, and now shall I die of thirst and must I fall into the hand of the uncircumcised?" 19 So God split open a mortar-shaped hollow that was in Le′hi, and water began to come out of it, and he proceeded to drink, after which his spirit returned and he revived. That is why he called its name En-hak·kor′e, which is in Le′hi down to this day.

20 And he continued to judge Israel in the days of the Phi·lis′tines twenty years.

16 Once Samson went to Ga′za and saw a prostitute woman there and came in to her. 2 And report was made to the Ga′zites, saying: "Samson has come in here." So they surrounded him and lay in wait for him all night long in the city gate. And they kept quiet the whole night, saying: "As soon as the morning gets light, we must also kill him."

3 However, Samson kept lying till midnight and then rose at midnight and grabbed hold of the doors of the city gate and the two side posts and pulled them out along with the bar and put them upon his shoulders and went carrying them up to the top of the mountain that is in front of He′bron.

4 And it came about after that that he fell in love with a woman in the torrent valley of So′rek, and her name was De·li′lah. 5 And the axis lords of the Phi·lis′tines proceeded to come up to her and to say to her: "Fool him and see in what his great power is and with what we can prevail over him and with what we are certain to tie him so as to master him; and we, for our part, shall give you each one thousand one hundred silver pieces."

6 Later De·li′lah said to Samson: "Do tell me, please, In what is your great power and with what can you be tied for one to master you?" 7 Then Samson said to her: "If they tie me with seven still-moist sinews that have not been dried out, I must also grow weak and become like an ordinary man." 8 So the axis lords of the Phi·lis′tines brought up to her seven still-moist sinews that had not been dried out. Later she tied him with them. 9 Now the ambush was sitting in the interior room of hers, and she began to say to him: "The Phi·lis′tines are upon you, Samson!" At that he tore the sinews in two, just as a twisted thread of tow is torn in two when it smells fire. And his power did not become known.

10 Subsequently De·li′lah said to Samson: "Look! You have trifled with me that you might speak lies to me. Now tell me, do please, with what you can be tied." 11 So he said to her: "If they tie me tight with new ropes with which no work has been done, I must also grow weak and become like an ordinary man." 12 So De·li′lah took new ropes and tied him with them and said to him: "The Phi·lis′tines are upon you, Samson!" All the while the ambush was sitting in the interior room. At that he tore them in two from off his arms like a thread.

13 After that De·li′lah said to Samson: "Up till now you have trifled with me that you might speak lies to me. Do tell me with what you can be tied." Then he said to her: "If you will weave the seven braids of my head with the warp thread." 14 Accordingly she fixed them with the pin, after which she said to him: "The Phi·lis′tines are upon you, Samson!" So he awoke from his sleep and pulled out the loom pin and the warp thread.

15 She now said to him: "How dare you say, 'I do love you,' when your heart is not with me? These three times you have trifled with me and have not told me in what your great power is." 16 And it came about that because she pressured him with her words all the time and kept urging him, his soul got to be impatient to the point of dying. 17 Finally he disclosed to her all his heart and said to her: "A razor has never come upon my head, because I am a Naz′i·rite of God from my mother's belly. If I did get shaved, my power also would certainly depart from me, and I should indeed grow weak and become like all other men."

18 When De·li′lah got to see that he had disclosed to her all his heart, she immediately sent and called the Phi·lis′tine axis lords, saying: "Come up this time, for he has disclosed to me all his heart." And the Phi·lis′tine axis lords

came up to her that they might bring up the money in their hand. 19 And she proceeded to make him sleep upon her knees. Then she called the man and had him shave off the seven braids of his head, after which she started to show the mastery of him, and his power kept departing from upon him. 20 Now she said: "The Phi·lis'tines are upon you, Samson!" At that he woke up from his sleep and said: "I shall go out as at other times and shake myself free." And he himself did not know that it was Jehovah that had departed from him. 21 So the Phi·lis'tines grabbed hold of him and bored his eyes out and brought him down to Ga'za and bound him with two fetters of copper; and he came to be a grinder in the prison house. 22 Meanwhile the hair of his head started to grow luxuriantly as soon as he had been shaved.

23 As for the Phi·lis'tine axis lords, they gathered together to sacrifice a great sacrifice to Da'gon their god and for rejoicing, and they kept saying: "Our god has given into our hand Samson our enemy!" 24 When the people got to see him, they at once gave way to praising their god, "because," said they, "our god has given into our hand our enemy and the devastator of our land and the one who multiplied our slain."

25 And it came about that because their heart was merry, they began to say: "Call Samson that he may offer us some amusement." So they called Samson out of the prison house that he might make sport before them; and they proceeded to stand him between the pillars. 26 Then Samson said to the boy that was holding him by his hand: "Do permit me to feel the pillars upon which the house is firmly established and let me lean against them." 27 (Incidentally, the house was full of men and women and all the Phi·lis'tine axis lords were there; and upon the roof there were about three thousand men and women who

were looking on while Samson offered some amusement.)

28 Samson now called to Jehovah and said: "Lord Jehovah, remember me, please, and strengthen me, please, just this once, O you the [true] God, and let me avenge myself upon the Phi·lis'tines with vengeance for one of my two eyes."

29 With that Samson braced himself against the two middle pillars upon which the house was firmly established, and got a grasp on them, one with his right and the other with his left hand. 30 And Samson proceeded to say: "Let my soul die with the Phi·lis'tines." Then he bent himself with power, and the house went falling upon the axis lords and upon all the people that were in it, so that the dead that he put to death in his own death came to be more than those he had put to death during his lifetime.

31 Later his brothers and all the household of his father came on down and lifted him up and brought him up and buried him between Zo'rah and Esh'ta·ol in the burial place of Ma·no'ah his father. As for him, he had judged Israel twenty years.

17 Now there happened to be a man of the mountainous region of E'phra·im whose name was Mi'cah. 2 In time he said to his mother: "The thousand one hundred silver pieces that were taken from you and over which you pronounced a curse and also said it in my hearing—look! the silver is with me. It was I who took it." At that his mother said: "Blessed may my son be of Jehovah." 3 Accordingly he gave back the thousand one hundred pieces of silver to his mother; and his mother went on to say: "I must without fail sanctify the silver to Jehovah from my hand for my son, so as to make a carved image and a molten statue; and now I shall give it back to you."

4 So he returned the silver to his mother, and his mother took

two hundred silver pieces and gave them to the silversmith. And he went making a carved image and a molten statue; and it got to be in Mi′cah's house. 5 As for the man Mi′cah, he had a house of gods, and he proceeded to make an eph′od and teraphim and to fill the hand of one of his sons with power, that he might serve as priest for him. 6 In those days there was no king in Israel. As for everybody, what was right in his own eyes he was accustomed to do.

7 Now there happened to be a young man of Beth′le·hem in Judah of the family of Judah, and he was a Levite. And he was residing there for a time. 8 And the man proceeded to go from the city of Beth′le·hem in Judah to reside for a time wherever he might find a place. At length while going his way he came into the mountainous region of E′phra·im as far as the house of Mi′cah. 9 Then Mi′cah said to him: "Where do you come from?" At that he said to him: "I am a Levite from Beth′le·hem in Judah, and I am on my way to reside for a time wherever I may find a place." 10 So Mi′cah said to him: "Do dwell with me and serve as a father and priest for me, and I, for my part, shall give you ten silver pieces a year and the usual outfit of garments and your sustenance." Accordingly the Levite went in. 11 Thus the Levite took it upon himself to dwell with the man, and the young man got to be as one of his sons to him. 12 Furthermore, Mi′cah filled the hand of the Levite with power, that the young man might serve as a priest for him and might continue in the house of Mi′cah. 13 Hence Mi′cah said: "Now I do know that Jehovah will do me good, because the Levite has become priest for me."

18 In those days there was no king in Israel. And in those days the tribe of the Dan′ites was looking for an inheritance for itself to dwell there; because up to that day an inheritance had not fallen to them in the midst of the tribes of Israel.

2 Eventually the sons of Dan sent five men of their family, men from among them, men who were valiant fellows, out from Zo′rah and Esh′ta·ol, to spy out the land and to explore it. So they said to them: "Go, explore the land." In time they came into the mountainous region of E′phra·im as far as the house of Mi′cah and got to spend the night there. 3 While they were close by the house of Mi′cah, they recognized the voice of the young man, the Levite, so that they turned aside there. And they proceeded to say to him: "Who brought you here, and what are you doing in this place, and what interest do you have here?" 4 In turn he said to them: "Thus and so Mi′cah did for me that he might hire me, and that I might serve as priest for him." 5 Then they said to him: "Inquire, please, of God that we may know whether our way on which we are going will be successful." 6 So the priest said to them: "Go in peace. It is before Jehovah that your way is in which you go."

7 Accordingly the five men went on and came to La′ish and saw how the people that were within it were dwelling in self-reliance according to the custom of the Si·do′ni·ans, quiet and unsuspecting, and there was no oppressive conqueror that was molesting a thing in the land, while they were far off from the Si·do′ni·ans and they had nothing to do with mankind.

8 At length they came to their brothers at Zo′rah and Esh′ta·ol, and their brothers began to say to them: "How was it with you?" 9 At this they said: "Do get up, and let us go up against them; for we have seen the land, and, look! it is very good. And you are hesitant. Do not be sluggish about walking to come in to take possession of the land. 10 When you come in, you will come to an unsuspecting people, and the land is quite wide; for God has given it

into YOUR hand, a place where there is no lack of any sort of thing that is in the earth."

11 Then six hundred men girded with weapons of war, out of the family of the Dan'ites, departed from there, that is, from Zo'rah and Esh'ta·ol. 12 And they got on their way up and went camping at Kir'i·ath-je'a·rim in Judah. That is why they have called that place Ma'ha·neh-dan down to this day. Look! It is west of Kir'i·ath-je'a·rim. 13 After that they passed along from there to the mountainous region of E'phra·im and came as far as the house of Mi'cah.

14 Then the five men that had gone to spy out the land of La'ish answered and said to their brothers: "Did YOU know that there are in these houses an eph'od and teraphim and a carved image and a molten statue? And now have in mind what YOU ought to do." 15 So they turned aside there and came to the house of the young man, the Levite, at the house of Mi'cah, and began to ask how he was getting along. 16 All the while the six hundred men girded with their weapons of war, who were of the sons of Dan, were standing at the entrance of the gate. 17 The five men that had gone to spy out the land now went on up, that they might enter in there to take the carved image and the eph'od and the teraphim and the molten image. (And the priest was standing at the entrance of the gate with the six hundred men girded with weapons of war.) 18 And these went into the house of Mi'cah and proceeded to take the carved image, the eph'od and the teraphim and the molten image. At that the priest said to them: "What are YOU doing?" 19 But they said to him: "Be quiet. Put your hand over your mouth, and go with us and become a father and a priest for us. Which is better, for you to continue a priest to the house of one man or for you to become a priest to a

tribe and family in Israel?" 20 At this the heart of the priest was pleased, and he now took the eph'od and the teraphim and the carved image and came into the midst of the people.

21 Then they turned and went their way and put the little ones and the livestock and the valuable things ahead of them. 22 They themselves had got a distance away from the house of Mi'cah when the men who were in the houses that were close by the house of Mi'cah were called together and tried to catch up with the sons of Dan. 23 When they kept crying out to the sons of Dan, then they turned their faces and said to Mi'cah: "What is the matter with you that you have been called together?" 24 So he said: "My gods that I made YOU have taken, the priest too, and YOU go YOUR way, and what do I have any more? How, then, is it that YOU can say to me, 'What is the matter with you?'" 25 At this the sons of Dan said to him: "Do not let your voice be heard close to us, for fear that men bitter of soul may assault YOU people, and you have to forfeit your own soul and the soul of your household." 26 And the sons of Dan kept going on their way; and Mi'cah got to see that they were stronger than he was, and so he turned and went back to his house.

27 As for them, they took what Mi'cah had made and the priest that had become his, and they kept going toward La'ish, against a people quiet and unsuspecting. And they proceeded to strike them with the edge of the sword, and the city they burned with fire. 28 And there was no deliverer, for it was far away from Si'don, and they had nothing at all to do with mankind; and it was in the low plain that belonged to Beth-re'hob. Then they built the city and took up dwelling in it. 29 Furthermore, they called the name of the city Dan by the name of their father, Dan, who had been born to Israel. Nevertheless, La'ish was the city's

name at first. 30 After that the sons of Dan stood up the carved image for themselves; and Jon'a-than the son of Ger'shom, Moses' son, he and his sons became priests to the tribe of the Dan'ites until the day of the land's being taken into exile. 31 And they kept the carved image of Mi'cah, which he had made, set up for them-selves all the days that the house of the [true] God continued in Shi'loh.

19 Now it happened in those days that there was no king in Israel. And it came about that a certain Levite was residing for a time in the remotest parts of the mountainous region of E'phra·im. In time he took as his wife a con-cubine from Beth'le·hem in Judah. 2 And his concubine began to com-mit fornication against him. Fi-nally she went away from him to the house of her father at Beth'le-hem in Judah and continued there fully four months. 3 Then her husband got up and went after her to speak consolingly to her so as to bring her back; and there were with him his attendant and a couple of he-asses. So she had him come into her father's house. When the father of the young woman got to see him, he at once rejoiced to meet him. 4 Consequently his father-in-law, the young woman's father, took hold of him, so that he continued to dwell with him three days; and they would eat and drink, and he would stay overnight there.

5 And it came about on the fourth day, when they got up early in the morning as usual, he now rose to go, but the father of the young woman said to his son-in-law: "Sustain your heart with a bit of bread and afterward you people may go." 6 So they sat down, and both of them began to eat and to drink together; after which the father of the young wom-an said to the man: "Come on, please, and stay overnight, and let your heart feel good." 7 When the man rose to go, his father-in-law

kept begging him, so that he stayed overnight there again.

8 When he got up early in the morning on the fifth day to go, the father of the young woman then said: "Please, take sustenance for your heart." And they lingered until the fading away of the day. And both of them kept eating. 9 The man now rose to go, he and his concubine and his attendant; but his father-in-law, the young woman's father, said to him: "Look, now! The day has declined to-ward becoming evening. Please, STAY overnight. Here the day is settling down. Stay here overnight, and let your heart feel good. And tomorrow YOU people must get up early for YOUR journey, and you must go to your tent." 10 How-ever, the man did not consent to stay overnight, but he rose and got on his way and came as far as in front of Je'bus, that is to say, Jerusalem; and with him there were the couple of he-asses saddled up, and his concubine and his at-tendant.

11 While they were close by Je'-bus, as the daylight had gone down considerably, the attendant now said to his master: "O come, now, and let us turn aside to this city of the Jeb'u·sites and stay in it overnight." 12 But his master said to him: "Let us not turn aside to a city of foreigners who are no part of the sons of Israel; and we have to pass on as far as Gib'e·ah." 13 And he went on to say to his attendant: "Come and let us ap-proach one of the places, and we must stay overnight either in Gib'-e·ah or in Ra'mah." 14 So they passed along and kept on their way, and the sun began to set upon them when near to Gib'e·ah, which belongs to Benjamin.

15 Consequently they turned aside there to go in to stay over-night in Gib'e·ah. And they pro-ceeded to go in and sit down in the public square of the city, and there was nobody taking them on into the house to stay overnight. 16 Eventually, look! an old man

coming in from his work in the field at evening, and the man was from the mountainous region of E'phra·im, and he was residing for a time in Gib'e·ah; but the men of the place were Ben'ja·mites. 17 When he raised his eyes he got to see the man, the traveler, in the public square of the city. So the old man said: "Where are you going, and where do you come from?" 18 In turn he said to him: "We are passing along from Beth'le·hem in Judah to the remotest parts of the mountainous region of E'phra·im. That is where I am from, but I went to Beth'le·hem in Judah; and it is to my own house that I am going, and there is nobody taking me on into the house. 19 And there are both straw and fodder for our he-asses, and there are both bread and wine for me and your slave girl and for the attendant with your servant. There is no lack of a single thing." 20 However, the old man said: "May you have peace! Just let any lack of yours be upon me. Only do not stay overnight in the public square." 21 With that he brought him into his house and threw mash to the he-asses. Then they washed their feet and began to eat and drink.

22 While they were making their hearts feel good, look! the men of the city, mere good-for-nothing men, surrounded the house, shoving one another against the door; and they kept saying to the old man, the owner of the house: "Bring out the man that came into your house, that we may have intercourse with him." 23 At that the owner of the house went on out to them and said to them: "No, my brothers, do not do anything wrong, please, since this man has come into my house. Do not commit this disgraceful folly. 24 Here are my virgin daughter and his concubine. Let me bring them out, please, and YOU rape them and do to them what is good in YOUR eyes. But to this man YOU must not do this disgraceful, foolish thing."

25 And the men did not want to listen to him. Hence the man took hold of his concubine and brought her forth to them outside; and they began to have intercourse with her, and kept on abusing her all night long until the morning, after which they sent her off at the ascending of the dawn. 26 Then the woman came as it was turning to morning, and fell down at the entrance of the man's house where her master was,—until daylight. 27 Later her master rose up in the morning and opened the doors of the house and went out to get on his way, and, look! the woman, his concubine, fallen at the entrance of the house with her hands upon the threshold! 28 So he said to her: "Rise up, and let us go." But there was no one answering. At that the man took her upon the ass and rose up and went to his place.

29 Then he entered his house and took the slaughtering knife and laid hold of his concubine and cut her up according to her bones into twelve pieces and sent her into every territory of Israel. 30 And it occurred that everybody seeing it said: "Such a thing as this has never been brought about or been seen from the day that the sons of Israel went up out of the land of Egypt down to this day. Set YOUR hearts upon it, take counsel and speak."

20 Consequently all the sons of Israel went out and the assembly congregated themselves as one man, from Dan down to Be'er-she'ba along with the land of Gil'e·ad, to Jehovah at Miz'pah. 2 So the key men of all the people and all the tribes of Israel took their station in the congregation of the people of the [true] God, four hundred thousand men on foot who drew the sword.

3 And the sons of Benjamin got to hear that the sons of Israel had gone up to Miz'pah.

Then the sons of Israel said: "SPEAK. How has this bad thing been brought about?" 4 At this the man, the Levite, the husband of the murdered woman, answered and said: "It was to Gib'e·ah, which belongs to Benjamin, that I came, I and my concubine, to stay overnight. 5 And the landowners of Gib'e·ah proceeded to rise up against me and to surround the house against me by night. It was I that they figured on killing, but it was my concubine that they raped, and she gradually died. 6 Hence I grasped my concubine and cut her up and sent her into every field of Israel's inheritance, because they had carried on loose conduct and disgraceful folly in Israel. 7 Look! All YOU sons of Israel, give YOUR word and counsel here."

8 So all the people rose up as one man, saying: "We shall not go any of us to his tent, nor shall we turn aside any of us to his house. 9 And now this is the thing that we shall do to Gib'e·ah. Let us go up by lot against it. 10 And we must take ten men out of a hundred of all the tribes of Israel, and a hundred out of a thousand, and a thousand out of ten thousand, to procure provisions for the people, that they may take action by going against Gib'e·ah of Benjamin, in view of all the disgraceful folly that they did in Israel." 11 Thus all the men of Israel were gathered against the city as one man, as allies.

12 Accordingly the tribes of Israel sent men to all the tribesmen of Benjamin, saying: "What is this bad thing that has been brought about among YOU? 13 And now give over the men, the good-for-nothing men, that are in Gib'e·ah, that we may put them to death, and let us clear out what is bad from Israel." And the sons of Benjamin did not want to listen to the voice of their brothers, the sons of Israel.

14 Then the sons of Benjamin went gathering together out of the cities to Gib'e·ah to go out to battle against the sons of Israel.

15 So the sons of Benjamin got to be mustered on that day from the cities, twenty-six thousand men drawing sword, apart from the inhabitants of Gib'e·ah, of whom seven hundred chosen men were mustered. 16 Out of all this people there were seven hundred chosen men left-handed. Every one of these was a slinger of stones to a hairbreadth and would not miss.

17 And the men of Israel were mustered apart from Benjamin, four hundred thousand men drawing sword. Every one of these was a man of war. 18 And they proceeded to rise up and go on up to Beth'el and to inquire of God. Then the sons of Israel said: "Who of us should go up in the lead to the battle against the sons of Benjamin?" To this Jehovah said: "Judah in the lead."

19 After that the sons of Israel rose up in the morning and camped against Gib'e·ah.

20 The men of Israel now went out to battle against Benjamin; and the men of Israel proceeded to draw up in battle formation against them at Gib'e·ah. 21 So the sons of Benjamin came on out from Gib'e·ah and brought twenty-two thousand men in Israel down to ruin to the earth on that day. 22 However, the people, the men of Israel, showed themselves courageous and again went drawing up in battle formation in the place where they had drawn up in formation on the first day. 23 Then the sons of Israel went up and wept before Jehovah until the evening and inquired of Jehovah, saying: "Shall I again approach for battle against the sons of Benjamin my brother?" To this Jehovah said: "Go up against him."

24 Accordingly the sons of Israel drew near to the sons of Benjamin on the second day. 25 In turn Benjamin came on out from Gib'e·ah to meet them on the second day and brought a further eighteen thousand men among the sons of Israel down to ruin to the earth, all

of these drawing sword. 26 At that all the sons of Israel, even all the people, went on up and came to Beth'el and wept and sat there before Jehovah and fasted on that day until the evening and offered up burnt offerings and communion offerings before Jehovah. 27 After that the sons of Israel inquired of Jehovah, as it was there that the ark of the covenant of the [true] God was in those days. 28 Now Phin'e·has the son of E·le·a'zar, the son of Aaron, was standing before it in those days, saying: "Shall I go out yet again to battle against the sons of Benjamin my brother or shall I cease to?" To this Jehovah said: "Go up, because tomorrow I shall give him into your hand." 29 Then Israel set men in ambush against Gib'e·ah all around.

30 And the sons of Israel proceeded to go up against the sons of Benjamin on the third day, and to draw up in formation against Gib'e·ah the same as at the other times. 31 When the sons of Benjamin went on out to meet the people, they were drawn away from the city. Then, the same as at the other times, they started to strike down some of the people mortally wounded on the highways, one of which goes up to Beth'el and the other to Gib'e·ah, in the field, about thirty men in Israel. 32 So the sons of Benjamin began to say: "They are suffering defeat before us the same as at the first." As for the sons of Israel, they said: "Let us flee, and we shall certainly draw them away from the city onto the highways." 33 And all the men of Israel rose up from their places and went drawing up in formation at Ba'al-ta'mar, while those of Israel in ambush were making a charge out of their places in the vicinity of Gib'e·ah. 34 Thus ten thousand chosen men out of all Israel came in front of Gib'e·ah, and the fighting was heavy; and the Ben'ja·mites did not know that calamity was impending over them.

35 And Jehovah proceeded to defeat Benjamin before Israel, so that the sons of Israel on that day brought down to ruin in Benjamin twenty-five thousand one hundred men, all of these drawing sword. 36 However, the sons of Benjamin imagined that the men of Israel faced defeat when they kept giving ground to Benjamin because they trusted in the ambush that they had set against Gib'e·ah. 37 As for the ambush, they acted quickly and went dashing toward Gib'e·ah. Then the ambush spread out and struck all the city with the edge of the sword. 38 Now the men of Israel had come to the arrangement with the ambush for them to make a smoke signal go up from the city. 39 When the sons of Israel turned around in the battle, Benjamin started to strike down about thirty men mortally wounded among the men of Israel, for they said: "They are unquestionably suffering nothing but defeat before us just as in the first battle." 40 And the signal started to go up from the city as a pillar of smoke. So when Benjamin turned his face back, look! the whole city went up heavenward. 41 And the men of Israel made an about-face, and the men of Benjamin were disturbed, for they saw that calamity had reached them. 42 Hence they turned before the men of Israel in the direction of the wilderness, and the battle followed them up closely, while the men from out of the cities were bringing them down to ruin in their midst. 43 They surrounded Benjamin. They pursued him without a place to rest. They trampled him down directly in front of Gib'e·ah toward the rising of the sun. 44 Finally there fell eighteen thousand men of Benjamin, all of these being valiant men.

45 Thus they turned and went fleeing to the wilderness to the crag of Rim'mon. And they made a gleaning of five thousand men of them on the highways, and they kept following closely after them

as far as Gi'dom and so struck down two thousand more men of them. 46 And all those of Benjamin that fell on that day amounted at last to twenty-five thousand men drawing sword, all these being valiant men. 47 But six hundred men turned and went fleeing to the wilderness to the crag of Rim'mon, and they continued to dwell on the crag of Rim'mon four months.

48 And the men of Israel came back against the sons of Benjamin and went striking with the edge of the sword those of the city, [from] men to domestic animal up to all that were found. Also, all the cities that were found they consigned to the fire.

21 Now the men of Israel had sworn in Miz'pah, saying: "Not a man of us will give his daughter to Benjamin as a wife." 2 Consequently the people came to Beth'el and kept sitting there before the [true] God until the evening and continued to raise their voice and indulge in a great deal of weeping. 3 And they would say: "Why, O Jehovah the God of Israel, has this occurred in Israel, for one tribe to be missing today from Israel?" 4 And it came about the next day that the people proceeded to get up early and to build an altar there and to offer up burnt offerings and communion offerings.

5 Then the sons of Israel said: "Who is there out of all the tribes of Israel that has not come up in the congregation to Jehovah, for there is a great oath that has taken place respecting the one that has not come up to Jehovah at Miz'pah, saying, 'Let him be put to death without fail.'" 6 And the sons of Israel began to feel regret over Benjamin their brother. So they said: "Today one tribe has been chopped off from Israel. 7 What shall we do to those who are left over as to wives, now that we ourselves have sworn by Jehovah not to give them any of our daughters as wives?"

8 And they went on to say: "Which one out of the tribes of Israel is it that has not come up to Jehovah at Miz'pah?" And, look! no one had come into the camp from Ja'besh-gil'e·ad to the congregation. 9 When the people were counted, well, look! there was not a man there from the inhabitants of Ja'besh-gil'e·ad. 10 Hence the assembly proceeded to send twelve thousand of the most valiant men there and to command them, saying: "Go, and you must strike the inhabitants of Ja'besh-gil'e·ad with the edge of the sword, even the women and the little ones. 11 And this is the thing that you should do: Every male and every woman that has experienced lying with a male you should devote to destruction." 12 However, they found out of the inhabitants of Ja'besh-gil'e·ad four hundred girls, virgins, that had not had intercourse with a man by lying with a male. So they brought them to the camp at Shi'loh, which is in the land of Ca'naan.

13 And all the assembly now sent and spoke to the sons of Benjamin that were on the crag of Rim'mon and offered them peace. 14 Accordingly Benjamin came back at that time. Then they gave them the women that they had preserved alive from the women of Ja'besh-gil'e·ad; but they did not find enough for them. 15 And the people felt regret over Benjamin because Jehovah had made a rupture between the tribes of Israel. 16 Consequently the older men of the assembly said: "What shall we do to the men that are left over as to wives, for womankind has been annihilated out of Benjamin?" 17 Then they said: "There should be a possession for those who have escaped of Benjamin, that a tribe might not be wiped out of Israel. 18 As for us, we are not allowed to give them wives from our daughters, because the sons of Israel have sworn, saying, 'Cursed is the one that gives a wife to Benjamin.'"

19 Finally they said: "Look! There is a festival of Jehovah from year to year in Shi′loh, which is to the north of Beth′el, toward the east of the highway that goes up from Beth′el to She′chem and toward the south of Le·bo′nah." 20 So they commanded the sons of Benjamin, saying: "Go, and YOU must lie in wait in the vineyards. 21 And YOU must look, and, there now, when the daughters of Shi′loh come on out to dance in circle dances, YOU must also come out from the vineyards and carry off for yourselves by force each one his wife from the daughters of Shi′loh, and YOU must go to the land of Benjamin. 22 And it must occur that should their fathers or their brothers come to conduct a legal case against us, we also shall certainly say to them, 'Do us a favor for their sakes, because we have not taken for each one his wife by war, for it was not YOU that did the giving to them at a time when YOU would become guilty.' "

23 Accordingly the sons of Benjamin did just that way, and they proceeded to carry off wives for their number from the women dancing around, whom they snatched away; after which they went off and returned to their inheritance and built the cities and took up dwelling in them.

24 And the sons of Israel began to disperse from there at that time, each one to his own tribe and his own family; and they went their way out from there, each one to his own inheritance.

25 In those days there was no king in Israel. What was right in his own eyes was what each one was accustomed to do.

RUTH

1 Now it came about in the days when the judges administered justice that a famine arose in the land, and a man proceeded to go from Beth′le·hem in Judah to reside as an alien in the fields of Mo′ab, he with his wife and his two sons. 2 And the man's name was E·lim′e·lech, and his wife's name Na′o·mi, and the names of his two sons were Mah′lon and Chil′i·on, Eph′rath·ites from Beth′le·hem in Judah. Eventually they came to the fields of Mo′ab and continued there.

3 In time E·lim′e·lech the husband of Na′o·mi died, so that she remained with her two sons. 4 Later the men took wives for themselves, Mo′ab·ite women. The name of the one was Or′pah, and the name of the other Ruth. And they went on dwelling there for about ten years. 5 In time the two of them, Mah′lon and Chil′i·on, also died, so that the woman remained without her two children and her husband. 6 And she proceeded to get up with her daughters-in-law and to return from the fields of Mo′ab, for she had heard in the field of Mo′ab that Jehovah had turned his attention to his people by giving them bread.

7 And she went her way out from the place where she had continued, and both of her daughters-in-law were with her, and they kept walking on the road to return to the land of Judah. 8 Finally Na′o·mi said to both of her daughters-in-law: "Go, return, each one to the house of her mother. May Jehovah exercise loving-kindness toward YOU, just as YOU have exercised it toward the men now dead and toward me. 9 May Jehovah make a gift to YOU, and do YOU find a resting place each one in the house of her husband." Then she kissed them,

and they began to raise their voices and weep. 10 And they kept saying to her: "No, but with you we shall return to your people." 11 But Na′o·mi said: "Return, my daughters. Why should you go with me? Do I still have sons in my inward parts, and will they have to become your husbands? 12 Return, my daughters, go, for I have grown too old to get to belong to a husband. If I had said I had hope also that I should certainly become a husband's tonight and also should certainly bear sons, 13 would you keep waiting for them until they could grow up? Would you keep yourselves secluded for them so as not to become a husband's? No, my daughters, for it is very bitter to me because of you, that the hand of Jehovah has gone out against me."

14 At that they raised their voices and wept some more, after which Or′pah kissed her mother-in-law. As for Ruth, she stuck with her. 15 So she said: "Look! Your widowed sister-in-law has returned to her people and her gods. Return with your widowed sister-in-law."

16 And Ruth proceeded to say: "Do not plead with me to abandon you, to turn back from accompanying you; for where you go I shall go, and where you spend the night I shall spend the night. Your people will be my people, and your God my God. 17 Where you die I shall die, and there is where I shall be buried. May Jehovah do so to me and add to it if anything but death should make a separation between me and you."

18 When she got to see that she was persistent about going with her, then she left off speaking to her. 19 And they both continued on their way until they came to Beth′le·hem. And it came about that as soon as they came to Beth′le·hem, all the city became stirred up over them, and the women kept saying: "Is this Na′o·mi?" 20 And she would say to the women: "Do not call me Na′o·mi. Call me Ma′ra, for the Almighty has made it very bitter for me. 21 I was full when I went, and it is empty-handed that Jehovah has made me return. Why should you call me Na′o·mi, when it is Jehovah that has humiliated me and the Almighty that has caused me calamity?"

22 Thus Na′o·mi made her return, Ruth the Mo′ab·ite woman, her daughter-in-law, being with her when returning from the fields of Mo′ab; and they came to Beth′-le·hem at the commencement of barley harvest.

2 Now Na′o·mi had a kinsman of her husband, a man mighty in wealth, of the family of E·lim′e-lech, and his name was Bo′az.

2 In time Ruth the Mo′ab·ite woman said to Na′o·mi: "Let me go, please, to the field and glean among the ears of grain following after whoever it is in whose eyes I may find favor." So she said to her: "Go, my daughter." 3 At that she went off and entered and began to glean in the field behind the harvesters. Thus by chance she lighted on the tract of the field belonging to Bo′az, who was of the family of E·lim′e·lech. 4 And, look! Bo′az came from Beth′le·hem and proceeded to say to the harvesters: "Jehovah be with you." In turn they would say to him: "Jehovah bless you."

5 Subsequently Bo′az said to the young man who was set over the harvesters: "To whom does this young woman belong?" 6 So the young man set over the harvesters answered and said: "The young woman is a Mo′ab·i·tess, who returned with Na′o·mi from the field of Mo′ab. 7 Then she said, 'Let me glean, please, and I shall certainly gather among the cut-off ears of grain behind the harvesters.' So she entered and kept on her feet from that time in the morning until her sitting down just now in the house a little while."

8 Later Bo′az said to Ruth: "You have heard, have you not, my

daughter? Do not go away to glean in another field, and you must also not cross over from this place, and in that way you should keep close by my young women. 9 Let your eyes be on the field that they will harvest, and you must go with them. Have I not commanded the young men not to touch you? When you are thirsty, you must also go to the vessels and drink from what the young men will draw."

10 At that she fell upon her face and bowed down to the earth and said to him: "How is it I have found favor in your eyes so that I am taken notice of, when I am a foreigner?" 11 Then Bo′az answered and said to her: "The report was fully made to me of all that you have done to your mother-in-law after the death of your husband, and how you proceeded to leave your father and your mother and the land of your relatives and to go to a people whom you had not known formerly. 12 May Jehovah reward the way you act, and may there come to be a perfect wage for you from Jehovah the God of Israel, under whose wings you have come to seek refuge." 13 To this she said: "Let me find favor in your eyes, my lord, because you have comforted me and because you have spoken reassuringly to your maidservant, although I myself may not happen to be like one of your maidservants."

14 And Bo′az proceeded to say to her at mealtime: "Approach here, and you must eat some of the bread and dip your piece in the vinegar." So she sat down beside the harvesters, and he would hold out roasted grain to her and she would eat, so that she was satisfied and yet had something left over. 15 Then she got up to glean. Bo′az now commanded his young men, saying: "Let her glean also among the cut-off ears of grain, and you must not molest her. 16 And you should also be sure to pull out some from the bundles of ears for her, and you must

leave them behind that she may glean them, and you must not rebuke her."

17 And she continued to glean in the field until the evening, after which she beat out what she had gleaned, and it came to be about an e′phah of barley. 18 Then she took it up and went into the city, and her mother-in-law got to see what she had gleaned. After that she took out what food she had left over when she had satisfied herself and gave it to her.

19 Her mother-in-law now said to her: "Where did you glean today, and where did you work? May the one who took notice of you become blessed." So she told her mother-in-law with whom she had worked; and she went on to say: "The name of the man with whom I worked today is Bo′az." 20 At that Na′o·mi said to her daughter-in-law: "Blessed be he of Jehovah, who has not left his loving-kindness toward the living and the dead." And Na′o·mi went on to say to her: "The man is related to us. He is one of our repurchasers." 21 Then Ruth the Mo′ab·i·tess said: "He also said to me, 'Close by the young people that are mine is where you should keep until they have finished the entire harvest that I have.'" 22 So Na′o·mi said to Ruth her daughter-in-law: "It is better, my daughter, that you should go out with his young women, that they may not annoy you in another field."

23 And she continued to keep close by the young women of Bo′az to glean until the harvest of the barley and the harvest of the wheat came to an end. And she kept on dwelling with her mother-in-law.

3 Na′o·mi her mother-in-law now said to her: "My daughter, ought I not to look for a resting place for you, that it may go well with you? 2 And now, is not Bo′az, with whose young women you have continued, our kinsman? Look! He is winnowing barley at the threshing floor tonight. 3 And you must wash and rub yourself with oil and put your mantles upon you and go down to the threshing floor. Do not make yourself known to the man until he has finished eating and drinking. 4 And it should occur that when he lies down, you must also take note of the place where he lies down; and you must come and uncover him at his feet and lie down; and he, for his part, will tell you what you ought to do."

5 At that she said to her: "All that you say to me I shall do." 6 And she proceeded to go down to the threshing floor and to do according to all that her mother-in-law had commanded her. 7 Meantime Bo'az ate and drank, and his heart was feeling good. Then he went to lie down at the extremity of the grain heap. After that she came stealthily and uncovered him at his feet and lay down. 8 And it came about at midnight that the man began to tremble. So he bent himself forward, and, look! a woman lying at his feet! 9 Then he said: "Who are you?" In turn she said: "I am Ruth your slave girl, and you must spread out your skirt over your slave girl, for you are a repurchaser." 10 At that he said: "Blessed may you be of Jehovah, my daughter. You have expressed your loving-kindness better in the last instance than in the first instance, in not going after the young fellows whether lowly or rich. 11 And now, my daughter, do not be afraid. All that you say I shall do for you, for everyone in the gate of my people is aware that you are an excellent woman. 12 And now while it is a fact that I am a repurchaser, there is also a repurchaser closer related than I am. 13 Lodge here tonight, and it must occur in the morning that if he will repurchase you, fine! Let him do the repurchasing. But if he does not take delight in repurchasing you, I will then repurchase you, I myself, as sure as Jehovah lives.

Keep lying down until the morning."

14 And she kept lying at his feet until the morning and then got up before anyone could recognize another. He now said: "Do not let it be known that a woman came to the threshing floor." 15 And he went on to say: "Bring the cloak that is on you, and hold it open." So she held it open, and he proceeded to measure out six measures of barley and to place it upon her, after which he went into the city.

16 And she went her way to her mother-in-law, who now said: "Who are you, my daughter?" Accordingly she told her everything that the man had done to her. 17 And she went on to say: "These six measures of barley he gave me, for he said to me, 'Do not come empty-handed to your mother-in-law.'" 18 At that she said: "Sit still, my daughter, until you know how the matter will turn out, for the man will have no rest unless he has brought the matter to an end today."

4 As for Bo'az, he went up to the gate and began to sit there. And, look! the repurchaser was passing by, whom Bo'az had mentioned. Then he said: "Do turn aside, do sit down here, So-and-so." Hence he turned aside and sat down. 2 After that he took ten men of the older men of the city and said: "Sit down here." So they sat down.

3 He now said to the repurchaser: "The tract of the field that belonged to our brother E·lim′e·lech, Na′o·mi, who has returned from the field of Mo′ab, must sell. 4 As for me, I thought that I should disclose it to you, saying, 'Buy it in front of the inhabitants and the older men of my people. If you will repurchase it, repurchase it; but if you will not repurchase it, do tell me, that I may know, for there is no one else but you to do the repurchasing, and I am next to you.'" At that he said: "I shall be the one to repurchase it." 5 Then Bo'az said: "On the day

that you buy the field from Na'o-mi's hand, it is also from Ruth the Mo'ab·i·tess, the wife of the dead man, that you must buy it so as to cause the name of the dead man to rise upon his inheritance." 6 To this the repurchaser said: "I am unable to repurchase it for myself, for fear I may ruin my own inheritance. You repurchase it for yourself with my right of repurchase, because I am not able to do the repurchasing."

7 Now this was the custom of former times in Israel concerning the right of repurchase and concerning the exchange, to establish every sort of thing: A man had to draw his sandal off and give it to his fellow, and this was the attestation in Israel. 8 So when the repurchaser said to Bo'az: "Buy it for yourself," he proceeded to draw his sandal off. 9 Then Bo'az said to the older men and all the people: "You are witnesses today that I do buy all that belonged to E·lim'e·lech and all that belonged to Chil'i·on and Mah'lon from the hand of Na'o·mi. 10 And also Ruth the Mo'ab·i·tess, the wife of Mah'lon, I do buy for myself as a wife to cause the name of the dead man to rise upon his inheritance and that the name of the dead man may not be cut off from among his brothers and from the gate of his place. You are witnesses today."

11 At this all the people that were in the gate and the older men said: "Witnesses! May Jehovah grant the wife who is coming into your house to be like Rachel and like Le'ah, both of whom built

the house of Israel; and you prove your worth in Eph'ra·thah and make a notable name in Beth'le-hem. 12 And may your house become like the house of Pe'rez, whom Ta'mar bore to Judah, from the offspring that Jehovah will give you out of this young woman."

13 Accordingly Bo'az took Ruth and she became his wife and he had relations with her. So Jehovah granted her conception and she bore a son. 14 And the women began to say to Na'o·mi: "Blessed be Jehovah, who has not let a repurchaser fail for you today; that his name may be proclaimed in Israel. 15 And he has become a restorer of your soul and one to nourish your old age, because your daughter-in-law who does love you, who is better to you than seven sons, has given birth to him." 16 And Na'o·mi proceeded to take the child and to put it in her bosom, and she came to be its nurse. 17 Then the neighbor ladies gave it a name, saying: "A son has been born to Na'o·mi." And they began to call his name O'bed. He is the father of Jes'se, David's father.

18 Now these are the generations of Pe'rez: Pe'rez became father to Hez'ron; 19 and Hez'ron became father to Ram; and Ram became father to Am·min'a·dab; 20 and Am·min'a·dab became father to Nah'shon; and Nah'shon became father to Sal'mon; 21 and Sal'mon became father to Bo'az; and Bo'az became father to O'bed; 22 and O'bed became father to Jes'se; and Jes'se became father to David.

THE FIRST OF

SAMUEL

or, according to the Greek *Septuagint*,

THE FIRST OF KINGS

1 Now there happened to be a certain man of Ra·math·a·'im-zo'phim of the mountainous region of E'phra·im, and his name was El·ka'nah, the son of Je·ro'ham, the son of E·li'hu, the son of To'hu, the son of Zuph, an E'phra·im·ite. **2** And he had two wives, the name of the one being Han'nah, and the name of the other being Pe·nin'nah. And Pe·nin'nah came to have children, but Han'nah had no children. **3** And that man went up out of his city from year to year to prostrate himself and to sacrifice to Jehovah of armies in Shi'loh. And there is where the two sons of E'li, Hoph'ni and Phin'e·has, were priests to Jehovah.

4 And there came to be a day when El·ka'nah proceeded to sacrifice, and he gave to Pe·nin'nah his wife and to all her sons and her daughters portions; **5** but to Han'nah he gave one portion. Nonetheless it was Han'nah that he loved, and, as for Jehovah, he had closed up her womb. **6** And her rival wife also vexed her sorely for the sake of making her feel disconcerted because Jehovah had closed up her womb. **7** And that was the way she would do year by year, as often as she went up into the house of Jehovah. That was the way she would vex her, so that she would weep and not eat. **8** And El·ka'nah her husband proceeded to say to her: "Han'nah, why do you weep, and why do you not eat, and why does your heart feel bad? Am I not better to you than ten sons?"

9 Then Han'nah got up after they had eaten in Shi'loh and after the drinking, while E'li the priest was sitting upon the seat by the doorpost of the temple of Jehovah. **10** And she was bitter of soul, and she began to pray to Jehovah and to weep greatly. **11** And she went on to make a vow and say: "O Jehovah of armies, if you will without fail look upon the affliction of your slave girl and actually remember me, and you will not forget your slave girl and actually give to your slave girl a male offspring, I will give him to Jehovah all the days of his life, and no razor will come upon his head."

12 And it occurred that while she prayed extendedly before Jehovah, E'li was watching her mouth. **13** As for Han'nah, she was speaking in her heart; only her lips were quivering, and her voice was not heard. But E'li took her for drunk. **14** So E'li said to her: "How long will you behave drunk? Put away your wine from upon you." **15** At this Han'nah answered and said: "No, my lord! A woman hard pressed in spirit I am; and wine and intoxicating liquor I have not drunk, but I pour out my soul before Jehovah. **16** Do not make your slave girl like a good-for-nothing woman, for it is out of the abundance of my concern and my vexation that I have spoken until now." **17** Then E'li answered and said: "Go in peace, and may the God of Israel grant your petition that you have asked of him." **18** To this she said: "Let your maidservant find favor in your eyes." And the woman proceeded to go on her way and to eat, and her face became self-concerned no more.

19 Then they got up early in the morning and prostrated themselves before Jehovah, after which they returned and came into their house at Ra'mah. El·ka'nah now had intercourse with Han'nah his wife, and Jehovah began remembering her. 20 So it came about at the rolling around of a year that Han'nah became pregnant and brought a son to birth and proceeded to call his name Samuel, because, said she, "it is from Jehovah that I have asked him."

21 In time the man El·ka'nah went up with all his household to sacrifice to Jehovah the yearly sacrifice and his vow offering. 22 As for Han'nah, she did not go up, for she had said to her husband: "As soon as the boy is weaned, I must bring him, and he must appear before Jehovah and dwell there to time indefinite." 23 At this El·ka'nah her husband said to her: "Do what is good in your eyes. Stay at home until you wean him. Only may Jehovah carry out his word." So the woman stayed at home and kept nursing her son until she weaned him.

24 Accordingly just as soon as she had weaned him, she brought him up with her, along with a three-year-old bull and one e'phah of flour and a large jar of wine, and she proceeded to enter the house of Jehovah in Shi'loh. And the boy was with her. 25 Then they slaughtered the bull and brought the boy to E'li. 26 With that she said: "Excuse me, my lord! By the life of your soul, my lord, I am the woman that was standing with you in this place to pray to Jehovah. 27 It was with reference to this boy that I prayed that Jehovah should grant me my petition that I asked of him. 28 And I, in my turn, have lent him to Jehovah. All the days that he does happen to be, he is one requested for Jehovah."

And he proceeded to bow down there to Jehovah.

2 And Han'nah went on to pray and say:
"My heart does exult in Jehovah,
My horn is indeed exalted in Jehovah.
My mouth is widened against my enemies,
For I do rejoice in the salvation from you.

2 There is no one holy like Jehovah, for there is no one but you;
And there is no rock like our God.
3 Do not you people speak very haughtily so much,
Let nothing go forth unrestrained from your mouth,
For a God of knowledge Jehovah is,
And by him deeds are rightly estimated.
4 The mighty men of the bow are filled with terror,
But those that are stumbling do gird on vital energy.
5 The satisfied must hire themselves out for bread,
But the hungry actually cease [to hunger].
Even the barren has given birth to seven,
But she that was abundant in sons has faded away.
6 Jehovah is a Killer and a Preserver of life,
A Bringer down to She'ol, and He brings up.
7 Jehovah is an Impoverisher and an Enricher,
An Abaser, also an Exalter,
8 A Raiser of a lowly one from the dust;
From the ashpit he lifts up a poor one,
To make them sit with nobles; and a throne of glory he gives to them as a possession.
For to Jehovah belong earth's supports,
And he places upon them the productive land.
9 The feet of his loyal ones he guards;
As for the wicked ones, they are silenced in darkness,
For not by power does a man prove superior.
10 As for Jehovah, those contending against him will be terrified;
Against them he will thunder in the heavens.
Jehovah himself will judge the ends of the earth,
That he may give strength to his king,

That he may exalt the horn of his anointed one."

11 Then El·ka′nah went to Ra′mah to his house; and as for the boy, he became a minister of Jehovah before E′li the priest.

12 Now the sons of E′li were good-for-nothing men; they did not acknowledge Jehovah. 13 As for the due right of the priests from the people, whenever any man was offering a sacrifice, an attendant of the priest came with the three-pronged fork in his hand, just when the meat was boiling, 14 and made a thrust into the basin or the two-handled cooking pot or the caldron or the one-handled cooking pot. Anything that the fork might bring up the priest would take for himself. That is the way they would do in Shi′loh to all the Israelites coming there. 15 Also, before ever they could make the fat smoke, an attendant of the priest came and said to the man sacrificing: "Do give meat to roast for the priest so that he may receive from you, not boiled meat, but raw." 16 When the man would say to him: "Let them be sure to make the fat smoke first of all. Then take for yourself just whatever your soul may crave," he actually said: "No, but you should give it now; and, if not, I shall have to take it by force!" 17 And the sin of the attendants came to be very great before Jehovah; for the men treated the offering of Jehovah with disrespect.

18 And Samuel was ministering before Jehovah, as a boy, having a linen eph′od girded on. 19 Also, a little sleeveless coat his mother would make for him, and she brought it up to him from year to year when she came up with her husband to sacrifice the yearly sacrifice. 20 And E′li blessed El·ka′nah and his wife and said: "May Jehovah appoint to you an offspring from this wife in place of the thing lent, that was lent to Jehovah." And they went to their place. 21 Accordingly Jehovah turned his attention to Han′nah, so that she had pregnancy and

gave birth to three sons and two daughters. And the boy Samuel continued growing up with Jehovah.

22 And E′li was very old, and he had heard of all that his sons kept doing to all Israel and how they would lie down with the women that were serving at the entrance of the tent of meeting. 23 And he used to say to them: "Why do you keep doing things like these? For the things I am hearing about you from all the people are bad. 24 No, my sons, because the report is not good that I am hearing, that the people of Jehovah are causing to circulate. 25 If a man should sin against a man, God will arbitrate for him; but if it is against Jehovah that a man should sin, who is there to pray for him?" But they would not listen to the voice of their father, because Jehovah was now pleased to put them to death. 26 All the while Samuel was growing bigger and more likable both from Jehovah's standpoint and from that of men.

27 And a man of God proceeded to come to E′li and say to him: "This is what Jehovah has said, 'Did I not for a fact reveal myself to the house of your forefather while they happened to be in Egypt as slaves to the house of Phar′aoh? 28 And there was a choosing of him out of all the tribes of Israel for me, to act as priest and go up upon my altar to make sacrificial smoke billow up, to bear an eph′od before me, that I might give to the house of your forefather all the offerings made by fire of the sons of Israel. 29 Why do you men keep kicking at my sacrifice and at my offering that I have commanded [in my] dwelling, and you keep honoring your sons more than me by fattening yourselves from the best of every offering of Israel my people?

30 " 'That is why the utterance of Jehovah the God of Israel is: "I did indeed say, As for your house and the house of your forefather, they will walk before me to

time indefinite." But now the utterance of Jehovah is: "It is unthinkable, on my part, because those honoring me I shall honor, and those despising me will be of little account." 31 Look! Days are coming when I shall certainly chop off your arm and the arm of the house of your forefather, so that there will not come to be an old man in your house. 32 And you will actually look upon an adversary [in my] dwelling amid all the good that is done to Israel; and never will there come to be an old man in your house. 33 And yet there is a man of yours that I shall not cut off from being at my altar so as to cause your eyes to fail and to make your soul pine away; but the greater number of your house will all die by the sword of men. 34 And this is the sign for you that will come to your two sons, Hoph'ni and Phin'e·has: On one day both of them will die. 35 And I shall certainly raise up for myself a faithful priest. In harmony with what is in my heart and in my soul he will do; and I shall certainly build for him a lasting house, and he will certainly walk before my anointed one always. 36 And it must occur that anyone left over in your house will come and bow down to him for the payment of money and a round loaf of bread, and will certainly say: "Attach me, please, to one of the priestly offices to eat a piece of bread." ' "

3 All the while the boy Samuel was ministering to Jehovah before E'li, and word from Jehovah had become rare in those days; there was no vision being spread abroad.

2 Now it came about on that day that E'li was lying in his place, and his eyes had begun to grow dim; he was not able to see. 3 And the lamp of God was not yet extinguished, and Samuel was lying in the temple of Jehovah, where the ark of God was. 4 And Jehovah proceeded to call Samuel. At this he said: "Here I am." 5 And

he went running to E'li and saying: "Here I am, for you called me." But he said: "I did not call. Lie down again." So he went and lay down. 6 And Jehovah went on to call yet again: "Samuel!" At this Samuel got up and went to E'li and said: "Here I am, for you did call me." But he said: "I did not call, my son. Lie down again." 7 (As regards Samuel, he had not yet come to know Jehovah, and the word of Jehovah had not yet begun to be revealed to him.) 8 So Jehovah called again for the third time: "Samuel!" At that he got up and went to E'li and said: "Here I am, for you must have called me."

And E'li began to discern that it was Jehovah that was calling the boy. 9 Consequently E'li said to Samuel: "Go, lie down, and it must occur that, if he should call you, you must say, 'Speak, Jehovah, for your servant is listening.' " So Samuel went and lay down in his place.

10 Then Jehovah came and took his position and called as at the other times: "Samuel, Samuel!" At this Samuel said: "Speak, for your servant is listening." 11 And Jehovah went on to say to Samuel: "Look! I am doing something in Israel which if anyone hears about, both his ears will tingle. 12 On that day I shall carry out toward E'li all that I have said respecting his house, from beginning to end. 13 And you must tell him that I am judging his house to time indefinite for the error that he has known, because his sons are calling down evil upon God, and he has not rebuked them. 14 And that is why I have sworn to the house of E'li that the error of the house of E'li will not be brought to exemption from punishment by sacrifice or by offering to time indefinite."

15 And Samuel continued lying down until the morning. Then he opened the doors of Jehovah's house. And Samuel was afraid to tell E'li of the appearing. 16 But E'li called Samuel and said: "Samuel, my son!" At this he said:

"Here I am." 17 And he went on to say: "What is the word that he has spoken to you? Do not, please, hide it from me. May God do so to you and so may he add to it if you should hide from me a word of all the word that he has spoken to you." 18 So Samuel told him all the words, and he did not hide anything from him. At that he said: "It is Jehovah. What is good in his eyes let him do."

19 And Samuel continued growing up, and Jehovah himself proved to be with him and did not cause any of all his words to fall to the earth. 20 And all Israel from Dan to Be′er-she′ba became aware that Samuel was one accredited for the position of prophet to Jehovah. 21 And Jehovah proceeded to appear again in Shi′loh, because Jehovah revealed himself to Samuel in Shi′loh by the word of Jehovah.

4 And the word of Samuel continued to come to all Israel.
Then Israel went out to meet the Phi·lis′tines in battle; and they took up camping alongside Eb·en-e′zer, and the Phi·lis′tines themselves encamped in A′phek. 2 And the Phi·lis′tines proceeded to draw up in formation to meet Israel, and the battle went badly, so that Israel was defeated before the Phi·lis′tines, who went striking down about four thousand men in closed battle line in the field. 3 When the people came to the camp the older men of Israel began to say: "Why did Jehovah defeat us today before the Phi·lis′tines? Let us take to ourselves from Shi′loh the ark of Jehovah's covenant, that it may come into our midst and may save us from the palm of our enemies." 4 So the people sent to Shi′loh and carried from there the ark of the covenant of Jehovah of armies, who is sitting upon the cherubs. And the two sons of E′li were there with the ark of the covenant of the [true] God, namely, Hoph′ni and Phin′e·has.

5 And it came about that as soon as the ark of the covenant of Jehovah came into the camp, all the Israelites broke out into loud shouting, so that the earth was in a stir. 6 The Phi·lis′tines also got to hear the sound of the shouting and began saying: "What does the sound of this loud shouting in the camp of the Hebrews mean?" Finally they got to know that the ark of Jehovah itself had come into the camp. 7 And the Phi·lis′tines became afraid, because they said: "God has come into the camp!" So they said: "Woe to us, for such a thing as this never occurred before! 8 Woe to us! Who will save us from the hand of this majestic God? This is the God that was the smiter of Egypt with every sort of slaughter in the wilderness. 9 Show yourselves courageous and prove yourselves men, you Phi·lis′tines, that you may not serve the Hebrews just as they have served you; and you must prove yourselves men and fight!" 10 Accordingly the Phi·lis′tines fought and Israel was defeated, and they went fleeing each one to his tent; and the slaughter came to be very great, so that out of Israel there fell thirty thousand men on foot. 11 And the ark of God itself was captured, and the two sons of E′li, Hoph′ni and Phin′e·has, died.

12 And a man of Benjamin went running from the battle line so that he arrived at Shi′loh on that day with his garments ripped apart and dirt on his head. 13 When he arrived, there was E′li sitting on the seat by the roadside, watching, because his heart had become atremble over the ark of the [true] God. And the man himself went in to report in the city, and the whole city began crying out. 14 And E′li got to hear the sound of the outcry. So he said: "What does the sound of this turmoil mean?" And the man himself hurried that he might go in and report to E′li. 15 (Now E′li was ninety-eight years old, and his eyes had set so that he was unable to see.) 16 And the man proceeded to say to E′li: "I am the one coming from the battle

line, and I—it is from the battle line that I have fled today." At this he said: "What is the thing that has happened, my son?" 17 So the news bearer answered and said: "Israel has fled before the Phi·lis'tines, and there has also occurred a great defeat among the people; and also your own two sons have died—Hoph'ni and Phin'e·has—and the very ark of the [true] God has been captured."

18 And it came about that at the moment that he mentioned the ark of the [true] God, he began to fall from the seat backward beside the gate, and his neck got broken so that he died, because the man was old and heavy; and he himself had judged Israel forty years. 19 And his daughter-in-law, the wife of Phin'e·has, was pregnant near to giving birth, and she got to hear the report that the ark of the [true] God was captured and that her father-in-law and her husband had died. At that she bowed herself and began giving birth, because her pangs came unexpectedly upon her. 20 And about the time of her death, the women standing by her began to speak: "Do not be afraid, because it is a son that you have borne." And she did not answer and did not set her heart on it. 21 But she called the boy Ich'a·bod, saying: "Glory has gone away from Israel into exile," [this] with reference to the ark of the [true] God's being captured and with reference to her father-in-law and her husband. 22 So she said: "Glory has gone away from Israel into exile, because the ark of the [true] God has been captured."

5 As for the Phi·lis'tines, they took the ark of the [true] God and then brought it from Eb·en-e'zer to Ash'dod. 2 And the Philis'tines proceeded to take the ark of the [true] God and bring it into the house of Da'gon and station it beside Da'gon. 3 Then the Ash'dod·ites got up early the very next day, and there Da'gon was fallen upon his face to the earth before the

ark of Jehovah. So they took Da'gon and returned him to his place. 4 When they got up early in the morning the very day after, there Da'gon was fallen upon his face to the earth before the ark of Jehovah, with the head of Da'gon and the palms of both his hands cut off, to the threshold. Only the fish part had been left upon him. 5 That is why the priests of Da'gon and all those going into the house of Da'gon do not tread upon the threshold of Da'gon in Ash'dod down to this day.

6 And the hand of Jehovah came to be heavy upon the Ash'dod·ites, and he began causing panic and striking them with piles, namely, Ash'dod and its territories. 7 And the men of Ash'dod came to see that it was so, and they said: "Do not let the ark of the God of Israel dwell with us, because his hand has been hard against us and against Da'gon our god." 8 Consequently they sent and gathered all the axis lords of the Philis'tines to them and said: "What shall we do to the ark of the God of Israel?" Finally they said: "Toward Gath let the ark of the God of Israel go around." So they brought the ark of the God of Israel around to there.

9 And it came about that after they had brought it around to there, the hand of Jehovah came to be upon the city with a very great confusion, and he began striking the men of the city, from small to great, and piles began breaking out on them. 10 Hence they sent the ark of the [true] God to Ek'ron. And it came about that as soon as the ark of the [true] God came to Ek'ron, the Ek'ron·ites began to cry out, saying: "They have brought the ark of the God of Israel around to me to put me and my people to death!" 11 Consequently they sent and gathered all the axis lords of the Phi·lis'tines and said: "SEND the ark of the God of Israel away that it may return to its place and may not put me and my people to death."

For a death-dealing confusion had occurred in the whole city; the hand of the [true] God had been very heavy there, 12 and the men that did not die had been struck with piles. And the cry of the city for help kept ascending to the heavens.

6 And the ark of Jehovah proved to be in the field of the Philis'tines seven months. 2 And the Phi·lis'tines proceeded to call the priests and the diviners, saying: "What shall we do with the ark of Jehovah? Let us know with what we should send it away to its place." 3 To this they said: "If you are sending the ark of the God of Israel away, do not send it away without an offering, for you should by all means return to him a guilt offering. Then it is that you will be healed, and it must become known to you why his hand would not turn away from you." 4 At this they said: "What is the guilt offering that we ought to return to him?" Then they said: "According to the number of the axis lords of the Phi·lis'tines, five golden piles and five golden jerboas, for every one of you and your axis lords have the same scourge. 5 And you must make images of your piles and images of your jerboas that are bringing the land to ruin, and you must give glory to the God of Israel. Perhaps he will lighten his hand from off you and your god and your land. 6 Also, why should you make your heart unresponsive just the way Egypt and Phar'aoh made their heart unresponsive? Was it not as soon as He dealt severely with them that they proceeded to send them away, and they went their way? 7 And now take and make a new wagon, and two cows that are giving suck, upon which no yoke has come up, and you must hitch the cows to the wagon, and you must make their young ones go back home from following them. 8 And you must take the ark of Jehovah and place it on the wagon, and the golden articles that you must re-turn to him as a guilt offering you should put into a box at the side of it. And you must send it away, and it must go. 9 And you must look: if it is the road to its territory that it goes up, to Beth-she'mesh, it is he that has done to us this great evil; but if not, we must know that it was not his hand that touched us; an accident it was that happened to us."

10 And the men proceeded to do accordingly. So they took two cows that were giving suck and hitched them to the wagon, and their young ones they shut up at home. 11 Then they put the ark of Jehovah upon the wagon, and also the box and the golden jerboas and the images of their piles. 12 And the cows began to go straight ahead on the road to Beth-she'-mesh. On the one highway they went, lowing as they went, and they did not turn aside to the right or to the left. All the while the axis lords of the Phi·lis'tines were walking after them as far as the boundary of Beth-she'mesh. 13 And people of Beth-she'mesh were reaping the wheat harvest in the low plain. When they raised their eyes and saw the Ark, they gave way to rejoicing at seeing it. 14 And the wagon itself came into the field of Joshua the Beth-she'-mite and kept standing there, where there was a large stone. And they went splitting up the wood of the wagon, and the cows they offered up as a burnt offering to Jehovah.

15 And the Levites themselves took the ark of Jehovah down and the box that was with it, in which the golden articles were, and they proceeded to put it upon the large stone. And the men of Beth-she'-mesh, for their part, offered up burnt offerings, and they continued rendering up sacrifices on that day to Jehovah.

16 And the five axis lords of the Phi·lis'tines themselves saw it and went their way back to Ek'ron on that day. 17 Now these are the golden piles that the Phi·lis'tines returned as a guilt offering to

Jehovah: for Ash'dod one, for Ga'za one, for Ash'ke·lon one, for Gath one, for Ek'ron one. 18 And the golden jerboas were to the number of all the cities of the Phi·lis'tines belonging to the five axis lords, from the fortified city to the village of the open country.

And the great stone upon which they rested the ark of Jehovah is a witness down to this day in the field of Joshua the Beth-she'mite. 19 And he went striking down the men of Beth-she'mesh, because they had looked upon the ark of Jehovah. So he struck down among the people seventy men—fifty thousand men—and the people began mourning because Jehovah had struck down the people with a great slaughter. 20 Further, the men of Beth-she'mesh said: "Who will be able to stand before Jehovah this holy God, and to whom will he withdraw from off us?" 21 Finally they sent messengers to the inhabitants of Kir'i·ath-je'a·rim, saying: "The Phi·lis'tines have returned the ark of Jehovah. Come down. Take it up to yourselves."

7 Accordingly the men of Kir'i·ath-je'a·rim came and brought the ark of Jehovah up and took it into the house of A·bin'a·dab on the hill, and E·le·a'zar his son was the one whom they sanctified to guard the ark of Jehovah.

2 And it came about that from the day of the Ark's dwelling in Kir'i·ath-je'a·rim the days kept multiplying, so that they amounted to twenty years, and all the house of Israel went lamenting after Jehovah. 3 And Samuel proceeded to say to all the house of Israel: "If it is with all YOUR heart YOU are returning to Jehovah, put away the foreign gods from YOUR midst and also the Ash'to·reth images, and direct YOUR heart unswervingly to Jehovah and serve him alone, and he will deliver YOU from the hand of the Phi·lis'tines." 4 At that the sons of Israel put away the Ba'als and the Ash'to·reth images and began serving Jehovah alone,

5 Then Samuel said: "Collect all Israel together at Miz'pah, that I may pray in YOUR behalf to Jehovah." 6 So they were collected together at Miz'pah, and they went drawing water and pouring it out before Jehovah and kept a fast on that day. And they began saying there: "We have sinned against Jehovah." And Samuel took up judging the sons of Israel in Miz'pah.

7 And the Phi·lis'tines came to hear that the sons of Israel had collected themselves together at Miz'pah, and the axis lords of the Phi·lis'tines got on their way up against Israel. When the sons of Israel heard of it, they began to be afraid on account of the Phi·lis'tines. 8 So the sons of Israel said to Samuel: "Do not keep silent for our sakes from calling to Jehovah our God for aid, that he may save us from the hand of the Phi·lis'tines." 9 Then Samuel took a sucking lamb and offered it up as a burnt offering, a whole offering, to Jehovah; and Samuel began calling to Jehovah for aid in behalf of Israel, and Jehovah proceeded to answer him. 10 And it came about that while Samuel was offering up the burnt offering, the Phi·lis'tines themselves drew near for battle against Israel. And Jehovah now caused it to thunder with a loud noise on that day against the Phi·lis'tines, that he might throw them into confusion; and they got defeated before Israel. 11 At that the men of Israel sallied forth from Miz'pah and went in pursuit of the Phi·lis'tines and kept striking them down as far as south of Beth-car. 12 Then Samuel took a stone and set it between Miz'pah and Jesh'a·nah and began to call its name Eb·en·e'zer. Accordingly he said: "Till now Jehovah has helped us." 13 Thus the Phi·lis'tines were subdued, and they did not come any more into the territory of Israel; and the hand of Jehovah continued to be against the Phi·lis'tines all the days of Samuel. 14 And the cities that

the Phi·lis'tines had taken from Israel kept coming back to Israel from Ek'ron to Gath, and the territory of them Israel delivered from the hand of the Phi·lis'tines.

And there came to be peace between Israel and the Am'or·ites.

15 And Samuel kept on judging Israel all the days of his life. 16 And he traveled from year to year and made the circuit of Beth'el and Gil'gal and Miz'pah and judged Israel at all these places. 17 But his return was to Ra'mah, because there was where his house was, and there he judged Israel. And he proceeded to build an altar there to Jehovah.

8 And it came about that as soon as Samuel had grown old he made appointments of his sons as judges for Israel. 2 Now the name of his first-born son happened to be Joel, and the name of his second A·bi'jah; they were judging in Be'er-she'ba. 3 And his sons did not walk in his ways, but they were inclined to follow unjust profit and would accept a bribe and pervert judgment.

4 In time all the older men of Israel collected themselves together and came to Samuel at Ra'mah 5 and said to him: "Look! You yourself have grown old, but your own sons have not walked in your ways. Now do appoint for us a king to judge us like all the nations." 6 But the thing was bad in the eyes of Samuel inasmuch as they had said: "Do give us a king to judge us," and Samuel began to pray to Jehovah. 7 Then Jehovah said to Samuel: "Listen to the voice of the people as respects all that they say to you; for it is not you whom they have rejected, but it is I whom they have rejected from being king over them. 8 In accord with all their doings that they have done from the day of my bringing them up out of Egypt until this day in that they kept leaving me and serving other gods, that is the way they are doing also to you. 9 And now listen to

their voice. Only this, that you should solemnly warn them, and you must tell them the rightful due of the king who will reign over them."

10 So Samuel said all the words of Jehovah to the people who were asking a king of him. 11 And he proceeded to say: "This will become the rightful due of the king that will reign over YOU: YOUR sons he will take and put them as his in his chariots and among his horsemen, and some will have to run before his chariots; 12 and to appoint for himself chiefs over thousands and chiefs over fifties, and [some] to do his plowing and to reap his harvest and to make his war instruments and his chariot instruments. 13 And YOUR daughters he will take for ointment mixers and cooks and bakers. 14 And YOUR fields and YOUR vineyards and YOUR olive groves, the best ones, he will take and actually give to his servants. 15 And of YOUR fields of seed and of YOUR vineyards he will take the tenth, and he will certainly give [them] to his court officials and his servants. 16 And YOUR menservants and YOUR maidservants and YOUR best herds, and YOUR asses he will take, and he will have to use them for his work. 17 Of YOUR flocks he will take the tenth, and YOU yourselves will become his as servants. 18 And YOU will certainly cry out in that day by reason of YOUR king, whom YOU have chosen for yourselves, but Jehovah will not answer YOU in that day."

19 However, the people refused to listen to the voice of Samuel and said: "No, but a king is what will come to be over us. 20 And we must become, we also, like all the nations, and our king must judge us and go out before us and fight our battles." 21 And Samuel gave a hearing to all the words of the people; then he spoke them in the ears of Jehovah. 22 And Jehovah proceeded to say to Samuel: "Listen to their voice, and you must cause a king to reign for

them." Accordingly Samuel said to the men of Israel: "Go each one to his city."

9 Now there happened to be a man of Benjamin, and his name was Kish, the son of A·bi′el, the son of Ze′ror, the son of Be·co′rath, the son of A·phi′ah, a Ben′ja·min·ite, a man mighty in wealth. 2 And he happened to have a son whose name was Saul, young and handsome, and there was no man of the sons of Israel that was handsomer than he; from his shoulders upward he was taller than all the people.

3 And the she-asses belonging to Kish the father of Saul got lost. So Kish said to Saul his son: "Take, please, with you one of the attendants and get up, go, look for the she-asses." 4 And he went passing through the mountainous region of E′phra·im and passing on through the land of Shal′i·shah, and they did not find them. And they went passing on through the land of Sha′a·lim, but they were not [there]. And he went passing on through the land of the Ben′ja·min·ites, and they did not find [them].

5 They themselves came into the land of Zuph; and Saul, for his part, said to his attendant that was with him: "Do come, and let us return, that my father may not quit attending to the she-asses and actually become anxious about us." 6 But he said to him: "Look, please! There is a man of God in this city, and the man is held in honor. All that he says comes true without fail. Let us go there now. Perhaps he can tell us our way that we must go." 7 At this Saul said to his attendant: "And if we should go, what shall we bring to the man? because the bread itself has disappeared from our receptacles, and, as a gift, there is nothing to bring to the man of the [true] God. What is there with us?" 8 So the attendant answered Saul once more and said: "Look! There is a quarter of a shekel of silver found in my hand, and I shall have to give it

to the man of the [true] God, and he will have to tell us our way." 9 (In former times in Israel this was the way the man would have talked on his going to seek God: "Come, and let us go to the seer." For the prophet of today used to be called a seer in former times.) 10 Then Saul said to his attendant: "Your word is good. Do come, let us go." And they went their way to the city where the man of the [true] God was.

11 While they were going up on the ascent to the city, they themselves found girls going out to draw water. So they said to them: "Is the seer in this place?" 12 Then they answered them and said: "He is. Look! He is ahead of you. Hurry now, because today he has come to the city, for there is a sacrifice today for the people on the high place. 13 As soon as you men come into the city, you will directly find him before he goes up to the high place to eat; because the people may not eat until his coming, for he is the one that blesses the sacrifice. First after that those who are invited may eat. And now go up, because him—just now you will find him." 14 Accordingly they went on up to the city. As they were coming into the middle of the city, why, there was Samuel coming out to meet them to go up to the high place.

15 As for Jehovah, he had uncovered the ear of Samuel the day before Saul came, saying: 16 "Tomorrow about this time I shall send to you a man from the land of Benjamin, and you must anoint him as leader over my people Israel; and he must save my people from the hand of the Phi·lis′tines, because I have seen [the affliction of] my people, for their outcry has come to me." 17 And Samuel himself saw Saul, and Jehovah, for his part, answered him: "Here is the man of whom I said to you, 'This is the one that will keep my people within bounds.'"

18 Then Saul approached Samuel in the middle of the gate and

said: "Do tell me, please, Just where is the house of the seer?" 19 And Samuel proceeded to answer Saul and say: "I am the seer. Go up before me to the high place, and YOU men must eat with me today, and I must send you away in the morning, and all that is in your heart I shall tell you. 20 As regards the she-asses that were lost to you three days ago, do not set your heart on them, for they have been found. And to whom does all that is desirable of Israel belong? Is it not to you and to the whole house of your father?" 21 At this Saul answered and said: "Am I not a Ben′ja·min·ite of the smallest of the tribes of Israel, and my family the most insignificant of all the families of the tribe of Benjamin? So why have you spoken to me a thing like this?"

22 Then Samuel took Saul and his attendant and brought them to the dining hall and gave them a place at the head of those invited; and they were about thirty men. 23 Later Samuel said to the cook: "Do give the portion that I have given to you, of which I said to you, 'Put it away by you.'" 24 At that the cook lifted off the leg and what was on it, and put it before Saul. And he went on to say: "Here is what has been reserved. Put it before yourself. Eat, because to the appointed time they have reserved it for you that you may eat with those invited." So Saul ate with Samuel on that day. 25 Subsequently they went down from the high place to the city, and he continued speaking with Saul on the housetop. 26 Then they rose early, and it came about that as soon as the dawn ascended Samuel proceeded to call to Saul on the housetop, saying: "Do get up, that I may send you away." So Saul got up and both of them, he and Samuel, went forth out-of-doors. 27 While they were descending by the edge of the city Samuel himself said to Saul: "Say to the attendant that he should pass on ahead of us"—so he passed on—

"and, as for you, stand still now that I may let you hear the word of God."

10 Samuel then took the flask of oil and poured it out upon his head and kissed him and said: "Is it not because Jehovah has anointed you as a leader over his inheritance? 2 On your going away from me today you will certainly find two men close by the tomb of Rachel in the territory of Benjamin at Zel′zah, and they will certainly say to you, 'The she-asses that you have gone to look for have been found, but now your father has given up the matter of the she-asses and has become anxious about YOU men, saying: "What shall I do about my son?"' 3 And you must pass on from there still farther and come as far as the big tree of Ta′bor, and there there must encounter you three men going up to the [true] God at Beth′el, one carrying three kids and one carrying three round loaves of bread and one carrying a large jar of wine. 4 And they will certainly ask about your welfare and give you two loaves, and you must accept them from their hand. 5 It is after that that you will come to the hill of the [true] God, where there is a garrison of the Phi·lis′tines. And it should come about that at the time of your coming there to the city, you will certainly meet a group of prophets coming down from the high place, and ahead of them a stringed instrument and tambourine and flute and harp, while they are speaking as prophets. 6 And the spirit of Jehovah will certainly become operative upon you, and you will certainly speak as a prophet along with them and be changed into another man. 7 And it must occur that when these signs come to you, do for yourself what your hand finds possible, because the [true] God is with you. 8 And you must go down ahead of me to Gil′gal; and, look! I am going down to you to offer up burnt sacrifices, to render up communion sacrifices. Seven days you should keep waiting until my coming to you, and I shall certainly let you know what you should do."

9 And it occurred that as soon as he turned his shoulder to go from Samuel, God began changing the heart of his into another; and all these signs proceeded to come true on that day. 10 So they went from there to the hill, and here there was a group of prophets to meet him; at once the spirit of God became operative upon him, and he began to speak as a prophet in the middle of them. 11 And it came about that when all those knowing him formerly saw him, look! it was with prophets that he prophesied. Consequently the people said one to another: "What is this that has happened to the son of Kish? Is Saul also among the prophets?" 12 Then a man from there answered and said: "But who is their father?" That is why it has become a proverbial saying: "Is Saul also among the prophets?"

13 At length he finished speaking as a prophet and came to the high place. 14 Later the brother of Saul's father said to him and to his attendant: "Where did you go?" Upon that he said: "To look for the she-asses, and we kept on going to see, but they were not [there]. So we came to Samuel." 15 At this Saul's uncle said: "Do tell me, please, What did Samuel say to you men?" 16 In turn Saul said to his uncle: "He told us unmistakably that the she-asses had been found." And the matter of the kingship about which Samuel had talked, he did not tell him.

17 And Samuel proceeded to call the people together to Jehovah at Miz′pah 18 and to say to the sons of Israel: "This is what Jehovah the God of Israel has said, 'It was I who brought Israel up out of Egypt and who went delivering you from the hand of Egypt and from the hand of all the kingdoms that were oppressing you. 19 But you—today you have rejected your God who was a savior

to you out of all your evils and your distresses, and you went on to say: "No, but a king is what you should put over us." And now take your stand before Jehovah by your tribes and by your thousands.'"

20 Accordingly Samuel had all the tribes of Israel draw near, and the tribe of Benjamin came to be picked. 21 Then he had the tribe of Benjamin draw near by its families, and the family of the Mat′rites came to be picked. Finally Saul the son of Kish came to be picked. And they went looking for him, and he was not to be found. 22 Hence they inquired further of Jehovah: "Has the man come here as yet?" To this Jehovah said: "Here he is, hidden among the luggage." 23 So they went running and took him from there. When he took his stand in the middle of the people, he was taller than all the other people from his shoulders upward. 24 Then Samuel said to all the people: "Have you seen the one whom Jehovah has chosen, that there is none like him among all the people?" And all the people began to shout and say: "Let the king live!"

25 Upon that Samuel spoke to the people about the rightful due of the kingship and wrote it in a book and deposited it before Jehovah. Then Samuel sent all the people away, each one to his house. 26 As for Saul himself, he went to his home at Gib′e·ah, and the valiant men whose heart God had touched proceeded to go with him. 27 As for the good-for-nothing men, they said: "How will this one save us?" Accordingly they despised him, and they did not bring any gift to him. But he continued like one grown speechless.

11 And Na′hash the Am′monite proceeded to go up and camp against Ja′besh in Gil′e·ad. At that all the men of Ja′besh said to Na′hash: "Conclude a covenant with us that we may serve you." 2 Then Na′hash the Am′mon·ite said to them: "On this condition

I shall conclude it with you, on the condition of boring out every right eye of yours, and I must put it as a reproach upon all Israel." 3 In turn the older men of Ja'besh said to him: "Give us seven days' time, and we will send messengers into all the territory of Israel and, if there is no savior of us, we must then go out to you." 4 In time the messengers came to Gib'e·ah of Saul and spoke the words in the ears of the people, and all the people began raising their voice and weeping.

5 But here is Saul coming after the herd from the field, and Saul proceeded to say: "What is the matter with the people, that they should weep?" And they began relating to him the words of the men of Ja'besh. 6 And the spirit of God became operative upon Saul on his hearing these words, and his anger got very hot. 7 So he took a pair of bulls and cut them in pieces and sent these into all the territory of Israel by the hand of the messengers, saying: "Whoever of us is not going out as a follower of Saul and of Samuel, this is the way it will be done to his cattle!" And the dread of Jehovah began to fall upon the people so that they came out as one man. 8 Then he took the sum of them in Be'zek, and the sons of Israel amounted to three hundred thousand, and the men of Judah thirty thousand. 9 They now said to the messengers that had come: "This is what you will say to the men of Ja'besh in Gil'e·ad, 'Tomorrow salvation will take place for you when the sun gets hot.'" With that the messengers came and told the men of Ja'besh, and they gave way to rejoicing. 10 Accordingly the men of Ja'besh said: "Tomorrow we shall come out to you people, and you must do to us in harmony with all that is good in your eyes."

11 And it came about on the next day that Saul proceeded to put the people into three bands; and they made their way into the middle of the camp during the morning watch and went striking down the Am'mon·ites till the day grew hot. When there proved to be some that were left over, then they were sent scattering and there were not left over among them two together. 12 And the people began to say to Samuel: "Who is it saying, 'Saul—is he to be king over us?' Give the men over, that we may put them to death." 13 However, Saul said: "Not a man should be put to death on this day, because today Jehovah has performed salvation in Israel."

14 Later Samuel said to the people: "Come and let us go to Gil'gal that we may there make the kingship anew." 15 So all the people went to Gil'gal, and there they proceeded to make Saul king before Jehovah in Gil'gal. Then they rendered up communion sacrifices there before Jehovah, and there Saul and all the men of Israel continued rejoicing to a great degree.

12 Finally Samuel said to all Israel: "Here I have listened to your voice as respects all that you have said to me, that I should cause a king to reign over you. 2 And now here is the king walking before you! As for me, I have grown old and gray, and my sons, here they are with you, and I—I have walked before you from my youth until this day. 3 Here I am. Answer against me in front of Jehovah and in front of his anointed one: Whose bull have I taken or whose ass have I taken or whom have I defrauded or whom have I crushed or from whose hand have I accepted hush money that I should hide my eyes with it? And I shall make restoration to you people." 4 To this they said: "You have not defrauded us, nor have you crushed us, nor have you accepted anything at all from the hand of a single one." 5 So he said to them: "Jehovah is a witness against you, and his anointed one is a witness this day that you have found nothing at all in my hand." To this they said: "He is a witness."

6 And Samuel went on to say to the people: "Jehovah [is a witness], who used Moses and Aaron and who brought YOUR forefathers up out of the land of Egypt. 7 And now take YOUR stand, and I will judge YOU before Jehovah [and recount to YOU] all the righteous acts of Jehovah that he has done with YOU and with YOUR forefathers.

8 "As soon as Jacob had come into Egypt and YOUR forefathers began calling to Jehovah for aid, Jehovah proceeded to send Moses and Aaron, that they might lead YOUR forefathers out from Egypt and cause them to dwell in this place. 9 And they went forgetting Jehovah their God, so that he sold them into the hand of Sis'e·ra the chief of the army of Ha'zor and into the hand of the Phi·lis'tines and into the hand of the king of Mo'ab, and they kept fighting against them. 10 And they began to call to Jehovah for aid and say, 'We have sinned, for we have left Jehovah that we might serve the Ba'als and the Ash'to·reth images; and now deliver us out of the hand of our enemies, that we may serve you.' 11 And Jehovah proceeded to send Jer·ub·ba'al and Be'dan and Jeph'thah and Samuel and deliver YOU out of the hand of YOUR enemies all around, that YOU might dwell in security. 12 When YOU saw that Na'hash the king of the sons of Am'mon had come against YOU, YOU kept saying to me, 'No, but a king is what should reign over us!' all the while Jehovah YOUR God being YOUR King. 13 And now here is the king whom YOU have chosen, for whom YOU asked; and here Jehovah has put over YOU a king. 14 If YOU will fear Jehovah and actually serve him and obey his voice, and YOU will not rebel against the order of Jehovah, both YOU and the king who must reign over YOU will certainly prove to be followers of Jehovah YOUR God. 15 But if YOU will not obey the voice of Jehovah and YOU will actually rebel against

the order of Jehovah, the hand of Jehovah will certainly prove to be against YOU and YOUR fathers. 16 Now, also, take YOUR stand and see this great thing that Jehovah is doing before YOUR eyes. 17 Is it not wheat harvest today? I shall call to Jehovah that he may give thunders and rain; then know and see that YOUR evil is abundant that YOU have done in the eyes of Jehovah in asking for yourselves a king."

18 Upon that Samuel called to Jehovah, and Jehovah proceeded to give thunders and rain on that day, so that all the people were greatly in fear of Jehovah and of Samuel. 19 And all the people began to say to Samuel: "Pray in behalf of your servants to Jehovah your God, as we do not want to die; because we have added to all our sins an evil in asking for ourselves a king."

20 So Samuel said to the people: "Do not be afraid. YOU—YOU have done all this evil. Only do not turn aside from following Jehovah, and YOU must serve Jehovah with all YOUR heart. 21 And YOU must not turn aside to follow the unrealities that are of no benefit and that do not deliver, because they are unrealities. 22 For Jehovah will not desert his people for the sake of his great name, because Jehovah has taken it upon himself to make YOU his people. 23 As for me also, it is unthinkable, on my part, to sin against Jehovah by ceasing to pray in YOUR behalf; and I must instruct YOU in the good and right way. 24 Only fear Jehovah, and YOU must serve him in truth with all YOUR heart; for see what great things he has done for YOU. 25 But if YOU flagrantly do what is bad, YOU will be swept away, both YOU and YOUR king."

13 Saul was [?] years old when he began to reign, and for two years he reigned over Israel. 2 And Saul proceeded to choose for himself three thousand men out of Israel; and two thousand came

to be with Saul at Mich'mash and in the mountainous region of Beth'el, and a thousand proved to be with Jon'a·than at Gib'e·ah of Benjamin, and the rest of the people he sent away, each one to his tent. 3 Then Jon'a·than struck down the garrison of the Phi·lis'tines that was in Ge'ba; and the Phi·lis'tines got to hear of it. As for Saul, he had the horn blown throughout all the land, saying: "Let the Hebrews hear!" 4 And all Israel itself heard tell: "Saul has struck down a garrison of the Phi·lis'tines, and now Israel has become foul-smelling among the Phi·lis'tines." So the people were called together to follow Saul to Gil'gal.

5 And the Phi·lis'tines, for their part, collected themselves together to fight against Israel, thirty thousand war chariots and six thousand horsemen and people like the grains of sand that are upon the seashore for multitude; and they went their way up and began camping in Mich'mash to the east of Beth-a'ven. 6 And the men of Israel themselves saw that they were in sore straits, because the people were hard pressed; and the people went hiding themselves in the caves and the hollows and the crags and the vaults and the waterpits. 7 Hebrews even crossed the Jordan to the land of Gad and Gil'e·ad. But Saul himself was yet in Gil'gal, and all the people trembled while following him. 8 And he continued waiting for seven days to the appointed time that Samuel [had said]; and Samuel did not come to Gil'gal, and the people were scattering from him. 9 Finally Saul said: "BRING near to me the burnt sacrifice and the communion sacrifices." With that he went offering up the burnt sacrifice.

10 And it came about that as soon as he had finished offering up the burnt sacrifice, why, there was Samuel coming in. So Saul went out to meet him and bless him. 11 Then Samuel said: "What is it you have done?" To this Saul said: "I saw that the people had been dispersed from me, and you—you did not come within the appointed days, and the Phi·lis'tines were being collected together at Mich'mash, 12 so I said to myself, 'Now the Phi·lis'tines will come down against me at Gil'gal, and the face of Jehovah I have not softened.' So I compelled myself and went offering up the burnt sacrifice."

13 At this Samuel said to Saul: "You have acted foolishly. You have not kept the commandment of Jehovah your God that he commanded you, because, if you had, Jehovah would have made your kingdom firm over Israel to time indefinite. 14 And now your kingdom will not last. Jehovah will certainly find for himself a man agreeable to his heart; and Jehovah will commission him as a leader over his people, because you did not keep what Jehovah commanded you."

15 Then Samuel rose and went his way up from Gil'gal to Gib'e·ah of Benjamin, and Saul proceeded to take the count of the people, those yet found with him, about six hundred men. 16 And Saul and Jon'a·than his son and the people yet found with them were dwelling in Ge'ba of Benjamin. As for the Phi·lis'tines, they had encamped in Mich'mash. 17 And the force of pillagers would sally forth from the camp of the Phi·lis'tines in three bands. The one band would turn to the road to Oph'rah, to the land of Shu'al, 18 and the other band would turn to the road of Beth-ho'ron, and the third band would turn to the road to the boundary that looks toward the valley of Ze·bo'im, toward the wilderness.

19 Now there was not a smith to be found in all the land of Israel, because the Phi·lis'tines had said: "That the Hebrews may not make a sword or a spear." 20 And all the Israelites would go down to the Phi·lis'tines to get each one his plowshare or his mattock or his ax or his sickle sharpened. 21 And the price for sharpening

proved to be a pim for the plow-shares and for the mattocks and for the three-toothed instruments and for the axes and for fixing fast the oxgoad. 22 And it happened on the day of battle that not a sword or a spear was found in the hand of any of the people that were with Saul and Jon′a·than; but there could be found one belonging to Saul and to Jon′a·than his son.

23 Now an outpost of the Phi-lis′tines would sally forth to the ravine pass of Mich′mash.

14 And it came about one day that Jon′a·than the son of Saul proceeded to say to the attendant carrying his weapons: "Do come and let us cross over to the outpost of the Phi·lis′tines who are across over there." But to his father he did not tell it. 2 And Saul was dwelling at the outskirts of Gib′e·ah under the pomegranate tree that is in Mig′ron; and the people that were with him were about six hundred men. 3 (And A·hi′jah the son of A·hi′tub, the brother of Ich′a·bod, the son of Phin′e·has, the son of E′li, the priest of Jehovah in Shi′loh, was carrying the eph′od.) And the people themselves did not know that Jon′a·than had gone. 4 Now between the passages that Jon′a·than looked for to cross over against the outpost of the Phi·lis′tines there was a toothlike crag here on this side and a toothlike crag there on that side, and the name of the one was Bo′zez and the name of the other was Se′neh. 5 The one tooth was a pillar on the north facing Mich′mash, and the other was on the south facing Ge′ba.

6 So Jon′a·than said to the attendant, his armor-bearer: "Do come and let us cross over to the outpost of these uncircumcised men. Perhaps Jehovah will work for us, for there is no hindrance to Jehovah to save by many or by few." 7 At this his armor-bearer said to him: "Do whatever is in your heart. Turn where you wish to. Here I am with you in accord

with your heart." 8 Then Jon′a·than said: "Here we are crossing over to the men, and let us expose ourselves to them. 9 If this is the way they should say to us, 'Stand still until we make contact with you!' we must then stand where we are, and we should not go on up to them. 10 But if this is the way they should say, 'Come up against us!' we must then go up, because Jehovah will certainly give them into our hand, and this is for us the sign."

11 With that the two of them exposed themselves to the outpost of the Phi·lis′tines. And the Phi-lis′tines proceeded to say: "Here are the Hebrews coming out from the holes where they have hidden themselves." 12 So the men of the outpost answered Jon′a·than and his armor-bearer and said: "Come on up to us, and we will let you know a thing!" At once Jon′a·than said to his armor-bearer: "Come up after me, because Jehovah will certainly give them into the hand of Israel." 13 And Jon′a·than kept going up on his hands and his feet, and his armor-bearer after him; and they began to fall before Jon′a·than, and his armor-bearer was putting them to death behind him. 14 And the first slaughter with which Jon′a·than and his armor-bearer struck them down amounted to about twenty men within about half the plowing line in an acre of field.

15 Then a trembling occurred in the camp in the field and among all the people of the outpost; and the force of pillagers trembled, even they, and the earth began quaking, and it developed into a trembling from God. 16 And the watchmen belonging to Saul in Gib′e·ah of Benjamin got to see it, and, look! the turmoil swayed this way and that.

17 And Saul proceeded to say to the people that were with him: "Take the count, please, and see who has gone out from us." When they took the count, why, look! Jon′a·than and his armor-bearer

were not there. 18 Saul now said to A·hi'jah: "Do bring the ark of the [true] God near!" (For the ark of the [true] God proved to be on that day with the sons of Israel.) 19 And it came about that while Saul was speaking to the priest, the turmoil that was in the camp of the Phi·lis'tines continued to go on, getting greater and greater. Then Saul said to the priest: "Withdraw your hand." 20 Thus Saul and all the people that were with him were called out. So they came as far as the battle, and there the sword of each one had come to be against his fellow man; the rout was very great. 21 And the Hebrews that had come to belong to the Phi·lis'tines as formerly and that had gone up with them into the camp round about, even they too were for proving themselves to be with Israel who was with Saul and Jon'a·than. 22 All the men of Israel also that were hidden in the mountainous region of E'phra·im heard that the Phi·lis'tines had taken to flight, and they too went pursuing closely after them into the battle. 23 And Jehovah proceeded on that day to save Israel, and the battle itself passed over to Beth-a'ven.

24 And the men of Israel themselves were hard pressed on that day, and yet Saul put the people under the pledge of an oath, saying: "Cursed is the man that eats bread before the evening and until I have taken vengeance upon my enemies!" And none of the people tasted bread.

25 And all those of the land came into the woods, when honey happened to be over all the surface of the field. 26 When the people came into the woods, why, look! there was a dripping of honey, but there was no one putting his hand to his mouth, because the people were afraid of the oath. 27 As for Jon'a·than, he had not been listening when his father put the people under an oath, so he stretched out the tip of the rod that was in his hand and dipped it into the honeycomb and drew his hand back to his mouth, and his eyes began to beam. 28 At this one of the people answered and said: "Your father solemnly put the people under oath, saying, 'Cursed is the man that eats bread today!'" (And the people began to get tired.) 29 However, Jon'a·than said: "My father has brought ostracism upon the land. SEE, please, how my eyes have beamed because I tasted this little bit of honey. 30 How much more so if the people had but eaten today from the spoil of their enemies that they found! For now the slaughter upon the Phi·lis'tines has not been great."

31 And on that day they kept striking down the Phi·lis'tines from Mich'mash to Ai'ja·lon, and the people got to be very tired. 32 And the people began darting greedily at the spoil and taking sheep and cattle and calves and slaughtering them on the earth, and the people fell to eating along with the blood. 33 So they told Saul, saying: "Look! The people are sinning against Jehovah by eating along with the blood." At this he said: "You have dealt treacherously. First of all, roll a great stone to me." 34 After that Saul said: "Scatter among the people, and you must say to them, 'Bring near to me, each one of you, his bull and, each one, his sheep, and you must do the slaughtering in this place and the eating, and you must not sin against Jehovah by eating along with the blood.'" Accordingly all the people brought near each one his bull that was in his hand that night and did the slaughtering there. 35 And Saul proceeded to build an altar to Jehovah. With it he started altar building to Jehovah.

36 Later Saul said: "Let us go down after the Phi·lis'tines by night and plunder them until the morning lightens up, and let us not leave a single one among them." To this they said: "Anything that is good in your eyes do." Then the

priest said: "Let us approach here to the [true] God." 37 And Saul began to inquire of God: "Shall I go down after the Phi·lis'tines? Will you give them into the hand of Israel?" And he did not answer him on that day. 38 So Saul said: "Come near here, all you key men of the people, and ascertain and see in what way this sin has come to be today. 39 For as Jehovah, who is the Deliverer of Israel, is alive, even if it is in Jon'a·than my son, yet he will positively die." But there was no one answering him out of all the people. 40 And he went on to say to all Israel: "You yourselves will come to be on the one side, and I and Jon'a·than my son—we will come to be on the other side." At this the people said to Saul: "What is good in your eyes do."

41 And Saul proceeded to say to Jehovah: "O God of Israel, do give Thum'mim!" Then Jon'a·than and Saul were taken, and the people themselves went out. 42 Saul now said: "CAST lots to decide between me and Jon'a·than my son." And Jon'a·than got to be taken. 43 Then Saul said to Jon'a·than: "Do tell me, What have you done?" So Jon'a·than told him and said: "I did for a fact taste a little honey on the tip of the rod that is in my hand. Here I am! Let me die!"

44 At this Saul said: "Thus may God do and thus may he add to it, if you do not positively die, Jon'a·than." 45 But the people said to Saul: "Is Jon'a·than to die, who has performed this great salvation in Israel? It is unthinkable! As Jehovah is alive, not as much as a single hair of his head will fall to the earth; for it was with God that he worked this day." With that the people redeemed Jon'a·than, and he did not die.

46 So Saul withdrew from following the Phi·lis'tines, and the Phi·lis'tines themselves went to their place.

47 And Saul himself took the kingship over Israel and went warring round about against all his enemies, against Mo'ab and against the sons of Am'mon and against E'dom and against the kings of Zo'bah and against the Phi·lis'tines; and wherever he would turn he administered condemnation. 48 And he went on acting valiantly and proceeded to strike down Am'a·lek and to deliver Israel out of the hand of their pillager.

49 And the sons of Saul came to be Jon'a·than and Ish'vi and Mal'chi-shu'a, and, as for the names of his two daughters, the name of the one born first was Me'rab and the name of the younger one Mi'chal. 50 And the name of Saul's wife was A·hin'o·am the daughter of A·him'a·az, and the name of the chief of his army was Ab'ner the son of Ner, the uncle of Saul. 51 And Kish was the father of Saul, and Ner the father of Ab'ner was the son of A·bi'el.

52 And the warfare continued heavy against the Phi·lis'tines all the days of Saul. When Saul saw any mighty man or any valiant person, he would gather him to himself.

15 Then Samuel said to Saul: "It was I whom Jehovah sent to anoint you as king over his people Israel, and now listen to the voice of the words of Jehovah. 2 This is what Jehovah of armies has said, 'I must call to account what Am'a·lek did to Israel when he set himself against him in the way while he was coming up out of Egypt. 3 Now go, and you must strike down Am'a·lek and devote him to destruction with all that he has, and you must not have compassion upon him, and you must put them to death, man as well as woman, child as well as suckling, bull as well as sheep, camel as well as ass.'" 4 Accordingly Saul summoned the people and took the count of them in Te·la'im, two hundred thousand men on foot and ten thousand men of Judah.

5 And Saul proceeded to come as far as the city of Am'a·lek and to lie in ambush by the torrent valley.

6 Meanwhile Saul said to the Ken'ites: "Go, DEPART, GO DOWN from the midst of the A·mal'ek·ites, that I may not sweep you away with them. As for you, you exercised loving-kindness with all the sons of Israel at the time of their coming up out of Egypt." So the Ken'ites departed from the midst of Am'a·lek. 7 After that Saul went striking down Am'a·lek from Hav'i·lah as far as Shur, which is in front of Egypt. 8 And he got to catch A'gag the king of Am'a·lek alive, and all the other people he devoted to destruction with the edge of the sword. 9 But Saul and the people had compassion upon A'gag and upon the best of the flock and the herd and the fat ones and upon the rams and upon all that was good, and they did not wish to devote them to destruction. As for all the goods that were despicable and rejected, these they devoted to destruction.

10 The word of Jehovah now came to Samuel, saying: 11 "I do regret that I have caused Saul to reign as king, because he has turned back from following me, and my words he has not carried out." And it was distressing to Samuel, and he kept crying out to Jehovah all night long. 12 Then Samuel got up early to meet Saul in the morning. But report was made to Samuel, saying: "Saul came to Car'mel, and, look! he was erecting a monument for himself, and he then turned around and went across and descended to Gil'gal." 13 At length Samuel came to Saul, and Saul began to say to him: "Blessed are you of Jehovah. I have carried out the word of Jehovah." 14 But Samuel said: "Then what does this sound of the flock in my ears mean, and the sound of the herd that I am hearing?" 15 To this Saul said: "From the A·mal'ek·ites they have brought them, because the people had compassion upon the best of the flock and of the herd, for the purpose of sacrificing to Jehovah your God; but what was

left over we have devoted to destruction." 16 At this Samuel said to Saul: "Stop! And I will tell you what Jehovah spoke to me last night." So he said to him: "Speak!"

17 And Samuel went on to say: "Was it not when you were little in your own eyes that you were head of the tribes of Israel, and Jehovah proceeded to anoint you as king over Israel? 18 Later Jehovah sent you on a mission and said, 'Go, and you must devote the sinners, the A·mal'ek·ites, to destruction, and you must fight against them until you will have exterminated them.' 19 So why is it you did not obey the voice of Jehovah but went darting greedily at the spoil and doing what was bad in the eyes of Jehovah?"

20 However, Saul said to Samuel: "But I have obeyed the voice of Jehovah in that I went on the mission on which Jehovah had sent me and I brought A'gag the king of Am'a·lek, but Am'a·lek I have devoted to destruction. 21 And the people went taking from the spoil sheep and cattle, the choicest of them as something devoted to destruction, to sacrifice to Jehovah your God in Gil'gal."

22 In turn Samuel said: "Does Jehovah have as much delight in burnt offerings and sacrifices as in obeying the voice of Jehovah? Look! To obey is better than a sacrifice, to pay attention than the fat of rams; 23 for rebelliousness is the same as the sin of divination, and pushing ahead presumptuously the same as [using] uncanny power and teraphim. Since you have rejected the word of Jehovah, he accordingly rejects you from being king."

24 Then Saul said to Samuel: "I have sinned; for I have overstepped the order of Jehovah and your words, because I feared the people and so obeyed their voice. 25 And now, please, pardon my sin and return with me that I may prostrate myself to Jehovah." 26 But Samuel said to Saul: "I shall not return with you, for you

have rejected the word of Jehovah, and Jehovah rejects you from continuing as king over Israel." 27 As Samuel was turning about to go, he immediately grabbed hold of the skirt of his sleeveless coat, but it ripped away. 28 At this Samuel said to him: "Jehovah has ripped away the royal rule of Israel from off you today, and he will certainly give it to a fellow man of yours who is better than you. 29 And, besides, the Excellency of Israel will not prove false, and He will not feel regrets, for He is not an earthling man so as to feel regrets."

30 At this he said: "I have sinned. Now honor me, please, in front of the older men of my people and in front of Israel and return with me, and I shall certainly prostrate myself to Jehovah your God." 31 So Samuel returned behind Saul, and Saul proceeded to prostrate himself to Jehovah. 32 After that Samuel said: "Bring A'gag the king of Am'a·lek near to me." Then A'gag went to him reluctantly, and A'gag began to say to himself: "Truly the bitter experience of death has departed." 33 However, Samuel said: "Just as your sword has bereaved women of children, in that way your mother will be most bereaved of children among women." With that Samuel went hacking A'gag to pieces before Jehovah in Gil'gal.

34 Samuel now went his way to Ra'mah, and Saul, for his part, went up to his own house at Gib'e·ah of Saul. 35 And Samuel did not see Saul again until the day of his death, because Samuel had gone into mourning for Saul. As for Jehovah, he regretted that he had made Saul king over Israel.

16 Eventually Jehovah said to Samuel: "For how long will you be mourning for Saul, while I, on the other hand, have rejected him from ruling as king over Israel? Fill your horn with oil and go. I shall send you to Jes'se the Beth'le·hem·ite, because I have provided among his sons a king for myself." 2 But Samuel said:

"How can I go? Once Saul has heard of it he will certainly kill me." And Jehovah went on to say: "A young cow of the herd you should take with you, and you must say, 'To sacrifice to Jehovah is why I have come.' 3 And you must call Jes'se to the sacrifice; and I, for my part, shall make known to you what you should do, and you must anoint for me the one whom I designate to you."

4 And Samuel proceeded to do what Jehovah spoke. When he came to Beth'le·hem the older men of the city began to tremble at meeting him, and so they said: "Does your coming mean peace?" 5 To this he said: "It means peace. To sacrifice to Jehovah is why I have come. Sanctify yourselves, and you must come with me to the sacrifice." Then he sanctified Jes'se and his sons, after which he called them to the sacrifice. 6 And it came about that, as they came in and he caught sight of E·li'ab, he at once said: "Surely his anointed one is before Jehovah." 7 But Jehovah said to Samuel: "Do not look at his appearance and at the height of his stature, for I have rejected him. For not the way man sees [is the way God sees], because mere man sees what appears to the eyes; but as for Jehovah, he sees what the heart is." 8 Then Jes'se called A·bin'a·dab and had him pass before Samuel, but he said: "Neither has Jehovah chosen this one." 9 Next Jes'se had Sham'mah pass by, but he said: "Neither has Jehovah chosen this one." 10 So Jes'se had seven of his sons pass before Samuel; still Samuel said to Jes'se: "Jehovah has not chosen these."

11 Finally Samuel said to Jes'se: "Are these all the boys?" To this he said: "The youngest one has till now been left out, and, look! he is pasturing the sheep." At that Samuel said to Jes'se: "Do send and fetch him, because we shall not sit down to meal until his coming here." 12 Accordingly he sent and had him come. Now he was

ruddy, a young man with beautiful eyes and handsome in appearance. Then Jehovah said: "Get up, anoint him, for this is he!" 13 Accordingly Samuel took the horn of oil and anointed him in the midst of his brothers. And the spirit of Jehovah began to be operative upon David from that day forward. Later Samuel rose and went his way to Ra′mah.

14 And the very spirit of Jehovah departed from Saul, and a bad spirit from Jehovah terrorized him. 15 And the servants of Saul began to say to him: "Here, now, God's bad spirit is terrorizing you. 16 Let our lord, please, command your servants before you that they should look for a skilled man playing upon the harp. And it must occur that, when God's bad spirit comes to be upon you, he will have to play with his hand, and it will certainly be well with you." 17 So Saul said to his servants: "Provide me, please, a man doing well at playing, and you must bring him to me."

18 And one of the attendants proceeded to answer and say: "Look! I have seen how a son of Jes′se the Beth′le·hem·ite is skilled at playing, and he is a valiant, mighty man and a man of war and an intelligent speaker and a well-formed man, and Jehovah is with him." 19 Then Saul sent messengers to Jes′se and said: "Do send to me David your son, who is with the flock." 20 So Jes′se took an ass, bread and a skin bottle of wine and a kid of the goats and sent them by the hand of David his son to Saul. 21 Thus David came to Saul and attended upon him; and he got to loving him very much, and he came to be his armor-bearer. 22 Consequently Saul sent to Jes′se, saying: "Let David, please, keep attending upon me, for he has found favor in my eyes." 23 And it occurred that, when God's spirit came to be upon Saul, David took the harp and played with his hand; and there was relief for Saul and it was well with him, and the bad spirit departed from upon him.

17 And the Phi·lis′tines went collecting their camps together for war. When they were collected together at So′coh, which belongs to Judah, then they took up camping between So′coh and A·ze′kah, in E′phes·dam′mim. 2 As for Saul and the men of Israel, they collected themselves together and took up camping in the low plain of E′lah, and they went drawing up in battle formation to meet the Phi·lis′tines. 3 And the Phi·lis′tines were standing on the mountain on this side, and the Israelites were standing on the mountain on that side, with the valley between them.

4 And a champion began to go out from the camps of the Phi·lis′tines, his name being Go·li′ath, from Gath, his height being six cubits and a span. 5 And there was a helmet of copper on his head, and he was clad with a coat of mail, of overlapping scales, and the weight of the coat of mail was five thousand shekels of copper. 6 And there were greaves of copper above his feet and a javelin of copper between his shoulders. 7 And the wooden shaft of his spear was like the beam of loom workers, and the blade of his spear was six hundred shekels of iron; and the bearer of the large shield was marching ahead of him. 8 Then he stood still and began to call to the battle lines of Israel and say to them: "Why do you come out to draw up in battle formation? Am I not the Phi·lis′tine and you servants belonging to Saul? Choose a man for yourselves, and let him come down to me. 9 If he is able to fight with me and he does strike me down, we must then become servants to you. But if I myself am a match for him and I do strike him down, you must also become servants to us, and you must serve us." 10 And the Phi·lis′tine went on to say: "I myself do taunt the battle lines of Israel this day. Give me a man, and let us fight together!"

11 When Saul and all Israel heard these words of the Phi·lis'-tine, then they became terrified and were greatly afraid.

12 Now David was the son of this Eph'rath·ite from Beth'le·hem of Judah whose name was Jes'se. And he had eight sons. And in the days of Saul the man was already old among men. **13** And the three oldest sons of Jes'se proceeded to go. They went after Saul to the war, and the names of his three sons that went into the war were E·li'ab the first-born, and his second son A·bin'a·dab and the third Sham'mah. **14** And David was the youngest, and the three oldest themselves went after Saul.

15 And David was going and returning from Saul to tend the sheep of his father at Beth'le·hem. **16** And the Phi·lis'tine kept coming forward at early morning and at evening and taking his position for forty days.

17 Then Jes'se said to David his son: "Take, please, to your brothers this e'phah of roasted grain and these ten loaves of bread, and carry them quickly to the camp to your brothers. **18** And these ten portions of milk you should bring to the chief of the thousand; also, you should look after your own brothers as regards their welfare, and a token from them you should take." **19** Meantime, Saul and they and all the other men of Israel were in the low plain of E'lah, fighting against the Phi·lis'tines.

20 Accordingly David got up early in the morning and left the sheep to the keeper's charge and picked up and went just as Jes'se had commanded him. When he came to the camp enclosure, the military forces were going out to the battle line, and they raised a shout for the battle. **21** And Israel and the Phi·lis'tines began drawing up battle line to meet battle line. **22** Immediately David left the baggage from off him to the care of the keeper of the baggage and went running to the battle line.

When he came, he began asking about the welfare of his brothers. **23** While he was speaking with them, why, here the champion, his name being Go·li'ath the Phi·lis'-tine from Gath, was coming up from the battle lines of the Phi·lis'tines, and he began speaking the same words as before, and David got to listen in. **24** As for all the men of Israel, on their seeing the man, why, they went fleeing on account of him and were very much afraid. **25** And the men of Israel began to say: "Have you seen this man that is coming up? For it is to taunt Israel that he is coming up. And it must occur that, the man who strikes him down, the king will enrich him with great riches, and his own daughter he will give him, and the house of his father he will set free in Israel."

26 And David began to say to the men that were standing close by him: "What will be done to the man that strikes down that Phi·lis'tine over there and actually turns away reproach from upon Israel? For who is this uncircumcised Phi·lis'tine that he has to taunt the battle lines of the living God?" **27** Then the people said to him the same words as before, saying: "This is the way it will be done to the man that strikes him down." **28** And E·li'ab his oldest brother got to hear as he spoke to the men, and E·li'ab's anger grew hot against David, so that he said: "Why is it that you have come down? And in whose charge did you leave those few sheep behind in the wilderness? I myself well know your presumptuousness and the badness of your heart, because you have come down for the purpose of seeing the battle." **29** To this David said: "What have I done now? Was it not just a word?" **30** With that he turned about from beside him toward someone else and went saying the same word as before; and, in turn, the people gave him the same reply as formerly.

31 So the words that David spoke came to be heard, and they went telling them before Saul. Hence he fetched him. 32 And David proceeded to say to Saul: "Do not let the heart of any man collapse within him. Your servant himself will go and actually fight with this Phi·lis'tine." 33 But Saul said to David: "You are not able to go against this Phi·lis'tine to fight with him, for you are but a boy, and he is a man of war from his boyhood." 34 And David went on to say to Saul: "Your servant became a shepherd of his father among the flock, and there came a lion, and also a bear, and [each] carried off a sheep from the drove. 35 And I went out after it and struck it down and made the rescue from its mouth. When it began rising against me, I grabbed hold of its beard and struck it down and put it to death. 36 Both the lion and the bear your servant struck down; and this uncircumcised Phi·lis'tine must become like one of them, for he has taunted the battle lines of the living God." 37 Then David added: "Jehovah, who delivered me from the paw of the lion and from the paw of the bear, he it is who will deliver me from the hand of this Phi·lis'tine." At this Saul said to David: "Go, and may Jehovah himself prove to be with you."

38 Saul now went clothing David with his garments, and he put a copper helmet upon his head, after which he clothed him with a coat of mail. 39 Then David girded his sword on over his garments and undertook to go [but could not], because he had not tried them out. Finally David said to Saul: "I am unable to go in these things, for I have not tried them out." So David removed them off him. 40 And he proceeded to take his staff in his hand and to choose for himself the five smoothest stones from the torrent valley and to place them in his shepherds' bag that served him as a receptacle, and in his hand was his sling.

And he began approaching the Phi·lis'tine.

41 And the Phi·lis'tine began to come, coming nearer and nearer to David, and the man carrying the large shield was ahead of him. 42 Now when the Phi·lis'tine looked and saw David, he began despising him because he proved to be a boy and ruddy, of beautiful appearance. 43 So the Phi·lis'tine said to David: "Am I a dog, so that you are coming to me with staves?" With that the Phi·lis'tine called down evil upon David by his gods. 44 And the Phi·lis'tine went on to say to David: "Just come to me, and I will give your flesh to the fowls of the heavens and to the beasts of the field."

45 In turn David said to the Phi·lis'tine: "You are coming to me with a sword and with a spear and with a javelin, but I am coming to you with the name of Jehovah of armies, the God of the battle lines of Israel, whom you have taunted. 46 This day Jehovah will surrender you into my hand, and I shall certainly strike you down and remove your head off you; and I shall certainly give the carcasses of the camp of the Phi·lis'tines this day to the fowls of the heavens and to the wild beasts of the earth; and people of all the earth will know that there exists a God belonging to Israel. 47 And all this congregation will know that neither with sword nor with spear does Jehovah save, because to Jehovah belongs the battle, and he must give YOU men into our hand."

48 And it occurred that the Phi·lis'tine rose and kept coming and drawing nearer to meet David, and David began hurrying and running toward the battle line to meet the Phi·lis'tine. 49 Then David thrust his hand into his bag and took a stone from there and slung it, so that he struck the Phi·lis'tine in his forehead and the stone sank into his forehead, and he went falling upon his face to the earth. 50 So David, with a sling and a

stone, proved stronger than the Phi·lis'tine and struck the Phi·lis'tine down and put him to death; and there was no sword in David's hand. 51 And David continued running and got to stand over the Phi·lis'tine. Then he took his sword and pulled it out of its sheath and definitely put him to death when he cut his head off with it. And the Phi·lis'tines got to see that their mighty one had died, and they took to flight.

52 At that the men of Israel and of Judah rose and broke into shouting and went in pursuit of the Phi·lis'tines clear to [the] valley and as far as the gates of Ek'ron, and the fatally wounded of the Phi·lis'tines kept falling on the way from Sha'a·ra'im, both as far as Gath and as far as Ek'ron. 53 Afterward the sons of Israel returned from hotly pursuing the Phi·lis'tines and went pillaging their camps.

54 Then David took the head of the Phi·lis'tine and brought it to Jerusalem, and his weapons he put in his tent.

55 Now at the moment that Saul saw David going out to meet the Phi·lis'tine, he said to Ab'ner the chief of the army: "Whose son is the boy, Ab'ner?" To this Ab'ner said: "By the life of your soul, O king, I do not know at all!" 56 So the king said: "You inquire whose son the lad is." 57 Accordingly, as soon as David returned from striking the Phi·lis'tine down, Ab'ner proceeded to take him and bring him before Saul with the head of the Phi·lis'tine in his hand. 58 Saul now said to him: "Whose son are you, boy?" to which David said: "The son of your servant Jes'se the Beth'le·hem·ite."

18 And it came about that, as soon as he had finished speaking to Saul, Jon'a·than's very soul became bound up with the soul of David, and Jon'a·than began to love him as his own soul. 2 Then Saul took him on that day, and he did not allow him to return to his father's house. 3 And Jon'a·than and David proceeded to conclude a covenant, because of his loving him as his own soul. 4 Further, Jon'a·than stripped himself of the sleeveless coat that was on him and gave it to David, and also his garments, and even his sword and his bow and his belt. 5 And David began going out. Wherever Saul would send him he would act prudently, so that Saul placed him over the men of war; and it seemed good in the eyes of all the people and also in the eyes of the servants of Saul.

6 And it came about that at their coming in, when David returned from striking the Phi·lis'tines down, the women began coming out from all the cities of Israel with song and dances to meet Saul the king, with tambourines, with rejoicing and with lutes. 7 And the women that were celebrating kept responding and saying:

"Saul has struck down his thousands,
And David his tens of thousands."

8 And Saul began to be very angry, and this saying was bad from his viewpoint, so that he said: "They have given David tens of thousands, but to me they have given the thousands, and there is yet only the kingship to give him!" 9 And Saul was continually looking suspiciously at David from that day forward.

10 And it came about the next day that God's bad spirit became operative upon Saul, so that he behaved like a prophet within the house, while David was playing music with his hand, as in former days; and the spear was in Saul's hand. 11 And Saul proceeded to hurl the spear and say: "I will pin David even to the wall!" but David turned aside from before him, twice. 12 And Saul grew afraid of David because Jehovah proved to be with him, but from Saul he had departed. 13 Consequently Saul removed him from his company and appointed him as chief of a thousand for him; and he regularly went out and

came in before the people. 14 And David was continually acting prudently in all his ways, and Jehovah was with him. 15 And Saul kept seeing that he was acting very prudently, so that he was scared of him. 16 And all Israel and Judah were lovers of David, because he was going out and coming in before them.

17 Finally Saul said to David: "Here is my oldest daughter Me′rab. She is the one that I shall give you as a wife. Only prove yourself a valiant person to me and fight the wars of Jehovah." But as for Saul, he said to himself: "Do not let my hand come to be upon him, but let the hand of the Phi·lis′tines come to be upon him." 18 At this David said to Saul: "Who am I and who are my kinsfolk, my father's family, in Israel, so that I should become son-in-law to the king?" 19 However, it came about that at the time for giving Me′rab, Saul's daughter, to David, she herself had already been given to A′dri·el the Me·hol′ath·ite as a wife.

20 Now Mi′chal, Saul's daughter, was in love with David, and they went reporting it to Saul, and the matter was to his liking. 21 So Saul said: "I shall give her to him that she may serve as a snare to him, and that the hand of the Phi·lis′tines may come to be upon him." Accordingly Saul said to David: "By [one of] the two women you will form a marriage alliance with me today." 22 Further, Saul commanded his servants: "Speak to David secretly, saying, 'Look! The king has found delight in you, and all his servants themselves have fallen in love with you. So now form a marriage alliance with the king.'" 23 And the servants of Saul began to speak these words in the ears of David, but David said: "Is it an easy thing in YOUR eyes to form a marriage alliance with the king, when I am a man of little means and lightly esteemed?" 24 Then the servants of Saul reported to him, saying: "It was

with words like these that David spoke."

25 At that Saul said: "This is what YOU men will say to David, 'The king has delight, not in marriage money, but in a hundred foreskins of the Phi·lis′tines, to avenge himself on the enemies of the king.'" But as for Saul, he had schemed to have David fall by the hand of the Phi·lis′tines. 26 So his servants reported these words to David, and the matter was to David's liking, to form a marriage alliance with the king, and the days had not yet expired. 27 So David rose and he and his men went and struck down among the Phi·lis′tines two hundred men, and David came bringing their foreskins and giving them in full number to the king, to form a marriage alliance with the king. In turn Saul gave him Mi′chal his daughter as a wife. 28 And Saul got to see and know that Jehovah was with David. As for Mi′chal, Saul's daughter, she loved him. 29 And again Saul felt still more fear because of David, and Saul came to be an enemy of David always.

30 And the princes of the Phi·lis′tines would go out, and it would happen that as often as they went out David acted most prudently of all the servants of Saul; and his name came to be very precious.

19 At length Saul spoke to Jon′a·than his son and to all his servants of putting David to death. 2 As for Jon′a·than, Saul's son, he took great delight in David. So Jon′a·than told David, saying: "Saul my father is seeking to have you put to death. And now be on your guard, please, in the morning, and you must dwell in secrecy and keep yourself hidden. 3 And I, for my part, shall go out and certainly stand at the side of my father in the field where you will be, and I myself shall speak for you to my father, and I shall certainly see what will happen, and I shall be sure to tell you."

4 Accordingly Jon′a·than spoke

well of David to Saul his father and said to him: "Do not let the king sin against his servant David, for he has not sinned toward you and his works have been very good toward you. 5 And he proceeded to put his soul in his palm and strike the Phi·lis′tine down, so that Jehovah performed a great salvation for all Israel. You saw it, and you gave way to rejoicing. So why should you sin against innocent blood in having David put to death for nothing?" 6 Then Saul obeyed the voice of Jon′a·than, and Saul swore: "As Jehovah is living, he will not be put to death." 7 Afterward Jon′a·than called David and Jon′a·than told him all these words. Then Jon′a·than brought David to Saul, and he continued before him the same as formerly.

8 In time war broke out again and David went sallying forth and fighting against the Phi·lis′tines and striking them down with a great slaughter, and they took to flight from before him.

9 And Jehovah's bad spirit came to be upon Saul when he was sitting in his house with his spear in his hand, while David was playing music with his hand. 10 Consequently Saul sought to pin David to the wall with the spear, but he dodged from before Saul, so that he struck the spear into the wall. And David himself fled that he might escape during that night. 11 Later Saul sent messengers to David's house to watch it and to have him put to death in the morning; but Mi′chal his wife told David, saying: "If you are not letting your soul escape tonight, tomorrow you will be a man put to death." 12 Immediately Mi′chal had David descend through the window, that he might go and run away and escape. 13 Then Mi′chal took the teraphim image and placed it on the couch, and a net of goats' hair she put at the place of his head, after which she covered it with a garment.

14 Saul now sent messengers to take David, but she said: "He is sick." 15 So Saul sent the messengers to see David, saying: "Bring him on his couch up to me to have him put to death." 16 When the messengers came in, why, there was the teraphim image on the couch and a net of goats' hair at the place of his head. 17 At this Saul said to Mi′chal: "Why did you trick me like this, so that you sent my enemy away that he might escape?" In turn Mi′chal said to Saul: "He himself said to me, 'Send me away! Why should I put you to death?'"

18 As for David, he ran away and made his escape and got to come to Samuel at Ra′mah. And he proceeded to tell him all that Saul had done to him. Then he and Samuel went away, and they took up dwelling in Nai′oth. 19 In time the report got to Saul, saying: "Look! David is in Nai′oth in Ra′mah." 20 At once Saul sent messengers to take David. When they got to see the elderly ones of the prophets prophesying, and Samuel standing in his position over them, the spirit of God came to be upon Saul's messengers, and they began behaving like prophets, they also.

21 When they told it to Saul, he immediately sent other messengers, and they began behaving like prophets, they also. So Saul sent messengers again, the third set, and they began behaving like prophets, they also. 22 Finally he too went to Ra′mah. When he got as far as the great cistern that is in Se′cu, he began to inquire and say: "Where are Samuel and David?" To this they said: "There in Nai′oth in Ra′mah." 23 And he kept on his way from there to Nai′oth in Ra′mah, and the spirit of God came to be upon him, yes, him, and he went on walking and continued behaving like a prophet until he came into Nai′oth in Ra′mah. 24 And he also proceeded to strip off his garments and behave, he also, like a prophet before Samuel, and he lay fallen naked all that day and all that night. That

is why they came to say: "Is Saul also among the prophets?"

20 And David went running away from Nai'oth in Ra'mah. However, he came and said in front of Jon'a·than: "What have I done? What is my error, and what sin have I committed before your father, for he is seeking for my soul?" 2 At this he said to him: "It is unthinkable! You will not die. Look! My father will not do a big thing or a little thing and not disclose it to my ear; and for what reason should my father conceal this matter from me? This does not happen." 3 But David swore in addition and said: "Your father must surely know that I have found favor in your eyes, and so would say, 'Do not let Jon'a·than know this for fear he may feel hurt.' But, in fact, as Jehovah is living and as your soul is living, there is just about a step between me and death!"

4 And Jon'a·than went on to say to David: "Whatever your soul may say I shall do for you." 5 At this David said to Jon'a·than: "Look! Tomorrow is new moon, and I myself ought, without fail, to be sitting with the king to eat; and you must send me away, and I must conceal myself in the field until the evening on the third day. 6 If your father should miss me at all, then you must say, 'David earnestly asked leave of absence of me to run to Beth'le·hem his city, because there is a yearly sacrifice there for all the family.' 7 If the way he should say is, 'It is all right!' it means peace to your servant. But if he should at all become angry, know that what is bad has been determined upon by him. 8 And you must render loving-kindness toward your servant, for it is into a covenant of Jehovah that you have brought your servant with you. But if there is error in me, put me to death yourself, since why should it be to your father that you should bring me?"

9 To this Jon'a·than said: "That is unthinkable respecting you! But if I should at all get to know that evil has been determined upon by my father to come upon you, shall I not tell it to you?" 10 Then David said to Jon'a·than: "Who will tell me whether what your father may answer you is harsh?" 11 In turn Jon'a·than said to David: "Just come, and let us go out into the field." So both of them went out into the field. 12 And Jon'a·than went on to say to David: "Jehovah the God of Israel [be a witness] that I shall sound out my father about this time tomorrow, or the third day, and if he is well-disposed toward David, shall I not then send to you and certainly disclose it to your ear? 13 So may Jehovah do to Jon'a·than and so may he add to it, if, in case it should seem good to my father to do evil against you, I do not indeed disclose it to your ear and send you away, and you do not certainly go in peace. And may Jehovah prove to be with you, just as he proved to be with my father. 14 And will you not, if I shall be still alive, yes, will you not exercise the loving-kindness of Jehovah toward me, that I may not die? 15 And you will not cut off your own loving-kindness from being with my household to time indefinite. Nor, when Jehovah cuts off the enemies of David, every one from the surface of the ground, 16 will [the name of] Jon'a·than be cut off from the house of David. And Jehovah must require it at the hand of David's enemies." 17 So Jon'a·than swore again to David because of his love for him; for as he loved his own soul he loved him.

18 And Jon'a·than went on to say to him: "Tomorrow is new moon, and you will certainly be missed, because your seat will be vacant. 19 And certainly on the third day you will be missed very much; and you must come to the place where you concealed yourself on the working day, and you must dwell near this stone here. 20 And as for me, I shall shoot

three arrows to one side of it, to send them where I will to a target. 21 And, look! I shall send the attendant, [saying,] 'Go, find the arrows.' If I should specifically say to the attendant, 'Look! The arrows are on this side of you, take them,' then you come, for it means peace for you and there is nothing the matter, as Jehovah is living. 22 But if this is the way I should say to the lad, 'Look! The arrows are farther away from you,' go, for Jehovah has sent you away. 23 And as for the word that we have spoken, I and you, why, may Jehovah be between me and you to time indefinite."

24 And David proceeded to conceal himself in the field. And it came to be new moon, and the king took his seat at the meal to eat. 25 And the king was sitting in his seat as at other times, in the seat by the wall; and Jon'a·than was facing him, and Ab'ner was sitting at Saul's side, but David's place was vacant. 26 And Saul did not say anything at all on that day, for he said to himself: "Something has happened so that he is not clean, for he has not been cleansed." 27 And it came about on the day after the new moon, on the second day, that David's place continued vacant. At this Saul said to Jon'a·than his son: "Why has not the son of Jes'se come to the meal either yesterday or today?" 28 So Jon'a·than answered Saul: "David earnestly asked leave of absence from me [to go] to Beth'le·hem. 29 And he went on to say, 'Send me away, please, because we have a family sacrifice in the city, and it was my own brother that commanded me. So now, if I have found favor in your eyes, let me slip away, please, that I may see my brothers.' That is why he has not come to the king's table." 30 Then Saul's anger grew hot against Jon'a·than and he said to him: "You son of a rebellious maid, do I not well know that you are choosing the son of Jes'se to your own shame

and to the shame of the secret parts of your mother? 31 For all the days that the son of Jes'se is alive on the ground, you and your kingship will not be firmly established. So now send and fetch him to me, for he is destined for death."

32 However, Jon'a·than answered Saul his father and said to him: "Why should he be put to death? What has he done?" 33 At that Saul went hurling the spear at him to strike him; and Jon'a·than came to know that it had been determined upon by his father to put David to death. 34 Immediately Jon'a·than rose up from the table in the heat of anger, and he did not eat bread on the second day after the new moon, for he had been hurt respecting David, because his own father had humiliated him.

35 And it came about in the morning that Jon'a·than made his way out to the field of David's appointed place, and a young attendant was with him. 36 And he proceeded to say to his attendant: "Run, please, find the arrows that I am shooting." The attendant ran, and he himself shot the arrow to make it pass beyond him. 37 When the attendant came as far as the place of the arrow that Jon'a·than had shot, Jon'a·than began to call from behind the attendant and say: "Is not the arrow farther away from you?" 38 And Jon'a·than went on calling from behind the attendant: "In haste! Act quickly! Do not stand still!" And the attendant of Jon'a·than went picking up the arrows and then came to his master. 39 As for the attendant, he did not know anything; only Jon'a·than and David themselves knew about the matter. 40 After that Jon'a·than gave his weapons to the attendant that belonged to him and he said to him: "Go, take them to the city."

41 The attendant went. As for David, he rose up from nearby to the south. Then he fell on his face

to the earth and bowed three times; and they began kissing each other and weeping for each other, until David had done it the most. 42 And Jon′a·than went on to say to David: "Go in peace, since we have sworn, both of us, in the name of Jehovah, saying, 'May Jehovah himself prove to be between me and you and between my offspring and your offspring to time indefinite.' "

Accordingly David rose up and went his way, and Jon′a·than himself came into the city.

21 Later David came into Nob to A·him′e·lech the priest; and A·him′e·lech began to tremble at meeting David and then said to him: "Why is it you are by yourself, and no one is with you?" 2 At this David said to A·him′e·lech the priest: "The king himself commanded me as to a matter, and he went on to say to me, 'Let no one know anything at all of the matter concerning which I am sending you and concerning which I have commanded you.' And I have made an appointment with the young men for such and such a place. 3 And now, if there are five loaves of bread at your disposal, just give them into my hand, or whatever may be found." 4 But the priest answered David and said: "There is no ordinary bread under my hand, but there is holy bread; provided that the young men have at least kept themselves from womankind." 5 So David answered the priest and said to him: "But womankind has been kept away from us the same as formerly when I went out, and the organisms of the young men continue holy, although the mission itself is ordinary. And how much more so today, when one becomes holy in [his] organism?" 6 At that the priest gave him what was holy, because there happened to be no bread there but the showbread that had been removed from before Jehovah so as to place fresh bread there on the day of its being taken away.

7 Now one of Saul's servants was there on that day, detained before Jehovah, and his name was Do′eg the E′dom·ite, the principal one of the shepherds that belonged to Saul.

8 And David went on to say to A·him′e·lech: "And is there nothing here at your disposal, a spear or a sword? For neither my own sword nor my weapons did I take in my hand, because the king's matter proved to be urgent." 9 To this the priest said: "The sword of Go·li′ath the Phi·lis′tine, whom you struck down in the low plain of E′lah—here it is, wrapped up in a mantle, behind the eph′od. If it is what you would take for yourself, take it, because there is no other here except it." And David went on to say: "There is none like it. Give it to me."

10 Then David rose up and continued running away on account of Saul on that day, and at length came to A′chish the king of Gath. 11 And the servants of A′chish began to say to him: "Is not this David the king of the land? Was it not to this one that they kept responding with dances, saying,

'Saul has struck down his thousands,
And David his tens of thousands'?"

12 And David began to take these words to his heart, and he became very much afraid on account of A′chish the king of Gath. 13 So he disguised his sanity under their eyes and began acting insane in their hand and kept making cross marks on the doors of the gate and let his saliva run down upon his beard. 14 Finally A′chish said to his servants: "Here you see a man behaving crazy. Why should you bring him to me? 15 Am I in need of people driven crazy, so that you have brought this one to behave crazy by me? Should this one come into my home?"

22 So David proceeded to go from there and escape to the cave of A·dul′lam; and his brothers and the entire house of his father got to hear of it and made their way down there to him. 2 And all men in distress and all men who had a creditor and all men bitter in soul began to collect together to him, and he came to be a chief over them; and there came to be with him about four hundred men.

3 Later David went from there to Miz'peh in Mo'ab and said to the king of Mo'ab: "Let my father and my mother, please, dwell with you people until I know what God will do to me." 4 Accordingly he settled them before the king of Mo'ab, and they continued dwelling with him all the days that David happened to be in the inaccessible place.

5 In time Gad the prophet said to David: "You must not keep dwelling in the inaccessible place. Go away, and you must come yourself into the land of Judah." Hence David went away and came into the forest of He'reth.

6 And Saul got to hear that David and the men that were with him had been discovered, while Saul was sitting in Gib'e·ah under the tamarisk tree on the high place with his spear in his hand and all his servants stationed about him. 7 Then Saul said to his servants stationed about him: "Listen, please, you Ben'ja·min·ites. Will the son of Jes'se also give to all of you fields and vineyards? Will he appoint all of you chiefs of thousands and chiefs of hundreds? 8 For you have conspired, all of you, against me; and there is no one disclosing it to my ear when my own son concludes [a covenant] with the son of Jes'se, and there is no one of you having sympathy for me and disclosing to my ear that my own son has raised up my own servant against me as a lier in ambush the way it is this day."

9 At this Do'eg the E'dom·ite, being stationed as he was over the servants of Saul, answered and said: "I saw the son of Jes'se come to Nob to A·him'e·lech the son of A·hi'tub. 10 And he proceeded to inquire of Jehovah for him; and provisions he gave him, and the sword of Go·li'ath the Phi·lis'tine he gave him." 11 At once the king sent to call A·him'e·lech the son of A·hi'tub the priest and all the house of his father, the priests that were in Nob. So all of them came to the king.

12 Saul now said: "Listen, please, you son of A·hi'tub!" to which he said: "Here I am, my lord." 13 And Saul went on to say to him: "Why have you men conspired against me, you and the son of Jes'se, by your giving him bread and a sword, and there being an inquiry of God for him, to rise up against me as a lier in ambush the way it is this day?" 14 At this A·him'e·lech answered the king and said: "And who among all your servants is like David, faithful, and the son-in-law of the king and a chief over your bodyguard and honored in your house? 15 Is it today that I have started to inquire of God for him? It is unthinkable on my part! Do not let the king lay anything against his servant [and] against the entire house of my father, for in all this your servant did not know a thing small or great."

16 But the king said: "You will positively die, A·him'e·lech, you with all the house of your father." 17 With that the king said to the runners stationed about him: "Turn and put to death the priests of Jehovah, because their hand also is with David and because they knew that he was a runaway and they did not disclose it to my ear!" And the servants of the king did not want to thrust out their hand to assault the priests of Jehovah. 18 Finally the king said to Do'eg: "You turn and assault the priests!" Immediately Do'eg the E'dom·ite turned and himself assaulted the priests and put to death on that day eighty-five men bearing an eph'od of linen. 19 Even Nob the city of the priests he struck with the edge of the sword, man as well

as woman, child as well as suckling and bull and ass and sheep with the edge of the sword.

20 However, one son of A·him′e·lech the son of A·hi′tub, whose name was A·bi′a·thar, made his escape and went running away to follow David. 21 Then A·bi′a·thar told David: "Saul has killed the priests of Jehovah." 22 At this David said to A·bi′a·thar: "I well knew on that day, because Do′eg the E′dom·ite was there, that he would without fail tell Saul. I personally have wronged every soul of the house of your father. 23 Just dwell with me. Do not be afraid, for whoever looks for my soul looks for your soul, for you are one needing protection with me."

23 In time they came reporting to David, saying: "Here the Phi·lis′tines are warring against Kei′lah, and they are pillaging the threshing floors." 2 And David proceeded to inquire of Jehovah, saying: "Shall I go, and must I strike down these Phi·lis′tines?" In turn Jehovah said to David: "Go, and you must strike down the Phi·lis′tines and save Kei′lah." 3 At this the men of David said to him: "Look! We are afraid while here in Judah, and how much more so in case we should go to Kei′lah against the battle lines of the Phi·lis′tines!" 4 So David inquired yet again of Jehovah. Jehovah now answered him and said: "Rise up, go down to Kei′lah, because I am giving the Phi·lis′tines into your hand." 5 Accordingly David went with his men to Kei′lah and fought against the Phi·lis′tines and drove off with their livestock, but struck them down with a great slaughter; and David came to be the savior of the inhabitants of Kei′lah.

6 Now it came about that when A·bi′a·thar the son of A·him′e·lech ran away to David at Kei′lah, there was an eph′od that went down in his hand. 7 In time the report was made to Saul: "David has come to Kei′lah." And Saul began to say: "God has sold him

into my hand, for he has shut himself up by coming into a city with doors and bar." 8 So Saul summoned all the people to war, to go down to Kei′lah, to besiege David and his men. 9 And David got to know that Saul was fabricating mischief against him. Hence he said to A·bi′a·thar the priest: "Do bring the eph′od near." 10 And David went on to say: "O Jehovah the God of Israel, your servant has definitely heard that Saul is seeking to come to Kei′lah to lay the city in ruin on my account. 11 Will the landowners of Kei′lah surrender me into his hand? Will Saul come down just as your servant has heard? O Jehovah the God of Israel, tell your servant, please." To this Jehovah said: "He will come down." 12 And David went on to say: "Will the landowners of Kei′lah surrender me and my men into Saul's hand?" In turn Jehovah said: "They will do the surrendering."

13 At once David rose up with his men, about six hundred men, and they went out of Kei′lah and continued walking about wherever they could walk about. And to Saul it was reported that David had escaped from Kei′lah, and so he gave up going out. 14 And David took up dwelling in the wilderness in places difficult to approach, and he kept dwelling in the mountainous region in the wilderness of Ziph. And Saul kept looking for him always, and God did not give him into his hand. 15 And David continued in fear because Saul had gone out to look for his soul while David was in the wilderness of Ziph at Ho′resh.

16 Jon′a·than the son of Saul now rose up and went to David at Ho′resh, that he might strengthen his hand in regard to God. 17 And he went on to say to him: "Do not be afraid; for the hand of Saul my father will not find you, and you yourself will be king over Israel, and I myself shall become second to you; and Saul my father also has knowledge to that effect."

18 Then the two of them concluded a covenant before Jehovah; and David kept dwelling in Ho'resh, and Jon'a·than himself went to his own home.

19 Later the men of Ziph went up to Saul at Gib'e·ah, saying: "Is not David concealing himself close by us in the places difficult to approach at Ho'resh, on the hill of Hach·i'lah, which is to the right side of Je·shi'mon? 20 And now in harmony with the craving of your soul, O king, to come down, come down, and our part will be to surrender him into the hand of the king." 21 At this Saul said: "Blessed are you of Jehovah, for you have had compassion on me. 22 Go, please, persevere some more and ascertain and see his place where his foot comes to be—whoever saw him there—for it has been said to me that he himself is surely cunning. 23 And see and ascertain about all the hiding places where he hides himself; and you must return to me with the evidence, and I will go with you; and it must occur that, if he is in the land, I will also search for him carefully among all the thousands of Judah."

24 So they rose up and went to Ziph ahead of Saul, while David and his men were in the wilderness of Ma'on in the Ar'a·bah to the south of Je·shi'mon. 25 Later Saul came with his men to look for him. When they told David, he at once went down to the crag and continued dwelling in the wilderness of Ma'on. When Saul got to hear of it, he went chasing after David into the wilderness of Ma'on. 26 Eventually Saul came to this side of the mountain, and David and his men were on that side of the mountain. So David became hurried to go away because of Saul; all the while Saul and his men were closing in on David and his men to grab hold of them. 27 But there was a messenger that came to Saul, saying: "Do hasten and go, for the Phi·lis'tines have made a raid on the land!" 28 At

that Saul turned back from chasing after David and went to meet the Phi·lis'tines. That is why they have called that place the Crag of the Divisions. 29 Then David made his way up from there and took up dwelling in the places difficult to approach at En·ge'di.

24 And it came about that, as soon as Saul returned from following the Phi·lis'tines, they came reporting to him, saying: "Look! David is in the wilderness of En·ge'di."

2 And Saul proceeded to take three thousand chosen men out of all Israel and to go looking for David and his men upon the bare rocks of the mountain goats. 3 At length he came to the stone sheepfolds along the road, where a cave was. So Saul came in to ease nature, while David and his men were in the parts of the cave farthest back, sitting down. 4 And David's men began to say to him: "Here is the day on which Jehovah does say to you, 'Look! I am giving your enemy into your hand, and you must do to him just as it may seem good in your eyes.'" So David rose up and quietly cut off the skirt of the sleeveless coat that belonged to Saul. 5 But it came about afterward that David's heart kept striking him for the reason that he had cut off the skirt [of the sleeveless coat] that belonged to Saul. 6 Hence he said to his men: "It is unthinkable, on my part, from Jehovah's standpoint, that I should do this thing to my lord, the anointed of Jehovah, by thrusting out my hand against him, for he is the anointed of Jehovah." 7 Accordingly David dispersed his men with these words, and he did not allow them to rise up against Saul. As for Saul, he rose up from the cave and kept going on his way.

8 So David rose up afterward and went out from the cave and called out after Saul, saying: "My lord the king!" At this Saul looked behind him, and David proceeded

to bow low with his face to the earth and prostrate himself. 9 And David went on to say to Saul: "Why do you listen to the words of man, saying, 'Look! David is seeking your hurt'? 10 Here this day your eyes have seen how Jehovah gave you today into my hand in the cave; and someone said to kill you, but I felt sorry for you and said, 'I shall not thrust out my hand against my lord, for he is the anointed of Jehovah.' 11 And, my father, see, yes, see the skirt of your sleeveless coat in my hand, for when I cut off the skirt of your sleeveless coat I did not kill you. Know and see that there is no badness or revolt in my hand, and I have not sinned against you, while you are lying in wait for my soul to take it away. 12 May Jehovah judge between me and you; and Jehovah must take vengeance for me from you, but my own hand will not come to be upon you. 13 Just as the proverb of the ancients says, 'From the wicked ones wickedness will go forth,' but my own hand will not come to be upon you. 14 After whom has the king of Israel gone out? After whom are you chasing? After a dead dog? After a single flea? 15 And Jehovah must become judge, and he must judge between me and you, and he will see and he will conduct the legal case for me and judge me [to free me] from your hand."

16 And it came about that, at the moment that David finished speaking these words to Saul, Saul proceeded to say: "Is this your voice, my son David?" And Saul began to raise his own voice and weep. 17 And he went on to say to David: "You are more righteous than I am, for it is you who have rendered me good, and it is I who have rendered you evil. 18 And you—you have told today what good you have done in connection with me in that Jehovah surrendered me into your hand and you did not kill me. 19 Now in the case where a man finds his enemy, will he send him away on a good road? So Jehovah himself will reward you with good, due to the fact that this day you have done it to me. 20 And now, look! I well know that you will, without fail, rule as king, and that in your hand the kingdom of Israel will certainly endure. 21 So now do swear to me by Jehovah that you will not cut off my seed after me and that you will not annihilate my name out of the house of my father." 22 Accordingly David swore to Saul, after which Saul went to his home. As for David and his men, they went up to the place difficult to approach.

25 In time Samuel died; and all Israel proceeded to collect together and bewail him and bury him at his house in Ra′mah. Then David rose up and went down to the wilderness of Pa′ran.

2 Now there was a man in Ma′on, and his work was in Car′mel. And the man was very great, and he had three thousand sheep and a thousand goats; and he came to be [engaged] in shearing his sheep at Car′mel. 3 And the man's name was Na′bal, and his wife's name was Ab′i·gail. And the wife was good in discretion and beautiful in form, but the husband was harsh and bad in his practices; and he was a Ca′leb·ite. 4 And David got to hear in the wilderness that Na′bal was shearing his sheep. 5 So David sent ten young men and David said to the young men: "Go up to Car′mel, and you must come to Na′bal and ask him in my name about his welfare. 6 And this is what you must say to my brother, 'May you be well and also your household be well and all that you have be well. 7 And now I have heard that you have shearers. Now the shepherds that belong to you happened themselves to be with us. We did not molest them, and nothing at all showed up missing of theirs all the days they happened to be in Car′mel. 8 Ask your own young men, and they will tell you, that my young

men may find favor in your eyes, because it was upon a good day that we came. Just give, please, whatever your hand may find to your servants and to your son David.'"

9 Accordingly David's young men came and spoke to Na'bal in accord with all these words in the name of David and then waited. 10 At this Na'bal answered David's servants and said: "Who is David, and who is the son of Jes'se? Nowadays the servants that are breaking away, each one from before his master, have become many. 11 And do I have to take my bread and my water and my slaughtered meat that I have butchered for my shearers and give it to men of whom I do not even know from where they are?"

12 Upon that David's young men turned around on their way and went back and came and reported to him in accord with all these words. 13 Immediately David said to his men: "Gird on every one his sword!" So they girded on every one his sword and David also girded on his own sword; and they began to go up after David, about four hundred men, while two hundred sat by the baggage.

14 Meanwhile, to Ab'i·gail, Na'bal's wife, one of the young men reported, saying: "Look! David sent messengers from the wilderness to wish our master well, but he screamed rebukes at them. 15 And the men were very good to us, and they did not molest us, and we did not miss a single thing all the days of our walking about with them while we happened to be in the field. 16 A wall was what they proved to be around us both by night and by day, all the days that we happened to be with them, shepherding the flock. 17 And now know and see what you are going to do, for calamity has been determined against our master and against all his house, as he is too much of a good-for-nothing fellow to speak to him."

18 At once Ab'i·gail hastened and took two hundred loaves of bread and two large jars of wine and five sheep dressed and five seah measures of roasted grain and a hundred cakes of raisins and two hundred cakes of pressed figs and put them upon the asses. 19 Then she said to her young men: "Pass on ahead of me. Look! I am coming after you." But to her husband Na'bal she told nothing.

20 And it occurred that while she was riding on the ass and secretly going down the mountain, why, there were David and his men coming down to meet her. So she encountered them. 21 As for David, he had said: "It was altogether for disappointment that I guarded everything that belongs to this fellow in the wilderness and not a single thing of all that belongs to him showed up missing, and yet he repays me evil in return for good. 22 So may God do to the enemies of David and so may he add to it if I shall let any one of all who are his that urinates against the wall remain until the morning."

23 When Ab'i·gail caught sight of David, she at once hastened and got down off the ass and fell upon her face before David and bowed to the earth. 24 She then fell at his feet and said: "Upon me myself, O my lord, be the error; and, please, let your slave girl speak in your ears, and listen to the words of your slave girl. 25 Please, do not let my lord set his heart upon this good-for-nothing man Na'bal, for, as his name is, so is he. Na'bal is his name, and senselessness is with him. As for me your slave girl, I did not see my lord's young men that you had sent. 26 And now, my lord, as Jehovah is living and as your soul is living, Jehovah has held you back from entering into bloodguilt and having your own hand come to your salvation. And now let your enemies and those seeking injury to my lord become like Na'bal. 27 And now as regards this gift blessing that your maidservant has brought to my lord, it must be given to the young

men that are walking about in the steps of my lord. 28 Pardon, please, the transgression of your slave girl, because Jehovah will without fail make for my lord a lasting house, because the wars of Jehovah are what my lord is fighting; and as for badness, it will not be found in you throughout your days. 29 When man rises up to pursue you and look for your soul, the soul of my lord will certainly prove to be wrapped up in the bag of life with Jehovah your God; but, as for the soul of your enemies, he will sling it forth as from inside the hollow of the sling. 30 And it must occur that, because Jehovah will do to my lord the good toward you according to all that he has spoken, he certainly will commission you as leader over Israel. 31 And let this not become to you a cause for staggering or a stumbling block to the heart of my lord, both by the shedding of blood without cause and by having [the hand of] my lord [itself] come to his salvation. And Jehovah will certainly do good to my lord, and you must remember your slave girl."

32 At this David said to Ab'i·gail: "Blessed be Jehovah the God of Israel, who has sent you this day to meet me! 33 And blessed be your sensibleness, and blessed be you who have restrained me this day from entering into bloodguilt and having my own hand come to my salvation. 34 And, on the other hand, as Jehovah the God of Israel is living, who has held me back from doing injury to you, if you had not hastened that you might come to meet me, there would certainly not have remained to Na'bal until the morning light anyone urinating against a wall." 35 With that David accepted from her hand what she had brought him, and to her he said: "Go up in peace to your house. See, I have listened to your voice that I may have consideration for your person."

36 Later Ab'i·gail came in to Na'bal, and there he was having a feast in his house like the feast of the king; and Na'bal's heart was feeling good within him, and he was as drunk as could be; and she did not tell him a thing, small or great, until the morning light. 37 And it came about in the morning, when the wine had gone out of Na'bal, that his wife went telling him these things. And his heart came to be dead inside him, and he himself became as a stone. 38 After that about ten days elapsed and then Jehovah struck Na'bal, so that he died.

39 And David got to hear that Na'bal had died, and so he said: "Blessed be Jehovah, who has conducted the legal case of my reproach [to free me] from Na'bal's hand and has kept his servant back from badness, and the badness of Na'bal Jehovah has turned back upon his own head!" And David proceeded to send and propose to Ab'i·gail to take her as his wife. 40 So David's servants came to Ab'i·gail at Car'mel and spoke to her, saying: "David himself has sent us to you to take you as his wife." 41 Immediately she rose up and bowed with her face to the earth and said: "Here is your slave girl as a maidservant to wash the feet of the servants of my lord." 42 Then Ab'i·gail hastened and rose up and went riding on the ass with five maids of hers walking behind her; and she went accompanying the messengers of David and then became his wife.

43 David had also taken A·hin'o·am from Jez're·el; and the women came to be, even both of them, his wives.

44 As for Saul, he had given Mi'chal his daughter, David's wife, to Pal'ti the son of La'ish, who was from Gal'lim.

26 In time the men of Ziph came to Saul at Gib'e·ah, saying: "Is not David concealing himself on the hill of Hach·i'lah, facing Je·shi'mon?" 2 And Saul proceeded to rise up and go down to the wilderness of Ziph, and with him three thousand men, the chosen ones of Israel, to look for David in the wilderness of Ziph. 3 And Saul took up camping on the hill of Hach·i'lah, which faces Je·shi'mon, by the road, while David was dwelling in the wilderness. And he got to see that Saul had come after him into the wilderness. 4 So David sent spies that he might know that Saul had for a fact come. 5 Later David rose up and went to the place where Saul had encamped, and David got to see the place where Saul had lain down, and also Ab'ner the son of Ner the chief of his army; and Saul was lying in the camp enclosure with the people camping all around him. 6 Then David answered and said to A·him'e·lech the Hit'tite and A·bish'ai the son of Ze·ru'iah, the brother of Jo'ab: "Who will go down with me to Saul into the camp?" To this A·bish'ai said: "I myself shall go down with you." 7 And David made his way with A·bish'ai to the people by night; and, look! Saul was lying asleep in the camp enclosure with his spear stuck into the earth at his head, and Ab'ner and the people were lying all around him.

8 A·bish'ai now said to David: "God has today surrendered your enemy into your hand. And now let me, please, pin him to the earth with the spear just once, and I shall not do it to him twice." 9 However, David said to A·bish'ai: "Do not bring him to ruin, for who is it that has thrust his hand out against the anointed of Jehovah and has remained innocent?" 10 And David went on to say: "As Jehovah is living, Jehovah himself will deal him a blow; or his day will come and he will have to die, or down into battle he will go, and he will certainly be swept away. 11 It is unthinkable, on my part, from Jehovah's standpoint, to thrust my hand out against the anointed of Jehovah! So now take, please, the spear that is at his head and the water jug, and let us get on our way." 12 Accord-

ingly David took the spear and the water jug from the place at Saul's head, and then they got on their way; and there was no one seeing nor anyone taking note nor anyone waking up, for all of them were asleep, because it was a deep sleep from Jehovah that had fallen upon them. 13 Then David passed on to the other side and stood upon the top of the mountain at a distance, the space between them being vast.

14 And David began to call out to the people and to Ab'ner the son of Ner, saying: "Will you not answer, Ab'ner?" And Ab'ner began to answer and say: "Who are you that have called out to the king?" 15 And David went on to say to Ab'ner: "Are you not a man? And who is like you in Israel? Why, then, did you not watch over your lord the king? For one of the people came in to bring the king your lord to ruin. 16 This thing that you have done is not good. As Jehovah is living, you men deserve to die, because you have not watched over your lord, over the anointed of Jehovah. And now see where the king's spear and the water jug are that were at his head."

17 And Saul began to recognize the voice of David and to say: "Is this your voice, my son David?" To this David said: "It is my voice, my lord the king." 18 And he added: "Why is this that my lord is chasing after his servant, for what have I done, and what badness is there in my hand? 19 And now let my lord the king, please, listen to the words of his servant: If it is Jehovah that has incited you against me, let him smell a grain offering. But if it is the sons of man, they are cursed before Jehovah, because they have driven me out today from feeling myself attached to the inheritance of Jehovah, saying, 'Go, serve other gods!' 20 And now do not let my blood fall to the earth before the face of Jehovah; for the king of Israel has gone out to look for a

single flea, just as one chases a partridge upon the mountains."

21 In turn Saul said: "I have sinned. Come back, my son David, for I shall no more do you injury, in view of the fact that my soul has been precious in your eyes this day. Look! I have acted foolishly and am very much mistaken." 22 Then David answered and said: "Here is the spear of the king, and let one of the young men come on over and fetch it. 23 And Jehovah it is who will repay to each one his own righteousness and his own faithfulness, in that Jehovah today gave you into my hand, and I was unwilling to thrust my hand out against the anointed of Jehovah. 24 And, look! just as your soul was great this day in my eyes, so may my soul be great in the eyes of Jehovah, that he may deliver me out of all distress." 25 At this Saul said to David: "Blessed may you be, my son David. Not only will you without fail work but you will also without fail come off the winner." And David proceeded to go on his way; and as for Saul, he returned to his place.

27 However, David said in his heart: "Now I shall be swept away one day by Saul's hand. There is nothing better for me than that I should escape without fail to the land of the Phi·lis′tines; and Saul must despair of me in looking for me any longer in all the territory of Israel, and I shall certainly escape from his hand." 2 So David rose up and he and six hundred men that were with him passed over to A′chish the son of Ma′och, the king of Gath. 3 And David continued to dwell with A′chish in Gath, he and his men, each one with his household, David and his two wives, A·hin′o·am the Jez′re·el·it·ess and Ab′i·gail, Na′bal's wife, the Car′mel·it·ess. 4 In time report was made to Saul that David had run away to Gath, and so he did not go looking for him still another time.

5 Then David said to A′chish: "If, now, I have found favor in your eyes, let them give me a place in one of the cities of the countryside, that I may dwell there; for why should your servant dwell in the royal city with you?" 6 Accordingly A′chish gave him Zik′lag on that day. That is why Zik′lag has come to belong to the kings of Judah down to this day.

7 And the number of the days that David dwelt in the countryside of the Phi·lis′tines came to be a year and four months. 8 And David proceeded to go up with his men that they might raid the Gesh′ur·ites and the Gir′zites and the A·mal′ek·ites; for they were inhabiting the land that [extended] from Te′lam as far as Shur and down to the land of Egypt. 9 And David struck the land, but he preserved neither man nor woman alive; and he took flocks and herds and asses and camels and garments, after which he returned and came to A′chish. 10 Then A′chish said: "Where did you men make a raid today?" To this David said: "Upon the south of Judah and upon the south of the Je·rah′me·el·ites and upon the south of the Ken′ites." 11 As for man and woman, David was not preserving any alive to bring them to Gath, saying: "That they may not tell on us, saying, 'This is the way David did.'" (And this way has been his procedure all the days that he dwelt in the countryside of the Phi·lis′tines.) 12 Consequently A′chish believed David, saying to himself: "He has unquestionably become a stench among his people Israel; and he will have to become my servant to time indefinite."

28 And it came about in those days that the Phi·lis′tines began to collect their camps for the army to make war against Israel. So A′chish said to David: "You undoubtedly know that it is with me that you should go out into the camp, you and your men." 2 At that David said to A′chish: "That is why you yourself know what your servant is to do." Accordingly A′chish said to David:

"That is why guardian of my head I shall appoint you always."

3 Now Samuel himself had died, and all Israel had proceeded to bewail him and bury him in Ra'mah his own city. As for Saul, he had removed the spirit mediums and the professional foretellers of events from the land.

4 Subsequently the Phi·lis'tines collected together and came and pitched camp in Shu'nem. So Saul collected all Israel together and they pitched camp in Gil·bo'a. 5 When Saul got to see the camp of the Phi·lis'tines he became afraid, and his heart began to tremble very much. 6 Although Saul would inquire of Jehovah, Jehovah never answered him, either by dreams or by the U'rim or by the prophets. 7 Finally Saul said to his servants: "Seek for me a woman who is a mistress of spirit mediumship, and I will go to her and consult her." Then his servants said to him: "Look! There is a woman who is a mistress of spirit mediumship in En·dor."

8 So Saul disguised himself and clothed himself with other garments and went, he and two men with him; and they came to the woman by night. He now said: "Employ divination, please, for me by spirit mediumship and bring up for me the one whom I shall designate to you." 9 However, the woman said to him: "Here you yourself well know what Saul did, how he cut off the spirit mediums and the professional foretellers of events from the land. Why, then, are you acting like a trapper against my soul to have me put to death?" 10 Immediately Saul swore to her by Jehovah, saying: "As Jehovah is alive, guilt for error will not befall you in this matter!" 11 At this the woman said: "Whom shall I bring up for you?" To this he said: "Bring up Samuel for me." 12 When the woman saw "Samuel" she began crying out at the top of her voice; and the woman went on to say to Saul: "Why did you trick me, when you yourself are Saul?"

13 But the king said to her: "Do not be afraid, but what did you see?" And the woman went on to say to Saul: "A god I saw coming up out of the earth." 14 At once he said to her: "What is his form?" to which she said: "It is an old man coming up, and he has himself covered with a sleeveless coat." At that Saul recognized that it was "Samuel," and he proceeded to bow low with his face to the earth and to prostrate himself.

15 And "Samuel" began to say to Saul: "Why have you disturbed me by having me brought up?" To this Saul said: "I am in very sore straits, as the Phi·lis'tines are fighting against me, and God himself has departed from me and has answered me no more, either by means of the prophets or by dreams; so that I am calling you to let me know what I shall do."

16 And "Samuel" went on to say: "Why, then, do you inquire of me, when Jehovah himself has departed from you and proves to be your adversary? 17 And Jehovah will do for himself just as he spoke by means of me, and Jehovah will rip the kingdom away from your hand and give it to your fellow man David. 18 As you did not obey the voice of Jehovah, and you did not execute his burning anger against Am'a·lek, that is why this is the thing that Jehovah will certainly do to you this day. 19 And Jehovah will also give Israel with you into the hand of the Phi·lis'tines, and tomorrow you and your sons will be with me. Even the camp of Israel Jehovah will give into the hand of the Phi·lis'tines."

20 At that Saul quickly fell down his full length to the earth and became very much afraid because of "Samuel's" words. Also, there happened to be no power in him, because he had not eaten food the whole day and the whole night. 21 The woman now came to Saul and saw that he had been greatly disturbed. So she said to him: "Here your maidservant has obeyed your voice, and I proceeded to put

my soul in my palm and obey the words that you spoke to me. 22 And now, please, you, in turn, obey the voice of your maidservant; and let me set before you a piece of bread, and you eat, that power may come to be in you, because you will go on your way." 23 But he refused and said: "I am not going to eat." However, his servants and also the woman kept urging him. Finally he obeyed their voice and rose up from the earth and sat on the couch. 24 Now the woman had a fattened calf in the house. So she quickly sacrificed it and took flour and kneaded dough and baked it into unfermented cakes. 25 Then she served them to Saul and his servants, and they ate. After that they rose up and went away during that night.

29 And the Phi·lis′tines proceeded to collect all their camps together at A′phek, while the Israelites were camping by the spring that was in Jez′re·el. 2 And the axis lords of the Phi·lis′tines were passing along by hundreds and by thousands, and David and his men were passing along afterward with A′chish. 3 And the princes of the Phi·lis′tines began to say: "What do these Hebrews mean?" At this A′chish said to the princes of the Phi·lis′tines: "Is this not David the servant of Saul king of Israel, who happened to be with me here a year or two, and I have not found in him a single thing from the day of his deserting [to me] until this day?" 4 And the princes of the Phi·lis′tines became indignant at him; and the princes of the Phi·lis′tines went on to say to him: "Make the man go back, and let him go back to his place where you assigned him; and do not let him go down with us into the battle, that he may not become a resister of us in the battle. And with what should this person put himself in favor with his lord? Is it not with the heads of those [our] men? 5 Is this not David to whom they kept responding in the dances, saying, 'Saul has struck down his

thousands, and David his tens of thousands'?"

6 Consequently A′chish called David and said to him: "As Jehovah is living, you are upright, and your going out and your coming in with me in the camp has been good in my eyes; for I have not found badness in you from the day of your coming to me until this day. But in the eyes of the axis lords you are not good. 7 And now return and go in peace, that you may not do anything bad in the eyes of the axis lords of the Phi·lis′tines." 8 However, David said to A′chish: "Why, what have I done, and what have you found in your servant from the day that I came to be before you until this day, that I should not come and actually fight against the enemies of my lord the king?" 9 At this A′chish answered and said to David: "I well know that you have been good in my own eyes, like an angel of God. Only it is the princes of the Phi·lis′tines that have said, 'Let him not go up with us into the battle.' 10 And now rise up early in the morning with the servants of your lord that came with you; and YOU men must rise up early in the morning when it has become light for YOU. Then go."

11 Accordingly David rose up early, he and his men, to go in the morning and return to the land of the Phi·lis′tines; and the Phi·lis′tines themselves went up to Jez′re·el.

30 And it came about while David and his men were coming to Zik′lag on the third day, that the A·mal′ek·ites made a raid on the south and on Zik′lag; and they proceeded to strike Zik′lag and burn it with fire, 2 and to carry off captive the women [and all] that were in it, from the smallest to the greatest. They did not put anyone to death, but they drove them along and went on their way. 3 When David came with his men to the city, why, there it was burned with fire, and, as for their wives and their sons and their daughters, they had been carried off captive. 4 And David and the people that were with him began to raise their voice and weep, until there was in them no power to weep [any more]. 5 And David's two wives had been carried off captive, A·hin′o·am the Jez′re·el·it·ess and Ab′i·gail the wife of Na′bal the Car′mel·ite. 6 And it became very distressing to David, because the people said to stone him; for the soul of all the people had become bitter, each one because of his sons and his daughters. So David took to strengthening himself by Jehovah his God.

7 Hence David said to A·bi′a·thar the priest, the son of A·him′e·lech: "Do, please, bring the eph′od near to me." And A·bi′a·thar came bringing the eph′od near to David. 8 And David began to inquire of Jehovah, saying: "Shall I chase after this marauder band? Shall I overtake them?" At this he said to him: "Go in chase, for you will without fail overtake them, and you will without fail make a deliverance."

9 Promptly David got on his way, he and the six hundred men that were with him, and they went on as far as the torrent valley of Be′sor, and the men that were to be left behind stood still. 10 And David kept up the chase, he and four hundred men, but two hundred men that were too tired to pass over the torrent valley of Be′sor stood still.

11 And they got to find a man, an Egyptian, in the field. So they took him to David and gave him bread that he might eat and gave him water to drink. 12 Further, they gave him a slice of a cake of pressed figs and two cakes of raisins. Then he ate and his spirit returned to him; for he had not eaten bread or drunk water for three days and three nights. 13 David now said to him: "To whom do you belong, and where are you from?" to which he said: "I am an Egyptian attendant, a slave of an A·mal′ek·ite man, but

my master left me because I took sick three days ago. 14 We were the ones that made a raid on the south of the Cher′e·thites and upon that which belongs to Judah and upon the south of Ca′leb; and Zik′lag we burned with fire." 15 At this David said to him: "Will you lead me down to this marauder band?" To this he said: "Do swear to me by God that you will not put me to death, and that you will not surrender me into the hand of my master, and I shall lead you down to this marauder band."

16 Accordingly he led him down, and there they were spread disorderly over the surface of all the land eating and drinking and having a feast on account of all the great spoil that they had taken from the land of the Phi·lis′tines and the land of Judah. 17 And David went striking them down from the morning darkness until the evening, that he might devote them to destruction; and not a man of them escaped except four hundred young men that rode upon camels and took to flight. 18 And David got to deliver all that the A·mal′ek·ites had taken, and his two wives David delivered. 19 And there was nothing of theirs lacking, from the smallest to the greatest and to sons and daughters and from the spoil, even to anything that they had taken for themselves. Everything David recovered. 20 So David took all the flocks and the herds, which they drove before that [other] livestock. Then they said: "This is David's spoil."

21 At length David came to the two hundred men who had been too tired to go along with David, and whom they had kept sitting by the torrent valley of Be′sor; and they came out to meet David and to meet the people that were with him. When David came near to the people he began to ask them how they were. 22 However, every bad and good-for-nothing man out of the men that had gone with David answered and kept saying: "For the reason that they did not

go with us, we will give them none of the spoil that we delivered, except to each one his wife and his sons, and let them lead them and go." 23 But David said: "You must not do that way, my brothers, with what Jehovah has given us, in that he safeguarded us and gave the marauder band that came against us into our hand. 24 And who will listen to YOU as to this saying? For as the share of the one that went down into the battle even so will the share of the one that sat by the baggage be. All will have a share together." 25 And it came about from that day forward that he kept it set as a regulation and a judicial decision for Israel down to this day.

26 When David came to Zik′lag he proceeded to send some of the spoil to the older men of Judah, his friends, saying: "Here is a gift blessing for YOU from the spoil of Jehovah's enemies." 27 To those who were in Beth′el, and to those in Ra′moth of the south, and to those in Jat′tir, 28 and to those in A·ro′er, and to those in Siph′moth, and to those in Esh·te·mo′a, 29 and to those in Ra′cal, and to those in the cities of the Je·rah′me·el·ites, and to those in the cities of the Ken′ites, 30 and to those in Hor′mah, and to those in Bor′a·shan, and to those in A′thach, 31 and to those in He′bron, and to all the places where David had walked about, he and his men.

31 Now the Phi·lis′tines were fighting against Israel, and the men of Israel took to flight from before the Phi·lis′tines, and they kept falling down slain in Mount Gil·bo′a. 2 And the Phi·lis′tines kept in close range of Saul and his sons; and the Phi·lis′tines at last struck down Jon′a·than and A·bin′a·dab and Mal′chi-shu′a, Saul's sons. 3 And the fighting became heavy against Saul, and the shooters, the bowmen, finally

found him, and he got severely wounded by the shooters. 4 Then Saul said to his armor-bearer: "Draw your sword and run me through with it, that these uncircumcised men may not come and certainly run me through and deal abusively with me." And his armor-bearer was unwilling, because he was very much afraid. So Saul took the sword and fell upon it. 5 When his armor-bearer saw that Saul had died, then he too fell upon his own sword and died with him. 6 Thus Saul and his three sons and his armor-bearer, even all his men, came to die together on that day. 7 When the men of Israel that were in the region of the low plain and that were in the region of the Jordan saw that the men of Israel had fled, and that Saul and his sons had died, then they began to leave the cities and flee, after which the Phi·lis′tines came on in and took up dwelling in them.

8 And it came about the next day that, when the Phi·lis′tines came to strip the slain, they got to find Saul and his three sons fallen upon Mount Gil·bo′a. 9 And they proceeded to cut off his head and strip off his armor and send into the land of the Phi·lis′tines all around to inform the houses of their idols and the people. 10 Finally they put his armor in the house of the Ash′to·reth images, and his corpse they fastened on the wall of Beth-shan. 11 And as regards him, the inhabitants of Ja′besh-gil′e·ad got to hear what the Phi·lis′tines had done to Saul. 12 Immediately all the valiant men rose up and went all night long and took the corpse of Saul and the corpses of his sons off the wall of Beth-shan and came to Ja′besh and burned them there. 13 Then they took their bones and buried them under the tamarisk tree in Ja′besh, and they went fasting for seven days.

THE SECOND OF

SAMUEL

or, according to the Greek *Septuagint,*

THE SECOND OF KINGS

1 And it came about after Saul's death, and when David himself had returned from striking down the A·mal′ek·ites, that David continued to dwell at Zik′lag two days. **2** And it came about on the third day that, look! a man was coming from the camp, from Saul, with his garments ripped apart and dirt upon his head; and it came about that when he came to David, he at once fell down to the earth and prostrated himself.

3 And David proceeded to say to him: "Where do you come from?" at which he said to him: "From the camp of Israel I have escaped." **4** And David went on to say to him: "How did the matter turn out? Tell me, please." To this he said: "The people have fled from the battle and also many of the people have fallen so that they died, and even Saul and Jon′a·than his son have died." **5** Then David said to the young man that was telling him: "How do you really know that Saul has died and also Jon′a·than his son?" **6** At this the young man that was telling him said: "I unexpectedly chanced to be on Mount Gil·bo′a, and there was Saul supporting himself upon his spear; and, look! the charioteers and the mounted men had caught up with him. **7** When he turned back and saw me, then he called me, and I said, 'Here I am!' **8** And he went on to say to me, 'Who are you?' at which I said to him, 'I am an A·mal′ek·ite.' **9** Then he said, 'Stand, please, over me and definitely put me to death, for the cramp has seized me, because all my soul is yet in me.' **10** So I stood over him and definitely put him to death, for I knew that he could not live after he had

fallen. Then I took the diadem that was upon his head and the bracelet that was upon his arm, that I might bring them to my lord here."

11 At this David took hold of his garments and ripped them apart, and so did all the men also that were with him. **12** And they began to wail and weep and fast until the evening over Saul and over Jon′a·than his son and over the people of Jehovah and over the house of Israel, because they had fallen by the sword.

13 David now said to the young man that was telling him: "Where are you from?" to which he said: "I am the son of an alien resident, an A·mal′ek·ite." **14** Then David said to him: "How was it that you did not fear to thrust your hand out to bring the anointed of Jehovah to ruin?" **15** With that David called one of the young men and said: "Go near. Smite him." Accordingly he struck him down so that he died. **16** David then said to him: "The bloodguilt for you be upon your own head, because your own mouth has testified against you, saying, 'I myself definitely put the anointed of Jehovah to death.'"

17 And David proceeded to chant this dirge over Saul and Jon′a·than his son **18** and to say that the sons of Judah should be taught "The Bow." Look! It is written in the book of Ja′shar:

19 "The beauty, O Israel, is slain upon your high places.
How have the mighty men fallen!
20 Do not, YOU people, tell it in Gath;
Do not announce it in the streets of Ash′ke·lon,

For fear that the daughters of
the Phi·lis′tines may rejoice,
For fear that the daughters of
the uncircumcised men may
exult.

21 You mountains of Gil·bo′a, let
no dew, let no rain be upon
you, nor let there be fields
of holy contributions;
Because there the shield of
mighty ones was befouled,
The shield of Saul, so that
there was none anointed
with oil.

22 From the blood of the slain,
from the fat of mighty ones,
The bow of Jon′a·than did
not turn back,
And the sword of Saul would
not return without success.

23 Saul and Jon′a·than, the lovable
ones and the pleasant ones
during their life,
And in their death they were
not separated.
Swifter than the eagles they
were,
Mightier than the lions they
were.

24 You daughters of Israel, weep
over Saul,
Who clothed you in scarlet
with finery,
Who put ornaments of gold
upon your clothing.

25 How have the mighty ones fallen
in the midst of the battle!
Jon′a·than slain upon your
high places!

26 I am distressed over you, my
brother Jon′a·than,
Very pleasant you were to me.
More wonderful was your love
to me than the love from
women.

27 How have the mighty ones fallen
And the weapons of war perished!"

2 And it came about afterward
that David proceeded to inquire
of Jehovah, saying: "Shall I go up
into one of the cities of Judah?"
At this Jehovah said to him: "Go
up." And David went on to say:
"Where shall I go up?" Then he
said: "To He′bron." 2 Accordingly
David went up there and also his
two wives, A·hin′o·am the Jez′-
re·el·it·ess and Ab′i·gail the wife
of Na′bal the Car′mel·ite. 3 And
the men that were with him David
brought up, each with his household; and they took up dwelling
in the cities of He′bron [territory].
4 Then the men of Judah came
and anointed David there as king
over the house of Judah.

And they came telling David,
saying: "The men of Ja′besh-
gil′e·ad were the ones that buried
Saul." 5 Hence David sent messengers to the men of Ja′besh-
gil′e·ad and said to them: "Blessed
may you be of Jehovah, because
you exercised this loving-kindness
toward your lord, toward Saul, in
that you buried him. 6 And now
may Jehovah exercise toward you
loving-kindness and trustworthiness, and I too shall exercise to you
this goodness because you have
done this thing. 7 And now let
your hands strengthen themselves
and prove yourselves valiant men,
because your lord Saul is dead,
and it is even I whom the house
of Judah have anointed as king
over them."

8 As for Ab′ner the son of Ner the
chief of the army that had belonged
to Saul, he took Ish-bo′sheth,
Saul's son, and proceeded to bring
him across to Ma·ha·na′im, 9 and
to make him king over Gil′e·ad
and the Ash′ur·ites and Jez′re·el
and over E′phra·im and Benjamin
and over Israel, all of it. 10 Forty
years old Ish-bo′sheth, Saul's son,
was when he became king over
Israel, and for two years he ruled
as king. Only the house of Judah
proved themselves followers of
David. 11 And the number of the
days that David proved to be king
in He′bron over the house of Judah
came to be seven years and six
months.

12 In time Ab′ner the son of
Ner and the servants of Ish-bo′-
sheth, Saul's son, went out from
Ma·ha·na′im to Gib′e·on. 13 As
for Jo′ab the son of Ze·ru′iah and
the servants of David, they went
out and later met together by the

pool of Gib'e·on; and they kept sitting, these on this side of the pool and those on that side of the pool. 14 Finally Ab'ner said to Jo'ab: "Let the young men rise up, please, and let them put on a combat before us." To this Jo'ab said: "Let them rise up." 15 So they rose up and went across by number, twelve belonging to Benjamin and Ish-bo'sheth, Saul's son, and twelve from the servants of David. 16 And they began grabbing hold of one another by the head, with the sword of each one in the side of the other, so that they fell down together. And that place came to be called Hel'kath-haz·zu'rim, which is in Gib'e·on.

17 And the fighting came to be extremely hard on that day, and Ab'ner and the men of Israel were finally defeated before the servants of David. 18 Now the three sons of Ze·ru'iah happened to be there, Jo'ab and A·bish'ai and As'a·hel; and As'a·hel was swift on his feet, like one of the gazelles that are in the open field. 19 And As'a·hel went chasing after Ab'ner, and he did not incline to go to the right or to the left from following Ab'ner. 20 At length Ab'ner looked behind him and said: "Is this you, As'a·hel?" to which he said: "It is I." 21 Then Ab'ner said to him: "Veer to your right or to your left and seize one of the young men as yours and take what you strip off him as yours." And As'a·hel did not want to turn aside from following him. 22 So Ab'ner said to As'a·hel yet again: "Turn your course aside from following me. Why should I strike you down to the earth? How, then, could I raise my face to Jo'ab your brother?" 23 But he kept refusing to turn aside; and Ab'ner got to strike him in the abdomen with the butt end of the spear, so that the spear came out from his back; and he fell there and died where he was. And it came about that all those who came to the place where As'a·hel fell and then died would stand still.

24 And Jo'ab and A·bish'ai went chasing after Ab'ner. As the sun was setting they themselves came to the hill of Am'mah, which is in front of Gi'ah on the way to the wilderness of Gib'e·on. 25 And the sons of Benjamin went collecting together behind Ab'ner, and they came to be one company and kept standing upon the top of one hill. 26 And Ab'ner began to call to Jo'ab and say: "Is the sword going to eat endlessly? Do you not really know that bitterness is what will develop at last? How long, then, will it be before you say to the people to turn back from following their brothers?" 27 At that Jo'ab said: "As the [true] God is living, if you had not spoken, then only by the morning would the people have been withdrawn, each one from following his brother." 28 Jo'ab now blew the horn, and all the people came to a halt and did not continue chasing after Israel any more, and they did not renew the fighting any more.

29 As for Ab'ner and his men, they marched through the Ar'a·bah all that night and went crossing the Jordan and marching through the entire gully and finally came to Ma·ha·na'im. 30 As for Jo'ab, he turned back from following Ab'ner and began to collect all the people together. And there were missing from the servants of David nineteen men and As'a·hel. 31 And the servants of David, for their part, had struck down those of Benjamin and of the men of Ab'ner—there were three hundred and sixty men that died. 32 And they proceeded to carry As'a·hel and bury him in the burial place of his father, which is at Beth'le·hem. Then Jo'ab and his men went marching on all night long, and it became daylight for them at He'bron.

3 And the war between the house of Saul and the house of David came to be long drawn out; and David kept getting stronger, and the house of Saul kept declining more and more.

2 Meantime, sons were born to David in He'bron, and his first-born came to be Am'non by A·hin'o·am the Jez're·el·it·ess. 3 And his second was Chil'e·ab by Ab'i·gail the wife of Na'bal the Car'mel·ite, and the third was Ab'sa·lom the son of Ma'a·cah the daughter of Tal'mai the king of Gesh'ur. 4 And the fourth was Ad·o·ni'jah the son of Hag'gith, and the fifth was Sheph·a·ti'ah the son of A·bi'tal. 5 And the sixth was Ith're·am by Eg'lah, David's wife. These were the ones born to David in He'bron.

6 And it came about that while the war between the house of Saul and the house of David kept up, Ab'ner himself was continually strengthening his position in the house of Saul. 7 Now Saul had had a concubine whose name was Riz'pah, the daughter of A'iah. Later Ish-bo'sheth said to Ab'ner: "Why was it that you had relations with the concubine of my father?" 8 And Ab'ner got very angry at the words of Ish-bo'sheth and went on to say: "Am I a dog's head that belongs to Judah? Today I keep exercising loving-kindness toward the house of Saul your father, to his brothers and his personal friends, and I have not let you find yourself in the hand of David; and yet you call me to account for an error concerning a woman today. 9 So may God do to Ab'ner and so may he add to it, if, just as Jehovah swore to David, that is not the way that I shall do to him, 10 so as to transfer the kingdom from the house of Saul and to establish the throne of David over Israel and over Judah from Dan to Be'er-she'ba." 11 And he was not able to say one word more in reply to Ab'ner because of being afraid of him.

12 Accordingly Ab'ner sent messengers to David on the spot, saying: "To whom does the land belong?" adding: "Do conclude your covenant with me, and, look! my hand will be with you to turn to your side the whole of Israel."

13 To this he said: "Good! I myself shall conclude a covenant with you. Only one thing there is that I am asking of you, saying, 'You may not see my face except first you bring Mi'chal, Saul's daughter, when you come to see my face.'" 14 Further, David sent messengers to Ish-bo'sheth, Saul's son, saying: "Do give over my wife Mi'chal, whom I engaged to myself for a hundred foreskins of the Phi·lis'tines." 15 So Ish-bo'sheth sent and took her from her husband, Pal'ti·el the son of La'ish. 16 But her husband kept walking with her, weeping as he walked after her as far as Ba·hu'rim. Then Ab'ner said to him: "Go, return!" At that he returned.

17 Meanwhile there had come to be communication by Ab'ner with the older men of Israel, saying: "Both yesterday and previously you proved yourselves seeking David as king over you. 18 And now act, for Jehovah himself said to David, 'By the hand of David my servant I shall save my people Israel from the hand of the Phi·lis'tines and from the hand of all their enemies.'" 19 Then Ab'ner also spoke in the ears of Benjamin, after which Ab'ner also went to speak in the ears of David at He'bron all that was good in the eyes of Israel and in the eyes of the whole house of Benjamin.

20 When Ab'ner came to David at He'bron, and with him twenty men, David proceeded to make a feast for Ab'ner and for the men that were with him. 21 Then Ab'ner said to David: "Let me rise up and go and collect all Israel together to my lord the king, that they may conclude a covenant with you, and you will certainly become king over all that your soul craves." So David sent Ab'ner off, and he got on his way in peace.

22 And here David's servants and Jo'ab were coming from a raid, and the spoil that they brought with them was abundant. As for Ab'ner, he was not with David in He'bron, for he had sent

him off, and he was on his way in peace. 23 And Jo'ab and all the army that was with him came in, and they now reported to Jo'ab, saying: "Ab'ner the son of Ner came to the king, and he proceeded to send him off, and he is on his way in peace." 24 So Jo'ab went in to the king and said: "What have you done? Look! Ab'ner has come to you. Why was it that you sent him off so that he successfully went away? 25 You well know Ab'ner the son of Ner, that it was to fool you that he came and to get to know your going out and your coming in and to get to know everything that you are doing."

26 With that Jo'ab went out from David and sent messengers after Ab'ner, and they then had him return from the cistern of Si'rah; and David himself did not know of it. 27 When Ab'ner returned to He'bron, Jo'ab now led him aside inside the gate to speak with him quietly. However, there he struck him in the abdomen, so that he died because of the blood of As'a·hel his brother. 28 When David heard of it afterward, he at once said: "I and my kingdom, from the standpoint of Jehovah, are innocent for time indefinite of bloodguilt for Ab'ner the son of Ner. 29 May it whirl back upon the head of Jo'ab and upon the entire house of his father, and let there not be cut off from Jo'ab's house a man with a running discharge or a leper or a man taking hold of the twirling spindle or one falling by the sword or one in need of bread!" 30 As for Jo'ab and A·bish'ai his brother, they killed Ab'ner over the fact that he had put As'a·hel their brother to death at Gib'e·on in the battle.

31 Then David said to Jo'ab and all the people that were with him: "Rip your garments apart and tie on sackcloth and wail before Ab'ner." Even King David was walking behind the couch. 32 And they had the burial of Ab'ner in He'bron; and the king began to raise his voice and weep at Ab'ner's

burial place, and all the people gave way to weeping. 33 And the king went on to chant over Ab'ner and say:

"As with the death of a senseless person should Ab'ner die?
34 Your hands had not been bound ones,
And your feet had not been put into fetters of copper.
As one falling before the sons of unrighteousness you have fallen."

At that all the people wept over him again.

35 Later all the people came to give David bread for consolation while it was yet that day, but David swore, saying: "So may God do to me and so may he add to it, if before the sun sets I shall taste bread or anything at all!" 36 And all the people themselves took notice, and it was good in their eyes. Like everything that the king did, it was in the eyes of all the people good. 37 And all the people and all Israel got to know on that day that it had not originated with the king to have Ab'ner the son of Ner put to death. 38 And the king went on to say to his servants: "Do you not know that it is a prince and a great man that has fallen this day in Israel? 39 And I today am weak although anointed as king, and these men, the sons of Ze·ru'iah, are too severe for me. May Jehovah repay the doer of what is bad according to his own badness."

4 When the son of Saul heard that Ab'ner had died in He'bron, then his hands became feeble and all the Israelites themselves were disturbed. 2 And there were two men, chiefs of the marauding bands, that happened to belong to the son of Saul, the name of the one being Ba'a·nah and the name of the other being Re'chab, the sons of Rim'mon the Be·er'oth·ite, of the sons of Benjamin; for Be·er'oth, too, used to be counted as part of Benjamin. 3 And the Be·er'oth·ites went running away to Git'ta·im, and they came to be

alien residents there down to this day.

4 Now Jon'a·than, the son of Saul, had a son lame in the feet. Five years old he happened to be when the report about Saul and Jon'a·than came from Jez're·el; and his nurse began to carry him and flee, but it came about that as she was running in panic to flee, he then had a fall and was lamed. And his name was Me·phib'o·sheth.

5 And the sons of Rim'mon the Be·er'oth·ite, Re'chab and Ba'a·nah, proceeded to go and come to the house of Ish-bo'sheth about when the day had heated up, as he was taking his noonday siesta. 6 And here they came into the middle of the house as men fetching wheat, and then struck him in the abdomen; and Re'chab and Ba'a·nah his brother themselves escaped detection. 7 When they went into the house, he was lying upon his couch in his inner bedroom, and then they struck him so that they put him to death, after which they removed his head and took his head and walked on the road to the Ar'a·bah all night long. 8 Eventually they came bringing the head of Ish-bo'sheth to David at He'bron and said to the king: "Here is the head of Ish-bo'sheth the son of Saul your enemy who looked for your soul; but Jehovah gives to my lord the king revenge this day upon Saul and his offspring."

9 However, David answered Re'-chab and Ba'a·nah his brother, the sons of Rim'mon the Be·er'-oth·ite, and said to them: "As Jehovah who redeemed my soul out of all distress is living, 10 when there was one reporting to me, saying, 'Here Saul is dead,' and he himself in his own eyes became like a bringer of good news, I, however, took hold of him and killed him in Zik'lag when it was due [for me] to give him the messenger's fee; 11 how much more so when wicked men themselves have killed a righteous man in his own

house upon his bed? And now should I not require his blood from YOUR hands, and must I not clear YOU out of the earth?" 12 With that David commanded the young men and they killed them and cut off their hands and their feet and hanged them by the pool in He'bron; and the head of Ish-bo'sheth they took and then buried in the burial place of Ab'ner in He'bron.

5 In time all the tribes of Israel came to David at He'bron and said: "Look! We ourselves are your bone and your flesh. 2 Both yesterday and previously while Saul happened to be king over us, you yourself became the one leading Israel out and bringing it in. And Jehovah proceeded to say to you, 'You yourself will shepherd my people Israel, and you yourself will become leader over Israel.'" 3 So all the older men of Israel came to the king at He'bron, and King David concluded a covenant with them in He'bron before Jehovah; after which they anointed David as king over Israel.

4 Thirty years old was David when he became king. For forty years he ruled as king. 5 In He'-bron he ruled as king over Judah for seven years and six months; and in Jerusalem he ruled as king for thirty-three years over all Israel and Judah. 6 Consequently the king and his men went to Jerusalem against the Jeb'u·sites inhabiting the land, and they began to say to David: "You will not come in here, but the blind and the lame ones will certainly turn you away," they thinking: "David will not come in here." 7 Just the same, David proceeded to capture the stronghold of Zion, that is, the city of David. 8 So David said on that day: "Anyone striking the Jeb'u·sites, let him, by means of the water tunnel, make contact with both the lame and the blind, hateful to the soul of David!" That is why they say: "The blind one and the lame one will not come into the house." 9 And David took up

dwelling in the stronghold, and it came to be called the city of David; and David began to build all around from the Mound and inward. 10 Thus David went on getting greater and greater, and Jehovah the God of armies was with him.

11 And Hi′ram the king of Tyre proceeded to send messengers to David, and also cedar trees and workers in wood and workers in stone for walls, and they began to build a house for David. 12 And David came to know that Jehovah had firmly established him as king over Israel and that he had exalted his kingdom for the sake of his people Israel.

13 Meantime, David went on taking more concubines and wives out of Jerusalem after he came from He′bron; and more sons and daughters continued to be born to David. 14 And these are the names of those born to him in Jerusalem: Sham·mu′a and Sho′bab and Na′than and Sol′o·mon, 15 and Ib′har and E·li′shu·a and Ne′pheg and Ja·phi′a, 16 and E·lish′a·ma and E·li′a·da and E·liph′e·let.

17 And the Phi·lis′tines got to hear that they had anointed David as king over Israel. At that all the Phi·lis′tines came up to look for David. When David heard of it, then he went down to the place hard to approach. 18 And the Phi·lis′tines, for their part, came in and kept tramping about in the low plain of Reph′a·im. 19 And David began to inquire of Jehovah, saying: "Shall I go up against the Phi·lis′tines? Will you give them into my hand?" At this Jehovah said to David: "Go up, for I shall without fail give the Phi·lis′tines into your hands." 20 So David came to Ba′al-pe·ra′zim, and David got to strike them down there. At that he said: "Jehovah has broken through my enemies ahead of me, like a gap made by waters." That is why he called the name of that place Ba′al-pe·ra′zim. 21 Consequently they left their idols there, and so David and his men took them away.

22 Later the Phi·lis′tines came up once again and tramped about in the low plain of Reph′a·im. 23 At that David inquired of Jehovah, but he said: "You must not go up. Go around to the rear of them, and you must come against them in front of the ba′ca bushes. 24 And let it occur that, when you hear the sound of a marching in the tops of the ba′ca bushes, at that time you act with decision, because at that time Jehovah will have gone out ahead of you to strike down the camp of the Phi·lis′tines." 25 Accordingly David did that way, just as Jehovah had commanded him, and he went striking down the Phi·lis′tines from Ge′ba to as far as Ge′zer.

6 And David proceeded again to gather all the choice men in Israel, thirty thousand. 2 Then David and all the people that were with him rose up and went to Ba′al·e·ju′dah to bring up from there the ark of the [true] God, where a name is called on, the name of Jehovah of armies, sitting on the cherubs. 3 However, they had the ark of the [true] God ride upon a new wagon, that they might carry it from the house of A·bin′a·dab, which was on the hill; and Uz′zah and A·hi′o, the sons of A·bin′a·dab, were leading the new wagon.

4 So they carried it from A·bin′a·dab's house, which was on the hill—with the ark of the [true] God; and A·hi′o was walking ahead of the Ark. 5 And David and all the house of Israel were celebrating before Jehovah with all sorts of instruments of juniper wood and with harps and with stringed instruments and with tambourines and with sistrums and with cymbals. 6 And they came gradually as far as the threshing floor of Na′con, and Uz′zah now thrust [his hand] out to the ark of the [true] God and grabbed hold of it, for the cattle nearly caused an upset. 7 At that Jehovah's anger blazed against Uz′zah and the [true] God struck him down there for the irreverent

act, so that he died there close by the ark of the [true] God. 8 And David became angry over the fact that Jehovah had broken through in a rupture against Uz′zah, and that place came to be called Pe′rez-uz′zah down to this day. 9 And David became afraid of Jehovah on that day and began to say: "How will the ark of Jehovah come to me?" 10 And David was not willing to remove the ark of Jehovah to him at the city of David. So David had it carried aside to the house of O′bed-e′dom the Git′tite.

11 And the ark of Jehovah kept dwelling at the house of O′bed-e′dom the Git′tite three months; and Jehovah kept blessing O′bed-e′dom and all his household. 12 Finally the report was made to King David, saying: "Jehovah has blessed the house of O′bed-e′dom and all that is his on account of the ark of the [true] God." At that David proceeded to go and bring the ark of the [true] God out of the house of O′bed-e′dom up to the city of David with rejoicing. 13 And it came about that when the carriers of the ark of Jehovah had marched six steps, he immediately sacrificed a bull and a fatling.

14 And David was dancing around before Jehovah with all his power, all the while David being girded with an eph′od of linen. 15 And David and all the house of Israel were bringing up the ark of Jehovah with joyful shouting and sound of horn. 16 And it occurred that when the ark of Jehovah came into the city of David, Mi′chal, Saul's daughter, herself looked down through the window and got to see King David leaping and dancing around before Jehovah; and she began to despise him in her heart. 17 So they brought the ark of Jehovah in and set it in its place inside the tent that David had pitched for it; after which David offered up burnt sacrifices and communion sacrifices before Jehovah. 18 When David

was finished with offering up the burnt sacrifices and the communion sacrifices, he then blessed the people in the name of Jehovah of armies. 19 Further, he apportioned to all the people, to the whole crowd of Israel, man as well as woman, to each one a ring-shaped cake of bread and a date cake and a raisin cake, after which all the people went each to his own house.

20 David now returned to bless his own household, and Mi′chal, Saul's daughter, came on out to meet David and then said: "How glorious the king of Israel made himself today when he uncovered himself today to the eyes of the slave girls of his servants, just as one of the empty-headed men uncovers himself outright!" 21 At this David said to Mi′chal: "It was before Jehovah, who chose me rather than your father and all his household to put me in command as leader over Jehovah's people Israel, and I will celebrate before Jehovah. 22 And I will make myself even more lightly esteemed than this, and I will become low in my eyes; and with the slave girls whom you mentioned, with them I am determined to glorify myself." 23 So, as regards Mi′chal, Saul's daughter, she came to have no child down to the day of her death.

7 And it came about that, when the king dwelt in his own house and Jehovah himself had given him rest from all his enemies round about, 2 then the king said to Nathan the prophet: "See, now, I am dwelling in a house of cedars while the ark of the [true] God is dwelling in the middle of tent cloths." 3 Upon that Nathan said to the king: "Everything that is in your heart—go, do, because Jehovah is with you."

4 And it came about on that night that the word of Jehovah came to Nathan, saying: 5 "Go, and you must say to my servant David, 'This is what Jehovah has said: "Should you yourself build me a house for me to dwell in?

6 For I have not dwelt in a house from the day of my bringing the sons of Israel up out of Egypt to this day, but I was continually walking about in a tent and in a tabernacle. 7 During all the time that I have walked about among all the sons of Israel, was there a word that I spoke with one of the tribes of Israel that I commanded to shepherd my people Israel, saying, 'Why did you people not build me a house of cedars?'"' 8 And now this is what you will say to my servant David, 'This is what Jehovah of armies has said: "I myself took you from the pasture ground from following the flock to become a leader over my people Israel. 9 And I shall prove to be with you wherever you do go, and I will cut off all your enemies from before you; and I shall certainly make for you a great name, like the name of the great ones that are in the earth. 10 And I shall certainly appoint a place for my people Israel and plant them, and they will indeed reside where they are, and no more will they be disturbed; and the sons of unrighteousness will not afflict them again as they did at the first, 11 even from the day that I put judges in command over my people Israel; and I will give you rest from all your enemies.

"'"And Jehovah has told you that a house is what Jehovah will make for you. 12 When your days come to the full, and you must lie down with your forefathers, then I shall certainly raise up your seed after you, which will come out of your inward parts; and I shall indeed firmly establish his kingdom. 13 He is the one that will build a house for my name, and I shall certainly establish the throne of his kingdom firmly to time indefinite. 14 I myself shall become his father, and he himself will become my son. When he does wrong, I will also reprove him with the rod of men and with the strokes of the sons of Adam. 15 As for my loving-kindness, it will not depart from him the way I removed it from Saul, whom I removed on account of you. 16 And your house and your kingdom will certainly be steadfast to time indefinite before you; your very throne will become one firmly established to time indefinite."'"

17 According to all these words and according to all this vision was the way that Nathan spoke to David.

18 At that King David came in and sat down before Jehovah and said: "Who am I, O Lord Jehovah? And what is my house that you have brought me thus far? 19 As though this should even be something little in your eyes, O Lord Jehovah, yet you also speak respecting the house of your servant down to a distant future time; and this is the law given for mankind, O Lord Jehovah. 20 And what more can David add and speak to you, when you yourself know your servant well, O Lord Jehovah? 21 For the sake of your word and in agreement with your own heart you have done all these great things to cause your servant to know them. 22 That is why you are indeed great, O Lord Jehovah; for there is no other like you, and there is no God except you among all of whom we have heard with our ears. 23 And what one nation in the earth is like your people Israel, whom God went to redeem to himself as a people and to assign himself a name and to do for them great and fear-inspiring things—to drive out because of your people, whom you have redeemed to yourself from Egypt, the nations and their gods? 24 And you proceeded to establish your people Israel firmly for yourself as your people to time indefinite; and you yourself, O Jehovah, have become their God.

25 "And now, Jehovah God, the word that you have spoken concerning your servant and concerning his house carry out to time indefinite and do just as you have spoken. 26 And let your own name become great to time indefinite, saying, 'Jehovah of armies is God

over Israel,' and let the very house of your servant David become firmly established before you. 27 For you, Jehovah of armies the God of Israel, have made a revelation to your servant's ear, saying, 'A house I shall build for you.' That is why your servant has taken heart to pray to you with this prayer. 28 And now, O Lord Jehovah, you are the [true] God; and as for your words, let them prove to be truth, since you promise to your servant this goodness. 29 And now take it upon yourself and bless the house of your servant [for it] to continue to time indefinite before you; for you yourself, O Lord Jehovah, have promised, and due to your blessing let the house of your servant be blessed to time indefinite."

8 And it came about afterward that David proceeded to strike the Phi·lis'tines down and subdue them, and David got to take Meth'eg-am'mah out of the hand of the Phi·lis'tines.

2 And he went on to strike down the Mo'ab·ites and measure them with a line, making them lie down on the earth, that he might measure two lines to put them to death, and a full line to preserve them alive; and the Mo'ab·ites came to be David's servants to carry tribute.

3 And David went on to strike down Had·ad·e'zer the son of Re'hob the king of Zo'bah as he was going his way to put his control back again at the river Eu·phra'tes. 4 And David got to capture from him one thousand seven hundred horsemen and twenty thousand men on foot; and David proceeded to hamstring all the chariot horses, but he let a hundred chariot horses of them remain.

5 When Syria of Damascus came to help Had·ad·e'zer the king of Zo'bah, David then struck down among the Syrians twenty-two thousand men. 6 Further, David put garrisons in Syria of Damascus; and the Syrians came to be David's servants to carry tribute.

And Jehovah continued to save David wherever he went. 7 Moreover, David took the circular shields of gold that happened to be on the servants of Had·ad·e'zer and brought them to Jerusalem. 8 And from Be'tah and Be·ro'thai, cities of Had·ad·e'zer, King David took copper in very great quantity.

9 Now To'i the king of Ha'math got to hear that David had struck down all the military force of Had·ad·e'zer. 10 So To'i sent Jo'ram his son to King David to ask him about his welfare and congratulate him over the fact that he had fought against Had·ad·e'zer so that he struck him down (for Had·ad·e'zer had become trained in warfare against To'i); and in his hand there proved to be articles of silver and articles of gold and articles of copper. 11 These also King David sanctified to Jehovah, together with the silver and the gold that he had sanctified from all the nations that he had subdued, 12 from Syria and from Mo'ab and from the sons of Am'mon and from the Phi·lis'tines and from Am'a·lek and from the spoil of Had·ad·e'zer the son of Re'hob the king of Zo'bah. 13 And David proceeded to make a name when he came back from striking down the E'dom·ites in the Valley of Salt—eighteen thousand. 14 And he kept garrisons placed in E'dom. In all E'dom he placed garrisons, and all the E'dom·ites came to be servants of David; and Jehovah kept saving David wherever he went.

15 And David kept reigning over all Israel; and David was continually rendering judicial decision and righteousness for all his people. 16 And Jo'ab the son of Ze·ru'iah was over the army; and Je·hosh'a·phat the son of A·hi'lud was recorder. 17 And Za'dok the son of A·hi'tub and A·him'e·lech the son of A·bi'a·thar were priests, and Se·rai'ah was secretary. 18 And Be·nai'ah the son of Je·hoi'a·da [was over] the Cher'e·thites and the Pel'e·thites. As for the sons of David, they became priests.

9 And David proceeded to say: "Is there yet anyone that is left over of the house of Saul, that I may exercise loving-kindness toward him for the sake of Jon´a·than?" 2 Now the house of Saul had a servant whose name was Zi´ba. So they called him to David, and the king then said to him: "Are you Zi´ba?" to which he said: "I am your servant." 3 And the king went on to say: "Is there nobody of the house of Saul any more, that I may exercise toward him the loving-kindness of God?" At this Zi´ba said to the king: "There is yet a son of Jon´a·than, lame in the feet." 4 Then the king said to him: "Where is he?" So Zi´ba said to the king: "Look! He is in the house of Ma´chir the son of Am´mi·el at Lo-de´bar."

5 Immediately King David sent and took him from the house of Ma´chir the son of Am´mi·el at Lo-de´bar. 6 When Me·phib´o·sheth the son of Jon´a·than the son of Saul came in to David, he at once fell upon his face and prostrated himself. Then David said: "Me·phib´o·sheth!" to which he said: "Here is your servant." 7 And David went on to say to him: "Do not be afraid, for without fail I shall exercise loving-kindness toward you for the sake of Jon´a·than your father; and I must return to you all the field of Saul your grandfather, and you yourself will eat bread at my table constantly."

8 At that he prostrated himself and said: "What is your servant, that you have turned your face to the dead dog such as I am?" 9 The king now called Zi´ba, Saul's attendant, and said to him: "Everything that had come to belong to Saul and to all his house I do give to the grandson of your master. 10 And you must cultivate the ground for him, you and your sons and your servants, and you must do the gathering in, and it must serve as food for [those belonging to] the grandson of your master, and they must eat; but Me·phib´o·sheth himself, the grand-son of your master, will eat bread at my table constantly."

Now Zi´ba had fifteen sons and twenty servants. 11 So Zi´ba said to the king: "In accord with all that my lord the king commands for his servant is the way that your servant will do; but Me·phib´o·sheth is eating at my table like one of the sons of the king." 12 Now Me·phib´o·sheth had a young son whose name was Mi´ca, and all those dwelling in the house of Zi´ba were servants to Me·phib´o·sheth. 13 And Me·phib´o·sheth himself was dwelling in Jerusalem, for it was constantly at the table of the king that he was eating; and he was lame in both of his feet.

10 And it came about afterward that the king of the sons of Am´mon came to die, and Ha´nun his son began to reign instead of him. 2 At this David said: "I shall exercise loving-kindness toward Ha´nun the son of Na´hash, just as his father exercised loving-kindness toward me." Accordingly David sent by means of his servants to comfort him over his father, and the servants of David proceeded to come into the land of the sons of Am´mon. 3 However, the princes of the sons of Am´mon said to Ha´nun their lord: "Is David honoring your father in your eyes in that he has sent to you comforters? Is it not for the sake of searching through the city and to spy it out and to overthrow it that David has sent his servants to you?" 4 So Ha´nun took the servants of David and shaved off half their beards and cut their garments in half to their buttocks and sent them away. 5 Later people reported it to David, and he at once sent to meet them, because the men had come to feeling very humiliated; and the king went on to say: "Dwell in Jer´i·cho until YOUR beards grow abundantly. Then YOU must return."

6 In time the sons of Am´mon saw that they had become foul-smelling to David, and the sons of Am´mon proceeded to send and

hire Syrians of Beth-re'hob and Syrians of Zo'bah, twenty thousand men on foot, and the king of Ma'a-cah, a thousand men, and Ish'tob, twelve thousand men. 7 When David heard of it, then he sent Jo'ab and all the army [and] the mighty men. 8 And the sons of Am'mon began to go out and draw up in battle formation at the entrance of the gate, also the Syrians of Zo'bah and of Re'hob, and Ish'-tob and Ma'a·cah by themselves in the open field.

9 When Jo'ab saw that the battle charges had come to be against him from the front and from the rear, he at once chose some of all the choice men in Israel and drew them up in formation to meet the Syrians. 10 And the rest of the people he gave into the hand of A·bish'ai his brother, that he might draw them up in formation to meet the sons of Am'mon. 11 And he went on to say: "If the Syrians become too strong for me, then you must serve as a salvation for me; but if the sons of Am'mon themselves become too strong for you, I must also come to save you. 12 Be strong, that we may show ourselves courageous in behalf of our people and in behalf of the cities of our God; and as for Jehovah, he will do what is good in his own eyes."

13 Then Jo'ab and the people that were with him advanced to the battle against the Syrians, and they went fleeing from before him. 14 As for the sons of Am'mon, they saw that the Syrians had fled, and they took to flight from before A·bish'ai and hence came into the city. After that Jo'ab returned from the sons of Am'mon and came to Jerusalem.

15 When the Syrians saw that they had been defeated before Israel, they proceeded to gather themselves together. 16 So Had-ad·e'zer sent and brought out the Syrians that were in the region of the River; and then they came to He'lam, with Sho'bach the chief of the army of Had·ad·e'zer before them.

17 When the report was made to David, he immediately gathered all Israel and crossed the Jordan and came to He'lam. The Syrians now drew up in formation to meet David and began to fight against him. 18 And the Syrians took to flight from before Israel; and David got to kill of the Syrians seven hundred charioteers and forty thousand horsemen, and Sho'bach the chief of their army he struck down so that he died there. 19 When all the kings, the servants of Had-ad·e'zer, saw that they had been defeated before Israel, they promptly made peace with Israel and began to serve them; and the Syrians were afraid to try saving the sons of Am'mon any more.

11 And it came about at the return of the year, at the time that kings sally forth, that David proceeded to send Jo'ab and his servants with him and all Israel, that they might bring the sons of Am'mon to ruin and lay siege to Rab'bah, while David was dwelling in Jerusalem.

2 And it came about at the time of evening that David proceeded to rise from his bed and walk about on the rooftop of the king's house; and from the rooftop he caught sight of a woman bathing herself, and the woman was very good in appearance. 3 Then David sent and inquired about the woman and someone said: "Is this not Bath-she'ba the daughter of E·li'am the wife of U·ri'ah the Hit'tite?" 4 After that David sent messengers that he might take her. So she came in to him and he lay down with her, while she was sanctifying herself from her uncleanness. Later she returned to her house.

5 And the woman became pregnant. Consequently she sent and told David and said: "I am pregnant." 6 At this David sent to Jo'ab, saying: "Send to me U·ri'ah the Hit'tite." So Jo'ab sent U·ri'ah to David. 7 When U·ri'ah came to him, David began to ask how Jo'ab was getting along and how the people were getting along and how the war was getting along.

8 Finally David said to U·ri′ah: "Go down to your house and bathe your feet." Accordingly U·ri′ah went out from the king's house, and the king's courtesy gift went out following him. 9 However, U·ri′ah lay down at the entrance of the king's house with all the other servants of his lord, and he did not go down to his own house. 10 So they told David, saying: "U·ri′ah did not go down to his own house." Upon that David said to U·ri′ah: "It is from a journey that you have come in, is it not? Why have you not gone down to your own house?" 11 At this U·ri′ah said to David: "The Ark and Israel and Judah are dwelling in booths, and my lord Jo′ab and the servants of my lord are camping on the face of the field, and I—shall I go into my own house to eat and drink and to lie down with my wife? As you are living and as your soul is living, I shall not do this thing!"

12 Then David said to U·ri′ah: "Dwell here also today, and tomorrow I shall send you away." Therefore U·ri′ah kept dwelling in Jerusalem on that day and the day following. 13 Further, David called him that he might eat before him and drink. So he got him drunk. Nevertheless, he went out in the evening to lie down on his bed with the servants of his lord, and to his own house he did not go down. 14 And it came about in the morning that David proceeded to write a letter to Jo′ab and send it by the hand of U·ri′ah. 15 So he wrote in the letter, saying: "Put U·ri′ah in front of the heaviest battle charges, and you men must retreat from behind him, and he must be struck down and die."

16 And it came about that while Jo′ab was keeping guard over the city he kept U·ri′ah put in the place where he knew that there were valiant men. 17 When the men of the city came on out and went fighting against Jo′ab, then some of the people, the servants of David, fell and U·ri′ah the Hit′tite also died. 18 Jo′ab now sent that

he might report to David all the matters of the war. 19 And he went on to command the messenger, saying: "As soon as you finish speaking to the king about all the matters of the war, 20 then it must occur that if the rage of the king comes up and he does say to you, 'Why did you have to go so near to the city to fight? Did you men not know that they would shoot from on top of the wall? 21 Who was it that struck down A·bim′e·lech the son of Je·rub′be·sheth? Was it not a woman that pitched an upper millstone upon him from on top of the wall so that he died at The′bez? Why did you men have to go so close to the wall?' you must also say, 'Your servant U·ri′ah the Hit′tite died too.'"

22 So the messenger went and came and told David all about which Jo′ab had sent him. 23 And the messenger went on to say to David: "The men proved superior to us, so that they came out against us into the field; but we kept pressing them right up to the entrance of the gate. 24 And the shooters kept shooting at your servants from on top of the wall, so that some of the servants of the king died; and your servant U·ri′ah the Hit′tite also died." 25 At that David said to the messenger: "This is what you will say to Jo′ab, 'Do not let this matter appear bad in your eyes, for the sword eats up one as well as another. Intensify your battle against the city and throw it down.' And encourage him."

26 And the wife of U·ri′ah got to hear that U·ri′ah her husband had died, and she began to wail over her owner. 27 When the mourning period was past, David immediately sent and took her home to his house, and she came to be his wife. In time she bore to him a son, but the thing that David had done appeared bad in the eyes of Jehovah.

12 And Jehovah proceeded to send Nathan to David. So he came in to him and said to him:

"There were two men that happened to be in one city, the one rich and the other of little means. 2 The rich man happened to have very many sheep and cattle; 3 but the man of little means had nothing but one female lamb, a small one, that he had bought. And he was preserving it alive, and it was growing up with him and with his sons, all together. From his morsel it would eat, and from his cup it would drink, and in his bosom it would lie, and it came to be as a daughter to him. 4 After a while a visitor came to the rich man, but he spared taking some from his own sheep and his own cattle to get such ready for the traveler that had come in to him. So he took the female lamb of the man of little means and got it ready for the man that had come in to him."

5 At this David's anger grew very hot against the man, so that he said to Nathan: "As Jehovah is living, the man doing this deserves to die! 6 And for the female lamb he should make compensation with four, as a consequence of the fact that he has done this thing and because he did not have compassion."

7 Then Nathan said to David: "You yourself are the man! This is what Jehovah the God of Israel has said, 'I myself anointed you as king over Israel, and I myself delivered you out of the hand of Saul. 8 And I was willing to give you the house of your lord and the wives of your lord into your bosom, and to give you the house of Israel and of Judah. And if it were not enough, I was willing to add to you things like these as well as other things. 9 Why did you despise the word of Jehovah by doing what is bad in his eyes? U·ri′ah the Hit′tite you struck down with the sword, and his wife you took as your wife, and him you killed by the sword of the sons of Am′mon. 10 And now a sword will not depart from your own house to time indefinite, as a consequence of the fact that you despised me so that you took the wife of U·ri′ah the Hit′tite to become your wife.'

11 This is what Jehovah has said, 'Here I am raising up against you calamity out of your own house; and I will take your wives under your own eyes and give them to your fellow man, and he will certainly lie down with your wives under the eyes of this sun. 12 Whereas you yourself acted in secret, I, for my part, shall do this thing in front of all Israel and in front of the sun.'"

13 David now said to Nathan: "I have sinned against Jehovah." At this Nathan said to David: "Jehovah, in turn, does let your sin pass by. You will not die. 14 Notwithstanding this, because you have unquestionably treated Jehovah with disrespect by this thing, also the son himself, just born to you, will positively die."

15 Then Nathan went to his own house.

And Jehovah proceeded to deal a blow to the child that the wife of U·ri′ah had borne to David so that it took sick. 16 And David began to seek the [true] God in behalf of the boy, and David went on a strict fast and came in and spent the night and lay down on the earth. 17 So the older men of his house stood up over him to raise him up from the earth, but he did not consent and did not take bread in company with them. 18 And it came about on the seventh day that the child gradually died. And the servants of David were afraid to tell him that the child had died; for they said: "Look! While the child continued alive we did speak to him, and he did not listen to our voice; so how can we say to him, 'The child has died'? Then he will certainly do something bad."

19 When David got to see that his servants were whispering together, David began to discern that the child had died. So David said to his servants: "Has the child died?" To this they said: "He has died." 20 Then David got up from the earth and washed and rubbed himself with oil and changed his mantles and came to the house of

Jehovah and prostrated himself; after which he came into his own house and asked, and they promptly set bread before him and he began to eat. 21 Consequently his servants said to him: "What does this thing mean that you have done? For the sake of the child while alive you fasted and kept weeping; and just as soon as the child had died you got up and began to eat bread." 22 To this he said: "While the child was yet alive I did fast and I kept weeping, because I said to myself, 'Who is there knowing whether Jehovah may show me favor, and the child will certainly live?' 23 Now that he has died, why is it I am fasting? Am I able to bring him back again? I am going to him, but, as for him, he will not return to me."

24 And David began to comfort Bath-she′ba his wife. Further, he came in to her and lay down with her. In time she bore a son, and his name came to be called Sol′o-mon. And Jehovah himself did love him. 25 So he sent by means of Nathan the prophet and called his name Jed·i·di′ah, for the sake of Jehovah.

26 And Jo′ab continued to fight against Rab′bah of the sons of Am′mon and got to capture the city of the kingdom. 27 So Jo′ab sent messengers to David and said: "I have fought against Rab′bah. I have also captured the city of waters. 28 And now gather the rest of the people and encamp against the city, and capture it; that I myself may not be the one to capture the city, and my name should not have to be called upon it."

29 Accordingly David gathered all the people and went to Rab′bah and fought against it and captured it. 30 And he got to take the crown of Mal′cam off its head, the weight of which was a talent of gold, along with precious stones; and it came to be upon David's head. And the spoil of the city that he brought out was very much. 31 And the people that were in it, he brought out that he might put

them at sawing stones and at sharp instruments of iron and at axes of iron, and he made them serve at brickmaking. And that was the way he proceeded to do to all the cities of the sons of Am′mon. Finally David and all the people returned to Jerusalem.

13 And it came about after such things that Ab′sa·lom the son of David had a beautiful sister whose name was Ta′mar, and Am′-non the son of David fell in love with her. 2 And it was so distressing to Am′non that he felt sick on account of Ta′mar his sister, because she was a virgin, and it was difficult in the eyes of Am′non to do anything at all to her. 3 Now Am′non had a companion whose name was Je·hon′a-dab, the son of Shim′e·ah, David's brother; and Je·hon′a·dab was a very wise man. 4 So he said to him: "Why are you, the son of the king, so downcast as this, morning by morning? Will you not tell me?" At this Am′non said to him: "With Ta′mar the sister of Ab′sa-lom my brother I am in love." 5 Upon that Je·hon′a·dab said to him: "Lie down on your bed and play sick. And your father will certainly come to see you, and you must say to him, 'Please, let Ta′mar my sister come in and give me bread as a patient, and she will have to make the bread of consolation under my eyes in order that I may see it, and I shall have to eat from her hand.'"

6 Accordingly Am′non lay down and played sick, and so the king came in to see him. Then Am′non said to the king: "Please, let Ta′-mar my sister come in and bake two heart-shaped cakes under my eyes, that I may take bread as a patient from her hand." 7 At that David sent to Ta′mar at the house, saying: "Go, please, to the house of Am′non your brother and make the bread of consolation for him." 8 So Ta′mar went to the house of Am′non her brother while he was lying down. Then she took the flour dough and kneaded it and made the cakes under his eyes and cooked

the heart-shaped cakes. 9 Finally she took the deep pan and poured it out before him, but Am'non refused to eat and said: "HAVE everybody go out from me!" Then everybody went out from him.

10 Am'non now said to Ta'mar: "Bring the bread of consolation to the interior room, that I may take it as a patient from your hand." So Ta'mar took the heart-shaped cakes that she had made and brought them in to Am'non her brother in the interior room. 11 When she came near to him for him to eat, he at once grabbed hold of her and said to her: "Come, lie down with me, my sister." 12 However, she said to him: "No, my brother! Do not humiliate me; for it is not usual to do that way in Israel. Do not do this disgraceful folly. 13 And I—where shall I cause my reproach to go? And you —you will become like one of the senseless men in Israel. And now speak, please, to the king; for he will not withhold me from you." 14 And he did not consent to listen to her voice, but used strength superior to hers and humiliated her and lay down with her. 15 And Am'non began hating her with a very great hatred, because the hatred with which he hated her was greater than the love with which he had loved her, so that Am'non said to her: "Get up, go away!" 16 At this she said to him: "No, my brother; for this badness in sending me away is greater than the other that you have done with me!" And he did not consent to listen to her.

17 With that he called his attendant who waited upon him and said: "Send this person away from me, please, to the outside, and lock the door behind her." 18 (Now upon her there was a striped robe; for that was the way the daughters of the king, the virgins, used to dress with sleeveless coats.) So his waiter proceeded to lead her clear outside, and he locked the door behind her. 19 Then Ta'mar placed ashes upon her head, and the striped robe

that was upon her she ripped apart; and she kept her hands put upon her head and went walking away, crying out as she walked.

20 At this Ab'sa·lom her brother said to her: "Was it Am'non your brother that happened to be with you? And now, my sister, keep silent. He is your brother. Do not set your heart on this matter." And Ta'mar began to dwell, while being kept from association [with others], at the house of Ab'sa·lom her brother. 21 And King David himself heard about all these things, and he became very angry. 22 And Ab'sa·lom did not speak with Am'non either bad or good; for Ab'sa·lom hated Am'non over the fact that he had humiliated Ta'mar his sister.

23 And it turned out after two full years that Ab'sa·lom came to have sheepshearers at Ba'al-ha'zor, which is close by E'phra·im; and Ab'sa·lom proceeded to invite all the sons of the king. 24 So Ab'sa·lom came in to the king and said: "Here, now, your servant has sheepshearers! Let the king go, please, and also his servants, with your servant." 25 But the king said to Ab'sa·lom: "No, my son! Do not let all of us go, please, that we may not be a burden upon you." Although he kept urging him, he did not consent to go but blessed him. 26 Finally Ab'sa·lom said: "If not [you], let Am'non my brother go with us, please." At this the king said to him: "Why should he go with you?" 27 And Ab'sa·lom began to urge him, so that he sent Am'non and all the sons of the king with him.

28 Then Ab'sa·lom commanded his attendants, saying: "See, please, that just as soon as Am'non's heart is in a merry mood with wine, and I shall certainly say to YOU, 'Strike down Am'non!' YOU must then put him to death. Do not be afraid. Have not I myself commanded YOU? Be strong and prove yourselves to be valiant men." 29 And Ab'sa·lom's attendants proceeded to do to Am'non just as Ab'sa·lom had commanded; and all the other sons

of the king began to rise up and mount each one his mule and take to flight. 30 And it came about that, while they were on the way, the report itself came to David, saying: "Ab'sa·lom has struck down all the sons of the king, and not one of them has been left over." 31 At this the king got up and ripped his clothes apart and lay upon the earth, and all his servants were standing by with their garments ripped apart.

32 However, Je·hon'a·dab the son of Shim'e·ah, David's brother, answered and said: "Do not let my lord think that it is all the young men the sons of the king that they have put to death, for it is Am'non alone that has died, because at the order of Ab'sa·lom it has occurred as something appointed from the day that he humiliated Ta'mar his sister. 33 And now do not let my lord the king take to his heart the word, saying, 'All the king's sons themselves have died'; but it is Am'non alone that has died."

34 Meantime, Ab'sa·lom went running away. Later the young man, the watchman, raised his eyes and saw, and, look! there were many people coming from the road behind him by the mountainside. 35 At this Je·hon'a·dab said to the king: "Look! The king's sons themselves have come in. In accord with the word of your servant so it has taken place." 36 And it came about that, as soon as he finished speaking, here the king's sons themselves came in, and they began to raise their voice and weep; and even the king and all his servants wept with a very great weeping. 37 As for Ab'sa·lom, he ran off that he might go to Tal'mai the son of Am·mi'hud the king of Gesh'ur. And David continued to mourn over his son all the days. 38 As for Ab'sa·lom, he ran off and made his way to Gesh'ur; and he came to be there three years. 39 Finally the soul of David the king longed to go out to Ab'sa·lom; for he had comforted himself concerning Am'non, because he was dead.

14 Now Jo'ab the son of Ze·ru'iah came to know that the king's heart was toward Ab'sa·lom. 2 Accordingly Jo'ab sent to Te·ko'a and took from there a wise woman and said to her: "Go in mourning, please, and dress yourself, please, with garments of mourning, and do not rub yourself with oil; and you must become like a woman here who has been mourning many days over someone dead. 3 And you must come in to the king and speak to him a word like this." And that Jo'ab put the words in her mouth.

4 And the Te·ko'ite woman proceeded to come in to the king and fall upon her face to the earth and prostrate herself and say: "Do save, O king!" 5 At this the king said to her: "What is the matter with you?" To this she said: "For a fact I am a widowed woman, now that my husband is dead. 6 And your maidservant had two sons, and the two of them began to struggle with each other in the field while there was no deliverer to part them. Finally the one struck the other down and put him to death. 7 And here all the family have risen up against your maidservant and keep saying, 'Give over the striker of his brother, that we may put him to death for the soul of his brother whom he killed, and let us even annihilate the heir!' And they will certainly extinguish the glow of my charcoals that has remained, so as to assign to my husband neither a name nor a remnant on the surface of the ground."

8 Then the king said to the woman: "Go to your house, and I myself shall give command regarding you." 9 At this the Te·ko'ite woman said to the king: "Upon me, O my lord the king, be the error, and also upon the house of my father, while the king and his throne are innocent." 10 And the king went on to say: "If there is anyone speaking to you, you must also bring him to me, and he will never hurt you again." 11 But she said: "Let the king, please, remem-

ber Jehovah your God, that the avenger of blood may not be continually causing ruin and that they may not annihilate my son." To this he said: "As Jehovah is living, not a single hair of your son will fall to the earth." 12 The woman now said: "Let your maidservant, please, speak a word to my lord the king." So he said: "Speak!"

13 And the woman went on to say: "Why, then, have you reasoned like this against the people of God? As the king is speaking this word he is like one that is guilty, in that the king does not bring back his own banished one. 14 For we shall die without fail and be like waters that are being poured down to the earth, which cannot be gathered. But God will not take away a soul, and he has thought out reasons why the one banished should not be banished from him. 15 And now that I have come in to speak this word to the king my lord, it is because the people made me afraid. So your maidservant said, 'Let me speak, please, to the king. Perhaps the king will act on the word of his slave girl. 16 Because the king proceeded to listen so as to deliver his slave girl out of the palm of the man [seeking] to annihilate me and my lone son from the inheritance given by God,' 17 then your maidservant said, 'Let the word of my lord the king serve, please, to give rest.' For just like an angel of the [true] God is the way my lord the king is, to distinguish what is good and what is bad, and may Jehovah your God himself prove to be with you."

18 The king now answered and said to the woman: "Do not, please, hide from me a thing about which I am asking you." To this the woman said: "Let my lord the king speak, please." 19 And the king went on to say: "Is the hand of Jo'ab with you in all this?" Then the woman answered and said: "As your soul is living, O my lord the king, no man can go to the right or go to the left from all that my lord the king has spoken; for it was your servant Jo'ab that com-

manded me, and he it was that put in the mouth of your maidservant all these words. 20 For the sake of altering the face of the matter your servant Jo'ab has done this thing, but my lord is wise as with the wisdom of the angel of the [true] God so as to know all that is in the earth."

21 Subsequently the king said to Jo'ab: "Here, now, I shall certainly do this thing. So go, bring the young man Ab'sa·lom back." 22 At this Jo'ab fell upon his face to the earth and prostrated himself and blessed the king; and Jo'ab went on to say: "Today your servant does know that I have found favor in your eyes, O my lord the king, because the king has acted on the word of his servant." 23 With that Jo'ab rose up and went to Gesh'ur and brought Ab'sa·lom to Jerusalem. 24 However, the king said: "Let him turn toward his own house, but my face he may not see." So Ab'sa·lom turned toward his own house, and the face of the king he did not see.

25 Now compared with Ab'sa·lom there proved to be no man so beautiful in all Israel as to be praised so much. From the sole of his foot to the crown of his head there proved to be no defect in him. 26 And when he shaved his head—and it occurred at the end of every year that he would shave it; because it was so heavy upon him, he shaved it—he weighed the hair of his head, two hundred shekels by the royal stone weight. 27 And there came to be born to Ab'sa·lom three sons and one daughter whose name was Ta'mar. She proved to be a woman most beautiful in appearance.

28 And Ab'sa·lom continued dwelling in Jerusalem for two full years, and the face of the king he did not see. 29 So Ab'sa·lom sent for Jo'ab to send him to the king, and he did not consent to come to him. Then he sent again, a second time, and he did not consent to come. 30 Finally he said to his servants: "See Jo'ab's tract of land beside mine, and there he has

barley. Go and set it ablaze with fire." Accordingly the servants of Ab'sa·lom set the tract of land ablaze with fire. 31 At this Jo'ab rose up and came to Ab'sa·lom at the house and said to him: "Why did your servants set the tract of land that is mine ablaze with fire?" 32 So Ab'sa·lom said to Jo'ab: "Look! I sent to you, saying, 'Come here and let me send you to the king, saying: "Why have I come from Gesh'ur? It would be better for me that I should still be there. And now let me see the face of the king and, if there is any error in me, he must then put me to death." ' "

33 Subsequently Jo'ab came in to the king and told him. Then he called Ab'sa·lom, who now came in to the king and prostrated himself to him, [falling] upon his face to the earth before the king; after which the king kissed Ab'sa·lom.

15 And it came about following such things that Ab'sa·lom proceeded to have a chariot made for himself, with horses and with fifty men running before him. 2 And Ab'sa·lom rose up early and stood at the side of the road to the gate. And it came about, when any man happened to have a legal case to come to the king for judgment, then Ab'sa·lom would call him and say: "From what city are you?" and he would say: "From one of the tribes of Israel your servant is." 3 And Ab'sa·lom would say to him: "See, your matters are good and straight; but there is no one from the king giving you a hearing." 4 And Ab'sa·lom would go on to say: "O that I were appointed judge in the land, that to me every man might come that happens to have a legal case or judgment! Then I should certainly do justice to him."

5 It also occurred that, when a man drew near to bow down to him, he thrust his hand out and grabbed hold of him and kissed him. 6 And Ab'sa·lom kept doing a thing like this to all Israelites that would come in for judgment to the king; and Ab'sa·lom kept stealing the hearts of the men of Israel.

7 And it came about at the end of forty years that Ab'sa·lom proceeded to say to the king: "Let me go, please, and pay in He'bron my vow that I solemnly made to Jehovah. 8 For your servant made a solemn vow when I was dwelling in Gesh'ur in Syria, saying, 'If Jehovah will without fail bring me back to Jerusalem, I must also render service to Jehovah.' " 9 So the king said to him: "Go in peace." With that he rose up and went to He'bron.

10 Ab'sa·lom now sent spies through all the tribes of Israel, saying: "As soon as YOU hear the sound of the horn, YOU must also say, 'Ab'sa·lom has become king in He'bron!' " 11 Now there had gone with Ab'sa·lom two hundred men from Jerusalem, being called and going unsuspectingly, and they did not know a single thing. 12 Further, when he offered the sacrifices, Ab'sa·lom sent for A·hith'o·phel the Gi'lon·ite, David's counselor, from his city Gi'loh. And the conspiracy kept getting stronger, and the people were continually growing in number with Ab'sa·lom.

13 In time an informer came to David, saying: "The heart of the men of Israel has come to be behind Ab'sa·lom." 14 At once David said to all his servants that were with him in Jerusalem: "Get up, and let us run away; for there will prove to be no escaping for us because of Ab'sa·lom! Go hurriedly, for fear he may hurry up and actually catch up with us and bring down upon us what is bad and strike the city with the edge of the sword!" 15 At this the king's servants said to the king: "According to all that my lord the king may choose, here are your servants." 16 So the king went out with all his household at his feet, and the king left ten women, concubines, to take care of the house. 17 And the king continued on his way out with all the people at his feet; and they came to a stop at Beth-mer'hak.

18 And all his servants were crossing at his side; and all the Cher′e·thites and all the Pel′e-thites and all the Git′tites, six hundred men that had followed him from Gath, were crossing before the king's face. **19** Then the king said to It′tai the Git′tite: "Why should you yourself also go with us? Go back and dwell with the king; for you are a foreigner and, besides, you are an exile from your place. **20** Yesterday was when you came and today shall I make you wander with us, to go when I am going wherever I am going? Go back and take your brothers back with you, [and may Jehovah exercise toward you] loving-kindness and trustworthiness!" **21** But It′-tai answered the king and said: "As Jehovah is living and as my lord the king is living, in the place where my lord the king may come to be, whether for death or for life, there is where your servant will come to be!" **22** At that David said to It′tai: "Go and cross over." So It′tai the Git′tite crossed over, and also all his men and all the little ones that were with him.

23 And all the people of the land were weeping with a loud voice, and all the people were crossing over, and the king was standing by the torrent valley of Kid′ron, and all the people were crossing over upon the open road to the wilderness. **24** And here also there were Za′dok and with him all the Levites carrying the ark of the covenant of the [true] God; and they proceeded to set the ark of the [true] God down by A·bi′a·thar until all the people completed crossing over from the city. **25** But the king said to Za′-dok: "Take the ark of the [true] God back to the city. If I shall find favor in the eyes of Jehovah, he will also certainly bring me back and let me see it and its abiding place. **26** But if this is what he should say, 'I have found no delight in you,' here I am, let him do to me just as it is good in his eyes." **27** And the king went on to say to Za′dok the priest: "You are a seer, are you? Do return to the city in

peace, and also A·him′a·az your son and Jon′a·than the son of A·bi′a·thar, the two sons of you men, with you. **28** See, I am lingering by the fords of the wilderness until word comes from you men to inform me." **29** Accordingly Za′dok and A·bi′a·thar took the ark of the [true] God back to Jerusalem, and they continued to dwell there.

30 And David was going up by the ascent of the Olives, weeping as he went up, with his head covered; and he was walking barefoot, and all the people that were with him covered each one his head, and they went up weeping as they went up. **31** And to David the report was made, saying: "A·hith′o-phel himself is among those conspiring with Ab′sa·lom." At this David said: "Turn, please, the counsel of A·hith′o·phel into foolishness, O Jehovah!"

32 And it came about that when David himself came to the summit where people used to bow down to God, here to meet him was Hu′shai the Ar′chite, with his robe ripped apart and dirt upon his head. **33** However, David said to him: "If you actually went across with me, you would then certainly become a load upon me. **34** But if you return to the city and you actually say to Ab′sa·lom, 'I am your servant, O King. I used to prove myself the servant of your father, even I at that time, but now even I am your servant,' you must then frustrate the counsel of A·hith′o·phel for me. **35** Are not Za′dok and A·bi′a·thar the priests there with you? And it must occur that everything that you may hear from the house of the king you should tell to Za′dok and A·bi′a-thar the priests. **36** Look! There with them are their two sons, A·him′a·az belonging to Za′dok and Jon′a·than belonging to A·bi′a-thar; and by means of them you men must send to me everything that you may hear." **37** So Hu′-shai, David's companion, came into the city. As for Ab′sa·lom, he proceeded to come into Jerusalem.

16 When David himself had crossed over a little beyond the summit, there was Zi′ba the attendant of Me·phib′o·sheth to meet him with a couple of asses saddled and upon them two hundred loaves of bread and a hundred cakes of raisins and a hundred loads of summer fruit and a large jar of wine. 2 Then the king said to Zi′ba: "What do these things mean on your part?" To this Zi′ba said: "The asses are for the household of the king to ride, and the bread and the load of summer fruit are for the young men to eat, and the wine is for the one tired out in the wilderness to drink." 3 The king now said: "And where is the son of your master?" At this Zi′ba said to the king: "There he is dwelling in Jerusalem; for he said, 'Today the house of Israel will give back to me the royal rule of my father.'" 4 The king then said to Zi′ba: "Look! Yours is everything that belongs to Me·phib′o·sheth." Upon that Zi′ba said: "I do bow down. Let me find favor in your eyes, my lord the king."

5 And King David came as far as Ba·hu′rim, and, look! coming out from there was a man of the family of Saul's house, and his name was Shim′e·i, the son of Ge′ra, coming out and calling down evil as he came out. 6 And he began throwing stones at David and at all the servants of King David; and all the people and all the mighty men were at his right and at his left. 7 And this is what Shim′e·i said as he called down evil: "Get out, get out, you bloodguilty man and good-for-nothing man! 8 Jehovah has brought back upon you all the bloodguilt for the house of Saul in place of whom you have ruled as king; and Jehovah gives the kingship into the hand of Ab′sa·lom your son. And here you are in your calamity, because you are a bloodguilty man!"

9 Finally A·bish′ai the son of Ze·ru′iah said to the king: "Why should this dead dog call down evil upon my lord the king? Let me go over, please, and take off his head." 10 But the king said: "What do I have to do with you men, you sons of Ze·ru′iah? Thus let him call down evil, because Jehovah himself has said to him, 'Call down evil upon David!' So who should say, 'Why did you do that way?'" 11 And David went on to say to A·bish′ai and all his servants: "Here my own son, who has come forth out of my own inward parts, is looking for my soul; and how much more now a Ben′ja·min·ite! Let him alone that he may call down evil, for Jehovah has said so to him! 12 Perhaps Jehovah will see with his eye, and Jehovah will actually restore to me goodness instead of his malediction this day." 13 With that David and his men kept going on in the road, while Shim′e·i was walking on the side of the mountain, walking abreast of him that he might call down evil; and he kept throwing stones while abreast of him, and he threw a lot of dust.

14 At length the king and all the people that were with him arrived tired. So they refreshed themselves there.

15 As for Ab′sa·lom and all the people, the men of Israel, they entered Jerusalem; and A·hith′o·phel was with him. 16 And it came about that, as soon as Hu′shai the Ar′chite, David's companion, came in to Ab′sa·lom, Hu′shai proceeded to say to Ab′sa·lom: "Let the king live! Let the king live!" 17 At this Ab′sa·lom said to Hu′shai: "This is the loving-kindness of yours toward your companion, is it? Why did you not go with your companion?" 18 So Hu′shai said to Ab′sa·lom: "No; but the one whom Jehovah has chosen and also this people and all the men of Israel, his I shall become, and with him I shall dwell. 19 And for the second time [I must say], Whom shall I myself serve? Is it not before his son? Just as I served before your father, so I shall prove to be before you."

20 Later Ab′sa·lom said to A·hith′o·phel: "You men, give

counsel on YOUR part. What shall we do?" 21 Then A·hith'o·phel said to Ab'sa·lom: "Have relations with the concubines of your father, whom he left behind to take care of the house. And all Israel will certainly hear that you have made yourself foul-smelling to your father, and the hands of all those who are with you will certainly become strong." 22 Accordingly they pitched a tent for Ab'sa·lom upon the roof, and Ab'sa·lom began to have relations with the concubines of his father under the eyes of all Israel.

23 And the counsel of A·hith'o·phel, with which he counseled in those days, was just as when a man would inquire of the word of the [true] God. That was the way all the counsel of A·hith'o·phel was both to David and to Ab'sa·lom.

17 And A·hith'o·phel proceeded to say to Ab'sa·lom: "Let me choose, please, twelve thousand men and rise up and chase after David tonight. 2 And I shall come upon him when he is weary and feeble in both hands, and I shall certainly drive him into trembling; and all the people that are with him will have to flee, and I shall certainly strike down the king by himself. 3 And let me bring all the people back to you. Equivalent to the returning of all is the man whom you are seeking; [and] all the people will themselves come to be at peace." 4 And the word was just right in the eyes of Ab'sa·lom and in the eyes of all the older men of Israel.

5 However, Ab'sa·lom said: "Call, please, Hu'shai the Ar'chite also, and let us hear what is in his mouth, even his." 6 So Hu'shai came in to Ab'sa·lom. Then Ab'sa·lom said to him: "According to this word is the way A·hith'o·phel spoke. Shall we act upon his word? If not, you yourself speak." 7 At this Hu'shai said to Ab'sa·lom: "The counsel with which A·hith'o·phel has counseled is not good in this instance!"

8 And Hu'shai went on to say: "You yourself well know your father and the men of his, that they are mighty, and they are bitter of soul, like a female bear that has lost her cubs in the field; and your father is a warrior, and he will not spend the night with the people. 9 Look! Now he is in hiding in one of the hollows or in one of the other places; and it will certainly occur that, just as soon as he falls upon them at the start, the one hearing of it will then be bound to hear and say, 'A defeat has taken place among the people that are following Ab'sa·lom!' 10 And even the valiant man whose heart is as the heart of the lion will himself surely soften in weakness; for all Israel is aware that your father is a mighty man and so, too, are the valiant men that are with him. 11 I myself do say in counsel: Let all Israel without fail be gathered to you, from Dan to Be'er-she'ba, as the sand particles that are by the sea for multitude, with your own person going into the fight. 12 And we must come against him in one of the places where he is certain to be found, and we ourselves will be upon him just as the dew falls upon the ground; and there will certainly not be left even a single one among him and all the men that are with him. 13 And if it is into some city that he will withdraw, all Israel must also carry ropes to that city, and we shall certainly drag it down to the torrent valley, until there shall not be found there even a pebble."

14 Then Ab'sa·lom and all the men of Israel said: "The counsel of Hu'shai the Ar'chite is better than the counsel of A·hith'o·phel!" And Jehovah himself had given command to frustrate the counsel of A·hith'o·phel although good, in order that Jehovah might bring calamity upon Ab'sa·lom.

15 Later Hu'shai said to Za'dok and A·bi'a·thar the priests: "This and that was the way that A·hith'o·phel counseled Ab'sa·lom and the older men of Israel; and this and that was the way that I myself counseled. 16 And now send speedily and tell David, saying, 'Do not lodge in the desert plains of

the wilderness tonight, but you also ought to cross over without fail, for fear that it may be communicated to the king and to all the people that are with him.'"

17 As Jon′a·than and A·him′a·az were standing at En-ro′gel, a maidservant went off and told them. So they themselves went off, as they had to tell King David; for they were not able to appear entering the city. 18 However, a young man got to see them and told Ab′sa·lom. So the two of them went off speedily and came to the house of a man in Ba·hu′rim, who had a well in his courtyard; and they went down into it. 19 After that the woman took and spread out a screen over the face of the well and heaped up cracked grain upon it; and not a thing became known of it. 20 The servants of Ab′sa·lom now came to the woman at her house and said: "Where are A·him′a·az and Jon′a·than?" At this the woman said to them: "They passed on from here to the waters." Then they kept on searching, and they did not find them and so returned to Jerusalem.

21 And it came about after their going away that then they came up out of the well and went on and told King David and said to David: "You people, rise up and speedily pass over the waters; for this is the way that A·hith′o·phel counseled against YOU." 22 Immediately David rose up and also all the people that were with him, and they kept crossing the Jordan until the morning became light, until not a one was lacking that had not passed over the Jordan.

23 As for A·hith′o·phel, he saw that his counsel had not been acted upon, and he proceeded to saddle an ass and rise up and go off to his house at his own city. Then he gave commands to his household and strangled himself and thus died. So he was buried in the burial place of his forefathers.

24 As for David, he came to Ma·ha·na′im, and Ab′sa·lom himself crossed the Jordan, he and all the men of Israel with him.

25 And A·ma′sa was the one whom Ab′sa·lom put in the place of Jo′ab over the army; and A·ma′sa was the son of a man whose name was Ith′ra the Israelite, who had relations with Ab′i·gail the daughter of Na′hash, the sister of Ze·ru′iah, Jo′ab's mother. 26 And Israel and Ab′sa·lom took up camping in the land of Gil′e·ad.

27 And it came about that, as soon as David came to Ma·ha·na′im, Sho′bi the son of Na′hash from Rab′bah of the sons of Am′mon, and Ma′chir the son of Am′mi·el from Lo-de′bar, and Bar·zil′lai the Gil′e·ad·ite from Ro·ge′lim 28 [brought] beds and basins and potter's vessels, and wheat and barley and flour and roasted grain and broad beans and lentils and parched grain; 29 and honey and butter and sheep and curds of cattle they brought forward for David and the people that were with him to eat, for they said: "The people are hungry and tired and thirsty in the wilderness."

18 And David proceeded to number the people that were with him and to place over them chiefs of thousands and chiefs of hundreds. 2 Further, David sent one third of the people under the hand of Jo′ab and one third under the hand of A·bish′ai the son of Ze·ru′iah, Jo′ab's brother, and one third under the hand of It′tai the Git′tite. Then the king said to the people: "I myself also shall without fail go out with YOU." 3 But the people said: "You must not go out, for if we should at all flee, they would not set heart upon us; and if half of us would die, they would not set heart upon us, because you are worth ten thousand of us; and now it would be better if you would be of service to us to give help from the city." 4 So the king said to them: "Whatever seems good in YOUR eyes I shall do." And the king kept standing at the side of the gate, and all the people themselves went out by hundreds and by thousands. 5 And the king went on to command Jo′ab and A·bish′ai and It′tai, saying: "Deal gently for my sake with the young man Ab'sa·lom." And all the people themselves heard when the king commanded all the chiefs over the matter of Ab'sa·lom.

6 And the people continued on their way out to the field to meet Israel; and the battle came to be in the forest of E'phra·im. 7 Finally the people of Israel were defeated there before the servants of David, and the slaughter there turned out to be great on that day, of twenty thousand men. 8 And the battle there got to be spread out over all the land that was in sight. Furthermore, the forest did more in eating up the people than the sword did in eating them up on that day.

9 Eventually Ab'sa·lom found himself before the servants of David. And Ab'sa·lom was riding upon a mule, and the mule got to come under the network of boughs of a massive big tree, so that his head got caught fast in the big tree, and he was taken up between the heavens and the earth, as the mule itself that was under him passed along. 10 Then a certain man saw it and told Jo'ab and said: "Look! I have seen Ab'sa·lom hung in a big tree." 11 At this Jo'ab said to the man who was telling him: "And here you saw it, and why did you not strike him down to the earth there? Then it would have been my obligation to give you ten pieces of silver and a belt." 12 But the man said to Jo'ab: "And although I were weighing upon my palms a thousand pieces of silver, I should not thrust my hand out against the king's son; for in our hearing it was that the king commanded you and A·bish'ai and It'tai, saying, 'WATCH, whoever [you are], over the young man, over Ab'sa·lom.' 13 Otherwise I should have dealt treacherously against his soul and the whole matter itself would not be hidden from the king, and you yourself would take a position off on the side." 14 To this Jo'ab said: "Let me not hold myself up this way before you!" With that he took three shafts in his palm and

proceeded to drive them through the heart of Ab'sa·lom while he was yet alive in the heart of the big tree. 15 Then ten attendants carrying Jo'ab's weapons came around and struck Ab'sa·lom, that they might put him to death. 16 Jo'ab now blew the horn, that the people might return from chasing after Israel; for Jo'ab had held back the people. 17 Finally they took Ab'sa·lom and pitched him in the forest into a big hollow and raised up over him a very big pile of stones. As for all Israel, they fled each man to his home.

18 Now Ab'sa·lom himself, while he was alive, had taken and proceeded to raise up for himself a pillar, which is in the Low Plain of the King, for he said: "I have no son in order to keep my name in remembrance." So he called the pillar by his own name, and it continues to be called Ab'sa·lom's Monument down to this day.

19 Now as regards A·him'a·az the son of Za'dok, he said: "Let me run, please, and break the news to the king, because Jehovah has judged him [to free him] from the hand of his enemies." 20 But Jo'ab said to him: "You are not a man of news this day, and you must break the news on another day; but this day you must not break the news, for the very reason that the king's own son has died." 21 Then Jo'ab said to the Cush'ite: "Go, tell the king what you have seen." At that the Cush'ite bowed to Jo'ab and began to run. 22 A·him'a·az the son of Za'dok now said once again to Jo'ab: "Let, now, happen whatever will, let me also myself, please, run behind the Cush'ite." However, Jo'ab said: "Why is it that you yourself have to run, my son, when there is no news being found for you?" 23 [Still he said:] "Let, now, happen whatever will, let me run." So he said to him: "Run!" And A·him'a·az began to run by the way of the District, and he eventually passed by the Cush'ite.

24 Now David was sitting between the two gates. Meantime, the

watchman went to the roof of the gate by the wall. At length he raised his eyes and saw and, look! there was a man running by himself. 25 So the watchman called and told the king, at which the king said: "If he is by himself, there is news in his mouth." And he kept coming, steadily getting nearer. 26 The watchman now saw another man running. The watchman therefore called to the gatekeeper and said: "Look! Another man running by himself!" at which the king said: "This one also is a news bearer." 27 And the watchman went on to say: "I am seeing that the running style of the first is like the running style of A·him′a·az the son of Za′dok," at which the king said: "This is a good man, and with good news he should come." 28 Eventually A·him′a·az called and said to the king: "It is well!" With that he bowed to the king with his face to the earth. And he went on to say: "Blessed be Jehovah your God, who has surrendered the men that lifted up their hand against my lord the king!"

29 However, the king said: "Is it well with the young man Ab′sa·lom?" To this A·him′a·az said: "I saw the great commotion at the time Jo′ab sent the king's servant and your servant, and I did not know what it was." 30 So the king said: "Step aside, take your position here." At that he stepped aside and kept standing still.

31 And here was the Cush′ite coming in, and the Cush′ite began to say: "Let my lord the king accept news, for Jehovah has judged you today [to free you] from the hand of all those rising up against you." 32 But the king said to the Cush′ite: "Is it well with the young man Ab′sa·lom?" To this the Cush′ite said: "May the enemies of my lord the king and all those who rose up against you for evil become as the young man."

33 Then the king became disturbed and went up to the roof chamber over the gateway and gave way to weeping; and this is what he said as he walked: "My son Ab′-sa·lom, my son, my son Ab′sa·lom! O that I might have died, I myself, instead of you, Ab′sa·lom my son, my son!"

19 Later it was reported to Jo′ab: "Look! The king is weeping, and he carries on mourning over Ab′sa·lom." 2 So the salvation on that day came to be an occasion of mourning on the part of all the people, because the people heard say on that day: "The king has felt hurt over his son." 3 And the people began to steal away on that day to come into the city, just as the people would steal away when they felt disgraced because they fled in the battle. 4 And the king himself covered up his face, and the king continued crying out with a loud voice: "My son Ab′sa·lom! Ab′sa·lom my son, my son!"

5 Finally Jo′ab came in to the king at the house and said: "You have today put to shame the face of all your servants, the ones providing escape for your soul today and for the soul of your sons and your daughters and the soul of your wives and the soul of your concubines, 6 by loving those hating you and by hating those loving you; for you have reported today that princes and servants are nothing to you, because I well know today that if only Ab′sa·lom were alive and all of us others were today dead, why, in that case it would be right in your eyes. 7 And now rise up, go out and speak straight to the heart of your servants, because, by Jehovah, I do swear that, in case you are not going out, not a man will lodge with you tonight; and this will certainly be worse for you than all the injury that has come upon you from your youth until now." 8 Accordingly the king rose up and seated himself in the gate, and to all the people they made the report, saying: "There is the king sitting in the gate." And all the people began to come before the king.

As for Israel, they had fled each one to his home. 9 And all the people came to be involved in dispute in all the tribes of Israel, saying: "It was the king that delivered us out of the palm of our enemies, and he it was that provided escape for us out of the palm of the Phi·lis'tines; and now he has run away out of the land from Ab'sa·lom. 10 As for Ab'sa·lom, whom we anointed over us, he has died in the battle. So now why are you doing nothing to bring the king back?"

11 As for King David, he sent to Za'dok and A·bi'a·thar the priests, saying: "Speak to the older men of Judah, saying, 'Why should you become the last ones to bring the king back to his house, when the word of all Israel itself has come to the king at his house? 12 My brothers you are; my bone and my flesh you are. So why should you become the last ones to bring the king back?' 13 And to A·ma'sa you should say, 'Are you not my bone and my flesh? So may God do to me and so may he add to it if you will not become the army chief before me always instead of Jo'ab.'"

14 And he proceeded to bend the heart of all the men of Judah as one man, so that they sent word to the king: "Come back, you and all your servants."

15 And the king began to go back and got to come as far as the Jordan. As for Judah, they came to Gil'gal to go and meet the king, to conduct the king across the Jordan. 16 Then Shim'e·i the son of Ge'ra the Ben'ja·min·ite, who was from Ba·hu'rim, hurried and went down with the men of Judah to meet King David. 17 And there were with him a thousand men from Benjamin. (And also Zi'ba the attendant of the house of Saul and his fifteen sons and twenty servants of his were with him, and they made it successfully to the Jordan before the king. 18 And he crossed the ford to conduct the household of the king across and to do what was good in his eyes.) As for Shim'e·i the son of Ge'ra, he fell down before the king when he was about to cross the Jordan.

19 He now said to the king: "Do not let my lord attribute error to me, and do not remember the wrong that your servant did on the day that my lord the king went out of Jerusalem, so that the king should lay it to his heart. 20 For your servant well knows that I am the one that sinned; and so here I have today come the first of all the house of Joseph to go down to meet my lord the king."

21 At once A·bish'ai the son of Ze·ru'iah answered and said: "In return for this should not Shim'e·i be put to death, in that he called evil down upon the anointed of Jehovah?" 22 But David said: "What do I have to do with you men, you sons of Ze·ru'iah, that you should become today a resister of me? Will anyone today be put to death in Israel? For do I not well know that today I am king over Israel?" 23 Then the king said to Shim'e·i: "You will not die." And the king went on to swear to him.

24 As for Me·phib'o·sheth the grandson of Saul, he came down to meet the king; and he had not attended to his feet nor had he attended to his mustache nor had he washed his garments from the day that the king went away until the day that he came in peace. 25 And it came about that, when he came to Jerusalem to meet the king, then the king said to him: "Why did you not go with me, Me·phib'o·sheth?" 26 To this he said: "My lord the king, it was my servant that tricked me. For your servant had said, 'Let me saddle the female ass for me that I may ride upon it and go with the king,' for your servant is lame. 27 So he slandered your servant to my lord the king. But my lord the king is as an angel of the [true] God, and so do what is good in your eyes. 28 For all the household of my father would have become nothing but doomed to death to my lord the king, and yet you placed your servant among those eating at your table. So what do I still have as

a just claim even for crying out further to the king?"

29 However, the king said to him: "Why do you yet keep speaking your words? I do say, You and Zi'ba should share in the field." 30 At this Me·phib'o·sheth said to the king: "Let him even take the whole, now that my lord the king has come in peace to his house."

31 And Bar·zil'lai the Gil'e·ad·ite himself came down from Ro·ge'lim that he might pass on to the Jordan with the king so as to escort him to the Jordan. 32 And Bar·zil'lai was very old, being eighty years of age; and he himself supplied the king with food while he was dwelling in Ma·ha·na'im, for he was a very great man. 33 So the king said to Bar·zil'lai: "You yourself cross over with me, and I shall certainly supply you with food with me in Jerusalem." 34 But Bar·zil'lai said to the king: "What are the days of the years of my life like, that I should go up with the king to Jerusalem? 35 I am eighty years old today. Could I discern between good and bad, or could your servant taste what I ate and what I drank, or could I listen any more to the voice of male and female singers? So why should your servant become a burden any more to my lord the king? 36 For it is just a little way that your servant could bring the king along to the Jordan, and why should the king repay me with this reward? 37 Let your servant return, please, and let me die in my city close by the burial place of my father and my mother. But here is your servant Chim'ham. Let him cross over with my lord the king; and you do to him what is good in your eyes."

38 Accordingly the king said: "With me Chim'ham will go across, and I myself shall do to him what is good in your eyes; and all that you may choose [to lay] upon me I shall do for you." 39 All the people now began to cross the Jordan, and the king himself crossed; but the king kissed Bar·zil'lai and blessed him, after which he returned to his place. 40 When the king went across to Gil'gal, Chim'ham himself crossed with him, and also all the people of Judah, and also half the people of Israel, that they might bring the king across.

41 And, look! all the men of Israel were coming to the king, and they proceeded to say to the king: "Why did our brothers the men of Judah steal you that they might bring the king and his household and all the men of David with him over the Jordan?" 42 At this all the men of Judah answered the men of Israel: "Because the king is closely related to us; and why is it that you have become angry over this thing? Have we eaten at all at the king's expense, or has a gift been carried to us?"

43 However, the men of Israel answered the men of Judah and said: "We have ten parts in the king, so that even in David we are more than you. Why, then, have you treated us with contempt, and why did not our matter become first for us to bring our king back?" But the word of the men of Judah was more severe than the word of the men of Israel.

20 Now there happened to be there a good-for-nothing man, whose name was She'ba, the son of Bich'ri a Ben'ja·min·ite; and he proceeded to blow the horn and say: "We have no share in David, and we have no inheritance in the son of Jes'se. Every one to his gods, O Israel!" 2 At that all the men of Israel began to go up from following David to follow She'ba the son of Bich'ri; but as for the men of Judah, they stuck to their king from the Jordan to Jerusalem.

3 Eventually David came to his house at Jerusalem. Then the king took the ten women, the concubines whom he had left behind to take care of the house, and he put them in a house of confinement, but he kept on supplying food to them. And with them he did not have any relations, but they continued shut up closely until the day of their dying, in a widowhood with a living [husband].

4 The king now said to A·ma'sa: "Call the men of Judah together to me within three days, and you yourself stand here." 5 So A·ma'sa went to call Judah together; but he came later than the fixed time that he had appointed for him. 6 Then David said to A·bish'ai: "Now She'ba the son of Bich'ri will be worse for us than Ab'sa·lom. You yourself take the servants of your lord and chase after him, that he may not actually find for himself fortified cities and escape before our eyes." 7 Accordingly the men of Jo'ab and the Cher'e·thites and the Pel'e·thites and all the mighty men went out after him; and they went on out of Jerusalem to chase after She'ba the son of Bich'ri. 8 They were close by the great stone that is in Gib'e·on, and A·ma'sa himself came to meet them. Now Jo'ab was girded, clothed with a garment; and upon him there was girded a sword attached to his hip, in its sheath. And he himself came forth, and so it fell out.

9 And Jo'ab proceeded to say to A·ma'sa: "Is it all right with you, my brother?" Then Jo'ab's right hand took hold of A·ma'sa's beard so as to kiss him. 10 As for A·ma'sa, he was not on guard against the sword that was in Jo'ab's hand; so that he struck him with it in the abdomen, and his intestines spilled out to the earth, and he did not have to do it to him again. So he died. And Jo'ab and A·bish'ai his brother, for their part, chased after She'ba the son of Bich'ri.

11 And a certain one of Jo'ab's young men stood over him and kept saying: "Whoever has found delight in Jo'ab and whoever belongs to David, let him follow Jo'ab!" 12 All the while A·ma'sa was wallowing in the blood in the middle of the highway. When the man saw that all the people stood still, then he moved A·ma'sa from the highway to the field. Finally he cast a garment over him, as he saw that everyone coming up to him stood still. 13 As soon as he had removed him from the highway,

each man passed by following Jo'ab to chase after She'ba the son of Bich'ri.

14 And [She'ba] went passing through all the tribes of Israel to A'bel of Beth-ma'a·cah. As for all the Bich'rites, they then congregated together and also went in after him.

15 And they proceeded to come and lay siege against him in A'bel of Beth-ma'a·cah and cast up a siege rampart against the city, as it was standing within a rampart. And all the people that were with Jo'ab were undermining the wall, to throw it down. 16 And a wise woman began to call from the city: "Listen, men, listen! Say, please, to Jo'ab, 'Come near as far as here, and let me speak to you.'" 17 So he went near to her, and the woman then said: "Are you Jo'ab?" to which he said: "I am." At this she said to him: "Listen to the words of your slave girl." In turn he said: "I am listening." 18 And she went on to say: "Without exception they used to speak in former times, saying, 'Let them but inquire in A'bel, and thus they will certainly end the matter.' 19 I represent the peaceable and faithful ones of Israel. You are seeking to put to death a city and a mother in Israel. Why should you swallow up the inheritance of Jehovah?" 20 To this Jo'ab answered and said: "It is altogether unthinkable on my part that I should swallow up and that I should bring to ruin. 21 The matter is not that way, but a man from the mountainous region of E'phra·im, whose name is She'ba the son of Bich'ri, has lifted up his hand against King David. You people, give him over by himself, and I will withdraw from the city." Then the woman said to Jo'ab: "Look! His head [will be] pitched to you over the wall!"

22 At once the woman went in her wisdom to all the people, and they proceeded to cut off the head of She'ba the son of Bich'ri and pitch it to Jo'ab. Upon that he blew the horn, and so they were

scattered from the city, each one to his home; and Jo′ab himself returned to Jerusalem to the king.

23 And Jo′ab was over all the army of Israel; and Be·nai′ah the son of Je·hoi′a·da was over the Cher′e·thites and over the Pel′e·thites. 24 And A·do′ram was over those conscripted for forced labor; and Je·hosh′a·phat the son of A·hi′lud was the recorder. 25 And She′va was secretary, and Za′dok and A·bi′a·thar were priests. 26 And I′ra the Ja′ir·ite also became a priest of David.

21 Now there came to be a famine in the days of David for three years, year after year; and David proceeded to consult the face of Jehovah. Then Jehovah said: "Upon Saul and upon his house there is bloodguilt, because he put the Gib′e·on·ites to death." 2 So the king called the Gib′e·on·ites and talked to them. (Incidentally, the Gib′e·on·ites were not of the sons of Israel, but of the remainder of the Am′or·ites; and the sons of Israel themselves had sworn to them, but Saul sought to strike them down in his feeling jealous for the sons of Israel and Judah.) 3 And David went on to say to the Gib′e·on·ites: "What shall I do to you, and with what shall I make atonement, that you may certainly bless the inheritance of Jehovah?" 4 So the Gib′e·on·ites said to him: "It is not a matter of silver or gold for us in connection with Saul and his household, neither is it ours to put a man to death in Israel." At that he said: "Whatever you are saying I shall do for you." 5 At this they said to the king: "The man that exterminated us and that schemed to annihilate us from subsisting in any of the territory of Israel, 6 let there be given to us seven men of his sons; and we must expose them to Jehovah in Gib′e·ah of Saul, the chosen one of Jehovah." Accordingly the king said: "I myself shall give them."

7 However, the king felt compassion upon Me·phib′o·sheth the son of Jon′a·than the son of Saul on account of the oath of Jehovah that was between them, between David and Jon′a·than the son of Saul. 8 Consequently the king took the two sons of Riz′pah the daughter of A′iah whom she bore to Saul, Ar·mo′ni and Me·phib′o·sheth, and the five sons of Mi′chal the daughter of Saul whom she bore to A′dri·el the son of Bar·zil′lai the Me·hol′ath·ite. 9 Then he gave them into the hand of the Gib′e·on·ites and they proceeded to expose them on the mountain before Jehovah, so that the seven of them fell together; and they themselves were put to death in the first days of harvest, at the start of the barley harvest. 10 However, Riz′pah the daughter of A′iah took sackcloth and spread it for herself upon the rock from the start of harvest until water poured down upon them from the heavens; and she did not allow the fowls of the heavens to rest upon them by day nor the wild beasts of the field by night.

11 At length it was reported to David what Riz′pah the daughter of A′iah, Saul's concubine, had done. 12 So David went and took the bones of Saul and the bones of Jon′a·than his son from the landowners of Ja′besh-gil′e·ad, who had stolen them from the public square of Beth-shan, where the Phi·lis′tines had hanged them on the day that the Phi·lis′tines struck down Saul on Gil·bo′a. 13 And he proceeded to bring up from there the bones of Saul and the bones of Jon′a·than his son; furthermore, they gathered the bones of the men being exposed. 14 Then they buried the bones of Saul and of Jon′a·than his son in the land of Benjamin in Ze′la in the burial place of Kish his father, that they might do everything that the king had commanded. So God let himself be entreated for the land after this.

15 And the Phi·lis′tines came to have war again with Israel. Accordingly David and his servants with him went down and fought the Phi·lis′tines; and David grew

tired. 16 And Ish'bi-be'nob, who was among those born of the Reph'a·im, the weight of whose spear was three hundred shekels of copper and who was girded with a new sword, got to think of striking David down. 17 At once A·bish'ai the son of Ze·ru'iah came to his help and struck the Phi·lis'tine down and put him to death. At that time the men of David swore to him, saying: "You must not go out with us to the battle any more, that you may not extinguish the lamp of Israel!"

18 And it came about after this that war arose once more with the Phi·lis'tines at Gob. Then it was that Sib'be·cai the Hu'shath·ite struck down Saph, who was among those born of the Reph'a·im.

19 And war arose once again with the Phi·lis'tines at Gob, and El·ha'nan the son of Ja'a·re·or'e·gim the Beth'le·hem·ite got to strike down Go·li'ath the Git'tite, the shaft of whose spear was like the beam of loom workers.

20 And war arose yet again at Gath, when there happened to be a man of extraordinary size, with six fingers on each of his hands and six toes on each of his feet, twenty-four in number; and he too had been born to the Reph'a·im. 21 And he kept taunting Israel. Finally Jon'a·than the son of Shim'e·i, David's brother, struck him down.

22 These four had been born to the Reph'a·im in Gath; and they came to fall by the hand of David and by the hand of his servants.

22 And David proceeded to speak to Jehovah the words of this song in the day that Jehovah had delivered him out of the palm of all his enemies and out of Saul's palm; 2 and he went on to say:

"Jehovah is my crag and my stronghold and the Provider of escape for me.

3 My God is my rock. I shall take refuge in him,
My shield and my horn of salvation, my secure height,

And my place for flight, my Savior; from violence you save me.

4 On the One to be praised, Jehovah, I shall call,
And from my enemies I shall be saved.

5 For deadly breaking waves encircled me;
There were flash floods of good-for-nothing [men] that kept terrifying me.

6 The ropes of She'ol themselves surrounded me;
The snares of death confronted me.

7 In my distress I kept calling upon Jehovah,
And to my God I kept calling.
Then out of his temple he heard my voice,
With my cry for help in his ears.

8 And back and forth the earth began to shake and to rock;
The foundations of the heavens themselves became agitated,
And they kept shaking back and forth because he had been angered.

9 Smoke went up at his nostrils, and fire itself from his mouth kept devouring;
Coals themselves blazed up from him.

10 And he proceeded to bend the heavens down and to descend;
And thick gloom was beneath his feet.

11 And he came riding upon a cherub and came flying;
And he was visible upon the wings of a spirit.

12 Then he put a darkness around him as booths,
Dark waters, thick clouds.

13 From the brightness in front of him burning coals of fire blazed up.

14 From heaven Jehovah began to thunder,
And the Most High himself began to give forth his voice.

15 And he kept sending out arrows, that he might scatter them;
Lightning, that he might throw them into confusion.

16 And the stream beds of the sea
became visible,
The foundations of the productive land became un-
covered,
At the rebuke of Jehovah,
from the blast of the breath
of his nostrils.
17 He was sending from on high,
he was taking me,
He was drawing me out of
great waters.
18 He was delivering me from my
strong enemy,
From those hating me; be-
cause they were stronger
than I was.
19 They kept confronting me in
the day of my disaster,
But Jehovah became my support.
20 And he proceeded to bring me
out into a roomy place;
He was rescuing me, because
he had found delight in me.
21 Jehovah rewards me according
to my righteousness;
According to the cleanness of
my hands he repays me.
22 For I have kept the ways of
Jehovah,
And I have not wickedly departed from my God.
23 For all his judicial decisions are
in front of me;
And as for his statutes, I shall
not turn aside from them.
24 And I shall prove myself faultless toward him,
And I will keep myself from
error on my part.
25 And let Jehovah repay me according to my righteousness,
According to my cleanness in
front of his eyes.
26 With someone loyal you will act
in loyalty;
With the faultless, mighty one
you will deal faultlessly;
27 With the one keeping clean
you will show yourself clean,
And with the crooked one you
will act as silly.
28 And the humble people you will
save;
But your eyes are against the
haughty ones, [that] you
may bring [them] low.

29 For you are my lamp, O Jehovah,
And it is Jehovah that makes
my darkness shine.
30 For by you I can run against a
marauder band;
By my God I can climb a wall.
31 As for the [true] God, perfect is
his way;
The saying of Jehovah is a
refined one.
A shield he is to all those
taking refuge in him.
32 For who is a God besides Jehovah,
And who is a rock besides our
God?
33 The [true] God is my strong
fortress,
And he will cause my way to
be perfect,
34 Making my feet like those of the
hinds;
And upon places high for me
he keeps me standing.
35 He is teaching my hands for
warfare;
And my arms have pressed
down a bow of copper.
36 And you will give me your shield
of salvation,
And it is your humility that
makes me great.
37 You will make room large
enough for my steps under
me;
And my ankles will certainly
not wobble.
38 I will pursue my enemies, that
I may annihilate them,
And I shall not return until
they are exterminated.
39 And I shall exterminate them
and break them in pieces,
that they may not rise up;
And they will fall under my
feet.
40 And you will gird me with vital
energy for the battle;
You will make those rising
against me collapse under
me.
41 And as for my enemies, you will
certainly give me the back
of their neck;
Those hating me intensely—I
shall also silence them.
42 They cry for help, but there is
no savior;

To Jehovah, but he actually
does not answer them.
43 And I shall pound them fine
like the dust of the earth;
Like the mire of the streets I
shall pulverize them;
I shall beat them flat.
44 And you will provide me escape
from the faultfinding of my
people.
You will safeguard me to be
the head of nations;
A people that I have not
known—they will serve me.
45 Foreigners themselves will come
cringing to me;
Ears will be obedient to hear
me.
46 Foreigners themselves will fade
away,
And they will come quaking
out from their bulwarks.
47 Jehovah is living; and blessed
be my Rock;
And let the God of the rock of
my salvation be exalted.
48 The [true] God is the Giver of
acts of vengeance to me
And the One bringing the
peoples down under me,
49 And the One bringing me out
from my enemies.
And above those who rise up
against me you will lift me
up;
From the man of violent deeds
you will deliver me.
50 That is why I shall thank you,
O Jehovah, among the na-
tions;
And to your name I shall
make melody:
51 The One doing great acts of
salvation for his king
And exercising loving-kindness
to his anointed one,
To David and to his seed for
time indefinite."

23 And these are the last words
of David:

"The utterance of David the
son of Jes'se,
And the utterance of the able-
bodied man that was raised
up on high,
The anointed of the God of
Jacob,

And the pleasant one of the
melodies of Israel.
2 The spirit of Jehovah it was
that spoke by me,
And his word was upon my
tongue.
3 The God of Israel said,
To me the Rock of Israel
spoke,
'When one ruling over mankind
is righteous,
Ruling in the fear of God,
4 Then it is as the light of morning, when the sun shines
forth,
A morning without clouds.
From brightness, from rain,
there is grass out of the
earth.'
5 For is not my household like
that with God?
Because it is an indefinitely
lasting covenant that he has
assigned to me,
Nicely put in order in everything and secured.
Because it is all my salvation
and all my delight,
Is that not why he will make
it grow?
6 But good-for-nothing persons
are chased away, like thornbushes, all of them;
For it is not by the hand that
they should be taken.
7 When a man touches them
He should be fully armed with
iron and the shaft of a spear,
And with fire they will thoroughly be burned up."

8 These are the names of the
mighty men that belonged to David: Jo'sheb-bas·she'beth a Tah-
che'mo·nite, the head of the three.
He was brandishing his spear over
eight hundred slain at one time.
9 Next to him E·le·a'zar the son of
Do'do the son of A·ho'hi was
among the three mighty men with
David when they taunted the Phi-
lis'tines. They had gathered themselves there for the battle, and so
the men of Israel retreated. 10 He
it was that rose up and kept striking down the Phi·lis'tines until his
hand wearied and his hand kept
cleaving to the sword, so that Jehovah performed a great salvation

on that day; and as for the people, they returned behind him only to strip [those struck down].

11 And next to him was Sham′mah the son of A′gee the Har′a·rite. And the Phi·lis′tines proceeded to gather themselves to Le′hi, where there then happened to be a tract of the field full of lentils; and the people themselves fled because of the Phi·lis′tines. 12 But he took his stand in the middle of the tract and delivered it and kept striking down the Phi·lis′tines, so that Jehovah performed a great salvation.

13 And three of the thirty head ones proceeded to go down and come at [the] harvest, to David at the cave of A·dul′lam; and a tent village of the Phi·lis′tines was encamped in the low plain of the Reph′a·im. 14 And David was then in the place hard to approach; and an outpost of the Phi·lis′tines was then in Beth′le·hem. 15 After a while David expressed his craving and said: "O that I might have a drink of the water from the cistern of Beth′le·hem that is at the gate!" 16 At that the three mighty men forced their way into the camp of the Phi·lis′tines and drew water from the cistern of Beth′le·hem that is at the gate and came carrying and bringing it to David; and he did not consent to drink it, but poured it out to Jehovah. 17 And he went on to say: "It is unthinkable on my part, O Jehovah, that I should do this! [Shall I drink] the blood of the men going at the risk of their souls?" And he did not consent to drink it.

These are the things the three mighty men did.

18 As for A·bish′ai the brother of Jo′ab the son of Ze·ru′iah, he was the head of the thirty, and he was brandishing his spear over three hundred slain ones, and he had a reputation like the three. 19 Although he was distinguished even more than the rest of the thirty, and he came to be their chief, to the rank of the [first] three he did not come.

20 As for Be·nai′ah the son of Je·hoi′a·da the son of a valiant man, who did many deeds in Kab′ze·el, he himself struck down the two sons of Ar′i·el of Mo′ab; and he himself descended and struck down a lion inside a waterpit on a day of snowfall. 21 And he it was that struck down the Egyptian man that was of extraordinary size. Though there was a spear in the hand of the Egyptian, yet he went on down to him with a rod and snatched the spear away from the Egyptian's hand and killed him with his own spear. 22 These things Be·nai′ah the son of Je·hoi′a·da did; and he had a reputation like the three mighty men. 23 Although he was distinguished even more than the thirty, to the rank of the three he did not come; but David appointed him to his own bodyguard.

24 As′a·hel the brother of Jo′ab was among the thirty; El·ha′nan the son of Do′do of Beth′le·hem, 25 Sham′mah the Ha′rod·ite, E·li′ka the Ha′rod·ite, 26 He′lez the Pal′tite, I′ra the son of Ik′kesh the Te·ko′ite, 27 A·bi·e′zer the An′a·thoth·ite, Me·bun′nai the Hu′shath·ite, 28 Zal′mon the A·ho′hite, Ma′ha·rai the Ne·toph′a·thite, 29 He′leb the son of Ba′a·nah the Ne·toph′a·thite, It′tai the son of Ri′bai of Gib′e·ah of the sons of Benjamin, 30 Be·nai′ah a Pir′a·thon·ite, Hid′dai of the torrent valleys of Ga′ash, 31 A′bi-al′bon the Ar′bath·ite, Az′ma·veth the Bar-hu′mite, 32 E·li′ah·ba the Sha·al′bo·nite, the sons of Ja′shen, Jon′a·than, 33 Sham′mah the Har′a·rite, A·hi′am the son of Sha′rar the Har′a·rite, 34 E·liph′e·let the son of A·has′bai the son of the Ma·ac′a·thite, E·li′am the son of A·hith′o·phel the Gi′lon·ite, 35 Hez′ro the Car′mel·ite, Pa′a·rai the Ar′bite, 36 I′gal the son of Nathan of Zo′bah, Ba′ni the Gad′ite, 37 Ze′lek the Am′mon·ite, Na′ha·rai the Be·er′oth·ite, armor-bearers of Jo′ab the son of Ze·ru′iah, 38 I′ra the Ith′rite, Ga′reb the Ith′rite, 39 U·ri′ah the Hit′tite—thirty-seven in all.

24 And again the anger of Jehovah came to be hot against Israel, when one incited David against them, saying: "Go, take a count of Israel and Judah." 2 So the king said to Jo'ab the chief of the military forces who was with him: "Move about, please, through all the tribes of Israel, from Dan to Be'er-she'ba, and YOU men register the people, and I shall certainly know the number of the people." 3 But Jo'ab said to the king: "May Jehovah your God even add to the people a hundred times as many as they are while the very eyes of my lord the king are seeing it. But as for my lord the king, why has he found delight in this thing?"

4 Finally the king's word prevailed upon Jo'ab and the chiefs of the military forces. So Jo'ab and the chiefs of the military forces went out from before the king to register the people Israel. 5 Then they crossed the Jordan and took up camping at A·ro'er to the right of the city that is in the middle of the torrent valley, toward the Gad'-ites, and to Ja'zer. 6 After that they came on to Gil'e·ad and the land of Tah'tim-hod'shi and continued on to Dan-ja'an and went around to Si'don. 7 Then they came to the fortress of Tyre and all the cities of the Hi'vites and of the Ca'naan·ites and came to the terminating point in the Neg'eb of Judah at Be'er-she'ba. 8 Thus they went moving about through all the land and came to Jerusalem at the end of nine months and twenty days. 9 Jo'ab now gave the number of the registration of the people to the king; and Israel amounted to eight hundred thousand valiant men drawing sword, and the men of Judah were five hundred thousand men.

10 And David's heart began to beat him after he had so numbered the people. Consequently David said to Jehovah: "I have sinned very much in what I have done. And now, Jehovah, let your servant's error pass by, please; for I have acted very foolishly."

11 When David proceeded to rise up in the morning, Jehovah's word itself came to Gad the prophet, David's visionary, saying: 12 "Go, and you must say to David, 'This is what Jehovah has said: "Three things I am laying upon you. Choose for yourself one of them that I may do it to you." ' " 13 Accordingly Gad came in to David and told him and said to him: "Should there come to you seven years of famine in your land, or three months of your fleeing before your adversaries, with them pursuing you, or the occurring of three days of pestilence in your land? Now know and see what I shall reply to the One sending me." 14 So David said to Gad: "It is very distressing to me. Let us fall, please, into the hand of Jehovah, for many are his mercies; but into the hand of man do not let me fall."

15 Then Jehovah gave a pestilence in Israel from the morning until the time appointed, so that out of the people from Dan to Be'er-she'ba seventy thousand persons died. 16 And the angel kept his hand thrust out toward Jerusalem to bring it to ruin; and Jehovah began to feel regret over the calamity, and so he said to the angel that was bringing ruin among the people: "It is enough! Now let your hand drop." And Jehovah's angel himself happened to be close by the threshing floor of A·rau'nah the Jeb'u·site.

17 And David proceeded to say to Jehovah, when he saw the angel that was striking the people down, yes, he proceeded to say: "Here it is I that have sinned and it is I that have done wrong; but these sheep—what have they done? Let your hand, please, come upon me and upon the house of my father."

18 Later Gad came in to David on that day and said to him: "Go up, set up for Jehovah an altar on the threshing floor of A·rau'nah the Jeb'u·site." 19 And David began to go up in accord with the word of Gad, according to what Jehovah had commanded. 20 When

A·rau'nah looked down and saw the king and his servants passing along toward him, A·rau'nah at once went out and bowed down to the king with his face to the earth. 21 Then A·rau'nah said: "Why has my lord the king come to his servant?" At that David said: "To buy from you the threshing floor for building an altar to Jehovah, that the scourge may be halted from upon the people." 22 But A·rau'nah said to David: "Let my lord the king take it and offer up what is good in his eyes. See the cattle for the burnt offering and the threshing sledge and the implements of the cattle for the wood. 23 Everything A·rau'nah, O king,

does give to the king." And A·rau'nah went on to say to the king: "May Jehovah your God show pleasure in you."

24 However, the king said to A·rau'nah: "No, but without fail I shall buy it from you for a price; and I shall not offer up to Jehovah my God burnt sacrifices without cost." Accordingly David bought the threshing floor and the cattle for fifty silver shekels. 25 And David proceeded to build there an altar to Jehovah and offer up burnt sacrifices and communion sacrifices, and Jehovah began letting himself be entreated for the land, so that the scourge was halted from upon Israel.

THE FIRST OF

KINGS

or, according to the Greek *Septuagint*,

THE THIRD OF KINGS

1 Now King David was old, advanced in days; and they would cover him with garments, but he would not feel warm. 2 So his servants said to him: "Let them look for a girl, a virgin, for my lord the king, and she will have to attend upon the king, that she may become his nurse; and she must lie in your bosom, and my lord the king will certainly feel warm." 3 And they went looking for a beautiful girl throughout all the territory of Israel, and finally found Ab'i·shag the Shu'nam·mite and then brought her in to the king. 4 And the girl was beautiful in the extreme; and she came to be the king's nurse and kept waiting upon him, and the king himself had no intercourse with her.

5 All the while Ad·o·ni'jah the son of Hag'gith was lifting himself up, saying: "I myself am going to rule as king!" And he proceeded to have a chariot made for himself

with horsemen and fifty men running before him. 6 And his father did not hurt his feelings at any time by saying: "Why is this the way you have done?" And he was also very good-looking in form, and [his mother] had borne him after Ab'sa·lom. 7 And he came to have dealings with Jo'ab the son of Ze·ru'iah and with A·bi'a·thar the priest, and they began offering help as followers of Ad·o·ni'jah. 8 As for Za'dok the priest and Be·nai'ah the son of Je·hoi'a·da and Nathan the prophet and Shim'e·i and Re'i and the mighty men that belonged to David, they did not become involved with Ad·o·ni'jah.

9 Eventually Ad·o·ni'jah held a sacrifice of sheep and cattle and fatlings close by the stone of Zo'he·leth, which is beside En·ro'gel, and he proceeded to invite all his brothers the king's sons and all the men of Judah the king's servants;

10 and Nathan the prophet and Be·nai′ah and the mighty men and Sol′o·mon his brother he did not invite. 11 Nathan now said to Bath-she′ba, Sol′o·mon's mother: "Have you not heard that Ad·o·ni′jah the son of Hag′gith has become king, and our lord David does not know of it at all? 12 So now come, let me, please, solemnly counsel you. And provide escape for your own soul and for the soul of your son Sol′o·mon. 13 Go and enter in to King David, and you must say to him, 'Was it not you, my lord the king, that swore to your slave girl, saying: "Sol′o·mon your son is the one that will become king after me, and he is the one that will sit upon my throne"? So why has Ad·o·ni′jah become king?' 14 Look! While you are yet speaking there with the king, then I myself shall come in after you, and I shall certainly confirm your words."

15 Accordingly Bath-she′ba went in to the king in the interior room, and the king was very old, and Ab′i·shag the Shu′nam·mite was waiting upon the king. 16 Then Bath-she′ba bowed low and prostrated herself to the king, upon which the king said: "What do you have [to ask]?" 17 At this she said to him: "My lord, it was you that swore by Jehovah your God to your slave girl, 'Sol′o·mon your son is the one that will become king after me, and he is the one that will sit upon my throne.' 18 And now, look! Ad·o·ni′jah himself has become king, and now my lord the king himself does not know of it at all. 19 So he sacrificed bulls and fatlings and sheep in great quantity and invited all the sons of the king and A·bi′a·thar the priest and Jo′ab the chief of the army; but Sol′o·mon your servant he has not invited. 20 And you my lord the king—the eyes of all Israel are upon you, to tell them who is going to sit upon the throne of my lord the king after him. 21 And it will certainly occur that as soon as my lord the king lies down with his forefathers, I myself and also my son Sol′o·mon shall certainly become offenders."

22 And, look! while she was yet speaking with the king, Nathan the prophet himself came in. 23 At once they told the king, saying: "Here is Nathan the prophet!" After that he came in before the king and prostrated himself to the king with his face to the earth. 24 Then Nathan said: "My lord the king, did you yourself say, 'Ad·o·ni′jah is the one that will become king after me, and he is the one that will sit upon my throne'? 25 For he has today gone down that he might sacrifice bulls and fatlings and sheep in great quantity and might invite all the sons of the king and the chiefs of the army and A·bi′a·thar the priest; and there they are eating and drinking before him and they keep saying, 'Let King Ad·o·ni′jah live!' 26 But as for me your servant, me and Za′dok the priest and Be·nai′ah the son of Je·hoi′a·da and Sol′o·mon your servant he has not invited. 27 If it is from my lord the king that this thing has been brought about, then you have not caused your servant to know who should sit upon the throne of my lord the king after him."

28 King David now answered and said: "You men, call Bath-she′ba for me." At that she came in before the king and stood before the king. 29 And the king proceeded to swear and say: "As Jehovah is living who redeemed my soul out of all distress, 30 just as I have sworn to you by Jehovah the God of Israel, saying, 'Sol′o·mon your son is the one that will become king after me, and he is the one that will sit upon my throne in place of me!' that is the way I shall do this day." 31 Then Bath-she′ba bowed low with her face to the earth and prostrated herself to the king and said: "Let my lord King David live to time indefinite!"

32 Immediately King David said: "You men, call for me Za′dok the priest and Nathan the prophet and Be·nai′ah the son of Je·hoi′a·da." So they came in be-

fore the king. 33 And the king went on to say to them: "Take with YOU the servants of YOUR lord, and YOU must make Sol′o·mon my son ride upon the she-mule that belongs to me and lead him down to Gi′hon. 34 And Za′dok the priest and Nathan the prophet must anoint him there as king over Israel; and YOU must blow the horn and say, 'Let King Sol′o·mon live!' 35 And YOU must come up following him, and he must come in and sit upon my throne; and he himself will be king in place of me, and him I shall have to commission to become leader over Israel and over Judah." 36 At once Be·nai′ah the son of Je·hoi′a·da answered the king and said: "Amen! Thus may Jehovah the God of my lord the king say. 37 Just as Jehovah proved to be with my lord the king, so let him prove to be with Sol′o·mon, and may he make his throne greater than the throne of my lord King David."

38 And Za′dok the priest and Nathan the prophet and Be·nai′ah the son of Je·hoi′a·da and the Cher′e·thites and the Pel′e·thites proceeded to go down and make Sol′o·mon ride upon the she-mule of King David, and then brought him to Gi′hon. 39 Za′dok the priest now took the horn of oil out of the tent and anointed Sol′o·mon; and they began to blow the horn, and all the people broke out saying: "Let King Sol′o·mon live!" 40 After that all the people came on up following him, and the people were playing on flutes and rejoicing with great joy, so that the earth was split by the noise of them.

41 And Ad·o·ni′jah and all the ones invited that were with him got to hear it, when they themselves had finished eating. When Jo′ab got to hear the sound of the horn, he at once said: "What does the noise of the town in an uproar mean?" 42 While he was yet speaking, why, here Jon′a·than the son of A·bi′a·thar the priest came. Then Ad·o·ni′jah said: "Come on

in, for you are a valiant man, and you bring good news." 43 But Jon′a·than answered and said to Ad·o·ni′jah: "No! Our lord King David himself has made Sol′o·mon king. 44 So the king sent with him Za′dok the priest and Nathan the prophet and Be·nai′ah the son of Je·hoi′a·da and the Cher′e·thites and the Pel′e·thites, and they made him ride upon the she-mule of the king. 45 Then Za′dok the priest and Nathan the prophet anointed him as king in Gi′hon; after which they came up from there rejoicing, and the town is in an uproar. That was the noise that YOU men heard. 46 And, besides, Sol′o·mon has sat down upon the throne of the kingship. 47 And, another thing, the servants of the king have come in to wish our lord King David well, saying, 'May your God make Sol′o·mon's name more splendid than your name, and may he make his throne greater than your throne!' At that the king bowed down upon the bed. 48 And too this is what the king said, 'Blessed be Jehovah the God of Israel, who has today given one to sit upon my throne, with my own eyes seeing it!' "

49 And all those invited that were with Ad·o·ni′jah began to tremble and rise up and go each one on his own way. 50 And Ad·o·ni′jah himself was afraid because of Sol′o·mon. So he rose up and went away and grabbed hold of the horns of the altar. 51 In time the report was made to Sol′o·mon, saying: "Here Ad·o·ni′jah himself has become afraid of King Sol′o·mon; and here he has taken hold on the horns of the altar, saying, 'Let King Sol′o·mon first of all swear to me that he will not put his servant to death by the sword.' " 52 To this Sol′o·mon said: "If he will become a valiant man, there will not fall a single hair of his to the earth; but if what is bad should be found in him, he will also have to die." 53 So King Sol′o·mon sent and they brought him down from off the altar. Then he came in and bowed down to King Sol′o-

mon; after which Sol'o·mon said to him: "Go to your own house."

2 And the days of David gradually drew near for him to die; and he proceeded to command Sol'o·mon his son, saying: 2 "I am going in the way of all the earth, and you must be strong and prove yourself to be a man. 3 And you must keep the obligation to Jehovah your God by walking in his ways, by keeping his statutes, his commandments and his judicial decisions and his testimonies, according to what is written in the law of Moses, in order that you may act prudently in everything that you do and everywhere that you turn; 4 in order that Jehovah may carry out his word that he spoke respecting me, saying, 'If your sons will take care of their way by walking before me in truth with all their heart and with all their soul, there will not be cut off a man of yours from [sitting] upon the throne of Israel.'

5 "And you yourself also well know what Jo'ab the son of Ze·ru'iah did to me in what he did to two chiefs of the armies of Israel, to Ab'ner the son of Ner and A·ma'sa the son of Je'ther, when he killed them and placed the blood of war in peacetime and put the blood of war on his belt that was about his hips and in his sandals that were on his feet. 6 And you must act according to your wisdom, and not let his gray hairs go down in peace to She'ol.

7 "And toward the sons of Bar·zil'lai the Gil'e·ad·ite you should exercise loving-kindness, and they must prove to be among those eating at your table; for that was the way they drew near to me when I ran away from before Ab'sa·lom your brother.

8 "And here there is with you Shim'e·i the son of Ge'ra the Ben'ja·min·ite from Ba·hu'rim, and he it was that called down evil upon me with a painful malediction on the day that I was going to Ma·ha·na'im; and he it was that came down to meet me at the Jordan, so that I swore to him by Jehovah, saying, 'I shall not put you to death by the sword.' 9 And now do not leave him unpunished, for you are a wise man and you well know what you ought to do to him, and you must bring his gray hairs down to She'ol with blood."

10 Then David lay down with his forefathers and was buried in the city of David. 11 And the days that David had reigned over Israel were forty years. In He'bron he had reigned seven years, and in Jerusalem he had reigned thirty-three years.

12 As for Sol'o·mon, he sat down upon the throne of David his father; and gradually his kingship became very firmly established.

13 In time Ad·o·ni'jah the son of Hag'gith came to Bath-she'ba, Sol'o·mon's mother. At this she said: "Is your coming peaceable?" to which he said: "It is peaceable." 14 And he went on to say: "There is a matter I have for you." So she said: "Speak." 15 And he continued: "You yourself well know that the kingship was to have become mine, and it was toward me that all Israel had set their face for me to become king; but the kingship turned and came to be my brother's, for it was from Jehovah that it became his. 16 And now there is one request that I am making of you. Do not turn my face away." Accordingly she said to him: "Speak." 17 And he went on to say: "Please, say to Sol'o·mon the king (for he will not turn your face away) that he should give me Ab'i·shag the Shu'nam·mite as a wife." 18 To this Bath-she'ba said: "Good! I myself shall speak for you to the king."

19 So Bath-she'ba came in to King Sol'o·mon to speak to him for Ad·o·ni'jah. At once the king rose to meet her and bowed down to her. Then he sat down upon his throne and had a throne set for the mother of the king, that she might sit at his right. 20 And she proceeded to say: "There is one little request that I am making of you. Do not turn my face away." So the king said to her: "Make it, my

mother; for I shall not turn your face away." 21 And she went on to say: "Let Ab′i·shag the Shu′nam·mite be given to Ad·o·ni′jah your brother as a wife." 22 At this King Sol′o·mon answered and said to his mother: "And why are you requesting Ab′i·shag the Shu′nam·mite for Ad·o·ni′jah? Request also for him the kingship (because he is my brother older than I am), even for him and for A·bi′a·thar the priest and for Jo′ab the son of Ze·ru′iah."

23 With that King Sol′o·mon swore by Jehovah, saying: "So may God do to me, and so may he add to it, if it was not against his own soul that Ad·o·ni′jah spoke this thing. 24 And now, as Jehovah is living who has firmly established me and keeps me seated upon the throne of David my father and who made a house for me just as he has spoken, today Ad·o·ni′jah will be put to death." 25 Immediately King Sol′o·mon sent by means of Be·nai′ah the son of Je·hoi′a·da; and he proceeded to fall upon him, so that he died.

26 And to A·bi′a·thar the priest the king said: "Go to An′a·thoth to your fields! For you are deserving of death; but on this day I shall not put you to death, because you carried the ark of the Lord Jehovah before David my father, and because you suffered affliction during all the time that my father suffered affliction." 27 So Sol′o·mon drove out A·bi′a·thar from serving as a priest of Jehovah, to fulfill Jehovah's word that he had spoken against the house of E′li in Shi′loh.

28 And the report itself came clear to Jo′ab—for Jo′ab himself had inclined to follow Ad·o·ni′jah, although Ab′sa·lom he had not inclined to follow—and Jo′ab went fleeing to the tent of Jehovah and began to hold fast to the horns of the altar. 29 Then King Sol′o·mon was told: "Jo′ab has fled to the tent of Jehovah, and there he is beside the altar." So Sol′o·mon sent Be·nai′ah the son of Je·hoi′a·da, saying: "Go, fall upon him!"

30 Accordingly Be·nai′ah came to the tent of Jehovah and said to him: "This is what the king has said, 'Come on out!'" But he said: "No! For here is where I shall die." At that Be·nai′ah brought word back to the king, saying: "This is what Jo′ab spoke, and this is what he answered me." 31 Then the king said to him: "Do just as he has spoken and fall upon him; and you must bury him and remove from off me and from off the house of my father the blood undeservedly shed that Jo′ab spilled. 32 And Jehovah will certainly bring back his blood upon his own head, because he fell upon two men more righteous and better than he was, and he proceeded to kill them with the sword, when my father David himself had not known of it, namely, Ab′ner the son of Ner the chief of the army of Israel and A·ma′sa the son of Je′ther the chief of the army of Judah. 33 And their blood must come back upon the head of Jo′ab and upon the head of his offspring to time indefinite; but for David and for his offspring and for his house and for his throne there will come to be peace to time indefinite from Jehovah." 34 Then Be·nai′ah the son of Je·hoi′a·da went on up and fell upon him and put him to death; and he got to be buried at his own house in the wilderness. 35 Upon that the king put Be·nai′ah the son of Je·hoi′a·da in place of him over the army; and Za′dok the priest the king put in the place of A·bi′a·thar.

36 Finally the king sent and called Shim′e·i and said to him: "Build yourself a house in Jerusalem, and you must dwell there and not go out from there to this place and that. 37 And it must occur that on the day of your going out and when you do pass over the torrent valley of Kid′ron, you should unmistakably know that you will positively die. Bloodguilt for you will itself come to be upon your own head." 38 At this Shim′e·i said to the king: "The word is good. Just as my lord the king has

spoken is the way that your servant will do." And Shim′e·i kept dwelling in Jerusalem many days.

39 And it came about at the end of three years that two slaves of Shim′e·i went running away to A′chish the son of Ma′a·cah the king of Gath; and people came telling Shim′e·i, saying: "Look! Your slaves are at Gath." 40 Immediately Shim′e·i got up and saddled his ass and went to Gath to A′chish to look for his slaves; after which Shim′e·i went and brought his slaves from Gath. 41 Then Sol′o·mon was told: "Shim′e·i has gone out of Jerusalem to Gath and is back." 42 At that the king sent and called Shim′e·i and said to him: "Did I not put you under oath by Jehovah that I might warn you, saying, 'On the day of your going outside and when you do go here and there you should unmistakably know that you will positively die,' and so did you not say to me, 'Good is the word that I have heard'? 43 Why, then, did you not keep the oath of Jehovah and the commandment that I solemnly laid upon you?" 44 And the king went on to say to Shim′e·i: "You yourself certainly know all the injury which your heart well knows that you did to David my father; and Jehovah will certainly return the injury by you upon your own head. 45 But King Sol′o·mon will be blessed, and the throne of David itself will prove to be firmly established before Jehovah forever." 46 With that the king commanded Be·nai′ah the son of Je·hoi′a·da, who then went out and fell upon him, so that he died.

And the kingdom was firmly established in the hand of Sol′o·mon.

3 And Sol′o·mon proceeded to form a marriage alliance with Phar′aoh the king of Egypt and to take Phar′aoh's daughter and bring her to the city of David, until he finished building his own house and the house of Jehovah and Jerusalem's wall all around. 2 Only the people were sacrificing on the high places, for a house had not been built to the name of Jehovah down to those days. 3 And Sol′o·mon continued to love Jehovah by walking in the statutes of David his father. Only it was on the high places that he was regularly sacrificing and making offerings smoke.

4 Accordingly the king went to Gib′e·on to sacrifice there, for that was the great high place. A thousand burnt sacrifices Sol′o·mon proceeded to offer upon that altar. 5 In Gib′e·on Jehovah appeared to Sol′o·mon in a dream by night; and God proceeded to say: "Request what I should give you." 6 At this Sol′o·mon said: "You yourself have exercised great loving-kindness toward your servant David my father according as he walked before you in truth and in righteousness and in uprightness of heart with you; and you continued keeping toward him this great loving-kindness, so that you gave him a son to sit upon his throne as at this day. 7 And now, Jehovah my God, you yourself have made your servant king in the place of David my father, and I am but a little boy. I do not know how to go out and how to come in. 8 And your servant is in the middle of your people whom you have chosen, a multitudinous people that cannot be numbered or counted for multitude. 9 And you must give to your servant an obedient heart to judge your people, to discern between good and bad; for who is able to judge this difficult people of yours?"

10 And the thing was pleasing in the eyes of Jehovah, because Sol′o·mon had requested this thing. 11 And God went on to say to him: "For the reason that you have requested this thing and have not requested for yourself many days nor requested for yourself riches nor requested the soul of your enemies, and you have requested for yourself understanding to hear judicial cases, 12 look! I shall certainly do according to your words. Look! I shall certainly give you a

wise and understanding heart, so that one like you there has not happened to be before you, and after you there will not rise up one like you. 13 And also what you have not requested I will give you, both riches and glory, so that there will not have happened to be any among the kings like you, all your days. 14 And if you will walk in my ways by keeping my regulations and my commandments, just as David your father walked, I will also lengthen your days."

15 When Sol'o·mon awoke, why, here it had been a dream. Then he came to Jerusalem and stood before the ark of the covenant of Jehovah and offered up burnt sacrifices and rendered up communion offerings and spread a feast for all his servants.

16 At that time two women, prostitutes, got to come in to the king and stand before him. 17 Then the one woman said: "Excuse me, my lord, I and this woman are dwelling in one house, so that I gave birth close by her in the house. 18 And it came about on the third day after I gave birth, this woman also proceeded to give birth. And we were together. There was no stranger with us in the house, no one but the two of us in the house. 19 Later the son of this woman died at night, because she lay upon him. 20 So she got up in the middle of the night and took my son from beside me while your slave girl herself was asleep and laid him in her own bosom, and her dead son she laid in my bosom. 21 When I got up in the morning to nurse my son, why, there he was dead. So I examined him closely in the morning, and, look! he did not prove to be my son that I had borne." 22 But the other woman said: "No, but my son is the living one and your son is the dead one!" All the while this woman was saying: "No, but your son is the dead one and my son is the living one." And they kept on speaking before the king.

23 Finally the king said: "This one is saying, 'This is my son, the living one, and your son is the dead one!' and that one is saying, 'No, but your son is the dead one and my son is the living one!'" 24 And the king went on to say: "You men, get me a sword." So they brought the sword before the king. 25 And the king proceeded to say: "You men, sever the living child in two and give the one half to the one woman and the other half to the other." 26 At once the woman whose son was the living one said to the king (for her inward emotions were excited toward her son, so that she said): "Excuse me, my lord! You men, give her the living child. Do not by any means put him to death." All the while this other woman was saying: "Neither mine nor yours will he become. You men, do the severing!" 27 At that the king answered and said: "You men, give her the living child, and you must by no means put him to death. She is his mother."

28 And all Israel got to hear of the judicial decision that the king had handed down; and they became fearful because of the king, for they saw that the wisdom of God was within him to execute judicial decision.

4 And King Sol'o·mon continued king over all Israel. 2 And these are the princes that he had: Az·a·ri'ah the son of Za'dok, the priest; 3 El·i·hor'eph and A·hi'jah, the sons of Shi'sha, secretaries; Je·hosh'a·phat the son of A·hi'lud, the recorder; 4 and Be·nai'ah the son of Je·hoi'a·da was over the army, and Za'dok and A·bi'a·thar were priests; 5 and Az·a·ri'ah the son of Nathan was over the deputies, and Za'bud the son of Nathan was a priest, the friend of the king; 6 and A·hi'shar was over the household, and Ad·o·ni'ram the son of Ab'da, over those conscripted for forced labor.

7 And Sol'o·mon had twelve deputies over all Israel, and they provided the king and his household with food. It would devolve upon each one to provide the food one

month in the year. 8 And these were their names: The son of Hur, in the mountainous region of E'phra·im; 9 the son of De'ker, in Ma'kaz and in Sha·al'bim and Beth-she'mesh and E'lon-beth-ha'-nan; 10 the son of He'sed, in A·rub'both (he had So'coh and all the land of He'pher); 11 the son of A·bin'a·dab, all the mountain ridge of Dor (Ta'phath, Sol'o·mon's daughter, herself became his wife); 12 Ba'a·na the son of A·hi'lud, in Ta'a·nach and Me·gid'do and all Beth-she'an, which is beside Zar'e-than below Jez're·el, from Beth-she'an to A'bel-me·ho'lah to the region of Jok'me·am; 13 the son of Ge'ber, in Ra'moth-gil'e·ad (he had the tent villages of Ja'ir the son of Ma·nas'seh, which are in Gil'e·ad; he had the region of Ar'gob, which is in Ba'shan: sixty large cities with wall and copper bar); 14 A·hin'a·dab the son of Id'do, in Ma·ha·na'im; 15 A·him'-a·az, in Naph'ta·li (he, too, took Bas'e·math, Sol'o·mon's daughter, as a wife); 16 Ba'a·na the son of Hu'shai, in Ash'er and Be'a·loth; 17 Je·hosh'a·phat the son of Pa-ru'ah, in Is'sa·char; 18 Shim'e·i the son of E'la, in Benjamin; 19 Ge'ber the son of U'ri, in the land of Gil'e·ad, the land of Si'hon the king of the Am'or·ites, and of Og the king of Ba'shan, and there was one deputy [over all the other deputies] that were in the land.

20 Judah and Israel were many, like the grains of sand that are by the sea for multitude, eating and drinking and rejoicing.

21 As for Sol'o·mon, he proved to be ruler over all the kingdoms from the River to the land of the Phi·lis'tines and to the boundary of Egypt. They were bringing gifts and serving Sol'o·mon all the days of his life.

22 And Sol'o·mon's food for each day regularly proved to be thirty cor measures of fine flour and sixty cor measures of flour, 23 ten fat cattle and twenty pastured cattle and a hundred sheep, besides some stags and gazelles and roebucks and fattened cuckoos. 24 For he was holding in subjection everything this side of the River, from Tiph'sah to Ga'za, even all the kings this side of the River; and peace itself became his in every region of his, all around. 25 And Judah and Israel continued to dwell in security, everyone under his own vine and under his own fig tree, from Dan to Be'er-she'ba, all the days of Sol'o·mon.

26 And Sol'o·mon came to have forty thousand stalls of horses for his chariots and twelve thousand horsemen.

27 And these deputies supplied food to King Sol'o·mon and every-one approaching the table of King Sol'o·mon, each one in his month. They left nothing lacking. 28 And the barley and the straw for the horses and for the teams of horses they kept bringing to wherever the place might prove to be, each one according to his commission.

29 And God continued giving Sol'o·mon wisdom and understand-ing in very great measure and a broadness of heart, like the sand that is upon the seashore. 30 And Sol'o·mon's wisdom was vaster than the wisdom of all the Orientals and than all the wisdom of Egypt. 31 And he was wiser than any other man, than E'than the Ez'ra-hite and He'man and Cal'col and Dar'da the sons of Ma'hol; and his fame came to be in all the nations all around. 32 And he could speak three thousand proverbs, and his songs came to be a thousand and five. 33 And he would speak about the trees, from the cedar that is in Leb'a·non to the hyssop that is coming forth on the wall; and he would speak about the beasts and about the flying creatures and about the moving things and about the fishes. 34 And they kept com-ing from all the peoples to hear Sol'o·mon's wisdom, even from all the kings of the earth who had heard of his wisdom.

5 And Hi'ram the king of Tyre proceeded to send his servants to Sol'o·mon, for he had heard that it was he that they had anoint-ed as king in place of his father;

for a lover of David Hi'ram had always proved to be. 2 In turn Sol'o·mon sent to Hi'ram, saying: 3 "You yourself well know that David my father was not able to build a house to the name of Jehovah his God because of the warfare with which they surrounded him, until Jehovah put them under the soles of his feet. 4 And now Jehovah my God has given me rest all around. There is no resister, and there is nothing bad happening. 5 And here I am thinking of building a house to the name of Jehovah my God, just as Jehovah promised to David my father, saying, 'Your son whom I shall put upon your throne in place of you, he is the one that will build the house to my name.' 6 And now command that they cut for me cedars from Leb'a·non; and my servants themselves will prove to be with your servants, and the wages of your servants I shall give to you according to all that you may say, for you yourself well know that there is among us no one knowing how to cut trees like the Si·do'ni·ans."

7 And it came about that as soon as Hi'ram heard the words of Sol'o·mon, he began to rejoice greatly, and he went on to say: "Blessed is Jehovah today in that he has given David a wise son over this numerous people!" 8 Accordingly Hi'ram sent to Sol'o·mon, saying: "I have heard what you sent to me. For my part, I shall do all your delight in the matter of timbers of cedar trees and timbers of juniper trees. 9 My servants themselves will bring them down out of Leb'a·non to the sea; and I, for my part, shall put them in log rafts [to go] by sea clear to the place that you will send me notice of; and I shall certainly have them broken up there, and you, for your part, will carry them; and you, for your part, will do my delight by giving the food for my household."

10 So Hi'ram became a giver of timbers of cedar trees and timbers of juniper trees to Sol'o·mon according to all his delight. 11 And Sol'o·mon, for his part, gave Hi'ram twenty thousand cor measures of wheat as food supplies for his household and twenty cor measures of beaten-out oil. That was what Sol'o·mon kept giving Hi'ram year by year. 12 And Jehovah, for his part, gave Sol'o·mon wisdom, just as he had promised him; and there came to be peace between Hi'ram and Sol'o·mon, and both of them proceeded to conclude a covenant.

13 And King Sol'o·mon kept bringing up those conscripted for forced labor out of all Israel; and those conscripted for forced labor amounted to thirty thousand men. 14 And he would send them to Leb'a·non in shifts of ten thousand a month. For a month they would continue in Leb'a·non, for two months at their homes; and Ad·o·ni'ram was over those conscripted for forced labor. 15 And Sol'o·mon came to have seventy thousand burden bearers and eighty thousand cutters in the mountain, 16 besides Sol'o·mon's princely deputies who were over the work, three thousand three hundred foremen over the people who were active in the work. 17 Accordingly the king commanded that they should quarry great stones, expensive stones, to lay the foundation of the house with hewn stones. 18 So Sol'o·mon's builders and Hi'ram's builders and the Ge'bal·ites did the cutting, and they kept preparing the timbers and the stones to build the house.

6 And it came about in the four hundred and eightieth year after the sons of Israel came out from the land of Egypt, in the fourth year, in the month of Ziv, that is, the second month, after Sol'o·mon became king over Israel, that he proceeded to build the house to Jehovah. 2 And the house that King Sol'o·mon built to Jehovah was sixty cubits in its length, and twenty in its width, and thirty cubits in its height. 3 And the porch in front of the temple of the house was twenty cubits in its length, in front of the width of

the house. Ten cubits it was in its depth, in front of the house.

4 And for the house he went on to make windows of narrowing frames. 5 Further, he built against the wall of the house a side structure all around, [against] the walls of the house all around the temple and the innermost room, and made side chambers all around. 6 The lowest side chamber was five cubits in its width, and the middle one was six cubits in its width, and the third one was seven cubits in its width; for there were cutbacks that he gave to the house all around outside, that it might not have a hold in the walls of the house.

7 As for the house, while it was being built, it was of quarry stone already completed that it was built; and as for hammers and axes or any tools of iron, they were not heard in the house while it was being built. 8 The entrance of the lowest side chamber was on the right side of the house, and by a winding staircase they would go up to the middle one, and from the middle one up to the third one. 9 Further, he continued building the house that he might finish it, and covered in the house with beams and rows in cedarwood. 10 Moreover, he built the side chambers against the whole house five cubits in their height, and they had a hold on the house by timbers of cedar trees.

11 Meantime, the word of Jehovah came to Sol'o·mon, saying: 12 "As regards this house that you are building, if you will walk in my statutes and perform my judicial decisions and actually keep all my commandments by walking in them, I also shall certainly carry out my word with you that I spoke to David your father; 13 and I shall indeed reside in the middle of the sons of Israel, and I shall not leave my people Israel."

14 And Sol'o·mon continued building the house that he might finish it. 15 And he proceeded to build the walls of the house inside it with boards of cedar. From the floor of the house up to the rafters of the ceiling he overlaid it with timber inside; and he went on to overlay the floor of the house with boards of juniper. 16 Further, he built twenty cubits at the rear sides of the house with boards of cedar, from the floor up to the rafters, and built for it inside the innermost room, the Most Holy. 17 And it was forty cubits that the house proved to be, that is, the temple in front of it. 18 And [the] cedarwood on the house inside was with carvings of gourd-shaped ornaments and garlands of blossoms. All of it was cedarwood; there was no stone to be seen.

19 And the innermost room in the interior of the house he prepared inside, to put there the ark of the covenant of Jehovah. 20 And the innermost room was twenty cubits in length, and twenty cubits in width, and twenty cubits in its height; and he proceeded to overlay it with pure gold, and to overlay the altar with cedarwood. 21 And Sol'o·mon went on to overlay the house inside with pure gold, and to make chainwork of gold pass across in front of the innermost room, and to overlay it with gold. 22 And the whole house he overlaid with gold, until all the house was completed; and all the altar that was toward the innermost room he overlaid with gold.

23 Further, he made in the innermost room two cherubs of oil-tree wood, ten cubits being the height of each one. 24 And five cubits was the one wing of the cherub, and five cubits was the other wing of the cherub. Ten cubits it was from the tip of his wing to the tip of his wing. 25 And the second cherub was ten cubits. The two cherubs had the same measure and the same shape. 26 The height of the one cherub was ten cubits, and that was so of the other cherub. 27 Then he put the cherubs inside the inner house, so that they spread out the wings of cherubs. Thus the wing of the one reached to the wall and the wing of the other cherub was reaching to the other wall; and their wings

were toward the middle of the house, reaching wing to wing. 28 Moreover, he overlaid the cherubs with gold.

29 And all the walls of the house round about he carved with engraved carvings of cherubs and palm-tree figures and engravings of blossoms, inside and outside; 30 and the floor of the house he overlaid with gold, inside and outside. 31 And the entrance of the innermost room he made with doors of oil-tree wood: side pillars, doorposts [and] a fifth. 32 And the two doors were of oil-tree wood, and he carved upon them carvings of cherubs and palm-tree figures and the engravings of blossoms, and he overlaid them with gold; and he proceeded to beat the gold down upon the cherubs and the palm-tree figures. 33 And that was the way he made for the entrance of the temple, the doorposts of oil-tree wood, foursquare, 34 And the two doors were of juniper wood. The two leaves of the one door turned on pivots, and the two leaves of the other door turned on pivots. 35 And he carved cherubs and palm-tree figures and engravings of blossoms, and overlaid gold foil upon the representations.

36 And he went on to build the inner courtyard with three rows of hewn stone and a row of beams of cedarwood.

37 In the fourth year the house of Jehovah had its foundation laid, in the lunar month of Ziv; 38 and in the eleventh year, in the lunar month of Bul, that is, the eighth month, the house was finished as regards all its details and all its plan; so that he was seven years at building it.

7 And his own house Sol′o·mon built in thirteen years, so that he finished all his own house.

2 And he proceeded to build the House of the Forest of Leb′a·non a hundred cubits in its length, and fifty cubits in its width, and thirty cubits in its height, upon four rows of pillars of cedarwood; and there were beams of cedarwood

upon the pillars. 3 And it was paneled in with cedarwood above upon the girders that were upon the forty-five pillars. There were fifteen to a row. 4 As for framed windows, there were three rows, and there was an illumination opening opposite an illumination opening in three tiers. 5 And all the entrances and the doorposts were squared [with the] frame, and also the forefront of the illumination opening opposite an illumination opening in three tiers.

6 And the Porch of Pillars he made fifty cubits in its length, and thirty cubits in its width; and another porch was in front of them with pillars and a canopy in front of them.

7 As for the Porch of the Throne where he would do judging, he made the porch of judgment; and they covered it in with cedarwood from the floor to the rafters.

8 As regards the house of his where he was to dwell, at the other courtyard, it was away from the house belonging to the Porch. It proved to be like this in workmanship. And there was a house like this Porch that he proceeded to build for Phar′aoh's daughter, whom Sol′o·mon had taken.

9 All these were [of] expensive stones according to measures, hewn, sawed with stone-saws, inside and outside, and from the foundation up to the coping, and outside as far as the great courtyard. 10 And the expensive stones laid as a foundation were great stones, stones of ten cubits, and stones of eight cubits. 11 And up above there were expensive stones according to measures, hewn, and also cedarwood. 12 As for the great courtyard, round about were three rows of hewn stone and a row of beams of cedarwood; and [this] also for the inner courtyard of the house of Jehovah, and for the porch of the house.

13 And King Sol′o·mon proceeded to send and fetch Hi′ram out of Tyre. 14 He was the son of a widowed woman from the tribe of Naph′ta·li, and his father was a

Tyr′i·an man, a worker in copper; and he was full of the wisdom and the understanding and the knowledge for doing every sort of work in copper. Accordingly he came to King Sol′o·mon and began to do all his work.

15 Then he cast the two pillars of copper, eighteen cubits being the height of each pillar, and a string of twelve cubits would measure around each of the two pillars. 16 And two capitals he made to put upon the tops of the pillars, cast in copper. Five cubits was the height of the one capital, and five cubits was the height of the other capital. 17 There were nets in network, twisted ornaments in chainwork, for the capitals that were upon the top of the pillars; seven for the one capital, and seven for the other capital. 18 And he went on to make the pomegranates and two rows round about upon the one network to cover the capitals that were upon the top of the pillars; and that was what he did for the other capital. 19 And the capitals that were upon the top of the pillars at the porch were of lily work, of four cubits. 20 And the capitals were upon the two pillars, also up close beside the belly that was adjoining the network; and there were two hundred pomegranates in rows all around upon each capital.

21 And he proceeded to set up the pillars belonging to the porch of the temple. So he set up the right-hand pillar and called its name Ja′chin, and then set up the left-hand pillar and called its name Bo′az. 22 And upon the top of the pillars there was lily work. And the work of the pillars was gradually completed.

23 And he proceeded to make the molten sea ten cubits from its one brim to its other brim, circular all around; and its height was five cubits, and it took a line of thirty cubits to circle all around it. 24 And there were gourd-shaped ornaments down below its brim all around, encircling it, ten in a cubit, enclosing the sea all around, with two rows of the gourd-shaped ornaments cast in its casting. 25 It was standing upon twelve bulls, three facing north, and three facing west, and three facing south, and three facing east; and the sea was above upon them, and all their hind parts were toward the center. 26 And its thickness was a handbreadth; and its brim was like the workmanship of the brim of a cup, a lily blossom. Two thousand bath measures were what it would contain.

27 And he went on to make the ten carriages of copper, four cubits being the length of each carriage, and four cubits its width, and three cubits its height. 28 And this was the workmanship of the carriages: they had side walls, and the side walls were between the crossbars. 29 And upon the side walls that were between the crossbars there were lions, bulls and cherubs, and over the crossbars it was like that. Up above and beneath the lions and the bulls there were wreaths in hanging work. 30 And there were four wheels of copper to each carriage, with axles of copper; and its four cornerpieces were supports for them. Beneath the basin were the supports, cast with wreaths across from each. 31 And its mouth from inside to the supports and upward was [?] cubits; and its mouth was round, the workmanship of a stand of one and a half cubits, and also upon its mouth there were carvings. And their side walls were squared, not round. 32 And the four wheels were down below the side walls, and the supports of the wheels were by the carriage; and the height of each wheel was one and a half cubits. 33 And the workmanship of the wheels was like the workmanship of a chariot wheel. Their supports and their felloes and their spokes and their hubs, they were all cast. 34 And there were four supports upon the four corners of each carriage; its supports were of one piece with the carriage. 35 And on top of the carriage there was [a stand] a half a cubit in height,

circular all around; and upon the top of the carriage its sides and its side walls were of one piece with it. 36 Further, he engraved upon the plates of its sides and upon its side walls cherubs, lions and palm-tree figures according to the clear space of each, and wreaths all around. 37 It was like this that he made the ten carriages; they all had one cast, one measure, one shape.

38 And he proceeded to make ten basins of copper. Forty bath measures were what each basin would contain. Each basin was four cubits. There was one basin upon each carriage for the ten carriages. 39 Then he put five carriages on the right side of the house, and five on the left side of the house; and the sea itself he put to the right side of the house eastward, toward the south.

40 And Hi′ram gradually made the basins and the shovels and the bowls. At length Hi′ram finished doing all the work that he did for King Sol′o·mon as respects the house of Jehovah: 41 The two pillars and the bowl-shaped capitals that were upon the top of the two pillars, and the two networks to cover the two round capitals that were upon the top of the pillars, 42 and the four hundred pomegranates for the two networks, two rows of pomegranates to each network, to cover the two bowl-shaped capitals that were upon the two pillars; 43 and the ten carriages and the ten basins upon the carriages, 44 and the one sea and the twelve bulls beneath the sea; 45 and the cans and the shovels and the bowls and all these utensils, which Hi′ram made of polished copper for King Sol′o·mon for the house of Jehovah. 46 In the District of the Jordan it was that the king cast them in the clay mold, between Suc′coth and Zar′e·than.

47 And Sol′o·mon left all the utensils [unweighed] because of so extraordinarily great a quantity. The weight of the copper was not ascertained. 48 And Sol′o·mon

gradually made all the utensils that pertained to the house of Jehovah, the altar of gold and the table on which was the showbread, of gold, 49 and the lampstands, five to the right and five to the left before the innermost room, of pure gold, and the blossoms and the lamps and the snuffers, of gold, 50 and the basins and the extinguishers and the bowls and the cups and the fire holders, of pure gold, and the sockets for the doors of the inner house, that is, the Most Holy, and for the doors of the house of the temple, of gold.

51 Finally all the work that King Sol′o·mon had to do as regards the house of Jehovah was at its completion; and Sol′o·mon began to bring in the things made holy by David his father; the silver and the gold and the articles he put in the treasures of the house of Jehovah.

8 At that time Sol′o·mon proceeded to congregate the older men of Israel, all the heads of the tribes, the chieftains of the fathers, of the sons of Israel, to King Sol′o·mon at Jerusalem, to bring up the ark of the covenant of Jehovah out of the city of David, that is to say, Zion. 2 So all the men of Israel congregated themselves to King Sol′o·mon in the lunar month of Eth′a·nim in the festival, that is, the seventh month. 3 So all the older men of Israel came, and the priests began to carry the Ark. 4 And they came bringing up the ark of Jehovah and the tent of meeting and all the holy utensils that were in the tent; and the priests and the Levites came bringing them up. 5 And King Sol′o·mon and with him all the assembly of Israel, those keeping their appointment with him, were before the Ark, sacrificing sheep and cattle that could not be counted or numbered for multitude.

6 Then the priests brought in the ark of the covenant of Jehovah to its place, to the innermost room of the house, the Most Holy, to underneath the wings of the cherubs. 7 For the cherubs were spreading out their wings over the place of

the Ark, so that the cherubs kept the Ark and its poles screened over from above. 8 But the poles proved to be long, so that the tips of the poles were visible from the Holy in front of the innermost room, but they were not visible outside. And there they continue down to this day. 9 There was nothing in the Ark but the two stone tablets which Moses had deposited there in Ho′reb, when Jehovah had covenanted with the sons of Israel while they were coming out from the land of Egypt.

10 And it came about that when the priests came out from the holy place, the cloud itself filled the house of Jehovah. 11 And the priests were unable to stand to do their ministering because of the cloud, for the glory of Jehovah filled the house of Jehovah. 12 At that time Sol′o·mon said: "Jehovah himself said he was to reside in the thick gloom. 13 I have successfully built a house of lofty abode for you, an established place for you to dwell in to time indefinite."

14 Then the king turned his face and began to bless all the congregation of Israel, while all the congregation of Israel were standing up. 15 And he went on to say: "Blessed is Jehovah the God of Israel, who spoke by his own mouth with David my father, and by his own hand has given fulfillment, saying, 16 'From the day that I brought my people Israel out from Egypt I have not chosen a city out of all the tribes of Israel to build a house for my name to continue there; but I shall choose David to come to be over my people Israel.' 17 And it came to be close to the heart of David my father to build a house to the name of Jehovah the God of Israel. 18 But Jehovah said to David my father, 'For the reason that it proved to be close to your heart to build a house to my name, you did well, because it proved to be close to your heart. 19 Only you yourself will not build the house, but your son who is coming forth from your loins is the one that will build the house to

my name.' 20 And Jehovah proceeded to carry out his word that he had spoken, that I might rise up in the place of David my father and sit upon the throne of Israel, just as Jehovah had spoken, and that I might build the house to the name of Jehovah the God of Israel, 21 and that I might locate a place there for the Ark where the covenant of Jehovah is that he concluded with our forefathers when he was bringing them out from the land of Egypt."

22 And Sol′o·mon began standing before the altar of Jehovah in front of all the congregation of Israel, and he now spread his palms out to the heavens; 23 and he went on to say: "O Jehovah the God of Israel, there is no God like you in the heavens above or on the earth beneath, keeping the covenant and the loving-kindness toward your servants who are walking before you with all their heart, 24 you who have kept toward your servant David my father that which you promised him, so that you made the promise with your own mouth, and with your own hand you have made the fulfillment, as at this day. 25 And now, O Jehovah the God of Israel, keep toward your servant David my father that which you promised him, saying, 'There will not be cut off a man of yours from before me to sit upon the throne of Israel, if only your sons will take care of their way by walking before me just as you have walked before me.' 26 And now, O God of Israel, let your promise that you have promised to your servant David my father prove trustworthy, please.

27 "But will God truly dwell upon the earth? Look! The heavens, yes, the heaven of the heavens, themselves cannot contain you; how much less, then, this house that I have built! 28 And you must turn toward the prayer of your servant and to his request for favor, O Jehovah my God, to listen to the entreating cry and to the prayer with which your servant is praying before you today; 29 that your

eyes may prove to be opened toward this house night and day, toward the place of which you said, 'My name will prove to be there,' to listen to the prayer with which your servant prays toward this place. 30 And you must listen to the request for favor on the part of your servant and of your people Israel with which they pray toward this place; and may you yourself hear at the place of your dwelling, in the heavens, and you must hear and forgive.

31 "When a man sins against his fellow man, and he actually lays a cursing upon him to bring him under liability to the curse, and he actually comes [within] the curse before your altar in this house, 32 then may you yourself hear from the heavens, and you must act and judge your servants by pronouncing the wicked one wicked by putting his way upon his own head, and by pronouncing the righteous one righteous by giving to him according to his own righteousness.

33 "When your people Israel are defeated before the enemy, because they kept sinning against you, and they indeed return to you and laud your name and pray and make request for favor toward you in this house, 34 then may you yourself hear from heaven, and you must forgive the sin of your people Israel and you must bring them back to the ground that you gave to their forefathers.

35 "When heaven is shut up so that no rain occurs, because they kept sinning against you, and they actually pray toward this place and laud your name, and from their sin they turn back, because you kept afflicting them, 36 then may you yourself hear from the heavens, and you must forgive the sin of your servants, even of your people Israel, because you teach them the good way in which they should walk; and you must give rain upon your land that you have given to your people as a hereditary possession.

37 "In case a famine occurs in the land, in case a pestilence occurs, in case scorching, mildew, locusts, cockroaches occur; in case their enemy besieges them in the land of their gates—any sort of plague, any sort of malady— 38 whatever prayer, whatever request for favor there may occur on the part of any man [or] of all your people Israel, because they know each one the plague of his own heart, and they actually spread out their palms to this house, 39 then may you yourself hear from the heavens, your established place of dwelling, and you must forgive and act and give to each one according to all his ways, because you know his heart (for you yourself alone well know the heart of all the sons of mankind); 40 to the end that they may fear you all the days that they are alive upon the surface of the ground that you gave to our forefathers.

41 "And also to the foreigner, who is no part of your people Israel and who actually comes from a distant land by reason of your name 42 (for they shall hear of your great name and of your strong hand and of your stretched-out arm), and he actually comes and prays toward this house, 43 may you yourself listen from the heavens, your established place of dwelling, and you must do according to all that for which the foreigner calls to you; in order that all the peoples of the earth may get to know your name so as to fear you the same as your people Israel do, and so as to know that your name itself has been called upon this house that I have built.

44 "In case your people go out to the war against their enemy in the way that you send them, and they indeed pray to Jehovah in the direction of the city that you have chosen and the house that I have built to your name, 45 you must also hear from the heavens their prayer and their request for favor, and you must execute judgment for them.

46 "In case they sin against you (for there is no man that does not sin), and you have to be incensed at them and abandon them to the enemy, and their captors actually carry them off captive to the land of the enemy distant or nearby; 47 and they indeed come to their senses in the land where they have been carried off captive, and they actually return and make request to you for favor in the land of their captors, saying, 'We have sinned and erred, we have acted wickedly'; 48 and they indeed return to you with all their heart and with all their soul in the land of their enemies who carried them off captive, and they indeed pray to you in the direction of their land that you gave to their forefathers, the city that you have chosen and the house that I have built to your name; 49 you must also hear from the heavens, your established place of dwelling, their prayer and their request for favor, and you must execute judgment for them, 50 and you must forgive your people who had sinned against you and all their transgressions with which they transgressed against you; and you must make them objects of pity before their captors and they must pity them 51 (for they are your people and your inheritance, whom you brought out from Egypt, from inside the iron furnace), 52 that your eyes may prove to be opened to the request for favor of your servant and to the request for favor of your people Israel, by listening to them in all for which they call to you. 53 For you yourself separated them as your inheritance out of all the peoples of the earth, just as you have spoken by means of Moses your servant when you were bringing our forefathers out from Egypt, O Lord Jehovah."

54 And it came about that, as soon as Sol′o·mon finished praying to Jehovah with all this prayer and request for favor, he rose up from before the altar of Jehovah, from bending down upon his knees with his palms spread out to the heavens; 55 and he began to stand and bless all the congregation of Israel with a loud voice, saying: 56 "Blessed be Jehovah, who has given a resting place to his people Israel according to all that he has promised. There has not failed one word of all his good promise that he has promised by means of Moses his servant. 57 May Jehovah our God prove to be with us just as he proved to be with our forefathers. May he neither leave us nor forsake us, 58 so as to incline our heart to himself to walk in all his ways and to keep his commandments and his regulations and his judicial decisions, which he gave in command to our forefathers. 59 And may these words of mine with which I have made request for favor before Jehovah prove to be near to Jehovah our God by day and night, that he may execute judgment for his servant and judgment for his people Israel as it may require day by day; 60 to the end that all the peoples of the earth may know that Jehovah is the [true] God. There is no other. 61 And YOUR heart must prove to be complete with Jehovah our God by walking in his regulations and by keeping his commandments as at this day."

62 And the king and all Israel with him were offering a grand sacrifice before Jehovah. 63 And Sol′o·mon proceeded to offer the communion sacrifices that he had to offer to Jehovah, twenty-two thousand cattle and a hundred and twenty thousand sheep, that the king and all the sons of Israel might inaugurate the house of Jehovah. 64 On that day the king had to sanctify the middle of the courtyard that is before the house of Jehovah, because there they had to render up the burnt sacrifice and the grain offering and the fat pieces of the communion sacrifices; for the copper altar that is before Jehovah was too small to contain the burnt sacrifice and the grain offering and the fat pieces of the communion sacrifices. 65 And Sol′o·mon proceeded to carry on at

that time the festival, and all Israel with him, a great congregation from the entering in of Ha'math down to the torrent valley of Egypt, before Jehovah our God seven days and another seven days, fourteen days. 66 On the eighth day he sent the people away; and they began to bless the king and to go to their homes, rejoicing and feeling merry of heart over all the goodness that Jehovah had performed for David his servant and for Israel his people.

9 And it came about that, as soon as Sol'o·mon had finished building the house of Jehovah and the house of the king and every desirable thing of Sol'o·mon that he took delight in making, 2 then Jehovah appeared to Sol'o·mon the second time, the same as he had appeared to him in Gib'e·on. 3 And Jehovah went on to say to him: "I have heard your prayer and your request for favor with which you requested favor before me. I have sanctified this house that you have built by putting my name there to time indefinite; and my eyes and my heart will certainly prove to be there always. 4 And you, if you will walk before me, just as David your father walked, with integrity of heart and with uprightness by doing according to all that I have commanded you, and you will keep my regulations and my judicial decisions, 5 I also shall indeed establish the throne of your kingdom over Israel to time indefinite, just as I promised David your father, saying, 'Not a man of yours will be cut off from [sitting] upon the throne of Israel.' 6 If you yourselves and your sons should definitely turn back from following me and not keep my commandments and my statutes that I have put before you men, and you actually go and serve other gods and bow down to them, 7 I will also cut Israel off from upon the surface of the ground that I have given to them; and the house that I have sanctified to my name I shall throw away from before me, and Israel will indeed become a proverbial saying and a taunt among all the peoples. 8 And this house itself will become heaps of ruins. Everyone passing by it will stare in amazement and will certainly whistle and say, 'For what reason did Jehovah do like that to this land and this house?' 9 And they will have to say, 'For the reason that they left Jehovah their God who had brought their forefathers out from the land of Egypt, and they proceeded to take hold of other gods and bow down to them and serve them. That is why Jehovah brought upon them all this calamity.'"

10 And it came about at the end of twenty years, in which Sol'o·mon built the two houses, the house of Jehovah and the house of the king, 11 (Hi'ram the king of Tyre had himself assisted Sol'o·mon with timbers of cedar trees and timbers of juniper trees and with gold as much as he delighted in,) that at that time King Sol'o·mon proceeded to give to Hi'ram twenty cities in the land of Gal'i·lee. 12 Accordingly Hi'ram went out from Tyre to see the cities that Sol'o·mon had given him, and they were not just right in his eyes. 13 So he said: "What sort of cities are these that you have given me, my brother?" And they came to be called the Land of Ca'bul down to this day. 14 In the meantime Hi'ram sent to the king a hundred and twenty talents of gold.

15 Now this is the account of those conscripted for forced labor that King Sol'o·mon levied to build the house of Jehovah and his own house and the Mound and the wall of Jerusalem and Ha'zor and Me·gid'do and Ge'zer. 16 (Phar'aoh the king of Egypt himself had come up and then captured Ge'zer and burned it with fire, and the Ca'naan·ites dwelling in the city he had killed. So he gave it as a parting gift to his daughter, the wife of Sol'o·mon.) 17 And Sol'o·mon went on to build Ge'zer and Lower Beth-ho'ron, 18 and Ba'al·ath and Ta'mar in the wilderness,

in the land, 19 and all the storage cities that became Sol'o·mon's and the chariot cities and the cities for the horsemen, and the desirable things of Sol'o·mon that he had desired to build in Jerusalem and in Leb'a·non and in all the land of his dominion. 20 As for all the people remaining over from the Am'or·ites, the Hit'tites, the Per'iz-zites, the Hi'vites and the Jeb'u-sites, who were no part of the sons of Israel, 21 their sons who had been left over after them in the land whom the sons of Israel had been unable to devote to destruc-tion, Sol'o·mon kept levying them for slavish forced labor until this day. 22 And there were none of the sons of Israel that Sol'o·mon constituted slaves; for they were the warriors and his servants and his princes and his adjutants and chiefs of his charioteers and of his horsemen. 23 These were the chiefs of the deputies who were over the work of Sol'o·mon, five hundred and fifty, the foremen over the people who were active in the work.

24 However, Phar'aoh's daughter herself came up out of the city of David to her own house that he had built for her. It was then that he built the Mound.

25 And Sol'o·mon continued three times in the year to offer up burnt sacrifices and communion sacrifices upon the altar that he had built for Jehovah, and there was a making of sacrificial smoke on the [altar], which was before Je-hovah; and he completed the house.

26 And there was a fleet of ships that King Sol'o·mon made in E'zi·on-ge'ber, which is by E'loth, upon the shore of the Red Sea in the land of E'dom. 27 And Hi'-ram kept sending in the fleet of ships his own servants, seamen, having a knowledge of the sea, along with the servants of Sol'o-mon. 28 And they proceeded to go to O'phir and take from there four hundred and twenty talents of gold and bring it in to King Sol'o·mon.

10 Now the queen of She'ba was hearing the report about Sol'-o·mon in connection with the name of Jehovah. So she came to test him with perplexing questions. 2 Finally she arrived at Jerusalem with a very impressive train, camels carrying balsam oil and very much gold and precious stones; and she came on in to Sol'o·mon and began to speak to him all that happened to be close to her heart. 3 Sol'o-mon, in turn, went on to tell her all her matters. There proved to be no matter hidden from the king that he did not tell her.

4 When the queen of She'ba got to see all the wisdom of Sol'o·mon and the house that he had built, 5 and the food of his table and the sitting of his servants and the table service of his waiters and their at-tire and his drinks and his burnt sacrifices that he regularly offered up at the house of Jehovah, then there proved to be no more spirit in her. 6 So she said to the king: "True has the word proved to be that I heard in my own land about your matters and about your wis-dom. 7 And I did not put faith in the words until I had come that my own eyes might see; and, look! I had not been told the half. You have surpassed in wisdom and pros-perity the things heard to which I listened. 8 Happy are your men; happy are these servants of yours who are standing before you con-stantly, listening to your wisdom! 9 May Jehovah your God come to be blessed, who has taken delight in you by putting you upon the throne of Israel; because Jehovah loves Israel to time indefinite, so that he appointed you as king to render judicial decision and right-eousness."

10 Then she gave the king a hundred and twenty talents of gold and a very great deal of balsam oil and precious stones. There never came any more the like of that balsam oil for quantity such as the queen of She'ba gave to King Sol'-o·mon.

11 And Hi'ram's fleet of ships that carried gold from O'phir also

21 When Re·ho·bo'am arrived at Jerusalem, he immediately congregated all the house of Judah and the tribe of Benjamin, a hundred and eighty thousand choice men able-bodied for war, to fight against the house of Israel, so as to bring the kingship back to Re·ho·bo'am the son of Sol'o·mon. 22 Then the word of the [true] God came to She·mai'ah the man of the [true] God, saying: 23 "Say to Re·ho·bo'am the son of Sol'o·mon the king of Judah and to all the house of Judah and Benjamin and the rest of the people, 24 'This is what Jehovah has said: "You must not go up and fight against your brothers the sons of Israel. Go back each one to his house, for it is at the instance of myself that this thing has been brought about." '" So they obeyed the word of Jehovah, and went back home according to the word of Jehovah.

25 And Jer·o·bo'am proceeded to build She'chem in the mountainous region of E'phra·im and to dwell in it. Then he went forth from there and built Pe·nu'el. 26 And Jer·o·bo'am began to say in his heart: "Now the kingdom will return to the house of David. 27 If this people continues going up to render sacrifices in the house of Jehovah in Jerusalem, the heart of this people will also be bound to return to their lord, Re·ho·bo'am the king of Judah; and they will certainly kill me and return to Re·ho·bo'am the king of Judah." 28 Consequently the king took counsel and made two golden calves and said to the people: "It is too much for you to go up to Jerusalem. Here is your God, O Israel, that brought you up out of the land of Egypt." 29 Then he placed the one in Beth'el, and the other he put in Dan. 30 And this thing came to be a cause for sin, and the people began to go before the one as far as Dan.

31 And he began to make a house of high places and to make priests from the people in general, who did not happen to be of the sons of Le'vi. 32 And Jer·o·bo'am went on to make a festival in the eighth month on the fifteenth day of the month, like the festival that was in Judah, that he might make offerings upon the altar that he had made in Beth'el, to sacrifice to the calves that he had made; and he put in attendance at Beth'el the priests of the high places that he had made. 33 And he began to make offerings upon the altar that he had made in Beth'el on the fifteenth day in the eighth month, in the month that he had invented by himself; and he proceeded to make a festival for the sons of Israel and to make offerings upon the altar to make sacrificial smoke.

13 And here there was a man of God that had come out of Judah by the word of Jehovah to Beth'el, while Jer·o·bo'am was standing by the altar to make sacrificial smoke. 2 Then he called out against the altar by the word of Jehovah and said: "O altar, altar, this is what Jehovah has said, 'Look! A son born to the house of David, whose name is Jo·si'ah! And he will certainly sacrifice upon you the priests of the high places that are making sacrificial smoke upon you, and men's bones he will burn upon you.' " 3 And he gave a portent on that day, saying: "This is the portent of which Jehovah has spoken: Look! The altar is ripped apart, and the fatty ashes that are upon it will certainly be spilled out."

4 And it came about that, as soon as the king heard the word of the man of the [true] God that he had called out against the altar in Beth'el, Jer·o·bo'am at once thrust out his hand from off the altar, saying: "You men, grab hold of him!" Immediately his hand that he had thrust out against him became dried up, and he was not able to draw it back to himself. 5 And the altar itself was ripped apart so that the fatty ashes were spilled out from the altar, according to the portent that the man of the [true] God had given by the word of Jehovah.

6 The king now answered and said to the man of the [true] God: "Soften, please, the face of Jehovah your God and pray in my behalf that my hand may be restored to me." At this the man of the [true] God softened the face of Jehovah, so that the king's hand was restored to him, and it came to be as at first. 7 And the king went on to say to the man of the [true] God: "Do come with me to the house and take sustenance, and let me give you a gift." 8 But the man of the [true] God said to the king: "If you gave me half of your house I would not come with you and eat bread or drink water in this place. 9 For that is the way he commanded me by the word of Jehovah, saying, 'You must not eat bread or drink water, and you must not return by the way that you went.'" 10 And he began to go by another way, and he did not return by the way by which he had come to Beth'el.

11 And a certain old prophet was dwelling in Beth'el, and his sons now came in and related to him all the work that the man of the [true] God had done that day in Beth'el [and] the words that he had spoken to the king, and they went on relating them to their father. 12 Then their father spoke to them: "Which way, then, did he go?" So his sons showed him the way that the man of the [true] God that had come out of Judah had gone. 13 He now said to his sons: "Saddle the ass for me." Accordingly they saddled the ass for him, and he went riding on it.

14 And he went following the man of the [true] God and got to find him sitting under the big tree. Then he said to him: "Are you the man of the [true] God who has come out of Judah?" to which he said: "I am." 15 And he went on to say to him: "Go with me to the house and eat bread." 16 But he said: "I am not able to go back with you or to come in with you, and I may not eat bread or drink water with you in this place. 17 For it has been spoken to me by the word of Jehovah, 'You must not eat bread or drink water there. You must not go back again by the way by which you went.'" 18 At this he said to him: "I too am a prophet like you, and an angel himself spoke to me by the word of Jehovah, saying, 'Have him come back with you to your house that he may eat bread and drink water.'" (He deceived him.) 19 So he went back with him that he might eat bread in his house and drink water.

20 And it came about, while they were sitting at the table, that the word of Jehovah came to the prophet that had brought him back; 21 and he began to call out to the man of the [true] God that had come out of Judah, saying: "This is what Jehovah has said, 'For the reason that you rebelled against the order of Jehovah and did not keep the commandment with which Jehovah your God commanded you, 22 but you went back that you might eat bread and drink water in the place about which he spoke to you: "Do not eat bread or drink water," your dead body will not come into the burial place of your forefathers.'"

23 And it came about after his eating bread and after his drinking that he at once saddled for him the ass, that is, for the prophet whom he had brought back. 24 And he got on his way. Later a lion found him on the road and put him to death, and his dead body came to be thrown onto the road. And the ass was standing beside it, and the lion was standing beside the dead body. 25 And here there were men passing by, so that they got to see the dead body thrown onto the road and the lion standing beside the dead body. Then they came in and spoke of it in the city in which the old prophet was dwelling.

26 When the prophet that had brought him back from the way heard of it, he immediately said: "It is the man of the [true] God that rebelled against the order of Jehovah; and so Jehovah gave him

to the lion, that he might crush him and put him to death, according to the word of Jehovah that he spoke to him." 27 And he went on to speak to his sons, saying: "Saddle the ass for me." So they saddled it. 28 Then he got on his way and found the dead body of him thrown onto the road with the ass and the lion standing beside the dead body. The lion had not eaten the dead body, nor had it crushed the ass. 29 And the prophet proceeded to lift up the dead body of the man of the [true] God and to deposit him upon the ass and to bring him back. Thus he came into the city of the old prophet to bewail and bury him. 30 Accordingly he deposited his dead body in his own burial place; and they kept wailing over him: "Too bad, my brother!" 31 And it came about after his burying him that he went on to say to his sons: "When I die you must bury me in the burial place in which the man of the [true] God is buried. Beside his bones deposit my own bones. 32 For without fail the word that he called out by the word of Jehovah against the altar that is in Beth'el and against all the houses of the high places that are in the cities of Sa·mar'i·a will take place."

33 After this thing Jer·o·bo'am did not turn back from his bad way, but he again went making priests of high places from the people in general. As for anyone delighting in it, he would fill his hand with power, [saying]: "And let him become [one of the] priests of high places." 34 And in this thing there came to be a cause of sin on the part of the household of Jer·o·bo'am and an occasion for effacing them and annihilating them off the surface of the ground.

14 At that particular time A·bi'jah the son of Jer·o·bo'am fell sick. 2 So Jer·o·bo'am said to his wife: "Rise up, please, and you must disguise yourself that they may not know that you are the wife of Jer·o·bo'am, and you must go to Shi'loh. Look! There is where A·hi'jah the prophet is. He is the one that spoke with reference to me as to becoming king over this people. 3 And you must take in your hand ten loaves of bread and sprinkled cakes and a flask of honey, and you must come in to him. He it is that will certainly tell you what is going to happen to the boy."

4 And the wife of Jer·o·bo'am proceeded to do so. Consequently she rose up and went to Shi'loh and came to the house of A·hi'jah. Now A·hi'jah himself was unable to see, for his eyes had set because of his age.

5 And Jehovah himself had said to A·hi'jah: "Here is the wife of Jer·o·bo'am coming to apply for a word from you regarding her son; for he is sick. This way and that is how you should speak to her. And it will occur that as soon as she arrives, she will be making herself unrecognizable."

6 And it came about that as soon as A·hi'jah heard the sound of her feet as she was coming into the entrance, he began to say: "Come in, you wife of Jer·o·bo'am. Why is it that you are making yourself unrecognizable while I am being sent to you with a severe message? 7 Go, say to Jer·o·bo'am, 'This is what Jehovah the God of Israel has said: "For the reason that I raised you up out of the middle of your people, that I might constitute you a leader over my people Israel, 8 and I went on to rip the kingdom away from the house of David and give it to you, and you have not become like my servant David, who kept my commandments and who walked after me with all his heart by doing only what was right in my eyes, 9 but you began to act worse than all those who happened to be prior to you, and you went and made for yourself another god and molten images to offend me, and it is I whom you have cast behind your back; 10 for that reason here I am bringing calamity upon the house of Jer·o·bo'am, and I shall certainly cut off from Jer·o·bo'am

anyone urinating against a wall, a helpless and worthless one in Israel; and I shall indeed make a clean sweep behind the house of Jer·o·bo′am, just as one clears away the dung until it is disposed of. 11 The one dying of Jer·o·bo′am's in the city, the dogs will eat; and the one dying in the field, the fowls of the heavens will eat, because Jehovah himself has spoken it." '

12 "And you yourself, rise up, go to your house. When your feet come into the city the child will certainly die. 13 And all Israel will indeed bewail him and bury him, because this one alone of Jer·o·bo′am's will come into a burial place; for the reason that something good toward Jehovah the God of Israel has been found in him in the house of Jer·o·bo′am. 14 And Jehovah will certainly raise up to himself a king over Israel who will cut off the house of Jer·o·bo′am the said day, and what if right now? 15 And Jehovah will indeed strike Israel down, just as the reed sways in the water; and he will certainly uproot Israel off this good ground that he gave to their forefathers, and he will indeed scatter them beyond the River, for the reason that they made their sacred poles, so offending Jehovah. 16 And he will give Israel up on account of the sins of Jer·o·bo′am with which he sinned and with which he caused Israel to sin."

17 At that Jer·o·bo′am's wife rose up and went her way and came to Tir′zah. As she was arriving at the threshold of the house, the boy himself died. 18 So they buried him, and all Israel went wailing for him, according to Jehovah's word that he had spoken by means of his servant A·hi′jah the prophet.

19 And the rest of the affairs of Jer·o·bo′am, how he warred and how he reigned, there they are written in the book of the affairs of the days of the kings of Israel. 20 And the days that Jer·o·bo′am reigned were twenty-two years,

after which he lay down with his forefathers; and Na′dab his son began to reign in place of him.

21 As for Re·ho·bo′am the son of Sol′o·mon, he had become king in Judah. Forty-one years old Re·ho·bo′am was when he began to reign, and seventeen years he reigned in Jerusalem, the city that Jehovah had chosen out of all the tribes of Israel to put his name there. And his mother's name was Na′a·mah the Am′mon·it·ess. 22 And Judah went on doing what was bad in the eyes of Jehovah, so that they incited him to jealousy more than all that their forefathers had done by their sins with which they sinned. 23 And they too kept building for themselves high places and sacred pillars and sacred poles upon every high hill and under every luxuriant tree. 24 And even the male temple prostitute proved to be in the land. They acted according to all the detestable things of the nations whom Jehovah had driven out from before the sons of Israel.

25 And it came about in the fifth year of King Re·ho·bo′am that Shi′shak the king of Egypt came up against Jerusalem. 26 And he got to take the treasures of the house of Jehovah and the treasures of the house of the king; and everything he took. And he went on to take all the gold shields that Sol′o·mon had made. 27 Consequently King Re·ho·bo′am made in place of them copper shields, and he committed them to the control of the chiefs of the runners, the guards of the entrance of the king's house. 28 And it would occur that as often as the king came to the house of Jehovah, the runners would carry them, and they returned them to the guard chamber of the runners.

29 And the rest of the affairs of Re·ho·bo′am and all that he did, are they not written in the book of the affairs of the times of the kings of Judah? 30 And warfare itself took place between Re·ho·bo′am and Jer·o·bo′am always. 31 Finally Re·ho·bo′am lay down

with his forefathers and was buried with his forefathers in the city of David. And his mother's name was Na'a·mah the Am'mon·it·ess. And A·bi'jam his son began to reign in place of him.

15 And in the eighteenth year of King Jer·o·bo'am the son of Ne'bat, A·bi'jam became king over Judah. 2 Three years he reigned in Jerusalem; and his mother's name was Ma'a·cah the granddaughter of A·bish'a·lom. 3 And he went on walking in all the sins of his father that he did prior to him; and his heart did not prove to be complete with Jehovah his God, like the heart of David his forefather. 4 For, on account of David, Jehovah his God gave him a lamp in Jerusalem by raising his son up after him and keeping Jerusalem in existence, 5 because David did what was right in the eyes of Jehovah, and he did not turn aside from anything that He had commanded him all the days of his life, only in the matter of U·ri'ah the Hit'tite. 6 And warfare itself took place between Re·ho·bo'am and Jer·o·bo'am all the days of his life.

7 As for the rest of the affairs of A·bi'jam and all that he did, are they not written in the book of the affairs of the days of the kings of Judah? There was warfare also that took place between A·bi'jam and Jer·o·bo'am. 8 Finally A·bi'jam lay down with his forefathers and they buried him in the city of David; and A'sa his son began to reign in place of him.

9 In the twentieth year of Jer·o·bo'am the king of Israel, A'sa reigned as king of Judah. 10 And forty-one years he reigned in Jerusalem; and his grandmother's name was Ma'a·cah the granddaughter of A·bish'a·lom. 11 And A'sa proceeded to do what was right in the eyes of Jehovah, like David his forefather. 12 Accordingly he had the male temple prostitutes pass out of the land and removed all the dungy idols that his forefathers had made. 13 As for even Ma'a·cah his grandmother, he went on

to remove her from [being] lady, because she had made a horrible idol to the sacred pole; after which A'sa cut down her horrible idol and burned it at the torrent valley of Kid'ron. 14 And the high places he did not remove. Nevertheless, A'sa's heart itself proved to be complete with Jehovah all his days. 15 And he began to bring in the things made holy by his father and the things made holy by himself into the house of Jehovah, silver and gold and articles.

16 And warfare itself took place between A'sa and Ba'a·sha the king of Israel all their days. 17 So Ba'a·sha the king of Israel came up against Judah and began to build Ra'mah, to allow no one to go out or come in to A'sa the king of Judah. 18 At that A'sa took all the silver and the gold that were left in the treasures of the house of Jehovah and the treasures of the house of the king and put them in the hand of his servants; and King A'sa now sent them to Ben-ha'dad the son of Tab·rim'mon the son of He'zi·on, the king of Syria, who was dwelling in Damascus, saying: 19 "There is a covenant between me and you, between my father and your father. Here I have sent you a present of silver and gold. Come, do break your covenant with Ba'a·sha the king of Israel, that he may withdraw from me." 20 Accordingly Ben-ha'dad listened to King A'sa and sent the chiefs of the military forces that were his against the cities of Israel and went striking down I'jon and Dan and A'bel-beth-ma'a·cah and all Chin'ne-reth, as far as all the land of Naph'ta·li. 21 And it came about that as soon as Ba'a·sha heard of it, he immediately quit building Ra'mah and continued dwelling in Tir'zah. 22 And King A'sa, for his part, summoned all Judah—there was none exempt—and they proceeded to carry the stones of Ra'-mah and the timbers of it, with which Ba'a·sha had been building; and King A'sa began to build with

them Ge'ba in Benjamin, and Miz'pah.

23 As for the rest of all the affairs of A'sa and all his mightiness and all that he did and the cities that he built, are they not written in the book of the affairs of the days of the kings of Judah? Only at the time of his growing old he got diseased in his feet. 24 Finally A'sa lay down with his forefathers and was buried with his forefathers in the city of David his forefather; and Je·hosh'a·phat his son began to reign in place of him.

25 As for Na'dab the son of Jer·o·bo'am, he became king over Israel in the second year of A'sa the king of Judah; and he continued to reign over Israel two years. 26 And he kept doing what was bad in the eyes of Jehovah and went on walking in the way of his father and in his sin with which he caused Israel to sin. 27 And Ba'a·sha the son of A·hi'jah of the house of Is'sa·char began to conspire against him; and Ba'a·sha got to strike him down at Gib'be·thon, which belonged to the Phi·lis'tines, while Na'dab and all Israel were besieging Gib'be·thon. 28 So Ba'a·sha put him to death in the third year of A'sa the king of Judah and began to reign in place of him. 29 And it came about that as soon as he became king, he struck down all the house of Jer·o·bo'am. He did not let anyone breathing remain of Jer·o·bo'am's until he had annihilated them, according to Jehovah's word that he had spoken by means of his servant A·hi'jah the Shi'lo·nite, 30 on account of the sins of Jer·o·bo'am with which he sinned and with which he caused Israel to sin [and] by his offensiveness with which he offended Jehovah the God of Israel. 31 As for the rest of the affairs of Na'dab and all that he did, are they not written in the book of the affairs of the days of the kings of Israel? 32 And warfare itself took place between A'sa and Ba'a·sha the king of Israel all their days.

33 In the third year of A'sa the king of Judah, Ba'a·sha the son of A·hi'jah became king over all Israel in Tir'zah for twenty-four years. 34 And he kept doing what was bad in the eyes of Jehovah and went walking in the way of Jer·o·bo'am and in his sin with which he caused Israel to sin.

16 The word of Jehovah now came to Je'hu the son of Ha·na'ni against Ba·a·sha, saying: 2 "Inasmuch as I raised you up out of the dust that I might constitute you leader over my people Israel, but you went walking in the way of Jer·o·bo'am and so caused my people Israel to sin by offending me with their sins, 3 here I am making a clean sweep after Ba'a·sha and after his house, and I shall certainly constitute his house like the house of Jer·o·bo'am the son of Ne'bat. 4 Anyone of Ba'a·sha that is dying in the city the dogs will eat; and anyone of his that is dying in the field the fowls of the heavens will eat."

5 As for the rest of the affairs of Ba'a·sha and what he did and his mightiness, are they not written in the book of the affairs of the days of the kings of Israel? 6 Finally Ba'a·sha lay down with his forefathers and was buried in Tir'zah; and E'lah his son began to reign in place of him. 7 And also by means of Je'hu the son of Ha·na'ni the prophet, Jehovah's word itself had come against Ba'a·sha and his house, both because of all the badness that he committed in the eyes of Jehovah by offending him with the work of his hands, that it might become like the house of Jer·o·bo'am, and because he struck him down.

8 In the twenty-sixth year of A'sa the king of Judah, E'lah the son of Ba'a·sha became king over Israel in Tir'zah for two years. 9 And his servant Zim'ri the chief of half the chariots began to conspire against him, while he was in Tir'zah drinking himself drunk at the house of Ar'zah, who was over the household in Tir'zah. 10 And Zim'ri proceeded to come in and

strike him down and put him to death in the twenty-seventh year of A'sa the king of Judah, and he began to reign in place of him. 11 And it came about that when he began to reign, as soon as he sat down upon his throne, he struck down all the house of Ba'a·sha. He did not let anyone of his remain that urinates against a wall or his avengers of blood or his friends. 12 Thus Zim'ri annihilated the whole house of Ba'a·sha, according to the word of Jehovah that he had spoken against Ba'a·sha by means of Je'hu the prophet, 13 on account of all the sins of Ba'a·sha and the sins of E'lah his son with which they caused Israel to sin by offending Jehovah the God of Israel with their vain idols. 14 As for the rest of the affairs of E'lah and all that he did, are they not written in the book of the affairs of the days of the kings of Israel?

15 In the twenty-seventh year of A'sa the king of Judah, Zim'ri became king for seven days in Tir'-zah, while the people were encamping against Gib'be·thon, which belonged to the Phi·lis'tines. 16 In time the people that were encamped heard it said: "Zim'ri has conspired and also struck down the king." So all Israel made Om'ri, the chief of the army, king over Israel on that day in the camp. 17 Om'ri and all Israel with him now went on up from Gib'be·thon and began to lay siege to Tir'zah. 18 And it came about that as soon as Zim'ri saw that the city had been captured, he then came into the dwelling tower of the king's house and burned the king's house over himself with fire, so that he died, 19 for the sins of his with which he had sinned by doing what was bad in the eyes of Jehovah by walking in the way of Jer·o·bo'am and in his sin which he did by causing Israel to sin. 20 As for the rest of the affairs of Zim'ri and his conspiracy with which he conspired, are they not written in the book of the affairs of the days of the kings of Israel? 21 It was then that the people

of Israel began to divide themselves into two parts. There was one part of the people that became followers of Tib'ni the son of Gi'nath, to make him king, and the other part followers of Om'ri. 22 Finally the people that were following Om'ri overcame the people that were following Tib'ni the son of Gi'nath; so that Tib'ni met death, and Om'ri began to reign.

23 In the thirty-first year of A'sa the king of Judah, Om'ri became king over Israel for twelve years. In Tir'zah he reigned six years. 24 And he proceeded to buy the mountain of Sa·mar'i·a from She'mer for two talents of silver, and began to build [on] the mountain and call the name of the city that he built by the name of She'-mer the master of the mountain, Sa·mar'i·a. 25 And Om'ri kept doing what was bad in the eyes of Jehovah and came to do worse than all who were prior to him. 26 And he went walking in all the way of Jer·o·bo'am the son of Ne'bat and in his sin with which he caused Israel to sin by offending Jehovah the God of Israel with their vain idols. 27 As for the rest of the affairs of Om'ri, what he did and his mightiness with which he acted, are they not written in the book of the affairs of the days of the kings of Israel? 28 Finally Om'ri lay down with his forefathers and was buried in Sa·mar'i·a; and A'hab his son began to reign in place of him.

29 And as for A'hab the son of Om'ri, he became king over Israel in the thirty-eighth year of A'sa the king of Judah; and A'hab the son of Om'ri continued to reign over Israel in Sa·mar'i·a twenty-two years. 30 And A'hab the son of Om'ri proceeded to do worse in the eyes of Jehovah than all those who were prior to him. 31 And it came about that, [as if it were] the most trivial thing for him to walk in the sins of Jer·o·bo'am the son of Ne'bat, he now took as wife Jez'e·bel the daughter of Eth·ba'al the king of the Si·do'ni·ans and

began to go and serve Ba′al and to bow down to him. 32 Further, he set up an altar to Ba′al at the house of Ba′al that he built in Sa·mar′i·a. 33 And A′hab went on to make the sacred pole; and A′hab came to do more to offend Jehovah the God of Israel than all the kings of Israel that happened to be prior to him.

34 In his days Hi′el the Beth′el·ite built Jer′i·cho. At the forfeit of A·bi′ram his first-born he laid the foundation of it, and at the forfeit of Se′gub his youngest he put up its doors, according to Jehovah's word that he spoke by means of Joshua the son of Nun.

17 And E·li′jah the Tish′bite from the inhabitants of Gil′e·ad proceeded to say to A′hab: "As Jehovah the God of Israel before whom I do stand is living, there will occur during these years neither dew nor rain, except at the order of my word!"

2 The word of Jehovah now came to him, saying: 3 "Go away from here, and you must turn your way eastward and conceal yourself at the torrent valley of Che′rith that is east of the Jordan. 4 And it must occur that from the torrent valley you should drink, and the ravens I shall certainly command to supply you food there." 5 Immediately he went and did according to the word of Jehovah, and so went and took up dwelling by the torrent valley of Che′rith that is east of the Jordan. 6 And the ravens themselves were bringing him bread and meat in the morning and bread and meat in the evening, and from the torrent valley he kept drinking. 7 But it came about at the end of some days that the torrent valley became dry, because there had occurred no downpour upon the earth.

8 The word of Jehovah now came to him, saying: 9 "Rise up, go to Zar′e·phath, which belongs to Si′don, and you must dwell there. Look! I shall certainly command there a woman, a widow, to supply you food." 10 Accordingly he rose up and went to Zar′e·phath and

came into the entrance of the city; and, look! a woman, a widow, was there gathering up pieces of wood. So he called to her and said: "Please, get me a sip of water in a vessel that I may drink." 11 When she began to go and get it, he went on to call to her and say: "Please, get me a bit of bread in your hand." 12 At this she said: "As Jehovah your God is living, I have no round cake, but a handful of flour in the large jar and a little oil in the small jar; and here I am gathering up a few pieces of wood, and I must go in and make something for myself and my son, and we shall have to eat it and die."

13 Then E·li′jah said to her: "Do not be afraid. Go in, do according to your word. Only from what is there make me a small round cake first, and you must bring it out to me, and for yourself and your son you can make something afterward. 14 For this is what Jehovah the God of Israel has said, 'The large jar of flour itself will not get exhausted, and the small jar of oil itself will not fail until the day of Jehovah's giving a downpour upon the surface of the ground.'" 15 So she went and did according to E·li′jah's word; and she continued to eat, she together with him and her household, for days. 16 The large jar of flour itself did not get exhausted, and the small jar of oil itself did not fail, according to Jehovah's word that he had spoken by means of E·li′jah.

17 And it came about after these things that the son of the woman, the mistress of the house, fell sick, and his sickness came to be so severe that there was no breath left in him. 18 At this she said to E·li′jah: "What do I have to do with you, O man of the [true] God? You have come to me to bring my error to mind and to put my son to death." 19 But he said to her: "Give me your son." Then he took him from her bosom and carried him up to the roof chamber, where he was dwelling, and laid him upon his own couch. 20 And he

began calling to Jehovah and saying: "O Jehovah my God, is it also upon the widow with whom I am residing as an alien that you must bring injury by putting her son to death?" 21 And he proceeded to stretch himself upon the child three times and call to Jehovah and say: "O Jehovah my God, please, cause the soul of this child to come back within him." 22 Finally Jehovah listened to E·li′jah's voice, so that the soul of the child came back within him and he came to life. 23 E·li′jah now took the child and brought him down from the roof chamber into the house and gave him to his mother; and E·li′jah then said: "See, your son is alive." 24 Upon that the woman said to E·li′jah: "Now, indeed, I do know that you are a man of God and that Jehovah's word in your mouth is true."

18 And it came about [after] many days that Jehovah's own word came to E·li′jah in the third year, saying: "Go, show yourself to A′hab, as I am determined to give rain upon the surface of the ground." 2 Accordingly E·li′jah went to show himself to A′hab, while the famine was severe in Sa·mar′i·a.

3 Meantime, A′hab called O·ba·di′ah, who was over the household. (Now O·ba·di′ah himself had proved to be one greatly fearing Jehovah. 4 Hence it came about that when Jez′e·bel cut off Jehovah's prophets, O·ba·di′ah proceeded to take a hundred prophets and keep them hid by fifties in a cave, and he supplied them bread and water.) 5 And A′hab went on to say to O·ba·di′ah: "Go through the land to all the springs of water and to all the torrent valleys. Perhaps we may find green grass, that we may preserve the horses and mules alive and may not have [any more] of the beasts cut off." 6 So they divided between themselves the land through which to pass. A′hab himself went alone by one way, and O·ba·di′ah himself went alone by another way.

7 As O·ba·di′ah continued on the way, why, there was E·li′jah to meet him. At once he recognized him and fell upon his face and said: "Is this you, my lord E·li′jah?" 8 At this he said to him: "It is I. Go, say to your lord, 'Here is E·li′jah.'" 9 But he said: "What sin have I committed that you should be putting your servant into the hand of A′hab to put me to death? 10 As Jehovah your God is living, there is not a nation or kingdom where my lord has not sent to look for you. After they had said, 'He is not [here],' he made the kingdom and the nation swear that they could not find you. 11 And now you are saying, 'Go, say to your lord: "Here is E·li′jah."' 12 And it is bound to occur that, when I myself go from you, then the spirit of Jehovah itself will carry you away to where I shall not know; and I shall have come to tell A′hab, and he will not find you, and he will be bound to kill me, as your servant himself has feared Jehovah from his youth. 13 Has not my lord been told what I did when Jez′e·bel killed the prophets of Jehovah, how I kept some of the prophets of Jehovah hid, a hundred men by fifties in a cave, and kept supplying them bread and water? 14 And now you are saying, 'Go, say to your lord: "Here is E·li′jah."' And he will be bound to kill me." 15 However, E·li′jah said: "As Jehovah of armies before whom I do stand is living, today I shall show myself to him."

16 Accordingly O·ba·di′ah went off to meet A′hab and told him; and so A′hab went to meet E·li′jah. 17 And it came about that, as soon as A′hab saw E·li′jah, A′hab immediately said to him: "Is this you, the bringer of ostracism upon Israel?" 18 To this he said: "I have not brought ostracism upon Israel, but you and the house of your father have, because you men have left the commandments of Jehovah, and you went following the Ba′als. 19 And now send, col-

lect together all Israel to me at Mount Car'mel and also the four hundred and fifty prophets of Ba'al and the four hundred prophets of the sacred pole, who are eating at the table of Jez'e·bel." 20 And A'hab proceeded to send among all the sons of Israel and collect the prophets together at Mount Car'mel.

21 Then E·li'jah approached all the people and said: "How long will YOU be limping upon two different opinions? If Jehovah is the [true] God, go following him; but if Ba'al is, go following him." And the people did not say a word in answer to him. 22 And E·li'jah went on to say to the people: "I myself have been left as a prophet of Jehovah, I alone, while the prophets of Ba'al are four hundred and fifty men. 23 Now let them give us two young bulls, and let them choose for themselves one young bull and cut it in pieces and put it upon the wood, but they should not put fire to it. And I myself shall dress the other young bull, and I must place it upon the wood, but I shall not put fire to it. 24 And YOU must call upon the name of YOUR god, and I, for my part, shall call upon the name of Jehovah; and it must occur that the [true] God that answers by fire is the [true] God." To this all the people answered and said: "The thing is good."

25 E·li'jah now said to the prophets of Ba'al: "Choose for yourselves one young bull and dress it first, because YOU are the majority; and call upon the name of YOUR god, but YOU must not put fire to it." 26 Accordingly they took the young bull that he gave them. Then they dressed it, and they kept calling upon the name of Ba'al from morning till noon, saying: "O Ba'al, answer us!" But there was no voice, and there was no one answering. And they kept limping around the altar that they had made. 27 And it came about at noon that E·li'jah began to mock them and say: "Call at the top of YOUR voice, for he is a god;

for he must be concerned with a matter, and he has excrement and has to go to the privy. Or maybe he is asleep and ought to wake up!" 28 And they began calling at the top of their voice and cutting themselves according to their custom with daggers and with lances, until they caused blood to flow out upon them. 29 And it came about that, as soon as noon was past and they continued behaving as prophets until the going up of the grain offering, there was no voice, and there was no one answering, and there was no paying of attention.

30 At length E·li'jah said to all the people: "Approach me." So all the people approached him. Then he proceeded to mend the altar of Jehovah that was torn down. 31 So E·li'jah took twelve stones, according to the number of the tribes of the sons of Jacob, to whom Jehovah's word had come, saying: "Israel is what your name will become." 32 And he went on to build the stones into an altar in the name of Jehovah and to make a trench, of about the area sowed with two seah measures of seed, all around the altar. 33 After that he put the pieces of wood in order and cut the young bull in pieces and placed it upon the pieces of wood. He now said: "FILL four large jars with water and pour it upon the burnt offering and upon the pieces of wood." 34 Then he said: "Do it again." So they did it again. But he said: "Do it a third time." So they did it a third time. 35 Thus the water went all around the altar, and the trench also he filled with water.

36 And it came about at the time that the grain offering goes up that E·li'jah the prophet began to approach and say: "O Jehovah, the God of Abraham, Isaac and Israel, today let it be known that you are God in Israel and I am your servant and it is by your word that I have done all these things. 37 Answer me, O Jehovah, answer me, that this people may know that you, Jehovah, are the [true] God

and you yourself have turned their heart back."

38 At that the fire of Jehovah came falling and went eating up the burnt offering and the pieces of wood and the stones and the dust, and the water that was in the trench it licked up. 39 When all the people saw it, they immediately fell upon their faces and said: "Jehovah is the [true] God! Jehovah is the [true] God!" 40 Then E·li′jah said to them: "Seize the prophets of Ba′al! Do not let a single one of them escape!" At once they seized them, and E·li′jah then brought them down to the torrent valley of Ki′shon and slaughtered them there.

41 E·li′jah now said to A′hab: "Go up, eat and drink; for there is the sound of the turmoil of a downpour." 42 And A′hab proceeded to go up to eat and drink. As for E·li′jah, he went up to the top of Car′mel and began crouching to the earth and keeping his face put between his knees. 43 Then he said to his attendant: "Go up, please. Look in the direction of the sea." So he went up and looked and then said: "There is nothing at all." And he went on to say, "Go back," for seven times. 44 And it came about at the seventh time that he got to say: "Look! There is a small cloud like a man's palm ascending out of the sea." He now said: "Go up, say to A′hab, 'Hitch up! And go down that the downpour may not detain you!'" 45 And it came about in the meantime that the heavens themselves darkened up with clouds and wind and a great downpour began to occur. And A′hab kept riding and made his way to Jez′re·el. 46 And the very hand of Jehovah proved to be upon E·li′jah, so that he girded up his hips and went running ahead of A′hab all the way to Jez′re·el.

19 Then A′hab told Jez′e·bel all that E·li′jah had done and all about how he had killed all the prophets with the sword. 2 At that Jez′e·bel sent a messenger to E·li′jah, saying: "So may the gods do, and so may they add to it, if at this time tomorrow I shall not make your soul like the soul of each one of them!" 3 And he became afraid. Consequently he rose up and began to go for his soul and came to Be′er-she′ba, which belongs to Judah. Then he left his attendant behind there. 4 And he himself went into the wilderness a day's journey, and at length came and sat down under a certain broom tree. And he began to ask that his soul might die and to say: "It is enough! Now, O Jehovah, take my soul away, for I am no better than my forefathers."

5 Finally he lay down and fell asleep under the broom tree. But, look! now an angel was touching him. Then he said to him: "Rise up, eat." 6 When he looked, why, there at his head was a round cake upon heated stones and a jug of water. And he began to eat and drink, after which he lay down again. 7 Later the angel of Jehovah came back a second time and touched him and said: "Rise up, eat, for the journey is too much for you." 8 So he rose up and ate and drank, and he kept going in the power of that nourishment for forty days and forty nights as far as the mountain of the [true] God, Ho′reb.

9 There he finally entered into a cave, that he might spend the night there; and, look! there was Jehovah's word for him, and it went on to say to him: "What is your business here, E·li′jah?" 10 To this he said: "I have been absolutely jealous for Jehovah the God of armies; for the sons of Israel have left your covenant, your altars they have torn down, and your prophets they have killed with the sword, so that I only am left; and they begin looking for my soul to take it away." 11 But it said: "Go out, and you must stand on the mountain before Jehovah." And, look! Jehovah was passing by, and a great and strong wind was rending mountains and breaking crags before Jehovah. (Jehovah was

not in the wind.) And after the wind there was a quaking. (Jehovah was not in the quaking.) 12 And after the quaking there was a fire. (Jehovah was not in the fire.) And after the fire there was a calm, low voice. 13 And it came about that as soon as E·li′jah heard it, he immediately wrapped his face in his official garment and went out and stood at the entrance of the cave; and, look! there was a voice for him, and it proceeded to say to him: "What is your business here, E·li′jah?" 14 To this he said: "I have been absolutely jealous for Jehovah the God of armies; for the sons of Israel have left your covenant, your altars they have torn down, and your prophets they have killed with the sword, so that I only am left; and they begin looking for my soul to take it away."

15 Jehovah now said to him: "Go, return on your way to the wilderness of Damascus; and you must come in and anoint Haz′a·el as king over Syria. 16 And Je′hu the grandson of Nim′shi you should anoint as king over Israel; and E·li′sha the son of Sha′phat from A′bel-me·ho′lah you should anoint as prophet in place of you. 17 And it must occur that the one escaping from Haz′a·el's sword, Je′hu will put to death; and the one escaping from Je′hu's sword, E·li′sha will put to death. 18 And I have let seven thousand remain in Israel, all the knees that have not bent down to Ba′al, and every mouth that has not kissed him."

19 Accordingly he went from there and found E·li′sha the son of Sha′phat while he was plowing with twelve spans before him, and he with the twelfth. So E·li′jah crossed over to him and threw his official garment upon him. 20 At that he left the bulls and went running after E·li′jah and said: "Let me, please, kiss my father and my mother. Then I will go following you." At this he said to him: "Go, return; for what have I done to you?" 21 So he returned from following him and then took a span of the bulls and sacrificed them, and with the implements of the bulls he boiled their flesh and then gave it to the people, and they proceeded to eat. After that he rose up and went following E·li′jah and began to minister to him.

20 As for Ben-ha′dad the king of Syria, he collected all his military forces together and also thirty-two kings with him and horses and chariots, and he proceeded to go up and lay siege to Sa·mar′i·a and fight against it. 2 Then he sent messengers to A′hab the king of Israel at the city. And he went on to say to him: "This is what Ben-ha′dad has said, 3 'Your silver and your gold are mine, and your wives and your sons, the best looking, are mine.'" 4 To this the king of Israel answered and said: "According to your word, my lord the king, yours I am with all that belongs to me."

5 Later the messengers came back and said: "This is what Ben-ha′dad has said, 'I sent to you, saying: "Your silver and your gold and your wives and your sons you will give me. 6 But about this time tomorrow I shall send my servants to you, and they must carefully search your house and the houses of your servants; and it must occur that everything desirable to your eyes they will put in their hand, and they must take it away."'"

7 At that the king of Israel called all the older men of the land and said: "Take note, please, and see that it is calamity that this one is seeking; for he sent to me for my wives and my sons and my silver and my gold, and I did not hold them back from him." 8 Then all the older men and all the people said to him: "Do not obey, and you should not consent." 9 So he said to the messengers of Ben-ha′dad: "Say to my lord the king, 'All that you sent to your servant at first I shall do; but this thing I am not able to do.'" With that the messengers went off and brought word back to him.

10 Ben-ha′dad now sent to him and said: "So may the gods do to me, and so may they add to it, if the dust of Sa·mar′i·a will be sufficient for handfuls for all the people that follow me!" 11 In turn the king of Israel answered and said: "YOU men, speak [to him], 'Do not let one girding on boast about himself like one unfastening.'" 12 And it came about that as soon as he heard this word, while he himself and the kings were drinking in the booths, he immediately said to his servants: "Get set!" And they began to get set against the city.

13 And, look! a certain prophet approached A′hab the king of Israel and then said: "This is what Jehovah has said, 'Have you seen all this great crowd? Here I am giving it into your hand today, and you will certainly know that I am Jehovah.'" 14 At this A′hab said: "By whom?" to which he said: "This is what Jehovah has said, 'By the young men of the princes of the jurisdictional districts.'" Finally he said: "Who will open the battle engagement?" to which he said: "YOU!"

15 And he proceeded to take the count of the young men of the princes of the jurisdictional districts, and they came to be two hundred and thirty-two; and after them he took the count of all the people, all the sons of Israel, seven thousand. 16 And they began to go out at noon while Ben-ha′dad was drinking himself drunk in the booths, he together with the kings, the thirty-two kings that were helping him. 17 When the young men of the princes of the jurisdictional districts came out first, Ben-ha′dad at once sent out; and they came telling him, saying: "There are men that have come out from Sa·mar′i·a." 18 At that he said: "Whether it is for peace that they have come out, YOU should seize them alive; or whether it is for battle that they have come out, alive is how YOU should seize them." 19 And these were the ones that came out from the city,

the young men of the princes of the jurisdictional districts and the military forces that were behind them. 20 And they began to strike down each one his man; and the Syrians took to flight, and Israel went in pursuit of them, but Ben-ha′dad the king of Syria got to escape upon a horse together with the horsemen. 21 But the king of Israel went out and kept striking down the horses and the chariots, and he struck down the Syrians with a great slaughter.

22 Later the prophet approached the king of Israel and said to him: "Go, strengthen yourself and take note and see what you are going to do; for at the return of the year the king of Syria is coming up against you."

23 As for the servants of the king of Syria, they said to him: "Their God is a God of mountains. That is why they proved stronger than we were. So, on the other hand, let us fight against them on the level land [and see] whether we shall not prove stronger than they are. 24 And do this thing: Remove the kings each one from his place and put in governors instead of them. 25 As for you, you should number a military force for yourself equal to the military force that fell from your side, with horse for horse and chariot for chariot; and let us fight against them on the level land [and see] whether we shall not prove stronger than they are." Accordingly he listened to their voice and did just that way.

26 And it came about at the return of the year that Ben-ha′dad proceeded to muster the Syrians and to go up to A′phek for battle against Israel. 27 As for the sons of Israel, they were mustered and supplied and began to go out to meet them; and the sons of Israel went into camp in front of them like two tiny flocks of goats, while the Syrians, for their part, filled the earth. 28 Then the man of the [true] God approached and said to the king of Israel, yes, he went on to say:

"This is what Jehovah has said, 'For the reason that the Syrians have said: "Jehovah is a God of mountains, and he is not a God of low plains," I shall have to give all this great crowd into your hand, and YOU men will certainly know that I am Jehovah.'"

29 And they continued encamped for seven days, these in front of those. And it came about on the seventh day that the engagement in battle began; and the sons of Israel went striking down the Syrians, a hundred thousand men on foot in one day. 30 And those that were left went fleeing to A'phek, to the city; and the wall came falling down upon twenty-seven thousand men that were left. As for Ben-ha'dad, he fled and finally came into the city into the innermost chamber.

31 So his servants said to him: "Here, now, we have heard that the kings of the house of Israel are kings of loving-kindness. Please, let us carry sackcloth upon our loins and ropes upon our heads, and let us go out to the king of Israel. Perhaps he will preserve your soul alive." 32 Accordingly they girded sackcloth about their loins, with ropes upon their heads, and came in to the king of Israel and said: "Your servant Ben-ha'dad has said, 'Please, let my soul live.'" To this he said: "Is he still alive? He is my brother." 33 So the men themselves took it as an omen and quickly took it as a decision of his own accord, and they went on to say: "Ben-ha'dad is your brother." At that he said: "Come, fetch him." Then Ben-ha'dad went out to him; and he at once had him get up into the chariot.

34 [Ben-ha'dad] now said to him: "The cities that my father took from your father I shall return; and streets you will assign to yourself in Damascus the same as my father assigned in Sa-mar'i·a."

"And as for me, in a covenant I shall send you away."

With that he concluded a covenant with him and sent him away.

35 And a certain man of the sons of the prophets said to his friend by the word of Jehovah: "Strike me, please." But the man refused to strike him. 36 Therefore he said to him: "For the reason that you did not listen to the voice of Jehovah, here you are going away from me, and a lion will certainly strike you down." After that he went away from beside him, and the lion got to find him and strike him down.

37 And he went on to find another man and to say: "Strike me, please." So the man struck him, striking and wounding.

38 Then the prophet went and stood still for the king by the road, and he kept himself disguised with a bandage over his eyes. 39 And it came about that as the king was passing by, he cried out to the king and proceeded to say: "Your servant himself went out into the thick of the battle; and, look! a man was leaving the line, and he came bringing a man to me and then said, 'Guard this man. If he should in any way be missing, your soul will also have to take the place of his soul, or else a talent of silver you will weigh out.' 40 And it came about that as your servant was active here and there, why, he himself was gone." At this the king of Israel said to him: "Thus your own judgment is. You yourself have decided." 41 Upon that he hurriedly removed the bandage from over his eyes, and the king of Israel got to recognize him, that he was from the prophets. 42 He now said to him: "This is what Jehovah has said, 'For the reason that you have let go out of your hand the man devoted to me for destruction, your soul must take the place of his soul, and your people the place of his people.'" 43 At that the king of Israel went on his way toward his house, sullen and dejected, and came to Sa·mar'i·a.

21 And it came about after these things that there was a vineyard that happened to belong to Na'both the Jez're·el·ite, which was

in Jez're·el, beside the palace of A'hab the king of Sa·mar'i·a. 2 So A'hab spoke to Na'both, saying: "Do give me your vineyard, that it may serve as a garden of vegetables to me, for it is close by my house; and let me give you in place of it a vineyard better than it. [Or] if it is good in your eyes, I will give you money as the price of this." 3 But Na'both said to A'hab: "It is unthinkable on my part, from Jehovah's standpoint, for me to give the hereditary possession of my forefathers to you." 4 Consequently A'hab came into his house, sullen and dejected over the word that Na'both the Jez're·el·ite had spoken to him, when he said: "I shall not give you the hereditary possession of my forefathers." Then he lay down upon his couch and kept his face turned, and he did not eat bread.

5 Finally Jez'e·bel his wife came in to him and spoke to him: "Why is it that your spirit is sad and you are not eating bread?" 6 At that he spoke to her: "Because I proceeded to speak to Na'both the Jez're·el·ite and say to him, 'Do give me your vineyard for money. Or, if you prefer, let me give you another vineyard in place of it.' But he said, 'I shall not give you my vineyard.'" 7 Then Jez'e·bel his wife said to him: "Is it you that now exercise the kingship over Israel? Rise up, eat bread and let your heart be merry. I myself shall give you the vineyard of Na'both the Jez're·el·ite." 8 Accordingly she wrote letters in A'hab's name and sealed them with his seal, and sent the letters to the older men and the nobles that were in his city dwelling with Na'both. 9 But she wrote in the letters, saying: "Proclaim a fast, and HAVE Na'both sit at the head of the people. 10 And MAKE two men, good-for-nothing fellows, sit in front of him, and let them bear witness against him. saying, 'You have cursed God and the king!' And BRING him out and stone him that he may die."

11 So the men of his city, the older men and the nobles that were

dwelling in his city, did just as Jez'e·bel had sent to them, just as it was written in the letters that she had sent to them. 12 They proclaimed a fast and had Na'both sit at the head of the people. 13 Then two of the men, good-for-nothing fellows, came in and sat down in front of him; and the good-for-nothing men began to bear witness against him, that is, Na'both, in front of the people, saying: "Na'both has cursed God and the king!" After that they brought him out to the outskirts of the city and stoned him with stones, so that he died. 14 They now sent to Jez'e·bel, saying: "Na'both has been stoned so that he is dead."

15 And it came about that, as soon as Jez'e·bel heard that Na'both had been stoned so that he died, Jez'e·bel immediately said to A'hab: "Rise up, take possession of the vineyard of Na'both the Jez're·el·ite, which he refused to give you for money; for Na'both is no longer alive, but dead." 16 And it came about that, as soon as A'hab heard that Na'both was dead, A'hab at once rose up to go down to the vineyard of Na'both the Jez're·el·ite, to take possession of it.

17 And Jehovah's word came to E·li'jah the Tish'bite, saying: 18 "Rise up, go down to meet A'hab the king of Israel, who is in Sa·mar'i·a. There he is in the vineyard of Na'both, where he has gone down to take possession of it. 19 And you must speak to him, saying, 'This is what Jehovah has said: "Have you murdered and also taken possession?"' And you must speak to him, saying, 'This is what Jehovah has said: "In the place where the dogs licked up the blood of Na'both, the dogs will lick up your blood, even yours."'"

20 And A'hab proceeded to say to E·li'jah: "Have you found me, O enemy of mine?" to which he said: "I have found you. 'For the reason that you have sold yourself to do what is bad in the eyes of Jehovah, 21 here I am bringing

calamity upon you; and I shall certainly make a clean sweep after you and cut off from A'hab anyone urinating against a wall and the helpless and worthless one in Israel. 22 And I shall certainly constitute your house like the house of Jer·o·bo'am the son of Ne'bat and like the house of Ba'a·sha the son of A·hi'jah, for the offense with which you have offended and then caused Israel to sin.' 23 And also as regards Jez'e·bel Jehovah has spoken, saying, 'The very dogs will eat up Jez'e·bel in the plot of land of Jez're·el. 24 Anyone of A'hab's that is dying in the city the dogs will eat up; and anyone dying in the field the fowls of the heavens will eat up. 25 Without exception no one has proved to be like A'hab, who sold himself to do what was bad in the eyes of Jehovah, whom Jez'e·bel his wife egged on. 26 And he went acting very detestably by going after the dungy idols, the same as all that the Am'or·ites had done, whom Jehovah drove out from before the sons of Israel.'"

27 And it came about that as soon as A'hab heard these words, he proceeded to rip his garments apart and to put sackcloth upon his flesh; and he went on a fast and kept lying down in sackcloth and walking despondently. 28 And Jehovah's word came to E·li'jah the Tish'bite, saying: 29 "Have you seen how A'hab has humbled himself on my account? For the reason that he has humbled himself because of me, I shall not bring the calamity in his own days. In the days of his son I shall bring the calamity upon his house."

22 And for three years they continued dwelling without war between Syria and Israel. 2 And it came about in the third year that Je·hosh'a·phat the king of Judah proceeded to go down to the king of Israel. 3 Then the king of Israel said to his servants: "Do you really know that Ra'moth-gil'e·ad belongs to us? Yet we are hesitating to take it out of the hand of the king of Syria." 4 And he went on to say to Je·hosh'a-phat: "Will you go with me to the fight at Ra'moth-gil'e·ad?" At this Je·hosh'a·phat said to the king of Israel: "I am the same as you. My people are the same as your people. My horses are the same as your horses."

5 However, Je·hosh'a·phat went on to say to the king of Israel: "Inquire, please, first of all for the word of Jehovah." 6 So the king of Israel collected the prophets together, about four hundred men, and said to them: "Shall I go against Ra'moth-gil'e·ad in war, or shall I refrain?" And they began to say: "Go up, and Jehovah will give it into the king's hand."

7 But Je·hosh'a·phat said: "Is there not here a prophet of Jehovah still? Then let us inquire through him." 8 At that the king of Israel said to Je·hosh'a·phat: "There is still one man through whom to inquire of Jehovah; but I myself certainly hate him, for he does not prophesy good things concerning me but bad—Mi·cai'ah the son of Im'lah." However, Je·hosh'a·phat said: "Do not let the king say a thing like that."

9 Accordingly the king of Israel called a certain court official and said: "Do bring Mi·cai'ah the son of Im'lah quickly." 10 Now the king of Israel and Je·hosh'a·phat the king of Judah were sitting each one on his throne, clothed in garments, in the threshing floor at the entrance of the gate of Sa·mar'i·a; and all the prophets were acting as prophets before them. 11 Then Zed·e·ki'ah the son of Che·na'a·nah made for himself horns of iron and said: "This is what Jehovah has said, 'With these you will push the Syrians until you exterminate them.'" 12 And all the other prophets were prophesying the same as that, saying: "Go up to Ra'moth-gil'e·ad and prove successful; and Jehovah will certainly give it into the king's hand."

13 And the messenger that had gone to call Mi·cai'ah spoke to him, saying: "Look, now! The words of the prophets are unanimously of good to the king. Let your word,

please, become like the word of one of them, and you must speak good." **14** But Mi·cai'ah said: "As Jehovah is living, what Jehovah will say to me, that is what I shall speak." **15** Then he came in to the king, and the king proceeded to say to him: "Mi·cai'ah, shall we go to Ra'moth-gil'e·ad in war, or shall we refrain?" At once he said to him: "Go up and prove successful; and Jehovah will certainly give it into the king's hand." **16** At that the king said to him: "For how many times am I putting you under oath that you should not speak to me anything but truth in the name of Jehovah?" **17** So he said: "I certainly see all the Israelites scattered on the mountains, like sheep that have no shepherd. And Jehovah went on to say: 'These have no masters. Let them go back each one to his house in peace.'"

18 Then the king of Israel said to Je·hosh'a·phat: "Did I not say to you, 'He will prophesy concerning me, not good things, but bad'?"

19 And he went on to say: "Therefore hear the word of Jehovah: I certainly see Jehovah sitting upon his throne and all the army of the heavens standing by him, to his right and to his left. **20** And Jehovah proceeded to say, 'Who will fool A'hab, that he may go up and fall at Ra'moth-gil'e·ad?' And this one began to say something like this, while that one was saying something like that. **21** Finally a spirit came out and stood before Jehovah and said, 'I myself shall fool him.' At that Jehovah said to him, 'By what means?' **22** To this he said, 'I shall go forth, and I shall certainly become a deceptive spirit in the mouth of all his prophets.' So he said, 'You will fool him, and, what is more, you will come off the winner. Go out and do that way.' **23** And now here Jehovah has put a deceptive spirit into the mouth of all these prophets of yours; but Jehovah himself has spoken calamity concerning you."

24 Zed·e·ki'ah the son of Che·na'a·nah now approached and struck Mi·cai'ah upon the cheek and said: "In just which [way] did the spirit of Jehovah pass along from me to speak with you?" **25** At that Mi·cai'ah said: "Look! You are seeing [which way] on that day when you will enter the innermost chamber to hide yourself." **26** Then the king of Israel said: "Take Mi·cai'ah and turn him back to A'mon the chief of the city and to Jo'ash the king's son. **27** And you must say, 'This is what the king has said: "Put this fellow in the house of detention and feed him with a reduced allowance of bread and a reduced allowance of water until I come in peace."'" **28** Upon that Mi·cai'ah said: "If you return at all in peace, Jehovah has not spoken with me." And he added: "Hear, all you peoples."

29 And the king of Israel and Je·hosh'a·phat the king of Judah proceeded to go up to Ra'moth-gil'e·ad. **30** The king of Israel now said to Je·hosh'a·phat: "There will be a disguising and entering into the battle [for me], but you, for your part, put on your garments." Accordingly, the king of Israel disguised himself and entered into the battle. **31** As for the king of Syria, he had commanded the thirty-two chiefs of the chariots that were his, saying: "You must fight, neither with the small nor the great, but with the king of Israel alone." **32** And it came about that, as soon as the chiefs of the chariots saw Je·hosh'a·phat, they, for their part, said to themselves: "Surely it is the king of Israel." So they turned aside against him to fight; and Je·hosh'a·phat began to cry for aid. **33** And it came about that, as soon as the chiefs of the chariots saw that it was not the king of Israel, they immediately came back from following him.

34 And there was a man that bent the bow in his innocence, but he got to strike the king of Israel between the appendages and the coat of mail, so that he said to his charioteer: "Turn your hand around, and take me out from the camp, because I have been badly wounded." 35 And the battle kept rising in intensity on that day, and the king himself had to be kept in a standing position in the chariot facing the Syrians, and gradually he died in the evening; and the blood of the wound kept pouring out upon the interior of the war chariot. 36 And the ringing cry began to pass through the camp about the setting of the sun, saying: "Everyone to his city, and everyone to his land!" 37 Thus the king died. When he was brought to Sa·mar′i·a, then they buried the king in Sa·mar′i·a. 38 And they began to wash off the war chariot by the pool of Sa·mar′i·a, and the dogs went licking up his blood (and the prostitutes themselves bathed there), according to Jehovah's word that he had spoken.

39 As for the rest of the affairs of A′hab and all that he did and the house of ivory that he built and all the cities that he built, are they not written in the book of the affairs of the days of the kings of Israel? 40 Finally A′hab lay down with his forefathers; and A·ha·zi′ah his son began to reign in place of him.

41 As for Je·hosh′a·phat the son of A′sa, he had become king over Judah in the fourth year of A′hab the king of Israel. 42 Je·hosh′a·phat was thirty-five years old when he began to reign, and for twenty-five years he reigned in Jerusalem; and his mother's name was A·zu′bah the daughter of Shil′hi. 43 And he kept walking in all the way of A′sa his father. He did not turn aside from it, by doing what was right in the eyes of Jehovah. Only the high places themselves did not disappear. The

people were still sacrificing and making sacrificial smoke on the high places. 44 And Je·hosh′a·phat kept peaceful relations with the king of Israel. 45 As for the rest of the affairs of Je·hosh′a·phat and the mightiness with which he acted and how he warred, are they not written in the book of the affairs of the days of the kings of Judah? 46 And the rest of the male temple prostitutes that had been left over in the days of A′sa his father he cleared out from the land.

47 As regards a king, there was none in E′dom; a deputy was king.

48 Je·hosh′a·phat, for his part, made Tar′shish ships to go to O′phir for gold; but they did not go, because the ships were wrecked at E′zi·on-ge′ber. 49 It was then that A·ha·zi′ah the son of A′hab said to Je·hosh′a·phat: "Let my servants go with your servants in the ships," but Je·hosh′a·phat did not consent.

50 Finally Je·hosh′a·phat lay down with his forefathers and was buried with his forefathers in the city of David his forefather; and Je·ho′ram his son began to reign in place of him.

51 As for A·ha·zi′ah the son of A′hab, he became king over Israel in Sa·mar′i·a in the seventeenth year of Je·hosh′a·phat the king of Judah, and he continued to reign over Israel for two years. 52 And he kept doing what was bad in Jehovah's eyes and went walking in the way of his father and in the way of his mother and in the way of Jer·o·bo′am the son of Ne′bat, who had caused Israel to sin. 53 And he continued serving Ba′al and bowing down to him and kept offending Jehovah the God of Israel according to all that his father had done.

THE SECOND OF

KINGS

or, according to the Greek *Septuagint*,

THE FOURTH OF KINGS

1 And Mo'ab began to revolt against Israel after the death of A'hab.

2 Then A·ha·zi'ah fell down through the grating in his roof chamber that was in Sa·mar'i·a and got sick. So he sent messengers and said to them: "Go, inquire of Ba'al-ze'bub the god of Ek'ron whether I shall revive from this sickness." 3 As for the angel of Jehovah, he spoke to E·li'jah the Tish'bite: "Rise up, go up to meet the messengers of the king of Sa·mar'i·a and say to them, 'Is it because there is no God at all in Israel that you are going to inquire of Ba'al-ze'bub the god of Ek'ron? 4 So therefore this is what Jehovah has said: "As regards the couch upon which you have gone up, you will not come down off it, because you will positively die." ' " With that E·li'jah went off.

5 When the messengers came back to him, he immediately said to them: "Why is it that you have come back?" 6 So they said to him: "There was a man that came up to meet us, and he proceeded to say to us, 'Go, return to the king who sent you, and you must speak to him: "This is what Jehovah has said, 'Is it because there is no God at all in Israel that you are sending to inquire of Ba'al-ze'bub the god of Ek'ron? Therefore, as regards the couch upon which you have gone up, you will not come down off it, because you will positively die.' " ' " 7 At this he spoke to them: "What was the appearance of the man that came up to meet you and then spoke these words to you?" 8 So they said to him: "A man possessing a hair garment, with a leather belt girded about his loins." Imme-

diately he said: "It was E·li'jah the Tish'bite."

9 And he proceeded to send to him a chief of fifty with his fifty. When he went up to him, there he was sitting upon the top of the mountain. He now spoke to him: "Man of the [true] God, the king himself has spoken, 'Do come down.' " 10 But E·li'jah answered and spoke to the chief of the fifty: "Well, if I am a man of God, let fire come down from the heavens and eat you up and your fifty." And fire came descending from the heavens and went eating up him and his fifty.

11 So he sent again to him another chief of fifty with his fifty. In turn he answered and spoke to him: "Man of the [true] God, this is what the king has said, 'Do come down quickly.' " 12 But E·li'jah answered and spoke to them: "If I am a man of the [true] God, let fire come down from the heavens and eat up you and your fifty." And fire of God came descending from the heavens and went eating up him and his fifty.

13 And he went sending again a third chief of fifty and his fifty. But the third chief of fifty went up and came and bent down upon his knees in front of E·li'jah and began to implore favor of him and speak to him: "Man of the [true] God, please let my soul and the soul of these fifty servants of yours be precious in your eyes. 14 Here fire came down from the heavens and went eating up the two former chiefs of fifty and their fifties, but now let my soul be precious in your eyes."

15 At that the angel of Jehovah spoke to E·li'jah: "Go down with him. Do not be afraid because of

him." So he rose and went down with him to the king. 16 Then he spoke to him: "This is what Jehovah has said, 'For the reason that you have sent messengers to inquire of Ba′al-ze′bub the god of Ek′ron, is it because there is no God at all in Israel of whose word to inquire? Therefore as regards the couch upon which you have gone up, you will not come down off it, because you will positively die.'" 17 And he gradually died, according to the word of Jehovah that E·li′jah had spoken; and Je·ho′ram began to reign in place of him, in the second year of Je·ho′ram the son of Je·hosh′a·phat the king of Judah, because he had not come to have a son.

18 As for the rest of A·ha·zi′ah's things that he did, are they not written in the book of the affairs of the days of the kings of Israel?

2 And it came about that when Jehovah was to take E·li′jah in a windstorm up to the heavens, E·li′jah and E·li′sha proceeded to go from Gil′gal. 2 And E·li′jah began to say to E·li′sha: "Sit here, please, because Jehovah himself has sent me clear to Beth′el." But E·li′sha said: "As Jehovah is living and as your soul is living, I will not leave you." So they went down to Beth′el. 3 Then the sons of the prophets that were at Beth′el came out to E·li′sha and said to him: "Do you really know that today Jehovah is taking your master from headship over you?" At this he said: "I too well know it. BE silent."

4 E·li′jah now said to him: "E·li′sha, sit here, please, because Jehovah himself has sent me to Jer′i·cho." But he said: "As Jehovah is living and as your soul is living, I will not leave you." So they came on to Jer′i·cho. 5 Then the sons of the prophets that were at Jer′i·cho approached E·li′sha and said to him: "Do you really know that today Jehovah is taking your master from headship over you?" At this he said: "I too well know it. BE silent."

6 E·li′jah now said to him: "Sit here, please, because Jehovah himself has sent me to the Jordan." But he said: "As Jehovah is living and as your soul is living, I will not leave you." So both of them went on. 7 And there were fifty men of the sons of the prophets that went and kept standing in view at a distance; but, as for both of them, they stood by the Jordan. 8 Then E·li′jah took his official garment and wrapped it up and struck the waters, and gradually they were divided this way and that way, so that both of them went across on the dry ground.

9 And it came about that as soon as they had gone across E·li′jah himself said to E·li′sha: "Ask what I should do for you before I am taken from you." To this E·li′sha said: "Please, that two parts in your spirit may come to me." 10 At that he said: "You have asked a difficult thing. If you see me when taken from you, it will happen to you that way; but if [you do] not, it will not happen."

11 And it came about that as they were walking along, speaking as they walked, why, look! a fiery war chariot and fiery horses, and they proceeded to make a separation between them both; and E·li′jah went ascending in the windstorm to the heavens. 12 All the while E·li′sha was seeing it, and he was crying out: "My father, my father, the war chariot of Israel and his horsemen!" And he did not see him any more. Consequently he took hold of his own garments and ripped them into two pieces. 13 After that he picked up the official garment of E·li′jah that had fallen off him, and went back and stood by the shore of the Jordan. 14 Then he took the official garment of E·li′jah that had fallen off him and struck the waters and said: "Where is Jehovah the God of E·li′jah, even He?" When he struck the waters, then they were gradually divided this way and that way, so that E·li′sha went across.

15 When the sons of the prophets that were at Jer′i·cho saw him some way off, they began to say: "The spirit of E·li′jah has settled down upon E·li′sha." Accordingly they came to meet him and bowed down to him to the earth. 16 And they went on to say to him: "Here, now, there are with your servants fifty men, valiant persons. Let them go, please, and look for your master. It may be that the spirit of Jehovah has lifted him up and then thrown him upon one of the mountains or in one of the valleys." But he said: "You must not send them." 17 And they kept urging him until he was embarrassed, so that he said: "Send." They now sent fifty men; and they kept looking for three days, but they did not find him. 18 When they returned to him, he was dwelling in Jer′i·cho. Then he said to them: "Did I not say to you, 'Do not go'?"

19 In time the men of the city said to E·li′sha: "Here, now, the situation of the city is good, just as my master is seeing; but the water is bad, and the land is causing miscarriages." 20 At that he said: "Fetch me a small new bowl and put salt in it." So they fetched it for him. 21 Then he went on out to the source of the water and threw salt in it and said: "This is what Jehovah has said, 'I do make this water healthful. No more will death or any causing of miscarriages result from it.'" 22 And the water continues healed down to this day, according to E·li′sha's word that he spoke.

23 And he proceeded to go up from there to Beth′el. As he was going up on the way, there were small boys that came out from the city and began to jeer him and that kept saying to him: "Go up, you baldhead! Go up, you baldhead!" 24 Finally he turned behind him and saw them and called down evil upon them in the name of Jehovah. Then two she-bears came out from the woods and went tearing to pieces forty-two children of their number. 25 And he kept going from there to Mount Car′mel,

and from there he returned to Sa·mar′i·a.

3 As for Je·ho′ram the son of A′hab, he became king over Israel in Sa·mar′i·a in the eighteenth year of Je·hosh′a·phat the king of Judah, and he continued to reign for twelve years. 2 And he kept on doing what was bad in Jehovah's eyes, only not like his father or like his mother, but he removed the sacred pillar of Ba′al that his father had made. 3 Only he stuck to the sins of Jer·o·bo′am the son of Ne′bat, with which he caused Israel to sin. He did not depart from them.

4 As regards Me′sha the king of Mo′ab, he became a sheep raiser, and he paid to the king of Israel a hundred thousand lambs and a hundred thousand unshorn male sheep. 5 And it came about that as soon as A′hab died, the king of Mo′ab began to revolt against the king of Israel. 6 Consequently King Je·ho′ram went out on that day from Sa·mar′i·a and mustered all Israel. 7 He went farther and now sent to Je·hosh′a·phat the king of Judah, saying: "The king of Mo′ab himself has revolted against me. Will you go with me to Mo′ab in war?" To this he said: "I shall go. I am the same as you are; my people are the same as your people; my horses are the same as your horses." 8 And he went on to say: "By which particular way shall we go up?" So he said: "By the way of the wilderness of E′dom."

9 And the king of Israel and the king of Judah and the king of E′dom proceeded to go, and they kept going their way around for seven days, and there proved to be no water for the camp and for the domestic animals that were following their steps. 10 At length the king of Israel said: "How unfortunate that Jehovah has called these three kings to give them into the hand of Mo′ab!" 11 At that Je·hosh′a·phat said: "Is there not here a prophet of Jehovah? Then let us inquire of Jehovah through him." So one of the servants of the king of Israel answered and

said: "There is here E·li'sha the son of Sha'phat, who poured out water upon the hands of E·li'jah." 12 Then Je·hosh'a·phat said: "The word of Jehovah exists with him." Accordingly the king of Israel and Je·hosh'a·phat and the king of E'dom went down to him.

13 And E·li'sha proceeded to say to the king of Israel: "What do I have to do with you? Go to the prophets of your father and to the prophets of your mother." But the king of Israel said to him: "No, for Jehovah has called these three kings to give them into the hand of Mo'ab." 14 To this E·li'sha said: "As Jehovah of armies before whom I do stand is living, if it were not that it is the face of Je·hosh'a·phat the king of Judah for which I am having consideration, I would not look at you or see you. 15 And now YOU men fetch me a string-instrument player." And it occurred that, as soon as the string-instrument player played, the hand of Jehovah came to be upon him. 16 And he went on to say: "This is what Jehovah has said, 'Let there be a making of this torrent valley full of ditches; 17 for this is what Jehovah has said: "YOU men will not see a wind, and YOU will not see a downpour; yet that torrent valley will be filled with water, and YOU men will certainly drink [from it], YOU and YOUR livestock and YOUR domestic animals."' 18 And this will indeed be a trivial thing in the eyes of Jehovah, and he will certainly give Mo'ab into YOUR hand. 19 And YOU must strike down every fortified city and every choice city, and every good tree YOU should fell, and all the springs of water YOU should stop up, and every good tract of land YOU should mar with stones."

20 And it came about in the morning, at the time of the going up of the grain offering, that, look! water was coming from the direction of E'dom, and the land came to be filled with the water.

21 As regards all the Mo'ab·ites, they heard that the kings had come up to fight against them. Consequently they called together [men] from as many as were girding on a belt and upward, and they began standing at the boundary. 22 When they got up early in the morning, the sun itself flashed upon the water, so that the Mo'ab·ites from the opposite side saw the water red like blood. 23 And they began to say: "This is blood! The kings have unquestionably been put to the sword, and they went striking one another down. So now, to the spoil, O Mo'ab!" 24 When they came into the camp of Israel, the Israelites immediately rose up and began striking the Mo'ab·ites down so that they took to flight from before them. Hence they came into Mo'ab, striking the Mo'ab·ites down as they came. 25 And the cities they went throwing down, and, as for every good tract of land, they would pitch each one his stone and actually fill it; and every spring of water they would stop up, and every good tree they would fell, until they left only the stones of Kir-har'e·seth remaining in it; and the slingers began going around it and striking it down.

26 When the king of Mo'ab saw that the battle had proved too strong for him, he at once took with him seven hundred men drawing sword to break through to the king of E'dom; but they were not able to. 27 Finally he took his first-born son who was going to reign in place of him and offered him up as a burnt sacrifice upon the wall. And there came to be great indignation against Israel, so that they pulled away from against him and returned to their land.

4 Now there was a certain woman of the wives of the sons of the prophets that cried out to E·li'sha, saying: "Your servant, my husband, is dead; and you yourself well know that your own servant had continually feared Jehovah, and the creditor himself has come to take both my children for his slaves." 2 At this E·li'sha said to her: "What shall I do for you?

Tell me; what do you have in the house?" To this she said: "Your maidservant has nothing at all in the house but a spouted jar of oil." 3 Then he said: "Go, ask for vessels for yourself from outside, from all your neighbors, empty vessels. Do not hold yourself to a few. 4 And you must go and close the door behind yourself and your sons, and you must pour out into all these vessels, and the full ones you should set aside." 5 Upon that she went away from him.

When she closed the door behind herself and her sons, they were bringing the vessels near to her, and she was doing the pouring out. 6 And it came about that as soon as the vessels were full she went on to say to her son: "Do bring still another vessel near to me." But he said to her: "There is no other vessel." At that the oil stopped. 7 So she came in and told the man of the [true] God, and he now said: "Go, sell the oil and pay off your debts, and you [and] your sons should live from what is left."

8 And it came about one day that E·li'sha went passing along to Shu'nem, where there was a prominent woman, and she began to constrain him to eat bread. And it came about that as often as he would pass by, he would turn aside there to eat bread. 9 At length she said to her husband: "Here, now, I well know that it is a holy man of God that is passing by us constantly. 10 Please, let us make a little roof chamber on the wall and put there for him a couch and a table and a chair and a lampstand; and it must occur that whenever he comes in to us he can turn aside there."

11 And it came about one day that as usual he came in there and turned aside to the roof chamber and lay down there. 12 So he said to Ge·ha'zi his attendant: "Call this Shu'nam·mite woman." At that he called her that she might stand before him. 13 Then he said to him: "Please, say to her, 'Here you have restricted yourself

for us with all this restriction. What is there to be done for you? Is there anything to speak to the king or to the chief of the army for you?'" To this she said: "In among my own people I am dwelling." 14 And he went on to say: "What, then, is there to be done for her?" Ge·ha'zi now said: "For a fact, a son she does not have, and her husband is old." 15 Immediately he said: "Call her." So he called her, and she kept standing at the entrance. 16 Then he said: "At this appointed time next year you will be embracing a son." But she said: "No, my master, O man of the [true] God! Do not tell lies in connection with your maidservant."

17 However, the woman became pregnant and gave birth to a son at this appointed time the next year, just as E·li'sha had spoken to her. 18 And the child kept on growing up, and it came about one day that he went out as usual to his father with the reapers. 19 And he kept saying to his father: "My head, O my head!" At last he said to the attendant: "Carry him to his mother." 20 Accordingly he carried him and brought him to his mother. And he kept sitting upon her knees until noon, and gradually he died. 21 Then she went up and laid him upon the couch of the man of the [true] God and closed the door upon him and went out. 22 She now called her husband and said: "Do send me, please, one of the attendants and one of the she-asses, and let me run as far as the man of the [true] God and return." 23 But he said: "Why are you going to him today? It is not a new moon nor a sabbath." However, she said: "It is all right." 24 So she saddled up the she-ass and said to her attendant: "Drive and go ahead. Do not hold back for my sake from riding unless I shall have said so to you."

25 And she proceeded to go and come to the man of the [true] God at Mount Car'mel. And it came about that, as soon as the man of

the [true] God saw her out ahead, he immediately said to Ge·ha′zi his attendant: "Look! The Shu′nam·mite woman over there. 26 Now run, please, to meet her and say to her, 'Is it all right with you? Is it all right with your husband? Is it all right with the child?'" To this she said: "It is all right." 27 When she came to the man of the [true] God at the mountain, she at once took hold of him by his feet. At this Ge·ha′zi came near to push her away, but the man of the [true] God said: "Let her alone, for her soul is bitter within her; and Jehovah himself has hidden it from me and not told me." 28 She now said: "Did I ask for a son through my lord? Did I not say, 'You must not lead me to a false hope'?"

29 Immediately he said to Ge·ha′zi: "Gird up your loins and take my staff in your hand and go. In case you encounter anyone, you must not greet him; and in case anyone should greet you, you must not answer him. And you must place my staff upon the face of the boy." 30 At this the mother of the boy said: "As Jehovah is living and as your soul is living, I will not leave you." Therefore he got up and went with her. 31 And Ge·ha′zi himself passed along before them and then put the staff upon the boy's face, but there was no voice nor paying of attention. So he went back to meet him and told him, saying: "The boy did not wake up."

32 At last E·li′sha came into the house, and there the boy was dead, being laid upon his couch. 33 Then he came in and closed the door behind them both and began to pray to Jehovah. 34 Finally he went up and lay down upon the child and put his own mouth upon his mouth and his own eyes upon his eyes and his own palms upon his palms and kept bent over him, and gradually the child's flesh grew warm. 35 Then he began walking again in the house, once this way and once that way, after which he went up and bent over him. And the boy began to sneeze as many as seven times, after which the boy opened his eyes. 36 He now called Ge·ha′zi and said: "Call this Shu′nam·mite woman." So he called her and she came in to him. Then he said: "Lift up your son." 37 And she proceeded to come in and fall at his feet and bow down to him to the earth, after which she lifted up her son and went out.

38 And E·li′sha himself returned to Gil′gal, and there was famine in the land. As the sons of the prophets were sitting before him, he in time said to his attendant: "Put the large cooking pot on and boil stew for the sons of the prophets." 39 Accordingly a certain one went out to the field to pick mallows, and he got to find a wild vine and went picking wild gourds from it, his garment full, and then came and sliced them into the stewpot, for they were not acquainted with them. 40 Later they poured it out for the men to eat. And it came about that, as soon as they ate from the stew, they themselves cried out and began saying: "There is death in the pot, O man of the [true] God." And they were not able to eat. 41 So he said: "FETCH, then, flour." After he threw it into the pot, he went on to say: "Pour out for the people that they may eat." And nothing injurious proved to be in the pot.

42 And there was a man that came from Ba′al-shal′i·shah, and he came bringing to the man of the [true] God bread of the first ripe fruits, twenty barley loaves, and new grain in his bread bag. Then he said: "Give it to the people that they may eat." 43 However, his waiter said: "How shall I put this before a hundred men?" To this he said: "Give it to the people that they may eat, for this is what Jehovah has said, 'There will be an eating and a having of leftovers.'" 44 At that he put it before them, and they began to eat, and they had leftovers according to the word of Jehovah.

5 Now a certain Na′a·man, the chief of the army of the king of Syria, had become a great man before his lord and held in esteem, because it was by him that Jehovah had given salvation to Syria; and the man himself had proved to be a valiant, mighty man, though a leper. 2 And the Syrians, for their part, had gone out as marauder bands, and they got to take captive from the land of Israel a little girl, and she came to be before Na′a·man's wife. 3 In time she said to her mistress: "If only my lord were before the prophet that is in Sa·mar′i·a! In that case he would recover him from his leprosy." 4 Subsequently someone came and reported to his lord, saying: "It was like this and that that the girl spoke who is from the land of Israel."

5 Then the king of Syria said: "Get going! Come, and let me send a letter to the king of Israel." So he proceeded to go and take in his hand ten talents of silver and six thousand pieces of gold and ten changes of garments. 6 And he came bringing the letter to the king of Israel, saying: "And now at the same time that this letter comes to you, here I do send to you Na′a·man my servant, that you may recover him from his leprosy." 7 And it came about that as soon as the king of Israel read the letter, he immediately ripped his garments apart and said: "Am I God, to put to death and to preserve alive? For this person is sending to me to recover a man from his leprosy; for just take note, please, you men, and see how he is seeking a quarrel with me."

8 And it came about that, as soon as E·li′sha the man of the [true] God heard that the king of Israel had ripped his garments apart, he at once sent to the king, saying: "Why did you rip your garments apart? Let him come, please, to me that he may know that there exists a prophet in Israel." 9 So Na′a·man came with his horses and his war chariots and stood at the entrance of the house of E·li′sha. 10 However, E·li′sha sent a messenger to him, saying: "Going there, you must bathe seven times in the Jordan that your flesh may come back to you; and be clean." 11 At this Na′a·man grew indignant and began to go away and say: "Here I had said [to myself], 'To me he will come out all the way and will certainly stand and call upon the name of Jehovah his God and move his hand to and fro over the place and actually give the leper recovery.' 12 Are not the A·ba′nah and the Phar′par, the rivers of Damascus, better than all the waters of Israel? Can I not bathe in them and certainly be clean?" With that he turned and went away in a rage.

13 His servants now approached and spoke to him and said: "My father, had it been a great thing that the prophet himself had spoken to you, would you not do it? How much more, then, since he said to you, 'Bathe and be clean'?" 14 At that he went down and began to plunge into the Jordan seven times according to the word of the man of the [true] God; after which his flesh came back like the flesh of a little boy and he became clean.

15 Then he went back to the man of the [true] God, he with all his camp, and came and stood before him and said: "Here, now, I certainly know that there is no God anywhere in the earth but in Israel. And now accept, please, a blessing gift from your servant." 16 However, he said: "As Jehovah before whom I do stand is living, I will not accept it." And he began to urge him to accept it, but he kept refusing. 17 Finally Na′a·man said: "If not, please, let there be given to your servant some ground, the load of a pair of mules; because your servant will no more render up a burnt offering or a sacrifice to any other gods but to Jehovah. 18 In this thing may Jehovah forgive your servant: When my lord comes into the

house of Rim′mon to bow down there, and he is supporting himself upon my hand, and I have to bow down at the house of Rim′mon, when I bow down at the house of Rim′mon may Jehovah, please, forgive your servant in this respect." 19 At this he said to him: "Go in peace." Accordingly he went away from him for a good stretch of the land.

20 Then Ge·ha′zi the attendant of E·li′sha the man of the [true] God said: "Here my master has spared Na′a·man this Syrian by not accepting from his hand what he brought. As Jehovah is living, I will run after him and take something from him." 21 And Ge·ha′zi went chasing after Na′a·man. When Na′a·man saw someone running after him, he at once got down from his chariot to meet him and then said: "Is all well?" 22 To this he said: "All is well. My master himself has sent me, saying, 'Look! Just now there have come to me two young men from the mountainous region of E′phra·im from the sons of the prophets. Do give them, please, a talent of silver and two changes of garments.'" 23 At that Na′a·man said: "Go on, take two talents." And he kept urging him and finally bound up two talents of silver in two bags, with two changes of garments, and gave them to two of his attendants, that they might carry them before him.

24 When he came to O′phel, he immediately took them from their hand and deposited them in the house and sent the men away. So off they went. 25 And he himself came in and then stood by his master. E·li′sha now said to him: "Where [did you come] from, Ge·ha′zi?" But he said: "Your servant did not go anywhere at all." 26 At that he said to him: "Did not my heart itself go along just as the man turned [to get down] off his chariot to meet you? Is it a time to accept silver or to accept garments or olive groves or vineyards or sheep or cattle or menservants or maidservants? 27 So the lep-

rosy of Na′a·man will stick to you and your offspring to time indefinite." Immediately he went out from before him, a leper white as snow.

6 And the sons of the prophets began to say to E·li′sha: "Look, now! The place where we are dwelling before you is too cramped for us. 2 Let us go, please, as far as the Jordan and take from there each one a beam and make for ourselves there a place in which to dwell." So he said: "Go." 3 And a certain one went on to say: "Come on, please, and go with your servants." At that he said: "I myself shall go." 4 Accordingly he went with them, and they finally came to the Jordan and began to cut down the trees. 5 And it came about that a certain one was felling his beam, and the axhead itself fell into the water. And he began to cry out and say: "Alas, my master, for it was borrowed!" 6 Then the man of the [true] God said: "Where did it fall?" So he showed him the place. Immediately he cut off a piece of wood and threw it there and made the axhead float. 7 He now said: "Lift it up for yourself." At once he thrust his hand out and took it.

8 And the king of Syria, for his part, became involved in war against Israel. Accordingly he took counsel with his servants, saying: "At such and such a place YOU will encamp with me." 9 Then the man of the [true] God sent to the king of Israel, saying: "Guard yourself against passing by this place, because there is where the Syrians are coming down." 10 So the king of Israel sent to the place that the man of the [true] God had said to him. And he warned him, and he kept away from there, not once or twice.

11 Consequently the heart of the king of Syria became enraged over this matter, so that he called his servants and said to them: "Will YOU not tell me who from those who belong to us is for the king of Israel?" 12 Then one of his servants said: "None, my lord the king,

but it is E·li'sha the prophet who is in Israel that tells the king of Israel the things that you speak in your inner bedroom." 13 So he said: "You men go and see where he is, that I may send and take him." Later the report was made to him, saying: "There he is in Do'than." 14 Immediately he sent horses and war chariots and a heavy military force there; and they proceeded to come by night and close in upon the city.

15 When the minister of the man of the [true] God rose early to get up, and went out, why, there a military force was surrounding the city with horses and war chariots. At once his attendant said to him: "Alas, my master! What shall we do?" 16 But he said: "Do not be afraid, for there are more who are with us than those who are with them." 17 And E·li'sha began to pray and say: "O Jehovah, open his eyes, please, that he may see." Immediately Jehovah opened the attendant's eyes, so that he saw; and, look! the mountainous region was full of horses and war chariots of fire all around E·li'sha.

18 When they began to come down to him, E·li'sha went on to pray to Jehovah and say: "Please, strike this nation with blindness." So he struck them with blindness according to the word of E·li'sha. 19 E·li'sha now said to them: "This is not the way, and this is not the city. Follow me, and let me conduct you to the man you look for." However, he conducted them to Sa·mar'i·a.

20 And it came about that as soon as they arrived at Sa·mar'i·a, E·li'sha then said: "O Jehovah, open the eyes of these that they may see." Immediately Jehovah opened their eyes, and they got to see; and here they were in the middle of Sa·mar'i·a. 21 The king of Israel now said to E·li'sha as soon as he saw them: "Shall I strike [them] down, shall I strike [them] down, my father?" 22 But he said: "You must not strike [them] down. Are those whom you have taken captive with your sword

and with your bow the ones that you are striking down? Set bread and water before them that they may eat and drink and go to their lord." 23 Accordingly he spread a great feast for them; and they began to eat and drink, after which he sent them away and they went to their lord. And not once did the marauding bands of the Syrians come again into the land of Israel.

24 And it came about afterward that Ben-ha'dad the king of Syria proceeded to collect all his camp together and to go up and besiege Sa·mar'i·a. 25 In time a great famine arose in Sa·mar'i·a, and, look! they were besieging it until an ass's head got to be worth eighty silver pieces, and the fourth of a cab measure of dove's dung was worth five silver pieces. 26 And it came about as the king of Israel was passing along upon the wall that a certain woman cried out to him, saying: "Do save, O my lord the king!" 27 To this he said: "If Jehovah does not save you, from what [source] shall I save you? either from the threshing floor or from the wine or oil press?" 28 And the king went on to say to her: "What is the matter with you?" So she said: "This very woman said to me, 'Give your son that we may eat him today, and my own son we shall eat tomorrow.' 29 Accordingly we boiled my son and ate him. Then I said to her on the next day, 'Give your son that we may eat him.' But she hid her son."

30 And it came about that as soon as the king heard the woman's words, he immediately ripped his garments apart; and as he was passing along upon the wall, the people got to see, and, look! sackcloth was underneath upon his flesh. 31 And he went on to say: "So may God do to me, and so may he add to it, if the head of E·li'sha the son of Sha'phat continues standing upon him today!"

32 And E·li'sha was sitting in his own house, and the older men were sitting with him, when he sent a man from before him. Before the

messenger could come in to him, he himself said to the older men: "Have you seen how this son of a murderer has sent to take off my head? See to it: as soon as the messenger comes, close the door, and you must press him back with the door. Is there not the sound of the feet of his lord behind him?" 33 While he was yet speaking with them, here was the messenger coming down to him, and [the king] proceeded to say: "Here this is the calamity from Jehovah. Why should I wait any longer for Jehovah?"

7 E·li′sha now said: "Listen, you men, to the word of Jehovah. This is what Jehovah has said, 'Tomorrow about this time a seah measure of fine flour will be worth a shekel, and two seah measures of barley worth a shekel in the gateway of Sa·mar′i·a.'" 2 At that the adjutant upon whose hand the king was supporting himself answered the man of the [true] God and said: "If Jehovah were making floodgates in the heavens, could this thing take place?" To this he said: "Here you are seeing it with your own eyes, but from it you will not eat."

3 And there were four men, lepers, that happened to be at the entrance of the gate; and they began to say the one to the other: "Why are we sitting here until we have died? 4 If we had said, 'Let us enter the city,' when the famine is in the city, we would also have to die there. And if we do sit here, we shall also have to die. So now come and let us invade the camp of the Syrians. If they preserve us alive, we shall live; but if they put us to death, then we shall have to die." 5 Accordingly they rose up in the evening darkness to enter the camp of the Syrians; and they got to come as far as the outskirts of the camp of the Syrians, and, look! nobody was there.

6 And Jehovah himself had caused the camp of the Syrians to hear the sound of war chariots, the sound of horses, the sound of a great military force, so that they said to one another: "Look! The king of Israel has hired against us the kings of the Hit′tites and the kings of Egypt to come against us!" 7 Immediately they got up and went fleeing in the evening darkness and leaving their tents and their horses and their asses—the camp just as it was—and they kept fleeing for their soul.

8 When these lepers came as far as the outskirts of the camp, they then entered into one tent and began to eat and drink and carry from there silver and gold and garments and go off and stick them away. After that they returned and entered into another tent and carried things from there and went off and stuck them away.

9 Finally they began to say the one to the other: "It is not right what we are doing. This day is a day of good news! If we are hesitating, and we actually wait until the morning light, guilt must also catch up with us. So now come and let us enter and make report at the king's house." 10 So they came and called to the gatekeepers of the city and reported to them, saying: "We came into the camp of the Syrians, and, look! there was nobody there nor sound of a man, but only the horses tied and the asses tied and the tents just as they were." 11 At once the gatekeepers called out and they reported to the king's house inside.

12 Immediately the king rose up by night and said to his servants: "Let me tell you, please, what the Syrians have done to us. They well know that we are hungry; and so they went out from the camp to hide themselves in the field, saying, 'They will come out from the city, and we shall catch them alive, and into the city we shall enter.'" 13 Then one of his servants answered and said: "Let them take, please, five of the remaining horses that have remained in the city. Look! They are the same as all the crowd of Israel that have remained in it. Look! They are the same as all the crowd of Israel that have perished. And let us send

out and see." 14 Accordingly they took two chariots with horses and the king sent them out after the camp of the Syrians, saying: "Go and see." 15 At that they went following them as far as the Jordan; and, look! all the way was full of garments and utensils that the Syrians had thrown away as they were hurrying away. Then the messengers returned and reported to the king.

16 And the people proceeded to go out and plunder the camp of the Syrians; and so a seah measure of fine flour came to be worth a shekel, and two seah measures of barley worth a shekel, according to the word of Jehovah. 17 And the king himself had appointed the adjutant upon whose hand he was supporting himself to have charge of the gateway; and the people kept trampling him in the gateway, so that he died, just as the man of the [true] God had spoken, when he spoke at the time that the king came down to him. 18 Thus it came about just as the man of the [true] God had spoken to the king, saying: "Two seah measures of barley worth a shekel and a seah measure of fine flour worth a shekel it will come to be tomorrow at this time in the gateway of Sa·mar'i·a." 19 But the adjutant answered the man of the [true] God and said: "Even if Jehovah were making floodgates in the heavens, could it take place according to this word?" To this he said: "Here you are seeing it with your own eyes, but from it you will not eat." 20 Thus it happened to him like that, when the people kept trampling him in the gateway, so that he died.

8 And E·li'sha himself had spoken to the woman whose son he had revived, saying: "Rise up and go, you with your household, and reside as an alien wherever you can reside as an alien; for Jehovah has called for a famine, and, besides, it must come upon the land for seven years." 2 So the woman got up and did according to the word of the man of the [true] God

and went, she with her household, and took up residence as an alien in the land of the Phi·lis'tines for seven years.

3 And it came about at the end of seven years that the woman proceeded to return from the land of the Phi·lis'tines and go forth to cry out to the king for her house and for her field. 4 Now the king was speaking to Ge·ha'zi the attendant of the man of the [true] God, saying: "Do relate to me, please, all the great things that E·li'sha has done." 5 And it came about that as he was relating to the king how he had revived the dead one, why, here the woman whose son he had revived was crying out to the king for her house and for her field. At once Ge·ha'zi said: "My lord the king, this is the woman, and this is her son whom E·li'sha revived." 6 At that the king asked the woman, and she went on to relate to him the story. Then the king gave her a court official, saying: "Return all that belongs to her and all the products of the field from the day of her leaving the land until now."

7 And E·li'sha proceeded to come to Damascus; and Ben·ha'dad the king of Syria was sick. Accordingly the report was made to him, saying: "The man of the [true] God has come as far as here." 8 At that the king said to Haz'a·el: "Take a gift in your hand and go and meet the man of the [true] God, and you must inquire of Jehovah through him, saying, 'Shall I revive from this sickness?'" 9 So Haz'a·el went to meet him and took a gift in his hand, even every sort of good thing of Damascus, the load of forty camels, and came and stood before him and said: "Your son, Ben·ha'dad, the king of Syria, has sent me to you, saying, 'Shall I revive from this sickness?'" 10 Then E·li'sha said to him: "Go, say to him, 'You will positively revive,' and Jehovah has shown me that he will positively die." 11 And he kept a fixed look and kept it set to the point of embarrassment.

Then the man of the [true] God gave way to weeping. 12 At this Haz·a'el said: "Why is my lord weeping?" To this he said: "Because I well know what injury you will do to the sons of Israel. Their fortified places you will consign to the fire, and their choice men you will kill with the sword, and their children you will dash to pieces, and their pregnant women you will rip up." 13 Upon that Haz·a'el said: "What is your servant, [who is a mere] dog, that he could do this great thing?" But E·li'sha said: "Jehovah has shown me you as king over Syria."

14 After that he went from E·li'sha and came to his own lord, who then said to him: "What did E·li'sha say to you?" To this he said: "He said to me, 'You will positively revive.'" 15 And it came about on the next day that he proceeded to take a coverlet and dip it in water and spread it out over his face, so that he died. And Haz·a'el began to reign in place of him.

16 And in the fifth year of Je·ho'ram the son of A'hab the king of Israel, while Je·hosh'a·phat was king of Judah, Je·ho'ram the son of Je·hosh'a·phat the king of Judah became king. 17 Thirty-two years old he happened to be when he became king, and for eight years he reigned in Jerusalem. 18 And he went walking in the way of the kings of Israel, just as those of the house of A'hab had done; for it was A'hab's daughter that became his wife, and he kept doing what was bad in Jehovah's eyes. 19 And Jehovah did not want to bring Judah to ruin for the sake of David his servant, just as he had promised him to give a lamp to him [and] to his sons always.

20 In his days E'dom revolted from under the hand of Judah, and then made a king reign over them. 21 Consequently Je·ho'ram passed over to Za'ir, also all the chariots with him. And it came about that he himself rose up by night and got to strike down the E'dom·ites that were surrounding him and the chiefs of the chariots; and the people went fleeing to their tents. 22 But E'dom kept up its revolt from under the hand of Judah down to this day. It was then that Lib'nah began to revolt at that time.

23 And the rest of the affairs of Je·ho'ram and all that he did, are they not written in the book of the affairs of the days of the kings of Judah? 24 Finally Je·ho'ram lay down with his forefathers and was buried with his forefathers in the city of David. And A·ha·zi'ah his son began to reign in place of him.

25 In the twelfth year of Je·ho'ram the son of A'hab the king of Israel, A·ha·zi'ah the son of Je·ho'ram the king of Judah became king. 26 Twenty-two years old was A·ha·zi'ah when he began to reign, and for one year he reigned in Jerusalem. And his mother's name was Ath·a·li'ah the granddaughter of Om'ri the king of Israel. 27 And he went walking in the way of the house of A'hab and kept doing what was bad in Jehovah's eyes, like the house of A'hab, for he was a relative of the house of A'hab by marriage. 28 Accordingly he went with Je·ho'ram the son of A'hab to the war against Haz·a'el the king of Syria at Ra'moth-gil'e·ad, but the Syrians struck down Je·ho'ram. 29 So Je·ho'ram the king returned to get healed at Jez're·el from the wounds that the Syrians got to inflict upon him at Ra'mah when he fought Haz·a'el the king of Syria. As for A·ha·zi'ah the son of Je·ho'ram the king of Judah, he went down to see Je·ho'ram the son of A'hab in Jez're·el, for he was sick.

9 And E·li'sha the prophet, for his part, called one of the sons of the prophets and then said to him: "Gird up your loins and take this flask of oil in your hand and go to Ra'moth-gil'e·ad. 2 When you have come in there, see Je'hu the son of Je·hosh'a·phat the son of Nim'shi there; and you must come in and make him get up from the midst of his brothers

and bring him into the innermost chamber. 3 And you must take the flask of oil and pour it out upon his head and say, 'This is what Jehovah has said: "I do anoint you as king over Israel."' And you must open the door and flee and not wait."

4 And the attendant, the prophet's attendant, got on his way to Ra′moth-gil′e·ad. 5 When he came in, why, there the chiefs of the military force were seated. He now said: "There is a word I have for you, O chief." At this Je′hu said: "For which one of all of us?" Then he said: "For you, O chief." 6 So he got up and came into the house; and he proceeded to pour the oil out upon his head and say to him: "This is what Jehovah the God of Israel has said, 'I do anoint you as king over Jehovah's people, that is, over Israel. 7 And you must strike down the house of A′hab your lord, and I must avenge the blood of my servants the prophets and the blood of all the servants of Jehovah at the hand of Jez′e·bel. 8 And the whole house of A′hab must perish; and I must cut off from A′hab anyone urinating against a wall and any helpless and worthless one in Israel. 9 And I must constitute the house of A′hab like the house of Jer·o·bo′am the son of Ne′bat and like the house of Ba′a·sha the son of A·hi′jah. 10 And Jez′e·bel the dogs will eat up in the tract of land at Jez′re·el, and there will be no one burying her.'" With that he opened the door and went fleeing.

11 As for Je′hu, he went out to the servants of his lord, and they began to say to him: "Is everything all right? Why did this crazy man come in to you?" But he said to them: "You yourselves well know the man and his sort of talk." 12 But they said: "It is false! Tell us, please." Then he said: "It was like this and like that that he talked to me, saying, 'This is what Jehovah has said: "I do anoint you as king over Israel."'" 13 At this they hurriedly took each one his garment and put it under him

upon the bare steps, and they began to blow the horn and say: "Je′hu has become king!" 14 And Je′hu the son of Je·hosh′a·phat the son of Nim′shi proceeded to conspire against Je·ho′ram.

And Je·ho′ram himself had happened to be keeping guard at Ra′moth-gil′e·ad, he with all Israel, because of Haz′a·el the king of Syria. 15 Later Je·ho′ram the king returned to get healed at Jez′-re·el from the wounds that the Syrians got to inflict upon him when he fought Haz′a·el the king of Syria.

Je′hu now said: "If your soul agrees, do not let anyone go out in escape from the city to go and make report in Jez′re·el." 16 And Je′hu began to ride and go to Jez′re·el; for Je·ho′ram was lying there, and A·ha·zi′ah the king of Judah himself had gone down to see Je·ho′ram. 17 And the watchman was standing upon the tower in Jez′re·el, and he got to see the heaving mass of Je′hu's [men] as he was coming, and he at once said: "There is a heaving mass [of men] that I am seeing." At that Je·ho′ram said: "Take a cavalryman and send him to meet them, and let him say, 'Is there peace?'" 18 Accordingly a rider on a horse went to meet him and said: "This is what the king has said, 'Is there peace?'" But Je′hu said: "What do you have to do with 'peace'? Get around to my rear!"

And the watchman went on to report, saying: "The messenger came as far as to them, but he has not returned." 19 So he sent out a second rider on a horse, who, when he came to them, proceeded to say: "This is what the king has said, 'Is there peace?'" But Je′hu said: "What do you have to do with 'peace'? Get around to my rear!"

20 And the watchman went on to report, saying: "He came as far as to them, but he has not returned; and the driving is like the driving of Je′hu the grandson of Nim′shi, for it is with madness that he drives." 21 At that Je·ho′-

ram said: "Hitch up!" So his war chariot was hitched up and Je·ho'ram the king of Israel and A·ha·zi'ah the king of Judah went out, each in his own war chariot. As they continued on out to meet Je'hu, they got to find him in the tract of land of Na'both the Jez're·el·ite.

22 And it came about that as soon as Je·ho'ram saw Je'hu, he immediately said: "Is there peace, Je'hu?" But he said: "What peace could there be as long as there are the fornications of Jez'e·bel your mother and her many sorceries?" 23 At once Je·ho'ram made a turn with his hands, that he might flee, and said to A·ha·zi'ah: "There is trickery, A·ha·zi'ah!" 24 And Je'hu himself filled his hand with a bow and proceeded to shoot Je·ho'ram between the arms, so that the arrow came out at his heart, and he collapsed in his war chariot. 25 He now said to Bid'kar his adjutant: "Lift him up; throw him into the tract of the field of Na'both the Jez're·el·ite; for remember: I and you were riding teams behind A'hab his father, and Jehovah himself lifted up this pronouncement against him: 26 ' "Certainly the blood of Na'both and the blood of his sons I saw yesterday," is the utterance of Jehovah, "and I shall certainly repay you in this tract of land," is the utterance of Jehovah.' So now, lift him up; throw him into the tract of land according to the word of Jehovah."

27 And A·ha·zi'ah the king of Judah himself saw it and took to flight by the way of the garden house. (Later Je'hu went in pursuit of him and said: "Him also! STRIKE him down!") So they struck him down while in the chariot on the way up to Gur, which is by Ib'le·am. And he continued his flight to Me·gid'do and got to die there. 28 Then his servants carried him in a chariot to Jerusalem, and so they buried him in his grave with his forefathers in the city of David. 29 And it was in the eleventh year of Je·ho'ram the son of A'hab that A·ha·zi'ah had become king over Judah.)

30 At length Je'hu came to Jez're·el, and Jez'e·bel herself heard of it. And she proceeded to paint her eyes with black paint and do her head up beautifully and to look down through the window. 31 And Je'hu himself came in by the gate. She now said: "Did it go all right with Zim'ri the killer of his lord?" 32 At that he raised his face toward the window and said: "Who is with me? Who?" Immediately two or three court officials looked down at him. 33 So he said: "Let her drop!" Then they let her drop, and some of her blood went spattering upon the wall and upon the horses; and he now trampled upon her. 34 After that he came on in and ate and drank and then said: "You men, please, take care of this accursed one and bury her, for she is the daughter of a king." 35 When they went to bury her, they did not find anything of her but the skull and the feet and the palms of the hands. 36 When they returned and told him, he went on to say: "It is the word of Jehovah that he spoke by means of his servant E·li'jah the Tish'bite, saying, 'In the tract of land of Jez're·el the dogs will eat the flesh of Jez'e·bel. 37 And the dead body of Jez'e·bel will certainly become as manure upon the face of the field in the tract of land of Jez're·el, that they may not say: "This is Jez'e·bel." ' "

10 Now A'hab had seventy sons in Sa·mar'i·a. Therefore Je'hu wrote letters and sent them to Sa·mar'i·a to the princes of Jez're·el, the older men and the caretakers of A'hab, saying: 2 "Now, then, at the very time that this letter comes to YOU there are with YOU the sons of YOUR lord, and there are with YOU the war chariots and the horses and a fortified city and the armor. 3 And YOU must see which is the best and most upright of the sons of YOUR lord and put him upon the throne of his father. Then fight for the house of YOUR lord."

4 And they became very greatly afraid and began to say: "Look! Two kings themselves did not stand before him, and how shall we ourselves stand?" **5** Consequently the one who was over the house and the one who was over the city and the older men and the caretakers sent to Je′hu, saying: "We are your servants, and everything that you say to us we shall do. We shall not make anyone king. What is good in your own eyes do."

6 At that he wrote them a second letter, saying: "If you belong to me, and it is my voice that you are obeying, take the heads of the men that are sons of your lord and come to me tomorrow at this time at Jez′re·el."

Now the sons of the king, seventy men, were with the distinguished men of the city that were bringing them up. **7** And it came about that as soon as the letter came to them, they went taking the sons of the king and slaughtering [them], seventy men, after which they put their heads in baskets and sent them to him at Jez′re·el. **8** Then the messenger came in and told him, saying: "They have brought the heads of the sons of the king." So he said: "Put them in two heaps at the entrance of the gate until morning." **9** And it came about in the morning that he proceeded to go out. Then he stood still and said to all the people: "You are righteous. Here I myself conspired against my lord, and I got to kill him; but who struck down all these? **10** Know, then, that nothing of Jehovah's word will fall [unfulfilled] to the earth that Jehovah has spoken against the house of A′hab; and Jehovah himself has done what he spoke by means of his servant E·li′jah." **11** Moreover, Je′hu went on to strike down all who were left over of the house of A′hab in Jez′re·el and all his distinguished men and his acquaintances and his priests, until he had let no survivor of his remain.

12 And he proceeded to rise and come in, then get on his way to Sa·mar′i·a. The binding house of the shepherds was on the way. **13** And Je′hu himself encountered the brothers of A·ha·zi′ah the king of Judah. When he said to them, "Who are you?" then they said: "We are the brothers of A·ha·zi′ah, and we are on our way down to ask if all is well with the sons of the king and the sons of the lady." **14** Immediately he said: "Seize them alive, you men!" So they seized them alive and slaughtered them at the cistern of the binding house, forty-two men, and he did not let a single one of them remain.

15 As he was going along from there he got to encounter Je·hon′a·dab the son of Re′chab [coming] to meet him. When he blessed him, he accordingly said to him: "Is your heart upright with me, just as my own heart is with your heart?"

To this Je·hon′a·dab said: "It is."

"If it is, do give me your hand."

So he gave him his hand. At that he made him get up into the chariot with him. **16** Then he said: "Do go along with me and look upon my toleration of no rivalry toward Jehovah." And they kept him riding with him in his war chariot. **17** Finally he came to Sa·mar′i·a. Now he went striking down all who were left over of A′hab's in Sa·mar′i·a, until he had annihilated them, according to Jehovah's word that he had spoken to E·li′jah.

18 Further, Je′hu collected all the people together and said to them: "A′hab, on the one hand, worshiped Ba′al a little. Je′hu, on the other hand, will worship him a great deal. **19** So now call all the prophets of Ba′al, all his worshipers and all his priests to me. Do not let a single one be missing, because I have a great sacrifice for Ba′al. Anyone that is missing will not keep living." As for Je′hu, he acted slyly, for the purpose of destroying the worshipers of Ba′al.

20 And Je′hu went on to say: "Sanctify a solemn assembly for Ba′al." Accordingly they proclaimed it. 21 After that Je′hu sent through all Israel, so that all the worshipers of Ba′al came in. And not a single one was left over that did not come in. And they kept coming into the house of Ba′al, and the house of Ba′al came to be full from end to end. 22 He now said to the one who was over the wardrobe: "Bring out garments for all the worshipers of Ba′al." So he brought the attire out for them. 23 Then Je′hu entered with Je·hon′a·dab the son of Re′chab into the house of Ba′al. He now said to the worshipers of Ba′al: "Search carefully and see that there may be here with you none of the worshipers of Jehovah, but only the worshipers of Ba′al." 24 Finally they came in to render up sacrifices and burnt offerings, and Je′hu himself stationed eighty men outside at his disposal and went on to say: "As for the man that escapes from the men whom I am bringing into your hands, the one′s soul will go for the other′s soul."

25 And it came about that as soon as he finished rendering up the burnt offering, Je′hu immediately said to the runners and the adjutants: "Come in, strike them down! Do not let a single one go out." And the runners and the adjutants began to strike them down with the edge of the sword and to throw them out, and they kept going as far as the city of the house of Ba′al. 26 Then they brought out the sacred pillars of the house of Ba′al and burned each one. 27 Further, they pulled down the sacred pillar of Ba′al and pulled down the house of Ba′al, and they kept it set aside for privies down to this day.

28 Thus Je′hu annihilated Ba′al out of Israel. 29 It was only the sins of Jer·o·bo′am the son of Ne′bat, with which he caused Israel to sin, that Je′hu did not turn aside from following, [that is,] the golden calves of which one was in Beth′el and one in Dan. 30 Consequently Jehovah said to Je′hu: "For the reason that you have acted well in doing what is right in my eyes,

[and] according to all that was in my heart you have done to the house of A′hab, sons themselves to the fourth generation will sit for you upon the throne of Israel." 31 And Je′hu himself did not take care to walk in the law of Jehovah the God of Israel with all his heart. He did not turn aside from the sins of Jer·o·bo′am with which he caused Israel to sin.

32 In those days Jehovah started to cut off Israel piece by piece; and Haz′a·el kept striking them in all the territory of Israel, 33 from the Jordan toward the rising of the sun, all the land of Gil′e·ad, the Gad′ites and the Reu′ben·ites and the Ma·nas′sites, from A·ro′er, which is by the torrent valley of Ar′non, even Gil′e·ad and Ba′shan.

34 And the rest of the affairs of Je′hu and all that he did and all his mightiness, are they not written in the book of the affairs of the days of the kings of Israel? 35 Finally Je′hu lay down with his forefathers, and they buried him in Sa·mar′i·a; and Je·ho′a·haz his son began to reign in place of him. 36 And the days that Je′hu had reigned over Israel were twenty-eight years in Sa·mar′i·a.

11 Now as regards Ath·a·li′ah the mother of A·ha·zi′ah, she saw that her son had died. So she rose up and destroyed all the offspring of the kingdom. 2 However, Je·hosh′e·ba the daughter of King Je·ho′ram, the sister of A·ha·zi′ah, took Je·ho′ash the son of A·ha·zi′ah and stole him from among the sons of the king that were to be put to death, even him and his nursing woman, into the inner room for the couches, and they kept him concealed from the face of Ath·a·li′ah, and he was not put to death. 3 And he continued with her at the house of Jehovah in hiding for six years, while Ath·a·li′ah was reigning over the land.

4 And in the seventh year Je·hoi′a·da sent and then took the chiefs of hundreds of the Ca′ri·an bodyguard and of the runners and brought them to himself at the

house of Jehovah and concluded a covenant with them and made them swear at the house of Jehovah, after which he showed them the son of the king. 5 And he went on to command them, saying: "This is the thing that YOU will do: One third of YOU are coming in on the sabbath and keeping strict watch over the king's house; 6 and one third will be at the gate of the Foundation, and one third will be at the gate behind the runners; and YOU must keep strict watch over the house by turns. 7 And there are two divisions among YOU that are all going out on the sabbath, and they must keep strict watch over the house of Jehovah in behalf of the king. 8 And YOU must encircle the king all around, each one with his weapons in his hand; and anyone entering within the rows will be put to death. And continue with the king when he goes out and when he comes in."

9 And the chiefs of hundreds proceeded to do according to all that Je·hoi′a·da the priest had commanded. So they took each one his men that were coming in on the sabbath, together with those that were going out on the sabbath, and then came in to Je·hoi′a·da the priest. 10 The priest now gave the chiefs of hundreds the spears and the circular shields that had belonged to King David, which were in the house of Jehovah. 11 And the runners kept standing each one with his weapons in his hand, from the right side of the house clear to the left side of the house, by the altar and by the house, all around near the king. 12 Then he brought the son of the king out and put upon him the diadem and the Testimony; and so they made him king and anointed him. And they began to clap their hands and say: "Let the king live!"

13 When Ath·a·li′ah heard the sound of the people running, she at once came to the people at the house of Jehovah. 14 Then she saw, and there the king was standing by the pillar according to the custom, and the chiefs and the trumpets by the king, and all the people of the land rejoicing and blowing the trumpets. Immediately Ath·a·li′ah ripped her garments apart and began crying: "Conspiracy! Conspiracy!" 15 But Je·hoi′a·da the priest commanded the chiefs of hundreds, the appointed ones of the military force, and said to them: "Take her out from inside the rows and, as for anyone coming after her, let there be an execution of death with the sword!" For the priest had said: "Do not let her be put to death in the house of Jehovah." 16 So they laid their hands upon her and she came by the way of the horse entry of the king's house, and she got put to death there.

17 Then Je·hoi′a·da concluded the covenant between Jehovah and the king and the people, that they should prove themselves the people of Jehovah; and also between the king and the people. 18 After that all the people of the land came to the house of Ba′al and pulled down his altars; and his images they broke up thoroughly, and Mat′tan the priest of Ba′al they killed before the altars.

And the priest proceeded to put overseers over the house of Jehovah. 19 Further, he took the chiefs of hundreds and the Ca′ri·an bodyguard and the runners and all the people of the land, that they might bring the king down from the house of Jehovah; and they came gradually by the way of the gate of the runners to the king's house; and he began to sit upon the throne of the kings. 20 And all the people of the land continued to rejoice; and the city, for its part, had no disturbance, and Ath·a·li′ah herself they had put to death with the sword at the king's house.

21 Seven years old Je·ho′ash was when he began to reign.

12 In the seventh year of Je′hu, Je·ho′ash became king, and for forty years he reigned in Jerusalem. And his mother's name was Zib′i·ah from Be′er-she′ba. 2 And

Je·ho′ash continued doing what was right in Jehovah's eyes all the days of his that Je·hoi′a·da the priest instructed him. 3 It was only the high places that did not disappear. The people were still sacrificing and making sacrificial smoke on the high places.

4 And Je·ho′ash proceeded to say to the priests: "All the money for the holy offerings that is brought to the house of Jehovah, the money at which each one is assessed, the money for the souls according to individual valuation, all the money that it comes up on the heart of each one to bring to the house of Jehovah, 5 let the priests take for themselves, each one from his acquaintance; and let them, for their part, repair the cracks of the house wherever any crack is found."

6 And it came about that by the twenty-third year of King Je·ho′ash, the priests had not yet repaired the cracks of the house. 7 So King Je·ho′ash called Je·hoi′a·da the priest and the priests and said to them: "Why is it that you are not repairing the cracks of the house? Now, then, do not take any more money from your acquaintances, but for the cracks of the house you should give it." 8 At that the priests consented not to take any more money from the people and not to repair the cracks of the house.

9 Je·hoi′a·da the priest now took a chest and bored a hole in its lid and put it beside the altar on the right as a person comes into the house of Jehovah, and there the priests, the doorkeepers, put all the money that was being brought into the house of Jehovah. 10 And it came about that as soon as they saw that there was a great deal of money in the chest, the secretary of the king and the high priest would come up, and they would bind it up and count the money that was being found at the house of Jehovah. 11 And they gave the money that had been counted off over to the hands of doers of the work that were appointed [to] the house of Jehovah. In turn they paid it out to the workers in wood and to the builders that were working at the house of Jehovah, 12 and to the masons and to the hewers of stone, and to buy timbers and hewn stones for repairing the cracks of the house of Jehovah and for all that was expended upon the house to repair it.

13 Only as respects the house of Jehovah there were not made basins of silver, extinguishers, bowls, trumpets, any sort of gold article and article of silver from the money that was being brought to the house of Jehovah; 14 for it was to the doers of the work that they would give it, and with it they repaired the house of Jehovah. 15 And they would not call for an accounting with the men into whose hand they would give the money to give to the doers of the work, because it was with faithfulness that they were working. 16 As for the money for guilt offerings and the money for sin offerings, it was not being brought to the house of Jehovah. So it came to belong to the priests.

17 Then it was that Haz′a·el the king of Syria proceeded to go up and fight against Gath and capture it, after which Haz′a·el set his face to go up against Jerusalem. 18 At that Je·ho′ash the king of Judah took all the holy offerings that Je·hosh′a·phat and Je·ho′ram and A·ha·zi′ah his forefathers, the kings of Judah, had sanctified and his own holy offerings and all the gold to be found in the treasures of the house of Jehovah and the house of the king and sent them to Haz′a·el the king of Syria. So he withdrew from against Jerusalem.

19 As for the rest of the affairs of Je·ho′ash and all that he did, are they not written in the book of the affairs of the days of the kings of Judah? 20 However, his servants rose up and leagued together in a conspiracy and struck Je·ho′ash down at the house of the Mound, [on the way] that goes down to Sil′la. 21 And Jo′za·car the son of Shim′e·ath and Je·hoz′-

a·bad the son of Sho′mer, his servants, were the ones that struck him down, so that he died. Accordingly they buried him with his forefathers in the city of David; and Am·a·zi′ah his son began to reign in place of him.

13 In the twenty-third year of Je·ho′ash the son of A·ha·zi′ah the king of Judah, Je·ho′a·haz the son of Je′hu became king over Israel in Sa·mar′i·a for seventeen years. 2 And he continued to do what was bad in Jehovah's eyes and went walking in pursuit of the sin of Jer·o·bo′am the son of Ne′bat, with which he caused Israel to sin. He did not turn aside from it. 3 And Jehovah's anger became hot against Israel, so that he gave them into the hand of Haz′a·el the king of Syria and into the hand of Ben-ha′dad the son of Haz′a·el all their days.

4 In time Je·ho′a·haz softened the face of Jehovah, so that Jehovah listened to him; for he had seen the oppression upon Israel, because the king of Syria had oppressed them. 5 Consequently Jehovah gave Israel a savior, so that they came out from under the hand of Syria, and the sons of Israel continued to dwell in their homes as formerly. 6 (Only they did not depart from the sin of the house of Jer·o·bo′am, with which he caused Israel to sin. In it he walked; and even the sacred pole itself stood in Sa·mar′i·a.) 7 For he had not left to Je·ho′a·haz any people but fifty horsemen and ten chariots and ten thousand men on foot, because the king of Syria had destroyed them, that he might make them like the dust at threshing.

8 As for the rest of the affairs of Je·ho′a·haz and all that he did and his mightiness, are they not written in the book of the affairs of the days of the kings of Israel? 9 Finally Je·ho′a·haz lay down with his forefathers, and they buried him in Sa·mar′i·a; and Je·ho′ash his son began to reign in place of him.

10 In the thirty-seventh year of Je·ho′ash the king of Judah, Je·ho′ash the son of Je·ho′a·haz became king over Israel in Sa·mar′i·a for sixteen years. 11 And he continued to do what was bad in Jehovah's eyes. He did not depart from all the sins of Jer·o·bo′am the son of Ne′bat, with which he made Israel sin. In them he walked.

12 As for the rest of the affairs of Je·ho′ash and all that he did and his mightiness [and] how he fought against Am·a·zi′ah the king of Judah, are they not written in the book of the affairs of the days of the kings of Israel? 13 Finally Je·ho′ash lay down with his forefathers, and Jer·o·bo′am himself sat upon his throne. In turn Je·ho′ash was buried in Sa·mar′i·a with the kings of Israel.

14 As regards E·li′sha, he had taken sick with the sickness with which he was to die. So Je·ho′ash the king of Israel came down to him and began to weep over his face and say: "My father, my father, the war chariot of Israel and his horsemen!" 15 And E·li′sha proceeded to say to him: "Take a bow and arrows." So he took to himself a bow and arrows. 16 And he went on to say to the king of Israel: "Put your hand to the bow." Accordingly he put his hand to it, after which E·li′sha laid his hands upon the hands of the king. 17 Then he said: "Open the window to the east." So he opened it. Finally E·li′sha said: "Shoot!" So he shot. He now said: "Jehovah's arrow of salvation, even the arrow of salvation against Syria! And you will certainly strike down Syria at A′phek to the finishing point."

18 And he went on to say: "Take the arrows." At that he took [them]. Then he said to the king of Israel: "Strike on the earth." So he struck three times and stopped. 19 And the man of the [true] God grew indignant at him; hence he said: "It was meant to strike five or six times! In that case you would certainly be striking down Syria to the finishing point,

but now it is three times that you will strike down Syria."

20 After that E·li′sha died and they buried him. And there were marauding bands of the Mo′ab·ites that regularly came into the land at the coming in of the year. 21 And it came about that as they were burying a man, why, here they saw the marauding band. At once they threw the man into E·li′sha's burial place and went off. When the man touched the bones of E·li′sha, he immediately came to life and stood upon his feet.

22 As for Haz′a·el the king of Syria, he oppressed Israel all the days of Je·ho′a·haz. 23 However, Jehovah showed them favor and had mercy upon them and turned to them for the sake of his covenant with Abraham, Isaac and Jacob; and he did not want to bring them to ruin, and he did not cast them away from before his face until now. 24 Finally Haz′a·el the king of Syria died, and Ben-ha′dad his son began to reign in place of him. 25 And Je·ho′ash the son of Je·ho′a·haz proceeded to take back again from the hand of Ben-ha′dad the son of Haz′a·el the cities that he had taken from the hand of Je·ho′a·haz his father in war. Three times Je·ho′ash struck him down, and he got to recover the cities of Israel.

14 In the second year of Je·ho′-ash the son of Je·ho′a·haz the king of Israel, Am·a·zi′ah the son of Je·ho′ash the king of Judah became king. 2 Twenty-five years old he happened to be when he began to reign, and for twenty-nine years he reigned in Jerusalem. And his mother's name was Je·ho·ad′-din of Jerusalem. 3 And he continued to do what was upright in Jehovah's eyes, only not like David his forefather. According to all that Je·ho′ash his father had done, he did. 4 It was only the high places that did not disappear. The people were still sacrificing and making sacrificial smoke on the high places. 5 And it came about that as soon as the kingdom had become firm in his hand, he began to strike down his servants that had struck down the king his father. 6 And the sons of the strikers he did not put to death, according to what is written in the book of Moses' law that Jehovah gave in command, saying: "Fathers should not be put to death for sons, and sons themselves should not be put to death for fathers; but for his own sin should each one be put to death." 7 He himself struck down the E′dom·ites in the Valley of Salt, ten thousand men, and got to seize Se′la in the war, and its name came to be called Jok′the·el down to this day.

8 Then it was that Am·a·zi′ah sent messengers to Je·ho′ash the son of Je·ho′a·haz the son of Je′hu the king of Israel, saying: "Do come. Let us look each other in the face." 9 At that Je·ho′ash the king of Israel sent to Am·a·zi′ah the king of Judah, saying: "The thorny weed itself that was in Leb′a·non sent to the cedar that was in Leb′a·non, saying, 'Do give your daughter to my son as a wife.' However, a wild beast of the field that was in Leb′a·non passed by and trampled the thorny weed down. 10 You have unmistakably struck down E′dom, and your heart has lifted you up. Enjoy your honor and dwell in your own house. Why, then, should you engage in strife under unfavorable conditions and have to fall, you and Judah with you?" 11 And Am·a·zi′ah did not listen.

So Je·ho′ash the king of Israel came up, and they proceeded to look each other in the face, he and Am·a·zi′ah the king of Judah, at Beth-she′mesh, which belongs to Judah. 12 And Judah came to be defeated before Israel, so that they took to flight, each one to his tent. 13 And it was Am·a·zi′ah the king of Judah the son of Je·ho′ash the son of A·ha·zi′ah that Je·ho′ash the king of Israel captured at Beth-she′mesh, after which they came to Jerusalem and he made a breach in the wall of Jerusalem at the gate of E′phra·im clear to the corner gate, four hundred cubits. 14 And he took all the gold and silver and all the articles to be found at the house of Jehovah and in the treasures of the house of the king and the hostages and then returned to Sa·mar′i·a.

15 As for the rest of the affairs of Je·ho′ash, what he did and his mightiness and how he fought against Am·a·zi′ah the king of Judah, are they not written in the book of the affairs of the days of the kings of Israel? 16 Finally Je·ho′ash lay down with his forefathers and was buried in Sa·mar′i·a with the kings of Israel, and Jer·o·bo′am his son began to reign in place of him.

17 And Am·a·zi′ah the son of Je·ho′ash the king of Judah continued to live after the death of Je·ho′ash the son of Je·ho′a·haz the king of Israel for fifteen years. 18 As for the rest of the affairs of Am·a·zi′ah, are they not written in the book of the affairs of the days of the kings of Judah? 19 At length they leagued against him in a conspiracy at Jerusalem, and he went fleeing to La′chish; but they sent in pursuit of him to La′chish and put him to death there. 20 So they carried him upon horses and he was buried in Jerusalem with his forefathers in the city of David. 21 Then all the people of Judah took Az·a·ri′ah, he at the time being sixteen years old, and they made him king in place of his father Am·a·zi′ah. 22 He himself built E′lath and got to restore it to Judah after the king lay down with his forefathers.

23 In the fifteenth year of Am·a·zi′ah the son of Je·ho′ash the king of Judah, Jer·o·bo′am the son of Je·ho′ash the king of Israel became king in Sa·mar′i·a for forty-one years. 24 And he continued to do what was bad in Jehovah's eyes. He did not depart from all the sins of Jer·o·bo′am the son of Ne′bat, with which he caused Israel to sin. 25 He it was that restored the boundary of Israel from the entering in of Ha′math clear to the sea of the Ar′a·bah,

according to the word of Jehovah the God of Israel who spoke by means of his servant Jo′nah the son of A·mit′tai, the prophet that was from Gath-he′pher. 26 For Jehovah had seen the very bitter affliction of Israel. There was neither any helpless one nor any worthless one, nor was there a helper for Israel. 27 And Jehovah had promised not to wipe out the name of Israel from under the heavens. Consequently he saved them by the hand of Jer·o·bo′am the son of Je·ho′ash.

28 As for the rest of the affairs of Jer·o·bo′am and all that he did and his mightiness, how he fought and how he restored Damascus and Ha′math to Judah in Israel, are they not written in the book of the affairs of the days of the kings of Israel? 29 Finally Jer·o·bo′am lay down with his forefathers, with the kings of Israel, and Zech·a·ri′ah his son began to reign in place of him.

15 In the twenty-seventh year of Jer·o·bo′am the king of Israel, Az·a·ri′ah the son of Am·a·zi′ah the king of Judah became king. 2 Sixteen years old he happened to be when he began to reign, and for fifty-two years he reigned in Jerusalem. And his mother's name was Je·co·li′ah of Jerusalem. 3 And he continued to do what was upright in Jehovah's eyes, according to all that Am·a·zi′ah his father had done. 4 It was only that the high places did not disappear. The people were still sacrificing and making sacrificial smoke on the high places. 5 Finally Jehovah plagued the king, and he continued to be a leper until the day of his death, and he kept dwelling in his house exempt from duties, while Jo′tham the king's son was over the house, judging the people of the land. 6 As for the rest of the affairs of Az·a·ri′ah and all that he did, are they not written in the book of the affairs of the days of the kings of Judah? 7 At length Az·a·ri′ah lay down with his forefathers, and they buried him with his forefathers in the

city of David; and Jo'tham his son began to reign in place of him.

8 In the thirty-eighth year of Az·a·ri'ah the king of Judah, Zech·a·ri'ah the son of Jer·o·bo'am became king over Israel in Sa·mar'i·a for six months. 9 And he went on doing what was bad in Jehovah's eyes, just as his forefathers had done. He did not depart from the sins of Jer·o·bo'am the son of Ne'bat, with which he caused Israel to sin. 10 Then Shal'lum the son of Ja'besh conspired against him and struck him down at Ib'le·am and put him to death and began to reign in place of him. 11 As for the rest of the affairs of Zech·a·ri'ah, there they are written in the book of the affairs of the days of the kings of Israel. 12 That was Jehovah's word that he had spoken to Je'hu, saying: "Sons themselves to the fourth generation will sit for you upon the throne of Israel." And it came to be that way.

13 As for Shal'lum the son of Ja'besh, he became king in the thirty-ninth year of Uz·zi'ah the king of Judah, and he continued to reign for a full lunar month in Sa·mar'i·a. 14 Then Men'a·hem the son of Ga'di came up from Tir'zah and came to Sa·mar'i·a and struck down Shal'lum the son of Ja'besh in Sa·mar'i·a and put him to death; and he began to reign in place of him. 15 As for the rest of the affairs of Shal'lum and his conspiracy with which he conspired, there they are written in the book of the affairs of the days of the kings of Israel. 16 It was then that Men'a·hem proceeded to strike down Tiph'sah and all that was in it and its territory out from Tir'zah, because it did not open up, and he went striking it down. All its pregnant women he ripped up.

17 In the thirty-ninth year of Az·a·ri'ah the king of Judah, Men'a·hem the son of Ga'di became king over Israel for ten years in Sa·mar'i·a. 18 And he continued to do what was bad in Jehovah's eyes. He did not depart

from all the sins of Jer·o·bo'am the son of Ne'bat, with which he caused Israel to sin, all his days. 19 Pul the king of As·syr'i·a came into the land. Consequently Men'a·hem gave Pul a thousand talents of silver, that his hands might prove to be with him to strengthen the kingdom in his own hand. 20 So Men'a·hem brought forth the silver at the expense of Israel, at the expense of all the valiant, mighty men, to give to the king of As·syr'i·a fifty silver shekels for each man. At that the king of As·syr'i·a turned back, and he did not stay there in the land. 21 As for the rest of the affairs of Men'a·hem and all that he did, are they not written in the book of the affairs of the days of the kings of Israel? 22 Finally Men'a·hem lay down with his forefathers, and Pek·a·hi'ah his son began to reign in place of him.

23 In the fiftieth year of Az·a·ri'ah the king of Judah, Pek·a·hi'ah the son of Men'a·hem became king over Israel in Sa·mar'i·a for two years. 24 And he continued to do what was bad in Jehovah's eyes. He did not depart from the sins of Jer·o·bo'am the son of Ne'bat, with which he caused Israel to sin. 25 Then Pe'kah the son of Rem·a·li'ah his adjutant conspired against him and struck him down in Sa·mar'i·a in the dwelling tower of the king's house with Ar'gob and A·ri'eh, and with him there were fifty men of the sons of Gil'e·ad. So he put him to death and began to reign in place of him. 26 As for the rest of the affairs of Pek·a·hi'ah and all that he did, there they are written in the book of the affairs of the days of the kings of Israel.

27 In the fifty-second year of Az·a·ri'ah the king of Judah, Pe'kah the son of Rem·a·li'ah became king over Israel in Sa·mar'i·a for twenty years. 28 And he continued to do what was bad in Jehovah's eyes. He did not depart from the sins of Jer·o·bo'am the son of Ne'bat, with which he caused Israel to sin. 29 In the days of

Pe'kah the king of Israel, Tig'lath-pil·e'ser the king of As·syr'i·a came in and proceeded to take I'jon and A'bel-beth-ma'a·cah and Ja·no'ah and Ke'desh and Ha'zor and Gil'e·ad and Gal'i·lee, all the land of Naph'ta·li, and to carry them into exile in As·syr'i·a. 30 Finally Ho·she'a the son of E'lah formed a conspiracy against Pe'kah the son of Rem·a·li'ah and struck him and put him to death; and he began to reign in place of him in the twentieth year of Jo'tham the son of Uz·zi'ah. 31 As for the rest of the affairs of Pe'kah and all that he did, there they are written in the book of the affairs of the days of the kings of Israel.

32 In the second year of Pe'kah the son of Rem·a·li'ah the king of Israel, Jo'tham the son of Uz·zi'ah the king of Judah became king. 33 Twenty-five years old he happened to be when he began to reign, and for sixteen years he reigned in Jerusalem. And his mother's name was Je·ru'sha the daughter of Za'dok. 34 And he continued to do what was right in Jehovah's eyes. According to all that Uz·zi'ah his father had done, he did. 35 It was only that the high places did not disappear. The people were still sacrificing and making sacrificial smoke on the high places. He it was that built the upper gate of the house of Jehovah. 36 As for the rest of the affairs of Jo'tham, what he did, are they not written in the book of the affairs of the days of the kings of Judah? 37 In those days Jehovah started to send against Judah Re'zin the king of Syria and Pe'kah the son of Rem·a·li'ah. 38 Finally Jo'tham lay down with his forefathers and was buried with his forefathers in the city of David his forefather; and A'haz his son began to reign in place of him.

16 In the seventeenth year of Pe'kah the son of Rem·a·li'ah, A'haz the son of Jo'tham the king of Judah became king. 2 Twenty years old was A'haz when he began to reign, and for sixteen years he reigned in Jerusalem; and he did not do what was right in the eyes of Jehovah his God like David his forefather. 3 And he went walking in the way of the kings of Israel, and even his own son he made pass through the fire, according to the detestable things of the nations whom Jehovah drove out because of the sons of Israel. 4 And he kept sacrificing and making sacrificial smoke on the high places and upon the hills and under every luxuriant tree.

5 It was then that Re'zin the king of Syria and Pe'kah the son of Rem·a·li'ah the king of Israel proceeded to come up against Jerusalem in war and laid siege against A'haz, but they were not able to fight. 6 At that time Re'zin the king of Syria restored E'lath to E'dom, after which he cleared out the Jews from E'lath; and the E'dom·ites, for their part, entered E'lath and kept dwelling there down to this day. 7 So A'haz sent messengers to Tig'lath-pil·e'ser the king of As·syr'i·a, saying: "I am your servant and your son. Come up and save me out of the palm of the king of Syria and out of the palm of the king of Israel, who are rising up against me." 8 Accordingly A'haz took the silver and the gold that was to be found at the house of Jehovah and in the treasures of the king's house and sent the king of As·syr'i·a a bribe. 9 At that the king of As·syr'i·a listened to him and the king of As·syr'i·a went up to Damascus and captured it and led its [people] into exile at Kir, and Re'zin he put to death.

10 Then King A'haz went to meet Tig'lath-pil·e'ser the king of As·syr'i·a at Damascus, and he got to see the altar that was in Damascus. So King A'haz sent U·ri'jah the priest the design of the altar and its pattern as respects all its workmanship. 11 And U·ri'jah the priest proceeded to build the altar. According to all that King A'haz had sent from Damascus was the way that U·ri'jah the priest

made it, pending the time that King A'haz came from Damascus. 12 When the king came from Damascus, the king got to see the altar; and the king began to go near to the altar and make offerings upon it. 13 And he continued to make his burnt offering and his grain offering smoke and to pour out his drink offering and to sprinkle the blood of the communion sacrifices that were his upon the altar. 14 And the copper altar that was before Jehovah he now brought near from in front of the house, from between his altar and the house of Jehovah, and put it at the north side of his altar. 15 And King A'haz went on to command him, even U·ri'jah the priest, saying: "Upon the great altar make the burnt offering of the morning smoke, also the grain offering of the evening and the burnt offering of the king and his grain offering and the burnt offering of all the people of the land and their grain offering and their drink offerings; and all the blood of burnt offering and all the blood of a sacrifice you should sprinkle upon it. As for the copper altar, it will become something for me to take under consideration." 16 And U·ri'jah the priest went doing according to all that King A'haz had commanded.

17 Furthermore, King A'haz cut the side walls of the carriages in pieces and removed from off them the basins; and the sea he took down off the copper bulls that were underneath it and then put it upon a stone pavement. 18 And the covered structure for the sabbath that they had built in the house and the king's outer entryway he shifted from the house of Jehovah because of the king of As·syr'i·a.

19 As for the rest of the affairs of A'haz, what he did, are they not written in the book of the affairs of the days of the kings of Judah? 20 Finally A'haz lay down with his forefathers and was buried with his forefathers in the city of David; and Hez·e·ki'ah his son began to reign in place of him.

17 In the twelfth year of A'haz the king of Judah, Ho·she'a the son of E'lah became king in Sa·mar'i·a over Israel for nine years. 2 And he continued to do what was bad in Jehovah's eyes, only not as the kings of Israel that happened to be prior to him. 3 It was against him that Shal·man·e'·ser the king of As·syr'i·a came up, and Ho·she'a came to be his servant and began to pay tribute to him. 4 However, the king of As·syr'i·a got to find conspiracy in Ho·she'a's case, in that he had sent messengers to So the king of Egypt and did not bring the tribute up to the king of As·syr'i·a as in former years. Hence the king of As·syr'i·a shut him up and kept him bound in the house of detention.

5 And the king of As·syr'i·a proceeded to come up against all the land and to come up to Sa·mar'i·a and lay siege against it for three years. 6 In the ninth year of Ho·she'a, the king of As·syr'i·a captured Sa·mar'i·a and then led Israel into exile in As·syr'i·a and kept them dwelling in Ha'lah and in Ha'bor at the river Go'zan and in the cities of the Medes.

7 And it came about because the sons of Israel had sinned against Jehovah their God, who brought them up out of the land of Egypt from under the hand of Phar'aoh the king of Egypt, and they began to fear other gods; 8 and they kept walking in the statutes of the nations whom Jehovah had driven out from before the sons of Israel, and [in the statutes of] the kings of Israel that they had made; 9 and the sons of Israel went searching into the things that were not right toward Jehovah their God and kept building themselves high places in all their cities, from the tower of the watchmen clear to the fortified city; 10 and they kept setting up for themselves sacred pillars and sacred poles upon every high hill and under every luxuriant tree; 11 and there on all the high places they continued to make sac-

rificial smoke the same as the nations whom Jehovah had taken into exile because of them, and they kept doing bad things to offend Jehovah;

12 And they continued to serve dungy idols, concerning which Jehovah had said to them: "You must not do this thing"; 13 and Jehovah kept warning Israel and Judah by means of all his prophets [and] every visionary, saying: "Turn back from YOUR bad ways and keep my commandments, my statutes, according to all the law that I commanded YOUR forefathers and that I have sent to YOU by means of my servants the prophets"; 14 and they did not listen but kept hardening their necks like the necks of their forefathers that had not exercised faith in Jehovah their God; 15 and they continued rejecting his regulations and his covenant that he had concluded with their forefathers and his reminders with which he had warned them, and they went following vain idols and became vain themselves, even in imitation of the nations that were all around them, concerning whom Jehovah had commanded them not to do like them;

16 And they kept leaving all the commandments of Jehovah their God and proceeded to make for themselves molten statues, two calves, and to make a sacred pole, and they began to bow down to all the army of the heavens and to serve Ba'al; 17 and they continued to make their sons and their daughters pass through the fire and to practice divination and to look for omens, and they kept selling themselves to do what was bad in the eyes of Jehovah, to offend him;

18 Therefore Jehovah got very incensed against Israel, so that he removed them from his sight. He did not let any remain but the tribe of Judah alone.

19 Even Judah itself did not keep the commandments of Jehovah their God, but they went walking in the statutes of Israel that they had made. 20 Consequently Jehovah rejected all the seed of Israel and kept afflicting them and giving them into the hand of pillagers, until he had cast them away from before him. 21 For he ripped Israel off from the house of David, and they proceeded to make Jer·o·bo'am the son of Ne'bat king; and Jer·o·bo'am proceeded to part Israel from following Jehovah, and he caused them to sin with a great sin. 22 And the sons of Israel went walking in all the sins of Jer·o·bo'am that he had done. They did not depart from them, 23 until Jehovah removed Israel from his sight, just as he had spoken by means of all his servants the prophets. So Israel went off its own soil into exile in As·syr'i·a down to this day.

24 Subsequently the king of As·syr'i·a brought people from Babylon and Cu'thah and Av'va and Ha'-math and Seph·ar·va'im and had them dwell in the cities of Sa·mar'i·a instead of the sons of Israel; and they began to take possession of Sa·mar'i·a and to dwell in its cities. 25 And it came about at the start of their dwelling there that they did not fear Jehovah. Therefore Jehovah sent lions among them, and they came to be killers among them. 26 So they sent word to the king of As·syr'i·a, saying: "The nations that you have taken into exile and then settled in the cities of Sa·mar'i·a have not known the religion of the God of the land, so that he keeps sending lions among them; and, look! they are putting them to death, inasmuch as there are none knowing the religion of the God of the land."

27 At that the king of As·syr'i·a commanded, saying: "Have one of the priests go there whom YOU led into exile from there, that he may go and dwell there and teach them the religion of the God of the land." 28 Accordingly one of the priests whom they had led into exile from Sa·mar'i·a came and began dwelling in Beth'el, and he came to be a teacher of them as to how they ought to fear Jehovah.

29 However, each different nation came to be a maker of its own god, which they then deposited in the house of the high places that the Sa·mar'i·tans had made, each different nation, in their cities where they were dwelling. 30 And the men of Babylon, for their part, made Suc'coth-be'noth, and the men of Cuth, for their part, made Ner'gal, and the men of Ha'math, for their part, made A·shi'ma. 31 As for the Av'vites, they made Nib'haz and Tar'tak; and the Se'phar·vites were burning their sons in the fire to A·dram'me·lech and A·nam'me·lech the gods of Seph·ar·va'im. 32 And they came to be fearers of Jehovah and went making for themselves from the people in general priests of high places, and they came to be functionaries for them in the house of the high places. 33 It was of Jehovah that they became fearers, but it was of their own gods that they proved to be worshipers, according to the religion of the nations from among whom they had led them into exile.

34 Down to this day they are doing according to their former religions. There were none fearing Jehovah and none doing according to his statutes and his judicial decisions and the law and the commandment that Jehovah had commanded the sons of Jacob, whose name he made Israel; 35 when Jehovah concluded a covenant with them and commanded them, saying: "You must not fear other gods, and you must not bow down to them nor serve them nor sacrifice to them. 36 But Jehovah, who brought you up out of the land of Egypt with great power and a stretched-out arm, is the One whom you should fear, and to him you should bow down, and to him you should sacrifice. 37 And the regulations and the judicial decisions and the law and the commandment that he wrote for you, you should take care to do always; and you must not fear other gods. 38 And the covenant that I have concluded with you, you must not forget; and you must not fear other

gods. 39 But it is Jehovah YOUR God that you should fear, as he is the one that will deliver you out of the hand of all YOUR enemies."

40 And they did not obey, but it was according to their former religion that they were doing. 41 And these nations came to be fearers of Jehovah, but it was their own graven images that they proved to be serving. As for both their sons and their grandsons, it was just as their forefathers had done that they themselves are doing down to this day.

18 And it came about in the third year of Ho·she'a the son of E'lah the king of Israel that Hez·e·ki'ah the son of A'haz the king of Judah became king. 2 Twenty-five years old he happened to be when he began to reign, and for twenty-nine years he reigned in Jerusalem. And his mother's name was A'bi the daughter of Zech·a·ri'ah. 3 And he continued to do what was right in Jehovah's eyes, according to all that David his forefather had done. 4 He it was that removed the high places and broke the sacred pillars to pieces and cut down the sacred pole and crushed to pieces the copper serpent that Moses had made; for down to those days the sons of Israel had continually been making sacrificial smoke to it, and it used to be called the copper serpent-idol. 5 In Jehovah the God of Israel he trusted; and after him there proved to be no one like him among all the kings of Judah, even those who had happened to be prior to him. 6 And he kept sticking to Jehovah. He did not turn aside from following him, but he continued keeping his commandments that Jehovah had commanded Moses. 7 And Jehovah proved to be with him. Wherever he would go out, he would act prudently; and he proceeded to rebel against the king of As·syr'i·a and did not serve him. 8 It was he that struck down the Phi·lis'tines clear to Ga'za and also its territories, from the tower of the watchmen clear to the fortified city.

9 And it came about in the fourth year of King Hez·e·ki′ah, that is, the seventh year of Ho·she′a the son of E′lah the king of Israel, that Shal·man·e′ser the king of As·syr′i·a came up against Sa·mar′i·a and began to lay siege to it. 10 And they got to capture it at the end of three years; in the sixth year of Hez·e·ki′ah, that is, the ninth year of Ho·she′a the king of Israel, Sa·mar′i·a was captured. 11 After that the king of As·syr′i·a took Israel into exile in As·syr′i·a and set them down in Ha′lah and in Ha′bor at the river Go′zan and in the cities of the Medes, 12 over the fact that they had not listened to the voice of Jehovah their God, but kept overstepping his covenant, even all that Moses the servant of Jehovah had commanded. They neither listened nor performed.

13 And in the fourteenth year of King Hez·e·ki′ah, Sen·nach′er·ib the king of As·syr′i·a came up against all the fortified cities of Judah and proceeded to seize them. 14 So Hez·e·ki′ah the king of Judah sent to the king of As·syr′i·a at La′chish, saying: "I have sinned. Turn back from against me. Whatever you may impose upon me I shall carry." Accordingly the king of As·syr′i·a laid upon Hez·e·ki′ah the king of Judah three hundred silver talents and thirty gold talents. 15 Therefore Hez·e·ki′ah gave all the silver that was to be found at the house of Jehovah and in the treasures of the king's house. 16 At that time Hez·e·ki′ah cut off the doors of the temple of Jehovah and the doorposts that Hez·e·ki′ah the king of Judah had overlaid and then gave them to the king of As·syr′i·a.

17 And the king of As·syr′i·a proceeded to send Tar′tan and Rab′sa·ris and Rab′sha·keh from La′chish to King Hez·e·ki′ah with a heavy military force to Jerusalem, that they might go up and come to Jerusalem. So they went up and came and stood still by the conduit of the upper pool, which is at the highway of the laundryman's field. 18 And they began to call out to the king, but there came out to them E·li′a·kim the son of Hil·ki′ah, who was over the household, and Sheb′nah the secretary and Jo′ah the son of A′saph the recorder.

19 Accordingly Rab′sha·keh said to them: "Please, say to Hez·e·ki′ah, 'This is what the great king, the king of As·syr′i·a, has said: "What is this confidence in which you have trusted? 20 You have said (but it is the word of lips), 'There are counsel and mightiness for the war.' Now in whom have you put your trust, that you have rebelled against me? 21 Now, look! you have put your trust in the support of this crushed reed, Egypt, which, if a man should brace himself upon it, would certainly enter into his palm and pierce it. That is the way Phar′aoh the king of Egypt is to all those putting their trust in him. 22 And in case you men should say to me, 'It is Jehovah our God in whom we have put our trust,' is he not the one whose high places and whose altars Hez·e·ki′ah has removed, while he says to Judah and Jerusalem, 'Before this altar you should bow down in Jerusalem'?" ' 23 Now, then, make a wager, please, with my lord the king of As·syr′i·a, and let me give you two thousand horses [to see] whether you are able, on your part, to put riders upon them. 24 How, then, could you turn back the face of one governor of the smallest servants of my lord, while you, for your part, put your trust in Egypt for chariots and for horsemen? 25 Now is it without authorization from Jehovah that I have come up against this place to bring it to ruin? Jehovah himself said to me, 'Go up against this land, and you must bring it to ruin.' "

26 At this E·li′a·kim the son of Hil·ki′ah and Sheb′nah and Jo′ah said to Rab′sha·keh: "Speak with your servants, please, in the Syrian language, for we can listen; and do not speak with us in the Jews' language in the ears of the people that are on the wall." 27 But Rab′sha·keh said to them: "Is it to your lord and to you that my lord

has sent me to speak these words? Is it not to the men sitting upon the wall, that they may eat their own excrement and drink their own urine with YOU men?"

28 And Rab'sha·keh continued to stand and call out in a loud voice in the Jews' language; and he went on to speak and say: "HEAR the word of the great king, the king of As·syr'i·a. 29 This is what the king has said, 'Do not let Hez·e·ki'ah deceive YOU people, for he is not able to deliver YOU out of my hand. 30 And do not let Hez·e·ki'ah cause YOU to trust in Jehovah, saying: "Without fail Jehovah will deliver us, and this city will not be given into the hand of the king of As·syr'i·a." 31 Do not listen to Hez·e·ki'ah; for this is what the king of As·syr'i·a has said: "Make a capitulation to me, and come out to me, and eat each one from his own vine and each one from his own fig tree and drink each one the water of his own cistern, 32 until I come and I actually take YOU to a land like YOUR own land, a land of grain and new wine, a land of bread and vineyards, a land of oil-olive trees and honey; and keep living that YOU may not die. And do not listen to Hez·e·ki'ah, for he allures YOU, saying, 'Jehovah himself will deliver us.' 33 Have the gods of the nations at all delivered each one his own land out of the hand of the king of As·syr'i·a? 34 Where are the gods of Ha'math and Ar'pad? Where are the gods of Seph·ar·va'im, He'na and Iv'vah? Have they delivered Sa·mar'i·a out of my hand? 35 Who are there among all the gods of the lands that have delivered their land out of my hand, so that Jehovah should deliver Jerusalem out of my hand?"'"

36 And the people kept silent and did not answer him a word, for the commandment of the king was, saying: "YOU must not answer him." 37 But E·li'a·kim the son of Hil·ki'ah, who was over the household, and Sheb'nah the secretary and Jo'ah the son of A'saph the recorder came to Hez·e·ki'ah

with their garments ripped apart and told him the words of Rab'-sha·keh.

19 And it came about that as soon as King Hez·e·ki'ah heard, he immediately ripped his garments apart and covered himself with sackcloth and came into the house of Jehovah. 2 Further, he sent E·li'a·kim, who was over the household, and Sheb'nah the secretary and the older men of the priests covered with sackcloth to Isaiah the prophet the son of A'moz. 3 And they proceeded to say to him: "This is what Hez·e·ki'ah has said, 'This day is a day of distress and of rebuke and of scornful insolence; for the sons have come as far as the womb's mouth, and there is no power to give birth. 4 Perhaps Jehovah your God will hear all the words of Rab'sha·keh, whom the king of As·syr'i·a his lord sent to taunt the living God, and he will actually call him to account for the words that Jehovah your God has heard. And you must lift up prayer in behalf of the remnant that are to be found.'"

5 So the servants of King Hez·e·ki'ah came in to Isaiah. 6 Then Isaiah said to them: "This is what YOU should say to YOUR lord, 'This is what Jehovah has said: "Do not be afraid because of the words that you have heard with which the attendants of the king of As·syr'i·a spoke abusively of me. 7 Here I am putting a spirit in him, and he must hear a report and return to his own land; and I shall certainly cause him to fall by the sword in his own land."'"

8 After that Rab'sha·keh returned and found the king of As·syr'i·a fighting against Lib'nah; for he had heard that he had pulled away from La'chish. 9 He heard it said respecting Tir·ha'kah the king of E·thi·o'pi·a: "Here he has come out to fight against you." Therefore he sent messengers again to Hez·e·ki'ah, saying: 10 "This is what YOU men should say to Hez·e·ki'ah the king of Judah, 'Do

not let your God in whom you are trusting deceive you, saying: "Jerusalem will not be given into the hand of the king of As·syr´i·a." 11 Look! You yourself have heard what the kings of As·syr´i·a did to all the lands by devoting them to destruction; and will you yourself be delivered? 12 Have the gods of the nations that my forefathers brought to ruin delivered them, even Go´zan and Ha´ran and Re´zeph and the sons of E´den that were in Tel-as´sar? 13 Where is he—the king of Ha´math and the king of Ar´pad and the king of the cities of Seph·ar·va´im, He´na and Iv´vah?' "

14 Then Hez·e·ki´ah took the letters out of the hand of the messengers and read them, after which Hez·e·ki´ah went up to the house of Jehovah and spread it out before Jehovah. 15 And Hez·e·ki´ah began to pray before Jehovah and say: "O Jehovah the God of Israel, sitting upon the cherubs, you alone are the [true] God of all the kingdoms of the earth. You yourself have made the heavens and the earth. 16 Incline your ear, O Jehovah, and hear. Open your eyes, O Jehovah, and see, and hear the words of Sen·nach´er·ib that he has sent to taunt the living God. 17 It is a fact, O Jehovah, the kings of As·syr´i·a have devastated the nations and their land. 18 And they have consigned their gods to the fire, because they were no gods, but the workmanship of man's hands, wood and stone; so that they destroyed them. 19 And now, O Jehovah our God, save us, please, out of his hand, that all the kingdoms of the earth may know that you, O Jehovah, are God alone."

20 And Isaiah the son of A´moz proceeded to send to Hez·e·ki´ah, saying: "This is what Jehovah the God of Israel has said, 'The prayer that you have made to me concerning Sen·nach´er·ib the king of As·syr´i·a I have heard. 21 This is the word that Jehovah has spoken against him:

"The virgin daughter of Zion has despised you, she has held you in derision.

Behind you the daughter of Jerusalem has wagged her head.

22 Whom have you taunted and spoken of abusively?
And against whom have you lifted up your voice
And do you raise your eyes on high?
It is against the Holy One of Israel!

23 By means of your messengers you have taunted Jehovah and you say,
'With the multitude of my war chariots I myself—
I shall certainly ascend the height of mountainous regions,
The remotest parts of Leb´a·non;
And I shall cut down its lofty cedars, its choice juniper trees.
And I will enter its final lodging place, the forest of its orchard.

24 I myself shall certainly dig and drink strange waters,
And I shall dry up with the soles of my feet all the Nile canals of Egypt.'

25 Have you not heard? From remote times it is what I will do.
From bygone days I have even formed it.
Now I will bring it in.
And you will serve to make fortified cities desolate as piles of ruins.

26 And their inhabitants will be feeble-handed;
They will simply be terrified and will be ashamed.
They must become as vegetation of the field and green tender grass,
Grass of the roofs, when there is a scorching before the east wind.

27 And your sitting quiet and your going out and your coming in I well know,

And your exciting yourself
against me,
28 Because your exciting yourself
against me and your roaring
have come up into my ears.
And I shall certainly put my
hook in your nose and my
bridle between your lips,
And I shall indeed lead you
back by the way by which
you have come."

29 "'And this will be the sign
for you: There will be an eating
this year of the growth from spilled
kernels, and in the second year
grain that shoots up of itself; but in
the third year sow seed, you people,
and reap and plant vineyards and
eat their fruitage. 30 And those who
escape of the house of Judah, those
who are left, will certainly take root
downward and produce fruitage upward. 31 For out of Jerusalem a
remnant will go forth, and those
who escape from Mount Zion. The
very zeal of Jehovah of armies will
do this.

32 "'That is why this is what
Jehovah has said concerning the
king of As·syr'i·a: "He will not
come into this city nor will he
shoot an arrow there nor confront
it with a shield nor cast up a siege
rampart against it. 33 By the way
by which he proceeded to come,
he will return, and into this city
he will not come, is the utterance
of Jehovah. 34 And I shall certainly defend this city to save it
for my own sake and for the sake
of David my servant."'"

35 And it came about on that
night that the angel of Jehovah
proceeded to go out and strike
down a hundred and eighty-five
thousand in the camp of the
As·syr'i·ans. When people rose up
early in the morning, why, there
all of them were dead carcasses.
36 Therefore Sen·nach'er·ib the
king of As·syr'i·a pulled away and
went and returned, and he took up
dwelling in Nin'e·veh. 37 And it
came about that as he was bowing
down at the house of Nis'roch his
god, A·dram'me·lech and Shar-
e'zer, his sons, themselves struck
him down with the sword, and they

themselves escaped to the land of
Ar'a·rat. And E'sar-had'don his
son began to reign in place of him.

20 In those days Hez·e·ki'ah got
sick to the point of dying.
Accordingly Isaiah the son of A'moz
the prophet came in to him and
said to him: "This is what Jehovah has said, 'Give commands to
your household, for you yourself
will indeed die and will not live.'"
2 At that he turned his face to the
wall and began to pray to Jehovah,
saying: 3 "I beseech you, O Jehovah, remember, please, how I have
walked before you in truthfulness
and with a complete heart, and
what was good in your eyes I have
done." And Hez·e·ki'ah began to
weep profusely.

4 And it came about that Isaiah
himself had not yet gone out to the
middle court when Jehovah's word
itself came to him, saying: 5 "Go
back, and you must say to Hez·e·
ki'ah the leader of my people,
'This is what Jehovah the God of
David your forefather has said:
"I have heard your prayer. I have
seen your tears. Here I am healing
you. On the third day you will go
up to the house of Jehovah. 6 And
I shall certainly add fifteen years to
your days, and out of the palm of
the king of As·syr'i·a I shall deliver you and this city, and I will
defend this city for my own sake
and for the sake of David my
servant."'"

7 And Isaiah went on to say:
"You men, take a cake of pressed
dried figs." So they took and put it
upon the boil, after which he
gradually revived.

8 Meantime, Hez·e·ki'ah said to
Isaiah: "What is the sign that
Jehovah will heal me and I shall
certainly go up on the third day to
the house of Jehovah?" 9 To this
Isaiah said: "This is the sign for
you from Jehovah that Jehovah will
perform the word that he has
spoken: Shall the shadow actually
go forward ten steps [of the stairs]
or should it go back ten steps?"
10 Then Hez·e·ki'ah said: "It is
an easy thing for the shadow to
extend itself ten steps, but not

that the shadow should go backward ten steps." 11 At that Isaiah the prophet began to call out to Jehovah; and he made the shadow that had gone down gradually go back on the steps, that is, on the steps [of the stairs] of A'haz, ten steps backward.

12 At that time Be·ro'dach-bal'a·dan the son of Bal'a·dan the king of Babylon sent letters and a gift to Hez·e·ki'ah; for he had heard that Hez·e·ki'ah had been sick. 13 And Hez·e·ki'ah proceeded to listen to them and show them all his treasure house, the silver and the gold and the balsam oil and the good oil and his armory and all that was to be found in his treasures. There proved to be nothing that Hez·e·ki'ah did not show them in his own house and in all his dominion.

14 After that Isaiah the prophet came in to King Hez·e·ki'ah and said to him: "What did these men say and from where did they proceed to come to you?" So Hez·e·ki'ah said: "From a distant land they came, from Babylon." 15 And he went on to say: "What did they see in your house?" To this Hez·e·ki'ah said: "Everything that is in my house they saw. There proved to be nothing that I did not show them in my treasures."

16 Isaiah now said to Hez·e·ki'ah: "Hear the word of Jehovah, 17 '"Look! Days are coming, and all that is in your own house and that your forefathers have stored up down to this day will actually be carried to Babylon. Nothing will be left," Jehovah has said. 18 "And some of your own sons that will come forth from you to whom you will become father will themselves be taken and actually become court officials in the palace of the king of Babylon." '"

19 At that Hez·e·ki'ah said to Isaiah: "The word of Jehovah that you have spoken is good." And he went on to say: "Is it not so, if peace and truth themselves will continue in my own days?"

20 As for the rest of the affairs of Hez·e·ki'ah and all his mighti-ness and how he made the pool and the conduit and then brought the water into the city, are they not written in the book of the affairs of the days of the kings of Judah? 21 Finally Hez·e·ki'ah lay down with his forefathers; and Ma·nas'seh his son began to reign in place of him.

21 Twelve years old was Ma·nas'seh when he began to reign, and for fifty-five years he reigned in Jerusalem. And his mother's name was Heph'zi·bah. 2 And he proceeded to do what was bad in Jehovah's eyes, according to the detestable things of the nations that Jehovah had driven out from before the sons of Israel. 3 So he built again the high places that Hez·e·ki'ah his father had destroyed, and set up altars to Ba'al and made a sacred pole, just as A'hab the king of Israel had done; and he began to bow down to all the army of the heavens and to serve them. 4 And he built altars in the house of Jehovah, respecting which Jehovah had said: "In Jerusalem I shall put my name." 5 And he went on to build altars to all the army of the heavens in two courtyards of the house of Jehovah. 6 And he made his own son pass through the fire, and he practiced magic and looked for omens and made spirit mediums and professional foretellers of events. He did on a large scale what was bad in Jehovah's eyes, to offend him.

7 Further, he put the carved image of the sacred pole that he had made in the house of which Jehovah had said to David and to Sol'o·mon his son: "In this house and in Jerusalem, which I have chosen out of all the tribes of Israel, I shall put my name to time indefinite. 8 And I shall not again make the foot of Israel wander from the ground that I gave to their forefathers, provided only they are careful to do according to all that I have commanded them, even concerning all the law that my servant Moses commanded them." 9 And they did not listen, but Ma·nas'seh kept seducing them to

do what was bad more than the nations whom Jehovah had annihilated from before the sons of Israel.

10 And Jehovah kept speaking by means of his servants the prophets, saying: 11 "For the reason that Ma·nas'seh the king of Judah has done these detestable things, he has acted more wickedly than all that the Am'or·ites did that were prior to him, and he proceeded to make even Judah sin with his dungy idols. 12 That is why this is what Jehovah the God of Israel has said, 'Here I am bringing a calamity upon Jerusalem and Judah, of which if anyone hears both his ears will tingle. 13 And I shall certainly stretch upon Jerusalem the measuring line applied to Sa·mar'i·a and also the leveling instrument applied to the house of A'hab; and I shall simply wipe Jerusalem clean just as one wipes the handleless bowl clean, wiping it clean and turning it upside down. 14 And I shall indeed forsake the remnant of my inheritance and give them into the hand of their enemies, and they will simply become plunder and pillage to all their enemies, 15 for the reason that they did what was bad in my eyes and were continually offending me from the day that their forefathers came out from Egypt down to this day.'"

16 And there was also innocent blood that Ma·nas'seh shed in very great quantity, until he had filled Jerusalem from end to end, besides his sin with which he caused Judah to sin by doing what was bad in the eyes of Jehovah. 17 As for the rest of the affairs of Ma·nas'seh and all that he did and his sin with which he sinned, are they not written in the book of the affairs of the days of the kings of Judah? 18 Finally Ma·nas'seh lay down with his forefathers and was buried in the garden of his house, in the garden of Uz'za; and A'mon his son began to reign in place of him.

19 Twenty-two years old was A'mon when he began to reign, and for two years he reigned in Jeru-salem. And his mother's name was Me·shul'le·meth the daughter of Ha'ruz from Jot'bah. 20 And he continued to do what was bad in Jehovah's eyes, just as Ma·nas'seh his father had done. 21 And he kept walking in all the way that his father had walked, and he continued serving the dungy idols that his father had served and bowing down to them. 22 Thus he left Jehovah the God of his forefathers, and he did not walk in the way of Jehovah. 23 Eventually servants of A'mon conspired against him and put the king to death in his own house. 24 But the people of the land struck down all the conspirators against King A'mon. Then the people of the land made Josi'ah his son king in place of him. 25 As for the rest of the affairs of A'mon, what he did, are they not written in the book of the affairs of the days of the kings of Judah? 26 So they buried him in his grave in the garden of Uz'za; and Jo·si'ah his son began to reign in place of him.

22 Eight years old was Jo·si'ah when he began to reign, and for thirty-one years he reigned in Jerusalem. And his mother's name was Je·di'dah the daughter of A·dai'ah from Boz'kath. 2 And he proceeded to do what was right in Jehovah's eyes and to walk in all the way of David his forefather, and he did not turn aside to the right or to the left.

3 And it came about in the eighteenth year of King Jo·si'ah that the king sent Sha'phan the son of Az·a·li'ah the son of Me·shul'lam the secretary to the house of Jehovah, saying: 4 "Go up to Hil·ki'ah the high priest, and let him complete the money that is being brought into the house of Jehovah that the doorkeepers have gathered from the people; 5 and let them put it into the hand of those doing the work, the appointed ones, in the house of Jehovah, that they may give it to those doing the work who are in the house of Jehovah to repair the cracks of the house, 6 to the craftsmen and the

builders and the masons, and to buy timbers and hewn stones to repair the house. 7 Only no accounting should be taken of the money with them into whose hand it is being put, for it is in faithfulness that they are working."

8 Later Hil·ki′ah the high priest said to Sha′phan the secretary: "The very book of the law I have found in the house of Jehovah." So Hil·ki′ah gave the book to Sha′-phan, and he began to read it. 9 Then Sha′phan the secretary came in to the king and replied to the king and said: "Your servants have poured out the money that was to be found in the house, and they keep putting it into the hand of the doers of the work, the ones appointed, in the house of Jeho-vah." 10 And Sha′phan the secre-tary went on to tell the king, say-ing: "There is a book that Hil·ki′ah the priest has given me." And Sha′phan began to read it before the king.

11 And it came about that as soon as the king heard the words of the book of the law, he imme-diately ripped his garments apart. 12 Then the king commanded Hil-ki′ah the priest and A·hi′kam the son of Sha′phan and Ach′bor the son of Mi·cai′ah and Sha′phan the secretary and A·sai′ah the king's servant, saying: 13 "Go, inquire of Jehovah in my own be-half and in behalf of the people and in behalf of all Judah con-cerning the words of this book that has been found; for great is Jeho-vah's rage that has been set afire against us over the fact that our forefathers did not listen to the words of this book by doing accord-ing to all that is written concern-ing us."

14 Accordingly Hil·ki′ah the priest and A·hi′kam and Ach′bor and Sha′phan and A·sai′ah went to Hul′dah the prophetess the wife of Shal′lum the son of Tik′vah the son of Har′has, the caretaker of the garments, as she was dwelling in Jerusalem in the second quarter; and they proceeded to speak to her. 15 In turn she said to them: "This

is what Jehovah the God of Israel has said, 'Say to the man that has sent YOU men to me: 16 "This is what Jehovah has said, 'Here I am bringing calamity upon this place and upon its inhabitants, even all the words of the book that the king of Judah has read; 17 due to the fact that they have left me and have gone making sacrificial smoke to other gods in order to offend me with all the work of their hands, and my rage has been set afire against this place and will not be extinguished.'"' 18 And as to the king of Judah who is sending YOU to inquire of Jehovah, this is what YOU should say to him, 'This is what Jehovah the God of Israel has said: "As regards the words that you have heard, 19 for the reason that your heart was soft so that you humbled yourself because of Jehovah at your hearing what I have spoken against this place and its inhabitants for it to become an object of astonishment and a mal-ediction, and then you ripped your garments apart and began weep-ing before me, I, even I, have heard," is the utterance of Jehovah. 20 "That is why here I am gather-ing you to your forefathers, and you will certainly be gathered to your own graveyard in peace, and your eyes will not look upon all the calamity that I am bringing upon this place."'" And they proceeded to bring the king the reply.

23 Then the king sent and they gathered together to him all the older men of Judah and Jeru-salem. 2 After that the king went up to the house of Jehovah, and also all the men of Judah and all the inhabitants of Jerusalem with him, and also the priests and the prophets and all the people, from small to great; and he began to read in their ears all the words of the book of the covenant that had been found in the house of Jeho-vah. 3 And the king kept standing by the pillar and now concluded the covenant before Jehovah, to walk after Jehovah and to keep his com-mandments and his testimonies and his statutes with all the heart and with all the soul by carrying out the words of this covenant that were written in this book. Accordingly all the people took their stand in the covenant.

4 And the king went on to command Hil·ki′ah the high priest and the priests of the second rank and the doorkeepers to bring out from the temple of Jehovah all the utensils made for Ba′al and for the sacred pole and for all the army of the heavens. Then he burned them outside Jerusalem on the terraces of Kid′ron, and he brought the dust of them to Beth′el. 5 And he put out of business the foreign-god priests, whom the kings of Judah had put in that they might make sacrificial smoke on the high places in the cities of Judah and the surroundings of Jerusalem, and also those making sacrificial smoke to Ba′al, to the sun and to the moon and to the constellations of the zodiac and to all the army of the heavens. 6 Furthermore, he brought out the sacred pole from the house of Jehovah to the outskirts of Jerusalem, to the torrent valley of Kid′ron, and burned it in the torrent valley of Kid′ron and ground it to dust and cast its dust upon the burial place of the sons of the people. 7 Further, he pulled down the houses of the male temple prostitutes that were in the house of Jehovah, where the women were weaving tent shrines for the sacred pole.

8 Then he brought all the priests from the cities of Judah, that he might make unfit for worship the high places where the priests had made sacrificial smoke, from Ge′ba as far as Be′er-she′ba; and he pulled down the high places of the gates that were at the entrance of the gate of Joshua, the chief of the city, which was at the left as a person came into the gate of the city. 9 Only the priests of the high places would not come up to the altar of Jehovah in Jerusalem, but they ate unfermented cakes in among their brothers. 10 And he made unfit for worship To′pheth, which is in the valley of the sons of Hin′nom, that no one might make his son or his daughter pass through the fire to Mo′lech. 11 Further, he caused the horses that the kings of Judah had given to the sun to cease from entering the house of Jehovah by the dining room of Na′than-me′lech the court official, which was in the porticoes; and the chariots of the sun he burned in the fire. 12 And the altars that were upon the roof of the roof chamber of A′haz that the kings of Judah had made, and the altars that Ma·nas′seh had made in two courtyards of the house of Jehovah, the king pulled down, after which he crushed them there, and he cast their dust into the torrent valley of Kid′ron. 13 And the high places that were in front of Jerusalem, that were to the right of the Mount of Ruination, that Sol′o·mon the king of Israel had built to Ash′to·reth the disgusting thing of the Si·do′ni·ans and to Che′mosh the disgusting thing of Mo′ab and to Mil′com the detestable thing of the sons of Am′mon, the king made unfit for worship. 14 And he broke the sacred pillars to pieces and went on to cut down the sacred poles and to fill their places with human bones. 15 And also the altar that was in Beth′el, the high place that Jer·o·bo′am the son of Ne′bat, who caused Israel to sin, had made, even that altar and the high place he pulled down. Then he burned the high place; he ground [it] to dust and burned the sacred pole.

16 When Jo·si′ah turned, he got to see the burial places that were there in the mountain. So he sent and took the bones from the burial places and burned them upon the altar, that he might make it unfit for worship, according to Jehovah's word that the man of the [true] God had proclaimed, who proclaimed these things. 17 Then he said: "What is the gravestone over there that I am seeing?" At this the men of the city said to him: "It is the burial place of the man of the [true] God that came from Judah and proceeded to proclaim

these things that you have done against the altar of Beth′el.″ **18** So he said: ″Let him rest. Do not let anyone disturb his bones.″ Consequently they let his bones alone along with the bones of the prophet that had come from Sa·mar′i·a.

19 And also all the houses of the high places that were in the cities of Sa·mar′i·a that the kings of Israel had built to cause offense Jo·si′ah removed, and he went on to do to them according to all the doings that he had done at Beth′el. **20** Accordingly he sacrificed all the priests of the high places that were there upon the altars and burned human bones upon them. After that he returned to Jerusalem.

21 The king now commanded all the people, saying: ″Hold a passover to Jehovah YOUR God according to what is written in this book of the covenant.″ **22** For no passover like this had been held from the days of the judges that had judged Israel, nor all the days of the kings of Israel and the kings of Judah. **23** But in the eighteenth year of King Jo·si′ah this passover was held to Jehovah in Jerusalem.

24 And also the spirit mediums and the professional foretellers of events and the teraphim and the dungy idols and all the disgusting things that had appeared in the land of Judah and in Jerusalem Jo·si′ah cleared out, in order that he might actually carry out the words of the law that were written in the book that Hil·ki′ah the priest had found at the house of Jehovah. **25** And like him there did not prove to be a king prior to him who returned to Jehovah with all his heart and with all his soul and with all his vital force, according to all the law of Moses; neither after him has there risen up one like him.

26 Nevertheless, Jehovah did not turn back from the great burning of his anger, with which his anger burned against Judah over all the offensive things with which Ma·nas′seh had made them offend. **27** But Jehovah said: ″Judah, too,

I shall remove from my sight, just as I have removed Israel; and I shall certainly reject this city that I have chosen, even Jerusalem, and the house of which I have said, ′My name will continue there.′ ″

28 As for the rest of the affairs of Jo·si′ah and all that he did, are they not written in the book of the affairs of the days of the kings of Judah? **29** In his days Phar′aoh Ne′choh the king of Egypt came up to the king of As·syr′i·a by the river Eu·phra′tes, and King Jo·si′ah proceeded to go to meet him; but he put him to death at Me·gid′do as soon as he saw him. **30** So his servants conveyed him dead in a chariot from Me·gid′do and brought him to Jerusalem and buried him in his grave. Then the people of the land took Je·ho′a·haz the son of Jo·si′ah and anointed him and made him king in place of his father.

31 Twenty-three years old was Je·ho′a·haz when he began to reign, and for three months he reigned in Jerusalem. And his mother's name was Ha·mu′tal the daughter of Jeremiah from Lib′nah. **32** And he began to do what was bad in Jehovah's eyes, according to all that forefathers of his had done. **33** And Phar′aoh Ne′choh got to put him in bonds at Rib′lah in the land of Ha′math, to keep him from reigning in Jerusalem, and then imposed a fine upon the land of a hundred silver talents and a gold talent. **34** Furthermore, Phar′aoh Ne′choh made E·li′a·kim the son of Jo·si′ah king in place of Jo·si′ah his father and changed his name to Je·hoi′a·kim; and Je·ho′a·haz he took and then brought to Egypt, where he eventually died. **35** And the silver and the gold Je·hoi′a·kim gave to Phar′aoh. Only he taxed the land, to give the silver at the order of Phar′aoh. According to each one's individual tax rate he exacted the silver and the gold from the people of the land, to give it to Phar′aoh Ne′choh.

36 Twenty-five years old was Je·hoi′a·kim when he began to reign, and for eleven years he reigned in Jerusalem. And his mother's name was Ze·bi′dah the daughter of Pe·dai′ah from Ru′mah. 37 And he continued to do what was bad in Jehovah's eyes, according to all that forefathers of his had done.

24 In his days Neb·u·chad·nez′zar the king of Babylon came up, and so Je·hoi′a·kim became his servant for three years. However, he turned back and rebelled against him. 2 And Jehovah began to send against him marauder bands of Chal·de′ans and marauder bands of Syrians and marauder bands of Mo′ab·ites and marauder bands of the sons of Am′mon, and he kept sending them against Judah to destroy it, according to Jehovah's word that he had spoken by means of his servants the prophets. 3 It was only by the order of Jehovah that it took place against Judah, to remove it from his sight for the sins of Ma·nas′seh, according to all that he had done; 4 and also [for] the innocent blood that he had shed, so that he filled Jerusalem with innocent blood, and Jehovah did not consent to grant forgiveness.

5 As for the rest of the affairs of Je·hoi′a·kim and all that he did, are they not written in the book of the affairs of the days of the kings of Judah? 6 Finally Je·hoi′a·kim lay down with his forefathers, and Je·hoi′a·chin his son began to reign in place of him.

7 And never again did the king of Egypt come out from his land, for the king of Babylon had taken all that happened to belong to the king of Egypt from the torrent valley of Egypt up to the river Eu·phra′tes.

8 Eighteen years old was Je·hoi′a·chin when he began to reign, and for three months he reigned in Jerusalem. And his mother's name was Ne·hush′ta the daughter of El·na′than of Jerusalem. 9 And he continued to do what was bad in Jehovah's eyes, according to all that his father had done. 10 During that time the servants of Neb·u·chad·nez′zar the king of Babylon

came up to Jerusalem, so that the city came under siege. 11 And Neb·u·chad·nez′zar the king of Babylon proceeded to come against the city, while his servants were laying siege against it.

12 At length Je·hoi′a·chin the king of Judah went out to the king of Babylon, he with his mother and his servants and his princes and his court officials; and the king of Babylon got to take him in the eighth year of his being king. 13 Then he brought out from there all the treasures of the house of Jehovah and the treasures of the king's house, and went on to cut to pieces all the gold utensils that Sol′o·mon the king of Israel had made in the temple of Jehovah, just as Jehovah had spoken. 14 And he took into exile all Jerusalem and all the princes and all the valiant, mighty men—ten thousand he was taking into exile—and also every craftsman and builder of bulwarks. No one had been left behind except the lowly class of the people of the land. 15 Thus he took Je·hoi′a·chin into exile to Babylon; and the king's mother and the king's wives and his court officials and the foremost men of the land he led away as exiled people from Jerusalem to Babylon. 16 As for all the valiant men, seven thousand, and the craftsmen and the builders of bulwarks, a thousand, all the mighty men carrying on war, the king of Babylon proceeded to bring them as exiled people to Babylon. 17 Further, the king of Babylon made Mat·ta·ni′ah his uncle king in place of him. Then he changed his name to Zed·e·ki′ah.

18 Twenty-one years old was Zed·e·ki′ah when he began to reign, and for eleven years he reigned in Jerusalem. And his mother's name was Ha·mu′tal the daughter of Jeremiah from Lib′nah. 19 And he continued to do what was bad in Jehovah's eyes, according to all that Je·hoi′a·kim had done. 20 For on account of the anger of Jehovah it took place in Jerusalem and in Judah, until he had cast them out of his sight. And Zed·e-

Bu'nah and O'ren and O'zem, A·hi'jah. 26 And Je·rah'me·el came to have another wife, whose name was At'a·rah. She was the mother of O'nam. 27 And the sons of Ram the first-born of Je·rah'me·el came to be Ma'az and Ja'min and E'ker. 28 And the sons of O'nam came to be Sham'mai and Ja'da. And the sons of Sham'mai were Na'dab and A·bi'shur. 29 And the name of A·bi'shur's wife was Ab'i·ha·il, who in time bore him Ah'-ban and Mo'lid. 30 And the sons of Na'dab were Se'led and Ap'pa·im. But Se'led died without sons. 31 And the sons of Ap'pa·im were Ish'i. And the sons of Ish'i were She'shan; and the sons of She'shan, Ah'-lai. 32 And the sons of Ja'da the brother of Sham'mai were Je'ther and Jon'a·than. But Je'ther died without sons. 33 And the sons of Jon'a·than were Pe'leth and Za'za. These became the sons of Je·rah'-me·el.

34 And She'shan came to have no sons, but daughters. Now She'shan had an Egyptian servant whose name was Jar'ha. 35 So She'shan gave his daughter to Jar'ha his servant as a wife, who in time bore him At'tai. 36 At'tai, in turn, became father to Nathan. Nathan, in turn, became father to Za'bad. 37 Za'bad, in turn, became father to Eph'lal. Eph'lal, in turn, became father to O'bed. 38 O'bed, in turn, became father to Je'hu. Je'hu, in turn, became father to Az·a·ri'ah. 39 Az·a·ri'ah, in turn, became father to He'lez. He'lez, in turn, became father to El·e·a'sah. 40 El·e·a'sah, in turn, became father to Sis'mai. Sis'mai, in turn, became father to Shal'-lum. 41 Shal'lum, in turn, became father to Jek·a·mi'ah. Jek·a·mi'ah, in turn, became father to E·lish'a·ma.

42 And the sons of Ca'leb the brother of Je·rah'me·el were Me'sha his first-born, who was the father of Ziph, and the sons of Ma·re'shah the father of He'bron. 43 And the sons of He'bron were Ko'rah and Tap'pu·ah and Re'kem and She'ma. 44 She'ma, in turn, became father to Ra'ham the father of Jor'ke·am. Re'kem, in turn, became father to Sham'mai. 45 And the son of Sham'mai was Ma'on; and Ma'on was the father of Beth-zur. 46 As for E'phah the concubine of Ca'leb, she gave birth to Ha'ran and Mo'za and Ga'-zez. As for Ha'ran, he became father to Ga'zez. 47 And the sons of Jah'dai were Re'gem and Jo'tham and Ge'shan and Pe'let and E'phah and Sha'aph. 48 As for Ca'leb's concubine Ma'a·cah, she gave birth to She'ber and Tir'ha·nah. 49 In time she bore Sha'aph the father of Mad·man'nah, She'va the father of Mach·be'nah and the father of Gib'e·a. And Ca'-leb's daughter was Ach'sah. 50 These became the sons of Ca'leb.

The sons of Hur the first-born of Eph'ra·thah: Sho'bal the father of Kir'i·ath-je'ar·im, 51 Sal'ma the father of Beth'-le·hem, Ha'reph the father of Beth-ga'der. 52 And Sho'bal the father of Kir'i·ath-je'ar·im came to have sons: Ha·ro'eh, half of the Me·nu'hoth. 53 And the families of Kir'i·ath-je'a·rim were the Ith'rites and the Pu'thites and Shu'math·ites and the Mish'ra·ites. It was from these that the Zo'rath·ites and the Esh'-ta·ol·ites came out. 54 The sons of Sal'ma were Beth'le·hem and the Ne·toph'a·thites, At'roth-beth-jo'ab and half of the Man·a·ha'thites, the Zor'-ites. 55 And the families of the scribes dwelling at Ja'bez were the Ti'rath·ites, the Shim'e·ath·ites, the Su'cath-ites. These were the Ken'ites that came from Ham'math the father of the house of Re'chab.

3 And these became the sons of David that were born to him in He'bron: the first-born Am'non, of A·hin'o·am the Jez're·el·it·ess, the second, Daniel, of Ab'i·gail the Car'mel·it·ess, 2 the third, Ab'sa·lom the son of Ma'a·cah the daughter of Tal'mai the king of Gesh'ur, the fourth, A·do·ni'jah the son of Hag'gith, 3 the fifth, Sheph·a·ti'ah, of A·bi'tal, the sixth, Ith're·am, of Eg'lah his wife. 4 There were six born to him in He'bron; and he continued to reign there seven years and six months, and for thirty-three years he reigned in Jerusalem.

5 And there were these born to him in Jerusalem: Shim'e·a and Sho'bab and Nathan and Sol'o·mon, four of Bath-she'ba the daughter of Am'mi·el, 6 and Ib'har and E·lish'a·ma and E·liph'e·let, 7 and No'gah and Ne'pheg and Ja·phi'a, 8 and E·lish'a·ma and E·li'a·da and E·liph'e·let, nine, 9 all the sons of David besides the sons of the concubines, and Ta'mar their sister.

10 And the son of Sol'o·mon was Re·ho·bo'am, A·bi'jah his son, A'sa his son, Je·hosh'a·phat his son, 11 Je·ho'ram his son, A·ha·zi'ah his son, Je·ho'ash his son, 12 Am·a·zi'ah his son, Az·a·ri'ah his son, Jo'tham his son, 13 A'haz his son, Hez·e·ki'ah his son, Ma·nas'seh his son, 14 A'mon his son, Jo·si'ah his son. 15 And the sons of Jo·si'ah were the first-born Jo·ha'nan, the second, Je·hoi'a·kim, the third, Zed·e·ki'ah, the fourth, Shal'lum. 16 And the sons of Je·hoi'a·kim were Jec·o·ni'ah his son, Zed·e·ki'ah his son. 17 And the sons of Jec·o·ni'ah as prisoner were She·al'ti·el his son 18 and Mal·chi'ram and Pe·dai'ah and She·naz'zar, Jek·a·mi'ah, Hosh'a·ma and Ned·a·bi'ah. 19 And the sons of Pe·dai'ah were Ze·rub'ba·bel and Shim'e·i; and the sons of Ze·rub'ba·bel were Me·shul'lam and Han·a·ni'ah (and She·lo'mith was their sister); 20 and Ha·shu'bah and O'hel and Ber·e·chi'ah and

Has·a·di'ah, Ju'shab-he'sed, five. 21 And the sons of Han·a·ni'ah were Pel·a·ti'ah and Je·sha'iah, the sons of [Je·sha'iah] Re·pha'iah, the sons of [Re·pha'iah] Ar'nan, the sons of [Ar'nan] O·ba·di'ah, the sons of [O·ba·di'ah] Shec·a·ni'ah; 22 and the sons of Shec·a·ni'ah, She·mai'ah, and the sons of She·mai'ah, Hat'tush and I'gal and Ba·ri'ah and Ne·a·ri'ah and Sha'phat, six. 23 And the sons of Ne·a·ri'ah were El·li·o·e'nai and Hiz·ki'ah and Az·ri'kam, three. 24 And the sons of El·li·o·e'nai were Hod·a·vi'ah and E·li'a·shib and Pe·la'iah and Ak'kub and Jo·ha'nan and De·la'iah and A·na'ni, seven.

4 The sons of Judah were Pe'rez, Hez'ron and Car'mi and Hur and Sho'bal. 2 As for Re·a'iah the son of Sho'bal, he became father to Ja'hath; Ja'hath, in turn, became father to A·hu'mai and La'had. These were the families of the Zo'rath·ites. 3 And these were [the sons of] the father of E'tam: Jez're·el and Ish'ma and Id'bash, (and the name of their sister was Haz·ze·lel·po'ni,) 4 and Pe·nu'el the father of Ge'dor and E'zer the father of Hu'shah. These were the sons of Hur the first-born of Eph'ra·thah the father of Beth'le·hem. 5 And Ash'hur the father of Te·ko'a came to have two wives, He'lah and Na'a·rah. 6 In time Na'a·rah bore to him A·huz'zam and He'pher and Te'me·ni and Ha·a·hash'ta·ri. These were the sons of Na'a·rah. 7 And the sons of He'lah were Ze'reth, Iz'har and Eth'nan. 8 As for Koz, he became father to A'nub and Zo·be'bah and the families of A·har'hel the son of Ha'rum.

9 And Ja'bez came to be more honorable than his brothers; and it was his mother that called his name Ja'bez, saying: "I have given him birth in pain." 10 And Ja'bez began to call upon the God of Israel, saying: "If you will without fail bless me and actually enlarge my territory and your hand really proves to be with me, and you really preserve [me] from calamity, that it may not hurt me,—" Ac-

cordingly God brought [to pass] what he had asked.

11 As for Che'lub the brother of Shu'hah, he became father to Me'hir, who was the father of Esh'ton. 12 Esh'ton, in turn, became father to Beth-ra'pha and Pa·se'ah and Te·hin'nah the father of Ir-na'hash. These were the men of Re'cah. 13 And the sons of Ke'naz were Oth'ni·el and Se·rai'ah, and the sons of Oth'ni·el, Ha'thath. 14 As for Me·o'no·thai, he became father to Oph'rah. As for Se·rai'ah, he became father to Jo'ab the father of Ge·har'a·shim; for craftsmen are what they became.

15 And the sons of Ca'leb the son of Je·phun'neh were I'ru, E'lah and Na'am; and the sons of E'lah, Ke'naz. 16 And the sons of Je·hal'le·lel were Ziph and Zi'phah, Tir'i·a and As'a·rel. 17 And the sons of Ez'rah were Je'ther and Me'red and E'pher and Ja'lon; and she got to conceive Mir'i·am and Sham'mai and Ish'bah the father of Esh·te·mo'a. 18 As for his Jewish wife, she gave birth to Je'red the father of Ge'dor and He'ber the father of So'co and Je·ku'thi·el the father of Za·no'ah. And these were the sons of Bi·thi'-ah the daughter of Phar'aoh, whom Me'red took.

19 And the sons of Ho·di'ah's wife, the sister of Na'ham, were the father of Kei'lah the Gar'mite and Esh·te·mo'a the Ma·ac'a·thite. 20 And the sons of Shi'mon were Am'non and Rin'nah, Ben-ha'nan and Ti'lon. And the sons of Ish'i were Zo'heth and Ben-zo'heth.

21 The sons of She'lah the son of Judah were Er the father of Le'cah and La'a·dah the father of Ma·re'shah and the families of the house of the workers of fine fabric of the house of Ash·be'a; 22 and Jo'kim and the men of Co·ze'ba and Jo'ash and Sa'raph, who became owners of Mo'ab·ite wives, and Jash'u·bi-le'hem. And the sayings are of old tradition. 23 They were the potters and the inhabitants of Ne·ta'im and Ge·de'rah. It was with the king in his work that they dwelt there.

24 The sons of Sim'e·on were Nem'u·el and Ja'min, Ja'rib, Ze'rah, Sha'ul, 25 Shal'lum his son, Mib'sam his son, Mish'ma his son. 26 And the sons of Mish'ma were Ham'mu·el his son, Zac'cur his son, Shim'e·i his son. 27 And Shim'e·i had sixteen sons and six daughters; but his brothers did not have many sons, and none of their families had as many as the sons of Judah. 28 And they continued to dwell in Be'er-she'ba and Mo·la'dah and Ha'zar-shu'al 29 and in Bil'hah and in E'zem and in To'lad 30 and in Be·thu'el and in Hor'mah and in Zik'lag 31 and in Beth-mar'ca·both and in Ha'zar-su'sim and in Beth-bir'i and in Sha'a·ra'im. These were their cities down till David reigned.

32 And their settlements were E'tam and A'in, Rim'mon and To'chen and A'shan, five cities. 33 And all their settlements that were all around these cities were as far as Ba'al. These were their dwelling places and their genealogical enrollments for them. 34 And Me·sho'bab and Jam'lech and Jo'shah the son of Am·a·zi'ah, 35 and Joel and Je'hu the son of Josh·i·bi'ah the son of Se·rai'ah the son of As'i·el, 36 and E·li·o·e'nai and Ja·a·ko'bah and Jesh·o·hai'ah and A·sai'ah and Ad'i·el and Je·sim'i·el and Be·nai'ah, 37 and Zi'za the son of Shi'phi the son of Al'lon the son of Je·da'iah the son of Shim'ri the son of She·mai'ah. 38 These who came in by names were the chieftains among their families, and the household itself of their forefathers increased in multitude. 39 And they proceeded to go to the entry-way of Ge'dor, clear to the east of the valley, to look for pasturage for their flocks. 40 Eventually they found fat and good pasturage, and the land was quite wide and having no disturbance but at ease; for those dwelling there in former times were of Ham. 41 And these written down by [their] names proceeded to come in in the days of Hez·e·ki'ah the king of Judah and strike down the tents of the

Ham'ites and the Me·u'nim that were to be found there, so that they devoted them to destruction down to this day; and they began to dwell in their place, because there was pasturage for their flocks there.

42 And from them there were some of the sons of Sim'e·on that went to Mount Se'ir, five hundred men, with Pel·a·ti'ah and Ne·a·ri'ah and Re·pha'iah and Uz'zi·el the sons of Ish'i at their head. 43 And they proceeded to strike down the remnant that had escaped of Am'a·lek, and they continued to dwell there down to this day.

5 And the sons of Reu'ben the first-born of Israel—for he was the first-born; but for his profaning the lounge of his father his right as first-born was given to the sons of Joseph the son of Israel, so that he was not to be enrolled genealogically for the right of the first-born. 2 For Judah himself proved to be superior among his brothers, and the one for leader was from him; but the right as first-born was Joseph's— 3 the sons of Reu'ben the first-born of Israel were Ha'noch and Pal'lu, Hez'ron and Car'mi. 4 The sons of Joel were She·mai'ah his son, Gog his son, Shim'e·i his son, 5 Mi'cah his son, Re·a'iah his son, Ba'al his son, 6 Be·er'ah his son, whom Til'gath-pil·ne'ser the king of As·syr'i·a took into exile, he being a chieftain of the Reu'ben·ites. 7 And his brothers by their families in the genealogical enrollment by their descendants were, as the head, Je·i'el, and Zech·a·ri'ah, 8 and Be'la the son of A'zaz the son of She'ma the son of Joel—he was dwelling in A·ro'er and as far as Ne'bo and Ba'al-me'on. 9 Even to the east he dwelt as far as where one enters the wilderness at the river Eu·phra'tes, for their livestock itself had become numerous in the land of Gil'e·ad. 10 And in the days of Saul they made war upon the Hag'rites, who came to fall by their hand; and so they dwelt in their tents throughout all the country east of Gil'e·ad.

11 As for the sons of Gad in front of them, they dwelt in the land of Ba'shan as far as Sal'e·cah. 12 Joel was the head, and Sha'-pham the second, and Ja'nai and Sha'phat in Ba'shan. 13 And their brothers belonging to the house of their forefathers were Mi'cha·el and Me·shul'lam and She'ba and Jo'rai and Ja'can and Zi'a and E'ber, seven. 14 These were the sons of Ab'i·ha·il the son of Hu'ri, the son of Ja·ro'ah, the son of Gil'e·ad, the son of Mi'cha·el, the son of Je·shish'ai, the son of Jah'do, the son of Buz; 15 A'hi the son of Ab'di·el, the son of Gu'-ni, head of the house of their forefathers. 16 And they continued to dwell in Gil'e·ad, in Ba'shan and in its dependent towns and in all the pasture grounds of Shar'on as far as their terminations. 17 They were all of them enrolled genealogically in the days of Jo'-tham the king of Judah and in the days of Jer·o·bo'am the king of Israel.

18 As for the sons of Reu'ben and the Gad'ites and the half tribe of Ma·nas'seh; of those who were valiant fellows, men carrying shield and sword and bending the bow and trained in war, there were forty-four thousand seven hundred and sixty going out to the army. 19 And they began to make war upon the Hag'rites, and Je'tur and Na'phish and No'dab. 20 And they came to be helped against them; so that the Hag'rites and all those who were with them were given into their hand, for it was to God that they called for aid in the war, and he let himself be entreated in their favor because they trusted in him. 21 And they got to take captive their livestock, their camels fifty thousand, and sheep two hundred and fifty thousand, and asses two thousand, and human souls a hundred thousand. 22 For there were many that had fallen slain, because it was on the part of the [true] God that the fighting was. And they continued to dwell

in their place down to the time of the exile.

23 As for the sons of the half tribe of Ma·nas′seh, they dwelt in the land from Ba′shan to Ba′al-her′mon and Se′nir and Mount Her′mon. They themselves became numerous. 24 And these were the heads of the house of their fore-fathers: E′pher and Ish′i and E′li·el and Az′ri·el and Jeremiah and Hod·a·vi′ah and Jah′di·el, men that were valiant, mighty fellows, men of fame, heads of the house of their forefathers. 25 And they began to act unfaithfully toward the God of their forefathers and went having immoral intercourse with the gods of the peoples of the land, whom God had annihilated from before them. 26 Consequently the God of Israel stirred up the spirit of Pul the king of As·syr′i·a even the spirit of Til′gath-pil·ne′ser the king of As·syr′i·a, so that he took into exile those of the Reu′-ben·ites and of the Gad′ites and of the half tribe of Ma·nas′seh and brought them to Ha′lah and Ha′bor and Ha′ra and the river Go′zan [to continue] until this day.

6 The sons of Le′vi were Ger′shon, Ko′hath and Me·rar′i. 2 And the sons of Ko′hath were Am′ram, Iz′har and He′bron and Uz′zi·el. 3 And the sons of Am′ram were Aaron and Moses, and there was Mir′i·am. And the sons of Aaron were Na′dab and A·bi′hu, E·le·a′zar and Ith′a·mar. 4 As for E·le·a′zar, he became father to Phin′e·has. Phin′e·has himself became father to Ab·i·shu′a. 5 Ab·i·shu′a, in turn, became father to Buk′ki; Buk′ki, in turn, became father to Uz′zi. 6 Uz′zi, in turn, became father to Zer·a·hi′ah; Zer·a·hi′ah, in turn, became father to Me·ra′-ioth. 7 Me·ra′ioth himself became father to Am·a·ri′ah; Am·a·ri′ah, in turn, became father to A·hi′tub. 8 A·hi′tub, in turn, became father to Za′dok; Za′dok, in turn, became father to A·him′a·az. 9 A·him′a·az, in turn, became father to Az·a·ri′ah. Az·a·ri′ah, in turn, be-came father to Jo·ha′nan. 10 Jo-ha′nan, in turn, became father to

Az·a·ri′ah. He was the one that acted as priest in the house that Sol′o·mon built in Jerusalem.

11 And Az·a·ri′ah came to be father to Am·a·ri′ah. Am·a·ri′ah, in turn, became father to A·hi′tub. 12 A·hi′tub, in turn, became father to Za′dok. Za′dok, in turn, became father to Shal′lum. 13 Shal′lum, in turn, became father to Hil·ki′ah. Hil·ki′ah, in turn, became father to Az·a·ri′ah. 14 Az·a·ri′ah, in turn, became father to Se·rai′ah. Se·rai′-ah, in turn, became father to Je·hoz′a·dak. 15 And Je·hoz′a·dak it was that went away when Jeho-vah took Judah and Jerusalem into exile by the hand of Neb·u·chad-nez′zar.

16 The sons of Le′vi were Ger′-shom, Ko′hath and Me·rar′i. 17 And these are the names of the sons of Ger′shom: Lib′ni and Shim′-e·i. 18 And the sons of Ko′hath were Am′ram and Iz′har and He′-bron and Uz′zi·el. 19 The sons of Me·rar′i were Mah′li and Mu′shi.

And these were the families of the Levites by their forefathers: 20 Of Ger′shom, Lib′ni his son, Ja′-hath his son, Zim′mah his son, 21 Jo′ah his son, Id′do his son, Ze′rah his son, Je·ath′e·rai his son. 22 The sons of Ko′hath were Am-min′a·dab his son, Ko′rah his son, As′sir his son, 23 El·ka′nah his son and E·bi′a·saph his son and As′sir his son; 24 Ta′hath his son, U·ri′el his son, Uz·zi′ah his son, and Sha′ul his son. 25 And the sons of El·ka′nah were A·ma′sai and A·hi′moth. 26 As for El·ka′-nah, the sons of El·ka′nah were Zo′phai his son and Na′hath his son, 27 E·li′ab his son, Je·ro′ham his son, El·ka′nah his son. 28 And the sons of Samuel were the first-born [Joel] and the second A·bi′-jah. 29 The sons of Me·rar′i were Mah′li, Lib′ni his son, Shim′-e·i his son, Uz′zah his son, 30 Shim′e·a his son, Hag·gi′ah his son, A·sai′ah his son.

31 And these were the ones to whom David gave positions for the direction of the singing at the house of Jehovah after the Ark had a resting place. 32 And they came

to be ministers in the singing before the tabernacle of the tent of meeting until Sol'o·mon built the house of Jehovah in Jerusalem; and they kept attending upon their service according to their commission. 33 And these were those in attendance and also their sons: Of the sons of the Ko'hath·ites He'man the singer, the son of Joel, the son of Samuel, 34 the son of El·ka'nah, the son of Je·ro'ham, the son of E'li·el, the son of To'ah, 35 the son of Zuph, the son of El·ka'nah, the son of Ma'hath, the son of A·ma'sai, 36 the son of El·ka'nah, the son of Joel, the son of Az·a·ri'ah, the son of Zeph·a·ni'ah, 37 the son of Ta'hath, the son of As'sir, the son of E·bi'a·saph, the son of Ko'rah, 38 the son of Iz'har, the son of Ko'hath, the son of Le'vi, the son of Israel.

39 As for his brother A'saph, who was attending at his right, A'saph was the son of Ber·e·chi'ah, the son of Shim'e·a, 40 the son of Mi'cha·el, the son of Ba·a·se'iah, the son of Mal·chi'jah, 41 the son of Eth'ni, the son of Ze'rah, the son of A·dai'ah, 42 the son of E'than, the son of Zim'mah, the son of Shim'e·i, 43 the son of Ja'hath, the son of Ger'shom, the son of Le'vi.

44 As regards the sons of Me·rar'i their brothers on the left hand, there was E'than the son of Kish'i, the son of Ab'di, the son of Mal'luch, 45 the son of Hash·a·bi'ah, the son of Am·a·zi'ah, the son of Hil·ki'ah, 46 the son of Am'zi, the son of Ba'ni, the son of She'mer, 47 the son of Mah'li, the son of Mu'shi, the son of Me·rar'i, the son of Le'vi.

48 And their brothers the Levites were the ones given for all the service of the tabernacle of the house of the [true] God. 49 And Aaron and his sons were making sacrificial smoke upon the altar of burnt offering and upon the altar of incense for all the work of the most holy things and to make atonement for Israel, according to all that Moses the servant of the [true] God had commanded.

50 And these were the sons of Aaron: E'le·a'zar his son, Phin'e·has his son, Ab·i·shu'a his son, 51 Buk'ki his son, Uz'zi his son, Zer·a·hi'ah his son, 52 Me·ra'ioth his son, Am·a·ri'ah his son, A·hi'tub his son, 53 Za'dok his son, A·him'a·az his son.

54 And these were their dwelling places by their walled camps in their territory, for the sons of Aaron belonging to the family of the Ko'hath·ites, for the lot had come to be theirs. 55 Accordingly they gave them He'bron in the land of Judah, with its pasture grounds all around it. 56 And the field of the city and its settlements they gave to Ca'leb the son of Je·phun'neh. 57 And to the sons of Aaron they gave the cities of refuge, He'bron, and Lib'nah with its pasture grounds and Jat'tir and Esh·te·mo'a with its pasture grounds, 58 and Hi'len with its pasture grounds, De'bir with its pasture grounds, 59 and A'shan with its pasture grounds and Beth-she'mesh with its pasture grounds; 60 and from the tribe of Benjamin Ge'ba with its pasture grounds and Al'e·meth with its pasture grounds and An'a·thoth with its pasture grounds. All their cities were thirteen cities among their families.

61 And to the sons of Ko'hath that were left over they gave from the family of the tribe, from the half tribe, the half of Ma·nas'seh, by the lot ten cities.

62 And to the sons of Ger'shom by their families they gave from the tribe of Is'sa·char and from the tribe of Ash'er and from the tribe of Naph'ta·li and from the tribe of Ma·nas'seh in Ba'shan, thirteen cities.

63 To the sons of Me·rar'i by their families they gave from the tribe of Reu'ben and from the tribe of Gad and from the tribe of Zeb'u·lun by the lot twelve cities.

64 Thus the sons of Israel gave the Levites the cities with their pasture grounds. 65 Furthermore, by the lot they gave from the tribe of the sons of Judah and from the tribe of the sons of Sim'e·on and

from the tribe of the sons of Benjamin these cities, which they proceeded to call by names.

66 And some of the families of the sons of Ko'hath came to have the cities of their territory from the tribe of E'phra·im. 67 Accordingly they gave them the cities of refuge, She'chem with its pasture grounds in the mountainous region of E'phra·im, and Ge'zer with its pasture grounds, 68 and Jok'me·am with its pasture grounds and Beth-ho'ron with its pasture grounds, 69 and Ai'ja·lon with its pasture grounds and Gath-rim'mon with its pasture grounds; 70 and from half of the tribe of Ma·nas'seh, A'ner with its pasture grounds and Bil'e·am with its pasture grounds, to the family of the sons of Ko'hath that were left over.

71 And to the sons of Ger'shom [they gave] from the family of the half tribe of Ma·nas'seh Go'lan in Ba'shan with its pasture grounds and Ash'ta·roth with its pasture grounds; 72 and from the tribe of Is'sa·char, Ke'desh with its pasture grounds and Dab'e·rath with its pasture grounds, 73 and Ra'moth with its pasture grounds and A'nem with its pasture grounds; 74 and from the tribe of Ash'er, Ma'shal with its pasture grounds and Ab'don with its pasture grounds, 75 and Hu'kok with its pasture grounds and Re'hob with its pasture grounds; 76 and from the tribe of Naph'ta·li, Ke'desh in Gal'i·lee with its pasture grounds and Ham'mon with its pasture grounds and Kir·i·a·tha'im with its pasture grounds.

77 To the sons of Me·rar'i that were left over [they gave] from the tribe of Zeb'u·lun Rim'mo·no with its pasture grounds, Ta'bor with its pasture grounds, 78 and in the region of the Jordan at Jer'i·cho to the east of the Jordan, from the tribe of Reu'ben, Be'zer in the wilderness with its pasture grounds and Ja'haz with its pasture grounds, 79 and Ked'e·moth with its pasture grounds and Meph'a·ath with its pasture grounds; 80 and from the tribe of Gad, Ra'moth in

Gil'e·ad with its pasture grounds and Ma·ha·na'im with its pasture grounds, 81 and Hesh'bon with its pasture grounds and Ja'zer with its pasture grounds.

7 Now the sons of Is'sa·char were To'la and Pu'ah, Ja'shub and Shim'ron, four. 2 And the sons of To'la were Uz'zi and Re·pha'iah and Je'ri·el and Jah'mai and Ib'sam and She·mu'el, heads of the house of their forefathers. Of To'la there were valiant, mighty men, by their descendants. Their number in the days of David was twenty-two thousand six hundred. 3 And the sons of Uz'zi were Iz·ra·hi'ah; and the sons of Iz·ra·hi'ah were Mi'cha·el and O·ba·di'ah and Joel, Is·shi'ah, , five, all of them being heads. 4 And with them by their descendants, according to the house of their forefathers, there were troops of the army for war, thirty-six thousand, for they had many wives and sons. 5 And their brothers of all the families of Is'sa·char were valiant, mighty men, eighty-seven thousand by the genealogical enrollment of them all.

6 [The sons of] Benjamin were Be'la and Be'cher and Je·di'a·el, three. 7 And the sons of Be'la were Ez'bon and Uz'zi and Uz'zi·el and Jer'i·moth and I'ri, five, heads of the house of their forefathers, valiant, mighty men; and their genealogical enrollment was twenty-two thousand and thirty-four. 8 And the sons of Be'cher were Ze·mi'rah and Jo'ash and E·li·e'zer and E·li·o·e'nai and Om'ri and Jer'e·moth and A·bi'jah and An'a·thoth and Al'e·meth, all these the sons of Be'cher. 9 And their genealogical enrollment by their descendants as respects the heads of the house of their forefathers, valiant, mighty men, was twenty thousand two hundred. 10 And the sons of Je·di'a·el were Bil'han; and the sons of Bil'han were Je'ush and Benjamin and E'hud and Che·na'a·nah and Ze'than and Tar'shish and A·hish'a·har. 11 All these were the sons of Je·di'a·el, according to the heads of their forefathers, valiant, mighty men,

seventeen thousand two hundred going out to the army for war.

12 And the Shup′pim and the Hup′pim were the sons of Ir; the Hu′shim were the sons of A′her.

13 The sons of Naph′ta·li were Jah′zi·el and Gu′ni and Je′zer and Shal′lum, the sons of Bil′hah.

14 The sons of Ma·nas′seh were As′ri·el, whom his Syrian concubine bore. (She bore Ma′chir the father of Gil′e·ad. 15 And Ma′chir himself took a wife for Hup′pim and for Shup′pim, and the name of his sister was Ma′a·cah.) And the name of the second was Ze·lo′phe·had, but Ze·lo′phe·had came to have daughters. 16 In time Ma′a·cah, Ma′chir's wife, bore a son and called his name Pe′resh; and the name of his brother was She′resh; and his sons were U′lam and Re′kem. 17 And the sons of U′lam were Be′dan. These were the sons of Gil′e·ad the son of Ma′chir the son of Ma·nas′seh. 18 And his sister was Ham·mo′le·cheth. She gave birth to Ish′hod and A·bi·e′zer and Mah′lah. 19 And the sons of She·mi′da came to be A·hi′an and She′chem and Lik′hi and A·ni′am.

20 And the sons of E′phra·im were Shu′the·lah and Be′red his son and Ta′hath his son and E·le·a′dah his son and Ta′hath his son, 21 and Za′bad his son and Shu′the·lah his son and E′zer and E′le·ad. And the men of Gath that were born in the land killed them because they came down to take their livestock. 22 And E′phra·im their father carried on mourning for many days, and his brothers kept coming in to comfort him. 23 Afterward he had relations with his wife, so that she became pregnant and gave birth to a son. But he called his name Be·ri′ah, because it was with calamity that she happened to be in his house. 24 And his daughter was She′e·rah, and she got to build Beth-ho′ron, the lower and the upper, and Uz′zen-she′e·rah. 25 And there was Re′phah his son, and Re′sheph, and Te′lah his son, and Ta′han his son, 26 La′dan his son, Am·mi′-

hud his son, E·lish′a·ma his son, 27 Nun his son, Je·hosh′u·a his son.

28 And their possession and their dwelling places were Beth′el and its dependent towns and, to the east, Na′a·ran and, to the west, Ge′zer and its dependent towns, and She′chem and its dependent towns clear to Ga′za and its dependent towns; 29 and by the side of the sons of Ma·nas′seh Beth-she′an and its dependent towns, Ta′a·nach and its dependent towns, Me·gid′do and its dependent towns, Dor and its dependent towns. In these the sons of Joseph the son of Israel dwelt.

30 The sons of Ash′er were Im′nah and Ish′vah and Ish′vi and Be·ri′ah; and Se′rah was their sister. 31 And the sons of Be·ri′ah were He′ber and Mal′chi·el, who was the father of Bir′za·ith. 32 As for He′ber, he became father to Japh′let and Sho′mer and Ho′tham, and to Shu′a their sister. 33 And the sons of Japh′let were Pa′sach and Bim′hal and Ash′vath. These were the sons of Japh′let. 34 And the sons of She′mer were A′hi and Roh′gah, Je·hub′bah and A′ram. 35 And the sons of He′lem his brother were Zo′phah and Im′na and She′lesh and A′mal. 36 The sons of Zo′phah were Su′ah and Har′ne·pher and Shu′al and Be′ri and Im′rah, 37 Be′zer and Hod and Sham′ma and Shil′shah and Ith′ran and Be·e′ra. 38 And the sons of Je′ther were Je·phun′neh and Pis′pah and A′ra. 39 And the sons of Ul′la were A′rah and Han′ni·el and Ri·zi′a. 40 All these were the sons of Ash′er, heads of the house of the forefathers, select, valiant, mighty men, heads of the chieftains; and their genealogical enrollment was in the army in the war. Their number was twenty-six thousand men.

8 As for Benjamin, he became father to Be′la his first-born, Ash′bel the second and A·har′ah the third, 2 No′hah the fourth and Ra′pha the fifth. 3 And Be′la came to have sons, Ad′dar and Ge′ra and A·bi′hud, 4 and Ab·i·shu′a and Na′a·man and A·ho′ah,

5 and Ge′ra and She·phu′phan and Hu′ram. 6 And these were the sons of E′hud. These were the heads of [the houses of] forefathers belonging to the inhabitants of Ge′ba, and they proceeded to take them into exile at Man′a·hath. 7 And Na′a·man and A·hi′jah; and Ge′ra—he was the one that took them into exile, and he became father to Uz′za and A·hi′hud. 8 As for Sha·ha·ra′im, he became father to [children] in the field of Mo′ab after he sent them away. Hu′shim and Ba′a·ra were his wives. 9 And by Ho′desh his wife he came to be father to Jo′bab and Zib′i·a and Me′sha and Mal′cam, 10 and Je′uz and Sa·chi′a and Mir′mah. These were his sons, heads of [the houses of] forefathers.

11 And by Hu′shim he became father to A·bi′tub and El·pa′al. 12 And the sons of El·pa′al were E′ber and Mi′sham and She′med, who built O′no and Lod and its dependent towns, 13 and Be·ri′ah and She′ma. These were heads of [the houses of] forefathers, belonging to the inhabitants of Ai′ja·lon. These were the ones that chased away the inhabitants of Gath. 14 And there were A·hi′o, Sha′shak and Jer′e·moth, 15 and Zeb·a·di′ah and A′rad and E′der, 16 and Mi′cha·el and Ish′pah and Jo′ha, the sons of Be·ri′ah, 17 and Zeb·a·di′ah and Me·shul′lam and Hiz′ki and He′ber, 18 and Ish′me·rai and Iz·li′ah and Jo′bab, the sons of El·pa′al, 19 and Ja′kim and Zich′ri and Zab′di, 20 and E·li·e′nai and Zil′le·thai and E′li·el, 21 and A·dai′ah and Be·ra′iah and Shim′rath, the sons of Shim′e·i, 22 and Ish′pan and E′ber and E′li·el, 23 and Ab′don and Zich′ri and Ha′nan, 24 and Han·a·ni′ah and E′lam and An·tho·thi′jah, 25 and Iph·de′iah and Pe·nu′el, the sons of Sha′shak, 26 and Sham′she·rai and She·ha·ri′ah and Ath·a·li′ah, 27 and Ja·a·re·shi′ah and E·li′jah and Zich′ri, the sons of Je·ro′ham. 28 These were heads of [the houses of] forefathers by their descendants, headmen. These were the ones that dwelt in Jerusalem.

29 And it was in Gib′e·on that the father of Gib′e·on, [Je·i′el,] dwelt, and his wife's name was Ma′a·cah. 30 And his son, the first-born, was Ab′don, and Zur and Kish and Ba′al and Na′dab, 31 and Ge′dor and A·hi′o and Ze′cher. 32 As for Mik′loth, he became father to Shim′e·ah. And these really were the ones that dwelt in front of their brothers in Jerusalem along with brothers of theirs.

33 As for Ner, he became father to Kish; Kish, in turn, became father to Saul; Saul, in turn, became father to Jon′a·than and Mal′chi-shu′a and A·bin′a·dab and Esh·ba′al. 34 And Jon′a·than's son was Mer′ib-ba′al. As for Mer′ib-ba′al, he became father to Mi′cah. 35 And the sons of Mi′cah were Pi′thon and Me′lech and Ta·re′a and A′haz. 36 As for A′haz, he became father to Je·ho′ad·dah; Je·ho′ad·dah, in turn, became father to Al′e·meth and Az′ma·veth and Zim′ri. Zim′ri, in turn, became father to Mo′za; 37 Mo′za, in turn, became father to Bin′e·a, Ra′phah his son, El·e·a′sah his son, A′zel his son. 38 And A′zel had six sons, and these were their names: Az·ri′kam, Bo′che·ru and Ish′ma·el and She·a·ri′ah and O·ba·di′ah and Ha′nan. All these were the sons of A′zel. 39 And the sons of E′shek his brother were U′lam his first-born, Je′ush the second and E·liph′e·let the third. 40 And the sons of U′lam came to be valiant, mighty men, bending the bow, and having many sons and grandsons, a hundred and fifty. All these were from the sons of Benjamin.

9 As for all Israelites, they were enrolled genealogically; and there they are written in the Book of the Kings of Israel. And Judah itself was taken into exile at Babylon for their unfaithfulness. 2 And the first inhabitants that were in their possession in their cities were the Israelites, the priests, the Levites and the Neth′i·nim. 3 And in Jerusalem there dwelt some of the sons of Judah and some of the sons of Benjamin and

some of the sons of E'phra·im and of Ma·nas'seh: 4 U'thai the son of Am·mi'hud the son of Om'ri the son of Im'ri the son of Ba'ni, of the sons of Pe'rez the son of Judah. 5 And of the Shi'lo·nites, A·sai'ah the first-born and his sons. 6 And of the sons of Ze'rah, Je·u'el, and six hundred and ninety brothers of theirs.

7 And of the sons of Benjamin, Sal'lu the son of Me·shul'lam the son of Hod·a·vi'ah the son of Has·se·nu'ah, 8 and Ib·ne'iah the son of Je·ro'ham, and E'lah the son of Uz'zi the son of Mich'ri, and Me·shul'lam the son of Sheph·a·ti'ah the son of Reu'el the son of Ib·ni'-jah. 9 And the brothers of theirs by their descendants were nine hundred and fifty-six. All these were men that were heads of the fathers by the house of their fore-fathers.

10 And of the priests there were Je·dai'ah and Je·hoi'a·rib and Ja'-chin, 11 and Az·a·ri'ah the son of Hil·ki'ah the son of Me·shul'-lam the son of Za'dok the son of Me·ra'ioth the son of A·hi'tub, a leader of the house of the [true] God, 12 and A·dai'ah the son of Je·ro'ham the son of Pash'hur the son of Mal·chi'jah, and Ma'a·sai the son of Ad'i·el the son of Jah'-ze·rah the son of Me·shul'lam the son of Me·shil'le·mith the son of Im'mer, 13 and their brothers, heads of the house of their fore-fathers, a thousand seven hundred and sixty, mighty men of ability for the work of the service of the house of the [true] God.

14 And of the Levites there were She·mai'ah the son of Has'shub the son of Az·ri'kam the son of Hash-a·bi'ah from the sons of Me·rar'i; 15 and Bak·bak'kar, He'resh and Ga'lal, and Mat·ta·ni'ah the son of Mi'ca the son of Zich'ri the son of A'saph, 16 and O·ba·di'ah the son of She·mai'ah the son of Ga'-lal the son of Je·du'thun, and Ber-e·chi'ah the son of A'sa the son of El·ka'nah, who was dwelling in the settlements of the Ne·toph'a·thites.

17 And the gatekeepers were Shal'lum and Ak'kub and Tal'mon and A·hi'man and their brother Shal'lum the head, 18 and up till then he was in the king's gate to the east. These were the gatekeep-ers of the camps of the sons of Le'vi. 19 And Shal'lum the son of Ko're the son of E·bi'a·saph the son of Ko'rah and his brothers of the house of his father the Ko'rah-ites, over the work of the service, the doorkeepers of the tent, and their fathers over the camp of Je-hovah, the keepers of the entry-way. 20 And it was Phin'e·has the son of E·le·a'zar that hap-pened to be leader over them in the past. Jehovah was with him. 21 Zech·a·ri'ah the son of Me·shel-e·mi'ah was the gatekeeper of the entrance of the tent of meeting.

22 All of them who were selected as gatekeepers at the thresholds were two hundred and twelve. They were in their settlements by their genealogical enrollment. These Da-vid and Samuel the seer ordained in their office of trust. 23 And they and their sons were over the gatekeepers of the house of Jeho-vah, even the house of the tent, for guard service. 24 It was to the four directions that the gatekeepers came to be, to the east, to the west, to the north and to the south. 25 And their brothers in their settlements were to come in for seven days, from time to time, along with these. 26 For in office of trust there were four mighty men of the gatekeepers. They were Levites, and they proved to be in charge of the dining rooms and of the treasures of the house of the [true] God. 27 And all around the house of the [true] God they would spend the night; for guard service was upon them, and they were in charge of the key, even [to open up] from morning to morning.

28 And some of them were in charge of the utensils of the service, for it was by number that they would bring them in and it was by number that they would take them out. 29 And some of them were men appointed over the utensils and over all the holy utensils and over the fine flour and the wine and

the oil and the frankincense and the balsam oil. 30 And some of the sons of the priests were makers of the ointment mixture of balsam oil. 31 And Mat·ti·thi'ah of the Levites, who was the first-born of Shal'lum the Ko'rah·ite, was in the office of trust over the things baked in pans. 32 And some of the sons of the Ko'hath·ites, their brothers, were in charge of the layer bread, to prepare it sabbath by sabbath.

33 And these were the singers, the heads of the fathers of the Levites in the dining rooms, those set free from duty; for by day and by night it was their responsibility to be in the work. 34 These were the heads of the fathers of the Levites by their descendants, headmen. These were the ones that dwelt in Jerusalem.

35 And in Gib'e·on was where the father of Gib'e·on, Je·i'el, dwelt. And his wife's name was Ma'a·cah. 36 And his son, the first-born, was Ab'don, and Zur and Kish and Ba'al and Ner and Na'dab, 37 and Ge'dor and A·hi'o and Zech·a·ri'ah and Mik'loth. 38 As for Mik'loth, he became father to Shim'e·am. And it was really they that dwelt in front of their brothers in Jerusalem along with brothers of theirs. 39 As for Ner, he became father to Kish; Kish, in turn, became father to Saul; Saul, in turn, became father to Jon'a·than and Mal'chi-shu'a and A·bin'a·dab and Esh-ba'al. 40 And the son of Jon'a·than was Mer'ib-ba'al. As for Mer'ib-ba'al, he became father to Mi'cah. 41 And the sons of Mi'cah were Pi'thon and Me'lech and Tahr'e·a [and A'haz]. 42 As for A'haz, he became father to Ja'rah; Ja'rah, in turn, became father to Al'e·meth and Az'ma·veth and Zim'ri. Zim'ri, in turn, became father to Mo'za. 43 As for Mo'za, he became father to Bin'e·a and Re·pha'iah his son, El·e·a'sah his son, A'zel his son. 44 And A'zel had six sons, and these were their names: Az·ri'kam, Bo'che·ru and Ish'ma·el and She·a·ri'ah and O·ba·di'ah and Ha'nan. These were the sons of A'zel.

10 And the Phi·lis'tines, for their part, made war upon Israel; and the men of Israel went fleeing from before the Phi·lis'tines and kept falling slain in Mount Gil·bo'a. 2 And the Phi·lis'tines kept in close range of Saul and his sons; and the Phi·lis'tines got to strike down Jon'a·than and A·bin'a·dab and Mal'chi-shu'a, sons of Saul. 3 And the fighting became heavy against Saul; and those shooting with the bow finally found him, and he got wounded by the shooters. 4 Then Saul said to his armor-bearer: "Draw your sword and run me through with it, that these uncircumcised men may not come and certainly deal abusively with me." And his armor-bearer was unwilling, because he was very much afraid. So Saul took the sword and fell upon it. 5 When his armor-bearer saw that Saul had died, then he too fell upon the sword and died. 6 Thus Saul and three sons of his died, and all those of his house died together. 7 When all the men of Israel that were in the low plain saw that they had fled and that Saul and his sons had died, then they began to leave their cities and flee; after which the Phi·lis'tines came on in and took up dwelling in them.

8 And it came about the next day that, when the Phi·lis'tines came to strip the slain, they got to find Saul and his sons fallen upon Mount Gil·bo'a. 9 And they proceeded to strip him and take off his head and his armor and send into the land of the Phi·lis'tines all around to inform their idols and the people. 10 Finally they put his armor in the house of their god, and his skull they fastened to the house of Da'gon.

11 And all those of Ja'besh in Gil'e·ad got to hear of all that the Phi·lis'tines had done to Saul. 12 So all the valiant men rose up and carried off the corpse of Saul and the corpses of his sons and brought them to Ja'besh and buried their bones under the big tree in Ja'besh; and they went fasting for seven days.

13 Thus Saul died for his unfaithfulness with which he had acted faithlessly against Jehovah concerning the word of Jehovah that he had not kept and also for asking of a spirit medium to make inquiry. 14 And he did not inquire of Jehovah. Consequently he put him to death and turned the kingship over to David the son of Jes'se.

11 In time all the Israelites collected themselves together to David at He'bron, saying: "Look! We are your bone and your flesh. 2 Both yesterday and previously, even while Saul happened to be king, you were the one leading Israel out and bringing it in; and Jehovah your God proceeded to say to you, 'You yourself will shepherd my people Israel, and you yourself will become leader over my people Israel.'" 3 So all the older men of Israel came to the king at He'bron and David concluded a covenant with them in He'bron before Jehovah; after which they anointed David as king over Israel, according to Jehovah's word by means of Samuel.

4 Later David and all Israel went to Jerusalem, that is to say, Je'bus, where the Jeb'u·sites were the inhabitants of the land. 5 And the inhabitants of Je'bus began to say to David: "You will not come in here." Just the same, David proceeded to capture the stronghold of Zion, that is to say, the city of David. 6 So David said: "Anyone striking the Jeb'u·sites first, he will become head and prince." And Jo'ab the son of Ze·ru'iah got to go up first, and he came to be head. 7 And David took up dwelling in the place difficult to approach. That is why they called it the city of David. 8 And he began to build the city all around, from the Mound even to the parts round about, but Jo'ab himself brought to life the rest of the city. 9 And David went on getting greater and greater, for Jehovah of armies was with him.

10 Now these are the heads of the mighty men that belonged to David, holding strongly with him in his kingship together with all

Israel, to make him king according to Jehovah's word concerning Israel. 11 And this is the list of the mighty men that belonged to David: Ja·sho'be·am the son of a Hach'mon·ite, the head of the three. He was brandishing his spear over three hundred slain at one time. 12 And after him there was E·le·a'zar the son of Do'do the A·ho'hite. He was among the three mighty men. 13 He it was that happened to be with David at Pas·dam'mim, where the Phi·lis'tines had gathered themselves together for war. Now there happened to be a tract of the field full of barley, and the people, for their part, had fled because of the Phi·lis'tines. 14 But he took his stand in the middle of the tract and delivered it, and kept striking down the Phi·lis'tines, so that Jehovah saved with a great salvation.

15 And three of the thirty head ones proceeded to go down to the rock, to David at the cave of A·dul'lam, while a camp of the Phi·lis'tines was camping in the low plain of Reph'a·im. 16 And David was then in the place hard to approach; and a garrison of the Phi·lis'tines was then in Beth'lehem. 17 After a while David showed his craving and said: "O that I might have a drink of the water from the cistern of Beth'le·hem, which is at the gate!" 18 At that the three forced their way into the camp of the Phi·lis'tines and drew water from the cistern of Beth'le·hem, which is at the gate, and came carrying and bringing it to David. And David did not consent to drink it, but poured it out to Jehovah. 19 And he went on to say: "It is unthinkable on my part, as regards my God, to do this! Is it the blood of these men that I should drink at the risk of their souls? For it was at the risk of their souls that they brought it." And he did not consent to drink it. These are the things that the three mighty men did.

20 As for A·bish'ai the brother of Jo'ab, he himself became head

of the three; and he was brandishing his spear over three hundred slain, and he had a reputation like the three. 21 Of the three he was more distinguished than the two others, and he came to be a chief to them; and yet he did not come up to the [first] three.

22 As for Be·nai′ah the son of Je·hoi′a·da, the son of a valiant man, who did many deeds in Kab′ze·el, he himself struck down the two [sons] of Ar′i·el of Moab; and he himself descended and struck down a lion inside a waterpit in the day of snowfall. 23 And he it was that struck down the Egyptian man, a man of extraordinary size, of five cubits. And in the hand of the Egyptian there was a spear like the beam of loom workers; yet he went on down to him with a rod and snatched the spear away from the Egyptian's hand and killed him with his own spear. 24 These things Be·nai′ah the son of Je·hoi′a·da did, and he had a name among the three mighty men. 25 Although he was more distinguished than the thirty, yet to the rank of the [first] three he did not come. However, David put him over his own bodyguard.

26 As for the mighty men of the military forces, there were As′a·hel the brother of Jo′ab, El·ha′nan the son of Do′do of Beth′le·hem, 27 Sham′moth the Ha′ro·rite, He′lez the Pel′o·nite, 28 I′ra the son of Ik′kesh the Te·ko′ite, A·bi·e′zer the An′a·thoth·ite, 29 Sib′be·cai the Hu′shath·ite, I′lai the A·ho′hite, 30 Ma′ha·rai the Ne·toph′a·thite, He′led the son of Ba′a·nah the Ne·toph′a·thite, 31 I′thai the son of Ri′bai of Gib′e·ah of the sons of Benjamin, Be·nai′ah the Pir′a·thon·ite, 32 Hu′rai from the torrent valleys of Ga′ash, A·bi′el the Ar′bath·ite, 33 Az′ma·veth the Ba·ha′rum·ite, E·li′ah·ba the Sha·al′bo·nite, 34 the sons of Ha′shem the Gi′zo·nite, Jon′a·than the son of Sha′gee the Har′a·rite, 35 A·hi′am the son of Sa′car the Har′a·rite, E·li′phal the son of Ur, 36 He′pher the Me·che′rath·ite, A·hi′jah the Pel′o·nite, 37 Hez′ro

the Car′mel·ite, Na′a·rai the son of Ez′bai, 38 Joel the brother of Nathan, Mib′har the son of Hag′ri, 39 Ze′lek the Am′mon·ite, Na′ha·rai the Be·roth′ite, the armorbearer of Jo′ab the son of Ze·ru′iah, 40 I′ra the Ith′rite, Ga′reb the Ith′rite, 41 U·ri′ah the Hit′tite, Za′bad the son of Ah′lai, 42 Ad′i·na the son of Shi′za the Reu′ben·ite, a head of the Reu′ben·ites, by whom there were thirty; 43 Ha′nan the son of Ma′a·cah, and Josh′a·phat the Mith′nite, 44 Uz·zi′a the Ash′te·rath·ite, Sha′ma and Je·i′el, the sons of Ho′tham the A·ro′er·ite, 45 Je·di′a·el the son of Shim′ri, and Jo′ha his brother the Ti′zite, 46 E′li·el the Ma′ha·vite, and Jer′i·bai and Josh·a·vi′ah the sons of El′na·am, and Ith′mah the Mo′ab·ite. 47 E′li·el and O′bed and Ja·a·si′el the Me·zo′ba·ite.

12 And these are the ones that came to David at Zik′lag while he was still under restrictions because of Saul the son of Kish; and they were among the mighty men, the helpers in the warfare, 2 armed with the bow, using the right hand and using the left hand with stones or with arrows in the bow. They were of the brothers of Saul, of Benjamin. 3 There was the head A·hi·e′zer and Jo′ash the sons of She·ma′ah the Gib′e·ath·ite, and Je′zi·el and Pe′let the sons of Az′ma·veth, and Ber′a·cah and Je′hu the An′a·thoth·ite, 4 and Ish·ma′iah the Gib′e·on·ite, a mighty man among the thirty and over the thirty; and Jeremiah and Ja·ha·zi′el and Jo·ha′nan and Jo′za·bad the Ge·de′rath·ite, 5 E·lu′zai and Jer′i·moth and Be·a·li′ah and Shem·a·ri′ah and Sheph·a·ti′ah the Har′i·phite, 6 El·ka′nah and Is·shi′ah and Az′ar·el and Jo·e′zer and Ja·sho′be·am, the Ko′rah·ites, 7 and Jo·e′lah and Zeb·a·di′ah the sons of Je·ro′ham of Ge′dor.

8 And there were some of the Gad′ites that separated themselves to David's side at the place difficult to approach in the wilderness, valiant, mighty men, army men for

the war, keeping the large shield and the lance ready, whose faces were the faces of lions, and they were like the gazelles upon the mountains for speed. 9 E′zer was the head, O·ba·di′ah the second, E·li′ab the third, 10 Mish·man′nah the fourth, Jeremiah the fifth, 11 At′tai the sixth, E′li·el the seventh, 12 Jo·ha′nan the eighth, El·za′bad the ninth, 13 Jeremiah the tenth, Mach′ban·nai the eleventh. 14 These were of the sons of Gad, heads of the army. The least one was equal to a hundred, and the greatest to a thousand. 15 These are the ones that crossed the Jordan in the first month when it was overflowing all its banks, and they then chased away all those of the low plains, to the east and to the west.

16 And some of the sons of Benjamin and Judah proceeded to come clear to the place difficult to approach, to David. 17 Then David went out before them and answered and said to them: "If it is for peace that you have come to me to help me, my own heart will become at unity with you. But if it is to betray me to my adversaries when there is no wrong on my palms, let the God of our forefathers see to it and set it in order." 18 And spirit itself enveloped A·ma′sai, the head of the thirty:

"Yours [we are], O David, and with you [we are], O son of Jes′se.

Peace, peace be yours, and peace to the one helping you,

For your God has helped you."

So David received them and put them among the heads of the troops.

19 And there were some of Ma·nas′seh that deserted to David when he came with the Phi·lis′tines against Saul for battle; but he did not help them, for on counsel the axis lords of the Phi·lis′tines sent him away, saying: "At the risk of our own heads he will desert to his lord Saul." 20 When he came to Zik′lag there deserted to him from Ma·nas′seh Ad′nah and Jo′za·bad and Je·di′a·el and Mi′cha·el

and Jo′za·bad and E·li′hu and Zil′le·thai, heads of the thousands that belonged to Ma·nas′seh. 21 And they, for their part, were of help to David against the marauder band, because all of them were mighty men of valor, and they came to be chiefs in the army; 22 for day by day people kept coming to David to help him, until it was a great camp, like the camp of God.

23 And these were the numbers of the heads of those equipped for the army that came to David at He′bron to turn the kingship of Saul over to him according to Jehovah's order. 24 The sons of Judah carrying the large shield and the lance were six thousand eight hundred, equipped for the army. 25 Of the sons of Sim′e·on the mighty men of valor of the army were seven thousand one hundred.

26 Of the sons of the Levites four thousand six hundred. 27 And Je·hoi′a·da was the leader [of the sons] of Aaron, and with him there were three thousand seven hundred. 28 Also Za′dok a young man, mighty in valor, and the house of his forefathers, twenty-two chiefs.

29 And of the sons of Benjamin, the brothers of Saul, there were three thousand, and up till then the greater number of them were keeping strict watch of the house of Saul. 30 And of the sons of E′phra·im there were twenty thousand eight hundred, mighty men of valor, men of fame, by the house of their forefathers.

31 And of the half tribe of Ma·nas′seh there were eighteen thousand that had been designated by name to come to make David king. 32 And of the sons of Is′sa·char having a knowledge of how to discern the times to know what Israel ought to do, there were two hundred head ones of theirs, and all their brothers were at their orders. 33 Of Zeb′u·lun those going out to the army, drawing up in battle formation with all the weapons of war, there were fifty thousand, and for flocking together [to

David] they were not of a double heart. 34 And of Naph'ta·li there were a thousand chiefs, and with them with the large shield and the spear there were thirty-seven thousand. 35 And of the Dan'ites those drawing up in battle formation were twenty-eight thousand six hundred. 36 And of Ash'er those going out to the army for drawing up in battle formation were forty thousand.

37 And from across the Jordan of the Reu'ben·ites and the Gad'-ites and the half tribe of Ma·nas'-seh with all the weapons of the military army there were a hundred and twenty thousand. 38 All these were men of war, flocking together in battle line; with a complete heart they came to He'bron to make David king over all Israel; and also all the remainder of Israel were of one heart for making David king. 39 And they continued there with David three days, eating and drinking, for their brothers had made preparation for them. 40 And also those near to them, as far as Is'sa·char and Zeb'u·lun and Naph'ta·li, were bringing food upon asses and upon camels and upon mules and upon cattle, eatables of flour, cakes of pressed figs and cakes of raisins and wine and oil and cattle and sheep in great quantity, for there was rejoicing in Israel.

13 And David proceeded to consult with the chiefs of the thousands and of the hundreds and with every leader; 2 and David went on to say to all the congregation of Israel: "If it seems good to YOU and it is acceptable with Jehovah our God, let us send to our brothers that are left over in all the lands of Israel and with them [to] the priests and the Levites in their cities with pasture grounds, that they may collect themselves together to us. 3 And let us bring the ark of our God around to ourselves." For they had not cared for it in the days of Saul. 4 So all the congregation said to do that way, for the thing seemed right in the eyes of all the people.

5 Accordingly David congregated all Israel from the river of Egypt as far as the entering of Ha'math, to bring the ark of the [true] God from Kir'i·ath-je·a·rim.

6 And David and all Israel proceeded to go up to Ba'al·ah, to Kir'i·ath-je·a·rim, which belongs to Judah, to bring up from there the ark of the [true] God, Jehovah, sitting on the cherubs, where [his] name is called on. 7 However, they had the ark of the [true] God ride upon a new wagon from the house of A·bin'a·dab, and Uz'zah and A·hi'o were leading the wagon. 8 And David and all Israel were celebrating before the [true] God with full power and with songs and with harps and with stringed instruments and with tambourines and with cymbals and with trumpets. 9 And they came gradually as far as the threshing floor of Chi'don, and Uz'zah now thrust his hand out to grab hold of the Ark, for the bulls nearly caused an upset. 10 At that Jehovah's anger blazed against Uz'zah, so that he struck him down because he had thrust his hand out upon the Ark, and he died there before God. 11 And David became angry because Jehovah had broken through in a rupture against Uz'zah; and that place came to be called Pe'rez-uz'zah down to this day.

12 And David became afraid of the [true] God on that day, saying: "How shall I bring the ark of the [true] God to me?" 13 And David did not remove the Ark to himself at the city of David, but he carried it aside to the house of O'bed-e'dom the Git'tite. 14 And the ark of the [true] God kept dwelling with the household of O'bed-e'dom, at his house three months; and Jehovah kept blessing the household of O'bed-e'dom and all that was his.

14 And Hi'ram the king of Tyre proceeded to send messengers to David and cedar timbers and builders of walls and workers in wood to build him a house. 2 And David came to know that Jehovah had firmly established him as king over Israel, for his kingship was highly exalted on account of his people Israel.

3 And David went on to take more wives in Jerusalem, and David came to be father to more sons and daughters. 4 And these are the names of the children that became his in Jerusalem: Sham·mu′a and Sho′bab, Nathan and Sol′o·mon, 5 and Ib′har and E·li′shu·a and El′pe·let, 6 and No′gah and Ne′pheg and Ja·phi′a, 7 and E·lish′a·ma and Be·e·li′a·da and E·liph′e·let.

8 And the Phi·lis′tines got to hear that David had been anointed as king over all Israel. At that all the Phi·lis′tines came up to look for David. When David heard of it, then he went out against them. 9 And the Phi·lis′tines, for their part, came in and kept making raids in the low plain of Reph′a·im. 10 And David began to inquire of God, saying: "Shall I go up against the Phi·lis′tines, and will you certainly give them into my hand?" At this Jehovah said to him: "Go up, and I shall certainly give them into your hand." 11 So David went up to Ba′al-pe·ra′zim and there got to strike them down. At that David said: "The [true] God has broken through my enemies by my hand like a gap made by waters." That is why they called the name of that place Ba′al-pe·ra′zim. 12 Consequently they left their gods there. Then David said the word, and so they were burned in the fire.

13 Later the Phi·lis′tines once again made a raid in the low plain. 14 At that David inquired again of God, and the [true] God now said to him: "You must not go up after them. Go around from directly against them, and you must come at them in front of the ba′ca bushes. 15 And let it occur that, when you hear the sound of the marching in the tops of the ba′ca bushes, then you go out into the fight, because the [true] God will have gone out before you to strike the camp of the Phi·lis′tines down." 16 So David did just as the [true] God had commanded

him, and they went striking down the camp of the Phi·lis′tines from Gib′e·on to Ge′zer. 17 And David's fame began to go out into all the lands, and Jehovah himself put the dread of him upon all the nations.

15 And he continued building houses for himself in the city of David; and he went on to prepare a place for the ark of the [true] God and pitch a tent for it. 2 It was then that David said: "No one is to carry the ark of the [true] God but the Levites, for they are the ones whom Jehovah has chosen to carry the ark of Jehovah and to minister to him to time indefinite." 3 Then David congregated all Israel at Jerusalem to bring the ark of Jehovah up to its place that he had prepared for it.

4 And David proceeded to gather the sons of Aaron and the Levites; 5 of the sons of Ko′hath, U·ri′el the chief and his brothers, a hundred and twenty; 6 of the sons of Me·rar′i, A·sai′ah the chief and his brothers, two hundred and twenty; 7 of the sons of Ger′shom, Joel the chief and his brothers, a hundred and thirty; 8 of the sons of E·li·za′phan, She·mai′ah the chief and his brothers, two hundred; 9 of the sons of He′bron, E′li·el the chief and his brothers, eighty; 10 of the sons of Uz′zi·el, Am·min′a·dab the chief and his brothers, a hundred and twelve. 11 Furthermore, David called Za′dok and A·bi′a·thar the priests, and the Levites U·ri′el, A·sai′ah and Joel, She·mai′ah and E′li·el and Am·min′a·dab, 12 and he went on to say to them: "You are the heads of the fathers of the Levites. Sanctify yourselves, you and your brothers, and you must bring the ark of Jehovah the God of Israel up to the place that I have prepared for it. 13 Because at the first time you did not, Jehovah our God broke through against us, for we did not search after him according to the custom." 14 So the priests and the Levites sanctified themselves to bring up the ark of Jehovah the God of Israel.

15 Then the sons of the Levites began to carry the ark of the [true] God, just as Moses had commanded by Jehovah's word, upon their shoulders with the rods upon them. 16 David now said to the chiefs of the Levites to station their brothers the singers with the instruments of song, stringed instruments and harps and cymbals, playing aloud to cause a sound of rejoicing to arise.

17 Accordingly the Levites stationed He'man the son of Joel and, of his brothers, A'saph the son of Ber·e·chi'ah; and, of the sons of Me·rar'i their brothers, E'than the son of Kush·a'iah; 18 and with them their brothers of the second division, Zech·a·ri'ah, Ben and Ja·a'zi·el and She·mir'a·moth and Je·hi'el and Un'ni, E·li'ab and Be·nai'ah and Ma·a·sei'ah and Mat·ti·thi'ah and E·liph'e·le·hu and Mik·ne'iah, and O'bed-e'dom and Je·i'el the gatekeepers, 19 and the singers He'man, A'saph and E'than, with the copper cymbals to play aloud; 20 and Zech·a·ri'ah and A'zi·el and She·mir'a·moth and Je·hi'el and Un'ni and E·li'ab and Ma·a·sei'ah and Be·nai'ah with stringed instruments tuned to Al'a·moth, 21 and Mat·ti·thi'ah and E·liph'e·le·hu and Mik·ne'iah and O'bed-e'dom and Je·i'el and Az·a·zi'ah with harps tuned to Shem'i·nith, to act as directors; 22 and Chen·a·ni'ah the chief of the Levites in carrying, he giving instruction in carrying, for he was expert; 23 and Ber·e·chi'ah and El·ka'nah the gatekeepers for the Ark; 24 and Sheb·a·ni'ah and Josh'a·phat and Ne·than'el and A·ma'sai and Zech·a·ri'ah and Be·nai'ah and E·li·e'zer the priests loudly sounding the trumpets before the ark of the [true] God, and O'bed-e'dom and Je·hi'ah the gatekeepers for the Ark.

25 And David and the older men of Israel and the chiefs of the thousands came to be the ones walking along to bring up the ark of the covenant of Jehovah from the house of O'bed-e'dom with rejoicing. 26 And it came about

when the [true] God helped the Levites while carrying the ark of the covenant of Jehovah that they proceeded to sacrifice seven young bulls and seven rams. 27 And David was dressed in a sleeveless coat of fine fabric, and also all the Levites carrying the Ark and the singers and Chen·a·ni'ah the chief of the carrying by the singers; but upon David there was an eph'od of linen. 28 And all the Israelites were bringing up the ark of the covenant of Jehovah with joyful shouting and with the sounding of the horn and with trumpets and with cymbals, playing aloud on stringed instruments and harps.

29 And it came about that, when the ark of the covenant of Jehovah came as far as the city of David, Mi'chal, Saul's daughter, herself looked down through the window and got to see King David skipping about and celebrating; and she began to despise him in her heart.

16 Thus they brought the ark of the [true] God in and placed it inside the tent that David had pitched for it; and they began to present burnt offerings and communion sacrifices before the [true] God. 2 When David finished offering up the burnt offering and the communion sacrifices, he went on to bless the people in the name of Jehovah. 3 Further, he apportioned to all the Israelites, man as well as woman, to each one a round loaf of bread and a date cake and a raisin cake. 4 Then he put before the ark of Jehovah some of the Levites as ministers, both to call to remembrance and to thank and praise Jehovah the God of Israel, 5 A'saph the head, and second to him Zech·a·ri'ah, and Je·i'el and She·mir'a·moth and Je·hi'el and Mat·ti·thi'ah and E·li'ab and Be·nai'ah and O'bed-e'dom and Je·i'el, with instruments of the string type and with harps, and A'saph with the cymbals playing aloud, 6 and Be·nai'ah and Ja·ha·zi'el the priests with the trumpets constantly before the ark of the covenant of the [true] God.

7 It was then on that day that

David made a contribution for the first time to thank Jehovah by means of A'saph and his brothers:

8 "Give thanks to Jehovah, YOU people; call upon his name, Make his deeds known among the peoples!

9 Sing to him, make melody to him, Concern yourselves with all his wonderful acts.

10 Make YOUR boast in his holy name, Let the heart of those seeking Jehovah rejoice.

11 Search after Jehovah and his strength, Seek his face constantly.

12 Remember his wonderful acts that he has performed, His miracles and the judicial decisions of his mouth,

13 O offspring of Israel his servant, YOU sons of Jacob, his chosen ones.

14 He is Jehovah our God; in all the earth are his judicial decisions.

15 Remember his covenant even to time indefinite, The word that he commanded, to a thousand generations,

16 Which [covenant] he concluded with Abraham, And his sworn statement to Isaac.

17 And which [statement] he kept standing as a regulation even to Jacob, As an indefinitely lasting covenant even to Israel,

18 Saying, 'To you I shall give the land of Ca'naan, As the allotment of YOUR inheritance.'

19 [This was] when YOU happened to be few in number, Yes, very few, and alien residents in it.

20 And they kept walking about from nation to nation, And from one kingdom to another people.

21 He did not allow anyone to defraud them, But on their account he reproved kings,

22 [Saying,] 'Do not YOU men touch my anointed ones, And to my prophets do nothing bad.'

23 Sing to Jehovah, all YOU of the earth! Announce from day to day the salvation he gives!

24 Relate among the nations his glory, Among all the peoples his wonderful acts.

25 For Jehovah is great and very much to be praised, And he is to be feared more than all other gods.

26 For all the gods of the peoples are valueless gods. As for Jehovah, he made the heavens.

27 Dignity and splendor are before him, Strength and joy are at his place.

28 Attribute to Jehovah, O families of peoples, Attribute to Jehovah glory and strength.

29 Attribute to Jehovah the glory of his name, Carry a gift and come in before him. Bow down to Jehovah in holy adornment.

30 Be in severe pains on account of him, all [YOU people of] the earth! Also the productive land is firmly established; Never will it be made to totter.

31 Let the heavens rejoice, let the earth be joyful, And let them say among the nations, 'Jehovah himself has become king!'

32 Let the sea thunder and also that which fills it, Let the field exult and all that is in it.

33 At the same time let the trees of the forest break out joyfully on account of Jehovah, For he has come to judge the earth.

34 Give thanks to Jehovah, YOU people, for he is good, For to time indefinite is his loving-kindness.

35 And say, 'Save us, O God of our
salvation,
And collect us together and
deliver us from the nations,
To give thanks to your holy
name, to speak exultingly
in your praise.
36 Blessed be Jehovah the God of
Israel from time indefinite
to time indefinite.' "

And all the people proceeded to
say, "Amen!" and a praise to Jehovah.

37 Then he left there before the
ark of the covenant of Jehovah
A'saph and his brothers to minister
before the Ark constantly, according to the requirement of each day;
38 and O'bed-e'dom and his brothers, sixty-eight, and O'bed-e'dom
the son of Je·du'thun and Ho'sah
as gatekeepers; 39 and Za'dok the
priest and his brothers the priests
before the tabernacle of Jehovah on
the high place that was at Gib'eon, 40 to offer up burnt offerings
to Jehovah on the altar of burnt
offering constantly morning and
evening and for all that is written
in the law of Jehovah that he laid
in command upon Israel; 41 and
with them He'man and Je·du'thun
and the rest of the select men that
were designated by names to thank
Jehovah, because "to time indefinite
is his loving-kindness"; 42 and
with them He'man and Je·du'thun,
to sound forth the trumpets and
cymbals and instruments of the
song of the [true] God; and the
sons of Je·du'thun at the gate.
43 And all the people proceeded
to go each one to his own house.
Accordingly David went around to
bless his own house.

17 And it came about that as
soon as David had begun
dwelling in his own house, David
proceeded to say to Nathan the
prophet: "Here I am dwelling in a
house of cedars, but the ark of the
covenant of Jehovah is under tent
cloths." 2 Upon that Nathan said
to David: "Everything that is in
your heart do, for the [true] God
is with you."

3 And it came about on that
night that the word of God came
to Nathan, saying: 4 "Go, and
you must say to David my servant,
'This is what Jehovah has said:
"It will not be you that will build
me the house in which to dwell.
5 For I have not dwelt in a house
from the day that I brought Israel
up until this day, but I continued
from tent to tent and from one
tabernacle [to another]. 6 During
all the time that I walked about
in all Israel, did I speak a single
word with one of the judges of
Israel whom I commanded to shepherd my people, saying, 'Why have
you men not built me a house of
cedars?' " '

7 "And now this is what you will
say to my servant David, 'This is
what Jehovah of armies has said:
"I myself took you from the pasture ground from following the flock
to become a leader over my people
Israel. 8 And I shall prove to be
with you wherever you do walk,
and I shall cut off all your enemies
from before you, and I shall certainly make for you a name like the
name of the great ones that are
upon the earth. 9 And I shall
certainly appoint a place for my
people Israel and plant them, and
they will indeed reside where they
are and no more will they be disturbed; and the sons of unrighteousness will not wear them out
again, just as they did at the first,
10 even since the days that I put
judges in command over my people
Israel. And I shall certainly humble
all your enemies. And I tell you,
'Also a house Jehovah will build
for you.'

11 " ' "And it must occur that
when your days have come to the
full [for you] to go [to be] with
your forefathers, I shall certainly
raise up your seed after you that
will come to be one of your sons,
and I shall indeed firmly establish
his kingship. 12 He is the one
that will build me a house, and I
shall certainly establish his throne
firmly to time indefinite. 13 I myself shall become his father, and
he himself will become my son;
and my loving-kindness I shall not
remove from him the way I re

moved it from the one that happened to be prior to you. 14 And I will cause him to stand in my house and in my kingship to time indefinite, and his throne will itself become one lasting to time indefinite.'"'

15 According to all these words and according to all this vision was the way that Nathan spoke to David.

16 After that King David came in and sat down before Jehovah and said: "Who am I, O Jehovah God, and what is my house that you have brought me thus far? 17 As though this should be something little in your eyes, O God, yet you speak concerning the house of your servant down to a distant future time, and you have looked on me according to the opportunity of the man in the ascendancy, O Jehovah God. 18 What more could David say to you as to honoring your servant, when you yourself know your servant well? 19 O Jehovah, for the sake of your servant and in agreement with your own heart you have done all these great things by making all the great achievements known. 20 O Jehovah, there is none like you, and there is no God except you in connection with all that we have heard with our ears. 21 And what other nation in the earth is like your people Israel, whom the [true] God went to redeem to himself as a people, to assign to yourself a name of great achievements and fear-inspiring things by driving out nations from before your people whom you have redeemed from Egypt? 22 And you proceeded to constitute your people Israel as your people to time indefinite, and you yourself, O Jehovah, became their God. 23 And now, O Jehovah, let the word that you have spoken concerning your servant and concerning his house prove faithful to time indefinite, and do just as you have spoken. 24 And let your name prove faithful and become great to time indefinite, saying, 'Jehovah of armies, the God of Israel, is God to Israel,' and let

the house of David your servant be one lasting before you. 25 For you yourself, my God, have revealed to your servant the purpose to build him a house. That is why your servant has found occasion to pray before you. 26 And now, O Jehovah, you are the [true] God, and you promise this goodness concerning your servant. 27 And now you must take it upon yourself and bless the house of your servant [for it] to continue to time indefinite before you; for you yourself, O Jehovah, have blessed, and it is blessed to time indefinite."

18 And it came about afterward that David proceeded to strike down the Phi·lis'tines and subdue them and take Gath and its dependent towns out of the hand of the Phi·lis'tines. 2 Then he struck Mo'ab down, and the Mo'ab·ites came to be David's servants bearing tribute.

3 And David went on to strike down Had·ad·e'zer the king of Zo'bah at Ha'math as he was going his way to set up his control at the river Eu·phra'tes. 4 Further, David captured from him a thousand chariots and seven thousand horsemen and twenty thousand men on foot. Then David hamstrung all the chariot horses, but he let a hundred chariot horses of them remain. 5 When Syria of Damascus came to help Had·ad·e'zer the king of Zo'bah, David went striking down among the Syrians twenty-two thousand men. 6 After that David put [garrisons] in Syria of Damascus, and the Syrians came to be David's servants bearing tribute. And Jehovah kept giving salvation to David wherever he went. 7 Moreover, David took the circular shields of gold that happened to be on the servants of Had·ad·e'zer and brought them to Jerusalem. 8 And from Tib'hath and Cun, cities of Had·ad·e'zer, David took very much copper. With it Sol'o·mon made the copper sea and the pillars and the copper utensils.

9 When To'u the king of Ha'math heard that David had struck down all the military force of Had-

ad·e′zer the king of Zo′bah, 10 he immediately sent Ha·do′ram his son to King David to ask him about his welfare and congratulate him over the fact that he had fought against Had·ad·e′zer so that he struck him down, (for Had·ad·e′zer had become trained in warfare against To′u,) and [there were with him] all sorts of articles of gold and silver and copper. 11 These also King David sanctified to Jehovah together with the silver and the gold that he had carried off from all the nations, from E′dom and from Mo′ab and from the sons of Am′mon and from the Phi·lis′tines and from Am′a·lek.

12 As for A·bish′ai the son of Ze·ru′iah, he struck down the E′dom·ites in the Valley of Salt, eighteen thousand. 13 So he put garrisons in E′dom, and all the E′dom·ites came to be David's servants. And Jehovah kept saving David wherever he went. 14 And David continued to reign over all Israel, and he was continually rendering judicial decision and righteousness for all his people. 15 And Jo′ab the son of Ze·ru′iah was over the army, and Je·hosh′a·phat the son of A·hi′lud was recorder. 16 And Za′dok the son of A·hi′tub and A·him′e·lech the son of A·bi′a·thar were priests, and Shav′sha was secretary. 17 And Be·nai′ah the son of Je·hoi′a·da was over the Cher′e·thites and the Pel′e·thites; and the sons of David were the first in position at the side of the king.

19 And it came about afterward that Na′hash the king of the sons of Am′mon came to die, and his son began to reign in place of him. 2 At that David said: "I shall exercise loving-kindness toward Ha′nun the son of Na′hash, because his father exercised loving-kindness toward me." Accordingly David sent messengers to comfort him over his father, and the servants of David proceeded to come into the land of the sons of Am′mon to Ha′nun to comfort him. 3 However, the princes of the sons of Am′mon said to Ha′nun: "Is David honoring your father in your eyes in that he has sent comforters to you? Is it not for the sake of making a thorough search and causing an overthrow and for spying out the land that his servants have come in to you?" 4 So Ha′nun took the servants of David and shaved them and cut their garments in half to their buttocks and sent them away. 5 Later people went and told David about the men; and he at once sent to meet them, because they had become men very much humiliated; and the king went on to say: "Dwell in Jer′i·cho until YOUR beards grow abundantly. Then YOU must return."

6 In time the sons of Am′mon saw that they had become foulsmelling to David, and Ha′nun and the sons of Am′mon proceeded to send a thousand silver talents to hire for themselves chariots and horsemen from Mes·o·po·ta′mi·a and from A′ram-ma′a·cah and from Zo′bah. 7 Thus they hired for themselves thirty-two thousand chariots and the king of Ma′a·cah and his people. Then they came in and camped before Med′e·ba; and as for the sons of Am′mon, they gathered together from their cities and now came in for the war.

8 When David heard of it, he immediately sent Jo′ab and all the army [and] the mighty men. 9 And the sons of Am′mon began to go out and draw up in battle formation at the entrance of the city, and the kings that had come were by themselves in the open field.

10 When Jo′ab saw that the battle charges had come to be against him from the front and from the rear, he at once chose some of all the choice men in Israel and drew them up in formation to meet the Syrians. 11 And the rest of the people he gave into the hand of A·bish′ai his brother, that they might draw up in formation to meet the sons of Am′mon. 12 And he went on to say: "If the Syrians become too strong for me, you must also serve as a salvation for me;

but if the sons of Am'mon themselves become too strong for you, I must also save you. 13 Be strong, that we may show ourselves courageous in behalf of our people and in behalf of the cities of our God; and as for Jehovah, what is good in his own eyes he will do."

14 Then Jo'ab and the people that were with him advanced before the Syrians to the battle, and they took to flight from before him. 15 As for the sons of Am'mon, they saw that the Syrians had fled, and they themselves also took to flight from before A·bish'ai his brother and then came into the city. Later Jo'ab came into Jerusalem.

16 When the Syrians saw that they had been defeated before Israel, they proceeded to send messengers and bring out the Syrians that were in the region of the River, with Sho'phach the chief of the army of Had·ad·e'zer before them. 17 When the report was made to David, he immediately gathered all Israel together and crossed the Jordan and came to them and drew up in formation against them. When David drew up in battle formation to meet the Syrians, they began to fight against him. 18 But the Syrians took to flight because of Israel; and David went killing of the Syrians seven thousand charioteers and forty thousand men on foot, and Sho'phach the chief of the army himself he put to death. 19 When the servants of Had·ad·e'zer saw that they had been defeated before Israel, they promptly made peace with David and began to serve him; and Syria did not want to try saving the sons of Am'mon any more.

20 And it came about at the time of the year's return, at the time that kings sally forth, that Jo'ab proceeded to lead the combat force of the army and lay the land of the sons of Am'mon in ruin and to come and besiege Rab'bah, while David was dwelling in Jerusalem; and Jo'ab went on to strike Rab'bah and throw it down. 2 But David took the crown of Mal'cam off its head, and found it to be a

talent of gold in weight, and in it there were precious stones; and it came to be on David's head. And the spoil of the city that he brought out was very much. 3 And the people that were in it he brought out, and he kept them employed at sawing stones and at sharp instruments of iron and at axes; and that was the way David proceeded to do to all the cities of the sons of Am'mon. Finally David and all the people returned to Jerusalem.

4 And it came about after this that war began breaking out at Ge'zer with the Phi·lis'tines. It was then that Sib'be·cai the Hu'shath-ite struck down Sip'pai of those born of the Reph'a·im, so that they were subdued.

5 And there came to be war again with the Phi·lis'tines; and El·ha'nan the son of Ja'ir got to strike down Lah'mi the brother of Go·li'ath the Git'tite, the shaft of whose spear was like the beam of loom workers.

6 And there came to be war again at Gath, when there happened to be a man of extraordinary size whose fingers and toes were in sixes, twenty-four; and he, too, had been born to the Reph'a·im. 7 And he kept taunting Israel. Finally Jon'a·than the son of Shim'e·a the brother of David struck him down.

8 These were the ones that had been born to the Reph'a·im in Gath; and they came to fall by the hand of David and by the hand of his servants.

21 And Satan proceeded to stand up against Israel and to incite David to number Israel. 2 So David said to Jo'ab and the chiefs of the people: "Go, count Israel from Be'er-she'ba to Dan and bring it to me that I may know their number." 3 But Jo'ab said: "May Jehovah add to his people a hundred times as many as they are. Do they not, O my lord the king, all of them belong to my lord as servants? Why does my lord seek this? Why should he become a cause of guilt to Israel?"

4 The king's word, however, pre-

vailed over Jo′ab, so that Jo′ab went out and walked through all Israel, after which he came to Jerusalem. 5 Jo′ab now gave the number of the registration of the people to David; and all Israel amounted to a million one hundred thousand men drawing sword, and Judah four hundred and seventy thousand men drawing sword. 6 And Le′vi and Benjamin he did not register in among them, because the king's word had been detestable to Jo′ab.

7 Now this thing was bad in the eyes of the [true] God, and so he struck down Israel. 8 Consequently David said to the [true] God: "I have sinned very much in that I have done this thing. And now, please, cause your servant's error to pass away; for I have acted very foolishly." 9 And Jehovah proceeded to speak to Gad, David's visionary, saying: 10 "Go, and you must speak to David, saying, 'This is what Jehovah has said: "There are three things that I am directing against you. Choose for yourself one of them, that I may do it to you."'" 11 Accordingly Gad went in to David and said to him: "This is what Jehovah has said, 'Take your pick, 12 whether for three years there is to be a famine; or for three months there is to be a sweeping away from before your adversaries and for the sword of your enemies to overtake [you], or for three days there is to be the sword of Jehovah, even pestilence, in the land, with Jehovah's angel bringing ruin in all the territory of Israel.' And now see what I should reply to the One sending me." 13 So David said to Gad: "It is very distressing to me. Please, let me fall into the hand of Jehovah, for very many are his mercies; but into the hand of man do not let me fall."

14 Then Jehovah gave a pestilence in Israel, so that out of Israel seventy thousand persons fell. 15 Moreover, the [true] God sent an angel to Jerusalem to bring ruin to it; and as soon as he began bringing the ruin, Jehovah saw it and began to feel regret over the calamity; and so he said to the angel that was bringing the ruin: "It is enough! Now let your hand drop." And Jehovah's angel was standing close by the threshing floor of Or′nan the Jeb′u·site.

16 When David raised his eyes, he got to see Jehovah's angel standing between the earth and the heavens with his drawn sword in his hand extended toward Jerusalem; and David and the older men, covered with sackcloth, at once fell down upon their faces. 17 And David proceeded to say to the [true] God: "Was it not I that said to make a numbering of the people, and is it not I that have sinned and have unquestionably done bad? As for these sheep, what have they done? O Jehovah my God, let your hand, please, come to be upon me and my father's house; but not upon your people, for a scourge."

18 And Jehovah's angel, for his part, said to Gad to say to David that David should go up to erect an altar to Jehovah on the threshing floor of Or′nan the Jeb′u·site. 19 Accordingly David went up at the word of Gad that he had spoken in the name of Jehovah. 20 Meantime, Or′nan turned back and saw the angel; and his four sons with him were hiding themselves. Now Or′nan had been threshing wheat. 21 So David came as far as Or′nan. When Or′nan looked and saw David, he immediately went out of the threshing floor and bowed down to David with his face to the earth. 22 Then David said to Or′nan: "Do give me the place of the threshing floor, that I may build in it an altar to Jehovah. For the money in full give it to me, that the scourge may be halted from upon the people." 23 But Or′nan said to David: "Take it as your own, and let my lord the king do what is good in his own eyes. See, I do give the cattle for burnt offerings and the threshing sledge for the wood and the wheat as a grain offering. The whole I do give."

24 However, King David said to Or'nan: "No, but without fail I shall make the purchase for the money in full, because I shall not carry what is yours to Jehovah to offer up burnt sacrifices without cost." 25 So David gave Or'nan for the place gold shekels to the weight of six hundred. 26 Then David built there an altar to Jehovah and offered up burnt sacrifices and communion sacrifices, and he proceeded to call upon Jehovah, who now answered him with fire from the heavens upon the altar of burnt offering. 27 Moreover, Jehovah said the word to the angel, who accordingly returned his sword to its sheath. 28 At that time, when David saw that Jehovah had answered him at the threshing floor of Or'nan the Jeb'u·site, he continued to sacrifice there. 29 But the tabernacle of Jehovah that Moses had made in the wilderness and the altar of burnt offering were at that time on the high place at Gib'e·on. 30 And David had not been able to go before it to consult God, for he had been terrified because of the sword of Jehovah's angel.

22 Then David said: "This is the house of Jehovah [true] God, and this is an altar for burnt offering for Israel."

2 David now said to bring together the alien residents that were in the land of Israel, and then he set them as stone hewers to hew squared stones for building the house of the [true] God. 3 And iron in great quantity for nails for the doors of the gates and for clamps David prepared, and also copper in such quantity as to be beyond weighing, 4 and also cedar timbers without number; for the Si·do'ni·ans and the Tyr'i·ans brought in cedar timbers in great quantity to David. 5 Accordingly David said: "Sol'o·mon my son is young and delicate, and the house to be built to Jehovah is to be surpassingly magnificent for beauteous distinction to all the lands. Let me, then, make preparation for him." So David made preparation in great quantities before his death.

6 Moreover, he called Sol'o·mon his son that he might command him to build a house to Jehovah the God of Israel. 7 And David went on to say to Sol'o·mon his son: "As for myself, it became close to my heart to build a house to the name of Jehovah my God. 8 But Jehovah's word came against me, saying, 'Blood in great quantity you have spilled, and great wars you have waged. You will not build a house to my name, for a great deal of blood you have spilled on the earth before me. 9 Look! There is a son being born to you. He himself will prove to be a restful man, and I shall certainly give him rest from all his enemies all around; for Sol'o·mon is what his name will become, and peace and quietness I shall bestow upon Israel in his days. 10 It is he that will build a house to my name, and he himself will become a son to me, and I a father to him. And I shall certainly establish the throne of his kingship firmly over Israel to time indefinite.'

11 "Now, my son, may Jehovah prove to be with you, and you must prove successful and build the house of Jehovah your God, just as he has spoken concerning you. 12 Only may Jehovah give you discretion and understanding, and may he give you commandment concerning Israel even to keep the law of Jehovah your God. 13 In that case you will prove successful if you take care to carry out the regulations and the judicial decisions that Jehovah commanded Moses respecting Israel. Be courageous and strong. Do not be afraid nor be terrified. 14 And here during my affliction I have prepared for Jehovah's house a hundred thousand talents of gold and a million talents of silver, and the copper and the iron there is no means of weighing because they have come to be in such quantity; and timbers and stones I have prepared, but to them you will make additions. 15 And with you there

are in great number doers of work, stone hewers and workers in stone and wood and every one skillful in every sort of work. 16 The gold, the silver and the copper and the iron there is no means of numbering. Rise and act, and may Jehovah prove to be with you."

17 And David went on to command all the princes of Israel to help Sol'o·mon his son: 18 "Is not Jehovah YOUR God with YOU, and has he not given YOU rest all around? For he has given into my hand the inhabitants of the land, and the land has been subdued before Jehovah and before his people. 19 Now set YOUR heart and YOUR soul to inquire after Jehovah YOUR God, and rise and build the sanctuary of Jehovah the [true] God, to bring the ark of the covenant of Jehovah and the holy utensils of the [true] God to the house built to the name of Jehovah."

23 And David himself had grown old and satisfied with days, and so he made Sol'o·mon his son king over Israel. 2 And he proceeded to gather all the princes of Israel and the priests and the Levites. 3 Accordingly the Levites were numbered from the age of thirty years upward; and their number, head by head of them, able-bodied man by able-bodied man, came to be thirty-eight thousand. 4 Of these for acting as supervisors over the work of the house of Jehovah there were twenty-four thousand; and as officers and judges six thousand; 5 and four thousand gatekeepers and four thousand givers of praise to Jehovah on the instruments that [David said] "I have made for giving praise."

6 Then David distributed them in divisions to the sons of Le'vi, to Ger'shon, Ko'hath and Me·rar'i. 7 To the Ger'shon·ites, La'dan and Shim'e·i. 8 The sons of La'dan were Je·hi'el the headman and Ze'tham and Joel, three. 9 The sons of Shim'e·i were She·lo'moth and Ha'zi·el and Ha'ran, three. These were the heads of the fa-

thers for La'dan. 10 And the sons of Shim'e·i were Ja'hath, Zi'na and Je'ush and Be·ri'ah. These four were the sons of Shim'e·i. 11 And Ja'hath came to be the head, and Zi'zah the second. As for Je'ush and Be·ri'ah, they did not have many sons; so they became a paternal house for one official class.

12 The sons of Ko'hath were Am'ram, Iz'har, He'bron and Uz'zi·el, four. 13 The sons of Am'ram were Aaron and Moses. But Aaron was separated that he might sanctify the Most Holy, he and his sons to time indefinite, to make sacrificial smoke before Jehovah, to minister to him and to pronounce blessing in his name to time indefinite. 14 As for Moses the man of the [true] God, his sons themselves continued to be called among the tribe of the Levites. 15 The sons of Moses were Ger'shom and E·li·e'zer. 16 The sons of Ger'shom were Sheb'u·el the head. 17 And the sons of E·li·e'zer came to be Re·ha·bi'ah the head; and E·li·e'zer did not come to have other sons, but the sons of Re·ha·bi'ah did themselves become exceedingly many. 18 The sons of Iz'har were She·lo'mith the headman. 19 The sons of He'bron were Je·ri'ah the head, Am·a·ri'ah the second, Ja·ha·zi'el the third and Jek·a·me'am the fourth. 20 The sons of Uz'zi·el were Mi'cah the head and Is·shi'ah the second.

21 The sons of Me·rar'i were Mah'li and Mu'shi. The sons of Mah'li were E·le·a'zar and Kish. 22 But E·le·a'zar died; and he had come to have, not sons, but daughters. So the sons of Kish their brothers took them [as wives]. 23 The sons of Mu'shi were Mah'li and E'der and Jer'e·moth, three.

24 These were the sons of Le'vi by the house of their fathers, the heads of the fathers, by their commissioned ones, in the number of the names, head by head of them, the doers of the work for the service of the house of Jehovah, from the age of twenty years upward. 25 For David had said: "Jehovah the God of Israel has given rest

to his people, and he will reside in Jerusalem to time indefinite. 26 And also the Levites will not have to carry the tabernacle or any of its utensils for its service." 27 For by the last words of David these were the number of the sons of Le′vi from the age of twenty years upward. 28 For their function was at the disposition of the sons of Aaron for the service of the house of Jehovah over the courtyards and over the dining rooms and over the purification of every holy thing and the work of the service of the house of the [true] God, 29 even for the layer bread and for the fine flour for the grain offering and for the wafers of unfermented bread and for the griddle [cakes] and for the mixed dough and for all measures of quantity and size; 30 and for standing morning by morning to thank and praise Jehovah, and likewise at evening; 31 and for every offering up of the burnt sacrifices to Jehovah at the sabbaths, at the new moons and at the festival seasons, by number according to the rule concerning them, constantly before Jehovah. 32 And they took care of the guarding of the tent of meeting and the guarding of the holy place and the guarding of the sons of Aaron their brothers for the service of the house of Jehovah.

24 Now the sons of Aaron had their divisions. The sons of Aaron were Na′dab and A·bi′hu, E·le·a′zar and Ith′a·mar. 2 However, Na′dab and A·bi′hu died before their father, and they did not happen to have any sons, but E·le·a′zar and Ith′a·mar continued to act as priests. 3 And David, and Za′dok from the sons of E·le·a′zar, and A·him′e·lech from the sons of Ith′a·mar proceeded to make divisions of them for their office in their service. 4 But the sons of E·le·a′zar were found to be more numerous in headmen than the sons of Ith′a·mar. So they distributed them to the sons of E·le·a′zar, as heads for [their] paternal houses, sixteen, and to the sons of Ith′a·mar, [as heads] for their paternal houses, eight.

5 Further, they distributed them by lots, these along with those, for there had to be chiefs of the holy place and chiefs of the [true] God from the sons of E·le·a′zar and from the sons of Ith′a·mar. 6 Then She·mai′ah the son of Ne·than′el the secretary of the Levites wrote them down before the king and the princes and Za′dok the priest and A·him′e·lech the son of A·bi′a·thar and the heads of the fathers of the priests and of the Levites, one paternal house being picked out for E·le·a′zar and one being picked out for Ith′a·mar.

7 And the lot proceeded to come out: the first for Je·hoi′a·rib; for Je·da′iah the second, 8 for Ha′rim the third, for Se·o′rim the fourth, 9 for Mal·chi′jah the fifth, for Mij′a·min the sixth, 10 for Hak′koz the seventh, for A·bi′jah the eighth, 11 for Jesh′u·a the ninth, for Shec·a·ni′ah the tenth, 12 for E·li′a·shib the eleventh, for Ja′kim the twelfth, 13 for Hup′pah the thirteenth, for Je·sheb′e·ab the fourteenth, 14 for Bil′gah the fifteenth, for Im′mer the sixteenth, 15 for He′zir the seventeenth, for Hap′piz·zez the eighteenth, 16 for Peth·a·hi′ah the nineteenth, for Je·hez′kel the twentieth, 17 for Ja′chin the twenty-first, for Ga′mul the twenty-second, 18 for De·la′iah the twenty-third, for Ma·a·zi′ah the twenty-fourth.

19 These were their offices for their service, to come into the house of Jehovah according to their due right by the hand of Aaron their forefather, just as Jehovah the God of Israel had commanded him.

20 And of the sons of Le′vi that were left over, of the sons of Am′ram there was Shu′ba·el; of the sons of Shu′ba·el, Jeh·de′iah; 21 of Re·ha·bi′ah: of the sons of Re·ha·bi′ah, Is·shi′ah the head; 22 of the Iz′har·ites, She·lo′moth; of the sons of She·lo′moth, Ja′hath; 23 and the sons [of He′bron], Je·ri′ah the head, Am·a·ri′ah the second, Ja·ha·zi′el the third, Jek-

a·me′am the fourth. 24 The sons of Uz′zi·el, Mi′cah; of the sons of Mi′cah, Sha′mir. 25 The brother of Mi′cah was Is·shi′ah; of the sons of Is·shi′ah, Zech·a·ri′ah.

26 The sons of Me·rar′i were Mah′li and Mu′shi; the sons of Ja·a·zi′ah, Be′no. 27 The sons of Me·rar′i: Of Ja·a·zi′ah, Be′no and Sho′ham and Zac′cur and Ib′ri. 28 Of Mah′li, E·le·a′zar, who did not come to have any sons. 29 Of Kish: the sons of Kish were Je·rah′me·el. 30 And the sons of Mu′shi were Mah′li and E′der and Jer′i·moth.

These were the sons of the Levites by their paternal houses. 31 And they themselves also proceeded to cast lots exactly as their brothers the sons of Aaron did before David the king and Za′dok and A·him′e·lech and the heads of the paternal houses of the priests and of the Levites. As respects paternal houses, the head one was exactly as his younger brother.

25 Further, David and the chiefs of the service groups separated for the service some of the sons of A′saph, He′man and Je·du′thun the ones prophesying with the harps, with the stringed instruments and with the cymbals. And from their number the official men for their service came to be. 2 Of the sons of A′saph, Zac′cur and Joseph and Neth·a·ni′ah and Ash·a·re′lah, the sons of A′saph under the control of A′saph the one prophesying under the control of the king. 3 Of Je·du′thun: the sons of Je·du′thun, Ged·a·li′ah and Ze′ri and Je·sha′iah, [and Shim′e·i] Hash·a·bi′ah and Mat·ti·thi′ah, six, under the control of their father Je·du′thun, who was prophesying with the harp for thanking and praising Jehovah. 4 Of He′man: the sons of He′man, Buk·ki′ah, Mat·ta·ni′ah, Uz′zi·el, Sheb′u·el and Jer′i·moth, Han·a·ni′ah, Ha·na′ni, E·li′a·thah, Gid·dal′ti and Ro·mam′ti-e′zer, Josh·be·kash′ah, Mal·lo′thi, Ho′thir, Ma·ha′zi·oth. 5 All these were sons of He′man, a visionary of the king in the things of the [true] God to raise up his horn; thus the [true] God proceeded to give He′man fourteen sons and three daughters. 6 All these were under the control of their father in song at the house of Jehovah, with cymbals, stringed instruments and harps for the service of the house of the [true] God.

Under the control of the king were A′saph and Je·du′thun and He′man.

7 And the number of them together with their brothers trained in song to Jehovah, all experts, came to be two hundred and eighty-eight. 8 So they cast lots as to the things to be taken care of, the little being just the same as the great, the expert along with the learner.

9 And the lot proceeded to come out: the first belonging to A′saph for Joseph, for Ged·a·li′ah the second (he and his brothers and his sons were twelve); 10 the third for Zac′cur, his sons and his brothers, twelve; 11 the fourth for Iz′ri, his sons and his brothers, twelve; 12 the fifth for Neth·a·ni′ah, his sons and his brothers, twelve; 13 the sixth for Buk·ki′ah, his sons and his brothers, twelve; 14 the seventh for Jesh·a·re′lah, his sons and his brothers, twelve; 15 the eighth for Je·sha′iah, his sons and his brothers, twelve; 16 the ninth for Mat·ta·ni′ah, his sons and his brothers, twelve; 17 the tenth for Shim′e·i, his sons and his brothers, twelve; 18 the eleventh for Az′ar·el, his sons and his brothers, twelve; 19 the twelfth for Hash·a·bi′ah, his sons and his brothers, twelve; 20 for the thirteenth, Shu′ba·el, his sons and his brothers, twelve; 21 for the fourteenth, Mat·ti·thi′ah, his sons and his brothers, twelve; 22 for the fifteenth, for Jer′e·moth, his sons and his brothers, twelve; 23 for the sixteenth, for Han·a·ni′ah, his sons and his brothers, twelve; 24 for the seventeenth, for Josh·be·kash′ah, his sons and his brothers, twelve; 25 for the eighteenth, for Ha·na′ni, his sons and his brothers, twelve; 26 for the

nineteenth, for Mal·lo'thi, his sons and his brothers, twelve; 27 for the twentieth, for E·li'a·thah, his sons and his brothers, twelve; 28 for the twenty-first, for Ho'thir, his sons and his brothers, twelve; 29 for the twenty-second, for Gid·dal'ti, his sons and his brothers, twelve; 30 for the twenty-third, for Ma·ha'zi·oth, his sons and his brothers, twelve; 31 for the twenty-fourth, for Ro·mam'ti-e'zer, his sons and his brothers, twelve.

26 For the divisions of gatekeepers: Of the Ko'rah·ites, Me·shel·e·mi'ah the son of Ko're of the sons of A'saph. 2 And Me·shel·e·mi'ah had sons: Zech·a·ri'ah the first-born, Je·di'a·el the second, Zeb·a·di'ah the third, Jath'ni·el the fourth, 3 E'lam the fifth, Je·ho·ha'nan the sixth, El'ie·ho·e'nai the seventh. 4 And O'bed-e'dom had sons: She·mai'ah the first-born, Je·hoz'a·bad the second, Jo'ah the third and Sa'car the fourth and Ne·than'el the fifth, 5 Am'mi·el the sixth, Is'sa·char the seventh, Pe·ul'le·thai the eighth; for God had blessed him. 6 And to She·mai'ah his son there were sons born that were rulers of the house of their father, for they were capable, mighty men. 7 The sons of She·mai'ah, Oth'ni and Reph'a·el and O'bed, El·za'bad, whose brothers were capable men, E·li'hu and Sem·a·chi'ah. 8 All these were of the sons of O'bed-e'dom, they and their sons and their brothers, capable men with the power for the service, sixty-two belonging to O'bed-e'dom. 9 And Me·shel·e·mi'ah had sons and brothers, capable men, eighteen. 10 And Ho'sah of the sons of Me·rar'i had sons. Shim'ri was the head, for he did not happen to be the first-born but his father appointed him as head; 11 Hil·ki'ah the second, Teb·a·li'ah the third, Zech·a·ri'ah the fourth. All the sons and brothers of Ho'sah were thirteen.

12 Of these divisions of the gatekeepers, the headmen had duties exactly as their brothers did, to minister at the house of Jehovah.

13 So they cast lots for the small the same as for the great by their paternal houses, for the different gates. 14 Then the lot to the east fell to Shel·e·mi'ah. For Zech·a·ri'ah his son, a counselor with discretion, they cast the lots, and his lot got to come out to the north. 15 O'bed-e'dom had his to the south, and his sons had the storehouses. 16 Shup'pim and Ho'sah had theirs to the west close by the gate Shal'lech·eth by the highway that goes up, guard group corresponding with guard group; 17 to the east there were six Levites; to the north for a day, four; to the south for a day, four; and for the stores, two by two; 18 for the portico to the west, four at the highway, two at the portico. 19 These were the divisions of the gatekeepers of the sons of the Ko'rah·ites and of the sons of Me·rar'i.

20 As regards the Levites, A·hi'jah was over the treasures of the house of the [true] God and over the treasures of the things made holy. 21 The sons of La'dan, the sons of the Ger'shon·ite belonging to La'dan; the heads of the paternal houses belonging to La'dan the Ger'shon·ite, Je·hi'e·li. 22 The sons of Je·hi'e·li, Ze'tham and Joel his brother, were over the treasures of the house of Jehovah. 23 For the Am'ram·ites, for the Iz'har·ites, for the He'bron·ites, for the Uz·zi'el·ites, 24 even Sheb'u·el the son of Ger'shom the son of Moses was a leader over the stores. 25 As regards his brothers, of E·li·e'zer there was Re·ha·bi'ah his son and Je·sha'iah his son and Jo'ram his son and Zich'ri his son and She·lo'moth his son. 26 This She·lo'moth and his brothers were over all the treasures of the things made holy, that David the king and the heads of the paternal houses, and the chiefs of the thousands and of the hundreds, and the chiefs of the army had made holy. 27 From the wars and from the spoil they had made [things] holy to maintain the house of Jehovah. 28 And also all that Samuel the seer and Saul the son of Kish and Ab'ner

the son of Ner and Jo'ab the son of Ze·ru'iah had made holy. What anyone made holy was under the control of She·lo'mith and his brothers.

29 Of the Iz'har·ites, Chen·a·ni'ah and his sons were for the outside business as officers and as judges over Israel.

30 Of the He'bron·ites, Hash·a·bi'ah and his brothers, capable men, a thousand seven hundred, were over the administration of Israel in the region of the Jordan to the west for all the work of Jehovah and for the king's service. 31 Of the He'bron·ites, Je·ri'jah was the head of the He'bron·ites by its generations by forefathers. In the fortieth year of David's kingship they were sought out, and valiant, mighty men came to be found among them in Ja'zer in Gil'e·ad. 32 And his brothers, capable men, were two thousand seven hundred, heads of the paternal houses. So David the king assigned them over the Reu'ben·ites and the Gad'ites and the half tribe of the Ma·nas'sites, for every matter of the [true] God and matter of the king.

27 As for the sons of Israel by their number, the heads of the paternal houses and the chiefs of the thousands and of the hundreds and their officers that were ministering to the king in every matter of the divisions of those that came in and that went out month by month for all the months of the year, each division was twenty-four thousand.

2 Over the first division of the first month there was Ja·sho'be·am the son of Zab'di·el, and in his division there were twenty-four thousand. 3 Some of the sons of Pe'rez the head of all the chiefs of the service groups were for the first month. 4 And over the division of the second month there was Do'dai the A·ho'hite with his division, and Mik'loth was the leader, and in his division there were twenty-four thousand. 5 The chief of the third service group for the third month was Be·nai'ah

the son of Je·hoi'a·da the chief priest, and in his division there were twenty-four thousand. 6 This Be·nai'ah was a mighty man of the thirty and over the thirty; and [over] his division there was Am·miz'a·bad his son. 7 The fourth for the fourth month was As'a·hel, Jo'ab's brother, and Zeb·a·di'ah his son after him, and in his division there were twenty-four thousand. 8 The fifth chief for the fifth month was Sham'huth the Iz'rah·ite, and in his division there were twenty-four thousand. 9 The sixth for the sixth month was I'ra the son of Ik'kesh the Te·ko'ite, and in his division there were twenty-four thousand. 10 The seventh for the seventh month was He'lez the Pel'o·nite of the sons of E'phra·im, and in his division there were twenty-four thousand. 11 The eighth for the eighth month was Sib'be·cai the Hu'shath·ite of the Ze'rah·ites, and in his division there were twenty-four thousand. 12 The ninth for the ninth month was A·bi·e'zer the An'a·thoth·ite of the Ben'ja·min·ites, and in his division there were twenty-four thousand. 13 The tenth for the tenth month was Ma'ha·rai the Ne·toph'a·thite of the Ze'rah·ites, and in his division there were twenty-four thousand. 14 The eleventh for the eleventh month was Be·nai'ah the Pir'a·thon·ite of the sons of E'phra·im, and in his division there were twenty-four thousand. 15 The twelfth for the twelfth month was Hel'dai the Ne·toph'a·thite, of Oth'ni·el, and in his division there were twenty-four thousand.

16 And over the tribes of Israel, of the Reu'ben·ites, E·li·e'zer the son of Zich'ri was leader; of the Sim'e·on·ites, Sheph·a·ti'ah the son of Ma'a·cah; 17 of Le'vi, Hash·a·bi'ah the son of Kem'u·el; of Aaron, Za'dok; 18 of Judah, E·li'hu, one of David's brothers; of Is'sa·char, Om'ri the son of Mi'cha·el; 19 of Zeb'u·lun, Ish·ma'·iah the son of O·ba·di'ah; of Naph'ta·li, Jer'i·moth the son of Az'ri·el; 20 of the sons of E'phra-

im, Ho·she'a the son of Az·a·zi'ah; of the half tribe of Ma·nas'seh, Joel the son of Pe·dai'ah; 21 of the half tribe of Ma·nas'seh in Gil'e·ad, Id'do the son of Zech·a·ri'ah; of Benjamin, Ja·a'si·el the son of Ab'ner; 22 of Dan, Az'ar·el the son of Je·ro'ham. These were the princes of the tribes of Israel.

23 And David did not take the number of those from twenty years of age and under, because Jehovah had promised to make Israel as many as the stars of the heavens. 24 Jo'ab the son of Ze·ru'iah had himself started to take the count, but he did not finish; and for this there came to be indignation against Israel, and the number did not come up into the account of the affairs of the days of King David.

25 And over the treasures of the king there was Az'ma·veth the son of Ad'i·el. And over the treasures in the field, in the cities and in the villages and in the towers there was Jon'a·than the son of Uz·zi'ah. 26 And over the doers of work in the field, for the cultivation of the soil, there was Ez'ri the son of Che'lub. 27 And over the vineyards there was Shim'e·i the Ra'math·ite; and over that which was in the vineyards for the wine supplies there was Zab'di the Shiph'mite. 28 And over the olive groves and the sycamore trees that were in the She·phe'lah there was Ba'al·ha'nan the Ge·de'rite; and over the oil supplies there was Jo'ash. 29 And over the herds that were grazing in Shar'on there was Shit'rai the Shar'on·ite; and over the herds in the low plains there was Sha'phat the son of Ad'lai. 30 And over the camels there was O'bil the Ish'ma·el·ite; and over the she-asses there was Jeh·de'iah the Me·ron'o·thite. 31 And over the flocks there was Ja'ziz the Hag'rite. All these were the chiefs of the goods that belonged to King David.

32 And Jon'a·than, David's nephew, was a counselor, a man of understanding, he being also a secretary; and Je·hi'el the son of Hach'mo·ni was with the king's sons. 33 And A·hith'o·phel was a counselor of the king; and Hu'shai the Ar'chite was the king's companion. 34 And after A·hith'o·phel there were Je·hoi'a·da the son of Be·nai'ah and A·bi'a·thar; and Jo'ab was chief of the army of the king.

28 And David proceeded to congregate all the princes of Israel, the princes of the tribes and the princes of the divisions of those ministering to the king and the chiefs of thousands and the chiefs of hundreds and the chiefs of all the goods and livestock of the king and of his sons, together with the court officials and the mighty men, even every valiant, mighty man, to Jerusalem. 2 Then David the king rose to his feet and said:

"Hear me, my brothers and my people. As for me, it was close to my heart to build a resting house for the ark of the covenant of Jehovah and as the footstool of our God, and I had made preparation to build. 3 And the [true] God himself said to me, 'You will not build a house to my name; for a man of wars you are, and blood you have spilled.' 4 Accordingly Jehovah the God of Israel chose me out of all the house of my father to become king over Israel to time indefinite; for it was Judah that he chose as leader, and in the house of Judah my father's house, and among my father's sons, I was the one whom he approved, to make me king over all Israel; 5 and out of all my sons (for many are the sons whom Jehovah has given me) he then chose Sol'o·mon my son to sit upon the throne of the kingship of Jehovah over Israel.

6 "Further, he said to me, 'Sol'o·mon your son is the one that will build my house and my courtyards; for I have chosen him as my son, and I myself shall become his father. 7 And I shall certainly establish his kingship firmly to time indefinite if he will be strongly resolved to do my commandments and my judicial decisions, as at this day.' 8 And now, before the eyes of all Israel, Jehovah's congregation, and in the ears of our

God, take care and search for all the commandments of Jehovah YOUR God, in order that YOU may possess the good land and may certainly pass it on as an inheritance to YOUR sons after YOU to time indefinite.

9 "And you, Sol′o·mon my son, know the God of your father and serve him with a complete heart and with a delightful soul; for all hearts Jehovah is searching, and every inclination of the thoughts he is discerning. If you search for him, he will let himself be found by you; but if you leave him, he will cast you off forever. 10 See, now, for Jehovah himself has chosen you to build a house as a sanctuary. Be courageous and act."

11 And David proceeded to give Sol′o·mon his son the architectural plan of the porch and of its houses and its storerooms and its roof chambers and its dark inner rooms and the house of the propitiatory cover; 12 even the architectural plan of everything that had come to be with him by inspiration for the courtyards of Jehovah's house and for all the dining rooms all around, for the treasures of the house of the [true] God and for the treasures of the things made holy; 13 and for the divisions of the priests and of the Levites and for all the work of the service of Jehovah's house and for all the utensils of the service of Jehovah's house; 14 for the gold by weight, the gold for all the utensils for the different services, for all the utensils of silver by weight, for all the utensils for the different services; 15 and the weight for the lampstands of gold and their lamps of gold, by weight of the different lampstands and their lamps, and for the lampstands of silver by weight for the lampstand and its lamps according to the service of the different lampstands; 16 and the gold by weight for the tables of the layer bread, for the different tables, and silver for the tables of silver; 17 and the forks and the bowls and the pitchers of pure gold, and for the small gold bowls by weight for the different small bowls, and for the small silver bowls by weight for the different small bowls; 18 and for the incense altar refined gold by weight and for the representation of the chariot, namely, the cherubs of gold for spreading [their wings] out and screening over the ark of the covenant of Jehovah. 19 "He gave insight for the entire thing in writing from the hand of Jehovah upon me, even for all the works of the architectural plan."

20 And David went on to say to Sol′o·mon his son: "Be courageous and strong and act. Do not be afraid nor be terrified, for Jehovah God, my God, is with you. He will not desert you or leave you until all the work of the service of Jehovah's house is finished. 21 And here are the divisions of the priests and of the Levites for all the service of the house of the [true] God; and with you in all the work there is every willing one with skill for all the service, and also the princes and all the people, for all your words."

29 David the king now said to all the congregation: "Sol′o·mon my son, the one [whom] God has chosen, is young and delicate, but the work is great; for the castle is not for man, but for Jehovah God. 2 And according to all my power I have prepared for the house of my God the gold for the gold-work, and the silver for the silver-work, and the copper for the copperwork, the iron for the iron-work, and the timbers for the timberwork; onyx stones, and stones to be set with hard mortar, and mosaic pebbles, and every precious stone, and alabaster stones in great quantity. 3 And since I am taking pleasure in the house of my God, there is yet a special property of mine, gold and silver; I do give it to the house of my God over and above all that I have prepared for the holy house: 4 three thousand talents of gold of the gold of O′phir, and seven thousand talents of refined silver, for coating the walls of the houses; 5 of the gold

for the goldwork, and of the silver for the silverwork and for all the work by the hand of the craftsmen. And who is there volunteering to fill his hand today [with a gift] for Jehovah?"

6 And the princes of the paternal houses and the princes of the tribes of Israel and the chiefs of thousands and of hundreds and the chiefs of the business of the king proceeded to volunteer. 7 Accordingly they gave to the service of the house of the [true] God gold worth five thousand talents and ten thousand darics and silver worth ten thousand talents and copper worth eighteen thousand talents and iron worth a hundred thousand talents. 8 And what stones were found with any persons they gave to the treasure of the house of Jehovah under the control of Je·hi′el the Ger′shon·ite. 9 And the people gave way to rejoicing over their making voluntary offerings, for it was with a complete heart that they made voluntary offerings to Jehovah; and even David the king himself rejoiced with great joy.

10 Consequently David blessed Jehovah before the eyes of all the congregation and David said: "Blessed may you be, O Jehovah the God of Israel our father, from time indefinite even to time indefinite. 11 Yours, O Jehovah, are the greatness and the mightiness and the beauty and the excellency and the dignity; for everything in the heavens and in the earth is [yours]. Yours is the kingdom, O Jehovah, the One also lifting yourself up as head over all. 12 The riches and the glory are on account of you, and you are dominating everything; and in your hand there are power and mightiness, and in your hand is [ability] to make great and to give strength to all. 13 And now, O our God, we are thanking you and praising your beauteous name.

14 "And yet, who am I and who are my people, that we should retain power to make voluntary offerings like this? For everything is from you, and out of your own hand we have given to you. 15 For we are alien residents before you and settlers the same as all our forefathers. Like a shadow our days are upon the earth and there is no hope. 16 O Jehovah our God, all this abundance that we have prepared to build for you a house for your holy name, from your hand it is, and to you it all belongs. 17 And I well know, O my God, that you are an examiner of the heart, and that it is in rectitude that you take pleasure. I, for my part, in the uprightness of my heart have voluntarily offered all these things, and now your people who are on hand here I have enjoyed seeing make offerings voluntarily to you. 18 O Jehovah the God of Abraham, Isaac and Israel our forefathers, do keep this to time indefinite as the inclination of the thoughts of the heart of your people, and direct their heart to you. 19 And to Sol′o·mon my son give a complete heart to keep your commandments, your testimonies and your regulations, and to do everything, and to build the castle for which I have made preparation."

20 And David went on to say to all the congregation: "Bless, now, Jehovah YOUR God." And all the congregation proceeded to bless Jehovah the God of their forefathers and bow low and prostrate themselves to Jehovah and to the king. 21 And they continued to sacrifice sacrifices to Jehovah and offer up burnt offerings to Jehovah on the day following that day, a thousand young bulls, a thousand rams, a thousand male lambs and their drink offerings, even sacrifices in great number for all Israel. 22 And they continued eating and drinking before Jehovah on that day with great rejoicing; and they proceeded a second time to make Sol′o·mon the son of David king and to anoint him to Jehovah as leader and also Za′dok as priest. 23 And Sol′o·mon began to sit upon Jehovah's throne as king in place of David his father and to make a success of it, and all the Israelites were

obedient to him. 24 As for all the princes and the mighty men and also all the sons of King David, they submitted themselves to Sol'o-mon the king. 25 And Jehovah continued to make Sol'o·mon surpassingly great before the eyes of all Israel and to put upon him such royal dignity as had not come to be upon any king before him over Israel.

26 As for David the son of Jes'se, he reigned over all Israel; 27 and the days that he reigned over Israel were forty years. In He'bron he reigned for seven years, and in Jerusalem he reigned for thirty-three [years]. 28 And gradually he died in a good old age, satisfied with days, riches and glory; and Sol'o·mon his son began to reign in place of him. 29 As for the affairs of David the king, the first ones and the last, there they are written among the words of Samuel the seer and among the words of Nathan the prophet and among the words of Gad the visionary, 30 together with all his kingship and his mightiness and the times that had passed over him and over Israel and over all the kingdoms of the lands.

THE SECOND OF
CHRONICLES

1 And Sol'o·mon the son of David continued to get strength in his kingship, and Jehovah his God was with him and kept making him surpassingly great.

2 And Sol'o·mon proceeded to say the word to all Israel, to the chiefs of the thousands and of the hundreds and to the judges and to all the chieftains of all Israel, the heads of the paternal houses. 3 Then Sol'o·mon and all the congregation with him went to the high place that was at Gib'e·on; for there was where the tent of meeting of the [true] God, which Moses the servant of Jehovah had made in the wilderness, happened to be. 4 However, the ark of the [true] God David had brought up from Kir'i·ath-je'a·rim to the place that David had prepared for it, for he had pitched a tent for it in Jerusalem. 5 And the copper altar that Bez'al·el the son of U'ri the son of Hur had made had been put before the tabernacle of Jehovah; and Sol'o·mon and the congregation applied as usual to it. 6 Sol'o·mon now made offerings there before Jehovah upon the copper altar that belonged to the tent of meeting, and he proceeded to offer upon it a thousand burnt offerings.

7 During that night God appeared to Sol'o·mon and then said to him: "Ask! What shall I give you?" 8 At that Sol'o·mon said to God: "You are the One that exercised great loving-kindness toward David my father and that have made me king in place of him. 9 Now, O Jehovah God, let your promise with David my father prove faithful, for you yourself have made me king over a people as numerous as the dust particles of the earth. 10 Give me now wisdom and knowledge that I may go out before this people and that I may come in, for who could judge this great people of yours?"

11 Then God said to Sol'o·mon: "For the reason that this has proved to be close to your heart and you have not asked for wealth, riches and honor or for the soul of those hating you, neither is it even many days that you have asked for, but you ask for wisdom and knowledge for yourself that you may judge my people over whom I have made you king, 12 the wisdom

and the knowledge are being given you; also wealth and riches and honor I shall give you such as no kings that were prior to you happened to have, and such as no one after you will come to have."

13 So Sol′o·mon came [from] the high place that was at Gib′e·on, from before the tent of meeting, to Jerusalem and continued to reign over Israel. 14 And Sol′o·mon kept gathering chariots and steeds so that he came to have a thousand four hundred chariots and twelve thousand steeds, and he kept them stationed in chariot cities and close by the king at Jerusalem. 15 And the king came to make the silver and the gold in Jerusalem like the stones; and cedarwood he made like the sycamore trees that are in the She·phe′lah for great quantity. 16 And there was the export of the horses that Sol′o·mon had from Egypt, and the company of the king's merchants would themselves take the horse drove for a price. 17 And they customarily brought up and exported from Egypt a chariot for six hundred silver pieces and a horse for a hundred and fifty; and that was the way it was for all the kings of the Hit′-tites and the kings of Syria. It was by means of them that they did the exporting.

2 Sol′o·mon now gave the word to build a house to Jehovah's name and a house for his kingship. 2 Accordingly Sol′o·mon counted off seventy thousand men as burden bearers and eighty thousand men as cutters in the mountain, and as overseers over them three thousand six hundred. 3 Further, Sol′o·mon sent to Hi′ram the king of Tyre, saying: "Just as you dealt with David my father and you kept sending him cedarwood to build himself a house in which to dwell,— 4 here I am building a house to the name of Jehovah my God to sanctify it to him, to burn perfumed incense before him, with the constant layer bread and burnt offerings in the morning and in the evening, on the sabbaths and on the new moons and at the festival seasons of Jehovah our God. To time indefinite this will be upon Israel. 5 And the house that I am building will be great, for our God is greater than all the [other] gods. 6 And who could retain power to build him a house? For the heavens and the heaven of the heavens cannot contain him, and who am I that I should build him a house except for making sacrificial smoke before him? 7 And now send me a skillful man to work in gold and in silver and in copper and in iron and in wool dyed reddish purple and crimson and blue thread, and knowing how to cut engravings, along with the skillful ones that are with me in Judah and in Jerusalem, whom David my father has prepared. 8 And send me timbers of cedar, juniper and almug from Leb′a·non, for I myself well know that your servants are experienced at cutting down the trees of Leb′a·non, (and here my servants are together with your servants,) 9 even for preparing timbers for me in great number, for the house that I am building will be great, yes, in a wonderful way. 10 And, look! to the gatherers of wood, the cutters of the trees, I do give wheat as food for your servants, twenty thousand cors, and barley twenty thousand cors, and wine twenty thousand baths, and oil twenty thousand baths."

11 At that Hi′ram the king of Tyre said [the word] in writing and sent [it] to Sol′o·mon: "Because Jehovah loved his people he has constituted you king over them." 12 And Hi′ram went on to say: "Blessed be Jehovah the God of Israel, who made the heavens and the earth, because he has given to David the king a wise son, experienced in discretion and understanding, who will build a house to Jehovah and a house for his kingship. 13 And now I do send a skillful man, experienced in understanding, belonging to Hi′ram-a′bi, 14 the son of a woman of the sons of Dan but whose father was a man of Tyre, experienced, to work in gold and in silver, in cop-

per, in iron, in stones and in timbers, in wool dyed reddish purple, in blue thread and in fine fabric and in crimson and at cutting every sort of engraving and at designing every sort of device that may be given to him along with your own skillful men and the skillful men of my lord David your father. 15 And now the wheat and the barley, the oil and the wine that my lord has promised, let him send to his servants. 16 As for ourselves, we shall cut down trees from Leb'a·non according to all your need, and we shall bring them to you as rafts by sea to Jop'pa, and you, for your part, will take them up to Jerusalem."

17 Then Sol'o·mon took a count of all the men that were alien residents, who were in the land of Israel, after the census that David his father had taken of them; and there came to be found a hundred and fifty-three thousand six hundred. 18 So he made seventy thousand of them burden bearers and eighty thousand cutters in the mountain and three thousand six hundred overseers for keeping the people in service.

3 Finally Sol'o·mon started to build the house of Jehovah in Jerusalem on Mount Mo·ri'ah, where [Jehovah] had appeared to David his father, in the place that David had prepared on the threshing floor of Or'nan the Jeb'u·site. 2 Accordingly he started to build in the second month on the second [day], in the fourth year of his reign. 3 And these things Sol'o·mon laid as a foundation for building the house of the [true] God, the length in cubits by the former measurement being sixty cubits, and the width twenty cubits. 4 And the porch that was in front of the length was twenty cubits in front of the width of the house, and its height was a hundred and twenty; and he proceeded to overlay it inside with pure gold. 5 And the great house he covered with juniper wood, after which he covered it with good gold, and then he brought up upon it palm-tree figures and chains. 6 Further, he overlaid the house with precious stone for beauty; and the gold was gold from the gold country. 7 And he went on to cover the house, the rafters, the thresholds and its walls and its doors with gold; and he engraved cherubs upon the walls.

8 And he proceeded to make the house of the Most Holy, its length in relation to the width of the house being twenty cubits, and its own width being twenty cubits; and then he covered it with good gold to the amount of six hundred talents. 9 And the weight for the nails was fifty gold shekels; and the roof chambers he covered with gold.

10 Then he made in the house of the Most Holy two cherubs in the workmanship of images, and overlaid them with gold. 11 As for the wings of the cherubs, their length was twenty cubits, the one wing of five cubits reaching to the wall of the house, and the other wing of five cubits reaching to the wing of the other cherub. 12 And the wing of the one cherub of five cubits was reaching to the wall of the house, and the other wing of five cubits was in contact with the wing of the other cherub. 13 The wings of these cherubs were spread out twenty cubits; and they were standing upon their feet with their faces inward.

14 Further, he made the curtain of blue thread and wool dyed reddish purple and crimson and fine fabric, and worked in cherubs upon it.

15 Then he made before the house two pillars, thirty-five cubits in length, and the capital that was upon the top of each one was five cubits. 16 Further, he made chains in necklace style and put them upon the tops of the pillars, and made a hundred pomegranates and put them on the chains. 17 And he proceeded to set up the pillars in front of the temple, one to the right and one to the left, after which he called the name of the right-hand one Ja'chin and the name of the left-hand one Bo'az.

4 Then he made the copper altar, twenty cubits being its length, and twenty cubits its width, and ten cubits its height.

2 And he proceeded to make the molten sea ten cubits from its one brim to its other brim, circular all around, and its height was five cubits, and it took a line of thirty cubits to circle all around it. 3 And there was the likeness of gourd-shaped ornaments under it clear around, surrounding it, ten in a cubit, enclosing the sea all around. The gourd-shaped ornaments were in two rows, being cast in its casting. 4 It was standing upon twelve bulls, three facing the north and three facing the west and three facing the south and three facing the east; and the sea was above upon them, and all their hind parts were inward. 5 And its thickness was a handbreadth; and its brim was like the workmanship of the brim of a cup, a lily blossom. As a receptacle, three thousand bath measures were what it could contain.

6 Further, he made ten basins, and put five to the right and five to the left, to wash in them. Things having to do with the burnt offering they would rinse in them. But the sea was for the priests to wash in it.

7 He then made lampstands of gold, ten of them of the same plan, and put them in the temple, five to the right and five to the left.

8 Further, he made ten tables, and stationed them in the temple, five to the right and five to the left, and made a hundred bowls of gold.

9 Then he made the courtyard of the priests and the great enclosure and the doors belonging to the enclosure, and their doors he overlaid with copper. 10 And the sea he placed at the right side, to the east, toward the south.

11 Finally Hi'ram made the cans and the shovels and the bowls.

So Hi'ram finished doing the work that he did for King Sol'o-mon on the house of the [true] God. 12 The two pillars and the round capitals upon the top of the two pillars and the two networks to cover the two round capitals that were upon the top of the pillars 13 and the four hundred pomegranates for the two networks, two rows of pomegranates for each network to cover the two round capitals that were upon the pillars, 14 and the ten carriages and the ten basins upon the carriages; 15 the one sea and the twelve bulls under it, 16 and the cans and the shovels and the forks and all their utensils Hi'ram-a'biv made for King Sol'o-mon for the house of Jehovah, of polished copper. 17 In the District of the Jordan the king cast them in the thick ground between Suc'coth and Zer'e·dah. 18 Thus Sol'o·mon made all these utensils in very great quantity, for the weight of the copper was not ascertained.

19 And Sol'o·mon proceeded to make all the utensils that were at the house of the [true] God and the golden altar and the tables with the showbread upon them, 20 and the lampstands and their lamps of pure gold, to light them up before the innermost room according to the rule; 21 and the blossoms and the lamps and the snuffers, of gold, (it was the purest gold,) 22 and the extinguishers and the bowls and the cups and the fire holders, of pure gold, and the entrance of the house, its inner doors for the Most Holy and the doors of the house of the temple, of gold.

5 Finally all the work that Sol'o-mon had to do for the house of Jehovah was at its completion, and Sol'o·mon began to bring in the things made holy by David his father; and the silver and the gold and all the utensils he put in the treasures of the house of the [true] God. 2 It was then that Sol'o·mon proceeded to congregate the older men of Israel and all the heads of the tribes, the chieftains of the paternal houses of the sons of Israel, to Jerusalem, to bring the ark of the covenant of Jehovah up from the city of David, that is to say, Zion. 3 So all the men of

Israel congregated themselves to the king at the festival, that of the seventh month.

4 So all the older men of Israel came, and the Levites began to carry the Ark. 5 And they came bringing up the Ark and the tent of meeting and all the holy utensils that were in the tent. The priests the Levites brought them up. 6 And King Sol'o·mon and all the assembly of Israelites that were keeping their appointment with him before the Ark were sacrificing sheep and cattle that could not be counted or numbered for multitude. 7 Then the priests brought the ark of the covenant of Jehovah into its place, into the innermost room of the house, into the Most Holy, to underneath the wings of the cherubs. 8 Thus the cherubs were continually spreading out their wings over the place of the Ark, so that the cherubs covered over the Ark and its poles from above. 9 But the poles were long, so that the tips of the poles were visible at the Holy in front of the innermost room, but they were not visible outside, and they continue there down to this day. 10 There was nothing in the Ark but the two tablets that Moses had given at Ho'reb, when Jehovah covenanted with the sons of Israel while they were coming out from Egypt.

11 And it came about when the priests came out from the holy place (for all the priests that were to be found had, for their part, sanctified themselves—there was no need to observe the divisions); 12 and the Levites that were singers belonging to all of them, namely, to A'saph, to He'man, to Je·du'thun and to their sons and to their brothers clothed in fine fabric with cymbals and with stringed instruments and harps, were standing to the east of the altar and along with them priests to [the number of] a hundred and twenty sounding the trumpets; 13 and it came about that as soon as the trumpeters and the singers were as one in causing one sound to be heard in praising

and thanking Jehovah, and as soon as they lifted up the sound with the trumpets and with the cymbals and with the instruments of song and with praising Jehovah, "for he is good, for to time indefinite is his loving-kindness," the house itself was filled with a cloud, the very house of Jehovah, 14 and the priests were not able to stand to minister because of the cloud; for the glory of Jehovah filled the house of the [true] God.

6 It was then that Sol'o·mon said: "Jehovah himself said he was to reside in the thick gloom; 2 and I, for my part, have built a house of lofty abode for you and an established place for you to dwell in to time indefinite."

3 Then the king turned his face and began to bless all the congregation of Israel, while all the congregation of Israel were standing up. 4 And he went on to say: "Blessed be Jehovah the God of Israel, who spoke with his own mouth with David my father and by his own hands has given fulfillment, saying, 5 'From the day that I brought my people out from the land of Egypt I have not chosen a city out of all the tribes of Israel to build a house for my name to prove to be there, and I have not chosen a man to become leader over my people Israel. 6 But I shall choose Jerusalem for my name to prove to be there, and I shall choose David to come to be over my people Israel.' 7 And it came to be close to the heart of David my father to build a house to the name of Jehovah the God of Israel. 8 But Jehovah said to David my father, 'For the reason that it proved to be close to your heart to build a house to my name, you did well because it proved to be close to your heart. 9 Only you yourself will not build the house, but your son who is coming forth from your loins is the one that will build the house to my name.' 10 And Jehovah proceeded to carry out his word that he had spoken, that I might rise up in the place of David my father and sit upon the

throne of Israel, just as Jehovah had spoken, and that I might build the house to the name of Jehovah the God of Israel, 11 and that I might place there the ark where the covenant of Jehovah is that he concluded with the sons of Israel."

12 And he began standing before the altar of Jehovah in front of all the congregation of Israel, and he now spread out his palms. 13 (For Sol'o·mon had made a platform of copper and then put it in the middle of the enclosure. Its length was five cubits, and its width five cubits, and its height three cubits; and he kept standing upon it.) And he proceeded to kneel upon his knees in front of all the congregation of Israel and to spread his palms out to the heavens. 14 And he went on to say: "O Jehovah the God of Israel, there is no God like you in the heavens or on the earth, keeping the covenant and the loving-kindness toward your servants who are walking before you with all their heart; 15 you who have kept toward your servant David my father what you promised him, so that you made the promise with your mouth, and with your own hand you have made fulfillment as at this day. 16 And now, O Jehovah the God of Israel, keep toward your servant David my father what you promised him, saying, 'There will not be cut off a man of yours from before me to sit upon the throne of Israel, if only your sons will take care of their way by walking in my law, just as you have walked before me.' 17 And now, O Jehovah the God of Israel, let your promise that you have promised to your servant David prove trustworthy.

18 "But will God truly dwell with mankind upon the earth? Look! Heaven, yes, the heaven of the heavens themselves, cannot contain you; how much less, then, this house that I have built? 19 And you must turn toward the prayer of your servant and to his request for favor, O Jehovah my God, by listening to the entreating cry and to the prayer with which your servant is praying before you, 20 that your eyes may prove to be opened toward this house day and night, toward the place where you said you would put your name, by listening to the prayer with which your servant prays toward this place. 21 And you must listen to the entreaties of your servant and of your people Israel when they pray toward this place, that you yourself may hear from the place of your dwelling, from the heavens; and you must hear and forgive.

22 "If a man sins against his fellow man and he actually lays a cursing upon him to bring him under liability to the curse, and he actually comes [within] the curse before your altar in this house, 23 then may you yourself hear from the heavens, and you must act and judge your servants so as to pay back the wicked by putting his course upon his own head and by pronouncing the righteous one righteous by giving to him according to his own righteousness.

24 "And if your people Israel are defeated before an enemy because they kept sinning against you, and they indeed return and laud your name and pray and make request for favor before you in this house, 25 then may you yourself hear from the heavens, and you must forgive the sin of your people Israel and bring them back to the ground that you gave to them and their forefathers.

26 "When the heavens are shut up so that no rain occurs because they kept sinning against you, and they actually pray toward this place and laud your name [and] from their sin they turn back because you kept afflicting them, 27 then may you yourself hear from the heavens, and you must forgive the sin of your servants, even of your people Israel, because you instruct them regarding the good way in which they should walk; and you must give rain upon your land that you have given to your people as a hereditary possession.

28 "In case a famine occurs in the land, in case a pestilence occurs, in case scorching and mildew, locusts and cockroaches occur; in case their enemies besiege them in the land of their gates—any sort of plague and any sort of malady— 29 whatever prayer, whatever request for favor there may occur on the part of any man or of all your people Israel, because they know each one his own plague and his own pain; when he actually spreads out his palms toward this house, 30 then may you yourself hear from the heavens, the place of your dwelling, and you must forgive and give to each one according to all his ways, because you know his heart (for you yourself alone well know the heart of the sons of mankind); 31 to the end that they may fear you by walking in your ways all the days that they are alive upon the surface of the ground that you gave to our forefathers.

32 "And also to the foreigner who is no part of your people Israel and who actually comes from a distant land by reason of your great name and your strong hand and your stretched-out arm, and they actually come and pray toward this house, 33 then may you yourself listen from the heavens, from your established place of dwelling, and you must do according to all for which the foreigner calls to you; in order that all the peoples of the earth may know your name and may fear you the same as your people Israel do, and may know that your name has been called upon this house that I have built.

34 "In case your people go out to the war against their enemies in the way that you send them, and they indeed pray to you in the direction of this city that you have chosen and the house that I have built to your name, 35 you must also hear from the heavens their prayer and their request for favor, and you must execute judgment for them.

36 "In case they sin against you (for there is no man that does not sin), and you have to be incensed at them and abandon them to an enemy, and their captors actually carry them off captive to a land distant or nearby; 37 and they indeed come to their senses in the land where they have been carried off captive, and they actually return and make request to you for favor in the land where they are captives, saying, 'We have sinned, we have erred and we have acted wickedly'; 38 and they indeed return to you with all their heart and with all their soul in the land where they are captives of those who carried them off captive, and they indeed pray in the direction of their land that you gave to their forefathers and the city that you have chosen and the house that I have built to your name; 39 you must also hear from the heavens, from your established place of dwelling, their prayer and their requests for favor, and you must execute judgment for them and forgive your people who have sinned against you.

40 "Now, O my God, please, let your eyes prove to be opened and your ears attentive to the prayer respecting this place. 41 And now do rise up, O Jehovah God, into your rest, you and the Ark of your strength. Let your priests themselves, O Jehovah God, be clothed with salvation, and let your loyal ones themselves rejoice in goodness. 42 O Jehovah God, do not turn back the face of your anointed one. O do remember the lovingkindnesses to David your servant."

7 Now as soon as Sol′o·mon finished praying, the fire itself came down from the heavens and proceeded to consume the burnt offering and the sacrifices, and Jehovah's glory itself filled the house. 2 And the priests were unable to enter into the house of Jehovah because Jehovah's glory had filled the house of Jehovah. 3 And all the sons of Israel were spectators when the fire came down and the glory of Jehovah was upon the house, and they immediately bowed low with their faces to the earth upon the pavement and prostrated themselves and thanked Jehovah, "for he is good, for his loving-kindness is to time indefinite."

4 And the king and all the people were offering sacrifice before Jehovah. 5 And King Sol'o·mon went on offering the sacrifice of twenty-two thousand cattle and a hundred and twenty thousand sheep. Thus the king and all the people inaugurated the house of the [true] God. 6 And the priests were standing at their posts of duty, and the Levites with the instruments of song to Jehovah that David the king had made to thank Jehovah, "for his loving-kindness is to time indefinite," when David would render praise by their hand; and the priests were loudly sounding the trumpets in front of them, while all the Israelites were standing.

7 Then Sol'o·mon sanctified the middle of the courtyard that was before the house of Jehovah, because there he rendered up the burnt offerings and the fat pieces of the communion sacrifices, for the copper altar that Sol'o·mon had made was itself not able to contain the burnt offering and the grain offering and the fat pieces. 8 And Sol'o·mon proceeded to hold the festival at that time for seven days, and all Israel with him, a very great congregation from the entering in of Ha'math down to the torrent valley of Egypt. 9 But on the eighth day they held a solemn assembly, because the inauguration of the altar they had held for seven days and the festival for seven days. 10 And on the twenty-third day of the seventh month he sent the people away to their homes, joyful and feeling good at heart over the goodness that Jehovah had performed toward David and toward Sol'o·mon and toward Israel his people.

11 Thus Sol'o·mon finished the house of Jehovah and the house of the king; and in everything that had come into Sol'o·mon's heart to do regarding the house of Jehovah and his own house he proved suc-

cessful. 12 Jehovah now appeared to Sol'o·mon during the night and said to him: "I have heard your prayer, and I have chosen this place for myself as a house of sacrifice. 13 When I shut up the heavens that no rain may occur and when I command the grasshoppers to eat up the land and if I send a pestilence among my people, 14 and my people upon whom my name has been called humble themselves and pray and seek my face and turn back from their bad ways, then I myself shall hear from the heavens and forgive their sin, and I shall heal their land. 15 Now my own eyes will prove to be opened and my ears attentive to prayer at this place. 16 And now I do choose and sanctify this house that my name may prove to be there to time indefinite, and my eyes and my heart will certainly prove to be there always.

17 "And if you yourself will walk before me, just as David your father walked, even by doing according to all that I have commanded you, and you will keep my regulations and my judicial decisions, 18 I will also establish the throne of your kingship, just as I covenanted with David your father, saying, 'There will not a man of yours be cut off from ruling over Israel.' 19 But if YOU yourselves turn back and actually leave my statutes and my commandments that I have put before YOU, and YOU actually go and serve other gods and bow down to them, 20 I will also uproot them from off my ground that I have given them; and this house that I have sanctified for my name, I shall throw away from before my face, and I shall make it a proverbial saying and a taunt among all the peoples. 21 As for this house that had become heaps of ruins, everyone passing by it will stare in amazement and be certain to say, 'For what reason did Jehovah do like that to this land and to this house?' 22 And they will have to say, 'It was for the reason that they left Jehovah the God of their fore-

fathers who had brought them out of the land of Egypt, and they proceeded to take hold of other gods and bow down to them and serve them. That is why he brought upon them all this calamity.'"

8 And it came about at the end of twenty years, in which Sol'o·mon had built the house of Jehovah and his own house, 2 that the cities that Hi'ram had given to Sol'o·mon—Sol'o·mon rebuilt them and then caused the sons of Israel to dwell there. 3 Furthermore, Sol'o·mon went to Ha'math-zo'bah and prevailed over it. 4 Then he rebuilt Tad'mor in the wilderness and all the storage cities that he had built in Ha'math. 5 And he went on to build Upper Beth-ho'ron and Lower Beth-ho'ron, fortified cities with walls, doors and bar, 6 and Ba'al·ath and all the storage cities that had become Sol'o·mon's and all the chariot cities and the cities for the horsemen and every desirable thing of Sol'o·mon that he had desired to build in Jerusalem and in Leb'a-non and in all the land of his dominion.

7 As for all the people that were left over of the Hit'tites and the Am'or·ites and the Per'iz·zites and the Hi'vites and the Jeb'u·sites, who were no part of Israel, 8 from their sons that had been left behind them in the land, whom the sons of Israel had not exterminated, Sol'o·mon kept levying men for forced labor until this day. 9 But there were none out of the sons of Israel that Sol'o·mon constituted slaves for his work; for they were warriors and chiefs of his adjutants and chiefs of his charioteers and of his horsemen. 10 These were the chiefs of the deputies that belonged to King Sol'o·mon, two hundred and fifty, the foremen over the people.

11 And Phar'aoh's daughter Sol'o·mon brought up out of the city of David to the house that he had built for her, for he said: "Although a wife of mine, she should not dwell in the house of David the king of Israel, for the places to which the ark of Jehovah has come are something holy."

12 It was then that Sol'o·mon offered up burnt sacrifices to Jehovah upon the altar of Jehovah that he had built before the porch, 13 even as a daily matter of course to make offerings according to the commandment of Moses for the sabbaths and for the new moons and for the appointed festivals three times in the year, at the festival of unfermented cakes and at the festival of the weeks and at the festival of the booths. 14 Further, he set the divisions of the priests over their services according to the rule of David his father, and the Levites at their posts of duty, to praise and to minister in front of the priests as a daily matter of course, and the gatekeepers in their divisions for the different gates, for such was the commandment of David the man of the [true] God. 15 And they did not turn aside from the king's commandment to the priests and the Levites concerning any matter and concerning the supplies. 16 So Sol'o·mon's work was all in a prepared state from the day of the foundation-laying of the house of Jehovah until it was finished. [So] the house of Jehovah was complete.

17 It was then that Sol'o·mon went to E'zi·on-ge'ber and to E'loth upon the shore of the sea in the land of E'dom. 18 And Hi'ram regularly sent to him by means of his servants ships and servants having a knowledge of the sea, and they would come with Sol'o·mon's servants to O'phir and take from there four hundred and fifty talents of gold and bring it to King Sol'o·mon.

9 And the queen of She'ba herself heard the report about Sol'o·mon, and she proceeded to come to test Sol'o·mon with perplexing questions at Jerusalem, along with a very impressive train and camels carrying balsam oil, and gold in great quantity, and precious stones. At length she came in to Sol'o·mon and spoke with him about everything that happened to be close to her heart. 2 Sol'o·mon, in turn, went on to tell her all her matters, and no matter was hidden from Sol'o·mon that he did not tell her.

3 When the queen of She'ba got to see Sol'o·mon's wisdom and the house that he had built, 4 and the food of his table and the sitting of his servants and the table service of his waiters and their attire and his drinking service and their attire, and his burnt sacrifices that he regularly offered up at the house of Jehovah, then there proved to be no more spirit in her. 5 So she said to the king: "True was the word that I heard in my own land about your matters and about your wisdom. 6 And I did not put faith in their words until I had come that my own eyes might see; and, look! there has not been told me the half of the abundance of your wisdom. You have surpassed the report that I have heard. 7 Happy are your men, and happy are these servants of yours who are standing before you constantly and listening to your wisdom. 8 May Jehovah your God come to be blessed, who has taken delight in you by putting you upon his throne as king for Jehovah your God; because your God loved Israel, to make it stand to time indefinite, so that he put you over them as king to execute judicial decision and righteousness."

9 Then she gave the king a hundred and twenty talents of gold, and balsam oil in very great quantity, and precious stones; and there had not come to be the like of that balsam oil which the queen of She'ba gave to King Sol'o·mon.

10 And, besides, the servants of Hi'ram and the servants of Sol'o·mon who brought gold from O'phir brought timbers of almug trees and precious stones. 11 And the king proceeded to make out of the timbers of the almug trees stairs for the house of Jehovah and for the king's house and also harps and stringed instruments for the singers, and the like of them had

never been seen before in the land of Judah.

12 And King Sol'o·mon himself gave the queen of She'ba all her delight for which she had asked, besides [the value of] what she brought to the king. So she turned about and went to her own land, she together with her servants.

13 And the weight of the gold that came to Sol'o·mon in one year amounted to six hundred and sixty-six talents of gold, 14 aside from the men of travel and the merchants who were bringing in and all the kings of the Arabs and the governors of the land who were bringing in gold and silver to Sol'o·mon.

15 And King Sol'o·mon went on to make two hundred large shields of alloyed gold (six hundred [shekels] of alloyed gold he proceeded to lay upon each large shield), 16 and three hundred bucklers of alloyed gold (three mi'nas of gold he proceeded to lay upon each buckler). Then the king put them in the House of the Forest of Leb'a·non.

17 Further, the king made a great ivory throne and overlaid it with pure gold. 18 And there were six steps to the throne, and there was a footstool in gold to the throne (they were attached), and there were armrests on this side and on that side by the place of sitting, and two lions were standing beside the armrests. 19 And there were twelve lions standing there upon the six steps on this side and on that side. No other kingdom had any made just like it. 20 And all the drinking vessels of King Sol'o·mon were of gold, and all the vessels of the House of the Forest of Leb'a·non were of pure gold. There was nothing of silver; it was considered as nothing at all in the days of Sol'o·mon. 21 For ships belonging to the king were going to Tar'shish with the servants of Hi'ram. Once every three years ships of Tar'shish would come in, carrying gold and silver, ivory, and apes and peacocks.

22 So King Sol'o·mon was greater than all the other kings of the earth in riches and wisdom. 23 And all the kings of the earth were seeking the face of Sol'o·mon to hear his wisdom, which the [true] God had put in his heart. 24 And they were bringing each his gift, articles of silver and articles of gold and garments, armor and balsam oil, horses and mules as a yearly matter of course. 25 And Sol'o·mon came to have four thousand stalls of horses and chariots and twelve thousand steeds, and he kept them stationed in the chariot cities and close by the king in Jerusalem. 26 And he came to be ruler over all the kings from the River down to the land of the Phi·lis'tines and down to the boundary of Egypt. 27 Furthermore, the king made the silver in Jerusalem like the stones; and cedarwood he made like the sycamore trees that are in the She'phe'lah for abundance. 28 And there were those bringing out horses to Sol'o·mon from Egypt and from all the other lands.

29 As for the rest of the affairs of Sol'o·mon, the first and the last, are they not written among the words of Nathan the prophet and in the prophecy of A·hi'jah the Shi'lo·nite and in the record of visions of Id'do the visionary concerning Jer·o·bo'am the son of Ne'bat? 30 And Sol'o·mon continued to reign in Jerusalem over all Israel for forty years. 31 Finally Sol'o·mon lay down with his forefathers. So they buried him in the city of David his father; and Re·ho·bo'am his son began to reign in place of him.

10 And Re·ho·bo'am proceeded to go to She'chem, for it was to She'chem that all the Israelites came to make him king. 2 And it came about that as soon as Jer·o·bo'am the son of Ne'bat heard of it while he was yet in Egypt, (because he had run away on account of Sol'o·mon the king,) Jer·o·bo'am immediately came back from Egypt. 3 So they sent and called him, and Jer·o·bo'am and

all Israel came and spoke to Re·ho·bo'am, saying: 4 "Your father, for his part, made our yoke hard; and now make the hard service of your father and the heavy yoke that he put upon us lighter, and we shall serve you."

5 At this he said to them: "Let there be yet three days. Then return to me." So the people went away. 6 And King Re·ho·bo'am began to take counsel with the older men that were continually attending upon Sol'o·mon his father while he continued alive, saying: "How are you advising to reply to this people?" 7 Accordingly they spoke to him, saying: "If you would prove yourself good to this people and actually be pleasing to them and indeed speak good words to them, they also will certainly become your servants always."

8 However, he left the counsel of the older men with which they had advised him, and he began to take counsel with the young men that had grown up with him, who were the ones attending upon him. 9 And he went on to say to them: "What is it that you are offering in counsel that we may reply to this people who have spoken to me, saying, 'Make the yoke that your father put upon us lighter'?" 10 In turn the young men that had grown up with him spoke with him, saying: "This is what you should say to the people who have spoken to you, saying, 'Your father, for his part, made our yoke heavy, but, as for you, make it lighter upon us'; this is what you should say to them, 'My own little finger will certainly be thicker than my father's hips. 11 And now my father, for his part, loaded upon you a heavy yoke, but I, for my part, shall add to your yoke. My father, for his part, chastised you with whips, but I, for my part, with scourges.'"

12 And Jer·o·bo'am and all the people proceeded to come to Re·ho·bo'am on the third day, just as the king had spoken, saying: "Return to me on the third day." 13 And the king began to answer them harshly. Thus King Re·ho·bo'am

left the counsel of the older men, 14 and he went on to speak to them according to the counsel of the young men, saying: "I shall make YOUR yoke heavier, and I, for my part, shall add to it. My father, for his part, chastised YOU with whips, but I, for my part, with scourges." 15 And the king did not listen to the people; for it proved to be a turn of affairs from the [true] God in order that Jehovah might carry out his word that he had spoken by means of A·hi′jah the Shi′lo·nite to Jer·o·bo′am the son of Ne′bat.

16 As for all Israel, because the king did not listen to them, the people now replied to the king, saying: "What share do we have in David? And there is no inheritance in the son of Jes′se. Each one to your gods, O Israel! Now see to your own house, O David." With that all Israel began to go to its tents.

17 As for the sons of Israel that were dwelling in the cities of Judah, Re·ho·bo′am continued to reign over them.

18 Subsequently King Re·ho·bo′am sent Ha·do′ram, who was over those conscripted for forced labor, but the sons of Israel pelted him with stones, so that he died. And King Re·ho·bo′am himself managed to get up into his chariot to flee to Jerusalem. 19 And the Israelites kept up their revolt against the house of David down to this day.

11 When Re·ho·bo′am arrived at Jerusalem, he immediately congregated the house of Judah and Benjamin, a hundred and eighty thousand choice men able-bodied for war, to fight against Israel so as to bring the kingdom back to Re·ho·bo′am. 2 Then the word of Jehovah came to She·mai′ah the man of the [true] God, saying: 3 "Say to Re·ho·bo′am the son of Sol′o·mon the king of Judah and to all Israel in Judah and Benjamin, saying, 4 'This is what Jehovah has said: "YOU must not go up and fight against YOUR brothers. Return each one to his house, for it is at my own instance that

this thing has been brought about." ' " So they obeyed the word of Jehovah and returned from going against Jer·o·bo′am.

5 And Re·ho·bo′am continued to dwell in Jerusalem and proceeded to build fortified cities in Judah. 6 Thus he rebuilt Beth′le·hem and E′tam and Te·ko′a, 7 and Beth-zur and So′co and A·dul′lam, 8 and Gath and Ma·re′shah and Ziph, 9 and Ad·o·ra′im and La′chish and A·ze′kah, 10 and Zo′rah and Ai′ja·lon and He′bron, fortified cities, which were in Judah and Benjamin. 11 Further, he reinforced the fortified places and put leaders in them and supplies of food and oil and wine, 12 and in all the different cities large shields and lances; and he went on reinforcing them to a very great degree. And Judah and Benjamin continued his.

13 And the priests and the Levites themselves that were in all Israel took their stand by him out of all their territories. 14 For the Levites left their pasture grounds and their possession and then came to Judah and Jerusalem, because Jer·o·bo′am and his sons had discharged them from acting as priests to Jehovah. 15 And he proceeded to put in office for himself priests for the high places and for the goat-shaped demons and for the calves that he had made. 16 And following them from all the tribes of Israel those that were giving their heart to seek Jehovah the God of Israel came themselves to Jerusalem to sacrifice to Jehovah the God of their forefathers. 17 And they kept strengthening the kingship of Judah and confirming Re·ho·bo′am the son of Sol′o·mon for three years, for they walked in the way of David and Sol′o·mon for three years.

18 Then Re·ho·bo′am took as his wife Ma′ha·lath the daughter of Jer′i·moth the son of David, and of Ab′i·ha·il the daughter of E·li′ab the son of Jes′se. 19 In time she bore him sons, Je′ush and Shem-a·ri′ah and Za′ham. 20 And after her he took Ma′a·cah the granddaughter of Ab′sa·lom. In time she

bore him A·bi'jah and At'tai and Zi'za and She·lo'mith. 21 And Re·ho·bo'am was more in love with Ma'a·cah the granddaughter of Ab'sa·lom than all his other wives and his concubines; for there were eighteen wives that he had taken, also sixty concubines, so that he became father to twenty-eight sons and sixty daughters. 22 Consequently Re·ho·bo'am put A·bi'jah the son of Ma'a·cah in office as head, as leader among his brothers, for [he thought] of making him king. 23 However, he acted understandingly and distributed some out of all his sons to all the lands of Judah and of Benjamin, to all the fortified cities, and gave them food in abundance and procured a multitude of wives [for them].

12 And it came about that, as soon as the kingship of Re·ho·bo'am was firmly established and as soon as he was strong, he left the law of Jehovah, and also all Israel with him. 2 And it came about in the fifth year of King Re·ho·bo'am that Shi'shak the king of Egypt came up against Jerusalem, (for they had behaved unfaithfully toward Jehovah,) 3 with twelve hundred chariots and with sixty thousand horsemen; and there was no number to the people that came with him out of Egypt— Lib'y·ans, Suk'ki·im and E·thi·o'pi·ans. 4 And he got to capture the fortified cities that belonged to Judah and finally came as far as Jerusalem.

5 Now as for She·mai'ah the prophet, he came to Re·ho·bo'am and the princes of Judah who had gathered themselves at Jerusalem because of Shi'shak, and he proceeded to say to them: "This is what Jehovah has said, 'YOU, for your part, have left me, and I, too, for my part, have left YOU to the hand of Shi'shak.'" 6 At that time the princes of Israel and the king humbled themselves and said: "Jehovah is righteous." 7 And when Jehovah saw that they had humbled themselves, the word of Jehovah came to She·mai'ah, saying: "They have humbled themselves.

I shall not bring them to ruin, and in a little while I shall certainly give them an escape, and my rage will not pour forth upon Jerusalem by the hand of Shi'shak. 8 But they will become servants of his, that they may know the difference between my service and the service of the kingdoms of the lands."

9 So Shi'shak the king of Egypt came up against Jerusalem and took the treasures of the house of Jehovah and the treasures of the king's house. Everything he took; and so he took the gold shields that Sol'o·mon had made. 10 Consequently King Re·ho·bo'am made in their place copper shields, and he committed them to the control of the chiefs of the runners, the guards of the entrance of the king's house. 11 And it would occur that as often as the king came to the house of Jehovah, the runners came in and carried them and returned them to the guard chamber of the runners. 12 And because he humbled himself, Jehovah's anger turned back from him, and he [did] not [think] of bringing them to ruin completely. And, besides, there happened to be good things in Judah.

13 And King Re·ho·bo'am continued to make his position strong in Jerusalem and kept reigning; for Re·ho·bo'am was forty-one years old when he began to reign, and for seventeen years he reigned in Jerusalem, the city that Jehovah had chosen out of all the tribes of Israel to put his name there. And his mother's name was Na'a·mah the Am'mon·it·ess. 14 But he did what was bad, for he had not firmly established his heart to search for Jehovah.

15 As for Re·ho·bo'am's affairs, the first and the last, are they not written among the words of She·mai'ah the prophet and of Id'do the visionary by genealogical enrollment? And there were wars between Re·ho·bo'am and Jer·o·bo'am all the time. 16 Finally Re·ho·bo'am lay down with his forefathers and was buried in the city of

David; and A·bi'jah his son began to reign in place of him.

13 In the eighteenth year of King Jer·o·bo'am it was that A·bi'jah began to reign over Judah. 2 Three years he reigned in Jerusalem, and his mother's name was Mi·cai'ah the daughter of U'ri·el of Gib'e·ah. And war itself took place between A·bi'jah and Jer·o·bo'am.

3 So A·bi'jah engaged in the war with a military force of four hundred thousand mighty men of war, chosen men. And Jer·o·bo'am himself drew up in battle formation against him with eight hundred thousand chosen men, valiant, mighty men. 4 A·bi'jah now rose up upon Mount Zem·a·ra'im, which is in the mountainous region of E'phra·im, and said: "Hear me, O Jer·o·bo'am and all Israel. 5 Is it not for you to know that Jehovah the God of Israel himself gave a kingdom to David over Israel to time indefinite, to him and to his sons, by a covenant of salt? 6 And Jer·o·bo'am the son of Ne'bat, the servant of Sol'o·mon the son of David, proceeded to rise up and rebel against his lord. 7 And idle men, good-for-nothing fellows, kept collecting themselves together by him. Finally they proved superior to Re·ho·bo'am the son of Sol'o·mon, when Re·ho·bo'am himself happened to be young and fainthearted, and he did not hold his own against them.

8 "And now you men are thinking of holding your own against the kingdom of Jehovah in the hand of the sons of David, when you are a large crowd and there are with you the golden calves that Jer·o·bo'am made for you as gods. 9 Have you not driven out Jehovah's priests, the sons of Aaron, and the Levites, and do you not keep making priests for yourselves like the peoples of the land? As for anyone that came and filled his hand with power by means of a young bull and seven rams, he became a priest of what are no gods. 10 As for us, Jehovah is our God, and we have not left him; but

priests are ministering to Jehovah, the sons of Aaron, and also the Levites in the work. 11 And they are making burnt offerings smoke to Jehovah morning by morning and evening by evening and also perfumed incense; and the layers of bread are upon the table of pure [gold], and there are the golden lampstands and its lamps to light up evening by evening; because we are keeping the obligation to Jehovah our God, but you yourselves have left him. 12 And, look! with us there is at the head the [true] God with his priests and the signal trumpets for sounding the battle alarm against you. O sons of Israel, do not fight against Jehovah the God of your forefathers, for you will not prove successful."

13 And Jer·o·bo'am, for his part, dispatched an ambush around to come behind them, so that they proved to be in front of Judah and the ambush behind them. 14 When those of Judah turned around, why, there they had the battle in front and behind. And they began to cry out to Jehovah, while the priests were loudly sounding the trumpets. 15 And the men of Judah broke out shouting a war cry. And it came about that, when the men of Judah shouted a war cry, then the [true] God himself defeated Jer·o·bo'am and all Israel before A·bi'jah and Judah. 16 And the sons of Israel took to flight from before Judah, and then God gave them into their hand. 17 And A·bi'jah and his people went striking them down with a vast slaughter; and the slain of Israel kept falling down, five hundred thousand chosen men. 18 Thus the sons of Israel were humbled at that time, but the sons of Judah proved superior because they leaned upon Jehovah the God of their forefathers. 19 And A·bi'jah kept chasing after Jer·o·bo'am and got to capture cities from him, Beth'el and its dependent towns, and Jesh'a·nah and its dependent towns, and E'phra·in and its dependent towns. 20 And Jer·o·bo'am did not retain any more power in the days of

A·bi′jah; but Jehovah dealt him a blow, so that he died.

21 And A·bi′jah continued to strengthen himself. In time he got fourteen wives for himself, and became father to twenty-two sons and sixteen daughters. 22 And the rest of A·bi′jah's affairs, even his ways and his words, are written in the exposition of the prophet Id′do.

14 Finally A·bi′jah lay down with his forefathers, and they buried him in the city of David; and A′sa his son began to reign in place of him. In his days the land had no disturbance for ten years.

2 And A′sa proceeded to do what was good and right in the eyes of Jehovah his God. 3 So he removed the foreign altars and the high places and broke up the sacred pillars and cut down the sacred poles. 4 Further, he said to Judah to search for Jehovah the God of their forefathers and to do the law and the commandment. 5 Accordingly he removed from all the cities of Judah the high places and the incense stands; and the kingdom continued without disturbance before him. 6 And he went on to build fortified cities in Judah, for the land had no disturbance; and there was no war against him during these years, for Jehovah gave him rest. 7 So he said to Judah: "Let us build these cities and make walls around and towers, double doors and bars. For us the land is yet available, because we have searched for Jehovah our God. We have searched, and he gives us rest all around." And they went building and proving successful.

8 And A′sa came to have a military force bearing the large shield and lance, three hundred thousand out of Judah. And out of Benjamin those bearing the buckler and bending the bow were two hundred and eighty thousand. All these were valiant, mighty men.

9 Later Ze′rah the E·thi·o′pi·an went out against them with a military force of a million men and three hundred chariots, and came as far as Ma·re′shah. 10 Then A′sa went out against him and they drew up in battle formation in the valley of Zeph′a·thah at Ma·re′shah. 11 And A′sa began to call to Jehovah his God and say: "O Jehovah, as to helping, it does not matter with you whether there are many or [those with] no power. Help us, O Jehovah our God, for upon you we do lean, and in your name we have come against this crowd. O Jehovah, you are our God. Do not let mortal man retain strength against you."

12 At that Jehovah defeated the E·thi·o′pi·ans before A′sa and before Judah, and the E·thi·o′pi·ans took to flight. 13 And A′sa and the people that were with him kept pursuing them as far as Ge′rar, and those of the E·thi·o′pi·ans continued falling down till there was no one alive of them; for they were broken to pieces before Jehovah and before his camp. Afterward they carried off a very great deal of spoil. 14 Further, they struck all the cities round about Ge′rar, for the dread of Jehovah had come to be upon them; and they went plundering all the cities, for there happened to be much to plunder in them. 15 And even the tents with livestock they struck so that they took captive flocks in great number and camels, after which they returned to Jerusalem.

15 Now for Az·a·ri′ah the son of O′ded, the spirit of God came to be upon him. 2 Consequently he went out before A′sa and said to him: "Hear me, O A′sa and all Judah and Benjamin! Jehovah is with YOU as long as YOU prove to be with him; and if YOU search for him, he will let himself be found by YOU, but if YOU leave him he will leave YOU. 3 And many were the days that Israel had been without a true God and without a priest teaching and without Law. 4 But when in their distress they returned to Jehovah the God of Israel and looked for him, then he let himself be found by them. 5 And in those times there was no peace for one going out or for one coming in, because there were many disorders among all the inhabitants of the lands. 6 And they were crushed to pieces, nation against nation and city against city, because God himself kept them in disorder with every sort of distress. 7 And YOU, be courageous and do not let YOUR hands drop down, because there exists a reward for YOUR activity."

8 And as soon as A′sa heard these words and the prophecy of O′ded the prophet, he took courage and proceeded to cause the disgusting things to vanish from all the land of Judah and Benjamin and from the cities that he had captured from the mountainous region of E′phra·im, and to renew Jehovah's altar that was before the porch of Jehovah. 9 And he began to collect together all Judah and Benjamin and the alien residents with them from E′phra·im and Ma·nas′seh and Sim′e·on, for they had deserted to him from Israel in great number when they saw that Jehovah his God was with him. 10 So they were collected together at Jerusalem in the third month of the fifteenth year of A′sa's reign. 11 Then they sacrificed to Jehovah on that day from the spoil they had brought, seven hundred cattle and seven thousand sheep. 12 Furthermore, they entered into a covenant to search for Jehovah the God of their forefathers with all their heart and with all their soul; 13 that anyone that would not search for Jehovah the God of Israel should be put to death, whether small or great, whether man or woman. 14 So they swore to Jehovah with a loud voice and with joyful shouting and with the trumpets and with horns. 15 And all Judah gave way to rejoicing over the thing sworn; for it was with all their heart that they had sworn and with full pleasure on their part that they had looked for him, so that he let himself be found by them; and Jehovah continued to give them rest all around.

16 As for even Ma′a·cah [his] grandmother, A′sa the king himself removed her from [being] lady, because she had made a horrible idol for the sacred pole; and then A′sa cut down her horrible idol and pulverized it and burned it in the torrent valley of Kid′ron. 17 And the high places themselves did not disappear from Israel. Only A′sa's heart itself proved to be complete all his days. 18 And he proceeded to bring the things made holy by his father and the things made holy by himself into the house of the [true] God, silver and gold and utensils. 19 As for war, it did not occur down to the thirty-fifth year of A′sa's reign.

16 In the thirty-sixth year of the reign of A′sa, Ba′a·sha the king of Israel came up against Judah and began to build Ra′mah, so as not to allow anyone to go out or come in to A′sa the king of Judah. 2 A′sa now brought out silver and gold from the treasures of Jehovah's house and the king's house and sent to Ben-ha′dad the king of Syria, who was dwelling at Damascus, saying: 3 "There is a covenant between me and you and between my father and your father. Here I do send you silver and gold. Go, break your covenant with Ba′-a·sha the king of Israel, that he may withdraw from me."

4 So Ben-ha′dad listened to King A′sa and sent the chiefs of the military forces that were his against the cities of Israel, so that they struck I′jon and Dan and A′bel-ma′im and all the storage places of the cities of Naph′ta·li. 5 And it came about that as soon as Ba′a·sha heard of it, he immediately quit building Ra′mah and stopped his work. 6 As for A′sa the king, he took all Judah, and they proceeded to carry away the stones of Ra′mah and its timbers with which Ba′a·sha had built, and he began to build with them Ge′ba and Miz′pah.

7 And at that time Ha·na′ni the seer came to A′sa the king of Judah and then said to him: "Because you leaned upon the king of Syria and did not lean upon Jehovah your God, for that reason the military force of the king of Syria has escaped out of your hand. 8 Did not the E·thi·o′pi·ans and the Lib′y·ans

themselves happen to be a very great military force in multitude, in chariots and in horsemen; and because of your leaning upon Jehovah did he not give them into your hand? 9 For, as regards Jehovah, his eyes are roving about through all the earth to show his strength in behalf of those whose heart is complete toward him. You have acted foolishly respecting this, for from now on there will exist wars against you."

10 However, A'sa became offended at the seer and put him in the house of the stocks, because he was in a rage at him over this. And A'sa began to crush some others of the people at that same time. 11 And, look! the affairs of A'sa, the first and the last, there they are written in the Book of the Kings of Judah and of Israel.

12 And A'sa in the thirty-ninth year of his reign developed an ailment in his feet until he was very sick; and even in his sickness he searched not for Jehovah but for the healers. 13 Finally A'sa lay down with his forefathers and died in the forty-first year of his reigning. 14 So they buried him in his grand burial place that he had excavated for himself in the city of David; and they laid him in the bed that had been filled with balsam oil and different sorts of ointment mixed in an ointment of special make. Further, they made an extraordinarily great funeral burning for him.

17 And Je·hosh'a·phat his son began to reign in place of him and to make his position strong over Israel. 2 And he proceeded to put military forces in all the fortified cities of Judah and to put garrisons in the land of Judah and in the cities of E'phra·im that A'sa his father had captured. 3 And Jehovah continued with Je·hosh'a·phat, because he walked in the former ways of David his forefather and did not search for the Ba'als. 4 For it was for the God of his father that he searched and in his commandment he walked, and not according to the doing of Israel. 5 And Jehovah kept the kingdom firmly established in his hand; and all Judah continued to give presents to Je·hosh'a·phat, and he came to have riches and glory in abundance. 6 And his heart became bold in the ways of Jehovah, and he even removed the high places and the sacred poles from Judah.

7 And in the third year of his reigning he sent for his princes, namely, Ben-ha'il and O·ba·di'ah and Zech·a·ri'ah and Ne·than'el and Mi·cai'ah, to teach in the cities of Judah, 8 and with them the Levites, She·mai'ah and Neth·a·ni'ah and Zeb·a·di'ah and As'a·hel and She·mir'a·moth and Je·hon'a·than and Ad·o·ni'jah and To·bi'jah and Tob-ad·o·ni'jah the Levites, and with them E·lish'a·ma and Je·ho'ram the priests. 9 And they began teaching in Judah, and with them there was the book of Jehovah's law; and they kept going around through all the cities of Judah and teaching among the people.

10 And the dread of Jehovah came to be upon all the kingdoms of the lands that were all around Judah, and they did not fight against Je·hosh'a·phat. 11 And from the Phi·lis'tines they were bringing to Je·hosh'a·phat presents and money as tribute. The Arabs also were bringing to him flocks, seven thousand seven hundred rams and seven thousand seven hundred he-goats.

12 And Je·hosh'a·phat continued advancing and growing great to a superior degree; and he went on building fortified places and storage cities in Judah. 13 And there were many interests that became his in the cities of Judah; and warriors, valiant, mighty men, were in Jerusalem. 14 And these were their offices by the house of their forefathers: Of Judah the chiefs of thousands, Ad'nah the chief, and with him there were three hundred thousand valiant, mighty men. 15 And under his control there was Je·ho·ha'nan the chief, and with him there were two hun-

dred and eighty thousand. 16 And under his control there was Am·a·si′ah the son of Zich′ri the volunteer for Jehovah, and with him there were two hundred thousand valiant, mighty men. 17 And out of Benjamin there was the valiant, mighty man E·li′a·da, and with him there were two hundred thousand men equipped with the bow and shield. 18 And under his control there was Je·hoz′a·bad, and with him there were a hundred and eighty thousand men outfitted for the army. 19 These were the ones ministering to the king apart from those whom the king put in the fortified cities throughout all Judah.

18 And Je·hosh′a·phat came to have riches and glory in abundance; but he formed a marriage alliance with A′hab. 2 So years later he went down to A′hab at Sa·mar′i·a; and A′hab proceeded to sacrifice sheep and cattle in abundance for him and for the people that were with him. And he began to allure him to go up against Ra′moth-gil′e·ad. 3 And A′hab the king of Israel went on to say to Je·hosh′a·phat the king of Judah: "Will you go with me to Ra′moth-gil′e·ad?" At this he said to him: "I am the same as you are, and my people are like your people and with you in the war."

4 However, Je·hosh′a·phat said to the king of Israel: "Please, inquire first of all for the word of Jehovah." 5 So the king of Israel collected the prophets together, four hundred men, and said to them: "Shall we go against Ra′moth-gil′e·ad in war, or shall I refrain?" And they began to say: "Go up, and the [true] God will give [it] into the king's hand."

6 But Je·hosh′a·phat said: "Is there not here a prophet of Jehovah still? Then let us inquire through him." 7 At that the king of Israel said to Je·hosh′a·phat: "There is still one man through whom to inquire of Jehovah, but I myself certainly hate him, for he is prophesying concerning me, not for good, but, all his days, for bad. He is Mi·cai′ah the son of Im′lah."

However, Je·hosh′a·phat said: "Do not let the king say a thing like that."

8 Accordingly the king of Israel called a court official and said: "Bring Mi·cai′ah the son of Im′lah quickly." 9 Now the king of Israel and Je·hosh′a·phat the king of Judah were sitting each one on his throne, clothed in garments, and were sitting in the threshing floor at the entrance of the gate of Sa·mar′i·a; and all the prophets were acting as prophets before them. 10 Then Zed·e·ki′ah the son of Che·na′a·nah made for himself horns of iron and said: "This is what Jehovah has said, 'With these you will push the Syrians until you exterminate them.' " 11 And all the other prophets were prophesying the same as that, saying: "Go up to Ra′moth-gil′e·ad and prove successful, and Jehovah will certainly give [it] into the king's hand."

12 And the messenger that went to call Mi·cai′ah spoke to him, saying: "Look! The words of the prophets are unanimously of good to the king; and let your word, please, become like one of them and you must speak good." 13 But Mi·cai′ah said: "As Jehovah is living, what my God will say, that is what I shall speak." 14 Then he came in to the king, and the king proceeded to say to him: "Mi·cai′ah, shall we go to Ra′moth-gil′e·ad in war, or shall I refrain?" At once he said: "Go up and prove successful; and they will be given into YOUR hand." 15 At that the king said to him: "For how many times am I putting you under oath that you should not speak to me anything but truth in the name of Jehovah?" 16 So he said: "I certainly see all the Israelites scattered upon the mountains, like sheep that have no shepherd. And Jehovah went on to say: 'These have no masters. Let them go back each one to his house in peace.' "

17 Then the king of Israel said to Je·hosh′a·phat: "Did I not say to you, 'He will prophesy concerning me, not good things, but bad'?"

18 And he went on to say: "Therefore HEAR the word of Jehovah: I certainly see Jehovah sitting upon his throne and all the army of the heavens standing at his right and his left. 19 And Jehovah proceeded to say, 'Who will fool A'hab the king of Israel that he may go up and fall at Ra'moth-gil'e·ad?' And there was talk, this one saying something like this, and that one saying something like that. 20 Finally a spirit came out and stood before Jehovah and said, 'I myself shall fool him.' At that Jehovah said to him, 'By what means?' 21 To this he said, 'I shall go forth and certainly become a deceptive spirit in the mouth of all his prophets.' So he said, 'You will fool him, and, what is more, you will come off the winner. Go out and do that way.' 22 And now here Jehovah has put a deceptive spirit in the mouth of these prophets of yours; but Jehovah himself has spoken calamity concerning you."

23 Zed·e·ki'ah the son of Chena'a·nah now approached and struck Mi·cai'ah on the cheek and said: "In just which way did the spirit of Jehovah pass along from me to speak with you?" 24 At that Mi·cai'ah said: "Look! You are seeing [which way] on that day when you will enter the innermost chamber to hide yourself." 25 Then the king of Israel said: "TAKE Mi·cai'ah and turn him back to A'mon the chief of the city and to Jo'ash the king's son. 26 And YOU men must say, 'This is what the king has said: "PUT this fellow in the house of detention and feed him with a reduced allowance of bread and a reduced allowance of water until I return in peace." '" 27 Upon that Mi·cai'ah said: "If you return at all in peace, Jehovah has not spoken with me." And he added: "Hear, all YOU peoples."

28 And the king of Israel and Je·hosh'a·phat the king of Judah proceeded to go up to Ra'moth-gil'e·ad. 29 The king of Israel now said to Je·hosh'a·phat: "There will be a disguising and entering into the battle [for me], but you, for your part, put on your garments." Accordingly the king of Israel disguised himself, after which they entered into the battle. 30 As for the king of Syria, he had commanded the chiefs of the chariots that were his, saying: "You must fight, neither with the small nor with the great, but with the king of Israel alone." 31 And it came about that, as soon as the chiefs of the chariots saw Je·hosh'a·phat, they, for their part, said to themselves: "It is the king of Israel." So they turned around against him to fight; and Je·hosh'a·phat began to cry for aid, and Jehovah himself helped him, and God at once allured them away from him. 32 And it came about that as soon as the chiefs of the chariots saw that it did not prove to be the king of Israel, they immediately came back from following him.

33 And there was a man that bent the bow in his innocence, but he got to strike the king of Israel between the appendages and the coat of mail, so that he said to the charioteer: "Turn your hand around, and you must take me out from the camp, because I have been badly wounded." 34 And the battle kept rising in intensity on that day, and the king of Israel himself had to be kept in a standing position in the chariot facing the Syrians until the evening; and gradually he died at the time of the setting of the sun.

19 Then Je·hosh'a·phat the king of Judah returned in peace to his own house at Jerusalem. 2 Je'hu the son of Ha·na'ni the visionary now went out before him and said to King Je·hosh'a·phat: "Is it to the wicked that help is to be given, and is it for those hating Jehovah that you should have love? And for this there is indignation against you from the person of Jehovah. 3 Nevertheless, there are good things that have been found with you, because you have cleared out the sacred poles from the land and you have prepared your heart to search for the [true] God."

4 And Je·hosh'a·phat continued dwelling in Jerusalem; and he began to go out again among the people from Be'er-she'ba to the mountainous region of E'phra·im, that he might bring them back to Jehovah the God of their forefathers. 5 And he proceeded to station judges throughout the land in all the fortified cities of Judah, city by city. 6 And he went on to say to the judges: "See what YOU are doing, because it is not for man that YOU judge but it is for Jehovah; and he is with YOU in the matter of judgment. 7 And now let the dread of Jehovah come to be upon YOU. Be careful and act, for with Jehovah our God there is no unrighteousness or partiality or taking of a bribe."

8 And in Jerusalem also Je·hosh'a·phat stationed some of the Levites and the priests and some of the heads of the paternal houses of Israel for the judgment of Jehovah and for the legal cases of the inhabitants of Jerusalem. 9 Further, he laid a command upon them, saying: "This is how YOU should do in the fear of Jehovah with faithfulness and with a complete heart. 10 As for every legal case that will come to YOU of YOUR brothers who are dwelling in their cities, involving the shedding of blood, involving law and commandment and regulations and judicial decisions, YOU must warn them that they may not do wrong against Jehovah and indignation may not have to take place against YOU and against YOUR brothers. This is how YOU should do that YOU may not incur guilt. 11 And here is Am·a·ri'ah the chief priest over YOU for every matter of Jehovah; and Zeb·a·di'ah the son of Ish'ma·el the leader of the house of Judah for every matter of the king; and as officers the Levites are available for YOU. Be strong and act, and let Jehovah prove to be with what is good."

20 And it came about afterward that the sons of Mo'ab and the sons of Am'mon and with them some of the Am'mon·im came against Je·hosh'a·phat in war.

2 So people came and told Je·hosh'a·phat, saying: "There has come against you a large crowd from the region of the sea, from E'dom; and there they are in Haz'a·zon-ta'mar, that is to say, En-ge'di." 3 At that Je·hosh'a·phat became afraid and set his face to search for Jehovah. So he proclaimed a fast for all Judah. 4 Eventually those of Judah were collected together to inquire of Jehovah. Even from all the cities of Judah they came to consult Jehovah.

5 Then Je·hosh'a·phat stood up in the congregation of Judah and of Jerusalem in the house of Jehovah before the new courtyard, 6 and he proceeded to say:

"O Jehovah the God of our forefathers, are you not God in the heavens, and are you not dominating over all the kingdoms of the nations, and are there not in your hand power and mightiness, with no one to hold his ground against you? 7 Did not you yourself, O God of ours, drive away the inhabitants of this land from before your people Israel and then give it to the seed of Abraham, your lover, to time indefinite? 8 And they took up dwelling in it, and they proceeded to build in it for you a sanctuary for your name, saying, 9 'If there should come upon us calamity, sword, adverse judgment, or pestilence or famine, let us stand before this house and before you (for your name is in this house), that we may call to you for aid out of our distress, and may you hear and save.' 10 And now here the sons of Am'mon, and Mo'ab and the mountainous region of Se'ir, whom you did not allow Israel to invade when they were coming out of the land of Egypt, but they turned away from them and did not annihilate them, 11 yes, here they are rewarding us by coming in to drive us out from your possession that you caused us to possess. 12 O our God, will you not execute judgment upon them? For in us there is no power before this large crowd that is coming against us; and we ourselves do not know what we ought to do, but our eyes are toward you."

13 All the while all those of Judah were standing before Jehovah, even their little ones, their wives and their sons.

14 Now as for Ja·ha·zi'el the son of Zech·a·ri'ah the son of Be·nai'ah the son of Je·i'el the son of Mat·ta·ni'ah the Levite of the sons of A'saph, the spirit of Jehovah came to be upon him in the middle of the congregation. 15 Consequently he said: "Pay attention, all Judah and you inhabitants of Jerusalem and King Je·hosh'a·phat! Here is what Jehovah has said to you, 'Do not you be afraid or be terrified because of this large crowd; for the battle is not yours, but God's. 16 Tomorrow go down against them. There they are coming up by the pass of Ziz; and you will be certain to find them at the end of the torrent valley in front of the wilderness of Je·ru'el. 17 You will not need to fight in this instance. Take your position, stand still and see the salvation of Jehovah in your behalf. O Judah and Jerusalem, do not be afraid or be terrified. Tomorrow go out against them, and Jehovah will be with you.'"

18 At once Je·hosh'a·phat bowed low with his face to the earth, and all Judah and the inhabitants of Jerusalem themselves fell down before Jehovah to do obeisance to Jehovah. 19 Then the Levites of the sons of the Ko'hath·ites and of the sons of the Ko'rah·ites rose up to praise Jehovah the God of Israel with an extraordinarily loud voice.

20 And they proceeded to rise early in the morning and go out to the wilderness of Te·ko'a. And as they went out, Je·hosh'a·phat stood up and then said: "Hear me, O Judah and you inhabitants of Jerusalem! Put faith in Jehovah your God that you may prove yourselves of long duration. Put faith in his prophets and so prove successful."

21 Further, he took counsel with the people and stationed singers to Jehovah and those offering praise in holy adornment as they went out ahead of the armed men, and saying: "Give praise to Jehovah, for to time indefinite is his lovingkindness."

22 And at the time that they started off with the joyful cry and praise, Jehovah set men in ambush against the sons of Am'mon, Mo'ab and the mountainous region of Se'ir who were coming into Judah, and they went smiting one another. 23 And the sons of Am'mon and Mo'ab proceeded to stand up against the inhabitants of the mountainous region of Se'ir to devote them to destruction and annihilate them; and as soon as they finished with the inhabitants of Se'ir, they helped each one to bring his own fellow to ruin.

24 But as for Judah, it came to the watchtower of the wilderness. When they turned their faces toward the crowd, why, there they were, their carcasses fallen to the earth without anyone escaping. 25 So Je·hosh'a·phat and his people came to plunder the spoil on them, and they got to find among them in abundance both goods and clothing and desirable articles; and they went stripping them off for themselves until they could carry no more. And it came to be three days that they were plundering the spoil, for it was abundant. 26 And on the fourth day they congregated together at the low plain of Ber'a·cah, for there they blessed Jehovah. That is why they called the name of that place Low Plain of Ber'a·cah—until today.

27 Then all the men of Judah and Jerusalem returned, with Je·hosh'a·phat at their head, to return to Jerusalem with rejoicing, for Jehovah had made them rejoice over their enemies. 28 So they came to Jerusalem with stringed instruments and with harps and with trumpets to the house of Jehovah. 29 And the dread of God came to be upon all the kingdoms of the lands when they heard that

Jehovah had fought against the enemies of Israel. 30 Thus the royal realm of Je·hosh′a·phat had no disturbance, and his God continued to give him rest all around.

31 And Je·hosh′a·phat went on reigning over Judah. Thirty-five years old he was when he began to reign, and for twenty-five years he reigned in Jerusalem. And his mother's name was A·zu′bah the daughter of Shil′hi. 32 And he kept walking in the way of his father A′sa, and he did not turn aside from it by doing what was right in Jehovah's eyes. 33 Only the high places themselves did not disappear; and the people themselves had not yet prepared their heart for the God of their forefathers.

34 As for the rest of the affairs of Je·hosh′a·phat, the first and the last, there they are written among the words of Je′hu the son of Ha·na′ni, which were inserted in the Book of the Kings of Israel. 35 And after this Je·hosh′a·phat the king of Judah had partnership with A·ha·zi′ah the king of Israel, who acted wickedly. 36 So he made him a partner with himself in making ships to go to Tar′shish and they made ships in E′zi·on-ge′ber. 37 However, E·li·e′zer the son of Dod·av′a·hu of Ma·re′sha spoke prophetically against Je·hosh′a·phat, saying: "Inasmuch as you have had partnership with A·ha·zi′ah, Jehovah will certainly break down your works." Accordingly the ships were wrecked, and they did not retain strength to go to Tar′shish.

21 Finally Je·hosh′a·phat lay down with his forefathers and was buried with his forefathers in the city of David; and Je·ho′ram his son began to reign in place of him. 2 And he had brothers, Je·hosh′a·phat's sons, Az·a·ri′ah and Je·hi′el and Zech·a·ri′ah and Az·a·ri′ah and Mi′cha·el and Sheph·a·ti′ah, all these being the sons of Je·hosh′a·phat the king of Israel. 3 Consequently their father gave them many gifts in silver and in gold and in choice things along with fortified cities in Judah; but the kingdom he gave to Je·ho′ram, for he was the first-born.

4 When Je·ho′ram rose up over the kingdom of his father he proceeded to make his position strong, and so he killed all his brothers with the sword and also some of the princes of Israel. 5 Thirty-two years old was Je·ho′ram when he began to reign, and for eight years he reigned in Jerusalem. 6 And he went on walking in the way of the kings of Israel, just as those of the house of A′hab had done; for A′hab's own daughter had become his wife, and he continued to do what was bad in Jehovah's eyes. 7 And Jehovah did not want to bring the house of David to ruin, for the sake of the covenant that he had concluded with David, and just as he had said he would give him and his sons a lamp always.

8 In his days E′dom revolted from under the hand of Judah and then made a king to reign over them. 9 So Je·ho′ram together with his chiefs passed over and also all the chariots with him. And it came about that he rose up by night and went striking down the E′dom·ites that were surrounding him and also the chiefs of the chariots. 10 But E′dom kept up its revolt from under the hand of Judah down to this day. It was then that Lib′nah began to revolt at the same time from under his hand, because he had left Jehovah the God of his forefathers. 11 He himself also had made high places on the mountains of Judah, that he might cause the inhabitants of Jerusalem to have immoral intercourse, and that he might drive Judah away.

12 Eventually there came a writing to him from E·li′jah the prophet, saying: "This is what Jehovah the God of David your forefather has said, 'Due to the fact that you have not walked in the ways of Je·hosh′a·phat your father or in the ways of A′sa the king of Judah, 13 but you walk in the way of the kings of Israel and cause Judah and the inhabitants of Jerusalem to

have immoral intercourse the same way that the house of A'hab caused the having of immoral intercourse, and even your own brothers, the household of your father, who were better than you, you have killed; 14 look! Jehovah is dealing a great blow to your people and to your sons and to your wives and to all your goods. 15 And you will be with many sicknesses, with a malady of your intestines, until your intestines have come out because of the sickness day by day.' "

16 Accordingly Jehovah aroused against Je·ho'ram the spirit of the Phi·lis'tines and the Arabs that were by the side of the E·thi·o'pi·ans. 17 So they came up into Judah and forced it open and took captive all the goods that were to be found in the king's house and also his sons and his wives, and there was not left to him a son but Je·ho'a·haz, his youngest son. 18 And after all this Jehovah plagued him in his intestines with a sickness for which there was no healing. 19 And it came about that in the days to come, even when the term of two full years had expired, his intestines came out during his sickness, and he gradually died in his bad maladies; and his people did not make a burning for him like the burning for his forefathers. 20 Thirty-two years old he happened to be when he began to reign, and for eight years he reigned in Jerusalem. Finally he went away without being desired. So they buried him in the city of David, but not in the burial places of the kings.

22 Then the inhabitants of Jerusalem made A·ha·zi'ah his youngest son king in place of him, (for the marauder band that came with the Arabs to the camp had killed all the older ones,) and A·ha·zi'ah the son of Je·ho'ram began to reign as king of Judah. 2 Twenty-two years old was A·ha·zi'ah when he began to reign, and for one year he reigned in Jerusalem. And his mother's name was Ath·a·li'ah the granddaughter of Om'ri.

3 He himself also walked in the ways of the house of A'hab, for his mother herself became his counselor in doing wickedly. 4 And he went on doing what was bad in Jehovah's eyes, the same as the house of A'hab, for they themselves became counselors to him after the death of his father, to his ruination. 5 It was also in their counsel that he walked, so that he went with Je·ho'ram the son of A'hab the king of Israel to the war against Haz'a·el the king of Syria at Ra'moth-gil'e·ad, at which the shooters got to strike Je·ho'ram. 6 Hence he returned to get healed at Jez're·el from the wounds that they had inflicted upon him at Ra'mah when he fought Haz'a·el the king of Syria.

As for Az·a·ri'ah the son of Je·ho'ram the king of Judah, he went down to see Je·ho'ram the son of A'hab in Jez're·el, for he was sick. 7 But it was from God that the downfall of A·ha·zi'ah occurred by [his] coming to Je·ho'ram; and when he came, he went out with Je·ho'ram to Je'hu the grandson of Nim'shi, whom Jehovah had anointed to cut off the house of A'hab. 8 And it came about that as soon as Je'hu had entered into controversy with the house of A'hab, he got to find the princes of Judah and the sons of the brothers of A·ha·zi'ah, ministers of A·ha·zi'ah, and he proceeded to kill them. 9 Then he went looking for A·ha·zi'ah, and they finally captured him, as he was hiding in Sa·mar'i·a, and brought him to Je'hu. Then they put him to death and buried him, for they said: "He is the grandson of Je·hosh'a·phat, who searched for Jehovah with all his heart." And there was no one of the house of A·ha·zi'ah to retain power for the kingdom.

10 As regards Ath·a·li'ah the mother of A·ha·zi'ah, she saw that her son had died. So she rose up and destroyed all the royal offspring of the house of Judah. 11 However, Je·ho·shab'e·ath the daughter of the king took Je·ho'ash the son of A·ha·zi'ah and stole

him away from among the sons of the king that were to be put to death, and put him and his nursing woman in the inner room for the couches. And Je·ho·shab'e·ath the daughter of King Je·ho'ram, the wife of Je·hoi'a·da the priest, (for she herself happened to be the sister of A·ha·zi'ah,) kept him concealed because of Ath·a·li'ah, and she did not put him to death. 12 And he continued with them in the house of the [true] God hidden for six years, while Ath·a·li'ah was ruling as queen over the land.

23 And in the seventh year Je·hoi'a·da showed himself courageous and proceeded to take the chiefs of hundreds, namely, Az·a·ri'ah the son of Je·ro'ham, and Ish'ma·el the son of Je·ho·ha'nan and Az·a·ri'ah the son of O'bed and Ma·a·sei'ah the son of A·dai'ah and E·li·sha'phat the son of Zich'ri, with him into the covenant. 2 Afterward they went around throughout Judah and collected together the Levites from all the cities of Judah and the heads of the paternal houses of Israel. So they came to Jerusalem. 3 Then all the congregation concluded a covenant with the king in the house of the [true] God, after which he said to them:

"Look! The son of the king himself will reign, just as Jehovah promised concerning the sons of David. 4 This is the thing that you will do: one third of you who are coming in on the sabbath, of the priests and of the Levites, will be for doorkeepers; 5 and one third will be at the house of the king; and one third will be at the gate of the Foundation; and all the people will be in the courtyards of the house of Jehovah. 6 And do not let anyone enter the house of Jehovah but the priests and those of the Levites ministering. These are the ones that will enter, because they are a holy group, and all the people themselves will keep the obligation to Jehovah. 7 And the Levites must encircle the king all around, each one with his weapons in his hands; and as for any-

one coming into the house, he should be put to death. And continue with the king when he comes in and when he goes out."

8 And the Levites and all Judah proceeded to do according to all that Je·hoi'a·da the priest had commanded. So they took each one his men that were coming in on the sabbath together with those going out on the sabbath, for Je·hoi'a·da the priest had not set the divisions free from duty. 9 Further, Je·hoi'a·da the priest gave the chiefs of hundreds the spears and the shields and the circular shields that had belonged to King David, which were in the house of the [true] God. 10 And he went on to station all the people, even each one with his missile in his hand, from the right side of the house clear to the left side of the house, by the altar and by the house, all around near the king. 11 Then they brought the king's son out and put upon him the diadem and the Testimony and made him king, and so Je·hoi'a·da and his sons anointed him and said: "Let the king live!"

12 When Ath·a·li'ah heard the sound of the people running and praising the king, she at once came to the people at the house of Jehovah. 13 Then she saw, and there was the king standing by his pillar at the entry, and the princes and the trumpets by the king, and all the people of the land were rejoicing and blowing the trumpets, and the singers with the instruments of song and those giving the signal for offering praise. Immediately Ath·a·li'ah ripped her garments apart and said: "Conspiracy! Conspiracy!" 14 But Je·hoi'a·da the priest brought out the chiefs of hundreds, the appointed ones of the military force, and said to them: "Take her out from inside the rows; and as for anyone coming after her, he should be put to death with the sword!" For the priest had said: "You must not put her to death at the house of Jehovah." 15 So they laid their hands upon her. When she came to the entry of the horse gate of the king's

house, they at once put her to death there.

16 Then Je·hoi′a·da concluded a covenant between himself and all the people and the king that they would continue as the people of Jehovah. 17 After that all the people came to the house of Ba′al and pulled it down; and his altars and his images they broke up, and Mat′tan the priest of Ba′al they killed before the altars. 18 Further, Je·hoi′a·da put the offices of the house of Jehovah in the hand of the priests [and] the Levites, whom David had put in divisions over the house of Jehovah to offer up the burnt sacrifices of Jehovah according to what is written in the law of Moses, with rejoicing and with song by the hands of David. 19 So he stationed the gatekeepers by the gates of the house of Jehovah that no one unclean in any respect might enter. 20 He now took the chiefs of hundreds and the lordly ones and the rulers over the people and all the people of the land and brought the king down from the house of Jehovah. Then they came right through the upper gate to the king's house and seated the king upon the throne of the kingdom. 21 And all the people of the land continued to rejoice; and the city itself had no disturbance, and Ath·a·li′ah they had put to death with the sword.

24 Seven years old was Je·ho′ash when he began to reign, and for forty years he reigned in Jerusalem. And his mother's name was Zib′i·ah from Be′er-she′ba. 2 And Je·ho′ash kept doing what was right in Jehovah's eyes all the days of Je·hoi′a·da the priest. 3 And Je·hoi′a·da proceeded to get two wives for him, and he came to be father to sons and daughters.

4 Now it occurred afterward that it became close to the heart of Je·ho′ash to renovate the house of Jehovah. 5 Accordingly he collected the priests and the Levites together and said to them: "Go out to the cities of Judah and collect money from all Israel to repair the house of YOUR God from year to year; and YOU, for YOUR part, should act quickly in the matter." And the Levites did not act quickly. 6 So the king called Je·hoi′a·da the head and said to him: "Why is it that you have not required an account of the Levites for bringing in from Judah and Jerusalem the sacred tax ordered by Moses the servant of Jehovah, even that of the congregation of Israel, for the tent of the Testimony? 7 For as regards Ath·a·li′ah the wicked woman, her sons themselves had broken into the house of the [true] God, and even all the holy things of the house of Jehovah they had rendered up to the Ba′als." 8 Then the king said [the word], and so they made a chest and put it outside at the gate of the house of Jehovah. 9 After that they issued a call throughout Judah and Jerusalem to bring to Jehovah the sacred tax ordered by Moses the servant of the [true] God upon Israel in the wilderness. 10 And all the princes and all the people began to rejoice, and they kept bringing and casting it into the chest until they all had given.

11 And it came about at the proper time he would bring the chest to the care of the king by the hand of the Levites, and, as soon as they saw that there was plenty of money, the secretary of the king and the commissioner of the chief priest came and emptied the chest and lifted it up and returned it to its place. That was the way they did from day to day, so that they gathered money in abundance. 12 Then the king and Je·hoi′a·da would give it to the doers of the work of the service of Jehovah's house, and they came to be hirers of the stone-cutters and of the craftsmen for renovating Jehovah's house, and also of the workers in iron and copper for repairing Jehovah's house. 13 And the doers of the work began operations, and the repair work kept advancing by their hand, and finally they made the house of the [true] God stand as it structurally should and made it strong. 14 And

as soon as they had finished they brought before the king and Je·hoi′a·da the rest of the money, and they proceeded to make utensils for the house of Jehovah, utensils for the ministry and for making offerings and cups and utensils of gold and of silver; and they came to be offerers of burnt sacrifices in the house of Jehovah constantly all the days of Je·hoi′a·da.

15 And Je·hoi′a·da got to be old and satisfied with years and gradually died, being a hundred and thirty years old at his death. 16 So they buried him in the city of David along with the kings, because he had done good in Israel and with the [true] God and His house.

17 And after Je·hoi′a·da's death the princes of Judah came in and proceeded to bow down to the king. At that time the king listened to them. 18 And gradually they left the house of Jehovah the God of their forefathers and began serving the sacred poles and the idols, so that there came to be indignation against Judah and Jerusalem because of this guilt of theirs. 19 And he kept sending prophets among them to bring them back to Jehovah; and they kept bearing witness against them, but they did not give ear.

20 And God's spirit itself enveloped Zech·a·ri′ah the son of Je·hoi′a·da the priest, so that he stood up above the people and said to them: "This is what the [true] God has said, 'Why are YOU overstepping the commandments of Jehovah, so that YOU cannot prove successful? Because YOU have left Jehovah, he will, in turn, leave YOU.'" 21 Finally they conspired against him and pelted him with stones at the king's commandment in the courtyard of Jehovah's house. 22 And Je·ho′ash the king did not remember the loving-kindness that Je·hoi′a·da his father had exercised toward him, so that he killed his son, who, when he was at the point of dying, said: "Let Jehovah see to it and ask it back."

23 And it came about at the turn of the year a military force of Syria came up against him, and they began to invade Judah and Jerusalem. Then they brought all the princes of the people to ruin from among the people, and all their spoil they sent to the king of Damascus. 24 For it was with a small number of men that the military force of the Syrians made an invasion, and Jehovah himself gave into their hand a military force of very great number, because they had left Jehovah the God of their forefathers; and upon Je·ho′ash they executed acts of judgment. 25 And when they went away from him (for they left him with many diseases), his own servants conspired against him because of the blood of the sons of Je·hoi′a·da the priest; and they got to kill him upon his own couch, so that he died. Then they buried him in the city of David, but they did not bury him in the burial places of the kings.

26 And these were the conspirators against him: Za′bad the son of Shim′e·ath the Am′mon·it·ess and Je·hoz′a·bad the son of Shim′rith the Mo′ab·i·tess. 27 As for his sons and the abundance of the pronouncement against him and the founding of the house of the [true] God, there they are written in the exposition of the Book of the Kings. And Am·a·zi′ah his son began to reign in place of him.

25 At the age of twenty-five years Am·a·zi′ah became king, and for twenty-nine years he reigned in Jerusalem. And his mother's name was Je·ho·ad′dan of Jerusalem. 2 And he continued to do what was right in Jehovah's eyes, only not with a complete heart. 3 And it came about that as soon as the kingdom had become strong upon him, he promptly killed his servants who had struck down the king his father. 4 And their sons he did not put to death, but [did] according to what is written in the law, in the book of Moses, that Jehovah commanded, saying: "Fathers should not die for sons, neither should sons themselves die for

fathers; but it is each one for his own sin that they should die."

5 And Am·a·zi′ah proceeded to collect Judah together and to have them stand according to the house of the forefathers, by the chiefs of thousands and by the chiefs of hundreds for all Judah and Benjamin; and he went on to register them from twenty years of age upward, and finally he found them [to be] three hundred thousand choice men going out to the army, handling lance and large shield. 6 Further, he hired from Israel a hundred thousand valiant, mighty men for a hundred silver talents. 7 And a certain man of the [true] God came to him, saying: "O king, do not let the army of Israel come with you, for Jehovah is not with Israel, [that is,] all the sons of E′phra·im. 8 But come you yourself, act, be courageous for the war. The [true] God could cause you to stumble before an enemy; for there exists power with God to help and to cause stumbling." 9 At this Am·a·zi′ah said to the man of the [true] God: "But what is there to do about the hundred talents that I have given to the troops of Israel?" To this the man of the [true] God said: "There exists with Jehovah the means to give you much more than this." 10 Accordingly Am·a·zi′ah separated them, namely, the troops that had come to him from E′phra·im, to go to their own place. However, their anger got very hot against Judah, so that they returned to their own place in the heat of anger.

11 And Am·a·zi′ah, for his part, took courage and proceeded to lead his own people and go to the Valley of Salt; and he went striking down the sons of Se′ir, ten thousand [of them]. 12 And there were ten thousand that the sons of Judah captured alive. So they brought them to the top of the crag, and proceeded to throw them from the top of the crag; and they, one and all, burst apart. 13 As for the members of the troop whom Am·a·zi′ah had sent back from going with him to the war, they began

making raids upon the cities of Judah, from Sa·mar′i·a clear to Beth-ho′ron, and went striking down three thousand of them and taking a great plunder.

14 But it occurred after Am·a·zi′ah came from striking down the E′dom·ites that he now brought the gods of the sons of Se′ir and set them up for himself as gods, and before them he began to bow down, and to them he began to make sacrificial smoke. 15 Consequently Jehovah's anger became hot against Am·a·zi′ah, and so he sent a prophet to him and said to him: "Why have you searched for the people's gods that did not deliver their own people out of your hand?" 16 And it came about when he spoke to him that [the king] immediately said to him: "Was it a counselor of the king that we constituted you? Quit for your own sake. Why should they strike you down?" Accordingly the prophet quit, but he said: "I certainly know that God has resolved to bring you to ruin, because you have done this and you have not listened to my counsel."

17 Then Am·a·zi′ah the king of Judah took counsel and sent to Je·ho′ash the son of Je·ho′a·haz the son of Je′hu the king of Israel, saying: "Come! Let us look each other in the face." 18 At that Je·ho′ash the king of Israel sent to Am·a·zi′ah the king of Judah, saying: "The thorny weed itself that was in Leb′a·non sent to the cedar that was in Leb′a·non, saying, 'Do give your daughter to my son as a wife.' However, a wild beast of the field that was in Leb′a·non passed by and trampled the thorny weed down. 19 You have said to yourself, Here you have struck down E′dom. And your heart has lifted you up to be glorified. Now do keep dwelling in your own house. Why should you engage in strife in a bad position and have to fall, you and Judah with you?"

20 But Am·a·zi′ah did not listen; for it was from the [true] God for the purpose of giving them into his hand, because they had searched

for the gods of E'dom. 21 So Je-ho'ash the king of Israel went up, and they proceeded to look each other in the face, he and Am·a·zi'ah the king of Judah, at Beth-she'mesh, which belongs to Judah. 22 And Judah came to be defeated before Israel, so that they took to flight each one to his tent. 23 And it was Am·a·zi'ah the king of Judah, the son of Je·ho'ash the son of Je·ho'a·haz, that Je·ho'ash the king of Israel seized at Beth-she'mesh, after which he brought him to Jerusalem and made a breach in the wall of Jerusalem, from the Gate of E'phra·im clear to the Corner Gate, four hundred cubits. 24 And [he took] all the gold and the silver and all the articles that were to be found in the house of the [true] God with O'bed-e'dom and the treasures of the king's house and the hostages, and then returned to Sa·mar'i·a.

25 And Am·a·zi'ah the son of Je·ho'ash the king of Judah continued to live after the death of Je·ho'ash the son of Je·ho'a·haz the king of Israel fifteen years. 26 As for the rest of the affairs of Am·a·zi'ah, the first and the last, look! are they not written in the Book of the Kings of Judah and Israel? 27 And from the time that Am·a·zi'ah turned aside from following Jehovah, they proceeded to form a conspiracy against him in Jerusalem. At length he fled to La'chish; but they sent after him to La'chish and put him to death there. 28 So they carried him upon horses and buried him with his forefathers in the city of Judah.

26 Then all the people of Judah took Uz·zi'ah, he being sixteen years old, and they made him king in place of his father Am·a·zi'ah. 2 He it was that rebuilt E'loth and then restored it to Judah after the king had lain down with his forefathers. 3 Sixteen years old was Uz·zi'ah when he began to reign, and for fifty-two years he reigned in Jerusalem. And his mother's name was Je·co·li'ah of Jerusalem. 4 And he kept doing what was right in Jehovah's eyes,

according to all that Am·a·zi'ah his father had done. 5 And he continually tended to search for God in the days of Zech·a·ri'ah, the instructor in the fear of the [true] God; and, in the days of his searching for Jehovah, the [true] God made him prosperous.

6 And he proceeded to go out and fight against the Phi·lis'tines and break through the wall of Gath and the wall of Jab'neh and the wall of Ash'dod, after which he built cities in Ash'dod [territory] and among the Phi·lis'tines. 7 And the [true] God continued to help him against the Phi·lis'tines and against the Arabians that were dwelling in Gur·ba'al and the Me·u'nim. 8 And the Am'mon·ites began to give tribute to Uz·zi'ah. Eventually his fame went even as far as Egypt, for he displayed strength to an extraordinary degree. 9 Moreover, Uz·zi'ah built towers in Jerusalem by the Corner Gate and by the Valley Gate and by the Buttress, and made them strong. 10 Further, he built towers in the wilderness, and hewed out many cisterns (for there was a great deal of livestock that became his), and also in the She·phe'lah and on the tableland. There were farmers and vinedressers in the mountains and in Car'mel, for a lover of agriculture he proved to be.

11 Moreover, Uz·zi'ah came to have a force engaging in war, those going out on military service in troops, by the number of their registration by the hand of Je·i'el the secretary and Ma·a·sei'ah the officer under the control of Ha·na·ni'ah of the king's princes. 12 The entire number of the heads of the paternal houses, of the valiant, mighty men, was two thousand six hundred. 13 And under their control the army forces were three hundred and seven thousand five hundred men engaging in war with the power of a military force to help the king against the enemy. 14 And Uz·zi'ah continued to prepare for them, for the entire army, shields and lances and helmets and coats of mail and bows and sling-

stones. 15 Further, he made in Jerusalem engines of war, the invention of engineers, that they might come to be upon the towers and upon the corners, to shoot arrows and great stones. Consequently his fame went out to a great distance, for he was helped wonderfully until he was strong.

16 However, as soon as he was strong, his heart became haughty even to the point of causing ruin, so that he acted unfaithfully against Jehovah his God and came into the temple of Jehovah to burn incense upon the altar of incense. 17 Immediately Az·a·ri′ah the priest and with him priests of Jehovah, eighty valiant men, came in after him. 18 Then they stood up against Uz·zi′ah the king and said to him: "It is not your business, O Uz·zi′ah, to burn incense to Jehovah, but it is the business of the priests the sons of Aaron, the ones sanctified, to burn incense. Go out from the sanctuary; for you have acted unfaithfully, and it is not for any glory to you on the part of Jehovah God."

19 But Uz·zi′ah became enraged while in his hand there was a censer for burning incense, and, during his rage against the priests, leprosy itself flashed up in his forehead before the priests in the house of Jehovah beside the altar of incense. 20 When Az·a·ri′ah the chief priest and all the priests turned toward him, why, there he was stricken with leprosy in his forehead! So they excitedly began to remove him from there, and he himself also hastened to go out, because Jehovah had smitten him.

21 And Uz·zi′ah the king continued to be a leper until the day of his death, and he kept dwelling in a house exempt from duties, as a leper; for he had been severed from the house of Jehovah, while Jo′tham his son was over the king's house, judging the people of the land.

22 And the rest of the affairs of Uz·zi′ah, the first and the last, Isaiah the son of A′moz the prophet has written. 23 Finally Uz·zi′ah

lay down with his forefathers; and so they buried him with his forefathers, [but] in the burial field that belonged to the kings, for they said: "He is a leper." And Jo′tham his son began to reign in place of him.

27 Twenty-five years old was Jo′tham when he began to reign, and for sixteen years he reigned in Jerusalem. And his mother's name was Je·ru′shah the daughter of Za′dok. 2 And he kept doing what was right in Jehovah's eyes, according to all that Uz·zi′ah his father had done. Only he did not invade the temple of Jehovah. However, the people were yet acting ruinously. 3 He himself built the upper gate of Jehovah's house, and on the wall of O′phel he did a great deal of building. 4 And cities he built in the mountainous region of Judah, and in the woodlands he built fortified places and towers. 5 And he himself warred against the king of the sons of Am′mon and eventually proved stronger than they were, so that the sons of Am′mon gave him in that year a hundred silver talents and ten thousand cor measures of wheat and ten thousand of barley. This was what the sons of Am′mon paid to him, also in the second year and the third. 6 So Jo′tham kept strengthening himself, for he prepared his ways before Jehovah his God.

7 As for the rest of the affairs of Jo′tham and all his wars and his ways, there they are written in the Book of the Kings of Israel and of Judah. 8 Twenty-five years old he happened to be when he began to reign, and for sixteen years he reigned in Jerusalem. 9 Finally Jo′tham lay down with his forefathers, and they buried him in the city of David. And A′haz his son began to reign in place of him.

28 Twenty years old was A′haz when he began to reign, and for sixteen years he reigned in Jerusalem, and he did not do what was right in Jehovah's eyes like David his forefather. 2 But he walked in the ways of the kings of

Israel, and even molten statues he made of the Ba′als. 3 And he himself made sacrificial smoke in the valley of the son of Hin′nom and proceeded to burn up his sons in the fire, according to the detestable things of the nations that Jehovah had driven out from before the sons of Israel. 4 And he regularly sacrificed and made sacrificial smoke on the high places and upon the hills and under every sort of luxuriant tree.

5 Consequently Jehovah his God gave him into the hand of the king of Syria, so that they struck him and carried off from him a great number of captives and brought them to Damascus. And also into the hand of the king of Israel he was given, so that he struck him with a great slaughter. 6 Accordingly Pe′kah the son of Rem·a·li′ah killed in Judah a hundred and twenty thousand in one day, all valiant men, because of their leaving Jehovah the God of their forefathers. 7 Further, Zich′ri, a mighty man of E′phra·im, killed Ma·a·sei′ah the son of the king and Az·ri′kam the leader of the household and El·ka′nah the one next to the king. 8 Moreover, the sons of Israel took two hundred thousand of their brothers captive, women, sons and daughters; and also a great deal of spoil they took from them as plunder, after which they brought the spoil to Sa·mar′i·a.

9 And there happened to be a prophet of Jehovah there whose name was O′ded. So he went out before the army that was coming to Sa·mar′i·a and said to them: "Look! It was because of the rage of Jehovah the God of your forefathers against Judah that he gave them into your hand, so that you did a killing among them with a raging that has reached clear to the heavens. 10 And now the sons of Judah and of Jerusalem you are thinking of reducing to menservants and maidservants for yourselves. Nevertheless, are there not with you yourselves cases of guilt against Jehovah your God? 11 And now listen to me and return the captives that you have captured from your brothers, for Jehovah's burning anger is against you."

12 At that [certain] men of the heads of the sons of E′phra·im, Az·a·ri′ah the son of Je·ho·ha′nan, Ber·e·chi′ah the son of Me·shil′le·moth and Je·hiz·ki′ah the son of Shal′lum and A·ma′sa the son of Had′lai, rose up against those coming in from the military campaign, 13 and they said to them: "You must not bring in the captives here, for it will result in guilt against Jehovah on our part. You are thinking of adding to our sins and to our guilt, for abundant is the guilt we have, and there is burning anger against Israel." 14 Accordingly the armed men left the captives and the plunder before the princes and all the congregation. 15 Then the men that were designated by their names rose up and took hold of the captives, and all their naked ones they clothed from the spoil. So they clothed them and furnished them with sandals and fed them and gave them drink and greased them. Furthermore, in the case of anyone tottering, they gave them transportation on the asses and brought them to Jer′i·cho, the city of palm trees, beside their brothers. After that they returned to Sa·mar′i·a.

16 At that time King A′haz sent to the kings of As·syr′i·a for them to help him. 17 And once again the E′dom·ites themselves came in and went striking down Judah and carrying off captives. 18 As for the Phi·lis′tines, they made a raid upon the cities of the She·phe′lah and the Neg′eb of Judah and got to capture Beth-she′mesh and Ai′ja·lon and Ge·de′roth and So′co and its dependent towns and Tim′nah and its dependent towns and Gim′zo and its dependent towns; and they took up dwelling there. 19 For Jehovah humbled Judah on account of A′haz the king of Israel, because he let unrestraint grow in Judah, and there was an acting with great unfaithfulness toward Jehovah.

20 Eventually Til′gath-pil·ne′ser

the king of As·syr'i·a came against him and caused him distress, and did not strengthen him. 21 For A'haz stripped the house of Jehovah and the house of the king and of the princes and thus made a gift to the king of As·syr'i·a; but it was of no assistance to him. 22 However, at the time that he was causing him distress, he acted unfaithfully still more toward Jehovah, that is, King A'haz did. 23 And he began to sacrifice to the gods of Damascus that were striking him, and he went on to say: "Because the gods of the kings of Syria are helping them, to them I shall sacrifice, that they may help me." And they themselves became to him a cause for making him and all Israel stumble. 24 Furthermore, A'haz gathered together the utensils of the house of the [true] God and cut to pieces the utensils of the house of the [true] God, and closed the doors of the house of Jehovah, and made altars for himself at every corner in Jerusalem. 25 And in all cities, even the cities of Judah, he made high places for making sacrificial smoke to other gods, so that he offended Jehovah the God of his forefathers.

26 As for the rest of his affairs and all his ways, the first and the last, there they are written in the Book of the Kings of Judah and of Israel. 27 Finally A'haz lay down with his forefathers, and they buried him in the city, in Jerusalem, for they did not bring him into the burial places of the kings of Israel. And Hez·e·ki'ah his son began to reign in place of him.

29 Hez·e·ki'ah himself became king at the age of twenty-five years, and for twenty-nine years he reigned in Jerusalem. And his mother's name was A·bi'jah the daughter of Zech·a·ri'ah. 2 And he kept doing what was right in Jehovah's eyes, according to all that David his forefather had done. 3 He himself, in the first year of his reigning, in the first month, opened the doors of the house of Jehovah and began to repair them. 4 Then he brought the priests and the Levites and gathered them to the open place to the east. 5 And he proceeded to say to them: "Listen to me, YOU Levites. Now sanctify yourselves and sanctify the house of Jehovah the God of YOUR forefathers, and bring the impure thing out from the holy place. 6 For our fathers have acted unfaithfully and have done what was bad in the eyes of Jehovah our God, so that they left him and turned around their face away from the tabernacle of Jehovah and offered the back of the neck. 7 They also closed the doors of the porch and kept the lamps extinguished, and incense they did not burn, and burnt sacrifice they did not offer up in the holy place to the God of Israel. 8 And Jehovah's indignation came to be against Judah and Jerusalem, so that he constituted them an object at which to quake, an object of astonishment and a cause for whistling, just as YOU are seeing with YOUR own eyes. 9 And here our forefathers fell by the sword, and our sons and our daughters and our wives were in captivity for this. 10 Now it is close to my heart to conclude a covenant with Jehovah the God of Israel, that his burning anger may turn back from us. 11 Now, my sons, do not give yourselves up to rest, for YOU are the ones whom Jehovah has chosen to stand before him to minister to him and to continue as his ministers and makers of sacrificial smoke."

12 At that the Levites rose up, Ma'hath the son of A·ma'sai and Joel the son of Az·a·ri'ah of the sons of the Ko'hath·ites; and from the sons of Me·rar'i, Kish the son of Ab'di and Az·a·ri'ah the son of Je·hal'le·lel; and from the Ger'shon·ites, Jo'ah the son of Zim'mah and E'den the son of Jo'ah; 13 and from the sons of E·li·za'phan, Shim'ri and Je·u'el; and from the sons of A'saph, Zech·a·ri'ah and Mat·ta·ni'ah; 14 and from the sons of He'man, Je·hi'el and Shim'e·i; and from the sons

of Je·du'thun, She·mai'ah and Uz'zi·el. 15 Then they gathered their brothers together and sanctified themselves and came according to the king's commandment in the words of Jehovah, to cleanse the house of Jehovah. 16 The priests now came inside the house of Jehovah to do the cleansing and brought out all the uncleanness that they found in the temple of Jehovah to the courtyard of the house of Jehovah. In turn the Levites received it to take it out to the torrent valley of Kid'ron outside. 17 Thus they got started on the first [day] of the first month at sanctifying, and on the eighth day of the month they came to the porch of Jehovah; so that they sanctified the house of Jehovah in eight days, and on the sixteenth day of the first month they finished.

18 After that they came inside to Hez·e·ki'ah the king and said: "We have cleansed the whole house of Jehovah, the altar of burnt offering and all its utensils, and the table of the layer bread and all its utensils. 19 And all the utensils that King A'haz removed from employment during his reign in his unfaithfulness we have prepared, and have sanctified them; and there they are before the altar of Jehovah."

20 And Hez·e·ki'ah the king proceeded to get up early and gather the princes of the city together and go up to the house of Jehovah. 21 And they came bringing seven bulls and seven rams and seven male lambs and seven male goats as a sin offering for the kingdom and for the sanctuary and for Judah. So he said to the sons of Aaron the priests to offer them up upon the altar of Jehovah. 22 Accordingly they slaughtered the cattle and the priests received the blood and sprinkled it upon the altar; after which they slaughtered the rams and sprinkled the blood upon the altar, and they slaughtered the male lambs and sprinkled the blood upon the altar. 23 Then they brought the male goats of the sin offering near before the king and

the congregation and laid their hands upon them. 24 The priests now slaughtered them and made a sin offering with their blood upon the altar, to make atonement for all Israel; because it was for all Israel that the king said the burnt offering and the sin offering [should be].

25 Meantime, he had the Levites stationed at the house of Jehovah, with cymbals, with stringed instruments and with harps, by the commandment of David and of Gad the king's visionary and of Nathan the prophet, for it was by the hand of Jehovah that the commandment was by means of his prophets. 26 So the Levites kept standing with the instruments of David, and also the priests with the trumpets.

27 Then Hez·e·ki'ah said to offer up the burnt sacrifice on the altar; and at the time that the burnt offering started, the song of Jehovah started and also the trumpets, even under the direction of the instruments of David the king of Israel. 28 And all the congregation were bowing down while the song was resounding and the trumpets were blaring—all this until the burnt offering was finished. 29 And as soon as they finished offering it up, the king and all those found with him bowed low and prostrated themselves. 30 Hez·e·ki'ah the king and the princes now said to the Levites to praise Jehovah in the words of David and of A'saph the visionary. So they began to offer praise even with rejoicing, and they kept bending down and prostrating themselves.

31 Finally Hez·e·ki'ah answered and said: "Now you have filled your hand with power for Jehovah. Approach, and bring sacrifices and thanksgiving sacrifices to the house of Jehovah." And the congregation began to bring sacrifices and thanksgiving sacrifices, and also every one willing of heart, burnt offerings. 32 And the number of the burnt offerings that the congregation brought came to be seventy cattle, a hundred rams, two hundred male lambs—all these

as a burnt offering to Jehovah; 33 and also the holy offerings, six hundred cattle and three thousand of the flock. 34 Only the priests themselves happened to be too few, and they were not able to skin all the burnt offerings. So their brothers the Levites helped them out until the work was finished and until the priests could sanctify themselves, for the Levites were more upright of heart for sanctifying themselves than the priests. 35 And, too, the burnt offerings were in great quantity with the fat pieces of the communion sacrifices and with the drink offerings for the burnt offerings. Thus the service of the house of Jehovah was prepared. 36 Consequently Hez·e·ki′ah and all the people rejoiced over the fact that the [true] God had made preparation for the people, because it was all of a sudden that the thing had occurred.

30 And Hez·e·ki′ah proceeded to send to all Israel and Judah, and even letters he wrote to E′phra·im and Ma·nas′seh, to come to the house of Jehovah in Jerusalem to hold the passover to Jehovah the God of Israel. 2 However, the king and his princes and all the congregation in Jerusalem resolved to hold the passover in the second month; 3 for they had not been able to hold it at that time, because not enough priests, on the one hand, had sanctified themselves and the people, on the other hand, had not gathered themselves to Jerusalem. 4 And the thing was right in the eyes of the king and in the eyes of all the congregation. 5 So they decided to have the call pass through all Israel, from Be′er-she′ba to Dan, to come and hold the passover to Jehovah the God of Israel at Jerusalem; for it was not as a multitude that they had done so according to what is written. 6 Accordingly the runners with the letters from the hand of the king and of his princes went throughout all Israel and Judah, even according to the commandment of the king, saying: "You sons of Israel, return to Jehovah the God of Abraham, Isaac and Israel, that he may return to the escaped ones that are left of you out of the palm of the kings of As·syr′i·a. 7 And do not become like your forefathers and like your brothers that acted unfaithfully toward Jehovah the God of their forefathers, so that he constituted them an object of astonishment, just as you are seeing. 8 Now do not stiffen your neck as your forefathers did. Give place to Jehovah and come to his sanctuary that he has sanctified to time indefinite and serve Jehovah your God, that his burning anger may turn back from you. 9 For when you return to Jehovah, your brothers and your sons will be objects of mercy before those holding them captive, and be allowed to return to this land; for Jehovah your God is gracious and merciful, and he will not turn away the face from you if you return to him."

10 So the runners continued on, passing along from city to city throughout the land of E′phra·im and Ma·nas′seh, even to Zeb′u·lun; but they were continually speaking in mockery of them and deriding them. 11 Only individuals from Ash′er and Ma·nas′seh and from Zeb′u·lun humbled themselves so that they came to Jerusalem. 12 The hand of the [true] God proved to be also in Judah to give them one heart to perform the commandment of the king and the princes in the matter of Jehovah.

13 And they proceeded to gather themselves together at Jerusalem, a numerous people, to hold the festival of the unfermented cakes in the second month, a congregation very multitudinous. 14 Then they rose up and removed the altars that were in Jerusalem, and all the incense altars they removed and then threw [them] into the torrent valley of Kid′ron. 15 After that they slaughtered the passover victim on the fourteenth [day] of the second month; and the priests and the Levites themselves had been humiliated, so that they sanctified themselves and brought burnt offerings to the house of Jehovah.

16 And they kept standing at their place according to their rule, according to the law of Moses the man of the [true] God, the priests sprinkling the blood received from the hand of the Levites. 17 For there were many in the congregation that had not sanctified themselves; and the Levites were in charge of slaughtering the passover victims for all that were not clean, to sanctify them to Jehovah. 18 For there was a great number of the people, many from E'phra·im and Ma·nas'seh, Is'sa·char and Zeb'u·lun, that had not cleansed themselves, for they did not eat the passover according to what is written; but Hez·e·ki'ah prayed for them, saying: "May the good Jehovah himself make allowance for 19 every one that has prepared his heart to search for the [true] God, Jehovah, the God of his forefathers, though without the purification for what is holy." 20 Accordingly Jehovah listened to Hez·e·ki'ah and healed the people.

21 So the sons of Israel that were found in Jerusalem held the festival of the unfermented cakes seven days with great rejoicing; and the Levites and the priests were offering praise to Jehovah day by day with loud instruments, even to Jehovah. 22 Moreover, Hez·e·ki'ah spoke to the heart of all the Levites who were acting with fine discretion toward Jehovah. And they proceeded to eat the appointed feast for seven days, sacrificing communion sacrifices and making confession to Jehovah the God of their forefathers.

23 Then all the congregation decided to hold it for seven more days, and so they held it for seven days with rejoicing. 24 For Hez·e·ki'ah the king of Judah himself contributed for the congregation a thousand bulls and seven thousand sheep, and the princes themselves contributed for the congregation a thousand bulls and ten thousand sheep; and priests kept sanctifying themselves in great number. 25 And all the congregation of Judah and the priests and the Levites and all the congregation that came from Israel and the alien residents that came from the land of Israel and those dwelling in Judah continued rejoicing. 26 And there came to be great rejoicing in Jerusalem, for from the days of Sol'o·mon the son of David the king of Israel there was none like this in Jerusalem. 27 Finally the priests, the Levites, stood up and blessed the people; and a hearing was granted to their voice, so that their prayer came to his holy dwelling, the heavens.

31 And as soon as they finished all this, all the Israelites that were found [there] went out to the cities of Judah, and they proceeded to break up the sacred pillars and cut down the sacred poles and pull down the high places and the altars out of all Judah and Benjamin and in E'phra·im and Ma·nas'seh until they had finished; after which all the sons of Israel returned to their cities, each one to his own possession.

2 Then Hez·e·ki'ah set the divisions of the priests and of the Levites in their divisions, each one in accordance with its service for the priests and for the Levites as regards the burnt offering and the communion sacrifices to minister and to give thanks and praise in the gates of the camps of Jehovah. 3 And there was a portion of the king from his own goods for the burnt offerings, for the burnt offerings of the morning and the evening, and also the burnt offerings for the sabbaths and for the new moons and for the festival seasons, according to what is written in the law of Jehovah.

4 Furthermore, he said to the people, the inhabitants of Jerusalem, to give the portion of the priests and of the Levites, in order that they might adhere strictly to the law of Jehovah. 5 And as soon as the word broke forth, the sons of Israel increased the first fruits of the grain, new wine, and oil and honey and all the produce of the field, and the tenth of everything they brought in abundantly.

6 And the sons of Israel and of Judah that were dwelling in the cities of Judah, even they themselves [brought in] the tenth of cattle and sheep and the tenth of the holy things, the things sanctified to Jehovah their God. They brought in and so gave heaps upon heaps. 7 In the third month they started the heaps by laying the lowest layer, and in the seventh month they finished. 8 When Hez·e·ki′ah and the princes came and saw the heaps, they proceeded to bless Jehovah and his people Israel.

9 In time Hez·e·ki′ah inquired of the priests and the Levites concerning the heaps. 10 Then Az·a·ri′ah the chief priest of the house of Za′dok said to him, yes, he said: "From the time they started to bring the contribution into the house of Jehovah there has been an eating and getting satisfied and having a surplus in abundance; for Jehovah himself has blessed his people, and what has been left over is this great plenty."

11 At this Hez·e·ki′ah said to prepare dining rooms in the house of Jehovah. Accordingly they prepared [them]. 12 And they kept bringing in the contribution and the tenth and the holy things in faithfulness; and Con·a·ni′ah the Levite was in charge of them as leader, and Shim′e·i his brother was second. 13 And Je·hi′el and Az·a·zi′ah and Na′hath and As′a·hel and Jer′i·moth and Jo′za·bad and E′li·el and Is·ma·chi′ah and Ma′hath and Be·nai′ah were commissioners at the side of Con·a·ni′ah and Shim′e·i his brother, by the order of Hez·e·ki′ah the king, and Az·a·ri′ah was the leading one of the house of the [true] God. 14 And Ko′re the son of Im′nah the Levite was the gatekeeper to the east, in charge of the voluntary offerings of the [true] God, to give Jehovah's contribution and the most holy things. 15 And under his control there were E′den and Mi·ni′a·min and Jesh′u·a and She·mai′ah, Am·a·ri′ah and Shec·a·ni′ah, in the cities of the priests, in office of trust, to give to their brothers in the divisions, equally to great and small; 16 apart from their genealogical enrollment of the males from three years of age upward, of all those coming to the house of Jehovah as a daily matter of course, for their service by their obligations according to their divisions.

17 This is the genealogical enrollment of the priests by the house of their fathers and also of the Levites, from the age of twenty years upward, by their obligations in their divisions; 18 both for the genealogical enrollment among all their little ones, their wives and their sons and their daughters, for all the congregation, because in their office of trust they proceeded to sanctify themselves for what was holy; 19 and for the sons of Aaron, the priests, in the fields of pasture ground of their cities. In all the different cities there were men that had been designated by [their] names, to give portions to every male among the priests and to the entire genealogical enrollment among the Levites.

20 And Hez·e·ki′ah proceeded to do like this in all Judah, and he continued to do what was good and right and faithful before Jehovah his God. 21 And in every work that he started in the service of the house of the [true] God and in the law and in the commandment to search for his God, it was with all his heart that he acted, and he proved successful.

32 After these things and this faithful course Sen·nach′er·ib the king of As·syr′i·a came and proceeded to invade Judah and camp against the fortified cities, and kept thinking of making them his by a break through. 2 When Hez·e·ki′ah saw that Sen·nach′er·ib had come with his face set for war against Jerusalem, 3 then he decided with his princes and his mighty men to stop up the waters of the springs that were outside the city; and so they helped him. 4 Accordingly many people were collected together, and they went stopping up all the fountains

and the torrent that floods through the middle of the land, saying: "Why should the kings of As·syr′i·a come and actually find a great deal of water?"

5 Furthermore, he took courage and built up all the broken-down wall and raised towers upon it, and on the outside another wall, and repaired the Mound of the city of David, and made missiles in abundance and shields. 6 And he proceeded to put military chiefs over the people and collect them to him at the public square of the gate of the city and speak to the heart of them, saying: 7 "Be courageous and strong. Do not be afraid nor be terrified because of the king of As·syr′i·a and on account of all the crowd that is with him; for with us there are more than there are with him. 8 With him there is an arm of flesh, but with us there is Jehovah our God to help us and to fight our battles." And the people began to brace themselves upon the words of Hez·e·ki′ah the king of Judah.

9 It was after this that Sen·nach′er·ib the king of As·syr′i·a sent his servants to Jerusalem, while he was at La′chish and all his imperial might with him, to Hez·e·ki′ah the king of Judah and to all the Judeans that were in Jerusalem, saying:

10 "This is what Sen·nach′er·ib the king of As·syr′i·a has said, 'In what is it that you are trusting while sitting quiet under siege in Jerusalem? 11 Is not Hez·e·ki′ah alluring you so as to give you over to die by famine and by thirst, saying: "Jehovah our God himself will deliver us out of the palm of the king of As·syr′i·a"? 12 Is it not Hez·e·ki′ah himself that removed his high places and his altars and then said to Judah and to Jerusalem: "Before one altar you should bow and upon it you should make sacrificial smoke"? 13 Do you not know what I myself and my forefathers did to all the peoples of the lands? Did the gods of the nations of the lands at all prove able to deliver their land out

of my hand? 14 Who was there among all the gods of these nations that my forefathers devoted to destruction that proved able to deliver his people out of my hand, so that your God should be able to deliver you out of my hand? 15 And now do not let Hez·e·ki′ah deceive you or allure you like this and do not put faith in him, for no god of any nation or kingdom was able to deliver his people out of my hand and out of the hand of my forefathers. How much less, then, will your own God deliver you out of my hand?'"

16 And his servants spoke yet further against Jehovah the [true] God and against Hez·e·ki′ah his servant. 17 Even letters he wrote to reproach Jehovah the God of Israel and to talk against him, saying: "Like the gods of the nations of the lands who did not deliver their people out of my hand, so the God of Hez·e·ki′ah will not deliver his people out of my hand." 18 And they kept calling with a loud voice in the Jews' language to the people of Jerusalem that were upon the wall, to make them afraid and to disturb them, in order that they might capture the city. 19 And they went on speaking against the God of Jerusalem the same way as against the gods of the peoples of the earth, the work of man's hands. 20 But Hez·e·ki′ah the king and Isaiah the son of A′moz, the prophet, kept praying over this and crying to the heavens for aid.

21 And Jehovah proceeded to send an angel and efface every valiant, mighty man and leader and chief in the camp of the king of As·syr′i·a, so that he went back with shame of face to his own land. Later on he entered the house of his god and there certain ones that had come out of his own inward parts felled him with the sword. 22 Thus Jehovah saved Hez·e·ki′ah and the inhabitants of Jerusalem out of the hand of Sen·nach′er·ib the king of As·syr′i·a and out of the hand of all others and gave them rest all around. 23 And

there were many bringing gifts to Jehovah at Jerusalem and choice things to Hez·e·ki′ah the king of Judah, and he came to be exalted in the eyes of all the nations after that.

24 In those days Hez·e·ki′ah fell sick to the point of dying, and he began to pray to Jehovah. So He talked to him, and a portent He gave him. 25 But according to the benefit rendered him Hez·e·ki′ah made no return, for his heart became haughty and there came to be indignation against him and against Judah and Jerusalem. 26 However, Hez·e·ki′ah humbled himself for the haughtiness of his heart, he and the inhabitants of Jerusalem, and Jehovah's indignation did not come upon them in the days of Hez·e·ki′ah.

27 And Hez·e·ki′ah came to have riches and glory to a very great amount; and storehouses he made for himself for silver and for gold and for precious stones and for balsam oil and for shields and for all the desirable articles; 28 and also storage places for the produce of grain and new wine and oil, and also stalls for all the different sorts of beasts and stalls for the droves. 29 And cities he acquired for himself, and also livestock of the flock and of the herd in abundance; for God gave him very many goods. 30 And Hez·e·ki′ah was the one that stopped up the upper source of the waters of Gi′hon and kept them directed straight along down to the west to the city of David, and Hez·e·ki′ah continued to prove successful in every work of his. 31 And thus it was that by the spokesmen of the princes of Babylon that were sent to him to inquire about the portent that had happened in the land, the [true] God left him to put him to the test, to get to know everything in his heart.

32 As for the rest of the affairs of Hez·e·ki′ah and his acts of loving-kindness, there they are written in the vision of Isaiah the prophet, the son of A′moz, in the Book of the Kings of Judah and Israel. 33 Finally Hez·e·ki′ah lay down with his forefathers, and they buried him in the ascent to the burial places of the sons of David; and honor was what all Judah and the inhabitants of Jerusalem rendered to him at his death. And Ma·nas′seh his son began to reign in place of him.

33 Twelve years old was Ma·nas′seh when he began to reign, and for fifty-five years he reigned in Jerusalem.

2 And he proceeded to do what was bad in Jehovah's eyes, according to the detestable things of the nations that Jehovah had driven out from before the sons of Israel. 3 So he built again the high places that Hez·e·ki′ah his father had pulled down, and set up altars to the Ba′als and made sacred poles, and he began to bow down to all the army of the heavens and serve them. 4 And he built altars in the house of Jehovah, respecting which Jehovah had said: "In Jerusalem my name will prove to be to time indefinite." 5 And he went on to build altars to all the army of the heavens in two courtyards of the house of Jehovah. 6 And he himself made his own sons pass through the fire in the valley of the son of Hin′nom, and practiced magic and used divination and practiced sorcery and made spiritistic mediums and professional foretellers of events. He did on a grand scale what was bad in the eyes of Jehovah, to offend him.

7 Furthermore, he put the carved image that he had made in the house of the [true] God, respecting which God had said to David and to Sol′o·mon his son: "In this house and in Jerusalem, which I have chosen out of all the tribes of Israel, I shall put my name to time indefinite. 8 And I shall not remove the foot of Israel again from off the ground that I assigned to their forefathers, provided only that they take care to do all that I have commanded them concerning all the law and the regulations and the judicial decisions by the hand of Moses." 9 And Ma·nas′seh kept

seducing Judah and the inhabitants of Jerusalem to do worse than the nations that Jehovah had annihilated from before the sons of Israel.

10 And Jehovah kept speaking to Ma·nas′seh and his people, but they paid no attention. 11 Finally Jehovah brought against them the chiefs of the army that belonged to the king of As·syr′i·a, and so they captured Ma·nas′seh in the hollows and bound him with two fetters of copper and took him to Babylon. 12 And as soon as it caused him distress, he softened the face of Jehovah his God and kept humbling himself greatly because of the God of his forefathers. 13 And he kept praying to Him, so that He let himself be entreated by him and He heard his request for favor and restored him to Jerusalem to his kingship; and Ma·nas′seh came to know that Jehovah is the [true] God.

14 And after this he built an outer wall for the city of David to the west of Gi′hon in the torrent valley and as far as the Fish Gate, and he ran [it] around to O′phel and proceeded to make it very high. Further, he put chiefs of the military force in all the fortified cities in Judah. 15 And he proceeded to remove the foreign gods and the idol image from the house of Jehovah and all the altars that he had built in the mountain of the house of Jehovah and in Jerusalem and then had them thrown outside the city. 16 Moreover, he prepared the altar of Jehovah and began to sacrifice upon it communion sacrifices and thanksgiving sacrifices and went on to say to Judah to serve Jehovah the God of Israel. 17 Nevertheless, the people were still sacrificing upon the high places; only it was to Jehovah their God.

18 As for the rest of the affairs of Ma·nas′seh and his prayer to his God and the words of the visionaries that kept speaking to him in the name of Jehovah the God of Israel, there they are among the affairs of the kings of Israel.

19 As for his prayer and how his entreaty was granted him and all his sin and his unfaithfulness and the locations in which he built high places and set up the sacred poles and the graven images before he humbled himself, there they are written among the words of his visionaries. 20 Finally Ma·nas′seh lay down with his forefathers, and they buried him at his house; and A′mon his son began to reign in place of him.

21 Twenty-two years old was A′mon when he began to reign, and for two years he reigned in Jerusalem. 22 And he proceeded to do what was bad in Jehovah's eyes, just as Ma·nas′seh his father had done; and to all the graven images that Ma·nas′seh his father had made A′mon sacrificed, and he continued serving them. 23 And he did not humble himself because of Jehovah the same as Ma·nas′seh his father humbled himself, for A′mon was one that made guiltiness increase. 24 Finally his servants conspired against him and put him to death in his own house. 25 But the people of the land struck down all the conspirators against King A′mon, and the people of the land then made Jo·si′ah his son king in place of him.

34 Eight years old was Jo·si′ah when he began to reign, and for thirty-one years he reigned in Jerusalem. 2 And he proceeded to do what was right in Jehovah's eyes and walk in the ways of David his forefather; and he did not turn aside to the right or to the left.

3 And in the eighth year of his reigning, while he was still a boy, he started to search for the God of David his forefather; and in the twelfth year he started to cleanse Judah and Jerusalem from the high places and the sacred poles and the graven images and the molten statues. 4 Further, they pulled down before him the altars of the Ba′als; and the incense stands that were up above he cut down from off them; and the sacred poles and the graven images and the molten statues he broke in

pieces and reduced to powder, and then sprinkled [it] upon the surface of the burial places of those that used to sacrifice to them. 5 And the bones of priests he burned upon their altars. Thus he cleansed Judah and Jerusalem.

6 Also, in the cities of Ma·nas′seh and E′phra·im and Sim′e·on and clear to Naph′ta·li, in their devastated places all around, 7 he even went pulling down the altars and the sacred poles, and the graven images he crushed and reduced to powder; and all the incense stands he cut down in all the land of Israel, after which he returned to Jerusalem.

8 And in the eighteenth year of his reigning, when he had cleansed the land and the house, he sent Sha′phan the son of Az·a·li′ah and Ma·a·sei′ah the chief of the city and Jo′ah the son of Jo′a·haz the recorder to repair the house of Jehovah his God. 9 And they proceeded to come to Hil·ki′ah the high priest and give the money that was being brought to the house of God, which the Levites the doorkeepers had gathered from the hand of Ma·nas′seh and E′phra·im and from all the rest of Israel and from all Judah and Benjamin and the inhabitants of Jerusalem. 10 Then they put [it] into the hand of the doers of the work that were appointed over the house of Jehovah. In turn the doers of the work who were active in the house of Jehovah applied it to mending and repairing the house. 11 So they gave it to the craftsmen and the builders to buy hewn stones and timbers for clamps and to build with beams the houses that the kings of Judah had brought to ruin.

12 And the men were acting in faithfulness in the work; and over them there were appointed Ja′hath and O·ba·di′ah the Levites, from the sons of Me·rar′i, and Zech·a·ri′ah and Me·shul′lam, from the sons of the Ko′hath·ites, to act as overseers. And the Levites, each of whom was expert with the instruments of song, 13 were over the

burden bearers, and the overseers of all the doers of the work for the different services; and from the Levites there were secretaries and officers and gatekeepers.

14 Now while they were bringing out the money that was being brought to the house of Jehovah, Hil·ki′ah the priest found the book of Jehovah's law by the hand of Moses. 15 So Hil·ki′ah answered and said to Sha′phan the secretary: "The very book of the law I have found in the house of Jehovah." With that Hil·ki′ah gave the book to Sha′phan. 16 Then Sha′phan brought the book to the king and replied further to the king, saying: "All that has been put in the hand of your servants they are doing. 17 And they pour out the money that is found in the house of Jehovah and put it in the hand of the appointed men and into the hand of the doers of the work." 18 And Sha′phan the secretary went on to report to the king, saying: "There is a book that Hil·ki′ah the priest gave me." And Sha′phan began to read out of it before the king.

19 And it came about that as soon as the king heard the words of the law, he immediately ripped his garments apart. 20 Then the king commanded Hil·ki′ah and A·hi′kam the son of Sha′phan and Ab′don the son of Mi′cah and Sha′phan the secretary and A·sai′ah the king's servant, saying: 21 "Go, inquire of Jehovah in my own behalf and in behalf of what is left in Israel and in Judah concerning the words of the book that has been found, for great is Jehovah's rage that must be poured out against us because of the fact that our forefathers did not keep the word of Jehovah by doing according to all that is written in this book."

22 Accordingly Hil·ki′ah along with those whom the king [had said] went to Hul′dah the prophetess, the wife of Shal′lum the son of Tik′vah the son of Har′has the caretaker of the garments, as she was dwelling in Jerusalem in the

second quarter; and they proceeded to speak to her like this. 23 In turn she said to them:

"This is what Jehovah the God of Israel has said, 'SAY to the man that sent YOU to me: 24 "This is what Jehovah has said, 'Here I am bringing calamity upon this place and its inhabitants, all the curses that are written in the book that they read before the king of Judah, 25 due to the fact that they have left me and gone making sacrificial smoke to other gods, in order to offend me with all the doings of their hands and that my rage may pour forth upon this place and not be extinguished.' " 26 And to the king of Judah, who is sending YOU to inquire of Jehovah, this is what YOU should say to him: "This is what Jehovah the God of Israel has said, 'As regards the words that you have heard, 27 for the reason that your heart was soft so that you humbled yourself because of God at your hearing his words concerning this place and its inhabitants, and you humbled yourself before me and ripped your garments apart and wept before me, I, even I, have heard, is the utterance of Jehovah. 28 Here I am gathering you to your forefathers, and you will certainly be gathered to your graveyard in peace, and your eyes will not look upon all the calamity that I am bringing upon this place and its inhabitants.' " ' "

Then they brought the reply to the king. 29 And the king proceeded to send and gather all the older men of Judah and of Jerusalem. 30 The king now went up to the house of Jehovah with all the men of Judah and the inhabitants of Jerusalem and the priests and the Levites and all the people, the great as well as the small; and he began to read in their ears all the words of the book of the covenant, which had been found at the house of Jehovah. 31 And the king kept standing in his place and proceeded to conclude the covenant before Jehovah to go following Jehovah and to keep his command-

ments and his testimonies and his regulations with all his heart and with all his soul, to perform the words of the covenant that were written in this book. 32 Furthermore, he had all those who were found in Jerusalem and Benjamin to take their stand [for it]. And the inhabitants of Jerusalem proceeded to do according to the covenant of God, the God of their forefathers. 33 After that Jo·si′ah removed all the detestable things out of all the lands that belonged to the sons of Israel, and he had all who were found in Israel take up service, to serve Jehovah their God. All his days they did not turn aside from following Jehovah the God of their forefathers.

35 Then Jo·si′ah held in Jerusalem a passover to Jehovah and they slaughtered the passover victim on the fourteenth day of the first month. 2 So he stationed the priests over the things under their care and encouraged them in the service of the house of Jehovah. 3 And he went on to say to the Levites, the instructors of all Israel, those holy to Jehovah: "Put the holy Ark in the house that Sol′o·mon the son of David the king of Israel built; it is not YOURS as a burden upon the shoulder. Now serve Jehovah YOUR God and his people Israel. 4 And make preparation by the house of YOUR forefathers according to YOUR divisions, by the writing of David the king of Israel and by the writing of Sol′o·mon his son. 5 And stand in the holy place by the classes of the house of the forefathers for YOUR brothers, the sons of the people, and the portion of a paternal house belonging to the Levites. 6 And slaughter the passover victim and sanctify yourselves and make preparation for YOUR brothers to do according to the word of Jehovah by means of Moses."

7 Jo·si′ah now contributed to the sons of the people flocks, male lambs and male kids, the whole for the passover victims for all who were to be found, to the number of thirty thousand, and cattle, three

thousand. These were from the goods of the king. 8 And his princes themselves made a contribution as a voluntary offering for the people, for the priests and for the Levites. Hil·ki'ah and Zech·a·ri'ah and Je·hi'el themselves as leaders of the house of the [true] God gave to the priests for the passover victims two thousand six hundred, and three hundred cattle. 9 And Con·a·ni'ah and She·mai'ah and Ne·than'el his brothers and Hash·a·bi'ah and Je·i'el and Jo'za·bad, the chiefs of the Levites, contributed to the Levites for passover victims five thousand, and five hundred cattle.

10 And the service was prepared and the priests kept standing at their places, and the Levites by their divisions, according to the king's commandment. 11 And the priests proceeded to slaughter the passover victim and sprinkle [the blood] from their hand, while the Levites were stripping the skins off. 12 Further, they prepared the burnt offerings so as to give them to the classes by the paternal house, to the sons of the people, so as to make a presentation to Jehovah according to what is written in the book of Moses; and thus also with the cattle. 13 And they went boiling the passover offering over the fire according to the custom; and the things made holy they boiled in cooking pots and in round-bottomed pots and in banquet bowls, after which they brought it quickly to all the sons of the people. 14 And afterward they prepared for themselves and for the priests, because the priests the sons of Aaron were engaged in offering up the burnt sacrifices and the fat pieces until night, and the Levites, for their part, prepared for themselves and for the priests the sons of Aaron.

15 And the singers the sons of A'saph were at their office according to the commandment of David and of A'saph and of He'man and of Je·du'thun the visionary of the king; and the gatekeepers were at the different gates. There was no

need for them to turn aside from their service, because their brothers the Levites themselves prepared for them. 16 And all the service of Jehovah was prepared on that day to hold the passover and to offer up the burnt offerings upon the altar of Jehovah, according to the commandment of King Jo·si'ah.

17 And the sons of Israel that were to be found proceeded to hold the passover at that time and also the festival of the unfermented cakes for seven days. 18 And there had never been held a passover like it in Israel since the days of Samuel the prophet, neither had any of the other kings of Israel themselves held a passover like that which Jo·si'ah and the priests and the Levites and all Judah and Israel that were to be found and the inhabitants of Jerusalem held. 19 In the eighteenth year of Jo·si'ah's reign this passover was held.

20 After all this when Jo·si'ah had prepared the house, Ne'cho the king of Egypt came up to fight at Car'che·mish by the Eu·phra'tes. Then Jo·si'ah went out to an encounter with him. 21 At that he sent messengers to him, saying: "What do I have to do with you, O king of Judah? It is not against you that I am coming today, but it is against another house that my fight is and that God himself said that I should cause disturbance. Refrain for your own sake because of God, who is with me, and do not let him bring you to ruin." 22 And Jo·si'ah did not turn his face away from him, but to fight against him he disguised himself and did not listen to the words of Ne'cho from the mouth of God. So he came to fight in the valley plain of Me·gid'do.

23 And the shooters got to shoot at King Jo·si'ah, so that the king said to his servants: "Take me down, for I have been very severely wounded." 24 Accordingly his servants took him down from the chariot and had him ride in the second war chariot that was his and brought him to Jerusalem. Thus he died and was buried in the

graveyard of his forefathers; and all Judah and Jerusalem were mourning over Jo·si'ah. 25 And Jeremiah began to chant over Jo·si'ah; and all the male singers and female singers keep talking about Jo·si'ah in their dirges down till today; and they have them set as a regulation over Israel, and there they are written among the dirges.

26 As for the rest of the affairs of Jo·si'ah and his acts of loving-kindness, according to what is written in the law of Jehovah, 27 and his affairs, the first and the last, there they are written in the Book of the Kings of Israel and Judah.

36 Then the people of the land took Je·ho'a·haz the son of Jo·si'ah and made him king in the place of his father in Jerusalem. 2 Twenty-three years old was Je·ho'a·haz when he began to reign, and for three months he reigned in Jerusalem. 3 However, the king of Egypt removed him in Jerusalem and fined the land a hundred silver talents and a gold talent. 4 Furthermore, the king of Egypt made E·li'a·kim his brother king over Judah and Jerusalem and changed his name to Je·hoi'a·kim; but his brother Je·ho'a·haz, Ne'cho took and brought to Egypt.

5 Twenty-five years old was Je·hoi'a·kim when he began to reign, and for eleven years he reigned in Jerusalem; and he continued to do what was bad in the eyes of Jehovah his God. 6 Against him Neb·u·chad·nez'zar the king of Babylon came up that he might bind him with two fetters of copper to carry him off to Babylon. 7 And some of the utensils of the house of Jehovah Neb·u·chad·nez'zar brought to Babylon and then put them in his palace in Babylon. 8 As for the rest of the affairs of Je·hoi'a·kim and his detestable things that he did and what was to be found against him, there they are written in the Book of the Kings of Israel and Judah; and Je·hoi'a·chin his son began to reign in place of him.

9 Eighteen years old was Je·hoi'a·chin when he began to reign, and for three months and ten days he reigned in Jerusalem; and he continued to do what was bad in Jehovah's eyes. 10 And at the return of the year King Neb·u·chad·nez'zar sent and proceeded to bring him to Babylon with desirable articles of the house of Jehovah. Further, he made Zed·e·ki'ah his [father's] brother king over Judah and Jerusalem.

11 Twenty-one years old was Zed·e·ki'ah when he began to reign, and for eleven years he reigned in Jerusalem. 12 And he continued to do what was bad in the eyes of Jehovah his God. He did not humble himself on account of Jeremiah the prophet at the order of Jehovah. 13 And even against King Neb·u·chad·nez'zar he rebelled, who had made him swear by God; and he kept stiffening his neck and hardening his heart so as not to return to Jehovah the God of Israel. 14 Even all the chiefs of the priests and the people themselves committed unfaithfulness on a large scale, according to all the detestable things of the nations, so that they defiled the house of Jehovah which he had sanctified in Jerusalem.

15 And Jehovah the God of their forefathers kept sending against them by means of his messengers, sending again and again, because he felt compassion for his people and for his dwelling. 16 But they were continually making jest at the messengers of the [true] God and despising his words and mocking at his prophets, until the rage of Jehovah came up against his people, until there was no healing.

17 So he brought up against them the king of the Chal·de'ans, who proceeded to kill their young men with the sword in the house of their sanctuary, neither did he feel compassion for young man or virgin, old or decrepit. Everything He gave into his hand. 18 And all the utensils, great and small, of the house of the [true] God and the treasures of the house of Jehovah and the treasures of the king and of his princes, everything he brought to Babylon. 19 And he

proceeded to burn the house of the [true] God and pull down the wall of Jerusalem; and all its dwelling towers they burned with fire and also all its desirable articles, so as to cause ruin. 20 Furthermore, he carried off those remaining from the sword captive to Babylon, and they came to be servants to him and his sons until the royalty of Persia began to reign; 21 to fulfill Jehovah's word by the mouth of Jeremiah, until the land had paid off its sabbaths. All the days of lying desolated it kept sabbath, to fulfill seventy years.

22 And in the first year of Cy′rus the king of Persia, that Jehovah's word by the mouth of Jeremiah might be accomplished, Jehovah roused the spirit of Cy′rus the king of Persia, so that he caused a cry to pass through all his kingdom, and also in writing, saying: 23 "This is what Cy′rus the king of Persia has said, 'All the kingdoms of the earth Jehovah the God of the heavens has given me, and he himself has commissioned me to build him a house in Jerusalem, which is in Judah. Whoever there is among you of all his people, Jehovah his God be with him. So let him go up.'"

EZRA

1 And in the first year of Cy′rus the king of Persia, that Jehovah's word from the mouth of Jeremiah might be accomplished, Jehovah roused the spirit of Cy′rus the king of Persia so that he caused a cry to pass through all his realm, and also in writing, saying:

2 "This is what Cy′rus the king of Persia has said, 'All the kingdoms of the earth Jehovah the God of the heavens has given me, and he himself has commissioned me to build him a house in Jerusalem, which is in Judah. 3 Whoever there is among you of all his people, may his God prove to be with him. So let him go up to Jerusalem, which is in Judah, and rebuild the house of Jehovah the God of Israel—he is the [true] God—which was in Jerusalem. 4 As for anyone that is left from all the places where he is residing as an alien, let the men of his place assist him with silver and with gold and with goods and with domestic animals along with the voluntary offering for the house of the [true] God, which was in Jerusalem.'"

5 Then the heads of the fathers of Judah and of Benjamin and the priests and the Levites rose up,

even everyone whose spirit the [true] God had roused, to go up and rebuild the house of Jehovah, which was in Jerusalem. 6 As for all those round about them, they strengthened their hands with utensils of silver, with gold, with goods and with domestic animals and with choice things, besides all that which was voluntarily offered.

7 Also, King Cy′rus himself brought forth the utensils of the house of Jehovah, which Neb·u·chad·nez′zar had brought out from Jerusalem and then put in the house of his god. 8 And Cy′rus the king of Persia proceeded to bring them forth under the control of Mith′re·dath the treasurer and to number them out to Shesh·baz′zar the chieftain of Judah.

9 Now these are the numbers of them: thirty basket-shaped vessels of gold, a thousand basket-shaped vessels of silver, twenty-nine replacement vessels, 10 thirty small bowls of gold, four hundred and ten small secondary bowls of silver, a thousand other utensils. 11 All the utensils of gold and of silver were five thousand four hundred. Everything Shesh·baz′zar brought up, along with the bringing up of the

exiled people out of Babylon to Jerusalem.

2 And these were the sons of the jurisdictional district that went up out of the captivity of the exiled people whom Neb·u·chad·nez'zar the king of Babylon had taken into exile at Babylon and who later returned to Jerusalem and Judah, each one to his own city; 2 those who came with Ze·rub'ba·bel, Jesh'u·a, Ne·he·mi'ah, Se·rai'ah, Re·el·ai'ah, Mor'de·cai, Bil'shan, Mis'par, Big'vai, Re'hum, Ba·a'nah.

The number of the men of the people of Israel: 3 The sons of Pa'rosh, two thousand one hundred and seventy-two; 4 the sons of Sheph·a·ti'ah, three hundred and seventy-two; 5 the sons of A'rah, seven hundred and seventy-five; 6 the sons of Pa'hath-mo'ab, of the sons of Jesh'u·a [and] Jo'ab, two thousand eight hundred and twelve; 7 the sons of E'lam, a thousand two hundred and fifty-four; 8 the sons of Zat'tu, nine hundred and forty-five; 9 the sons of Zac'cai, seven hundred and sixty, 10 the sons of Ba'ni, six hundred and forty-two; 11 the sons of Be'bai, six hundred and twenty-three; 12 the sons of Az'gad, a thousand two hundred and twenty-two; 13 the sons of Ad·o·ni'kam, six hundred and sixty-six; 14 the sons of Big'vai, two thousand and fifty-six; 15 the sons of A'din, four hundred and fifty-four; 16 the sons of A'ter, of Hez·e·ki'ah, ninety-eight; 17 the sons of Be'zai, three hundred and twenty-three; 18 the sons of Jo'rah, a hundred and twelve; 19 the sons of Ha'shum, two hundred and twenty-three; 20 the sons of Gib'bar, ninety-five; 21 the sons of Beth'le·hem, a hundred and twenty-three; 22 the men of Ne·to'phah, fifty-six; 23 the men of An'a·thoth, a hundred and twenty-eight; 24 the sons of Az'ma·veth, forty-two; 25 the sons of Kir'i·ath·je·a'rim, Che·phi'rah and Be·er'oth, seven hundred and forty-three; 26 the sons of Ra'mah and Ge'ba, six hundred and twenty-one; 27 the men of Mich'mas, a hun-

dred and twenty-two; 28 the men of Beth'el and A'i, two hundred and twenty-three; 29 the sons of Ne'bo, fifty-two; 30 the sons of Mag'bish, a hundred and fifty-six; 31 the sons of the other E'lam, a thousand two hundred and fifty-four; 32 the sons of Ha'rim, three hundred and twenty; 33 the sons of Lod, Ha'did and O'no, seven hundred and twenty-five; 34 the sons of Jer'i·cho, three hundred and forty-five; 35 the sons of Se·na'ah, three thousand six hundred and thirty.

36 The priests: The sons of Je·da'iah of the house of Jesh'u·a nine hundred and seventy-three; 37 the sons of Im'mer, a thousand and fifty-two; 38 the sons of Pash'hur, a thousand two hundred and forty-seven; 39 the sons of Ha'rim, a thousand and seventeen.

40 The Levites: The sons of Jesh'u·a and Kad'mi·el, of the sons of Hod·a·vi'ah, seventy-four. 41 The singers, the sons of A'saph, a hundred and twenty-eight. 42 The sons of the gatekeepers, the sons of Shal'lum, the sons of A'ter, the sons of Tal'mon, the sons of Ak'kub, the sons of Ha·ti'ta, the sons of Sho'bai, all together, a hundred and thirty-nine.

43 The Neth'i·nim: The sons of Zi'ha, the sons of Ha·su'pha, the sons of Tab·ba'oth, 44 the sons of Ke'ros, the sons of Si'a·ha, the sons of Pa'don, 45 the sons of Le·ba'nah, the sons of Hag'a·bah, the sons of Ak'kub, 46 the sons of Ha'gab, the sons of Sal'mai, the sons of Ha'nan, 47 the sons of Gid'del, the sons of Ga'har, the sons of Re·a'iah, 48 the sons of Re'zin, the sons of Ne·ko'da, the sons of Gaz'zam, 49 the sons of Uz'za, the sons of Pa·se'ah, the sons of Be'sai, 50 the sons of As'nah, the sons of Me·u'nim, the sons of Ne·phu'sim; 51 the sons of Bak'buk, the sons of Ha·ku'pha, the sons of Har'hur, 52 the sons of Baz'luth, the sons of Me·hi'da, the sons of Har'sha, 53 the sons of Bar'kos, the sons of Sis'e·ra, the sons of Te'mah, 54 the sons of Ne·zi'ah, the sons of Ha·ti'pha.

55 The sons of the servants of Sol'o·mon: The sons of So'tai, the sons of So·phe'reth, the sons of Pe·ru'da, 56 the sons of Ja'a·lah, the sons of Dar'kon, the sons of Gid'del, 57 the sons of Sheph·a·ti'ah, the sons of Hat'til, the sons of Po'che·reth-haz·ze·ba'im, the sons of A'mi.

58 All the Neth'i·nim and the sons of the servants of Sol'o·mon were three hundred and ninety-two.

59 And these were the ones going up from Tel-me'lah, Tel-har'sha, Che'rub, Ad'don [and] Im'mer, and they proved unable to tell the house of their fathers and their origin, whether they were of Israel: 60 the sons of De·la'iah, the sons of To·bi'ah, the sons of Ne·ko'da, six hundred and fifty-two. 61 And of the sons of the priests: the sons of Ha·bai'ah, the sons of Hak'koz, the sons of Bar·zil'lai, who took a wife from the daughters of Bar·zil'lai the Gil'e·ad·ite and came to be called by their name. 62 These were the ones that looked for their register to establish their genealogy publicly, and they did not find themselves, so that they were barred as polluted from the priesthood. 63 Consequently the Tir·sha'tha said to them that they could not eat from the most holy things until a priest stood up with U'rim and Thum'mim.

64 The entire congregation as one group was forty-two thousand three hundred and sixty, 65 apart from their men slaves and their slave girls, these being seven thousand three hundred and thirty-seven; and they had two hundred male singers and female singers. 66 Their horses were seven hundred and thirty-six, their mules two hundred and forty-five, 67 their camels four hundred and thirty-five, [their] asses six thousand seven hundred and twenty.

68 And certain ones of the heads of the paternal houses, on coming to the house of Jehovah, which was in Jerusalem, made voluntary offerings to the house of the [true] God, to cause it to stand on its own site. 69 According to their power they gave gold for the working supplies, sixty-one thousand drachmas, and silver, five thousand mi'nas, and a hundred robes of priests. 70 And the priests and the Levites and some of the people, and the singers and the gatekeepers and the Neth'i·nim took up dwelling in their cities, and all Israel in their cities.

3 When the seventh month arrived the sons of Israel were in [their] cities. And the people began to gather themselves as one man to Jerusalem. 2 And Jesh'u·a the son of Je·hoz'a·dak and his brothers the priests and Ze·rub'ba·bel the son of She·al'ti·el and his brothers proceeded to rise up and build the altar of the God of Israel, to offer up burnt sacrifices upon it, according to what is written in the law of Moses the man of the [true] God.

3 So they established the altar firmly upon its own site, for fright [came] upon them because of the peoples of the lands, and they began offering up burnt sacrifices to Jehovah upon it, the burnt sacrifices of the morning and of the evening. 4 Then they held the festival of booths according to what is written, with the burnt sacrifices day by day in number according to the rule of what was due each day. 5 And afterward there was the constant burnt offering and that for the new moons and for all the sanctified festival seasons of Jehovah and for everyone that willingly offered a voluntary offering to Jehovah. 6 From the first day of the seventh month on they started to offer up burnt sacrifices to Jehovah, when the foundation of Jehovah's temple itself had not yet been laid.

7 And they proceeded to give money to the cutters and to the craftsmen, and eatables and drink and oil to the Si·do'ni·ans and the Tyr'i·ans, to bring cedar timbers from Leb'a·non to the sea at Jop'pa, according to the permission granted by Cy'rus the king of Persia to them.

8 And in the second year of their coming to the house of the [true] God at Jerusalem, in the second month, Ze·rub′ba·bel the son of She·al′ti·el and Jesh′u·a the son of Je·hoz′a·dak and the rest of their brothers, the priests and the Levites, and all those who had come out of the captivity to Jerusalem started; and they now put in positions the Levites from twenty years of age upward to act as supervisors over the work of the house of Jehovah. 9 Accordingly Jesh′u·a, his sons and his brothers, [and] Kad′mi·el and his sons, the sons of Judah, stood up as one group to act as supervisors over the doers of the work in the house of the [true] God, [also] the sons of Hen′a·dad, their sons and their brothers, the Levites.

10 When the builders laid the foundation of the temple of Jehovah, then the priests in official clothing, with the trumpets, and the Levites the sons of A′saph, with the cymbals, stood up to praise Jehovah according to the direction of David the king of Israel. 11 And they began to respond by praising and giving thanks to Jehovah, "for he is good, for his loving-kindness toward Israel is to time indefinite." As for all the people, they shouted with a loud shout in praising Jehovah over the laying of the foundation of the house of Jehovah. 12 And many of the priests and the Levites and the heads of the paternal houses, the old men that had seen the former house, were weeping with a loud voice at the laying of the foundation of this house before their eyes, while many others were raising the voice in shouting for joy. 13 Hence the people were not distinguishing the sound of the shout of rejoicing from the sound of the weeping of the people, for the people were shouting with a loud shout, and the sound itself was heard even to a great distance.

4 When the adversaries of Judah and Benjamin heard that the sons of the Exile were building a temple to Jehovah the God of Israel, 2 they immediately approached Ze·rub′ba·bel and the heads of the paternal houses and said to them: "Let us build along with YOU; for, just like YOU, we search for YOUR God and to him we are sacrificing since the days of E′sar-had′don the king of As·syr′i·a, who brought us up here." 3 However, Ze·rub′ba·bel and Jesh′u·a and the rest of the heads of the paternal houses of Israel said to them: "YOU have nothing to do with us in building a house to our God, for we ourselves shall together build to Jehovah the God of Israel, just as King Cy′rus the king of Persia has commanded us."

4 At that the people of the land were continually weakening the hands of the people of Judah and disheartening them from building, 5 and hiring counselors against them to frustrate their counsel all the days of Cy′rus the king of Persia down till the reign of Da·ri′us the king of Persia. 6 And in the reign of A·has·u·e′rus, at the start of his reign, they wrote an accusation against the inhabitants of Judah and Jerusalem. 7 Also, in the days of Ar·ta·xerx′es, Bish′lam, Mith′re·dath, Tab′e·el and the rest of his colleagues wrote to Ar·ta·xerx′es the king of Persia, and the writing of the letter was written in Ar·a·ma′ic characters and translated into the Ar·a·ma′ic language.

8 Re′hum the chief government official and Shim′shai the scribe wrote a letter against Jerusalem to Ar·ta·xerx′es the king, as follows: 9 Then Re′hum the chief government official and Shim′shai the scribe and the rest of their colleagues, the judges and the lesser governors across the River, the secretaries, the people of E′rech, the Babylonians, the inhabitants of Su′sa, that is, the E′lam·ites, 10 and the rest of the nations whom the great and honorable As′e·nap·par took into exile and settled in the cities of Sa·mar′i·a, and the rest beyond the River, ——; and now 11 this is a copy of the letter that they sent concerning it:

"To Ar·ta·xerx'es the king your servants, the men beyond the River: And now 12 let it become known to the king that the Jews who came up here from you to us have come to Jerusalem. They are building the rebellious and bad city, and they proceed to finish the walls and to repair the foundations. 13 Now let it become known to the king that, if this city should be rebuilt and its walls be finished, neither tax nor tribute nor toll will they give, and it will cause loss to the treasuries of the kings. 14 Now inasmuch as we do eat the salt of the palace, and it is not proper for us to see the denuding of the king, on this account we have sent and made [it] known to the king, 15 that there may be an investigation of the book of records of your ancestors. Then you will find in the book of records and learn that that city is a city rebellious and causing loss to kings and jurisdictional districts, and within it there were movers of revolt from the days of old. For this reason that city has been laid waste. 16 We are making known to the king that, if that city should be rebuilt and its walls be finished, you also will certainly have no share beyond the River."

17 The king sent word to Re'hum the chief government official and Shim'shai the scribe and the rest of their colleagues who were dwelling in Sa·mar'i·a and the rest beyond the River:

"Greetings! And now 18 the official document that you have sent us has been distinctly read before me. 19 So an order has been put through by me, and they have investigated and found that that city has from the days of old been one rising up against kings and one in which rebellion and revolt have been carried on. 20 And there proved to be strong kings over Jerusalem and governing all beyond the River, and tax, tribute and toll were being given to them. 21 Now PUT an order through for these able-bodied men to stop, that that city may not be rebuilt until the

order is put through by me. 22 So be careful that there be no negligence about acting in this regard, that the harm may not increase to the injury of kings."

23 Now after the copy of the official document of Ar·ta·xerx'es the king had been read before Re'hum and Shim'shai the scribe and their colleagues, they went in a hurry to Jerusalem to the Jews and stopped them by force of arms. 24 It was then that the work on the house of God, which was in Jerusalem, stopped; and it continued stopped until the second year of the reign of Da·ri'us the king of Persia.

5 And Hag'gai the prophet and Zech·a·ri'ah the grandson of Id'do the prophet prophesied to the Jews who were in Judah and in Jerusalem, in the name of the God of Israel [who was] over them. 2 It was then that Ze·rub'ba·bel the son of She·al'ti·el and Jesh'u·a the son of Je·hoz'a·dak got up and started to rebuild the house of God, which was in Jerusalem; and with them there were God's prophets giving them aid. 3 At that time Tat'te·nai the governor beyond the River and She'thar-boz'e·nai and their colleagues came to them, and this is what they were saying to them: "Who put an order through to you to build this house and to finish this beam structure?" 4 Then they said to them this: "What are the names of the able-bodied men that are building this building?" 5 And the eye of their God proved to be upon the older men of the Jews, and they did not stop them until the report could go to Da·ri'us and then an official document concerning this could be sent back.

6 [Here] is a copy of the letter that Tat'te·nai the governor beyond the River and She'thar-boz'e·nai and his colleagues, the lesser governors that were beyond the River, sent to Da·ri'us the king; 7 they sent the word to him, and the writing in it was in this manner:

"To Da·ri'us the king:

"All peace! 8 Let it become

known to the king that we went to the jurisdictional district of Judah to the house of the great God, and it is being built with stones rolled [into place], and timbers are being laid in the walls; and that work is being eagerly done and is making progress in their hands. 9 Then we asked these older men. This is what we said to them: 'Who put an order through to you to build this house and to finish this beam structure?' 10 And we also asked them their names, so as to let you know, that we might write the names of the able-bodied men that are at their head.

11 "And this is the word that they gave back to us, saying: 'We are the servants of the God of the heavens and the earth, and we are rebuilding the house that had been built many years before this, which a great king of Israel built and finished. 12 However, because our fathers irritated the God of the heavens, he gave them into the hand of Neb·u·chad·nez'zar the king of Babylon, the Chal·de'an, and he demolished this house and took the people into exile at Babylon. 13 Nevertheless, in the first year of Cy'rus the king of Babylon, Cy'rus the king put an order through to rebuild this house of God. 14 And also the gold and silver vessels of the house of God that Neb·u·chad·nez'zar had taken out of the temple, which was in Jerusalem, and brought to the temple of Babylon, these Cy'rus the king took out of the temple of Babylon, and they were given to Shesh·baz'zar, the name of the one whom he made governor. 15 And he said to him: "Take these vessels. Go, deposit them in the temple that is in Jerusalem, and let the house of God be rebuilt upon its place." 16 When that Shesh·baz'zar came he laid the foundations of the house of God, which is in Jerusalem; and from then until now it is being rebuilt but it has not been completed.'

17 "And now if to the king it seems good, let there be an investigation in the king's house of treasures that is there in Babylon, whether it is so that from Cy'rus the king an order was put through to rebuild that house of God in Jerusalem; and the decision of the king concerning this let him send to us."

6 It was then that Da·ri'us the king put an order through, and they made an investigation in the house of the records of the treasures deposited there in Babylon. 2 And at Ec·bat'a·na, in the fortified place that was in the jurisdictional district of Me'di·a, there was found a scroll, and the memorandum to this effect was written within it:

3 "In the first year of Cy'rus the king, Cy'rus the king put an order through concerning the house of God in Jerusalem: Let the house be rebuilt as the place where they are to offer sacrifices, and its foundations are to be fixed, its height being sixty cubits, its width sixty cubits, 4 with three layers of stones rolled [into place] and one layer of timbers; and let the expense be given from the king's house. 5 And also let the gold and silver vessels of the house of God that Neb·u·chad·nez'zar took out of the temple that was in Jerusalem and brought to Babylon be returned, that they may reach the temple that is in Jerusalem at its place and be deposited in the house of God.

6 "Now Tat'te·nai the governor beyond the River, She'thar-boz'e·nai and their colleagues, the lesser governors that are beyond the River, keep your distance from there. 7 Let the work on that house of God alone. The governor of the Jews and the older men of the Jews will rebuild that house of God upon its place. 8 And by me an order has been put through as to what you will do with these older men of the Jews, for rebuilding that house of God; and from the royal treasury of the tax beyond the River the expense will promptly be given to these able-bodied men without cessation. 9 And what is needed, young bulls as well as rams

and lambs for the burnt offerings to the God of heaven, wheat, salt, wine and oil, just as the priests that are in Jerusalem say, let there be given them continually day by day without fail; 10 that they may continually be presenting soothing offerings to the God of the heavens and praying for the life of the king and his sons. 11 And by me an order has been put through that, as for anybody that violates this decree, a timber will be pulled out of his house and he will be impaled upon it, and his house will be turned into a public privy on this account. 12 And may the God who has caused his name to reside there overthrow any king and people that thrusts his hand out to commit a violation and destroy that house of God, which is in Jerusalem. I, Da·ri′us, do put through an order. Let it be done promptly.''

13 Then Tat′te·nai the governor beyond the River, She′thar-boz′e·nai and their colleagues, just as Da·ri′us the king had sent [word], so they did promptly. 14 And the older men of the Jews were building and making progress under the prophesying of Hag′gai the prophet and Zech·a·ri′ah the grandson of Id′do, and they built and finished [it] due to the order of the God of Israel and due to the order of Cy′rus and Da·ri′us and Ar·ta·xerx′es the king of Persia. 15 And they completed this house by the third day of the lunar month A·dar′, that is, in the sixth year of the reign of Da·ri′us the king.

16 And the sons of Israel, the priests and the Levites and the rest of the former exiles held the inauguration of this house of God with joy. 17 And they presented for the inauguration of this house of God a hundred bulls, two hundred rams, four hundred lambs, and as a sin offering for all Israel twelve male goats, according to the number of the tribes of Israel. 18 And they appointed the priests in their classes and the Levites in their divisions, for the service of God which is in Jerusalem, according

to the prescription of the book of Moses.

19 And the former exiles proceeded to hold the passover on the fourteenth [day] of the first month. 20 As the priests and the Levites had cleansed themselves as one group, they were all of them clean, and so they slaughtered the passover victim for all the former exiles and for their brothers the priests and for themselves. 21 Then the sons of Israel that had returned from the Exile ate, and everyone that had separated himself to them from the uncleanness of the nations of the land, to search for Jehovah the God of Israel. 22 And they went on to hold the festival of unfermented cakes seven days with rejoicing; for Jehovah caused them to rejoice, and he had turned the heart of the king of As·syr′i·a around toward them to strengthen their hands in the work of the house of the [true] God, the God of Israel.

7 And after these things in the reign of Ar·ta·xerx′es the king of Persia, Ez′ra the son of Se·rai′ah the son of Az·a·ri′ah the son of Hil·ki′ah 2 the son of Shal′lum the son of Za′dok the son of A·hi′-tub 3 the son of Am·a·ri′ah the son of Az·a·ri′ah the son of Me-ra′ioth 4 the son of Zer·a·hi′ah the son of Uz′zi the son of Buk′ki 5 the son of Ab·i·shu′a the son of Phin′e·has the son of E·le·a′zar the son of Aaron the chief priest— 6 the said Ez′ra himself went up from Babylon; and he was a skilled copyist in the law of Moses, which Jehovah the God of Israel had given, so that the king granted him, according to the hand of Jehovah his God upon him, all his request.

7 Consequently some of the sons of Israel and of the priests and the Levites and the singers and the gatekeepers and the Neth′i·nim went up to Jerusalem in the seventh year of Ar·ta·xerx′es the king. 8 At length he came to Jerusalem in the fifth month, that is, in the seventh year of the king. 9 For on the first [day] of the first month

he himself appointed the going up from Babylon, and on the first [day] of the fifth month he came to Jerusalem, according to the good hand of his God upon him. 10 For Ez′ra himself had prepared his heart to consult the law of Jehovah and to do [it] and to teach in Israel regulation and justice.

11 And this is a copy of the letter that King Ar·ta·xerx′es gave Ez′ra the priest the copyist, a copyist of the words of the commandments of Jehovah and of his regulations toward Israel:

12 "Ar·ta·xerx′es, the king of kings, to Ez′ra the priest, the copyist of the law of the God of the heavens: [Peace] be perfected. And now 13 by me an order has been put through that everyone in my realm of the people of Israel and their priests and Levites that is willing to go to Jerusalem with you should go. 14 Inasmuch as from before the king and his seven counselors [an order] was sent to investigate concerning Judah and Jerusalem in the law of your God that is in your hand, 15 and to bring the silver and the gold that the king and his counselors have voluntarily given to the God of Israel, whose residence is in Jerusalem, 16 with all the silver and the gold that you find in all the jurisdictional district of Babylon along with the gift of the people and the priests who are voluntarily giving to the house of their God, which is in Jerusalem; 17 accordingly you will promptly buy with this money bulls, rams, lambs and their grain offerings and their drink offerings and you will present them upon the altar of the house of YOUR God, which is in Jerusalem.

18 "And whatever it seems good to you and to your brothers to do with the rest of the silver and gold, according to the will of YOUR God, YOU men will do. 19 And the vessels that are being given to you for the service of the house of your God deliver in full before God at Jerusalem. 20 And the rest of the necessities of the house of your God that it devolves upon you to give, you will give out of the king's house of treasures.

21 "And by me myself, Ar·ta·xerx′es the king, an order has been put through to all the treasurers that are beyond the River, that everything that Ez′ra the priest, the copyist of the law of the God of the heavens, requests of YOU men it will be done promptly, 22 even to a hundred talents of silver and a hundred cor measures of wheat and a hundred bath measures of wine and a hundred bath measures of oil, and salt without limit. 23 Let all that is by the order of the God of the heavens be done with zeal for the house of the God of the heavens, that there may occur no wrath against the king's realm and his sons. 24 And to YOU men it is being made known that, as respects any of the priests and the Levites, the musicians, the doorkeepers, the Neth′i·nim, and the workers of this house of God, no tax, tribute or toll is allowed to be imposed upon them.

25 "And you, Ez′ra, according to the wisdom of your God that is in your hand appoint magistrates and judges that they may continually judge all the people that are beyond the River, even all those knowing the laws of your God; and anyone that has not known [them] YOU men will instruct. 26 And as for everyone that does not become a doer of the law of your God and the law of the king, let judgment be promptly executed upon him, whether for death or for banishment, or for money fine or for imprisonment."

27 Blessed be Jehovah the God of our forefathers, who has put such a thing into the heart of the king, to beautify the house of Jehovah, which is in Jerusalem! 28 And toward me he has extended loving-kindness before the king and his counselors and as respects all the mighty princes of the king. And I, for my part, strengthened myself according to the hand of Jehovah my God upon me, and I proceeded

to collect out of Israel the head ones to go up with me.

8 Now these were the heads of their paternal houses and the genealogical enrollment of those going up with me during the reign of Ar·ta·xerx´es the king out of Babylon: 2 Of the sons of Phin´e·has, Ger´shom; of the sons of Ith´a·mar, Daniel; of the sons of David, Hat´tush; 3 of the sons of Shec·a·ni´ah, of the sons of Pa´rosh, Zech·a·ri´ah, and with him there was an enrollment of a hundred and fifty males; 4 of the sons of Pa´hath-mo´ab, El´ie·ho·e´nai the son of Zer·a·hi´ah, and with him two hundred males; 5 of the sons [of Zat´tu], Shec·a·ni´ah the son of Ja·ha·zi´el, and with him three hundred males; 6 and of the sons of A´din, E´bed the son of Jon´a·than, and with him fifty males; 7 and of the sons of E´lam, Je·sha´iah the son of Ath·a·li´ah, and with him seventy males; 8 and of the sons of Sheph·a·ti´ah, Zeb·a·di´ah the son of Mi´cha·el, and with him eighty males; 9 of the sons of Jo´ab, O·ba·di´ah the son of Je·hi´el, and with him two hundred and eighteen males; 10 and of the sons of [Ba´ni], She·lo´mith the son of Jo·si·phi´ah, and with him a hundred and sixty males; 11 and of the sons of Be´bai, Zech·a·ri´ah the son of Be´bai, and with him twenty-eight males; 12 and of the sons of Az´gad, Jo·ha´nan the son of Hak´ka·tan, and with him a hundred and ten males; 13 and of the sons of A·do·ni´kam, those who were the last, and these were their names: E·liph´e·let, Je·i´el and She·mai´ah, and with them sixty males; 14 and of the sons of Big´vai, U´thai and Zab´bud, and with them seventy males.

15 And I proceeded to collect them at the river that comes to A·ha´va; and we kept encamped there three days, that I might scrutinize the people and the priests, but none of the sons of Le´vi did I find there. 16 Accordingly I sent for E·li·e´zer, Ar´i·el, She·mai´ah and El·na´than and Ja´rib and El·na´than and Nathan and Zech·a-

ri´ah and Me·shul´lam, head ones, and for Joi´a·rib and El·na´than, instructors. 17 Then I gave them a command concerning Id´do the head one in the place Ca·si·phi´a, and I put in their mouth words to speak to Id´do [and] his brothers the Neth´i·nim in the place Ca·si·phi´a, to bring to us ministers for the house of our God. 18 So they brought to us, according to the good hand of our God upon us, a man of discretion from the sons of Mah´li the grandson of Le´vi the son of Israel, namely, She·re·bi´ah and his sons and his brothers, eighteen; 19 and Hash·a·bi´ah and with him Je·sha´iah from the sons of Me·rar´i, his brothers, and their sons, twenty. 20 And from the Neth´i·nim, whom David and the princes gave to the service of the Levites, two hundred and twenty Neth´i·nim, all of whom had been designated by [their] names.

21 Then I proclaimed a fast there at the river A·ha´va, to humble ourselves before our God, to seek from him the right way for us and for our little ones and for all our goods. 22 For I felt ashamed to ask a military force and horsemen from the king to help us against the enemy in the way, because we had said to the king: "The hand of our God is over all those seeking him for good, but his strength and his anger are against all those leaving him." 23 Therefore we fasted and made request of our God concerning this, so that he let himself be entreated by us.

24 I now separated from the chiefs of the priests twelve, namely, She·re·bi´ah, Hash·a·bi´ah, and with them ten of their brothers. 25 And I proceeded to weigh out to them the silver and the gold and the utensils, the contribution to the house of our God that the king and his counselors and his princes and all the Israelites who were to be found had contributed. 26 Thus I weighed out into their hand six hundred and fifty talents of silver and a hundred silver utensils worth [two] talents, [and] gold a hundred talents, 27 and twenty small

gold bowls worth a thousand darics and two utensils of good copper, gleaming red, as desirable as gold. 28 Then I said to them: "You are something holy to Jehovah, and the utensils are something holy, and the silver and the gold are a voluntary offering to Jehovah the God of YOUR forefathers. 29 Keep awake and be on guard until YOU weigh [them] out before the chiefs of the priests and the Levites and the princes of the fathers of Israel in Jerusalem, in the dining halls of the house of Jehovah." 30 And the priests and the Levites received the weight of the silver and the gold and the utensils, to bring [them] to Jerusalem to the house of our God.

31 Finally we pulled away from the river A·ha′va on the twelfth [day] of the first month to go to Jerusalem, and the very hand of our God proved to be over us, so that he delivered us out of the palm of the enemy and the ambush by the way. 32 So we came to Jerusalem and dwelt there three days. 33 And on the fourth day we proceeded to weigh out the silver and the gold and the utensils in the house of our God into the hand of Mer′e·moth the son of U·ri′jah the priest and with him E·le·a′zar the son of Phin′e·has and with them Jo′za·bad the son of Jesh′u·a and No·a·di′ah the son of Bin′nu·i the Levites, 34 by number [and] by weight for everything, after which all the weight was written down at that time. 35 Those coming out of the captivity, the former exiles, themselves presented burnt sacrifices to the God of Israel, twelve bulls for all Israel, ninety-six rams, seventy-seven male lambs, twelve he-goats as a sin offering, everything as a burnt offering to Jehovah.

36 Then we gave the laws of the king to the satraps of the king and the governors beyond the River, and they assisted the people and the house of the [true] God.

9 And as soon as these things were finished, the princes approached me, saying: "The people of Israel and the priests and the Levites have not separated themselves from the peoples of the lands as regards their detestable things, namely, the Ca′naan·ites, the Hit′tites, the Per′iz·zites, the Jeb′u·sites, the Am′mon·ites, the Mo′ab·ites, the Egyptians and the Am′or·ites. 2 For they have accepted some of their daughters for themselves and for their sons; and they, the holy seed, have become mingled with the peoples of the lands, and the hand of the princes and the deputy rulers has proved to be foremost in this unfaithfulness."

3 Now as soon as I heard of this thing I ripped apart my garment and my sleeveless coat, and I began to pull out some of the hair of my head and of my beard, and I kept sitting stunned. 4 Also to me they came gathering themselves, everyone trembling because of the words of the God of Israel against the unfaithfulness of the exiled people, while I was sitting stunned until the grain offering of the evening.

5 And at the grain offering of the evening I stood up from my humiliation, with my garment and my sleeveless coat torn apart, and I proceeded to kneel upon my knees and spread out my palms to Jehovah my God. 6 And I went on to say: "O my God, I do feel ashamed and embarrassed to raise my face to you, O my God, for our errors themselves have multiplied over our head and our guiltiness has grown great even to the heavens. 7 From the days of our forefathers we have been in great guiltiness until this day; and because of our errors we have been given, we ourselves, our kings, our priests, into the hand of the kings of the lands with the sword, with the captivity and with the plunder and with shame of face, just as this day. 8 And now for a little moment favor from Jehovah our God has come by leaving over for us those who escape and by giving us a peg in his holy place, to make our eyes shine, O our God, and to give us a little reviving in our servitude. 9 For we are servants; and in our servitude our

God has not left us, but he extends toward us loving-kindness before the kings of Persia, to give us a reviving so as to raise up the house of our God and to restore its desolated places and to give us a stone wall in Judah and in Jerusalem.

10 "And now what shall we say, O our God, after this? For we have left your commandments, 11 which you commanded by means of your servants the prophets, saying, 'The land that YOU people are going in to take possession of is an impure land because of the impurity of the peoples of the lands, because of their detestable things with which they have filled it from end to end by their uncleanness. 12 And now YOUR daughters do not YOU people give to their sons, neither their daughters do YOU accept for YOUR sons; and to time indefinite YOU must not work for their peace and their prosperity, in order that YOU may grow strong and certainly eat the good of the land and indeed take possession [of it] for YOUR sons to time indefinite.' 13 And after all that has come upon us for our bad deeds and our great guiltiness—for you yourself, O our God, have underestimated our error, and you have given us those who have escaped such as these— 14 shall we go breaking your commandments again and forming marriage alliances with the peoples of these detestable things? Will you not get incensed at us to the limit so that there will be none remaining and none escaping? 15 O Jehovah the God of Israel, you are righteous, because we have been left over as an escaped people as at this day. Here we are before you in our guiltiness, for it is impossible to stand before you on account of this."

10 Now as soon as Ez′ra had prayed and he had made confession while weeping and lying prostrate before the house of the [true] God, those of Israel collected themselves together to him, a very large congregation, men and women and children, for the people had wept profusely. 2 Then Shec·a-

ni′ah the son of Je·hi′el of the sons of E′lam answered and said to Ez′ra: "We—we have acted unfaithfully against our God, so that we gave a dwelling to foreign wives from the peoples of the land. Yet now there exists a hope for Israel concerning this. 3 And now let us conclude a covenant with our God to put away all the wives and those born from them according to the counsel of Jehovah and of those trembling at the commandment of our God, that it may be done according to the law. 4 Get up, for the matter devolves upon you, and we are with you. Be strong and act."

5 At that Ez′ra rose and had the chiefs of the priests, the Levites and all Israel take an oath to do according to this word. Accordingly they took an oath. 6 Ez′ra now rose from before the house of the [true] God and went to the dining hall of Je·ho·ha′nan the son of E·li′a·shib. Although he went there, he ate no bread and drank no water, for he was mourning over the unfaithfulness of the exiled people.

7 Then they caused a call to pass throughout Judah and Jerusalem for all the former exiles to collect themselves together at Jerusalem; 8 and anyone that did not come in three days' time according to the counsel of the princes and the older men—all his goods would be put under a ban and he himself be separated from the congregation of the exiled people. 9 So all the men of Judah and Benjamin collected themselves together at Jerusalem within three days, that is, in the ninth month on the twentieth [day] of the month, and all the people kept sitting in the open place of the house of the [true] God, shivering because of the matter and on account of the showers of rain.

10 At length Ez′ra the priest rose and said to them: "You yourselves have acted unfaithfully in that YOU gave a dwelling to foreign wives so as to add to the guiltiness of Israel. 11 And now make confession to Jehovah the

God of YOUR forefathers and do his pleasure and separate yourselves from the peoples of the land and from the foreign wives." 12 To this all the congregation answered and said with a loud voice: "Exactly according to your word it devolves upon us to do. 13 However, the people are many, and it is the season of showers of rain, and it is not possible to stand outside; and the business will not take one day or two, for we have rebelled to a great extent in this matter. 14 So, please, let our princes act representatively for all the congregation; and, as for all in our cities who have given a dwelling to foreign wives, let them come at the times appointed and along with them the older men of each individual city and its judges, until we have turned back the burning anger of our God from us, on account of this matter."

15 (However, Jon'a·than the son of As'a·hel and Jah·zei'ah the son of Tik'vah themselves stood up against this, and Me·shul'lam and Shab'be·thai the Levites were the ones that helped them.) 16 And the former exiles proceeded to do that way; and Ez'ra the priest [and] the men that were the heads of the fathers for their paternal house, even all of them by [their] names, now separated themselves and began sitting on the first day of the tenth month to inquire into the matter; 17 and gradually they finished with all the men that had given a dwelling to foreign wives by the first day of the first month. 18 And some of the sons of the priests came to be found that had given a dwelling to foreign wives; of the sons of Jesh'u·a the son of Je·hoz'a·dak and his brothers, Ma·a·sei'ah and E·li·e'zer and Ja'rib and Ged·a·li'ah. 19 But they promised by shaking hands to put their wives away, and that, they being guilty, there should be a ram of the flock for their guiltiness.

20 And of the sons of Im'mer there were Ha·na'ni and Zeb·a·di'ah; 21 and of the sons of Ha'-rim, Ma·a·sei'ah and E·li'jah and She·mai'ah and Je·hi'el and Uz·zi'ah; 22 and of the sons of Pash'hur, E·li·o·e'nai, Ma·a·sei'ah, Ish'ma·el, Ne·than'el, Jo'za·bad and El·e·a'sah. 23 And of the Levites, Jo'za·bad and Shim'e·i and Ke·lai'ah (that is, Ke·li'ta), Peth·a·hi'ah, Judah and E·li·e'zer; 24 and of the singers, E·li'a·shib; and of the gatekeepers, Shal'lum and Te'lem and U'ri.

25 And of Israel, of the sons of Pa'rosh there were Ra·mi'ah and Iz·zi'ah and Mal·chi'jah and Mij'a·min and E·le·a'zer and Mal·chi'jah and Be·nai'ah; 26 and of the sons of E'lam, Mat·ta·ni'ah, Zech·a·ri'ah and Je·hi'el and Ab'di and Jer'e·moth and E·li'jah; 27 and of the sons of Zat'tu, E·li·o·e'nai, E·li'a·shib, Mat·ta·ni'ah and Jer'e·moth and Za'bad and A·zi'za; 28 and of the sons of Be'bai, Je·ho·ha'nan, Han·a·ni'ah, Zab'bai, Ath'lai; 29 and of the sons of Ba'ni, Me·shul'lam, Mal'luch and A·dai'ah, Ja'shub and She'al [and] Jer'e·moth; 30 and of the sons of Pa'hath-mo'ab, Ad'na and Che'lal, Be·nai'ah, Ma·a·sei'ah, Mat·ta·ni'ah, Bez·a'lel and Bin'nu·i and Ma·nas'seh; 31 and [of] the sons of Ha'rim, E·li·e'zer, Is·shi'jah, Mal·chi'jah, She·mai'ah, Shim'e·on, 32 Benjamin, Mal'luch [and] Shem·a·ri'ah; 33 of the sons of Ha'shum, Mat·te'nai, Mat'tat·tah, Za'bad, E·liph'e·let, Jer'e·mai, Ma·nas'seh [and] Shim'e·i; 34 of the sons of Ba'ni, Ma·a·da'i, Am'ram and U'el, 35 Be·nai'ah, Be·dei'ah, Chel'u·hi, 36 Va·ni'ah, Mer'e·moth, E·li'a·shib, 37 Mat·ta·ni'ah, Mat·te'nai and Ja'a·su; 38 and of the sons of Bin'nu·i, Shim'e·i 39 and Shel·e·mi'ah and Nathan and A·dai'ah, 40 Mach·nad'e·bai, Sha'shai, Sha'rai, 41 Az'ar·el and Shel·e·mi'ah, Shem·a·ri'ah, 42 Shal'lum, Am·a·ri'ah, Joseph; 43 of the sons of Ne'bo, Je·i'el, Mat·ti·thi'ah, Za'bad, Ze·bi'na, Jad'dai and Joel [and] Be·nai'ah. 44 These all had accepted foreign wives, and they proceeded to send away wives along with sons.

NEHEMIAH

1 The words of Ne·he·mi'ah the son of Hac·a·li'ah: Now it came about in the month Chis'lev, in the twentieth year, that I myself happened to be in Shu'shan the castle. **2** Then Ha·na'ni, one of my brothers, came in, he and other men from Judah, and I proceeded to ask about the Jews, those who had escaped, who had been left over of the captivity, and also about Jerusalem. **3** Accordingly they said to me: "Those left over, who have been left over from the captivity, there in the jurisdictional district, are in a very bad plight and in reproach; and the wall of Jerusalem is broken down, and its very gates have been burned with fire."

4 And it came about that, as soon as I heard these words, I sat down and began to weep and mourn for days, and I was continually fasting and praying before the God of the heavens. **5** And I went on to say: "Ah, Jehovah the God of the heavens, the God great and fear-inspiring, keeping the covenant and loving-kindness toward those loving him and keeping his commandments, **6** please, let your ear become attentive and your eyes opened, to listen to the prayer of your servant, which I am praying before you today, day and night, concerning the sons of Israel your servants, all the while making confession concerning the sins of the sons of Israel with which we have sinned against you. We have sinned, both I and the house of my father. **7** We have unquestionably acted corruptly against you and have not kept the commandments and the regulations and the judicial decisions that you gave in command to Moses your servant.

8 "Remember, please, the word that you commanded Moses your servant, saying, 'Should YOU, for YOUR part, act unfaithfully, I, for my part, shall scatter YOU among the peoples. **9** When YOU will

have returned to me and kept my commandments and done them, though YOUR dispersed people should happen to be at the end of the heavens, from there I shall collect them and certainly bring them to the place that I have chosen to have my name reside there.' **10** And they are your servants and your people, whom you redeemed by your great power and by your strong hand. **11** Ah, Jehovah, please, let your ear become attentive to the prayer of your servant and to the prayer of your servants who take delight in fearing your name; and, please, do grant success to your servant today and make him an object of pity before this man."

Now I myself happened to be cupbearer to the king.

2 And it came about in the month Ni'san, in the twentieth year of Ar·ta·xerx'es the king, that wine was before him, and I as usual took up the wine and gave it to the king. But never had I happened to be gloomy before him. **2** So the king said to me: "Why is your face gloomy when you yourself are not sick? This is nothing but a gloominess of heart." At this I became very much afraid.

3 Then I said to the king: "Let the king himself live to time indefinite! Why should not my face become gloomy when the city, the house of the burial places of my forefathers, is devastated, and its very gates have been eaten up with fire?" **4** In turn the king said to me: "What is this that you are seeking to secure?" At once I prayed to the God of the heavens. **5** After that I said to the king: "If to the king it does seem good, and if your servant seems good before you, that you would send me to Judah, to the city of the burial places of my forefathers, that I may rebuild it." **6** At this the king said to me, as his queenly

561

consort was sitting beside him: "How long will your journey come to be and when will you return?" So it seemed good before the king that he should send me, when I gave him the appointed time.

7 And I went on to say to the king: "If to the king it does seem good, let letters be given me to the governors beyond the River, that they may let me pass until I come to Judah; 8 also a letter to A'saph the keeper of the park that belongs to the king, that he may give me trees to build with timber the gates of the Castle that belongs to the house, and for the wall of the city and for the house into which I am to enter." So the king gave [them] to me, according to the good hand of my God upon me.

9 Eventually I came to the governors beyond the River and gave them the letters of the king. Moreover, the king sent with me chiefs of the military force and horsemen. 10 When San·bal'lat the Hor'o·nite and To·bi'ah the servant, the Am'mon·ite, got to hear [of it], then it seemed to them something very bad that a man had come to seek something good for the sons of Israel.

11 At length I came to Jerusalem, and I continued there for three days. 12 Then I rose up by night, I and a few men with me, and I did not tell a man what my God was putting into my heart to do for Jerusalem, and there was no domestic animal with me except the domestic animal on which I was riding. 13 And I proceeded to go out by the Valley Gate by night and in front of the Fountain of the Big Snake and to the Gate of the Ash-heaps, and I was constantly examining the walls of Jerusalem, how they were broken down and the gates of it had been eaten up by fire. 14 And I went passing along to the Fountain Gate and to the King's Pool, and there was no place for the domestic animal under me to pass along. 15 But I kept on ascending in the torrent valley by night, and I kept

on examining the wall; after which I came back and entered by the Valley Gate, and so got back.

16 And the deputy rulers themselves did not know where I had gone and what I was doing; and to the Jews and the priests and the nobles and the deputy rulers and the rest of the doers of the work I had not yet told anything. 17 Finally I said to them: "You are seeing the bad plight in which we are, how Jerusalem is devastated and its gates have been burned with fire. Come and let us rebuild the wall of Jerusalem, that we may no longer continue to be a reproach." 18 And I went on to tell them of the hand of my God, how it was good upon me, and also of the king's words that he had said to me. At this they said: "Let us get up, and we must build." So they strengthened their hands for the good work.

19 Now when San·bal'lat the Hor'o·nite and To·bi'ah the servant, the Am'mon·ite, and Ge'shem the Arabian heard of it, they began to deride us and look on us despisingly and say: "What is this thing that YOU are doing? Is it against the king that YOU are rebelling?" 20 However, I replied to them and said to them: "The God of the heavens is the One that will grant us success, and we ourselves, his servants, shall get up, and we must build; but YOU yourselves have no share, nor just claim, nor memorial in Jerusalem."

3 And E·li'a·shib the high priest and his brothers, the priests, proceeded to get up and build the Sheep Gate. They themselves sanctified it and went setting up its doors; and as far as the Tower of Me'ah they sanctified it, as far as the Tower of Ha·nan'el. 2 And at their side the men of Jer'i·cho did building. And at their side Zac'cur the son of Im'ri did building.

3 And the Fish Gate was what the sons of Has·se·na'ah built; they themselves timbered it and then set up its doors, its bolts and its bars. 4 And at their side Mer'e·moth the son of U·ri'jah the son

of Hak′koz did repair work, and at their side Me·shul′lam the son of Ber·e·chi′ah the son of Me-shez′a·bel did repair work; and at their side Za′dok the son of Ba′a·na did repair work. 5 And at their side the Te·ko′ites did repair work; but their majestic ones themselves did not bring the back of their neck into the service of their masters.

6 And the Gate of the Old [City] was what Joi′a·da the son of Pa-se′ah and Me·shul′lam the son of Bes·o·dei′ah repaired; they them-selves timbered it and then set up its doors and its bolts and its bars. 7 And at their side Mel·a·ti′ah the Gib′e·on·ite and Ja′don the Me-ron′o·thite, did repair work, men of Gib′e·on and Miz′pah, belong-ing to the throne of the governor beyond the River. 8 At his side Uz′zi·el the son of Har·hai′ah, goldsmiths, did repair work; and at his side Han·a·ni′ah a member of the ointment mixers did repair work; and they proceeded to flag-stone Jerusalem as far as the Broad Wall. 9 And at their side Re·pha′-iah the son of Hur, a prince of half the district of Jerusalem, did repair work. 10 And at their side Je·da′iah the son of Ha·ru′maph did repair work in front of his own house; and at his side Hat′-tush the son of Hash·ab·nei′ah did repair work.

11 Another measured section was what Mal·chi′jah the son of Ha′rim and Has′shub the son of Pa′hath-mo′ab repaired, and also the Tower of the Bake Ovens. 12 And at his side Shal′lum the son of Hal-lo′hesh, a prince of half the district of Jerusalem, did repair work, he and his daughters.

13 The Valley Gate was what Ha′nun and the inhabitants of Za·no′ah repaired; they themselves built it and then set up its doors, its bolts and its bars, also a thou-sand cubits in the wall as far as the Gate of the Ash-heaps. 14 And the Gate of the Ash-heaps was what Mal·chi′jah the son of Re′chab, a prince of the district of Beth-hac·che′rem, repaired; he

himself went building it and setting up its doors, its bolts and its bars.

15 And the Fountain Gate was what Shal′lun the son of Col·ho′-zeh, a prince of the district of Miz′pah, repaired; he himself pro-ceeded to build it and to roof it over and to set up its doors, its bolts and its bars, and also the wall of the Pool of the Canal to the King's Garden and as far as the Stairway that goes down from the City of David.

16 After him Ne·he·mi′ah the son of Az′buk, a prince of half the district of Beth-zur, did repair work as far as in front of the Burial Places of David and as far as the pool that had been made and as far as the House of the Mighty Ones.

17 After him the Levites did re-pair work, Re′hum the son of Ba′ni; at his side Hash·a·bi′ah, a prince of half the district of Kei′-lah, did repair work for his district. 18 After him their brothers did re-pair work, Bav′vai the son of Hen′-a·dad, a prince of half the district of Kei′lah.

19 And E′zer the son of Jesh′u·a, a prince of Miz′pah, proceeded at his side to repair another meas-ured section in front of the going up to the Armory at the Buttress.

20 After him Bar′uch the son of Zab′bai worked with fervor [and] repaired another measured section, from the Buttress as far as the entrance of the house of E·li′a·shib the high priest.

21 After him Mer′e·moth the son of U·ri′jah the son of Hak′koz repaired another measured section, from the entrance of the house of E·li′a·shib as far as the end of E·li′a·shib's house.

22 And after him the priests, men of the [Jordan] District, did repair work. 23 After them Ben-jamin and Has′shub did repair work in front of their own house. After them Az·a·ri′ah the son of Ma·a·sei′ah the son of A·na·ni′ah did repair work close by his own house. 24 After him Bin′nu·i the son of Hen′a·dad repaired another measured section, from the house

of Az·a·ri′ah as far as the Buttress and as far as the corner.

25 [After him] Pa′lal the son of U′zai [did repair work] in front of the Buttress and the tower that goes out from the King's House, the upper one that belongs to the Courtyard of the Guard. After him there was Pe·dai′ah the son of Pa′rosh.

26 And the Neth′i·nim themselves happened to be dwellers in O′phel; [they did repair work] as far as in front of the Water Gate on the east and the protruding tower.

27 After them the Te·ko′ites repaired another measured section, from in front of the great protruding tower as far as the wall of O′phel.

28 Above the Horse Gate the priests did repair work, each one in front of his own house.

29 After them Za′dok the son of Im′mer did repair work in front of his own house.

And after him She·mai′ah the son of Shec·a·ni′ah, the keeper of the East Gate, did repair work.

30 After him Han·a·ni′ah the son of Shel·e·mi′ah and Ha′nun the sixth son of Za′laph repaired another measured section.

After him Me·shul′lam the son of Ber·e·chi′ah did repair work in front of his own hall.

31 After him Mal·chi′jah, a member of the goldsmith guild, did repair work as far as the house of the Neth′i·nim and the traders, in front of the Inspection Gate and as far as the roof chamber of the corner.

32 And between the roof chamber of the corner and the Sheep Gate the goldsmiths and the traders did repair work.

4 Now it came about that, as soon as San·bal′lat heard that we were rebuilding the wall, he became angry and highly offended, and he kept deriding the Jews. 2 And he began to say before his brothers and the military force of Sa·mar′i·a, yes, he began to say: "What are the feeble Jews doing? Will they depend upon themselves? Will they sacrifice? Will they finish up in a day? Will they bring the stones to life out of the heaps of dusty rubbish when they are burned?"

3 Now To·bi′ah the Am′mon·ite was alongside him, and he went on to say: "Even what they are building, if a fox went up [against it], he would certainly break down their wall of stones."

4 Hear, O our God, for we have become an object of contempt; and make their reproach return upon their own head, and give them to the plunder in the land of captivity. 5 And do not cover over their error and their sin from before you. Let it not be wiped out, for they have committed offense against the builders.

6 So we kept building the wall, and the entire wall came to be joined together clear to half its [height], and the people continued to have a heart for working.

7 Now it came about that, as soon as San·bal′lat and To·bi′ah and the Arabians and the Am′mon·ites and the Ash′dod·ites heard that the repairing of the walls of Jerusalem had gone forward, for the gaps had started to be stopped up, they became very angry. 8 And all of them began to conspire together to come and fight against Jerusalem and cause me disturbance. 9 But we prayed to our God and kept a guard posted against them day and night on account of them.

10 And Judah began to say: "The power of the burden bearer has stumbled, and there is a great deal of rubbish; and we ourselves are not able to build on the wall."

11 Moreover, our adversaries kept saying: "They will not know and they will not see until we come right in among them, and we shall certainly kill them and put a stop to the work."

12 And it came about that, whenever the Jews dwelling close by them came in, they proceeded to say to us ten times: "[They will come up] from all the places

where YOU people will return to us."

13 So I kept [men] posted at the lowest parts of the place behind the wall at the open places, and I kept the people posted by families with their swords, their lances and their bows. 14 When I saw [their fear] I immediately rose and said to the nobles and the deputy rulers and the rest of the people: "Do not be afraid on their account. Jehovah the great and the fear-inspiring One keep in YOUR mind; and fight for YOUR brothers, YOUR sons and YOUR daughters, YOUR wives and YOUR homes."

15 Now it came about that as soon as our enemies heard that it had become known to us, so that the [true] God had frustrated their counsel and we had all of us gone back to the wall, each one to his work, 16 yes, it came about that from that day forward half of my young men were active in the work and half of them were holding the lances, the shields and the bows and the coats of mail; and the princes were behind the whole house of Judah. 17 As for the builders on the wall and those who were carrying the burden of load bearers, [each] one was active in the work with his one hand while the other [hand] was holding the missile. 18 And the builders were girded, each one with his sword upon his hip, while building; and the one to blow the horn was alongside me.

19 And I proceeded to say to the nobles and the deputy rulers and the rest of the people: "The work is large and extensive, and we are spread about upon the wall far apart from one another. 20 In the place where YOU hear the sound of the horn, there is where YOU will collect yourselves together to us. Our God himself will fight for us."

21 While we were active in the work, the other half of them also were holding the lances, from the ascending of the dawn until the stars came out. 22 Besides, at that time I said to the people: "Let the men spend the night, each one with his attendant, in the midst of Jerusalem, and they must become for us a guard by night and workers by day." 23 As for me and my brothers and my attendants and the men of the guard who were behind me, we were not taking off our garments, each one [having] his missile in his right hand.

5 However, there came to be a great outcry of the people and their wives against their Jewish brothers. 2 And there were those who were saying: "Our sons and our daughters we are giving as security that we may get grain and eat and keep alive." 3 And there were those who were saying: "Our fields and our vineyards and our houses we are giving as security that we may get grain during the food shortage." 4 And there were those who were saying: "We have borrowed money for the king's tribute on our fields and our vineyards. 5 And now our flesh is the same as the flesh of our brothers; our sons are the same as their sons, but here we are reducing our sons and our daughters to slaves, and there are some of our daughters already reduced; and there is no power in our hands while our fields and our vineyards belong to others."

6 Now I became very angry as soon as I heard their outcry and these words. 7 So my heart took consideration within me, and I began finding fault with the nobles and the deputy rulers, and went on to say to them: "Usury is what YOU are exacting, each one from his own brother."

Further, I arranged a great assembly on their account. 8 And I proceeded to say to them: "We ourselves have bought back our own Jewish brothers who were sold to the nations, as far as it was in our power; and at the same time will YOU yourselves sell YOUR own brothers, and must they be sold to us?" At this they became speechless, and they did not find a word.

9 And I went on to say: "The thing that you are doing is not good. Is it not in the fear of our God that you should walk because of the reproach of the nations, our enemies? 10 And also I, my brothers and my attendants are giving money and grain on loan among them. Let us, please, leave off this lending on interest. 11 Please, restore to them on this day their fields, their vineyards, their olive groves and their houses, and the hundredth of the money and the grain, the new wine and the oil that you are exacting as interest from them."

12 To this they said: "We shall make restoration, and from them we shall ask nothing back. We shall do precisely as you are saying." So I called the priests and made them swear to do according to this word. 13 Also, my bosom I shook out and then said: "In this manner may the [true] God shake out from his house and from his acquired property every man that does not carry out this word; and in this manner may he become shaken out and empty." To this all the congregation said: "Amen!" And they began to praise Jehovah. And the people proceeded to do according to this word.

14 Another thing: From the day that he commissioned me to become their governor in the land of Judah, from the twentieth year to the thirty-second year of Ar·ta·xerx′es the king, twelve years, I myself and my brothers did not eat the bread due the governor. 15 As for the former governors that were prior to me, they had made it heavy upon the people, and they kept taking from them for bread and wine daily forty silver shekels. Also, their attendants themselves domineered over the people. As for me, I did not do that way on account of the fear of God. 16 And, what is more, in the work of this wall I took a hand, and not a field did we acquire; and all my attendants were collected together there for the work.

17 And the Jews and the deputy rulers, a hundred and fifty men, and those coming in to us from the nations that were around us were at my table. 18 As for that which happened to be made ready daily, one bull, six select sheep and birds were made ready for me, and once every ten days every sort of wine in abundance. And along with this the bread due the governor I did not demand, because the service upon this people was heavy. 19 Do remember for me, O my God, for good, all that I have done in behalf of this people.

6 Now it came about that, as soon as it was told to San·bal′lat and To·bi′ah and to Ge′shem the Arabian and to the rest of our enemies that I had rebuilt the wall and there had not been left in it a gap (although up to that time the doors themselves I had not set up in the gates), 2 San·bal′lat and Ge′shem immediately sent to me, saying: "Do come, and let us meet together by appointment in the villages of the valley plain of O′no." But they were scheming to do me harm. 3 So I sent messengers to them, saying: "It is a great work that I am doing, and I am not able to go down. Why should the work cease while I take off from it and have to go down to you?" 4 However, they sent me the same word four times, and I kept replying to them with the same word.

5 Finally San·bal′lat sent his attendant to me with the same word a fifth time, with an open letter in his hand. 6 There was written in it: "Among the nations it has been heard, and Ge′shem is saying [it], that you and the Jews are scheming to rebel. That is why you are building the wall; and you are becoming a king to them, according to these words. 7 And there are even prophets that you have appointed to call out concerning you throughout Jerusalem, saying, 'There is a king in Judah!' And now things like these will be told to the king. So now do come, and let us consult together."

8 However, I sent to him, saying: "Things such as you are saying have not been brought about, but it is out of your own heart that you are inventing them." 9 For all of them were trying to make us afraid, saying: "Their hands will drop down from the work so that it will not be done." But now strengthen my hands.

10 And I myself entered the house of She·mai'ah the son of De·la'iah the son of Me·het'a·bel while he was shut up. And he proceeded to say: "Let us meet by appointment at the house of the [true] God, within the temple, and let us close the doors of the temple; for they are coming in to kill you, even by night they are coming in to kill you." 11 But I said: "Should a man like me run away? And who is there like me that could enter into the temple and live? I shall not enter!" 12 So I investigated, and here it was not God that had sent him, but he had spoken this prophecy against me as To·bi'ah and San·bal'lat themselves had hired him. 13 For this reason he had been hired in order that I might be afraid and do that way, and I should certainly sin and it should certainly become in their possession a bad reputation, in order that they might reproach me.

14 Do remember, O my God, To·bi'ah and San·bal'lat, according to these deeds of [each] one, and also No·a·di'ah the prophetess and the rest of the prophets that were continually trying to make me afraid.

15 At length the wall came to completion on the twenty-fifth [day] of E'lul, in fifty-two days.

16 And it came about that, as soon as all our enemies heard [of it] and all the nations that were around us got to see it, they at once fell very much in their own eyes, and they got to know that it was from our God that this work had been done. 17 In those days also the nobles of Judah were making numerous their letters that were going to To·bi'ah and those of To·bi'ah that were coming in to

them. 18 For many in Judah were sworn to him, for a son-in-law he was to Shec·a·ni'ah the son of A'rah; and Je·ho·ha'nan his son had himself taken the daughter of Me·shul'lam the son of Ber·e·chi'-ah. 19 Also, good things about him they were continually saying before me. And my own words they were continually taking out to him. There were letters that To·bi'ah sent to make me afraid.

7 And it came about that, as soon as the wall had been rebuilt, I at once set up the doors. Then there were appointed the gatekeepers and the singers and the Levites. 2 And I went on to put in command of Jerusalem Ha·na'ni my brother and Han·a·ni'ah the prince of the Castle, for he was such a trustworthy man and feared the [true] God more than many others. 3 So I said to them: "The gates of Jerusalem should not be opened until the sun gets hot; and while they are standing by they should shut the doors and bolt [them]. And station guards of the inhabitants of Jerusalem, each one at his own guardpost and each one in front of his own house." 4 Now the city was wide and great, and there were few people inside it, and there were no houses built.

5 But my God put [it] into my heart that I should collect together the nobles and the deputy rulers and the people to get themselves enrolled genealogically. Then I found the book of genealogical enrollment of those who came up at the first, and found written in it:

6 These are the sons of the jurisdictional district who came up out of the captivity of the exiled people whom Neb·u·chad·nez'zar the king of Babylon had taken into exile and who later returned to Jerusalem and to Judah, each to his own city; 7 those who came in with Ze·rub'ba·bel, Jesh'u·a, Ne·he·mi'ah, Az·a·ri'ah, Ra·a·mi'-ah, Na·ham'a·ni, Mor'de·cai, Bil'-shan, Mis'pe·reth, Big'vai, Ne'hum, Ba'a·nah.

The number of the men of the people of Israel: 8 The sons of

Pa′rosh, two thousand one hundred and seventy-two; 9 the sons of Sheph·a·ti′ah, three hundred and seventy-two; 10 the sons of A′rah, six hundred and fifty-two; 11 the sons of Pa′hath-mo′ab, of the sons of Jesh′u·a and Jo′ab, two thousand eight hundred and eighteen; 12 the sons of E′lam, a thousand two hundred and fifty-four; 13 the sons of Zat′tu, eight hundred and forty-five; 14 the sons of Zac′cai, seven hundred and sixty; 15 the sons of Bin′nu·i, six hundred and forty-eight; 16 the sons of Be′bai, six hundred and twenty-eight; 17 the sons of Az′gad, two thousand three hundred and twenty-two; 18 the sons of Ad·o·ni′kam, six hundred and sixty-seven; 19 the sons of Big′vai, two thousand and sixty-seven; 20 the sons of A′din, six hundred and fifty-five; 21 the sons of A′ter, of Heze·ki′ah, ninety-eight; 22 the sons of Ha′shum, three hundred and twenty-eight; 23 the sons of Be′zai, three hundred and twenty-four; 24 the sons of Ha′riph, a hundred and twelve; 25 the sons of Gib′e·on, ninety-five; 26 the men of Beth′le·hem and Ne·to′phah, a hundred and eighty-eight; 27 the men of An′a·thoth, a hundred and twenty-eight; 28 the men of Beth-az′ma·veth, forty-two; 29 the men of Kir′i·ath-je′a·rim, Che·phi′rah and Be·er′oth, seven hundred and forty-three; 30 the men of Ra′mah and Ge′ba, six hundred and twenty-one; 31 the men of Mich′mas, a hundred and twenty-two; 32 the men of Beth′el and A′i, a hundred and twenty-three; 33 the men of the other Ne′bo, fifty-two; 34 the sons of the other E′lam, a thousand two hundred and fifty-four; 35 the sons of Ha′rim, three hundred and twenty; 36 the sons of Jer′i·cho, three hundred and forty-five; 37 the sons of Lod, Ha′did and O′no, seven hundred and twenty-one; 38 the sons of Se·na′ah, three thousand nine hundred and thirty.

39 The priests: The sons of Jeda′iah of the house of Jesh′u·a, nine hundred and seventy-three; 40 the sons of Im′mer, a thousand and fifty-two; 41 the sons of Pash′hur, a thousand two hundred and forty-seven; 42 the sons of Ha′rim, a thousand and seventeen.

43 The Levites: The sons of Jesh′u·a, of Kad′mi·el, of the sons of Ho′de·vah, seventy-four. 44 The singers, the sons of A′saph, a hundred and forty-eight. 45 The gatekeepers, the sons of Shal′lum, the sons of A′ter, the sons of Tal′mon, the sons of Ak′kub, the sons of Ha·ti′ta, the sons of Sho′bai, a hundred and thirty-eight.

46 The Neth′i·nim: The sons of Zi′ha, the sons of Ha·su′pha, the sons of Tab·ba′oth, 47 the sons of Ke′ros, the sons of Si′a, the sons of Pa′don, 48 the sons of Le·ba′nah, the sons of Hag′a·bah, the sons of Sal′mai, 49 the sons of Ha′nan, the sons of Gid′del, the sons of Ga′har, 50 the sons of Re·a′iah, the sons of Re′zin, the sons of Ne·ko′da, 51 the sons of Gaz′zam, the sons of Uz′za, the sons of Pa·se′ah, 52 the sons of Be′sai, the sons of Me·u′nim, the sons of Ne·phush′e·sim, 53 the sons of Bak′buk, the sons of Ha·ku′pha, the sons of Har′hur, 54 the sons of Baz′lith, the sons of Me·hi′da, the sons of Har′sha, 55 the sons of Bar′kos, the sons of Sis′e·ra, the sons of Te′mah, 56 the sons of Ne·zi′ah, the sons of Ha·ti′pha.

57 The sons of the servants of Sol′o·mon: The sons of So′tai, the sons of So·phe′reth, the sons of Pe·ri′da, 58 the sons of Ja′a·la, the sons of Dar′kon, the sons of Gid′del, 59 the sons of Sheph·a·ti′ah, the sons of Hat′til, the sons of Po′che·reth-haz·ze·ba′im, the sons of A′mon. 60 All the Neth′i·nim and the sons of the servants of Sol′o·mon were three hundred and ninety-two.

61 And these were the ones going up from Tel-me′lah, Tel-har′sha, Che′rub, Ad′don and Im′mer, and they were not able to tell the house of their fathers and their origin, whether they were of Israel: 62 the sons of De·la′iah, the sons of To·bi′ah, the sons of Ne·ko′da,

six hundred and forty-two. 63 And of the priests: the sons of Ha·bai'-ah, the sons of Hak'koz, the sons of Bar·zil'lai, who took a wife from the daughters of Bar·zil'lai the Gil'e·ad·ite and came to be called by their name. 64 These were the ones that looked for their register, to establish their genealogy publicly, and it was not found, so that they were barred as polluted from the priesthood. 65 Consequently the Tir·sha'tha said to them that they should not eat from the most holy things until the priest with U'rim and Thum'mim stood up.

66 The entire congregation as one group was forty-two thousand three hundred and sixty, 67 apart from their men slaves and their slave girls, these being seven thousand three hundred and thirty-seven; and they had two hundred and forty-five male singers and female singers. [68 Their horses were seven hundred and thirty-six, their mules two hundred and forty-five.] 69 The camels were four hundred and thirty-five. The asses were six thousand seven hundred and twenty.

70 And there was a part of the heads of the paternal houses that gave to the work. The Tir·sha'tha himself gave to the treasure a thousand gold drachmas, fifty bowls, five hundred and thirty priests' robes. 71 And there were some of the heads of the paternal houses that gave to the treasure for the work twenty thousand gold drachmas and two thousand two hundred silver mi'nas. 72 And what the rest of the people gave was twenty thousand gold drachmas and two thousand silver mi'nas and sixty-seven priests' robes.

73 And the priests and the Levites and the gatekeepers and the singers and some of the people and the Neth'i·nim and all Israel took up dwelling in their cities. When the seventh month arrived, the sons of Israel were then in their cities.

8 And all the people proceeded to gather themselves as one man at the public square that was before the Water Gate. Then they said to Ez'ra the copyist to bring the book of the law of Moses, which Jehovah had commanded Israel. 2 Accordingly Ez'ra the priest brought the law before the congregation of men as well as of women and of all intelligent enough to listen, on the first day of the seventh month. 3 And he continued to read aloud from it before the public square that is before the Water Gate, from daybreak till midday, in front of the men and the women and the other intelligent ones; and the ears of all the people were [attentive] to the book of the law. 4 And Ez'ra the copyist kept standing upon a wooden podium, which they had made for the occasion; and there were standing alongside him Mat·ti·thi'ah and She'ma and A·nai'ah and U·ri'ah and Hil·ki'ah and Ma·a·sei'ah to his right hand, and at his left Pe·dai'ah and Mish'a·el and Mal·chi'jah and Ha'-shum and Hash-bad'da·nah, Zech-a·ri'ah [and] Me·shul'lam.

5 And Ez'ra proceeded to open the book before the eyes of all the people, for he happened to be above all the people; and as he opened it all the people stood up. 6 Then Ez'ra blessed Jehovah the [true] God, the great One, at which all the people answered, "Amen! Amen!" with the lifting up of their hands. They then bowed low and prostrated themselves to Jehovah with [their] faces to the earth. 7 And Jesh'u·a and Ba'ni and She-re·bi'ah, Ja'min, Ak'kub, Shab'be-thai, Ho·di'ah, Ma·a·sei'ah, Ke·li'-ta, Az·a·ri'ah, Jo'za·bad, Ha'nan, Pe·la'iah, even the Levites, were explaining the law to the people, while the people were in a standing position. 8 And they continued reading aloud from the book, from the law of the [true] God, it being expounded, and there being a putting of meaning [into it]; and they continued giving understanding in the reading.

9 And Ne·he·mi'ah, that is, the Tir·sha'tha, and Ez'ra the priest, the copyist, and the Levites who were instructing the people pro-

ceeded to say to all the people: "This very day is holy to Jehovah YOUR God. Do not mourn or weep." For all the people were weeping as they were hearing the words of the law. 10 And he went on to say to them: "Go, eat the fatty things and drink the sweet things, and send portions to the one for whom nothing has been prepared; for this day is holy to our Lord, and do not feel hurt, for the joy of Jehovah is YOUR stronghold." 11 And the Levites were ordering all the people to be silent, saying: "Keep quiet! for this day is holy; and do not feel hurt." 12 So all the people went away to eat and drink and to send out portions and to carry on a great rejoicing, for they had understood the words that had been made known to them.

13 And on the second day the heads of the fathers of all the people, the priests and the Levites, gathered themselves together to Ez′ra the copyist, even to gain insight into the words of the law. 14 Then they found written in the law that Jehovah had commanded by means of Moses that the sons of Israel should dwell in booths during the festival in the seventh month, 15 and that they should make proclamation and cause a call to pass throughout all their cities and throughout Jerusalem, saying: "Go out to the mountainous region and bring in olive leaves and the leaves of oil trees and myrtle leaves and palm leaves and the leaves of branchy trees to make booths, according to what is written."

16 And the people proceeded to go out and bring [them] in and make booths for themselves, each one upon his own roof and in their courtyards and in the courtyards of the house of the [true] God and in the public square of the Water Gate and in the public square of the Gate of E′phra·im. 17 Thus all the congregation of those who had come back from the captivity made booths and took up dwelling in the booths; for the sons of Israel had not done that way from the days of Joshua the son of Nun

until that day, so that there came to be very great rejoicing. 18 And there was a reading aloud of the book of the law of the [true] God day by day, from the first day until the last day; and they went on holding the festival seven days, and on the eighth day there was a solemn assembly, according to the rule.

9 And on the twenty-fourth day of this month the sons of Israel gathered themselves together with fasting and with sackcloth and dirt upon themselves. 2 And the seed of Israel proceeded to separate themselves from all the foreigners, and to stand and make confession of their own sins and the errors of their fathers. 3 Then they rose up at their place and they read aloud from the book of the law of Jehovah their God a fourth part of the day; and a fourth part they were making confession and bowing down to Jehovah their God.

4 And Jesh′u·a and Ba′ni, Kad′-mi·el, Sheb·a·ni′ah, Bun′ni, She-re·bi′ah, Ba′ni [and] Che·na′ni proceeded to rise on the platform of the Levites and cry out with a loud voice to Jehovah their God. 5 And the Levites Jesh′u·a and Kad′mi·el, Ba′ni, Hash·ab·nei′ah, She·re·bi′ah, Ho·di′ah, Sheb·a·ni′-ah [and] Peth·a·hi′ah went on to say: "Rise, bless Jehovah YOUR God from time indefinite to time indefinite. And let them bless your glorious name, which is exalted above all blessing and praise.

6 "You are Jehovah alone; you yourself have made the heavens, [even] the heaven of the heavens, and all their army, the earth and all that is upon it, the seas and all that is in them; and you are preserving all of them alive; and the army of the heavens are bowing down to you. 7 You are Jehovah the [true] God, who chose A′bram and brought him out of Ur of the Chal·de′ans and constituted his name Abraham. 8 And you found his heart faithful before you; so there was a contracting of the covenant with him to give [him] the land of the Ca′naan·ites, the

Hit'tites, the Am'or·ites and the Per'iz·zites and the Jeb'u·sites and the Gir'ga·shites, to give [it] to his seed; and you proceeded to carry out your words, because you are righteous.

9 "So you saw the affliction of our forefathers in Egypt, and their outcry at the Red Sea you heard. 10 Then you gave signs and miracles against Phar'aoh and all his servants and all the people of his land, for you knew that they acted presumptuously against them; and you proceeded to make a name for yourself as at this day. 11 And the sea you split before them, so that they crossed over through the midst of the sea on the dry land; and their pursuers you hurled into the depths like a stone in the strong waters. 12 And by a pillar of cloud you led them by day, and by a pillar of fire by night, to light up for them the way in which they should go. 13 And upon Mount Si'nai you came down and spoke with them out of heaven and went on to give them upright judicial decisions and laws of truth, good regulations and commandments. 14 And your holy sabbath you made known to them, and commandments and regulations and a law you commanded them by means of Moses your servant. 15 And bread from heaven you gave them for their hunger, and waters out of the crag you brought forth to them for their thirst, and you went on to say to them to enter and possess the land that you had lifted your hand [in an oath] to give to them.

16 "And they themselves, even our forefathers, acted presumptuously and proceeded to harden their neck, and they did not listen to your commandments. 17 So they refused to listen, and they did not remember your wonderful acts that you performed with them, but they hardened their neck and appointed a head to return to their servitude in Egypt. But you are a God of acts of forgiveness, gracious and merciful, slow to anger and abundant in loving-kindness, and you did not leave them. 18 Yes, when they had made for themselves a molten statue of a calf and began to say, 'This is your God who led you up out of Egypt,' and they went on to commit great acts of disrespect, 19 you, even you, in your abundant mercy did not leave them in the wilderness. The pillar of cloud itself did not depart from over them by day to lead them in the way, nor the pillar of fire by night to light up for them the way in which they should go. 20 And your good spirit you gave to make them prudent, and your manna you did not hold back from their mouth, and water you gave them for their thirst. 21 And for forty years you provided them with food in the wilderness. They lacked nothing. Their very garments did not wear out, and their feet themselves did not become swollen.

22 "And you proceeded to give them kingdoms and peoples, and to apportion them piece by piece; so that they took possession of the land of Si'hon, even the land of the king of Hesh'bon, and the land of Og the king of Ba'shan. 23 And their sons you made as many as the stars of the heavens. Then you brought them into the land that you had promised to their forefathers that [they] should enter to take possession. 24 So their sons came in and took the land in possession, and you proceeded to subdue before them the inhabitants of the land, the Ca'naan·ites, and to give them into their hand, even their kings and the peoples of the land, to do with them according to their liking. 25 And they went capturing fortified cities and a fat soil and taking in possession houses full of all good things, cisterns hewn out, vineyards and olive groves and trees for food in abundance, and they began to eat and to be satisfied and to grow fat and to luxuriate in your great goodness.

26 "However, they became disobedient and rebelled against you and kept casting your law behind their back, and your own prophets they killed, who bore witness against

them to bring them back to you; and they went on committing acts of great disrespect. 27 For this you gave them into the hand of their adversaries, who kept causing them distress; but in the time of their distress they would cry out to you, and you yourself would hear from the very heavens; and in accord with your abundant mercy you would give them saviors who would save them out of the hand of their adversaries.

28 "But as soon as they were at rest, they would again do what is bad before you, and you would leave them to the hand of their enemies, who would tread them down. Then they would return and call to you for aid, and you yourself would hear from the very heavens and deliver them in accord with your abundant mercy, time and again. 29 Although you would bear witness against them to bring them back to your law, they themselves even acted presumptuously and did not listen to your commandments; and against your own judicial decisions they sinned, which, if a man will do, he must also live by means of them. And they kept giving a stubborn shoulder, and their neck they hardened, and they did not listen. 30 But you were indulgent with them for many years and kept bearing witness against them by your spirit by means of your prophets, and they did not give ear. Finally you gave them into the hand of the peoples of the lands. 31 And in your abundant mercy you did not make an extermination of them or leave them; for you are a God gracious and merciful.

32 "And now, O our God, the God great, mighty and fear-inspiring, keeping the covenant and loving-kindness, do not let all the hardship that has found us, our kings, our princes and our priests and our prophets and our forefathers and all your people from the days of the kings of As·syr′i·a down to this day, seem little before you. 33 And you are righteous as regards all that has come upon us,

for faithfully is how you have acted, but we are the ones that have done wickedly. 34 As for our kings, our princes, our priests and our forefathers, they have not performed your law, nor paid attention to your commandments or to your testimonies with which you bore witness against them. 35 And they themselves—during their kingdom and amid your abundant good things that you gave to them and in the broad and fat land that you made available for them, they did not serve you and did not turn back from their bad practices. 36 Look! We are today slaves; and as for the land that you gave to our forefathers to eat its fruitage and its good things, look! we are slaves upon it, 37 and its produce is abounding for the kings that you have put over us because of our sins, and over our bodies they are ruling and over our domestic animals, according to their liking, and we are in great distress.

38 "So in view of all this we are contracting a trustworthy arrangement, both in writing and attested by the seal of our princes, our Levites [and] our priests."

10 Now attesting it by seal there were:

Ne·he·mi′ah the Tir·sha′tha, the son of Hac·a·li′ah,

And Zed·e·ki′ah, 2 Se·rai′ah, Az·a·ri′ah, Jeremiah, 3 Pash′hur, Am·a·ri′ah, Mal·chi′jah, 4 Hat′-tush, Sheb·a·ni′ah, Mal′luch, 5 Ha′rim, Mer′e·moth, O·ba·di′ah, 6 Daniel, Gin′ne·thon, Bar′uch, 7 Me·shul′lam, A·bi′jah, Mij′a·min, 8 Ma·a·zi′ah, Bil′gai [and] She-mai′ah, these being the priests.

9 Also the Levites: Jesh′u·a the son of Az·a·ni′ah, Bin′nu·i of the sons of Hen′a·dad, Kad′mi·el 10 and their brothers Sheb·a·ni′ah, Ho·di′ah, Ke·li′ta, Pe·la′iah, Ha′-nan, 11 Mi′ca, Re′hob, Hash·a-bi′ah, 12 Zac′cur, She·re·bi′ah, Sheb·a·ni′ah, 13 Ho·di′ah, Ba′ni [and] Be·ni′nu.

14 The heads of the people: Pa′rosh, Pa′hath-mo′ab, E′lam, Zat′tu, Ba′ni, 15 Bun′ni, Az′gad, Be′bai, 16 Ad·o·ni′jah, Big′vai,

A'din, 17 A'ter, Hez·e·ki'ah, Az'-zur, 18 Ho·di'ah, Ha'shum, Be'zai, 19 Ha'riph, An'a·thoth, Ne'bai, 20 Mag'pi·ash, Me·shul'lam, He'-zir, 21 Me·shez'a·bel, Za'dok, Jad'du·a, 22 Pe·la·ti'ah, Ha'nan, A·nai'ah, 23 Ho·she'a, Han·a·ni'-ah, Has'shub, 24 Hal·lo'hesh, Pil'-ha, Sho'bek, 25 Re'hum, Ha-shab'nah, Ma·a·sei'ah, 26 and A·hi'jah, Ha'nan, A'nan, 27 Mal'-luch, Ha'rim, Ba'a·nah.

28 As for the rest of the people, the priests, the Levites, the gate-keepers, the singers, the Neth'i·nim and everyone separating himself from the peoples of the lands to the law of the [true] God, their wives, their sons and their daugh-ters, everyone having knowledge [and] understanding, 29 they were adhering to their brothers, their majestic ones, and coming into [liability to] a curse and into an oath, to walk in the law of the [true] God, which had been given by the hand of Moses the servant of the [true] God, and to keep and to perform all the commandments of Jehovah our Lord and his ju-dicial decisions and his regula-tions; 30 and that we should not give our daughters to the peoples of the land, and their daughters we should not take for our sons.

31 As for the peoples of the land who were bringing in wares and every kind of cereal on the sab-bath day to sell, we should take nothing from them on the sabbath or on a holy day, and we should forego the seventh year and the debt of every hand.

32 Also, we imposed upon our-selves commandments to give, each of us, a third of a shekel yearly for the service of the house of our God, 33 for the layer bread and the constant grain offering and the constant burnt offering of the sab-baths, the new moons, for the ap-pointed feasts and for the holy things and for the sin offerings to make atonement for Israel and all the work of the house of our God.

34 Also, the lots we cast con-cerning the supply of the wood that the priests, the Levites and

the people should bring to the house of our God, by the house of our forefathers, at the appointed times, year by year, to burn upon the altar of Jehovah our God, ac-cording to what is written in the law; 35 and to bring the first ripe fruits of our ground and the first ripe fruits of all the fruitage of every sort of tree, year by year, to the house of Jehovah; 36 and the first-born of our sons and of our domestic animals, according to what is written in the law, and the first-born of our herds and of our flocks, to bring [them] to the house of our God, to the priests that were ministering in the house of our God. 37 Also, the first fruits of our coarse meal and our contribu-tions and the fruitage of every sort of tree, new wine and oil we should bring to the priests to the dining halls of the house of our God, also the tenth from our soil to the Le-vites, as they, the Levites, are the ones receiving a tenth in all our agricultural cities.

38 And the priest, the son of Aaron, must prove to be with the Levites when the Levites receive a tenth; and the Levites themselves should offer up a tenth of the tenth to the house of our God to the dining halls of the supply house. 39 For it is to the dining halls that the sons of Israel and the sons of the Levites should bring the con-tribution of the grain, the new wine and the oil, and there is where the utensils of the sanctuary and the priests that were ministering, and the gatekeepers and the singers are; and we should not neglect the house of our God.

11 Now the princes of the peo-ple had their dwelling in Jerusalem; but as for the rest of the people, they cast lots to bring in one out of every ten to dwell in Jerusalem the holy city, and the nine other parts in the other cities. 2 Moreover, the people blessed all the men who volunteered to dwell in Jerusalem.

3 And these are the heads of the jurisdictional district who dwelt in Jerusalem; but in the cities of Ju-

dah there dwelt, each one in his own possession, in their cities, Israel, the priests and the Levites, and the Neth'i·nim and the sons of the servants of Sol'o·mon.

4 Also, in Jerusalem there dwelt some of the sons of Judah and some of the sons of Benjamin. Of the sons of Judah there were A·thai'-ah the son of Uz·zi'ah the son of Zech·a·ri'ah the son of Am·a·ri'ah the son of Sheph·a·ti'ah the son of Ma·hal'a·lel of the sons of Pe'rez; 5 and Ma·a·sei'ah the son of Bar'uch the son of Col·ho'zeh the son of Ha·zai'ah the son of A·dai'ah the son of Joi'a·rib the son of Zech·a·ri'ah the son of the She·la'nite. 6 All the sons of Pe'rez who were dwelling in Jerusalem were four hundred and sixty-eight, capable men.

7 And these were the sons of Benjamin: Sal'lu the son of Me·shul'lam the son of Jo'ed the son of Pe·dai'ah the son of Ko·lai'ah the son of Ma·a·sei'ah the son of Ith'i·el the son of Je·sha'iah; 8 and after him Gab·ba'i [and] Sal·la'i, nine hundred and twenty-eight; 9 and Joel the son of Zich'ri, an overseer over them, and Judah the son of Has·se·nu'ah over the city as second.

10 Of the priests: Je·da'iah the son of Joi'a·rib, Ja'chin, 11 Se·rai'ah the son of Hil·ki'ah the son of Me·shul'lam the son of Za'dok the son of Me·ra'ioth the son of A·hi'tub, a leader of the house of the [true] God; 12 and their brothers the doers of the work of the house, eight hundred and twenty-two; and A·dai'ah the son of Je·ro'ham the son of Pel·a·li'ah the son of Am'zi the son of Zech·a·ri'ah the son of Pash'hur the son of Mal·chi'jah, 13 and his brothers, heads of paternal houses, two hundred and forty-two, and A·mash'sai the son of Az'ar·el the son of Ah'zai the son of Me·shil'le·moth the son of Im'mer, 14 and their brothers, mighty men of valor, a hundred and twenty-eight, and there was an overseer over them, Zab'di·el the son of the great ones.

15 And of the Levites: She-

mai'ah the son of Has'shub the son of Az·ri'kam the son of Hash·a·bi'ah the son of Bun'ni, 16 and Shab'be·thai and Jo'za·bad, of the heads of the Levites, over the outside business of the house of the [true] God; 17 and Mat·ta·ni'ah himself, the son of Mi'cah the son of Zab'di the son of A'saph, the conductor of the praise [singing], did the lauding at prayer, and Bak·bu·ki'ah was second of his brothers, and Ab'da the son of Sham·mu'a the son of Ga'lal the son of Je·du'thun. 18 All the Levites in the holy city were two hundred and eighty-four.

19 And the gatekeepers were Ak'kub, Tal'mon and their brothers who were keeping guard in the gates, a hundred and seventy-two.

20 And the rest of Israel, of the priests [and] of the Levites, were in all the other cities of Judah, each one in his own hereditary possession. 21 And the Neth'i·nim were dwelling in O'phel; and Zi'ha and Gish'pa were over the Neth'i·nim.

22 And the overseer of the Levites in Jerusalem was Uz'zi the son of Ba'ni the son of Hash·a·bi'ah the son of Mat·ta·ni'ah the son of Mi'ca of the sons of A'saph, the singers, concerning the work of the house of the [true] God. 23 For there was a commandment of the king in behalf of them, and there was a fixed provision for the singers as each day required. 24 And Peth·a·hi'ah the son of Me·shez'a·bel of the sons of Ze'rah the son of Judah was at the side of the king for every matter of the people.

25 And as regards the settlements in their fields, there were some of the sons of Judah that dwelt in Kir'i·ath-ar'ba and its dependent towns and in Di'bon and its dependent towns and in Je·kab'ze·el and its settlements, 26 and in Jesh'u·a and in Mo·la'dah and in Beth-pel'et 27 and in Ha'zar-shu'al and in Be'er-she'ba and its dependent towns 28 and in Zik'lag and in Me·co'nah and its dependent towns 29 and in En-rim'mon and

in Zo′rah and in Jar′muth, 30 Za-no′ah, A·dul′lam and their settle-ments, La′chish and its fields, A·ze′kah and its dependent towns. And they took up camping from Be′er-she′ba clear to the valley of Hin′nom.

31 And the sons of Benjamin were from Ge′ba, Mich′mash and Ai′ja and Beth′el and its depend-ent towns, 32 An′a·thoth, Nob, A·na·ni′ah, 33 Ha′zor, Ra′mah, Git′ta·im, 34 Ha′did, Ze·bo′im, Ne·bal′lat, 35 Lod and O′no, the valley of the craftsmen. 36 And of the Levites there were divisions of Judah for Benjamin.

12 And these were the priests and the Levites that went up with Ze·rub′ba·bel the son of She-al′ti·el and Jesh′u·a: Se·rai′ah, Jeremiah, Ez′ra, 2 Am·a·ri′ah, Mal′luch, Hat′tush, 3 Shec·a·ni′-ah, Re′hum, Mer′e·moth, 4 Id′do, Gin′ne·thoi, A·bi′jah, 5 Mij′a·min, Ma·a·di′ah, Bil′gah, 6 She·mai′-ah, and Joi′a·rib, Je·da′iah, 7 Sal′-lu, A′mok, Hil′ki′ah, Je·da′iah. These were the heads of the priests and their brothers in the days of Jesh′u·a.

8 And the Levites were Jesh′u·a, Bin′nu·i, Kad′mi·el, She·re·bi′ah, Judah, Mat·ta·ni′ah, over the giv-ing of thanks, he and his brothers. 9 And Bak·bu·ki′ah and Un′ni their brothers were opposite them for guard duties. 10 Jesh′u·a him-self became father to Joi′a·kim, and Joi′a·kim himself became fa-ther to E·li′a·shib, and E·li′a·shib to Joi′a·da. 11 And Joi′a·da him-self became father to Jon′a·than, and Jon′a·than himself became father to Jad′du·a.

12 And in the days of Joi′a·kim there happened to be priests, the heads of the paternal houses: for Se·rai′ah, Me·rai′ah; for Jeremiah, Han·a·ni′ah; 13 for Ez′ra, Me-shul′lam; for Am·a·ri′ah, Je·ho-ha′nan; 14 for Mal′lu·chi, Jon′a-than; for Sheb·a·ni′ah, Joseph; 15 for Ha′rim, Ad′na; for Me·ra′-ioth, Hel′kai; 16 for Id′do, Zech-a·ri′ah; for Gin′ne·thon, Me·shul′-lam; 17 for A·bi′jah, Zich′ri; for Mi·ni′a·min, ——; for Mo·a·di′ah,

Pil′tai; 18 for Bil′gah, Sham·mu′a; for She·mai′ah, Je·hon′a·than; 19 and for Joi′a·rib, Mat·te′nai; for Je·da′iah, Uz′zi; 20 for Sal-la′i, Kal′lai; for A′mok, E′ber; 21 for Hil·ki′ah, Hash·a·bi′ah; for Je·da′iah, Ne·than′el.

22 The Levites in the days of E·li′a·shib, Joi′a·da and Jo·ha′nan and Jad′du·a were recorded as heads of paternal houses, also the priests, down till the kingship of Da·ri′us the Persian.

23 The sons of Le′vi as heads of the paternal houses were recorded in the book of the affairs of the times, even down till the days of Jo·ha′nan the son of E·li′a·shib. 24 And the heads of the Levites were Hash·a·bi′ah, She·re·bi′ah and Jesh′u·a the son of Kad′mi·el and their brothers opposite them to offer praise [and] give thanks according to the commandment of David the man of the [true] God, guard group corresponding with guard group. 25 Mat·ta-ni′ah and Bak·bu·ki′ah, O·ba·di′ah, Me·shul′lam, Tal′mon, Ak′kub were keeping guard as gatekeepers, a guard group by the stores of the gates. 26 These were in the days of Joi′a·kim the son of Jesh′u·a the son of Jo′za·dak and in the days of Ne·he·mi′ah the governor and Ez′ra the priest, the copyist.

27 And at the inauguration of the wall of Jerusalem they looked for the Levites, to bring them out of all their places to Jerusalem to carry on an inauguration and a rejoicing even with thanksgivings and with song, cymbals [and] stringed instruments and with harps. 28 And the sons of the singers proceeded to gather them-selves even from the District, from all around Jerusalem and from the settlements of the Ne·toph′a·thites, 29 and from Beth-gil′gal and from the fields of Ge′ba and Az′ma·veth, for there were settlements that the singers had built for themselves all around Jerusalem. 30 And the priests and the Levites proceeded to cleanse themselves and cleanse the people and the gates and the wall.

31 Then I brought up the princes of Judah upon the wall. Further, I appointed two large thanksgiving choirs and processions, [and the one was walking] to the right upon the wall to the Gate of the Ash-heaps. 32 And Ho·shai′ah and half of the princes of Judah began to walk behind them, 33 also Az·a·ri′ah, Ez′ra and Me·shul′lam, 34 Judah and Benjamin and She-mai′ah and Jeremiah; 35 also of the sons of the priests with the trumpets Zech·a·ri′ah the son of Jon′a·than the son of She·mai′ah the son of Mat·ta·ni′ah the son of Mi·cai′ah the son of Zac′cur the son of A′saph, 36 and his brothers She·mai′ah and Az′ar·el, Mil′a·lai, Gil′a·lai, Ma′ai, Ne·than′-el and Judah, Ha·na′ni, with the instruments of song of David the man of the [true] God; and Ez′ra the copyist before them. 37 And at the Fountain Gate and straight ahead of them they went up on the Stairway of the City of David by the ascent of the wall above the House of David and clear to the Water Gate to the east.

38 And the other thanksgiving choir was walking in front, and I after it, also half of the people, upon the wall up over the Tower of the Bake Ovens and on to the Broad Wall, 39 and up over the Gate of E′phra·im and on to the Gate of the Old [City] and clear to the Fish Gate and the Tower of Ha·nan′el and the Tower of Me′ah and on to the Sheep Gate; and they came to a stand at the Gate of the Guard.

40 At length the two thanks-giving choirs came to a stand at the house of the [true] God, also I and half of the deputy rulers with me, 41 and the priests E·li′a·kim, Ma·a·sei′ah, Mi·ni′a·min, Mi·cai′-ah, E·li·o·e′nai, Zech·a·ri′ah, Han-a·ni′ah with the trumpets, 42 and Ma·a·sei′ah and She·mai′ah, and E·le·a′zar and Uz′zi and Je·ho·ha′-nan and Mal·chi′jah and E′lam and E′zer. And the singers with Iz·ra·hi′ah the overseer kept mak-ing themselves heard.

43 And they proceeded to sacri-fice on that day great sacrifices and to rejoice, for the [true] God him-self caused them to rejoice with great joy. And also the women and the children themselves re-joiced, so that the rejoicing of Jeru-salem could be heard far away.

44 Further, there were appointed on that day men over the halls for the stores, for the contributions, for the first fruits and for the tenths, to gather into them out of the fields of the cities the portions [called for by] the law for the priests and the Levites; for the re-joicing of Judah was because of the priests and of the Levites who were in attendance. 45 And they began taking care of the obligation of their God and the obligation of the purification, also the singers and the gatekeepers, according to the commandment of David [and] Sol′o·mon his son. 46 For in the days of David and A′saph in bygone time there were heads of the sing-ers and the song of praise and thanksgivings to God. 47 And all Israel during the days of Ze·rub′-ba·bel and during the days of Ne-he·mi′ah were giving the portions of the singers and of the gate-keepers according to the daily need and were sanctifying [them] to the Levites; and the Levites were sanc-tifying [them] to the sons of Aaron.

13 On that day there was a read-ing from the book of Moses in the ears of the people; and there was found written in it that the Am′mon·ite and the Mo′ab·ite should not come into the congre-gation of the [true] God to time indefinite, 2 for they had not met the sons of Israel with bread and with water, but went hiring against them Ba′laam to call down evil upon them. However, our God changed the malediction into a benediction. 3 So it came about that, as soon as they heard the law, they began to separate all the mixed company from Israel.

4 Now before this, E·li′a·shib the priest in charge of a dining hall of the house of our God was a relative of To·bi′ah; 5 and he proceeded to make for him a large dining

hall, where previously they were regularly putting the grain offering, the frankincense and the utensils and the tenth of the grain, the new wine and the oil, to which the Levites and the singers and the gatekeepers are entitled, and the contribution for the priests.

6 And during all this [time] I did not happen to be in Jerusalem, for in the thirty-second year of Ar·ta·xerx′es the king of Babylon I came to the king, and some time later I asked leave of absence from the king. 7 Then I came to Jerusalem and got to notice the badness that E·li′a·shib had committed for To·bi′ah by making for him a hall in the courtyard of the house of the [true] God. 8 And it seemed very bad to me. So I threw all the furniture of To·bi′-ah's house outside the dining hall. 9 After that I said [the word] and they cleansed the dining halls; and I proceeded to put back there the utensils of the house of the [true] God, with the grain offering and the frankincense.

10 And I got to find out that the very portions of the Levites had not been given [them], so that the Levites and the singers doing the work went running off, each one to his own field. 11 And I began to find fault with the deputy rulers and say: "Why has the house of the [true] God been neglected?" Consequently I collected them together and stationed them at their standing place. 12 And all Judah, for their part, brought in the tenth of the grain and of the new wine and of the oil to the stores. 13 Then I put Shel·e·mi′ah the priest and Za′dok the copyist and Pe·dai′ah of the Levites in charge of the stores; and under their control there was Ha′nan the son of Zac′cur the son of Mat·ta·ni′ah, for they were considered faithful; and upon them it devolved to do the distributing to their brothers.

14 Do remember me, O my God, concerning this, and do not wipe out my acts of loving-kindness that I have performed in connection with the house of my God and the guardianship of it.

15 In those days I saw in Judah people treading wine presses on the sabbath and bringing in grain heaps and loading [them] upon asses, and also wine, grapes and figs and every sort of burden, and bringing [them] into Jerusalem on the sabbath day; and I proceeded to bear witness [against them] on the day of their selling provisions. 16 And the Tyr′i·ans themselves dwelt in [the city], bringing in fish and every sort of merchandise and making sales on the sabbath to the sons of Judah and in Jerusalem. 17 So I began to find fault with the nobles of Judah and say to them: "What is this bad thing that you are doing, even profaning the sabbath day? 18 Was it not this way that your forefathers did, so that our God brought upon us all this calamity, and also upon this city? Yet you are adding to the burning anger against Israel by profaning the sabbath."

19 And it came about that, as soon as the gates of Jerusalem had grown shadowy before the sabbath, I immediately said [the word] and the doors began to be closed. I said further that they should not open them until after the sabbath; and some of my own attendants I stationed at the gates that no burden might come in on the sabbath day. 20 Consequently the traders and the sellers of every sort of merchandise spent the night outside Jerusalem once and a second time. 21 Then I proceeded to bear witness against them and say to them: "Why are you spending the night in front of the wall? If you do it again, a hand I shall lay on you." From that time on they did not come on the sabbath.

22 And I went on to say to the Levites that they should be regularly purifying themselves and coming in, keeping guard of the gates to sanctify the sabbath day. This, also, do remember to my account, O my God, and do feel sorry for me according to the abundance of your loving-kindness.

23 Also, in those days I saw the Jews that had given a dwelling to Ash′dod·ite, Am′mon·ite [and] Mo′ab·ite wives. **24** And as for their sons, half were speaking Ash′dod·ite, and there were none of them knowing how to speak Jewish, but in the tongue of the different peoples. **25** And I began to find fault with them and call down evil upon them and strike some men of them and pull out their hair and make them swear by God: "You should not give YOUR daughters to their sons, and you should not accept any of their daughters for YOUR sons or yourselves. **26** Was it not because of these that Sol′o·mon the king of Israel sinned? And among the many nations there proved to be no king like him; and loved of his God he happened to be, so that God constituted him king over all Israel. Even him

the foreign wives caused to sin. **27** And is it not something unheard of for YOU to commit all this great badness in acting unfaithfully against our God by giving a dwelling to foreign wives?"

28 And one of the sons of Joi′a·da the son of E·li′a·shib the high priest was a son-in-law of San·bal′lat the Hor′o·nite. So I chased him away from me.

29 Do remember them, O my God, on account of the defilement of the priesthood and the covenant of the priesthood and of the Levites.

30 And I purified them from everything foreign and proceeded to assign duties to the priests and to the Levites, each one in his own work, **31** even for the supply of the wood at appointed times and for the first ripe fruits.

Do remember me, O my God, for good.

ESTHER

1 Now it came about in the days of A·has·u·e′rus, that is, the A·has·u·e′rus who was ruling as king from In′di·a to E·thi·o′pi·a, [over] a hundred and twenty-seven jurisdictional districts, **2** [that] in those days as King A·has·u·e′rus was sitting upon his royal throne, which was in Shu′shan the castle, **3** in the third year of his reigning he held a banquet for all his princes and his servants, the military force of Persia and Me′di·a, the nobles and the princes of the jurisdictional districts before himself, **4** when he showed the riches of his glorious kingdom and the honor [and] the beauty of his greatness for many days, a hundred and eighty days. **5** And when these days had come to the full, the king held a banquet for seven days for all the people that were found in Shu′shan the castle, for the great as well as the small, in the courtyard of the garden of the king's palace. **6** There

were linen, fine cotton and blue held fast in ropes of fine fabric, and wool dyed reddish purple in silver rings and pillars of marble, couches of gold and silver upon a pavement of porphyry and marble and pearl and black marble.

7 And there was a passing of wine to drink in gold vessels; and the vessels were different from one another, and the royal wine was in great quantity, according to the means of the king. **8** As regards the time of drinking according to the law, there was no one compelling, for that was the way the king had arranged for every great man of his household, to do according to the liking of each and every one.

9 Also, Vash′ti the queen herself held a banquet for the women at the royal house that belonged to King A·has·u·e′rus.

10 On the seventh day, when the king's heart was in a merry mood with wine, he said to Me·hu′man,

Biz′tha, Har·bo′na, Big′tha and A·bag′tha, Ze′thar and Car′kas, the seven court officials that were ministering to the person of King A·has·u·e′rus, 11 to bring Vash′ti the queen in the royal headdress before the king, to show the peoples and the princes her loveliness; for she was beautiful in appearance. 12 But Queen Vash′ti kept refusing to come at the king's word that was [conveyed] by means of the court officials. At this the king grew highly indignant and his very rage flared up within him.

13 And the king proceeded to say to the wise men having knowledge of the times (for in this way the king's matter [came] before all those versed in law and legal cases, 14 and those closest to him were Car·she′na, She′thar, Ad·ma′tha, Tar′shish, Me′res, Mar·se′na, [and] Me·mu′can, seven princes of Persia and Me′di·a, having access to the king, [and] who were sitting first in the kingdom): 15 "According to law what is to be done with Queen Vash′ti because she has not performed the saying of King A·has·u·e′rus by means of the court officials?"

16 To this Me·mu′can said before the king and the princes: "It is not against the king alone that Vash′ti the queen has done wrong, but against all the princes and against all the peoples that are in all the jurisdictional districts of King A·has·u·e′rus. 17 For the affair of the queen will go out to all the wives so that they will despise their owners in their own eyes, when they say, 'King A·has·u·e′rus himself said to bring in Vash′ti the queen before him, and she did not come in.' 18 And this day the princesses of Persia and Me′di·a, who have heard the affair of the queen, will talk to all the princes of the king, and there will be plenty of contempt and indignation. 19 If to the king it does seem good, let a royal word go out from his person, and let it be written among the laws of Persia and Me′di·a, that it may not pass away, that Vash′ti may not come in before King

A·has·u·e′rus; and her royal dignity let the king give to a companion of hers, a woman better than she is. 20 And the decree of the king that he will make must be heard in all his realm (for it is vast), and all the wives themselves will give honor to their owners, the great as well as the small."

21 And the thing was pleasing in the eyes of the king and the princes, and the king proceeded to do according to the word of Me·mu′can. 22 So he sent written documents to all the king's jurisdictional districts, to each jurisdictional district in its own style of writing and to each people in its own tongue, for every husband to be continually acting as prince in his own house and speaking in the tongue of his own people.

2 After these things, when the rage of King A·has·u·e′rus had subsided, he remembered Vash′ti and what she had done and what had been decided against her. 2 Then the king's attendants, his ministers, said: "Let them seek young women, virgins, beautiful in appearance, for the king, 3 and let the king appoint commissioners in all the jurisdictional districts of his realm, and let them collect together all the young women, virgins, beautiful in appearance, at Shu′shan the castle, at the house of the women in charge of Heg′a·i the king's eunuch, the guardian of the women; and let there be a giving of their massages. 4 And that young woman who seems pleasing in the king's eyes will be queen instead of Vash′ti." And the thing was pleasing in the king's eyes, and he proceeded to do that way.

5 A certain man, a Jew, happened to be in Shu′shan the castle, and his name was Mor′de·cai the son of Ja′ir the son of Shim′e·i the son of Kish a Ben′ja·min·ite, 6 who had been taken into exile from Jerusalem with the deported people who were taken into exile with Jec·o·ni′ah the king of Judah whom Neb·u·chad·nez′zar the king of Babylon took into exile. 7 And he came to be the caretaker of

Ha·das'sah, that is, Esther, the daughter of his father's brother, for she had neither father nor mother; and the young woman was pretty in form and beautiful in appearance, and at the death of her father and her mother Mor'de·cai took her as his daughter. 8 And it came about that, when the king's word and his law were heard, and when many young women were collected together at Shu'shan the castle in charge of Heg'a·i, then Esther was taken to the king's house in charge of Heg'a·i the guardian of the women.

9 Now the young woman was pleasing in his eyes, so that she gained loving-kindness before him and he made haste to give her her massages and her appropriate food, and to give her seven selected young women from the king's house, and he proceeded to transfer her and her young women to the best place of the house of the women. 10 Esther had not told about her people or about her relatives, for Mor'de·cai himself had laid the command upon her that she should not tell. 11 And day after day Mor'de·cai was walking before the courtyard of the house of the women to know of Esther's welfare and what was being done with her.

12 And when the turn of each young woman arrived to go in to King A·has·u·e'rus after it had happened to her according to the women's regulation for twelve months, for that was the way the days of their massage procedure were gradually fulfilled, six months with oil of myrrh and six months with balsam oil and with the massages of the women; 13 then on these conditions the young woman herself came in to the king. Everything that she would mention would be given her, to come with her from the house of the women to the king's house. 14 In the evening she herself came in, and in the morning she herself returned to the second house of the women in charge of Sha·ash'gaz the king's eunuch, the guardian of the concubines. She would not come in any more to the king unless the king had taken delight in her and she had been called by name.

15 And when the turn of Esther the daughter of Ab'i·ha·il the uncle of Mor'de·cai, whom he had taken as his daughter, arrived to come in to the king, she did not request anything except what Heg'a·i the king's eunuch, the guardian of the women, proceeded to mention (all the while Esther was continually gaining favor in the eyes of everyone seeing her). 16 Then Esther was taken to King A·has·u·e'rus at his royal house in the tenth month, that is, the month Te'beth, in the seventh year of his reign. 17 And the king came to love Esther more than all the other women, so that she gained more favor and loving-kindness before him than all the other virgins. And he proceeded to put the royal headdress upon her head and make her queen instead of Vash'ti. 18 And the king went on to hold a great banquet for all his princes and his servants, the banquet of Esther; and an amnesty for the jurisdictional districts he granted, and he kept giving presents according to the means of the king.

19 Now when virgins were collected together a second time, Mor'de·cai was sitting in the king's gate. 20 Esther was not telling about her relatives and her people, just as Mor'de·cai had laid the command upon her; and the saying of Mor'de·cai Esther was performing, just as when she happened to be under care by him.

21 In those days while Mor'de·cai was sitting in the king's gate, Big'than and Te'resh, two court officials of the king, doorkeepers, became indignant and kept seeking to lay hand on King A·has·u·e'rus. 22 And the thing came to be known to Mor'de·cai, and he immediately told Esther the queen. In turn Esther talked to the king in Mor'de·cai's name. 23 So the matter was sought out and eventually found out, and both of them got to be hanged on a stake; after which it

was written in the book of the affairs of the days before the king.

3 After these things King A·has·u·e′rus magnified Ha′man the son of Ham·me·da′tha the Ag′ag·ite and proceeded to exalt him and to put his throne above all the other princes that were with him. 2 And all the king's servants that were in the king's gate were bowing low and prostrating themselves to Ha′man, for so the king had commanded respecting him. But as for Mor′de·cai, he would neither bow low nor prostrate himself. 3 And the king's servants who were in the king's gate began to say to Mor′de·cai: "Why are you side-stepping the king's commandment?" 4 And it came about that, as they talked to him day by day, and he did not listen to them, then they told Ha′man to see whether Mor′de·cai's affairs would stand; for he had told them that he was a Jew.

5 Now Ha′man kept seeing that Mor′de·cai was not bowing low and prostrating himself to him, and Ha′man became filled with rage. 6 But it was despicable in his eyes to lay hand upon Mor′de·cai alone, for they had told him about Mor′de·cai's people; and Ha′man began seeking to annihilate all the Jews who were in all the realm of A·has·u·e′rus, Mor′de·cai's people.

7 In the first month, that is, the month Ni′san, in the twelfth year of King A·has·u·e′rus, someone cast Pur, that is, the Lot, before Ha′man from day to day and from month to month, [to] the twelfth, that is, the month A·dar′. 8 And Ha′man proceeded to say to King A·has·u·e′rus: "There is one certain people scattered and separated among the peoples in all the jurisdictional districts of your realm; and their laws are different from all other people's, and the king's own laws they are not performing, and for the king it is not appropriate to let them alone. 9 If to the king it does seem good, let there be a writing that they be destroyed; and ten thousand silver talents I shall pay into the hands of those doing the work by bringing [it] into the king's treasury."

10 At that the king removed his signet ring from his own hand and gave it to Ha′man the son of Ham·me·da′tha the Ag′ag·ite, the one showing hostility to the Jews. 11 And the king went on to say to Ha′man: "The silver is given to you, also the people, to do with them according to what is good in your own eyes." 12 The king's secretaries were then called in the first month on the thirteenth day of it, and writing went on according to all that Ha′man commanded the king's satraps and the governors who were over the different jurisdictional districts, and the princes of the different peoples, of each jurisdictional district, in its own style of writing, and each people in its own tongue; in the name of King A·has·u·e′rus it was written and it was sealed with the king's signet ring.

13 And there was a sending of the letters by means of couriers to all the king's jurisdictional districts, to annihilate, to kill and to destroy all the Jews, young man as well as old man, little ones and women, on one day, on the thirteenth [day] of the twelfth month, that is, the month A·dar′, and to plunder the spoil of them. 14 A copy of the writing to be given as law in all the different jurisdictional districts was being published to all the peoples, [for them] to become ready for this day. 15 The couriers themselves went out, being moved to speed because of the king's word, and the law itself was given in Shu′shan the castle. As for the king and Ha′man, they sat down to drink; but as for the city of Shu′shan, it was in confusion.

4 And Mor′de·cai himself got knowledge of everything that had been done; and Mor′de·cai proceeded to rip his garments apart and put on sackcloth and ashes and go out into the middle of the city and cry out with a loud and bitter outcry. 2 Finally he came as far as in front of the king's gate, for no one was to come into the king's gate in clothing of sackcloth. 3 And in all the different jurisdictional districts, wherever the king's word and his law were reaching, there was great mourning among the Jews, and fasting and weeping and wailing. Sackcloth and ashes themselves came to be spread out as a couch for many. 4 And Esther's young women and her eunuchs began to come in and tell her. And the queen was very much pained. Then she sent garments to clothe Mor'de·cai and to remove his sackcloth off him. And he did not accept [them]. 5 At this Esther called Ha'thach, one of the king's eunuchs, whom he had made to attend upon her, and she proceeded to give him a command concerning Mor'de·cai, to know what this meant and what this was all about.

6 So Ha'thach went out to Mor'-de·cai into the public square of the city that was before the king's gate. 7 Then Mor'de·cai told him about all the things that had befallen him and the exact statement of the money that Ha'man had said to pay to the king's treasury against the Jews, to destroy them. 8 And a copy of the writing of the law that had been given in Shu'-shan to have them annihilated he gave him to show Esther and to tell her and to lay the command upon her to come in to the king and implore favor of him and make request directly before him for her own people.

9 Ha'thach now came in and told Esther Mor'de·cai's words. 10 Then Esther said to Ha'thach and commanded him concerning Mor'de·cai: 11 "All the king's servants and the people of the king's jurisdictional districts are aware that, as regards any man or woman that comes in to the king at the inner courtyard who is not called, his one law is to have [him] put to death; only in case the king holds out to him the golden scepter, he will also certainly stay alive. As for me, I have not been called to come in to the king now for thirty days."

12 And they proceeded to tell Mor'de·cai the words of Esther. 13 Then Mor'de·cai said to reply to Esther: "Do not imagine within your own soul that the king's household will escape any more than all the other Jews. 14 For if you are altogether silent at this time, relief and deliverance themselves will stand up for the Jews from another place; but as for you and your father's house, you people will perish. And who is there knowing whether it is for a time like this that you have attained to royal dignity?"

15 Accordingly Esther said to reply to Mor'de·cai: 16 "Go, gather all the Jews that are to be found in Shu'shan and fast in my behalf and neither eat nor drink for three days, night and day. I too with my young women, I shall fast likewise, and upon that I shall come in to the king, which is not according to the law; and in case I must perish, I must perish." 17 At this Mor'-de·cai passed along and proceeded to do according to all that Esther had laid in command upon him.

5 And it came about on the third day that Esther went dressing up royally, after which she took her stand in the inner courtyard of the king's house opposite the king's house, while the king was sitting on his royal throne in the royal house opposite the entrance of the house. 2 And it came about that, as soon as the king saw Esther the queen standing in the courtyard, she gained favor in his eyes, so that the king held out to Esther the golden scepter that was in his hand. Esther now came near and touched the top of the scepter.

3 Then the king said to her: "What do you have, O Esther the queen, and what is your request? To the half of the kingship—let it even be given to you!" 4 In turn Esther said: "If to the king it does seem good, let the king with Ha'-man come today to the banquet that I have made for him." 5 Accordingly the king said: "You men, have Ha'man act quickly on the

word of Esther." Later the king and Ha′man came to the banquet that Esther had made.

6 In time the king said to Esther during the banquet of wine: "What is your petition? Let it even be granted you! And what is your request? To the half of the kingship—let it even be done!" 7 To this Esther answered and said: "My petition and my request is, 8 If I have found favor in the king's eyes and if to the king it does seem good to grant my petition and to act on my request, let the king and Ha′man come to the banquet that I shall hold for them [tomorrow], and tomorrow I shall do according to the king's word."

9 Consequently Ha′man went out on that day joyful and merry of heart; but as soon as Ha′man saw Mor′de·cai in the king's gate and that he did not rise and did not quake on account of him, Ha′man was immediately filled with rage against Mor′de·cai. 10 However, Ha′man kept control of himself and came into his house. Then he sent and had his friends and Ze′resh his wife brought in; 11 and Ha′man proceeded to declare to them the glory of his riches and the large number of his sons and everything with which the king had magnified him and how he had exalted him over the princes and the servants of the king.

12 And Ha′man went on to say: "What is more, Esther the queen brought in with the king to the banquet that she had made no one but me, and tomorrow also I am invited to her with the king. 13 But all this—none of it suits me as long as I am seeing Mor′de·cai the Jew sitting in the king's gate." 14 At that Ze′resh his wife and all his friends said to him: "Let them make a stake fifty cubits high. Then in the morning say to the king that they should hang Mor′de·cai on it. Then go in with the king to the banquet joyful." So the thing seemed good before Ha′man, and he proceeded to have the stake made.

6 During that night the king's sleep fled. Therefore he said to bring the book of the records of the affairs of the times. Thus there came to be a reading of them before the king. 2 At length there was found written what Mor′de·cai had reported concerning Big·tha′na and Te′resh, two court officials of the king, doorkeepers, who had sought to lay hand on King A·has·u·e′rus. 3 Then the king said: "What honor and great thing has been done to Mor′de·cai for this?" To this the king's attendants, his ministers, said: "Nothing has been done with him."

4 Later the king said: "Who is in the courtyard?" Now Ha′man himself had come into the outer courtyard of the king's house to say to the king to hang Mor′de·cai on the stake that he had prepared for him. 5 Accordingly the king's attendants said to him: "Here is Ha′man standing in the courtyard." So the king said: "Let him come in."

6 When Ha′man came in, the king proceeded to say to him: "What is to be done to the man in whose honor the king himself has taken a delight?" At this Ha′man said in his heart: "To whom would the king take delight in rendering an honor more than me?" 7 So Ha′man said to the king: "As for the man in whose honor the king himself has taken a delight, 8 let them bring royal apparel with which the king does clothe himself and a horse upon which the king does ride and on the head of which the royal headdress has been put. 9 And let there be a putting of the apparel and the horse into the charge of one of the king's noble princes; and they must clothe the man in whose honor the king himself has taken a delight, and they must make him ride on the horse in the public square of the city, and they must call out before him, 'This is how it is done to the man in whose honor the king himself has taken a delight.' " 10 At once the king said to Ha′man: "Quickly, take the apparel and the horse, just as you have

said, and do that way to Mor'de-cai the Jew who is sitting in the king's gate. Do not let anything go unfulfilled of all that you have spoken."

11 And Ha'man proceeded to take the apparel and the horse and clothe Mor'de·cai and make him ride in the public square of the city and call out before him: "This is how it is done to the man in whose honor the king himself has taken a delight." 12 Afterward Mor'de·cai returned to the king's gate. As for Ha'man, he hurried to his house, mourning and with his head covered. 13 And Ha'man went on to relate to Ze'resh his wife and to all his friends everything that had befallen him. At that his wise men and Ze'resh his wife said to him: "If it is from the seed of the Jews that Mor'de·cai is before whom you have started to fall, you will not prevail against him, but you will without fail fall before him."

14 While they were yet speaking with him the king's court officials themselves arrived and proceeded hastily to bring Ha'man to the banquet that Esther had made.

7 Then the king and Ha'man came in to banquet with Esther the queen. 2 The king now said to Esther also on the second day during the banquet of wine: "What is your petition, O Esther the queen? Let it even be given to you. And what is your request? To the half of the kingship—let it even be done!" 3 At this Esther the queen answered and said: "If I have found favor in your eyes, O king, and if to the king it does seem good, let there be given me my own soul at my petition and my people at my request. 4 For we have been sold, I and my people, to be annihilated, killed and destroyed. Now if we had been sold for mere men slaves and for mere maidservants, I should have kept silent. But the distress is not appropriate when with damage to the king."

5 King A·has·u·e'rus now said, yes, he went on to say to Esther the queen: "Who is this, and just where is the one who has emboldened himself to do that way?" 6 Then Esther said: "The man, the adversary and enemy, is this bad Ha'man."

As for Ha'man, he became terrified because of the king and the queen. 7 As for the king, he rose up in his rage from the banquet of wine [to go] to the garden of the palace; and Ha'man himself stood up to make request for his soul from Esther the queen, for he saw that bad had been determined against him by the king. 8 And the king himself returned from the garden of the palace to the house of the wine banquet; and Ha'man was fallen upon the couch on which Esther was. Consequently the king said: "Is there also to be a raping of the queen, with me in the house?" The word itself went out of the king's mouth, and Ha'man's face they covered. 9 Har·bo'na, one of the court officials before the king, now said: "Also, there is the stake that Ha'man made for Mor'-de·cai, who had spoken good concerning the king, standing in Ha'-man's house—fifty cubits high." At that the king said: "You men, hang him on it." 10 And they proceeded to hang Ha'man on the stake that he had prepared for Mor'de·cai; and the king's rage itself subsided.

8 On that day King A·has·u·e'rus gave to Esther the queen the house of Ha'man, the one showing hostility to the Jews; and Mor'de-cai himself came in before the king, because Esther had told what he was to her. 2 Then the king removed his signet ring that he had taken away from Ha'man and gave it to Mor'de·cai; and Esther went on to place Mor'de·cai over the house of Ha'man.

3 Moreover, Esther spoke again before the king and fell down before his feet and wept and implored favor of him to turn away the badness of Ha'man the Ag'ag-ite and his scheme that he had schemed against the Jews. 4 Then the king held the golden scepter out

to Esther, at which Esther rose and stood before the king. 5 She now said: "If to the king it does seem good, and if I have found favor before him and the thing is proper before the king and I am good in his eyes, let it be written to undo the written documents, the scheme of Ha′man the son of Ham·me·da′tha the Ag′ag·ite, which he wrote to destroy the Jews that are in all the king's jurisdictional districts. 6 For how can I [bear it] when I must look upon the calamity that will find my people, and how can I [bear it] when I must look upon the destruction of my relatives?"

7 So King A·has·u·e′rus said to Esther the queen and to Mor′de·cai the Jew: "Look! The house of Ha′man I have given to Esther, and him they have hanged on the stake, for the reason that he thrust out his hand against the Jews. 8 And YOU yourselves write in behalf of the Jews according to what is good in YOUR own eyes in the king's name and seal [it] with the king's signet ring; for a writing that is written in the king's name and sealed with the king's signet ring it is not possible to undo."

9 Accordingly the secretaries of the king were called at that time in the third month, that is, the month of Si′van, on the twenty-third [day] of it; and writing went on according to all that Mor′de·cai commanded to the Jews and to the satraps and the governors and the princes of the jurisdictional districts that were from In′di·a to E·thi·o′pi·a, a hundred and twenty-seven jurisdictional districts, [to] each jurisdictional district in its own style of writing and [to] each people in its own tongue, and to the Jews in their own style of writing and in their own tongue.

10 And he proceeded to write in the name of King A·has·u·e′rus and do the sealing with the king's signet ring and send written documents by the hand of the couriers on horses, riding post horses used in the royal service, sons of speedy mares, 11 that the king granted to the Jews that were in all the dif-

ferent cities to congregate themselves and stand for their souls, to annihilate and kill and destroy all the force of the people and jurisdictional district that were showing hostility to them, little ones and women, and to plunder their spoil, 12 on the one day in all the jurisdictional districts of King A·has·u·e′rus, on the thirteenth [day] of the twelfth month, that is, the month of A·dar′. 13 A copy of the writing was to be given as law throughout all the different jurisdictional districts, published to all the peoples, that the Jews should become ready for this day to avenge themselves upon their enemies. 14 The couriers themselves, riding post horses used in the royal service, went forth, being urged forward and being moved with speed by the king's word; and the law itself was given out in Shu′shan the castle.

15 As for Mor′de·cai, he went forth from before the king in royal apparel of blue and linen, with a great crown of gold, and a fine-fabric cloak, even of wool dyed reddish purple. And the city of Shu′shan itself cried out shrilly and was joyful. 16 For the Jews there occurred light and rejoicing and exultation and honor. 17 And in all the different jurisdictional districts and in all the different cities wherever the word of the king and his law were reaching there were rejoicing and exultation for the Jews, a banquet and a good day; and many of the peoples of the land were declaring themselves Jews, for the dread of the Jews had fallen upon them.

9 And in the twelfth month, that is, the month of A·dar′, on the thirteenth day of it, when the king's word and his law came due to be performed, on the day for which the enemies of the Jews had waited to domineer over them, there was even a turning to the contrary, in that the Jews themselves domineered over those hating them. 2 The Jews congregated themselves in their cities in all the jurisdictional districts of King A·has·u-

e'rus to lay hand on those seeking their injury, and not a man stood his ground before them, for the dread of them had fallen upon all the peoples. 3 And all the princes of the jurisdictional districts and the satraps and the governors and the doers of the business that belonged to the king were assisting the Jews, for the dread of Mor'de·cai had fallen upon them. 4 For Mor'de·cai was great in the king's house and his fame was traveling throughout all the jurisdictional districts, because the man Mor'de·cai was steadily growing greater.

5 And the Jews went striking down all their enemies with a slaughter by the sword and with a killing and destruction, and they went doing to those hating them according to their liking. 6 And in Shu'shan the castle the Jews killed and there was a destroying of five hundred men. 7 Also, Par·shan·da'tha and Dal'phon and As·pa'tha 8 and Po·ra'tha and A·da'li·a and A·ri·da'tha 9 and Par·mash'ta and Ar'i·sai and Ar'i·dai and Vai·za'tha, 10 the ten sons of Ha'man the son of Ham·me·da'tha, the one showing hostility to the Jews, they killed; but on the plunder they did not lay their hand.

11 On that day the number of those killed in Shu'shan the castle came before the king.

12 And the king proceeded to say to Esther the queen: "In Shu'shan the castle the Jews have killed, and there has been a destroying of five hundred men and the ten sons of Ha'man. In the rest of the jurisdictional districts of the king what have they done? And what is your petition? Let it even be given to you. And what is your further request? Let it even be done." 13 Accordingly Esther said: "If to the king it does seem good, let it be granted tomorrow also to the Jews that are in Shu'shan to do according to the law of today; and let the ten sons of Ha'man be hanged upon the stake." 14 So the king said for it to be done that way. Then a law was given out

in Shu'shan, and the ten sons of Ha'man were hanged.

15 And the Jews that were in Shu'shan proceeded to congregate themselves also on the fourteenth day of the month A·dar', and they got to kill in Shu'shan three hundred men; but on the plunder they did not lay their hand.

16 As for the rest of the Jews that were in the jurisdictional districts of the king, they congregated themselves, and there was a stand for their souls, and there was an avenging of themselves upon their enemies and a killing among those hating them of seventy-five thousand; but on the plunder they did not lay their hand, 17 on the thirteenth day of the month A·dar'; and there was a rest on the fourteenth [day] of it, and there was a making of it a day of banqueting and of rejoicing.

18 As for the Jews that were in Shu'shan, they congregated themselves on the thirteenth [day] of it and on the fourteenth [day] of it, and there was a rest on the fifteenth [day] of it, and there was a making of it a day of banqueting and of rejoicing. 19 That is why the country Jews, inhabiting the cities of the outlying districts, were making the fourteenth day of the month A·dar' a rejoicing and a banqueting and a good day and a sending of portions to one another.

20 And Mor'de·cai proceeded to write these things and send written documents to all the Jews that were in all the jurisdictional districts of King A·has·u·e'rus, the nearby and the distant ones, 21 to impose upon them the obligation to be regularly holding the fourteenth day of the month A·dar' and the fifteenth day of it in each and every year, 22 according to the days on which the Jews had rested from their enemies and the month that was changed for them from grief to rejoicing and from mourning to a good day, to hold them as days of banqueting and rejoicing and sending of portions to one another and of gifts to the poor people.

23 And the Jews accepted what they had started to do and what Mor'de·cai had written to them. 24 For Ha'man the son of Ham·me·da'tha, the Ag'ag·ite, the one showing hostility to all the Jews, had himself schemed against the Jews to destroy them, and he had had Pur, that is, the Lot, cast, to disquiet them and destroy them. 25 But when Esther came in before the king he said with the written document: "Let his bad scheme that he has schemed against the Jews come back upon his own head"; and they hanged him and his sons upon the stake. 26 That is why they called these days Pu'rim, by the name of the Pur. That is why, according to all the words of this letter and what they had seen as to this and what had come upon them, 27 the Jews imposed and accepted upon themselves and upon their offspring and upon all those joining themselves to them, that it should not pass away, the obligation to be regularly holding these two days according to what was written concerning them and according to their appointed time in each and every year. 28 And these days were to be remembered and held in each and every generation, each family, each jurisdictional district and each city, and these days of Pu'rim themselves should not pass away from the midst of the Jews and the commemoration itself of them not come to an end among their offspring.

29 And Esther the queen, the daughter of Ab'i·ha·il, and Mor'de·cai the Jew proceeded to write with all forcefulness to confirm this second letter concerning Pu'rim. 30 Then he sent written documents to all the Jews in the one hundred and twenty-seven jurisdictional districts, the realm of A·has·u·e'rus, [in] words of peace and truth, 31 to confirm these days of Pu'rim at their appointed times, just as Mor'de·cai the Jew and Esther the queen had imposed upon them, and just as they had imposed upon their own soul and upon their offspring, the matters of the fasts and their cry for aid. 32 And the very saying of Esther confirmed these matters of Pu'rim, and it was written down in a book.

10 And King A·has·u·e'rus proceeded to lay forced labor upon the land and the isles of the sea. 2 As for all his energetic work and his mightiness and the exact statement of Mor'de·cai's greatness with which the king magnified him, are they not written in the Book of the affairs of the times of the kings of Me'di·a and Persia? 3 For Mor'de·cai the Jew was second to King A·has·u·e'rus and was great among the Jews and approved by the multitude of his brothers, working for the good of his people and speaking peace to all their offspring.

JOB

1 There happened to be a man in the land of Uz whose name was Job; and that man proved to be blameless and upright, and fearing God and turning aside from bad. 2 And seven sons and three daughters came to be born to him. 3 And his livestock got to be seven thousand sheep and three thousand camels and five hundred spans of cattle and five hundred she-asses, along with a very large body of servants; and that man came to be the greatest of all the Orientals. 4 And his sons went and held a banquet at the house of each one on his own day; and they sent and invited their three sisters to eat and drink with them. 5 And it would occur that when the banquet days had gone round the circuit, Job would send and sanctify them; and he got up early in the morning and offered up burnt sacrifices according to the number of all of them; for, said Job, "maybe my sons have sinned and have cursed God in their heart." That is the way Job would do always.

6 Now it came to be the day when the sons of the [true] God entered to take their station before Jehovah, and even Satan proceeded to enter right among them.

7 Then Jehovah said to Satan: "Where do you come from?" At that Satan answered Jehovah and said: "From roving about in the earth and from walking about in it." 8 And Jehovah went on to say to Satan: "Have you set your heart upon my servant Job, that there is no one like him in the earth, a man blameless and upright, fearing God and turning aside from bad?" 9 At that Satan answered Jehovah and said: "Is it for nothing that Job has feared God? 10 Have not you yourself put up a hedge about him and about his house and about everything that he has all around? The work of his hands you have blessed, and his livestock itself has spread abroad in the earth. 11 But, for a change, thrust out your hand, please, and touch everything he has [and see] whether he will not curse you to your very face." 12 Accordingly Jehovah said to Satan: "Look! Everything that he has is in your hand. Only against him himself do not thrust out your hand!" So Satan went out away from the person of Jehovah.

13 Now it came to be the day when his sons and his daughters were eating and drinking wine in the house of their brother the first-born. 14 And there came a messenger to Job, and he proceeded to say: "The cattle themselves happened to be plowing and the she-asses were grazing at the side of them 15 when the Sa·be'ans came making a raid and taking them, and the attendants they struck down with the edge of the sword; and I got to escape, only I by myself, to tell you."

16 While this one was yet speaking that one came and proceeded to say: "The very fire of God fell from the heavens and went blazing among the sheep and the attendants and eating them up; and I got to escape, only I by myself, to tell you."

17 While that one was yet speaking another one came and proceeded to say: "The Chal·de'ans made up three bands and went dashing against the camels and taking them, and the attendants they struck down with the edge of the sword; and I got to escape, only I by myself, to tell you."

18 While this other one was yet speaking, still another one came and proceeded to say: "Your sons and your daughters were eating and drinking wine in the house of their brother the first-born. 19 And, look! there came a great wind from the region of the wilderness, and it went striking the four corners of the house, so that it fell upon the young people and they died. And I got to escape, only I by myself, to tell you."

20 And Job proceeded to get up and rip his sleeveless coat apart and cut the hair off his head and fall to the earth and bow down 21 and say:

"Naked I came out of my mother's belly,
  And naked shall I return there.
Jehovah himself has given, and Jehovah himself has taken away.
  Let the name of Jehovah continue to be blessed."

22 In all this Job did not sin or ascribe anything improper to God.

2 Afterward it came to be the day when the sons of the [true] God entered to take their station before Jehovah, and Satan also proceeded to enter right among them to take his station before Jehovah.

2 Then Jehovah said to Satan: "Just where do you come from?" At that Satan answered Jehovah and said: "From roving about in the earth and from walking about in it." 3 And Jehovah went on

to say to Satan: "Have you set your heart upon my servant Job, that there is no one like him in the earth, a man blameless and upright, fearing God and turning aside from bad? Even yet he is holding fast his integrity, although you incite me against him to swallow him up without cause." 4 But Satan answered Jehovah and said: "Skin in behalf of skin, and everything that a man has he will give in behalf of his soul. 5 For a change, thrust out your hand, please, and touch as far as his bone and his flesh [and see] whether he will not curse you to your very face."

6 Accordingly Jehovah said to Satan: "There he is in your hand! Only watch out for his soul itself!" 7 So Satan went out away from the person of Jehovah and struck Job with a malignant boil from the sole of his foot to the crown of his head. 8 And he proceeded to take for himself a fragment of earthenware with which to scrape himself; and he was sitting in among the ashes.

9 Finally his wife said to him: "Are you yet holding fast your integrity? Curse God and die!" 10 But he said to her: "As one of the senseless women speaks, you speak also. Shall we accept merely what is good from the [true] God and not accept also what is bad?" In all this Job did not sin with his lips.

11 And three companions of Job got to hear of all this calamity that had come upon him, and they proceeded to come, each one from his own place, El′i·phaz the Te′man·ite and Bil′dad the Shu′hite and Zo′phar the Na′a·ma·thite. So they met together by appointment to come and sympathize with him and comfort him. 12 When they raised their eyes from far off they did not then recognize him. And they proceeded to raise their voice and weep and rip each one his sleeveless coat apart and toss dust toward the heavens upon their heads. 13 And they kept sitting with him on the earth seven days

and seven nights, and there was no one speaking a word to him, for they saw that the pain was very great.

3 It was after this that Job opened his mouth and began to call down evil upon his day. 2 Job now answered and said:

3 "Let the day perish on which I
       came to be born,
    Also the night that someone
       said, 'An able-bodied man
       has been conceived!'
4 As for that day, let it become
       darkness.
    Let not God look for it from
       above,
    Nor let daylight beam upon it.
5 Let darkness and deep shadow
       reclaim it.
    Let a rain cloud reside over it.
    Let the things that darken a
       day terrorize it.
6 That night—let gloom take it;
    Let it not feel glad among the
       days of a year;
    Among the number of the
       lunar months let it not
       enter.
7 Look! That night—let it become
       sterile;
    Let no joyful cry come in it.
8 Let curses of the day execrate it,
    Those ready to awaken Le-
       vi′a·than.
9 Let the stars of its twilight
       grow dark;
    Let it wait for the light and
       there be none;
    And let it not see the beams
       of dawn.
10 For it did not close the doors
       of my mother's belly,
    And so conceal trouble from
       my eyes.
11 Why from the womb did I not
       proceed to die?
    [Why did I not] come forth
       from the belly itself and
       then expire?
12 Why was it that knees con-
       fronted me,
    And why breasts that I should
       take suck?
13 For by now I should have lain
       down that I might be un-
       disturbed;

I should have slept then; I should be at rest

14 With kings and counselors of the earth,
Those building desolate places for themselves,

15 Or with princes who have gold, Those who fill their houses with silver;

16 Or, like a hidden miscarriage, I should not come to be, Like children that have seen no light.

17 There the wicked themselves have ceased from agitation, And there those weary in power are at rest.

18 Together prisoners themselves are at ease; They actually do not hear the voice of one driving them to work.

19 Small and great are there the same, And the slave is set free from his master.

20 Why does he give light to one having trouble, And life to those bitter of soul?

21 Why are there those waiting for death, and it is not, Although they keep digging for it more than for hidden treasures?

22 Those who are rejoicing to glee-fulness, They exult because they find a burial place.

23 [Why does he give light] to able-bodied man, whose way has been concealed, And whom God hedges in?

24 For before my food my sighing comes, And like waters my roaring cries pour forth;

25 Because a dreadful thing I have dreaded, and it comes upon me; And what I have been scared of comes to me.

26 I have not been carefree, nor have I been undisturbed, Nor been at rest, and yet agitation comes."

4 And El'i·phaz the Te'man·ite proceeded to reply and say:

2 "If one does try out a word to you, will you become weary? But to put a restraint on words who is able?

3 Look! You have corrected many, And the weak hands you used to strengthen.

4 Anyone stumbling, your words would raise up; And knees giving way you would make firm.

5 But this time it comes to you, and you become weary; It touches even you, and you get disturbed.

6 Is not your reverence [the basis of] your confidence? Is not your hope even the integrity of your ways?

7 Remember, please: Who that is innocent has ever perished? And where have the upright ever been effaced?

8 According to what I have seen, those devising what is hurtful And those sowing trouble will themselves reap it.

9 Through the breath of God they perish, And through the spirit of his anger they come to an end.

10 There is the roaring of a lion, and the voice of a young lion, But the teeth of maned young lions do get broken down.

11 A lion is perishing from there being no prey, And the cubs of a lion are separated from one another.

12 Now to me a word was stealthily brought, And my ear proceeded to get a whisper of it,

13 In disquieting thoughts from visions of the night, When deep sleep falls upon men.

14 A dread came over me, and a trembling, And the multitude of my bones it filled with dread.

15 And a spirit itself went passing over my face; The hair of my flesh began to bristle.

16 It began to stand still,
   But I did not recognize its
      appearance;
   A form was in front of my eyes;
   There was a calm, and I now
      heard a voice:
17 'Mortal man—can he be more
      just than God himself?
   Or can able-bodied man
      be cleaner than his own
      Maker?'
18 Look! In his servants he has no
      faith,
   And his messengers he charges
      with faultiness.
19 How much more so with those
      dwelling in houses of clay,
   Whose foundation is in the
      dust!
   One crushes them more quickly
      than a moth.
20 From morning to evening they
      are crushed to pieces;
   Without anyone's taking [it to
      heart] they perish forever.
21 Has not their tent cord within
      them been pulled out?
   They die for lack of wisdom.

5 "Call, please! Is there anyone
      answering you?
   And to which one of the holy
      ones will you turn?
2 For the foolish one vexation
      will kill,
   And the one easily enticed
      envying will put to death.
3 I myself have seen the foolish
      one taking root,
   But suddenly I began to exe-
      crate his abiding place.
4 His sons remain far from sal-
      vation,
   And they are crushed in the
      gate without a deliverer.
5 What he harvests the hungry
      one eats;
   And even from butcher hooks
      one takes it,
   And a snare actually snaps
      at their means of main-
      tenance.
6 For not from mere dust does
      what is hurtful go forth,
   And from mere ground trouble
      does not spring up.
7 For man himself is born for
      trouble,
   As the very sparks fly upward.

8 However, I myself would apply
      to God,
   And to God I would submit
      my cause,
9 [To the] One doing great things
      unsearchable,
   Wonderful things without
      number;
10 [To] the One giving rain upon
      the surface of the earth
   And sending waters upon the
      open fields;
11 [To] the One putting those who
      are low on a high place,
   So that those who are sad are
      high up in salvation;
12 [To the] One frustrating the
      schemes of the shrewd,
   So that their hands do not
      work with effect;
13 [To the] One catching the wise
      in their own cunning,
   So that the counsel of astute
      ones is carried headlong;
14 They encounter darkness even
      by day,
   And they grope about at mid-
      day as if at night;
15 And [to the] One saving
      from the sword out of their
      mouth,
   And from the hand of the
      strong one, a poor one,
16 So that for the lowly one there
      comes to be hope,
   But unrighteousness actually
      shuts its mouth.
17 Look! Happy is the man whom
      God reproves;
   And the discipline of the
      Almighty do not you reject!
18 For he himself causes pain, but
      binds up [the wound];
   He breaks to pieces, but his
      own hands do the healing.
19 In six distresses he will deliver
      you,
   And in seven nothing inju-
      rious will touch you.
20 During famine he will certainly
      redeem you from death,
   And during war from the
      power of a sword.
21 From the whip of a tongue you
      will be hidden,
   And you will not be afraid of
      despoiling when it comes.

22 At despoiling and hunger you
will laugh,
And of the wild beast of
the earth you need not be
afraid.

23 For with the stones of the field
your covenant will be,
And the wild beast of the
field himself will be made
to live at peace with you.

24 And you will certainly know that
peace itself is your tent,
And you will be bound to go
and see your pasture ground,
and you will miss nothing.

25 And you will certainly know
that your offspring are many
And your descendants like the
vegetation of the earth.

26 You will come in vigor to the
burial place,
As when sheaves pile up in
their time.

27 Look! This is what we have
investigated. So is it.
Hear it, and you—know it
for yourself."

6 And Job proceeded to answer
and say:

2 "O that my vexation were altogether weighed,
And that at the same time
my adversity they would
put on scales themselves!

3 For now it is heavier even than
the sands of the seas.
That is why my own words
have been wild talk.

4 For the arrows of the Almighty
are with me,
The venom of which my spirit
is drinking;
The terrors from God range
themselves up against me.

5 Will a zebra cry out over grass,
Or a bull low over its fodder?

6 Will tasteless things be eaten
without salt,
Or is there any taste in the
slimy juice of marsh mallow?

7 My soul has refused to touch
[anything].
They are like disease in my
food.

8 O that my request would come
And that God would grant
even my hope!

9 And that God would go ahead
and crush me,
That he would release his
hand and cut me off!

10 Even it would still be my comfort;
And I should leap [for joy]
at [my] labor pains,
[Though] he would have no
compassion, for I have not
hidden the sayings of the
Holy One.

11 What is my power, that I should
keep waiting?
And what is my end, that I
should keep prolonging my
soul?

12 Is my power the power of stones?
Or is my flesh of copper?

13 Is it that self-assistance is not
in me,
And effectual working itself
has been chased away from
me?

14 As regards anyone who with-
holds loving-kindness from
his own fellow,
He will also leave off even
the fear of the Almighty.

15 My own brothers have dealt
treacherously, like a winter
torrent,
Like the channel of winter
torrents that keep passing
away.

16 They are dark from ice,
Upon them snow hides itself.

17 In due season they become
waterless, they have been
silenced;
When it grows hot they are
dried up from their place.

18 The paths of their way are
turned aside;
They go up into the empty
place and perish.

19 The caravans of Te′ma have
looked,
The traveling company of
Sa·be′ans have waited for
them.

20 They certainly are ashamed because they had trusted;
They have come clear to the
place and they get disap-
pointed.

21 For now you men have
amounted to nothing;

You see terror, and YOU become afraid.

22 Is it because I have said, 'GIVE me [something],
Or from some of the power of YOU men make a present in my behalf;

23 And rescue me out of the hand of an adversary,
And out of the hand of tyrants YOU men should redeem me'?

24 Instruct me, and I, for my part, shall be silent;
And what mistake I have committed make me understand.

25 The sayings of uprightness have been—O not painful!
But what does reproving on the part of YOU men reprove?

26 Is it to reprove words that YOU men scheme,
When the sayings of one in despair are for mere wind?

27 How much more will YOU cast lots even over someone fatherless,
And barter over YOUR companion!

28 And now GO ahead, pay attention to me,
[And see] whether I shall lie to YOUR very faces.

29 Return, please—let no unrighteousness arise—
Yes, return—my righteousness is yet in it.

30 Is there unrighteousness on my tongue,
Or does my own palate not discern adversity?

7 "Is there not a compulsory labor for mortal man on earth,
And are not his days like the days of a hired laborer?

2 Like a slave he pants for the shadow,
And like a hired laborer he waits for his wages.

3 Thus I have been made to possess worthless lunar months,
And nights of trouble they have counted out to me.

4 When I have lain down I have also said, 'When shall I get up?'

And [when] evening actually goes its measure, I have also been glutted with restlessness until morning twilight.

5 My flesh has become clothed with maggots and lumps of dust;
My skin itself has formed crusts and dissolves.

6 My days themselves have become swifter than a weaver's shuttle,
And they come to an end in hopelessness.

7 Remember that my life is wind;
That my eye will not see good again.

8 The eye of him that sees me will not behold me;
Your eyes will be upon me, but I shall not be.

9 The cloud certainly comes to its end and goes away;
So he that is going down to She'ol will not come up.

10 He will not return any more to his house,
And his place will not acknowledge him any more.

11 I, also, I shall not hold back my mouth.
I will speak in the distress of my spirit;
I will be concerned with the bitterness of my soul!

12 Am I a sea or a sea monster,
That you should set a guard over me?

13 When I said, 'My divan will comfort me,
My bed will help carry my concern,'

14 You even have terrified me with dreams,
And by visions you make me start up in fright,

15 So that my soul chooses suffocation,
Death rather than my bones.

16 I have rejected [it]; to time indefinite I would not live.
Cease from me, for my days are an exhalation.

17 What is mortal man that you should rear him,
And that you should set YOUR heart upon him,

18 And that you should pay attention to him every morning,
That every moment you should test him?
19 Why will you not turn your gaze from me,
Nor let me alone until I swallow my saliva?
20 If I have sinned, what can I accomplish against you, the Observer of mankind?
Why is it that you have set me as your target, so that I should become a burden to you?
21 And why do you not pardon my transgression
And overlook my error?
For now in dust I shall lie down;
And you will certainly look for me, and I shall not be."

8 And Bil'dad the Shu'hite proceeded to answer and say:
2 "How long will you keep uttering these things,
When the sayings of your mouth are but a powerful wind?
3 Will God himself pervert judgment,
Or will the Almighty himself pervert righteousness?
4 If your own sons have sinned against him,
So that he lets them go into the hand of their revolt,
5 If you yourself will look for God,
And [if] of the Almighty you will implore favor,
6 If you are pure and upright,
By now he would awake for you
And he would certainly restore your righteous abiding place.
7 Also, your beginning may have proved to be a small thing,
But your own end afterward would grow very great.
8 Indeed, ask, please, of the former generation,
And direct [your attention] to the things searched out by their fathers.
9 For we were only yesterday, and we know nothing,
Because our days on earth are a shadow.
10 Will not they themselves instruct you, tell you,
And from their heart will they not bring forth words?
11 Will a papyrus plant grow tall without a swampy place?
Will a reed grow big without water?
12 While it is yet in its bud, not plucked off,
Even ahead of all other grass it will dry up.
13 Thus are the pathways of all those forgetting God,
And the very hope of an apostate will perish,
14 Whose confidence is cut off,
And whose trust is a spider's house.
15 He will lean upon his house, but it will not keep standing;
He will take hold of it, but it will not last.
16 He is full of sap before the sun,
And in his garden his own twig goes forth.
17 In a stone heap his roots become interwoven,
A house of stones he beholds.
18 If one swallows him up from his place,
It will also certainly deny him, [saying,] 'I have not seen you.'
19 Look! That is the dissolving of his way;
And from the dust others spring up.
20 Look! God himself will not reject anyone blameless,
Neither will he take hold of the hand of evildoers,
21 Until he fills your mouth with laughter,
And your lips with joyful shouting.
22 The very ones hating you will be clothed with shame,
And the tent of wicked ones will not be."

9 And Job proceeded to answer and say:
2 "For a fact I do know that it is so.

But how can mortal man be in the right in a case with God?

3 If he should find delight in contending with him,
He cannot answer him once out of a thousand.

4 He is wise in heart and strong in power.
Who can show stubbornness to him and come off un-injured?

5 He is moving mountains away, so that people do not even know [of them],
He who has overthrown them in his anger.

6 He is making the earth go quaking from its place,
So that its very pillars shudder.

7 He is saying to the sun that it should not shine forth,
And around stars he puts a seal,

8 Stretching out the heavens by himself
And treading upon the high waves of the sea;

9 Making the Ash constellation, the Ke′sil constellation,
And the Ki′mah constellation and the interior rooms of the South;

10 Doing great things unsearchable, And wonderful things without number.

11 Look! He passes by me and I do not see [him],
And he moves on and I do not discern him.

12 Look! He snatches away. Who can resist him?
Who will say to him, 'What are you doing?'

13 God himself will not turn back his anger;
Beneath him the helpers of a stormer must bow down.

14 How much more so in case I myself answer him!
I will choose my words with him,

15 Whom I would not answer, even though I were really in the right.
Of my opponent-at-law I would implore favor.

16 If I called him, would he answer me?
I do not believe that he would give ear to my voice;

17 Who with a storm bruises me And certainly makes my wounds many for no reason.

18 He will not grant me my taking of a fresh breath,
For he keeps glutting me with bitter things.

19 If in power anyone is strong, there [he is];
And if in justice [anyone is strong], O that I may be summoned!

20 If I were in the right, my own mouth would pronounce me wicked;
Were I blameless, then he would declare me crooked.

21 Were I blameless, I would not know my soul;
I would refuse my life.

22 One thing there is. That is why I do say,
'One blameless, also a wicked one, he is bringing to their end.'

23 If a flash flood itself should cause death suddenly,
At the very despair of the innocent ones he would mock.

24 Earth itself has been given into the hand of the wicked one;
The face of its judges he covers.
If not, who, then, is it?

25 Also my own days have become swifter than a runner;
They have run away, they will certainly not see good.

26 They have moved on like reed boats,
Like an eagle that darts to and fro for something to eat.

27 If I have said, 'Let me forget my concern,
Let me alter my countenance and brighten up,'

28 I have been scared of all my pains;
I do know that you will not hold me innocent.

29 I myself am to become wicked. Why is it that I toil merely in vain?

30 If I actually washed myself in snow water,
And I actually cleansed my hands in potash,
31 Then in a pit you would dip me,
And my garments would certainly detest me.
32 For he is not a man like me [that] I should answer him,
That we should come together in judgment.
33 There exists no person to decide between us,
That he should put his hand upon both of us.
34 Let him remove his rod from upon me,
And his frightfulness, let it not terrify me.
35 Let me speak and not be afraid of him,
For I am not so disposed in myself.

10 "My soul certainly feels a loathing toward my life.
I will give vent to my concern about myself.
I will speak in the bitterness of my soul!
2 I shall say to God, 'Do not pronounce me wicked.
Cause me to know why it is that you are contending with me.
3 Is it good for you that you should do wrong,
That you should reject [the product of] the hard work of your hands,
And that upon the counsel of wicked ones you should actually beam?
4 Do you have eyes of flesh,
Or is it as a mortal man sees that you see?
5 Are your days like the days of mortal man,
Or your years just like the days of an able-bodied man,
6 That you should try to find my error
And for my sin you should keep looking?
7 This in spite of your own knowledge that I am not in the wrong,
And there is no one delivering out of your own hand?

8 Your own hands have shaped me so that they made me
In entirety round about, and yet you would swallow me up.
9 Remember, please, that out of clay you have made me
And to dust you will make me return.
10 Did you not proceed to pour me out as milk itself
And like cheese to curdle me?
11 With skin and flesh you proceeded to clothe me
And with bones and sinews to weave me together.
12 Life and loving-kindness you have worked with me;
And your own care has guarded my spirit.
13 And these things you have concealed in your heart.
I well know that these things are with you.
14 If I have sinned and you have kept watching me
And of my error you do not hold me innocent.
15 If I am actually in the wrong, too bad for me!
And [if] I am actually in the right, I may not raise my head,
Glutted with dishonor and saturated with affliction.
16 And [if] it acts haughtily, like a young lion you will hunt for me,
And you will again show yourself marvelous in my case.
17 You will bring forth new witnesses of yours in front of me,
And you will make your vexation with me greater;
Hardship after hardship is with me.
18 So why from a womb did you bring me out?
Could I have expired, that not even an eye could see me,
19 There as though I had not come to be I should have become;
From the belly to the burial place I should have been brought.'
20 Are not my days few? Let him leave off,

Let him turn his gaze from
me, that I may brighten
up a little
21 Before I go away—and I shall
not come back—
To the land of darkness and
deep shadow,
22 To the land of obscurity like
gloom, of deep shadow
And disorder, where it beams
no more than gloom does."

11 And Zo'phar the Na'a·ma-
thite proceeded to answer and
say:
2 "Will a multitude of words go
unanswered,
Or will a mere boaster be in
the right?
3 Will your empty talk itself put
men to silence,
And will you keep deriding
without having anyone re-
buke [you]?
4 Also, you say, 'My instruction
is pure,
And I have proved really clean
in your eyes.'
5 Yet O if only God himself
would speak
And open his lips with you!
6 Then he would tell you the
secrets of wisdom,
For the things of practical
wisdom are manifold.
Also, you would know that
God allows some of your
error to be forgotten for
you.
7 Can you find out the deep
things of God,
Or can you find out to the
very limit of the Almighty?
8 It is higher than heaven. What
can you accomplish?
It is deeper than She'ol. What
can you know?
9 It is longer than the earth in
measure,
And broader than the sea.
10 If he moves on and hands
[someone] over
And calls a court, then who
can resist him?
11 For he himself well knows men
who are untrue.
When he sees what is hurtful,
will he not also show himself attentive?

12 Even a hollow-minded man
himself will get good motive
As soon as an asinine zebra
be born a man.
13 If you yourself will really prepare your heart
And actually spread out your
palms to him,
14 If what is hurtful is in your
hand, put it far away,
And let no unrighteousness
dwell in your tents.
15 For then you will raise your
face without defect
And you will certainly become
established, and you will
not fear.
16 For you—you will forget trouble
itself;
As waters that have passed
along you will remember
[it].
17 And brighter than midday will
[your] life's duration arise;
Darkness will become like the
morning itself.
18 And you will be bound to trust
because there exists hope;
And you will certainly look
carefully around—in secu-
rity you will lie down.
19 And you will indeed stretch
yourself out, with no one to
make [you] tremble.
And many people will certainly
put you in a gentle mood;
20 And the very eyes of the wicked
will fail;
And a place for flight will
certainly perish from them,
And their hope will be an
expiring of the soul."

12 And Job proceeded to answer
and say:
2 "For a fact you men are the
people,
And with you wisdom will
die out!
3 I too have a heart as well as
you.
I am not inferior to you,
And with whom are there not
things like these?
4 [One who is] a laughingstock
to his fellow man I become,
One calling to God that he
should answer him.

A laughingstock is the righteous, unblamable one.
5 In thought, the carefree one
has contempt for extinction
itself;
It is made ready for those of
wobbling feet.
6 The tents of the despoilers are
unworried,
And the ones enraging God
have the safety
Belonging to one who has
brought a god in his hand.
7 However, ask, please, the domestic animals, and they
will instruct you;
Also the winged creatures
of the heavens, and they
will tell you.
8 Or show your concern to the
earth, and it will instruct
you;
And the fishes of the sea will
declare it to you.
9 Who among all these does not
well know
That the hand of Jehovah
itself has done this,
10 In whose hand is the soul of
everyone alive
And the spirit of all flesh of
man?
11 Does not the ear itself test out
words
As the palate tastes food?
12 Is there not wisdom among the
aged
And understanding [in] length
of days?
13 With him there are wisdom and
mightiness;
He has counsel and under-
standing.
14 Look! He tears down, that there
may be no building up;
He makes it shut to man,
that it may not be opened
up.
15 Look! He puts a restraint upon
the waters and they dry up;
And he sends them, and they
change the earth.
16 With him there are strength and
practical wisdom;
To him belong the one making
a mistake and the one leading astray;

17 He is making counselors go
barefoot,
And he makes judges them-
selves go crazy.
18 The bonds of kings he actually
loosens,
And he binds a belt upon
their hips.
19 He is making priests walk barefoot,
And permanently seated ones
he subverts;
20 He is removing speech from the
faithful ones,
And the sensibleness of old
men he takes away;
21 He is pouring out contempt upon
nobles,
And the girdle of powerful
ones he actually weakens;
22 He is uncovering deep things
from the darkness,
And he brings forth to the
light deep shadow;
23 Making the nations grow great,
that he may destroy them;
Spreading out the nations,
that he may lead them
away;
24 Taking away the heart of the
head ones of the people of
the land,
That he may make them
wander about in an empty
place, where there is no way.
25 They grope in darkness, where
there is no light,
That he may make them
wander about like a drunken
man.

13 "Look! All this my eye has
seen,
My ear has heard and con-
siders it.
2 What you men know I myself
well know also;
I am not inferior to you.
3 However, I, for my part, would
speak to the Almighty himself,
And in arguing with God I
would find delight.
4 On the other hand, you men
are smearers of falsehood;
All of you are physicians of
no value.
5 If only you would absolutely
keep silent,

That it might prove to be
wisdom on YOUR part!
6 Hear, please, my counterarguments,
And to the pleadings of my
lips pay attention.
7 Will YOU men speak unrighteousness for God himself,
And for him will YOU speak
deceit?
8 Will YOU be treating him with
partiality,
Or for the [true] God will
YOU contend at law?
9 Would it be good that he sound
YOU out?
Or as one trifles with mortal
man will YOU trifle with
him?
10 He will positively reprove YOU
If in secrecy YOU try to show
partiality,
11 Will not his very dignity make
YOU start up with fright,
And the very dread of him
fall upon YOU?
12 YOUR memorable sayings are
proverbs of ashes;
YOUR shield bosses are as
shield bosses of clay.
13 KEEP silent before me, that I
myself may speak.
Then let come upon me whatever it may be!
14 Why do I carry my flesh in my
teeth
And place my own soul in my
palm?
15 Even if he would slay me, would
I not wait?
I would only argue to his face
for my own ways.
16 He would also be my salvation,
For before him no apostate
will come in.
17 HEAR my word clear through,
And let my declaration be in
YOUR ears.
18 Look! Please, I have presented
a case of justice;
I well know that I myself am
in the right.
19 Who is the one that will contend with me?
For now were I to become
silent I should simply expire!
20 Only two things do not do to
me;

In that case I shall not conceal myself just on your
account;
21 Put your own hand far away
from upon me,
And the fright of you—may
it not terrify me.
22 Either call that I myself may
answer;
Or may I speak, and you
return me answer.
23 In what way do I have errors
and sins?
Make me to know my own
revolt and my own sin.
24 Why do you conceal your very
face
And regard me as an enemy
of yours?
25 Will you make a mere leaf driven
about quiver,
Or keep chasing after mere
dry stubble?
26 For you keep writing against me
bitter things
And you make me possess [the
consequences of] the errors
of my youth.
27 You also keep my feet put in
the stocks,
And you watch all my paths;
For the soles of my feet you
mark your own line.
28 And he is like something rotten
that wears out;
Like a garment that a moth
actually eats up.

14 "Man, born of woman,
Is short-lived and glutted
with agitation.
2 Like a blossom he has come
forth and is cut off,
And he runs away like the
shadow and does not keep
existing.
3 Yes, upon this one you have
opened your eye,
And me you bring into judgment with you.
4 Who can produce someone clean
out of someone unclean?
There is not one.
5 If his days are decided,
The number of his months is
with you;
A decree for him you have
made that he may not go
beyond.

6 Turn your gaze from upon him
    that he may have rest,
  Until he finds pleasure as a
    hired laborer does in his day.
7 For there exists hope for even
    a tree.
  If it gets cut down, it will
    even sprout again,
  And its own twig will not
    cease to be.
8 If its root grows old in the earth
  And in the dust its stump dies,
9 At the scent of water it will
    sprout
  And it will certainly produce
    a bough like a new plant.
10 But an able-bodied man dies
    and lies vanquished;
  And an earthling man expires,
    and where is he?
11 Waters do disappear from a sea,
  And a river itself drains off
    and dries up.
12 Man also has to lie down and
    does not get up.
  Until heaven is no more they
    will not wake up,
  Nor will they be aroused from
    their sleep.
13 O that in She'ol you would
    conceal me,
  That you would keep me
    secret until your anger
    turns back,
  That you would set a time
    limit for me and remember
    me!
14 If an able-bodied man dies can
    he live again?
  All the days of my compulsory
    service I shall wait,
  Until my relief comes.
15 You will call, and I myself shall
    answer you.
  For the work of your hands
    you will have a yearning.
16 For now you keep counting my
    very steps;
  You watch for nothing but
    my sin.
17 Sealed up in a bag is my revolt,
  And you apply glue over my
    error.
18 However, a mountain itself, fall-
    ing, will fade away,
  And even a rock will be moved
    away from its place.

19 Water certainly rubs away even
    stones;
  Its outpouring washes off
    earth's dust.
  So you have destroyed the
    very hope of mortal man.
20 You overpower him forever so
    that he goes away;
  You are disfiguring his face
    so that you send him away.
21 His sons get honored, but he
    does not know [it];
  And they become insignificant,
    but he does not consider
    them.
22 Only his own flesh while upon
    him will keep aching,
  And his own soul while within
    him will keep mourning."

15 And El'i·phaz the Te'man·ite
    proceeded to answer and say:
2 "Will a wise person himself
    answer with windy knowl-
    edge,
  Or will he fill his belly with
    the east wind?
3 Merely reproving with a word
    will be of no use,
  And mere utterances will be of
    no benefit by themselves.
4 However, you yourself make
    fear [before God] to have
    no force,
  And you diminish the having
    of any concern before God.
5 For your error trains your
    mouth,
  And you choose the tongue of
    shrewd people.
6 Your mouth pronounces you
    wicked, and not I;
  And your own lips answer
    against you.
7 Were you the very first man to
    be born,
  Or before the hills were you
    brought forth with labor
    pains?
8 To the confidential talk of God
    do you listen,
  And do you limit wisdom to
    yourself?
9 What do you actually know that
    we do not know?
  What do you understand that
    is not also with us?
10 Both the gray-headed and the
    aged one are with us,

The one greater than your father in days.

11 Are the consolations of God not enough for you,
Or a word [spoken] gently with you?

12 Why does your heart carry you away,
And why do your eyes flash?

13 For you turn your spirit against God himself,
And you have caused words to go forth from your own mouth.

14 What is mortal man that he should be clean,
Or that anyone born of a woman should be in the right?

15 Look! In his holy ones he has no faith,
And the heavens themselves are actually not clean in his eyes.

16 How much less so when one is detestable and corrupt,
A man who is drinking in unrighteousness just like water!

17 I shall declare it to you. Listen to me!
Even this I have beheld, so let me relate [it],

18 That which wise ones themselves tell
And which they did not hide, [it being] from their fathers.

19 To them alone the land was given,
And no stranger passed through the midst of them.

20 All his days a wicked one is suffering torture,
Even the very number of years that have been reserved for the tyrant.

21 The sound of dreadful things is in his ears;
During peace a despoiler himself comes upon him.

22 He does not believe that he will come back out of darkness,
And he is reserved for a sword.

23 He is straying about in search of bread—where is it?

He well knows that the day of darkness is ready at his hand.

24 Distress and anguish keep terrifying him;
They overpower him like a king in readiness for the assault.

25 Because he stretches out his hand against God himself,
And over the Almighty he tries to show himself superior;

26 [Because] he runs against him stiff-neckedly,
With the thick bosses of his shields;

27 Because he actually covers his face with his fattiness
And he puts on fat upon his loins,

28 He merely resides in cities that are to be effaced;
In houses in which people will not keep dwelling,
Which certainly prove destined for heaps of stones.

29 He will not grow rich and his wealth will not mount up,
Nor will he spread out the acquisition of them over the earth.

30 He will not turn away from darkness;
His twig a flame will dry up,
And he will turn aside by a blast of His mouth.

31 Let him put no faith in worthlessness, being led astray,
For mere worthlessness will prove to be what he gets in exchange;

32 Before his day will it be fulfilled.
And his shoot itself will certainly not grow luxuriantly.

33 He will thrust away his unripe grapes just like a vine,
And cast off his blossoms just like an olive tree.

34 For the assembly of apostates is sterile,
And fire itself must eat up the tents of bribery.

35 There is a conceiving of trouble and a giving birth to what is hurtful,
And their belly itself prepares deceit."

16 And Job proceeded to answer and say:

2 "I have heard many things like these.
All of YOU are troublesome comforters!

3 Is there an end to windy words?
Or what galls you, that you answer?

4 I myself also could well speak as YOU men do.
If only YOUR souls existed where my soul is,
Would I be brilliant in words against YOU,
And would I wag my head against YOU?

5 I would strengthen YOU with the words of my mouth,
And the consolation of my own lips would hold back—.

6 If I do speak, my own pain is not held back,
And if I do cease doing so, what goes away from me?

7 Only now he has made me weary;
He has made all those assembling with me desolate.

8 You also seize me. It has become a witness,
So that my leanness rises up against me. In my face it testifies.

9 His very anger has torn me to pieces, and he harbors animosity against me.
He actually grinds his teeth against me.
My adversary himself sharpens his eyes against me.

10 They have opened their mouth wide against me,
With reproach they have struck my cheeks,
In large number they mass themselves against me.

11 God hands me over to young boys,
And into the hands of wicked ones he throws me headlong.

12 I had come to be at ease, but he proceeded to shake me up;
And he grabbed me by the back of the neck and proceeded to smash me,
And he sets me up as a target for himself.

13 His archers encircle me;
He splits open my kidneys and feels no compassion;
He pours out my gall bladder to the very earth.

14 He keeps breaking through me with breach after breach;
He runs at me like a mighty one.

15 Sackcloth I have sewed together over my skin,
And I have thrust my horn in the very dust.

16 My face itself has become reddened from weeping,
And upon my eyelids there is deep shadow,

17 Although there is no violence upon my palms,
And my prayer is pure.

18 O earth, do not cover my blood!
And let there prove to be no place for my outcry!

19 Also now, look! in the heavens is one testifying about me,
And my witness is in the heights.

20 My companions are spokesmen against me;
To God my eye has looked sleeplessly.

21 And the decision is to be made between an able-bodied man and God,
The same as between a son of man and his fellow.

22 For just a few years are to come,
And by the path by which I shall not return I shall go away.

17 "My very spirit has been broken, my own days have been extinguished;
The graveyard is for me.

2 Certainly there is mockery at me,
And amid their rebellious behavior my eye lodges.

3 Please, do put my security with yourself.
Who else is there that will shake hands with me in pledge?

4 For their heart you have closed to discretion,

That is why you do not exalt them.

5 He may tell companions to take their shares,
But the very eyes of his sons will fail.

6 And he has set me forth as a proverbial saying of peoples,
So that I become someone into whose face to spit.

7 And from vexation my eye grows dimmer
And my members are all of them like the shadow.

8 Upright people stare in amazement at this,
And even the innocent one gets excited over the apostate.

9 The righteous one keeps holding fast to his way,
And the one with clean hands keeps increasing in strength.

10 However, YOU men may all of YOU resume. So come on, please,
As I do not find anyone wise among YOU.

11 My own days have passed along, my own plans have been torn apart,
The wishes of my heart.

12 Night they keep putting for day: 'Light is near on account of darkness.'

13 If I keep waiting, She'ol is my house;
In the darkness I shall have to spread out my lounge.

14 To the pit I shall have to call out, 'You are my father!'
To the maggot, 'My mother and my sister!'

15 So where, then, is my hope?
And my hope—who is it that beholds it?

16 To the bars of She'ol they will go down,
When we, all together, must descend to the very dust.''

18 And Bil'dad the Shu'hite proceeded to answer and say:

2 "How long will YOU people be at putting an end to words?
YOU should understand, that afterward we may speak.

3 Why should we be reckoned as beasts

[And] be regarded as unclean in YOUR eyes?

4 He is tearing his soul to pieces in his anger.
For your sake will the earth be abandoned,
Or a rock move away from its place?

5 The light also of wicked ones will be extinguished
And the spark of his fire will not shine.

6 A light itself will certainly grow dark in his tent,
And in it his own lamp will be extinguished.

7 His steps of vigor will become cramped.
Even his counsel will cast him off.

8 For he will indeed be let go into a net by his feet,
And onto a network he will walk.

9 A trap will seize [him] by the heel;
A snare keeps hold upon him.

10 A cord for him is hidden on the earth,
And a catching device for him on [his] pathway.

11 Round about, sudden terrors certainly make him start up in fright,
And indeed chase him at his feet.

12 His vigor becomes famished,
And disaster stands ready to make him limp.

13 It will eat the pieces of his skin;
The first-born of death will eat his limbs.

14 His confidence will be torn away from his own tent
And it will march him to the king of terrors.

15 There will reside in his tent something that is not his;
Sulphur will be strewed upon his own abiding place.

16 Underneath will his very roots dry up,
And, up above, his bough will wither.

17 The very mentioning of him will certainly perish from the earth,

And he will have no name out in the street.

18 They will push him out of the light into the darkness,
And from the productive land they will chase him away.

19 He will have no posterity and no progeny among his people,
And there will be no survivor in his place of alien residence.

20 At his day the people in the West will indeed stare in amazement,
And a shudder will certainly seize even the people in the East.

21 Only these are the tabernacles of a wrongdoer,
And this is the place of one that has not known God."

19 And Job proceeded to answer and say:

2 "How long will YOU men keep irritating my soul
And keep crushing me with words?

3 These ten times YOU proceeded to rebuke me;
You are not ashamed [that] YOU deal so hard with me.

4 And, granted that I have made a mistake,
It is with me that my mistake will lodge.

5 If for a fact against me YOU men do put on great airs,
And YOU show my reproach to be proper against me,

6 KNOW, then, that God himself has misled me,
And his hunting net he has closed in upon me.

7 Look! I keep crying out, 'Violence!' but I get no answer;
I keep crying for help, but there is no justice.

8 My very path he has blocked with a stone wall, and I cannot pass over;
And upon my roadways he puts darkness itself.

9 My own glory he has stripped from me,
And he takes away the crown of my head.

10 He pulls me down on all sides, and I go away;
And he pulls my hope out just like a tree.

11 His anger also grows hot against me,
And he keeps reckoning me as an adversary of his.

12 Unitedly his troops come and cast up their way against me,
And they camp round about my tent.

13 My own brothers he has put far away from me,
And the very ones knowing me have even turned aside from me.

14 My intimate acquaintances have ceased to be,
And those known by me have themselves forgotten me,

15 Those residing as aliens in my house; and my slave girls themselves reckon me as a stranger;
A real foreigner I have become in their eyes.

16 To my servant I have called, but he does not answer.
With my own mouth I keep imploring him for compassion.

17 My breath itself has become loathsome to my wife,
And I have become foul-smelling to the sons of my [mother's] belly.

18 Also young boys themselves have rejected me;
Let me but rise up, and they begin to speak against me.

19 All the men of my intimate group detest me,
And those whom I loved have turned against me.

20 To my skin and to my flesh my bones actually cleave,
And I escape with the skin of my teeth.

21 Show me some favor, show me some favor, O YOU my companions,
For God's own hand has touched me.

22 Why do YOU men keep persecuting me as God does,

And not become satisfied with
my very flesh?

23 O that now my words were
written down!
O that in a book they were
even inscribed!

24 With an iron stylus and [with]
lead,
Forever in the rock O that
they were hewn!

25 And I myself well know that my
redeemer is alive,
And that, coming after [me],
he will rise up over [the]
dust.

26 And after my skin, [which]
they have skinned off,—this!
Yet reduced in my flesh I
shall behold God,

27 Whom even I shall behold for
myself,
And [whom] my very eyes
will certainly see, but not
some stranger.
My kidneys have failed deep
within me.

28 For you men say, 'Why do we
keep persecuting him?'
When the very root of [the]
matter is found in me.

29 Be frightened for yourselves
because of a sword,
For the sword means a raging
against errors,
In order that you men may
know there is a judge."

20 And Zo'phar the Na'a·ma-
thite proceeded to reply and
say:

2 "Therefore do my own disquieting thoughts themselves
answer me,
Even on account of my in-
ward excitement.

3 An insulting exhortation to me
I hear;
And a spirit without the
understanding that I have
replies to me.

4 Have you at all times known
this very thing,
Since man was put upon the
earth,

5 That the joyful cry of wicked
people is short
And the rejoicing of an apostate is for a moment?

6 Although his excellency ascends
to heaven itself
And his very head reaches to
the clouds,

7 Like his manure cakes he perishes forever;
The very ones seeing him
will say, 'Where is he?'

8 Like a dream he will fly off,
and they will not find him;
And he will be chased away
like a vision of the night.

9 The eye that has caught sight
of him will not do so again,
And no more will his place
behold him.

10 His own sons will seek the favor
of lowly people,
And his own hands will give
back his valuable things.

11 His own bones have been full
of his youthful vigor,
But with him it will lie down
in mere dust.

12 If what is bad tastes sweet in
his mouth,
If he causes it to melt away
under his tongue,

13 If he has compassion upon it
and does not leave it,
And if he keeps holding it
back in the midst of his
palate,

14 His food itself will certainly be
changed in his own in-
testines;
It will be the gall of cobras
within him.

15 Wealth he has swallowed down,
but he will vomit it up;
God will drive it out from his
very belly.

16 The venom of cobras he will
suck;
The tongue of a viper will
kill him.

17 He will never see the watercourses,
Torrential streams of honey
and butter.

18 He will be giving back [his]
acquired property and will
not swallow [it] down;
Like wealth from his trade,
but which he will not enjoy.

19 For he has crushed to pieces,
he has left lowly ones;
He has snatched away a house

itself that he did not proceed to build.

20 For he will certainly know no ease in his belly;
By means of his desirable things he will not escape.

21 There is nothing left over for him to devour;
That is why his well-being will not endure.

22 While his plenty is at its peak he will be feeling anxious;
All the power of misfortune itself will come against him.

23 Let it occur that, to fill his belly,
He will send his burning anger upon him
And will rain [it] upon him, into his bowels.

24 He will run away from armor of iron;
A bow of copper will cut him up.

25 A missile itself will even go out through his back,
And a glittering weapon out through his gall;
Frightful objects will go against him.

26 All darkness will be reserved for his treasured things;
A fire that no one fanned will eat him up;
It will go badly with a survivor in his tent.

27 Heaven will uncover his error,
And earth will be in revolt against him.

28 A heavy shower will roll his house away;
There will be things poured forth on the day of his anger.

29 This is the share of the wicked man from God,
Even his stated inheritance from God."

21 And Job proceeded to answer and say:

2 "Listen, YOU men, attentively to my word,
And let this become YOUR consolation.

3 Put up with me, and I myself shall speak;
And after my speaking you may [each] deride.

4 As for me, is my concern [expressed] to man?
Or why is it that my spirit does not get impatient?

5 Turn YOUR faces to me and stare in amazement,
And put [YOUR] hand upon [YOUR] mouth.

6 And if I have remembered, I have also become disturbed,
And shuddering has taken hold of my flesh.

7 Why is it that the wicked themselves keep living,
Have grown old, also have become superior in wealth?

8 Their offspring are firmly established with them in their sight,
And their descendants before their eyes.

9 Their houses are peace itself, free from dread,
And the rod of God is not upon them.

10 His own bull actually impregnates, and it does not waste semen;
His cows bring forth and suffer no abortion.

11 They keep sending out their young boys just like a flock,
And their own male children go skipping about.

12 They continue raising [their voice] with the tambourine and harp,
And keep rejoicing at the sound of the pipe.

13 They spend their days in good times,
And in a moment down to She'ol they descend.

14 And they say to the [true] God, 'Turn away from us!
And in the knowledge of your ways we have found no delight.

15 What does the Almighty amount to, that we should serve him,
And how do we benefit ourselves in that we have come in touch with him?'

16 Look! Their well-being is not in their own power.
The very counsel of wicked ones has kept far from me.

17 How many times is the lamp
   of the wicked ones extinguished,
   And [how many times] does
   their disaster come upon
   them?
   [How many times] in his
   anger does he apportion
   destruction?
18 Do they become like straw before a wind,
   And like chaff that a stormwind has stolen away?
19 God himself will store up one's
   hurtfulness for one's own
   sons;
   He will reward him that he
   may know [it].
20 His eyes will see his decay,
   And from the rage of the
   Almighty he will drink.
21 For what will his delight be in
   his house after him,
   When the number of his
   months will really be cut in
   two?
22 Will he teach knowledge even to
   God,
   When that One himself judges
   high ones?
23 This very one will die during
   his full self-sufficiency,
   When he is altogether carefree
   and at ease;
24 [When] his own thighs have
   become full of fat
   And the very marrow of his
   bones is being kept moist.
25 And this other one will die with
   a bitter soul
   When he has not eaten of
   good things.
26 Together in the dust they will
   lie down
   And maggots themselves will
   form a cover over them.
27 Look! I well know the thoughts
   of you men
   And the schemes with which
   you would act violently
   against me.
28 For you say, 'Where is the house
   of the noble one,
   And where is the tent, the
   tabernacles of wicked ones?'
29 Have you not asked those traveling over the roads?

And do you not carefully inspect their very signs,
30 That at the day of disaster an
   evil one is spared,
   At the day of fury he is
   delivered?
31 Who will tell him of his way
   to his very face?
   And for what he himself has
   done who will reward him?
32 As for him, to the graveyard
   he will be brought,
   And over a tomb a vigil will
   be kept.
33 To him the clods of earth of a
   torrent valley will certainly
   become sweet,
   And after him he will drag
   all mankind,
   And those before him were
   without number.
34 So how vainly you men try to
   comfort me,
   And your very replies do remain as unfaithfulness!"

22 And Eli·phaz the Te′man·ite
   proceeded to answer and say:
2 "Can an able-bodied man be of
   use to God himself,
   That anyone having insight
   should be of use toward
   him?
3 Does the Almighty have any
   delight in that you are
   righteous,
   Or any gain in that you make
   your way blameless?
4 For your reverence will he reprove you,
   Will he come with you into
   the judgment?
5 Is not your own badness too
   much already,
   And will there be no end to
   your errors?
6 For you seize a pledge from
   your brothers without cause,
   And you strip off even the
   garments of naked people.
7 You do not give the tired one
   a drink of water,
   And from the hungry one you
   hold back bread.
8 As for a man of strength, the
   land is his,
   And one who is treated with
   partiality himself dwells in
   it.

9 Widows you have sent away
    empty-handed,
    And the arms of fatherless
    boys are crushed.
10 That is why bird traps are all
    around you,
    And sudden dread disturbs
    you;
11 Or darkness, [so that] you can-
    not see,
    And a heaving mass of water
    itself covers you.
12 Is not God the height of heaven?
    Also see the sum total of the
    stars, that they are high.
13 And yet you have said: 'What
    does God really know?
    Through thick gloom can he
    judge?
14 Clouds are a concealment place
    for him so that he does not
    see,
    And on the vault of heaven he
    walks about.'
15 Will you keep to the very way
    of long ago
    That hurtful men have
    trodden,
16 [Men] who have been snatched
    away before their time,
    Whose foundation is poured
    away just as a river,
17 Who are saying to the [true]
    God: 'Turn away from us!
    And what can the Almighty
    accomplish against us?'
18 Yet he himself has filled their
    houses with good things;
    And the very counsel of wicked
    ones has kept far from me.
19 The righteous ones will see and
    rejoice,
    And the innocent one him-
    self will hold them in de-
    rision:
20 'Truly our antagonists have been
    effaced;
    And what is left of them a
    fire will certainly eat up.'
21 Acquaint yourself, please, with
    him, and keep peace;
    Thereby good things will come
    to you.
22 Take, please, the law from his
    own mouth,
    And put his sayings in your
    heart.

23 If you return to the Almighty,
    you will be built up;
    [If] you will keep unright-
    eousness far from your tent,
24 And [if] there is a placing of
    precious ore in the dust
    And gold of O'phir in the rock
    of torrent valleys,
25 The Almighty also will indeed
    become your precious ores,
    And silver, the choicest, to
    you.
26 For then in the Almighty you
    will find your exquisite de-
    light,
    And you will raise your face
    to God himself.
27 You will make entreaty to him,
    and he will hear you;
    And your vows you will pay.
28 And you will decide on some-
    thing, and it will stand for
    you;
    And upon your ways light will
    certainly shine.
29 For there must be a humiliation
    when you speak arrogantly;
    But one with downcast eyes
    he will save.
30 He will rescue an innocent man,
    And you will certainly be
    rescued for the cleanness of
    your hands."

23 And Job proceeded to answer
    and say:
2 "Even today my state of concern
    is rebelliousness;
    My own hand is heavy on
    account of my sighing.
3 O that I really knew where I
    might find him!
    I would come clear to his
    fixed place.
4 I would present before him a
    case of justice,
    And my mouth I would fill
    with counterarguments;
5 I would know the words with
    which he answers me,
    And I would consider what
    he says to me.
6 Would he with an abundance
    of power contend with me?
    O no! Surely he himself would
    pay heed to me.
7 There the upright one himself
    will certainly set matters
    straight with him,

And I would go safe forever
from my judge.
8 Look! To the east I go, and he
is not there;
And back again, and I cannot
discern him;
9 To the left where he is working,
but I cannot behold [him];
He turns aside to the right,
but I do not see [him].
10 For he well knows the way I
take.
[After] he has tested me out,
I shall come forth as gold
itself.
11 Of his steps my foot has laid
hold;
His way I have kept, and I
do not deviate.
12 [From] the commandment of
his lips I do not move away.
I have treasured up the sayings of his mouth more
than what is prescribed for
me.
13 And he is in one [mind], and
who can resist him?
And his own soul has a desire,
and he will do [it].
14 For he will carry out completely
what is prescribed for me,
And things like these are
many with him.
15 That is why I feel disturbed
because of him;
I show myself attentive and
am in dread of him.
16 Even God himself has made my
heart timid,
And the Almighty himself
has disturbed me.
17 For I have not been put to
silence because of darkness,
Nor because gloom has covered
my own face.

24 "Why is it that times have
not been stored up by the
Almighty himself,
And the very ones knowing
him have not beheld his
days?
2 There are those who move back
boundary marks;
A drove they have snatched
away, that they may shep-
herd [it].
3 They drive off even the male
ass of fatherless boys;

They seize the widow's bull
as a pledge.
4 They turn aside the poor ones
from the way;
At the same time the afflicted
of the earth have kept
themselves hidden.
5 Look! [As] zebras in the wilderness
They have gone forth in their
activity, looking for food.
The desert plain [gives] to
each one bread for the boys.
6 In the field its fodder they
harvest,
And the vineyard of the wicked
one they hastily despoil.
7 Naked, they pass the night without a garment,
And without any covering in
the cold.
8 From the rainstorm of the mountains they get drenched,
And because there is no shelter they have to hug a rock.
9 They snatch away a fatherless
boy even from the breast,
And what is on the afflicted
one they take as a pledge.
10 Naked, they have to go about
without a garment,
And, hungry, they have to
carry the reaped ears.
11 Between the terrace walls they
pass the noontime;
Wine presses they have to
tread, and yet they go
thirsty.
12 From out of the city the dying
keep groaning,
And the soul of deadly
wounded ones cries for help;
And God himself considers
[it] not as anything im-
proper.
13 As for them, they proved to be
among the rebels against
light;
They did not recognize its
ways,
And they did not dwell in its
roadways.
14 At daylight the murderer gets
up,
He proceeds to slay the afflicted
and the poor one;
And during the night he becomes a regular thief.

15 As for the eye of the adulterer,
it has watched for evening
darkness,
Saying, 'No eye will behold
me!'
And over his face he puts a
covering.

16 In the darkness he has dug
into houses;
By day they must keep themselves locked in.
They have not known day-
light.

17 For morning is the same as
deep shadow for them,
For they recognize the
sudden terrors of deep shadow are.

18 He is swift on the surface of the
waters.
Their tract of land will be
cursed in the earth.
He will not turn toward the
way of the vineyards.

19 The drought, also the heat,
snatch away the snow
waters;
So does She'ol those who have
sinned!

20 The womb will forget him, the
maggot will sweetly suck
him,
He will be remembered no
more.
And unrighteousness will be
broken just like a tree.

21 He is having dealings with a
barren woman who does
not bear,
And with a widow, to whom
he does no good.

22 And he will certainly draw
away strong people by his
power;
He will rise up and not be
sure of his life.

23 He will grant him to become
confident that he may support himself;
And his eyes will be upon
their ways.

24 They have become high up a
little while, then they are
no more,
And they have been brought
low; like everyone else they
are plucked off,

And like the head of an ear
of grain they are cut off.

25 So really now, who will make
me out a liar
Or reduce my word to nothing?"

25 And Bil′dad the Shu′hite proceeded to answer and say:

2 "Rulership and dreadfulness are
with him;
He is making peace on his
heights.

3 Is there any number to his
troops?
And upon whom does his light
not rise?

4 So how can mortal man be in
the right before God,
Or how can one born of a
woman be clean?

5 Look! There is even the moon,
and it is not bright;
And the stars themselves have
not proved clean in his eyes.

6 How much less so mortal man,
who is a maggot,
And a son of man, who is a
worm!"

26 And Job proceeded to answer
and say:

2 "O how much help you have
been to one without power!
O [how] you have saved
an arm that is without
strength!

3 How much you have advised
one that is without wisdom,
And you have made practical
wisdom itself known to the
multitude!

4 To whom have you told words,
And whose breath has come
forth from you?

5 Those impotent in death keep
trembling
Beneath the waters and those
residing in them.

6 She'ol is naked in front of him,
And [the place of] destruction
has no covering.

7 He is stretching out the north
over the empty place,
Hanging the earth upon
nothing;

8 Wrapping up the waters in his
clouds,
So that the cloud mass is not
split under them;

9 Enclosing the face of the throne,
Spreading out over it his
cloud.
10 He has described a circle upon
the face of the waters,
To where light ends in darkness.
11 The very pillars of heaven shake,
And they are amazed because
of his rebuke.
12 By his power he has stirred up
the sea,
And by his understanding he
has broken the stormer to
pieces.
13 By his wind he has polished up
heaven itself,
His hand has pierced the
gliding serpent.
14 Look! These are the fringes of
his ways,
And what a whisper of a
matter has been heard of
him!
But of his mighty thunder
who can show an under-
standing?"

27 And Job proceeded again to
lift up his proverbial utterance
and went on to say:

2 "As God lives, who has taken
away my judgment,
And as the Almighty [lives],
who has made my soul
bitter,
3 While my breath is yet whole
within me,
And the spirit of God is in
my nostrils,
4 My lips will speak no unrighteousness
And my own tongue will mutter no deceit!
5 It is unthinkable on my part
that I should declare you
men righteous!
Until I expire I shall not take
away my integrity from myself!
6 On my justness I have laid
hold, and I shall not let it
go;
My heart will not taunt [me]
for any of my days.
7 Let my enemy become in every
way a wicked man,
And the one revolting against
me really a wrongdoer.

8 For what is the hope of an
apostate in case he cuts
[him] off,
In case God carries off his
soul from him?
9 Will God hear an outcry of his
In case distress comes upon
him?
10 Or in the Almighty will he find
exquisite delight?
Will he call to God at all
times?
11 I shall instruct you men by the
hand of God;
That which is with the Almighty I shall not hide.
12 Look! You yourselves have all
of you seen visions;
So why is it that you show
yourselves utterly vain?
13 This is the share of the wicked
man from God;
And the inheritance of the
tyrants they will receive
from the Almighty himself.
14 If his sons become many, it is
for a sword;
And his descendants them-
selves will not have enough
food.
15 His own survivors will be buried
during a deadly plague,
And their own widows will
not weep.
16 If he should pile up silver like
dust itself,
And he should prepare attire
just as if clay,
17 He would prepare, but the righteous would be the one to
clothe himself,
And in the silver the innocent
would be the one to have a
share.
18 He has built his house like a
mere moth,
And like a booth that a watchman has made.
19 Rich he will lie down, but nothing will be gathered;
His eyes he has opened, but
there will be nothing.
20 Like waters sudden terrors will
overtake him;
At night a stormwind will
certainly steal him away.
21 An east wind will carry him
off and he will go away,

And it will whirl him away from his place.

22 And it will hurl itself at him and have no compassion;
From its power he will without fail try to run away.

23 One will clap his hands at him
And will whistle at him from his place.

28 "Indeed, for silver there exists a place to find it
And a place for gold that they refine;

2 Iron itself is taken from the very dust
And [from] stone copper is being poured out.

3 An end to the darkness he has set;
And to every limit he is searching out
Stone in the gloom and deep shadow.

4 He has sunk a shaft far from where [people] reside as aliens,
Places forgotten far from the foot;
Some of mortal men have swung down, they have dangled.

5 As for the earth, out of it food goes forth;
But underneath it, it has been upturned as if by fire.

6 Its stones are the place of the sapphire,
And it has gold dust.

7 A pathway—no bird of prey has known it,
Nor has the eye of a black kite caught sight of it.

8 The majestic wild beasts have not trodden it down solid;
The young lion has not paced over it.

9 Upon the flint he has thrust out his hand;
He has overthrown mountains from [their] root;

10 Into the rocks he has channeled water-filled galleries,
And all precious things his eye has seen.

11 The places from which rivers trickled he has dammed up,
And the concealed thing he brings forth to the light.

12 But wisdom—where can it be found,
And where, now, is the place of understanding?

13 Mortal man has not come to know its valuation,
And it is not found in the land of those living.

14 The watery deep itself has said, 'It is not in me!'
The sea too has said, 'It is not with me!'

15 Pure gold cannot be given in exchange for it,
And silver cannot be weighed out as its price.

16 It cannot be paid for with gold of O'phir,
With the rare onyx stone and the sapphire.

17 Gold and glass cannot be compared to it,
Nor is any vessel of refined gold an exchange for it.

18 Coral and rock crystal themselves will not be mentioned,
But a bagful of wisdom is worth more than [one full of] pearls.

19 The topaz of Cush cannot be compared to it;
It cannot be paid for even with gold in its purity.

20 But wisdom itself—from where does it come,
And where, now, is the place of understanding?

21 It has been hidden even from the eyes of everyone alive,
And from the flying creatures of the heavens it has been concealed.

22 Destruction and death themselves have said,
'With our ears we have heard a report of it.'

23 God is the One who has understood its way,
And he himself has known its place,

24 For he himself looks to the very ends of the earth;
Under the whole heavens he sees,

25 To make a weight for the wind,
While he has proportioned the waters themselves by a measure;

26 When he made for the rain a regulation,
And a way for the thunderous storm cloud,
27 Then it was that he saw [wisdom] and proceeded to tell about it;
He prepared it and also searched it through.
28 And he went on to say to man, 'Look! The fear of Jehovah—that is wisdom,
And to turn away from bad is understanding.'"

29 And Job proceeded again to lift up his proverbial utterance and went on to say:
2 "O that I were as in the lunar months of long ago,
As in the days when God was guarding me;
3 When he caused his lamp to shine upon my head,
[When] I would walk [through] darkness by his light;
4 Just as I happened to be in the days of my prime,
When intimacy with God was at my tent;
5 When the Almighty was yet with me,
[When] my attendants were all around me!
6 When I washed my steps in butter,
And the rock kept pouring out streams of oil for me;
7 When I went forth to the gate by the town,
In the public square I would prepare my seat!
8 The boys saw me and hid themselves,
And even the aged ones rose up, they stood.
9 Princes themselves restrained words,
And the palm they would put upon their mouth.
10 The voice of the leaders themselves was hidden,
And their very tongue cleaved to their palate.
11 For the ear itself listened and proceeded to pronounce me happy,

And the eye itself saw and proceeded to bear witness for me.
12 For I would rescue the afflicted one crying for help,
And the fatherless boy and anyone that had no helper.
13 The blessing of the one about to perish—upon me it would come,
And the heart of the widow I would make glad.
14 With righteousness I clothed myself, and it was clothing me.
My justice was like a sleeveless coat—and a turban.
15 Eyes I became to the blind one;
And feet to the lame one I was.
16 I was a real father to the poor ones;
And the legal case of one whom I did not know—I would examine it.
17 And I would break the jawbones of the wrongdoer,
And from his teeth I would tear away the prey.
18 And I used to say, 'Within my nest I shall expire,
And like the grains of sand I shall multiply [my] days.
19 My root is opened for the waters,
And dew itself will stay overnight upon my bough.
20 My glory is fresh with me,
And my bow in my hand will shoot repeatedly.'
21 To me they listened; and they waited,
And they would keep silent for my counsel.
22 After my word they would not speak again,
And upon them my word would drip.
23 And they waited for me as for the rain,
And their mouth they opened wide for the spring rain.
24 I would smile at them—they would not believe [it]—
And the light of my face they would not cast down.
25 I would choose the way for them, and I was sitting as head;

And I resided as a king among [his] troops,
As one who comforts the mourners.

30 "And now they have laughed at me,
Those younger in days than I am,
Whose fathers I would have refused
To place with the dogs of my flock.

2 Even the power of their hands—
of what use was it to me?
In them vigor has perished.

3 Because of want and hunger they are sterile,
Gnawing at a waterless region,
[Where] yesterday there were storm and desolation.

4 They were plucking the salt herb by the bushes,
And the root of broom trees was their food.

5 From the community they would be driven away;
People would shout at them as at a thief.

6 [They have] to reside on the very slope of torrent valleys,
In holes of the dust and in rocks.

7 Among the bushes they would cry out;
Under the nettles they would huddle together.

8 Sons of the senseless one, also sons of the nameless one,
They have been scourged out of the land.

9 And now I have become even the theme of their song,
And I am to them for a byword.

10 They have detested me, they have kept themselves far from me;
And from my face they did not hold back [their] spit.

11 For he loosened [my] own bow-string and proceeded to humble me,
And the bridle they left loose on my account.

12 At [my] right hand they rise up as a brood;
My feet they have let go,
But they proceeded to cast up against me their disastrous barriers.

13 They have torn down my road-ways;
They were beneficial only for adversity to me,
Without their having any helper.

14 As through a wide gap they proceed to come;
Under a storm they have rolled along.

15 Sudden terrors have been turned upon me;
My noble bearing is chased like the wind,
And like a cloud my salvation has passed away.

16 And now my soul is poured out within me;
Days of affliction take hold upon me.

17 At night my very bones have been bored through [and dropped] from off me,
And [pains] gnawing me do not take any rest.

18 By the abundance of power my garment takes on a change;
Like the collar of my long garment it engirdles me.

19 He has brought me down to the clay,
So that I show myself like dust and ashes.

20 I cry to you for help, but you do not answer me;
I have stood, that you might show yourself attentive to me.

21 You change yourself to become cruel to me;
With the full might of your hand you harbor animosity toward me.

22 You lift me to the wind, you cause me to ride [it];
Then you dissolve me with a crash.

23 For I well know that to death you will make me turn back,
And to the house of meeting for everyone living.

24 Only no one thrusts his hand out against a mere heap of ruins,

Nor during one's decay is there a cry for help respecting those things.

25 Certainly I have wept for the one having a hard day;
My soul has grieved for the poor one.

26 Although for good I waited, yet bad came;
And I kept awaiting the light, but gloom came.

27 My own intestines were made to boil and did not keep silent;
Days of affliction confronted me.

28 Saddened I walked about when there was no sunlight;
I got up in the congregation, I kept crying for help.

29 A brother to jackals I became,
And a companion to the daughters of the ostrich.

30 My very skin became black [and dropped] off me,
And my very bones became hot from dryness.

31 And my harp came to be merely for mourning,
And my pipe for the voice of weeping ones.

31 "A covenant I have concluded with my eyes.
So how could I show myself attentive to a virgin?

2 And what portion is there from God above,
Or inheritance from the Almighty from on high?

3 Is there not disaster for a wrongdoer,
And misfortune for those practicing what is hurtful?

4 Does he not himself see my ways
And count even all my steps?

5 If I have walked with [men of] untruth,
And my foot hastens to deception,

6 He will weigh me in accurate scales
And God will get to know my integrity.

7 If my stepping deviates from the way,
Or my heart has walked merely after my eyes,

Or any defect has stuck in my own palms,

8 Let me sow seed and someone else eat,
And let my own descendants be rooted out.

9 If my heart has been enticed toward a woman,
And I kept lying in wait at the very entranceway of my companion,

10 Let my wife do the grinding for another man,
And over her let other men kneel down.

11 For that would be loose conduct,
And that would be an error for [attention by] the justices.

12 For that is a fire that would eat clear to destruction,
And among all my produce it would take root.

13 If I used to refuse the judgment of my slave man
Or of my slave girl in their case at law with me,

14 Then what can I do when God rises up?
And when he calls for an accounting, what can I answer him?

15 Did not the One making me in the belly make him,
And did not just One proceed to prepare us in the womb?

16 If I used to hold back the lowly ones from [their] delight,
And the eyes of the widow I would cause to fail,

17 And I used to eat my morsel by myself,
While the fatherless boy did not eat from it

18 (For from my youth he grew up with me as with a father,
And from the belly of my mother I kept leading her);

19 If I used to see anyone perishing from having no garment,
Or that the poor one had no covering;

20 If his loins did not bless me,
Nor from the shorn wool of my young rams he would warm himself;

21 If I waved my hand to and fro against the fatherless boy,

When I would see [need of]
my assistance in the gate,
22 Let my own shoulder blade fall
from its shoulder,
And let my own arm be
broken from its upper bone.
23 For disaster from God was a
dread to me,
And against his dignity I
could not hold out.
24 If I have put gold as my confidence,
Or to gold I have said, 'You
are my trust!'
25 If I used to rejoice because my
property was much,
And because my hand had
found a lot of things;
26 If I used to see the light when
it would flash forth,
Or the precious moon walking
along,
27 And my heart began to be enticed in secrecy
And my hand proceeded to
kiss my mouth,
28 That too would be an error for
[attention by] the justices,
For I should have denied the
[true] God above.
29 If I used to rejoice at the extinction of one intensely
hating me,
Or I felt excited because evil
had found him—
30 And I did not allow my palate
to sin
By asking for an oath against
his soul.
31 If the men of my tent did not
say,
'Who can produce anyone that
has not been satisfied from
food of his?'—
32 Outside no alien resident would
spend the night;
My doors I kept open to the
path.
33 If like an earthling man I
covered over my trans-
gressions
By hiding my error in my
shirt pocket—
34 Because I would suffer a shock
at a large crowd,
Or the contempt itself of
families would terrorize me

And I would keep silent, I
would not go out of the
entrance.
35 O that I had someone listening
to me,
That according to my signature the Almighty himself
would answer me!
Or that the individual in the
case at law with me had
written a document itself!
36 Surely upon my shoulder I would
carry it;
I would bind it around me like
a grand crown.
37 The number of my steps I
would tell him;
Like a leader I would approach
him.
38 If against me my own ground
would cry for aid,
And together its furrows themselves would weep;
39 If its fruitage I have eaten without money,
And the soul of its owners I
have caused to pant,
40 Instead of wheat let the thorny
weed go forth,
And instead of barley stinking
weeds."

The words of Job have come
to an end.

32 So these three men ceased
from answering Job, for he
was righteous in his own eyes.
2 But the anger of E·li′hu the son
of Bar′a·chel the Buz′ite of the
family of Ram came to be hot.
Against Job his anger blazed over
his declaring his own soul righteous
rather than God. 3 Also, against
his three companions his anger
blazed over the fact that they had
not found an answer but they proceeded to pronounce God wicked.
4 And E·li′hu himself had waited
for Job with words, because they
were older than he was in days.
5 And E·li′hu gradually saw that
there was no answer in the mouth
of the three men, and his anger
kept getting hotter. 6 And E·li′hu
the son of Bar′a·chel the Buz′ite
proceeded to answer and say:

"Young I am in days
And you men are aged.

That is why I drew back and was afraid
To declare my knowledge to YOU men.

7 I said, 'Days themselves should speak,
And a multitude of years are what should make wisdom known.'

8 Surely it is the spirit in mortal men
And the breath of the Almighty [that] gives them understanding.

9 It is not those merely abundant in days that prove wise,
Nor those just old that understand judgment.

10 Therefore I said, 'Do listen to me.
I shall declare my knowledge, even I.'

11 Look! I have waited for the words of YOU men,
I kept giving ear to YOUR reasonings,
Until YOU could search for words [to say].

12 And to YOU I kept my attention turned,
And here there is no one reproving Job,
None of YOU answering his sayings,

13 That YOU may not say, 'We have found wisdom;
It is God that drives him away, not a man.'

14 As he has not arrayed words against me,
So with the sayings of YOU men I shall not reply to him.

15 They have been terrified, they have answered no more;
Words have moved away from them.

16 And I have waited, for they do not continue speaking;
For they stood still, they answered no more.

17 I shall give in answer my part, even I;
I shall declare my knowledge, even I;

18 For I have become full of words;
Spirit has brought pressure upon me in my belly.

19 Look! My belly is like wine that has no vent;
Like new skin bottles it wants to burst open.

20 Let me speak that it may be a relief to me.
I shall open my lips that I may answer.

21 Let me not, please, show partiality to a man;
And on an earthling man I shall not bestow a title;

22 For I certainly do not know how I can bestow a title;
Easily my Maker would carry me away.

33 "Now, however, O Job, please hear my words,
And to all my speaking do give ear.

2 Look, Please! I have to open my mouth;
My tongue with my palate has to speak.

3 My sayings are the uprightness of my heart,
And knowledge is what my lips do utter sincerely.

4 God's own spirit made me,
And the Almighty's own breath proceeded to bring me to life.

5 If you are able, make reply to me,
Array [words] before me; do take your station.

6 Look! I am to the [true] God just what you are;
From the clay I was shaped, I too.

7 Look! No frightfulness in me will terrify you,
And no pressure by me will be heavy upon you.

8 Only you have said in my ears,
And the sound of [your] words I kept hearing,

9 'I am pure without transgression;
Clean I am, and I have no error.

10 Look! Occasions for opposition to me he finds,
He takes me for an enemy of his.

11 He puts my feet in the stocks,
He watches all my paths.'

12 Look! In this you have not been in the right, I answer you;

For God is much more than mortal man.

13 Why is it against him that you contended,
Because all your words he does not answer?

14 For God speaks once,
And twice—though one does not regard it—

15 In a dream, a vision of the night,
When deep sleep falls upon men,
During slumbers upon the bed.

16 It is then that he uncovers the ear of men,
And on exhortation to them he puts his seal,

17 To turn aside a man from his deed,
And that he may cover pride itself from an able-bodied man.

18 He keeps his soul back from the pit
And his life from passing away by a missile.

19 And he is actually reproved with pain upon his bed,
And the quarreling of his bones is continual.

20 And his life certainly makes bread loathsome,
And his own soul desirable food.

21 His flesh wastes away from sight,
And his bones that were not seen certainly grow bare.

22 And his soul draws near to the pit,
And his life to those inflicting death.

23 If there exists for him a messenger,
A spokesman, one out of a thousand,
To tell to man his uprightness,

24 Then he favors him and says,
'Let him off from going down into the pit!
I have found a ransom!

25 Let his flesh become fresher than in youth;
Let him return to the days of his youthful vigor.'

26 He will make entreaty to God that he may take pleasure in him,
And he will see his face with joyful shouting,
And He will restore His righteousness to mortal man.

27 He will sing to men and say, 'I have sinned; and what is upright I have perverted,
And it certainly was not the proper thing for me.

28 He has redeemed my soul from passing into the pit,
And my life itself will see the light.'

29 Look! All these things God performs,
Two times, three times, in the case of an able-bodied man,

30 To turn his soul back from the pit,
That he may be enlightened with the light of those living.

31 Pay attention, O Job! Listen to me!
Keep silent, and I myself shall continue speaking.

32 If there are any words [to say], make reply to me;
Speak, for I have taken delight in your righteousness.

33 If there are none, you yourself listen to me;
Keep silent, and I shall teach you wisdom."

34 And E·li'hu continued to answer and say:

2 "Listen, you wise ones, to my words;
And you who know, give ear to me.

3 For the ear itself makes a test of words,
Just as the palate tastes when eating.

4 Judgment let us choose for ourselves;
Let us know among ourselves what is good.

5 For Job has said, 'I certainly am in the right,
But God himself has turned aside the judgment of me.

6 Against my own judgment do I tell lies?
My severe wound is incurable though there is no transgression.'

7 What able-bodied man is like Job,
[Who] drinks up derision like water?
8 And he is certainly on his way to companionship with practicers of what is hurtful
And to walking with men of wickedness.
9 For he has said, 'An able-bodied man does not profit
By his taking pleasure in God.'
10 Therefore, YOU men of heart, listen to me.
Far be it from the [true] God to act wickedly,
And the Almighty to act unjustly!
11 For [according to] the way earthling man acts he will reward him,
And according to the path of man he will cause it to come upon him.
12 Yes, for a fact, God himself does not act wickedly,
And the Almighty himself does not pervert judgment.
13 Who has assigned to him the earth,
And who has appointed [to him] the productive land, even all of it?
14 If he sets his heart upon anyone,
[If] that one's spirit and breath he gathers to himself,
15 All flesh will expire together,
And earthling man himself will return to the very dust.
16 So if [you have] understanding, do listen to this;
Do give ear to the sound of my words.
17 Really will anyone hating justice control,
And if a powerful one is righteous will you pronounce [him] wicked?
18 Shall one say to a king, 'You are good for nothing'?
To nobles, 'You are wicked'?
19 [There is One] who has not shown partiality to princes
And has not given more consideration to the noble one than to the lowly one,

For all of them are the work of his hands.
20 In a moment they die, even in the middle of the night;
The people shake back and forth and pass away,
And powerful ones depart by no hand.
21 For his eyes are upon the ways of man,
And all his steps he sees.
22 There is no darkness nor any deep shadow
For those practicing what is hurtful to conceal themselves there.
23 For he sets no appointed time for any man
To go to God in judgment.
24 He breaks powerful ones without any investigation,
And he makes others stand up instead of them.
25 Therefore he recognizes what their works are,
And he does overthrow [them] at night, and they get crushed.
26 As wicked ones he does slap them
In the place of onlookers;
27 For the reason that they have turned aside from following him,
And none of his ways have they considered,
28 So as to cause the outcry of the lowly one to come to him;
And so he hears the outcry of the afflicted ones.
29 When he himself causes quietness, who, then, can condemn?
And when he conceals [his] face, who can behold him,
Whether it is toward a nation or toward a man, it being the same thing?
30 So that an apostate man may not reign,
Nor there be snares of the people.
31 For will anyone actually say to God himself,
'I have borne, although I do not act corruptly;
32 Although I behold nothing, instruct me yourself;

If any unrighteousness I have committed,
I shall not do [it] again'?

33 Will he make good for it from your standpoint because you do refuse [judgment],
Because you yourself choose, and not I?
Even what you well know, speak.

34 Men of heart themselves will say to me—
Even a wise able-bodied man that is listening to me,

35 'Job himself speaks without knowledge,
And his words are without [his] having insight.'

36 My father, let Job be tested out to the limit
Over his replies among men of hurtfulness.

37 For on top of his sin he adds revolt;
Among us he claps [his hands] and multiplies his sayings against the [true] God!"

35 And E·li′hu continued answering and saying:

2 "Is this what you have regarded as justice?
You have said, 'My righteousness is more than God's.'

3 For you say, 'Of what use is it to you?
What benefit do I have more than by my sinning?'

4 I myself shall reply to you
And to your companions with you.

5 Look up to heaven and see,
And behold the clouds, [that] they are indeed higher than you.

6 If you actually sin, what do you accomplish against him?
And [if] your revolts actually increase, what do you do to him?

7 If you are really in the right, what do you give him,
Or what does he receive from your own hand?

8 Your wickedness may be against a man like you,
And your righteousness to a son of earthling man.

9 Because of the multitude of oppressions they keep calling for aid;
They keep crying for help because of the arm of the great ones.

10 And yet no one has said, 'Where is God my grand Maker,
The One giving melodies in the night?'

11 He is the One teaching us more than the beasts of the earth,
And he makes us wiser than even the flying creatures of the heavens.

12 There they keep crying out, but he does not answer,
Because of the pride of the bad ones.

13 Only the untruth God does not hear,
And the Almighty himself does not behold it.

14 How much less, then, when you say you do not behold him!
The legal case is before him, and so you should wait anxiously for him.

15 And now because his anger has not called for an accounting,
He has also not taken note of the extreme rashness.

16 And Job himself opens his mouth wide simply for nothing;
Without knowledge he multiplies mere words."

36 And E·li′hu proceeded to say further:

2 "Have patience with me a little while, and I shall declare to you
That there are yet words [to say] for God.

3 I shall carry my knowledge from far off,
And to my Fashioner I shall ascribe righteousness.

4 For my words are for a fact no falsehood;
The One perfect in knowledge is with you.

5 Look! God is mighty and will not reject;
[He is] mighty in power of heart;

6 He will not preserve anyone wicked alive,

But the judgment of the afflicted ones he will give.

7 He will not take away his eyes
from anyone righteous;
Even kings on the throne—
He will also seat them forever,
and they will be exalted.

8 And if they are bound in fetters,
They are captured with ropes
of affliction.

9 Then he will tell them about
the way they act
And their transgressions, because they take a superior
air.

10 And he will uncover their ear
to exhortation,
And he will say that they
should turn back from what
is hurtful.

11 If they obey and serve,
They will finish their days in
what is good
And their years in pleasantness.

12 But if they do not obey, they
will pass away even by a
missile,
And they will expire without
knowledge.

13 And those apostate in heart will
themselves lay up anger.
They should not cry for help
because he has bound them.

14 Their soul will die in youth itself,
And their life among male
temple prostitutes.

15 He will rescue the afflicted one
in his affliction,
And he will uncover their ear
in the oppression.

16 And he will also certainly allure
you from the mouth of
distress!
Broader space, not constraint,
will be in its place,
And the consolation of your
table will be full of fatness.

17 With the judicial sentence upon
the wicked one you will certainly be filled;
Judicial sentence and justice
will themselves take hold.

18 For [take care] that rage does
not allure you into [spiteful] hand clapping,

And let not a large ransom itself lead you astray.

19 Will your cry for help take
effect? No, nor in distress
Even all [your] powerful
efforts.

20 Do not pant for the night,
For peoples to retreat [from]
where they are.

21 Be on your guard that you do
not turn to what is hurtful,
For this you have chosen
rather than affliction.

22 Look! God himself acts exaltedly
with his power;
Who is an instructor like him?

23 Who has called his way to account against him,
And who has said, 'You have
committed unrighteousness'?

24 Remember that you should magnify his activity
Of which men have sung.

25 All mankind themselves have
gazed upon it;
Mortal man himself keeps
looking from far off.

26 Behold! God is more exalted
than we can know;
In number his years are beyond searching.

27 For he draws up the drops of
water;
They filter as rain for his
mist,

28 So that the clouds trickle,
They drip upon mankind
abundantly.

29 Indeed, who can understand the
cloud layers,
The crashings from his booth?

30 Look! He has spread out over
it his light,
And the roots of the sea he
has covered.

31 For by them he pleads the cause
of peoples;
He gives food in abundance.

32 In his hands he has covered
over the lightning,
And he lays a command upon
it against an assailant.

33 His booming tells about him,
The livestock also concerning the one coming up.

37 "Indeed at this my heart
begins to tremble,
And it leaps up from its place.

2 Listen attentively, you men, to
    the rumbling of his voice,
  And the growling that goes
    forth from his mouth.
3 Under the whole heavens he lets
    it loose,
  And his lightning is to the
    extremities of the earth.
4 After it a sound roars;
  He thunders with the sound
    of his superiority,
  And he does not hold them
    back when his voice is
    heard.
5 God thunders with his voice in
    a wonderful way,
  Doing great things that we
    cannot know.
6 For to the snow he says, 'Fall
    earthward,'
  And [to] the downpour of
    rain, even [to] the down-
    pour of his strong rains.
7 On the hand of every earthling
    man he puts a seal
  For every mortal man to know
    his work.
8 And the wild beast comes into
    the ambush,
  And in its hiding places it
    dwells.
9 Out of the interior room comes
    the stormwind
  And out of the north winds
    the cold.
10 By the breath of God the ice is
    given
  And the breadth of waters is
    under constraint.
11 Yes, with moisture he burdens
    the cloud,
  His light scatters the cloud
    mass,
12 And it is being turned round
    about by his steering [them]
    for their performance
  Wherever he commands them
    upon the face of the pro-
    ductive land of the earth.
13 Whether for a rod or for his
    land
  Or for loving-kindness, he
    makes it produce effects.
14 Do give ear to this, O Job;
  Stand still and show yourself
    attentive to the wonderful
    works of God.

15 Do you know when God laid
    an appointment upon them,
  And when he caused the light
    of his cloud to beam?
16 Do you know about the poisings
    of the cloud,
  The wonderful works of the
    One perfect in knowledge?
17 How your garments are hot
  When the earth shows quiet-
    ness from the south?
18 With him can you beat out the
    skies
  Hard like a molten mirror?
19 Let us know what we should
    say to him;
  We cannot produce [words]
    because of darkness.
20 Should it be related to him that
    I would speak?
  Or has any man said that it
    will be communicated?
21 And now they do not really see
    the light;
  It is brilliant in the skies,
  When a wind itself has passed
    by and proceeded to cleanse
    them.
22 Out of the north golden splendor
    comes.
  Upon God dignity is fear-
    inspiring.
23 As for the Almighty, we have
    not found him out;
  He is exalted in power,
  And justice and abundance
    of righteousness he will not
    belittle.
24 Therefore let men fear him.
  He does not regard any who
    are wise in [their own]
    heart."

38 And Jehovah proceeded to
    answer Job out of the wind-
    storm and say:
2 "Who is this that is obscuring
    counsel
  By words without knowledge?
3 Gird up your loins, please, like
    an able-bodied man,
  And let me question you, and
    you inform me.
4 Where did you happen to be
    when I founded the earth?
  Tell [me], if you do know
    understanding.
5 Who set its measurements, in
    case you know,

Or who stretched out upon it
the measuring line?

6 Into what have its socket pedestals been sunk down,
Or who laid its cornerstone,

7 When the morning stars joyfully cried out together,
And all the sons of God began
shouting in applause?

8 And [who] barricaded the sea
with doors,
Which began to go forth as
when it burst out from the
womb;

9 When I put the cloud as its
garment
And thick gloom as its swaddling band,

10 And I proceeded to break up
my regulation upon it
And to set a bar and doors,

11 And I went on to say, 'This
far you may come, and no
farther;
And here your proud waves
are limited'?

12 Was it from your days onward
that you commanded the
morning?
Did you cause the dawn to
know its place,

13 To take hold on the extremities
of the earth,
That the wicked ones might
be shaken out from it?

14 It transforms itself like clay
under a seal,
And things take their station
as in clothing.

15 And from the wicked ones their
light is held back,
And the high arm itself gets
broken.

16 Have you come to the sources
of the sea,
Or in search of the watery
deep have you walked about?

17 Have the gates of death been
uncovered to you,
Or the gates of deep shadow
can you see?

18 Have you intelligently considered
the broad spaces of the
earth?
Tell, if you have come to
know it all.

19 Where, now, is the way to where
light resides?

As for darkness, where, now,
is its place,

20 That you should take it to its
boundary
And that you should understand the roadways to its
house?

21 Have you come to know because
at that time you were being
born,
And [because] in number
your days are many?

22 Have you entered into the storehouses of the snow,
Or do you see even the storehouses of the hail,

23 Which I have kept back for the
time of distress,
For the day of fight and war?

24 Where, now, is the way by which
the light distributes itself,
[And] the east wind scatters
about upon the earth?

25 Who has divided a channel for
the flood
And a way for the thunderous
storm cloud,

26 To make it rain upon the land
where there is no man,
[Upon] the wilderness in
which there is no earthling
man,

27 To satisfy storm-stricken and
desolate places
And to cause the growth of
grass to sprout?

28 Does there exist a father for the
rain,
Or who gave birth to the
dewdrops?

29 Out of whose belly does the ice
actually come forth,
And as for the hoarfrost of
heaven, who indeed brings
it to birth?

30 The very waters keep themselves
hidden as by stone,
And the surface of the watery
deep makes itself compact.

31 Can you tie fast the bonds of
the Ki'mah constellation,
Or can you loosen the very
cords of the Ke'sil constellation?

32 Can you bring forth the Maz'-
za·roth constellation in its
appointed time?

And as for the Ash constellation alongside its sons, can you conduct them?

33 Have you come to know the statutes of the heavens,
Or could you put its authority in the earth?

34 Can you raise your voice even to the cloud,
So that a heaving mass of water itself may cover you?

35 Can you send forth lightnings that they may go
And say to you, 'Here we are!'?

36 Who put wisdom in the cloud layers,
Or who gave understanding to the sky phenomenon?

37 Who can exactly number the clouds in wisdom,
Or the water jars of heaven—who can tip [them] over,

38 When the dust pours out as into a molten mass,
And the clods of earth themselves get stuck together?

39 Can you hunt prey for a lion itself
And can you satisfy the lively appetite of young lions,

40 When they crouch in the hiding places,
[Or] keep lying in the covert for an ambush?

41 Who prepares for the raven its food
When its own young ones cry to God for help,
[When] they keep wandering about because there is nothing to eat?

39 "Have you come to know the appointed time for the mountain goats of the crag to give birth?
Do you observe just when the hinds bring forth with birth pangs?

2 Do you count the lunar months that they fulfill,
Or have you come to know the appointed time that they give birth?

3 They bow down when they cast forth their young ones,
[When] they get rid of their pangs.

4 Their sons become robust, they get big in the open field;
They actually go forth and do not return to them.

5 Who sent forth the zebra free,
And who loosened the very bands of the wild ass,

6 Whose house I have appointed the desert plain
And whose dwelling places the salt country?

7 It laughs at the turmoil of a town;
The noises of a stalker it does not hear.

8 It explores mountains for its pasturage
And after every sort of green plant it seeks.

9 Does a wild bull want to serve you,
Or will it spend the night by your manger?

10 Will you bind a wild bull fast with its ropes in the furrow,
Or will it harrow low plains after you?

11 Will you trust in it because its power is abundant,
And will you leave your toil to it?

12 Will you rely on it that it will bring back your seed
And that it will gather to your threshing floor?

13 Has the wing of the female ostrich flapped joyously,
Or [has she] the pinions of a stork and the plumage?

14 For she leaves her eggs to the earth itself
And in the dust she keeps them warm,

15 And she forgets that some foot may crush them
Or even a wild beast of the field may tread on them.

16 She does treat her sons roughly, as if not hers—
In vain is her toil [because she has] no dread.

17 For God has made her forget wisdom,
And he has not given her a share in understanding.

18 At the time she flaps [her wings] on high,

She laughs at the horse and at its rider.

19 Can you give to the horse mightiness?
   Can you clothe its neck with a rustling mane?

20 Can you cause it to leap like a locust?
   The dignity of its snorting is frightful.

21 It paws in the low plain and exults in power;
   It goes forth to meet armor.

22 It laughs at dread, and is not terrified;
   Nor does it turn back on account of a sword.

23 Against it a quiver rattles,
   The blade of a spear and a javelin.

24 With pounding and excitement it swallows up the earth,
   And it does not believe that it is the sound of a horn.

25 As soon as the horn blows it says Aha!
   And from far off it smells the battle,
   The uproar of chiefs and the war cry.

26 Is it owing to your understanding that the falcon soars up,
   That it spreads its wings to the south wind?

27 Or is it at your order that an eagle flies upward
   And that it builds its nest high up,

28 That on a crag it resides and stays during the night
   Upon the tooth of a crag and an inaccessible place?

29 From there it has to search for food;
   Far into the distance its eyes keep looking.

30 And its young ones themselves keep sipping up blood;
   And where the slain are, there it is."

40 And Jehovah proceeded to answer Job and say:

2 "Should there be any contending of a faultfinder with the Almighty?
   Let the reprover of God himself answer it."

3 And Job went on to answer Jehovah and say:

4 "Look! I have become of little account.
   What shall I reply to you?
   My hand I have put over my mouth.

5 Once have I spoken, and I will not answer;
   And twice, and I will add nothing."

6 And Jehovah went on to answer Job out of the windstorm and say:

7 "Gird up your loins, please, like an able-bodied man;
   I shall question you, and you inform me.

8 Really, will you invalidate my justice?
   Will you pronounce me wicked in order that you may be in the right?

9 Or do you have an arm like that of the [true] God,
   And with a voice like his can you make it thunder?

10 Deck yourself, please, with superiority and highness;
   And with dignity and splendor may you clothe yourself.

11 Let flow the furious outbursts of your anger,
   And see every one haughty and bring him low.

12 See every one haughty, humble him,
   And tread down the wicked right where they are.

13 Hide them together in the dust,
   Bind their very faces in the hidden place,

14 And I, even I, shall commend you,
   Because your right hand can save you.

15 Here, now, is Be·he'moth that I have made as well as you.
   Green grass it eats just as a bull does.

16 Here, now, its power is in its hips,
   And its dynamic energy in the tendons of its belly.

17 It bends down its tail like a cedar;
   The sinews of its thighs are interwoven.

18 Its bones are tubes of copper;
Its strong bones are like wrought-iron rods.
19 It is the beginning of the ways of God;
Its Maker can bring near his sword.
20 For the mountains themselves bear their produce for it,
And all the wild beasts of the field themselves play there.
21 Under the thorny lotus trees it lies down,
In the concealed place of reeds and the swampy place.
22 The thorny lotus trees keep it blocked off with their shadow;
The poplars of the torrent valley surround it.
23 If the river acts violently, it does not run in panic.
It is confident, although the Jordan should burst forth against its mouth.
24 Before its eyes can anyone take it?
With snares can anyone bore [its] nose?

41 "Can you draw out Le·vi′a·than with a fishhook,
Or with a rope can you hold down its tongue?
2 Can you put a rush in its nostrils,
Or with a thorn can you bore its jaws?
3 Will it make many entreaties to you,
Or will it say soft words to you?
4 Will it conclude a covenant with you,
That you may take it as a slave to time indefinite?
5 Will you play with it as with a bird,
Or will you tie it for your young girls?
6 Will partners barter for it?
Will they divide it up among tradesmen?
7 Will you fill its skin with harpoons,
Or its head with fish spears?
8 Put your hands upon it.
Remember the battle. Do not do it again.

9 Look! One's expectation about it will certainly be disappointed.
One will also be hurled down at the mere sight of it.
10 None is so audacious that he should stir it up.
And who is it that can hold his ground before me?
11 Who has given me something first, that I ought to reward him?
Under the whole heavens it is mine.
12 I shall not keep silent about its parts
Or the matter of [its] mightiness and the grace of its proportions.
13 Who has uncovered the face of its clothing?
Into its double jaw who will enter?
14 The doors of its face who has opened?
Its teeth round about are frightful.
15 Furrows of scales are its haughtiness,
Closed as with a tight seal.
16 One to the other they fit closely,
And not even air can come in between them.
17 Each one to the other they are stuck together;
They grasp one another and cannot be separated.
18 Its very sneezings flash forth light,
And its eyes are like the beams of dawn.
19 Out of its mouth there go lightning flashes,
Even sparks of fire make their escape.
20 Out of its nostrils smoke goes forth,
Like a furnace set aflame even with rushes.
21 Its soul itself sets coals ablaze,
And even a flame goes forth out of its mouth.
22 In its neck lodges strength,
And before it despair leaps.
23 The folds of its flesh do cling together;
They are as a casting upon it, immovable.

24 Its heart is cast like stone,
Yes, cast like a lower millstone.
25 Due to its rising up the strong get frightened;
Due to consternation they get bewildered.
26 Overtaking it, the sword itself does not prove equal,
Nor spear, dart or arrowhead.
27 It regards iron as mere straw,
Copper as mere rotten wood.
28 An arrow does not chase it away;
The slingstones have been changed for it into mere stubble.
29 A club has been regarded by it as mere stubble,
And it laughs at the rattling of a javelin.
30 As pointed earthenware fragments are its under parts;
It spreads out a threshing instrument upon the mire.
31 It causes the depths to boil just like a pot;
It makes the very sea like an ointment pot.
32 Behind itself it makes a pathway shine;
One would regard the watery deep as gray-headedness.
33 Upon the dust there is not the like of it,
The one made to be without terror.
34 Everything high it sees.
It is king over all majestic wild beasts."

42 And Job proceeded to answer Jehovah and say:
2 "I have come to know that you are able to do all things,
And there is no idea that is unattainable for you.
3 'Who is this that is obscuring counsel without knowledge?'
Therefore I talked, but I was not understanding
Things too wonderful for me, which I do not know.
4 'Hear, please, and I myself shall speak.
I shall question you, and you inform me.'
5 In hearsay I have heard about you,
But now my own eye does see you.
6 That is why I make a retraction,
And I do repent in dust and ashes."

7 And it came about after Jehovah had spoken these words to Job, that Jehovah proceeded to say to El′i·phaz the Te′man·ite: "My anger has grown hot against you and your two companions, for YOU men have not spoken concerning me what is truthful as has my servant Job. 8 And now take for yourselves seven bulls and seven rams and go to my servant Job, and YOU men must offer up a burnt sacrifice in YOUR own behalf; and Job my servant will himself pray for YOU. His face only I shall accept so as not to commit disgraceful folly with YOU, for YOU have not spoken concerning me what is truthful, as has my servant Job."

9 Accordingly El′i·phaz the Te′man·ite and Bil′dad the Shu′hite [and] Zo′phar the Na′a·ma·thite went and did just as Jehovah had spoken to them; and so Jehovah accepted Job's face.

10 And Jehovah himself turned back the captive condition of Job when he prayed in behalf of his companions, and Jehovah began to give in addition all that had been Job's, in double amount. 11 And there kept coming to him all his brothers and all his sisters and all those formerly knowing him, and they began to eat bread with him in his house and to sympathize with him and to comfort him over all the calamity that Jehovah had let come upon him; and they proceeded each one to give him a piece of money and each one a gold ring.

12 As for Jehovah, he blessed the end of Job afterward more than his beginning, so that he came to have fourteen thousand sheep and six thousand camels and a thousand spans of cattle and a thousand she-asses. 13 He also came to have seven sons and three daughters. 14 And he went calling the name of the first Je·mi′mah and the name of the second Ke-

 zi'ah and the name of the third Ker'en-hap'puch. 15 And no women were found as pretty as Job's daughters in all the land, and their father proceeded to give them an inheritance in among their brothers.

16 And Job continued living after this a hundred and forty years and came to see his sons and his grandsons—four generations. 17 And gradually Job died, old and satisfied with days.

PSALMS

BOOK ONE
(Psalms 1 – 41)

1 Happy is the man that has not walked in the counsel of the wicked ones,
And in the way of sinners has not stood,
And in the seat of ridiculers has not sat.
2 But his delight is in the law of Jehovah,
And in his law he reads in an undertone day and night.
3 And he will certainly become like a tree planted by streams of water,
That gives its own fruit in its season
And the foliage of which does not wither,
And everything he does will succeed.
4 The wicked are not like that,
But are like the chaff that the wind drives away.
5 That is why the wicked ones will not stand up in the judgment,
Nor sinners in the assembly of righteous ones.
6 For Jehovah is taking knowledge of the way of righteous ones,
But the very way of wicked ones will perish.

2 Why have the nations been in tumult
And the national groups themselves kept muttering an empty thing?
2 The kings of earth take their stand
And high officials themselves have massed together as one

Against Jehovah and against his anointed one,
3 [Saying:] "Let us tear their bands apart
And cast their cords away from us!"
4 The very One sitting in the heavens will laugh;
Jehovah himself will hold them in derision.
5 At that time he will speak to them in his anger
And in his hot displeasure he will disturb them,
6 [Saying:] "I, even I, have installed my king
Upon Zion, my holy mountain."
7 Let me refer to the decree of Jehovah;
He has said to me: "You are my son;
I, today, I have become your father.
8 Ask of me, that I may give nations as your inheritance
And the ends of the earth as your own possession.
9 You will break them with an iron scepter,
As though a potter's vessel you will dash them to pieces."
10 And now, O kings, exercise insight;
Let yourselves be corrected, O judges of the earth.
11 Serve Jehovah with fear
And be joyful with trembling.
12 Kiss the son, that He may not become incensed

And YOU may not perish [from] the way,
For his anger flares up easily.
Happy are all those taking refuge in him.

A melody of David when he was running away on account of Ab'sa.lom his son.

3 O Jehovah, why have my adversaries become many?
Why are many rising up against me?

2 Many are saying of my soul: "There is no salvation for him by God." *Se'lah.*

3 And yet you, O Jehovah, are a shield about me,
My glory and the One lifting up my head.

4 With my voice I shall call to Jehovah himself,
And he will answer me from his holy mountain. *Se'lah.*

5 As for me, I will lie down that I may sleep;
I shall certainly awake, for Jehovah himself keeps supporting me.

6 I shall not be afraid of ten thousands of people
Who have set themselves in array against me round about.

7 Do arise, O Jehovah! Save me, O my God!
For you will have to strike all my enemies on the jaw.
The teeth of wicked ones you will have to break.

8 Salvation belongs to Jehovah.
Your blessing is upon your people. *Se'lah.*

To the director on stringed instruments. A melody of David.

4 When I call, answer me, O my righteous God.
In the distress you must make broad space for me.
Show me favor and hear my prayer.

2 You sons of men, how long must my glory be for insult,
[While] YOU keep loving empty things,
[While] YOU keep seeking to find a lie? *Se'lah.*

3 So take knowledge that Jehovah will certainly distinguish his loyal one;
Jehovah himself will hear when I call to him.

4 BE agitated, but do not sin.
Have YOUR say in YOUR heart, upon YOUR bed, and keep silent. *Se'lah.*

5 Sacrifice the sacrifices of righteousness,
And trust in Jehovah.

6 There are many saying: "Who will show us good?"
Lift up the light of your face upon us, O Jehovah.

7 You will certainly give a rejoicing in my heart
Greater than in the time when their grain and their new wine have abounded.

8 In peace I will both lie down and sleep,
For you yourself alone, O Jehovah, make me dwell in security.

To the director for Ne'hi.loth.
A melody of David.

5 To my sayings do give ear, O Jehovah;
Do understand my sighing.

2 Do pay attention to the sound of my cry for help,
O my King and my God, because to you I pray.

3 O Jehovah, in the morning you will hear my voice;
In the morning I shall address myself to you and be on the watch.

4 For you are not a God taking delight in wickedness;
No one bad may reside for any time with you.

5 No boasters may take their stand in front of your eyes.
You do hate all those practicing what is hurtful;

6 You will destroy those speaking a lie.
A man of bloodshed and deception Jehovah detests.

7 As for me, in the abundance of your loving-kindness
I shall come into your house,
I shall bow down toward

your holy temple in fear of you.

8 O Jehovah, lead me in your righteousness by reason of my foes;
Make your way smooth before me.

9 For in their mouth there is nothing trustworthy;
Their inward part is adversity indeed.
Their throat is an opened burial place;
A smooth tongue they use.

10 God will certainly hold them guilty;
They will fall due to their own counsels.
In the multitude of their transgressions let there be a dispersing of them,
Because they have rebelled against you.

11 But all those taking refuge in you will rejoice;
To time indefinite they will cry out joyfully.
And you will block approach to them,
And those loving your name will exult in you.

12 For you yourself will bless anyone righteous, O Jehovah;
As with a large shield, with approval you will surround them.

To the director on stringed instruments on the lower octave. A melody of David.

6 O Jehovah, do not in your anger reprove me,
And do not in your rage correct me.

2 Show me favor, O Jehovah, for I am fading away.
Heal me, O Jehovah, for my bones have been disturbed.

3 Yes, my own soul has been very much disturbed;
And you, O Jehovah—how long?

4 Do return, O Jehovah, do rescue my soul;
Save me for the sake of your loving-kindness.

5 For in death there is no mention of you;
In She'ol who will laud you?

6 I have grown weary with my sighing;
All night long I make my couch swim;
With my tears I make my own divan overflow.

7 From vexation my eye has become weak,
It has grown old because of all those showing hostility to me.

8 Get away from me, all you practicers of what is hurtful,
For Jehovah will certainly hear the sound of my weeping.

9 Jehovah will indeed hear my request for favor;
Jehovah himself will accept my own prayer.

10 All my enemies will be very much ashamed and disturbed;
They will turn back, they will be ashamed instantly.

A dirge of David that he sang to Jehovah concerning the words of Cush the Ben'ja·min·ite.

7 O Jehovah my God, in you I have taken refuge.
Save me from all those persecuting me and deliver me,

2 That no one may tear my soul to pieces as a lion does,
Snatching [me] away when there is no deliverer.

3 O Jehovah my God, if I have done this,
If there exists any injustice in my hands,

4 If I have repaid the one rewarding me with what is bad,
Or [if] I have despoiled anyone showing hostility to me without success,

5 Let an enemy pursue my soul
And let him overtake and trample my life down to the very earth
And cause my own glory to reside in the dust itself. *Se'lah.*

6 Do arise, O Jehovah, in your anger;
Lift yourself up at the out-

bursts of fury of those showing hostility to me,
And do awake for me, [since] you have given command for judgment itself.

7 And let the very assembly of national groups surround you,
And against it do you return on high.

8 Jehovah himself will pass sentence on the peoples.
Judge me, O Jehovah, according to my righteousness
And according to my integrity in me.

9 Please, may the badness of wicked ones come to an end,
And may you establish the righteous one;
And God as righteous is testing out heart and kidneys.

10 The shield for me is upon God, a Savior of those upright in heart.

11 God is a righteous Judge,
And God is hurling denunciations every day.

12 If anyone will not return, His sword he will sharpen,
His bow he will certainly bend, and he will make it ready [for shooting].

13 And for himself he must prepare the instruments of death;
His arrows he will make flaming ones.

14 Look! There is one that is pregnant with what is hurtful,
And he has conceived trouble and is bound to give birth to falsehood.

15 A pit he has excavated, and he proceeded to dig it;
But he will fall into the hole [that] he went making.

16 His trouble will return upon his own head,
And upon the crown of his head his own violence will descend.

17 I shall laud Jehovah according to his righteousness,
And I will make melody to the name of Jehovah the Most High.

To the director upon the Git′tith.
A melody of David.

8 O Jehovah our Lord, how majestic your name is in all the earth,
You whose dignity is recounted above the heavens!

2 Out of the mouth of children and sucklings you have founded strength,
On account of those showing hostility to you,
So as to make the enemy and the one taking his vengeance desist.

3 When I see your heavens, the works of your fingers,
The moon and the stars that you have prepared,

4 What is mortal man that you keep him in mind,
And the son of earthling man that you take care of him?

5 You also proceeded to make him a little less than godlike ones,
And with glory and splendor you then crowned him.

6 You make him dominate over the works of your hands;
Everything you have put under his feet:

7 Small cattle and oxen, all of them,
And also the beasts of the open field,

8 The birds of heaven and the fish of the sea,
Anything passing through the paths of the seas.

9 O Jehovah our Lord, how majestic your name is in all the earth!

To the director upon Muth-lab′ben.
A melody of David.

א [Aleph]

9 I will laud [you], O Jehovah, with all my heart;
I will declare all your wonderful works.

2 I will rejoice and exult in you,
I will make melody to your name, O Most High.

ב [Beth]

3 When my enemies turn back,

They will stumble and perish
from before you.
4 For you have executed my judgment and my cause;
You have sat on the throne
judging with righteousness.

♪ [*Gimel*]

5 You have rebuked nations, you
have destroyed the wicked
one.
Their name you have wiped
out to time indefinite, even
forever.
6 O you enemy, [your] desolations have come to their
perpetual finish,
And the cities that you have
uprooted.
The very mention of them
will certainly perish.

ה [*He*]

7 As for Jehovah, he will sit to
time indefinite,
Firmly establishing his throne
for judgment itself.
8 And he himself will judge the
productive land in right-
eousness;
He will judicially try national
groups in uprightness.

ו [*Waw*]

9 And Jehovah will become a
secure height for anyone
crushed,
A secure height in times of
distress.
10 And those knowing your name
will trust in you,
For you will certainly not
leave those looking for you,
O Jehovah.

ז [*Zayin*]

11 Make melody, you people, to
Jehovah, who is dwelling
in Zion;
Tell among the peoples his
deeds.
12 For, when looking for bloodshed, he will certainly remember those very ones;
He is sure not to forget the
outcry of the afflicted ones.

ח [*Heth*]

13 Show me favor, O Jehovah; see

my affliction by those hating
me,
O you who are lifting me up
from the gates of death,
14 In order that I may declare all
your praiseworthy deeds
In the gates of the daughter
of Zion,
That I may be joyful in your
salvation.

ט [*Teth*]

15 The nations have sunk down
into the pit that they have
made;
In the net that they hid, their
own foot has been caught.
16 Jehovah is known by the judgment that he has executed.
By the activity of his own
hands the wicked one has
been ensnared.
Hig·ga'ion. Se'lah.

י [*Yod*]

17 Wicked people will turn back
to She'ol,
Even all the nations forgetting God.
18 For not always will the poor
one be forgotten,
Nor will the hope of the meek
ones ever perish.

כ [*Kaph*]

19 Do arise, O Jehovah! Let not
mortal man prove superior
in strength.
Let the nations be judged before your face.
20 Do put fear into them, O Jehovah,
That the nations may know
that they are but mortal
men. Se'lah.

ל [*Lamed*]

10 Why, O Jehovah, do you keep
standing afar off?
[Why] do you keep yourself
hid in times of distress?
2 In his haughtiness the wicked
one hotly pursues the af-
flicted one;
They get caught by the ideas
that they have thought up.
3 For the wicked has praised himself over the selfish longing
of his soul,

And the one making undue profit has blessed himself;

ב [*Nun*]

He has disrespected Jehovah.
4 The wicked one according to his superciliousness makes no search;
All his ideas are: "There is no God."
5 His ways keep prospering all the time.
Your judicial decisions are high up out of his range;
As for all those showing hostility to him, he puffs at them.
6 He has said in his heart: "I shall not be made to totter;
For generation after generation [I shall be] one who is in no calamity."

פ [*Pe*]

7 His mouth is full of oaths and of deceptions and of oppression.
Under his tongue are trouble and what is hurtful.
8 He sits in an ambush of settlements;
From concealed places he will kill someone innocent.

ע [*Ayin*]

His eyes are on the lookout for someone unfortunate.
9 He keeps lying in wait in the concealed place like a lion in his covert.
He keeps lying in wait to carry off some afflicted one by force.
He carries off the afflicted one by force when he draws his net shut.
10 He is crushed, he bows down,
And the army of dejected ones has to fall into his strong [claws].
11 He has said in his heart: "God has forgotten.
He has concealed his face.
He will certainly never see [it]."

ק [*Qoph*]

12 Do arise, O Jehovah. O God, lift up your hand.
Do not forget the afflicted ones.
13 Why is it that the wicked one has disrespected God?
He has said in his heart: "You will not require an accounting."

ר [*Resh*]

14 For you yourself have seen trouble and vexation.
You keep looking on, to get [them] into your hand.
To you the unfortunate one, the fatherless boy, commits [himself].
You yourself have become [his] helper.

ש [*Shin*]

15 Break the arm of the wicked and bad one.
May you search after his wickedness [until] you find no more.
16 Jehovah is King to time indefinite, even forever.
The nations have perished out of his earth.

ת [*Taw*]

17 The desire of the meek ones you will certainly hear, O Jehovah.
You will prepare their heart.
You will pay attention with your ear,
18 To judge the fatherless boy and the crushed one,
That mortal man who is of the earth may no more cause trembling.

To the director. Of David.

11 In Jehovah I have taken refuge.
How dare you men say to my soul:
"Flee as a bird to your mountain!"
2 For, look! the wicked ones themselves bend the bow,
They do make ready their arrow upon the bowstring,
To shoot in the gloom at the ones upright in heart.
3 When the foundations themselves are torn down,
What must anyone righteous do?

4 Jehovah is in his holy temple.
Jehovah—in the heavens is
his throne.
His own eyes behold, his own
beaming eyes examine the
sons of men.
5 Jehovah himself examines the
righteous one as well as the
wicked one,
And anyone loving violence
His soul certainly hates.
6 He will rain down upon the
wicked ones traps, fire and
sulphur
And a scorching wind, as the
portion of their cup.
7 For Jehovah is righteous; he
does love righteous acts.
The upright are the ones that
will behold his face.

To the director on the lower octave.
A melody of David.

12 Do save [me], O Jehovah, for
the loyal one has come to
an end;
For faithful people have vanished from the sons of men.
2 Untruth they keep speaking one
to the other;
With a smooth lip they keep
speaking even with a double
heart.
3 Jehovah will cut off all smooth
lips,
The tongue speaking great
things,
4 Those who have said: "With
our tongue we shall prevail.
Our lips are with us. Who
will be a master to us?"
5 "Because of the despoiling of the
afflicted ones, because of the
sighing of the poor ones,
I shall at this time arise,"
says Jehovah.
"I shall put [him] in safety
from anyone that puffs at
him."
6 The sayings of Jehovah are
pure sayings,
As silver refined in a smelting
furnace of earth, clarified
seven times.
7 You yourself, O Jehovah, will
guard them;
You will preserve each one

from this generation to time
indefinite.
8 The wicked ones walk all
around,
Because vileness is exalted
among the sons of men.

To the director. A melody of David.

13 How long, O Jehovah, will you
forget me? Forever?
How long will you conceal
your face from me?
2 How long shall I set resistance
in my soul,
Grief in my heart by day?
How long will my enemy be
exalted over me?
3 Do look [upon me]; answer me,
O Jehovah my God.
Do make my eyes shine, that
I may not fall asleep in
death,
4 That my enemy may not say:
"I have won out over him!"
[That] my adversaries themselves may [not] be joyful
because I am made to
stagger.
5 As for me, in your loving-
kindness I have trusted;
Let my heart be joyful in your
salvation.
6 I will sing to Jehovah, for he
has dealt rewardingly with
me.

To the director. Of David.

14 The senseless one has said
in his heart:
"There is no Jehovah."
They have acted ruinously, they
have acted detestably in
[their] dealing.
There is no one doing good.
2 As for Jehovah, he has looked
down from heaven itself
upon the sons of men,
To see whether there exists
anyone having insight, anyone seeking Jehovah.
3 They have all turned aside, they
are [all] alike corrupt;
There is no one doing good,
Not even one.
4 Have none of the practicers of
what is hurtful got knowledge,
Eating up my people as they
have eaten bread?

They have not called even
upon Jehovah.
5 There they were filled with a
great dread,
For Jehovah is among the
generation of the righteous
one.
6 The counsel of the afflicted one
YOU people would put to
shame,
Because Jehovah is his refuge.
7 O that out of Zion there were
the salvation of Israel!
When Jehovah gathers back
the captive ones of his
people,
Let Jacob be joyful, let Israel rejoice.

A melody of David.

15 O Jehovah, who will be a
guest in your tent?
Who will reside in your holy
mountain?
2 He who is walking faultlessly
and practicing righteous-
ness
And speaking the truth in his
heart.
3 He has not slandered with his
tongue.
To his companion he has done
nothing bad,
And no reproach has he taken
up against his intimate acquaintance.
4 In his eyes anyone contemptible
is certainly rejected,
But those fearing Jehovah he
honors.
He has sworn to what is bad
[for himself], and yet he
does not alter.
5 His money he has not given out
on interest,
And a bribe against the innocent one he has not taken.
He that is doing these things
will never be made to totter.

A mik'tam of David.

16 Keep me, O God, for I have
taken refuge in you.
2 I have said to Jehovah: "You
are Jehovah; my goodness
is, not for your sake,
3 [But] to the holy ones that are
in the earth.

They, even the majestic ones,
are the ones in whom is all
my delight."
4 Pains become many to those
[who], when there is someone else, do hurry [after
him].
I shall not pour out their
drink offerings of blood,
And I shall not carry their
names upon my lips.
5 Jehovah is the portion of my
allotted share and of my
cup.
You are holding fast my lot.
6 The measuring lines themselves
have fallen for me in pleasant places.
Really, [my own] possession
has proved agreeable to me.
7 I shall bless Jehovah, who has
given me advice.
Really, during the nights my
kidneys have corrected me.
8 I have placed Jehovah in front
of me constantly.
Because [he] is at my right
hand, I shall not be made
to totter.
9 Therefore my heart does rejoice, and my glory is inclined to be joyful.
Also, my own flesh will reside
in security.
10 For you will not leave my soul
in She'ol.
You will not allow your loyal
one to see the pit.
11 You will cause me to know the
path of life.
Rejoicing to satisfaction is
with your face;
There is pleasantness at your
right hand forever.

A prayer of David.

17 Do hear what is righteous, O
Jehovah; do pay attention
to my entreating cry;
Do give ear to my prayer
without lips of deception.
2 From before you may my judgment go forth;
May your own eyes behold
uprightness.
3 You have examined my heart,
you have made inspection
by night,

You have refined me; you will
discover [that] I have not
schemed.
My mouth will not transgress.
4 As for the activities of men,
By the word of your lips I
myself have watched against
the paths of the robber.
5 Let my steps take hold on your
tracks,
[In which] my footsteps will
certainly not be made to
totter.
6 I myself do call upon you, because you will answer me,
O God.
Incline your ear to me. Hear
my saying.
7 Make your acts of loving-
kindnesses wonderful, O
Savior of those seeking refuge
From the revolters against
your right hand.
8 Keep me as the pupil of the
eyeball,
In the shadow of your wings
may you conceal me,
9 Because of the wicked who have
despoiled me.
The enemies against my soul
themselves keep closing in
upon me.
10 They have enclosed [themselves]
with their own fat;
With their mouth they have
spoken in haughtiness;
11 As regards our steps, now they
have surrounded us;
They fix their eyes to incline
to the earth.
12 His likeness is that of a lion
that yearns to tear to pieces
And that of a young lion sitting in concealed places.
13 Do rise up, O Jehovah; do confront him to the face;
Make him bow down; do provide escape for my soul from
the wicked one with your
sword,
14 From men, [by] your hand, O
Jehovah,
From men of [this] system of
things, whose share is in
[this] life,
And whose belly you fill with
your concealed treasure,

Who are satisfied with sons
And who do lay up for their
children what they leave
over.
15 As for me, in righteousness I
shall behold your face;
I will be satisfied when
awakening [to see] your
form.

To the director. Of Jehovah's
servant, of David, who spoke to
Jehovah the words of this song
in the day that Jehovah had
delivered him out of the palm of
all his enemies and out of the
hand of Saul. And he proceeded
to say:

18 I shall have affection for you,
O Jehovah my strength.
2 Jehovah is my crag and my
stronghold and the Provider
of escape for me.
My God is my rock. I shall
take refuge in him,
My shield and my horn of
salvation, my secure height.
3 On the One to be praised, Jehovah, I shall call,
And from my enemies I shall
be saved.
4 The ropes of death encircled me;
Flash floods of good-for-
nothing [men] also kept
terrifying me.
5 The very ropes of She'ol surrounded me;
The snares of death con-
fronted me.
6 In my distress I kept calling
upon Jehovah,
And to my God I kept crying
for help.
Out of his temple he proceeded
to hear my voice,
And my own cry before him
for help now came into his
ears.
7 And the earth began to shake
and rock,
And the foundations of the
mountains themselves be-
came agitated,
And they kept shaking back
and forth because he had
been angered.
8 Smoke went up at his nostrils,
and fire itself from his
mouth kept devouring;

Coals themselves blazed forth from him.

9 And he proceeded to bend the heavens down and descend. And thick gloom was beneath his feet.

10 And he came riding upon a cherub and came flying, And he came darting upon the wings of a spirit.

11 He then made darkness his concealment place, All around him as his booth, Dark waters, thick clouds.

12 Out of the brightness in front of him there were his clouds that passed by, Hail and burning coals of fire.

13 And in the heavens Jehovah began to thunder, And the Most High himself began to give his voice, Hail and burning coals of fire.

14 And he kept sending out his arrows, that he might scatter them; And lightnings he shot out, that he might throw them into confusion.

15 And the stream beds of waters became visible, And the foundations of the productive land became uncovered From your rebuke, O Jehovah, from the blast of the breath of your nostrils.

16 He was sending from on high, he was taking me, He was drawing me out of great waters.

17 He was delivering me from my strong enemy, And from those hating me; because they were stronger than I was.

18 They kept confronting me in the day of my disaster, But Jehovah came to be as a support for me.

19 And he proceeded to bring me out into a roomy place; He was rescuing me, because he had found delight in me.

20 Jehovah rewards me according to my righteousness; According to the cleanness of my hands he repays me.

21 For I have kept the ways of Jehovah, And I have not wickedly departed from my God.

22 For all his judicial decisions are in front of me, And his statutes I shall not remove from myself.

23 And I will prove myself faultless with him, And I shall keep myself from error on my part.

24 And let Jehovah repay me according to my righteousness, According to the cleanness of my hands in front of his eyes.

25 With someone loyal you will act in loyalty; With the faultless, able-bodied man you will deal faultlessly;

26 With the one keeping clean you will show yourself clean; And with the crooked one you will show yourself tortuous;

27 Because the afflicted people you yourself will save; But the haughty eyes you will abase.

28 For you yourself will light my lamp, O Jehovah; My God himself will make my darkness shine.

29 For by you I can run against a marauder band; And by my God I can climb a wall.

30 As for the [true] God, perfect is his way; The saying of Jehovah is a refined one. A shield he is to all those taking refuge in him.

31 For who is a God besides Jehovah? And who is a rock except our God?

32 The [true] God is the One girding me closely with vital energy, And he will grant my way to be perfect,

33 Making my feet like those of the hinds, And upon places high for me he keeps me standing.

34 He is teaching my hands for
   warfare,
   And my arms have pressed
   down a bow of copper.
35 And you will give me your
   shield of salvation,
   And your own right hand will
   sustain me,
   And your own humility will
   make me great.
36 You will make room large
   enough for my steps under
   me,
   And my ankles will certainly
   not wobble.
37 I shall pursue my enemies and
   overtake them;
   And I shall not return until
   they are exterminated.
38 I shall break them in pieces so
   that they will not be able
   to rise up;
   They will fall under my feet.
39 And you will gird me with vital
   energy for warfare;
   You will make those rising
   against me collapse under
   me.
40 And as for my enemies, you
   will certainly give me the
   back of [their] neck;
   And as for those hating me
   intensely, I shall silence
   them.
41 They cry for help, but there is
   no savior,
   To Jehovah, but he actually
   does not answer them.
42 And I shall pound them fine
   like dust before the wind;
   Like the mire of the streets I
   shall pour them out.
43 You will provide me escape
   from the faultfinding of the
   people.
   You will appoint me the head
   of the nations.
   A people that I have not
   known—they will serve me.
44 At mere hearsay they will be
   obedient to me;
   Foreigners themselves will
   come cringing to me.
45 Foreigners themselves will fade
   away,
   And they will come quaking
   out from their bulwarks.

46 Jehovah is living, and blessed
   be my Rock,
   And let the God of my salvation be exalted.
47 The [true] God is the Giver of
   acts of vengeance to me;
   And he subdues the peoples
   under me.
48 He is providing escape for me
   from my angry enemies;
   Above those who rise up
   against me you will lift me
   up,
   From the man of violence you
   will deliver me.
49 That is why I shall laud you
   among the nations, O Jehovah,
   And to your name I will make
   melody.
50 He is doing great acts of salvation for his king
   And exercising loving-kindness
   to his anointed one,
   To David and to his seed to
   time indefinite.

To the director. A melody of David.

19

The heavens are declaring the
   glory of God;
   And of the work of his hands
   the expanse is telling.
2 One day after another day
   causes speech to bubble
   forth,
   And one night after another
   night shows forth knowledge.
3 There is no speech, and there
   are no words;
   No voice on their part is being
   heard.
4 Into all the earth their measuring line has gone out,
   And to the extremity of the
   productive land their utterances.
   In them he has set a tent for
   the sun,
5 And it is like a bridegroom when
   coming out of his nuptial
   chamber;
   It exults as a mighty man
   does to run in a path.
6 From one extremity of the heavens is its going forth,
   And its [finished] circuit is
   to their [other] extremities;

And there is nothing concealed from its heat.

7 The law of Jehovah is perfect, bringing back the soul.
The reminder of Jehovah is trustworthy, making the inexperienced one wise.

8 The orders from Jehovah are upright, causing the heart to rejoice;
The commandment of Jehovah is clean, making the eyes shine.

9 The fear of Jehovah is pure, standing forever.
The judicial decisions of Jehovah are true; they have proved altogether righteous.

10 They are more to be desired than gold, yes, than much refined gold;
And sweeter than honey and the flowing honey of the combs.

11 Also, your own servant has been warned by them;
In the keeping of them there is a large reward.

12 Mistakes—who can discern?
From concealed sins pronounce me innocent.

13 Also from presumptuous acts hold your servant back;
Do not let them dominate me.
In that case I shall be complete,
And I shall have remained innocent from much transgression.

14 Let the sayings of my mouth and the meditation of my heart
Become pleasurable before you,
O Jehovah my Rock and my Redeemer.

To the director. A melody of David.

20 May Jehovah answer you in the day of distress.
May the name of the God of Jacob protect you.

2 May he send your help out of the holy place,
And sustain you out of Zion itself.

3 May he remember all your gift offerings,
And may he accept your burnt offering as being fat. *Se'lah.*

4 May he give to you according to your heart,
And all your counsel may he fulfill.

5 We will cry out joyfully because of your salvation,
And in the name of our God we shall lift our banners.
May Jehovah fulfill all your requests.

6 Now I do know that Jehovah certainly saves his anointed one.
He answers him from his holy heavens
With the saving mighty acts of his right hand.

7 Some concerning chariots and others concerning horses,
But, as for us, concerning the name of Jehovah our God we shall make mention.

8 Those very ones have broken down and fallen;
But as for us, we have risen up, that we may be restored.

9 O Jehovah, do save the king!
He will answer us in the day that we call.

To the director. A melody of David.

21 O Jehovah, in your strength the king rejoices;
And in your salvation how very joyful he wants to be!

2 The desire of his heart you have given him,
And the wish of his lips you have not withheld. *Se'lah.*

3 For you proceeded to meet him with blessings of good,
[And] to place on his head a crown of refined gold.

4 Life he asked of you. You gave [it] to him,
Length of days to time indefinite, even forever.

5 His glory is great in your salvation.
Dignity and splendor you put upon him.

6 For you constitute him highly blessed forever;
You make him feel glad with the rejoicing at your face.

7 For the king is trusting in Jehovah,

Even in the loving-kindness of the Most High. He will not be caused to totter.

8 Your hand will find all your enemies;
Your own right hand will find those hating you.

9 You will constitute them as a fiery furnace at the appointed time for your attention.
Jehovah in his anger will swallow them up, and the fire will devour them.

10 Their fruitage you will destroy from the very earth,
And their offspring from the sons of men.

11 For they have directed against you what is bad;
They have thought out ideas that they are unable to carry out.

12 For you will make them turn their backs in flight
By your bowstrings that you make ready against their face.

13 O be exalted in your strength, O Jehovah.
We will sing and make melody to your mightiness.

To the director upon the Hind of the Dawn. A melody of David.

22 My God, my God, why have you left me?
[Why are you] far from saving me,
[From] the words of my roaring?

2 O my God, I keep calling by day, and you do not answer;
And by night, and there is no silence on my part.

3 But you are holy,
Inhabiting the praises of Israel.

4 In you our fathers trusted;
They trusted, and you kept providing them with escape.

5 To you they cried out, and they got away safe;
In you they trusted, and they did not come to shame.

6 But I am a worm, and not a man,

A reproach to men and despicable to the people.

7 As for all those seeing me, they hold me in derision;
They keep opening their mouths wide, they keep wagging [their] head:

8 "He committed himself to Jehovah. Let Him provide him with escape!
Let him deliver him, since he has taken delight in him!"

9 For you were the One drawing me forth from the belly,
The One making me trust while upon the breasts of my mother.

10 Upon you I have been thrown from the womb;
From the belly of my mother you have been my God.

11 Do not keep far off from me, because distress is nearby,
Because there is no other helper.

12 Many young bulls have surrounded me;
The powerful ones of Ba'shan themselves have got around me.

13 They have opened against me their mouth,
As a lion tearing in pieces and roaring.

14 Like water I have been poured out,
And all my bones have been separated from one another.
My heart has become like wax;
It has melted deep in my inward parts.

15 My power has dried up just like a fragment of earthenware,
And my tongue is made to stick to my gums;
And in the dust of death you are setting me.

16 For dogs have surrounded me;
The assembly of evildoers themselves have enclosed me.
Like a lion [they are at] my hands and my feet.

17 I can count all my bones.
They themselves look, they gaze upon me.

18 They apportion my garments among themselves,

And upon my clothing they cast lots.

19 But you, O Jehovah, O do not keep far off.

O you my strength, do make haste to my assistance.

20 Do deliver from the sword my soul,

My only one from the very paw of the dog;

21 Save me from the mouth of the lion,

And from the horns of wild bulls you must answer [and save] me.

22 I will declare your name to my brothers;

In the middle of the congregation I shall praise you.

23 You fearers of Jehovah, praise him!

All you the seed of Jacob, glorify him!

And be frightened at him, all you the seed of Israel.

24 For he has neither despised Nor loathed the affliction of the afflicted one;

And he has not concealed his face from him,

And when he cried to him for help he heard.

25 From you my praise will be in the large congregation;

My vows I shall pay in front of those fearing him.

26 The meek ones will eat and be satisfied;

Those seeking him will praise Jehovah.

May your hearts live forever.

27 All the ends of the earth will remember and turn back to Jehovah.

And all the families of the nations will bow down before you.

28 For the kingship belongs to Jehovah,

And he is dominating the nations.

29 All the fat ones of the earth shall eat and will bow down;

Before him all those going down to the dust will bend down,

And no one will ever preserve his own soul alive.

30 A seed itself will serve him;

It will be declared concerning Jehovah to the generation.

31 They will come and tell of his righteousness

To the people that is to be born, that he has done [this].

A melody of David.

23 Jehovah is my Shepherd.

I shall lack nothing.

2 In grassy pastures he makes me lie down;

By well-watered resting places he conducts me.

3 My soul he refreshes.

He leads me in the tracks of righteousness for his name's sake.

4 Even though I walk in the valley of deep shadow,

I fear nothing bad,

For you are with me;

Your rod and your staff are the things that comfort me.

5 You arrange before me a table in front of those showing hostility to me.

With oil you have greased my head;

My cup is well filled.

6 Surely goodness and lovingkindness themselves will pursue me all the days of my life;

And I will dwell in the house of Jehovah to the length of days.

Of David. A melody.

24 To Jehovah belong the earth and that which fills it,

The productive land and those dwelling in it.

2 For upon the seas he himself has solidly fixed it,

And upon the rivers he keeps it firmly established.

3 Who may ascend into the mountain of Jehovah,

And who may rise up in his holy place?

4 Anyone innocent in his hands and clean in heart,

Who has not carried My soul to sheer worthlessness,

Nor taken an oath deceitfully.

5 He will carry away blessing from
    Jehovah
    And righteousness from his
        God of salvation.
6 This is the generation of those
    seeking him,
    Of those searching for your
        face, O [God of] Jacob.
        Se'lah.
7 Raise YOUR heads, O YOU gates,
    And raise yourselves up, O
        YOU long-lasting entrances,
    That the glorious King may
        come in!
8 Who, then, is this glorious King?
    Jehovah strong and mighty,
    Jehovah mighty in battle.
9 Raise YOUR heads, O YOU gates;
    Yes, raise [them] up, O YOU
        long-lasting entrances,
    That the glorious King may
        come in!
10 Who, then, is he, this glorious
        King?
    Jehovah of armies—he is the
        glorious King. *Se'lah.*

                Of David.

              א [*Aleph*]

25 To you, O Jehovah, I raise my
        very soul.

              ב [*Beth*]

2 O my God, in you have I put
        my trust;
    O may I not be ashamed.
    May my enemies not exult
        over me.

              ג [*Gimel*]

3 Also, none of those hoping in
        you will be ashamed.
    They will be ashamed who
        are dealing treacherously
        without success.

              ד [*Daleth*]

4 Make me know your own ways,
        O Jehovah;
    Teach me your own paths.

              ה [*He*]

5 Make me walk in your truth
        and teach me,
    For you are my God of salva-
        tion.

              ו [*Waw*]

    In you I have hoped all day
        long.

              ז [*Zayin*]

6 Remember your mercies, O Je-
        hovah, and your loving-
        kindnesses,
    For they are from time in-
        definite.

              ח [*Heth*]

7 The sins of my youth and my
        revolts O do not remember.
    According to your loving-
        kindness do you yourself
        remember me,
    For the sake of your goodness,
        O Jehovah.

              ט [*Teth*]

8 Good and upright is Jehovah.
    That is why he instructs
        sinners in the way.

              י [*Yod*]

9 He will cause the meek ones to
        walk in [his] judicial de-
        cision,
    And he will teach the meek
        ones his way.

              כ [*Kaph*]

10 All the paths of Jehovah are
        loving-kindness and true-
        ness
    For those observing his cove-
        nant and his reminders.

              ל [*Lamed*]

11 For your name's sake, O Jeho-
        vah,
    You must even forgive my
        error, for it is considerable.

              מ [*Mem*]

12 Who, now, is the man fearful of
        Jehovah?
    He will instruct him in the
        way [that] he will choose.

              נ [*Nun*]

13 His own soul will lodge in good-
        ness itself,
    And his own offspring will
        take possession of the earth.

              ס [*Samekh*]

14 The intimacy with Jehovah be-
        longs to those fearful of
        him,
    Also his covenant, to cause
        them to know it.

ע [Ayin]

15 My eyes are constantly toward Jehovah,
For he it is that brings my feet out of the net.

פ [Pe]

16 Turn your face to me, and show me favor;
For I am solitary and afflicted.

צ [Tsade]

17 Distresses of my heart have multiplied;
From the stresses upon me O bring me out.

ר [Resh]

18 See my affliction and my trouble,
And pardon all my sins.
19 See how many my enemies have become,
And with a violent hatred they have hated me.

ש [Shin]

20 Do guard my soul and deliver me.
May I not be ashamed, for I have taken refuge in you.

ת [Taw]

21 Let integrity and uprightness themselves safeguard me,
For I have hoped in you.
22 O God, redeem Israel out of all his distresses.

Of David.

26 Judge me, O Jehovah, for I myself have walked in my own integrity,
And in Jehovah I have trusted, that I may not wobble.
2 Examine me, O Jehovah, and put me to the test;
Refine my kidneys and my heart.
3 For your loving-kindness is in front of my eyes,
And I have walked in your truth.
4 For I have not sat with men of untruth;
And with those who hide what they are I do not come in.
5 I have hated the congregation of evildoers,

And with the wicked ones I do not sit.
6 I shall wash my hands in innocency itself,
And I will march around your altar, O Jehovah,
7 To cause thanksgiving to be heard aloud,
And to declare all your wonderful works.
8 Jehovah, I have loved the dwelling of your house
And the place of the residing of your glory.
9 Do not take away my soul along with sinners,
Nor my life along with bloodguilty men,
10 In whose hands there is loose conduct,
And whose right hand is full of bribery.
11 As for me, in my integrity I shall walk.
O redeem me and show me favor.
12 My own foot will certainly stand on a level place;
Among the congregated throngs I shall bless Jehovah.

Of David.

27 Jehovah is my light and my salvation.
Of whom shall I be in fear?
Jehovah is the stronghold of my life.
Of whom shall I be in dread?
2 When the evildoers approached against me to eat up my flesh,
They being my adversaries and my enemies personally,
They themselves stumbled and fell.
3 Though against me an encampment should pitch tent,
My heart will not fear.
Though against me war should rise,
Even then I shall be trusting.
4 One thing I have asked from Jehovah—
It is what I shall look for,

That I may dwell in the house
of Jehovah all the days of
my life,
To behold the pleasantness
of Jehovah
And to look with appreciation
upon his temple.
5 For he will hide me in his covert
in the day of calamity;
He will conceal me in the
secret place of his tent;
High on a rock he will put me.
6 And now my head will be high
above my enemies all around
me;
And I will sacrifice at his
tent sacrifices of joyful
shouting;
I will sing and make melody
to Jehovah.
7 Hear, O Jehovah, when I call
with my voice,
And show me favor and an-
swer me.
8 Concerning you my heart has
said: "Seek to find my face,
you people."
Your face, O Jehovah, I shall
seek to find.
9 Do not conceal your face from
me.
Do not in anger turn your
servant away.
My assistance you must become.
Do not forsake me and do
not leave me, O my God of
salvation.
10 In case my own father and my
own mother did leave me,
Even Jehovah himself would
take me up.
11 Instruct me, O Jehovah, in your
way,
And lead me in the path of
uprightness on account of
my foes.
12 Do not give me over to the soul
of my adversaries;
For against me false witnesses
have risen up,
And he who launches forth
violence.
13 If I had not had faith in seeing
the goodness of Jehovah in
the land of those alive—!

14 Hope in Jehovah; be courageous
and let your heart be strong.
Yes, hope in Jehovah.

Of David.

28 To you, O Jehovah, I keep
calling.
O my Rock, do not be deaf
to me,
That you may not keep still
toward me
And I do not have to become
like those going down to the
pit.
2 Hear the voice of my entreaties
when I cry to you for help,
When I raise my hands to the
innermost room of your holy
place.
3 Do not draw me along with
wicked people and with
practicers of what is hurtful,
Those who are speaking peace
with their companions but
in whose hearts is what is
bad.
4 Give to them according to their
acting
And according to the badness
of their practices.
According to the work of their
hands do you give to them.
Pay back to them their own
doing.
5 For they have no regard for the
activities of Jehovah,
Nor for the work of his hands.
He will tear them down and
not build them up.
6 Blessed be Jehovah, for he has
heard the voice of my en-
treaties.
7 Jehovah is my strength and my
shield.
In him my heart has trusted,
And I have been helped, so
that my heart exults,
And with my song I shall laud
him.
8 Jehovah is a strength to his
people,
And he is a stronghold of the
grand salvation of his
anointed one.
9 Do save your people, and bless
your inheritance;
And shepherd them and carry
them to time indefinite.

A melody of David.

29 Ascribe to Jehovah, O YOU
sons of strong ones,
Ascribe to Jehovah glory and
strength.

2 Ascribe to Jehovah the glory of
his name.
Bow down to Jehovah in holy
adornment.

3 The voice of Jehovah is over the
waters;
The glorious God himself has
thundered.
Jehovah is over many waters.

4 The voice of Jehovah is powerful;
The voice of Jehovah is splendid.

5 The voice of Jehovah is breaking the cedars;
Yes, Jehovah breaks the cedars of Leb′a·non in pieces,

6 And he makes them skip about
like a calf,
Leb′a·non and Sir′i·on like
the sons of wild bulls.

7 The voice of Jehovah is hewing
with the flames of fire;

8 The voice of Jehovah itself
makes the wilderness writhe,
Jehovah makes the wilderness
of Ka′desh writhe.

9 The voice of Jehovah itself
makes the hinds writhe
with birth pains
And strips bare the forests.
And in his temple each one
is saying: "Glory!"

10 Upon the deluge Jehovah has
seated himself;
And Jehovah sits as king to
time indefinite.

11 Jehovah himself will give
strength indeed to his
people.
Jehovah himself will bless his
people with peace.

A melody. A song of inauguration
of the house. Of David.

30 I shall exalt you, O Jehovah,
for you have drawn me up
And you have not let my
enemies rejoice over me.

2 O Jehovah my God, I cried to
you for help, and you proceeded to heal me.

3 O Jehovah, you have brought
up my soul from She′ol
itself;
You have kept me alive, that
I should not go down into
the pit.

4 Make melody to Jehovah, O YOU
loyal ones of his,
Give thanks to his holy memorial;

5 Because being under his anger
is for a moment,
Being under his good will is
for a lifetime.
In the evening weeping may
take up lodging, but in the
morning there is a joyful
cry.

6 As for me, I have said in my
ease:
"Never shall I be made to
totter."

7 O Jehovah, in your good will
you have made my moun-
tain to stand in strength.
You concealed your face; I
became one that is disturbed.

8 To you, O Jehovah, I kept
calling;
And to Jehovah I kept making
entreaty for favor.

9 What profit is there in my blood
when I go down to the pit?
Will the dust laud you? Will
it tell of your trueness?

10 Hear, O Jehovah, and show me
favor.
O Jehovah, prove yourself my
helper.

11 You have changed my mourning into dancing for me;
You have loosened my sackcloth, and you keep me
girded with rejoicing,

12 In order that [my] glory may
make melody to you and
not keep silent.
O Jehovah my God, to time
indefinite I will laud you.

To the director. A melody of David.

31 In you, O Jehovah, have I
taken refuge.
O may I never be ashamed.
In your righteousness provide
escape for me.

2 Incline to me your ear.
Deliver me speedily.

Become for me a rocky stronghold,
A house of strongholds to save
me.
3 For you are my crag and my
stronghold;
And for the sake of your
name you will lead me and
conduct me.
4 You will bring me out of the
net that they have hidden
for me,
For you are my fortress.
5 Into your hand I entrust my
spirit.
You have redeemed me, O
Jehovah the God of truth.
6 I do hate those paying regard
to worthless, vain idols;
But as for me, in Jehovah I
do trust.
7 I will be joyful and rejoice in
your loving-kindness,
In that you have seen my
affliction,
You have known about the
distresses of my soul,
8 And you have not surrendered
me into the hand of the
enemy.
You have made my feet stand
in a roomy place.
9 Show me favor, O Jehovah, for
I am in sore straits.
With vexation my eye has become weak, my soul and my
belly.
10 For with grief my life has come
to an end,
And my years in sighing.
Because of my error my power
has stumbled,
And my very bones have become weak.
11 From the standpoint of all those
showing hostility to me I
have become a reproach,
And to my neighbors very
much so,
And a dread to my acquaintances.
When seeing me out of doors,
they have fled from me.
12 Like someone dead [and] not in
the heart, I have been forgotten;
I have become like a damaged
vessel;

13 For I have heard the bad report
by many,
Fright being on all sides.
When they mass together as
one against me,
It is to take away my soul
that they do scheme.
14 But I—in you I have put my
trust, O Jehovah.
I have said: "You are my
God."
15 My times are in your hand.
Deliver me from the hand of
my enemies and from those
pursuing me.
16 Do cause your face to shine
upon your servant.
Save me in your loving-
kindness.
17 O Jehovah, may I not be
ashamed, for I have called
on you.
May the wicked ones be
ashamed;
May they keep silent in She'ol.
18 May false lips become speechless,
That are speaking against the
righteous one, unrestrainedly
in haughtiness and con-
tempt.
19 How abundant your goodness is,
which you have treasured
up for those fearing you!
[Which] you have rendered to
those taking refuge in you,
In front of the sons of men.
20 You will conceal them in the
secret place of your person
From the banding together of
men.
You will hide them in your
booth from the quarreling
of tongues.
21 Blessed be Jehovah,
For he has rendered wonderful loving-kindness to me in
a city under stress.
22 As for me, I said when I became panicky:
"I shall certainly be exterminated from in front of
your eyes."
Surely you have heard the
voice of my entreaties when
I cried to you for help.
23 O love Jehovah, all you loyal
ones of his.

The faithful ones Jehovah is safeguarding,
But he is rewarding exceedingly anyone showing haughtiness.
24 Be courageous, and may YOUR heart be strong,
All YOU who are waiting for Jehovah.

Of David. Mas′kil.

32 Happy is the one whose revolt is pardoned, whose sin is covered.

2 Happy is the man to whose account Jehovah does not put error,
And in whose spirit there is no deceit.

3 When I kept silent my bones wore out through my groaning all day long.

4 For day and night your hand was heavy upon me.
My life's moisture has been changed as in the dry heat of summer. *Se′lah.*

5 My sin I finally confessed to you, and my error I did not cover.
I said: "I shall make confession over my transgressions to Jehovah."
And you yourself pardoned the error of my sins. *Se′lah.*

6 On this account every loyal one will pray to you
At such a time only as you may be found.
As for the flood of many waters, they will not touch him himself.

7 You are a place of concealment for me; you will safeguard me from distress itself.
With joyful cries at providing escape you will surround me. *Se′lah.*

8 "I shall make you have insight and instruct you in the way you should go.
I will give advice with my eye upon you.

9 Do not make yourselves like a horse or mule without understanding,
Whose spiritedness is to be curbed even by bridle or halter
Before [they] will come near to you."

10 Many are the pains that the wicked one has;
But as for the one trusting in Jehovah, loving-kindness itself surrounds him.

11 Rejoice in Jehovah and be joyful, YOU righteous ones;
And cry out joyfully, all YOU who are upright in heart.

33 Cry out joyfully, O YOU righteous ones, because of Jehovah.
On the part of the upright ones praise is fitting.

2 Give thanks to Jehovah on the harp;
On an instrument of ten strings make melody to him.

3 Sing to him a new song;
Do YOUR best at playing on the strings along with joyful shouting.

4 For the word of Jehovah is upright,
And all his work is in faithfulness.

5 He is a lover of righteousness and justice.
With the loving-kindness of Jehovah the earth is filled.

6 By the word of Jehovah the heavens themselves were made,
And by the spirit of his mouth all their army.

7 He is gathering as by a dam the waters of the sea,
Putting in storehouses the surging waters.

8 Let all [those of] the earth be in fear of Jehovah.
At him let all the inhabitants of the productive land be frightened.

9 For he himself said, and it came to be;
He himself commanded, and it proceeded to stand so.

10 Jehovah himself has broken up the counsel of the nations;
He has thwarted the thoughts of the peoples.

11 To time indefinite the very counsel of Jehovah will stand;

The thoughts of his heart are
to one generation after another generation.
12 Happy is the nation whose God
is Jehovah,
The people whom he has
chosen as his inheritance.
13 From the heavens Jehovah has
looked,
He has seen all the sons of
men.
14 From the established place
where he dwells
He has gazed at all those
dwelling on the earth.
15 He is forming their hearts all
together;
He is considering all their
works.
16 There is no king saved by
the abundance of military
forces;
A mighty man himself is not
delivered by the abundance
of power.
17 The horse is a deception for
salvation,
And by the abundance of its
vital energy it does not
afford escape.
18 Look! The eye of Jehovah is
toward those fearing him,
To those waiting for his loving-
kindness,
19 To deliver their soul from death
itself,
And to preserve them alive in
famine.
20 Our very soul has been in expectation of Jehovah.
Our helper and our shield he
is.
21 For in him our heart rejoices;
For in his holy name we have
put our trust.
22 Let your loving-kindness, O Jehovah, prove to be upon us,
Even as we have kept waiting
for you.

Of David, at the time of his
disguising his sanity before
A.bim′e.lech, so that he drove
him out, and he went away.

א [Aleph]

34 I will bless Jehovah at all
times;
Constantly his praise will be
in my mouth.

ב [Beth]

2 In Jehovah my soul will make
its boast;
The meek ones will hear and
will rejoice.

ג [Gimel]

3 O magnify Jehovah with me,
you people,
And let us exalt his name
together.

ד [Daleth]

4 I inquired of Jehovah, and he
answered me,
And out of all my frights he
delivered me.

ה [He]

5 They looked to him and became
radiant,
And their very faces could
not possibly be ashamed.

ז [Zayin]

6 This afflicted one called, and Je-
hovah himself heard,
And out of all his distresses
He saved him.

ח [Heth]

7 The angel of Jehovah is camping all around those fearing
him,
And he rescues them.

ט [Teth]

8 Taste and see that Jehovah is
good, O you people;
Happy is the able-bodied man
that takes refuge in him.

י [Yod]

9 Fear Jehovah, you holy ones of
his,
For there is no lack to those
fearing him.

כ [Kaph]

10 The maned young lions themselves have had little on
hand and gone hungry;
But as for those seeking Jehovah, they will not lack anything good.

ל [Lamed]

11 Come, you sons, listen to me;
The fear of Jehovah is what
I shall teach you.

מ [*Mem*]

12 Who is the man that is delighting in life,
  That is loving enough days
  to see what is good?

נ [*Nun*]

13 Safeguard your tongue against
  what is bad,
  And your lips against speaking
  deception.

ס [*Samekh*]

14 Turn away from what is bad,
  and do what is good;
  Seek to find peace, and pursue
  it.

ע [*Ayin*]

15 The eyes of Jehovah are toward
  the righteous ones,
  And his ears are toward their
  cry for help.

פ [*Pe*]

16 The face of Jehovah is against
  those doing what is bad,
  To cut off the mention of
  them from the very earth.

צ [*Tsade*]

17 They cried out, and Jehovah
  himself heard,
  And out of all their distresses
  he delivered them.

ק [*Qoph*]

18 Jehovah is near to those that
  are broken at heart;
  And those who are crushed in
  spirit he saves.

ר [*Resh*]

19 Many are the calamities of the
  righteous one,
  But out of them all Jehovah
  delivers him.

ש [*Shin*]

20 He is guarding all the bones of
  that one;
  Not one of them has been
  broken.

ת [*Taw*]

21 Calamity will put the wicked
  one himself to death;
  And the very ones hating the
  righteous one will be held
  guilty.

22 Jehovah is redeeming the soul of
  his servants;
  And none of those taking
  refuge in him will be held
  guilty.

Of David.

35 Do conduct my case, O Jehovah, against my opponents;
  War against those warring
  against me.

2 Take hold of buckler and large
  shield,
  And do rise up in assistance
  of me,

3 And draw spear and double ax
  to meet those pursuing me.
  Say to my soul: "I am your
  salvation."

4 May those be shamed and humiliated who are hunting
  for my soul.
  May those be turned back and
  be abashed who are scheming calamity for me.

5 May they become like chaff before the wind,
  And let Jehovah's angel be
  pushing [them] along.

6 Let their way become darkness
  and slippery places,
  And let Jehovah's angel be
  pursuing them.

7 For without cause they have
  hid for me their netted pit;
  Without cause they have dug
  it for my soul.

8 Let ruin come upon him without
  his knowing,
  And let his own net that he
  hid catch him;
  With ruin let him fall into it.

9 But let my own soul be joyful
  in Jehovah;
  Let it exult in his salvation.

10 Let all my bones themselves say:
  "O Jehovah, who is there like
  you,
  Delivering the afflicted one from
  one stronger than he is,
  And the afflicted and poor
  one from the one robbing
  him?"

11 Violent witnesses rise up;
  What I have not known they
  ask me.

12 They reward me with bad for
good,
Bereavement to my soul.

13 As for me, when they became
ill, my clothing was sackcloth,
With fasting I afflicted my
soul,
And upon my bosom my own
prayer would return.

14 As for a companion, as for a
brother of mine,
I walked about like one mourning for a mother,
Saddened, I bowed down.

15 But at my limping they rejoiced
and gathered together;
They gathered together
against me,
Striking [me] down when I did
not know it;
They ripped [me] to pieces
and did not keep silent.

16 Among the apostate mockers
for a cake
There was a grinding of their
teeth even against me.

17 O Jehovah, how long will you
keep seeing [it]?
Do bring back my soul from
their ravages,
Even my only one from the
maned young lions.

18 I will laud you in the big congregation;
Among a numerous people I
shall praise you.

19 O may those who for no reason
are my enemies not rejoice
over me;
As for those hating me without cause, let them not
wink the eye.

20 For it is not peace that they
speak;
But against the quiet ones
of the earth
Things of deception they keep
scheming.

21 And they open wide their mouth
even against me.
They have said: "Aha! Aha!
our eye has seen [it]."

22 You have seen, O Jehovah. Do
not keep silent.
O Jehovah, do not keep yourself far from me.

23 Do arouse yourself and awake
to my judgment,
O my God, even Jehovah, to
my case at law.

24 Judge me according to your
righteousness, O Jehovah
my God,
And may they not rejoice
over me.

25 O may they not say in their
heart: "Aha, our soul!"
May they not say: "We have
swallowed him up."

26 Let those be ashamed and
abashed all together
Who are joyful at my calamity.
Let those be clothed with
shame and humiliation who
are assuming great airs
against me.

27 Let those cry out joyfully and
rejoice who are delighting
in my righteousness,
And let them say constantly:
"Let Jehovah be magnified,
who takes delight in the
peace of his servant."

28 And let my own tongue utter
in an undertone your righteousness,
All day long your praise.

To the director.
Of Jehovah's servant, David.

36 The utterance of transgression
to the wicked one is in the
midst of his heart;
There is no dread of God in
front of his eyes.

2 For he has acted too smoothly
to himself in his own eyes
To find out his error so as
to hate [it].

3 The words of his mouth are
hurtfulness and deception;
He has ceased to have insight
for doing good.

4 Hurtfulness is what he keeps
scheming upon his bed.
He stations himself on a way
that is not good.
What is bad he does not
reject.

5 O Jehovah, your loving-kindness
is in the heavens;
Your faithfulness is up to the
clouds.

6 Your righteousness is like mountains of God;
   Your judicial decision is a
   vast watery deep.
   Man and beast you save, O
   Jehovah.
7 How precious your loving-
   kindness is, O God!
   And in the shadow of your
   wings the sons of men themselves take refuge.
8 They drink their fill of the fatness of your house;
   And of the torrent of your
   pleasures you cause them
   to drink.
9 For with you is the source of
   life;
   By light from you we can see
   light.
10 Continue your loving-kindness
   to those knowing you,
   And your righteousness to
   those upright in heart.
11 O may not the foot of haughtiness come [against] me;
   As for the hand of wicked
   people, let it not make me
   a wanderer.
12 There the practicers of hurtfulness have fallen;
   They have been pushed down
   and have been unable to
   get up.

Of David.

א [Aleph]

37 Do not show yourself heated
   up because of the evildoers.
   Do not be envious of those
   doing unrighteousness.
2 For like grass they will speedily
   wither,
   And like green new grass
   they will fade away.

ב [Beth]

3 Trust in Jehovah and do good;
   Reside in the earth, and deal
   with faithfulness.
4 Also take exquisite delight in
   Jehovah,
   And he will give you the
   requests of your heart.

ג [Gimel]

5 Roll upon Jehovah your way,
   And rely upon him, and he
   himself will act.

6 And he will certainly bring forth
   your righteousness as the
   light itself,
   And your justice as the midday.

ד [Daleth]

7 Keep silent before Jehovah
   And wait longingly for him.
   Do not show yourself heated up
   at anyone making his way
   successful,
   At the man carrying out [his]
   ideas.

ה [He]

8 Let anger alone and leave rage;
   Do not show yourself heated
   up only to do evil.
9 For evildoers themselves will be
   cut off,
   But those hoping in Jehovah
   are the ones that will possess the earth.

ו [Waw]

10 And just a little while longer,
   and the wicked one will be
   no more;
   And you will certainly give
   attention to his place, and
   he will not be.
11 But the meek ones themselves
   will possess the earth,
   And they will indeed find
   their exquisite delight in the
   abundance of peace.

ז [Zayin]

12 The wicked one is plotting
   against the righteous one,
   And at him he is grinding
   his teeth.
13 Jehovah himself will laugh at
   him,
   For he certainly sees that his
   day will come.

ח [Heth]

14 The wicked ones have drawn a
   sword itself and have bent
   their bow,
   To cause the afflicted and poor
   one to fall,
   To slaughter those who are
   upright in [their] way.
15 Their own sword will enter into
   their heart,
   And their own bows will be
   broken.

ט [Teth]

16 Better is the little of the right-
    eous one
        Than the abundance of the
        many wicked ones.
17 For the very arms of the wicked
    ones will be broken,
        But Jehovah will be support-
        ing the righteous ones.

י [Yod]

18 Jehovah is aware of the days of
    the faultless ones,
        And their very inheritance
        will continue even to time
        indefinite.
19 They will not be ashamed in the
    time of calamity,
        And in the days of famine
        they will be satisfied.

כ [Kaph]

20 For the wicked themselves will
    perish,
        And the enemies of Jehovah
        will be like the preciousness
        of pastures;
        They must come to their end.
        In smoke they must come to
        their end.

ל [Lamed]

21 The wicked one is borrowing
    and does not pay back,
        But the righteous one is show-
        ing favor and is making
        gifts.
22 For those being blessed by him
    will themselves possess the
    earth,
        But those upon whom evil is
        called by him will be cut off.

מ [Mem]

23 By Jehovah the very steps of an
    able-bodied man have been
    made ready,
        And in his way He takes de-
        light.
24 Although he may fall, he will
    not be hurled down,
        For Jehovah is supporting his
        hand.

נ [Nun]

25 A young man I used to be, I
    have also grown old,
        And yet I have not seen any-
        one righteous left entirely,

Nor his offspring looking for
    bread.
26 All day long he is showing favor
    and lending,
        And so his offspring are in
        line for a blessing.

ס [Samekh]

27 Turn away from what is bad
    and do what is good,
        And so reside to time in-
        definite.
28 For Jehovah is a lover of jus-
    tice,
        And he will not leave his loyal
        ones.

ע [Ayin]

To time indefinite they will
    certainly be guarded;
        But as for the offspring of the
        wicked ones, they will in-
        deed be cut off.
29 The righteous themselves will
    possess the earth,
        And they will reside forever
        upon it.

פ [Pe]

30 The mouth of the righteous is
    the one that utters wisdom
    in an undertone,
        And his is the tongue that
        speaks justly.
31 The law of his God is in his
    heart;
        His steps will not wobble.

צ [Tsade]

32 The wicked one is keeping on
    the watch for the righteous
        And is seeking to put him to
        death.
33 As for Jehovah, he will not leave
    him to the hand of that
    one,
        And he will not pronounce
        him wicked when he is
        being judged.

ק [Qoph]

34 Hope in Jehovah and keep his
    way,
        And he will exalt you to take
        possession of the earth.
        When the wicked ones are
        cut off, you will see [it].

ר [Resh]

35 I have seen the wicked a tyrant

And spreading himself as a luxuriant [tree] in native soil.

36 And yet he proceeded to pass away, and there he was not; And I kept seeking him, and he was not found.

ש [Shin]

37 Watch the blameless one and keep the upright one in sight, For the future of [that] man will be peaceful.

38 But the transgressors themselves will certainly be annihilated together; The future of wicked people will indeed be cut off.

ת [Taw]

39 And the salvation of the righteous ones is from Jehovah; He is their fortress in the time of distress.

40 And Jehovah will help them and provide them with escape. He will provide them with escape from wicked people and save them, Because they have taken refuge in him.

A melody of David, to bring to remembrance.

38 O Jehovah, do not in your indignation reprove me, Nor in your rage correct me.

2 For your own arrows have sunk themselves deep into me, And upon me your hand is come down.

3 There is no sound spot in my flesh because of your denunciation. There is no peace in my bones on account of my sin.

4 For my own errors have passed over my head; Like a heavy load they are too heavy for me.

5 My wounds have become stinky, they have festered, Because of my foolishness.

6 I have become disconcerted, I have bowed low to an extreme degree; All day long I have walked about sad.

7 For my very loins have become full of burning, And there is no sound spot in my flesh.

8 I have grown numb and become crushed to an extreme degree; I have roared due to the groaning of my heart.

9 O Jehovah, in front of you is all my desire, And from you my sighing itself has not been concealed.

10 My own heart has palpitated heavily, my power has left me, And the light of my own eyes also is not with me.

11 As for my lovers and my companions, they keep standing away from my plague, And my close acquaintances themselves have stood off at a distance.

12 But those seeking my soul lay out traps, And those working for a calamity to me have spoken of adversities, And deceptions they keep muttering all day long.

13 As for me, like someone deaf, I would not listen; And like someone speechless, I would not open my mouth.

14 And I came to be like a man that was not hearing, And in my mouth there were no counterarguments.

15 For on you, O Jehovah, I waited; You yourself proceeded to answer, O Jehovah my God.

16 For I said: "Otherwise they would rejoice at me; When my foot moved unsteadily, they would certainly assume great airs against me."

17 For I was ready to limp, And my pain was in front of me constantly.

18 For I proceeded to tell about my own error; I began to be anxious over my sin.

19 And my enemies who are alive became mighty,

And those hating me for no
reason became many.

20 And they were rewarding me
with bad for good;
They kept resisting me in return for my pursuing what
is good.

21 Do not leave me, O Jehovah.
O my God, do not keep far
away from me.

22 Do make haste to my assistance,
O Jehovah my salvation.

To the director of Je.du'thun.
A melody of David.

39 I said: "I will guard my ways
To keep from sinning with
my tongue.
I will set a muzzle as a guard
to my own mouth,
As long as anyone wicked is in
front of me."

2 I became speechless with silence;
I kept quiet from what is good,
And my being pained was
ostracized.

3 My heart grew hot inside me;
During my sighing the fire
kept burning.
I spoke with my tongue:

4 "Cause me, O Jehovah, to know
my end,
And the measure of my days
—what it is,
That I may know how tran-
sient I am.

5 Look! You have made my days
just a few;
And my life's duration is as
nothing in front of you.
Surely every earthling man,
though standing firm, is
nothing but an exhalation.
Se'lah.

6 Surely in a semblance man
walks about.
Surely they are boisterous in
vain.
One piles up things and does
not know who will be gathering them.

7 And now for what have I hoped,
O Jehovah?
My expectation is toward you.

8 From all my transgressions deliver me.
Do not set me as a reproach
of the senseless one.

9 I kept speechless; I could not
open my mouth,
For you yourself acted.

10 Remove from off me your plague.
Due to the hostility of your
hand I myself have come to
an end.

11 By reproofs against error you
have corrected man,
And you consume his desirable
things just as a moth does.
Surely every earthling man is
an exhalation. *Se'lah.*

12 Do hear my prayer, O Jehovah,
And to my cry for help do
give ear.
At my tears do not keep
silent.
For I am but an alien resident
with you,
A settler the same as all my
forefathers.

13 Look away from me, that I may
brighten up
Before I go away and I am
not."

To the director.
Of David, a melody.

40 I earnestly hoped in Jehovah,
And so he inclined [his ear]
to me and heard my cry
for help.

2 He also proceeded to bring me
up out of a roaring pit,
Out of the mire of [the]
sediment.
Then he raised up my feet upon
a crag;
He firmly established my steps.

3 Further, he put in my mouth a
new song,
Praise to our God.
Many will see [it] and will fear,
And they will trust in Jehovah.

4 Happy is the able-bodied man
that has put Jehovah as
his trust
And that has not turned his
face to defiant people,
Nor to those falling away to
lies.

5 Many things you yourself have
done,
O Jehovah my God, even your
wonderful works and your
thoughts toward us;
There is none to be compared
to you.

Were I inclined to tell and speak
[of them],
They have become more nu-
merous than I can recount.

6 Sacrifice and offering you did
not delight in;
These ears of mine you opened
up.
Burnt offering and sin offering you did not ask for.

7 In view of that, I said: "Here
I have come,
In the roll of the book it
being written about me.

8 To do your will, O my God, I
have delighted,
And your law is within my
inward parts.

9 I have told the good news of
righteousness in the big
congregation.
Look! My lips I do not restrain.
O Jehovah, you yourself know
that well.

10 Your righteousness I have not
covered over within my
heart.
Your faithfulness and your
salvation I have declared.
I have not hidden your loving-
kindness and your trueness
in the big congregation."

11 You yourself, O Jehovah, do not
restrain your pity from me.
Let your loving-kindness and
your trueness themselves
constantly safeguard me.

12 For calamities encircled me until
there was no numbering of
them.
More errors of mine overtook
me than I was able to see;
They became more numerous
than the hairs of my head,
And my own heart left me.

13 Be pleased, O Jehovah, to deliver me.
O Jehovah, to my assistance
do make haste.

14 May those be ashamed and
abashed all together
Who are seeking my soul to
sweep it away.
May those turn back and be
humiliated who are delighting in my calamity.

15 Let those stare in amazement
in consequence of their
shame
Who are saying to me: "Aha!
Aha!"

16 Let those exult and rejoice in
you,
All those who are seeking you.
Let those say constantly: "May
Jehovah be magnified,"
Those who are loving salva-
tion by you.

17 But I am afflicted and poor.
Jehovah himself takes ac-
count of me.
You are my assistance and the
Provider of escape for me.
O my God, do not be too late.

To the director.
A melody of David.

41 Happy is anyone acting with
consideration toward the
lowly one;
In the day of calamity Jehovah will provide escape for
him.

2 Jehovah himself will guard him
and preserve him alive.
He will be pronounced happy
in the earth;
And you cannot possibly give
him over to the soul of his
enemies.

3 Jehovah himself will sustain
him upon a divan of illness;
All his bed you will certainly
change during his sickness.

4 As for me, I said: "O Jehovah,
show me favor.
Do heal my soul, for I have
sinned against you."

5 As for my enemies, they say
what is bad concerning me:
"When will he die and his
name actually perish?"

6 And if one does come to see
[me], untruth is what his
heart will speak;
He will gather up for himself
something hurtful;
He will go out; on the outside he will speak [of it].

7 Unitedly against me all those
hating me whisper to one
another;
Against me they keep scheming something bad for me:

8 "A good-for-nothing thing is
    poured out upon him;
    Now that he has lain down,
    he will not get up again."
9 Also the man at peace with me,
    in whom I trusted,
    Who was eating my bread, has
    magnified [his] heel against
    me.
10 As for you, O Jehovah, show me
    favor and cause me to get
    up,
    That I may pay them back.

11 By this I do know that you
    have found delight in me,
    Because my enemy does not
    shout in triumph over me.
12 As for me, because of my in-
    tegrity you have upheld me,
    And you will set me before
    your face to time indefinite.
13 Blessed be Jehovah the God of
    Israel
    From time indefinite even to
    time indefinite.
    Amen and Amen.

BOOK TWO
(Psalms 42 – 72)

To the director.
Mas'kil for the sons of Ko'rah.

42 As the hind that longs for the
    water streams,
    So my very soul longs for you,
    O God.
2 My soul indeed thirsts for God,
    for the living God.
    When shall I come and ap-
    pear [before] God?
3 To me my tears have become
    food day and night,
    While [they] say to me all
    day long: "Where is your
    God?"
4 These things I will remember,
    and I will pour out my soul
    within me.
    For I used to pass along with
    the throng,
    I used to walk slowly before
    them to the house of God,
    With the voice of a joyful cry
    and thanksgiving,
    Of a crowd celebrating a fes-
    tival.
5 Why are you in despair, O my
    soul,
    And why are you boisterous
    within me?
    Wait for God,
    For I shall yet laud him as
    the grand salvation of my
    person.
6 O my God, within me my very
    soul is in despair.
    That is why I remember you,
    From the land of Jordan and
    the peaks of Her'mon,
    From the little mountain.
7 Watery deep to watery deep is
    calling

At the sound of your (water-)
    spouts.
    All your breakers and your
    waves—
    Over me they have passed.
8 By day Jehovah will command
    his loving-kindness,
    And by night his song will be
    with me;
    There will be prayer to the
    God of my life.
9 I will say to God my crag:
    "Why have you forgotten me?
    Why do I walk sad because
    of the oppression of the
    enemy?"
10 With murder against my bones
    those showing hostility to
    me have reproached me,
    While they say to me all day
    long: "Where is your God?"
11 Why are you in despair, O my
    soul,
    And why are you boisterous
    within me?
    Wait for God,
    For I shall yet laud him as
    the grand salvation of my
    person and as my God.

43 Judge me, O God,
    And do conduct my legal
    case against a nation not
    loyal.
    From the man of deception
    and unrighteousness may
    you provide me with escape.
2 For you are the God of my for-
    tress.
    Why have you cast me off?
    Why do I walk about sad be-

cause of the oppression by the enemy?

3 Send out your light and your truth.
    May these themselves lead me.
    May they bring me to your holy mountain and to your grand tabernacle.

4 And I will come to the altar of God,
    To God, my exultant rejoicing.
    And I will laud you on the harp, O God, my God.

5 Why are you in despair, O my soul,
    And why are you boisterous within me?
    Wait for God,
    For I shall yet laud him as the grand salvation of my person and as my God.

To the director.
Of the sons of Ko'rah. Mas'kil.

44 O God, with our ears we have heard,
    Our forefathers themselves have recounted to us
    The activity that you performed in their days,
    In the days of long ago.

2 You yourself by your hand drove away even nations,
    And you proceeded to plant them [instead].
    You went breaking national groups and sending them away.

3 For it was not by their own sword that they took possession of the land,
    And their own arm was not what brought them salvation.
    For it was your right hand and your arm and the light of your face,
    Because you took pleasure in them.

4 You yourself are my King, O God.
    Command grand salvation for Jacob.

5 By you we shall push our adversaries themselves;
    In your name we shall tread down those rising up against us.

6 For it was not in my bow that I kept trusting
    And it was not my sword that was saving me.

7 For you saved us from our adversaries,
    And those intensely hating you put to shame.

8 In God we will offer praise all day long,
    And to time indefinite your name we shall laud. *Se'lah*.

9 But now you have cast off and keep humiliating us,
    And you do not go forth with our armies.

10 You keep making us turn back from the adversary,
    And the very ones intensely hating us have pillaged for themselves.

11 You give us up like sheep, as something to eat,
    And among the nations you have scattered us.

12 You sell your people for no value at all,
    And you have made no wealth by the price for them.

13 You set us as a reproach to our neighbors,
    A derision and jeering to those all around us.

14 You set us as a proverbial saying among the nations,
    A shaking of the head among the national groups.

15 All day long my humiliation is in front of me,
    And the shame of my own face has covered me,

16 Due to the voice of the one reproaching and speaking abusively,
    Because of the enemy and the one taking his revenge.

17 All this is what has come upon us, and we have not forgotten you,
    And we have not acted falsely in your covenant.

18 Our heart has not turned faithlessly back,
    Nor do our footsteps deviate from your path.

19 For you have crushed us in the place of jackals,

And you cover us over with deep shadow.

20 If we have forgotten the name of our God,
Or we spread out our palms to a strange god,

21 Will not God himself search this out?
For he is aware of the secrets of the heart.

22 But for your sake we have been killed all day long;
We have been accounted as sheep for slaughtering.

23 Do arouse yourself. Why do you keep sleeping, O Jehovah?
Do awake. Do not keep casting off forever.

24 Why do you keep your very face concealed?
Why do you forget our affliction and our oppression?

25 For our soul has bowed down to the dust itself;
Our belly has clung to the very earth.

26 Do arise in assistance to us
And redeem us for the sake of your loving-kindness.

To the director upon The Lilies.
Of the sons of Ko'rah. Mas'kil.
A song of the beloved women.

45 My heart has become astir with a goodly matter.
I am saying: "My works are concerning a king."
May my tongue be the stylus of a skilled copyist.

2 You are indeed more handsome than the sons of men.
Charm has been poured out upon your lips.
That is why God has blessed you to time indefinite.

3 Gird your sword upon [your] thigh, O mighty one,
[With] your dignity and your splendor.

4 And in your splendor go on to success;
Ride in the cause of truth and humility [and] righteousness,
And your right hand will instruct you in fear-inspiring things.

5 Your arrows are sharp—under you peoples keep falling—
In the heart of the enemies of the king.

6 God is your throne to time indefinite, even forever;
The scepter of your kingship is a scepter of uprightness.

7 You have loved righteousness and you hate wickedness.
That is why God, your God, has anointed you with the oil of exultation more than your partners.

8 All your garments are myrrh and aloeswood [and] cassia;
Out from the grand ivory palace stringed instruments themselves have made you rejoice.

9 The daughters of kings are among your precious women.
The queenly consort has taken her stand at your right hand in gold of O'phir.

10 Listen, O daughter, and see, and incline your ear;
And forget your people and your father's house.

11 And the king will long for your prettiness,
For he is your lord,
So bow down to him.

12 The daughter of Tyre also with a gift—
The rich ones of the people will soften your own face.

13 The king's daughter is all glorious within [the house];
Her clothing is with settings of gold.

14 In woven apparel she will be brought to the king.
The virgins in her train as her companions are being brought in to you.

15 They will be brought with rejoicing and joyfulness;
They will enter into the palace of the king.

16 In place of your forefathers there will come to be your sons,
Whom you will appoint as princes in all the earth.

17 I will make mention of your

name throughout all generations to come.
That is why peoples themselves will laud you to time indefinite, even forever.

To the director.
Of the sons of Ko′rah upon
The Maidens. A song.

46 God is for us a refuge and strength,
A help that is readily to be found during distresses.
2 That is why we shall not fear, though the earth undergo change
And though the mountains totter into the heart of the vast sea;
3 Though its waters be boisterous, foam over,
Though the mountains rock at its uproar. *Se′lah.*
4 There is a river the streams of which make the city of God rejoice,
The holiest grand tabernacle of the Most High.
5 God is in the midst of [the city]; it will not be made to totter.
God will help it at the appearance of morning.
6 The nations became boisterous, the kingdoms tottered;
He sounded with his voice, the earth proceeded to melt.
7 Jehovah of armies is with us;
The God of Jacob is a secure height for us. *Se′lah.*
8 Come, you people, behold the activities of Jehovah,
How he has set astonishing events on the earth.
9 He is making wars to cease to the extremity of the earth.
The bow he breaks apart and does cut the spear in pieces;
The wagons he burns in the fire.
10 "Give in, you people, and know that I am God.
I will be exalted among the nations,
I will be exalted in the earth."
11 Jehovah of armies is with us;
The God of Jacob is a secure height for us. *Se′lah.*

To the director.
Of the sons of Ko′rah.
A melody.

47 All you peoples, clap your hands.
Shout in triumph to God with the sound of a joyful cry.
2 For Jehovah, the Most High, is fear-inspiring,
A great King over all the earth.
3 He will subdue peoples under us
And national groups under our feet.
4 He will choose for us our inheritance,
The pride of Jacob, whom he has loved. *Se′lah.*
5 God has ascended with joyful shouting,
Jehovah with the sound of the horn.
6 MAKE melody to God, make melody.
Make melody to our King, make melody.
7 For God is King of all the earth;
MAKE melody, acting with discretion.
8 God has become king over the nations.
God himself has taken his seat upon his holy throne.
9 The nobles of the peoples themselves have gathered together,
[With] the people of the God of Abraham.
For to God the shields of the earth belong.
He is very high in his ascent.

A song.
A melody of the sons of Ko′rah.

48 Jehovah is great and much to be praised
In the city of our God, [in] his holy mountain.
2 Pretty for loftiness, the exultation of the whole earth,
Is Mount Zion on the remote sides of the north,
The town of the grand King.
3 In her dwelling towers God himself has become known as a secure height.
4 For, look! the kings themselves have met by appointment,
They have passed by together.

5 They themselves saw; [and] so
    they were amazed.
  They got disturbed, they were
    sent running in panic.
6 Trembling itself took hold of
    them there,
  Birth pangs like those of a
    woman giving birth.
7 With an east wind you wreck
    the ships of Tar'shish.
8 Just as we have heard, so we
    have seen
  In the city of Jehovah of
    armies, in the city of our
    God.
  God himself will firmly es-
    tablish it to time indefinite.
    Se'lah.
9 We have pondered, O God, over
    your loving-kindness
  In the midst of your temple.
10 Like your name, O God, so your
    praise is
  To the borders of the earth.
  Your right hand is full of
    righteousness itself.
11 May Mount Zion rejoice,
  May the dependent towns of
    Judah be joyful, on account
    of your judicial decisions.
12 March around Zion, you people,
    and go about it,
  Count its towers.
13 Set your hearts upon its ram-
    part,
  Inspect its dwelling towers,
  In order that you may re-
    count it to the future gen-
    eration.
14 For this God is our God to time
    indefinite, even forever.
  He himself will guide us until
    [we] die.

To the director.
Of the sons of Ko'rah. A melody.

49 Hear this, all you peoples.
  Give ear, all you inhabit-
    ants of the system of
    things,
2 You sons of humankind as well
    as you sons of man,
  You rich one and you poor
    one together.
3 My own mouth will speak things
    of wisdom,
  And the meditation of my
    heart will be of things of
    understanding.

4 To a proverbial utterance I shall
    incline my ear;
  On a harp I shall open up
    my riddle.
5 Why should I be afraid in the
    days of evil,
  [When] the very error of my
    supplanters surrounds me?
6 Those who are trusting in their
    means of maintenance,
  And who keep boasting about
    the abundance of their
    riches,
7 Not one of them can by
    any means redeem even a
    brother,
  Nor give to God a ransom for
    him;
8 (And the redemption price of
    their soul is so precious
  That it has ceased to time
    indefinite)
9 That he should still live forever
    [and] not see the pit.
10 For he sees that even the wise
    ones die,
  Together the stupid one and
    the unreasoning one perish,
  And they must leave to others
    their means of maintenance.
11 Their inward wish is that their
    houses may be to time in-
    definite,
  Their tabernacles to genera-
    tion after generation.
  They have called their landed
    estates by their names.
12 And yet earthling man, though
    in honor, cannot keep
    lodging;
  He is indeed comparable with
    the beasts that have been
    destroyed.
13 This is the way of those who
    have stupidity,
  And of those coming after
    them who take pleasure in
    their very mouthings. Se'lah.
14 Like sheep they have been ap-
    pointed to She'ol itself;
  Death itself will shepherd
    them;
  And the upright ones will have
    them in subjection in the
    morning,
  And their forms are due to
    wear away;

She'ol rather than a lofty
abode is for each one.

15 However, God himself will redeem my soul from the
hand of She'ol,
For he will receive me. *Se'lah*.

16 Do not be afraid because some
man gains riches,
Because the glory of his house
increases,

17 For at his death he cannot take
along anything at all;
His glory will not go down
along with him himself.

18 For during his lifetime he kept
blessing his own soul;
(And people will laud you because you do well for yourself,)

19 [His soul] finally comes only as
far as the generation of his
forefathers.
Nevermore will they see the
light.

20 Earthling man, although in
honor, who does not understand,
Is indeed comparable with the
beasts that have been de-
stroyed.

A melody of A'saph.

50 The Divine One, God, Jehovah, has himself spoken,
And he proceeds to call the
earth,
From the rising of the sun
until its setting.

2 Out of Zion, the perfection of
prettiness, God himself has
beamed forth.

3 Our God will come and cannot
possibly keep silent.
Before him there devours a
fire,
And all around him it has
become exceedingly stormy
weather.

4 He calls to the heavens above
and to the earth
So as to execute judgment on
his people:

5 "Gather to me my loyal ones,
Those concluding my cove-
nant over sacrifice."

6 And the heavens tell of his
righteousness,

For God himself is Judge.
Se'lah.

7 "Do listen, O my people, and I
will speak,
O Israel, and I will bear witness against you.
I am God, your God.

8 Not concerning your sacrifices
do I reprove you,
Nor [concerning] your whole
burnt offerings [that are]
in front of me constantly.

9 I will not take out of your house
a bull,
Out of your pens he-goats.

10 For to me belongs every wild
animal of the forest,
The beasts upon a thousand
mountains.

11 I well know every winged creature of the mountains,
And the animal throngs of
the open field are with me.

12 If I were hungry, I would not
say it to you;
For to me the productive land
and its fullness belong.

13 Shall I eat the flesh of powerful [bulls],
And the blood of he-goats
shall I drink?

14 Offer thanksgiving as your sacrifice to God,
And pay to the Most High
your vows;

15 And call me in the day of distress.
I shall rescue you, and you
will glorify me."

16 But to the wicked one God will
have to say:
"What right do you have to
enumerate my regulations,
And that you may bear my
covenant in your mouth?

17 Why, you—you have hated discipline,
And you keep throwing my
words behind you.

18 Whenever you saw a thief, you
were even pleased with him;
And your sharing was with
adulterers.

19 Your mouth you have let loose
to what is bad,
And your tongue you keep attached to deception.

20 You sit [and] speak against your own brother,
   Against the son of your mother you give away a fault.

21 These things you have done, and I kept silent.
   You imagined that I would positively become like you.
   I am going to reprove you, and I will set things in order before your eyes.

22 Understand this, please, YOU forgetters of God,
   That I may not tear [YOU] to pieces without there being any deliverer.

23 The one offering thanksgiving as his sacrifice is the one that glorifies me;
   And as for the one keeping a set way,
   I will cause him to see salvation by God."

To the director. A melody of David. When Nathan the prophet came in to him after he had had relations with Bath-she′ba.

51 Show me favor, O God, according to your loving-kindness.
   According to the abundance of your mercies wipe out my transgressions.

2 Thoroughly wash me from my error,
   And cleanse me even from my sin.

3 For my transgressions I myself know,
   And my sin is in front of me constantly.

4 Against you, you alone, I have sinned,
   And what is bad in your eyes I have done,
   In order that you may prove to be righteous when you speak,
   That you may be in the clear when you judge.

5 Look! With error I was brought forth with birth pains,
   And in sin my mother conceived me.

6 Look! You have taken delight in truthfulness itself in the inward parts;
   And in the secret self may you cause me to know sheer wisdom.

7 May you purify me from sin with hyssop, that I may be clean;
   May you wash me, that I may become whiter even than snow.

8 May you cause me to hear exultation and rejoicing,
   That the bones that you have crushed may be joyful.

9 Conceal your face from my sins,
   And wipe out even all my errors.

10 Create in me even a pure heart, O God,
   And put within me a new spirit, a steadfast one.

11 Do not throw me away from before your face;
   And your holy spirit O do not take away from me.

12 Do restore to me the exultation of salvation by you,
   And may you support me even with a willing spirit.

13 I will teach transgressors your ways,
   That sinners themselves may turn right back to you.

14 Deliver me from bloodguiltiness, O God the God of my salvation,
   That my tongue may joyfully tell about your righteousness.

15 O Jehovah, may you open these lips of mine,
   That my own mouth may tell forth your praise.

16 For you do not take delight in sacrifice—otherwise I would give [it];
   In whole burnt offering you do not find pleasure.

17 The sacrifices to God are a broken spirit;
   A heart broken and crushed, O God, you will not despise.

18 In your good will do deal well with Zion;
   May you build the walls of Jerusalem.

19 In that case you will be delighted with sacrifices of
righteousness,
With burnt sacrifice and
whole offering;
In that case bulls will be offered up on your very own
altar.

To the director. Mas'kil. Of
David, when Do'eg the E'dom-
ite came and proceeded to tell
Saul and say to him that David
had come to the house of
A.him'e.lech.

52 Why do you make your boast
over what is bad, O you
mighty one?
The loving-kindness of God
is all day long.

2 Adversities your tongue schemes
up, sharpened like a razor,
Working deceitfully.

3 You have loved what is bad
more than what is good,
Falsehood more than speaking righteousness. *Se'lah.*

4 You have loved all devouring
words,
O you deceitful tongue.

5 God himself will also pull you
down forever;
He will knock you down and
tear you away from [your]
tent,
And he will certainly root you
out of the land of the living
ones. *Se'lah.*

6 And the righteous ones will see
[it] and will be afraid,
And over him they will laugh.

7 Here is the able-bodied man
that does not put God as
his fortress,
But that trusts in the abundance of his riches,
That takes shelter in adversities by him.

8 But I shall be like a luxuriant
olive tree in God's house;
I do trust in the loving-
kindness of God to time
indefinite, even forever.

9 I will laud you to time indefinite,
for you have taken action;
And I shall hope in your name,
because it is good, in front
of your loyal ones.

To the director over Ma'ha.lath.
Mas'kil. Of David.

53 The senseless one has said in
his heart:
"There is no Jehovah."
They have acted ruinously and
have acted detestably in unrighteousness;
There is no one doing good.

2 As for God, he has looked down
from heaven itself upon the
sons of men,
To see whether there exists
anyone having insight, anyone seeking Jehovah.

3 They have all of them turned
back, they are [all] alike
corrupt;
There is no one doing good,
Not even one.

4 Have none of the practicers of
what is hurtful got knowledge,
Eating up my people as they
have eaten bread?
They have not called even
upon Jehovah.

5 There they were filled with a
great dread,
Where there had proved to be
no dread;
For God himself will certainly
scatter the bones of anyone
camping against you.
You will certainly put [them]
to shame, for Jehovah himself has rejected them.

6 O that out of Zion there were
the grand salvation of Israel!
When Jehovah gathers back
the captive ones of his
people,
Let Jacob be joyful, let Israel
rejoice.

To the director on stringed instruments. Mas'kil. Of David.
When the Ziph'ites came in and
proceeded to say to Saul: "Is
not David concealing himself
with us?"

54 O God, by your name save me,
And with your mightiness
may you plead my cause.

2 O God, hear my prayer;
Do give ear to the sayings
of my mouth.

3 For there are strangers that
   have risen up against me,
   And tyrants that do seek my
   soul.
   They have not set God in
   front of them. *Se'lah.*
4 Look! God is my helper;
   Jehovah is among those supporting my soul.
5 He will repay the bad to my
   foes;
   In your trueness silence them.
6 In willingness I will sacrifice to
   you.
   I shall laud your name, O
   Jehovah, for it is good.
7 For out of every distress he delivered me,
   And upon my enemies my eye
   has looked.

To the director on stringed instruments. Mas'kil. Of David.

55 Do give ear, O God, to my
     prayer;
     And do not hide yourself
     from my request for favor.
2 Do pay attention to me and
   answer me.
   I am driven restlessly about
   by my concern,
   And I cannot but show disquietude,
3 Due to the voice of the enemy,
   because of the pressure of
   the wicked one.
   For they keep dropping upon
   me what is hurtful,
   And in anger they harbor
   animosity against me.
4 My very heart is in severe pain
   within me,
   And the frights of death itself
   have fallen upon me.
5 Fear, yes, trembling itself enters
   into me,
   And shuddering covers me.
6 And I keep saying: "O that I
   had wings as a dove has!
   I would fly away and reside.
7 Look! I would go far away in
   flight;
   I would lodge in the wilderness.—*Se'lah*—
8 I would hasten to a place of
   escape for me
   From the rushing wind, from
   the tempest."

9 Confuse, O Jehovah, divide their
   tongue,
   For I have seen violence and
   disputing in the city.
10 Day and night they go round
   about it upon its walls;
   And hurtfulness and trouble
   are within it.
11 Adversities are within it;
   And from its public square
   oppression and deception
   have not moved away.
12 For it was not an enemy that
   proceeded to reproach me;
   Otherwise I could put up with
   it.
   It was not an intense hater of
   me that assumed great airs
   against me;
   Otherwise I could conceal myself from him.
13 But it was you, a mortal man
   who was as my equal,
   One familiar to me and my
   acquaintance,
14 Because we used to enjoy sweet
   intimacy together;
   Into the house of God we
   used to walk with the
   throng.
15 Desolations [be] upon them!
   Let them go down into She'ol
   alive;
   For during their alien residence bad things have been
   within them.
16 As for me, to God I shall call
   out;
   And Jehovah himself will save
   me.
17 Evening and morning and noontime I cannot but show
   concern and I moan,
   And he hears my voice.
18 He will certainly redeem [and
   put] my soul in peace from
   the fight that is against me,
   For in multitudes they have
   come to be against me.
19 God will hear and answer them,
   Even He that is sitting [en-
   throned] as in the past—
   Se'lah—
   Those with whom there are no
   changings
   And who have not feared God.
20 He has thrust out his hands

against those at peace with
him;
He has profaned his covenant.
21 Smoother than butter are [the
words of] his mouth,
But his heart is disposed to
fight.
His words are softer than oil,
But they are drawn swords.
22 Throw your burden upon Jehovah himself,
And he himself will sustain
you.
Never will he allow the righteous one to totter.
23 But you yourself, O God, will
bring them down to the
lowest pit.
As for bloodguilty and deceitful men, they will not live
out half their days.
But as for me, I shall trust
in you.

To the director on the Silent
Dove among those far away.
Of David. Mik'tam. When the
Phi·lis'tines laid hold of him
in Gath.

56 Show me favor, O God,
because mortal man has
snapped at me.
Warring all day long, he keeps
oppressing me.
2 My foes have kept snapping
all day long,
For there are many warring
against me high-mindedly.
3 Whatever day I get afraid, I, for
my part, shall trust even
in you.
4 In union with God I shall praise
his word.
In God I have put my trust;
I shall not be afraid.
What can flesh do to me?
5 All day long they keep hurting
my personal affairs;
All their thoughts are against
me for bad.
6 They attack, they conceal themselves,
They, for their part, keep
observing my very steps,
While they have waited for
my soul.
7 On account of [their] hurtfulness cast them forth.

In anger bring down even the
peoples, O God.
8 My being a fugitive you yourself have reported.
Do put my tears in your skin
bottle.
Are they not in your book?
9 At that time my enemies will
turn back, on the day that
I call;
This I well know, that God
is for me.
10 In union with God I shall praise
[his] word;
In union with Jehovah I shall
praise [his] word.
11 In God I have put my trust.
I shall not be afraid.
What can earthling man do
to me?
12 Upon me, O God, there are vows
to you.
I shall render expressions of
thanksgiving to you.
13 For you have delivered my soul
from death—
[Have you] not [delivered]
my feet from stumbling?—
That [I] may walk about before God in the light of
those alive.

To the director. "Do not bring
to ruin." Of David. Mik'tam.
When he ran away because of
Saul, into the cave.

57 Show me favor, O God, show
me favor,
For in you my soul has taken
refuge;
And in the shadow of your
wings I take refuge until
the adversities pass over.
2 I call to God the Most High, to
the [true] God who is
bringing [them] to an end
on my account.
3 He will send from heaven and
save me.
He will certainly confuse the
one snapping at me. Se'lah.
God will send his loving-
kindness and his trueness.
4 My soul is in the middle of
lions;
I cannot but lie down among
devourers, [even] the sons
of men,

Whose teeth are spears and
arrows,
And whose tongue is a sharp
sword.
5 O be exalted above the heavens,
O God;
Let your glory be above all
the earth.
6 A net they have prepared for
my steps;
My soul has become bowed
down.
They excavated before me a
pitfall;
They have fallen into the
midst of it. Se′lah.
7 My heart is steadfast, O God,
My heart is steadfast.
I will sing and make melody.
8 Do awake, O my glory;
Do awake, O stringed instrument; you too, O harp.
I will awaken the dawn.
9 I shall laud you among the
peoples, O Jehovah;
I shall make melody to you
among the national groups.
10 For your loving-kindness is great
up to the heavens,
And your trueness up to the
skies.
11 Do be exalted above the heavens, O God;
Let your glory be above all
the earth.

To the director. "Do not bring
to ruin." Of David. Mik′tam.

58 [In your] silence can you
really speak about right-
eousness itself?
Can you judge in uprightness
itself, O you sons of men?
2 How much, rather, do you with
the heart practice outright
unrighteousness in the
earth,
[And] prepare the road for
the very violence of your
hands!
3 The wicked ones have been
perverts from the womb;
They have wandered about
from the belly onward;
They are speaking lies.
4 The venom of theirs is like the
venom of the serpent,

Deaf like the cobra that stops
up its ear,
5 That will not listen to the voice
of charmers,
Though someone wise is binding with spells.
6 O God, knock out their teeth
in their mouth.
Break down the very jawbones
of maned young lions, O Jehovah.
7 May they dissolve as into waters
that go their way;
May he bend [the bow for]
his arrows as they collapse.
8 Like a snail melting away he
walks;
Like a miscarriage of a woman they will certainly not
behold the sun.
9 Before your pots feel the [kin-
dled] bramble,
The live green as well as the
burning, he will carry them
off as a stormy wind.
10 The righteous one will rejoice
because he has beheld the
vengeance.
His steps he will bathe in the
blood of the wicked one.
11 And mankind will say: "Surely
there is fruitage for the
righteous one.
Surely there exists a God that
is judging in the earth."

To the director. "Do not bring
to ruin." Of David. Mik′tam.
When Saul sent, and they kept
watching the house, to put him
to death.

59 Deliver me from my enemies,
O my God;
From those rising up against
me may you protect me.
2 Deliver me from the practicers
of what is hurtful,
And from bloodguilty men
save me.
3 For, look! they have lain in wait
for my soul;
Strong ones make an attack
upon me,
For no revolt on my part, nor
any sin on my part, O Je-
hovah.
4 Though there is no error, they
run and get themselves
ready.

Do rouse yourself at my calling and see.
5 And you, O Jehovah God of armies, are the God of Israel.
Do wake up to turn your attention to all the nations.
Do not show favor to any hurtful traitors. *Se'lah.*
6 They keep returning at evening-time;
They keep barking like a dog and go all around the city.
7 Look! They make a bubbling forth with their mouth;
Swords are on their lips,
For who is listening?
8 But you yourself, O Jehovah, will laugh at them;
You will hold all the nations in derision.
9 O my Strength, toward you I will keep watch;
For God is my secure height.
10 The God of loving-kindness to me will himself confront me;
God himself will cause me to look upon my foes.
11 Do not kill them, that my people may not forget.
By your vital energy make them wander about,
And bring them down, O our shield Jehovah,
12 [For] the sin of their mouth, the word of their lips;
And may they be caught in their pride,
Even for the cursing and the deception that they rehearse.
13 Bring [them] to an end in rage;
Bring [them] to an end, that they may not be;
And may they know that God is ruling in Jacob to the ends of the earth. *Se'lah.*
14 And let them return at evening-time;
Let them bark like a dog and go all around the city.
15 Let those very ones wander about for something to eat;
Let them not be satisfied or stay overnight.

16 But as for me, I shall sing of your strength,
And in the morning I shall joyfully tell about your loving-kindness.
For you have proved to be a secure height for me
And a place to which to flee in the day of my distress.
17 O my Strength, to you I will make melody,
For God is my secure height, the God of loving-kindness to me.

To the director on The Lily of Reminder. Mik'tam. Of David. For teaching. When he engaged in a struggle with A'ram-na.ha-ra'im and A'ram-Zo'bah, and Jo'ab proceeded to return and strike down E'dom in the Valley of Salt, even twelve thousand.

60 O God, you have cast us off, you have broken through us,
You have become incensed. You should restore us.
2 You have caused the earth to rock, you have split it open.
Heal its breaches, for it has tottered.
3 You have caused your people to see hardship.
You have made us drink wine sending us reeling.
4 You have given to those fearing you a signal
To flee zigzag on account of the bow. *Se'lah.*
5 In order that your beloved ones may be rescued,
O do save with your right hand and answer us.
6 God himself has spoken in his holiness:
"I will exult, I will give out She'chem as a portion;
And the low plain of Suc'coth I shall measure off.
7 Gil'e·ad belongs to me and Ma-nas'seh belongs to me,
And E'phra·im is the fortress of my head one;
Judah is my commander's staff.
8 Mo'ab is my washing pot.
Over E'dom I shall throw my sandal.

Over Phi·lis'ti·a I shall shout
in triumph."

9 Who will bring me to the besieged city?
Who will certainly lead me as
far as E'dom?

10 Is it not you, O God, who have
cast us off
And who do not go forth with
our armies as God?

11 Do give us assistance from distress,
As salvation by earthling man
is worthless.

12 By God we shall gain vital
energy,
And he himself will tread
down our adversaries.

To the director on stringed
instruments. Of David.

61 Do hear, O God, my entreating cry.
Do pay attention to my prayer.

2 From the extremity of the earth
I shall cry, even to you,
when my heart grows feeble.
Onto a rock that is higher
than I am may you lead
me.

3 For you have proved to be a
refuge for me,
A strong tower in the face of
the enemy.

4 I will be a guest in your tent
for times indefinite;
I will take refuge in the concealment of your wings.
Se'lah.

5 For you yourself, O God, have
listened to my vows.
You have given [me] the
possession of those fearing
your name.

6 Days you will add to the days
of the king;
His years will be like generation after generation.

7 He will dwell to time indefinite
before God;
O assign loving-kindness and
trueness, that these may
safeguard him.

8 So I will make melody to your
name forever,
That I may pay my vows day
after day.

To the director of Je.du'thun.
A melody of David.

62 Indeed toward God is my soul
[waiting in] silence.
From him my salvation is.

2 Indeed he is my rock and my
salvation, my secure height;
I shall not be made to totter
very much.

3 How long will you carry on
frantically against the man
whom you would murder?
All of you are like a leaning
wall, a stone wall that is
being pushed in.

4 Indeed they give advice so as to
allure from one's own dignity;
They take pleasure in a lie.
With their mouth they bless,
but inside themselves they
call down evil. Se'lah.

5 Indeed toward God wait silently,
O my soul,
Because from him is my hope.

6 Indeed he is my rock and my
salvation, my secure height;
I shall not be made to totter.

7 Upon God are my salvation and
my glory.
My strong rock, my refuge
is in God.

8 Trust in him at all times, O
people.
Before him pour out your
heart.
God is a refuge for us. Se'lah.

9 Indeed the sons of earthling
man are an exhalation,
The sons of mankind are a
lie.
When laid upon the scales
they are all together lighter
than an exhalation.

10 Do not put your trust in defrauding,
Nor become vain in sheer
robbery.
In case the means of maintenance should thrive, do
not set your heart [on
them].

11 Once God has spoken, twice I
have heard even this,
That strength belongs to God.

12 Also loving-kindness belongs to
you, O Jehovah,

For you yourself pay back to each one according to his work.

A melody of David, when he happened to be in the wilderness of Judah.

63 O God, you are my God, I keep looking for you.
My soul does thirst for you.
For you my flesh has grown faint [with longing]
In a land dry and exhausted, where there is no water.

2 Thus I have beheld you in the holy place,
At seeing your strength and your glory.

3 Because your loving-kindness is better than life,
My own lips will commend you.

4 Thus I shall bless you during my lifetime;
In your name I shall raise my palms.

5 As with the best part, even fatness, my soul is satisfied,
And with lips of joyful cries my mouth offers praise.

6 When I have remembered you upon my lounge,
During the night watches I meditate on you.

7 For you have proved to be of assistance to me,
And in the shadow of your wings I cry out joyfully.

8 My soul has closely followed you;
On me your right hand keeps fast hold.

9 As for those who keep seeking my soul for [its] ruin,
They will come into the lowest parts of the earth.

10 They will be delivered over to the power of the sword;
They will become a mere portion for foxes.

11 And the king himself will rejoice in God.
Every one swearing by him will boast,
For the mouth of those speaking falsehood will be stopped up.

To the director. A melody of David.

64 Hear, O God, my voice in my concern.
From the dreadfulness of the enemy may you safeguard my life.

2 May you conceal me from the confidential talk of evildoers,
From the tumult of practicers of hurtfulness,

3 Who have sharpened their tongue just like a sword,
Who have aimed their arrow, bitter speech,

4 To shoot from concealed places at someone blameless.
All of a sudden they shoot at him and do not fear.

5 They hold themselves down to bad speech;
They make statements about hiding traps.
They have said: "Who sees them?"

6 They keep searching out unrighteous things;
They have hidden a shrewd device well searched out,
And the inward part of each one, even [his] heart, is deep.

7 But God will shoot at them with an arrow suddenly.
Wounds have resulted to them,

8 And they cause one to stumble.
[But] their tongue is against their own selves.
All those looking upon them will shake their head,

9 And all earthling men will become afraid;
And they will tell of the activity of God,
And they will certainly have insight into his work.

10 And the righteous one will rejoice in Jehovah and will indeed take refuge in him;
And all the upright in heart will boast.

To the director. A melody of David.
A song.

65 For you there is praise—silence—, O God, in Zion;
And to you the vow will be paid.

2 O Hearer of prayer, even to you
people of all flesh will come.
3 Things of error have proved
mightier than I am.
As for our transgressions, you
yourself will cover them.
4 Happy is the one you choose and
cause to approach,
That he may reside in your
courtyards.
He will certainly be satisfied
with the goodness of your
house,
The holy place of your temple.
5 With fear-inspiring things in
righteousness you will answer us,
O God of our salvation,
The Trust of all the borders
of the earth and those far
away on the sea.
6 He is firmly establishing the
mountains with his power;
He is indeed girded with
mightiness.
7 He is stilling the noise of the
seas,
The noise of their waves and
the turmoil of the national
groups.
8 And the inhabitants of the utter-
most parts will be afraid
of your signs;
The goings forth of the morning and evening you cause
to cry out joyfully.
9 You have turned your attention
to the earth, that you may
give it abundance;
You enrich it very much.
The stream from God is full of
water.
You prepare their grain,
For that is the way you prepare the earth.
10 There is a drenching of its
furrows, a leveling off of its
clods;
With copious showers you
soften it; you bless its very
sprouts.
11 You have crowned the year with
your goodness,
And your very tracks drip
with fatness.
12 The pasture grounds of the wilderness keep dripping,

And with joyfulness the very
hills gird themselves.
13 The pastures have become
clothed with flocks,
And the low plains themselves
are enveloped with grain.
They shout in triumph, yes,
they sing.

To the director. A song, a melody.

66 Shout in triumph to God, all
[you people of] the earth.
2 Make melody to the glory of
his name.
Render his praise glorious.
3 Say to God: "How fear-inspiring
your works are!
Because of the abundance of
your strength your enemies
will come cringing to you.
4 All [people of] the earth will
bow down to you,
And they will make melody to
you, they will make melody
to your name." Se'lah.
5 Come, you people, and see the
activities of God.
His dealing with the sons of
men is fear-inspiring.
6 He has changed the sea into dry
land;
Through the river they went
crossing over on foot.
There we began to rejoice in
him.
7 He is ruling by his mightiness
to time indefinite.
Upon the nations his own eyes
keep watch.
As for those who are stubborn,
let them not be exalted in
themselves. Se'lah.
8 Bless our God, O you peoples,
And cause the voice of praise
to him to be heard.
9 He is setting our soul in life,
And he has not allowed our
foot to totter.
10 For you have examined us, O
God;
You have refined us as when
refining silver.
11 You have brought us into a
hunting net;
You have put pressure on our
hips.
12 You have made mortal man to
ride over our head;

We have come through fire
and through water,
And you proceeded to bring
us forth to relief.
13 I shall come into your house
with whole burnt offerings;
I shall pay to you my vows
14 That my lips have opened up to
say
And that my mouth has
spoken when I was in sore
straits.
15 Whole burnt offerings of fatlings I shall offer up to you,
With the sacrificial smoke of
rams.
I shall render up a bull with
he-goats. Se'lah.
16 Come, listen, all you who fear
God, and I will relate
What he has done for my soul.
17 To him I called with my mouth,
And there was an extolling
with my tongue.
18 If I have regarded anything
hurtful in my heart,
Jehovah will not hear [me].
19 Truly God has heard;
He has paid attention to the
voice of my prayer.
20 Blessed be God, who has not
turned aside my prayer,
Nor his loving-kindness from
me.

To the director on stringed instruments. A melody, a song.

67 God himself will show us
favor and bless us;
He will make his face shine
upon us—Se'lah—
2 That your way may be known
in the earth,
Your salvation even among
all the nations.
3 Let peoples laud you, O God;
Let the peoples, all of them,
laud you.
4 Let national groups rejoice and
cry out joyfully,
For you will judge the peoples
with uprightness;
And as for national groups,
on the earth you will lead
them. Se'lah.
5 Let peoples laud you, O God;
Let peoples, all of them, laud
you.

6 The earth itself will certainly
give its produce;
God, our God, will bless us.
7 God will bless us,
And all the ends of the earth
will fear him.

To the director.
Of David. A melody, a song.

68 Let God arise, let his enemies
be scattered,
And let those who intensely
hate him flee because of
him.
2 As smoke is driven away, may
you drive [them] away;
As wax melts because of the
fire,
Let the wicked ones perish
from before God.
3 But as for the righteous, let
them rejoice,
Let them be elated before
God,
And let them exult with rejoicing.
4 Sing you to God, make melody
to his name;
Raise up [a song] to the One
riding through the desert
plains
As Jah, which is his name;
and jubilate before him;
5 A father of fatherless boys and
a judge of widows
Is God in his holy dwelling.
6 God is causing the solitary ones
to dwell in a house;
He is bringing forth prisoners
into full prosperity.
However, as for the stubborn,
they have to reside in a
scorched land.
7 O God, when you went forth
before your people,
When you marched through
the desert—Se'lah—
8 The earth itself rocked,
Heaven itself also dripped because of God;
This Si'nai [rocked] because
of God, the God of Israel.
9 A copious downpour you began
causing to fall, O God;
Your inheritance, even when
it was weary—you yourself
reinvigorated it.
10 Your tent community—they
have dwelt in it;

With your goodness you proceeded to make it ready for the afflicted one, O God.

11 Jehovah himself gives the saying;
The women telling the good news are a large army.

12 Even the kings of armies flee, they flee.
As for her who abides at home, she shares in the spoil.

13 Although you men kept lying between the [camp] ash heaps,
There will be the wings of a dove covered with silver
And its pinions with yellowish-green gold.

14 When the Almighty One scattered abroad the kings in it,
It began to snow in Zal'mon.

15 The mountainous region of Ba'shan is a mountain of God;
The mountainous region of Ba'shan is a mountain of peaks.

16 Why do you, O you mountains of peaks, keep watching enviously
The mountain that God has desired for himself to dwell in?
Even Jehovah himself will reside [there] forever.

17 The war chariots of God are in tens of thousands, thousands over and over again.
Jehovah himself has come from Si'nai into the holy place.

18 You have ascended on high;
You have carried away captives;
You have taken gifts in the form of men,
Yes, even the stubborn ones, to reside [among them], O Jah God.

19 Blessed be Jehovah, who daily carries the load for us,
The [true] God of our salvation. Se'lah.

20 The [true] God is for us a God of saving acts;
And to Jehovah the Sovereign Lord belong the ways out from death.

21 Indeed God himself will break the head of his enemies in pieces,
The hairy crown of the head of anyone walking about in his guiltiness.

22 Jehovah has said: "From Ba'shan I shall bring back,
I shall bring [them] back from the depths of the sea,

23 In order that you may wash your foot in blood,
That the tongue of your dogs may have its portion from the enemies."

24 They have seen your processions, O God,
The processions of my God, my King, into the holy place.

25 The singers went in front, the players on stringed instruments after them;
In between were the maidens beating tambourines.

26 In congregated throngs bless God,
Jehovah, [O you who are] from the Source of Israel.

27 There is little Benjamin subduing them,
The princes of Judah with their shouting crowd,
The princes of Zeb'u·lun, the princes of Naph'ta·li.

28 Your God has laid command upon your strength.
Do show strength, O God, you who have acted for us.

29 Because of your temple at Jerusalem,
Kings will bring gifts to you yourself.

30 Rebuke the wild beast of the reeds, the assembly of bulls,
With the calves of the peoples, each one stamping down on pieces of silver.
He has scattered the peoples that take delight in fights.

31 Bronzeware things will come out of Egypt;
Cush itself will quickly stretch out its hands [with gifts] to God.

32 O you kingdoms of the earth, sing to God,
Make melody to Jehovah—
Se'lah—

33 To the One riding on the ancient heaven of heavens.
Lo! He sounds with his voice,
a strong voice.
34 ASCRIBE strength to God.
Over Israel his eminence is
and his strength is in the
clouds.
35 God is fear-inspiring out of
your grand sanctuary.
The God of Israel he is,
giving strength, even might
to the people.
Blessed be God.

To the director on The Lilies.
Of David.

69 Save me, O God, for the
waters have come clear to
the soul.
2 I have sunk down in deep mire,
where there is no standing
ground.
I have come into profound
waters,
And a flowing stream itself
has washed me away.
3 I have become tired by my
calling out;
My throat has become hoarse.
My eyes have failed while
waiting for my God.
4 Those hating me without a
cause have become even
more than the hairs of my
head.
Those bringing me to silence,
being my enemies for no
reason, have become nu-
merous.
What I had not taken by robbery I then proceeded to
give back.
5 O God, you yourself have come
to know my foolishness,
And from you my own guiltiness has not been hidden.
6 O may those hoping in you not
be ashamed because of me,
O Sovereign Lord, Jehovah of
armies.
O may those seeking you not be
humiliated because of me,
O God of Israel.
7 For on your account I have
borne reproach,
Humiliation has covered my
face.

8 I have become one estranged
to my brothers,
And a foreigner to the sons
of my mother.
9 For sheer zeal for your house
has eaten me up,
And the very reproaches of
those reproaching you have
fallen upon me.
10 And I proceeded to weep with
the fasting of my soul,
But it came to be for re-
proaches to me.
11 When I made sackcloth my
clothing,
Then I became to them a
proverbial saying.
12 Those sitting in the gate began
concerning themselves about
me,
And [I was] the subject of the
songs of drinkers of intoxicating liquor.
13 But as for me, my prayer was
to you, O Jehovah,
At an acceptable time, O God.
In the abundance of your
loving-kindness answer me
with the truth of salvation
by you.
14 Deliver me from the mire, that
I may not sink down.
O may I be delivered from
those hating me and from
the deep waters.
15 O may not the flowing stream
of waters wash me away,
Nor the depth swallow me up,
Nor the well close its mouth
over me.
16 Answer me, O Jehovah, for your
loving-kindness is good.
According to the multitude
of your mercies turn to me,
17 And do not conceal your face
from your servant.
Because I am in sore straits,
answer me quickly.
18 Do come near to my soul, reclaim it;
On account of my enemies
redeem me.
19 You yourself have come to know
my reproach and my shame
and my humiliation.
All those showing hostility to
me are in front of you.
20 Reproach itself has broken my

heart, and [the wound] is incurable.
And I kept hoping for someone to show sympathy, but there was none;
And for comforters, but I found none.

21 But for food they gave [me] a poisonous plant,
And for my thirst they tried to make me drink vinegar.

22 Let their table before them become a trap,
And what is for their welfare a snare.

23 Let their eyes become darkened so as not to see;
And cause their very hips to wobble constantly.

24 Pour out upon them your denunciation,
And may your own burning anger overtake them.

25 Let their walled camp become desolate;
In their tents may there come to be no dweller.

26 For the one whom you yourself have struck they have pursued,
And the pains of those pierced by you they keep recounting.

27 Do give error upon their error,
And may they not come into your righteousness.

28 Let them be wiped out of the book of the living ones,
And with the righteous ones may they not be written in.

29 But I am afflicted and aching.
May your own salvation, O God, protect me.

30 I will praise the name of God with song,
And I will magnify him with thanksgiving.

31 This will also be more pleasing to Jehovah than a bull,
Than a young bull displaying horns, splitting the hoof.

32 The meek ones will certainly see [it]; they will rejoice.
You who are seeking God, let YOUR heart also keep alive.

33 For Jehovah is listening to the poor ones,
And he will indeed not despise his very own prisoners.

34 Let heaven and earth praise him,
The seas and everything moving about in them.

35 For God himself will save Zion
And will build the cities of Judah;
And they will certainly dwell there and take possession of it.

36 And the offspring of his servants themselves will inherit it,
And those loving his name will be the ones to reside in it.

To the director.
Of David, to bring to remembrance.

70 O God, to deliver me,
O Jehovah, to my assistance do make haste.

2 May those be ashamed and abashed who are seeking my soul.
May those turn back and be humiliated who are taking delight in my calamity.

3 May those go back by reason of their shame who are saying: "Aha, aha!"

4 May those exult and rejoice in you, all of whom are seeking you,
And may they say constantly: "God be magnified!"—those loving your salvation.

5 But I am afflicted and poor.
O God, do act quickly for me.
You are my help and the Provider of escape for me.
O Jehovah, do not be too late.

71 In you, O Jehovah, I have taken refuge.
O may I never be ashamed.

2 In your righteousness may you deliver me and provide me with escape.
Incline to me your ear and save me.

3 Become to me a rock fortress into which to enter constantly.
You must command to save me,
For you are my crag and my stronghold.

4 O my God, provide me with

escape from the hand of
the wicked one,
From the palm of the one
acting unjustly and op-
pressively,
5 For you are my hope, O Sovereign Lord Jehovah, my
confidence from my youth.
6 Upon you I have supported myself from the belly;
You are the One severing me
even from the inward parts
of my mother.
In you my praise is constantly.
7 I have become just like a miracle to many people;
But you are my strong refuge.
8 My mouth is filled with your
praise,
All day long with your beauty.
9 Do not throw me away in the
time of old age;
Just when my power is failing, do not leave me.
10 For my enemies have said in
regard to me,
And the very ones keeping
watch for my soul have
jointly exchanged counsel,
11 Saying: "God himself has left
him.
Pursue and catch him, for
there is no deliverer."
12 O God, do not keep far away
from me.
O my God, do hurry to my
assistance.
13 May those be ashamed, may
those come to their end,
who are resisting my soul.
May those cover themselves
with reproach and humiliation who are seeking calamity for me.
14 But as for me, I shall wait constantly,
And I will add to all your
praise.
15 My own mouth will recount your
righteousness,
All day long your salvation,
For I have not come to know
the numbers [of them].
16 I shall come in grand mightiness, O Sovereign Lord Jehovah;
I shall mention your righteousness, yours alone.

17 O God, you have taught me
from my youth on,
And until now I keep telling
about your wonderful works.
18 And even until old age and
gray-headedness, O God, do
not leave me,
Until I may tell about your
arm to the generation,
To all those who are to come,
about your mightiness.
19 Your righteousness, O God, is
up to the height;
As respects the great things
that you have done,
O God, who is like you?
20 Because you have made me see
many distresses and calamities,
May you revive me again;
And from the watery deeps
of the earth may you again
bring me up.
21 May you enlarge my greatness,
And may you surround [and]
comfort me.
22 I too, I shall laud you on an
instrument of a stringed
sort,
As regards your trueness, O
my God.
I will make melody to you on
the harp, O Holy One of
Israel.
23 My lips will cry out joyfully
when I am inclined to make
melody to you,
Even my soul that you have
redeemed.
24 Also, my own tongue, all day
long, will utter in an undertone your righteousness,
For they have become
ashamed, for they have become abashed, who are
seeking calamity for me.

Regarding Solomon.

72 O God, give your own judicial
decisions to the king,
And your righteousness to the
son of the king.
2 May he plead the cause of your
people with righteousness
And of your afflicted ones with
judicial decision.
3 Let the mountains carry peace
to the people,

Also the hills, through righteousness.

4 Let him judge the afflicted ones
of the people,
Let him save the sons of the
poor one,
And let him crush the de-
frauder.

5 They will fear you as long as
there is a sun,
And before the moon for
generation after generation.

6 He will descend like the rain
upon the mown grass,
Like copious showers that wet
the earth.

7 In his days the righteous one
will sprout,
And the abundance of peace
until the moon is no more.

8 And he will have subjects from
sea to sea
And from the River to the
ends of the earth.

9 Before him the inhabitants of
waterless regions will bow
down,
And his very enemies will lick
the dust itself.

10 The kings of Tar′shish and of
the islands—
Tribute they will pay.
The kings of She′ba and of
Se′ba—
A gift they will present.

11 And to him all the kings will
prostrate themselves;
All the nations, for their part,
will serve him.

12 For he will deliver the poor one
crying for help,
Also the afflicted one and whoever has no helper.

13 He will feel sorry for the lowly
one and the poor one,
And the souls of the poor ones
he will save.

14 From oppression and from violence he will redeem their
soul,
And their blood will be precious in his eyes.

15 And let him live, and to him let
some of the gold of She′ba
be given.
And in his behalf let prayer
be made constantly;
All day long let him be blessed.

16 There will come to be plenty of
grain on the earth;
On the top of the mountains
there will be an overflow.
His fruit will be as in Leb′a·non,
And those who are from the
city will blossom like the
vegetation of the earth.

17 Let his name prove to be to time
indefinite;
Before the sun let his name
have increase,
And by means of him let them
bless themselves;
Let all nations pronounce him
happy.

18 Blessed be Jehovah God, Israel's
God,
Who alone is doing wonderful
works.

19 And blessed be his glorious name
to time indefinite,
And let his glory fill the whole
earth.
Amen and Amen.

20 The prayers of David, the son
of Jes′se, have come to their
end.

BOOK THREE
(Psalms 73 – 89)

A melody of A′saph.

73 God is indeed good to Israel,
to those clean in heart.

2 As for me, my feet had almost
turned aside,
My steps had nearly been
made to slip.

3 For I became envious of the
boasters,
[When] I would see the very
peace of wicked people.

4 For they have no deathly pangs;
And their paunch is fat.

5 They are not even in the trouble
of mortal man,
And they are not plagued the
same as other men.

6 Therefore haughtiness has
served as a necklace to
them;
Violence envelops them as a
garment.

7 Their eye has bulged from fatness;
They have exceeded the imaginations of the heart.
8 They scoff and speak about what is bad;
About defrauding they speak in an elevated style.
9 They have put their mouth in the very heavens,
And their tongue itself walks about in the earth.
10 Therefore he brings his people back hither,
And the waters of what is full are drained out for them.
11 And they have said: "How has God come to know?
And does there exist knowledge in the Most High?"
12 Look! These are the wicked, who are at ease indefinitely.
They have increased [their] means of maintenance.
13 Surely it is in vain that I have cleansed my heart
And that I wash my hands in innocence itself.
14 And I came to be plagued all day long,
And my correction is every morning.
15 If I had said: "I will tell a story like that,"
Look! against the generation of your sons
I should have acted treacherously.
16 And I kept considering so as to know this;
It was a trouble in my eyes,
17 Until I proceeded to come into the grand sanctuary of God.
I wanted to discern their future.
18 Surely on slippery ground is where you place them.
You have made them fall to ruins.
19 O how they have become an object of astonishment as in a moment!
[How] they have reached their end, have been brought to their finish through sudden terrors!

20 Like a dream after awaking, O Jehovah,
[So] when arousing [yourself] you will despise their very image.
21 For my heart was soured
And in my kidneys I was sharply pained,
22 And I was unreasoning and I could not know;
I became as mere beasts from your standpoint.
23 But I am constantly with you;
You have taken hold of my right hand.
24 With your counsel you will lead me,
And afterward you will take me even to glory.
25 Whom do I have in the heavens?
And besides you I do have no other delight on the earth.
26 My organism and my heart have failed.
God is the rock of my heart and my share to time indefinite.
27 For, look! the very ones keeping away from you will perish.
You will certainly silence every one immorally leaving you.
28 But as for me, the drawing near to God is good for me.
In the Sovereign Lord Jehovah I have placed my refuge,
To declare all your works.

A mas′kil. Of A′saph.

74 Why, O God, have you cast off forever?
Why does your anger keep smoking against the flock of your pasturage?
2 Remember your assembly that you acquired long ago,
The tribe that you redeemed as your inheritance,
This Mount Zion in which you have resided.
3 Do lift up your steps to the long-lasting desolations.
Everything the enemy has treated badly in the holy place.
4 Those showing hostility to you have roared in the middle of your meeting place.

They have set their own signs as [the] signs.

5 One is notorious in being like him that brings up axes on high against a thicket of trees.

6 And now the very engravings of it, one and all, they strike even with hatchet and iron-tipped beams.

7 They have thrust your sanctuary into the fire itself.

They have profaned the tabernacle of your name to the very earth.

8 They, even their offspring, have said together in their own heart:

"All the meeting places of God must be burned in the land."

9 Our signs we have not seen; there is no prophet any more,

And there is no one with us knowing how long.

10 How long, O God, will the adversary keep reproaching?

Will the enemy keep treating your name with disrespect forever?

11 Why do you keep your hand, even your right hand, withdrawn

From the midst of your bosom to make an end [of us]?

12 And yet God is my King from long ago,

The One performing grand salvation in the midst of the earth.

13 You yourself stirred up the sea with your own strength;

You broke the heads of the sea monsters in the waters.

14 You yourself crushed to pieces the heads of Le·vi'a·than.

You proceeded to give it as food to the people, to those inhabiting the waterless regions.

15 You were the One that split the spring and the torrent;

You yourself dried up ever-flowing rivers.

16 To you the day belongs; also, to you the night belongs.

You yourself prepared the luminary, even the sun.

17 It was you that set up all the boundaries of the earth;

Summer and winter—you yourself formed them.

18 Remember this: The enemy himself has reproached, O Jehovah,

And a senseless people have treated your name with disrespect.

19 Do not give to the wild beast the soul of your turtledove.

Do not forget the very life of your afflicted ones forever.

20 Take a look at the covenant,

For the dark places of the earth have become full of the abodes of violence.

21 O may the crushed one not return humiliated.

May the afflicted one and the poor one praise your name.

22 Do arise, O God, do conduct your own case at law.

Remember your reproach from the senseless one all day long.

23 Do not forget the voice of those showing hostility to you.

The noise of those rising up against you is ascending constantly.

To the director. "Do not bring to ruin." A melody. Of A'saph. A song.

75 We give thanks to you, O God; we give thanks to you,

And your name is near.

Men have to declare your wondrous works.

2 "For I proceeded to take a set time;

I myself began judging with uprightness.

3 The earth and all its inhabitants being dissolved,

It was I that adjusted its pillars." Se'lah.

4 I said to the foolish ones: "Do not be foolish,"

And to the wicked ones: "Do not exalt the horn.

5 Do not exalt YOUR horn on high.

Do not speak with an arrogant neck.

6 For neither from the east nor from the west,

Nor from the south is there an exalting.

7 For God is the judge.
This one he abases, and that one he exalts.

8 For there is a cup in the hand of Jehovah,
And the wine is foaming, it is full of mixture.
And surely its dregs will be poured out from it;
All the wicked ones of the earth will drain [them] out, drink [them]."

9 But as for me, I shall tell [of it] to time indefinite;
I will make melody to the God of Jacob.

10 And all the horns of the wicked ones I shall cut down.
The horns of the righteous one will be exalted.

To the director on stringed instruments. A melody of A'saph. A song.

76 God is known in Judah;
In Israel his name is great.

2 And his covert proves to be in Sa'lem itself,
And his dwelling place in Zion.

3 There he broke the flaming shafts of the bow,
The shield and the sword and the battle. Se'lah.

4 You are enveloped with light, more majestic than the mountains of prey.

5 The ones powerful in heart have been despoiled,
They have drowsed away to their sleep,
And none of all the valiant men have found their hands.

6 From your rebuke, O God of Jacob, both the charioteer and the horse have fallen fast asleep.

7 You—fear-inspiring you are,
And who can stand before you because of the strength of your anger?

8 From heaven you caused the legal contest to be heard;
The earth itself feared and kept quiet

9 When God rose up to judgment,
To save all the meek of the earth. Se'lah.

10 For the very rage of man will laud you;
The remainder of raging you will gird upon yourself.

11 Vow and pay to Jehovah YOUR God, all YOU who are round about him.
Let them bring a gift in fear.

12 He will humble the spirit of leaders;
Fear-inspiring he is to the kings of the earth.

To the director on Je.du'thun.
Of A'saph. A melody.

77 With my voice I will even cry out to God himself,
With my voice to God, and he will certainly give ear to me.

2 In the day of my distress I have searched for Jehovah himself.
At night my very hand has been stretched out and does not grow numb;
My soul has refused to be comforted.

3 I will remember God and be boisterous;
I will show concern, that my spirit may faint away. Se'lah.

4 You have seized hold of my eyelids;
I have become agitated, and I cannot speak.

5 I have thought upon the days of long ago,
On the years in the indefinite past.

6 I will remember my string music in the night;
With my heart I will show concern,
And my spirit will carefully search.

7 Will it be to times indefinite that Jehovah keeps casting off,
And will he no more be pleased again?

8 Has his loving-kindness terminated forever?

Has [his] saying come to
nothing for generation after
generation?
9 Has God forgotten to be favorable,
Or has he shut off his mercies
in anger? *Se'lah.*
10 And shall I keep saying: "This
is what pierces me through,
The changing of the right
hand of the Most High"?
11 I shall remember the practices
of Jah;
For I will remember your
marvelous doing of long ago.
12 And I shall certainly meditate
on all your activity,
And with your dealings I will
concern myself.
13 O God, your way is in the holy
place.
Who is a great God like God?
14 You are the [true] God, doing
marvelously.
Among the peoples you have
made your strength known.
15 With [your] arm you have recovered your people,
The sons of Jacob and of
Joseph. *Se'lah.*
16 The waters have seen you, O
God,
The waters have seen you;
they began to be in severe
pains.
Also, the watery deeps began
to be agitated.
17 The clouds have thunderously
poured down water;
A sound the cloudy skies have
given forth.
Also, your own arrows proceeded to go here and there.
18 The sound of your thunder was
like chariot wheels;
Lightnings have lighted up
the productive land;
The earth became agitated
and began to rock.
19 Through the sea your way was,
And your path was through
many waters;
And your very footprints have
not come to be known.
20 You have led your people just
like a flock,
By the hand of Moses and
Aaron.

Mas'kil. Of A'saph.

78 Do give ear, O my people, to
my law;
Incline YOUR ear to the sayings
of my mouth.
2 In a proverbial saying I will
open my mouth;
I will cause riddles of long
ago to bubble forth,
3 Which we have heard and know,
And which our own fathers
have related to us;
4 Which we do not hide from
their sons,
Relating [them] even to the
generation to come,
The praises of Jehovah and his
strength
And his wonderful things that
he has done.
5 And he proceeded to raise up a
reminder in Jacob,
And a law he set in Israel,
Things that he commanded our
forefathers,
To make them known to their
sons;
6 In order that the generation to
come, the sons that were to
be born, might know [them],
That they might rise up and
relate [them] to their sons,
7 And that they might set their
confidence in God himself
And not forget the practices
of God but observe his own
commandments.
8 And they should not become
like their forefathers,
A generation stubborn and
rebellious,
A generation who had not prepared their heart
And whose spirit was not
trustworthy with God.
9 The sons of E'phra·im, though
armed shooters of the bow,
Retreated in the day of fight.
10 They did not keep the covenant
of God,
And in his law they refused
to walk.
11 They also began to forget his
dealings
And his wonderful works that
he caused them to see.
12 In front of their forefathers he
had done marvelously

In the land of Egypt, the field of Zo'an.

13 He split the sea, that he might let them pass over,
And he caused the waters to stand like a dam.

14 And he continued to lead them with a cloud by day
And the whole night with a light of fire.

15 He proceeded to split rocks in the wilderness,
That he might cause [them] to drink an abundance just like watery deeps.

16 And he went bringing forth streams out of a crag
And causing waters to descend just like rivers.

17 And they kept sinning still more against him
By rebelling against the Most High in the waterless region;

18 And they proceeded to test God in their heart
By asking for something to eat for their soul.

19 So they began to speak against God.
They said: "Is God able to arrange a table in the wilderness?"

20 Look! He struck a rock
That waters might flow and torrents themselves might flood forth.
"Is he able also to give bread itself,
Or can he prepare sustenance for his people?"

21 That was why Jehovah heard and began to be furious;
And fire itself was kindled against Jacob,
And anger also ascended against Israel.

22 For they did not put faith in God,
And they did not trust in salvation by him.

23 And he proceeded to command the cloudy skies above,
And he opened the very doors of heaven.

24 And he kept raining upon them manna to eat,
And the grain of heaven he gave to them.

25 Men ate the very bread of powerful ones;
Provisions he sent them to satisfaction.

26 He began making an east wind burst forth in the heavens
And making a south wind blow by his own strength.

27 And he proceeded to make sustenance rain upon them just like dust,
Even winged flying creatures just like the sand grains of the seas.

28 And he kept making [them] fall in the middle of his camp,
All around his tabernacles.

29 And they went eating and satisfying themselves very much,
And what they desired he proceeded to bring to them.

30 They had not turned aside from their desire,
While their food was yet in their mouth,

31 When God's wrath itself ascended against them.
And he went killing among their stout ones;
And the young men of Israel he made collapse.

32 Despite all this they sinned some more
And did not put faith in his wonderful works.

33 So he brought their days to an end as if a mere exhalation,
And their years by the disturbance.

34 As often as he killed them, they also inquired for him,
And they returned and looked for God.

35 And they began to remember that God was their Rock,
And that God the Most High was their Avenger.

36 And they tried to fool him with their mouth;
And with their tongue they tried to lie to him.

37 And their heart was not steadfast with him;
And they did not prove faithful in his covenant.

38 But he was merciful; he would
cover the error and not
bring ruin.
And many times he made his
anger turn back,
And he would not rouse up
all his rage.
39 And he kept remembering that
they were flesh,
That the spirit is going forth
and does not come back.
40 How often they would rebel
against him in the wilderness,
They would make him feel
hurt in the desert!
41 And again and again they would
put God to the test,
And they pained even the
Holy One of Israel.
42 They did not remember his hand,
The day that he redeemed
them from the adversary,
43 How he put his signs in Egypt
itself
And his miracles in the field
of Zo'an;
44 And how he began changing to
blood their Nile canals,
So that they could not drink
from their own streams.
45 He proceeded to send upon them
gadflies, that these might
eat them up;
And frogs, that these might
bring them to ruin.
46 And he began to give to the
cockroaches their yield,
And their toil to the locusts.
47 He went killing their vine even
by the hail
And their sycamore trees by
hailstones.
48 And he proceeded to hand over
their beasts of burden even
to the hail
And their livestock to the
flaming fever.
49 He went sending upon them his
burning anger,
Fury and denunciation and
distress,
Deputations of angels bringing
calamity.
50 He proceeded to prepare a pathway for his anger.
He did not hold back their
soul from death itself;

And their life he handed over
even to the pestilence.
51 Finally he struck down all the
first-born in Egypt,
The beginning of their generative power in the tents of
Ham.
52 Afterward he caused his people
to depart just like a flock,
And conducted them like a
drove in the wilderness.
53 And he kept leading them in
security, and they felt no
dread;
And the sea covered their
enemies themselves.
54 And he proceeded to bring them
to his holy territory,
This mountainous region that
his right hand acquired.
55 And because of them he gradually drove out the nations,
And by the measuring line he
went allotting them an inheritance,
So that he caused the tribes
of Israel to reside in their
own homes.
56 And they began to test and rebel
against God the Most High,
And his reminders they did
not keep.
57 They also kept turning back and
acting treacherously like
their forefathers;
They turned around like a
loose bow.
58 And they kept offending him
with their high places,
And with their graven images
they kept inciting him to
jealousy.
59 God heard and got to be furious,
And so he contemned Israel
very much.
60 And he finally forsook the tabernacle of Shi'loh,
The tent in which he resided
among earthling men.
61 And he proceeded to give his
strength even to captivity
And his beauty into the hand
of the adversary.
62 And he kept handing over his
people to the sword itself,
And against his inheritance
he became furious.

63 His young men a fire ate up,
   And his virgins were not
      praised.
64 As for his priests, they fell by
      the very sword,
   And their own widows did not
      give way to weeping.
65 Then Jehovah began to awake
      as from sleeping,
   Like a mighty one sobering
      up from wine.
66 And he went striking down his
      adversaries from behind;
   A reproach of indefinite dura-
      tion he gave to them.
67 And he proceeded to reject the
      tent of Joseph;
   And the tribe of E'phra·im he
      did not choose.
68 But he chose the tribe of Judah,
      Mount Zion, which he loved.
69 And he began to build his
      sanctuary just like the
      heights,
   Like the earth that he has
      founded to time indefinite.
70 And so he chose David his
      servant
   And took him from the pens
      of the flock.
71 From following the females giv-
      ing suck
   He brought him in to be a
      shepherd over Jacob his
      people
   And over Israel his inherit-
      ance.
72 And he began to shepherd them
      according to the integrity
      of his heart,
   And with the skillfulness of
      his hands he began leading
      them.

      A melody of A'saph.

79 O God, the nations have come
      into your inheritance;
   They have defiled your holy
      temple;
   They have laid Jerusalem in
      a heap of ruins.
2 They have given the dead body
      of your servants as food to
      the fowls of the heavens,
   The flesh of your loyal ones
      to the wild beasts of the
      earth.

3 They have poured out their
      blood like water
   All around Jerusalem, and
      there is no one to do the
      burying.
4 We have become a reproach to
      our neighbors,
   A derision and a jeering to
      those round about us.
5 How long, O Jehovah, will you
      be incensed? Forever?
   How long will your ardor burn
      just like fire?
6 Pour out your rage upon the
      nations that have not
      known you,
   And upon the kingdoms that
      have not called upon your
      own name.
7 For they have eaten up Jacob,
   And they have caused his own
      abiding place to be desolated.
8 Do not remember against us the
      errors of ancestors.
   Hurry! Let your mercies con-
      front us,
   For we have become greatly
      impoverished.
9 Help us, O God of our salvation,
   For the sake of the glory of
      your name;
   And deliver us and cover over
      our sins on account of your
      name.
10 Why should the nations say:
      "Where is their God?"
   Among the nations let there
      be known before our eyes
   The avenging of the blood
      of your servants that has
      been shed.
11 May the sighing of the prisoner
      come in even before you.
   According to the greatness of
      your arm preserve those ap-
      pointed to death.
12 And repay to our neighbors
      seven times into their bosom
   Their reproach with which
      they have reproached you,
      O Jehovah.
13 As for us your people and the
      flock of your pasturage,
   We shall give thanks to you
      to time indefinite;
   From generation to generation
      we shall declare your praise.

To the director upon The Lilies.
A reminder. Of A'saph.
A melody.

80 O Shepherd of Israel, do give
ear,
You who are conducting Joseph just like a flock.
O you who are sitting upon
the cherubs, do beam forth.

2 Before E'phra·im and Benjamin
and Ma·nas'seh do rouse up
your mightiness,
And do come to our salvation.

3 O God, bring us back;
And light up your face, that
we may be saved.

4 O Jehovah God of armies, how
long must you fume against
the prayer of your people?

5 You have made them eat the
bread of tears,
And you keep making them
drink tears upon tears in
[great] measure.

6 You set us for strife to our
neighbors,
And our very enemies keep
deriding as they please.

7 O God of armies, bring us back;
And light up your face, that
we may be saved.

8 You proceeded to make a vine
depart from Egypt.
You kept driving out the nations, that you might plant
it.

9 You made a clearing before it,
that it might take root and
fill the land.

10 The mountains were covered
with its shadow,
And the cedars of God with
its boughs.

11 It gradually sent forth its boughs
as far as the sea,
And to the River its twigs.

12 Why have you broken down its
stone walls,
And [why] have all those
passing by on the road
plucked at it?

13 A boar out of the woods keeps
eating it away,
And the animal throngs of the
open field keep feeding upon
it.

14 O God of armies, return, please;
Look down from heaven and
see and take care of this
vine,

15 And the stock that your right
hand has planted,
And [look] upon the son
whom you have made strong
for yourself.

16 It is burned with fire, cut off.
From the rebuke of your face
they perish.

17 Let your hand prove to be upon
the man of your right hand,
Upon the son of mankind
whom you have made strong
for yourself,

18 And we shall not turn back from
you.
May you preserve us alive,
that we may call upon your
own name.

19 O Jehovah God of armies, bring
us back;
Light up your face, that we
may be saved.

To the director upon the Git'tith.
Of A'saph.

81 O cry out joyfully, you people,
to God our strength;
Shout in triumph to the God
of Jacob.

2 Strike up a melody and take a
tambourine,
The pleasant harp together
with the stringed instru-
ment.

3 On the new moon, BLOW the
horn;
On the full moon, for the day
of our festival.

4 For it is a regulation for Israel,
A judicial decision of the God
of Jacob.

5 As a reminder he laid it upon
Joseph himself,
When he was going forth over
the land of Egypt.
A language that I did not
know I kept hearing.

6 "I turned aside his shoulder
even from [the] burden;
His own hands got to be free
even from the basket.

7 In distress you called, and I
proceeded to rescue you;
I began to answer you in the
concealed place of thunder.

I went examining you at the waters of Mer'i·bah. Se'lah.

8 Hear, O my people, and I will bear witness against you, O Israel, if you will listen to me.

9 Among you there will prove to be no strange god; And you will not bow down to a foreign god.

10 I, Jehovah, am your God, The One bringing you up out of the land of Egypt. Open your mouth wide, and I shall fill it.

11 But my people has not listened to my voice; And Israel itself has not showed any willingness toward me.

12 And so I let them go in the stubbornness of their heart; They went walking in their own counsels.

13 O that my people were listening to me, O that Israel itself would walk in my very ways!

14 Their enemies I would easily subdue, And against their adversaries I would turn my hand.

15 As for those intensely hating Jehovah, they will come cringing to him, And their time will prove to be to time indefinite.

16 And he will keep feeding him off the fat of the wheat, And out of the rock I shall satisfy you with honey itself."

A melody of A'saph.

82 God is stationing himself in the assembly of the Divine One; In the middle of the gods he judges:

2 "How long will you keep on judging with injustice And showing partiality to the wicked themselves? Se'lah.

3 Be judges for the lowly one and the fatherless boy. To the afflicted one and the one of little means do justice.

4 Provide escape for the lowly one and the poor one; Out of the hand of the wicked ones deliver [them]."

5 They have not known, and they do not understand; In darkness they keep walking about; All the foundations of the earth are made to totter.

6 "I myself have said, 'You are gods, And all of you are sons of the Most High.

7 Surely you will die just as men do; And like any one of the princes you will fall!' "

8 Do rise up, O God, do judge the earth; For you yourself should take possession of all the nations.

A song. A melody of A'saph.

83 O God, let there be no silence on your part; Do not keep speechless, and do not stay quiet, O Divine One.

2 For, look! your very enemies are in an uproar; And the very ones intensely hating you have raised [their] head.

3 Against your people they cunningly carry on their confidential talk; And they conspire against your concealed ones.

4 They have said: "Come and let us efface them from being a nation, That the name of Israel may be remembered no more."

5 For with the heart they have unitedly exchanged counsel; Against you they proceeded to conclude even a covenant,

6 The tents of E'dom and the Ish'ma·el·ites, Mo'ab and the Hag'rites,

7 Ge'bal and Am'mon and Am'a·lek, Phi·lis'ti·a together with the inhabitants of Tyre.

8 Also, As·syr'i·a itself has become joined with them;

They have become an arm to the sons of Lot. *Se'lah.*

9 Do to them as to Mid'i·an, as to Sis'e·ra,

As to Ja'bin at the torrent valley of Ki'shon.

10 They were annihilated at En'dor; They became manure for the ground.

11 As for their nobles, make these like O'reb and like Ze'eb, And like Ze'bah and like Zal·mun'na all their dukes,

12 Who have said: "Let us take possession of the abiding places of God for ourselves."

13 O my God, make them like a thistle whirl, Like stubble before a wind.

14 Like a fire that burns up the forest And like a flame that scorches the mountains,

15 In just that way may you pursue them with your tempest And may you disturb them with your own stormwind.

16 Fill their faces with dishonor, That people may search for your name, O Jehovah.

17 O may they be ashamed and be disturbed for all times, And may they become abashed and perish;

18 That people may know that you, whose name is Jehovah, You alone are the Most High over all the earth.

For the director upon the Git'tith. Of the sons of Ko'rah. A melody.

84 How lovely your grand tabernacle is, O Jehovah of armies!

2 My soul has yearned and also pined away for the courtyards of Jehovah. My own heart and my very flesh cry out joyfully to the living God.

3 Even the bird itself has found a house, And the swallow a nest for herself, Where she has put her young ones— Your grand altar, O Jehovah of armies, my King and my God!

4 Happy are those dwelling in your house! They still keep on praising you. *Se'lah.*

5 Happy are the men whose strength is in you, In whose heart are the highways.

6 Passing along through the low plain of the ba'ca bushes, They turn it into a spring itself; Even with blessings the instructor enwraps himself.

7 They will walk on from vital energy to vital energy; Each one appears to God in Zion.

8 O Jehovah God of armies, do hear my prayer; Do give ear, O God of Jacob. *Se'lah.*

9 O shield of ours, see, O God, And look upon the face of your anointed one.

10 For a day in your courtyards is better than a thousand [elsewhere]. I have chosen to stand at the threshold in the house of my God Rather than to move around in the tents of wickedness.

11 For Jehovah God is a sun and a shield; Favor and glory are what he gives. Jehovah himself will not hold back anything good from those walking in faultlessness.

12 O Jehovah of armies, happy is the man that is trusting in you.

For the director. Of the sons of Ko'rah. A melody.

85 You have taken pleasure, O Jehovah, in your land; You have brought back the ones taken captive of Jacob.

2 You have pardoned the error of your people; You have covered all their sin. *Se'lah.*

3 You have controlled all your fury; You have turned back from the heat of your anger.

4 Gather us back, O God of our
    salvation,
    And break off your vexation
    with us.
5 Is it to time indefinite that you
    will be incensed at us?
    Will you draw out your anger
    to generation after genera-
    tion?
6 Will you yourself not enliven us
    again,
    That your people themselves
    may rejoice in you?
7 Show us, O Jehovah, your loving-
    kindness,
    And your salvation may you
    give to us.
8 I will hear what the [true] God
    Jehovah will speak,
    For he will speak peace to his
    people and to his loyal ones,
    But let them not return to
    self-confidence.
9 Surely his salvation is near to
    those fearing him,
    For glory to reside in our land.
10 As for loving-kindness and true-
    ness, they have met each
    other;
    Righteousness and peace—
    they have kissed each other.
11 Trueness itself will sprout out
    of the very earth,
    And righteousness itself will
    look down from the very
    heavens.
12 Also, Jehovah, for his part, will
    give what is good,
    And our own land will give
    its yield.
13 Before him righteousness itself
    will walk,
    And it will make a way by his
    steppings.

    A prayer of David.

86 Incline, O Jehovah, your ear.
    Answer me,
    For I am afflicted and poor.
2 O do guard my soul, for I am
    loyal.
    Save your servant—you are
    my God—that is trusting in
    you.
3 Show me favor, O Jehovah,
    For to you I keep calling all
    day long.
4 Make the soul of your servant
    rejoice,

For to you, O Jehovah, I lift
    up my very soul.
5 For you, O Jehovah, are good
    and ready to forgive;
    And the loving-kindness to
    all those calling upon you is
    abundant.
6 Do give ear, O Jehovah, to my
    prayer;
    And do pay attention to the
    voice of my entreaties.
7 In the day of my distress I will
    call upon you,
    For you will answer me.
8 There is none like you among
    the gods, O Jehovah,
    Neither are there any works
    like yours.
9 All the nations whom you have
    made will themselves come,
    And they will bow down be-
    fore you, O Jehovah,
    And will give glory to your
    name.
10 For you are great and are do-
    ing wondrous things;
    You are God, you alone.
11 Instruct me, O Jehovah, about
    your way.
    I shall walk in your truth.
    Unify my heart to fear your
    name.
12 I laud you, O Jehovah my God,
    with all my heart,
    And I will glorify your name
    to time indefinite,
13 For your loving-kindness is great
    toward me,
    And you have delivered my
    soul out of She'ol, its lowest
    place.
14 O God, the presumptuous ones
    themselves have risen up
    against me;
    And the very assembly of
    tyrannical ones have looked
    for my soul,
    And they have not set you in
    front of themselves.
15 But you, O Jehovah, are a God
    merciful and gracious,
    Slow to anger and abundant
    in loving-kindness and true-
    ness.
16 Turn to me and show me favor.
    Do give your strength to your
    servant,

And do save the son of your
slave girl.
17 Work out with me a sign meaning goodness,
That those hating me may see
[it] and be ashamed.
For you yourself, O Jehovah,
have helped me and com-
forted me.

Of the sons of Ko'rah.
A melody, a song.

87 His foundation is in the holy
mountains.
2 Jehovah is more in love with
the gates of Zion
Than with all the tabernacles
of Jacob.
3 Glorious things are being spoken
about you, O city of the
[true] God. Se'lah.
4 I shall make mention of Ra'hab
and Babylon as among those
knowing me;
Here are Phi·lis'ti·a and Tyre,
together with Cush:
"This is one who was born
there."
5 And respecting Zion it will be
said:
"Each and every one was born
in her."
And the Most High himself
will firmly establish her.
6 Jehovah himself will declare,
when recording the peoples:
"This is one who was born
there." Se'lah.
7 There will also be singers as
well as dancers of circle
dances:
"All my springs are in you."

A song, a melody of the sons
of Ko'rah. To the director over
Ma'ha.lath for making responses.
Mas'kil of He'man the Ez'ra.hite.

88 O Jehovah, the God of my
salvation,
By day I have cried out,
In the night [also] in front
of you.
2 Before you my prayer will come.
Incline your ear to my entreating cry.
3 For my soul has had enough of
calamities,
And my very life has come
in touch even with She'ol.

4 I have been reckoned in among
those going down to the pit;
I have become like an
able-bodied man without
strength,
5 Set free among the dead themselves,
Like slain ones lying in the
burial place,
Whom you have remembered no
longer
And who have been severed
from your own [helping]
hand.
6 You have put me in a pit of
the lowest depths,
In dark places, in a large
abyss.
7 Upon me your rage has thrown
itself,
And with all your breaking
waves you have afflicted
[me]. Se'lah.
8 You have put my acquaintances
far away from me;
You have set me as something
very detestable to them.
I am under restraint and cannot go forth.
9 My own eye has languished because of my affliction.
I have called on you, O Jehovah, all day long;
To you I have spread out my
palms.
10 For those who are dead will you
do a marvel?
Or will those impotent in
death themselves arise,
Will they laud you? Se'lah.
11 Will your loving-kindness be
declared in the burial place
itself,
Your faithfulness in [the place
of] destruction?
12 Will a marvel by you be known
in the darkness itself,
Or your righteousness in the
land of oblivion?
13 And yet to you, O Jehovah, I
myself have cried for help,
And in the morning my own
prayer keeps confronting
you.
14 Why is it, O Jehovah, that you
cast off my soul?
Why do you keep your face
concealed from me?

15 I am afflicted and about to expire from boyhood on;
I have borne frightful things from you very much.

16 Over me your flashes of burning anger have passed;
Terrors from you yourself have brought me to silence.

17 They have surrounded me like waters all day long;
They have closed in upon me all at one time.

18 You have put far away from me friend and companion;
My acquaintances are a dark place.

Mas'kil. Of E'than the Ez'ra.hite.

89 Jehovah's expressions of loving-kindness I will sing about even to time indefinite.
For generation after generation I shall make your faithfulness known with my mouth.

2 For I have said: "Loving-kindness will stay built even to time indefinite;
As for the heavens, you keep your faithfulness firmly established in them."

3 "I have concluded a covenant toward my chosen one;
I have sworn to David my servant,

4 'Even to time indefinite I shall firmly establish your seed,
And I will build your throne to generation after generation.'" Se'lah.

5 And the heavens will laud your marvelous act, O Jehovah,
Yes, your faithfulness in the congregation of the holy ones.

6 For who in the skies can be compared to Jehovah?
Who can resemble Jehovah among the sons of God?

7 God is to be held in awe among the intimate group of holy ones;
He is grand and fear-inspiring over all who are round about him.

8 O Jehovah God of armies,
Who is vigorous like you, O Jah?
And your faithfulness is all around you.

9 You are ruling over the swelling of the sea;
When it raises up its waves you yourself calm them.

10 You yourself have crushed Ra'-hab, even as someone slain.
By the arm of your strength you have scattered your enemies.

11 Heaven is yours, the earth also is yours;
The productive land and what fills it—you yourself have founded them.

12 The north and the south—you yourself created them;
Ta'bor and Her'mon—in your name they cry out joyfully.

13 An arm with mightiness is yours,
Your hand is strong,
Your right hand is exalted.

14 Righteousness and judgment are the established place of your throne;
Loving-kindness and trueness themselves come in before your face.

15 Happy are the people knowing the joyful shouting.
O Jehovah, in the light of your face they keep walking.

16 In your name they are joyful all day long
And in your righteousness they are exalted.

17 For you are the beauty of their strength;
And by your good will our horn is exalted.

18 For our shield belongs to Jehovah,
And our king belongs to the Holy One of Israel.

19 At that time you spoke in a vision to your loyal ones,
And you proceeded to say:
"I have placed help upon a mighty one;
I have exalted a chosen one from among the people.

20 I have found David my servant;
With my holy oil I have anointed him,

21 With whom my own hand will
be firm,
Whom my own arm also will
strengthen.
22 No enemy will make exactions
upon him,
Neither will any son of unrighteousness afflict him.
23 And from before him I crushed
his adversaries to pieces,
And to those intensely hating
him I kept dealing out blows.
24 And my faithfulness and my
loving-kindness are with
him,
And in my name his horn is
exalted.
25 And on the sea I have put his
hand
And on the rivers his right
hand.
26 He himself calls out to me, 'You
are my Father,
My God and the Rock of my
salvation.'
27 Also, I myself shall place him as
first-born,
The most high of the kings of
the earth.
28 To time indefinite I shall preserve my loving-kindness toward him,
And my covenant will be
faithful to him.
29 And I shall certainly set up his
seed forever
And his throne as the days of
heaven.
30 If his sons leave my law
And in my judicial decisions
they do not walk,
31 If they profane my own statutes
And they do not keep my own
commandments,
32 I must also turn my attention
to their transgression even
with a rod
And to their error even with
strokes.
33 But my loving-kindness I shall
not break off from him,
Nor shall I prove false with
regard to my faithfulness.
34 I shall not profane my covenant,
And the expression out of my
lips I shall not change.

35 Once I have sworn in my holiness,
To David I will not tell lies.
36 His seed itself will prove to be
even to time indefinite,
And his throne as the sun in
front of me.
37 As the moon it will be firmly
established for time indefinite,
And [as] a faithful witness in
the skies." *Se'lah*.
38 But you—you have cast off and
you keep contemning;
You have become furious toward your anointed one.
39 You have spurned the covenant
of your servant;
You have profaned his diadem
to the very earth.
40 You have broken down all his
stone pens;
You have laid his fortifications in ruin.
41 All those passing along the way
have pillaged him;
He has become a reproach to
his neighbors.
42 You have exalted the right hand
of his adversaries;
You have caused all his enemies to rejoice.
43 What is more, you again treat
his sword as a foe,
And you have caused him not
to gain ground in the battle.
44 You have made [him] cease
from his luster,
And his throne you have
hurled to the very earth.
45 You have shortened the days of
his youth;
You have enwrapped him with
shame. *Se'lah*.
46 How long, O Jehovah, will
you keep yourself concealed?
For all time?
Will your rage keep on burning just like a fire?
47 Remember of what duration of
life I am.
Is it all in vain that you have
created all the sons of men?
48 What able-bodied man is there
alive who will not see death?
Can he provide escape for his

soul from the hand of She'-
ol? Se'lah.

49 Where are your former acts of
loving-kindness, O Jehovah,
About which you swore to
David in your faithfulness?

50 Remember, O Jehovah, the reproach upon your servants,
My carrying in my bosom [the

reproach of] all the many
peoples,

51 How your enemies have reproached, O Jehovah,
How they have reproached the
footprints of your anointed
one.

52 Blessed be Jehovah to time indefinite. Amen and Amen.

BOOK FOUR
(Psalms 90 – 106)

A prayer of Moses,
the man of the [true] God.

90 O Jehovah, you yourself have
proved to be a real dwelling
for us
During generation after generation.

2 Before the mountains themselves
were born,
Or you proceeded to bring
forth as with labor pains
the earth and the produc-
tive land,
Even from time indefinite to
time indefinite you are God.

3 You make mortal man go back
to crushed matter,
And you say: "Go back, YOU
sons of men."

4 For a thousand years are in your
eyes but as yesterday when
it is past,
And as a watch during the
night.

5 You have swept them away;
they become a mere sleep;
In the morning [they are]
just like green grass that
changes.

6 In the morning it puts forth
blossoms and must change;
At evening it withers and
certainly dries up.

7 For we have come to an end in
your anger,
And by your rage we have
been disturbed.

8 You have set our errors right
in front of you,
Our hidden things before your
bright face.

9 For all our days have come to
their decline in your fury;
We have finished our years
just like a whisper.

10 In themselves the days of our
years are seventy years;
And if because of special
mightiness they are eighty
years,
Yet their insistence is on trouble
and hurtful things;
For it must quickly pass by,
and away we fly.

11 Who is there knowing the
strength of your anger
And your fury according to
the fear of you?

12 Show [us] just how to count
our days in such a way
That we may bring a heart
of wisdom in.

13 Do return, O Jehovah! How long
will it be?
And feel regret over your
servants.

14 Satisfy us in the morning with
your loving-kindness,
That we may cry out joyfully
and may rejoice during all
our days.

15 Make us rejoice correspondingly
to the days that you have
afflicted us,
The years that we have seen
calamity.

16 May your activity appear to
your own servants
And your splendor upon their
sons.

17 And let the pleasantness of Jehovah our God prove to be
upon us,
And the work of our hands do
you firmly establish upon us.
Yes, the work of our hands,
do you firmly establish it.

91 Anyone dwelling in the secret
place of the Most High
Will procure himself lodging

under the very shadow of the Almighty One.

2 I will say to Jehovah: "[You are] my refuge and my stronghold,
My God, in whom I will trust."

3 For he himself will deliver you from the trap of the bird-catcher,
From the pestilence causing adversities.

4 With his pinions he will block approach to you,
And under his wings you will take refuge.
His trueness will be a large shield and bulwark.

5 You will not be afraid of anything dreadful by night,
Nor of the arrow that flies by day,

6 Nor of the pestilence that walks in the gloom,
Nor of the destruction that despoils at midday.

7 A thousand will fall at your very side
And ten thousand at your right hand;
To you it will not come near.

8 Only with your eyes will you look on
And see the retribution itself of the wicked ones.

9 Because you [said]: "Jehovah is my refuge,"
You have made the Most High himself your dwelling;

10 No calamity will befall you,
And not even a plague will draw near to your tent.

11 For he will give his own angels a command concerning you,
To guard you in all your ways.

12 Upon their hands they will carry you,
That you may not strike your foot against any stone.

13 Upon the young lion and the cobra you will tread;
You will trample down the maned young lion and the big snake.

14 Because on me he has set his affection,
I shall also provide him with escape.
I shall protect him because he has come to know my name.

15 He will call upon me, and I shall answer him.
I shall be with him in distress.
I shall rescue him and glorify him.

16 With length of days I shall satisfy him,
And I shall cause him to see salvation by me.

A melody, a song, for the sabbath day.

92 It is good to give thanks to Jehovah
And to make melody to your name, O Most High;

2 To tell in the morning about your loving-kindness
And about your faithfulness during the nights,

3 Upon a ten-stringed instrument and upon the lute,
By resounding music on the harp.

4 For you have made me rejoice, O Jehovah, because of your activity;
Because of the works of your hands I cry out joyfully.

5 How great your works are, O Jehovah!
Very deep your thoughts are.

6 No unreasoning man himself can know [them],
And no one stupid can understand this.

7 When the wicked ones sprout as the vegetation
And all the practicers of what is hurtful blossom forth,
It is that they may be annihilated forever.

8 But you are on high to time indefinite, O Jehovah.

9 For, look! your enemies, O Jehovah,
For, look! your own enemies will perish;
All the practicers of what is hurtful will be separated from one another.

10 But you will exalt my horn like that of a wild bull;
I shall moisten [myself] with fresh oil.

11 And my eye will look on my foes;
My ears will hear about the very ones who rise up against me, the evildoers.
12 The righteous himself will blossom forth as a palm tree does;
As a cedar in Leb′a·non does, he will grow big.
13 Those who are planted in the house of Jehovah,
In the courtyards of our God, they will blossom forth.
14 They will still keep on thriving during gray-headedness,
Fat and fresh they will continue to be
15 To tell that Jehovah is upright.
[He is] my Rock, in whom there is no unrighteousness.

93 Jehovah himself has become king!
With eminence he is clothed;
Jehovah is clothed—with strength he has girded himself.
The productive land also becomes firmly established so that it cannot be made to totter.
2 Your throne is firmly established from long ago;
You are from time indefinite.
3 The rivers have raised, O Jehovah,
The rivers have raised their sound;
The rivers keep raising their pounding.
4 Above the sounds of vast waters, the majestic breaking waves of the sea,
Jehovah is majestic in the height.
5 Your own reminders have proved very trustworthy.
Holiness is befitting to your own house, O Jehovah, for length of days.

94 O God of acts of vengeance, Jehovah,
O God of acts of vengeance, beam forth!
2 Raise yourself up, O Judge of the earth.
Bring back a retribution upon the haughty ones.

3 How long are the wicked, O Jehovah,
How long are the wicked themselves going to exult?
4 They keep bubbling forth, they keep speaking unrestrained;
All the practicers of what is hurtful keep bragging about themselves.
5 Your people, O Jehovah, they keep crushing,
And your inheritance they keep afflicting.
6 The widow and the alien resident they kill,
And the fatherless boys they murder.
7 And they keep saying: "Jah does not see;
And the God of Jacob does not understand [it]."
8 Understand, YOU who are unreasoning among the people;
And as for YOU stupid ones, when will YOU have any insight?
9 The One planting the ear, can he not hear?
Or the One forming the eye, can he not look?
10 The One correcting the nations, can he not reprove,
Even the One teaching men knowledge?
11 Jehovah is knowing the thoughts of men, that they are as an exhalation.
12 Happy is the able-bodied man whom you correct, O Jah,
And whom you teach out of your own law,
13 To give him quietness from days of calamity,
Until for the wicked one a pit is excavated.
14 For Jehovah will not forsake his people,
Nor will he leave his own inheritance.
15 For judicial decision will return even to righteousness,
And all the upright in heart will follow it.
16 Who will rise up for me against the evildoers?
Who will take his stand for me against the practicers of hurtfulness?

17 Unless Jehovah had been of assistance to me,
　　In a little while my soul would have resided in silence.
18 When I said: "My foot will certainly move unsteadily,"
　　Your own loving-kindness, O Jehovah, kept sustaining me.
19 When my disquieting thoughts became many inside of me,
　　Your own consolations began to fondle my soul.
20 Will the throne causing adversities be allied with you
　　While it is framing trouble by decree?
21 They make sharp attacks on the soul of the righteous one
　　And pronounce wicked even the blood of the innocent one.
22 But Jehovah will become a secure height for me,
　　And my God the rock of my refuge.
23 And he will turn back upon them their hurtfulness
　　And will silence them with their own calamity.
　　Jehovah our God will silence them.

95 O come let us cry out joyfully to Jehovah!
　　Let us shout in triumph to our Rock of salvation.
2 Let us come before his person with thanksgiving;
　　Let us with melodies shout in triumph to him.
3 For Jehovah is a great God
　　And a great King over all other gods,
4 He in whose hand are the inmost depths of the earth
　　And to whom the peaks of the mountains belong;
5 To whom the sea, which he himself made, belongs
　　And whose own hands formed the dry land itself.
6 O come in, let us worship and bow down;
　　Let us kneel before Jehovah our Maker.
7 For he is our God, and we are the people of his pasturage and the sheep of his hand.

Today if you people listen to his own voice,
8 Do not harden your heart as at Mer′i·bah,
　　As in the day of Mas′sah in the wilderness,
9 When your forefathers put me to the proof;
　　They examined me, they also saw my activity.
10 For forty years I kept feeling a loathing toward [that] generation,
　　And I proceeded to say: "They are a people wayward at heart,
　　And they themselves have not come to know my ways";
11 Concerning whom I swore in my anger:
　　"They shall not enter into my resting place."

96 Sing to Jehovah a new song.
　　Sing to Jehovah, all [you people of] the earth.
2 Sing to Jehovah, bless his name.
　　From day to day tell the good news of salvation by him.
3 Declare among the nations his glory,
　　Among all the peoples his wonderful works.
4 For Jehovah is great and very much to be praised.
　　He is fear-inspiring above all other gods.
5 For all the gods of the peoples are valueless gods;
　　But as for Jehovah, he has made the very heavens.
6 Dignity and splendor are before him;
　　Strength and beauty are in his sanctuary.
7 Ascribe to Jehovah, O you families of the peoples,
　　Ascribe to Jehovah glory and strength.
8 Ascribe to Jehovah the glory belonging to his name;
　　Carry a gift and come into his courtyards.
9 Bow down to Jehovah in holy adornment;
　　Be in severe pains because of him, all [you people of] the earth.

10 Say among the nations: "Jehovah himself has become
king.
The productive land also becomes firmly established so
that it cannot be made to
totter.
He will plead the cause of the
peoples in uprightness."
11 Let the heavens rejoice, and let
the earth be joyful.
Let the sea thunder and that
which fills it.
12 Let the open field exult and all
that is in it.
At the same time let all the
trees of the forest break out
joyfully
13 Before Jehovah. For he has
come;
For he has come to judge the
earth.
He will judge the productive
land with righteousness
And the peoples with his
faithfulness.

97 Jehovah himself has become
king! Let the earth be joyful.
Let the many islands rejoice.
2 Clouds and thick gloom are all
around him;
Righteousness and judgment
are the established place of
his throne.
3 Before him a very fire goes,
And it consumes his adversaries all around.
4 His lightnings lighted up the
productive land;
The earth saw and came to be
in severe pains.
5 The mountains themselves proceeded to melt just like wax
on account of Jehovah,
On account of the Lord of the
whole earth.
6 The heavens have told forth his
righteousness,
And all the peoples have seen
his glory.
7 Let all those serving any carved
image be ashamed,
Those who are making their
boast in valueless gods.
Bow down to him, all you
gods.

8 Zion heard and began to rejoice,
And the dependent towns of
Judah began to be joyful
By reason of your judicial decisions, O Jehovah.
9 For you, O Jehovah, are the
Most High over all the
earth;
You are very high in your
ascent over all other gods.
10 O you lovers of Jehovah, hate
what is bad.
He is guarding the souls of his
loyal ones;
Out of the hand of the wicked
ones he delivers them.
11 Light itself has flashed up for
the righteous one,
And rejoicing even for the
ones upright in heart.
12 Rejoice in Jehovah, O you
righteous ones,
And give thanks to his holy
memorial.

A melody.

98 Sing to Jehovah a new song,
For wonderful are the things
that he has done.
His right hand, even his holy
arm, has gained salvation
for him.
2 Jehovah has made his salvation known;
In the eyes of the nations he
has revealed his righteousness.
3 He has remembered his loving-
kindness and his faithfulness to the house of Israel.
All the ends of the earth have
seen the salvation by our
God.
4 Shout in triumph to Jehovah,
all [you people of] the
earth.
Be cheerful and cry out joyfully and make melody.
5 Make melody to Jehovah with
the harp,
With the harp and the voice
of melody.
6 With the trumpets and the
sound of the horn
Shout in triumph before the
King, Jehovah.
7 Let the sea thunder and that
which fills it,

The productive land and those dwelling in it.

8 Let the rivers themselves clap their hands;
  All together let the very mountains cry out joyfully
9 Before Jehovah, for he has come to judge the earth.
  He will judge the productive land with righteousness
  And the peoples with uprightness.

99 Jehovah himself has become king. Let the peoples be agitated.
  He is sitting upon the cherubs. Let the earth quiver.

2 Jehovah is great in Zion,
  And he is high over all the peoples.
3 Let them laud your name.
  Great and fear-inspiring, holy it is.
4 And with the strength of a king judgment he has loved.
  You yourself have firmly established uprightness.
  Judgment and righteousness in Jacob are what you yourself have effected.
5 Exalt Jehovah our God and bow down yourselves at his footstool;
  He is holy.
6 Moses and Aaron were among his priests,
  And Samuel was among those calling upon his name.
  They were calling to Jehovah, and he himself kept answering.
7 In the pillar of cloud he continued speaking to them.
  They kept his reminders and the regulation that he gave to them.
8 O Jehovah our God, you yourself answered them.
  A God granting pardon you proved to be to them,
  And executing vengeance against their notorious deeds.
9 Exalt Jehovah our God
  And bow down yourselves at his holy mountain.
  For Jehovah our God is holy.

A melody of thanksgiving.

100 Shout in triumph to Jehovah, all [YOU people of] the earth.

2 Serve Jehovah with rejoicing.
  Come in before him with a joyful cry.
3 Know that Jehovah is God.
  It is he that has made us, and not we ourselves.
  [We are] his people and the sheep of his pasturage.
4 Come into his gates with thanksgiving,
  Into his courtyards with praise.
  Give thanks to him, bless his name.
5 For Jehovah is good;
  His loving-kindness is to time indefinite,
  And his faithfulness to generation after generation.

Of David. A melody.

101 About loving-kindness and judgment I will sing.
  To you, O Jehovah, I will make melody.

2 I will act with discretion in a faultless way.
  When will you come to me?
  I shall walk about in the integrity of my heart inside my house.
3 I shall not set in front of my eyes any good-for-nothing thing.
  The doing of those who fall away I have hated;
  It does not cling to me.
4 A crooked heart departs from me;
  Nothing bad do I know.
5 Anyone slandering his companion in secrecy,
  Him I silence.
  Anyone of haughty eyes and of arrogant heart,
  Him I cannot endure.
6 My eyes are upon the faithful ones of the earth,
  That they may dwell with me.
  The one walking in a faultless way,
  He it is who will minister to me.

7 There will dwell inside my house
no worker of trickiness.
As for anyone speaking falsehoods, he will not be firmly
established
In front of my eyes.
8 Every morning I shall silence
all the wicked ones of the
earth,
To cut off from the city of
Jehovah all the practicers
of what is hurtful.

A prayer of the afflicted in case
he grows feeble and pours out
his concern before Jehovah himself.

102 O Jehovah, do hear my
prayer;
And to you may my own cry
for help come.
2 Do not conceal your face from
me on the day that I am
in sore straits.
Incline to me your ear;
On the day that I call, hurry,
answer me.
3 For my days have come to an
end just like smoke,
And my very bones have been
made red-hot just like a
fireplace.
4 My heart has been struck just
like vegetation and is dried
up,
For I have forgotten to eat
my food.
5 Because of the sound of my
sighing
My bones have stuck to my
flesh.
6 I do resemble the pelican of
the wilderness.
I have become like a little
owl of desolated places.
7 I have grown emaciated,
And I am become like a bird
isolated upon a roof.
8 All day long my enemies have
reproached me.
Those making a fool of me
have sworn even by me.
9 For I have eaten ashes themselves just like bread;
And the things I drink I have
mingled even with weeping,
10 Because of your denunciation
and your indignation;
For you have lifted me up,

that you might throw me
away.
11 My days are like a shadow that
has declined,
And I myself am dried up
like mere vegetation.
12 As for you, O Jehovah, to time
indefinite you will dwell,
And your memorial will be
for generation after generation.
13 You yourself will arise, you will
have mercy on Zion,
For it is the season to be
favorable to her,
For the appointed time has
come.
14 For your servants have found
pleasure in her stones,
And to her dust they direct
their favor.
15 And the nations will fear the
name of Jehovah,
And all the kings of the earth
your glory.
16 For Jehovah will certainly build
up Zion;
He must appear in his glory.
17 He will certainly turn to the
prayer of those stripped [of
everything],
And not despise their prayer.
18 This is written for the future
generation;
And the people that is to be
created will praise Jah.
19 For he has looked down from
his holy height,
From the very heavens Jehovah himself has looked even
at the earth,
20 To hear the sighing of the
prisoner,
To loosen those appointed to
death;
21 For the name of Jehovah to be
declared in Zion
And his praise in Jerusalem,
22 When the peoples are collected
all together,
And the kingdoms to serve
Jehovah.
23 On the way he afflicted my
power,
He cut short my days.
24 I proceeded to say: "O my God,
Do not take me off at the
half of my days;

Your years are throughout all generations.

25 Long ago you laid the foundations of the earth itself,
And the heavens are the work of your hands.

26 They themselves will perish, but you yourself will keep standing;
And just like a garment they will all of them wear out.
Just like clothing you will replace them, and they will finish their turn.

27 But you are the same, and your own years will not be completed.

28 The sons of your servants will continue residing;
And before you their own offspring will be firmly established."

Of David.

103 Bless Jehovah, O my soul,
Even everything within me, his holy name.

2 Bless Jehovah, O my soul,
And do not forget all his doings,

3 Him who is forgiving all your error,
Who is healing all your maladies,

4 Who is reclaiming your life from the very pit,
Who is crowning you with loving-kindness and mercies,

5 Who is satisfying your lifetime with what is good;
Your youth keeps renewing itself just like that of an eagle.

6 Jehovah is executing acts of righteousness
And judicial decisions for all those being defrauded.

7 He made known his ways to Moses,
His dealings even to the sons of Israel.

8 Jehovah is merciful and gracious,
Slow to anger and abundant in loving-kindness.

9 He will not for all time keep finding fault,

Neither will he to time indefinite keep resentful.

10 He has not done to us even according to our sins;
Nor according to our errors has he brought upon us what we deserve.

11 For as the heavens are higher than the earth,
His loving-kindness is superior toward those fearing him.

12 As far off as the sunrise is from the sunset,
So far off from us he has put our transgressions.

13 As a father shows mercy to his sons,
Jehovah has shown mercy to those fearing him.

14 For he himself well knows the formation of us,
Remembering that we are dust.

15 As for mortal man, his days are like those of green grass;
Like a blossom of the field is the way he blossoms forth.

16 For a mere wind has to pass over it, and it is no more;
And its place will acknowledge it no further.

17 But the loving-kindness of Jehovah is from time indefinite even to time indefinite
Toward those fearing him,
And his righteousness to the sons of sons,

18 Toward those keeping his covenant
And toward those remembering his orders so as to carry them out.

19 Jehovah himself has firmly established his throne in the very heavens;
And over everything his own kingship has held domination.

20 Bless Jehovah, O you angels of his, mighty in power, carrying out his word,
By listening to the voice of his word.

21 Bless Jehovah, all you armies of his,
You ministers of his, doing his will.

22 Bless Jehovah, all you his works,

In all places of his domination.
Bless Jehovah, O my soul.

104 Bless Jehovah, O my soul.
O Jehovah my God, you
have proved very great.
With dignity and splendor
you have clothed yourself,
2 Enwrapping yourself with light
as with a garment,
Stretching out the heavens
like a tent cloth,
3 The One building his upper
chambers with beams in the
very waters,
Making the clouds his chariot,
Walking upon the wings of
the wind,
4 Making his angels spirits,
His ministers a devouring fire.
5 He has founded the earth upon
its established places;
It will not be made to totter
to time indefinite, or forever.
6 With a watery deep just like a
garment you covered it.
The waters were standing
above the very mountains.
7 At your rebuke they began to
flee;
At the sound of your thunder
they were sent running in
panic—
8 Mountains proceeded to ascend,
Valley plains proceeded to descend—
To the place that you have
founded for them.
9 A boundary you set, beyond
which they should not pass,
That they should not again
cover the earth.
10 He is sending springs into the
torrent valleys;
Between the mountains they
keep going on.
11 They continually give drink to
all the wild beasts of the
open field;
The zebras regularly quench
their thirst.
12 Above them roost the flying
creatures of the heavens;
From among the thick foliage they keep giving forth
sound.
13 He is watering the mountains
from his upper chambers.

With the fruitage of your
works the earth is satisfied.
14 He is making green grass sprout
for the beasts,
And vegetation for the service
of mankind,
To cause food to go forth
from the earth,
15 And wine that makes the heart
of mortal man rejoice,
To make the face shine with
oil,
And bread that sustains the
very heart of mortal man.
16 The trees of Jehovah are satisfied,
The cedars of Leb'a·non that
he planted,
17 Where the birds themselves
make nests.
As for the stork, the juniper
trees are its house.
18 The high mountains are for the
mountain goats;
The crags are a refuge for
the rock badgers.
19 He has made the moon for appointed times;
The sun itself knows well
where it sets.
20 You cause darkness, that it may
become night;
In it all the wild animals of
the forest move forth.
21 The maned young lions are
roaring for the prey
And for seeking their food
from God himself.
22 The sun begins to shine—they
withdraw
And they lie down in their
own hiding places.
23 Man goes forth to his activity
And to his service until evening.
24 How many your works are, O
Jehovah!
All of them in wisdom you
have made.
The earth is full of your pro-
ductions.
25 As for this sea so great and
wide,
There there are moving things
without number,
Living creatures, small as well
as great.
26 There the ships go;

As for Le·vi'a·than, him you
have formed to play about
in it.
27 All of them—for you they keep
waiting
To give [them] their food in
its season.
28 What you give them they pick
up.
You open your hand—they
get satisfied with good
things.
29 If you conceal your face, they
get disturbed.
If you take away their spirit,
they expire,
And back to their dust they
go.
30 If you send forth your spirit,
they are created;
And you make the face of the
ground new.
31 The glory of Jehovah will prove
to be to time indefinite.
Jehovah will rejoice in his
works.
32 He is looking at the earth, and
it trembles;
He touches the mountains,
and they smoke.
33 I will sing to Jehovah throughout my life;
I will make melody to my God
as long as I am.
34 Let my musing about him be
pleasurable.
I, for my part, shall rejoice
in Jehovah.
35 The sinners will be finished off
from the earth;
And as for the wicked, they
will be no longer.
Bless Jehovah, O my soul.
Praise Jah, you people!

105 Give thanks to Jehovah, call
upon his name,
Make known among the peo-
ples his dealings.
2 Sing to him, make melody to
him,
Concern yourselves with all
his wonderful works.
3 Make your boast in his holy
name.
Let the heart of those seeking Jehovah rejoice.

4 Search for Jehovah and his
strength.
Seek his face constantly.
5 Remember his wonderful works
that he has performed,
His miracles and the judicial
decisions of his mouth,
6 O you seed of Abraham his
servant,
You sons of Jacob, his chosen
ones.
7 He is Jehovah our God.
His judicial decisions are in
all the earth.
8 He has remembered his covenant even to time indefinite,
The word that he commanded,
to a thousand generations,
9 Which [covenant] he concluded
with Abraham,
And his sworn statement to
Isaac,
10 And which [statement] he kept
standing as a regulation
even to Jacob,
As an indefinitely lasting covenant even to Israel,
11 Saying: "To you I shall give the
land of Ca'naan
As the allotment of your
inheritance."
12 [This was] when they happened to be few in number,
Yes, very few, and alien residents in it.
13 And they kept walking about
from nation to nation,
From one kingdom to another
people.
14 He did not allow any human
to defraud them,
But on their account he reproved kings,
15 [Saying:] "Do not you men
touch my anointed ones,
And to my prophets do nothing bad."
16 And he proceeded to call for a
famine upon the land;
He broke every rod around
which ring-shaped loaves
were suspended.
17 He sent ahead of them a man
Who was sold to be a slave,
Joseph.
18 With fetters they afflicted his
feet,
Into irons his soul came;

19 Until the time that his word
   came,
   The saying of Jehovah itself
      refined him.
20 The king sent that he might
   release him,
   The ruler of the peoples, that
      he might let him loose.
21 He set him as master to his
   household
   And as ruler over all his
      property,
22 To bind his princes agreeably
   to his soul
   And that he might teach wis-
      dom to even his elderly men.
23 And Israel proceeded to come
   into Egypt,
   And Jacob himself resided as
      an alien in the land of Ham.
24 And he kept making his people
   very fruitful,
   And gradually made them
      mightier than their adver-
      saries.
25 He let their heart change to
   hate his people,
   To behave cunningly against
      his servants.
26 He sent Moses his servant,
   Aaron whom he had chosen.
27 They set among them the matters of his signs,
   And the miracles in the land
      of Ham.
28 He sent darkness and so made
   it dark;
   And they did not rebel against
      his words.
29 He changed their waters into
   blood,
   And proceeded to put their
      fish to death.
30 Their land swarmed with frogs,
   In the interior rooms of their
      kings.
31 He said that the gadflies should
   come in,
   Gnats in all their territories.
32 He made their downpours hail,
   A flaming fire on their land.
33 And he proceeded to strike
   their vines and their fig
      trees
   And to break the trees of
      their territory.
34 He said that the locusts should
   come in,

And a species of locust, even
   without number.
35 And they went eating all the
   vegetation in their land;
   They also went eating the
      fruitage of their ground.
36 And he proceeded to strike down
   every first-born in their
      land,
   The beginning of all their
      generative power.
37 And he began to bring them
   out with silver and gold;
   And among his tribes there
      was no one stumbling along.
38 Egypt rejoiced when they went
   out,
   For the dread of them had
      fallen upon them.
39 He spread out a cloud for a
   screen,
   And fire to give light by night.
40 They asked, and he proceeded
   to bring quails,
   And with bread from heaven
      he kept satisfying them.
41 He opened a rock, and waters
   began to flow out;
   These went through the water-
      less regions as a river.
42 For he remembered his holy
   word with Abraham his
      servant.
43 So he brought out his people
   with exultation,
   His chosen ones even with a
      joyful cry.
44 And gradually he gave them
   the lands of the nations,
   And they kept taking pos-
      session of the product of
      the hard work of national
      groups,
45 To the end that they might
   keep his regulations
   And observe his own laws.
   Praise Jah, you people!

106 Praise Jah, you people!
   Give thanks to Jehovah,
      for he is good;
   For his loving-kindness is to
      time indefinite.
2 Who can utter the mighty performances of Jehovah,
   [Or] can make all his praise
      to be heard?
3 Happy are those observing
   justice,

Doing righteousness all the time.

4 Remember me, O Jehovah, with the good will toward your people.
Take care of me with your salvation,

5 That I may see the goodness to your chosen ones,
That I may rejoice with the rejoicing of your nation,
That I may make my boast with your inheritance.

6 We have sinned just the same as our forefathers;
We have done wrong; we have acted wickedly.

7 As for our forefathers in Egypt,
They did not show any insight into your wonderful works.
They did not remember the abundance of your grand loving-kindness,
But they behaved rebelliously at the sea, by the Red Sea.

8 And he proceeded to save them for the sake of his name,
So as to make his mightiness known.

9 Accordingly he rebuked the Red Sea, and it was gradually dried up;
And he went walking them through the surging waters as through the wilderness;

10 And so he saved them from the hand of the hater
And reclaimed them from the hand of the enemy.

11 And the waters came covering their adversaries;
Not one of them was left.

12 Then they had faith in his word;
They began to sing his praise.

13 Quickly they forgot his works;
They did not wait for his counsel.

14 But they showed their selfish desire in the wilderness
And went putting God to the proof in the desert.

15 And he proceeded to give them their request
And to send a wasting disease into their soul.

16 And they began to envy Moses in the camp,
Even Aaron the holy one of Jehovah.

17 The earth then opened up and swallowed down Da'than,
And covered over the assembly of A·bi'ram.

18 And a fire went burning among their assembly;
A flame itself went devouring the wicked ones.

19 Furthermore, they made a calf in Ho'reb
And bowed down to a molten image,

20 So that they exchanged my glory
For a representation of a bull, an eater of vegetation.

21 They forgot God their Savior,
The Doer of great things in Egypt,

22 Wonderful works in the land of Ham,
Fear-inspiring things at the Red Sea.

23 And he was about to say to annihilate them,
If it had not been for Moses his chosen one,
Who stood in the gap before him,
To turn back his rage from bringing [them] to ruin.

24 And they got to contemning the desirable land;
They had no faith in his word.

25 And they kept grumbling in their tents;
They did not listen to the voice of Jehovah.

26 So he proceeded to raise his hand [in an oath] concerning them,
That he would make them fall in the wilderness,

27 And that he would make their offspring fall among the nations,
And that he would scatter them among the lands.

28 And they began to attach themselves to Ba'al of Pe'or
And to eat the sacrifices of the dead ones.

29 As they were causing offense by
their dealings,
A scourge now broke out
among them.
30 When Phin'e·has stood up and
intervened,
Then the scourge was halted.
31 And it came to be counted to
him as righteousness
For generation after generation to time indefinite.
32 Further, they caused provocation at the waters of Mer'-
i·bah,
So that it went badly with
Moses by reason of them.
33 For they embittered his spirit
And he began to speak rashly
with his lips.
34 They did not annihilate the
peoples,
As Jehovah had said to them.
35 And they went mingling with
the nations
And took up learning their
works.
36 And they kept serving their
idols,
And these came to be a snare
to them.
37 And they would sacrifice their
sons
And their daughters to demons.
38 So they kept spilling innocent
blood,
The blood of their sons and
their daughters,
Whom they sacrificed to the
idols of Ca'naan;
And the land came to be
polluted with bloodshed.
39 And they got to be unclean by
their works
And kept having immoral intercourse by their dealings.

40 And the anger of Jehovah began
to blaze against his people,
And he came to detest his
inheritance.
41 And he repeatedly gave them
into the hand of the na-
tions,
That those hating them might
rule over them,
42 And that their enemies might
oppress them,
And that they might be subdued under their hand.
43 Many times he would deliver
them,
But they themselves would
behave rebelliously in their
disobedient course,
And they would be brought
low for their error.
44 And he would see the distress
of theirs
When he heard their entreating cry.
45 And he would remember concerning them his covenant,
And he would feel regret according to the abundance of
his grand loving-kindness.
46 And he would grant them to
be objects of pity
Before all those holding them
captive.
47 Save us, O Jehovah our God,
And collect us together from
the nations
To give thanks to your holy
name,
To speak exultingly in your
praise.
48 Blessed be Jehovah the God of
Israel
From time indefinite even to
time indefinite;
And all the people must say
Amen.
Praise Jah, you people!

BOOK FIVE
(Psalms 107 – 150)

107 O give thanks to Jehovah,
you people, for he is good;
For his loving-kindness is
to time indefinite.
2 Let the reclaimed ones of Jehovah say so,
Whom he has reclaimed from
the hand of the adversary,

3 And whom he has collected together even from the lands,
From the sunrise and from
the sunset,
From the north and from the
south.
4 They wandered about in the
wilderness, in the desert;

They did not find any way to a city of habitation.

5 They were hungry, also thirsty;
Their very soul within them began to faint away.

6 And they kept crying out to Jehovah in their distress;
Out of the stresses upon them he proceeded to deliver them,

7 And to have them walk in the right way,
So as to come to a city of habitation.

8 O let people give thanks to Jehovah for his loving-kindness
And for his wonderful works to the sons of men.

9 For he has satisfied the dried-out soul;
And the hungry soul he has filled with good things.

10 There were those dwelling in darkness and deep shadow,
Prisoners in affliction and irons.

11 For they had behaved rebelliously against the sayings of God;
And the counsel of the Most High they had disrespected.

12 So with trouble he proceeded to subdue their heart;
They stumbled, and there was no one helping.

13 And they began calling to Jehovah for help in their distress;
Out of the stresses upon them he as usual saved them.

14 He went bringing them out from darkness and deep shadow,
And tearing even their bands apart.

15 O let people give thanks to Jehovah for his loving-kindness
And for his wonderful works to the sons of men.

16 For he has broken the doors of copper,
And he has cut down even the bars of iron.

17 Those who were foolish, due to the way of their transgression

And due to their errors, finally caused themselves affliction.

18 Their soul got to detest even every sort of food,
And they were arriving at the gates of death.

19 And they began calling to Jehovah for help in their distress;
Out of the stresses upon them he as usual saved them.

20 He proceeded to send his word and heal them
And to provide [them] escape out of their pits.

21 O let people give thanks to Jehovah for his loving-kindness
And for his wonderful works to the sons of men.

22 And let them offer the sacrifices of thanksgiving
And declare his works with a joyful cry.

23 Those going down to the sea in the ships,
Doing business on vast waters,

24 They are the ones that have seen the works of Jehovah
And his wonderful works in the depths;

25 How he says [the word] and causes a tempestuous wind to arise,
So that it lifts up its waves.

26 They go up to the heavens,
They go down to the bottoms.
Because of the calamity their very soul finds itself melting.

27 They reel and move unsteadily like a drunken man,
And even all their wisdom proves confused.

28 And they begin crying out to Jehovah in their distress,
And out of the stresses upon them he brings them forth.

29 He causes the windstorm to stand at a calm,
So that the waves of the sea keep quiet.

30 And they rejoice because these become still,
And he leads them to the haven of their delight.

31 O let people give thanks to Jehovah for his loving-kindness
And for his wonderful works to the sons of men.

32 And let them extol him in the congregation of the people;
And in the seat of the elderly men let them praise him.

33 He converts rivers into a wilderness,
And the outflows of water into thirsty ground,

34 Fruitful land into salt country, Owing to the badness of those dwelling in it.

35 He converts a wilderness into a reedy pool of water,
And the land of a waterless region into outflows of water.

36 And there he causes the hungry ones to dwell,
So that they firmly establish a city of habitation.

37 And they sow fields and plant vineyards,
That they may yield fruitful crops.

38 And he blesses them so that they become very many;
And he does not let their cattle become few.

39 Again they become few and crouch down
Owing to restraint, calamity and grief.

40 He is pouring out contempt upon nobles,
So that he makes them wander about in a featureless place, where there is no way.

41 But he protects the poor one from affliction
And converts him into families just like a flock.

42 The upright ones see and rejoice;
But as for all unrighteousness, it has to shut its mouth.

43 Who is wise? He will both observe these things
And show himself attentive toward Jehovah's acts of loving-kindness.

A song. A melody of David.

108 My heart is steadfast, O God.
I will sing and make melody, Even my glory.

2 Do awake, O stringed instrument; you too, O harp.
I will awaken the dawn.

3 I shall laud you among the peoples, O Jehovah;
And I shall make melody to you among the national groups.

4 For your loving-kindness is great up to the heavens,
And your trueness up to the skies.

5 O be exalted above the heavens, O God;
And let your glory be above all the earth.

6 In order that your beloved ones may be rescued,
O do save with your right hand and answer me.

7 God himself has spoken in his holiness:
"I will exult, I will give out She'chem as a portion;
And the low plain of Suc'coth I shall measure off.

8 Gil'e·ad belongs to me; Manas'seh belongs to me;
And E'phra·im is the fortress of my head one;
Judah is my commander's staff.

9 Mo'ab is my washing pot.
Over E'dom I shall throw my sandal.
Over Phi·lis'ti·a I shall shout in triumph."

10 Who will bring me to the fortified city?
Who will actually lead me as far as E'dom?

11 Is it not [you], O God, who have cast us off
And who do not go forth with our armies as God?

12 Do give us assistance from distress,
As salvation by earthling man is worthless.

13 By God we shall gain vital energy,
And he himself will tread down our adversaries.

To the director. Of David.
A melody.

109 O God of my praise, do not
keep silent.
2 For the mouth of the wicked
one and the mouth of de-
ception have opened against
me.
They have spoken about me
with the tongue of false-
hood;
3 And with words of hatred they
have surrounded me,
And they keep fighting against
me without cause.
4 For my love they keep resisting
me;
But on my part there is
prayer.
5 And they render to me bad for
good
And hatred for my love.
6 Appoint over him someone
wicked,
And may a resister himself
keep standing at his right
hand.
7 When he is judged, let him go
forth as someone wicked;
And let his very prayer become a sin.
8 Let his days prove to be few;
His office of oversight let
someone else take.
9 Let his sons become fatherless
boys
And his wife be a widow.
10 And without fail let his sons go
wandering about;
And they must do begging,
And they must look for [food]
from their desolate places.
11 Let the usurer lay out traps for
all that he has,
And let strangers make plunder of his product of toil.
12 May he come to have no one
extending loving-kindness,
And may there prove to be
no one showing favor to his
fatherless boys.
13 Let his posterity be for cutting
off.
In the following generation let
their name be wiped out.
14 Let the error of his forefathers
be remembered to Jehovah,

And the sin of his mother—
may it not be wiped out.
15 Let them prove to be in front
of Jehovah constantly;
And may he cut off the remembrance of them from
the very earth;
16 For the reason that he did not
remember to exercise loving-
kindness,
But he kept pursuing the
afflicted and poor man
And the one dejected at heart,
to put [him] to death.
17 And he kept loving the malediction, so that it came
upon him;
And he did not take delight
in the blessing,
So that it became far away
from him;
18 And he came to be clothed with
malediction as his garment.
So it came like waters into
the midst of him
And like oil into his bones.
19 May it prove to be for him like
a garment with which he
enwraps himself
And as a girdle that he keeps
girded about himself con-
stantly.
20 This is the wages from Jehovah
of the one resisting me
And of those speaking evil
against my soul.
21 But you are Jehovah the Sovereign Lord.
Deal with me for the sake of
your name.
Because your loving-kindness
is good, deliver me.
22 For I am afflicted and poor,
And my heart itself has been
pierced within me.
23 Like a shadow when it declines,
I am obliged to go away;
I have been shaken off like a
locust.
24 My knees themselves have
swayed from fasting,
And my very flesh has grown
lean, without any oil.
25 And to them I myself have become something reproach-
able.
They see me—they begin wagging their head.

26 Help me, O Jehovah my God;
　　Save me according to your
　　　loving-kindness.
27 And may they know that this
　　is your hand;
　　That you yourself, O Jehovah,
　　　have done it.
28 Let them, for their part, pro-
　　nounce a malediction,
　　But may you, for your part,
　　pronounce a blessing.
　　They have risen up, but let
　　　them be ashamed,
　　And let your own servant re-
　　　joice.
29 Let those resisting me be clothed
　　with humiliation,
　　And let them enwrap them-
　　selves with their shame
　　just as with a sleeveless coat.
30 I shall laud Jehovah very much
　　with my mouth,
　　And in among many people
　　I shall praise him.
31 For he will stand at the right
　　hand of the poor,
　　To save [him] from those
　　judging his soul.

Of David. A melody.

110 The utterance of Jehovah to
my Lord is:
　　"Sit at my right hand
　　Until I place your enemies
　　as a stool for your feet."
2 The rod of your strength Jeho-
　vah will send out of Zion,
　[saying:]
　　"Go subduing in the midst of
　　your enemies."
3 Your people will offer them-
　selves willingly on the day
　of your military force.
　　In the splendors of holiness,
　　from the womb of the dawn,
　　You have your company of
　　young men just like dew-
　　drops.
4 Jehovah has sworn (and he will
　feel no regret):
　　"You are a priest to time in-
　　definite
　　According to the manner of
　　Mel·chiz′e·dek!"
5 Jehovah himself at your right
　hand
　　Will certainly break kings to

pieces on the day of his
anger.
6 He will execute judgment among
　the nations;
　　He will cause a fullness of
　　dead bodies.
　　He will certainly break to
　　pieces the head one over a
　　populous land.
7 From the torrent valley in the
　way he will drink.
　　That is why he will raise
　　high [his] head.

111 Praise Jah, YOU people!

א [Aleph]
　I shall laud Jehovah with all
　[my] heart

ב [Beth]
　In the intimate group of up-
　right ones and the assembly.

ג [Gimel]
2 The works of Jehovah are great,

ד [Daleth]
　Searched for on the part of
　all those delighting in them.

ה [He]
3 His activity is dignity and
　splendor themselves,

ו [Waw]
　And his righteousness is
　standing forever.

ז [Zayin]
4 A memorial he has made for
　his wonderful works.

ח [Heth]
　Jehovah is gracious and mer-
　ciful.

ט [Teth]
5 Food he has given to those
　fearing him.

י [Yod]
　To time indefinite he will re-
　member his covenant.

כ [Kaph]
6 The power of his works he has
　told to his people,

ל [Lamed]
　In giving them the inherit-
　ance of the nations.

מ [Mem]

7 The works of his hands are truth and judgment;

נ [Nun]

Trustworthy are all the orders he gives,

ס [Samekh]

8 Well supported forever, to time indefinite,

ע [Ayin]

Done in truth and uprightness.

פ [Pe]

9 He has sent redemption itself to his people.

צ [Tsade]

To time indefinite he has commanded his covenant.

ק [Qoph]

His name is holy and fear-inspiring.

ר [Resh]

10 The fear of Jehovah is the beginning of wisdom.

שׂ [Sin]

All those doing them have a good insight.

ת [Taw]

His praise is standing forever.

112 Praise Jah, you people!

א [Aleph]

Happy is the man in fear of Jehovah,

ב [Beth]

In whose commandments he has taken very much delight.

ג [Gimel]

2 Mighty in the earth his offspring will become.

ד [Daleth]

As for the generation of the upright ones, it will be blessed.

ה [He]

3 Valuable things and riches are in his house;

ו [Waw]

And his righteousness is standing forever.

ז [Zayin]

4 He has flashed up in the darkness as a light to the upright ones.

ח [Heth]

He is gracious and merciful and righteous.

ט [Teth]

5 The man is good who is gracious and is lending.

י [Yod]

He sustains his affairs with justice.

כ [Kaph]

6 For at no time will he be made to totter.

ל [Lamed]

The righteous one will prove to be for remembrance to time indefinite.

מ [Mem]

7 He will not be afraid even of bad news.

נ [Nun]

His heart is steadfast, made reliant upon Jehovah.

ס [Samekh]

8 His heart is unshakable; he will not be afraid,

ע [Ayin]

Until he looks on his adversaries.

פ [Pe]

9 He has distributed widely; he has given to the poor ones.

צ [Tsade]

His righteousness is standing forever.

ק [Qoph]

His own horn will be exalted with glory.

ר [Resh]

10 The wicked one himself will see and certainly become vexed.

צ׳ [*Shin*]
He will grind his very teeth
and actually melt away.

ת [*Taw*]
The desire of the wicked ones
will perish.

113 Praise Jah, YOU people!
Offer praise, O YOU serv-
ants of Jehovah,
Praise the name of Jehovah.
2 May Jehovah's name become
blessed
From now on and to time indefinite.
3 From the rising of the sun until
its setting
Jehovah's name is to be
praised.
4 Jehovah has become high above
all the nations;
His glory is above the heavens.
5 Who is like Jehovah our God,
Him who is making his dwelling on high?
6 He is condescending to look on
heaven and earth,
7 Raising up the lowly one from
the very dust;
He exalts the poor one from
the ashpit itself,
8 To make [him] sit with nobles,
With the nobles of his people.
9 He is causing the barren woman
to dwell in a house
As a joyful mother of sons.
Praise Jah, YOU people!

114 When Israel went forth
from Egypt,
The house of Jacob from a
people speaking unintelligibly,
2 Judah became his holy place,
Israel his grand dominion.
3 The sea itself saw and took to
flight;
As for the Jordan, it began to
turn back.
4 The mountains themselves
skipped about like rams,
The hills like lambs.
5 What was the matter with you,
O sea, that you took to
flight,
O Jordan, that you began to
turn back?

6 O mountains, that YOU went
skipping about like rams;
O hills, like lambs?
7 Because of the Lord be in severe pains, O earth,
Because of the God of Jacob,
8 Who is changing the rock into
a reedy pool of water,
A flinty rock into a spring of
water.

115 To us belongs nothing, O
Jehovah, to us belongs
nothing,
But to your name give glory
According to your loving-
kindness, according to your
trueness.
2 Why should the nations say:
"Where, now, is their God?"
3 But our God is in the heavens;
Everything that he delighted
[to do] he has done.
4 Their idols are silver and gold,
The work of the hands of
earthling man.
5 A mouth they have, but they
cannot speak;
Eyes they have, but they cannot see;
6 Ears they have, but they cannot hear.
A nose they have, but they
cannot smell.
7 Hands are theirs, but they cannot feel.
Feet are theirs, but they cannot walk;
They utter no sound with
their throat.
8 Those making them will become
just like them,
All those who are trusting in
them.
9 O Israel, trust in Jehovah;
He is their help and their
shield.
10 O house of Aaron, put YOUR
trust in Jehovah;
He is their help and their
shield.
11 You that fear Jehovah, trust in
Jehovah;
He is their help and their
shield.
12 Jehovah himself has remembered us; he will bless,
He will bless the house of Israel,

He will bless the house of
Aaron.

13 He will bless those fearing Jehovah,
The small ones as well as the
great ones.

14 Jehovah will give increase to
YOU,
To YOU and to YOUR sons.

15 YOU are the ones blessed by
Jehovah,
The Maker of heaven and
earth.

16 As regards the heavens, to Jehovah the heavens belong,
But the earth he has given
to the sons of men.

17 The dead themselves do not
praise Jah,
Nor do any going down into
silence.

18 But we ourselves will bless Jah
From now on and to time
indefinite.
Praise Jah, YOU people!

116 I do love, because Jehovah
hears
My voice, my entreaties.

2 For he has inclined his ear to
me,
And throughout my days I
shall call.

3 The ropes of death encircled me
And the distressing circumstances of She'ol themselves
found me.
Distress and grief I kept
finding.

4 But upon the name of Jehovah
I proceeded to call:
"Ah, Jehovah, do provide my
soul with escape!"

5 Jehovah is gracious and righteous;
And our God is One showing
mercy.

6 Jehovah is guarding the inexperienced ones.
I was impoverished, and he
proceeded to save even me.

7 Return to your resting place,
O my soul,
For Jehovah himself has acted
appropriately toward you.

8 For you have rescued my soul
from death,
My eye from tears, my foot
from stumbling.

9 I will walk before Jehovah in
the lands of those living.

10 I had faith, for I proceeded to
speak.
I myself was very much afflicted.

11 I, for my part, said, when I
became panicky:
"Every man is a liar."

12 What shall I repay to Jehovah
For all his benefits to me?

13 The cup of grand salvation I
shall take up,
And on the name of Jehovah
I shall call.

14 My vows I shall pay to Jehovah,
Yes, in front of all his people.

15 Precious in the eyes of Jehovah
Is the death of his loyal ones.

16 Ah, now, O Jehovah,
I am your servant.
I am your servant, the son of
your slave girl.
You have loosened my bands.

17 To you I shall offer the sacri-
fice of thanksgiving,
And on the name of Jehovah
I shall call.

18 My vows I shall pay to Jehovah,
Yes, in front of all his people,

19 In the courtyards of the house
of Jehovah,
In the midst of you, O Jerusalem.
Praise Jah, YOU people!

117 Praise Jehovah, all YOU nations;
Commend him, all YOU clans.

2 For toward us his loving-
kindness has proved mighty;
And the trueness of Jehovah
is to time indefinite.
Praise Jah, YOU people!

118 Give thanks to Jehovah, YOU
people, for he is good;
For his loving-kindness is
to time indefinite.

2 Let Israel now say:
"For his loving-kindness is to
time indefinite."

3 Let those of the house of Aaron
now say:
"For his loving-kindness is to
time indefinite."

4 Let those fearing Jehovah now
say:
"For his loving-kindness is to
time indefinite."

5 Out of the distressing circumstances I called upon Jah;
  Jah answered [and put] me into a roomy place.
6 Jehovah is on my side; I shall not fear.
  What can earthling man do to me?
7 Jehovah is on my side among those helping me,
  So that I myself shall look upon those hating me.
8 It is better to take refuge in Jehovah
  Than to trust in earthling man.
9 It is better to take refuge in Jehovah
  Than to trust in nobles.
10 All the nations themselves surrounded me.
  It was in the name of Jehovah that I kept holding them off.
11 They surrounded me, yes, they had me surrounded.
  It was in the name of Jehovah that I kept holding them off.
12 They surrounded me like bees;
  They were extinguished like a fire of thornbushes.
  It was in the name of Jehovah that I kept holding them off.
13 You pushed me hard that I should fall,
  But Jehovah himself helped me.
14 Jah is my shelter and my might,
  And to me he becomes salvation.
15 The voice of a joyful cry and salvation
  Is in the tents of the righteous ones.
  The right hand of Jehovah is demonstrating vital energy.
16 The right hand of Jehovah is exalting [itself];
  The right hand of Jehovah is demonstrating vital energy.
17 I shall not die, but I shall keep living,
  That I may declare the works of Jah.
18 Jah corrected me severely,
  But he did not give me over to death itself.

19 Open to me the gates of righteousness, you people.
  I shall go into them; I shall laud Jah.
20 This is the gate of Jehovah.
  The righteous themselves will go into it.
21 I shall laud you, for you answered me
  And you came to be my salvation.
22 The stone that the builders rejected
  Has become the head of the corner.
23 This has come to be from Jehovah himself;
  It is wonderful in our eyes.
24 This is the day that Jehovah has made;
  We will be joyful and rejoice in it.
25 Ah, now, Jehovah, do save, please!
  Ah, now, Jehovah, do grant success, please!
26 Blessed be the One coming in the name of Jehovah;
  We have blessed you people out of the house of Jehovah.
27 Jehovah is the Divine One,
  And he gives us light.
  Bind the festival procession with boughs, O you people,
  As far as the horns of the altar.
28 You are my Divine One, and I shall laud you;
  My God—I shall exalt you.
29 Give thanks to Jehovah, you people, for he is good;
  For his loving-kindness is to time indefinite.

א [Aleph]

119 Happy are the ones faultless in [their] way,
  The ones walking in the law of Jehovah.
2 Happy are those observing his reminders;
  With all the heart they keep searching for him.
3 Really they have practiced no unrighteousness.
  In his ways they have walked.

4 You yourself have command-
ingly given your orders
To be carefully kept.
5 O that my ways were firmly
established
To keep your regulations!
6 In that case I should not be
ashamed,
When I look to all your
commandments.
7 I shall laud you in uprightness
of heart,
When I learn your righteous
judicial decisions.
8 Your regulations I continue to
keep.
O do not leave me entirely.

ב [Beth]

9 How will a young man cleanse
his path?
By keeping on guard ac-
cording to your word.
10 With my whole heart I have
searched for you.
Do not cause me to go
astray from your com-
mandments.
11 In my heart I have treasured
up your saying,
In order that I may not sin
against you.
12 Blessed you are, O Jehovah.
Teach me your regulations.
13 With my lips I have declared
All the judicial decisions of
your mouth.
14 In the way of your reminders
I have exulted,
Just as over all other valuable things.
15 With your orders I will concern myself,
And I will look to your paths.
16 For your statutes I shall show
a fondness.
I shall not forget your word.

ג [Gimel]

17 Act appropriately toward your
servant, that I may live
And that I may keep your
word.
18 Uncover my eyes, that I may
look
At the wonderful things out
of your law.

19 I am but an alien resident in
the land.
Do not conceal from me your
commandments.
20 My soul is crushed with longing
For your judicial decisions
all the time.
21 You have rebuked the cursed
presumptuous ones,
Who are straying from your
commandments.
22 Roll off me reproach and contempt,
For I have observed your
own reminders.
23 Even princes have sat; against
me they have spoken with
one another.
As for your servant, he concerns himself with your
regulations.
24 Also, your reminders are what
I am fond of,
As men of my counsel.

ד [Daleth]

25 My soul has been cleaving to
the very dust.
Preserve me alive according
to your word.
26 I have declared my own ways,
that you may answer me.
Teach me your regulations.
27 Make me understand the way
of your own orders,
That I may concern myself
with your wonderful works.
28 My soul has been sleepless from
grief.
Raise me up according to
your word.
29 Remove from me even the
false way,
And favor me with your own
law.
30 The way of faithfulness I have
chosen.
Your judicial decisions I
have considered appropri-
ate.
31 I have cleaved to your reminders.
O Jehovah, do not put me to
shame.
32 I shall run the very way of
your commandments,
Because you make my heart
have the room.

ה [*He*]

33 Instruct me, O Jehovah, in the
way of your regulations,
That I may observe it down
to the last.

34 Make me understand, that I
may observe your law
And that I may keep it with
the whole heart.

35 Cause me to tread in the pathway of your command-
ments,
For in it I have taken delight.

36 Incline my heart to your reminders,
And not to profits.

37 Make my eyes pass on from
seeing what is worthless;
Preserve me alive in your
own way.

38 Carry out to your servant your
saying
That [tends] to the fear of
you.

39 Make my reproach pass away,
of which I have been
scared,
For your judicial decisions
are good.

40 Look! I have longed for your
orders.
In your righteousness preserve me alive.

ו [*Waw*]

41 And may your loving-
kindnesses come to me,
O Jehovah,
Your salvation according to
your saying,

42 That I may answer the one
reproaching me with a
word,
For I have trusted in your
word.

43 And do not take away from
my mouth the word of
truth entirely,
For I have waited for your
own judicial decision.

44 And I will keep your law constantly,
To time indefinite, even forever.

45 And I will walk about in a
roomy place,
For I have searched even
for your orders.

46 I will also speak about your
reminders in front of
kings,
And I shall not be ashamed.

47 And I shall show a fondness
for your commandments
That I have loved.

48 And I shall raise my palms
to your commandments
that I have loved,
And I will concern myself
with your regulations.

ז [*Zayin*]

49 Remember the word to your
servant,
For which you have made
me wait.

50 This is my comfort in my
affliction,
For your own saying has
preserved me alive.

51 The presumptuous ones themselves have derided me to
the extreme.
From your law I have not
deviated.

52 I have remembered your judicial decisions from time
indefinite, O Jehovah,
And I find comfort for myself.

53 A raging heat itself has taken
hold of me because of the
wicked,
Who are leaving your law.

54 Melodies your regulations have
become to me
In the house of my alien
residences.

55 In the night I have remembered your name, O Je-
hovah,
That I may keep your law.

56 Even this has become mine,
Because your orders I have
observed.

ח [*Heth*]

57 Jehovah is my share;
I have promised to keep
your words.

58 I have softened your face with
all [my] heart.
Show me favor according to
your saying.

59 I have considered my ways,
That I may turn back my
feet to your reminders.

60 I hurried up, and I did not
delay
To keep your command-
ments.
61 The very ropes of the wicked
ones surrounded me.
Your law I did not forget.
62 At midnight I get up to give
thanks to you
For your righteous judicial
decisions.
63 A partner I am of all those
who do fear you,
And of those keeping your
orders.
64 Your loving-kindness, O Jehovah, has filled the earth.
Teach me your own regu-
lations.

ט [Teth]

65 You have dealt well indeed
with your servant,
O Jehovah, according to your
word.
66 Teach me goodness, sensibleness and knowledge them-
selves,
For in your commandments
I have exercised faith.
67 Before I was under affliction
I was sinning by mistake,
But now I have kept your
very saying.
68 You are good and are doing
good.
Teach me your regulations.
69 The presumptuous have
smeared me with falsehood.
As for me, with all [my]
heart I shall observe your
orders.
70 Their heart has become un-
feeling just like fat.
I, for my part, have been
fond of your own law.
71 It is good for me that I have
been afflicted,
In order that I may learn
your regulations.
72 The law of your mouth is good
for me,
More so than thousands of
pieces of gold and silver.

י [Yod]

73 Your own hands have made
me, and they proceeded
to fix me solidly.

Make me understand, that
I may learn your com-
mandments.
74 Those fearing you are the
ones that see me and re-
joice,
For I have waited for your
own word.
75 I well know, O Jehovah, that
your judicial decisions are
righteousness
And that with faithfulness
you have afflicted me.
76 May your loving-kindness serve,
please, to comfort me,
According to your saying to
your servant.
77 Let your mercies come to me,
that I may keep living;
For your law is what I am
fond of.
78 Let the presumptuous ones be
ashamed, for without cause
they have misled me.
As for me, I concern myself
with your orders.
79 Let those fearing you turn
back to me,
Those also knowing your
reminders.
80 Let my heart prove faultless in
your regulations,
In order that I may not be
ashamed.

כ [Kaph]

81 For your salvation my soul has
pined away;
For your word I have waited.
82 My eyes have pined away for
your saying,
While I say: "When will you
comfort me?"
83 For I have become like a skin
bottle in the smoke.
Your regulations I have not
forgotten.
84 How many are the days of your
servant?
When will you execute judgment against those per-
secuting me?
85 The presumptuous have excavated pitfalls to get me,
Those who are not in accord
with your law.
86 All your commandments are
faithfulness itself.

Without cause they have
persecuted me. O help me.
87 In a little while they would
have exterminated me in
the earth;
But I myself did not leave
your orders.
88 According to your loving-
kindness preserve me alive,
That I may keep the re-
minder of your mouth.

ל [*Lamed*]

89 To time indefinite, O Jehovah,
Your word is stationed in
the heavens.
90 Your faithfulness is for generation after generation.
You have solidly fixed the
earth, that it may keep
standing.
91 According to your judicial
decisions they have stood
[till] today,
For they are all your servants.
92 If your law had not been what
I am fond of,
Then I should have perished
in my affliction.
93 To time indefinite I shall not
forget your orders,
Because by them you have
preserved me alive.
94 I am yours. O save me,
Because I have searched for
your own orders.
95 For me the wicked have waited,
to destroy me.
To your reminders I keep
showing myself attentive.
96 To all perfection I have seen
an end.
Your commandment is very
broad.

מ [*Mem*]

97 How I do love your law!
All day long it is my concern.
98 Wiser than my enemies your
commandment makes me,
Because to time indefinite it
is mine.
99 More insight than all my
teachers I have come to
have,
Because your reminders are
a concern to me.

100 With more understanding than
older men I behave,
Because I have observed your
own orders.
101 From every bad path I have
restrained my feet,
For the purpose that I may
keep your word.
102 From your judicial decisions I
have not turned aside,
For you yourself have in-
structed me.
103 How smooth to my palate your
sayings have been,
More so than honey to my
mouth!
104 Owing to your orders I behave
with understanding.
That is why I have hated
every false path.

נ [*Nun*]

105 Your word is a lamp to my foot,
And a light to my roadway.
106 I have made a sworn statement, and I will carry it
out,
To keep your righteous judicial decisions.
107 I have been afflicted to a great
extent.
O Jehovah, preserve me alive
according to your word.
108 Please take pleasure in the
voluntary offerings of my
mouth, O Jehovah,
And teach me your own judicial decisions.
109 My soul is in my palm constantly;
But your law I have not
forgotten.
110 The wicked have set a trap
for me,
But from your orders I have
not wandered.
111 I have taken your reminders as
a possession to time in-
definite,
For they are the exultation
of my heart.
112 I have inclined my heart to
do your regulations
To time indefinite, down to
the last.

ס [*Samekh*]

113 The halfhearted ones I have
hated,

But your law I have loved.

114 You are my place of concealment and my shield.
For your word I have waited.

115 Get away from me, you evildoers,
That I may observe the commandments of my God.

116 Support me according to your
saying, that I may keep
living,
And do not put me to shame
for my hope.

117 Sustain me, that I may be
saved,
And I shall gaze upon your
regulations constantly.

118 You have tossed away all those
straying from your regulations;
For their trickiness is falsehood.

119 As scummy dross you have
made all the wicked ones
of the earth to cease.
Therefore I have loved your
reminders.

120 From the dread of you my
flesh has had a creepy
feeling;
And because of your judi-
cial decisions I have been
afraid.

ע [Ayin]

121 I have executed judgment and
righteousness.
O do not abandon me to
those defrauding me!

122 Act as a surety for your servant for what is good.
May the presumptuous ones
not defraud me.

123 My very eyes have pined away
for your salvation
And for your righteous saying.

124 Do with your servant according
to your loving-kindness,
And teach me your own
regulations.

125 I am your servant. Make me
understand,
That I may know your re-
minders.

126 It is the time for Jehovah to
act.
They have broken your law.

127 That is why I have loved your
commandments
More than gold, even refined
gold.

128 That is why I have considered
all orders regarding all
things to be right;
Every false path I have
hated.

פ [Pe]

129 Your reminders are wonderful.
That is why my soul has observed them.

130 The very disclosure of your
words gives light,
Making the inexperienced
ones understand.

131 My mouth I have opened wide,
that I may pant,
Because for your command-
ments I have longed.

132 Turn to me and show me favor,
According to [your] judicial
decision toward those loving your name.

133 Fix my own steps solidly in
your saying,
And may no kind of hurtful
thing domineer over me.

134 Redeem me from any defrauder of mankind,
And I will keep your orders.

135 Make your own face shine upon
your servant,
And teach me your regula-
tions.

136 Streams of water have run
down my eyes
Over the fact that they have
not kept your law.

צ [Tsade]

137 You are righteous, O Jehovah,
And your judicial decisions
are upright.

138 You have commanded your reminders in righteousness
And in exceeding faithfulness.

139 My ardor has made an end of
me,
Because my adversaries have
forgotten your words.

140 Your saying is very much refined,
And your own servant loves
it.

141 I am insignificant and contemptible.
    Your orders I have not forgotten.
142 Your righteousness is a righteousness to time indefinite,
    And your law is truth.
143 Distress and difficulty themselves found me.
    Your commandments I was fond of.
144 The righteousness of your reminders is to time indefinite.
    Make me understand, that I may keep living.

      ק [*Qoph*]

145 I have called with [my] whole heart. Answer me, O Jehovah.
    Your regulations I will observe.
146 I have called upon you. O save me!
    And I will keep your reminders.
147 I have been up early in the morning twilight, that I may cry for help.
    For your words I have waited.
148 My eyes have been ahead of the night watches,
    [For me] to concern myself with your saying.
149 O do hear my own voice according to your loving-kindness.
    O Jehovah, according to your judicial decision preserve me alive.
150 Those in pursuit of loose conduct have come near;
    They have got far away from your own law.
151 You are near, O Jehovah,
    And all your commandments are truth.
152 Long ago I have known some of your reminders,
    For to time indefinite you have founded them.

      ר [*Resh*]

153 O see my affliction, and rescue me;
    For I have not forgotten your own law.

154 O do conduct my legal case and recover me;
    Preserve me alive in agreement with your saying.
155 Salvation is far away from the wicked ones,
    For they have not searched for your own regulations.
156 Many are your mercies, O Jehovah.
    According to your judicial decisions, O preserve me alive.
157 My persecutors and my adversaries are many.
    From your reminders I have not deviated.
158 I have seen those who are treacherous in dealing,
    And I do feel a loathing, because they have not kept your own saying.
159 O see that I have loved your own orders.
    O Jehovah, according to your loving-kindness preserve me alive.
160 The substance of your word is truth,
    And every righteous judicial decision of yours is to time indefinite.

      ש [*Sin or Shin*]

161 Princes themselves have persecuted me for no cause,
    But my heart has been in dread of your own words.
162 I am exulting over your saying
    Just as one does when finding much spoil.
163 Falsehood I have hated, and I do keep detesting it.
    Your law I have loved.
164 Seven times in the day I have praised you
    Because of your righteous judicial decisions.
165 Abundant peace belongs to those loving your law,
    And for them there is no stumbling block.
166 I have hoped for your salvation, O Jehovah,
    And I have done your own commandments.
167 My soul has kept your reminders,
    And I love them exceedingly.

168 I have kept your orders and your reminders,
　For all my ways are in front of you.

ת [*Taw*]

169 May my entreating cry come near before you, O Jehovah.
　According to your word, O make me understand.
170 May my request for favor enter in before you.
　According to your saying, O deliver me.
171 May my lips bubble forth praise,
　For you teach me your regulations.
172 May my tongue sing forth your saying,
　For all your commandments are righteousness.
173 May your hand serve to help me,
　Because your orders I have chosen.
174 I have longed for your salvation, O Jehovah,
　And your law I am fond of.
175 May my soul keep living and praising you,
　And may your own judicial decisions help me.
176 I have wandered like a lost sheep. O look for your servant,
　For I have not forgotten your own commandments.

A Song of the Ascents.

120 To Jehovah I called in the distress of mine,
　And he proceeded to answer me.
2 O Jehovah, do deliver my soul from false lips,
　From the tricky tongue.
3 What will one give to you, and what will one add to you, O you tricky tongue?
4 Sharpened arrows of a mighty man,
　Along with burning coals of the broom trees.
5 Woe to me, for I have resided as an alien in Me'shech!
　I have tabernacled together with the tents of Ke'dar.

6 For too long a time my soul has tabernacled
　With the haters of peace.
7 I stand for peace; but when I speak,
　They are for war.

A Song for the Ascents.

121 I shall raise my eyes to the mountains.
　From where will my help come?
2 My help is from Jehovah,
　The Maker of heaven and earth.
3 He cannot possibly allow your foot to totter.
　The One guarding you cannot possibly be drowsy.
4 Look! He will not be drowsy nor go to sleep,
　He that is guarding Israel.
5 Jehovah is guarding you.
　Jehovah is your shade on your right hand.
6 By day the sun itself will not strike you,
　Nor the moon by night.
7 Jehovah himself will guard you against all calamity.
　He will guard your soul.
8 Jehovah himself will guard your going out and your coming in
　From now on and to time indefinite.

A Song of the Ascents. Of David.

122 I rejoiced when they were saying to me:
　"To the house of Jehovah let us go."
2 Our feet proved to be standing Within your gates, O Jerusalem.
3 Jerusalem is one that is built like a city
　That has been joined together in oneness,
4 To which the tribes have gone up,
　The tribes of Jah,
　As a reminder to Israel
　To give thanks to the name of Jehovah.
5 For there the thrones for judgment have been sitting,
　Thrones for the house of David.

6 Ask, O YOU people, for the
  peace of Jerusalem.
    Those loving you, [O city,]
    will be free from care.
7 May peace continue within your
  rampart,
    Freedom from care within
    your dwelling towers.
8 For the sake of my brothers
  and my companions I will
  now speak:
    "May there be peace within
    you."
9 For the sake of the house of
  Jehovah our God
    I will keep seeking good for
    you.

A Song of the Ascents.

123 To you I have raised my
       eyes,
    O You who are dwelling in
    the heavens.
2 Look! As the eyes of servants
  are toward the hand of
  their master,
    As the eyes of a maidservant
    are toward the hand of her
    mistress,
  So our eyes are toward Jehovah
  our God
    Until he shows us favor.
3 Show us favor, O Jehovah, show
  us favor;
    For to an abundance we have
    been glutted with contempt.
4 Abundantly our soul has been
  glutted with the derision of
  those who are at ease,
    Of the contempt on the part
    of the arrogant ones.

A Song of the Ascents. Of David.

124 "Had it not been that Jeho-
       vah proved to be for us,"
    Let Israel now say,
2 "Had it not been that Jehovah
  proved to be for us
    When men rose up against us,
3 Then they would have swallowed
  us up even alive,
    When their anger was burning
    against us.
4 Then the very waters would
  have washed us away,
    The torrent itself would have
    passed over our soul.
5 Then there would have passed
  over our soul

The waters of presumptuousness.
6 Blessed be Jehovah, who has
  not given us
    As a prey to their teeth.
7 Our soul is like a bird that is
  escaped
    From the trap of baiters.
  The trap is broken,
    And we ourselves have es-
    caped.
8 Our help is in the name of
  Jehovah,
    The Maker of heaven and
    earth."

A Song of the Ascents.

125 Those trusting in Jehovah
       Are like Mount Zion, which
       cannot be made to totter,
       but dwells even to time
       indefinite.
2 Jerusalem—as mountains are all
  around it,
    So Jehovah is all around his
    people
  From now on and to time
  indefinite.
3 For the scepter of wickedness
  will not keep resting upon
  the lot of the righteous ones,
    In order that the righteous
    ones may not thrust out
    their hand upon any wrong-
    doing.
4 O do good, O Jehovah, to the
  good ones,
    Even to the ones upright in
    their hearts.
5 As for those turning aside to
  their crooked ways,
    Jehovah will make them go
    away with the practicers
    of what is hurtful.
  There will be peace upon
  Israel.

A Song of the Ascents.

126 When Jehovah gathered back
       the captive ones of Zion,
       We became like those who
       were dreaming.
2 At that time our mouth came
  to be filled with laughter,
    And our tongue with a joyful
    cry.
  At that time they proceeded to
  say among the nations:

"Jehovah has done a great
thing in what he has done
with them."
3 Jehovah has done a great thing
in what he has done with us.
We have become joyful.
4 Do gather back, O Jehovah, our
company of captives,
Like stream beds in the Neg′eb.
5 Those sowing seed with tears
Will reap even with a joyful
cry.
6 The one that without fail goes
forth, even weeping,
Carrying along a bagful of
seed,
Will without fail come in with
a joyful cry,
Carrying along his sheaves.

A Song of the Ascents.
Of Solomon.

127 Unless Jehovah himself
builds the house,
It is to no avail that its
builders have worked hard
on it.
Unless Jehovah himself guards
the city,
It is to no avail that the
guard has kept awake.
2 To no avail it is for you men
that you are rising up early,
That you are sitting down
late,
That you are eating food with
pains.
Just like this he gives sleep
even to his beloved one.
3 Look! Sons are an inheritance
from Jehovah;
The fruitage of the belly is a
reward.
4 Like arrows in the hand of a
mighty man,
So are the sons of youth.
5 Happy is the able-bodied man
that has filled his quiver
with them.
They will not be ashamed,
For they will speak with
enemies in the gate.

A Song of the Ascents.

128 Happy is everyone fearing
Jehovah,
Who is walking in his ways.
2 For you will eat the toil of your
own hands.

Happy you will be and it will
be well with you.
3 Your wife will be like a fruit-
bearing vine
In the innermost parts of your
house.
Your sons will be like slips of
olive trees all around your
table.
4 Look! That is how the able-
bodied man will be blessed
Who fears Jehovah.
5 Jehovah will bless you out of
Zion.
See also the good of Jerusalem
all the days of your life,
6 And see the sons of your sons.
May there be peace upon
Israel.

A Song of the Ascents.

129 "Long enough they have
shown hostility to me from
my youth,'
Let Israel now say,
2 "Long enough they have shown
hostility to me from my
youth;
Yet they have not prevailed
over me.
3 Plowmen have plowed upon my
very back;
They have lengthened their
furrows.''
4 Jehovah is righteous.
He has cut in pieces the ropes
of the wicked ones.
5 They will be ashamed and turn
themselves back,
All those hating Zion.
6 They will become like green
grass of the roofs,
Which before it has been
torn out has dried up,
7 With which the reaper has not
filled his own hand,
Nor anyone gathering sheaves
his own bosom.
8 Nor have those passing by said:
"The blessing of Jehovah be
upon you men.
We have blessed you in the
name of Jehovah.''

A Song of the Ascents.

130 Out of the depths I have
called upon you, O Je-
hovah.
2 O Jehovah, do hear my voice.

May your ears prove to be attentive to the voice of my entreaties.
3 If errors were what you watch, O Jah,
O Jehovah, who could stand?
4 For there is the [true] forgiveness with you,
In order that you may be feared.
5 I have hoped, O Jehovah, my soul has hoped,
And for his word I have waited.
6 My soul [has waited] for Jehovah
More than watchmen for the morning,
Watching for the morning.
7 Let Israel keep waiting for Jehovah.
For there is loving-kindness with Jehovah,
And abundantly so is there redemption with him.
8 And he himself will redeem Israel out of all his errors.

A Song of the Ascents. Of David.

131 O Jehovah, my heart has not been haughty,
Nor have my eyes been lofty;
Nor have I walked in things too great,
Nor in things too wonderful for me.
2 Surely I have soothed and quieted my soul
Like a weanling upon his mother.
My soul is like a weanling upon me.
3 Let Israel wait for Jehovah
From now on and to time indefinite.

A Song of the Ascents.

132 Remember, O Jehovah, concerning David
All his humiliations;
2 How he swore to Jehovah,
How he vowed to the Powerful One of Jacob:
3 "I will not go into the tent of my house,
I will not go up on the divan of my grand lounge,
4 I will not give sleep to my eyes,

Nor slumber to my own beaming eyes,
5 Until I find a place for Jehovah,
A grand tabernacle for the Powerful One of Jacob."
6 Look! We have heard it in Eph'ra·thah,
We have found it in the fields of the forest.
7 Let us come into his grand tabernacle;
Let us bow down at his footstool.
8 Do arise, O Jehovah, to your resting place,
You and the ark of your strength.
9 Let your priests themselves be clothed with righteousness,
And let your own loyal ones cry out joyfully.
10 On account of David your servant,
Do not turn back the face of your anointed one.
11 Jehovah has sworn to David,
Truly he will not draw back from it:
"Of the fruitage of your belly I shall set on your throne.
12 If your sons will keep my covenant
And my reminders that I shall teach them,
Their sons also forever
Will sit upon your throne."
13 For Jehovah has chosen Zion;
He has longed for it as a dwelling for himself:
14 "This is my resting place forever;
Here I shall dwell, for I have longed for it.
15 Its provisions I shall bless without fail.
Its poor ones I shall satisfy with bread.
16 And its priests I shall clothe with salvation;
And its loyal ones will without fail cry out joyfully.
17 There I shall cause the horn of David to grow.
I have set in order a lamp for my anointed one.
18 His enemies I shall clothe with shame;

But upon him his diadem
will flourish."

A Song of the Ascents. Of David.

133 Look! How good and how
pleasant it is
For brothers to dwell to-
gether in unity!
2 It is like the good oil upon the
head,
That is running down upon
the beard,
Aaron's beard,
That is running down to the
collar of his garments,
3 It is like the dew of Her'mon
That is descending upon the
mountains of Zion.
For there Jehovah commanded
the blessing [to be],
[Even] life to time indefinite.

A Song of the Ascents.

134 O bless Jehovah,
All you servants of Je-
hovah,
You who are standing in the
house of Jehovah during
the nights.
2 Raise your hands in holiness
And bless Jehovah.
3 May Jehovah bless you out of
Zion,
He the Maker of heaven and
earth.

135 Praise Jah, you people!
Praise the name of Jehovah,
Offer praise, O servants of
Jehovah,
2 You who are standing in the
house of Jehovah,
In the courtyards of the house
of our God.
3 Praise Jah, for Jehovah is good.
Make melody to his name, for
it is pleasant.
4 For Jah has chosen even Jacob
for himself,
Israel for his special property.
5 For I myself well know that
Jehovah is great,
And our Lord is more than
all other gods.
6 Everything that Jehovah delighted [to do] he has done
In the heavens and in the
earth, in the seas and all
the watery deeps.

7 He is causing vapors to ascend
from the extremity of the
earth;
He has made even sluices for
the rain;
He is bringing forth the wind
from his storehouses,
8 He who struck down the first-
born ones of Egypt,
Both man and beast.
9 He sent signs and miracles into
the midst of you, O Egypt,
Upon Phar'aoh and upon all
his servants;
10 He who struck down many
nations
And killed potent kings,
11 Even Si'hon the king of the
Am'or·ites
And Og the king of Ba'shan
And all the kingdoms of
Ca'naan,
12 And who gave their land as an
inheritance,
An inheritance to Israel his
people.
13 O Jehovah, your name is to
time indefinite.
O Jehovah, your memorial is
to generation after generation.
14 For Jehovah will plead the
cause of his people,
And he will feel regret even
over his servants.
15 The idols of the nations are
silver and gold,
The work of the hands of
earthling man.
16 A mouth they have, but they
can speak nothing;
Eyes they have, but they can
see nothing;
17 Ears they have, but they can
give ear to nothing.
Also there exists no spirit in
their mouth.
18 Those making them will become
just like them,
Everyone who is trusting in
them.
19 O house of Israel, do you men
bless Jehovah.
O house of Aaron, do you
men bless Jehovah.
20 O house of Le'vi, do you men
bless Jehovah.

You fearers of Jehovah, bless Jehovah.
21 Blessed out of Zion be Jehovah, Who is residing in Jerusalem. Praise Jah, YOU people!

136 Give thanks to Jehovah, O YOU people, for he is good:
For his loving-kindness is to time indefinite;
2 Give thanks to the God of the gods:
For his loving-kindness is to time indefinite;
3 Give thanks to the Lord of the lords:
For his loving-kindness is to time indefinite;
4 To the Doer of wonderful, great things by himself:
For his loving-kindness is to time indefinite;
5 To the One making the heavens with understanding:
For his loving-kindness is to time indefinite;
6 To the One laying out the earth above the waters:
For his loving-kindness is to time indefinite;
7 To the One making the great lights:
For his loving-kindness is to time indefinite;
8 Even the sun for dominion by day:
For his loving-kindness is to time indefinite;
9 The moon and the stars for combined dominion by night:
For his loving-kindness is to time indefinite;
10 To the One striking down Egypt in their first-born ones:
For his loving-kindness is to time indefinite;
11 And the One bringing Israel out of the midst of them:
For his loving-kindness is to time indefinite;
12 By a strong hand and by an arm stretched out:
For his loving-kindness is to time indefinite;
13 To the One severing the Red Sea into parts:
For his loving-kindness is to time indefinite;

14 And who caused Israel to pass through the middle of it:
For his loving-kindness is to time indefinite;
15 And who shook off Phar'aoh and his military force into the Red Sea:
For his loving-kindness is to time indefinite;
16 To the One making his people walk through the wilderness:
For his loving-kindness is to time indefinite;
17 To the One striking down great kings:
For his loving-kindness is to time indefinite;
18 And who proceeded to kill majestic kings:
For his loving-kindness is to time indefinite;
19 Even Si'hon the king of the Am'or·ites:
For his loving-kindness is to time indefinite;
20 And Og the king of Ba'shan:
For his loving-kindness is to time indefinite;
21 And who gave their land as an inheritance:
For his loving-kindness is to time indefinite;
22 An inheritance to Israel his servant:
For his loving-kindness is to time indefinite;
23 Who during our low condition remembered us:
For his loving-kindness is to time indefinite;
24 And who repeatedly tore us away from our adversaries:
For his loving-kindness is to time indefinite;
25 The One giving food to all flesh:
For his loving-kindness is to time indefinite;
26 Give thanks to the God of the heavens:
For his loving-kindness is to time indefinite.

137 By the rivers of Babylon— there we sat down.
We also wept when we remembered Zion.
2 Upon the poplar trees in the midst of her We hung our harps.

3 For there those holding us captive asked us for the words
of a song,
And those mocking us—for
rejoicing:
"SING for us one of the songs
of Zion."
4 How can we sing the song of
Jehovah
Upon foreign ground?
5 If I should forget you, O Jerusalem,
Let my right hand be for-
getful.
6 Let my tongue stick to my
palate,
If I were not to remember
you,
If I were not to make Jerusalem ascend
Above my chief cause for rejoicing.
7 Remember, O Jehovah, regarding the sons of E'dom the
day of Jerusalem,
Who were saying: "Lay [it]
bare! Lay [it] bare to the
foundation within it!"
8 O daughter of Babylon, who are
to be despoiled,
Happy will he be that rewards
you
With your own treatment with
which you treated us.
9 Happy will he be that grabs
ahold and does dash to
pieces
Your children against the
crag.

Of David.

138 I shall laud you with all
my heart.
In front of other gods I shall
make melody to you.
2 I shall bow down toward your
holy temple,
And I shall laud your name,
Because of your loving-kindness
and because of your true-
ness.
For you have magnified your
saying even above all your
name.
3 On the day that I called, you
also proceeded to answer
me;
You began to make me bold
in my soul with strength.

4 All the kings of the earth will
laud you, O Jehovah,
For they will have heard the
sayings of your mouth.
5 And they will sing about the
ways of Jehovah,
For the glory of Jehovah is
great.
6 For Jehovah is high, and yet the
humble one he sees;
But the lofty one he knows
only from a distance.
7 If I should walk in the midst
of distress, you will preserve
me alive.
Because of the anger of my
enemies you will thrust out
your hand,
And your right hand will save
me.
8 Jehovah himself will complete
what is in my behalf.
O Jehovah, to time indefinite
is your loving-kindness.
Do not desert the works of
your own hands.

For the director.
Of David. A melody.

139 O Jehovah, you have
searched through me, and
you know [me].
2 You yourself have come to know
my sitting down and my
rising up.
You have considered my
thought from far off.
3 My journeying and my lying
outstretched you have measured off,
And you have become familiar
even with all my ways.
4 For there is not a word on my
tongue,
But, look! O Jehovah, you
already know it all.
5 Behind and before, you have
besieged me;
And you place your hand
upon me.
6 [Such] knowledge is too wonderful for me.
It is so high up that I cannot
attain to it.
7 Where can I go from your spirit,
And where can I run away
from your face?
8 If I should ascend to heaven,
there you would be;

And if I should spread out my couch in She'ol, look! you [would be there].

9 Were I to take the wings of the dawn,
That I might reside in the most remote sea,

10 There, also, your own hand would lead me
And your right hand would lay hold of me.

11 And were I to say: "Surely darkness itself will hastily seize me!"
Then night would be light about me.

12 Even the darkness itself would not prove too dark for you,
But night itself would shine just as the day does;
The darkness might just as well be the light.

13 For you yourself produced my kidneys;
You kept me screened off in the belly of my mother.

14 I shall laud you because in a fear-inspiring way I am wonderfully made.
Your works are wonderful,
As my soul is very well aware.

15 My bones were not hidden from you
When I was made in secret,
When I was woven in the lowest parts of the earth.

16 Your eyes saw even the embryo of me,
And in your book all its parts were down in writing,
As regards the days when they were formed
And there was not yet one among them.

17 So, to me how precious your thoughts are!
O God, how much does the grand sum of them amount to!

18 Were I to try to count them, they are more than even the grains of sand.
I have awaked, and yet I am still with you.

19 O that you, O God, would slay the wicked one!
Then even the bloodguilty men will certainly depart from me,

20 Who say things about you according to [their] idea;
They have taken up [your name] in a worthless way— your adversaries.

21 Do I not hate those who are intensely hating you, O Jehovah,
And do I not feel a loathing for those revolting against you?

22 With a complete hatred I do hate them.
They have become to me real enemies.

23 Search through me, O God, and know my heart.
Examine me, and know my disquieting thoughts,

24 And see whether there is in me any painful way,
And lead me in the way of time indefinite.

For the director. A melody of David.

140 Rescue me, O Jehovah, from bad men;
May you safeguard me even from the man of deeds of violence,

2 Those who have schemed bad things in [their] heart,
Who all day long keep attacking as in wars.

3 They have sharpened their tongue like that of a serpent;
The venom of the horned viper is under their lips. *Se'lah.*

4 Keep me, O Jehovah, from the hands of the wicked one;
May you safeguard me even from the man of deeds of violence,
Those who have schemed to push my steps.

5 The self-exalted ones have hidden a trap for me;
And ropes they have spread out as a net at the side of the track.
Snares they have set for me. *Se'lah.*

6 I have said to Jehovah: "You are my God,

Do give ear, O Jehovah, to the
voice of my entreaties."

7 O Jehovah the Sovereign Lord,
the strength of my salvation,
You have screened over my
head in the day of the
armed force.

8 Do not grant, O Jehovah, the
cravings of the wicked one.
Do not promote his plotting,
that they may not be ex-
alted. *Se'lah.*

9 As for the heads of those surrounding me,
May the trouble of their own
lips cover them.

10 May burning coals be dropped
upon them.
Let them be made to fall into
the fire, into watery pits,
that they may not get up.

11 The big talker—let him not be
firmly established in the
earth.
The man of violence—let evil
itself hunt him with re-
peated thrusts.

12 I well know that Jehovah will
execute
The legal claim of the afflicted
one, the judgment of the
poor ones.

13 Surely the righteous themselves
will give thanks to your
name;
The upright ones will dwell
before your face.

A melody of David.

141 O Jehovah, I have called
upon you.
Do make haste to me.
Do give ear to my voice when
I call to you.

2 May my prayer be prepared as
incense before you,
The raising up of my palms
as the evening grain offering.

3 Do set a guard, O Jehovah, for
my mouth;
Do set a watch over the door
of my lips.

4 Do not incline my heart to anything bad,
So as to carry on notorious
deeds in wickedness
With men who are practicing
what is hurtful,

That I may not feed myself
on their dainties.

5 Should the righteous one strike
me, it would be a loving-
kindness;
And should he reprove me,
it would be oil upon the
head,
Which my head would not want
to refuse.
For still there would be even
my prayer during their
calamities.

6 Their judges have been thrown
down by the sides of the
crag,
But they have heard my sayings, that they are pleasant.

7 As when one is doing cleaving
and splitting on the earth,
Our bones have been scattered
at the mouth of She'ol.

8 However, my eyes are to you,
O Jehovah the Sovereign
Lord.
In you I have taken refuge.
Do not pour out my soul.

9 Keep me from the clutches of
the trap that they have
laid for me
And from the snares of those
practicing what is hurtful.

10 The wicked will fall into their
own nets all together,
While I, for my part, pass by.

Mas'kil. Of David, when he
happened to be in the cave.
A prayer.

142 With my voice, to Jehovah
I proceeded to call for aid;
With my voice, to Jehovah
I began to cry for favor.

2 Before him I kept pouring out
my concern;
Before him I continued to tell
about my own distress,

3 When my spirit fainted away
within me.
Then you yourself knew my
roadway.
In the path in which I walk
They have hidden a trap for
me.

4 Look to the right hand and see
That there is no one giving
any recognition to me.

My place for flight has perished
from me;
There is no one inquiring for
my soul.
5 I called to you, O Jehovah, for
aid.
I said: "You are my refuge,
My share in the land of the
living ones."
6 Do pay attention to my entreating cry,
For I have become very much
impoverished.
Deliver me from my persecutors,
For they are stronger than I
am.
7 Do bring my soul out of the
very dungeon
To laud your name.
Around me let the righteous
ones gather,
Because you deal appropriately
with me.

A melody of David.

143 O Jehovah, hear my prayer;
Do give ear to my entreaty.
In your faithfulness answer
me in your righteousness.
2 And do not enter into judgment with your servant;
For before you no one alive
can be righteous.
3 For the enemy has pursued my
soul;
He has crushed my life to the
very earth.
He has caused me to dwell
in dark places like those
dead for time indefinite.
4 And my spirit faints away within me;
In the midst of me my heart
shows itself numbed.
5 I have remembered days of
long ago;
I have meditated on all your
activity;
I willingly kept myself concerned with the work of
your own hands.
6 I have spread out my hands to
you,
My soul is like an exhausted
land to you. Se'lah.
7 O hurry, answer me, O Jehovah.
My spirit has come to an end.

Do not conceal your face from
me,
Or else I must become comparable with those going
down into the pit.
8 In the morning cause me to
hear your loving-kindness,
For in you I have put my
trust.
Make known to me the way in
which I should walk,
For to you I have lifted up
my soul.
9 Deliver me from my enemies,
O Jehovah.
I have taken cover even with
you.
10 Teach me to do your will,
For you are my God.
Your spirit is good;
May it lead me in the land
of uprightness.
11 For the sake of your name,
O Jehovah, may you pre-
serve me alive.
In your righteousness may you
bring forth my soul out
of distress.
12 And in your loving-kindness
may you silence my enemies;
And you must destroy all
those showing hostility to
my soul,
For I am your servant.

Of David.

144 Blessed be Jehovah my Rock,
Who is teaching my hands
for fighting,
My fingers for warfare;
2 My loving-kindness and my
stronghold,
My secure height and my
Provider of escape for me,
My shield and the One in whom
I have taken refuge,
The One subduing peoples
under me.
3 O Jehovah, what is man that
you should notice him,
The son of mortal man that
you should take account of
him?
4 Man himself bears resemblance
to a mere exhalation;
His days are like a passing
shadow.

5 O Jehovah, bend down your heavens that you may descend;
Touch the mountains that they may smoke.

6 Lighten with lightning that you may scatter them;
Send out your arrows that you may throw them into confusion.

7 Thrust your hands out from the height;
Set me free and deliver me from the many waters,
From the hand of the foreigners,

8 Whose mouth has spoken what is untrue
And whose right hand is a right hand of falsehood.

9 O God, a new song I will sing to you.
On an instrument of ten strings I will make melody to you,

10 The One giving salvation to kings,
The One setting David his servant free from the injurious sword.

11 Set me free and deliver me from the hand of the foreigners,
Whose mouth has spoken what is untrue
And whose right hand is a right hand of falsehood,

12 Who [say]: "Our sons are like little plants grown up in their youth,
Our daughters like corners carved in palace style,

13 Our garners full, furnishing products of one sort after another,
Our flocks multiplying by thousands, ten thousand to one, in our streets,

14 Our cattle loaded down, without any rupture and with no abortion,
And with no outcry in our public squares.

15 Happy is the people for whom it is just like [that]!"
Happy is the people whose God is Jehovah!

A praise, of David.

א [Aleph]

145 **1** I will exalt you, O my God the King,
And I will bless your name to time indefinite, even forever.

ב [Beth]

2 All day long I will bless you,
And I will praise your name to time indefinite, even forever.

ג [Gimel]

3 Jehovah is great and very much to be praised,
And his greatness is unsearchable.

ד [Daleth]

4 Generation after generation will commend your works,
And about your mighty acts they will tell.

ה [He]

5 The glorious splendor of your dignity
And the matters of your wonderful works I will make my concern.

ו [Waw]

6 And they will talk about the strength of your own fear-inspiring things;
And as for your greatness, I will declare it.

ז [Zayin]

7 With the mention of the abundance of your goodness they will bubble over,
And [because of] your righteousness they will cry out joyfully.

ח [Heth]

8 Jehovah is gracious and merciful,
Slow to anger and great in loving-kindness.

ט [Teth]

9 Jehovah is good to all,
And his mercies are over all his works.

י [Yod]

10 All your works will laud you, O Jehovah,

And your loyal ones will bless you.

 כ [Kaph]

11 About the glory of your kingship they will talk,
And about your mightiness they will speak,

ל [Lamed]

12 To make known to the sons of men his mighty acts
And the glory of the splendor of his kingship.

מ [Mem]

13 Your kingship is a kingship for all times indefinite,
And your dominion is throughout all successive generations.

ס [Samekh]

14 Jehovah is giving support to all who are falling,
And is raising up all who are bowed down.

ע [Ayin]

15 To you the eyes of all look hopefully,
And you are giving them their food in its season.

פ [Pe]

16 You are opening your hand
And satisfying the desire of every living thing.

צ [Tsade]

17 Jehovah is righteous in all his ways
And loyal in all his works.

ק [Qoph]

18 Jehovah is near to all those calling upon him,
To all those who call upon him in trueness.

ר [Resh]

19 The desire of those fearing him he will perform,
And their cry for help he will hear, and he will save them.

ש [Shin]

20 Jehovah is guarding all those loving him,
But all the wicked ones he will annihilate.

ת [Taw]

21 The praise of Jehovah my mouth will speak;
And let all flesh bless his holy name to time indefinite, even forever.

146 Praise Jah, YOU people!
Praise Jehovah, O my soul.

2 I will praise Jehovah during my lifetime.
I will make melody to my God as long as I am.

3 Do not put YOUR trust in nobles,
Nor in the son of earthling man, to whom no salvation belongs.

4 His spirit goes out, he goes back to his ground;
In that day his thoughts do perish.

5 Happy is the one who has the God of Jacob for his help,
Whose hope is in Jehovah his God,

6 The Maker of heaven and earth,
Of the sea, and of all that is in them,
The One keeping trueness to time indefinite,

7 The One executing judgment for the defrauded ones,
The One giving bread to the hungry ones.
Jehovah is releasing those who are bound.

8 Jehovah is opening the eyes of the blind ones;
Jehovah is raising up the ones bowed down;
Jehovah is loving the righteous ones.

9 Jehovah is guarding the alien residents;
The fatherless boy and the widow he relieves,
But the way of the wicked ones he makes crooked.

10 Jehovah will be king to time indefinite,
Your God, O Zion, for generation after generation.
Praise Jah, YOU people!

147 Praise Jah, YOU people,
For it is good to make melody to our God;
For it is pleasant—praise is fitting.

2 Jehovah is building Jerusalem;
     The dispersed ones of Israel
     he brings together.
3 He is healing the brokenhearted
     ones,
     And is binding up their pain-
     ful spots.
4 He is counting the number of
     the stars;
     All of them he calls by [their]
     names.
5 Our Lord is great and is abun-
     dant in power;
     His understanding is beyond
     recounting.
6 Jehovah is relieving the meek
     ones;
     He is abasing the wicked ones
     to the earth.
7 Respond to Jehovah with
     thanksgiving, you people;
     Make melody to our God on
     the harp,
8 The One who is covering the
     heavens with clouds,
     The One preparing rain for
     the earth,
     The One making the moun-
     tains to sprout green grass.
9 To the beasts he is giving their
     food,
     To the young ravens that keep
     calling.
10 Not in the mightiness of the
     horse does he take delight,
     Nor in the legs of the man
     does he find pleasure.
11 Jehovah is finding pleasure in
     those fearing him,
     In those waiting for his
     loving-kindness.
12 Commend Jehovah, O Jeru-
     salem.
     Praise your God, O Zion.
13 For he has made the bars of
     your gates strong;
     He has blessed your sons in
     the midst of you.
14 He is putting peace in your
     territory;
     With the fat of the wheat he
     keeps satisfying you.
15 He is sending his saying to the
     earth;
     With speed his word runs.
16 He is giving snow like wool;
     Hoarfrost he scatters just
     like ashes.

17 He is throwing his ice like
     morsels.
     Before his cold who can stand?
18 He sends forth his word and
     melts them.
     He causes his wind to blow;
     The waters trickle.
19 He is telling his word to Jacob,
     His regulations and his judi-
     cial decisions to Israel.
20 He has not done that way to
     any other nation;
     And as for [his] judicial
     decisions, they have not
     known them.
     Praise Jah, you people!

148 Praise Jah, you people!
     Praise Jehovah from the
     heavens,
     Praise him in the heights.
2 Praise him, all you his angels.
     Praise him, all you his army.
3 Praise him, you sun and moon.
     Praise him, all you stars of
     light.
4 Praise him, you heavens of the
     heavens,
     And you waters that are
     above the heavens.
5 Let them praise the name of
     Jehovah;
     For he himself commanded,
     and they were created.
6 And he keeps them standing
     forever, to time indefinite.
     A regulation he has given, and
     it will not pass away.
7 Praise Jehovah from the earth,
     You sea monsters and all you
     watery deeps,
8 You fire and hail, snow and
     thick smoke,
     You tempestuous wind, ac-
     complishing his word,
9 You mountains and all you
     hills,
     You fruit trees and all you
     cedars,
10 You wild animals and all you
     domestic animals,
     You creeping things and
     winged birds,
11 You kings of the earth and all
     you national groups,
     You princes and all you
     judges of the earth,
12 You young men and also you
     virgins,

You old men together with
boys.
13 Let them praise the name of
Jehovah,
For his name alone is un-
reachably high.
His dignity is above earth
and heaven.
14 And he will exalt the horn of
his people,
The praise of all his loyal ones,
Of the sons of Israel, the people near to him.
Praise Jah, YOU people!

149 Praise Jah, YOU people!
Sing to Jehovah a new
song,
His praise in the congregation of loyal ones.
2 Let Israel rejoice in its grand
Maker,
The sons of Zion—let them be
joyful in their King.
3 Let them praise his name with
dancing.
With the tambourine and the
harp let them make melody
to him.
4 For Jehovah is taking pleasure
in his people.
He beautifies the meek ones
with salvation.
5 Let the loyal ones exult in glory;
Let them cry out joyfully on
their beds.
6 Let the songs extolling God be
in their throat,

And a two-edged sword be in
their hand,
7 To execute vengeance upon the
nations,
Rebukes upon the national
groups,
8 To bind their kings with shackles
And their glorified ones with
fetters of iron,
9 To execute upon them the judicial decision written.
Such splendor belongs to all
his loyal ones.
Praise Jah, YOU people!

150 Praise Jah, YOU people!
Praise God in his holy
place.
Praise him in the expanse of
his strength.
2 Praise him for his works of
mightiness.
Praise him according to the
abundance of his greatness.
3 Praise him with the blowing of
the horn.
Praise him with the stringed
instrument and the harp.
4 Praise him with the tambourine
and the circle dance.
Praise him with strings and
the pipe.
5 Praise him with the cymbals of
melodious sound.
Praise him with the clashing
cymbals.
6 Every breathing thing—let it
praise Jah.
Praise Jah, YOU people!

PROVERBS

1 The proverbs of Sol'o·mon the
son of David, the king of Israel,
2 for one to know wisdom and
discipline, to discern the sayings
of understanding, 3 to receive the
discipline that gives insight, righteousness and judgment and uprightness, 4 to give to the inexperienced ones shrewdness, to a
young man knowledge and thinking ability.
5 A wise person will listen and
take in more instruction, and a

man of understanding is the one
who acquires skillful direction,
6 to understand a proverb and a
puzzling saying, the words of wise
persons and their riddles.
7 The fear of Jehovah is the beginning of knowledge. Wisdom and
discipline are what mere fools
have despised.
8 Listen, my son, to the discipline of your father, and do not
forsake the law of your mother.
9 For they are a wreath of at-

tractiveness to your head and a fine necklace to your throat.

10 My son, if sinners try to seduce you, do not consent. 11 If they keep saying: "Do go with us. Do let us lie in ambush for blood. Do let us lie in concealment for the innocent men without any cause. 12 Let us swallow them down alive just like She'ol, even whole, like those going down into a pit. 13 Let us find all sorts of precious valuables. Let us fill our houses with spoil. 14 Your lot you ought to cast in among us. Let there come to be just one bag belonging to all of us"— 15 my son, do not go in the way with them. Hold back your foot from their roadway. 16 For their feet are those that run to sheer badness, and they keep hastening to shed blood. 17 For it is for nothing that the net is spread before the eyes of anything owning wings. 18 Consequently they themselves lie in ambush for the very blood of these; they lie in concealment for their souls. 19 Thus are the paths of everyone making unjust profit. It takes away the very soul of its owners.

20 True wisdom itself keeps crying aloud in the very street. In the public squares it keeps giving forth its voice. 21 At the upper end of the noisy streets it calls out. At the entrances of the gates into the city it says its own sayings:

22 "How long will YOU inexperienced ones keep loving inexperience, and [how long] must YOU ridiculers desire for yourselves outright ridicule, and [how long] will YOU stupid ones keep hating knowledge? 23 Turn back at my reproof. Then to YOU I will cause my spirit to bubble forth; I will make my words known to YOU. 24 Because I have called out but YOU keep refusing, I have stretched out my hand but there is no one paying attention, 25 and YOU keep neglecting all my counsel, and my reproof YOU have not accepted, 26 I also, for my part, shall laugh at YOUR own disaster, I shall mock when what YOU dread comes, 27 when what YOU dread comes

just like a storm, and YOUR own disaster gets here just like a stormwind, when distress and hard times come upon YOU. 28 At that time they will keep calling me, but I shall not answer; they will keep looking for me, but they will not find me, 29 for the reason that they hated knowledge, and the fear of Jehovah they did not choose. 30 They did not consent to my counsel; they disrespected all my reproof. 31 So they will eat from the fruitage of their way, and they will be glutted with their own counsels. 32 For the renegading of the inexperienced ones is what will kill them, and the easygoingness of the stupid is what will destroy them. 33 As for the one listening to me, he will reside in security and be undisturbed from dread of calamity."

2 My son, if you will receive my sayings and treasure up my own commandments with yourself, 2 so as to pay attention to wisdom with your ear, that you may incline your heart to discernment; 3 if, moreover, you call out for understanding itself and you give forth your voice for discernment itself, 4 if you keep seeking for it as for silver, and as for hid treasures you keep searching for it, 5 in that case you will understand the fear of Jehovah, and you will find the very knowledge of God. 6 For Jehovah himself gives wisdom; out of his mouth there are knowledge and discernment. 7 And for the upright ones he will treasure up practical wisdom; for those walking in integrity he is a shield, 8 by observing the paths of judgment, and he will guard the very way of his loyal ones. 9 In that case you will understand righteousness and judgment and uprightness, the entire course of what is good.

10 When wisdom enters into your heart and knowledge itself becomes pleasant to your very soul, 11 thinking ability itself will keep guard over you, discernment itself will safeguard you, 12 to deliver you from the bad way, from the man speaking perverse things,

13 from those leaving the paths of uprightness to walk in the ways of darkness, 14 from those who are rejoicing in doing bad, who are joyful in the perverse things of badness; 15 those whose paths are crooked and who are devious in their general course; 16 to deliver you from the strange woman, from the foreign woman who has made her own sayings smooth, 17 who is leaving the confidential friend of her youth and who has forgotten the very covenant of her God. 18 For down to death her house does sink and down to those impotent in death her tracks. 19 None of those having relations with her will come back, nor will they regain the paths of those living.

20 The purpose is that you may walk in the way of good people and that the paths of the righteous ones you may keep. 21 For the upright are the ones that will reside in the earth, and the blameless are the ones that will be left over in it. 22 As regards the wicked, they will be cut off from the very earth; and as for the treacherous, they will be torn away from it.

3 My son, my law do not forget, and my commandments may your heart observe, 2 because length of days and years of life and peace will be added to you. 3 May loving-kindness and trueness themselves not leave you. Tie them about your throat. Write them upon the tablet of your heart, 4 and so find favor and good insight in the eyes of God and of earthling man. 5 Trust in Jehovah with all your heart and do not lean upon your own understanding. 6 In all your ways take notice of him, and he himself will make your paths straight.

7 Do not become wise in your own eyes. Fear Jehovah and turn away from bad. 8 May it become a healing to your navel and a refreshment to your bones.

9 Honor Jehovah with your valuable things and with the first fruits of all your produce. 10 Then your stores of supply will be filled with plenty; and with new wine your own press vats will overflow.

11 The discipline of Jehovah, O my son, do not reject; and do not abhor his reproof, 12 because the one whom Jehovah loves he reproves, even as a father does a son in whom he finds pleasure.

13 Happy is the man that has found wisdom, and the man that gets discernment, 14 for having it as gain is better than having silver as gain and having it as produce than gold itself. 15 It is more precious than corals, and all other delights of yours cannot be made equal to it. 16 Length of days is in its right hand; in its left hand there are riches and glory. 17 Its ways are ways of pleasantness, and all its roadways are peace. 18 It is a tree of life to those taking hold of it, and those keeping fast hold of it are to be called happy.

19 Jehovah himself in wisdom founded the earth. He solidly fixed the heavens in discernment. 20 By his knowledge the watery deeps themselves were split apart, and the cloudy skies keep dripping down light rain. 21 My son, may they not get away from your eyes. Safeguard practical wisdom and thinking ability, 22 and they will prove to be life to your soul and charm to your throat. 23 In that case you will walk in security on your way, and even your foot will not strike against anything. 24 Whenever you lie down you will feel no dread; and you will certainly lie down, and your sleep must be pleasurable. 25 You will not need to be afraid of any sudden dreadful thing, nor of the storm upon the wicked ones, because it is coming. 26 For Jehovah himself will prove to be, in effect, your confidence, and he will certainly keep your foot against capture.

27 Do not hold back good from those to whom it is owing, when it happens to be in the power of your hand to do [it]. 28 Do not say to your fellow man: "Go, and come back and tomorrow I shall give," when there is something with you. 29 Do not fabricate against

your fellow man anything bad, when he is dwelling in a sense of security with you. 30 Do not quarrel with a man without cause, if he has rendered no bad to you.

31 Do not become envious of the man of violence, nor choose any of his ways. 32 For the devious person is a detestable thing to Jehovah, but His intimacy is with the upright ones. 33 The curse of Jehovah is on the house of the wicked one, but the abiding place of the righteous ones he blesses. 34 If it has to do with ridiculers, he himself will deride; but to the meek ones he will show favor. 35 Honor is what the wise ones will come to possess, but the stupid ones are exalting dishonor.

4 Listen, O sons, to the discipline of a father and pay attention, so as to know understanding. 2 For good instruction is what I certainly shall give to you. My law do not leave. 3 For I proved to be a real son to my father, tender and the only one before my mother. 4 And he would instruct me and say to me: "May your heart keep fast hold of my words. Keep my commandments and continue living. 5 Acquire wisdom, acquire understanding. Do not forget, and do not turn aside from the sayings of my mouth. 6 Do not leave it, and it will keep you. Love it, and it will safeguard you. 7 Wisdom is the prime thing. Acquire wisdom; and with all that you acquire, acquire understanding. 8 Highly esteem it, and it will exalt you. It will glorify you because you embrace it. 9 To your head it will give a wreath of charm; a crown of beauty it will bestow upon you."

10 Hear, my son, and accept my sayings. Then for you the years of life will become many. 11 I will instruct you even in the way of wisdom; I will cause you to tread in the tracks of uprightness. 12 When you walk, your pace will not be cramped; and if you run, you will not stumble. 13 Take hold on discipline; do not let go. Safeguard it, for it itself is your life.

14 Into the path of the wicked ones do not enter, and do not walk straight on into the way of the bad ones. 15 Shun it, do not pass along by it; turn aside from it, and pass along. 16 For they do not sleep unless they do badness, and their sleep has been snatched away unless they cause someone to stumble. 17 For they have fed themselves with the bread of wickedness, and the wine of acts of violence is what they drink. 18 But the path of the righteous ones is like the bright light that is getting lighter and lighter until the day is firmly established. 19 The way of the wicked ones is like the gloom; they have not known at what they keep stumbling.

20 My son, to my words do pay attention. To my sayings incline your ear. 21 May they not get away from your eyes. Keep them in the midst of your heart. 22 For they are life to those finding them and health to all their flesh. 23 More than all else that is to be guarded, safeguard your heart, for out of it are the sources of life. 24 Remove from yourself the crookedness of speech; and the deviousness of lips put far away from yourself. 25 As for your eyes, straight ahead they should look, yes, your own beaming eyes should gaze straight in front of you. 26 Smooth out the course of your foot, and may all your own ways be firmly established. 27 Do not incline to the right hand or to the left. Remove your foot from what is bad.

5 My son, to my wisdom O do pay attention. To my discernment incline your ears, 2 so as to guard thinking abilities; and may your own lips safeguard knowledge itself.

3 For as a honeycomb the lips of a strange woman keep dripping, and her palate is smoother than oil. 4 But the aftereffect from her is as bitter as wormwood; it is as sharp as a two-edged sword. 5 Her feet are descending to death. Her steps take hold on She'ol itself. 6 The path of life she does not contemplate. Her tracks

of my mouth. 25 May your heart not turn aside to her ways. Do not wander into her roadways. 26 For many are the ones she has caused to fall down slain, and all those being killed by her are numerous. 27 The ways to She'ol her house is; they are descending to the interior rooms of death.

8 Does not wisdom keep calling out, and discernment keep giving forth its voice? 2 On top of the heights, by the way, at the crossing of the roadways it has stationed itself. 3 At the side of the gates, at the mouth of the town, at the going in of the entrances it keeps crying loudly: 4 "To you, O men, I am calling, and my voice is to the sons of men. 5 O inexperienced ones, understand shrewdness; and you stupid ones, understand heart. 6 Listen, for it is about the foremost things that I speak, and the opening of my lips is about uprightness. 7 For my palate in low tones utters truth itself; and wickedness is something detestable to my lips. 8 All the sayings of my mouth are in righteousness. Among them there is nothing twisted or crooked. 9 All of them are straight to the discerning one, and upright to the ones finding knowledge. 10 TAKE my discipline and not silver, and knowledge rather than choice gold. 11 For wisdom is better than corals, and all other delights themselves cannot be made equal to it.

12 "I, wisdom, I have resided with shrewdness and I find even the knowledge of thinking abilities. 13 The fear of Jehovah means the hating of bad. Self-exaltation and pride and the bad way and the perverse mouth I have hated. 14 I have counsel and practical wisdom. I—understanding; I have mightiness. 15 By me kings themselves keep reigning, and high officials themselves keep decreeing righteousness. 16 By me princes themselves keep ruling as princes, and nobles are all judging in righteousness. 17 Those loving me I myself love, and those looking for me are the ones that find me.

18 Riches and glory are with me, hereditary values and righteousness. 19 My fruitage is better than gold, even than refined gold, and my produce than choice silver. 20 In the path of righteousness I walk, in the middle of the roadways of judgment, 21 to cause those loving me to take possession of substance; and their storehouses I keep filled.

22 "Jehovah himself produced me as the beginning of his way, the earliest of his achievements of long ago. 23 From time indefinite I was installed, from the start, from times earlier than the earth. 24 When there were no watery deeps I was brought forth as with labor pains, when there were no springs heavily charged with water. 25 Before the mountains themselves had been settled down, ahead of the hills, I was brought forth as with labor pains, 26 when as yet he had not made the earth and the open spaces and the first part of the dust masses of the productive land. 27 When he prepared the heavens I was there; when he decreed a circle upon the face of the watery deep, 28 when he made firm the cloud masses above, when he caused the fountains of the watery deep to be strong, 29 when he set for the sea his decree that the waters themselves should not pass beyond his order, when he decreed the foundations of the earth, 30 then I came to be beside him as a master worker, and I came to be the one he was specially fond of day by day, I being glad before him all the time, 31 being glad at the productive land of his earth, and the things I was fond of were with the sons of men.

32 "And now, O sons, listen to me; yes, happy are the ones that keep my very ways. 33 Listen to discipline and become wise, and do not show any neglect. 34 Happy is the man that is listening to me by keeping awake at my doors day by day, by watching at the posts of my entrances. 35 For the one finding me will certainly find life, and gets good will from Jehovah. 36 But the one missing me is doing

violence to his soul; all those intensely hating me are the ones that do love death."

9 True wisdom has built its house; it has hewn out its seven pillars. 2 It has organized its meat slaughtering; it has mixed its wine; more than that, it has set in order its table. 3 It has sent forth its lady attendants, that it may call out on top of the heights of the town: 4 "Whoever is inexperienced, let him turn aside here." Whoever is in want of heart—she has said to him: 5 "Come, feed yourselves with my bread and share in drinking the wine that I have mixed. 6 Leave the inexperienced ones and keep living, and walk straight in the way of understanding."

7 He that is correcting the ridiculer is taking to himself dishonor, and he that is giving a reproof to someone wicked—a defect in him. 8 Do not reprove a ridiculer, that he may not hate you. Give a reproof to a wise person and he will love you. 9 Give to a wise person and he will become still wiser. Impart knowledge to someone righteous and he will increase in learning.

10 The fear of Jehovah is the start of wisdom, and the knowledge of the Most Holy One is what understanding is. 11 For by me your days will become many, and to you years of life will be added. 12 If you have become wise, you have become wise in your own behalf; and if you have ridiculed, you will bear [it], just you alone.

13 A woman of stupidity is boisterous. She is simple-mindedness itself and has come to know nothing whatever. 14 And she has seated herself at the entrance of her house, upon a seat, [in] the high places of the town, 15 to call out to those passing along the way, those who are going straight ahead on their paths: 16 "Whoever is inexperienced, let him turn aside here." And whoever is in want of heart—she has also said to him: 17 "Stolen waters themselves are sweet, and bread [eaten] in secrecy

—it is pleasant." 18 But he has not come to know that those impotent in death are there, that those called in by her are in the low places of She'ol.

10 Proverbs of Sol'o·mon. A wise son is the one that makes a father rejoice, and a stupid son is the grief of his mother. 2 The treasures of the wicked one will be of no benefit, but righteousness is what will deliver from death. 3 Jehovah will not cause the soul of the righteous one to go hungry, but the craving of the wicked ones he will push away.

4 The one working with a slack hand will be of little means, but the hand of the diligent one is what will make one rich.

5 The son acting with insight is gathering during the summertime; the son acting shamefully is fast asleep during the harvest.

6 Blessings are for the head of the righteous one, but as regards the mouth of the wicked ones, it covers up violence. 7 The remembrance of the righteous one is due for a blessing, but the very name of the wicked ones will rot.

8 The one wise in heart will accept commandments, but the one foolish with his lips will be trodden down.

9 He that is walking in integrity will walk in security, but he that is making his ways crooked will make himself known.

10 The one winking his eye will give pain, and the one foolish with his lips will be trodden down. 11 The mouth of the righteous one is a source of life; but as regards the mouth of the wicked ones, it covers up violence.

12 Hatred is what stirs up contentions, but love covers over even all transgressions.

13 On the lips of the understanding person wisdom is found, but the rod is for the back of one in want of heart.

14 The wise are the ones that treasure up knowledge, but the mouth of the foolish one is near to ruin itself.

15 The valuable things of a rich

man are his strong town. The ruin of the lowly ones is their poverty.

16 The activity of the righteous one results in life; the produce of the wicked one results in sin.

17 He that is holding to discipline is a path to life, but he that is leaving reproof is causing to wander.

18 Where there is one covering over hatred there are lips of falsehood, and the one bringing forth a bad report is stupid.

19 In the abundance of words there does not fail to be transgression, but the one keeping his lips in check is acting discreetly.

20 The tongue of the righteous one is choice silver; the heart of the wicked one is worth little.

21 The very lips of the righteous one keep pasturing many, but for want of heart the foolish themselves keep dying.

22 The blessing of Jehovah— that is what makes rich, and he adds no pain with it.

23 To the stupid one the carrying on of loose conduct is like sport, but wisdom is for the man of discernment.

24 The thing frightful to the wicked one—that is what will come to him; but the desire of the righteous ones will be granted. 25 As when the stormwind passes over, so the wicked one is no more; but the righteous one is a foundation to time indefinite.

26 As vinegar to the teeth and as smoke to the eyes, so the lazy man is to those sending him forth.

27 The very fear of Jehovah will add days, but the years themselves of the wicked ones will be cut short.

28 The expectation of the righteous ones is a rejoicing, but the very hope of the wicked ones will perish.

29 The way of Jehovah is a stronghold for the blameless one, but ruin is for the practicers of what is hurtful.

30 As for the righteous one, to time indefinite he will not be caused to stagger; but as for the wicked ones, they will not keep residing on the earth.

31 The mouth of the righteous one—it bears the fruit of wisdom, but the tongue of perverseness will be cut off.

32 The lips of the righteous one—they come to know good will, but the mouth of the wicked ones is perverseness.

11 A cheating pair of scales is something detestable to Jehovah, but a complete stone-weight is a pleasure to him.

2 Has presumptuousness come? Then dishonor will come; but wisdom is with the modest ones.

3 The integrity of the upright ones is what leads them, but distortion by those dealing treacherously will despoil them.

4 Valuable things will be of no benefit on the day of fury, but righteousness itself will deliver from death.

5 The righteousness of the blameless one is what will make his way straight, but in his own wickedness the wicked one will fall. 6 The righteousness of the upright ones is what will deliver them, but by their craving those dealing treacherously will themselves be caught.

7 When a wicked man dies, [his] hope perishes, and even expectation [based] on powerfulness has perished.

8 The righteous is the one rescued even from distress, and the wicked one comes in instead of him.

9 By [his] mouth the one who is an apostate brings his fellow man to ruin, but by knowledge are the righteous rescued.

10 Because of the goodness of the righteous ones a town is elated, but when the wicked ones perish there is a joyful cry.

11 Because of the blessing of the upright ones a town is exalted, but because of the mouth of the wicked ones it gets torn down.

12 The one in want of heart has despised his own fellow man, but the man of broad discernment is one that keeps silent.

13 The one walking about as a slanderer is uncovering confidential talk, but the one faithful in spirit is covering over a matter.

14 When there is no skillful direction, the people fall; but there is salvation in the multitude of counselors.

15 One will positively fare badly because he has gone surety for a stranger, but the one hating handshaking is keeping carefree.

16 A woman of charm is the one that takes hold of glory; but the tyrants, for their part, take hold of riches.

17 A man of loving-kindness is dealing rewardingly with his own soul, but the cruel person is bringing ostracism upon his own organism.

18 The wicked one is making false wages, but the one sowing righteousness, true earnings.

19 The one firmly standing for righteousness is in line for life, but the one chasing after what is bad is in line for his own death.

20 Those crooked at heart are something detestable to Jehovah, but the ones blameless in [their] way are a pleasure to him.

21 Though hand be to hand, a bad person will not go unpunished; but the offspring of the righteous ones will certainly escape.

22 As a gold nose ring in the snout of a pig, so is a woman that is pretty but that is turning away from sensibleness.

23 The desire of the righteous ones is surely good; the hope of the wicked ones is fury.

24 There exists the one that is scattering and yet is being increased; also the one that is keeping back from what is right, but it results only in want.

25 The generous soul will itself be made fat, and the one freely watering [others] will himself also be freely watered.

26 The one holding back grain— the populace will execrate him, but there is a blessing for the head of the one letting it be bought.

27 He that is looking for good, will keep seeking good will; but as for the one searching for bad, it will come upon him.

28 The one trusting in his riches —he himself will fall; but just like foliage the righteous ones will flourish.

29 As for anyone bringing ostracism upon his own house, he will take possession of wind; and a foolish person will be a servant to the one wise in heart.

30 The fruitage of the righteous one is a tree of life, and he that is winning souls is wise.

31 Look! The righteous one—in the earth he will be rewarded. How much more should the wicked one and the sinner be!

12 A lover of discipline is a lover of knowledge, but a hater of reproof is unreasoning.

2 One that is good gets approval from Jehovah, but the man of [wicked] ideas he pronounces wicked.

3 No man will be firmly established by wickedness; but as for the root-foundation of the righteous ones, it will not be caused to stagger.

4 A capable wife is a crown to her owner, but as rottenness in his bones is she that acts shamefully.

5 The thoughts of the righteous ones are judgment; the steering by the wicked ones is deception.

6 The words of the wicked ones are a lying in wait for blood, but the mouth of the upright ones is what will deliver them.

7 There is an overthrowing of the wicked ones and they are no more, but the very house of the righteous ones will keep standing.

8 For his mouth of discretion a man will be praised, but one who is twisted at heart will come to be for contempt.

9 Better is the one lightly esteemed but having a servant than the one glorifying himself but in want of bread.

10 The righteous one is caring for the soul of his domestic animal, but the mercies of the wicked ones are cruel.

11 The one cultivating his ground will himself be satisfied with bread, but the one pursuing valueless things is in want of heart.

12 The wicked one has desired the netted prey of bad men; but as for the root of the righteous ones, it yields.

13 By the transgression of the lips the bad person is ensnared, but the righteous one gets out of distress.

14 From the fruitage of a man's mouth he is satisfied with good, and the very doing of a man's hands will come back to him.

15 The way of the foolish one is right in his own eyes, but the one listening to counsel is wise.

16 It is a foolish person that makes known his vexation in the [same] day, but the shrewd one is covering over a dishonor.

17 He that launches forth faithfulness will tell what is righteous, but a false witness, deception.

18 There exists the one speaking thoughtlessly as with the stabs of a sword, but the tongue of the wise ones is a healing.

19 It is the lip of truth that will be firmly established forever, but the tongue of falsehood will be only as long as a moment.

20 Deception is in the heart of those fabricating mischief, but those counseling peace have rejoicing.

21 Nothing hurtful will befall the righteous one, but the wicked are the ones that will certainly be filled with calamity.

22 False lips are something detestable to Jehovah, but those acting in faithfulness are a pleasure to him.

23 A shrewd man is covering knowledge, but the heart of the stupid ones is one that calls out foolishness.

24 The hand of the diligent ones is the one that will rule, but the slack hand will come to be for forced labor.

25 Anxious care in the heart of a man is what will cause it to bow down, but the good word is what makes it rejoice.

26 The righteous one spies out his own pasturage, but the very way of wicked ones causes them to wander about.

27 Slackness will not start up one's game animals, but the diligent one is a man's precious wealth.

28 In the path of righteousness there is life, and the journey in its pathway means no death.

13 A son is wise where there is a father's discipline, but the ridiculer is one that has not heard rebuke.

2 From the fruitage of his mouth a man will eat good, but the very soul of those dealing treacherously is violence.

3 The one guarding his mouth is keeping his soul. The one opening wide his lips—he will have ruin.

4 The lazy one is showing himself desirous, but his soul [has] nothing. However, the very soul of the diligent ones will be made fat.

5 A false word is what the righteous hates, but the wicked ones act shamefully and cause disgrace for themselves.

6 Righteousness itself safeguards the one who is harmless in his way, but wickedness is what subverts the sinner.

7 There exists the one that is pretending to be rich and yet he has nothing at all; there is the one that is pretending to be of little means and yet [he has] many valuable things.

8 The ransom for a man's soul is his riches, but the one of little means has not heard rebuke.

9 The very light of the righteous ones will rejoice; but the lamp of the wicked ones—it will be extinguished.

10 By presumptuousness one only causes a struggle, but with those consulting together there is wisdom.

11 Valuable things resulting from vanity become fewer, but the one collecting by the hand is the one that makes increase.

12 Expectation postponed is making the heart sick, but the thing desired is a tree of life when it does come.

13 He that has despised the word, from him a [debtor's] pledge will be seized; but the one fearing the commandment is the one that will be rewarded.

14 The law of the wise one is a source of life, to turn one away from the snares of death.

15 Good insight itself gives favor, but the way of those dealing treacherously is rugged.

16 Everyone shrewd will act with knowledge, but the one that is stupid will spread abroad foolishness.

17 A messenger that is wicked will fall into bad, but a faithful envoy is a healing.

18 The one neglecting discipline [comes to] poverty and dishonor, but the one keeping a reproof is the one that is glorified.

19 Desire when realized is pleasurable to the soul; but it is something detestable to the stupid ones to turn away from bad.

20 He that is walking with wise persons will become wise, but he that is having dealings with the stupid ones will fare badly.

21 Sinners are the ones whom calamity pursues, but the righteous are the ones whom good rewards.

22 One who is good will leave an inheritance to sons of sons, and the wealth of the sinner is something treasured up for the righteous one.

23 Plowed ground of persons of little means [yields] a great deal of food, but there exists the one that is swept away for lack of judgment.

24 The one holding back his rod is hating his son, but the one loving him is he that does look for him with discipline.

25 The righteous is eating to the satisfaction of his soul, but the belly of the wicked ones will be empty.

14 The truly wise woman has built up her house, but the foolish one tears it down with her own hands.

2 The one walking in his uprightness is fearing Jehovah, but the one crooked in his ways is despising Him.

3 The rod of haughtiness is in the mouth of the foolish one, but the very lips of the wise ones will guard them.

4 Where there are no cattle the manger is clean, but the crop is abundant because of the power of a bull.

5 A faithful witness is one that will not lie, but a false witness launches forth mere lies.

6 The ridiculer has sought to find wisdom, and there is none; but to the understanding one knowledge is an easy thing.

7 Go away from in front of the stupid man, for you will certainly not take note of the lips of knowledge.

8 The wisdom of the shrewd is to understand his way, but the foolishness of stupid ones is deception.

9 Foolish are those who make a derision of guilt, but among the upright ones there is agreement.

10 The heart is aware of the bitterness of one's soul, and with its rejoicing no stranger will intermeddle.

11 The house of wicked people will be annihilated, but the tent of the upright ones will flourish.

12 There exists a way that is upright before a man, but the ways of death are the end of it afterward.

13 Even in laughter the heart may be in pain; and grief is what rejoicing ends up in.

14 The one faithless at heart will be satisfied with the results of his own ways, but the good man with the results of his dealings.

15 Anyone inexperienced puts faith in every word, but the shrewd one considers his steps.

16 The wise one fears and is turning away from badness, but the stupid is becoming furious and self-confident.

17 He that is quick to anger will commit foolishness, but the man of thinking abilities is hated.

18 The inexperienced ones will certainly take possession of foolishness, but the shrewd ones will bear knowledge as a headdress.

19 Bad people will have to bow down before the good ones, and the wicked people at the gates of the righteous one.

20 Even to his fellow man one who is of little means is an object of hatred, but many are the friends of the rich person.

21 The one despising his own fellow man is sinning, but happy is he who is showing favor to the afflicted ones.

22 Will not those devising mischief go wandering about? But there are loving-kindness and trueness as regards those devising good.

23 By every kind of toil there comes to be an advantage, but merely the word of the lips [tends] to want.

24 The crown of the wise is their riches; the foolishness of the stupid ones is foolishness.

25 A true witness is delivering souls, but a deceitful one launches forth mere lies.

26 In the fear of Jehovah there is strong confidence, and for his sons there will come to be a refuge.

27 The fear of Jehovah is a well of life, to turn away from the snares of death.

28 In the multitude of people there is an adornment of a king, but in the lack of population is the ruin of a high official.

29 He that is slow to anger is abundant in discernment, but one that is impatient is exalting foolishness.

30 A calm heart is the life of the fleshly organism, but jealousy is rottenness to the bones.

31 He that is defrauding the lowly one has reproached his Maker, but the one showing favor to the poor one is glorifying Him.

32 Because of his badness the wicked will be pushed down, but the righteous will be finding refuge in his integrity.

33 In the heart of the understanding one there rests wisdom, and in the midst of stupid ones it becomes known.

34 Righteousness is what exalts a nation, but sin is something disgraceful to national groups.

35 The pleasure of a king is in the servant who is acting with insight, but his fury comes to be toward one acting shamefully.

15 An answer, when mild, turns away rage, but a word causing pain makes anger to come up.

2 The tongue of wise ones does good with knowledge, but the mouth of the stupid ones bubbles forth with foolishness.

3 The eyes of Jehovah are in every place, keeping watch upon the bad ones and the good ones.

4 The calmness of the tongue is a tree of life, but distortion in it means a breaking down in the spirit.

5 Anyone foolish disrespects the discipline of his father, but anyone regarding reproof is shrewd.

6 In the house of the righteous one there is an abundant store, but in the produce of the wicked one there is a becoming ostracized.

7 The lips of the wise ones keep scattering knowledge about, but the heart of the stupid ones is not like that.

8 The sacrifice of the wicked ones is something detestable to Jehovah, but the prayer of the upright ones is a pleasure to him.

9 The way of the wicked one is something detestable to Jehovah, but the one pursuing righteousness he loves.

10 Discipline is bad to the one leaving the path; anyone hating reproof will die.

11 She'ol and [the place of] destruction are in front of Jehovah. How much more so the hearts of the sons of mankind!

12 The ridiculer does not love the one reproving him. To the wise ones he will not go.

13 A joyful heart has a good effect on the countenance, but because of the pain of the heart there is a stricken spirit.

14 The understanding heart is one that searches for knowledge, but the mouth of stupid people is one that aspires to foolishness.

15 All the days of the afflicted one are bad; but the one that is good at heart [has] a feast constantly.

16 Better is a little in the fear of Jehovah than an abundant supply and confusion along with it.

17 Better is a dish of vegetables where there is love than a manger-fed bull and hatred along with it.

18 An enraged man stirs up contention, but one that is slow to anger quiets down quarreling.

19 The way of the lazy one is like a brier hedge, but the path of the upright ones is a way cast up.

20 A wise son is the one that makes a father rejoice, but a stupid man is despising his mother.

21 Foolishness is a rejoicing to one who is in want of heart, but the man of discernment is one who goes straight ahead.

22 There is a frustrating of plans where there is no confidential talk, but in the multitude of counselors there is accomplishment.

23 A man has rejoicing in the answer of his mouth, and a word at its right time is O how good!

24 The path of life is upward to one acting with insight, in order to turn away from She′ol down below.

25 The house of the self-exalted ones Jehovah will tear down, but he will fix the boundary of the widow.

26 The schemes of the bad one are something detestable to Jehovah, but pleasant sayings are clean.

27 The one making unjust profit is bringing ostracism upon his own house, but the hater of gifts is the one that will keep living.

28 The heart of the righteous one meditates so as to answer, but the mouth of the wicked ones bubbles forth with bad things.

29 Jehovah is far away from the wicked ones, but the prayer of the righteous ones he hears.

30 The brightness of the eyes makes the heart rejoice; a report that is good makes the bones fat.

31 The ear that is listening to the reproof of life lodges right in among wise people.

32 Anyone shunning discipline is rejecting his own soul, but the one listening to reproof is acquiring heart.

33 The fear of Jehovah is a discipline toward wisdom, and before glory there is humility.

16 To earthling man belong the arrangings of the heart, but from Jehovah is the answer of the tongue.

2 All the ways of a man are pure in his own eyes, but Jehovah is making an estimate of spirits.

3 Roll your works upon Jehovah himself and your plans will be firmly established.

4 Everything Jehovah has made for his purpose, yes, even the wicked one for the evil day.

5 Everyone that is proud in heart is something detestable to Jehovah. Hand [may join] to hand, [yet] one will not be free from punishment.

6 By loving-kindness and true-ness error is atoned for, and in the fear of Jehovah one turns away from bad.

7 When Jehovah takes pleasure in the ways of a man he causes even his enemies themselves to be at peace with him.

8 Better is a little with righteousness than an abundance of products without justice.

9 The heart of earthling man may think out his way, but Jehovah himself does the directing of his steps.

10 Inspired decision should be upon the lips of a king; in judgment his mouth should not prove unfaithful.

11 The just indicator and scales belong to Jehovah; all the stone weights of the bag are his work.

12 The doing of wickedness is something detestable to kings, for by righteousness is the throne firmly established.

13 The lips of righteousness are a pleasure to a grand king; and the speaker of upright things he loves.

14 The rage of a king means messengers of death, but the wise man is one that averts it.

15 In the light of the king's face there is life, and his good will is like the cloud of spring rain.

16 The getting of wisdom is O how much better than gold! And the getting of understanding is to be chosen more than silver.

17 The highway of the upright ones is to turn away from bad. One who is safeguarding his way is keeping his soul.

18 Pride is before a crash, and a haughty spirit before stumbling.

19 Better is it to be lowly in spirit with the meek ones than to divide spoil with the self-exalted ones.

20 He that is showing insight in a matter will find good, and happy is he that is trusting in Jehovah.

21 The one that is wise in heart will be called understanding, and he that is sweet in [his] lips adds persuasiveness.

22 To its owners insight is a well of life; and the discipline of the foolish ones is foolishness.

23 The heart of the wise one causes his mouth to show insight, and to his lips it adds persuasiveness.

24 Pleasant sayings are a honeycomb, sweet to the soul and a healing to the bones.

25 There exists a way that is upright before a man, but the ways of death are the end of it afterward.

26 The soul of the hard worker has worked hard for him, because his mouth has pressed him hard.

27 A good-for-nothing man is digging up what is bad, and upon his lips there is, as it were, a scorching fire.

28 A man of intrigues keeps sending forth contention, and a slanderer is separating those familiar with one another.

29 A man of violence will seduce his fellow, and certainly causes him to go in a way that is not good.

30 He is blinking with his eyes to scheme up intrigues. Pinching his lips together, he certainly brings mischief to completion.

31 Gray-headedness is a crown of beauty when it is found in the way of righteousness.

32 He that is slow to anger is better than a mighty man, and he that is controlling his spirit than the one capturing a city.

33 Into the lap the lot is cast down, but every decision by it is from Jehovah.

17 Better is a dry piece of bread with which there is quietness than a house full of the sacrifices of quarreling.

2 A servant that is showing insight will rule over the son who is acting shamefully, and in among the brothers he will have a share of the inheritance.

3 The refining pot is for silver and the furnace for gold, but Jehovah is the examiner of hearts.

4 The evildoer is paying attention to the lip of hurtfulness. A falsifier is giving ear to the tongue causing adversities.

5 He that is holding the one of little means in derision has reproached his Maker. He that is joyful at [another's] disaster will not be free from punishment.

6 The crown of old men is the grandsons, and the beauty of sons is their fathers.

7 For anyone senseless the lip of uprightness is not fitting. How much less so for a noble the lip of falsehood!

8 The gift is a stone winning favor in the eyes of its grand owner. Everywhere that he turns he has success.

9 The one covering over transgression is seeking love, and he that keeps talking about a matter is separating those familiar with one another.

10 A rebuke works deeper in one having understanding than striking a stupid one a hundred times.

11 Only rebellion is what the bad one keeps seeking, and cruel is the messenger that is sent against him.

12 Let there be an encountering by a man of a bear bereaved of its cubs rather than anyone stupid in his foolishness.

13 As for anyone repaying bad for good, bad will not move away from his house.

14 The beginning of contention is as one letting out waters; so before the quarrel has burst forth, take your leave.

15 Anyone pronouncing the wicked one righteous and anyone pronouncing the righteous one wicked

—even both of them are something detestable to Jehovah.

16 Why is it that there is in the hand of a stupid one the price to acquire wisdom, when he has no heart?

17 A true companion is loving all the time, and is a brother that is born for when there is distress.

18 A man that is wanting in heart shakes hands, going full surety before his companion.

19 Anyone loving transgression is loving a struggle. Anyone making his entryway high is seeking a crash.

20 He that is crooked at heart will not find good, and he that is turned around in his tongue will fall into calamity.

21 Anyone becoming father to a stupid child—it is a grief to him; and the father of a senseless child does not rejoice.

22 A heart that is joyful does good as a curer, but a spirit that is stricken makes the bones dry.

23 One who is wicked will take even a bribe from the bosom to bend the paths of judgment.

24 Wisdom is before the face of the understanding one, but the eyes of the stupid one are at the extremity of the earth.

25 A stupid son is a vexation to his father and a bitterness to her that gave him birth.

26 Furthermore, the laying of a fine upon the righteous one is not good. To strike nobles is against what is upright.

27 Anyone holding back his sayings is possessed of knowledge, and a man of discernment is cool of spirit.

28 Even anyone foolish, when keeping silent, will be regarded as wise; anyone closing up his own lips, as having understanding.

18 One isolating himself will seek his own selfish longing; against all practical wisdom he will break forth.

2 Anyone stupid finds no delight in discernment, except that his heart should uncover itself.

3 When a wicked one comes in, contempt also must come in; and along with dishonor there is reproach.

4 The words of a man's mouth are deep waters. The well of wisdom is a torrent bubbling forth.

5 The showing of partiality to the wicked one is not good, nor the turning aside of the righteous one in judgment.

6 The lips of one who is stupid enter into quarreling, and his very mouth calls even for strokes.

7 The mouth of the stupid one is the ruin of him, and his lips are a snare for his soul.

8 The words of the slanderer are like things to be swallowed greedily, which do go down into the innermost parts of the belly.

9 Also, the one showing himself slack in his work—he is a brother to the one causing ruin.

10 The name of Jehovah is a strong tower. Into it the righteous runs and is given protection.

11 The valuable things of the rich are his strong town, and they are like a protective wall in his imagination.

12 Before a crash the heart of a man is lofty, and before glory there is humility.

13 When anyone is replying to a matter before he hears [it], that is foolishness on his part and a humiliation.

14 The spirit of a man can put up with his malady; but as for a stricken spirit, who can bear it?

15 The heart of the understanding one acquires knowledge, and the ear of wise ones seeks to find knowledge.

16 A man's gift will make a large opening for him, and it will lead him even before great people.

17 The one first in his legal case is righteous; his fellow comes in and certainly searches him through.

18 The lot puts even contentions to rest, and it separates even the mighty from one another.

19 A brother who is transgressed against is more than a strong town; and there are contentions that are like the bar of a dwelling tower.

20 From the fruitage of a man's mouth his belly will be satisfied; he will be satisfied even with the produce of his lips.

21 Death and life are in the power of the tongue, and he that is loving it will eat its fruitage.

22 Has one found a [good] wife? One has found a good thing, and one gets good will from Jehovah.

23 Entreaties the one of little means speaks out, but one that is rich answers in a strong way.

24 There exist companions disposed to break one another to pieces, but there exists a friend sticking closer than a brother.

19 Anyone of little means who is walking in his integrity is better than the one crooked in his lips, and the one that is stupid.

2 Also, that the soul should be without knowledge is not good, and he that is hastening with his feet is sinning.

3 It is the foolishness of an earthling man that distorts his way, and so his heart becomes enraged against Jehovah himself.

4 Wealth is what adds many companions, but one that is lowly gets separated even from his companion.

5 A false witness will not be free from punishment, and he that launches forth lies will not escape.

6 Many are those who soften the face of a noble, and everybody is a companion to the man making gifts.

7 The brothers of one of little means have all hated him. How much farther have his personal friends kept away from him! He is pursuing with things to say; they are not.

8 He that is acquiring heart is loving his own soul. He that is guarding discernment is going to find good.

9 The false witness will not be free from punishment, and he that launches forth lies will perish.

10 Luxury is not fitting for anyone stupid. How much less for a servant to rule over princes!

11 The insight of a man certainly slows down his anger, and it is beauty on his part to pass over transgression.

12 The raging of a king is a growling like that of a maned young lion, but his good will is like the dew upon the vegetation.

13 A stupid son means adversities to his father, and the contentions of a wife are as a leaking roof that drives one away.

14 The inheritance from fathers is a house and wealth, but a discreet wife is from Jehovah.

15 Laziness causes a deep sleep to fall, and a slack soul goes hungry.

16 He that is keeping the commandment is keeping his soul; he that is despising his ways will be put to death.

17 He that is showing favor to the lowly one is lending to Jehovah, and his treatment He will repay to him.

18 Chastise your son while there exists hope; and to the putting of him to death do not lift up your soul[ful desire].

19 He that is of great rage will be bearing the fine; for if you would deliver [him], you will also keep doing it again and again.

20 Listen to counsel and accept discipline, in order that you may become wise in your future.

21 Many are the plans in the heart of a man, but the counsel of Jehovah is what will stand.

22 The desirable thing in earthling man is his loving-kindness; and one of little means is better than a lying man.

23 The fear of Jehovah tends toward life, and one will spend the night satisfied; one will not be visited with what is bad.

24 The lazy one has hidden his hand in the banquet bowl; he cannot bring it back even to his own mouth.

25 The ridiculer you should strike, that the inexperienced one may become shrewd; and there should be a reproving of the understanding one, that he may discern knowledge.

26 He that is maltreating a father [and] that chases a mother away

is a son acting shamefully and disgracefully.

27 Cease, my son, to listen to discipline [and it will mean] to stray from the sayings of knowledge.

28 A good-for-nothing witness derides justice, and the very mouth of wicked people swallows down what is hurtful.

29 Judgments have been firmly established for ridiculers, and strokes for the back of stupid ones.

20 Wine is a ridiculer, intoxicating liquor is boisterous, and everyone going astray by it is not wise.

2 The frightfulness of a king is a growling like that of a maned young lion. Anyone drawing his fury against himself is sinning against his own soul.

3 It is a glory for a man to desist from disputing, but everyone foolish will burst out [in it].

4 Because of winter the lazy one will not plow; he will be begging in reaping time, but there will be nothing.

5 Counsel in the heart of a man is as deep waters, but the man of discernment is one that will draw it up.

6 A multitude of men will proclaim each one his own lovingkindness, but a faithful man who can find?

7 The righteous is walking in his integrity. Happy are his sons after him.

8 The king is sitting upon the throne of judgment, scattering all badness with his own eyes.

9 Who can say: "I have cleansed my heart; I have become pure from my sin"?

10 Two sorts of weights and two sorts of e'phah measures—they are both of them together something detestable to Jehovah.

11 Even by his practices a boy makes himself recognized as to whether his activity is pure and upright.

12 The hearing ear and the seeing eye—Jehovah himself has made even both of them.

13 Do not love sleep, that you may not come to poverty. Open your eyes; be satisfied with bread.

14 "It is bad, bad!" says the buyer, and he is going his way. Then it is that he boasts about himself.

15 There exists gold, also an abundance of corals; but the lips of knowledge are precious vessels.

16 Take one's garment, in case one has gone surety for a stranger; and in the instance of a foreign woman, seize from him a pledge.

17 Bread [gained by] falsehood is pleasurable to a man, but afterward his mouth will be filled with gravel.

18 By counsel plans themselves are firmly established, and by skillful direction carry on your war.

19 He that is going about as a slanderer is uncovering confidential talk; and with one that is enticed with his lips you must have no fellowship.

20 As for anyone calling down evil upon his father and his mother, his lamp will be extinguished at the approach of darkness.

21 An inheritance is being got by greed at first, but its own future will not be blessed.

22 Do not say: "I will pay back evil!" Hope in Jehovah, and he will save you.

23 Two sorts of weights are something detestable to Jehovah, and a cheating pair of scales is not good.

24 From Jehovah are the steppings of an able-bodied man. As regards earthling man, how can he discern his way?

25 It is a snare when earthling man has rashly cried out, "Holy!" and after vows [he is disposed] to make examination.

26 A wise king is scattering wicked people, and he turns around upon them a wheel.

27 The breath of earthling man is the lamp of Jehovah, carefully searching all the innermost parts of the belly.

28 Loving-kindness and trueness —they safeguard the king; and by loving-kindness he has sustained his throne.

29 The beauty of young men is their power, and the splendor of old men is their gray-headedness.

30 Bruising wounds are what scours away the bad; and strokes, the innermost parts of the belly.

21 A king's heart is as streams of water in the hand of Jehovah. Everywhere that he delights to, he turns it.

2 Every way of a man is upright in his own eyes, but Jehovah is making an estimate of hearts.

3 To carry on righteousness and judgment is more preferable to Jehovah than sacrifice.

4 Haughty eyes and an arrogant heart, the lamp of the wicked ones, are sin.

5 The plans of the diligent one surely make for advantage, but everyone that is hasty surely heads for want.

6 The getting of treasures by a false tongue is an exhalation driven away, in the case of those seeking death.

7 The very despoiling by the wicked ones will drag them away, for they have refused to do justice.

8 A man, even a stranger, is crooked in [his] way; but the pure one is upright in his activity.

9 Better is it to dwell upon a corner of a roof than with a contentious wife, although in a house in common.

10 The very soul of the wicked one has craved what is bad; his fellow will be shown no favor in his eyes.

11 By the laying of a fine on the ridiculer the inexperienced becomes wise; and by one's giving insight to a wise person he gets knowledge.

12 The Righteous One is giving consideration to the house of the wicked one, subverting the wicked ones to [their] calamity.

13 As for anyone stopping up his ear from the complaining cry of the lowly one, he himself also will call and not be answered.

14 A gift made in secrecy subdues anger; and a bribe in the bosom, strong rage.

15 It is a rejoicing for the righteous one to do justice, but there is something terrible for those practicing what is hurtful.

16 As for a man wandering from the way of insight, he will rest in the very congregation of those impotent in death.

17 He that is loving merriment will be an individual in want; he that is loving wine and oil will not gain riches.

18 The wicked is a ransom for the righteous one; and the one dealing treacherously takes the place of the upright ones.

19 Better is it to dwell in a wilderness land than with a contentious wife along with vexation.

20 Desirable treasure and oil are in the abode of the wise one, but the man that is stupid will swallow it up.

21 He that is pursuing righteousness and loving-kindness will find life, righteousness and glory.

22 A wise one has scaled even the city of mighty men, that he might bring down the strength of its confidence.

23 He that is keeping his mouth and his tongue is keeping his soul from distresses.

24 Presumptuous, self-assuming braggart is the name of the one who is acting in a fury of presumptuousness.

25 The very craving of the lazy will put him to death, for his hands have refused to work. 26 All the day he has shown himself eagerly craving, but the righteous one gives and holds nothing back.

27 The sacrifice of the wicked ones is something detestable. How much more so when one brings it along with loose conduct.

28 A lying witness will perish, but the man that is listening will speak even forever.

29 A wicked man has put on a bold face, but the upright is the one that will firmly establish his ways.

30 There is no wisdom, nor any discernment, nor any counsel in opposition to Jehovah.

31 The horse is something prepared for the day of battle, but salvation belongs to Jehovah.

22 A name is to be chosen rather than abundant riches; favor is better than even silver and gold.

2 The rich one and the one of little means have met each other. The Maker of them all is Jehovah.

3 Shrewd is the one that has seen the calamity and proceeds to conceal himself, but the inexperienced have passed along and must suffer the penalty.

4 The result of humility [and] the fear of Jehovah is riches and glory and life.

5 Thorns [and] traps are in the way of the crooked one; he that is guarding his soul keeps far away from them.

6 Train up a boy according to the way for him; even when he grows old he will not turn aside from it.

7 The rich is the one that rules over those of little means, and the borrower is servant to the man doing the lending.

8 He that is sowing unrighteousness will reap what is hurtful, but the very rod of his fury will come to its end.

9 He that is kindly in eye will be blessed, for he has given of his food to the lowly one.

10 Drive away the ridiculer, that contention may go out and that legal contest and dishonor may cease.

11 The one loving purity of heart —for the charm of his lips the king will be his companion.

12 The eyes of Jehovah himself have safeguarded knowledge, but he subverts the words of the treacherous one.

13 The lazy one has said: "There is a lion outside! In the midst of the public squares I shall be murdered!"

14 The mouth of strange women is a deep pit. The one denounced by Jehovah will fall into it.

15 Foolishness is tied up with the heart of a boy; the rod of discipline is what will remove it far from him.

16 He that is defrauding the lowly one to supply many things to himself, he also that is giving to the rich one, is surely destined for want.

17 Incline your ear and hear the words of the wise ones, that you may apply your very heart to my knowledge. 18 For it is pleasant that you should keep them in your belly, that they may be firmly established together upon your lips.

19 For your confidence to come to be in Jehovah himself I have given you knowledge today, even you.

20 Have I not written you heretofore with counselings and knowledge, 21 to show you the truthfulness of true sayings, so as to return sayings that are the truth— to the one sending you forth?

22 Do not rob the lowly one because he is lowly, and do not crush the afflicted one in the gate. 23 For Jehovah himself will plead their cause, and he will certainly rob of soul those robbing them.

24 Do not have companionship with anyone given to anger; and with a man having fits of rage you must not enter in, 25 that you may not get familiar with his paths and certainly take a snare for your soul.

26 Do not get to be among those striking hands, among those who go security for loans. 27 If you have nothing to pay, why should he take your bed from under you?

28 Do not move back a boundary of long ago, which your forefathers have made.

29 Have you beheld a man skillful in his work? Before kings is where he will station himself; he will not station himself before commonplace men.

23 In case you should sit down to feed yourself with a king, you should diligently consider what is before you, 2 and you must put a knife to your throat if you are the owner of soul[ful desire]. 3 Do not show yourself craving his tasty dishes, as it is the food of lies.

4 Do not toil to gain riches. Cease from your own understanding. 5 Have you caused your eyes to glance at it, when it is nothing?

For without fail it makes wings for itself like those of an eagle and flies away toward the heavens.

6 Do not feed yourself with the food of anyone of ungenerous eye, nor show yourself craving his tasty dishes. 7 For as one that has calculated within his soul, so he is. "Eat and drink," he says to you, but his heart itself is not with you. 8 Your morsel that you have eaten, you will vomit it out, and you will have wasted your pleasant words.

9 Into the ears of a stupid one do not speak, for he will despise your discreet words.

10 Do not move back the boundary of long ago, and into the field of fatherless boys do not enter. 11 For their Redeemer is strong; he himself will plead their cause with you.

12 Do bring your heart to discipline and your ear to the sayings of knowledge.

13 Do not hold back discipline from the mere boy. In case you beat him with the rod, he will not die. 14 With the rod you yourself should beat him, that you may deliver his very soul from She'ol itself.

15 My son, if your heart has become wise, my heart will rejoice, even mine. 16 And my kidneys will exult when your lips speak uprightness.

17 Let your heart not be envious of sinners, but be in the fear of Jehovah all day long. 18 For in that case there will exist a future, and your own hope will not be cut off.

19 You, O my son, hear and become wise, and lead your heart on in the way.

20 Do not come to be among heavy drinkers of wine, among those who are gluttonous eaters of flesh. 21 For a drunkard and a glutton will come to poverty, and drowsiness will clothe one with mere rags.

22 Listen to your father who caused your birth, and do not despise your mother just because she has grown old. 23 Buy truth itself and do not sell it—wisdom and discipline and understanding. 24 The father of a righteous one will without fail be joyful; the one becoming father to a wise one will also rejoice in him. 25 Your father and your mother will rejoice, and she that gave birth to you will be joyful.

26 My son, do give your heart to me, and may those eyes of yours take pleasure in my own ways. 27 For a prostitute is a deep pit and a foreign woman is a narrow well. 28 Surely she, just like a robber, lies in wait; and among men she increases the treacherous ones.

29 Who has woe? Who has uneasiness? Who has contentions? Who has concern? Who has wounds for no reason? Who has dullness of eyes? 30 Those staying a long time with the wine, those coming in to search out mixed wine. 31 Do not look at wine when it exhibits a red color, when it gives off its sparkle in the cup, [when] it goes with a slickness. 32 At its end it bites just like a serpent, and it secretes poison just like a viper. 33 Your own eyes will see strange things, and your own heart will speak perverse things. 34 And you will certainly become like one lying down in the heart of the sea, even like one lying down at the top of a mast. 35 "They have struck me, but I did not become sick; they have smitten me, but I did not know it. When shall I wake up? I shall seek it yet some more."

24 Do not be envious of bad men, and do not show yourself craving to get in with them. 2 For despoiling is what their heart keeps meditating, and trouble is what their own lips keep speaking.

3 By wisdom a household will be built up, and by discernment it will prove firmly established. 4 And by knowledge will the interior rooms be filled with all precious and pleasant things of value.

5 One wise in strength is an able-bodied man, and a man of knowledge is reinforcing power. 6 For by skillful direction you will carry on your war, and in the

multitude of counselors there is salvation.

7 For a foolish one true wisdom is too high; in the gate he will not open his mouth.

8 As for anyone scheming to do bad, he will be called a mere master at evil ideas.

9 The loose conduct of foolishness is sin, and a ridiculer is something detestable to mankind.

10 Have you shown yourself discouraged in the day of distress? Your power will be scanty.

11 Deliver those who are being taken away to death; and those staggering to the slaughter, O may you hold [them] back. 12 In case you should say: "Look! We did not know of this," will not he himself that is making an estimate of hearts discern it, and he himself that is observing your soul know and certainly pay back to earthling man according to his activity?

13 My son, eat honey, for it is good; and let sweet comb honey be upon your palate. 14 In the same way, do know wisdom for your soul. If you have found [it], then there exists a future, and your own hope will not be cut off.

15 Do not, as a wicked one, lie in wait for the abiding place of the righteous one; do not despoil his resting place. 16 For the righteous one may fall even seven times, and he will certainly get up; but the wicked ones will be made to stumble by calamity.

17 When your enemy falls, do not rejoice; and when he is caused to stumble, may your heart not be joyful, 18 that Jehovah may not see and it be bad in his eyes and he certainly turn back his anger from against him.

19 Do not show yourself heated up at evildoers. Do not become envious of wicked people. 20 For there will prove to be no future for anyone bad; the very lamp of wicked people will be extinguished.

21 My son, fear Jehovah and the king. With those who are for a change, do not intermeddle. 22 For their disaster will arise so suddenly,

that who is aware of the extinction of those who are for a change?

23 These [sayings] also are for the wise ones: The showing of partiality in judgment is not good.

24 He that is saying to the wicked one: "You are righteous," the peoples will execrate him, national groups will denounce him. 25 But for those reproving [him] it will be pleasant, and upon them there will come the blessing of good. 26 Lips will he kiss who is replying in a straightforward way.

27 Prepare your work out of doors, and make it ready for yourself in the field. Afterward you must also build up your household.

28 Do not become a witness against your fellow man without grounds. Then you would have to be foolish with your lips. 29 Do not say: "Just as he did to me, so I am going to do to him. I shall repay to each one according to his acting."

30 I passed along by the field of the lazy individual and by the vineyard of the man in need of heart. 31 And, look! all of it produced weeds. Nettles covered its very surface, and its stone wall itself had been torn down.

32 So I proceeded to behold, I myself; I began taking [it] to heart; I saw, I took the discipline: 33 A little sleeping, a little slumbering, a little folding of the hands to lie down, 34 and as a highwayman your poverty will certainly come and your neediness as an armed man.

25 These also are the proverbs of Sol′o·mon that the men of Hez·e·ki′ah the king of Judah transcribed:

2 The glory of God is the keeping of a matter secret, and the glory of kings is the searching through a matter.

3 The heavens for height and the earth for depth, and the heart of kings, that is unsearchable.

4 Let there be a removing of scummy dross from the silver, and all of it will come forth refined.

5 Let there be the removing of the wicked one before the king, and his throne will be firmly established by righteousness itself.

6 Do not do yourself honor before the king, and in the place of great ones do not stand. 7 For it is better [for him] to say to you: "Come up here," than to abase you before a noble whom your eyes have seen.

8 Do not go forth to conduct a legal case hastily, that it may not be a question of what you will do in the culmination of it when your fellow man now humiliates you. 9 Plead your own cause with your fellow man, and do not reveal the confidential talk of another; 10 that the one listening may not put you to shame and the bad report by you can have no recall.

11 As apples of gold in silver carvings is a word spoken at the right time for it.

12 An earring of gold, and an ornament of special gold, is a wise reprover upon the hearing ear.

13 Just like the coolness of snow in the day of harvest is the faithful envoy to those sending him, for he restores the very soul of his masters.

14 As vaporous clouds and a wind without any downpour is a man boasting himself about a gift in falsehood.

15 By patience a commander is induced, and a mild tongue itself can break a bone.

16 Is it honey that you have found? Eat what is sufficient for you, that you may not take too much of it and have to vomit it up.

17 Make your foot rare at the house of your fellow man, that he may not have his sufficiency of you and certainly hate you.

18 As a war club and a sword and a sharpened arrow is a man testifying against his fellow man as a false witness.

19 As a broken tooth and a wobbling foot is the confidence in one proving treacherous in the day of distress.

20 He that is removing a garment on a cold day is as vinegar upon alkali and as a singer with songs upon a gloomy heart.

21 If the one hating you is hungry, give him bread to eat; and if he is thirsty, give him water to drink. 22 For coals are what you are raking together upon his head, and Jehovah himself will reward you.

23 The wind from the north brings forth as with labor pains a downpour; and a tongue [giving away] a secret, a denounced face.

24 Better is it to dwell upon a corner of a roof than with a contentious wife, although in a house in common.

25 As cold water upon a tired soul, so is a good report from a distant land.

26 A fouled spring and a ruined well is the righteous one when staggering before the wicked one.

27 The eating of too much honey is not good; and for people to search out their own glory, is it glory?

28 As a city broken through, without a wall, is the man that has no restraint for his spirit.

26 Like snow in summer and like rain in harvesttime, so glory is not fitting for a stupid one.

2 Just as a bird has cause for fleeing [and] just as a swallow for flying, so a malediction itself does not come without real cause.

3 A whip is for the horse, a bridle is for the ass, and the rod is for the back of stupid people.

4 Do not answer anyone stupid according to his foolishness, that you yourself also may not become equal to him.

5 Answer someone stupid according to his foolishness, that he may not become someone wise in his own eyes.

6 As one that is mutilating [his] feet, as one that is drinking mere violence, is he that is thrusting matters into the hand of someone stupid.

7 Have the legs of the lame one drawn up water? Then there is a proverb in the mouth of stupid people.

8 Like one shutting up a stone in a heap of stones, so is the one giving glory to a mere stupid one.

9 As a thorny weed has come up into the hand of a drunkard, so a proverb into the mouth of stupid people.

10 As an archer piercing everything is the one hiring someone stupid or the one hiring passers-by.

11 Just like a dog returning to its vomit, the stupid one is repeating his foolishness.

12 Have you seen a man wise in his own eyes? There is more hope for the stupid one than for him.

13 The lazy one has said: "There is a young lion in the way, a lion in among the public squares."

14 A door keeps turning upon its pivot, and the lazy one upon his couch.

15 The lazy one has hidden his hand in the banquet bowl; he has become too weary to bring it back to his mouth.

16 The lazy one is wiser in his own eyes than seven giving a sensible reply.

17 As one grabbing hold of the ears of a dog is anyone passing by that is becoming furious at the quarrel that is not his.

18 Just like someone mad that is shooting fiery missiles, arrows and death, 19 so is the man that has tricked his fellow man and has said: "Was I not having fun?"

20 Where there is no wood the fire goes out, and where there is no slanderer contention grows still.

21 As charcoal for the embers and wood for the fire, so is a contentious man for causing a quarrel to glow.

22 The words of a slanderer are like things to be swallowed greedily, which do go down into the innermost parts of the belly.

23 As a silver glazing overlaid upon a fragment of earthenware are fervent lips along with a bad heart.

24 With his lips the hater makes himself unrecognizable, but inside of him he puts deception. 25 Although he makes his voice gracious,

do not believe in him, for there are seven detestable things in his heart. 26 Hatred is covered over by deceit. His badness will be uncovered in the congregation.

27 He that is excavating a pit will fall into the same, and he that is rolling away a stone—back to him it will return.

28 A tongue that is false hates the one crushed by it, and a flattering mouth causes an overthrow.

27 Do not make your boast about the next day, for you do not know what a day will give birth to.

2 May a stranger, and not your own mouth, praise you; may a foreigner, and not your own lips, do so.

3 The heaviness of a stone and a load of sand—but the vexation by someone foolish is heavier than both of them.

4 There is the cruelty of rage, also the flood of anger, but who can stand before jealousy?

5 Better is a revealed reproof than a concealed love.

6 The wounds inflicted by a lover are faithful, but the kisses of a hater are things to be entreated.

7 A soul that is satisfied will tread down comb honey, but to a hungry soul every bitter thing is sweet.

8 Just like a bird fleeing away from its nest, so is a man fleeing away from his place.

9 Oil and incense are what make the heart rejoice, also the sweetness of one's companion due to the counsel of the soul.

10 Do not leave your own companion or the companion of your father, and do not enter the house of your own brother on the day of your disaster. Better is a neighbor that is near than a brother that is far away.

11 Be wise, my son, and make my heart rejoice, that I may make a reply to him that is taunting me.

12 The shrewd one that has seen the calamity has concealed himself; the inexperienced that have passed along have suffered the penalty.

13 Take one's garment, in case one has gone surety for a stranger;

and in the instance of a foreign woman, seize from him a pledge.

14 He that is blessing his fellow man with a loud voice early in the morning, as a malediction it will be accounted on his part.

15 A leaking roof that drives away in the day of a steady rain and a contentious wife are comparable. 16 Anyone sheltering her has sheltered the wind, and oil is what his right hand encounters.

17 By iron, iron itself is sharpened. So one man sharpens the face of another.

18 He that is safeguarding the fig tree will himself eat its fruit, and he that is guarding his master will be honored.

19 As in water face corresponds with face, so the heart of a man with [that of] a man.

20 She'ol and [the place of] destruction themselves do not get satisfied; neither do the eyes of a man get satisfied.

21 The refining pot is for silver, and the furnace is for gold; and an individual is according to his praise.

22 Even if you should pound the foolish one fine with a pestle in a mortar, in among cracked grain, his foolishness will not depart from him.

23 You ought to know positively the appearance of your flock. Set your heart to your droves; 24 for treasure will not be to time indefinite, nor a diadem for all generations.

25 The green grass has departed, and the new grass has appeared, and the vegetation of the mountains has been gathered. 26 The young rams are for your clothing, and the he-goats are the price of the field. 27 And there is a sufficiency of goats' milk for your food, for the food of your household, and the means of life for your girls.

28 The wicked do flee when there is no pursuer, but the righteous are like a young lion that is confident.

2 Because of the transgression of a land many are its [successive] princes, but by a discerning man having knowledge of right [the prince] will remain long.

3 An able-bodied man that is of little means and that is defrauding the lowly ones is as a rain that washes away so that there is no food.

4 Those who are leaving the law praise the wicked one, but those who are keeping the law excite themselves against them.

5 Men given to badness cannot understand judgment, but those who are seeking Jehovah can understand everything.

6 Better is the one of little means who is walking in his integrity than anyone crooked in [his] ways, although he is rich.

7 An understanding son is observing the law, but one having companionship with gluttons humiliates his father.

8 He that is multiplying his valuables by interest and usury collects them merely for the one showing favor to the lowly ones.

9 He that is turning his ear away from hearing the law—even his prayer is something detestable.

10 He that is causing the upright ones to go astray into the bad way will himself fall into his own pit, but the faultless ones themselves will come into possession of good.

11 A rich man is wise in his own eyes, but the lowly one who is discerning searches him through.

12 When the righteous ones are exulting, there is abundant beauty; but when the wicked ones rise up, a man disguises himself.

13 He that is covering over his transgressions will not succeed, but he that is confessing and leaving [them] will be shown mercy.

14 Happy is the man that is feeling dread constantly, but he that is hardening his heart will fall into calamity.

15 As a growling lion and an onrushing bear is a wicked ruler over a lowly people.

16 A leader that is in want of true discernment is also abundant in fraudulent practices, but he that is hating unjust profit will prolong [his] days.

17 A man burdened with the bloodguilt for a soul will himself flee even to the pit. Let them not get hold of him.

18 He that is walking faultless will be saved, but he that is made crooked in [his] ways will fall at once.

19 He that is cultivating his own ground will have his sufficiency of bread, and he that is pursuing valueless things will have his sufficiency of poverty.

20 A man of faithful acts will get many blessings, but he that is hastening to gain riches will not remain innocent.

21 The showing of partiality is not good, nor that an able-bodied man should transgress over a mere piece of bread.

22 A man of envious eye is bestirring himself after valuable things, but he does not know that want itself will come upon him.

23 He that is reproving a man will afterward find more favor than he will that is flattering with his tongue.

24 He that is robbing his father and his mother and is saying: "It is no transgression," is a partner of a man causing ruination.

25 He that is arrogant in soul stirs up contention, but he that is relying upon Jehovah will be made fat.

26 He that is trusting in his own heart is stupid, but he that is walking in wisdom is the one that will escape.

27 He that is giving to the one of little means will have no want, but he that is hiding his eyes will get many curses.

28 When the wicked rise up, a man conceals himself; but when they perish, the righteous become many.

29 A man repeatedly reproved but making his neck hard will suddenly be broken, and that without healing.

2 When the righteous become many, the people rejoice; but when anyone wicked bears rule, the people sigh.

3 A man that is loving wisdom makes his father rejoice, but he that is having companionship with prostitutes destroys valuable things.

4 By justice a king makes a land keep standing, but a man out for bribes tears it down.

5 An able-bodied man that is flattering his companion is spreading out a mere net for his steps.

6 In the transgression of a bad man there is a snare, but he that is righteous cries out joyfully and is glad.

7 The righteous one is knowing the legal claim of the lowly ones. He that is wicked does not consider such knowledge.

8 Men of boastful talk inflame a town, but those who are wise turn back anger.

9 A wise man having entered into judgment with a foolish man—he has become excited and has also laughed, and there is no rest.

10 Bloodthirsty men hate anyone blameless; and as for the upright ones, they keep seeking for the soul of each one.

11 All his spirit is what a stupid one lets out, but he that is wise keeps it calm to the last.

12 Where a ruler is paying attention to false speech, all those waiting on him will be wicked.

13 The one of little means and the man of oppressions have met each other; but Jehovah is lighting up the eyes of them both.

14 Where a king is judging the lowly ones in trueness, his throne will be firmly established for all time.

15 The rod and reproof are what give wisdom; but a boy let on the loose will be causing his mother shame.

16 When the wicked become many, transgression abounds; but those who are righteous will look on their very downfall.

17 Chastise your son and he will bring you rest and give much pleasure to your soul.

18 Where there is no vision the people go unrestrained, but happy are they that are keeping the law.

19 A servant will not let himself be corrected by mere words, for he understands but he is paying no heed.

20 Have you beheld a man hasty with his words? There is more hope for someone stupid than for him.

21 If one is pampering one's servant from youth on, in his later life he will even become a thankless one.

22 A man given to anger stirs up contention, and anyone disposed to rage has many a transgression.

23 The very haughtiness of earthling man will humble him, but he that is humble in spirit will take hold of glory.

24 He that is partner with a thief is hating his own soul. An oath involving a curse he may hear, but he reports nothing.

25 Trembling at men is what lays a snare, but he that is trusting in Jehovah will be protected.

26 Many are those seeking the face of a ruler, but the judgment of a man is from Jehovah.

27 A man of injustice is something detestable to the righteous ones, and one who is upright in his way is something detestable to a wicked one.

30 The words of A'gur the son of Ja'keh, the weighty message. The utterance of the able-bodied man to Ith'i·el, to Ith'i·el and U'cal.

2 For I am more unreasoning than anyone else, and I do not have the understanding of mankind; 3 and I have not learned wisdom; and the knowledge of the Most Holy One I do not know.

4 Who has ascended to heaven that he may descend? Who has gathered the wind in the hollow of both hands? Who has wrapped up the waters in a mantle? Who has made all the ends of the earth to rise? What is his name and what the name of his son, in case you know?

5 Every saying of God is refined. He is a shield to those taking refuge in him. 6 Add nothing to his words, that he may not reprove you, and that you may not have to be proved a liar.

7 Two things I have asked of you. Do not withhold them from me before I die. 8 Untruth and the lying word put far away from me. Give me neither poverty nor riches. Let me devour the food prescribed for me, 9 that I may not become satisfied and I actually deny [you] and say: "Who is Jehovah?" and that I may not come to poverty and I actually steal and assail the name of my God.

10 Do not slander a servant to his master, that he may not call down evil upon you, and that you may not have to be held guilty.

11 There is a generation that calls down evil even upon its father and that does not bless even its mother.

12 There is a generation that is pure in its own eyes but that has not been washed from its own excrement.

13 There is a generation whose eyes have become O how lofty! and whose beaming eyes are lifted up.

14 There is a generation whose teeth are swords and whose jawbones are slaughtering knives, to eat up the afflicted ones off the earth and the poor ones from among mankind.

15 The leeches have two daughters [that cry]: "Give! Give!" There are three things that do not get satisfied, four that have not said: "Enough!" 16 She'ol and a restrained womb, a land that has not been satisfied with water, and fire that has not said: "Enough!"

17 The eye that holds a father in derision and that despises obedience to a mother—the ravens of the torrent valley will pick it out and the sons of the eagle will eat it up.

18 There are three things that have proved too wonderful for me, and four that I have not come to know: 19 the way of an eagle in the heavens, the way of a serpent on a rock, the way of a ship in the heart of the sea and the way of an able-bodied man with a maiden.

20 Here is the way of an adulterous woman: she has eaten and

has wiped her mouth and she has said: "I have committed no wrong."

21 Under three things the earth has been agitated, and under four it is not able to endure: 22 under a slave when he rules as king, and someone senseless when he has his sufficiency of food; 23 under a hated woman when she is taken possession of as a wife, and a maidservant when she dispossesses her mistress.

24 There are four things that are the smallest of the earth, but they are instinctively wise: 25 the ants are a people not strong, and yet in the summer they prepare their food; 26 the rock badgers are a people not mighty, and yet upon a crag is where they put their house; 27 the locusts have no king, and yet they go forth all of them divided into groups; 28 the gecko lizard takes hold with its own hands and it is in the grand palace of a king.

29 There are three that do well in [their] pacing, and four that do well in [their] moving along: 30 the lion, which is the mightiest among the beasts and which does not turn back from before anyone; 31 the greyhound or the he-goat, and a king of a band of soldiers of his own people.

32 If you have acted senselessly by lifting yourself up, and if you have fixed your thought [upon it], [put] the hand to the mouth. 33 For the churning of milk is what brings forth butter, and the squeezing of the nose is what brings forth blood, and the squeezing out of anger is what brings forth quarreling.

31 The words of Lem′u·el the king, the weighty message that his mother gave to him in correction:

2 What [am I saying], O son of mine, and what, O son of my belly, and what, O son of my vows?

3 Do not give your vital energy to women, nor your ways to [what leads to] wiping out kings.

4 It is not for kings, O Lem′u·el, it is not for kings to drink wine or

for high officials [to say:] "Where is intoxicating liquor?" 5 that one may not drink and forget what is decreed and pervert the cause of any of the sons of affliction. 6 Give intoxicating liquor, ʏᴏᴜ people, to the one about to perish and wine to those who are bitter of soul. 7 Let one drink and forget one's poverty, and let one remember one's own trouble no more.

8 Open your mouth for the speechless one, in the cause of all those passing away. 9 Open your mouth, judge righteously and plead the cause of the afflicted one and the poor one.

א [Aleph]

10 A capable wife who can find? Her value is far more than that of corals.

ב [Beth]

11 In her the heart of her owner has put trust, and there is no gain lacking.

ג [Gimel]

12 She has rewarded him with good, and not bad, all the days of her life.

ד [Daleth]

13 She has sought wool and linen, and she works at whatever is the delight of her hands.

ה [He]

14 She has proved to be like the ships of a merchant. From far away she brings in her food.

ו [Waw]

15 She also gets up while it is still night, and gives food to her household and the prescribed portion to her young women.

ז [Zayin]

16 She has considered a field and proceeded to obtain it; from the fruitage of her hands she has planted a vineyard.

ח [Heth]

17 She has girded her hips with strength, and she invigorates her arms.

ט [Teth]

18 She has sensed that her trading is good; her lamp does not go out at night.

י [Yod]

19 Her hands she has thrust out to the distaff, and her own hands take hold of the spindle.

כ [Kaph]

20 Her palm she has stretched out to the afflicted one, and her hands she has thrust out to the poor one.

ל [Lamed]

21 She does not fear for her household because of the snow, for all her household are clothed with double garments.

מ [Mem]

22 Coverlets she has made for herself. Her clothing is of linen and wool dyed reddish purple.

נ [Nun]

23 Her owner is someone known in the gates, when he sits down with the older men of the land.

ס [Samekh]

24 She has made even undergarments and proceeded to sell [them], and belts she has given to the tradesmen.

ע [Ayin]

25 Strength and splendor are her clothing, and she laughs at a future day.

פ [Pe]

26 Her mouth she has opened in wisdom, and the law of loving-kindness is upon her tongue.

צ [Tsade]

27 She is watching over the goings on of her household, and the bread of laziness she does not eat.

ק [Qoph]

28 Her sons have risen up and proceeded to pronounce her happy; her owner [rises up], and he praises her.

ר [Resh]

29 There are many daughters that have shown capableness, but you—you have ascended above them all.

ש [Shin]

30 Charm may be false, and prettiness may be vain; [but] the woman that fears Jehovah is the one that procures praise for herself.

ת [Taw]

31 GIVE her of the fruitage of her hands, and let her works praise her even in the gates.

ECCLESIASTES

1 The words of the congregator, the son of David the king in Jerusalem. 2 "The greatest vanity!" the congregator has said, "the greatest vanity! Everything is vanity!" 3 What profit does a man have in all his hard work at which he works hard under the sun? 4 A generation is going, and a generation is coming; but the earth is standing even to time indefinite. 5 And the sun also has flashed forth, and the sun has set, and it is coming panting to its place where it is going to flash forth.

6 The wind is going to the south, and it is circling around to the north. Round and round it is continually circling, and right back to its circlings the wind is returning.

7 All the winter torrents are going forth to the sea, yet the sea itself is not full. To the place where the winter torrents are going

forth, there they are returning so as to go forth. 8 All things are wearisome; no one is able to speak of it. The eye is not satisfied at seeing, neither is the ear filled from hearing. 9 That which has come to be, that is what will come to be; and that which has been done, that is what will be done; and so there is nothing new under the sun. 10 Does anything exist of which one may say: "See this; it is new"? It has already had existence for time indefinite; what has come into existence is from time prior to us. 11 There is no remembrance of people of former times, nor will there be of those also who will come to be later. There will prove to be no remembrance even of them among those who will come to be still later on.

12 I, the congregator, happened to be king over Israel in Jerusalem. 13 And I set my heart to seek and explore wisdom in relation to everything that has been done under the heavens—the calamitous occupation that God has given to the sons of mankind in which to be occupied. 14 I saw all the works that were done under the sun, and, look! everything was vanity and a striving after wind.

15 That which is made crooked cannot be made straight, and that which is wanting cannot possibly be counted. 16 I, even I, spoke with my heart, saying: "Look! I myself have greatly increased in wisdom more than anyone that happened to be before me in Jerusalem, and my own heart saw a great deal of wisdom and knowledge." 17 And I proceeded to give my heart to knowing wisdom and to knowing madness, and I have come to know folly, that this too is a striving after wind. 18 For in the abundance of wisdom there is an abundance of vexation, so that he that increases knowledge increases pain.

2 I said, even I, in my heart: "Do come now, let me try you out with rejoicing. Also, see good." And, look! that too was vanity. 2 I said

to laughter: "Insanity!" and to rejoicing: "What is this doing?"

3 I explored with my heart by cheering my flesh even with wine, while I was leading my heart with wisdom, even to lay hold on folly until I could see what good there was to the sons of mankind in what they did under the heavens for the number of the days of their life. 4 I engaged in greater works. I built houses for myself; I planted vineyards for myself. 5 I made gardens and parks for myself, and I planted in them fruit trees of all sorts. 6 I made pools of water for myself, to irrigate with them the forest, springing up with trees. 7 I acquired menservants and maidservants, and I came to have sons of the household. Also, livestock, cattle and flocks in great quantity I came to have, more so than all those who happened to be before me in Jerusalem. 8 I accumulated also silver and gold for myself, and property peculiar to kings and the jurisdictional districts. I made male singers and female singers for myself and the exquisite delights of the sons of mankind, a lady, even ladies. 9 And I became greater and increased more than anyone that happened to be before me in Jerusalem. Moreover, my own wisdom remained mine.

10 And anything that my eyes asked for I did not keep away from them. I did not hold back my heart from any sort of rejoicing, for my heart was joyful because of all my hard work, and this came to be my portion from all my hard work. 11 And I, even I, turned toward all the works of mine that my hands had done and toward the hard work that I had worked hard to accomplish, and, look! everything was vanity and a striving after wind, and there was nothing of advantage under the sun.

12 And I, even I, turned to see wisdom and madness and folly; for what can the earthling man do who comes in after the king? The thing that people have already done. 13 And I saw, even I, that there exists more advantage for

wisdom than for folly, just as there is more advantage for light than for darkness.

14 As regards anyone wise, his eyes are in his head; but the stupid one is walking on in sheer darkness. And I have come to know, I too, that there is one eventuality that eventuates to them all. 15 And I myself said in my heart: "An eventuality like that upon the stupid one will eventuate to me, yes, me." Why, then, had I become wise, I overmuch so at that time? And I spoke in my heart: "This too is vanity." 16 For there is no more remembrance of the wise one than of the stupid one to time indefinite. In the days that are already coming in, everyone is certainly forgotten; and how will the wise one die? Along with the stupid one.

17 And I hated life, because the work that has been done under the sun was calamitous from my standpoint, for everything was vanity and a striving after wind. 18 And I, even I, hated all my hard work at which I was working hard under the sun, that I would leave behind for the man who would come to be after me. 19 And who is there knowing whether he will prove to be wise or foolish? Yet he will take control over all my hard work at which I worked hard and at which I showed wisdom under the sun. This too is vanity. 20 And I myself turned around toward making my heart despair over all the hard work at which I had worked hard under the sun. 21 For there exists the man whose hard work has been with wisdom and with knowledge and with proficiency, but to a man that has not worked hard at such a thing will be given the portion of that one. This too is vanity and a big calamity.

22 For what does a man come to have for all his hard work and for the striving of his heart with which he is working hard under the sun? 23 For all his days his occupation means pains and vexation, also during the night his

heart just does not lie down. This too is mere vanity.

24 With a man there is nothing better [than] that he should eat and indeed drink and cause his soul to see good because of his hard work. This too I have seen, even I, that this is from the hand of the [true] God. 25 For who eats and who drinks better than I do?

26 For to the man that is good before him he has given wisdom and knowledge and rejoicing, but to the sinner he has given the occupation of gathering and bringing together merely to give to the one that is good before the [true] God. This too is vanity and a striving after wind.

3 For everything there is an appointed time, even a time for every affair under the heavens: 2 a time for birth and a time to die; a time to plant and a time to uproot what was planted; 3 a time to kill and a time to heal; a time to break down and a time to build; 4 a time to weep and a time to laugh; a time to wail and a time to skip about; 5 a time to throw stones away and a time to bring stones together; a time to embrace and a time to keep away from embracing; 6 a time to seek and a time to give up as lost; a time to keep and a time to throw away; 7 a time to rip apart and a time to sew together; a time to keep quiet and a time to speak; 8 a time to love and a time to hate; a time for war and a time for peace. 9 What advantage is there for the doer in what he is working hard at?

10 I have seen the occupation that God has given to the sons of mankind in which to be occupied. 11 Everything he has made pretty in its time. Even time indefinite he has put in their heart, that mankind may never find out the work that the [true] God has made from the start to the finish. 12 I have come to know that there is nothing better for them than to rejoice and to do good during one's life; 13 and also that every man

should eat and indeed drink and see good for all his hard work. It is the gift of God.

14 I have come to know that everything that the [true] God makes, it will prove to be to time indefinite. To it there is nothing to add and from it there is nothing to subtract; but the [true] God himself has made it, that people may be afraid on account of him.

15 What has happened to be, it had already been, and what is to come to be has already proved to be; and the [true] God himself keeps seeking that which is pursued.

16 And I have further seen under the sun the place of justice where there was wickedness and the place of righteousness where wickedness was. 17 I myself have said in my heart: "The [true] God will judge both the righteous one and the wicked one, for there is a time for every affair and concerning every work there."

18 I, even I, have said in my heart with regard to the sons of mankind that the [true] God is going to select them, that they may see that they themselves are beasts. 19 For there is an eventuality as respects the sons of mankind and an eventuality as respects the beast, and they have the same eventuality. As the one dies, so the other dies; and they all have but one spirit, so that there is no superiority of the man over the beast, for everything is vanity. 20 All are going to one place. They have all come to be from the dust, and they are all returning to the dust. 21 Who is there knowing the spirit of the sons of mankind, whether it is ascending upward; and the spirit of the beast, whether it is descending downward to the earth? 22 And I have seen that there is nothing better than that the man should rejoice in his works, for that is his portion; because who will bring him in to look on what is going to be after him?

4 And I myself returned that I might see all the acts of oppression that are being done under the sun, and, look! the tears of those being oppressed, but they had no comforter; and on the side of their oppressors there was power, so that they had no comforter. 2 And I congratulated the dead who had already died rather than the living who were still alive. 3 So better than both of them [is] the one who has not yet come to be, who has not seen the calamitous work that is being done under the sun.

4 And I myself have seen all the hard work and all the proficiency in work, that it means the rivalry of one toward another; this also is vanity and a striving after the wind.

5 The stupid one is folding his hands and is eating his own flesh.

6 Better is a handful of rest than a double handful of hard work and striving after the wind.

7 I myself returned that I might see the vanity under the sun: 8 There exists one, but not a second one; also no son or brother does he have, but there is no end to all his hard work. Also, his eyes themselves are not satisfied with riches: "And for whom am I working hard and causing my soul to lack in good things?" This too is vanity, and it is a calamitous occupation.

9 Two are better than one, because they have a good reward for their hard work. 10 For if one of them should fall, the other one can raise his partner up. But how will it be with just the one who falls when there is not another to raise him up?

11 Moreover, if two lie down together, they also will certainly get warm; but how can just one keep warm? 12 And if somebody could overpower one alone, two together could make a stand against him. And a threefold cord cannot quickly be torn in two.

13 Better is a needy but wise child than an old but stupid king, who has not come to know enough to be warned any longer. 14 For he has gone forth from the prison house itself to become king, although in the kingship of this one he had been born as one of little means. 15 I have seen all those alive who

are walking about under the sun, [how it goes] with the child, who is second, that stands up in the other one's place. 16 There is no end to all the people, to all those before whom he happened to be; neither will people afterward rejoice in him, for this too is vanity and a striving after the wind.

5 Guard your feet whenever you go to the house of the [true] God; and let there be a drawing near to hear, rather than to give a sacrifice as the stupid ones do, for they are not aware of doing what is bad.

2 Do not hurry yourself as regards your mouth; and as for your heart, let it not be hasty to bring forth a word before the [true] God. For the [true] God is in the heavens but you are on the earth. That is why your words should prove to be few. 3 For a dream certainly comes in because of abundance of occupation, and the voice of a stupid one because of the abundance of words. 4 Whenever you vow a vow to God, do not hesitate to pay it, for there is no delight in the stupid ones. What you vow, pay. 5 Better is it that you vow not than that you vow and do not pay. 6 Do not allow your mouth to cause your flesh to sin, neither say before the angel that it was a mistake. Why should the [true] God become indignant on account of your voice and have to wreck the work of your hands? 7 For because of abundance [of occupation] there are dreams, and there are vanities and words in abundance. But fear the [true] God himself.

8 If you see any oppression of the one of little means and the violent taking away of judgment and of righteousness in a jurisdictional district, do not be amazed over the affair, for one that is higher than the high one is watching, and there are those who are high above them.

9 Also, the profit of the earth is among them all; for a field the king himself has been served.

10 A mere lover of silver will not be satisfied with silver, neither any lover of wealth with income. This too is vanity.

11 When good things become many, those eating them certainly become many. And what advantage is there to the grand owner of them, except looking [at them] with his eyes?

12 Sweet is the sleep of the one serving, regardless of whether it is little or much that he eats; but the plenty belonging to the rich one is not permitting him to sleep.

13 There exists a grave calamity that I have seen under the sun: riches being kept for their grand owner to his calamity. 14 And those riches have perished because of a calamitous occupation, and he has become father to a son when there is nothing at all in his hand.

15 Just as one has come forth from his mother's belly, naked will one go away again, just as one came; and nothing at all can one carry away for his hard work, which he can take along with his hand.

16 And this too is a grave calamity: exactly as one has come, so one will go away; and what profit is there to the one who keeps working hard for the wind? 17 Also, all his days he eats in darkness itself, with a great deal of vexation, with sickness on his part and [cause for] indignation.

18 Look! The best thing that I myself have seen, which is pretty, is that one should eat and drink and see good for all his hard work with which he works hard under the sun for the number of the days of his life that the [true] God has given him, for that is his portion. 19 Also every man to whom the [true] God has given riches and material possessions, he has even empowered him to eat from it and to carry off his portion and to rejoice in his hard work. This is the gift of God. 20 For not often will he remember the days of his life, because the [true] God is preoccupying [him] with the rejoicing of his heart.

6 There exists a calamity that I have seen under the sun, and it is frequent among mankind: 2 a man to whom the [true] God gives riches and material possessions and glory and who, for his soul, is in no need of anything that he shows himself longing for, and yet the [true] God does not enable him to eat from it, although a mere foreigner may eat it. This is vanity and it is a bad sickness. 3 If a man should become a father a hundred times, and he should live many years, so that numerous the days of his years should become, yet his own soul is not satisfied with good things and even the grave has not become his, I must say that one prematurely born is better off than he is. 4 For in vain has this one come and in darkness he goes away, and with darkness his own name will be covered. 5 Even the sun itself he has not seen, neither known. This one has rest rather than the former one. 6 Even supposing that he has lived a thousand years twice over and yet he has not seen what is good, is it not to just one place that everyone is going?

7 All the hard work of mankind is for their mouth, but even their own soul does not get filled. 8 For what advantage does the wise have over the stupid one? What does the afflicted one have in knowing how to walk in front of the living ones? 9 Better is the seeing by the eyes than the walking about of the soul. This too is vanity and a striving after the wind.

10 Whatever has come to be, its name has already been pronounced, and it has become known what man is; and he is not able to plead his cause with one that is more powerful than he is.

11 Because there exist many things that are causing much vanity, what advantage does a man have? 12 For who is there knowing what good a man has in life for the number of the days of his vain life, when he spends them like a shadow? For who can tell man what will happen after him under the sun?

7 A name is better than good oil, and the day of death than the day of one's being born. 2 Better is it to go to the house of mourning than to go to the banquet house, because that is the end of all mankind; and the one alive should take [it] to his heart. 3 Better is vexation than laughter, for by the crossness of the face the heart becomes better. 4 The heart of the wise ones is in the house of mourning, but the heart of the stupid ones is in the house of rejoicing.

5 Better is it to hear the rebuke of someone wise than to be the man hearing the song of the stupid ones. 6 For as the sound of thorns under the pot, so is the laughter of the stupid one; and this too is vanity. 7 For mere oppression may make a wise one act crazy, and a gift can destroy the heart.

8 Better is the end afterward of a matter than its beginning. Better is one who is patient than one who is haughty in spirit. 9 Do not hurry yourself in your spirit to become offended, for the taking of offense is what rests in the bosom of the stupid ones.

10 Do not say: "Why has it happened that the former days proved to be better than these?" for it is not due to wisdom that you have asked about this.

11 Wisdom along with an inheritance is good and is advantageous for those seeing the sun. 12 For wisdom is for a protection [the same as] money is for a protection; but the advantage of knowledge is that wisdom itself preserves alive its owners.

13 See the work of the [true] God, for who is able to make straight what he has made crooked? 14 On a good day prove yourself to be in goodness, and on a calamitous day see that the [true] God has made even this exactly as that, to the intent that mankind may not discover anything at all after them.

15 Everything I have seen during my vain days. There exists the

righteous one perishing in his righteousness, and there exists the wicked one continuing long in his badness.

16 Do not become righteous overmuch, nor show yourself excessively wise. Why should you cause desolation to yourself? 17 Do not be wicked overmuch, nor become foolish. Why should you die when it is not your time? 18 It is better that you should take hold of the one, but from the other also do not withdraw your hand; for he that fears God will go forth with them all.

19 Wisdom itself is stronger for the wise one than ten men in power who happened to be in a city. 20 For there is no man righteous in the earth that keeps doing good and does not sin.

21 Also, do not give your heart to all the words that people may speak, that you may not hear your servant calling down evil upon you. 22 For your own heart well knows even many times that you, even you, have called down evil upon others.

23 All this I have tested with wisdom. I said: "I will become wise." But it was far from me. 24 What has come to be is far off and exceedingly deep. Who can find it out? 25 I myself turned around, even my heart did, to know and to explore and to search for wisdom and the reason of things, and to know about the wickedness of stupidity and the foolishness of madness; 26 and I was finding out: More bitter than death [I found] the woman who is herself nets for hunting and whose heart is dragnets [and] whose hands are fetters. One is good before the [true] God if one escapes from her, but one is sinning if one is captured by her.

27 "See! This I have found," said the congregator, "one thing [taken] after another, to find out the sumup, 28 which my soul has continuously sought, but I have not found. One man out of a thousand I have found, but a woman among all these I have not found. 29 See!

This only I have found, that the [true] God made mankind upright, but they themselves have sought out many plans."

8 Who is there like the wise one? And who is there knowing the interpretation of a thing? The wisdom of a man itself causes his face to shine, and even the sternness of his face is changed [for the better].

2 I [say:] "Keep the very order of the king, and that out of regard for the oath of God. 3 Do not hurry yourself, that you may go out from before him. Do not stand in a bad thing. For all that he delights [to do] he will do, 4 because the word of the king is the power of control; and who may say to him: 'What are you doing?'"

5 He that is keeping the commandment will not know any calamitous thing, and the wise heart will know both time and judgment. 6 For there exists a time and judgment even for every affair, because the calamity of mankind is abundant upon them. 7 For there is no one knowing what will come to be, because who can tell him just how it will come to be?

8 There is no man having power over the spirit to restrain the spirit; neither is there any power of control in the day of death; nor is there any discharge in the war. And wickedness will provide no escape for those indulging in it.

9 All this I have seen, and there was an applying of my heart to every work that has been done under the sun, [during] the time that man has dominated man to his injury. 10 But, though this is so, I have seen the wicked ones being buried, how they came in and how they would go away from the holy place itself and be forgotten in the city where they acted that way. This too is vanity.

11 Because sentence against a bad work has not been executed speedily, that is why the heart of the sons of men has become fully set in them to do bad. 12 Although a sinner may be doing bad a hundred times and continuing a

long time as he pleases, yet I am also aware that it will turn out well with those fearing the [true] God, because they were in fear of him. 13 But it will not turn out well at all with the wicked one, neither will he prolong his days that are like a shadow, because he is not in fear of God.

14 There exists a vanity that is carried out on the earth, that there exist righteous ones to whom it is happening as if for the work of the wicked ones, and there exist wicked ones to whom it is happening as if for the work of the righteous ones. I said that this too is vanity.

15 And I myself commended rejoicing, because mankind have nothing better under the sun than to eat and drink and rejoice, and that it should accompany them in their hard work for the days of their life, which the [true] God has given them under the sun. 16 In accord with this I applied my heart to know wisdom and to see the occupation that is carried on in the earth, because there is one seeing no sleep with his eyes, either by day or by night.

17 And I saw all the work of the [true] God, how mankind are not able to find out the work that has been done under the sun; however much mankind keep working hard to seek, yet they do not find out. And even if they should say they are wise enough to know, they would be unable to find out.

9 For I took all this to my heart, even to search out all this, that the righteous ones and the wise ones and their works are in the hand of the [true] God. Mankind are not aware of either the love or the hate that were all prior to them. 2 All are the same in what all have. One eventuality there is to the righteous one and the wicked one, the good one and the clean one and the unclean one, and the one sacrificing and the one that is not sacrificing. The good one is the same as the sinner; the one swearing is the same as whoever has been afraid of a sworn oath. 3 This is what is calamitous in all that has been done under the sun, that, because there is one eventuality to all, the heart of the sons of men is also full of bad; and there is madness in their heart during their lifetime, and after it—to the dead ones!

4 For as respects whoever is joined to all the living there exists confidence, because a live dog is better off than a dead lion. 5 For the living are conscious that they will die; but as for the dead, they are conscious of nothing at all, neither do they any more have wages, because the remembrance of them has been forgotten. 6 Also, their love and their hate and their jealousy have already perished, and they have no portion any more to time indefinite in anything that has to be done under the sun.

7 Go, eat your food with rejoicing and drink your wine with a good heart, because already the [true] God has found pleasure in your works. 8 On every occasion let your garments prove to be white, and let oil not be lacking upon your head. 9 See life with the wife whom you love all the days of your vain life that He has given you under the sun, all the days of your vanity, for that is your portion in life and in your hard work with which you are working hard under the sun. 10 All that your hand finds to do, do with your very power, for there is no work nor devising nor knowledge nor wisdom in She'ol, the place to which you are going.

11 I returned to see under the sun that the swift do not have the race, nor the mighty ones the battle, nor do the wise also have the food, nor do the understanding ones also have the riches, nor do even those having knowledge have the favor; because time and unforeseen occurrence befall them all. 12 For man also does not know his time. Just like fishes that are being taken in an evil net, and like birds that are being taken in a trap, so the sons of men themselves are being ensnared at a calamitous time, when it falls upon them suddenly.

13 Also this I saw as respects wisdom under the sun—and it was great to me: 14 There was a little city, and the men in it were few; and there came to it a great king, and he surrounded it and built against it great strongholds. 15 And there was found in it a man, needy [but] wise, and that one provided escape for the city by his wisdom. But no man remembered that needy man. 16 And I myself said: "Wisdom is better than mightiness; yet the wisdom of the needy one is despised, and his words are not listened to."

17 The words of the wise ones in quietness are more to be heard than the cry of one ruling among stupid people.

18 Wisdom is better than implements for fighting, and merely one sinner can destroy much good.

10 Dead flies are what cause the oil of the ointment maker to stink, to bubble forth. [So] a little foolishness does to one who is precious for wisdom and glory.

2 The heart of the wise is at his right hand, but the heart of the stupid at his left hand. 3 And also in whatever way the foolish one is walking, his own heart is lacking, and he certainly says to everybody that he is foolish.

4 If the spirit of a ruler should mount up against you, do not leave your own place, for calmness itself allays great sins.

5 There exists something calamitous that I have seen under the sun, as when there is a mistake going forth on account of the one in power: 6 Foolishness has been put in many high positions, but the rich ones themselves keep dwelling merely in a low condition.

7 I have seen servants on horses but princes walking on the earth just like servants.

8 He that is digging a pit will himself fall right into it; and he that is breaking through a stone wall, a serpent will bite him.

9 He that is quarrying out stones will hurt himself with them. He that is splitting logs will have to be careful with them.

10 If an iron tool has become blunt and someone has not whetted its edge, then he will exert his own vital energies. So the using of wisdom to success means advantage.

11 If the serpent bites when no charming results, then there is no advantage to the one indulging in the tongue.

12 The words of the mouth of the wise one mean favor, but the lips of the stupid one swallow him up. 13 The start of the words of his mouth is foolishness, and the end afterward of his mouth is calamitous madness. 14 And the foolish one speaks many words.

Man does not know what will come to be; and that which will come to be after him, who can tell him?

15 The hard work of the stupid ones makes them weary, because not one has come to know how to go to the city.

16 How will it be with you, O land, when your king is a boy and your own princes keep eating even in the morning? 17 Happy are you, O land, when your king is the son of noble ones and your own princes eat at the proper time for mightiness, not for mere drinking.

18 Through great laziness the beamwork sinks in, and through the letting down of the hands the house leaks.

19 Bread is for the laughter of the workers, and wine itself makes life rejoice; but money is what meets a response in all things.

20 Even in your bedroom do not call down evil upon the king himself, and in the interior rooms where you lie down do not call down evil upon anyone rich; for a flying creature of the heavens will convey the sound and something owning wings will tell the matter.

11 Send out your bread upon the surface of the waters, for in the course of many days you will find it again. 2 Give a portion to seven, or even to eight, for you do not know what calamity will occur on the earth.

3 If the clouds are filled [with water], they empty out a sheer downpour upon the earth; and if a tree falls to the south or if to the north, in the place where the tree falls there it will prove to be.

4 He that is watching the wind will not sow seed; and he that is looking at the clouds will not reap.

5 Just as you are not aware of what is the way of the spirit in the bones in the belly of her that is pregnant, in like manner you do not know the work of the [true] God, who does all things.

6 In the morning sow your seed and until the evening do not let your hand rest; for you are not knowing where this will have success, either here or there, or whether both of them will alike be good.

7 The light is also sweet, and it is good for the eyes to see the sun; **8** for if a man should live even many years, in all of them let him rejoice. And let him remember the days of darkness, though they could be many; every [day] that has come in is vanity.

9 Rejoice, young man, in your youth, and let your heart do you good in the days of your young manhood, and walk in the ways of your heart and in the things seen by your eyes. But know that on account of all these the [true] God will bring you into judgment. **10** So remove vexation from your heart, and ward off calamity from your flesh; for youth and the prime of life are vanity.

12 Remember, now, your grand Creator in the days of your young manhood, before the calamitous days proceed to come, or the years have arrived when you will say: "I have no delight in them"; **2** before the sun and the light and the moon and the stars grow dark, and the clouds have returned, afterward the downpour; **3** in the day when the keepers of the house tremble, and the men of vital energy have bent themselves, and the grinding women have quit working because they have become few, and

the ladies seeing at the windows have found it dark; **4** and the doors onto the street have been closed, when the sound of the grinding mill becomes low, and one gets up at the sound of a bird, and all the daughters of song sound low. **5** Also, they have become afraid merely at what is high, and there are terrors in the way. And the almond tree carries blossoms, and the grasshopper drags itself along, and the caper berry bursts, because man is walking to his long-lasting house and the wailers have marched around in the street; **6** before the silver cord is removed, and the golden bowl gets crushed, and the jar at the spring is broken, and the water wheel for the cistern has been crushed. **7** Then the dust returns to the earth just as it happened to be and the spirit itself returns to the [true] God who gave it.

8 "The greatest vanity!" said the congregator, "Everything is vanity."

9 And besides the fact that the congregator had become wise, he also taught the people knowledge continually, and he pondered and made a thorough search, that he might arrange many proverbs in order. **10** The congregator sought to find the delightful words and the writing of correct words of truth.

11 The words of the wise ones are like oxgoads, and just like nails driven in are those indulging in collections [of sentences]; they have been given from one shepherd. **12** As regards anything besides these, my son, take a warning: To the making of many books there is no end, and much devotion [to them] is wearisome to the flesh.

13 The conclusion of the matter, everything having been heard, is: Fear the [true] God and keep his commandments. For this is the whole [obligation] of man. **14** For the [true] God himself will bring every sort of work into the judgment in relation to every hidden thing, as to whether it is good or bad.

THE SONG OF SOLOMON

1 The superlative song, which is Sol′o·mon's: 2 "May he kiss me with the kisses of his mouth, for your expressions of endearment are better than wine. 3 For fragrance your oils are good. Like an oil that is poured out is your name. That is why maidens themselves have loved you. 4 Draw me with you; let us run. The king has brought me into his interior rooms! Do let us be joyful and rejoice in you. Do let us mention your expressions of endearment more than wine. Deservedly they have loved you.

5 "A black girl I am, but comely, O YOU daughters of Jerusalem, like the tents of Ke′dar, [yet] like the tent cloths of Sol′o·mon. 6 Do not YOU look at me because I am swarthy, because the sun has caught sight of me. The sons of my own mother grew angry with me; they appointed me the keeper of the vineyards, [although] my vineyard, one that was mine, I did not keep.

7 "Do tell me, O you whom my soul has loved, where you do shepherding, where you make the flock lie down at midday. Just why should I become like a woman wrapped in mourning among the droves of your partners?"

8 "If you do not know for yourself, O you most beautiful one among women, go out yourself in the footprints of the flock and pasture your kids of the goats alongside the tabernacles of the shepherds."

9 "To a mare of mine in the chariots of Phar′aoh I have likened you, O girl companion of mine. 10 Your cheeks are comely among the hair braids, your neck in a string of beads. 11 Circlets of gold we shall make for you, along with studs of silver."

12 "As long as the king is at his round table my own spikenard has given out its fragrance. 13 As a bag of myrrh my dear one is to me; between my breasts he will spend the night. 14 As a cluster of henna my dear one is to me, among the vineyards of En-ge′di."

15 "Look! You are beautiful, O girl companion of mine. Look! You are beautiful. Your eyes are [those of] doves."

16 "Look! You are beautiful, my dear one, also pleasant. Our divan also is one of foliage. 17 The beams of our grand house are cedars, our rafters juniper trees.

2 "A mere saffron of the coastal plain I am, a lily of the low plains."

2 "Like a lily among thorny weeds, so is my girl companion among the daughters."

3 "Like an apple tree among the trees of the forest, so is my dear one among the sons. His shade I have passionately desired, and there I have sat down, and his fruit has been sweet to my palate. 4 He brought me into the house of wine, and his banner over me was love. 5 Do YOU people refresh me with cakes of raisins, sustain me with apples; for I am lovesick. 6 His left hand is under my head; and his right hand—it embraces me. 7 I have put YOU under oath, O daughters of Jerusalem, by the female gazelles or by the hinds of the field, that YOU try not to awaken or arouse love [in me] until it feels inclined.

8 "The sound of my dear one! Look! This one is coming, climbing upon the mountains, leaping upon the hills. 9 My dear one is resembling a gazelle or the young of the stags. Look! This one is standing behind our wall, gazing through the windows, glancing through the lattices. 10 My dear one has answered and said to me, 'Rise up, you girl companion of mine, my beautiful one, and come away.

11 For, look! the rainy season itself has passed, the downpour itself is over, it has gone its way. **12** Blossoms themselves have appeared in the land, the very time of vine trimming has arrived, and the voice of the turtledove itself has been heard in our land. **13** As for the fig tree, it has gained a mature color for its early figs; and the vines are abloom, they have given [their] fragrance. Rise up, come, O girl companion of mine, my beautiful one, and come away. **14** O my dove in the retreats of the crag, in the concealed place of the steep way, show me your form, let me hear your voice, for your voice is pleasurable and your form is comely.'"

15 "Do you people grab hold of the foxes for us, the little foxes that are making spoil of the vineyards, as our vineyards are abloom."

16 "My dear one is mine and I am his. He is shepherding among the lilies. **17** Until the day breathes and the shadows have fled, turn around, O my dear one; be like the gazelle or like the young of the stags upon the mountains of separation.

3 "On my bed during the nights I have sought the one whom my soul has loved. I sought him, but I did not find him. **2** Let me rise up, please, and go round about in the city; in the streets and in the public squares let me seek the one whom my soul has loved. I sought him, but I did not find him. **3** The watchmen who were going around in the city found me, 'The one whom my soul has loved have you men seen?' **4** Hardly had I passed on from them until I found the one whom my soul has loved. I grabbed hold of him, and I would not let go of him, until I had brought him into my mother's house and into the interior room of her that had been pregnant with me. **5** I have put you under oath, O daughters of Jerusalem, by the female gazelles or by the hinds of the field, that you try not to awaken or arouse love [in me] until it feels inclined."

6 "What is this thing that is coming up from the wilderness like columns of smoke, being perfumed with myrrh and frankincense, even with every sort of scent powder of a trader?"

7 "Look! It is his couch, the one belonging to Sol′o·mon. Sixty mighty men are all around it, from the mighty men of Israel, **8** all of them in possession of a sword, being taught in warfare, each one with his sword upon his thigh because of dread during the nights."

9 "It is the litter that King Sol′o·mon has made for himself from the trees of Leb′a·non. **10** Its pillars he has made of silver, its supports of gold. Its seat is of wool dyed reddish purple, its interior being fitted out lovingly by the daughters of Jerusalem."

11 "Go out and look, O you daughters of Zion, on King Sol′o·mon with the wreath that his mother wove for him on the day of his marriage and on the day of the rejoicing of his heart."

4 "Look! You are beautiful, O girl companion of mine. Look! You are beautiful. Your eyes are [those of] doves, behind your veil. Your hair is like a drove of goats that have hopped down from the mountainous region of Gil′e·ad. **2** Your teeth are like a drove of freshly-shorn [ewes] that have gone up from the washing, all of which are bearing twins, with none among them having lost its young ones. **3** Your lips are just like a scarlet thread, and your speaking is agreeable. Like a segment of pomegranate are your temples behind your veil. **4** Your neck is like the tower of David, built in courses of stone, upon which are hung a thousand shields, all the circular shields of the mighty men. **5** Your two breasts are like two young ones, the twins of a female gazelle, that are feeding among the lilies."

6 "Until the day breathes and the shadows have fled, I shall go my way to the mountain of myrrh and to the hill of frankincense."

7 "You are altogether beautiful, O girl companion of mine, and there is no defect in you. 8 With me from Leb′a·non, O bride, with me from Leb′a·non may you come. May you descend from the top of Anti-Leb′a·non, from the top of Se′nir, even Her′mon, from the lairs of lions, from the mountains of leopards. 9 You have made my heart beat, O my sister, [my] bride, you have made my heart beat by one of your eyes, by one pendant of your necklace. 10 How beautiful your expressions of endearment are, O my sister, my bride! How much better are your expressions of endearment than wine and the fragrance of your oils than all sorts of perfume! 11 With comb honey your lips keep dripping, O [my] bride. Honey and milk are under your tongue, and the fragrance of your garments is like the fragrance of Leb′a·non. 12 A garden barred in is my sister, [my] bride, a garden barred in, a spring sealed up. 13 Your skin is a paradise of pomegranates, with the choicest fruits, henna plants along with spikenard plants; 14 spikenard and saffron, cane and cinnamon, along with all sorts of trees of frankincense, myrrh and aloes, along with all the finest perfumes; 15 [and] a spring of gardens, a well of fresh water, and trickling streams from Leb′a·non. 16 Awake, O north wind, and come in, O south wind. Breathe upon my garden. Let its perfumes trickle."

"Let my dear one come into his garden and eat its choicest fruits."

5 "I have come into my garden, O my sister, [my] bride. I have plucked my myrrh along with my spice. I have eaten my honeycomb along with my honey; I have drunk my wine along with my milk."

"Eat, O companions! Drink and become drunk with expressions of endearment!"

2 "I am asleep, but my heart is awake. There is the sound of my dear one knocking!"

"Open to me, O my sister, my girl companion, my dove, my blameless one! For my head is filled with dew, the locks of my hair with the drops of the night."

3 "'I have put off my robe. How can I put it back on? I have washed my feet. How can I soil them?' 4 My dear one himself pulled back his hand from the hole [of the door], and my inward parts themselves became boisterous within me. 5 I got up, even I, to open to my dear one, and my own hands dripped with myrrh and my fingers with liquid myrrh, upon the hollows of the lock. 6 I opened, even I, to my dear one, but my dear one himself had turned away, he had passed along. My very soul had gone out [of me] when he spoke. I sought him, but I did not find him. I called him, but he did not answer me. 7 The watchmen that were going about in the city found me. They struck me, they wounded me. The watchmen of the walls lifted my wide wrap off me.

8 "I have put you under oath, O daughters of Jerusalem, that, if you find my dear one, you should tell him that I am lovesick."

9 "How is your dear one more than any other dear one, O you most beautiful one among women? How is your dear one more than any other dear one, that you have put us under such an oath as this?"

10 "My dear one is dazzling and ruddy, the most conspicuous of ten thousand. 11 His head is gold, refined gold. The locks of his hair are date clusters. His black [hair] is like the raven. 12 His eyes are like doves by the channels of water, which are bathing themselves in milk, sitting within the rims. 13 His cheeks are like a garden bed of spice, towers of scented herbs. His lips are lilies, dripping with liquid myrrh. 14 His hands are cylinders of gold, filled with chrysolite. His abdomen is an ivory plate covered with sapphires. 15 His legs are pillars of marble based on socket pedestals of refined gold. His appearance is like Leb′a·non, choice like the cedars. 16 His palate is sheer sweetness, and everything about him is altogether desirable. This is my dear one, and this is my boy companion, O daughters of Jerusalem."

6 "Where has your dear one gone, O most beautiful one among women? Where has your dear one turned, that we may seek him with you?"

2 "My own dear one has gone down to his garden, to the garden beds of spice plants, to shepherd among the gardens, and to pick lilies. 3 I am my dear one's, and my dear one is mine. He is shepherding among the lilies."

4 "You are beautiful, O girl companion of mine, like Pleasant City, comely like Jerusalem, awesome as companies gathered around banners. 5 Turn your eyes away from in front of me, for they themselves have alarmed me. Your hair is like a drove of goats that have hopped down from Gil'e·ad. 6 Your teeth are like a drove of ewes that have come up from the washing, all of which are bearing twins, none among them having lost its young ones. 7 Like a segment of pomegranate are your temples behind your veil. 8 There may be sixty queens and eighty concubines and maidens without number. 9 One there is who is my dove, my blameless one. One there is who belongs to her mother. She is the pure one of the one giving birth to her. The daughters have seen her, and they proceeded to pronounce her happy; queens and concubines, and they proceeded to praise her, 10 'Who is this woman that is looking down like the dawn, beautiful like the full moon, pure like the glowing sun, awesome as companies gathered around banners?'"

11 "To the garden of nut trees I had gone down, to see the buds in the torrent valley, to see whether the vine had sprouted, whether the pomegranate trees had blossomed. 12 Before I knew it, my own soul had put me at the chariots of my willing people."

13 "Come back, come back, O Shu'lam·mite! Come back, come back, that we may behold you!"

"What do you people behold in the Shu'lam·mite?"

"Something like the dance of two camps!"

7 "How beautiful your steps have become in [your] sandals, O willing daughter! The curvings of your thighs are like ornaments, the work of an artisan's hands. 2 Your navel roll is a round bowl. Let not the mixed wine be lacking [from it]. Your belly is a heap of wheat, fenced about with lilies. 3 Your two breasts are like two young ones, the twins of a female gazelle. 4 Your neck is like an ivory tower. Your eyes are like the pools in Hesh'bon, by the gate of Bath·rab'bim. Your nose is like the tower of Leb'a·non, which is looking out toward Damascus. 5 Your head upon you is like Car'mel, and the tresses of your head are like wool dyed reddish purple. The king is held bound by the flowings. 6 How beautiful you are, and how pleasant you are, O beloved girl, among exquisite delights! 7 This stature of yours does resemble a palm tree, and your breasts, date clusters. 8 I have said, 'I shall go up on the palm tree, that I may take hold of its fruit stalks of dates.' And, please, may your breasts become like clusters of the vine, and the fragrance of your nose like apples, 9 and your palate like the best wine that is going with a slickness for my dear one, softly flowing over the lips of sleeping ones."

10 "I am my dear one's, and toward me is his craving. 11 Do come, O my dear one, let us go forth to the field; do let us lodge among the henna plants. 12 Do let us rise early and go to the vineyards, that we may see whether the vine has sprouted, the blossom has burst open, the pomegranate trees have bloomed. There I shall give my expressions of endearment to you. 13 The mandrakes themselves have given [their] fragrance, and by our entranceways there are all sorts of the choicest fruits. The new ones as well as the old, O my dear one, I have treasured up for you.

8 "O that you were like a brother of mine, sucking the breasts of my mother! Should I find you outside, I would kiss you. People would not even despise me. 2 I would lead you, I would bring you into the house of my mother, who used to teach me. I would give you a drink of spiced wine, the fresh juice of pomegranates. 3 His left hand would be under my head; and his right hand—it would embrace me.

4 "I have put you under oath, O daughters of Jerusalem, that you try not to awaken or arouse love [in me] until it feels inclined."

5 "Who is this woman coming up from the wilderness, leaning upon her dear one?"

"Under the apple tree I aroused you. There your mother was in birth pangs with you. There she that was giving birth to you experienced birth pangs.

6 "Place me as a seal upon your heart, as a seal upon your arm; because love is as strong as death is, insistence on exclusive devotion is as unyielding as She'ol is. Its blazings are the blazings of a fire, the flame of Jah. 7 Many waters themselves are not able to extinguish love, nor can rivers themselves wash it away. If a man would give all the valuable things of his house for love, persons would positively despise them."

8 "We have a little sister that does not have any breasts. What shall we do for our sister on the day that she will be spoken for?"

9 "If she should be a wall, we shall build upon her a battlement of silver; but if she should be a door, we shall block her up with a cedar plank."

10 "I am a wall, and my breasts are like towers. In this case I have become in his eyes like her that is finding peace.

11 "There was a vineyard that Sol'o·mon happened to have in Ba'al-ha'mon. He gave the vineyard over to the keepers. Each one would bring in for its fruitage a thousand silver pieces.

12 "My vineyard, which belongs to me, is at my disposal. The thousand belong to you, O Sol'o·mon, and two hundred to those keeping its fruitage."

13 "O you who are dwelling in the gardens, the partners are paying attention to your voice. Let me hear it."

14 "Run away, my dear one, and make yourself like a gazelle or like a young one of the stags upon the mountains of spices."

ISAIAH

1 The vision of Isaiah the son of A'moz that he visioned concerning Judah and Jerusalem in the days of Uz·zi'ah, Jo'tham, A'haz [and] Hez·e·ki'ah, kings of Judah:

2 Hear, O heavens, and give ear, O earth, for Jehovah himself has spoken: "Sons I have brought up and raised, but they themselves have revolted against me. 3 A bull well knows its buyer, and the ass the manger of its owner; Israel itself has not known, my own people have not behaved understandingly."

4 Woe to the sinful nation, the people heavy with error, an evil-doing seed, ruinous sons! They have left Jehovah, they have treated the Holy One of Israel with disrespect, they have turned backwards. 5 Where else will you be struck still more, in that you add more revolt? The whole head is in a sick condition, and the whole heart is feeble. 6 From the sole of the foot even to the head there is no sound spot in it. Wounds and bruises and fresh stripes—they have not been squeezed out or bound up, nor has there been a softening with oil.

7 YOUR land is a desolation, YOUR cities are burned with fire; YOUR ground—right in front of YOU strangers are eating it up, and the desolation is like an overthrow by strangers. 8 And the daughter of Zion has been left remaining like a booth in a vineyard, like a lookout hut in a field of cucumbers, like a blockaded city. 9 Unless Jehovah of armies himself had left remaining to us just a few survivors, we should have become just like Sod'om, we should have resembled Go·mor'rah itself.

10 Hear the word of Jehovah, YOU dictators of Sod'om. Give ear to the law of our God, YOU people of Go·mor'rah. 11 "Of what benefit to me is the multitude of YOUR sacrifices?" says Jehovah. "I have had enough of whole burnt offerings of rams and the fat of well-fed animals; and in the blood of young bulls and male lambs and he-goats I have taken no delight. 12 When YOU people keep coming in to see my face, who is it that has required this from YOUR hand, to trample my courtyards? 13 Stop bringing in any more valueless grain offerings. Incense—it is something detestable to me. New moon and sabbath, the calling of a convention—I cannot put up with the [use of] uncanny power along with the solemn assembly. 14 YOUR new moons and YOUR festal seasons my soul has hated. To me they have become a burden; I have become tired of bearing [them]. 15 And when YOU spread out YOUR palms, I hide my eyes from YOU. Even though YOU make many prayers, I am not listening; with bloodshed YOUR very hands have become filled. 16 Wash yourselves; make yourselves clean; remove the badness of YOUR dealings from in front of my eyes; cease to do bad. 17 Learn to do good; search for justice; set right the oppressor; render judgment for the fatherless boy; plead the cause of the widow."

18 "Come, now, YOU people, and let us set matters straight between us," says Jehovah. "Though the sins of YOU people should prove to be as scarlet, they will be made white just like snow; though they should be red like crimson cloth, they will become even like wool. 19 If YOU people show willingness and do listen, the good of the land YOU will eat. 20 But if YOU people refuse and are actually rebellious, with a sword YOU will be eaten up; for the very mouth of Jehovah has spoken [it]."

21 O how the faithful town has become a prostitute! She was full of justice; righteousness itself used to lodge in her, but now murderers. 22 Your silver itself has become scummy dross. Your wheat beer is diluted with water. 23 Your princes are stubborn and partners with thieves. Every one of them is a lover of a bribe and a chaser after gifts. For a fatherless boy they do not render judgment; and even the legal case of a widow does not get admittance to them.

24 Therefore the utterance of the [true] Lord, Jehovah of armies, the Powerful One of Israel, is: "Aha! I shall relieve myself of my adversaries, and I will avenge myself on my enemies. 25 And I will turn back my hand upon you, and I shall smelt away your scummy dross as with lye, and I will remove all your waste products. 26 And I will bring back again judges for you as at the first, and counselors for you as at the start. After this you will be called City of Righteousness, Faithful Town. 27 With justice Zion herself will be redeemed, and those returning of her, with righteousness. 28 And the crash of revolters and that of sinful ones will be at the same time, and those leaving Jehovah will come to their finish. 29 For they will be ashamed of the mighty trees that YOU people desired, and YOU will be abashed because of the gardens that YOU have chosen. 30 For YOU will become like a big tree the foliage of which is withering, and like a garden that has no water. 31 And the vigorous man will certainly become tow, and the product of his activity a spark; and both of them will certainly go up in

flames at the same time, with no one to do the extinguishing."

2 The thing that Isaiah the son of A'moz visioned concerning Judah and Jerusalem: 2 And it must occur in the final part of the days [that] the mountain of the house of Jehovah will become firmly established above the top of the mountains, and it will certainly be lifted up above the hills; and to it all the nations must stream. 3 And many peoples will certainly go and say: "Come, YOU people, and let us go up to the mountain of Jehovah, to the house of the God of Jacob; and he will instruct us about his ways, and we will walk in his paths." For out of Zion law will go forth, and the word of Jehovah out of Jerusalem. 4 And he will certainly render judgment among the nations and set matters straight respecting many peoples. And they will have to beat their swords into plowshares and their spears into pruning shears. Nation will not lift up sword against nation, neither will they learn war any more.

5 O men of the house of Jacob, come and let us walk in the light of Jehovah.

6 For you have forsaken your people, the house of Jacob. For they have become full of what is from the East, and they are practicers of magic like the Phi·lis'tines, and with the children of foreigners they abound. 7 And their land is filled with silver and gold, and there is no limit to their treasures. And their land is filled with horses, and there is no limit to their chariots. 8 And their land is filled with valueless gods. To the work of one's hands they bow down, to that which one's fingers have made. 9 And earthling man bows down, and man becomes low, and you cannot possibly pardon them.

10 Enter into the rock and hide yourself in the dust because of the dreadfulness of Jehovah, and from his splendid superiority. 11 The haughty eyes of earthling man must become low, and the loftiness of men must bow down; and Jehovah alone must be put on high in that day. 12 For it is the day belonging to Jehovah of armies. It is upon everyone self-exalted and lofty and upon everyone lifted up or low; 13 and upon all the cedars of Leb'a·non that are lofty and lifted up and upon all the massive trees of Ba'shan; 14 and upon all the lofty mountains and upon all the hills that are lifted up; 15 and upon every high tower and upon every fortified wall; 16 and upon all the ships of Tar'shish and upon all desirable boats. 17 And the haughtiness of the earthling man must bow down, and the loftiness of men must become low; and Jehovah alone must be put on high in that day.

18 And the valueless gods themselves will pass away completely. 19 And people will enter into the caves of the rocks and into the holes of the dust because of the dreadfulness of Jehovah and from his splendid superiority, when he rises up for the earth to suffer shocks. 20 In that day the earthling man will throw his worthless gods of silver and his valueless gods of gold that they had made for him to bow before to the shrewmice and to the bats, 21 in order to enter into the holes in the rocks and into the clefts of the crags, because of the dreadfulness of Jehovah and from his splendid superiority, when he rises up for the earth to suffer shocks. 22 For YOUR own sakes, hold off from the earthling man, whose breath is in his nostrils, for on what basis is he himself to be taken into account?

3 For, look! the [true] Lord, Jehovah of armies, is removing from Jerusalem and from Judah support and stay, the whole support of bread and the whole support of water, 2 mighty man and warrior, judge and prophet, and practicer of divination and elderly man, 3 chief of fifty and highly respected man and counselor and expert in magical arts, and the skilled charmer. 4 And I shall certainly make boys their princes, and mere arbitrary power will rule over them. 5 And the people will actually tyrannize one over the other, even each one over his fellow man. They will storm, the boy against the old man, and the lightly esteemed one against the one to be honored. 6 For each one will lay hold of his brother in the house of his father, [saying:] "You have a mantle. A dictator you ought to become to us, and this overthrown mass should be under your hand." 7 He will raise [his voice] in that day, saying: "I shall not become a wound dresser; and in my house there is neither bread nor a mantle. You men must not set me as dictator over the people."

8 For Jerusalem has stumbled, and Judah itself has fallen, because their tongue and their dealings are against Jehovah, in behaving rebelliously in the eyes of his glory. 9 The very expression of their faces actually testifies against them, and of their sin like that of Sod'om they do tell. They have not hidden [it]. Woe to their soul! For they have dealt out to themselves calamity.

10 Say, you men, that it [will be] well with the righteous one, for they will eat the very fruitage of their dealings. 11 Woe to the wicked one!—Calamity; for the treatment [rendered] by his own hands will be rendered to him! 12 As for my people, its task assigners are dealing severely, and mere women actually rule over it. O my people, those leading you on are causing [you] to wander, and the way of your paths they have confused.

13 Jehovah is stationing himself to contend and is standing up to pass sentence upon peoples. 14 Jehovah himself will enter into judgment with the elderly ones of his people and its princes.

"And you yourselves have burned down the vineyard. What was taken by robbery from the afflicted one is in your houses. 15 What do you men mean in that you crush my people, and that you grind the very faces of the afflicted ones?" is the utterance of the Sovereign Lord, Jehovah of armies.

16 And Jehovah says: "For the reason that the daughters of Zion have become haughty and they walk with their throats stretched forth and ogling with their eyes, they go walking with tripping steps, and with their feet they make a tinkling sound, 17 Jehovah also will actually make the crown of the head of the daughters of Zion scabby, and Jehovah himself will lay their very forehead bare. 18 In that day Jehovah will take away the beauty of the bangles and the headbands and the moon-shaped ornaments, 19 the eardrops and the bracelets and the veils, 20 the headdresses and the step chains and the breastbands and the 'houses of the soul' and the ornamental humming shells, 21 the finger rings and the nose rings, 22 the robes of state and the overtunics and the cloaks and the purses, 23 and the hand mirrors and the undergarments and the turbans and the large veils.

24 "And it must occur that instead of balsam oil there will come to be merely a musty smell; and instead of a belt, a rope; and instead of an artistic hair arrangement, baldness; and instead of a rich garment, a girding of sackcloth; a brand mark instead of prettiness. 25 By the sword your own men will fall, and your mightiness by war. 26 And her entrances will have to mourn and express sorrow, and she will certainly be cleaned out. She will sit down on the very earth."

4 And seven women will actually grab hold of one man in that day, saying: "We shall eat our own bread and wear our own mantles; only may we be called by your name to take away our reproach."

2 In that day what Jehovah makes sprout will come to be for decoration and for glory, and the fruitage of the land will be something to be proud of and something beautiful for those of Israel who have escaped. 3 And it must occur that the ones remaining in Zion and the ones left over in

Jerusalem will be said to be holy to him, everyone written down for life in Jerusalem.

4 When Jehovah will have washed away the excrement of the daughters of Zion and he will rinse away even the bloodshed of Jerusalem from within her by the spirit of judgment and by the spirit of burning down, 5 Jehovah will also certainly create over every established place of Mount Zion and over her convention place a cloud by day and a smoke, and the brightness of a flaming fire by night; because over all the glory there will be a shelter. 6 And there will come to be a booth for a shade by day from the dry heat, and for a refuge and for a hiding place from the rainstorm and from the precipitation.

5 Let me sing, please, to my beloved one a song of my loved one concerning his vineyard. There was a vineyard that my beloved one came to have on a fruitful hillside. 2 And he proceeded to dig it up and to rid it of stones and to plant it with a choice red vine, and to build a tower in the middle of it. And there was also a wine press that he hewed out in it. And he kept hoping for it to produce grapes, but it gradually produced wild grapes.

3 "And now, O you inhabitants of Jerusalem and you men of Judah, please judge between me and my vineyard. 4 What is there yet to do for my vineyard that I have not already done in it? Why is it that I hoped for it to produce grapes, but it gradually produced wild grapes? 5 And now, please, may I make known to you men what I am doing to my vineyard: There will be a removing of its hedge, and it must be destined for burning down. There must be a breaking down of its stone wall, and it must be destined for a place of trampling. 6 And I shall set it as a thing destroyed. It will not be pruned, nor will it be hoed. And it must come up with the thornbush and weeds; and upon the clouds I shall lay a command to keep from precipitating any rain upon it. 7 For the vineyard of Jehovah of armies is the house of Israel, and the men of Judah are the plantation of which he was fond. And he kept hoping for judgment, but, look! the breaking of law; for righteousness, but, look! an outcry."

8 Woe to the ones joining house to house, [and] those who annex field to field until there is no more room and you men have been made to dwell all by yourselves in the midst of the land! 9 In my ears Jehovah of armies [has sworn that] many houses, though great and good, will become an outright object of astonishment, without an inhabitant. 10 For even ten acres of vineyard will produce but one bath measure, and even a homer measure of seed will produce but an e'phah measure.

11 Woe to those who are getting up early in the morning that they may seek just intoxicating liquor, who are lingering till late in the evening darkness so that wine itself inflames them! 12 And there must prove to be harp and stringed instrument, tambourine and flute, and wine at their feasts; but the activity of Jehovah they do not look at, and the work of his hands they have not seen.

13 Therefore my people will have to go into exile for lack of knowledge; and their glory will be famished men, and their crowd will be parched with thirst. 14 Therefore She'ol has made its soul spacious and has opened its mouth wide beyond bounds; and what is splendid in her, also her crowd and her uproar and the exultant one, will certainly go down into it. 15 And earthling man will bow down, and man will become low, and even the eyes of the high ones will become low. 16 And Jehovah of armies will become high through judgment, and the [true] God, the Holy One, will certainly sanctify himself through righteousness. 17 And the male lambs will actually graze as in their pasture; and the desolate places of well-fed animals alien residents will eat.

18 Woe to those drawing error with ropes of untruth, and as with wagon cords sin; 19 those who are saying: "Let his work hasten; do let it come quickly, in order that we may see [it]; and let the counsel of the Holy One of Israel draw near and come, that we may know [it]!"

20 Woe to those who are saying that good is bad and bad is good, those who are putting darkness for light and light for darkness, those who are putting bitter for sweet and sweet for bitter!

21 Woe to those wise in their own eyes and discreet even in front of their own faces!

22 Woe to those who are mighty in drinking wine, and to the men with vital energy for mixing intoxicating liquor, 23 those who are pronouncing the wicked one righteous in consideration of a bribe, and who take away even the righteousness of the righteous one from him!

24 Therefore just as a tongue of fire eats up the stubble and into the flames mere dried grass sinks down, their very rootstock will become just like a musty smell, and their blossom itself will go up just like powder, because they have rejected the law of Jehovah of armies, and the saying of the Holy One of Israel they have disrespected. 25 That is why the anger of Jehovah has grown hot against his people, and he will stretch out his hand against them and strike them. And the mountains will be agitated, and their dead bodies will become like the offal in the midst of the streets.

In view of all this his anger has not turned back, but his hand is stretched out still. 26 And he has raised up a signal to a great nation far away, and he has whistled to it at the extremity of the earth; and, look! in haste it will swiftly come in. 27 There is no one tired nor is anyone stumbling among them. No one is drowsy and no one sleeps. And the belt around their loins will certainly not be opened, nor the laces of their sandals be torn in two; 28 because their arrows are sharpened and all their bows are bent. The very hoofs of their horses will have to be accounted as flint itself, and their wheels as a stormwind. 29 The roaring of theirs is like that of a lion, and they roar like maned young lions. And they will growl and grab hold of the prey and bring [it] safely away, and there will be no deliverer. 30 And they will growl over it in that day as with the growling of the sea. And one will actually gaze at the land, and, look! there is distressing darkness; and even the light has grown dark because of the drops falling on it.

6 In the year that King Uz·zi′ah died I, however, got to see Jehovah, sitting on a throne lofty and lifted up, and his skirts were filling the temple. 2 Seraphs were standing above him. Each one had six wings. With two he kept his face covered, and with two he kept his feet covered, and with two he would fly about. 3 And this one called to that one and said: "Holy, holy, holy is Jehovah of armies. The fullness of all the earth is his glory." 4 And the pivots of the thresholds began to quiver at the voice of the one calling, and the house itself gradually filled with smoke.

5 And I proceeded to say: "Woe to me! For I am as good as brought to silence, because a man unclean in lips I am, and in among a people unclean in lips I am dwelling; for my eyes have seen the King, Jehovah of armies, himself!"

6 At that, one of the seraphs flew to me, and in his hand there was a glowing coal that he had taken with tongs off the altar. 7 And he proceeded to touch my mouth and to say: "Look! This has touched your lips, and your error has departed and your sin itself is atoned for."

8 And I began to hear the voice of Jehovah saying: "Whom shall I send, and who will go for us?" And I proceeded to say: "Here I am! Send me." 9 And he went on to say: "Go, and you must say to this

people, 'Hear again and again, O men, but do not understand; and see again and again, but do not get any knowledge.' 10 Make the heart of this people unreceptive, and make their very ears unresponsive, and paste their very eyes together, that they may not see with their eyes and with their ears they may not hear, and that their own heart may not understand and that they may not actually turn back and get healing for themselves."

11 At this I said: "How long, O Jehovah?" Then he said: "Until the cities actually crash in ruins, to be without an inhabitant, and the houses be without earthling man, and the ground itself is ruined into a desolation; 12 and Jehovah actually removes earthling men far away, and the deserted condition does become very extensive in the midst of the land. 13 And there will still be in it a tenth, and it must again become something for burning down, like a big tree and like a massive tree in which, when there is a cutting down [of them], there is a stump; a holy seed will be the stump of it."

7 Now it came about in the days of A'haz the son of Jo'tham the son of Uz·zi'ah, the king of Judah, that Re'zin the king of Syria and Pe'kah the son of Rem·a·li'ah, the king of Israel, came up to Jerusalem for war against it, and he proved unable to war against it. 2 And a report was made to the house of David, saying: "Syria has leaned upon E'phra·im."

And his heart and the heart of his people began to quiver, like the quivering of the trees of the forest because of a wind.

3 And Jehovah proceeded to say to Isaiah: "Go out, please, to meet A'haz, you and She'ar-jash'ub your son, to the end of the conduit of the upper pool by the highway of the laundryman's field. 4 And you must say to him, 'Watch yourself and keep undisturbed. Do not be afraid, and do not let your heart itself be timid because of the two tail-ends of these smoking logs,

because of the hot anger of Re'zin and Syria and the son of Rem·a·li'ah, 5 for the reason that Syria [with] E'phra·im and the son of Rem·a·li'ah has advised what is bad against you, saying: 6 "Let us go up against Judah and tear it apart and by breakthroughs take it for ourselves; and let us make another king reign inside it, the son of Ta'be·el."'

7 " 'This is what the Lord Jehovah has said: "It will not stand, neither will it take place. 8 For the head of Syria is Damascus, and the head of Damascus is Re'zin; and within just sixty-five years E'phra·im will be shattered to pieces so as not to be a people. 9 And the head of E'phra·im is Sa·mar'i·a, and the head of Sa·mar'i·a is the son of Rem·a·li'ah. Unless you people have faith, you will in that case not be of long duration." ' "

10 And Jehovah went on speaking some more to A'haz, saying: 11 "Ask for yourself a sign from Jehovah your God, making it as deep as She'ol or making it high as the upper regions." 12 But A'haz said: "I shall not ask, neither shall I put Jehovah to the test."

13 And he proceeded to say: "Listen, please, O house of David. Is it such a little thing for you to tire out men, that you should also tire out my God? 14 Therefore Jehovah himself will give you men a sign: Look! The maiden herself will actually become pregnant, and she is giving birth to a son, and she will certainly call his name Im·man'u·el. 15 Butter and honey he will eat by the time that he knows how to reject the bad and choose the good. 16 For before the boy will know how to reject the bad and choose the good, the ground of whose two kings you are feeling a sickening dread will be left entirely. 17 Jehovah will bring against you and against your people and against the house of your father days such as have not come since the day of E'phra·im's turning away from alongside Judah, namely, the king of As·syr'i·a.

18 "And it must occur in that day that Jehovah will whistle for the flies that are at the extremity of the Nile canals of Egypt and for the bees that are in the land of As·syr'i·a, 19 and they will certainly come in and settle down, all of them, upon the precipitous torrent valleys and upon the clefts of the crags and upon all the thorn thickets and upon all the watering places.

20 "In that day, by means of a hired razor in the region of the River, even by means of the king of As·syr'i·a, Jehovah will shave the head and the hair of the feet, and it will sweep away even the beard itself.

21 "And it must occur in that day that an individual will preserve alive a young cow of the herd and two sheep. 22 And it must occur that, due to the abundance of the producing of milk, he will eat butter; because butter and honey are what everyone left remaining in the midst of the land will eat.

23 "And it must occur in that day that every place where there used to be a thousand vines, worth a thousand pieces of silver, will come to be—for the thornbushes and for the weeds it will come to be. 24 With arrows and the bow he will come there, because all the land will become mere thornbushes and weeds. 25 And all the mountains that used to be cleared of troublesome plants with a hoe—you will not come there for fear of thornbushes and weeds; and it will certainly become a place for letting bulls loose and a trampling ground of sheep."

8 And Jehovah proceeded to say to me: "Take for yourself a large tablet and write upon it with the stylus of mortal man, 'Ma'her-shal'al-hash-baz.' 2 And let me have attestation for myself by faithful witnesses, U·ri'ah the priest and Zech·a·ri'ah the son of Je·ber·e·chi'ah."

3 Then I went near to the prophetess, and she came to be pregnant and in time gave birth to a son. Jehovah now said to me: "Call his name Ma'her-shal'al-hash-baz, 4 for before the boy will know how to call out, 'My father!' and 'My mother!' one will carry away the resources of Damascus and the spoil of Sa·mar'i·a before the king of As·syr'i·a."

5 And Jehovah proceeded to speak yet further to me, saying: 6 "For the reason that this people has rejected the waters of the Shi·lo'ah that are going gently, and there is exultation over Re'zin and the son of Rem·a·li'ah; 7 even therefore, look! Jehovah is bringing up against them the mighty and the many waters of the River, the king of As·syr'i·a and all his glory. And he will certainly come up over all his stream beds and go over all his banks 8 and move on through Judah. He will actually flood and pass over. Up to the neck he will reach. And the outspreading of his wings must occur to fill the breadth of your land, O Im·man'u·el!"

9 Be injurious, O you peoples, and be shattered to pieces; and give ear, all you in distant parts of the earth! Gird yourselves, and be shattered to pieces! Gird yourselves, and be shattered to pieces! 10 Plan out a scheme, and it will be broken up! Speak any word, and it will not stand, for God is with us! 11 For this is what Jehovah has said to me with strongness of the hand, that he may make me turn aside from walking in the way of this people, saying: 12 "You men must not say, 'A conspiracy!' respecting all that of which this people keep saying, 'A conspiracy!' and the object of their fear you men must not fear, nor must you tremble at it. 13 Jehovah of armies—he is the One whom you should treat as holy, and he should be the object of your fear, and he should be the One causing you to tremble."

14 And he must become as a sacred place; but as a stone to strike against and as a rock over which to stumble to both the houses

of Israel, as a trap and as a snare to the inhabitants of Jerusalem. 15 And many among them will be certain to stumble and to fall and be broken, and to be snared and caught.

16 Wrap up the attestation, put a seal about the law among my disciples! 17 And I will keep in expectation of Jehovah, who is concealing his face from the house of Jacob, and I will hope in him.

18 Look! I and the children whom Jehovah has given me are as signs and as miracles in Israel from Jehovah of armies, who is residing in Mount Zion.

19 And in case they should say to YOU people: "Apply to the spiritistic mediums or to those having a spirit of prediction who are chirping and making utterances in low tones," is it not to its God that any people should apply? [Should there be application] to dead persons in behalf of living persons? 20 To the law and to the attestation!

Surely they will keep saying what is according to this statement that will have no light of dawn. 21 And each one will certainly pass through the land hard pressed and hungry; and it must occur that because he is hungry and has made himself feel indignant, he will actually call down evil upon his king and upon his God and will certainly peer upward. 22 And to the earth he will look, and, lo! distress and darkness, obscurity, hard times and gloominess with no brightness.

9 However, the obscureness will not be as when the land had stress, as at the former time when one treated with contempt the land of Zeb'u·lun and the land of Naph'ta·li and when at the later time one caused [it] to be honored—the way by the sea, in the region of the Jordan, Gal'i·lee of the nations. 2 The people that were walking in the darkness have seen a great light. As for those dwelling in the land of deep shadow, light itself has shone upon them. 3 You have made the nation populous; for it

you have made the rejoicing great. They have rejoiced before you as with the rejoicing in the harvesttime, as those who are joyful when they divide up the spoil.

4 For the yoke of their load and the rod upon their shoulders, the staff of the one driving them to work, you have shattered to pieces as in the day of Mid'i·an. 5 For every boot of the one tramping with tremors and the mantle rolled in blood have even come to be for burning as food for fire. 6 For there has been a child born to us, there has been a son given to us; and the princely rule will come to be upon his shoulder. And his name will be called Wonderful Counselor, Mighty God, Eternal Father, Prince of Peace. 7 To the abundance of the princely rule and to peace there will be no end, upon the throne of David and upon his kingdom in order to establish it firmly and to sustain it by means of justice and by means of righteousness, from now on and to time indefinite. The very zeal of Jehovah of armies will do this.

8 There was a word that Jehovah sent against Jacob, and it fell upon Israel. 9 And the people will certainly know [it], even all of them, E'phra·im and the inhabitant of Sa·mar'i·a, because of [their] haughtiness and because of [their] insolence of heart in saying: 10 "Bricks are what have fallen, but with hewn stone we shall build. Sycamore trees are what have been cut down, but with cedars we shall make replacement." 11 And Jehovah will set the adversaries of Re'zin on high against him, and the enemies of that one he will goad on, 12 Syria from the east and the Phi·lis'tines from behind, and they will eat up Israel with open mouth. In view of all this his anger has not turned back, but his hand is stretched out still.

13 And the people themselves have not returned to the One striking them, and Jehovah of armies they have not sought. 14 And Jehovah will cut off from Israel head and tail, shoot and rush, in

one day. 15 The aged and highly respected one is the head, and the prophet giving false instruction is the tail. 16 And those who are leading this people on prove to be the ones causing [them] to wander; and those of them who are being led on, the ones who are being confused. 17 That is why Jehovah will not rejoice even over their young men, and upon their fatherless boys and upon their widows he will have no mercy; because all of them are apostates and evildoers and every mouth is speaking senselessness. In view of all this his anger has not turned back, but his hand is stretched out still.

18 For wickedness has become aflame just like a fire; thornbushes and weeds it will eat up. And it will catch fire in the thickets of the forest, and they will be borne aloft as the billowing of smoke. 19 In the fury of Jehovah of armies the land has been set afire, and the people will become as food for the fire. No one will show compassion even on his brother. 20 And one will cut down on the right and will certainly be hungry; and one will eat on the left, and they will certainly not be satisfied. They will each one eat the flesh of his own arm, 21 Ma·nas'seh E'phra·im, and E'phra·im Ma·nas'seh. Together they will be against Judah. In view of all this his anger has not turned back, but his hand is stretched out still.

10 Woe to those who are enacting harmful regulations and those who, constantly writing, have written out sheer trouble, 2 in order to push away the lowly ones from a legal case and to wrest away justice from the afflicted ones of my people, for the widows to become their spoil, and that they may plunder even the fatherless boys! 3 And what will you men do at the day of being given attention and at the ruin, when it comes from far away? Toward whom will you flee for assistance, and where will you leave your glory, 4 except it be that one must bow down under the prisoners and that people

keep falling under those who have been killed? In view of all this his anger has not turned back, but his hand is stretched out still.

5 "Aha, the As·syr'i·an, the rod for my anger, and the stick that is in their hand for my denunciation! 6 Against an apostate nation I shall send him, and against the people of my fury I shall issue a command to him, to take much spoil and to take much plunder and to make it a trampling place like the clay of the streets. 7 Though he may not be that way, he will feel inclined; though his heart may not be that way, he will scheme, because to annihilate is in his heart, and to cut off nations not a few. 8 For he will say, 'Are not my princes at the same time kings? 9 Is not Cal'no just like Car'che·mish? Is not Ha'math just like Ar'pad? Is not Sa·mar'i·a just like Damascus? 10 Whenever my hand has reached the kingdoms of the valueless god whose graven images are more than those at Jerusalem and at Sa·mar'i·a, 11 will it not be that just as I shall have done to Sa·mar'i·a and to her valueless gods, even so I shall do to Jerusalem and to her idols?'

12 "And it must occur that when Jehovah terminates all his work in Mount Zion and in Jerusalem, I shall make an accounting for the fruitage of the insolence of the heart of the king of As·syr'i·a and for the self-importance of his loftiness of eyes. 13 For he has said, 'With the power of my hand I shall certainly act, and with my wisdom, for I do have understanding; and I shall remove the boundaries of peoples, and their things stored up I shall certainly pillage, and I shall bring down the inhabitants just like a powerful one. 14 And just as if a nest, my hand will reach the resources of the peoples; and just as when one gathers eggs that have been left, I myself will gather up even all the earth, and there will certainly be no one fluttering [his] wings or opening [his] mouth or chirping.' "

15 Will the ax enhance itself over the one chopping with it, or the saw magnify itself over the one moving it back and forth, as though the staff moved back and forth the ones raising it on high, as though the rod raised on high the one who is not wood? 16 Therefore the [true] Lord, Jehovah of armies, will keep sending upon his fat ones a wasting disease, and under his glory a burning will keep burning away like the burning of a fire. 17 And Israel's Light must become a fire, and his Holy One a flame; and it must blaze up and eat up his weeds and his thornbushes in one day. 18 And the glory of his forest and of his orchard He will bring to an end, even from the soul clear to the flesh, and it must become like the melting away of one that is ailing. 19 And the rest of the trees of his forest—they will become such a number that a mere boy will be able to write them down.

20 And it will certainly occur in that day that those remaining over of Israel and those who have escaped of the house of Jacob will never again support themselves upon the one striking them, and they will certainly support themselves upon Jehovah, the Holy One of Israel, in trueness. 21 A mere remnant will return, the remnant of Jacob, to the Mighty God. 22 For although your people, O Israel, would prove to be like the grains of sand of the sea, a mere remnant among them will return. An extermination decided upon will be flooding through in righteousness, 23 because an exterminating and a strict decision the Sovereign Lord, Jehovah of armies, will be executing in the midst of the whole land.

24 Therefore this is what the Sovereign Lord, Jehovah of armies, has said: "Do not be afraid, O my people who are dwelling in Zion, because of the As·syr′i·an, who with the rod used to strike [you] and who used to lift up his own staff against you in the way that Egypt did. 25 For yet a very little while—and the denunciation will have come to an end, and my anger, in their wearing away. 26 And Jehovah of armies will certainly brandish against him a whip as at the defeat of Mid′i·an by the rock O′reb; and his staff will be upon the sea, and he will certainly lift it up in the way that he did with Egypt.

27 "And it must occur in that day that his load will depart from upon your shoulder, and his yoke from upon your neck, and the yoke will certainly be wrecked because of the oil."

28 He has come upon Ai′ath; he has passed along through Mig′ron; at Mich′mash he deposits his articles. 29 They have passed over the ford, Ge′ba is a place for them to spend the night, Ra′mah has trembled, Gib′e·ah of Saul itself has fled. 30 Let your voice out in shrill cries, O daughter of Gal′lim. Pay attention, O La′i·shah. O you afflicted one, An′a·thoth! 31 Mad·me′nah has run away. The inhabitants of Ge′bim themselves have taken to shelter. 32 It is yet day in Nob to make a halt. He waves his hand [threateningly] at the mountain of the daughter of Zion, the hill of Jerusalem.

33 Look! The [true] Lord, Jehovah of armies, is lopping off boughs with a terrible crash; and those tall in growth are being cut down, and the high ones themselves become low. 34 And he has struck down the thickets of the forest with an iron tool, and by a powerful one Leb′a·non itself will fall.

11 And there must go forth a twig out of the stump of Jes′se; and out of his roots a sprout will be fruitful. 2 And upon him the spirit of Jehovah must settle down, the spirit of wisdom and of understanding, the spirit of counsel and of mightiness, the spirit of knowledge and of the fear of Jehovah; 3 and there will be enjoyment by him in the fear of Jehovah.

And he will not judge by any mere appearance to his eyes, nor reprove simply according to the thing heard by his ears. 4 And with righteousness he must judge the lowly ones, and with uprightness he must give reproof in behalf of the meek ones of the earth. And he must strike the earth with the rod of his mouth; and with the spirit of his lips he will put the wicked one to death. 5 And righteousness must prove to be the belt of his hips, and faithfulness the belt of his loins.

6 And the wolf will actually reside for a while with the male lamb, and with the kid the leopard itself will lie down, and the calf and the maned young lion and the well-fed animal all together; and a mere little boy will be leader over them. 7 And the cow and the bear themselves will feed; together their young ones will lie down. And even the lion will eat straw just like the bull. 8 And the sucking child will certainly play upon the hole of the cobra; and upon the light aperture of a poisonous snake will a weaned child actually put his own hand. 9 They will not do any harm or cause any ruin in all my holy mountain; because the earth will certainly be filled with the knowledge of Jehovah as the waters are covering the very sea.

10 And it must occur in that day that there will be the root of Jes'se that will be standing up as a signal for the peoples. To him even the nations will turn inquiringly, and his resting place must become glorious.

11 And it must occur in that day that Jehovah will again offer his hand, a second time, to acquire the remnant of his people who will remain over from As·syr'i·a and from Egypt and from Path'ros and from Cush and from E'lam and from Shi'nar and from Ha'math and from the islands of the sea. 12 And he will certainly raise up a signal for the nations and gather the dispersed ones of Israel; and the scattered ones of Judah he will collect together from the four extremities of the earth.

13 And the jealousy of E'phra·im must depart, and even those showing hostility to Judah will be cut off. E'phra·im itself will not be jealous of Judah, nor will Judah show hostility toward E'phra·im. 14 And they must fly at the shoulder of the Phi·lis'tines to the west; together they will plunder the sons of the East. E'dom and Mo'ab will be those upon whom they will thrust out their hand, and the sons of Am'mon will be their subjects. 15 And Jehovah will certainly cut off the tongue of the Egyptian sea, and wave his hand at the River in the glow of his spirit. And he must strike it in [its] seven torrents, and he will actually cause people to walk in [their] sandals. 16 And there must come to be a highway out of As·syr'i·a for the remnant of his people who will remain over, just as there came to be [one] for Israel in the day of his coming up out of the land of Egypt.

12 And in that day you will be sure to say: "I shall thank you, O Jehovah, for [although] you got incensed at me, your anger gradually turned back, and you proceeded to comfort me. 2 Look! God is my salvation. I shall trust and be in no dread; for Jah Jehovah is my strength and [my] might, and he came to be the salvation of me."

3 With exultation you people will be certain to draw water out of the springs of salvation. 4 And in that day you will certainly say: "Give thanks to Jehovah, you people! Call upon his name. Make known among the peoples his dealings. Make mention that his name is put on high. 5 Make melody to Jehovah, for he has done surpassingly. This is made known in all the earth.

6 "Cry out shrilly and shout for joy, O you inhabitress of Zion, for great in the midst of you is the Holy One of Israel."

13 The pronouncement against Babylon that Isaiah the son of A'moz saw in vision: 2 "Upon a mountain of bare rocks raise up a signal, you men. Lift up the voice to them, wave the hand, that they may come into the entrances of the nobles. 3 I myself have issued the command to my sanctified ones. I have also called my mighty ones for [expressing] my anger, my eminently exultant ones. 4 Listen! A crowd in the mountains, something like a numerous people! Listen! The uproar of kingdoms, of nations gathered together! Jehovah of armies is mustering the army of war. 5 They are coming from the land far away, from the extremity of the heavens, Jehovah and the weapons of his denunciation, to wreck all the earth.

6 "Howl, YOU people, for the day of Jehovah is near! As a despoiling from the Almighty it will come. 7 That is why all hands themselves will drop down, and the whole heart itself of mortal man will melt. 8 And people have become disturbed. Convulsions and birth pains themselves grab hold; like a woman that is giving birth they have labor pains. They look at each other in amazement. Their faces are inflamed faces.

9 "Look! The day of Jehovah itself is coming, cruel both with fury and with burning anger, in order to make the land an object of astonishment, and that it may annihilate [the land's] sinners out of it. 10 For the very stars of the heavens and their constellations of Ke'sil will not flash forth their light; the sun will actually grow dark at its going forth, and the moon itself will not cause its light to shine. 11 And I shall certainly bring home [its own] badness upon the productive land, and their own error upon the wicked themselves. And I shall actually cause the pride of the presumptuous ones to cease, and the haughtiness of the tyrants I shall abase. 12 I shall make mortal man rarer than refined gold, and earthling man [rarer] than the gold of O'phir. 13 That is why I shall cause heaven itself to become agitated, and the earth will rock out of its place at the fury of Jehovah of armies and at the day of his burning anger. 14 And it must occur that, like a gazelle chased away and like a flock without anyone to collect them together, they will turn, each one to his own people; and they will flee, each one to his own land. 15 Every one that is found will be pierced through, and every one that is caught in the sweep will fall by the sword; 16 and their very children will be dashed to pieces before their eyes. Their houses will be pillaged, and their own wives will be raped.

17 "Here I am arousing against them the Medes, who account silver itself as nothing and who, as respects gold, take no delight in it. 18 And [their] bows will dash even young men to pieces. And the fruitage of the belly they will not pity; for sons their eye will not feel sorry. 19 And Babylon, the decoration of kingdoms, the beauty of the pride of the Chal·de'ans, must become as when God overthrew Sod'om and Go·mor'rah. 20 She will never be inhabited, nor will she reside for generation after generation. And there the Arab will not pitch his tent, and no shepherds will let [their flocks] lie down there. 21 And there the haunters of waterless regions will certainly lie down, and their houses must be filled with eagle owls. And there the ostriches must reside, and goat-shaped demons themselves will go skipping about there. 22 And jackals must howl in her dwelling towers, and the big snake will be in the palaces of exquisite delight. And the season for her is near to come, and her days themselves will not be postponed."

14 For Jehovah will show mercy to Jacob, and he is yet certain to choose Israel; and he will actually give them rest upon their soil, and the alien resident must be joined to them, and they must attach themselves to the house of Jacob. 2 And peoples will actually take them and bring them to their own place, and the house of Israel must take them to themselves as a possession upon the soil of Jehovah as menservants and as maidservants; and they must become the

captors of those holding them captive, and they must have in subjection those who were driving them to work.

3 And it must occur in the day when Jehovah gives you rest from your pain and from your agitation and from the hard slavery in which you were made a slave, 4 that you must raise up this proverbial saying against the king of Babylon and say:

"How has the one driving [others] to work come to a stop, the oppression come to a stop! 5 Jehovah has broken the rod of the wicked ones, the staff of the ruling ones, 6 the one striking peoples in fury with a stroke incessantly, the one subduing nations in sheer anger with a persecution without restraint. 7 The whole earth has come to rest, has become free of disturbance. People have become cheerful with joyful cries. 8 Even the juniper trees have also rejoiced at you, the cedars of Leb'a·non, [saying,] 'Ever since you have lain down, no [wood]cutter comes up against us.'

9 "Even She'ol underneath has become agitated at you in order to meet you on coming in. At you it has awakened those impotent in death, all the goatlike leaders of the earth. It has made all the kings of the nations get up from their thrones. 10 All of them speak up and say to you, 'Have you yourself also been made weak like us? Is it to us that you have been made comparable? 11 Down to She'ol your pride has been brought, the din of your stringed instruments. Beneath you, maggots are spread out as a couch; and worms are your covering.'

12 "O how you have fallen from heaven, you shining one, son of the dawn! How you have been cut down to the earth, you who were disabling the nations! 13 As for you, you have said in your heart, 'To the heavens I shall go up. Above the stars of God I shall lift up my throne, and I shall sit down upon the mountain of meeting, in the remotest parts of the north. 14 I shall go up above the high places of the clouds; I shall make myself resemble the Most High.'

15 "However, down to She'ol you will be brought, to the remotest parts of the pit. 16 Those seeing you will gaze even at you; they will give close examination even to you, [saying,] 'Is this the man that was agitating the earth, that was making kingdoms rock, 17 that made the productive land like the wilderness and that overthrew its very cities, that did not open the way homeward even for his prisoners?' 18 All other kings of the nations, yes, all of them, have lain down in glory, each one in his own house. 19 But as for you, you have been thrown away without a burial place for you, like a detested sprout, clothed with killed men stabbed with the sword that are going down to the stones of a pit, like a carcass trodden down. 20 You will not become united with them in a grave, because you brought your own land to ruin, you killed your own people. To time indefinite the offspring of evildoers will not be named.

21 "Make ready, you men, a slaughtering block for his own sons because of the error of their forefathers, that they may not rise up and actually take possession of the earth and fill the face of the productive land with cities."

22 "And I will rise up against them," is the utterance of Jehovah of armies.

"And I will cut off from Babylon name and remnant and progeny and posterity," is the utterance of Jehovah.

23 "And I will make her a possession of porcupines and reedy pools of water, and I will sweep her with the broom of annihilation," is the utterance of Jehovah of armies.

24 Jehovah of armies has sworn, saying: "Surely just as I have figured, so it must occur; and just as I have counseled, that is what will come true, 25 in order to break the As·syr'i·an in my land and that I may tread him down on

my own mountains; and that his yoke may actually depart from upon them and that his very load may depart from upon their shoulder."

26 This is the counsel that is counseled against all the earth, and this is the hand that is stretched out against all the nations. 27 For Jehovah of armies himself has counseled, and who can break [it] up? And his hand is the one stretched out, and who can turn it back?

28 In the year that King A'haz died this pronouncement occurred: 29 "Do not rejoice, O Phi·lis'ti·a, any one of you, just because the staff of the one striking you has been broken. For out of the root of the serpent there will come forth a poisonous snake, and its fruit will be a flying fiery snake. 30 And the first-born ones of the lowly ones will certainly feed, and in security the poor ones themselves will lie down. And with famine I will put your root to death, and what remains over of you will be killed. 31 Howl, O gate! Cry out, O city! All of you must become disheartened, O Phi·lis'ti·a! For out of the north a smoke is coming, and there is no one getting isolated from his ranks."

32 And what will anyone say in answer to the messengers of the nation? That Jehovah himself has laid the foundation of Zion, and in her the afflicted ones of his people will take refuge.

15 The pronouncement against Mo'ab: Because in the night it has been despoiled, Ar of Mo'ab itself has been silenced. Because in the night it has been despoiled, Kir of Mo'ab itself has been silenced. 2 He has gone up to The House and to Di'bon, to the high places, to a weeping. Over Ne'bo and over Med'e·ba Mo'ab itself howls. On all heads in it there is baldness; every beard is clipped. 3 In its streets they have girded on sackcloth. Upon the roofs thereof and in the public squares thereof everyone thereof howls, going down with weeping. 4 And Hesh'-bon and E·le·a'leh cry out. As far as Ja'haz their voice has been heard. That is why the armed men of Mo'ab themselves keep shouting. His very soul has quivered within him.

5 My own heart cries out over Mo'ab himself. The runaways thereof are as far along as Zo'ar [and] Eg'lath-she·li'shi·yah. For on the ascent of Lu'hith—with weeping [each] one goes up on it; for on the way to Hor·o·na'im they arouse the outcry about the catastrophe. 6 For the very waters of Nim'rim become sheer desolations. For the green grass has dried up, the grass has come to an end; nothing has become green. 7 That is why the leftovers and their stored goods that they have put up, they keep carrying them away right over the torrent valley of the poplars. 8 For the outcry has gone around the territory of Mo'ab. The howling thereof is clear to E·gla'im; the howling thereof is clear to Be'er-e'lim. 9 because the very waters of Di'mon have become full of blood. For upon Di'mon I shall place additional things, such as a lion for the escapees of Mo'ab who escape and for the remaining ones of the ground.

16 Send a ram, you men, to the ruler of the land, from Se'la toward the wilderness, to the mountain of the daughter of Zion.

2 And it must occur [that] like a fleeing winged creature, chased away from [its] nest, the daughters of Mo'ab will become at the fords of Ar'non.

3 "Bring in counsel, you men, execute the decision.

"Make your shadow just like the night in the midst of noontime. Conceal the dispersed ones; do not betray anyone fleeing. 4 May my dispersed ones reside as aliens even in you, O Mo'ab. Become a place of concealment to them because of the despoiler. For the oppressor has reached his end; the despoiling has terminated; those trampling down [others] have been finished off the earth.

5 "And in loving-kindness a throne will certainly be firmly established; and one must sit down upon it in trueness in the tent of David, judging and seeking justice and being prompt in righteousness."

6 We have heard of the pride of Mo′ab, that he is very proud; his haughtiness and his pride and his fury—his empty talk will not be so. 7 Therefore Mo′ab will howl for Mo′ab; even all of it will howl. For the raisin cakes of Kir-har′e·seth the stricken ones indeed will moan, 8 because the terraces themselves of Hesh′bon have withered. The vine of Sib′mah—the owners of the nations themselves have smitten down its bright-red [branches]. As far as Ja′zer they had reached; they had wandered about in the wilderness. Its own shoots had been left to luxuriate for themselves; they had gone over to the sea.

9 That is why I shall weep with the weeping of Ja′zer over the vine of Sib′mah. With my tears I shall drench you, O Hesh′bon and E·le-a′leh, because shouting even over your summer and over your harvest has fallen down. 10 And rejoicing and joyfulness have been taken away from the orchard; and in the vineyards there is no joyful crying out, there is no shouting done. No wine in the presses does the treader tread out. Shouting I have caused to cease.

11 That is why my very inwards are boisterous just like a harp even over Mo′ab, and the midst of me over Kir-har′e·seth.

12 And it occurred that it was seen that Mo′ab was made weary upon the high place; and he came to his sanctuary to pray, and he could not accomplish anything.

13 This is the word that Jehovah spoke concerning Mo′ab formerly. 14 And now Jehovah has spoken, saying: "Within three years, according to the years of a hired laborer, the glory of Mo′ab must also be disgraced with much commotion of every sort, and those who remain over will be a trifling few, not mighty."

17 The pronouncement against Damascus: "Look! Damascus removed from being a city, and she has become a heap, a decaying ruin. 2 The cities of A·ro′er that have been left behind become mere places for droves, where they actually lie down, with no one to make [them] tremble. 3 And the fortified city has been made to cease out of E′phra·im, and the kingdom out of Damascus; and those of Syria remaining over will become just like the glory of the sons of Israel," is the utterance of Jehovah of armies.

4 "And it must occur in that day that the glory of Jacob will become lowly, and even the fatness of his flesh will be made lean. 5 And it must occur that when the harvester is gathering the standing grain and his own arm harvests the ears of grain, he must even become like one gleaning ears of grain in the low plain of Reph′a·im. 6 And there must remain in it a gleaning as when there is a beating off of the olive tree: two [or] three ripe olives in the top of the branch; four [or] five on the fruit-bearing boughs thereof," is the utterance of Jehovah the God of Israel.

7 In that day earthling man will look up to his Maker, and his own eyes will gaze at the Holy One of Israel himself. 8 And he will not look to the altars, the work of his hands; and at what his fingers have made he will not gaze, either at the sacred poles or at the incense stands. 9 In that day his fortress cities will become like a place left entirely in the woodland, even the branch that they have left entirely on account of the sons of Israel; and it must become a desolate waste. 10 For you have forgotten the God of your salvation; and the Rock of your fortress you have not remembered. That is why you plant pleasant plantations, and with the shoot of a stranger you set it. 11 In the day you may carefully fence about the plantation of yours, and in the morning you may cause the seed of yours to sprout, [but]

the harvest will certainly flee in the day of the disease and incurable pain.

12 Ha for the commotion of many peoples, who are boisterous as with the boisterousness of the seas! And for the noise of national groups, who make a din just like the noise of mighty waters! 13 The national groups themselves will make a din just like the noise of many waters. And He will certainly rebuke it, and it must flee far away and be chased like the chaff of the mountains before a wind and like a thistle whirl before a stormwind. 14 At evening time, why, look! there is sudden terror. Before morning—it is no more. This is the share of those pillaging us, and the lot belonging to those plundering us.

18 Ha for the land of the whirring insects with wings, which is in the region of the rivers of E·thi·o'pi·a! 2 It is the one sending forth envoys by means of the sea, and by means of vessels of papyrus upon the surface of the waters, [saying:] "Go, you swift messengers, to a nation drawn out and scoured, to a people fear-inspiring everywhere, a nation of tensile strength and of treading down, whose land the rivers have washed away."

3 All you inhabitants of the productive land and you residents of the earth, you will see a sight just as when there is the raising up of a signal upon the mountains, and you will hear a sound just as when there is the blowing of a horn. 4 For this is what Jehovah has said to me: "I will keep undisturbed and look upon my established place, like the dazzling heat along with the light, like the cloud of dew in the heat of harvest. 5 For before the harvest, when the blossom comes to perfection and the bloom becomes a ripening grape, one must also cut off the sprigs with pruning shears and must remove the tendrils, must lop [them] off. 6 They will be left all together for the bird of prey of the mountains and for the beast of the earth. And upon it the bird of prey will certainly pass the summer, and upon it even every beast of the earth will pass the harvesttime.

7 "In that time a gift will be brought to Jehovah of armies, [from] a people drawn out and scoured, even from a people fear-inspiring everywhere, a nation of tensile strength and of treading down, whose land the rivers have washed away, to the place of the name of Jehovah of armies, Mount Zion."

19 The pronouncement against Egypt: Look! Jehovah is riding on a swift cloud and coming into Egypt. And the valueless gods of Egypt will certainly quiver because of him, and the very heart of Egypt will melt in the midst of it.

2 "And I will goad Egyptians against Egyptians, and they will certainly war each one against his brother, and each one against his companion, city against city, kingdom against kingdom. 3 And the spirit of Egypt must become bewildered in the midst of it, and I shall confuse its own counsel. And they will be certain to resort to the valueless gods and to the charmers and to the spirit mediums and to the professional foretellers of events. 4 And I will deliver up Egypt into the hand of a hard master, and strong will be the king that will rule over them," is the utterance of the [true] Lord, Jehovah of armies.

5 And the water will certainly be dried up from the sea, and the river itself will become parched and actually run dry. 6 And the rivers must stink; the Nile canals of Egypt must become low and parched. The reed and the rush themselves must molder. 7 The bare places by the Nile River, at the mouth of the Nile River, and every seedland of the Nile River will dry up. It will certainly be driven away, and it will be no more. 8 And the fishers will have to mourn, and all those casting fishhooks into the Nile River must express sorrow, and even those

spreading fishing nets upon the surface of the water will actually fade away. 9 And the workers in carded flax must become ashamed; also the loom workers on white fabrics. 10 And her weavers must become crushed, all the wage workers grieved in soul.

11 The princes of Zo'an are indeed foolish. As regards the wise ones of Phar'aoh's counselors, [their] counsel is something unreasonable. How will you men say to Phar'aoh: "I am the son of wise ones, the son of kings of ancient time"? 12 Where, then, are they—the wise men of yours—that they may now tell you and that they may know what Jehovah of armies has counseled concerning Egypt? 13 The princes of Zo'an have acted foolishly, the princes of Noph have been deceived, the key men of her tribes have caused Egypt to wander about. 14 Jehovah himself has mingled in the midst of her the spirit of disconcertedness; and they have caused Egypt to wander about in all its work, just as someone drunk is made to wander about in his vomit. 15 And Egypt will not come to have any work that the head or the tail, the shoot or the rush, can do.

16 In that day Egypt will become like women, and it will certainly tremble and be in dread because of the waving of the hand of Jehovah of armies which he is waving against it. 17 And the ground of Judah must become to Egypt a cause for reeling. Everybody to whom one mentions it is in dread because of the counsel of Jehovah of armies that he is counseling against him.

18 In that day there will prove to be five cities in the land of Egypt speaking the language of Ca'naan and swearing to Jehovah of armies. The City of Tearing Down will one [city] be called.

19 In that day there will prove to be an altar to Jehovah in the midst of the land of Egypt, and a pillar to Jehovah beside its boundary. 20 And it must prove to be for a sign and for a witness to Jehovah of armies in the land of Egypt; for they will cry out to Jehovah because of the oppressors, and he will send them a savior, even a grand one, who will actually deliver them. 21 And Jehovah will certainly become known to the Egyptians; and the Egyptians must know Jehovah in that day, and they must render sacrifice and gift and must make a vow to Jehovah and pay it. 22 And Jehovah will certainly deal Egypt a blow. There will be a dealing of a blow and a healing; and they must return to Jehovah, and he must let himself be entreated by them and must heal them.

23 In that day there will come to be a highway out of Egypt to As·syr'i·a, and As·syr'i·a will actually come into Egypt, and Egypt into As·syr'i·a; and they will certainly render service, Egypt with As·syr'i·a. 24 In that day Israel will come to be the third with Egypt and with As·syr'i·a, namely, a blessing in the midst of the earth, 25 because Jehovah of armies will have blessed it, saying: "Blessed be my people, Egypt, and the work of my hands, As·syr'i·a, and my inheritance, Israel."

20 In the year that Tar'tan came to Ash'dod, when Sar'gon the king of As·syr'i·a sent him, and he proceeded to war against Ash'dod and to capture it; 2 at that time Jehovah spoke by the hand of Isaiah the son of A'moz, saying: "Go, and you must loosen the sackcloth from off your hips; and your sandals you should draw from off your feet." And he proceeded to do so, walking about naked and barefoot.

3 And Jehovah went on to say: "Just as my servant Isaiah has walked about naked and barefoot three years as a sign and a portent against Egypt and against E·thi·o'pi·a, 4 so the king of As·syr'i·a will lead the body of captives of Egypt and the exiles of E·thi·o'pi·a, boys and old men, naked and barefoot, and with buttocks stripped, the nakedness of Egypt. 5 And they will certainly be terrified and

be ashamed of E·thi·o′pi·a their looked-for hope and of Egypt their beauty. 6 And the inhabitant of this coastland will be certain to say in that day, "There is how our looked-for hope is, to which we fled for assistance, in order to be delivered because of the king of As·syr′i·a! And how shall we ourselves escape?' "

21 The pronouncement against the wilderness of the sea: Like stormwinds in the south in moving onward, from the wilderness it is coming, from a fear-inspiring land. 2 There is a hard vision that has been told to me: The treacherous dealer is dealing treacherously, and the despoiler is despoiling. Go up, O E′lam! Lay siege, O Me′di·a! All sighing due to her I have caused to cease. 3 That is why my hips have become full of severe pains. Convulsions themselves have grabbed hold of me, like the convulsions of a woman that is giving birth. I have become disconcerted so that I do not hear; I have become disturbed so that I do not see. 4 My heart has wandered about; a shuddering itself has terrified me. The twilight for which I had an attachment has been made for me a trembling.

5 Let there be a setting of the table in order, an arranging of the location of seats, an eating, a drinking! Get up, you princes, anoint the shield. 6 For this is what Jehovah has said to me: "Go, post a lookout that he may tell just what he sees."

7 And he saw a war chariot [with] a span of steeds, a war chariot of asses, a war chariot of camels. And he paid strict attention, with much attentiveness. 8 And he proceeded to call out like a lion: "Upon the watchtower, O Jehovah, I am standing constantly by day, and at my guardpost I am stationed all the nights. 9 And here, now, there is coming a war chariot of men, [with] a span of steeds!"

And he began to speak up and say: "She has fallen! Babylon has fallen, and all the graven images of her gods he has broken to the earth!"

10 O my threshed ones and the son of my threshing floor, what I have heard from Jehovah of armies, the God of Israel, I have reported to you people.

11 The pronouncement against Du′mah: To me there is one calling out from Se′ir: "Watchman, what about the night? Watchman, what about the night?" 12 The watchman said: "The morning has to come, and also the night. If you people would inquire, inquire. Come again!"

13 The pronouncement against the desert plain: In the forest in the desert plain you will spend the night, O caravans of men of De′dan. 14 To meet the thirsty one BRING water. O you inhabitants of the land of Te′ma, confront the one fleeing away with bread for him. 15 For because of the swords they have fled away, because of the drawn sword, and because of the bent bow and because of the heaviness of the war.

16 For this is what Jehovah has said to me: "Within yet a year, according to the years of a hired laborer, all the glory of Ke′dar must even come to its end. 17 And the ones remaining over of the number of bow[men], the mighty men of the sons of Ke′dar, will become few, for Jehovah himself, the God of Israel, has spoken [it]."

22 The pronouncement of the valley of the vision: What is the matter with you, then, that you have gone up in your entirety to the roofs? 2 With turmoil you were full, a boisterous city, an exultant town. Your slain ones are not those slain with the sword, nor those dead in battle. 3 All your dictators themselves have fled at one time. Without [need of] a bow they have been taken prisoner. All those of you who have been found have been taken prisoner together. Far off they had run away.

4 That is why I have said: "Turn your gaze away from me. I will show bitterness in weeping. Do not you people insist on comforting

me over the despoiling of the daughter of my people. 5 For it is the day of confusion and of downtreading and of confounding that the Sovereign Lord, Jehovah of armies, has in the valley of the vision. There is the demolisher of the wall, and the cry to the mountain. 6 And E′lam itself has taken up the quiver, in the war chariot of earthling man, [with] steeds; and Kir itself has uncovered the shield. 7 And it will occur that the choicest of your low plains must become full of war chariots, and the very steeds must without fail set themselves in position at the gate, 8 and one will remove the screen of Judah. And you will look in that day toward the armory of the house of the forest, 9 and you people will certainly see the very breaches of the city of David, for they will actually be many. And you will collect the waters of the lower pool. 10 And the houses of Jerusalem you will actually count. You will also pull down the houses to make the wall unattainable. 11 And there will be a collecting basin that you must make between the two walls for the waters of the old pool. And you will certainly not look at the grand maker of it, and the one forming it long ago you will certainly not see.

12 "And the Sovereign Lord, Jehovah of armies, will call in that day for weeping and for mourning and for baldness and for girding on sackcloth. 13 But, look! exultation and rejoicing, the killing of cattle and the slaughtering of sheep, the eating of flesh and the drinking of wine, 'Let there be eating and drinking, for tomorrow we shall die.' "

14 And in my ears Jehovah of armies has revealed himself: " 'This error will not be atoned for in your behalf until you people die,' the Sovereign Lord, Jehovah of armies, has said."

15 This is what the Sovereign Lord, Jehovah of armies, has said: "Go, enter in to this steward, to Sheb′na, who is over the house, 16 'What is there of interest to you

here, and who is there of interest to you here, that you have hewed out for yourself here a burial place?' On a height he is hewing out his burial place; in a crag he is cutting out a residence for himself. 17 'Look! Jehovah is hurling you down with violent hurling, O able-bodied man, and grasping you forcibly. 18 Without fail he will wrap you up tightly, like a ball for a wide land. There you will die, and there the chariots of your glory will be the dishonor of the house of your master. 19 And I will push you away from your position; and from your official standing one will tear you down.

20 " 'And it must occur in that day that I will call my servant, namely, E·li′a·kim the son of Hil·ki′ah. 21 And I will clothe him with your robe, and your sash I shall firmly bind about him, and your dominion I shall give into his hand; and he must become a father to the inhabitant of Jerusalem and to the house of Judah. 22 And I will put the key of the house of David upon his shoulder, and he must open without anyone's shutting, and he must shut without anyone's opening. 23 And I will drive him in as a peg in a lasting place, and he must become as a throne of glory to the house of his father. 24 And they must hang upon him all the glory of the house of his father, the descendants and the offshoots, all the vessels of the small sort, the vessels of the bowl sort as well as all the vessels of the large jars.

25 " 'In that day,' is the utterance of Jehovah of armies, 'the peg that is driven in a lasting place will be removed, and it must be hewn down and fall, and the load that is upon it must be cut off, for Jehovah himself has spoken [it].' "

23 The pronouncement of Tyre: Howl, you ships of Tar′shish! for it has been despoiled from [being] a port, from [being a place] to enter in. From the land of Kit′tim it has been revealed to them. 2 Be silent, you inhabitants of the coastland. The merchants from

Si'don, the ones crossing over the sea—they have filled you. 3 And on many waters has been the seed of Shi'hor, the harvest of the Nile, your revenue; and it came to be the profit of the nations.

4 Be ashamed, O Si'don; because the sea, O you stronghold of the sea, has said: "I have not had birth pains, and I have not given birth, nor have I brought up young men, raised up virgins." 5 Just as at the report pertaining to Egypt, people will likewise be in severe pains at the report on Tyre. 6 Cross over to Tar'shish; howl, you inhabitants of the coastland. 7 Is this your [city] that was exultant from days of long ago, [from] her early times? Her feet used to bring her far away to reside as an alien.

8 Who is it that has given this counsel against Tyre, the bestower of crowns, whose merchants were princes, whose tradesmen were the honorable ones of the earth?

9 Jehovah of armies himself has given this counsel, to profane the pride of all beauty, to treat with contempt all the honorable ones of the earth.

10 Cross over your land like the Nile River, O daughter of Tar'shish. There is no shipyard any longer. 11 His hand he has stretched out over the sea; he has caused kingdoms to be agitated. Jehovah himself has given a command against Phoenicia, to annihilate her strongholds. 12 And he says: "You must never again exult, O oppressed one, the virgin daughter of Si'don. Get up, cross over to Kit'tim itself. Even there it will not be restful for you."

13 Look! The land of the Chal·de'ans. This is the people—As·syr'i·a did not prove to be [the one]—they founded her for the desert haunters. They have erected their siege towers; they have stripped bare her dwelling towers; one has set her as a crumbling ruin.

14 Howl, you ships of Tar'shish, for your stronghold has been despoiled.

15 And it must occur in that day that Tyre must be forgotten seventy years, the same as the days of one king. At the end of seventy years it will happen to Tyre as in the song of a prostitute: 16 "Take a harp, go around the city, O forgotten prostitute. Do your best at playing on the strings; make your songs many, in order that you may be remembered."

17 And it must occur at the end of seventy years that Jehovah will turn his attention to Tyre, and she must return to her hire and commit prostitution with all the kingdoms of the earth upon the surface of the ground. 18 And her profit and her hire must become something holy to Jehovah. It will not be stored up, nor be laid up, because her hire will come to be for those dwelling before Jehovah, for eating to satisfaction and for elegant covering.

24 Look! Jehovah is emptying the land and laying it waste, and he has twisted the face of it and scattered its inhabitants. 2 And it must come to be the same for the people as for the priest; the same for the servant as for his master; the same for the maidservant as for her mistress; the same for the buyer as for the seller; the same for the lender as for the borrower; the same for the interest taker as for the one paying the interest. 3 Without fail the land will be emptied, and without fail it will be plundered, for Jehovah himself has spoken this word. 4 The land has gone to mourning, has faded away. The productive land has withered, has faded away. The high ones of the people of the land have withered. 5 And the very land has been polluted under its inhabitants, for they have bypassed the laws, changed the regulation, broken the indefinitely lasting covenant. 6 That is why the curse itself has eaten up the land, and those inhabiting it are held guilty. That is why the inhabitants of the land have decreased in number, and very few mortal men have remained over.

7 The new wine has gone to mourning, the vine has withered, all those glad at heart have gone to sighing. **8** The exultation of the tambourines has ceased, the noise of the highly elated ones has discontinued, the exultation of the harp has ceased. **9** It is with no song that they drink wine; the intoxicating liquor becomes bitter to those drinking it. **10** The deserted town has been broken down; every house has been shut up from entering. **11** There is an outcry in the streets for [want of] wine. All rejoicing has passed away; the exultation of the land has departed. **12** In the city an astonishing condition has been left behind; the gate has been crushed to a mere rubble heap.

13 For thus it will become in the midst of the land, in among the peoples, like the beating off of the olive tree, like the gleaning when the grape gathering has come to an end. **14** They themselves will raise their voice, they will cry out joyfully. In the superiority of Jehovah they will certainly cry out shrilly from the sea. **15** That is why in the region of light they must glorify Jehovah, in the islands of the sea the name of Jehovah, the God of Israel. **16** From the extremity of the land there are melodies that we have heard: "Decoration to the Righteous One!"

But I say: "For me there is leanness, for me there is leanness! Woe to me! The treacherous dealers have dealt treacherously. Even with treachery the treacherous dealers have dealt treacherously."

17 Dread and the hollow and the trap are upon you, you inhabitant of the land. **18** And it must occur that anyone fleeing from the sound of the dreaded thing will fall into the hollow, and anyone coming up from inside the hollow will be caught in the trap. For the very floodgates on high will actually be opened, and the foundations of the land will rock. **19** The land has absolutely burst apart, the land has absolutely been shaken up, the land has

absolutely been sent staggering. **20** The land absolutely moves unsteadily like a drunken man, and it has swayed to and fro like a lookout hut. And its transgression has become heavy upon it, and it must fall, so that it will not rise up again.

21 And it must occur in that day that Jehovah will turn his attention upon the army of the height in the height, and upon the kings of the ground upon the ground. **22** And they will certainly be gathered with a gathering as of prisoners into the pit, and be shut up in the dungeon; and after an abundance of days they will be given attention. **23** And the full moon has become abashed, and the glowing [sun] has become ashamed, for Jehovah of armies has become king in Mount Zion and in Jerusalem and in front of his elderly men with glory.

25 O Jehovah, you are my God. I exalt you, I laud your name, for you have done wonderful things, counsels from early times, in faithfulness, in trustworthiness. **2** For you have made a city a pile of stones, a fortified town a crumbling ruin, a dwelling tower of strangers to be no city, which will not be rebuilt even to time indefinite. **3** That is why those who are a strong people will glorify you; the town of the tyrannical nations, they will fear you. **4** For you have become a stronghold to the lowly one, a stronghold to the poor one in the distress that he has, a refuge from the rainstorm, a shade from the heat, when the blast of the tyrannical ones is like a rainstorm against a wall. **5** Like the heat in a waterless country, the noise of strangers you subdue, the heat with the shadow of a cloud. The melody itself of the tyrannical ones becomes suppressed.

6 And Jehovah of armies will certainly make for all the peoples, in this mountain, a banquet of well-oiled dishes, a banquet of [wine kept on] the dregs, of well-oiled dishes filled with marrow, of [wine kept on] the dregs, filtered. **7** And in this mountain he will certainly swallow up the face of the envelopment that is enveloping over all the peoples, and the woven work that is interwoven upon all the nations. 8 He will actually swallow up death forever, and the Lord Jehovah will certainly wipe the tears from all faces. And the reproach of his people he will take away from all the earth, for Jehovah himself has spoken [it].

9 And in that day one will certainly say: "Look! This is our God. We have hoped in him, and he will save us. This is Jehovah. We have hoped in him. Let us be joyful and rejoice in the salvation by him."

10 For the hand of Jehovah will settle down on this mountain, and Mo'ab must be trodden down in its place as when a straw heap is trodden down in a manure place. 11 And he must slap out his hands in the midst of it as when a swimmer slaps [them] out to swim, and he must abase its haughtiness with the tricky movements of his hands. 12 And the fortified city, with your high walls of security, he must lay low; he must abase [it], bring [it] into contact with the earth, to the dust.

26 In that day this song will be sung in the land of Judah: "We have a strong city. He sets salvation itself for walls and rampart. 2 Open the gates, you men, that the righteous nation that is keeping faithful conduct may enter. 3 The inclination that is well supported you will safeguard in continuous peace, because it is in you that one is made to trust. 4 Trust in Jehovah, you people, for all times, for in Jah Jehovah is the Rock of times indefinite.

5 "For he has laid low those inhabiting the height, the elevated town. He abases it, he abases it to the earth; he brings it in touch with the dust. 6 The foot will trample it down, the feet of the afflicted one, the steps of the lowly ones."

7 The path of the righteous one is uprightness. You being upright, you will smooth out the very course of a righteous one. 8 Yes, for the path of your judgments, O Jehovah, we have hoped in you. For your name and for your memorial the desire of the soul has been. 9 With my soul I have desired you in the night; yes, with my spirit within me I keep looking for you; because, when there are judgments from you for the earth, righteousness is what the inhabitants of the productive land will certainly learn. 10 Though the wicked one should be shown favor, he simply will not learn righteousness. In the land of straightforwardness he will act unjustly and will not see the eminence of Jehovah.

11 O Jehovah, your hand has become high, [but] they do not behold [it]. They will behold and be ashamed at the zeal for [your] people. Yes, the very fire for your own adversaries will eat them up. 12 O Jehovah, you will adjudge peace to us, because even all our works you have performed for us. 13 O Jehovah our God, other masters besides you have acted as owners of us. By you only shall we make mention of your name. 14 They are dead; they will not live. Impotent in death, they will not rise up. Therefore you have turned your attention that you might annihilate them and destroy all mention of them.

15 You have added to the nation; O Jehovah, you have added to the nation; you have glorified yourself. You have extended afar all the borders of the land. 16 O Jehovah, during distress they have turned their attention to you; they have poured out a whisper [of prayer] when they had your disciplining. 17 Just as a pregnant woman draws near to giving birth, has labor pains, cries out in her birth pangs, so we have become because of you, O Jehovah. 18 We have become pregnant, we have had labor pains; as it were, we have given birth to wind. No real salvation do we accomplish as regards the land, and no inhabitants for the productive land proceed to fall [in birth].

19 "Your dead ones will live. A corpse of mine—they will rise up. Awake and cry out joyfully, you residents in the dust! For your dew is as the dew of mallows, and the earth itself will let even those impotent in death drop [in birth].

20 "Go, my people, enter into your interior rooms, and shut your doors behind you. Hide yourself for but a moment until the denunciation passes over. 21 For, look! Jehovah is coming forth from his place to call to account the error of the inhabitant of the land against him, and the land will certainly expose her bloodshed and will no longer cover over her killed ones."

27 In that day Jehovah, with his hard and great and strong sword, will turn his attention to Le·vi'a·than, the gliding serpent, even to Le·vi'a·than, the crooked serpent, and he will certainly kill the sea monster that is in the sea.

2 In that day sing to her, you people: "A vineyard of foaming wine! 3 I, Jehovah, am safeguarding her. Every moment I shall water her. In order that no one may turn his attention against her, I shall safeguard her even night and day. 4 There is no rage that I have. Who will give me thornbushes [and] weeds in the battle? I will step on such. I will set such on fire at the same time. 5 Otherwise let him take hold of my stronghold, let him make peace with me; peace let him make with me."

6 In the coming [days] Jacob will take root, Israel will put forth blossoms and actually sprout; and they will simply fill the surface of the productive land with produce.

7 As with the stroke of one striking him does one have to strike him? Or as with the slaughter of his killed ones does he have to be killed? 8 With a scare cry you will contend with her when sending her forth. He must expel [her] with his blast, a hard one in the day of the east wind. 9 Therefore by this means the error of Jacob will be atoned for, and this is all the fruit [when] he takes away his sin, when he makes all the stones of the altar like chalkstones that have been pulverized, so that the sacred poles and the incense stands will not rise up. 10 For the fortified city will be solitary, the pasture ground will be left to itself and abandoned like a wilderness. There the calf will graze, and there it will lie down; and he will actually consume her boughs. 11 When her sprigs have dried up, women coming in will break [them] off, lighting them up. For it is not a people of keen understanding. That is why its Maker will show it no mercy, and its own Former will show it no favor.

12 And it must occur in that day that Jehovah will beat off [the fruit], from the flowing stream of the River to the torrent valley of Egypt, and so you yourselves will be picked up one after the other, O sons of Israel. 13 And it must occur in that day that there will be a blowing on a great horn, and those who are perishing in the land of As·syr'i·a and those who are dispersed in the land of Egypt will certainly come and bow down to Jehovah in the holy mountain in Jerusalem.

28 Woe to the eminent crown of the drunkards of E'phra·im, and the fading blossom of its decoration of beauty that is upon the head of the fertile valley of those overpowered by wine! 2 Look! Jehovah has someone strong and vigorous. Like a thunderous storm of hail, a destructive storm, like a thunderous storm of powerful, flooding waters, he will certainly do a casting down to the earth with force. 3 With the feet the eminent crowns of the drunkards of E'phra·im will be trampled down. 4 And the fading flower of its decoration of beauty that is upon the head of the fertile valley must become like the early fig before summer, that, when the seer sees it, while it is yet in his palm, he swallows it down.

5 In that day Jehovah of armies will become as a crown of decora-

tion and as a garland of beauty to the ones remaining over of his people, 6 and as a spirit of justice to the one sitting in the judgment, and as mightiness [to] those turning away the battle from the gate. 7 And these also—because of wine they have gone astray and because of intoxicating liquor they have wandered about. Priest and prophet—they have gone astray because of intoxicating liquor, they have become confused as a result of the wine, they have wandered about as a result of the intoxicating liquor; they have gone astray in their seeing, they have reeled as to decision. 8 For the tables themselves have all become full of filthy vomit—there is no place [without it].

9 Whom will one instruct in knowledge, and whom will one make understand what has been heard? Those who have been weaned from the milk, those moved away from the breasts? 10 For it is "command upon command, command upon command, measuring line upon measuring line, measuring line upon measuring line, here a little, there a little." 11 For by those stammering with their lips and by a different tongue he will speak to this people, 12 those to whom he has said:"This is the resting place. GIVE rest to the weary one. And this is the place of ease," but who were not willing to hear. 13 And to them the word of Jehovah will certainly become "command upon command, command upon command, measuring line upon measuring line, measuring line upon measuring line, here a little, there a little," in order that they may go and certainly stumble backwards and actually be broken and ensnared and caught.

14 Therefore hear the word of Jehovah, YOU braggarts, YOU rulers of this people who are in Jerusalem: 15 Because YOU men have said: "We have concluded a covenant with Death; and with She′ol we have effected a vision; the overflowing flash flood, in case it should pass through, will not come to

us, for we have made a lie our refuge and in falsehood we have concealed ourselves"; 16 therefore this is what the Lord Jehovah has said: "Here I am laying as a foundation in Zion a stone, a tried stone, the precious corner of a sure foundation. No one exercising faith will get panicky. 17 And I will make justice the measuring line and righteousness the leveling instrument; and the hail must sweep away the refuge of a lie, and the waters themselves will flood out the very place of concealment. 18 And YOUR covenant with Death will certainly be dissolved, and that vision of YOURS with She′ol will not stand. The overflowing flash flood, when it passes through—YOU must also become for it a trampling place. 19 As often as it passes through, it will take YOU men away, because morning by morning it will pass through, during the day and during the night; and it must become nothing but a reason for quaking to make [others] understand what has been heard."

20 For the couch has proved too short for stretching oneself on, and the woven sheet itself is [too] narrow when wrapping oneself up. 21 For Jehovah will rise up just as at Mount Pe·ra′zim, he will be agitated just as in the low plain near Gib′e·on, that he may do his deed—his deed is strange—and that he may work his work—his work is unusual. 22 And now do not show yourselves scoffers, in order that YOUR bands may not grow strong, for there is an extermination, even something decided upon, that I have heard of from the Sovereign Lord, Jehovah of armies, for all the land.

23 Give ear, YOU men, and listen to my voice; pay attention and listen to my saying. 24 Is it all day long that the plower plows in order to sow seed, that he loosens and harrows his ground? 25 Does he not, when he has smoothed out its surface, then scatter black cummin and sprinkle the cummin, and must he not put in wheat, millet, and barley in the appointed place,

and spelt as his boundary? 26 And one corrects him according to what is right. His own God instructs him. 27 For it is not with a threshing instrument that black cummin is given a treading; and upon cummin no wheel of a wagon is turned. For it is with a rod that black cummin is generally beaten out, and cummin with a staff. 28 Is breadstuff itself generally crushed? For never does one incessantly keep treading it out. And he must set the roller of his wagon in motion, and his own steeds, [but] he will not crush it. 29 This also is what has come forth from Jehovah of armies himself, who has been wonderful in counsel, who has done greatly in effectual working.

29 "Woe to Ar′i·el, to Ar′i·el, the town where David encamped! Add year upon year, you people; let the festivals run the round. 2 And I have to make things tight for Ar′i·el, and there must come to be mourning and lamentation, and she must become to me as the altar hearth of God. 3 And I must encamp on all sides against you, and I must lay siege to you with a palisade and raise up against you siegeworks. 4 And you must become low so that you will speak from the very earth, and as from the dust your saying will sound low. And like a spirit medium your voice must become even from the earth, and from the dust your own saying will chirp. 5 And the crowd of those strange to you must become just like fine powder, and the crowd of the tyrants just like the chaff that is passing away. And it must occur in an instant, suddenly. 6 From Jehovah of armies you will have attention with thunder and with quaking and with a great sound, stormwind and tempest, and the flame of a devouring fire."

7 And it must occur just as in a dream, in a vision of the night, regarding the crowd of all the nations that are waging war against Ar′i·el, even all those waging war against her, and the siege towers against her and those making things tight for her. 8 Yes, it must occur just as when someone hungry dreams and here he is eating, and he actually awakes and his soul is empty; and just as when someone thirsty dreams and here he is drinking, and he actually awakes and here he is tired and his soul is dried out; thus it will occur with the crowd of all the nations that are waging war against Mount Zion.

9 Linger, you men, and be amazed; blind yourselves, and be blinded. They have become intoxicated, but not with wine; they have moved unsteadily, but not because of intoxicating liquor.

10 For upon you men Jehovah has poured a spirit of deep sleep; and he closes your eyes, the prophets, and he has covered even your heads, the visionaries. 11 And for you men the vision of everything becomes like the words of the book that has been sealed up, which they give to someone knowing the writing, saying: "Read this out loud, please," and he has to say: "I am unable, for it is sealed up"; 12 and the book must be given to someone that does not know writing, [somebody] saying: "Read this out loud, please," and he has to say: "I do not know writing at all."

13 And Jehovah says: "For the reason that this people have come near with their mouth, and they have glorified me merely with their lips, and they have removed their heart itself far away from me, and their fear toward me becomes men's commandment that is being taught, 14 therefore here I am, the One that will act wonderfully again with this people, in a wonderful manner and with something wonderful; and the wisdom of their wise men must perish, and the very understanding of their discreet men will conceal itself."

15 Woe to those who are going very deep in concealing counsel from Jehovah himself, and whose deeds have occurred in a dark place, while they say: "Who is seeing us, and who is knowing of us?" 16 The perversity of you men! Should the potter himself be

accounted just like the clay? For should the thing made say respecting its maker: "He did not make me"? And does the very thing formed actually say respecting its former: "He showed no understanding"?

17 Is it not yet but a very little time and Leb'a·non must be turned into an orchard and the orchard itself will be accounted just as a forest? 18 And in that day the deaf ones will certainly hear the words of the book, and out of the gloom and out of the darkness even the eyes of the blind ones will see. 19 And the meek ones will certainly increase their rejoicing in Jehovah himself, and even the poor ones of mankind will be joyful in the Holy One of Israel himself, 20 because the tyrant must reach his end, and the bragger must come to his finish, and all those keeping alert to do harm must be cut off, 21 those bringing a man into sin by [his] word, and those who lay bait even for the one reproving in the gate, and those who push aside the righteous one with empty arguments.

22 Therefore this is what Jehovah has said to the house of Jacob, he that redeemed Abraham: "Jacob will not now be ashamed, nor will his own face now grow pale; 23 for when he sees his children, the work of my hands, in the midst of him, they will sanctify my name, and they will certainly sanctify the Holy One of Jacob, and the God of Israel they will regard with awe. 24 And those who are erring in [their] spirit will actually get to know understanding, and even those who are grumbling will learn instruction."

30 "Woe to the stubborn sons," is the utterance of Jehovah, "[those disposed] to carry out counsel, but not that from me; and to pour out a libation, but not with my spirit, in order to add sin to sin; 2 those who are setting out to go down to Egypt and who have not inquired of my own mouth, to take shelter in the stronghold of Phar'aoh and to take refuge in

the shadow of Egypt! 3 And the stronghold of Phar'aoh must become even for you men a reason for shame, and the refuge in the shadow of Egypt a cause for humiliation. 4 For his princes have come to be in Zo'an itself, and his own envoys reach even Ha'nes. 5 Every one will certainly become ashamed of a people that bring no benefit to one, that are of no help and bring no benefit, but are a reason for shame and also a cause for reproach."

6 The pronouncement against the beasts of the south: Through the land of distress and hard conditions, of the lion and the leopard growling, of the viper and the flying fiery snake, on the shoulders of full-grown asses they carry their resources, and on the humps of camels their supplies. In behalf of the people they will prove of no benefit. 7 And the Egyptians are mere vanity, and they will help simply for nothing. Therefore I have called this one: "Ra'hab—they are for sitting still."

8 "Now come, write it upon a tablet with them, and inscribe it even in a book, that it may serve for a future day, for a witness to time indefinite. 9 For it is a rebellious people, untruthful sons, sons who have been unwilling to hear the law of Jehovah; 10 who have said to the ones seeing, 'You must not see,' and to the ones having visions, 'You must not envision for us any straightforward things. Speak to us smooth things; envision deceptive things. 11 Turn aside from the way; deviate from the path. Cause the Holy One of Israel to cease just on account of us.'"

12 Therefore this is what the Holy One of Israel has said: "In view of your rejecting of this word, and [since] you men trust in defrauding and in what is devious and you support yourselves on it, 13 therefore for you this error will become like a broken section about to fall down, a swelling out in a highly raised wall, the breakdown of which may come suddenly, in an

instant. 14 And one will certainly break it as in the breaking of a large jar of the potters, crushed to pieces without one's sparing [it], so that there cannot be found among its crushed pieces a fragment of earthenware with which to rake the fire from the fireplace or to skim water from a marshy place."

15 For this is what the Lord Jehovah, the Holy One of Israel, has said: "By coming back and resting YOU people will be saved. YOUR mightiness will prove to be simply in keeping undisturbed and in trustfulness." But YOU were not willing. 16 And YOU proceeded to say: "No, but on horses we shall flee!" That is why YOU will flee. "And on swift [horses] we shall ride!" That is why those pursuing YOU will show themselves swift. 17 A thousand will tremble on account of the rebuke of one; on account of the rebuke of five YOU will flee until YOU will have remained over like a mast on the top of a mountain and like a signal on a hill.

18 And therefore Jehovah will keep in expectation of showing YOU favor, and therefore he will rise up to show YOU mercy. For Jehovah is a God of judgment. Happy are all those keeping in expectation of him. 19 When the very people in Zion will dwell in Jerusalem, you will by no means weep. He will without fail show you favor at the sound of your outcry; as soon as he hears it he will actually answer you. 20 And Jehovah will certainly give YOU people bread in the form of distress and water in the form of oppression; yet your Grand Instructor will no longer hide himself, and your eyes must become [eyes] seeing your Grand Instructor. 21 And your own ears will hear a word behind you saying: "This is the way. Walk in it, YOU people," in case YOU people should go to the right or in case YOU should go to the left.

22 And YOU people must defile the overlaying of your graven images of silver and the close-fitting covering of your molten statue of gold. You will scatter them. Like a menstruating woman, you will say to it: "Mere dirt!" 23 And he will certainly give the rain for your seed with which you sow the ground, and as the produce of the ground bread, which must become fat and oily. Your livestock will graze in that day in a spacious pasture. 24 And the cattle and the full-grown asses cultivating the ground will eat fodder seasoned with sorrel, which was winnowed with the shovel and with the fork. 25 And upon every high mountain and upon every elevated hill there must come to be streams, water ditches, in the day of the big slaughter when the towers fall. 26 And the light of the full moon must become as the light of the glowing [sun]; and the very light of the glowing [sun] will become seven times as much, like the light of seven days, in the day that Jehovah binds up the breakdown of his people and heals even the severe wound resulting from the stroke by him.

27 Look! The name of Jehovah is coming from far away, burning with his anger and with heavy clouds. As for his lips, they have become full of denunciation, and his tongue is like a devouring fire. 28 And his spirit is like a flooding torrent that reaches clear to the neck, to swing the nations to and fro with a sieve of worthlessness; and a bridle that causes one to wander about will be in the jaws of the peoples. 29 YOU people will come to have a song like that in the night that one sanctifies oneself for a festival, and rejoicing of heart like that of one walking with a flute to enter into the mountain of Jehovah, to the Rock of Israel.

30 And Jehovah will certainly make the dignity of his voice to be heard and will make the descending of his arm to be seen, in the raging of anger and the flame of a devouring fire [and] cloudburst and rainstorm and hailstones. 31 For because of the voice of Jehovah As·syr′i·a will be struck with

terror; he will strike [it] even with a staff. 32 And every swing of his rod of chastisement that Jehovah will cause to settle down upon [As·syr′i·a] will certainly prove to be with tambourines and with harps; and with battles of brandishing he will actually fight against them. 33 For his To′pheth is set in order from recent times; it is also prepared for the king himself. He has made its pile deep. Fire and wood are in abundance. The breath of Jehovah, like a torrent of sulphur, is burning against it.

31 Woe to those going down to Egypt for assistance, those who rely on mere horses, and who put their trust in war chariots, because they are numerous, and in steeds, because they are very mighty, but who have not looked to the Holy One of Israel and have not searched for Jehovah himself. 2 And he is also wise and will bring in what is calamitous, and he has not called back his own words; and he will certainly rise up against the house of evildoers and against the assistance of those practicing what is hurtful.

3 The Egyptians, though, are earthling men, and not God; and their horses are flesh, and not spirit. And Jehovah himself will stretch out his hand, and he that is offering help will have to stumble, and he that is being helped will have to fall, and at the same time they will all of them come to an end.

4 For this is what Jehovah has said to me: "Just as the lion growls, even the maned young lion, over its prey, when there is called out against it a full number of shepherds, [and] in spite of their voice he will not be terrified and in spite of their commotion he will not stoop; in the same way Jehovah of armies will come down to wage war over Mount Zion and over her hill. 5 Like birds flying, Jehovah of armies will in the same way defend Jerusalem. Defending [her], he will also certainly deliver [her]. Sparing [her], he must also cause [her] to escape."

6 "Return, you people, to the One against whom the sons of Israel have gone deep in their revolt. 7 For in that day they will reject each one his worthless gods of silver and his valueless gods of gold, that your hands have made for yourselves as a sin. 8 And the As·syr′i·an must fall by the sword, not [that of] a man; and a sword, not [that of] earthling man, will devour him. And he must flee because of the sword, and his own young men will come to be for forced labor itself. 9 And his own crag will pass away out of sheer fright, and because of the signal his princes must be terrified," is the utterance of Jehovah, whose light is in Zion and whose furnace is in Jerusalem.

32 Look! A king will reign for righteousness itself; and as respects princes, they will rule as princes for justice itself. 2 And each one must prove to be like a hiding place from the wind and a place of concealment from the rainstorm, like streams of water in a waterless country, like the shadow of a heavy crag in an exhausted land.

3 And the eyes of those seeing will not be pasted together, and the very ears of those hearing will pay attention. 4 And the heart itself of those who are overhasty will consider knowledge, and even the tongue of the stammerers will be quick in speaking clear things. 5 The senseless one will no longer be called generous; and as for the unprincipled man, he will not be said to be noble; 6 because the senseless one himself will speak mere senselessness, and his very heart will work at what is hurtful, to work at apostasy and to speak against Jehovah what is wayward, to cause the soul of the hungry one to go empty, and he causes even the thirsty one to go without drink itself. 7 As for the unprincipled man, his instruments are bad; he himself has given counsel for acts of loose conduct, to wreck the afflicted ones with false sayings, even when someone poor speaks what is right.

8 As regards the generous one, it is for generous things that he has given counsel; and in favor of generous things he himself will rise up.

9 "You women who are at ease, rise up, listen to my voice! You careless daughters, give ear to my saying! 10 Within a year and some days you careless ones will be agitated, because the grape picking will have come to an end [but] no [fruit] gathering will come in. 11 Tremble, you women who are at ease! Be agitated, you careless ones! Undress and make yourselves naked, and gird [sack-cloth] upon the loins. 12 Beat yourselves upon the breasts in lamentation over the desirable fields, over the fruit-bearing vine. 13 Upon the ground of my people merely thorns, spiny bushes come up, for they are upon all the houses of exultation, yes, the highly elated town. 14 For the dwelling tower itself has been forsaken, the very hubbub of the city has been abandoned; O'phel and the watchtower themselves have become bare fields, for time indefinite the exultation of zebras, the pasture of droves; 15 until upon us the spirit is poured out from on high, and the wilderness will have become an orchard, and the orchard itself is accounted as a real forest.

16 "And in the wilderness justice will certainly reside, and in the orchard righteousness itself will dwell. 17 And the work of the [true] righteousness must become peace; and the service of the [true] righteousness, quietness and security to time indefinite. 18 And my people must dwell in a peaceful abiding place and in residences of full confidence and in undisturbed resting places. 19 And it will certainly hail when the forest goes down and the city becomes low in an abased state.

20 "Happy are you people who are sowing seed alongside all waters, sending forth the feet of the bull and of the ass."

33 Woe to you who are despoiling, without you yourself being despoiled, and to you who are dealing treacherously, without [others] having dealt treacherously with you! As soon as you have finished as a despoiler, you will be despoiled. As soon as you have done with dealing treacherously, they will deal treacherously with you.

2 O Jehovah, show us favor. In you we have hoped. Become our arm every morning, yes, our salvation in the time of distress. 3 At the sound of turmoil peoples have fled. At your arising nations have been dispersed. 4 And the spoil of you people will actually be gathered [like] the cockroaches when gathering in, like the onrush of locust swarms that is rushing against one. 5 Jehovah will certainly be put on high, for he is residing in the height. He must fill Zion with justice and righteousness. 6 And the trustworthiness of your times must prove to be a wealth of salvations—wisdom and knowledge, the fear of Jehovah, which is his treasure.

7 Look! Their very heroes have cried out in the street; the very messengers of peace will weep bitterly. 8 The highways have been made desolate; the one passing over the path has ceased. He has broken the covenant; he has contemned the cities; he has taken no account of mortal man. 9 The land has gone mourning, has withered away. Leb'a·non has become abashed; it has moldered. Shar'on has become like the desert plain; and Ba'shan and Car'mel are shaking off [their leaves].

10 "Now I will rise up," says Jehovah, "now I will exalt myself; now I will lift myself up. 11 You people conceive dried grass; you will give birth to stubble. Your own spirit, as a fire, will eat you up. 12 And peoples must become as the burnings of lime. As thorns cut away, they will be set ablaze even with fire. 13 Hear, you men who are far away, what I must do! And know, you who are nearby, my mightiness. 14 In Zion the sinners

have come to be in dread; shivering has grabbed hold of the apostates: 'Who of us can reside for any time with a devouring fire? Who of us can reside for any time with long-lasting conflagrations?'

15 "There is one who is walking in continual righteousness and speaking what is upright, who is rejecting the unjust gain from frauds, who is shaking his hands clear from taking hold on a bribe, who is stopping up his ear from listening to bloodshed, and who is closing his eyes so as not to see what is bad. 16 He is the one that will reside on the heights themselves; his secure height will be craggy places difficult to approach. His own bread will certainly be given [him]; his water supply will be unfailing."

17 A king in his handsomeness is what your eyes will behold; they will see a land far away. 18 Your own heart will comment in low tones on a frightful thing: "Where is the secretary? Where is the one that does the paying out? Where is the one counting the towers?" 19 No insolent people will you see, a people too deep in language to listen to, of a stammering tongue without [your] understanding. 20 Behold Zion, the town of our festal occasions! Your own eyes will see Jerusalem an undisturbed abiding place, a tent that no one will pack up. Never will its tent pins be pulled out, and none of its ropes will be torn in two. 21 But there the Majestic One, Jehovah, will be for us a place of rivers, of wide canals. On it no galley fleet will go, and no majestic ship will pass over it. 22 For Jehovah is our Judge, Jehovah is our Statute-giver, Jehovah is our King; he himself will save us.

23 Your ropes must hang loose; their mast they will not hold firmly erect; they have not spread a sail. At that time even spoil in abundance will have to be divided up; the lame ones themselves will actually take a big plunder. 24 And no resident will say: "I am sick." The people that are dwelling in [the land] will be those pardoned for their error.

34 Come up close, YOU nations, to hear; and YOU national groups, pay attention. Let the earth and that which fills it listen, the productive land and all its produce. 2 For Jehovah has indignation against all the nations, and rage against all their army. He must devote them to destruction; he must give them to the slaughter. 3 And their slain ones will be thrown out; and as for their carcasses, their stink will ascend; and the mountains must melt because of their blood. 4 And all those of the army of the heavens must rot away. And the heavens must be rolled up, just like a book scroll; and their army will all shrivel away, just as the leafage shrivels off the vine and like a shriveled [fig] off the fig tree.

5 "For in the heavens my sword will certainly be drenched. Look! Upon E'dom it will descend, and upon the people devoted by me to destruction in justice. 6 Jehovah has a sword; it must be filled with blood; it must be made greasy with the fat, with the blood of young rams and he-goats, with the fat of the kidneys of rams. For Jehovah has a sacrifice in Boz'rah, and a great slaughtering in the land of E'dom. 7 And the wild bulls must come down with them, and young bulls with the powerful ones; and their land must be drenched with blood, and their very dust will be made greasy with the fat."

8 For Jehovah has a day of vengeance, a year of retributions for the legal case over Zion.

9 And her torrents must be changed into pitch, and her dust into sulphur; and her land must become as burning pitch. 10 By night or by day it will not be extinguished; to time indefinite its smoke will keep ascending. From generation to generation she will be parched; forever and ever no one will be passing across her. 11 And the pelican and the porcupine must take possession of her,

and long-eared owls and ravens themselves will reside in her; and he must stretch out over her the measuring line of emptiness and the stones of wasteness. 12 Her nobles—there are none there whom they will call to the kingship itself, and her very princes will all become nothing. 13 On her dwelling towers thorns must come up, nettles and thorny weeds in her fortified places; and she must become an abiding place of jackals, the courtyard for the ostriches. 14 And haunters of waterless regions must meet up with howling animals, and even the goat-shaped demon will call to its companion. Yes, there the nightjar will certainly take its ease and find for itself a resting place. 15 There the arrow snake has made its nest and lays [eggs], and it must hatch [them] and gather [them] together under its shadow. Yes, there the gledes must collect themselves together, each one with her mate.

16 Search for yourselves in the book of Jehovah and read out loud: not one has been missing of them; they actually do not fail to have each one her mate, for it is the mouth of Jehovah that has given the command, and it is his spirit that has collected them together. 17 And it is He that has cast for them the lot, and his own hand has apportioned the place to them by the measuring line. To time indefinite they will take possession of it; for generation after generation they will reside in it.

35 The wilderness and the waterless region will exult, and the desert plain will be joyful and blossom as the saffron. 2 Without fail it will blossom, and it will really be joyful with joyousness and with glad crying out. The glory of Leb′a·non itself must be given to it, the splendor of Car′mel and of Shar′on. There will be those who will see the glory of Jehovah, the splendor of our God.

3 Strengthen the weak hands, you people, and make the knees that are wobbling firm. 4 Say to those who are anxious at heart:

"Be strong. Do not be afraid. Look! Your own God will come with vengeance itself, God even with a repayment. He himself will come and save you people."

5 At that time the eyes of the blind ones will be opened, and the very ears of the deaf ones will be unstopped. 6 At that time the lame one will climb up just as a stag does, and the tongue of the speechless one will cry out in gladness. For in the wilderness waters will have burst out, and torrents in the desert plain. 7 And the heat-parched ground will have become as a reedy pool, and the thirsty ground as springs of water. In the abiding place of jackals, a resting place for [them], there will be green grass with reeds and papyrus plants.

8 And there will certainly come to be a highway there, even a way; and the Way of Holiness it will be called. The unclean one will not pass over it. And it will be for the one walking on the way, and no foolish ones will wander about [on it]. 9 No lion will prove to be there, and the rapacious sort of wild beasts will not come up on it. None will be found there; and the repurchased ones must walk [there]. 10 And the very ones redeemed by Jehovah will return and certainly come to Zion with a joyful cry; and rejoicing to time indefinite will be upon their head. To exultation and rejoicing they will attain, and grief and sighing must flee away.

36 Now it came about in the fourteenth year of King Hez·e·ki′ah that Sen·nach′er·ib king of As·syr′i·a came up against all the fortified cities of Judah and proceeded to seize them. 2 And the king of As·syr′i·a finally sent Rab′sha·keh from La′chish to Jerusalem, to King Hez·e·ki′ah, with a heavy military force, and he proceeded to stand still by the conduit of the upper pool at the highway of the laundryman's field. 3 Then there came out to him E·li′a·kim the son of Hil·ki′ah, who was over the household, and Sheb′na the secretary and Jo′ah the son of A′saph the recorder.

4 Accordingly Rab′sha·keh said to them: "Please, say to Hez·e·ki′ah, 'This is what the great king, the king of As·syr′i·a, has said: "What is this confidence in which you have trusted? 5 You have said (but it is the word of lips), 'There are counsel and mightiness for the war.' Now in whom have you put trust, that you have rebelled against me? 6 Look! You have trusted in the support of this crushed reed, in Egypt, which, if a man should brace himself upon it, would certainly enter into his palm and pierce it. That is the way Phar′aoh the king of Egypt is to all those putting their trust in him. 7 And in case you should say to me, 'It is Jehovah our God in whom we have trusted,' is he not the one whose high places and whose altars Hez·e·ki′ah has removed, while he says to Judah and Jerusalem, 'Before this altar you should bow down'?" ' 8 Now, then, make a wager, please, with my lord the king of As·syr′i·a, and let me give you two thousand horses [to see] whether you are able, on your part, to put riders upon them. 9 How, then, could you turn back the face of one governor of the smallest servants of my lord, while you, for your part, put your trust in Egypt for chariots and for horsemen? 10 And now is it without authorization from Jehovah that I have come up against this land to bring it to ruin? Jehovah himself said to me, 'Go up against this land, and you must bring it to ruin.' "

11 At this E·li′a·kim and Sheb′na and Jo′ah said to Rab′sha·keh: "Speak, please, to your servants in the Syrian language, for we are listening; and do not speak to us in the Jews' language in the ears of the people that are on the wall." 12 But Rab′sha·keh said: "Is it to your lord and to you that my lord has sent me to speak these words? Is it not to the men sitting upon the wall, that they may eat their own excrement and drink their own urine with you men?"

13 And Rab′sha·keh continued to stand and call out in a loud voice in the Jews' language, and he went on to say: "HEAR the words of the great king, the king of As·syr′i·a. 14 This is what the king has said, 'Do not let Hez·e·ki′ah deceive you people, for he is not able to deliver you. 15 And do not let Hez·e·ki′ah cause you to trust in Jehovah, saying: "Without fail Jehovah will deliver us. This city will not be given into the hand of the king of As·syr′i·a." 16 Do not listen to Hez·e·ki′ah, for this is what the king of As·syr′i·a has said: "Make a capitulation to me and come out to me and eat each one from his own vine and each one from his own fig tree and drink each one the water of his own cistern, 17 until I come and actually take you to a land like your own land, a land of grain and new wine, a land of bread and vineyards; 18 in order that Hez·e·ki′ah may not allure you, saying, 'Jehovah himself will deliver us.' Have the gods of the nations delivered each one his own land out of the hand of the king of As·syr′i·a? 19 Where are the gods of Ha′math and Ar′pad? Where are the gods of Seph·ar·va′im? And have they delivered Sa·mar′i·a out of my hand? 20 Who are there among all the gods of these lands that have delivered their land out of my hand so that Jehovah should deliver Jerusalem out of my hand?" ' "

21 And they continued to keep silent and did not answer him a word, for the commandment of the king was, saying: "You must not answer him." 22 But E·li′a·kim the son of Hil·ki′ah, who was over the household, and Sheb′na the secretary and Jo′ah the son of A′saph the recorder came to Hez·e·ki′ah with their garments ripped apart, and told him the words of Rab′sha·keh.

37 And it came about that as soon as King Hez·e·ki′ah heard, he immediately ripped his garments apart and covered himself with sackcloth and came into the house of Jehovah. 2 Further, he sent E·li'a·kim, who was over the household, and Sheb'na the secretary and the older men of the priests covered with sackcloth to Isaiah the son of A'moz the prophet. 3 And they proceeded to say to him: "This is what Hez·e·ki'ah has said, 'This day is a day of distress and of rebuke and of scornful insolence, for the sons have come as far as the womb's mouth, and there is no power to give birth. 4 Perhaps Jehovah your God will hear the words of Rab'sha·keh, whom the king of As·syr'i·a his lord sent to taunt the living God, and he will actually call him to account for the words that Jehovah your God has heard. And you must lift up prayer in behalf of the remnant that are to be found.'"

5 So the servants of King Hez·e·ki'ah came in to Isaiah. 6 Then Isaiah said to them: "This is what you should say to your lord, 'This is what Jehovah has said: "Do not be afraid because of the words that you have heard with which the attendants of the king of As·syr'i·a spoke abusively of me. 7 Here I am putting a spirit in him, and he must hear a report and return to his own land; and I shall certainly cause him to fall by the sword in his own land."'"

8 After that Rab'sha·keh returned and found the king of As·syr'i·a fighting against Lib'nah, for he had heard that he had pulled away from La'chish. 9 Now he heard it said concerning Tir·ha'kah the king of E·thi·o'pi·a: "He has come out to fight against you." When he heard, he at once sent messengers to Hez·e·ki'ah, saying: 10 "This is what you men should say to Hez·e·ki'ah the king of Judah, 'Do not let your God in whom you are trusting deceive you, saying: "Jerusalem will not be given into the hand of the king of As·syr'i·a." 11 Look! You yourself have heard what the kings of As·syr'i·a did to all the lands by devoting them to destruction, and will you yourself be delivered? 12 Have the gods of the nations that my forefathers brought to ruin delivered them,

even Go'zan and Ha'ran and Re'zeph and the sons of E'den that were in Tel-as'sar? 13 Where is the king of Ha'math and the king of Ar'pad and the king of the city of Seph·ar·va'im—of He'na and of Iv'vah?'"

14 Then Hez·e·ki'ah took the letters out of the hand of the messengers and read them, after which Hez·e·ki'ah went up to the house of Jehovah and spread it out before Jehovah. 15 And Hez·e·ki'ah began to pray to Jehovah, saying: 16 "O Jehovah of armies, the God of Israel, sitting upon the cherubs, you alone are the [true] God of all the kingdoms of the earth. You yourself have made the heavens and the earth. 17 Incline your ear, O Jehovah, and hear. Open your eyes, O Jehovah, and see, and hear all the words of Sen·nach'er·ib that he has sent to taunt the living God. 18 It is a fact, O Jehovah, that the kings of As·syr'i·a have devastated all the lands, and their own land. 19 And there was a consigning of their gods to the fire, because they were no gods, but the workmanship of man's hands, wood and stone, so that they destroyed them. 20 And now, O Jehovah our God, save us out of his hand, that all the kingdoms of the earth may know that you, O Jehovah, are [God] alone."

21 And Isaiah the son of A'moz proceeded to send to Hez·e·ki'ah, saying: "This is what Jehovah the God of Israel has said, 'Because you have prayed to me concerning Sen·nach'er·ib the king of As·syr'i·a, 22 this is the word that Jehovah has spoken against him:

"The virgin daughter of Zion has despised you, she has held you in derision.

Behind you the daughter of Jerusalem has wagged [her] head.

23 Whom have you taunted and spoken of abusively?

And against whom have you lifted up [your] voice

And do you raise your eyes on high?

It is against the Holy One of Israel!

24 By means of your servants you have taunted Jehovah and you say,

'With the multitude of my war chariots I myself—

I shall certainly ascend the height of mountainous regions,

The remotest parts of Leb'a·non;

And I shall cut down its lofty cedars, its choice juniper trees.

And I shall enter its final height, the forest of its orchard.

25 I myself shall certainly dig and drink waters,

And I shall dry up with the soles of my feet all the Nile canals of Egypt.'

26 Have you not heard? From remote times it is what I will do.

From bygone days I have even formed it. Now I will bring it in.

And you will serve to make fortified cities become desolate as piles of ruins.

27 And their inhabitants will be feeble-handed;

They will simply be terrified and ashamed.

They must become as vegetation of the field and green tender grass,

Grass of the roofs and of the terrace before the east wind.

28 And your sitting quiet and your going out and your coming in I well know,

And your exciting yourself against me,

29 Because your exciting yourself against me and your roaring have come up into my ears.

And I shall certainly put my hook in your nose and my bridle between your lips,

And I shall indeed lead you back by the way by which you have come."

30 "'And this will be the sign for you: There will be an eating this year of the growth from spilled kernels, and in the second year grain that shoots up of itself; but in the third year sow seed, you people, and reap, and plant vineyards and eat their fruitage. 31 And those who escape of the house of Judah, those who are left remaining, will certainly take root downward and produce fruitage upward. 32 For out of Jerusalem a remnant will go forth and those who escape out of Mount Zion. The very zeal of Jehovah of armies will do this.

33 "'Therefore this is what Jehovah has said concerning the king of As·syr'i·a: "He will not come into this city, nor will he shoot an arrow there, nor confront it with a shield, nor cast up a siege rampart against it."'

34 "'By the way by which he came he will return, and into this city he will not come,' is the utterance of Jehovah. 35 'And I shall certainly defend this city to save it for my own sake and for the sake of David my servant.'"

36 And the angel of Jehovah proceeded to go forth and strike down a hundred and eighty-five thousand in the camp of the As·syr'i·ans. When people rose up early in the morning, why, there all of them were dead carcasses. 37 Hence Sennach'er·ib the king of As·syr'i·a pulled away and went and returned and took up dwelling in Nin'e·veh. 38 And it came about that as he was bowing down at the house of Nis'roch his god, A·dram'me·lech and Shar·e'zer, his own sons, struck him down with the sword, and they themselves escaped to the land of Ar'a·rat. And E'sar-had'don his son began to reign in place of him.

38 In those days Hez·e·ki'ah got sick to the point of dying. Accordingly Isaiah the son of A'moz the prophet came in to him and said to him: "This is what Jehovah has said, 'Give commands to your household, for you yourself will indeed die and will not live.'" 2 At that Hez·e·ki'ah turned his face to the wall and began to pray to Jehovah 3 and to say: "I beseech you, O Jehovah, remember, please, how I have walked before you in truthfulness and with a complete heart, and what was good in your eyes I have done." And Hez·e·ki′ah began to weep profusely.

4 And the word of Jehovah now occurred to Isaiah, saying: 5 "Go, and you must say to Hez·e·ki′ah, 'This is what Jehovah the God of David your forefather has said: "I have heard your prayer. I have seen your tears. Here I am adding onto your days fifteen years; 6 and out of the palm of the king of As·syr′i·a I shall deliver you and this city, and I will defend this city. 7 And this is the sign for you from Jehovah that Jehovah will perform this word that he has spoken: 8 Here I am making the shadow of the steps that had gone down on the steps [of the stairs] of A′haz by the sun retrace backward ten steps."'" And the sun gradually went back ten steps on the steps [of the stairs] that it had gone down.

9 A writing of Hez·e·ki′ah the king of Judah, when he got sick and revived from his sickness.

10 I myself said: "In the midst of my days I will go into the gates of She′ol.
I must be deprived of the remainder of my years."

11 I have said: "I shall not see Jah, even Jah, in the land of the living ones.
I shall no more look on mankind—with the inhabitants of [the land of] cessation.

12 My own habitation has been pulled out and removed from me like the tent of shepherds.
I have rolled up my life just like a loom worker;
One proceeds to cut me off from the very threads of the warp.
From daylight till night you keep handing me over.

13 I have soothed myself until the morning.
Like a lion, so he keeps breaking all my bones;

From daylight till night you keep handing me over.

14 Like the swift, the bulbul, so I keep chirping;
I keep cooing like the dove.
My eyes have looked languishingly to the height:
'O Jehovah, I am under oppression. Stand good for me.'

15 What shall I speak, and [what] will he actually say to me?
He himself has also acted.
I keep walking solemnly all my years in the bitterness of my soul.

16 O Jehovah, on that account they keep living; and as with everybody, thereby is the life of my spirit.
And you will restore me to health and certainly preserve me alive.

17 Look! For peace I had what was bitter, yes, bitter;
And you yourself have become attached to my soul [and kept it] from the pit of disintegration.
For you have thrown behind your back all my sins.

18 For it is not She′ol that can laud you; death itself cannot praise you.
Those going down into the pit cannot look hopefully to your trueness.

19 The living, the living, he is the one that can laud you,
Just as I can this day.
The father himself can give knowledge to his own sons concerning your trueness.

20 O Jehovah, [undertake] to save me, and we shall play my string selections
All the days of our life at the house of Jehovah."

21 And Isaiah proceeded to say: "Let them take a cake of pressed dried figs and rub [it] in upon the boil, that he may revive." 22 Meantime, Hez·e·ki′ah said: "What is the sign that I shall go up to the house of Jehovah?"

39 At that time Mer′o·dach-bal′a·dan the son of Bal′a·dan the king of Babylon sent letters and a gift to Hez·e·ki′ah, after he heard that he had been sick but was strong again. 2 So Hez·e·ki′ah began to rejoice over them and proceeded to show them his treasure house, the silver and the gold and the balsam oil and the good oil and all his armory and all that was to be found in his treasures. There proved to be nothing that Hez·e·ki′ah did not show them in his own house and in all his dominion.

3 After that Isaiah the prophet came in to King Hez·e·ki′ah and said to him: "What did these men say, and from where did they proceed to come to you?" So Hez·e·ki′ah said: "From a distant land they came to me, from Babylon." 4 And he went on to say: "What did they see in your house?" To this Hez·e·ki′ah said: "Everything that is in my house they saw. There proved to be nothing that I did not show them in my treasures." 5 Isaiah now said to Hez·e·ki′ah: "Hear the word of Jehovah of armies, 6 'Look! Days are coming, and all that is in your own house and that your forefathers have stored up down to this day will actually be carried to Babylon.' 'Nothing will be left,' Jehovah has said. 7 'And some of your own sons that will come forth from you, to whom you will become father, will themselves be taken and actually become court officials in the palace of the king of Babylon.'"

8 At that Hez·e·ki′ah said to Isaiah: "The word of Jehovah that you have spoken is good." And he went on to say: "Because peace and truth will continue in my own days."

40 "Comfort, comfort my people," says the God of you men. 2 "Speak to the heart of Jerusalem and call out to her that her military service has been fulfilled, that her error has been paid off. For from the hand of Jehovah she has received a full amount for all her sins."

3 Listen! Someone is calling out in the wilderness: "Clear up the way of Jehovah, you people! Make the highway for our God through the desert plain straight. 4 Let every valley be raised up, and every mountain and hill be made low. And the knobby ground must become level land, and the rugged ground a valley plain. 5 And the glory of Jehovah will certainly be revealed, and all flesh must see [it] together, for the very mouth of Jehovah has spoken [it]."

6 Listen! Someone is saying: "Call out!" And one said: "What shall I call out?"

"All flesh is green grass, and all their loving-kindness is like the blossom of the field. 7 The green grass has dried up, the blossom has withered, because the very spirit of Jehovah has blown upon it. Surely the people are green grass. 8 The green grass has dried up, the blossom has withered; but as for the word of our God, it will last to time indefinite."

9 Make your way up even onto a high mountain, you woman bringing good news for Zion. Raise your voice even with power, you woman bringing good news for Jerusalem. Raise [it]. Do not be afraid. Say to the cities of Judah: "Here is your God." 10 Look! The Lord Jehovah himself will come even as a strong one, and his arm will be ruling for him. Look! His reward is with him, and the wage he pays is before him. 11 Like a shepherd he will shepherd his own drove. With his arm he will collect together the lambs; and in his bosom he will carry [them]. Those giving suck he will conduct [with care].

12 Who has measured the waters in the mere hollow of his hand, and taken the proportions of the heavens themselves with a mere span and included in a measure the dust of the earth, or weighed with an indicator the mountains, and the hills in the scales? 13 Who has taken the proportions of the spirit of Jehovah, and who as his man of counsel can make him know anything? 14 With whom did he consult together that one might make him understand, or who teaches him in the path of justice, or teaches him knowledge,

or makes him know the very way of real understanding?

15 Look! The nations are as a drop from a bucket; and as the film of dust on the scales they have been accounted. Look! He lifts the islands themselves as mere fine [dust]. 16 Even Leb′a·non is not sufficient for keeping a fire burning, and its wild animals are not sufficient for a burnt offering. 17 All the nations are as something nonexistent in front of him; as nothing and an unreality they have been accounted to him.

18 And to whom can YOU people liken God, and what likeness can YOU put alongside him? 19 The craftsman has cast a mere molten image, and with gold the metalworker overlays it, and silver chains he is forging. 20 A certain tree as a contribution, a tree that is not rotten, he chooses. A skillful craftsman he searches out for himself, to prepare a carved image that may not be made to totter.

21 Do YOU people not know? Do YOU not hear? Has it not been told to YOU from the outset? Have YOU not applied understanding from the foundations of the earth? 22 There is One who is dwelling above the circle of the earth, the dwellers in which are as grasshoppers, the One who is stretching out the heavens just as a fine gauze, who spreads them out like a tent in which to dwell, 23 the One who is reducing high officials to nothing, who has made the very judges of the earth as a mere unreality.

24 Never yet have they been planted; never yet have they been sown; never yet has their stump taken root in the earth. And one has only to blow upon them and they dry up; and like stubble the windstorm itself will carry them away.

25 "But to whom can YOU people liken me so that I should be made his equal?" says the Holy One. 26 "Raise YOUR eyes high up and see. Who has created these things? It is the One who is bringing forth the army of them even by number, all of whom he calls even by name. Due to the abundance of dynamic energy, he also being vigorous in power, not one [of them] is missing.

27 "For what reason do you say, O Jacob, and do you speak out, O Israel, 'My way has been concealed from Jehovah, and justice to me eludes my God himself'? 28 Have you not come to know or have you not heard? Jehovah, the Creator of the extremities of the earth, is a God to time indefinite. He does not tire out or grow weary. There is no searching out of his understanding. 29 He is giving to the tired one power; and to the one without dynamic energy he makes full might abound. 30 Boys will both tire out and grow weary, and young men themselves will without fail stumble, 31 but those who are hoping in Jehovah will regain power. They will mount up with wings like eagles. They will run and not grow weary; they will walk and not tire out."

41 "Attend to me in silence, YOU islands; and let national groups themselves regain power. Let them approach. At that time let them speak. Let us come up close together for the judgment itself.

2 "Who has roused up [someone] from the sunrise? [Who] proceeded in righteousness to call him to His feet, to give before him the nations, and to make [him] go subduing even kings? [Who] kept giving [them] like dust to his sword, so that they have been driven about like mere stubble with his bow? 3 [Who] kept pursuing them, kept peacefully passing along on his feet over the path [by which] he did not proceed to come? 4 Who has been active and has done [this], calling out the generations from the start?

"I, Jehovah, the First One; and with the last ones I am the same."

5 The islands saw and began to fear. The very extremities of the earth began trembling. They drew near and kept coming. 6 They went helping each one his companion, and one would say to his brother: "Be strong." 7 So the

craftsman went strengthening the metalworker; the one doing the smoothing out with the forge hammer him that is hammering away at the anvil, saying regarding the soldering: "It is good." Finally one fastened it with nails that it could not be made to totter.

8 "But you, O Israel, are my servant, you, O Jacob, whom I have chosen, the seed of Abraham my friend; 9 you, whom I have taken hold of from the extremities of the earth, and you, whom I have called even from the remote parts of it. And so I said to you, 'You are my servant; I have chosen you, and I have not rejected you. 10 Do not be afraid, for I am with you. Do not gaze about, for I am your God. I will fortify you. I will really help you. I will really keep fast hold of you with my right hand of righteousness.'

11 "Look! All those getting heated up against you will become ashamed and be humiliated. The men in a quarrel with you will become as nothing and will perish. 12 You will search for them, but you will not find them, those men in a struggle with you. They will become as something nonexistent and as nothing, those men at war with you. 13 For I, Jehovah your God, am grasping your right hand, the One saying to you, 'Do not be afraid. I myself will help you.'

14 "Do not be afraid, you worm Jacob, you men of Israel. I myself will help you," is the utterance of Jehovah, even your Repurchaser, the Holy One of Israel. 15 "Look! I have made you a threshing sledge, a new threshing instrument having double-edged [teeth]. You will tread down the mountains and crush [them]; and the hills you will make just like the chaff. 16 You will winnow them, and a wind itself will carry them away, and a windstorm itself will drive them different ways. And you yourself will be joyful in Jehovah. In the Holy One of Israel you will boast about yourself."

17 "The afflicted ones and the poor ones are seeking for water, but there is none. Because of thirst their very tongue has become dry. I myself, Jehovah, shall answer them. I, the God of Israel, shall not leave them. 18 Upon bare hills I shall open up rivers, and in the midst of the valley plains, springs. I shall make the wilderness into a reedy pool of water, and the waterless land into sources of water. 19 In the wilderness I shall set the cedar tree, the acacia and the myrtle and the oil tree. In the desert plain I shall place the juniper tree, the ash and the cypress at the same time; 20 in order that people may see and know and pay heed and have insight at the same time, that the very hand of Jehovah has done this, and the Holy One of Israel has himself created it.

21 "Bring YOUR controversial case forward, YOU people," says Jehovah. "Produce YOUR arguments," says the King of Jacob. 22 "Produce and tell to us the things that are going to happen. The first things— what they were—do tell, that we may apply our heart and know the future of them. Or cause us to hear even the things that are coming. 23 Tell the things that are to come afterward, that we may know that YOU are gods. Yes, YOU ought to do good or do bad, that we may gaze about and see [it] at the same time. 24 Look! YOU men are something nonexistent, and YOUR achievement is nothing. A detestable thing is anyone that chooses YOU.

25 "I have roused up [someone] from the north, and he will come. From the rising of the sun he will call upon my name. And he will come upon deputy rulers as [if they were] clay and just as a potter that tramples down the moist material.

26 "Who has told anything from the start, that we may know, or from times past, that we may say, 'He is right'? Really there is no one telling. Really there is no one causing [one] to hear. Really there is no one that is hearing any sayings of YOU men."

27 There is one first, [saying] to Zion: "Look! Here they are!" and

to Jerusalem I shall give a bringer of good news.

28 And I kept seeing, and there was not a man; and out of these there was also no one that was giving counsel. And I kept asking them, that they might make a reply. 29 Look! All of them are something nonexistent. Their works are nothing. Their molten images are wind and unreality.

42 Look! My servant, on whom I keep fast hold! My chosen one, [whom] my soul has approved! I have put my spirit in him. Justice to the nations is what he will bring forth. 2 He will not cry out or raise [his voice], and in the street he will not let his voice be heard. 3 No crushed reed will he break; and as for a dim flaxen wick, he will not extinguish it. In trueness he will bring forth justice. 4 He will not grow dim nor be crushed until he sets justice in the earth itself; and for his law the islands themselves will keep waiting.

5 This is what the [true] God, Jehovah, has said, the Creator of the heavens and the grand One stretching them out; the One laying out the earth and its produce, the One giving breath to the people on it, and spirit to those walking in it: 6 "I myself, Jehovah, have called you in righteousness, and I proceeded to take hold of your hand. And I shall safeguard you and give you as a covenant of the people, as a light of the nations, 7 [for you] to open the blind eyes, to bring forth out of the dungeon the prisoner, out of the house of detention those sitting in darkness.

8 "I am Jehovah. That is my name; and to no one else shall I give my own glory, neither my praise to graven images.

9 "The first things—here they have come, but new things I am telling out. Before they begin to spring up, I cause YOU people to hear [them]."

10 Sing to Jehovah a new song, his praise from the extremity of the earth, YOU men that are going down to the sea and to that which

fills it, YOU islands and YOU inhabiting them. 11 Let the wilderness and its cities raise [their voice], the settlements that Ke'dar inhabits. Let the inhabitants of the crag cry out in joy. From the top of the mountains let people cry aloud. 12 Let them attribute to Jehovah glory, and in the islands let them tell forth even his praise.

13 Like a mighty man Jehovah himself will go forth. Like a warrior he will awaken zeal. He will shout, yes, he will let out a war cry; over his enemies he will show himself mightier.

14 "I have kept quiet for a long time. I continued silent. I kept exercising self-control. Like a woman giving birth I am going to groan, pant, and gasp at the same time. 15 I shall devastate mountains and hills, and all their vegetation I shall dry up. And I will turn rivers into islands, and reedy pools I shall dry up. 16 And I will make the blind ones walk in a way that they have not known; in a roadway that they have not known I shall cause them to tread. I shall turn a dark place before them into light, and rugged terrain into level land. These are the things that I will do for them, and I will not leave them."

17 They must be turned back, they will be very much ashamed, those who are putting trust in the carved image, those who are saying to a molten image: "YOU are our gods."

18 Hear, YOU deaf ones; and look forth to see, YOU blind ones. 19 Who is blind, if not my servant, and who is deaf as my messenger whom I send? Who is blind as the one rewarded, or blind as the servant of Jehovah? 20 It was a case of seeing many things, but you did not keep watching. It was a case of opening the ears, but you did not keep listening. 21 Jehovah himself for the sake of his righteousness has taken a delight in that he should magnify the law and make it majestic. 22 But it is a people plundered and pillaged, all of them being trapped in the holes,

and in the houses of detention they have been kept hidden. They have come to be for plunder without a deliverer, for pillage without anyone to say: "Bring back!"

23 Who among you people will give ear to this? Who will pay attention and listen for later times? 24 Who has given Jacob for mere pillage, and Israel to the plunderers? Is it not Jehovah, the One against whom we have sinned, and in whose ways they did not want to walk and to whose law they did not listen? 25 So He kept pouring out upon him rage, his anger, and the strength of war. And it kept consuming him all around, but he took no note; and it kept blazing up against him, but he would lay nothing to heart.

43 And now this is what Jehovah has said, your Creator, O Jacob, and your Former, O Israel: "Do not be afraid, for I have repurchased you. I have called [you] by your name. You are mine. 2 In case you should pass through the waters, I will be with you; and through the rivers, they will not flood over you. In case you should walk through the fire, you will not be scorched, neither will the flame itself singe you. 3 For I am Jehovah your God, the Holy One of Israel your Savior. I have given Egypt as a ransom for you, E·thi·o′pi·a and Se′ba in place of you. 4 Owing to the fact that you have been precious in my eyes, you have been considered honorable, and I myself have loved you. And I shall give men in place of you, and national groups in place of your soul.

5 "Do not be afraid, for I am with you. From the sunrising I shall bring your seed, and from the sunset I shall collect you together. 6 I shall say to the north, 'Give up!' and to the south, 'Do not keep back. Bring my sons from far off, and my daughters from the extremity of the earth, 7 everyone that is called by my name and that I have created for my own glory, that I have formed, yes, that I have made.'

8 "Bring forth a people blind though eyes themselves exist, and the ones deaf though they have ears. 9 Let the nations all be collected together at one place, and let national groups be gathered together. Who is there among them that can tell this? Or can they cause us to hear even the first things? Let them furnish their witnesses, that they may be declared righteous, or let them hear and say, 'It is the truth!'"

10 "You are my witnesses," is the utterance of Jehovah, "even my servant whom I have chosen, in order that you may know and have faith in me, and that you may understand that I am the same One. Before me there was no God formed, and after me there continued to be none. 11 I—I am Jehovah, and besides me there is no savior."

12 "I myself have told forth and have saved and have caused [it] to be heard, when there was among you no strange [god]. So you are my witnesses," is the utterance of Jehovah, "and I am God. 13 Also, all the time I am the same One; and there is no one effecting deliverance out of my own hand. I shall get active, and who can turn it back?"

14 This is what Jehovah has said, the Repurchaser of you people, the Holy One of Israel: "For your sakes I will send to Babylon and cause the bars of the prisons to come down, and the Chal·de′ans in the ships with whining cries on their part. 15 I am Jehovah your Holy One, the Creator of Israel, your King."

16 This is what Jehovah has said, the One making a way through the sea itself and a roadway even through strong waters, 17 the One bringing forth the war chariot and the horse, the military force and the strong ones at the same time: "They will lie down. They will not get up. They will certainly be extinguished. Like a flaxen wick they must be put out."

18 "Do not remember the first things, and to the former things

do not turn YOUR consideration. 19 Look! I am doing something new. Now it will spring up. You people will know it, will YOU not? Really, through the wilderness I shall set a way, through the desert rivers. 20 The wild beast of the field will glorify me, the jackals and the ostriches; because I shall have given water even in the wilderness, rivers in the desert, to cause my people, my chosen one, to drink, 21 the people whom I have formed for myself, that they should recount the praise of me.

22 "But you have not called even me, O Jacob, because you have grown weary of me, O Israel. 23 You have not brought me the sheep of your whole burnt offerings, and with your sacrifices you have not glorified me. I have not compelled you to serve me with a gift, nor have I made you weary with frankincense. 24 For me you have bought no [sweet] cane with any money; and with the fat of your sacrifices you have not saturated me. In reality you have compelled me to serve because of your sins; you have made me weary with your errors.

25 "I—I am the One that is wiping out your transgressions for my own sake, and your sins I shall not remember. 26 Remind me; let us put ourselves on judgment together; tell your own account of it in order that you may be in the right. 27 Your own father, the first one, has sinned, and your own spokesmen have transgressed against me. 28 So I shall profane the princes of the holy place, and I will give Jacob over as a man devoted to destruction and Israel over to words of abuse.

44 "And now listen, O Jacob my servant, and you, O Israel, whom I have chosen. 2 This is what Jehovah has said, your Maker and your Former, who kept helping you even from the belly, 'Do not be afraid, O my servant Jacob, and you, Jesh'u·run, whom I have chosen. 3 For I shall pour out water upon the thirsty one, and trickling streams upon the dry place. I shall pour out my spirit upon your seed, and my blessing upon your descendants. 4 And they will certainly spring up as among the green grass, like poplars by the water ditches. 5 This one will say: "I belong to Jehovah." And that one will call [himself] by the name of Jacob, and another will write upon his hand: "Belonging to Jehovah." And by the name of Israel one will betitle [himself].'

6 "This is what Jehovah has said, the King of Israel and the Repurchaser of him, Jehovah of armies, 'I am the first and I am the last, and besides me there is no God. 7 And who is there like me? Let him call out, that he may tell it and present it to me. From when I appointed the people of long ago, both the things coming and the things that will enter in let them tell on their part. 8 Do not be in dread, YOU people, and do not become stupefied. Have I not from that time on caused you individually to hear and told [it] out? And YOU are my witnesses. Does there exist a God besides me? No, there is no Rock. I have recognized none.'"

9 The formers of the carved image are all of them an unreality, and their darlings themselves will be of no benefit; and as their witnesses they see nothing and know nothing, in order that they may be ashamed. 10 Who has formed a god or cast a mere molten image? Of no benefit at all has it been. 11 Look! All his partners themselves will be ashamed, and the craftsmen are from earthling men. They will all of them collect themselves together. They will stand still. They will be in dread. They will be ashamed at the same time.

12 As for the carver of iron with the billhook, he has been busy [at it] with the coals; and with the hammers he proceeds to form it, and he keeps busy at it with his powerful arm. Also, he has become hungry, and so without power. He has not drunk water; so he gets tired.

13 As for the wood carver, he has stretched out the measuring line; he traces it out with red chalk; he works it up with a wood scraper; and with a compass he keeps tracing it out, and gradually he makes it like the representation of a man, like the beauty of mankind, to sit in a house.

14 There is one whose business is to cut down cedars; and he takes a certain species of tree, even a massive tree, and he lets it become strong for himself among the trees of the forest. He planted the laurel tree, and the pouring rain itself keeps making it get big. 15 And it has become [something] for man to keep a fire burning. So he takes part of it that he may warm himself. In fact he builds a fire and actually bakes bread. He also works on a god to which he may bow down. He has made it into a carved image, and he prostrates himself to it. 16 Half of it he actually burns up in a fire. Upon half of it he roasts well the flesh that he eats, and he becomes satisfied. He also warms himself and says: "Aha! I have warmed myself. I have seen the firelight." 17 But the remainder of it he actually makes into a god itself, into his carved image. He prostrates himself to it and bows down and prays to it and says: "Deliver me, for you are my God."

18 They have not come to know, nor do they understand, because their eyes have been besmeared so as not to see, their heart so as to have no insight. 19 And no one recalls to his heart or has knowledge or understanding, saying: "The half of it I have burned up in a fire, and upon its coals I have also baked bread; I roast flesh and eat. But the rest of it shall I make into a mere detestable thing? To the dried-out wood of a tree shall I prostrate myself?" 20 He is feeding on ashes. His own heart that has been trifled with has led him astray. And he does not deliver his soul, nor does he say: "Is there not a falsehood in my right hand?"

21 "Remember these things, O Jacob, and you, O Israel, because you are my servant. I have formed you. You are a servant belonging to me. O Israel, you will not be forgotten on my part. 22 I will wipe out your transgressions just as with a cloud, and your sins just as with a cloud mass. Do return to me, for I will repurchase you.

23 "Joyfully cry out, YOU heavens, for Jehovah has taken action! Shout in triumph, YOU lowest parts of the earth! Become cheerful, YOU mountains, with joyful outcry, you forest and all YOU trees in it! For Jehovah has repurchased Jacob, and on Israel he shows his beauty."

24 This is what Jehovah has said, your Repurchaser and the Former of you from the belly: "I, Jehovah, am doing everything, stretching out the heavens by myself, laying out the earth. Who was with me? 25 [I am] frustrating the signs of the empty talkers, and [I am] the One that makes diviners themselves act crazily; the One turning wise men backwards, and the One that turns even their knowledge into foolishness; 26 the One making the word of his servant come true, and the One that carries out completely the counsel of his own messengers; the One saying of Jerusalem, 'She will be inhabited,' and of the cities of Judah, 'They will be rebuilt, and her desolated places I shall raise up'; 27 the One saying to the watery deep, 'Be evaporated; and all your rivers I shall dry up'; 28 the One saying of Cyrus, 'He is my shepherd, and all that I delight in he will completely carry out'; even in [my] saying of Jerusalem, 'She will be rebuilt,' and of the temple, 'You will have your foundation laid.'"

45 This is what Jehovah has said to his anointed one, to Cyrus, whose right hand I have taken hold of, to subdue before him nations, so that I may ungird even the hips of kings; to open before him the two-leaved doors, so that even the gates will not be shut: 2 "Before

you I myself shall go, and the swells of land I shall straighten out. The copper doors I shall break in pieces, and the iron bars I shall cut down. 3 And I will give you the treasures in the darkness and the hidden treasures in the concealment places, in order that you may know that I am Jehovah, the One calling [you] by your name, the God of Israel. 4 For the sake of my servant Jacob and of Israel my chosen one, I even proceeded to call you by your name; I proceeded to give you a name of honor, although you did not know me. 5 I am Jehovah, and there is no one else. With the exception of me there is no God. I shall closely gird you, although you have not known me, 6 in order that people may know from the rising of the sun and from its setting that there is none besides me. I am Jehovah, and there is no one else. 7 Forming light and creating darkness, making peace and creating calamity, I, Jehovah, am doing all these things.

8 "O YOU heavens, cause a dripping from above; and let the cloudy skies themselves trickle with righteousness. Let the earth open up, and let it be fruitful with salvation, and let it cause righteousness itself to spring up at the same time. I myself, Jehovah, have created it."

9 Woe to the one that has contended with his Former, as an earthenware fragment with the other earthenware fragments of the ground! Should the clay say to its former: "What do you make?" And your achievement [say]: "He has no hands"? 10 Woe to the one saying to a father: "What do you become father to?" and to the wife: "What are you in birth pains with?"

11 This is what Jehovah has said, the Holy One of Israel and the Former of him: "Ask me even about the things that are coming concerning my sons; and concerning the activity of my hands YOU people should command me. 12 I myself have made the earth and have created even man upon it. I—my own hands have stretched out the heavens, and all the army of them I have commanded."

13 "I myself have roused up someone in righteousness, and all his ways I shall straighten out. He is the one that will build my city, and those of mine in exile he will let go, not for a price nor for bribery," Jehovah of armies has said.

14 This is what Jehovah has said: "The unpaid laborers of Egypt and the merchants of E·thi·o'pi·a and the Sa·be'ans, tall men, will themselves come over even to you, and yours they will become. Behind you they will walk; in fetters they will come over, and to you they will bow down. To you they will pray, [saying,] 'Indeed God is in union with you, and there is no one else; there is no [other] God.'"

15 Truly you are a God keeping yourself concealed, the God of Israel, a Savior. 16 They will certainly be ashamed and even be humiliated, all of them. Together in humiliation the manufacturers of [idol] forms will have to walk. 17 As for Israel, he will certainly be saved in union with Jehovah with a salvation for times indefinite. YOU people will not be ashamed, nor will YOU be humiliated for the indefinite times of eternity.

18 For this is what Jehovah has said, the Creator of the heavens, He the [true] God, the Former of the earth and the Maker of it, He the One who firmly established it, who did not create it simply for nothing, who formed it even to be inhabited: "I am Jehovah, and there is no one else. 19 In a place of concealment I spoke not, in a dark place of the earth; nor said I to the seed of Jacob, 'Seek me simply for nothing, YOU people.' I am Jehovah, speaking what is righteous, telling what is upright.

20 "Collect yourselves and come. Bring yourselves up close together, YOU escapees from the nations. Those carrying the wood of their carved image have not come to any knowledge, neither have those

praying to a god that cannot save. 21 Make YOUR report and YOUR presentation. Yes, let them consult together in unity. Who has caused this to be heard from a long time ago? [Who] has reported it from that very time? Is it not I, Jehovah, besides whom there is no other God; a righteous God and a Savior, there being none excepting me? 22 "Turn to me and be saved, all YOU [at the] ends of the earth; for I am God, and there is no one else. 23 By my own self I have sworn—out of my own mouth in righteousness the word has gone forth, so that it will not return— that to me every knee will bend down, every tongue will swear, 24 saying, 'Surely in Jehovah there are full righteousness and strength. All those getting heated up against him will come straight to him and be ashamed. 25 In Jehovah all the seed of Israel will prove to be right and will boast about themselves.'"

46 Bel has bent down, Ne'bo is stooping over; their idols have come to be for the wild beasts and for the domestic animals, their loads, pieces of luggage, a burden for the tired animals. 2 They must stoop over; they must each alike bend down; they are simply unable to furnish escape for the burden, but into captivity their own soul must go.

3 "Listen to me, O house of Jacob, and all YOU remaining ones of the house of Israel, YOU the ones conveyed [by me] from the belly, the ones carried from the womb. 4 Even to [one's] old age I am the same One; and to [one's] gray-headedness I myself shall keep bearing up. I myself shall certainly act, that I myself may carry and that I myself may bear up and furnish escape.

5 "To whom will YOU people liken me or make [me] equal or compare that we may resemble each other? 6 There are those who are lavishing out the gold from the purse, and with the scale beam they weigh out the silver. They hire a metalworker, and he

makes it into a god. They prostrate themselves, yes, they bow down. 7 They carry it upon the shoulder, they bear it and deposit it in its place that it may stand still. From its standing place it does not move away. One even cries out to it, but it does not answer; out of one's distress it does not save one.

8 "Remember this, that YOU people may muster up courage. Lay it to heart, YOU transgressors. 9 Remember the first things of a long time ago, that I am the Divine One and there is no other God, nor anyone like me; 10 the One telling from the beginning the finale, and from long ago the things that have not been done; the One saying, 'My own counsel will stand, and everything that is my delight I shall do'; 11 the One calling from the sunrising a bird of prey, from a distant land the man to execute my counsel. I have even spoken [it]; I shall also bring it in. I have formed [it], I shall also do it.

12 "Listen to me, YOU the ones powerful at heart, YOU the ones far away from righteousness. 13 I have brought near my righteousness. It is not far away, and my own salvation will not be late. And I will give in Zion salvation, to Israel my beauty."

47 Come down and sit down in the dust, O virgin daughter of Babylon. Sit down on the earth where there is no throne, O daughter of the Chal·de'ans. For you will not experience again that people call you delicate and dainty. 2 Take a hand mill and grind out flour. Uncover your veil. Strip off the flowing skirt. Uncover the leg. Cross over the rivers. 3 You ought to uncover your nakedness. Also, your reproach ought to be seen. Vengeance is what I shall take, and I shall not meet any man [kindly].

4 "There is One repurchasing us. Jehovah of armies is his name, the Holy One of Israel."

5 Sit down silently and come into the darkness, O daughter of the Chal·de'ans; for you will not experience again that people call you Mistress of Kingdoms. 6 I grew

indignant at my people. I profaned my inheritance, and I proceeded to give them into your hand. You showed them no mercies. Upon the old man you made your yoke very heavy. 7 And you kept saying: "To time indefinite I shall prove to be Mistress, forever." You did not take these things to your heart; you did not remember the finale of the matter.

8 And now hear this, you pleasure-given [woman], the one sitting in security, the one saying in her heart: "I am, and there is nobody else. I shall not sit as a widow, and I shall not know the loss of children." 9 But to you these two things will come suddenly, in one day: loss of children and widowhood. In their complete measure they must come upon you, for the abundance of your sorceries, for the full might of your spells—exceedingly. 10 And you kept trusting in your badness. You have said: "There is no one seeing me." Your wisdom and your knowledge—this is what has led you away; and you keep saying in your heart: "I am, and there is nobody else." 11 And upon you calamity must come; you will know no charming against it. And upon you adversity will fall; you will not be able to avert it. And upon you there will suddenly come a ruin that you are not accustomed to know.

12 Stand still, now, with your spells and with the abundance of your sorceries, in which you have toiled from your youth; that perhaps you might be able to benefit, that perhaps you might strike people with awe. 13 You have grown weary with the multitude of your counselors. Let them stand up, now, and save you, the worshipers of the heavens, the lookers at the stars, those giving out knowledge at the new moons concerning the things that will come upon you. 14 Look! They have become like stubble. A fire itself will certainly burn them up. They will not deliver their soul from the power of the flame. There will be no glow of charcoals for people to warm themselves, no fire-

light in front of which to sit down. 15 Thus they will certainly become to you, with whom you have toiled as your charmers from your youth. They will actually wander, each one to his own region. There will be no one to save you.

48 Hear this, O house of Jacob, you who are calling yourselves by the name of Israel and who have come forth from the very waters of Judah, you who are swearing by the name of Jehovah and who make mention even of the God of Israel, not in truth and not in righteousness. 2 For they have called themselves as being from the holy city, and upon the God of Israel they have supported themselves, Jehovah of armies being his name.

3 "The first things I have told even from that time, and out of my own mouth they went forth, and I kept making them heard. Suddenly I acted, and the things proceeded to come in. 4 Due to my knowing that you are hard and that your neck is an iron sinew and that your forehead is copper, 5 I also kept telling you from that time. Before it could come in, I caused you to hear [it], that you might not say, 'My own idol has done them, and my own carved image and my own molten image have commanded them.' 6 You have heard. Behold it all. As for you people, will you not tell [it]? I have made you hear new things from the present time, even things kept in reserve, that you have not known. 7 At the present time they must be created, and not from that time, even things that before today you have not heard, that you may not say, 'Look! I have already known them.'

8 "Moreover, you have not heard, neither have you known, nor from that time on has your ear been opened. For I well know that without fail you kept dealing treacherously, and a 'transgressor from the belly' you have been called. 9 For the sake of my name I shall check my anger, and for my praise I shall restrain myself toward you that there may be no cutting you off. 10 Look! I have refined you, but

not in [the form of] silver. I have made choice of you in the smelting furnace of affliction. 11 For my own sake, for my own sake I shall act, for how could one let oneself be profaned? And to no one else shall I give my own glory.

12 "Listen to me, O Jacob, and you Israel my called one. I am the same One. I am the first. Moreover, I am the last. 13 Moreover, my own hand laid the foundation of the earth, and my own right hand extended out the heavens. I am calling to them, that they may keep standing together.

14 "Be collected together, all YOU people, and hear. Who among them has told these things? Jehovah himself has loved him. He will do what is his delight upon Babylon, and his own arm will be upon the Chal·de′ans. 15 I—I myself have spoken. Moreover, I have called him. I have brought him in, and there will be a making of his way successful.

16 "Come near to me, YOU people. Hear this. From the start I have spoken in no place of concealment at all. From the time of its occurring I have been there."

And now the Lord Jehovah himself has sent me, even his spirit. 17 This is what Jehovah has said, your Repurchaser, the Holy One of Israel: "I, Jehovah, am your God, the One teaching you to benefit [yourself], the One causing you to tread in the way in which you should walk. 18 O if only you would actually pay attention to my commandments! Then your peace would become just like a river, and your righteousness like the waves of the sea. 19 And your offspring would become just like the sand, and the descendants from your inward parts like the grains of it. One's name would not be cut off or be annihilated from before me."

20 Go forth, YOU people, out of Babylon! Run away from the Chal·de′ans. Tell forth even with the sound of a joyful cry, cause this to be heard. Make it to go forth to the extremity of the earth. Say: "Jehovah has repurchased his servant Jacob. 21 And they did not get thirsty when he was making them walk even through devastated places. Water out of the rock he caused to flow forth for them, and he proceeded to split a rock that the water might stream forth."

22 "There is no peace," Jehovah has said, "for the wicked ones."

49 Listen to me, O YOU islands, and pay attention, YOU national groups far away. Jehovah himself has called me even from the belly. From the inward parts of my mother he has made mention of my name. 2 And he proceeded to make my mouth like a sharp sword. In the shadow of his hand he has hidden me. And he gradually made me a polished arrow. He concealed me in his own quiver. 3 And he went on to say to me: "You are my servant, O Israel, you the one in whom I shall show my beauty."

4 But as for me, I said: "It is for nothing that I have toiled. For unreality and vanity I have used up my own power. Truly my judgment is with Jehovah, and my wages with my God." 5 And now Jehovah, the One forming me from the belly as a servant belonging to him, has said [for me] to bring back Jacob to him, in order that to him Israel itself may be gathered. And I shall be glorified in the eyes of Jehovah, and my own God will have become my strength. 6 And he proceeded to say: "It has been more than a trivial matter for you to become my servant to raise up the tribes of Jacob and to bring back even the safeguarded ones of Israel; I also have given you for a light of the nations, that my salvation may come to be to the extremity of the earth."

7 This is what Jehovah, the Repurchaser of Israel, his Holy One, has said to him that is despised in soul, to him that is detested by the nation, to the servant of rulers: "Kings themselves will see and certainly rise up, [and] princes, and they will bow down, by reason of Jehovah, who is faithful, the Holy One of Israel, who chooses you."

8 This is what Jehovah has said: "In an acceptable time I have answered you, and in a day of salvation I have helped you; and I kept safeguarding you that I might give you as a covenant for the people, to rehabilitate the land, to bring about the repossessing of the desolated hereditary possessions, 9 to say to the prisoners, 'Come out!' to those who are in the darkness, 'Reveal yourselves!' By the ways they will pasture, and on all beaten paths their pasturing will be. 10 They will not go hungry, neither will they go thirsty, nor will parching heat or sun strike them. For the One who is having pity upon them will lead them, and by the springs of water he will conduct them. 11 And I will make all my mountains a way, and my highways themselves will be on an elevation. 12 Look! These will come even from far away, and, look! these from the north and from the west, and these from the land of Si′nim."

13 Give a glad cry, YOU heavens, and be joyful, you earth. Let the mountains become cheerful with a glad outcry. For Jehovah has comforted his people, and he shows pity upon his own afflicted ones.

14 But Zion kept saying: "Jehovah has left me, and Jehovah himself has forgotten me." 15 Can a wife forget her suckling so that she should not pity the son of her belly? Even these women can forget, yet I myself shall not forget you. 16 Look! Upon [my] palms I have engraved you. Your walls are in front of me constantly. 17 Your sons have hurried up. The very ones tearing you down and devastating you will go forth even from you. 18 Raise your eyes all around and see. They have all of them been collected together. They have come to you. "As I am living," is the utterance of Jehovah, "with all of them you will clothe yourself just as with ornaments, and you will bind them on yourself like a bride. 19 Although there are your devastated places and your desolated places and the land of your ruins, although now you are too cramped

to be dwelling, and those swallowing you down have been far away, 20 yet in your own ears the sons of your bereaved state will say, 'The place has become too cramped for me. Do make room for me, that I may dwell.' 21 And you will for certain say in your heart, 'Who has become father to these for me, since I am a woman bereaved of children and sterile, gone into exile and taken prisoner? As for these, who has brought [them] up? Look! I myself had been left behind alone. These—where have they been?' "

22 This is what the Lord Jehovah has said: "Look! I shall raise up my hand even to the nations, and to the peoples I shall lift up my signal. And they will bring your sons in the bosom, and upon the shoulder they will carry your own daughters. 23 And kings must become caretakers for you, and their princesses nursing women for you. With faces to the earth they will bow down to you, and the dust of your feet they will lick up; and you will have to know that I am Jehovah, of whom those hoping in me will not be ashamed."

24 Can those already taken be taken from a mighty man himself, or can the body of captives of the tyrant make their escape? 25 But this is what Jehovah has said: "Even the body of captives of the mighty man will be taken away, and those already taken by the tyrant himself will make their escape. And against anyone contending against you I myself shall contend, and your own sons I myself shall save. 26 And I will make those maltreating you eat their own flesh; and as with the sweet wine they will become drunk with their own blood. And all flesh will have to know that I, Jehovah, am your Savior and your Repurchaser, the Powerful One of Jacob."

50 This is what Jehovah has said: "Where, then, is the divorce certificate of the mother of YOU people, whom I sent away? Or which one of my creditors is it to whom I have sold YOU people? Look! Because of YOUR own errors

YOU have been sold, and because of YOUR own transgressions YOUR mother has been sent away. 2 Why is it that, when I came in, there was no one? When I called, there was nobody answering? Has my hand become in fact so short that it cannot redeem, or is there in me no power to deliver? Look! With my rebuke I dry up the sea; I make rivers a wilderness. Their fish stink due to there being no water, and they die because of thirst. 3 I clothe the heavens with obscurity, and I make sackcloth itself their covering."

4 The Lord Jehovah himself has given me the tongue of the taught ones, that I may know how to answer the tired one with a word. He awakens morning by morning; he awakens my ear to hear like the taught ones. 5 The Lord Jehovah himself has opened my ear, and I, for my part, was not rebellious. I did not turn in the opposite direction. 6 My back I gave to the strikers, and my cheeks to those plucking off [the hair]. My face I did not conceal from humiliating things and spit.

7 But the Lord Jehovah himself will help me. That is why I shall not have to feel humiliated. That is why I have set my face like a flint, and I know that I shall not be ashamed. 8 The One declaring me righteous is near. Who can contend with me? Let us stand up together. Who is my judicial antagonist? Let him approach me. 9 Look! The Lord Jehovah himself will help me. Who is there that can pronounce me wicked? Look! All of them, like a garment, will wear out. A mere moth will eat them up.

10 Who among YOU people is in fear of Jehovah, listening to the voice of his servant, who has walked in continual darkness and for whom there has been no brightness? Let him trust in the name of Jehovah and support himself upon his God.

11 "Look! All YOU who are igniting a fire, making sparks light up, walk in the light of YOUR fire, and amid the sparks that YOU have set ablaze. From my hand YOU will certainly come to have this: In sheer pain YOU will lie down.

51 "Listen to me, YOU people who are pursuing after righteousness, YOU who are seeking to find Jehovah. Look to the rock from which YOU were hewn out, and to the hollow of the pit from which YOU were dug out. 2 Look to Abraham YOUR father and to Sarah who gradually brought YOU forth with childbirth pains. For he was one when I called him, and I proceeded to bless him and to make him many. 3 For Jehovah will certainly comfort Zion. He will for certain comfort all her devastated places, and he will make her wilderness like Eden and her desert plain like the garden of Jehovah. Exultation and rejoicing themselves will be found in her, thanksgiving and the voice of melody.

4 "Pay attention to me, O my people; and you national group of mine, to me give ear. For from me a law itself will go forth, and my judicial decision I shall cause to repose even as a light to the peoples. 5 My righteousness is near. My salvation will certainly go forth, and my own arms will judge even the peoples. In me the islands themselves will hope, and for my arm they will wait.

6 "Raise YOUR eyes to the heavens themselves, and look at the earth beneath. For the very heavens must be dispersed in fragments just like smoke, and like a garment the earth itself will wear out, and its inhabitants themselves will die like a mere gnat. But as for my salvation, it will prove to be even to time indefinite, and my own righteousness will not be shattered.

7 "Listen to me, YOU the ones knowing righteousness, the people in whose heart is my law. Do not be afraid of the reproach of mortal men, and do not be struck with terror just because of their abusive words. 8 For the moth will eat them up just as if a garment, and the clothes moth will eat them up just as if wool. But as for my righteousness, it will prove to be even

to time indefinite, and my salvation to unnumbered generations."

9 Awake, awake, clothe yourself with strength, O arm of Jehovah! Awake as in the days of long ago, as during the generations of times long past. Are you not the one that broke Ra'hab to pieces, that pierced the sea monster? 10 Are you not the one that dried up the sea, the waters of the vast deep? The one that made the depths of the sea a way for the repurchased ones to go across? 11 Then the redeemed ones of Jehovah themselves will return and must come to Zion with a joyful outcry, and rejoicing to time indefinite will be upon their head. To exultation and rejoicing they will attain. Grief and sighing will certainly flee away.

12 "I—I myself am the One that is comforting you people.

"Who are you that you should be afraid of a mortal man that will die, and of a son of mankind that will be rendered as mere green grass? 13 And that you should forget Jehovah your Maker, the One stretching out the heavens and laying the foundation of the earth, so that you were in dread constantly the whole day long on account of the rage of the one hemming [you] in, as though he was all set to bring [you] to ruin? And where is the rage of the one hemming [you] in?

14 "The one stooping in chains will certainly be loosened speedily, that he may not go in death to the pit and that his bread may not be lacking.

15 "But I, Jehovah, am your God, the One stirring up the sea that its waves may be boisterous. Jehovah of armies is his name. 16 And I shall put my words in your mouth, and with the shadow of my hand I shall certainly cover you, in order to plant the heavens and lay the foundation of the earth and say to Zion, 'You are my people.'

17 "Rouse yourself, rouse yourself, rise up, O Jerusalem, you who have drunk at the hand of Jehovah his cup of rage. The goblet, the cup causing reeling, you have drunk, you have drained out. 18 There was none of all the sons that she brought to birth conducting her, and there was none of all the sons that she brought up taking hold of her hand. 19 Those two things were befalling you. Who will sympathize with you? Despoiling and breakdown, and hunger and sword! Who will comfort you? 20 Your own sons have swooned away. They have lain down at the head of all the streets like the wild sheep in the net, as those who are full of the rage of Jehovah, the rebuke of your God."

21 Therefore listen to this, please, O woman afflicted and drunk, but not with wine. 22 This is what your Lord, Jehovah, even your God, who contends for his people, has said: "Look! I will take away from your hand the cup causing reeling. The goblet, my cup of rage—you will not repeat the drinking of it any more. 23 And I will put it in the hand of the ones irritating you, who have said to your soul, 'Bow down that we may cross over,' so that you used to make your back just like the earth, and like the street for those crossing over."

52 Wake up, wake up, put on your strength, O Zion! Put on your beautiful garments, O Jerusalem, the holy city! For no more will there come again into you the uncircumcised and unclean one. 2 Shake yourself free from the dust, rise up, take a seat, O Jerusalem. Loosen for yourself the bands on your neck, O captive daughter of Zion.

3 For this is what Jehovah has said: "It was for nothing that you people were sold, and it will be without money that you will be repurchased."

4 For this is what the Lord Jehovah has said: "It was to Egypt that my people went down in the first instance to reside there as aliens; and without cause As·syr'-i·a, for its part, oppressed them."

5 "And now, what interest do I have here?" is the utterance of Jehovah. "For my people were taken for nothing. The very ones

ruling over them kept howling," is the utterance of Jehovah, "and constantly, all day long, my name was being treated with disrespect. 6 For that reason my people will know my name, even for that reason in that day, because I am the One that is speaking. Look! It is I."

7 How comely upon the mountains are the feet of the one bringing good news, the one publishing peace, the one bringing good news of something better, the one publishing salvation, the one saying to Zion: "Your God has become king!"

8 Listen! Your own watchmen have raised [their] voice. In unison they keep crying out joyfully; for it will be eye into eye that they will see when Jehovah gathers back Zion.

9 Become cheerful, cry out joyfully in unison, YOU devastated places of Jerusalem, for Jehovah has comforted his people; he has repurchased Jerusalem. 10 Jehovah has bared his holy arm before the eyes of all the nations; and all the ends of the earth must see the salvation of our God.

11 Turn away, turn away, get out of there, touch nothing unclean; get out from the midst of her, keep yourselves clean, YOU who are carrying the utensils of Jehovah. 12 For YOU people will get out in no panic, and YOU will go in no flight. For Jehovah will be going even before YOU, and the God of Israel will be YOUR rear guard.

13 Look! My servant will act with insight. He will be in high station and will certainly be elevated and exalted very much. 14 To the extent that many have stared at him in amazement—so much was the disfigurement as respects his appearance more than that of any other man and as respects his stately form more than that of the sons of mankind— 15 he will likewise startle many nations. At him kings will shut their mouth, because what had not been recounted to them they will actually see, and to what they had not heard they must turn their consideration.

53 Who has put faith in the thing heard by us? And as for the arm of Jehovah, to whom has it been revealed? 2 And he will come up like a twig before one, and like a root out of waterless land. No stately form does he have, nor any splendor; and when we shall see him, there is not the appearance so that we should desire him.

3 He was despised and was avoided by men, a man meant for pains and for having acquaintance with sickness. And there was as if the concealing of one's face from us. He was despised, and we held him as of no account. 4 Truly our sicknesses were what he himself carried; and as for our pains, he bore them. But we ourselves accounted him as plagued, stricken by God and afflicted. 5 But he was being pierced for our transgression; he was being crushed for our errors. The chastisement meant for our peace was upon him, and because of his wounds there has been a healing for us. 6 Like sheep we have all of us wandered about; it was each one to his own way that we have turned; and Jehovah himself has caused the error of us all to meet up with that one. 7 He was hard pressed, and he was letting himself be afflicted; yet he would not open his mouth. He was being brought just like a sheep to the slaughtering; and like a ewe that before her shearers has become mute, he also would not open his mouth.

8 Because of restraint and of judgment he was taken away; and who will concern himself even with [the details of] his generation? For he was severed from the land of the living ones. Because of the transgression of my people he had the stroke. 9 And he will make his burial place even with the wicked ones, and with the rich class in his death, despite the fact that he had done no violence and there was no deception in his mouth.

10 But Jehovah himself took delight in crushing him; he made him sick. If you will set his soul as a guilt offering, he will see his offspring, he will prolong [his] days, and in his hand what is the delight of Jehovah will succeed. 11 Because of the trouble of his soul he will see, he will be satisfied. By means of his knowledge the righteous one, my servant, will bring a righteous standing to many people; and their errors he himself will bear. 12 For that reason I shall deal him a portion among the many, and it will be with the mighty ones that he will apportion the spoil, due to the fact that he poured out his soul to the very death, and it was with the transgressors that he was counted in; and he himself carried the very sin of many people, and for the transgressors he proceeded to interpose.

54 "Cry out joyfully, you barren woman that did not give birth! Become cheerful with a joyful outcry and cry shrilly, you that had no childbirth pains, for the sons of the desolated one are more numerous than the sons of the woman with a husbandly owner," Jehovah has said. 2 "Make the place of your tent more spacious. And let them stretch out the tent cloths of your grand tabernacle. Do not hold back. Lengthen out your tent cords, and make those tent pins of yours strong. 3 For to the right and to the left you will break forth, and your own offspring will take possession even of nations, and they will inhabit even the desolated cities. 4 Do not be afraid, for you will not be put to shame; and do not feel humiliated, for you will not be disappointed. For you will forget even the shame of your time of youth, and the reproach of your continuous widowhood you will remember no more."

5 "For your grand Maker is your husbandly owner, Jehovah of armies being his name; and the Holy One of Israel is your Repurchaser. The God of the whole earth he will be called. 6 For Jehovah called you as if you were a wife left entirely and hurt in spirit, and as a wife of the time of youth who was then rejected," your God has said.

7 "For a little moment I left you entirely, but with great mercies I shall collect you together. 8 With a flood of indignation I concealed my face from you for but a moment, but with loving-kindness to time indefinite I will have mercy upon you," your Repurchaser, Jehovah, has said.

9 "This is just as the days of Noah to me. Just as I have sworn that the waters of Noah shall no more pass over the earth, so I have sworn that I will not become indignant toward you nor rebuke you. 10 For the mountains themselves may be removed, and the very hills may stagger, but my loving-kindness itself will not be removed from you, nor will my covenant of peace itself stagger," Jehovah, the One having mercy upon you, has said.

11 "O woman afflicted, tempest-tossed, uncomforted, here I am laying with hard mortar your stones, and I will lay your foundation with sapphires. 12 And I will make your battlements of rubies, and your gates of fiery glowing stones, and all your boundaries of delightsome stones. 13 And all your sons will be persons taught by Jehovah, and the peace of your sons will be abundant. 14 You will prove to be firmly established in righteousness itself. You will be far away from oppression—for you will fear none—and from anything terrifying, for it will not come near you. 15 If anyone should at all make an attack, it will not be at my orders. Whoever is making an attack upon you will fall even on account of you."

16 "Look! I myself have created the craftsman, the one blowing upon the fire of charcoal and bringing forth a weapon as his workmanship. I myself, too, have created the ruinous man for wrecking work. 17 Any weapon whatever that will be formed against you will have no success, and any

tongue at all that will rise up against you in the judgment you will condemn. This is the hereditary possession of the servants of Jehovah, and their righteousness is from me," is the utterance of Jehovah.

55 Hey there, all YOU thirsty ones! Come to the water. And the ones that have no money! Come, buy and eat. Yes, come, buy wine and milk even without money and without price. 2 Why do YOU people keep paying out money for what is not bread, and why is YOUR toil for what results in no satisfaction? Listen intently to me, and eat what is good, and let YOUR soul find its exquisite delight in fatness itself. 3 Incline YOUR ear and come to me. Listen, and YOUR soul will keep alive, and I shall readily conclude with YOU people an indefinitely lasting covenant respecting the loving-kindnesses to David that are faithful. 4 Look! As a witness to the national groups I have given him, as a leader and commander to the national groups.

5 Look! A nation that you do not know you will call, and those of a nation who have not known you will run even to you, for the sake of Jehovah your God, and for the Holy One of Israel, because he will have beautified you.

6 Search for Jehovah, YOU people, while he may be found. Call to him while he proves to be near. 7 Let the wicked man leave his way, and the harmful man his thoughts; and let him return to Jehovah, who will have mercy upon him, and to our God, for he will forgive in a large way.

8 "For the thoughts of YOU people are not my thoughts, nor are my ways YOUR ways," is the utterance of Jehovah. 9 "For as the heavens are higher than the earth, so my ways are higher than YOUR ways, and my thoughts than YOUR thoughts. 10 For just as the pouring rain descends, and the snow, from the heavens and does not return to that place, unless it actually saturates the earth and

makes it produce and sprout, and seed is actually given to the sower and bread to the eater, 11 so my word that goes forth from my mouth will prove to be. It will not return to me without results, but it will certainly do that in which I have delighted, and it will have certain success in that for which I have sent it.

12 "For with rejoicing YOU people will go forth, and with peace YOU will be brought in. The mountains and the hills themselves will become cheerful before YOU with a joyful outcry, and the very trees of the field will all clap their hands. 13 Instead of the thicket of thorns the juniper tree will come up. Instead of the stinging nettle the myrtle tree will come up. And it must become for Jehovah something famous, a sign to time indefinite that will not be cut off."

56 This is what Jehovah has said: "Keep justice, YOU people, and do what is righteous. For my salvation is at hand to come in, and my righteousness to be revealed. 2 Happy is the mortal man that does this, and the son of mankind that lays hold of it, keeping the sabbath in order not to profane it, and keeping his hand in order not to do any kind of badness. 3 And let not the foreigner that has joined himself to Jehovah say, 'Without doubt Jehovah will divide me off from his people.' Neither let the eunuch say, 'Look! I am a dry tree.'"

4 For this is what Jehovah has said to the eunuchs that keep my sabbaths and that have chosen what I have delighted in and that are laying hold of my covenant: 5 "I will even give to them in my house and within my walls a monument and a name, something better than sons and daughters. A name to time indefinite I shall give them, one that will not be cut off.

6 "And the foreigners that have joined themselves to Jehovah to minister to him and to love the name of Jehovah, in order to become servants to him, all those

keeping the sabbath in order not to profane it and laying hold of my covenant, 7 I will also bring them to my holy mountain and make them rejoice inside my house of prayer. Their whole burnt offerings and their sacrifices will be for acceptance upon my altar. For my own house will be called even a house of prayer for all the peoples."

8 The utterance of the Lord Jehovah, who is collecting together the dispersed ones of Israel, is: "I shall collect together to him others besides those already collected together of his."

9 All you wild animals of the open field, come to eat, all you wild animals in the forest. 10 His watchmen are blind. None of them have taken note. All of them are speechless dogs; they are not able to bark, panting, lying down, loving to slumber. 11 They are even dogs strong in soul[ful desire]; they have known no satisfaction. They are also shepherds that have not known how to understand. They have all of them turned to their own way, each one for his unjust gain from his own border: 12 "Come, men! Let me take some wine; and let us drink intoxicating liquor to the limit. And tomorrow will certainly turn out just as today, great in a very much larger way."

57 The righteous one himself has perished, but there is no one taking [it] to heart. And men of loving-kindness are being gathered [to the dead], while no one discerns that it is because of the calamity that the righteous one has been gathered away. 2 He enters into peace; they take rest upon their beds, [each] one that is walking straightforwardly.

3 "As for you men, come up close here, you sons of a soothsaying woman, the seed of an adulterous person and of a woman that commits prostitution: 4 Over whom is it that you have a jolly good time? Against whom do you keep opening wide the mouth, keep sticking out the tongue? Are you not the children of transgression, the seed of falsehood, 5 those who are working up passion among big trees, under every luxuriant tree, slaughtering the children in the torrent valleys under the clefts of the crags?

6 "With the smooth stones of the torrent valley was your portion. They—they were your lot. Moreover, to them you poured out a drink offering, you offered up a gift. For these things shall I comfort myself? 7 Upon a mountain high and lifted up you set your bed. There also you went up to offer sacrifice. 8 And behind the door and the doorpost you set your memorial. For apart from me you uncovered [yourself] and proceeded to go up; you made your bed spacious. And for yourself you went concluding a covenant with them. You loved a bed with them. The male organ you beheld. 9 And you proceeded to descend toward Mel′ech with oil, and kept making your ointments abundant. And you continued sending your envoys far off, so that you lowered matters to She′ol. 10 In the multitude of your ways you have toiled. You have not said, 'It is hopeless!' You have found a revival of your own power. That is why you have not grown sick.

11 "Whom did you become frightened at and begin to fear, so that you took up lying? But I was not the one that you remembered. You took nothing to your heart. Was I not keeping silent and hiding matters? So you were in no fear even of me. 12 I myself shall tell forth your righteousness and your works, that they will not benefit you. 13 When you cry for aid your collection of things will not deliver you, but a wind will carry even all of them away. An exhalation will take them away, but the one taking refuge in me will inherit the land and will take possession of my holy mountain. 14 And one will certainly say, 'Bank up, you people, bank up! Clear the way. Remove any obstacle from the way of my people.'"

15 For this is what the High and Lofty One, who is residing forever and whose name is holy, has said: "In the height and in the holy place is where I reside, also with the one crushed and lowly in spirit, to revive the spirit of the lowly ones and to revive the heart of the ones being crushed. **16** For it will not be to time indefinite that I shall contend, nor perpetually that I shall be indignant; for because of me the spirit itself would grow feeble, even the breathing creatures that I myself have made.

17 "At the erroneousness of his unjust gain I grew indignant, and I proceeded to strike him, concealing [my face], while I was indignant. But he kept walking as a renegade in the way of his heart. **18** I have seen his very ways; and I began to heal him and conduct him and make compensation with comfort to him and to his mourning ones."

19 "I am creating the fruit of the lips. Continuous peace there will be to the one that is far away and to the one that is near," Jehovah has said, "and I will heal him."

20 "But the wicked are like the sea that is being tossed, when it is unable to calm down, the waters of which keep tossing up seaweed and mire. **21** There is no peace," my God has said, "for the wicked ones."

58 "Call out full-throated; do not hold back. Raise your voice just like a horn, and tell my people their revolt, and the house of Jacob their sins. **2** Yet day after day it was I whom they kept seeking, and it was in the knowledge of my ways that they would express delight, like a nation that carried on righteousness itself and that had not left the very justice of their God, in that they kept asking me for righteous judgments, drawing near to God in whom they had delight,

3 " 'For what reason did we fast and you did not see, and did we afflict our soul and you would take no note?'

"Indeed you people were finding delight in the very day of your fasting, when there were all your toilers that you kept driving to work. **4** Indeed for quarreling and struggle you would fast, and for striking with the fist of wickedness. Did you not keep fasting as in the day for making your voice to be heard in the height? **5** Should the fast that I choose become like this, as a day for earthling man to afflict his soul? For bowing down his head just like a rush, and that he should spread out mere sackcloth and ashes as his couch? Is it this that you call a fast and a day acceptable to Jehovah?

6 "Is not this the fast that I choose? To loosen the fetters of wickedness, to release the bands of the yoke bar, and to send away the crushed ones free, and that you people should tear in two every yoke bar? **7** Is it not the dividing of your bread out to the hungry one, and that you should bring the afflicted, homeless people into [your] house? That, in case you should see someone naked, you must cover him, and that you should not hide yourself from your own flesh?

8 "In that case your light would break forth just like the dawn; and speedily would recuperation spring up for you. And before you your righteousness would certainly walk; the very glory of Jehovah would be your rear guard. **9** In that case you would call, and Jehovah himself would answer; you would cry for help, and he would say, 'Here I am!'

"If you will remove from your midst the yoke bar, the poking out of the finger and the speaking of what is hurtful; **10** and you will grant to the hungry one your own soul[ful desire], and you will satisfy the soul that is being afflicted, your light also will certainly flash up even in the darkness, and your gloom will be like midday. **11** And Jehovah will be bound to lead you constantly and to satisfy your soul even in a scorched land, and he will invigorate your very bones;

and you must become like a well-watered garden, and like the source of water, the waters of which do not lie. 12 And at your instance men will certainly build up the places devastated a long time; you will raise up even the foundations of continuous generations. And you will actually be called the repairer of [the] gap, the restorer of roadways by which to dwell.

13 "If in view of the sabbath you will turn back your foot as regards doing your own delights on my holy day, and will actually call the sabbath an exquisite delight, a holy [day] of Jehovah, one being glorified, and will actually glorify it rather than doing your own ways, rather than finding what delights you and speaking a word; 14 you will in that case find your exquisite delight in Jehovah, and I will make you ride upon the high places of the earth; and I will cause you to eat from the hereditary possession of Jacob your forefather, for the mouth of Jehovah itself has spoken [it]."

59 Look! The hand of Jehovah has not become too short that it cannot save, nor has his ear become too heavy that it cannot hear. 2 No, but the very errors of YOU people have become the things causing division between YOU and YOUR God, and YOUR own sins have caused the concealing of [his] face from YOU to keep from hearing. 3 For YOUR own palms have become polluted with blood, and YOUR fingers with error. YOUR own lips have spoken falsehood. YOUR own tongue kept muttering sheer unrighteousness. 4 There is no one calling out in righteousness, and no one at all has gone to court in faithfulness. There has been a trusting in unreality, and a speaking of worthlessness. There has been a conceiving of trouble, and a bringing of what is hurtful to birth.

5 The eggs of a poisonous snake are what they have hatched, and they kept weaving the mere cobweb of a spider. Anyone eating some of their eggs would die, and the [egg]

that was smashed would be hatched into a viper. 6 Their mere cobweb will not serve as a garment, nor will they cover themselves with their works. Their works are hurtful works, and the activity of violence is in their palms. 7 Their own feet keep running to sheer badness, and they are in a hurry to shed innocent blood. Their thoughts are hurtful thoughts; despoiling and breakdown are in their highways. 8 The way of peace they have ignored, and there is no justice in their tracks. Their roadways they have made crooked for themselves. No one at all treading in them will actually know peace.

9 That is why justice has come to be far away from us, and righteousness does not catch up with us. We keep hoping for light, but, look! darkness; for brightness, [but] in continuous gloom we kept walking. 10 We keep groping for the wall just like blind men, and like those without eyes we keep groping. We have stumbled at high noon just as in evening darkness; among the stout ones [we are] just like dead people. 11 We keep groaning, all of us, just like bears; and like doves we mournfully keep cooing. We kept hoping for justice, but there was none; for salvation, [but] it has stayed far away from us. 12 For our revolts have become many in front of you; and as for our sins, each one has testified against us. For our revolts are with us; and as for our errors, we well know them. 13 There have been transgressing and a denying of Jehovah; and there was a moving back from our God, a speaking of oppression and revolt, a conceiving and a muttering of words of falsehood from the very heart. 14 And justice was forced to move back, and righteousness itself kept standing simply far off. For truth has stumbled even in the public square, and what is straightforward is unable to enter. 15 And the truth proves to be missing, and anyone turning away from badness is being despoiled.

And Jehovah got to see, and it was bad in his eyes that there was no justice. 16 And when he saw that there was no man, he began to show himself astonished that there was no one interposing. And his arm proceeded to save for him, and his own righteousness was the thing that supported him. 17 Then he put on righteousness as a coat of mail, and the helmet of salvation upon his head. Furthermore, he put on the garments of vengeance as raiment and enwrapped himself with zeal as if a sleeveless coat. 18 In accordance with the dealings he will reward correspondingly, rage to his adversaries, due treatment to his enemies. To the islands he will recompense due treatment. 19 And from the sunset they will begin to fear the name of Jehovah, and from the rising of the sun the glory of him, for he will come in like a distressing river, which the very spirit of Jehovah has driven along.

20 "And to Zion the Repurchaser will certainly come, and to those turning from transgression in Jacob," is the utterance of Jehovah.

21 "And as for me, this is my covenant with them," Jehovah has said.

"My spirit that is upon you and my words that I have put in your mouth—they will not be removed from your mouth or from the mouth of your offspring or from the mouth of the offspring of your offspring," Jehovah has said, "from now on even to time indefinite."

60 "Arise, O woman, shed forth light, for your light has come and upon you the very glory of Jehovah has shone forth. 2 For, look! darkness itself will cover the earth, and thick gloom the national groups; but upon you Jehovah will shine forth, and upon you his own glory will be seen. 3 And nations will certainly go to your light, and kings to the brightness of your shining forth.

4 "Raise your eyes all around and see! They have all of them been collected together; they have come to you. From far away your own sons keep coming, and your daughters who will be taken care of on the flank. 5 At that time you will see and certainly become radiant, and your heart will actually quiver and expand, because to you the wealthiness of the sea will direct itself; the very resources of the nations will come to you. 6 The heaving mass of camels itself will cover you, the young male camels of Mid'i·an and of E'phah. All those from She'ba—they will come. Gold and frankincense they will carry. And the praises of Jehovah they will announce. 7 All the flocks of Ke'dar—they will be collected together to you. The rams of Ne·ba'ioth—they will minister to you. With approval they will come up upon my altar, and I shall beautify my own house of beauty.

8 "Who are these that come flying just like a cloud, and like doves to their birdhouse holes? 9 For in me the islands themselves will keep hoping, the ships of Tar'shish also as at the first, in order to bring your sons from far away, their silver and their gold being with them, to the name of Jehovah your God and to the Holy One of Israel, for he will have beautified you. 10 And foreigners will actually build your walls, and their own kings will minister to you; for in my indignation I shall have struck you, but in my good will I shall certainly have mercy upon you.

11 "And your gates will actually be kept open constantly; they will not be closed even by day or by night, in order to bring to you the resources of the nations, and their kings will be taking the lead. 12 For any nation and any kingdom that will not serve you will perish; and the nations themselves will without fail come to devastation.

13 "To you the very glory of Leb'a·non will come, the juniper tree, the ash tree and the cypress at the same time, in order to beautify the place of my sanctuary;

and I shall glorify the very place of my feet.

14 "And to you the sons of those afflicting you must go, bowing down; and all those treating you disrespectfully must bend down at the very soles of your feet, and they will have to call you the city of Jehovah, Zion of the Holy One of Israel.

15 "Instead of your proving to be one left entirely and hated, with nobody passing through, I will even set you as a thing of pride to time indefinite, an exultation for generation after generation. 16 And you will actually suck the milk of nations, and the breast of kings you will suck; and you will be certain to know that I, Jehovah, am your Savior, and the Powerful One of Jacob is your Repurchaser. 17 Instead of the copper I shall bring in gold, and instead of the iron I shall bring in silver, and instead of the wood, copper, and instead of the stones, iron; and I will appoint peace as your overseers and righteousness as your task assigners.

18 "No more will violence be heard in your land, despoiling or breakdown within your boundaries. And you will certainly call your own walls Salvation and your gates Praise. 19 For you the sun will no more prove to be a light by day, and for brightness the moon itself will no more give you light. And Jehovah must become to you an indefinitely lasting light, and your God your beauty. 20 No more will your sun set, nor will your moon go on the wane; for Jehovah himself will become for you an indefinitely lasting light, and the days of your mourning will have come to completion. 21 And as for your people, all of them will be righteous; to time indefinite they will hold possession of the land, the sprout of my planting, the work of my hands, for [me] to be beautified. 22 The little one himself will become a thousand, and the small one a mighty nation. I myself, Jehovah, shall speed it up in its own time."

61 The spirit of the Lord Jehovah is upon me, for the reason that Jehovah has anointed me to tell good news to the meek ones. He has sent me to bind up the brokenhearted, to proclaim liberty to those taken captive and the wide opening [of the eyes] even to the prisoners; 2 to proclaim the year of good will on the part of Jehovah and the day of vengeance on the part of our God; to comfort all the mourning ones; 3 to assign to those mourning over Zion, to give them a headdress instead of ashes, the oil of exultation instead of mourning, the mantle of praise instead of the downhearted spirit; and they must be called big trees of righteousness, the planting of Jehovah, for [him] to be beautified. 4 And they must rebuild the long-standing devastated places; they will raise up even the desolated places of former times, and they will certainly make anew the devastated cities, the places desolate for generation after generation.

5 "And strangers will actually stand and shepherd the flocks of YOU people, and the foreigners will be YOUR farmers and YOUR vinedressers. 6 And as for YOU, the priests of Jehovah YOU will be called; the ministers of our God YOU will be said to be. The resources of the nations YOU people will eat, and in their glory YOU will speak elatedly about yourselves. 7 Instead of YOUR shame there will be a double portion, and instead of humiliation they will cry out joyfully over their share. Therefore in their land they will take possession of even a double portion. Rejoicing to time indefinite is what will come to be theirs. 8 For I, Jehovah, am loving justice, hating robbery along with unrighteousness. And I will give their wages in trueness, and an indefinitely lasting covenant I shall conclude toward them. 9 And their offspring will actually be known even among the nations, and their descendants in among the peoples. All those seeing them will recognize them, that they

are the offspring whom Jehovah has blessed."

10 Without fail I shall exult in Jehovah. My soul will be joyful in my God. For he has clothed me with the garments of salvation; with the sleeveless coat of righteousness he has enwrapped me, like the bridegroom who, in a priestly way, puts on a headdress, and like the bride who decks herself with her ornamental things. 11 For as the earth itself brings forth its sprout, and as the garden itself makes the things that are sown in it sprout, in like manner Jehovah himself will cause the sprouting of righteousness and of praise in front of all the nations.

62 For the sake of Zion I shall not keep still, and for the sake of Jerusalem I shall not stay quiet until her righteousness goes forth just like the brightness, and her salvation like a torch that burns.

2 "And the nations will certainly see your righteousness, O woman, and all kings your glory. And you will actually be called by a new name, which the very mouth of Jehovah will designate. 3 And you must become a crown of beauty in the hand of Jehovah, and a kingly turban in the palm of your God. 4 No more will you be said to be a woman left entirely; and your own land will no more be said to be desolate; but you yourself will be called My Delight Is in Her, and your land Owned as a Wife. For Jehovah will have taken delight in you, and your own land will be owned as a wife. 5 For just as a young man takes ownership of a virgin as his wife, your sons will take ownership of you as a wife. And with the exultation of a bridegroom over a bride, your God will exult even over you. 6 Upon your walls, O Jerusalem, I have commissioned watchmen. All day long and all night long, constantly, let them not keep still.

"You who are making mention of Jehovah, let there be no silence on YOUR part, 7 and do not give him any silence until he fixes sol-idly, yes, until he sets Jerusalem as a praise in the earth."

8 Jehovah has sworn with his right hand and with his strong arm: "I will no more give your grain as food to your enemies, nor will foreigners drink your new wine, for which you have toiled. 9 But the very ones gathering it will eat it, and they will be certain to praise Jehovah; and the very ones collecting it will drink it in my holy courtyards."

10 Pass out, pass out through the gates, YOU men. Clear the way of the people. Bank up, bank up the highway. Rid [it] of stones. Raise up a signal for the peoples. 11 Look! Jehovah himself has caused [it] to be heard to the farthest part of the earth: "Say, YOU people, to the daughter of Zion, 'Look! Your salvation is coming. Look! The reward he gives is with him, and the wages he pays are before him.'"

12 And men will certainly call them the holy people, those repurchased by Jehovah; and you yourself will be called Searched For, a City Not Left Entirely.

63 Who is this one coming from E'dom, the one with garments of glowing colors from Boz'rah, this one who is honorable in his clothing, marching in the abundance of his power?

"I, the One speaking in righteousness, the One abounding [in power] to save."

2 Why is it that your clothing is red, and your garments are like those of one treading in the wine press?

3 "The wine trough I have trodden by myself, while there was no man with me from the peoples. And I kept treading them in my anger, and I kept trampling them down in my rage. And their spurting blood kept spattering upon my garments, and all my clothing I have polluted. 4 For the day of vengeance is in my heart, and the very year of my repurchased ones has come. 5 And I kept looking, but there was no helper; and I began to show myself astonished, but there was no

one offering support. So my arm furnished me salvation, and my rage was what supported me. 6 And I kept stamping down peoples in my anger, and I proceeded to make them drunk with my rage and to bring down to the earth their spurting blood."

7 The loving-kindnesses of Jehovah I shall mention, the praises of Jehovah, according to all that Jehovah has rendered to us, even the abundant goodness to the house of Israel that he has rendered to them according to his mercies and according to the abundance of his loving-kindnesses. 8 And he went on to say: "Surely they are my people, sons that will not prove false." So it was to them that he came to be a Savior. 9 During all their distress it was distressing to him. And his own personal messenger saved them. In his love and in his compassion he himself repurchased them, and he proceeded to lift them up and carry them all the days of long ago.

10 But they themselves rebelled and made his holy spirit feel hurt. He now was changed into an enemy of theirs; he himself warred against them. 11 And one began to remember the days of long ago, Moses his servant: "Where is the One that brought them up out of the sea with the shepherds of his flock? Where is the One that put within him His own holy spirit? 12 The One making His beautiful arm go at the right hand of Moses; the One splitting the waters from before them in order to make an indefinitely lasting name for his own self; 13 the One making them walk through the surging waters so that, like a horse in the wilderness, they did not stumble? 14 Just as when a beast itself goes down into the valley plain, the very spirit of Jehovah proceeded to make them rest."

Thus you led your people in order to make a beautiful name for your own self.

15 Look from heaven and see out of your lofty abode of holiness and beauty. Where are your zeal and your full might, the commotion of your inward parts, and your mercies? Toward me they have restrained themselves. 16 For you are our Father; although Abraham himself may not have known us and Israel himself may not recognize us, you, O Jehovah, are our Father. Our Repurchaser of long ago is your name. 17 Why do you, O Jehovah, keep making us wander from your ways? Why do you make our heart hard against the fear of you? Come back for the sake of your servants, the tribes of your hereditary possession. 18 For a little while your holy people had possession. Our own adversaries have stamped down your sanctuary. 19 We have for a long time become as those over whom you did not rule, as those upon whom your name had not been called.

64 O if only you had ripped the heavens apart, that you had come down, that on account of you the very mountains had quaked, 2 as when a fire ignites the brushwood, [and] the fire makes the very water boil up, in order to make your name known to your adversaries, that on account of you the nations might be agitated! 3 When you did fear-inspiring things for which we could not hope, you came down. On account of you the mountains themselves quaked. 4 And from time long ago none have heard, nor have any given ear, nor has an eye itself seen a God, except you, that acts for the one that keeps in expectation of him. 5 You have met up with the one exulting and doing righteousness, those who keep remembering you in your own ways.

Look! You yourself became indignant, while we kept sinning—in them a long time, and should we be saved? 6 And we become like someone unclean, all of us, and all our acts of righteousness are like a garment for periods of menstruation; and we shall fade away like leafage, all of us, and our errors themselves will carry us away just like a wind. 7 And there is no one calling upon your name, no one rousing himself to lay hold on you; for you have concealed your face from us, and you cause us to melt by the power of our error.

8 And now, O Jehovah, you are our Father. We are the clay, and you are our Potter; and all of us are the work of your hand. 9 Do not be indignant, O Jehovah, to the extreme, and do not forever remember [our] error. Look, now, please: we are all your people. 10 Your own holy cities have become a wilderness. Zion itself has become a sheer wilderness, Jerusalem a desolate waste. 11 Our house of holiness and beauty, in which our forefathers praised you, has itself become something for burning in the fire; and every one of our desirable things has become a devastation. 12 In the face of these things will you continue keeping yourself in check, O Jehovah? Will you stay still and let us be afflicted to the extreme?

65 "I have let myself be searched for by those who had not asked [for me]. I have let myself be found by those who had not looked for me. I have said, 'Here I am, here I am!' to a nation that was not calling upon my name.

2 "I have spread out my hands all day long to a stubborn people, those who are walking in the way that is not good, after their thoughts; 3 the people [made up of] those offending me right to my face constantly, sacrificing in the gardens and making sacrificial smoke upon the bricks, 4 seating themselves among the burial places, who also pass the night even in the watch huts, eating the flesh of the pig, even the broth of foul things being in their vessels; 5 those who are saying, 'Keep close to yourself. Do not approach me, for I shall certainly convey holiness to you.' These are a smoke in my nostrils, a fire burning all day long.

6 "Look! It is written before me. I shall not keep still, but I will render a reward; I will even render the reward into their own bosom, 7 for their own errors and for the errors of their forefathers at the same time," Jehovah has said. "Because they have made sacrificial smoke upon the mountains, and upon the hills they have reproached me, I will also measure out their wages first of all into their own bosom."

8 This is what Jehovah has said: "In the same way that the new wine is found in the cluster and someone has to say, 'Do not ruin it, because there is a blessing in it,' so I shall do for the sake of my servants in order not to bring everybody to ruin. 9 And I will bring forth out of Jacob an offspring and out of Judah the hereditary possessor of my mountains; and my chosen ones must take possession of it, and my own servants will reside there. 10 And Shar′on must become a pasture ground for sheep and the low plain of A′chor a resting place for cattle, for my people who will have looked for me.

11 "But you men are those leaving Jehovah, those forgetting my holy mountain, those setting in order a table for the god of Good Luck and those filling up mixed wine for the god of Destiny. 12 And I will destine you men to the sword, and you will all of you bow down to being slaughtered; for the reason that I called, but you did not answer; I spoke, but you did not listen; and you kept doing what was bad in my eyes, and the thing in which I took no delight you chose."

13 Therefore this is what the Lord Jehovah has said: "Look! My own servants will eat, but you yourselves will go hungry. Look! My own servants will drink, but you yourselves will go thirsty. Look! My own servants will rejoice, but you yourselves will suffer shame. 14 Look! My own servants will cry out joyfully because of the good condition of the heart, but you yourselves will make outcries because of the pain of heart and you will howl because of sheer breakdown of spirit. 15 And you men will certainly lay up your name

for an oath by my chosen ones, and the Lord Jehovah will actually put [YOU] individually to death, but his own servants he will call by another name; 16 so that anyone blessing himself in the earth will bless himself by the God of faith, and anyone making a sworn statement in the earth will swear by the God of faith; because the former distresses will actually be forgotten and because they will actually be concealed from my eyes.

17 "For here I am creating new heavens and a new earth; and the former things will not be called to mind, neither will they come up into the heart. 18 But exult, YOU people, and be joyful forever in what I am creating. For here I am creating Jerusalem a cause for joyfulness and her people a cause for exultation. 19 And I will be joyful in Jerusalem and exult in my people; and no more will there be heard in her the sound of weeping or the sound of a plaintive cry."

20 "No more will there come to be a suckling a few days old from that place, neither an old man that does not fulfill his days; for one will die as a mere boy, although a hundred years of age; and as for the sinner, although a hundred years of age he will have evil called down upon him. 21 And they will certainly build houses and have occupancy; and they will certainly plant vineyards and eat [their] fruitage. 22 They will not build and someone else have occupancy; they will not plant and someone else do the eating. For like the days of a tree will the days of my people be; and the work of their own hands my chosen ones will use to the full. 23 They will not toil for nothing, nor will they bring to birth for disturbance; because they are the offspring made up of the chosen ones of Jehovah, and their descendants with them. 24 And it will actually occur that before they call out I myself shall answer; while they are yet speaking, I myself shall hear.

25 "The wolf and the lamb themselves will feed as one, and the lion will eat straw just like the bull; and as for the serpent, his food will be dust. They will do no harm nor cause any ruin in all my holy mountain," Jehovah has said.

66 This is what Jehovah has said: "The heavens are my throne, and the earth is my footstool. Where, then, is the house that YOU people can build for me, and where, then, is the place as a resting place for me?"

2 "Now all these things my own hand has made, so that all these came to be," is the utterance of Jehovah. "To this one, then, I shall look, to the one afflicted and contrite in spirit and trembling at my word.

3 "The one slaughtering the bull is as one striking down a man. The one sacrificing the sheep is as one breaking the neck of a dog. The one offering up a gift—the blood of a pig! The one presenting a memorial of frankincense is as one saying a blessing with uncanny words. They are also the ones that have chosen their own ways, and in their disgusting things their very soul has taken a delight. 4 I myself, in turn, shall choose ways of ill-treating them; and the things frightful to them I shall bring upon them; for the reason that I called, but there was no one answering; I spoke, but there were none that listened; and they kept on doing what was bad in my eyes, and the thing in which I took no delight they chose."

5 Hear the word of Jehovah, YOU men who are trembling at his word: "YOUR brothers that are hating YOU, that are excluding YOU by reason of my name, said, 'May Jehovah be glorified!' He must also appear with rejoicing on YOUR part, and they are the ones that will be put to shame."

6 There is a sound of uproar out of the city, a sound out of the temple! It is the sound of Jehovah repaying what is deserved to his enemies.

7 Before she began to come into labor pains she gave birth. Before

birth pangs could come to her, she even gave deliverance to a male child. 8 Who has heard of a thing like this? Who has seen things like these? Will a land be brought forth with labor pains in one day? Or will a nation be born at one time? For Zion has come into labor pains as well as given birth to her sons.

9 "As for me, shall I cause the breaking through and not cause the giving birth?" says Jehovah. "Or am I causing a giving birth and do I actually cause a shutting up?" your God has said.

10 Rejoice with Jerusalem and be joyful with her, all you lovers of her. Exult greatly with her, all you keeping yourselves in mourning over her; 11 for the reason that you will suck and certainly get satisfaction from the breast of full consolation by her; for the reason that you will sip and experience exquisite delight from the teat of her glory. 12 For this is what Jehovah has said: "Here I am extending to her peace just like a river and the glory of nations just like a flooding torrent, and you will certainly suck. Upon the flank you will be carried, and upon the knees you will be fondled. 13 Like a man whom his own mother keeps comforting, so I myself shall keep comforting you people; and in the case of Jerusalem you will be comforted. 14 And you will certainly see, and your heart will be bound to exult, and your very bones will sprout just like tender grass. And the hand of Jehovah will certainly be made known to his servants, but he will actually denounce his enemies."

15 "For here Jehovah himself comes as a very fire, and his chariots are like a stormwind, in order to pay back his anger with sheer rage and his rebuke with flames of fire. 16 For as fire Jehovah himself will for a fact take up the controversy, yes, with his sword, against all flesh; and the slain of Jehovah will certainly become many. 17 Those sanctifying themselves and cleansing themselves for the gardens behind one in the center, eating the flesh of the pig and the loathsome thing, even the jumping rodent, they will all together reach their end," is the utterance of Jehovah. 18 "And as regards their works and their thoughts, I am coming in order to collect all the nations and tongues together; and they will have to come and see my glory."

19 "And I will set among them a sign, and I will send some of those who are escaped to the nations, [to] Tar'shish, Pul, and Lud, those drawing the bow, Tu'bal and Ja'van, the faraway islands, who have not heard a report about me or seen my glory; and they will for certain tell about my glory among the nations. 20 And they will actually bring all your brothers out of all the nations as a gift to Jehovah, on horses and in chariots and in covered wagons and on mules and on swift she-camels, up to my holy mountain, Jerusalem," Jehovah has said, "just as when the sons of Israel bring the gift in a clean vessel into the house of Jehovah."

21 "And from them also I shall take some for the priests, for the Levites," Jehovah has said.

22 "For just as the new heavens and the new earth that I am making are standing before me," is the utterance of Jehovah, "so the offspring of you people and the name of you people will keep standing."

23 "And it will certainly occur that from new moon to new moon and from sabbath to sabbath all flesh will come in to bow down before me," Jehovah has said. 24 "And they will actually go forth and look upon the carcasses of the men that were transgressing against me; for the very worms upon them will not die and their fire itself will not be extinguished, and they must become something repulsive to all flesh."

birth things could come to the birth, even gave severance those gave birth to them, child. 8 Who has heard

JEREMIAH

1 The words of Jeremiah the son of Hil·ki′ah, one of the priests that were in An′a·thoth in the land of Benjamin; 2 to whom the word of Jehovah occurred in the days of Jo·si′ah the son of A′mon, the king of Judah, in the thirteenth year of his reigning. 3 And it kept on occurring in the days of Je·hoi′a·kim the son of Jo·si′ah, the king of Judah, until the completion of the eleventh year of Zed·e·ki′ah the son of Jo·si′ah, the king of Judah, until Jerusalem went into exile in the fifth month.

4 And the word of Jehovah began to occur to me, saying: 5 "Before I was forming you in the belly I knew you, and before you proceeded to come forth from the womb I sanctified you. Prophet to the nations I made you."

6 But I said: "Alas, O Lord Jehovah! Here I actually do not know how to speak, for I am but a boy."

7 And Jehovah went on to say to me: "Do not say, 'I am but a boy.' But to all those to whom I shall send you, you should go; and everything that I shall command you, you should speak. 8 Do not be afraid because of their faces, for 'I am with you to deliver you,' is the utterance of Jehovah."

9 At that Jehovah thrust his hand out and caused it to touch my mouth. Then Jehovah said to me: "Here I have put my words in your mouth. 10 See, I have commissioned you this day to be over the nations and over the kingdoms, in order to uproot and to pull down and to destroy and to tear down, to build and to plant."

11 And the word of Jehovah continued to occur to me, saying: "What are you seeing, Jeremiah?"

So I said: "An offshoot of an almond tree is what I am seeing."

12 And Jehovah went on to say to me: "You have seen well, for I am keeping awake concerning my word in order to carry it out."

13 And the word of Jehovah proceeded to occur to me the second time, saying: "What are you seeing?"

So I said: "A widemouthed cooking pot blown upon is what I am seeing, and its mouth is away from the north."

14 At this Jehovah said to me: "Out of the north the calamity will be loosened against all the inhabitants of the land. 15 For 'here I am calling for all the families of the kingdoms of the north,' is the utterance of Jehovah; 'and they will certainly come and place each one his throne at the entrance of the gates of Jerusalem, and against all her walls round about and against all the cities of Judah. 16 And I will speak with them my judgments over all their badness, in that they have left me and they keep making sacrificial smoke to other gods and bowing down to the works of their own hands.'

17 "And as for you, you should gird up your hips, and you must rise up and speak to them everything that I myself command you. Do not be struck with any terror because of them, in order that I may not strike you with terror before them. 18 But as for me, here I have made you today a fortified city and an iron pillar and copper walls against all the land, toward the kings of Judah, toward her princes, toward her priests and toward the people of the land. 19 And they will be certain to fight against you, but they will not prevail against you, for 'I am with you,' is the utterance of Jehovah, 'to deliver you.'"

2 And the word of Jehovah proceeded to occur to me, saying: 2 "Go, and you must call out in the ears of Jerusalem, saying, 'This is what Jehovah has said: "I well remember, on your part, the loving-kindness of your youth, the love during your being engaged to marry, your walking after me in the wilderness, in a land not sown with seed. 3 Israel was something holy to Jehovah, the first yield to Him." ' 'Any persons devouring him would make themselves guilty. Calamity itself would come upon them,' was the utterance of Jehovah."

4 Hear the word of Jehovah, O house of Jacob, and all YOU families of the house of Israel. 5 This is what Jehovah has said: "What have YOUR fathers found in me that was unjust, so that they have become far off from me, and they kept walking after the vain idol and becoming vain themselves? 6 And they have not said, 'Where is Jehovah, the One bringing us up out of the land of Egypt, the One walking us through the wilderness, through a land of desert plain and pit, through a land of no water and of deep shadow, through a land through which no man passed and in which no earthling man dwelt?'

7 "And I gradually brought YOU to a land of the orchard, to eat its fruitage and its good things. But YOU came in and defiled my land; and my own inheritance YOU made something detestable. 8 The priests themselves did not say, 'Where is Jehovah?' And the very ones handling the law did not know me; and the shepherds themselves transgressed against me, and even the prophets prophesied by Ba′al, and after those who could bring no benefit they walked.

9 "Therefore I shall contend further with YOU people,' is the utterance of Jehovah, 'and with the sons of YOUR sons I shall contend.'

10 " 'But pass over to the coastlands of the Kit′tim and see. Yes, send even to Ke′dar and give YOUR special consideration, and see whether anything like this has happened. 11 Has a nation exchanged gods, even for those that are no gods? But my own people have exchanged my glory for what can bring no benefit. 12 Stare in

amazement, O YOU heavens, at this; and bristle up in very great horror,' is the utterance of Jehovah, 13 'because there are two bad things that my people have done: They have left even me, the source of living water, in order to hew out for themselves cisterns, broken cisterns, that cannot contain the water.'

14 " 'Is Israel a servant, or a slave born in the household? Why is it that he has come to be for plunder? 15 Against him maned young lions roar; they have given out their voice. And they went making his land an object of astonishment. His own cities have been set afire, so that there is no inhabitant. 16 Even the sons of Noph and Tah′pa·nes themselves kept feeding on you at the crown of the head. 17 Is not this what you proceeded to do to yourself by your leaving Jehovah your God during the time of [his] walking you in the way? 18 And now what concern should you have for the way of Egypt in order to drink the waters of Shi′hor? And what concern should you have for the way of As·syr′i·a in order to drink the waters of the River? 19 Your badness should correct you, and your own acts of unfaithfulness should reprove you. Know, then, and see that your leaving Jehovah your God is something bad and bitter, and no dread of me [has resulted] to you,' is the utterance of the Sovereign Lord, Jehovah of armies.

20 " 'For long ago I broke your yoke to pieces; I tore your bands apart. But you said: "I am not going to serve," for upon every high hill and under every luxuriant tree you were lying sprawled out, prostituting yourself. 21 And as for me, I had planted you as a choice red vine, all of it a true seed. So how have you been changed toward me into the degenerate [shoots] of a foreign vine?'

22 " 'But though you should do the washing with alkali and take to yourself large quantities of lye, your error would certainly be a

stain before me,' is the utterance of the Lord Jehovah. 23 How can you say, 'I have not defiled myself. After the Ba'als I have not walked'? See your way in the valley. Take note of what you have done. A swift young she-camel aimlessly running to and fro in her ways; 24 a zebra accustomed to the wilderness, at the craving of her soul, snuffing up the wind; at her time for copulation, who can turn her back? All those who are looking for her will not go tiring themselves out. In her month they will find her. 25 Hold your foot back from [becoming] barefoot, and your throat from thirst. But you proceeded to say, 'It is hopeless! No, but I have fallen in love with strangers, and after them I am going to walk.'

26 "As with the shame of a thief when he is found out, so those of the house of Israel have felt shame, they, their kings, their princes and their priests and their prophets. 27 They are saying to a tree, 'You are my father,' and to a stone, 'You yourself brought me to birth.' But to me they have turned the back of the neck and not the face. And in the time of their calamity they will say, 'Do rise up and save us!'

28 "But where are your gods that you have made for yourself? Let them rise up if they can save you in the time of your calamity. For as the number of your cities your gods have become, O Judah.

29 " 'Why do YOU people keep contending against me? Why have YOU transgressed, all of YOU, against me?' is the utterance of Jehovah. 30 To no effect I have struck YOUR sons. No discipline did they take. YOUR sword has devoured YOUR prophets, like a lion that is causing ruin. 31 O generation, see for yourselves the word of Jehovah.

"Have I become a mere wilderness to Israel or a land of intense darkness? Why is it that these, my people, have said, 'We have roamed. We shall come to you no more'? 32 Can a virgin forget her ornaments, a bride her breast-bands? And yet my own people— they have forgotten me days without number.

33 "Why do you, O woman, improve your way in order to look for love? Therefore it has also been in bad things that you have taught your ways. 34 Also, in your skirts there have been found the blood marks of the souls of the innocent poor ones. Not in the act of breaking in have I found them, but [they are] upon all these.

35 "But you say, 'I have remained innocent. Surely his anger has turned back from me.'

"Here I am entering into controversy with you on account of your saying, 'I have not sinned.' 36 Why do you treat as very insignificant the changing of your way? Of Egypt, too, you will become ashamed, just as you became ashamed of As·syr'i·a. 37 For this cause also you will go forth with your hands upon your head, because Jehovah has rejected the objects of your confidence, and you will have no success with them."

3 There is a saying: "If a man should send away his wife and she should actually go away from him and become another man's, should he return to her any more?"

Has that land not positively been polluted?

"And you yourself have committed prostitution with many companions; and should there be a returning to me?" is the utterance of Jehovah. 2 "Raise your eyes to the beaten paths and see. Where is it that you have not been raped? Alongside the ways you have sat for them, like an Arabian in the wilderness; and you keep polluting the land with your acts of prostitution and with your badness. 3 So copious showers are withheld, and not even a spring rain has occurred. And the forehead of a wife committing prostitution is what has become yours. You have refused to feel humiliated. 4 Have you from now on called out to me, 'My Father, you are the confidential friend of my youth! 5 Should one stay resentful to time indefinite, or keep watching [something] forever?' Look! You have spoken, and you went on to do bad things and prevail."

6 And Jehovah proceeded to say to me in the days of Jo·si′ah the king: " 'Have you seen what unfaithful Israel has done? She is going upon every high mountain and underneath every luxuriant tree, that she may commit prostitution there. 7 And after her doing all these things I kept saying that she should return even to me, but she did not return; and Judah kept looking at her own treacherous sister. 8 When I got to see that, for the very reason that unfaithful Israel had committed adultery, I sent her away and proceeded to give the certificate of her full divorce to her, yet treacherously dealing Judah her sister did not become afraid, but she herself also began to go and commit prostitution. 9 And her prostitution occurred because of [her] frivolous view, and she kept polluting the land and committing adultery with stones and with trees; 10 and even for all this her treacherous sister Judah did not return to me with all her heart, only falsely,' is the utterance of Jehovah."

11 And Jehovah went on to say to me: "Unfaithful Israel has proved her own soul to be more righteous than treacherously dealing Judah. 12 Go, and you must proclaim these words to the north and say:

" ' "Do return, O renegade Israel," is the utterance of Jehovah.'

' "I shall not have my face drop [angrily] upon you people, for I am loyal," is the utterance of Jehovah.' ' "I shall not stay resentful to time indefinite. 13 Only take note of your error, for it is against Jehovah your God that you have transgressed. And you continued scattering your ways to the strangers under every luxuriant tree, but to my voice you people did not listen," is the utterance of Jehovah.' "

14 "Return, O YOU renegade sons," is the utterance of Jehovah. "For I myself have become the husbandly owner of YOU people; and I will take YOU, one out of a city and two out of a family, and I will bring YOU to Zion. 15 And I will give YOU shepherds in agreement with my heart, and they will certainly feed YOU with knowledge and insight. 16 And it must occur that YOU will become many and certainly bear fruit in the land in those days," is the utterance of Jehovah. "No more will they say, 'The ark of the covenant of Jehovah!' nor will it come up into the heart, nor will they remember it or miss it, and no more will it be made. 17 In that time they will call Jerusalem the throne of Jehovah; and to her all the nations must be brought together to the name of Jehovah at Jerusalem, and they will no more walk after the stubbornness of their bad heart."

18 "In those days they will walk, the house of Judah alongside the house of Israel, and together they will come out of the land of the north into the land that I gave as a hereditary possession to YOUR forefathers. 19 And I myself have said, 'O how I proceeded to place you among the sons and to give you the desirable land, the hereditary possession of the ornament of the armies of the nations!' And I further said, ' "My Father!" YOU people will call out to me, and from following me YOU people will not turn back.' 20 'Truly [as] a wife has treacherously gone from her companion, so YOU, O house of Israel, have dealt treacherously with me,' is the utterance of Jehovah."

21 On the beaten paths there has been heard a sound, the weeping, the entreaties of the sons of Israel. For they have twisted their way; they have forgotten Jehovah their God. 22 "Return, YOU renegade sons. I shall heal YOUR renegade condition."

"Here we are! We have come to you, for you, O Jehovah, are our God. 23 Truly the hills as well as the turmoil on the mountains belong to falsehood. Truly in Jehovah our God is the salvation of Israel. 24 But the shameful thing itself has eaten up the toil of our forefathers from our youth, their flocks and their herds, their sons and their daughters. 25 We lie down in our shame, and our humiliation keeps covering us; for it is toward Jehovah our God that we have sinned, we and our fathers from our youth on and down to this day, and we have not obeyed the voice of Jehovah our God."

4 "If you would return, O Israel," is the utterance of Jehovah, "you may return even to me. And if you will take away your disgusting things on my account, then you will not go as a fugitive. 2 And [if] you will certainly swear, 'As Jehovah is alive in truth, in justice and in righteousness!' then in him the nations will actually bless themselves, and in him they will boast about themselves."

3 For this is what Jehovah has said to the men of Judah and to Jerusalem: "Plow for yourselves arable land, and do not keep sowing among thorns. 4 Get yourselves circumcised to Jehovah, and take away the foreskins of YOUR hearts, YOU men of Judah and inhabitants of Jerusalem; that my rage may not go forth just like a fire, and it certainly burn with no one to do the extinguishing, on account of the badness of YOUR dealings."

5 Tell [it] in Judah, YOU men, and publish [it] even in Jerusalem, and say [it] out, and blow a horn throughout the land. Call out loudly and say: "Gather yourselves together, and let us enter into the fortified cities. 6 Raise a signal toward Zion. Make provision for shelter. Do not stand still." For there is a calamity that I am bringing in from the north, even a great crash. 7 He has gone up as a lion out of his thicket, and the one who is bringing the nations to ruin has pulled away; he has gone forth from his place in order to render your land as an object of astonishment. Your own cities will fall in ruins so that there will be no inhabitant. 8 On this account gird on sackcloth, YOU people. Beat YOUR breasts and howl, because the burning anger of Jehovah has not turned back from us.

9 "And it must occur in that day," is the utterance of Jehovah, "that the heart of the king will perish, also the heart of the princes; and the priests will certainly be driven to astonishment, and the prophets themselves will be amazed."

10 And I proceeded to say: "Alas, O Lord Jehovah! Truly you have absolutely deceived this people and Jerusalem, saying, 'Peace itself will become YOURS,' and the sword has reached clear to the soul."

11 At that time it will be said to this people and to Jerusalem: "There is a searing wind of the beaten paths through the wilderness [on] the way to the daughter of my people; it is not for winnowing, nor for cleansing. 12 The full wind itself comes even from these to me. Now I myself also shall speak forth the judgments with them. 13 Look! Like rain clouds he will come up, and his chariots are like a stormwind. His horses are swifter than eagles. Woe to us, because we have been despoiled! 14 Wash your heart clean of sheer badness, O Jerusalem, in order that you may be saved. How long will your erroneous thoughts lodge within you? 15 For a voice is telling from Dan and is publishing something hurtful from the mountainous region of E'phra·im. 16 Make mention [of it], YOU people, yes, to the nations. Publish [it] against Jerusalem."

"Watchers are coming from a land far away, and they will let out their voice against the very cities of Judah. 17 Like guards of the open field they have become against her on all sides, because she has rebelled even against me," is the utterance of Jehovah. 18 "Your way and your dealings —there will be a rendering of these to you. This is the calamity upon you, for it is bitter; because it has reached clear to your heart."

19 O my intestines, my intestines! I am in severe pains in the walls of my heart. My heart is boisterous within me. I cannot keep silent, for the sound of the horn is what my soul has heard, the alarm signal of war. 20 Crash upon crash is what has been called out, for the whole land has been despoiled. Suddenly my tents have been despoiled, in a moment my tent cloths. 21 How long shall I keep seeing the signal, keep hearing the sound of the horn? 22 For my people is foolish. Of me they have not taken note. They are unwise sons; and they are not those having understanding. Wise they are for doing bad, but for doing good they actually have no knowledge.

23 I saw the land, and, look! [it was] empty and waste; and into the heavens, and their light was no more. 24 I saw the mountains, and, look! they were rocking, and the hills themselves were all given a shaking. 25 I saw, and, look! there was not an earthling man, and the flying creatures of the heavens had all fled. 26 I saw, and, look! the orchard itself was a wilderness, and the very cities of it had all been torn down. It was because of Jehovah, because of his burning anger.

27 For this is what Jehovah has said: "A desolate waste is what the whole land will become, and shall I not carry out a sheer extermination? 28 On this account the land will mourn, and the heavens above will certainly become dark. It is because I have spoken, I have considered, and I have not felt regret, nor shall I turn back from it. 29 Because of the sound of the horsemen and bow shooters the entire city is running away. They have entered into the thickets, and into the rocks they have gone up. Every city is left, and there is no man dwelling in them."

30 Now that you are despoiled, what will you do, since you used to clothe yourself with scarlet, since you used to deck yourself with ornaments of gold, since you used to enlarge your eyes with black paint? It is in vain that you used to make yourself pretty. Those lusting after [you] have rejected you; they keep seeking for your very soul. 31 For a voice like that of a sick woman I have heard, the distress like that of a woman giving birth to her first child, the voice of the daughter of Zion who keeps gasping for breath. She keeps spreading out her palms: "Woe, now, to me, for my soul is tired of the killers!"

5 Go roving about in the streets of Jerusalem and see, now, and know, and seek for yourselves in her public squares whether YOU can find a man, whether there exists anyone doing justice, anyone seeking faithfulness, and I shall forgive her. 2 Even if they should say: "As Jehovah is alive!" they would thereby be swearing to sheer falsehood.

3 O Jehovah, are not those eyes of yours toward faithfulness? You have struck them, but they did not become ill. You exterminated them. They refused to take discipline. They made their faces harder than a crag. They refused to turn back. 4 Even I myself had said: "Surely they are of low class. They acted foolishly, for they have ignored the way of Jehovah, the judgment of their God. 5 I will go my way to the great ones and speak with them; for they themselves must have taken note of the way of Jehovah, the judgment of their God. Surely they themselves must have all together broken the yoke; they must have torn apart the bands."

6 That is why a lion out of the forest has struck them, a wolf itself of the desert plains keeps despoiling them, a leopard is keeping awake at their cities. Everyone going forth from them gets torn to pieces. For their transgressions have become many; their acts of unfaithfulness have become numerous.

7 How can I forgive you for this very thing? Your own sons have

left me, and they keep swearing by what is no God. And I kept satisfying them, but they continued committing adultery, and to the house of a prostitute woman they go in troops. 8 Horses seized with sexual heat, having [strong] testicles, they have become. They neigh each one to the wife of his companion.

9 "Should I not take an accounting because of these very things?" is the utterance of Jehovah. "Or upon a nation that is like this should not my soul avenge itself?"

10 "Come up against her [vine] rows and cause ruin, but do not YOU men make an actual extermination. Take away her luxuriating shoots, for they do not belong to Jehovah. 11 For the house of Israel and the house of Judah have positively dealt treacherously with me," is the utterance of Jehovah. 12 "They have denied Jehovah, and they keep saying, 'He is not. And upon us no calamity will come, and no sword or famine shall we see.' 13 And the prophets themselves become a wind, and the word is not in them. That is how it will be done to them."

14 Therefore this is what Jehovah, the God of armies, has said: "For the reason that YOU men are saying this thing, here I am making my words in your mouth a fire, and this people will be pieces of wood, and it will certainly devour them."

15 "Here I am bringing in upon YOU men a nation from far away, O house of Israel," is the utterance of Jehovah. "It is an enduring nation. It is a nation of long ago, a nation whose language you do not know, and you cannot hear [understandingly] what they speak. 16 Their quiver is like an open burial place; all of them are mighty men. 17 They will also certainly eat up your harvest and your bread. The men will eat up your sons and your daughters. They will eat up your flocks and your herds. They will eat up your vine and your fig tree. They will shatter with the sword your fortified cities in which you are trusting."

18 "And even in those days," is the utterance of Jehovah, "I shall not carry out an extermination of YOU men. 19 And it must occur that YOU will say, 'Due to what fact has Jehovah our God done to us all these things?' And you must say to them, 'Just as YOU have left me and have gone serving a foreign god in YOUR land, so YOU will serve strangers in a land that is not YOURS.'"

20 TELL this in the house of Jacob, and publish it in Judah, saying: 21 "Hear, now, this, O unwise people that is without heart: They have eyes, but they cannot see; they have ears, but they cannot hear. 22 'Do YOU not fear even me,' is the utterance of Jehovah, 'or are YOU in no severe pains even because of me, who have set the sand as the boundary for the sea, an indefinitely lasting regulation that it cannot pass over? Although its waves toss themselves, still they cannot prevail; and [although] they do become boisterous, still they cannot pass over it. 23 But this very people has come to have a stubborn and rebellious heart; they have turned aside and keep walking in their course. 24 But they have not said in their heart: "Let us, now, fear Jehovah our God, the One who is giving the downpour and the autumn rain and the spring rain in its season, the One who guards even the prescribed weeks of the harvest for us." 25 YOUR own errors have turned these things away, and YOUR own sins have held back what is good from YOU people.

26 "For among my people there have been found wicked men. They keep peering, as when birdcatchers crouch down. They have set a ruinous [trap]. It is men that they catch. 27 As a cage is full of flying creatures, so their houses are full of deception. That is why they have become great and they gain riches. 28 They have grown fat; they have become shiny. They have also overflowed with bad

things. No legal case have they pleaded, even the legal case of the fatherless boy, that they may gain success; and the judgment of the poor ones they have not taken up.' "

29 "Should I not hold an accounting because of these very things," is the utterance of Jehovah, "or on a nation that is like this should not my soul avenge itself? 30 An astonishing situation, even a horrible thing, has been brought to be in the land: 31 The prophets themselves actually prophesy in falsehood; and as for the priests, they go subduing according to their powers. And my own people have loved [it] that way; and what will YOU men do in the finale of it?"

6 Take shelter, O YOU sons of Benjamin, from the midst of Jerusalem; and in Te·ko′a blow the horn. And over Beth-hac·che′rem raise a fire signal; because calamity itself has looked down out of the north, even a great crash. 2 The daughter of Zion has resembled indeed a comely and daintily bred woman. 3 To her the shepherds and their droves proceeded to come. Against her they pitched [their] tents all around. They grazed off each one his own part. 4 Against her they have sanctified war: "Rise up, and let us go up at midday!"

"Woe to us, for the day has declined, for the shadows of evening keep extending themselves!"

5 "Rise up, and let us go up during the night and bring to ruin her dwelling towers."

6 For this is what Jehovah of armies has said: "Cut down wood and throw up against Jerusalem a siege rampart. She is the city with which an accounting must be held. She is nothing but oppression in the midst of her. 7 As a cistern keeps its waters cool, so she has kept her badness cool. Violence and despoiling are heard in her; sickness and plague are before my face constantly. 8 Be corrected, O Jerusalem, that my soul may not turn away disgusted from you; that I

may not set you as a desolate waste, a land not inhabited."

9 This is what Jehovah of armies has said: "They will without fail glean the remnant of Israel just like a vine. Put your hand back like one that is gathering grapes upon the vine tendrils."

10 "To whom shall I speak and give warning, that they may hear? Look! Their ear is uncircumcised, so that they are unable to pay attention. Look! The very word of Jehovah has become to them a reproach, in which [word] they can take no delight. 11 And with the rage of Jehovah I have become full. I have become weary with holding in."

"Pour [it] out upon the child in the street and upon the intimate group of young men at the same time; for they will also be caught, a man along with his wife, an old man along with one that is full of days. 12 And their houses will certainly be turned over to others for possession, the fields and the wives at the same time. For I shall stretch my hand out against the inhabitants of the land," is the utterance of Jehovah.

13 "For from the least one of them even to the greatest one of them, every one is making for himself unjust gain; and from the prophet even to the priest, each one is acting falsely. 14 And they try to heal the breakdown of my people lightly, saying, 'There is peace! There is peace!' when there is no peace. 15 Did they feel shame because it was something detestable that they had done? For one thing, they positively do not feel any shame; for another thing, they have not come to know even how to feel humiliated. Therefore they will fall among those who are falling; in the time that I must hold an accounting with them they will stumble," Jehovah has said.

16 This is what Jehovah has said: "Stand still in the ways, YOU people, and see, and ask for the roadways of long ago, where, now, the good way is; and walk in it, and find ease for YOUR souls." But

they kept saying: "We are not going to walk." 17 "And I raised up over YOU people watchmen, 'Pay attention to the sound of the horn!'" But they kept saying: "We are not going to pay attention." 18 "Therefore hear, O YOU nations! And know, O you assembly, what will be among them. 19 Listen, O earth! Here I am bringing in calamity upon this people as the fruitage of their thoughts, for they paid no attention to my very own words; and my law—they also kept rejecting it."

20 "What does this matter to me that you bring in even frankincense from She′ba and the good cane from the land far away? The whole burnt offerings of YOU people serve for no pleasure, and YOUR very sacrifices have not been gratifying to me." 21 Therefore this is what Jehovah has said: "Here I am setting for this people stumbling blocks, and they will certainly stumble over them, father and sons together; the neighbor and his companion—they will perish."

22 This is what Jehovah has said: "Look! A people is coming from the land of the north, and there is a great nation that will be awakened from the remotest parts of the earth. 23 The bow and the javelin they will grab hold of. It is a cruel one, and they will have no pity. Their very voice will resound just like the sea, and upon horses they will ride. It is drawn up in battle order like a man of war against you, O daughter of Zion."

24 We have heard the report about it. Our hands have dropped. Distress itself has seized hold of us, labor pains like those of a woman giving birth. 25 Do not go out into the field, and do not walk even in the way; for there is the sword belonging to the enemy, there is fright all around. 26 O daughter of my people, gird on sackcloth and wallow in the ashes. Make your mourning that for an only [son], the wailing of bitterness; because suddenly the despoiler will come upon us.

27 "I have made you a metal tester among my people, one making a thorough search; and you will take note and you must examine their way. 28 All of them are the most stubborn men, walking about as slanderers—copper and iron. They are all of them ruinous. 29 The bellows have been scorched. Out from their fire there is lead. One has kept refining intensely simply for nothing, and those who are bad have not been separated. 30 Rejected silver is what people will certainly call them, for Jehovah has rejected them."

7 The word that occurred to Jeremiah from Jehovah, saying: 2 "Stand in the gate of the house of Jehovah, and you must proclaim there this word, and you must say, 'Hear the word of Jehovah, all YOU of Judah, who are entering into these gates to bow down to Jehovah. 3 This is what Jehovah of armies, the God of Israel, has said: "Make YOUR ways and YOUR dealings good, and I will keep YOU people residing in this place. 4 Do not put YOUR trust in fallacious words, saying, 'The temple of Jehovah, the temple of Jehovah, the temple of Jehovah they are!' 5 For if YOU will positively make YOUR ways and YOUR dealings good, if YOU will positively carry out justice between a man and his companion, 6 if no alien resident, no fatherless boy and no widow YOU will oppress, and innocent blood YOU will not shed in this place, and after other gods YOU will not walk for calamity to yourselves, 7 I, in turn, shall certainly keep YOU residing in this place, in the land that I gave to YOUR forefathers, from time indefinite even to time indefinite."'"

8 "Here YOU are putting YOUR trust in fallacious words—it will certainly be of no benefit at all. 9 Can there be stealing, murdering and committing a d u l t e r y and swearing falsely and making sacrificial smoke to Ba′al and walking after other gods whom YOU had not known, 10 and must YOU come and stand before me in this house

upon which my name has been called, and must YOU say, 'We shall certainly be delivered,' in the face of doing all these detestable things? 11 Has this house upon which my name has been called become a mere cave of robbers in YOUR eyes? Here I myself also have seen [it]," is the utterance of Jehovah.

12 "'However, GO, now, to my place that was in Shi′loh, where I caused my name to reside at first, and see what I did to it because of the badness of my people Israel. 13 And now for the reason that YOU kept doing all these works,' is the utterance of Jehovah, 'and I kept speaking to YOU, getting up early and speaking, but YOU did not listen, and I kept calling YOU, but YOU did not answer, 14 I will do also to the house upon which my name has been called, in which YOU are trusting, and to the place that I gave to YOU and to YOUR forefathers, just as I did to Shi′loh. 15 And I will throw YOU out from before my face, just as I threw out all YOUR brothers, the whole offspring of E′phra·im.'

16 "And as for you, do not pray in behalf of this people, neither raise in their behalf an entreating cry or a prayer nor beseech me, for I shall not be listening to you. 17 Are you not seeing what they are doing in the cities of Judah and in the streets of Jerusalem? 18 The sons are picking up sticks of wood, and the fathers are lighting the fire, and the wives are kneading flour dough in order to make sacrificial cakes to the 'queen of the heavens'; and there is a pouring out of drink offerings to other gods for the purpose of offending me. 19 'Is it I whom they are offending?' is the utterance of Jehovah. 'Is it not they themselves, for the purpose of shame to their faces?' 20 Therefore this is what the Lord Jehovah has said, 'Look! My anger and my rage are being poured forth upon this place, upon mankind and upon domestic animal, and upon the tree of the field and upon the fruitage of the

ground; and it must burn, and it will not be extinguished.'

21 "This is what Jehovah of armies, the God of Israel, has said, 'Add those whole burnt offerings of YOURS to YOUR sacrifices and eat flesh. 22 For I did not speak with YOUR forefathers, nor did I command them in the day of my bringing them out from the land of Egypt concerning the matters of whole burnt offering and sacrifice. 23 But this word I did express in command upon them, saying: "Obey my voice, and I will become YOUR God, and YOU yourselves will become my people; and YOU must walk in all the way that I shall command YOU, in order that it may go well with YOU."' 24 But they did not listen, neither did they incline their ear, but they went walking in the counsels in the stubbornness of their bad heart, so that they became backward in direction and not forward, 25 from the day that YOUR forefathers came forth out of the land of Egypt until this day; and I kept sending to YOU all my servants the prophets, daily getting up early and sending [them]. 26 But they did not listen to me, and they did not incline their ear, but they kept hardening their neck. They acted worse than their forefathers!

27 "And you must speak to them all these words, but they will not listen to you; and you must call to them, but they will not answer you. 28 And you must say to them, 'This is the nation whose people have not obeyed the voice of Jehovah its God, and have not taken discipline. Faithfulness has perished, and it has been cut off from their mouth.'

29 "Shear off your uncut hair and throw [it] away, and upon the bare hills raise a dirge, for Jehovah has rejected and will desert the generation with which he is furious. 30 'For the sons of Judah have done what is bad in my eyes,' is the utterance of Jehovah. 'They have set their disgusting things in the house upon which my name has been called, in order

to defile it. 31 And they have built the high places of To'pheth, which is in the valley of the son of Hin'nom, in order to burn their sons and their daughters in the fire, a thing that I had not commanded and that had not come up into my heart.'

32 "'Therefore, look! days are coming,' is the utterance of Jehovah, 'when it will no more be said [to be] To'pheth and the valley of the son of Hin'nom, but the valley of the killing; and they will have to bury in To'pheth without there being enough place. 33 And the dead bodies of this people must become food for the flying creatures of the heavens and for the beasts of the earth, with nobody to make [them] tremble. 34 And I will cause to cease from the cities of Judah and from the streets of Jerusalem the voice of exultation and the voice of rejoicing, the voice of the bridegroom and the voice of the bride; for the land will become nothing but a devastated place.'"

8 "At that time," is the utterance of Jehovah, "people will also bring forth the bones of the kings of Judah and the bones of its princes and the bones of the priests and the bones of the prophets and the bones of the inhabitants of Jerusalem from their graves. 2 And they will actually spread them out to the sun and to the moon and to all the army of the heavens that they have loved and that they have served and that they have walked after and that they have sought and that they have bowed down to. They will not be gathered, nor will they be buried. As manure upon the face of the ground they will become."

3 "And death will certainly be chosen rather than life on the part of all the remnant of those remaining out of this bad family in all the places of the remaining ones, where I will have dispersed them," is the utterance of Jehovah of armies.

4 "And you must say to them, 'This is what Jehovah has said:

"Will they fall and not get up again? If one would turn back, will the other not also turn back? 5 Why is it that this people, Jerusalem, is unfaithful with an enduring unfaithfulness? They have taken hold of trickiness; they have refused to turn back. 6 I have paid attention, and I kept listening. It was not right the way they kept speaking. There was not a man repenting over his badness, saying, 'What have I done?' Each one is going back into the popular course, like a horse that is dashing into the battle. 7 Even the stork in the heavens—it well knows its appointed times; and the turtledove and the swift and the bulbul—they observe well the time of each one's coming in. But as for my people, they have not come to know the judgment of Jehovah." '

8 "'How can YOU men say: "We are wise, and the law of Jehovah is with us"? Surely, now, the false stylus of the secretaries has worked in sheer falsehood. 9 The wise ones have become ashamed. They have become terrified and will be caught. Look! They have rejected the very word of Jehovah, and what wisdom do they have? 10 Therefore I shall give their wives to other men, their fields to those taking possession; for, from the least one even to the greatest one, each one is making unjust gain; from the prophet even to the priest, each one is acting falsely. 11 And they try to heal the breakdown of the daughter of my people lightly, saying: "There is peace! There is peace!" when there is no peace. 12 Did they feel shame because they had done even what was detestable? For one thing, they positively could not feel ashamed; for another thing, they did not know even how to feel humiliated.

"'Therefore they will fall among those who are falling. In the time of their being given attention, they will stumble,' Jehovah has said.

13 "'When doing the gathering, I shall bring them to their finish,' is the utterance of Jehovah. 'There will be no grapes on the vine, and

there will be no figs on the fig tree, and the foliage itself will certainly wither. And things that I give to them will pass by them.'"

14 "Why are we sitting still? Gather yourselves together, and let us enter into the fortified cities and be silent there. For Jehovah our God has himself put us to silence, and he gives us poisoned water to drink, because we have sinned against Jehovah. 15 There was a hoping for peace, but no good [came]; for a time of healing, but, look! terror! 16 From Dan has been heard the snorting of his horses. Due to the sound of the neighing of his stallions the whole land has begun to rock. And they come in and eat up the land and what fills it, the city and its inhabitants."

17 "For here I am sending in among YOU serpents, poisonous snakes, for which there is no charming, and they will certainly bite YOU," is the utterance of Jehovah.

18 A grief that is beyond curing has come up into me. My heart is ill. 19 Here there is the sound of the cry for help of the daughter of my people from a land far away: "Is Jehovah not in Zion? Or is her king not in her?"

"Why is it that they have offended me with their graven images, with their vain foreign gods?"

20 "The harvest has passed, the summer has come to an end; but as for us, we have not been saved!"

21 Over the breakdown of the daughter of my people I have become shattered. I have grown sad. Outright astonishment has seized hold of me. 22 Is there no balsam in Gil′e·ad? Or is there no healer there? Why is it, then, that the recuperation of the daughter of my people has not come up?

9 O that my head were waters, and that my eyes were a source of tears! Then I could weep day and night for the slain ones of the daughter of my people.

2 O that I had in the wilderness a lodging place of travelers! Then I would leave my people and go away from them, for all of them are adulterers, a solemn assembly of treacherous dealers; 3 and they bend their tongue as their bow in falsehood; but not for faithfulness have they proved mighty in the land.

"For from badness to badness they went forth, and they ignored even me," is the utterance of Jehovah.

4 "Guard yourselves each one against his own companion, and put YOUR trust in no brother at all. For even every brother would positively supplant, and every companion himself would walk around as a mere slanderer, 5 and they keep trifling each one with his companion; and they speak no truth at all. They have taught their tongue to speak falsehood. They have tired themselves out merely in doing wrong.

6 "Your sitting is in the midst of deception. Through deception they have refused to know me," is the utterance of Jehovah.

7 Therefore this is what Jehovah of armies has said: "Here I am smelting them, and I have to examine them, because how otherwise shall I act on account of the daughter of my people? 8 Their tongue is a slaughtering arrow. Deception is what it has spoken. With his mouth, peace is what [a person] keeps speaking with his own companion; but within himself he sets his ambush."

9 "Because of these things should I not hold an accounting with them?" is the utterance of Jehovah. "Or upon a nation that is like this should not my soul avenge itself? 10 Over the mountains I shall raise a weeping and lamentation, and over the pasture grounds of the wilderness a dirge; for they will have been burned so that there is no man passing through and people actually will not hear the sound of livestock. Both the flying creature of the heavens and the beast will have fled; they will have gone. 11 And I will make Jerusalem piles of stones, the lair of jackals; and the cities of Judah I shall make a

desolate waste, without an inhabitant.

12 "Who is the man that is wise, that he may understand this, even the one to whom the mouth of Jehovah has spoken, that he may tell it? On what account should the land actually perish, be actually burned like the wilderness without anyone passing through?"

13 And Jehovah proceeded to say: "On account of their leaving my law that I gave [to be] before them, and [because] they have not obeyed my voice and have not walked in it, 14 but they kept on walking after the stubbornness of their heart and after the Ba'al images, about which their fathers had taught them; 15 therefore this is what Jehovah of armies, the God of Israel, has said, 'Here I am making them, that is, this people, eat wormwood, and I will make them drink poisoned water; 16 and I will scatter them among the nations that neither they nor their fathers have known, and I will send after them the sword until I shall have exterminated them.'

17 "This is what Jehovah of armies has said, 'Behave with understanding, YOU people, and call the dirge-chanting women, that they may come; and send even to the skilled women, that they may come, 18 and that they may hurry and raise up over us a lamentation. And may our eyes run down with tears and our own beaming eyes trickle with waters. 19 For the voice of lamentation is what has been heard from Zion: "How we have been despoiled! How much we have felt shame! For we have left the land; for they have thrown away our residences." 20 But hear, O YOU women, the word of Jehovah, and may YOUR ear take the word of his mouth. Then teach YOUR daughters a lamentation, and each woman her companion a dirge. 21 For death has come up through our windows; it has come into our dwelling towers, in order to cut off the child from the street, the young men from the public squares.'

22 "Speak, 'This is what the utterance of Jehovah is: "The dead bodies of mankind must also fall like manure upon the face of the field and like a row of newly cut grain after the reaper, with no one to do the gathering up." ' "

23 This is what Jehovah has said: "Let not the wise man brag about himself because of his wisdom, and let not the mighty man brag about himself because of his mightiness. Let not the rich man brag about himself because of his riches."

24 "But let the one bragging about himself brag about himself because of this very thing, the having of insight and the having of knowledge of me, that I am Jehovah, the One exercising lovingkindness, justice and righteousness in the earth; for in these things I do take delight," is the utterance of Jehovah.

25 "Look! Days are coming," is the utterance of Jehovah, "and I will hold an accounting with everyone circumcised [but still] in uncircumcision, 26 upon Egypt and upon Judah and upon E'dom and upon the sons of Am'mon and upon Mo'ab and upon all those with hair clipped at the temples who are dwelling in the wilderness; for all the nations are uncircumcised, and all the house of Israel are uncircumcised in heart."

10 Hear the word that Jehovah has spoken against YOU people, O house of Israel. 2 This is what Jehovah has said: "Do not learn the way of the nations at all, and do not be struck with terror even at the signs of the heavens, because the nations are struck with terror at them. 3 For the customs of the peoples are just an exhalation, because it is a mere tree out of the forest that one has cut down, the work of the hands of the craftsman with the billhook. 4 With silver and with gold one makes it pretty. With nails and with hammers they fasten them down, that none may reel. 5 They are like a scarecrow of a cucumber field, and cannot speak. Without fail they are carried, for they cannot take any steps. Do not be afraid because of them, for they can do nothing calamitous and, what is more, the doing of any good is not with them."

6 In no way is there anyone like you, O Jehovah. You are great, and your name is great in mightiness. 7 Who should not fear you, O King of the nations, for to you it is fitting; because among all the wise ones of the nations and among all their kingships there is in no way anyone like you. 8 And at one and the same time they prove to be unreasoning and stupid. A tree is a mere exhortation of vanities. 9 Silver beaten into plates is what is brought in even from Tar'shish, and gold from U'phaz, the workmanship of a craftsman and of the hands of a metalworker; their clothing is blue thread and wool dyed reddish purple. They are all the workmanship of skilled people.

10 But Jehovah is in truth God. He is the living God and the King to time indefinite. Because of his indignation the earth will rock, and no nations will hold up under his denunciation. 11 This is what you men will say to them: "The gods that did not make the very heavens and the earth are the ones who will perish from the earth and from under these heavens." 12 He is the Maker of the earth by his power, the One firmly establishing the productive land by his wisdom, and the One who by his understanding stretched out the heavens. 13 At [his] voice there is a giving by him of a turmoil of waters in the heavens, and he causes vapors to ascend from the extremity of the earth. He has made even sluices for the rain, and he brings forth the wind from his storehouses.

14 Every man has behaved so unreasoningly as not to know. Every metalworker will certainly feel shame because of the carved image; for his molten image is a falsehood, and there is no spirit in them. 15 They are vanity, a

work of mockery. In the time of their being given attention they will perish.

16 The Share of Jacob is not like these things, for he is the Former of everything, and Israel is the staff of his inheritance. Jehovah of armies is his name.

17 Gather up from the earth your pack load, O woman dwelling under stress. 18 For this is what Jehovah has said: "Here I am slinging out the inhabitants of the earth on this occasion, and I will cause them distress in order that they may find out."

19 Woe to me on account of my breakdown! My stroke has become sickish. And I myself have said: "Surely this is my sickness, and I shall carry it. 20 My own tent has been despoiled, and my own tent cords have all been torn in two. My own sons have gone forth from me, and they are no more. There is no one stretching out my tent any more or raising up my tent cloths. 21 For the shepherds have behaved unreasoningly, and they have not looked even for Jehovah. That is why they have not acted with insight, and all their pastured animals have been scattered."

22 Listen! A report! Here it has come, also a great pounding from the land of the north, in order to make the cities of Judah a desolate waste, the lair of jackals.

23 I well know, O Jehovah, that to earthling man his way does not belong. It does not belong to man who is walking even to direct his step. 24 Correct me, O Jehovah, however with judgment; not in your anger, that you may not reduce me to nothing. 25 Pour out your rage upon the nations who have ignored you, and upon the families who have not called even upon your name. For they have eaten up Jacob. Yes, they have eaten him up, and they keep at exterminating him; and his abiding place they have desolated.

11 The word that occurred to Jeremiah from Jehovah, saying: 2 "Hear the words of this covenant, you men!

"And you must speak them to the men of Judah and to the inhabitants of Jerusalem, 3 and you must say to them, 'This is what Jehovah the God of Israel has said: "Cursed is the man that does not listen to the words of this covenant, 4 which I commanded YOUR forefathers in the day of my bringing them out of the land of Egypt, out of the furnace of iron, saying, 'Obey my voice, and YOU must do things according to all that I command YOU; and YOU will certainly become my people and I myself shall become YOUR God, 5 for the purpose of carrying out the oath that I swore to YOUR forefathers, to give them the land flowing with milk and honey, as in this day.' " ' "

And I proceeded to answer and say: "Amen, O Jehovah."

6 And Jehovah went on to say to me: "Proclaim all these words in the cities of Judah and in the streets of Jerusalem, saying, 'Hear, YOU people, the words of this covenant, and YOU must do them. 7 For I solemnly admonished YOUR forefathers in the day of my bringing them up out of the land of Egypt and down to this day, rising up early and admonishing, saying: "Obey my voice." 8 But they did not listen or incline their ear, but they kept walking each one in the stubbornness of their bad heart; and so I brought upon them all the words of this covenant that I commanded [them] to do, but that they did not do.' "

9 Furthermore, Jehovah said to me: "Conspiracy has been found among the men of Judah and among the inhabitants of Jerusalem. 10 They have returned to the errors of their forefathers, the first ones, who refused to obey my words, but who themselves have walked after other gods in order to serve them. The house of Israel and the house of Judah have broken my covenant that I concluded with their forefathers. 11 Therefore this is what Jehovah has said, 'Here I am bringing upon them a calamity that they will not be able to get out of; and they will certainly call to me for aid, but I shall not listen to them. 12 And the cities of Judah and the inhabitants of Jerusalem will have to go and call for aid to the gods to which they are making sacrificial smoke, but which will positively bring no salvation to them in the time of their calamity. 13 For your gods have become as many as your cities, O Judah; and as many altars as the streets of Jerusalem YOU people have placed for the shameful thing, altars to make sacrificial smoke to Ba'al.'

14 "And as for you, do not pray in behalf of this people, and do not lift up in their behalf an entreating cry or a prayer, for I shall not be listening in the time of their calling out to me in regard to their calamity.

15 "What business does my beloved one have in my house, that many of them should do this thing, the [evil] device? And with holy flesh will they make [it] pass over from upon you, when your calamity [comes]? At that time will you exult? 16 'A luxuriant olive tree, pretty with fruit [and] in form,' is what Jehovah has called your name. With sound of the great roaring, he has set a fire blazing against her, and they have broken its branches.

17 "And Jehovah of armies himself, the Planter of you, has spoken against you a calamity on account of the badness of the house of Israel and the house of Judah that they have committed on their own part to offend me in making sacrificial smoke to Ba'al."

18 And Jehovah himself has informed me that I may know. At that time you caused me to see their dealings. 19 And I was like a male lamb, an intimate one, that is brought to slaughter; and I did not know that it was against me that they thought out schemes: "Let us bring to ruin the tree with its food, and let us cut him off from the land of the living ones, that his very name may no more be remembered." 20 But Jehovah of armies is judging with righteous-

ness; he is examining the kidneys and the heart. O may I see your vengeance on them, for it is to you that I have revealed my case at law. 21 Therefore this is what Jehovah has said against the men of An′a·thoth who are seeking for your soul, saying: "You must not prophesy in the name of Jehovah, that you may not die at our hand"; 22 therefore this is what Jehovah of armies has said: "Here I am turning my attention upon them. The young men themselves will die by the sword. Their sons and their daughters themselves will die by the famine. 23 And not even a remnant will there come to be for them, because I shall bring calamity upon the men of An′a·thoth, the year of their being given attention."

12 You are righteous, O Jehovah, when I make my complaint to you, indeed when I speak even about matters of judgment with you. Why is it that the way of wicked ones is what has succeeded, that all those who are committing treachery are the unworried ones? 2 You have planted them; they have also taken root. They keep going ahead; they have also produced fruit. You are near in their mouth, but far away from their kidneys. 3 And you yourself, O Jehovah, know me well; you see me, and you have examined my heart in union with yourself. Single them out like sheep for the slaughtering, and set them apart for the day of killing. 4 How long should the land keep withering away, and the very vegetation of all the field dry up? Because of the badness of those dwelling in it the beasts and the flying creatures have been swept away. For they have said: "He does not see our future."

5 Because with footmen you have run, and they would tire you out, how, then, can you run a race with horses? And in the land of peace are you confident? So how will you act among the proud [thickets] along the Jordan? 6 For even your own brothers and the household of your own father, even they

themselves have dealt treacherously with you. Even they themselves have called out loudly behind you. Do not put any faith in them, just because they speak to you good things.

7 "I have left my house; I have deserted my inheritance; I have given the beloved one of my soul into the palm of her enemies. 8 My inheritance has become to me like a lion in the forest. She has let loose her voice even against me. That is why I have hated her. 9 My inheritance is as a many-colored bird of prey to me; the birds of prey are round about upon it. Come, gather together, all you wild beasts of the field; bring [them] to eat. 10 Many shepherds themselves have brought my vineyard to ruin; they have stamped down my share. They have turned my desirable share into a wilderness of a desolate waste. 11 One has made it a desolate waste; it has withered away; it is desolated to me. The whole land has been made desolate, because there is no man that has taken [it] to heart. 12 On all the beaten paths through the wilderness the despoilers have come. For the sword belonging to Jehovah is devouring from one end of the land even to the other end of the land. There is no peace for any flesh. 13 They have sown wheat, but thorns are what they have reaped. They have worked themselves sick; they will be of no benefit. And they will certainly be ashamed of the products of you people because of the burning anger of Jehovah."

14 This is what Jehovah has said against all my bad neighbors, who are touching the hereditary possession that I caused my people, even Israel, to possess: "Here I am uprooting them from off their ground; and the house of Judah I shall uproot from the midst of them. 15 And it must occur that after my uprooting them I shall again certainly have mercy upon them and will bring them back, each one to his hereditary possession and each one to his land."

16 "And it must occur that if they will without fail learn the ways of my people in swearing by my name, 'As Jehovah is alive!' just as they taught my people to swear by Ba'al, they will also be built up in the midst of my people. 17 But if they will not obey, I will also uproot that nation, up-rooting and destroying [it]," is the utterance of Jehovah.

13 This is what Jehovah has said to me: "Go, and you must get for yourself a linen belt and put it upon your hips, but you must not bring it into any water." 2 So I got the belt in accord with the word of Jehovah and put it upon my hips. 3 And the word of Jehovah proceeded to occur to me a second time, saying: 4 "Take the belt that you got, that is upon your hips, and rise up, go to the Eu·phra'tes, and hide it there in a cleft of the crag." 5 So I went and hid it by the Eu·phra'tes, just as Jehovah had commanded me.

6 But it came about at the end of many days that Jehovah pro-ceeded to say to me: "Rise up, go to the Eu·phra'tes and take from there the belt that I com-manded you to hide there." 7 Ac-cordingly I went to the Eu·phra'tes and dug and took the belt from the place in which I had hid it, and, look! the belt had been ruined; it was not fit for anything.

8 Then the word of Jehovah occurred to me, saying: 9 "This is what Jehovah has said, 'In the same way I shall bring to ruin the pride of Judah and the abundant pride of Jerusalem. 10 This bad people who are refusing to obey my words, who are walking in the stubbornness of their heart and who keep walking after other gods in order to serve them and to bow down to them, will also become just like this belt that is fit for nothing.' 11 'For just as a belt clings to the hips of a man, so I caused the whole house of Israel and the whole house of Judah to cling even to me,' is the utterance of Jehovah, 'in order to become to me a people and a name and a praise and something beautiful; but they did not obey.'

12 "And you must say to them this word, 'This is what Jehovah the God of Israel has said: "Every large jar is something that gets filled with wine."' And they will certainly say to you, 'Do we not positively know that every large jar is something that gets filled with wine?' 13 And you must say to them, 'This is what Jehovah has said: "Here I am filling all the inhabitants of this land and the kings that are sitting for David upon his throne and the priests and the prophets and all the inhabitants of Jerusalem with drunkenness. 14 And I will dash them one against another, both the fathers and the sons, at the same time," is the utterance of Jehovah. "I shall show no compassion, nor feel any sorrow, and I shall not have the mercy to keep from bringing them to ruin."'

15 "Hear, YOU people, and give ear. Do not be haughty, for Jeho-vah himself has spoken. 16 Give to Jehovah YOUR God glory, before he causes darkness and before YOUR feet strike up against each other on the mountains at dusk. And YOU will certainly hope for the light, and he will actually make it deep shadow; he will turn [it] into thick gloom. 17 And if YOU will not hear it, in places of con-cealment my soul will weep because of pride and will positively shed tears; and my eye will run down with tears, because the drove of Jehovah will have been carried captive.

18 "Say to the king and to the lady, 'Seat yourselves in a lower place, for down from YOUR heads YOUR crown of beauty will certainly come.' 19 The cities of the south themselves have been shut up, so that there is no one opening [them]. Judah in its entirety has been taken into exile. It has been taken into exile completely."

20 "Raise your eyes and see those who are coming from the north. Where is the drove that one gave to you, your beautiful flock? 21 What will you say when

one turns his attention upon you, when you yourself have taught them as confidential friends right alongside you at the start? Will not birth pangs themselves seize hold of you, like those of a wife giving birth? 22 And when you will say in your heart, 'Why is it that these things have befallen me?' because of the abundance of your error your skirts have been taken off as a cover; your heels have been treated violently.

23 "Can a Cush'ite change his skin? or a leopard its spots? You yourselves would also be able to do good, who are persons taught to do bad. 24 So I shall scatter them like stubble that is passing along in the wind from the wilderness. 25 This is your lot, your measured portion from me," is the utterance of Jehovah, "because you have forgotten me and you keep putting your trust in falsehood. 26 And I myself also will lift up your skirts over your face, and your dishonor will certainly be seen, 27 your acts of adultery and your neighings, your loose conduct in prostitution. Upon the hills, in the field, I have seen your disgusting things. Woe to you, O Jerusalem! You cannot be clean—after how much longer?"

14 [This is] what occurred as the word of Jehovah to Jeremiah concerning the matters of the droughts: 2 Judah has gone mourning, and its very gates have faded away. They have become dejected to the earth, and even the outcry of Jerusalem has gone up. 3 And their majestic ones themselves have sent their insignificant ones for water. They have come to the ditches. They have found no water. They have returned with their vessels empty. They have been put to shame and have been disappointed, and they have covered their head. 4 On account of the soil that has been shattered because there has occurred no downpour upon the land, the farmers have become ashamed; they have covered their head. 5 For even the hind in the field has given birth, but leaving [it], because there

proved to be no tender grass. 6 And the zebras themselves have stood still upon the bare hills; they have snuffed up the wind like the jackals; their eyes have failed because there is no vegetation. 7 Even if our own errors do testify against us, O Jehovah, act for the sake of your name; for our acts of unfaithfulness have become many; it is against you that we have sinned.

8 O you the hope of Israel, the Savior of him in the time of distress, why do you become like an alien resident in the land, and like a traveler that has turned aside to spend the night? 9 Why do you become like a man astounded, like a mighty man that is unable to do any saving? Yet you yourself are in the midst of us, O Jehovah, and upon us it is that your own name has been called. Do not let us down.

10 This is what Jehovah has said concerning this people: "Thus they have loved to wander about; their feet they have not kept in check. So Jehovah himself has taken no pleasure in them. Now he will remember their error and will give attention to their sins."

11 And Jehovah proceeded to say to me: "Do not pray in behalf of this people for any good. 12 When they fast, I am not listening to their entreating cry; and when they offer up the whole burnt offering and the grain offering, I am taking no pleasure in them; for by the sword and by famine and by pestilence I am bringing them to their end."

13 At this I said: "Alas, O Lord Jehovah! Here the prophets are saying to them, 'You will see no sword, and there will be no famine to happen to you, but true peace is what I shall give you in this place.'"

14 And Jehovah went on to say to me: "Falsehood is what the prophets are prophesying in my name. I have not sent them, nor have I commanded them or spoken to them. A false vision and divina-

tion and a valueless thing and the trickiness of their heart they are speaking prophetically to you people. 15 Therefore this is what Jehovah has said concerning the prophets who are prophesying in my name and whom I myself did not send and who are saying that no sword or famine will occur in this land, 'By sword and by famine those prophets will come to their finish. 16 And the very people to whom they are prophesying will become people cast out into the streets of Jerusalem because of the famine and the sword, with no one to do the burying of them—them, their wives and their sons and their daughters. And I will pour out upon them their calamity.'

17 "And you must say to them this word, 'Let my eyes run down with tears night and day and let them not keep still, for with a great crash the virgin daughter of my people has been broken, with an extremely sickish stroke. 18 If I actually go out into the field, look, now, those slain by the sword! And if I actually come into the city, look, also, the maladies from the famine! For both the prophet and the priest themselves have gone around to a land that they have not known.'"

19 Have you absolutely rejected Judah, or has your soul abhorred even Zion? Why is it that you have struck us, so that there is no healing for us? There was a hoping for peace, but no good [came]; and for a time of healing, and, look! terror! 20 We do acknowledge, O Jehovah, our wickedness, the error of our forefathers, for we have sinned against you. 21 Do not disrespect [us] for the sake of your name; do not despise your glorious throne. Remember; do not break your covenant with us. 22 Do there exist among the vain idols of the nations any that can pour down rain, or can even the heavens themselves give copious showers? Are you not the One, O Jehovah our God? And we hope in you, for you yourself have done all these things.

15 And Jehovah proceeded to say to me: "If Moses and Samuel were standing before me, my soul would not be toward this people. There would be a sending of them away from before my face, that they might go out. 2 And it must occur that should they say to you, 'Where shall we go out to?' you must also say to them, 'This is what Jehovah has said: "Whoever is for deadly plague, to deadly plague! And whoever is for the sword, to the sword! And whoever is for the famine, to the famine! And whoever is for the captivity, to the captivity!"'

3 "'And I will commission over them four families,' is the utterance of Jehovah, 'the sword to kill, and the dogs to drag away, and the flying creatures of the heavens and the beasts of the earth to eat and to bring to ruin. 4 And I will give them for a quaking to all the kingdoms of the earth on account of Ma·nas′seh the son of Hez·e·ki′ah, the king of Judah, for what he did in Jerusalem. 5 For who will show compassion upon you, O Jerusalem, and who will sympathize with you, and who will turn aside to ask about your welfare?'

6 "'You yourself have deserted me,' is the utterance of Jehovah. 'Backwards is the way you keep walking. And I shall stretch out my hand against you and bring you to ruin. I have got tired of feeling regret. 7 And I shall winnow them with a fork in the gates of the land. I shall certainly bereave [them] of children. I will destroy my people, [since] they have not turned back from their own ways. 8 To me their widows have become more numerous than the sand grains of the seas. I will bring for them, upon mother, young man, the despoiler at midday. I will cause to fall upon them suddenly excitement and disturbances. 9 The woman giving birth to seven has faded away; her soul has struggled for breath. Her sun has set while it is yet day; it has become ashamed and felt abashed.' 'And to the sword I shall give the mere

remnant of them before their enemies,' is the utterance of Jehovah."

10 Woe to me, O my mother, because you have given birth to me, a man subject to quarrel and a man subject to strife with all the earth. I have given no loan, and they have given me no loan. All of them are calling down evil upon me.

11 Jehovah has said: "Surely I will minister to you for good. Surely I will intercede for you in the time of calamity and in the time of distress, against the enemy. 12 Can one break iron in pieces, iron out of the north, and copper? 13 Your resources and your treasures I shall give for mere plunder, not for a price, but for all your sins, even in all your territories. 14 And I will cause [them] to pass over with your enemies into a land that you have not known. For a fire itself has been ignited in my anger. Against you people it is kindled."

15 You yourself have known. O Jehovah, remember me and turn your attention to me and avenge me upon my persecutors. In your slowness to anger do not take me away. Take note of my bearing reproach on account of your own self. 16 Your words were found, and I proceeded to eat them; and your word becomes to me the exultation and the rejoicing of my heart; for your name has been called upon me, O Jehovah God of armies. 17 I have not sat down in the intimate group of those playing jokes and begun exulting. Because of your hand I have sat down all by myself, for it is with denunciation that you have filled me. 18 Why has my pain become chronic and my stroke incurable? It has refused to be healed. You positively become to me like something deceitful, like waters that have proved untrustworthy.

19 Therefore this is what Jehovah has said: "If you will come back, then I shall bring you back. Before me you will stand. And if you will bring forth what is precious from valueless things, you will become like my own mouth. They themselves will come back to you, but you yourself will not come back to them."

20 "And I have made you to this people a fortified copper wall; and they will certainly fight against you, but they will not prevail over you. For I am with you, to save you and to deliver you," is the utterance of Jehovah. 21 "And I will deliver you out of the hand of the bad ones, and I will redeem you out of the palm of the tyrannical ones."

16 And the word of Jehovah continued to occur to me, saying: 2 "You must not take for yourself a wife, and you must not come to have sons and daughters in this place. 3 For this is what Jehovah has said concerning the sons and concerning the daughters that are born in this place, and concerning their mothers who are giving them birth and concerning their fathers who are causing their birth in this land, 4 'With deaths from maladies they will die. They will not be bewailed, neither will they be buried. As manure upon the surface of the ground they will become; and by the sword and by famine they will come to an end, and their dead bodies will actually serve as food for the flying creatures of the heavens and for the beasts of the earth.'

5 "For this is what Jehovah has said, 'Do not enter into the house of a mourners' feast, and do not go to bewail and do not sympathize with them.'

"'For I have taken away my peace from this people,' is the utterance of Jehovah, 'even lovingkindness and mercies. 6 And they will certainly die, the great ones and the small ones, in this land. They will not be buried, neither will people beat themselves for them, nor will anyone make cuts upon himself or make himself bald for them. 7 And they will not deal out to them any bread on account of mourning to comfort someone over the dead; neither will they give them the cup of consolation to drink on account of one's father and on account of one's mother.

8 And you must enter no house of banqueting at all to sit down with them to eat and to drink.'

9 "For this is what Jehovah of armies, the God of Israel, has said, 'Here I am causing to cease out of this place before the eyes of YOU people and in YOUR days the voice of exultation and the voice of rejoicing, the voice of the bridegroom and the voice of the bride.'

10 "And it must occur that, when you tell to this people all these words and they actually say to you, 'On what account has Jehovah spoken against us all this great calamity, and what is our error and what is our sin with which we have sinned against Jehovah our God?' 11 you must also say to them, '"On account of the fact that YOUR fathers left me," is the utterance of Jehovah, "and they kept going after other gods and serving them and bowing down to them. But me they left, and my law they did not keep. 12 And YOU yourselves have acted worse in YOUR doing than YOUR fathers, and here YOU are walking each one after the stubbornness of his bad heart in not obeying me. 13 And I will hurl YOU out from off this land into the land that YOU yourselves have not known, neither YOUR fathers, and there YOU will have to serve other gods day and night, because I shall not give YOU any favor."'

14 "'Therefore, look! days are coming,' is the utterance of Jehovah, 'when it will no more be said: "As Jehovah is alive who brought the sons of Israel up out of the land of Egypt!" 15 but: "As Jehovah is alive who brought the sons of Israel up out of the land of the north and out of all the lands to which he had dispersed them!" and I shall certainly bring them back to their soil, which I gave to their forefathers.'

16 "'Here I am sending for many fishers,' is the utterance of Jehovah, 'and they will certainly fish for them; and afterward I shall send for many hunters, and they will certainly hunt them from every mountain and from every hill

and out of the clefts of the crags. 17 For my eyes are upon all their ways. They have not been concealed from before me, neither has their error been hid from in front of my eyes. 18 And, first of all, I will repay the full amount of their error and of their sin, on account of their profaning my land. With the corpses of their disgusting things and their detestable things they had filled my inheritance.'"

19 O Jehovah my strength and my stronghold, and my place for flight in the day of distress, to you the nations themselves will come from the ends of the earth, and they will say: "Indeed our forefathers came to possess sheer falsehood, vanity and things in which there was nothing beneficial." 20 Can earthling man make for himself gods when they are no gods?

21 "Therefore here I am causing them to know; at this one time I shall cause them to know my hand and my mightiness, and they will have to know that my name is Jehovah."

17 "The sin of Judah is written down with an iron stylus. With a diamond point it is engraved on the tablet of their heart, and on the horns of their altars, 2 when their sons remember their altars and their sacred poles beside a luxuriant tree, upon the high hills, 3 [on] the mountains in the field. Your resources, all your treasures, I shall give for mere plunder— your high places because of sin throughout all your territories. 4 And you let loose, even of your own accord, from your hereditary possession that I had given you. I also will make you serve your enemies in the land that you have not known; for as a fire YOU people have been ignited in my anger. To time indefinite it will keep kindled."

5 This is what Jehovah has said: "Cursed is the able-bodied man who puts his trust in earthling man and actually makes flesh his arm, and whose heart turns away from Jehovah himself. 6 And he will certainly become like a solitary tree in

the desert plain and will not see when good comes; but he must reside in parched places in the wilderness, in a salt country that is not inhabited. 7 Blessed is the able-bodied man who puts his trust in Jehovah, and whose confidence Jehovah has become. 8 And he will certainly become like a tree planted by the waters, that sends out its roots right by the watercourse; and he will not see when heat comes, but his foliage will actually prove to be luxuriant. And in the year of drought he will not become anxious, nor will he leave off from producing fruit.

9 "The heart is more treacherous than anything else and is desperate. Who can know it? 10 I, Jehovah, am searching the heart, examining the kidneys, even to give to each one according to his ways, according to the fruitage of his dealings. 11 [As] the partridge that has gathered together what it has not laid is the one making riches, but not with justice. At the half of his days he will leave them, and in his finale he will prove to be senseless."

12 There is the glorious throne on high from the start; it is the place of our sanctuary. 13 O Jehovah, the hope of Israel, all those who are leaving you will be put to shame. Those apostatizing from me will be written down even in the earth, because they have left the source of living water, Jehovah. 14 Heal me, O Jehovah, and I shall be healed. Save me, and I will be saved; for you are my praise.

15 Look! There are those saying to me: "Where is the word of Jehovah? Let it come in, please." 16 But as for me, I did not hasten from being a shepherd following you, and for the desperate day I did not show any craving. You yourself have known the expression of my lips; in front of your face it has occurred. 17 Do not become something terrifying to me. You are my refuge in the day of calamity. 18 Let my persecutors be put to shame, but let me personally be put to no shame. Let them be the ones to be struck with terror, but let me personally not be struck with terror. Bring upon them the day of calamity, and break them even with twice as much breakdown.

19 This is what Jehovah has said to me: "Go, and you must stand in the gate of the sons of the people by which the kings of Judah enter in and by which they go out, and in all the gates of Jerusalem. 20 And you must say to them, 'Hear the word of Jehovah, YOU kings of Judah and all Judah and all YOU inhabitants of Jerusalem, who are entering in by these gates. 21 This is what Jehovah has said: "Watch out for YOUR souls, and do not carry on the sabbath day any load that YOU must bring in through the gates of Jerusalem. 22 And YOU must bring no load out of YOUR homes on the sabbath day; and no work at all must YOU do. And YOU must sanctify the sabbath day, just as I commanded YOUR forefathers; 23 but they did not listen or incline their ear, and they proceeded to harden their neck in order not to hear and in order to receive no discipline." '

24 " ' "And it must occur that, if YOU strictly obey me," is the utterance of Jehovah, "to bring in no load through the gates of this city on the sabbath day and to sanctify the sabbath day by not doing on it any work, 25 there will also certainly enter in by the gates of this city kings with princes, sitting on the throne of David, riding in the chariot and upon horses, they and their princes, the men of Judah and the inhabitants of Jerusalem; and this city will certainly be inhabited to time indefinite. 26 And people will actually come from the cities of Judah and from round about Jerusalem and from the land of Benjamin and from the lowland and from the mountainous region and from the Neg'eb, bringing whole burnt offering and sacrifice and grain offering and frankincense and bringing thanksgiving sacrifice into the house of Jehovah.

27 " ' "But if YOU will not obey me by sanctifying the sabbath day and not carrying a load, but there is a coming in [with it] through the gates of Jerusalem on the sabbath day, I will also set a fire ablaze in her gates, and it will certainly devour the dwelling towers of Jerusalem and will not be extinguished." ' "

18 The word that occurred to Jeremiah from Jehovah, saying: 2 "Rise up, and you must go down to the house of the potter, and there I shall cause you to hear my words."

3 And I proceeded to go down to the house of the potter, and there he was doing work upon the potter's wheels. 4 And the vessel that he was making with the clay was spoiled by the potter's hand, and he turned back and went making it into another vessel, just as it looked right in the eyes of the potter to make.

5 And the word of Jehovah continued to occur to me, saying: 6 " 'Am I not able to do just like this potter to YOU people, O house of Israel?' is the utterance of Jehovah. 'Look! As the clay in the hand of the potter, so YOU are in my hand, O house of Israel. 7 At any moment that I may speak against a nation and against a kingdom to uproot [it] and to pull [it] down and to destroy [it], 8 and that nation actually turns back from its badness against which I spoke, I will also feel regret over the calamity that I had thought to execute upon it. 9 But at any moment that I may speak concerning a nation and concerning a kingdom to build [it] up and to plant [it], 10 and it actually does what is bad in my eyes by not obeying my voice, I will also feel regret over the good that I said [to myself] to do for its good.'

11 "And now say, please, to the men of Judah and to the inhabitants of Jerusalem, 'This is what Jehovah has said: "Here I am forming against YOU a calamity and thinking against YOU a thought. Turn back, please, each one from his bad way, and make YOUR ways and YOUR dealings good." ' "

12 And they said: "It is hopeless! For after our own thoughts we shall walk, and we are going to carry out each one the stubbornness of his bad heart."

13 Therefore this is what Jehovah has said: "Ask for yourselves, please, among the nations. Who has heard things like these? There is a horrible thing that the virgin of Israel has done to an excess. 14 Will the snow of Leb'a·non go away from the rock of the open field? Or will strange waters, cool, trickling, be dried up? 15 For my people have forgotten me in that they make sacrificial smoke to something worthless, and in that they make men stumble in their ways, the paths of long ago, to walk in roadways, a way not banked up, 16 in order to make their land an object of astonishment, for whistling at to time indefinite. Every last one passing along by it will stare in astonishment and shake his head. 17 As with an east wind I shall scatter them before the enemy. The back, and not the face, I shall show them in the day of their disaster."

18 And they proceeded to say: "Come, men, and let us think out against Jeremiah some thoughts, for the law will not perish from the priest or counsel from the wise one or the word from the prophet. Come and let us strike him with the tongue, and let us pay no attention to any of his words."

19 Do pay attention to me, O Jehovah, and listen to the voice of my opponents. 20 Should bad be repaid for good? For they have excavated a pit for my soul. Remember my standing before you to speak good even concerning them, to turn back your rage from them. 21 Therefore give their sons over to the famine, and deliver them over to the power of the sword; and may their wives become women bereaved of children, and widows. And may their own men become those killed with deadly plague, their young men those struck down with the sword in the battle. 22 Let a cry be

heard out of their houses, when you bring upon them suddenly a marauder band. For they have excavated a pit to capture me, and traps they have hid for my feet.

23 But you yourself, O Jehovah, well know all their counsel against me for [my] death. Do not cover over their error, and do not wipe out that sin of theirs from before you; but let them become those who are made to stumble before you. In the time of your anger take action against them.

19 This is what Jehovah said: "Go, and you must get an earthenware flask of a potter and some of the older men of the people and some of the older men of the priests. 2 And you must go out to the valley of the son of Hin′nom, which is at the entrance of the Gate of the Potsherds. And there you must proclaim the words that I shall speak to you. 3 And you must say, 'Hear the word of Jehovah, O YOU kings of Judah and YOU inhabitants of Jerusalem. This is what Jehovah of armies, the God of Israel, has said:

" ' "Here I am bringing a calamity upon this place, of which when anyone hears, his ears will tingle; 4 for the reason that they have left me and have proceeded to make this place unrecognizable and to make sacrificial smoke in it to other gods whom they had not known, they and their forefathers and the kings of Judah; and they have filled this place with the blood of the innocent ones. 5 And they built the high places of the Ba′al in order to burn their sons in the fire as whole burnt offerings to the Ba′al, something that I had not commanded or spoken of, and that had not come up into my heart." '

6 " ' "Therefore, look! there are days coming," is the utterance of Jehovah, "when this place will be called no more To′pheth and the valley of the son of Hin′nom, but the valley of the killing. 7 And I will make void the counsel of Judah and of Jerusalem in this place, and I will cause them to fall by the sword before their enemies and by

the hand of those seeking for their soul. And I will give their dead bodies as food to the flying creatures of the heavens and to the beasts of the earth. 8 And I will make this city an object of astonishment and something to be whistled at. Every last one passing along by it will stare in astonishment and whistle over all its plagues. 9 And I will make them eat the flesh of their sons and the flesh of their daughters; and they will eat each one the flesh of his fellow man, because of the tightness and because of the stress with which their enemies and those seeking for their soul will hem them in." '

10 "And you must break the flask before the eyes of the men who are going with you. 11 And you must say to them, 'This is what Jehovah of armies has said: "In the same way I shall break this people and this city as someone breaks the vessel of the potter so that it is no more able to be repaired; and in To′pheth they will bury until there is no more place to bury." '

12 " 'That is how I shall do to this place,' is the utterance of Jehovah, 'and to the inhabitants of it, even to make this city like To′pheth. 13 And the houses of Jerusalem and the houses of the kings of Judah must become like the place of To′pheth, unclean ones, that is, all the houses upon the roofs of which they made sacrificial smoke to all the army of the heavens and there was a pouring out of drink offerings to other gods.' "

14 And Jeremiah proceeded to come from To′pheth, to which Jehovah had sent him to prophesy, and to stand in the courtyard of the house of Jehovah and say to all the people: 15 "This is what Jehovah of armies, the God of Israel, has said, 'Here I am bringing upon this city and upon all its cities all the calamity that I have spoken against it, because they have hardened their neck in order not to obey my words.' "

20 Now Pash′hur the son of Im′mer, the priest, who was also the leading commissioner in the house of Jehovah, kept listening to Jeremiah while prophesying these words. 2 Then Pash′hur struck Jeremiah the prophet and put him into the stocks that were in the upper gate of Benjamin, which was in the house of Jehovah. 3 But it came about on the following day that Pash′hur proceeded to let Jeremiah out from the stocks, and Jeremiah now said to him:

"Jehovah has called your name, not Pash′hur, but Fright all around. 4 For this is what Jehovah has said, 'Here I am making you a fright to yourself and to all your lovers, and they will certainly fall by the sword of their enemies while your eyes will be looking on; and all Judah I shall give into the hand of the king of Babylon, and he will actually take them into exile in Babylon and strike them down with the sword. 5 And I will give all the stored-up things of this city and all its product and all its precious things; and all the treasures of the kings of Judah I am going to give into the hand of their enemies. And they will certainly plunder them and take them and bring them to Babylon. 6 And as for you, O Pash′hur, and all the inhabitants of your house, YOU will go into captivity; and to Babylon you will come and there you will die and there you yourself will be buried with all your lovers, because you have prophesied to them in falsehood.'"

7 You have fooled me, O Jehovah, so that I was fooled. You used your strength against me, so that you prevailed. I became an object of laughter all day long; everyone is holding me in derision. 8 For as often as I speak, I cry out. Violence and despoiling are what I call out. For the word of Jehovah became for me a cause for reproach and for jeering all day long. 9 And I said: "I am not going to make mention of him, and I shall speak no more in his name." And in my heart it proved to be like a burning fire shut up in my bones; and I got tired of holding in, and I was unable [to endure it]. 10 For I heard the bad report of many. There was

fright all around. "TELL out, that we may tell out about him." Every mortal man bidding me "Peace!"— they are watching for my limping: "Perhaps he will be fooled, so that we may prevail against him and take our revenge upon him." 11 But Jehovah was with me like a terrible mighty one. That is why the very ones persecuting me will stumble and not prevail. They will certainly be put to much shame, because they will not have prospered. [Their] indefinitely lasting humiliation will be one that will not be forgotten.

12 But you, O Jehovah of armies, are examining the righteous one; you are seeing the kidneys and the heart. May I see your vengeance upon them, for to you I have revealed my case at law.

13 Sing to Jehovah, YOU people! Praise Jehovah! For he has delivered the soul of the poor one out of the hand of evildoers.

14 Cursed be the day on which I was born! May the day that my mother gave me birth not become blessed! 15 Cursed be the man that brought good news to my father, saying: "There has been born to you a son, a male!" He positively made him rejoice. 16 And that very man must become like cities that Jehovah has overthrown while He has felt no regret. And he must hear an outcry in the morning and an alarm signal at the time of midday.

17 Why did he not definitely put me to death from the womb, that my mother should become to me my burial place and her womb be pregnant to time indefinite? 18 Why is it that I have come forth from the very womb in order to see hard work and grief and that my days should come to their end in mere shame?

21 The word that occurred to Jeremiah from Jehovah, when King Zed·e·ki′ah sent to him Pash′hur the son of Mal·chi′ah and Zeph·a·ni′ah the son of Ma·a·sei′ah, the priest, saying: 2 "Please inquire in our behalf of Jehovah, because Neb·u·chad·rez′zar the king

of Babylon is making war against us. Perhaps Jehovah will do with us according to all his wonderful works, so that he will withdraw from us."

3 And Jeremiah proceeded to say to them: "This is what YOU will say to Zed·e·ki′ah, 4 'This is what Jehovah the God of Israel has said: "Here I am turning in reverse the weapons of war that are in the hand of YOU people, with which YOU are fighting the king of Babylon, and the Chal·de′ans who are laying siege against YOU outside the wall, and I will gather them into the middle of this city. 5 And I myself will fight against YOU with a stretched-out hand and with a strong arm and with anger and with rage and with great indignation. 6 And I will strike the inhabitants of this city, both man and beast. With a great pestilence they will die."'

7 "'"And after that," is the utterance of Jehovah, "I shall give Zed·e·ki′ah the king of Judah and his servants and the people and those who are remaining over in this city from the pestilence, from the sword and from the famine, into the hand of Neb·u·chad·rez′zar the king of Babylon, even into the hand of their enemies and into the hand of those who are seeking for their soul, and he will certainly strike them with the edge of the sword. He will not feel sorry for them, nor will he show compassion or have any mercy."'

8 "And to this people you will say, 'This is what Jehovah has said: "Here I am putting before YOU people the way of life and the way of death. 9 The one sitting still in this city will die by the sword and by the famine and by the pestilence; but the one who is going out and who actually falls away to the Chal·de′ans who are laying siege against YOU will keep living, and his soul will certainly come to be his as a spoil."'

10 "'"For I have set my face against this city for calamity and not for good," is the utterance of Jehovah. "Into the hand of the king of Babylon it will be given, and he will certainly burn it with fire."

11 "'And as regards the household of the king of Judah, hear, O men, the word of Jehovah. 12 O house of David, this is what Jehovah has said: "Every morning render sentence in justice, and deliver the one being robbed out of the hand of the defrauder, that my rage may not go forth just like a fire and actually burn and there be no one to extinguish it because of the badness of YOUR dealings."'

13 "'Here I am against you, O inhabitress of the low plain, O rock of the level land,' is the utterance of Jehovah. 'As for YOU who are saying: "Who will descend against us? And who will come into our dwellings?" 14 I will also hold an accounting against YOU according to the fruitage of YOUR dealings,' is the utterance of Jehovah. 'And I will set a fire ablaze in her forest, and it will certainly devour all the things round about her.'"

22 This is what Jehovah has said: "Go down to the house of the king of Judah, and you must speak there this word. 2 And you must say, 'Hear the word of Jehovah, O king of Judah who are sitting on the throne of David, you with your servants and your people, those who are coming in through these gates. 3 This is what Jehovah has said: "RENDER justice and righteousness, and deliver the one that is being robbed out of the hand of the defrauder; and do not maltreat any alien resident, fatherless boy or widow. Do [them] no violence. And do not shed any innocent blood in this place. 4 For if YOU will by all means perform this word, there will also certainly come in through the gates of this house the kings sitting for David upon his throne, riding in chariots and on horses, he with his servants and his people." 5 "'But if YOU will not obey these words, by myself I do swear,' is the utterance of Jehovah, 'that this house will become a mere devastated place.'

6 "For this is what Jehovah has said concerning the house of the king of Judah, 'You are as Gil′e·ad to me, the head of Leb′a·non. Assuredly I shall make you a wilderness; as for the cities, not one will be inhabited. 7 And I will sanctify against you those bringing ruin, each one and his weapons; and they must cut down the choicest of your cedars and cause them to fall into the fire. 8 And many nations will actually pass along by this city and say one to the other: "On what account did Jehovah do like this to this great city?" 9 And they will have to say: "On account of the fact that they left the covenant of Jehovah their God and proceeded to bow down to other gods and to serve them." '

10 "Do not weep for the dead one, and do not sympathize with him, you people. Weep profusely for the one going away, for he will return no more and he will actually not see the land of his relatives. 11 For this is what Jehovah has said concerning Shal′lum the son of Jo·si′ah, the king of Judah who is reigning instead of Jo·si′ah his father, who has gone forth from this place, 'He will return there no more. 12 For in the place where they have taken him into exile he will die, and this land he will see no more.'

13 "Woe to the one building his house, but not with righteousness, and his upper chambers, but not with justice, by use of his fellow man who serves for nothing, and whose wages he does not give him; 14 the one saying, 'I am going to build for myself a roomy house and commodious upper chambers; and my windows must be widened out for it, and the paneling will be with cedar and smeared with vermilion.' 15 Will you continue reigning because you are competing by use of cedar? As for your father, did he not eat and drink and execute justice and righteousness? In that case it went well with him. 16 He pleaded the legal claim of the afflicted one and the poor one. In that case it went well. 'Was not

that a case of knowing me?' is the utterance of Jehovah. 17 'Assuredly your eyes and your heart are upon nothing but upon your unjust gain, and upon the blood of the innocent one in order to shed [it], and upon defrauding and upon extortion in order to carry [them] on.'

18 "Therefore this is what Jehovah has said concerning Je·hoi′a·kim the son of Jo·si′ah, the king of Judah, 'They will not wail for him: "Alas, my brother! And alas, [my] sister!" They will not wail for him: "Alas, O master! And alas, his dignity!" 19 With the burial of a he-ass he will be buried, with a dragging about and a throwing away, out beyond the gates of Jerusalem.'

20 "Go up onto Leb′a·non and cry out, and on Ba′shan let your voice out. And cry out from Ab′a·rim, because all those intensely loving you have been broken. 21 I spoke to you during your freedom from care. You said, 'I shall not obey.' This has been your way since your youth, for you did not obey my voice. 22 A wind will shepherd all your own shepherds; and as for those intensely loving you, they will go into captivity itself. For at that time you will be ashamed and certainly feel humiliated because of all your calamity. 23 O you who are dwelling in Leb′a·non, being nested in the cedars, how you will certainly sigh when there come to you birth pangs, the labor pains like those of a woman giving birth!"

24 " 'As I am alive,' is the utterance of Jehovah, 'even if Co·ni′ah the son of Je·hoi′a·kim, the king of Judah, happened to be the seal ring on my right hand, from there I would pull you off! 25 And I will give you into the hand of those who are seeking for your soul and into the hand of those of whom you are scared and into the hand of Neb·u·chad·rez′zar the king of Babylon and into the hand of the Chal·de′ans. 26 And I will hurl you and your mother who gave you birth out into another land in

which you people were not born, and there is where you will die. 27 And into the land to which they will be lifting up their soul to return, there they will not return. 28 Is this man Co·ni′ah a mere form despised, dashed to pieces, or a vessel in which there is no delight? Why is it that he himself and his offspring must be hurled down and thrown into the land that they have not known?′

29 "O earth, earth, earth, hear the word of Jehovah. 30 This is what Jehovah has said, 'WRITE down this man as childless, as an able-bodied man who will not have any success in his days; for from his offspring not a single one will have any success, sitting upon the throne of David and ruling any more in Judah.'"

23 "Woe to the shepherds who are destroying and scattering the sheep of my pasturage!" is the utterance of Jehovah.

2 Therefore this is what Jehovah the God of Israel has said against the shepherds who are shepherding my people: "You yourselves have scattered my sheep; and you kept dispersing them, and you have not turned your attention to them."

"Here I am turning my attention upon you for the badness of your dealings," is the utterance of Jehovah.

3 "And I myself shall collect together the remnant of my sheep out of all the lands to which I had dispersed them, and I will bring them back to their pasture ground, and they will certainly be fruitful and become many. 4 And I will raise up over them shepherds who will actually shepherd them; and they will be afraid no more, neither will they be struck with any terror, and none will be missing," is the utterance of Jehovah.

5 "Look! There are days coming," is the utterance of Jehovah, "and I will raise up to David a righteous sprout. And a king will certainly reign and act with discretion and execute justice and righteousness in the land. 6 In his days Judah will be saved, and Israel itself will reside in security. And this is his name with which he will be called, Jehovah Is Our Righteousness."

7 "Therefore, look! there are days coming," is the utterance of Jehovah, "and they will no more say, 'Jehovah is alive who brought the sons of Israel up out of the land of Egypt,' 8 but, 'Jehovah is alive who brought up and who brought in the offspring of the house of Israel out of the land of the north and out of all the lands to which I have dispersed them,' and they will certainly dwell on their own ground."

9 As regards the prophets, my heart has been broken within me. All my bones have begun shaking. I have become like a man that is drunk, and like an able-bodied man whom wine has overcome, because of Jehovah and because of his holy words. 10 For it is with adulterers that the land has become full. For because of the curse the land has gone to mourning, the pasture grounds of the wilderness have dried up; and their course of action proves to be bad, and their mightiness is not right.

11 "For both the prophet and the priest themselves have become polluted. Also in my own house I have found their badness," is the utterance of Jehovah. 12 "Therefore their way will become for them like slippery places in the gloom, into which they will be pushed and certainly fall."

"For I shall bring upon them a calamity, the year of their being given attention," is the utterance of Jehovah. 13 "And in the prophets of Sa·mar′i·a I have seen impropriety. They have acted as prophets [incited] by Ba′al, and they keep making my people, even Israel, wander about. 14 And in the prophets of Jerusalem I have seen horrible things, committing adultery and walking in falsehood; and they have strengthened the hands of evildoers in order that they should not return, each one from his own badness. To me all of them have become like Sod′om, and the inhabitants of her like Go·mor′rah."

15 Therefore this is what Jehovah of armies has said against the prophets: "Here I am making them eat wormwood, and I will give them poisoned water to drink. For from the prophets of Jerusalem apostasy has gone forth to all the land."

16 This is what Jehovah of armies has said: "Do not listen to the words of the prophets who are prophesying to you people. They are making you become vain. The vision of their own heart is what they speak—not from the mouth of Jehovah. 17 They are saying again and again to those who are disrespectful of me, 'Jehovah has spoken: "Peace is what you people will come to have." ' And [to] every one walking in the stubbornness of his heart they have said, 'No calamity will come upon you people.' 18 For who has stood in the intimate group of Jehovah that he might see and hear his word? Who has given attention to his word that he might hear it? 19 Look! The windstorm of Jehovah, rage itself, will certainly go forth, even a whirling tempest. Upon the head of the wicked ones it will whirl itself. 20 The anger of Jehovah will not turn back until he will have carried out and until he will have made the ideas of his heart come true. In the final part of the days you people will give your consideration to it with understanding.

21 "I did not send the prophets, yet they themselves ran. I did not speak to them, yet they themselves prophesied. 22 But if they had stood in my intimate group, then they would have made my people hear my own words, and they would have caused them to turn back from their bad way and from the badness of their dealings."

23 "Am I a God nearby," is the utterance of Jehovah, "and not a God far away?"

24 "Or can any man be concealed in places of concealment and I myself not see him?" is the utterance of Jehovah.

"Is it not the heavens and the earth that I myself actually fill?" is the utterance of Jehovah. 25 "I have heard what the prophets who are prophesying falsehood in my own name have said, saying, 'I have had a dream! I have had a dream!' 26 How long will it exist in the heart of the prophets who are prophesying the falsehood and who are prophets of the trickiness of their own heart? 27 They are thinking of making my people forget my name by means of their dreams that they keep relating each one to the other, just as their fathers forgot my name by means of Ba′al. 28 The prophet with whom there is a dream, let him relate the dream; but the one with whom my own word is, let him speak forth my word truthfully."

"What does the straw have to do with the grain?" is the utterance of Jehovah. 29 "Is not my word correspondingly like a fire," is the utterance of Jehovah, "and like a forge hammer that smashes the crag?"

30 "Therefore here I am against the prophets," is the utterance of Jehovah, "the ones who are stealing away my words, each one from his companion."

31 "Here I am against the prophets," is the utterance of Jehovah, "the ones who are employing their tongue that they may utter forth, 'An utterance!' "

32 "Here I am against the prophets of false dreams," is the utterance of Jehovah, "who relate them and cause my people to wander about because of their falsehoods and because of their boasting."

"But I myself did not send them or command them. So they will by no means benefit this people," is the utterance of Jehovah.

33 "And when this people or the prophet or priest asks you, saying, 'What is the burden of Jehovah?' you must also say to them, ' "You people are—O what a burden! And I shall certainly abandon you," is the utterance of Jehovah.' 34 As for the prophet or the priest or the people who say, 'The burden of

Jehovah!' I will also turn my attention upon that man and upon his household. 35 This is what YOU keep saying each one to his fellow and each one to his brother, 'What has Jehovah answered? And what has Jehovah spoken?' 36 But the burden of Jehovah YOU people remember no more, for the burden itself becomes to each one his own word, and YOU have changed the words of the living God, Jehovah of armies, our God.

37 "This is what you will say to the prophet, 'What answer has Jehovah given you? And what has Jehovah spoken? 38 And if "The burden of Jehovah!" is what YOU keep on saying, therefore this is what Jehovah has said: "By reason of YOUR saying, 'This word is the very burden of Jehovah,' when I kept sending to YOU, saying, 'YOU must not say: "The burden of Jehovah!"' 39 therefore here I am! And I will give YOU people to neglect, with finality, and I will desert YOU and the city that I gave to YOU and to YOUR forefathers—from before me. 40 And I will put upon YOU reproach to time indefinite and humiliation to time indefinite, which will not be forgotten." '"

24 And Jehovah showed me, and, look! two baskets of figs set before the temple of Jehovah, after Neb·u·chad·rez′zar the king of Babylon had carried into exile Jec·o·ni′ah the son of Je·hoi′a·kim, the king of Judah, and the princes of Judah and the craftsmen and the builders of bulwarks, from Jerusalem that he might bring them to Babylon. 2 As for the one basket, the figs were very good, like early figs; and as for the other basket, the figs were very bad, so that they could not be eaten for badness.

3 And Jehovah proceeded to say to me: "What are you seeing, Jeremiah?" So I said: "Figs, the good figs being very good, and the bad ones being very bad, so that they cannot be eaten for badness."

4 Then the word of Jehovah occurred to me, saying: 5 "This is what Jehovah the God of Israel has said, 'Like these good figs, so

I shall regard the exiles of Judah, whom I will send away from this place to the land of the Chal·de′ans, in a good way. 6 And I will set my eye upon them in a good way, and I shall certainly cause them to return to this land. And I will build them up, and I shall not tear down; and I will plant them, and I shall not uproot. 7 And I will give them a heart to know me, that I am Jehovah; and they must become my people, and I myself shall become their God, for they will return to me with all their heart.

8 "'And like the bad figs that cannot be eaten for badness, this in fact is what Jehovah has said: "So I shall give Zed·e·ki′ah the king of Judah and his princes and the remnant of Jerusalem who are remaining over in this land and those who are dwelling in the land of Egypt— 9 I will also give them over for quaking, for calamity, in all the kingdoms of the earth, for reproach and for a proverbial saying, for a taunt and for a malediction, in all the places to which I shall disperse them. 10 And I will send against them the sword, the famine and the pestilence, until they come to their finish off the ground that I gave to them and to their forefathers."'"

25 The word that occurred to Jeremiah concerning all the people of Judah in the fourth year of Je·hoi′a·kim the son of Jo·si′ah, the king of Judah, that is, the first year of Neb·u·chad·rez′zar the king of Babylon; 2 which Jeremiah the prophet spoke concerning all the people of Judah and concerning all the inhabitants of Jerusalem, saying:

3 "From the thirteenth year of Jo·si′ah the son of A′mon, the king of Judah, and down to this day, these twenty-three years the word of Jehovah has occurred to me, and I kept speaking to YOU people, rising up early and speaking, but YOU did not listen. 4 And Jehovah sent to YOU all his servants the prophets, rising up early and sending [them], but YOU did not listen,

neither did YOU incline YOUR ear to listen, 5 they saying, "Turn back, please, every one from his bad way and from the badness of YOUR dealings, and continue dwelling upon the ground that Jehovah gave to YOU and to YOUR forefathers from long ago and to a long time to come. 6 And do not walk after other gods in order to serve them and to bow down to them, that YOU may not offend me with the work of YOUR hands, and that I may not cause calamity to YOU.'

7 " 'But YOU did not listen to me,' is the utterance of Jehovah, 'to the intent that YOU might offend me with the work of YOUR hands, for calamity to yourselves.'

8 "Therefore this is what Jehovah of armies has said, ' "For the reason that YOU did not obey my words, 9 here I am sending and I will take all the families of the north," is the utterance of Jehovah, "even [sending] to Neb·u·chad·rez'zar the king of Babylon, my servant, and I will bring them against this land and against its inhabitants and against all these nations round about; and I will devote them to destruction and make them an object of astonishment and something to whistle at and places devastated to time indefinite. 10 And I will destroy out of them the sound of exultation and the sound of rejoicing, the voice of the bridegroom and the voice of the bride, the sound of the hand mill and the light of the lamp. 11 And all this land must become a devastated place, an object of astonishment, and these nations will have to serve the king of Babylon seventy years." '

12 " 'And it must occur that when seventy years have been fulfilled I shall call to account against the king of Babylon and against that nation,' is the utterance of Jehovah, 'their error, even against the land of the Chal·de'ans, and I will make it desolate wastes to time indefinite. 13 And I will bring in upon that land all my words that I have spoken against it, even all that is written in this

book that Jeremiah has prophesied against all the nations. 14 For even they themselves, many nations and great kings, have exploited them as servants; and I will repay them according to their activity and according to the work of their hands.' "

15 For this is what Jehovah the God of Israel said to me: "Take this cup of the wine of rage out of my hand, and you must make all the nations to whom I am sending you drink it. 16 And they must drink and shake back and forth and act like crazed men because of the sword that I am sending among them."

17 And I proceeded to take the cup out of the hand of Jehovah and to make all the nations drink to whom Jehovah had sent me: 18 namely, Jerusalem and the cities of Judah and her kings, her princes, to make them a devastated place, an object of astonishment, something to whistle at and a malediction, just as at this day; 19 Phar'aoh the king of Egypt and his servants and his princes and all his people; 20 and all the mixed company, and all the kings of the land of Uz, and all the kings of the land of the Phi·lis'tines and Ash'ke·lon and Ga'za and Ek'ron and the remnant of Ash'dod; 21 E'dom and Mo'ab and the sons of Am'mon; 22 and all the kings of Tyre and all the kings of Si'don and the kings of the island that is in the region of the sea; 23 and De'dan and Te'ma and Buz and all those with hair clipped at the temples; 24 and all the kings of the Arabs and all the kings of the mixed company who are residing in the wilderness; 25 and all the kings of Zim'ri and all the kings of E'lam and all the kings of the Medes; 26 and all the kings of the north who are near and far away, one after the other, and all the [other] kingdoms of the earth that are on the surface of the ground; and the king of She'shach himself will drink after them.

27 "And you must say to them, 'This is what Jehovah of armies,

the God of Israel, has said: "Drink and get drunk and puke and fall so that YOU cannot get up because of the sword that I am sending among YOU." ' 28 And it must occur that in case they refuse to take the cup out of your hand to drink, you must also say to them, 'This is what Jehovah of armies has said: "YOU will drink without fail. 29 For, look! it is upon the city upon which my name is called that I am starting off in bringing calamity, and should YOU yourselves in any way go free of punishment?" '

" 'YOU will not go free of punishment, for there is a sword that I am calling against all the inhabitants of the earth,' is the utterance of Jehovah of armies.

30 "And as for you, you will prophesy to them all these words, and you must say to them, 'From on high Jehovah himself will roar, and from his holy dwelling he will give forth his voice. Without fail he will roar upon his abiding place. A shout like that of those treading [the wine press] he will sing out against all the inhabitants of the earth.'

31 " 'A noise will certainly come clear to the farthest part of the earth, for there is a controversy that Jehovah has with the nations. He must personally put himself in judgment with all flesh. As regards the wicked ones, he must give them to the sword,' is the utterance of Jehovah.

32 "This is what Jehovah of armies has said, 'Look! A calamity is going forth from nation to nation, and a great tempest itself will be roused up from the remotest parts of the earth. 33 And those slain by Jehovah will certainly come to be in that day from one end of the earth clear to the other end of the earth. They will not be bewailed, neither will they be gathered up or be buried. As manure on the surface of the ground they will become.'

34 "Howl, YOU shepherds, and cry out! And wallow about, YOU majestic ones of the flock, because

YOUR days for slaughtering and for YOUR scatterings have been fulfilled, and YOU must fall like a desirable vessel! 35 And a place to flee to has perished from the shepherds, and a means of escape from the majestic ones of the flock. 36 Listen! The outcry of the shepherds, and the howling of the majestic ones of the flock, for Jehovah is despoiling their pasturage. 37 And the peaceful abiding places have been rendered lifeless because of the burning anger of Jehovah. 38 He has left his covert just like a maned young lion, for their land has become an object of astonishment because of the maltreating sword and because of his burning anger."

26 In the beginning of the royal rule of Je·hoi'a·kim the son of Jo·si'ah, the king of Judah, this word occurred from Jehovah, saying: 2 "This is what Jehovah has said, 'Stand in the courtyard of the house of Jehovah, and you must speak concerning all the cities of Judah that are coming in to bow down at the house of Jehovah all the words that I will command you to speak to them. Do not take away a word. 3 Perhaps they will listen and return, each one from his bad way, and I shall have to feel regret for the calamity that I am thinking to execute upon them because of the badness of their dealings. 4 And you must say to them: "This is what Jehovah has said, 'If YOU will not listen to me by walking in my law that I have put before YOU, 5 by listening to the words of my servants the prophets, whom I am sending to YOU, even rising up early and sending [them], whom YOU have not listened to, 6 I will, in turn, make this house like that in Shi'loh, and this city I shall make a malediction to all the nations of the earth.' " ' "

7 And the priests and the prophets and all the people began to hear Jeremiah speaking these words in the house of Jehovah. 8 So it came about that when Jeremiah had completed speaking all that

Jehovah had commanded [him] to speak to all the people, then the priests and the prophets and all the people laid hold of him, saying: "You will positively die. 9 Why is it that you have prophesied in the name of Jehovah, saying, 'Like that in Shi'loh is how this house will become, and this very city will be devastated so as to be without an inhabitant'?" And all the people kept congregating themselves about Jeremiah in the house of Jehovah.

10 In time the princes of Judah got to hear these words, and they proceeded to come up from the house of the king to the house of Jehovah and to sit down in the entrance of the new gate of Jehovah. 11 And the priests and the prophets began to say to the princes and to all the people: "To this man the judgment of death belongs, because he has prophesied concerning this city just as you have heard with your own ears."

12 At that Jeremiah said to all the princes and to all the people: "It was Jehovah that sent me to prophesy concerning this house and concerning this city all the words that you have heard. 13 And now make your ways and your dealings good, and obey the voice of Jehovah your God, and Jehovah will feel regret for the calamity that he has spoken against you. 14 And as for me, here I am in your hand. Do to me according to what is good and according to what is right in your eyes. 15 Only you should by all means know that, if you are putting me to death, it is innocent blood that you are putting upon yourselves and upon this city and upon her inhabitants, for in truth Jehovah did send me to you to speak in your ears all these words."

16 Then the princes and all the people said to the priests and to the prophets: "There is no judgment of death belonging to this man, for it was in the name of Jehovah our God that he spoke to us."

17 Furthermore, certain ones of the older men of the land rose up and began saying to all the congregation of the people: 18 "Mi'cah of Mo'resh·eth himself happened to be prophesying in the days of Hez·e·ki'ah the king of Judah and went on to say to all the people of Judah, 'This is what Jehovah of armies has said: "Zion herself will be plowed up as a mere field, and Jerusalem herself will become mere heaps of ruins, and the mountain of the House will be for high places of a forest." ' 19 Did Hez·e·ki'ah the king of Judah and all those of Judah by any means put him to death? Did he not fear Jehovah and proceed to soften the face of Jehovah, so that Jehovah got to feeling regret for the calamity that he had spoken against them? So we are working up a great calamity against our souls.

20 "And there also happened to be a man prophesying in the name of Jehovah, U·ri'jah the son of She·mai'ah from Kir'i·ath-je'a·rim. And he kept prophesying against this city and against this land in accord with all the words of Jeremiah. 21 And King Je·hoi'a·kim and all his mighty men and all the princes got to hear his words, and the king began seeking to put him to death. When U·ri'jah got to hear [of it] he at once became afraid and ran away and came into Egypt. 22 But King Je·hoi'a·kim sent men to Egypt, El·na'than the son of Ach'bor and other men with him to Egypt. 23 And they proceeded to bring U·ri'jah out from Egypt and to bring him to King Je·hoi'a·kim, who then struck him down with the sword and cast his dead body into the graveyard of the sons of the people."

24 Moreover, it was the hand of A·hi'kam the son of Sha'phan that proved to be with Jeremiah, in order not to give him into the hand of the people to have him put to death.

27 In the beginning of the kingdom of Je·hoi'a·kim the son of Jo·si'ah, the king of Judah, this

word occurred to Jeremiah from Jehovah, saying: 2 "This is what Jehovah has said to me, 'Make for yourself bands and yoke bars, and you must put them upon your neck. 3 And you must send them to the king of E'dom and to the king of Mo'ab and to the king of the sons of Am'mon and to the king of Tyre and to the king of Si'don by the hand of the messengers who are coming to Jerusalem to Zed·e·ki'ah the king of Judah. 4 And you must give them a command for their masters, saying:

" ' "This is what Jehovah of armies, the God of Israel, has said; this is what you should say to your masters, 5 'I myself have made the earth, mankind and the beasts that are upon the surface of the earth by my great power and by my stretched-out arm; and I have given it to whom it has proved right in my eyes. 6 And now I myself have given all these lands into the hand of Neb·u·chad·nez'-zar the king of Babylon, my servant; and even the wild beasts of the field I have given him to serve him. 7 And all the nations must serve even him and his son and his grandson until the time even of his own land comes, and many nations and great kings must exploit him as a servant.'

8 " ' "And it must occur that the nation and the kingdom that will not serve him, even Neb·u·chad·nez'zar the king of Babylon; and the one that will not put its neck under the yoke of the king of Babylon, with the sword and with the famine and with the pestilence I shall turn my attention upon that nation,' is the utterance of Jehovah, 'until I shall have finished them off by his hand.'

9 " ' "And as for you men, do not listen to your prophets and to your practicers of divination and to your dreamers and to your practicers of magic and to your sorcerers, who are saying to you: "You men will not serve the king of Babylon." 10 For falsehood is what they are prophesying to you, for the purpose of having you taken far away from off your ground; and I shall have to disperse you, and you will have to perish.

11 " ' "And as for the nation that will bring its neck under the yoke of the king of Babylon and actually serve him, I will also let it rest upon its ground,' is the utterance of Jehovah, 'and it will certainly cultivate it and dwell in it.' " ' "

12 Even to Zed·e·ki'ah the king of Judah I spoke according to all these words, saying: "Bring your necks under the yoke of the king of Babylon and serve him and his people and keep on living. 13 Why should you yourself and your people die by the sword, by the famine and by the pestilence according to what Jehovah has spoken to the nation that does not serve the king of Babylon? 14 And do not listen to the words of the prophets that are saying to you men, 'You will not serve the king of Babylon,' because falsehood is what they are prophesying to you.

15 " 'For I have not sent them,' is the utterance of Jehovah, 'but they are prophesying in my name falsely, to the end that I shall disperse you, and you will have to perish, you men and the prophets that are prophesying to you.' "

16 And to the priests and to all this people I spoke, saying: "This is what Jehovah has said, 'Do not listen to the words of your prophets that are prophesying to you, saying: "Look! The utensils of the house of Jehovah are being brought back from Babylon soon now!" For falsehood is what they are prophesying to you. 17 Do not listen to them. Serve the king of Babylon and keep on living. Why should this city become a devastated place? 18 But if they are prophets and if the word of Jehovah does exist with them, let them, please, beseech Jehovah of armies, that the utensils that are remaining over in the house of Jehovah and the house of the king of Judah and in Jerusalem may not come into Babylon.'

19 "For this is what Jehovah of armies has said concerning the pillars and concerning the sea and concerning the carriages and concerning the remainder of the utensils that are remaining over in this city, 20 that Neb·u·chad·nez′zar the king of Babylon had not taken when he carried Jec·o·ni′ah the son of Je·hoi′a·kim, the king of Judah, into exile from Jerusalem to Babylon, together with all the nobles of Judah and Jerusalem; 21 for this is what Jehovah of armies, the God of Israel, has said concerning the utensils that are remaining over at the house of Jehovah and the house of the king of Judah and Jerusalem, 22 ' "To Babylon is where they will be brought and there they will continue to be until the day of my turning my attention to them," is the utterance of Jehovah. "And I will bring them up and restore them to this place." ' "

28 Then it came about in that year, in the beginning of the kingdom of Zed·e·ki′ah the king of Judah, in the fourth year, in the fifth month, that Han·a·ni′ah the son of Az′zur, the prophet who was from Gib′e·on, said to me in the house of Jehovah before the eyes of the priests and of all the people: 2 "This is what Jehovah of armies, the God of Israel, has said, 'I will break the yoke of the king of Babylon. 3 Within two full years more I am bringing back to this place all the utensils of the house of Jehovah that Neb·u·chad·nez′zar the king of Babylon took from this place that he might bring them to Babylon.' " 4 " 'And Jec·o·ni′ah the son of Je·hoi′a·kim, the king of Judah, and all the exiles of Judah who have come to Babylon I am bringing back to this place,' is the utterance of Jehovah, 'for I shall break the yoke of the king of Babylon.' "

5 And Jeremiah the prophet proceeded to say to Han·a·ni′ah the prophet before the eyes of the priests and before the eyes of all the people who were standing in the house of Jehovah; 6 yes, Jeremiah the prophet proceeded to say: "Amen! Thus may Jehovah do! May Jehovah establish your words that you have prophesied by bringing back the utensils of the house of Jehovah and all the exiled people from Babylon to this place! 7 However, hear, please, this word that I am speaking in your ears and in the ears of all the people. 8 As regards the prophets that happened to be prior to me and prior to you from long ago, they also used to prophesy concerning many lands and concerning great kingdoms, of war and of calamity and of pestilence. 9 As regards the prophet that prophesies of peace, when the word of the prophet comes true the prophet whom Jehovah has sent in truth will become known."

10 At that Han·a·ni′ah the prophet took the yoke bar from off the neck of Jeremiah the prophet and broke it. 11 And Han·a·ni′ah went on to say before the eyes of all the people: "This is what Jehovah has said, 'Just like this I shall break the yoke of Neb·u·chad·nez′zar the king of Babylon within two full years more from off the neck of all the nations.' " And Jeremiah the prophet proceeded to go his way.

12 Then the word of Jehovah occurred to Jeremiah, after Han·a·ni′ah the prophet had broken the yoke bar from off the neck of Jeremiah the prophet, saying: 13 "Go, and you must say to Han·a·ni′ah, 'This is what Jehovah has said: "Yoke bars of wood you have broken, and instead of them you will have to make yoke bars of iron." 14 For this is what Jehovah of armies, the God of Israel, has said: "A yoke of iron I will put upon the neck of all these nations, to serve Neb·u·chad·nez′zar the king of Babylon; and they must serve him. And even the wild beasts of the field I will give him." ' "

15 And Jeremiah the prophet went on to say to Han·a·ni′ah the prophet: "Listen, please, O Han·a·ni′ah! Jehovah has not sent you,

but you yourself have caused this people to trust in a falsehood. 16 Therefore this is what Jehovah has said, 'Look! I am sending you away from off the surface of the ground. This year you yourself must die, for you have spoken outright revolt against Jehovah.' "

17 So Han·a·ni'ah the prophet died in that year, in the seventh month.

29 And these are the words of the letter that Jeremiah the prophet sent from Jerusalem to the remainder of the older men of the exiled people and to the priests and to the prophets and to all the people, whom Neb·u·chad·nez'zar had carried into exile from Jerusalem to Babylon, 2 after Jec·o·ni'ah the king and the lady and the court officials, the princes of Judah and Jerusalem, and the craftsmen and the builders of bulwarks had gone forth from Jerusalem. 3 It was by the hand of El·a'sah the son of Sha'phan and Gem·a·ri'ah the son of Hil·ki'ah, whom Zed·e·ki'ah the king of Judah sent to Babylon to Neb·u·chad·nez'zar the king of Babylon, saying:

4 "This is what Jehovah of armies, the God of Israel, has said to all the exiled people, whom I have caused to go into exile from Jerusalem to Babylon, 5 'Build houses and inhabit [them], and plant gardens and eat their fruitage. 6 Take wives and become father to sons and to daughters; and take wives for YOUR own sons and give YOUR own daughters to husbands, that they may give birth to sons and to daughters; and become many there, and do not become few. 7 Also, seek the peace of the city to which I have caused YOU to go into exile, and pray in its behalf to Jehovah, for in its peace there will prove to be peace for YOU yourselves. 8 For this is what Jehovah of armies, the God of Israel, has said: "Let not YOUR prophets who are in among YOU and YOUR practicers of divination deceive YOU, and do not YOU listen to their dreams that they are dreaming. 9 For 'it is in false-hood that they are prophesying to YOU in my name. I have not sent them,' is the utterance of Jehovah."'"

10 "For this is what Jehovah has said, 'In accord with the fulfilling of seventy years at Babylon I shall turn my attention to YOU people, and I will establish toward YOU my good word in bringing YOU back to this place.'

11 "'For I myself well know the thoughts that I am thinking toward YOU,' is the utterance of Jehovah, 'thoughts of peace, and not of calamity, to give YOU a future and a hope. 12 And YOU will certainly call me and come and pray to me, and I will listen to YOU.'

13 "'And YOU will actually seek me and find [me], for YOU will search for me with all YOUR heart. 14 And I will let myself be found by YOU,' is the utterance of Jehovah. 'And I will gather YOUR body of captives and collect YOU together out of all the nations and out of all the places to which I have dispersed YOU,' is the utterance of Jehovah. 'And I will bring YOU back to the place from which I caused YOU to go into exile.'

15 "But YOU have said, 'Jehovah has raised up for us prophets in Babylon.'

16 "For this is what Jehovah has said to the king sitting on the throne of David and to all the people dwelling in this city, YOUR brothers that have not gone forth with YOU into exile, 17 'This is what Jehovah of armies has said: "Here I am sending against them the sword, the famine and the pestilence, and I will make them like the burst-open figs that cannot be eaten for badness." '

18 "'And I will pursue after them with the sword, with the famine and with the pestilence, and I will give them for a quaking to all the kingdoms of the earth, for a curse and for an object of astonishment and for a whistling at and for a reproach among all the nations to which I shall certainly disperse them, 19 due to the fact that they have not listened to my

words,' is the utterance of Jehovah, 'that I have sent to them with my servants the prophets, getting up early and sending [them].'

"'But YOU have not listened,' is the utterance of Jehovah.

20 "And as for YOU, hear the word of Jehovah, all YOU exiled people, whom I have sent away from Jerusalem to Babylon. 21 This is what Jehovah of armies, the God of Israel, has said concerning A'hab the son of Ko·lai'ah and to Zed·e·ki'ah the son of Ma·a·sei'ah, who are prophesying to YOU falsehood in my own name, 'Here I am giving them into the hand of Neb·u·chad·rez'zar the king of Babylon, and he must strike them down before YOUR eyes. 22 And from them a malediction will certainly be taken on the part of the entire body of exiles of Judah that is in Babylon, saying: "May Jehovah make you like Zed·e·ki'ah and like A'hab, whom the king of Babylon roasted in the fire!" 23 for the reason that they have carried on senselessness in Israel, and they keep committing adultery with the wives of their companions and keep speaking falsely in my own name the word that I did not command them.

"'"And I am the One knowing and am a witness," is the utterance of Jehovah.'"

24 "And to She·mai'ah of Ne·hel'am you will say, 25 'This is what Jehovah of armies, the God of Israel, has said: "For the reason that you yourself have sent in your name letters to all the people who are in Jerusalem, and to Zeph·a·ni'ah the son of Ma·a·sei'ah, the priest, and to all the priests, saying, 26 'Jehovah himself has made you priest instead of Je·hoi'a·da the priest, in order to become the grand overseer of the house of Jehovah toward any man maddened and behaving like a prophet, and you must put him into the stocks and into the pillory; 27 now, then, why have you not rebuked Jeremiah of An'a·thoth, who is behaving as a prophet to YOU people? 28 For that is why he has sent to us at Babylon, saying: "It is long drawn out! Build houses and inhabit [them], and plant gardens and eat their fruitage,—"'"'"

29 And Zeph·a·ni'ah the priest proceeded to read this letter in the ears of Jeremiah the prophet.

30 Then the word of Jehovah occurred to Jeremiah, saying: 31 "Send to all the exiled people, saying, 'This is what Jehovah has said concerning She·mai'ah of Ne·hel'am: "For the reason that She·mai'ah has prophesied to YOU people, but I myself did not send him, and he tried to make YOU trust in falsehood, 32 therefore this is what Jehovah has said, 'Here I am turning my attention upon She·mai'ah of Ne·hel'am and upon his offspring.'

"'"'He will not come to have a man dwelling in the midst of this people; and he will not look upon the good that I am doing for my people,' is the utterance of Jehovah, 'for he has spoken outright revolt against Jehovah.'"'"

30 The word that occurred to Jeremiah from Jehovah, saying: 2 "This is what Jehovah the God of Israel has said, 'Write for yourself in a book all the words that I will speak to you. 3 For, "look! there are days coming," is the utterance of Jehovah, "and I will gather the captive ones of my people, Israel and Judah," Jehovah has said, "and I will bring them back to the land that I gave to their forefathers, and they will certainly repossess it."'"

4 And these are the words that Jehovah has spoken to Israel and to Judah. 5 For this is what Jehovah has said: "The sound of trembling we have heard, dread, and there is no peace. 6 Ask, please, O men, and see whether a male is giving birth. Why is it that I have seen every able-bodied man with his hands upon his loins like a female that is giving birth, and all faces have turned pale? 7 Alas! For that day is a great one, so that there is no other like it, and it is the time of distress for Jacob. But he will be saved even out of it."

8 "And it must occur in that day," is the utterance of Jehovah of armies, "that I shall break one's yoke from off your neck, and your bands I shall tear in two, and no more will strangers exploit him as a servant. 9 And they will certainly serve Jehovah their God and David their king, whom I shall raise up for them."

10 "And as for you, do not be afraid, O my servant Jacob," is the utterance of Jehovah, "and do not be struck with terror, O Israel. For here I am saving you from far off and your offspring from the land of their captivity. And Jacob will certainly return and be free of disturbance and be at ease, and there will be no one causing trembling."

11 "For I am with you," is the utterance of Jehovah, "to save you; but I shall make an extermination among all the nations to which I have scattered you. However, in your case I shall make no extermination. And I shall have to correct you to the proper degree, as I shall by no means leave you unpunished."

12 For this is what Jehovah has said: "There is no cure for your breakdown. Your stroke is chronic. 13 There is no one pleading your cause, for [your] ulcer. There are no means of healing, no mending, for you. 14 All those intensely loving you are the ones that have forgotten you. You are not the one for whom they keep searching. For with the stroke of an enemy I have struck you, with the chastisement of someone cruel, on account of the abundance of your error; your sins have become numerous. 15 Why do you cry out on account of your breakdown? Your pain is incurable on account of the abundance of your error; your sins have become numerous. I have done these things to you. 16 Therefore all those devouring you will themselves be devoured; and as for all your adversaries, into captivity they will all of them go. And those pillaging you will certainly come to be for pillaging, and all those plundering you I shall give over to plundering."

17 "For I shall bring up a recuperation for you, and from your strokes I shall heal you," is the utterance of Jehovah. "For a woman chased away is what they called you: 'That is Zion, for whom no one is searching.'"

18 This is what Jehovah has said: "Here I am gathering the captive ones of the tents of Jacob, and for his tabernacles I shall have pity. And the city will actually be rebuilt upon her mound; and upon its rightful site the dwelling tower itself will sit. 19 And from them there will certainly go forth thanksgiving, and the sound of those who are laughing. And I will multiply them, and they will not become few; and I will make them heavy in number, and they will not become insignificant. 20 And his sons must become as in former times, and before me his own assembly will be firmly established. And I will turn my attention upon all his oppressors. 21 And his majestic one will certainly come to be from him, and from the midst of him his own ruler will go forth; and I will cause him to come near, and he must approach to me."

"For who, now, is this one that has given his heart in pledge in order to approach to me?" is the utterance of Jehovah. 22 "And YOU will certainly become my people, and I myself shall become YOUR God."

23 Look! A windstorm of Jehovah, rage itself, has gone forth, an onward-sweeping tempest. Upon the head of the wicked ones it will whirl. 24 The burning anger of Jehovah will not turn back until he will have executed and until he will have carried out the ideas of his heart. In the final part of the days YOU people will give YOUR consideration to it.

31 "At that time," is the utterance of Jehovah, "I shall become God to all the families of Israel; and as for them, they will become my people."

2 This is what Jehovah has said: "The people made up of survivors from the sword found favor in the

wilderness, when Israel was walking to get his repose." 3 From far away Jehovah himself appeared to me, [saying:] "And with a love to time indefinite I have loved you. That is why I have drawn you with loving-kindness. 4 Yet shall I rebuild you, and you will actually be rebuilt, O virgin of Israel. You will yet deck yourself with your tambourines and actually go forth in the dance of those who are laughing. 5 You will yet plant vineyards in the mountains of Sa·mar′i·a. The planters will certainly plant and start to use [them]. 6 For there exists a day when the lookouts in the mountainous region of E′phra·im will actually call out, 'Rise up, O men, and let us go up to Zion, to Jehovah our God.' "

7 For this is what Jehovah has said: "Cry out loudly to Jacob with rejoicing, and cry shrilly at the head of nations. Publish [it]. Give praise and say, 'Save, O Jehovah, your people, the remnant of Israel.' 8 Here I am bringing them from the land of the north, and I will collect them together from the remotest parts of the earth. Among them will be the blind and the lame, the pregnant woman and the one giving birth, all together. As a great congregation they will return here. 9 With weeping they will come, and with [their] entreaties for favor I shall bring them. I shall make them walk to torrent valleys of water, in a right way in which they will not be caused to stumble. For I have become to Israel a Father; and as for E′phra·im, he is my first-born."

10 Hear the word of Jehovah, O you nations, and tell [it] among the islands far away, and say: "The One scattering Israel will himself collect him together, and he will certainly keep him as a shepherd does his drove. 11 For Jehovah will actually redeem Jacob and reclaim him out of the hand of the one stronger than he is. 12 And they will certainly come and cry out joyfully on the height of Zion and become radiant over the goodness of Jehovah, over

the grain and over the new wine and over the oil and over the young ones of the flock and the cattle. And their soul will simply become like a well-watered garden, and no more will they languish again."

13 "At that time the virgin will rejoice in the dance, also the young men and the old men, all together. And I will change their mourning into exultation, and I will comfort them and make them rejoice away from their grief. 14 And I will saturate the soul of the priests with fatness, and with my goodness my own people will become satisfied," is the utterance of Jehovah.

15 "This is what Jehovah has said, 'In Ra′mah a voice is being heard, lamentation and bitter weeping; Ra′chel weeping over her sons. She has refused to be comforted over her sons, because they are no more.' "

16 This is what Jehovah has said: " 'Hold back your voice from weeping, and your eyes from tears, for there exists a reward for your activity,' is the utterance of Jehovah, 'and they will certainly return from the land of the enemy.'

17 " 'And there exists a hope for your future,' is the utterance of Jehovah, 'and the sons will certainly return to their own territory.' "

18 "I have positively heard E′phra·im bemoaning himself, 'You have corrected me, that I may be corrected, like a calf that has not been trained. Cause me to turn back, and I shall readily turn back, for you are Jehovah my God. 19 For after my turning back I felt regret; and after my being led to know I made a slap upon the thigh. I became ashamed, and I also felt humiliated, for I had carried the reproach of my youth.' "

20 "Is E′phra·im a precious son to me, or a fondly treated child? For to the extent of my speaking against him I shall without fail remember him further. That is why my intestines have become boisterous for him. By all means I shall have pity upon him," is the utterance of Jehovah.

21 "Set up road marks for yourself. Place signposts for yourself. Fix your heart upon the highway, the way that you will have to go. Come back, O virgin of Israel. Come back to these cities of yours. 22 How long will you turn this way and that, O unfaithful daughter? For Jehovah has created a new thing in the earth: A mere female will press around an able-bodied man."

23 This is what Jehovah of armies, the God of Israel, has said: "They will yet say this word in the land of Judah and in his cities, when I shall gather their captives, 'May Jehovah bless you, O righteous dwelling place, O holy mountain.' 24 And in it Judah and all his cities will certainly dwell all together, farmers and those who have set out with the drove. 25 For I will saturate the tired soul, and every languishing soul I will fill."

26 At this thing I awoke and began to see; and as for my sleep, it had been pleasurable to me.

27 "Look! There are days coming," is the utterance of Jehovah, "and I will sow the house of Israel and the house of Judah with the seed of man and with the seed of domestic animal."

28 "And it must occur that just as I had kept alert toward them to uproot and to pull down and to tear down and to destroy and to do damage, so I shall keep alert toward them to build up and to plant," is the utterance of Jehovah. 29 "In those days they will no more say, 'The fathers were the ones that ate the unripe grape, but it was the teeth of the sons that got set on edge.' 30 But it will be each one for his own error that one will die. Any man eating the unripe grape, his will be the teeth that will be set on edge."

31 "Look! There are days coming," is the utterance of Jehovah, "and I will conclude with the house of Israel and with the house of Judah a new covenant; 32 not one like the covenant that I concluded with their forefathers in the day of my taking hold of their hand to bring them forth out of the land of Egypt, 'which covenant of mine they themselves broke, although I myself had husbandly ownership of them,' is the utterance of Jehovah."

33 "For this is the covenant that I shall conclude with the house of Israel after those days," is the utterance of Jehovah. "I will put my law within them, and in their heart I shall write it. And I will become their God, and they themselves will become my people."

34 "And they will no more teach each one his companion and each one his brother, saying, 'KNOW Jehovah!' for they will all of them know me, from the least one of them even to the greatest one of them," is the utterance of Jehovah. "For I shall forgive their error, and their sin I shall remember no more."

35 This is what Jehovah, the Giver of the sun for light by day, the statutes of the moon and the stars for light by night, the One stirring up the sea that its waves may become boisterous, the One whose name is Jehovah of armies, has said: 36 "'If these regulations could be removed from before me,' is the utterance of Jehovah, 'those who are the seed of Israel could likewise cease from proving to be a nation before me always.'"

37 This is what Jehovah has said: "'If the heavens up above could be measured and the foundations of the earth below could be searched out, I myself also could reject the entire seed of Israel on account of all that they have done,' is the utterance of Jehovah."

38 "Look! There are days coming," is the utterance of Jehovah, "and the city will certainly be built to Jehovah from the tower of Ha·nan′el to the Corner Gate. 39 And the line for measurement will yet actually go forth straight ahead to the hill of Ga′reb, and it will certainly go around to Go′ah. 40 And all the low plain of the carcasses and of the fatty ashes, and all the terraces as far as the torrent valley of Kid′ron, clear to

the corner of the Horse Gate toward the sunrising, will be something holy to Jehovah. It will not be uprooted, neither will it be torn down any more to time indefinite."

32 The word that occurred to Jeremiah from Jehovah in the tenth year of Zed·e·ki′ah the king of Judah, that is, the eighteenth year of Neb·u·chad·rez′zar. 2 And at that time the military forces of the king of Babylon were laying siege to Jerusalem; and as for Jeremiah the prophet, he happened to be under restraint in the Courtyard of the Guard that is in the house of the king of Judah; 3 because Zed·e·ki′ah the king of Judah had restrained him, saying:

"Why is it that you are prophesying, saying, 'This is what Jehovah has said: "Here I am giving this city into the hand of the king of Babylon, and he will certainly capture it; 4 and Zed·e·ki′ah himself, the king of Judah, will not escape from the hand of the Chal·de′ans, for he will without fail be given into the hand of the king of Babylon. and his mouth will actually speak with the mouth of that one, and his own eyes will see even the eyes of that one"'; 5 'and to Babylon he will take Zed·e·ki′ah, and there he will continue until I turn my attention to him,' is the utterance of Jehovah; 'although YOU men keep warring against the Chal·de′ans, YOU will not succeed'?"

6 And Jeremiah proceeded to say: "The word of Jehovah has occurred to me, saying, 7 'Here is Han′a·mel the son of Shal′lum your paternal uncle coming in to you, saying: "Buy for yourself the field of mine that is in An′a·thoth, because the right of repurchase belongs to you for buying [it]." ' "

8 In time Han′a·mel the son of my paternal uncle came in to me, according to the word of Jehovah, into the Courtyard of the Guard, and proceeded to say to me: "Buy, please, the field of mine that is in An′a·thoth, which is in the land of Benjamin. for the right of hereditary possession is yours, and the repurchasing power is yours. Buy [it] for yourself." At that I knew that it had been the word of Jehovah.

9 So I proceeded to buy from Han·a·mel the son of my paternal uncle the field that was in An′a·thoth. And I began to weigh out to him the money, seven shekels and ten silver pieces. 10 Then I wrote in a deed and affixed the seal and took witnesses as I went weighing the money in the scales. 11 After that I took the deed of purchase, the one sealed according to the commandment and the regulations, and the one left open; 12 and I then gave the deed of purchase to Bar′uch the son of Ne·ri′ah the son of Mah·sei′ah before the eyes of Han′a·mel [the son of] my paternal uncle and before the eyes of the witnesses, those writing in the deed of purchase, before the eyes of all the Jews who were sitting in the Courtyard of the Guard.

13 I now commanded Bar′uch before their eyes, saying: 14 "This is what Jehovah of armies, the God of Israel, has said, 'Taking these deeds, this deed of purchase, even the sealed one, and the other deed left open, you must also put them into an earthenware vessel, in order that they may last for many days.' 15 For this is what Jehovah of armies, the God of Israel, has said, 'Houses and fields and vineyards will yet be bought in this land.' "

16 And I began to pray to Jehovah after my having given the deed of purchase to Bar′uch the son of Ne·ri′ah, saying: 17 "Alas, O Lord Jehovah! Here you yourself have made the heavens and the earth by your great power and by your outstretched arm. The whole matter is not too wonderful for you yourself, 18 the One exercising loving-kindness toward thousands, and repaying the error of the fathers into the bosom of their sons after them, the [true] God, the great One, the mighty One, Jehovah of armies being his name, 19 great in counsel and abundant

in acts, you whose eyes are opened upon all the ways of the sons of men, in order to give to each one according to his ways and according to the fruitage of his dealings; 20 you who set signs and miracles in the land of Egypt down to this day and in Israel and among men, that you might make a name for your own self, just as at this day. 21 And you proceeded to bring forth your people Israel out of the land of Egypt, with signs and with miracles and with a strong hand and with a stretched-out arm and with great fearsomeness.

22 "In time you gave them this land that you swore to their forefathers to give to them, a land flowing with milk and honey. 23 And they proceeded to come in and take possession of it, but they did not obey your voice, and in your law they did not walk. All the things that you commanded them to do they did not do, so that you caused all this calamity to befall them. 24 Look! With siege ramparts men have come to the city to capture it, and the very city will certainly be given into the hand of the Chal·de′ans who are fighting against it, because of the sword and the famine and the pestilence; and what you have said has happened, and here you are seeing [it]. 25 Yet you yourself have said to me, O Lord Jehovah, 'Buy for yourself the field with money and take witnesses,' although the city itself must be given into the hand of the Chal·de′ans."

26 At that the word of Jehovah occurred to Jeremiah, saying: 27 "Here I am, Jehovah, the God of all flesh. For me is there any matter at all too wonderful? 28 Therefore this is what Jehovah has said, 'Here I am giving this city into the hand of the Chal·de′ans and into the hand of Neb·u·chad·rez′zar the king of Babylon, and he must capture it. 29 And the Chal·de′ans who are fighting against this city must come in and set this city aflame with fire and must burn it down and the houses upon the roofs of which

they have made sacrificial smoke to Ba′al and have poured out drink offerings to other gods for the purpose of offending me.'

30 " 'For the sons of Israel and the sons of Judah have proved to be mere doers of what was bad in my eyes, from their youth on up; for the sons of Israel are even offending me by the work of their hands,' is the utterance of Jehovah. 31 'For this city, from the day that they built it, clear down to this day, has proved to be nothing but a cause of anger in me and a cause of rage in me, in order to remove it from before my face, 32 on account of all the badness of the sons of Israel and of the sons of Judah that they have done to offend me, they, their kings, their princes, their priests and their prophets, and the men of Judah and the inhabitants of Jerusalem. 33 And they kept turning to me the back and not the face; though there was a teaching of them, a rising up early and teaching, but there were none of them listening to receive discipline. 34 And they went putting their disgusting things in the house upon which my own name has been called, in order to defile it. 35 Furthermore, they built the high places of Ba′al that are in the valley of the son of Hin′nom, in order to make their sons and their daughters pass through [the fire] to Mo′lech, a thing that I did not command them, neither did it come up into my heart to do this detestable thing, for the purpose of making Judah sin.'

36 "And now, therefore, this is what Jehovah the God of Israel has said concerning this city which YOU persons are saying will certainly be given into the hand of the king of Babylon by the sword and by the famine and by the pestilence, 37 'Here I am collecting them together out of all the lands to which I shall have dispersed them in my anger and in my rage and in great indignation; and I will bring them back to this place and make them dwell in security. 38 And they

will certainly become my people, and I myself shall become their God. 39 And I will give them one heart and one way in order to fear me always, for good to them and to their sons after them. 40 And I will conclude with them an indefinitely lasting covenant, that I shall not turn back from behind them, for me to do them good; and the fear of me I shall put in their heart in order not to turn aside from me. 41 And I will exult over them to do them good, and I will plant them in this land in trueness with all my heart and with all my soul.' "

42 "For this is what Jehovah has said, 'Just as I have brought in upon this people all this great calamity, so I am bringing in upon them all the goodness that I am speaking concerning them. 43 And fields will certainly be bought in this land of which YOU people will be saying: "It is a desolate waste without man and domestic animal. It has been given into the hand of the Chal·de'ans." '

44 " 'With money people will buy fields themselves, and there will be a recording in the deed and a sealing and a taking of witnesses in the land of Benjamin and in the surroundings of Jerusalem and in the cities of Judah and in the cities of the mountainous region and in the cities of the lowland and in the cities of the south, because I shall bring back their captives,' is the utterance of Jehovah."

33 And the word of Jehovah proceeded to occur to Jeremiah the second time, while he was yet shut up in the Courtyard of the Guard, saying: 2 "This is what Jehovah the Maker of [earth] has said, Jehovah the Former of it to establish it firmly, Jehovah being his name, 3 'Call to me, and I shall answer you and readily tell you great and incomprehensible things that you have not known.' "

4 "For this is what Jehovah the God of Israel has said concerning the houses of this city and concerning the houses of the kings of Judah that are pulled down on account of the siege ramparts and on account of the sword; 5 [concerning] those who are coming to fight against the Chal·de'ans and to fill places with the carcasses of the men whom I have struck down in my anger and in my rage, and on account of all whose badness I have concealed my face from this city, 6 'Here I am bringing up for her a recuperation and health; and I will heal them and reveal to them an abundance of peace and truth. 7 And I will bring back the captives of Judah and the captives of Israel, and I will build them just as at the start. 8 And I will purify them from all their error with which they have sinned against me, and I will forgive all their errors with which they have sinned against me and with which they have transgressed against me. 9 And she will certainly become to me a name of exultation, a praise and a beauty toward all the nations of the earth who will hear of all the goodness that I am rendering to them. And they will certainly be in dread and be agitated on account of all the goodness and on account of all the peace that I am rendering to her.' "

10 "This is what Jehovah has said, 'In this place that YOU people will be saying is waste without man and without domestic animal, in the cities of Judah and in the streets of Jerusalem that are desolated without man and without inhabitant and without domestic animal, there will yet be heard 11 the sound of exultation and the sound of rejoicing, the voice of the bridegroom and the voice of the bride, the voice of those saying: "LAUD Jehovah of armies, for Jehovah is good; for to time indefinite is his loving-kindness!" '

" 'They will be bringing a thanksgiving offering into the house of Jehovah, for I shall bring back the captives of the land just as at the start,' Jehovah has said."

12 "This is what Jehovah of armies has said, 'In this waste place without man and even domestic animal and in all its cities there will yet come to be the pasture

ground of the shepherds who are making the flock lie down.'

13 " 'In the cities of the mountainous region, in the cities of the lowland and in the cities of the south and in the land of Benjamin and in the surroundings of Jerusalem and in the cities of Judah flocks will yet pass by under the hands of the one taking the count,' Jehovah has said."

14 " 'Look! There are days coming,' is the utterance of Jehovah, 'and I shall certainly carry out the good word that I have spoken, concerning the house of Israel and concerning the house of Judah. 15 In those days and at that time I shall make sprout for David a righteous sprout, and he will certainly execute justice and righteousness in the land. 16 In those days Judah will be saved and Jerusalem itself will reside in security. And this is what she will be called, Jehovah Is Our Righteousness.' "

17 "For this is what Jehovah has said, 'There will not be cut off in David's case a man to sit upon the throne of the house of Israel. 18 And in the case of the priests, the Levites, there will not be cut off a man from before me to offer up whole burnt offering and to make smoke with a grain offering and to render sacrifice always.' "

19 And the word of Jehovah came further to Jeremiah, saying: 20 "This is what Jehovah has said, 'If you people could break my covenant of the day and my covenant of the night, even in order for day and night not to occur in their time, 21 likewise could my own covenant be broken with David my servant so that he should not come to have a son ruling as king upon his throne; also with the Levites, the priests, my ministers. 22 Just as the army of the heavens cannot be counted, neither the sand of the sea be measured, so I shall multiply the seed of David my servant and the Levites who are ministering to me.' "

23 And the word of Jehovah continued to occur to Jeremiah, saying: 24 "Have you not seen what those of this people have spoken, saying, 'The two families whom Jehovah has chosen, he will also reject them'? And my own people they keep treating with disrespect, so that it should no more continue being a nation before them.

25 "This is what Jehovah has said, 'If it was not a fact that I had appointed my own covenant of the day and night, the statutes of heaven and earth, 26 so too I would reject even the seed of Jacob and of David my servant, so that I should not take from his seed rulers over the seed of Abraham, Isaac and Jacob. For I shall gather their captives and will have pity upon them.' "

34 The word that occurred to Jeremiah from Jehovah, when Neb·u·chad·rez′zar the king of Babylon and all his military force and all the kingdoms of the earth, the dominion under his hand, and all the peoples were fighting against Jerusalem and against all her cities, saying:

2 "This is what Jehovah the God of Israel has said, 'Go, and you must say to Zed·e·ki′ah the king of Judah, yes, you must say to him: "This is what Jehovah has said, 'Here I am giving this city into the hand of the king of Babylon, and he must burn it with fire. 3 And you yourself will not escape out of his hand, because you will without fail be caught and into his hand you will be given. And your own eyes will see even the eyes of the king of Babylon, and his own mouth will speak even with your mouth, and to Babylon you will come.' 4 However, hear the word of Jehovah, O Zed·e·ki′ah king of Judah, 'This is what Jehovah has said concerning you: "You will not die by the sword. 5 In peace you will die; and as with the burnings for your fathers, the former kings who happened to be prior to you, so they will make a burning for you, and 'Alas, O master!' is what they will say in lament for you, for 'I myself have spoken the very

word,' is the utterance of Jehovah.'"'"'"

6 And Jeremiah the prophet proceeded to speak to Zed·e·ki′ah the king of Judah all these words in Jerusalem, 7 when the military forces of the king of Babylon were fighting against Jerusalem and against all the cities of Judah that were left remaining, against La′chish and against A·ze′kah; for they, the fortified cities, were the ones that remained over among the cities of Judah.

8 The word that occurred to Jeremiah from Jehovah after King Zed·e·ki′ah concluded a covenant with all the people who were in Jerusalem to proclaim to them liberty, 9 to let each one his manservant and each one his maidservant, Hebrew man and Hebrew woman, go free, in order not to use them as servants, that is, a Jew, who is his brother. 10 So all the princes obeyed, and all the people who had entered into the covenant to let each one his manservant and each one his maidservant go free, in order to use them no more as servants, and they proceeded to obey and to let [them] go. 11 But they turned about after that and began to bring back the menservants and the maidservants whom they had let go free, and they went subjecting them as menservants and as maidservants. 12 Consequently the word of Jehovah occurred to Jeremiah from Jehovah, saying:

13 "This is what Jehovah the God of Israel has said, 'I myself concluded a covenant with YOUR forefathers in the day of my bringing them out of the land of Egypt, out of the house of servants, saying: 14 "At the end of seven years YOU men should let go each one his brother, a Hebrew man, who came to be sold to you and who has served you six years; and you must let him go free from being with you." But YOUR forefathers did not listen to me, neither did they incline their ear. 15 And YOU yourselves turn around today and do what is upright in my eyes in proclaiming liberty each one to his companion, and YOU conclude a covenant before me in the house upon which my name has been called. 16 Then YOU turn back and profane my name and bring back each one his manservant and each one his maidservant, whom YOU let go free agreeably to their soul, and YOU subject them to become YOUR menservants and maidservants.'

17 "Therefore this is what Jehovah has said, 'YOU yourselves have not obeyed me in keeping on proclaiming liberty each one to his brother and each one to his companion. Here I am proclaiming to YOU a liberty,' is the utterance of Jehovah, 'to the sword, to the pestilence and to the famine, and I shall certainly give YOU for a quaking to all the kingdoms of the earth. 18 And I will give the men side-stepping my covenant, in that they did not carry out the words of the covenant that they concluded before me [with] the calf that they cut in two that they might pass between its pieces; 19 [namely,] the princes of Judah and the princes of Jerusalem, the court officials and the priests and all the people of the land who went passing between the pieces of the calf— 20 yes, I will give them into the hand of their enemies and into the hand of those seeking for their soul; and their dead bodies must become food for the flying creatures of the heavens and for the beasts of the earth. 21 And Zed·e·ki′ah the king of Judah and his princes I shall give into the hand of their enemies and into the hand of those seeking for their soul and into the hand of the military forces of the king of Babylon who are withdrawing from against YOU men.'

22 "'Here I am commanding,' is the utterance of Jehovah, 'and I shall certainly bring them back to this city, and they must fight against it and capture it and burn it with fire; and the cities of Judah I shall make a desolate waste without an inhabitant.' "

35 The word that occurred to Jeremiah from Jehovah in the days of Je·hoi'a·kim the son of Jo·si'ah, the king of Judah, saying: 2 "Go to the house of the Re'chabites, and you must speak with them and bring them into the house of Jehovah, to one of the dining rooms, and you must give them wine to drink."

3 So I took Ja·az·a·ni'ah the son of Jeremiah the son of Habaz·zi·ni'ah and his brothers, and all his sons, and all the household of the Re'cha·bites, 4 and I proceeded to bring them into the house of Jehovah, to the dining room of the sons of Ha'nan the son of Ig·da·li'ah, a man of the [true] God, which was beside the dining room of the princes that was above the dining room of Ma·a·sei'ah the son of Shal'lum the doorkeeper. 5 Then I put before the sons of the house of the Re'cha·bites cups full of wine and goblets and said to them: "Drink wine."

6 But they said: "We shall drink no wine, because Jon'a·dab the son of Re'chab, our forefather, was the one that laid the command upon us, saying, 'You must drink no wine, neither you nor your sons, to time indefinite. 7 And no house must you build, and no seed must you sow; and no vineyard must you plant, nor must it come to be yours. But in tents you should dwell all your days, in order that you may keep living many days upon the surface of the ground where you are residing as aliens.' 8 So we keep obeying the voice of Je·hon'a·dab the son of Re'chab our forefather in everything that he commanded us by drinking no wine all our days, we, our wives, our sons and our daughters, 9 and by not building houses for us to dwell in, so that no vineyard or field or seed should become ours. 10 And we keep dwelling in tents and obeying and doing according to all that Jon'a·dab our forefather commanded us. 11 But it came about when Neb·u·chad·rez'zar the king of Babylon came up against the land that we began to say, 'Come, and let us enter into Jerusalem because of the military force of the Chal·de'ans and because of the military force of the Syrians, and let us dwell in Jerusalem.' "

12 And the word of Jehovah proceeded to occur to Jeremiah, saying: 13 "This is what Jehovah of armies, the God of Israel, has said, 'Go, and you must say to the men of Judah and to the inhabitants of Jerusalem: "Did you not continually receive exhortation to obey my words?" is the utterance of Jehovah. 14 "There has been a carrying out of the words of Je·hon'a·dab the son of Re'chab, that he commanded his sons, to drink no wine, and they have drunk none down to this day, because they have obeyed the commandment of their forefather. And as for me, I have spoken to you men, rising up early and speaking, but you have not obeyed me. 15 And I kept sending to you all my servants the prophets, rising up early and sending [them], saying, 'Turn back, please, each one from his bad way, and make your dealings good, and do not walk after other gods to serve them. And keep dwelling on the ground that I have given to you and to your forefathers.' But you did not incline your ear, nor did you listen to me. 16 But the sons of Je·hon'a·dab the son of Re'chab have carried out the commandment of their forefather that he commanded them; but as for this people, they have not listened to me." ' "

17 "Therefore this is what Jehovah the God of armies, the God of Israel, has said, 'Here I am bringing upon Judah and upon all the inhabitants of Jerusalem all the calamity that I have spoken against them, for the reason that I have spoken to them but they did not listen, and I kept calling to them but they did not answer.' "

18 And to the household of the Re'cha·bites Jeremiah said: "This is what Jehovah of armies, the God of Israel, has said, 'For the reason that you have obeyed the commandment of Je·hon'a·dab your

forefather and continue keeping all his commandments and doing according to all that he commanded YOU, 19 therefore this is what Jehovah of armies, the God of Israel, has said: "There will not be cut off from Jon'a·dab the son of Re'chab a man to stand before me always." ' "

36 Now it came about in the fourth year of Je·hoi'a·kim the son of Jo·si'ah, the king of Judah, that this word occurred to Jeremiah from Jehovah, saying: 2 "Take for yourself a roll of a book, and you must write in it all the words that I have spoken to you against Israel and against Judah and against all the nations, since the day that I spoke to you, since the days of Jo·si'ah, clear down to this day. 3 Perhaps those of the house of Judah will listen to all the calamity that I am thinking of doing to them, to the end that they may return, each one from his bad way, and that I may actually forgive their error and their sin."

4 And Jeremiah proceeded to call Bar'uch the son of Ne·ri'ah that Bar'uch might write at the mouth of Jeremiah all the words of Jehovah that He had spoken to him, on the roll of the book. 5 Then Jeremiah commanded Bar'uch, saying: "I am shut up. I am unable to enter into the house of Jehovah. 6 And you yourself must enter in and read aloud from the roll that you have written at my mouth the words of Jehovah in the ears of the people at the house of Jehovah in the day of fast; and also in the ears of all Judah who are coming in from their cities you should read them aloud. 7 Perhaps their request for favor will fall before Jehovah and they will return, each one from his bad way, for great is the anger and the rage that Jehovah has spoken against this people."

8 And Bar'uch the son of Ne·ri'ah proceeded to do according to all that Jeremiah the prophet had commanded him, to read aloud from the book the words of Jehovah at the house of Jehovah.

9 Now it came about in the fifth year of Je·hoi'a·kim the son of Jo·si'ah, the king of Judah, in the ninth month, that all the people in Jerusalem and all the people that were coming in from the cities of Judah into Jerusalem proclaimed a fast before Jehovah. 10 And Bar'uch began to read aloud from the book the words of Jeremiah at the house of Jehovah, in the dining room of Gem·a·ri'ah the son of Sha'phan the copyist, in the upper courtyard, at the entrance of the new gate of the house of Jehovah, in the ears of all the people.

11 And Mi·cai'ah the son of Gem·a·ri'ah the son of Sha'phan got to hear all the words of Jehovah from out of the book. 12 At that he went down to the house of the king, to the dining room of the secretary, and, look! there is where all the princes were sitting, E·lish'a·ma the secretary and De·la'iah the son of She·mai'ah and El·na'than the son of Ach'bor and Gem·a·ri'ah the son of Sha'phan and Zed·e·ki'ah the son of Han·a·ni'ah and all the other princes. 13 And Mi·cai'ah proceeded to tell them all the words that he had heard when Bar'uch read aloud from the book in the ears of the people.

14 Then all the princes sent out to Bar'uch Je·hu'di the son of Neth·a·ni'ah the son of Shel·e·mi'ah the son of Cush'i, saying: "The roll from which you read aloud in the ears of the people—take it in your hand and come." Accordingly Bar'uch the son of Ne·ri'ah took the roll in his hand and came in to them. 15 Then they said to him: "Sit down, please, and read it aloud in our ears." So Bar'uch read aloud in their ears.

16 Now it came about that as soon as they heard all the words, they looked at one another in dread; and they proceeded to say to Bar'uch: "We shall without fail tell the king all these words." 17 And Bar'uch they asked, saying: "Tell us, please, How did you write all

these words from his mouth?"
18 Then Bar'uch said to them:
"Out of his mouth he kept declaring to me all these words, and
I was writing in the book with ink."
19 Finally the princes said to Bar'-uch: "Go, conceal yourself, you
and Jeremiah, so that no one at
all will know where YOU men are."
20 Then they came in to the
king, to the courtyard, and the roll
they entrusted to the dining room
of E·lish'a·ma the secretary; and
they began to tell all the words in
the ears of the king.

21 So the king sent Je·hu'di out
to get the roll. Accordingly he got
it out of the dining room of
E·lish'a·ma the secretary. And Je-hu'di began to read it aloud in the
ears of the king and in the ears
of all the princes standing by the
king. **22** And the king was sitting
in the winter house, in the ninth
month, with a brazier burning before him. **23** Then it came about
that as soon as Je·hu'di had read
three or four page-columns, he proceeded to tear it apart with the
secretary's knife, pitching [it] also
into the fire that was in the brazier
until all the roll ended up in the
fire that was in the brazier.
24 And they felt no dread; neither
did the king and all his servants,
who were listening to all these
words, rip their garments apart.
25 And even El·na'than and De-la'iah and Gem·a·ri'ah themselves
pleaded with the king not to burn
the roll, but he did not listen to
them. **26** Further, the king commanded Je·rah'me·el the son of
the king and Se·rai'ah the son of
Az'ri·el and Shel·e·mi'ah the son
of Ab'de·el to get Bar'uch the
secretary and Jeremiah the prophet. But Jehovah kept them concealed.

27 And the word of Jehovah occurred further to Jeremiah after
the king had burned up the roll
with the words that Bar'uch had
written at the mouth of Jeremiah,
saying: **28** "Take again for yourself a roll, another one, and write
on it all the first words that proved
to be on the first roll, which Je-

hoi'a·kim the king of Judah burned
up. **29** And against Je·hoi'a·kim
the king of Judah you should say,
'This is what Jehovah has said:
"You yourself have burned up this
roll, saying, 'Why is it that you
have written on it, saying: "The
king of Babylon will come without
fail and will certainly bring this
land to ruin and cause man and
beast to cease from it"?' **30** Therefore this is what Jehovah has said
against Je·hoi'a·kim the king of
Judah, 'He will come to have no
one sitting upon the throne of
David, and his own dead body will
become something thrown out to
the heat by day and to the frost
by night. **31** And I will call to
account against him and against
his offspring and against his servants their error, and I will bring
upon them and upon the inhabitants of Jerusalem and upon the
men of Judah all the calamity that
I have spoken against them, and
they did not listen.' " '"

32 And Jeremiah himself took
another roll and then gave it to
Bar'uch the son of Ne·ri'ah the
secretary, who proceeded to write
upon it at the mouth of Jeremiah
all the words of the book that Je-hoi'a·kim the king of Judah had
burned in the fire; and there were
added to them many more words
like those.

37 And King Zed·e·ki'ah the son
of Jo·si'ah began to reign in
place of Co·ni'ah the son of Je-hoi'a·kim, whom Neb·u·chad·rez'-zar the king of Babylon made king
in the land of Judah. **2** And he
himself and his servants and the
people of the land did not listen
to the words of Jehovah that he
spoke by means of Jeremiah the
prophet.

3 And King Zed·e·ki'ah proceeded to send Je·hu'cal the son
of Shel·e·mi'ah and Zeph·a·ni'ah
the son of Ma·a·sei'ah the priest
to Jeremiah the prophet, saying:
"Pray, please, in our behalf to Je-hovah our God." **4** And Jeremiah
was coming in and going out into
the midst of the people, as they
had not put him in the house of

detention. 5 And there was a military force of Phar'aoh that came out of Egypt; and the Chal·de'ans that were laying siege to Jerusalem got to hear the report about them. So they withdrew from against Jerusalem. 6 Then the word of Jehovah occurred to Jeremiah the prophet, saying: 7 "This is what Jehovah the God of Israel has said, 'This is what YOU men should say to the king of Judah, the one sending YOU to me to inquire of me: "Look! The military force of Phar'aoh that is coming forth to YOU people for the purpose of assistance will have to go back to their land, Egypt. 8 And the Chal·de'ans will certainly come back and fight against this city and capture it and burn it with fire." 9 This is what Jehovah has said: "Do not deceive YOUR souls, saying, 'The Chal·de'ans will without fail go away from against us,' because they will not go away. 10 For if YOU men had struck down all the military force of the Chal·de'ans who are fighting YOU and there remained over among them men pierced through, they would each one in his tent rise up and actually burn this city with fire." ' "

11 And it occurred when the military force of the Chal·de'ans had withdrawn themselves from against Jerusalem because of the military force of Phar'aoh, 12 that Jeremiah began to go forth from Jerusalem to go to the land of Benjamin and to get [his] portion from there in the midst of the people. 13 So it came about when he was in the gate of Benjamin that the officer holding the oversight, whose name was I·ri'jah the son of Shel·e·mi'ah the son of Han·a·ni'ah, was there. At once he took hold of Jeremiah the prophet, saying: "It is to the Chal·de'ans that you are falling away!" 14 But Jeremiah said: "It is false! I am not falling away to the Chal·de'ans." But he did not listen to him. So I·ri'jah kept hold of Jeremiah and brought him in to the princes. 15 And the princes began to get indignant at Jeremiah, and they

struck him and put him into the house of fetters, in the house of Je·hon'a·than the secretary, for this was what they had made the house of detention. 16 When Jeremiah came into the house of the cistern and into the vaulted rooms, then Jeremiah continued dwelling there many days.

17 And King Zed·e·ki'ah proceeded to send and take him, and the king began asking him questions in his house in a place of concealment. And he went on to say: "Does there exist a word from Jehovah?" To this Jeremiah said: "There does exist!" And he said further: "Into the hand of the king of Babylon you will be given!"

18 Then Jeremiah said to King Zed·e·ki'ah: "In what way have I sinned against you and against your servants and against this people, so that YOU men have put me into the house of detention? 19 Where, now, are YOUR prophets who prophesied to YOU, saying, 'The king of Babylon will not come against YOU men and against this land'? 20 And now listen, please, O my lord the king. May my request for favor, please, fall before you, and do not send me back to the house of Je·hon'a·than the secretary, that I may not die there." 21 Accordingly King Zed·e·ki'ah commanded, and they then put Jeremiah in custody in the Courtyard of the Guard; and there was a giving of a round loaf of bread to him daily from the street of the bakers, until all the bread was exhausted from the city. And Jeremiah continued dwelling in the Courtyard of the Guard.

38 And Sheph·a·ti'ah the son of Mat'tan and Ged·a·li'ah the son of Pash'hur and Ju'cal the son of Shel·e·mi'ah and Pash'hur the son of Mal·chi'jah got to hear the words that Jeremiah was speaking to all the people, saying: 2 "This is what Jehovah has said, 'The one continuing to dwell in this city is the one that will die by the sword, by the famine and by the pestilence. But the one going out to the Chal·de'ans is the one that will

keep living and that will certainly come to have his soul as a spoil and alive.' 3 This is what Jehovah has said, 'Without fail this city will be given into the hand of the military force of the king of Babylon, and he will certainly capture it.'"

4 And the princes began to say to the king: "Let this man, please, be put to death, for that is how he is weakening the hands of the men of war who are left remaining in this city and the hands of all the people, by speaking to them according to these words. For this man is one seeking not for the peace of this people but for calamity." 5 So King Zed·e·ki'ah said: "Look! He is in YOUR hands. For there is nothing at all in which the king himself can prevail against YOU."

6 And they proceeded to take Jeremiah and throw him into the cistern of Mal·chi'jah the son of the king, which was in the Courtyard of the Guard. So they let Jeremiah down by means of ropes. Now in the cistern there was no water, but mire; and Jeremiah began to sink down into the mire.

7 And E'bed-me'lech the E·thi·o'pi·an, a man who was a eunuch and who was in the house of the king, got to hear that they had put Jeremiah into the cistern; and the king was sitting in the gate of Benjamin. 8 So E'bed-me'lech went out of the house of the king and spoke to the king, saying: 9 "O my lord the king, these men have done bad in all that they have done to Jeremiah the prophet, whom they have thrown into the cistern, so that he will die where he is because of the famine. For there is no bread any more in the city."

10 Then the king commanded E'bed-me'lech the E·thi·o'pi·an, saying: "Take in your charge from this place thirty men, and you must get Jeremiah the prophet up out of the cistern before he dies." 11 Accordingly E'bed-me'lech took the men in his charge and went into the house of the king to beneath the treasury and took from there worn-out rags and worn-out pieces

of cloth and let them down to Jeremiah into the cistern by means of the ropes. 12 Then E'bed-me'lech the E·thi·o'pi·an said to Jeremiah: "Put, please, the worn-out rags and the pieces of cloth under your armpits beneath the ropes." Jeremiah now did so. 13 Finally they drew out Jeremiah by means of the ropes and brought him up out of the cistern. And Jeremiah continued to dwell in the Courtyard of the Guard.

14 And King Zed·e·ki'ah proceeded to send and take Jeremiah the prophet to him to the third entryway, which is in the house of Jehovah, and then the king said to Jeremiah: "I am asking something of you. Do not hide from me anything." 15 At this Jeremiah said to Zed·e·ki'ah: "In case I should tell you, will you not without fail put me to death? And in case I advise you, you will not listen to me." 16 At that King Zed·e·ki'ah swore to Jeremiah in the place of concealment, saying: "As Jehovah is alive, who has made for us this soul, I will not put you to death, and I will not give you into the hand of these men who are seeking for your soul."

17 Jeremiah now said to Zed·e·ki'ah: "This is what Jehovah, the God of armies, the God of Israel, has said, 'If you will without fail go out to the princes of the king of Babylon, your soul will also certainly keep living and this city itself will not be burned with fire, and you yourself and your household will certainly keep living. 18 But if you will not go out to the princes of the king of Babylon, this city must also be given into the hand of the Chal·de'ans, and they will actually burn it with fire, and you yourself will not escape out of their hand.'"

19 Then King Zed·e·ki'ah said to Jeremiah: "I am in fright of the Jews that have fallen away to the Chal·de'ans, for fear that they might give me into their hand and they might actually deal abusively with me." 20 But Jeremiah said:

"They will do no such giving. Obey, please, the voice of Jehovah in what I am speaking to you, and it will go well with you, and your soul will continue to live. 21 But if you are refusing to go out, this is the thing that Jehovah has caused me to see: 22 And, look! all the women that have been left remaining in the house of the king of Judah are being brought out to the princes of the king of Babylon, and they are saying,

'The men at peace with you
     have allured you and pre-
     vailed over you.
They have caused your foot to
     sink down into the very
     ooze; they have retreated in
     the opposite direction.'

23 And all your wives and your sons they are bringing out to the Chal·de'ans, and you yourself will not escape out of their hand, but by the hand of the king of Babylon you will be seized, and because of you this city will be burned with fire."

24 And Zed·e·ki'ah proceeded to say to Jeremiah: "May no man at all get to know about these things, so that you do not die. 25 And in case the princes hear that I have spoken with you and they actually come in to you and say to you, 'Do tell us, please, What did you speak about to the king? Do not hide anything from us, and we shall not put you to death. And what did the king speak about to you?' 26 you must also say to them, 'I was letting my request for favor fall before the king, that he should not send me back to the house of Je·hon'a·than to die there.'"

27 In time all the princes came in to Jeremiah and began questioning him. In turn, he told them according to all these words that the king had commanded. So they became silent before him, for the matter was not heard. 28 And Jeremiah continued to dwell in the Courtyard of the Guard until the day that Jerusalem was captured. And it occurred just when Jerusalem was captured.

39 In the ninth year of Zed·e·ki'ah the king of Judah, in the tenth month, Neb·u·chad·rez'zar the king of Babylon and all his military force came to Jerusalem and began to lay siege to it. 2 In the eleventh year of Zed·e·ki'ah, in the fourth month, on the ninth day of the month, the city was broken through. 3 And all the princes of the king of Babylon proceeded to come in and sit down in the Middle Gate, [namely,] Ner'gal-sha·re'zer, Sam'gar-ne'bo, Sar'se-chim, Rab'sa·ris, Ner'gal-sha·re'zer the Rab'mag and all the rest of the princes of the king of Babylon.

4 Now it came about that as soon as Zed·e·ki'ah the king of Judah and all the men of war saw them, they began to run away and to go out by night from the city by the way of the garden of the king, by the gate between the double wall; and they kept going out by the way of the Ar'a·bah. 5 And a military force of the Chal·de'ans went chasing after them, and they got to overtake Zed·e·ki'ah in the desert plains of Jer'i·cho. Then they took him and brought him up to Neb·u·chad-rez'zar the king of Babylon at Rib'-lah in the land of Ha'math that he might pronounce upon him judicial decisions. 6 And the king of Babylon proceeded to slaughter the sons of Zed·e·ki'ah in Rib'lah before his eyes, and all the nobles of Judah the king of Babylon slaughtered. 7 And the eyes of Zed·e·ki'ah he blinded, after which he bound him with copper fetters, in order to bring him to Babylon.

8 And the house of the king and the houses of the people the Chal·de'ans burned with fire, and the walls of Jerusalem they pulled down. 9 And the rest of the people who were left remaining in the city, and the deserters that had fallen away to him, and the rest of the people who were left remaining Neb·u'zar·ad'an the chief of the bodyguard took into exile to Babylon.

10 And some of the people, the lowly ones who had nothing at all,

Neb·u'zar·ad'an the chief of the bodyguard let remain in the land of Judah; and he went on to give them vineyards and compulsory services on that day.

11 Furthermore, Neb·u·chad·rez'zar the king of Babylon gave command concerning Jeremiah by means of Neb·u'zar·ad'an the chief of the bodyguard, saying: 12 "Take him and keep your own eyes set upon him, and do not do to him anything bad at all. But just as he may speak to you, so do with him."

13 Accordingly Neb·u'zar·ad'an the chief of the bodyguard and Neb·u·shaz'ban the Rab'sa·ris, and Ner'gal-sha·re'zer the Rab'mag and all the principal men of the king of Babylon sent; 14 they even proceeded to send and take Jeremiah out of the Courtyard of the Guard and give him over to Ged·a·li'ah the son of A·hi'kam the son of Sha'phan, in order to bring him forth to [his] house, that he might dwell in the midst of the people.

15 And to Jeremiah the word of Jehovah occurred while he happened to be shut up in the Courtyard of the Guard, saying: 16 "Go, and you must say to E'bed-me'lech the E·thi·o'pi·an, 'This is what Jehovah of armies, the God of Israel, has said: "Here I am bringing true my words upon this city for calamity and not for good, and they will certainly happen before you in that day." '

17 " 'And I will deliver you in that day,' is the utterance of Jehovah, 'and you will not be given into the hand of the men of whom you yourself are scared.'

18 " 'For I shall without fail furnish you an escape, and by the sword you will not fall; and you will certainly come to have your soul as a spoil, because you have trusted in me,' is the utterance of Jehovah."

40 The word that occurred to Jeremiah from Jehovah after Neb·u'zar·ad'an the chief of the bodyguard sent him from Ra'mah, when he took him while he was bound with handcuffs in the midst of all the exiles of Jerusalem and of Judah, who were being taken into exile in Babylon. 2 Then the chief of the bodyguard took Jeremiah and said to him: "Jehovah your God himself spoke this calamity against this place, 3 that Jehovah might bring [it] true and do just as he has spoken, because you people have sinned against Jehovah and have not obeyed his voice. And this thing has happened to you. 4 And now, look! I have let you loose today from the handcuffs that were upon your hands. If it is good in your eyes to come with me to Babylon, come, and I shall keep my eye upon you. But if it is bad in your eyes to come with me to Babylon, refrain. See! The entire land is before you. To wherever it is good and right in your eyes to go, go there."

5 And he was yet not one that would return, when [Neb·u'zar·ad'an said]: "Do return to Ged·a·li'ah the son of A·hi'kam the son of Sha'phan, whom the king of Babylon has commissioned over the cities of Judah, and dwell with him in the midst of the people; or to wherever it is right in your eyes to go, go."

And the chief of the bodyguard then gave him a food allowance and a present and let him go. 6 Accordingly Jeremiah came to Ged·a·li'ah the son of A·hi'kam at Miz'pah and took up dwelling with him in the midst of the people who were left remaining in the land.

7 In time all the chiefs of the military forces who were in the field, they and their men, got to hear that the king of Babylon had commissioned Ged·a·li'ah the son of A·hi'kam over the land and that he had commissioned him [over] the men and women and little children and some of the lowly people of the land, who had not been taken into exile in Babylon. 8 So they came to Ged·a·li'ah at Miz'pah, even Ish'ma·el the son of Neth·a·ni'ah and Jo·ha'nan and Jon'a·than, the sons of Ka·re'ah, and Se·rai'ah the son of Tan·hu'-

meth and the sons of E'phai the Ne·toph'a·thite and Jez·a·ni'ah the son of the Ma·ac'a·thite, they and their men. 9 And Ged·a·li'ah the son of A·hi'kam the son of Sha'-phan proceeded to swear to them and to their men, saying: "Do not be afraid of serving the Chal·de'-ans. Continue dwelling in the land and serve the king of Babylon, and it will go well with you. 10 And as for me, here I am dwelling in Miz'pah, in order to stand before the Chal·de'ans who will come to us. And as for you yourselves, gather wine and summer fruits and oil and put [them] in your vessels and dwell in your cities that you have seized."

11 And all the Jews that were in Mo'ab and among the sons of Am'-mon and in E'dom and those who were in all the [other] lands, they also heard that the king of Babylon had given a remnant to Judah and that he had commissioned over them Ged·a·li'ah the son of A·hi'-kam the son of Sha'phan. 12 And all the Jews began to return from all the places to which they had been dispersed, and they kept coming into the land of Judah to Ged·a·li'ah at Miz'pah. And they went gathering wine and summer fruits in very great quantity.

13 As for Jo·ha'nan the son of Ka·re'ah and all the chiefs of the military forces who were in the field, they came to Ged·a·li'ah at Miz'pah. 14 And they proceeded to say to him: "Do you not at all know that Ba'a·lis, the king of the sons of Am'mon, himself has sent Ish'ma·el the son of Neth·a·ni'ah to strike you to the soul?" But Ged·a·li'ah the son of A·hi'kam did not believe them.

15 And Jo·ha'nan the son of Ka·re'ah himself said to Ged·a·li'ah, in a place of concealment in Miz'-pah: "I want to go, now, and strike down Ish'ma·el the son of Neth·a·ni'ah, as no one at all will know. Why should he strike you to the soul, and why must all those of Judah who are being collected together to you be scattered and the remnant of Judah perish?" 16 But

Ged·a·li'ah the son of A·hi'kam said to Jo·ha'nan the son of Ka·re'ah: "Do not do this thing, for it is a falsehood that you are speaking concerning Ish'ma·el."

41 So it came about in the seventh month that Ish'ma·el the son of Neth·a·ni'ah the son of E·lish'a·ma of the royal offspring and [of the] principal men of the king and ten other men with him came to Ged·a·li'ah the son of A·hi'kam at Miz'pah. And there they began to eat bread together in Miz'pah. 2 Then Ish'ma·el the son of Neth·a·ni'ah and the ten men that happened to be with him rose up and struck down Ged·a·li'ah the son of A·hi'kam the son of Sha'phan with the sword. So he put to death the one whom the king of Babylon had commissioned over the land. 3 And all the Jews who happened to be with him, that is, with Ged·a·li'ah, in Miz'pah, and the Chal·de'ans who were found there, that is, the men of war, Ish'ma·el struck down.

4 And it came about on the second day of the putting of Ged·a·li'ah to death, when there was no one at all that knew [it], 5 then there came men from She'chem, from Shi'loh and from Sa·mar'i·a, eighty men with their beards shaved off and with their garments ripped apart and with cuts made upon themselves, and there were grain offering and frankincense in their hand to bring to the house of Jehovah. 6 So Ish'ma·el the son of Neth·a·ni'ah went out from Miz'-pah to meet them, weeping while he was walking along. And it came about that as soon as he encountered them he proceeded to say to them: "Come to Ged·a·li'ah the son of A·hi'kam." 7 But it occurred that as soon as they came into the midst of the city, Ish'ma·el the son of Neth·a·ni'ah went slaughtering them [and throwing them] into the midst of the cistern, he and the men that were with him.

8 But there were ten men that were found among them who immediately said to Ish'ma·el: "Do

not put us to death, for there exist in our possession hidden treasures in the field, wheat and barley and oil and honey." So he refrained, and he did not put them to death in the midst of their brothers. 9 Now the cistern into which Ish′ma·el threw all the carcasses of the men that he had struck down was a great cistern, the one that King A′sa had made because of Ba′a·sha the king of Israel. It was the one that Ish′ma·el the son of Neth·a·ni′ah filled with those slain.

10 Then Ish′ma·el took captive all the remnant of the people who were in Miz′pah, the daughters of the king and all the people who were remaining over in Miz′pah, whom Neb·u′zar·ad′an the chief of the bodyguard had put in the custody of Ged·a·li′ah the son of A·hi′kam. So Ish′ma·el the son of Neth·a·ni′ah took them captive and went off to cross over to the sons of Am′mon.

11 In time Jo·ha′nan the son of Ka·re′ah and all the chiefs of the military forces who were with him got to hear all the bad that Ish′ma·el the son of Neth·a·ni′ah had done. 12 Consequently they took all the men and went off to fight against Ish′ma·el the son of Neth·a·ni′ah and found him by the abundant waters that were in Gib′e·on.

13 Then it came about that as soon as all the people that were with Ish′ma·el saw Jo·ha′nan the son of Ka·re′ah and all the chiefs of the military forces who were with him, they began to rejoice. 14 And all the people whom Ish′ma·el had led captive from Miz′pah proceeded to turn around and return and go to Jo·ha′nan the son of Ka·re′ah. 15 And as for Ish′ma·el the son of Neth·a·ni′ah, he escaped with eight men from before Jo·ha′nan, that he might go to the sons of Am′mon.

16 Jo·ha′nan the son of Ka·re′ah and all the chiefs of the military forces who were with him now took all the remnant of the people whom they brought back from Ish′ma·el the son of Neth·a·ni′ah, from Miz′-pah, after he had struck down Ged·a·li′ah the son of A·hi′kam, able-bodied men, men of war, and the wives and the little children and the court officials, whom he brought back from Gib′e·on. 17 So they went and took up dwelling in the lodging place of Chim′ham that was beside Beth′le·hem, in order to go on and enter into Egypt, 18 because of the Chal·de′ans; for they had become afraid because of them, since Ish′ma·el the son of Neth·a·ni′ah had struck down Ged·a·li′ah the son of A·hi′kam, whom the king of Babylon had commissioned over the land.

42 Then all the chiefs of the military forces and Jo·ha′nan the son of Ka·re′ah and Jez·a·ni′ah the son of Ho·shai′ah and all the people, from the smallest one even to the greatest one, approached 2 and said to Jeremiah the prophet: "May our request for favor, please, fall before you, and do you pray in our behalf to Jehovah your God, in behalf of all this remnant, for we have been left remaining, a few out of many, just as your eyes are seeing us. 3 And may Jehovah your God tell us the way in which we should walk and the thing that we should do."

4 At that Jeremiah the prophet said to them: "I have heard. Here I am praying to Jehovah your God according to your words; and it will certainly occur that every word that Jehovah gives in answer to you I shall tell you. I shall not hold back from you a word."

5 And they, for their part, said to Jeremiah: "May Jehovah prove to be a true and faithful witness against us if it is not according to every word with which Jehovah your God sends you to us that we shall exactly do. 6 Whether good or bad, it is the voice of Jehovah our God to whom we are sending you that we shall obey, to the intent that it may go well with us because we obey the voice of Jehovah our God."

7 Now it came about at the end of ten days that the word of Jehovah proceeded to occur to Jere-

miah. 8 So he called for Jo·ha'-nan the son of Ka·re'ah and for all the chiefs of the military forces who were with him and for all the people, from the smallest one even to the greatest one; 9 and he went on to say to them: "This is what Jehovah the God of Israel, to whom YOU sent me to cause YOUR request for favor to fall before him, has said, 10 'If YOU will without fail keep dwelling in this land, I will also build YOU up and I shall not tear [YOU] down, and I will plant YOU and I shall not uproot [YOU]; for I shall certainly feel regret over the calamity that I have caused to YOU. 11 Do not be afraid because of the king of Babylon, of whom YOU are in fear.'

"'Do not be afraid because of him,' is the utterance of Jehovah, 'for I am with YOU, in order to save YOU and to deliver YOU out of his hand. 12 And I shall give to YOU mercies, and he will certainly have mercy upon YOU and return YOU to YOUR own soil.

13 "'But if YOU are saying: "No; we are not going to dwell in this land!" in order to disobey the voice of Jehovah YOUR God, 14 saying: "No, but into the land of Egypt we shall enter, where we shall see no war and the sound of the horn we shall not hear and for bread we shall not go hungry; and there is where we shall dwell"; 15 even now therefore hear the word of Jehovah, O remnant of Judah. This is what Jehovah of armies, the God of Israel, has said: "If YOU yourselves positively set YOUR faces to enter into Egypt and YOU actually enter in to reside there as aliens, 16 it must also occur that the very sword of which YOU are afraid will there catch up with YOU in the land of Egypt, and the very famine at which YOU are in a fright will there closely follow after YOU to Egypt; and there is where YOU will die. 17 And it will come about that all the men that have set their faces to enter into Egypt to reside there as aliens will be the ones to die by the sword, by the famine and by the pestilence; and they will not come to have a survivor or an escapee, because of the calamity that I am bringing in upon them."'

18 "For this is what Jehovah of armies, the God of Israel, has said, 'Just as my anger and my rage have been poured out upon the inhabitants of Jerusalem, so my rage will be poured out upon YOU because of YOUR entering into Egypt, and YOU will certainly become a curse and an object of astonishment and a malediction and a reproach, and you will no more see this place.'

19 "Jehovah has spoken against YOU, O remnant of Judah. Do not enter into Egypt. YOU should positively know that I have borne witness against YOU today, 20 that YOU have committed error against YOUR souls; for YOU yourselves have sent me to Jehovah YOUR God, saying, 'Pray in our behalf to Jehovah our God; and according to everything that Jehovah our God says tell us that way, and we shall certainly do.' 21 And I tell YOU today, but YOU will certainly not obey the voice of Jehovah YOUR God or anything with which he has sent me to YOU. 22 And now YOU should positively know that by the sword, by the famine and by the pestilence YOU will die in the place into which YOU do delight to enter to reside as aliens."

43 Now it came about that as soon as Jeremiah finished speaking to all the people all the words of Jehovah their God with which Jehovah their God had sent him to them, even all these words, 2 Az·a·ri'ah the son of Ho·shai'ah and Jo·ha'nan the son of Ka·re'ah and all the presumptuous men proceeded to say to Jeremiah: "It is a falsehood that you are speaking. Jehovah our God has not sent you, saying, 'Do not enter into Egypt to reside there as aliens.' 3 But Bar'uch the son of Ne·ri'ah is instigating you against us for the purpose of giving us into the hand of the Chal·de'ans, to put us to death or to take us into exile in Babylon."

4 And Jo·ha'nan the son of Ka-re'ah and all the chiefs of the mili-

tary forces and all the people did not obey the voice of Jehovah, to keep on dwelling in the land of Judah. 5 So Jo·ha′nan the son of Ka·re′ah and all the chiefs of the military forces took all the remnant of Judah that had returned from all the nations to which they had been dispersed, in order to reside for a while in the land of Judah, 6 even the able-bodied men and the wives and the little children and the daughters of the king and every soul that Neb·u′zar·ad′an the chief of the bodyguard had let stay with Ged·a·li′ah the son of A·hi′kam the son of Sha′phan, and Jeremiah the prophet and Bar′uch the son of Ne·ri′ah. 7 And they finally came into the land of Egypt, for they did not obey the voice of Jehovah; and they came gradually as far as Tah′pan·hes.

8 Then the word of Jehovah occurred to Jeremiah in Tah′pan·hes, saying: 9 "Take in your hand great stones, and you must hide them in the mortar in the terrace of bricks that is at the entrance of the house of Phar′aoh in Tah′panhes before the eyes of the Jewish men. 10 And you must say to them, 'This is what Jehovah of armies, the God of Israel, has said: "Here I am sending and I will take Neb·u·chad·rez′zar the king of Babylon, my servant, and I will place his throne right above these stones that I have hidden, and he will certainly extend his state tent over them. 11 And he must come in and strike the land of Egypt. Whoever is [due] for deadly plague will be for deadly plague, and whoever is [due] for captivity will be for captivity, and whoever is [due] for the sword will be for the sword. 12 And I will set a fire ablaze in the houses of the gods of Egypt; and he will certainly burn them and lead them captive and wrap himself up in the land of Egypt, just as a shepherd wraps himself up in his garment, and he will actually go out from there in peace. 13 And he will certainly break to pieces the pillars of Beth-she′mesh, which is in the land of Egypt; and

the houses of the gods of Egypt he will burn with fire." ' "

44 The word that occurred to Jeremiah for all the Jews that were dwelling in the land of Egypt, the ones dwelling in Mig′dol and in Tah′pan·hes and in Noph and in the land of Path′ros, saying: 2 "This is what Jehovah of armies, the God of Israel, has said, 'YOU yourselves have seen all the calamity that I have brought in upon Jerusalem and upon all the cities of Judah, and here they are a devastated place this day, and in them there is no inhabitant. 3 It is because of their badness that they did in order to offend me by going and making sacrificial smoke and rendering service to other gods whom they themselves had not known, neither YOU nor YOUR forefathers. 4 And I kept sending to YOU all my servants the prophets, rising up early and sending, saying: "Do not do, please, this detestable sort of thing that I have hated." 5 But they did not listen, nor did they incline their ear to turn back from their badness by not making sacrificial smoke to other gods. 6 So my rage, and my anger, was poured out and it burned in the cities of Judah and in the streets of Jerusalem; and they came to be a devastated place, a desolate waste, as at this day.'

7 "And now this is what Jehovah, the God of armies, the God of Israel, has said, 'Why are YOU causing a great calamity to YOUR souls, in order to cut off from yourselves man and woman, child and suckling, out of the midst of Judah, so that YOU do not leave over for yourselves a remnant; 8 by offending me with the works of YOUR hands by making sacrificial smoke to other gods in the land of Egypt, into which YOU are entering to reside as aliens; for the purpose of causing a cutting off of yourselves and for the purpose of YOUR becoming a malediction and a reproach among all the nations of the earth? 9 Have YOU forgotten the bad deeds of YOUR forefathers and the bad deeds of the kings of Judah

and the bad deeds of their wives and YOUR own bad deeds and the bad deeds of YOUR wives, that they have done in the land of Judah and in the streets of Jerusalem? 10 And down to this day they did not feel crushed, and they did not become afraid, nor did they walk in my law and in my statutes that I put before YOU and before YOUR forefathers.'

11 "Therefore this is what Jehovah of armies, the God of Israel, has said, 'Here I am setting my face against YOU for calamity and for cutting off all Judah. 12 And I will take the remnant of Judah who set their faces to enter into the land of Egypt to reside there as aliens, and they will all certainly come to their finish in the land of Egypt. They will fall by the sword; [and] by the famine they will come to their finish, from the smallest one even to the greatest one; by the sword and by the famine they will die. And they must become a curse, an object of astonishment and a malediction and a reproach. 13 And I will hold an accounting against those dwelling in the land of Egypt, just as I held an accounting against Jerusalem, with the sword, with the famine and with the pestilence. 14 And there will come to be no escapee or survivor for the remnant of Judah who are entering to reside there as aliens, in the land of Egypt, even to return to the land of Judah to which they are lifting up their soul[ful desire] to return in order to dwell; for they will not return, except some escaped ones.'"

15 And all the men who were knowing that their wives had been making sacrificial smoke to other gods, and all the wives who were standing as a great congregation, and all the people who were dwelling in the land of Egypt, in Path'-ros, proceeded to answer Jeremiah, saying: 16 "As regards the word that you have spoken to us in the name of Jehovah, we are not listening to you; 17 but we shall positively do every word that has gone forth from our mouth, in order to make sacrificial smoke to the 'queen of the heavens' and to pour out to her drink offerings, just as we ourselves and our forefathers, our kings and our princes did in the cities of Judah and in the streets of Jerusalem, when we used to be satisfied with bread and to be well off, and we did not see any calamity at all. 18 And from the time that we ceased to make sacrificial smoke to the 'queen of the heavens' and pour out drink offerings to her we have lacked everything, and by the sword and by the famine we have come to our finish.

19 "Also, when we were making sacrificial smoke to the 'queen of the heavens' and [were disposed] to pour out drink offerings to her, did we without asking our husbands make for her sacrificial cakes, in order to make an image of her, and to pour out drink offerings to her?"

20 In turn Jeremiah said to all the people, to the able-bodied men and to the wives and to all the people, who were answering him with a word, saying: 21 "As for the sacrificial smoke that YOU made in the cities of Judah and in the streets of Jerusalem, YOU and YOUR forefathers, YOUR kings and YOUR princes and the people of the land, was it not this that Jehovah remembered and that proceeded to come up into his heart? 22 Finally Jehovah was no longer able to put up with it because of the badness of YOUR dealings, because of the detestable things that YOU had done, and so YOUR land came to be a devastated place and an object of astonishment and a malediction, without an inhabitant, as at this day. 23 Because of the fact that YOU made sacrificial smoke and that YOU sinned against Jehovah and did not obey the voice of Jehovah and in his law and in his statutes and in his reminders YOU did not walk, that is why there has befallen YOU this calamity as at this day."

24 And Jeremiah continued on to say to all the people and to all the women: "Hear the word of Je-

hovah, all Judah who are in the land of Egypt. 25 This is what Jehovah of armies, the God of Israel, has said, 'As for YOU men and YOUR wives, YOU women also speak with YOUR mouths, (and with YOUR hands YOU people have made a fulfillment,) saying: "We shall without fail perform our vows that we have vowed, to make sacrificial smoke to the 'queen of the heavens' and to pour out drink offerings to her." YOU women will without fail carry out YOUR vows, and YOU will without fail perform YOUR vows.'

26 "Therefore hear the word of Jehovah, all Judah who are dwelling in the land of Egypt, ' "Here I myself have sworn by my great name," Jehovah has said, "that my name will no more prove to be something called out by the mouth of any man of Judah, saying, 'As the Lord Jehovah is alive!' in all the land of Egypt. 27 Here I am keeping alert toward them for calamity and not for good; and all the men of Judah that are in the land of Egypt will certainly come to their finish by the sword and by the famine, until they cease to be. 28 And as for the ones escaping from the sword, they will return from the land of Egypt to the land of Judah, few in number; and all those of the remnant of Judah, who are coming into the land of Egypt to reside there as aliens, will certainly know whose word comes true, that from me or that from them." ' "

29 " 'And this is the sign for YOU,' is the utterance of Jehovah, 'that I am turning my attention upon YOU in this place, in order that YOU may know that my words will without fail come true upon YOU for calamity. 30 This is what Jehovah has said: "Here I am giving Phar'aoh Hoph'ra, the king of Egypt, into the hand of his enemies and into the hand of those seeking for his soul, just as I have given Zed·e·ki'ah the king of Judah into the hand of Neb·u·chad·rez'-zar the king of Babylon, his enemy and the one seeking for his soul." ' "

45 The word that Jeremiah the prophet spoke to Bar'uch the son of Ne·ri'ah when he wrote in a book these words from the mouth of Jeremiah in the fourth year of Je·hoi'a·kim the son of Jo·si'ah, the king of Judah, saying:

2 "This is what Jehovah the God of Israel has said concerning you, O Bar'uch, 3 'You have said: "Woe, now, to me, for Jehovah has added grief to my pain! I have grown weary because of my sighing, and no resting place have I found." '

4 "This is what you should say to him, 'This is what Jehovah has said: "Look! What I have built up I am tearing down, and what I have planted I am uprooting, even all the land itself. 5 But as for you, you keep seeking great things for yourself. Do not keep on seeking." '

" 'For here I am bringing in a calamity upon all flesh,' is the utterance of Jehovah, 'and I will give you your soul as a spoil in all the places to which you may go.' "

46 This is what occurred as the word of Jehovah to Jeremiah the prophet concerning the nations: 2 For Egypt, concerning the military force of Phar'aoh Ne'cho the king of Egypt, who happened to be by the river Eu·phra'tes at Car'-che·mish, whom Neb·u·chad·rez'zar the king of Babylon defeated in the fourth year of Je·hoi'a·kim the son of Jo·si'ah, the king of Judah: 3 "Set in array, O men, buckler and large shield, and approach to battle. 4 Harness the horses, and mount, O YOU horsemen, and station yourselves with the helmet. Polish the lances. Clothe yourselves with coats of mail.

5 " 'Why is it that I have seen them terror-stricken? They are turning back, and their mighty men themselves are crushed to pieces; and they have positively fled, and they have not turned around. There is fright all around,' is the utterance of Jehovah. 'Let not the swift one try to flee, and let not the mighty man try to escape. Up north by the bank of the

river Eu·phra′tes they have stumbled and fallen.'

7 "Who is this one that comes up just like the Nile River, like the rivers the waters of which toss themselves? 8 Egypt itself comes up just like the Nile River, and like rivers the waters toss themselves. And it says, 'I shall go up. I shall cover the earth. I shall readily destroy the city and those inhabiting it.' 9 Go up, O YOU horses; and drive madly, O YOU chariots! And let the mighty men go forth, Cush and Put, who are handling the shield, and the Lu′dim, who are handling [and] treading the bow.

10 "And that day belongs to the Sovereign Lord, Jehovah of armies, the day of vengeance for avenging himself upon his adversaries. And the sword will certainly devour and satisfy itself and take its fill of their blood, for the Sovereign Lord, Jehovah of armies, has a sacrifice in the land of the north by the river Eu·phra′tes.

11 "Go up to Gil′e·ad and get some balsam, O virgin daughter of Egypt. In vain you have multiplied the means of healing. There is no mending for you. 12 The nations have heard your dishonor, and your own outcry has filled the land. For they have stumbled, mighty man against mighty man. Together they have fallen down, both of them."

13 The word that Jehovah spoke to Jeremiah the prophet as regards the coming of Neb·u·chad·rez′zar the king of Babylon to strike down the land of Egypt: 14 "Tell [it] in Egypt, O men, and publish [it] in Mig′dol, and publish [it] in Noph and in Tah′pan·hes. Say, 'Station yourself, making preparation also for yourself, for a sword will certainly devour all around you. 15 Why is it that your powerful ones have been washed away? They have made no stand, for Jehovah himself has pushed them away. 16 In great numbers they are stumbling. They also actually fall. And they keep saying one to the other: "Do rise up, and do let us return to our people and to the land of our relatives because of

the maltreating sword." ' 17 There they have proclaimed, 'Phar′aoh the king of Egypt is a mere noise. He has let the festal time pass by.'

18 " 'As I am alive,' is the utterance of the King, whose name is Jehovah of armies, 'like Ta′bor among the mountains and like Car′mel by the sea he will come in. 19 Make for yourself mere baggage for exile, O inhabitress, the daughter of Egypt. For Noph itself will become a mere object of astonishment and will actually be set afire, so as to be without an inhabitant. 20 Egypt is as a very pretty heifer. From the north a mosquito itself will certainly come against her. 21 Furthermore, her hired [soldiers] in the midst of her are like fattened calves. But they themselves also have given way; they have fled together. They have not made a stand. For the very day of their disaster has come in upon them, the time of their being given attention.'

22 " 'Her voice is like that of a serpent that goes along; for with vital energy men will go, and with axes they will actually come in to her, like those who are gathering pieces of wood. 23 They will certainly cut down her forest,' is the utterance of Jehovah, 'for it could not be penetrated. For they have become more numerous than the locust, and they are without number. 24 The daughter of Egypt will certainly feel shame. She will actually be given into the hand of the people of the north.'

25 "Jehovah of armies, the God of Israel, has said, 'Here I am turning my attention upon A′mon from No and upon Phar′aoh and upon Egypt and upon her gods and upon her kings, even upon Phar′aoh and upon all those trusting in him.'

26 " 'And I will give them into the hand of those seeking for their soul and into the hand of Neb·u·chad·rez′zar the king of Babylon and into the hand of his servants; and afterward she will be resided in as in the days of old,' is the utterance of Jehovah.

27 "'And as for you, do not be afraid, O my servant Jacob, and do not be terror-stricken, O Israel. For here I am saving you from far away and your offspring from the land of their captivity. And Jacob will certainly return and have no disturbance and be at ease and without anyone causing trembling. 28 As for you, do not be afraid, O my servant Jacob,' is the utterance of Jehovah, 'for I am with you. For I shall make an extermination among all the nations to which I have dispersed you, but with you I shall make no extermination. Yet I shall have to chastise you to the proper degree, and I shall absolutely not leave you unpunished.'"

47 This is what proved to be the word of Jehovah to Jeremiah the prophet concerning the Phi·lis′tines before Phar′aoh proceeded to strike down Ga′za. 2 This is what Jehovah has said:

"Look! Waters are coming up from the north and have become a flooding torrent. And they will flood the land and what fills it, the city and those inhabiting it. And the men will certainly cry out, and everyone dwelling in the land must howl. 3 At the sound of the stamping of the hoofs of his stallions, at the rattling of his war chariots, the turmoil of his wheels, the fathers will actually not turn around to the sons, because of the dropping down of [their] hands, 4 on account of the day that is coming to despoil all the Phi·lis′tines, to cut off from Tyre and from Si′don every survivor that was helping. For Jehovah is despoiling the Phi·lis′tines, who are the remaining ones from the island of Caph′tor. 5 Baldness must come to Ga′za. Ash′ke·lon has been put to silence. O remnant of their low plain, how long will you keep making cuts upon yourself?

6 "Aha, the sword of Jehovah! How long will you not stay quiet? Be shoved into your sheath. Take your repose and keep silent.

7 "How can it stay quiet, when Jehovah himself has given a command to it? It is for Ash′ke·lon and for the coast of the sea. There is where he has designated it to be."

48 For Mo′ab this is what Jehovah of armies, the God of Israel, has said: "Woe to Ne′bo, for she has been despoiled! Kir·i·a·tha′im has been put to shame, has been captured. The secure height has been put to shame and been put in terror. 2 No more is there any praise of Mo′ab. In Hesh′bon they have thought out against her a calamity: 'Come, men, and let us cut her off from being a nation.'

"You, too, O Mad′men, should keep silent. After you there walks a sword. 3 There is the sound of an outcry from Hor·o·na′im, a despoiling and great breaking down. 4 Mo′ab has been broken down. Her little ones have caused a cry to be heard. 5 For on the way up to Lu′hith it is with weeping that one goes up—there is a weeping. For on the way down from Hor·o·na′im there is a distressing outcry over the breakdown that people have heard.

6 "Take to flight; provide escape for YOUR souls, and YOU should become like a juniper tree in the wilderness. 7 Because your trust is in your works and in your treasures, you yourself will also be captured. And Che′mosh will certainly go forth into exile, his priests and his princes at the same time. 8 And the despoiler will come in on every city, and there will be no city that can make its escape. And the low plain will certainly perish and the level land be annihilated, a thing that Jehovah has said.

9 "Give a road mark to Mo′ab, YOU people, for at the falling in ruins she will go forth; and her very cities will become a mere object of astonishment, with no one dwelling in them.

10 "Cursed be the one that is carrying out the mission of Jehovah neglectfully; and cursed be the one that is holding back his sword from blood!

11 "The Mo′ab·ites have been at ease since their youth, and they are keeping undisturbed on their dregs.

And they have not been emptied from one vessel into another vessel, and into exile they have not gone. That is why their taste has stood still within them, and their very scent has not been changed.

12 "'Therefore, look! there are days coming,' is the utterance of Jehovah, 'and I will send to them [vessel] tilters, and they will certainly tilt them; and their vessels they will empty out, and their large jars they will dash to pieces. 13 And the Mo'ab·ites will have to be ashamed of Che'mosh, just as those of the house of Israel have become ashamed of Beth'el their confidence. 14 How dare YOU people say: "We are mighty men and men of vital energy for the war"?'

15 "'Mo'ab has been despoiled, and one has gone up against her own cities. And their choicest young men themselves have gone down to the slaughtering,' is the utterance of the King, whose name is Jehovah of armies.

16 "The disaster on the Mo'ab·ites is near to come, and their very calamity is actually hurrying up very much. 17 All those round about them will have to sympathize with them, even all those knowing their name. Say, YOU people, 'O how the rod of strength has been broken, the staff of beauty!'

18 "Get down from glory, and sit down in thirst, O inhabitress of the daughter of Di'bon; for the despoiler of Mo'ab has come up against you. He will actually bring your fortified places to ruin.

19 "Stand still and look out for the way itself, O inhabitress of A·ro'er. Ask him that is fleeing and her that is making her escape. Say, 'What has been brought about?' 20 Mo'ab has been put to shame, for she has been struck with terror. Howl and cry out. Tell in Ar'non, O men, that Mo'ab has been despoiled. 21 And judgment itself has come to the land of level country, to Ho'lon and to Ja'haz and against Meph'a·ath, 22 and against Di'bon and against Ne'bo and against Beth-dib·la·tha'im, 23 and against Kir·i·a·tha'im and

against Beth-ga'mul and against Beth-me'on 24 and against Ke'ri·oth and against Boz'rah and against all the cities of the land of Mo'ab, those far away and those near.

25 "'The horn of Mo'ab has been cut down, and his own arm has been broken,' is the utterance of Jehovah. 26 'Make him drunk, O men, for he has put on great airs against Jehovah himself; and Mo'ab has slapped around in his vomit, and he has become an object of ridicule, even he himself.

27 "'And did not Israel become a mere object of ridicule to you? Or was he found among outright thieves? For you would shake yourself just as often as you spoke against him.

28 "'Leave the cities and reside on the crag, YOU inhabitants of Mo'ab, and become like the dove that makes its nest in the regions of the mouth of the hollow.'"

29 "We have heard of the pride of Mo'ab—he is very haughty—of his highness and of his pride and of his haughtiness and of the loftiness of his heart."

30 "'I myself have known his fury,' is the utterance of Jehovah, 'and that is not the way it will be; his empty talk—they will not actually do in just that way. 31 That is why it is over Mo'ab that I shall howl, and for Mo'ab in his entirety I shall cry out. For the men of Kir-he'res one shall moan.

32 "'With more than the weeping for Ja'zer I shall weep for you, O vine of Sib'mah. Your own flourishing shoots have crossed over the sea. To the sea—[to] Ja'zer—they have reached. Upon your summer fruitage and upon your grape gathering the despoiler himself has fallen. 33 And rejoicing and joyfulness have been taken away from the orchard and from the land of Mo'ab. And from the wine presses I have caused the wine itself to cease. No one will be doing the treading with shouting. The shouting will be no shouting.'"

34 "'From the cry in Hesh'bon clear to E·le·a'leh, clear to Ja'haz

they have given forth their voice, from Zo'ar clear to Hor·o·na'im, to Eg'lath-she·li'shi·yah; for even the waters of Nim'rim themselves will become mere desolations. 35 And I will cause to cease from Mo'ab,' is the utterance of Jehovah, 'the one bringing up an offering upon the high place and the one making sacrificial smoke to his god. 36 That is why my own heart will be boisterous for Mo'ab himself, just like flutes; and for the men of Kir-he'res my very heart will be boisterous, just like flutes. That is why the very abundance that he has produced will certainly perish. 37 For upon every head there is baldness, and every beard is clipped. Upon all hands there are cuts, and upon the hips there is sackcloth!' "

38 " 'On all the roofs of Mo'ab and in her public squares—all of it—there is wailing; for I have broken Mo'ab just like a vessel in which there is no delight,' is the utterance of Jehovah. 39 'O how she has become terrified! Howl, YOU people! O how Mo'ab has turned the back! He has become ashamed. And Mo'ab has become an object of ridicule and something terrifying to all those round about him.' "

40 "For this is what Jehovah has said, 'Look! Just like an eagle that pounces, someone must also spread his wings over Mo'ab. 41 The towns will actually be captured, and her own strong places will certainly be seized. And the heart of the mighty men of Mo'ab must become in that day like the heart of a wife having childbirth distress.' "

42 " 'And Mo'ab will certainly be annihilated from being a people, for it is against Jehovah that he has put on great airs. 43 Dread and the hollow and the trap are upon you, O inhabitant of Mo'ab,' is the utterance of Jehovah. 44 'Anyone fleeing because of the dread will fall into the hollow; and anyone coming up out of the hollow will be caught in the trap.'

" 'For I shall bring upon her, upon Mo'ab, the year of their being given attention,' is the utterance of Jehovah. 45 'In the shadow of Hesh'bon those fleeing have stood still without power. For a very fire will certainly go forth out of Hesh'-bon, and a flame from the midst of Si'hon; and it will devour the temples of Mo'ab and the crown of the head of the sons of uproar.'

46 " 'Woe to you, O Mo'ab! The people of Che'mosh have perished. For your sons have been taken as captives and your daughters as captives. 47 And I will gather the captive ones of Mo'ab in the final part of the days,' is the utterance of Jehovah. 'Down to this point is the judgment upon Mo'ab.' "

49 For the sons of Am'mon this is what Jehovah has said: "Are there no sons that Israel has, or is there no inheritor that he has? Why is it that Mal'cham has taken possession of Gad, and his own people have taken up dwelling in [Israel's] very cities?"

2 " 'Therefore, look! there are days coming,' is the utterance of Jehovah, 'and I will cause the alarm signal of war to be heard even against Rab'bah of the sons of Am'mon; and she will certainly become a mound of a desolate waste, and her dependent towns themselves will be set aflame in the very fire.'

" 'And Israel will actually take possession of those in possession of him,' Jehovah has said.

3 " 'Howl, O Hesh'bon, for A'i has been despoiled! Cry out, O dependent towns of Rab'bah. Gird sackcloth on yourselves. Wail, and rove about among the stone pens, for Mal'cham himself will go even into exile, his priests and his princes, all together. 4 Why do you brag about the low plains, your flowing low plain, O daughter unfaithful, you the one trusting in her treasures, [saying:] "Who will come to me?" ' "

5 " 'Here I am bringing in upon you a dreadful thing,' is the utterance of the Sovereign Lord, Jehovah of armies, 'from all those round about you. And YOU people will certainly be dispersed, each one in his own direction, and there will

be no one collecting together those running away.' "

6 " 'But afterward I shall gather the captive ones of the sons of Am'mon,' is the utterance of Jehovah."

7 For E'dom this is what Jehovah of armies has said: "Is there no longer any wisdom in Te'man? Has counsel perished from those having understanding? Has their wisdom gone to putrefying? 8 Flee! Let yourselves give way! Go down deep in order to dwell, O inhabitants of De'dan! For the disaster of E'sau I will bring in upon him, the time that I must turn my attention to him. 9 If grape gatherers themselves actually came in to you, would they not let some gleanings remain? If thieves [came in] by night, they would certainly cause only as much ruin as they wanted. 10 But as for me, I will strip E'sau bare. I will uncover his places of concealment, and one will not be able to hide oneself. His offspring and his brothers and his neighbors will certainly be despoiled, and he will not be. 11 Do leave your fatherless boys. I myself shall preserve [them] alive, and your own widows will trust even in me."

12 For this is what Jehovah has said: "Look! Although it is not their custom to drink the cup, they will drink without fail. And you yourself, will you be absolutely left unpunished? You will not be left unpunished, for you will drink without fail."

13 "For by my own self I have sworn," is the utterance of Jehovah, "that nothing but an object of astonishment, a reproach, a devastation and a malediction will Boz'-rah become; and all her own cities will become devastated places to time indefinite."

14 There is a report that I have heard from Jehovah, and there is an envoy that is sent among the nations, [saying:] "Collect yourselves together, and come against her, and rise up to battle."

15 "For, look! I have made you small indeed among the nations, despised among mankind. 16 The shuddering you caused has deceived you, the presumptuousness of your heart, O you who are residing in the retreats of the crag, holding the height of the hill. Although you build your nest high up just like an eagle, down from there I shall bring you," is the utterance of Jehovah. 17 "And E'dom must become an object of astonishment. Everyone passing along by her will stare in astonishment and whistle on account of all her plagues. 18 Just as in the overthrow of Sod'om and Go·mor'rah and her neighbor [towns]," Jehovah has said, "no man will dwell there, and no son of mankind will reside in her as an alien.

19 "Look! Someone will come up just like a lion from the proud [thickets] along the Jordan to the durable abiding place, but in a moment I will make him run away from her. And the one who is chosen I shall appoint over her. For who is like me, and who will challenge me, and who, now, is the shepherd that can stand before me? 20 Therefore hear, O men, the counsel of Jehovah that he has formulated against E'dom, and his thoughts that he has thought out against the inhabitants of Te'man: Surely the little ones of the flock will be dragged about. Surely on account of them he will make their dwelling place become desolate. 21 At the sound of their falling earth has begun to rock. There is an outcry! The sound of it has been heard even at the Red Sea. 22 Look! Just like an eagle someone will ascend and pounce down, and he will spread out his wings over Boz'rah; and the heart of the mighty men of E'dom will actually become in that day like the heart of the wife having distress in childbirth."

23 For Damascus: "Ha'math and Ar'pad have become ashamed, for it is a bad report that they have heard. They have disintegrated. In the sea there is anxious care; it is not able to keep undisturbed. 24 Damascus has lost courage. She has turned to flee, and sheer panic

has seized her. Distress and birth pangs themselves have taken hold of her, as with a woman that is giving birth. 25 How is it that the city of praise has not been abandoned, the town of exultation?

26 "Therefore her young men will fall in her public squares, and all the men of war themselves will be brought to silence in that day," is the utterance of Jehovah of armies. 27 "And I will set a fire ablaze on the wall of Damascus, and it will certainly devour the dwelling towers of Ben-ha′dad."

28 For Ke′dar and the kingdoms of Ha′zor, which Neb·u·chad·rez′-zar the king of Babylon struck down, this is what Jehovah has said: "Rise up, go up to Ke′dar, O men, and despoil the sons of the East. 29 Their own tents and their own flocks will be taken, their tent cloths and all their articles. And their own camels will be carried off from them. And they will certainly cry out to them, 'Fright is all around!'"

30 "Flee, take flight far away; go down deep in order to dwell, O inhabitants of Ha′zor," is the utterance of Jehovah. "For Neb·u·chad·rez′zar the king of Babylon has formulated a counsel even against you and has thought out against you a thought."

31 "Rise up, O men, go up against the nation that is at ease, dwelling in security!" is the utterance of Jehovah.

"No doors and no bar does it have. Solitary they reside. 32 And their camels must become a plunder, and the multitude of their livestock a spoil. And I will scatter them to every wind, those who have their hair clipped at the temples; and from all regions near it I shall bring in their disaster," is the utterance of Jehovah. 33 "And Ha′zor must become the lair of jackals, a desolate waste to time indefinite. No man will dwell there, and in her no son of mankind will reside as an alien."

34 This is what occurred as the word of Jehovah to Jeremiah the prophet concerning E′lam in the beginning of the kingship of Zed·e-ki′ah the king of Judah, saying: 35 "This is what Jehovah of armies has said, 'Here I am breaking the bow of E′lam, the beginning of their mightiness. 36 And I will bring in upon E′lam the four winds from the four extremities of the heavens. And I will scatter them to all these winds, and there will prove to be no nation to which the dispersed ones of E′lam will not come.'"

37 "And I will shatter the E′lam-ites before their enemies and before those seeking for their soul; and I will bring upon them a calamity, my burning anger," is the utterance of Jehovah. "And I will send after them the sword until I shall have exterminated them."

38 "And I will set my throne in E′lam, and I will destroy out of there the king and the princes," is the utterance of Jehovah.

39 "And it will certainly occur in the final part of the days that I shall gather the captive ones of E′lam," is the utterance of Jehovah.

50 The word that Jehovah spoke concerning Babylon, concerning the land of the Chal·de′ans, by means of Jeremiah the prophet: 2 "Tell [it] among the nations and publish [it]. And lift up a signal; publish [it]. Hide nothing, O men. Say, 'Babylon has been captured. Bel has been put to shame. Mer′o-dach has become terrified. Her images have been put to shame. Her dungy idols have become terrified.' 3 For against her a nation has come up from the north. It is the one that makes her land an object of astonishment, so that there proves to be no one dwelling in her. Both man and domestic animal have taken flight. They have gone away."

4 "In those days and at that time," is the utterance of Jehovah, "the sons of Israel, they and the sons of Judah together, will come. They will walk, weeping as they walk, and for Jehovah their God they will seek. 5 To Zion they will keep asking the way, with their faces in that direction, [saying,] 'Come and let us join ourselves to

Jehovah in an indefinitely lasting covenant that will not be forgotten.' 6 A flock of perishing creatures my people has become. Their own shepherds have caused them to wander about. On the mountains they have led them away. From mountain to hill they have gone. They have forgotten their resting place. 7 All those finding them have eaten them up, and their own adversaries have said, 'We shall not become guilty, due to the fact that they have sinned against Jehovah the abiding place of righteousness and the hope of their forefathers, Jehovah.'"

8 "Take YOUR flight out of the midst of Babylon, and go forth even out of the land of the Chalde'ans, and become like the leading animals before the flock. 9 For here I am arousing and bringing up against Babylon a congregation of great nations from the land of the north, and they will certainly array themselves against her. From there she will be captured. One's arrows are like those of a mighty man causing bereavement of children, who does not come back without results. 10 And Chal·de'a must become a spoil. All those making spoil of her will satisfy themselves," is the utterance of Jehovah.

11 "For YOU men kept rejoicing, for YOU men kept exulting when pillaging my own inheritance. For YOU kept pawing like a heifer in the tender grass, and YOU kept neighing like stallions. 12 The mother of YOU men has become very much ashamed. She that gave YOU birth has been disappointed. Look! She is the least important of the nations, a waterless wilderness and a desert plain. 13 Because of the indignation of Jehovah she will not be inhabited, and she must become a desolate waste in her entirety. As for anyone passing along by Babylon, he will stare in astonishment and whistle on account of all her plagues.

14 "Array yourselves against Babylon on every side, all YOU who are treading the bow. Shoot at her. Spare no arrow, for it is against Jehovah that she has sinned. 15 Shout a war cry against her on every side. She has given her hand. Her pillars have fallen. For it is the vengeance of Jehovah. Take YOUR vengeance on her. Just as she has done, do to her. 16 Cut off the sower from Babylon, and the one handling the sickle in the time of harvest. Because of the maltreating sword they will turn each one to his own people, and they will flee each one to his own land.

17 "Israel is a scattered sheep. Lions themselves have done the dispersing. In the first instance the king of As·syr'i·a has devoured him, and in this latter instance Neb·u·chad·rez'zar the king of Babylon has gnawed on his bones. 18 Therefore this is what Jehovah of armies, the God of Israel, has said, 'Here I am turning my attention upon the king of Babylon and upon his land in the same way that I turned my attention upon the king of As·syr'i·a. 19 And I will bring Israel back to his pasture ground, and he will certainly graze on Car'mel and on Ba'shan; and in the mountainous region of E'phra·im and of Gil'e·ad his soul will be satisfied.'"

20 "And in those days and at that time," is the utterance of Jehovah, "the error of Israel will be searched for, but it will not be; and the sins of Judah, and they will not be found, for I shall forgive those whom I let remain."

21 "Against the land of Mer·a·tha'im—come up against her and against the inhabitants of Pe'kod. Let there be a massacre and a devoting to destruction close upon them," is the utterance of Jehovah, "and do according to all that I have commanded you. 22 There is the sound of war in the land, and a great breakdown. 23 O how the forge hammer of all the earth has been cut down and gets broken! O how Babylon has become a mere object of astonishment among the nations! 24 I have laid a snare for you and you have also been caught, O Babylon, and you yourself did not

know [it]. You were found and also taken hold of, for it was against Jehovah that you excited yourself.

25 "Jehovah has opened his storehouse, and he brings forth the weapons of his denunciation. For there is a work that the Sovereign Lord, Jehovah of armies, has in the land of the Chal·de′ans. 26 Come in to her from the farthest part. Open up her granaries. Bank her up, just like those making heaps, and devote her to destruction. May she not come to have any remaining ones. 27 Massacre all her young bulls. May they go down to the slaughter. Woe to them, for their day has come, the time for their being given attention!

28 "There is the sound of those fleeing and those escaping from the land of Babylon to tell out in Zion the vengeance of Jehovah our God, the vengeance for his temple.

29 "Summon against Babylon archers, all who are treading the bow. Encamp against her all around. May there prove to be no escapees. Pay back to her according to her activity. According to all that she has done, do to her. For it is against Jehovah that she has acted presumptuously, against the Holy One of Israel. 30 Therefore her young men will fall in her public squares, and even all her men of war will be brought to silence in that day," is the utterance of Jehovah.

31 "Look! I am against you, O Presumptuousness," is the utterance of the Sovereign Lord, Jehovah of armies, "for your day must come, the time that I must give you attention. 32 And Presumptuousness will certainly stumble and fall, and it will have no one to cause it to rise up. And I will set a fire ablaze in its cities, and it must devour all its surroundings."

33 This is what Jehovah of armies has said: "The sons of Israel and the sons of Judah are being oppressed together, and all those taking them captive have laid hold on them. They have refused to let them go. 34 Their Repurchaser is strong, Jehovah of armies being his name. Without fail he will conduct their legal case, in order that he may actually give repose to the land and cause agitation to the inhabitants of Babylon."

35 "There is a sword against the Chal·de′ans," is the utterance of Jehovah, "and against the inhabitants of Babylon and against her princes and against her wise ones. 36 There is a sword against the empty talkers, and they will certainly act foolishly. There is a sword against her mighty men, and they will actually become terrified. 37 There is a sword against their horses and against their war chariots and against all the mixed company that are in the midst of her, and they will certainly become women. There is a sword against her treasures, and they will actually be plundered. 38 There is a devastation upon her waters, and they must be dried up. For it is a land of graven images, and because of [their] frightful visions they keep acting crazy. 39 Therefore the haunters of waterless regions will dwell with the howling animals, and in her the ostriches must dwell; and she will nevermore be dwelt in, nor will she reside for generation after generation."

40 "Just as with God's overthrow of Sod′om and of Go·mor′rah and of her neighbor [towns]," is the utterance of Jehovah, "no man will dwell there, nor will the son of mankind reside in her as an alien.

41 "Look! A people is coming in from the north; and a great nation and grand kings themselves will be roused up from the remotest parts of the earth. 42 Bow and javelin they handle. They are cruel and will show no mercy. The sound of them is like the sea that is boisterous, and upon horses they will ride; set in array as one man for war against you, O daughter of Babylon.

43 "The king of Babylon has heard the report about them, and his hands have dropped down. There is distress! Severe pains have seized hold of him, just like a woman giving birth.

44 "Look! Someone will come up just like a lion from the proud [thickets] along the Jordan to the durable abiding place, but in a moment I shall make them run away from her. And the one who is chosen I shall appoint over her. For who is like me, and who will challenge me, and who, now, is the shepherd that can stand before me? 45 Therefore hear, O men, the counsel of Jehovah that he has formulated against Babylon and his thoughts that he has thought out against the land of the Chal·de´ans. Surely the little ones of the flock will be dragged about. Surely on account of them he will cause their abiding place to be desolated. 46 At the sound [when] Babylon has been seized, the earth will certainly be set rocking, and among the nations an outcry itself be heard."

51 This is what Jehovah has said: "Here I am rousing up against Babylon and against the inhabitants of Leb-ka'mai a ruinous wind; 2 and I will send to Babylon winnowers who will certainly winnow her and who will make her land empty; for they will actually prove to be against her on all sides in the day of calamity.

3 "Let the one treading his bow do no treading. And let no one raise himself up in his coat of mail.

"And do not you men show any compassion for her young men. Devote to destruction all her army. 4 And they must fall slain in the land of the Chal·de´ans and pierced through in her streets.

5 "For Israel and Judah are not widowed from their God, from Jehovah of armies. For the land of those has been full of guilt from the standpoint of the Holy One of Israel.

6 "FLEE out of the midst of Babylon, and provide escape each one for his own soul. Do not be rendered inanimate through her error. For it is the time of vengeance belonging to Jehovah. There is treatment that he is paying back to her. 7 Babylon has been a golden cup in the hand of Jehovah, she making all the earth drunk. From her wine the nations have drunk. That is why the nations keep acting crazed. 8 Suddenly Babylon has fallen, so that she is broken. Howl over her, you people. Take balsam for her pain. Perhaps she may be healed."

9 "We would have healed Babylon, but she has not been healed. Leave her, you people, and let us go each one to his own land. For clear to the heavens her judgment has reached, and it has been lifted up to the cloudy skies. 10 Jehovah has brought forth deeds of righteousness for us. Come and do let us recount in Zion the work of Jehovah our God."

11 "Polish the arrows. Fill the circular shields, O men. Jehovah has aroused the spirit of the kings of the Medes, because it is against Babylon that his idea is, in order to bring her to ruin. For it is the vengeance of Jehovah, the vengeance for his temple. 12 Against the walls of Babylon lift up a signal. Make strong the watch. Post the watchmen. Make ready those lying in ambush. For Jehovah both has formed the idea and will certainly do what he has spoken against the inhabitants of Babylon."

13 "O woman residing on abounding waters, abundant in treasures, your end has come, the measure of your profit making. 14 Jehovah of armies has sworn by his own soul, 'I will fill you with men, like the locusts, and they will certainly sing forth over you a shout.' 15 He is the Maker of the earth by his power, the One firmly establishing the productive land by his wisdom, and the One who by his understanding stretched out the heavens. 16 At [his] voice there is a giving by him of a turmoil of waters in the heavens, and he causes vapors to ascend from the extremity of the earth. He has made even sluices for the rain, and he brings forth the wind from his storehouses. 17 Every man has behaved so unreasonably as not to know. Every metalworker will feel ashamed because of the carved image; for his molten image is a falsehood, and there is no spirit in them. 18 They

are vanity, a work of mockery. In the time of their being given attention they will perish.

19 "The Share of Jacob is not like these things, for he is the Former of everything, even the staff of his inheritance. Jehovah of armies is his name.

20 "You are a club for me, as weapons of war, and by you I shall certainly dash nations to pieces, and by you I will bring kingdoms to ruin. 21 And by you I will dash the horse and his rider to pieces, and by you I will dash the war chariot and its rider to pieces. 22 And by you I will dash man and woman to pieces, and by you I will dash old man and boy to pieces, and by you I will dash young man and virgin to pieces. 23 And by you I will dash shepherd and his drove to pieces, and by you I will dash farmer and his span [of animals] to pieces, and by you I will dash governors and deputy rulers to pieces. 24 And I will pay back to Babylon and to all the inhabitants of Chal·de′a all their badness that they have committed in Zion before the eyes of you people," is the utterance of Jehovah.

25 "Here I am against you, O ruinous mountain," is the utterance of Jehovah, "you ruiner of the whole earth; and I will stretch out my hand against you and roll you away from the crags and make you a burnt-out mountain."

26 "And people will not take from you a stone for a corner or a stone for foundations, because desolate wastes to time indefinite are what you will become," is the utterance of Jehovah.

27 "Lift up a signal in the land, O men. Blow a horn among the nations. Sanctify against her the nations. Summon against her the kingdoms of Ar′a·rat, Min′ni and Ash′ke·naz. Commission against her a recruiting officer. Make the horses come up like bristly locusts. 28 Sanctify against her the nations, the kings of Me′di·a, its governors and all its deputy rulers and all the land of each one's dominion. 29 And let the earth rock and be in se-

vere pain, for against Babylon the thoughts of Jehovah have risen up to make the land of Babylon an object of astonishment, without an inhabitant.

30 "The mighty men of Babylon have ceased to fight. They have kept sitting in the strong places. Their mightiness has run dry. They have become women. Her residences have been set on fire. Her bars have been broken.

31 "One runner runs to meet another runner, and one reporter to meet another reporter, to report to the king of Babylon that his city has been captured at every end, 32 and that the fords themselves have been seized, and the papyrus boats they have burned with fire, and the men of war themselves have become disturbed."

33 For this is what Jehovah of armies, the God of Israel, has said: "The daughter of Babylon is like a threshing floor. It is the time to tread her down solid. Yet a little while and the time of the harvest must come for her."

34 "Neb·u·chad·rez′zar the king of Babylon has eaten me up; he has thrown me into confusion. He has set me as an empty vessel. He has swallowed me down like a big snake; he has filled his abdomen with my pleasant things. He has rinsed me away. 35 'The violence done to me and [to] my organism be upon Babylon!' the inhabitress of Zion will say. 'And my blood be upon the inhabitants of Chal·de′a!' Jerusalem will say."

36 Therefore this is what Jehovah has said: "Here I am conducting your legal case, and I shall certainly execute vengeance for you. And I will dry up her sea, and I will make her wells dry. 37 And Babylon must become piles of stones, the lair of jackals, an object of astonishment and something to whistle at, without an inhabitant. 38 All together they will roar just like maned young lions. They will certainly growl like the whelps of lions."

39 "When they are heated I shall set their banquets and I will make

them drunk, in order that they may exult; and they must sleep an indefinitely lasting sleep, from which they will not wake up," is the utterance of Jehovah. 40 "I shall bring them down like male sheep to the slaughtering, like rams along with the he-goats."

41 "O how She'shach has been captured, and how the Praise of the whole earth gets to be seized! How Babylon has become a mere object of astonishment among the nations! 42 The sea has come up even over Babylon. By the multitude of its waves she has been covered. 43 Her cities have become an object of astonishment, a waterless land and a desert plain. As a land, in them no man will dwell, and through them no son of mankind will pass. 44 And I will turn my attention upon Bel in Babylon, and I will bring forth out of his mouth what he has swallowed. And to him nations will stream no more. Also, the wall itself of Babylon must fall.

45 "Get out of the midst of her, O my people, and provide each one his soul with escape from the burning anger of Jehovah. 46 Or otherwise YOUR heart will be timid, and YOU will become afraid because of the report that is to be heard in the land. And in one year the report will actually come, and after it in another year there will be the report and violence in the earth and ruler against ruler. 47 Therefore, look! there are days coming, and I will turn my attention upon the graven images of Babylon; and all her own land will become ashamed, and all her own slain ones will fall in the midst of her.

48 "And over Babylon the heavens and the earth and all that is in them will certainly cry out joyfully, for out of the north there will come to her the despoilers," is the utterance of Jehovah. 49 "Not only was Babylon the cause for the slain ones of Israel to fall but also at Babylon the slain ones of all the earth have fallen.

50 "YOU escapees from the sword, keep going. Do not stand still. From far away remember Jehovah, and

may Jerusalem herself come up into YOUR heart."

51 "We have been put to shame, for we have heard reproach. Humiliation has covered our faces, for strangers have come against the holy places of the house of Jehovah."

52 "Therefore, look! there are days coming," is the utterance of Jehovah, "and I will turn my attention upon her graven images, and throughout all her land the pierced one will groan."

53 "Even if Babylon should ascend to the heavens and even if she should make the height of her strength unapproachable, from me the despoilers will come to her," is the utterance of Jehovah.

54 "Listen! There is an outcry from Babylon, and a great crash from the land of the Chal·de'ans, 55 for Jehovah is despoiling Babylon, and he will certainly destroy out of her the great voice, and their waves will actually be boisterous like many waters. The noise of their voice will certainly be given out. 56 For there must come upon her, upon Babylon, the despoiler, and her mighty men will certainly be captured. Their bows must be shattered, for Jehovah is a God of recompenses. Without fail he will repay. 57 And I will make her princes and her wise ones, her governors and her deputy rulers and her mighty men drunk, and they must sleep an indefinitely lasting sleep, from which they will not wake up," is the utterance of the King, whose name is Jehovah of armies.

58 This is what Jehovah of armies has said: "The wall of Babylon, although broad, will without fail be demolished; and her gates, although high, will be set aflame with fire. And the peoples will have to toil for simply nothing, and national groups simply for the fire; and they will just tire themselves out."

59 The word that Jeremiah the prophet commanded Se·rai'ah the son of Ne·ri'ah the son of Mahsei'ah when he went with Zed·e-

ki'ah the king of Judah to Babylon in the fourth year of his being king; and Se·rai'ah was the quartermaster. 60 And Jeremiah proceeded to write in one book all the calamity that would come upon Babylon, even all these words written against Babylon. 61 Furthermore, Jeremiah said to Se·rai'ah: "As soon as you come to Babylon and actually see [her], you must also read aloud all these words. 62 And you must say, 'O Jehovah, you yourself have spoken against this place, in order to cut it off so that there may come to be in it no inhabitant, either man or even domestic animal, but that she may become mere desolate wastes to time indefinite.' 63 And it must occur that when you will have completed reading this book, you will tie to it a stone, and you must pitch it into the midst of the Eu·phra'tes. 64 And you must say, 'This is how Babylon will sink down and never rise up because of the calamity that I am bringing in upon her; and they will certainly tire themselves out.' "

Down to this point are the words of Jeremiah.

52 Zed·e·ki'ah was twenty-one years old when he began to reign, and for eleven years he reigned in Jerusalem. And the name of his mother was Ha·mu'tal the daughter of Jeremiah of Lib'nah. 2 And he continued to do what was bad in the eyes of Jehovah, according to all that Je·hoi'a·kim had done. 3 For on account of the anger of Jehovah it occurred in Jerusalem and Judah, until he had cast them out from before his face. And Zed·e·ki'ah proceeded to rebel against the king of Babylon. 4 Finally it came about in the ninth year of his being king, in the tenth month, on the tenth day of the month, that Neb·u·chad·rez'zar the king of Babylon came, he and all his military force, against Jerusalem, and they began to camp against her and to build against her a siege wall all around. 5 So the city came under siege until the eleventh year of King Zed·e·ki'ah.

6 In the fourth month, on the ninth day of the month, the famine also got to be severe in the city and there proved to be no bread for the people of the land. 7 Finally the city was broken through; and as regards all the men of war, they began to run away and go forth from the city by night by the way of the gate between the double wall that is by the king's garden, while the Chal·de'ans were all around against the city; and they kept going by the way of the Ar'a·bah. 8 And a military force of the Chal·de'ans went chasing after the king, and they got to overtake Zed·e·ki'ah in the desert plains of Jer'i·cho; and all his own military force was scattered from his side. 9 Then they seized the king and brought him up to the king of Babylon at Rib'lah in the land of Ha'math, that he might pronounce upon him judicial decisions. 10 And the king of Babylon proceeded to slaughter the sons of Zed·e·ki'ah before his eyes, and also all the princes of Judah he slaughtered in Rib'lah. 11 And the eyes of Zed·e·ki'ah he blinded, after which the king of Babylon bound him with copper fetters and brought him to Babylon and put him in the house of custody until the day of his death.

12 And in the fifth month, on the tenth day of the month, that is, [in] the nineteenth year of King Neb·u·chad·rez'zar, the king of Babylon, Neb·u'zar·ad'an the chief of the bodyguard, who was standing before the king of Babylon, came into Jerusalem. 13 And he proceeded to burn the house of Jehovah and the house of the king and all the houses of Jerusalem; and every great house he burned with fire. 14 And all the walls of Jerusalem, round about, all the military forces of the Chal·de'ans that were with the chief of the bodyguard pulled down.

15 And some of the lowly ones of the people and the rest of the people that were left remaining in the city and the deserters that had fallen away to the king of Babylon and the rest of the master workmen

Neb·u'zar·ad'an the chief of the bodyguard took into exile. 16 And some of the lowly ones of the land Neb·u'zar·ad'an the chief of the bodyguard let remain as vinedressers and as compulsory laborers.

17 And the copper pillars that belonged to the house of Jehovah and the carriages and the copper sea that was in the house of Jehovah the Chal·de'ans broke to pieces and went carrying all the copper of them to Babylon. 18 And the cans and the shovels and the extinguishers and the bowls and the cups and all the copper utensils with which they used to minister they took. 19 And the basins and the fire holders and the bowls and the cans and the lampstands and the cups and the bowls that were of genuine gold, and those that were of genuine silver, the chief of the bodyguard took. 20 And the two pillars, the one sea, and the twelve copper bulls that were under [the sea], the carriages, that King Sol'o·mon had made for the house of Jehovah. There happened to be no weight [taken] of the copper of them—all these articles.

21 And as regards the pillars, eighteen cubits in height was each pillar, and a thread of twelve cubits itself would go around it; and its thickness was four fingerbreadths, it being hollow. 22 And the capital upon it was of copper, and the height of the one capital was five cubits; and as regards the network and the pomegranates upon the capital, all around, the whole was of copper; and the second pillar had just the same as these, also the pomegranates. 23 And the pomegranates came to be ninety-six, on the sides, all the pomegranates being one hundred upon the network round about.

24 Furthermore, the chief of the bodyguard took Se·rai'ah the chief priest and Zeph·a·ni'ah the second priest and the three doorkeepers, 25 and from the city he took one court official that happened to be

commissioner over the men of war, and seven men of those having access to the king, who were found in the city, and the secretary of the chief of the army, the one mustering the people of the land, and sixty men of the people of the land, who were found in the midst of the city. 26 So these Neb·u'zar·ad'an the chief of the bodyguard took and conducted them to the king of Babylon at Rib'lah. 27 And these the king of Babylon proceeded to strike down and to put them to death in Rib'lah in the land of Ha'math. Thus Judah went into exile from off its soil.

28 These are the people whom Neb·u·chad·rez'zar took into exile: in the seventh year, three thousand and twenty-three Jews.

29 In the eighteenth year of Neb·u·chad·rez'zar, from Jerusalem there were eight hundred and thirty-two souls.

30 In the twenty-third year of Neb·u·chad·rez'zar, Neb·u'zar·ad'an the chief of the bodyguard took Jews into exile, seven hundred and forty-five souls.

All the souls were four thousand and six hundred.

31 At length it came about in the thirty-seventh year of the exile of Je·hoi'a·chin the king of Judah, in the twelfth month, on the twenty-fifth day of the month, that E'vil-me·ro'dach the king of Babylon, in the year of his becoming king, raised up the head of Je·hoi'a·chin the king of Judah and proceeded to bring him forth from the prison house. 32 And he began to speak with him good things and to put his throne higher than the thrones of the [other] kings that were with him in Babylon. 33 And he took off his prison garments, and he ate bread before him constantly all the days of his life. 34 And as for his allowance, there was a constant allowance given him from the king of Babylon, daily as due, until the day of his death, all the days of his life.

LAMENTATIONS

א [Aleph]

1 O how she has come to sit solitary, the city that was abundant with people!

How she has become like a widow, she that was populous among the nations!

How she that was a princess among the jurisdictional districts has come to be for forced labor!

ב [Beth]

2 Profusely she weeps during the night, and her tears are upon her cheeks.

She has no one to comfort her from among all her lovers.

All her very own companions have dealt treacherously with her. They have become enemies to her.

ג [Gimel]

3 Judah has gone into exile because of the affliction and because of the abundance of servitude.

She herself has had to dwell among the nations. No resting place has she found.

All those who were persecuting her have overtaken her among distressing circumstances.

ד [Daleth]

4 The ways of Zion are mourning, because there are none coming to the festival.

All her gates are laid desolate; her priests are sighing.

Her virgins are grief-stricken, and she herself has bitterness.

ה [He]

5 Her adversaries have become the head. Those who are her enemies are unconcerned.

Because Jehovah himself has brought grief to her on account of the abundance of her transgressions,

Her own children have walked captive before the adversary.

ו [Waw]

6 And from the daughter of Zion there goes out all her splendor.

Her princes have proved to be like stags that have found no pasturage;

And they keep walking without power before the pursuer.

ז [Zayin]

7 Jerusalem has remembered [in] the days of her affliction and of her homeless people

All her desirable things that happened to be from days of long ago.

When her people fell into the hand of the adversary and she had no helper,

The adversaries saw her. They laughed over her collapse.

ח [Heth]

8 Jerusalem has committed outright sin. That is why she has become a mere abhorrent thing.

All who were honoring her have treated her as something cheap, for they have seen her nakedness.

She herself is also sighing and turns her back.

ט [Teth]

9 Her uncleanness is in her skirts. She did not remember the future for her,

And down she goes in a wondrous manner. No comforter does she have.

O Jehovah, see my affliction, for the enemy has put on great airs.

י [Yod]

10 The adversary has spread out his own hand against all her desirable things.

For she has seen nations that
have come into her sanc-
tuary,
Whom you commanded that
they should not come into
the congregation belonging
to you.

 כ [Kaph]

11 All her people are sighing; they
are looking for bread.
They have given their de-
sirable things for something
to eat, in order to refresh
the soul.
See, O Jehovah, and do look,
for I have become as a
valueless woman.

ל [Lamed]

12 Is it nothing to all YOU who
are passing along the way?
Look and see.
Does there exist any pain like
my pain that has been se-
verely dealt out to me,
With which Jehovah has
caused grief in the day of
his burning anger?

מ [Mem]

13 From the height he has sent
fire into my bones, and he
subdues each one.
He has spread out a net for
my feet. He has turned me
backward.
He has made me a woman
laid desolate. All the day I
am ill.

נ [Nun]

14 He has kept himself alert
against my transgressions.
In his hand they intertwine
one another.
They have come up upon my
neck. My power has stum-
bled.
Jehovah has given me into
the hand of those against
whom I am unable to
rise up.

ס [Samekh]

15 All my powerful ones Jehovah
has tossed aside from the
midst of me.

He has called against me a
meeting, in order to break
my young men to pieces.
Jehovah has trodden the very
wine press belonging to the
virgin daughter of Judah.

ע [Ayin]

16 Over these things I am weeping as a woman. My eye,
my eye is running down
with waters.
For a comforter has become
far away from me, someone
to refresh my soul.
My sons have become those
laid desolate, for the enemy
has put on great airs.

פ [Pe]

17 Zion has spread out her hands.
No comforter does she have.
Jehovah has given a com-
mand concerning Jacob to
all who are around him as
his adversaries.
Jerusalem has become an abhorrent thing in among
them.

צ [Tsade]

18 Jehovah is righteous, for it is
against his mouth that I
have rebelled.
Listen, now, all YOU peoples,
and see my pain.
My own virgins and my own
young men have gone into
captivity.

ק [Qoph]

19 I have called to those intensely
loving me. They themselves
have tricked me.
In the city my own priests
and my own old men have
expired,
While they had to look for
something to eat for themselves that they might refresh their soul.

ר [Resh]

20 See, O Jehovah, for I am in
sore straits. My very in-
testines are in a ferment.
My heart has been overturned
in the midst of me, for I
have been absolutely re-
bellious.

Outside the sword caused bereavement of children. Within the house it is the same as death.

ש [*Shin*]

21 People have heard how I myself am sighing as a woman. There is no comforter for me.

All my enemies themselves have heard of my calamity. They have exulted, because you yourself have done [it].

You will certainly bring the day that you have proclaimed, that they may become like me.

ת [*Taw*]

22 May all their badness come before you, and deal severely with them,

Just as you have dealt severely with me on account of all my transgressions.

For my sighs are many, and my heart is ill.

א [*Aleph*]

2 O how Jehovah in his anger beclouds the daughter of Zion!

He has thrown down from heaven to earth the beauty of Israel.

And he has not remembered his footstool in the day of his anger.

ב [*Beth*]

2 Jehovah has swallowed up, he has shown no compassion upon any abiding places of Jacob.

In his fury he has torn down the fortified places of the daughter of Judah.

He has brought into contact with the earth, he has profaned the kingdom and her princes.

ג [*Gimel*]

3 In the heat of anger he has cut down every horn of Israel.

He has turned his right hand back from before the enemy;

And in Jacob he keeps burning like a flaming fire that has devoured all around.

ד [*Daleth*]

4 He has trodden his bow like an enemy. His right hand has taken its position

Like an adversary, and he kept killing all those desirable to the eyes.

Into the tent of the daughter of Zion he has poured out his rage, just like fire.

ה [*He*]

5 Jehovah has become like an enemy. He has swallowed down Israel.

He has swallowed down all her dwelling towers; he has brought his fortified places to ruin.

And in the daughter of Judah he makes mourning and lamentation abound.

ו [*Waw*]

6 And he treats his booth violently like that in a garden. He has brought his festival to ruin.

Jehovah has caused to be forgotten in Zion festival and sabbath,

And in his angry denunciation he shows no respect for king and priest.

ז [*Zayin*]

7 Jehovah has cast off his altar. He has spurned his sanctuary.

Into the hand of the enemy he has surrendered the walls of her dwelling towers.

In the house of Jehovah they have let out [their] own voice, as in the day of a festival.

ח [*Heth*]

8 Jehovah has thought of bringing the wall of the daughter of Zion to ruin.

He has stretched out the measuring line. He has not turned back his hand from swallowing up.

And he causes rampart and wall to go mourning. Together they have faded away.

ט [Teth]

9 Her gates have sunk down into the very earth. He has destroyed and broken her bars in pieces.

Her king and her princes are among the nations. There is no law.

Her own prophets also have found no vision from Jehovah.

י [Yod]

10 The older men of the daughter of Zion sit down on the earth, [where] they keep silence.

They have brought up dust upon their head. They have girded on sackcloth.

The virgins of Jerusalem have brought their head down to the very earth.

כ [Kaph]

11 My eyes have come to their end in sheer tears. My intestines are in a ferment.

My liver has been poured out to the very earth, on account of the crash of the daughter of my people,

Because of the fainting away of child and suckling in the public squares of the town.

ל [Lamed]

12 To their mothers they kept saying: "Where are grain and wine?"

Because of their fainting away like someone slain in the public squares of the city,

Because of their soul being poured out into the bosom of their mothers.

מ [Mem]

13 Of what shall I use you as a witness? What shall I liken to you, O daughter of Jerusalem?

What shall I make equal to you, that I may comfort you, O virgin daughter of Zion?

For your breakdown is just as great as the sea. Who can bring healing to you?

נ [Nun]

14 Your own prophets have visioned for you worthless and unsatisfying things,

And they have not uncovered your error in order to turn back your captivity,

But they kept visioning for you worthless and misleading pronouncements.

ס [Samekh]

15 At you all those passing along on the road have clapped their hands.

They have whistled and kept wagging their head at the daughter of Jerusalem, [saying:]

"Is this the city of which they used to say, 'It is the perfection of prettiness, an exultation for all the earth'?"

פ [Pe]

16 At you all your enemies have opened their mouth.

They have whistled and kept grinding the teeth. They have said: "We will swallow [her] down.

This indeed is the day that we have hoped for. We have found! We have seen!"

ע [Ayin]

17 Jehovah has done what he had in mind. He has accomplished his saying,

What he had commanded from the days of long ago. He has torn down and shown no compassion.

And over you he causes the enemy to rejoice. He has made the horn of your adversaries high.

צ [Tsade]

18 Their heart has cried out to

Jehovah, O wall of the
daughter of Zion.
Cause tears to descend just
like a torrent day and night.
Give no numbness to your-
self. May the pupil of your
eye not keep quiet.

ק [Qoph]

19 Rise up! Whine during the
night at the start of the
morning watches.
Pour out your heart before
the face of Jehovah just
like water.
Raise to him your palms on
account of the soul of your
children,
Who are fainting away be-
cause of famine at the head
of all the streets.

ר [Resh]

20 See, O Jehovah, and do look to
the one to whom you have
dealt severely in this manner.
Should the women keep eating their own fruitage, the
children born fully formed,
Or in the sanctuary of Jehovah should priest and
prophet be killed?

ש [Shin]

21 Boy and old man have lain
down on the earth of the
streets.
My virgins and my young men
themselves have fallen by
the sword.
You have killed in the day
of your anger. You have
slaughtered; you have had
no compassion.

ת [Taw]

22 As in the day of a festival you
proceeded to call out my
places of alien residence
all around.
And in the day of the wrath
of Jehovah there proved to
be no escapee or survivor;
Those whom I brought forth
fully formed and reared, my
enemy himself exterminated
them.

א [Aleph]

3 I am the able-bodied man that
has seen affliction because of
the staff of his fury.

2 It is I whom he has led and
makes to walk in darkness
and not in light.

3 Indeed, it is against me that he
repeatedly turns his hand
all day long.

ב [Beth]

4 He has caused my flesh and my
skin to wear away. He has
broken my bones.

5 He has built against me, that
he may encircle [me] with
poisonous plant and hard-
ship.

6 In dark places he has made
me sit like men dead for a
long time.

ג [Gimel]

7 He has blocked me up as with a
stone wall, that I may not
go forth. He has made my
copper fetters heavy.

8 Also, when I call for aid and
cry for help, he actually
hampers my prayer.

9 He has blocked up my ways
with hewn stone. My road-
ways he has twisted.

ד [Daleth]

10 As a bear lying in wait he is
to me, as a lion in places
of concealment.

11 My ways he has disarranged,
and he makes me lie fallow.
He has made me one laid
desolate.

12 He has trodden his bow, and
he sets me up as the target
for the arrow.

ה [He]

13 He has brought into my kidneys
the sons of his quiver.

14 I have become an object
of laughter to all people
against me, the theme of
their song all day long.

15 He has given me a sufficiency
of bitter things. He has
saturated me with worm-
wood.

ו [Waw]

16 And with gravel he makes my teeth get broken. He has made me cower in the ashes.

17 You also do a casting off so that there is no peace for my soul. I have lost memory of what good is.

18 And I keep saying: "My excellency has perished, and my expectation from Jehovah."

ז [Zayin]

19 Remember my affliction and my homeless state, the wormwood and the poisonous plant.

20 Without fail your soul will remember and bow low over me.

21 This is what I shall bring back to my heart. That is why I shall show a waiting attitude.

ח [Heth]

22 It is the acts of loving-kindness of Jehovah that we have not come to our finish, because his mercies will certainly not come to an end.

23 They are new each morning. Your faithfulness is abundant.

24 "Jehovah is my share," my soul has said, "that is why I shall show a waiting attitude for him."

ט [Teth]

25 Good is Jehovah to the one hoping in him, to the soul that keeps seeking for him.

26 Good it is that one should wait, even silently, for the salvation of Jehovah.

27 Good it is for an able-bodied man that he should carry the yoke during his youth.

י [Yod]

28 Let him sit solitary and keep silent, because he has laid [something] upon him.

29 Let him put his mouth in the very dust. Perhaps there exists a hope.

30 Let him give [his] cheek to the very one striking him. Let him have his sufficiency of reproach.

כ [Kaph]

31 For not to time indefinite will Jehovah keep on casting off.

32 For although he has caused grief, he will also certainly show mercy according to the abundance of his loving-kindness.

33 For not out of his own heart has he afflicted or does he grieve the sons of men.

ל [Lamed]

34 For crushing beneath one's feet all the prisoners of the earth,

35 For turning aside the judgment of an able-bodied man before the face of the Most High,

36 For making a man crooked in his legal case, Jehovah himself has had no countenance.

מ [Mem]

37 Who, now, has said that something should occur [when] Jehovah himself has not commanded?

38 From the mouth of the Most High bad things and what is good do not go forth.

39 How can a living man indulge in complaints, an able-bodied man on account of his sin?

נ [Nun]

40 Do let us search out our ways and explore them, and do let us return clear to Jehovah.

41 Let us raise our heart along with [our] palms to God in the heavens:

42 "We ourselves have transgressed, and we have behaved rebelliously. You yourself have not forgiven.

ס [Samekh]

43 You have blocked approach with anger, and you keep pursuing us. You have killed;

you have shown no compassion.

44 You have blocked approach to yourself with a cloud mass, that prayer may not pass through.

45 You make us mere offscouring and refuse in the midst of the peoples."

ס [Pe]

46 Against us all our enemies have opened their mouth.

47 Dread and the hollow themselves have become ours, desolateness and breakdown.

48 With streams of water my eye keeps running down on account of the breakdown of the daughter of my people.

ע [Ayin]

49 My very eye has been poured forth and will not keep still, so that there are no pauses,

50 Until Jehovah looks down and sees from heaven.

51 My own eye has dealt severely with my soul, because of all the daughters of my city.

צ [Tsade]

52 My enemies have positively hunted for me just as for a bird, for no cause.

53 They have silenced my life in the pit itself, and they kept hurling stones at me.

54 Waters have flowed over my head. I have said: "I shall certainly be cut off!"

ק [Qoph]

55 I have called out your name, O Jehovah, from a pit of the lowest sort.

56 My voice you must hear. Do not hide your ear to my relief, to my cry for help.

57 You have drawn near in the day that I kept calling you. You said: "Do not be afraid."

ר [Resh]

58 You have taken up, O Jehovah, the contests of my soul. You have repurchased my life.

59 You have seen, O Jehovah, the wrong done to me. O do conduct the judgment for me.

60 You have seen all their vengeance, all their thoughts against me.

ש [Shin]

61 You have heard their reproach, O Jehovah, all their thoughts against me,

62 The lips of those rising up against me and their whispering against me all day long.

63 Do look at their very sitting down and their rising up. I am the subject of their song.

ת [Taw]

64 You will give back to them a treatment, O Jehovah, according to the work of their hands.

65 You will give to them the insolence of heart, your curse to them.

66 You will pursue in anger and annihilate them from under the heavens of Jehovah.

א [Aleph]

4 O how the gold that shines becomes dim, the good gold! O how the holy stones are poured out at the head of all the streets!

ב [Beth]

2 As for the precious sons of Zion, those who were weighed against refined gold, O how they have been reckoned as large jars of earthenware, the work of the hands of a potter!

ג [Gimel]

3 Even jackals themselves have presented the udder. They have suckled their cubs. The daughter of my people becomes cruel, like ostriches in the wilderness.

ד [Daleth]

4 The tongue of the suckling has

cleaved to its palate because of thirst.
Children themselves have asked for bread. There is no one dealing [it] out to them.

ה [He]

5 The very ones that were eating pleasant things have been struck with astonishment in the streets.
The very ones that were being reared in scarlet have had to embrace ash heaps.

ו [Waw]

6 The [punishment for the] error of the daughter of my people also becomes greater than the [punishment for the] sin of Sod'om,
Which was overthrown as in a moment, and to which no hands turned [helpfully].

ז [Zayin]

7 Her Naz'i·rites were purer than snow; they were whiter than milk.
They were in fact more ruddy than corals; their polish was as the sapphire.

ח [Heth]

8 Their aspect has become darker than blackness itself. They have not been recognized in the streets.
Their skin has shriveled upon their bones. It has become just as dry as a tree.

ט [Teth]

9 Better have those slain with the sword proved to be than those slain by famine,
Because these pine away, pierced through for lack of the produce of the open field.

י [Yod]

10 The very hands of compassionate women have boiled their own children.
They have become as bread of consolation to one during the breakdown of the daughter of my people.

כ [Kaph]

11 Jehovah has accomplished his rage. He has poured out his burning anger.
And he sets a fire ablaze in Zion, which eats up her foundations.

ל [Lamed]

12 The kings of the earth and all the inhabitants of the productive land had not believed
That the adversary and the enemy would come into the gates of Jerusalem.

מ [Mem]

13 Because of the sins of her prophets, the errors of her priests.
There were in the midst of her those pouring out the blood of righteous ones.

נ [Nun]

14 They have wandered about as blind in the streets. They have become polluted with blood,
So that none are able to touch their garments.

ס [Samekh]

15 "Get out of the way! Unclean!" they have called out to them. "Get out of the way! Get out of the way! Do not touch!"
For they have gone homeless. They have also wandered about. People have said among the nations: "They will not reside again as aliens."

פ [Pe]

16 The face of Jehovah has divided them up. He will not look upon them again.
Men will certainly show no consideration even for the priests. They will certainly show no favor even to the old men."

ע [Ayin]

17 While we yet are, our eyes keep pining away in vain for assistance to us.

During our looking about we have looked out to a nation that can bring no salvation.

צ [Tsade]

18 They have hunted our steps so that there is no walking in our public squares.
Our end has drawn near. Our days have come to their full, for our end has come.

ק [Qoph]

19 Swifter than the eagles of the heavens our pursuers have proved to be.
Upon the mountains they have hotly pursued us. In the wilderness they have lain in wait for us.

ר [Resh]

20 The very breath of our nostrils, the anointed one of Jehovah, has been captured in their large pit,
The one of whom we have said: "In his shade we shall live among the nations."

שׂ [Sin]

21 Exult and rejoice, O daughter of E'dom, dwelling as you do in the land of Uz.
To you also the cup will pass along. You will become drunk and show yourself in nakedness.

ת [Taw]

22 Your error, O daughter of Zion, has come to its finish. He will not carry you off into exile again.
He has turned his attention to your error, O daughter of E'dom. He has uncovered your sins.

5 Remember, O Jehovah, what has happened to us. Do look and see our reproach.

2 Our own hereditary possession has been turned over to strangers, our houses to foreigners.

3 We have become mere orphans without a father. Our mothers are like widows.

4 For money we have had to drink our own water. For a price our own wood comes in.

5 Close onto our neck we have been pursued. We have grown weary. No rest has been left for us.

6 To Egypt we have given the hand; to As·syr'i·a, in order to get satisfaction with bread.

7 Our forefathers are the ones that have sinned. They are no more. As for us, it is their errors that we have had to bear.

8 Mere servants have ruled over us. There is no one tearing us away from their hand.

9 At the risk of our soul we bring in our bread, because of the sword of the wilderness.

10 Our very skin has grown hot just like a furnace, because of the pangs of hunger.

11 The wives in Zion they have humbled, the virgins in the cities of Judah.

12 Princes themselves have been hanged by just their hand. The faces of even old men have not been honored.

13 Even young men have lifted up a hand mill itself, and under the wood mere boys have stumbled.

14 Old men themselves have ceased even out of the gate, young men from their instrumental music.

15 The exultation of our heart has ceased. Our dancing has been changed into mere mourning.

16 The crown of our head has fallen. Woe, now, to us, because we have sinned!

17 On this account our heart has become ill. On account of these things our eyes have grown dim,

18 On account of Zion's mountain that is desolated; foxes themselves have walked on it.

19 As for you, O Jehovah, to time indefinite you will sit. Your

throne is for generation after generation.

20 Why is it that forever you forget us, that you leave us for the length of days?

21 Bring us back, O Jehovah, to yourself, and we shall readily come back. Bring new days for us as in the long ago.

22 However, you have positively rejected us. You have been indignant toward us very much.

EZEKIEL

1 Now it came about in the thirtieth year, in the fourth [month], on the fifth [day] of the month, while I was in the midst of the exiled people by the river Che′bar, that the heavens were opened and I began to see visions of God. 2 On the fifth [day] of the month, that is, [in] the fifth year of the exile of King Je·hoi′a·chin, 3 the word of Jehovah occurred specifically to Ezekiel the son of Bu′zi the priest in the land of the Chal·de′ans by the river Che′bar, and upon him in that place the hand of Jehovah came to be.

4 And I began to see, and, look! there was a tempestuous wind coming from the north, a great cloud mass and quivering fire, and it had a brightness all around, and out of the midst of it there was something like the look of electrum, out of the midst of the fire. 5 And out of the midst of it there was the likeness of four living creatures, and this was how they looked: they had the likeness of earthling man. 6 And [each] one had four faces, and [each] one of them four wings. 7 And their feet were straight feet, and the sole of their feet was like the sole of the foot of a calf; and they were gleaming as with the glow of burnished copper. 8 And there were the hands of a man under their wings on their four sides, and the four of them had their faces and their wings. 9 Their wings were joining one to the other. They would not turn when they went; they would go each one straight forward.

10 And as for the likeness of their faces, the four of them had a man's face with a lion's face to the right, and the four of them had a bull's face on the left; the four of them also had an eagle's face. 11 That is the way their faces were. And their wings were spreading out upward. Each one had two joining to each other, and two were covering their bodies.

12 And they would go each one straight forward. To wherever the spirit would incline to go, they would go. They would not turn as they went. 13 And as for the likeness of the living creatures, their appearance was like burning coals of fire. Something like the appearance of torches was moving back and forth between the living creatures, and the fire was bright, and out of the fire there was lightning going forth. 14 And on the part of the living creatures there was a going forth and a returning as with the appearance of the lightning.

15 As I kept seeing the living creatures, why, look! there was one wheel on the earth beside the living creatures, by the four faces of each. 16 As for the appearance of the wheels and their structure, it was like the glow of chrysolite; and the four of them had one likeness. And their appearance and their structure were just as when a wheel proved to be in the midst of a wheel. 17 When they went they would go on their four respective sides. They would not turn another way when they went. 18 And as for their rims, they had such height that they caused fearfulness; and

their rims were full of eyes all around the four of them. 19 And when the living creatures went, the wheels would go beside them, and when the living creatures were lifted up from the earth, the wheels would be lifted up. 20 Wherever the spirit inclined to go, they would go, the spirit [inclining] to go there; and the wheels themselves would be lifted up close alongside them, for the spirit of the living creature was in the wheels. 21 When they went, these would go; and when they stood still, these would stand still; and when they were lifted up from the earth, the wheels would be lifted up close alongside them, for the spirit of the living creature was in the wheels.

22 And over the heads of the living creatures there was the likeness of an expanse like the sparkle of awesome ice, stretched out over their heads up above. 23 And under the expanse their wings were straight, one to the other. Each one had two wings covering on this side and each one had two covering on that side their bodies. 24 And I got to hear the sound of their wings, a sound like that of vast waters, like the sound of the Almighty One, when they went, the sound of a tumult, like the sound of an encampment. When they stood still, they would let their wings down.

25 And there came to be a voice above the expanse that was over their head. (When they stood still, they would let their wings down.) 26 And above the expanse that was over their head there was something in appearance like sapphire stone, the likeness of a throne. And upon the likeness of the throne there was a likeness of someone in appearance like an earthling man upon it, up above. 27 And I got to see something like the glow of electrum, like the appearance of fire all around inside thereof, from the appearance of his hips and upward; and from the appearance of his hips and downward I saw something like the appearance of fire, and he had a brightness all around. 28 There was something like the appearance of the bow that occurs in a cloud mass on the day of a pouring rain. That is how the appearance was of the brightness round about. It was the appearance of the likeness of the glory of Jehovah. When I got to see [it], then I fell upon my face, and I began to hear the voice of one speaking.

2 And he proceeded to say to me: "Son of man, stand up upon your feet that I may speak with you." 2 And spirit began to come into me as soon as he spoke to me, and it finally made me stand up upon my feet that I might hear the One speaking to me.

3 And he went on to say to me: "Son of man, I am sending you to the sons of Israel, to rebellious nations that have rebelled against me. They themselves and their forefathers have transgressed against me down to this selfsame day. 4 And the sons insolent of face and hard of heart—I am sending you to them, and you must say to them, 'This is what the Lord Jehovah has said.' 5 And as for them, whether they will hear or will refrain—for they are a rebellious house—they will certainly know also that a prophet himself happened to be in the midst of them.

6 "And you, O son of man, do not be afraid of them; and of their words do not be afraid, because there are obstinate ones and things pricking you and it is among scorpions that you are dwelling. Of their words do not you be afraid, and at their faces do not you be struck with terror, for they are a rebellious house. 7 And you must speak my words to them, regardless of whether they hear or they refrain, for they are a case of rebellion.

8 "And you, O son of man, hear what I am speaking to you. Do not become rebellious like the rebellious house. Open your mouth and eat what I am giving you."

9 And I began to see, and, look! there was a hand thrust out to me,

and, look! in it there was the roll of a book. 10 And he gradually spread it out before me, and it was written upon in front and on the back; and there were written in it dirges and moaning and wailing.

3 And he proceeded to say to me: "Son of man, what you find, eat. Eat this roll, and go, speak to the house of Israel."

2 So I opened my mouth, and he gradually made me eat this roll. 3 And he went on to say to me: "Son of man, you should cause your own belly to eat, that you may fill your very intestines with this roll that I am giving you." And I began to eat it, and it came to be in my mouth like honey for sweetness.

4 And he continued saying to me: "Son of man, go, enter in among the house of Israel, and you must speak with my words to them. 5 For it is not to a people who are unintelligible in language or heavy of tongue that you are being sent—to the house of Israel, 6 not to numerous peoples unintelligible in language or heavy in tongue, whose words you cannot hear [understandingly]. If it was to them that I had sent you, those very ones would listen to you. 7 But as for the house of Israel, they will not want to listen to you, for they are not wanting to listen to me; because all those of the house of Israel are hardheaded and hardhearted. 8 Look! I have made your face exactly as hard as their faces and your forehead exactly as hard as their foreheads. 9 Like a diamond, harder than flint, I have made your forehead. You must not be afraid of them, and you must not be struck with terror at their faces, for they are a rebellious house."

10 And he went on to say to me: "Son of man, all my words that I shall speak to you, take into your heart and hear with your own ears. 11 And go, enter in among the exiled people, among the sons of your people, and you must speak to them and say to them, 'This is what the Lord Jehovah has said,'

regardless of whether they hear or they refrain."

12 And a spirit proceeded to bear me along and I began to hear behind me the sound of a great rushing: "Blessed be the glory of Jehovah from his place." 13 And there was the sound of the wings of the living creatures that were closely touching each other, and the sound of the wheels close beside them, and the sound of a great rushing. 14 And [the] spirit bore me along and proceeded to take me, so that I went bitterly in the rage of my spirit, and the hand of Jehovah upon me was strong. 15 So I entered in among the exiled people at Tel-a′bib, who were dwelling by the river Che′bar, and I began to dwell where they were dwelling; and I kept dwelling there for seven days, stunned in the midst of them.

16 And it came about at the end of seven days that the word of Jehovah proceeded to occur to me, saying:

17 "Son of man, a watchman is what I have made you to the house of Israel, and you must hear from my mouth speech and you must warn them from me. 18 When I say to someone wicked, 'You will positively die,' and you do not actually warn him and speak in order to warn the wicked one from his wicked way to preserve him alive, he being wicked, in his error he will die, but his blood I shall ask back from your own hand. 19 But as for you, in case you have warned someone wicked and he does not actually turn back from his wickedness and from his wicked way, he himself for his error will die; but as for you, you will have delivered your own soul. 20 And when someone righteous turns back from his righteousness and actually does injustice and I must put a stumbling block before him, he himself will die because you did not warn him. For his sin he will die, and his righteous acts that he did will not be remembered, but his blood I shall ask back from your own hand. 21 And as for

you, in case you have warned someone righteous that the righteous one should not sin, and he himself does not actually sin, he will without fail keep on living because he had been warned, and you yourself will have delivered your own soul."

22 And the hand of Jehovah came to be upon me there and he proceeded to say to me: "Get up, go forth to the valley plain, and there I shall speak with you." 23 So I got up and went forth to the valley plain, and, look! the glory of Jehovah was standing there, like the glory that I had seen by the river Che'bar, and I went falling upon my face. 24 Then spirit entered into me and made me stand up on my feet, and he began to speak with me and say to me:

"Come, be shut up inside your house. 25 And you, O son of man, look! they will certainly put cords upon you and bind you with them so that you cannot go forth into the midst of them. 26 And your very tongue I will make stick to the roof of your mouth, and you will certainly become mute, and you will not become to them a man administering reproof, because they are a rebellious house. 27 And when I speak with you I shall open your mouth, and you must say to them, 'This is what the Lord Jehovah has said.' Let the one hearing hear, and let the one refraining refrain, because they are a rebellious house.

4 "And you, O son of man, take for yourself a brick, and you must put it before you and engrave upon it a city, even Jerusalem. 2 And you must lay siege against it and build a siege wall against it and throw up a siege rampart against it and set encampments against it and put battering rams all around against it. 3 And as for you, take to yourself an iron griddle, and you must put it as an iron wall between you and the city, and you must fix your face against it, and it must get to be in a siege,

and you must besiege it. It is a sign to the house of Israel.

4 "And as for you, lie upon your left side, and you must lay the error of the house of Israel upon it. For the number of the days that you will lie upon it you will carry their error. 5 And I myself must give to you the years of their error to the number of three hundred and ninety days, and you must carry the error of the house of Israel. 6 And you must complete them.

"And you must lie upon your right side in the second case, and you must carry the error of the house of Judah forty days. A day for a year, a day for a year, is what I have given you. 7 And to the siege of Jerusalem you will fix your face, with your arm bared, and you must prophesy against it.

8 "And, look! I will put cords upon you that you may not turn yourself from your one side to your other side, until you will have completed the days of your siege.

9 "And as for you, take for yourself wheat and barley and broad beans and lentils and millet and spelt, and you must put them in one utensil and make them into bread for you, for the number of the days that you are lying upon your side; three hundred and ninety days you will eat it. 10 And your food that you will eat will be by weight—twenty shekels a day. From time to time you will eat it.

11 "And water you will drink merely by measure, the sixth part of a hin. From time to time you will drink.

12 "And as a round cake of barley you will eat it; and as for it, upon dung cakes of the excrement of mankind you will bake it before their eyes." 13 And Jehovah went on to say: "Just like this the sons of Israel will eat their bread unclean among the nations to which I shall disperse them."

14 And I proceeded to say: "Alas, O Lord Jehovah! Look! My soul is not a defiled one; neither a body [already] dead nor a torn animal have I eaten from my youth up,

even until now, and into my mouth there has come no foul flesh."

15 Accordingly he said to me: "See, I have given you cattle manure instead of the dung cakes of mankind, and you must make your bread upon it." 16 And he continued saying to me: "Son of man, here I am breaking the rods around which ring-shaped loaves are suspended, in Jerusalem, and they will have to eat bread by weight and in anxious care, and it will be by measure and in horror that they will drink water itself, 17 to the intent that they may be lacking bread and water and they may look astonished at one another and rot away in their error.

5 "And as for you, O son of man, take for yourself a sharp sword. As a barbers' razor you will take it for yourself, and you must make it pass along upon your head and upon your beard, and you must take for yourself weighing scales and divide [the hair] in portions. 2 A third you will burn in the very fire in the midst of the city as soon as the days of the siege have come to the full. And you must take another third. You will strike [it] with the sword all around her, and the [last] third you will scatter to the wind, and I shall draw out a sword itself after them.

3 "And you must take therefrom a few in number and wrap them up in your skirts. 4 And others of them you will take and you must pitch them into the midst of the fire and incinerate them in the fire. From one a fire will go forth to all the house of Israel.

5 "This is what the Lord Jehovah has said, 'This is Jerusalem. In the midst of the nations I have set her, with lands all around her. 6 And she proceeded to behave rebelliously against my judicial decisions in wickedness more than the nations, and against my statutes more than the lands that are all around her, for my judicial decisions they rejected and, as for my statutes, they did not walk in them.'

7 "Therefore this is what the Lord Jehovah has said, 'For the reason that YOU people were more turbulent than the nations that are all around YOU, in my statutes YOU did not walk and my judicial decisions YOU did not perform; but according to the judicial decisions of the nations that are all around YOU, YOU performed, did YOU not? 8 therefore this is what the Lord Jehovah has said: "Here I am against you, [O city,] even I, and I will execute in the midst of you judicial decisions in the eyes of the nations. 9 And I will do in you that which I have not done and the like of which I shall not do any more by reason of all your detestable things.

10 " ' "Therefore fathers themselves will eat sons in the midst of you, and sons themselves will eat their fathers, and I will execute in you acts of judgment and scatter all the remainder of you to every wind." '

11 " ' "Therefore as I am alive,' is the utterance of the Lord Jehovah, 'surely for the reason that it was my sanctuary that you defiled with all your disgusting things and with all your detestable things, I myself also am the One that will diminish [you] and my eye will not feel sorry and I myself also will not show compassion. 12 A third of you—by the pestilence they will die, and by famine they will come to their end in the midst of you. And another third—by the sword they will fall all around you. And the [last] third I shall scatter even to every wind, and a sword is what I shall draw out after them. 13 And my anger will certainly come to its finish and I will appease my rage on them and comfort myself; and they will have to know that I myself, Jehovah, have spoken in my insistence on exclusive devotion, when I bring my rage to its finish upon them.

14 " 'And I shall make you a devastated place and a reproach among the nations that are all around you before the eyes of every passer-by. 15 And you must be-

come a reproach and an object of reviling words, a warning example and a horror to the nations that are all around you, when I do in you acts of judgment in anger and in rage and in raging reproofs. I myself, Jehovah, have spoken.

16 " 'When I send the injurious arrows of the famine upon them, which must prove to be for ruination, which [arrows] I shall send to bring you people to ruin, even famine I shall increase upon you people and I will break your rods around which ring-shaped loaves are suspended. 17 And I will send upon you people famine and injurious wild beasts, and they must bereave you of children, and pestilence and blood themselves will pass along through you, and a sword I shall bring in upon you. I myself, Jehovah, have spoken.' "

6 And the word of Jehovah continued to occur to me, saying: 2 "Son of man, set your face toward the mountains of Israel and prophesy to them. 3 And you must say, 'O mountains of Israel, hear the word of the Lord Jehovah: This is what the Lord Jehovah has said to the mountains and to the hills, to the stream beds and to the valleys: "Here I am! I am bringing upon you a sword, and I shall certainly destroy your high places. 4 And your altars must be made desolate and your incense stands must be broken, and I will cause your slain ones to fall before your dungy idols. 5 And I will put the carcasses of the sons of Israel before their dungy idols, and I will scatter your bones all around your altars. 6 In all your dwelling places the very cities will become devastated and the high places themselves will become desolated, in order that they may lie devastated and your altars may lie desolated and be actually broken and your dungy idols may be actually made to cease and your incense stands cut down and your works wiped out. 7 And the slain one will certainly fall in the midst of you, and you will have to know that I am Jehovah.

8 " ' "And when it occurs I will let you have as a remnant the ones escaping from the sword among the nations, when you get scattered among the lands. 9 And your escaped ones will certainly remember me among the nations to which they will have been taken captive, because I have been broken up at their fornicating heart that has turned aside from me and at their eyes that are going in fornication after their dungy idols; and they will certainly feel a loathing in their faces at the bad things that they have done in all their detestable things. 10 And they will have to know that I am Jehovah; not in vain did I speak about doing to them this calamitous thing." '

11 "This is what the Lord Jehovah has said, 'Clap your hands and stamp with your foot, and say: "Alas!" on account of all the bad detestable things of the house of Israel, because by the sword, by the famine and by the pestilence they will fall. 12 As for the one far away, by the pestilence he will die; and as for the one that is nearby, by the sword he will fall; and as for the one that has been left remaining and that has been safeguarded, by the famine he will die, and I will bring to its finish my rage against them. 13 And you people will have to know that I am Jehovah, when their slain ones come to be in the midst of their dungy idols, all around their altars, upon every high hill, on all the tops of the mountains and under every luxuriant tree and under every branchy big tree, the place where they have offered a restful odor to all their dungy idols. 14 And I will stretch out my hand against them and make the land a desolate waste, even a desolation worse than the wilderness toward Dib'lah, in all their dwelling places. And they will have to know that I am Jehovah.' "

7 And the word of Jehovah continued to occur to me, saying: 2 "And as for you, O son of man, this is what the Lord Jehovah has said to the soil of Israel, 'An end,

the end, has come upon the four extremities of the land. 3 Now the end is upon you, and I must send my anger against you, and I will judge you according to your ways and bring upon you all your detestable things. 4 And my eye will not feel sorry for you, neither will I feel compassion, for upon you I shall bring your own ways, and in the midst of you your own detestable things will come to be; and you people will have to know that I am Jehovah.'

5 "This is what the Lord Jehovah has said, 'A calamity, a unique calamity, look! it is coming. 6 An end itself must come. The end must come; it must awaken for you. Look! It is coming. 7 The garland must come to you, O inhabiter of the land, the time must come, the day is near. There is confusion, and not the shouting of the mountains.

8 "'Now shortly I shall pour out my rage upon you, and I will bring my anger against you to its finish, and I will judge you according to your ways and bring upon you all your detestable things. 9 Neither will my eye feel sorry nor shall I feel compassion. According to your ways shall I do the bringing upon you yourself, and your own detestable things will come to be right in the midst of you; and you people will have to know that I, Jehovah, am doing the striking.

10 "'Look! The day! Look! It is coming. The garland has gone forth. The rod has blossomed. Presumptuousness has sprouted. 11 Violence itself has risen up into a rod of wickedness. It is not from them, nor is it from their wealth; and it is not from their own selves, nor is there any eminency in them. 12 The time must come, the day must arrive. As regards the buyer, let him not rejoice; and as regards the seller, let him not go into mourning, for there is hot feeling against all its crowd. 13 For to what was sold the seller himself will not return, while their life is yet among the living ones; for the vision is for all its crowd. No one

will return, and they will not possess themselves each one of his own life by his own error.

14 "'They have blown the trumpet and there has been a preparing of everybody, but there is no one going to the battle, because my hot feeling is against all its crowd. 15 The sword is outside, and the pestilence and the famine are inside. Whoever is in the field, by the sword he will die, and whoever are in the city, famine and pestilence themselves will devour them. 16 And their escapees will certainly make their escape and become on the mountains like the doves of the valleys, all of which are moaning, each one in his own error. 17 As for all the hands, they keep dropping down; and as for all knees, they keep dripping with water. 18 And they have girded on sackcloth, and shuddering has covered them; and on all faces there is shame and on all their heads there is baldness.

19 "'Into the streets they will throw their very silver, and an abhorrent thing their own gold will become. Neither their silver nor their gold will be able to deliver them in the day of Jehovah's fury. Their souls they will not satisfy, and their intestines they will not fill, for it has become a stumbling block causing their error. 20 And the decoration of one's ornament —one has set it as reason for pride; and their detestable images, their disgusting things, they have made with it. That is why I will make it to them an abhorrent thing. 21 And I will give it into the hand of the strangers for plunder and to the wicked ones of the earth for spoil, and they will certainly profane it.

22 "'And I shall have to turn away my face from them, and they will actually profane my concealed place, and into it robbers will really come and profane it.

23 "'Make the chain, for the land itself has become full of bloodstained judgment and the city itself has become full of violence. 24 And I will bring in the worst

ones of the nations, and they will certainly take possession of their houses, and I will cause the pride of the strong ones to cease, and their sanctuaries must be profaned. 25 There will come anguish, and they will certainly seek peace but there will be none. 26 There will come adversity upon adversity, and there will occur report upon report, and people will actually seek a vision from a prophet, and the law itself will perish from a priest and counsel from elderly men. 27 The king himself will go into mourning; even a chieftain will clothe himself with desolation, and the very hands of the people of the land will get disturbed. According to their way I shall act toward them, and with their judgments I shall judge them; and they will have to know that I am Jehovah.'"

8 And it came about in the sixth year, in the sixth [month], on the fifth day of the month, that I was sitting in my house and the older men of Judah were sitting before me, when the hand of the Lord Jehovah fell upon me there. 2 And I began to see, and, look! a likeness similar to the appearance of fire; from the appearance of his hips even downward there was fire, and from his hips even upward there was something like the appearance of a shining, like the glow of electrum. 3 Then he thrust out the representation of a hand and took me by a tuft of hair of my head, and a spirit carried me between the earth and the heavens and brought me to Jerusalem in the visions of God, to the entrance of the inner gate that is facing northward, where the dwelling place is of the symbol of jealousy that is inciting to jealousy. 4 And, look! the glory of the God of Israel was there, like the appearance that I had seen in the valley plain.

5 And he proceeded to say to me: "Son of man, please, raise your eyes in the direction of the north." So I raised my eyes in the direction of the north, and, look! to the north of the gate of the altar there was this symbol of jealousy in the entranceway. 6 And he went on to say to me: "Son of man, are you seeing what great detestable things they are doing, the things that the house of Israel are doing here [for me] to become far off from my sanctuary? And yet you will see again great detestable things."

7 Accordingly he brought me to the entrance of the courtyard, and I began to see, and, look! a certain hole in the wall. 8 He now said to me: "Son of man, bore, please, through the wall." And I gradually bored through the wall, and, look! there was a certain entrance. 9 And he further said to me: "Go in and see the bad detestable things that they are doing here." 10 So I went in and began to see, and, look! there was every representation of creeping things and loathsome beasts, and all the dungy idols of the house of Israel, the carving being upon the wall all round about. 11 And seventy men of the elderly ones of the house of Israel, with Ja·az·a·ni'ah the son of Sha'phan standing in among them, were standing before them, each one with his censer in his hand, and the perfume of the cloud of the incense was ascending. 12 And he proceeded to say to me: "Have you seen, O son of man, what the elderly ones of the house of Israel are doing in the darkness, each one in the inner rooms of his showpiece? For they are saying, 'Jehovah is not seeing us. Jehovah has left the land.'"

13 And he continued on to say to me: "You will yet see again great detestable things that they are doing." 14 So he brought me to the entrance of the gate of the house of Jehovah, which is toward the north, and, look! there the women were sitting, weeping over the [god] Tam'muz.

15 And he further said to me: "Have you seen [this], O son of man? You will yet see again great detestable things worse than these." 16 So he brought me to the inner courtyard of the house of Jehovah,

and, look! at the entrance of the temple of Jehovah, between the porch and the altar, there were about twenty-five men with their backs to the temple of Jehovah and their faces to the east, and they were bowing down to the east, to the sun.

17 And he went on to say to me: "Have you seen [this], O son of man? Is it such a light thing to the house of Judah to do the detestable things that they have done here, that they have to fill the land with violence and that they should offend me again, and here they are thrusting out the shoot to my nose? 18 And I myself also shall act in rage. My eye will not feel sorry, neither shall I feel compassion. And they will certainly call out in my ears with a loud voice, but I shall not hear them."

9 And he proceeded to call out in my ears with a loud voice, saying: "HAVE those giving their attention to the city come near, each one with his weapon in his hand for bringing ruin!"

2 And, look! there were six men coming from the direction of the upper gate that faces to the north, each one with his weapon for smashing in his hand; and there was one man in among them clothed with linen, with a recorder's inkhorn at his hips, and they proceeded to come in and stand beside the copper altar.

3 And as regards the glory of the God of Israel, it was taken up from over the cherubs over which it happened to be to the threshold of the house, and he began calling out to the man that was clothed with the linen, at whose hips there was the recorder's inkhorn. 4 And Jehovah went on to say to him: "Pass through the midst of the city, through the midst of Jerusalem, and you must put a mark on the foreheads of the men that are sighing and groaning over all the detestable things that are being done in the midst of it."

5 And to these [others] he said in my ears: "Pass through the city after him and strike. Let not your eye feel sorry, and do not feel any compassion. 6 Old man, young man and virgin and little child and women YOU should kill off—to a ruination. But to any man upon whom there is the mark do not go near, and from my sanctuary YOU should start." So they started with the old men that were before the house. 7 And he said further to them: "Defile the house and fill the courtyards with the slain ones. Go forth!" And they went forth and struck in the city.

8 And it came about that, while they were striking and I was left remaining, I proceeded to fall upon my face and cry out and say: "Alas, O Lord Jehovah! Are you bringing to ruin all the remaining ones of Israel while you are pouring out your rage upon Jerusalem?"

9 So he said to me: "The error of the house of Israel and Judah is very, very great, and the land is filled with bloodshed and the city is full of crookedness; for they have said, 'Jehovah has left the land, and Jehovah is not seeing.' 10 And as for me also, my eye will not feel sorry, neither shall I show compassion. Their way I shall certainly bring upon their own head."

11 And, look! the man clothed with the linen, at whose hips there was the inkhorn, was bringing back word, saying: "I have done just as you have commanded me."

10 And I continued to see, and, look! upon the expanse that was over the head of the cherubs there was something like sapphire stone, like the appearance of the likeness of a throne, appearing above them. 2 And he proceeded to say to the man clothed with the linen, even to say: "Enter in between the wheelwork, in under the cherubs, and fill the hollows of both your hands with coals of fire from between the cherubs and toss [them] over the city." So he entered in before my eyes.

3 And the cherubs were standing to the right of the house when the man entered, and the cloud was filling the inner courtyard. 4 And the glory of Jehovah began to rise

up from the cherubs by the threshold of the house, and the house gradually became filled with the cloud, and the courtyard itself was full of the brightness of the glory of Jehovah. 5 And the very sound of the wings of the cherubs made itself heard to the outer courtyard, like the sound of God Almighty when he speaks.

6 And it came about, when he commanded the man clothed with the linen, saying: "Take fire from between the wheelwork, from between the cherubs," that he proceeded to enter and stand beside the wheel. 7 Then the cherub thrust his hand out from between the cherubs to the fire that was between the cherubs and carried and put [it] into the hollows of the hands of the one clothed with the linen, who now took [it] and went out. 8 And there was seen belonging to the cherubs the representation of a hand of earthling man under their wings.

9 And I continued to see, and, look! there were four wheels beside the cherubs, one wheel beside the one cherub and one wheel beside the other cherub, and the appearance of the wheels was like the glow of a chrysolite stone. 10 And as for their appearance, the four of them had one likeness, just as when a wheel proves to be in the midst of a wheel. 11 When they would go, to their four sides they would go. They would not change direction when they went, because the place to which the head would face, after it they would go. They would not change direction when they went. 12 And all their flesh and their backs and their hands and their wings and the wheels were full of eyes all around. The four of them had their wheels. 13 As regards the wheels, to them it was called out in my ears, "O wheelwork!"

14 And [each] one had four faces. The first face was the face of the cherub, and the second face was the face of earthling man, and the third was the face of a lion, and the fourth was the face of an eagle.

15 And the cherubs would rise —it was the [same] living creature that I had seen at the river Che′bar— 16 and when the cherubs went, the wheels would go alongside them; and when the cherubs lifted up their wings to be high above the earth, the wheels would not change direction, even they themselves, from alongside them. 17 When these stood still, they would stand still; and when these rose, they would rise with them, for the spirit of the living creature was in them.

18 And the glory of Jehovah proceeded to go forth from over the threshold of the house and to stand still over the cherubs. 19 And the cherubs now lifted up their wings and rose from the earth before my eyes. When they went forth, the wheels also were close alongside them; and they began standing at the eastern entrance of the gate of the house of Jehovah, and the glory of the God of Israel was over them, from above.

20 This is the living creature that I had seen under the God of Israel at the river Che′bar, so that I came to know that they were cherubs. 21 As for the four, [each] one had four faces and [each] one had four wings, and the likeness of the hands of earthling man was under their wings. 22 And as for the likeness of their faces, they were the faces the appearance of which I had seen by the river Che′bar, the very ones. They would go each one straight forward.

11 And a spirit proceeded to lift me up and bring me to the eastern gate of the house of Jehovah that is facing eastward, and, look! in the entrance of the gate there were twenty-five men, and I got to see in the midst of them Ja·az·a·ni′ah the son of Az′zur and Pel·a·ti′ah the son of Be·nai′ah, princes of the people. 2 Then he said to me: "Son of man, these are the men that are scheming hurtfulness and advising bad counsel against this city; 3 that are saying, 'Is not the building of houses close at hand? She is the widemouthed cooking pot, and we are the flesh.'

4 "Therefore prophesy against them. Prophesy, O son of man."

5 Then the spirit of Jehovah fell upon me, and he went on to say to me: "Say, 'This is what Jehovah has said: "You people said the right thing, O house of Israel; and as regards the things that come up in YOUR spirit, I myself have known it. 6 You have caused YOUR slain ones in this city to be many, and YOU have filled her streets with the slain [ones]." ' ' 7 "Therefore this is what the Lord Jehovah has said, 'As regards YOUR slain ones whom YOU people have put in the midst of her, they are the flesh, and she is the widemouthed cooking pot; and there will be a bringing forth of YOU yourselves out of the midst of her.' "

8 " 'A sword YOU have feared, and a sword I shall bring upon YOU,' is the utterance of the Lord Jehovah. 9 'And I shall certainly bring YOU forth out of the midst of her and give YOU into the hand of strangers and execute upon YOU acts of judgment. 10 By the sword YOU will fall. On the territory of Israel I shall judge YOU people; and YOU will have to know that I am Jehovah. 11 She herself will not prove to be for YOU a widemouthed cooking pot, and YOU yourselves will not prove to be flesh in the midst of her. On the territory of Israel I shall judge YOU, 12 and YOU will have to know that I am Jehovah, because in my regulations YOU did not walk and my judgments YOU did not do, but according to the judgments of the nations that are round about YOU, YOU have done.' "

13 And it came about that as soon as I prophesied Pel·a·ti'ah the son of Be·nai'ah himself died, and I proceeded to fall upon my face and cry with a loud voice and say: "Alas, O Lord Jehovah! Is it an extermination that you are executing with the remaining ones of Israel?"

14 And the word of Jehovah continued to occur to me, saying: 15 "Son of man, as regards your brothers, your brothers, the men concerned with your right to repurchase, and all the house of Israel, all of it, are the ones to whom the inhabitants of Jerusalem have said, 'Get far away from Jehovah. To us it belongs; the land has been given [us] as a thing to possess'; 16 therefore say, 'This is what the Lord Jehovah has said: "Although I have put them far away among the nations, and although I have scattered them among the lands, yet I shall become to them a sanctuary for a little while among the lands to which they have come." '

17 "Therefore say, 'This is what the Lord Jehovah has said: "I will also collect YOU from the peoples and gather YOU from the lands among which YOU have been scattered, and I will give YOU the soil of Israel. 18 And they will certainly come there and remove all its disgusting things and all its detestable things out of it. 19 And I will give them one heart, and a new spirit I shall put inside them; and I shall certainly remove the heart of stone from their flesh and give them a heart of flesh, 20 in order that they may walk in my own statutes and keep my own judicial decisions and actually carry them out; and they may really become my people and I myself may become their God." '

21 " ' "But as for those whose heart is walking in their disgusting things and their detestable things, upon their head I shall certainly bring their own way," is the utterance of the Lord Jehovah.' "

22 And the cherubs now lifted up their wings, and the wheels were close by them, and the glory of the God of Israel was over them, from above. 23 And the glory of Jehovah went ascending from over the midst of the city and began to stand over the mountain that is to the east of the city. 24 And a

spirit itself lifted me up and finally brought me to Chal·de′a to the exiled people, in the vision by the spirit of God; and the vision that I had seen went ascending from upon me. 25 And I began to speak to the exiled people all the things of Jehovah that he had caused me to see.

12 And the word of Jehovah continued to occur to me, saying: 2 "Son of man, in the midst of a rebellious house is where you are dwelling, that have eyes to see but they actually do not see, that have ears to hear but they actually do not hear, for they are a rebellious house. 3 As for you, O son of man, make up for yourself luggage for exile and go into exile in the daytime before their eyes, and you must go into exile from your place to another place before their eyes. Perhaps they will see, though they are a rebellious house. 4 And you must bring out your luggage like luggage for exile in the daytime before their eyes, and you yourself will go out in the evening before their eyes like those being brought forth for exile.

5 "Before their eyes, bore your way through the wall, and you must do the bringing out through it. 6 Before their eyes you will do the carrying on the shoulder itself. During the darkness you will do the bringing out. You will cover your very face that you may not see the earth, because a portent is what I have made you to the house of Israel."

7 And I proceeded to do just the way that I had been commanded. My luggage I brought out, just like luggage for exile, in the daytime; and in the evening I bored my way through the wall by hand. During the darkness I did the bringing out. On my shoulder I did the carrying, before their eyes.

8 And the word of Jehovah continued to occur to me in the morning, saying: 9 "Son of man, did not those of the house of Israel, the rebellious house, say to you, 'What are you doing?' 10 Say to them, 'This is what the Lord Je-

hovah has said: "As regards the chieftain, there is this pronouncement against Jerusalem and all the house of Israel who are in the midst of them." '

11 "Say, 'I am a portent for you. Just as I have done, that is the way it will be done to them. Into exile, into captivity they will go. 12 And as regards the chieftain who is in the midst of them, on the shoulder he will do carrying in the darkness and go out; through the wall they will bore in order to do the bringing forth through it. His face he will cover in order that he may not see with his own eye the earth.' 13 And I shall certainly spread my net over him, and he must be caught in my hunting net; and I will bring him to Babylon, to the land of the Chal·de′ans, but it he will not see; and there he will die. 14 And all who are round about him as a help, and all his military bands, I shall scatter to every wind; and a sword I shall draw out after them. 15 And they will have to know that I am Jehovah when I disperse them among the nations and I actually scatter them among the lands. 16 And I will leave remaining from them a few men from the sword, from the famine and from the pestilence, in order that they may recount all their detestable things among the nations to whom they must come in; and they will have to know that I am Jehovah."

17 And the word of Jehovah continued to occur to me, saying: 18 "Son of man, with quaking your bread you should eat, and with agitation and with anxious care your water you should drink. 19 And you must say to the people of the land, 'This is what the Lord Jehovah has said to the inhabitants of Jerusalem upon the soil of Israel: "With anxious care their bread they will eat, and with horror their water they will drink, in order that its land may be laid desolate of its fullness because of the violence of all those dwelling in it. 20 And the inhabited cities themselves will be devastated, and the

land itself will become a mere desolate waste; and you will have to know that I am Jehovah.' ' "

21 And the word of Jehovah occurred further to me, saying: 22 "Son of man, what is this proverbial saying that you people have on the soil of Israel, saying, 'The days are prolonged, and every vision has perished'? 23 Therefore say to them, 'This is what the Lord Jehovah has said: "I shall certainly cause this proverbial saying to cease, and they will no more say it as a proverb in Israel." ' But speak to them, 'The days have drawn near, and the matter of every vision.' 24 For there will no more prove to be any valueless vision nor double-faced divination in the midst of the house of Israel. 25 ' "For I myself, Jehovah, shall speak what word I shall speak, and it will be done. There will be no postponement any more, for in your days, O rebellious house, I shall speak a word and certainly do it," is the utterance of the Lord Jehovah.' "

26 And the word of Jehovah continued to occur to me, saying: 27 "Son of man, look! those of the house of Israel are saying, 'The vision that he is visioning is many days off, and respecting times far off he is prophesying.' 28 Therefore say to them, 'This is what the Lord Jehovah has said: " 'There will be no postponement any more as to any words of mine. What word I shall speak, it will even be done,' is the utterance of the Lord Jehovah." ' "

13 And the word of Jehovah continued to occur to me, saying: 2 "Son of man, prophesy concerning the prophets of Israel who are prophesying, and you must say to those prophesying out of their own heart, 'Hear the word of Jehovah. 3 This is what the Lord Jehovah has said: "Woe to the stupid prophets, who are walking after their own spirit, when there is nothing that they have seen! 4 Like foxes in the devastated places are what your own prophets have become, O Israel. 5 You men will certainly

not go up into the gaps, neither will you build up a stone wall in behalf of the house of Israel, in order to stand in the battle in the day of Jehovah." 6 "They have visioned what is untrue and a lying divination, those who are saying, 'The utterance of Jehovah is,' when Jehovah himself has not sent them, and they have waited to have a word come true. 7 Is it not an untrue vision that you men have visioned, and a lying divination that you have said, when saying, 'The utterance of Jehovah is,' when I myself have spoken nothing?" '

8 " 'Therefore this is what the Lord Jehovah has said: " 'For the reason that you men have spoken untruth and you have visioned a lie, therefore here I am against you,' is the utterance of the Lord Jehovah." 9 And my hand has come to be against the prophets that are visioning untruth and that are divining a lie. In the intimate group of my people they will not continue on, and in the register of the house of Israel they will not be written, and to the soil of Israel they will not come; and you people will have to know that I am the Lord Jehovah, 10 for the reason, yes, for the reason that they have led my people astray, saying, "There is peace!" when there is no peace, and there is one that is building a partition wall, but in vain there are those plastering it with whitewash.'

11 "Say to those plastering with whitewash that it will fall. A flooding downpour will certainly occur, and you, O hailstones, will fall, and a blast of windstorms itself will cause a splitting. 12 And, look! the wall must fall. Will it not be said to you men, 'Where is the coating with which you did the plastering?'

13 "Therefore this is what the Lord Jehovah has said, 'I will also cause a blast of windstorms to burst forth in my rage, and in my anger there will occur a flooding downpour, and in rage there will be hailstones for an extermination. 14 And I will tear down the

wall that you men have plastered with whitewash and bring it into contact with the earth, and its foundation must be exposed. And she will certainly fall, and you must come to an end in the midst of her; and you will have to know that I am Jehovah.'

15 "'And I will bring my rage to its finish upon the wall and upon those plastering it with whitewash, and I shall say to you men: "The wall is no more, and those plastering it are no more, 16 the prophets of Israel that are prophesying to Jerusalem and that are visioning for her a vision of peace, when there is no peace," ' is the utterance of the Lord Jehovah.

17 "And as for you, O son of man, set your face against the daughters of your people who are acting as prophetesses out of their own heart, and prophesy against them. 18 And you must say, 'This is what the Lord Jehovah has said: "Woe to the women sewing bands together upon all elbows and making veils upon the head of every size in order to hunt souls! Are the souls that you women hunt down the ones belonging to my people, and the souls belonging to you the ones that you preserve alive? 19 And will you profane me toward my people for the handfuls of barley and for the morsels of bread, in order to put to death the souls that ought not to die and in order to preserve alive the souls that ought not to live by your lie to my people, the hearers of a lie?" '

20 "Therefore this is what the Lord Jehovah has said, 'Here I am against the bands of you women, with which you are hunting down the souls as though they were flying things, and I will rip them from off your arms and let go the souls that you are hunting down, souls as though they were flying things. 21 And I will rip away your veils and deliver my people out of your hand, and they will no more prove to be in your hand something caught in the hunt; and you will have to know that I am Jehovah. 22 By reason of deject-

ing the heart of a righteous one with falsehood, when I myself had not caused him pain, and for making the hands of a wicked one strong so that he would not turn back from his bad way in order to preserve him alive, 23 therefore untruth you women will not keep on visioning, and divination you will divine no longer; and I will deliver my people out of your hand, and you will have to know that I am Jehovah.' "

14 And men from the elderly ones of Israel proceeded to come to me and sit down before me. 2 Then the word of Jehovah occurred to me, saying: 3 "Son of man, as regards these men, they have brought up their dungy idols upon their heart, and the stumbling block causing their error they have put in front of their faces. Shall I be inquired of at all by them? 4 Therefore speak with them and you must say to them, 'This is what the Lord Jehovah has said: "Any man at all of the house of Israel that brings up his dungy idols upon his heart and that places the very stumbling block causing his error in front of his face and that actually comes to the prophet, I, Jehovah, I will let myself be brought to answer him in the matter according to the multitude of his dungy idols, 5 for the purpose of catching the house of Israel by their heart, because they have withdrawn themselves from me through their dungy idols—all of them." '

6 "Therefore say to the house of Israel, 'This is what the Lord Jehovah has said: "Come back and turn yourselves back from your dungy idols and turn your faces back even from all your detestable things; 7 for any man at all from the house of Israel or from the alien residents that reside as aliens in Israel, that withdraws himself from following me and that brings up his dungy idols upon his heart and that sets the very stumbling block causing his error in front of his face and that actually comes to the prophet to make inquiry for

himself by me, I, Jehovah, I am letting myself be brought to answer him by myself. 8 And I must set my face against that man and place him for a sign and for proverbial sayings, and I must cut him off from the midst of my people; and you people will have to know that I am Jehovah."'

9 "'And as for the prophet, in case he gets fooled and actually speaks a word, I myself, Jehovah, have fooled that prophet; and I will stretch out my hand against him and annihilate him from the midst of my people Israel. 10 And they will have to bear their error. The error of the inquirer will prove to be just the same as the error of the prophet, 11 in order that those of the house of Israel may no more go wandering off from following me and may no more go defiling themselves with all their transgressions. And they must become my people and I myself shall become their God,' is the utterance of the Lord Jehovah."

12 And the word of Jehovah continued to come to me, saying: 13 "Son of man, as regards a land, in case it commits sin against me in acting unfaithfully, I will also stretch out my hand against it and break for it the rods around which ring-shaped loaves are suspended, and I will send upon it famine and cut off from it earthling man and domestic animal." 14 "'And had these three men proved to be in the midst of it, Noah, Daniel and Job, they themselves because of their righteousness would deliver their soul,' is the utterance of the Lord Jehovah."

15 "'Or if I should make injurious wild beasts pass through the land and they actually bereaved it of children and it actually became a desolate waste without anybody passing through on account of the wild beasts, 16 were these three men in the midst of it, as I am alive,' is the utterance of the Lord Jehovah, 'neither sons nor daughters would they deliver; they, only they themselves, would be

delivered and the land itself would become a desolate waste.'"

17 "'Or were it a sword that I should bring upon that land, and should I actually say: "Let a sword itself pass through the land," and should I actually cut off from it earthling man and domestic animal, 18 even were these three men in the midst of it, as I am alive,' is the utterance of the Lord Jehovah, 'they would deliver neither sons nor daughters, but they, only they themselves, would be delivered.'"

19 "'Or were it pestilence that I should send upon that land and should I actually pour out my rage upon it with blood, in order to cut off from it earthling man and domestic animal, 20 even were Noah, Daniel and Job in the midst of it, as I am alive,' is the utterance of the Lord Jehovah, 'neither son nor daughter would they deliver; they themselves because of their righteousness would deliver their soul.'"

21 "For this is what the Lord Jehovah has said, 'So, too, [it will be] when there will be my four injurious acts of judgment—sword and famine and injurious wild beast and pestilence—that I shall actually send upon Jerusalem in order to cut off from it earthling man and domestic animal. 22 But, look! there will certainly be left remaining in it an escaped company, those being brought forth. Sons and daughters, here they are! They are going forth to you people, and you will have to see their way and their dealings. And you will certainly be comforted over the calamity that I shall have brought upon Jerusalem, even all that I shall have brought upon her.'"

23 "'And they will certainly comfort you people when you see their way and their dealings; and you will have to know that it was not without cause that I shall have done all that I must do against her,' is the utterance of the Lord Jehovah."

15 And the word of Jehovah continued to occur to me, saying: 2 "Son of man, in what

way does the vine tree happen to be different from every other tree, the shoot, that has come to be among the trees of the forest? 3 Is there taken from it a pole with which to do some work? Or do people take from it a peg on which to hang any kind of utensil? 4 Look! Into the fire is where it must be put for fuel. Both ends of it the fire certainly devours, and the very middle of it does get scorched. Is it fit for any work? 5 Look! When it happens to be intact, it is not used for any work. How much less so, when fire itself has devoured it and it gets scorched, can it actually be used for any further work!"

6 "Therefore this is what the Lord Jehovah has said, 'Just like the vine tree among the trees of the forest, that I have given to the fire as fuel, so I have given the inhabitants of Jerusalem. 7 And I have set my face against them. Out of the fire they have gone forth, but the fire itself will devour them. And you people will have to know that I am Jehovah, when I direct my face against them.'"

8 "'And I will make the land a desolate waste, for the reason that they have acted unfaithfully,' is the utterance of the Lord Jehovah."

16 And the word of Jehovah came further to me, saying: 2 "Son of man, make known to Jerusalem her detestable things. 3 And you must say, 'This is what the Lord Jehovah has said to Jerusalem: "Your origin and your birth were from the land of the Ca·naan·ite. Your father was the Am'or·ite, and your mother was a Hit'tite. 4 And as regards your birth, on the day of your being born your navel string had not been cut, and in water you had not been washed for cleansing, and with salt you had not at all been rubbed, and by no means had you been swaddled. 5 No eye felt sorry for you to do for you one of these things in compassion upon you, but you were thrown upon the surface of the field because there was an abhorring of your soul in the day of your being born.

6 "'"And I came passing along by you and got to see you kicking about in your blood, and I proceeded to say to you in your blood, 'Keep living!' yes, to say to you in your blood, 'Keep living!' 7 A very big multitude like the sprouting of the field is what I made you so that you would grow big and become great and come in with the finest ornament. The two breasts themselves were firmly developed, and your own hair grew luxuriantly, when you had been naked and nude."'

8 "'And I came passing along by you and got to see you, and look! your time was the time for love's expressions. So I proceeded to spread my skirt over you and to cover your nudeness and to make a sworn statement to you and enter into a covenant with you,' is the utterance of the Lord Jehovah, 'and so you became mine. 9 Furthermore, I washed you with water and rinsed away your blood from off you and greased you with oil. 10 And I went on to clothe you with an embroidered garment and to shoe you with sealskin and to wrap you in fine linen and to cover you with costly material. 11 And I went on to deck you with ornaments and to put bracelets upon your hands and a necklace about your throat. 12 Furthermore, I put a nose ring in your nostril and earrings on your ears and a beautiful crown on your head. 13 And you kept decking yourself with gold and silver, and your attire was fine linen and costly material and an embroidered garment. Fine flour and honey and oil were what you ate, and you grew to be very, very pretty, and gradually you became fit for royal position.'"

14 "'And for you a name began to go forth among the nations because of your prettiness, for it was perfect because of my splendor that I placed upon you,' is the utterance of the Lord Jehovah."

15 " 'But you began to trust in your prettiness and become a prostitute on account of your name and to pour out your acts of prostitution on every passer-by; his it came to be. 16 And you proceeded to take some of your garments and make for yourself high places of varied colors and you would prostitute yourself on them —such things are not coming in, and it should not happen. 17 And you would take your beautiful articles from my gold and from my silver that I had given to you and you would make for yourself images of a male and prostitute yourself with them. 18 And you would take your embroidered garments and cover them; and my oil and my incense you would actually put before them. 19 And my bread that I had given to you—fine flour and oil and honey that I had had you eat—you also actually put it before them as a restful odor, and it continued to occur,' is the utterance of the Lord Jehovah."

20 " 'And you would take your sons and your daughters whom you had borne to me, and you would sacrifice these to them to be devoured—is that not enough of your acts of prostitution? 21 And you would slaughter my sons, and by making them pass through [the fire] you would give these to them. 22 And in all your detestable things and your acts of prostitution you did not remember the days of your youth when you happened to be naked and nude; kicking about in your blood you happened to be. 23 So it came about after all your badness ("woe, woe to you," is the utterance of the Lord Jehovah) 24 that you went building for yourself a mound and making for yourself a height in every public square. 25 At every head of the way you built your height and you began to make your prettiness something detestable and sprawl out your feet to every passer-by and multiply your acts of prostitution. 26 And you went prostituting yourself to the sons of Egypt, your neighbors great of flesh, and you continued making your prostitution abound in order to offend me. 27 And, look! I shall certainly stretch out my hand against you and I shall diminish your allowance and give you to the soul[ful desire] of the women hating you, the daughters of the Phi·lis'tines, the women humiliated on account of your way as regards loose conduct.

28 " 'And you went on to prostitute yourself to the sons of As·syr'i·a because there was no satisfying of you, and you kept prostituting yourself with them and also did not get satisfaction. 29 So you kept making your prostitution abound toward the land of Ca'naan, toward the Chal·de'ans; and even in this you did not get satisfaction. 30 O how I am filled up with rage against you,' is the utterance of the Lord Jehovah, 'by your doing all these things, the work of a woman, a domineering prostitute! 31 When you built your mound at the head of every way and you made your own height in every public square, yet you became unlike a prostitute in disdaining hire. 32 In the case of the wife that commits adultery, she takes strangers instead of her own husband. 33 To all prostitutes they are accustomed to give a present, but you —you have given your presents to all those passionately loving you, and you offer a bribe to them to come in to you from all around in your acts of prostitution. 34 And in your case the opposite thing takes place from that of other women in your acts of prostitution, and after your style no prostitution has been committed, even in your giving hire when no hire has been given to you, and so it occurs in the opposite way.'

35 "Therefore, O prostitute, hear the word of Jehovah. 36 This is what the Lord Jehovah has said, 'For the reason that your lustfulness has been poured out and your private parts are uncovered in your acts of prostitution toward those passionately loving you and toward all your detestable dungy idols, even with the blood of your sons whom

you gave to them, 37 therefore here I am collecting together all those passionately loving you toward whom you were pleasurable and all those whom you loved along with all those whom you hated, and I will collect them together against you from all around and uncover your private parts to them, and they must see all your private parts.

38 "'And I will judge you with the judgments of adulteresses and women shedding blood, and I will give you the blood of rage and jealousy. 39 And I will give you into their hand, and they will certainly tear down your mound and your heights will certainly be pulled down, and they must strip you of your garments and take your beautiful articles and leave you behind naked and nude. 40 And they must bring up against you a congregation and pelt you with stones and slaughter you with their swords. 41 And they must burn your houses with fire and execute in you acts of judgment before the eyes of many women; and I will cause you to cease from [being] a prostitute, and also no more hire will you give. 42 And I will bring my rage to its rest in you, and my jealousy must turn away from you; and I will stay quiet and I shall no more feel offended.'

43 "'For the reason that you did not remember the days of your youth and you would cause me agitation because of all these things, even here I also, for my part, will put your own way upon [your] very head,' is the utterance of the Lord Jehovah, 'and you will certainly not carry on any loose conduct alongside all your detestable things.

44 "'Look! Everyone using a proverb against you will use the proverb, saying: "Like mother is her daughter!" 45 You are the daughter of your mother, one abhorring her husband and her sons. And you are the sister of your sisters, who abhorred their husbands and their sons. The mother

of YOU women was a Hit'tite, and YOUR father was an Am'or·ite.'"

46 "'And your older sister is Sa·mar'i·a herself with her dependent towns, who is dwelling on your left, and your sister younger than you, who is dwelling on your right, is Sod'om with her dependent towns. 47 And it was not in their ways that you walked, nor according to their detestable things that you did. In a very little while you even began to act more ruinously than they did in all your ways. 48 As I am alive,' is the utterance of the Lord Jehovah, 'Sod'om your sister, she with her dependent towns, has not done according to what you did, you and your dependent towns. 49 Look! This is what proved to be the error of Sod'om your sister: Pride, sufficiency of bread and the carefreeness of keeping undisturbed were what happened to belong to her and her dependent towns, and the hand of the afflicted one and the poor one she did not strengthen. 50 And they continued to be haughty and to carry on a detestable thing before me, and I finally removed them, just as I saw [fit].

51 "'And as for Sa·mar'i·a, she has not sinned even up to half of your sins, but you kept making your detestable things abound more than they did, so that you made your sisters appear righteous because of all your detestable things that you carried on. 52 You also, bear your humiliation when you must argue in favor of your sisters. Because of your sins in which you acted more detestably than they did, they are more righteous than you. And you also, be ashamed and bear your humiliation in that you make your sisters appear righteous.'

53 "'And I will gather their captive ones, the captive ones of Sod'om and of her dependent towns, and the captive ones of Sa·mar'i·a and of her dependent towns; I will also gather your captive ones in the midst of them, 54 in order that you may bear your humiliation; and you must feel humiliated owing to all that you have done, in that you comforted them. 55 And your

own sisters, Sod'om and her dependent towns, will return to their former state, and Sa·mar'i·a and her dependent towns will return to their former state, and you yourself and your own dependent towns will return to YOUR former state. 56 And Sod'om your sister did not prove to be anything worth hearing about from your mouth in the day of your pride, 57 before your own badness got to be exposed, just as at the time of the reproach of the daughters of Syria and of all round about her, the daughters of the Phi·lis'tines, those treating you with scorn on all sides. 58 Your loose conduct and your detestable things, you yourself must bear them,' is the utterance of Jehovah."

59 "For this is what the Lord Jehovah has said, 'I also must do with you just as you have done, because you despised the oath in breaking [my] covenant. 60 And I, I myself, must remember my covenant with you in the days of your youth, and I must establish for you an indefinitely lasting covenant. 61 And you will certainly remember your ways and feel humiliated when you receive your sisters, the ones older than you as well as the ones younger than you, and I shall certainly give them to you as daughters, but not owing to your covenant.'

62 "'And I, I myself, will establish my covenant with you; and you will have to know that I am Jehovah, 63 in order that you may remember and actually be ashamed and you may no more come to have any reason to open [your] mouth because of your humiliation, when I make an atonement for you for all that you have done,' is the utterance of the Lord Jehovah."

17 And the word of Jehovah continued to occur to me, saying: 2 "Son of man, propound a riddle and compose a proverbial saying toward the house of Israel. 3 And you must say, 'This is what the Lord Jehovah has said: "The great eagle, having great wings, with long pinions, full of plumage, which had

color variety, came to Leb'a·non and proceeded to take the treetop of the cedar. 4 He plucked off the very top of its young shoots and came bringing it to the land of Ca'naan; in a city of traders he placed it. 5 Furthermore, he took some of the seed of the land and put it in a field for seed. As a willow by vast waters, as a willow tree he placed it. 6 And it began to sprout and gradually became a luxuriantly growing vine low in height, inclined to turn its foliage inward; and as for its roots, they gradually came to be under it. And it finally became a vine and produced shoots and sent forth branches.

7 "'"And there came to be another great eagle, having great wings, and having large pinions, and, look! this very vine stretched its roots hungrily toward him. And its foliage it thrust out to him in order [for him] to irrigate it, away from the garden beds where it was planted. 8 Into a good field, by vast waters, it was already transplanted, in order to produce boughs and to bear fruit, to become a majestic vine."'

9 "Say, 'This is what the Lord Jehovah has said: "Will it have success? Will not someone tear out its very roots and make its very fruit scaly? And must [not] all its freshly plucked sprouts become dry? It will become dry. Neither by a great arm nor by a multitudinous people will it have to be lifted up from its roots. 10 And, look! although transplanted, will it have success? Will it not dry up completely, even as when the east wind touches it? In the garden beds of its sprout it will dry up."'"

11 And the word of Jehovah continued to occur to me, saying: 12 "Say, please, to the rebellious house, 'Do YOU people actually not know what these things mean?' Say, 'Look! The king of Babylon came to Jerusalem and proceeded to take its king and its princes and bring them to himself at Babylon. 13 Furthermore, he took one of the royal seed and concluded a cove-

nant with him and brought him into an oath; and the foremost men of the land he took away, 14 in order that the kingdom might become low, unable to lift itself up, that by keeping his covenant it might stand. 15 But he finally rebelled against him in sending his messengers to Egypt, [for it] to give him horses and a multitudinous people. Will he have success? Will he escape, he who is doing these things, and who has broken a covenant? And will he actually escape?'

16 " ' "As I am alive," ' is the utterance of the Lord Jehovah, "in the place of the king who put in as king the one that despised his oath and that broke his covenant, with him in the midst of Babylon he will die. 17 And by a great military force and by a multitudinous congregation Phar'aoh will not make him effective in the war, by throwing up a siege rampart and by building a siege wall, in order to cut off many souls. 18 And he has despised an oath in breaking a covenant, and, look! he had given his hand and has done even all these things. He will not make his escape." '

19 " 'Therefore this is what the Lord Jehovah has said: "As I am alive, surely my oath that he has despised and my covenant that he has broken—I will even bring it upon his head. 20 And I will spread over him my net, and he will certainly be caught in my hunting net; and I will bring him to Babylon and put myself on judgment with him there respecting his unfaithfulness with which he acted against me. 21 And as regards all the fugitives of his in all his bands, by the sword they will fall, and the ones left remaining will be spread abroad even to every wind. And YOU people will have to know that I myself, Jehovah, have spoken [it]." '

22 " 'This is what the Lord Jehovah has said: "I myself will also take and put some of the lofty treetop of the cedar; from the top of its twigs I shall pluck off a tender one and I will myself transplant [it] upon a high and lofty mountain. 23 On the mountain of the height of Israel I shall transplant it, and it will certainly bear boughs and produce fruit and become a majestic cedar. And under it there will actually reside all the birds of every wing; in the shadow of its foliage they will reside. 24 And all the trees of the field will have to know that I myself, Jehovah, have abased the high tree, have put on high the low tree, have dried up the still-moist tree and have made the dry tree blossom. I myself, Jehovah, have spoken and have done [it]." ' "

18 And the word of Jehovah continued to occur to me, saying: 2 "What does it mean to YOU people that YOU are expressing this proverbial saying on the soil of Israel, saying, 'Fathers are the ones that eat unripe grapes, but it is the teeth of the sons that get set on edge'?

3 " 'As I am alive,' is the utterance of the Lord Jehovah, 'it will no more continue to be YOURS to express this proverbial saying in Israel. 4 Look! All the souls—to me they belong. As the soul of the father so likewise the soul of the son—to me they belong. The soul that is sinning—it itself will die.

5 " 'And as regards a man, in case he happens to be righteous and he has executed justice and righteousness; 6 on the mountains he did not eat and his eyes he did not raise to the dungy idols of the house of Israel, and his companion's wife he did not defile and to a woman in her impurity he would not go near; 7 and no man would he maltreat; the pledge that he took for indebtedness, he would return; nothing would he wrest away in robbery; to the hungry one he would give his own bread and the naked one he would cover with a garment; 8 nothing would he give on interest and no usury would he take; from injustice he would draw back his hand; true justice he would execute between man and man; 9 in my statutes he kept walking and my judicial

decisions he kept in order to execute truth, he is righteous. He will positively keep living,' is the utterance of the Lord Jehovah.

10 "'And [if] one has become father to a son who is a robber, a shedder of blood, who has done the like of one of these things 11 (but he himself has done none of these very things); in case he has eaten also upon the mountains, and his companion's wife he has defiled; 12 the afflicted and poor one he has maltreated; things he has wrested away in robbery, a pledged thing he would not return; and to the dungy idols he lifted up his eyes, a detestable thing is what he has done. 13 On usury he has given, and interest he has taken, and he positively will not keep living. All these detestable things he has done. He will positively be put to death. On him his own blood will come to be.

14 "'And, look! one has become father to a son, who keeps seeing all the sins of his father that he has done, and he sees and does not do things like them. 15 On the mountains he has not eaten, and his eyes he has not lifted up to the dungy idols of the house of Israel; his companion's wife he has not defiled; 16 and no man has he maltreated, no pledge has he seized, and nothing has he taken in robbery; to the hungry one he has given his own bread, and the naked one he has covered with a garment; 17 from the afflicted one he has drawn back his hand; no usury and interest has he taken; my judicial decisions he has carried out; in my statutes he has walked; he himself will not die because of the error of his father. He will positively keep living. 18 As for his father, because he committed outright defrauding, wrested something away in robbery of a brother, and whatever is not good he has done in the midst of his peoples, look! then he must die for his error.

19 "'And YOU people will certainly say: "Why is it that the son does not have to bear anything because of the error of the father?" Now as regards the son, justice and righteousness he has executed, all the statutes of mine he has kept and he keeps doing them. He will positively keep living. 20 The soul that is sinning—it itself will die. A son himself will bear nothing because of the error of the father, and a father himself will bear nothing because of the error of the son. Upon his own self the very righteousness of the righteous one will come to be, and upon his own self the very wickedness of a wicked one will come to be.

21 "'Now as regards someone wicked, in case he should turn back from all his sins that he has committed and he should actually keep all my statutes and execute justice and righteousness, he will positively keep living. He will not die. 22 All his transgressions that he has committed—they will not be remembered against him. For his righteousness that he has done he will keep living.'

23 "'Do I take any delight at all in the death of someone wicked,' is the utterance of the Lord Jehovah, '[and] not in that he should turn back from his ways and actually keep living?'

24 "'Now when someone righteous turns back from his righteousness and actually does injustice; according to all the detestable things that the wicked one has done he keeps doing and he is living, none of all his righteous acts that he has done will be remembered. For his unfaithfulness that he has committed and for his sin with which he has sinned, for them he will die.

25 "'And YOU people will certainly say: "The way of Jehovah is not adjusted right." Hear, please, O house of Israel. Is not my own way adjusted right? Are not the ways of YOU people not adjusted right?

26 "'When someone righteous turns back from his righteousness and he actually does injustice and dies on account of them, for his

injustice that he has done he will die.

27 "'And when someone wicked turns back from his wickedness that he has committed and proceeds to execute justice and righteousness, he is the one that will preserve his own soul alive. 28 When he sees and he turns back from all his transgressions that he has done, he will positively keep living. He will not die.

29 "'And the house of Israel will certainly say: "The way of Jehovah is not adjusted right." As for my ways, are they not adjusted right, O house of Israel? Are not the ways of YOU people the ones that are not adjusted right?'

30 "'Therefore each one according to his ways is how I shall judge YOU, O house of Israel,' is the utterance of the Lord Jehovah. 'Turn back, yes, cause a turning back from all YOUR transgressions, and let nothing prove to be for YOU people a stumbling block causing error. 31 Throw off from yourselves all YOUR transgressions in which YOU have transgressed and make for yourselves a new heart and a new spirit, for why should YOU die, O house of Israel?'

32 "'For I do not take any delight in the death of someone dying,' is the utterance of the Lord Jehovah. 'So cause a turning back and keep living, O YOU people.'"

19 "And as for you, raise a dirge concerning the chieftains of Israel, 2 and you must say, 'What was your mother? A lioness among lions. She lay down in among maned young lions. She reared her cubs.

3 "'And gradually she brought up one of her cubs. A maned young lion is what he became, and he began to learn how to tear apart prey. He devoured even earthling man. 4 And nations kept hearing about him. In their pit he was caught, and they proceeded to bring him by means of hooks to the land of Egypt.

5 "'When she got to see that she had waited [and] her hope had perished, then she took another of her cubs. As a maned young lion she put him forth. 6 And he began to walk about in the midst of lions. A maned young lion is what he became. And he gradually learned how to tear apart prey. He devoured even earthling man. 7 And he got to know his dwelling towers, and he devastated even their cities, so that the land was laid desolate and he filled it with the sound of his roaring. 8 And nations all around from the jurisdictional districts began to set against him and got to spread over him their net. In their pit he was caught. 9 Finally they put him in the cage by means of hooks and brought him to the king of Babylon. They got to bring him by means of hunting nets, in order that his voice might no more be heard on the mountains of Israel.

10 "'Your mother was like a vine in your blood, planted by waters. A bearer of fruit and full of branches she became because of abundant water. 11 And they came to be for her strong rods, meant for the scepters of rulers. And its height gradually became tall up among branches, and it got to be visible because of its tallness, because of the abundance of its foliage. 12 But she was finally uprooted in fury. To the earth she was thrown, and there was an east wind that dried up her fruit. Her strong rod was torn off and became dry. Fire itself devoured it. 13 And now she is planted in the wilderness, in a waterless and thirsty land. 14 And fire proceeded to come forth from [her] rod. It devoured her very shoots, her very fruit, and there proved to be in her no strong rod, no scepter for ruling.

"'That is a dirge, and it will become a dirge.'"

20 Now it came about in the seventh year, in the fifth [month], on the tenth [day] of the month, [that] men from the elderly ones of Israel came in to inquire of Jehovah, and they proceeded to sit down before me. 2 Then the word of Jehovah occurred to me, saying: 3 "Son of man, speak with the elderly men of Israel, and you must say to them, 'This is what the Lord Jehovah has said: "Is it in order to inquire of me that YOU men are coming? 'As I am alive, I will not be inquired of by YOU,' is the utterance of the Lord Jehovah."'

4 "Will you judge them? Will you judge [them], O son of man? Cause them to know the detestable things of their forefathers. 5 And you must say to them, 'This is what the Lord Jehovah has said: "In the day of my choosing Israel, I also proceeded to lift up my hand [in an oath] to the seed of the house of Jacob and to make myself known to them in the land of Egypt. Yes, I proceeded to lift up my hand [in an oath] to them, saying, 'I am Jehovah YOUR God.' 6 In that day I lifted up my hand [in an oath] to them to bring them forth from the land of Egypt to a land that I had spied out for them, one flowing with milk and honey. It was the decoration of all the lands. 7 And I went on to say to them, 'Throw away, each one of YOU, the disgusting things of his eyes, and with the dungy idols of Egypt do not defile yourselves. I am Jehovah YOUR God.'

8 "'"And they began to rebel against me, and they did not consent to listen to me. The disgusting things of their eyes they did not individually throw away, and the dungy idols of Egypt they did not leave, so that I promised to pour out my rage upon them, in order to bring my anger to its finish upon them in the midst of the land of Egypt. 9 And I went acting for the sake of my own name that [it] might not be profaned before the eyes of the nations in among whom they were, because I had made myself known to them before their eyes on bringing them forth from the land of Egypt. 10 So I brought them forth from the land of Egypt and brought them into the wilderness.

11 "'"And I proceeded to give them my statutes; and my judicial decisions I made known to them, in order that the man who keeps doing them might also keep living by them. 12 And my sabbaths I also gave to them, to become a sign between me and them, in order [for them] to know that I am Jehovah who is sanctifying them.

13 "'"But they, the house of Israel, rebelled against me in the wilderness. In my statutes they did not walk, and my judicial decisions they rejected, which, should the man keep doing, he will also keep living by them. And my sabbaths they profaned very much, so that I promised to pour out my fury upon them in the wilderness, in order to exterminate them. 14 But I acted for the sake of my own name that [it] might not be profaned before the eyes of the nations, before whose eyes I had brought them forth. 15 And I myself also lifted up my hand [in an oath] to them in the wilderness, not to bring them into the land that I had given, one flowing with milk and honey, (it is the decoration of all the lands,) 16 for the reason that they rejected my own judicial decisions; and as regards my statutes, they did not walk in them, and my sabbaths they profaned, because it was after their dungy idols that their heart was going.

17 "'"And my eye began to feel sorry for them [to keep me] from bringing them to ruin, and I did not make an extermination of them in the wilderness. 18 And I proceeded to say to their sons in the wilderness, 'In the regulations of YOUR forefathers do not YOU walk, and their judgments do not YOU keep, and with their dungy idols do not YOU defile yourselves. 19 I am Jehovah YOUR God. Walk in my own statutes, and keep my own judicial decisions and do them. 20 And sanctify my own sabbaths, and they must serve as a sign between me and YOU, [for YOU] to know that I am Jehovah YOUR God.'

21 "'"And the sons began to rebel against me. In my statutes they did not walk, and my judicial decisions they did not keep by doing

them, which, should the man keep doing, he will also keep living by them. My sabbaths they profaned. So I promised to pour out my rage upon them, in order to bring my anger to its finish upon them in the wilderness. 22 And I drew back my hand and went acting for the sake of my own name, that [it] should not be profaned before the eyes of the nations, before whose eyes I had brought them out. 23 Also, I myself lifted up my hand [in an oath] to them in the wilderness, to scatter them among the nations and to disperse them among the lands, 24 for the reason that they did not carry out my own judicial decisions and they rejected my own statutes and they profaned my own sabbaths, and it was after the dungy idols of their forefathers that their eyes proved to be. 25 And I myself also let them have regulations that were not good and judicial decisions by which they could not keep living. 26 And I would let them become defiled by their gifts when [they] made every child opening the womb pass through [the fire], in order that I might make them desolate, in order that they might know that I am Jehovah." '

27 "Therefore speak to the house of Israel, O son of man, and you must say to them, 'This is what the Lord Jehovah has said: "Yet in this respect, YOUR forefathers spoke abusively of me, in their acting against me with unfaithfulness. 28 And I proceeded to bring them into the land that I had lifted up my hand [in an oath] to give them. When they got to see every exalted hill and every branchy tree, then they began sacrificing there their sacrifices and giving there their offensive offering, and presenting there their restful odors and pouring out there their drink offerings. 29 So I said to them, 'What does the high place mean to which YOU are coming, that its name should be called a High Place down to this day?' " '

30 "Therefore say to the house of Israel, 'This is what the Lord Je-hovah has said: "In the way of YOUR forefathers are YOU people defiling yourselves, and after their disgusting things are YOU going in immoral intercourse? 31 And in lifting up YOUR gifts by making YOUR sons pass through the fire, are YOU defiling yourselves for all YOUR dungy idols down till today? At the same time shall I myself be inquired of by YOU people, O house of Israel?" '

" 'As I am alive,' is the utterance of the Lord Jehovah, 'I will not be inquired of by YOU. 32 And that which is coming up into YOUR spirit will itself positively not happen, in that YOU are saying: "Let us become like the nations, like the families of the lands, in ministering to wood and stone." ' "

33 " 'As I am alive,' is the utter-ance of the Lord Jehovah, 'it will be with a strong hand and with a stretched-out arm and with out-poured rage that I will rule as king over YOU people. 34 And I will bring YOU forth from the peoples, and I will collect YOU together out of the lands to which YOU have been scattered with a strong hand and with a stretched-out arm and with outpoured rage. 35 And I will bring YOU into the wilderness of the peoples and put myself on judgment with YOU there face to face.

36 " 'Just as I put myself on judgment with YOUR forefathers in the wilderness of the land of Egypt, so I shall put myself on judgment with YOU,' is the utterance of the Lord Jehovah. 37 'And I will make YOU pass under the rod and bring YOU into the bond of the covenant. 38 And I will clean out from YOU the revolters and the transgressors, for out of the land of their alien residence I shall bring them forth, but onto the soil of Israel they will not come; and YOU people will have to know that I am Jehovah.'

39 "And YOU, O house of Israel, this is what the Lord Jehovah has said, 'Go serve each one of YOU his own dungy idols. And after-ward if YOU are not listening to me,

then my holy name you will no more profane by your gifts and by your dungy idols.'

40 " 'For in my holy mountain, in the mountain of the height of Israel,' is the utterance of the Lord Jehovah, 'there is where they, the whole house of Israel in its entirety, will serve me, in the land. There I shall take pleasure in them, and there I shall require your contributions and the first fruits of your presentations in all your holy things. 41 Because of the restful odor I shall take pleasure in you, when I bring you forth from the peoples and I actually collect you together from the lands to which you have been scattered, and I will be sanctified in you before the eyes of the nations.'

42 " 'And you people will have to know that I am Jehovah, when I bring you onto the soil of Israel, into the land that I lifted up my hand [in an oath] to give to your forefathers. 43 And you will certainly remember there your ways and all your dealings by which you defiled yourselves, and you will actually feel a loathing at your own faces because of all your bad things that you did. 44 And you will have to know that I am Jehovah when I take action with you for the sake of my name, not according to your bad ways or according to your corrupted dealings, O house of Israel,' is the utterance of the Lord Jehovah."

45 And the word of Jehovah continued to occur to me, saying: 46 "Son of man, set your face in the direction of the southern quarter and drip [words] to the south, and prophesy to the forest of the field of [the] south. 47 And you must say to the forest of the south, 'Hear the word of Jehovah. This is what the Lord Jehovah has said: "Here I am setting a fire ablaze against you, and it must devour in you every still-moist tree and every dry tree. The kindling flame will not be extinguished, and by it all faces must be scorched from [the] south to the north. 48 And all those of flesh must see that

I myself, Jehovah, have set it afire, so that it will not be extinguished." ' "

49 And I proceeded to say: "Alas, O Lord Jehovah! They are saying respecting me, 'Is he not composing proverbial sayings?' "

21 And the word of Jehovah continued to occur to me, saying: 2 "Son of man, set your face toward Jerusalem and drip [words] toward the holy places, and prophesy against the soil of Israel. 3 And you must say to the soil of Israel, 'This is what Jehovah has said: "Here I am against you, and I will bring forth my sword out of its sheath and cut off from you righteous one and wicked one. 4 In order that I may actually cut off from you righteous one and wicked one, therefore my sword will go forth from its sheath against all flesh from south to north. 5 And all those of flesh will have to know that I myself, Jehovah, have brought forth my sword from its sheath. No more will it go back." '

6 "And as for you, O son of man, sigh with shaking hips. Even with bitterness you should sigh before their eyes. 7 And it must occur that, in case they say to you, 'On account of what are you sighing?' you must say, 'At a report.' For it will certainly come, and every heart must melt and all hands must drop down and every spirit must become dejected and all knees themselves will drip with water. 'Look! It will certainly come and be brought to occur,' is the utterance of the Lord Jehovah."

8 And the word of Jehovah continued to occur to me, saying: 9 "Son of man, prophesy, and you must say, 'This is what Jehovah has said: "Say, 'A sword, a sword! It has been sharpened, and it is also polished. 10 For the purpose of organizing a slaughter it has been sharpened; for the purpose of its getting a glitter it has been polished.' " '

"Or shall we exult?"

" 'Is it rejecting the scepter of my own son, as [it does] every tree?

11 "'And one gives it to be polished, in order to wield [it] with the hand. It—a sword has been sharpened, and it—it has been polished, in order to give it into the hand of a killer.

12 "'Cry out and howl, O son of man, for it itself has come to be against my people; it is against all the chieftains of Israel. The very ones hurled to the sword have come to be with my people. Therefore make a slap on [the] thigh. **13** For an extermination has been made, and what [of it] if it is rejecting also the scepter? This will not continue existing,' is the utterance of the Lord Jehovah.

14 "And you, O son of man— prophesy, and strike palm against palm, and 'A sword!' should be repeated for three times. The sword of the slain ones it is. It is the sword of someone slain who is great, which is making an encirclement of them. **15** In order for the heart to melt and [in order] to multiply those who are overthrown at all their gates, I will make a slaughter by the sword. Alas, it is made for a glittering, polished for a slaughter! **16** Show yourself sharp; go to the right! Set your position; go to the left! To wherever your face is directed! **17** And I myself also shall strike my one palm against my other palm, and I will bring my rage to its rest. I myself, Jehovah, have spoken."

18 And the word of Jehovah continued to occur to me, saying: **19** "And as for you, O son of man, set for yourself two ways for the sword of the king of Babylon to enter. From the one land both of them should go forth, and an [index] hand should be cut out; at the head of the way to the city it should be cut out. **20** A way you should set for [the] sword to enter against Rab'bah of the sons of Am'mon, and [one] against Judah, against Jerusalem fortified. **21** For the king of Babylon stood still at the crossways, at the head of the two ways, in order to resort to divination. He has shaken the ar-

rows. He has asked by means of the teraphim; he has looked into the liver. **22** In his right hand the divination proved to be for Jerusalem, to set battering-rams, to open one's mouth for a slaying, to raise the sound in an alarm signal, to set battering-rams against gates, to throw up a siege rampart, to build a siege wall. **23** And it has become to them like an untrue divination in their eyes— those who are sworn with oaths to them; and he is calling error to remembrance, in order [for them] to be caught.

24 "Therefore this is what the Lord Jehovah has said, 'By reason of YOUR causing YOUR error to be remembered by YOUR transgressions being uncovered, in order that YOUR sins may be seen according to all YOUR dealings, by reason of YOUR being called to remembrance YOU people will be seized even by the hand.'

25 "And as for you, O deadly wounded, wicked chieftain of Israel, whose day has come in the time of the error of [the] end, **26** this is what the Lord Jehovah has said, 'Remove the turban, and lift off the crown. This will not be the same. Put on high even what is low, and bring low even the high one. **27** A ruin, a ruin, a ruin I shall make it. As for this also, it will certainly become no [one's] until he comes who has the legal right, and I must give [it] to him.'

28 "And you, O son of man, prophesy, and you must say, 'This is what the Lord Jehovah has said concerning the sons of Am'mon and concerning the reproach from them.' And you must say, 'A sword, a sword drawn for a slaughter, polished to cause [it] to devour, in order to glitter, **29** because of [their] beholding for you an unreality, because of [their] divining for you a lie, in order to put you on the necks of the slain ones, the wicked men whose day has come in the time of the error of [the] end. **30** Return [it] to its sheath. In the place that you were created, in the land of your origin, I shall judge you. 31 And I will pour out upon you my denunciation. With the fire of my fury I shall blow upon you, and I will give you into the hand of men who are unreasoning, the craftsmen of ruination. 32 For the fire you will become fuel. Your own blood will prove to be in the midst of the land. You will not be remembered, for I myself, Jehovah, have spoken.'"

22 And the word of Jehovah continued to occur to me, saying: 2 "And as for you, O son of man, will you judge, will you judge the bloodguilty city and certainly cause her to know all her detestable things? 3 And you must say, 'This is what the Lord Jehovah has said: "O city that is shedding blood in her midst till her time comes, and that has made dungy idols within herself in order to become unclean, 4 by your blood that you have shed you have become guilty, and by your dungy idols that you have made you have become unclean. And you bring your days near, and you will come to your years. That is why I must make you an object of reproach to the nations and of jeering to all the lands. 5 The [lands] nearby and those far away from you will jeer you, O you unclean in name, abounding in confusion. 6 Look! The chieftains of Israel have proved to be in you, each one [given over] to his arm for the purpose of shedding blood. 7 Father and mother they have treated with contempt in you. Toward the alien resident they have acted with defrauding in the midst of you. Fatherless boy and widow they have maltreated in you." '"

8 " 'My holy places you have despised, and my sabbaths you have profaned. 9 Outright slanderers have proved to be in you, for the purpose of shedding blood; and on the mountains they have eaten in you. Loose conduct they have carried on in the midst of you. 10 The nakedness of a father they have uncovered in you; a woman unclean in [her] menstruation they

have humiliated in you. 11 And with the wife of his companion a man has done a detestable thing, and his own daughter-in-law a man has defiled with loose conduct; and his sister, the daughter of his own father, a man has humiliated in you. 12 A bribe they have taken in you for the purpose of shedding blood. Interest and usury you have taken, and you violently keep making gain of your companions with defrauding, and me you have forgotten,' is the utterance of the Lord Jehovah.

13 " 'And, look! I have struck my hand at your unjust gain that you have made, and over your acts of bloodshed that have proved to be in the midst of you. 14 Will your heart keep enduring or your hands furnish strength in the days when I am taking action toward you? I myself, Jehovah, have spoken and I will take action. 15 And I will scatter you among the nations and disperse you among the lands, and I will destroy your uncleanness out of you. 16 And you will certainly be profaned within yourself before the eyes of [the] nations, and you will have to know that I am Jehovah.' "

17 And the word of Jehovah continued to come to me, saying: 18 "Son of man, to me those of the house of Israel have become as scummy dross. All of them are copper and tin and iron and lead in the midst of a furnace. Much scummy dross, [that of] silver, they have become.

19 "Therefore this is what the Lord Jehovah has said, 'For the reason that all of you have become as much scummy dross, therefore here I am collecting you together into the midst of Jerusalem. 20 As in collecting silver and copper and iron and lead and tin into the midst of a furnace, in order to blow upon it with fire to cause a liquifying, so I shall collect [them] together in my anger and in my rage, and I will blow and cause you people to liquify. 21 And I will bring you together and blow

upon YOU with the fire of my fury, and YOU must be liquified in the midst of her. 22 As in the liquifying of silver in the midst of a furnace, so YOU people will be liquified in the midst of her; and YOU will have to know that I myself, Jehovah, have poured out my rage upon YOU.'"

23 And the word of Jehovah continued to come to me, saying: 24 "Son of man, say to her, 'You are a land not being cleansed, one not rained down upon in the day of denunciation. 25 There is a conspiracy of her prophets in the midst of her, like the roaring lion, tearing prey. A soul they actually devour. Treasure and precious things they keep taking. Her widows they have multiplied in the midst of her. 26 Her priests themselves have done violence to my law, and they keep profaning my holy places. Between the holy thing and the common they have made no distinction, and between the unclean thing and the clean they have made nothing known, and from my sabbaths they have hidden their eyes, and I am profaned in the midst of them. 27 Her princes in the midst of her are like wolves tearing prey in shedding blood, in destroying souls for the purpose of making unjust gain. 28 And her prophets have plastered for them with whitewash, visioning an unreality and divining for them a lie, saying: "This is what the Lord Jehovah has said," when Jehovah himself has not spoken. 29 The people of the land themselves have carried on a scheme of defrauding and have done a tearing away in robbery, and the afflicted one and the poor one they have maltreated, and the alien resident they have defrauded without justice.'

30 "'And I kept looking for a man from among them who would be repairing the stone wall and standing in the gap before me in behalf of the land, in order [for me] not to bring it to ruin; and I found no one. 31 So I shall pour out my denunciation upon them. With the fire of my fury I will exterminate them. Their way I will bring upon their own head,' is the utterance of the Lord Jehovah."

23 And the word of Jehovah proceeded to come to me, saying: 2 "Son of man, two women, the daughters of one mother, there happened to be. 3 And they began to prostitute themselves in Egypt. In their youth they committed prostitution. There their breasts were squeezed, and there they pressed the bosoms of their virginity. 4 And their names were O·ho'lah the older one and O·hol'i·bah her sister, and they came to be mine and began to give birth to sons and daughters. And as for their names, O·ho'lah is Sa·mar'i·a, and O·hol'i·bah is Jerusalem.

5 "And O·ho'lah began to prostitute herself, while subject to me, and kept lusting after those passionately loving her, after the As·syr'i·ans, who were near, 6 governors clothed with blue material, and their deputy rulers—desirable young men all of them, cavalrymen riding horses. 7 And she continued giving forth her prostitutions upon them, the choicest sons of As·syr'i·a all of them; and with all those after whom she lusted—with their dungy idols—she defiled herself. 8 And her prostitutions [carried] from Egypt she did not leave, for with her they had lain down in her youth, and they were the ones that pressed the bosoms of her virginity and they kept pouring out their immoral intercourse upon her. 9 Therefore I gave her into the hand of those passionately loving her, into the hand of the sons of As·syr'i·a, toward whom she had lusted. 10 They were the ones that uncovered her nakedness. Her sons and her daughters they took, and her they killed even with sword. And she came to be infamy to women, and acts of judgment were what they executed upon her.

11 "When her sister O·hol'i·bah got to see [it], then she exercised her sensual desire more ruinously than she, and her prostitution more than the fornication of her

sister. 12 For the sons of As·syr'-i·a she lusted, governors and deputy rulers who were near, clothed with perfect taste, cavalrymen riding horses—desirable young men all of them. 13 And I got to see that, because she had defiled herself, both of them had one way. 14 And she kept adding to her acts of prostitution when she got to see the men in carvings upon the wall, images of Chal·de'ans carved in vermilion, 15 girded with belts on their hips, with pendant turbans on their heads, having the appearance of warriors, all of them, the likeness of the sons of Babylon, Chal·de'ans as respects the land of their birth. 16 And she began to lust after them at the sight of her eyes and proceeded to send messengers to them in Chal·de'a. 17 And the sons of Babylon kept coming in to her, to the bed of expressions of love, and defiling her with their immoral intercourse; and she continued getting defiled by them, and her soul began to turn away disgusted from them.

18 "And she went on uncovering her acts of prostitution and uncovering her nakedness, so that my soul turned away disgusted from company with her, just as my soul had turned away disgusted from company with her sister. 19 And she kept multiplying her acts of prostitution to the point of calling to mind the days of her youth, when she prostituted herself in the land of Egypt. 20 And she kept lusting in the style of concubines belonging to those whose fleshly member is as the fleshly member of male asses and whose genital organ is as the genital organ of male horses. 21 And you continued calling attention to the loose conduct of your youth by the pressing of your bosoms from Egypt onward, for the sake of the breasts of your youth.

22 "Therefore, O O·hol'i·bah, this is what the Lord Jehovah has said, 'Here I am rousing up your passionate lovers against you, those from whom your soul has turned away in disgust, and I will bring them in against you on all sides, 23 the sons of Babylon and all the Chal·de'ans, Pe'kod and Sho'a and Ko'a, all the sons of As·syr'i·a with them, desirable young men, governors and deputy rulers all of them, warriors and summoned ones, riding on horses, all of them. 24 And they must come in against you with rattling of war chariots and wheels, and with a congregation of peoples, with large shield and buckler and helmet. They will set themselves against you all around, and I will give judgment over to them, and they must judge you with their judgments. 25 And I will express my ardor against you, and they must take action against you in rage. Your nose and your ears they will remove, and the remainder of you will fall even by the sword. Your sons and your daughters they themselves will take, and the remainder of you will be devoured by the fire. 26 And they will certainly strip off you your garments and take away your beautiful articles. 27 And I shall actually cause your loose conduct to cease from you, and your prostitution [carried] from the land of Egypt; and you will not raise your eyes to them, and Egypt you will remember no more.'

28 "For this is what the Lord Jehovah has said, 'Here I am giving you into the hand of those whom you have hated, into the hand of those from whom your soul has turned away disgusted. 29 And they must take action against you in hatred and take away all your product of toil and leave you naked and nude; and the nudeness of your acts of fornication and your loose conduct and your acts of prostitution must be uncovered. 30 There will be a doing of these things to you because of your going like a prostitute after [the] nations, on account of the fact that you defiled yourself with their dungy idols. 31 In the way of your sister you have walked; and I shall have to give her cup into your hand.'

32 "This is what the Lord Jehovah has said, 'The cup of your sister you will drink, the deep and wide one. You will become an object of laughter and derision, [the cup] containing much. 33 With drunkenness and grief you will be filled, with the cup of astonishment and of desolation, the cup of your sister Sa·mar′i·a. 34 And you will have to drink it and drain [it] out, and its earthenware fragments you will gnaw, and your breasts you will tear out. "For I myself have spoken," is the utterance of the Lord Jehovah.'

35 "Therefore this is what the Lord Jehovah has said, 'For the reason that you have forgotten me and you proceeded to cast me behind your back, then you yourself also bear your loose conduct and your acts of prostitution.' "

36 And Jehovah went on to say to me: "Son of man, will you judge O·ho′lah and O·hol′i·bah and tell them their detestable things? 37 For they have committed adultery and there is blood on their hands, and with their dungy idols they have committed adultery. And, besides that, their sons whom they had borne to me they made pass through [the fire] to them as food. 38 What is more, this is what they have done to me: They have defiled my sanctuary in that day, and my sabbaths they have profaned. 39 And when they had slaughtered their sons to their dungy idols they even proceeded to come into my sanctuary on that day to profane it, and, look! that is what they have done in the midst of my house. 40 And in addition to that, when they began to send to the men coming from far away, to whom there was sent a messenger, then, look! they came, for whom you had washed yourself, painted your eyes and decked yourself with ornaments. 41 And you sat down upon a glorious couch, with a table set in order before it, and my incense and my oil you put upon it. 42 And the sound of a crowd at ease was in her, and to the men out of the mass of mankind there were drunk-ards being brought in from the wilderness, and they proceeded to put bracelets on the hands of the women and beautiful crowns upon their heads.

43 "Then I said respecting her who was worn out with adultery, 'Now she will keep on committing her prostitution, even she herself.' 44 And they kept on coming in to her, just as one comes in to a woman that is a prostitute; in that manner they came in to O·ho′lah and to O·hol′i·bah as women of loose conduct. 45 But as regards righteous men, they are the ones that will judge her with the judgment for adulteresses and with the judgment for female shedders of blood; for adulteresses are what they are, and there is blood on their hands.

46 "For this is what the Lord Jehovah has said, 'There will be the bringing up of a congregation against them and a making of them a frightful object and something to plunder. 47 And the congregation must pelt them with stones, and there will be a cutting of them down with their swords. Their sons and their daughters they will kill, and with fire their houses they will burn. 48 And I shall certainly cause loose conduct to cease out of the land, and all the women will have to let themselves be corrected, so that they will not do according to YOUR loose conduct. 49 And they must bring YOUR loose conduct upon YOU, and the sins of YOUR dungy idols YOU will bear; and YOU people will have to know that I am the Lord Jehovah.' "

24 And the word of Jehovah continued to occur to me in the ninth year, in the tenth month, on the tenth [day] of the month, saying: 2 "Son of man, write down for yourself the name of the day, this selfsame day. The king of Babylon has thrown himself against Jerusalem on this selfsame day. 3 And compose a proverbial saying concerning the rebellious house, and you must say concerning them,

" 'This is what the Lord Jehovah has said: "Put the widemouthed cooking pot on; put [it] on, and also pour water into it. 4 Gather pieces in it, every good piece, thigh and shoulder; fill [it] even with the choicest bones. 5 Let there be a taking of the choicest sheep, and also stack the logs in a circle under it. Boil its pieces, also cook its bones in the midst of it." ' "

6 "Therefore this is what the Lord Jehovah has said, 'Woe to the city of deeds of bloodshed, the widemouthed cooking pot, the rust of which is in it, and the very rust of which has not gone forth from it! Piece by piece of it, bring it out; no lot must be cast over it. 7 For its very blood has come to be right in the midst of it. Upon the shining, bare surface of a crag she placed it. She did not pour it out upon the earth, in order to cover it over with dust. 8 In order to bring up rage for the executing of vengeance, I have put her blood upon the shining, bare surface of a crag, in order that it may not be covered over.'

9 "Therefore this is what the Lord Jehovah has said, 'Woe to the city of deeds of bloodshed! I myself also shall make the pile great. 10 Make the logs many. Kindle the fire. Boil the flesh thoroughly. And empty out the broth, and let the bones themselves become piping hot. 11 Stand it empty upon its coals in order that it may get hot; and its copper must become heated up, and its uncleanness must be liquified in the midst of it. Let its rust get consumed. 12 Troubles! It has made [one] tired, but the great amount of its rust does not go forth from it. Into [the] fire with its rust!'

13 " 'There was loose conduct in your uncleanness. For that reason I had to cleanse you, but you did not become clean from your uncleanness. You will become clean no more until I cause my rage to come to its rest in your case. 14 I myself, Jehovah, have spoken. It must come, and I will act. I shall not neglect, neither shall I feel sorry nor feel regret. According to your ways and according to your dealings they will certainly judge you,' is the utterance of the Lord Jehovah."

15 And the word of Jehovah continued to occur to me, saying: 16 "Son of man, here I am taking away from you the thing desirable to your eyes by a blow, and you should not beat your breast, neither should you weep nor should your tears come on. 17 Sigh without words. For the dead ones no mourning should you make. Your headdress bind on yourself, and your sandals you should put upon your feet. And you should not cover over [the] mustache, and the bread of men you should not eat."

18 And I proceeded to speak to the people in the morning, and my wife gradually died in the evening. So I did in the morning just as I had been commanded. 19 And the people kept saying to me: "Will you not tell us what these things have to do with us, that you are doing?" 20 Then I said to them: "The very word of Jehovah has occurred to me, saying, 21 'Say to the house of Israel: "This is what the Lord Jehovah has said, 'Here I am profaning my sanctuary, the pride of YOUR strength, the thing desirable to YOUR eyes and the object of YOUR soul's compassion, and YOUR sons and YOUR daughters whom YOU people have left behind—by the sword they will fall. 22 And YOU will have to do just as I have done. Mustaches YOU will not cover over, and the bread of men YOU will not eat. 23 And YOUR headdress will be on YOUR heads, and YOUR sandals be upon YOUR feet. YOU will not beat yourselves nor will YOU weep, and YOU will have to rot away in YOUR errors, and YOU will actually groan over one another. 24 And Ezekiel has become for YOU a portent. In accord with all that he has done, YOU will do. When it comes, YOU will also have to know that I am the Lord Jehovah.' " ' "

25 "And as for you, O son of man, will it not be in the day of my taking away from them their fortress, the beautiful object of their exultation, the thing desirable

to their eyes and the longing of their soul, their sons and their daughters, that 26 in that day there will come to you the escaped one for making the ears hear? 27 In that day your mouth will be opened to the escaped one, and you will speak and be mute no longer; and you will certainly become to them a portent, and they will have to know that I am Jehovah."

25 And the word of Jehovah continued to occur to me, saying: 2 "Son of man, set your face toward the sons of Am'mon and prophesy against them. 3 And you must say concerning the sons of Am'mon, 'Hear the word of the Lord Jehovah. This is what the Lord Jehovah has said: "For the reason that you have said Aha! against my sanctuary, because it has been profaned, and against the soil of Israel, because it has been laid desolate, and against the house of Judah, because they have gone into exile, 4 therefore here I am giving you to the Orientals as something to possess, and they will set up their walled camps in you and will certainly put in you their tabernacles. They themselves will eat your fruitage, and they themselves will drink your milk. 5 And I will make Rab'bah a pasture ground of camels and the sons of Am'mon a resting place of a flock; and you people will have to know that I am Jehovah." '"

6 "For this is what the Lord Jehovah has said, 'For the reason that you clapped the hands and you stamped with the feet and you kept rejoicing with all scorn in your part in [your] soul against the soil of Israel, 7 therefore here I am; I have stretched out my hand against you, and I will give you as something to plunder to the nations; and I will cut you off from the peoples and destroy you from the lands. I shall annihilate you, and you will have to know that I am Jehovah.'

8 "This is what the Lord Jehovah has said, 'For the reason that Mo'ab and Se'ir have said: "Look!

The house of Judah is like all the other nations," 9 therefore here I am opening the slope of Mo'ab at the cities, at his cities to his frontier, the decoration of [the] land, Beth-jesh'i·moth, Ba'al-me'on, even to Kir·i·a·tha'im, 10 to the Orientals, alongside the sons of Am'mon; and I will make it something to possess, in order that it may not be remembered, [that is,] the sons of Am'mon, among the nations. 11 And in Mo'ab I shall execute acts of judgment; and they will have to know that I am Jehovah.'

12 "This is what the Lord Jehovah has said, 'For the reason that E'dom has acted in taking vengeance upon the house of Judah and they kept doing wrong extensively and avenged themselves on them, 13 therefore this is what the Lord Jehovah has said: "I will also stretch out my hand against E'dom and cut off from it man and domestic animal, and I will make it a devastated place from Te'man, even to De'dan. By the sword they will fall. 14 'And I will bring my vengeance on E'dom by the hand of my people Israel; and they must do in E'dom according to my anger and according to my rage; and they will have to know what my vengeance is,' is the utterance of the Lord Jehovah." '

15 "This is what the Lord Jehovah has said, 'For the reason that the Phi·lis'tines have acted with vengeance and they kept avenging themselves with a vengeance with scorn in [the] soul, in order to cause ruin, with an indefinitely lasting enmity, 16 therefore this is what the Lord Jehovah has said: "Here I am stretching out my hand against the Phi·lis'tines, and I will cut off the Cher'e·thites and destroy the rest of the seacoast. 17 And I will execute in them great acts of vengeance, with raging reproofs; and they will have to know that I am Jehovah when I bring my vengeance on them." '"

26 And it came about in the eleventh year, on the first [day] of the month, that the word of Jehovah occurred to me, saying: 2 "Son of man, for the reason that Tyre has said against Jerusalem, 'Aha! She has been broken, the doors of the peoples! The trend will certainly be to me. I shall be filled—she has been devastated,' 3 therefore this is what the Lord Jehovah has said, 'Here I am against you, O Tyre, and I will bring up against you many nations, just as the sea brings up its waves. 4 And they will certainly bring the walls of Tyre to ruin and tear down her towers, and I will scrape her dust away from her and make her a shining, bare surface of a crag. 5 A drying yard for dragnets is what she will become in the midst of the sea.'

" ' "For I myself have spoken," is the utterance of the Lord Jehovah, "and she must become an object of plunder for the nations. 6 And her dependent towns that are in the field—by the sword they will be killed, and people will have to know that I am Jehovah." '

7 "For this is what the Lord Jehovah has said, 'Here I am bringing against Tyre Neb·u·chad·rez'zar the king of Babylon from the north, a king of kings, with horses and war chariots and cavalrymen and a congregation, even a multitudinous people. 8 Your dependent towns in the field he will kill even with the sword, and he must make against you a siege wall and throw up against you a siege rampart and raise up against you a large shield; 9 and the strike of his attack engine he will direct against your walls, and your towers he will pull down, with his swords. 10 Owing to the heaving mass of his horses their dust will cover you. Owing to the sound of cavalryman and wheel and war chariot your walls will rock, when he comes in through your gates, as in the cases of entering into a city opened by breaches. 11 With the hoofs of his horses he will trample down all your streets. Your people he will kill even with the sword, and to the earth your own pillars of strength will go down. 12 And

they will certainly spoil your resources and plunder your sales goods, and tear down your walls, and your desirable houses they will pull down. And your stones and your woodwork and your dust they will place in the very midst of the water.'

13 " 'And I will cause the turmoil of your singing to cease, and the very sound of your harps will be heard no more. 14 And I will make you a shining, bare surface of a crag. A drying yard for dragnets is what you will become. Never will you be rebuilt; for I myself, Jehovah, have spoken,' is the utterance of the Lord Jehovah.

15 "This is what the Lord Jehovah has said to Tyre, 'At the sound of your downfall, when the fatally wounded one groans, when there is a killing with slaughter in the midst of you, will not the islands rock? 16 And down from their thrones all the chieftains of the sea will certainly come and remove their sleeveless coats, and they will strip off their own embroidered garments. They will put on trembling spells. Upon the earth they will sit down, and they will certainly tremble every moment and stare in amazement at you. 17 And they must raise up over you a dirge and say to you:

" ' "How you have perished, that used to be inhabited from the seas, O praised city, who became a strong one in the sea, she and those inhabiting her, those who gave their terror to all the inhabitants [of the earth]! 18 Now the islands will tremble in the day of your downfall. And the islands that are in the sea must be disturbed owing to your going out." '

19 "For this is what the Lord Jehovah has said, 'When I make you a devastated city, like the cities that are actually not inhabited, when [I] bring up over you the watery deep, and the vast waters will have covered you, 20 I will also bring you down with those going down into the pit to the people of long ago, and I will cause you to dwell in the lowest

land, like places devastated for a long time, with those going down into the pit, in order that you may not be inhabited; and I will put decoration in the land of those alive.

21 "'Sudden terrors are what I shall make you, and you will not be; and you will be sought for, but you will no more be found to time indefinite,' is the utterance of the Lord Jehovah."

27 And the word of Jehovah continued to occur to me, saying: 2 "And as for you, O son of man, raise up concerning Tyre a dirge, 3 and you must say to Tyre,

"'O you who are dwelling at the entrances of [the] sea, the tradeswoman of the peoples for many islands, this is what the Lord Jehovah has said: "O Tyre, you yourself have said, 'I am perfect in prettiness.' 4 In the heart of [the] seas are your territories. Your own builders have perfected your prettiness. 5 Out of juniper timbers from Se'nir they built for you all the planks. A cedar from Leb'a·non they took to make a mast upon you. 6 Out of massive trees from Ba'shan they made your oars. Your prow they made with ivory in cypress wood, from the islands of Kit'tim. 7 Linen in various colors from Egypt your cloth expanse happened to be, in order for [it] to serve as your sail. Blue thread and wool dyed reddish purple from the islands of E·li'shah are what your deck covering proved to be.

8 "'"The inhabitants of Si'don and of Ar'vad themselves became rowers for you. Your skilled ones, O Tyre, happened to be in you; they were your sailors. 9 Even old men of Ge'bal and her skilled ones happened to be in you as calkers for your seams. All the ships of the sea and their mariners themselves proved to be in you, in order to exchange articles of merchandise. 10 Persians and Lu'dim and men of Put—they happened to be in your military force, your men of war. Shield and helmet they hung up in you. They were the ones that caused your splendor. 11 The sons of Ar'vad, even your military force, were upon your walls all around, and valorous men were the ones that happened to be in your own towers. Their circular shields they hung up on your walls all around. They themselves perfected your prettiness.

12 "'"Tar'shish was your merchant because of the abundance of all sorts of valuable things. For [its] silver, iron, tin and lead, your stores were given. 13 Ja'van, Tu'bal and Me'shech themselves were your traders. For the souls of mankind and articles of copper your articles of exchange were given. 14 From the house of To·gar'mah there were horses and steeds and mules, [for which] your stores were given. 15 The sons of De'dan were your traders; many islands were merchants in your employ; horns of ivory and ebony they have paid back as gift to you. 16 E'dom was your merchant because of the abundance of your works. For turquoise, wool dyed reddish purple and material of various colors and fine fabric and corals and rubies, your stores were given in exchange.

17 "'"Judah and the land of Israel themselves were your traders. For the wheat of Min'nith and special foodstuff and honey and oil and balsam, your articles of exchange were given.

18 "'"Damascus was your merchant in the abundance of your works, because of the abundance of all your valuable things, with the wine of Hel'bon and the wool of reddish gray. 19 Ve'dan and Ja'van from U'zal—for your stores they gave. Iron in wrought works, cassia and cane—for your articles of exchange they proved to be. 20 De'dan was your trader in garments of woven material for riding. 21 The Arabs and all the chieftains of Ke'dar themselves were merchants in your employ. In male lambs and rams and he-goats—in them they were your merchants. 22 The traders of She'ba and Ra'amah themselves were your traders; for the finest of all sorts of per-

fumes and for all sorts of precious stones and gold, your stores were given. 23 Ha'ran and Can'neh and E'den, the traders of She'ba, As'shur [and] Chil'mad were your traders. 24 They were your traders in gorgeous garments, in wraps of blue material and material of various colors and in carpets of two-colored stuff, in ropes twined and solidly made, in your trading center.

25 "'"The ships of Tar'shish were your caravans for your articles of exchange, so that you get filled and become very glorious in the heart of the open sea.

26 "'"Into vast waters those rowing you have brought you. The east wind itself has broken you in the heart of the open sea. 27 Your valuable things and your stores, your articles of exchange, your mariners and your sailors, the calkers of your seams and those exchanging your articles of merchandise and all your men of war, who are in you and in all your congregation, who are in the midst of you,—they will fall in the heart of the open sea in the day of your downfall.

28 "'"At the sound of the outcry of your sailors the open country will rock. 29 And all those handling an oar, mariners, all the sailors of the sea, will certainly go down from their ships; upon the land they will stand. 30 And over you they will certainly let themselves be heard with their voice and will cry out bitterly. And they will bring up dust upon their heads. In the ashes they will wallow. 31 And they will have to make [themselves] bald with a baldness for you, and gird on sackcloth and weep over you in bitterness of soul, with bitter wailing. 32 And for you in their lamentation they will certainly lift up a dirge and chant over you,

"'"Who is like Tyre, like her that has been brought to silence in the midst of the sea? 33 When your stores went forth from the open sea, you satisfied many peoples. With the abundance of your valuable things and your articles of exchange you made earth's kings

rich. 34 Now you have been broken by the open sea, in the depths of the waters. As for your articles of exchange and all your congregation, in the midst of you they have fallen. 35 All the inhabitants of the islands—in amazement they will certainly stare at you, and their kings themselves will have to shudder in horror. Faces must become perturbed. 36 As for merchants among the peoples, they will certainly whistle over you. Sudden terrors are what you must become, and you will be no more to time indefinite.'"'"

28 And the word of Jehovah continued to occur to me, saying: 2 "Son of man, say to the leader of Tyre, 'This is what the Lord Jehovah has said:

"'"For the reason that your heart has become haughty, and you keep saying, 'I am a god. In the seat of god I have seated myself, in the heart of the open sea,' whereas an earthling man is what you are, and not a god, and you keep making your heart like the heart of god— 3 look! you are wiser than Daniel. There are no secrets that have proved a match for you. 4 By your wisdom and by your discernment you have made wealth for your own self, and you keep getting gold and silver in your storehouses. 5 By the abundance of your wisdom, by your sales goods, you have made your wealth abound, and your heart began to be haughty because of your wealth."'

6 "Therefore this is what the Lord Jehovah has said: "For the reason that you make your heart like the heart of god, 7 therefore here I am bringing upon you strangers, the tyrants of [the] nations, and they will certainly draw their swords against the beauty of your wisdom and profane your beaming splendor. 8 Down to the pit they will bring you, and you must die the death of someone slain in the heart of the open sea. 9 Will you without fail say, 'I am god,' before the one killing you, whereas you are a mere earthling

man, and not a god, in the hand of those profaning you?"'

10 "'The deaths of uncircumcised ones you will die by the hand of strangers, for I myself have spoken,' is the utterance of the Lord Jehovah."

11 And the word of Jehovah continued to occur to me, saying: 12 "Son of man, lift up a dirge concerning the king of Tyre, and you must say to him, 'This is what the Lord Jehovah has said:

"'"You are sealing up a pattern, full of wisdom and perfect in beauty. 13 In Eden, the garden of God, you proved to be. Every precious stone was your covering, ruby, topaz and jasper; chrysolite, onyx and jade; sapphire, turquoise and emerald; and of gold was the workmanship of your settings and your sockets in you. In the day of your being created they were made ready. 14 You are the anointed cherub that is covering, and I have set you. On the holy mountain of God you proved to be. In the midst of fiery stones you walked about. 15 You were faultless in your ways from the day of your being created until unrighteousness was found in you.

16 "'"Because of the abundance of your sales goods they filled the midst of you with violence, and you began to sin. And I shall put you as profane out of the mountain of God, and I shall destroy you, O cherub that is covering, from the midst of the fiery stones.

17 "'"Your heart became haughty because of your beauty. You brought your wisdom to ruin on account of your beaming splendor. Onto the earth I will throw you. Before kings I will set you, [for them] to look upon you.

18 "'"Owing to the abundance of your errors, because of the injustice of your sales goods, you have profaned your sanctuaries. And I shall bring forth a fire from the midst of you. It is what must devour you. And I shall make you ashes upon the earth before the eyes of all those seeing you. 19 As for all those knowing you among the peoples, they will certainly stare in amazement at you. Sudden terrors are what you must become, and you will be no more to time indefinite."'"

20 And the word of Jehovah continued to occur to me, saying: 21 "Son of man, set your face toward Si'don, and prophesy against her. 22 And you must say, 'This is what the Lord Jehovah has said: "Here I am against you, O Si'don, and I shall certainly be glorified in the midst of you; and people will have to know that I am Jehovah when I execute acts of judgment in her and I am actually sanctified in her. 23 And I will send pestilence into her and blood into her streets. And the slain one must fall in the midst of her by the sword against her on every side; and people will have to know that I am Jehovah. 24 And no more will there prove to be to the house of Israel a malignant prickle or a painful thorn out of all those round about them, those who are treating them with scorn; and people will have to know that I am the Lord Jehovah."'

25 "'This is what the Lord Jehovah has said: "When I collect together the house of Israel out from the peoples among whom they have been scattered, I will also be sanctified among them in the eyes of the nations. And they will certainly dwell upon their soil that I gave to my servant, to Jacob. 26 And they will actually dwell upon it in security and build houses and plant vineyards, and they must dwell in security when I execute acts of judgment upon all those treating them with scorn all round about them; and they will have to know that I am Jehovah their God."'"

29 In the tenth year, in the tenth [month], on the twelfth [day] of the month, the word of Jehovah occurred to me, saying: 2 "Son of man, set your face against Phar'aoh the king of Egypt and prophesy against him and against Egypt in its entirety. 3 Speak, and you must say, 'This is what the Lord

Jehovah has said: "Here I am against you, O Phar'aoh, king of Egypt, the great sea monster lying stretched out in the midst of his Nile canals, that has said, 'My Nile River belongs to me, and I—I have made [it] for myself.' 4 And I will put hooks in your jaws and cause the fish of your Nile canals to cling to your scales. And I will bring you up out of the midst of your Nile canals and all the fish of your Nile canals that cling to your very scales. 5 And I will abandon you to the wilderness, you and all the fish of your Nile canals. Upon the surface of the field you will fall. You will not be gathered up nor be collected together. To the wild beasts of the earth and to the flying creatures of the heavens I will give you for food. 6 And all the inhabitants of Egypt will have to know that I am Jehovah, for the reason that they proved to be, as a support, a reed to the house of Israel. 7 When they took hold of you by the hand, you got to be crushed, and you caused a split in their entire shoulder. And when they supported themselves upon you, you got to be broken, and you caused all their hips to wobble."

8 "'Therefore this is what the Lord Jehovah has said: "Here I am bringing upon you a sword, and I will cut off from you earthling man and domestic animal. 9 And the land of Egypt must become a desolate waste and a devastated place; and they will have to know that I am Jehovah, for the reason that he has said, 'To me the Nile River belongs, and I myself have made [it].' 10 Therefore here I am against you and against your Nile canals, and I will make the land of Egypt devastated places, dryness, a desolated waste, from Mig'dol to Sy-e'ne and to the boundary of E·thi-o'pi·a. 11 There will not pass through it the foot of earthling man, nor will the foot of domestic animal pass through it, and for forty years it will not be inhabited. 12 And I will make the land of Egypt a desolate waste in the midst of desolated lands; and its own cities will become a desolate waste in the very midst of devastated cities for forty years; and I will scatter the Egyptians among the nations and disperse them among the lands."'

13 "'For this is what the Lord Jehovah has said: "At the end of forty years I shall collect the Egyptians together out of the peoples among whom they will have been scattered, 14 and I will bring back the captive group of the Egyptians; and I will bring them back to the land of Path'ros, to the land of their origin, and there they must become a lowly kingdom. 15 Lower than the [other] kingdoms it will become, and it will no more lift itself up over the [other] nations, and I will make them so few as not to have the [other] nations in subjection. 16 And it will no more prove to be the house of Israel's confidence, bringing error to remembrance by their turning after them. And they will have to know that I am the Lord Jehovah."'"

17 Now it came about in the twenty-seventh year, in the first [month], on the first [day] of the month, that the word of Jehovah occurred to me, saying: 18 "Son of man, Neb·u·chad·rez'zar himself, the king of Babylon, made his military force perform a great service against Tyre. Every head was one made bald, and every shoulder was one rubbed bare. But as for wages, there proved to be none for him and his military force from Tyre for the service that he had performed against her.

19 "Therefore this is what the Lord Jehovah has said, 'Here I am giving to Neb·u·chad·rez'zar the king of Babylon the land of Egypt, and he must carry off its wealth and make a big spoil of it and do a great deal of plundering of it; and it must become wages for his military force.'

20 "'As his compensation for service that he did against her I have given him the land of Egypt, because they acted for me,' is the utterance of the Lord Jehovah.

21 "In that day I shall cause a horn to sprout for the house of Israel, and to you I shall give occasion to open the mouth in the midst of them; and they will have to know that I am Jehovah."

30 And the word of Jehovah continued to occur to me, saying: 2 "Son of man, prophesy, and you must say, 'This is what the Lord Jehovah has said: "Howl, YOU people, 'Alas for the day!' 3 for a day is near, yes, a day belonging to Jehovah is near. A day of clouds, an appointed time of nations it will prove to be. 4 And a sword will certainly come into Egypt, and severe pains must occur in E·thi·o'pi·a when one falls slain in Egypt and they actually take its wealth and its foundations are actually torn down. 5 E·thi·o'pi·a and Put and Lud and all the mixed company and Chub and the sons of the land of the covenant—with them they will fall by the very sword." '

6 "This is what Jehovah has said, 'The supporters of Egypt must also fall, and the pride of its strength must come down.'

" 'From Mig'dol to Sy·e'ne they will fall in it even by the sword,' is the utterance of the Lord Jehovah. 7 'They must also be made desolate in the midst of desolated lands, and its own cities will come to be right in the midst of devastated cities. 8 And they will have to know that I am Jehovah when I set a fire in Egypt and all its helpers are actually broken. 9 In that day messengers will go forth from before me in the ships, in order to drive self-confident E·thi·o'pi·a into trembling. And severe pains must occur among them in the day of Egypt, for, look! it must come.'

10 "This is what the Lord Jehovah has said, 'I will also cause the crowd of Egypt to cease by the hand of Neb·u·chad·rez'zar the king of Babylon. 11 He and his people with him, the tyrants of [the] nations, are being brought in to reduce the land to ruin. And they must draw their swords against Egypt and fill the land with the slain. 12 And I will make the Nile canals dry ground and will sell the land into the hand of bad men, and I will cause the land and its fullness to be desolated by the hand of strangers. I myself, Jehovah, have spoken.'

13 "This is what the Lord Jehovah has said, 'I will also destroy the dungy idols and cause the valueless gods to cease out of Noph, and there will no more prove to be a chieftain out of the land of Egypt; and I shall certainly put fear in the land of Egypt. 14 And I will bring Path'ros to desolation and set a fire in Zo'an and execute acts of judgment in No. 15 And I will pour out my rage upon Sin, the fortress of Egypt, and cut off the crowd of No. 16 And I will set a fire in Egypt. Sin will without fail be in severe pains, and No itself will come to be for capture by breaches; and as regards Noph— there will be adversaries during the daytime! 17 As for the young men of On and Pi·be'seth, by the sword they will fall, and into captivity the [cities] themselves will go. 18 And in Te·haph'ne·hes the day will actually grow dark, when I break there the yoke bars of Egypt. And in her the pride of her strength will actually be made to cease. As for her, clouds themselves will cover her, and into captivity her own dependent towns will go. 19 And I will execute acts of judgment in Egypt; and they will have to know that I am Jehovah.' "

20 And it occurred further that in the eleventh year, in the first [month], on the seventh [day] of the month, the word of Jehovah occurred to me, saying: 21 "Son of man, the arm of Phar'aoh the king of Egypt I shall certainly break, and, look! it will not be bound up at all in order to give [it] healing by putting a bandage on for binding it up, for it to become strong to take hold of the sword."

22 "Therefore this is what the Lord Jehovah has said, 'Here I am

against Phar'aoh the king of Egypt, and I will break his arms, the strong one and the broken one, and I will cause the sword to fall out of his hand. 23 And I will scatter the Egyptians among the nations and disperse them among the lands. 24 And I will strengthen the arms of the king of Babylon and give my sword into his hand, and I will break the arms of Phar'aoh, and as a deadly wounded one he will certainly do a great deal of groaning before him. 25 And I will strengthen the arms of the king of Babylon, and the very arms of Phar'aoh will fall; and they will have to know that I am Jehovah when I give my sword into the hand of the king of Babylon and he actually extends it out against the land of Egypt. 26 And I will scatter the Egyptians among the nations and disperse them among the lands; and they will have to know that I am Jehovah.'"

31 And it occurred further that in the eleventh year, in the third [month], on the first [day] of the month, the word of Jehovah occurred to me, saying: 2 "Son of man, say to Phar'aoh the king of Egypt and to his crowd,

" 'Whom have you come to resemble in your greatness? 3 Look! An As·syr'i·an, a cedar in Leb'a·non, pretty in bough, with a woody thicket offering shadow, and high in stature, so that among the clouds its treetop proved to be. 4 Waters were what made it get big; the watery deep caused it to grow high. With its streams it was going all around its planting place; and its channels it sent forth to all the trees of the field. 5 That is why it grew higher in its stature than all the [other] trees of the field.

" 'And its boughs kept multiplying, and its branches continued getting longer because of much water in its watercourses. 6 On its boughs all the flying creatures of the heavens made their nests, and under its branches all the wild beasts of the field gave birth, and

in its shade all the populous nations would dwell. 7 And it came to be pretty in its greatness, in the length of its foliage, for its root system proved to be over many waters. 8 [Other] cedars were no match for it in the garden of God. As for juniper trees, they bore no resemblance as respects its boughs. And plane trees themselves did not prove to be like it in branches. No [other] tree in the garden of God resembled it in its prettiness. 9 Pretty is the way that I made it in the abundance of its foliage, and all the [other] trees of Eden that were in the garden of the [true] God kept envying it.'

10 "Therefore this is what the Lord Jehovah has said, 'For the reason that you became high in stature, so that it put its treetop even among the clouds and its heart became exalted because of its height, 11 I shall also give it into the hand of the despot of [the] nations. Without fail he will act against it. According to its wickedness I will drive it out. 12 And strangers, the tyrants of [the] nations, will cut it down, and people will abandon it upon the mountains; and in all the valleys its foliage will certainly fall, and its branches will be broken among all the stream beds of the earth. And out from its shade all the peoples of the earth will come down and abandon it. 13 Upon its fallen trunk all the flying creatures of the heavens will reside, and upon its branches there will certainly come to be all the wild beasts of the field; 14 to the end that none of the watered trees may become high in their stature, or put their treetops even among the clouds, and that none drinking water may stand up against them in their height, for they will certainly all of them be given to death, to the land down below, in the midst of the sons of mankind, to those going down into the pit.'

15 "This is what the Lord Jehovah has said, 'On the day of its going down to She'ol I shall certainly cause a mourning. On its

account I will cover the watery deep, that I may hold back its streams and [that] the many waters may be restrained; and on its account I shall darken Leb'a·non, and on its account the trees of the field will all swoon away. 16 At the sound of its downfall I shall certainly cause nations to rock when I bring it down to She'ol with those going down into the pit, and in the land down below all the trees of Eden, the choicest and the best of Leb'a·non, all those drinking water, will be comforted. 17 With him they themselves also have gone down to She'ol, to those slain by the sword, and those who as his seed have dwelt in his shadow in the midst of nations.'

18 "'Whom have you come to resemble thus in glory and greatness among the trees of Eden? But you will certainly be brought down with the trees of Eden to the land down below. In the midst of the uncircumcised ones you will lie down with those slain by the sword. This is Phar'aoh and all his crowd,' is the utterance of the Lord Jehovah."

32 And it occurred further that in the twelfth year, in the twelfth month, on the first [day] of the month, the word of Jehovah occurred to me, saying: 2 "Son of man, lift up a dirge concerning Phar'aoh the king of Egypt, and you must say to him, 'As a maned young lion of nations you have been silenced.

"'And you have been like the marine monster in the seas, and you kept gushing in your rivers and kept muddying the waters with your feet and fouling their rivers.'

3 "This is what the Lord Jehovah has said, 'I will also spread over you my net by means of a congregation of many peoples, and they will certainly bring you in my dragnet. 4 And I must abandon you on the land. Upon the surface of the field I shall hurl you. And on you I will cause all the flying creatures of the heavens to reside, and off you I will satisfy the wild beasts of the whole earth. 5 And

I will put your flesh upon the mountains and fill the valleys with the refuse of you. 6 And I will cause [the] land to drink up your discharged matter, from your blood, upon the mountains; and stream beds themselves will be filled up from you.'

7 "'And when you get extinguished I will cover [the] heavens and darken their stars. As for [the] sun, with clouds I shall cover it, and [the] moon itself will not let its light shine. 8 All the luminaries of light in the heavens— I shall darken them on your account, and I will put darkness upon your land,' is the utterance of the Lord Jehovah.

9 "'And I will offend the heart of many peoples when I bring the captives from you among the nations to lands that you have not known. 10 And at you I shall certainly cause many peoples to be awe-struck, and their kings themselves will shudder in horror at you when I brandish my sword in their faces, and they will have to tremble every moment, each one for his own soul, on the day of your downfall.'

11 "For this is what the Lord Jehovah has said, 'The very sword of the king of Babylon will come upon you. 12 I shall cause your crowd to fall by the very swords of mighty ones, the tyrants of [the] nations, all of them; and they will actually despoil the pride of Egypt, and all her crowd must be annihilated. 13 And I will destroy all her domestic animals from beside many waters, and the foot of earthling man will no more muddy them, nor will even the hoofs of a domestic animal muddy them.'

14 "'At that time I shall make their waters clear up, and their rivers I shall make go just like oil,' is the utterance of the Lord Jehovah.

15 "'When I make the land of Egypt a desolate waste and the land is desolated of its fullness, when I strike down all the inhabitants in it, they will also have to know that I am Jehovah.

16 " 'This is a dirge, and people will certainly chant it. Even the daughters of the nations will chant it; over Egypt and over all its crowd they will chant it,' is the utterance of the Lord Jehovah."

17 And it occurred further that in the twelfth year, on the fifteenth [day] of the month, the word of Jehovah occurred to me, saying: 18 "Son of man, lament over the crowd of Egypt and bring it down, her and the daughters of majestic nations, to the land down below, with those going down into [the] pit.

19 " 'Compared with whom are you more pleasant? Do go down, and you must be laid with the uncircumcised ones!'

20 " 'In the midst of those slain by the sword they will fall. [To] a sword she has been given. Drag her away and all her crowds, YOU men.

21 " 'The foremost men of the mighty ones will speak out of the midst of She'ol even to him, with his helpers. They will certainly go down; they must lie down as the uncircumcised, slain by the sword. 22 There is where As·syr'i·a and all her congregation are. His burial places are round about him. All of them are slain, those falling by the sword. 23 For her burial places have been put in the innermost parts of a pit, and her congregation proves to be round about her grave, all of them slain, falling by the sword, because they had caused terror in the land of those alive.

24 " 'There are E'lam and all her crowd round about her grave, all of them slain ones, those falling by the sword, who have gone down uncircumcised to the land down below, those who have caused their terror in the land of those alive; and they will bear their humiliation with those going down into [the] pit. 25 In the midst of slain ones they have set a bed for her among all her crowd. Her burial places are round about it. All of them are uncircumcised, slain by the sword, because their terror was caused in

the land of those alive; and they will bear their humiliation with those going down into [the] pit. In the midst of slain ones he has been put.

26 " 'There is where Me'shech [and] Tu'bal and all her crowd are. Her burial places are round about him. All of them are uncircumcised, pierced through by the sword, because they have caused their terror in the land of those alive. 27 And will they not lie down with mighty ones, falling from among the uncircumcised, who have gone down to She'ol with their weapons of war? And they will put their swords under their heads, and their errors will come to be upon their bones, because mighty ones were a terror in the land of those alive. 28 And as for you, in the midst of uncircumcised ones you will be broken, and you will lie down with those slain by the sword.

29 " 'There is where E'dom, her kings and all her chieftains are, who, in their mightiness, were put with those slain by the sword; they themselves will lie down even with the uncircumcised ones and with those going down into [the] pit.

30 " 'There is where the dukes of the north are, all of them, and all the Si·do'ni·ans, who have gone down with the slain ones, in their terribleness because of their mightiness, ashamed. And they will lie down uncircumcised with those slain by the sword and will bear their humiliation with those going down into [the] pit.

31 " 'These are the ones that Phar'aoh will see, and he will certainly be comforted over all his crowd. Phar'aoh and all his military force will be people slain by the sword,' is the utterance of the Lord Jehovah.

32 " 'For he has caused his terror in the land of those alive, and he must be laid in the midst of the uncircumcised ones, with those slain by the sword, even Phar'aoh and all his crowd,' is the utterance of the Lord Jehovah."

33 And the word of Jehovah proceeded to occur to me, saying: 2 "Son of man, speak to the sons of your people, and you must say to them,

" 'As regards a land, in case I bring upon it a sword and the people of the land, one and all, actually take a man and set him as their watchman, 3 and he really sees the sword coming upon the land and blows the horn and warns the people, 4 and the hearer actually hears the sound of the horn but he takes no warning at all, and a sword comes and takes him away, his own blood will come to be upon his own head. 5 The sound of the horn he heard, but he took no warning. His own blood will come to be upon his own self. And had he himself taken warning, his own soul would have escaped. 6 " 'Now as regards the watchman, in case he sees the sword coming and he actually does not blow the horn and the people itself gets no warning at all and a sword comes and takes away from them soul, for its own error it itself must be taken away, but its blood I shall ask back from the hand of the watchman himself.'

7 "Now as regards you, O son of man, a watchman is what I have made you to the house of Israel, and at my mouth you must hear [the] word and give them warning from me. 8 When I say to someone wicked, 'O wicked one, you will positively die!' but you actually do not speak out to warn the wicked one from his way, he himself as a wicked one will die in his own error, but his blood I shall ask back at your own hand. 9 But as regards you, in case you actually warn someone wicked from his way [for him] to turn back from it but he actually does not turn back from his way, he himself will die in his own error, whereas you yourself will certainly deliver your own soul.

10 "Now as regards you, O son of man, say to the house of Israel, 'Thus YOU people have said: "Because our revolts and our sins are upon us and in them we are rotting away, how, then, shall we keep living?" ' 11 Say to them, ' "As I am alive," is the utterance of the Lord Jehovah, "I take delight, not in the death of the wicked one, but in that someone wicked turns back from his way and actually keeps living. Turn back, turn back from YOUR bad ways, for why is it that YOU should die, O house of Israel?" '

12 "And as for you, O son of man, say to the sons of your people, 'The righteousness of the righteous one will not itself deliver him in the day of his revolt. But as regards the wickedness of the wicked one, he will not be made to stumble by it in the day of his turning back from his wickedness. Nor will even anyone having righteousness be able to keep living because of it in the day of his sinning. 13 When I say to the righteous one: "You will positively keep living," and he himself actually trusts in his own righteousness and does injustice, all his own righteous acts will not be remembered, but for his injustice that he has done—for this he will die.

14 " 'And when I say to the wicked one: "You will positively die," and he actually turns back from his sin and carries on justice and righteousness, 15 [and] the wicked one returns the very thing pledged, pays back the very things taken by robbery, [and] actually walks in the very statutes of life by not doing injustice, he will positively keep living. He will not die. 16 None of his sins with which he has sinned will be remembered against him. Justice and righteousness are what he has carried on. He will positively keep living.'

17 "And the sons of your people have said, 'The way of Jehovah is not adjusted right,' but, as for them, it is their way that is not adjusted right.

18 "When someone righteous turns back from his righteousness and actually does injustice, he must also die for them. 19 And when someone wicked turns back from his wickedness and actually carries

on justice and righteousness, it will be on account of them that he himself will keep living.

20 "And you people have said, 'The way of Jehovah is not adjusted right.' It will be each one according to his ways that I shall judge you, O house of Israel."

21 At length it occurred in the twelfth year, in the tenth [month], on the fifth day of the month of our exile, that there came to me the escaped one from Jerusalem, saying: "The city has been struck down!"

22 Now the very hand of Jehovah had come to be upon me in the evening before the coming of the escaped one, and He proceeded to open my mouth prior to [that one's] coming to me in the morning, and my mouth was opened and I proved to be speechless no longer.

23 And the word of Jehovah began to occur to me, saying: 24 "Son of man, the inhabitants of these devastated places are saying even concerning the soil of Israel, 'Abraham happened to be just one and yet he took possession of the land. And we are many; to us the land has been given as something to possess.'

25 "Therefore say to them, 'This is what the Lord Jehovah has said: "With the blood you keep eating, and your eyes you keep lifting to your dungy idols, and blood you keep pouring out. So should you possess the land? 26 You have depended upon your sword. You have done a detestable thing, and you have defiled each one the wife of his companion. So should you possess the land?"'

27 "This is what you should say to them, 'This is what the Lord Jehovah has said: "As I am alive, surely the ones who are in the devastated places will fall by the sword itself; and the one who is upon the surface of the field, to the wild beast I shall certainly give him for food; and those who are in the strong places and in the caves will die by the pestilence itself. 28 And I shall actually make the land a desolate waste,

even a desolation, and the pride of its strength must be made to cease and the mountains of Israel must be laid desolate, with no one passing through. 29 And they will have to know that I am Jehovah when I make the land a desolate waste, even a desolation, on account of all their detestable things that they have done."'

30 "And as for you, O son of man, the sons of your people are speaking with one another about you beside the walls and in the entrances of the houses, and the one has spoken with the other, each one with his brother, saying, 'Come, please, and hear what the word is that is going forth from Jehovah.' 31 And they will come in to you, like the coming in of people, and sit before you as my people; and they will certainly hear your words but these they will not do, for with their mouth they are expressing lustful desires [and] after their unjust gain is where their heart is going. 32 And, look! you are to them like a song of sensuous loves, like one with a pretty voice and playing a stringed instrument well. And they will certainly hear your words, but there are none doing them. 33 And when it comes true—look! it must come true—they will also have to know that a prophet himself had proved to be in the midst of them."

34 And the word of Jehovah continued to occur to me, saying: 2 "Son of man, prophesy against the shepherds of Israel. Prophesy, and you must say to them, to the shepherds, 'This is what the Lord Jehovah has said: "Woe to the shepherds of Israel, who have become feeders of themselves! Is it not the flock that the shepherds ought to feed? 3 The fat is what you eat, and with the wool you clothe your own selves. The plump animal is what you slaughter. The flock itself you do not feed. 4 The sickened ones you have not strengthened, and the ailing one you have not healed, and the broken one you have not bandaged, and the dispersed one

multiplied against me YOUR words. I myself have heard [them].'

14 "This is what the Lord Jehovah has said, 'At the same time that all the earth rejoices, a desolate waste is what I shall make of you. 15 Just as there was rejoicing on your part at the inheritance of the house of Israel because it was laid desolate, the same thing I shall make of you. A desolate waste is what you will become, O mountainous region of Se'ir, even all E'dom, all of it; and they will have to know that I am Jehovah.' "

36 "And as for you, O son of man, prophesy concerning the mountains of Israel, and you must say, 'O mountains of Israel, hear the word of Jehovah. 2 This is what the Lord Jehovah has said: "For the reason that the enemy has said against YOU, 'Aha! Even the high places of old time—as a possession it has become ours!' " '

3 "Therefore prophesy, and you must say, 'This is what the Lord Jehovah has said: "For the reason, even for the reason that there has been a lying desolate and a snapping at YOU people from all sides, in order for YOU to become a possession to the remaining ones of the nations and YOU continue being talked about with the tongue and there is a bad report among people, 4 therefore, O mountains of Israel, hear the word of the Lord Jehovah! This is what the Lord Jehovah has said to the mountains and to the hills, to the stream beds and to the valleys and to the devastated places that were laid desolate and to the abandoned cities that have come to be for plunder and for ridicule to the remaining ones of the nations that are round about; 5 therefore this is what the Lord Jehovah has said, 'Certainly in the fire of my zeal I will speak against the remaining ones of the nations and against E'dom, all of it, those who have given my land to themselves as a possession with the rejoicing of all the heart, with scorn in [the] soul, for the sake of its pasture ground [and] for the plunder.' " '

6 "Therefore prophesy concerning the soil of Israel, and you must say to the mountains and to the hills, to the stream beds and to the valleys, 'This is what the Lord Jehovah has said: "Look! I myself in my zeal and in my rage must speak, for the reason that humiliation by nations is what YOU have borne." '

7 "Therefore this is what the Lord Jehovah has said, 'I myself have raised my hand [in an oath] that the nations that YOU have round about—they themselves will bear their own humiliation. 8 And YOU yourselves, O mountains of Israel, will give forth YOUR very own boughs and bear YOUR own fruitage for my people Israel, for they have drawn near to the point of coming in. 9 For here I am in favor of YOU, and I shall certainly turn toward YOU, and YOU will actually be cultivated and sown with seed. 10 And I will multiply upon YOU humankind, the whole house of Israel, all of it, and the cities must become inhabited, and the devastated places themselves will be rebuilt. 11 Yes, I will multiply upon YOU humankind and animalkind, and they will certainly multiply and become fruitful, and I shall actually cause YOU to be inhabited as in YOUR former condition and I will do more good than in YOUR initial state; and YOU will have to know that I am Jehovah. 12 And upon YOU I will cause humankind to walk, even my people Israel, and they must take possession of YOU, and YOU must become a hereditary possession to them, and YOU will not bereave them again of any more children.' "

13 "This is what the Lord Jehovah has said, 'For the reason that there are those saying to YOU: "A devourer of humankind is what you yourself are, and [a land] bereaving your nations of children is what you have become," ' 14 'therefore humankind you will no more devour, and your nations you will no more bereave of children,' is the utterance of the Lord Jehovah. 15 'And I shall cause no

further humiliating talk by the nations to be heard concerning you, and reproach by peoples you will bear no more, and your nations you will no more cause to stumble,' is the utterance of the Lord Jehovah."

16 And the word of Jehovah continued to occur to me, saying: 17 "Son of man, the house of Israel are dwelling upon their soil, and they keep making it unclean with their way and with their dealings. Like the uncleanness of menstruation their way has become before me. 18 And I shall pour out my rage upon them on account of the blood that they have poured out upon the land, which [land] they have made unclean with their dungy idols. 19 And I shall scatter them among the nations, so that they will be dispersed among the lands. According to their way and according to their dealings I shall have to judge them. 20 And they will come in to the nations where they will have to come in, and people will profane my holy name in saying with reference to them, 'These are the people of Jehovah, and from his land they have gone out.' 21 And I shall have compassion on my holy name, which the house of Israel have profaned among the nations where they have come in."

22 "Therefore say to the house of Israel, 'This is what the Lord Jehovah has said: "Not for your sakes am I doing [it], O house of Israel, but for my holy name, which you have profaned among the nations where you have come in."' 23 'And I shall certainly sanctify my great name, which was being profaned among the nations, which you profaned in the midst of them; and the nations will have to know that I am Jehovah,' is the utterance of the Lord Jehovah, 'when I am sanctified among you before their eyes. 24 And I will take you out of the nations and collect you together out of all the lands and bring you in upon your soil. 25 And I will sprinkle upon you clean water, and you will become clean; from all

your impurities and from all your dungy idols I shall cleanse you. 26 And I will give you a new heart, and a new spirit I shall put inside you, and I will take away the heart of stone from your flesh and give you a heart of flesh. 27 And my spirit I shall put inside you, and I will act so that in my regulations you will walk, and my judicial decisions you will keep and actually carry out. 28 And you will certainly dwell in the land that I gave to your forefathers, and you must become my people and I myself shall become your God.'

29 " 'And I will save you from all your impurities and call to the grain and make it abound, and I shall put upon you no famine. 30 And I shall certainly make the fruitage of the tree abound, and the produce of the field, in order that you may no more receive among the nations the reproach of famine. 31 And you will be bound to remember your bad ways and your dealings that were not good, and you will be bound to feel a loathing at your own person on account of your errors and on account of your detestable things. 32 Not for your sakes am I doing [this],' is the utterance of the Lord Jehovah, 'let it be known to you. Be ashamed and feel humiliation because of your ways, O house of Israel.'

33 "This is what the Lord Jehovah has said, 'In the day of my cleansing you from all your errors I will also cause the cities to be inhabited, and the devastated places must be rebuilt. 34 And the desolated land itself will be cultivated, whereas it had become a desolate waste before the eyes of every passer-by. 35 And people will certainly say: "That land yonder which was laid desolate has become like the garden of Eden, and the cities that were a waste and that were laid desolate and that were torn down are fortified; they have become inhabited." 36 And the nations that will be left remaining round about you will have to know that I myself, Jeho-

vah, have built the things torn down, I have planted what has been laid desolate. I myself, Jehovah, have spoken and I have done [it].'

37 "This is what the Lord Jehovah has said, 'This is what I shall yet let myself be searched for by the house of Israel to do for them: I shall multiply them like a flock with men. 38 Like a flock of holy persons, like the flock of Jerusalem in her festal seasons, thus the cities that had been a waste will become full of a flock of men; and people will have to know that I am Jehovah.'"

37 The hand of Jehovah proved to be upon me, so that he brought me forth in the spirit of Jehovah and set me down in the midst of the valley plain, and it was full of bones. 2 And he had me pass along by them all round about, and, look! there were very many on the surface of the valley plain and, look! they were very dry. 3 And he began to say to me: "Son of man, can these bones come to life?" To that I said: "Lord Jehovah, you yourself well know." 4 And he went on to say to me: "Prophesy over these bones, and you must say to them, 'O you dry bones, hear the word of Jehovah:

5 "'This is what the Lord Jehovah has said to these bones: "Here I am bringing into you breath, and you must come to life. 6 And I will put upon you sinews and cause to come upon you flesh, and I will overlay upon you skin and put in you breath, and you must come to life; and you will have to know that I am Jehovah."'"

7 And I prophesied just as I had been commanded. And a sound began to occur as soon as I prophesied, and here there was a rattling, and bones began to approach, bone to its bone. 8 And I saw, and, look! upon them sinews themselves and flesh itself came up and skin began to be overlaid upon them above. But as regards breath, there was none in them.

9 And he went on saying to me: "Prophesy to the wind. Prophesy, O son of man, and you must say to the wind, 'This is what the Lord Jehovah has said: "From the four winds come in, O wind, and blow upon these killed people, that they may come to life."'"

10 And I prophesied just as he had commanded me, and the breath proceeded to come into them, and they began to live and stand upon their feet, a very, very great military force.

11 And he went on to say to me: "Son of man, as regards these bones, they are the whole house of Israel. Here they are saying, 'Our bones have become dry, and our hope has perished. We have been severed off to ourselves.' 12 Therefore prophesy, and you must say to them, 'This is what the Lord Jehovah has said: "Here I am opening your burial places, and I will bring you up out of your burial places, O my people, and bring you in upon the soil of Israel. 13 And you will have to know that I am Jehovah when I open your burial places and when I bring you up out of your burial places, O my people."' 14 'And I will put my spirit in you, and you must come to life, and I will settle you upon your soil; and you will have to know that I myself, Jehovah, have spoken and I have done [it],' is the utterance of Jehovah."

15 And the word of Jehovah continued to occur to me, saying: 16 "And as for you, O son of man, take for yourself a stick and write upon it, 'For Judah and for the sons of Israel his partners.' And take another stick and write upon it, 'For Joseph, the stick of E′phra-im, and all the house of Israel his partners.' 17 And cause them to approach each other into one stick for yourself, and they will actually become just one in your hand. 18 And when the sons of your people begin to say to you, 'Will you not tell us what these things mean to you?' 19 speak to them, 'This is what the Lord Jehovah has said: "Here I am taking the stick of

Joseph, which is in the hand of E′phra·im, and the tribes of Israel his partners, and I will put them upon it, that is, the stick of Judah, and I shall actually make them one stick, and they must become one in my hand."' 20 And the sticks upon which you write must prove to be in your hand before their eyes.

21 "And speak to them, 'This is what the Lord Jehovah has said: "Here I am taking the sons of Israel from among the nations to which they have gone, and I will collect them together from round about and bring them onto their soil. 22 And I shall actually make them one nation in the land, on the mountains of Israel, and one king is what all of them will come to have as king, and they will no longer continue to be two nations, nor will they be divided any longer into two kingdoms. 23 And they will no longer defile themselves with their dungy idols and with their disgusting things and with all their transgressions; and I shall certainly save them from all their dwelling places in which they have sinned, and I will cleanse them, and they must become my people, and I myself shall become their God.

24 "'"And my servant David will be king over them, and one shepherd is what they will all come to have; and in my judicial decisions they will walk, and my statutes they will keep, and they will certainly carry them out. 25 And they will actually dwell upon the land that I gave to my servant, to Jacob, in which YOUR forefathers dwelt, and they will actually dwell upon it, they and their sons and their sons' sons to time indefinite, and David my servant will be their chieftain to time indefinite.

26 "'"And I will conclude with them a covenant of peace; an indefinitely lasting covenant is what there will come to be with them. And I will place them and multiply them and place my sanctuary in the midst of them to time indefinite. 27 And my tabernacle will actually prove to be over them, and I shall certainly become their God, and they themselves will become my people. 28 And the nations will have to know that I, Jehovah, am sanctifying Israel when my sanctuary comes to be in the midst of them to time indefinite."'"

38 And the word of Jehovah continued to occur to me, saying: 2 "Son of man, set your face against Gog [of] the land of Ma′gog, the head chieftain of Me′shech and Tu′bal, and prophesy against him. 3 And you must say, 'This is what the Lord Jehovah has said: "Here I am against you, O Gog, you head chieftain of Me′shech and Tu′bal. 4 And I shall certainly turn you around and put hooks in your jaws and bring you forth with all your military force, horses and horsemen, all of them clothed in perfect taste, a numerous congregation, with large shield and buckler, all of them handling swords; 5 Persia, E·thi·o′pi·a and Put with them, all of them with buckler and helmet; 6 Go′mer and all its bands, the house of To·gar′mah, [of] the remotest parts of the north, and all its bands, many peoples with you.

7 "'"Be ready, and let there be preparation on your part, you with all your congregation, those congregated alongside you, and you must become their guard.

8 "'"After many days you will be given attention. In the final part of the years you will come to the land [of people] brought back from the sword, collected together out of many peoples, onto the mountains of Israel, that have proved to be a constantly devastated place; even [a land] that has been brought forth from the peoples, [where] they have dwelt in security, all of them. 9 And you will be bound to come up. Like a storm you will come in. Like clouds to cover the land you will become, you and all your bands and many peoples with you."'

10 "This is what the Lord Jehovah has said, 'And it must occur in that day that things will come

up into your heart, and you will certainly think up an injurious scheme; 11 and you must say: "I shall go up against the land of open rural country. I shall come in upon those having no disturbance, dwelling in security, all of them dwelling without wall, and they do not have even bar and doors." 12 It will be to get a big spoil and to do much plundering, in order to turn your hand back upon devastated places reinhabited and upon a people gathered together out of the nations, [one] that is accumulating wealth and property, [those] who are dwelling in the center of the earth.

13 " 'She′ba and De′dan and the merchants of Tar′shish and all its maned young lions—they will say to you: "Is it to get a big spoil that you are coming in? Is it to do much plundering that you have congregated your congregation, in order to carry off silver and gold, to take wealth and property, to get a very great spoil?" '

14 "Therefore prophesy, O son of man, and you must say to Gog, 'This is what the Lord Jehovah has said: "Will it not be in that day when my people Israel are dwelling in security that you will know [it]? 15 And you will certainly come from your place, from the remotest parts of the north, you and many peoples with you, all of them riding on horses, a great congregation, even a numerous military force. 16 And you will be bound to come up against my people Israel, like clouds to cover the land. In the final part of the days it will occur, and I shall certainly bring you against my land, for the purpose that the nations may know me when I sanctify myself in you before their eyes, O Gog." '

17 "This is what the Lord Jehovah has said, 'Are you the same one of whom I spoke in the former days by the hand of my servants the prophets of Israel, who were prophesying in those days—years —as to bringing you in upon them?'

18 " 'And it must occur in that day, in the day when Gog comes in upon the soil of Israel,' is the utterance of the Lord Jehovah, 'that my rage will come up into my nose. 19 And in my ardor, in the fire of my fury, I shall have to speak. Surely in that day a great quaking will occur in the soil of Israel. 20 And because of me the fish of the sea and the flying creatures of the heavens and the wild beasts of the field and all the creeping things that are creeping on the ground and all mankind that are upon the surface of the ground will be bound to shiver, and the mountains will actually be thrown down and the steep ways will have to fall, and to the earth even every wall will fall.'

21 " 'And I will call forth against him throughout all my mountainous region a sword,' is the utterance of the Lord Jehovah. 'Against his own brother the sword of each one will come to be. 22 And I will bring myself into judgment with him, with pestilence and with blood; and a flooding downpour and hailstones, fire and sulphur I shall rain down upon him and upon his bands and upon the many peoples that will be with him. 23 And I shall certainly magnify myself and sanctify myself and make myself known before the eyes of many nations; and they will have to know that I am Jehovah.'

39 "And as regards you, O son of man, prophesy against Gog, and you must say, 'This is what the Lord Jehovah has said: "Here I am against you, O Gog, you head chieftain of Me′shech and Tu′bal. 2 And I will turn you around and lead you on and cause you to come up from the remotest parts of the north and bring you in upon the mountains of Israel. 3 And I will strike your bow out of your left hand, and your arrows I shall cause to fall out of your own right hand. 4 On the mountains of Israel you will fall, you and all your bands and the peoples that will be with you. To birds of prey, birds of every sort of wing, and the wild beasts of the field I will give you for food." '

5 " 'Upon the surface of the field you will fall, for I myself have spoken,' is the utterance of the Lord Jehovah.

6 " 'And I will send fire upon Ma'gog and upon those who are inhabiting the islands in security; and people will have to know that I am Jehovah. 7 And my holy name I shall make known in the midst of my people Israel, and I shall no more let my holy name be profaned; and the nations will have to know that I am Jehovah, the Holy One in Israel.'

8 " 'Look! It must come and it must be brought to be,' is the utterance of the Lord Jehovah. 'This is the day of which I have spoken. 9 And the inhabitants of the cities of Israel will certainly go forth and burn and build fires with the armor and bucklers and large shields,— with the bows and with the arrows and with the handstaves and with the lances; and with them they will have to light fires seven years. 10 And they will not carry sticks of wood from the field, nor will they gather firewood out of the forests, for with the armor they will light fires.'

" 'And they will certainly make spoil of those who had been making spoil of them, and plunder those who had been plundering them,' is the utterance of the Lord Jehovah.

11 " 'And it must occur in that day that I shall give to Gog a place there, a burial place in Israel, the valley of those passing through on the east of the sea, and it will be stopping up those passing through. And there they will have to bury Gog and all his crowd, and they will be certain to call [it] the Valley of Gog's Crowd. 12 And those of the house of Israel will have to bury them for the purpose of cleansing the land, for seven months. 13 And all the people of the land will have to do the burying, and it will certainly become for them a matter of fame in the day that I glorify myself,' is the utterance of the Lord Jehovah.

14 " 'And there will be men for continual [employment] whom they will divide off, passing along through the land, burying, with those passing through, those left remaining on the surface of the earth, in order to cleanse it. To the end of seven months they will keep making search. 15 And those passing through must pass along through the land, and should one actually see the bone of a man he must also build beside it a marker, until those who do the burying will have buried it in the Valley of Gog's Crowd. 16 And the name of [the] city will also be Ha·mo'-nah. And they will have to cleanse the land.'

17 "And as regards you, O son of man, this is what the Lord Jehovah has said, 'Say to the birds of every sort of wing and to all the wild beasts of the field: "Collect your-selves together and come. Gather yourselves together all around to my sacrifice, which I am sacrific-ing for you, a great sacrifice on the mountains of Israel. And you will certainly eat flesh and drink blood. 18 The flesh of mighty ones you will eat, and the blood of the chieftains of the earth you will drink, rams, young male sheep, and he-goats, young bulls, the fatlings of Ba'shan all of them. 19 And you will be certain to eat fat to satisfaction and to drink blood to drunkenness, from my sacrifice that I will sacrifice for you." '

20 " 'And you must get satisfied at my table on horses and chariot-eers, mighty persons and all sorts of warriors,' is the utterance of the Lord Jehovah.

21 " 'And I will set my glory among the nations; and all the nations will have to see my judg-ment that I have executed and my hand that I have placed among them. 22 And those of the house of Israel will have to know that I, Jehovah, am their God from that day and forward. 23 And the nations will have to know that it was because of their error that they, the house of Israel, went into exile, on account of the fact that they behaved unfaithfully toward me, so that I concealed my face

from them and gave them into the hand of their adversaries, and they kept falling, all of them, by the sword. 24 According to their uncleanness and according to their transgressions I did with them, and I kept concealing my face from them.'

25 "Therefore this is what the Lord Jehovah has said, 'Now is when I shall bring back the captive ones of Jacob and actually have mercy upon all the house of Israel; and I will show exclusive devotion for my holy name. 26 And they will have borne their humiliation and all their unfaithfulness with which they have acted toward me, when they dwell on their soil in security, with no one to make [them] tremble. 27 When I bring them back from the peoples and I actually collect them together out of the lands of their enemies, I will also sanctify myself among them before the eyes of many nations.'

28 "'And they will have to know that I, Jehovah, am their God, when I send them in exile to the nations and actually bring them together upon their soil, so that I shall leave none of them remaining there any longer. 29 And I shall no longer conceal my face from them, because I will pour out my spirit upon the house of Israel,' is the utterance of the Lord Jehovah."

40 In the twenty-fifth year of our exile, in the start of the year, on the tenth [day] of the month, in the fourteenth year after the city had been struck down, on this very same day the hand of Jehovah proved to be upon me, so that he brought me to that place. 2 In the visions of God he brought me to the land of Israel and gradually set me down upon a very high mountain, on which there was something like the structure of a city to the south.

3 And he proceeded to bring me there, and, look! there was a man. His appearance was like the appearance of copper, and there was a flax cord in his hand, and a meas-

uring reed, and he was standing in the gate. 4 And the man began to speak to me: "Son of man, see with your eyes, and with your ears hear, and set your heart upon all that I am showing you, because for the purpose of [my] showing you, you have been brought here. Tell everything that you are seeing to the house of Israel."

5 And, look! there was a wall outside the house all round about. And in the hand of the man there was the measuring reed of six cubits, by a cubit and a handbreadth. And he began to measure the breadth of the thing built, one reed; and the height, one reed.

6 Then he came to the gate, the front of which is toward the east, and went up by its steps. And he began to measure the threshold of the gate, one reed in width, and the other threshold, one reed in width. 7 And the guard chamber was one reed in length and one reed in width, and between the guard chambers there were five cubits; and the threshold of the gate beside the porch of the gate toward the interior was one reed.

8 And he proceeded to measure the porch of the gate toward the interior, one reed. 9 So he measured the porch of the gate, eight cubits; and its side pillars, two cubits; and the porch of the gate was toward the interior.

10 And the guard chambers of the gate toward the east were three on this side and three on that side. The three of them were of the same measurement, and the side pillars were of the same measurement, on this side and on that side.

11 Then he measured the width of the entrance of the gate, ten cubits; the length of the gate, thirteen cubits.

12 And the fenced area in front of the guard chambers was one cubit, and there was a fenced area of one cubit on [either] side. And the guard chamber was six cubits on this side and six cubits on that side.

13 And he went on to measure the gate from the roof of the [one]

guard chamber to the roof of the other, a width of twenty-five cubits; entrance was across from entrance. 14 Then he made side pillars of sixty cubits, even to the side pillar[s] of the courtyard in the gate[s] all around. 15 And by the front of the gate of the entryway [to] the front of the porch of the inner gate was fifty cubits.

16 And there were windows of narrowing frames for the guard chambers and for their side pillars toward the inside of the gate all around, and that is the way it was for the porches. And the windows were all around toward the inside, and on the side pillars there were palm-tree figures.

17 And he gradually brought me into the outer courtyard, and, look! there were dining rooms, and a pavement made for the courtyard all around. There were thirty dining rooms upon the pavement. 18 And the pavement at the side of the gates was exactly as the length of the gates—the lower pavement.

19 And he proceeded to measure the width from in front of the lower gate to the front of the inner courtyard. Outside it was a hundred cubits, to the east and to the north.

20 And the outer courtyard had a gate the front of which was toward the north. He measured its length and its width. 21 And its guard chambers were three on this side and three on that side. And its own side pillars and its own porch proved to be according to the measurement of the first gate. Fifty cubits was its length, and its width was twenty-five in cubits. 22 And its windows and its porch and its palm-tree figures were of the same measurement as those of the gate the front of which is toward the east. And by seven steps people could go up into it, and its porch was to their front.

23 And the gate of the inner courtyard was opposite the gate to the north; also [one] to the east. And he proceeded to measure from gate to gate a hundred cubits.

24 And he gradually brought me toward the south, and, look! there was a gate toward the south, and he measured its side pillars and its porch as of the same measurements as these. 25 And it and its porch had windows all around, like these windows. Fifty cubits was the length, and the breadth was twenty-five cubits. 26 And there were seven steps for going up to it, and its porch was to their front. And it had palm-tree figures, one on this side and one on that side on its side pillars.

27 And the inner courtyard had a gate toward the south. And he measured from gate to gate toward the south a hundred cubits. 28 And he gradually brought me into the inner courtyard by the gate of the south. And he proceeded to measure the gate of the south as of the same measurements as these. 29 And its guard chambers and its side pillars and its porch were of the same measurements as these. And it and its porch had windows round about. Fifty cubits was the length, and the width was twenty-five cubits. 30 And there were porches all around; the length was twenty-five cubits, and the width five cubits. 31 And its porch was to the outer courtyard, and palm-tree figures were on its side pillars, and its ascent was eight steps.

32 And he gradually brought me into the inner courtyard by way of the east, and he proceeded to measure the gate as of the same measurements as these. 33 And its guard chambers and its side pillars and its porch were of the same measurements as these, and it and its porch had windows all around. The length was fifty cubits, and the width twenty-five cubits. 34 And its porch was toward the outer courtyard, and palm-tree figures were on its side pillars on this side and on that side. And its ascent was eight steps.

35 And he proceeded to bring me into the north gate, and he measured, with the same measurements as these, 36 its guard chambers, its side pillars and its porch. And

it had windows all around. The length was fifty cubits, and the width twenty-five cubits. 37 And to the outer courtyard were its side pillars, and palm-tree figures were on its side pillars on this side and on that side. And its ascent was eight steps.

38 And a dining room with its entrance was by the side pillars of the gates. There it was that they would rinse the whole burnt offering.

39 And in the porch of the gate there were two tables on this side and two tables on that side, for slaughtering upon them the whole burnt offering and the sin offering and the guilt offering. 40 And on the outer side, as one goes up to the entrance of the north gate, there were two tables. And on the other side that belongs to the porch of the gate there were two tables. 41 There were four tables over here and four tables over there at the side of the gate—eight tables, upon which they would do the slaughtering. 42 And the four tables for the whole burnt offering were of hewn stone. The length was one cubit and a half, and the width one cubit and a half, and the height one cubit. Upon them they would also deposit the implements with which they would slaughter the whole burnt offering and the sacrifice. 43 And the ledges for setting down things were of one handbreadth, firmly fixed on the interior, all around; and upon the tables [they would deposit] the flesh of the gift offering.

44 And on the outside of the inner gate there were the dining rooms of the singers, in the inner courtyard, which is on the side of the north gate. And their front side was toward the south. There was one on the side of the east gate. The front was toward the north.

45 And he proceeded to speak to me: "This one, the dining room the front of which is toward the south, is for the priests who are taking care of the obligation of the house. 46 And the dining room

the front of which is toward the north is for the priests who are taking care of the obligation of the altar. They are the sons of Za′dok, who, from the sons of Le′vi, are approaching Jehovah to minister to him."

47 And he went measuring the [inner] courtyard. The length was a hundred cubits, and the width a hundred cubits, foursquare. And the altar was before the house.

48 And he proceeded to bring me into the porch of the house, and he went measuring the side pillar of the porch, five cubits on this side and five cubits on that side. And the width of the gate was three cubits on this side and three cubits on that side.

49 The length of the porch was twenty cubits, and the width eleven cubits. And by steps was how they would go up to it. And there were pillars by the side posts, one over here and one over there.

41 And he proceeded to bring me into the temple, and he went measuring the side pillars, six cubits being the width over here and six cubits the width over there, the width of the side pillar. 2 And the width of the entrance was ten cubits, and the sides of the entrance were five cubits over here and five cubits over there. And he went measuring its length, forty cubits; and the width, twenty cubits.

3 And he went inside and proceeded to measure the side pillar of the entrance, two cubits; and the entrance, six cubits; and the width of the entrance was seven cubits. 4 And he went measuring its length, twenty cubits; and [its] width, twenty cubits, before the temple. Then he said to me: "This is the Most Holy."

5 And he proceeded to measure the wall of the house, six cubits. And the width of the side chamber was four cubits, round about; all around the house it was, round about. 6 And the side chambers were side chamber upon side chamber, three [stories], and for thirty times; and they were entering into

the wall that belonged to the house, that is, the side chambers all around, in order that they might be held in, but they were not held in in the wall of the house. 7 And there was a widening out and turning around upward and upward to the side chambers, for the winding passage of the house was upward and upward all around the house. Therefore there was a widening to the house upward, and from the lowest [story] one could go up to the uppermost [story], by the middle [story].

8 And I saw that there was a high platform for the house all around. As regards the foundations of the side chambers, there was a full reed of six cubits to the joining. 9 The width of the wall that belonged to the side chamber, to the outside, was five cubits. And there was a space left open [by] the construction of the side chambers that belonged to the house.

10 And between the dining rooms the width was twenty cubits round about the house, all around. 11 And the entrance of the side chamber was to the space left open, one entrance being toward the north and one entrance to the south; and the width of the area of the space left open was five cubits, all around.

12 And the building that was before the separated area, the side [of which] was toward the west, was seventy cubits wide. And the wall of the building was five cubits in width, it being all around; and its length was ninety cubits.

13 And he measured the house, a hundred cubits in length; and the separated area and the building and its walls, a hundred cubits in length. 14 And the width of the front of the house and the separated area to the east was a hundred cubits.

15 And he measured the length of the building before the separated area that was behind it and its galleries on this side and on that side, a hundred cubits.

Also the temple [and] the inner place and the porches of the court-

yard; 16 the thresholds, and the windows with narrowing frames, and the galleries were round about the three of them. In front of the threshold there was paneling of wood all around, and [from] the floor up to the windows; and the windows were covered ones. 17 To above the entrance and as far as the inner house and on the outside and upon the whole wall all around, on the inner [house] and on the outside, there were measurements, 18 even carved cherubs and palm-tree figures, with a palm-tree figure between a cherub and a cherub, and the cherub had two faces. 19 And the face of a man was toward the palm-tree figure on this side, and the face of a maned young lion was toward the palm-tree figure on that side, they being carved on the whole house all around. 20 From the floor to above the entrance there were carved cherubs and palm-tree figures, [on] the wall of the temple.

21 As for the temple, the doorpost was squared; and [in] front of the holy place there was an appearance like the [following] appearance: 22 the wooden altar was three cubits high, and its length was two cubits, and it had its corner posts. And its length and its walls were of wood. And he proceeded to speak to me: "This is the table that is before Jehovah."

23 And the temple and the holy place had two doors. 24 And two door leaves belonged to the doors, the two being turnable. One door had two door leaves, and the other had two door leaves. 25 And there were made upon them, upon the doors of the temple, cherubs and palm-tree figures, like those made for the walls, and there was a canopy of wood over the front of the porch outside. 26 And there were windows of narrowing frames and palm-tree figures over here and over there along the sides of the porch and the side chambers of the house and the canopies.

42 And he gradually brought me forth to the outer courtyard by the way toward the north. And

he proceeded to bring me to the dining-room [block] that was in front of the separated area and that was in front of the building to the north. 2 Before the length of a hundred cubits there was the north entrance, and the width was fifty cubits. 3 In front of the twenty [cubits] that belonged to the inner courtyard and in front of the pavement that belonged to the outer courtyard there was gallery opposite gallery in three [stories]. 4 And before the dining rooms there was a walkway ten cubits in width to the inside, a way of one cubit, and their entrances were to the north. 5 And as for the dining rooms, the uppermost ones were shorter, for the galleries took away from them, more than the lowest ones and than the middle ones, as regards [the] building. 6 For they were in three stories, and they had no pillars like the pillars of the courtyards. That is why more room was taken away than from the lowest ones and from the middle ones from the floor.

7 And the stone wall that was outside was close by the dining rooms toward the outer courtyard before the [other] dining rooms. Its length was fifty cubits. 8 For the length of the dining rooms that were toward the outer courtyard was fifty cubits, and, look! before the temple it was a hundred cubits. 9 And from below these dining rooms the entryway was to the east, when one comes in to them from the outer courtyard.

10 In the width of the stone wall of the courtyard toward the east, before the separated area and before the building, there were dining rooms. 11 And there was a way before them like the appearance of the dining rooms that were toward the north, so their length was [and] so their width was; and all their exits [were alike], and their plans alike and their entrances alike. 12 And like the entrances of the dining rooms that were toward the south was the entrance at the head of the way, the way

before the corresponding stone wall toward the east, when one comes in to them.

13 And he proceeded to say to me: "The dining rooms of the north [and] the dining rooms of the south that are before the separated area, they are the holy dining rooms, where the priests who are approaching Jehovah eat the most holy things. There they deposit the most holy things and the grain offering and the sin offering and the guilt offering, because the place is holy. 14 When they, the priests, have come in, they will not also go out from the holy place to the outer courtyard, but there they will deposit their garments in which they customarily minister, for they are something holy. They will clothe themselves with other garments, and must approach to what has to do with the people."

15 And he finished the measurements of the inner house, and he brought me out by the way of the gate the front of which was toward the east, and he measured it all around.

16 He measured the eastern side with the measuring reed. It was five hundred reeds, by the measuring reed, round about.

17 He measured the northern side, five hundred reeds, by the measuring reed, round about.

18 The southern side he measured, five hundred reeds, by the measuring reed.

19 He went around to the western side. He measured five hundred reeds, by the measuring reed.

20 For the four sides he measured it. It had a wall all around, with a length of five hundred [reeds] and a width of five hundred [reeds], to make a division between what is holy and what is profane.

43 Then he made me go to the gate, the gate that is facing toward the east. 2 And, look! the glory of the God of Israel was coming from the direction of the east, and his voice was like the voice of vast waters; and the earth itself shone because of his glory.

3 And it was like the appearance of the vision that I had seen, like the vision that I saw when I came to bring the city to ruin; and there were appearances like the appearance that I saw by the river Che′bar, and I went falling upon my face.

4 And the glory of Jehovah itself came into the house by way of the gate the front of which was toward the east. 5 And a spirit proceeded to raise me up and bring me into the inner courtyard, and, look! the house had become full of the glory of Jehovah. 6 And I began to hear someone speaking to me out of the house, and [the] man himself had come to be standing beside me. 7 And He went on to say to me:

"Son of man, [this is] the place of my throne and the place of the soles of my feet, where I shall reside in the midst of the sons of Israel to time indefinite; and no more will they, the house of Israel, defile my holy name, they and their kings, by their fornication and by the carcasses of their kings at their death, 8 by their putting their threshold with my threshold and their doorpost beside my doorpost, with the wall between me and them. And they defiled my holy name by their detestable things that they did, so that I went exterminating them in my anger. 9 Now let them remove their fornication and the carcasses of their kings far from me, and I shall certainly reside in the midst of them to time indefinite.

10 "As for you, O son of man, inform the house of Israel about the House, that they may feel humiliated because of their errors, and they must measure the pattern. 11 And if they actually feel humiliated because of all that they have done, the ground plan of the House, and its arrangement and its exits and its entryways, and all its ground plans and all its specifications, and all its ground plans and all its laws do you make known to them and write before their eyes, in order that they may observe all its ground plan and all its specifications and may actually carry them out. 12 This is the law of the House. On the top of the mountain its entire territory all around is something most holy. Look! This is the law of the House.

13 "And these are the measurements of the altar in cubits, a cubit being a cubit and a handbreadth. And [its] bottom is a cubit. And a cubit is the width. And its border is upon its lip round about, one span. And this is the base of the altar. 14 And from the bottom on the floor to the lower surrounding ledge there are two cubits, and the width is one cubit. And from the small surrounding ledge to the big surrounding ledge there are four cubits, and [its] width is a cubit. 15 And the altar hearth is four cubits, and out from the altar hearth and upward there are the four horns. 16 And the altar hearth is twelve [cubits] in length, with twelve [cubits] of width, squared on its four sides. 17 And the surrounding ledge is fourteen [cubits] in length, with fourteen [cubits] of width, on its four sides; and the border surrounding it is half a cubit, and its bottom is a cubit round about.

"And its steps are facing east."

18 And he proceeded to say to me: "Son of man, this is what the Lord Jehovah has said, 'These are the statutes of the altar on the day of its being made, in order to offer upon it whole burnt offerings and to sprinkle upon it blood.'

19 "'And you must give to the Levitical priests, who are of the offspring of Za′dok, the ones approaching me,' is the utterance of the Lord Jehovah, 'to minister to me, a young bull, the son of [the] herd, as a sin offering. 20 And you must take some of its blood and put [it] upon its four horns and upon the four corners of the surrounding ledge and upon the border round about and purify it from sin and make atonement for it. 21 And you must take the young bull, the sin offering, and one must burn it in the appointed

place of the House, outside the sanctuary. 22 And on the second day you will bring near a buck of the goats, a sound one, as a sin offering; and they must purify the altar from sin the same as they purified [it] from sin with the young bull.'

23 " 'On your making an end of the purifying from sin you will bring near a young bull, the son of [the] herd, a sound one, and a ram from the flock, a sound one. 24 And you must bring them near before Jehovah, and the priests must throw salt upon them and offer them up as a whole burnt offering to Jehovah. 25 For seven days you will render up a he-goat as a sin offering for the day; and a young bull, the son of [the] herd, and a ram out of the flock, perfect ones, they will render up. 26 For seven days they will make atonement for the altar, and they must cleanse it and install it. 27 And they will complete the days. And it must occur on the eighth day and from then on that the priests will render upon the altar the whole burnt offerings of you people and your communion sacrifices; and I shall certainly find pleasure in you,' is the utterance of the Lord Jehovah."

44 And he proceeded to bring me back by way of the gate of the sanctuary, the outer one facing east, and it was shut. 2 Then Jehovah said to me: "As regards this gate, shut is how it will continue. It will not be opened, and no mere man will come in by it; for Jehovah himself, the God of Israel, has come in by it, and it must continue shut. 3 However, the chieftain—as chieftain he himself will sit in it, in order to eat bread before Jehovah. By way of the porch of the gate he will come in, and by way of it he will go out."

4 And he now brought me by way of the north gate to before the house, that I might see, and, look! the glory of Jehovah had filled the house of Jehovah. And I went falling on my face. 5 Then Jehovah said to me: "Son of man, set your heart and see with your eyes, and

with your ears hear all that I am speaking with you regarding all the statutes of the house of Jehovah and regarding all its laws, and you must set your heart upon the entryway of the house with all the exits of the sanctuary. 6 And you must say to Rebelliousness, to the house of Israel, 'This is what the Lord Jehovah has said: "That is enough of you because of all your detestable things, O house of Israel, 7 when you bring in the foreigners uncircumcised in heart and uncircumcised in flesh, in order to come to be in my sanctuary so as to profane it, even my house; when you present my bread, fat and blood, while they keep breaking my covenant on account of all your detestable things. 8 Neither have you taken care of the obligation of my holy things, nor would you post [others] as caretakers of my obligation in my sanctuary for yourselves." '

9 " 'This is what the Lord Jehovah has said: "No foreigner, uncircumcised in heart and uncircumcised in flesh, may come into my sanctuary, that is, any foreigner who is in the midst of the sons of Israel." '

10 " 'But as for the Levites who got far away from me when Israel, who wandered away from me, wandered after their dungy idols, they must also bear their error. 11 And in my sanctuary they must become ministers at posts of oversight over the gates of the house and ministers at the house. They themselves will slaughter the whole burnt offering and the sacrifice for the people, and they themselves will stand before them to minister to them. 12 For the reason that they kept ministering to them before their dungy idols and became to the house of Israel a stumbling block into error, that is why I have raised my hand against them,' is the utterance of the Lord Jehovah, 'and they must bear their error. 13 And they will not approach to me to act as priest to me or to approach to any holy things of mine, to the most holy things, and

they must bear their humiliation and their detestable things that they did. 14 And I shall certainly make them caretakers of the obligation of the house, as regards all its service and as regards all that should be done in it.'

15 "'And as for the Levitical priests, the sons of Za'dok, who took care of the obligation of my sanctuary when the sons of Israel wandered away from me, they themselves will come near to me to minister to me, and they must stand before me to present to me fat and the blood,' is the utterance of the Lord Jehovah. 16 'They are the ones that will come into my sanctuary, and they themselves will come near to my table to minister to me, and they must take care of the obligation to me.

17 "'And it must occur that when they come into the gates of the inner courtyard, linen garments they should wear, and no wool should come up on them when they minister in the gates of the inner courtyard and inside. 18 Linen headdresses are what should prove to be on their head, and linen drawers are what should prove to be upon their hips. They should not gird themselves with [what causes] sweat. 19 And when they go forth to the outer courtyard, [even] to the outer courtyard to the people, they should strip off their garments in which they were ministering, and they must deposit them in the holy dining rooms and put on other garments, that they may not sanctify the people with their garments. 20 And their head they should not shave, and the hair of the head they should not wear loose. They should by all means clip [the hair of] their heads. 21 And no wine should any priests drink when they come into the inner courtyard. 22 And no widow or divorced woman should they take for themselves as wives, but virgins the offspring of the house of Israel or the widow who happens to be the widow of a priest they may take.'

23 "'And my people they should instruct in the difference between a holy thing and a profane thing; and the difference between what is unclean and what is clean they should cause them to know. 24 And in a legal case they themselves should stand in order to judge; with my judicial decisions they must also judge it. And my laws and my statutes in regard to all my festal seasons they should keep, and my sabbaths they should sanctify. 25 And to a dead person of mankind he should not come in so as to become unclean, but for father or for mother or for son or for daughter [or] for brother or for a sister that has not become a husband's they may make themselves unclean. 26 And after his purification, seven days they should number off for him. 27 And on the day of his coming into the holy place, into the inner courtyard, to minister in the holy place, he should present his sin offering,' is the utterance of the Lord Jehovah.

28 "'And it must become theirs as an inheritance: I am their inheritance. And no possession should you people give them in Israel: I am their possession. 29 The grain offering and the sin offering and the guilt offering—they are the ones who will eat them. And every devoted thing in Israel—theirs it will become. 30 And the first of all the first ripe fruits of everything and every contribution of everything out of all your contributions —to the priests it will come to belong; and the first fruits of your coarse meals you should give to the priest, in order to cause a blessing to rest upon your house. 31 No body [already] dead and no creature torn to pieces of the flying creatures or of the beasts should the priests eat.'

45 "'And when you people allot the land as an inheritance, you should offer a contribution to Jehovah, a holy portion out of the land; as to length, twenty-five thousand [cubits] in length, and as to width, ten thousand. It will be a holy portion in all its boundaries round about. 2 From this there will prove to be for the holy place five hundred by five hundred, it being made square round about; and fifty cubits it will have as pasture ground on each side. 3 And out of this measurement you should measure the length of twenty-five thousand and the width of ten thousand, and in it the sanctuary will come to be, something most holy. 4 As a holy portion out of the land it will come to be for the priests themselves, the ministers of the sanctuary, those approaching to minister to Jehovah. And for them it must prove to be a place for houses, and a sacred place for the sanctuary.

5 "There will be twenty-five thousand in length and ten thousand in width. It will become the Levites', the ministers of the house. As a possession they will have twenty dining rooms.

6 "'And as the possession of the city, you people will give five thousand in width and a length of twenty-five thousand, exactly as the holy contribution. To all the house of Israel it will come to belong.

7 "'And for the chieftain there will be on this side and on that side of the holy contribution and of the possession of the city, beside the holy contribution and beside the possession of the city, something on the west side westward and something on the east side eastward. And the length will be exactly as one of the shares, from the western boundary to the eastern boundary. 8 As regards the land, it will become his as a possession in Israel. And no more will my chieftains maltreat my people, and the land they will give to the house of Israel with respect to their tribes.'

9 "This is what the Lord Jehovah has said, 'That is enough of you, O chieftains of Israel!'

"'Remove the violence and the despoiling, and do justice and righteousness themselves. Lift your expropriations off my people,' is the utterance of the Lord Jehovah. 10 'Accurate scales and an accurate e'phah and an accurate bath measure you men should come to have. 11 As regards the e'phah and the bath measure, there should come to be but one fixed amount, for the bath to carry a tenth of a ho'mer and the tenth of the ho'mer an e'phah; with reference to the ho'mer, its required amount should prove to be. 12 And the shekel is twenty ge'rahs. Twenty shekels, twenty-five shekels, fifteen shekels should prove to be the ma'neh for you.'

13 "'This is the contribution that you should offer, the sixth part of the e'phah from the ho'mer of wheat, and the sixth part of the e'phah from the ho'mer of barley; 14 and as for the allowance of the oil, there is the bath measure of the oil. The bath is a tenth of the cor. Ten baths are a ho'mer; because ten baths are a ho'mer. 15 And one sheep out of the flock, out of two hundred from the livestock of Israel, for the grain offering and for the whole burnt offering and for the communion sacrifices, in order to make atonement for them,' is the utterance of the Lord Jehovah.

16 "'As for all the people of the land, they will be responsible for this contribution to the chieftain in Israel. 17 And upon the chieftain will devolve the whole burnt offerings and the grain offering and the drink offering during the festivals and during the new moons and during the sabbaths, during all the festal seasons of the house of Israel. He will be the one to provide the sin offering and the grain offering and the whole burnt offering and the communion sacrifices, in order to make atonement in behalf of the house of Israel.'

18 "This is what the Lord Jehovah has said, 'In the first [month], on the first [day] of the month, you should take a young bull, a son of the herd, a sound one, and you must purify the sanctuary from sin. 19 And the priest must take some of the blood of the sin offering and put it upon the doorpost of the house and upon the four corners of the surrounding ledge belonging

to the altar and upon the doorpost of the gate of the inner courtyard. 20 And that is how you will do on the seventh [day] in the month because of any man making a mistake and because of any inexperienced one; and you people must make atonement for the House.

21 " 'In the first [month], on the fourteenth day of the month, there should occur for you the passover. As a festival for seven days unfermented cakes are what should be eaten. 22 And on that day, in his own behalf and in behalf of all the people of the land, the chieftain must provide a young bull as a sin offering. 23 And for the seven days of the festival he should provide as a whole burnt offering to Jehovah seven young bulls and seven rams, sound ones, daily for the seven days, and as a sin offering a buck of the goats daily. 24 And as a grain offering an e'phah for the young bull and an e'phah for the ram he should provide, and, as regards oil, a hin to the e'phah.

25 " 'In the seventh [month], on the fifteenth day of the month, during the festival, he should provide the same as these for the seven days, the same as the sin offering, as the whole burnt offering, and as the grain offering and as the oil.' "

46 "This is what the Lord Jehovah has said, 'As regards the gate of the inner courtyard that is facing east, it should continue shut for the six workdays, and on the sabbath day it should be opened, and on the day of the new moon it should be opened. 2 And the chieftain must come in by the way of the porch of the gate, from outside, and stand by the doorpost of the gate; and the priests must render up his whole burnt offering and his communion sacrifices, and he must bow down upon the threshold of the gate, and he must go out, but the gate itself should not be shut until the evening. 3 And the people of the land must bow down at the entrance of that gate on the sabbaths and on the new moons, before Jehovah.

4 " 'And the whole burnt offering that the chieftain should present to Jehovah on the sabbath day should be six sound male lambs and a sound ram; 5 and as a grain offering an e'phah for the ram, and for the male lambs a grain offering as he is able to give, and, as regards oil, a hin to the e'phah. 6 And on the day of the new moon there should be a young bull, the son of the herd, a sound one, and six male lambs and a ram; sound ones they should prove to be. 7 And an e'phah for the young bull and an e'phah for the ram he should render up as a grain offering, and for the male lambs according to what he is able to afford; and, as regards oil, a hin to the e'phah.

8 " 'And when the chieftain comes in, by the way of the porch of the gate he should come in, and by the way of it he should go out. 9 And when the people of the land come in before Jehovah in the festal seasons, the one coming in by the way of the north gate in order to bow down should go out by the way of the south gate; and the one coming in by the way of the south gate should go out by the way of the gate to the north. No one should go back by the way of the gate by which he came in, for he should go out straight ahead of him. 10 And as regards the chieftain in their midst, when they come in, he should come in; and when they go out, he should go out. 11 And in the festivals and in the festal seasons the grain offering should prove to be an e'phah for the young bull and an e'phah for the ram, and for the male lambs as he is able to give; and, as regards oil, a hin to the e'phah.

12 " 'And in case the chieftain should provide as a voluntary offering a whole burnt offering, or communion sacrifices as a voluntary offering to Jehovah, one must also open to him the gate that is facing east, and he must provide his whole burnt offering and his communion sacrifices just as he does on the sabbath day. And he must go out,

and one must shut the gate after his going out.

13 "'And a sound male lamb, in its first year, you should provide as a whole burnt offering daily to Jehovah. Morning by morning you should provide it. 14 And as a grain offering you should provide with it morning by morning the sixth of an e'phah and, as regards oil, the third of a hin for sprinkling the fine flour. The grain offering to Jehovah is an indefinitely lasting statute, constantly. 15 And they must provide the male lamb and the grain offering and the oil morning by morning as a constant whole burnt offering.'

16 "This is what the Lord Jehovah has said, 'In case the chieftain should give a gift to each one of his sons as his inheritance, it itself will become the property of his sons themselves. It is their possession by inheritance. 17 And in case he should give a gift from his inheritance to one of his servants, it must also become his until the year of liberty; and it must return to the chieftain. Only his inheritance—as regards his sons— is what should continue to belong to their own selves. 18 And the chieftain should not take any of the inheritance of the people so as to force them out of their possession. From his own possession he should give his sons an inheritance, to the end that my people may not be scattered each one from his possession.'"

19 And he proceeded to bring me in by the entryway that was by the side of the gate to the holy dining rooms, those belonging to the priests, that were facing to the north, and, look! there was a place there on both rear sides to the west. 20 And he proceeded to say to me: "This is the place where the priests will boil the guilt offering and the sin offering, [and] where they will bake the grain offering, in order to carry nothing out to the outer courtyard so as to sanctify the people."

21 And he proceeded to bring me out to the outer courtyard and make me pass along to the four corner posts of the courtyard, and, look! there was a courtyard by [this] corner post of the courtyard, a courtyard by [that] corner post of the courtyard. 22 At the four corner posts of the courtyard there were small courtyards, forty [cubits] in length and thirty in width. The four of them with corner structures had the same measurement. 23 And there was a row round about them, round about the four of them, and there were boiling places made beneath the rows round about. 24 Then he said to me: "These are the houses of those doing the boiling, where the ministers of the House boil the sacrifice of the people."

47 And gradually he brought me back to the entrance of the House, and, look! there was water going forth from under the threshold of the House eastward, for the front of the House was east. And the water was going down from under, from the right-hand side of the House, south of the altar.

2 And he gradually brought me forth by the way of the north gate and took me around by the way outside to the outer gate that is facing toward the east, and, look! water was trickling from the right-hand side.

3 When the man went forth eastward with a measuring line in his hand, he also proceeded to measure a thousand in cubits and to make me pass through the water, water [up] to the ankles.

4 And he continued measuring a thousand and then made me pass through the water, water [up] to the knees.

And he continued measuring a thousand and now made me pass through—water [up] to the hips.

5 And he continued measuring a thousand. It was a torrent that I was not able to pass through, for the water had got high, water [permitting] swimming, a torrent that could not be passed through.

6 At that he said to me: "Have you seen [this], O son of man?"

Then he had me walk and had me return [to] the bank of the

torrent. 7 When I returned, why, look! on the bank of the torrent there were very many trees, on this side and on that side. 8 And he went on to say to me: "This water is going forth to the eastern region and must go down through the Ar′a·bah. And it must come to the sea. It being brought forth into the sea itself, [its] water is also actually healed. 9 And it must occur that every living soul that swarms, in every place to which the double-size torrent comes, will get life. And it must occur that there will be very many fish, because there is where this water will certainly come, and the [sea water] will be healed, and everything will be alive where the torrent comes.

10 "And it must occur that fishers will actually stand alongside it from En-ge′di even up to En-eg′la·im. There will come to be a drying yard for dragnets. In their kinds their fish will prove to be, like the fish of the Great Sea, very many.

11 "There are its swampy places and its marshy places, and they will not be healed. To salt they will certainly be given.

12 "And alongside the torrent there will come up, along its bank on this side and on that side, all sorts of trees for food. Their leafage will not wither, nor will their fruitage be consumed. In their months they will bear new fruit, because the water for them—it is coming forth from the very sanctuary. And their fruitage must prove to be for food and their leafage for healing."

13 This is what the Lord Jehovah has said: "This is the territory that YOU will assign to yourselves for inheritance as the land for the twelve tribes of Israel, with two pieces of field to Joseph. 14 And YOU people must inherit it, each one the same as his brother, which [land] I raised my hand [in an oath] to give to YOUR forefathers; and this land must fall to YOU [by lot] for inheritance.

15 "And this is the boundary of the land to the northern side,

from the Great Sea by the way to Heth′lon, as one comes to Ze′dad, 16 Ha′math, Be·ro′thah, Sib′ra·im, which is between the boundary of Damascus and the boundary of Ha′math; Ha′zer-hat′ti·con, which is toward the boundary of Ha·u·ran′. 17 And the boundary from the sea must prove to be Ha′zar-e′non, the boundary of Damascus and north—northward, and the boundary of Ha′math. This is the northern side.

18 "And the eastern side is from between Ha·u·ran′ and Damascus and between Gil′e·ad and the land of Israel; the Jordan, from the boundary to the eastern sea YOU people should measure. This is the eastern side.

19 "And the southern side is to the south, from Ta′mar to the waters of Mer′i·bath-ka′desh, the torrent valley to the Great Sea. This is the side to the south, toward the Neg′eb.

20 "And the western side is the Great Sea, from the boundary straight ahead to the entering in to Ha′math. This is the western side."

21 "And YOU must apportion this land to yourselves, to the twelve tribes of Israel. 22 And it must occur that YOU should allot it for inheritance to yourselves and to the alien residents who are residing as aliens in YOUR midst, who have become father to sons in the midst of YOU. And they must become to YOU like a native among the sons of Israel. With YOU people they will fall [by lot] into an inheritance in the midst of the tribes of Israel. 23 And it must occur that in the tribe with which the alien resident has taken up residence as an alien, there is where YOU should give his inheritance," is the utterance of the Lord Jehovah.

48 "And these are the names of the tribes. From the northern extremity, on the side by the way of Heth′lon to the entering in to Ha′math, Ha′zar-e′nan, the boundary of Damascus northward, on the side of Ha′math; and it must prove to have an eastern border [and] the western, Dan one [por-

tion]. 2 And on the boundary of Dan, from the eastern border to the western border, Ash'er one. 3 And on the boundary of Ash'er, from the eastern border even to the western border, Naph'ta·li one. 4 And on the boundary of Naph'ta·li, from the eastern border to the western border, Ma·nas'seh one. 5 And on the boundary of Ma·nas'seh, from the eastern border to the western border, E'phra·im one. 6 And on the boundary of E'phra·im, from the eastern border even to the western border, Reu'ben one. 7 And on the boundary of Reu'ben, from the eastern border to the western border, Judah one. 8 And on the boundary of Judah, from the eastern border to the western border, the contribution that you people should contribute should prove to be twenty-five thousand [cubits] in width, and [the] length according to one of the portions from the eastern border to the western border. And the sanctuary must prove to be in the midst of it.

9 "As regards the contribution that you should contribute to Je-hovah, [the] length will be twenty-five thousand [cubits] and [the] width ten thousand. 10 And as to these there should prove to be the holy contribution for the priests, to the north twenty-five thousand [cubits], and to the west a width of ten thousand, and to the east a width of ten thousand, and to the south a length of twenty-five thou-sand. And the sanctuary of Jeho-vah must prove to be in the midst of it. 11 It will be for the priests, those who are sanctified from the sons of Za'dok, who took care of the obligation toward me, who did not wander away when the sons of Israel wandered away, just as the Levites wandered away. 12 And they must come to have a contribu-tion from the contribution of the land as something most holy, on the boundary of the Levites.

13 "And the Levites should have, right next to the territory of the priests, twenty-five thousand [cu-bits] in length, and in width ten thousand; the whole length being twenty-five thousand and width being ten thousand. 14 And they should not sell any of it, nor should one make an exchange, nor should one cause the choicest of the land to pass away [from them]; for it is something holy to Jehovah.

15 "As regards the five thousand [cubits] that is left remaining in width alongside the twenty-five thousand, it is something profane for the city, for a dwelling place and for pasture ground. And the city must come to be in the midst of it. 16 And these are the [city's] measurements: the northern border four thousand five hundred [cubits], and the southern border four thou-sand five hundred, and the eastern border four thousand five hundred, and the western border four thou-sand five hundred. 17 And the city must come to have a pasture ground, to the north two hundred and fifty [cubits], and to the south two hundred and fifty, and to the east two hundred and fifty, and to the west two hundred and fifty.

18 "And what is left remaining over in length will be exactly as the holy contribution, ten thousand [cubits] to the east, and ten thou-sand to the west; and it must prove to be exactly as the holy contribu-tion, and its produce must come to be for bread for the ones serving the city. 19 And those who are serving the city out of all the tribes of Israel will cultivate it.

20 "The whole contribution is twenty-five thousand [cubits] by twenty-five thousand. A four-square part you people should contribute as the holy contribution with the possession of the city.

21 "And what is left over will belong to the chieftain, on this side and on that side of the holy contribution and of the possession of the city, alongside the twenty-five thousand [cubits] [of] the contribution to the eastern bound-ary; and on the west alongside the twenty-five thousand [cubits] to the western boundary. Exactly like the portions, [it will be] for the chieftain. And the holy con-tribution and the sanctuary of the

house must prove to be in the midst of it.

22 "And as regards the possession of the Levites and the possession of the city, in between what belongs to the chieftain it should prove to be. Between the boundary of Judah and the boundary of Benjamin it should come to belong to the chieftain.

23 "And as regards the rest of the tribes, from the eastern border to the western border, Benjamin one [portion]. 24 And by the boundary of Benjamin, from the eastern border to the western border, Sim′e·on one. 25 And by the boundary of Sim′e·on, from the eastern border to the western border, Is′sa·char one. 26 And by the boundary of Is′sa·char, from the eastern border to the western border, Zeb′u·lun one. 27 And by the boundary of Zeb′u·lun, from the eastern border to the western border, Gad one. 28 And by the boundary of Gad, to the southern border, it will be southward; and the boundary must prove to be from Ta′mar to the waters of Mer′i·bath-ka′desh, to the torrent valley, as far as the Great Sea.

29 "This will be the land that you people should cause to fall [by lot] for inheritance to the tribes of Israel, and these will be their shares," is the utterance of the Lord Jehovah.

30 "And these will be the outlets of the city: On the northern border, four thousand five hundred [cubits] will be [the] measurement.

31 "And the gates of the city will be according to the names of the tribes of Israel, three gates being on the north, the gate of Reu′ben, one; the gate of Judah, one; the gate of Le′vi, one.

32 "And on the eastern border there will be four thousand five hundred [cubits], and three gates, even the gate of Joseph, one; the gate of Benjamin, one; the gate of Dan, one.

33 "And the southern border will be four thousand five hundred [cubits] as to measurement, with three gates, the gate of Sim′e·on, one; the gate of Is′sa·char, one; the gate of Zeb′u·lun, one.

34 "The western border will be four thousand five hundred [cubits], there being three gates, the gate of Gad, one; the gate of Ash′er, one; the gate of Naph′ta·li, one.

35 "Round about it will be eighteen thousand [cubits]; and the name of the city from [that] day on will be Jehovah Himself Is There."

DANIEL

1 In the third year of the kingship of Je·hoi′a·kim the king of Judah, Neb·u·chad·nez′zar the king of Babylon came to Jerusalem and proceeded to lay siege to it. 2 In time Jehovah gave into his hand Je·hoi′a·kim the king of Judah and a part of the utensils of the house of the [true] God, so that he brought them to the land of Shi′nar to the house of his god; and the utensils he brought to the treasure house of his god.

3 Then the king said to Ash′pe·naz his chief court-official to bring some of the sons of Israel and of the royal offspring and of the nobles, 4 children in whom there was no defect at all, but good in appearance and having insight into all wisdom and being acquainted with knowledge, and having discernment of what is known, in whom also there was ability to stand in the palace of the king; and to teach them the writing and the tongue of the Chal·de′ans. 5 Furthermore, to them the king appointed a daily allowance from the delicacies of the king and from

his drinking wine, even to nourish them for three years, that at the end of these they might stand before the king.

6 Now there happened to be among them some of the sons of Judah, Daniel, Han·a·ni′ah, Mish′a·el and Az·a·ri′ah. 7 And to them the principal court-official went assigning names. So he assigned to Daniel [the name of] Bel·te·shaz′zar; and to Han·a·ni′ah, Sha′drach; and to Mish′a·el, Me′shach; and to Az·a·ri′ah, A·bed′ne·go.

8 But Daniel determined in his heart that he would not pollute himself with the delicacies of the king and with his drinking wine. And he kept requesting of the principal court-official that he might not pollute himself. 9 Accordingly the [true] God gave Daniel over to loving-kindness and to mercy before the principal court-official. 10 So the principal court-official said to Daniel: "I am in fear of my lord the king, who has appointed YOUR food and YOUR drink. Why, then, should he see YOUR faces dejected-looking in comparison with the children who are of the same age as YOURS, and [why] should you have to make my head guilty to the king?" 11 But Daniel said to the guardian whom the principal court-official had appointed over Daniel, Han·a·ni′ah, Mish′a·el and Az·a·ri′ah: 12 "Please, put your servants to the test for ten days, and let them give us some vegetables that we may eat and water that we may drink; 13 and let our countenances and the countenance of the children who are eating the delicacies of the king appear before you, and according to what you see do with your servants."

14 Finally he listened to them as regards this matter and to put them to the test for ten days. 15 And at the end of ten days their countenances appeared better and fatter in flesh than all the children who were eating the delicacies of the king. 16 So the guardian kept on taking away their delicacies and their drinking wine and giving them vegetables. 17 And as for these children, the four of them, to them the [true] God gave knowledge and insight in all writing and wisdom; and Daniel himself had understanding in all sorts of visions and dreams.

18 And at the end of the days that the king had said to bring them in, the principal court-official also proceeded to bring them in before Neb·u·chad·nez′zar. 19 And the king began to speak with them, and out of them all no one was found like Daniel, Han·a·ni′ah, Mish′a·el and Az·a·ri′ah; and they continued to stand before the king. 20 And as regards every matter of wisdom [and] understanding that the king inquired about from them, he even got to find them ten times better than all the magic-practicing priests [and] the conjurers that were in all his royal realm. 21 And Daniel continued on until the first year of Cy′rus the king.

2 And in the second year of the kingship of Neb·u·chad·nez′zar, Neb·u·chad·nez′zar dreamed dreams; and his spirit began to feel agitated, and his very sleep was made to be something beyond him. 2 So the king said to call the magic-practicing priests and the conjurers and the sorcerers and the Chal·de′ans to tell the king his dreams. And they proceeded to come in and to stand before the king. 3 Then the king said to them: "There is a dream that I have dreamed, and my spirit is agitated to know the dream." 4 At that the Chal·de′ans spoke to the king in the Ar·a·ma′ic language: "O king, live on even for times indefinite. Say what the dream is to your servants, and we shall show the very interpretation."

5 The king was answering and saying to the Chal·de′ans: "The word is being promulgated by me: If YOU men do not make the dream known to me, and its interpretation, dismembered is what YOU will be, and into public privies YOUR own houses will be turned. 6 But if the dream and its interpretation

you will show, gifts and a present and much dignity you will receive on my part. Therefore show me the very dream and its interpretation."

7 They answered a second time and were saying: "Let the king say what the dream is to his servants, and we shall show its very interpretation."

8 The king was answering and saying: "For a fact, I am aware that time is what you men are trying to gain, forasmuch as you have perceived that the word is being promulgated by me. 9 For if you do not make known to me the very dream, this one and only sentence is upon you. But it is a lying and wrong word that you have agreed to say before me, until the time itself is changed. Therefore tell me the very dream, and I shall know that you can show the very interpretation of it."

10 The Chal·de′ans answered before the king, and they were saying: "There does not exist a man on the dry land that is able to show the matter of the king, forasmuch as no grand king or governor has asked such a thing as this of any magic-practicing priest or conjurer or Chal·de′an. 11 But the thing that the king himself is asking is difficult, and nobody else exists who can show it before the king except the gods, whose own dwelling does not exist with flesh at all."

12 Because of this the king himself became angry and got very furious, and he said to destroy all the wise men of Babylon. 13 And the order itself went out, and the wise men were about to be killed; and they looked for Daniel and his companions, for them to be killed.

14 At that time Daniel, for his part, addressed himself with counsel and sensibleness to Ar′i·och the chief of the king's bodyguard, who had gone out to kill the wise men of Babylon. 15 He was answering and saying to Ar′i·och the officer of the king: "For what reason is there such a harsh order on the part of the king?" Then it was that Ar′i·och made known the matter itself to Daniel. 16 So Daniel himself went in and asked from the king that he should give him time expressly to show the very interpretation to the king.

17 After that Daniel went to his own house; and to Han·a·ni′ah, Mish′a·el and Az·a·ri′ah his companions he made known the matter, 18 even [for them] to ask for mercies on the part of the God of heaven concerning this secret, in order that they might not destroy Daniel and his companions with the remainder of the wise men of Babylon.

19 Then it was that to Daniel in a night vision the secret was revealed. Consequently Daniel himself blessed the God of heaven. 20 Daniel was answering and saying: "Let the name of God become blessed from time indefinite even to time indefinite, for wisdom and mightiness—for they belong to him. 21 And he is changing times and seasons, removing kings and setting up kings, giving wisdom to the wise ones and knowledge to those knowing discernment. 22 He is revealing the deep things and the concealed things, knowing what is in the darkness; and with him the light does dwell. 23 To you, O God of my forefathers, I am giving praise and commendation, because wisdom and mightiness you have given to me. And now you have made known to me what we requested of you, for you have made known to us the very matter of the king."

24 Because of this Daniel himself went in to Ar′i·och, whom the king had appointed to destroy the wise men of Babylon. He went, and this is what he said to him: "Do not destroy any wise men of Babylon. Take me in before the king, that I may show the interpretation itself to the king."

25 Then it was that Ar′i·och, in a hurry, took Daniel in before the king, and this is what he said to him: "I have found an able-bodied man of the exiles of Judah who

can make known the interpretation itself to the king." 26 The king was answering and saying to Daniel, whose name was Bel·te·shaz'-zar: "Are you competent enough to make known to me the dream that I beheld, and its interpretation?" 27 Daniel was answering before the king and saying: "The secret that the king himself is asking, the wise men, the conjurers, the magic-practicing priests [and] the astrologers themselves are unable to show to the king. 28 However, there exists a God in the heavens who is a Revealer of secrets, and he has made known to King Neb·u·chad·nez'zar what is to occur in the final part of the days. Your dream and the visions of your head upon your bed—this it is:

29 "As for you, O king, on your bed your own thoughts came up as regards what is to occur after this, and the One who is the Revealer of secrets has made known to you what is to occur. 30 And as for me, it is not through any wisdom that exists in me more than in any others alive that this secret is revealed to me, except to the intent that the interpretation may be made known to the king himself and that the thoughts of your heart you may know.

31 "You, O king, happened to be beholding, and, look! a certain immense image. That image, which was large and the brightness of which was extraordinary, was standing in front of you, and its appearance was dreadful. 32 As regards that image, its head was of good gold, its breasts and its arms were of silver, its belly and its thighs were of copper, 33 its legs were of iron, its feet were partly of iron and partly of molded clay. 34 You kept on looking until a stone was cut out not by hands, and it struck the image on its feet of iron and of molded clay and crushed them. 35 At that time the iron, the molded clay, the copper, the silver and the gold were, all together, crushed and became like the chaff from the summer thresh-

ing floor, and the wind carried them away so that no trace at all was found of them. And as for the stone that struck the image, it became a large mountain and filled the whole earth.

36 "This is the dream, and its interpretation we shall say before the king. 37 You, O king, the king of kings, you to whom the God of heaven has given the kingdom, the might, and the strength and the dignity, 38 and into whose hand he has given, wherever the sons of mankind are dwelling, the beasts of the field and the winged creatures of the heavens, and whom he has made ruler over all of them, you yourself are the head of gold.

39 "And after you there will rise another kingdom inferior to you; and another kingdom, a third one, of copper, that will rule over the whole earth.

40 "And as for the fourth kingdom, it will prove to be strong like iron. Forasmuch as iron is crushing and grinding everything else, so, like iron that shatters, it will crush and shatter even all these.

41 "And whereas you beheld the feet and the toes to be partly of molded clay of a potter and partly of iron, the kingdom itself will prove to be divided, but somewhat of the hardness of iron will prove to be in it, forasmuch as you beheld the iron mixed with moist clay. 42 And as for the toes of the feet being partly of iron and partly of molded clay, the kingdom will partly prove to be strong and will partly prove to be fragile. 43 Whereas you beheld iron mixed with moist clay, they will come to be mixed with the offspring of mankind; but they will not prove to be sticking together, this one to that one, just as iron is not mixing with molded clay.

44 "And in the days of those kings the God of heaven will set up a kingdom that will never be brought to ruin. And the kingdom itself will not be passed on to any other people. It will crush and put an end to all these kingdoms, and

it itself will stand to times indefinite; 45 forasmuch as you beheld that out of the mountain a stone was cut not by hands, and [that] it crushed the iron, the copper, the molded clay, the silver and the gold. The grand God himself has made known to the king what is to occur after this. And the dream is reliable, and the interpretation of it is trustworthy."

46 At that time King Neb·u·chad·nez'zar himself fell down upon his face, and to Daniel he paid homage, and he said to offer even a present and incense to him. 47 The king was answering Daniel and saying: "Truly the God of you men is a God of gods and a Lord of kings and a Revealer of secrets, because you were able to reveal this secret." 48 Consequently the king made Daniel someone great, and many big gifts he gave to him, and he made him the ruler over all the jurisdictional district of Babylon and the chief prefect over all the wise men of Babylon. 49 And Daniel, for his part, made a request of the king, and he appointed over the administration of the jurisdictional district of Babylon Sha'drach, Me'shach and A·bed'ne·go, but Daniel was in the court of the king.

3 Neb·u·chad·nez'zar the king made an image of gold, the height of which was sixty cubits [and] the breadth of which was six cubits. He set it up in the plain of Du'ra in the jurisdictional district of Babylon. 2 And Neb·u·chad·nez'zar himself as king sent to assemble the satraps, the prefects and the governors, the counselors, the treasurers, the judges, the police magistrates and all the administrators of the jurisdictional districts to come to the inauguration of the image that Neb·u·chad·nez'zar the king had set up.

3 At that time the satraps, the prefects and the governors, the counselors, the treasurers, the judges, the police magistrates and all the administrators of the jurisdictional districts were assembling themselves for the inauguration of the image that Neb·u·chad·nez'zar the king had set up, and they were standing in front of the image that Neb·u·chad·nez'zar had set up. 4 And the herald was crying out loudly: "To you it is being said, O peoples, national groups and languages, 5 that at the time that you hear the sound of the horn, the pipe, the zither, the triangular harp, the stringed instrument, the bagpipe and all sorts of musical instruments, you fall down and worship the image of gold that Neb·u·chad·nez'zar the king has set up. 6 And whoever does not fall down and worship will at the same moment be thrown into the burning fiery furnace." 7 Because of this, at the same time as all the peoples were hearing the sound of the horn, the pipe, the zither, the triangular harp, the stringed instrument and all sorts of musical instruments, all the peoples, national groups and languages were falling down [and] worshiping the image of gold that Neb·u·chad·nez'zar the king had set up.

8 Because of this, at that same time certain Chal·de'ans approached and accused the Jews. 9 They answered, and they were saying to Neb·u·chad·nez'zar the king: "O king, live on even for times indefinite. 10 You yourself, O king, set forth the command that every man that hears the sound of the horn, the pipe, the zither, the triangular harp, the stringed instrument, and the bagpipe and all sorts of musical instruments, should fall down and worship the image of gold; 11 and that whoever would not fall down and worship should be thrown into the burning fiery furnace. 12 There exist certain Jews whom you appointed over the administration of the jurisdictional district of Babylon, Sha'drach, Me'shach and A·bed'ne·go; these able-bodied men have paid no regard to you, O king, they are not serving your own gods, and the image of gold that you have set up they are not worshiping."

13 At that time Neb·u·chad·nez'-zar, in a rage and fury, said to bring in Sha'drach, Me'shach and A·bed'ne·go. Consequently these able-bodied men were brought in before the king. **14** Neb·u·chad-nez'zar was answering and saying to them: "Is it really so, O Sha'-drach, Me'shach and A·bed'ne·go, that YOU are not serving my own gods, and the image of gold that I have set up YOU are not wor-shiping? **15** Now if YOU are ready so that when YOU hear the sound of the horn, the pipe, the zither, the triangular harp, the stringed instrument, and the bagpipe and all sorts of musical instruments, YOU fall down and worship the image that I have made, [all right]. But if YOU do not worship, at that same moment YOU will be thrown into the burning fiery furnace. And who is that god that can rescue YOU out of my hands?"

16 Sha'drach, Me'shach and A·bed'ne·go answered, and they were saying to the king: "O Neb·u·chad·nez'zar, we are under no necessity in this regard to say back a word to you. **17** If it is to be, our God whom we are serving is able to rescue us. Out of the burn-ing fiery furnace and out of your hand, O king, he will rescue [us]. **18** But if not, let it become known to you, O king, that your gods are not the ones we are serving, and the image of gold that you have set up we will not worship."

19 Then it was that Neb·u·chad-nez'zar himself got filled with fury, and the very expression of his face was changed toward Sha'drach, Me'shach and A·bed'ne·go. He was answering and saying to heat up the furnace seven times more than it was customary to heat it up. **20** And to certain able-bodied men of vital energy who were in his military force he said to bind Sha'-drach, Me'shach and A·bed'ne·go, in order to throw [them] into the burning fiery furnace. **21** Then it was that these able-bodied men were bound in their mantles, their garments and their caps and their other clothing and were thrown into the burning fiery furnace. **22** Just because the king's word was harsh and the fur-nace was heated to excess, these able-bodied men that took up Sha'-drach, Me'shach and A·bed'ne·go were the ones that the fiery flame killed. **23** But these [other] able-bodied men, the three of them, Sha'drach, Me'shach and A·bed'-ne·go, fell down bound in the midst of the burning fiery furnace.

24 At that time Neb·u·chad·nez'-zar the king himself became fright-ened and he rose up in a hurry. He was answering and saying to his high royal officials: "Was it not three able-bodied men that we threw bound into the midst of the fire?" They were answering and saying to the king: "Yes, O king." **25** He was answering and saying: "Look! I am beholding four able-bodied men walking about free in the midst of the fire, and there is no hurt to them, and the appear-ance of the fourth one is resem-bling a son of the gods."

26 Then it was that Neb·u·chad-nez'zar approached the door of the burning fiery furnace. He was an-swering and saying: "Sha'drach, Me'shach and A·bed'ne·go, YOU servants of the Most High God, step out and come here!" At that time Sha'drach, Me'shach and A·bed'ne·go were stepping out from the midst of the fire. **27** And the satraps, the prefects and the gover-nors and the high officials of the king that were assembled were be-holding these able-bodied men, that the fire had had no power over their bodies, and not a hair of their head had been singed, and even their mantles had not been changed and the smell of fire itself had not come onto them.

28 Neb·u·chad·nez'zar was an-swering and saying: "Blessed be the God of Sha'drach, Me'shach and A·bed'ne·go, who sent his angel and rescued his servants that trusted in him and that changed the very word of the king and gave over their bodies, because they would not serve and would not worship any god at all except their own

God. 29 And from me an order is being put through, that any people, national group or language that says anything wrong against the God of Sha′drach, Me′shach and A·bed′ne·go should be dismembered, and its house should be turned into a public privy; forasmuch as there does not exist another god that is able to deliver like this one."

30 At that time the king himself caused Sha′drach, Me′shach and A·bed′ne·go to prosper in the jurisdictional district of Babylon.

4 "Neb·u·chad·nez′zar the king, to all the peoples, national groups and languages that are dwelling in all the earth: May YOUR peace grow great. 2 The signs and wonders that the Most High God has performed with me, it has seemed good to me to declare. 3 How grand his signs are, and how mighty his wonders are! His kingdom is a kingdom to time indefinite, and his rulership is for generation after generation.

4 "I, Neb·u·chad·nez′zar, happened to be at ease in my house and flourishing in my palace. 5 There was a dream that I beheld, and it began to make me afraid. And there were mental images upon my bed and visions of my head that began to frighten me. 6 And from me an order was being put through to bring in before me all the wise men of Babylon, that they might make known to me the very interpretation of the dream.

7 "At that time the magic-practicing priests, the conjurers, the Chal·de′ans and the astrologers were entering; and I was saying before them what the dream was, but its interpretation they were not making known to me. 8 And at last there came in before me Daniel, whose name is Bel·te·shaz′zar according to the name of my god and in whom there is the spirit of the holy gods; and before him I said what the dream was:

9 "'O Bel·te·shaz′zar the chief of the magic-practicing priests, because I myself well know that the spirit of the holy gods is in you and that there is no secret at all that is troubling you, tell [me] the visions of my dream that I have beheld and its interpretation.

10 "'Now the visions of my head upon my bed I happened to be beholding, and, look! a tree in the midst of the earth, the height of which was immense. 11 The tree grew up and became strong, and its very height finally reached the heavens, and it was visible to the extremity of the whole earth. 12 Its foliage was fair, and its fruit was abundant, and there was food for all on it. Under it the beast of the field would seek shade, and on its boughs the birds of the heavens would dwell, and from it all flesh would feed itself.

13 "'I continued beholding in the visions of my head upon my bed, and, look! a watcher, even a holy one, coming down from the heavens themselves. 14 He was calling out loudly, and this is what he was saying: "CHOP the tree down, and cut off its boughs. SHAKE off its foliage, and scatter its fruitage. Let the beast flee from under it, and the birds from its boughs. 15 However, LEAVE its rootstock itself in the earth, even with a banding of iron and of copper, among the grass of the field; and with the dew of the heavens let it be wet, and with the beast let its portion be among the vegetation of the earth. 16 Let its heart be changed from that of mankind, and let the heart of a beast be given to it, and let seven times pass over it. 17 By the decree of watchers the thing is, and [by] the saying of holy ones the request is, to the intent that people living may know that the Most High is Ruler in the kingdom of mankind and that to the one whom he wants to, he gives it and he sets up over it even the lowliest one of mankind."

18 "'This was the dream that I myself, King Neb·u·chad·nez′zar, beheld; and you yourself, O Bel·te·shaz′zar, say what the interpretation is, forasmuch as all the [other]

wise men of my kingdom are unable to make known to me the interpretation itself. But you are competent, because the spirit of holy gods is in you.'

19 "At that time Daniel himself, whose name is Bel·te·shaz′zar, was astonished for a moment, and his very thoughts began to frighten him.

"The king was answering and saying, 'O Bel·te·shaz′zar, do not let the dream and the interpretation themselves frighten you.'

"Bel·te·shaz′zar was answering and saying, 'O my lord, may the dream [apply] to those hating you, and its interpretation to your adversaries.

20 " 'The tree that you beheld, that grew great and became strong and the height of which finally reached the heavens and which was visible to all the earth, 21 and the foliage of which was fair, and the fruit of which was abundant, and on which there was food for all; under which the beasts of the field would dwell, and on the boughs of which the birds of the heavens would reside, 22 it is you, O king, because you have grown great and become strong, and your grandeur has grown great and reached to the heavens, and your rulership to the extremity of the earth.

23 " 'And because the king beheld a watcher, even a holy one, coming down from the heavens, who was also saying: "CHOP the tree down, and RUIN it. However, LEAVE its rootstock itself in the earth, but with a banding of iron and of copper, among the grass of the field, and with the dew of the heavens let it become wet, and with the beasts of the field let its portion be until seven times themselves pass over it," 24 this is the interpretation, O king, and the decree of the Most High is that which must befall my lord the king. 25 And you they will be driving away from men, and with the beasts of the field your dwelling will come to be, and the vegetation is what they will give even to you to eat just like bulls; and with the

dew of the heavens you yourself will be getting wet, and seven times themselves will pass over you, until you know that the Most High is Ruler in the kingdom of mankind, and that to the one whom he wants to he gives it.

26 " 'And because they said to leave the rootstock of the tree, your kingdom will be sure to you after you know that the heavens are ruling. 27 Therefore, O king, may my counsel seem good to you, and remove your own sins by righteousness, and your iniquity by showing mercy to the poor ones. Maybe there will occur a lengthening of your prosperity.' "

28 All this befell Neb·u·chad·nez′zar the king.

29 At the end of twelve lunar months he happened to be walking upon the royal palace of Babylon. 30 The king was answering and saying: "Is not this Babylon the Great, that I myself have built for the royal house with the strength of my might and for the dignity of my majesty?"

31 While the word was yet in the king's mouth, there was a voice that fell from the heavens: "To you it is being said, O Neb·u·chad·nez′zar the king, 'The kingdom itself has gone away from you, 32 and from mankind they are driving even you away, and with the beasts of the field your dwelling will be. Vegetation they will give even to you to eat just like bulls, and seven times themselves will pass over you, until you know that the Most High is Ruler in the kingdom of mankind, and that to the one whom he wants to he gives it.' "

33 At that moment the word itself was fulfilled upon Neb·u·chad·nez′zar, and from mankind he was being driven away, and vegetation he began to eat just like bulls, and with the dew of the heavens his own body got to be wet, until his very hair grew long just like eagles' [feathers] and his nails like birds' [claws].

34 "And at the end of the days I, Neb·u·chad·nez′zar, lifted up to the heavens my eyes, and my own

understanding began to return to me; and I blessed the Most High himself, and the One living to time indefinite I praised and glorified, because his rulership is a rulership to time indefinite and his kingdom is for generation after generation. 35 And all the inhabitants of the earth are being considered as merely nothing, and he is doing according to his own will among the army of the heavens and the inhabitants of the earth. And there exists no one that can check his hand or that can say to him, 'What have you been doing?'

36 "At the same time my understanding itself began to return to me, and for the dignity of my kingdom my majesty and my brightness themselves began to return to me; and for me even my high royal officers and my grandees began eagerly searching, and I was re-established upon my own kingdom, and greatness extraordinary was added to me.

37 "Now I, Neb·u·chad·nez'zar, am praising and exalting and glorifying the King of the heavens, because all his works are truth and his ways are justice, and because those who are walking in pride he is able to humiliate."

5 As regards Bel·shaz'zar the king, he made a big feast for a thousand of his grandees, and in front of the thousand he was drinking wine. 2 Bel·shaz'zar, under the influence of the wine, said to bring in the vessels of gold and of silver that Neb·u·chad·nez'zar his father had taken away from the temple that was in Jerusalem, that from them the king and his grandees, his concubines and his secondary wives might drink. 3 At that time they brought in the vessels of gold that they had taken away from the temple of the house of God that was in Jerusalem, and from them the king and his grandees, his concubines and his secondary wives drank. 4 They drank wine, and they praised the gods of gold and of silver, copper, iron, wood and stone.

5 At that moment the fingers of a man's hand came forth and were writing in front of the lampstand upon the plaster of the wall of the palace of the king, and the king was beholding the back of the hand that was writing. 6 At that time, as regards the king, his very complexion was changed in him, and his own thoughts began to frighten him, and his hip joints were loosening and his very knees were knocking each other.

7 The king was calling out loudly to bring in the conjurers, the Chal·de'ans and the astrologers. The king was answering and saying to the wise men of Babylon: "Any man that will read this writing and show me its very interpretation, with purple he will be clothed, with a necklace of gold about his neck, and as the third one in the kingdom he will rule."

8 At that time all the wise men of the king were coming in, but they were not competent enough to read the writing itself or to make known to the king the interpretation. 9 Consequently King Bel·shaz'zar was very much frightened and his complexion was changing within him; and his grandees were perplexed.

10 As regards the queen, because of the words of the king and his grandees she entered right into the banqueting hall. The queen answered and said: "O king, keep living even to times indefinite. Do not let your thoughts frighten you, nor let your complexion be changed. 11 There exists a capable man in your kingdom in whom there is the spirit of holy gods; and in the days of your father illumination and insight and wisdom like the wisdom of gods were found in him, and King Neb·u·chad·nez'zar your father himself set him up as chief of the magic-practicing priests, the conjurers, the Chal·de'-ans [and] the astrologers, [even] your father, O king; 12 forasmuch as an extraordinary spirit and knowledge and insight to interpret dreams and the explanation of riddles and the untying of knots had

been found in him, in Daniel, whom the king himself named Bel·te·shaz′zar. Now let Daniel himself be called, that he may show the very interpretation."

13 Accordingly Daniel himself was brought in before the king. The king was speaking up and saying to Daniel: "Are you the Daniel that is of the exiles of Judah, whom the king my father brought out of Judah? 14 I have also heard concerning you that the spirit of gods is in you, and illumination and insight and wisdom extraordinary have been found in you. 15 And now there have been brought in before me the wise men [and] the conjurers, that they may read this very writing, even to make known to me its interpretation; but they are not competent enough to show the very interpretation of the word. 16 And I myself have heard concerning you, that you are able to furnish interpretations and to untie knots themselves. Now, if you are able to read the writing and to make known to me its very interpretation, with purple you will be clothed, with a necklace of gold around your neck, and as the third one in the kingdom you will rule."

17 At that time Daniel was answering and saying before the king: "Let your gifts prove to be to you yourself, and your presents do you give to others. However, I shall read the writing itself to the king, and the interpretation I shall make known to him. 18 As for you, O king, the Most High God himself gave to Neb·u·chad·nez′zar your father the kingdom and the greatness and the dignity and the majesty. 19 And because of the greatness that He gave him, all peoples, national groups and languages proved to be quaking and showing fear before him. Whom he happened to want to, he was killing; and whom he happened to want to, he was striking; and whom he happened to want to, he was exalting; and whom he happened to want to, he was humiliating. 20 But when his heart became

haughty and his own spirit became hard, so as to act presumptuously, he was brought down from the throne of his kingdom, and his own dignity was taken away from him. 21 And from the sons of mankind he was driven away, and his very heart was made like that of a beast, and with the wild asses his dwelling was. Vegetation they would give him to eat just like bulls, and with the dew of the heavens his own body got to be wet, until he knew that the Most High God is Ruler in the kingdom of mankind, and that the one whom he wants to, he sets up over it.

22 "And as for you, his son Bel·shaz′zar, you have not humbled your heart, although you knew all this. 23 But against the Lord of the heavens you exalted yourself, and they brought before you even the vessels of his house; and you yourself and your grandees, your concubines and your secondary wives have been drinking wine from them, and you have praised mere gods of silver and of gold, copper, iron, wood and stone, that are beholding nothing or hearing nothing or knowing nothing; but the God in whose hand your breath is and to whom all your ways belong you have not glorified. 24 Consequently from before him there was being sent the back of a hand, and this very writing was inscribed. 25 And this is the writing that was inscribed: ME′NE, ME′NE, TE′KEL and PAR′SIN.

26 "This is the interpretation of the word: ME′NE, God has numbered [the days of] your kingdom and has finished it.

27 "TE′KEL, you have been weighed in the balances and have been found deficient.

28 "PE′RES, your kingdom has been divided and given to the Medes and the Persians."

29 At that time Bel·shaz′zar commanded, and they clothed Daniel with purple, with a necklace of gold about his neck; and they heralded concerning him that he was to become the third ruler in the kingdom.

30 In that very night Bel·shaz'-zar the Chal·de'an king was killed, **31** and Da·ri'us the Mede himself received the kingdom, being about sixty-two years old.

6 It seemed good to Da·ri'us, and he set up over the kingdom one hundred and twenty satraps, who were to be over the whole kingdom; **2** and over them three high officials, of whom Daniel was one, in order that these satraps might continually be giving to them the report and the king himself might not become the loser. **3** Then it was that this Daniel was steadily distinguishing himself over the high officials and the satraps, forasmuch as an extraordinary spirit was in him; and the king was intending to elevate him over all the kingdom.

4 At that time the high officials and the satraps themselves were constantly seeking to find some pretext against Daniel respecting the kingdom; but there was no pretext or corrupt thing at all that they were able to find, forasmuch as he was trustworthy and no negligence or corrupt thing at all was found in him. **5** Consequently these able-bodied men were saying: "We shall find in this Daniel no pretext at all, except we have to find [it] against him in the law of his God."

6 Accordingly these high officials and satraps themselves entered as a throng to the king, and this is what they were saying to him: "O Da·ri'us the king, live on even for times indefinite. **7** All the high officials of the kingdom, the prefects and the satraps, the high royal officers and the governors, have taken counsel together to establish a royal statute and to enforce an interdict, that whoever makes a petition to any god or man for thirty days except to you, O king, should be thrown to the lions' pit. **8** Now, O king, may you establish the statute and sign the writing, in order for [it] not to be changed, according to the law of the Medes and the Persians, which is not annulled."

9 In accord with this, King Da·ri'us himself signed the writing and the interdict.

10 But Daniel, as soon as he knew that the writing had been signed, entered into his house, and, the windows in his roof chamber being open for him toward Jerusalem, even three times in a day he was kneeling on his knees and praying and offering praise before his God, as he had been regularly doing prior to this. **11** At that time these able-bodied men themselves crowded in and found Daniel petitioning and imploring favor before his God.

12 Then it was that they approached and were saying before the king concerning the interdict of the king: "Is there not an interdict that you have signed that any man that asks a petition from any god or man for thirty days except from you, O king, he should be thrown to the lions' pit?" The king was answering and saying: "The matter is well established according to the law of the Medes and the Persians, which is not annulled." **13** Immediately they answered, and they were saying before the king: "Daniel, who is of the exiles of Judah, has paid no regard to you, O king, nor to the interdict that you signed, but three times in a day he is making his petition." **14** Consequently the king, as soon as he heard the word, it was very displeasing to him, and toward Daniel he set [his] mind in order to rescue him; and till the setting of the sun he kept on striving to deliver him. **15** Finally these able-bodied men themselves entered as a throng to the king, and they were saying to the king: "Take note, O king, that the law belonging to the Medes and the Persians is that any interdict or statute that the king himself establishes is not to be changed."

16 Accordingly the king himself commanded, and they brought Daniel and threw him into the pit of the lions. The king was answering and saying to Daniel: "Your God whom you are serving with constancy, he himself will rescue you."

17 And a stone was brought and placed on the mouth of the pit, and the king sealed it with his signet ring and with the signet ring of his grandees, in order that nothing should be changed in the case of Daniel.

18 At that time the king went to his palace and spent the night fasting, and no musical instruments were brought in before him, and his very sleep fled from him. 19 Finally the king himself, at dawn, proceeded to get up in the daylight, and in a hurry he went right to the lions' pit. 20 And as he got near to the pit, he cried out with a sad voice even to Daniel. The king was speaking up and saying to Daniel: "O Daniel, servant of the living God, has your God whom you are serving with constancy been able to rescue you from the lions?" 21 Immediately Daniel himself spoke even with the king: "O king, live on even to times indefinite. 22 My own God sent his angel and shut the mouth of the lions, and they have not brought me to ruin, forasmuch as before him innocence itself was found in me; and also before you, O king, no hurtful act have I done."

23 Then it was that the king himself became very glad, and Daniel himself he commanded to be lifted up out of the pit. And Daniel was lifted up out of the pit, and there was no hurt at all found on him, because he had trusted in his God.

24 And the king commanded, and they brought these able-bodied men who had accused Daniel, and into the lions' pit they threw them, their sons and their wives; and they had not reached the bottom of the pit before the lions had got the mastery over them, and all their bones they crushed.

25 Then it was that Da·ri′us the king himself wrote to all the people, the national groups and the tongues that are dwelling in all the earth: "May YOUR peace grow very much! 26 From before me there has been put through an order that, in every dominion of my kingdom, people are to be quaking and fearing before the God of Daniel. For he is the living God and One enduring to times indefinite, and his kingdom is one that will not be brought to ruin, and his dominion is forever. 27 He is rescuing and delivering and performing signs and wonders in the heavens and on the earth, for he has rescued Daniel from the paw of the lions."

28 And as for this Daniel, he prospered in the kingdom of Da·ri′us and in the kingdom of Cy′rus the Persian.

7 In the first year of Bel·shaz′zar the king of Babylon, Daniel himself beheld a dream and visions of his head upon his bed. At that time he wrote down the dream itself. The complete account of the matters he told. 2 Daniel was speaking up and saying:

"I happened to be beholding in my visions during the night, and, see there! the four winds of the heavens were stirring up the vast sea. 3 And four huge beasts were coming up out of the sea, each one being different from the others.

4 "The first one was like a lion, and it had the wings of an eagle. I kept on beholding until its wings were plucked out, and it was lifted up from the earth and was made to stand up on two feet just like a man, and there was given to it the heart of a man.

5 "And, see there! another beast, a second one, it being like a bear. And on one side it was raised up, and there were three ribs in its mouth between its teeth; and this is what they were saying to it, 'Get up, eat much flesh.'

6 "After this I kept on beholding, and, see there! another [beast], one like a leopard, but it had four wings of a flying creature on its back. And the beast had four heads, and there was given to it rulership indeed.

7 "After this I kept on beholding in the visions of the night, and, see there! a fourth beast, fearsome and terrible and unusually strong. And it had teeth of iron, big ones.

It was devouring and crushing, and what was left it was treading down with its feet. And it was something different from all the [other] beasts that were prior to it, and it had ten horns. 8 I kept on considering the horns, and, look! another horn, a small one, came up in among them, and there were three of the first horns that were plucked up from before it. And, look! there were eyes like the eyes of a man in this horn, and there was a mouth speaking grandiose things.

9 "I kept on beholding until there were thrones placed and the Ancient of Days sat down. His clothing was white just like snow, and the hair of his head was like clean wool. His throne was flames of fire; its wheels were a burning fire. 10 There was a stream of fire flowing and going out from before him. There were a thousand thousands that kept ministering to him, and ten thousand times ten thousand that kept standing right before him. The Court took its seat, and there were books that were opened.

11 "I kept on beholding at that time because of the sound of the grandiose words that the horn was speaking; I kept on beholding until the beast was killed and its body was destroyed and it was given to the burning fire. 12 But as for the rest of the beasts, their rulerships were taken away, and there was a lengthening in life given to them for a time and a season.

13 "I kept on beholding in the visions of the night, and, see there! with the clouds of the heavens someone like a son of man happened to be coming; and to the Ancient of Days he gained access, and they brought him up close even before that One. 14 And to him there were given rulership and dignity and kingdom, that the peoples, national groups and languages should all serve even him. His rulership is an indefinitely lasting rulership that will not pass away, and his kingdom one that will not be brought to ruin.

15 "As for me, Daniel, my spirit was distressed within on account of it, and the very visions of my head began to frighten me. 16 I went up close to one of those who were standing, that I might request from him reliable information on all this. And he said to me, as he went on to make known to me the very interpretation of the matters,

17 " 'As for these huge beasts, because they are four, there are four kings that will stand up from the earth. 18 But the holy ones of the Supreme One will receive the kingdom, and they will take possession of the kingdom for time indefinite, even for time indefinite upon times indefinite.'

19 "Then it was that I desired to make certain concerning the fourth beast, which proved to be different from all the others, extraordinarily fearsome, the teeth of which were of iron and the claws of which were of copper, which was devouring [and] crushing, and which was treading down even what was left with its feet; 20 and concerning the ten horns that were on its head, and the other [horn] that came up and before which three fell, even that horn that had eyes and a mouth speaking grandiose things and the appearance of which was bigger than that of its fellows.

21 "I kept on beholding when that very horn made war upon the holy ones, and it was prevailing against them, 22 until the Ancient of Days came and judgment itself was given in favor of the holy ones of the Supreme One, and the definite time arrived that the holy ones took possession of the kingdom itself.

23 "This is what he said, 'As for the fourth beast, there is a fourth kingdom that will come to be on the earth, that will be different from all the [other] kingdoms; and it will devour all the earth and will trample it down and crush it. 24 And as for the ten horns, out of that kingdom there are ten kings that will rise up; and still another

one will rise up after them, and he himself will be different from the first ones, and three kings he will humiliate. 25 And he will speak even words against the Most High, and he will harass continually the holy ones themselves of the Supreme One. And he will intend to change times and law, and they will be given into his hand for a time, and times and half a time. 26 And the Court itself proceeded to sit, and his own rulership they finally took away, in order to annihilate [him] and to destroy [him] totally.

27 " 'And the kingdom and the rulership and the grandeur of the kingdoms under all the heavens were given to the people who are the holy ones of the Supreme One. Their kingdom is an indefinitely lasting kingdom, and all the rulerships will serve and obey even them.'

28 "Up to this point is the end of the matter. As for me, Daniel, my own thoughts kept frightening me a great deal, so that my very complexion changed in me; but the matter itself I kept in my own heart."

8 In the third year of the kingship of Bel·shaz′zar the king, there was a vision that appeared to me, even me, Daniel, after the one appearing to me at the start. 2 And I began to see in the vision; and it came about, while I was seeing, that I was in Shu′shan the castle, which is in E′lam the jurisdictional district; and I proceeded to see in the vision, and I myself happened to be by the watercourse of U′lai. 3 When I raised my eyes, then I saw, and, look! a ram standing before the watercourse, and it had two horns. And the two horns were tall, but the one was taller than the other, and the taller was the one that came up afterward. 4 I saw the ram making thrusts to the west and to the north and to the south, and no wild beasts kept standing before it, and there was no one doing any delivering out of its hand. And it did according to its will, and it put on great airs.

5 And I, for my part, kept on considering, and, look! there was a male of the goats coming from the sunset upon the surface of the whole earth, and it was not touching the earth. And as regards the he-goat, there was a conspicuous horn between its eyes. 6 And it kept coming all the way to the ram possessing the two horns, which I had seen standing before the watercourse; and it came running toward it in its powerful rage.

7 And I saw it coming into close touch with the ram, and it began showing bitterness toward it, and it proceeded to strike down the ram and to break its two horns, and there proved to be no power in the ram to stand before it. So it threw it to the earth and trampled it down, and the ram proved to have no deliverer out of its hand.

8 And the male of the goats, for its part, put on great airs to an extreme; but as soon as it became mighty, the great horn was broken, and there proceeded to come up conspicuously four instead of it, toward the four winds of the heavens.

9 And out of one of them there came forth another horn, a small one, and it kept getting very much greater toward the south and toward the sunrising and toward the Decoration. 10 And it kept getting greater all the way to the army of the heavens, so that it caused some of the army and some of the stars to fall to the earth, and it went trampling them down. 11 And all the way to the Prince of the army it put on great airs, and from him the constant [feature] was taken away, and the established place of his sanctuary was thrown down. 12 And an army itself was gradually given over, together with the constant [feature], because of transgression; and it kept throwing truth to the earth, and it acted and had success.

13 And I got to hear a certain holy one speaking, and another holy one proceeded to say to the particular one who was speaking: "How long will the vision be of

the constant [feature] and of the transgression causing desolation, to make both [the] holy place and [the] army things to trample on?" 14 So he said to me: "Until two thousand three hundred evenings [and] mornings; and [the] holy place will certainly be brought into its right condition."

15 Then it came about that, while I myself, Daniel, was seeing the vision and seeking an understanding, why, look! there was standing in front of me someone in appearance like an able-bodied man. 16 And I began to hear the voice of an earthling man in the midst of the U'lai, and he proceeded to call out and say: "Ga'bri·el, make that one there understand the thing seen." 17 So he came beside where I was standing, but when he came I got terrified so that I fell upon my face. And he proceeded to say to me: "Understand, O son of man, that the vision is for the time of [the] end." 18 And while he was speaking with me, I had become fast asleep on my face on the earth. So he touched me and made me stand up where I had been standing. 19 And he went on to say: "Here I am causing you to know what will occur in the final part of the denunciation, because it is for the appointed time of [the] end.

20 "The ram that you saw possessing the two horns [stands for] the kings of Me'di·a and Persia. 21 And the hairy he-goat [stands for] the king of Greece; and as for the great horn that was between its eyes, it [stands for] the first king. 22 And that one having been broken, so that there were four that finally stood up instead of it, there are four kingdoms from [his] nation that will stand up, but not with his power.

23 "And in the final part of their kingdom, as the transgressors act to a completion, there will stand up a king fierce in countenance and understanding ambiguous sayings. 24 And his power must become mighty, but not by his own power. And in a wonderful way he will cause ruin, and he will cer-

tainly prove successful and do effectively. And he will actually bring mighty ones to ruin, also the people made up of [the] holy ones. 25 And according to his insight he will also certainly cause deception to succeed in his hand. And in his heart he will put on great airs, and during a freedom from care he will bring many to ruin. And against the Prince of princes he will stand up, but it will be without hand that he will be broken.

26 "And the thing seen concerning the evening and the morning, which has been said, it is true. And you, for your part, keep secret the vision, because it is yet for many days."

27 And as for me, Daniel, I felt exhausted and was made sick for [some] days. Then I got up and did the work of the king; but I kept showing myself numbed on account of the thing seen, and there was nobody understanding [it].

9 In the first year of Da·ri'us the son of A·has·u·e'rus of the seed of the Medes, who had been made king over the kingdom of the Chal·de'ans; 2 in the first year of his reigning I myself, Daniel, discerned by the books the number of the years concerning which the word of Jehovah had occurred to Jeremiah the prophet, for fulfilling the devastations of Jerusalem, [namely,] seventy years. 3 And I proceeded to set my face to Jehovah the [true] God, in order to seek [him] with prayer and with entreaties, with fasting and sackcloth and ashes. 4 And I began to pray to Jehovah my God and to make confession and to say:

"Ah Jehovah the [true] God, the great One and the fear-inspiring One, keeping the covenant and the loving-kindness to those loving him and to those keeping his commandments, 5 we have sinned and done wrong and acted wickedly and rebelled; and there has been a turning aside from your commandments and from your judicial decisions. 6 And we have not listened to your servants the prophets, who have spoken in your name to our kings, our princes and our forefathers and to all the people of the land. 7 To you, O Jehovah, there belongs the righteousness, but to us the shame of face as at this day, to the men of Judah and to the inhabitants of Jerusalem and to all those of Israel, those nearby and those far away in all the lands to which you dispersed them because of their unfaithfulness with which they acted against you.

8 "O Jehovah, to us belongs the shame of face, to our kings, to our princes and to our forefathers, because we have sinned against you. 9 To Jehovah our God belong the mercies and the acts of forgiveness, for we have rebelled against him. 10 And we have not obeyed the voice of Jehovah our God by walking in his laws that he set before us by the hand of his servants the prophets. 11 And all those of Israel have overstepped your law, and there has been a turning aside by not obeying your voice, so that you poured out upon us the curse and the sworn oath that is written in the law of Moses the servant of the [true] God, for we have sinned against Him. 12 And he proceeded to carry out his words that he had spoken against us and against our judges who judged us, by bringing upon us great calamity, such as was not done under the whole heavens as what has been done in Jerusalem. 13 Just as it is written in the law of Moses, all this calamity—it has come upon us, and we have not softened the face of Jehovah our God by turning back from our error and by showing insight into your trueness.

14 "And Jehovah kept alert to the calamity and finally brought it upon us, for Jehovah our God is righteous in all his works that he has done; and we have not obeyed his voice.

15 "And now, O Jehovah our God, you who brought your people out from the land of Egypt by a strong hand and proceeded to make a name for yourself as at this day, we have sinned, we have acted wickedly. 16 O Jehovah, accord-ing to all your acts of righteousness, please, may your anger and your rage turn back from your city Jerusalem, your holy mountain; for, because of our sins and because of the errors of our forefathers, Jerusalem and your people are an object of reproach to all those round about us. 17 And now listen, O our God, to the prayer of your servant and to his entreaties, and cause your face to shine upon your sanctuary that is desolated, for the sake of Jehovah. 18 Incline your ear, O my God, and hear. Do open your eyes and see our desolated conditions and the city that has been called by your name; for not according to our righteous acts are we letting our entreaties fall before you, but according to your many mercies. 19 O Jehovah, do hear. O Jehovah, do forgive. O Jehovah, do pay attention and act. Do not delay, for your own sake, O my God, for your own name has been called upon your city and upon your people."

20 While I was yet speaking and praying and confessing my sin and the sin of my people Israel and letting my request for favor fall before Jehovah my God concerning the holy mountain of my God, 21 and [while] I was yet speaking in the prayer, why, the man Ga'-bri·el, whom I had seen in the vision at the start, having been made weary with tiredness, was arriving by me at the time of the evening gift offering. 22 And he proceeded to impart understanding and speak with me and say:

"O Daniel, now I have come forth to make you have insight with understanding. 23 At the start of your entreaties a word went forth, and I myself have come to make report, because you are someone very desirable. So give consideration to the matter, and have understanding in the thing seen.

24 "There are seventy weeks that have been determined upon your people and upon your holy city, in order to terminate the transgression, and to finish off sin, and to make atonement for error, and to

bring in righteousness for times indefinite, and to imprint a seal upon vision and prophet, and to anoint the Holy of Holies. 25 And you should know and have the insight [that] from the going forth of [the] word to restore and to rebuild Jerusalem until Mes·si′ah [the] Leader, there will be seven weeks, also sixty-two weeks. She will return and be actually rebuilt, with a public square and moat, but in the straits of the times.

26 "And after the sixty-two weeks Mes·si′ah will be cut off, with nothing for himself.

"And the city and the holy place the people of a leader that is coming will bring to their ruin. And the end of it will be by the flood. And until [the] end there will be war; what is decided upon is desolations.

27 "And he must keep [the] covenant in force for the many for one week; and at the half of the week he will cause sacrifice and gift offering to cease.

"And upon the wing of disgusting things there will be the one causing desolation; and until an extermination, the very thing decided upon will go pouring out also upon the one lying desolate."

10 In the third year of Cy′rus the king of Persia there was a matter revealed to Daniel, whose name was called Bel·te·shaz′zar; and the matter was true, and there was a great military service. And he understood the matter, and he had understanding in the thing seen.

2 In those days I myself, Daniel, happened to be mourning for three full weeks. 3 Dainty bread I did not eat, and no flesh or wine entered into my mouth, and in no way did I grease myself until the completing of the three full weeks. 4 And on the twenty-fourth day of the first month, while I myself happened to be on the bank of the great river, that is, Hid′de·kel, 5 I also proceeded to raise my eyes and see, and here was a certain man clothed in linen, with his hips girded with gold of U′phaz. 6 And his body was like chrysolite, and

his face like the appearance of lightning, and his eyes like fiery torches, and his arms and the place of his feet were like the sight of burnished copper, and the sound of his words was like the sound of a crowd. 7 And I saw, I Daniel by myself, the appearance; but as for the men that happened to be with me, they did not see the appearance. However, there was a great trembling that fell upon them, so that they went running away in hiding themselves.

8 And I—I was left remaining by myself, so that I saw this great appearance. And there was left remaining in me no power, and my own dignity became changed upon me to ruination, and I retained no power. 9 And I began hearing the sound of his words; and while I was hearing the sound of his words, I myself also happened to be fast asleep upon my face, with my face to the earth. 10 And, look! there was a hand that touched me, and it gradually stirred me up to [get] upon my knees and the palms of my hands. 11 And he proceeded to say to me:

"O Daniel, you very desirable man, have understanding in the words that I am speaking to you, and stand up where you were standing, for now I have been sent to you."

And when he spoke with me this word, I did stand up, shivering.

12 And he went on to say to me: "Do not be afraid, O Daniel, for from the first day that you gave your heart to understanding and humbling yourself before your God your words have been heard, and I myself have come because of your words. 13 But the prince of the royal realm of Persia was standing in opposition to me for twenty-one days, and, look! Mi′cha·el, one of the foremost princes, came to help me; and I, for my part, remained there beside the kings of Persia. 14 And I have come to cause you to discern what will befall your people in the final part of the days, because it is a vision yet for the days [to come]."

15 Now when he spoke with me words like these, I had set my face to the earth and had become speechless. **16** And, look! one similar to the likeness of the sons of mankind was touching my lips, and I began to open my mouth and speak and say to the one who was standing in front of me: "O my lord, because of the appearance my convulsions were turned within me, and I did not retain any power. **17** So how was the servant of this my lord able to speak with this my lord? And as for me, up to now there kept standing in me no power, and no breath at all was left remaining in me."

18 And the one like the appearance of an earthling man proceeded to touch me again and strengthen me. **19** Then he said: "Do not be afraid, O very desirable man. May you have peace. Be strong, yes, be strong." And as soon as he spoke with me I exerted my strength and finally said: "Let my lord speak, because you have strengthened me." **20** So he went on to say:

"Do you really know why I have come to you? And now I shall go back to fight with the prince of Persia. When I am going forth, look! also the prince of Greece is coming. **21** However, I shall tell you the things noted down in the writing of truth, and there is no one holding strongly with me in these [things] but Mi·cha·el, the prince of you people.

11 "And as for me, in the first year of Da·ri'us the Mede I stood up as a strengthener and as a fortress to him. **2** And now what is truth I shall tell to you:

"Look! There will yet be three kings standing up for Persia, and the fourth one will amass greater riches than all [others]. And as soon as he has become strong in his riches, he will rouse up everything against the kingdom of Greece.

3 "And a mighty king will certainly stand up and rule with extensive dominion and do according to his will. **4** And when he will have stood up, his kingdom will be broken and be divided toward the four winds of the heavens, but not to his posterity and not according to his dominion with which he had ruled; because his kingdom will be uprooted, even for others than these.

5 "And the king of the south will become strong, even [one] of his princes; and he will prevail against him and will certainly rule with extensive dominion [greater than] that one's ruling power.

6 "And at the end of [some] years they will ally themselves with each other, and the very daughter of the king of the south will come to the king of the north in order to make an equitable arrangement. But she will not retain the power of her arm; and he will not stand, neither his arm; and she will be given up, she herself, and those bringing her in, and he who caused her birth, and the one making her strong in [those] times. **7** And one from the sprout of her roots will certainly stand up in his position, and he will come to the military force and come against the fortress of the king of the north and will certainly act against them and prevail. **8** And also with their gods, with their molten images, with their desirable articles of silver and of gold, [and] with the captives he will come to Egypt. And he himself will for [some] years stand off from the king of the north.

9 "And he will actually come into the kingdom of the king of the south and go back to his own soil.

10 "Now as for his sons, they will excite themselves and actually gather together a crowd of large military forces. And in coming he will certainly come and flood over and pass through. But he will go back, and he will excite himself all the way to his fortress.

11 "And the king of the south will embitter himself and will have to go forth and fight with him, [that is,] with the king of the north; and he will certainly have a large crowd stand up, and the crowd will actually be given into the hand of that one. 12 And the crowd will certainly be carried away. His heart will become exalted, and he will actually cause tens of thousands to fall; but he will not use his strong position.

13 "And the king of the north must return and set up a crowd larger than the first; and at the end of the times, [some] years, he will come, doing so with a great military force and with a great deal of goods. 14 And in those times there will be many who will stand up against the king of the south.

"And the sons of the robbers belonging to your people will, for their part, be carried along to try making a vision come true; and they will have to stumble.

15 "And the king of the north will come and throw up a siege rampart and actually capture a city with fortifications. And as for the arms of the south, they will not stand, neither the people of his picked ones; and there will be no power to keep standing. 16 And the one coming against him will do according to his will, and there will be no one standing before him. And he will stand in the land of the Decoration, and there will be extermination in his hand. 17 And he will set his face to come with the forcefulness of his entire kingdom, and there will be equitable [terms] with him; and he will act effectively. And as regards the daughter of womankind, it will be granted to him to bring her to ruin. And she will not stand, and she will not continue to be his. 18 And he will turn his face back to the coastlands and will actually capture many. And a commander will have to make the reproach from him cease for himself, [so that] his reproach will not be. He will make it turn back upon that one. 19 And he will turn his face back to the fortresses of his [own] land, and he will certainly stumble and fall, and he will not be found.

20 "And there must stand up in his position one who is causing an exacter to pass through the splen-

did kingdom, and in a few days he will be broken, but not in anger nor in warfare.

21 "And there must stand up in his position one who is to be despised, and they will certainly not set upon him the dignity of [the] kingdom; and he will actually come in during a freedom from care and take hold of [the] kingdom by means of smoothness. 22 And as regards the arms of the flood, they will be flooded over on account of him, and they will be broken; as will also the Leader of [the] covenant. 23 And because of their allying themselves with him he will carry on deception and actually come up and become mighty by means of a little nation. 24 And during freedom from care, even into the fatness of the jurisdictional district he will enter in and actually do what his fathers and the fathers of his fathers have not done. Plunder and spoil and goods he will scatter among them; and against fortified places he will scheme out his schemes, but only until a time.

25 "And he will arouse his power and his heart against the king of the south with a great military force; and the king of the south, for his part, will excite himself for the war with an exceedingly great and mighty military force. And he will not stand, because they will scheme out against him schemes. 26 And the very ones eating his delicacies will bring his breakdown.

"And as for his military force, it will be flooded away, and many will certainly fall down slain. 27 "And as regards these two kings, their heart will be inclined to doing what is bad, and at one table a lie is what they will keep speaking. But nothing will succeed, because [the] end is yet for the time appointed.

28 "And he will go back to his land with a great amount of goods, and his heart will be against the holy covenant. And he will act effectively and certainly go back to his land.

29 "At the time appointed he will go back, and he will actually come against the south; but it will not prove to be at the last the same as at the first. 30 And there will certainly come against him the ships of Kit'tim, and he will have to become dejected.

"And he will actually go back and hurl denunciations against the holy covenant and act effectively; and he will have to go back and will give consideration to those leaving the holy covenant. 31 And there will be arms that will stand up, proceeding from him; and they will actually profane the sanctuary, the fortress, and remove the constant [feature].

"And they will certainly put in place the disgusting thing that is causing desolation.

32 "And those who are acting wickedly against [the] covenant, he will lead into apostasy by means of smooth words. But as regards the people who are knowing their God, they will prevail and act effectively. 33 And as regards those having insight among the people, they will impart understanding to the many. And they will certainly be made to stumble by sword and by flame, by captivity and by plundering, for [some] days. 34 But when they are made to stumble they will be helped with a little help; and many will certainly join themselves to them by means of smoothness. 35 And some of those having insight will be made to stumble, in order to do a refining work because of them and to do a cleansing and to do a whitening, until the time of [the] end; because it is yet for the time appointed.

36 "And the king will actually do according to his own will, and he will exalt himself and magnify himself above every god; and against the God of gods he will speak marvelous things. And he will certainly prove successful until [the] denunciation will have come to a finish; because the thing decided upon must be done. 37 And to the god of his fathers he will give no consideration; and to the desire of women and to every other god he will give no consideration, but over everyone he will magnify himself. 38 But to the god of fortresses, in his position he will give glory; and to a god that his fathers did not know he will give glory by means of gold and by means of silver and by means of precious stone and by means of desirable things. 39 And he will act effectively against the most fortified strongholds, along with a foreign god. Whoever has given [him] recognition he will make abound with glory, and he will actually make them rule among many; and [the] ground he will apportion out for a price.

40 "And in the time of [the] end the king of the south will engage with him in a pushing, and against him the king of the north will storm with chariots and with horsemen and with many ships; and he will certainly enter into the lands and flood over and pass through. 41 He will also actually enter into the land of the Decoration, and there will be many [lands] that will be made to stumble. But these are the ones that will escape out of his hand, E'dom and Mo'ab and the main part of the sons of Am'mon. 42 And he will keep thrusting out his hand against the lands; and as regards the land of Egypt, she will not prove to be an escapee. 43 And he will actually rule over the hidden treasures of the gold and the silver and over all the desirable things of Egypt. And the Lib'y·ans and the E·thi·o'pi·ans will be at his steps.

44 "But there will be reports that will disturb him, out of the sunrising and out of the north, and he will certainly go forth in a great rage in order to annihilate and to devote many to destruction. 45 And he will plant his palatial tents between [the] grand sea and the holy mountain of Decoration; and he will have to come all the way to his end, and there will be no helper for him.

12 "And during that time Mi'-cha·el will stand up, the great prince who is standing in behalf of the sons of your people. And there will certainly occur a time of distress such as has not been made to occur since there came to be a nation until that time. And during that time your people will escape, every one who is found written down in the book. **2** And there will be many of those asleep in the ground of dust who will wake up, these to indefinitely lasting life and those to reproaches [and] to indefinitely lasting abhorrence.

3 "And the ones having insight will shine like the brightness of the expanse; and those who are bringing the many to righteousness, like the stars to time indefinite, even forever.

4 "And as for you, O Daniel, make secret the words and seal up the book, until the time of [the] end. Many will rove about, and the [true] knowledge will become abundant."

5 And I saw, I Daniel, and, look! there were two others standing, one on the bank here of the stream and the other on the bank there of the stream. **6** Then one said to the man clothed with the linen, who was up above the waters of the stream: "How long will it be to the end of the wonderful things?" **7** And I began to hear the man clothed with the linen, who was up above the waters of the stream, as he proceeded to raise his right [hand] and his left [hand] to the heavens and to swear by the One who is alive for time indefinite: "It will be for an appointed time, appointed times and a half. And as soon as there will have been a finishing of the dashing of the power of the holy people to pieces, all these things will come to their finish."

8 Now as for me, I heard, but I could not understand; so that I said: "O my lord, what will be the final part of these things?"

9 And he went on to say: "Go, Daniel, because the words are made secret and sealed up until the time of [the] end. **10** Many will cleanse themselves and whiten themselves and will be refined. And the wicked ones will certainly act wickedly, and no wicked ones at all will understand; but the ones having insight will understand.

11 "And from the time that the constant [feature] has been removed and there has been a placing of the disgusting thing that is causing desolation, there will be one thousand two hundred and ninety days.

12 "Happy is the one who is keeping in expectation and who arrives at the one thousand three hundred and thirty-five days! **13** "And as for you yourself, go toward the end; and you will rest, but you will stand up for your lot at the end of the days."

HOSEA

1 The word of Jehovah that occurred to Ho·se'a the son of Be·e'ri in the days of Uz·zi'ah, Jo'tham, A'haz [and] Hez·e·ki'ah, kings of Judah, and in the days of Jer·o·bo'am the son of Jo'ash, the king of Israel. **2** There was a start of the word of Jehovah by Ho·se'a, and Jehovah proceeded to say to Ho·se'a: "Go, take to yourself a wife of fornication and chil-dren of fornication, because by fornication the land positively turns from following Jehovah."

3 And he proceeded to go and take Go'mer the daughter of Dib·la'im, so that she became pregnant and in time bore to him a son.

4 And Jehovah went on to say to him: "Call his name Jez're·el, for yet a little while and I must hold an accounting for the acts of bloodshed of Jez're·el against the house of Je'hu, and I must cause the royal rule of the house of Israel to cease. 5 And it must occur in that day that I must break the bow of Israel in the low plain of Jez're·el."

6 And she proceeded to become pregnant another time and to give birth to a daughter. And He went on to say to him: "Call her name Lo-ru·ha'mah, for I shall no more show mercy again to the house of Israel, because I shall positively take them away. 7 But to the house of Judah I shall show mercy, and I will save them by Jehovah their God; but I shall not save them by a bow or by a sword or by war, by horses or by horsemen."

8 And she gradually weaned Loru·ha'mah, and she proceeded to become pregnant and give birth to a son. 9 So He said: "Call his name Lo-am'mi, because you men are not my people and I myself shall prove to be not yours.

10 "And the number of the sons of Israel must become like the grains of the sand of the sea that cannot be measured or numbered. And it must occur that in the place in which it used to be said to them, 'You men are not my people,' it will be said to them, 'The sons of the living God.' 11 And the sons of Judah and the sons of Israel will certainly be collected together into a unity and will actually set up for themselves one head and go up out of the land, because great will be the day of Jez're·el.

2 "Say to your brothers, 'My people!' and to your sisters, 'O woman shown mercy!' 2 Carry on a legal case with your mother; carry on a legal case, for she is not my wife and I am not her husband. And she should put away her fornication from before herself and her acts of adultery from between her breasts, 3 that I may not strip her naked and actually place her as in the day of her being born, and actually set her like a wilderness and place her like a waterless land and put her to death with

thirst. 4 And to her sons I shall not show mercy, for they are the sons of fornication. 5 For their mother has committed fornication. She that was pregnant with them has acted shamefully, for she has said, 'I want to go after those passionately loving me, those giving my bread and my water, my wool and my linen, my oil and my drink.'

6 "Therefore here I am hedging your way about with thorns; and I will heap up a stone wall against her, so that her own roadways she will not find. 7 And she will actually chase after her passionate lovers, but she will not overtake them; and she will certainly look for them, but she will not find [them]. And she will have to say, 'I want to go and return to my husband, the first one, for I had it better at that time than now.' 8 But she herself did not recognize that it was I who had given to her the grain and the sweet wine and the oil, and that I had made silver itself abound for her, and gold, [which] they made use of for Ba'al.

9 "Therefore I shall turn back and certainly take away my grain in its time and my sweet wine in its season, and I will snatch away my wool and my linen for covering her nakedness. 10 And now I shall uncover her private parts to the eyes of her passionate lovers, and there will be no man to snatch her out of my hand. 11 And I shall certainly cause all her exultation, her festival, her new moon and her sabbath and her every festal season to cease. 12 And I will lay desolate her vine and her fig tree, of which she has said: "They are a gift to me, which my passionate lovers have given to me"; and I will set them as a forest, and the wild beast of the field will certainly devour them. 13 And I will hold an accounting against her for all the days of the Ba'al images to which she kept making sacrificial smoke, when she kept decking herself with her ring and her ornament and kept going after her passionate lovers, and I was the one

that she forgot,' is the utterance of Jehovah.

14 "'Therefore here I am prevailing upon her, and I will cause her to go into the wilderness, and I will speak to her heart. 15 And I will give her her vineyards from then onward, and the low plain of A'chor as an entrance to hope; and she will certainly answer there as in the days of her youth and as in the day of her coming up out of the land of Egypt. 16 And it must occur in that day,' is the utterance of Jehovah, 'that you will call [me] My husband, and you will no longer call me My owner.'

17 "'And I will remove the names of the Ba'al images from her mouth, and they will no longer remember [them] by their name. 18 And for them I shall certainly conclude a covenant in that day in connection with the wild beast of the field and with the flying creature of the heavens and the creeping thing of the ground, and the bow and the sword and war I shall break out of the land, and I will make them lie down in security. 19 And I will engage you to me for time indefinite, and I will engage you to me in righteousness and in justice and in loving-kindness and in mercies. 20 And I will engage you to me in faithfulness; and you will certainly know Jehovah.

21 "'And it must occur in that day that I shall answer,' is the utterance of Jehovah, 'I shall answer the heavens, and they, for their part, will answer the earth; 22 and the earth, for its part, will answer the grain and the sweet wine and the oil; and they, for their part, will answer Jez're·el [=God will sow seed]. 23 And I shall certainly sow her like seed for me in the earth, and I will show mercy to her who was not shown mercy, and I will say to those not my people: "You are my people"; and they, for their part, will say: "[You are] my God."'"

3 And Jehovah went on to say to me: "Go once again, love a woman loved by a companion and committing adultery, as in the case of Jehovah's love for the sons of Israel while they are turning to other gods and are loving raisin cakes."

2 And I proceeded to purchase her for myself for fifteen silver [pieces] and a ho'mer measure of barley and a half-ho'mer of barley. 3 Then I said to her: "For many days you will dwell as mine. You must not commit fornication, and you must not come to belong to [another] man; and I also will be for you."

4 It is because for many days the sons of Israel will dwell without a king and without a prince and without a sacrifice and without a pillar and without an eph'od and teraphim. 5 Afterwards the sons of Israel will come back and certainly look for Jehovah their God, and for David their king; and they will certainly come quivering to Jehovah and to his goodness in the final part of the days.

4 Hear the word of Jehovah, O sons of Israel, for Jehovah has a legal case with the inhabitants of the land, for there is no truth nor loving-kindness nor knowledge of God in the land. 2 There are the pronouncing of curses and practicing of deception and murdering and stealing and committing of adultery that have broken forth, and acts of bloodshed have touched other acts of bloodshed. 3 That is why the land will mourn and every inhabitant in it will have to fade away with the wild beast of the field and with the flying creature of the heavens, and even the fishes of the sea themselves will be gathered [in death].

4 "However, let no man contend, neither let a man reprove, as your people are like those who are contending against a priest. 5 And you will certainly stumble in the daytime, and even a prophet must stumble with you, as at night. And I will put your mother to silence. 6 My people will certainly be silenced, because there is no knowledge. Because the knowledge is what you yourself have rejected, I

shall also reject you from serving as a priest to me; and [because] you keep forgetting the law of your God, I shall forget your sons, even I. 7 In proportion to the multitude of them, so they have sinned against me. My own glory they have exchanged for mere dishonor. 8 The sin of my people is what they keep devouring, and to their error they keep lifting up their soul.

9 "And it will have to become for the people the same as for the priest; and I shall certainly hold an accounting against them for their ways; and their dealings I shall bring back upon them. 10 And they will actually eat, but will not get satisfied. They will actually treat [women] as harlots; but they will not increase, because they have left off paying regard to Jehovah himself. 11 Fornication and wine and sweet wine are what take away good motive. 12 Of their wooden [idol] my own people keep inquiring, and their own [hand]staff keeps telling them; because the very spirit of fornication has caused them to wander off, and by fornication they go out from under their God. 13 On the tops of the mountains they sacrifice, and on the hills they make sacrificial smoke, under massive tree and storax tree and big tree, because its shade is good. That is why YOUR daughters commit fornication and YOUR own daughters-in-law commit adultery.

14 "I shall not hold an accounting against YOUR daughters because they commit fornication, and against YOUR daughters-in-law because they commit adultery. For, as to the [men], it is with the harlots that they get off to themselves, and with the female temple prostitutes that they sacrifice; and a people [that] does not understand will be trodden down. 15 Although you are committing fornication, O Israel, let not Judah become guilty, and do not YOU people come to Gil'gal, neither go up to Beth-a'ven nor swear 'As Jehovah is alive!' 16 For, like a stubborn

cow, Israel has become stubborn. Is it now that Jehovah will shepherd them like a young ram in a roomy place? 17 E'phra·im is joined with idols. Let him be to himself! 18 Their wheat beer being gone, they have positively treated [woman] as a harlot. Her shielders have positively loved dishonor. 19 A wind has wrapped her up in its wings. And they will be ashamed of their sacrifices."

5 "Hear this, O priests, and pay attention, O house of Israel, and YOU, O house of the king, give ear, for with YOU people the judgment has to do; because a trap is what YOU have become to Miz'pah and as a net spread over Ta'bor. 2 And in slaughter work those falling away have gone deep down, and I was an exhortation to all of them. 3 I personally have known E'phra·im, and Israel itself has not been hidden from me. For now, O E'phra·im, you have treated [women] like harlots; Israel has defiled itself. 4 Their dealings do not permit of a returning to their God, because there is a spirit of fornication in the midst of them; and Jehovah himself they have not acknowledged. 5 And the pride of Israel has testified to his face; and Israel and E'phra·im themselves are made to stumble in their error. Judah has also stumbled with them. 6 With their flock and with their herd they proceeded to go and look for Jehovah, but they could not find [him]. He had drawn away from them. 7 With Jehovah himself they have dealt treacherously, for it is to strange sons that they have become father. Now a month will devour them with their portions.

8 "BLOW a horn against Gib'e-ah, a trumpet against Ra'mah! SHOUT a war cry at Beth-a'ven —after you, O Benjamin! 9 O E'phra·im, a mere object of astonishment you will become in the day of rebuke. Among the tribes of Israel I have made known trustworthy words. 10 The princes of Judah have become just like those moving back a boundary. Upon

them I shall pour out my fury just like water. 11 E′phra·im is oppressed, crushed in justice, for he had taken it upon himself to walk after his adversary. 12 And I was like the moth to E′phra·im and just like rottenness to the house of Judah.

13 "And E′phra·im got to see his sickness, and Judah his ulcer. And E′phra·im proceeded to go to As·syr′i·a and send to a great king. But that one himself was unable to give healing to you people, and he could not take from you an ulcer with any cure. 14 For I shall be like a young lion to E′phra·im and like a maned young lion to the house of Judah. I, I myself shall tear to pieces and I shall go [and] carry off, and there will be no deliverer. 15 I shall go, I will return to my place until they bear their guilt; and they will certainly seek my face. When they are in sore straits, they will seek me."

6 "Come, you people, and do let us return to Jehovah, for he himself has torn in pieces but he will heal us. He kept striking, but he will bind us up. 2 He will make us alive after two days. On the third day he will make us get up, and we shall live before him. 3 And we will know, we will pursue to know Jehovah. Like dawn, his going forth is firmly established. And he will come in like a pouring rain to us; like a spring rain that saturates [the] earth."

4 "What shall I do to you, O E′phra·im? What shall I do to you, O Judah, when the loving-kindness of you people is like the morning clouds and like the dew that early goes away? 5 That is why I shall have to hew [them] by the prophets; I shall have to kill them by the sayings of my mouth. And the judgments upon you will be as the light that goes forth. 6 For in loving-kindness I have taken delight, and not in sacrifice; and in the knowledge of God rather than in whole burnt offerings. 7 But they themselves, like earthling man, have overstepped [the] covenant.

There is where they have dealt treacherously with me. 8 Gil′e·ad is a town of practicers of what is harmful; their footprints are blood. 9 And as in the lying in wait for a man, the association of priests are marauding bands. By the wayside they commit murder at She′chem, because they have carried on nothing but loose conduct. 10 In the house of Israel I have seen a horrible thing. There there is fornication on the part of E′phra·im. Israel has defiled itself. 11 Furthermore, O Judah, a harvest has been fixed for you, when I gather back the captive ones of my people."

7 "At the time that I would bring healing to Israel, the error of E′phra·im is also actually uncovered, and the bad things of Sa·mar′i·a; for they have practiced falsehood, and a thief himself comes in; a marauder band actually makes a dash on the outside. 2 And they do not say to their own heart that all their badness I will remember. Now their dealings have surrounded them. In front of my face they have come to be. 3 By their badness they make [the] king rejoice, and, by their deceptions, princes. 4 All of them are adulterers, like a furnace set burning by a baker, [who] ceases poking after kneading dough until it is leavened. 5 On the day of our king, princes have sickened themselves—there is a rage because of wine. He has drawn his hand along with deriders. 6 For they have brought their heart near as to a furnace; it is burning inside them. All night long their baker is sleeping; by morning [the furnace] is burning as with a flaming fire. 7 They get hot, all of them, like the furnace, and they actually devour their judges. Their own kings have all fallen; none among them is calling out to me.

8 "As for E′phra·im, it is among the peoples that he personally mingles himself. E′phra·im himself has become a round cake not turned on the other side. 9 Strangers have eaten up his power, and he himself has not come to know

[it]. Also, gray hairs themselves have become white on him, but he himself has not come to know [it]. 10 And the pride of Israel has testified to his face, and they have not returned to Jehovah their God, nor have they looked for him because of all this. 11 And E′phra·im proves to be like a simple-minded dove without heart. To Egypt they have called; to As·syr′i·a they have gone. 12 Whichever way they go, I shall spread out over them my net. Like flying creatures of the heavens I shall bring them down. I shall discipline them in agreement with the report to their assembly. 13 Woe to them, for they have fled from me! Despoiling to them, for they have transgressed against me! And I myself proceeded to redeem them, but they themselves have spoken lies even against me. 14 And they did not call to me for aid with their heart, although they kept howling on their beds. On account of their grain and sweet wine they kept loafing about; they kept turning against me. 15 And I, for my part, did disciplining; I strengthened their arms, but against me they kept scheming what was bad. 16 And they proceeded to return, not to anything higher; they had become like a loose bow. By the sword their princes will fall because of the denunciation of their tongue. This will be their derision in the land of Egypt."

8 "To your mouth—a horn! [One comes] like an eagle against the house of Jehovah, for the reason that they have overstepped my covenant, and against my law they have transgressed. 2 To me they keep crying, 'O my God, we, Israel, have known you.'

3 "Israel has cast off good. Let one who is an enemy pursue him. 4 They themselves have set up kings, but not because of me. They have set up princes, but I did not know [it]. With their silver and their gold they have made for themselves idols, to the end that they may be cut off. 5 Your calf has been cast off, O Sa·mar′i·a.

My anger has grown hot against them. How long will they be incapable of innocency? 6 For from Israel was even this. A mere craftsman made it, and it is not God; because the calf of Sa·mar′i·a will become mere splinters.

7 "For it is wind that they keep sowing, and a stormwind is what they will reap. Nothing has standing grain. No sprout produces flour. Should any perhaps produce [it], strangers themselves will swallow it down.

8 "Israel must be swallowed down. Now they must come to be among the nations, like a vessel in which there is no delight. 9 For they themselves have gone up to As·syr′i·a, as a zebra isolated to itself. In E′phra·im's case, they have hired lovers. 10 Also, although they keep hiring [them] among the nations, I shall now collect them together; and they will be a little while in severe pains because of the burden of king [and] princes.

11 "For E′phra·im has multiplied altars in order to sin. He has come to have altars in order to sin. 12 I proceeded to write for him many things of my law; just like something strange they have been accounted. 13 As my gift sacrifices they kept sacrificing flesh, and they kept eating what Jehovah himself took no pleasure in. Now he will remember their error and hold an accounting for their sins. To Egypt they themselves proceeded to return. 14 And Israel began forgetting his Maker and building temples; and Judah, for his part, multiplied fortified cities. And I shall certainly send fire into his cities and it must devour the dwelling towers of [each] one."

9 "Do not rejoice, O Israel. Do not act joyful like the peoples. For by fornication you have gone from alongside your God. You have loved gifts of hire on all the threshing floors of grain. 2 Threshing floor and wine press do not feed them, and sweet wine itself proves disappointing to her. 3 They will not continue dwelling

in the land of Jehovah, and E'phra·im must return to Egypt, and in As·syr'i·a they will eat what is unclean. 4 They will not continue pouring out wine to Jehovah. And their sacrifices will not be gratifying to him; they are like the bread of times of mourning to them; all those eating it will defile themselves. For their bread is for their own soul; it will not come into the house of Jehovah. 5 What will you people do in the day of meeting and in the day of the festival of Jehovah? 6 For, look! they will have to go because of despoiling. Egypt itself will collect them together; Mem'phis, for its part, will bury them. As for their desirable things of silver, nettles themselves will take possession of them; thorny bushes will be in their tents.

7 "The days of being given attention must come; the days of the due payment must come. Those of Israel will know [it]. The prophet will be foolish, the man of inspired expression will be maddened on account of the abundance of your error, even animosity being abundant."

8 The watchman of E'phra·im was with my God. As regards a prophet, there is the trap of a birdcatcher on all his ways; there is an animosity in the house of his God. 9 They have gone down deep in bringing ruin, as in the days of Gib'e·ah. He will remember their error; he will give attention to their sins.

10 "Like grapes in the wilderness I found Israel. Like the early fig on a fig tree in its beginning I saw the forefathers of you people. They themselves went in to Ba'al of Pe'or, and they proceeded to dedicate themselves to the shameful thing, and they came to be disgusting like [the thing of] their love. 11 As regards E'phra·im, like a flying creature their glory flies away, so that there is no giving birth, and no [pregnant] belly and no conception. 12 For although they bring up their sons, I will also bereave them of children so that there will be no man; because—woe also to them when I turn away from them! 13 E'phra·im, whom I have seen like Tyre planted in a pasture ground, even E'phra·im is destined to a bringing out of his sons even to a killer."

14 Give to them, O Jehovah, what you should give. Give them a miscarrying womb and breasts shriveling up.

15 "All their badness was in Gil'gal, for there I had to hate them. On account of the evil of their dealings I shall drive them away from my own house. I will not continue on loving them. All their princes are acting stubborn. 16 E'phra·im must be struck down. Their very root must dry up. There will be no fruit that they produce. Also, in case they bring to birth, I will even put to death the desirable things of their belly."

17 My God will reject them, for they have not listened to him, and they will become fugitives among the nations.

10 "Israel is a degenerating vine. Fruit he keeps putting forth for himself. In proportion to the abundance of his fruit he has multiplied [his] altars. In proportion to the goodness of his land, they put up good pillars. 2 Their heart has become hypocritical; now they will be found guilty.

"There is one who will break their altars; he will despoil their pillars. 3 For now they will say, 'We have no king, for we have not feared Jehovah. And as regards the king, what will he do for us?' 4 "They speak words, making false oaths, concluding a covenant; and judgment has sprouted like a poisonous plant in the furrows of the open field. 5 For the calf [idol] of Beth-a'ven the residents of Sa·mar'i·a will get frightened; for over it its people will certainly mourn, as well as its foreign-god priests [who] used to be joyful over it, on account of its glory, because it will have gone into exile away from it. 6 Even it someone will bring to As·syr'i·a itself as a gift to a great king. Shame is what

E'phra·im himself will get, and Israel will be ashamed of its counsel. 7 Sa·mar'i·a [and] her king will certainly be silenced, like a snapped-off twig on the surface of waters. 8 And the high places of [Beth-]a'ven, the sin of Israel, will actually be annihilated. Thorns and thistles themselves will come up upon their altars. And people will in fact say to the mountains, 'Cover us!' and to the hills, 'Fall over us!'

9 "From the days of Gib'e·ah you have sinned, O Israel. There they stood still. In Gib'e·ah war against the sons of unrighteousness did not get to overtake them. 10 When it is my craving I shall also discipline them. And against them peoples will certainly be gathered when there is a harnessing of them to their two errors.

11 "And E'phra·im was a trained heifer loving to thresh; and I, for my part, passed over her good-looking neck. I make [someone] ride E'phra·im. Judah plows; Jacob harrows for him. 12 Sow seed for yourselves in righteousness; reap in accord with loving-kindness. Till for yourselves arable land, when there is time for searching for Jehovah until he comes and gives instruction in righteousness to you.

13 "You people have plowed wickedness. Unrighteousness is what you have reaped. You have eaten the fruitage of deception, for you have trusted in your way, in the multitude of your mighty ones. 14 And an uproar has risen among your people, and your own fortified cities will all be despoiled, as with the despoiling by Shal'man of the house of Ar'bel, in the day of battle [when] a mother herself was dashed to pieces alongside [her] own sons. 15 In this way one will certainly do to you people, O Beth'el, because of your extreme badness. In the dawn the king of Israel will positively have to be silenced."

11 "When Israel was a boy, then I loved him, and out of Egypt I called my son.

2 "They called them. To that same extent they went away from before them. To the Ba'al images they took up sacrificing, and to the graven images they began making sacrificial smoke. 3 But as for me, I taught E'phra·im to walk, taking them upon [my] arms; and they did not recognize that I had healed them. 4 With the ropes of earthling man I kept drawing them, with the cords of love, so that I became to them as those lifting off a yoke on their jaws, and gently I brought food to [each] one. 5 He will not return to the land of Egypt, but As·syr'i·a will be his king, because they refused to return. 6 And a sword will certainly whirl about in his cities and make an end of his bars and devour because of their counsels. 7 And my people are tending toward unfaithfulness to me. And upward they call it; no one at all does any rising up.

8 "How can I give you up, O E'phra·im? [How] can I deliver you up, O Israel? How can I set you as Ad'mah? [How] can I place you like Ze·boi'im? My heart has changed within me; at the same time my compassions have grown hot. 9 I shall not express my burning anger. I shall not bring E'phra·im to ruin again, for I am God and not man, the Holy One in the midst of you; and I shall not come in excitement. 10 After Jehovah they will walk. Like a lion he will roar; for he himself will roar, and sons will come trembling from the west. 11 Like a bird they will come trembling out of Egypt, and like a dove out of the land of As·syr'i·a; and I shall certainly make them dwell in their houses," is the utterance of Jehovah.

12 "With lying, E'phra·im has surrounded me, and with deception the house of Israel. But Judah is yet roaming with God, and with the Most Holy One he is trustworthy."

12 "E'phra·im is feeding on wind and chasing after the east wind all day long. Lying and despoiling are what he multiplies. And a covenant with As·syr'i·a they conclude, and to Egypt oil itself is brought.

2 "And Jehovah has a legal case with Judah, even to hold an accounting against Jacob according to his ways; according to his dealings he will repay him. 3 In the belly he seized his brother by the heel, and with his dynamic energy he contended with God. 4 And he kept contending with an angel and gradually prevailed. He wept, that he might implore favor for himself."

At Beth'el He got to find him, and there he began talking with us. 5 And Jehovah the God of the armies, Jehovah is his memorial.

6 "And as respects you, to your God you should return, keeping loving-kindness and justice; and let there be a hoping in your God constantly. 7 As regards [the] tradesman, in his hand are the scales of deception; to defraud is what he has loved. 8 And E'phra·im keeps saying, 'Indeed, I have become rich; I have found valuable things for myself. As regards all my toiling, they will find, on my part, no error that is sin.'

9 "But I am Jehovah your God from the land of Egypt. Yet I shall make you dwell in the tents as in the days of an appointed time. 10 And I spoke to the prophets, and visions I myself multiplied, and by the hand of the prophets I kept making likenesses.

11 "With Gil'e·ad what is uncanny, also untruth, have occurred. In Gil'gal they have sacrificed even bulls. Moreover, their altars are like piles of stones in the furrows of the open field. 12 And Jacob proceeded to run away to the field of Syria, and Israel kept serving for a wife, and for a wife he guarded [sheep]. 13 And by a prophet Jehovah brought up Israel out of Egypt, and by a prophet he was guarded. 14 E'phra·im caused offense to bitterness, and his deeds of bloodshed he leaves upon his own self, and his reproach his grand Master will repay to him."

13 "When E'phra·im spoke, there was trembling; he himself carried [weight] in Israel. But he proceeded to become guilty in regard to Ba'al and die. 2 And now they commit additional sin and make for themselves a molten statue from their silver, idols according to their own understanding, the work of craftsmen, all of it. To them they are saying, 'Let the sacrificers who are men kiss mere calves.' 3 Therefore they will become like the clouds of morning and like the dew that early goes away; like chaff that is stormed away from the threshing floor and like smoke from the [roof] hole.

4 "But I am Jehovah your God from the land of Egypt, and there was no God except me that you used to know; and there was no savior but I. 5 I myself knew you in the wilderness, in the land of fevers. 6 According to their pasturage they also came to be satisfied. They became satisfied and their heart began to be exalted. That is why they forgot me. 7 And I shall become to them like a young lion. Like a leopard by [the] way I shall keep looking. 8 I shall encounter them like a bear that has lost its cubs, and I shall rip apart the enclosure of their heart. And I shall devour them there like a lion; a wild beast of the field itself will tear them to pieces. 9 It will certainly bring you to ruin, O Israel, because it was against me, against your helper.

10 "Where, then, is your king, that he may save you in all your cities, and your judges, [concerning] whom you said, 'Do give me a king and princes'? 11 I proceeded to give you a king in my anger, and I shall take [him] away in my fury.

12 "The error of E'phra·im is wrapped up, his sin is treasured up. 13 The labor pangs of a woman giving birth are what will come to him. He is a son not wise, for in season he will not stand still at the breaking forth of sons [from the womb].

14 "From the hand of She'ol I shall redeem them; from death I shall recover them. Where are your stings, O Death? Where is your destructiveness, O She'ol? Compassion itself will be concealed from my eyes.

15 "In case he himself as the son of reed plants should show fruitfulness, an east wind, the wind of Jehovah, will come. From a wilderness it is coming up, and it will dry up his well and drain his spring. That one will pillage the treasure of all desirable articles.

16 "Sa·mar'i·a will be held guilty, for she is actually rebellious against her God. By the sword they will fall. Their own children will be dashed to pieces, and their pregnant women themselves will be ripped up."

14 "Do come back, O Israel, to Jehovah your God, for you have stumbled in your error. 2 Take with yourselves words and come back to Jehovah. Say to him, all you people, 'May you pardon error; and accept what is good, and we will offer in return the young bulls of our lips. 3 As·syr'i·a itself will not save us. Upon horses we shall not ride. And no more shall we say: "O our God!" to the work of our hands, because it is by you that a fatherless boy is shown mercy.'

4 "I shall heal their unfaithfulness. I shall love them of [my] own free will, because my anger has turned back from him. 5 I shall become like the dew to Israel. He will blossom like the lily, and will strike his roots like Leb'a·non. 6 His twigs will go forth, and his dignity will become like that of the olive tree, and his fragrance will be like that of Leb'a·non. 7 They will again be dwellers in his shadow. They will grow grain, and will bud like the vine. His memorial will be like the wine of Leb'a·non.

8 "E'phra·im [will say], 'What do I have to do any longer with the idols?'

"I myself shall certainly give an answer and I shall keep looking on him. I am like a luxuriant juniper tree. From me must fruit for you be found."

9 Who is wise, that he may understand these things? Discreet, that he may know them? For the ways of Jehovah are upright, and the righteous are the ones who will walk in them; but the transgressors are the ones who will stumble in them.

JOEL

1 The word of Jehovah that occurred to Joel the son of Pe·thu'el:

2 "Hear this, you older men, and give ear, all you inhabitants of the land. Has this occurred in your days, or even in the days of your forefathers? 3 Concerning it give an account to your own sons, and your sons to their sons, and their sons to the following generation. 4 What was left by the caterpillar, the locust has eaten; and what was left by the locust, the creeping, unwinged locust has eaten; and what the creeping, unwinged locust has left, the cockroach has eaten.

5 "Wake up, you drunkards, and weep; and howl, all you wine drinkers, on account of sweet wine, for it has been cut off from your mouths. 6 For there is a nation that has come up into my land, mighty and without number. Its teeth are the teeth of a lion, and it has the jawbones of a lion. 7 It has set my vine as an object of astonishment, and my fig tree as a stump. It has positively stripped it bare and thrown [it] away. The twigs of it have become white. 8 Wail, as a virgin girded with sackcloth does over the owner of her youth.

9 "Grain offering and drink offering have been cut off from the house of Jehovah; the priests, the ministers of Jehovah, have mourned. 10 [The] field has been despoiled, [the] ground has gone to mourning; for [the] grain has been despoiled, [the] new wine has been dried up, [the] oil has faded away. 11 Farmers have felt shame; vinedressers have howled, on account of wheat and on account of barley; for the harvest of [the] field has perished. 12 The vine itself has shown dryness, and even the fig tree has faded away. As for [the] pomegranate tree, also [the] palm tree and [the] apple tree, all the trees of the field, they have dried up; for exultation has gone ashamed away from the sons of mankind.

13 "Gird yourselves, and beat YOUR breasts, YOU priests. Howl, YOU ministers of [the] altar. Come in, spend the night in sackcloth, YOU ministers of my God; for from the house of YOUR God grain offering and drink offering have been withheld. 14 Sanctify a time of fasting. Call together a solemn assembly. Gather together [the] older men, all the inhabitants of the land, to the house of Jehovah YOUR God, and cry to Jehovah for aid.

15 "Alas for the day; because the day of Jehovah is near, and like a despoiling from the Almighty One it will come! 16 Has not food itself been cut off before our very eyes; from the house of our God, rejoicing and joyfulness? 17 Dried figs have shriveled under their shovels. Storehouses have been laid desolate. Barns have been torn down, for [the] grain has dried up. 18 O how the domestic animal has sighed! [How] the droves of cattle have wandered in confusion! For there is no pasturage for them. Also, the droves of the sheep have been the ones made to bear guilt.

19 "To you, O Jehovah, I shall call; for fire itself has devoured the pasture grounds of [the] wilderness, and a very flame has consumed all the trees of the field. 20 The beasts of the field also keep longing for you, because the channels of water have dried up, and fire itself has devoured the pasture grounds of the wilderness."

2 "Blow a horn in Zion, O men, and shout a war cry in my holy mountain. Let all the inhabitants of the land get agitated; for the day of Jehovah is coming, for it is near! 2 It is a day of darkness and gloominess, a day of clouds and thick gloom, like light of dawn spread out upon the mountains.

"There is a people numerous and mighty; one like it has not been made to exist from the indefinite past, and after it there will be none again to the years of generation after generation. 3 Ahead of it a fire has devoured, and behind it a flame consumes. Like the garden of Eden the land is ahead of it; but behind it is a desolate wilderness, and there has also proved to be nothing thereof escaping.

4 "Its appearance is like the appearance of horses, and like steeds is the way they keep running. 5 As with the sound of chariots on the tops of the mountains they keep skipping about, as with the sound of a flaming fire that is devouring stubble. It is like a mighty people, drawn up in battle order. 6 Because of it, peoples will be in severe pains. As for all faces, they will certainly collect a glow [of excitement].

7 "Like powerful men they run. Like men of war they go up a wall. And they go each one in his own ways, and they do not alter their paths. 8 And one another they do not shove. As an able-bodied man in his course, they keep going; and should some fall even among the missiles, the [others] do not break off course.

9 "Into the city they rush. On the wall they run. On the houses they go up. Through the windows they go in like the thief. 10 Before it [the] land has become agitated, [the] heavens have rocked. Sun and moon themselves have become dark, and the very stars have withdrawn their brightness. 11 And Jehovah himself will cer-

tainly give forth his voice before his military force, for his camp is very numerous. For he who is carrying out his word is mighty; for the day of Jehovah is great and very fear-inspiring, and who can hold up under it?

12 "And now also," the utterance of Jehovah is, "come back to me with all YOUR hearts, and with fasting and with weeping and with wailing. 13 And rip apart YOUR hearts, and not YOUR garments; and come back to Jehovah YOUR God, for he is gracious and merciful, slow to anger and abundant in loving-kindness, and he will certainly feel regret on account of the calamity. 14 Who is there knowing whether he will turn back and actually feel regret and let remain after it a blessing, a grain offering and a drink offering for Jehovah YOUR God?

15 "Blow a horn in Zion, O men. Sanctify a time of fasting. Call together a solemn assembly. 16 Gather [the] people together. Sanctify a congregation. Collect [the] old men together. Gather children and those sucking the breasts together. Let [the] bridegroom go forth from his interior room, and [the] bride from her nuptial chamber.

17 "Between the porch and the altar let the priests, the ministers of Jehovah, weep and say, 'Do feel sorry, O Jehovah, for your people, and do not make your inheritance a reproach, for nations to rule over them. Why should they say among the peoples: "Where is their God?"' 18 And Jehovah will be zealous for his land and will show compassion upon his people. 19 And Jehovah will answer and say to his people, 'Here I am sending to YOU the grain and the new wine and the oil, and YOU people will certainly be satisfied with it; and I shall not make YOU any more a reproach among the nations. 20 And the northerner I shall put far away from upon YOU, and I shall actually disperse him to a waterless land and desolated waste, with his face to the eastern sea and his rear

section to the western sea. And the stink from him will certainly ascend, and the stench from him will keep ascending; for He will actually do a great thing in what He does.'

21 "Do not be fearful, O ground. Be joyful and rejoice; for Jehovah will actually do a great thing in what He does. 22 Do not be fearful, YOU beasts of the open field, for the pasture grounds of [the] wilderness will certainly grow green. For the tree will actually give its fruitage. The fig tree and the vine must give their vital energy. 23 And, YOU sons of Zion, be joyful and rejoice in Jehovah YOUR God; for he will be bound to give YOU the autumn rain in right measure, and he will bring down upon YOU people a downpour, autumn rain and spring rain, as at the first. 24 And the threshing floors must be full of [cleansed] grain, and the press vats must overflow with new wine and oil. 25 And I will make compensation to YOU for the years that the locust, the creeping, unwinged locust, and the cockroach and the caterpillar have eaten, my great military force that I have sent among YOU. 26 And YOU will certainly eat, eating and becoming satisfied, and YOU will be bound to praise the name of Jehovah YOUR God, who has done with YOU so wonderfully; and my people will not be ashamed to time indefinite. 27 And YOU people will have to know that I am in the midst of Israel, and that I am Jehovah YOUR God and there is no other. And my people will not be ashamed to time indefinite.

28 "And after that it must occur that I shall pour out my spirit on every sort of flesh, and YOUR sons and YOUR daughters will certainly prophesy. As for YOUR old men, dreams they will dream. As for YOUR young men, visions they will see. 29 And even on the menservants and on the maidservants in those days I shall pour out my spirit.

30 "And I will give portents in the heavens and on the earth, blood

and fire and columns of smoke. 31 The sun itself will be turned into darkness, and the moon into blood, before the coming of the great and fear-inspiring day of Jehovah. 32 And it must occur that everyone who calls on the name of Jehovah will get away safe; for in Mount Zion and in Jerusalem there will prove to be the escaped ones, just as Jehovah has said, and in among the survivors, whom Jehovah is calling."

3 "For, look! in those days and in that time, when I shall bring back the captive ones of Judah and Jerusalem, 2 I will also collect together all the nations and bring them down to the low plain of Je·hosh′a·phat; and I will put myself on judgment with them there on account of my people and my inheritance Israel, whom they scattered among the nations; and they apportioned out my own land. 3 And for my people they kept casting lots; and they would give the male child for a prostitute, and the female child they sold for wine, that they might drink.

4 "And, also, what do you have to do with me, O Tyre and Si′don and all you regions of Phi·lis′ti·a? Is it the treatment that you are giving me as a reward? And if you are giving such treatment to me, swiftly, speedily I shall pay back your treatment upon your heads. 5 Because you men have taken my own silver and my own gold, and you have brought my own desirable good things into your temples; 6 and the sons of Judah and the sons of Jerusalem you have sold to the sons of the Greeks, for the purpose of removing them far from their own territory; 7 here I am arousing them [to come] from the place where you have sold them, and I will pay back your treatment upon your own heads. 8 And I will sell your sons and your daughters into the hand of the sons of Judah, and they must sell them to the men of She′ba, to a nation far away; for Jehovah himself has spoken [it].

9 "Proclaim this, you people, among the nations, 'Sanctify war! Arouse the powerful men! Let them draw near! Let them come up, all the men of war! 10 Beat your plowshares into swords and your pruning shears into lances. As for the weak one, let him say: "I am a powerful man." 11 Lend your aid and come, all you nations round about, and collect yourselves together.'"

To that place, O Jehovah, bring your powerful ones down.

12 "Let the nations be aroused and come up to the low plain of Je·hosh′a·phat; for there I shall sit in order to judge all the nations round about.

13 "Thrust in a sickle, for harvest has grown ripe. Come, descend, for [the] wine press has become full. The press vats actually overflow; for their badness has become abundant. 14 Crowds, crowds are in the low plain of the decision, for the day of Jehovah is near in the low plain of the decision. 15 Sun and moon themselves will certainly become dark, and the very stars will actually withdraw their brightness. 16 And out of Zion Jehovah himself will roar, and out of Jerusalem he will give forth his voice. And heaven and earth certainly will rock; but Jehovah will be a refuge for his people, and a fortress for the sons of Israel. 17 And you people will have to know that I am Jehovah your God, residing in Zion my holy mountain. And Jerusalem must become a holy place; and as regards strangers, they will no more pass through her.

18 "And it must occur in that day that the mountains will drip with sweet wine, and the very hills will flow with milk, and the very stream beds of Judah will all flow with water. And out of the house of Jehovah there will go forth a spring, and it must irrigate the torrent valley of the Acacia Trees. 19 As regards Egypt, a desolate waste it will become; and as regards E′dom, a wilderness of desolate waste it will become, because of the violence to the sons of Judah,

in whose land they shed innocent blood. 20 But as for Judah, to time indefinite it will be inhabited, and Jerusalem to generation after generation. 21 And I will consider innocent their blood that I had not considered innocent; and Jehovah will be residing in Zion."

AMOS

1 The words of A′mos, who happened to be among the sheep raisers from Te·ko′a, which he visioned concerning Israel in the days of Uz·zi′ah the king of Judah and in the days of Jer·o·bo′am the son of Jo′ash, the king of Israel, two years before the earthquake. 2 And he proceeded to say:
"Jehovah—out of Zion he will roar, and out of Jerusalem he will give forth his voice; and the pasture grounds of the shepherds must go to mourning, and the summit of Car′mel must dry up."
3 "This is what Jehovah has said, ‘ "On account of three revolts of Damascus, and on account of four, I shall not turn it back, on account of their threshing Gil′e·ad even with iron threshing instruments. 4 And I will send a fire onto the house of Haz′a·el, and it must devour the dwelling towers of Ben-ha′dad. 5 And I will break the bar of Damascus and cut off [the] inhabitant from Bik′-ath-a′ven, and the holder of [the] scepter from Beth-e′den; and the people of Syria will have to go as exiles to Kir," Jehovah has said.'
6 "This is what Jehovah has said, ‘ "On account of three revolts of Ga′za, and on account of four, I shall not turn it back, on account of their taking into exile a complete body of exiles to hand over to E′dom. 7 And I will send a fire onto the wall of Ga′za, and it must devour her dwelling towers. 8 And I will cut off [the] inhabitant from Ash′dod, and the holder of [the] scepter from Ash′ke·lon; and I will turn my hand back upon Ek′ron, and the remaining ones of the Phi·lis′tines must perish," the Lord Jehovah has said.'

9 "This is what Jehovah has said, ‘On account of three revolts of Tyre, and on account of four, I shall not turn it back, on account of their handing over a complete body of exiles to E′dom, and [because] they did not remember the covenant of brothers. 10 And I will send a fire onto the wall of Tyre, and it must devour her dwelling towers.'
11 "This is what Jehovah has said, ‘On account of three revolts of E′dom, and on account of four, I shall not turn it back, on account of his pursuing his own brother with the sword, and [because] he ruined his [own] merciful qualities, and his anger keeps tearing away forever; and his fury—he has kept it perpetually. 12 And I will send a fire into Te′man, and it must devour the dwelling towers of Boz′rah.'
13 "This is what Jehovah has said, ‘ "On account of three revolts of the sons of Am′mon, and on account of four, I shall not turn it back, on account of their slitting open the pregnant women of Gil′e·ad, for the purpose of widening out their own territory. 14 And I will set fire to the wall of Rab′bah, and it must devour her dwelling towers, with an alarm signal in the day of battle, with a tempest in the day of stormwind. 15 And their king must go into exile, he and his princes together," Jehovah has said.'
2 "This is what Jehovah has said, ‘ "On account of three revolts of Mo′ab, and on account of four, I shall not turn it back, on account of his burning the bones of the king of E′dom for lime. 2 And I will send a fire into Mo′ab, and it must devour the dwelling towers

of Ke′ri·oth; and with noise Mo′ab must die, with an alarm signal, with the sound of a horn. 3 And I will cut off [the] judge from the midst of her, and all her princes I shall kill with him," Jehovah has said.'

4 "This is what Jehovah has said, 'On account of three revolts of Judah, and on account of four, I shall not turn it back, on account of their rejecting the law of Jehovah, and [because] they did not keep his own regulations; but their lies, after which their forefathers had walked, kept making them wander. 5 And I will send a fire into Judah, and it must devour the dwelling towers of Jerusalem.'

6 "This is what Jehovah has said, 'On account of three revolts of Israel, and on account of four, I shall not turn it back, on account of their selling someone righteous for mere silver, and someone poor for [the price of] a pair of sandals. 7 They are panting for the dust of [the] earth on the head of lowly persons; and the way of meek people they turn aside; and a man and his own father have gone to the [same] girl, for the purpose of profaning my holy name. 8 And on garments seized as a pledge they stretch themselves out beside every altar; and the wine of those who have been fined they drink at the house of their gods.'

9 " 'But as for me, I had annihilated the Am′o·rite on account of them, whose height was like the height of cedars, and who was vigorous like the massive trees; and I went annihilating his fruitage above and his roots below. 10 And I myself brought you people up out of the land of Egypt, and I kept making you walk through the wilderness forty years, in order to take possession of the land of the Am′o·rite. 11 And I kept raising up some of your sons as prophets and some of your young men as Naz′i·rites. Should this really not be, O sons of Israel?' is the utterance of Jehovah.

12 " 'But you kept giving the Naz′i·rites wine to drink, and upon the prophets you laid a command, saying: "You must not prophesy." 13 Here I am making what is under you sway, just as the wagon sways that is full up with a row of newly cut grain. 14 And a place to which to flee must perish from the swift one, and no one strong will reinforce his power, and no mighty man will provide his soul with escape. 15 And no one handling the bow will stand, and no one swift on his feet will escape, and no rider of the horse will provide his soul with escape. 16 And as for one strong in his heart among the mighty men, naked is how he will flee in that day,' is the utterance of Jehovah."

3 "Hear this word that Jehovah has spoken concerning you, O sons of Israel, concerning the whole family that I brought up out of the land of Egypt, saying, 2 'You people only have I known out of all the families of the ground. That is why I shall hold an accounting against you for all your errors.

3 " 'Will two walk together unless they have met by appointment? 4 Will a lion roar in the forest when it has no prey? Will a young maned lion give forth its voice from its hiding place if it has caught nothing at all? 5 Will a bird fall into a trap on the earth when there is no snare for it? Does a trap go up from the ground when it has absolutely caught nothing? 6 If a horn is blown in a city, do not also the people themselves tremble? If a calamity occurs in the city, is it not also Jehovah who has acted? 7 For the Lord Jehovah will not do a thing unless he has revealed his confidential matter to his servants the prophets. 8 There is a lion that has roared! Who will not be afraid? The Lord Jehovah himself has spoken! Who will not prophesy?'

9 " 'Publish it on [the] dwelling towers in Ash′dod and on [the] dwelling towers in the land of Egypt, and say: "Be gathered together against the mountains of Sa·mar′i·a, and see the many dis-

orders in the midst of her and cases of defrauding inside her. 10 And they have not known how to do what is straightforward," is the utterance of Jehovah, "those who are storing up violence and despoiling in their dwelling towers."'

11 "Therefore this is what the Lord Jehovah has said, 'There is an adversary even round about the land, and he will certainly bring your strength down from you, and your dwelling towers will actually be plundered.'

12 "This is what Jehovah has said, 'Just as the shepherd snatches away from the mouth of the lion two shanks or a piece of an ear, so the sons of Israel will be snatched away, those sitting in Sa·mar′i·a on a splendid couch and on a Damascene divan.'

13 "'HEAR and give witness in the house of Jacob,' is the utterance of the Lord Jehovah, the God of the armies. 14 'For, in the day of my holding an accounting for the revolts of Israel against him, I will also hold an accounting against the altars of Beth′el; and the horns of the altar will certainly be cut off and must fall to the earth. 15 And I will strike down the winter house in addition to the summer house.'

"'And the houses of ivory will have to perish, and many houses will have to come to their finish,' is the utterance of Jehovah."

4 "Hear this word, you cows of Ba′shan, who are on the mountain of Sa·mar′i·a, who are defrauding the lowly ones, who are crushing the poor ones, who are saying to their masters, 'Do bring, and let us drink!' 2 The Lord Jehovah has sworn by his holiness, '"Look! There are days coming upon you, and he will certainly lift you up with butcher hooks and the last part of you with fishhooks. 3 And [by] breaches you will go forth, each one straight ahead; and you will certainly be thrown out to Har′mon," is the utterance of Jehovah.'

4 "'Come, you people, to Beth′el and commit transgression. At Gil′gal be frequent in committing transgression, and bring your sacrifices in the morning; on the third day, your tenth parts. 5 And from what is leavened make a thanksgiving sacrifice to smoke, and proclaim voluntary offerings; publish [it], for that is the way you have loved, O sons of Israel,' is the utterance of the Lord Jehovah.

6 "'And I also, for my part, gave you people cleanness of teeth in all your cities and want of bread in all your places; but you did not come back to me,' is the utterance of Jehovah.

7 "'And as for me, I also withheld from you people the downpour when there were yet three months to the harvest; and I made it rain on one city, but on another city I would not make it rain. There was one tract of land that would be rained on, but a tract of land on which I would not make it rain would be dried up. 8 And two or three cities staggered to one city in order to drink water, and they would not get satisfied; but you did not come back to me,' is the utterance of Jehovah.

9 "'I struck you people with scorching and mildew. There was a multiplying of your gardens and of your vineyards, but your fig trees and your olive trees the caterpillar would devour; yet you did not come back to me,' is the utterance of Jehovah.

10 "'I sent among you people a pestilence in the nature of that of Egypt. With the sword I killed your young men, along with the taking captive of your horses. And I kept making the stink of your camps ascend even into your nostrils; but you did not come back to me,' is the utterance of Jehovah.

11 "'I caused an overthrow among you people, like God's overthrow of Sod′om and Go·mor′rah. And you came to be like a log snatched out of [the] burning; but you did not come back to me,' is the utterance of Jehovah.

12 "Therefore that is what I shall do to you, O Israel. As a consequence of the fact that I

shall do this very thing to you, get ready to meet your God, O Israel. 13 For, look! the Former of [the] mountains and the Creator of [the] wind, and the One telling to earthling man what his mental concern is, the One making dawn into obscurity, and the One treading on earth's high places, Jehovah the God of armies is his name."

5 "Hear this word that I am taking up over you people as a dirge, O house of Israel:

2 "The virgin, Israel, has fallen; She cannot get up again. She has been forsaken upon her own ground; There is no one raising her up.

3 "For this is what the Lord Jehovah has said, 'The very city that was going forth with a thousand will have a hundred left; and the one going forth with a hundred will have ten left, for the house of Israel.'

4 "For this is what Jehovah has said to the house of Israel, 'Search for me, and keep living. 5 And do not search for Beth'el, and to Gil'gal you must not come, and to Be'er-she'ba you must not pass over; because Gil'gal itself will without fail go into exile; and as regards Beth'el, it will become something uncanny. 6 Search for Jehovah, and keep living, that he may not become operative just like fire, O house of Joseph, and it may not actually devour, and Beth'el may not be with no one to extinguish [it], 7 O you who are turning justice into mere wormwood, and the ones who have cast righteousness itself to the earth. 8 The Maker of the Ki'mah constellation and the Ke'sil constellation, and the One turning deep shadow into the morning itself, and the One who has made day itself dark as night, the One calling for the waters of the sea, that he may pour them out upon the surface of the earth—Jehovah is his name; 9 who is causing a despoiling to flash forth upon someone strong, that despoiling itself may come upon even a fortified place.

10 "'In the gate they have hated a reprover, and a speaker of perfect things they detest. 11 Therefore, for the reason that you are extracting farm rent from someone lowly, and the tribute of grain you keep taking from him; houses of hewn stone you have built, but you will not keep dwelling in them; and desirable vineyards you have planted, but you will not keep drinking the wine of them. 12 For I have known how many your revolts are and how mighty your sins are, O you who are showing hostility toward someone righteous, you who are taking hush money, and the ones who have turned aside poor people even in the gate. 13 Therefore the very one having insight will in that time keep silent, for it will be a calamitous time.

14 "'Search for what is good, and not what is bad, to the end that you people may keep living; and that thus Jehovah the God of armies may come to be with you, just as you have said. 15 Hate what is bad, and love what is good, and give justice a place in the gate. It may be that Jehovah the God of armies will show favor to the remaining ones of Joseph.'

16 "Therefore this is what Jehovah the God of armies, Jehovah, has said, 'In all the public squares there will be wailing, and in all the streets people will be saying: "Ah! Ah!" And they will have to call a farmer to mourning, and to wailing those experienced in lamentation.' 17 'And in all vineyards there will be wailing; for I shall pass through the midst of you,' Jehovah has said.

18 "'Woe to those who are craving the day of Jehovah! What, then, will the day of Jehovah mean to you people? It will be darkness, and no light, 19 just as when a man flees because of the lion, and the bear actually meets him; and [as when] he went into the house and supported his hand against the wall, and the serpent bit him. 20 Will not the day of Jehovah be darkness, and not light; and will it not have gloom, and not brightness? 21 I have hated, I have re-

jected YOUR festivals, and I shall not enjoy the smell of YOUR solemn assemblies. 22 But if YOU people offer up to me whole burnt offerings, even in YOUR gift offerings I shall find no pleasure, and on YOUR communion sacrifices of fatlings I shall not look. 23 Remove from me the turmoil of your songs; and the melodious sound of your stringed instruments may I not hear. 24 And let justice roll forth just like waters, and righteousness like a constantly flowing torrent. 25 Was it sacrifices and gift offerings that YOU people brought near to me in the wilderness for forty years, O house of Israel? 26 And YOU will certainly carry Sak'kuth YOUR king and Kai'wan, YOUR images, the star of YOUR god, whom YOU made for yourselves. 27 And I will cause YOU to go into exile beyond Damascus,' he whose name is Jehovah the God of armies has said."

6 "Woe to those who are at ease in Zion and to those trusting in the mountain of Sa·mar'i·a! They are the distinguished ones of the chief part of the nations, and to them the house of Israel have come. 2 Make YOUR way over to Cal'neh, and see; and go from there to populous Ha'math, and go down to Gath of the Phi·lis'tines. Are they better than these kingdoms, or is their territory bigger than YOUR territory? 3 [Are YOU] putting out of [YOUR] mind the calamitous day, and do YOU bring near the dwelling of violence? 4 [YOU men] that are lying down on couches of ivory and are sprawling on their divans, and are eating the rams out of a flock and the young bulls from among fattened calves; 5 that are improvising according to the sound of the stringed instrument; that, like David, have devised for themselves instruments for song; 6 that are drinking out of bowls of wine, and that with the choicest oils do their anointing, and that have not been made sick at the catastrophe of Joseph.

7 "Therefore now they will go into exile at the head of those going into exile, and the revelry of sprawling ones must depart.

8 " 'The Lord Jehovah has sworn by his own soul,' is the utterance of Jehovah the God of armies, ' "I am detesting the pride of Jacob, and his dwelling towers I have hated, and I will deliver up [the] city and what fills it. 9 And it must occur that if ten men should be left remaining in one house, they must also die. 10 And his father's brother will have to carry them forth one by one, and will be burning them one by one, in order to bring out [the] bones from the house. And he will have to say to whoever is in the innermost parts of the house, 'Are there any more with you?' And he will certainly say, 'Nobody!' And he will have to say, 'Keep silence! For it is not the occasion for making any mention of the name of Jehovah.' "

11 " 'For here is Jehovah commanding, and he will certainly strike down the great house into rubble and the small house into debris.

12 " 'On a crag will horses run, or will one plow [there] with cattle? For into a poisonous plant YOU people have turned justice, and the fruitage of righteousness into wormwood, 13 [YOU who] are rejoicing in a thing that is not; who are saying: "Have we not in our strength taken horns to ourselves?" 14 Look! I am raising up against YOU, O house of Israel,' is the utterance of Jehovah the God of the armies, 'a nation, and they must oppress YOU people from the entering in of Ha'math down to the torrent valley of the Ar'a·bah.' "

7 This is what the Lord Jehovah caused me to see, and, look! he was forming a [locust] swarm at the start of the coming up of the later sowing. And, look! it was the later sowing after the mown grass of the king. 2 And it occurred that when it had finished eating up the vegetation of the land, I proceeded to say: "O Lord Jehovah, forgive, please. Who will rise up of Jacob? For he is small!"

3 Jehovah felt regret over this. "It shall not occur," Jehovah said.

4 This is what the Lord Jehovah caused me to see, and, look! the Lord Jehovah was calling for a contention by means of fire; and it went eating up the vast watery deep and ate up the tract of land. 5 And I proceeded to say: "O Lord Jehovah, hold off, please. Who will rise up of Jacob? For he is small!"

6 Jehovah felt regret over this. "That, too, will not occur," the Lord Jehovah said.

7 This is what he caused me to see, and, look! Jehovah was stationed on a wall [made with] a plummet, and there was a plummet in his hand. 8 Then Jehovah said to me: "What are you seeing, A′mos?" So I said: "A plummet." And Jehovah went on to say: "Here I am setting a plummet in the midst of my people Israel. I shall no more do any further excusing of it. 9 And the high places of Isaac will certainly be laid desolate, and the sanctuaries themselves of Israel will be devastated; and I will rise up against the house of Jer·o·bo′am with a sword."

10 And Am·a·zi′ah the priest of Beth′el proceeded to send to Jer′o·bo′am the king of Israel, saying: "A′mos has conspired against you right inside the house of Israel. The land is not able to put up with all his words. 11 For this is what A′mos has said, 'By the sword Jer·o·bo′am will die; and as regards Israel, it will without fail go into exile from its own ground.'"

12 And Am·a·zi′ah proceeded to say to A′mos: "O visionary, go, run your way off to the land of Judah, and there eat bread, and there you may prophesy. 13 But at Beth′el you must no longer do any further prophesying, for it is the sanctuary of a king and it is the house of a kingdom."

14 Then A′mos answered and said to Am·a·zi′ah: "I was not a prophet, neither was I the son of a prophet; but I was a herdsman and a nipper of figs of sycamore trees. 15 And Jehovah proceeded to take me from following the flock,

and Jehovah went on to say to me, 'Go, prophesy to my people Israel.' 16 And now hear the word of Jehovah, 'Are you saying: "You must not prophesy against Israel, and you must let no [word] drop against the house of Isaac"? 17 Therefore this is what Jehovah has said: "As regards your wife, in the city she will become a prostitute. And as regards your sons and your daughters, by the sword they will fall. And as regards your ground, by the measuring rope it will be apportioned out. And as regards you yourself, on unclean ground you will die; and as regards Israel, it will without fail go into exile from its own ground."'"

8 This is what the Lord Jehovah caused me to see, and, look! there was a basket of summer fruit. 2 Then he said: "What are you seeing, A′mos?" So I said: "A basket of summer fruit." And Jehovah went on to say to me: "The end has come to my people Israel. I shall no more do any further excusing of them. 3 'And the songs of [the] temple will actually be a howling in that day,' is the utterance of the Lord Jehovah. 'There will be many a carcass. In every place one will certainly throw [them] out—hush!'

4 "Hear this, you men snapping at someone poor, even in order to cause the meek ones of the earth to cease, 5 saying, 'How long will it be before the new moon passes and we may sell cereals? Also, the sabbath, and we may offer grain for sale; in order to make the e′phah small and to make the shekel great and to falsify the scales of deception; 6 in order to buy lowly people for mere silver and someone poor for [the price of] a pair of sandals, and that we may sell mere refuse of grain?'

7 "Jehovah has sworn by the Superiority of Jacob, 'Never will I forget all their works. 8 Will it not be on this account that the land will be agitated, and every inhabitant in it will have to mourn; and it will, all of it, certainly come up just like the Nile and be tossed

and sink down like the Nile of Egypt?'

9 "'And it must occur in that day,' is the utterance of the Lord Jehovah, 'that I will make the sun go down at high noon, and I will cause darkness for the land on a bright day. 10 And I will turn YOUR festivals into mourning and all YOUR songs into a dirge, and I will bring up upon all hips sackcloth and upon every head baldness; and I will make the situation like the mourning for an only [son], and the end result of it as a bitter day.'

11 "'Look! There are days coming,' is the utterance of the Lord Jehovah, 'and I will send a famine into the land, a famine, not for bread, and a thirst, not for water, but for hearing the words of Jehovah. 12 And they will certainly stagger from sea all the way to sea, and from north even to the sunrise. They will keep roving about while searching for the word of Jehovah, but they will not find [it]. 13 In that day the pretty virgins will swoon away, also the young men, because of the thirst; 14 those who are swearing by the guiltiness of Sa·mar'i·a, and who actually say: "As your god is alive, O Dan!" and, "As the way of Be'er-she'ba is alive!" And they will certainly fall, and they will rise up no more.'"

9 I saw Jehovah stationed above the altar, and he proceeded to say: "Strike the pillar head, so that the thresholds will rock. And cut them off at the head, all of them. And the last part of them I shall kill with the sword itself. No one fleeing of them will make good his flight, and no one escaping of them will make his getaway. 2 If they dig down into She'ol, from there my own hand will take them; and if they go up to the heavens, from there I shall bring them down. 3 And if they hide themselves on the top of Car'mel, from there I shall carefully search and be certain to take them. And if they conceal themselves from in front of my eyes on the floor of the sea, down there I shall com-

mand the serpent, and it must bite them. 4 And if they go into captivity before their enemies, from there I shall command the sword, and it must kill them; and I will set my eyes upon them for bad, and not for good. 5 And the Sovereign Lord, Jehovah of the armies, is the One touching the land, so that it melts; and all the inhabitants in it will have to mourn; and it will certainly come up like the Nile, all of it, and sink down like the Nile of Egypt.

6 "'He who is building in the heavens his stairs, and his structure over the earth that he founded; he who is calling for the waters of the sea, that he may pour them out upon the surface of the earth—Jehovah is his name.'

7 "'Are YOU not like the sons of the Cush'ites to me, O sons of Israel?' is the utterance of Jehovah. 'Did I not bring Israel itself up out of the land of Egypt, and the Phi·lis'tines out of Crete, and Syria out of Kir?'

8 "'Look! The eyes of the Lord Jehovah are upon the sinful kingdom, and he will certainly annihilate it from upon the surface of the ground. Nevertheless, I shall not completely annihilate the house of Jacob,' is the utterance of Jehovah. 9 'For, look! I am commanding, and I will jiggle the house of Israel among all the nations, just as one jiggles the sieve, so that not a pebble falls to the earth. 10 By the sword they will die—all the sinners of my people, those who are saying: "The calamity will not come near or reach as far as us."'

11 "'In that day I shall raise up the booth of David that is fallen, and I shall certainly repair their breaches. And its ruins I shall raise up, and I shall certainly build it up as in the days of long ago, 12 to the end that they may take possession of what is left remaining of E'dom, and all the nations upon whom my name has been called,' is the utterance of Jehovah, who is doing this.

13 "'Look! There are days coming,' is the utterance of Jehovah,

'and the plowman will actually overtake the harvester, and the treader of grapes, the carrier of the seed; and the mountains must drip with sweet wine, and the very hills will all find themselves melting. 14 And I will gather back the captive ones of my people Israel, and they will actually build [the] desolated cities and inhabit [them], and plant vineyards and drink the wine of them, and make gardens and eat the fruit of them.'

15 "'And I shall certainly plant them upon their ground, and they will no more be uprooted from their ground that I have given them,' Jehovah your God has said."

OBADIAH

1 The vision of O·ba·di'ah:

This is what the Lord Jehovah has said regarding E'dom: "There is a report that we have heard from Jehovah, and there is an envoy that has been sent among the nations, 'Rise up, you people, and let us rise up against her in battle.' "

2 "Look! Small is what I have made you among the nations. You are despised very much. **3** The presumptuousness of your heart is what has deceived you, you who are residing in the retreats of the crag, the height where he dwells, saying in his heart, 'Who will bring me down to [the] earth?' **4** If you should make your position high like the eagle, or if among the stars there were a placing of your nest, down from there I would bring you," is the utterance of Jehovah.

5 "If it were thieves that came in to you, if despoilers [came in] by night, to what extent would you have been silenced? Would they not steal as much as they wanted? Or if it were grape gatherers that came in to you, would they not let some gleanings remain? **6** O the extent to which those of E'sau have been searched out! [How] his concealed treasures have been sought out! **7** As far as the boundary they have sent you. The very men in covenant with you have all deceived you. The men at peace with you have prevailed against you. Those [eating] food with you will place a net under you as one in whom there is no discernment.

8 Will it not be in that day?" is the utterance of Jehovah.

"And I shall certainly destroy the wise ones out of E'dom, and discernment out of the mountainous region of E'sau. **9** And your mighty men must become terrified, O Te'man, for the reason that each one will be cut off from the mountainous region of E'sau, because of a killing. **10** Because of the violence to your brother Jacob, shame will cover you, and you will have to be cut off to time indefinite. **11** In the day when you stood off on the side, in the day when strangers took his military force into captivity and [when] outright foreigners entered his gate and over Jerusalem they cast lots, you also were like one of them.

12 "And you ought not to watch the sight in the day of your brother, in the day of his misfortune; and you ought not to rejoice at the sons of Judah in the day of their perishing; and you ought not to maintain a big mouth in the day of [their] distress. **13** You ought not to come into the gate of my people in the day of their disaster. You, even you, ought not to peer at his calamity in the day of his disaster; and you ought not to thrust out a hand upon his wealth in the day of his disaster. **14** And you ought not to stand at the parting of the ways, in order to cut off his escapees; and you ought not to hand over his survivors in the day of distress. **15** For the day of Jehovah against all the nations is near. In the way that you have done, it will be done to you. Your sort of treatment will return upon your own head. 16 For in the way that you people have drunk upon my holy mountain, all the nations will keep drinking constantly. And they will certainly drink and gulp down and become as though they had never happened to be.

17 "And in Mount Zion is where those escaping will prove to be, and it must become something holy; and the house of Jacob must take possession of the things for them to possess. 18 And the house of Jacob must become a fire, and the house of Joseph a flame, and the house of E′sau as stubble; and they must set them ablaze and devour them. And there will prove to

be no survivor to the house of E′sau; for Jehovah himself has spoken [it]. 19 And they must take possession of the Neg′eb, even of the mountainous region of E′sau, and of the She·phe′lah, even of the Phi·lis′tines. And they must take possession of the field of E′phra·im and of the field of Sa·mar′i·a; and Benjamin [must take possession of] Gil′e·ad. 20 And as for the exiles of this rampart, to the sons of Israel will belong what the Ca′naan·ites [possessed] as far as Zar′e·phath. And the exiles of Jerusalem, who were in Se′phar′ad, will take possession of the cities of the Neg′eb.

21 "And saviors will certainly come up onto Mount Zion, in order to judge the mountainous region of E′sau; and the kingship must become Jehovah's."

JONAH

1 And the word of Jehovah began to occur to Jo′nah the son of A·mit′tai, saying: 2 "Get up, go to Nin′e·veh the great city, and proclaim against her that their badness has come up before me."

3 And Jo′nah proceeded to get up and run away to Tar′shish from before Jehovah; and he finally came down to Jop′pa and found a ship going to Tar′shish. So he paid its fare and went down into it, in order to go with them to Tar′shish from before Jehovah.

4 And Jehovah himself hurled forth a great wind at the sea, and there came to be a great tempest on the sea; and as for the ship, it was about to be wrecked. 5 And the mariners began to fear and to call for aid, each one to his god. And they kept hurling out the articles that were in the ship to the sea, in order to lighten [it] of them. But Jo′nah himself had gone down to the innermost parts of the decked vessel, and he proceeded to lie down and go fast asleep. 6 At

length the ship captain came near to him and said to him: "What is the matter with you, sleeper? Get up, call out to your god! Perhaps the [true] God will show himself caring about us, and we shall not perish."

7 And they began to say to one another: "Come, and let us cast lots, that we may know on whose account we have this calamity." And they kept casting lots, and finally the lot fell upon Jo′nah. 8 So they said to him: "Do tell us, please, on whose account it is that we are having this calamity? What is your work, and from where do you come? What is your country, and from which people are you?"

9 At that he said to them: "I am a Hebrew, and Jehovah the God of the heavens I am fearing, the One who made the sea and the dry land."

10 And the men began to fear greatly, and they went on to say to him: "What is this that you have done?" For the men had come

to know that it was from before Jehovah that he was running away, because he had told them. **11** Finally they said to him: "What should we do to you, in order that the sea may become still for us?" For the sea was continually growing more tempestuous. **12** So he said to them: "Lift me up and hurl me into the sea, and the sea will become still for you; because I am aware that it is on my account that this great tempest is upon you." **13** But the men tried to work their way through, in order to bring [the ship] back to the dry land; yet they were unable, because the sea was continually growing more tempestuous against them.

14 And they proceeded to call out to Jehovah and to say: "Ah, now, O Jehovah, may we, please, not perish because of the soul of this man! And do not put upon us innocent blood, since you yourself, O Jehovah, have done according to what you have delighted in!" **15** Then they lifted up Jo′nah and hurled him into the sea; and the sea began to halt from its raging. **16** At that the men began to fear Jehovah greatly, and so they offered a sacrifice to Jehovah and made vows.

17 Now Jehovah appointed a great fish to swallow Jo′nah, so that Jo′nah came to be in the inward parts of the fish three days and three nights.

2 Then Jo′nah prayed to Jehovah his God from the inward parts of the fish **2** and said:

"Out of my distress I called out to Jehovah, and he proceeded to answer me.
Out of the belly of She′ol I cried for help.
You heard my voice.
3 When you threw me [to] the depths, into the heart of the open sea,
Then a very river encircled me.
All your breakers and your waves—over me they passed on.
4 And as for me, I said, 'I have been driven away from in front of your eyes!

How shall I gaze again upon your holy temple?'
5 Waters encircled me clear to [the] soul; the watery deep itself kept enclosing me.
Weeds were wound around my head.
6 To the bottoms of [the] mountains I went down.
As for the earth, its bars were upon me for time indefinite.
But out of [the] pit you proceeded to bring up my life, O Jehovah my God.
7 When my soul fainted away within me, Jehovah was the One whom I remembered.
Then my prayer came in to you, into your holy temple.
8 As for those who are observing the idols of untruth, they leave their own lovingkindness.
9 But as for me, with the voice of thanksgiving I will sacrifice to you.
What I have vowed, I will pay.
Salvation belongs to Jehovah."

10 In time Jehovah commanded the fish, so that it vomited out Jo′nah onto the dry land.

3 Then the word of Jehovah occurred to Jo′nah the second time, saying: **2** "Get up, go to Nin′e·veh the great city, and proclaim to her the proclamation that I am speaking to you."

3 At that, Jo′nah got up and went to Nin′e·veh in accord with the word of Jehovah. Now Nin′e·veh herself proved to be a city great to God, with a walking distance of three days. **4** Finally Jo′nah started to enter into the city the walking distance of one day, and he kept proclaiming and saying: "Only forty days more, and Nin′e·veh will be overthrown."

5 And the men of Nin′e·veh began to put faith in God, and they proceeded to proclaim a fast and to put on sackcloth, from the greatest one of them even to the least one of them. **6** When the word reached the king of Nin′e·veh, then he rose up from his throne and put off his official garment from himself and covered himself with sackcloth and sat down in the ashes. 7 Furthermore, he had the cry made, and he had it said in Nin′e·veh, by the decree of the king and his great ones, saying: "No man and no domestic animal, no herd and no flock, should taste anything at all. None should take food. Even water they should not drink. 8 And let them cover themselves with sackcloth, man and domestic animal; and let them call out to God with strength and come back, each one from his bad way and from the violence that was in their hands. 9 Who is there knowing whether the [true] God may turn back and actually feel regret and turn back from his burning anger, so that we may not perish?"

10 And the [true] God got to see their works, that they had turned back from their bad way; and so the [true] God felt regret over the calamity that he had spoken of causing to them; and he did not cause [it].

4 To Jo′nah, though, it was highly displeasing, and he got to be hot with anger. 2 Hence he prayed to Jehovah and said: "Ah, now, O Jehovah, was not this an affair of mine, while I happened to be on my own ground? That is why I went ahead and ran away to Tar′shish; for I knew that you are a God gracious and merciful, slow to anger and abundant in loving-kindness, and feeling regret over the calamity. 3 And now, O Jehovah, take away, please, my soul from me, for my dying is better than my being alive."

4 In turn Jehovah said: "Have you rightly become hot with anger?"

5 Then Jo′nah went out of the city and sat down east of the city;

and gradually he made for himself there a booth, that he might sit under it in the shade until he would see what would become of the city. 6 Accordingly Jehovah God appointed a bottle-gourd plant, that it should come up over Jo′nah, in order to become a shade over his head, to deliver him from his calamitous state. And Jo′nah began to rejoice greatly over the bottle-gourd plant.

7 But the [true] God appointed a worm at the ascending of the dawn on the next day, that it should strike the bottle-gourd plant; and it gradually dried up. 8 And it came about that, as soon as the sun shone forth, God also went on to appoint a parching east wind, and the sun kept striking upon the head of Jo′nah, so that he was swooning away; and he kept asking that his soul might die, and he repeatedly said: "My dying off is better than my being alive."

9 And God proceeded to say to Jo′nah: "Have you rightly become hot with anger over the bottle-gourd plant?"

At that he said: "I have rightly become hot with anger, to the point of death." 10 But Jehovah said: "You, for your part, felt sorry for the bottle-gourd plant, which you did not toil upon or make get big, which proved to be a mere growth of a night and perished as a mere growth of a night. 11 And, for my part, ought I not to feel sorry for Nin′e·veh the great city, in which there exist more than one hundred and twenty thousand men who do not at all know the difference between their right hand and their left, besides many domestic animals?"

MICAH

1 The word of Jehovah that occurred to Mi′cah of Mo′resh-eth, in the days of Jo′tham, A′haz, Hez·e·ki′ah, kings of Judah, that he visioned concerning Sa·mar′i·a and Jerusalem:

2 "Hear, O you peoples, all of you; pay attention, O earth and what fills you, and let the Lord Jehovah serve against you as a witness, Jehovah from his holy temple. 3 For, look! Jehovah is going forth from his place, and he will certainly come down and tread upon earth's high places. 4 And the mountains must melt under him, and the low plains themselves will split apart, like wax because of the fire, like waters being poured down a steep place.

5 "It is because of the revolt of Jacob that there is all this, even because of the sins of the house of Israel. What is the revolt of Jacob? Is it not Sa·mar′i·a? And what are the high places of Judah? Are they not Jerusalem? 6 And I shall certainly make Sa·mar′i·a a heap of ruins of the field, the planting places of a vineyard; and I will pour down into the valley her stones, and her foundations I shall lay bare. 7 And her graven images will all be crushed to pieces, and all the gifts [made] to her as her hire will be burned in the fire; and all her idols I shall make a desolate waste. For from the things given as the hire of a prostitute she collected [them], and to the thing given as the hire of a prostitute they will return."

8 On this account I will wail and howl; I will walk barefoot and naked. I shall make a wailing like the jackals, and a mourning like female ostriches. 9 For the stroke upon her is unhealable; for it has come as far as Judah, [the] plague as far as the gate of my people, as far as Jerusalem.

10 "In Gath do not you men tell [it] out; positively do not weep. "In the house of Aph′rah wallow in the very dust. 11 Make your way across, O inhabitress of Sha′phir, in shameful nudity. The inhabitress of Za′a·nan has not gone forth. The wailing of Beth-e′zel will take from you people [its] standing place. 12 For the inhabitress of Ma′roth has waited for good, but what is bad has come down from Jehovah to the gate of Jerusalem. 13 Attach the chariot to the team of horses, O inhabitress of La′chish. The beginning of sin was what she was to the daughter of Zion, for in you the revolts of Israel have been found. 14 Therefore you will give parting gifts to Mo′resh·eth-gath. The houses of Ach′zib were as something deceitful to the kings of Israel. 15 The dispossessor I shall yet bring to you, O inhabitress of Ma·re′shah. As far as A·dul′lam the glory of Israel will come. 16 Cause baldness, and shear [your hair] off on account of your sons of exquisite delight. Broaden out your baldness like [that of] the eagle, because they have gone away from you into exile."

2 "Woe to those who are scheming what is harmful, and to those practicing what is bad, upon their beds! By the light of the morning they proceed to do it, because it is in the power of their hand. 2 And they have desired fields and have seized [them]; also houses, and have taken [them]; and they have defrauded an able-bodied man and his household, a man and his hereditary possession.

3 "Therefore this is what Jehovah has said, 'Here I am thinking up against this family a calamity from which you people will not remove your necks, so that you will not walk haughtily; because it is a time of calamity. 4 In that day one will raise up concerning you people a proverbial saying and will certainly lament a lamentation, even a lamentation. One will have

1024

to say: "We have positively been despoiled! The very portion of my people he alters. How he removes [it] from me! To the unfaithful one he apportions out our own fields." 5 Therefore you will come to have no one casting out the cord, by lot, in the congregation of Jehovah. 6 Do not you people let [words] drop. They let [words] drop. They will not let [words] drop concerning these [things]. Humiliations will not move away.

7 "'Is it being said, O house of Jacob: "Has the spirit of Jehovah become discontented, or are these his dealings?" Do not my own words do good in the case of the one walking uprightly?

8 "'And yesterday my own people proceeded to rise up as an outright enemy. From the front of a garment you men strip off the majestic ornament, from the ones passing by confidently, [like] those returning from war. 9 The women of my people you drive out from the house in which a woman has exquisite delight. From off her children you take my splendor, to time indefinite. 10 Get up and go, because this is not a resting place. Because of the fact that she has become unclean, there is a wrecking; and [the] wrecking work is painful. 11 If a man, walking by wind and falsehood, has told the lie: "I shall let [words] drop to you concerning wine and concerning intoxicating liquor," he also will certainly become the one letting [words] drop for this people.

12 "'I shall positively gather Jacob, all of you; I shall without fail collect the remaining ones of Israel together. In unity I shall set them, like a flock in the pen, like a drove in the midst of its pasture; they will be noisy with men.'

13 "The one making a breakthrough will certainly come up before them: they will actually break through. And they will pass through a gate, and they will go out by it. And their king will pass through before them, with Jehovah at the head of them."

3 And I proceeded to say: "Hear, please, you heads of Jacob and you commanders of the house of Israel. Is it not your business to know justice? 2 You haters of what is good and lovers of badness, tearing off their skin from people and their organism from off their bones; 3 you the ones who have also eaten the organism of my people, and have stripped their very skin from off them, and smashed to pieces their very bones, and crushed [them] to pieces like what is in a widemouthed pot and like flesh in the midst of a cooking pot. 4 At that time they will call to Jehovah for aid, but he will not answer them. And he will conceal his face from them in that time, according as they committed badness in their dealings.

5 "This is what Jehovah has said against the prophets that are causing my people to wander, that are biting with their teeth and that actually call out, 'Peace!' that, when anyone does not put [something] into their mouths, also actually sanctify war against him, 6 'Therefore you men will have night, so that there will be no vision; and darkness you will have, so as not to practice divination. And the sun will certainly set upon the prophets, and the day must get dark upon them. 7 And the visionaries will have to be ashamed, and the diviners will certainly have to be disappointed. And they will have to cover over the mustache, all of them, for there is no answer from God.'"

8 And, on the other hand, I myself have become full of power, with the spirit of Jehovah, and of justice and mightiness, in order to tell to Jacob his revolt and to Israel his sin.

9 Hear, please, this, you head ones of the house of Jacob and you commanders of the house of Israel, the ones detesting justice and the ones who make even everything that is straight crooked; 10 building Zion with acts of bloodshed and Jerusalem with unrighteousness. 11 Her own head ones

judge merely for a bribe, and her own priests instruct just for a price, and her own prophets practice divination simply for money; yet upon Jehovah they keep supporting themselves, saying: "Is not Jehovah in the midst of us? There will come upon us no calamity." **12** Therefore on account of you men Zion will be plowed up as a mere field, and Jerusalem herself will become mere heaps of ruins, and the mountain of the house will be as the high places of a forest.

4 And it must occur in the final part of the days [that] the mountain of the house of Jehovah will become firmly established above the top of the mountains, and it will certainly be lifted up above the hills; and to it peoples must stream. **2** And many nations will certainly go and say: "Come, you people, and let us go up to the mountain of Jehovah and to the house of the God of Jacob; and he will instruct us about his ways, and we will walk in his paths." For out of Zion law will go forth, and the word of Jehovah out of Jerusalem. **3** And he will certainly render judgment among many peoples, and set matters straight respecting mighty nations far away. And they will have to beat their swords into plowshares and their spears into pruning shears. They will not lift up sword, nation against nation, neither will they learn war any more. **4** And they will actually sit, each one under his vine and under his fig tree, and there will be no one making [them] tremble; for the very mouth of Jehovah of armies has spoken [it].

5 For all the peoples, for their part, will walk each one in the name of its god; but we, for our part, shall walk in the name of Jehovah our God to time indefinite, even forever.

6 "In that day," is the utterance of Jehovah, "I will gather her that was limping; and her that was dispersed I will collect together, even her whom I have treated badly. **7** And I shall certainly make her that was limping a remnant, and her that was removed far off a mighty nation; and Jehovah will actually rule as king over them in Mount Zion, from now on and into time indefinite.

8 "And as for you, O tower of the drove, the mound of the daughter of Zion, as far as to you it will come, yes, the first dominion will certainly come, the kingdom belonging to the daughter of Jerusalem.

9 "Now why is it that you keep shouting loudly? Is there no king in you, or has your own counselor perished, so that pangs like those of a woman giving birth have grabbed hold of you? **10** Be in severe pains and burst forth, O daughter of Zion, like a woman giving birth, for now you will go forth from a town, and you will have to reside in the field. And you will have to come as far as to Babylon. There you will be delivered. There Jehovah will buy you back out of the palm of your enemies.

11 "And now there will certainly be gathered against you many nations, those who are saying, 'Let her be polluted, and may our eyes look upon Zion.' **12** But as for them, they have not come to know the thoughts of Jehovah, and they have not come to understand his counsel; because he will certainly collect them together like a row of newly cut grain to the threshing floor.

13 "Get up and thresh, O daughter of Zion; for your horn I shall change into iron, and your hoofs I shall change into copper, and you will certainly pulverize many peoples; and by a ban you will actually devote to Jehovah their unjust profit, and their resources to the [true] Lord of the whole earth."

5 "At this time you make cuttings upon yourself, O daughter of an invasion; a siege he has laid against us. With the rod they will strike upon the cheek the judge of Israel.

2 "And you, O Beth'le·hem Eph'ra·thah, the one too little to get to be among the thousands of Judah, from you there will come out to me the one who is to become ruler in Israel, whose origin is from early times, from the days of time indefinite.

3 "Therefore he will give them up until the time that she who is giving birth actually gives birth. And the rest of his brothers will return to the sons of Israel.

4 "And he will certainly stand and do shepherding in the strength of Jehovah, in the superiority of the name of Jehovah his God. And they will certainly keep dwelling, for now he will be great as far as the ends of the earth. 5 And this one must become peace. As for the As·syr´i·an, when he comes into our land and when he treads upon our dwelling towers, we shall also have to raise up against him seven shepherds, yes, eight dukes of mankind. 6 And they will actually shepherd the land of As·syr´i·a with the sword, and the land of Nim´rod in its entrances. And he will certainly bring about deliverance from the As·syr´i·an, when he comes into our land and when he treads upon our territory.

7 "And the remaining ones of Jacob must become in the midst of many peoples like dew from Jehovah, like copious showers upon vegetation, that does not hope for man or wait for the sons of earthling man. 8 And the remaining ones of Jacob must become among the nations, in the midst of many peoples, like a lion among the beasts of a forest, like a maned young lion among droves of sheep, which, when it actually passes through, certainly both tramples down and tears in pieces; and there is no deliverer. 9 Your hand will be high above your adversaries, and all enemies of yours will be cut off."

10 "And it must occur in that day," is the utterance of Jehovah, "that I will cut off your horses from the midst of you and destroy your chariots. 11 And I will cut off the cities of your land and tear down all your fortified places. 12 And I will cut off sorceries out of your hand, and no practicers of

magic will you continue to have. 13 And I will cut off your graven images and your pillars from the midst of you, and you will no more bow down to the work of your hands. 14 And I will uproot your sacred poles from the midst of you and annihilate your cities. 15 And in anger and in rage I will execute vengeance upon the nations that have not obeyed."

6 Hear, please, you people, what Jehovah is saying. Get up, conduct a legal case with the mountains, and may the hills hear your voice. 2 Hear, O you mountains, the legal case of Jehovah, also you durable objects, you foundations of [the] earth; for Jehovah has a legal case with his people, and it is with Israel that he will argue:

3 "O my people, what have I done to you? And in what way have I tired you out? Testify against me. 4 For I brought you up out of the land of Egypt, and from the house of slaves I redeemed you; and I proceeded to send before you Moses, Aaron and Mir´i·am. 5 O my people, remember, please, what Ba´lak the king of Mo´ab counseled, and what Ba´laam the son of Be´or answered him. From Shit´tim it was, all the way to Gil´gal, to the intent that the righteous acts of Jehovah might be known."

6 With what shall I confront Jehovah? [With what] shall I bow myself to God on high? Shall I confront him with whole burnt offerings, with calves a year old? 7 Will Jehovah be pleased with thousands of rams, with tens of thousands of torrents of oil? Shall I give my first-born son for my revolt, the fruitage of my belly for the sin of my soul? 8 He has told you, O earthling man, what is good. And what is Jehovah asking back from you but to exercise justice and to love kindness and to be modest in walking with your God?

9 To the city the very voice of Jehovah calls out, and [the person of] practical wisdom will fear your name. Hear [the] rod and who it was that designated it, O you people. 10 Do there yet exist [in] the

house of a wicked one the treasures of wickedness, and the scrimped e'phah measure that is denounced? 11 Can I be [morally] clean with wicked scales and with a bag of deceptive stone weights? 12 For her own rich men have become full of violence, and her own inhabitants have spoken falsehood, and their tongue is tricky in their mouth.

13 "And I also, for my part, shall certainly make [you] sick by striking you; there will be a desolating [of you], on account of your sins. 14 You, for your part, will eat and not get satisfied, and your emptiness will be in the midst of you. And you will remove [things], but you will not carry [them] safely away; and whatever you would carry away safely, I shall give to the sword itself. 15 You, for your part, will sow seed, but you will not reap. You, for your part, will tread olives, but you will not grease yourself with oil; also sweet wine, but you will not drink wine. 16 And the statutes of Om'ri and all the work of the house of A'hab are observed, and you people walk in their counsels; to the end that I may make you an object of astonishment and her inhabitants something to be whistled at; and the reproach of peoples you men will bear."

7 Too bad for me, for I have become like the gatherings of summer fruit, like the gleaning of a grape gathering! There is no grape cluster to eat, no early fig, that my soul would desire! 2 The loyal one has perished from the earth, and among mankind there is no upright one. All of them, for bloodshed they lie in wait. They hunt, everyone his own brother, with a dragnet. 3 [Their] hands are upon what is bad, to do [it] well; the prince is asking [for something], and the one who is judging [does so] for the reward, and the great one is speaking forth the craving of his soul, his very own; and they interweave it. 4 Their best one is like a brier, [their] most upright one is worse

than a thorn hedge. The day of your watchmen, [of] your being given attention, must come. Now will occur the confounding of them.

5 Do not put your faith in a companion. Do not put your trust in a confidential friend. From her who is lying in your bosom guard the openings of your mouth. 6 For a son is despising a father; a daughter is rising up against her mother; a daughter-in-law against her mother-in-law; a man's enemies are the men of his household.

7 But as for me, it is for Jehovah that I shall keep on the lookout. I will show a waiting attitude for the God of my salvation. My God will hear me.

8 Do not rejoice over me, O you woman enemy of mine. Although I have fallen, I shall certainly rise up; although I dwell in the darkness, Jehovah will be a light to me. 9 The raging of Jehovah I shall bear—for I have sinned against him—until he conducts my legal case and actually executes justice for me. He will bring me forth to the light; I shall look upon his righteousness. 10 And my enemy will see, and shame will cover her, who was saying to me: "Where is he, Jehovah your God?" My own eyes will look upon her. Now she will become a place of trampling, like the mire of streets.

11 The day for building your stone walls, at that day [the] decree will be far away. 12 At that day even all the way to you they will come from As·syr'i·a and the cities of Egypt, and from Egypt even all the way to [the] River; and from sea to sea, and [from] mountain to the mountain. 13 And the land must become a desolate waste on account of its inhabitants, because of the fruit of their dealings.

14 Shepherd your people with your staff, the flock of your inheritance, the one who was residing alone in a forest—in the midst of an orchard. Let them feed on Ba'shan and Gil'e·ad as in the days of a long time ago.

15 "As in the days of your coming forth from the land of Egypt I shall show him wonderful things. **16** Nations will see and become ashamed of all their mightiness. They will put [their] hand upon [their] mouth; their very ears will become deaf. **17** They will lick up dust like the serpents; like reptiles of [the] earth they will come in agitation out of their bulwarks. To Jehovah our God they will come quivering, and they will be afraid of you."

18 Who is a God like you, one pardoning error and passing over transgression of the remnant of his inheritance? He will certainly not hold onto his anger forever, for he is delighting in loving-kindness. **19** He will again show us mercy; he will subject our errors. And you will throw into the depths of [the] sea all their sins. **20** You will give [the] trueness [given] to Jacob, [the] loving-kindness [given] to Abraham, which you swore to our forefathers from the days of long ago.

NAHUM

1 The pronouncement against Nin′e·veh: The book of the vision of Na′hum the El′kosh·ite:

2 Jehovah is a God exacting exclusive devotion and taking vengeance; Jehovah is taking vengeance and is disposed to rage. Jehovah is taking vengeance against his adversaries, and he is resentful toward his enemies.

3 Jehovah is slow to anger and great in power, and by no means will Jehovah hold back from punishing.

In destructive wind and in storm is his way, and the cloud mass is the powder of his feet.

4 He is rebuking the sea, and he dries it up; and all the rivers he actually makes run dry.

Ba′shan and Car′mel have withered, and the very blossom of Leb′a·non has withered.

5 Mountains themselves have rocked because of him, and the very hills found themselves melting.

And the earth will be upheaved because of his face; the productive land also, and all those dwelling in it.

6 In the face of his denunciation who can stand? And who can rise up against the heat of his anger?

His own rage will certainly be poured out like fire, and the very rocks will actually be pulled down because of him.

7 Jehovah is good, a stronghold in the day of distress.

And he is cognizant of those seeking refuge in him.

8 And by the flood that is passing along he will make an outright extermination of her place, and darkness will pursue his very enemies.

9 What will you men think up against Jehovah? He is causing an outright extermination.

Distress will not rise up a second time.

10 Although they are being interwoven even as thorns and they are drunken as with their wheat beer, they will certainly be devoured like stubble fully dry.

11 Out of you there will actually go forth one who is thinking up against Jehovah what is bad, counseling what is not worth while.

12 This is what Jehovah has said: "Although they were in complete form and there were many in that state, even in that state they must be cut down; and one must pass through. And I shall certainly afflict you, so that I shall not afflict you any more. **13** And now I shall break his carrying bar from upon you, and the bands upon you I shall tear in two. **14** And concerning you Jehovah has commanded, 'Nothing of your name will be sown any more. Out of the house of your gods I shall cut off carved image and molten statue. I shall make a burial place for you, because you have been of no account.'

15 "Look! Upon the mountains the feet of one bringing good news, one publishing peace. O Judah, celebrate your festivals. Pay your vows; because no more will any good-for-nothing person pass again through you. In his entirety he will certainly be cut off."

2 One that does a scattering has come up before your face. Let there be a safeguarding of the fortified place. Watch [the] way. Strengthen [the] hips. Reinforce power very much.

2 For Jehovah will certainly gather the pride of Jacob, like the pride of Israel, because those emptying out have emptied them out; and the shoots of them they have ruined.

3 The shield of his mighty men is dyed red; [his] men of vital energy are dressed in crimson stuff. With the fire of iron [fittings] is the war chariot in the day of his getting ready, and the juniper tree [spears] have been made to quiver. 4 In the streets the war chariots keep driving madly. They keep rushing up and down in the public squares. Their appearances are like torches. Like the lightnings they keep running.

5 He will remember his majestic ones. They will stumble in their walking. They will hasten to her wall, and the barricade will have to be firmly established. 6 The very gates of the rivers will certainly be opened, and the palace itself will actually be dissolved. 7 And it has been fixed; she has been uncovered; she will certainly be carried away, and her slave girls will be moaning, like the sound of doves, beating repeatedly upon their hearts. 8 And Nin′e·veh, from the days [that] she [has been], was like a pool of waters; but they are fleeing. "Stand still, you men! Stand still!" But there is no one turning back.

9 Plunder silver, you men; plunder gold; as there is no limit to the [things in] arrangement. There is a heavy amount of all sorts of desirable articles.

10 Emptiness and voidness, and [a city] laid waste! And the heart is melting, and there is a tottering of [the] knees, and severe pains are in all hips; and as for the faces of all of them, they have collected a glow [of excitement]. 11 Where is the lair of lions, and the cave that belongs to the maned young lions, where the lion walked and entered, where the lion's cub was, and no one was making [them] tremble? 12 [The] lion was tearing to pieces enough for his whelps, and was strangling for his lionesses. And he kept his holes filled with prey and his hiding places with animals torn to pieces.

13 "Look! I am against you," is the utterance of Jehovah of armies, "and I will burn up her war chariot in the smoke. And a sword will devour your own maned young lions. And I will cut off from the earth your prey, and no more will the voice of your messengers be heard."

3 Woe to the city of bloodshed. She is all full of deception [and] of robbery. Prey does not depart! 2 There is the sound of [the] whip and the sound of the rattling of [the] wheel, and the dashing horse and the leaping chariot. 3 The mounted horseman, and the flame of [the] sword, and the lightning of [the] spear, and the multitude of slain ones, and the heavy mass of carcasses; and there is no end to the dead bodies. They keep stumbling among their dead bodies; 4 owing to the abundance of the acts of prostitution of the prostitute, attractive with charm, a mistress of sorceries, she who is ensnaring nations by her acts of prostitution and families by her sorceries.

5 "Look! I am against you," is the utterance of Jehovah of armies, "and I will put the covering of your skirts over your face, and I will cause nations to see your naked-

ness, and kingdoms your dishonor. 6 And I will throw disgusting things upon you, and I will make you despicable; and I will set you as a spectacle. 7 And it must occur that everyone seeing you will flee away from you and will certainly say, 'Nin'e·veh has been despoiled! Who will sympathize with her?' From where shall I seek comforters for you? 8 Are you better than No-a'mon, that was sitting by the Nile canals? Waters were all around her, whose wealth was [the] sea, whose wall was from [the] sea. 9 E·thi·o'pi·a was her full might, also Egypt; and that without limit. Put and the Lib'y·ans themselves proved to be of assistance to you. 10 She, too, was meant for exile; she went into captivity. Her own children also came to be dashed to pieces at the head of all the streets; and over her glorified men they cast lots, and her great ones have all been bound with fetters.

11 "You yourself will also become drunk; you will become something hidden. You yourself also will seek a stronghold from [the] enemy. 12 All your fortified places are as fig trees with the first ripe fruits, which, if they get wiggled, will certainly fall into the mouth of an eater.

13 "Look! Your people are women in the midst of you. To your enemies the gates of your land must without fail be opened. Fire will certainly devour your bars. 14 Water for a siege draw out for yourself. Strengthen your fortified places. Get into the mire, and trample down in the clay; grab hold of [the] brick mold. 15 Even there fire will devour you. A sword will cut you off. It will devour you like the locust species. Make yourself heavy in numbers like the locust species; make yourself heavy in numbers like the locust. 16 You have multiplied your tradesmen more than the stars of the heavens.

"As for the locust species, it actually strips off its skin; then it flies away. 17 Your guardsmen are like the locust, and your recruiting officers like the locust swarm. They are camping in the stone pens in a cold day. The sun itself has but to shine forth, and away they certainly flee; and their place is really unknown where they are.

18 "Your shepherds have become drowsy, O king of As·syr'i·a; your majestic ones stay in their residences. Your people have been scattered upon the mountains, and there is no one collecting [them] together. 19 There is no relief for your catastrophe. Your stroke has become unhealable. All those hearing the report about you will certainly clap their hands at you; because upon whom was it that your badness did not pass over constantly?"

HABAKKUK

1 The pronouncement that Ha-bak'kuk the prophet visioned: 2 How long, O Jehovah, must I cry for help, and you do not hear? [How long] shall I call to you for aid from violence, and you do not save? 3 Why is it that you make me see what is hurtful, and you keep looking upon mere trouble? And [why] are despoiling and violence in front of me, and [why] does quarreling occur, and [why] is strife carried?

4 Therefore law grows numb, and justice never goes forth. Because the wicked one is surrounding the righteous one, for that reason justice goes forth crooked.

5 "See, YOU people, among the nations, and look on, and stare in amazement at one another. Be amazed; for there is an activity that one is carrying on in YOUR days, [which] YOU people will not believe although it is related. 6 For here I am raising up the Chal·de'-

ans, the nation bitter and impetuous, which is going to the wide-open places of earth in order to take possession of residences not belonging to it. 7 Frightful and fear-inspiring it is. From itself its own justice and its own dignity go forth. 8 And its horses have proved swifter than leopards, and they have proved fiercer than evening wolves. And its steeds have pawed the ground, and from far away its own steeds come. They fly like the eagle speeding to eat [something]. 9 In its entirety it comes for mere violence. The assembling of their faces is as [the] east wind, and it gathers up captives just like the sand. 10 And for its part, it jeers kings themselves, and high officials are something laughable to it. For its part, it laughs even at every fortified place, and it piles up dust and captures it. 11 At that time it will certainly move onward [like] wind and will pass through and will actually become guilty. This its power is due to its god."

12 Are you not from long ago, O Jehovah? O my God, my Holy One, you do not die. O Jehovah, for a judgment you have set it; and, O Rock, for a reproving you have founded it.

13 You are too pure in eyes to see what is bad; and to look on trouble you are not able. Why is it that you look on those dealing treacherously, that you keep silent when someone wicked swallows up someone more righteous than he is? 14 And [why] do you make earthling man like the fishes of the sea, like creeping things over whom no one is ruling? 15 All these he has brought up with a mere fish-hook; he drags them away in his dragnet, and he gathers them in his fishing net. That is why he rejoices and is joyful. 16 That is why he offers sacrifice to his dragnet and makes sacrificial smoke to his fishing net; for by them his portion is well oiled, and his food is healthful. 17 Is that why he will empty out his dragnet, and does he have to kill nations

constantly, while he shows no compassion?

2 At my guard post I will keep standing, and I will keep myself stationed upon [the] bulwark; and I shall keep watch, to see what he will speak by me and what I shall reply at the reproof of me.

2 And Jehovah proceeded to answer me and to say: "Write down [the] vision, and set [it] out plainly upon tablets, in order that the one reading aloud from it may do so fluently. 3 For [the] vision is yet for the appointed time, and it keeps panting on to the end, and it will not tell a lie. Even if it should delay, keep in expectation of it; for it will without fail come true. It will not be late.

4 "Look! His soul has been swelled up; it has not been upright within him. But as for the righteous one, by his faithfulness he will keep living. 5 And, indeed, because the wine is dealing treacherously, an able-bodied man is self-assuming; and he will not reach his goal, he who has made his soul spacious just like She'ol, and who is like death and cannot be satisfied. And he keeps gathering to himself all the nations and collecting together to himself all the peoples. 6 Will not these very ones, all of them, lift up against him a proverbial saying and an alluding remark, insinuations at him? And one will say,

" 'Woe to him who is multiplying what is not his own—O how long! —and who is making debt heavy against himself! 7 Will not those claiming interest of you rise up suddenly, and those wake up who are violently shaking you, and you certainly become to them something to pillage? 8 Because you yourself despoiled many nations, all the remaining ones of [the] peoples will despoil you, because of the shedding of blood of mankind and the violence to [the] earth, [the] town and all those dwelling in it.

9 " 'Woe to the one that is making evil gain for his house, in order to set his nest on the height,

so as to be delivered from the grasp of what is calamitous! 10 You have counseled something shameful to your house, the cutting off of many peoples; and your soul is sinning. 11 For out of [the] wall a stone itself will cry out plaintively, and from the woodwork a rafter itself will answer it.

12 "'Woe to the one that is building a city by bloodshed, and that has solidly established a town by unrighteousness! 13 Look! Is it not from Jehovah of armies that peoples will toil on only for the fire, and that national groups will tire themselves out merely for nothing? 14 For the earth will be filled with the knowing of the glory of Jehovah as the waters themselves cover over [the] sea.

15 "'Woe to the one giving his companions something to drink, attaching [to it] your rage and anger, in order to make [them] drunk, for the purpose of looking upon their parts of shame. 16 You will certainly be satiated with dishonor instead of glory. Drink also, you yourself, and be considered uncircumcised. The cup of the right hand of Jehovah will come around to you, and there will be disgrace upon your glory; 17 because the violence [done] to Leb′a·non is what will cover you, and the rapacity upon [the] beasts that terrifies them, because of the shedding of blood of mankind and the violence [done] to [the] earth, the town and all those dwelling in it. 18 Of what benefit has a carved image been, when the former of it has carved it, a molten statue, and an instructor in falsehood? when the former of its form has trusted in it, to the extent of making valueless gods that are speechless?

19 "'Woe to the one saying to the piece of wood: "O do awake!" to a dumb stone: "O wake up! It itself will give instruction"! Look! It is sheathed in gold and silver, and there is no breath at all in the midst of it. 20 But Jehovah is in his holy temple. Keep silence before him, all the earth!'"

3 The prayer of Ha·bak′kuk the prophet in dirges: 2 O Jehovah, I have heard the report about you. I have become afraid, O Jehovah, of your activity.

In the midst of [the] years O bring it to life! In the midst of [the] years may you make it known. During the agitation, to show mercy may you remember.

3 God himself proceeded to come from Te′man, even a Holy One from Mount Pa′ran. Se′lah.

His dignity covered [the] heavens; and with his praise the earth became filled.

4 As for [his] brightness, it got to be just like the light. He had two rays [issuing] out of his hand, and there the hiding of his strength was.

5 Before him pestilence kept going, and burning fever would go forth at his feet.

6 He stood still, that he might shake up [the] earth. He saw, and then caused nations to leap.

And the eternal mountains got to be smashed; the indefinitely lasting hills bowed down. The walkings of long ago are his.

7 Under what is hurtful I saw the tents of Cu′shan. The tent cloths of the land of Mid′i·an began to be agitated.

8 Is it against the rivers, O Jehovah, is it against the rivers that your anger has become hot, or is your fury against the sea? For you went riding upon your horses; your chariots were salvation.

9 In [its] nakedness your bow comes to be uncovered. The sworn oaths of [the] tribes are the thing said. Se′lah. With rivers you proceeded to split [the] earth.

10 Mountains saw you; they got to be in severe pains. A thunderstorm of waters passed through. The watery deep gave forth its sound. On high its hands it lifted up.

11 Sun—moon—stood still, in the lofty abode thereof. Like light your own arrows kept going. The lightning of your spear served for brightness.

12 With denunciation you went marching [through] the earth. In anger you went threshing [the] nations.

13 And you went forth for the salvation of your people, to save your anointed one. You broke to pieces the head one out of the house of the wicked one. There was a laying of the foundation bare, clear up to the neck. *Se'lah.*

14 With his own rods you pierced [the] head of his warriors [when] they moved tempestuously to scatter me. Their high glee was as of those bent on devouring an afflicted one in a place of concealment.

15 Through the sea you trod [with] your horses, [through] the heap of vast waters.

16 I heard, and my belly began to be agitated; at the sound my lips quivered; rottenness began to enter into my bones; and in my situation I was agitated, that I should quietly wait for the day of distress, for [his] coming up to the people, [that] he may raid them.

17 Although [the] fig tree itself may not blossom, and there may be no yield on the vines; the work of [the] olive tree may actually turn out a failure, and the terraces themselves may actually produce no food; [the] flock may actually be severed from [the] pen, and there may be no herd in the enclosures;

18 Yet, as for me, I will exult in Jehovah himself; I will be joyful in the God of my salvation.

19 Jehovah the Sovereign Lord is my vital energy; and he will make my feet like those of the hinds, and upon my high places he will cause me to tread.

To the director on my stringed instruments.

ZEPHANIAH

1 The word of Jehovah that occurred to Zeph·a·ni'ah the son of Cush'i the son of Ged·a·li'ah the son of Am·a·ri'ah the son of Hez·e·ki'ah in the days of Jo·si'ah the son of A'mon the king of Judah:

2 "I shall without fail finish everything off the surface of the ground," is the utterance of Jehovah.

3 "I shall finish off earthling man and beast. I shall finish off the flying creature of the heavens and the fishes of the sea, and the stumbling blocks with the wicked ones; and I will cut off mankind from the surface of the ground," is the utterance of Jehovah. **4** "And I will stretch out my hand against Judah and against all the inhabitants of Jerusalem, and I will cut off from this place the remaining ones of the Ba'al, the name of the foreign-god priests along with the priests, **5** and those who are bowing down upon the roofs to the army of the heavens, and those who are bowing down, making sworn oaths to Jehovah and making sworn oaths by Mal'cham; **6** and those who are drawing back from following Jehovah and who have not sought Jehovah and have not inquired of him."

7 Keep silence before the Lord Jehovah; for the day of Jehovah is near, for Jehovah has prepared a sacrifice; he has sanctified his invited ones.

8 "And it must occur on the day of Jehovah's sacrifice that I will give attention to the princes, and to the sons of the king, and to all those wearing foreign attire. **9** And I will give attention to everyone that is climbing upon the platform in that day, those who are filling the house of their masters with violence and deception. **10** And there must occur on that day," is the utterance of Jehovah, "the sound of an outcry from the Fish Gate, and a howling from the second quarter, and a great crashing from the hills. 11 Howl, you inhabitants of Mak′tesh, for all the people who are tradesmen have been silenced; all those weighing out silver have been cut off.

12 "And it must occur at that time that I shall carefully search Jerusalem with lamps, and I will give attention to the men who are congealing upon their dregs [and] who are saying in their heart, 'Jehovah will not do good, and he will not do bad.' 13 And their wealth must come to be for pillage and their houses for a desolate waste. And they will build houses, but they will not have occupancy; and they will plant vineyards, but they will not drink the wine of them.

14 "The great day of Jehovah is near. It is near, and there is a hurrying [of it] very much. The sound of the day of Jehovah is bitter. There a mighty man is letting out a cry. 15 That day is a day of fury, a day of distress and of anguish, a day of storm and of desolation, a day of darkness and of gloominess, a day of clouds and of thick gloom, 16 a day of horn and of alarm signal, against the fortified cities and against the high corner towers. 17 And I will cause distress to mankind, and they will certainly walk like blind men; because it is against Jehovah that they have sinned. And their blood will actually be poured out like dust, and their bowels like the dung. 18 Neither their silver nor their gold will be able to deliver them in the day of Jehovah's fury; but by the fire of his zeal the whole earth will be devoured, because he will make an extermination, indeed a terrible one, of all the inhabitants of the earth."

2 Gather yourselves together, yes, do the gathering, O nation not paling in shame. 2 Before [the] statute gives birth to [anything], [before the] day has passed by just like chaff, before there comes upon you people the burning anger of Jehovah, before there comes upon you the day of Jehovah's anger, 3 seek Jehovah, all you meek ones of the earth, who have practiced His own judicial decision. Seek righteousness, seek meekness. Probably you may be concealed in the day of Jehovah's anger. 4 For, as regards Ga′za, an abandoned [city] is what she will become; and Ash′ke·lon is to be a desolate waste. As regards Ash′dod, at high noon they will drive her out; and as regards Ek′ron, she will be uprooted.

5 "Woe to those inhabiting the region of the sea, the nation of Cher′e·thites! The word of Jehovah is against you people. O Ca′naan, the land of the Phi·lis′tines, I will also destroy you, so that there will be no inhabitant. 6 And the region of the sea must become pasture grounds, [with] wells for shepherds and stone pens for sheep. 7 And it must become a region for the remaining ones of the house of Judah. Upon them they will feed. In the houses of Ash′ke·lon, in the evening, they will lie stretched out. For Jehovah their God will turn his attention to them and certainly gather back the captive ones of them."

8 "I have heard the reproach by Mo′ab and the abusive words of the sons of Am′mon, with which they have reproached my people and kept putting on great airs against their territory. 9 Therefore, as I am alive," is the utterance of Jehovah of armies, the God of Israel, "Mo′ab herself will become just like Sod′om, and the sons of Am′mon like Go·mor′rah, a place possessed by nettles, and a salt pit, and a desolate waste, even to time indefinite. The remaining ones of my people will plunder them, and the remnant of my own nation will take possession of them. 10 This is what they will have instead of their pride, because they reproached and kept putting on great airs against the people of Jehovah of armies. 11 Jehovah will be fear-inspiring against them; for he will certainly emaciate all the gods of the earth, and people will bow down to him, each one from his place, all the islands of the nations.

12 "You also, you E·thi·o'pi·ans, you yourselves will be people slain by my sword.

13 "And he will stretch out his hand toward the north, and he will destroy As·syr'i·a. And he will make Nin'e·veh a desolate waste, a waterless region like the wilderness. 14 And in the midst of her, droves will certainly lie stretched out, all the wild animals of a nation. Both pelican and porcupine will spend the night right among her pillar capitals. A voice will keep singing in the window. There will be devastation at the threshold; for he will certainly lay bare the very wainscoting. 15 This is the exultant city that was sitting in security, that was saying in her heart, 'I am, and there is nobody else.' O how she has become an object of astonishment, a place for the wild animals to lie stretched out! Everyone passing along by her will whistle; he will wag his hand."

3 Woe to her that is rebelling and polluting herself, the oppressive city! 2 She did not listen to a voice; she did not accept discipline. In Jehovah she did not trust. To her God she did not draw near. 3 Her princes in the midst of her were roaring lions. Her judges were evening wolves that did not gnaw [bones] till the morning. 4 Her prophets were insolent, were men of treachery. Her priests themselves profaned what was holy; they did violence to [the] law. 5 Jehovah was righteous in the midst of her; he would do no unrighteousness. Morning by morning he kept giving his own judicial decision. At daylight it did not prove lacking. But the unrighteous one was knowing no shame.

6 "I cut off nations; their corner towers were desolated. I devastated their streets, so that there was no one passing through. Their cities were laid waste, so that there was no man, so that there was no inhabitant. 7 I said, 'Surely you will fear me; you will accept discipline'; so that her dwelling might not be cut off—all that I must call to account against her. Truly they acted promptly in making all their dealings ruinous.

8 " 'Therefore keep yourselves in expectation of me,' is the utterance of Jehovah, 'till the day of my rising up to [the] booty, for my judicial decision is to gather nations, for me to collect together kingdoms, in order to pour out upon them my denunciation, all my burning anger; for by the fire of my zeal all the earth will be devoured. 9 For then I shall give to peoples the change to a pure language, in order for them all to call upon the name of Jehovah, in order to serve him shoulder to shoulder.'

10 "From the region of the rivers of E·thi·o'pi·a the ones entreating me, [namely,] the daughter of my scattered ones, will bring a gift to me. 11 In that day you will not be ashamed because of all your dealings with which you transgressed against me, for then I shall remove from the midst of you your haughtily exultant ones; and you will never again be haughty in my holy mountain. 12 And I shall certainly let remain in the midst of you a people humble and lowly, and they will actually take refuge in the name of Jehovah. 13 As regards the remaining ones of Israel, they will do no unrighteousness, nor speak a lie, nor will there be found in their mouths a tricky tongue; for they themselves will feed and actually lie stretched out, and there will be no one making [them] tremble."

14 Joyfully cry out, O daughter of Zion! Break out in cheers, O Israel! Rejoice and exult with all the heart, O daughter of Jerusalem! 15 Jehovah has removed the judgments upon you. He has turned away your enemy. The king of Israel, Jehovah, is in the midst of you. You will fear calamity no more. 16 In that day it will be said to Jerusalem: "Do not be afraid, O Zion. May your hands not drop down. 17 Jehovah your God is in the midst of you. As a mighty One, he will save. He will exult over you with rejoicing. He will become silent

in his love. He will be joyful over you with happy cries.

18 "The ones grief-stricken in absence from your festal season I shall certainly gather together; absent from you they happened to be, because of bearing reproach on her account. 19 Here I am acting against all those afflicting you, at that time; and I will save her that is limping, and her that is dispersed I shall collect together. And I will set them as a praise and as a name in all the land of their shame. 20 At that time I shall bring YOU people in, even in the time of my collecting YOU together. For I shall make YOU people to be a name and a praise among all the peoples of the earth, when I gather back YOUR captive ones before YOUR eyes," Jehovah has said.

HAGGAI

1 In the second year of Da·ri′us the king, in the sixth month, on the first day of the month, the word of Jehovah occurred by means of Hag′gai the prophet to Ze·rub′ba·bel the son of She·al′ti·el, the governor of Judah, and to Joshua the son of Je·hoz′a·dak the high priest, saying:

2 "This is what Jehovah of armies has said, 'As regards this people, they have said: "The time has not come, the time of the house of Jehovah, for [it] to be built." ' "

3 And the word of Jehovah continued to come by means of Hag′gai the prophet, saying: 4 "Is it the time for YOU yourselves to dwell in YOUR paneled houses, while this house is waste? 5 And now this is what Jehovah of armies has said, 'Set YOUR heart upon YOUR ways. 6 YOU have sown much seed, but there is a bringing of little in. There is an eating, but it is not to satisfaction. There is a drinking, but not to the point of getting intoxicated. There is a putting on of clothes, but it is not with anyone's getting warm; and he that is hiring himself out is hiring himself out for a bag having holes.' "

7 "This is what Jehovah of armies has said, 'Set YOUR heart upon YOUR ways.'

8 " 'Go up to the mountain, and YOU must bring in lumber. And build the house, that I may take pleasure in it and I may be glorified,' Jehovah has said."

9 " 'There was a looking for much, but here there was just a little; and YOU have brought [it] into the house, and I blew upon it—for what reason?' is the utterance of Jehovah of armies. 'By reason of my house that is waste, while YOU are on the run, each one in behalf of his own house. 10 Therefore over YOU [the] heavens kept back [their] dew, and the earth itself kept back its yield. 11 And I kept calling for dryness upon the earth, and upon the mountains, and upon the grain, and upon the new wine, and upon the oil, and upon what the ground would bring forth, and upon earthling man, and upon domestic animal, and upon all the toil of [the] hands.' "

12 And Ze·rub′ba·bel the son of She·al′ti·el, and Joshua the son of Je·hoz′a·dak the high priest, and all the remaining ones of the people began to listen to the voice of Jehovah their God, and to the words of Hag′gai the prophet, as Jehovah their God had sent him; and the people began to fear because of Jehovah.

13 And Hag′gai the messenger of Jehovah went on to say to the people according to the messenger's commission from Jehovah, saying: " 'I am with YOU people,' is the utterance of Jehovah."

14 And Jehovah proceeded to rouse up the spirit of Ze·rub′ba·bel the son of She·al′ti·el, the governor of Judah, and the spirit of Joshua the son of Je·hoz′a·dak the high priest, and the spirit of all the remaining ones of the people; and they began to enter in and to do the work in the house of Jehovah of armies their God. 15 It was on the twenty-fourth day of the sixth month in the second year of Da·ri′us the king.

2 In the seventh [month], on the twenty-first [day] of the month, the word of Jehovah occurred by means of Hag′gai the prophet, saying: 2 "Say, please, to Ze·rub′ba·bel the son of She·al′ti·el, the governor of Judah, and to Joshua the son of Je·hoz′a·dak the high priest, and to the remaining ones of the people, saying, 3 'Who is there among you that is remaining over who saw this house in its former glory? And how are you people seeing it now? Is it not, in comparison with that, as nothing in your eyes?'

4 "'But now be strong, O Ze·rub′ba·bel,' is the utterance of Jehovah, 'and be strong, O Joshua the son of Je·hoz′a·dak the high priest.'

"'And be strong, all you people of the land,' is the utterance of Jehovah, 'and work.'

"'For I am with you people,' is the utterance of Jehovah of armies. 5 '[Remember] the thing that I concluded with you people when you came forth from Egypt, and [when] my spirit was standing in among you. Do not be afraid.'"

6 "For this is what Jehovah of armies has said, 'Yet once—it is a little while—and I am rocking the heavens and the earth and the sea and the dry ground.'

7 "'And I will rock all the nations, and the desirable things of all the nations must come in; and I will fill this house with glory,' Jehovah of armies has said.

8 "'The silver is mine, and the gold is mine,' is the utterance of Jehovah of armies.

9 "'Greater will the glory of this later house become than [that of] the former,' Jehovah of armies has said.

"'And in this place I shall give peace,' is the utterance of Jehovah of armies."

10 In the twenty-fourth [day] of the ninth [month], in the second year of Da·ri′us, the word of Jehovah occurred to Hag′gai the prophet, saying: 11 "This is what Jehovah of armies has said, 'Ask, please, the priests as to [the] law, saying: 12 "If a man carries holy flesh in the skirt of his garment, and he actually touches with his skirt bread or stew or wine or oil or any sort of food, will it become holy?"'"

And the priests proceeded to answer and say: "No!"

13 And Hag′gai went on to say: "If someone unclean by a deceased soul touches any of these things, will it become unclean?"

In turn the priests answered and said: "It will become unclean."

14 Accordingly Hag′gai answered and said: "'That is how this people is, and that is how this nation is before me,' is the utterance of Jehovah, 'and that is how all the work of their hands is, and whatever they present there. It is unclean.'

15 "'But now, please, set your heart [on this] from this day and forward, before there was the placing of a stone upon a stone in the temple of Jehovah, 16 from when those things happened to be —one came to a heap of twenty [measures], and it proved to be ten; one came to the press vat to draw off fifty [measures] of the wine trough, and it proved to be twenty; 17 I struck you people with scorching and with mildew and with hail, even all the work of your hands, and there was no one with you [turning] to me,' is the utterance of Jehovah—

18 "'Set your heart, please, [on this] from this day and forward, from the twenty-fourth [day] of the ninth [month], from the day that the foundation of the temple of Jehovah was laid; set your heart [on this]: 19 Is there as yet the

seed in the grain pit? And as yet, the vine and the fig tree and the pomegranate tree and the olive tree—it has not borne, has it? From this day I shall bestow blessing.' "

20 And the word of Jehovah proceeded to occur a second time to Hag'gai on the twenty-fourth [day] of the month, saying: 21 "Say to Ze·rub'ba·bel the governor of Judah, 'I am rocking the heavens and the earth. 22 And I shall certainly overthrow the throne of kingdoms and annihilate the strength of the kingdoms of the nations; and I will overthrow [the] chariot and its riders, and [the] horses and their riders will certainly come down, each one by the sword of his brother.' "

23 " 'In that day,' is the utterance of Jehovah of armies, 'I shall take you, O Ze·rub'ba·bel the son of She·al'ti·el, my servant,' is the utterance of Jehovah; 'and I shall certainly set you as a seal ring, because you are the one whom I have chosen,' is the utterance of Jehovah of armies."

ZECHARIAH

1 In the eighth month in the second year of Da·ri'us the word of Jehovah occurred to Zech·a·ri'ah the son of Ber·e·chi'ah the son of Id'do the prophet, saying: 2 "Jehovah grew indignant at YOUR fathers—very much so.

3 "And you must say to them, 'This is what Jehovah of armies has said: " 'Return to me,' is the utterance of Jehovah of armies, 'and I shall return to YOU,' Jehovah of armies has said." '

4 " 'Do not become like YOUR fathers to whom the former prophets called, saying: "This is what Jehovah of armies has said, 'Return, please, from YOUR bad ways and from YOUR bad dealings.' " '

" 'But they did not listen, and they paid no attention to me,' is the utterance of Jehovah.

5 " 'As for YOUR fathers, where are they? And as for the prophets, was it to time indefinite that they continued to live? 6 However, as regards my words and my regulations that I commanded my servants, the prophets, did they not catch up with YOUR fathers?' "

So they returned and said: "According to what Jehovah of armies had in mind to do to us, according to our ways and according to our dealings, that is how he has done with us."

7 On the twenty-fourth [day] of the eleventh month, that is, the month She'bat, in the second year of Da·ri'us, the word of Jehovah occurred to Zech·a·ri'ah the son of Ber·e·chi'ah the son of Id'do the prophet, saying: 8 "I saw [in] the night, and, look! a man riding on a red horse, and he was standing still among the myrtle trees that were in the deep place; and behind him there were horses red, bright red, and white."

9 And so I said: "Who are these, my lord?"

At that the angel who was speaking with me said to me: "I myself shall show you who these very ones are."

10 Then the man who was standing still among the myrtle trees answered and said: "These are the ones whom Jehovah has sent forth to walk about in the earth." 11 And they proceeded to answer the angel of Jehovah who was standing among the myrtle trees and to say: "We have walked about in the earth, and, look! the whole earth is sitting still and having no disturbance."

12 So the angel of Jehovah answered and said: "O Jehovah of armies, how long will you yourself not show mercy to Jerusalem and to the cities of Judah, whom

you have denounced these seventy years?"

13 And Jehovah proceeded to answer the angel who was speaking with me, with good words, comforting words; 14 and the angel who was speaking with me went on to say to me: "Call out, saying, 'This is what Jehovah of armies has said: "I have been jealous for Jerusalem and for Zion with great jealousy. 15 With great indignation I am feeling indignant against the nations that are at ease; because I, for my part, felt indignant to only a little extent, but they, for their part, helped toward calamity."'

16 "Therefore this is what Jehovah has said, '"I shall certainly return to Jerusalem with mercies. My own house will be built in her," is the utterance of Jehovah of armies, "and a measuring line itself will be stretched out over Jerusalem."'

17 "Call out further, saying, 'This is what Jehovah of armies has said: "My cities will yet overflow with goodness; and Jehovah will yet certainly feel regrets over Zion and yet actually choose Jerusalem."'"

18 And I proceeded to raise my eyes and see; and, look! there were four horns. 19 So I said to the angel who was speaking with me: "What are these?" In turn he said to me: "These are the horns that dispersed Judah, Israel and Jerusalem."

20 Furthermore, Jehovah showed me four craftsmen. 21 At that I said: "What are these coming to do?"

And he went on to say: "These are the horns that dispersed Judah to such an extent that no one at all raised his head; and these others will come to set them trembling, to cast down the horns of the nations that are lifting up a horn against the land of Judah, in order to disperse her."

2 And I proceeded to raise my eyes and see; and, look! there was a man, and in his hand a measuring rope. 2 So I said: "Where are you going?"

In turn he said to me: "To measure Jerusalem, in order to see what her breadth amounts to and what her length amounts to."

3 And, look! the angel who was speaking with me was going forth, and there was another angel going forth to meet him. 4 Then he said to him: "Run, speak to the young man over there, saying, '"As open rural country Jerusalem will be inhabited, because of the multitude of men and domestic animals in the midst of her. 5 And I myself shall become to her," is the utterance of Jehovah, "a wall of fire all around, and a glory is what I shall become in the midst of her."'

6 "Hey there! Hey there! Flee, then, you people, from the land of the north," is the utterance of Jehovah.

"For in the direction of the four winds of the heavens I have spread you people abroad," is the utterance of Jehovah.

7 "Hey there, Zion! Make your escape, you who are dwelling with the daughter of Babylon. 8 For this is what Jehovah of armies has said, 'Following after [the] glory he has sent me to the nations that were despoiling you people; for he that is touching you is touching my eyeball. 9 For here I am waving my hand against them, and they will have to become spoil to their slaves.' And you people will certainly know that Jehovah of armies himself has sent me.

10 "Cry out loudly and rejoice, O daughter of Zion; for here I am coming, and I will reside in the midst of you," is the utterance of Jehovah. 11 "And many nations will certainly become joined to Jehovah in that day, and they will actually become my people; and I will reside in the midst of you." And you will have to know that Jehovah of armies himself has sent me to you. 12 And Jehovah will certainly take possession of Judah as his portion upon the holy ground, and he must yet choose Jerusalem. 13 Keep silence, all flesh, before Jehovah, for he has

aroused himself from his holy dwelling.

3 And he proceeded to show me Joshua the high priest standing before the angel of Jehovah, and Satan standing at his right hand in order to resist him. 2 Then [the angel of] Jehovah said to Satan: "Jehovah rebuke you, O Satan, yes, Jehovah rebuke you, he who is choosing Jerusalem! Is this one not a log snatched out of the fire?"

3 Now as for Joshua, he happened to be clothed in befouled garments and standing before the angel. 4 Then he answered and said to those standing before him: "Remove the befouled garments from upon him." And he went on to say to him: "See, I have caused your error to pass away from upon you, and there is a clothing of you with robes of state."

5 At that I said: "Let them put a clean turban upon his head." And they proceeded to put the clean turban upon his head and to clothe him with garments; and the angel of Jehovah was standing by. 6 And the angel of Jehovah began to bear witness to Joshua, saying: 7 "This is what Jehovah of armies has said, 'If it is in my ways that you will walk, and if it is my obligation that you will keep, then also it will be you that will judge my house and also keep my courtyards; and I shall certainly give you free access among these who are standing by.'

8 "Hear, please, O Joshua the high priest, you and your companions who are sitting before you, for they are men [serving] as portents; for here I am bringing in my servant Sprout! 9 For, look! the stone that I have put before Joshua! Upon the one stone there are seven eyes. Here I am engraving its engraving,' is the utterance of Jehovah of armies, 'and I will take away the error of that land in one day.'

10 "'In that day,' is the utterance of Jehovah of armies, 'you will call, each one to the other, while under [the] vine and while under [the] fig tree.'"

4 And the angel who was speaking with me proceeded to come back and wake me up, like a man that is awakened from his sleep. 2 Then he said to me: "What are you seeing?"

So I said: "I have seen, and, look! there is a lampstand, all of it of gold, with a bowl on top of it. And its seven lamps are upon it, even seven; and the lamps that are at the top of it have seven pipes. 3 And there are two olive trees alongside it, one on the right side of the bowl and one on its left side."

4 Then I answered and said to the angel who was speaking with me, saying: "What do these [things] mean, my lord?" 5 So the angel who was speaking with me answered and said to me: "Do you not really know what these things mean?"

In turn I said: "No, my lord."

6 Accordingly he answered and said to me: "This is the word of Jehovah to Ze·rub′ba·bel, saying, 'Not by a military force, nor by power, but by my spirit,' Jehovah of armies has said. 7 Who are you, O great mountain? Before Ze·rub′ba·bel [you will become] a level land. And he will certainly bring forth the headstone. There will be shoutings to it: "How charming! How charming!"'"

8 And the word of Jehovah continued to occur to me, saying: 9 "The very hands of Ze·rub′ba·bel have laid the foundation of this house, and his own hands will finish [it]. And you will have to know that Jehovah of armies himself has sent me to you people. 10 For who has despised the day of small things? And they will certainly rejoice and see the plummet in the hand of Ze·rub′ba·bel. These seven are the eyes of Jehovah. They are roving about in all the earth."

11 And I proceeded to answer and say to him: "What do these two olive trees on the right side of the lampstand and on its left side mean?" 12 Then I answered the

second time and said to him: "What are the two bunches of twigs of the olive trees that, by means of the two golden tubes, are pouring forth from within themselves the golden [liquid]?"

13 So he said to me: "Do you not really know what these [things] mean?"

In turn I said: "No, my lord."

14 Accordingly he said: "These are the two anointed ones who are standing alongside the Lord of the whole earth."

5 Then I raised my eyes again and saw; and, look! a flying scroll. 2 So he said to me: "What are you seeing?"

In turn I said: "I am seeing a flying scroll, the length of which is twenty cubits, and the breadth of which is ten cubits."

3 Then he said to me: "This is the curse that is going forth over the surface of all the earth, because everyone that is stealing, according to it on this side, has gone free of punishment; and everyone making a sworn oath, according to it on that side, has gone free of punishment. 4 'I have caused it to go forth,' is the utterance of Jehovah of armies, 'and it must enter into the house of the thief and into the house of the one making a sworn oath in my name falsely; and it must lodge in the midst of his house and exterminate it and its timbers and its stones.'"

5 Then the angel who was speaking with me went forth and said to me: "Raise your eyes, please, and see what this is that is going forth."

6 So I said: "What is it?"

In turn he said: "This is the e'phah measure that is going forth." And he went on to say: "This is their aspect in all the earth."

7 And, look! the circular lid of lead was lifted up; and this is a certain woman sitting in the midst of the e'phah. 8 So he said: "This is Wickedness." And he proceeded to throw her [back] into the midst of the e'phah, after which he threw the lead weight upon its mouth.

9 Then I raised my eyes and saw, and here there were two women coming forth, and wind was in their wings. And they had wings like the wings of the stork. And they gradually raised the e'phah up between the earth and the heavens. 10 So I said to the angel who was speaking with me: "Where are they taking the e'phah?"

11 In turn he said to me: "In order to build for her a house in the land of Shi'nar; and it must be firmly established, and she must be deposited there upon her proper place."

6 Then I raised my eyes again and saw; and, look! there were four chariots coming forth from between two mountains, and the mountains were copper mountains. 2 In the first chariot there were red horses; and in the second chariot, black horses. 3 And in the third chariot there were white horses; and in the fourth chariot, horses speckled, parti-colored.

4 And I proceeded to answer and say to the angel who was speaking with me: "What are these, my lord?"

5 So the angel answered and said to me: "These are the four spirits of the heavens that are going forth after having taken their station before the Lord of the whole earth. 6 As for the one in which the black horses are, they are going forth to the land of the north; and as for the white ones, they must go forth to behind the sea; and as for the speckled ones, they must go forth to the land of the south. 7 And as for the parti-colored ones, they must go forth and keep seeking [where] to go, in order to walk about in the earth." Then he said: "Go, walk about in the earth." And they began walking about in the earth.

8 And he proceeded to cry out to me and speak to me, saying: "See, those going forth to the land of the north are the ones that have caused the spirit of Jehovah to rest in the land of the north."

9 And the word of Jehovah continued to occur to me, saying:

10 "Let there be a taking of something from the exiled people, [even] from Hel′dai and from To·bi′jah and from Je·da′iah; and you yourself must come in that day, and you must come into the house of Jo·si′ah the son of Zeph·a·ni′ah [with these] who have come from Babylon. **11** And you must take silver and gold and make a grand crown and put [it] upon the head of Joshua the son of Je·hoz′a·dak the high priest. **12** And you must say to him,

"'This is what Jehovah of armies has said: "Here is the man whose name is Sprout. And from his own place he will sprout, and he will certainly build the temple of Jehovah. **13** And he himself will build the temple of Jehovah, and he, for his part, will carry [the] dignity; and he must sit down and rule on his throne, and he must become a priest upon his throne, and the very counsel of peace will prove to be between both of them. **14** And the grand crown itself will come to belong to He′lem and to To·bi′jah and to Je·da′iah and to Hen the son of Zeph·a·ni′ah as a memorial in the temple of Jehovah. **15** And those who are far away will come and actually build in the temple of Jehovah." And you people will have to know that Jehovah of armies himself has sent me to you. And it must occur—if you will without fail listen to the voice of Jehovah your God.'"

7 Furthermore, it came about that in the fourth year of Da·ri′us the king the word of Jehovah occurred to Zech·a·ri′ah, on the fourth [day] of the ninth month, [that is,] in Chis′lev. **2** And Beth′el proceeded to send Shar·e′zer and Reg′em-mel′ech and his men to soften the face of Jehovah, **3** saying to the priests who belonged to the house of Jehovah of armies, and to the prophets, even saying: "Shall I weep in the fifth month, practicing an abstinence, the way I have done these O how many years?"

4 And the word of Jehovah of armies continued to occur to me,

saying: **5** "Say to all the people of the land and to the priests, 'When you fasted and there was a wailing in the fifth [month] and in the seventh [month], and this for seventy years, did you really fast to me, even me? **6** And when you would eat and when you would drink, were not you the ones doing the eating, and were not you the ones doing the drinking? **7** [Should you] not [obey] the words that Jehovah called out by means of the former prophets, while Jerusalem happened to be inhabited, and at ease, with her cities all around her, and [while] the Neg′eb and the She·phe′lah were inhabited?'"

8 And the word of Jehovah continued to occur to Zech·a·ri′ah, saying: **9** "This is what Jehovah of armies has said, 'With true justice do your judging; and carry on with one another loving-kindness and mercies; **10** and defraud no widow or fatherless boy, no alien resident or afflicted one, and scheme out nothing bad against one another in your hearts.' **11** But they kept refusing to pay attention, and they kept giving a stubborn shoulder, and their ears they made too unresponsive to hear. **12** And their heart they set as an emery stone to keep from obeying the law and the words that Jehovah of armies sent by his spirit, by means of the former prophets; so that there occurred great indignation on the part of Jehovah of armies."

13 "'And so it occurred that, just as he called and they did not listen, so they would call and I would not listen,' Jehovah of armies has said. **14** 'And I proceeded tempestuously to hurl them throughout all the nations that they had not known; and the land itself has been left desolate behind them, with no one passing through and with no one returning; and they proceeded to make the desirable land an object of astonishment.'"

8 And the word of Jehovah of armies continued to occur, saying: **2** "This is what Jehovah of armies has said, 'I will be jealous for Zion with great jealousy, and with great rage I will be jealous for her.'"

3 "This is what Jehovah has said, 'I will return to Zion and reside in the midst of Jerusalem; and Jerusalem will certainly be called the city of trueness, and the mountain of Jehovah of armies, the holy mountain.'"

4 "This is what Jehovah of armies has said, 'There will yet sit old men and old women in the public squares of Jerusalem, each one also with his staff in his hand because of the abundance of [his] days. 5 And the public squares of the city themselves will be filled with boys and girls playing in her public squares.'"

6 "This is what Jehovah of armies has said, 'Although it should seem too difficult in the eyes of the remaining ones of this people in those days, should it seem too difficult also in my eyes?' is the utterance of Jehovah of armies."

7 "This is what Jehovah of armies has said, 'Here I am saving my people from the land of the sunrise and from the land of the setting of the sun. 8 And I shall certainly bring them in, and they must reside in the midst of Jerusalem; and they must become my people, and I myself shall become their God in trueness and in righteousness.'"

9 "This is what Jehovah of armies has said, 'Let the hands of you people be strong, you who are hearing in these days these words from the mouth of the prophets, on the day on which the foundation of the house of Jehovah of armies was laid, for the temple to be built. 10 For before those days there were no wages for mankind made to exist; and as for the wages of domestic animals, there was no such thing; and to the one going out and to the one coming in there was no peace because of the adversary, as I kept thrusting all mankind against one another.'

11 "'And now I shall not be as in the former days to the remaining ones of this people,' is the

utterance of Jehovah of armies. 12 'For there will be the seed of peace; the vine itself will give its fruitage, and the earth itself will give its yield, and the heavens themselves will give their dew; and I shall certainly cause the remaining ones of this people to inherit all these [things]. 13 And it must occur that just as YOU became a malediction among the nations, O house of Judah and house of Israel, so I shall save YOU, and YOU must become a blessing. Do not be afraid. May YOUR hands be strong.'

14 "For this is what Jehovah of armies has said, ' "Just as I had in mind to do what was calamitous to YOU people because of YOUR forefathers' making me indignant," Jehovah of armies has said, "and I felt no regret, 15 so I will again have in mind in these days to deal well with Jerusalem and with the house of Judah. Do not be afraid." '

16 " 'These are the things that YOU people should do: Speak truthfully with one another. With truth and the judgment of peace do YOUR judging in YOUR gates. 17 And calamity to one another do not YOU scheme up in YOUR hearts, and do not love any false oath; for these are all things that I have hated,' is the utterance of Jehovah."

18 And the word of Jehovah of armies continued to occur to me, saying: 19 "This is what Jehovah of armies has said, 'The fast of the fourth [month], and the fast of the fifth [month], and the fast of the seventh [month], and the fast of the tenth [month] will become for the house of Judah an exultation and a rejoicing and good festal seasons. So love truth and peace.'

20 "This is what Jehovah of armies has said, 'It will yet be that peoples and the inhabitants of many cities will come; 21 and the inhabitants of one [city] will certainly go to [those of] another, saying: "Let us earnestly go to soften the face of Jehovah and to seek Jehovah of armies. I myself will go also." 22 And many peoples and mighty nations will actually come to seek Jehovah of

armies in Jerusalem and to soften the face of Jehovah.'

23 "This is what Jehovah of armies has said, 'It will be in those days that ten men out of all the languages of the nations will take hold, yes, they will actually take hold of the skirt of a man who is a Jew, saying: "We will go with YOU people, for we have heard [that] God is with YOU people."'"

9 A pronouncement:
"The word of Jehovah is against the land of Ha'drach, and Damascus is where it rests; for Jehovah has an eye on earthling man and on all the tribes of Israel. 2 And Ha'math itself will also border upon her; Tyre and Si'don, for she is very wise. 3 And Tyre proceeded to build a rampart for herself, and to pile up silver like dust and gold like the mire of [the] streets. 4 Look! Jehovah himself will dispossess her, and into the sea he will certainly strike down her military force; and in the fire she herself will be devoured. 5 Ash'ke·lon will see and get afraid; and as for Ga'za, she will also feel very severe pains; Ek'ron also, because her looked-for hope will have to experience shame. And a king will certainly perish from Ga'za, and Ash'ke·lon herself will not be inhabited. 6 And an illegitimate son will actually seat himself in Ash'dod, and I shall certainly cut off the pride of the Phi·lis'tine. 7 And I will remove his bloodstained things from his mouth and his disgusting things from between his teeth, and he himself also will certainly be left remaining for our God; and he must become like a sheik in Judah, and Ek'ron like the Jeb'u·site. 8 And I will encamp as an outpost for my house, so that there will be no one passing through and no one returning; and there will no more pass through them a taskmaster, for now I have seen [it] with my eyes.

9 "Be very joyful, O daughter of Zion. Shout in triumph, O daughter of Jerusalem. Look! Your king himself comes to you. He is righteous, yes, saved; humble, and riding upon an ass, even upon a full-grown animal the son of a she-ass. 10 And I shall certainly cut off [the] war chariot from E'phra·im and [the] horse from Jerusalem. And the battle bow must be cut off. And he will actually speak peace to the nations; and his rulership will be from sea to sea and from the River to the ends of [the] earth.

11 "Also, you, O woman, by the blood of your covenant I will send your prisoners out of the pit in which there is no water. 12 "Return to the stronghold, YOU prisoners of the hope.

"Also, today [I am] telling [you], 'I shall repay to you, O woman, a double portion. 13 For I will tread as my [bow] Judah. The bow I will fill with E'phra·im, and I will awaken your sons, O Zion, against your sons, O Greece, and I will make you as the sword of a mighty man.' 14 And over them Jehovah himself will be seen, and his arrow will certainly go forth just like lightning. And on the horn the Lord Jehovah himself will blow, and he will certainly go with the windstorms of the south. 15 Jehovah of armies himself will defend them, and they will actually devour and subdue the slingstones. And they will certainly drink—be boisterous—as if there were wine; and they will actually become filled like the bowl, like the corners of [the] altar.

16 "And Jehovah their God will certainly save them in that day like the flock of his people; for they will be as the stones of a diadem glittering over his soil. 17 For O how [great] his goodness is, and how [great] his handsomeness is! Grain is what will make the young men thrive, and new wine the virgins."

10 "Make YOUR requests of Jehovah for rain in the time of the spring rain, even of Jehovah who is making the storm clouds, and [who] gives a downpour of rain to them, to each one vegetation in the field. 2 For the teraphim themselves have spoken what

is uncanny; and the practicers of divination, for their part, have visioned falsehood, and valueless dreams are what they keep speaking, and in vain they try to comfort. That is why they will certainly depart like a flock; they will become afflicted, because there is no shepherd.

3 "Against the shepherds my anger has grown hot, and against the goatlike leaders I shall hold an accounting; for Jehovah of armies has turned his attention to his drove, the house of Judah, and has made them like his horse of dignity in the battle. 4 Out of him is the keyman, out of him is the supporting ruler, out of him is the battle bow; out of him goes forth every taskmaster, all together. 5 And they must become like mighty men stamping down in the mire of [the] streets in the battle. And they must get engaged in battle, for Jehovah is with them; and the riders of horses will have to experience shame. 6 And I will make the house of Judah superior, and the house of Joseph I shall save. And I will give them a dwelling, for I will show them mercy; and they must become like those whom I had not cast off; for I am Jehovah their God, and I shall answer them. 7 And those of E'phra·im must become just like a mighty man, and their heart must rejoice as though from wine. And their own sons will see and certainly rejoice; their heart will be joyful in Jehovah.

8 "'I will whistle for them and collect them together; for I shall certainly redeem them, and they must become many, just like those who have become many. 9 And I shall scatter them like seed among the peoples, and in the distant places they will remember me; and they must revive with their sons and return. 10 And I must bring them back from the land of Egypt; and from As·syr'i·a I shall collect them together; and to the land of Gil'e·ad and Leb'a·non I shall bring them, and no [room] will be found for them. 11 And he must pass through the sea [with] dis-

tress; and in the sea he must strike down [the] waves, and all the depths of the Nile must dry up. And the pride of As·syr'i·a must be brought down, and the very scepter of Egypt will depart. 12 And I will make them superior in Jehovah, and in his name they will walk about,' is the utterance of Jehovah."

11 "Open up your doors, O Leb'a·non, that a fire may devour among your cedars. 2 Howl, O juniper tree, for the cedar has fallen; because the majestic ones themselves have been despoiled! Howl, you massive trees of Ba'shan, for the impenetrable forest has come down! 3 Listen! The howling of shepherds, for their majesty has been despoiled. Listen! The roaring of maned young lions, for the proud [thickets] along the Jordan have been despoiled.

4 "This is what Jehovah my God has said, 'Shepherd the flock [meant] for the killing, 5 the buyers of which proceed to kill [them] although they are not held guilty. And those who are selling them say: "May Jehovah be blessed, while I shall gain riches." And their own shepherds do not show any compassion upon them.'

6 "'For I shall show compassion no more upon the inhabitants of the land,' is the utterance of Jehovah. 'So here I am causing mankind to find themselves, each one in the hand of his companion and in the hand of his king; and they will certainly crush to pieces the land, and I shall do no delivering out of their hand.'"

7 And I proceeded to shepherd the flock [meant] for the killing, in your behalf, O afflicted ones of the flock. So I took for myself two staffs. The one I called Pleasantness, and the other I called Union, and I went shepherding the flock. 8 And I finally effaced three shepherds in one lunar month, as my soul gradually became impatient with them, and also their own soul felt a loathing toward me. 9 At length I said: "I shall not keep shepherding you. The one that is dying, let her die. And the one that

is being effaced, let her be effaced. And as for the ones left remaining, let them devour, each one the flesh of her companion." 10 So I took my staff Pleasantness and cut it to pieces, in order to break my covenant that I had concluded with all the peoples. 11 And it came to be broken in that day, and the afflicted ones of the flock who were watching me got to know in this way that it was the word of Jehovah.

12 Then I said to them: "If it is good in YOUR eyes, give [me] my wages; but if not, refrain." And they proceeded to pay my wages, thirty pieces of silver.

13 At that, Jehovah said to me: "Throw it to the treasury—the majestic value with which I have been valued from their standpoint." Accordingly I took the thirty pieces of silver and threw it into the treasury at the house of Jehovah.

14 Then I cut in pieces my second staff, the Union, in order to break the brotherhood between Judah and Israel.

15 And Jehovah went on to say to me: "Take yet for yourself the implements of a useless shepherd. 16 For here I am letting a shepherd rise up in the land. To the [sheep] being effaced he will give no attention. The young one he will not seek, and the broken [sheep] he will not heal. The one stationing herself he will not supply [with food], and the flesh of the fat one he will eat, and the hoofs of the [sheep] he will tear off. 17 Woe to my valueless shepherd, who is leaving the flock! A sword will be upon his arm and upon his right eye. His own arm will without fail dry up, and his own right eye will without fail grow dim."

12 A pronouncement:
"The word of Jehovah concerning Israel," is the utterance of Jehovah, the One who is stretching out [the] heavens and laying the foundation of [the] earth and forming the spirit of man inside him. 2 "Here I am making Jerusalem a bowl [causing] reeling to all the peoples round about; and also against Judah he will come

to be in the siege, [even] against Jerusalem. 3 And it must occur in that day [that] I shall make Jerusalem a burdensome stone to all the peoples. All those lifting it will without fail get severe scratches for themselves; and against her all the nations of the earth will certainly be gathered. 4 In that day," is the utterance of Jehovah, "I shall strike every horse with bewilderment and its rider with madness; and upon the house of Judah I shall open my eyes, and every horse of the peoples I shall strike with loss of sight. 5 And the sheiks of Judah will have to say in their heart, 'The inhabitants of Jerusalem are a strength to me by Jehovah of armies their God.' 6 In that day I shall make the sheiks of Judah like a fire pot among trees and like a fiery torch in a row of newly cut grain, and they must devour on the right [hand] and on the left all the peoples round about; and Jerusalem must yet be inhabited in her [own] place, in Jerusalem.

7 "And Jehovah will certainly save the tents of Judah first, to the end that the beauty of the house of David and the beauty of the inhabitants of Jerusalem may not become too great over Judah. 8 In that day Jehovah will be a defense around the inhabitants of Jerusalem; and the one that is stumbling among them must become in that day like David, and the house of David like God, like Jehovah's angel before them. 9 And it must occur in that day [that] I shall seek to annihilate all the nations that are coming against Jerusalem.

10 "And I will pour out upon the house of David and upon the inhabitants of Jerusalem the spirit of favor and entreaties, and they will certainly look to the One whom they pierced through, and they will certainly wail over him as in the wailing over an only [son]; and there will be a bitter lamentation over him as when there is bitter lamentation over the first-born [son]. 11 In that day the wailing

in Jerusalem will be great, like the wailing of Ha·dad·rim'mon in the valley plain of Me·gid'do. 12 And the land will certainly wail, each family by itself; the family of the house of David by itself, and their women by themselves; the family of the house of Nathan by itself, and their women by themselves; 13 the family of the house of Le'vi by itself; and their women by themselves; the family of the Shim'e·ites by itself, and their women by themselves; 14 all the families that are left remaining, each family by itself, and their women by themselves.

13 "In that day there will come to be a well opened to the house of David and to the inhabitants of Jerusalem for sin and for an abhorrent thing.

2 "And it must occur in that day," is the utterance of Jehovah of armies, "[that] I shall cut off the names of the idols out of the land, and they will no more be remembered; and also the prophets and the spirit of uncleanness I shall cause to pass out of the land. 3 And it must occur [that] in case a man should prophesy any more, his father and his mother, the ones who caused his birth, must also say to him, 'You will not live, because falsehood is what you have spoken in the name of Jehovah.' And his father and his mother, the ones who caused his birth, must pierce him through because of his prophesying.

4 "And it must occur in that day [that] the prophets will become ashamed, each one of his vision when he prophesies; and they will not wear an official garment of hair for the purpose of deceiving. 5 And he will certainly say, 'I am no prophet. I am a man cultivating [the] soil, because an earthling man himself acquired me from my youth on.' 6 And one must say to him, 'What are these wounds [on your person] between your hands?' And he will have to say, 'Those with which I was struck in the house of my intense lovers.'"

7 "O sword, awake against my shepherd, even against the able-bodied man who is my associate," is the utterance of Jehovah of armies. "Strike the shepherd, and let those of the flock be scattered; and I shall certainly turn my hand back upon those who are insignificant."

8 "And it must occur in all the land," is the utterance of Jehovah, "[that] two parts in it are what will be cut off [and] expire; and as for the third [part], it will be left remaining in it. 9 And I shall certainly bring the third [part] through the fire; and I shall actually refine them as in the refining of silver, and examine them as in the examining of gold. It, for its part, will call upon my name, and I, for my part, will answer it. I will say, 'It is my people,' and it, in its turn, will say, 'Jehovah is my God.'"

14 "Look! There is a day coming, belonging to Jehovah, and the spoil of you will certainly be apportioned out in the midst of you. 2 And I shall certainly gather all the nations against Jerusalem for the war; and the city will actually be captured and the houses be pillaged, and the women themselves will be raped. And half of the city must go forth into the exile; but as for the remaining ones of the people, they will not be cut off from the city.

3 "And Jehovah will certainly go forth and war against those nations as in the day of his warring, in the day of fight. 4 And his feet will actually stand in that day upon the mountain of the olive trees, which is in front of Jerusalem, on the east; and the mountain of the olive trees must be split at its middle, from the sunrising and to the west. There will be a very great valley; and half of the mountain will actually be moved to the north, and half of it to the south. 5 And you people will certainly flee to the valley of my mountains; because the valley of [the] mountains will reach all the way to A'zel. And you will have to flee, just as you

fled because of the [earth]quake in the days of Uz·zi′ah the king of Judah. And Jehovah my God will certainly come, all the holy ones being with him.

6 "And it must occur in that day [that] there will prove to be no precious light—things will be congealed. 7 And it must become one day that is known as belonging to Jehovah. It will not be day, neither will it be night; and it must occur [that] at evening time it will become light. 8 And it must occur in that day [that] living waters will go forth from Jerusalem, half of them to the eastern sea and half of them to the western sea. In summer and in winter it will occur. 9 And Jehovah must become king over all the earth. In that day Jehovah will prove to be one, and his name one.

10 "The whole land will be changed like the Ar′a·bah, from Ge′ba to Rim′mon to the south of Jerusalem; and she must rise and become inhabited in her place, from the gate of Benjamin all the way to the place of the First Gate, all the way to the Corner Gate, and [from] the Tower of Ha·nan′el all the way to the press vats of the king. 11 And people will certainly inhabit her; and there will occur no more any banning [to destruction], and Jerusalem must be inhabited in security.

12 "And this is what will prove to be the scourge with which Jehovah will scourge all the peoples that will actually do military service against Jerusalem: There will be a rotting away of one's flesh, while one is standing upon one's feet; and one's very eyes will rot away in their sockets, and one's very tongue will rot away in one's mouth.

13 "And it must occur in that day [that] confusion from Jehovah will become widespread among them; and they will actually grab hold, each one of the hand of his companion, and his hand will ac-

tually come up against the hand of his companion. 14 And Judah itself also will be warring at Jerusalem; and the wealth of all the nations round about will certainly be gathered, gold and silver and garments in excessive abundance.

15 "And this is how the scourge of the horse, the mule, the camel, and the male ass, and every sort of domestic animal that happens to be in those camps, will prove to be, like this scourge.

16 "And it must occur [that], as regards everyone who is left remaining out of all the nations that are coming against Jerusalem, they must also go up from year to year to bow down to the King, Jehovah of armies, and to celebrate the festival of the booths. 17 And it must occur that, as regards anyone that does not come up out of the families of the earth to Jerusalem to bow down to the King, Jehovah of armies, even upon them no pouring rain will occur. 18 And if the family of Egypt itself does not come up and does not actually enter, upon them also there shall be none. The scourge will occur with which Jehovah scourges the nations that do not come up to celebrate the festival of the booths. 19 This itself will prove to be the [punishment for the] sin of Egypt and the sin of all the nations that do not come up to celebrate the festival of the booths.

20 "In that day there will prove to be upon the bells of the horse 'Holiness belongs to Jehovah!' And the widemouthed cooking pots in the house of Jehovah must become like the bowls before the altar. 21 And every widemouthed cooking pot in Jerusalem and in Judah must become something holy belonging to Jehovah of armies, and all those who are sacrificing must come in and take from them and must do boiling in them. And there will no more prove to be a Ca′naan·ite in the house of Jehovah of armies in that day."

MALACHI

1 A pronouncement: The word of Jehovah concerning Israel by means of Mal′a·chi:

2 "I have loved YOU people," Jehovah has said.

And YOU have said: "In what way have you loved us?"

"Was not E′sau the brother of Jacob?" is the utterance of Jehovah. "But I loved Jacob, 3 and E′sau I have hated; and I finally made his mountains a desolated waste and his inheritance for the jackals of [the] wilderness."

4 "Because E′dom keeps saying, 'We have been shattered, but we shall return and build [the] devastated places,' this is what Jehovah of armies has said, 'They, for their part, will build; but I, for my part, shall tear down. And people will certainly call them "the territory of wickedness" and "the people whom Jehovah has denounced to time indefinite." 5 And YOUR own eyes will see [it], and YOU yourselves will say: "May Jehovah be magnified over the territory of Israel."'"

6 " 'A son, for his part, honors a father; and a servant, his grand master. So if I am a father, where is the honor to me? And if I am a grand master, where is the fear of me?' Jehovah of armies has said to YOU, O priests who are despising my name.

" 'And YOU have said: "In what way have we despised your name?" '

7 " '[By] presenting upon my altar polluted bread.'

" 'And YOU have said: "In what way have we polluted you?" '

" 'By YOUR saying: "The table of Jehovah is something to be despised." 8 And when YOU present a blind [animal] for sacrificing: "It is nothing bad." And when YOU present a lame [animal] or a sick one: "It is nothing bad." ' "

"Bring it near, please, to your governor. Will he find pleasure in you, or will he receive you kindly?" Jehovah of armies has said.

9 "And now, please, soften the face of God, that he may show us favor. From YOUR hand this has occurred. Will he receive any of YOU men kindly?" Jehovah of armies has said.

10 "Who also is there among YOU that will shut the doors? And YOU men will not light my altar—for nothing. No delight do I have in YOU," Jehovah of armies has said, "and in the gift offering from YOUR hand I take no pleasure."

11 "For from the sun's rising even to its setting my name will be great among the nations, and in every place sacrificial smoke will be made, a presentation will be made to my name, even a clean gift; because my name will be great among the nations," Jehovah of armies has said.

12 "But YOU men are profaning me by YOUR saying, 'The table of Jehovah is something polluted, and its fruit is something to be despised, its food.' 13 And YOU have said, 'Look! What a weariness!' and YOU have caused a sniffing at it," Jehovah of armies has said. "And YOU have brought something torn away, and the lame one, and the sick one; yes, YOU have brought [it] as a gift. Can I take pleasure in it at YOUR hand?" Jehovah has said.

14 "And cursed is the one acting cunningly when there exists in his drove a male animal, and he is making a vow and sacrificing a ruined one to Jehovah. For I am a great King," Jehovah of armies has said, "and my name will be fear-inspiring among the nations."

2 "And now this commandment is to YOU, O priests. 2 If YOU will not listen, and if YOU will not lay [it] to heart to give glory to my name," Jehovah of armies has said, "I shall also certainly send upon

YOU the curse, and I will curse YOUR blessings. Yes, I have even cursed the [blessing], because YOU are not laying [it] to heart."

3 "Look! I am rebuking on YOUR account the [sown] seed, and I will scatter dung upon YOUR faces, the dung of YOUR festivals; and someone will actually carry YOU away to it. 4 And YOU will have to know that I have sent to YOU this commandment, in order that my covenant with Le′vi may continue," Jehovah of armies has said.

5 "As for my covenant, it proved to be with him, [one] of life and of peace, and I kept giving them to him, with fear. And he continued fearing me; yes, because of my name he himself was struck with terror. 6 The very law of truth proved to be in his mouth, and there was no unrighteousness to be found on his lips. In peace and in uprightness he walked with me, and many were those whom he turned back from error. 7 For the lips of a priest are the ones that should keep knowledge, and [the] law is what people should seek from his mouth; for he is the messenger of Jehovah of armies.

8 "But YOU men—YOU have turned aside from the way. YOU have caused many to stumble in the law. YOU have ruined the covenant of Le′vi," Jehovah of armies has said. 9 "And I also, for my part, shall certainly make YOU to be despised and low to all the people, according as YOU were not keeping my ways, but were showing partiality in the law."

10 "Is it not one father that all of us have? Is it not one God that has created us? Why is it that we deal treacherously with one another, in profaning the covenant of our forefathers? 11 Judah has dealt treacherously, and a detestable thing has been committed in Israel and in Jerusalem; for Judah has profaned the holiness of Jehovah, which He has loved, and he has taken possession of the daughter of a foreign god as a bride. 12 Jehovah will cut off each one that does it, one who is awake and one who

is answering, from the tents of Jacob, and one who is presenting a gift offering to Jehovah of armies."

13 "And this is the second thing that YOU people do, [this resulting in] covering with tears the altar of Jehovah, with weeping and sighing, so that there is no more a turning toward the gift offering or a taking of pleasure [in anything] from YOUR hand. 14 And YOU have said, 'On what account?' On this account, that Jehovah himself has borne witness between you and the wife of your youth, with whom you yourself have dealt treacherously, although she is your partner and the wife of your covenant. 15 And there was one who did not do [it], as he had what was remaining of [the] spirit. And what was that one seeking? The seed of God. And YOU people must guard yourselves respecting YOUR spirit, and with the wife of your youth may no one deal treacherously. 16 For he has hated a divorcing," Jehovah the God of Israel has said; "and the one who with violence has covered over his garment," Jehovah of armies has said. "And YOU must guard yourselves respecting YOUR spirit, and YOU must not deal treacherously.

17 "YOU people have made Jehovah weary by YOUR words, and YOU have said, 'In what way have we made [him] weary?' By YOUR saying, 'Everyone that is doing bad is good in the eyes of Jehovah, and in such ones he himself has taken delight'; or, 'Where is the God of justice?' "

3 "Look! I am sending my messenger, and he must clear up a way before me. And suddenly there will come to His temple the [true] Lord, whom YOU people are seeking, and the messenger of the covenant in whom YOU are delighting. Look! He will certainly come," Jehovah of armies has said.

2 "But who will be putting up with the day of his coming, and who will be the one standing when he appears? For he will be like the fire of a refiner and like the lye of laundrymen. 3 And he must sit

as a refiner and cleanser of silver and must cleanse the sons of Le'vi; and he must clarify them like gold and like silver, and they will certainly become to Jehovah people presenting a gift offering in righteousness. 4 And the gift offering of Judah and of Jerusalem will actually be gratifying to Jehovah, as in the days of long ago and as in the years of antiquity.

5 "And I will come near to you people for the judgment, and I will become a speedy witness against the sorcerers, and against the adulterers, and against those swearing falsely, and against those acting fraudulently with the wages of a wage worker, with [the] widow and with [the] fatherless boy, and those turning away the alien resident, while they have not feared me," Jehovah of armies has said.

6 "For I am Jehovah; I have not changed. And you are sons of Jacob; you have not come to your finish. 7 From the days of your forefathers you have turned aside from my regulations and have not kept [them]. Return to me, and I will return to you," Jehovah of armies has said.

And you have said: "In what way shall we return?"

8 "Will earthling man rob God? But you are robbing me."

And you have said: "In what way have we robbed you?"

"In the tenth parts and in the contributions. 9 With the curse you are cursing [me], and me you are robbing—the nation in its entirety. 10 Bring all the tenth parts into the storehouse, that there may come to be food in my house; and test me out, please, in this respect," Jehovah of armies has said, "whether I shall not open to you people the floodgates of the heavens and actually empty out upon you a blessing until there is no more want."

11 "And I will rebuke for you the devouring one, and it will not ruin for you the fruit of the ground, nor will the vine in the field prove fruitless for you," Jehovah of armies has said.

12 "And all the nations will have to pronounce you happy, for you yourselves will become a land of delight," Jehovah of armies has said.

13 "Strong have been your words against me," Jehovah has said.

And you have said: "What have we spoken with one another against you?"

14 "You have said, 'It is of no value to serve God. And what profit is there in that we have kept the obligation to him, and that we have walked dejectedly on account of Jehovah of armies? 15 And at present we are pronouncing presumptuous people happy. Also, the doers of wickedness have been built up. Also, they have tested God out and keep getting away.'"

16 At that time those in fear of Jehovah spoke with one another, each one with his companion, and Jehovah kept paying attention and listening. And a book of remembrance began to be written up before him for those in fear of Jehovah and for those thinking upon his name.

17 "And they will certainly become mine," Jehovah of armies has said, "at the day when I am producing a special property. And I will show compassion upon them, just as a man shows compassion upon his son who is serving him. 18 And you people will again certainly see [the distinction] between a righteous one and a wicked one, between one serving God and one who has not served him."

4 "For, look! the day is coming that is burning like the furnace, and all the presumptuous ones and all those doing wickedness must become as stubble. And the day that is coming will certainly devour them," Jehovah of armies has said, "so that it will not leave to them either root or bough. 2 And to you who are in fear of my name the sun of righteousness will certainly shine forth, with healing in its wings; and you will actually go forth and paw the ground like fattened calves."

3 "And you people will certainly

tread down [the] wicked ones, for they will become as powder under the soles of YOUR feet in the day on which I am acting," Jehovah of armies has said.

4 "Remember, YOU people, the law of Moses my servant with which I commanded him in Ho'reb concerning all Israel, even regulations and judicial decisions.

5 "Look! I am sending to YOU people E·li'jah the prophet before the coming of the great and fear-inspiring day of Jehovah. 6 And he must turn the heart of fathers back toward sons, and the heart of sons back toward fathers; in order that I may not come and actually strike the earth with a devoting [of it] to destruction."

(End of the translation of the Hebrew-Aramaic Scriptures, to be followed by that of the Christian Greek Scriptures)

MATTHEW

1 The book of the history of Jesus Christ, son of David, son of Abraham:

2 Abraham became father to Isaac;

Isaac became father to Jacob;

Jacob became father to Judah and his brothers;

3 Judah became father to Pe'rez and to Ze'rah by Ta'mar;

Pe'rez became father to Hez'ron;

Hez'ron became father to Ram;

4 Ram became father to Am·min'a·dab;

Am·min'a·dab became father to Nah'shon;

Nah'shon became father to Sal'mon;

5 Sal'mon became father to Bo'az by Ra'hab;

Bo'az became father to O'bed by Ruth;

O'bed became father to Jes'se;

6 Jes'se became father to David the king.

David became father to Sol'o·mon by the wife of U·ri'ah;

7 Sol'o·mon became father to Re·ho·bo'am;

Re·ho·bo'am became father to A·bi'jah;

A·bi'jah became father to A'sa;

8 A'sa became father to Je·hosh'a·phat;

Je·hosh'a·phat became father to Je·ho'ram;

Je·ho'ram became father to Uz·zi'ah;

9 Uz·zi'ah became father to Jo'tham;

Jo'tham became father to A'haz;

A'haz became father to Hez·e·ki'ah;

10 Hez·e·ki'ah became father to Ma·nas'seh;

Ma·nas'seh became father to A'mon;

A'mon became father to Jo·si'ah;

11 Jo·si'ah became father to Jec·o·ni'ah and to his brothers at the time of the deportation to Babylon.

12 After the deportation to Babylon Jec·o·ni'ah became father to She·al'ti·el;

She·al'ti·el became father to Ze·rub'ba·bel;

13 Ze·rub'ba·bel became father to A·bi'ud;

A·bi'ud became father to E·li'a·kim;

E·li'a·kim became father to A'zor;

14 A'zor became father to Za'dok;

Za'dok became father to A'chim;

A'chim became father to E·li'ud;

15 E·li'ud became father to El·e·a'zar;

El·e·a'zar became father to Mat'than;

Mat'than became father to Jacob;

16 Jacob became father to Joseph the husband of Mary, of whom Jesus was born, who is called Christ.

17 All the generations, then, from Abraham until David were fourteen generations, and from David until the deportation to Babylon fourteen generations, and from the deportation to Babylon until the Christ fourteen generations.

18 But the birth of Jesus Christ was in this way. During the time his mother Mary was promised in marriage to Joseph, she was found to be pregnant by holy spirit before they were united. 19 However, Joseph her husband, because he was righteous and did not want to make her a public spectacle, intended to divorce her secretly. 20 But after he had thought these things over, look! Jehovah's angel appeared to him in a dream, saying: "Joseph, son of David, do not be afraid to take Mary your wife home, for that which has been begotten in her is by holy spirit. 21 She will give birth to a son, and you must call

worship, and it is to him alone you must render sacred service.'"
11 Then the Devil left him, and, look! angels came and began to minister to him.

12 Now when he heard that John had been arrested, he withdrew into Gal'i·lee. 13 Further, after leaving Naz'a·reth, he came and took up residence in Ca·per'na·um beside the sea in the districts of Zeb'u·lun and Naph'ta·li, 14 that there might be fulfilled what was spoken through Isaiah the prophet, saying: 15 "O land of Zeb'u·lun and land of Naph'ta·li, along the road of the sea, on the other side of the Jordan, Gal'i·lee of the nations! 16 the people sitting in darkness saw a great light, and as for those sitting in a region of deathly shadow, light rose upon them." 17 From that time on Jesus commenced preaching and saying: "Repent, YOU people, for the kingdom of the heavens has drawn near."

18 Walking alongside the sea of Gal'i·lee he saw two brothers, Simon who is called Peter and Andrew his brother, letting down a fishing net into the sea, for they were fishers. 19 And he said to them: "Come after me, and I will make YOU fishers of men." 20 At once abandoning the nets, they followed him. 21 Going on also from there he saw two others [who were] brothers, James [the son] of Zeb'e·dee and John his brother, in the boat with Zeb'e·dee their father, mending their nets, and he called them. 22 At once leaving the boat and their father, they followed him.

23 Then he went around throughout the whole of Gal'i·lee, teaching in their synagogues and preaching the good news of the kingdom and curing every sort of disease and every sort of infirmity among the people. 24 And the report about him went out into all Syria; and they brought him all those faring badly, distressed with various diseases and torments, demon-possessed and epileptic and paralyzed persons, and he cured them. 25 Consequently great crowds followed him from Gal'i·lee and De·cap'o·lis and Jerusalem and Ju·de'a and from the other side of the Jordan.

5 When he saw the crowds he went up into the mountain; and after he sat down his disciples came to him; 2 and he opened his mouth and began teaching them, saying:

3 "Happy are those conscious of their spiritual need, since the kingdom of the heavens belongs to them.

4 "Happy are those who mourn, since they will be comforted.

5 "Happy are the mild-tempered ones, since they will inherit the earth.

6 "Happy are those hungering and thirsting for righteousness, since they will be filled.

7 "Happy are the merciful, since they will be shown mercy.

8 "Happy are the pure in heart, since they will see God.

9 "Happy are the peaceable, since they will be called 'sons of God.'

10 "Happy are those who have been persecuted for righteousness' sake, since the kingdom of the heavens belongs to them.

11 "Happy are YOU when people reproach YOU and persecute YOU and lyingly say every sort of wicked thing against YOU for my sake. 12 Rejoice and leap for joy, since YOUR reward is great in the heavens; for in that way they persecuted the prophets prior to YOU.

13 "YOU are the salt of the earth; but if the salt loses its strength, how will its saltness be restored? It is no longer usable for anything but to be thrown outside to be trampled on by men.

14 "YOU are the light of the world. A city cannot be hid when situated upon a mountain. 15 People light a lamp and set it, not under the measuring basket, but upon the lampstand, and it shines upon all those in the house. 16 Likewise let YOUR light shine before men, that they may see YOUR fine works and give glory to YOUR Father who is in the heavens.

17 "Do not think I came to destroy the Law or the Prophets. I came, not to destroy, but to fulfill; 18 for truly I say to you that sooner would heaven and earth pass away than for one smallest letter or one particle of a letter to pass away from the Law by any means and not all things take place. 19 Whoever, therefore, breaks one of these least commandments and teaches mankind to that effect, he will be called 'least' in relation to the kingdom of the heavens. As for anyone who does them and teaches them, this one will be called 'great' in relation to the kingdom of the heavens. 20 For I say to you that if your righteousness does not abound more than that of the scribes and Pharisees, you will by no means enter into the kingdom of the heavens.

21 "You heard that it was said to those of ancient times, 'You must not murder; but whoever commits a murder will be accountable to the court of justice.' 22 However, I say to you that everyone who continues wrathful with his brother will be accountable to the court of justice; but whoever addresses his brother with an unspeakable word of contempt will be accountable to the Supreme Court; whereas whoever says, 'You despicable fool!' will be liable to the fiery Ge·hen′na.

23 "If, then, you are bringing your gift to the altar and you there remember that your brother has something against you, 24 leave your gift there in front of the altar, and go away; first make your peace with your brother, and then, when you have come back, offer up your gift.

25 "Be about settling matters quickly with the one complaining against you at law, while you are with him on the way there, that somehow the complainant may not turn you over to the judge, and the judge to the court attendant, and you get thrown into prison. 26 I say to you for a fact, You will certainly not come out from there until you have paid over the last coin of very little value.

27 "You heard that it was said, 'You must not commit adultery.' 28 But I say to you that everyone that keeps on looking at a woman so as to have a passion for her has already committed adultery with her in his heart. 29 If, now, that right eye of yours is making you stumble, tear it out and throw it away from you. For it is more beneficial to you for one of your members to be lost to you than for your whole body to be pitched into Ge·hen′na. 30 Also, if your right hand is making you stumble, cut it off and throw it away from you. For it is more beneficial for one of your members to be lost to you than for your whole body to land in Ge·hen′na.

31 "Moreover it was said, 'Whoever divorces his wife, let him give her a certificate of divorce.' 32 However, I say to you that everyone divorcing his wife, except on account of fornication, makes her a subject for adultery, seeing that whoever marries a divorced woman commits adultery.

33 "Again you heard that it was said to those of ancient times, 'You must not swear without performing, but you must pay your vows to Jehovah.' 34 However, I say to you: Do not swear at all, neither by heaven, because it is God's throne; 35 nor by earth, because it is the footstool of his feet; nor by Jerusalem, because it is the city of the great King. 36 Nor by your head must you swear, because you cannot turn one hair white or black. 37 Just let your word Yes mean Yes, your No, No; for what is in excess of these is from the wicked one.

38 "You heard that it was said, 'Eye for eye and tooth for tooth.' 39 However, I say to you: Do not resist him that is wicked; but whoever slaps you on your right cheek, turn the other also to him. 40 And if a person wants to go to court with you and get possession of your inner garment, let your outer garment also go to him; 41 and if someone under authority impresses you into service for a

mile, go with him two miles. 42 Give to the one asking you, and do not turn away from one that wants to borrow from you [without interest].

43 "You heard that it was said, 'You must love your neighbor and hate your enemy.' 44 However, I say to you: Continue to love your enemies and to pray for those persecuting you; 45 that you may prove yourselves sons of your Father who is in the heavens, since he makes his sun rise upon wicked people and good and makes it rain upon righteous people and unrighteous. 46 For if you love those loving you, what reward do you have? Are not also the tax collectors doing the same thing? 47 And if you greet your brothers only, what extraordinary thing are you doing? Are not also the people of the nations doing the same thing? 48 You must accordingly be perfect, as your heavenly Father is perfect.

6 "Take good care not to practice your righteousness in front of men in order to be observed by them; otherwise you will have no reward with your Father who is in the heavens. 2 Hence when you go making gifts of mercy, do not blow a trumpet ahead of you, just as the hypocrites do in the synagogues and in the streets, that they may be glorified by men. Truly I say to you, They are having their reward in full. 3 But you, when making gifts of mercy, do not let your left hand know what your right is doing, 4 that your gifts of mercy may be in secret; then your Father who is looking on in secret will repay you.

5 "Also, when you pray, you must not be as the hypocrites; because they like to pray standing in the synagogues and on the corners of the broad ways to be visible to men. Truly I say to you, They are having their reward in full. 6 You, however, when you pray, go into your private room and, after shutting your door, pray to your Father who is in secret; then your Father who looks on in secret will repay

you. 7 But when praying, do not say the same things over and over again, just as the people of the nations do, for they imagine they will get a hearing for their use of many words. 8 So, do not make yourselves like them, for God your Father knows what things you are needing before ever you ask him.

9 "You must pray, then, this way:

" 'Our Father in the heavens, let your name be sanctified. 10 Let your kingdom come. Let your will take place, as in heaven, also upon earth. 11 Give us today our bread for this day; 12 and forgive us our debts, as we also have forgiven our debtors. 13 And do not bring us into temptation, but deliver us from the wicked one.'

14 "For if you forgive men their trespasses, your heavenly Father will also forgive you; 15 whereas if you do not forgive men their trespasses, neither will your Father forgive your trespasses.

16 "When you are fasting, stop becoming sad-faced like the hypocrites, for they disfigure their faces that they may appear to men to be fasting. Truly I say to you, They are having their reward in full. 17 But you, when fasting, grease your head and wash your face, 18 that you may appear to be fasting, not to men, but to your Father who is in secrecy; then your Father who is looking on in secrecy will repay you.

19 "Stop storing up for yourselves treasures upon the earth, where moth and rust consume, and where thieves break in and steal. 20 Rather, store up for yourselves treasures in heaven, where neither moth nor rust consumes, and where thieves do not break in and steal. 21 For where your treasure is, there your heart will be also.

22 "The lamp of the body is the eye. If, then, your eye is simple, your whole body will be bright; 23 but if your eye is wicked, your whole body will be dark. If in reality the light that is in you is darkness, how great that darkness is!

24 "No one can slave for two masters; for either he will hate the one and love the other, or he will stick to the one and despise the other. You cannot slave for God and for Riches.

25 "On this account I say to you: Stop being anxious about your souls as to what you will eat or what you will drink, or about your bodies as to what you will wear. Does not the soul mean more than food and the body than clothing? 26 Observe intently the birds of heaven, because they do not sow seed or reap or gather into storehouses; still your heavenly Father feeds them. Are you not worth more than they are? 27 Who of you by being anxious can add one cubit to his life span? 28 Also, on the matter of clothing, why are you anxious? Take a lesson from the lilies of the field, how they are growing; they do not toil, nor do they spin; 29 but I say to you that not even Sol'o·mon in all his glory was arrayed as one of these. 30 If, now, God thus clothes the vegetation of the field, which is here today and tomorrow is thrown into the oven, will he not much rather clothe you, you with little faith? 31 So never be anxious and say, 'What are we to eat?' or, 'What are we to drink?' or, 'What are we to put on?' 32 For all these are the things the nations are eagerly pursuing. For your heavenly Father knows you need all these things.

33 "Keep on, then, seeking first the kingdom and his righteousness, and all these [other] things will be added to you. 34 So, never be anxious about the next day, for the next day will have its own anxieties. Sufficient for each day is its own badness.

7 "Stop judging that you may not be judged; 2 for with what judgment you are judging, you will be judged; and with the measure that you are measuring out, they will measure out to you. 3 Why, then, do you look at the straw in your brother's eye, but do not consider the rafter in your own eye?

4 Or how can you say to your brother, 'Allow me to extract the straw from your eye'; when, look! a rafter is in your own eye? 5 Hypocrite! First extract the rafter from your own eye, and then you will see clearly how to extract the straw from your brother's eye.

6 "Do not give what is holy to dogs, neither throw your pearls before swine, that they may never trample them under their feet and turn around and rip you open.

7 "Keep on asking, and it will be given you; keep on seeking, and you will find; keep on knocking, and it will be opened to you. 8 For everyone asking receives, and everyone seeking finds, and to everyone knocking it will be opened. 9 Indeed, who is the man among you whom his son asks for bread—he will not hand him a stone, will he? 10 Or, perhaps, he will ask for a fish—he will not hand him a serpent, will he? 11 Therefore, if you, although being wicked, know how to give good gifts to your children, how much more so will your Father who is in the heavens give good things to those asking him?

12 "All things, therefore, that you want men to do to you, you also must likewise do to them; this, in fact, is what the Law and the Prophets mean.

13 "Go in through the narrow gate; because broad and spacious is the road leading off into destruction, and many are the ones going in through it; 14 whereas narrow is the gate and cramped the road leading off into life, and few are the ones finding it.

15 "Be on the watch for the false prophets that come to you in sheep's covering, but inside they are ravenous wolves. 16 By their fruits you will recognize them. Never do people gather grapes from thorns or figs from thistles, do they? 17 Likewise every good tree produces fine fruit, but every rotten tree produces worthless fruit; 18 a good tree cannot bear worthless fruit, neither can a rotten tree produce fine fruit. 19 Every tree not

producing fine fruit gets cut down and thrown into the fire. 20 Really, then, by their fruits YOU will recognize those [men].

21 "Not everyone saying to me, 'Lord, Lord,' will enter into the kingdom of the heavens, but the one doing the will of my Father who is in the heavens will. 22 Many will say to me in that day, 'Lord, Lord, did we not prophesy in your name, and expel demons in your name, and perform many powerful works in your name?' 23 And yet then I will confess to them: I never knew YOU! Get away from me, YOU workers of lawlessness.

24 "Therefore everyone that hears these sayings of mine and does them will be likened to a discreet man, who built his house upon the rock-mass. 25 And the rain poured down and the floods came and the winds blew and lashed against that house, but it did not cave in, for it had been founded upon the rock-mass. 26 Furthermore, everyone hearing these sayings of mine and not doing them will be likened to a foolish man, who built his house upon the sand. 27 And the rain poured down and the floods came and the winds blew and struck against that house and it caved in, and its collapse was great."

28 Now when Jesus finished these sayings, the effect was that the crowds were astounded at his way of teaching; 29 for he was teaching them as a person having authority, and not as their scribes.

8 After he had come down from the mountain great crowds followed him. 2 And, look! a leprous man came up and began doing obeisance to him, saying: "Lord, if you just want to, you can make me clean." 3 And so, stretching out [his] hand, he touched him, saying: "I want to. Be made clean." And immediately his leprosy was cleansed away. 4 Then Jesus said to him: "See that you tell no one, but go, show yourself to the priest, and offer the gift that Moses appointed, for the purpose of a witness to them."

5 When he entered into Ca·per'-na·um, an army officer came to him, entreating him 6 and saying: "Sir, my manservant is laid up in the house with paralysis, being terribly tormented." 7 He said to him: "When I get there I will cure him." 8 In reply the army officer said: "Sir, I am not a fit man for you to enter under my roof, but just say the word and my manservant will be healed. 9 For I too am a man placed under authority, having soldiers under me, and I say to this one, 'Be on your way!' and he is on his way, and to another, 'Come!' and he comes, and to my slave, 'Do this!' and he does it." 10 Hearing that, Jesus became amazed and said to those following him: "I tell YOU the truth, With no one in Israel have I found so great a faith. 11 But I tell YOU that many from eastern parts and western parts will come and recline at the table with Abraham and Isaac and Jacob in the kingdom of the heavens; 12 whereas the sons of the kingdom will be thrown into the darkness outside. There is where [their] weeping and the gnashing of [their] teeth will be." 13 Then Jesus said to the army officer: "Go. Just as it has been your faith, so let it come to pass for you." And the manservant was healed in that hour.

14 And Jesus, on coming into Peter's house, saw his mother-in-law lying down and sick with fever. 15 So he touched her hand, and the fever left her, and she got up and began ministering to him. 16 But after it became evening, people brought him many demon-possessed persons; and he expelled the spirits with a word, and he cured all who were faring badly; 17 that there might be fulfilled what was spoken through Isaiah the prophet, saying: "He himself took our sicknesses and carried our diseases."

18 When Jesus saw a crowd around him, he gave the command to shove off for the other side. 19 And a certain scribe came up and said to him: "Teacher, I will follow you wherever you are about

to go." 20 But Jesus said to him: "Foxes have dens and birds of heaven have roosts, but the Son of man has nowhere to lay down his head." 21 Then another of the disciples said to him: "Lord, permit me first to leave and bury my father." 22 Jesus said to him: "Keep following me, and let the dead bury their dead."

23 And when he got aboard a boat, his disciples followed him. 24 Now, look! a great agitation arose in the sea, so that the boat was being covered by the waves; he, however, was sleeping. 25 And they came and woke him up, saying: "Lord, save us, we are about to perish!" 26 But he said to them: "Why are YOU fainthearted, YOU with little faith?" Then, getting up, he rebuked the winds and the sea, and a great calm set in. 27 So the men became amazed and said: "What sort of person is this, that even the winds and the sea obey him?"

28 When he got to the other side, into the country of the Gad·a·renes', there met him two demon-possessed men coming out from among the memorial tombs, unusually fierce, so that nobody had the courage to pass by on that road. 29 And, look! they screamed, saying: "What have we to do with you, Son of God? Did you come here to torment us before the appointed time?" 30 But a long way off from them a herd of many swine was at pasture. 31 So the demons began to entreat him, saying: "If you expel us, send us forth into the herd of swine." 32 Accordingly he said to them: "Go!" They came out and went off into the swine; and, look! the entire herd rushed over the precipice into the sea and died in the waters. 33 But the herders fled and, going into the city, they reported everything, including the affair of the demon-possessed men. 34 And, look! all the city turned out to meet Jesus; and after having seen him, they earnestly urged him to move out from their districts.

9 So, boarding the boat, he proceeded across and went into his own city. 2 And, look! they were bringing him a paralyzed man lying on a bed. On seeing their faith Jesus said to the paralytic: "Take courage, child; your sins are forgiven." 3 And, look! certain of the scribes said to themselves: "This fellow is blaspheming." 4 And Jesus, knowing their thoughts, said: "Why are YOU thinking wicked things in YOUR hearts? 5 For instance, which is easier, to say, Your sins are forgiven, or to say, Get up and walk? 6 However, in order for YOU to know that the Son of man has authority on earth to forgive sins—" then he said to the paralytic: "Get up, pick up your bed, and go to your home." 7 And he got up and went off to his home. 8 At the sight of this the crowds were struck with fear, and they glorified God, who gave such authority to men.

9 Next, while passing along from there, Jesus caught sight of a man named Matthew seated at the tax office, and he said to him: "Be my follower." Thereupon he did rise up and follow him. 10 Later, while he was reclining at the table in the house, look! many tax collectors and sinners came and began reclining with Jesus and his disciples. 11 But on seeing this the Pharisees began to say to his disciples: "Why is it that YOUR teacher eats with tax collectors and sinners?" 12 Hearing [them], he said: "Persons in health do not need a physician, but the ailing do. 13 Go, then, and learn what this means, 'I want mercy, and not sacrifice.' For I came to call, not righteous people, but sinners."

14 Then John's disciples came to him and asked: "Why is it that we and the Pharisees practice fasting but your disciples do not fast?" 15 At this Jesus said to them: "The friends of the bridegroom have no reason to mourn as long as the bridegroom is with them, do they? But days will come when the bridegroom will be taken away from them, and then they will fast.

16 Nobody sews a patch of unshrunk cloth upon an old outer garment; for its full strength would pull from the outer garment and the tear would become worse. 17 Neither do people put new wine into old wineskins; but if they do, then the wineskins burst and the wine spills out and the wineskins are ruined. But people put new wine into new wineskins, and both things are preserved."

18 While he was telling them these things, look! a certain ruler who had approached began to do obeisance to him, saying: "By now my daughter must be dead; but come and lay your hand upon her and she will come to life."

19 Then Jesus, getting up, began to follow him; also his disciples did. 20 And, look! a woman suffering twelve years from a flow of blood came up behind and touched the fringe of his outer garment; 21 for she kept saying to herself: "If I only touch his outer garment I shall get well." 22 Jesus turned around and, noticing her, said: "Take courage, daughter; your faith has made you well." And from that hour the woman became well.

23 When, now, he came into the ruler's house and caught sight of the flute players and the crowd in noisy confusion, 24 Jesus began to say: "Leave the place, for the little girl did not die, but she is sleeping." At this they began to laugh at him scornfully. 25 As soon as the crowd had been sent outside, he went in and took hold of her hand, and the little girl got up. 26 Of course, the talk about this spread out into all that region.

27 As Jesus was passing along from there, two blind men followed him, crying out and saying: "Have mercy on us, Son of David." 28 After he had gone into the house, the blind men came to him, and Jesus asked them: "Do you have faith that I can do this?" They answered him: "Yes, Lord." 29 Then he touched their eyes, saying: "According to your faith let it happen to you." 30 And their eyes received sight. Moreover,

Jesus sternly charged them, saying: "See that nobody gets to know it." 31 But they, after getting outside, made it public about him in all that region.

32 Now when they were leaving, look! people brought him a dumb man possessed of a demon; 33 and after the demon had been expelled the dumb man spoke. Well, the crowds felt amazement and said: "Never was anything like this seen in Israel." 34 But the Pharisees began to say: "It is by the ruler of the demons that he expels the demons."

35 And Jesus set out on a tour of all the cities and villages, teaching in their synagogues and preaching the good news of the kingdom and curing every sort of disease and every sort of infirmity. 36 On seeing the crowds he felt pity for them, because they were skinned and thrown about like sheep without a shepherd. 37 Then he said to his disciples: "Yes, the harvest is great, but the workers are few. 38 Therefore, beg the Master of the harvest to send out workers into his harvest."

10 So he summoned his twelve disciples and gave them authority over unclean spirits, in order to expel these and to cure every sort of disease and every sort of infirmity.

2 The names of the twelve apostles are these: First, Simon, the one called Peter, and Andrew his brother; and James the [son] of Zeb'e-dee and John his brother; 3 Philip and Bar·thol'o·mew; Thomas and Matthew the tax collector; James the [son] of Al·phae'us, and Thaddae'us; 4 Simon the Ca·na·nae'an, and Judas Is·car'i·ot, who later betrayed him.

5 These twelve Jesus sent forth, giving them these orders: "Do not go off into the road of the nations, and do not enter into a Sa·mar'i·tan city; 6 but, instead, go continually to the lost sheep of the house of Israel. 7 As you go, preach, saying, 'The kingdom of the heavens has drawn near.' 8 Cure sick people, raise up dead persons, make lepers

clean, expel demons. You received free, give free. 9 Do not procure gold or silver or copper for YOUR girdle purses, 10 or a food pouch for the trip, or two undergarments, or sandals or a staff; for the worker deserves his food.

11 "Into whatever city or village YOU enter, search out who in it is deserving, and stay there until YOU leave. 12 When YOU are entering into the house, greet the household; 13 and if the house is deserving, let the peace YOU wish it come upon it; but if it is not deserving, let the peace from YOU return upon YOU. 14 Wherever anyone does not take YOU in or listen to YOUR words, on going out of that house or that city shake the dust off YOUR feet. 15 Truly I say to YOU, It will be more endurable for the land of Sod'om and Go·mor'rah on Judgment Day than for that city.

16 "Look! I am sending YOU forth as sheep amidst wolves; therefore prove yourselves cautious as serpents and yet innocent as doves. 17 Be on YOUR guard against men; for they will deliver YOU up to local courts, and they will scourge YOU in their synagogues. 18 Why, YOU will be haled before governors and kings for my sake, for a witness to them and the nations. 19 However, when they deliver YOU up, do not become anxious about how or what YOU are to speak; for what YOU are to speak will be given YOU in that hour; 20 for the ones speaking are not just YOU, but it is the spirit of YOUR Father that speaks by YOU. 21 Further, brother will deliver up brother to death, and a father his child, and children will rise up against parents and will have them put to death. 22 And YOU will be objects of hatred by all people on account of my name; but he that has endured to the end is the one that will be saved. 23 When they persecute YOU in one city, flee to another; for truly I say to YOU, YOU will by no means complete the circuit of the cities of Israel until the Son of man arrives.

24 "A disciple is not above his teacher, nor a slave above his lord. 25 It is enough for the disciple to become as his teacher, and the slave as his lord. If people have called the householder Be·el'ze·bub, how much more [will they call] those of his household so? 26 Therefore do not fear them; for there is nothing covered over that will not become uncovered, and secret that will not become known. 27 What I tell YOU in the darkness, say in the light; and what YOU hear whispered, preach from the housetops. 28 And do not become fearful of those who kill the body but cannot kill the soul; but rather be in fear of him that can destroy both soul and body in Ge·hen'na. 29 Do not two sparrows sell for a coin of small value? Yet not one of them will fall to the ground without YOUR Father's [knowledge]. 30 But the very hairs of YOUR head are all numbered. 31 Therefore have no fear: YOU are worth more than many sparrows.

32 "Everyone, then, that confesses union with me before men, I will also confess union with him before my Father who is in the heavens; 33 but whoever disowns me before men, I will also disown him before my Father who is in the heavens. 34 Do not think I came to put peace upon the earth; I came to put, not peace, but a sword. 35 For I came to cause division, with a man against his father, and a daughter against her mother, and a young wife against her mother-in-law. 36 Indeed, a man's enemies will be persons of his own household. 37 He that has greater affection for father or mother than for me is not worthy of me; and he that has greater affection for son or daughter than for me is not worthy of me. 38 And whoever does not accept his torture stake and follow after me is not worthy of me. 39 He that finds his soul will lose it, and he that loses his soul for my sake will find it.

40 "He that receives YOU receives me also, and he that receives me receives him also that

sent me forth. 41 He that receives a prophet because he is a prophet will get a prophet's reward, and he that receives a righteous man because he is a righteous man will get a righteous man's reward. 42 And whoever gives one of these little ones only a cup of cold water to drink because he is a disciple, I tell YOU truly, he will by no means lose his reward."

11 Now when Jesus had finished giving instructions to his twelve disciples, he set out from there to teach and preach in their cities.

2 But John, having heard in jail about the works of the Christ, sent by means of his own disciples 3 and said to him: "Are you the Coming One, or are we to expect a different one?" 4 In reply Jesus said to them: "Go YOUR way and report to John what YOU are hearing and seeing: 5 The blind are seeing again, and the lame are walking about, the lepers are being cleansed and the deaf are hearing, and the dead are being raised up, and the poor are having the good news declared to them; 6 and happy is he that finds no cause for stumbling in me."

7 While these were on their way, Jesus started to say to the crowds respecting John: "What did YOU go out into the wilderness to behold? A reed being tossed by a wind? 8 What, then, did YOU go out to see? A man dressed in soft garments? Why, those wearing soft garments are in the houses of kings. 9 Really, then, why did YOU go out? To see a prophet? Yes, I tell YOU, and far more than a prophet. 10 This is he concerning whom it is written, 'Look! I myself am sending forth my messenger before your face, who will prepare your way ahead of you!' 11 Truly I say to YOU people, Among those born of women there has not been raised up a greater than John the Baptist; but a person that is a lesser one in the kingdom of the heavens is greater than he is. 12 But from the days of John the Baptist until now the kingdom of the heavens

is the goal toward which men press, and those pressing forward are seizing it. 13 For all, the Prophets and the Law, prophesied until John; 14 and if YOU want to accept it, He himself is 'E·li′jah who is destined to come.' 15 Let him that has ears listen.

16 "With whom shall I compare this generation? It is like young children sitting in the market places who cry out to their playmates, 17 saying, 'We played the flute for YOU, but YOU did not dance; we wailed, but YOU did not beat yourselves in grief.' 18 Correspondingly, John came neither eating nor drinking, yet people say, 'He has a demon'; 19 the Son of man did come eating and drinking, still people say, 'Look! A man gluttonous and given to drinking wine, a friend of tax collectors and sinners.' All the same, wisdom is proved righteous by its works."

20 Then he started to reproach the cities in which most of his powerful works had taken place, because they did not repent: 21 "Woe to you, Cho·ra′zin! Woe to you, Beth·sa′i·da! because if the powerful works had taken place in Tyre and Si′don that took place in YOU, they would long ago have repented in sackcloth and ashes. 22 Consequently I say to YOU, It will be more endurable for Tyre and Si′don on Judgment Day than for YOU. 23 And you, Ca·per′na·um, will you perhaps be exalted to heaven? Down to Ha′des you will come; because if the powerful works that took place in you had taken place in Sod′om, it would have remained until this very day. 24 Consequently I say to YOU people, It will be more endurable for the land of Sod′om on Judgment Day than for you."

25 At that time Jesus said in response: "I publicly praise you, Father, Lord of heaven and earth, because you have hidden these things from the wise and intellectual ones and have revealed them to babes. 26 Yes, O Father, because to do thus came to be the way approved by you. 27 All things have

been delivered to me by my Father, and no one fully knows the Son but the Father, neither does anyone fully know the Father but the Son and anyone to whom the Son is willing to reveal him. 28 Come to me, all you who are toiling and loaded down, and I will refresh you. 29 Take my yoke upon you and become my disciples, for I am mildtempered and lowly in heart, and you will find refreshment for your souls. 30 For my yoke is kindly and my load is light."

12 At that season Jesus went through the grainfields on the sabbath. His disciples got hungry and started to pluck heads of grain and to eat. 2 At seeing this the Pharisees said to him: "Look! Your disciples are doing what it is not lawful to do on the sabbath." 3 He said to them: "Have you not read what David did when he and the men with him got hungry? 4 How he entered into the house of God and they ate the loaves of presentation, something that it was not lawful for him to eat, nor for those with him, but for the priests only? 5 Or, have you not read in the Law that on the sabbaths the priests in the temple treat the sabbath as not sacred and continue guiltless? 6 But I tell you that something greater than the temple is here. 7 However, if you had understood what this means, 'I want mercy, and not sacrifice,' you would not have condemned the guiltless ones. 8 For Lord of the sabbath is what the Son of man is."

9 After departing from that place he went into their synagogue; 10 and, look! a man with a withered hand! So they asked him, "Is it lawful to cure on the sabbath?" that they might get an accusation against him. 11 He said to them: "Who will be the man among you that has one sheep and, if this falls into a pit on the sabbath, will not get hold of it and lift it out? 12 All considered, of how much more worth is a man than a sheep! So it is lawful to do a fine thing on the sabbath." 13 Then he said to the

man: "Stretch out your hand." And he stretched it out, and it was restored sound like the other hand. 14 But the Pharisees went out and took counsel against him that they might destroy him. 15 Having come to know [this], Jesus withdrew from there. Many also followed him, and he cured them all, 16 but he strictly charged them not to make him manifest; 17 that there might be fulfilled what was spoken through Isaiah the prophet, who said:

18 "Look! My servant whom I chose, my beloved, whom my soul approved! I will put my spirit upon him, and what justice is he will make clear to the nations. 19 He will not wrangle, nor cry aloud, nor will anyone hear his voice in the broad ways. 20 No bruised reed will he crush, and no smoldering flaxen wick will he extinguish, until he sends out justice with success. 21 Indeed, in his name nations will hope."

22 Then they brought him a demon-possessed man, blind and dumb; and he cured him, so that the dumb man spoke and saw. 23 Well, all the crowds were simply carried away and began to say: "May this not perhaps be the Son of David?" 24 At hearing this, the Pharisees said: "This fellow does not expel the demons except by means of Be·el′ze·bub, the ruler of the demons." 25 Knowing their thoughts, he said to them: "Every kingdom divided against itself comes to desolation, and every city or house divided against itself will not stand. 26 In the same way, if Satan expels Satan, he has become divided against himself; how, then, will his kingdom stand? 27 Moreover, if I expel the demons by means of Be·el′ze·bub, by means of whom do your sons expel them? This is why they will be judges of you. 28 But if it is by means of God's spirit that I expel the demons, the kingdom of God has really overtaken you. 29 Or how can anyone invade the house of a strong man and seize his movable goods, unless first he binds the

strong man? And then he will plunder his house. 30 He that is not on my side is against me, and he that does not gather with me scatters.

31 "On this account I say to YOU, Every sort of sin and blasphemy will be forgiven men, but the blasphemy against the spirit will not be forgiven. 32 For example, whoever speaks a word against the Son of man, it will be forgiven him; but whoever speaks against the holy spirit, it will not be forgiven him, no, not in this system of things nor in that to come.

33 "Either YOU people make the tree fine and its fruit fine or make the tree rotten and its fruit rotten; for by its fruit the tree is known. 34 Offspring of vipers, how can YOU speak good things, when YOU are wicked? For out of the abundance of the heart the mouth speaks. 35 The good man out of his good treasure sends out good things, whereas the wicked man out of his wicked treasure sends out wicked things. 36 I tell YOU that every unprofitable saying that men speak, they will render an account concerning it on Judgment Day; 37 for by your words you will be declared righteous, and by your words you will be condemned."

38 Then as an answer to him some of the scribes and Pharisees said: "Teacher, we want to see a sign from you." 39 In reply he said to them: "A wicked and adulterous generation keeps on seeking for a sign, but no sign will be given it except the sign of Jo′nah the prophet. 40 For just as Jo′nah was in the belly of the huge fish three days and three nights, so the Son of man will be in the heart of the earth three days and three nights. 41 Men of Nin′e·veh will rise up in the judgment with this generation and will condemn it; because they repented at what Jo′nah preached, but, look! something more than Jo′nah is here. 42 The queen of the south will be raised up in the judgment with this generation and will condemn it; because she came from the ends of the earth to hear the wisdom of Sol′o·mon, but, look! something more than Sol′o·mon is here.

43 "When an unclean spirit comes out of a man, it passes through parched places in search of a resting place, and finds none. 44 Then it says, 'I will go back to my house out of which I moved'; and on arriving it finds it unoccupied but swept clean and adorned. 45 Then it goes its way and takes along with it seven different spirits more wicked than itself, and, after getting inside, they dwell there; and the final circumstances of that man become worse than the first. That is how it will be also with this wicked generation."

46 While he was yet speaking to the crowds, look! his mother and brothers took up a position outside seeking to speak to him. 47 So someone said to him: "Look! Your mother and your brothers are standing outside, seeking to speak to you." 48 As an answer he said to the one telling him: "Who is my mother, and who are my brothers?" 49 And extending his hand toward his disciples, he said: "Look! My mother and my brothers! 50 For whoever does the will of my Father who is in heaven, the same is my brother, and sister, and mother."

13 On that day Jesus, having left the house, was sitting by the sea; 2 and great crowds gathered to him, so that he went aboard a boat and sat down, and all the crowd was standing on the beach. 3 Then he told them many things by illustrations, saying: "Look! A sower went out to sow; 4 and as he was sowing, some [seeds] fell alongside the road, and the birds came and ate them up. 5 Others fell upon the rocky places where they did not have much soil, and at once they sprang up because of not having depth of soil. 6 But when the sun rose they were scorched, and because of not having root they withered. 7 Others, too, fell among the thorns, and the thorns came up and choked them. 8 Still others fell upon the fine soil and they began to yield fruit, this one a hundredfold, that one sixty, the other thirty. 9 Let him that has ears listen."

10 So the disciples came up and said to him: "Why is it you speak to them by the use of illustrations?" 11 In reply he said: "To YOU it is granted to understand the sacred secrets of the kingdom of the heavens, but to those people it is not granted. 12 For whoever has, more will be given him and he will be made to abound; but whoever does not have, even what he has will be taken from him. 13 This is why I speak to them by the use of illustrations, because, looking, they look in vain, and hearing, they hear in vain, neither do they get the sense of it; 14 and toward them the prophecy of Isaiah is having fulfillment, which says, 'By hearing, YOU will hear but by no means get the sense of it; and, looking, YOU will look but by no means see. 15 For the heart of this people has grown thick, and with their ears they have heard with annoyance, and they have shut their eyes; that they might never see with their eyes and hear with their ears and get the sense of it with their hearts and turn back, and I heal them.'

16 "However, happy are YOUR eyes because they behold, and YOUR ears because they hear. 17 For I truly say to YOU, Many prophets and righteous men desired to see the things YOU are beholding and did not see them, and to hear the things YOU are hearing and did not hear them.

18 "YOU, then, listen to the illustration of the man that sowed. 19 Where anyone hears the word of the kingdom but does not get the sense of it, the wicked one comes and snatches away what has been sown in his heart; this is the one sown alongside the road. 20 As for the one sown upon the rocky places, this is the one hearing the word and at once accepting it with joy. 21 Yet he has no root in himself but continues for a time, and after tribulation or persecution has arisen on account of the word

he is at once stumbled. 22 As for the one sown among the thorns, this is the one hearing the word, but the anxiety of this system of things and the deceptive power of riches choke the word, and he becomes unfruitful. 23 As for the one sown upon the fine soil, this is the one hearing the word and getting the sense of it, who really does bear fruit and produces, this one a hundredfold, that one sixty, the other thirty."

24 Another illustration he set before them, saying: "The kingdom of the heavens has become like a man that sowed fine seed in his field. 25 While men were sleeping, his enemy came and oversowed weeds in among the wheat, and left. 26 When the blade sprouted and produced fruit, then the weeds appeared also. 27 So the slaves of the householder came up and said to him, 'Master, did you not sow fine seed in your field? How, then, does it come to have weeds?' 28 He said to them, 'An enemy, a man, did this.' They said to him, 'Do you want us, then, to go out and collect them?' 29 He said, 'No; that by no chance, while collecting the weeds, YOU uproot the wheat with them. 30 Let both grow together until the harvest; and in the harvest season I will tell the reapers, First collect the weeds and bind them in bundles to burn them up, then go to gathering the wheat into my storehouse.'"

31 Another illustration he set before them, saying: "The kingdom of the heavens is like a mustard grain, which a man took and planted in his field; 32 which is, in fact, the tiniest of all the seeds, but when it has grown it is the largest of the vegetables and becomes a tree, so that the birds of heaven come and find lodging among its branches."

33 Another illustration he spoke to them: "The kingdom of the heavens is like leaven, which a woman took and hid in three large measures of flour, until the whole mass was fermented."

34 All these things Jesus spoke

to the crowds by illustrations. Indeed, without an illustration he would not speak to them; 35 that there might be fulfilled what was spoken through the prophet who said: "I will open my mouth with illustrations, I will publish things hidden since the founding."

36 Then after dismissing the crowds he went into the house. And his disciples came to him and said: "Explain to us the illustration of the weeds in the field." 37 In response he said: "The sower of the fine seed is the Son of man; 38 the field is the world; as for the fine seed, these are the sons of the kingdom; but the weeds are the sons of the wicked one, 39 and the enemy that sowed them is the Devil. The harvest is a conclusion of a system of things, and the reapers are angels. 40 Therefore, just as the weeds are collected and burned with fire, so it will be in the conclusion of the system of things. 41 The Son of man will send forth his angels, and they will collect out from his kingdom all things that cause stumbling and persons who are doing lawlessness, 42 and they will pitch them into the fiery furnace. There is where [their] weeping and the gnashing of [their] teeth will be. 43 At that time the righteous ones will shine as brightly as the sun in the kingdom of their Father. Let him that has ears listen.

44 "The kingdom of the heavens is like a treasure hidden in the field, which a man found and hid; and for the joy he has he goes and sells what things he has and buys that field.

45 "Again the kingdom of the heavens is like a traveling merchant seeking fine pearls. 46 Upon finding one pearl of high value, away he went and promptly sold all the things he had and bought it.

47 "Again the kingdom of the heavens is like a dragnet let down into the sea and gathering up [fish] of every kind. 48 When it got full they hauled it up onto the beach and, sitting down, they collected the fine ones into vessels, but the unsuitable they threw away. 49 That is how it will be in the conclusion of the system of things: the angels will go out and separate the wicked from among the righteous 50 and will cast them into the fiery furnace. There is where [their] weeping and the gnashing of [their] teeth will be.

51 "Did you get the sense of all these things?" They said to him: "Yes." 52 Then he said to them: "That being the case, every public instructor, when taught respecting the kingdom of the heavens, is like a man, a householder, who brings out of his treasure store things new and old."

53 Now when Jesus had finished these illustrations he went across country from there. 54 And after coming into his home territory he began to teach them in their synagogue, so that they were astounded and said: "Where did this man get this wisdom and these powerful works? 55 Is this not the carpenter's son? Is not his mother called Mary, and his brothers James and Joseph and Simon and Judas? 56 And his sisters, are they not all with us? Where, then, did this man get all these things?" 57 So they began to stumble at him. But Jesus said to them: "A prophet is not unhonored except in his home territory and in his own house." 58 And he did not do many powerful works there on account of their lack of faith.

14 At that particular time Herod, the district ruler, heard the report about Jesus 2 and said to his servants: "This is John the Baptist. He was raised up from the dead, and this is why the powerful works are operating in him." 3 For Herod had arrested John and bound him and put him away in prison on account of He·ro'di·as the wife of Philip his brother. 4 For John had been saying to him: "It is not lawful for you to be having her." 5 However, although he wanted to kill him, he feared the crowd, because they took him for a prophet. 6 But when Herod's birthday was being celebrated the

daughter of He·ro′di·as danced at it and pleased Herod so much 7 that he promised with an oath to give her whatever she asked. 8 Then she, under her mother's coaching, said: "Give me here upon a platter the head of John the Baptist." 9 Grieved though he was, the king out of regard for his oaths and for those reclining with him commanded it to be given; 10 and he sent and had John beheaded in the prison. 11 And his head was brought on a platter and given to the maiden, and she brought it to her mother. 12 Finally his disciples came up and removed the corpse and buried him and came and reported to Jesus. 13 At hearing this Jesus withdrew from there by boat into a lonely place for isolation; but the crowds, getting to hear of it, followed him on foot from the cities.

14 Now when he came forth he saw a great crowd; and he felt pity for them, and he cured their sick ones. 15 But when evening fell his disciples came to him and said: "The place is lonely and the hour is already far advanced; send the crowds away, that they may go into the villages and buy themselves things to eat." 16 However, Jesus said to them: "They do not have to leave; YOU give them something to eat." 17 They said to him: "We have nothing here but five loaves and two fishes." 18 He said: "BRING them here to me." 19 Next he commanded the crowds to recline on the grass and took the five loaves and two fishes and, looking up to heaven, he said a blessing and, after breaking the loaves, he distributed them to the disciples, the disciples in turn to the crowds. 20 So all ate and were satisfied, and they took up the surplus of fragments, twelve baskets full. 21 Yet those eating were about five thousand men, besides women and young children. 22 Then, without delay, he compelled his disciples to board the boat and go ahead of him to the other side, while he sent the crowds away.

23 Eventually, having sent the crowds away, he went up into the mountain by himself to pray. Though it became late, he was there alone. 24 By now the boat was many hundreds of yards away from land, being hard put to it by the waves, because the wind was against them. 25 But in the fourth watch period of the night he came to them, walking over the sea. 26 When they caught sight of him walking on the sea, the disciples were troubled, saying: "It is an apparition!" And they cried out in their fear. 27 At once Jesus spoke to them with the words: "Take courage, it is I; have no fear." 28 In reply Peter said to him: "Lord, if it is you, command me to come to you over the waters." 29 He said: "Come!" Thereupon Peter, getting down off the boat, walked over the waters and went toward Jesus. 30 But looking at the windstorm, he got afraid and, after starting to sink, he cried out: "Lord, save me!" 31 Immediately stretching out his hand Jesus caught hold of him and said to him: "You with little faith, why did you give way to doubt?" 32 And after they got up into the boat, the windstorm abated. 33 Then those in the boat did obeisance to him, saying: "You are really God's Son." 34 And they got across and came to land in Gen·nes′a·ret.

35 Upon recognizing him the men of that place sent forth into all that surrounding country, and people brought him all those who were ill. 36 And they went entreating him that they might just touch the fringe of his outer garment; and all those who touched it were made completely well.

15 Then there came to Jesus from Jerusalem Pharisees and scribes, saying: 2 "Why is it your disciples overstep the tradition of the men of former times? For example, they do not wash their hands when about to eat a meal."

3 In reply he said to them: "Why is it YOU also overstep the commandment of God because of

YOUR tradition? 4 For example, God said, 'Honor your father and your mother'; and, 'Let him that reviles father or mother end up in death.' 5 But you say, 'Whoever says to his father or mother: "Whatever I have by which you might get benefit from me is a gift dedicated to God," 6 he must not honor his father at all.' And so YOU have made the word of God invalid because of YOUR tradition. 7 You hypocrites, Isaiah aptly prophesied about YOU, when he said, 8 'This people honors me with their lips, yet their heart is far removed from me. 9 It is in vain that they keep worshiping me, because they teach commands of men as doctrines.'" 10 With that he called the crowd near and said to them: "Listen and get the sense of it: 11 Not what enters into [his] mouth defiles a man; but it is what proceeds out of [his] mouth that defiles a man."

12 Then the disciples came up and said to him: "Do you know that the Pharisees stumbled at hearing what you said?" 13 In reply he said: "Every plant that my heavenly Father did not plant will be uprooted. 14 LET them be. Blind guides is what they are. If, then, a blind man guides a blind man, both will fall into a pit." 15 By way of response Peter said to him: "Make the illustration plain to us." 16 At this he said: "Are YOU also yet without understanding? 17 Are YOU not aware that everything entering into the mouth passes along into the intestines and is discharged into the sewer? 18 However, the things proceeding out of the mouth come out of the heart, and those things defile a man. 19 For example, out of the heart come wicked reasonings, murders, adulteries, fornications, thieveries, false testimonies, blasphemies. 20 These are the things defiling a man; but to take a meal with unwashed hands does not defile a man."

21 Leaving there, Jesus now withdrew into the parts of Tyre and Si'don. 22 And, look! a Phoeni'cian woman from those regions came out and cried aloud, saying: "Have mercy on me, Lord, Son of David. My daughter is badly demonized." 23 But he did not say a word in answer to her. So his disciples came up and began to request him: "Send her away; because she keeps crying out after us." 24 In answer he said: "I was not sent forth to any but to the lost sheep of the house of Israel." 25 When the woman came she began doing obeisance to him, saying: "Lord, help me!" 26 In answer he said: "It is not right to take the bread of the children and throw it to little dogs." 27 She said: "Yes, Lord; but really the little dogs do eat of the crumbs falling from the table of their masters." 28 Then Jesus said in reply to her: "O woman, great is your faith; let it happen to you as you wish." And her daughter was healed from that hour on.

29 Crossing country from there, Jesus next came near the sea of Gal'i·lee, and, after going up into the mountain, he was sitting there. 30 Then great crowds approached him, having along with them people that were lame, maimed, blind, dumb, and many otherwise, and they fairly threw them at his feet, and he cured them; 31 so that the crowd felt amazement as they saw the dumb speaking and the lame walking and the blind seeing, and they glorified the God of Israel.

32 But Jesus called his disciples to him and said: "I feel pity for the crowd, because it is already three days that they have stayed with me and they have nothing to eat; and I do not want to send them away fasting. They may possibly give out on the road." 33 However, the disciples said to him: "Where are we in this lonely place going to get sufficient loaves to satisfy a crowd of this size?" 34 At this Jesus said to them: "How many loaves have YOU?" They said: "Seven, and a few little fishes." 35 So, after instructing the crowd to recline upon the ground, 36 he took the seven loaves and the fishes and, after

offering thanks, he broke them and began distributing to the disciples, the disciples in turn to the crowds. 37 And all ate and were satisfied, and as a surplus of fragments they took up seven provision baskets full. 38 Yet those eating were four thousand men, besides women and young children. 39 Finally, after sending the crowds away, he got into the boat and came into the regions of Mag'a·dan.

16 Here the Pharisees and Sadducees approached him and, to tempt him, they asked him to display to them a sign from heaven. 2 In reply he said to them: [["When evening falls you are accustomed to say, 'It will be fair weather, for the sky is fire-red'; 3 and at morning, 'It will be wintry, rainy weather today, for the sky is fire-red, but gloomy-looking.' You know how to interpret the appearance of the sky, but the signs of the times you cannot interpret.]] 4 A wicked and adulterous generation keeps on seeking for a sign, but no sign will be given it except the sign of Jo'nah." With that he went away, leaving them behind.

5 Now the disciples crossed to the other side and forgot to take loaves along. 6 Jesus said to them: "Keep your eyes open and watch out for the leaven of the Pharisees and Sadducees." 7 So they began to reason among themselves, saying: "We did not take any loaves along." 8 Knowing this, Jesus said: "Why are you doing this reasoning among yourselves, because you have no loaves, you with little faith? 9 Do you not yet see the point, or do you not remember the five loaves in the case of the five thousand and how many baskets you took up? 10 Or the seven loaves in the case of the four thousand and how many provision baskets you took up? 11 How is it you do not discern that I did not talk to you about loaves? But watch out for the leaven of the Pharisees and Sadducees." 12 Then they grasped that he said

to watch out, not for the leaven of the loaves, but for the teaching of the Pharisees and Sadducees.

13 Now when he had come into the parts of Caes·a·re'a Phi·lip'pi, Jesus went asking his disciples: "Who are men saying the Son of man is?" 14 They said: "Some say John the Baptist, others E·li'jah, still others Jeremiah or one of the prophets." 15 He said to them: "You, though, who do you say I am?" 16 In answer Simon Peter said: "You are the Christ, the Son of the living God." 17 In response Jesus said to him: "Happy you are, Simon son of Jo'nah, because flesh and blood did not reveal [it] to you, but my Father who is in the heavens did. 18 Also, I say to you, You are Peter, and on this rock-mass I will build my congregation, and the gates of Ha'des will not overpower it. 19 I will give you the keys of the kingdom of the heavens, and whatever you may bind on earth will be the thing bound in the heavens, and whatever you may loose on earth will be the thing loosed in the heavens." 20 Then he sternly charged the disciples not to say to anybody that he was the Christ.

21 From that time forward Jesus Christ commenced showing his disciples that he must go to Jerusalem and suffer many things from the older men and chief priests and scribes, and be killed, and on the third day be raised up. 22 At this Peter took him aside and commenced rebuking him, saying: "Be kind to yourself, Lord; you will not have this [destiny] at all." 23 But, turning his back, he said to Peter: "Get behind me, Satan! You are a stumbling block to me, because you think, not God's thoughts, but those of men."

24 Then Jesus said to his disciples: "If anyone wants to come after me, let him disown himself and pick up his torture stake and continually follow me. 25 For whoever wants to save his soul will lose it; but whoever loses his soul for my sake will find it. 26 For what benefit will it be to a man

if he gains the whole world but forfeits his soul? or what will a man give in exchange for his soul? 27 For the Son of man is destined to come in the glory of his Father with his angels, and then he will recompense each one according to his behavior. 28 Truly I say to you that there are some of those standing here that will not taste death at all until first they see the Son of man coming in his kingdom."

17 Six days later Jesus took Peter and James and John his brother along and brought them up into a lofty mountain by themselves. 2 And he was transfigured before them, and his face shone as the sun, and his outer garments became brilliant as the light. 3 And, look! there appeared to them Moses and E·li′jah, conversing with him. 4 Responsively Peter said to Jesus: "Lord, it is fine for us to be here. If you wish, I will erect three tents here, one for you and one for Moses and one for E·li′jah." 5 While he was yet speaking, look! a bright cloud overshadowed them, and, look! a voice out of the cloud, saying: "This is my Son, the beloved, whom I have approved; listen to him." 6 At hearing this the disciples fell upon their faces and became very much afraid. 7 Then Jesus came near and, touching them, said: "Get up and have no fear." 8 When they raised their eyes, they saw no one but Jesus himself only. 9 And as they were descending from the mountain, Jesus commanded them, saying: "Tell the vision to no one until the Son of man is raised up from the dead."

10 However, the disciples put the question to him: "Why, then, do the scribes say that E·li′jah must come first?" 11 In reply he said: "E·li′jah, indeed, is coming and will restore all things. 12 However, I say to you that E·li′jah has already come and they did not recognize him but did with him the things they wanted. In this way also the Son of man is destined to suffer at their hands." 13 Then the disciples perceived that he

spoke to them about John the Baptist.

14 And when they came toward the crowd, a man approached him, kneeling down to him and saying: 15 "Lord, have mercy on my son, because he is an epileptic and is ill, for he falls often into the fire and often into the water; 16 and I brought him to your disciples, but they could not cure him." 17 In reply Jesus said: "O faithless and twisted generation, how long must I continue with you? How long must I put up with you? Bring him here to me." 18 Then Jesus rebuked it, and the demon came out of him; and the boy was cured from that hour. 19 Thereupon the disciples came up to Jesus privately and said: "Why is it we could not expel it?" 20 He said to them: "Because of your little faith. For truly I say to you, If you have faith the size of a mustard grain, you will say to this mountain, 'Transfer from here to there,' and it will transfer, and nothing will be impossible for you." 21 ——

22 It was while they were gathered together in Gal′i·lee that Jesus said to them: "The Son of man is destined to be betrayed into men's hands, 23 and they will kill him, and the third day he will be raised up." Consequently they were very much grieved.

24 After they arrived in Ca·per′na·um the men collecting the two drachmas [tax] approached Peter and said: "Does your teacher not pay the two drachmas [tax]?" 25 He said: "Yes." However, when he entered the house Jesus got ahead of him by saying: "What do you think, Simon? From whom do the kings of the earth receive duties or head tax? From their sons or from the strangers?" 26 When he said: "From the strangers," Jesus said to him: "Really, then, the sons are tax-free. 27 But that we do not cause them to stumble, you go to the sea, cast a fishhook, and take the first fish coming up and, when you open its mouth, you will find a stater coin. Take that

and give it to them for me and you."

18 In that hour the disciples came near to Jesus and said: "Who really is greatest in the kingdom of the heavens?" 2 So, calling a young child to him, he set it in their midst 3 and said: "Truly I say to YOU, Unless YOU turn around and become as young children, YOU will by no means enter into the kingdom of the heavens. 4 Therefore, whoever will humble himself like this young child is the one that is the greatest in the kingdom of the heavens; 5 and whoever receives one such young child on the basis of my name receives me [also]. 6 But whoever stumbles one of these little ones who put faith in me, it is more beneficial for him to have hung around his neck a millstone such as is turned by an ass and to be sunk in the wide, open sea.

7 "Woe to the world due to the stumbling blocks! Of course, the stumbling blocks must of necessity come, but woe to the man through whom the stumbling block comes! 8 If, then, your hand or your foot is making you stumble, cut it off and throw it away from you; it is finer for you to enter into life maimed or lame than to be thrown with two hands or two feet into the everlasting fire. 9 Also, if your eye is making you stumble, tear it out and throw it away from you; it is finer for you to enter one-eyed into life than to be thrown with two eyes into the fiery Ge·hen′na. 10 See to it that YOU men do not despise one of these little ones; for I tell YOU that their angels in heaven always behold the face of my Father who is in heaven. 11 ——

12 "What do YOU think? If a certain man comes to have a hundred sheep and one of them gets strayed, will he not leave the ninety-nine upon the mountains and set out on a search for the one that is straying? 13 And if he happens to find it, I certainly tell YOU, he rejoices more over it than over the ninety-nine that have not

strayed. 14 Likewise it is not a desirable thing with my Father who is in heaven for one of these little ones to perish.

15 "Moreover, if your brother commits a sin, go lay bare his fault between you and him alone. If he listens to you, you have gained your brother. 16 But if he does not listen, take along with you one or two more, in order that at the mouth of two or three witnesses every matter may be established. 17 If he does not listen to them, speak to the congregation. If he does not listen even to the congregation, let him be to you just as a man of the nations and as a tax collector.

18 "Truly I say to YOU men, Whatever things YOU may bind on earth will be things bound in heaven, and whatever things YOU may loose on earth will be things loosed in heaven. 19 Again I truly say to YOU, If two of YOU on earth agree concerning anything of importance that they should request, it will take place for them due to my Father in heaven. 20 For where there are two or three gathered together in my name, there I am in their midst."

21 Then Peter came up and said to him: "Lord, how many times is my brother to sin against me and am I to forgive him? Up to seven times?" 22 Jesus said to him: "I say to you, not, Up to seven times, but, Up to seventy-seven times.

23 "That is why the kingdom of the heavens has become like a man, a king, that wanted to settle accounts with his slaves. 24 When he started to settle them, there was brought in a man who owed him ten thousand talents [=60,-000,000 de·nar′i·i]. 25 But because he did not have the means to pay [it] back, his master ordered him and his wife and his children and all the things he had to be sold and payment to be made. 26 Therefore the slave fell down and began to do obeisance to him, saying, 'Be patient with me and I will pay back everything to you.' 27 Moved to pity at this, the master of that

slave let him off and canceled his debt. 28 But that slave went out and found one of his fellow slaves that was owing him a hundred de·nar′i·i; and, grabbing him, he began to choke him, saying, ‘Pay back whatever you owe.’ 29 Therefore his fellow slave fell down and began to entreat him, saying, ‘Be patient with me and I will pay you back.’ 30 However, he was not willing, but went off and had him thrown into prison until he should pay back what was owing. 31 When, therefore, his fellow slaves saw the things that had happened, they became very much grieved, and they went and made clear to their master all the things that had happened. 32 Then his master summoned him and said to him, ‘Wicked slave, I canceled all that debt for you, when you entreated me. 33 Ought you not, in turn, to have had mercy on your fellow slave, as I also had mercy on you?’ 34 With that his master, provoked to wrath, delivered him to the jailers, until he should pay back all that was owing. 35 In like manner my heavenly Father will also deal with YOU if YOU do not forgive each one his brother from YOUR hearts.”

19 Now when Jesus had finished these words, he departed from Gal′i·lee and came to the frontiers of Ju·de′a across the Jordan. 2 Also, great crowds followed him, and he cured them there.

3 And Pharisees came up to him, intent on tempting him and saying: “Is it lawful for a man to divorce his wife on every sort of ground?” 4 In reply he said: “Did YOU not read that he who created them from [the] beginning made them male and female 5 and said, ‘For this reason a man will leave his father and his mother and will stick to his wife, and the two will be one flesh’? 6 So that they are no longer two, but one flesh. Therefore, what God has yoked together let no man put apart.” 7 They said to him: “Why, then, did Moses prescribe giving a certificate of dismissal and divorcing her?” 8 He

said to them: “Moses, out of regard for YOUR hardheartedness, made the concession to YOU of divorcing YOUR wives, but such has not been the case from [the] beginning. 9 I say to YOU that whoever divorces his wife, except on the ground of fornication, and marries another commits adultery.”

10 The disciples said to him: “If such is the situation of a man with his wife, it is not advisable to marry.” 11 He said to them: “Not all men make room for the saying, but only those who have the gift. 12 For there are eunuchs that were born such from their mother’s womb, and there are eunuchs that were made eunuchs by men, and there are eunuchs that have made themselves eunuchs on account of the kingdom of the heavens. Let him that can make room for it make room for it.”

13 Then young children were brought to him, for him to put his hands upon them and offer prayer; but the disciples reprimanded them. 14 Jesus, however, said: “Let the young children alone, and stop hindering them from coming to me, for the kingdom of the heavens belongs to suchlike ones.” 15 And he put his hands upon them and went from there.

16 Now, look! a certain one came up to him and said: “Teacher, what good must I do in order to get everlasting life?” 17 He said to him: “Why do you ask me about what is good? One there is that is good. If, though, you want to enter into life, observe the commandments continually.” 18 He said to him: “Which ones?” Jesus said: “Why, You must not murder, You must not commit adultery, You must not steal, You must not bear false witness, 19 Honor [your] father and [your] mother, and, You must love your neighbor as yourself.” 20 The young man said to him: “I have kept all these; what yet am I lacking?” 21 Jesus said to him: “If you want to be perfect, go sell your belongings and give to the poor and you will have treasure in heaven, and come be

my follower." 22 When the young man heard this saying, he went away grieved, for he was holding many possessions. 23 But Jesus said to his disciples: "Truly I say to YOU that it will be a difficult thing for a rich man to get into the kingdom of the heavens. 24 Again I say to YOU, It is easier for a camel to get through a needle's eye than for a rich man to get into the kingdom of God."

25 When the disciples heard that, they expressed very great surprise, saying: "Who really can be saved?" 26 Looking them in the face, Jesus said to them: "With men this is impossible, but with God all things are possible."

27 Then Peter said to him in reply: "Look! We have left all things and followed you; what actually will there be for us?" 28 Jesus said to them: "Truly I say to YOU, In the re-creation, when the Son of man sits down upon his glorious throne, YOU who have followed me will also yourselves sit upon twelve thrones, judging the twelve tribes of Israel. 29 And everyone that has left houses or brothers or sisters or father or mother or children or lands for the sake of my name will receive many times more and will inherit everlasting life.

30 "But many that are first will be last and the last first.

20 "For the kingdom of the heavens is like a man, a householder, who went out early in the morning to hire workers for his vineyard. 2 When he had agreed with the workers for a de·nar′i·us a day, he sent them forth into his vineyard. 3 Going out also about the third hour, he saw others standing unemployed in the market place; 4 and to those he said, 'YOU also, go into the vineyard, and whatever is just I will give YOU.' 5 So off they went. Again he went out about the sixth and the ninth hour and did likewise. 6 Finally, about the eleventh hour he went out and found others standing, and he said to them, 'Why have YOU been standing here all day unem-

ployed?' 7 They said to him, 'Because nobody has hired us.' He said to them, 'YOU too go into the vineyard.'

8 "When it became evening, the master of the vineyard said to his man in charge, 'Call the workers and pay them their wages, proceeding from the last to the first.' 9 When the eleventh-hour men came, they each received a de·nar′-i·us. 10 So, when the first came, they concluded they would receive more; but they also received pay at the rate of a de·nar′i·us. 11 On receiving it they began to murmur against the householder 12 and said, 'These last put in one hour's work; still you made them equal to us who bore the burden of the day and the burning heat!' 13 But in reply to one of them he said, 'Fellow, I do you no wrong. You agreed with me for a de·nar′i·us, did you not? 14 Take what is yours and go. I want to give to this last one the same as to you. 15 Is it not lawful for me to do what I want with my own things? Or is your eye wicked because I am good?' 16 In this way the last ones will be first, and the first ones last."

17 Being now about to go up to Jerusalem, Jesus took the twelve disciples off privately and said to them on the road: 18 "Look! We are going up to Jerusalem, and the Son of man will be delivered up to the chief priests and scribes, and they will condemn him to death, 19 and will deliver him up to [men of] the nations to make fun of and to scourge and to impale, and the third day he will be raised up."

20 Then the mother of the sons of Zeb′e·dee approached him with her sons, doing obeisance and asking for something from him. 21 He said to her: "What do you want?" She said to him: "Give the word that these my two sons may sit down, one at your right hand and one at your left, in your kingdom." 22 Jesus said in answer: "YOU men do not know what YOU are asking for. Can YOU drink the cup that I am about to drink?" They

said to him: "We can." 23 He said to them: "You will indeed drink my cup, but this sitting down at my right hand and at my left is not mine to give, but it belongs to those for whom it has been prepared by my Father."

24 When the ten others heard of this, they became indignant at the two brothers. 25 But Jesus, calling them to him, said: "You know that the rulers of the nations lord it over them and the great men wield authority over them. 26 This is not the way among you; but whoever wants to become great among you must be your minister, 27 and whoever wants to be first among you must be your slave. 28 Just as the Son of man came, not to be ministered to, but to minister and to give his soul a ransom in exchange for many."

29 Now as they were going out of Jer'i·cho a great crowd followed him. 30 And, look! two blind men sitting beside the road, when they heard that Jesus was passing by, cried out, saying: "Lord, have mercy on us, Son of David!" 31 But the crowd sternly told them to keep silent; yet they cried all the louder, saying: "Lord, have mercy on us, Son of David!" 32 So Jesus stopped, called them and said: "What do you want me to do for you?" 33 They said to him: "Lord, let our eyes be opened." 34 Moved with pity, Jesus touched their eyes, and immediately they received sight, and they followed him.

21 Well, when they got close to Jerusalem and arrived at Beth'pha·ge on the Mount of Olives, then Jesus sent forth two disciples, 2 saying to them: "Be on your way into the village that is within sight of you, and you will at once find an ass tied, and a colt with her; untie them and bring them to me. 3 And if someone says anything to you, you must say, 'The Lord needs them.' At that he will immediately send them forth."

4 This actually took place that there might be fulfilled what was spoken through the prophet, saying:

5 "Tell the daughter of Zion, 'Look! Your King is coming to you, mild-tempered, and mounted upon an ass, yes, upon a colt, the offspring of a beast of burden.' "

6 So the disciples got on their way and did just as Jesus ordered them. 7 And they brought the ass and its colt, and they put upon these their outer garments, and he seated himself upon them. 8 Most of the crowd spread their outer garments on the road, while others began cutting down branches from the trees and spreading them on the road. 9 As for the crowds, those going ahead of him and those following kept crying out: "Save, we pray, the Son of David! Blessed is he that comes in Jehovah's name! Save him, we pray, in the heights above!"

10 Now when he entered into Jerusalem, the whole city was set in commotion, saying: "Who is this?" 11 The crowds kept telling: "This is the prophet Jesus, from Naz'a·reth of Gal'i·lee!"

12 And Jesus entered into the temple and threw out all those selling and buying in the temple, and overturned the tables of the money-changers and the benches of those selling doves. 13 And he said to them: "It is written, 'My house will be called a house of prayer,' but you are making it a cave of robbers." 14 Also, blind and lame persons came up to him in the temple, and he cured them.

15 When the chief priests and the scribes saw the marvelous things he did and the boys that were crying out in the temple and saying: "Save, we pray, the Son of David!" they became indignant 16 and said to him: "Do you hear what these are saying?" Jesus said to them: "Yes. Did you never read this, 'Out of the mouth of babes and sucklings you have furnished praise'?" 17 And leaving them behind he went outside the city to Beth'a·ny and passed the night there.

18 While returning to the city early in the morning, he got hungry. 19 And he caught sight of a fig

tree by the road and went to it, but he found nothing on it except leaves only, and he said to it: "Let no fruit come from you any more forever." And the fig tree withered instantly. 20 But when the disciples saw this, they wondered, saying: "How is it that the fig tree withered instantly?" 21 In answer Jesus said to them: "Truly I say to YOU, If only YOU have faith and do not doubt, not only will YOU do what I did to the fig tree, but also if YOU say to this mountain, 'Be lifted up and cast into the sea,' it will happen. 22 And all the things YOU ask in prayer, having faith, YOU will receive."

23 Now after he went into the temple, the chief priests and the older men of the people came up to him while he was teaching and said: "By what authority do you do these things? And who gave you this authority?" 24 In reply Jesus said to them: "I, also, will ask YOU one thing. If YOU tell it to me, I also will tell YOU by what authority I do these things: 25 The baptism by John, from what source was it? From heaven or from men?" But they began to reason among themselves, saying: "If we say, 'From heaven,' he will say to us, 'Why, then, did YOU not believe him?' 26 If, though, we say, 'From men,' we have the crowd to fear, for they all hold John as a prophet." 27 So in answer to Jesus they said: "We do not know." He, in turn, said to them: "Neither am I telling YOU by what authority I do these things.

28 "What do YOU think? A man had two children. Going up to the first, he said, 'Child, go work today in the vineyard.' 29 In answer this one said, 'I will, sir,' but did not go out. 30 Approaching the second, he said the same. In reply this one said, 'I will not.' Afterwards he felt regret and went out. 31 Which of the two did the will of [his] father?" They said: "The latter." Jesus said to them: "Truly I say to YOU that the tax collectors and the harlots are going ahead of YOU into the kingdom of God.

32 For John came to YOU in a way of righteousness, but YOU did not believe him. However, the tax collectors and the harlots believed him, and YOU, although YOU saw [this], did not feel regret afterwards so as to believe him.

33 "Hear another illustration: There was a man, a householder, who planted a vineyard and put a fence around it and dug a wine press in it and erected a tower, and let it out to cultivators, and traveled abroad. 34 When the season of the fruits came around, he dispatched his slaves to the cultivators to get his fruits. 35 However, the cultivators took his slaves, and one they beat up, another they killed, another they stoned. 36 Again he dispatched other slaves, more than the first, but they did the same to these. 37 Lastly he dispatched his son to them, saying, 'They will respect my son.' 38 On seeing the son the cultivators said among themselves, 'This is the heir; come, let us kill him and get his inheritance!' 39 So they took him and threw him out of the vineyard and killed him. 40 Therefore, when the owner of the vineyard comes, what will he do to those cultivators?" 41 They said to him: "Because they are evil, he will bring an evil destruction upon them and will let out the vineyard to other cultivators, who will render him the fruits when they become due."

42 Jesus said to them: "Did YOU never read in the Scriptures, 'The stone that the builders rejected is the one that has become the chief cornerstone. From Jehovah this has come to be, and it is marvelous in our eyes'? 43 This is why I say to YOU, The kingdom of God will be taken from YOU and be given to a nation producing its fruits. 44 Also, the person falling upon this stone will be shattered. As for anyone upon whom it falls, it will pulverize him."

45 Now when the chief priests and the Pharisees had heard his illustrations, they took note that he was speaking about them. 46 But,

although they were seeking to seize him, they feared the crowds, because these held him to be a prophet.

22 In further reply Jesus again spoke to them with illustrations, saying: 2 "The kingdom of the heavens has become like a man, a king, that made a marriage feast for his son. 3 And he sent forth his slaves to call those invited to the marriage feast, but they were unwilling to come. 4 Again he sent forth other slaves, saying, 'Tell those invited: "Look! I have prepared my dinner, my bulls and fattened animals are slaughtered, and all things are ready. Come to the marriage feast."' 5 But unconcerned they went off, one to his own field, another to his commercial business; 6 but the rest, laying hold of his slaves, treated them insolently and killed them. 7 "But the king grew wrathful, and sent his armies and destroyed those murderers and burned their city. 8 Then he said to his slaves, 'The marriage feast indeed is ready, but those invited were not worthy. 9 Therefore go to the roads leading out of the city, and anyone you find invite to the marriage feast.' 10 Accordingly those slaves went out to the roads and gathered together all they found, both wicked and good; and the room for the wedding ceremonies was filled with those reclining at the table.

11 "When the king came in to inspect the guests he caught sight there of a man not clothed with a marriage garment. 12 So he said to him, 'Fellow, how did you get in here not having on a marriage garment?' He was rendered speechless. 13 Then the king said to his servants, 'Bind him hand and foot and throw him out into the darkness outside. There is where [his] weeping and the gnashing of [his] teeth will be.'

14 "For there are many invited, but few chosen."

15 Then the Pharisees went their way and took counsel together in order to trap him in his speech. 16 So they dispatched to him their disciples, together with party followers of Herod, saying: "Teacher, we know you are truthful and teach the way of God in truth, and you do not care for anybody, for you do not look upon men's outward appearance. 17 Tell us, therefore, What do you think? Is it lawful to pay head tax to Caesar or not?" 18 But Jesus, knowing their wickedness, said: "Why do you put me to the test, hypocrites? 19 Show me the head tax coin." They brought him a de·nar′i·us. 20 And he said to them: "Whose image and inscription is this?" 21 They said: "Caesar's." Then he said to them: "Pay back, therefore, Caesar's things to Caesar, but God's things to God." 22 Well, when they heard [that], they marveled, and leaving him they went off.

23 On that day Sadducees, who say there is no resurrection, came up to him and asked him: 24 "Teacher, Moses said, 'If any man dies without having children, his brother must take his wife in marriage and raise up offspring for his brother.' 25 Now there were seven brothers with us; and the first married and deceased, and, not having offspring, he left his wife for his brother. 26 It went the same way also with the second and the third, until through all seven, 27 Last of all the woman died. 28 Consequently, in the resurrection, to which of the seven will she be wife? For they all got her."

29 In reply Jesus said to them: "You are mistaken, because you know neither the Scriptures nor the power of God; 30 for in the resurrection neither do men marry nor are women given in marriage, but are as angels in heaven. 31 As regards the resurrection of the dead, did you not read what was spoken to you by God, saying, 32 'I am the God of Abraham and the God of Isaac and the God of Jacob'? He is the God, not of the dead, but of the living." 33 On hearing [that], the crowds were astounded at his teaching.

34 After the Pharisees heard that he had put the Sadducees to silence,

they came together in one group. 35 And one of them, versed in the Law, asked, testing him: 36 "Teacher, which is the greatest commandment in the Law?" 37 He said to him: "'You must love Jehovah your God with your whole heart and with your whole soul and with your whole mind.' 38 This is the greatest and first commandment. 39 The second, like it, is this, 'You must love your neighbor as yourself.' 40 On these two commandments the whole Law hangs, and the Prophets."

41 Now while the Pharisees were gathered together Jesus asked them: 42 "What do you think about the Christ? Whose son is he?" They said to him: "David's." 43 He said to them: "How, then, is it that David by inspiration calls him 'Lord,' saying, 44 'Jehovah said to my Lord: "Sit at my right hand until I put your enemies beneath your feet"'? 45 If, therefore, David calls him 'Lord,' how is he his son?" 46 And nobody was able to say a word in reply to him, nor did anyone dare from that day on to question him any further.

23 Then Jesus spoke to the crowds and to his disciples, saying: 2 "The scribes and the Pharisees have seated themselves in the seat of Moses. 3 Therefore all the things they tell you, do and observe, but do not do according to their deeds, for they say but do not perform. 4 They bind up heavy loads and put them upon the shoulders of men, but they themselves are not willing to budge them with their finger. 5 All the works they do they do to be viewed by men; for they broaden the [scripture-containing] cases that they wear as safeguards, and enlarge the fringes of their garments. 6 They like the most prominent place at evening meals and the front seats in the synagogues, 7 and the greetings in the market places and to be called Rabbi by men. 8 But you, do not you be called Rabbi, for one is your teacher, whereas all you are broth-ers. 9 Moreover, do not call anyone your father on earth, for one is your Father, the heavenly One. 10 Neither be called 'leaders,' for your Leader is one, the Christ. 11 But the greatest one among you must be your minister. 12 Whoever exalts himself will be humbled, and whoever humbles himself will be exalted.

13 "Woe to you, scribes and Pharisees, hypocrites! because you shut up the kingdom of the heavens before men; for you yourselves do not go in, neither do you permit those on their way in to go in. 14 ——

15 "Woe to you, scribes and Pharisees, hypocrites! because you traverse sea and dry land to make one proselyte, and when he becomes one you make him a subject for Ge·hen'na twice as much so as yourselves.

16 "Woe to you, blind guides, who say, 'If anyone swears by the temple, it is nothing; but if anyone swears by the gold of the temple, he is under obligation.' 17 Fools and blind ones! Which, in fact, is greater, the gold or the temple that has sanctified the gold? 18 Also, 'If anyone swears by the altar, it is nothing; but if anyone swears by the gift on it, he is under obligation.' 19 Blind ones! Which, in fact, is greater, the gift or the altar that sanctifies the gift? 20 Therefore he that swears by the altar is swearing by it and by all the things on it; 21 and he that swears by the temple is swearing by it and by him that is inhabiting it; 22 and he that swears by heaven is swearing by the throne of God and by him that is sitting on it.

23 "Woe to you, scribes and Pharisees, hypocrites! because you give the tenth of the mint and the dill and the cummin, but you have disregarded the weightier matters of the Law, namely, justice and mercy and faithfulness. These things it was binding to do, yet not to disregard the other things. 24 Blind guides, who strain out the gnat but gulp down the camel!

25 "Woe to YOU, scribes and Pharisees, hypocrites! because YOU cleanse the outside of the cup and of the dish, but inside they are full of plunder and immoderateness. 26 Blind Pharisee, cleanse first the inside of the cup and of the dish, that the outside of it also may become clean.

27 "Woe to YOU, scribes and Pharisees, hypocrites! because YOU resemble whitewashed graves, which outwardly indeed appear beautiful but inside are full of dead men's bones and of every sort of uncleanness. 28 In that way YOU also, outwardly indeed, appear righteous to men, but inside YOU are full of hypocrisy and lawlessness.

29 "Woe to YOU, scribes and Pharisees, hypocrites! because YOU build the graves of the prophets and decorate the memorial tombs of the righteous ones, 30 and YOU say, 'If we were in the days of our forefathers, we would not be sharers with them in the blood of the prophets.' 31 Therefore YOU are bearing witness against yourselves that YOU are sons of those who murdered the prophets. 32 Well, then, fill up the measure of YOUR forefathers.

33 "Serpents, offspring of vipers, how are YOU to flee from the judgment of Ge·hen′na? 34 For this reason, here I am sending forth to YOU prophets and wise men and public instructors. Some of them YOU will kill and impale, and some of them YOU will scourge in YOUR synagogues and persecute from city to city; 35 that there may come upon YOU all the righteous blood spilled on earth, from the blood of righteous Abel to the blood of Zech·a·ri′ah son of Bar·a·chi′ah, whom YOU murdered between the sanctuary and the altar. 36 Truly I say to YOU, All these things will come upon this generation.

37 "Jerusalem, Jerusalem, the killer of the prophets and stoner of those sent forth to her,—how often I wanted to gather your children together, the way a hen gathers her chicks together under her wings! But YOU people did not want it. 38 Look! YOUR house is abandoned to YOU. 39 For I say to YOU, YOU will by no means see me from henceforth until YOU say, 'Blessed is he that comes in Jehovah's name!'"

24 Departing now, Jesus was on his way from the temple, but his disciples approached to show him the buildings of the temple. 2 In response he said to them: "Do YOU not behold all these things? Truly I say to YOU, By no means will a stone be left here upon a stone and not be thrown down."

3 While he was sitting upon the Mount of Olives, the disciples approached him privately, saying: "Tell us, When will these things be, and what will be the sign of your presence and of the conclusion of the system of things?"

4 And in answer Jesus said to them: "Look out that nobody misleads YOU; 5 for many will come on the basis of my name, saying, 'I am the Christ,' and will mislead many. 6 YOU are going to hear of wars and reports of wars; see that YOU are not terrified. For these things must take place, but the end is not yet.

7 "For nation will rise against nation and kingdom against kingdom, and there will be food shortages and earthquakes in one place after another. 8 All these things are a beginning of pangs of distress.

9 "Then people will deliver YOU up to tribulation and will kill YOU, and YOU will be objects of hatred by all the nations on account of my name. 10 Then, also, many will be stumbled and will betray one another and will hate one another. 11 And many false prophets will arise and mislead many; 12 and because of the increasing of lawlessness the love of the greater number will cool off. 13 But he that has endured to the end is the one that will be saved. 14 And this good news of the kingdom will be preached in all the inhabited earth for a witness to all the nations; and then the end will come.

15 "Therefore, when you catch sight of the disgusting thing that causes desolation, as spoken of through Daniel the prophet, standing in a holy place, (let the reader use discernment,) **16** then let those in Ju·de′a begin fleeing to the mountains. **17** Let the man on the housetop not come down to take the goods out of his house; **18** and let the man in the field not return to the house to pick up his outer garment. **19** Woe to the pregnant women and those suckling a baby in those days! **20** Keep praying that your flight may not occur in wintertime, nor on the sabbath day; **21** for then there will be great tribulation such as has not occurred since the world's beginning until now, no, nor will occur again. **22** In fact, unless those days were cut short, no flesh would be saved; but on account of the chosen ones those days will be cut short.

23 "Then if anyone says to you, 'Look! Here is the Christ,' or, 'There!' do not believe it. **24** For false Christs and false prophets will arise and will give great signs and wonders so as to mislead, if possible, even the chosen ones. **25** Look! I have forewarned you. **26** Therefore, if people say to you, 'Look! He is in the wilderness,' do not go out; 'Look! He is in the inner chambers,' do not believe it. **27** For just as the lightning comes out of eastern parts and shines over to western parts, so the presence of the Son of man will be. **28** Wherever the carcass is, there the eagles will be gathered together.

29 "Immediately after the tribulation of those days the sun will be darkened, and the moon will not give its light, and the stars will fall from heaven, and the powers of the heavens will be shaken. **30** And then the sign of the Son of man will appear in heaven, and then all the tribes of the earth will beat themselves in lamentation, and they will see the Son of man coming on the clouds of heaven with power and great glory. **31** And he will send forth his angels with a great trumpet sound, and they will gather his chosen ones together from the four winds, from one extremity of the heavens to their other extremity.

32 "Now learn from the fig tree as an illustration this point: Just as soon as its young branch grows tender and it puts forth leaves, you know that summer is near. **33** Likewise also you, when you see all these things, know that he is near at the doors. **34** Truly I say to you that this generation will by no means pass away until all these things occur. **35** Heaven and earth will pass away, but my words will by no means pass away.

36 "Concerning that day and hour nobody knows, neither the angels of the heavens nor the Son, but only the Father. **37** For just as the days of Noah were, so the presence of the Son of man will be. **38** For as they were in those days before the flood, eating and drinking, men marrying and women being given in marriage, until the day that Noah entered into the ark; **39** and they took no note until the flood came and swept them all away, so the presence of the Son of man will be. **40** Then two men will be in the field: one will be taken along and the other be abandoned; **41** two women will be grinding at the hand mill: one will be taken along and the other be abandoned. **42** Keep on the watch, therefore, because you do not know on what day your Lord is coming.

43 "But know one thing, that if the householder had known in what watch the thief was coming, he would have kept awake and not allowed his house to be broken into. **44** On this account you too prove yourselves ready, because at an hour that you do not think to be it, the Son of man is coming.

45 "Who really is the faithful and discreet slave whom his master appointed over his domestics, to give them their food at the proper time? **46** Happy is that slave if his master on arriving finds him doing so. 47 Truly I say to YOU, He will appoint him over all his belongings.

48 "But if that evil slave should say in his heart, 'My master is delaying,' 49 and should start to beat his fellow slaves and should eat and drink with the confirmed drunkards, 50 the master of that slave will come on a day that he does not expect and in an hour that he does not know, 51 and will punish him with the greatest severity and will assign him his part with the hypocrites. There is where [his] weeping and the gnashing of [his] teeth will be.

25 "Then the kingdom of the heavens will become like ten virgins that took their lamps and went out to meet the bridegroom. 2 Five of them were foolish, and five were discreet. 3 For the foolish took their lamps but took no oil with them, 4 whereas the discreet took oil in their receptacles with their lamps. 5 While the bridegroom was delaying, they all nodded and went to sleep. 6 Right in the middle of the night there arose a cry, 'Here is the bridegroom! Be on YOUR way out to meet him.' 7 Then all those virgins rose and put their lamps in order. 8 The foolish said to the discreet, 'Give us some of YOUR oil, because our lamps are about to go out.' 9 The discreet answered with the words, 'Perhaps there may not be quite enough for us and YOU. Be on YOUR way, instead, to those who sell it and buy for yourselves.' 10 While they were going off to buy, the bridegroom arrived, and the virgins that were ready went in with him to the marriage feast; and the door was shut. 11 Afterwards the rest of the virgins also came, saying, 'Sir, sir, open to us!' 12 In answer he said, 'I tell YOU the truth, I do not know YOU.'

13 "Keep on the watch, therefore, because YOU know neither the day nor the hour.

14 "For it is just as when a man, about to travel abroad, summoned slaves of his and committed to them his belongings. 15 And

to one he gave five talents, to another two, to still another one, to each one according to his own ability, and he went abroad. 16 Immediately the one that received the five talents went his way and did business with them and gained five more. 17 In the same way the one that received the two gained two more. 18 But the one that received just one went off, and dug in the ground and hid the silver money of his master.

19 "After a long time the master of those slaves came and settled accounts with them. 20 So the one that had received five talents came forward and brought five additional talents, saying, 'Master, you committed five talents to me; see, I gained five talents more.' 21 His master said to him, 'Well done, good and faithful slave! You were faithful over a few things. I will appoint you over many things. Enter into the joy of your master.' 22 Next the one that had received the two talents came forward and said, 'Master, you committed to me two talents; see, I gained two talents more.' 23 His master said to him, 'Well done, good and faithful slave! You were faithful over a few things. I will appoint you over many things. Enter into the joy of your master.'

24 "Finally the one that had received the one talent came forward and said, 'Master, I knew you to be an exacting man, reaping where you did not sow and gathering where you did not winnow. 25 So I grew afraid and went off and hid your talent in the ground. Here you have what is yours.' 26 In reply his master said to him, 'Wicked and sluggish slave, you knew, did you, that I reaped where I did not sow and gathered where I did not winnow? 27 Well, then, you ought to have deposited my silver monies with the bankers, and on my arrival I would be receiving what is mine with interest.

28 "Therefore TAKE away the talent from him and give it to him that has the ten talents. 29 For to everyone that has, more will be

given and he will have abundance; but as for him that does not have, even what he has will be taken away from him. 30 And throw the good-for-nothing slave out into the darkness outside. There is where [his] weeping and the gnashing of [his] teeth will be.'

31 "When the Son of man arrives in his glory, and all the angels with him, then he will sit down on his glorious throne. 32 And all the nations will be gathered before him, and he will separate people one from another, just as a shepherd separates the sheep from the goats. 33 And he will put the sheep on his right hand, but the goats on his left.

34 "Then the king will say to those on his right, 'Come, you who have been blessed by my Father, inherit the kingdom prepared for you from the founding of the world. 35 For I became hungry and you gave me something to eat; I got thirsty and you gave me something to drink. I was a stranger and you received me hospitably; 36 naked, and you clothed me. I fell sick and you looked after me. I was in prison and you came to me.' 37 Then the righteous ones will answer him with the words, 'Lord, when did we see you hungry and feed you, or thirsty, and give you something to drink? 38 When did we see you a stranger and receive you hospitably, or naked, and clothe you? 39 When did we see you sick or in prison and go to you?' 40 And in reply the king will say to them, 'Truly I say to you, To the extent that you did it to one of the least of these my brothers, you did it to me.'

41 "Then he will say, in turn, to those on his left, 'Be on your way from me, you who have been cursed, into the everlasting fire prepared for the Devil and his angels. 42 For I became hungry, but you gave me nothing to eat, and I got thirsty, but you gave me nothing to drink. 43 I was a stranger, but you did not receive me hospitably; naked, but you did not clothe me; sick and in prison, but you did

not look after me.' 44 Then they also will answer with the words, 'Lord, when did we see you hungry or thirsty or a stranger or naked or sick or in prison and did not minister to you?' 45 Then he will answer them with the words, 'Truly I say to you, To the extent that you did not do it to one of these least ones, you did not do it to me.' 46 And these will depart into everlasting cutting-off, but the righteous ones into everlasting life."

26 Now when Jesus had finished all these sayings, he said to his disciples: 2 "You know that two days from now the passover occurs, and the Son of man is to be delivered up to be impaled."

3 Then the chief priests and the older men of the people gathered together in the courtyard of the high priest who was called Ca·ia·phas, 4 and took counsel together to seize Jesus by crafty device and kill him. 5 However, they kept saying: "Not at the festival, in order that no uproar may arise among the people."

6 While Jesus happened to be in Beth'a·ny in the house of Simon the leper, 7 a woman with an alabaster case of costly perfumed oil approached him, and she began pouring it upon his head as he was reclining at the table. 8 On seeing this the disciples became indignant and said: "Why this waste? 9 For this could have been sold for a great deal and been given to poor people." 10 Aware of this, Jesus said to them: "Why do you try to make trouble for the woman? For she did a fine deed toward me. 11 For you always have the poor with you, but you will not always have me. 12 For when this woman put this perfumed oil upon my body, she did it for the preparation of me for burial. 13 Truly I say to you, Wherever this good news is preached in all the world, what this woman did shall also be told as a remembrance of her."

14 Then one of the twelve, the one called Judas Is·car'i·ot, went to the chief priests 15 and said: "What will you give me to betray

him to you?" They stipulated to him thirty silver pieces. 16 So from then on he kept seeking a good opportunity to betray him.

17 On the first day of the unfermented cakes the disciples came up to Jesus, saying: "Where do you want us to prepare for you to eat the passover?" 18 He said: "Go into the city to So-and-so and say to him, The Teacher says, 'My appointed time is near; I will celebrate the passover with my disciples at your home.'" 19 And the disciples did as Jesus ordered them, and they got things ready for the passover.

20 When, now, it had become evening, he was reclining at the table with the twelve disciples. 21 While they were eating, he said: "Truly I say to you, One of you will betray me." 22 Being very much grieved at this, they commenced each and every one to say to him: "Lord, it is not I, is it?" 23 In reply he said: "He that dips his hand with me in the bowl is the one that will betray me. 24 True, the Son of man is going away, just as it is written concerning him, but woe to that man through whom the Son of man is betrayed! It would have been finer for him if that man had not been born." 25 By way of reply Judas, who was about to betray him, said: "It is not I, is it, Rabbi?" He said to him: "You yourself said [it]."

26 As they continued eating, Jesus took a loaf and, after saying a blessing, he broke it and, giving it to the disciples, he said: "TAKE, eat. This means my body." 27 Also, he took a cup and, having given thanks, he gave it to them, saying: "Drink out of it, all of you; 28 for this means my 'blood of the covenant,' which is to be poured out in behalf of many for forgiveness of sins. 29 But I tell you, I will by no means drink henceforth any of this product of the vine until that day when I drink it new with you in the kingdom of my Father." 30 Finally, after singing praises, they went out to the Mount of Olives.

31 Then Jesus said to them: "All of you will be stumbled in connection with me on this night, for it is written, 'I will strike the shepherd, and the sheep of the flock will be scattered about.' 32 But after I have been raised up, I will go ahead of you into Gal'i·lee." 33 But Peter, in answer, said to him: "Although all the others are stumbled in connection with you, never will I be stumbled!" 34 Jesus said to him: "Truly I say to you, On this night, before a cock crows, you will disown me three times." 35 Peter said to him: "Even if I should have to die with you, I will by no means disown you." All the other disciples also said the same thing.

36 Then Jesus came with them to the spot called Geth·sem'a·ne, and he said to the disciples: "Sit down here while I go over there and pray." 37 And taking along Peter and the two sons of Zeb'e·dee, he started to be grieved and to be sorely troubled. 38 Then he said to them: "My soul is deeply grieved, even to death. Stay here and keep on the watch with me." 39 And going a little way forward, he fell upon his face, praying and saying: "My Father, if it is possible, let this cup pass away from me. Yet, not as I will, but as you will."

40 And he came to the disciples and found them sleeping, and he said to Peter: "Could you men not so much as watch one hour with me? 41 Keep on the watch and pray continually, that you may not enter into temptation. The spirit, of course, is eager, but the flesh is weak." 42 Again, for the second time, he went off and prayed, saying: "My Father, if it is not possible for this to pass away except I drink it, let your will take place." 43 And he came again and found them sleeping, for their eyes were heavy. 44 So leaving them, he again went off and prayed for the third time, saying once more the same word. 45 Then he came to the disciples and said to them: "At such a time as this you are sleeping and taking your rest! Look! The hour has drawn near

for the Son of man to be betrayed into the hands of sinners. 46 Get up, let us go. Look! My betrayer has drawn near." 47 And while he was yet speaking, look! Judas, one of the twelve, came and with him a great crowd with swords and clubs from the chief priests and older men of the people.

48 Now his betrayer had given them a sign, saying: "Whoever it is I kiss, this is he; take him into custody." 49 And going straight up to Jesus he said: "Good day, Rabbi!" and kissed him very tenderly. 50 But Jesus said to him: "Fellow, for what purpose are you present?" Then they came forward and laid hands on Jesus and took him into custody. 51 But, look! one of those with Jesus reached out his hand and drew his sword and struck the slave of the high priest and took off his ear. 52 Then Jesus said to him: "Return your sword to its place, for all those who take the sword will perish by the sword. 53 Or do you think that I cannot appeal to my Father to supply me at this moment more than twelve legions of angels? 54 In that case, how would the Scriptures be fulfilled that it must take place this way?" 55 In that hour Jesus said to the crowds: "Have you come out with swords and clubs as against a robber to arrest me? Day after day I used to sit in the temple teaching, and yet you did not take me into custody. 56 But all this has taken place for the scriptures of the prophets to be fulfilled." Then all the disciples abandoned him and fled.

57 Those who took Jesus into custody led him away to Ca'ia·phas the high priest, where the scribes and the older men were gathered together. 58 But Peter kept following him at a good distance, as far as the courtyard of the high priest, and, after going inside, he was sitting with the house attendants to see the outcome. 59 Meantime the chief priests and the entire San'he·drin were looking for false witness against

Jesus in order to put him to death, 60 but they found none, although many false witnesses came forward. Later on two came forward 61 and said: "This man said, 'I am able to throw down the temple of God and build it up in three days.'" 62 With that the high priest stood up and said to him: "Have you no answer? What is it these are testifying against you?" 63 But Jesus kept silent. So the high priest said to him: "By the living God I put you under oath to tell us whether you are the Christ the Son of God!" 64 Jesus said to him: "You yourself said [it]. Yet I say to you men, From henceforth you will see the Son of man sitting at the right hand of power and coming on the clouds of heaven." 65 Then the high priest ripped his outer garments, saying: "He has blasphemed! What further need do we have of witnesses? See! Now you have heard the blasphemy. 66 What is your opinion?" They returned answer: "He is liable to death." 67 Then they spit into his face and hit him with their fists. Others slapped him in the face, 68 saying: "Prophesy to us, you Christ. Who is it that struck you?"

69 Now Peter was sitting outside in the courtyard; and a servant girl came up to him, saying: "You, too, were with Jesus the Gal·i·le'an!" 70 But he denied it before them all, saying: "I do not know what you are talking about." 71 After he had gone out to the gatehouse, another girl noticed him and said to those there: "This man was with Jesus the Naz·a·rene'." 72 And again he denied it, with an oath: "I do not know the man!" 73 After a little while those standing around came up and said to Peter: "Certainly you also are one of them, for, in fact, your dialect gives you away." 74 Then he started to curse and swear: "I do not know the man!" And immediately a cock crowed. 75 And Peter called to mind the saying Jesus spoke, namely: "Before a cock crows, you will disown me three times." And he went outside and wept bitterly.

to the people, 'He was raised up from the dead!' and this last imposture will be worse than the first." 65 Pilate said to them: "You have a guard. Go make it as secure as you know how." 66 So they went and made the grave secure by sealing the stone and having the guard.

28 After the sabbath, when it was growing light on the first day of the week, Mary Mag'da·lene and the other Mary came to view the grave.

2 And, notice! a great earthquake had taken place; for Jehovah's angel had descended from heaven and approached and rolled away the stone, and was sitting on it. 3 His outward appearance was as lightning, and his clothing as white as snow. 4 Yes, for fear of him the watchmen trembled and became as dead men.

5 But the angel in answer said to the women: "Do not you be fearful, for I know you are looking for Jesus who was impaled. 6 He is not here, for he was raised up, as he said. Come, see the place where he was lying. 7 And go quickly and tell his disciples that he was raised up from the dead, and, look! he is going ahead of you into Gal'i·lee; there you will see him. Look! I have told you."

8 So, quickly leaving the memorial tomb, with fear and great joy, they ran to report to his disciples. 9 And, look! Jesus met them and said: "Good day!" They approached and caught him by his feet and did obeisance to him. 10 Then Jesus said to them: "Have no fear! Go, report to my brothers, that they may go off into Gal'i·lee; and there they will see me."

11 While they were on their way, look! some of the guard went into the city and reported to the chief priests all the things that had happened. 12 And after these had gathered together with the older men and taken counsel, they gave a sufficient number of silver pieces to the soldiers 13 and said: "Say, 'His disciples came in the night and stole him while we were sleeping.' 14 And if this gets to the governor's ears, we will persuade [him] and will set you free from worry." 15 So they took the silver pieces and did as they were instructed; and this saying has been spread abroad among the Jews up to this very day.

16 However, the eleven disciples went into Gal'i·lee to the mountain where Jesus had arranged for them, 17 and when they saw him they did obeisance, but some doubted. 18 And Jesus approached and spoke to them, saying: "All authority has been given me in heaven and on the earth. 19 Go therefore and make disciples of people of all the nations, baptizing them in the name of the Father and of the Son and of the holy spirit, 20 teaching them to observe all the things I have commanded you. And, look! I am with you all the days until the conclusion of the system of things."

ACCORDING TO

MARK

1 [The] beginning of the good news about Jesus Christ: 2 Just as it is written in Isaiah the prophet: "(Look! I am sending forth my messenger before your face, who will prepare your way;) 3 listen! someone is crying out in the wilderness, 'Prepare the way of Jeho- vah, you people, make his roads straight,'" 4 John the baptizer turned up in the wilderness, preaching baptism [in symbol] of repentance for forgiveness of sins. 5 Consequently all the territory of Ju·de'a and all the inhabitants of Jerusalem made their way out to him, and they were baptized by him in the Jordan River, openly confessing their sins. 6 Now John was clothed with camel's hair and with a leather girdle around his loins, and was eating insect locusts and wild honey. 7 And he would preach, saying: "After me someone stronger than I am is coming; I am not fit to stoop and untie the laces of his sandals. 8 I baptized YOU with water, but he will baptize YOU with holy spirit."

9 In the course of those days Jesus came from Naz·a·reth of Gal'i·lee and was baptized in the Jordan by John. 10 And immediately on coming up out of the water he saw the heavens being parted, and, like a dove, the spirit coming down upon him; 11 and a voice came out of the heavens: "You are my Son, the beloved; I have approved you."

12 And immediately the spirit impelled him to go into the wilderness. 13 So he continued in the wilderness forty days, being tempted by Satan, and he was with the wild beasts, but the angels were ministering to him.

14 Now after John was put under arrest Jesus went into Gal'i·lee, preaching the good news of God 15 and saying: "The appointed time has been fulfilled, and the kingdom of God has drawn near. Be repentant, YOU people, and have faith in the good news."

16 While walking alongside the sea of Gal'i·lee he saw Simon and Andrew the brother of Simon casting [their nets] about in the sea, for they were fishers. 17 So Jesus said to them: "Come after me, and I shall cause YOU to become fishers of men." 18 And at once they abandoned their nets and followed him. 19 And after going a little farther he saw James the [son] of Zeb'e·dee and John his brother, in fact, while they were in their boat mending their nets; 20 and without delay he called them. In turn they left their father Zeb'e·dee in the boat with the hired men and went off after him. 21 And they went their way into Ca·per'na·um.

No sooner was it the sabbath than he entered into the synagogue and began to teach. 22 And they became astounded at his way of teaching, for there he was teaching them as one having authority, and not as the scribes. 23 Also, at that immediate time there was in their synagogue a man under the power of an unclean spirit, and he shouted, 24 saying: "What have we to do with you, Jesus you Naz·a·rene'? Did you come to destroy us? I know exactly who you are, the Holy One of God." 25 But Jesus rebuked it, saying: "Be silent, and come on out of him!" 26 And the unclean spirit, after throwing him into a convulsion and yelling at the top of its voice, came on out of him. 27 Well, the people were all so astonished that they began a discussion among themselves, saying: "What is this? A new teaching! He authoritatively orders even the unclean spirits, and they obey him." 28 So the report about him spread out immediately in all directions through all the country round about in Gal'i·lee.

29 And immediately they went out of the synagogue and went into the home of Simon and Andrew with James and John. 30 Now Simon's mother-in-law was lying down sick with a fever, and they at once told him about her. 31 And going to her he raised her up, taking her by the hand; and the fever left her, and she began ministering to them.

32 After evening had fallen, when the sun had set, the people began bringing him all those who were ill and those demon-possessed; 33 and the whole city was gathered right at the door. 34 So he cured many that were ill with various sicknesses, and he expelled many demons, but he would not let the demons speak, because they knew him to be Christ.

35 And early in the morning, while it was still dark, he rose up and went outside and left for a lonely place, and there he began praying. 36 However, Simon and those with him hunted him down

37 and found him, and they said to him: "All are looking for you." 38 But he said to them: "Let us go somewhere else, into the village towns nearby, that I may preach there also, for it is for this purpose I have gone out." 39 And he did go, preaching in their synagogues throughout the whole of Gal'i·lee and expelling the demons.

40 There also came to him a leper, entreating him even on bended knee, saying to him: "If you just want to, you can make me clean." 41 At that he was moved with pity, and he stretched out his hand and touched him, and said to him: "I want to. Be made clean." 42 And immediately the leprosy vanished from him, and he became clean. 43 Furthermore, he gave him strict orders and at once sent him away, 44 and said to him: "See that you tell nobody a thing, but go show yourself to the priest and offer in behalf of your cleansing the things Moses directed, for a witness to them." 45 But after going away the man started to proclaim it a great deal and to spread the account abroad, so that [Jesus] was no longer able to enter openly into a city, but he continued outside in lonely places. Yet they kept coming to him from all sides.

2 However, after some days he again entered into Ca·per'na·um and he was reported to be at home. 2 Consequently many gathered, so much so that there was no more room, not even about the door, and he began to speak the word to them. 3 And men came bringing him a paralytic carried by four. 4 But not being able to bring him right to [Jesus] on account of the crowd, they removed the roof over where he was, and having dug an opening they lowered the cot on which the paralytic was lying. 5 And when Jesus saw their faith he said to the paralytic: "Child, your sins are forgiven." 6 Now there were some of the scribes there, sitting and reasoning in their hearts: 7 "Why is this man talking in this manner? He is blaspheming. Who can forgive sins except one, God?" 8 But Jesus, having discerned immediately by his spirit that they were reasoning that way in themselves, said to them: "Why are YOU reasoning these things in YOUR hearts? 9 Which is easier, to say to the paralytic, 'Your sins are forgiven,' or to say, 'Get up and pick up your cot and walk'? 10 But in order for YOU men to know that the Son of man has authority to forgive sins upon the earth,"—he said to the paralytic: 11 "I say to you, Get up, pick up your cot, and go to your home." 12 At that he did get up, and immediately picked up his cot and walked out in front of them all, so that they were all simply carried away, and they glorified God, saying: "We never saw the like of it."

13 Again he went out beside the sea; and all the crowd kept coming to him, and he began to teach them. 14 But as he was passing along, he caught sight of Le'vi the [son] of Al·phae'us sitting at the tax office, and he said to him: "Be my follower." And rising up he followed him. 15 Later he happened to be reclining at the table in his house, and many tax collectors and sinners were reclining with Jesus and his disciples, for there were many of them and they began following him. 16 But the scribes of the Pharisees, when they saw he was eating with the sinners and tax collectors, began saying to his disciples: "Does he eat with the tax collectors and sinners?" 17 Upon hearing this Jesus said to them: "Those who are strong do not need a physician, but those who are ill do. I came to call, not righteous people, but sinners."

18 Now John's disciples and the Pharisees practiced fasting. So they came and said to him: "Why is it the disciples of John and the disciples of the Pharisees practice fasting, but your disciples do not practice fasting?" 19 And Jesus said to them: "While the bridegroom is with them the friends of the bridegroom cannot fast, can they? As long as they have the

bridegroom with them they cannot fast. 20 But days will come when the bridegroom will be taken away from them, and then they will fast in that day. 21 Nobody sews a patch of unshrunk cloth upon an old outer garment; if he does, its full strength pulls from it, the new from the old, and the tear becomes worse. 22 Also, nobody puts new wine into old wineskins; if he does, the wine bursts the skins, and the wine is lost as well as the skins. But people put new wine into new wineskins."

23 Now it happened that he was proceeding through the grainfields on the sabbath, and his disciples started to make their way plucking the heads of grain. 24 So the Pharisees went saying to him: "Look here! Why are they doing on the sabbath what is not lawful?" 25 But he said to them: "Have you never once read what David did when he fell in need and got hungry, he and the men with him? 26 How he entered into the house of God, in the account about A·bi'a·thar the chief priest, and ate the loaves of presentation, which it is not lawful for anybody to eat except the priests, and he gave some also to the men who were with him?" 27 So he went on to say to them: "The sabbath came into existence for the sake of man, and not man for the sake of the sabbath; 28 hence the Son of man is Lord even of the sabbath."

3 Once again he entered into a synagogue, and a man was there with a dried-up hand. 2 So they were watching him closely to see whether he would cure the man on the sabbath, in order that they might accuse him. 3 And he said to the man with the withered hand: "Get up [and come] to the center." 4 Next he said to them: "Is it lawful on the sabbath to do a good deed or to do a bad deed, to save or to kill a soul?" But they kept silent. 5 And after looking around upon them with indignation, being thoroughly grieved at the insensibility of their hearts, he said to the man: "Stretch out your hand."

And he stretched it out, and his hand was restored. 6 At that the Pharisees went out and immediately began holding council with the party followers of Herod against him, in order to destroy him.

7 But Jesus with his disciples withdrew to the sea; and a great multitude from Gal'i·lee and from Ju·de'a followed him. 8 Even from Jerusalem and from Id·u·me'a and from across the Jordan and around Tyre and Si'don, a great multitude, on hearing of how many things he was doing, came to him. 9 And he told his disciples to have a little boat continually at his service so that the crowd might not press upon him. 10 For he cured many, with the result that all those who had grievous diseases were falling upon him to touch him. 11 Even the unclean spirits, whenever they would behold him, would prostrate themselves before him and cry out, saying: "You are the Son of God." 12 But many times he sternly charged them not to make him known.

13 And he ascended a mountain and summoned those he wanted, and they went off to him. 14 And he formed [a group of] twelve, whom he also named "apostles," that they might continue with him and that he might send them out to preach 15 and to have authority to expel the demons.

16 And the [group of] twelve that he formed were Simon, to whom he also gave the surname Peter, 17 and James the [son] of Zeb'e·dee and John the brother of James (he also gave these the surname Bo·a·ner'ges, which means Sons of Thunder), 18 and Andrew and Philip and Bar·thol'o·mew and Matthew and Thomas and James the son of Al·phae'us and Thad·dae'us and Simon the Ca·na·nae'an 19 and Judas Is·car'i·ot, who later betrayed him.

And he went into a house. 20 Once more the crowd gathered, so that they were not able even to eat a meal. 21 But when his relatives heard about it, they went out to lay hold of him, for they were saying: "He has gone out of his mind." 22 Also, the scribes that came down from Jerusalem were saying: "He has Be·el′ze·bub, and he expels the demons by means of the ruler of the demons." 23 So, after calling them to him, he began to say to them with illustrations: "How can Satan expel Satan? 24 Why, if a kingdom becomes divided against itself, that kingdom cannot stand; 25 and if a house becomes divided against itself, that house will not be able to stand. 26 Also, if Satan has risen up against himself and become divided, he cannot stand, but is coming to an end. 27 In fact, no one that has got into the house of a strong man is able to plunder his movable goods unless first he binds the strong man, and then he will plunder his house. 28 Truly I say to you that all things will be forgiven the sons of men, no matter what sins and blasphemies they blasphemously commit. 29 However, whoever blasphemes against the holy spirit has no forgiveness forever, but is guilty of everlasting sin." 30 This, because they were saying: "He has an unclean spirit."

31 Now his mother and his brothers came, and, as they were standing on the outside, they sent in to him to call him. 32 As it was, a crowd was sitting around him, so they said to him: "Look! Your mother and your brothers outside are seeking you." 33 But in reply he said to them: "Who are my mother and my brothers?" 34 And having looked about upon those sitting around him in a circle, he said: "See, my mother and my brothers! 35 Whoever does the will of God, this one is my brother and sister and mother."

4 And he again started teaching beside the sea. And a very great crowd gathered near him, so that he went aboard a boat and sat out on the sea, but all the crowd beside the sea were on the shore. 2 So he began to teach them many things with illustrations and to say to them in his teaching: 3 "Listen. Look! The sower went

out to sow. 4 And as he was sowing, some [seed] fell alongside the road, and the birds came and ate it up. 5 And other [seed] fell upon the rocky place where it, of course, did not have much soil, and it immediately sprang up because of not having depth of soil. 6 But when the sun rose, it was scorched, and for not having root it withered. 7 And other [seed] fell among the thorns, and the thorns came up and choked it, and it yielded no fruit. 8 But others fell upon the fine soil, and, coming up and increasing, they began to yield fruit, and they were bearing thirtyfold, and sixty and a hundred." 9 So he added the word: "Let him that has ears to listen listen."

10 Now when he got to be alone, those around him with the twelve began questioning him on the illustrations. 11 And he proceeded to say to them: "To you the sacred secret of the kingdom of God has been given, but to those outside all things occur in illustrations, 12 in order that, though looking, they may look and yet not see, and, though hearing, they may hear and yet not get the sense of it, nor ever turn back and forgiveness be given them." 13 Further, he said to them: "You do not know this illustration, and so how will you understand all the other illustrations?

14 "The sower sows the word. 15 These, then, are the ones alongside the road where the word is sown; but as soon as they have heard [it] Satan comes and takes away the word that was sown in them. 16 And likewise these are the ones sown upon the rocky places: as soon as they have heard the word, they accept it with joy. 17 Yet they have no root in themselves, but they continue for a time; then as soon as tribulation or persecution arises because of the word, they are stumbled. 18 There are still others who are sown among the thorns; these are the ones that have heard the word, 19 but the anxieties of this system of things

and the deceptive power of riches and the desires for the rest of the things make inroads and choke the word, and it becomes unfruitful. 20 Finally, the ones that were sown on the fine soil are those who listen to the word and favorably receive it and bear fruit thirtyfold and sixty and a hundred."

21 And he went on to say to them: "A lamp is not brought to be put under a measuring basket or under a bed, is it? It is brought to be put upon a lampstand, is it not? 22 For there is nothing hidden except for the purpose of being exposed; nothing has become carefully concealed but for the purpose of coming into the open. 23 Whoever has ears to listen, let him listen."

24 He further said to them: "Pay attention to what YOU are hearing. With the measure that YOU are measuring out, YOU will have it measured out to YOU, yes, YOU will have more added to YOU. 25 For he that has will have more given to him; but he that does not have, even what he has will be taken away from him."

26 So he went on to say: "In this way the kingdom of God is just as when a man casts the seed upon the ground, 27 and he sleeps at night and rises up by day, and the seed sprouts and grows tall, just how he does not know. 28 Of its own self the ground bears fruit gradually, first the grass blade, then the stalk head, finally the full grain in the head. 29 But as soon as the fruit permits it, he thrusts in the sickle, because the harvest time has come."

30 And he went on to say: "With what are we to liken the kingdom of God, or in what illustration shall we set it out? 31 Like a mustard grain, which at the time it was sown in the ground was the tiniest of all the seeds that are on the earth— 32 but when it has been sown, it comes up and becomes greater than all other vegetables and produces great branches, so that the birds of the heaven are able to find lodging under its shadow."

33 So with many illustrations of that sort he would speak the word to them, as far as they were able to listen. 34 Indeed, without an illustration he would not speak to them, but privately to his disciples he would explain all things.

35 And on that day, when evening had fallen, he said to them: "Let us cross to the other shore." 36 So, after they had dismissed the crowd, they took him in the boat, just as he was, and there were other boats with him. 37 Now a great violent windstorm broke out, and the waves kept dashing into the boat, so that the boat was close to being swamped. 38 But he was in the stern, sleeping upon a pillow. So they woke him up and said to him: "Teacher, do you not care that we are about to perish?" 39 With that he roused himself and rebuked the wind and said to the sea: "Hush! Be quiet!" And the wind abated, and a great calm set in. 40 So he said to them: "Why are YOU fainthearted? Do YOU not yet have any faith?" 41 But they felt an unusual fear, and they would say to one another: "Who really is this, because even the wind and the sea obey him?"

5 Well, they got to the other side of the sea into the country of the Ger′a·senes. 2 And immediately after he got out of the boat a man under the power of an unclean spirit met him from among the memorial tombs. 3 He had his haunt among the tombs; and up to that time absolutely nobody was able to bind him fast even with a chain, 4 because he had oftentimes been bound with fetters and chains, but the chains were snapped apart by him and the fetters were actually smashed; and nobody had the strength to subdue him. 5 And continually, night and day, he was crying out in the tombs and in the mountains and slashing himself with stones. 6 But on catching sight of Jesus from a distance he ran and did obeisance to him, 7 and, when he had cried

out with a loud voice, he said: "What have I to do with you, Jesus, Son of the Most High God? I put you under oath by God not to torment me." 8 For he had been telling it: "Come out of the man, you unclean spirit." 9 But he began to ask him: "What is your name?" And he said to him: "My name is Legion, because there are many of us." 10 And he entreated him many times not to send the spirits out of the country.

11 Now a great herd of swine was there at the mountain feeding. 12 So they entreated him, saying: "Send us into the swine, that we may enter into them." 13 And he permitted them. With that the unclean spirits came out and entered into the swine; and the herd rushed over the precipice into the sea, about two thousand of them, and they drowned one after another in the sea. 14 But the herders of them fled and reported it in the city and in the countryside; and people came to see what it was that had happened. 15 So they came to Jesus, and they beheld the demon-possessed [man] sitting clothed and in his sound mind, this [man] that had had the legion; and they grew fearful. 16 Also, those who had seen it related to them how this had happened to the demon-possessed [man] and about the swine. 17 And so they started to entreat him to go away from their districts.

18 Now as he was boarding the boat, the [man] that had been demon-possessed began entreating him that he might continue with him. 19 However, he did not let him, but said to him: "Go home to your relatives, and report to them all the things Jehovah has done for you and the mercy he had on you." 20 And he went away and started to proclaim in the Decap'o·lis all the things Jesus did for him; and all the people began to wonder.

21 After Jesus had crossed back again in the boat to the opposite shore a great crowd gathered together to him; and he was beside the sea. 22 Now one of the presiding officers of the synagogue, Ja'i·rus by name, came and, on catching sight of him, he fell at his feet 23 and entreated him many times, saying: "My little daughter is in an extreme condition. Would you please come and put your hands upon her that she may get well and live." 24 At that he went off with him. And a great crowd was following him and pressing against him.

25 Now there was a woman subject to a flow of blood twelve years, 26 and she had been put to many pains by many physicians and had spent all her resources and had not been benefited but, rather, had got worse. 27 When she heard the things about Jesus, she came behind in the crowd and touched his outer garment; 28 for she kept saying: "If I touch just his outer garments I shall get well." 29 And immediately her fountain of blood dried up, and she sensed in her body that she had been healed of the grievous sickness.

30 Immediately, also, Jesus recognized in himself that power had gone out of him, and he turned about in the crowd and began to say: "Who touched my outer garments?" 31 But his disciples began to say to him: "You see the crowd pressing in upon you, and do you say, 'Who touched me?'" 32 However, he was looking around to see her that had done this. 33 But the woman, frightened and trembling, knowing what had happened to her, came and fell down before him and told him the whole truth. 34 He said to her: "Daughter, your faith has made you well. Go in peace, and be in good health from your grievous sickness."

35 While he was yet speaking, some men from the home of the presiding officer of the synagogue came and said: "Your daughter died! Why bother the teacher any longer?" 36 But Jesus, overhearing the word being spoken, said to the presiding officer of the synagogue: "Have no fear, only exercise faith." 37 Now he did not

let anyone follow along with him except Peter and James and John the brother of James.

38 So they came to the house of the presiding officer of the synagogue, and he beheld the noisy confusion and those weeping and letting out many wails, 39 and, after stepping in, he said to them: "Why are YOU causing noisy confusion and weeping? The young child has not died, but is sleeping." 40 At this they began to laugh scornfully at him. But, having put them all out, he took along the young child's father and mother and those with him, and he went in where the young child was. 41 And, taking the hand of the young child, he said to her: "Tal′i·tha cu′mi," which, translated, means: "Maiden, I say to you, Get up!" 42 And immediately the maiden rose and began walking, for she was twelve years old. And at once they were beside themselves with great ecstasy. 43 But he ordered them again and again to let no one learn of this, and he said that something should be given her to eat.

6 And he departed from there and came into his home territory, and his disciples followed him. 2 When it became sabbath, he started teaching in the synagogue; and the greater number of those listening were astounded and said: "Where did this man get these things? And why should this wisdom have been given this man, and such powerful works be performed through his hands? 3 This is the carpenter the son of Mary and the brother of James and Joseph and Judas and Simon, is it not? And his sisters are here with us, are they not?" So they began to stumble at him. 4 But Jesus went on to say to them: "A prophet is not unhonored except in his home territory and among his relatives and in his own house." 5 So he was able to do no powerful work there except to lay his hands upon a few sickly ones and cure them. 6 Indeed, he wondered at their lack of faith. And he went

round about to the villages in a circuit, teaching.

7 Now he summoned the twelve, and he initiated sending them out two by two, and he began to give them authority over the unclean spirits. 8 Also, he gave them orders to carry nothing for the trip except a staff alone, no bread, no food pouch, no copper money in their girdle purses, 9 but to bind on sandals, and not to wear two undergarments. 10 Further, he said to them: "Wherever YOU enter into a home, stay there until YOU go out of that place. 11 And wherever a place will not receive YOU nor hear YOU, on going out from there shake off the dirt that is beneath YOUR feet for a witness to them." 12 So they set out and preached in order that people might repent; 13 and they would expel many demons and grease many sickly people with oil and cure them.

14 Now it got to the ears of King Herod, for the name of [Jesus] became public, and people were saying: "John the baptizer has been raised from the dead, and on that account the powerful works are operating in him." 15 But others were saying: "It is E·li′jah." Still others were saying: "It is a prophet like one of the prophets." 16 But when Herod heard it he began to say: "The John that I beheaded, this one has been raised up." 17 For Herod himself had sent out and arrested John and bound him in prison on account of He·ro′di·as the wife of Philip his brother, because he had married her. 18 For John had repeatedly said to Herod: "It is not lawful for you to be having the wife of your brother." 19 But He·ro′di·as was nursing a grudge against him and was wanting to kill him, but could not. 20 For Herod stood in fear of John, knowing him to be a righteous and holy man; and he was keeping him safe. And after hearing him he was at a great loss what to do, yet he continued to hear him gladly.

21 But a convenient day came along when Herod spread an eve-

ning meal on his birthday for his top-ranking men and the military commanders and the foremost ones of Gal'i·lee. 22 And the daughter of this very He·ro'di·as came in and danced and pleased Herod and those reclining with him. The king said to the maiden: "Ask me for whatever you want, and I will give it to you." 23 Yes, he swore to her: "Whatever you ask me for, I will give it to you, up to half my kingdom." 24 And she went out and said to her mother: "What should I ask for?" She said: "The head of John the baptizer." 25 Immediately she went in with haste to the king and made her request, saying: "I want you to give me right away on a platter the head of John the Baptist." 26 Although he became deeply grieved, yet the king did not want to disregard her, in view of the oaths and those reclining at the table. 27 So the king immediately dispatched a body guardsman and commanded him to bring his head. And he went off and beheaded him in the prison 28 and brought his head on a platter, and he gave it to the maiden, and the maiden gave it to her mother. 29 When his disciples heard of it they came and took up his corpse and laid it in a memorial tomb.

30 And the apostles gathered together before Jesus and reported to him all the things they had done and taught. 31 And he said to them: "Come, you yourselves, privately into a lonely place and rest up a bit." For there were many coming and going, and they had no leisure time even to eat a meal. 32 So off they went in the boat for a lonely place to themselves. 33 But people saw them going and many got to know it, and from all the cities they ran there together on foot and got ahead of them. 34 Well, on getting out, he saw a great crowd, but he was moved with pity for them, because they were as sheep without a shepherd. And he started to teach them many things.

35 By now the hour had grown late, and his disciples came up to him and began to say: "The place is isolated, and the hour is already late. 36 Send them away, that they may go off into the country-side and villages round about and buy themselves something to eat." 37 In reply he said to them: "You give them something to eat." At this they said to him: "Shall we go off and buy two hundred de·nar'i·i worth of loaves and give [them] to the people to eat?" 38 He said to them: "How many loaves have you? Go see!" After ascertaining it, they said: "Five, besides two fishes." 39 And he instructed all the people to recline by companies on the green grass. 40 And they laid themselves down in groups of a hundred and of fifty. 41 Taking now the five loaves and the two fishes he looked up to heaven and said a blessing, and broke the loaves up and began giving them to the disciples, that these might place them before the people; and he divided up the two fishes for all. 42 So they all ate and were satisfied; 43 and they took up fragments, twelve baskets full, aside from the fishes. 44 Furthermore, those who ate of the loaves were five thousand men.

45 And, without delay, he compelled his disciples to board the boat and go on ahead to the opposite shore toward Beth·sa'i·da, while he himself dismissed the crowd. 46 But after saying good-by to them he went off into a mountain to pray. 47 Evening having now fallen, the boat was in the midst of the sea, but he was alone on the land. 48 And when he saw them being hard put to it in their rowing, for the wind was against them, about the fourth watch of the night he came toward them, walking on the sea; but he was inclined to pass them by. 49 At catching sight of him walking on the sea they thought: "It is an apparition!" and they cried aloud. 50 For they all saw him and were troubled. Immediately he spoke with them, and he said to

them: "Take courage, it is I; have no fear." 51 And he got up into the boat with them, and the wind abated. At this they were very much amazed within themselves, 52 for they had not grasped the meaning of the loaves, but their hearts continued dull of understanding.

53 And when they got across to land, they came into Gen·nes′a·ret and anchored ship nearby. 54 But as soon as they got out of the boat, people recognized him, 55 and they ran around all that region and started to carry about on cots those who were ailing to where they heard he was. 56 And wherever he would enter into villages or cities or countryside they would place the sick ones in the market places, and they would plead with him that they might touch just the fringe of his outer garment. And as many as did touch it were made well.

7 Now the Pharisees and some of the scribes that had come from Jerusalem gathered about him. 2 And when they saw some of his disciples eat their meal with defiled hands, that is, unwashed ones— 3 for the Pharisees and all the Jews do not eat unless they wash their hands up to the elbow, holding fast the tradition of the men of former times, 4 and, when back from market, they do not eat unless they cleanse themselves by sprinkling; and there are many other traditions that they have received to hold fast; baptisms of cups and pitchers and copper vessels;— 5 so these Pharisees and scribes asked him: "Why is it your disciples do not conduct themselves according to the tradition of the men of former times, but they take their meal with defiled hands?" 6 He said to them: "Isaiah aptly prophesied about you hypocrites, as it is written, 'This people honor me with [their] lips, but their hearts are far removed from me. 7 It is in vain that they keep worshiping me, because they teach as doctrines commands of men.' 8 Letting go the commandment of God, you hold fast the tradition of men."

9 Further, he went on to say to them: "Adroitly you set aside the commandment of God in order to retain your tradition. 10 For example, Moses said, 'Honor your father and your mother,' and, 'Let him that reviles father or mother end up in death.' 11 But you men say, 'If a man says to his father or his mother: "Whatever I have by which you may get benefit from me is corban, (that is, a gift dedicated to God,)"'— 12 you men no longer let him do a single thing for his father or his mother, 13 and thus you make the word of God invalid by your tradition which you handed down. And many things similar to this you do." 14 So, calling the crowd to him again, he proceeded to say to them: "Listen to me, all of you, and get the meaning. 15 There is nothing from outside a man that passes into him that can defile him; but the things that issue forth out of a man are the things that defile a man." 16 ——

17 Now when he had entered a house away from the crowd, his disciples began to question him respecting the illustration. 18 So he said to them: "Are you also without perception like them? Are you not aware that nothing from outside that passes into a man can defile him, 19 since it passes, not into [his] heart, but into [his] intestines, and it passes out into the sewer?" Thus he declared all foods clean. 20 Further, he said: "That which issues forth out of a man is what defiles a man; 21 for from inside, out of the heart of men, injurious reasonings issue forth: fornications, thieveries, murders, 22 adulteries, covetings, acts of wickedness, deceit, loose conduct, an envious eye, blasphemy, haughtiness, unreasonableness. 23 All these wicked things issue forth from within and defile a man."

24 From there he rose up and went into the regions of Tyre and Si′don. And he entered into a house and did not want anyone to get to know it. Yet he could not escape

notice; 25 but immediately a woman whose little daughter had an unclean spirit heard about him and came and prostrated herself at his feet. 26 The woman was a Grecian, a Sy·ro·phoe·ni'cian nationally; and she kept asking him to expel the demon from her daughter. 27 But he began by saying to her: "First let the children be satisfied, for it is not right to take the bread of the children and throw it to the little dogs." 28 In reply, however, she said to him: "Yes, sir, and yet the little dogs underneath the table eat of the crumbs of the little children." 29 At that he said to her: "Because of saying this, go; the demon has gone out of your daughter." 30 So she went away to her home and found the young child laid on the bed and the demon gone out.

31 Now coming back out of the regions of Tyre he went through Si'don to the sea of Gal'i·lee in the midst of the regions of De·cap'o·lis. 32 Here they brought him a man deaf and with a speech impediment, and they entreated him to lay his hand upon him. 33 And he took him away from the crowd privately and put his fingers into the man's ears and, after spitting, he touched his tongue. 34 And with a look up into heaven he sighed deeply and said to him: *"Eph'pha·tha,"* that is, "Be opened." 35 Well, his hearing powers were opened, and the impediment of his tongue was loosed, and he began speaking normally. 36 With that he charged them not to tell anyone; but the more he would charge them, that much more they would proclaim it. 37 Indeed, they were being astounded in a most extraordinary way and they said: "He has done all things well. He even makes the deaf hear and the speechless speak."

8 In those days, when there was again a big crowd and they had nothing to eat, he summoned the disciples and said to them: 2 "I feel pity for the crowd, because it is already three days that they have remained near me and they have

nothing to eat; 3 and if I should send them off to their homes fasting, they will give out on the road. Indeed, some of them are from far away." 4 But his disciples answered him: "From where will anybody here in an isolated place be able to satisfy these people with loaves?" 5 Still he went on to ask them: "How many loaves have you?" They said: "Seven." 6 And he instructed the crowd to recline on the ground, and he took the seven loaves, gave thanks, broke them, and began to give them to his disciples to serve, and they served them to the crowd. 7 They also had a few little fishes; and, having blessed these, he told them also to serve these. 8 Accordingly they ate and were satisfied, and they took up surpluses of fragments, seven provision baskets full. 9 Yet there were about four thousand [men]. Finally he sent them away.

10 And immediately he boarded the boat with his disciples and came into the parts of Dal·ma·nu'tha. 11 Here the Pharisees came out and started disputing with him, seeking from him a sign from heaven, to put him to the test. 12 So he groaned deeply with his spirit, and said: "Why does this generation seek a sign? Truly I say, No sign will be given to this generation." 13 With that he left them, got aboard again, and went off to the opposite shore.

14 As it was, they forgot to take loaves along, and except for one loaf they had nothing with them in the boat. 15 And he began to order them expressly and say: "Keep YOUR eyes open, look out for the leaven of the Pharisees and the leaven of Herod." 16 So they went arguing with one another over the fact that they had no loaves. 17 Noting this, he said to them: "Why do YOU argue over your having no loaves? Do YOU not yet perceive and get the meaning? Do YOU have YOUR hearts dull of understanding? 18 'Though having eyes, do YOU not see; and though having ears, do YOU not hear?'

And do you not remember, 19 when I broke the five loaves for the five thousand [men], how many baskets full of fragments you took up?" They said to him: "Twelve." 20 "When I broke the seven for the four thousand [men], how many provision baskets full of fragments did you take up?" And they said to him: "Seven." 21 With that he said to them: "Do you not yet get the meaning?"

22 Now they put in at Beth·sa'-i·da. Here people brought him a blind man, and they entreated him to touch him. 23 And he took the blind man by the hand, brought him outside the village, and, having spit upon his eyes, he laid his hands upon him and began to ask him: "Do you see anything?" 24 And the man looked up and began saying: "I see men, because I observe what seem to be trees, but they are walking about." 25 Then he laid his hands again upon the man's eyes, and the man saw clearly, and he was restored, and he was seeing everything distinctly. 26 So he sent him off home, saying: "But do not enter into the village."

27 Jesus and his disciples now left for the villages of Caes·a·re'a Phi·lip'pi, and on the way he began questioning his disciples, saying to them: "Who are men saying that I am?" 28 They said to him: "John the Baptist, and others, E·li'-jah, still others, One of the prophets." 29 And he put the question to them: "You, though, who do you say I am?" In answer Peter said to him: "You are the Christ." 30 At that he strictly charged them not to tell anyone about him. 31 Also, he started teaching them that the Son of man must undergo many sufferings and be rejected by the older men and the chief priests and the scribes and be killed, and rise three days later. 32 Indeed, with outspokenness he was making that statement. But Peter took him aside and started rebuking him. 33 He turned, looked at his disciples and rebuked Peter, and said: "Get be-

hind me, Satan, because you think, not God's thoughts, but those of men."

34 He now called the crowd to him with his disciples and said to them: "If anyone wants to come after me, let him disown himself and pick up his torture stake and follow me continually. 35 For whoever wants to save his soul will lose it; but whoever loses his soul for the sake of me and the good news will save it. 36 Really, of what benefit is it for a man to gain the whole world and to forfeit his soul? 37 What, really, would a man give in exchange for his soul? 38 For whoever becomes ashamed of me and my words in this adulterous and sinful generation, the Son of man will also be ashamed of him when he arrives in the glory of his Father with the holy angels."

9 Furthermore, he went on to say to them: "Truly I say to you, There are some of those standing here that will not taste death at all until first they see the kingdom of God already come in power." 2 Accordingly six days later Jesus took Peter and James and John along, and brought them up into a lofty mountain to themselves alone. And he was transfigured before them, 3 and his outer garments became glistening, far whiter than any clothes cleaner on earth could whiten them. 4 Also, E·li'jah with Moses appeared to them, and they were conversing with Jesus. 5 And responsively Peter said to Jesus: "Rabbi, it is fine for us to be here, so let us erect three tents, one for you and one for Moses and one for E·li'jah." 6 In fact, he did not know what response he should make, for they became quite fearful. 7 And a cloud formed, overshadowing them, and a voice came out of the cloud: "This is my Son, the beloved; listen to him." 8 Suddenly, however, they looked around and saw no one with them any longer, except Jesus alone.

9 As they were coming down out of the mountain, he expressly ordered them not to relate to any-

body what they saw, until after the Son of man had risen from the dead. 10 And they took the word to heart, but discussed among themselves what this rising from the dead meant. 11 And they began to question him, saying: "Why do the scribes say that first E·li'jah must come?" 12 He said to them: "E·li'jah does come first and restore all things; but how is it that it is written respecting the Son of man that he must undergo many sufferings and be treated as of no account? 13 But I say to YOU, E·li'jah, in fact, has come, and they did to him as many things as they wanted, just as it is written respecting him."

14 When, now, they came toward the other disciples, they noticed a great crowd about them and scribes disputing with them. 15 But as soon as all the crowd caught sight of him they were stunned, and, running up to him, they began to greet him. 16 And he asked them: "What are YOU disputing with them?" 17 And one of the crowd answered him: "Teacher, I brought my son to you because he has a speechless spirit; 18 and wherever it seizes him it dashes him to the ground, and he foams and grinds his teeth and loses his strength. And I told your disciples to expel it, but they were not capable." 19 In response he said to them: "O faithless generation, how long must I continue with YOU? How long must I put up with YOU? Bring him to me." 20 So they brought him to him. But at the sight of him the spirit at once threw [the child] into convulsions, and after falling on the ground he kept rolling about, foaming. 21 And he asked his father: "How long has this been happening to him?" He said: "From childhood on; 22 and time and again it would throw him both into the fire and into the water to destroy him. But if you can do anything, have pity on us and help us." 23 Jesus said to him: "That expression, 'If you can'! Why, all things can be to one if one has faith." 24 Immediately

crying out, the father of the young child was saying: "I have faith! Help me out where I need faith!" 25 Jesus, now noticing that a crowd was running together upon [them], rebuked the unclean spirit, saying to it: "You speechless and deaf spirit, I order you, get out of him and enter into him no more." 26 And after crying out and going through many convulsions it got out; and he became as dead, so that the greater number of them were saying: "He is dead!" 27 But Jesus took him by the hand and raised him up, and he rose. 28 So after he entered into a house his disciples proceeded to ask him privately: "Why could we not expel it?" 29 And he said to them: "This kind cannot get out by anything except by prayer."

30 From there they departed and went their way through Gal'i·lee, but he did not want anyone to get to know it. 31 For he was teaching his disciples and telling them: "The Son of man is to be delivered into men's hands, and they will kill him, but, despite being killed, he will rise three days later." 32 However, they were not understanding the saying, and they were afraid to question him.

33 And they came into Ca·per'-na·um. Now when he was inside the house he put the question to them: "What were YOU arguing over on the road?" 34 They kept silent, for on the road they had argued among themselves who is greater. 35 So he sat down and called the twelve and said to them: "If anyone wants to be first, he must be last of all and minister of all." 36 And he took a young child, stood it in their midst and put his arms around it and said to them: 37 "Whoever receives one of such young children on the basis of my name, receives me; and whoever receives me, receives, not me only, but also him that sent me forth."

38 John said to him: "Teacher, we saw a certain man expelling demons by the use of your name and we tried to prevent him, be-

cause he was not accompanying us." **39** But Jesus said: "Do not try to prevent him, for there is no one that will do a powerful work on the basis of my name that will quickly be able to revile me; **40** for he that is not against us is for us. **41** For whoever gives you a cup of water to drink on the ground that you belong to Christ, I truly tell you, he will by no means lose his reward. **42** But whoever stumbles one of these little ones that believe, it would be finer for him if a millstone such as is turned by an ass were put around his neck and he were actually pitched into the sea.

43 "And if ever your hand makes you stumble, cut it off; it is finer for you to enter into life maimed than with two hands to go off into Ge·hen′na, into the fire that cannot be put out. **44** —— **45** And if your foot makes you stumble, cut it off; it is finer for you to enter into life lame than with two feet to be pitched into Ge·hen′na. **46** —— **47** And if your eye makes you stumble, throw it away; it is finer for you to enter one-eyed into the kingdom of God than with two eyes to be pitched into Ge·hen′na, **48** where their maggot does not die and the fire is not put out.

49 "For everyone must be salted with fire. **50** Salt is fine; but if ever the salt loses its strength, with what will you season it itself? Have salt in yourselves, and keep peace between one another."

10 From there he rose and came to the frontiers of Ju·de′a and across the Jordan, and again crowds came together to him, and as he was accustomed to do he again went teaching them. **2** Pharisees now approached and, to put him to the test, began questioning him whether it was lawful for a man to divorce a wife. **3** In answer he said to them: "What did Moses command you?" **4** They said: "Moses allowed the writing of a certificate of dismissal and divorcing [her]." **5** But Jesus said to them: "Out of regard for your hardheartedness he wrote you this commandment. **6** However, from [the] beginning of creation 'He made them male and female. **7** On this account a man will leave his father and mother, **8** and the two will be one flesh'; so that they are no longer two, but one flesh. **9** Therefore what God yoked together let no man put apart." **10** When again in the house the disciples began to question him concerning this. **11** And he said to them: "Whoever divorces his wife and marries another commits adultery against her, **12** and if ever a woman, after divorcing her husband, marries another, she commits adultery."

13 Now people began bringing him young children for him to touch these; but the disciples reprimanded them. **14** At seeing this Jesus was indignant and said to them: "Let the young children come to me; do not try to stop them, for the kingdom of God belongs to suchlike ones. **15** Truly I say to you, Whoever does not receive the kingdom of God like a young child will by no means enter into it." **16** And he took the children into his arms and began blessing them, laying his hands upon them.

17 And as he was going out on his way, a certain man ran up and fell upon his knees before him and put the question to him: "Good Teacher, what must I do to inherit everlasting life?" **18** Jesus said to him: "Why do you call me good? Nobody is good, except one, God. **19** You know the commandments, 'Do not murder, Do not commit adultery, Do not steal, Do not bear false witness, Do not defraud, Honor your father and mother.'" **20** The man said to him: "Teacher, all these things I have kept from my youth on." **21** Jesus looked upon him and felt love for him and said to him: "One thing is missing about you: Go, sell what things you have and give to the poor, and you will have treasure in heaven, and come be my follower." **22** But he grew sad at the saying and went off grieved, for he was holding many possessions.

23 After looking around Jesus said to his disciples: "How difficult a thing it will be for those with money to enter into the kingdom of God!" 24 But the disciples gave way to surprise at his words. In response Jesus again said to them: "Children, how difficult a thing it is to enter into the kingdom of God! 25 It is easier for a camel to go through a needle's eye than for a rich man to enter into the kingdom of God." 26 They became still more astounded and said to him: "Who, in fact, can be saved?" 27 Looking straight at them Jesus said: "With men it is impossible, but not so with God, for all things are possible with God." 28 Peter started to say to him: "Look! We left all things and have been following you." 29 Jesus said: "Truly I say to you men, No one has left house or brothers or sisters or mother or father or children or fields for my sake and for the sake of the good news 30 who will not get a hundredfold now in this period of time, houses and brothers and sisters and mothers and children and fields, with persecutions, and in the coming system of things everlasting life. 31 However, many that are first will be last, and the last first."

32 Now they were advancing on the road up to Jerusalem, and Jesus was going in front of them, and they felt amazement; but those who followed began to fear. Once again he took the twelve aside and started to tell them these things destined to befall him: 33 "Here we are, advancing up to Jerusalem, and the Son of man will be delivered to the chief priests and the scribes, and they will condemn him to death and will deliver him to men of the nations, 34 and they will make fun of him and will spit upon him and scourge him and kill him, but three days later he will rise."

35 And James and John, the two sons of Zeb′e·dee, stepped up to him and said to him: "Teacher, we want you to do for us whatever it is we ask you for." 36 He said to them: "What do you want me to do for you?" 37 They said to him: "Grant us to sit down, one at your right hand and one at your left, in your glory." 38 But Jesus said to them: "You do not know what you are asking for. Are you able to drink the cup which I am drinking, or to be baptized with the baptism with which I am being baptized?" 39 They said to him: "We are able." At that Jesus said to them: "The cup I am drinking you will drink, and with the baptism with which I am being baptized you will be baptized. 40 However, this sitting down at my right or at my left is not mine to give, but it belongs to those for whom it has been prepared."

41 Well, when the ten others heard about it, they started to be indignant at James and John. 42 But Jesus, after calling them to him, said to them: "You know that those who appear to be ruling the nations lord it over them and their great ones wield authority over them. 43 This is not the way among you; but whoever wants to become great among you must be your minister, 44 and whoever wants to be first among you must be the slave of all. 45 For even the Son of man came, not to be ministered to, but to minister and to give his soul a ransom in exchange for many."

46 And they came into Jer′i·cho. But as he and his disciples and a considerable crowd were going out of Jer′i·cho, Bar·ti·mae′us (the son of Ti·mae′us), a blind beggar, was sitting beside the road. 47 When he heard that it was Jesus the Naz·a·rene′, he started shouting and saying: "Son of David, Jesus, have mercy on me!" 48 At this many began sternly telling him to be silent; but he kept shouting that much more: "Son of David, have mercy on me!" 49 So Jesus stopped and said: "Call him." And they called the blind man, saying to him: "Take courage, get up, he is

calling you." 50 Throwing off his outer garment, he leaped to his feet and went to Jesus. 51 And in answer to him Jesus said: "What do you want me to do for you?" The blind man said to him: "*Rab·bo'ni*, let me recover sight." 52 And Jesus said to him: "Go, your faith has made you well." And immediately he recovered sight, and he began to follow him on the road.

11 Now when they were getting near to Jerusalem, to Beth'pha·ge and Beth'a·ny at the Mount of Olives, he dispatched two of his disciples 2 and told them: "Go into the village that is within sight of you, and as soon as you pass into it you will find a colt tied, on which none of mankind has yet sat; loose it and bring it. 3 And if anyone says to you, 'Why are you doing this?' say, 'The Lord needs it, and will at once send it off back here.'" 4 So they went away and found the colt tied at the door, outside on the side street, and they loosed it. 5 But some of those standing there began to say to them: "What are you doing loosing the colt?" 6 They said to these just as Jesus had said; and they let them go.

7 And they brought the colt to Jesus, and they put their outer garments upon it, and he sat on it. 8 Also, many spread their outer garments on the road, but others cut down foliage from the fields. 9 And those going in front and those coming behind kept crying out: "Save, we pray! Blessed is he that comes in Jehovah's name! 10 Blessed is the coming kingdom of our father David! Save, we pray, in the heights above!" 11 And he entered into Jerusalem, into the temple; and he looked around upon all things, and, as the hour was already late, he went out to Beth'a·ny with the twelve.

12 The next day, when they had come out from Beth'a·ny, he became hungry. 13 And from a distance he caught sight of a fig tree that had leaves, and he went to see whether he would perhaps find something on it. But, on coming to it, he found nothing but leaves, for it was not the season of figs. 14 So, in response, he said to it: "Let no one eat fruit from you any more forever." And his disciples were listening.

15 Now they came to Jerusalem. There he entered into the temple and started to throw out those selling and buying in the temple, and he overturned the tables of the money-changers and the benches of those selling doves; 16 and he would not let anyone carry a utensil through the temple, 17 but he kept teaching and saying: "Is it not written, 'My house will be called a house of prayer for all the nations'? But you have made it a cave of robbers." 18 And the chief priests and the scribes heard it, and they began to seek how to destroy him; for they were in fear of him, for all the crowd was continually being astounded at his teaching.

19 And when it became late in the day, they would go out of the city. 20 But when they were passing by early in the morning, they saw the fig tree already withered up from the roots. 21 So Peter, remembering it, said to him: "Rabbi, see! the fig tree that you cursed has withered up." 22 And in reply Jesus said to them: "Have faith in God. 23 Truly I say to you that whoever tells this mountain, 'Be lifted up and thrown into the sea,' and does not doubt in his heart but has faith that what he says is going to occur, he will have it so. 24 This is why I tell you, All the things you pray and ask for have faith that you have practically received, and you will have them. 25 And when you stand praying, forgive whatever you have against anyone; in order that your Father who is in the heavens may also forgive you your trespasses." 26 ——

27 And they came again to Jerusalem. And as he was walking in the temple, the chief priests and the scribes and the older men came to him 28 and began to say to him: "By what authority do you

do these things? or who gave you this authority to do these things?" 29 Jesus said to them: "I will ask YOU one question. YOU answer me, and I will also tell YOU by what authority I do these things. 30 Was the baptism by John from heaven or from men? Answer me." 31 So they began to reason among themselves, saying: "If we say, 'From heaven,' he will say, 'Why is it, therefore, YOU did not believe him?' 32 But dare we say, 'From men'?" —They were in fear of the crowd, for these all held that John had really been a prophet. 33 Well, in reply to Jesus they said: "We do not know." And Jesus said to them: "Neither am I telling YOU by what authority I do these things."

12 Also, he started to speak to them with illustrations: "A man planted a vineyard, and put a fence around it, and dug a vat for the wine press and erected a tower, and let it out to cultivators, and traveled abroad. 2 Now in due season he sent forth a slave to the cultivators, that he might get some of the fruits of the vineyard from the cultivators. 3 But they took him, beat him up and sent him away empty. 4 And again he sent forth another slave to them; and that one they struck on the head and dishonored. 5 And he sent forth another, and that one they killed; and many others, some of whom they beat up and some of whom they killed. 6 One more he had, a beloved son. He sent him forth last to them, saying, 'They will respect my son.' 7 But those cultivators said among themselves, 'This is the heir. Come, let us kill him, and the inheritance will be ours.' 8 So they took him and killed him, and threw him outside the vineyard. 9 What will the owner of the vineyard do? He will come and destroy the cultivators, and will give the vineyard to others. 10 Did YOU never read this scripture, 'The stone that the builders rejected, this has become the chief cornerstone. 11 From Jehovah this has come to be, and it is marvelous in our eyes'?"

12 At that they began seeking how to seize him, but they feared the crowd, for they took note that he spoke the illustration with them in mind. So they left him and went away.

13 Next they sent forth to him some of the Pharisees and of the party followers of Herod, to catch him in his speech. 14 On arrival these said to him: "Teacher, we know you are truthful and you do not care for anybody, for you do not look upon men's outward appearance, but you teach the way of God in line with truth: Is it lawful to pay head tax to Caesar or not? 15 Shall we pay, or shall we not pay?" Detecting their hypocrisy, he said to them: "Why do YOU put me to the test? Bring me a de·nar'i·us to look at." 16 They brought one. And he said to them: "Whose image and inscription is this?" They said to him: "Caesar's." 17 Jesus then said: "Pay back Caesar's things to Caesar, but God's things to God." And they began to marvel at him.

18 Now Sadducees came to him, who say there is no resurrection, and they put the question to him: 19 "Teacher, Moses wrote us that if someone's brother dies and leaves a wife behind but does not leave a child, his brother should take the wife and raise up offspring from her for his brother. 20 There were seven brothers; and the first took a wife, but when he died he left no offspring. 21 And the second took her, but died without leaving offspring; and the third the same way. 22 And the seven did not leave any offspring. Last of all the woman also died. 23 In the resurrection to which of them will she be wife? For the seven got her as wife." 24 Jesus said to them: "Is not this why YOU are mistaken, YOUR not knowing either the Scriptures or the power of God? 25 For when they rise from the dead, neither do men marry nor are women given in marriage, but are as angels in the heavens. 26 But concerning the dead, that they are raised up, did YOU not read in the book of

Moses, in the account about the thornbush, how God said to him, 'I am the God of Abraham and God of Isaac and God of Jacob'? 27 He is a God, not of the dead, but of the living. You are much mistaken."

28 Now one of the scribes that had come up and heard them disputing, knowing that he had answered them in a fine way, asked him: "Which commandment is first of all?" 29 Jesus answered: "The first is, 'Hear, O Israel, Jehovah our God is one Jehovah, 30 and you must love Jehovah your God with your whole heart and with your whole soul and with your whole mind and with your whole strength.' 31 The second is this, 'You must love your neighbor as yourself.' There is no other commandment greater than these." 32 The scribe said to him: "Teacher, you well said in line with truth, 'He is One, and there is no other than He'; 33 and this loving him with one's whole heart and with one's whole understanding and with one's whole strength and this loving one's neighbor as oneself is worth far more than all the whole burnt offerings and sacrifices." 34 At this Jesus, discerning he had answered intelligently, said to him: "You are not far from the kingdom of God." But nobody had the courage any more to question him.

35 However, when making a reply, Jesus began to say as he taught in the temple: "How is it that the scribes say that the Christ is David's son? 36 By the holy spirit David himself said, 'Jehovah said to my Lord: "Sit at my right hand until I put your enemies beneath your feet."' 37 David himself calls him 'Lord,' but how does it come that he is his son?"

And the great crowd was listening to him with pleasure. 38 And in his teaching he went on to say: "Look out for the scribes that want to walk around in robes and want greetings in the market places 39 and front seats in the synagogues and most prominent places at evening meals. 40 They are the ones devouring the houses of the widows and for a pretext making long prayers; these will receive a heavier judgment."

41 And he sat down with the treasury chests in view and began observing how the crowd was dropping money into the treasury chests; and many rich people were dropping in many coins. 42 Now a poor widow came and dropped in two small coins, which have very little value. 43 So he called his disciples to him and said to them: "Truly I say to you that this poor widow dropped in more than all those dropping money into the treasury chests; 44 for they all dropped in out of their surplus, but she, out of her want, dropped in all of what she had, her whole living."

13 As he was going out of the temple one of his disciples said to him: "Teacher, see! what sort of stones and what sort of buildings!" 2 However, Jesus said to him: "Do you behold these great buildings? By no means will a stone be left here upon a stone and not be thrown down."

3 And as he was sitting on the Mount of Olives with the temple in view, Peter and James and John and Andrew began to ask him privately: 4 "Tell us, When will these things be, and what will be the sign when all these things are destined to come to a conclusion?" 5 So Jesus started to say to them: "Look out that nobody misleads you. 6 Many will come on the basis of my name, saying, 'I am he,' and will mislead many. 7 Moreover, when you hear of wars and reports of wars, do not be terrified; [these things] must take place, but the end is not yet.

8 "For nation will rise against nation and kingdom against kingdom, there will be earthquakes in one place after another, there will be food shortages. These are a beginning of pangs of distress.

9 "As for you, look out for yourselves; people will deliver you up to local courts, and you will be beaten in synagogues and be put on

the stand before governors and kings for my sake, for a witness to them. 10 Also, in all the nations the good news has to be preached first. 11 But when they are leading YOU along to deliver YOU up, do not be anxious beforehand about what to speak; but whatever is given YOU in that hour, speak this, for YOU are not the ones speaking, but the holy spirit is. 12 Furthermore, brother will deliver brother over to death, and a father a child, and children will rise up against parents and have them put to death; 13 and YOU will be objects of hatred by all people on account of my name. But he that has endured to the end is the one that will be saved.

14 "However, when YOU catch sight of the disgusting thing that causes desolation standing where it ought not (let the reader use discernment), then let those in Ju-de'a begin fleeing to the mountains. 15 Let the man on the housetop not come down, nor go inside to take anything out of his house; 16 and let the man in the field not return to the things behind to pick up his outer garment. 17 Woe to the pregnant women and those suckling a baby in those days! 18 Keep praying that it may not occur in wintertime; 19 for those days will be [days of] a tribulation such as has not occurred from[the] beginning of the creation which God created until that time, and will not occur again. 20 In fact, unless Jehovah had cut short the days, no flesh would be saved. But on account of the chosen ones whom he has chosen he has cut short the days.

21 "Then, too, if anyone says to YOU, 'See! Here is the Christ,' 'See! There he is,' do not believe [it]. 22 For false Christs and false prophets will arise and will give signs and wonders to lead astray, if possible, the chosen ones. 23 You, then, watch out; I have told YOU all things beforehand.

24 "But in those days, after that tribulation, the sun will be darkened, and the moon will not give

its light, 25 and the stars will be falling out of heaven, and the powers that are in the heavens will be shaken. 26 And then they will see the Son of man coming in clouds with great power and glory. 27 And then he will send forth the angels and will gather his chosen ones together from the four winds, from earth's extremity to heaven's extremity.

28 "Now from the fig tree learn the illustration: Just as soon as its young branch grows tender and puts forth its leaves, YOU know that summer is near. 29 Likewise also YOU, when YOU see these things happening, know that he is near, at the doors. 30 Truly I say to YOU that this generation will by no means pass away until all these things happen. 31 Heaven and earth will pass away, but my words will not pass away.

32 "Concerning that day or the hour nobody knows, neither the angels in heaven nor the Son, but the Father. 33 Keep looking, keep awake, for YOU do not know when the appointed time is. 34 It is like a man traveling abroad that left his house and gave the authority to his slaves, to each one his work, and commanded the doorkeeper to keep on the watch. 35 Therefore keep on the watch, for YOU do not know when the master of the house is coming, whether late in the day or at midnight or at cock-crowing or early in the morning; 36 in order that when he arrives suddenly, he does not find YOU sleeping. 37 But what I say to YOU I say to all, Keep on the watch."

14 Now the passover and the [festival of] unfermented cakes was two days later. And the chief priests and the scribes were seeking how to seize him by crafty device and kill him; 2 for they repeatedly said: "Not at the festival; perhaps there might be an uproar of the people."

3 And while he was at Beth'a·ny in the house of Simon the leper, as he was reclining at the meal, a woman came with an alabaster case of perfumed oil, genuine nard, very

expensive. Breaking open the alabaster case she began to pour it upon his head. 4 At this there were some expressing indignation among themselves: "Why has this waste of the perfumed oil taken place? 5 For this perfumed oil could have been sold for upward of three hundred de·nar'i·i and been given to the poor!" And they were feeling great displeasure at her. 6 But Jesus said: "Let her alone. Why do you try to make trouble for her? She did a fine deed toward me. 7 For you always have the poor with you, and whenever you want to you can always do them good, but me you do not have always. 8 She did what she could; she undertook beforehand to put perfumed oil on my body in view of the burial. 9 Truly I say to you, Wherever the good news is preached in all the world, what this woman did shall also be told as a remembrance of her."

10 And Judas Is·car'i·ot, one of the twelve, went off to the chief priests in order to betray him to them. 11 When they heard it, they rejoiced and promised to give him silver money. So he began seeking how to betray him conveniently.

12 Now on the first day of unfermented cakes, when they customarily sacrificed the passover victim, his disciples said to him: "Where do you want us to go and prepare for you to eat the passover?" 13 With that he sent forth two of his disciples and said to them: "Go into the city, and a man carrying an earthenware vessel of water will encounter you. Follow him, 14 and wherever he goes inside say to the householder, 'The Teacher says: "Where is the guest room for me where I may eat the passover with my disciples?"' 15 And he will show you a large upper room, furnished in preparation; and there prepare for us." 16 So the disciples went out, and they entered the city and found it just as he said to them; and they prepared for the passover.

17 After evening had fallen he came with the twelve. 18 And as they were reclining at the table and eating, Jesus said: "Truly I say to you, One of you, who is eating with me, will betray me." 19 They started to be grieved and to say to him one by one: "It is not I, is it?" 20 He said to them: "It is one of the twelve, who is dipping with me into the common bowl. 21 True, the Son of man is going away, just as it is written concerning him, but woe to that man through whom the Son of man is betrayed! It would have been finer for that man if he had not been born."

22 And as they continued eating, he took a loaf, said a blessing, broke it and gave it to them, and said: "Take it, this means my body." 23 And taking a cup, he offered thanks and gave it to them, and they all drank out of it. 24 And he said to them: "This means my 'blood of the covenant,' which is to be poured out in behalf of many. 25 Truly I say to you, I shall by no means drink any more of the product of the vine until that day when I drink it new in the kingdom of God." 26 Finally, after singing praises, they went out to the Mount of Olives.

27 And Jesus said to them: "You will all be stumbled, because it is written, 'I will strike the shepherd, and the sheep will be scattered about.' 28 But after I have been raised up I will go ahead of you into Gal'i·lee." 29 But Peter said to him: "Even if all the others are stumbled, yet I will not be." 30 At that Jesus said to him: "Truly I say to you, You today, yes, this night, before a cock crows twice, even you will disown me three times." 31 But he began to say profusely: "If I have to die with you, I will by no means disown you." Also, all the others began saying the same thing.

32 So they came to a spot named Geth·sem'a·ne, and he said to his disciples: "Sit down here while I pray." 33 And he took Peter and James and John along with him, and he started to be stunned and to be sorely troubled. 34 And he

said to them: "My soul is deeply grieved, even to death. Stay here and keep on the watch." 35 And going a little way forward he proceeded to fall on the ground and began praying that, if it were possible, the hour might pass away from him. 36 And he went on to say: "*Abba*, Father, all things are possible to you; remove this cup from me. Yet not what I want, but what you want." 37 And he came and found them sleeping, and he said to Peter: "Simon, are you sleeping? Did you not have strength to keep on the watch one hour? 38 Men, keep on the watch and praying, in order that YOU do not come into temptation. The spirit, of course, is eager, but the flesh is weak." 39 And he went away again and prayed, saying the same word. 40 And again he came and found them sleeping, for their eyes were weighed down, and so they did not know what to answer him. 41 And he came the third time and said to them: "At such a time as this YOU are sleeping and taking YOUR rest! It is enough! The hour has come! Look! The Son of man is betrayed into the hands of sinners. 42 Get up, let us go. Look! My betrayer has drawn near."

43 And immediately, while he was yet speaking, Judas, one of the twelve, arrived and with him a crowd with swords and clubs from the chief priests and the scribes and the older men. 44 Now his betrayer had given them an agreed sign, saying: "Whoever it is I kiss, this is he; take him into custody and lead him away safely." 45 And he came straight up and approached him and said: "Rabbi!" and kissed him very tenderly. 46 So they laid their hands upon him and took him into custody. 47 However, a certain one of those standing by drew his sword and struck the slave of the high priest and took his ear off. 48 But in response Jesus said to them: "Did YOU come out with swords and clubs as against a robber to arrest me? 49 Day after day I was with YOU in the temple teaching, and

yet YOU did not take me into custody. Nevertheless, it is in order that the Scriptures may be fulfilled."

50 And they all abandoned him and fled. 51 But a certain young man wearing a fine linen garment over his naked body began to follow him nearby; and they tried to seize him, 52 but he left his linen garment behind and got away naked.

53 They now led Jesus away to the high priest, and all the chief priests and the older men and the scribes assembled. 54 But Peter, from a good distance, followed him as far as in the courtyard of the high priest; and he was sitting together with the house attendants and warming himself before a bright fire. 55 Meantime the chief priests and the whole San′he·drin were looking for testimony against Jesus to put him to death, but they were not finding any. 56 Many, indeed, were giving false witness against him, but their testimonies were not in agreement. 57 Also, certain ones were rising and bearing false witness against him, saying: 58 "We heard him say, 'I will throw down this temple that was made with hands and in three days I will build another not made with hands.'" 59 But neither on these grounds was their testimony in agreement.

60 Finally the high priest rose in their midst and questioned Jesus, saying: "Do you say nothing in reply? What is it these are testifying against you?" 61 But he kept silent and made no reply at all. Again the high priest began to question him and said to him: "Are you the Christ the Son of the Blessed One?" 62 Then Jesus said: "I am; and YOU persons will see the Son of man sitting at the right hand of power and coming with the clouds of heaven." 63 At this the high priest ripped his inner garments and said: "What further need do we have of witnesses? 64 YOU heard the blasphemy. What is evident to YOU?" They all condemned him to be liable to death.

65 And some started to spit on him and some to cover his whole face and hit him with their fists and say to him: "Prophesy!" And, slapping him in the face, the court attendants took him.

66 Now while Peter was below in the courtyard, one of the servant girls of the high priest came, 67 and, seeing Peter warming himself, she looked straight at him and said: "You, too, were with the Naz·a·rene', this Jesus." 68 But he denied it, saying: "Neither do I know him nor do I understand what you are saying," and he went outside to the vestibule. 69 There the servant girl, at the sight of him, started again to say to those standing by: "This is one of them." 70 Again he was denying it. And once more after a little while those standing by began saying to Peter: "Certainly you are one of them, for, in fact, you are a Gal·i·le'an." 71 But he commenced to curse and swear: "I do not know this man of whom you speak." 72 And immediately a cock crowed a second time; and Peter recalled the saying that Jesus spoke to him: "Before a cock crows twice, you will disown me three times." And he broke down and gave way to weeping.

15 And immediately at dawn the chief priests with the older men and the scribes, even the whole San'he·drin, conducted a consultation, and they bound Jesus and led him off and handed him over to Pilate. 2 So Pilate put the question to him: "Are you the king of the Jews?" In answer to him he said: "You yourself say [it]." 3 But the chief priests proceeded to accuse him of many things. 4 Now Pilate began questioning him again, saying: "Have you no reply to make? See how many charges they are bringing against you." 5 But Jesus made no further answer, so that Pilate began to marvel.

6 Well, from festival to festival he used to release to them one prisoner, whom they petitioned for. 7 At the time there was the so-called Bar·ab'bas in bonds with the seditionists, who in their sedition

had committed murder. 8 So the crowd came on up and started to make petition according to what he used to do for them. 9 Pilate responded to them, saying: "Do you want me to release to you the king of the Jews?" 10 For he was aware that because of envy the chief priests had handed him over. 11 But the chief priests stirred up the crowd to have him release Bar·ab'bas to them, instead. 12 Again in reply Pilate was saying to them: "What, then, shall I do with him whom you call the king of the Jews?" 13 Once more they cried out: "Impale him!" 14 But Pilate went on to say to them: "Why, what bad thing did he do?" Still they cried out all the more: "Impale him!" 15 At that Pilate, wishing to satisfy the crowd, released Bar·ab'bas to them, and, after having Jesus whipped, he handed him over to be impaled.

16 The soldiers now led him off into the courtyard, that is, into the governor's palace; and they called the whole body of troops together, 17 and they decked him with purple and braided a crown of thorns and put it on him. 18 And they started greeting him: "Good day, you King of the Jews!" 19 Also, they would hit him on the head with a reed and spit upon him and, bending their knees, they would do obeisance to him. 20 Finally, when they had made fun of him, they stripped him of the purple and put his outer garments upon him. And they led him out to impale him. 21 Also, they impressed into service a passer-by, a certain Simon of Cy·re'ne, coming from the country, the father of Alexander and Rufus, that he should lift up his torture stake.

22 So they brought him to the place Gol'go·tha, which means, when translated, Skull Place. 23 Here they tried to give him wine drugged with myrrh, but he would not take it. 24 And they impaled him and distributed his outer garments by casting the lot over them as to who takes what. 25 It was now the third hour, and

they impaled him. 26 And the inscription of the charge against him was written above, "The King of the Jews." 27 Moreover, they impaled two robbers with him, one on his right and one on his left. 28 —— 29 And those going by would speak abusively to him, wagging their heads and saying: "Bah! You would-be thrower-down of the temple and builder of it in three days' time, 30 save yourself by coming down off the torture stake." 31 In like manner also the chief priests were making fun among themselves with the scribes and saying: "Others he saved; himself he cannot save!" 32 Let the Christ the King of Israel now come down off the torture stake, that we may see and believe." Even those impaled together with him were reproaching him.

33 When it became the sixth hour a darkness fell over the whole land until the ninth hour. 34 And at the ninth hour Jesus called out with a loud voice: *"E′li, E′li, la′ma sa·bach·tha′ni?"* which means, when translated: "My God, my God, why have you forsaken me?" 35 And some of those standing near, on hearing it, began to say: "See! He is calling E·li′jah." 36 But a certain one ran, soaked a sponge with sour wine, put it on a reed, and began giving him a drink, saying: "LET [him] be! Let us see whether E·li′jah comes to take him down." 37 But Jesus let out a loud cry and expired. 38 And the curtain of the sanctuary was rent in two from top to bottom. 39 Now, when the army officer that was standing by with him in view saw he had expired under these circumstances, he said: "Certainly this man was God's Son."

40 There were also women viewing from a distance, among them Mary Mag′da·lene as well as Mary the mother of James the Less and of Jo′ses, and Sa·lo′me, 41 who used to accompany him and minister to him when he was in Gal′i·lee, and many other women who had come up together with him to Jerusalem.

42 Now as it was already late in the afternoon, and since it was Preparation, that is, the day before the sabbath, 43 there came Joseph of Ar·i·ma·the′a, a reputable member of the San′he·drin, who also himself was waiting for the kingdom of God. He took courage to go in before Pilate and asked for the body of Jesus. 44 But Pilate wondered whether he was already dead, and, summoning the army officer, he asked him whether he had already died. 45 So after making certain from the army officer, he granted the corpse to Joseph. 46 Accordingly he bought fine linen and took him down, wrapped him in the fine linen and laid him in a tomb which was quarried out of a rock-mass; and he rolled a stone up to the door of the memorial tomb. 47 But Mary Mag′da·lene and Mary the mother of Jo′ses continued looking at where he had been laid.

16 So when the sabbath had passed, Mary Mag′da·lene, and Mary the mother of James, and Sa·lo′me bought spices in order to come and grease him. 2 And very early on the first day of the week they came to the memorial tomb, when the sun had risen. 3 And they were saying one to another: "Who will roll the stone away from the door of the memorial tomb for us?" 4 But when they looked up, they beheld that the stone had been rolled away, although it was very large. 5 When they entered into the memorial tomb, they saw a young man sitting on the right side clothed in a white robe, and they were stunned. 6 He said to them: "Stop being stunned. YOU are looking for Jesus the Naz·a·rene′, who was impaled. He was raised up, he is not here. See! The place where they laid him. 7 But go, tell his disciples and Peter, 'He is going ahead of YOU into Gal′i·lee; there YOU will see him, just as he told YOU.' " 8 So when they came out they fled from the memorial tomb, for trembling and strong emotion were gripping them. And they told nobody anything, for they were in fear.

LONG CONCLUSION

Certain ancient manuscripts (ACD) and versions (VgSyᵉˑᵖ) add the following long conclusion, but which אBSyˢArm omit:

9 After he rose early on the first day of the week he appeared first to Mary Mag′da·lene, from whom he had expelled seven demons. 10 She went and reported to those who had been with him, as they were mourning and weeping. 11 But they, when they heard he had come to life and had been viewed by her, did not believe. 12 Moreover, after these things he appeared in another form to two of them walking along, as they were going into the country; 13 and they came back and reported to the rest. Neither did they believe these. 14 But later he appeared to the eleven themselves as they were reclining at the table, and he reproached their lack of faith and hardheartedness, because they did not believe those who had beheld him now raised up from the dead. 15 And he said to them: ''Go into all the world and preach the good news to all creation. 16 He that believes and is baptized will be saved, but he that does not believe will be condemned. 17 Furthermore, these signs will accompany those believing: By the use of my name they will expel demons, they will speak with tongues, 18 and with their hands they will pick up serpents, and if they drink anything deadly it will not hurt them at all. They will lay their hands upon sick persons, and these will become well.''

19 So, then, the Lord Jesus, after having spoken to them, was taken up to heaven and sat down at the right hand of God. 20 They, accordingly, went out and preached everywhere, while the Lord worked with them and backed up the message through the accompanying signs.

SHORT CONCLUSION

Some late manuscripts and versions contain a short conclusion after Mark 16:8, as follows:

But all the things that had been commanded they related briefly to those around Peter. Further, after these things, Jesus himself sent out through them from the east to the west the holy and incorruptible proclamation of everlasting salvation.

ACCORDING TO

LUKE

1 Whereas many have undertaken to compile a statement of the facts that are given full credence among us, 2 just as those who from [the] beginning became eyewitnesses and attendants of the message delivered these to us, 3 I resolved also, because I have traced all things from the start with accuracy, to write them in logical order to you, most excellent The·oph′i·lus, 4 that you may know fully the certainty of the things that you have been taught orally.

5 In the days of Herod, king of Ju·de′a, there happened to be a certain priest named Zech·a·ri′ah of the division of A·bi′jah, and he had a wife from the daughters of Aaron, and her name was Elizabeth. 6 They both were righteous before God because of walking blamelessly in accord with all the commandments and legal requirements of Jehovah. 7 But they had no child, because Elizabeth was barren, and they both were well along in years.

8 Now as he was acting as priest in the assignment of his division before God, 9 according to the solemn practice of the priestly office it became his turn to offer incense when he entered into the sanctuary of Jehovah; 10 and all the multitude of the people was praying outside at the hour of offering incense. 11 To him Jehovah's angel appeared, standing at the right side of the incense altar. 12 But Zech·a·ri′ah became troubled at the sight, and fear fell upon him. 13 How-

ever, the angel said to him: "Have no fear, Zech·a·ri'ah, because your supplication has been favorably heard, and your wife Elizabeth will become mother to a son to you, and you are to call his name John. 14 And you will have joy and great gladness, and many will rejoice over his birth; 15 for he will be great before Jehovah. But he must drink no wine and strong drink at all, and he will be filled with holy spirit right from his mother's womb; 16 and many of the sons of Israel will he turn back to Jehovah their God. 17 Also, he will go before him with E·li'jah's spirit and power, to turn back the hearts of fathers to children and the disobedient ones to the practical wisdom of righteous ones, to get ready for Jehovah a prepared people."

18 And Zech·a·ri'ah said to the angel: "How am I to be sure of this? For I am aged and my wife is well along in years." 19 In reply the angel said to him: "I am Ga'bri·el, who stands near before God, and I was sent forth to speak with you and declare the good news of these things to you. 20 But, look! you will be silent and not able to speak until the day that these things take place, because you did not believe my words, which will be fulfilled in their appointed time." 21 Meanwhile the people continued waiting for Zech·a·ri'ah, and they began to wonder at his delaying in the sanctuary. 22 But when he came out he was not able to speak to them, and they perceived that he had just seen a supernatural sight in the sanctuary; and he kept making signs to them, but remained dumb. 23 When, now, the days of his public service were fulfilled, he went off to his home.

24 But after these days Elizabeth his wife became pregnant; and she kept herself secluded for five months, saying: 25 "This is the way Jehovah has dealt with me in these days when he has given me his attention to take away my reproach among men."

26 In her sixth month the angel Ga'bri·el was sent forth from God to a city of Gal'i·lee named Naz'-a·reth, 27 to a virgin promised in marriage to a man named Joseph of David's house; and the name of the virgin was Mary. 28 And when he went in before her he said: "Good day, highly favored one, Jehovah is with you." 29 But she was deeply disturbed at the saying and began to reason out what sort of greeting this might be. 30 So the angel said to her: "Have no fear, Mary, for you have found favor with God; 31 and, look! you will conceive in your womb and give birth to a son, and you are to call his name Jesus. 32 This one will be great and will be called Son of the Most High; and Jehovah God will give him the throne of David his father, 33 and he will rule as king over the house of Jacob forever, and there will be no end of his kingdom."

34 But Mary said to the angel: "How is this to be, since I am having no intercourse with a man?" 35 In answer the angel said to her: "Holy spirit will come upon you, and power of the Most High will overshadow you. For that reason also what is born will be called holy, God's Son. 36 And, look! Elizabeth your relative has also herself conceived a son, in her old age, and this is the sixth month for her, the so-called barren woman; 37 because with God no declaration will be an impossibility." 38 Then Mary said: "Look! Jehovah's slave girl! May it take place with me according to your declaration." At that the angel departed from her.

39 So Mary rose in these days and went into the mountainous country with haste, to a city of Judah, 40 and she entered into the home of Zech·a·ri'ah and greeted Elizabeth. 41 Well, as Elizabeth heard the greeting of Mary, the infant in her womb leaped; and Elizabeth was filled with holy spirit, 42 and she called out with a loud cry and said: "Blessed are you among women, and blessed is the

fruit of your womb! 43 So how is it that this [privilege] is mine, to have the mother of my Lord come to me? 44 For, look! as the sound of your greeting fell upon my ears, the infant in my womb leaped with great gladness. 45 Happy too is she that believed, because there will be a complete performance of those things spoken to her from Jehovah."

46 And Mary said: "My soul magnifies Jehovah, 47 and my spirit cannot keep from being overjoyed at God my Savior; 48 because he has looked upon the low position of his slave girl. For, look! from now on all generations will pronounce me happy; 49 because the powerful One has done great deeds for me, and holy is his name; 50 and for generations after generations his mercy is upon those who fear him. 51 He has performed mightily with his arm, he has scattered abroad those who are haughty in the intention of their hearts. 52 He has brought down men of power from thrones and exalted lowly ones; 53 he has fully satisfied hungry ones with good things and he has sent away empty those who had wealth. 54 He has come to the aid of Israel his servant, to call to mind mercy, 55 just as he told to our forefathers, to Abraham and to his seed, forever." 56 Then Mary remained with her about three months, and returned to her own home.

57 The time now became due for Elizabeth to give birth, and she became mother to a son. 58 And the neighbors and her relatives heard that Jehovah had magnified his mercy to her, and they began to rejoice with her. 59 And on the eighth day they came to circumcise the young child, and they were going to call it by the name of its father, Zech·a·ri'ah. 60 But its mother answered and said: "No, indeed! but he shall be called John." 61 At this they said to her: "There is no one among your relatives that is called by this name." 62 Then they went asking its father by signs what he wanted

it to be called. 63 And he asked for a tablet and wrote: "John is its name." At this they all marveled. 64 Instantly his mouth was opened and his tongue loosed and he began to speak, blessing God. 65 And fear fell upon all those living in their neighborhood; and in the whole mountainous country of Ju·de'a all these things began to be talked around, 66 and all that heard made note of it in their hearts, saying: "What really will this young child be?" For the hand of Jehovah was indeed with it.

67 And Zech·a·ri'ah its father was filled with holy spirit, and he prophesied, saying: 68 "Blessed be Jehovah the God of Israel, because he has turned his attention and performed deliverance toward his people. 69 And he has raised up a horn of salvation for us in the house of David his servant, 70 just as he, through the mouth of his holy prophets from of old, has spoken 71 of a salvation from our enemies and from the hand of all those hating us; 72 to perform the mercy in connection with our forefathers and to call to mind his holy covenant, 73 the oath that he swore to Abraham our forefather, 74 to grant us, after we have been rescued from the hands of enemies, the privilege of fearlessly rendering sacred service to him 75 with loyalty and righteousness before him all our days. 76 But as for you, young child, you will be called a prophet of the Most High, for you will go in advance before Jehovah to make his ways ready, 77 to give knowledge of salvation to his people by forgiveness of their sins, 78 because of the tender compassion of our God. With this [compassion] a daybreak will visit us from on high, 79 to give light to those sitting in darkness and death's shadow, to direct our feet prosperously in the way of peace."

80 And the young child went on growing and getting strong in spirit, and he continued in the deserts until the day of showing himself openly to Israel.

2 Now in those days a decree went forth from Caesar Au·gus′tus for all the inhabited earth to be registered; 2 (this first registration took place when Qui·rin′i·us was governor of Syria;) 3 and all people went traveling to be registered, each one to his own city. 4 Of course, Joseph also went up from Gal′i·lee, out of the city of Naz′a·reth, into Ju·de′a, to David's city, which is called Beth′le·hem, because of his being a member of the house and family of David, 5 to get registered with Mary, who had been given him in marriage as promised, at present heavy with child. 6 While they were there, the days came to the full for her to give birth. 7 And she gave birth to her son, the first-born, and she bound him with cloth bands and laid him in a manger, because there was no place for them in the lodging room.

8 There were also in that same country shepherds living out of doors and keeping watches in the night over their flocks. 9 And suddenly Jehovah's angel stood by them, and Jehovah's glory gleamed around them, and they became very fearful. 10 But the angel said to them: "Have no fear, for, look! I am declaring to you good news of a great joy that all the people will have, 11 because there was born to you today a Savior, who is Christ the Lord, in David's city. 12 And this is a sign for you: you will find an infant bound in cloth bands and lying in a manger." 13 And suddenly there came to be with the angel a multitude of the heavenly army, praising God and saying: 14 "Glory in the heights above to God, and upon earth peace among men of good will."

15 So when the angels had departed from them into heaven, the shepherds began saying to one another: "Let us by all means go clear to Beth′le·hem and see this thing that has taken place, which Jehovah has made known to us." 16 And they went with haste and found Mary as well as Joseph, and the infant lying in the manger.

17 When they saw it, they made known the saying that had been spoken to them concerning this young child. 18 And all that heard marveled over the things told them by the shepherds, 19 but Mary began to preserve all these sayings, drawing conclusions in her heart. 20 Then the shepherds went back, glorifying and praising God for all the things they heard and saw, just as these had been told them.

21 Now when eight days came to the full for circumcising him, his name was also called Jesus, the name called by the angel before he was conceived in the womb.

22 Also, when the days for purifying them according to the law of Moses came to the full, they brought him up to Jerusalem to present him to Jehovah, 23 just as it is written in Jehovah's law: "Every male opening a womb must be called holy to Jehovah," 24 and to offer sacrifice according to what is said in the law of Jehovah: "A pair of turtledoves or two young pigeons."

25 And, look! there was a man in Jerusalem named Sim′e·on, and this man was righteous and reverent, waiting for Israel's consolation, and holy spirit was upon him. 26 Furthermore, it had been divinely revealed to him by the holy spirit that he would not see death before he had seen the Christ of Jehovah. 27 Under the power of the spirit he now came into the temple; and as the parents brought the young child Jesus in to do for it according to the customary practice of the law, 28 he himself received it into his arms and blessed God and said: 29 "Now, Sovereign Lord, you are letting your slave go free in peace according to your declaration; 30 because my eyes have seen your means of saving 31 that you have made ready in the sight of all the peoples, 32 a light for removing the veil from the nations and a glory of your people Israel." 33 And its father and mother continued wondering at the things being spoken about it. 34 Also, Sim′e·on blessed them, but

said to Mary its mother: "Look! This one is laid for the fall and the rising again of many in Israel and for a sign to be talked against 35 (yes, a long sword will be run through the soul of you yourself), in order that the reasonings of many hearts may be uncovered."

36 Now there was Anna a prophetess, Phan'u·el's daughter, of Ash'er's tribe (this woman was well along in years, and had lived with a husband for seven years from her virginity, 37 and she was a widow now eighty-four years old), who was never missing from the temple, rendering sacred service night and day with fastings and supplications. 38 And in that very hour she came near and began returning thanks to God and speaking about [the child] to all those waiting for Jerusalem's deliverance.

39 So when they had carried out all the things according to the law of Jehovah, they went back into Gal'i·lee to their own city Naz'a·reth. 40 And the young child continued growing and getting strong, being filled with wisdom, and God's favor continued upon him.

41 Now his parents were accustomed to go from year to year to Jerusalem for the festival of the passover. 42 And when he became twelve years old, they went up according to the custom of the festival 43 and completed the days. But when they were returning, the boy Jesus remained behind in Jerusalem, and his parents did not notice it. 44 Assuming that he was in the company traveling together, they covered a day's distance and then began to hunt him up among the relatives and acquaintances. 45 But, not finding him, they returned to Jerusalem, making a diligent search for him. 46 Well, after three days they found him in the temple, sitting in the midst of the teachers and listening to them and questioning them. 47 But all those listening to him were in constant amazement at his understanding and his answers. 48 Now when they saw

him they were astounded, and his mother said to him: "Child, why did you treat us this way? Here your father and I in mental distress have been looking for you." 49 But he said to them: "Why did you have to go looking for me? Did you not know that I must be in the [house] of my Father?" 50 However, they did not grasp the saying that he spoke to them.

51 And he went down with them and came to Naz'a·reth, and he continued subject to them. Also, his mother carefully kept all these sayings in her heart. 52 And Jesus went on progressing in wisdom and in physical growth and in favor with God and men.

3 In the fifteenth year of the reign of Ti·be'ri·us Caesar, when Pontius Pilate was governor of Ju·de'a, and Herod was district ruler of Gal'i·lee, but Philip his brother was district ruler of the country of It·u·rae'a and Trach·o·ni'tis, and Ly·sa'ni·as was district ruler of Ab·i·le'ne, 2 in the days of chief priest An'nas and of Ca'ia·phas, God's declaration came to John the son of Zech·a·ri'ah in the wilderness.

3 So he came into all the country around the Jordan, preaching baptism [in symbol] of repentance for forgiveness of sins, 4 just as it is written in the book of the words of Isaiah the prophet: "Listen! Someone is crying out in the wilderness, 'Prepare the way of Jehovah, you people, make his roads straight. 5 Every gully must be filled up, and every mountain and hill leveled down, and the curves must become straight ways and the rough places smooth ways; 6 and all flesh will see the saving means of God.'"

7 Therefore he began to say to the crowds coming out to be baptized by him: "You offspring of vipers, who has shown you how to flee from the coming wrath? 8 Therefore produce fruits that befit repentance. And do not start saying within yourselves, 'As a father we have Abraham.' For I say to you that God has power to raise

36 Further, he went on to give an illustration to them: "No one cuts a patch from a new outer garment and sews it onto an old outer garment; but if he does, then both the new patch tears away and the patch from the new garment does not match the old. 37 Moreover, no one puts new wine into old wineskins; but if he does, then the new wine will burst the wineskins, and it will be spilled out and the wineskins will be ruined. 38 But new wine must be put into new wineskins. 39 No one that has drunk old wine wants new; for he says, 'The old is nice.'"

6 Now on a sabbath he happened to be passing through grain-fields, and his disciples were pluck-ing and eating the heads of grain, rubbing them with their hands. 2 At this some of the Pharisees said: "Why are you doing what is not lawful on the sabbath?" 3 But Jesus said in reply to them: "Have you never read the very thing David did when he and the men with him got hungry? 4 How he entered into the house of God and received the loaves of presentation and ate and gave some to the men with him, which it is lawful for no one to eat but for the priests only?" 5 And he went on to say to them: "Lord of the sabbath is what the Son of man is."

6 In the course of another sab-bath he entered into the synagogue and began teaching. And there was a man present whose right hand was withered. 7 The scribes and the Pharisees were now watch-ing him closely to see whether he would cure on the sabbath, in order to find some way to accuse him. 8 He, however, knew their reasonings, yet he said to the man with the withered hand: "Get up and stand in the center." And he rose and took his stand. 9 Then Jesus said to them: "I ask you men, Is it lawful on the sabbath to do good or to do injury, to save or to destroy a soul?" 10 And after looking around at them all, he said to the man: "Stretch out your hand." He did so, and his hand was restored. 11 But they became filled with madness, and they began to talk over with one another what they might do to Jesus.

12 In the progress of these days he went out into the mountain to pray, and he continued the whole night in prayer to God. 13 But when it became day he called his disciples to him and chose from among them twelve, whom he also named apostles: 14 Simon, whom he also named Peter, and Andrew his brother, and James and John, and Philip and Bar·thol′o·mew, 15 and Matthew and Thomas, and James [the son] of Al·phae′us, and Simon who is called "the zealous one," 16 and Judas [the son] of James, and Judas Is·car′i·ot, who turned traitor.

17 And he came down with them and took his station on a level place, and there was a great crowd of his disciples, and a great multi-tude of people from all of Ju·de′a and Jerusalem and the maritime country of Tyre and Si′don, who came to hear him and be healed of their sicknesses. 18 Even those troubled with unclean spirits were cured. 19 And all the crowd were seeking to touch him, because power was going out of him and healing them all.

20 And he lifted up his eyes upon his disciples and began to say:

"Happy are you poor, because yours is the kingdom of God.

21 "Happy are you who hunger now, because you will be filled.

"Happy are you who weep now, because you will laugh.

22 "Happy are you whenever men hate you, and whenever they exclude you and reproach you and cast out your name as wicked for the sake of the Son of man. 23 Re-joice in that day and leap, for, look! your reward is great in heav-en, for those are the same things their forefathers used to do to the prophets.

24 "But woe to you rich per-sons, because you are having your consolation in full.

25 "Woe to YOU who are filled up now, because YOU will go hungry.

"Woe, YOU who are laughing now, because YOU will mourn and weep.

26 "Woe, whenever all men speak well of YOU, for things like these are what their forefathers did to the false prophets.

27 "But I say to YOU who are listening, Continue to love YOUR enemies, to do good to those hating YOU, 28 to bless those cursing YOU, to pray for those who are insulting YOU. 29 To him that strikes you on the one cheek, offer the other also; and from him that takes away your outer garment, do not withhold even the undergarment. 30 Give to everyone asking you, and from the one taking your things away do not ask [them] back.

31 "Also, just as YOU want men to do to YOU, do the same way to them.

32 "And if YOU love those loving YOU, of what credit is it to YOU? For even the sinners love those loving them. 33 And if YOU do good to those doing good to YOU, really of what credit is it to YOU? Even the sinners do the same. 34 Also, if YOU lend [without interest] to those from whom YOU hope to receive, of what credit is it to YOU? Even sinners lend [without interest] to sinners that they may get back as much. 35 To the contrary, continue to love YOUR enemies and to do good and to lend [without interest], not hoping for anything back; and YOUR reward will be great, and YOU will be sons of the Most High, because he is kind toward the unthankful and wicked. 36 Continue becoming merciful, just as YOUR Father is merciful.

37 "Moreover, stop judging, and YOU will by no means be judged; and stop condemning, and YOU will by no means be condemned. Keep on releasing, and YOU will be released. 38 Practice giving, and people will give to YOU. They will pour into YOUR laps a fine measure, pressed down, shaken together and overflowing. For with the measure that YOU are measuring out, they will measure out to YOU in return."

39 Then he also spoke an illustration to them: "A blind man cannot guide a blind man, can he? Both will tumble into a pit, will they not? 40 A pupil is not above his teacher, but everyone that is perfectly instructed will be like his teacher. 41 Why, then, do you look at the straw that is in your brother's eye, but do not observe the rafter that is in your own eye? 42 How can you say to your brother, 'Brother, allow me to extract the straw that is in your eye,' while you yourself are not looking at the rafter in that eye of yours? Hypocrite! First extract the rafter from your own eye, and then you will see clearly how to extract the straw that is in your brother's eye.

43 "For there is not a fine tree producing rotten fruit; again there is not a rotten tree producing fine fruit. 44 For each tree is known by its own fruit. For example, people do not gather figs from thorns, nor do they cut grapes off a thornbush. 45 A good man brings forth good out of the good treasure of his heart, but a wicked man brings forth what is wicked out of his wicked [treasure]; for out of the heart's abundance his mouth speaks.

46 "Why, then, do YOU call me 'Lord! Lord!' but do not do the things I say? 47 Everyone that comes to me and hears my words and does them, I will show YOU whom he is like: 48 He is like a man building a house, who dug and went down deep and laid a foundation upon the rock-mass. Consequently, when a flood arose, the river dashed against that house, but was not strong enough to shake it, because of its being well built. 49 On the other hand, he who hears and does not do, is like a man who built a house upon the ground without a foundation. Against it the river dashed, and immediately it collapsed, and the ruin of that house became great."

7 When he had completed all his sayings in the hearing of the people, he entered into Ca·per′na·um. 2 Now a certain army officer's slave, who was dear to him, was ailing and was about to pass away. 3 When he heard about Jesus, he sent forth older men of the Jews to him to ask him to come and bring his slave safely through. 4 Then those that came up to Jesus began to entreat him earnestly, saying: "He is worthy of your conferring this upon him, 5 for he loves our nation and he himself built the synagogue for us." 6 So Jesus started off with them. But when he was not far from the house, the army officer had already sent friends to say to him: "Sir, do not bother, for I am not fit to have you come in under my roof. 7 For that reason I did not consider myself worthy to come to you. But say the word, and let my servant be healed. 8 For I too am a man placed under authority, having soldiers under me, and I say to this one, 'Be on your way!' and he is on his way, and to another, 'Come!' and he comes, and to my slave, 'Do this!' and he does it." 9 Well, when Jesus heard these things he marveled at him, and he turned to the crowd following him and said: "I tell you, Not even in Israel have I found so great a faith." 10 And those that had been sent, on getting back to the house, found the slave in good health.

11 Closely following this he traveled to a city called Na′in, and his disciples and a great crowd were traveling with him. 12 As he got near the gate of the city, why, look! there was a dead man being carried out, the only-begotten son of his mother. Besides, she was a widow. A considerable crowd from the city was also with her. 13 And when the Lord caught sight of her, he was moved with pity for her, and he said to her: "Stop weeping." 14 With that he approached and touched the bier, and the bearers stood still, and he said: "Young man, I say to you,

Get up!" 15 And the dead man sat up and started to speak, and he gave him to his mother. 16 Now fear seized them all, and they began to glorify God, saying: "A great prophet has been raised up among us," and, "God has turned his attention to his people." 17 And this news concerning him spread out into all Ju·de′a and all the surrounding country.

18 Now John's disciples reported to him about all these things. 19 So John summoned a certain two of his disciples and sent them to the Lord to say: "Are you the Coming One or are we to expect a different one?" 20 When they came up to him the men said: "John the Baptist dispatched us to you to say, 'Are you the Coming One or are we to expect another?'" 21 In that hour he cured many of sicknesses and grievous diseases and wicked spirits, and granted many blind persons the favor of seeing. 22 Hence in answer he said to the [two]: "Go YOUR way, report to John what YOU saw and heard: the blind are receiving sight, the lame are walking, the lepers are being cleansed and the deaf are hearing, the dead are being raised up, the poor are being told the good news. 23 And happy is he who has not stumbled over me."

24 When the messengers of John had gone away, he started to say to the crowds concerning John: "What did YOU go out into the wilderness to behold? A reed being tossed by the wind? 25 What, then, did YOU go out to see? A man dressed in soft outer garments? Why, those in splendid dress and existing in luxury are in royal houses. 26 Really, then, what did YOU go out to see? A prophet? Yes, I tell YOU, and far more than a prophet. 27 This is he concerning whom it is written, 'Look! I am sending forth my messenger before your face, who will prepare your way ahead of you.' 28 I tell YOU, Among those born of women there is none greater than John; but a person that is a

lesser one in the kingdom of God is greater than he is." 29 (And all the people and the tax collectors, when they heard [this], declared God to be righteous, they having been baptized with the baptism of John. 30 But the Pharisees and those versed in the Law disregarded the counsel of God to them, they not having been baptized by him.)

31 "With whom, therefore, shall I compare the men of this generation, and whom are they like? 32 They are like young children sitting in a market place and crying out to one another, and who say, 'We played the flute for you, but you did not dance; we wailed, but you did not weep.' 33 Correspondingly, John the Baptist has come neither eating bread nor drinking wine, but you say, 'He has a demon.' 34 The Son of man has come eating and drinking, but you say, 'Look! A man gluttonous and given to drinking wine, a friend of tax collectors and sinners!' 35 All the same, wisdom is proved righteous by all its children."

36 Now a certain one of the Pharisees kept asking him to dine with him. Accordingly he entered into the house of the Pharisee and reclined at the table. 37 And, look! a woman who was known in the city to be a sinner, learned that he was taking a meal in the house of the Pharisee, and she brought an alabaster case of perfumed oil, 38 and, taking a position behind at his feet, she wept and started to wet his feet with her tears and she would wipe them off with the hair of her head. Also, she tenderly kissed his feet and greased them with the perfumed oil. 39 At the sight the Pharisee that invited him said within himself: "This man, if he were a prophet, would know who and what kind of woman it is that is touching him, that she is a sinner." 40 But in reply Jesus said to him: "Simon, I have something to say to you." He said: "Teacher, say it!"

41 "Two men were debtors to a certain lender; the one was in debt for five hundred de·nar′i·i, but the other for fifty. 42 When they did not have anything with which to pay back, he freely forgave them both. Therefore, which of them will love him the more?" 43 In answer Simon said: "I suppose it is the one to whom he freely forgave the more." He said to him: "You judged correctly." 44 With that he turned to the woman and said to Simon: "Do you behold this woman? I entered into your house; you gave me no water for my feet. But this woman wet my feet with her tears and wiped them off with her hair. 45 You gave me no kiss; but this woman, from the hour that I came in, did not leave off tenderly kissing my feet. 46 You did not grease my head with oil; but this woman greased my feet with perfumed oil. 47 By virtue of this, I tell you, her sins, many though they are, are forgiven, because she loved much; but he who is forgiven little, loves little." 48 Then he said to her: "Your sins are forgiven." 49 At this those reclining at the table with him started to say within themselves: "Who is this man who even forgives sins?" 50 But he said to the woman: "Your faith has saved you; go your way in peace."

8 Shortly afterwards he went journeying from city to city and from village to village, preaching and declaring the good news of the kingdom of God. And the twelve were with him, 2 and certain women that had been cured of wicked spirits and sicknesses, Mary the so-called Mag′da·lene, from whom seven demons had come out, 3 and Jo·an′na the wife of Chu′za, Herod's man in charge, and Su·san′na and many other women, who were ministering to them from their belongings.

4 Now when a great crowd had collected together with those that went to him from city after city, he spoke by means of an illustration: 5 "A sower went out to sow his seed. Well, as he was sowing, some of it fell alongside the road and was trampled down, and the

birds of heaven ate it up. 6 Some other landed upon the rock-mass, and, after sprouting, it dried up because of not having moisture. 7 Some other fell among the thorns, and the thorns that grew up with it choked it off. 8 Some other fell upon the good soil, and, after sprouting, it produced fruit a hundredfold." As he told these things, he proceeded to call out: "Let him that has ears to listen, listen."

9 But his disciples began to ask him what this illustration might mean. 10 He said: "To YOU it is granted to understand the sacred secrets of the kingdom of God, but for the rest it is in illustrations, in order that, though looking, they may look in vain and, though hearing, they may not get the meaning. 11 Now the illustration means this: The seed is the word of God. 12 Those alongside the road are the ones that have heard, then the Devil comes and takes the word away from their hearts in order that they may not believe and be saved. 13 Those upon the rock-mass are the ones who, when they hear it, receive the word with joy, but these have no root; they believe for a season, but in a season of testing they fall away. 14 As for that which fell among the thorns, these are the ones that have heard, but, by being carried away by anxieties and riches and pleasures of this life, they are completely choked and bring nothing to perfection. 15 As for that on the fine soil, these are the ones that, after hearing the word with a fine and good heart, retain it and bear fruit with endurance.

16 "No one, after lighting a lamp, covers it with a vessel or puts it underneath a bed, but he puts it on a lampstand, that those stepping in may behold the light. 17 For there is nothing hidden that will not become manifest, neither anything carefully concealed that will never become known and never come into the open. 18 Therefore, pay attention to how YOU listen; for whoever has, more will be given him, but whoever does not have,

even what he imagines he has will be taken away from him."

19 Now his mother and brothers came toward him, but they were unable to get to him because of the crowd. 20 However, it was reported to him: "Your mother and your brothers are standing outside wanting to see you." 21 In reply he said to them: "My mother and my brothers are these who hear the word of God and do it."

22 In the course of one of the days he and his disciples got into a boat, and he said to them: "Let us cross to the other side of the lake." So they set sail. 23 But as they were sailing he fell asleep. Now a violent windstorm descended upon the lake, and they began to fill up with [water] and to be in danger. 24 Finally they went to him and roused him, saying: "Instructor, Instructor, we are about to perish!" Rousing himself, he rebuked the wind and the raging of the water, and they subsided, and a calm set in. 25 Then he said to them: "Where is YOUR faith?" But struck with fear, they marveled, saying to one another: "Who really is this, for he orders even the winds and the water, and they obey him?"

26 And they put in to shore in the country of the Ger′a·senes, which is on the side opposite Gal′i·lee. 27 But as he got out onto land a certain man from the city who had demons met him. And for a considerable time he had not worn clothing, and he was staying, not at home, but among the tombs. 28 At the sight of Jesus he cried aloud and fell down before him, and with a loud voice he said: "What have I to do with you, Jesus Son of the Most High God? I beg you, do not torment me." 29 (For he had been ordering the unclean spirit to come out of the man. For over a long time it had held him fast, and he was repeatedly bound with chains and fetters under guard, but he would burst the bonds and be driven by the demon into the lonely places.) 30 Jesus asked him: "What is your

name?" He said: "Legion," because many demons had entered into him. 31 And they kept entreating him not to order them to go away into the abyss. 32 Now a herd of a considerable number of swine was feeding there on the mountain; so they entreated him to permit them to enter into those. And he gave them permission. 33 Then the demons went out of the man and entered into the swine, and the herd rushed over the precipice into the lake and drowned. 34 But when the herders saw what had happened, they fled and reported it to the city and to the country-side.

35 Then people turned out to see what had happened, and they came to Jesus and found the man from whom the demons came out, clothed and in his sound mind, sitting at the feet of Jesus; and they became fearful. 36 Those who had seen it reported to them how the demon-possessed man had been made well. 37 So all the multitude from the surrounding country of the Ger′a·senes asked him to get away from them, because they were in the grip of great fear. Then he went aboard the boat and turned away. 38 However, the man from whom the demons had gone out kept begging to continue with him; but he dismissed the man, saying: 39 "Be on your way back home, and keep on relating what things God did for you." Accordingly he went away, proclaiming throughout the whole city what things Jesus did for him.

40 When Jesus got back, the crowd received him kindly, for they were all expecting him. 41 But, look! a man named Ja′i·rus came, and this man was a presiding officer of the synagogue. And he fell at the feet of Jesus and began to entreat him to enter into his house, 42 because he had an only-begotten daughter about twelve years old and she was dying.

As he was going the crowds thronged him. 43 And a woman, subject to a flow of blood for twelve years, who had not been able to get a cure from anyone, 44 approached from behind and touched the fringe of his outer garment, and instantly her flow of blood stopped. 45 So Jesus said: "Who was it that touched me?" When they were all denying it, Peter said: "Instructor, the crowds are hemming you in and closely pressing you." 46 Yet Jesus said: "Someone touched me, for I perceived that power went out of me." 47 Seeing that she had not escaped notice, the woman came trembling and fell down before him and disclosed before all the people the cause for which she touched him and how she was healed instantly. 48 But he said to her: "Daughter, your faith has made you well; go your way in peace."

49 While he was yet speaking, a certain representative of the presiding officer of the synagogue came, saying: "Your daughter has died; do not bother the teacher any longer." 50 On hearing this, Jesus answered him: "Have no fear, only put forth faith, and she will be saved." 51 When he reached the house he did not let anyone go in with him except Peter and John and James and the girl's father and mother. 52 But people were all weeping and beating themselves in grief for her. So he said: "STOP weeping, for she did not die but is sleeping." 53 At this they began to laugh at him scornfully, because they knew she had died. 54 But he took her by the hand and called, saying: "Girl, get up!" 55 And her spirit returned, and she rose instantly, and he ordered something to be given her to eat. 56 Well, her parents were beside themselves; but he instructed them to tell no one what had happened.

9 Then he called the twelve together and gave them power and authority over all the demons and to cure sicknesses. 2 And so he sent them forth to preach the kingdom of God and to heal, 3 and he said to them: "Carry nothing for the trip, neither staff nor food pouch, nor bread nor silver money; neither have two undergarments.

4 But wherever you enter into a home, stay there and leave from there. 5 And wherever people do not receive you, on going out of that city shake the dust off your feet for a witness against them." 6 Then starting out they went through the territory from village to village, declaring the good news and performing cures everywhere.

7 Now Herod the district ruler heard of all the things happening, and he was in great perplexity because of its being said by some that John had been raised up from the dead, 8 but by others that E·li'jah had appeared, but by still others that a certain one of the ancient prophets had risen. 9 Herod said: "John I beheaded. Who, then, is this about whom I am hearing such things?" So he was seeking to see him.

10 And when the apostles returned they recounted to him what things they had done. With that he took them along and withdrew to privacy into a city called Beth·sa'i·da. 11 But the crowds, getting to know it, followed him. And he received them kindly and began to speak to them about the kingdom of God, and he healed those needing a cure. 12 Then the day started to decline. The twelve now came up and said to him: "Dismiss the crowd, that they may go into the villages and countryside round about and procure lodging and find provisions, because out here we are in a lonely place." 13 But he said to them: "You give them something to eat." They said: "We have nothing more than five loaves and two fishes, unless perhaps we ourselves go and buy foodstuffs for all these people." 14 They were, in fact, about five thousand men. But he said to his disciples: "Have them recline as at meals, in groups of about fifty each." 15 And they did so and had them all recline. 16 Then taking the five loaves and the two fishes, he looked up to heaven, blessed them and broke them up and began to give them to the disciples to set before the crowd. 17 So they all

ate and were satisfied, and the surplus that they had was taken up, twelve baskets of fragments. 18 Later, while he was praying alone, the disciples came together to him, and he questioned them, saying: "Who are the crowds saying that I am?" 19 In reply they said: "John the Baptist; but others, E·li'jah, and still others, that one of the ancient prophets has risen." 20 Then he said to them: "You, though, who do you say I am?" Peter said in reply: "The Christ of God." 21 Then in a stern talk to them he instructed them not to be telling this to anybody, 22 but said: "The Son of man must undergo many sufferings and be rejected by the older men and chief priests and scribes, and be killed, and on the third day be raised up."

23 Then he went on to say to all: "If anyone wants to come after me, let him disown himself and pick up his torture stake day after day and follow me continually. 24 For whoever wants to save his soul will lose it; but whoever loses his soul for my sake is the one that will save it. 25 Really, what does a man benefit himself if he gains the whole world but loses his own self or suffers damage? 26 For whoever becomes ashamed of me and of my words, the Son of man will be ashamed of this one when he arrives in his glory and that of the Father and of the holy angels. 27 But I tell you truthfully, There are some of those standing here that will not taste death at all until first they see the kingdom of God."

28 In actual fact, about eight days after these words, he took Peter and John and James along and climbed up into the mountain to pray. 29 And as he was praying the appearance of his face became different and his apparel became glitteringly white. 30 Also, look! two men were conversing with him, who were Moses and E·li'jah. 31 These appeared with glory and began talking about his departure that he was destined to fulfill at Jerusalem. 32 Now Peter and

those with him were weighed down with sleep; but when they got fully awake they saw his glory and the two men standing with him. 33 And as these were being separated from him, Peter said to Jesus: "Instructor, it is fine for us to be here, so let us erect three tents, one for you and one for Moses and one for E·li'jah," he not realizing what he was saying. 34 But as he was saying these things a cloud formed and began to overshadow them. As they entered into the cloud, they became fearful. 35 And a voice came out of the cloud, saying: "This is my Son, the one that has been chosen. Listen to him." 36 And as the voice occurred Jesus was found alone. But they kept quiet and did not report to anyone in those days any of the things they saw.

37 On the succeeding day, when they got down from the mountain, a great crowd met him. 38 And, look! a man cried out from the crowd, saying: "Teacher, I beg you to take a look at my son, because he is my only-begotten, 39 and, look! a spirit takes him, and suddenly he cries out, and it throws him into convulsions with foam, and it scarcely withdraws from him after bruising him. 40 And I begged your disciples to expel it, but they could not." 41 In response Jesus said: "O faithless and twisted generation, how long must I continue with you and put up with you? Lead your son over here." 42 But even as he was approaching, the demon dashed him to the ground and violently convulsed him. However, Jesus rebuked the unclean spirit and healed the boy and delivered him to his father. 43 Well, they all began to be astounded at the majestic power of God.

Now as they were all marveling at all the things he was doing, he said to his disciples: 44 "Give lodgment to these words in your ears, for the Son of man is destined to be delivered into the hands of men." 45 But they continued without understanding of this saying.

In fact, it was concealed from them that they might not see through it, and they were afraid to question him about this saying.

46 Then a reasoning entered among them as to who would be the greatest of them. 47 Jesus, knowing the reasoning of their hearts, took a young child, set it beside him 48 and said to them: "Whoever receives this young child on the basis of my name receives me [too], and whoever receives me receives him [also] that sent me forth. For he that conducts himself as a lesser one among all of you is the one that is great."

49 In response John said: "Instructor, we saw a certain man expelling demons by the use of your name and we tried to prevent him, because he is not following with us." 50 But Jesus said to him: "Do not you men try to prevent [him], for he that is not against you is for you."

51 As the days were now coming to the full for him to be taken up, he firmly set his face to go to Jerusalem. 52 So he sent forth messengers in advance of him. And they went their way and entered into a village of Sa·mar'i·tans, to make preparation for him; 53 but they did not receive him, because his face was set for going to Jerusalem. 54 When the disciples James and John saw this they said: "Lord, do you want us to tell fire to come down from heaven and annihilate them?" 55 But he turned and rebuked them. 56 So they went to a different village.

57 Now as they were going on the road, someone said to him: "I will follow you to wherever you may depart." 58 And Jesus said to him: "Foxes have dens and birds of heaven have roosts, but the Son of man has nowhere to lay down his head." 59 Then he said to another: "Be my follower." The man said: "Permit me first to leave and bury my father." 60 But he said to him: "Let the dead bury their dead, but you go away and declare abroad the kingdom of God." 61 And still another said:

"I will follow you, Lord; but first permit me to say good-by to those in my household." 62 Jesus said to him: "No man that has put his hand to a plow and looks at the things behind is well fitted for the kingdom of God."

10 After these things the Lord designated seventy others and sent them forth by twos in advance of him into every city and place to which he himself was going to come. 2 Then he began to say to them: "The harvest, indeed, is great, but the workers are few. Therefore beg the Master of the harvest to send out workers into his harvest. 3 Go forth. Look! I am sending YOU forth as lambs in among wolves. 4 Do not carry a purse, nor a food pouch, nor sandals, and do not embrace anybody in greeting along the road. 5 Wherever YOU enter into a house say first, 'May this house have peace.' 6 And if a friend of peace is there, YOUR peace will rest upon him. But if there is not, it will turn back to YOU. 7 So stay in that house, eating and drinking the things they provide, for the worker is worthy of his wages. Do not be transferring from house to house.

8 "Also, wherever YOU enter into a city and they receive YOU, eat the things set before YOU, 9 and cure the sick ones in it, and go on telling them, 'The kingdom of God has come near to YOU.' 10 But wherever YOU enter into a city and they do not receive YOU, go out into its broad ways and say, 11 'Even the dust that got stuck to our feet from YOUR city we wipe off against YOU. Nevertheless, keep this in mind, that the kingdom of God has come near.' 12 I tell YOU that it will be more endurable for Sod'om in that day than for that city.

13 "Woe to you, Cho·ra'zin! Woe to you, Beth·sa'i·da! because if the powerful works that have taken place in YOU had taken place in Tyre and Si'don, they would long ago have repented sitting in sackcloth and ashes. 14 Consequently it will be more endurable for Tyre and Si'don in the judgment than for YOU. 15 And you, Ca·per'na·um, will you perhaps be exalted to heaven? Down to Ha'des you will come!

16 "He that listens to YOU listens to me [too]. And he that disregards YOU disregards me [too]. Moreover, he that disregards me disregards [also] him that sent me forth."

17 Then the seventy returned with joy, saying: "Lord, even the demons are made subject to us by the use of your name." 18 At that he said to them: "I began to behold Satan already fallen like lightning from heaven. 19 Look! I have given YOU the authority to trample underfoot serpents and scorpions, and over all the power of the enemy, and nothing will by any means do YOU hurt. 20 Nevertheless, do not rejoice over this, that the spirits are made subject to YOU, but rejoice because YOUR names have been inscribed in the heavens." 21 In that very hour he became overjoyed in the holy spirit and said: "I publicly praise you, Father, Lord of heaven and earth, because you have carefully hidden these things from wise and intellectual ones, and have revealed them to babes. Yes, O Father, because to do thus came to be the way approved by you. 22 All things have been delivered to me by my Father, and who the Son is no one knows but the Father; and who the Father is, no one [knows] but the Son, and he to whom the Son is willing to reveal him."

23 With that he turned to the disciples by themselves and said: "Happy are the eyes that behold the things YOU are beholding. 24 For I say to YOU, Many prophets and kings desired to see the things YOU are beholding but did not see them, and to hear the things YOU are hearing but did not hear them."

25 Now, look! a certain man versed in the Law rose up, to test him out, and said: "Teacher, by doing what shall I inherit everlasting life?" 26 He said to him:

"What is written in the Law? How do you read?" 27 In answer he said: "'You must love Jehovah your God with your whole heart and with your whole soul and with your whole strength and with your whole mind,' and, 'your neighbor as yourself.'" 28 He said to him: "You answered correctly; 'keep on doing this and you will get life.'"

29 But, wanting to prove himself righteous, the man said to Jesus: "Who really is my neighbor?" 30 In reply Jesus said: "A certain man was going down from Jerusalem to Jer'i·cho and fell among robbers, who both stripped him and inflicted blows, and went off, leaving him half-dead. 31 Now, by coincidence, a certain priest was going down over that road, but, when he saw him, he went by on the opposite side. 32 Likewise, a Levite also, when he got down to the place and saw him, went by on the opposite side. 33 But a certain Sa·mar'i·tan traveling the road came upon him and, at seeing him, he was moved with pity. 34 So he approached him and bound up his wounds, pouring oil and wine upon them. Then he mounted him upon his own beast and brought him to an inn and took care of him. 35 And the next day he took out two de·nar'i·i, gave them to the innkeeper, and said, 'Take care of him, and whatever you spend besides this, I will repay you when I come back here.' 36 Who of these three seems to you to have made himself neighbor to the man that fell among the robbers?" 37 He said: "The one that acted mercifully toward him." Jesus then said to him: "Go your way and be doing the same yourself."

38 Now as they were going their way he entered into a certain village. Here a certain woman named Martha received him as guest into the house. 39 This woman also had a sister called Mary, who, however, sat down at the feet of the Lord and kept listening to his word. 40 Martha, on the other hand, was distracted with attending to many duties. So, she came near and said: "Lord, does it not matter to you that my sister has left me alone to attend to things? Tell her, therefore, to join in helping me." 41 In answer the Lord said to her: "Martha, Martha, you are anxious and disturbed about many things. 42 A few things, though, are needed, or just one. For her part, Mary chose the good portion, and it will not be taken away from her."

11 Now on the occasion of his being in a certain place praying, when he stopped, a certain one of his disciples said to him: "Lord, teach us how to pray, just as John also taught his disciples."

2 Then he said to them: "Whenever you pray, say, 'Father, let your name be sanctified. Let your kingdom come. 3 Give us our bread for the day according to the day's requirement. 4 And forgive us our sins, for we ourselves also forgive everyone that is in debt to us; and do not bring us into temptation.'"

5 Further, he said to them: "Who of you will have a friend and will go to him at midnight and say to him, 'Friend, loan me three loaves, 6 because a friend of mine has just come to me on a journey and I have nothing to set before him'? 7 And that one from inside says in reply, 'Quit making me trouble. The door is already locked, and my young children are with me in bed; I cannot rise up and give you anything.' 8 I tell you, Although he will not rise up and give him anything because of being his friend, certainly because of his bold persistence he will get up and give him what things he needs. 9 Accordingly I say to you, Keep on asking, and it will be given you; keep on seeking, and you will find; keep on knocking, and it will be opened to you. 10 For everyone asking receives, and everyone seeking finds, and to everyone knocking it will be opened. 11 Indeed, which father is there among you who, if his son asks for a fish,

will perhaps hand him a serpent instead of a fish? **12** Or if he also asks for an egg, will hand him a scorpion? **13** Therefore, if YOU, although being wicked, know how to give good gifts to YOUR children, how much more so will the Father in heaven give holy spirit to those asking him!"

14 Later he was expelling a dumb demon. After the demon came out, the dumb man spoke. And the crowds marveled. **15** But certain ones of them said: "He expels the demons by means of Be·el′ze·bub the ruler of the demons." **16** However, others, to tempt him, began seeking a sign out of heaven from him. **17** Knowing their imaginations he said to them: "Every kingdom divided against itself comes to desolation, and a house [divided] against itself falls. **18** So if Satan is also divided against himself, how will his kingdom stand? Because YOU say I expel the demons by means of Be·el′ze·bub. **19** If it is by means of Be·el′ze·bub I expel the demons, by whom do YOUR sons expel them? Because of this they will be judges of YOU. **20** But if it is by means of God's finger I expel the demons, the kingdom of God has really overtaken YOU. **21** When a strong man, well armed, guards his palace, his belongings continue in peace. **22** But when someone stronger than he is comes against him and conquers him, he takes away his full armament in which he was trusting, and he divides out the things he despoiled him of. **23** He that is not on my side is against me, and he that does not gather with me scatters.

24 "When an unclean spirit comes out of a man, it passes through parched places in search of a resting place, and, after finding none, it says, 'I will return to my house out of which I moved.' **25** And on arriving it finds it swept clean and adorned. **26** Then it goes its way and takes along seven different spirits more wicked than itself, and, after getting inside, they dwell there; and the final circumstances of that man become worse than the first."

27 Now as he was saying these things a certain woman out of the crowd raised her voice and said to him: "Happy is the womb that carried you and the breasts that you sucked!" **28** But he said: "No, rather, Happy are those hearing the word of God and keeping it!"

29 When the crowds were massing together, he started to say: "This generation is a wicked generation; it looks for a sign. But no sign will be given it except the sign of Jo′nah. **30** For just as Jo′nah became a sign to the Nin′e·vites, in the same way will the Son of man be also to this generation. **31** The queen of the south will be raised up in the judgment with the men of this generation and will condemn them; because she came from the ends of the earth to hear the wisdom of Sol′o·mon, but, look! something more than Sol′o·mon is here. **32** The men of Nin′e·veh will rise in the judgment with this generation and will condemn it; because they repented at what Jo′nah preached; but, look! something more than Jo′nah is here. **33** After lighting a lamp, a person puts it, not in a vault nor under a measuring basket, but upon the lampstand, that those stepping in may behold the light. **34** The lamp of the body is your eye. When your eye is simple, your whole body is also bright; but when it is wicked, your body is also dark. **35** Be alert, therefore. Perhaps the light that is in you is darkness. **36** Therefore, if your whole body is bright with no part at all dark, it will all be as bright as when a lamp gives you light by its rays."

37 When he had spoken this, a Pharisee requested him to dine with him. So he went in and reclined at the table. **38** However, the Pharisee was surprised at seeing that he did not first wash before the dinner. **39** But the Lord said to him: "Now YOU Pharisees, YOU cleanse the outside of the cup and dish, but the inside of you is full of plunder and wickedness. **40** Unreasonable persons! He that made the outside made also the inside, did he not? **41** Nevertheless, give as gifts of mercy the things that are inside, and, look! all [other] things are clean about you. **42** But woe to you Pharisees, because you give the tenth of the mint and the rue and of every [other] vegetable, but you pass by the justice and the love of God! These things you were under obligation to do, but those other things not to omit. **43** Woe to you Pharisees, because you love the front seats in the synagogues and the greetings in the market places! **44** Woe to you, because you are as those memorial tombs which are not in evidence, so that men walk upon them and do not know [it]!"

45 In answer a certain one of those versed in the Law said to him: "Teacher, in saying these things you also insult us." **46** Then he said: "Woe also to you who are versed in the Law, because you load men with loads hard to be borne, but you yourselves do not touch the loads with one of your fingers!

47 "Woe to you, because you build the memorial tombs of the prophets, but your forefathers killed them! **48** Certainly you are witnesses of the deeds of your forefathers and yet you give consent to them, because these killed the prophets but you are building [their tombs]. **49** On this account the wisdom of God also said, 'I will send forth to them prophets and apostles, and they will kill and persecute some of them, **50** so that the blood of all the prophets spilled from the founding of the world may be required from this generation, **51** from the blood of Abel down to the blood of Zech·a·ri′ah, who was slain between the altar and the house.' Yes, I tell you, it will be required from this generation.

52 "Woe to you who are versed in the Law, because you took away the key of knowledge; you your-

selves did not go in, and those going in you hindered!"

53 So when he went out from there the scribes and the Pharisees started in to press upon him terribly and to ply him with questions about further things, **54** lying in wait for him, to catch something out of his mouth.

12 In the meantime, when the crowd had gathered together in so many thousands that they were stepping upon one another, he started out by saying first to his disciples: "Watch out for the leaven of the Pharisees, which is hypocrisy. **2** But there is nothing carefully concealed that will not be revealed, and secret that will not become known. **3** Wherefore what things you say in the darkness will be heard in the light, and what you whisper in private rooms will be preached from the housetops. **4** Moreover, I say to you, my friends, Do not fear those who kill the body and after this are not able to do anything more. **5** But I will indicate to you whom to fear: Fear him who after killing has authority to throw into Ge·hen′na. Yes, I tell you, fear this One. **6** Five sparrows sell for two coins of small value, do they not? Yet not one of them goes forgotten before God. **7** But even the hairs of your heads are all numbered. Have no fear; you are worth more than many sparrows.

8 "I say, then, to you, Everyone that confesses union with me before men, the Son of man will also confess union with him before the angels of God. **9** But he that disowns me before men will be disowned before the angels of God. **10** And everyone that says a word against the Son of man, it will be forgiven him; but he that blasphemes against the holy spirit will not be forgiven it. **11** But when they bring you in before public assemblies and government officials and authorities, do not become anxious about how or what you will speak in defense or what you will say; **12** for the holy spirit will teach you in that very hour the things you ought to say."

13 Then a certain one of the crowd said to him: "Teacher, tell my brother to divide the inheritance with me." 14 He said to him: "Man, who appointed me judge or apportioner over you persons?" 15 Then he said to them: "Keep your eyes open and guard against every sort of covetousness, because even when a person has an abundance his life does not result from the things he possesses." 16 With that he spoke an illustration to them, saying: "The land of a certain rich man produced well. 17 Consequently he began reasoning within himself, saying, 'What shall I do, now that I have nowhere to gather my crops?' 18 So he said, 'I will do this: I will tear down my storehouses and build bigger ones, and there I will gather all my grain and all my good things; 19 and I will say to my soul: "Soul, you have many good things laid up for many years; take your ease, eat, drink, enjoy yourself." ' 20 But God said to him, 'Unreasonable one, this night they are demanding your soul from you. Who, then, is to have the things you stored up?' 21 So it goes with the man that lays up treasure for himself but is not rich toward God."

22 Then he said to his disciples: "On this account I say to you, Quit being anxious about your souls as to what you will eat or about your bodies as to what you will wear. 23 For the soul is worth more than food and the body than clothing. 24 Mark well that the ravens neither sow seed nor reap, and they have neither barn nor storehouse, and yet God feeds them. Of how much more worth are you than birds? 25 Who of you by being anxious can add a cubit to his life span? 26 If, therefore, you cannot do the least thing, why be anxious about the remaining things? 27 Mark well how the lilies grow; they neither toil nor spin; but I tell you, Not even Sol′o·mon in all his glory

was arrayed as one of these. 28 If, now, God thus clothes the vegetation in the field that today exists and tomorrow is cast into an oven, how much rather will he clothe you, you with little faith! 29 So quit seeking what you might eat and what you might drink, and quit being in anxious suspense; 30 for all these are the things the nations of the world are eagerly pursuing, but your Father knows you need these things. 31 Nevertheless, seek continually his kingdom, and these things will be added to you.

32 "Have no fear, little flock, because your Father has approved of giving you the kingdom. 33 Sell the things belonging to you and give gifts of mercy. Make purses for yourselves that do not wear out, a never-failing treasure in the heavens, where a thief does not get near nor moth consumes. 34 For where your treasure is, there your hearts will be also.

35 "Let your loins be girded and your lamps be burning, 36 and you yourselves be like men waiting for their master when he returns from the marriage, so that at his arriving and knocking they may at once open to him. 37 Happy are those slaves whom the master on arriving finds watching! Truly I say to you, He will gird himself and make them recline at the table and will come alongside and minister to them. 38 And if he arrives in the second watch, even if in the third, and finds them thus, happy are they! 39 But know this, that if the householder had known at what hour the thief would come, he would have kept watching and not have let his house be broken into. 40 You also, keep ready, because at an hour that you do not think likely the Son of man is coming."

41 Then Peter said: "Lord, are you saying this illustration to us or also to all?" 42 And the Lord said: "Who really is the faithful steward, the discreet one, whom his master will appoint over his body of attendants to keep giving them their measure of food sup-

plies at the proper time? 43 Happy is that slave, if his master on arriving finds him doing so! 44 I tell you truthfully, He will appoint him over all his belongings. 45 But if ever that slave should say in his heart, 'My master delays coming,' and should start to beat the menservants and the maidservants, and to eat and drink and get drunk, 46 the master of that slave will come on a day that he is not expecting [him] and in an hour that he does not know, and he will punish him with the greatest severity and assign him a part with the unfaithful ones. 47 Then that slave that understood the will of his master but did not get ready or do in line with his will will be beaten with many strokes. 48 But the one that did not understand and so did things deserving of strokes will be beaten with few. Indeed, everyone to whom much was given, much will be demanded of him; and the one whom people put in charge of much, they will demand more than usual of him.

49 "I came to start a fire on the earth, and what more is there for me to wish if it has already been lighted? 50 Indeed, I have a baptism with which to be baptized, and how I am being distressed until it is finished! 51 Do you imagine I came to give peace on the earth? No, indeed, I tell you, but rather division. 52 For from now on there will be five in one house divided, three against two and two against three. 53 They will be divided, father against son and son against father, mother against daughter and daughter against [her] mother, mother-in-law against [her] daughter-in-law and daughter-in-law against [her] mother-in-law."

54 Then he went on to say also to the crowds: "When you see a cloud rising in western parts, at once you say, 'A storm is coming,' and it turns out so. 55 And when you see that a south wind is blowing, you say, 'There will be a heat wave,' and it occurs. 56 Hypocrites, you know how to examine the outward appearance of earth and sky, but how is it you do not know how to examine this particular time? 57 Why do you not judge also for yourselves what is righteous? 58 For example, when you are going with your adversary at law to a ruler, get to work, while on the way, to rid yourself of the dispute with him, that he may never hale you before the judge, and the judge deliver you to the court officer, and the court officer throw you into prison. 59 I tell you, You will certainly not get out from there until you pay over the last small coin of very little value."

13 At that very season there were certain ones present that reported to him about the Gal·i·le'ans whose blood Pilate had mixed with their sacrifices. 2 So in reply he said to them: "Do you imagine that these Gal·i·le'ans were proved worse sinners than all other Gal·i·le'ans because they have suffered these things? 3 No, indeed, I tell you; but, unless you repent, you will all likewise be destroyed. 4 Or those eighteen upon whom the tower in Si·lo'am fell, thereby killing them, do you imagine that they were proved greater debtors than all other men inhabiting Jerusalem? 5 No, indeed, I tell you; but, unless you repent, you will all be destroyed in the same way."

6 Then he went on to tell this illustration: "A certain man had a fig tree planted in his vineyard, and he came looking for fruit on it, but found none. 7 Then he said to the vinedresser, 'Here it is three years that I have come looking for fruit on this fig tree, but have found none. Cut it down! Why really should it keep the ground useless?' 8 In reply he said to him, 'Master, let it alone also this year, until I dig around it and put on manure; 9 and if then it produces fruit in the future, [well and good]; but if not, you shall cut it down.' "

10 Now he was teaching in one of the synagogues on the sabbath. 11 And, look! a woman with a

spirit of weakness for eighteen years, and she was bent double and was unable to raise herself up at all. 12 When he saw her, Jesus addressed her and said to her: "Woman, you are released from your weakness." 13 And he laid his hands on her; and instantly she straightened up, and began to glorify God. 14 But in response the presiding officer of the synagogue, indignant because Jesus did the cure on the sabbath, began to say to the crowd: "There are six days on which work ought to be done; on them, therefore, come and be cured, and not on the sabbath day." 15 However, the Lord answered him and said: "Hypocrites, does not each one of you on the sabbath untie his bull or his ass from the stall and lead it away to give it drink? 16 Was it not due, then, for this woman who is a daughter of Abraham, and whom Satan held bound, look! eighteen years, to be loosed from this bond on the sabbath day?" 17 Well, when he said these things, all his opposers began to feel shame; but all the crowd began to rejoice at all the glorious things done by him.

18 Therefore he went on to say: "What is the kingdom of God like, and with what shall I compare it? 19 It is like a mustard grain that a man took and put in his garden, and it grew and became a tree, and the birds of heaven took up lodging in its branches."

20 And again he said: "With what shall I compare the kingdom of God? 21 It is like leaven, which a woman took and hid in three large measures of flour until the whole mass was fermented."

22 And he journeyed through from city to city and from village to village, teaching and continuing on his journey to Jerusalem. 23 Now a certain man said to him: "Lord, are those who are being saved few?" He said to them: 24 "Exert yourselves vigorously to get in through the narrow door, because many, I tell you, will seek to get in but will not be able, 25 when once the householder has

got up and locked the door, and you start to stand outside and to knock at the door, saying, 'Sir, open to us.' But in answer he will say to you, 'I do not know where you are from.' 26 Then you will start saying, 'We ate and drank in front of you, and you taught in our broad ways.' 27 But he will speak and say to you, 'I do not know where you are from. Get away from me, all you workers of unrighteousness!' 28 There is where [your] weeping and the gnashing of [your] teeth will be, when you see Abraham and Isaac and Jacob and all the prophets in the kingdom of God, but yourselves thrown outside. 29 Furthermore, people will come from eastern parts and western, and from north and south, and will recline at the table in the kingdom of God. 30 And, look! there are those last who will be first, and there are those first who will be last."

31 In that very hour certain Pharisees came up, saying to him: "Get out and be on your way from here, because Herod wants to kill you." 32 And he said to them: "Go and tell that fox, 'Look! I am casting out demons and accomplishing healing today and tomorrow, and the third day I shall be finished.' 33 Nevertheless, I must go on my way today and tomorrow and the following day, because it is not admissible for a prophet to be destroyed outside of Jerusalem. 34 Jerusalem, Jerusalem, the killer of the prophets and stoner of those sent forth to her—how often I wanted to gather your children together in the manner that a hen gathers her brood of chicks under her wings, but you people did not want [it]! 35 Look! Your house is abandoned to you. I tell you, You will by no means see me until you say, 'Blessed is he that comes in Jehovah's name.'"

14 And on an occasion when he went into the house of a certain one of the rulers of the Pharisees on the sabbath to eat a meal, they were closely watching him. 2 And, look! there was before him

a certain man who had dropsy. 3 So in response Jesus spoke to those versed in the Law and to the Pharisees, saying: "Is it lawful on the sabbath to cure or not?" 4 But they kept silent. With that he took hold of [the man], healed him and sent [him] away. 5 And he said to them: "Who of YOU, if his son or bull falls into a well, will not immediately pull him out on the sabbath day?" 6 And they were not able to answer back on these things.

7 He then went on to tell the invited men an illustration, as he marked how they were choosing the most prominent places for themselves, saying to them: 8 "When you are invited by someone to a marriage feast, do not lie down in the most prominent place. Perhaps someone more distinguished than you may at the time have been invited by him, 9 and he that invited you and him will come and say to you, 'Let this man have the place.' And then you will start off with shame to occupy the lowest place. 10 But when you are invited, go and recline in the lowest place, that when the man that has invited you comes he will say to you, 'Friend, go on up higher.' Then you will have honor in front of all your fellow guests. 11 For everyone that exalts himself will be humbled and he that humbles himself will be exalted."

12 Next he proceeded to say also to the man that invited him: "When you spread a dinner or evening meal, do not call your friends or your brothers or your relatives or rich neighbors. Perhaps some time they might also invite you in return and it would become a repayment to you. 13 But when you spread a feast, invite poor people, crippled, lame, blind; 14 and you will be happy, because they have nothing with which to repay you. For you will be repaid in the resurrection of the righteous ones."

15 On hearing these things a certain one of the fellow guests said to him: "Happy is he who eats bread in the kingdom of God."

16 [Jesus] said to him: "A certain man was spreading a grand evening meal, and he invited many. 17 And he sent his slave out at the hour of the evening meal to say to the invited ones, 'Come, because things are now ready.' 18 But they all in common started to beg off. The first said to him, 'I bought a field and need to go out and see it; I ask you, Have me excused.' 19 And another said, 'I bought five yoke of cattle and am going to examine them; I ask you, Have me excused.' 20 Still another said, 'I just married a wife and for this reason I cannot come.' 21 So the slave came up and reported these things to his master. Then the householder became wrathful and said to his slave, 'Go out quickly into the broad ways and the lanes of the city, and bring in here the poor and crippled and blind and lame.' 22 In time the slave said, 'Master, what you ordered has been done, and yet there is room.' 23 And the master said to the slave, 'Go out into the roads and the fenced-in places, and compel them to come in, that my house may be filled. 24 For I say to YOU people, None of those men that were invited shall have a taste of my evening meal.'"

25 Now great crowds were traveling with him, and he turned and said to them: 26 "If anyone comes to me and does not hate his father and mother and wife and children and brothers and sisters, yes, and even his own soul, he cannot be my disciple. 27 Whoever is not carrying his torture stake and coming after me cannot be my disciple. 28 For example, who of YOU that wants to build a tower does not first sit down and calculate the expense, to see if he has enough to complete it? 29 Otherwise, he might lay its foundation but not be able to finish it, and all the onlookers might start to ridicule him, 30 saying, 'This man started to build but was not able to finish.' 31 Or what king, marching to meet another king in war does not first sit down and take counsel whether

he is able with ten thousand troops to cope with the one that comes against him with twenty thousand? 32 If, in fact, he cannot do so, then while that one is yet far away he sends out a body of ambassadors and sues for peace. 33 Thus, you may be sure, none of YOU that does not say good-by to all his belongings can be my disciple.

34 "Salt, to be sure, is fine. But if even the salt loses its strength, with what will it be seasoned? 35 It is suitable neither for soil nor for manure. People throw it outside. Let him that has ears to listen, listen."

15 Now all the tax collectors and the sinners kept drawing near to him to hear him. 2 Consequently both the Pharisees and the scribes kept muttering, saying: "This man welcomes sinners and eats with them." 3 Then he spoke this illustration to them, saying: 4 "What man of YOU with a hundred sheep, on losing one of them, will not leave the ninety-nine behind in the wilderness and go for the lost one until he finds it? 5 And when he has found it he puts it upon his shoulders and rejoices. 6 And when he gets home he calls his friends and his neighbors together, saying to them, 'Rejoice with me, because I have found my sheep that was lost.' 7 I tell YOU that thus there will be more joy in heaven over one sinner that repents than over ninety-nine righteous ones who have no need of repentance.

8 "Or what woman with ten drachma coins, if she loses one drachma coin, does not light a lamp and sweep her house and search carefully until she finds it? 9 And when she has found it she calls the women who are her friends and neighbors together, saying, 'Rejoice with me, because I have found the drachma coin that I lost.' 10 Thus, I tell YOU, joy arises among the angels of God over one sinner that repents."

11 Then he said: "A certain man had two sons. 12 And the younger of them said to his father, 'Father,

give me the part of the property that falls to my share.' Then he divided his means of living to them. 13 Later, after not many days, the younger son gathered all things together and traveled abroad into a distant country, and there squandered his property by living a debauched life. 14 When he had spent everything, a severe famine occurred throughout that country, and he started to be in need. 15 He even went and attached himself to one of the citizens of that country, and he sent him into his fields to herd swine. 16 And he used to desire to be filled with the carob pods which the swine were eating, and no one would give him [anything].

17 "When he came to his senses, he said, 'How many hired men of my father are abounding with bread, while I am perishing here from famine! 18 I will rise and journey to my father and say to him: "Father, I have sinned against heaven and against you. 19 I am no longer worthy of being called your son. Make me as one of your hired men."' 20 So he rose and went to his father. While he was yet a long way off, his father caught sight of him and was moved with pity, and he ran and fell upon his neck and tenderly kissed him. 21 Then the son said to him, 'Father, I have sinned against heaven and against you. I am no longer worthy of being called your son. Make me as one of your hired men.' 22 But the father said to his slaves, 'Quick! bring out a robe, the best one, and clothe him with it, and put a ring on his hand and sandals on his feet. 23 And bring the fattened young bull, slaughter it and let us eat and enjoy ourselves, 24 because this my son was dead and came to life again; he was lost and was found.' And they started to enjoy themselves.

25 "Now his older son was in the field; and as he came and got near the house he heard a music concert and dancing. 26 So he called one of the servants to

him and inquired what these things meant. 27 He said to him, 'Your brother has come, and your father slaughtered the fattened young bull, because he got him back in good health.' 28 But he became wrathful and was unwilling to go in. Then his father came out and began to entreat him. 29 In reply he said to his father, 'Here it is so many years I have slaved for you and never once did I transgress your commandment, and yet to me you never once gave a kid for me to enjoy myself with my friends. 30 But as soon as this your son who ate up your means of living with harlots arrived, you slaughtered the fattened young bull for him.' 31 Then he said to him, 'Child, you have always been with me, and all the things that are mine are yours; 32 but we just had to enjoy ourselves and rejoice, because this your brother was dead and came to life, and he was lost and was found.' "

16 Then he went on to say also to the disciples: "A certain man was rich and he had a steward, and this one was accused to him as handling his goods wastefully. 2 So he called him and said to him, 'What is this I hear about you? Hand in the account of your stewardship, for you can no longer manage the house.' 3 Then the steward said to himself, 'What am I to do, seeing that my master will take the stewardship away from me? I am not strong enough to dig, I am ashamed to beg. 4 Ah! I know what I shall do, so that, when I am put out of the stewardship, people will receive me into their homes.' 5 And calling to him each one of the debtors of his master he proceeded to say to the first, 'How much are you owing my master?' 6 He said, 'A hundred bath measures of olive oil.' He said to him, 'Take your written agreement back and sit down and quickly write fifty.' 7 Next, he said to another one, 'Now you, how much are you owing?' He said, 'A hundred cor measures of wheat.' He said to him, 'Take your written agreement back

and write eighty.' 8 And his master commended the steward, though unrighteous, because he acted with practical wisdom; for the sons of this system of things are wiser in a practical way toward their own generation than the sons of the light are.

9 "Also, I say to you, Make friends for yourselves by means of the unrighteous riches, so that, when such fail, they may receive you into the everlasting dwelling places. 10 The person faithful in what is least is faithful also in much, and the person unrighteous in what is least is unrighteous also in much. 11 Therefore, if you have not proved yourselves faithful in connection with the unrighteous riches, who will entrust you with what is true? 12 And if you have not proved yourselves faithful in connection with what is another's, who will give you what is for yourselves? 13 No house servant can be a slave to two masters; for, either he will hate the one and love the other, or he will stick to the one and despise the other. You cannot be slaves to God and to riches."

14 Now the Pharisees, who were money lovers, were listening to all these things, and they began to sneer at him. 15 Consequently he said to them: "You are those who declare yourselves righteous before men, but God knows your hearts; because what is lofty among men is a disgusting thing in God's sight.

16 "The Law and the Prophets were until John. From then on the kingdom of God is being declared as good news, and every sort of person is pressing forward toward it. 17 Indeed, it is easier for heaven and earth to pass away than for one particle of a letter of the Law to go unfulfilled.

18 "Everyone that divorces his wife and marries another commits adultery, and he that marries a woman divorced from a husband commits adultery.

19 "But a certain man was rich, and he used to deck himself with purple and linen, enjoying himself

from day to day with magnificence. 20 But a certain beggar named Laz'a·rus used to be put at his gate, full of ulcers 21 and desiring to be filled with the things dropping from the table of the rich man. Yes, too, the dogs would come and lick his ulcers. 22 Now in course of time the beggar died and he was carried off by the angels to the bosom [position] of Abraham.

"Also, the rich man died and was buried. 23 And in Ha'des he lifted up his eyes, he existing in torments, and he saw Abraham afar off and Laz'a·rus in the bosom [position] with him. 24 So he called and said, 'Father Abraham, have mercy on me and send Laz'a·rus to dip the tip of his finger in water and cool my tongue, because I am in anguish in this blazing fire.' 25 But Abraham said, 'Child, remember that you received in full your good things in your lifetime, but Laz'a·rus correspondingly the injurious things. Now, however, he is having comfort here but you are in anguish. 26 And besides all these things, a great chasm has been fixed between us and YOU people, so that those wanting to go over from here to YOU people cannot, neither may people cross over from there to us.' 27 Then he said, 'In that event I ask you, father, to send him to the house of my father, 28 for I have five brothers, in order that he may give them a thorough witness, that they also should not get into this place of torment.' 29 But Abraham said, 'They have Moses and the Prophets; let them listen to these.' 30 Then he said, 'No, indeed, father Abraham, but if someone from the dead goes to them they will repent.' 31 But he said to him, 'If they do not listen to Moses and the Prophets, neither will they be persuaded if someone rises from the dead.' "

17 Then he said to his disciples: "It is unavoidable that causes for stumbling should come. Nevertheless, woe to the one through whom they come! 2 It would be of more advantage to him if a millstone were suspended from his neck and he were thrown into the sea than for him to stumble one of these little ones. 3 Pay attention to yourselves. If your brother commits a sin give him a rebuke, and if he repents forgive him. 4 Even if he sins seven times a day against you and he comes back to you seven times, saying, 'I repent,' you must forgive him."

5 Now the apostles said to the Lord: "Give us more faith." 6 Then the Lord said: "If YOU had faith the size of a mustard grain, YOU would say to this black mulberry tree, 'Be uprooted and planted in the sea!' and it would obey YOU.

7 "Who of YOU is there that has a slave plowing or minding the flock who will say to him when he gets in from the field, 'Come here at once and recline at the table'? 8 Rather, will he not say to him, 'Get something ready for me to have my evening meal, and put on an apron and minister to me until I am through eating and drinking, and afterward you can eat and drink'? 9 He will not feel gratitude to the slave because he did the things assigned, will he? 10 So YOU, also, when YOU have done all the things assigned to YOU, say, 'We are good-for-nothing slaves. What we have done is what we ought to have done.' "

11 And while he was going to Jerusalem he was passing through the midst of Sa·mar'i·a and Gal'i-lee. 12 And as he was entering into a certain village ten leprous men met him, but they stood up afar off. 13 And they raised their voices and said: "Jesus, Instructor, have mercy on us!" 14 And when he got sight of them he said to them: "Go and show yourselves to the priests." Then as they were going off their cleansing occurred. 15 One of them, when he saw he was healed, turned back, glorifying God with a loud voice. 16 And he fell upon his face at Jesus' feet, thanking him; furthermore, he was a Sa·mar'i·tan. 17 In reply Jesus said: "The ten were cleansed, were they not? Where, then, are the other nine? 18 Were none found

that turned back to give glory to God but this man of another nation?" 19 And he said to him: "Rise and be on your way; your faith has made you well."

20 But on being asked by the Pharisees when the kingdom of God was coming, he answered them and said: "The kingdom of God is not coming with striking observableness, 21 neither will people be saying, 'See here!' or, 'There!' For, look! the kingdom of God is in YOUR midst."

22 Then he said to the disciples: "Days will come when YOU will desire to see one of the days of the Son of man but YOU will not see [it]. 23 And people will say to YOU, 'See there!' or, 'See here!' Do not go out or chase after [them]. 24 For even as the lightning, by its flashing, shines from one part under heaven to another part under heaven, so the Son of man will be. 25 First, however, he must undergo many sufferings and be rejected by this generation. 26 Moreover, just as it occurred in the days of Noah, so it will be also in the days of the Son of man: 27 they were eating, they were drinking, men were marrying, women were being given in marriage, until that day when Noah entered into the ark, and the flood arrived and destroyed them all. 28 Likewise, just as it occurred in the days of Lot: they were eating, they were drinking, they were buying, they were selling, they were planting, they were building. 29 But on the day that Lot came out of Sod'om it rained fire and sulphur from heaven and destroyed them all. 30 The same way it will be on that day when the Son of man is to be revealed. 31 "On that day let the person that is on the housetop but whose movable things are in the house not come down to pick these up, and the person out in the field, let him likewise not return to the things behind. 32 REMEMBER the wife of Lot. 33 Whoever seeks to keep his soul safe for himself will lose it, but whoever loses it will preserve it alive. 34 I tell YOU,

In that night two [men] will be in one bed; the one will be taken along, but the other will be abandoned. 35 There will be two [women] grinding at the same mill; the one will be taken along, but the other will be abandoned." 36 —— 37 So in response they said to him: "Where, Lord?" He said to them: "Where the body is, there also the eagles will be gathered together."

18 Then he went on to tell them an illustration with regard to the need for them always to pray and not to give up, 2 saying: "In a certain city there was a certain judge that had no fear of God and had no respect for man. 3 But there was a widow in that city and she kept going to him, saying, 'See that I get justice from my adversary at law.' 4 Well, for a while he was unwilling, but afterward he said to himself, 'Although I do not fear God or respect a man, 5 at any rate, because of this widow's continually making me trouble, I will see that she gets justice, so that she will not keep coming and pummeling me to a finish.' " 6 Then the Lord said: "HEAR what the judge, although unrighteous, said! 7 Certainly, then, shall not God cause justice to be done for his chosen ones who cry out to him day and night, even though he is long-suffering toward them? 8 I tell YOU, He will cause justice to be done to them speedily. Nevertheless, when the Son of man arrives, will he really find the faith on the earth?"

9 But he spoke this illustration also to some who trusted in themselves that they were righteous and who considered the rest as nothing: 10 "Two men went up into the temple to pray, the one a Pharisee and the other a tax collector. 11 The Pharisee stood and began to pray these things to himself, 'O God, I thank you I am not as the rest of men, extortioners, unrighteous, adulterers, or even as this tax collector. 12 I fast twice a week, I give the tenth of all things I acquire.' 13 But the tax

collector standing at a distance was not willing even to raise his eyes heavenward, but kept beating his breast, saying, 'O God, be gracious to me a sinner.' 14 I tell YOU, This man went down to his home proved more righteous than that man; because everyone that exalts himself will be humiliated, but he that humbles himself will be exalted."

15 Now people began to bring him also their infants for him to touch these; but on seeing it the disciples began to reprimand them. 16 However, Jesus called the infants to him, saying: "Let the young children come to me, and do not try to stop them. For the kingdom of God belongs to such-like ones. 17 Truly I say to YOU, Whoever does not receive the kingdom of God like a young child will by no means get into it."

18 And a certain ruler questioned him, saying: "Good Teacher, by doing what shall I inherit everlasting life?" 19 Jesus said to him: "Why do you call me good? Nobody is good, except one, God. 20 You know the commandments, 'Do not commit adultery, Do not murder, Do not steal, Do not bear false witness, Honor your father and mother.'" 21 Then he said: "All these I have kept from youth on." 22 After hearing that, Jesus said to him: "There is yet one thing lacking about you: Sell all the things you have and distribute to poor people, and you will have treasure in the heavens; and come be my follower." 23 When he heard this, he became deeply grieved, for he was very rich.

24 Jesus looked at him and said: "How difficult a thing it will be for those having money to make their way into the kingdom of God! 25 It is easier, in fact, for a camel to get through the eye of a sewing needle than for a rich man to get into the kingdom of God." 26 Those who heard this said: "Who possibly can be saved?" 27 He said: "The things impossible with men are possible with God." 28 But Peter said: "Look! We have

left our own things and followed you." 29 He said to them: "Truly I say to YOU, There is no one who has left house or wife or brothers or parents or children for the sake of the kingdom of God 30 who will not in any way get many times more in this period of time, and in the coming system of things everlasting life."

31 Then he took the twelve aside and said to them: "Look! We are going up to Jerusalem, and all the things written by means of the prophets as to the Son of man will be completed. 32 For instance, he will be delivered up to men of the nations and will be made fun of and be treated insolently and spit upon; 33 and after scourging him they will kill him, but on the third day he will rise." 34 However, they did not get the meaning of any of these things; but this utterance was hidden from them, and they were not knowing the things said.

35 Now as he was getting near to Jer′i·cho a certain blind man was sitting beside the road begging. 36 Because he heard a crowd moving through he began to inquire what this might mean. 37 They reported to him: "Jesus the Naz·a-rene′ is passing by!" 38 At that he cried out, saying: "Jesus, Son of David, have mercy on me!" 39 And those going in advance began to tell him sternly to keep quiet, but that much more he kept shouting: "Son of David, have mercy on me." 40 Then Jesus stood still and commanded the [man] to be led to him. After he got near, Jesus asked him: 41 "What do you want me to do for you?" He said: "Lord, let me recover sight." 42 So Jesus said to him: "Recover your sight; your faith has made you well." 43 And instantly he recovered sight, and he began to follow him, glorifying God. Also, all the people, at seeing [it], gave praise to God.

19 And he entered Jer′i·cho and was going through. 2 Now here there was a man called by the name Zac·chae′us; and he was a

chief tax collector, and he was rich. 3 Well, he was seeking to see who this Jesus was, but he could not for the crowd, because he was small in size. 4 So he ran ahead to an advance position and climbed a fig-mulberry tree in order to see him, because he was about to go through that way. 5 Now when Jesus got to the place, he looked up and said to him: "Zac·chae′us, hurry and get down, for today I must stay in your house." 6 With that he hurried and got down and with rejoicing he received him as guest. 7 But when they saw [it], they all fell to muttering, saying: "With a man that is a sinner he went in to lodge." 8 But Zac·chae′us stood up and said to the Lord: "Look! The half of my belongings, Lord, I am giving to the poor, and whatever I extorted from anyone by false accusation I am restoring fourfold." 9 At this Jesus said to him: "This day salvation has come to this house, because he also is a son of Abraham. 10 For the Son of man came to seek and to save what was lost."

11 While they were listening to these things he spoke in addition an illustration, because he was near Jerusalem and they were imagining that the kingdom of God was going to display itself instantly. 12 Therefore he said: "A certain man of noble birth traveled to a distant land to secure kingly power for himself and to return. 13 Calling ten slaves of his he gave them ten mi′nas and told them, 'Do business till I come.' 14 But his citizens hated him and sent out a body of ambassadors after him, to say, 'We do not want this [man] to become king over us.'

15 "Eventually when he got back after having secured the kingly power, he commanded to be called to him these slaves to whom he had given the silver money, in order to ascertain what they had gained by business activity. 16 Then the first one presented himself, saying, 'Lord, your mi′na gained ten mi′nas.' 17 So he said

to him, 'Well done, good slave! Because in a very small matter you have proved yourself faithful, hold authority over ten cities.' 18 Now the second came, saying, 'Your mi′na, Lord, made five mi′nas.' 19 He said to this one also, 'You, too, be in charge of five cities.' 20 But a different one came, saying, 'Lord, here is your mi′na, that I kept laid away in a cloth. 21 You see, I was in fear of you, because you are a harsh man; you take up what you did not deposit and you reap what you did not sow.' 22 He said to him, 'Out of your own mouth I judge you, wicked slave. You knew, did you, that I am a harsh man, taking up what I did not deposit and reaping what I did not sow? 23 Hence why is it you did not put my silver money in a bank? Then on my arrival I would have collected it with interest.'

24 "With that he said to those standing by, 'Take the mi′na from him and give it to him that has the ten mi′nas.' 25 But they said to him, 'Lord, he has ten mi′nas!'— 26 'I say to YOU, To everyone that has, more will be given; but from the one that does not have, even what he has will be taken away. 27 Moreover, these enemies of mine that did not want me to become king over them BRING here and slaughter them before me.' "

28 So, after he had said these things, he began to go on ahead, going up to Jerusalem. 29 And when he got near to Beth′pha·ge and Beth′a·ny at the mountain called Mount of Olives, he sent forth two of the disciples, 30 saying: "Go into the village that is within sight of YOU, and in it after YOU pass in YOU will find a colt tied, on which none of mankind ever sat. Loose it and bring it. 31 But if anyone asks YOU, 'Why is it YOU are loosing it?' YOU must speak in this way, 'The Lord needs it.' " 32 So those who were sent forth departed and found it just as he said to them. 33 But as they were loosing the colt the owners of it said to them: "Why are YOU

loosing the colt?" 34 They said: "The Lord needs it." 35 And they led it to Jesus, and they threw their outer garments upon the colt and set Jesus upon [it].

36 As he moved along they kept spreading their outer garments on the road. 37 As soon as he got near the road down the Mount of Olives all the multitude of the disciples started to rejoice and praise God with a loud voice concerning all the powerful works they had seen, 38 saying: "Blessed is the One coming as the King in Jehovah's name! Peace in heaven, and glory in the highest places!" 39 However, some of the Pharisees from the crowd said to him: "Teacher, rebuke your disciples." 40 But in reply he said: "I tell you, If these remained silent, the stones would cry out."

41 And when he got nearby, he viewed the city and wept over it, 42 saying: "If you, even you, had discerned in this day the things having to do with peace—but now they have been hid from your eyes. 43 Because the days will come upon you when your enemies will build around you a fortification with pointed stakes and will encircle you and distress you from every side, 44 and they will dash you and your children within you to the ground, and they will not leave a stone upon a stone in you, because you did not discern the time of your being inspected."

45 And he entered into the temple and started to throw out those who were selling, 46 saying to them: "It is written, 'And my house will be a house of prayer,' but you made it a cave of robbers."

47 Furthermore, he went teaching daily in the temple. But the chief priests and the scribes and the principal ones of the people were seeking to destroy him; 48 and yet they did not find the effective thing for them to do, for the people one and all kept hanging onto him to hear him.

20 On one of the days while he was teaching the people in the temple and declaring the good news, the chief priests and the scribes with the older men came near, 2 and they spoke up, saying to him: "Tell us by what authority you do these things, or who it is that gave you this authority." 3 In reply he said to them: "I will also ask you a question, and you tell me: 4 Was the baptism of John from heaven or from men?" 5 Then among themselves they drew conclusions, saying: "If we say, 'From heaven,' he will say, 'Why is it you did not believe him?' 6 But if we say, 'From men,' the people one and all will stone us, for they are persuaded that John was a prophet." 7 So they replied that they did not know its source. 8 And Jesus said to them: "Neither am I telling you by what authority I do these things."

9 Then he started to tell the people this illustration: "A man planted a vineyard and let it out to cultivators, and he traveled abroad for considerable time. 10 But in due season he sent out a slave to the cultivators, that they might give him some of the fruit of the vineyard. The cultivators, however, sent him away empty, after beating him up. 11 But he repeated and sent them a different slave. That one also they beat up and dishonored and sent away empty. 12 Yet again he sent a third; this one also they wounded and threw out. 13 At this the owner of the vineyard said, 'What shall I do? I will send my son the beloved. Likely they will respect this one.' 14 When the cultivators caught sight of him they went reasoning with one another, saying, 'This is the heir; let us kill him, that the inheritance may become ours.' 15 With that they threw him outside the vineyard and killed him. What, therefore, will the owner of the vineyard do to them? 16 He will come and destroy these cultivators and will give the vineyard to others."

On hearing [this] they said: "Never may that happen!" 17 But he looked upon them and said: "What, then, does this that is written mean, 'The stone which the builders rejected, this has become the chief cornerstone'? 18 Everyone falling upon that stone will be shattered. As for anyone upon whom it falls, it will pulverize him."

19 The scribes and the chief priests now sought to get their hands on him in that very hour, but they feared the people; for they perceived that he spoke this illustration with them in mind. 20 And, after observing him closely, they sent out men secretly hired to pretend that they were righteous, in order that they might catch him in speech, so as to turn him over to the government and to the authority of the governor. 21 And they questioned him, saying: "Teacher, we know you speak and teach correctly and show no partiality, but you teach the way of God in line with truth: 22 Is it lawful for us to pay tax to Caesar or not?" 23 But he detected their cunning and said to them: 24 "Show me a de·nar'i·us. Whose image and inscription does it have?" They said: "Caesar's." 25 He said to them: "By all means, then, pay back Caesar's things to Caesar, but God's things to God." 26 Well, they were not able to catch him in this saying before the people, but, in amazement at his answer, they said nothing.

27 However, some of the Sadducees, those who say there is no resurrection, came up and questioned him, 28 saying: "Teacher, Moses wrote us, 'If a man's brother dies having a wife, but this one remained childless, his brother should take the wife and raise up offspring from her for his brother.' 29 Accordingly there were seven brothers; and the first took a wife and died childless. 30 So the second, 31 and the third took her. Likewise even the seven: they did not leave children behind, but died off. 32 Lastly, the woman also died. 33 Consequently, in the resurrection, of which one of them does she become [the] wife? For the seven got her as wife."

34 Jesus said to them: "The children of this system of things marry and are given in marriage, 35 but those who have been counted worthy of gaining that system of things and the resurrection from the dead neither marry nor are given in marriage. 36 In fact, neither can they die any more, for they are like the angels, and they are God's children by being children of the resurrection. 37 But that the dead are raised up even Moses disclosed, in the account about the thornbush, when he calls Jehovah 'the God of Abraham and God of Isaac and God of Jacob.' 38 He is a God, not of the dead, but of the living, for they are all living to him." 39 In response some of the scribes said: "Teacher, you spoke well." 40 For no longer did they have the courage to ask him a single question.

41 In turn he said to them: "How is it they say that the Christ is David's son? 42 For David himself says in the book of Psalms, 'Jehovah said to my Lord, Sit at my right hand 43 until I place your enemies as a stool for your feet.' 44 David, therefore, calls him 'Lord'; so how is he his son?"

45 Then, while all the people were listening he said to the disciples: 46 "Look out for the scribes who desire to walk around in robes and like greetings in the market places and front seats in the synagogues and most prominent places at evening meals, 47 and who devour the houses of the widows and for a pretext make long prayers. These will receive a heavier judgment."

21 Now as he looked up he saw the rich dropping their gifts into the treasury chests. 2 Then he saw a certain needy widow drop two small coins of very little value there, 3 and he said: "I tell you truthfully, This widow, although poor, dropped in more than they all did. 4 For all these dropped in gifts out of their surplus, but this [woman] out of her want dropped in all the means of living she had."

5 Later, as certain ones were speaking concerning the temple, how it was adorned with fine stones and dedicated things, **6** he said: "As for these things that YOU are beholding, the days will come in which not a stone upon a stone will be left here and not be thrown down." **7** Then they questioned him, saying: "Teacher, when will these things actually be, and what will be the sign when these things are destined to occur?" **8** He said: "Look out that YOU are not misled; for many will come on the basis of my name, saying, 'I am he,' and, 'The due time has approached.' Do not go after them. **9** Furthermore, when YOU hear of wars and disorders, do not be terrified. For these things must occur first, but the end does not [occur] immediately."

10 Then he went on to say to them: "Nation will rise against nation, and kingdom against kingdom; **11** and there will be great earthquakes, and in one place after another pestilences and food shortages; and there will be fearful sights and from heaven great signs.

12 "But before all these things people will lay their hands upon YOU and persecute YOU, delivering YOU up to the synagogues and prisons, YOU being haled before kings and governors for the sake of my name. **13** It will turn out to YOU for a witness. **14** Therefore settle it in YOUR hearts not to rehearse beforehand how to make YOUR defense, **15** for I will give YOU a mouth and wisdom, which all YOUR opposers together will not be able to resist or dispute. **16** Moreover, YOU will be delivered up even by parents and brothers and relatives and friends, and they will put some of YOU to death; **17** and YOU will be objects of hatred by all people because of my name. **18** And yet not a hair of YOUR heads will by any means perish. **19** By endurance on YOUR part YOU will acquire YOUR souls.

20 "Furthermore, when YOU see Jerusalem surrounded by encamped armies, then know that the des- olating of her has drawn near. **21** Then let those in Ju·de′a begin fleeing to the mountains, and let those in the midst of her withdraw, and let those in the country places not enter into her; **22** because these are days for meting out justice, that all the things written may be fulfilled. **23** Woe to the pregnant women and the ones suckling a baby in those days! For there will be great necessity upon the land and wrath on this people; **24** and they will fall by the edge of the sword and be led captive into all the nations; and Jerusalem will be trampled on by the nations, until the appointed times of the nations are fulfilled.

25 "Also, there will be signs in sun and moon and stars, and on the earth anguish of nations, not knowing the way out because of the roaring of the sea and [its] agitation, **26** while men become faint out of fear and expectation of the things coming upon the inhabited earth; for the powers of the heavens will be shaken. **27** And then they will see the Son of man coming in a cloud with power and great glory. **28** But as these things start to occur, raise yourselves erect and lift YOUR heads up, because YOUR deliverance is getting near."

29 With that he spoke an illustration to them: "Note the fig tree and all the other trees: **30** When they are already in the bud, by observing it YOU know for yourselves that now the summer is near. **31** In this way YOU also, when YOU see these things occurring, know that the kingdom of God is near. **32** Truly I say to YOU, This generation will by no means pass away until all things occur. **33** Heaven and earth will pass away, but my words will by no means pass away.

34 "But pay attention to yourselves that YOUR hearts never become weighed down with overeating and heavy drinking and anxieties of life, and suddenly that day be instantly upon YOU **35** as a snare. For it will come in upon all those dwelling upon the face of all the earth. 36 Keep awake, then, all the time making supplication that YOU may succeed in escaping all these things that are destined to occur, and in standing before the Son of man."

37 So by day he would be teaching in the temple, but by night he would go out and lodge on the mountain called the Mount of Olives. 38 And all the people would come early in the day to him in the temple to hear him.

22 Now the festival of the unfermented cakes, the so-called Passover, was getting near. 2 Also, the chief priests and the scribes were seeking the effective way for them to get rid of him, for they were in fear of the people. 3 But Satan entered into Judas, the one called Is·car'i·ot, who was numbered among the twelve; 4 and he went off and talked with the chief priests and [temple] captains about the effective way to betray him to them. 5 Well, they rejoiced and agreed to give him silver money. 6 So he consented, and he began to seek a good opportunity to betray him to them without a crowd around.

7 The day of the unfermented cakes now arrived, on which the passover [victim] must be sacrificed; 8 and he dispatched Peter and John, saying: "Go and get the passover ready for us to eat." 9 They said to him: "Where do you want us to get [it] ready?" 10 He said to them: "Look! When YOU enter into the city a man carrying an earthenware vessel of water will meet YOU. Follow him into the house into which he enters. 11 And YOU must say to the landlord of the house, 'The Teacher says to you: "Where is the guest room in which I may eat the passover with my disciples?"' 12 And that [man] will show YOU a large upper room furnished. Get [it] ready there." 13 So they departed and found it just as he had said to them, and they got the passover ready.

14 At length when the hour came, he reclined at the table, and the apostles with him. 15 And he said to them: "I have greatly desired to eat this passover with YOU before I suffer; 16 for I tell YOU, I will not eat it again until it becomes fulfilled in the kingdom of God." 17 And, accepting a cup, he gave thanks and said: "Take this and pass it from one to the other among yourselves; 18 for I tell YOU, From now on I will not drink again from the product of the vine until the kingdom of God arrives."

19 Also, he took a loaf, gave thanks, broke it, and gave it to them, saying: "This means my body which is to be given in YOUR behalf. Keep doing this in remembrance of me." 20 Also, the cup in the same way after they had the evening meal, he saying: "This cup means the new covenant by virtue of my blood, which is to be poured out in YOUR behalf.

21 "But, look! the hand of my betrayer is with me at the table. 22 Because the Son of man is going his way according to what is marked out; all the same, woe to that man through whom he is betrayed!" 23 So they started to discuss among themselves the question of which of them would really be the one that was about to do this.

24 However, there also arose a heated dispute among them over which one of them seemed to be greatest. 25 But he said to them: "The kings of the nations lord it over them, and those having authority over them are called Benefactors. 26 YOU, though, are not to be that way. But let him that is the greatest among YOU become as the youngest, and the one acting as chief as the one ministering. 27 For which one is greater, the one reclining at the table or the one ministering? Is it not the one reclining at the table? But I am in YOUR midst as the one ministering.

28 "However, YOU are the ones that have stuck with me in my trials; 29 and I make a covenant with YOU, just as my Father has

made a covenant with me, for a kingdom, 30 that YOU may eat and drink at my table in my kingdom, and sit on thrones to judge the twelve tribes of Israel.

31 "Simon, Simon, look! Satan has demanded to have YOU men to sift YOU as wheat. 32 But I have made supplication for you that your faith may not give out; and you, when once you have returned, strengthen your brothers." 33 Then he said to him: "Lord, I am ready to go with you both into prison and into death." 34 But he said: "I tell you, Peter, A cock will not crow today until you have three times denied knowing me."

35 He also said to them: "When I sent YOU forth without purse and food pouch and sandals, YOU did not want for anything, did YOU?" They said: "No!" 36 Then he said to them: "But now let the one that has a purse take it up, likewise also a food pouch; and let the one having no sword sell his outer garment and buy one. 37 For I tell YOU that this which is written must be accomplished in me, namely, 'And he was reckoned with lawless ones.' For that which concerns me is having an accomplishment." 38 Then they said: "Lord, look! here are two swords." He said to them: "It is enough."

39 On going out he went as customarily to the Mount of Olives; and the disciples also followed him. 40 Having come to the place he said to them: "Carry on prayer, that YOU do not enter into temptation." 41 And he himself drew away from them about a stone's throw, and bent his knees and began to pray, 42 saying: "Father, if you wish, remove this cup from me. Nevertheless, let, not my will, but yours take place." 43 Then an angel from heaven appeared to him and strengthened him. 44 But getting into an agony he continued praying more earnestly; and his sweat became as drops of blood falling to the ground. 45 And he rose from prayer, went to the disciples and found them slumbering

from grief; 46 and he said to them: "Why are YOU sleeping? Rise and carry on prayer, that YOU do not enter into temptation."

47 While he was yet speaking, look! a crowd, and the [man] called Judas, one of the twelve, was going before them; and he approached Jesus to kiss him. 48 But Jesus said to him: "Judas, do you betray the Son of man with a kiss?" 49 When those about him saw what was going to happen, they said: "Lord, shall we strike with the sword?" 50 A certain one of them even did strike the slave of the high priest and took off his right ear. 51 But in reply Jesus said: "LET it go as far as this." And he touched the ear and healed him. 52 Jesus then said to the chief priests and captains of the temple and older men that had come there for him: "Did YOU come out with swords and clubs as against a robber? 53 While I was with YOU in the temple day after day YOU did not stretch out YOUR hands against me. But this is YOUR hour and the authority of darkness."

54 Then they arrested him and led him off and brought him into the house of the high priest; but Peter was following at a distance. 55 When they lit a fire in the midst of the courtyard and sat down together, Peter was sitting in among them. 56 But a certain servant girl saw him sitting by the bright fire and looked him over and said: 57 "This man also was with him." But he denied it, saying: "I do not know him, woman." 58 And after a short time another person seeing him said: "You also are one of them." But Peter said: "Man, I am not." 59 And after about an hour intervened a certain other [man] began insisting strongly: "For a certainty this [man] also was with him; for, in fact, he is a Gal·i·le′an!" 60 But Peter said: "Man, I do not know what you are saying." And instantly, while he was yet speaking, a cock crowed. 61 And the Lord turned and looked upon Peter, and Peter recalled the

utterance of the Lord when he said to him: "Before a cock crows today you will disown me three times." 62 And he went outside and wept bitterly.

63 Now the men that had him in custody began to make fun of him, hitting him; 64 and after covering him over they would ask and say: "Prophesy. Who is it that struck you?" 65 And they went on saying many other things in blasphemy against him.

66 At length when it became day, the assembly of older men of the people, both chief priests and scribes, gathered together, and they haled him into their San'he·drin hall, saying: 67 "If you are the Christ, tell us." But he said to them: "Even if I told you, you would not believe it at all. 68 Moreover, if I questioned you, you would not answer at all. 69 However, from now on the Son of man will be sitting at the powerful right hand of God." 70 At this they all said: "Are you, therefore, the Son of God?" He said to them: "You yourselves are saying that I am." 71 They said: "Why do we need further witness? For we ourselves have heard [it] out of his own mouth."

23 So the multitude of them rose, one and all, and led him to Pilate. 2 Then they started to accuse him, saying: "This man we found subverting our nation and forbidding the paying of taxes to Caesar and saying he himself is Christ a king." 3 Now Pilate asked him the question: "Are you the king of the Jews?" In answer he said: "You yourself are saying [it]." 4 Then Pilate said to the chief priests and the crowds: "I find no crime in this man." 5 But they began to be insistent, saying: "He stirs up the people by teaching throughout all Ju·de'a, even starting out from Gal'i·lee to here." 6 On hearing that, Pilate asked whether the man was a Gal·i·le'an, 7 and, after ascertaining that he was from the jurisdiction of Herod, he sent him on to Herod, who

was also himself in Jerusalem in these days.

8 When Herod saw Jesus he rejoiced greatly, for over a considerable time he was wanting to see him because of having heard about him, and he was hoping to see some sign performed by him. 9 Now he began to question him with a good many words; but he made him no answer. 10 However, the chief priests and the scribes kept standing up and vehemently accusing him. 11 Then Herod together with his soldier guards discredited him, and he made fun of him by clothing him with a bright garment and sent him back to Pilate. 12 Both Herod and Pilate now became friends with each other on that very day; for before that they had continued at enmity between themselves.

13 Pilate then called the chief priests and the rulers and the people together 14 and said to them: "You brought this man to me as one inciting the people to revolt, and, look! I examined him in front of you but found in this man no ground for the charges you are bringing against him. 15 In fact, neither did Herod, for he sent him back to us; and, look! nothing deserving of death has been committed by him. 16 I will therefore chastise him and release him." 17 —— 18 But with their whole multitude they cried out, saying: "Take this one away, but release Bar·ab'bas to us!" 19 (Which [man] had been thrown into prison for a certain sedition occurring in the city and for murder.) 20 Again Pilate called out to them, because he wanted to release Jesus. 21 Then they began to yell, saying: "Impale! Impale him!" 22 The third time he said to them: "Why, what bad thing did this [man] do? I found nothing deserving of death in him; I will therefore chastise and release him." 23 At this they began to be urgent, with loud voices, demanding that he be impaled; and their voices began to win out. 24 So Pilate gave sentence for their demand to be met: 25 he released

the man that had been thrown into prison for sedition and murder and whom they were demanding, but he surrendered Jesus to their will.

26 Now as they led him away, they laid hold of Simon, a certain native of Cy·re′ne, coming from the country, and they placed the torture stake upon him to bear it behind Jesus. 27 But there was following him a great multitude of the people and of women who kept beating themselves in grief and bewailing him. 28 Jesus turned to the women and said: "Daughters of Jerusalem, stop weeping for me. On the contrary, weep for yourselves and for YOUR children; 29 because, look! days are coming in which people will say, 'Happy are the barren women, and the wombs that did not give birth and the breasts that did not nurse!' 30 Then they will start to say to the mountains, 'Fall over us!' and to the hills, 'Cover us over!' 31 Because if they do these things when the tree is moist, what will occur when it is withered?"

32 But two other men, evildoers, were also being led to be executed with him. 33 And when they got to the place called Skull, there they impaled him and the evildoers, one on his right and one on his left. 34 [But Jesus was saying: "Father, forgive them, for they do not know what they are doing."] Furthermore, to distribute his garments, they cast lots. 35 And the people stood looking on. But the rulers were sneering, saying: "Others he saved; let him save himself, if this one is the Christ of God, the Chosen One." 36 Even the soldiers made fun of him, coming close and offering him sour wine 37 and saying: "If you are the king of the Jews, save yourself." 38 There was also an inscription over him: "This is the king of the Jews."

39 But one of the hung evildoers began to say abusively to him: "You are the Christ, are you not? Save yourself and us." 40 In reply the other rebuked him and said:

"Do you not fear God at all, now that you are in the same judgment? 41 And we, indeed, justly so, for we are receiving in full what we deserve for things we did; but this [man] did nothing out of the way." 42 And he went on to say: "Jesus, remember me when you get into your kingdom." 43 And he said to him: "Truly I tell you today, You will be with me in Paradise."

44 Well, by now it was about the sixth hour, and yet a darkness fell over all the earth until the ninth hour, 45 because the sunlight failed; then the curtain of the sanctuary was rent down the middle. 46 And Jesus called with a loud voice and said: "Father, into your hands I entrust my spirit." When he had said this, he expired. 47 Because of seeing what occurred the army officer began to glorify God, saying: "Really this man was righteous." 48 And all the crowds that were gathered together there for this spectacle, when they beheld the things that occurred, began to return, beating their breasts. 49 Moreover, all those acquainted with him were standing at a distance. Also, women, who together had followed him from Gal′i·lee, were standing beholding these things.

50 And, look! a man named Joseph, who was a member of the Council, a good and righteous man— 51 this [man] had not voted in support of their design and action—he was from Ar·i·ma·the′a, a city of the Ju·de′ans, and was waiting for the kingdom of God; 52 this man went to Pilate and asked for the body of Jesus. 53 And he took it down and wrapped it up in fine linen, and he laid him in a tomb carved in the rock, in which no man had yet lain. 54 Now it was the day of Preparation, and the evening light of the sabbath was approaching. 55 But the women, who had come with him out of Gal′i·lee, followed along and took a look at the memorial tomb and how his body was laid; 56 and they went back to prepare spices and perfumed oils.

But, of course, they rested on the sabbath according to the commandment.

24 On the first day of the week, however, they went very early to the tomb, bearing the spices they had prepared. 2 But they found the stone rolled away from the memorial tomb, 3 and when they entered they did not find the body of the Lord Jesus. 4 While they were in perplexity over this, look! two men in flashing clothing stood by them. 5 As the [women] became frightened and kept their faces turned to the ground, the [men] said to them: "Why are you looking for the living One among the dead? 6 [[He is not here, but has been raised up.]] Recall how he spoke to you while he was yet in Gal'i·lee, 7 saying that the Son of man must be delivered into the hands of sinful men and be impaled and yet on the third day rise." 8 So they called his sayings to mind, 9 and they returned from the memorial tomb and reported all these things to the eleven and to all the rest. 10 They were the Mag'da·lene Mary, and Jo·an'na, and Mary the mother of James. Also, the rest of the women with them were telling the apostles these things. 11 However, these sayings appeared as nonsense to them and they would not believe the [women].

12 [[But Peter rose and ran to the memorial tomb, and, stooping forward, he beheld the bandages alone. So he went off. wondering within himself at what had occurred.]]

13 But, look! on that very day two of them were journeying to a village about seven miles distant from Jerusalem [and] named Em·ma'us, 14 and they were conversing with each other over all these things that had come about. 15 Now as they were conversing and discussing, Jesus himself approached and began walking with them; 16 but their eyes were kept from recognizing him. 17 He said to them: "What are these matters that you are debating between yourselves as you walk along?"

And they stood still with sad faces. 18 In answer the one named Cle'o·pas said to him: "Are you dwelling as an alien by yourself in Jerusalem and so do not know the things that have occurred in her in these days?" 19 And he said to them: "What things?" They said to him: "The things concerning Jesus the Naz·a·rene', who became a prophet powerful in work and word before God and all the people; 20 and how our chief priests and rulers handed him over to the sentence of death and impaled him. 21 But we were hoping that this [man] was the one destined to deliver Israel; yes, and besides all these things, this makes the third day since these things occurred. 22 Moreover, certain women from among us also astonished us, because they had been early to the memorial tomb 23 but did not find his body and they came saying they had also seen a supernatural sight of angels, who said he is alive. 24 Further, some of those with us went off to the memorial tomb; and they found it so, just as the women had said, but they did not see him."

25 So he said to them: "O senseless ones and slow in heart to believe on all the things the prophets spoke! 26 Was it not necessary for the Christ to suffer these things and to enter into his glory?" 27 And commencing at Moses and all the Prophets he interpreted to them things pertaining to himself in all the Scriptures.

28 Finally they got close to the village where they were journeying, and he made as if he was journeying on farther. 29 But they used pressure upon him, saying: "Stay with us, because it is toward evening and the day has already declined." With that he went in to stay with them. 30 And as he was reclining with them at the meal he took the loaf, blessed it, broke it and began to hand it to them. 31 At that their eyes were fully opened and they recognized him; and he disappeared from them. 32 And they said to each

to Jesus. When Jesus looked upon him he said: "You are Simon the son of John; you will be called Ce'phas" (which is translated Peter).

43 The next day he desired to depart for Gal'i·lee. So Jesus found Philip and said to him: "Be my follower." 44 Now Philip was from Beth·sa'i·da, from the city of Andrew and Peter. 45 Philip found Na·than'a·el and said to him: "We have found the one of whom Moses, in the Law, and the Prophets wrote, Jesus, the son of Joseph, from Naz'a·reth." 46 But Na·than'a·el said to him: "Can anything good come out of Naz'a·reth?" Philip said to him: "Come and see." 47 Jesus saw Na·than'a·el coming toward him and said about him: "See, an Israelite for a certainty, in whom there is no deceit." 48 Na·than'a·el said to him: "How does it come that you know me?" Jesus in answer said to him: "Before Philip called you, while you were under the fig tree, I saw you." 49 Na·than'a·el answered him: "Rabbi, you are the Son of God, you are King of Israel." 50 Jesus in answer said to him: "Because I told you I saw you underneath the fig tree do you believe? You will see things greater than these." 51 He further said to him: "Most truly I say to you men, You will see heaven opened up and the angels of God ascending and descending to the Son of man."

2 Now on the third day a marriage feast took place in Ca'na of Gal'i·lee, and the mother of Jesus was there. 2 Jesus and his disciples were also invited to the marriage feast. 3 When the wine ran short the mother of Jesus said to him: "They have no wine." 4 But Jesus said to her: "What have I to do with you, woman? My hour has not yet come." 5 His mother said to those ministering: "Whatever he tells you, do." 6 As it was, there were six stone water jars sitting there as required by the purification rules of the Jews, each able to hold two or three liquid measures. 7 Jesus said to them: "Fill the water jars with water." And they filled them to the brim. 8 And he said to them: "Draw some out now and take it to the director of the feast." So they took it. 9 When, now, the director of the feast tasted the water that had been turned into wine but did not know what its source was, although those ministering who had drawn out the water knew, the director of the feast called the bridegroom 10 and said to him: "Every other man puts out the fine wine first, and when people are intoxicated, the inferior. You have reserved the fine wine until now." 11 Jesus performed this in Ca'na of Gal'i·lee as [the] beginning of his signs, and he made his glory manifest; and his disciples put their faith in him.

12 After this he and his mother and brothers and his disciples went down to Ca·per'na·um, but they did not stay there many days.

13 Now the passover of the Jews was near, and Jesus went up to Jerusalem. 14 And he found in the temple those selling cattle and sheep and doves and the money brokers in their seats. 15 So, after making a whip of ropes, he drove all those with the sheep and cattle out of the temple, and he poured out the coins of the money-changers and overturned their tables. 16 And he said to those selling the doves: "Take these things away from here! Stop making the house of my Father a house of merchandise!" 17 His disciples called to mind that it is written: "The zeal for your house will eat me up." 18 Therefore, in answer, the Jews said to him: "What sign have you to show us, since you are doing these things?" 19 In answer Jesus said to them: "Break down this temple, and in three days I will raise it up." 20 Therefore the Jews said: "This temple was built in forty-six years, and will you raise it up in three days?" 21 But he was talking about the temple of his body. 22 When, though, he was raised up from the dead, his disciples called to mind that he

used to say this; and they believed the Scripture and the saying that Jesus said.

23 However, when he was in Jerusalem at the passover, at its festival, many people put their faith in his name, viewing his signs that he was performing. 24 But Jesus himself was not entrusting himself to them because of his knowing them all 25 and because he was in no need to have anyone bear witness about man, for he himself knew what was in man.

3 Now there was a man of the Pharisees, Nic·o·de′mus was his name, a ruler of the Jews. 2 This one came to him in the night and said to him: "Rabbi, we know that you as a teacher have come from God; for no one can perform these signs that you perform unless God is with him." 3 In answer Jesus said to him: "Most truly I say to you, Unless anyone is born again, he cannot see the kingdom of God." 4 Nic·o·de′mus said to him: "How can a man be born when he is old? He cannot enter into the womb of his mother a second time and be born, can he?" 5 Jesus answered: "Most truly I say to you, Unless anyone is born from water and spirit, he cannot enter into the kingdom of God. 6 What has been born from the flesh is flesh, and what has been born from the spirit is spirit. 7 Do not marvel because I told you, You people must be born again. 8 The wind blows where it wants to, and you hear the sound of it, but you do not know where it comes from and where it is going. So is everyone that has been born from the spirit."

9 In answer Nic·o·de′mus said to him: "How can these things come about?" 10 In answer Jesus said to him: "Are you a teacher of Israel and yet do not know these things? 11 Most truly I say to you, What we know we speak and what we have seen we bear witness of, but you people do not receive the witness we give. 12 If I have told you earthly things and yet you do not believe, how will you believe if I tell you heavenly things? 13 Moreover, no man has ascended into heaven but he that descended from heaven, the Son of man. 14 And just as Moses lifted up the serpent in the wilderness, so the Son of man must be lifted up, 15 that everyone believing in him may have everlasting life.

16 "For God loved the world so much that he gave his only-begotten Son, in order that everyone exercising faith in him might not be destroyed but have everlasting life. 17 For God sent forth his Son into the world, not for him to judge the world, but for the world to be saved through him. 18 He that exercises faith in him is not to be judged. He that does not exercise faith has been judged already, because he has not exercised faith in the name of the only-begotten Son of God. 19 Now this is the basis for judgment, that the light has come into the world but men have loved the darkness rather than the light, for their works were wicked. 20 For he that practices vile things hates the light and does not come to the light, in order that his works may not be reproved. 21 But he that does what is true comes to the light, in order that his works may be made manifest as having been worked in harmony with God."

22 After these things Jesus and his disciples went into Ju·de′an country, and there he spent some time with them and did baptizing. 23 But John also was baptizing in Ae′non near Sa′lim, because there was a great quantity of water there, and people kept coming and being baptized; 24 for John had not yet been thrown into prison.

25 Therefore a dispute arose on the part of the disciples of John with a Jew concerning purification. 26 So they came to John and said to him: "Rabbi, the man that was with you across the Jordan, to whom you have borne witness, see, this one is baptizing and all are going to him." 27 In answer John said: "A man cannot receive a single thing unless it has been

given him from heaven. 28 You yourselves bear me witness that I said, I am not the Christ, but, I have been sent forth in advance of that one. 29 He that has the bride is the bridegroom. However, the friend of the bridegroom, when he stands and hears him, has a great deal of joy on account of the voice of the bridegroom. Therefore this joy of mine has been made full. 30 That one must go on increasing, but I must go on decreasing."

31 He that comes from above is over all others. He that is from the earth is from the earth and speaks of things of the earth. He that comes from heaven is over all others. 32 What he has seen and heard, of this he bears witness, but no man is accepting his witness. 33 He that has accepted his witness has put his seal to it that God is true. 34 For the one whom God sent forth speaks the sayings of God, for he does not give the spirit by measure. 35 The Father loves the Son and has given all things into his hand. 36 He that exercises faith in the Son has everlasting life; he that disobeys the Son will not see life, but the wrath of God remains upon him.

4 When, now, the Lord became aware that the Pharisees had heard that Jesus was making and baptizing more disciples than John — 2 although, indeed, Jesus himself did no baptizing but his disciples did— 3 he left Ju·de'a and departed again for Gal'i·lee. 4 But it was necessary for him to go through Sa·mar'i·a. 5 Accordingly he came to a city of Sa·mar'i·a called Sy'char near the field that Jacob gave to Joseph his son. 6 In fact, Jacob's fountain was there. Now Jesus, tired out from the journey, was sitting at the fountain just as he was. The hour was about the sixth.

7 A woman of Sa·mar'i·a came to draw water. Jesus said to her: "Give me a drink." 8 (For his disciples had gone off into the city to buy foodstuffs.) 9 Therefore the Sa·mar'i·tan woman said to him:

"How is it that you, despite being a Jew, ask me for a drink, when I am a Sa·mar'i·tan woman?" (For Jews have no dealings with Samar'i·tans.) 10 In answer Jesus said to her: "If you had known the free gift of God and who it is that says to you, 'Give me a drink,' you would have asked him, and he would have given you living water." 11 She said to him: "Sir, you have not even a bucket for drawing water, and the well is deep. From what source, therefore, do you have this living water? 12 You are not greater than our forefather Jacob, who gave us the well and who himself together with his sons and his cattle drank out of it, are you?" 13 In answer Jesus said to her: "Everyone drinking from this water will get thirsty again. 14 Whoever drinks from the water that I will give him will never get thirsty at all, but the water that I will give him will become in him a fountain of water bubbling up to impart everlasting life." 15 The woman said to him: "Sir, give me this water, so that I may neither thirst nor keep coming over to this place to draw water."

16 He said to her: "Go, call your husband and come to this place." 17 In answer the woman said: "I do not have a husband." Jesus said to her: "You said well, 'A husband I do not have.' 18 For you have had five husbands, and the [man] you now have is not your husband. This you have said truthfully." 19 The woman said to him: "Sir, I perceive you are a prophet. 20 Our forefathers worshiped in this mountain; but you people say that in Jerusalem is the place where persons ought to worship." 21 Jesus said to her: "Believe me, woman, The hour is coming when neither in this mountain nor in Jerusalem will you people worship the Father. 22 You worship what you do not know; we worship what we know, because salvation originates with the Jews. 23 Nevertheless, the hour is coming, and it is now, when the true worshipers will worship the Father with spirit and

truth, for, indeed, the Father is looking for suchlike ones to worship him. 24 God is a Spirit, and those worshiping him must worship with spirit and truth." 25 The woman said to him: "I know that Mes·si′ah is coming, who is called Christ. Whenever that one arrives, he will declare all things to us openly." 26 Jesus said to her: "I who am speaking to you am he."

27 Now at this point his disciples arrived, and they began to wonder because he was speaking with a woman. Of course, no one said: "What are you looking for?" or, "Why do you talk with her?" 28 The woman, therefore, left her water jar and went off into the city and told the men: 29 "Come here, see a man that told me all the things I did. This is not perhaps the Christ, is it?" 30 They went out of the city and began coming to him.

31 Meanwhile the disciples were urging him, saying: "Rabbi, eat." 32 But he said to them: "I have food to eat of which you do not know." 33 Therefore the disciples began saying to one another: "No one has brought him anything to eat, has he?" 34 Jesus said to them: "My food is for me to do the will of him that sent me and to finish his work. 35 Do you not say that there are yet four months before the harvest comes? Look! I say to you: Lift up your eyes and view the fields, that they are white for harvesting. Already 36 the reaper is receiving wages and gathering fruit for everlasting life, so that the sower and the reaper may rejoice together. 37 In this respect, indeed, the saying is true, One is the sower and another the reaper. 38 I dispatched you to reap what you have spent no labor on. Others have labored, and you have entered into the benefit of their labor."

39 Now many of the Sa·mar′i·tans out of that city put faith in him on account of the word of the woman who said in witness: "He told me all the things I did."

40 Therefore when the Sa·mar′i·tans came to him, they began asking him to stay with them; and he stayed there two days. 41 Consequently many more believed on account of what he said, 42 and they began to say to the woman: "We do not believe any longer on account of your talk; for we have heard for ourselves and we know that this man is for a certainty the savior of the world."

43 After the two days he left there for Gal′i·lee. 44 Jesus himself, however, bore witness that in his own home land a prophet has no honor. 45 When, therefore, he arrived in Gal′i·lee, the Gal·i·le′ans received him, because they had seen all the things he did in Jerusalem at the festival, for they also had gone to the festival.

46 Accordingly he came again to Ca′na of Gal′i·lee, where he had turned the water into wine. Now there was a certain attendant of the king whose son was sick in Ca·per′na·um. 47 When this man heard that Jesus had come out of Ju·de′a into Gal′i·lee, he went off to him and began asking him to come down and heal his son, for he was at the point of dying. 48 However, Jesus said to him: "Unless you people see signs and wonders, you will by no means believe." 49 The attendant of the king said to him: "Lord, come down before my young child dies." 50 Jesus said to him: "Go your way; your son lives." The man believed the word that Jesus spoke to him and went his way. 51 But already while he was on his way down his slaves met him to say that his boy was living. 52 Therefore he began to inquire of them the hour in which he got better in health. Accordingly they said to him: "Yesterday at the seventh hour the fever left him." 53 Therefore the father knew it was in the very hour that Jesus said to him: "Your son lives." And he and his whole household believed. 54 Again this was the second sign Jesus performed when he came out of Ju·de′a into Gal′i·lee.

5 After these things there was a festival of the Jews, and Jesus went up to Jerusalem. 2 Now in Jerusalem at the sheepgate there is a pool designated in Hebrew Beth·za′tha, with five colonnades. 3 In these a multitude of the sick, blind, lame and those with withered members, was lying down. 4 —— 5 But a certain man was there who had been in his sickness for thirty-eight years. 6 Seeing this man lying down, and being aware that he had already been [sick] a long time, Jesus said to him: "Do you want to become sound in health?" 7 The sick man answered him: "Sir, I do not have a man to put me into the pool when the water is disturbed; but while I am coming another steps down ahead of me." 8 Jesus said to him: "Get up, pick up your cot and walk." 9 With that the man immediately became sound in health, and he picked up his cot and began to walk.

Now on that day it was a sabbath. 10 Therefore the Jews began to say to the cured man: "It is Sabbath, and it is not lawful for you to carry the cot." 11 But he answered them: "The very one that made me sound in health said to me, 'Pick up your cot and walk.'" 12 They asked him: "Who is the man that told you, 'Pick it up and walk'?" 13 But the healed man did not know who he was, for Jesus had turned aside, there being a crowd in the place.

14 After these things Jesus found him in the temple and said to him: "See, you have become sound in health. Do not sin any more, in order that something worse does not happen to you." 15 The man went away and told the Jews it was Jesus that made him sound in health. 16 So on this account the Jews went persecuting Jesus, because he was doing these things during Sabbath. 17 But he answered them: "My Father has kept working until now, and I keep working." 18 On this account, indeed, the Jews began seeking all the more to kill him, because not only was he breaking the Sabbath but he was also calling God his own Father, making himself equal to God.

19 Therefore, in answer, Jesus went on to say to them: "Most truly I say to you, The Son cannot do a single thing of his own initiative, but only what he beholds the Father doing. For whatever things that One does, these things the Son also does in like manner. 20 For the Father has affection for the Son and shows him all the things he himself does, and he will show him works greater than these, in order that you may marvel. 21 For just as the Father raises the dead up and makes them alive, so the Son also makes those alive whom he wants to. 22 For the Father judges no one at all, but he has committed all the judging to the Son, 23 in order that all may honor the Son just as they honor the Father. He that does not honor the Son does not honor the Father who sent him. 24 Most truly I say to you, He that hears my word and believes him that sent me has everlasting life, and he does not come into judgment but has passed over from death to life.

25 "Most truly I say to you, The hour is coming, and it is now, when the dead will hear the voice of the Son of God and those who have given heed will live. 26 For just as the Father has life in himself, so he has granted also to the Son to have life in himself. 27 And he has given him authority to do judging, because Son of man he is. 28 Do not marvel at this, because the hour is coming in which all those in the memorial tombs will hear his voice 29 and come out, those who did good things to a resurrection of life, those who practiced vile things to a resurrection of judgment. 30 I cannot do a single thing of my own initiative; just as I hear, I judge; and the judgment that I render is righteous, because I seek, not my own will, but the will of him that sent me.

31 "If I alone bear witness about myself, my witness is not true.

32 There is another that bears witness about me, and I know that the witness which he bears about me is true. 33 You have dispatched men to John, and he has borne witness to the truth. 34 However, I do not accept the witness from man, but I say these things that you may be saved. 35 That man was a burning and shining lamp, and you for a short time were willing to rejoice greatly in his light. 36 But I have the witness greater than that of John, for the very works that my Father assigned me to accomplish, the works themselves that I am doing, bear witness about me that the Father dispatched me. 37 Also, the Father who sent me has himself borne witness about me. You have neither heard his voice at any time nor seen his figure; 38 and you do not have his word remaining in you, because the very one whom he dispatched you do not believe.

39 "You are searching the Scriptures, because you think that by means of them you will have everlasting life; and these are the very ones that bear witness about me. 40 And yet you do not want to come to me that you may have life. 41 I do not accept glory from men, 42 but I well know that you do not have the love of God in you. 43 I have come in the name of my Father, but you do not receive me; if someone else arrived in his own name, you would receive that one. 44 How can you believe, when you are accepting glory from one another and you are not seeking the glory that is from the only God? 45 Do not think that I will accuse you to the Father; there is one that accuses you, Moses, in whom you have put your hope. 46 In fact, if you believed Moses you would believe me, for that one wrote about me. 47 But if you do not believe the writings of that one, how will you believe my sayings?"

6 After these things Jesus departed across the sea of Gal'i·lee, or Ti·be'ri·as. 2 But a great crowd kept following him, because

they were beholding the signs he was performing upon those who were ill. 3 So Jesus went up into a mountain, and there he was sitting with his disciples. 4 Now the passover, the festival of the Jews, was near. 5 When, therefore, Jesus raised his eyes and observed that a great crowd was coming to him, he said to Philip: "Where shall we buy loaves for these to eat?" 6 However, he was saying this to test him, for he himself knew what he was about to do. 7 Philip answered him: "Two hundred de·nar'i·i worth of loaves is not enough for them, so that each one may get a little." 8 One of his disciples, Andrew the brother of Simon Peter, said to him: 9 "Here is a little boy that has five barley loaves and two small fishes. But what are these among so many?"

10 Jesus said: "HAVE the men recline as at meal." Now there was a lot of grass in the place. Therefore the men reclined, about five thousand in number. 11 So Jesus took the loaves and, after giving thanks, he distributed them to those reclining, likewise also as much of the small fishes as they wanted. 12 But when they had their fill he said to his disciples: "Gather together the fragments that remain over, so that nothing is wasted." 13 Therefore they gathered them together, and they filled twelve baskets with fragments from the five barley loaves, which were left over by those who had eaten.

14 Hence when the men saw the signs he performed, they began to say: "This is for a certainty the prophet that was to come into the world." 15 Therefore Jesus, knowing they were about to come and seize him to make him king, withdrew again into the mountain all alone.

16 When evening fell, his disciples went down to the sea, 17 and, boarding a boat, they set out across the sea for Ca·per'na·um. Well, by now it had grown dark and Jesus had not yet come to them. 18 Also, the sea began to

be stirred up because a strong wind was blowing. 19 However, when they had rowed about three or four miles, they beheld Jesus walking upon the sea and getting near the boat; and they became fearful. 20 But he said to them: "It is I; have no fear!" 21 Therefore they were willing to take him into the boat, and directly the boat was at the land to which they were trying to go.

22 The next day the crowd that was standing on the other side of the sea saw that there was no boat there except a little one, and that Jesus had not entered into the boat with his disciples but that only his disciples had left; 23 but boats from Ti·be′ri·as arrived near the place where they ate the bread after the Lord had given thanks. 24 Therefore when the crowd saw that neither Jesus was there nor his disciples, they boarded their little boats and came to Ca·per′na·um to look for Jesus.

25 So when they found him across the sea they said to him: "Rabbi, when did you get here?" 26 Jesus answered them and said: "Most truly I say to you, You are looking for me, not because you saw signs, but because you ate from the loaves and were satisfied. 27 Work, not for the food that perishes, but for the food that remains for life everlasting, which the Son of man will give you; for upon this one the Father, even God, has put his seal [of approval]."

28 Therefore they said to him: "What shall we do to work the works of God?" 29 In answer Jesus said to them: "This is the work of God, that you exercise faith in him whom that One sent forth." 30 Therefore they said to him: "What, then, are you performing as a sign, in order for us to see [it] and believe you? What work are you doing? 31 Our forefathers ate the manna in the wilderness, just as it is written, 'He gave them bread from heaven to eat.'" 32 Hence Jesus said to them: "Most truly I say to you,

Moses did not give you the bread from heaven, but my Father does give you the true bread from heaven. 33 For the bread of God is the one who comes down from heaven and gives life to the world." 34 Therefore they said to him: "Lord, always give us this bread."

35 Jesus said to them: "I am the bread of life. He that comes to me will not get hungry at all, and he that exercises faith in me will never get thirsty at all. 36 But I have said to you, You have even seen me and yet do not believe. 37 Everything the Father gives me will come to me, and the one that comes to me I will by no means drive away; 38 because I have come down from heaven to do, not my will, but the will of him that sent me. 39 This is the will of him that sent me, that I should lose nothing out of all that he has given me but that I should resurrect it at the last day. 40 For this is the will of my Father, that everyone that beholds the Son and exercises faith in him should have everlasting life, and I will resurrect him at the last day."

41 Therefore the Jews began to murmur at him because he said: "I am the bread that came down from heaven"; 42 and they began saying: "Is this not Jesus the son of Joseph, whose father and mother we know? How is it that now he says, 'I have come down from heaven'?" 43 In answer Jesus said to them: "Stop murmuring among yourselves. 44 No man can come to me unless the Father, who sent me, draws him; and I will resurrect him in the last day. 45 It is written in the Prophets, 'And they will all be taught by Jehovah.' Everyone that has heard from the Father and has learned comes to me. 46 Not that any man has seen the Father, except he who is from God; this one has seen the Father. 47 Most truly I say to you, He that believes has everlasting life.

48 "I am the bread of life. 49 Your forefathers ate the manna in the wilderness and yet died.

50 This is the bread that comes down from heaven, so that anyone may eat of it and not die. 51 I am the living bread that came down from heaven; if anyone eats of this bread he will live forever; and, for a fact, the bread that I shall give is my flesh in behalf of the life of the world."

52 Therefore the Jews began contending with one another, saying: "How can this man give us his flesh to eat?" 53 Accordingly Jesus said to them: "Most truly I say to you, Unless you eat the flesh of the Son of man and drink his blood, you have no life in yourselves. 54 He that feeds on my flesh and drinks my blood has everlasting life, and I shall resurrect him at the last day; 55 for my flesh is true food, and my blood is true drink. 56 He that feeds on my flesh and drinks my blood remains in union with me, and I in union with him. 57 Just as the living Father sent me forth and I live because of the Father, he also that feeds on me, even that one will live because of me. 58 This is the bread that came down from heaven. It is not as when YOUR forefathers ate and yet died. He that feeds on this bread will live forever." 59 These things he said as he was teaching in public assembly at Ca·per′na·um.

60 Therefore many of his disciples, when they heard this, said: "This speech is shocking; who can listen to it?" 61 But Jesus, knowing in himself that his disciples were murmuring about this, said to them: "Does this stumble you? 62 What, therefore, if you should behold the Son of man ascending to where he was before? 63 It is the spirit that is life-giving; the flesh is of no use at all. The sayings that I have spoken to you are spirit and are life. 64 But there are some of you that do not believe." For from [the] beginning Jesus knew who were the ones not believing and who was the one that would betray him. 65 So he went on to say: "This is why I have said to you, No one can come to

me unless it is granted him by the Father."

66 Owing to this many of his disciples went off to the things behind and would no longer walk with him. 67 Therefore Jesus said to the twelve: "You do not want to go also, do you?" 68 Simon Peter answered him: "Lord, whom shall we go away to? You have sayings of everlasting life; 69 and we have believed and come to know that you are the Holy One of God." 70 Jesus answered them: "I chose you twelve, did I not? Yet one of you is a slanderer." 71 He was, in fact, speaking of Judas the son of Simon Is·car′i·ot; for this one was going to betray him, although one of the twelve.

7 Now after these things Jesus continued walking about in Gal′i·lee, for he did not want to walk about in Ju·de′a, because the Jews were seeking to kill him. 2 However, the festival of the Jews, the festival of tabernacles, was near. 3 Therefore his brothers said to him: "Pass on over from here and go into Ju·de′a, in order that your disciples also may behold the works you do. 4 For nobody does anything in secret while himself seeking to be known publicly. If you do these things, manifest yourself to the world." 5 His brothers were, in fact, not exercising faith in him. 6 Therefore Jesus said to them: "My due time is not yet present, but YOUR due time is always at hand. 7 The world has no reason to hate you, but it hates me, because I bear witness concerning it that its works are wicked. 8 You go up to the festival; I am not yet going up to this festival, because my due time has not yet fully come." 9 So after he told them these things, he remained in Gal′i·lee.

10 But when his brothers had gone up to the festival, then he also went up himself, not openly but as in secret. 11 Therefore the Jews began looking for him at the festival and saying: "Where is that [man]?" 12 And there was a lot of subdued talk about him among

the crowds. Some would say: "He is a good man." Others would say: "He is not, but he misleads the crowd." 13 No one, of course, would speak about him publicly because of the fear of the Jews.

14 When by now the festival was half over, Jesus went up into the temple and began teaching. 15 Therefore the Jews fell to wondering, saying: "How does this man have a knowledge of letters, when he has not studied at the schools?" 16 Jesus, in turn, answered them and said: "What I teach is not mine, but belongs to him that sent me. 17 If anyone desires to do His will, he will know concerning the teaching whether it is from God or I speak of my own originality. 18 He that speaks of his own originality is seeking his own glory; but he that seeks the glory of him that sent him, this one is true, and there is no unrighteousness in him. 19 Moses gave you the Law, did he not? But not one of you obeys the Law. Why are you seeking to kill me?" 20 The crowd answered: "You have a demon. Who is seeking to kill you?" 21 In answer Jesus said to them: "One deed I performed, and you are all wondering. 22 For this reason Moses has given you the circumcision—not that it is from Moses, but that it is from the forefathers—and you circumcise a man on a sabbath. 23 If a man receives circumcision on a sabbath in order that the law of Moses may not be broken, are you violently angry at me because I made a man completely sound in health on a sabbath? 24 Stop judging from the outward appearance, but judge with righteous judgment."

25 Therefore some of the inhabitants of Jerusalem began to say: "This is the man they are seeking to kill, is it not? 26 And yet, see! he is speaking in public, and they say nothing to him. The rulers have not come to know for a certainty that this is the Christ, have they? 27 On the contrary, we know where this man is from; yet when the Christ comes, no one

is to know where he is from." 28 Therefore Jesus cried out as he was teaching in the temple and said: "You both know me and know where I am from. Also, I have not come of my own initiative, but he that sent me is real, and you do not know him. 29 I know him, because I am a representative from him, and that One sent me forth." 30 Hence they began seeking to get hold of him, but no one laid a hand upon him, because his hour had not yet come. 31 Still, many of the crowd put faith in him; and they commenced saying: "When the Christ arrives, he will not perform more signs than this man has performed, will he?"

32 The Pharisees heard the crowd murmuring these things about him, and the chief priests and the Pharisees dispatched officers to get hold of him. 33 Therefore Jesus said: "I continue a little while longer with you before I go to him that sent me. 34 You will look for me, but you will not find me, and where I am you cannot come." 35 Therefore the Jews said among themselves: "Where does this [man] intend going, so that we shall not find him? He does not intend to go to the [Jews] dispersed among the Greeks and teach the Greeks, does he? 36 What does this saying mean that he said, 'You will look for me, but you will not find me, and where I am you cannot come'?"

37 Now on the last day, the great day of the festival, Jesus was standing up and he cried out, saying: "If anyone is thirsty, let him come to me and drink. 38 He that puts faith in me, just as the Scripture has said, 'Out from his inmost part streams of living water will flow.'" 39 However, he said this concerning the spirit which those who put faith in him were about to receive; for as yet there was no spirit, because Jesus had not yet been glorified. 40 Therefore some of the crowd that heard these words began saying: "This is for a certainty The Prophet." 41 Others were saying: "This is the Christ."

But some were saying: "The Christ is not actually coming out of Gal'i·lee, is he? 42 Has not the Scripture said that the Christ is coming from the offspring of David, and from Beth'le·hem the village where David used to be?" 43 Therefore a division over him developed among the crowd. 44 Some of them, though, were wanting to get hold of him, but no one did lay [his] hands upon him.

45 Therefore the officers went back to the chief priests and Pharisees, and the latter said to them: "Why is it you did not bring him in?" 46 The officers replied: "Never has [another] man spoken like this." 47 In turn the Pharisees answered: "You have not been misled also, have you? 48 Not one of the rulers or of the Pharisees has put faith in him, has he? 49 But this crowd that does not know the Law are accursed people. 50 Nic·o·de'mus, who had come to him previously, and who was one of them, said to them: 51 "Our law does not judge a man unless first it has heard from him and come to know what he is doing, does it?" 52 In answer they said to him: "You are not also out of Gal'i·lee, are you? Search and see that no prophet is to be raised up out of Gal'i·lee."[a]

8 12 Therefore Jesus spoke again to them, saying: "I am the light of the world. He that follows me will by no means walk in darkness, but will possess the light of life." 13 Hence the Pharisees said to him: "You bear witness about yourself; your witness is not true." 14 In answer Jesus said to them: "Even if I do bear witness about myself, my witness is true, because I know where I came from and where I am going. But you do not know where I came from and where I am going. 15 You judge according to the flesh; I do not judge any man at all. 16 And yet if I do judge, my judgment is truthful, because I am not alone, but the Father who sent me is with me. 17 Also, in your own Law it is written, 'The witness of two men is true.' 18 I am one that bears witness about myself, and the Father who sent me bears witness about me." 19 Therefore they went on to say to him: "Where is your Father?" Jesus answered: "You know neither me nor my Father. If you did know me, you would know my Father also." 20 These sayings he spoke in the treasury as he was teaching in the temple. But no one laid hold of him, because his hour had not yet come.

21 Hence he said to them again: "I am going away, and you will look for me, and yet you will die in your sin. Where I am going you cannot come." 22 Therefore the

---

[a] Manuscripts אBSy^s omit verses 53 to chapter 8, verse 11, which read (with some variations in the various Greek texts and versions) as follows:

53 So they went each one to his home. **8** But Jesus went to the Mount of Olives. 2 At daybreak, however, he again presented himself at the temple, and all the people began coming to him, and he sat down and began to teach them. 3 Now the scribes and the Pharisees brought a woman caught at adultery, and, after standing her in their midst, 4 they said to him: "Teacher, this woman has been caught in the act of committing adultery. 5 In the Law Moses prescribed for us to stone such sort of women. What, really, do you say?" 6 Of course, they were saying this to put him to the test, in order to have something with which to accuse him. But Jesus bent down and began to write with his finger in the ground. 7 When they persisted in asking him, he straightened up and said to them: "Let the one of you that is sinless be the first to throw a stone at her." 8 And bending over again he kept on writing in the ground. 9 But those who heard this began going out, one by one, starting with the older men, and he was left alone, and the woman that was in their midst. 10 Straightening up, Jesus said to her: "Woman, where are they? Did no one condemn you?" 11 She said: "No one, sir." Jesus said: "Neither do I condemn you. Go your way; from now on practice sin no more."

Jews began to say: "He will not kill himself, will he? Because he says, 'Where I am going YOU cannot come.'" 23 So he went on to say to them: "YOU are from the realms below; I am from the realms above. YOU are from this world; I am not from this world. 24 Therefore I said to YOU, YOU will die in YOUR sins. For if YOU do not believe that I am he, YOU will die in YOUR sins." 25 Therefore they began to say to him: "Who are you?" Jesus said to them: "Why am I even speaking to YOU at all? 26 I have many things to speak concerning YOU and to pass judgment upon. As a matter of fact, he that sent me is true, and the very things I heard from him I am speaking in the world." 27 They did not grasp that he was talking to them about the Father. 28 Therefore Jesus said: "When once YOU have lifted up the Son of man, then YOU will know that I am he, and that I do nothing of my own initiative; but just as the Father taught me I speak these things. 29 And he that sent me is with me; he did not abandon me to myself, because I always do the things pleasing to him." 30 As he was speaking these things, many put faith in him.

31 And so Jesus went on to say to the Jews that had believed him: "If YOU remain in my word, YOU are really my disciples, 32 and YOU will know the truth, and the truth will set YOU free." 33 They replied to him: "We are Abraham's offspring and never have we been slaves to anybody. How is it you say, 'YOU will become free'?" 34 Jesus answered them: "Most truly I say to YOU, Every doer of sin is a slave of sin. 35 Moreover, the slave does not remain in the household forever; the son remains forever. 36 Therefore if the Son sets YOU free, YOU will be actually free. 37 I know that YOU are Abraham's offspring; but YOU are seeking to kill me, because my word makes no progress among YOU. 38 What things I have seen with my Father I speak; and YOU, there-

fore, do the things YOU have heard from [YOUR] father." 39 In answer they said to him: "Our father is Abraham." Jesus said to them: "If YOU are Abraham's children, do the works of Abraham. 40 But now YOU are seeking to kill me, a man that has told YOU the truth that I heard from God. Abraham did not do this. 41 YOU do the works of YOUR father." They said to him: "We were not born from fornication; we have one Father, God."

42 Jesus said to them: "If God were YOUR Father, YOU would love me, for from God I came forth and am here. Neither have I come of my own initiative at all, but that One sent me forth. 43 Why is it YOU do not know what I am speaking? Because YOU cannot listen to my word. 44 YOU are from YOUR father the Devil, and YOU wish to do the desires of YOUR father. That one was a manslayer when he began, and he did not stand fast in the truth, because truth is not in him. When he speaks the lie, he speaks according to his own disposition, because he is a liar and the father of [the lie]. 45 Because I, on the other hand, tell the truth, YOU do not believe me. 46 Who of YOU convicts me of sin? If I speak truth, why is it YOU do not believe me? 47 He that is from God listens to the sayings of God. This is why YOU do not listen, because YOU are not from God."

48 In answer the Jews said to him: "Do we not rightly say, You are a Sa·mar'i·tan and have a demon?" 49 Jesus answered: "I do not have a demon, but I honor my Father, and YOU dishonor me. 50 But I am not seeking glory for myself; there is One that is seeking and judging. 51 Most truly I say to YOU, If anyone observes my word, he will never see death at all." 52 The Jews said to him: "Now we do know you have a demon. Abraham died, also the prophets; but you say, 'If anyone observes my word, he will never taste death at all.' 53 You are not greater than our father Abraham, who died,

are you? Also, the prophets died. Who do you claim to be?" 54 Jesus answered: "If I glorify myself, my glory is nothing. It is my Father that glorifies me, he who YOU say is YOUR God; 55 and yet YOU have not known him. But I know him. And if I said I do not know him I should be like YOU, a liar. But I do know him and am observing his word. 56 Abraham YOUR father rejoiced greatly in the prospect of seeing my day, and he saw it and rejoiced." 57 Therefore the Jews said to him: "You are not yet fifty years old, and still you have seen Abraham?" 58 Jesus said to them: "Most truly I say to YOU, Before Abraham came into existence, I have been." 59 Therefore they picked up stones to hurl [them] at him; but Jesus hid and went out of the temple.

9 Now as he was passing along he saw a man blind from birth. 2 And his disciples asked him: "Rabbi, who sinned, this man or his parents, so that he was born blind?" 3 Jesus answered: "Neither this man sinned nor his parents, but it was in order that the works of God might be made manifest in his case. 4 We must work the works of him that sent me while it is day; the night is coming when no man can work. 5 As long as I am in the world, I am the world's light." 6 After he said these things, he spit on the ground and made a clay with the saliva, and put his clay upon the [man's] eyes 7 and said to him: "Go wash in the pool of Si·lo'am" (which is translated 'Sent forth'). And so he went off and washed, and came back seeing.

8 Therefore the neighbors and those who formerly used to see he was a beggar began to say: "This is the man that used to sit and beg, is it not?" 9 Some would say: "This is he." Others would say: "Not at all, but he is like him." The man would say: "I am he." 10 Consequently they began to say to him: "How, then, were your eyes opened?" 11 He answered: "The man called Jesus made a clay

and smeared [it] on my eyes and said to me, 'Go to Si·lo'am and wash.' I therefore went and washed and gained sight." 12 At this they said to him: "Where is that [man]?" He said: "I do not know."

13 They led the once-blind man himself to the Pharisees. 14 Incidentally it was Sabbath on the day that Jesus made the clay and opened his eyes. 15 This time, therefore, the Pharisees also took up asking him how he gained sight. He said to them: "He put a clay upon my eyes, and I washed and have sight." 16 Therefore some of the Pharisees began to say: "This is not a man from God, because he does not observe the Sabbath." Others began to say: "How can a man that is a sinner perform signs of that sort?" So there was a division among them. 17 Hence they said to the blind man again: "What do you say about him, seeing that he opened your eyes?" The [man] said: "He is a prophet."

18 However, the Jews did not believe concerning him that he had been blind and had gained sight, until they called the parents of the man that gained sight. 19 And they asked them: "Is this YOUR son who YOU say was born blind? How, then, is it he sees at present?" 20 Then in answer his parents said: "We know that this is our son and that he was born blind. 21 But how it is he now sees we do not know, or who opened his eyes we do not know. ASK him. He is of age. He must speak for himself." 22 His parents said these things because they were in fear of the Jews, for the Jews had already come to an agreement that, if anyone confessed him as Christ, he should get expelled from the synagogue. 23 This is why his parents said: "He is of age. QUESTION him."

24 Therefore a second time they called the man that had been blind and said to him: "Give glory to God; we know that this man is a sinner." 25 In turn he answered: "Whether he is a sinner I do not know. One thing I do know, that,

whereas I was blind, I see at present." 26 Therefore they said to him: "What did he do to you? How did he open your eyes?" 27 He answered them: "I told you already, and yet you did not listen. Why do you want to hear it again? You do not want to become his disciples also, do you?" 28 At this they reviled him and said: "You are a disciple of that [man], but we are disciples of Moses. 29 We know that God has spoken to Moses; but as for this [man], we do not know where he is from." 30 In answer the man said to them: "This certainly is a marvel, that you do not know where he is from, and yet he opened my eyes. 31 We know that God does not listen to sinners, but if anyone is God-fearing and does his will, he listens to this one. 32 From of old it has never been heard that anyone opened the eyes of one born blind. 33 If this [man] were not from God, he could do nothing at all." 34 In answer they said to him: "You were altogether born in sins, and yet are you teaching us?" And they threw him out!

35 Jesus heard that they had thrown him out, and, on finding him, he said: "Are you putting faith in the Son of man?" 36 The [man] answered: "And who is he, sir, that I may put faith in him?" 37 Jesus said to him: "You have seen him and, besides, he that is speaking with you is that one." 38 Then he said: "I do put faith in him, Lord." And he did obeisance to him. 39 And Jesus said: "For [this] judgment I came into this world: that those not seeing might see and those seeing might become blind." 40 Those of the Pharisees who were with him heard these things, and they said to him: "We are not blind also, are we?" 41 Jesus said to them: "If you were blind, you would have no sin. But now you say, 'We see.' Your sin remains."

10 "Most truly I say to you, He that does not enter into the sheepfold through the door but climbs up some other place, that one is a thief and a plunderer. 2 But he that enters through the door is shepherd of the sheep. 3 The doorkeeper opens to this one, and the sheep listen to his voice, and he calls his own sheep by name and leads them out. 4 When he has got all his own out, he goes before them, and the sheep follow him, because they know his voice. 5 A stranger they will by no means follow but will flee from him, because they do not know the voice of strangers." 6 Jesus spoke this comparison to them; but they did not know what the things meant that he was speaking to them.

7 Therefore Jesus said again: "Most truly I say to you, I am the door of the sheep. 8 All those that have come in place of me are thieves and plunderers; but the sheep have not listened to them. 9 I am the door; whoever enters through me will be saved, and he will go in and out and find pasturage. 10 The thief does not come unless it is to steal and slay and destroy. I have come that they might have life and have it in abundance. 11 I am the fine shepherd; the fine shepherd surrenders his soul in behalf of the sheep. 12 The hired man, who is no shepherd and to whom the sheep do not belong as his own, beholds the wolf coming and abandons the sheep and flees—and the wolf snatches them and scatters them— 13 because he is a hired man and does not care for the sheep. 14 I am the fine shepherd, and I know my sheep and my sheep know me, 15 just as the Father knows me and I know the Father; and I surrender my soul in behalf of the sheep.

16 "And I have other sheep, which are not of this fold; those also I must bring, and they will listen to my voice, and they will become one flock, one shepherd. 17 This is why the Father loves me, because I surrender my soul, in order that I may receive it again. 18 No man has taken it away from me, but I surrender it of my own initiative. I have authority to

surrender it, and I have authority to receive it again. The commandment on this I received from my Father."

19 Again a division resulted among the Jews because of these words. 20 Many of them were saying: "He has a demon and is mad. Why do you listen to him?" 21 Others would say: "These are not the sayings of a demonized man. A demon cannot open blind people's eyes, can it?"

22 At that time the festival of dedication took place in Jerusalem. It was wintertime, 23 and Jesus was walking in the temple in the colonnade of Sol'o·mon. 24 Therefore the Jews encircled him and began to say to him: "How long are you to keep our souls in suspense? If you are the Christ, tell us outspokenly." 25 Jesus answered them: "I told you, and yet you do not believe. The works that I am doing in the name of my Father, these bear witness about me. 26 But you do not believe, because you are none of my sheep. 27 My sheep listen to my voice, and I know them, and they follow me. 28 And I give them everlasting life, and they will by no means ever be destroyed, and no one will snatch them out of my hand. 29 What my Father has given me is something greater than all other things, and no one can snatch them out of the hand of the Father. 30 I and the Father are one."

31 Once more the Jews lifted up stones to stone him. 32 Jesus replied to them: "I displayed to you many fine works from the Father. For which of those works are you stoning me?" 33 The Jews answered him: "We are stoning you, not for a fine work, but for blasphemy, even because you, although being a man, make yourself a god." 34 Jesus answered them: "Is it not written in your Law, 'I said: "You are gods" '? 35 If he called 'gods' those against whom the word of God came, and yet the Scripture cannot be nullified, 36 do you say to me whom the Father sanctified and dispatched into the world, 'You

blaspheme,' because I said, I am God's Son? 37 If I am not doing the works of my Father, do not believe me. 38 But if I am doing them, even though you do not believe me, believe the works, in order that you may come to know and may continue knowing that the Father is in union with me and I am in union with the Father." 39 Therefore they tried again to seize him; but he got out of their reach.

40 So he went off again across the Jordan to the place where John was baptizing at first, and he stayed there. 41 And many people came to him, and they began saying: "John, indeed, did not perform a single sign, but as many things as John said about this man were all true." 42 And many put faith in him there.

11 Now there was a certain man sick, Laz'a·rus of Beth'a·ny, of the village of Mary and of Martha her sister. 2 It was, in fact, the Mary that greased the Lord with perfumed oil and wiped his feet dry with her hair, whose brother Laz'a·rus was sick. 3 Therefore his sisters dispatched word to him, saying: "Lord, see! the one for whom you have affection is sick." 4 But when Jesus heard it he said: "This sickness is not with death as its object, but is for the glory of God, in order that the Son of God may be glorified through it."

5 Now Jesus loved Martha and her sister and Laz'a·rus. 6 However, when he heard that he was sick, then he actually remained two days in the place where he was. 7 Then after this he said to the disciples: "Let us go into Ju·de'a again." 8 The disciples said to him: "Rabbi, just lately the Ju·de'ans were seeking to stone you, and are you going there again?" 9 Jesus answered: "There are twelve hours of daylight, are there not? If anyone walks in daylight he does not bump against anything, because he sees the light of this world. 10 But if anyone walks in the night, he bumps

against something, because the light is not in him."

11 He said these things, and after this he said to them: "Laz'a-rus our friend has gone to rest, but I am journeying there to awaken him from sleep." 12 Therefore the disciples said to him: "Lord, if he has gone to rest, he will get well." 13 Jesus had spoken, however, about his death. But they imagined he was speaking about taking rest in sleep. 14 At that time, therefore, Jesus said to them outspokenly: "Laz'a·rus has died, 15 and I rejoice on YOUR account that I was not there, in order for YOU to believe. But let us go to him." 16 Therefore Thomas, who was called The Twin, said to his fellow disciples: "Let us also go, that we may die with him."

17 Consequently when Jesus arrived, he found he had already been four days in the memorial tomb. 18 Now Beth'a·ny was near Jerusalem at a distance of about two miles. 19 Accordingly many of the Jews had come to Martha and Mary in order to console them concerning their brother. 20 Therefore Martha, when she heard that Jesus was coming, met him; but Mary kept sitting at home. 21 Martha therefore said to Jesus: "Lord, if you had been here my brother would not have died. 22 And yet at present I know that as many things as you ask God for, God will give you." 23 Jesus said to her: "Your brother will rise." 24 Martha said to him: "I know he will rise in the resurrection on the last day." 25 Jesus said to her: "I am the resurrection and the life. He that exercises faith in me, even though he dies, will come to life; 26 and everyone that is living and exercises faith in me will never die at all. Do you believe this?" 27 She said to him: "Yes, Lord; I have believed that you are the Christ the Son of God, the One coming into the world." 28 And when she had said this, she went off and called Mary her sister, saying secretly: "The Teacher is present and is calling you." 29 The

latter, when she heard this, got up quickly and was on her way to him.

30 Jesus had not yet, in fact, come into the village, but he was still in the place where Martha met him. 31 Therefore the Jews that were with her in the house and that were consoling her, on seeing Mary rise quickly and go out, followed her, supposing that she was going to the memorial tomb to weep there. 32 And so Mary, when she arrived where Jesus was and caught sight of him, fell at his feet, saying to him: "Lord, if you had been here, my brother would not have died." 33 Jesus, therefore, when he saw her weeping and the Jews that came with her weeping, groaned in the spirit and became troubled; 34 and he said: "Where have YOU laid him?" They said to him: "Lord, come and see." 35 Jesus gave way to tears. 36 Therefore the Jews began to say: "See, what affection he used to have for him!" 37 But some of them said: "Was not this [man] that opened the eyes of the blind man able to prevent this one from dying?"

38 Hence Jesus, after groaning again within himself, came to the memorial tomb. It was, in fact, a cave, and a stone was lying against it. 39 Jesus said: "TAKE the stone away." Martha, the sister of the deceased, said to him: "Lord, by now he must smell, for it is four days." 40 Jesus said to her: "Did I not tell you that if you would believe you would see the glory of God?" 41 Therefore they took the stone away. Now Jesus raised his eyes heavenward and said: "Father, I thank you that you have heard me. 42 True, I knew that you always hear me; but on account of the crowd standing around I spoke, in order that they might believe that you sent me forth." 43 And when he had said these things, he cried out with a loud voice: "Laz'a·rus, come on out!" 44 The [man] that had been dead came out with his feet and hands bound with wrappings, and his countenance was bound

about with a cloth. Jesus said to them: "Loose him and let him go."

45 Therefore many of the Jews that had come to Mary and that beheld what he did put faith in him; 46 but some of them went off to the Pharisees and told them the things Jesus did. 47 Consequently the chief priests and the Pharisees gathered the San'he·drin together and began to say: "What are we to do, because this man performs many signs? 48 If we let him alone this way, they will all put faith in him, and the Romans will come and take away both our place and our nation." 49 But a certain one of them, Ca'ia·phas, who was high priest that year, said to them: "You do not know anything at all, 50 and you do not reason out that it is to your benefit for one man to die in behalf of the people and not for the whole nation to be destroyed." 51 This, though, he did not say of his own originality; but because he was high priest that year, he prophesied that Jesus was destined to die for the nation, 52 and not for the nation only, but in order that the children of God who are scattered about he might also gather together in one. 53 Therefore from that day on they took counsel to kill him.

54 Hence Jesus no longer walked about publicly among the Jews, but he departed from there to the country near the wilderness, into a city called E'phra·im, and there he remained with the disciples. 55 Now the passover of the Jews was near, and many people went up out of the country to Jerusalem before the passover in order to cleanse themselves ceremonially. 56 Therefore they went looking for Jesus and they would say to one another as they stood around in the temple: "What is your opinion? That he will not come to the festival at all?" 57 As it was, the chief priests and the Pharisees had given orders that if anyone got to know where he was, he should disclose [it], in order that they might seize him.

12 Accordingly Jesus, six days before the passover, arrived at Beth'a·ny, where Laz'a·rus was whom Jesus had raised up from the dead. 2 Therefore they spread an evening meal for him there, and Martha was ministering, but Laz'a·rus was one of those reclining at the table with him. 3 Mary, therefore, took a pound of perfumed oil, genuine nard, very costly, and she greased the feet of Jesus and wiped his feet dry with her hair. The house became filled with the scent of the perfumed oil. 4 But Judas Is·car'i·ot, one of his disciples, who was about to betray him, said: 5 "Why was it this perfumed oil was not sold for three hundred de·nar'i·i and given to the poor people?" 6 He said this, though, not because he was concerned about the poor, but because he was a thief and had the money box and used to carry off the monies put in it. 7 Therefore Jesus said: "Let her alone, that she may keep this observance in view of the day of my burial. 8 For you have the poor always with you, but me you will not have always."

9 Therefore a great crowd of the Jews got to know he was there, and they came, not on account of Jesus only, but also to see Laz'a·rus, whom he raised up from the dead. 10 The chief priests now took counsel to kill Laz'a·rus also, 11 because on account of him many of the Jews were going there and putting faith in Jesus.

12 The next day the great crowd that had come to the festival, on hearing that Jesus was coming to Jerusalem, 13 took the branches of palm trees and went out to meet him. And they began to shout: "Save, we pray you! Blessed is he that comes in Jehovah's name, even the king of Israel!" 14 But when Jesus had found a young ass, he sat on it, just as it is written: 15 "Have no fear, daughter of Zion. Look! Your king is coming, seated upon an ass's colt." 16 These things his disciples took no note of at first, but when Jesus became glorified, then they called

to mind that these things were written respecting him and that they did these things to him.

17 Accordingly the crowd that was with him when he called Laz'a·rus out of the memorial tomb and raised him up from the dead kept bearing witness. 18 On this account the crowd, because they heard he had performed this sign, also met him. 19 Therefore the Pharisees said among themselves: "YOU observe YOU are getting absolutely nowhere. See! The world has gone after him."

20 Now there were some Greeks among those that came up to worship at the festival. 21 These, therefore, approached Philip who was from Beth·sa'i·da of Gal'i·lee, and they began to request him, saying: "Sir, we want to see Jesus." 22 Philip came and told Andrew. Andrew and Philip came and told Jesus.

23 But Jesus answered them, saying: "The hour has come for the Son of man to be glorified. 24 Most truly I say to YOU, Unless a grain of wheat falls into the ground and dies, it remains just one [grain]; but if it dies, it then bears much fruit. 25 He that is fond of his soul destroys it, but he that hates his soul in this world will safeguard it for everlasting life. 26 If anyone would minister to me, let him follow me, and where I am there my minister will be also. If anyone would minister to me, the Father will honor him. 27 Now my soul is troubled, and what shall I say? Father, save me out of this hour. Nevertheless, this is why I have come to this hour. 28 Father, glorify your name." Therefore a voice came out of heaven: "I both glorified [it] and will glorify [it] again."

29 Hence the crowd that stood about and heard it began to say that it had thundered. Others began to say: "An angel has spoken to him." 30 In answer Jesus said: "This voice has occurred, not for my sake, but for YOUR sakes. 31 Now there is a judging of this world; now the ruler of this world

will be cast out. 32 And yet I, if I am lifted up from the earth, will draw men of all sorts to me." 33 This he was really saying to signify what sort of death he was about to die. 34 Therefore the crowd answered him: "We heard from the Law that the Christ remains forever; and how is it you say that the Son of man must be lifted up? Who is this Son of man?" 35 Jesus therefore said to them: "The light will be among YOU a little while longer. Walk while YOU have the light, so that darkness does not overpower YOU; and he that walks in the darkness does not know where he is going. 36 While YOU have the light, exercise faith in the light, in order to become sons of light."

Jesus spoke these things and went off and hid from them. 37 But although he had performed so many signs before them, they were not putting faith in him, 38 so that the word of Isaiah the prophet was fulfilled which he said: "Jehovah, who has put faith in the thing heard by us? And as for the arm of Jehovah, to whom has it been revealed?" 39 The reason why they were not able to believe is that again Isaiah said: 40 "He has blinded their eyes and he has made their hearts hard, that they should not see with their eyes and get the thought with their hearts and turn around and I should heal them." 41 Isaiah said these things because he saw his glory, and he spoke about him. 42 All the same, many even of the rulers actually put faith in him, but because of the Pharisees they would not confess [him], in order not to be expelled from the synagogue; 43 for they loved the glory of men more than even the glory of God.

44 However, Jesus cried out and said: "He that puts faith in me puts faith, not in me [only], but in him [also] that sent me; 45 and he that beholds me beholds [also] him that sent me. 46 I have come as a light into the world, in order that everyone putting faith in me

may not remain in the darkness. 47 But if anyone hears my sayings and does not keep them, I do not judge him; for I came, not to judge the world, but to save the world. 48 He that disregards me and does not receive my sayings has one to judge him. The word that I have spoken is what will judge him in the last day; 49 because I have not spoken out of my own impulse, but the Father himself who sent me has given me a commandment as to what to tell and what to speak. 50 Also, I know that his commandment means everlasting life. Therefore the things I speak, just as the Father has told me [them], so I speak [them]."

13 Now, because he knew before the festival of the passover that his hour had come for him to move out of this world to the Father, Jesus, having loved his own that were in the world, loved them to the end. 2 So, while the evening meal was going on, the Devil having already put it into the heart of Judas Is·car'i·ot, the son of Simon, to betray him, 3 he, knowing that the Father had given all things into [his] hands and that he came forth from God and was going to God, 4 got up from the evening meal and laid aside his outer garments. And, taking a towel, he girded himself. 5 After that he put water into a basin and started to wash the feet of the disciples and to dry them off with the towel with which he was girded. 6 And so he came to Simon Peter. He said to him: "Lord, are you washing my feet?" 7 In answer Jesus said to him: "What I am doing you do not understand at present, but you will understand after these things." 8 Peter said to him: "You will certainly never wash my feet." Jesus answered him: "Unless I wash you, you have no part with me." 9 Simon Peter said to him: "Lord, not my feet only, but also my hands and my head." 10 Jesus said to him: "He that has bathed does not need to have more than his feet washed, but is wholly clean. And

you men are clean, but not all." 11 He knew, indeed, the man betraying him. This is why he said: "Not all of you are clean."

12 When, now, he had washed their feet and had put his outer garments on and laid himself down at the table again, he said to them: "Do you know what I have done to you? 13 You address me, 'Teacher,' and, 'Lord,' and you speak rightly, for I am such. 14 Therefore, if I, although Lord and Teacher, washed your feet, you also ought to wash the feet of one another. 15 For I set the pattern for you, that, just as I did to you, you should do also. 16 Most truly I say to you, A slave is not greater than his master, nor is one that is sent forth greater than the one that sent him. 17 If you know these things, happy you are if you do them. 18 I am not talking about all of you; I know the ones I have chosen. But it is in order that the Scripture might be fulfilled, 'He that used to feed on my bread has lifted up his heel against me.' 19 From this moment on I am telling you before it occurs, in order that when it does occur you may believe that I am he. 20 Most truly I say to you, He that receives anyone I send receives me [also]. In turn he that receives me, receives [also] him that sent me."

21 After saying these things, Jesus became troubled in spirit, and he bore witness and said: "Most truly I say to you, One of you will betray me." 22 The disciples began to look at one another, being at a loss as to which one he was saying [it] about. 23 There was reclining in front of Jesus' bosom one of his disciples, and Jesus loved him. 24 Therefore Simon Peter nodded to this one and said to him: "Tell who it is about whom he is saying [it]." 25 So the latter leaned back upon the breast of Jesus and said to him: "Lord, who is it?" 26 Therefore Jesus answered: "It is that one to whom I shall give the morsel that I dip." And so, having dipped the morsel, he took and gave it to Judas, the

son of Simon Is·car′i·ot. 27 And after the morsel then Satan entered into the latter. Jesus, therefore, said to him: "What you are doing get done more quickly." 28 However, none of those reclining at the table knew for what purpose he said this to him. 29 Some, in fact, were imagining, since Judas was holding the money box, that Jesus was telling him: "Buy what things we need for the festival," or that he should give something to the poor. 30 Therefore, after he received the morsel, he went out immediately. And it was night.

31 Hence when he had gone out, Jesus said: "Now the Son of man is glorified, and God is glorified in connection with him. 32 And God will himself glorify him, and he will glorify him immediately. 33 Little children, I am with you a little longer. You will look for me; and just as I said to the Jews, 'Where I go you cannot come,' I say also to you at present. 34 I am giving you a new commandment, that you love one another; just as I have loved you, that you also love one another. 35 By this all will know that you are my disciples, if you have love among yourselves."

36 Simon Peter said to him: "Lord, where are you going?" Jesus answered: "Where I am going you cannot follow me now, but you will follow afterwards." 37 Peter said to him: "Lord, why is it I cannot follow you at present? I will surrender my soul in your behalf." 38 Jesus answered: "Will you surrender your soul in my behalf? Most truly I say to you, A cock will by no means crow until you have disowned me three times."

14 "Do not let your hearts be troubled. Exercise faith in God, exercise faith also in me. 2 In the house of my Father there are many abodes. Otherwise, I would have told you, because I am going my way to prepare a place for you. 3 Also, if I go my way and prepare a place for you, I am coming again and will receive you home to myself, that where I

am you also may be. 4 And where I am going you know the way."

5 Thomas said to him: "Lord, we do not know where you are going. How do we know the way?" 6 Jesus said to him: "I am the way and the truth and the life. No one comes to the Father except through me. 7 If you men had known me, you would have known my Father also; from this moment on you know him and have seen him."

8 Philip said to him: "Lord, show us the Father, and it is enough for us."

9 Jesus said to him: "Have I been with you men so long a time, and yet, Philip, you have not come to know me? He that has seen me has seen the Father [also]. How is it you say, 'Show us the Father'? 10 Do you not believe that I am in union with the Father and the Father is in union with me? The things I say to you men I do not speak of my own originality; but the Father who remains in union with me is doing his works. 11 Believe me that I am in union with the Father and the Father is in union with me; otherwise, believe on account of the works themselves. 12 Most truly I say to you, He that exercises faith in me, that one also will do the works that I do; and he will do works greater than these, because I am going my way to the Father. 13 Also, whatever it is that you ask in my name, I will do this, in order that the Father may be glorified in connection with the Son. 14 If you ask anything in my name, I will do it.

15 "If you love me, you will observe my commandments; 16 and I will request the Father and he will give you another helper to be with you forever, 17 the spirit of the truth, which the world cannot receive, because it neither beholds it nor knows it. You know it, because it remains with you and is in you. 18 I shall not leave you bereaved. I am coming to you. 19 A little longer and the world will behold me no more, but you will behold me, because I live and

YOU will live. 20 In that day YOU will know that I am in union with my Father and YOU are in union with me and I am in union with YOU. 21 He that has my commandments and observes them, that one is he who loves me. In turn he that loves me will be loved by my Father, and I will love him and will plainly show myself to him."

22 Judas, not Is·car'i·ot, said to him: "Lord, what has happened that you intend to show yourself plainly to us and not to the world?"

23 In answer Jesus said to him: "If anyone loves me, he will observe my word, and my Father will love him, and we shall come to him and make our abode with him. 24 He that does not love me does not observe my words; and the word that YOU are hearing is not mine, but belongs to the Father who sent me.

25 "While remaining with YOU I have spoken these things to YOU. 26 But the helper, the holy spirit, which the Father will send in my name, that one will teach YOU all things and bring back to YOUR minds all the things I told YOU. 27 I leave YOU peace, I give YOU my peace. I do not give it to YOU the way that the world gives it. Do not let YOUR hearts be troubled nor let them shrink for fear. 28 You heard that I said to YOU, I am going away and I am coming [back] to YOU. If YOU loved me, YOU would rejoice that I am going my way to the Father, because the Father is greater than I am. 29 So now I have told YOU before it occurs, in order that, when it does occur, YOU may believe. 30 I shall not speak much with YOU any more, for the ruler of the world is coming. And he has no hold on me, 31 but, in order for the world to know that I love the Father, even as the Father has given me commandment [to do], so I am doing. Get up, let us go from here.

15 "I am the true vine, and my Father is the cultivator. 2 Every branch in me not bearing fruit he takes away, and every one bearing fruit he cleans, that it may bear more fruit. 3 YOU are already clean because of the word that I have spoken to YOU. 4 Remain in union with me, and I in union with YOU. Just as the branch cannot bear fruit of itself unless it remains in the vine, in the same way neither can YOU, unless YOU remain in union with me. 5 I am the vine, YOU are the branches. He that remains in union with me, and I in union with him, this one bears much fruit; because apart from me YOU can do nothing at all. 6 If anyone does not remain in union with me, he is cast out as a branch and is dried up; and men gather those branches up and pitch them into the fire and they are burned. 7 If YOU remain in union with me and my sayings remain in YOU, ask whatever YOU wish and it will take place for YOU. 8 My Father is glorified in this, that YOU keep bearing much fruit and prove yourselves my disciples. 9 Just as the Father has loved me and I have loved YOU, remain in my love. 10 If YOU observe my commandments, YOU will remain in my love, just as I have observed the commandments of the Father and remain in his love.

11 "These things I have spoken to YOU, that my joy may be in YOU and YOUR joy may be made full. 12 This is my commandment, that YOU love one another just as I have loved YOU. 13 No one has love greater than this, that someone should surrender his soul in behalf of his friends. 14 YOU are my friends if YOU do what I am commanding YOU. 15 I no longer call YOU slaves, because a slave does not know what his master does. But I have called YOU friends, because all the things I have heard from my Father I have made known to YOU. 16 YOU did not choose me, but I chose YOU, and I appointed YOU to go on and keep bearing fruit and that YOUR fruit should remain; in order that no matter what YOU ask the Father in my name he might give it to YOU.

17 "These things I command YOU, that YOU love one another. 18 If the world hates YOU, YOU know that it has hated me before it hated YOU. 19 If YOU were part of the world, the world would be fond of what is its own. Now because YOU are no part of the world, but I have chosen YOU out of the world, on this account the world hates YOU. 20 Bear in mind the word I said to YOU, A slave is not greater than his master. If they have persecuted me, they will persecute YOU also; if they have observed my word, they will observe YOURS also. 21 But they will do all these things against YOU on account of my name, because they do not know him that sent me. 22 If I had not come and spoken to them, they would have no sin; but now they have no excuse for their sin. 23 He that hates me hates also my Father. 24 If I had not done among them the works that no one else did, they would have no sin; but now they have both seen and hated me as well as my Father. 25 But it is that the word written in their Law may be fulfilled, 'They hated me without cause.' 26 When the helper arrives that I will send YOU from the Father, the spirit of the truth, which proceeds from the Father, that one will bear witness about me; 27 and YOU, in turn, are to bear witness, because YOU have been with me from when I began.

16 "I have spoken these things to YOU that YOU may not be stumbled. 2 Men will expel YOU from the synagogue. In fact, the hour is coming when everyone that kills YOU will imagine he has rendered a sacred service to God. 3 But they will do these things because they have not come to know either the Father or me. 4 Nevertheless, I have spoken these things to YOU that, when the hour for them arrives, YOU may remember I told them to YOU.

"These things, however, I did not tell YOU at first, because I was with YOU. 5 But now I am going to him that sent me, and yet not one of YOU asks me, 'Where are you going?' 6 But because I have spoken these things to YOU grief has filled YOUR hearts. 7 Nevertheless, I am telling YOU the truth, It is for YOUR benefit I am going away. For if I do not go away, the helper will by no means come to YOU; but if I do go my way, I will send him to YOU. 8 And when that one arrives he will give the world convincing evidence concerning sin and concerning righteousness and concerning judgment: 9 in the first place, concerning sin, because they are not exercising faith in me; 10 then concerning righteousness, because I am going to the Father and YOU will behold me no longer; 11 then concerning judgment, because the ruler of this world has been judged.

12 "I have many things yet to say to YOU, but YOU are not able to bear them at present. 13 However, when that one arrives, the spirit of the truth, he will guide YOU into all the truth, for he will not speak of his own impulse, but what things he hears he will speak, and he will declare to YOU the things coming. 14 That one will glorify me, because he will receive from what is mine and will declare it to YOU. 15 All the things that the Father has are mine. That is why I said he receives from what is mine and declares [it] to YOU. 16 In a little while YOU will behold me no longer, and, again, in a little while YOU will see me."

17 Therefore some of his disciples said to one another: "What does this mean that he says to us, 'In a little while YOU will not behold me, and, again, in a little while YOU will see me,' and, 'because I am going to the Father'?" 18 Hence they were saying: "What does this mean that he says, 'a little while'? We do not know what he is talking about." 19 Jesus knew they were wanting to question him, so he said to them: "Are YOU inquiring among yourselves over this, because I said, In a little while YOU will not behold me, and, again, in a little while YOU

will see me? 20 Most truly I say to you, You will weep and wail, but the world will rejoice; you will be grieved, but your grief will be turned into joy. 21 A woman, when she is giving birth, has grief, because her hour has arrived; but when she has brought forth the young child, she remembers the tribulation no more because of the joy that a man has been born into the world. 22 You also, therefore, are now, indeed, having grief; but I shall see you again and your hearts will rejoice, and your joy no one will take from you. 23 And in that day you will ask me no question at all. Most truly I say to you, If you ask the Father for anything he will give it to you in my name. 24 Until this present time you have not asked a single thing in my name. Ask and you will receive, that your joy may be made full.

25 "I have spoken these things to you in comparisons. The hour is coming when I will speak to you no more in comparisons, but I will report to you with plainness concerning the Father. 26 In that day you will ask in my name, and I do not say to you that I shall make request of the Father concerning you. 27 For the Father himself has affection for you, because you have had affection for me and have believed that I came out as the Father's representative. 28 I came out from the Father and have come into the world. Further, I am leaving the world and am going my way to the Father."

29 His disciples said: "See! Now you are speaking with plainness, and are uttering no comparison. 30 Now we know that you know all things and you do not need to have anyone question you. By this we believe that you came out from God." 31 Jesus answered them: "Do you believe at present? 32 Look! The hour is coming, indeed, it has come, when you will be scattered each one to his own house and you will leave me alone; and yet I am not alone, because the Father is with me. 33 I have said these things to you that by means of me you may have peace. In the world you are having tribulation, but take courage! I have conquered the world."

17 Jesus spoke these things, and, raising his eyes to heaven, he said: "Father, the hour has come; glorify your son, that your son may glorify you, 2 according as you have given him authority over all flesh, that, as regards the whole [number] whom you have given him, he may give them everlasting life. 3 This means everlasting life, their taking in knowledge of you, the only true God, and of the one whom you sent forth, Jesus Christ. 4 I have glorified you on the earth, having finished the work you have given me to do. 5 So now you, Father, glorify me alongside yourself with the glory that I had alongside you before the world was.

6 "I have made your name manifest to the men you gave me out of the world. They were yours, and you gave them to me, and they have observed your word. 7 They have now come to know that all the things you gave me are from you; 8 because the sayings that you gave me I have given to them, and they have received them and have certainly come to know that I came out as your representative, and they have believed that you sent me forth. 9 I make request concerning them; I make request, not concerning the world, but concerning those you have given me; because they are yours, 10 and all my things are yours and yours are mine, and I have been glorified among them.

11 "Also, I am no longer in the world, but they are in the world and I am coming to you. Holy Father, watch over them on account of your own name which you have given me, in order that they may be one just as we are. 12 When I was with them I used to watch over them on account of your own name which you have given me; and I have kept them, and not one of them is destroyed except the son of destruction, in order that the

scripture might be fulfilled. 13 But now I am coming to you, and I am speaking these things in the world in order that they may have my joy in themselves to the full. 14 I have given your word to them, but the world has hated them, because they are no part of the world, just as I am no part of the world.

15 "I request you, not to take them out of the world, but to watch over them because of the wicked one. 16 They are no part of the world, just as I am no part of the world. 17 Sanctify them by means of the truth; your word is truth. 18 Just as you sent me forth into the world, I also sent them forth into the world. 19 And I am sanctifying myself in their behalf, that they also may be sanctified by means of truth.

20 "I make request, not concerning these only, but also concerning those putting faith in me through their word; 21 in order that they may all be one, just as you, Father, are in union with me and I am in union with you, that they also may be in union with us, in order that the world may believe that you sent me forth. 22 Also, I have given them the glory that you have given me, in order that they may be one just as we are one. 23 I in union with them and you in union with me, in order that they may be perfected into one, that the world may have the knowledge that you sent me forth and that you loved them just as you loved me. 24 Father, as to what you have given me, I wish that, where I am, they also may be with me, in order to behold my glory that you have given me, because you loved me before the founding of the world. 25 Righteous Father, the world has, indeed, not come to know you; but I have come to know you, and these have come to know that you sent me forth. 26 And I have made your name known to them and will make it known, in order that the love with which you loved me may be in them and I in union with them."

18 Having said these things, Jesus went out with his disciples across the winter torrent of Kid'ron to where there was a garden, and he and his disciples entered into it. 2 Now Judas, his betrayer, also knew the place, because Jesus had many times met there with his disciples. 3 Therefore Judas took the soldier band and officers of the chief priests and of the Pharisees and came there with torches and lamps and weapons. 4 Jesus, therefore, knowing all the things coming upon him, went forth and said to them: "Whom are you looking for?" 5 They answered him: "Jesus the Naz·a·rene'." He said to them: "I am he." Now Judas, his betrayer, was also standing with them.

6 However, when he said to them: "I am he," they drew back and fell to the ground. 7 Therefore he asked them again: "Whom are you looking for?" They said: "Jesus the Naz·a·rene'." 8 Jesus answered: "I told you I am he. If, therefore, it is I you are looking for, let these go"; 9 in order that the word might be fulfilled which he said: "Of those whom you have given me I have not lost a single one."

10 Then Simon Peter, as he had a sword, drew it and struck the slave of the high priest and cut his right ear off. The name of the slave was Malchus. 11 Jesus, however, said to Peter: "Put the sword into [its] sheath. The cup that the Father has given me, should I not by all means drink it?"

12 Then the soldier band and the military commander and the officers of the Jews seized Jesus and bound him, 13 and they led him first to An'nas; for he was father-in-law to Ca'ia·phas, who was high priest that year. 14 Ca'ia·phas was, in fact, the one that counseled the Jews that it was to their benefit for one man to die in behalf of the people.

15 Now Simon Peter as well as another disciple was following Jesus. That disciple was known to the high priest, and he went in

with Jesus into the courtyard of the high priest, 16 but Peter was standing outside at the door. Therefore the other disciple, who was known to the high priest, went out and spoke to the doorkeeper and brought Peter in. 17 The servant girl, the doorkeeper, then said to Peter: "You are not also one of this man's disciples, are you?" He said: "I am not." 18 Now the slaves and the officers were standing about, as they had built a charcoal fire, because it was cold, and they were warming themselves. Peter also was standing with them and warming himself.

19 And so the chief priest questioned Jesus about his disciples and about his teaching. 20 Jesus answered him: "I have spoken to the world publicly. I always taught in a synagogue and in the temple, where all the Jews come together; and I spoke nothing in secret. 21 Why do you question me? Question those who have heard what I spoke to them. See! These know what I said." 22 After he said these things, one of the officers that was standing by gave Jesus a slap in the face and said: "Is that the way you answer the chief priest?" 23 Jesus answered him: "If I spoke wrongly, bear witness concerning the wrong; but if rightly, why do you hit me?" 24 Then An'nas sent him away bound to Ca'ia·phas the high priest.

25 Now Simon Peter was standing and warming himself. Then they said to him: "You are not also one of his disciples, are you?" He denied it and said: "I am not." 26 One of the slaves of the high priest, being a relative of the man whose ear Peter cut off, said: "I saw you in the garden with him, did I not?" 27 However, Peter denied it again; and immediately a cock crowed.

28 Then they led Jesus from Ca'ia·phas to the governor's palace. It was now early in the day. But they themselves did not enter into the governor's palace, that they might not get defiled but might eat the passover. 29 Therefore Pilate

came outside to them and said: "What accusation do you bring against this man?" 30 In answer they said to him: "If this man were not a wrongdoer, we would not have delivered him up to you." 31 Hence Pilate said to them: "Take him yourselves and judge him according to your law." The Jews said to him: "It is not lawful for us to kill anyone." 32 This, in order that the word of Jesus might be fulfilled which he said to signify what sort of death he was destined to die.

33 So Pilate entered into the governor's palace again and called Jesus and said to him: "Are you the king of the Jews?" 34 Jesus answered: "Is it of your own originality that you say this, or did others tell you about me?" 35 Pilate answered: "I am not a Jew, am I? Your own nation and the chief priests delivered you up to me. What did you do?" 36 Jesus answered: "My kingdom is no part of this world. If my kingdom were part of this world, my attendants would have fought that I should not be delivered up to the Jews. But, as it is, my kingdom is not from this source." 37 Therefore Pilate said to him: "Well, then, are you a king?" Jesus answered: "You yourself are saying that I am a king. For this I have been born, and for this I have come into the world, that I should bear witness to the truth. Everyone that is on the side of the truth listens to my voice." 38 Pilate said to him: "What is truth?"

And after saying this, he went out again to the Jews and said to them: "I find no fault in him. 39 Moreover, you have a custom that I should release a man to you at the passover. Do you, therefore, wish me to release to you the king of the Jews?" 40 Then they shouted again, saying: "Not this man, but Bar·ab'bas!" Now Bar·ab'bas was a robber.

19 At that time, therefore, Pilate took Jesus and scourged him. 2 And the soldiers braided a crown of thorns and put it on his head and arrayed him with a purple outer garment; 3 and they began coming up to him and saying: "Good day, you king of the Jews!" Also, they would give him slaps in the face. 4 And Pilate went outside again and said to them: "See! I bring him outside to YOU in order for YOU to know I find no fault in him." 5 Accordingly Jesus came outside, wearing the thorny crown and the purple outer garment. And he said to them: "Look! The man!" 6 However, when the chief priests and the officers saw him, they shouted, saying: "Impale [him]! Impale [him]!" Pilate said to them: "Take him yourselves and impale him, for I do not find any fault in him." 7 The Jews answered him: "We have a law, and according to the law he ought to die, because he made himself God's son."

8 When, therefore, Pilate heard this saying, he became more fearful; 9 and he entered into the governor's palace again and said to Jesus: "Where are you from?" But Jesus gave him no answer. 10 Hence Pilate said to him: "Are you not speaking to me? Do you not know I have authority to release you and I have authority to impale you?" 11 Jesus answered him: "You would have no authority at all against me unless it had been granted to you from above. This is why the man that handed me over to you has greater sin."

12 For this reason Pilate kept on seeking how to release him. But the Jews shouted, saying: "If you release this [man], you are not a friend of Caesar. Every man making himself a king speaks against Caesar." 13 Therefore Pilate, after hearing these words, brought Jesus outside, and he sat down on a judgment seat in a place called The Stone Pavement, but, in Hebrew, Gab'ba·tha. 14 Now it was preparation of the passover; it was about the sixth hour. And he said to the Jews: "See! YOUR king!" 15 However, they shouted: "Take [him] away! Take [him] away! Impale him!"

Pilate said to them: "Shall I impale YOUR king?" The chief priests answered: "We have no king but Caesar." 16 At that time, therefore, he handed him over to them to be impaled.

Then they took charge of Jesus. 17 And, bearing the torture stake for himself, he went out to the so-called Skull Place, which is called Gol'go·tha in Hebrew; 18 and there they impaled him, and two other [men] with him, one on this side and one on that, but Jesus in the middle. 19 Pilate wrote a title also and put it on the torture stake. It was written: "Jesus the Naz·a·rene' the King of the Jews." 20 Therefore many of the Jews read this title, because the place where Jesus was impaled was near the city; and it was written in Hebrew, in Latin, in Greek. 21 However, the chief priests of the Jews began to say to Pilate: "Do not write 'The King of the Jews,' but that he said, 'I am King of the Jews.'" 22 Pilate answered: "What I have written I have written."

23 Now when the soldiers had impaled Jesus, they took his outer garments and made four parts, for each soldier a part, and the inner garment. But the inner garment was without a seam, being woven from the top throughout its length. 24 Therefore they said to one another: "Let us not tear it, but let us determine by lots over it whose it will be." This was that the scripture might be fulfilled: "They apportioned my outer garments among themselves, and upon my apparel they cast lots." And so the soldiers really did these things.

25 By the torture stake of Jesus, however, there were standing his mother and the sister of his mother; Mary the wife of Clo'pas, and Mary Mag'da·lene. 26 Therefore Jesus, seeing his mother and the disciple whom he loved standing by, said to his mother: "Woman, see! your son!" 27 Next he said to the disciple: "See! Your mother!" And from that hour on

the disciple took her to his own home.

28 After this, when Jesus knew that by now all things had been accomplished, in order that the scripture might be accomplished he said: "I am thirsty." 29 A vessel was sitting there full of sour wine. Therefore they put a sponge full of the sour wine upon a hyssop [stalk] and brought it to his mouth. 30 When, now, he had received the sour wine, Jesus said: "It has been accomplished!" and, bowing his head, he delivered up [his] spirit.

31 Then the Jews, since it was Preparation, in order that the bodies might not remain upon the torture stakes on the sabbath, (for the day of that sabbath was a great one,) requested Pilate to have their legs broken and the bodies taken away. 32 The soldiers came, therefore, and broke the legs of the first [man] and those of the other [man] that had been impaled with him. 33 But on coming to Jesus, as they saw that he was already dead, they did not break his legs. 34 Yet one of the soldiers jabbed his side with a spear, and immediately blood and water came out. 35 And he that has seen [it] has borne witness, and his witness is true, and that man knows he tells true things, in order that you also may believe. 36 In fact, these things took place in order for the scripture to be fulfilled: "Not a bone of his will be crushed." 37 And, again, a different scripture says: "They will look to the One whom they pierced."

38 Now after these things Joseph from Ar·i·ma·the′a, who was a disciple of Jesus but a secret one out of [his] fear of the Jews, requested Pilate that he might take away the body of Jesus; and Pilate gave him permission. Therefore he came and took his body away. 39 Nic·o·de′mus also, the man that came to him in the night the first time, came bringing a roll of myrrh and aloes, about a hundred pounds [of it]. 40 So they took the body of Jesus and bound it up with bandages with the spices, just the way the Jews have the custom of preparing for burial. 41 Incidentally, at the place where he was impaled there was a garden, and in the garden a new memorial tomb, in which no one had ever yet been laid. 42 There, then, on account of the preparation of the Jews, they laid Jesus, because the memorial tomb was nearby.

20 On the first day of the week Mary Mag′da·lene came to the memorial tomb early, while there was still darkness, and she beheld the stone already taken away from the memorial tomb. 2 Therefore she ran and came to Simon Peter and to the other disciple, for whom Jesus had affection, and she said to them: "They have taken away the Lord out of the memorial tomb, and we do not know where they have laid him."

3 Then Peter and the other disciple went out and started for the memorial tomb. 4 Yes, the two together began to run; but the other disciple ran ahead of Peter with greater speed and reached the memorial tomb first. 5 And, stooping forward, he beheld the bandages lying, yet he did not go in. 6 Then Simon Peter also came following him, and he entered into the memorial tomb. And he viewed the bandages lying, 7 also the cloth that had been upon his head not lying with the bandages but separately rolled up in one place. 8 At that time, therefore, the other disciple who had reached the memorial tomb first also went in, and he saw and believed. 9 For they did not yet discern the scripture that he must rise from the dead. 10 And so the disciples went back to their homes.

11 Mary, however, kept standing outside near the memorial tomb, weeping. Then, while she was weeping, she stooped forward to look into the memorial tomb 12 and she viewed two angels in white sitting one at the head and one at the feet where the body of Jesus had been lying. 13 And they said to her: "Woman, why are you weeping?" She said to them: "They

have taken my Lord away, and I do not know where they have laid him." 14 After saying these things, she turned back and viewed Jesus standing, but she did not discern it was Jesus. 15 Jesus said to her: "Woman, why are you weeping? Whom are you looking for?" She, imagining it was the gardener, said to him: "Sir, if you have carried him off, tell me where you have laid him, and I will take him away." 16 Jesus said to her: "Mary!" Upon turning around, she said to him, in Hebrew: *"Rab·bo'-ni!"* (which means "Teacher!") 17 Jesus said to her: "Stop clinging to me. For I have not yet ascended to the Father. But be on your way to my brothers and say to them, 'I am ascending to my Father and YOUR Father and to my God and YOUR God.'" 18 Mary Mag'da·lene came and brought the news to the disciples: "I have seen the Lord!" and that he said these things to her.

19 Therefore, when it was late on that day, the first of the week, and, although the doors were locked where the disciples were for fear of the Jews, Jesus came and stood in their midst and said to them: "May YOU have peace." 20 And after he said this he showed them both his hands and his side. Then the disciples rejoiced at seeing the Lord. 21 Jesus, therefore, said to them again: "May YOU have peace. Just as the Father has sent me forth, I also am sending YOU." 22 And after he said this he blew upon them and said to them: "Receive holy spirit. 23 If YOU forgive the sins of any persons, they stand forgiven to them; if YOU retain those of any persons, they stand retained."

24 But Thomas, one of the twelve, who was called The Twin, was not with them when Jesus came. 25 Consequently the other disciples would say to him: "We have seen the Lord!" But he said to them: "Unless I see in his hands the print of the nails and stick my finger into the print of the nails and stick my hand into his side, I will certainly not believe."

26 Well, eight days later his disciples were again indoors, and Thomas with them. Jesus came, although the doors were locked, and he stood in their midst and said: "May YOU have peace." 27 Next he said to Thomas: "Put your finger here, and see my hands, and take your hand and stick it into my side, and stop being unbelieving but become believing." 28 In answer Thomas said to him: "My Lord and my God!" 29 Jesus said to him: "Because you have seen me have you believed? Happy are those who do not see and yet believe."

30 To be sure, Jesus performed many other signs also before the disciples, which are not written down in this scroll. 31 But these have been written down that YOU may believe that Jesus is the Christ the Son of God, and that, because of believing, YOU may have life by means of his name.

21 After these things Jesus manifested himself again to the disciples at the sea of Ti·be'ri·as; but he made the manifestation in this way. 2 There were in company Simon Peter and Thomas, who was called The Twin, and Na·than'a·el from Ca'na of Gal'i·lee and the sons of Zeb'e·dee and two others of his disciples. 3 Simon Peter said to them: "I am going fishing." They said to him: "We also are coming with you." Out they went and got aboard the boat, but during that night they caught nothing.

4 However, just as it was getting to be morning, Jesus stood on the beach, but the disciples did not, of course, discern that it was Jesus. 5 Then Jesus said to them: "Young children, YOU do not have anything to eat, do YOU?" They answered "No!" to him. 6 He said to them: "Cast the net on the right side of the boat and YOU will find [some]." Then they cast it, but they were no longer able to draw it in because of the multitude of the fishes. 7 Therefore that disciple whom Jesus used to love said to

Peter: "It is the Lord!" Hence Simon Peter, upon hearing that it was the Lord, girded about himself his top garment, for he was naked, and plunged into the sea. 8 But the other disciples came in the little boat, for they were not a long way from land, only about three hundred feet away, dragging the net of fishes.

9 However, when they disembarked onto land they beheld lying there a charcoal fire and fish lying upon it and bread. 10 Jesus said to them: "Bring some of the fish YOU just now caught." 11 Simon Peter, therefore, went on board and drew the net to land full of big fishes, one hundred and fifty-three of them. But although there were so many the net did not burst. 12 Jesus said to them: "Come, take YOUR breakfast." Not one of the disciples had the courage to inquire of him: "Who are you?" because they knew it was the Lord. 13 Jesus came and took the bread and gave it to them, and the fish likewise. 14 This was now the third time that Jesus appeared to the disciples after his being raised up from the dead.

15 When, now, they had breakfasted, Jesus said to Simon Peter: "Simon son of John, do you love me more than these?" He said to him: "Yes, Lord, you know I have affection for you." He said to him: "Feed my lambs." 16 Again he said to him, a second time: "Simon son of John, do you love me?" He said to him: "Yes, Lord, you know I have affection for you." He said to him: "Shepherd my little sheep." 17 He said to him the third time: "Simon son of John, do you have affection for me?" Peter became grieved that he said to him the third time: "Do you have affection for me?" So he said to him: "Lord, you know all things; you are aware that I have affection for you." Jesus said to him: "Feed my little sheep. 18 Most truly I say to you, When you were younger, you used to gird yourself and walk about where you wanted. But when you grow old you will stretch out your hands and another [man] will gird you and bear you where you do not wish." 19 This he said to signify by what sort of death he would glorify God. So, when he had said this, he said to him: "Continue following me."

20 Upon turning about Peter saw the disciple whom Jesus used to love following, the one who at the evening meal had also leaned back upon his breast and said: "Lord, who is the one betraying you?" 21 Accordingly, when he caught sight of him, Peter said to Jesus: "Lord, what will this [man do]?" 22 Jesus said to him: "If it is my will for him to remain until I come, of what concern is that to you? You continue following me." 23 In consequence, this saying went out among the brothers, that that disciple would not die. However, Jesus did not say to him that he would not die, but: "If it is my will for him to remain until I come, of what concern is that to you?"

24 This is the disciple that bears witness about these things and that wrote these things, and we know that the witness he gives is true.

25 There are, in fact, many other things also which Jesus did, which, if ever they were written in full detail, I suppose, the world itself could not contain the scrolls written.

ACTS OF APOSTLES

1 The first account, O The·oph′i·lus, I composed about all the things Jesus started both to do and to teach, 2 until the day that he was taken up, after he had given commandment through holy spirit to the apostles whom he chose. **3** To these also by many positive proofs he showed himself alive after he had suffered, being seen by them throughout forty days and telling the things about the kingdom of God. **4** And while he was meeting with them he gave them the orders: "Do not withdraw from Jerusalem, but keep waiting for what the Father has promised, about which YOU heard from me; **5** because John, indeed, baptized with water, but YOU will be baptized in holy spirit not many days after this."

6 When, now, they had assembled, they went asking him: "Lord, are you restoring the kingdom to Israel at this time?" **7** He said to them: "It does not belong to YOU to get knowledge of the times or seasons which the Father has placed in his own jurisdiction; **8** but YOU will receive power when the holy spirit arrives upon YOU, and YOU will be witnesses of me both in Jerusalem and in all Ju·de′a and Sa·mar′i·a and to the most distant part of the earth." **9** And after he had said these things, while they were looking on, he was lifted up and a cloud caught him up from their vision. **10** And as they were gazing into the sky while he was on his way, also, look! two men in white garments stood alongside them, **11** and they said: "Men of Gal′i·lee, why do YOU stand looking into the sky? This Jesus who was received up from YOU into the sky will come thus in the same manner as YOU have beheld him going into the sky."

12 Then they returned to Jerusalem from a mountain called the Mount of Olives, which is near Jerusalem, being a sabbath day's journey away. **13** So, when they had entered, they went up into the upper chamber, where they were staying, Peter as well as John and James and Andrew, Philip and Thomas, Bar·thol′o·mew and Matthew, James the son of Al·phae′us and Simon the zealous one, and Judas the son of James. **14** With one accord all these were persisting in prayer, together with some women and Mary the mother of Jesus and with his brothers.

15 Now during these days Peter rose up in the midst of the brothers and said (the crowd of persons was all together about one hundred and twenty): **16** "Men, brothers, it was necessary for the scripture to be fulfilled, which the holy spirit spoke beforehand by David's mouth about Judas, who became a guide to those who arrested Jesus, **17** because he had been numbered among us and he obtained a share in this ministry. **18** (This very man, therefore, purchased a field with the wages for unrighteousness, and pitching head foremost he noisily burst in his midst and all his intestines were poured out. **19** It also became known to all the inhabitants of Jerusalem, so that that field was called in their language A·kel′da·ma, that is, Field of Blood.) **20** For it is written in the book of Psalms, 'Let his lodging place become desolate, and let there be no dweller in it,' and, 'His office of oversight let someone else take.' **21** It is therefore necessary that of the men that assembled with us during all the time in which the Lord Jesus went in and out among us, **22** starting with his baptism by John and until the day he was received up from us, one of these men should become a witness with us of his resurrection."

23 So they put up two, Joseph called Bar′sab·bas, who was surnamed Justus, and Mat·thi′as. 24 And they prayed and said: "You, O Jehovah, who know the hearts of all, designate which one of these two men you have chosen, 25 to take the place of this ministry and apostleship, from which Judas deviated to go to his own place." 26 So they cast lots over them, and the lot fell upon Mat·thi′as; and he was reckoned along with the eleven apostles.

2 Now while the day of the [festival of] Pentecost was in progress they were all together at the same place, 2 and suddenly there occurred from heaven a noise just like that of a rushing stiff breeze, and it filled the whole house in which they were sitting. 3 And tongues as if of fire became visible to them and were distributed about, and one sat upon each one of them, 4 and they all became filled with holy spirit and started to speak with different tongues, just as the spirit was granting them to make utterance.

5 As it was, there were dwelling in Jerusalem Jews, reverent men, from every nation of those under heaven. 6 So, when this sound occurred, the multitude came together and were bewildered, because each one heard them speaking in his own language. 7 Indeed, they were astonished and began to wonder and say: "See here, all these who are speaking are Gal·i·le′ans, are they not? 8 And yet how is it we are hearing, each one of us, his own language in which we were born? 9 Par′thi·ans and Medes and E′lam·ites, and the inhabitants of Mes·o·po·ta′mi·a, and Ju·de′a and Cap·pa·do′ci·a, Pon′tus and the [district of] Asia, 10 and Phryg′i·a and Pam·phyl′i·a, Egypt and the parts of Lib′y·a, which is toward Cy·re′ne, and sojourners from Rome, both Jews and proselytes, 11 Cre′tans and Arabians, we hear them speaking in our tongues about the magnificent things of God." 12 Yes, they were all astonished and were in perplexity, saying one to another: "What does this thing pur-

port to be?" 13 However, different ones mocked at them and began to say: "They are full of sweet wine."

14 But Peter stood up with the eleven and raised his voice and made this utterance to them: "Men of Ju·de′a and all YOU inhabitants of Jerusalem, let this be known to YOU and give ear to my sayings. 15 These [people] are, in fact, not drunk, as YOU suppose, for it is the third hour of the day. 16 On the contrary, this is what was said through the prophet Joel, 17 ' "And in the last days," God says, "I shall pour out some of my spirit upon every sort of flesh, and YOUR sons and YOUR daughters will prophesy and YOUR young men will see visions and YOUR old men will dream dreams; 18 and even upon my men slaves and upon my women slaves I will pour out some of my spirit in those days, and they will prophesy. 19 And I will give portents in heaven above and signs on earth below, blood and fire and smoke mist; 20 the sun will be turned into darkness and the moon into blood before the great and illustrious day of Jehovah arrives. 21 And everyone who calls on the name of Jehovah will be saved." '

22 "Men of Israel, hear these words: Jesus the Naz·a·rene′, a man publicly shown by God to YOU through powerful works and portents and signs that God did through him in YOUR midst, just as YOU yourselves know, 23 this [man], as one delivered up by the determined counsel and foreknowledge of God, YOU fastened to a stake by the hand of lawless men and did away with. 24 But God resurrected him by loosing the pangs of death, because it was not possible for him to continue to be held fast by it. 25 For David says respecting him, 'I had Jehovah constantly before my eyes; because he is at my right hand that I may never be shaken. 26 On this account my heart became cheerful and my tongue rejoiced greatly. Moreover, even my flesh will reside in hope; 27 be-

Naz·a·rene', whom you impaled but whom God raised up from the dead, by this one does this man stand here sound in front of you. 11 This is 'the stone that was treated by you builders as of no account that has become the head of the corner.' 12 Furthermore, there is no salvation in anyone else, for there is not another name under heaven that has been given among men by which we must get saved."

13 Now when they beheld the outspokenness of Peter and John, and perceived that they were men unlettered and ordinary, they got to wondering. And they began to recognize about them that they used to be with Jesus; 14 and as they were looking at the man that had been cured standing with them, they had nothing to say in rebuttal. 15 So they commanded them to go outside the San'he·drin hall, and they began consulting with one another, 16 saying: "What shall we do with these men? Because, for a fact, a noteworthy sign has occurred through them, one manifest to all the inhabitants of Jerusalem; and we cannot deny it. 17 Nevertheless, in order that it may not be spread abroad further among the people, let us tell them with threats not to speak any more upon the basis of this name to any man at all."

18 With that they called them and charged them, nowhere to make any utterance or to teach upon the basis of the name of Jesus. 19 But in reply Peter and John said to them: "Whether it is righteous in the sight of God to listen to you rather than to God, judge for yourselves. 20 But as for us, we cannot stop speaking about the things we have seen and heard." 21 So, when they had further threatened them, they released them, since they did not find any ground on which to punish them and on account of the people, because they were all glorifying God over what had occurred; 22 for the man upon whom this sign of healing had occurred was more than forty years old.

23 After being released they went to their own people and reported what things the chief priests and the older men had said to them. 24 Upon hearing this they with one accord raised their voices to God and said:

"Sovereign Lord, you are the One who made the heaven and the earth and the sea and all the things in them, 25 and who through holy spirit said by the mouth of our forefather David, your servant, 'Why did nations become tumultuous and peoples meditate upon empty things? 26 The kings of the earth took their stand and the rulers massed together as one against Jehovah and against his anointed one.' 27 Even so, both Herod and Pontius Pilate with men of nations and with peoples of Israel were in actuality gathered together in this city against your holy servant Jesus, whom you anointed, 28 in order to do what things your hand and counsel had foreordained to occur. 29 And now, Jehovah, give attention to their threats, and grant your slaves to keep speaking your word with all boldness, 30 while you stretch out your hand for healing and while signs and portents occur through the name of your holy servant Jesus."

31 And when they had made supplication, the place in which they were gathered together was shaken; and they were one and all filled with the holy spirit and were speaking the word of God with boldness.

32 Moreover, the multitude of those who had believed had one heart and soul, and not even one would say that any of the things he possessed was his own; but they had all things in common. 33 Also, with great power the apostles continued giving forth the witness concerning the resurrection of the Lord Jesus; and undeserved kindness in large measure was upon them all. 34 In fact, there was not one in need among them; for all those who were possessors of fields or houses would sell them and bring the values of the things sold 35 and they would

deposit them at the feet of the apostles. In turn distribution would be made to each one, just as he would have the need. 36 So Joseph, who was surnamed Bar'-na·bas by the apostles, which means, when translated, Son of Comfort, a Levite, a native of Cy'prus, 37 possessing a piece of land, sold it and brought the money and deposited it at the feet of the apostles.

5 However, a certain man, An·a-ni'as by name, together with Sap·phi'ra his wife, sold a possession 2 and secretly held back some of the price, his wife also knowing about it, and he brought just a part and deposited it at the feet of the apostles. 3 But Peter said: "An·a·ni'as, why has Satan emboldened you to play false to the holy spirit and to hold back secretly some of the price of the field? 4 As long as it remained with you did it not remain yours, and after it was sold did it not continue in your control? Why was it that you purposed such a deed as this in your heart? You have played false, not to men, but to God." 5 On hearing these words An·a·ni'as fell down and expired. And great fear came over all those hearing of it. 6 But the younger men rose, wrapped him in cloths, and carried him out and buried him.

7 Now after an interval of about three hours his wife came in, not knowing what had happened. 8 Peter said to her: "Tell me, did YOU [two] sell the field for so much?" She said: "Yes, for so much." 9 So Peter said to her: "Why was it agreed upon between YOU [two] to make a test of the spirit of Jehovah? Look! The feet of those who buried your husband are at the door, and they will carry you out." 10 Instantly she fell down at his feet and expired. When the young men came in they found her dead, and they carried her out and buried her alongside her husband. 11 Consequently great fear came over the whole congregation and over all those hearing about these things.

12 Moreover, through the hands of the apostles many signs and portents continued to occur among the people; and they were all with one accord in Sol'o·mon's colonnade. 13 True, not a one of the others had the courage to join himself to them; nevertheless, the people were extolling them. 14 More than that, believers in the Lord kept on being added, multitudes both of men and of women; 15 so that they brought the sick out even into the broad ways and laid them there upon little beds and cots, in order that, as Peter would go by, at least his shadow might fall upon some one of them. 16 Also, the multitude from the cities around Jerusalem kept coming together, bearing sick people and those troubled with unclean spirits, and they would one and all be cured.

17 But the high priest and all those with him, the then existing sect of the Sadducees, rose and became filled with jealousy, 18 and they laid hands upon the apostles and put them in the public place of custody. 19 But during the night Jehovah's angel opened the doors of the prison, brought them out and said: 20 "Be on YOUR way, and, having taken a stand in the temple, keep on speaking to the people all the sayings about this life." 21 After hearing this, they entered into the temple at daybreak and began to teach.

Now when the high priest and those with him arrived, they called together the San'he·drin and the assembly of older men of the sons of Israel, and they sent out to the jail to have them brought. 22 But when the officers got there they did not find them in the prison. So they returned and made report, 23 saying: "The jail we found locked with all security and the guards standing at the doors, but on opening up we found no one inside." 24 Well, when both the captain of the temple and the chief priests heard these words, they fell into a quandary over these matters as to what this would come to. 25 But a certain man arrived and reported to them: "Look! The men YOU put in the prison are in the temple, standing and teaching the people." 26 Then the captain went off with his officers and proceeded to bring them, but without violence, as they were afraid of being stoned by the people.

27 So they brought them and stood them in the San'he·drin hall. And the high priest questioned them 28 and said: "We positively ordered YOU not to keep teaching upon the basis of this name, and yet, look! YOU have filled Jerusalem with YOUR teaching, and YOU are determined to bring the blood of this man upon us." 29 In answer Peter and the [other] apostles said: "We must obey God as ruler rather than men. 30 The God of our forefathers raised up Jesus, whom YOU slew, hanging him upon a stake. 31 God exalted this one as Chief Agent and Savior to his right hand, to give repentance to Israel and forgiveness of sins. 32 And we are witnesses of these matters, and so is the holy spirit, which God has given to those obeying him as ruler."

33 When they heard this, they felt deeply cut and were wanting to do away with them. 34 But a certain man rose in the San'he·drin, a Pharisee named Ga·ma'li·el, a Law teacher esteemed by all the people, and gave the command to put the men outside for a little while. 35 And he said to them: "Men of Israel, pay attention to yourselves as to what YOU intend to do respecting these men. 36 For instance, before these days Theu'das rose, saying he himself was somebody, and a number of men, about four hundred, joined his party. But he was done away with, and all those who were obeying him were dispersed and came to nothing. 37 After him Judas the Gal·i·le'an rose in the days of the registration, and he drew off people after him. And yet that man perished, and all those who were obeying him were scattered abroad. 38 And so, under the present cir-

cumstances, I say to YOU, Do not meddle with these men, but let them alone; (because, if this scheme or this work is from men, it will be overthrown; 39 but if it is from God, YOU will not be able to overthrow them;) otherwise, YOU may perhaps be found fighters actually against God." 40 At this they gave heed to him, and they summoned the apostles, flogged them, and ordered them to stop speaking upon the basis of Jesus' name, and let them go.

41 These, therefore, went their way from before the San'he·drin, rejoicing because they had been counted worthy to be dishonored in behalf of his name. 42 And every day in the temple and from house to house they continued without letup teaching and declaring the good news about the Christ, Jesus.

6 Now in these days, when the disciples were increasing, a murmuring arose on the part of the Greek-speaking Jews against the Hebrew-speaking Jews, because their widows were being overlooked in the daily distribution. 2 So the twelve called the multitude of the disciples to them and said: "It is not pleasing for us to leave the word of God to distribute [food] to tables. 3 So, brothers, search out for yourselves seven certified men from among YOU, full of spirit and wisdom, that we may appoint them over this necessary business; 4 but we shall devote ourselves to prayer and to the ministry of the word." 5 And the thing spoken was pleasing to the whole multitude, and they selected Stephen, a man full of faith and holy spirit, and Philip and Proch'o·rus and Ni·ca'nor and Ti'mon and Par'me·nas and Ni·co·la'us, a proselyte of Antioch; 6 and they placed them before the apostles, and, after having prayed, these laid their hands upon them.

7 Consequently the word of God went on growing, and the number of the disciples kept multiplying in Jerusalem very much; and a great crowd of priests began to be obedient to the faith.

8 Now Stephen, full of graciousness and power, was performing great portents and signs among the people. 9 But certain men rose up of those from the so-called Synagogue of the Freedmen, and of the Cy·re'ni·ans and Alexandrians and of those from Ci·li'cia and Asia, to dispute with Stephen; 10 and yet they could not hold their own against the wisdom and the spirit with which he was speaking. 11 Then they secretly induced men to say: "We have heard him speaking blasphemous sayings against Moses and God." 12 And they stirred up the people and the older men and the scribes, and, coming upon him suddenly, they took him by force and led him to the San'he·drin. 13 And they brought forward false witnesses, who said: "This man does not stop speaking things against this holy place and against the Law. 14 For instance, we have heard him say that this Jesus the Naz·a·rene' will throw down this place and change the customs that Moses handed down to us."

15 And as all those sitting in the San'he·drin gazed at him, they saw that his face was as an angel's face.

7 But the high priest said: "Are these things so?" 2 He said: "Men, brothers and fathers, hear. The God of glory appeared to our forefather Abraham while he was in Mes·o·po·ta'mi·a, before he took up residence in Ha'ran, 3 and he said to him, 'Go out from your land and from your relatives and come on into the land I shall show you.' 4 Then he went out from the land of the Chal·de'ans and took up residence in Ha'ran. And from there, after his father died, [God] caused him to change his residence to this land in which you now dwell. 5 And yet he did not give him any inheritable possession in it, no, not a footbreadth; but he promised to give it to him as a possession, and after him to his seed, while as yet he had no child. 6 Moreover, God spoke to this effect, that his seed would be alien residents in a foreign land and [the people] would enslave them and afflict [them] for four hundred years. 7 'And that nation for which they will slave I shall judge,' God said, 'and after these things they will come out and will render sacred service to me in this place.'

8 "He also gave him a covenant of circumcision; and thus he became the father of Isaac and circumcised him on the eighth day, and Isaac of Jacob, and Jacob of the twelve family heads. 9 And the family heads became jealous of Joseph and sold him into Egypt. But God was with him, 10 and he delivered him out of all his tribulations and gave him graciousness and wisdom in the sight of Phar'aoh king of Egypt. And he appointed him to govern Egypt and his whole house. 11 But a famine came upon the whole of Egypt and Ca'naan, even a great tribulation; and our forefathers were not finding any provisions. 12 But Jacob heard there were foodstuffs in Egypt and he sent our forefathers out the first time. 13 And during the second time Joseph was made known to his brothers; and the family stock of Joseph became manifest to Phar'aoh. 14 So Joseph sent out and called Jacob his father and all his relatives from that place, to the number of seventy-five souls. 15 Jacob went down into Egypt. And he deceased; and so did our forefathers, 16 and they were transferred to She'chem and were laid in the tomb that Abraham had bought for a price with silver money from the sons of Ha'mor in She'chem.

17 "Just as the time was approaching for [fulfillment of] the promise that God had openly declared to Abraham, the people grew and multiplied in Egypt, 18 until there rose a different king over Egypt, who did not know of Joseph. 19 This one used statecraft against our race and wrongfully forced the fathers to expose their infants, that they might not be preserved alive. 20 In that particular time Moses was born, and he

was divinely beautiful. And he was nursed three months in [his] father's home. 21 But when he was exposed, the daughter of Phar'-aoh picked him up and brought him up as her own son. 22 Consequently Moses was instructed in all the wisdom of the Egyptians. In fact, he was powerful in his words and deeds.

23 "Now when the time of his fortieth year was being fulfilled, it came into his heart to make an inspection of his brothers, the sons of Israel. 24 And when he caught sight of a certain one being unjustly treated, he defended him and executed vengeance for the one being abused by striking the Egyptian down. 25 He was supposing his brothers would grasp that God was giving them salvation by his hand, but they did not grasp [it]. 26 And the next day he appeared to them as they were fighting, and he tried to bring them together again in peace, saying, 'Men, you are brothers. Why do you treat each other unjustly?' 27 But the one that was treating his neighbor unjustly thrust him away, saying, 'Who appointed you ruler and judge over us? 28 You do not want to do away with me in the same manner that you did away with the Egyptian yesterday, do you?' 29 At this speech Moses took to flight and became an alien resident in the land of Mid'i·an, where he became the father of two sons.

30 "And when forty years were fulfilled, there appeared to him in the wilderness of Mount Si'nai an angel in the fiery flame of a thornbush. 31 Now when Moses saw it he marveled at the sight. But as he was approaching to investigate, Jehovah's voice came, 32 'I am the God of your forefathers, the God of Abraham and of Isaac and of Jacob.' Seized with trembling, Moses did not dare to investigate further. 33 Jehovah said to him, 'Take the sandals off your feet, for the place on which you are standing is holy ground. 34 I have certainly seen the wrongful treatment of my people who are in Egypt,

and I have heard their groaning and have come down to deliver them. And now come, I will send you off to Egypt.' 35 This Moses, whom they disowned, saying, 'Who appointed you ruler and judge?' this man God sent off as both ruler and deliverer by the hand of the angel that appeared to him in the thornbush. 36 This man led them out after doing portents and signs in Egypt and in the Red Sea and in the wilderness for forty years.

37 "This is the Moses that said to the sons of Israel, 'God will raise up for you from among your brothers a prophet like me.' 38 This is he that came to be among the congregation in the wilderness with the angel that spoke to him on Mount Si'nai and with our forefathers, and he received living sacred pronouncements to give you. 39 To him our forefathers refused to become obedient, but they thrust him aside and in their hearts they turned back to Egypt, 40 saying to Aaron, 'Make gods for us to go ahead of us. For this Moses, who led us out of the land of Egypt, we do not know what has happened to him.' 41 So they made a calf in those days and brought up a sacrifice to the idol and began to enjoy themselves in the works of their hands. 42 So God turned and handed them over to render sacred service to the army of heaven, just as it is written in the book of the prophets, 'It was not to me that you offered victims and sacrifices for forty years in the wilderness, was it, O house of Israel? 43 But it was the tent of Mo'loch and the star of the god Re'phan that you took up, the figures which you made to worship them. Consequently I will deport you beyond Babylon.'

44 "Our forefathers had the tent of the witness in the wilderness, just as he gave orders when speaking to Moses to make it according to the pattern he had seen. 45 And our forefathers who succeeded to it also brought it in with Joshua into the land possessed by

the nations, whom God thrust out from before our forefathers. Here it remained until the days of David. 46 He found favor in the sight of God and asked for [the privilege of] providing a habitation for the God of Jacob. 47 However, Sol·o·mon built a house for him. 48 Nevertheless, the Most High does not dwell in houses made with hands; just as the prophet says, 49 'The heaven is my throne, and the earth is my footstool. What sort of house will you build for me? Jehovah says. Or what is the place for my resting? 50 My hand made all these things, did it not?'

51 "Obstinate men and uncircumcised in hearts and ears, you are always resisting the holy spirit; as your forefathers did, so you do. 52 Which one of the prophets did your forefathers not persecute? Yes, they killed those who made announcement in advance concerning the coming of the righteous One, whose betrayers and murderers you have now become, 53 you who received the Law as transmitted by angels but have not kept it."

54 Well, at hearing these things they felt cut to their hearts and began to gnash their teeth at him. 55 But he, being full of holy spirit, gazed into heaven and caught sight of God's glory and of Jesus standing at God's right hand, 56 and he said: "Look! I behold the heavens opened up and the Son of man standing at God's right hand." 57 At this they cried out at the top of the voice and put their hands over their ears and rushed upon him with one accord. 58 And after throwing him outside the city, they began casting stones at him. And the witnesses laid down their outer garments at the feet of a young man called Saul. 59 And they went on casting stones at Stephen as he made appeal and said: "Lord Jesus, receive my spirit." 60 Then, bending his knees, he cried out with a strong voice: "Jehovah, do not charge this sin against them." And after saying this he fell asleep [in death].

8 Saul, for his part, was approving of the murder of him.

On that day great persecution arose against the congregation that was in Jerusalem; all except the apostles were scattered throughout the regions of Ju·de'a and Sa·mar'i·a. 2 But reverent men carried Stephen to the burial, and they made a great lamentation over him. 3 Saul, though, began to deal outrageously with the congregation. Invading one house after another and, dragging out both men and women, he would turn them over to prison.

4 However, those who had been scattered went through the land declaring the good news of the word. 5 Philip, for one, went down to the city of Sa·mar'i·a and began to preach the Christ to them. 6 With one accord the crowds were paying attention to the things said by Philip while they listened and looked at the signs he was performing. 7 For there were many that had unclean spirits, and these would cry out with a loud voice and come out. Moreover, many that were paralyzed and lame were cured. 8 So there came to be a great deal of joy in that city.

9 Now in the city there was a certain man named Simon, who, prior to this, had been practicing magical arts and amazing the nation of Sa·mar'i·a, saying he himself was somebody great. 10 And all of them, from the least to the greatest, would pay attention to him and say: "This man is the Power of God, which can be called Great." 11 So they would pay attention to him because of his having amazed them for quite a while by his magical arts. 12 But when they believed Philip, who was declaring the good news of the kingdom of God and of the name of Jesus Christ, they proceeded to be baptized, both men and women. 13 Simon himself also became a believer, and, after being baptized, he was in constant attendance upon Philip; and he was amazed at beholding great signs and powerful works taking place.

14 When the apostles in Jerusalem heard that Sa·mar′i·a had accepted the word of God, they dispatched Peter and John to them; 15 and these went down and prayed for them to get holy spirit. 16 For it had not yet fallen upon any one of them, but they had only been baptized in the name of the Lord Jesus. 17 Then they went laying their hands upon them, and they began to receive holy spirit.

18 Now when Simon saw that through the laying on of the hands of the apostles the spirit was given, he offered them money, 19 saying: "Give me also this authority, that anyone upon whom I lay my hands may receive holy spirit." 20 But Peter said to him: "May your silver perish with you, because you thought through money to get possession of the free gift of God. 21 You have neither part nor lot in this matter, for your heart is not straight in the sight of God. 22 Repent, therefore, of this badness of yours, and supplicate Jehovah that, if possible, the device of your heart may be forgiven you; 23 for I see you are a poisonous gall and a bond of unrighteousness." 24 In answer Simon said: "You men, make supplication for me to Jehovah that none of the things you have said may come upon me."

25 Therefore, when they had given the witness thoroughly and had spoken the word of Jehovah, they turned back to Jerusalem, and they went declaring the good news to many villages of the Sa·mar′i·tans.

26 However, Jehovah's angel spoke to Philip, saying: "Rise and go to the south to the road that runs down from Jerusalem to Ga′za." (This is a desert road.) 27 With that he rose and went, and, look! an Ethiopian eunuch, a man in power under Can·da′ce queen of the Ethiopians, and who was over all her treasure. He had gone to Jerusalem to worship, 28 but he was returning and was sitting in his chariot and reading aloud the prophet Isaiah. 29 So the spirit said to Philip: "Approach and join yourself to this chariot." 30 Philip ran alongside and heard him reading aloud Isaiah the prophet, and he said: "Do you actually know what you are reading?" 31 He said: "Really, how could I ever do so, unless someone guided me?" And he entreated Philip to get on and sit down with him. 32 Now the passage of Scripture that he was reading aloud was this: "As a sheep he was brought to the slaughter, and as a lamb that is voiceless before its shearer, so he does not open his mouth. 33 During his humiliation the judgment was taken away from him. Who will tell the details of his generation? Because his life is taken away from the earth."

34 In answer the eunuch said to Philip: "I beg you, About whom does the prophet say this? About himself or about some other man?" 35 Philip opened his mouth and, starting with this Scripture, he declared to him the good news about Jesus. 36 Now as they were going over the road, they came to a certain body of water, and the eunuch said: "Look! A body of water; what prevents me from getting baptized?" 37 —— 38 With that he commanded the chariot to halt, and they both went down into the water, both Philip and the eunuch; and he baptized him. 39 When they had come up out of the water, Jehovah's spirit quickly led Philip away, and the eunuch did not see him any more, for he kept going on his way rejoicing. 40 But Philip was found to be in Ash′dod, and he went through the territory and kept on declaring the good news to all the cities until he got to Caes·a·re′a.

9 But Saul, still breathing threat and murder against the disciples of the Lord, went to the high priest 2 and asked him for letters to the synagogues in Damascus, in order that he might bring bound to Jerusalem any whom he found who belonged to The Way, both men and women.

3 Now as he was traveling he approached Damascus, when sud-

denly a light from heaven flashed around him, 4 and he fell to the ground and heard a voice say to him: "Saul, Saul, why are you persecuting me?" 5 He said: "Who are you, Lord?" He said: "I am Jesus, whom you are persecuting. 6 Nevertheless, rise and enter into the city, and what you must do will be told you." 7 Now the men that were journeying with him were standing speechless, hearing, indeed, the sound of a voice, but not beholding any man. 8 But Saul got up from the ground, and though his eyes were opened he was seeing nothing. So they led him by the hand and conducted him into Damascus. 9 And for three days he did not see anything, and he neither ate nor drank.

10 There was in Damascus a certain disciple named An·a·ni'as, and the Lord said to him in a vision: "An·a·ni'as!" He said: "Here I am, Lord." 11 The Lord said to him: "Rise, go to the street called Straight, and at the house of Judas look for a man named Saul, from Tarsus. For, look! he is praying, 12 and in a vision he has seen a man named An·a·ni'as come in and lay his hands upon him that he might recover sight." 13 But An·a·ni'as answered: "Lord, I have heard from many about this man, how many injurious things he did to your holy ones in Jerusalem. 14 And here he has authority from the chief priests to put in bonds all those calling upon your name." 15 But the Lord said to him: "Be on your way, because this man is a chosen vessel to me to bear my name to the nations as well as to kings and the sons of Israel. 16 For I shall show him plainly how many things he must suffer for my name."

17 So An·a·ni'as went off and entered into the house, and he laid his hands upon him and said: "Saul, brother, the Lord, the Jesus that appeared to you on the road over which you were coming, has sent me forth, in order that you may recover sight and be filled with holy spirit." 18 And immediately there fell from his eyes what looked like scales, and he recovered sight; and he rose and was baptized, 19 and he took food and gained strength.

He got to be for some days with the disciples in Damascus, 20 and immediately in the synagogues he began to preach Jesus, that this One is the Son of God. 21 But all those hearing him gave way to astonishment and would say: "Is this not the man that ravaged those in Jerusalem who call upon this name, and that had come here for this very purpose, that he might lead them bound to the chief priests?" 22 But Saul kept on acquiring power all the more and was confounding the Jews that dwelt in Damascus as he proved logically that this is the Christ.

23 Now when a good many days were coming to a close, the Jews took counsel together to do away with him. However, their plot against him became known to Saul. 24 But they were closely watching also the gates both day and night in order to do away with him. 25 So his disciples took him and let him down by night through an opening in the wall, lowering him in a basket.

26 On arriving in Jerusalem he made efforts to join himself to the disciples; but they were all afraid of him, because they did not believe he was a disciple. 27 So Bar'na·bas came to his aid and led him to the apostles, and he told them in detail how on the road he had seen the Lord and that he had spoken to him, and how in Damascus he had spoken boldly in the name of Jesus. 28 And he continued with them, walking in and out at Jerusalem, speaking boldly in the name of the Lord; 29 and he was talking and disputing with the Greek-speaking Jews. But these made attempts to do away with him. 30 When the brothers detected this, they brought him down to Caes·a·re'a and sent him off to Tarsus.

31 Then, indeed, the congregation throughout the whole of Ju-

de'a and Gal'i·lee and Sa·mar'i·a entered into a period of peace, being built up; and as it walked in the fear of Jehovah and in the comfort of the holy spirit it kept on multiplying.

32 Now as Peter was going through all [parts] he came down also to the holy ones that dwelt in Lyd'da. **33** There he found a certain man named Ae·ne'as, who had been lying flat on his cot for eight years, as he was paralyzed. **34** And Peter said to him: "Ae·ne'-as, Jesus Christ heals you. Rise and make up your bed." And he rose immediately. **35** And all those who inhabited Lyd'da and the [plain of] Shar'on saw him, and these turned to the Lord.

36 But in Jop'pa there was a certain disciple named Tab'i·tha, which, when translated, means Dor'cas. She abounded in good deeds and gifts of mercy that she was rendering. **37** But in those days she happened to fall sick and die. So they bathed her and laid her in an upper chamber. **38** Now as Lyd'da was near Jop'pa, when the disciples heard that Peter was in this city they dispatched two men to him to entreat [him]: "Please do not hesitate to come on as far as us." **39** At that Peter rose and went with them. And when he arrived, they led him up into the upper chamber; and all the widows presented themselves to him weeping and exhibiting many inner garments and outer garments that Dor'cas used to make while she was with them. **40** But Peter put everybody outside and, bending his knees, he prayed, and, turning to the body, he said: "Tab'i·tha, rise!" She opened her eyes and, as she caught sight of Peter, she sat up. **41** Giving her his hand, he raised her up, and he called the holy ones and the widows and presented her alive. **42** This became known throughout all Jop'pa, and many became believers on the Lord. **43** For quite a few days he remained in Jop'pa with a certain Simon, a tanner.

10 Now in Caes·a·re'a there was a certain man named Cornelius, an army officer of the Italian band, as it was called, **2** a devout man and one fearing God together with all his household, and he made many gifts of mercy to the people and made supplication to God continually. **3** Just about the ninth hour of the day he saw plainly in a vision an angel of God come in to him and say to him: "Cornelius!" **4** The man gazed at him and, becoming frightened, said: "What is it, Lord?" He said to him: "Your prayers and gifts of mercy have ascended as a remembrance before God. **5** So now send men to Jop'pa and summon a certain Simon who is surnamed Peter. **6** This man is being entertained by a certain Simon, a tanner, who has a house by the sea." **7** As soon as the angel that spoke to him had left, he called two of his house servants and a devout soldier from among those who were in constant attendance upon him, **8** and he related everything to them and dispatched them to Jop'pa.

9 The next day as they were pursuing their journey and were approaching the city, Peter went up to the housetop about the sixth hour to pray. **10** But he became very hungry and wanted to eat. While they were preparing, he fell into a trance **11** and beheld heaven opened and some sort of vessel descending like a great linen sheet being let down by its four extremities upon the earth; **12** and in it there were all sorts of four-footed creatures and creeping things of the earth and birds of heaven. **13** And a voice came to him: "Rise, Peter, slaughter and eat!" **14** But Peter said: "Not at all, Lord, because never have I eaten anything defiled and unclean." **15** And the voice [spoke] again to him, the second time: "You stop calling defiled the things God has cleansed." **16** This occurred a third time, and immediately the vessel was taken up into heaven.

17 Now while Peter was in great perplexity inwardly over what the vision he had seen might mean, look! the men dispatched by Cornelius had made inquiries for Simon's house and stood there at the gate. 18 And they called out and inquired whether Simon who was surnamed Peter was being entertained there. 19 As Peter was going over in his mind about the vision, the spirit said: "Look! Three men are seeking you. 20 However, rise, go downstairs and be on your way with them, not doubting at all, because I have dispatched them." 21 So Peter went downstairs to the men and said: "Look! I am the one you are seeking. What is the cause for which you are present?" 22 They said: "Cornelius, an army officer, a man righteous and fearing God and well reported by the whole nation of the Jews, was given divine instructions by a holy angel to send for you to come to his house and to hear the things you have to say." 23 Therefore he invited them in and entertained them.

The next day he rose and went off with them, and some of the brothers that were from Jop'pa went with him. 24 On the day after that he entered into Caes·a·re'a. Cornelius, of course, was expecting them and had called together his relatives and intimate friends. 25 As Peter entered, Cornelius met him, fell down at his feet and did obeisance to him. 26 But Peter lifted him up, saying: "Rise; I myself am also a man." 27 And as he conversed with him he went in and found many people assembled, 28 and he said to them: "You well know how unlawful it is for a Jew to join himself to or approach a man of another race; and yet God has shown me I should call no man defiled or unclean. 29 Hence I came, really without objection, when I was sent for. Therefore I inquire the reason that you have sent for me."

30 Accordingly Cornelius said: "Four days ago counting from this hour I was praying in my house at the ninth hour, when, look! a man in bright raiment stood before me 31 and said, 'Cornelius, your prayer has been favorably heard and your gifts of mercy have been remembered before God. 32 Send, therefore, to Jop'pa and call for Simon, who is surnamed Peter. This man is being entertained in the house of Simon, a tanner, by the sea.' 33 Therefore I at once sent to you, and you did well in coming here. And so at this time we are all present before God to hear all the things you have been commanded by Jehovah to say."

34 At this Peter opened his mouth and said: "For a certainty I perceive that God is not partial, 35 but in every nation the man that fears him and works righteousness is acceptable to him. 36 He sent out the word to the sons of Israel to declare to them the good news of peace through Jesus Christ: this One is Lord of all [others]. 37 You know the subject that was talked about throughout the whole of Ju·de'a, starting from Gal'i·lee after the baptism that John preached, 38 namely, Jesus who was from Naz'a·reth, how God anointed him with holy spirit and power, and he went through the land doing good and healing all those oppressed by the Devil; because God was with him. 39 And we are witnesses of all the things he did both in the country of the Jews and in Jerusalem; but they also did away with him by hanging him on a stake. 40 God raised this One up on the third day and granted him to become manifest, 41 not to all the people, but to witnesses appointed beforehand by God, to us, who ate and drank with him after his rising from the dead. 42 Also, he ordered us to preach to the people and to give a thorough witness that this is the One decreed by God to be judge of the living and the dead. 43 To him all the prophets bear witness, that everyone putting faith in him gets forgiveness of sins through his name."

44 While Peter was yet speaking about these matters the holy spirit fell upon all those hearing the word. **45** And the faithful ones that had come with Peter who were of those circumcised were amazed, because the free gift of the holy spirit was being poured out also upon people of the nations. **46** For they heard them speaking with tongues and glorifying God. Then Peter responded: **47** "Can anyone forbid water so that these might not be baptized who have received the holy spirit even as we have?" **48** With that he commanded them to be baptized in the name of Jesus Christ. Then they requested him to remain for some days.

11 Now the apostles and the brothers that were in Ju·de′a heard that people of the nations had also received the word of God. **2** So when Peter came up to Jerusalem, the [supporters] of circumcision began to contend with him, **3** saying he had gone into the house of men that were not circumcised and had eaten with them. **4** At this Peter commenced and went on to explain the particulars to them, saying:

5 "I was in the city of Jop′pa praying, and in a trance I saw a vision, some sort of vessel descending like a great linen sheet being let down by its four extremities from heaven, and it came clear to me. **6** Gazing into it, I made observations and saw four-footed creatures of the earth and wild beasts and creeping things and birds of heaven. **7** I also heard a voice say to me, 'Rise, Peter, slaughter and eat!' **8** But I said, 'Not at all, Lord, because a defiled or unclean thing has never entered into my mouth.' **9** The second time the voice from heaven answered, 'You stop calling defiled the things God has cleansed.' **10** This occurred for a third time, and everything was pulled up again into heaven. **11** Also, look! at that instant there were three men standing at the house in which we were, they having been dispatched from Caes·a·re′a to me. **12** So the spirit told me to go with them, not doubting at all. But these six brothers also went with me, and we entered into the house of the man. **13** "He reported to us how he saw the angel stand in his house and say, 'Dispatch men to Jop′pa and send for Simon who is surnamed Peter, **14** and he will speak those things to you by which you and all your household may get saved.' **15** But when I started to speak, the holy spirit fell upon them just as it did also upon us in [the] beginning. **16** At this I called to mind the saying of the Lord, how he used to say, 'John, for his part, baptized with water, but you will be baptized in holy spirit.' **17** If, therefore, God gave the same free gift to them as he also did to us who have believed upon the Lord Jesus Christ, who was I that I should be able to hinder God?"

18 Now when they heard these things, they acquiesced, and they glorified God, saying: "Well, then, God has granted repentance for the purpose of life to people of the nations also."

19 Consequently those who had been scattered by the tribulation that arose over Stephen went through as far as Phoe·ni′cia and Cy′prus and Antioch, but speaking the word to no one except to Jews only. **20** However, out of them there were some men of Cy′prus and Cy·re′ne that came to Antioch and began talking to the Greek-speaking people, declaring the good news of the Lord Jesus. **21** Furthermore, the hand of Jehovah was with them, and a great number that became believers turned to the Lord.

22 The account about them got to the ears of the congregation that was in Jerusalem, and they sent out Bar′na·bas as far as Antioch. **23** When he arrived and saw the undeserved kindness of God, he rejoiced and began to encourage them all to continue in the Lord with hearty purpose; **24** for he was a good man and full of holy spirit and of faith. And a considerable crowd was added to the Lord. 25 So he went off to Tarsus to make a thorough search for Saul 26 and, after he found him, he brought him to Antioch. It thus came about that for a whole year they gathered together with them in the congregation and taught quite a crowd, and it was first in Antioch that the disciples were by divine providence called Christians.

27 Now in these days prophets came down from Jerusalem to Antioch. 28 One of them named Ag′a·bus rose and proceeded to indicate through the spirit that a great famine was about to come upon the entire inhabited earth; which, for that matter, did take place in the time of Claudius. 29 So those of the disciples determined, each of them according as anyone could afford it, to send a relief ministration to the brothers dwelling in Ju·de′a; 30 and this they did, dispatching it to the older men by the hand of Bar′na·bas and Saul.

12 About that particular time Herod the king applied his hands to mistreating some of those of the congregation. 2 He did away with James the brother of John by the sword. 3 As he saw it was pleasing to the Jews, he went on to arrest Peter also. (As it was, those were days of the unfermented cakes.) 4 And laying hold of him, he put him in prison, turning him over to four shifts of four soldiers each to guard him, as he intended to produce him for the people after the passover. 5 Consequently Peter was being kept in the prison; but prayer to God for him was being carried on intensely by the congregation.

6 Now when Herod was about to produce him, that night Peter was sleeping bound with two chains between two soldiers, and guards before the door were keeping the prison. 7 But, look! Jehovah's angel stood by, and a light shone in the prison cell. Striking Peter on the side, he roused him, saying: "Rise quickly!" And his chains fell off his hands. 8 The angel said to

him: "Gird yourself and bind your sandals on." He did so. Finally he said to him: "Put your outer garment on and keep following me." 9 And he went out and kept following him, but he did not know that what was happening through the angel was real. In fact, he supposed he was seeing a vision. 10 Going through the first sentinel guard and the second they got to the iron gate leading into the city, and this opened to them of its own accord. And after they went out they advanced down one street, and immediately the angel departed from him. 11 And Peter, coming to himself, said: "Now I actually know that Jehovah sent his angel forth and delivered me out of Herod's hand and from all that the people of the Jews were expecting."

12 And after he considered it, he went to the house of Mary the mother of John who was surnamed Mark, where quite a few were gathered together and praying. 13 When he knocked at the door of the gateway, a servant girl named Rhoda came to attend to the call, 14 and, upon recognizing the voice of Peter, out of joy she did not open the gate, but ran inside and reported that Peter was standing before the gateway. 15 They said to her: "You are mad." But she kept on strongly asserting it was so. They began to say: "It is his angel." 16 But Peter remained there knocking. When they opened, they saw him and were astonished. 17 But he motioned to them with his hand to be silent and told them in detail how Jehovah brought him out of the prison, and he said: "Report these things to James and the brothers." With that he went out and journeyed to another place.

18 Well, when it became day, there was no little stir among the soldiers over what really had become of Peter. 19 Herod made diligent search for him and, when not finding him, he examined the guards and commanded them to be led off [to punishment]; and he

went down from Ju·de′a to Caes-a·re′a and spent some time there.

20 Now he was in a fighting mood against the people of Tyre and of Si′don. So with one accord they came to him and, after persuading Blastus, who was in charge of the bedchamber of the king, they began suing for peace, because their country was supplied with food from that of the king. 21 But on a set day Herod clothed himself with royal raiment and sat down upon the judgment seat and began giving them a public address. 22 In turn the assembled people began shouting: "A god's voice, and not a man's!" 23 Instantly the angel of Jehovah struck him, because he did not give the glory to God; and he became eaten up with worms and expired.

24 But the word of Jehovah went on growing and spreading.

25 As for Bar′na·bas and Saul, after having fully carried out the relief ministration in Jerusalem, they returned and took along with them John, the one surnamed Mark.

13 Now in Antioch there were prophets and teachers in the local congregation, Bar′na·bas as well as Sym′e·on who was called Ni′ger, and Lucius of Cy·re′ne, and Man′a·en who was educated with Herod the district ruler, and Saul. 2 As they were publicly ministering to Jehovah and fasting, the holy spirit said: "Of all persons set Bar′na·bas and Saul apart for me for the work to which I have called them." 3 Then they fasted and prayed and laid their hands upon them and let them go.

4 Accordingly these men, sent out by the holy spirit, went down to Se·leu′cia, and from there they sailed away to Cy′prus. 5 And when they got to be in Sal′a·mis they began publishing the word of God in the synagogues of the Jews. They had John also as an attendant.

6 When they had gone through the whole island as far as Pa′phos, they met up with a certain man, a sorcerer, a false prophet, a Jew whose name was Bar-Je′sus, 7 and

he was with the proconsul Sergius Paulus, an intelligent man. Calling Bar′na·bas and Saul to him, this man earnestly sought to hear the word of God. 8 But El′y·mas the sorcerer (that, in fact, is the way his name is translated) began opposing them, seeking to turn the proconsul away from the faith. 9 Saul, who is also Paul, becoming filled with holy spirit, looked at him intently 10 and said: "O man full of every sort of fraud and every sort of villainy, you son of the Devil, you enemy of everything righteous, will you not quit distorting the right ways of Jehovah? 11 Well, then, look! Jehovah's hand is upon you, and you will be blind, not seeing the sunlight for a period of time." Instantly a thick mist and darkness fell upon him, and he went around seeking men to lead him by the hand. 12 Then the proconsul, upon seeing what had happened, became a believer, as he was astounded at the teaching of Jehovah.

13 The men, together with Paul, now put out to sea from Pa′phos and arrived at Perga in Pam-phyl′i·a. But John withdrew from them and returned to Jerusalem. 14 They, however, went on from Perga and came to Antioch in Pi-sid′i·a and, going into the synagogue on the sabbath day, they took a seat. 15 After the public reading of the Law and of the Prophets the presiding officers of the synagogue sent out to them, saying: "Men, brothers, if there is any word of encouragement for the people that you have, tell it." 16 So Paul rose, and motioning with his hand, he said:

"Men, Israelites and you [others] that fear God, hear. 17 The God of this people Israel chose our forefathers, and he exalted the people during their alien residence in the land of Egypt and brought them out of it with an uplifted arm. 18 And for a period of about forty years he put up with their manner of action in the wilderness. 19 After destroying seven nations in the land of Ca′naan, he distributed the land of them by lot; 20 all that during about four hundred and fifty years.

"And after these things he gave them judges until Samuel the prophet. 21 But from then on they demanded a king, and God gave them Saul son of Kish, a man of the tribe of Benjamin, for forty years. 22 And after removing him, he raised up for them David as king, respecting whom he bore witness and said, 'I have found David the son of Jes'se, a man agreeable to my heart, who will do all the things I desire.' 23 From the offspring of this [man] according to his promise God has brought to Israel a savior, Jesus, 24 after John, in advance of the entry of that One, had preached publicly to all the people of Israel the baptism of those repenting. 25 But as John was fulfilling his course, he would say, 'What do you suppose I am? I am not he. But, look! one is coming after me the sandals of whose feet I am not worthy to untie.'

26 "Men, brothers, you sons of the stock of Abraham and those [others] among you who fear God, the word of this salvation has been sent forth to us. 27 For the inhabitants of Jerusalem and their rulers did not know this One, but, when acting as judges, they fulfilled the things voiced by the Prophets, which things are read aloud every Sabbath, 28 and, although they found no cause for death, they demanded of Pilate that he be executed. 29 When, now, they had accomplished all the things written about him, they took him down from the stake and laid him in a memorial tomb. 30 But God raised him up from the dead; 31 and for many days he became visible to those who had gone up with him from Gal'i·lee to Jerusalem, who are now his witnesses to the people.

32 "And so we are declaring to you the good news about the promise made to the forefathers, 33 that God has entirely fulfilled it to us their children in that he resurrected Jesus; even as it is written in the second psalm, 'You are my son, I have become your Father this day.' 34 And that fact that he resurrected him from the dead destined no more to return to corruption, he has stated in this way, 'I will give you people the loving-kindnesses to David that are faithful.' 35 Hence he also says in another psalm, 'You will not allow your loyal one to see corruption.' 36 For David, on the one hand, served the express will of God in his own generation and fell asleep [in death] and was laid with his forefathers and did see corruption. 37 On the other hand, he whom God raised up did not see corruption.

38 "Let it therefore be known to you, brothers, that through this One a forgiveness of sins is being published to you; 39 and that from all the things from which you could not be declared guiltless by means of the law of Moses, everyone who believes is declared guiltless by means of this One. 40 Therefore see to it that what is said in the Prophets does not come upon you, 41 'Behold it, you scorners, and wonder at it, and vanish away, because I am working a work in your days, a work that you will by no means believe even if anyone relates it to you in detail.'"

42 Now when they were going out, the people began entreating for these matters to be spoken to them on the following sabbath. 43 So after the synagogue assembly was dissolved, many of the Jews and of the proselytes who worshiped [God] followed Paul and Bar'na·bas, who in speaking to them began urging them to continue in the undeserved kindness of God.

44 The next sabbath nearly all the city gathered together to hear the word of Jehovah. 45 When the Jews got sight of the crowds, they were filled with jealousy and began blasphemously contradicting the things being spoken by Paul. 46 And so, talking with boldness, Paul and Bar'na·bas said: "It was

necessary for the word of God to be spoken first to you. Since you are thrusting it away from you and do not judge yourselves worthy of everlasting life, look! we turn to the nations. 47 In fact, Jehovah has laid commandment upon us in these words, 'I have appointed you as a light of nations, for you to be a salvation to the extremity of the earth.'"

48 When those of the nations heard this, they began to rejoice and to glorify the word of Jehovah, and all those who were rightly disposed for everlasting life became believers. 49 Furthermore, the word of Jehovah went on being carried throughout the whole country. 50 But the Jews stirred up the reputable women who worshiped [God] and the principal men of the city, and they raised up a persecution against Paul and Bar′na·bas and threw them outside their boundaries. 51 These shook the dust off their feet against them and went to I·co′ni·um. 52 And the disciples continued to be filled with joy and holy spirit.

14 Now in I·co′ni·um they entered together into the synagogue of the Jews and spoke in such a manner that a great multitude of both Jews and Greeks became believers. 2 But the Jews that did not believe stirred up and wrongly influenced the souls of people of the nations against the brothers. 3 Therefore they spent considerable time speaking with boldness by the authority of Jehovah, who bore witness to the word of his undeserved kindness by granting signs and portents to occur through their hands. 4 However, the multitude of the city was split, and some were for the Jews but others for the apostles. 5 Now when a violent attempt took place on the part of both people of the nations and Jews with their rulers, to treat them insolently and pelt them with stones. 6 they, on being informed of it, fled to the cities of Lyc·a·o′ni·a, Lys′tra and Der′be and the country round about;

7 and there they went on declaring the good news.

8 Now in Lys′tra there was sitting a certain man disabled in his feet, lame from his mother's womb, and he had never walked at all. 9 This man was listening to Paul speak, who, on looking at him intently and seeing he had faith to be made well, 10 said with a loud voice: "Stand up erect on your feet." And he leaped up and began walking. 11 And the crowds, seeing what Paul had done, raised their voices, saying in the Lyc·a·o′ni·an tongue: "The gods have become like humans and have come down to us!" 12 And they went calling Bar′na·bas Zeus, but Paul Her′mes, since he was the one taking the lead in speaking. 13 And the priest of Zeus, whose [temple] was before the city, brought bulls and garlands to the gates and was desiring to offer sacrifices with the crowds.

14 However, when the apostles Bar′na·bas and Paul heard of it, they ripped their outer garments and leaped out into the crowd, crying out 15 and saying: "Men, why are you doing these things? We also are humans having the same infirmities as you do, and are declaring the good news to you, for you to turn from these vain things to the living God, who made the heaven and the earth and the sea and all the things in them. 16 In the past generations he permitted all the nations to go on in their ways, 17 although, indeed, he did not leave himself without witness in that he did good, giving you rains from heaven and fruitful seasons, filling your hearts to the full with food and good cheer." 18 And yet by saying these things they scarcely restrained the crowds from sacrificing to them.

19 But Jews arrived from Antioch and I·co′ni·um and persuaded the crowds, and they stoned Paul and dragged him outside the city, imagining he was dead. 20 However, when the disciples surrounded him, he rose up and entered into the city. And on the next day he

left with Bar'na·bas for Der'be. 21 And after declaring the good news to that city and making quite a few disciples, they returned to Lys'tra and to I·co'ni·um and to Antioch, 22 strengthening the souls of the disciples, encouraging them to remain in the faith and [saying]: "We must enter into the kingdom of God through many tribulations." 23 Moreover, they appointed older men to office for them in the congregation and, offering prayer with fastings, they committed them to Jehovah in whom they had become believers.

24 And they went through Pi·sid'i·a and came into Pam·phyl'i·a, 25 and, after speaking the word in Perga, they went down to At·ta·li'a. 26 And from there they sailed off for Antioch, where they had been entrusted to the undeserved kindness of God for the work they had fully performed.

27 When they had arrived and had gathered the congregation together, they proceeded to relate the many things God had done by means of them, and that he had opened to the nations the door to faith. 28 So they spent not a little time with the disciples.

15 And certain men came down from Ju·de'a and began to teach the brothers: "Unless you get circumcised according to the custom of Moses, you cannot be saved." 2 But when there had occurred no little dissension and disputing by Paul and Bar'na·bas with them, they arranged for Paul and Bar'na·bas and some others of them to go up to the apostles and older men in Jerusalem regarding this dispute.

3 Accordingly, after being conducted part way by the congregation, these men continued on their way through both Phoe·ni'cia and Sa·mar'i·a, relating in detail the conversion of people of the nations, and they were causing great joy to all the brothers. 4 On arriving in Jerusalem they were kindly received by the congregation and the apostles and the older men, and they recounted the many things

God had done by means of them. 5 Yet, some of those of the sect of the Pharisees that had believed rose up from their seats and said: "It is necessary to circumcise them and charge them to observe the law of Moses."

6 And the apostles and the older men gathered together to see about this affair. 7 Now when much disputing had taken place, Peter rose and said to them: "Men, brothers, you well know that from early days God made the choice among you that through my mouth people of the nations should hear the word of the good news and believe; 8 and God, who knows the heart, bore witness by giving them the holy spirit, just as he did to us also. 9 And he made no distinction at all between us and them, but purified their hearts by faith. 10 Now, therefore, why are you making a test of God by imposing upon the neck of the disciples a yoke that neither our forefathers nor we were capable of bearing? 11 On the contrary, we trust to get saved through the undeserved kindness of the Lord Jesus in the same way as those people also."

12 At that the entire multitude became silent, and they began to listen to Bar'na·bas and Paul relate the many signs and portents that God did through them among the nations. 13 After they quit speaking, James answered, saying: "Men, brothers, hear me. 14 Sym'e·on has related thoroughly how God for the first time turned his attention to the nations to take out of them a people for his name. 15 And with this the words of the Prophets agree, just as it is written, 16 'After these things I shall return and rebuild the booth of David that is fallen down; and I shall rebuild its ruins and erect it again, 17 in order that those who remain of the men may earnestly seek Jehovah, together with people of all the nations, people who are called by my name, says Jehovah, who is doing these things, 18 known from of old.' 19 Hence my decision is not to trouble those from

the nations who are turning to God, 20 but to write them to abstain from things polluted by idols and from fornication and from what is strangled and from blood. 21 For from ancient times Moses has had in city after city those who preach him, because he is read aloud in the synagogues on every sabbath."

22 Then the apostles and the older men together with the whole congregation favored sending chosen men from among them to Antioch along with Paul and Bar'nabas, namely, Judas who was called Bar'sab·bas and Silas, leading men among the brothers; 23 and by their hand they wrote:

"The apostles and the older brothers to those brothers in Antioch and Syria and Ci·li'cia who are from the nations: Greetings! 24 Since we have heard that some from among us have caused YOU trouble with speeches, trying to subvert YOUR souls, although we did not give them any instructions, 25 we have come to a unanimous accord and have favored choosing men to send to YOU together with our loved ones, Bar'na·bas and Paul, 26 men that have delivered up their souls for the name of our Lord Jesus Christ. 27 We are therefore dispatching Judas and Silas, that they also may report the same things by word. 28 For the holy spirit and we ourselves have favored adding no further burden to YOU, except these necessary things, 29 to keep abstaining from things sacrificed to idols and from blood and from things strangled and from fornication. If YOU carefully keep yourselves from these things, YOU will prosper. Good health to YOU!"

30 Accordingly, when these men were let go, they went down to Antioch, and they gathered the multitude together and handed them the letter. 31 After reading it, they rejoiced over the encouragement. 32 And Judas and Silas, since they themselves were also prophets, encouraged the brothers with many a discourse and strengthened them. 33 So, when they had

passed some time, they were let go in peace by the brothers to those who had sent them out. 34 —— 35 However, Paul and Bar'na·bas continued spending time in Antioch teaching and declaring, with many others also, the good news of the word of Jehovah.

36 Now after some days Paul said to Bar'na·bas: "Above all things, let us return and visit the brothers in every one of the cities in which we published the word of Jehovah to see how they are." 37 For his part, Bar'na·bas was determined to take along also John, who was called Mark. 38 But Paul did not think it proper to be taking this one along with them, seeing that he had departed from them from Pamphyl'i·a and had not gone with them to the work. 39 At this there occurred a sharp burst of anger, so that they separated from each other; and Bar'na·bas took Mark along and sailed away to Cy'prus. 40 Paul selected Silas and went off after he had been entrusted by the brothers to the undeserved kindness of Jehovah. 41 But he went through Syria and Ci·li'cia, strengthening the congregations.

16 So he arrived at Der'be and also at Lys'tra. And, look! a certain disciple was there by the name of Timothy, the son of a believing Jewish woman but of a Greek father, 2 and he was well reported on by the brothers in Lys'tra and I·co'ni·um. 3 Paul expressed the desire for this man to go out with him, and he took him and circumcised him because of the Jews that were in those places, for one and all knew that his father was a Greek. 4 Now as they traveled on through the cities they would deliver to those there for observance the decrees that had been decided upon by the apostles and older men who were in Jerusalem. 5 Therefore, indeed, the congregations continued to be made firm in the faith and to increase in number from day to day.

6 Moreover, they went through Phryg'i·a and the country of Ga·la'ti·a, because they were forbidden

by the holy spirit to speak the word in the [district of] Asia. 7 Further, when getting down to Mys'i·a they made efforts to go into Bi·thyn'i·a, but the spirit of Jesus did not permit them. 8 So they passed Mys'i·a by and came down to Tro'as. 9 And during the night a vision appeared to Paul: a certain Mac·e·do'ni·an man was standing and entreating him and saying: "Step over into Mac·e·do'ni·a and help us." 10 Now as soon as he had seen the vision, we sought to go forth into Mac·e·do'ni·a, drawing the conclusion that God had summoned us to declare the good news to them.

11 Therefore we put out to sea from Tro'as and came with a straight run to Sam'o·thrace, but on the following day to Ne·ap'o·lis, 12 and from there to Phi·lip'pi, a colony, which is the principal city of the district of Mac·e·do'ni·a. We continued in this city, spending some days. 13 And on the sabbath day we went forth outside the gate beside a river, where we were thinking there was a place of prayer; and we sat down and began speaking to the women that had assembled. 14 And a certain woman named Lyd'i·a, a seller of purple, of the city of Thy·a·ti'ra and a worshiper of God, was listening, and Jehovah opened her heart wide to pay attention to the things being spoken by Paul. 15 Now when she and her household got baptized, she said with entreaty: "If YOU men have judged me to be faithful to Jehovah, enter into my house and stay." And she just made us come.

16 And it happened that as we were going to the place of prayer, a certain servant girl with a spirit, a demon of divination, met us. She used to furnish her masters with much gain by practicing the art of prediction. 17 This [girl] kept following Paul and us and crying out with the words: "These men are slaves of the Most High God, who are publishing to YOU the way of salvation." 18 This she kept doing for many days. Finally Paul got tired of it and turned and said to the spirit: "I order you in the name of Jesus Christ to come out of her." And it came out that very hour.

19 Well, when her masters saw that their hope of gain had left, they laid hold of Paul and Silas and dragged them into the market place to the rulers, 20 and, leading them up to the civil magistrates, they said: "These men are disturbing our city very much, they being Jews, 21 and they are publishing customs that it is not lawful for us to take up or practice, seeing we are Romans." 22 And the crowd rose up together against them; and the civil magistrates, after tearing the outer garments off them, gave the command to beat them with rods. 23 After they had inflicted many blows upon them, they threw them into prison, ordering the jailer to keep them securely. 24 Because he got such an order, he threw them into the inner prison and made their feet fast in the stocks.

25 But about the middle of the night Paul and Silas were praying and praising God with song; yes, the prisoners were hearing them. 26 Suddenly a great earthquake occurred, so that the foundations of the jail were shaken. Moreover, all the doors were instantly opened, and the bonds of all were loosened. 27 The jailer, being awakened out of sleep and seeing the prison doors were open, drew his sword and was about to do away with himself, imagining that the prisoners had escaped. 28 But Paul called out with a loud voice, saying: "Do not hurt yourself, for we are all here!" 29 So he asked for lights and leaped in and, seized with trembling, he fell down before Paul and Silas. 30 And he brought them outside and said: "Sirs, what must I do to get saved?" 31 They said: "Believe on the Lord Jesus and you will get saved, you and your household." 32 And they spoke the word of Jehovah to him together with all those in his house. 33 And he took them along in that hour of the night and bathed their stripes;

and, one and all, he and his were baptized without delay. 34 And he brought them into his house and set a table before them, and he rejoiced greatly with all his household now that he had believed God.

35 When it became day, the civil magistrates dispatched the constables to say: "Release those men." 36 So the jailer reported their words to Paul: "The civil magistrates have dispatched men that YOU [two] might be released. Now, therefore, come out and go YOUR way in peace." 37 But Paul said to them: "They flogged us publicly uncondemned, men who are Romans, and threw us into prison; and are they now throwing us out secretly? No, indeed! but let them come themselves and bring us out." 38 So the constables reported these sayings to the civil magistrates. These grew fearful when they heard that the men were Romans. 39 Consequently they came and entreated them and, after bringing them out, they requested them to depart from the city. 40 But they came out of the prison and went to the home of Lyd′i·a, and when they saw the brothers they encouraged them and departed.

17 They now journeyed through Am·phip′o·lis and Ap·ol·lo′ni·a and came to Thes·sa·lo·ni′ca, where there was a synagogue of the Jews. 2 So according to Paul's custom he went inside to them, and for three sabbaths he reasoned with them from the Scriptures, 3 explaining and proving by references that it was necessary for the Christ to suffer and to rise from the dead, and [saying]: "This is the Christ, this Jesus whom I am publishing to YOU." 4 As a result some of them became believers and associated themselves with Paul and Silas, and a great multitude of the Greeks who worshiped [God] and not a few of the principal women did so.

5 But the Jews, getting jealous, took into their company certain wicked men of the market-place idlers and formed a mob and proceeded to throw the city into an uproar. And they assaulted the house of Ja′son and went seeking to have them brought forth to the rabble. 6 When they did not find them they dragged Ja′son and certain brothers to the city rulers, crying out: "These men that have overturned the inhabited earth are present here also, 7 and Ja′son has received them with hospitality. And all these [men] act in opposition to the decrees of Caesar, saying there is another king, Jesus." 8 They indeed agitated the crowd and the city rulers when they heard these things; 9 and first after taking sufficient security from Ja′son and the others they let them go.

10 Immediately by night the brothers sent both Paul and Silas out to Be·roe′a, and these, upon arriving, went into the synagogue of the Jews. 11 Now the latter were more noble-minded than those in Thes·sa·lo·ni′ca, for they received the word with the greatest eagerness of mind, carefully examining the Scriptures daily as to whether these things were so. 12 Therefore many of them became believers, and so did not a few of the reputable Greek women and of the men. 13 But when the Jews from Thes·sa·lo·ni′ca learned that the word of God was published also in Be·roe′a by Paul, they came there also to incite and agitate the masses. 14 Then the brothers immediately sent Paul off to go as far as the sea; but both Silas and Timothy remained behind there. 15 However, those conducting Paul brought him as far as Athens and, after receiving a command for Silas and Timothy to come to him as quickly as possible, they departed.

16 Now while Paul was waiting for them in Athens, his spirit within him came to be irritated at beholding that the city was full of idols. 17 Consequently he began to reason in the synagogue with the Jews and the other people who worshiped [God] and every day in the market place with those who happened to be on hand. 18 But

certain ones of both the Ep·i·cu·re′an and the Sto′ic philosophers took to conversing with him controversially, and some would say: "What is it this chatterer would like to tell?" Others: "He seems to be a publisher of foreign deities." This was because he was declaring the good news of Jesus and the resurrection. 19 So they laid hold of him and led him to the Ar·e·op′a·gus, saying: "Can we get to know what this new teaching is which is spoken by you? 20 For you are introducing some things that are strange to our ears. Therefore we desire to get to know what these things purport to be." 21 In fact, all Athenians and the foreigners sojourning there would spend their leisure time at nothing but telling something or listening to something new. 22 Paul now stood in the midst of the Ar·e·op′a·gus and said:

"Men of Athens, I behold that in all things you seem to be more given to the fear of the deities than others are. 23 For instance, while passing along and carefully observing your objects of veneration I also found an altar on which had been inscribed 'To an Unknown God.' Therefore what you are unknowingly giving godly devotion to, this I am publishing to you. 24 The God that made the world and all the things in it, being, as this One is, Lord of heaven and earth, does not dwell in handmade temples, 25 neither is he attended to by human hands as if he needed anything, because he himself gives to all [persons] life and breath and all things. 26 And he made out of one [man] every nation of men, to dwell upon the entire surface of the earth, and he decreed the appointed times and the set limits of the dwelling of [men], 27 for them to seek God, if they might grope for him and really find him, although, in fact, he is not far off from each one of us. 28 For by him we have life and move and exist, even as certain ones of the poets among you have said, 'For we are also his progeny.'

29 "Seeing, therefore, that we are the progeny of God, we ought not to imagine that the Divine Being is like gold or silver or stone, like something sculptured by the art and contrivance of man. 30 True, God has overlooked the times of such ignorance, yet now he is telling mankind that they should all everywhere repent. 31 Because he has set a day in which he purposes to judge the inhabited earth in righteousness by a man whom he has appointed, and he has furnished a guarantee to all men in that he has resurrected him from the dead."

32 Well, when they heard of a resurrection of the dead, some began to mock, while others said: "We will hear you about this even another time." 33 Thus Paul went out from their midst, but some men joined themselves to him and became believers, 34 among whom also were Di·o·nys′i·us, a judge of the court of the Ar·e·op′a·gus, and a woman named Dam′a·ris, and others besides them.

18 After these things he departed from Athens and came to Corinth. 2 And he found a certain Jew named Aq′ui·la, a native of Pontus who had recently come from Italy, and Pris·cil′la his wife, because of the fact that Claudius had ordered all the Jews to depart from Rome. So he went to them 3 and on account of being of the same trade he stayed at their home, and they worked, for they were tentmakers by trade. 4 However, he would give a talk in the synagogue every sabbath and would persuade Jews and Greeks.

5 When, now, both Silas and Timothy came down from Mac·e·do′ni·a, Paul began to be intensely occupied with the word, witnessing to the Jews to prove that Jesus is the Christ. 6 But after they kept on opposing and speaking abusively, he shook out his garments and said to them: "Let your blood be upon your own heads. I am clean. From now on I will go to people of the nations." 7 Accordingly he transferred from there and went into the house of a man named Titius

Justus, a worshiper of God, whose house was adjoining the synagogue. 8 But Crispus the presiding officer of the synagogue became a believer in the Lord, and so did all his household. And many of the Corinthians that heard began to believe and be baptized. 9 Moreover, by night the Lord said to Paul through a vision: "Have no fear, but keep on speaking and do not keep silent, 10 because I am with you and no man will assault you so as to do you injury; for I have many people in this city." 11 So he stayed set there a year and six months, teaching among them the word of God.

12 Now while Gal'li·o was proconsul of A·cha'ia, the Jews rose up with one accord against Paul and led him to the judgment seat, 13 saying: "Contrary to the law this person leads men to another persuasion in worshiping God." 14 But as Paul was going to open his mouth, Gal'li·o said to the Jews: "If it were, indeed, some wrong or a wicked act of villainy, O Jews, I would with reason put up patiently with you. 15 But if it is controversies over speech and names and the law among you, you yourselves must see to it. I do not wish to be a judge of these things." 16 With that he drove them away from the judgment seat. 17 So they all laid hold of Sos'the·nes the presiding officer of the synagogue and went to beating him in front of the judgment seat. But Gal'li·o would not concern himself at all with these things.

18 However, after staying quite some days longer, Paul said goodby to the brothers and proceeded to sail away for Syria, and with him Pris·cil'la and Aq'ui·la, as he had the hair of his head clipped short in Cen'chre·ae, for he had a vow. 19 So they arrived at Eph'e·sus, and he left them there; but he himself entered into the synagogue and reasoned with the Jews. 20 Although they kept requesting him to remain for a longer time, he would not consent 21 but said good-by and told them: "I will return to you again, if Je-

hovah is willing." And he put out to sea from Eph'e·sus 22 and came down to Caes·a·re'a. And he went up and greeted the congregation, and went down to Antioch.

23 And when he had passed some time there he departed and went from place to place through the country of Ga·la'ti·a and Phryg'i·a, strengthening all the disciples.

24 Now a certain Jew named A·pol'los, a native of Alexandria, an eloquent man, arrived in Eph'e·sus; and he was well versed in the Scriptures. 25 This [man] had been orally instructed in the way of Jehovah and, as he was aglow with the spirit, he went speaking and teaching with correctness the things about Jesus, but being acquainted with only the baptism of John. 26 And this [man] started to speak boldly in the synagogue. When Pris·cil'la and Aq'ui·la heard him, they took him into their company and expounded the way of God more correctly to him. 27 Further, because he was desiring to go across into A·cha'ia, the brothers wrote the disciples, exhorting them to receive him kindly. So when he got there, he greatly helped those who had believed on account of God's undeserved kindness; 28 for with intensity he thoroughly proved the Jews to be wrong publicly, while he demonstrated by the Scriptures that Jesus was the Christ.

19 In the course of events, while A·pol'los was in Corinth, Paul went through the inland parts and came down to Eph'e·sus, and found some disciples; 2 and he said to them: "Did you receive holy spirit when you became believers?" They said to him: "Why, we have never heard whether there is a holy spirit." 3 And he said: "In what, then, were you baptized?" They said: "In John's baptism." 4 Paul said: "John baptized with the baptism [in symbol] of repentance, telling the people to believe in the one coming after him, that is, in Jesus." 5 On hearing this, they got baptized in the name of the Lord Jesus. 6 And when Paul

laid his hands upon them, the holy spirit came upon them, and they began speaking with tongues and prophesying. 7 All together, there were about twelve men.

8 Entering into the synagogue, he spoke with boldness for three months, giving talks and using persuasion concerning the kingdom of God. 9 But when some went on hardening themselves and not believing, speaking injuriously about The Way before the multitude, he withdrew from them and separated the disciples from them, daily giving talks in the school [auditorium] of Ty·ran′nus. 10 This took place for two years, so that all those inhabiting the [district of] Asia heard the word of the Lord, both Jews and Greeks.

11 And God kept performing extraordinary works of power through the hands of Paul, 12 so that even cloths and aprons were borne from his body to the ailing people, and the diseases left them, and the wicked spirits came out. 13 But certain ones of the roving Jews who practiced the casting out of demons also undertook to name the name of the Lord Jesus over those having the wicked spirits, saying: "I solemnly charge you by Jesus whom Paul preaches." 14 Now there were seven sons of a certain Sce′va, a Jewish chief priest, doing this. 15 But in answer the wicked spirit said to them: "I know Jesus and I am acquainted with Paul; but who are you?" 16 With that the man in whom the wicked spirit was leaped upon them, got the mastery of one after the other, and prevailed against them, so that they fled naked and wounded out of that house. 17 This became known to all, both the Jews and the Greeks that dwelt in Eph′e·sus; and a fear fell upon them all, and the name of the Lord Jesus went on being magnified. 18 And many of those who had become believers would come and confess and report their practices openly. 19 Indeed, quite a number of those who practiced magical arts brought their books together and burned them up before everybody. And they calculated together the prices of them and found them worth fifty thousand pieces of silver. 20 Thus in a mighty way the word of Jehovah kept growing and prevailing.

21 Now when these things had been completed, Paul purposed in his spirit that, after going through Mac·e·do′ni·a and A·cha′ia, he would journey to Jerusalem, saying: "After I get there I must also see Rome." 22 So he dispatched to Mac·e·do′ni·a two of those who ministered to him, Timothy and E·ras′tus, but he himself delayed for some time in the [district of] Asia.

23 At that particular time there arose no little disturbance concerning The Way. 24 For a certain man named De·me′tri·us, a silversmith, by making silver shrines of Ar′te·mis furnished the craftsmen no little gain; 25 and he gathered them and those who worked at such things and said: "Men, you well know that from this business we have our prosperity. 26 Also, you behold and hear how not only in Eph′e·sus but in nearly all the [district of] Asia this Paul has persuaded a considerable crowd and turned them to another opinion, saying that the ones that are made by hands are not gods. 27 Moreover, the danger exists not only that this occupation of ours will come into disrepute but also that the temple of the great goddess Ar′te·mis will be esteemed as nothing and even her magnificence which the whole [district of] Asia and the inhabited earth worships is about to be brought down to nothing." 28 Hearing this and becoming full of anger, the men began crying out, saying: "Great is Ar′te·mis of the E·phe′sians!"

29 So the city became filled with confusion, and with one accord they rushed into the theater, taking forcibly along with them Ga′ius and Ar·is·tar′chus, Mac·e·do′ni·ans, traveling companions of Paul. 30 For his part, Paul was willing to go inside to the people, but the disciples would not permit him.

31 Even some of the commissioners of festivals and games, who were friendly to him, sent to him and began pleading for him not to risk himself in the theater. 32 The fact is, some were crying out one thing and others another; for the assembly was in confusion, and the majority of them did not know the reason why they had come together. 33 So together they brought Alexander out of the crowd, the Jews thrusting him up front; and Alexander motioned with his hand and was wanting to make his defense to the people. 34 But when they recognized that he was a Jew, one cry arose from them all as they shouted for about two hours: "Great is Ar'te·mis of the E·phe'-sians!"

35 When, finally, the city recorder had quieted the crowd, he said: "Men of Eph'e·sus, who really is there of mankind that does not know that the city of the E·phe'-sians is the temple keeper of the great Ar'te·mis and of the image that fell from heaven? 36 Therefore since these things are indisputable, it is becoming for you to keep calm and not act rashly. 37 For you have brought these men who are neither robbers of temples nor blasphemers of our goddess. 38 Therefore if De·me'-tri·us and the craftsmen with him do have a case against someone, court days are held and there are proconsuls; let them bring charges against one another. 39 If, though, you are searching for anything beyond that, it must be decided in a regular assembly. 40 For we are really in danger of being charged with sedition over today's affair, no single cause existing that will permit us to render a reason for this disorderly mob." 41 And when he had said these things, he dismissed the assembly.

20 Now after the uproar had subsided, Paul sent for the disciples, and when he had encouraged them and bidden them farewell, he went forth to journey into Mac·e·do'ni·a. 2 After going through those parts and encourag-ing the ones there with many a word, he came into Greece. 3 And when he had spent three months there, because a plot was hatched against him by the Jews as he was about to set sail for Syria, he made up his mind to return through Mac·e·do'ni·a. 4 There were accompanying him Sop'a·ter the son of Pyr'rhus of Be·roe'a, Ar·is·tar'-chus and Se·cun'dus of the Thessa·lo'ni·ans, and Ga'ius of Der'be, and Timothy, and from the [district of] Asia Tych'i·cus and Troph'i·mus. 5 These went on and were waiting for us in Tro'as; 6 but we put out to sea from Phi·lip'pi after the days of the unfermented cakes, and we came to them in Tro'as within five days; and there we spent seven days.

7 On the first day of the week, when we were gathered together to have a meal, Paul began discoursing to them, as he was going to depart the next day; and he prolonged his speech until midnight. 8 So there were quite a few lamps in the upper chamber where we were gathered together. 9 Seated at the window, a certain young man named Eu'ty·chus fell into a deep sleep while Paul kept talking on, and, collapsing in sleep, he fell down from the third story and was picked up dead. 10 But Paul went downstairs, threw himself upon him and embraced him and said: "Stop raising a clamor, for his soul is in him." 11 He now went upstairs and began the meal and took food, and after conversing for quite a while, until daybreak, he at length departed. 12 So they took the boy away alive and were comforted beyond measure.

13 We now went ahead to the boat and set sail to As'sos, where we were intending to take Paul aboard, for, after giving instructions to this effect, he himself was intending to go on foot. 14 So when he caught up with us in As'sos, we took him aboard and went to Mit-y·le'ne; 15 and, sailing away from there the succeeding day, we arrived opposite Chi'os, but the next day we touched at Sa'mos, and on

the following day we arrived at Mi·le′tus. 16 For Paul had decided to sail past Eph′e·sus, in order that he might not spend any time in the [district of] Asia; for he was hastening to get to Jerusalem on the day of the [festival of] Pentecost if he possibly could.

17 However, from Mi·le′tus he sent to Eph′e·sus and called for the older men of the congregation. 18 When they got to him he said to them: "You well know how from the first day that I stepped into the [district of] Asia I was with you the whole time, 19 slaving for the Lord with the greatest lowliness of mind and tears and trials that befell me by the plots of the Jews; 20 while I did not hold back from telling you any of the things that were profitable nor from teaching you publicly and from house to house. 21 But I thoroughly bore witness both to Jews and to Greeks about repentance toward God and faith in our Lord Jesus. 22 And now, look! bound in the spirit, I am journeying to Jerusalem, although not knowing the things that will happen to me in it, 23 except that from city to city the holy spirit repeatedly bears witness to me as it says that bonds and tribulations are waiting for me. 24 Nevertheless, I do not make my soul of any account as dear to me, if only I may finish my course and the ministry that I received of the Lord Jesus, to bear thorough witness to the good news of the undeserved kindness of God.

25 "And now, look! I know that all of you among whom I went preaching the kingdom will see my face no more. 26 Hence I call you to witness this very day that I am clean from the blood of all men, 27 for I have not held back from telling you all the counsel of God. 28 Pay attention to yourselves and to all the flock, among which the holy spirit has appointed you overseers, to shepherd the congregation of God, which he purchased with the blood of his own [Son]. 29 I know that after my going away oppressive wolves will enter in among you and will not treat the flock with tenderness, 30 and from among you yourselves men will rise and speak twisted things to draw away the disciples after themselves.

31 "Therefore keep awake, and bear in mind that for three years, night and day, I did not quit admonishing each one with tears. 32 And now I commit you to God and to the word of his undeserved kindness, which [word] can build you up and give you the inheritance among all the sanctified ones. 33 I have coveted no man's silver or gold or apparel. 34 You yourselves know that these hands have attended to the needs of me and of those with me. 35 I have exhibited to you in all things that by thus laboring you must assist those who are weak, and must bear in mind the words of the Lord Jesus, when he himself said, 'There is more happiness in giving than there is in receiving.'"

36 And when he had said these things, he kneeled down with all of them and prayed. 37 Indeed, quite a bit of weeping broke out among them all, and they fell upon Paul's neck and tenderly kissed him, 38 because they were especially pained at the word he had spoken that they were going to behold his face no more. So they proceeded to conduct him to the boat.

21 Now when we had torn ourselves away from them and put out to sea, we ran with a straight course and came to Cos, but on the next [day] to Rhodes, and from there to Pat′a·ra. 2 And when we had found a boat that was crossing to Phoe·ni′cia, we went aboard and sailed away. 3 After coming in sight of the island of Cy′prus we left it behind on the left side and sailed on to Syria, and landed at Tyre, for there the boat was to unload [its] cargo. 4 By a search we found the disciples and remained here seven days. But through the spirit they repeatedly told Paul not to set foot in Jerusalem. 5 So when we had

completed the days, we went forth and started on our way; but they all, together with the women and children, conducted us as far as outside the city. And kneeling down on the beach we had prayer 6 and said good-by to one another, and we went up into the boat but they returned to their homes.

7 We then completed the voyage from Tyre and arrived at Ptol·e·ma'is, and we greeted the brothers and stayed one day with them. 8 The next day we set out and arrived in Caes·a·re'a, and we entered into the house of Philip the evangelizer, who was one of the seven men, and we stayed with him. 9 This man had four daughters, virgins, that prophesied. 10 But while we were remaining quite a number of days, a certain prophet named Ag'a·bus came down from Ju·de'a, 11 and he came to us and took up the girdle of Paul, bound his own feet and hands and said: "Thus says the holy spirit, 'The man to whom this girdle belongs the Jews will bind in this manner in Jerusalem and deliver into the hands of people of the nations.' " 12 Now when we heard this, both we and those of that place began entreating him not to go up to Jerusalem. 13 Then Paul answered: "What are you doing by weeping and making me weak at heart? Rest assured, I am ready not only to be bound but also to die at Jerusalem for the name of the Lord Jesus." 14 When he would not be dissuaded, we acquiesced with the words: "Let the will of Jehovah take place."

15 Now after these days we prepared for the journey and began going up to Jerusalem. 16 But some of the disciples from Caes·a·re'a also went with us, to bring us to the man at whose home we were to be entertained, a certain Mna'son of Cy'prus, an early disciple. 17 When we got into Jerusalem, the brothers received us gladly. 18 But on the following [day] Paul went in with us to James; and all the older men were present. 19 And he greeted them and began

giving in detail an account of the things God did among the nations through his ministry.

20 After hearing this they began to glorify God, and they said to him: "You behold, brother, how many thousands of believers there are among the Jews; and they are all zealous for the Law. 21 But they have heard it rumored about you that you have been teaching all the Jews among the nations an apostasy from Moses, telling them neither to circumcise their children nor to walk in the [solemn] customs. 22 What, then, is to be done about it? In any case they are going to hear you have arrived. 23 Therefore do this which we tell you: We have four men with a vow upon themselves. 24 Take these men along and cleanse yourself ceremonially with them and take care of their expenses, that they may have their heads shaved. And so everybody will know that there is nothing to the rumors they were told about you, but that you are walking orderly, you yourself also keeping the Law. 25 As for the believers from among the nations, we have sent out, rendering our decision that they should keep themselves from what is sacrificed to idols as well as from blood and what is strangled and from fornication."

26 Then Paul took the men along the next day and cleansed himself ceremonially with them and went into the temple, to give notice of the days to be fulfilled for the ceremonial cleansing, until the offering should be presented for each one of them.

27 Now when the seven days were about to be concluded, the Jews from Asia on beholding him in the temple began to throw all the crowd into confusion, and they laid their hands upon him, 28 crying out: "Men of Israel, help! This is the man that teaches everybody everywhere against the people and the Law and this place and, what is more, he even brought Greeks into the temple and has defiled this holy place." 29 For they had pre-

viously seen Troph'i·mus the E·phe'sian in the city with him, but they were imagining Paul had brought him into the temple. 30 And the whole city was set in an uproar, and a running together of the people occurred; and they laid hold of Paul and dragged him outside the temple. And immediately the doors were closed. 31 And while they were seeking to kill him, information came up to the commander of the band that all Jerusalem was in confusion; 32 and he at once took soldiers and army officers and ran down to them. When they caught sight of the military commander and the soldiers, they quit beating Paul.

33 Then the military commander came near and took hold of him and gave command for him to be bound with two chains; and he proceeded to inquire who he might be and what he had done. 34 But some in the crowd began shouting out one thing, and others another. So, being unable himself to learn anything certain because of the tumult, he commanded him to be brought to the soldiers' quarters. 35 But when he got upon the stairs, the situation became such that he was being carried along by the soldiers because of the violence of the crowd; 36 for the multitude of the people kept following, crying out: "Take him away!"

37 And as he was about to be led into the soldiers' quarters, Paul said to the military commander: "Am I allowed to say something to you?" He said: "Can you speak Greek? 38 Are you not really the Egyptian who before these days stirred up a sedition and led the four thousand dagger men out into the wilderness?" 39 Then Paul said: "I am, in fact, a Jew, of Tarsus in Ci·li'cia, a citizen of no obscure city. So I beg you, permit me to speak to the people." 40 After he gave permission, Paul, standing on the stairs, motioned with his hand to the people. When a great silence fell, he addressed them in the Hebrew language, saying:

22 "Men, brothers and fathers, hear my defense to you now." 2 (Well, when they heard he was addressing them in the Hebrew language, they kept all the more silent, and he said:) 3 "I am a Jew, born in Tarsus of Ci·li'cia, but educated in this city at the feet of Ga·ma'li·el, instructed according to the strictness of the ancestral Law, being zealous for God just as all of you are this day. 4 And I persecuted this Way to the death, binding and handing over to prisons both men and women, 5 as both the high priest and all the assembly of older men can bear me witness. From them I also procured letters to the brothers in Damascus, and I was on my way to bring also those who were there bound to Jerusalem to be punished.

6 "But as I was journeying and drawing close to Damascus, about midday, suddenly out of heaven a great light flashed all around me, 7 and I fell to the ground and heard a voice say to me, 'Saul, Saul, why are you persecuting me?' 8 I answered, 'Who are you, Lord?' And he said to me, 'I am Jesus the Naz·a·rene', whom you are persecuting.' 9 Now the men that were with me beheld, indeed, the light but did not hear the voice of the one speaking to me. 10 At that I said, 'What shall I do, Lord?' The Lord said to me, 'Rise, go your way into Damascus, and there you will be told about everything it is appointed for you to do.' 11 But as I could not see anything for the glory of that light, I arrived in Damascus, being led by the hand of those who were with me.

12 "Now An·a·ni'as, a certain man reverent according to the Law, well reported on by all the Jews dwelling there, 13 came to me and, standing by me, he said to me, 'Saul, brother, have your sight again!' And I looked up at him that very hour. 14 He said, 'The God of our forefathers has chosen you to come to know his will and to see the righteous One and to hear the voice of his mouth, 15 because

you are to be a witness for him to all men of things you have seen and heard. 16 And now why are you delaying? Rise, get baptized and wash your sins away by your calling upon his name.'

17 "But when I had returned to Jerusalem and was praying in the temple, I fell into a trance 18 and saw him saying to me, 'Hurry up and get out of Jerusalem quickly, because they will not agree to your witness concerning me.' 19 And I said, 'Lord, they themselves well know that I used to imprison and flog in one synagogue after another those believing upon you; 20 and when the blood of Stephen your witness was being spilled, I myself was also standing by and approving and guarding the outer garments of those doing away with him.' 21 And yet he said to me, 'Get on your way, because I shall send you out to nations far off.' "

22 Now they kept listening to him down to this word, and they raised their voices, saying: "Take such a [man] away from the earth, for he was not fit to live!" 23 And because they were crying out and throwing their outer garments about and tossing dust into the air, 24 the military commander ordered him to be brought into the soldiers' quarters and said he should be examined under scourging, that he might know fully for what cause they were shouting against him this way. 25 But when they had stretched him out for the whipping, Paul said to the army officer standing there: "Is it lawful for you men to scourge a man that is a Roman and uncondemned?" 26 Well, when the army officer heard this, he went to the military commander and made report, saying: "What are you intending to do? Why, this man is a Roman." 27 So the military commander approached and said to him: "Tell me, Are you a Roman?" He said: "Yes." 28 The military commander responded: "I purchased these rights as a citizen for a large sum [of money]." Paul said: "But I was even born [in them]."

29 Immediately, therefore, the men that were about to examine him with torture withdrew from him; and the military commander became afraid on ascertaining that he was a Roman and that he had bound him.

30 So, the next day, as he desired to know for sure just why he was being accused by the Jews, he let him loose and commanded the chief priests and all the San'-he·drin to assemble. And he brought Paul down and stood him among them.

23 Looking intently at the San'-he·drin Paul said: "Men, brothers, I have behaved before God with a perfectly clear conscience down to this day." 2 At this the high priest An·a·ni'as ordered those standing by him to strike him on the mouth. 3 Then Paul said to him: "God is going to strike you, you whitewashed wall. Do you at one and the same time sit to judge me in accord with the Law and, transgressing the Law, command me to be struck?" 4 Those standing by said: "Are you reviling the high priest of God?" 5 And Paul said: "Brothers, I did not know he was high priest. For it is written, 'You must not speak injuriously of a ruler of your people.' "

6 Now when Paul took note that the one part was of Sadducees but the other of Pharisees, he proceeded to cry out in the San'he-drin: "Men, brothers, I am a Pharisee, a son of Pharisees. Over the hope of resurrection of the dead I am being judged." 7 Because he said this, a dissension arose between the Pharisees and Sadducees, and the multitude was split. 8 For Sadducees say there is neither resurrection nor angel nor spirit, but the Pharisees publicly declare them all. 9 So there broke out a loud screaming, and some of the scribes of the party of the Pharisees rose and began contending fiercely, saying: "We find nothing wrong in this man; but if a spirit or an angel spoke to him,—." 10 Now when the dissension grew great, the military commander became

afraid that Paul would be pulled to pieces by them, and he commanded the force of soldiers to go down and snatch him from their midst and bring him into the soldiers' quarters.

11 But the following night the Lord stood by him and said: "Be of good courage! For as you have been giving a thorough witness on the things about me in Jerusalem, so you must also bear witness in Rome."

12 Now when it became day, the Jews formed a conspiracy and bound themselves with a curse, saying they would neither eat nor drink until they had killed Paul. 13 There were more than forty men that formed this oathbound conspiracy; 14 and they went to the chief priests and the older men and said: "We have solemnly bound ourselves with a curse not to take a bite of food until we have killed Paul. 15 Now, therefore, you together with the San'he·drin make it clear to the military commander why he should bring him down to you as though you intended to determine more accurately the matters involving him. But before he gets near we will be ready to do away with him."

16 However, the son of Paul's sister heard of their lying in wait, and he came and entered into the soldiers' quarters and reported it to Paul. 17 So Paul called one of the army officers to him and said: "Lead this young man off to the military commander, for he has something to report to him." 18 Therefore this man took him and led him to the military commander and said: "The prisoner Paul called me to him and requested me to lead this young man to you, as he has something to tell you." 19 The military commander took him by the hand and withdrew and began inquiring privately: "What is it you have to report to me?" 20 He said: "The Jews have agreed to request you to bring Paul down to the San'he·drin tomorrow as though intending to learn something more accurate about him.

21 Above all things, do not let them persuade you, for more than forty men of theirs are lying in wait for him, and they have bound themselves with a curse neither to eat nor to drink until they have done away with him; and they are now ready, waiting for the promise from you." 22 Therefore the military commander let the young man go after ordering him: "Do not blab to anyone that you have made these things clear to me."

23 And he summoned a certain two of the army officers and said: "Get two hundred soldiers ready to march clear to Caes·a·re'a, also seventy horsemen and two hundred spearmen, at the third hour of the night. 24 Also, provide beasts of burden that they may have Paul ride and convey him safely to Felix the governor." 25 And he wrote a letter having this form:

26 "Claudius Lys'i·as to his excellency, Governor Felix: Greetings! 27 This man was seized by the Jews and was about to be done away with by them, but I came suddenly with a force of soldiers and rescued him, because I learned he was a Roman. 28 And wishing to ascertain the cause for which they were accusing him, I brought him down into their San'he·drin. 29 I found him to be accused about questions of their Law, but not charged with a single thing deserving of death or bonds. 30 But because a plot that is to be laid against the man has been disclosed to me, I am at once sending him to you, and commanding the accusers to speak against him before you."

31 Therefore these soldiers took Paul according to their orders and brought him by night to An·tip'a·tris. 32 The next day they permitted the horsemen to go on with him, and they returned to the soldiers' quarters. 33 The [horsemen] entered into Caes·a·re'a and delivered the letter to the governor and also presented Paul to him. 34 So he read it and inquired from what province he was, and ascer-

tained that he was from Ci·li′cia. 35 "I shall give you a thorough hearing," he said, "when your accusers arrive also." And he commanded that he be kept under guard in the prae·to′ri·an palace of Herod.

24 Five days later the high priest An·a·ni′as came down with some older men and a public speaker, a certain Ter·tul′lus, and they gave information to the governor against Paul. 2 When he was called, Ter·tul′lus started accusing him, saying:

"Seeing that we enjoy great peace through you and that reforms are taking place in this nation through your forethought, 3 at all times and also in all places we receive it, Your Excellency Felix, with the greatest thankfulness. 4 But that I may not hinder you any further, I beseech you to hear us briefly in your kindliness. 5 For we have found this man a pestilent fellow and stirring up seditions among all the Jews throughout the inhabited earth and a spearhead of the sect of the Naz·a·renes′, 6 one who also tried to profane the temple and whom we seized. 7 —— 8 From him you yourself can by examination find out about all these things of which we are accusing him."

9 With that the Jews also joined in the attack, asserting that these things were so. 10 And Paul, when the governor nodded to him to speak, answered:

"Knowing well that this nation has had you as judge for many years, I readily speak in my defense the things about myself, 11 as you are in a position to find out that for me it has not been more than twelve days since I went up to worship in Jerusalem; 12 and they found me neither in the temple arguing with anyone nor causing a mob to rush together, either in the synagogues or throughout the city. 13 Nor can they prove to you the things of which they are accusing me right now. 14 But I do admit this to you, that, according to the way that they call a 'sect,' in this manner I am rendering sacred

service to the God of my forefathers, as I believe all the things set forth in the Law and written in the Prophets; 15 and I have hope toward God, which hope these [men] themselves also entertain, that there is going to be a resurrection of both the righteous and the unrighteous. 16 In this respect, indeed, I am exercising myself continually to have a consciousness of committing no offense against God and men. 17 So after quite a number of years I arrived to bring gifts of mercy to my nation, and offerings. 18 While I was at these matters they found me ceremonially cleansed in the temple, but not with a crowd or with a tumult. But there were certain Jews from the [district of] Asia, 19 who ought to be present before you and to accuse me if they might have anything against me. 20 Or, let the [men] here say for themselves what wrong they found as I stood before the San′he·drin, 21 except with respect to this one utterance which I cried out while standing among them, 'Over the resurrection of the dead I am today being judged before YOU!'"

22 However, Felix, knowing quite accurately the matters concerning this Way, began to put the [men] off and said: "Whenever Lys′i·as the military commander comes down, I shall decide upon these matters involving YOU." 23 And he ordered the army officer that the man be kept and have some relaxation [of custody], and that he forbid no one of his people to wait upon him.

24 Some days later Felix arrived with Dru·sil′la his wife, who was a Jewess, and he sent for Paul and listened to him on the belief in Christ Jesus. 25 But as he talked about righteousness and self-control and the judgment to come, Felix became frightened and answered: "For the present go your way, but when I get an opportune time I shall send for you again." 26 At the same time, though, he was hoping for money to be given him by Paul. On that account he sent for

him even more frequently and would converse with him. 27 But, when two years had elapsed, Felix was succeeded by Porcius Festus; and because Felix desired to gain favor with the Jews, he left Paul bound.

25 Therefore Festus, after entering upon the [government of] the province, went up three days later to Jerusalem from Caes·a·re′a; 2 and the chief priests and the principal men of the Jews gave him information against Paul. So they began to entreat him, 3 asking for themselves as a favor against the [man] that he would send for him to come to Jerusalem, as they were laying an ambush to do away with him along the road. 4 However, Festus answered that Paul was to be kept in Caes·a·re′a and that he himself was about to depart shortly for there. 5 "Hence let those who are in power among you," he said, "come down with me and accuse him, if there is anything out of the way about the man."

6 So when he had spent not more than eight or ten days among them, he went down to Caes·a·re′a, and the next day he sat down on the judgment seat and commanded Paul to be brought in. 7 When he arrived, the Jews that had come down from Jerusalem stood round about him, leveling against him many and serious charges for which they were unable to show evidence.

8 But Paul said in defense: "Neither against the Law of the Jews nor against the temple nor against Caesar have I committed any sin." 9 Festus, desiring to gain favor with the Jews, said in reply to Paul: "Do you wish to go up to Jerusalem and be judged there before me concerning these things?" 10 But Paul said: "I am standing before the judgment seat of Caesar, where I ought to be judged. I have done no wrong to the Jews, as you also are finding out quite well. 11 If, on the one hand, I am really a wrongdoer and have committed anything deserving of death, I do not beg off from

dying; if, on the other hand, none of those things exists of which these [men] accuse me, no man can hand me over to them as a favor. I appeal to Caesar!" 12 Then Festus, after speaking with the assembly of counselors, replied: "To Caesar you have appealed; to Caesar you shall go."

13 Now when some days had passed, A·grip′pa the king and Ber·ni′ce arrived in Caes·a·re′a for a visit of courtesy to Festus. 14 So, as they were spending a number of days there, Festus laid before the king the matters respecting Paul, saying:

"There is a certain man left prisoner by Felix, 15 and when I was in Jerusalem the chief priests and the older men of the Jews brought information about him, asking a judgment of condemnation against him. 16 But I replied to them that it is not Roman procedure to hand any man over as a favor before the accused man meets his accusers face to face and gets a chance to speak in his defense concerning the complaint. 17 Therefore when they got together here, I made no delay, but the next day I sat down on the judgment seat and commanded the man to be brought in. 18 Taking the stand, the accusers produced no charge of the wicked things I had supposed concerning him. 19 They simply had certain disputes with him concerning their own worship of the deity and concerning a certain Jesus who was dead but who Paul kept asserting was alive. 20 So, being perplexed as to the dispute over these matters, I proceeded to ask if he would like to go to Jerusalem and there be judged concerning these matters. 21 But when Paul appealed to be kept for the decision by the August One, I commanded him to be kept until I should send him on up to Caesar."

22 Here A·grip′pa [said] to Festus: "I myself would also like to hear the man." "Tomorrow," he said, "you shall hear him." 23 Therefore, on the next day,

concerning you from Ju·de′a, nor has anyone of the brothers that has arrived reported or spoken anything wicked about you. 22 But we think it proper to hear from you what your thoughts are, for truly as regards this sect it is known to us that everywhere it is spoken against."

23 They now arranged for a day with him, and they came in greater numbers to him in his lodging place. And he explained the matter to them by bearing thorough witness concerning the kingdom of God and by using persuasion with them concerning Jesus from both the law of Moses and the Prophets, from morning till evening. 24 And some began to believe the things said; others would not believe. 25 So, because they were at disagreement with one another, they began to depart, while Paul made this one comment:

"The holy spirit aptly spoke through Isaiah the prophet to YOUR forefathers, 26 saying, 'Go to this people and say: "By hearing, YOU will hear but by no means understand; and, looking, YOU will look but by no means see. 27 For the heart of this people has grown unreceptive, and with their ears they have heard without response, and they have shut their eyes; that they should never see with their eyes and hear with their ears and understand with their heart and turn back, and I should heal them."' 28 Therefore let it be known to YOU that this, the means by which God saves, has been sent out to the nations; they will certainly listen to it." 29 ——

30 So he remained for an entire two years in his own hired house, and he would kindly receive all those who came in to him, 31 preaching the kingdom of God to them and teaching the things concerning the Lord Jesus Christ with the greatest freeness of speech, without hindrance.

TO THE
ROMANS

1 Paul, a slave of Jesus Christ and called to be an apostle, separated to God's good news, 2 which he promised aforetime through his prophets in the holy Scriptures, 3 concerning his Son, who sprang from the seed of David according to the flesh, 4 but who with power was declared God's Son according to the spirit of holiness by means of resurrection from the dead—yes, Jesus Christ our Lord, 5 through whom we received undeserved kindness and an apostleship in order that there might be obedience of faith among all the nations respecting his name, 6 among which [nations] YOU also are those called to belong to Jesus Christ— 7 to all those who are in Rome as God's beloved ones, called to be holy ones:

May YOU have undeserved kindness and peace from God our Father and [the] Lord Jesus Christ. 8 First of all, I give thanks to my God through Jesus Christ concerning all of YOU, because YOUR faith is talked about throughout the whole world. 9 For God, to whom I render sacred service with my spirit in connection with the good news about his Son, is my witness of how without ceasing I always make mention of YOU in my prayers, 10 begging that if at all possible I may now at last be prospered in the will of God so as to come to YOU. 11 For I am longing to see YOU, that I may impart some spiritual gift to YOU in order for YOU to be made firm; 12 or, rather, that there may be an interchange of encouragement among you, by each one through the other's faith, both YOURS and mine. 13 But I do not want YOU to fail to know, brothers, that I many times purposed to come to YOU, but I have been hindered until now, in order that I might acquire some fruitage also among YOU even as among the rest of the nations. 14 Both to Greeks and to Barbarians, both to wise and to senseless ones I am a debtor; 15 so there is eagerness on my part to declare the good news also to YOU there in Rome. 16 For I am not ashamed of the good news; it is, in fact, God's power for salvation to everyone having faith, to the Jew first and also to the Greek; 17 for in it God's righteousness is being revealed by reason of faith and toward faith, just as it is written: "But the righteous one— by means of faith he will live."

18 For God's wrath is being revealed from heaven against all ungodliness and unrighteousness of men who are suppressing the truth in an unrighteous way, 19 because what may be known about God is manifest among them, for God made it manifest to them. 20 For his invisible [qualities] are clearly seen from the world's creation onward, because they are perceived by the things made, even his eternal power and Godship, so that they are inexcusable; 21 because, although they knew God, they did not glorify him as God nor did they thank him, but they became empty-headed in their reasonings and their unintelligent heart became darkened. 22 Although asserting they were wise, they became foolish 23 and turned the glory of the incorruptible God into something like the image of corruptible man and of birds and four-footed creatures and creeping things.

24 Therefore God, in keeping with the desires of their hearts, gave them up to uncleanness, that their bodies might be dishonored among them, 25 even those who exchanged the truth of God for the lie and venerated and rendered sacred service to the creation rather than the One who created, who is blessed forever. Amen. 26 That is why God gave them up to disgraceful sexual appetites, for both their females changed the natural use of themselves into one contrary to nature; 27 and likewise even the males left the natural use of the female and became violently inflamed in their lust toward one another, males with males, working what is obscene and receiving in themselves the full recompense, which was due for their error.

28 And just as they did not approve of holding God in accurate knowledge, God gave them up to a disapproved mental state, to do the things not fitting, 29 filled as they were with all unrighteousness, wickedness, covetousness, badness, being full of envy, murder, strife, deceit, malicious disposition, being whisperers, 30 backbiters, haters of God, insolent, haughty, self-assuming, inventors of injurious things, disobedient to parents, 31 without understanding, false to agreements, having no natural affection, merciless. 32 Although these know full well the righteous decree of God, that those practicing such things are deserving of death, they not only keep on doing them but also consent with those practicing them.

2 Therefore you are inexcusable, O man, whoever you are, if you judge; for in the thing in which you judge another, you condemn yourself, inasmuch as you that judge practice the same things. 2 Now we know that the judgment of God is, in accord with truth, against those who practice such things.

3 But do you have this idea, O man, while you judge those who practice such things and yet you do them, that you will escape the judgment of God? 4 Or do you despise the riches of his kindness and forbearance and long-suffering, because you do not know that the kindly [quality] of God is trying to lead you to repentance? 5 But according to your hardness and unrepentant heart you are storing up

wrath for yourself on the day of wrath and of the revealing of God's righteous judgment. 6 And he will render to each one according to his works: 7 everlasting life to those who are seeking glory and honor and incorruptibleness by endurance in work that is good; 8 however, for those who are contentious and who disobey the truth but obey unrighteousness there will be wrath and anger, 9 tribulation and distress, upon the soul of every man who works what is injurious, of the Jew first and also of the Greek; 10 but glory and honor and peace for everyone who works what is good, for the Jew first and also for the Greek. 11 For there is no partiality with God.

12 For instance, all those who sinned without law will also perish without law; but all those who sinned under law will be judged by law. 13 For the hearers of law are not the ones righteous before God, but the doers of law will be declared righteous. 14 For whenever people of the nations that do not have law do by nature the things of the law, these people, although not having law, are a law to themselves. 15 They are the very ones who demonstrate the matter of the law to be written in their hearts, while their conscience is bearing witness with them and, between their own thoughts, they are being accused or even excused. 16 This will be in the day when God through Christ Jesus judges the secret things of mankind, according to the good news I declare.

17 If, now, you are a Jew in name and are resting upon law and taking pride in God, 18 and you know his will and approve of things that are excellent because you are orally instructed out of the Law; 19 and you are persuaded that you are a guide of the blind, a light for those in darkness, 20 a corrector of the unreasonable ones, a teacher of babes, and having the framework of the knowledge and of the truth in the Law— 21 do you, however, the one teaching someone else, not teach yourself? You, the one preaching "Do not steal," do you steal? 22 You, the one saying "Do not commit adultery," do you commit adultery? You, the one expressing abhorrence of the idols, do you rob temples? 23 You, who take pride in law, do you by your transgressing of the Law dishonor God? 24 For "the name of God is being blasphemed on account of you people among the nations"; just as it is written.

25 Circumcision is, in fact, of benefit only if you practice law; but if you are a transgressor of law, your circumcision has become uncircumcision. 26 If, therefore, an uncircumcised person keeps the righteous requirements of the Law, his uncircumcision will be counted as circumcision, will it not? 27 And the uncircumcised [person] that is such by nature will, by carrying out the Law, judge you who with its written code and circumcision are a transgressor of law. 28 For he is not a Jew who is one on the outside, nor is circumcision that which is on the outside upon the flesh. 29 But he is a Jew who is one on the inside, and [his] circumcision is that of the heart by spirit, and not by a written code. The praise of that one comes, not from men, but from God.

3 What, then, is the superiority of the Jew, or what is the benefit of the circumcision? 2 A great deal in every way. First of all, because they were entrusted with the sacred pronouncements of God. 3 What, then, [is the case]? If some did not express faith, will their lack of faith perhaps make the faithfulness of God without effect? 4 Never may that happen! But let God be found true, though every man be found a liar, even as it is written: "That you might be proved righteous in your words and might win when you are being judged." 5 However, if our unrighteousness brings God's righteousness to the fore, what shall we say? God is not unjust when he vents his wrath, is he? (I am speaking as a man does.) 6 Never

may that happen! How, otherwise, will God judge the world?

7 Yet if by reason of my lie the truth of God has been made more prominent to his glory, why am I also yet being judged as a sinner? 8 And [why] not [say], just as it is falsely charged to us and just as some men state that we say: "Let us do the bad things that the good things may come"? The judgment against those [men] is in harmony with justice.

9 What then? Are we in a better position? Not at all! For above we have made the charge that Jews as well as Greeks are all under sin; 10 just as it is written: "There is not a righteous [man], not even one; 11 there is no one that has any insight, there is no one that seeks for God. 12 All [men] have deflected, all of them together have become worthless; there is no one that does kindness, there is not so much as one." 13 "Their throat is an opened grave, they have used deceit with their tongues." "Poison of asps is behind their lips." 14 "And their mouth is full of cursing and bitter expression." 15 "Their feet are speedy to shed blood." 16 "Ruin and misery are in their ways, 17 and they have not known the way of peace." 18 "There is no fear of God before their eyes."

19 Now we know that all the things the Law says it addresses to those under the Law, so that every mouth may be stopped and all the world may become liable to God for punishment. 20 Therefore by works of law no flesh will be declared righteous before him, for by law is the accurate knowledge of sin.

21 But now apart from law God's righteousness has been made manifest, as it is borne witness to by the Law and the Prophets; 22 yes, God's righteousness through the faith in Jesus Christ, for all those having faith. For there is no distinction. 23 For all have sinned and fall short of the glory of God, 24 and it is as a free gift that they are being declared righteous by his undeserved kindness through the release by the ransom [paid] by Christ Jesus. 25 God set him forth as an offering for propitiation through faith in his blood. This was in order to exhibit his own righteousness, because he was forgiving the sins that occurred in the past while God was exercising forbearance; 26 so as to exhibit his own righteousness in this present season, that he might be righteous even when declaring righteous the man that has faith in Jesus.

27 Where, then, is the boasting? It is shut out. Through what law? That of works? No indeed, but through the law of faith. 28 For we reckon that a man is declared righteous by faith apart from works of law. 29 Or is he the God of the Jews only? Is he not also of people of the nations? Yes, of people of the nations also, 30 if truly God is one, who will declare circumcised people righteous as a result of faith and uncircumcised people righteous by means of their faith. 31 Do we, then, abolish law by means of our faith? Never may that happen! On the contrary, we establish law.

4 That being so, what shall we say about Abraham our forefather according to the flesh? 2 If, for instance, Abraham were declared righteous as a result of works, he would have ground for boasting; but not with God. 3 For what does the scripture say? "Abraham exercised faith in Jehovah, and it was counted to him as righteousness." 4 Now to the man that works the pay is counted, not as an undeserved kindness, but as a debt. 5 On the other hand, to the man that does not work but puts faith in him who declares the ungodly one righteous, his faith is counted as righteousness. 6 Just as David also speaks of the happiness of the man to whom God counts righteousness apart from works: 7 "Happy are those whose lawless deeds have been pardoned and whose sins have been covered; 8 happy is the man whose sin Je-

hovah will by no means take into account."

9 Does this happiness, then, come upon circumcised people or also upon uncircumcised people? For we say: "His faith was counted to Abraham as righteousness." 10 Under what circumstances, then, was it counted? When he was in circumcision or in uncircumcision? Not in circumcision, but in uncircumcision. 11 And he received a sign, namely, circumcision, as a seal of the righteousness by the faith he had while in his uncircumcised state, that he might be the father of all those having faith while in uncircumcision, in order for righteousness to be counted to them; 12 and a father of circumcised offspring, not only to those who adhere to circumcision, but also to those who walk orderly in the footsteps of that faith while in the uncircumcised state which our father Abraham had.

13 For it was not through law that Abraham or his seed had the promise that he should be heir of a world, but it was through the righteousness by faith. 14 For if those who adhere to law are heirs, faith has been made useless and the promise has been abolished. 15 In reality the Law produces wrath, but where there is no law, neither is there any transgression.

16 On this account it was as a result of faith, that it might be according to undeserved kindness, in order for the promise to be sure to all his seed, not only to that which adheres to the Law, but also to that which adheres to the faith of Abraham. (He is the father of us all, 17 just as it is written: "I have appointed you a father of many nations.") This was in the sight of the One in whom he had faith, even of God, who makes the dead alive and calls the things that are not as though they were. 18 Although beyond hope, yet based on hope he had faith, that he might become the father of many nations in accord with what had been said: "So your seed will be."

19 And, although he did not grow weak in faith, he considered his own body, now already deadened, as he was about one hundred years old, also the deadness of the womb of Sarah. 20 But because of the promise of God he did not waver in a lack of faith, but became powerful by his faith, giving God glory 21 and being fully convinced that what he had promised he was also able to do. 22 Hence "it was counted to him as righteousness."

23 That "it was counted to him" was written, however, not for his sake only, 24 but also for the sake of us to whom it is destined to be counted, because we believe on him who raised Jesus our Lord up from the dead. 25 He was delivered up for the sake of our trespasses and was raised up for the sake of declaring us righteous.

5 Therefore, now that we have been declared righteous as a result of faith, let us enjoy peace with God through our Lord Jesus Christ, 2 through whom also we have gained our approach by faith into this undeserved kindness in which we now stand; and let us exult, based on hope of the glory of God. 3 And not only that, but let us exult while in tribulations, since we know that tribulation produces endurance; 4 endurance, in turn, an approved condition; the approved condition, in turn, hope, 5 and the hope does not lead to disappointment; because the love of God has been poured out into our hearts through the holy spirit, which was given us.

6 For, indeed, Christ, while we were yet weak, died for ungodly men at the appointed time. 7 For hardly will anyone die for a righteous [man]; indeed, for the good [man], perhaps, someone even dares to die. 8 But God recommends his own love to us in that, while we were yet sinners, Christ died for us. 9 Much more, therefore, since we have been declared righteous now by his blood, shall we be saved through him from wrath. 10 For if, when we were enemies, we be-

came reconciled to God through the death of his Son, much more, now that we have become reconciled, we shall be saved by his life. 11 And not only that, but we are also exulting in God through our Lord Jesus Christ, through whom we have now received the reconciliation.

12 That is why, just as through one man sin entered into the world and death through sin, and thus death spread to all men because they had all sinned—. 13 For until the Law sin was in the world, but sin is not charged against anyone when there is no law. 14 Nevertheless, death ruled as king from Adam down to Moses, even over those who had not sinned after the likeness of the transgression by Adam, who bears a resemblance to him that was to come.

15 But it is not with the gift as it was with the trespass. For if by one man's trespass many died, the undeserved kindness of God and his free gift with the undeserved kindness by the one man Jesus Christ abounded much more to many. 16 Also, it is not with the free gift as it was with the way things worked through the one [man] that sinned. For the judgment resulted from one trespass in condemnation, but the gift resulted from many trespasses in a declaration of righteousness. 17 For if by the trespass of the one [man] death ruled as king through that one, much more will those who receive the abundance of the undeserved kindness and of the free gift of righteousness rule as kings in life through the one [person], Jesus Christ.

18 So, then, as through one trespass the result to men of all sorts was condemnation, likewise also through one act of justification the result to men of all sorts is a declaring of them righteous for life. 19 For just as through the disobedience of the one man many were constituted sinners, likewise also through the obedience of the one [person] many will be constituted righteous. 20 Now the Law

came in beside in order that trespassing might abound. But where sin abounded, undeserved kindness abounded still more. 21 To what end? That, just as sin ruled as king with death, likewise also undeserved kindness might rule as king through righteousness with everlasting life in view through Jesus Christ our Lord.

6 Consequently, what shall we say? Shall we continue in sin, that undeserved kindness may abound? 2 Never may that happen! Seeing that we died with reference to sin, how shall we keep on living any longer in it? 3 Or do you not know that all of us who were baptized into Christ Jesus were baptized into his death? 4 Therefore we were buried with him through our baptism into his death, in order that, just as Christ was raised up from the dead through the glory of the Father, we also should likewise walk in a newness of life. 5 For if we have become united with him in the likeness of his death, we shall certainly also be [united with him in the likeness] of his resurrection; 6 because we know that our old personality was impaled with [him], that our sinful body might be made inactive, that we should no longer go on being slaves to sin. 7 For he who has died has been acquitted from [his] sin.

8 Moreover, if we have died with Christ, we believe that we shall also live with him. 9 For we know that Christ, now that he has been raised up from the dead, dies no more; death is master over him no more. 10 For [the death] that he died, he died with reference to sin once for all time; but [the life] that he lives, he lives with reference to God. 11 Likewise also you: reckon yourselves to be dead indeed with reference to sin but living with reference to God by Christ Jesus.

12 Therefore do not let sin continue to rule as king in your mortal bodies that you should obey their desires. 13 Neither go on presenting your members to sin as

weapons of unrighteousness, but present yourselves to God as those alive from the dead, also YOUR members to God as weapons of righteousness. 14 For sin must not be master over YOU, seeing that YOU are not under law but under undeserved kindness.

15 What follows? Shall we commit a sin because we are not under law but under undeserved kindness? Never may that happen! 16 Do YOU not know that if YOU keep presenting yourselves to anyone as slaves to obey him, YOU are slaves of him because YOU obey him, either of sin with death in view or of obedience with righteousness in view? 17 But thanks to God that YOU were the slaves of sin but YOU became obedient from the heart to that form of teaching to which YOU were handed over. 18 Yes, since YOU were set free from sin, YOU became slaves to righteousness. 19 I am speaking in human terms because of the weakness of YOUR flesh: for even as YOU presented YOUR members as slaves to uncleanness and lawlessness with lawlessness in view, so now present YOUR members as slaves to righteousness with holiness in view. 20 For when YOU were slaves of sin, YOU were free as to righteousness.

21 What, then, was the fruit that YOU used to have at that time? Things of which YOU are now ashamed. For the end of those things is death. 22 However, now, because YOU were set free from sin but became slaves to God, YOU are having YOUR fruit in the way of holiness, and the end everlasting life. 23 For the wages sin pays is death, but the gift God gives is everlasting life by Christ Jesus our Lord.

7 Can it be that YOU do not know, brothers, (for I am speaking to those who know law,) that the Law is master over a man as long as he lives? 2 For instance, a married woman is bound by law to her husband while he is alive; but if her husband dies, she is discharged from the law of her husband.

3 So, then, while her husband is living, she would be styled an adulteress if she became another man's. But if her husband dies, she is free from his law, so that she is not an adulteress if she becomes another man's.

4 So, my brothers, YOU also were made dead to the Law through the body of the Christ, that YOU might become another's, the one's who was raised up from the dead, that we should bear fruit to God. 5 For when we were in accord with the flesh, the sinful passions that were excited by the Law were at work in our members that we should bring forth fruit to death. 6 But now we have been discharged from the Law, because we have died to that by which we were being held fast, that we might be slaves in a new sense by the spirit, and not in the old sense by the written code.

7 What, then, shall we say? Is the Law sin? Never may that become so! Really I would not have come to know sin if it had not been for the Law; and, for example, I would not have known covetousness if the Law had not said: "You must not covet." 8 But sin, receiving an inducement through the commandment, worked out in me covetousness of every sort, for apart from law sin was dead. 9 In fact, I was once alive apart from law; but when the commandment arrived, sin came to life again, but I died. 10 And the commandment which was to life, this I found to be to death. 11 For sin, receiving an inducement through the commandment, seduced me and killed me through it. 12 Wherefore, on its part, the Law is holy, and the commandment is holy and righteous and good.

13 Did, then, what is good become death to me? Never may that happen! But sin did, that it might be shown as sin working out death for me through that which is good; that sin might become far more sinful through the commandment. 14 For we know that the Law is spiritual; but I am fleshly, sold

under sin. 15 For what I am working out I do not know. For what I wish, this I do not practice; but what I hate is what I do. 16 However, if what I do not wish is what I do, I agree that the Law is fine. 17 But now the one working it out is no longer I, but sin that resides in me. 18 For I know that in me, that is, in my flesh, there dwells nothing good; for ability to wish is present with me, but ability to work out what is fine is not [present]. 19 For the good that I wish I do not do, but the bad that I do not wish is what I practice. 20 If, now, what I do not wish is what I do, the one working it out is no longer I, but the sin dwelling in me.

21 I find, then, this law in my case: that when I wish to do what is right, what is bad is present with me. 22 I really delight in the law of God according to the man I am within, 23 but I behold in my members another law warring against the law of my mind and leading me captive to sin's law that is in my members. 24 Miserable man that I am! Who will rescue me from the body undergoing this death? 25 Thanks to God through Jesus Christ our Lord! So, then, with [my] mind I myself am a slave to God's law, but with [my] flesh to sin's law.

8 Therefore those in union with Christ Jesus have no condemnation. 2 For the law of that spirit which gives life in union with Christ Jesus has set you free from the law of sin and of death. 3 For, there being an incapability on the part of the Law, while it was weak through the flesh, God, by sending his own Son in the likeness of sinful flesh and concerning sin, condemned sin in the flesh, 4 that the righteous requirement of the Law might be fulfilled in us who walk, not in accord with the flesh, but in accord with the spirit. 5 For those who are in accord with the flesh set their minds on the things of the flesh, but those in accord with the spirit on the things of the spirit. 6 For

the minding of the flesh means death, but the minding of the spirit means life and peace; 7 because the minding of the flesh means enmity with God, for it is not under subjection to the law of God, nor, in fact, can it be. 8 So those who are in harmony with the flesh cannot please God.

9 However, you are in harmony, not with the flesh, but with the spirit, if God's spirit truly dwells in you. But if anyone does not have Christ's spirit, this one does not belong to him. 10 But if Christ is in union with you, the body indeed is dead on account of sin, but the spirit is life on account of righteousness. 11 If, now, the spirit of him that raised up Jesus from the dead dwells in you, he that raised up Christ Jesus from the dead will also make your mortal bodies alive through his spirit that resides in you.

12 So, then, brothers, we are under obligation, not to the flesh to live in accord with the flesh; 13 for if you live in accord with the flesh you are sure to die; but if you put the practices of the body to death by the spirit, you will live. 14 For all who are led by God's spirit, these are God's sons. 15 For you did not receive a spirit of slavery causing fear again, but you received a spirit of adoption as sons, by which spirit we cry out: "*Abba*, Father!" 16 The spirit itself bears witness with our spirit that we are God's children. 17 If, then, we are children, we are also heirs: heirs indeed of God, but joint heirs with Christ, provided we suffer together that we may also be glorified together.

18 Consequently I reckon that the sufferings of the present season do not amount to anything in comparison with the glory that is going to be revealed in us. 19 For the eager expectation of the creation is waiting for the revealing of the sons of God. 20 For the creation was subjected to futility, not by its own will but through him that subjected it, on the basis of hope 21 that the creation itself also will

be set free from enslavement to corruption and have the glorious freedom of the children of God. 22 For we know that all creation keeps on groaning together and being in pain together until now. 23 Not only that, but we ourselves also who have the first fruits, namely, the spirit, yes, we ourselves groan within ourselves, while we are earnestly waiting for adoption as sons, the release from our bodies by ransom. 24 For we were saved in [this] hope; but hope that is seen is not hope, for when a man sees a thing, does he hope for it? 25 But if we hope for what we do not see, we keep on waiting for it with endurance.

26 In like manner the spirit also joins in with help for our weakness; for the [problem of] what we should pray for as we need to we do not know, but the spirit itself pleads for us with groanings unuttered. 27 Yet he who searches the hearts knows what the meaning of the spirit is, because it is pleading in accord with God for holy ones.

28 Now we know that God makes all his works co-operate together for the good of those who love God, those who are the ones called according to his purpose; 29 because those whom he gave his first recognition he also foreordained to be patterned after the image of his Son, that he might be the first-born among many brothers. 30 Moreover, those whom he foreordained are the ones he also called; and those whom he called are the ones he also declared to be righteous. Finally those whom he declared righteous are the ones he also glorified.

31 What, then, shall we say to these things? If God is for us, who will be against us? 32 He who did not even spare his own Son but delivered him up for us all, why will he not also with him kindly give us all other things? 33 Who will file accusation against God's chosen ones? God is the One who declares [them] righteous. 34 Who is he that will condemn?

Christ Jesus is the one who died, yes, rather the one who was raised up from the dead, who is on the right hand of God, who also pleads for us. 35 Who will separate us from the love of the Christ? Will tribulation or distress or persecution or hunger or nakedness or danger or sword? 36 Just as it is written: "For your sake we are being put to death all day long, we have been accounted as sheep for slaughtering." 37 To the contrary, in all these things we are coming off completely victorious through him that loved us. 38 For I am convinced that neither death nor life nor angels nor governments nor things now here nor things to come nor powers 39 nor height nor depth nor any other creation will be able to separate us from God's love that is in Christ Jesus our Lord.

9 I am telling the truth in Christ; I am not lying, since my conscience bears witness with me in holy spirit, 2 that I have great grief and unceasing pain in my heart. 3 For I could wish that I myself were separated as the cursed one from the Christ in behalf of my brothers, my relatives according to the flesh, 4 who, as such, are Israelites, to whom belong the adoption as sons and the glory and the covenants and the giving of the Law and the sacred service and the promises; 5 to whom the forefathers belong and from whom Christ [sprang] according to the flesh: God, who is over all, [be] blessed forever. Amen.

6 However, it is not as though the word of God had failed. For not all who [spring] from Israel are really "Israel." 7 Neither because they are Abraham's seed are they all children, but: "What will be called 'your seed' will be through Isaac." 8 That is, the children in the flesh are not really the children of God, but the children by the promise are counted as the seed. 9 For the word of promise was as follows: "At this time I will come and Sarah will have a son." 10 Yet not that case alone, but also

when Rebekah conceived twins from the one [man], Isaac our forefather: 11 for when they had not yet been born nor had practiced anything good or vile, in order that the purpose of God respecting the choosing might continue dependent, not upon works, but upon the One who calls, 12 it was said to her: "The older will be the slave of the younger." 13 Just as it is written: "I loved Jacob, but Esau I hated."

14 What shall we say, then? Is there injustice with God? Never may that become so! 15 For he says to Moses: "I will have mercy upon whomever I do have mercy, and I will show compassion to whomever I do show compassion." 16 So, then, it depends, not upon the one wishing nor upon the one running, but upon God, who has mercy. 17 For the Scripture says to Phar'aoh: "For this very cause I have let you remain, that in connection with you I may show my power, and that my name may be declared in all the earth." 18 So, then, upon whom he wishes he has mercy, but whom he wishes he lets become obstinate.

19 You will therefore say to me: "Why does he yet find fault? For who has withstood his express will?" 20 O man, who, then, really are you to be answering back to God? Shall the thing molded say to him that molded it, "Why did you make me this way?" 21 What? Does not the potter have authority over the clay to make from the same lump one vessel for an honorable use, another for a dishonorable use? 22 If, now, God, although having the will to demonstrate his wrath and to make his power known, tolerated with much longsuffering vessels of wrath made fit for destruction, 23 in order that he might make known the riches of his glory upon vessels of mercy, which he prepared beforehand for glory, 24 namely, us, whom he called not only from among Jews but also from among nations, [what of it]? 25 It is as he says also in Ho·se'a: "Those not my

people I will call 'my people,' and her who was not beloved 'beloved'; 26 and in the place where it was said to them, 'You are not my people,' there they will be called 'sons of the living God.'"

27 Moreover, Isaiah cries out concerning Israel: "Although the number of the sons of Israel may be as the sand of the sea, it is the remnant that will be saved. 28 For Jehovah will make an accounting on the earth, concluding it and cutting it short." 29 Also, just as Isaiah had said aforetime: "Unless Jehovah of armies had left a seed to us, we should have become just like Sod'om, and we should have been made just like Go·mor'rah."

30 What shall we say, then? That people of the nations, although not pursuing righteousness, caught up with righteousness, the righteousness that results from faith; 31 but Israel, although pursuing a law of righteousness, did not attain to the law. 32 For what reason? Because he pursued it, not by faith, but as by works. They stumbled on the "stone of stumbling"; 33 as it is written: "Look! I am laying in Zion a stone of stumbling and a rock-mass of offense, but he that rests his faith on it will not come to disappointment."

10 Brothers, the good will of my heart and my supplication to God for them are, indeed, for their salvation. 2 For I bear them witness that they have a zeal for God; but not according to accurate knowledge; 3 for, because of not knowing the righteousness of God but seeking to establish their own, they did not subject themselves to the righteousness of God. 4 For Christ is the end of the Law, so that everyone exercising faith may have righteousness.

5 For Moses writes that the man that has done the righteousness of the Law will live by it. 6 But the righteousness resulting from faith speaks in this manner: "Do not say in your heart, 'Who will ascend into heaven?' that is, to bring Christ down; 7 or, 'Who will descend into the abyss?' that is, to

bring Christ up from the dead." 8 But what does it say? "The word is near you, in your own mouth and in your own heart"; that is, the "word" of faith, which we are preaching. 9 For if you publicly declare that 'word in your own mouth,' that Jesus is Lord, and exercise faith in your heart that God raised him up from the dead, you will be saved. 10 For with the heart one exercises faith for righteousness, but with the mouth one makes public declaration for salvation.

11 For the Scripture says: "None that rests his faith on him will be disappointed." 12 For there is no distinction between Jew and Greek, for there is the same Lord over all, who is rich to all those calling upon him. 13 For "everyone who calls on the name of Jehovah will be saved." 14 However, how will they call on him in whom they have not put faith? How, in turn, will they put faith in him of whom they have not heard? How, in turn, will they hear without someone to preach? 15 How, in turn, will they preach unless they have been sent forth? Just as it is written: "How comely are the feet of those who declare good news of good things!"

16 Nevertheless, they did not all obey the good news. For Isaiah says: "Jehovah, who put faith in the thing heard by us?" 17 So faith follows the thing heard. In turn the thing heard is through the word about Christ. 18 Nevertheless I ask, They did not fail to hear, did they? Why, in fact, "into all the earth their sound went out, and to the extremities of the inhabited earth their utterances." 19 Nevertheless I ask, Israel did not fail to know, did they? First Moses says: "I will incite YOU people to jealousy through that which is not a nation; I will incite YOU to violent anger through a stupid nation." 20 But Isaiah becomes very bold and says: "I was found by those who were not seeking me; I became manifest to those who were not asking for me." 21 But as respects Israel he says:

"All day long I have spread out my hands toward a people that is disobedient and talks back."

11 I ask, then, God did not reject his people, did he? Never may that happen! For I also am an Israelite, of the seed of Abraham, of the tribe of Benjamin. 2 God did not reject his people, whom he first recognized. Why, do YOU not know what the Scripture says in connection with E·li′jah, as he pleads with God against Israel? 3 "Jehovah, they have killed your prophets, they have dug up your altars, and I alone am left, and they are looking for my soul." 4 Yet, what does the divine pronouncement say to him? "I have left seven thousand men over for myself, [men] who have not bent the knee to Ba′al." 5 In this way, therefore, at the present season also a remnant has turned up according to a choosing due to undeserved kindness. 6 Now if it is by undeserved kindness, it is no longer due to works; otherwise, the undeserved kindness no longer proves to be undeserved kindness.

7 What, then? The very thing Israel is earnestly seeking he did not obtain, but the ones chosen obtained it. The rest had their sensibilities blunted; 8 just as it is written: "God has given them a spirit of deep sleep, eyes so as not to see and ears so as not to hear, down to this very day." 9 Also, David says: "Let their table become for them a snare and a trap and a stumbling block and a retribution; 10 let their eyes become darkened so as not to see, and always bow down their back."

11 Therefore I ask, Did they stumble so that they fell completely? Never may that happen! But by their false step there is salvation to people of the nations, to incite them to jealousy. 12 Now if their false step means riches to the world, and their decrease means riches to people of the nations, how much more will the full number of them mean it!

13 Now I speak to YOU who are people of the nations. Forasmuch as

I am, in reality, an apostle to the nations, I glorify my ministry, 14 if I may by any means incite [those who are] my own flesh to jealousy and save some from among them. 15 For if the casting of them away means reconciliation for the world, what will the receiving of them mean but life from the dead? 16 Further, if the [part taken as] first fruits is holy, the lump is also; and if the root is holy, the branches are also.

17 However, if some of the branches were broken off but you, although being a wild olive, were grafted in among them and became a sharer of the olive's root of fatness, 18 do not be exulting over the branches. If, though, you are exulting over them, it is not you that bear the root, but the root [bears] you. 19 You will say, then: "Branches were broken off that I might be grafted in." 20 All right! For [their] lack of faith they were broken off, but you are standing by faith. Quit having lofty ideas, but be in fear. 21 For if God did not spare the natural branches, neither will he spare you. 22 See, therefore, God's kindness and severity. Toward those who fell there is severity, but toward you there is God's kindness, provided you remain in his kindness; otherwise, you also will be lopped off. 23 They also, if they do not remain in their lack of faith, will be grafted in; for God is able to graft them in again. 24 For if you were cut out of the olive tree that is wild by nature and were grafted contrary to nature into the garden olive tree, how much rather will these who are natural be grafted into their own olive tree!

25 For I do not want you, brothers, to be ignorant of this sacred secret, in order for you not to be discreet in your own eyes: that a dulling of sensibilities has happened in part to Israel until the full number of people of the nations has come in, 26 and in this manner all Israel will be saved. Just as it is written: "The deliverer will come out of Zion and turn away ungodly practices from Jacob. 27 And this is the covenant on my part with them, when I take their sins away." 28 True, with reference to the good news they are enemies for YOUR sakes, but with reference to God's choosing they are beloved for the sake of their forefathers. 29 For the gifts and the calling of God are not things he will regret. 30 For just as YOU were once disobedient to God but have now been shown mercy because of their disobedience, 31 so also these now have been disobedient with mercy resulting to YOU, that they themselves also may now be shown mercy. 32 For God has shut them all up together in disobedience, that he might show all of them mercy.

33 O the depth of God's riches and wisdom and knowledge! How unsearchable his judgments [are] and past tracing out his ways [are]! 34 For "who has come to know Jehovah's mind, or who has become his counselor?" 35 Or, "Who has first given to him, so that it must be repaid to him?" 36 Because from him and by him and for him are all things. To him be the glory forever. Amen.

12 Consequently I entreat YOU by the compassions of God, brothers, to present YOUR bodies a sacrifice living, holy, acceptable to God, a sacred service with YOUR power of reason. 2 And quit being fashioned after this system of things, but be transformed by making YOUR mind over, that YOU may prove to yourselves the good and acceptable and perfect will of God.

3 For through the undeserved kindness given to me I tell everyone there among YOU not to think more of himself than it is necessary to think; but to think so as to have a sound mind, each one as God has distributed to him a measure of faith. 4 For just as we have in one body many members, but the members do not all have the same function, 5 so we, although many, are one body in union with Christ, but members belong-

ing individually to one another. 6 Since, then, we have gifts differing according to the undeserved kindness given to us, whether prophecy, [let us prophesy] according to the faith proportioned [to us]; 7 or a ministry, [let us be] at this ministry; or he that teaches, [let him be] at his teaching; 8 or he that exhorts, [let him be] at his exhortation; he that distributes, [let him do it] with liberality; he that presides, [let him do it] in real earnest; he that shows mercy, [let him do it] with cheerfulness.

9 Let [YOUR] love be without hypocrisy. Abhor what is wicked, cling to what is good. 10 In brotherly love have tender affection for one another. In showing honor to one another take the lead. 11 Do not loiter at YOUR business. Be aglow with the spirit. Slave for Jehovah. 12 Rejoice in the hope. Endure under tribulation. Persevere in prayer. 13 Share with the holy ones according to their needs. Follow the course of hospitality. 14 Keep on blessing those who persecute; be blessing and do not be cursing. 15 Rejoice with people who rejoice; weep with people who weep. 16 Be minded the same way toward others as to yourselves; do not be minding lofty things, but be led along with the lowly things. Do not become discreet in YOUR own eyes.

17 Return evil for evil to no one. Provide fine things in the sight of all men. 18 If possible, as far as it depends upon YOU, be peaceable with all men. 19 Do not avenge yourselves, beloved, but yield place to the wrath; for it is written: "Vengeance is mine; I will repay, says Jehovah." 20 But, "if your enemy is hungry, feed him; if he is thirsty, give him something to drink; for by doing this you will heap fiery coals upon his head." 21 Do not let yourself be conquered by the evil, but keep conquering the evil with the good.

13 Let every soul be in subjection to the superior authorities, for there is no authority except by God; the existing authorities stand placed in their relative positions by God. 2 Therefore he who opposes the authority has taken a stand against the arrangement of God; those who have taken a stand against it will receive judgment to themselves. 3 For those ruling are an object of fear, not to the good deed, but to the bad. Do you, then, want to have no fear of the authority? Keep doing good, and you will have praise from it; 4 for it is God's minister to you for your good. But if you are doing what is bad, be in fear: for it is not without purpose that it bears the sword; for it is God's minister, an avenger to express wrath upon the one practicing what is bad.

5 There is therefore compelling reason for YOU people to be in subjection, not only on account of that wrath but also on account of [YOUR] conscience. 6 For that is why YOU are also paying taxes; for they are God's public servants constantly serving this very purpose. 7 Render to all their dues, to him who [calls for] the tax, the tax; to him who [calls for] the tribute, the tribute; to him who [calls for] fear, such fear; to him who [calls for] honor, such honor.

8 Do not YOU people be owing anybody a single thing, except to love one another; for he that loves his fellow man has fulfilled [the] law. 9 For the [law code], "You must not commit adultery, You must not murder, You must not steal, You must not covet," and whatever other commandment there is, is summed up in this word, namely, "You must love your neighbor as yourself." 10 Love does not work evil to one's neighbor; therefore love is the law's fulfillment.

11 [Do] this, too, because YOU people know the season, that it is already the hour for YOU to awake from sleep, for now our salvation is nearer than at the time when we became believers. 12 The night is well along; the day has drawn near. Let us therefore put off the

works belonging to darkness and let us put on the weapons of the light. 13 As in the daytime let us walk decently, not in revelries and drunken bouts, not in illicit intercourse and loose conduct, not in strife and jealousy. 14 But put on the Lord Jesus Christ, and do not be planning ahead for the desires of the flesh.

14 Welcome the [man] having weaknesses in [his] faith, but not to make decisions on inward questionings. 2 One [man] has faith to eat everything, but the [man] who is weak eats vegetables. 3 Let the one eating not look down on the one not eating, and let the one not eating not judge the one eating, for God has welcomed that one. 4 Who are you to judge the house servant of another? To his own master he stands or falls. Indeed, he will be made to stand, for Jehovah can make him stand.

5 One [man] judges one day as above another; another [man] judges one day as all others; let each [man] be fully convinced in his own mind. 6 He who observes the day observes it to Jehovah. Also, he who eats, eats to Jehovah, for he gives thanks to God; and he who does not eat does not eat to Jehovah, and yet gives thanks to God. 7 None of us, in fact, lives with regard to himself only, and no one dies with regard to himself only; 8 for both if we live, we live to Jehovah, and if we die, we die to Jehovah. Therefore both if we live and if we die, we belong to Jehovah. 9 For to this end Christ died and came to life again, that he might be Lord over both the dead and the living.

10 But why do you judge your brother? Or why do you also look down on your brother? For we shall all stand before the judgment seat of God; 11 for it is written: " 'As I live,' says Jehovah, 'to me every knee will bend down, and every tongue will make open acknowledgment to God.' " 12 So, then, each of us will render an account for himself to God.

13 Therefore let us not be judging one another any longer, but rather make this YOUR decision, not to put before a brother a stumbling block or a cause for tripping. 14 I know and am persuaded in the Lord Jesus that nothing is defiled in itself; only where a man considers something to be defiled, to him it is defiled. 15 For if because of food your brother is being grieved, you are no longer walking in accord with love. Do not by your food ruin that one for whom Christ died. 16 Do not, therefore, let the good YOU people do be spoken of with injury to YOU. 17 For the kingdom of God does not mean eating and drinking, but [means] righteousness and peace and joy with holy spirit. 18 For he who in this regard slaves for Christ is acceptable to God and has approval with men.

19 So, then, let us pursue the things making for peace and the things that are upbuilding to one another. 20 Stop tearing down the work of God just for the sake of food. True, all things are clean, but it is injurious to the man who with an occasion for stumbling eats. 21 It is well not to eat flesh or to drink wine or do anything over which your brother stumbles. 22 The faith that you have, have it in accord with yourself in the sight of God. Happy is the man that does not put himself on judgment by what he approves. 23 But if he has doubts, he is already condemned if he eats, because [he does] not [eat] out of faith. Indeed, everything that is not out of faith is sin.

15 We, though, who are strong ought to bear the weaknesses of those not strong, and not to be pleasing ourselves. 2 Let each of us please [his] neighbor in what is good for [his] upbuilding. 3 For even Christ did not please himself; but just as it is written: "The reproaches of those who were reproaching you have fallen upon me." 4 For all the things that were written aforetime were written for our instruction, that through

our endurance and through the comfort from the Scriptures we might have hope. 5 Now may the God who supplies endurance and comfort grant YOU to have among yourselves the same mental attitude that Christ Jesus had, 6 that with one accord YOU may with one mouth glorify the God and Father of our Lord Jesus Christ.

7 Therefore welcome one another, just as the Christ also welcomed us, with glory to God in view. 8 For I say that Christ actually became a minister of those who are circumcised in behalf of God's truthfulness, so as to verify the promises He made to their forefathers, 9 and that the nations might glorify God for his mercy. Just as it is written: "That is why I will openly acknowledge you among the nations and to your name I will make melody." 10 And again he says: "Be glad, YOU nations, with his people." 11 And again: "Praise Jehovah, all YOU nations, and let all the peoples praise him." 12 And again Isaiah says: "There will be the root of Jes'se, and there will be one arising to rule nations; on him nations will rest their hope." 13 May the God who gives hope fill YOU with all joy and peace by YOUR believing, that YOU may abound in hope with power of holy spirit.

14 Now I myself also am persuaded about YOU, my brothers, that YOU yourselves are also full of goodness, as YOU have been filled with all knowledge, and that YOU can also admonish one another. 15 However, I am writing YOU the more outspokenly on some points, as if reminding YOU again, because of the undeserved kindness given to me from God 16 for me to be a public servant of Christ Jesus to the nations, engaging in the holy work of the good news of God, in order that the offering, namely, these nations, might prove to be acceptable, it being sanctified with holy spirit.

17 Therefore I have cause for exulting in Christ Jesus when it comes to things pertaining to God.

18 For I will not venture to tell one thing if it is not of those things which Christ worked through me for the nations to be obedient, by [my] word and deed, 19 with the power of signs and portents, with the power of holy spirit; so that from Jerusalem and in a circuit as far as Il·lyr'i·cum I have thoroughly preached the good news about the Christ. 20 In this way, indeed, I made it my aim not to declare the good news where Christ had already been named, in order that I might not be building on another man's foundation; 21 but, just as it is written: "Those to whom no announcement has been made about him will see, and those who have not heard will understand."

22 Therefore also I was many times hindered from getting to YOU. 23 But now that I no longer have [untouched] territory in these regions, and for some years having had a longing to get to YOU 24 whenever I am on my way to Spain, I hope, above all, when I am on the journey there, to get a look at YOU and to be escorted part way there by YOU after I have first in some measure been satisfied with your company. 25 But now I am about to journey to Jerusalem to minister to the holy ones. 26 For those in Mac·e·do'ni·a and A·cha'ia have been pleased to share up their things by a contribution to the poor of the holy ones in Jerusalem. 27 True, they have been pleased to do so, and yet they were debtors to them; for if the nations have shared in their spiritual things, they also owe it to minister publicly to these with things for the fleshly body. 28 Hence after I have finished with this and have got this fruit securely to them, I shall depart by way of YOU for Spain. 29 Moreover, I know that when I do come to YOU I shall come with a full measure of blessing from Christ.

30 Now I exhort YOU, brothers, through our Lord Jesus Christ and through the love of the spirit, that YOU exert yourselves with me in prayers to God for me, 31 that I

may be delivered from the unbelievers in Ju·de′a and that my ministry which is for Jerusalem may prove to be acceptable to the holy ones, 32 so that when I get to YOU with joy by God's will I shall be refreshed together with YOU. 33 May the God who gives peace be with all of YOU. Amen.

16 I recommend to YOU Phoe′be our sister, who is a minister of the congregation that is in Cen′chre·ae, 2 that YOU may welcome her in [the] Lord in a way worthy of the holy ones, and that YOU may assist her in any matter where she may need YOU, for she herself also proved to be a defender of many, yes, of me myself.

3 Give my greetings to Pris′ca and Aq′ui·la my fellow workers in Christ Jesus, 4 who have risked their own necks for my soul, to whom not only I but also all the congregations of the nations render thanks; 5 and [greet] the congregation that is in their house. Greet my beloved E·pae′ne·tus, who is a first fruits of Asia for Christ. 6 Greet Mary, who has performed many labors for YOU. 7 Greet An·dron′i·cus and Ju′ni·as my relatives and my fellow captives, who are men of note among the apostles and who have been in union with Christ longer than I have.

8 Give my greetings to Am·pli·a′tus my beloved in [the] Lord. 9 Greet Ur·ba′nus our fellow worker in Christ, and my beloved Sta′chys. 10 Greet A·pel′les, the approved one in Christ. Greet those from the household of A·ris·tob′u·lus. 11 Greet He·ro′di·on my relative. Greet those from the household of Nar·cis′sus who are in [the] Lord. 12 Greet Try·phae′na and Try·pho′sa, [women] who are working hard in [the] Lord. Greet Per′sis our beloved one, for she performed many labors in [the] Lord. 13 Greet Ru′fus the chosen one in [the] Lord, and his mother and mine. 14 Greet A·syn′cri·tus,

Phle′gon, Her′mes, Pat′ro·bas, Her′mas, and the brothers with them. 15 Greet Phi·lol′o·gus and Julia, Ne′reus and his sister, and O·lym′pas, and all the holy ones with them. 16 Greet one another with a holy kiss. All the congregations of the Christ greet YOU.

17 Now I exhort YOU, brothers, to keep your eye on those who cause divisions and occasions for stumbling contrary to the teaching that YOU have learned, and avoid them. 18 For men of that sort are slaves, not of our Lord Christ, but of their own bellies; and by smooth talk and complimentary speech they seduce the hearts of guileless ones. 19 For YOUR obedience has come to the notice of all. I therefore rejoice over YOU. But I want YOU to be wise as to what is good, but innocent as to what is evil. 20 For his part, the God who gives peace will crush Satan under YOUR feet shortly. May the undeserved kindness of our Lord Jesus be with YOU.

21 Timothy my fellow worker greets YOU, and so do Lucius and Ja′son and So·sip′a·ter my relatives.

22 I, Ter′tius, who have done the writing of this letter, greet YOU in [the] Lord.

23 Ga′ius, my host and that of all the congregation, greets YOU. E·ras′tus the city steward greets YOU, and so does Quar′tus his brother. 24 ——

25 Now to him who can make YOU firm in accord with the good news I declare and the preaching of Jesus Christ, according to the revelation of the sacred secret which has been kept in silence for long-lasting times 26 but has now been made manifest and has been made known through the prophetic scriptures among all the nations in accord with the command of the everlasting God to promote obedience by faith; 27 to God, wise alone, be the glory through Jesus Christ forever. Amen.

CORINTHIANS

1 Paul, called to be an apostle of Jesus Christ through God's will, and Sos'the·nes our brother 2 to the congregation of God that is in Corinth, to you who have been sanctified in union with Christ Jesus, called to be holy ones, together with all who everywhere are calling upon the name of our Lord, Jesus Christ, their Lord and ours:

3 May you have undeserved kindness and peace from God our Father and [the] Lord Jesus Christ.

4 I always thank God for you in view of the undeserved kindness of God given to you in Christ Jesus; 5 that in everything you have been enriched in him, in full ability to speak and in full knowledge, 6 even as the witness about the Christ has been rendered firm among you, 7 so that you do not fall short in any gift at all, while you are eagerly waiting for the revelation of our Lord Jesus Christ. 8 He will also make you firm to the end, that you may be open to no accusation in the day of our Lord Jesus Christ. 9 God is faithful, by whom you were called into a sharing with his Son Jesus Christ our Lord.

10 Now I exhort you, brothers, through the name of our Lord Jesus Christ that you should all speak in agreement, and that there should not be divisions among you, but that you may be fitly united in the same mind and in the same line of thought. 11 For the disclosure was made to me about you, my brothers, by those of [the house of] Chlo'e, that dissensions exist among you. 12 What I mean is this, that each one of you says: "I belong to Paul," "But I to A·pol'los," "But I to Ce'phas," "But I to Christ." 13 The Christ exists divided. Paul was not impaled for you, was he? Or were you baptized in the name of Paul? 14 I am thankful I baptized none of you except Cris'-

pus and Ga'ius, 15 so that no one may say that you were baptized in my name. 16 Yes, I also baptized the household of Steph'a·nas. As for the rest, I do not know whether I baptized anybody else. 17 For Christ dispatched me, not to go baptizing, but to go declaring the good news, not with wisdom of speech, that the torture stake of the Christ should not be made useless.

18 For the speech about the torture stake is foolishness to those who are perishing, but to us who are being saved it is God's power. 19 For it is written: "I will make the wisdom of the wise [men] perish, and the intelligence of the intellectual [men] I will shove aside." 20 Where is the wise man? Where is the scribe? Where the debater of this system of things? Did not God make the wisdom of the world foolish? 21 For since, in the wisdom of God, the world through its wisdom did not get to know God, God saw good through the foolishness of what is preached to save those believing.

22 For both the Jews ask for signs and the Greeks look for wisdom; 23 but we preach Christ impaled, to the Jews a cause for stumbling but to the nations foolishness; 24 however, to those who are the called, both Jews and Greeks, Christ the power of God and the wisdom of God. 25 Because a foolish thing of God is wiser than men, and a weak thing of God is stronger than men.

26 For you behold his calling of you, brothers, that not many wise in a fleshly way were called, not many powerful, not many of noble birth; 27 but God chose the foolish things of the world, that he might put the wise men to shame; and God chose the weak things of the world, that he might put the strong things to shame; 28 and God chose the ignoble things of the

world and the things looked down upon, the things that are not, that he might bring to nothing the things that are, 29 in order that no flesh might boast in the sight of God. 30 But it is due to him that you are in union with Christ Jesus, who has become to us wisdom from God, also righteousness and sanctification and release by ransom; 31 that it may be just as it is written: "He that boasts, let him boast in Jehovah."

2 And so I, when I came to you, brothers, did not come with an extravagance of speech or of wisdom declaring the sacred secret of God to you. 2 For I decided not to know anything among you except Jesus Christ, and him impaled. 3 And I came to you in weakness and in fear and with much trembling; 4 and my speech and what I preached were not with persuasive words of wisdom but with a demonstration of spirit and power, 5 that your faith might be, not in men's wisdom, but in God's power.

6 Now we speak wisdom among those who are mature, but not the wisdom of this system of things nor that of the rulers of this system of things, who are to come to nothing. 7 But we speak God's wisdom in a sacred secret, the hidden wisdom, which God foreordained before the systems of things for our glory. 8 This [wisdom] not one of the rulers of this system of things came to know, for if they had known [it] they would not have impaled the glorious Lord. 9 But just as it is written: "Eye has not seen and ear has not heard, neither have there been conceived in the heart of man the things that God has prepared for those who love him." 10 For it is to us God has revealed them through his spirit, for the spirit searches into all things, even the deep things of God.

11 For who among men knows the things of a man except the spirit of man that is in him? So, too, no one has come to know the things of God, except the spirit of God. 12 Now we received, not the spirit of the world, but the spirit which is from God, that we might know the things that have been kindly given us by God. 13 These things we also speak, not with words taught by human wisdom, but with those taught by [the] spirit, as we combine spiritual [matters] with spiritual [words].

14 But a physical man does not receive the things of the spirit of God, for they are foolishness to him; and he cannot get to know [them], because they are examined spiritually. 15 However, the spiritual man examines indeed all things, but he himself is not examined by any man. 16 For "who has come to know the mind of Jehovah, that he may instruct him?" But we do have the mind of Christ.

3 And so, brothers, I was not able to speak to you as to spiritual men, but as to fleshly men, as to babes in Christ. 2 I fed you milk, not something to eat, for you were not yet strong enough. In fact, neither are you strong enough now, 3 for you are yet fleshly. For whereas there are jealousy and strife among you, are you not fleshly and are you not walking as men do? 4 For when one says: "I belong to Paul," but another says: "I to A·pol'los," are you not simply men?

5 What, then, is A·pol'los? Yes, what is Paul? Ministers through whom you became believers, even as the Lord granted each one. 6 I planted, A·pol'los watered, but God kept making [it] grow; 7 so that neither is he that plants anything nor is he that waters, but God who makes [it] grow. 8 Now he that plants and he that waters are one, but each [person] will receive his own reward according to his own labor. 9 For we are God's fellow workers. You people are God's field under cultivation, God's building.

10 According to the undeserved kindness of God that was given to me, as a wise director of works I laid a foundation, but someone else is building on it. But let each one keep watching how he is

building on it. 11 For no man can lay any other foundation than what is laid, which is Jesus Christ. 12 Now if anyone builds on the foundation gold, silver, precious stones, wood materials, hay, stubble, 13 each one's work will become manifest, for the day will show it up, because it will be revealed by means of fire; and the fire itself will prove what sort of work each one's is. 14 If anyone's work that he has built on it remains, he will receive a reward; 15 if anyone's work is burned up, he will suffer loss, but he himself will be saved; yet, if so, [it will be] as through fire.

16 Do YOU not know that YOU people are God's temple, and that the spirit of God dwells in YOU? 17 If anyone destroys the temple of God, God will destroy him; for the temple of God is holy, which [temple] YOU people are.

18 Let no one be seducing himself: If anyone among YOU thinks he is wise in this system of things, let him become a fool, that he may become wise. 19 For the wisdom of this world is foolishness with God; for it is written: "He catches the wise in their own cunning." 20 And again: "Jehovah knows that the reasonings of the wise men are futile." 21 Hence let no one be boasting in men; for all things belong to YOU, 22 whether Paul or A·pol'los or Ce'phas or the world or life or death or things now here or things to come, all things belong to YOU; 23 in turn YOU belong to Christ; Christ, in turn, belongs to God.

4 Let a man so appraise us as being subordinates of Christ and stewards of sacred secrets of God. 2 Besides, in this case, what is looked for in stewards is for a man to be found faithful. 3 Now to me it is a very trivial matter that I should be examined by YOU or by a human tribunal. Even I do not examine myself. 4 For I am not conscious of anything against myself. Yet by this I am not proved righteous, but he that examines me is Jehovah. 5 Hence do not judge anything before the due time, until the Lord comes, who will both bring the secret things of darkness to light and make the counsels of the hearts manifest, and then each one will have his praise come to him from God.

6 Now, brothers, these things I have transferred so as to apply to myself and A·pol'los for YOUR good, that in our case YOU may learn the [rule]: "Do not go beyond the things that are written," in order that YOU may not be puffed up individually in favor of the one against the other. 7 For who makes you to differ from another? Indeed, what do you have that you did not receive? If, now, you did indeed receive [it], why do you boast as though you did not receive [it]?

8 YOU men already have YOUR fill, do YOU? YOU are rich already, are YOU? YOU have begun ruling as kings without us, have YOU? And I wish indeed that YOU had begun ruling as kings, that we also might rule with YOU as kings. 9 For it seems to me that God has put us the apostles last on exhibition as men appointed to death, because we have become a theatrical spectacle to the world, both to angels and to men. 10 We are fools because of Christ, but YOU are discreet in Christ; we are weak, but YOU are strong; YOU are in good repute, but we are in dishonor. 11 Down to this very hour we continue to hunger and also to thirst and to be scantily clothed and to be knocked about and to be homeless 12 and to toil, working with our own hands. When being reviled, we bless; when being persecuted, we bear up; 13 when being defamed, we entreat; we have become as the refuse of the world, the offscouring of all things, until now.

14 I am writing these things, not to shame YOU, but to admonish YOU as my beloved children. 15 For though YOU may have ten thousand tutors in Christ, [YOU] certainly [do] not [have] many fathers; for in Christ Jesus I have become YOUR father through the good news. 16 I entreat YOU, therefore, become

imitators of me. 17 That is why I am sending Timothy to you, as he is my beloved and faithful child in [the] Lord; and he will put you in mind of my methods in connection with Christ Jesus, just as I am teaching everywhere in every congregation.

18 Some are puffed up as though I were in fact not coming to you. 19 But I will come to you shortly, if Jehovah wills, and I shall get to know, not the speech of those who are puffed up, but [their] power. 20 For the kingdom of God [lies] not in speech, but in power. 21 What do you want? Shall I come to you with a rod, or with love and mildness of spirit?

5 Actually fornication is reported among you, and such fornication as is not even among the nations, that a wife a certain [man] has of [his] father. 2 And are you puffed up, and did you not rather mourn, in order that the man that committed this deed should be taken away from your midst? 3 I for one, although absent in body but present in spirit, have certainly judged already, as if I were present, the man who has worked in such a way as this, 4 that in the name of our Lord Jesus, when you are gathered together, also my spirit with the power of our Lord Jesus, 5 you hand such a man over to Satan for the destruction of the flesh, in order that the spirit may be saved in the day of the Lord.

6 Your [cause for] boasting is not fine. Do you not know that the little leaven ferments the whole lump? 7 Clear away the old leaven, that you may be a new lump, according as you are free from ferment. For, indeed, Christ our passover has been sacrificed. 8 Consequently let us keep the festival, not with old leaven, neither with leaven of badness and wickedness, but with unfermented cakes of sincerity and truth.

9 In my letter I wrote you to quit mixing in company with fornicators, 10 not [meaning] entirely with the fornicators of this world or the greedy persons and extortioners or idolaters. Otherwise, you would actually have to get out of the world. 11 But now I am writing you to quit mixing in company with anyone called a brother that is a fornicator or a greedy person or an idolater or a reviler or a drunkard or an extortioner, not even eating with such a man. 12 For what do I have to do with judging those outside? Do you not judge those inside, 13 while God judges those outside? "Remove the wicked [man] from among yourselves."

6 Does anyone of you that has a case against the other dare to go to court before unrighteous men, and not before the holy ones? 2 Or do you not know that the holy ones will judge the world? And if the world is to be judged by you, are you unfit to try very trivial matters? 3 Do you not know that we shall judge angels? Why, then, not matters of this life? 4 If, then, you do have matters of this life to be tried, is it the men looked down upon in the congregation that you put in as judges? 5 I am speaking to move you to shame. Is it true that there is not one wise man among you that will be able to judge between his brothers, 6 but brother goes to court with brother, and that before unbelievers?

7 Really, then, it means altogether a defeat for you that you are having lawsuits with one another. Why do you not rather let yourselves be wronged? Why do you not rather let yourselves be defrauded? 8 To the contrary, you wrong and defraud, and your brothers at that.

9 What! Do you not know that unrighteous persons will not inherit God's kingdom? Do not be misled. Neither fornicators, nor idolaters, nor adulterers, nor men kept for unnatural purposes, nor men who lie with men, 10 nor thieves, nor greedy persons, nor drunkards, nor revilers, nor extortioners will inherit God's kingdom. 11 And yet that is what some of you were. But you have

been washed clean, but YOU have been sanctified, but YOU have been declared righteous in the name of our Lord Jesus Christ and with the spirit of our God.

12 All things are lawful for me; but not all things are advantageous. All things are lawful for me; but I will not let myself be brought under authority by anything. 13 Foods for the belly, and the belly for foods; but God will bring both it and them to nothing. Now the body is not for fornication, but for the Lord; and the Lord is for the body. 14 But God both raised up the Lord and will raise us up out of [death] through his power.

15 Do YOU not know that YOUR bodies are members of Christ? Shall I, then, take the members of the Christ away and make them members of a harlot? Never may that happen! 16 What! Do YOU not know that he who is joined to a harlot is one body? For, "The two," says he, "will be one flesh." 17 But he who is joined to the Lord is one spirit. 18 Flee from fornication. Every other sin that a man may commit is outside his body, but he that practices fornication is sinning against his own body. 19 What! Do YOU not know that the body of YOU people is [the] temple of the holy spirit within YOU, which YOU have from God? Also, YOU do not belong to yourselves, 20 for YOU were bought with a price. By all means, glorify God in the body of YOU people.

7 Now concerning the things about which YOU wrote, it is well for a man not to touch a woman; 2 yet, because of prevalence of fornication, let each man have his own wife and each woman have her own husband. 3 Let the husband render to [his] wife her due; but let the wife also do likewise to [her] husband. 4 The wife does not exercise authority over her own body, but her husband does; likewise, also, the husband does not exercise authority over his own body, but his wife does. 5 Do not be depriving each other [of it], except by mutual consent for an

appointed time, that YOU may devote time to prayer and may come together again, that Satan may not keep tempting YOU for YOUR lack of self-regulation. 6 However, I say this by way of concession, not in the way of a command. 7 But I wish all men were as I myself am. Nevertheless, each one has his own gift from God, one in this way, another in that way.

8 Now I say to the unmarried persons and the widows, it is well for them that they remain even as I am. 9 But if they do not have self-control, let them marry, for it is better to marry than to be inflamed [with passion].

10 To the married people I give instructions, yet not I but the Lord, that a wife should not depart from her husband; 11 but if she should actually depart, let her remain unmarried or else make up again with her husband; and a husband should not leave his wife.

12 But to the others I say, yes, I, not the Lord: If any brother has an unbelieving wife, and yet she is agreeable to dwelling with him, let him not leave her; 13 and a woman who has an unbelieving husband, and yet he is agreeable to dwelling with her, let her not leave her husband. 14 For the unbelieving husband is sanctified in relation to [his] wife, and the unbelieving wife is sanctified in relation to the brother; otherwise, YOUR children would really be unclean, but now they are holy. 15 But if the unbelieving one proceeds to depart, let him depart; a brother or a sister is not in servitude under such circumstances, but God has called YOU to peace. 16 For, wife, how do you know but that you will save [your] husband? Or, husband, how do you know but that you will save [your] wife?

17 Only, as Jehovah has given each one a portion, let each one so walk as God has called him. And thus I ordain in all the congregations. 18 Was any man called circumcised? Let him not become uncircumcised. Has any man been called in uncircumcision? Let him

not get circumcised. 19 Circumcision does not mean a thing, and uncircumcision means not a thing, but observance of God's commandments [does]. 20 In whatever state each one was called, let him remain in it. 21 Were you called when a slave? Do not let it worry you; but if you can also become free, rather seize the opportunity. 22 For anyone in [the] Lord that was called when a slave is the Lord's freedman; likewise he that was called when a free man is a slave of Christ. 23 You were bought with a price; stop becoming slaves of men. 24 In whatever condition each one was called, brothers, let him remain in it associated with God.

25 Now concerning virgins I have no command from the Lord, but I give my opinion as one who had mercy shown him by the Lord to be faithful. 26 Therefore I think this to be well in view of the necessity here with us, that it is well for a man to continue as he is. 27 Are you bound to a wife? Stop seeking a release. Are you loosed from a wife? Stop seeking a wife. 28 But even if you did marry, you would commit no sin. And if a virgin [person] married, such one would commit no sin. However, those who do will have tribulation in their flesh. But I am sparing you.

29 Moreover, this I say, brothers, the time left is reduced. Henceforth let those who have wives be as though they had none, 30 and also those who weep be as those who do not weep, and those who rejoice as those who do not rejoice, and those who buy as those not possessing, 31 and those making use of the world as those not using it to the full; for the scene of this world is changing. 32 Indeed, I want you to be free from anxiety. The unmarried man is anxious for the things of the Lord, how he may gain the Lord's approval. 33 But the married man is anxious for the things of the world, how he may gain the approval of his wife, 34 and he is divided. Further,

the unmarried woman, and the virgin, is anxious for the things of the Lord, that she may be holy both in her body and in her spirit. However, the married woman is anxious for the things of the world, how she may gain the approval of her husband. 35 But this I am saying for YOUR personal advantage, not that I may cast a noose upon YOU, but to move YOU to that which is becoming and that which means constant attendance upon the Lord without distraction.

36 But if anyone thinks he is behaving improperly toward his virginity, if that is past the bloom of youth, and this is the way it should take place, let him do what he wants; he does not sin. Let them marry. 37 But if anyone stands settled in his heart, having no necessity, but has authority over his own will and has made this decision in his own heart, to keep his own virginity, he will do well. 38 Consequently he also that gives his virginity in marriage does well, but he that does not give it in marriage will do better.

39 A wife is bound during all the time her husband is alive. But if her husband should fall asleep [in death], she is free to be married to whom she wants, only in [the] Lord. 40 But she is happier if she remains as she is, according to my opinion. I certainly think I also have God's spirit.

8 Now concerning foods offered to idols: we know we all have knowledge. Knowledge puffs up, but love builds up. 2 If anyone thinks he has acquired knowledge of something, he does not yet know [it] just as he ought to know [it]. 3 But if anyone loves God, this one is known by him.

4 Now concerning the eating of foods offered to idols, we know that an idol is nothing in the world, and that there is no God but one. 5 For even though there are those who are called "gods," whether in heaven or on earth, just as there are many "gods" and many "lords," 6 there is actually to us one God the Father, out of whom all things

are, and we for him; and there is one Lord, Jesus Christ, through whom all things are, and we through him.

7 Nevertheless, there is not this knowledge in all persons; but some, being accustomed until now to the idol, eat food as something sacrificed to an idol, and their conscience, being weak, is defiled. 8 But food will not commend us to God; if we do not eat, we do not fall short, and, if we eat, we have no credit to ourselves. 9 But keep watching that this authority of YOURS does not somehow become a stumbling block to those who are weak. 10 For if anyone should see you, the one having knowledge, reclining at a meal in an idol temple, will not the conscience of that one who is weak be built up to the point of eating foods offered to idols? 11 Really, by your knowledge, the man that is weak is being ruined, [your] brother for whose sake Christ died. 12 But when YOU people thus sin against YOUR brothers and wound their conscience that is weak, YOU are sinning against Christ. 13 Therefore, if food makes my brother stumble, I will never again eat flesh at all, that I may not make my brother stumble.

9 Am I not free? Am I not an apostle? Have I not seen Jesus our Lord? Are not YOU my work in [the] Lord? 2 If I am not an apostle to others, I most certainly am to YOU, for YOU are the seal confirming my apostleship in relation to [the] Lord.

3 My defense to those who examine me is as follows: 4 We have authority to eat and drink, do we not? 5 We have authority to lead about a sister as a wife, even as the rest of the apostles and the Lord's brothers and Ce′phas, do we not? 6 Or is it only Bar′na·bas and I that do not have authority to refrain from [secular] work? 7 Who is it that ever serves as a soldier at his own expense? Who plants a vineyard and does not eat of its fruit? Or who shepherds a flock and does not eat some of the milk of the flock?

8 Am I speaking these things by human standards? Or does not the Law also say these things? 9 For in the law of Moses it is written: "You must not muzzle a bull when it is threshing out the grain." Is it bulls God is caring for? Or is it altogether for our sakes he says it? 10 Really for our sakes it was written, because the man who plows ought to plow in hope and the man who threshes ought to do so in hope of being a partaker.

11 If we have sown spiritual things to YOU, is it something great if we shall reap things for the flesh from YOU? 12 If other men partake of this authority over YOU, do we not much more so? Nevertheless, we have not made use of this authority, but we are bearing all things, in order that we might not offer any hindrance to the good news about the Christ. 13 Do YOU not know that the men performing sacred duties eat the things of the temple, and those constantly attending at the altar have a portion for themselves with the altar? 14 In this way, too, the Lord ordained for those proclaiming the good news to live by means of the good news.

15 But I have not made use of a single one of these [provisions]. Indeed, I have not written these things that it should become so in my case, for it would be finer for me to die than—no man is going to make my reason for boasting void! 16 If, now, I am declaring the good news, it is no reason for me to boast, for necessity is laid upon me. Really, woe is me if I did not declare the good news! 17 If I perform this willingly, I have a reward; but if I do it against my will, all the same I have a stewardship entrusted to me. 18 What, then, is my reward? That while declaring the good news I may furnish the good news without cost, to the end that I may not abuse my authority in the good news.

19 For, though I am free from all persons, I have made myself the slave to all, that I may gain the

most persons. 20 And so to the Jews I became as a Jew, that I might gain Jews; to those under law I became as under law, though I myself am not under law, that I might gain those under law. 21 To those without law I became as without law, although I am not without law toward God but under law toward Christ, that I might gain those without law. 22 To the weak I became weak, that I might gain the weak. I have become all things to people of all sorts, that I might by all means save some. 23 But I do all things for the sake of the good news, that I may become a sharer of it with [others].

24 Do you not know that the runners in a race all run, but only one receives the prize? Run in such a way that you may attain it. 25 Moreover, every man taking part in a contest exercises self-control in all things. Now they, of course, do it that they may get a corruptible crown, but we an incorruptible one. 26 Therefore, the way I am running is not uncertainly; the way I am directing my blows is so as not to be striking the air; 27 but I pummel my body and lead it as a slave, that, after I have preached to others, I myself should not become disapproved somehow.

10 Now I do not want you to be ignorant, brothers, that our forefathers were all under the cloud and all passed through the sea 2 and all got baptized into Moses by means of the cloud and of the sea; 3 and all ate the same spiritual food 4 and all drank the same spiritual drink. For they used to drink from the spiritual rock-mass that followed them, and that rock-mass meant the Christ. 5 Nevertheless, on most of them God did not express his approval, for they were laid low in the wilderness.

6 Now these things became our examples, for us not to be persons desiring injurious things, even as they desired them. 7 Neither become idolaters, as some of them did; just as it is written: "The people sat down to eat and drink, and they got up to have a good time." 8 Neither let us practice fornication, as some of them committed fornication, only to fall, twenty-three thousand [of them] in one day. 9 Neither let us put Jehovah to the test, as some of them put [him] to the test, only to perish by the serpents. 10 Neither be murmurers, just as some of them murmured, only to perish by the destroyer. 11 Now these things went on befalling them as examples, and they were written for a warning to us upon whom the ends of the systems of things have arrived.

12 Consequently let him that thinks he is standing beware that he does not fall. 13 No temptation has taken you except what is common to men. But God is faithful, and he will not let you be tempted beyond what you can bear, but along with the temptation he will also make the way out in order for you to be able to endure it.

14 Therefore, my beloved ones, flee from idolatry. 15 I speak as to men with discernment; judge for yourselves what I say. 16 The cup of blessing which we bless, is it not a sharing in the blood of the Christ? The loaf which we break, is it not a sharing in the body of the Christ? 17 Because there is one loaf, we, although many, are one body, for we are all partaking of that one loaf.

18 Look at that which is Israel in a fleshly way: Are not those who eat the sacrifices sharers with the altar? 19 What, then, am I to say? That what is sacrificed to an idol is anything, or that an idol is anything? 20 No; but I say that the things which the nations sacrifice they sacrifice to demons, and not to God; and I do not want you to become sharers with the demons. 21 You cannot be drinking the cup of Jehovah and the cup of demons; you cannot be partaking of "the table of Jehovah" and the table of demons. 22 Or "are we inciting Jehovah to jealousy"? We are not stronger than he is, are we?

23 All things are lawful; but not all things are advantageous. All things are lawful; but not all things build up. 24 Let each one keep seeking, not his own [advantage], but that of the other person.

25 Everything that is sold in a meat market keep eating, making no inquiry on account of YOUR conscience; 26 for "to Jehovah belong the earth and that which fills it." 27 If anyone of the unbelievers invites YOU and YOU wish to go, proceed to eat everything that is set before YOU, making no inquiry on account of YOUR conscience. 28 But if anyone should say to YOU: "This is something offered in sacrifice," Do not eat on account of the one that disclosed it and on account of conscience. 29 "Conscience," I say, not your own, but that of the other person. For why should it be that my freedom is judged by another person's conscience? 30 If I am partaking with thanks, why am I to be spoken of abusively over that for which I give thanks?

31 Therefore, whether YOU are eating or drinking or doing anything else, do all things for God's glory. 32 Keep from becoming causes for stumbling to Jews as well as Greeks and to the congregation of God, 33 even as I am pleasing all people in all things, not seeking my own advantage but that of the many, in order that they might get saved.

11 Become imitators of me, even as I am of Christ.

2 Now I commend YOU because in all things YOU have me in mind and YOU are holding fast the traditions just as I handed [them] on to YOU. 3 But I want YOU to know that the head of every man is the Christ; in turn the head of a woman is the man; in turn the head of the Christ is God. 4 Every man that prays or prophesies having something on his head shames his head; 5 but every woman that prays or prophesies with her head uncovered shames her head, for it is one and the same as if she were a [woman] with a shaved head. 6 For if a woman does not cover herself, let her also be shorn; but if it is disgraceful for a woman to be shorn or shaved, let her be covered.

7 For a man ought not to have his head covered, as he is God's image and glory; but the woman is man's glory. 8 For man is not out of woman, but woman out of man; 9 and, what is more, man was not created for the sake of the woman, but woman for the sake of the man. 10 That is why the woman ought to have a sign of authority upon her head because of the angels.

11 Besides, in connection with [the] Lord neither is woman without man nor man without woman. 12 For just as the woman is out of the man, so also the man is through the woman; but all things are out of God. 13 Judge for YOUR own selves: Is it fitting for a woman to pray uncovered to God? 14 Does not nature itself teach YOU that if a man has long hair, it is a dishonor to him; 15 but if a woman has long hair, it is a glory to her? Because her hair is given her instead of a headdress. 16 However, if any man seems to dispute for some other custom, we have no other, neither do the congregations of God.

17 But, while giving these instructions, I do not commend YOU because it is, not for the better, but for the worse that YOU meet together. 18 For first of all, when YOU come together in a congregation, I hear divisions exist among YOU; and in some measure I believe it. 19 For there must also be sects among YOU, that the persons approved may also become manifest among YOU.

20 Therefore, when YOU come together to one place, it is not possible to eat the Lord's evening meal. 21 For, when YOU eat [it], each one takes his own evening meal beforehand, so that one is hungry but another is intoxicated. 22 Certainly YOU do have houses for eating and drinking, do YOU not? Or

do you despise the congregation of God and make those who have nothing ashamed? What shall I say to you? Shall I commend you? In this I do not commend you.

23 For I received from the Lord that which I also handed on to you, that the Lord Jesus in the night in which he was going to be handed over took a loaf 24 and, after giving thanks, he broke it and said: "This means my body which is in your behalf. Keep doing this in remembrance of me." 25 He did likewise respecting the cup also, after he had the evening meal, saying: "This cup means the new covenant by virtue of my blood. Keep doing this, as often as you drink it, in remembrance of me." 26 For as often as you eat this loaf and drink this cup, you keep proclaiming the death of the Lord, until he arrives.

27 Consequently whoever eats the loaf or drinks the cup of the Lord unworthily will be guilty respecting the body and the blood of the Lord. 28 First let a man approve himself after scrutiny, and thus let him eat of the loaf and drink of the cup. 29 For he that eats and drinks eats and drinks judgment against himself if he does not discern the body. 30 That is why many among you are weak and sickly, and quite a few are sleeping [in death]. 31 But if we would discern what we ourselves are, we would not be judged. 32 However, when we are judged, we are disciplined by Jehovah, that we may not become condemned with the world. 33 Consequently, my brothers, when you come together to eat [it], wait for one another. 34 If anyone is hungry, let him eat at home, that you may not come together for judgment. But the remaining matters I will set in order when I get there.

12 Now concerning the spiritual gifts, brothers, I do not want you to be ignorant. 2 You know that when you were people of the nations, you were being led away to those voiceless idols just as you happened to be led. 3 Therefore I

would have you know that nobody when speaking by God's spirit says: "Jesus is accursed!" and nobody can say: "Jesus is Lord!" except by holy spirit.

4 Now there are varieties of gifts, but there is the same spirit; 5 and there are varieties of ministries, and yet there is the same Lord; 6 and there are varieties of operations, and yet it is the same God who performs all the operations in all persons. 7 But the manifestation of the spirit is given to each one for a beneficial purpose. 8 For example, to one there is given through the spirit speech of wisdom, to another speech of knowledge according to the same spirit, 9 to another faith by the same spirit, to another gifts of healings by that one spirit, 10 to yet another operations of powerful works, to another prophesying, to another discernment of inspired utterances, to another different tongues, and to another interpretation of tongues. 11 But all these operations the one and the same spirit performs, making a distribution to each one respectively just as it wills.

12 For just as the body is one but has many members, and all the members of that body, although being many, are one body, so also is the Christ. 13 For truly by one spirit we were all baptized into one body, whether Jews or Greeks, whether slaves or free, and we were all made to drink one spirit.

14 For the body, indeed, is not one member, but many. 15 If the foot should say: "Because I am not a hand, I am no part of the body," it is not for this reason no part of the body. 16 And if the ear should say: "Because I am not an eye, I am no part of the body," it is not for this reason no part of the body. 17 If the whole body were an eye, where would the [sense of] hearing be? If it were all hearing, where would the smelling be? 18 But now God has set the members in the body, each one of them, just as he pleased.

19 If they were all one member, where would the body be? 20 But

now they are many members, yet one body. 21 The eye cannot say to the hand: "I have no need of you"; or, again, the head [cannot say] to the feet: "I have no need of you." 22 But much rather is it the case that the members of the body which seem to be weaker are necessary, 23 and the parts of the body which we think to be less honorable, these we surround with more abundant honor, and so our unseemly parts have the more abundant comeliness, 24 whereas our comely parts do not need anything. Nevertheless, God compounded the body, giving honor more abundant to the part which had a lack, 25 so that there should be no division in the body, but that its members should have the same care for one another. 26 And if one member suffers, all the other members suffer with it; or if a member is glorified, all the other members rejoice with it.

27 Now you are Christ's body, and members individually. 28 And God has set the respective ones in the congregation, first, apostles; second, prophets; third, teachers; then powerful works; then gifts of healings; helpful services, abilities to direct, different tongues. 29 Not all are apostles, are they? Not all are prophets, are they? Not all are teachers, are they? Not all perform powerful works, do they? 30 Not all have gifts of healings, do they? Not all speak in tongues, do they? Not all are translators, are they? 31 But keep zealously seeking the greater gifts. And yet I show you a surpassing way.

13 If I speak in the tongues of men and of angels but do not have love, I have become a sounding [piece of] brass or a clashing cymbal. 2 And if I have the gift of prophesying and am acquainted with all the sacred secrets and all knowledge, and if I have all the faith so as to transplant mountains, but do not have love, I am nothing. 3 And if I give all my belongings to feed others, and if I hand over my body, that I may boast, but do not have love, I am not profited at all.

4 Love is long-suffering and kind. Love is not jealous, it does not brag, does not get puffed up, 5 does not behave indecently, does not look for its own interests, does not become provoked. It does not keep account of the injury. 6 It does not rejoice over unrighteousness, but rejoices with the truth. 7 It bears all things, believes all things, hopes all things, endures all things.

8 Love never fails. But whether there are [gifts of] prophesying, they will be done away with; whether there are tongues, they will cease; whether there is knowledge, it will be done away with. 9 For we have partial knowledge and we prophesy partially; 10 but when that which is complete arrives, that which is partial will be done away with. 11 When I was a babe, I used to speak as a babe, to think as a babe, to reason as a babe; but now that I have become a man, I have done away with the [traits] of a babe. 12 For at present we see in hazy outline by means of a metal mirror, but then it will be face to face. At present I know partially, but then I shall know accurately even as I am accurately known. 13 Now, however, there remain faith, hope, love, these three; but the greatest of these is love.

14 Pursue love, yet keep zealously seeking the spiritual gifts, but preferably that you may prophesy. 2 For he that speaks in a tongue speaks, not to men, but to God, for no one listens, but he speaks sacred secrets by the spirit. 3 However, he that prophesies upbuilds and encourages and consoles men by his speech. 4 He that speaks in a tongue upbuilds himself, but he that prophesies upbuilds a congregation. 5 Now I would like for all of you to speak in tongues, but I prefer that you prophesy. Indeed, he that prophesies is greater than he that speaks in tongues, unless, in fact, he translates, that the congregation may receive upbuilding. 6 But at this time, brothers, if I should come speaking to YOU in tongues, what good would I do YOU unless I spoke to YOU either with a revelation or with knowledge or with a prophecy or with a teaching?

7 As it is, the inanimate things give off sound, whether a flute or a harp; unless it makes an interval to the tones, how will it be known what is being played on the flute or on the harp? 8 For truly, if the trumpet sounds an indistinct call, who will get ready for battle? 9 In the same way also, unless YOU through the tongue utter speech easily understood, how will it be known what is being spoken? YOU will, in fact, be speaking into the air. 10 It may be that there are so many kinds of speech sounds in the world, and yet no [kind] is without meaning. 11 If, then, I do not understand the force of the speech sound, I shall be a foreigner to the one speaking, and the one speaking will be a foreigner to me. 12 So also YOU yourselves, since YOU are zealously desirous of [gifts of the] spirit, seek to abound in them for the upbuilding of the congregation.

13 Therefore let the one who speaks in a tongue pray that he may translate. 14 For if I am praying in a tongue, it is my [gift of the] spirit that is praying, but my mind is unfruitful. 15 What is to be done, then? I will pray with the [gift of the] spirit, but I will also pray with [my] mind. I will sing praise with the [gift of the] spirit, but I will also sing praise with [my] mind. 16 Otherwise, if you offer praise with a [gift of the] spirit, how will the man occupying the seat of the ordinary person say Amen to your giving of thanks, since he does not know what you are saying? 17 True, you give thanks in a fine way, but the other man is not being built up. 18 I thank God, I speak in more tongues than all of YOU do. 19 Nevertheless, in a congregation I would rather speak five words with my mind, that I might also instruct others verbally,

than ten thousand words in a tongue.

20 Brothers, do not become young children in powers of understanding, but be babes as to badness; yet become full-grown in powers of understanding. 21 In the Law it is written: " 'With the tongues of foreigners and with the lips of strangers I will speak to this people, and yet not even then will they give heed to me,' says Jehovah." 22 Consequently tongues are for a sign, not to the believers, but to the unbelievers, whereas prophesying is, not for the unbelievers, but for the believers. 23 Therefore, if the whole congregation comes together to one place and they all speak in tongues, but ordinary people or unbelievers come in, will they not say that YOU are mad? 24 But if YOU are all prophesying and any unbeliever or ordinary person comes in, he is reproved by them all, he is closely examined by all; 25 the secrets of his heart become manifest, so that he will fall upon [his] face and worship God, declaring: "God is really among YOU."

26 What is to be done, then, brothers? When YOU come together, one has a psalm, another has a teaching, another has a revelation, another has a tongue, another has an interpretation. Let all things take place for upbuilding. 27 And if someone speaks in a tongue, let it be limited to two or three at the most, and in turns; and let someone translate. 28 But if there be no translator, let him keep silent in the congregation and speak to himself and to God. 29 Further, let two or three prophets speak, and let the others discern the meaning. 30 But if there is a revelation to another one while sitting there, let the first one keep silent. 31 For YOU can all prophesy one by one, that all may learn and all be encouraged. 32 And [gifts of] the spirit of the prophets are to be controlled by the prophets. 33 For God is [a God], not of disorder, but of peace.

As in all the congregations of the holy ones, 34 let the women

movable, always having plenty to do in the work of [the] Lord, knowing that YOUR labor is not in vain in connection with the Lord.

16 Now concerning the collection that is for the holy ones, just as I gave orders to the congregations of Ga·la′ti·a, do that way also yourselves. 2 Every first day of the week let each of YOU at his own house set something aside in store as he may be prospering, so that when I arrive collections will not take place then. 3 But when I get there, whatever men YOU approve of by letters, these I shall send to carry YOUR kind gift to Jerusalem. 4 However, if it is fitting for me to go there also, they will go there with me.

5 But I shall come to YOU when I have gone through Mac·e·do′ni·a, for I am going through Mac·e·do′ni·a; 6 and perhaps I shall stay or even pass the winter with YOU, that YOU may conduct me part way to where I may be going. 7 For I do not want to see YOU just now on [my] passing through, for I hope to remain some time with YOU, if Jehovah permits. 8 But I am remaining in Eph′e·sus until the [festival of] Pentecost; 9 for a large door that leads to activity has been opened to me, but there are many opposers.

10 However, if Timothy arrives, see that he becomes free of fear among YOU, for he is performing the work of Jehovah, even as I am. 11 Let no one, therefore, look down upon him. Conduct him part way in peace, that he may get here

to me, for I am waiting for him with the brothers.

12 Now concerning A·pol′los our brother, I entreated him very much to come to YOU with the brothers, and yet it was not his will at all to come now; but he will come when he has the opportunity.

13 Stay awake, stand firm in the faith, carry on as men, grow mighty. 14 Let all YOUR affairs take place with love.

15 Now I exhort YOU, brothers: YOU know that the household of Steph′a·nas is the first fruits of A·cha′ia and that they set themselves to minister to the holy ones. 16 May YOU also keep submitting yourselves to persons of that kind and to everyone co-operating and laboring. 17 But I rejoice over the presence of Steph′a·nas and For·tu·na′tus and A·cha′i·cus, because they have made up for YOUR not being here. 18 For they have refreshed my spirit and YOURS. Therefore recognize men of that sort.

19 The congregations of Asia send YOU their greetings. Aq′ui·la and Pris′ca together with the congregation that is in their house greet YOU heartily in [the] Lord. 20 All the brothers greet YOU. Greet one another with a holy kiss.

21 [Here is] my greeting, Paul's, in my own hand.

22 If anyone has no affection for the Lord, let him be accursed. O our Lord, come! 23 May the undeserved kindness of the Lord Jesus be with YOU. 24 May my love be with all of YOU in union with Christ Jesus.

THE SECOND TO THE

CORINTHIANS

1 Paul, an apostle of Christ Jesus through God's will, and Timothy [our] brother to the congregation of God that is in Corinth, together with all the holy ones who are in all of A·cha′ia: 2 May YOU have undeserved kind-

ness and peace from God our Father and [the] Lord Jesus Christ.

3 Blessed be the God and Father of our Lord Jesus Christ, the Father of tender mercies and the God of all comfort, 4 who comforts us in all our tribulation, that we may

be able to comfort those in any sort of tribulation through the comfort with which we ourselves are being comforted by God. 5 For just as the sufferings for the Christ abound in us, so the comfort we get also abounds through the Christ. 6 Now whether we are in tribulation, it is for YOUR comfort and salvation; or whether we are being comforted, it is for YOUR comfort that operates to make YOU endure the same sufferings that we also suffer. 7 And so our hope for YOU is unwavering, knowing as we do that, just as YOU are sharers of the sufferings, in the same way YOU will also share the comfort.

8 For we do not wish YOU to be ignorant, brothers, about the tribulation that happened to us in the [district of] Asia, that we were under extreme pressure beyond our strength, so that we were very uncertain even of our lives. 9 In fact, we felt within ourselves that we had received the sentence of death. This was that we might have our trust, not in ourselves, but in the God who raises up the dead. 10 From such a great thing as death he did rescue us and will rescue us; and our hope is in him that he will also rescue us further. 11 YOU also can help along by YOUR supplication for us, in order that thanks may be given by many in our behalf for what is kindly given to us due to many [prayerful] faces.

12 For the thing we boast of is this, to which our conscience bears witness, that with holiness and godly sincerity, not with fleshly wisdom but with God's undeserved kindness, we have conducted ourselves in the world, but more especially toward YOU. 13 For we are really not writing YOU things except those which YOU well know or also recognize; and which I hope YOU will continue to recognize to the end, 14 just as YOU have also recognized, to an extent, that we are a cause for YOU to boast, just as YOU will also be for us in the day of our Lord Jesus.

15 So, with this confidence, I was intending before to come to YOU, that YOU might have a second [occasion for] joy, 16 and after a stopover with YOU to go to Mac·e·do'ni·a, and to come back from Mac·e·do'ni·a to YOU and be conducted part way by YOU to Ju·de'a. 17 Well, when I had such an intention, I did not indulge in any lightness, did I? Or what things I purpose, do I purpose [them] according to the flesh, that with me there should be "Yes, Yes" and "No, No"? 18 But God can be relied upon that our speech addressed to YOU is not Yes and yet No. 19 For the Son of God, Christ Jesus, who was preached among YOU through us, that is, through me and Sil·va'nus and Timothy, did not become Yes and yet No, but Yes has become Yes in his case. 20 For no matter how many the promises of God are, they have become Yes by means of him. Therefore also through him is the Amen [said] to God for glory through us. 21 But he who guarantees that YOU and we belong to Christ and he who has anointed us is God. 22 He has also put his seal upon us and has given us the token of what is to come, that is, the spirit, in our hearts.

23 Now I call upon God as a witness against my own soul that it is to spare YOU that I have not yet come to Corinth. 24 Not that we are the masters over YOUR faith, but we are fellow workers for YOUR joy, for it is by [YOUR] faith that YOU are standing.

2 For this is what I have decided for myself, not to come to YOU again in sadness. 2 For if I make YOU sad, who indeed is there to cheer me except the one that is made sad by me? 3 And so I wrote this very thing, that, when I come, I may not get sad because of those over whom I ought to rejoice; because I have confidence in all of YOU that the joy I have is that of all of YOU. 4 For out of much tribulation and anguish of heart I wrote YOU with many tears, not that YOU might be saddened,

but that you might know the love that I have more especially for you.

5 Now if anyone has caused sadness, he has saddened, not me, but all of you to an extent—not to be too harsh in what I say. 6 This rebuke given by the majority is sufficient for such a man, 7 so that, on the contrary now, you should kindly forgive and comfort [him], that somehow such a man may not be swallowed up by his being overly sad. 8 Therefore I exhort you to confirm your love for him. 9 For to this end also I write to ascertain the proof of you, whether you are obedient in all things. 10 Anything you kindly forgive anyone, I do too. In fact, as for me, whatever I have kindly forgiven, if I have kindly forgiven anything, it has been for your sakes in Christ's sight; 11 that we may not be overreached by Satan, for we are not ignorant of his designs.

12 Now when I arrived in Tro'as to declare the good news about the Christ, and a door was opened to me in [the] Lord, 13 I got no relief in my spirit on account of not finding Titus my brother, but I said good-by to them and departed for Mac·e·do'ni·a.

14 But thanks be to God who always leads us in a triumphal procession in company with the Christ and makes the odor of the knowledge of him perceptible through us in every place! 15 For to God we are a sweet odor of Christ among those who are being saved and among those who are perishing; 16 to the latter ones an odor issuing from death to death, to the former ones an odor issuing from life to life. And who is adequately qualified for these things? 17 [We are;] for we are not peddlers of the word of God as many men are, but as out of sincerity, yes, as sent from God, under God's view, in company with Christ, we are speaking.

3 Are we starting again to recommend ourselves? Or do we, perhaps, like some men, need letters of recommendation to you or from you? 2 You yourselves are our letter, inscribed on our hearts and known and being read by all mankind. 3 For you are shown to be a letter of Christ written by us as ministers, inscribed not with ink but with spirit of a living God, not on stone tablets, but on fleshly tablets, on hearts.

4 Now through the Christ we have this sort of confidence toward God. 5 Not that we of ourselves are adequately qualified to reckon anything as issuing from ourselves, but our being adequately qualified issues from God, 6 who has indeed adequately qualified us to be ministers of a new covenant, not of a written code, but of spirit; for the written code condemns to death, but the spirit makes alive.

7 Moreover, if the code which administers death and which was engraved in letters in stones came about in a glory, so that the sons of Israel could not gaze intently at the face of Moses because of the glory of his face, [a glory] that was to be done away with, 8 why should not the administering of the spirit be much more with glory? 9 For if the code administering condemnation was glorious, much more does the administering of righteousness abound with glory. 10 In fact, even that which has once been made glorious has been stripped of glory in this respect, because of the glory that excels it. 11 For if that which was to be done away with was brought in with glory, much more would that which remains be with glory.

12 Therefore, as we have such a hope, we are using great freeness of speech, 13 and not doing as when Moses would put a veil upon his face, that the sons of Israel might not gaze intently at the end of that which was to be done away with. 14 But their mental powers were dulled. For to this present day the same veil remains unlifted at the reading of the old covenant, because it is done away with by means of Christ. 15 In fact, down till today whenever

Moses is read, a veil lies upon their hearts. 16 But when there is a turning to Jehovah, the veil is taken away. 17 Now Jehovah is the Spirit; and where the spirit of Jehovah is, there is freedom. 18 And all of us, while we with unveiled faces reflect like mirrors the glory of Jehovah, are transformed into the same image from glory to glory, exactly as done by Jehovah [the] Spirit.

4 That is why, since we have this ministry according to the mercy that was shown us, we do not give up; 2 but we have renounced the underhanded things of which to be ashamed, not walking with cunning, neither adulterating the word of God, but by making the truth manifest recommending ourselves to every human conscience in the sight of God. 3 If, now, the good news we declare is in fact veiled, it is veiled among those who are perishing, 4 among whom the god of this system of things has blinded the minds of the unbelievers, that the illumination of the glorious good news about the Christ, who is the image of God, might not shine through. 5 For we are preaching, not ourselves, but Christ Jesus as Lord, and ourselves as YOUR slaves for Jesus' sake. 6 For God is he who said: "Let the light shine out of darkness," and he has shone on our hearts to illuminate [them] with the glorious knowledge of God by the face of Christ.

7 However, we have this treasure in earthen vessels, that the power beyond what is normal may be God's and not that out of ourselves. 8 We are pressed in every way, but not cramped beyond movement; we are perplexed, but not absolutely with no way out; 9 we are persecuted, but not left in the lurch; we are thrown down, but not destroyed. 10 Always we endure everywhere in our body the death-dealing treatment given to Jesus, that the life of Jesus may also be made manifest in our body. 11 For we who live are ever being brought face to face with death for Jesus' sake, that the life of Jesus

may also be made manifest in our mortal flesh. 12 Consequently death is at work in us, but life in YOU.

13 Now because we have the same spirit of faith as that of which it is written: "I exercised faith, therefore I spoke," we too exercise faith and therefore we speak, 14 knowing that he who raised Jesus up will raise us up also together with Jesus and will present us together with YOU. 15 For all things are for YOUR sakes, in order that the undeserved kindness which was multiplied should abound because of the thanksgiving of many more to the glory of God.

16 Therefore we do not give up, but even if the man we are outside is wasting away, certainly the man we are inside is being renewed from day to day. 17 For though the tribulation is momentary and light, it works out for us a glory that is of more and more surpassing weight and is everlasting; 18 while we keep our eyes, not on the things seen, but on the things unseen. For the things seen are temporary, but the things unseen are everlasting.

5 For we know that if our earthly house, this tent, should be dissolved, we are to have a building from God, a house not made with hands, everlasting in the heavens. 2 For in this dwelling house we do indeed groan, earnestly desiring to put on the one for us from heaven, 3 so that, having really put it on, we shall not be found naked. 4 In fact, we who are in this tent groan, being weighed down; because we want, not to put it off, but to put on the other, that what is mortal may be swallowed up by life. 5 Now he that produced us for this very thing is God, who gave us the token of what is to come, that is, the spirit.

6 We are therefore always of good courage and know that, while we have our home in the body, we are absent from the Lord, 7 for we are walking by faith, not by sight. 8 But we are of good cour-

age and are well pleased rather to become absent from the body and to make our home with the Lord. 9 Therefore we are also making it our aim that, whether having our home with him or being absent from him, we may be acceptable to him. 10 For we must all be made manifest before the judgment seat of the Christ, that each one may get his award for the things done through the body, according to the things he has practiced, whether it is good or vile.

11 Knowing, therefore, the fear of the Lord, we keep persuading men, but we have been made manifest to God. However, I hope that we have been made manifest also to YOUR consciences. 12 We are not again recommending ourselves to YOU, but giving YOU an inducement for boasting in respect to us, that YOU may have [an answer] for those who boast over the outward appearance but not over the heart. 13 For if we were out of our mind, it was for God; if we are sound in mind, it is for YOU. 14 For the love the Christ has compels us, because this is what we have judged, that one man died for all; so, then, all had died; 15 and he died for all that those who live might live no longer for themselves, but for him who died for them and was raised up.

16 Consequently from now on we know no man according to the flesh. Even if we have known Christ according to the flesh, certainly we now know him so no more. 17 Consequently if anyone is in union with Christ, he is a new creation; the old things passed away, look! new things have come into existence. 18 But all things are from God, who reconciled us to himself through Christ and gave us the ministry of the reconciliation, 19 namely, that God was by means of Christ reconciling a world to himself, not reckoning to them their trespasses, and he committed the word of the reconciliation to us.

20 We are therefore ambassadors substituting for Christ, as though God were making entreaty through us. As substitutes for Christ we beg: "Become reconciled to God." 21 The one who did not know sin he made to be sin for us, that we might become God's righteousness by means of him.

6 Working together with him, we also entreat YOU not to accept the undeserved kindness of God and miss its purpose. 2 For he says: "In an acceptable time I heard you, and in a day of salvation I helped you." Look! Now is the especially acceptable time. Look! Now is the day of salvation.

3 In no way are we giving any cause for stumbling, that our ministry might not be found fault with; 4 but in every way we recommend ourselves as God's ministers, by the endurance of much, by tribulations, by cases of need, by difficulties, 5 by beatings, by prisons, by disorders, by labors, by sleepless nights, by times without food, 6 by purity, by knowledge, by long-suffering, by kindness, by holy spirit, by love free from hypocrisy, 7 by truthful speech, by God's power; through the weapons of righteousness on the right hand and on the left, 8 through glory and dishonor, through bad report and good report; as deceivers and yet truthful, 9 as being unknown and yet being recognized, as dying and yet, look! we live, as disciplined and yet not delivered to death, 10 as sorrowing but ever rejoicing, as poor but making many rich, as having nothing and yet possessing all things.

11 Our mouth has been opened to YOU, Corinthians, our heart has widened out. 12 You are not cramped for room within us, but YOU are cramped for room in YOUR own tender affections. 13 So, as a recompense in return—I speak as to children—YOU, too, widen out.

14 Do not become unevenly yoked with unbelievers. For what fellowship do righteousness and lawlessness have? Or what sharing does light have with darkness? 15 Further, what harmony is there between Christ and Be'li·al? Or what

portion does a faithful person have with an unbeliever? 16 And what agreement does God's temple have with idols? For we are a temple of a living God; just as God said: "I shall reside among them and walk among [them], and I shall be their God, and they will be my people." 17 " 'Therefore get out from among them, and separate yourselves,' says Jehovah, 'and quit touching the unclean thing' "; " 'and I will take YOU in.' " 18 " 'And I shall be a father to YOU, and YOU will be sons and daughters to me,' says Jehovah the Almighty."

7 Therefore, since we have these promises, beloved ones, let us cleanse ourselves of every defilement of flesh and spirit, perfecting holiness in God's fear.

2 ALLOW room for us. We have wronged no one, we have corrupted no one, we have taken advantage of no one. 3 I do not say this to condemn YOU. For I have said before that YOU are in our hearts to die and to live with us. 4 I have great freeness of speech toward YOU. I have great boasting in regard to YOU. I am filled with comfort, I am overflowing with joy in all our affliction.

5 In fact, when we arrived in Mac·e·do'ni·a, our flesh got no relief, but we continued to be afflicted in every manner—there were fights without, fears within. 6 Nevertheless God, who comforts those laid low, comforted us by the presence of Titus; 7 yet not alone by his presence, but also by the comfort with which he had been comforted over YOU, as he brought us word again of YOUR longing, YOUR mourning, YOUR zeal for me; so that I rejoiced yet more.

8 Hence even if I saddened YOU by my letter, I do not regret it. Even if I did at first regret it, (I see that that letter saddened YOU, though but for a little while,) 9 now I rejoice, not because YOU were just saddened, but because YOU were saddened into repenting; for YOU were saddened in a godly way, that YOU might suffer no damage in anything due to us.

10 For sadness in a godly way makes for repentance to salvation that is not to be regretted; but the sadness of the world produces death. 11 For, look! this very thing, YOUR being saddened in a godly way, what a great earnestness it produced in YOU, yes, clearing of yourselves, yes, indignation, yes, fear, yes, longing, yes, zeal, yes, righting of the wrong! In every respect YOU demonstrated yourselves to be chaste in this matter. 12 Certainly, although I wrote YOU, I did it, neither for the one who did the wrong, nor for the one who was wronged, but that YOUR earnestness for us might be made manifest among YOU in the sight of God. 13 That is why we have been comforted.

However, in addition to our comfort we rejoiced still more abundantly due to the joy of Titus, because his spirit has been refreshed by all of YOU. 14 For if we have made any boast to him about YOU, I have not been put to shame; but as we have spoken all things to YOU in truth, so also our boasting before Titus has proved to be true. 15 Also, his tender affections are more abundant toward YOU, while he calls to mind the obedience of all of YOU, how YOU received him with fear and trembling. 16 I rejoice that in every way I may have good courage by reason of YOU.

8 Now we let YOU know, brothers, about the undeserved kindness of God that has been bestowed upon the congregations of Mac·e·do'ni·a, 2 that during a great test under affliction their abundance of joy and their deep poverty made the riches of their generosity abound. 3 For according to their actual ability, yes, I testify, beyond their actual ability this was, 4 while they of their own accord kept begging us with much entreaty for the [privilege of] kindly giving and for a share in the ministry destined for the holy ones. 5 And not merely as we had hoped, but first they gave themselves to the Lord and to us through God's will. 6 This led us to encourage Titus

that, just as he had been the one to initiate it among you, so too he should complete this same kind giving on your part. 7 Nevertheless, just as you are abounding in everything, in faith and word and knowledge and all earnestness and in this love of ours to you, may you also abound in this kind giving.

8 It is not in the way of commanding you, but in view of the earnestness of others and to make a test of the genuineness of your love, that I am speaking. 9 For you know the undeserved kindness of our Lord Jesus Christ, that though he was rich he became poor for your sakes, that you might become rich through his poverty.

10 And in this I render an opinion: for this matter is of benefit to you, seeing that already a year ago you initiated not only the doing but also the wanting [to do]; 11 now, then, finish up also the doing of it, in order that, just as there was a readiness to want to do, so also there should be a finishing up of it out of what you have. 12 For if the readiness is there first, it is especially acceptable according to what a person has, not according to what a person does not have. 13 For I do not mean for it to be easy for others, but hard on you; 14 but that by means of an equalizing your surplus just now might offset their deficiency, in order that their surplus might also come to offset your deficiency, that an equalizing might take place. 15 Just as it is written: "The person with much did not have too much, and the person with little did not have too little."

16 Now thanks be to God for putting the same earnestness for you in the heart of Titus, 17 because he has indeed responded to the encouragement, but, being very earnest, he is going forth of his own accord to you. 18 But we are sending along with him the brother whose praise in connection with the good news has spread through all the congregations. 19 Not only that, but he was also appointed by the congregations to be our travel-

ing companion in connection with this kind gift to be administered by us for the glory of the Lord and in proof of our ready mind. 20 Thus we are avoiding having any man find fault with us in connection with this liberal contribution to be administered by us. 21 For we "make honest provision, not only in the sight of Jehovah, but also in the sight of men."

22 Moreover, we are sending with them our brother whom we have often proved in many things to be earnest, but now much more earnest due to his great confidence in you. 23 If, though, there is any question about Titus, he is a sharer with me and a fellow worker for your interests; or if about our brothers, they are apostles of congregations and a glory of Christ. 24 Therefore demonstrate to them the proof of your love and of what we boasted about you, before the face of the congregations.

9 Now concerning the ministry that is for the holy ones, it is superfluous for me to write you, 2 for I know your readiness of mind of which I am boasting to the Mac·e·do′ni·ans about you, that A·cha′ia has stood ready now for a year, and your zeal has stirred up the majority of them. 3 But I am sending the brothers, that our boasting about you might not prove empty in this respect, but that you may really be ready, just as I used to say you would be. 4 Otherwise, in some way, if Mac·e·do′ni·ans should come with me and find you not ready, we—not to say you—should be put to shame in this assurance of ours. 5 Therefore I thought it necessary to encourage the brothers to come to you in advance and to get ready in advance your bountiful gift previously promised, that thus this might be ready as a bountiful gift and not as something extorted.

6 But as to this, he that sows sparingly will also reap sparingly; and he that sows bountifully will also reap bountifully. 7 Let each one do just as he has resolved in

his heart, not grudgingly or under compulsion, for God loves a cheerful giver. 8 God, moreover, is able to make all his undeserved kindness abound toward you, that, while you always have full self-sufficiency in everything, you may have plenty for every good work. 9 (Just as it is written: "He has distributed widely, he has given to the poor ones, his righteousness continues forever." 10 Now he that abundantly supplies seed to the sower and bread for eating will supply and multiply the seed for you to sow and will increase the products of your righteousness.) 11 In everything you are being enriched for every sort of generosity, which produces through us an expression of thanks to God; 12 because the ministry of this public service is not only to supply abundantly the wants of the holy ones but also to be rich with many expressions of thanks to God. 13 Through the proof that this ministry gives, they glorify God because you are submissive to the good news about the Christ, as you publicly declare you are, and because you are generous in your contribution to them and to all; 14 and with supplication for you they long for you because of the surpassing undeserved kindness of God upon you. 15 Thanks be to God for his indescribable free gift.

10 Now I myself, Paul, entreat you by the mildness and kindness of the Christ, lowly though I am in appearance among you, whereas when absent I am bold toward you. 2 Indeed I beg that, when present, I may not use boldness with that confidence with which I am counting on taking bold measures against some who appraise us as if we walked according to [what we are in the] flesh. 3 For though we walk in the flesh, we do not wage warfare according to [what we are in the] flesh. 4 For the weapons of our warfare are not fleshly, but powerful by God for overturning strongly entrenched things. 5 For we are overturning reasonings and every lofty thing raised up against the knowledge of God; and we are bringing every thought into captivity to make it obedient to the Christ; 6 and we are holding ourselves in readiness to inflict punishment for every disobedience, as soon as your own obedience has been fully carried out.

7 You look at things according to their face value. If anyone trusts in himself that he belongs to Christ, let him again take this fact into account for himself, that, just as he belongs to Christ, so do we also. 8 For even if I should boast a bit too much about the authority that the Lord gave us to build you up and not to tear you down, I would not be put to shame, 9 that I may not seem to want to terrify you by [my] letters. 10 For, say they: "[his] letters are weighty and forceful, but [his] presence in person is weak and [his] speech contemptible." 11 Let such a man take this into account, that what we are in our word by letters when absent, such we shall also be in action when present. 12 For we do not dare to class ourselves among some or compare ourselves with some who recommend themselves. Certainly they in measuring themselves by themselves and comparing themselves with themselves have no understanding.

13 For our part we will boast, not outside our assigned boundaries, but according to the boundary of the territory that God apportioned to us by measure, making it reach even as far as you. 14 Really we are not overstretching ourselves as if we did not reach to you, for we were the first to come even as far as you in declaring the good news about the Christ. 15 No, we are not boasting outside our assigned boundaries in the labors of someone else, but we entertain hope that, as your faith is being increased, we may be made great among you with reference to our territory. Then we will abound still more, 16 to declare the good news to the countries beyond you, so as not to

boast in someone else's territory where things are already prepared. 17 "But he that boasts, let him boast in Jehovah." 18 For not the one who recommends himself is approved, but the man whom Jehovah recommends.

11 I wish you would put up with me in some little unreasonableness. But, in fact, you are putting up with me! 2 For I am jealous over you with a godly jealousy, for I personally promised you in marriage to one husband that I might present you as a chaste virgin to the Christ. 3 But I am afraid that somehow, as the serpent seduced Eve by its cunning, your minds might be corrupted away from the sincerity and the chastity that are due the Christ. 4 For, as it is, if someone comes and preaches a Jesus other than the one we preached, or you receive a spirit other than what you received, or good news other than what you accepted, you easily put up [with him]. 5 For I consider that I have not in a single thing proved inferior to your superfine apostles. 6 But even if I am unskilled in speech, I certainly am not in knowledge; but in every way we manifested [it] to you in all things.

7 Or did I commit a sin by humbling myself that you might be exalted, because without cost I gladly declared the good news of God to you? 8 Other congregations I robbed by accepting provisions in order to minister to you; 9 and yet when I was present with you and I fell in need, I did not become a burden to a single one, for the brothers that came from Mac·e·do'ni·a abundantly supplied my deficiency. Yes, in every way I kept myself unburdensome to you and will keep myself so. 10 It is a truth of Christ in my case that no stop shall be put to this boasting of mine in the regions of A·cha'ia. 11 For what reason? Because I do not love you? God knows [I do].

12 Now what I am doing I will still do, that I may cut off the pretext from those who are wanting a pretext for being found equal to us in the office of which they boast. 13 For such men are false apostles, deceitful workers, transforming themselves into apostles of Christ. 14 And no wonder, for Satan himself keeps transforming himself into an angel of light. 15 It is therefore nothing great if his ministers also keep transforming themselves into ministers of righteousness. But their end shall be according to their works.

16 I say again, Let no man think I am unreasonable. Still, if you really do, accept me even if as unreasonable, that I too may do some little boasting. 17 What I speak I speak, not after the Lord's example, but as in unreasonableness, in this cocksureness peculiar to boasting. 18 Since many are boasting according to the flesh, I too will boast. 19 For you gladly put up with the unreasonable persons, seeing you are reasonable. 20 In fact, you put up with whoever enslaves you, whoever devours [what you have], whoever grabs [what you have], whoever exalts himself over [you], whoever strikes you in the face.

21 I say this to [our] dishonor, as though our position had been weak.

But if anyone else acts bold in something—I am talking unreasonably—I too am acting bold in it. 22 Are they Hebrews? I am one also. Are they Israelites? I am one also. Are they Abraham's seed? I am also. 23 Are they ministers of Christ? I reply like a madman, I am more outstandingly one: in labors more plentifully, in prisons more plentifully, in blows to an excess, in near-deaths often. 24 By Jews I five times received forty strokes less one, 25 three times I was beaten with rods, once I was stoned, three times I experienced shipwreck, a night and a day I have spent in the deep; 26 in journeys often, in dangers from rivers, in dangers from highwaymen, in dangers from [my own] race, in dangers from the nations, in dangers in the city, in dangers in the wilderness, in dangers at sea, in dangers among false brothers, 27 in labor and toil, in sleepless nights often, in hunger and thirst, in abstinence from food many times, in cold and nakedness. 28 Besides those things of an external kind, there is what rushes in on me from day to day, the anxiety for all the congregations. 29 Who is weak, and I am not weak? Who is stumbled, and I am not incensed?

30 If boasting there must be, I will boast of the things having to do with my weakness. 31 The God and Father of the Lord Jesus, even the One who is to be praised forever, knows I am not lying. 32 In Damascus the governor under A·re′tas the king was guarding the city of the Dam·a·scenes′ to seize me, 33 but through a window in the wall I was lowered in a wicker basket and escaped his hands.

12 I have to boast. It is not beneficial; but I shall pass on to supernatural visions and revelations of [the] Lord. 2 I know a man in union with Christ who, fourteen years ago—whether in the body I do not know, or out of the body I do not know; God knows—was caught away as such to the third heaven. 3 Yes, I know such a man—whether in the body or apart from the body, I do not know, God knows— 4 that he was caught away into paradise and heard unutterable words which it is not lawful for a man to speak. 5 Over such a man I will boast, but I will not boast over myself, except as respects [my] weaknesses. 6 For if I ever do want to boast, I shall not be unreasonable, for I shall say the truth. But I abstain, in order that no one should put to my credit more than what he sees I am or he hears from me, 7 just because of the excess of the revelations.

Therefore, that I might not feel overly exalted, there was given me a thorn in the flesh, an angel of Satan, to keep slapping me, that I might not be overly exalted. 8 In this behalf I three times entreated the Lord that it might depart from me; 9 and yet he really said to me: "My undeserved kindness is sufficient for you; for [my] power is being made perfect in weakness." Most gladly, therefore, will I rather boast as respects my weaknesses, that the power of the Christ may like a tent remain over me. 10 Therefore I take pleasure in weaknesses, in insults, in cases of need, in persecutions and difficulties, for Christ. For when I am weak, then I am powerful.

11 I have become unreasonable. You compelled me to, for I ought to have been recommended by you. For I did not prove to be inferior to [your] superfine apostles in a single thing, even if I am nothing. 12 Indeed, the signs of an apostle were produced among you by all endurance, and by signs and portents and powerful works. 13 For in what respect is it that you became less than the rest of the congregations, except that I myself did not become a burden to you? Kindly forgive me this wrong.

14 Look! This is the third time I am ready to come to you, and yet I will not become a burden. For I am seeking, not your possessions, but you; for the children ought not to lay up for [their] parents, but the parents for [their] children. 15 For my part I will most gladly spend and be completely spent for your souls. If I love you the more abundantly, am I to be loved the less? 16 But be that as it may, I did not burden you down. Nevertheless, you say, I was "crafty" and I caught you "by trickery." 17 As for any one of those I have dispatched to you, I did not take advantage of you through him, did I? 18 I urged Titus and I dispatched the brother with him. Titus did not take advantage of you at all, did he? We walked in the same spirit, did we not? In the same footsteps, did we not?

19 Have you been thinking all this while that we have been making our defense to you? It is before

God that we are speaking in connection with Christ. But, beloved ones, all things are for YOUR upbuilding. 20 For I am afraid that somehow, when I arrive, I may find YOU not as I could wish and I may prove to be to YOU not as YOU could wish, but, instead, there should somehow be strife, jealousy, cases of anger, contentions, backbitings, whisperings, cases of being puffed up, disorders. 21 Perhaps, when I come again, my God might humiliate me among YOU, and I might mourn over many of those who formerly sinned but have not repented over their uncleanness and fornication and loose conduct that they have practiced.

13 This is the third time I am coming to YOU. "At the mouth of two witnesses or of three every matter must be established." 2 I have said previously and, as if present the second time and yet absent now, I say in advance to those who have sinned before and to all the rest, that if ever I come again I will not spare, 3 since YOU are seeking a proof of Christ speaking in me, [Christ] who is not weak toward YOU but is powerful among YOU. 4 True, indeed, he was impaled owing to weakness, but he is alive owing to God's power. True, also, we are weak with him, but we shall live together with him owing to God's power toward YOU.

5 Keep testing whether YOU are in the faith, keep proving what YOU yourselves are. Or do YOU not recognize that Jesus Christ is in union with YOU? Unless YOU are disapproved. 6 I truly hope YOU will come to know we are not disapproved.

7 Now we pray to God that YOU may do nothing wrong, not that we ourselves may appear approved, but that YOU may be doing what is fine, though we ourselves may appear disapproved. 8 For we can do nothing against the truth, but only for the truth. 9 We certainly rejoice whenever we are weak but YOU are powerful; and for this we are praying, YOUR being readjusted. 10 That is why I write these things while absent, that, when I am present, I may not act with severity according to the authority that the Lord gave me, to build up and not to tear down.

11 Finally, brothers, continue to rejoice, to be readjusted, to be comforted, to think in agreement, to live peaceably; and the God of love and of peace will be with YOU. 12 Greet one another with a holy kiss. 13 All the holy ones send YOU their greetings.

14 The undeserved kindness of the Lord Jesus Christ and the love of God and the sharing in the holy spirit be with all of YOU.

TO THE

GALATIANS

1 Paul, an apostle, neither from men nor through a man, but through Jesus Christ and God the Father, who raised him up from the dead, 2 and all the brothers with me, to the congregations of Ga·la′ti·a:

3 May YOU have undeserved kindness and peace from God our Father and [the] Lord Jesus Christ. 4 He gave himself for our sins that he might deliver us from the present wicked system of things according to the will of our God and Father, 5 to whom be the glory forever and ever. Amen.

6 I marvel that YOU are being so quickly removed from the One who called YOU with Christ's undeserved kindness over to another sort of good news. 7 But it is not another; only there are certain ones who are causing YOU trouble and wanting to pervert the good news

about the Christ. 8 However, even if we or an angel out of heaven were to declare to YOU as good news something beyond what we declared to YOU as good news, let him be accursed. 9 As we have said above, I also now say again, Whoever it is that is declaring to YOU as good news something beyond what YOU accepted, let him be accursed.

10 Is it, in fact, men I am now trying to persuade or God? Or am I seeking to please men? If I were yet pleasing men, I would not be Christ's slave. 11 For I put YOU on notice, brothers, that the good news which was declared by me as good news is not something human; 12 for neither did I receive it from man, nor was I taught [it], except through revelation by Jesus Christ.

13 YOU, of course, heard about my conduct formerly in Ju′da·ism, that to the point of excess I kept on persecuting the congregation of God and devastating it, 14 and I was making greater progress in Ju′da·ism than many of my own age in my race, as I was far more zealous for the traditions of my fathers. 15 But when God, who separated me from my mother's womb and called [me] through his undeserved kindness, thought good 16 to reveal his Son in connection with me, that I might declare the good news about him to the nations, I did not go at once into conference with flesh and blood. 17 Neither did I go up to Jerusalem to those who were apostles previous to me, but I went off into Arabia, and I came back again to Damascus.

18 Then three years later I went up to Jerusalem to visit Ce′phas, and I stayed with him for fifteen days. 19 But I saw no one else of the apostles, only James the brother of the Lord. 20 Now as to the things I am writing YOU, look! in the sight of God, I am not lying.

21 After that I went into the regions of Syria and of Ci·li′ci·a. 22 But I was unknown by face to the congregations of Ju·de′a that were in union with Christ; 23 they only used to hear: "The man that formerly persecuted us is now declaring the good news about the faith which he formerly devastated." 24 So they began glorifying God because of me.

2 Then after fourteen years I again went up to Jerusalem with Bar′na·bas, taking also Titus along with me. 2 But I went up as a result of a revelation. And I laid before them the good news which I am preaching among the nations, privately, however, before those who were outstanding men, for fear that somehow I was running or had run in vain. 3 Nevertheless, not even Titus, who was with me, was compelled to be circumcised, although he was a Greek. 4 But because of the false brothers brought in quietly, who sneaked in to spy upon our freedom which we have in union with Christ Jesus, that they might completely enslave us— 5 to these we did not yield by way of submission, no, not for an hour, in order that the truth of the good news might continue with YOU.

6 But on the part of those who seemed to be something—whatever sort of men they formerly were makes no difference to me—God does not go by a man's outward appearance—to me, in fact, those outstanding men imparted nothing new. 7 But, on the contrary, when they saw that I had entrusted to me the good news for those who are uncircumcised, just as Peter [had it] for those who are circumcised— 8 for He who gave Peter powers necessary for an apostleship to those who are circumcised gave powers also to me for those who are of the nations; 9 yes, when they came to know the undeserved kindness that was given me, James and Ce′phas and John, the ones who seemed to be pillars, gave me and Bar′na·bas the right hand of sharing together, that we should go to the nations, but they to those who are circumcised. 10 Only we should keep the poor in mind. This very thing I have also earnestly endeavored to do.

11 However, when Ce'phas came to Antioch, I resisted him face to face, because he stood condemned. 12 For before the arrival of certain men from James, he used to eat with people of the nations; but when they arrived, he went withdrawing and separating himself, in fear of those of the circumcised class. 13 The rest of the Jews also joined him in putting on this pretense, so that even Bar'na·bas was led along with them in their pretense. 14 But when I saw they were not walking straight according to the truth of the good news, I said to Ce'phas before them all: "If you, though you are a Jew, live as the nations do, and not as Jews do, how is it that you are compelling people of the nations to live according to Jewish practice?"

15 We who are Jews by nature, and not sinners from the nations, 16 knowing as we do that a man is declared righteous, not due to works of law, but only through faith toward Christ Jesus, even we have put our faith in Christ Jesus, that we may be declared righteous due to faith toward Christ, and not due to works of law, because due to works of law no flesh will be declared righteous. 17 Now if we, in seeking to be declared righteous by means of Christ, have also ourselves been found sinners, is Christ in reality sin's minister? May that never happen! 18 For if the very things that I once threw down I build up again, I demonstrate myself to be a transgressor. 19 As for me, through law I died toward law, that I might become alive toward God. 20 I am impaled along with Christ. It is no longer I that live, but it is Christ that is living in union with me. Indeed, the life that I now live in flesh I live by the faith that is toward the Son of God, who loved me and handed himself over for me. 21 I do not shove aside the undeserved kindness of God; for if righteousness is through law, Christ actually died for nothing.

3 O senseless Ga·la'tians, who is it that brought you under evil influence, you before whose eyes Jesus Christ was openly portrayed impaled? 2 This alone I want to learn from you: Did you receive the spirit due to works of law or due to a hearing by faith? 3 Are you so senseless? After starting in spirit are you now being completed in flesh? 4 Did you undergo so many sufferings to no purpose? If it really was to no purpose. 5 He, therefore, who supplies you the spirit and performs powerful works among you, does he do it owing to works of law or owing to a hearing by faith? 6 Just as Abraham "put faith in Jehovah, and it was counted to him as righteousness."

7 Surely you know that those who adhere to faith are the ones who are sons of Abraham. 8 Now the Scripture, seeing in advance that God would declare people of the nations righteous due to faith, declared the good news beforehand to Abraham, namely: "By means of you all the nations will be blessed." 9 Consequently those who adhere to faith are being blessed together with faithful Abraham.

10 For all those who depend upon works of law are under a curse; for it is written: "Cursed is every one that does not continue in all the things written in the scroll of the Law in order to do them." 11 Moreover, that by law no one is declared righteous with God is evident, because "the righteous one will live by reason of faith." 12 Now the Law does not adhere to faith, but "he that does them shall live by means of them." 13 Christ by purchase released us from the curse of the Law by becoming a curse instead of us, because it is written: "Accursed is every man hanged upon a stake." 14 The purpose was that the blessing of Abraham might come to be by means of Jesus Christ for the nations, that we might receive the promised spirit through our faith.

15 Brothers, I speak with a human illustration: A validated cove-

nant, though it is a man's, no one sets aside or attaches additions to it. 16 Now the promises were spoken to Abraham and to his seed. It says, not: "And to seeds," as in the case of many such, but as in the case of one: "And to your seed," who is Christ. 17 Further, I say this: As to the covenant previously validated by God, the Law that has come into being four hundred and thirty years later does not invalidate it, so as to abolish the promise. 18 For if the inheritance is due to law, it is no longer due to promise; whereas God has kindly given it to Abraham through a promise.

19 Why, then, the Law? It was added to make transgressions manifest, until the seed should arrive to whom the promise had been made; and it was transmitted through angels by the hand of a mediator. 20 Now there is no mediator where only one person is concerned, but God is only one. 21 Is the Law, therefore, against the promises of God? May that never happen! For if a law had been given that was able to give life, righteousness would actually have been by means of law. 22 But the Scripture delivered up all things together to the custody of sin, that the promise resulting from faith toward Jesus Christ might be given to those exercising faith.

23 However, before the faith arrived, we were being guarded under law, being delivered up together into custody, looking to the faith that was destined to be revealed. 24 Consequently the Law has become our tutor leading to Christ, that we might be declared righteous due to faith. 25 But now that the faith has arrived, we are no longer under a tutor.

26 You are all, in fact, sons of God through your faith in Christ Jesus. 27 For all of you who were baptized into Christ have put on Christ. 28 There is neither Jew nor Greek, there is neither slave nor freeman, there is neither male nor female; for you are all one [person] in union with Christ Jesus. 29 Moreover, if you belong to Christ, you are really Abraham's seed, heirs with reference to a promise.

4 Now I say that as long as the heir is a babe he does not differ at all from a slave, lord of all things though he is, 2 but he is under men in charge and under stewards until the day his father appointed beforehand. 3 Likewise we also, when we were babes, continued enslaved by the elementary things belonging to the world. 4 But when the full limit of the time arrived, God sent forth his Son, who came to be out of a woman and who came to be under law, 5 that he might release by purchase those under law, that we, in turn, might receive the adoption as sons.

6 Now because you are sons, God has sent forth the spirit of his Son into our hearts and it cries out: "Abba, Father!" 7 So, then, you are no longer a slave but a son; and if a son, also an heir through God.

8 Nevertheless, when you did not know God, then it was that you slaved for those who by nature are not gods. 9 But now that you have come to know God, or rather now that you have come to be known by God, how is it that you are turning back again to the weak and beggarly elementary things and want to slave for them over again? 10 You are scrupulously observing days and months and seasons and years. 11 I fear for you, that somehow I have toiled to no purpose respecting you.

12 Brothers, I beg you, Become as I am, because I used to be also as you are. You did me no wrong. 13 But you know that it was through a sickness of my flesh I declared the good news to you the first time. 14 And what was a trial to you in my flesh, you did not treat with contempt or spit at in disgust; but you received me like an angel of God, like Christ Jesus. 15 Where, then, is that happiness you had? For I bear you witness that, if it had been possible, you would have gouged out your

eyes and given them to me. 16 Well, then, have I become YOUR enemy because I tell YOU the truth? 17 They zealously seek YOU, not in a fine way, but they want to shut YOU off [from me], that YOU may zealously seek them. 18 However, it is fine for YOU to be zealously sought for in a fine cause at all times, and not only when I am present with YOU, 19 my little children, with whom I am again in childbirth pains until Christ is formed in YOU. 20 But I could wish to be present with YOU just now and to speak in a different way, because I am perplexed over YOU.

21 Tell me, YOU who want to be under law, Do YOU not hear the Law? 22 For example, it is written that Abraham acquired two sons, one by the servant girl and one by the free woman; 23 but the one by the servant girl was actually born in the manner of flesh, the other by the free woman through a promise. 24 These things stand as a symbolic drama; for these [women] mean two covenants, the one from Mount Si'nai, which brings forth children for slavery, and which is Ha'gar. 25 Now this Ha'gar means Si'nai, a mountain in Arabia, and she corresponds with the Jerusalem today, for she is in slavery with her children. 26 But the Jerusalem above is free, and she is our mother.

27 For it is written: "Be glad, you barren woman who does not give birth; break out and cry aloud, you woman who does not have childbirth pains; for the children of the desolate woman are more numerous than [those] of her who has the husband." 28 Now we, brothers, are children belonging to the promise the same as Isaac was. 29 But just as then the one born in the manner of flesh began persecuting the one born in the manner of spirit, so also now. 30 Nevertheless, what does the Scripture say? "Drive out the servant girl and her son, for by no means shall the son of the servant girl be an heir with the son of the free woman." 31 Wherefore, brothers, we are children, not of a servant girl, but of the free woman.

5 For such freedom Christ set us free. Therefore stand fast, and do not let yourselves be confined again in a yoke of slavery.

2 See! I, Paul, am telling YOU that if YOU become circumcised, Christ will be of no benefit to YOU. 3 Moreover, I bear witness again to every man getting circumcised that he is under obligation to perform the whole Law. 4 YOU are parted from Christ, whoever YOU are that try to be declared righteous by means of law; YOU have fallen away from his undeserved kindness. 5 For our part we by spirit are eagerly waiting for the hoped-for righteousness as a result of faith. 6 For as regards Christ Jesus neither circumcision is of any value nor is uncircumcision, but faith operating through love [is].

7 YOU were running well. Who hindered YOU from keeping on obeying the truth? 8 This sort of persuasion is not from the One calling YOU. 9 A little leaven ferments the whole lump. 10 I am confident about YOU who are in union with [the] Lord that YOU will not come to think otherwise; but the one who is causing YOU trouble will bear [his] judgment, no matter who he may be. 11 As for me, brothers, if I am still preaching circumcision, why am I still being persecuted? Then, indeed, the stumbling block of the torture stake has been abolished. 12 I wish the men who are trying to overturn YOU would even get themselves emasculated.

13 YOU were, of course, called for freedom, brothers; only do not use this freedom as an inducement for the flesh, but through love slave for one another. 14 For the entire Law stands fulfilled in one saying, namely: "You must love your neighbor as yourself." 15 If, though, YOU keep on biting and devouring one another, look out that YOU do not get annihilated by one another.

16 But I say, Keep walking by spirit and YOU will carry out no fleshly desire at all. 17 For the flesh is against the spirit in its desire, and the spirit against the flesh; for these are opposed to each other, so that the very things that YOU would like to do YOU do not do. 18 Furthermore, if YOU are being led by spirit, YOU are not under law.

19 Now the works of the flesh are manifest, and they are fornication, uncleanness, loose conduct, 20 idolatry, practice of spiritism, enmities, strife, jealousy, fits of anger, contentions, divisions, sects, 21 envies, drunken bouts, revelries, and things like these. As to these things I am forewarning YOU, the same way as I did forewarn YOU, that those who practice such things will not inherit God's kingdom.

22 On the other hand, the fruitage of the spirit is love, joy, peace, long-suffering, kindness, goodness, faith, 23 mildness, self-control. Against such things there is no law. 24 Moreover, those who belong to Christ Jesus impaled the flesh together with its passions and desires.

25 If we are living by spirit, let us go on walking orderly also by spirit. 26 Let us not become egotistical, stirring up competition with one another, envying one another.

6 Brothers, even though a man takes some false step before he is aware of it, YOU who have spiritual qualifications try to readjust such a man in a spirit of mildness, as you each keep an eye on yourself, for fear you also may be tempted. 2 Go on carrying the burdens of one another, and thus fulfill the law of the Christ. 3 For if anyone thinks he is something when he is nothing, he is deceiving his own mind. 4 But let him prove what his own work is, and then he will have cause for exultation in regard to himself alone, and not in comparison with the other person.

5 For each one will carry his own load.

6 Moreover, let anyone who is being orally taught the word share in all good things with the one who gives such oral teaching.

7 Do not be misled: God is not one to be mocked. For whatever a man is sowing, this he will also reap; 8 because he who is sowing with a view to his flesh will reap corruption from his flesh, but he who is sowing with a view to the spirit will reap everlasting life from the spirit. 9 So let us not give up in doing what is fine, for in due season we shall reap if we do not tire out. 10 Really, then, as long as we have time favorable for it, let us work what is good toward all, but especially toward those related to [us] in the faith.

11 SEE with what large letters I have written YOU with my own hand.

12 All those who want to make a pleasing appearance in the flesh are the ones that try to compel YOU to get circumcised, only that they may not be persecuted for the torture stake of the Christ, Jesus. 13 For not even do those who are getting circumcised keep the Law themselves, but they want YOU to be circumcised that they may have cause for boasting in YOUR flesh. 14 Never may it occur that I should boast, except in the torture stake of our Lord Jesus Christ, through whom the world has been impaled to me and I to the world. 15 For neither is circumcision anything nor is uncircumcision, but a new creation [is something]. 16 And all those who will walk orderly by this rule of conduct, upon them be peace and mercy, even upon the Israel of God.

17 Henceforth let no one be making trouble for me, for I am carrying on my body the brand marks [of a slave] of Jesus.

18 The undeserved kindness of our Lord Jesus Christ be with the spirit YOU show, brothers. Amen.

EPHESIANS

1 Paul, an apostle of Christ Jesus through God's will, to the holy ones who are in Eph'e·sus and faithful ones in union with Christ Jesus:

2 May YOU have undeserved kindness and peace from God our Father and [the] Lord Jesus Christ.

3 Blessed be the God and Father of our Lord Jesus Christ, for he has blessed us with every spiritual blessing in the heavenly places in union with Christ, 4 just as he chose us in union with him before the founding of the world, that we should be holy and without blemish before him in love. 5 For he foreordained us to the adoption through Jesus Christ as sons to himself, according to the good pleasure of his will, 6 in praise of his glorious undeserved kindness which he kindly conferred upon us by means of [his] loved one. 7 By means of him we have the release by ransom through the blood of that one, yes, the forgiveness of [our] trespasses, according to the riches of his undeserved kindness.

8 This he caused to abound toward us in all wisdom and good sense, 9 in that he made known to us the sacred secret of his will. It is according to his good pleasure which he purposed in himself 10 for an administration at the full limit of the appointed times, namely, to gather all things together again in the Christ, the things in the heavens and the things on the earth. [Yes,] in him, 11 in union with whom we were also assigned as heirs, in that we were foreordained according to the purpose of him who operates all things according to the way his will counsels, 12 that we should serve for the praise of his glory, we who have been first to hope in the Christ. 13 But YOU also hoped in him after YOU heard the word of truth, the good news about YOUR salvation. By means of him also, after YOU believed, YOU were sealed with the promised holy spirit, 14 which is a token in advance of our inheritance, for the purpose of releasing by a ransom God's own possession, to his glorious praise.

15 That is why I also, since I have heard of the faith YOU have in the Lord Jesus and toward all the holy ones, 16 do not cease giving thanks for YOU. I continue mentioning YOU in my prayers, 17 that the God of our Lord Jesus Christ, the Father of glory, may give YOU a spirit of wisdom and of revelation in the accurate knowledge of him; 18 the eyes of YOUR heart having been enlightened, that YOU may know what is the hope to which he called YOU, what the glorious riches which he holds as an inheritance for the holy ones, 19 and what the surpassing greatness of his power is toward us believers. It is according to the operation of the mightiness of his strength, 20 with which he has operated in the case of the Christ when he raised him up from the dead and seated him at his right hand in the heavenly places, 21 far above every government and authority and power and lordship and every name named, not only in this system of things, but also in that to come. 22 He also subjected all things under his feet, and made him head over all things to the congregation, 23 which is his body, the fullness of him who fills up all things in all.

2 Furthermore, [it is] YOU [God made alive] though YOU were dead in YOUR trespasses and sins, 2 in which YOU at one time walked according to the system of things of this world, according to the ruler of the authority of the air, the spirit that now operates in the sons of disobedience. 3 Yes, among them we all at one time conducted ourselves in harmony with the desires of our flesh, doing the things willed by the flesh and the thoughts, and we were naturally children of wrath even as the rest. 4 But God, who is rich in mercy, for his great love with which he loved us, 5 made us alive together with the Christ, even when we were dead in trespasses—by undeserved kindness you have been saved— 6 and he raised us up together and seated us together in the heavenly places in union with Christ Jesus, 7 that in the coming systems of things there might be demonstrated the surpassing riches of his undeserved kindness in his graciousness toward us in union with Christ Jesus.

8 By this undeserved kindness, indeed, you have been saved through faith; and this not owing to you, it is God's gift. 9 No, it is not owing to works, in order that no man should have ground for boasting. 10 For we are a product of his work and were created in union with Christ Jesus for good works, which God prepared in advance for us to walk in them.

11 Therefore keep bearing in mind that formerly you were people of the nations as to flesh; "uncircumcision" you were called by that which is called "circumcision" made in the flesh with hands— 12 that you were at that particular time without Christ, alienated from the state of Israel and strangers to the covenants of the promise, and you had no hope and were without God in the world. 13 But now in union with Christ Jesus you who were once far off have come to be near by the blood of the Christ. 14 For he is our peace, he who made the two parties one and destroyed the wall in between that fenced them off. 15 By means of his flesh he abolished the enmity, the Law of commandments consisting in decrees, that he might create the two peoples in union with himself into one new man and make peace; 16 and that he might

fully reconcile both peoples in one body to God through the torture stake, because he had killed off the enmity by means of himself. 17 And he came and declared the good news of peace to you, the ones far off, and peace to those near, 18 because through him we, both peoples, have the approach to the Father by one spirit.

19 Certainly, therefore, you are no longer strangers and alien residents, but you are fellow citizens of the holy ones and are members of the household of God, 20 and you have been built up upon the foundation of the apostles and prophets, while Christ Jesus himself is the foundation cornerstone. 21 In union with him the whole building, being harmoniously joined together, is growing into a holy temple for Jehovah. 22 In union with him you, too, are being built up together into a place for God to inhabit by spirit.

3 On account of this I, Paul, the prisoner of Christ Jesus in behalf of you, the people of the nations— 2 if, really, you have heard about the stewardship of the undeserved kindness of God that was given me with you in view, 3 that by way of a revelation the sacred secret was made known to me, just as I wrote previously in brief. 4 In the face of this you, when you read this, can realize the comprehension I have in the sacred secret of the Christ. 5 In other generations this [secret] was not made known to the sons of men as it has now been revealed to his holy apostles and prophets by spirit, 6 namely, that people of the nations should be joint heirs and fellow members of the body and partakers with us of the promise in union with Christ Jesus through the good news. 7 I became a minister of this according to the free gift of the undeserved kindness of God that was given me according to the way his power operates.

8 To me, a man less than the least of all holy ones, this undeserved kindness was given, that I should declare to the nations the

good news about the unfathomable riches of the Christ 9 and should make men see how the sacred secret is administered which has from the indefinite past been hidden in God, who created all things. 10 [This was] to the end that now to the governments and the authorities in the heavenly places there might be made known through the congregation the greatly diversified wisdom of God, 11 according to the eternal purpose that he formed in connection with the Christ, Jesus our Lord, 12 by means of whom we have this freeness of speech and an approach with confidence through our faith in him. 13 Wherefore I ask you not to give up on account of these tribulations of mine in your behalf, for these mean glory for you.

14 On account of this I bend my knees to the Father, 15 to whom every family in heaven and on earth owes its name, 16 to the end that he may grant you according to the riches of his glory to be made mighty in the man you are inside with power through his spirit, 17 to have the Christ dwell through [your] faith in your hearts with love; that you may be rooted and established on the foundation, 18 in order that you may be thoroughly able to grasp mentally with all the holy ones what is the breadth and length and height and depth, 19 and to know the love of the Christ which surpasses knowledge, that you may in everything be filled with all the fullness that God gives.

20 Now to the one who can, according to his power which is operating in us, do more than superabundantly beyond all the things we ask or conceive, 21 to him be the glory by means of the congregation and by means of Christ Jesus to all generations forever and ever. Amen.

4 I, therefore, the prisoner in [the] Lord, entreat you to walk worthily of the calling with which you were called, 2 with complete lowliness of mind and mildness, with long-suffering, putting up with one another in love, 3 earnestly endeavoring to observe the oneness of the spirit in the uniting bond of peace. 4 One body there is, and one spirit, even as you were called in the one hope to which you were called; 5 one Lord, one faith, one baptism; 6 one God and Father of all [persons], who is over all and through all and in all.

7 Now to each one of us undeserved kindness was given according to how the Christ measured out the free gift. 8 Wherefore he says: "When he ascended on high he carried away captives; he gave gifts [in] men." 9 Now the expression "he ascended," what does it mean but that he also descended into the lower regions, that is, the earth? 10 The very one that descended is also the one that ascended far above all the heavens, that he might give fullness to all things.

11 And he gave some as apostles, some as prophets, some as evangelizers, some as shepherds and teachers, 12 with a view to the readjustment of the holy ones, for ministerial work, for the building up of the body of the Christ, 13 until we all attain to the oneness in the faith and in the accurate knowledge of the Son of God, to a full-grown man, to the measure of stature that belongs to the fullness of the Christ; 14 in order that we should no longer be babes, tossed about as by waves and carried hither and thither by every wind of teaching by means of the trickery of men, by means of cunning in contriving error. 15 But speaking the truth, let us by love grow up in all things into him who is the head, Christ. 16 From him all the body, by being harmoniously joined together and being made to co-operate through every joint that gives what is needed, according to the functioning of each respective member in due measure, makes for the growth of the body for the building up of itself in love.

17 This, therefore, I say and bear witness to in [the] Lord, that

YOU no longer go on walking just as the nations also walk in the unprofitableness of their minds, 18 while they are in darkness mentally, and alienated from the life that belongs to God, because of the ignorance that is in them, because of the insensibility of their hearts. 19 Having come to be past all moral sense, they gave themselves over to loose conduct to work uncleanness of every sort with greediness.

20 But YOU did not learn the Christ to be so, 21 provided, indeed, that YOU heard him and were taught by means of him, just as truth is in Jesus, 22 that YOU should put away the old personality which conforms to YOUR former course of conduct and which is being corrupted according to his deceptive desires; 23 but that YOU should be made new in the force actuating YOUR mind, 24 and should put on the new personality which was created according to God's will in true righteousness and loyalty.

25 Wherefore, now that YOU have put away falsehood, speak truth each one of YOU with his neighbor, because we are members belonging to one another. 26 Be wrathful, and yet do not sin; let the sun not set with YOU in a provoked state, 27 neither allow place for the Devil. 28 Let the stealer steal no more, but rather let him do hard work, doing with his hands what is good work, that he may have something to distribute to someone in need. 29 Let a rotten saying not proceed out of YOUR mouth, but whatever saying is good for building up as the need may be, that it may impart what is favorable to the hearers. 30 Also, do not be grieving God's holy spirit, with which YOU have been sealed for a day of releasing by ransom. 31 Let all malicious bitterness and anger and wrath and screaming and abusive speech be taken away from YOU along with all badness. 32 But become kind to one another, tenderly compassionate, freely forgiving one another just as God also by Christ freely forgave YOU.

5 Therefore, become imitators of God, as beloved children, 2 and go on walking in love, just as the Christ also loved YOU and delivered himself up for YOU as an offering and a sacrifice to God for a sweet-smelling odor.

3 Let fornication and uncleanness of every sort or greediness not even be mentioned among YOU, just as it befits holy people; 4 neither shameful conduct nor foolish talking nor obscene jesting, things which are not becoming, but rather the giving of thanks. 5 For YOU know this, recognizing it for yourselves, that no fornicator or unclean person or greedy person—which means being an idolater—has any inheritance in the kingdom of the Christ and of God.

6 Let no man deceive YOU with empty words, for because of the aforesaid things the wrath of God is coming upon the sons of disobedience. 7 Therefore do not become partakers with them; 8 for YOU were once darkness, but YOU are now light in connection with [the] Lord. Go on walking as children of light, 9 for the fruitage of the light consists of every sort of goodness and righteousness and truth. 10 Keep on making sure of what is acceptable to the Lord; 11 and quit sharing with them in the unfruitful works that belong to the darkness, but, rather, even be reproving [them], 12 for the things that take place in secret by them it is shameful even to relate. 13 Now all the things that are being reproved are made manifest by the light, for everything that is being made manifest is light. 14 Wherefore he says: "Awake, O sleeper, and arise from the dead, and the Christ will shine upon you."

15 So keep strict watch that how YOU walk is not as unwise but as wise [persons], 16 buying out the opportune time for yourselves, because the days are wicked. 17 On this account cease becoming unreasonable, but go on perceiving what the will of Jehovah is. 18 Also,

do not be getting drunk with wine, in which there is debauchery, but keep getting filled with spirit, 19 speaking to yourselves with psalms and praises to God and spiritual songs, singing and accompanying yourselves with music in YOUR hearts to Jehovah, 20 in the name of our Lord Jesus Christ giving thanks always for all things to our God and Father.

21 Be in subjection to one another in fear of Christ. 22 Let wives be in subjection to their husbands as to the Lord, 23 because a husband is head of his wife as the Christ also is head of the congregation, he being a savior of [this] body. 24 In fact, as the congregation is in subjection to the Christ, so let wives also be to their husbands in everything. 25 Husbands, continue loving YOUR wives, just as the Christ also loved the congregation and delivered up himself for it, 26 that he might sanctify it, cleansing it with the bath of water by means of the word, 27 that he might present the congregation to himself in its splendor, not having a spot or a wrinkle or any of such things, but that it should be holy and without blemish.

28 In this way husbands ought to be loving their wives as their own bodies. He who loves his wife loves himself, 29 for no man ever hated his own flesh; but he feeds and cherishes it, as the Christ also does the congregation, 30 because we are members of his body. 31 "For this reason a man will leave [his] father and [his] mother and he will stick to his wife, and the two will become one flesh." 32 This sacred secret is great. Now I am speaking with respect to Christ and the congregation. 33 Nevertheless, also, let each one of YOU individually so love his wife as he does himself; on the other hand, the wife should have deep respect for her husband.

6 Children, be obedient to YOUR parents in union with [the] Lord, for this is righteous: 2 "Honor your father and [your] mother"; which is the first command with a promise: 3 "That it may go well with you and you may endure a long time on the earth." 4 And YOU, fathers, do not be irritating YOUR children, but go on bringing them up in the discipline and mental-regulating of Jehovah.

5 YOU slaves, be obedient to those who are [YOUR] masters in a fleshly sense, with fear and trembling in the sincerity of YOUR hearts, as to the Christ, 6 not by way of eyeservice as men pleasers, but as Christ's slaves, doing the will of God whole-souled. 7 Be slaves with good inclinations, as to Jehovah, and not to men, 8 for YOU know that each one, whatever good he may do, will receive this back from Jehovah, whether he be slave or freeman. 9 Also, YOU masters, keep doing the same things to them, letting up on the threatening, for YOU know that the Master of both them and YOU is in the heavens, and there is no partiality with him.

10 Finally, go on acquiring power in [the] Lord and in the mightiness of his strength. 11 Put on the complete suit of armor from God that YOU may be able to stand firm against the machinations of the Devil; 12 because we have a wrestling, not against blood and flesh, but against the governments, against the authorities, against the world rulers of this darkness, against the wicked spirit forces in the heavenly places. 13 On this account take up the complete suit of armor from God, that YOU may be able to resist in the wicked day and, after YOU have done all things thoroughly, to stand firm.

14 Stand firm, therefore, with YOUR loins girded about with truth, and having on the breastplate of righteousness, 15 and with YOUR feet shod with the equipment of the good news of peace. 16 Above all things, take up the large shield of faith, with which YOU will be able to quench all the wicked one's burning missiles. 17 Also, accept the helmet of salvation, and the sword of the spirit, that is, God's

word, 18 while with every form of prayer and supplication YOU carry on prayer on every occasion in spirit. And to that end keep awake with all constancy and with supplication in behalf of all the holy ones, 19 also for me, that ability to speak may be given me with the opening of my mouth, with all freeness of speech to make known the sacred secret of the good news, 20 for which I am acting as an ambassador in chains; that I may speak in connection with it with boldness as I ought to speak.

21 Now in order that YOU may also know about my affairs, as to how I am doing, Tych'i·cus, a beloved brother and faithful minister in [the] Lord, will make everything known to YOU. 22 I am sending him to YOU for this very purpose, that YOU may know of the things having to do with us and that he may comfort YOUR hearts.

23 May the brothers have peace and love with faith from God the Father and the Lord Jesus Christ. 24 May the undeserved kindness be with all those loving our Lord Jesus Christ in incorruptness.

TO THE

PHILIPPIANS

1 Paul and Timothy, slaves of Christ Jesus, to all the holy ones in union with Christ Jesus who are in Phi·lip'pi, along with overseers and ministerial servants:

2 May YOU have undeserved kindness and peace from God our Father and [the] Lord Jesus Christ.

3 I thank my God always upon every remembrance of YOU 4 in every supplication of mine for all of YOU, as I offer my supplication with joy, 5 because of the contribution YOU have made to the good news from the first day until this moment. 6 For I am confident of this very thing, that he who started a good work in YOU will carry it to completion until the day of Jesus Christ. 7 It is altogether right for me to think this regarding all of YOU, on account of my having YOU in my heart, all of YOU being sharers with me in the undeserved kindness, both in the defending and legally establishing of the good news.

8 For God is my witness of how I am yearning for all of YOU in such tender affection as Christ Jesus has. 9 And this is what I continue praying, that YOUR love may abound yet more and more

with accurate knowledge and full discernment; 10 that YOU may make sure of the more important things, so that YOU may be flawless and not be stumbling others up to the day of Christ, 11 and may be filled with righteous fruit, which is through Jesus Christ, to God's glory and praise.

12 Now I desire YOU to know, brothers, that my affairs have turned out for the advancement of the good news rather than otherwise, 13 so that my prison bonds have become public knowledge in association with Christ among all the prae·to'ri·an guard and all the rest; 14 and most of the brothers in [the] Lord, feeling confidence by reason of my prison bonds, are showing all the more courage to speak the word of God fearlessly.

15 True, some are preaching the Christ through envy and rivalry, but others also through good will. 16 The latter are publicizing the Christ out of love, for they know I am set here for the defense of the good news; 17 but the former do it out of contentiousness, not with a pure motive, for they are supposing to stir up tribulation [for me] in my prison bonds.

18 What then? [Nothing,] except that in every way, whether in pretense or in truth, Christ is being publicized, and in this I rejoice. In fact, I will also keep on rejoicing, **19** for I know this will result in my salvation through YOUR supplication and a supply of the spirit of Jesus Christ, **20** in harmony with my eager expectation and hope that I shall not be ashamed in any respect, but that in all freeness of speech Christ will, as always before, so now be magnified by means of my body, whether through life or through death.

21 For in my case to live is Christ, and to die, gain. **22** Now if it be to live on in the flesh, this is a fruitage of my work—and yet which thing to select I do not make known. **23** I am under pressure from these two things; but what I do desire is the releasing and the being with Christ, for this, to be sure, is far better. **24** However, for me to remain in the flesh is more necessary on YOUR account. **25** So, being confident of this, I know I shall remain and shall abide with all of YOU for YOUR advancement and the joy that belongs to [YOUR] faith, **26** so that YOUR exultation may overflow in Christ Jesus by reason of me through my presence again with YOU.

27 Only behave in a manner worthy of the good news about the Christ, in order that, whether I come and see YOU or be absent, I may hear about the things which concern YOU, that YOU are standing firm in one spirit, with one soul striving side by side for the faith of the good news, **28** and in no respect being frightened by YOUR opponents. This very thing is a proof of destruction for them, but of salvation for YOU; and this [indication] is from God, **29** because to YOU the privilege was given in behalf of Christ, not only to put YOUR faith in him, but also to suffer in his behalf. **30** For YOU have the same struggle as YOU saw in my case and as YOU now hear about in my case.

2 If, then, there is any encouragement in Christ, if any consolation of love, if any sharing of spirit, if any tender affections and compassions, **2** make my joy full in that YOU are of the same mind and have the same love, being joined together in soul, holding the one thought in mind, **3** doing nothing out of contentiousness or out of egotism, but with lowliness of mind considering that the others are superior to YOU, **4** keeping an eye, not in personal interest upon just YOUR own matters, but also in personal interest upon those of the others.

5 Keep this mental attitude in YOU that was also in Christ Jesus, **6** who, although he was existing in God's form, gave no consideration to a seizure, namely, that he should be equal to God. **7** No, but he emptied himself and took a slave's form and came to be in the likeness of men. **8** More than that, when he found himself in fashion as a man, he humbled himself and became obedient as far as death, yes, death on a torture stake. **9** For this very reason also God exalted him to a superior position and kindly gave him the name that is above every other name, **10** so that in the name of Jesus every knee should bend of those in heaven and those on earth and those under the ground, **11** and every tongue should openly acknowledge that Jesus Christ is Lord to the glory of God the Father.

12 Consequently, my beloved ones, in the way that YOU have always obeyed, not during my presence only, but now much more readily during my absence, keep working out YOUR own salvation with fear and trembling; **13** for God is the one that, for the sake of [his] good pleasure, is acting within YOU in order for YOU both to will and to act. **14** Keep doing all things free from murmurings and arguments, **15** that YOU may come to be blameless and innocent, children of God without a blemish in among a crooked and twisted generation, among whom YOU are shining as illuminators in the world. 16 keeping a tight grip on the word of life, that I may have cause for exultation in Christ's day, that I did not run in vain or work hard in vain. 17 Notwithstanding, even if I am being poured out like a drink offering upon the sacrifice and public service to which faith has led YOU, I am glad and I rejoice with all of YOU. 18 Now in the same way YOU yourselves also be glad and rejoice with me.

19 For my part I am hoping in the Lord Jesus to send Timothy to YOU shortly, that I may be a cheerful soul when I get to know about the things pertaining to YOU. 20 For I have no one else of a disposition like his who will genuinely care for the things pertaining to YOU. 21 For all the others are seeking their own interests, not those of Christ Jesus. 22 But YOU know the proof he gave of himself, that like a child with a father he slaved with me in furtherance of the good news. 23 This, therefore, is the man I am hoping to send just as soon as I have seen how things stand concerning me. 24 Indeed, I am confident in [the] Lord that I myself shall also come shortly.

25 However, I consider it necessary to send to YOU E·paph·ro·di′tus, my brother and fellow worker and fellow soldier, but YOUR envoy and private servant for my need, 26 since he is longing to see all of YOU and is depressed because YOU heard he had fallen sick. 27 Yes, indeed, he fell sick nearly to the point of death; but God had mercy on him, in fact, not only on him, but also on me, that I should not get grief upon grief. 28 Therefore with the greater haste I am sending him, that on seeing him YOU may rejoice again and I may be the more free from grief. 29 Therefore give him the customary welcome in [the] Lord with all joy; and keep holding men of that sort dear, 30 because on account of the Lord's work he came quite near to death, exposing his soul to danger, that he might fully make up for YOUR not being here to render private service to me.

3 Finally, my brothers, continue rejoicing in [the] Lord. To be writing the same things to YOU is not troublesome for me, but it is of safety to YOU.

2 Look out for the dogs, look out for the workers of injury, look out for those who mutilate the flesh. 3 For we are those with the real circumcision, who are rendering sacred service by God's spirit and have our boasting in Christ Jesus and do not have our confidence in the flesh, 4 though I, if anyone, do have grounds for confidence also in the flesh.

If any other man thinks he has grounds for confidence in the flesh, I the more so: 5 circumcised the eighth day, out of the family stock of Israel, of the tribe of Benjamin, a Hebrew [born] from Hebrews; as respects law, a Pharisee; 6 as respects zeal, persecuting the congregation; as respects righteousness that is by means of law, one who proved himself blameless. 7 Yet what things were gains to me, these I have considered loss on account of the Christ. 8 Why, for that matter, I do indeed also consider all things to be loss on account of the excelling value of the knowledge of Christ Jesus my Lord. On account of him I have taken the loss of all things and I consider them as a lot of refuse, that I may gain Christ 9 and be found in union with him, having, not my own righteousness, which results from law, but that which is through faith in Christ, the righteousness that issues from God on the basis of faith, 10 so as to know him and the power of his resurrection and a sharing in his sufferings, submitting myself to a death like his, 11 to see if I may by any means attain to the earlier resurrection from the dead.

12 Not that I have already received it or am already made perfect, but I am pursuing to see if I may also lay hold on that for which I have also been laid hold on by Christ Jesus. 13 Brothers,

I do not yet consider myself as having laid hold on [it]; but there is one thing about it: Forgetting the things behind and stretching forward to the things ahead, 14 I am pursuing down toward the goal for the prize of the upward call of God by means of Christ Jesus. 15 Let us, then, as many of us as are mature, be of this mental attitude; and if you are mentally inclined otherwise in any respect, God will reveal the above [attitude] to you. 16 At any rate, to what extent we have made progress, let us go on walking orderly in this same routine.

17 Unitedly become imitators of me, brothers, and keep your eye on those who are walking in a way that accords with the example you have in us. 18 For there are many, I used to mention them often but now I mention them also with weeping, who are walking as the enemies of the torture stake of the Christ, 19 and their finish is destruction, and their god is their belly, and their glory consists in their shame, and they have their minds upon things on the earth. 20 As for us, our citizenship exists in the heavens, from which place also we are eagerly waiting for a savior, the Lord Jesus Christ, 21 who will refashion our humiliated body to be conformed to his glorious body according to the operation of the power that he has, even to subject all things to himself.

4 Consequently, my brothers beloved and longed for, my joy and crown, stand firm in this way in [the] Lord, beloved ones.

2 Eu·o'di·a I exhort and Syn'ty·che I exhort to be of the same mind in [the] Lord. 3 Yes, I request you too, genuine yokefellow, keep assisting these [women] who have striven side by side with me in the good news along with Clement as well as the rest of my fellow workers, whose names are in the book of life.

4 Always rejoice in [the] Lord. Once more I will say, Rejoice! 5 Let your reasonableness become known to all men. The Lord is near. 6 Do not be anxious over anything, but in everything by prayer and supplication along with thanksgiving let your petitions be made known to God; 7 and the peace of God that excels all thought will guard your hearts and your mental powers by means of Christ Jesus.

8 Finally, brothers, whatever things are true, whatever things are of serious concern, whatever things are righteous, whatever things are chaste, whatever things are lovable, whatever things are well spoken of, whatever virtue there is and whatever praiseworthy thing there is, continue considering these things. 9 The things that you learned as well as accepted and heard and saw in connection with me, practice these; and the God of peace will be with you.

10 I do rejoice greatly in [the] Lord that now at last you have revived your thinking in my behalf, to which you were really giving thought, but you lacked opportunity. 11 Not that I am speaking with regard to being in want, for I have learned, in whatever circumstances I am, to be self-sufficient. 12 I know indeed how to be low [on provisions], I know indeed how to have an abundance. In everything and in all circumstances I have learned the secret of both how to be full and how to hunger, both how to have an abundance and how to suffer want. 13 For all things I have the strength by virtue of him who imparts power to me.

14 Nevertheless, you acted well in becoming sharers with me in my tribulation. 15 In fact, you Philip'pi·ans, also know that at [the] start of declaring the good news, when I departed from Mac·e·do'ni·a, not a congregation took a share with me in the matter of giving and receiving, except you alone; 16 because, even in Thes·sa·lo·ni'ca, you sent something to me both once and a second time for my need. 17 Not that I am earnestly seeking the gift, but that I am earnestly seeking the fruitage

that brings more credit to YOUR account. 18 However, I have all things in full and have an abundance. I am filled, now that I have received from E·paph·ro·di′tus the things from YOU, a sweet-smelling odor, an acceptable sacrifice, well-pleasing to God. 19 In turn, my God will fully supply all YOUR need to the extent of his riches in glory by means of Christ Jesus. 20 Now to our God and Father

be the glory forever and ever. Amen.

21 Give my greetings to every holy one in union with Christ Jesus. The brothers who are with me send YOU their greetings. 22 All the holy ones, but especially those of the household of Caesar, send YOU their greetings.

23 The undeserved kindness of the Lord Jesus Christ be with the spirit YOU [show].

TO THE

COLOSSIANS

1 Paul, an apostle of Christ Jesus through God's will, and Timothy [our] brother 2 to the holy ones and faithful brothers in union with Christ at Co·los′sae:

May YOU have undeserved kindness and peace from God our Father.

3 We thank God the Father of our Lord Jesus Christ always when we pray for YOU, 4 since we heard of YOUR faith in connection with Christ Jesus and the love YOU have for all the holy ones 5 because of the hope that is being reserved for YOU in the heavens. This [hope] YOU heard of before by the telling of the truth of that good news 6 which has presented itself to YOU, even as it is bearing fruit and increasing in all the world just as [it is doing] also among YOU, from the day YOU heard and accurately knew the undeserved kindness of God in truth. 7 That is what YOU have learned from Ep′a·phras our beloved fellow slave, who is a faithful minister of the Christ on our behalf, 8 who also disclosed to us YOUR love in a spiritual way.

9 That is also why we, from the day we heard [of it], have not ceased praying for YOU and asking that YOU may be filled with the accurate knowledge of his will in all wisdom and spiritual comprehension, 10 in order to walk worthily of Jehovah to the end of fully

pleasing [him] as YOU go on bearing fruit in every good work and increasing in the accurate knowledge of God, 11 being made powerful with all power to the extent of his glorious might so as to endure fully and be long-suffering with joy, 12 thanking the Father who rendered YOU suitable for YOUR participation in the inheritance of the holy ones in the light.

13 He delivered us from the authority of the darkness and transferred us into the kingdom of the Son of his love, 14 by means of whom we have our release by ransom, the forgiveness of our sins. 15 He is the image of the invisible God, the first-born of all creation; 16 because by means of him all [other] things were created in the heavens and upon the earth, the things visible and the things invisible, no matter whether they are thrones or lordships or governments or authorities. All [other] things have been created through him and for him. 17 Also, he is before all [other] things and by means of him all [other] things were made to exist, 18 and he is the head of the body, the congregation. He is the beginning, the first-born from the dead, that he might become the one who is first in all things; 19 because God saw good for all fullness to dwell in him, 20 and through him

to reconcile again to himself all [other] things by making peace through the blood [he shed] on the torture stake, no matter whether they are the things upon the earth or the things in the heavens.

21 Indeed, you who were once alienated and enemies because your minds were on the works that were wicked, 22 he now has again reconciled by means of that one's fleshly body through [his] death, in order to present you holy and unblemished and open to no accusation before him, 23 provided, of course, that you continue in the faith, established on the foundation and steadfast and not being shifted away from the hope of that good news which you heard, and which was preached in all creation that is under heaven. Of this [good news] I Paul became a minister.

24 I am now rejoicing in my sufferings for you, and I, in my turn, am filling up what is lacking of the tribulations of the Christ in my flesh on behalf of his body, which is the congregation. 25 I became a minister of this [congregation] in accordance with the stewardship from God which was given me in your interest to preach the word of God fully, 26 the sacred secret that was hidden from the past systems of things and from the past generations. But now it has been made manifest to his holy ones, 27 to whom God has been pleased to make known what are the glorious riches of this sacred secret among the nations. It is Christ in union with you, the hope of [his] glory. 28 He is the one we are publicizing, admonishing every man and teaching every man in all wisdom, that we may present every man complete in union with Christ. 29 To this end I am indeed working hard, exerting myself in accordance with the operation of him and which is at work in me with power.

2 For I want you to realize how great a struggle I am having in behalf of you and of those at La·o·di·ce′a and of all those who have not seen my face in the flesh,

2 that their hearts may be comforted, that they may be harmoniously joined together in love and with a view to all the riches of the full assurance of [their] understanding, with a view to an accurate knowledge of the sacred secret of God, namely, Christ. 3 Carefully concealed in him are all the treasures of wisdom and of knowledge. 4 This I am saying that no man may delude you with persuasive arguments. 5 For though I am absent in the flesh, all the same I am with you in the spirit, rejoicing and beholding your good order and the firmness of your faith toward Christ.

6 Therefore, as you have accepted Christ Jesus the Lord, go on walking in union with him, 7 rooted and being built up in him and being stabilized in the faith, just as you were taught, overflowing with [faith] in thanksgiving.

8 Look out: perhaps there may be someone who will carry you off as his prey through the philosophy and empty deception according to the tradition of men, according to the elementary things of the world and not according to Christ; 9 because it is in him that all the fullness of the divine quality dwells bodily. 10 And so you are possessed of a fullness by means of him, who is the head of all government and authority. 11 By relationship with him you were also circumcised with a circumcision [performed] without hands by the stripping off the body of the flesh, by the circumcision that belongs to the Christ, 12 for you were buried with him in [his] baptism, and by relationship with him you were also raised up together through [your] faith in the operation of God, who raised him up from the dead.

13 Furthermore, though you were dead in your trespasses and in the uncircumcised state of your flesh, [God] made you alive together with him. He kindly forgave us all our trespasses 14 and blotted out the handwritten document against

us, which consisted of decrees and which was in opposition to us; and He has taken it out of the way by nailing it to the torture stake. 15 Stripping the governments and the authorities bare, he exhibited them in open public as conquered, leading them in a triumphal procession by means of it.

16 Therefore let no man judge you in eating and drinking or in respect of a festival or of an observance of the new moon or of a sabbath; 17 for those things are a shadow of the things to come, but the reality belongs to the Christ. 18 Let no man deprive you of the prize who takes delight in a [mock] humility and a form of worship of the angels, "taking his stand on" the things he has seen, puffed up without proper cause by his fleshly frame of mind, 19 whereas he is not holding fast to the head, to the one from whom all the body, being supplied and harmoniously joined together by means of its joints and ligaments, goes on growing with the growth that God gives.

20 If you died together with Christ toward the elementary things of the world, why do you, as if living in the world, further subject yourselves to the decrees: 21 "Do not handle, nor taste, nor touch." 22 respecting things that are all destined to destruction by being used up, in accordance with the commands and teachings of men? 23 Those very things are, indeed, possessed of an appearance of wisdom in a self-imposed form of worship and [mock] humility, a severe treatment of the body; but they are of no value in combating the satisfying of the flesh.

3 If, however, you were raised up with the Christ, go on seeking the things above, where the Christ is seated at the right hand of God. 2 Keep your minds fixed on the things above, not on the things upon the earth. 3 For you died, and your life has been hidden with the Christ in union with God. 4 When the Christ, our life, is made manifest, then you also will be made manifest with him in glory.

5 Deaden, therefore, your body members that are upon the earth as respects fornication, uncleanness, sexual appetite, hurtful desire, and covetousness, which is idolatry. 6 On account of those things the wrath of God is coming. 7 In those very things you, too, once walked when you used to live in them. 8 But now really put them all away from you, wrath, anger, badness, abusive speech, and obscene talk out of your mouth. 9 Do not be lying to one another. Strip off the old personality with its practices, 10 and clothe yourselves with the new [personality], which through accurate knowledge is being made new according to the image of the One who created it, 11 where there is neither Greek nor Jew, circumcision nor uncircumcision, foreigner, Scyth'i·an, slave, freeman, but Christ is all things and in all.

12 Accordingly, as God's chosen ones, holy and loved, clothe yourselves with the tender affections of compassion, kindness, lowliness of mind, mildness, and longsuffering. 13 Continue putting up with one another and forgiving one another freely if anyone has a cause for complaint against another. Even as Jehovah freely forgave you, so do you also. 14 But, besides all these things, clothe yourselves with love, for it is a perfect bond of union.

15 Also, let the peace of the Christ control in your hearts, for you were, in fact, called to it in one body. And show yourselves thankful. 16 Let the word of the Christ reside in you richly in all wisdom. Keep on teaching and admonishing one another with psalms, praises to God, spiritual songs with graciousness, singing in your hearts to Jehovah. 17 And whatever it is that you do in word or in work, do everything in the name of the Lord Jesus, thanking God the Father through him.

18 You wives, be in subjection to [your] husbands, as it is becoming

in [the] Lord. 19 You husbands, keep on loving [YOUR] wives and do not be bitterly angry with them. 20 You children, be obedient to [YOUR] parents in everything, for this is well-pleasing in [the] Lord. 21 You fathers, do not be exasperating YOUR children, so that they do not become downhearted. 22 You slaves, be obedient in everything to those who are [YOUR] masters in a fleshly sense, not with acts of eyeservice, as men pleasers, but with sincerity of heart, with fear of Jehovah. 23 Whatever you are doing, work at it whole-souled as to Jehovah, and not to men, 24 for you know that it is from Jehovah you will receive the due reward of the inheritance. SLAVE for the Master, Christ. 25 Certainly the one that is doing wrong will receive back what he wrongly did, and there is no partiality.

4 You masters, keep dealing out what is righteous and what is fair to [YOUR] slaves, knowing that you also have a Master in heaven.

2 Be persevering in prayer, remaining awake in it with thanksgiving, 3 at the same time praying also for us, that God may open a door of utterance to us, to speak the sacred secret about the Christ, for which, in fact, I am in prison bonds; 4 so that I shall make it manifest as I ought to speak.

5 Go on walking in wisdom toward those on the outside, buying out the opportune time for yourselves. 6 Let YOUR utterance be always with graciousness, seasoned with salt, so as to know how you ought to give an answer to each one.

7 All my affairs Tych'i·cus, [my] beloved brother and faithful minister and fellow slave in [the] Lord, will make known to you. 8 For the very purpose of YOUR knowing the things having to do with us and that he may comfort YOUR hearts, I am sending him to you 9 along with O·nes'i·mus, my faithful and beloved brother, who is from among you. All the things here they will make known to you.

10 Ar·is·tar'chus my fellow captive sends you his greetings, and so does Mark the cousin of Bar'na·bas, (concerning whom you received commands to welcome him if ever he comes to you,) 11 and Jesus who is called Justus, these being of those circumcised. Only these are my fellow workers for the kingdom of God, and these very ones have become a strengthening aid to me. 12 Ep'a·phras, who is from among you, a slave of Christ Jesus, sends you his greetings, always exerting himself in YOUR behalf in [his] prayers, that you may finally stand complete and with firm conviction in all the will of God. 13 I indeed bear him witness that he puts himself to great effort in behalf of you and of those at La·o·di·ce'a and of those at Hi·e·rap'o·lis.

14 Luke the beloved physician sends you his greetings, and so does De'mas. 15 Give my greetings to the brothers at La·o·di·ce'a and to Nym'pha and to the congregation at her house. 16 And when this letter has been read among you, arrange that it also be read in the congregation of the La·o·di·ce'ans and that you also read the one from La·o·di·ce'a. 17 Also, tell Ar·chip'pus: "Keep watching the ministry which you accepted in [the] Lord, that you fulfill it."

18 [Here is] my greeting, Paul's, in my own hand. Continue bearing my [prison] bonds in mind. The undeserved kindness be with you.

THE FIRST TO THE
THESSALONIANS

1 Paul and Sil·va′nus and Tim-
othy to the congregation of the
Thes·sa·lo′ni·ans in union with
God the Father and [the] Lord
Jesus Christ:

May you have undeserved kindness and peace.

2 We always thank God when
we make mention concerning all of
you in our prayers, 3 for we bear
incessantly in mind your faithful
work and your loving labor and
[your] endurance due to [your]
hope in our Lord Jesus Christ before our God and Father. 4 For
we know, brothers loved by God,
his choosing of you, 5 because the
good news we preach did not turn
up among you with speech alone
but also with power and with holy
spirit and strong conviction, just
as you know what sort of men we
became to you for your sakes;
6 and you became imitators of us
and of the Lord, seeing that you
accepted the word under much
tribulation with joy of holy spirit,
7 so that you came to be an example to all the believers in Mac-
e·do′ni·a and in A·cha′ia.

8 The fact is, not only has the
word of Jehovah sounded forth
from you in Mac·e·do′ni·a and
A·cha′ia, but in every place your
faith toward God has spread
abroad, so that we do not need to
say anything. 9 For they themselves keep reporting about the way
we first entered in among you and
how you turned to God from
[your] idols to slave for a living
and true God, 10 and to wait for
his Son from the heavens, whom he
raised up from the dead, namely,
Jesus, who delivers us from the
wrath which is coming.

2 To be sure, you yourselves know,
brothers, how our visit to you
has not been without results, 2 but
how, after we had first suffered
and been insolently treated (just

as you know) in Phi·lip′pi, we
mustered up boldness by means of
our God to speak to you the good
news of God with a great deal of
struggling. 3 For the exhortation
we give does not arise from error
or from uncleanness or with deceit,
4 but, just as we have been proved
by God as fit to be entrusted with
the good news, so we speak, as
pleasing, not men, but God, who
makes proof of our hearts.

5 In fact, at no time have we
turned up either with flattering
speech, (just as you know) or
with a false front for covetousness,
God is witness! 6 Neither have
we been seeking glory from men,
no, either from you or from
others, though we could be an expensive burden as apostles of
Christ. 7 To the contrary, we became gentle in the midst of you,
as when a nursing mother cherishes
her own children. 8 So, having a
tender affection for you, we were
well pleased to impart to you,
not only the good news of God,
but also our own souls, because
you became beloved to us.

9 Certainly you bear in mind,
brothers, our labor and toil. It was
with working night and day, so as
not to put an expensive burden
upon any one of you, that we
preached the good news of God to
you. 10 You are witnesses, God
is also, how loyal and righteous and
unblamable we proved to be to
you believers. 11 In harmony with
that you well know how, as a
father does his children, we kept
exhorting each one of you, and
consoling and bearing witness to
you, 12 to the end that you
should go on walking worthily of
God who is calling you to his
kingdom and glory.

13 Indeed, that is why we also
thank God incessantly, because
when you received God's word,
which you heard from us, you ac-

cepted it, not as the word of men, but, just as it truthfully is, as the word of God, which is also at work in YOU believers. 14 For YOU became imitators, brothers, of the congregations of God that are in Ju·de′a in union with Christ Jesus, because YOU also began suffering at the hands of YOUR own countrymen the same things as they also [are suffering] at the hands of the Jews, 15 who killed even the Lord Jesus and the prophets and persecuted us. Furthermore, they are not pleasing God, but are against [the interests of] all men, 16 as they try to hinder us from speaking to people of the nations that these might be saved, with the result that they always fill up the measure of their sins. But his wrath has at length come upon them.

17 As for ourselves, brothers, when we were bereaved of YOU for but a short time, in person, not in heart, we endeavored far more than is usual to see YOUR faces with great desire. 18 For this reason we wanted to come to YOU, yes, I Paul, both once and a second time, but Satan cut across our path. 19 For what is our hope or joy or crown of exultation—why, is it not in fact YOU?—before our Lord Jesus at his presence? 20 YOU certainly are our glory and joy.

3 Hence, when we could bear it no longer, we saw good to be left alone in Athens; 2 and we sent Timothy, our brother and God's minister in the good news about the Christ, in order to make YOU firm and comfort YOU in behalf of YOUR faith, 3 that no one might be swayed by these tribulations. For YOU yourselves know we are appointed to this very thing. 4 In fact, too, when we were with YOU, we used to tell YOU beforehand that we were destined to suffer tribulation, just as it has also happened and as YOU know. 5 That is why, indeed, when I could bear it no longer, I sent to know of YOUR faithfulness, as perhaps in some way the tempter might have tempted YOU, and our labor might have turned out to be in vain.

6 But Timothy has just now come to us from YOU and given us the good news about YOUR faithfulness and love, and that YOU continue having good remembrance of us always, yearning to see us in the same way, indeed, as we also do YOU. 7 That is why, brothers, we have been comforted over YOU in all our necessity and tribulation through the faithfulness YOU show, 8 because now we live if YOU stand firm in [the] Lord. 9 For what thanksgiving can we render to God concerning YOU in return for all the joy with which we are rejoicing on YOUR account before our God, 10 while night and day we make more than extraordinary supplications to see YOUR faces and to make good the things that are lacking about YOUR faith?

11 Now may our God and Father himself and our Lord Jesus direct our way prosperously to YOU. 12 Moreover, may the Lord cause YOU to increase, yes, make YOU abound, in love to one another and to all, even as we also do to YOU; 13 to the end that he may make YOUR hearts firm, unblamable in holiness before our God and Father at the presence of our Lord Jesus with all his holy ones.

4 Finally, brothers, we request YOU and exhort YOU by the Lord Jesus, just as YOU received [the instruction] from us on how YOU ought to walk and please God, just as YOU are in fact walking, that YOU would keep on doing it more fully. 2 For YOU know the orders we gave YOU through the Lord Jesus.

3 For this is what God wills, the sanctifying of YOU, that YOU abstain from fornication; 4 that each one of YOU should know how to get possession of his own vessel in sanctification and honor, 5 not in covetous sexual appetite such as also those nations have which do not know God; 6 that no one go to the point of harming and encroach upon the rights of his brother in this matter, because Jehovah is one who exacts punishment for all these things, just as we told

YOU beforehand and also gave YOU a thorough witness. 7 For God called us, not with allowance for uncleanness, but in connection with sanctification. 8 So, then, the man that shows disregard is disregarding, not man, but God, who puts his holy spirit in YOU.

9 However, with reference to brotherly love, YOU do not need us to be writing YOU, for YOU yourselves are taught by God to love one another; 10 and, in fact, YOU are doing it to all the brothers in all of Mac·e·do′ni·a. But we exhort YOU, brothers, to go on doing it in fuller measure, 11 and to make it YOUR aim to live quietly and to mind YOUR own business and work with YOUR hands, just as we ordered YOU; 12 so that YOU may be walking decently as regards people outside and not be needing anything.

13 Moreover, brothers, we do not want YOU to be ignorant concerning those who are sleeping [in death]; that YOU may not sorrow just as the rest also do who have no hope. 14 For if our faith is that Jesus died and rose again, so, too, those who have fallen asleep [in death] through Jesus God will bring with him. 15 For this is what we tell YOU by Jehovah's word, that we the living who survive to the presence of the Lord shall in no way precede those who have fallen asleep [in death]; 16 because the Lord himself will descend from heaven with a commanding call, with an archangel's voice and with God's trumpet, and those who are dead in union with Christ will rise first. 17 Afterward we the living who are surviving will, together with them, be caught away in clouds to meet the Lord in the air; and thus we shall always be with [the] Lord. 18 Consequently keep comforting one another with these words.

5 Now as for the times and the seasons, brothers, YOU need nothing to be written to YOU. 2 For YOU yourselves know quite well that Jehovah's day is coming exactly as a thief in the night. 3 Whenever it is that they are say-

ing: "Peace and security!" then sudden destruction is to be instantly upon them just as the pang of distress upon a pregnant woman; and they will by no means escape. 4 But YOU, brothers, YOU are not in darkness, so that that day should overtake YOU as it would thieves, 5 for YOU are all sons of light and sons of day. We belong neither to night nor to darkness.

6 So, then, let us not sleep on as the rest do, but let us stay awake and keep our senses. 7 For those who sleep are accustomed to sleep at night, and those who get drunk are usually drunk at night. 8 But as for us who belong to the day, let us keep our senses and have on the breastplate of faith and love and as a helmet the hope of salvation; 9 because God assigned us, not to wrath, but to the acquiring of salvation through our Lord Jesus Christ. 10 He died for us, that, whether we stay awake or are asleep, we should live together with him. 11 Therefore keep comforting one another and building one another up, just as YOU are in fact doing.

12 Now we request YOU, brothers, to have regard for those who are working hard among YOU and presiding over YOU in [the] Lord and admonishing YOU; 13 and to give them more than extraordinary consideration in love because of their work. Be peaceable with one another. 14 On the other hand, we exhort YOU, brothers, admonish the disorderly, speak consolingly to the depressed souls, support the weak, be long-suffering toward all. 15 See that no one renders injury for injury to anyone else, but always pursue what is good toward one another and to all others.

16 Always be rejoicing. 17 Pray incessantly. 18 In connection with everything give thanks. For this is the will of God in union with Christ Jesus respecting YOU. 19 Do not put out the fire of the spirit. 20 Do not treat prophesyings with contempt. 21 Make sure of all things; hold fast to what is fine.

himself give you peace constantly in every way. The Lord be with all of you.

17 [Here is] my greeting, Paul's, in my own hand, which is a sign in every letter; this is the way I write.

18 The undeserved kindness of our Lord Jesus Christ be with all of you.

THE FIRST TO

TIMOTHY

1 Paul, an apostle of Christ Jesus under command of God our Savior and of Christ Jesus, our hope, 2 to Timothy, a genuine child in the faith:

May there be undeserved kindness, mercy, peace from God [the] Father and Christ Jesus our Lord.

3 Just as I encouraged you to stay in Eph'e·sus when I was about to go my way into Mac·e·do'ni·a, so I do now, that you might command certain ones not to teach different doctrine, 4 nor to pay attention to false stories and to genealogies, which end up in nothing, but which furnish questions for research rather than a dispensing of anything by God in connection with faith. 5 Really the objective of this mandate is love out of a clean heart and out of a good conscience and out of faith without hypocrisy. 6 By deviating from these things certain ones have been turned aside into idle talk, 7 wanting to be teachers of law, but not perceiving either the things they are saying or the things about which they are making strong assertions.

8 Now we know that the Law is fine provided one handles it lawfully 9 in the knowledge of this fact, that law is promulgated, not for a righteous man, but for persons lawless and unruly, ungodly and sinners, lacking loving-kindness, and profane, murderers of fathers and murderers of mothers, manslayers, 10 fornicators, men who lie with males, kidnapers, liars, false swearers, and whatever other thing is in opposition to the healthful teaching 11 according to the glorious good news of the happy God, with which I was entrusted.

12 I am grateful to Christ Jesus our Lord, who imparted power to me, because he considered me faithful by assigning me to a ministry, 13 although formerly I was a blasphemer and a persecutor and an insolent man. Nevertheless, I was shown mercy, because I was ignorant and acted with a lack of faith. 14 But the undeserved kindness of our Lord abounded exceedingly along with faith and love that is in connection with Christ Jesus. 15 Faithful and deserving of full acceptance is the saying that Christ Jesus came into the world to save sinners. Of these I am foremost. 16 Nevertheless, the reason why I was shown mercy was that by means of me as the foremost case Christ Jesus might demonstrate all his long-suffering for a sample of those who are going to rest their faith on him for everlasting life.

17 Now to the King of eternity, incorruptible, invisible, [the] only God, be honor and glory forever and ever. Amen.

18 This mandate I commit to you, child, Timothy, in accord with the predictions that led directly on to you, that by these you may go on waging the fine warfare; 19 holding faith and a good conscience, which some have thrust aside and have experienced shipwreck concerning [their] faith. 20 Hy·me·nae'us and Alexander belong to these, and I have handed them over to Satan that they may be taught by discipline not to blaspheme.

2 I therefore exhort, first of all, that supplications, prayers, intercessions, offerings of thanks, be made concerning all sorts of men, 2 concerning kings and all those who are in high station; in order that we may go on leading a calm and quiet life with full godly devotion and seriousness. 3 This is fine and acceptable in the sight of our Savior, God, 4 whose will is that all sorts of men should be saved and come to an accurate knowledge of truth. 5 For there is one God, and one mediator between God and men, a man, Christ Jesus, 6 who gave himself a corresponding ransom for all—[this is] what is to be witnessed to at its own particular times. 7 For the purpose of this witness I was appointed a preacher and an apostle—I am telling the truth, I am not lying—a teacher of nations in the matter of faith and truth.

8 Therefore I desire that in every place the men carry on prayer, lifting up loyal hands, apart from wrath and debates. 9 Likewise I desire the women to adorn themselves in well-arranged dress, with modesty and soundness of mind, not with styles of hair braiding and gold or pearls or very expensive garb, 10 but in the way that befits women professing to reverence God, namely, through good works.

11 Let a woman learn in silence with full submissiveness. 12 I do not permit a woman to teach, or to exercise authority over a man, but to be in silence. 13 For Adam was formed first, then Eve. 14 Also, Adam was not deceived, but the woman was thoroughly deceived and came to be in transgression. 15 However, she will be kept safe through childbearing, provided they continue in faith and love and sanctification along with soundness of mind.

3 That statement is faithful. If any man is reaching out for an office of overseer, he is desirous of a fine work. 2 The overseer should therefore be irreprehensible, a husband of one wife, moderate in habits, sound in mind, orderly, hospitable, qualified to teach, 3 not a drunken brawler, not a smiter, but reasonable, not belligerent, not a lover of money, 4 a man presiding over his own household in a fine manner, having children in subjection with all seriousness; 5 (if indeed any man does not know how to preside over his own household, how will he take care of God's congregation?) 6 not a newly converted man, for fear that he might get puffed up [with pride] and fall into the judgment passed upon the Devil. 7 Moreover, he should also have a fine testimony from people on the outside, in order that he might not fall into reproach and a snare of the Devil.

8 Ministerial servants should likewise be serious, not double-tongued, not giving themselves to a lot of wine, not greedy of dishonest gain, 9 holding the sacred secret of the faith with a clean conscience.

10 Also, let these be tested as to fitness first, then let them serve as ministers, as they are free from accusation.

11 Women should likewise be serious, not slanderous, moderate in habits, faithful in all things.

12 Let ministerial servants be husbands of one wife, presiding in a fine manner over children and their own households. 13 For the men who minister in a fine manner are acquiring for themselves a fine standing and great freeness of speech in the faith in connection with Christ Jesus.

14 I am writing you these things, though I am hoping to come to you shortly, 15 but in case I am delayed, that you may know how you ought to conduct yourself in God's household, which is the congregation of [the] living God, a pillar and support of the truth. 16 Indeed, the sacred secret of this godly devotion is admittedly great: 'He was made manifest in flesh, was declared righteous in spirit, appeared to angels, was preached about among nations, was believed

upon in [the] world, was received up in glory.'

4 However, the inspired utterance says definitely that in later periods of time some will fall away from the faith, paying attention to misleading inspired utterances and teachings of demons, 2 by the hypocrisy of men who speak lies, marked in their conscience as with a branding iron; 3 forbidding to marry, commanding to abstain from foods which God created to be partaken of with thanksgiving by those who have faith and accurately know the truth. 4 The reason for this is that every creation of God is fine, and nothing is to be rejected if it is received with thanksgiving, 5 for it is sanctified through God's word and prayer over [it].

6 By giving these advices to the brothers you will be a fine minister of Christ Jesus, one nourished with the words of the faith and of the fine teaching which you have followed closely. 7 But turn down the false stories which violate what is holy and which old women tell. On the other hand, be training yourself with godly devotion as your aim. 8 For bodily training is beneficial for a little; but godly devotion is beneficial for all things, as it holds promise of the life now and that which is to come. 9 Faithful and deserving of full acceptance is that statement. 10 For to this end we are working hard and exerting ourselves, because we have rested our hope on a living God, who is a Savior of all sorts of men, especially of faithful ones.

11 Keep on giving these commands and teaching them. 12 Let no man ever look down on your youth. On the contrary, become an example to the faithful ones in speaking, in conduct, in love, in faith, in chasteness. 13 While I am coming, continue applying yourself to public reading, to exhortation, to teaching. 14 Do not be neglecting the gift in you that was given you through a prediction and when the body of older men laid their hands upon you. 15 Ponder

over these things; be absorbed in them, that your advancement may be manifest to all [persons]. 16 Pay constant attention to yourself and to your teaching. Stay by these things, for by doing this you will save both yourself and those who listen to you.

5 Do not severely criticize an older man. To the contrary, entreat him as a father, younger men as brothers, 2 older women as mothers, younger women as sisters with all chasteness.

3 Honor widows that are actually widows. 4 But if any widow has children or grandchildren, let these learn first to practice godly devotion in their own household and to keep paying a due compensation to their parents and grandparents, for this is acceptable in God's sight. 5 Now the woman who is actually a widow and left destitute has put her hope in God and persists in supplications and prayers night and day. 6 But the one that goes in for sensual gratification is dead though she is living. 7 So keep on giving these commands, that they may be irreprehensible. 8 Certainly if anyone does not provide for those who are his own, and especially for those who are members of his household, he has disowned the faith and is worse than a person without faith.

9 Let a widow be put on the list who has become not less than sixty years old, a wife of one husband, 10 having a witness borne to her for fine works, if she reared children, if she entertained strangers, if she washed the feet of holy ones, if she relieved those in tribulation, if she diligently followed every good work.

11 On the other hand, turn down younger widows, for when their sexual impulses have come between them and the Christ, they want to marry, 12 having a judgment because they have disregarded their first [expression of] faith. 13 At the same time they also learn to be unoccupied, gadding about to the houses; yes, not only unoccupied, but also gossipers and med-

dlers in other people's affairs, talking of things they ought not. 14 Therefore I desire the younger widows to marry, to bear children, to manage a household, to give no inducement to the opposer to revile. 15 Already, in fact, some have been turned aside to follow Satan. 16 If any believing woman has widows, let her relieve them, and let the congregation not be under the burden. Then it can relieve those who are actually widows.

17 Let the older men who preside in a fine way be reckoned worthy of double honor, especially those who work hard in speaking and teaching. 18 For the scripture says: "You must not muzzle a bull when it threshes out the grain"; also: "The workman is worthy of his wages." 19 Do not admit an accusation against an older man, except only on the evidence of two or three witnesses. 20 Reprove before all onlookers persons who practice sin, that the rest also may have fear. 21 I solemnly charge you before God and Christ Jesus and the chosen angels to keep these things without prejudgment, doing nothing according to a biased leaning.

22 Never lay your hands hastily upon any man; neither be a sharer in the sins of others; preserve yourself chaste.

23 Do not drink water any longer, but use a little wine for the sake of your stomach and your frequent cases of sickness.

24 The sins of some men are publicly manifest, leading directly to judgment, but as for other men [their sins] also become manifest later. 25 In the same way also the fine works are publicly manifest and those that are otherwise cannot be kept hid.

6 Let as many as are slaves under a yoke keep on considering their owners worthy of full honor, that the name of God and the teaching may never be spoken of injuriously. 2 Moreover, let those having believing owners not look down on them, because they are brothers.

On the contrary, let them the more readily be slaves, because those receiving the benefit of their good service are believers and beloved.

Keep on teaching these things and giving these exhortations. 3 If any man teaches other doctrine and does not assent to healthful words, those of our Lord Jesus Christ, nor to the teaching that accords with godly devotion, 4 he is puffed up [with pride], not understanding anything, but being mentally diseased over questionings and debates about words. From these things spring envy, strife, abusive speeches, wicked suspicions, 5 violent disputes about trifles on the part of men corrupted in mind and despoiled of the truth, thinking that godly devotion is a means of gain. 6 To be sure, it is a means of great gain, [this] godly devotion along with self-sufficiency. 7 For we have brought nothing into the world, and neither can we carry anything out. 8 So, having sustenance and covering, we shall be content with these things.

9 However, those who are determined to be rich fall into temptation and a snare and many senseless and hurtful desires, which plunge men into destruction and ruin. 10 For the love of money is a root of all sorts of injurious things, and by reaching out for this love some have been led astray from the faith and have stabbed themselves all over with many pains.

11 However, you, O man of God, flee from these things. But pursue righteousness, godly devotion, faith, love, endurance, mildness of temper. 12 Fight the fine fight of the faith, get a firm hold on the everlasting life for which you were called and you offered the fine public declaration in front of many witnesses.

13 In the sight of God, who preserves all things alive, and of Christ Jesus, who as a witness made the fine public declaration before Pontius Pilate, I give you orders 14 that you observe the commandment in a spotless and irreprehen-

sible way until the manifestation of our Lord Jesus Christ. 15 This [manifestation] the happy and only Potentate will show in its own appointed times, [he] the King of those who rule as kings and Lord of those who rule as lords, 16 the one alone having immortality, who dwells in unapproachable light, whom not one of men has seen or can see. To him be honor and might everlasting. Amen.

17 Give orders to those who are rich in the present system of things not to be high-minded, and to rest their hope, not on uncertain riches, but on God, who furnishes us all

things richly for our enjoyment; 18 to work at good, to be rich in fine works, to be liberal, ready to share, 19 safely treasuring up for themselves a fine foundation for the future, in order that they may get a firm hold on the real life.

20 O Timothy, guard what is laid up in trust with you, turning away from the empty speeches that violate what is holy and from the contradictions of the falsely called "knowledge." 21 For making a show of such [knowledge] some have deviated from the faith.

May the undeserved kindness be with you people.

THE SECOND TO
TIMOTHY

1 Paul, an apostle of Christ Jesus through God's will according to the promise of the life that is in union with Christ Jesus, 2 to Timothy, a beloved child:

May there be undeserved kindness, mercy, peace from God [the] Father and Christ Jesus our Lord.

3 I am grateful to God, to whom I am rendering sacred service as my forefathers did and with a clean conscience, that I never leave off remembering you in my supplications, night and day 4 longing to see you, as I remember your tears, that I may get filled with joy. 5 For I recollect the faith which is in you without any hypocrisy, and which dwelt first in your grandmother Lo'is and your mother Eu'nice, but which I am confident is also in you.

6 For this very cause I remind you to stir up like a fire the gift of God which is in you through the laying of my hands upon you. 7 For God gave us not a spirit of cowardice, but that of power and of love and of soundness of mind. 8 Therefore do not become ashamed of the witness about our Lord, neither of me a prisoner for his sake, but take your part in suffering evil

for the good news according to the power of God. 9 He saved us and called us with a holy calling, not by reason of our works, but by reason of his own purpose and undeserved kindness. This was given us in connection with Christ Jesus before times long lasting, 10 but now it has been made clearly evident through the manifestation of our Savior, Christ Jesus, who has abolished death but has shed light upon life and incorruption through the good news, 11 for which I was appointed a preacher and apostle and teacher.

12 For this very cause I am also suffering these things, but I am not ashamed. For I know the one whom I have believed, and I am confident he is able to guard what I have laid up in trust with him until that day. 13 Keep holding the pattern of healthful words that you heard from me with the faith and love that are in connection with Christ Jesus. 14 This fine trust guard through the holy spirit which is dwelling in us.

15 You know this, that all the men in the [district of] Asia have turned away from me. Phy·gel'us and Her·mog'e·nes are of that num-

ber. 16 May the Lord grant mercy to the household of On·e·siph'o·rus, because he often brought me refreshment, and he did not become ashamed of my chains. 17 On the contrary, when he happened to be in Rome, he diligently looked for me and found me. 18 May the Lord grant him to find mercy from Jehovah in that day. And all the services he rendered in Eph'e·sus you know well enough.

2 You, therefore, my child, keep on acquiring power in the undeserved kindness that is in connection with Christ Jesus, 2 and the things you heard from me with the support of many witnesses, these things commit to faithful men, who, in turn, will be adequately qualified to teach others. 3 As a fine soldier of Christ Jesus take your part in suffering evil. 4 No man serving as a soldier involves himself in the commercial businesses of life, in order that he may gain the approval of the one who enrolled him as a soldier. 5 Moreover, if anyone contends even in the games, he is not crowned unless he has contended according to the rules. 6 The hard-working farmer must be the first to partake of the fruits. 7 Give constant thought to what I am saying; the Lord will really give you discernment in all things.

8 Remember that Jesus Christ was raised up from the dead and was of David's seed, according to the good news I preach; 9 in connection with which I am suffering evil to the point of prison bonds as an evildoer. Nevertheless, the word of God is not bound. 10 On this account I go on enduring all things for the sake of the chosen ones, that they too may obtain the salvation that is in union with Christ Jesus along with everlasting glory. 11 Faithful is the saying: Certainly if we died together, we shall also live together; 12 if we go on enduring, we shall also rule together as kings; if we deny, he also will deny us; 13 if we are unfaithful, he remains faithful, for he cannot deny himself.

14 Keep reminding them of these things, charging them before God as witness, not to fight about words, a thing of no usefulness at all because it overturns those listening. 15 Do your utmost to present yourself approved to God, a workman with nothing to be ashamed of, handling the word of the truth aright. 16 But shun empty speeches that violate what is holy; for they will advance to more and more ungodliness, 17 and their word will spread like gangrene. Hy·me·nae'us and Phi·le'tus are of that number. 18 These very [men] have deviated from the truth, saying that the resurrection has already occurred; and they are subverting the faith of some. 19 For all that, the solid foundation of God stays standing, having this seal: "Jehovah knows those who belong to him," and: "Let everyone naming the name of Jehovah renounce unrighteousness."

20 Now in a large house there are vessels not only of gold and silver but also of wood and earthenware, and some for an honorable purpose but others for a purpose lacking honor. 21 If, therefore, anyone keeps clear of the latter ones, he will be a vessel for an honorable purpose, sanctified, useful to his owner, prepared for every good work. 22 So, flee from the desires incidental to youth, but pursue righteousness, faith, love, peace, along with those who call upon the Lord out of a clean heart.

23 Further, turn down foolish and ignorant questionings, knowing they produce fights. 24 But a slave of the Lord does not need to fight, but needs to be gentle toward all, qualified to teach, keeping himself restrained under evil, 25 instructing with mildness those not favorably disposed; as perhaps God may give them repentance leading to an accurate knowledge of truth, 26 and they may come back to their proper senses out from the snare of the Devil, seeing that they have been caught alive by him for the will of that one.

3 But know this, that in the last days critical times hard to deal with will be here. 2 For men will be lovers of themselves, lovers of money, self-assuming, haughty, blasphemers, disobedient to parents, unthankful, disloyal, 3 having no natural affection, not open to any agreement, slanderers, without self-control, fierce, without love of goodness, 4 betrayers, headstrong, puffed up [with pride], lovers of pleasures rather than lovers of God, 5 having a form of godly devotion but proving false to its power; and from these turn away. 6 For from these arise those men who slyly work their way into households and lead as their captives weak women loaded down with sins, led by various desires, 7 always learning and yet never able to come to an accurate knowledge of truth.

8 Now in the way that Jan'nes and Jam'bres resisted Moses, so these also go on resisting the truth, men completely corrupted in mind, disapproved as regards the faith. 9 Nevertheless, they will make no further progress, for their madness will be very plain to all, even as the [madness] of those [two men] became. 10 But you have closely followed my teaching, my course of life, my purpose, my faith, my long-suffering, my love, my endurance, 11 my persecutions, my sufferings, the sort of things that happened to me in Antioch, in I·co'ni·um, in Lys'tra, the sort of persecutions I have borne; and yet out of them all the Lord delivered me. 12 In fact, all those desiring to live with godly devotion in association with Christ Jesus will also be persecuted. 13 But wicked men and impostors will advance from bad to worse, misleading and being misled.

14 You, however, continue in the things that you learned and were persuaded to believe, knowing from what persons you learned them 15 and that from infancy you have known the holy writings, which are able to make you wise for salvation through the faith in connection with Christ Jesus. 16 All Scripture is inspired of God and bene-ficial for teaching, for reproving, for setting things straight, for disciplining in righteousness, 17 that the man of God may be fully competent, completely equipped for every good work.

4 I solemnly charge you before God and Christ Jesus, who is destined to judge the living and the dead, and by his manifestation and his kingdom, 2 preach the word, be at it urgently in favorable season, in troublesome season, reprove, reprimand, exhort, with all long-suffering and [art of] teaching. 3 For there will be a period of time when they will not put up with the healthful teaching, but, in accord with their own desires, they will accumulate teachers for themselves to have their ears tickled; 4 and they will turn their ears away from the truth, whereas they will be turned aside to false stories. 5 You, though, keep your senses in all things, suffer evil, do [the] work of an evangelizer, fully accomplish your ministry.

6 For I am already being poured out like a drink offering, and the due time for my releasing is imminent. 7 I have fought the fine fight, I have run the course to the finish, I have observed the faith. 8 From this time on there is reserved for me the crown of righteousness, which the Lord, the righteous judge, will give me as a reward in that day, yet not only to me, but also to all those who have loved his manifestation.

9 Do your utmost to come to me shortly. 10 For De'mas has forsaken me because he loved the present system of things, and he has gone to Thes·sa·lo·ni'ca; Cres'cens to Ga·la'tia, Titus to Dal·ma'tia. 11 Luke alone is with me. Take Mark and bring him with you, for he is useful to me for ministering. 12 But I have sent Tych'i·cus off to Eph'e·sus. 13 When you come, bring the cloak I left at Tro'as with Carpus, and the scrolls, especially the parchments.

14 Alexander the coppersmith did me many injuries—Jehovah will repay him according to his deeds—

15 and you too be on guard against him, for he resisted our words to an excessive degree.

16 In my first defense no one came to my side, but they all proceeded to forsake me—may it not be put to their account— 17 but the Lord stood near me and infused power into me, that through me the preaching might be fully accomplished and all the nations might hear it; and I was delivered from the lion's mouth. 18 The Lord will deliver me from every wicked work and will save [me]

for his heavenly kingdom. To him be the glory forever and ever. Amen.

19 Give my greetings to Pris'ca and Aq'ui·la and the household of On·e·siph'o·rus.

20 E·ras'tus stayed in Corinth, but I left Troph'i·mus sick at Mi·le'tus. 21 Do your utmost to arrive before winter.

Eu·bu'lus sends you his greetings, and [so do] Pu'dens and Li'nus and Clau'di·a and all the brothers.

22 The Lord [be] with the spirit you show. His undeserved kindness [be] with you people.

TO

TITUS

1 Paul, a slave of God and an apostle of Jesus Christ according to the faith of God's chosen ones and the accurate knowledge of the truth which accords with godly devotion 2 upon the basis of a hope of the everlasting life which God, who cannot lie, promised before times long lasting, 3 whereas in his own due times he made his word manifest in the preaching with which I was entrusted, under command of our Savior, God; 4 to Titus, a genuine child according to a faith shared in common:

May there be undeserved kindness and peace from God [the] Father and Christ Jesus our Savior.

5 For this reason I left you in Crete, that you might correct the things that were defective and might make appointments of older men in city after city, as I gave you orders; 6 if there is any man free from accusation, a husband of one wife, having believing children that were not under a charge of debauchery nor unruly. 7 For an overseer must be free from accusation as God's steward, not self-willed, not prone to wrath, not a drunken brawler, not a smiter, not greedy of dishonest gain, 8 but hospitable, a lover of goodness,

sound in mind, righteous, loyal, self-controlled, 9 holding firmly to the faithful word as respects his [art of] teaching, that he may be able both to exhort by the teaching that is healthful and to reprove those who contradict.

10 For there are many unruly men, profitless talkers, and deceivers of the mind, especially those men who adhere to the circumcision. 11 It is necessary to shut the mouths of these, as these very men keep on subverting entire households by teaching things they ought not for the sake of dishonest gain. 12 A certain one of them, their own prophet, said: "Cre'tans are always liars, injurious wild beasts, unemployed gluttons."

13 This witness is true. For this very cause keep on reproving them with severity, that they may be healthy in the faith, 14 paying no attention to Jewish fables and commandments of men who turn themselves away from the truth. 15 All things are clean to clean [persons]. But to [persons] defiled and faithless nothing is clean, but both their minds and their consciences are defiled. 16 They publicly declare they know God, but they disown him by their works, because they are detestable and

disobedient and not approved for good work of any sort.

2 You, however, keep on speaking what things are fitting for healthful teaching. 2 Let the aged men be moderate in habits, serious, sound in mind, healthy in faith, in love, in endurance. 3 Likewise let the aged women be reverent in behavior, not slanderous, neither enslaved to a lot of wine, teachers of what is good; 4 that they may recall the young women to their senses to love their husbands, to love their children, 5 to be sound in mind, chaste, workers at home, good, subjecting themselves to their own husbands, so that the word of God may not be spoken of abusively.

6 Likewise keep on exhorting the younger men to be sound in mind, 7 in all things showing yourself an example of fine works; showing uncorruptness in your teaching, seriousness, 8 wholesome speech which cannot be condemned; so that the man on the opposing side may get ashamed, having nothing vile to say about us. 9 Let slaves be in subjection to their owners in all things, and please them well, not talking back, 10 not committing theft, but exhibiting good fidelity to the full, so that they may adorn the teaching of our Savior, God, in all things.

11 For the undeserved kindness of God which brings salvation to all sorts of men has been manifested, 12 instructing us to repudiate ungodliness and worldly desires and to live with soundness of mind and righteousness and godly devotion amid this present system of things, 13 while we wait for the happy hope and glorious manifestation of the great God and of [the] Savior of us, Christ Jesus, 14 who gave himself for us that he might deliver us from every sort of lawlessness and cleanse for himself a people peculiarly his own, zealous for fine works.

15 Keep on speaking these things and exhorting and reproving with full authority to command. Let no man ever despise you.

3 Continue reminding them to be in subjection and be obedient to governments and authorities as rulers, to be ready for every good work, 2 to speak injuriously of no one, not to be belligerent, to be reasonable, exhibiting all mildness toward all men. 3 For even we were once senseless, disobedient, being misled, being slaves to various desires and pleasures, carrying on in badness and envy, abhorrent, hating one another.

4 However, when the kindness and the love for man on the part of our Savior, God, was manifested, 5 owing to no works in righteousness that we had performed, but according to his mercy he saved us through the bath that brought us to life and through the making of us new by holy spirit. 6 This [spirit] he poured out richly upon us through Jesus Christ our Savior, 7 that, after being declared righteous by virtue of the undeserved kindness of that one, we might become heirs according to a hope of everlasting life.

8 Faithful is the saying, and concerning these things I desire you to make firm assertions constantly, in order that those who have believed God may keep their minds on maintaining fine works. These things are fine and beneficial to men.

9 But shun foolish questionings and genealogies and strife and fights over the Law, for they are unprofitable and futile. 10 As for a man that promotes a sect, reject him after a first and a second admonition; 11 knowing that such a man has been turned out of the way and is sinning, he being self-condemned.

12 When I send Ar'te·mas or Tych'i·cus to you, do your utmost to come to me at Ni·cop'o·lis, for there is where I have decided to winter. 13 Carefully supply Ze'nas, who is versed in the Law, and A·pol'los for their trip, that they may not lack anything. 14 But let our people also learn to maintain fine works so as to meet their

pressing needs, that they may not be unfruitful.

15 All those with me send you their greetings. Give my greetings to those who have affection for us in the faith.

May the undeserved kindness be with all of YOU people.

TO

PHILEMON

1 Paul, a prisoner for the sake of Christ Jesus, and Timothy, [our] brother, to Phi·le'mon, our beloved one and fellow worker, 2 and to Ap'phi·a, our sister, and to Ar·chip'pus, our fellow soldier, and to the congregation that is in your house:

3 May YOU people have undeserved kindness and peace from God our Father and [the] Lord Jesus Christ.

4 I always thank my God when I make mention of you in my prayers, 5 as I keep hearing of your love and faith which you have toward the Lord Jesus and toward all the holy ones; 6 in order that the sharing of your faith may go into action by your acknowledging of every good thing among us as related to Christ. 7 For I got much joy and comfort over your love, because the tender affections of the holy ones have been refreshed through you, brother.

8 For this very reason, though I have great freeness of speech in connection with Christ to order you to do what is proper, 9 I am exhorting you rather on the basis of love, seeing that I am such as I am, Paul an aged man, yes, now also a prisoner for the sake of Christ Jesus; 10 I am exhorting you concerning my child, to whom I became a father while in my prison bonds, O·nes'i·mus, 11 formerly useless to you but now useful to you and to me. 12 This very one I am sending back to you, yes, him, that is, my own tender affections.

13 I would like to hold him back for myself that in place of you he might keep on ministering to me in the prison bonds I bear for the sake of the good news. 14 But without your consent I do not want to do anything, so that your good act may be, not as under compulsion, but of your own free will. 15 Perhaps really on this account he broke away for an hour, that you may have him back forever, 16 no longer as a slave but as more than a slave, as a brother beloved, especially so to me, yet how much more so to you both in fleshly relationship and in [the] Lord. 17 If, therefore, you consider me a sharer, receive him kindly the way you would me. 18 Moreover, if he did you any wrong or owes you anything, keep this charged to my account. 19 I Paul am writing with my own hand: I will pay it back—not to be telling you that, besides, you owe me even yourself. 20 Yes, brother, may I derive profit from you in connection with [the] Lord: refresh my tender affections in connection with Christ.

21 Trusting in your compliance, I am writing you, knowing you will even do more than the things I say. 22 But along with that, also get lodging ready for me, for I am hoping that through the prayers of YOU people I shall be set at liberty for YOU.

23 Sending you greetings is Ep'a·phras my fellow captive in union with Christ, 24 [also] Mark, Ar·is·tar'chus, De'mas, Luke, my fellow workers.

25 The undeserved kindness of the Lord Jesus Christ be with the spirit YOU people show.

HEBREWS

1 God, who long ago spoke on many occasions and in many ways to our forefathers by means of the prophets, **2** has at the end of these days spoken to us by means of a Son, whom he appointed heir of all things, and through whom he made the systems of things. **3** He is the reflection of [his] glory and the exact representation of his very being, and he sustains all things by the word of his power; and after he had made a purification for our sins he sat down on the right hand of the Majesty in lofty places. **4** So he has become better than the angels, to the extent that he has inherited a name more excellent than theirs.

5 For example, to which one of the angels did he ever say: "You are my son; I, today, I have become your father"? And again: "I myself shall become his father, and he himself will become my son"? **6** But when he again brings his First-born into the inhabited earth, he says: "And let all God's angels worship him."

7 Also, with reference to the angels he says: "And he makes his angels spirits, and his public servants a flame of fire." **8** But with reference to the Son: "God is your throne forever, and [the] scepter of your kingdom is the scepter of uprightness. **9** You loved righteousness, and you hated lawlessness. That is why God, your God, anointed you with [the] oil of exultation more than your partners." **10** And: "You at [the] beginning, O Lord, laid the foundations of the earth itself, and the heavens are [the] works of your hands. **11** They themselves will perish, but you yourself are to remain continually; and just like an outer garment they will all grow old, **12** and you will wrap them up just as a cloak, as an outer garment; and they will be changed, but you are the same, and your years will never run out."

13 But with reference to which one of the angels has he ever said: "Sit at my right hand, until I place your enemies as a stool for your feet"? **14** Are they not all spirits for public service, sent forth to minister for those who are going to inherit salvation?

2 That is why it is necessary for us to pay more than the usual attention to the things heard by us, that we may never drift away. **2** For if the word spoken through angels proved to be firm, and every transgression and disobedient act received a retribution in harmony with justice; **3** how shall we escape if we have neglected a salvation of such greatness in that it began to be spoken through [our] Lord and was verified for us by those who heard him, **4** while God joined in bearing witness with signs as well as portents and various powerful works and with distributions of holy spirit according to his will?

5 For it is not to angels that he has subjected the inhabited earth to come, about which we are speaking. **6** But a certain witness has given proof somewhere, saying: "What is man that you keep him in mind, or [the] son of man that you take care of him? **7** You made him a little lower than angels; with glory and honor you crowned him, and appointed him over the works of your hands. **8** All things you subjected under his feet." For in that he subjected all things to him God left nothing that is not subject to him. Now, though, we do not yet see all things in subjection to him; **9** but we behold Jesus, who has been made a little lower than angels, crowned with glory and honor for having suffered death, that he by God's undeserved kindness might taste death for every [man].

10 For it was fitting for the one for whose sake all things are and through whom all things are, in bringing many sons to glory, to make the Chief Agent of their salvation perfect through sufferings. 11 For both he who is sanctifying and those who are being sanctified all [stem] from one, and for this cause he is not ashamed to call them "brothers," 12 as he says: "I will declare your name to my brothers; in the middle of [the] congregation I will praise you with song." 13 And again: "I will have my trust in him." And again: "Look! I and the young children, whom Jehovah gave me."

14 Therefore, since the "young children" are sharers of blood and flesh, he also similarly partook of the same things, that through his death he might bring to nothing the one having the means to cause death, that is, the Devil; 15 and [that] he might emancipate all those who for fear of death were subject to slavery all through their lives. 16 For he is really not assisting angels at all, but he is assisting Abraham's seed. 17 Consequently he was obliged to become like his "brothers" in all respects, that he might become a merciful and faithful high priest in things pertaining to God, in order to offer propitiatory sacrifice for the sins of the people. 18 For in that he himself has suffered when being put to the test, he is able to come to the aid of those who are being put to the test.

3 Consequently, holy brothers, partakers of the heavenly calling, consider the apostle and high priest whom we confess—Jesus. 2 He was faithful to the One that made him such, as Moses was also in all the house of that One. 3 For the latter is counted worthy of more glory than Moses, inasmuch as he who constructs it has more honor than the house. 4 Of course, every house is constructed by someone, but he that constructed all

things is God. 5 And Moses as an attendant was faithful in all the house of that One as a testimony of the things that were to be spoken afterwards, 6 but Christ [was faithful] as a Son over the house of that One. We are the house of that One, if we make fast our hold on our freeness of speech and our boasting over the hope firm to the end.

7 For this reason, just as the holy spirit says: "Today if you people listen to his own voice, 8 do not harden your hearts as on the occasion of causing bitter anger, as in the day of making the test in the wilderness, 9 in which your forefathers made a test of me with a trial, and yet they had seen my works for forty years. 10 For this reason I became disgusted with this generation and said, 'They always go astray in their hearts, and they themselves have not come to know my ways.' 11 So I swore in my anger, 'They shall not enter into my rest.'"

12 Beware, brothers, for fear there should ever develop in any one of you a wicked heart lacking faith by drawing away from the living God; 13 but keep on exhorting one another each day, as long as it may be called "Today," for fear any one of you should become hardened by the deceptive power of sin. 14 For we actually become partakers of the Christ only if we make fast our hold on the confidence we had at the beginning firm to the end, 15 while it is being said: "Today if you people listen to his own voice, do not harden your hearts as on the occasion of causing bitter anger."

16 For who were they that heard and yet provoked to bitter anger? Did not, in fact, all do so who went out of Egypt under Moses? 17 Moreover, with whom did [God] become disgusted for forty years? Was it not with those who sinned, whose carcasses fell in the wilderness? 18 But to whom did he swear that they should not enter into his rest except to those who acted disobediently? 19 So we see

that they could not enter in because of lack of faith.

4 Therefore, since a promise is left of entering into his rest, let us fear that sometime someone of YOU may seem to have fallen short of it. 2 For we have had the good news declared to us also, even as they also had; but the word which was heard did not benefit them, because they were not united by faith with those who did hear. 3 For we who have exercised faith do enter into the rest, just as he has said: "So I swore in my anger, 'They shall not enter into my rest,'" although his works were finished from the founding of the world. 4 For in one place he has said of the seventh day as follows: "And God rested on the seventh day from all his works," 5 and again in this place: "They shall not enter into my rest."

6 Since, therefore, it remains for some to enter into it, and those to whom the good news was first declared did not enter in because of disobedience, 7 he again marks off a certain day by saying after so long a time in David's [psalm] "Today"; just as it has been said above: "Today if YOU people listen to his own voice, do not harden YOUR hearts." 8 For if Joshua had led them into a place of rest, [God] would not afterward have spoken of another day. 9 So there remains a sabbath resting for the people of God. 10 For the man that has entered into [God's] rest has also himself rested from his own works, just as God did from his own.

11 Let us therefore do our utmost to enter into that rest, for fear anyone should fall in the same pattern of disobedience. 12 For the word of God is alive and exerts power and is sharper than any two-edged sword and pierces even to the dividing of soul and spirit, and of joints and [their] marrow, and [is] able to discern thoughts and intentions of [the] heart. 13 And there is not a creation that is not manifest to his sight, but all things are naked and openly exposed to

the eyes of him with whom we have an accounting.

14 Seeing, therefore, that we have a great high priest who has passed through the heavens, Jesus the Son of God, let us hold onto [our] confessing of [him]. 15 For we have as high priest, not one who cannot sympathize with our weaknesses, but one who has been tested in all respects like ourselves, but without sin. 16 Let us, therefore, approach with freeness of speech to the throne of undeserved kindness, that we may obtain mercy and find undeserved kindness for help at the right time.

5 For every high priest taken from among men is appointed in behalf of men over the things pertaining to God, that he may offer gifts and sacrifices for sins. 2 He is able to deal moderately with the ignorant and erring ones since he also is surrounded with his own weakness, 3 and on its account he is obliged to make offerings for sins as much for himself as for the people.

4 Also, a man takes this honor, not of his own accord, but only when he is called by God, just as Aaron also [was]. 5 So too the Christ did not glorify himself by becoming a high priest, but [was glorified by him] who spoke with reference to him: "You are my son; I, today, I have become your father." 6 Just as he says also in another place: "You are a priest forever according to the manner of Mel·chiz'e·dek."

7 In the days of his flesh [Christ] offered up supplications and also petitions to the one who was able to save him out of death, with strong outcries and tears, and he was favorably heard for his godly fear. 8 Although he was a Son, he learned obedience from the things he suffered; 9 and after he had been made perfect he became responsible for everlasting salvation to all those obeying him, 10 because he has been specifically called by God a high priest according to the manner of Mel·chiz'e·dek.

11 Concerning him we have much to say and hard to be explained, since you have become dull in your hearing. **12** For, indeed, although you ought to be teachers in view of the time, you again need someone to teach you from the beginning the elementary things of the sacred pronouncements of God; and you have become such as need milk, not solid food. **13** For everyone that partakes of milk is unacquainted with the word of righteousness, for he is a babe. **14** But solid food belongs to mature people, to those who through use have their perceptive powers trained to distinguish both right and wrong.

6 For this reason, now that we have left the primary doctrine about the Christ, let us press on to maturity, not laying a foundation again, namely, repentance from dead works, and faith toward God, **2** the teaching on baptisms and the laying on of the hands, the resurrection of the dead and everlasting judgment. **3** And this we will do, if God indeed permits.

4 For it is impossible as regards those who have once for all been enlightened, and who have tasted the heavenly free gift, and who have become partakers of holy spirit, **5** and who have tasted the fine word of God and powers of the coming system of things, **6** but who have fallen away, to revive them again to repentance, because they impale the Son of God afresh for themselves and expose him to public shame. **7** For example, the ground that drinks in the rain which often comes upon it, and that then brings forth vegetation suitable to those for whom it is also cultivated, receives in return a blessing from God. **8** But if it produces thorns and thistles, it is rejected and is near to being cursed; and it ends up with being burned.

9 However, in your case, beloved ones, we are convinced of better things and things accompanied with salvation, although we are speaking in this way. **10** For God is not unrighteous so as to forget your work and the love you showed

for his name, in that you have ministered to the holy ones and continue ministering. **11** But we desire each one of you to show the same industriousness so as to have the full assurance of the hope down to the end, **12** in order that you may not become sluggish, but be imitators of those who through faith and patience inherit the promises.

13 For when God made his promise to Abraham, since he could not swear by anyone greater, he swore by himself, **14** saying: "Assuredly in blessing I will bless you, and in multiplying I will multiply you." **15** And thus after [Abraham] had shown patience, he obtained [this] promise. **16** For men swear by the one greater, and their oath is the end of every dispute, as it is a legal guarantee to them. **17** In this manner God, when he purposed to demonstrate more abundantly to the heirs of the promise the unchangeableness of his counsel, stepped in with an oath, **18** in order that, through two unchangeable things in which it is impossible for God to lie, we who have fled to the refuge may have strong encouragement to lay hold on the hope set before us. **19** This [hope] we have as an anchor for the soul, both sure and firm, and it enters in within the curtain, **20** where a forerunner has entered in our behalf, Jesus, who has become a high priest according to the manner of Mel·chiz′e·dek forever.

7 For this Mel·chiz′e·dek, king of Sa′lem, priest of the Most High God, who met Abraham returning from the slaughter of the kings and blessed him **2** and to whom Abraham apportioned a tenth from all things, is first of all, by translation, "King of Righteousness," and is then also king of Sa′lem, that is, "King of Peace." **3** In being fatherless, motherless, without genealogy, having neither a beginning of days nor an end of life, but having been made like the Son of God, he remains a priest perpetually.

4 BEHOLD, then, how great this man was to whom Abraham, the family head, gave a tenth out of the chief spoils. 5 True, the men from the sons of Le'vi who receive their priestly office have a commandment to collect tithes from the people according to the Law, that is, from their brothers, even if these have issued from the loins of Abraham; 6 but the man who did not trace his genealogy from them took tithes from Abraham and blessed him who had the promises. 7 Now without any dispute, the less is blessed by the greater. 8 And in the one case it is men who are dying that receive tithes, but in the other case it is someone of whom it is witnessed that he lives. 9 And, if I may use the expression, through Abraham even Le'vi who receives tithes has paid tithes, 10 for he was still in the loins of his forefather when Mel·chiz'e·dek met him.

11 If, then, perfection were really through the Levitical priesthood, (for with it as a feature the people were given the Law,) what further need would there be for another priest to arise according to the manner of Mel·chiz'e·dek and not said to be according to the manner of Aaron? 12 For since the priesthood is being changed, there comes to be of necessity a change also of the law. 13 For the man respecting whom these things are said has been a member of another tribe, from which no one has officiated at the altar. 14 For it is quite plain that our Lord has sprung up out of Judah, a tribe about which Moses spoke nothing concerning priests.

15 And it is still more abundantly clear that with a similarity to Mel·chiz'e·dek there arises another priest, 16 who has become such, not according to the law of a commandment depending upon the flesh, but according to the power of an indestructible life, 17 for in witness it is said: "You are a priest forever according to the manner of Mel·chiz'e·dek."

18 Certainly, then, there occurs a setting aside of the preceding commandment on account of its weakness and ineffectiveness. 19 For the Law made nothing perfect, but the bringing in besides of a better hope did, through which we are drawing near to God. 20 Also, to the extent that it was not without a sworn oath, 21 (for there are indeed men that have become priests without a sworn oath, but there is one with an oath sworn by the One who said respecting him: "Jehovah has sworn (and he will feel no regret), 'You are a priest forever,'") 22 to that extent also Jesus has become the one given in pledge of a better covenant. 23 Furthermore, many had to become priests [in succession] because of being prevented by death from continuing as such, 24 but he because of continuing alive forever has his priesthood without any successors. 25 Consequently he is able also to save completely those who are approaching God through him, because he is always alive to plead for them.

26 For such a high priest as this was suitable for us, loyal, guileless, undefiled, separated from the sinners, and become higher than the heavens. 27 He does not need daily, as those high priests do, to offer up sacrifices, first for his own sins and then for those of the people: (for this he did once for all time when he offered himself up;) 28 for the Law appoints men high priests having weakness, but the word of the sworn oath that came after the Law appoints a Son, who is perfected forever.

8 Now as to the things being discussed this is the main point: We have such a high priest as this, and he has sat down at the right hand of the throne of the Majesty in the heavens, 2 a public servant of the holy place and of the true tent, which Jehovah put up, and not man. 3 For every high priest is appointed to offer both gifts and sacrifices; wherefore it was necessary for this one also to have something to offer. 4 If, now, he were upon earth, he would not be a priest, there being [men] who offer the gifts according to the Law,

5 but which [men] are rendering sacred service in a typical representation and a shadow of the heavenly things; just as Moses, when about to make the tent in completion, was given the divine command: For says he: "See that you make all things after [their] pattern that was shown to you in the mountain." 6 But now Jesus has obtained a more excellent public service, so that he is also the mediator of a correspondingly better covenant, which has been legally established upon better promises.

7 For if that first covenant had been faultless, no place would have been sought for a second; 8 for he does find fault with the people when he says: "'Look! There are days coming,' says Jehovah, 'and I will conclude with the house of Israel and with the house of Judah a new covenant; 9 not according to the covenant that I made with their forefathers in [the] day of my taking hold of their hand to bring them forth out of the land of Egypt, because they did not continue in my covenant, so that I stopped caring for them,' says Jehovah."

10 "'For this is the covenant that I shall covenant with the house of Israel after those days,' says Jehovah. 'I will put my laws in their mind, and in their hearts I shall write them. And I will become their God, and they themselves will become my people.

11 "'And they will by no means teach each one his fellow citizen and each one his brother, saying: "Know Jehovah!" For they will all know me, from [the] least one to [the] greatest one of them. 12 For I shall be merciful to their unrighteous deeds, and I shall by no means call their sins to mind any more.'"

13 In his saying "a new [covenant]" he has made the former one obsolete. Now that which is made obsolete and growing old is near to vanishing away.

9 For its part, then, the former [covenant] used to have ordinances of sacred service and [its]

holy place upon this earth. 2 For there was constructed a first tent [compartment] in which were the lampstand and also the table and the display of the loaves; and it is called "the Holy Place." 3 But behind the second curtain was the tent [compartment] called "the Most Holy." 4 This had a golden censer and the ark of the covenant overlaid all around with gold, in which were the golden jar having the manna and the rod of Aaron that budded and the tablets of the covenant; 5 but up above it were the glorious cherubs overshadowing the propitiatory [cover]. But now is not the time to speak in detail concerning these things.

6 After these things had been constructed this way, the priests enter the first tent [compartment] at all times to perform the sacred services; 7 but into the second [compartment] the high priest alone enters once a year, not without blood, which he offers for himself and for the sins of ignorance of the people. 8 Thus the holy spirit makes it plain that the way into the holy place had not yet been made manifest while the first tent was standing. 9 This very [tent] is an illustration for the appointed time that is now here, and in keeping with it both gifts and sacrifices are offered. However, these are not able to make the [man] doing sacred service perfect as respects his conscience, 10 but have to do only with foods and drinks and various baptisms. They were legal requirements pertaining to the flesh and were imposed until the appointed time to set things straight.

11 However, when Christ came as a high priest of the good things that have come to pass, through the greater and more perfect tent not made with hands, that is, not of this creation, 12 he entered, no, not with the blood of goats and of young bulls, but with his own blood, once for all time into the holy place and obtained an everlasting deliverance [for us]. 13 For if the blood of goats and of bulls and the ashes

of a heifer sprinkled on those who have been defiled sanctifies to the extent of cleanness of the flesh, 14 how much more will the blood of the Christ, who through an ever-lasting spirit offered himself without blemish to God, cleanse our consciences from dead works that we may render sacred service to [the] living God?

15 So that is why he is a mediator of a new covenant, in order that, because a death has occurred for [their] release by ransom from the transgressions under the former covenant, the ones who have been called might receive the promise of the everlasting inheritance. 16 For where there is a covenant, the death of the [human] covenanter needs to be furnished. 17 For a covenant is valid over dead [victims], since it is not in force at any time while the [human] covenanter is living. 18 Consequently neither was the former [covenant] inaugurated without blood. 19 For when every commandment according to the Law had been spoken by Moses to all the people, he took the blood of the young bulls and of the goats with water and scarlet wool and hyssop and sprinkled the book itself and all the people, 20 saying: "This is the blood of the covenant that God has laid as a charge upon you." 21 And he sprinkled the tent and all the vessels of the public service likewise with the blood. 22 Yes, nearly all things are cleansed with blood according to the Law, and unless blood is poured out no forgiveness takes place.

23 Therefore it was necessary that the typical representations of the things in the heavens should be cleansed by these means, but the heavenly things themselves with sacrifices that are better than such sacrifices. 24 For Christ entered, not into a holy place made with hands, which is a copy of the reality, but into heaven itself, now to appear before the person of God for us. 25 Neither is it in order that he should offer himself often, as indeed the high priest enters into the holy place from year to year with blood not his own. 26 Otherwise, he would have to suffer often from the founding of the world. But now he has manifested himself once for all time at the conclusion of the systems of things to put sin away through the sacrifice of himself. 27 And as it is reserved for men to die once for all time, but after this a judgment, 28 so also the Christ was offered once for all time to bear the sins of many; and the second time that he appears it will be apart from sin and to those earnestly looking for him for [their] salvation.

10 For since the Law has a shadow of the good things to come, but not the very substance of the things, [men] can never with the same sacrifices from year to year which they offer continually make those who approach perfect. 2 Otherwise, would the [sacrifices] not have stopped being offered, because those rendering sacred service who had been cleansed once for all time would have no consciousness of sins any more? 3 To the contrary, by these sacrifices there is a reminding of sins from year to year, 4 for it is not possible for the blood of bulls and of goats to take sins away.

5 Hence when he comes into the world he says: "'Sacrifice and offering you did not want, but you prepared a body for me. 6 You did not approve of whole burnt offerings and sin [offering].' 7 Then I said, 'Look! I am come (in the roll of the book it is written about me) to do your will, O God.'" 8 After first saying: "You did not want nor did you approve of sacrifices and offerings and whole burnt offerings and sin [offering]"—[sacrifices] that are offered according to the Law— 9 then he actually says: "Look! I am come to do your will." He does away with what is first that he may establish what is second. 10 By the said "will" we have been sanctified through the offering of the body of Jesus Christ once for all time.

11 Also, every priest takes his

station from day to day to render public service and to offer the same sacrifices often, as these are at no time able to take sins away completely. 12 But this [man] offered one sacrifice for sins perpetually and sat down at the right hand of God, 13 from then on awaiting until his enemies should be placed as a stool for his feet. 14 For it is by one [sacrificial] offering that he has made those who are being sanctified perfect perpetually. 15 Moreover, the holy spirit also bears witness to us, for after it has said: 16 "'This is the covenant that I shall covenant toward them after those days,' says Jehovah. 'I will put my laws in their hearts, and in their minds I shall write them,'" 17 it says afterwards: "And I shall by no means call their sins and their lawless deeds to mind any more." 18 Now where there is forgiveness of these, there is no longer an offering for sin.

19 Therefore, brothers, since we have boldness for the way of entry into the holy place by the blood of Jesus, 20 which he inaugurated for us as a new and living way through the curtain, that is, his flesh, 21 and since we have a great priest over the house of God, 22 let us approach with true hearts in the full assurance of faith, having had our hearts sprinkled from a wicked conscience and our bodies bathed with clean water. 23 Let us hold fast the public declaration of our hope without wavering, for he is faithful that promised. 24 And let us consider one another to incite to love and fine works, 25 not forsaking the gathering of ourselves together, as some have the custom, but encouraging one another, and all the more so as you behold the day drawing near.

26 For if we practice sin willfully after having received the accurate knowledge of the truth, there is no longer any sacrifice for sins left, 27 but [there is] a certain fearful expectation of judgment and [there is] a fiery jealousy that is going to consume those in opposition. 28 Any man that has

disregarded the law of Moses dies without compassion, upon the testimony of two or three. 29 Of how much more severe a punishment, do you think, will the man be counted worthy who has trampled upon the Son of God and who has esteemed as of ordinary value the blood of the covenant by which he was sanctified, and who has outraged the spirit of undeserved kindness with contempt? 30 For we know him that said: "Vengeance is mine; I will recompense"; and again: "Jehovah will judge his people." 31 It is a fearful thing to fall into the hands of [the] living God.

32 However, keep on remembering the former days in which, after you were enlightened, you endured a great contest under sufferings, 33 sometimes while you were being exposed as in a theater both to reproaches and tribulations, and sometimes while you became sharers with those who were having such an experience. 34 For you both expressed sympathy for those in prison and joyfully took the plundering of your belongings, knowing you yourselves have a better and an abiding possession.

35 Do not, therefore, throw away your freeness of speech, which has a great reward to be paid it. 36 For you have need of endurance, in order that, after you have done the will of God, you may receive the [fulfillment of the] promise. 37 For yet "a very little while," and "he who is coming will arrive and will not delay." 38 "But my righteous one will live by reason of faith," and, "if he shrinks back, my soul has no pleasure in him." 39 Now we are not the sort that shrink back to destruction, but the sort that have faith to the preserving alive of the soul.

11 Faith is the assured expectation of things hoped for, the evident demonstration of realities though not beheld. 2 For by means of this the men of old times had witness borne to them.

3 By faith we perceive that the systems of things were put in order

by God's word, so that what is beheld has come to be out of things that do not appear.

4 By faith Abel offered God a sacrifice of greater worth than Cain, through which [faith] he had witness borne to him that he was righteous, God bearing witness respecting his gifts; and through it he, although he died, yet speaks.

5 By faith Enoch was transferred so as not to see death, and he was nowhere to be found because God had transferred him; for before his transference he had the witness that he had pleased God well. 6 Moreover, without faith it is impossible to please [him] well, for he that approaches God must believe that he is and that he becomes the rewarder of those earnestly seeking him.

7 By faith Noah, after being given divine warning of things not yet beheld, showed godly fear and constructed an ark for the saving of his household; and through this [faith] he condemned the world, and he became an heir of the righteousness that is according to faith.

8 By faith Abraham, when he was called, obeyed in going out into a place he was destined to receive as an inheritance; and he went out, although not knowing where he was going. 9 By faith he resided as an alien in the land of the promise as in a foreign land, and dwelt in tents with Isaac and Jacob, the heirs with him of the very same promise. 10 For he was awaiting the city having real foundations, the builder and maker of which [city] is God.

11 By faith also Sarah herself received power to conceive seed, even when she was past the age limit, since she esteemed him faithful who had promised. 12 Hence also from one [man], and him as good as dead, there were born [children] just as the stars of heaven for multitude and as the sands that are by the seaside, innumerable.

13 In faith all these died, although they did not get the [fulfillment of the] promises, but they saw them afar off and welcomed them and publicly declared that they were strangers and temporary residents in the land. 14 For those who say such things give evidence that they are earnestly seeking a place of their own. 15 And yet, if they had indeed kept remembering that [place] from which they had gone forth, they would have had opportunity to return. 16 But now they are reaching out for a better [place], that is, one belonging to heaven. Hence God is not ashamed of them, to be called upon as their God, for he has made a city ready for them.

17 By faith Abraham, when he was tested, as good as offered up Isaac, and the man that had gladly received the promises attempted to offer up [his] only-begotten [son], 18 although it had been said to him: "What will be called 'your seed' will be through Isaac." 19 But he reckoned that God was able to raise him up even from the dead; and from there he did receive him also in an illustrative way.

20 By faith also Isaac blessed Jacob and Esau concerning things to come.

21 By faith Jacob, when about to die, blessed each of the sons of Joseph and worshiped leaning upon the top of his staff.

22 By faith Joseph, nearing his end, made mention of the exodus of the sons of Israel; and he gave a command concerning his bones.

23 By faith Moses was hid for three months by his parents after his birth, because they saw the young child was beautiful and they did not fear the order of the king. 24 By faith Moses, when grown up, refused to be called the son of the daughter of Phar'aoh, 25 choosing to be ill-treated with the people of God rather than to have the temporary enjoyment of sin, 26 because he esteemed the reproach of the Christ as riches greater than the treasures of Egypt; for he looked intently toward the payment of the reward. 27 By faith he left

Egypt, but not fearing the anger of the king, for he continued steadfast as seeing the One who is invisible. 28 By faith he had celebrated the passover and the splashing of the blood, that the destroyer might not touch their firstborn ones.

29 By faith they passed through the Red Sea as on dry land, but on venturing out upon it the Egyptians were swallowed up.

30 By faith the walls of Jer'i·cho fell down after they had been encircled for seven days. 31 By faith Ra'hab the harlot did not perish with those who acted disobediently, because she received the spies in a peaceable way.

32 And what more shall I say? For the time will fail me if I go on to relate about Gid'e·on, Ba'rak, Samson, Jeph'thah, David as well as Samuel and the [other] prophets. 33 who through faith defeated kingdoms in conflict, effected righteousness, obtained promises, stopped the mouths of lions, 34 stayed the force of fire, escaped the edge of the sword, from a weak state were made powerful, became valiant in war, routed the armies of foreigners. 35 Women received their dead by resurrection; but other [men] were tortured because they would not accept release by some ransom, in order that they might attain a better resurrection. 36 Yes, others received their trial by mockings and scourgings, indeed, more than that, by bonds and prisons. 37 They were stoned, they were tried, they were sawn asunder, they died by slaughter with the sword, they went about in sheepskins, in goatskins, while they were in want, in tribulation, under ill-treatment; 38 and the world was not worthy of them. They wandered about in deserts and mountains and dens and caves of the earth.

39 And yet all these, although they had witness borne to them through their faith, did not get the [fulfillment of the] promise, 40 as God foresaw something better for us, in order that they might not be made perfect apart from us.

12 So, then, because we have so great a cloud of witnesses surrounding us, let us also put off every weight and the sin that easily entangles us, and let us run with endurance the race that is set before us, 2 as we look intently at the Chief Agent and Perfecter of our faith, Jesus. For the joy that was set before him he endured a torture stake, despising shame, and has sat down at the right hand of the throne of God. 3 Indeed, consider closely the one who has endured such contrary talk by sinners against their own interests, that you may not get tired and give out in your souls.

4 In carrying on your contest against that sin you have never yet resisted as far as blood, 5 but you have entirely forgotten the exhortation which addresses you as sons: "My son, do not belittle [the] discipline from Jehovah, neither give out when you are corrected by him; 6 for whom Jehovah loves he disciplines; in fact, he scourges every one whom he receives as a son."

7 It is for discipline you are enduring. God is dealing with you as with sons. For what son is he that a father does not discipline? 8 But if you are without the discipline of which all have become partakers, you are really illegitimate children, and not sons. 9 Furthermore, we used to have fathers who were of our flesh to discipline us, and we used to give them respect. Shall we not much more subject ourselves to the Father of our spiritual life and live? 10 For they for a few days used to discipline us according to what seemed good to them, but he does so for our profit that we may partake of his holiness. 11 True, no discipline seems for the present to be joyous, but grievous; yet afterward to those who have been trained by it it yields peaceable fruit, namely, righteousness.

12 Hence straighten up the hands that hang down and the enfeebled knees, 13 and keep making straight paths for your feet, that what is

lame may not be put out of joint, but rather that it may be healed. 14 Pursue peace with all people, and the sanctification without which no man will see the Lord, 15 carefully watching that no one may be deprived of the undeserved kindness of God; that no poisonous root may spring up and cause trouble and that many may not be defiled by it; 16 that there may be no fornicator nor anyone not appreciating sacred things, like Esau, who in exchange for one meal gave away his rights as first-born. 17 For you know that afterward also when he wanted to inherit the blessing he was rejected, for, although he earnestly sought a change of mind with tears, he found no place for it.

18 For you have not approached that which can be felt and which has been set aflame with fire, and a dark cloud and thick darkness and a tempest, 19 and the blare of a trumpet and the voice of words; on hearing which voice the people implored that no word should be added to them. 20 For the command was not bearable to them: "And if a beast touches the mountain, it must be stoned." 21 Also, the display was so fearsome that Moses said: "I am fearful and trembling." 22 But you have approached a Mount Zion and a city of [the] living God, heavenly Jerusalem, and myriads of angels, 23 in general assembly, and the congregation of the first-born who have been enrolled in the heavens, and God the Judge of all, and the spiritual lives of righteous ones who have been made perfect, 24 and Jesus the mediator of a new covenant, and the blood of sprinkling, which speaks in a better way than Abel's [blood].

25 See that you do not beg off from him who is speaking. For if they did not escape who begged off from him who was giving divine warning upon earth, much more shall we not if we turn away from him who speaks from the heavens. 26 At that time his voice shook the earth, but now he has promised,

saying: "Yet once more I will set in commotion not only the earth but also the heaven." 27 Now the expression "Yet once more" signifies the removal of the things being shaken as things that have been made, in order that the things not being shaken may remain. 28 Wherefore, seeing that we are to receive a kingdom that cannot be shaken, let us continue to have undeserved kindness, through which we may acceptably render God sacred service with godly fear and awe. 29 For our God is also a consuming fire.

13 Let your brotherly love continue. 2 Do not forget hospitality, for through it some, unknown to themselves, entertained angels. 3 Keep in mind those in prison bonds as though you have been bound with them, and those being ill-treated, since you yourselves also are still in a body. 4 Let marriage be honorable among all, and the marriage bed be without defilement, for God will judge fornicators and adulterers. 5 Let [your] manner of life be free of the love of money, while you are content with the present things. For he has said: "I will by no means leave you nor by any means forsake you." 6 So that we may be of good courage and say: "Jehovah is my helper; I will not be afraid. What can man do to me?"

7 Remember those who are taking the lead among you, who have spoken the word of God to you, and as you contemplate how [their] conduct turns out imitate [their] faith.

8 Jesus Christ is the same yesterday and today, and forever.

9 Do not be carried away with various and strange teachings; for it is fine for the heart to be given firmness by undeserved kindness, not by eatables, by which those who occupy themselves with them have not been benefited.

10 We have an altar from which those who do sacred service at the tent have no authority to eat. 11 For the bodies of those animals whose blood is taken into the holy

place by the high priest for sin are burned up outside the camp. 12 Hence Jesus also, that he might sanctify the people with his own blood, suffered outside the gate. 13 Let us, then, go forth to him outside the camp, bearing the reproach he bore, 14 for we do not have here a city that continues, but we are earnestly seeking the one to come. 15 Through him let us always offer to God a sacrifice of praise, that is, the fruit of lips which make public declaration to his name. 16 Moreover, do not forget the doing of good and the sharing of things with others, for with such sacrifices God is well pleased.

17 Be obedient to those who are taking the lead among you and be submissive, for they are keeping watch over your souls as those who will render an account; that they may do this with joy and not with sighing, for this would be damaging to you.

18 Carry on prayer for us, for we trust we have an honest con-science, as we wish to conduct ourselves honestly in all things. 19 But I exhort you more especially to do this, that I may be restored to you the sooner.

20 Now may the God of peace, who brought up from the dead the great shepherd of the sheep with the blood of an everlasting covenant, our Lord Jesus, 21 equip you with every good thing to do his will, performing in us through Jesus Christ that which is well-pleasing in his sight; to whom be the glory forever and ever. Amen.

22 Now I exhort you, brothers, to bear with this word of encouragement, for I have, indeed, composed a letter to you in few words. 23 Take note that our brother Timothy has been released, with whom, if he comes quite soon, I shall see you.

24 Give my greetings to all those who are taking the lead among you and to all the holy ones. Those in Italy send you their greetings.

25 The undeserved kindness be with all of you.

THE LETTER OF

JAMES

1 James, a slave of God and of [the] Lord Jesus Christ, to the twelve tribes that are scattered about:

Greetings!

2 Consider it all joy, my brothers, when you meet with various trials, 3 knowing as you do that this tested quality of your faith works out endurance. 4 But let endurance have its work complete, that you may be complete and sound in all respects, not lacking in anything.

5 So, if any one of you is lacking in wisdom, let him keep on asking God, for he gives generously to all and without reproaching; and it will be given him. 6 But let him keep on asking in faith, not doubting at all, for he who doubts is like a wave of the sea driven by the wind and blown about. 7 In fact, let not that man suppose that he will receive anything from Jehovah; 8 he is an indecisive man, unsteady in all his ways.

9 But let the lowly brother exult over his exaltation, 10 and the rich one over his humiliation, because like a flower of the vegetation he will pass away. 11 For the sun rises with its burning heat and withers the vegetation, and its flower drops off and the beauty of its outward appearance perishes. So, too, the rich man will fade away in his ways of life.

12 Happy is the man that keeps on enduring trial, because on becoming approved he will receive the crown of life, which Jehovah

promised to those who continue loving him. 13 When under trial, let no one say: "I am being tried by God." For with evil things God cannot be tried nor does he himself try anyone. 14 But each one is tried by being drawn out and enticed by his own desire. 15 Then the desire, when it has become fertile, gives birth to sin; in turn, sin, when it has been accomplished, brings forth death.

16 Do not be misled, my beloved brothers. 17 Every good gift and every perfect present is from above, for it comes down from the Father of the [celestial] lights, and with him there is not a variation of the turning of the shadow. 18 Because he willed it, he brought us forth by the word of truth, for us to be certain first fruits of his creatures.

19 Know this, my beloved brothers. Every man must be swift about hearing, slow about speaking, slow about wrath; 20 for man's wrath does not work out God's righteousness. 21 Hence put away all filthiness and that superfluous thing, badness, and accept with mildness the implanting of the word which is able to save your souls.

22 However, become doers of the word, and not hearers only, deceiving yourselves with false reasoning. 23 For if anyone is a hearer of the word, and not a doer, this one is like a man looking at his natural face in a mirror. 24 For he looks at himself, and off he goes and immediately forgets what sort of man he is. 25 But he who peers into the perfect law that belongs to freedom and who persists in [it], this [man], because he has become, not a forgetful hearer, but a doer of the work, will be happy in his doing [it].

26 If any man seems to himself to be a formal worshiper and yet does not bridle his tongue, but goes on deceiving his own heart, this man's form of worship is futile. 27 The form of worship that is clean and undefiled from the standpoint of our God and Father is this: to look after orphans and widows in their tribulation, and to keep oneself without spot from the world.

2 My brothers, you are not holding the faith of our Lord Jesus Christ, our glory, with acts of favoritism, are you? 2 For, if a man with gold rings on his fingers and in splendid clothing enters into a gathering of you, but a poor [man] in filthy clothing also enters, 3 yet you look with favor upon the one wearing the splendid clothing and say: "You take this seat here in a fine place," and you say to the poor one: "You keep standing," or: "Take that seat there under my footstool," 4 you have class distinctions among yourselves and you have become judges rendering wicked decisions, is that not so?

5 Listen, my beloved brothers. God chose the ones who are poor respecting the world to be rich in faith and heirs of the kingdom, which he promised to those who love him, did he not? 6 You, though, have dishonored the poor [man]. The rich oppress you, and they drag you before law courts, do they not? 7 They blaspheme the fine name by which you were called, do they not? 8 If, now, you practice carrying out the kingly law according to the scripture: "You must love your neighbor as yourself," you are doing quite well. 9 But if you continue showing favoritism, you are working a sin, for you are reproved by the law as transgressors.

10 For whoever observes all the Law but makes a false step in one point, he has become an offender against them all. 11 For he who said: "You must not commit adultery," said also: "You must not murder." If, now, you do not commit adultery but you do murder, you have become a transgressor of law. 12 Keep on speaking in such a way and keep on doing in such a way as those do who are going to be judged by the law of a free people. 13 For the one that does not practice mercy will have [his]

judgment without mercy. Mercy exults triumphantly over judgment. **14** Of what benefit is it, my brothers, if a certain one says he has faith but he does not have works? That faith cannot save him, can it? **15** If a brother or a sister is in a naked state and lacking the food sufficient for the day, **16** yet a certain one of YOU says to them: "Go in peace, keep warm and well fed," but YOU do not give them the necessities for [their] body, of what benefit is it? **17** Thus, too, faith, if it does not have works, is dead in itself.

18 Nevertheless, a certain one will say: "You have faith, and I have works. Show me your faith apart from the works, and I shall show you my faith by my works." **19** You believe there is one God, do you? You are doing quite well. And yet the demons believe and shudder. **20** But do you care to know, O empty man, that faith apart from works is inactive? **21** Was not Abraham our father declared righteous by works after he had offered up Isaac his son upon the altar? **22** You behold that [his] faith worked along with his works and by [his] works [his] faith was perfected, **23** and the scripture was fulfilled which says: "Abraham put faith in Jehovah, and it was counted to him as righteousness," and he came to be called "Jehovah's friend."

24 You see that a man is to be declared righteous by works, and not by faith alone. **25** In the same manner was not also Ra'hab the harlot declared righteous by works, after she had received the messengers hospitably and sent them out by another way? **26** Indeed, as the body without spirit is dead, so also faith without works is dead.

3 Not many of YOU should become teachers, my brothers, knowing that we shall receive heavier judgment. **2** For we all stumble many times. If anyone does not stumble in word, this one is a perfect man, able to bridle also [his] whole body. **3** If we put bridles in the mouths of horses for them to obey us, we manage also their whole body. **4** Look! Even boats, although they are so big and are driven by hard winds, are steered by a very small rudder to where the inclination of the man at the helm wishes.

5 So, too, the tongue is a little member and yet makes great brags. Look! How little a fire it takes to set so great a woodland on fire! **6** Well, the tongue is a fire. The tongue is constituted a world of unrighteousness among our members, for it spots up all the body and sets the wheel of natural life aflame and it is set aflame by Gehenna. **7** For every species of wild beast as well as bird and creeping thing and sea creature is to be tamed and has been tamed by humankind. **8** But the tongue, not one of mankind can get it tamed. An unruly injurious thing, it is full of death-dealing poison. **9** With it we bless Jehovah, even [the] Father, and yet with it we curse men who have come into existence "in the likeness of God." **10** Out of the same mouth come forth blessing and cursing.

It is not proper, my brothers, for these things to go on occurring this way. **11** A fountain does not cause the sweet and the bitter to bubble out of the same opening, does it? **12** My brothers, a fig tree cannot produce olives or a vine figs, can it? Neither can salt water produce sweet water.

13 Who is wise and understanding among YOU? Let him show out of his fine conduct his works with a meekness that belongs to wisdom. **14** But if YOU have bitter jealousy and contentiousness in YOUR hearts, do not be bragging and lying against the truth. **15** This is not the wisdom that comes down from above, but is [the] earthly, animal, demonic. **16** For where jealousy and contentiousness are, there disorder and every vile thing are.

17 But the wisdom from above is first of all chaste, then peaceable, reasonable, ready to obey, full of mercy and good fruits, not making partial distinctions, not hypocritical. 18 Moreover, the fruit of righteousness has its seed sown under peaceful conditions for those who are making peace.

4 From what source are there wars and from what source are there fights among you? Are they not from this source, namely, from your cravings for sensual pleasure that carry on a conflict in your members? 2 You desire, and yet you do not have. You go on murdering and coveting, and yet you are not able to obtain. You go on fighting and waging war. You do not have because of your not asking. 3 You do ask, and yet you do not receive, because you are asking for a wrong purpose, that you may expend [it] upon your cravings for sensual pleasure.

4 Adulteresses, do you not know that the friendship with the world is enmity with God? Whoever, therefore, wants to be a friend of the world is constituting himself an enemy of God. 5 Or does it seem to you that the scripture says to no purpose: "It is with a tendency to envy that the spirit which has taken up residence within us keeps longing"? 6 However, the undeserved kindness which he gives is greater. Hence it says: "God opposes the haughty ones, but he gives undeserved kindness to the humble ones."

7 Subject yourselves, therefore, to God; but oppose the Devil, and he will flee from you. 8 Draw close to God, and he will draw close to you. Cleanse your hands, you sinners, and purify your hearts, you indecisive ones. 9 Give way to misery and mourn and weep. Let your laughter be turned into mourning, and [your] joy into dejection. 10 Humble yourselves in the eyes of Jehovah, and he will exalt you.

11 Quit speaking against one another, brothers. He who speaks against a brother or judges his brother speaks against law and judges law. Now if you judge law, you are, not a doer of law, but a judge. 12 One there is that is lawgiver and judge, he who is able to save and to destroy. But you, who are you to be judging [your] neighbor?

13 Come, now, you who say: "Today or tomorrow we will journey to this city and will spend a year there, and we will engage in business and make profits," 14 whereas you do not know what your life will be tomorrow. For you are a mist appearing for a little while and then disappearing. 15 Instead, you ought to say: "If Jehovah wills, we shall live and also do this or that." 16 But now you take pride in your self-assuming brags. All such taking of pride is wicked. 17 Therefore, if one knows how to do what is right and yet does not do it, it is a sin for him.

5 Come, now, you rich [men], weep, howling over your miseries that are coming upon you. 2 Your riches have rotted, and your outer garments have become moth-eaten. 3 Your gold and silver are rusted away, and their rust will be as a witness against you and will eat your fleshy parts. Something like fire is what you have stored up in the last days. 4 Look! The wages due the workers who harvested your fields but which are held up by you, keep crying out, and the calls for help on the part of the reapers have entered into the ears of Jehovah of armies. 5 You have lived in luxury upon the earth and have gone in for sensual pleasure. You have fattened your hearts on the day of slaughter. 6 You have condemned, you have murdered the righteous one. Is he not opposing you?

7 Exercise patience, therefore, brothers, until the presence of the Lord. Look! The farmer keeps waiting for the precious fruit of the earth, exercising patience over it until he gets the early rain and the late rain. 8 You too exercise patience; make your hearts firm, because the presence of the Lord has drawn close.

9 Do not heave sighs against one another, brothers, so that you do not get judged. Look! The Judge is standing before the doors.

10 Brothers, take as a pattern of the suffering of evil and the exercising of patience the prophets, who spoke in the name of Jehovah. 11 Look! We pronounce happy those who have endured. You have heard of the endurance of Job and have seen the outcome Jehovah gave, that Jehovah is very tender in affection and merciful.

12 Above all things, though, my brothers, stop swearing, yes, either by heaven or by earth or by any other oath. But let YOUR Yes mean Yes, and YOUR No, No, so that YOU do not fall under judgment.

13 Is there anyone suffering evil among YOU? Let him carry on prayer. Is there anyone in good spirits? Let him sing psalms. 14 Is there anyone sick among YOU? Let him call the older men of the congregation to [him], and let them pray over him, greasing [him] with oil in the name of Jehovah.

15 And the prayer of faith will make the indisposed one well, and Jehovah will raise him up. Also, if he has committed sins, it will be forgiven him.

16 Therefore openly confess YOUR sins to one another and pray for one another, that YOU may get healed. A righteous man's supplication, when it is at work, has much force. 17 E·li'jah was a man with feelings like ours, and yet in prayer he prayed for it not to rain; and it did not rain upon the land for three years and six months. 18 And he prayed again, and the heaven gave rain and the land put forth its fruit.

19 My brothers, if anyone among YOU is misled from the truth and another turns him back, 20 know that he who turns a sinner back from the error of his way will save his soul from death and will cover a multitude of sins.

THE FIRST OF

PETER

1 Peter, an apostle of Jesus Christ, to the temporary residents scattered about in Pontus, Ga·la'-tia, Cap·pa·do'ci·a, Asia, and Bi-thyn'i·a, to the ones chosen 2 according to the foreknowledge of God the Father, with sanctification by the spirit, for the purpose of their being obedient and sprinkled with the blood of Jesus Christ:

May undeserved kindness and peace be increased to YOU.

3 Blessed be the God and Father of our Lord Jesus Christ, for according to his great mercy he gave us a new birth to a living hope through the resurrection of Jesus Christ from the dead, 4 to an incorruptible and undefiled and unfading inheritance. It is reserved in the heavens for YOU, 5 who are being safeguarded by God's power through faith for a salvation ready to be revealed in the last period of time. 6 In this fact YOU are

greatly rejoicing, though for a little while at present, if it must be, YOU have been grieved by various trials, 7 in order that the tested quality of YOUR faith, of much greater value than gold that perishes despite its being proved by fire, may be found a cause for praise and glory and honor at the revelation of Jesus Christ. 8 Though YOU never saw him, YOU love him. Though YOU are not looking upon him at present, yet YOU exercise faith in him and are greatly rejoicing with an unspeakable and glorified joy, 9 as YOU receive the end of YOUR faith, the salvation of YOUR souls.

10 Concerning this very salvation a diligent inquiry and a careful search were made by the prophets who prophesied about the undeserved kindness meant for YOU. 11 They kept on investigating what particular season or what sort of

[season] the spirit in them was indicating concerning Christ when it was bearing witness beforehand about the sufferings for Christ and about the glories to follow these. 12 It was revealed to them that, not to themselves, but to YOU, they were ministering the things that have now been announced to YOU through those who have declared the good news to YOU with holy spirit sent forth from heaven. Into these very things angels are desiring to peer.

13 Hence brace up YOUR minds for activity, keep YOUR senses completely; set YOUR hope upon the undeserved kindness that is to be brought to YOU at the revelation of Jesus Christ. 14 As obedient children, quit being fashioned according to the desires YOU formerly had in YOUR ignorance, 15 but, in accord with the Holy One who called YOU, do YOU also become holy yourselves in all [YOUR] conduct, 16 because it is written: "YOU must be holy, because I am holy."

17 Furthermore, if YOU are calling upon the Father who judges impartially according to each one's work, conduct yourselves with fear during the time of YOUR alien residence. 18 For YOU know that it was not with corruptible things, with silver or gold, that YOU were delivered from YOUR fruitless form of conduct received by tradition from YOUR forefathers. 19 But it was with precious blood, like that of an unblemished and spotless lamb, even Christ's. 20 True, he was foreknown before the founding of the world, but he was made manifest at the end of the times for the sake of YOU 21 who through him are believers in God, the one who raised him up from the dead and gave him glory; so that YOUR faith and hope might be in God.

22 Now that YOU have purified YOUR souls by [YOUR] obedience to the truth with unhypocritical brotherly love as the result, love one another intensely from the heart. 23 For YOU have been given a new birth, not by corruptible, but by incorruptible [reproductive] seed, through the word of [the] living and enduring God. 24 For "all flesh is like grass, and all its glory is like a blossom of grass; the grass becomes withered, and the flower falls off, 25 but the saying of Jehovah endures forever." Well, this is the "saying," this which has been declared to YOU as good news.

2 Accordingly, put away all badness and all deceitfulness and hypocrisy and envies and all sorts of backbiting, 2 [and,] as newborn infants, form a longing for the unadulterated milk belonging to the word, that through it YOU may grow to salvation, 3 provided YOU have tasted that the Lord is kind.

4 Coming to him as to a living stone, rejected, it is true, by men, but chosen, precious, with God, 5 YOU yourselves also as living stones are being built up a spiritual house for the purpose of a holy priesthood, to offer up spiritual sacrifices acceptable to God through Jesus Christ. 6 For it is contained in Scripture: "Look! I am laying in Zion a stone, chosen, a foundation cornerstone, precious; and no one exercising faith in it will by any means come to disappointment."

7 It is to YOU, therefore, that he is precious, because YOU are believers; but to those not believing, "the identical stone that the builders rejected has become [the] head of [the] corner," 8 and "a stone of stumbling and a rock-mass of offense." These are stumbling because they are disobedient to the word. To this very end they were also appointed. 9 But YOU are "a chosen race, a royal priesthood, a holy nation, a people for special possession, that YOU should declare abroad the excellencies" of the one that called YOU out of darkness into his wonderful light. 10 For YOU were once not a people, but are now God's people; YOU were those who had not been shown mercy, but are now those who have been shown mercy.

11 Beloved, I exhort YOU as aliens and temporary residents to keep

abstaining from fleshly desires, which are the very ones that carry on a conflict against the soul. 12 Maintain YOUR conduct fine among the nations, that, in the thing in which they are speaking against YOU as evildoers, they may as a result of YOUR fine works of which they are eyewitnesses glorify God in the day for [his] inspection.

13 For the Lord's sake subject yourselves to every human creation: whether to a king as being superior 14 or to governors as being sent by him to inflict punishment on evildoers but to praise doers of good. 15 For so the will of God is, that by doing good YOU may muzzle the ignorant talk of the unreasonable men. 16 Be as free people, and yet holding YOUR freedom, not as a blind for badness, but as slaves of God. 17 Honor [men] of all sorts, have love for the whole association of brothers, be in fear of God, have honor for the king.

18 Let house servants be in subjection to [their] owners with all [due] fear, not only to the good and reasonable, but also to those hard to please. 19 For if someone, because of conscience toward God, bears up under grievous things and suffers unjustly, this is an agreeable thing. 20 For what merit is there in it if, when YOU are sinning and being slapped, YOU endure it? But if, when YOU are doing good and YOU suffer, YOU endure it, this is a thing agreeable with God.

21 In fact, to this [course] YOU were called, because even Christ suffered for YOU, leaving YOU a model for YOU to follow his steps closely. 22 He committed no sin, nor was deception found in his mouth. 23 When he was being reviled, he did not go reviling in return. When he was suffering, he did not go threatening, but kept on committing himself to the one who judges righteously. 24 He himself bore our sins in his own body upon the stake, in order that we might be done with sins and live to righteousness. And "by his stripes YOU were healed." 25 For YOU were

like sheep, going astray; but now YOU have returned to the shepherd and overseer of YOUR souls.

3 In like manner, YOU wives, be in subjection to YOUR own husbands, in order that, if any are not obedient to the word, they may be won without a word through the conduct of [their] wives, 2 because of having been eyewitnesses of YOUR chaste conduct together with deep respect. 3 And do not let YOUR adornment be that of the external braiding of the hair and of the putting on of gold ornaments or the wearing of outer garments, 4 but let it be the secret person of the heart in the incorruptible [apparel] of the quiet and mild spirit, which is of great value in the eyes of God. 5 For so, too, formerly the holy women who were hoping in God used to adorn themselves, subjecting themselves to their own husbands, 6 as Sarah used to obey Abraham, calling him "lord." And YOU have become her children, provided YOU keep on doing good and not fearing any cause for terror.

7 YOU husbands, continue dwelling in like manner with them according to knowledge, assigning them honor as to a weaker vessel, the feminine one, since YOU are also heirs with them of the undeserved favor of life, in order for YOUR prayers not to be hindered.

8 Finally, all of YOU be likeminded, showing fellow feeling, having brotherly affection, tenderly compassionate, humble in mind, 9 not paying back injury for injury or reviling for reviling, but, to the contrary, bestowing a blessing, because YOU were called to this [course], so that YOU might inherit a blessing.

10 For, "he that would love life and see good days, let him restrain his tongue from what is bad and [his] lips from speaking deception, 11 but let him turn away from what is bad and do what is good; let him seek peace and pursue it. 12 For [the] eyes of Jehovah are upon the righteous ones, and his ears are toward their supplication;

but [the] face of Jehovah is against those doing bad things."

13 Indeed, who is the man that will harm YOU if YOU become zealous for what is good? 14 But even if YOU should suffer for the sake of righteousness, YOU are happy. However, the object of their fear do not YOU fear, neither become agitated. 15 But sanctify the Christ as Lord in YOUR hearts, always ready to make a defense before everyone that demands of YOU a reason for the hope in YOU, but doing so together with a mild temper and deep respect.

16 Hold a good conscience, so that in the particular in which YOU are spoken against they may get ashamed who are speaking slightingly of YOUR good conduct in connection with Christ. 17 For it is better to suffer because YOU are doing good, if the will of God wishes it, than because YOU are doing evil. 18 Why, even Christ died once for all time concerning sins, a righteous [person] for unrighteous ones, that he might lead YOU to God, he being put to death in the flesh, but being made alive in the spirit. 19 In this [state] also he went his way and preached to the spirits in prison, 20 who had once been disobedient when the patience of God was waiting in Noah's days, while the ark was being constructed, in which a few people, that is, eight souls, were carried safely through the water.

21 That which corresponds to this is also now saving YOU, namely, baptism, (not the putting away of the filth of the flesh, but the request made to God for a good conscience,) through the resurrection of Jesus Christ. 22 He is at God's right hand, for he went his way to heaven; and angels and authorities and powers were made subject to him.

4 Therefore since Christ suffered in the flesh, YOU too arm yourselves with the same mental disposition; because the person that has suffered in the flesh has desisted from sins, 2 to the end that he may live the remainder of [his] time in the flesh, no more for the desires of men, but for God's will. 3 For the time that has passed by is sufficient for YOU to have worked out the will of the nations when YOU proceeded in deeds of loose conduct, lusts, excesses with wine, revelries, drinking matches, and illegal idolatries. 4 Because YOU do not continue running with them in this course to the same low sink of debauchery, they are puzzled and go on speaking abusively of YOU. 5 But these people will render an account to the one ready to judge those living and those dead. 6 In fact, for this purpose the good news was declared also to the dead, that they might be judged as to the flesh from the standpoint of men but might live as to the spirit from the standpoint of God.

7 But the end of all things has drawn close. Be sound in mind, therefore, and be vigilant with a view to prayers. 8 Above all things, have intense love for one another, because love covers a multitude of sins. 9 Be hospitable to one another without grumbling. 10 In proportion as each one has received a gift, use it in ministering to one another as fine stewards of God's undeserved kindness expressed in various ways. 11 If anyone speaks, let him speak as it were [the] sacred pronouncements of God; if anyone ministers, [let him minister] as dependent on the strength that God supplies; so that in all things God may be glorified through Jesus Christ. The glory and the might are his forever and ever. Amen.

12 Beloved ones, do not be puzzled at the burning among YOU, which is happening to YOU for a trial, as though a strange thing were befalling YOU. 13 On the contrary, go on rejoicing forasmuch as YOU are sharers in the sufferings of the Christ, that YOU may rejoice and be overjoyed also during the revelation of his glory. 14 If YOU are being reproached for the name of Christ, YOU are happy, because the [spirit] of glory, even the spirit of God, is resting upon YOU.

15 However, let none of you suffer as a murderer or a thief or an evildoer or as a busybody in other people's matters. 16 But if [he suffers] as a Christian, let him not feel shame, but let him keep on glorifying God in this name. 17 For it is the appointed time for the judgment to start with the house of God. Now if it starts first with us, what will the end be of those who are not obedient to the good news of God? 18 "And if the righteous [man] is being saved with difficulty, where will the ungodly [man] and the sinner make a showing?" 19 So, then, also let those who are suffering in harmony with the will of God keep on commending their souls to a faithful Creator while they are doing good.

5 Therefore, to the older men among you I give this exhortation, for I too am an older man like them and a witness of the sufferings of the Christ, a sharer even of the glory that is to be revealed: 2 Shepherd the flock of God in your care, not under compulsion, but willingly; neither for love of dishonest gain, but eagerly; 3 neither as lording it over those who are God's inheritance, but becoming examples to the flock. 4 And when the chief shepherd has been made manifest, you will receive the unfadable crown of glory.

5 In like manner, you younger men, be in subjection to the older men. But all of you gird yourselves with lowliness of mind toward one another, because God opposes the haughty ones, but he gives undeserved kindness to the humble ones.

6 Humble yourselves, therefore, under the mighty hand of God, that he may exalt you in due time; 7 while you throw all your anxiety upon him, because he cares for you. 8 Keep your senses, be watchful. Your adversary, the Devil, walks about like a roaring lion, seeking to devour [someone]. 9 But take your stand against him, solid in the faith, knowing that the same things in the way of sufferings are being accomplished in the entire association of your brothers in the world. 10 But, after you have suffered a little while, the God of all undeserved kindness, who called you to his everlasting glory in union with Christ, will himself finish your training, he will make you firm, he will make you strong. 11 To him be the might forever. Amen.

12 Through Sil·va'nus, a faithful brother, as I account him, I have written you in few [words], to give encouragement and an earnest witness that this is the true undeserved kindness of God; in which stand firm. 13 She who is in Babylon, a chosen one like [you], sends you her greetings, and so does Mark my son. 14 Greet one another with a kiss of love.

May all of you who are in union with Christ have peace.

THE SECOND OF
PETER

1 Simon Peter, a slave and apostle of Jesus Christ, to those who have obtained a faith, held in equal privilege with ours, by the righteousness of our God and [the] Savior Jesus Christ:

2 May undeserved kindness and peace be increased to you by an accurate knowledge of God and of Jesus our Lord, 3 forasmuch as his divine power has given us freely all the things that concern life and godly devotion, through the accurate knowledge of the one who called us through glory and virtue. 4 Through these things he has freely given us the precious and very grand promises, that through

these you may become sharers in divine nature, having escaped from the corruption that is in the world through lust.

5 Yes, for this very reason, by your contributing in response all earnest effort, supply to your faith virtue, to [your] virtue knowledge, 6 to [your] knowledge self-control, to [your] self-control endurance, to [your] endurance godly devotion, 7 to [your] godly devotion brotherly affection, to [your] brotherly affection love. 8 For if these things exist in you and overflow, they will prevent you from being either inactive or unfruitful regarding the accurate knowledge of our Lord Jesus Christ.

9 For if these things are not present in anyone, he is blind, shutting his eyes [to the light], and has become forgetful of his cleansing from his sins of long ago. 10 For this reason, brothers, all the more do your utmost to make the calling and choosing of you sure for yourselves; for if you keep on doing these things you will by no means ever fail. 11 In fact, thus there will be richly supplied to you the entrance into the everlasting kingdom of our Lord and Savior Jesus Christ.

12 For this reason I shall be disposed always to remind you of these things, although you know [them] and are firmly set in the truth that is present [in you]. 13 But I consider it right, as long as I am in this tabernacle, to rouse you up by way of reminding you, 14 knowing as I do that the putting off of my tabernacle is soon to be, just as also our Lord Jesus Christ signified to me. 15 So I will do my utmost also at every time that, after my departure, you may be able to make mention of these things for yourselves.

16 No, it was not by following artfully contrived false stories that we acquainted you with the power and presence of our Lord Jesus Christ, but it was by having become eyewitnesses of his magnificence. 17 For he received from God the Father honor and glory,

when words such as these were borne to him by the magnificent glory: "This is my son, my beloved, whom I myself have approved." 18 Yes, these words we heard borne from heaven while we were with him in the holy mountain.

19 Consequently we have the prophetic word [made] more sure; and you are doing well in paying attention to it as to a lamp shining in a dark place, until day dawns and a daystar rises, in your hearts. 20 For you know this first, that no prophecy of Scripture springs from any private interpretation. 21 For prophecy was at no time brought by man's will, but men spoke from God as they were borne along by holy spirit.

2 However, there also came to be false prophets among the people, as there will also be false teachers among you. These very ones will quietly bring in destructive sects and will disown even the owner that bought them, bringing speedy destruction upon themselves. 2 Furthermore, many will follow their acts of loose conduct, and on account of these the way of the truth will be spoken of abusively. 3 Also, with covetousness they will exploit you with counterfeit words. But as for them, the judgment from of old is not moving slowly, and the destruction of them is not slumbering.

4 Certainly if God did not hold back from punishing the angels that sinned, but, by throwing them into Tar′ta·rus, delivered them to pits of dense darkness to be reserved for judgment; 5 and he did not hold back from punishing an ancient world, but kept Noah, a preacher of righteousness, safe with seven others when he brought a deluge upon a world of ungodly people; 6 and by reducing the cities Sod′om and Go·mor′rah to ashes he condemned them, setting a pattern for ungodly persons of things to come; 7 and he delivered righteous Lot, who was greatly distressed by the indulgence of the law-defying people in loose conduct— 8 for that righteous man

by what he saw and heard while dwelling among them from day to day was tormenting his righteous soul by reason of their lawless deeds— 9 Jehovah knows how to deliver people of godly devotion out of trial, but to reserve unrighteous people for the day of judgment to be cut off, 10 especially, however, those who go on after flesh with the desire to defile [it] and who look down on lordship.

Daring, self-willed, they do not tremble at glorious ones but speak abusively, 11 whereas angels, although they are greater in strength and power, do not bring against them an accusation in abusive terms, [not doing so] out of respect for Jehovah. 12 But these [men], like unreasoning animals born naturally to be caught and destroyed, will, in the things of which they are ignorant and speak abusively, even suffer destruction in their own [course of] destruction, 13 wronging themselves as a reward for wrongdoing.

They consider luxurious living in the daytime a pleasure. They are spots and blemishes, indulging with unrestrained delight in their deceptive teachings while feasting together with you. 14 They have eyes full of adultery and unable to desist from sin, and they entice unsteady souls. They have a heart trained in covetousness. They are accursed children. 15 Abandoning the straight path, they have been misled. They have followed the path of Ba'laam, [the son] of Be'or, who loved the reward of wrongdoing, 16 but got a reproof for his own violation of what was right. A voiceless beast of burden, making utterance with the voice of a man, hindered the prophet's mad course.

17 These are fountains without water, and mists driven by a violent storm, and for them the blackness of darkness has been reserved. 18 For they utter swelling expressions of no profit, and by the desires of the flesh and by loose habits they entice those who are just escaping from people who conduct themselves in error. 19 While they are promising them freedom, they themselves are existing as slaves of corruption. For whoever is overcome by another is enslaved by this one. 20 Certainly if, after having escaped from the defilements of the world by an accurate knowledge of the Lord and Savior Jesus Christ, they get involved again with these very things and are overcome, the final conditions have become worse for them than the first. 21 For it would have been better for them not to have accurately known the path of righteousness than after knowing it accurately to turn away from the holy commandment delivered to them. 22 The saying of the true proverb has happened to them: "The dog has returned to its own vomit, and the sow that was bathed to rolling in the mire."

3 Beloved ones, this is now the second letter I am writing you, in which, as in my first one, I am arousing your clear thinking faculties by way of a reminder, 2 that you should remember the sayings previously spoken by the holy prophets and the commandment of the Lord and Savior through your apostles. 3 For you know this first, that in the last days there will come ridiculers with their ridicule, proceeding according to their own desires 4 and saying: "Where is this promised presence of his? Why, from the day our forefathers fell asleep [in death], all things are continuing exactly as from creation's beginning."

5 For, according to their wish, this fact escapes their notice, that there were heavens from of old and an earth standing compactly out of water and in the midst of water by the word of God; 6 and by those [means] the world of that time suffered destruction when it was deluged with water. 7 But by the same word the heavens and the earth that are now are stored up for fire and are being reserved to the day of judgment and of destruction of the ungodly men.

8 However, let this one fact not be escaping YOUR notice, beloved ones, that one day is with Jehovah as a thousand years and a thousand years as one day. 9 Jehovah is not slow respecting his promise, as some people consider slowness, but he is patient with YOU because he does not desire any to be destroyed but desires all to attain to repentance. 10 Yet Jehovah's day will come as a thief, in which the heavens will pass away with a hissing noise, but the elements being intensely hot will be dissolved, and earth and the works in it will be discovered.

11 Since all these things are thus to be dissolved, what sort of persons ought YOU to be in holy acts of conduct and deeds of godly devotion, 12 awaiting and keeping close in mind the presence of the day of Jehovah, through which [the] heavens being on fire will be dissolved and [the] elements being intensely hot will melt! 13 But there are new heavens and a new earth that we are awaiting according to his promise, and in these righteousness is to dwell.

14 Hence, beloved ones, since YOU are awaiting these things, do YOUR utmost to be found finally by him spotless and unblemished and in peace. 15 Furthermore, consider the patience of our Lord as salvation, just as our beloved brother Paul according to the wisdom given him also wrote YOU, 16 speaking about these things as he does also in all [his] letters. In them, however, are some things hard to understand, which the untaught and unsteady are twisting, as [they do] also the rest of the Scriptures, to their own destruction.

17 YOU, therefore, beloved ones, having this advance knowledge, be on YOUR guard that YOU may not be led away with them by the error of the law-defying people and fall from YOUR own steadfastness. 18 No, but go on growing in the undeserved kindness and knowledge of our Lord and Savior Jesus Christ. To him [be] the glory both now and to the day of eternity.

THE FIRST OF

JOHN

1 That which was from [the] beginning, which we have heard, which we have seen with our eyes, which we have viewed attentively and our hands felt, concerning the word of life, 2 (yes, the life was made manifest, and we have seen and are bearing witness and reporting to YOU the everlasting life which was with the Father and was made manifest to us,) 3 that which we have seen and heard we are reporting also to YOU, that YOU too may be having a sharing with us. Furthermore, this sharing of ours is with the Father and with his Son Jesus Christ. 4 And so we are writing these things that our joy may be in full measure.

5 And this is the message which we have heard from him and are announcing to YOU, that God is light and there is no darkness at all in union with him. 6 If we make the statement: "We are having a sharing with him," and yet we go on walking in the darkness, we are lying and are not practicing the truth. 7 However, if we are walking in the light as he himself is in the light, we do have a sharing with one another, and the blood of Jesus his Son cleanses us from all sin.

8 If we make the statement: "We have no sin," we are misleading ourselves and the truth is not in us. 9 If we confess our sins, he is faithful and righteous so as to forgive us our sins and to cleanse us from all unrighteousness. 10 If we make the statement: "We have not

sinned," we are making him a liar, and his word is not in us.

2 My little children, I am writing you these things that you may not commit a sin. And yet, if anyone does commit a sin, we have a helper with the Father, Jesus Christ, a righteous one. 2 And he is a propitiatory sacrifice for our sins, yet not for ours only but also for the whole world's. 3 And by this we have the knowledge that we have come to know him, namely, if we continue observing his commandments. 4 He that says: "I have come to know him," and yet is not observing his commandments, is a liar, and the truth is not in this [person]. 5 But whoever does observe his word, truthfully in this [person] the love of God has been made perfect. By this we have the knowledge that we are in union with him. 6 He that says he remains in union with him is under obligation himself also to go on walking just as that one walked.

7 Beloved ones, I am writing you, not a new commandment, but an old commandment which you have had from [the] beginning. This old commandment is the word which you heard. 8 Again, I am writing you a new commandment, a fact that is true in his case and in yours, because the darkness is passing away and the true light is already shining.

9 He that says he is in the light and yet hates his brother is in the darkness up to right now. 10 He that loves his brother remains in the light, and there is no cause for stumbling in his case. 11 But he that hates his brother is in the darkness and is walking in the darkness, and he does not know where he is going, because the darkness has blinded his eyes.

12 I am writing you, little children, because your sins have been forgiven you for the sake of his name. 13 I am writing you, fathers, because you have come to know him who is from [the] beginning. I am writing you, young men, because you have conquered the wicked one. I write you, young children, because you have come to know the Father. 14 I write you, fathers, because you have come to know him who is from [the] beginning. I write you, young men, because you are strong and the word of God remains in you and you have conquered the wicked one.

15 Do not be loving either the world or the things in the world. If anyone loves the world, the love of the Father is not in him; 16 because everything in the world—the desire of the flesh and the desire of the eyes and the showy display of one's means of life—does not originate with the Father, but originates with the world. 17 Furthermore, the world is passing away and so is its desire, but he that does the will of God remains forever.

18 Young children, it is the last hour, and, just as you have heard that antichrist is coming, even now there have come to be many antichrists; from which fact we gain the knowledge that it is the last hour. 19 They went out from us, but they were not of our sort; for if they had been of our sort, they would have remained with us. But [they went out] that it might be shown up that not all are of our sort. 20 And you have an anointing from the holy one; all of you have knowledge. 21 I write you, not because you do not know the truth, but because you know it, and because no lie originates with the truth.

22 Who is the liar if it is not the one that denies that Jesus is the Christ? This is the antichrist, the one that denies the Father and the Son. 23 Everyone that denies the Son does not have the Father either. He that confesses the Son has the Father also. 24 As for you, let that which you have heard from [the] beginning remain in you. If that which you have heard from [the] beginning remains in you, you will also abide in union with the Son and in union with the Father. 25 Furthermore, this is the promised thing that he himself promised us, the life everlasting.

26 These things I write you about those who are trying to mislead you. 27 And as for you, the anointing that you received from him remains in you, and you do not need anyone to be teaching you; but, as the anointing from him is teaching you about all things, and is true and is no lie, and just as it has taught you, remain in union with him. 28 So now, little children, remain in union with him, that when he is made manifest we may have freeness of speech and not be shamed away from him at his presence. 29 If you know that he is righteous, you gain the knowledge that everyone who practices righteousness has been born from him.

3 See what sort of love the Father has given us, so that we should be called children of God; and such we are. That is why the world does not have a knowledge of us, because it has not come to know him. 2 Beloved ones, now we are children of God, but as yet it has not been made manifest what we shall be. We do know that whenever he is made manifest we shall be like him, because we shall see him just as he is. 3 And everyone who has this hope set upon him purifies himself just as that one is pure.

4 Everyone who practices sin is also practicing lawlessness, and so sin is lawlessness. 5 You know too that that one was made manifest to take away [our] sins, and there is no sin in him. 6 Everyone remaining in union with him does not practice sin; no one that practices sin has either seen him or come to know him. 7 Little children, let no one mislead you; he who carries on righteousness is righteous, just as that one is righteous. 8 He who carries on sin originates with the Devil, because the Devil has been sinning from [the] beginning. For this purpose the Son of God was made manifest, namely, to break up the works of the Devil.

9 Everyone who has been born from God does not carry on sin, because His [reproductive] seed remains in such one, and he cannot practice sin, because he has been born from God. 10 The children of God and the children of the Devil are evident by this fact: Everyone who does not carry on righteousness does not originate with God, neither does he who does not love his brother. 11 For this is the message which you have heard from [the] beginning, that we should have love for one another; 12 not like Cain, who originated with the wicked one and slaughtered his brother. And for the sake of what did he slaughter him? Because his own works were wicked, but those of his brother [were] righteous.

13 Do not marvel, brothers, that the world hates you. 14 We know we have passed over from death to life, because we love the brothers. He who does not love remains in death. 15 Everyone who hates his brother is a manslayer, and you know that no manslayer has everlasting life remaining in him. 16 By this we have come to know love, because that one surrendered his soul for us; and we are under obligation to surrender [our] souls for [our] brothers. 17 But whoever has this world's means for supporting life and beholds his brother having need and yet shuts the door of his tender compassions upon him, in what way does the love of God remain in him? 18 Little children, let us love, neither in word nor with the tongue, but in deed and truth.

19 By this we shall know that we originate with the truth, and we shall assure our hearts before him 20 as regards whatever our hearts may condemn us in, because God is greater than our hearts and knows all things. 21 Beloved ones, if [our] hearts do not condemn [us], we have freeness of speech toward God; 22 and whatever we ask we receive from him, because we are observing his commandments and are doing the things that are pleasing in his eyes. 23 Indeed, this is his command-

ment, that we have faith in the name of his Son Jesus Christ and be loving one another, just as he gave us commandment. 24 Moreover, he who observes his commandments remains in union with him, and he in union with such one; and by this we gain the knowledge that he is remaining in union with us, owing to the spirit which he gave us.

4 Beloved ones, do not believe every inspired expression, but test the inspired expressions to see whether they originate with God, because many false prophets have gone forth into the world.

2 You gain the knowledge of the inspired expression from God by this: Every inspired expression that confesses Jesus Christ as having come in the flesh originates with God, 3 but every inspired expression that does not confess Jesus does not originate with God. Furthermore, this is the antichrist's [inspired expression] which you have heard was coming, and now it is already in the world.

4 You originate with God, little children, and you have conquered those [persons], because he that is in union with you is greater than he that is in union with the world. 5 They originate with the world; that is why they speak [what proceeds] from the world and the world listens to them. 6 We originate with God. He that gains the knowledge of God listens to us; he that does not originate with God does not listen to us. This is how we take note of the inspired expression of truth and the inspired expression of error.

7 Beloved ones, let us continue loving one another, because love is from God, and everyone who loves has been born from God and gains the knowledge of God. 8 He that does not love has not come to know God, because God is love. 9 By this the love of God was made manifest in our case, because God sent forth his only-begotten Son into the world that we might gain life through him. 10 The love is

in this respect, not that we have loved God, but that he loved us and sent forth his Son as a propitiatory sacrifice for our sins.

11 Beloved ones, if this is how God loved us, then we are ourselves under obligation to love one another. 12 At no time has anyone beheld God. If we continue loving one another, God remains in us and his love is made perfect in us. 13 By this we gain the knowledge that we are remaining in union with him and he in union with us, because he has imparted his spirit to us. 14 In addition, we ourselves have beheld and are bearing witness that the Father has sent forth his Son as Savior of the world. 15 Whoever makes the confession that Jesus Christ is the Son of God, God remains in union with such one and he in union with God. 16 And we ourselves have come to know and have believed the love that God has in our case.

God is love, and he that remains in love remains in union with God and God remains in union with him. 17 This is how love has been made perfect with us, that we may have freeness of speech in the day of judgment, because, just as that one is, so are we ourselves in this world. 18 There is no fear in love, but perfect love throws fear outside, because fear exercises a restraint. Indeed, he that is under fear has not been made perfect in love. 19 As for us, we love, because he first loved us.

20 If anyone makes the statement: "I love God," and yet is hating his brother, he is a liar. For he who does not love his brother, whom he has seen, cannot be loving God, whom he has not seen. 21 And this commandment we have from him, that the one who loves God should be loving his brother also.

5 Everyone believing that Jesus is the Christ has been born from God, and everyone who loves the one that caused to be born loves him who has been born from that

one. 2 By this we gain the knowledge that we are loving the children of God, when we are loving God and doing his commandments. 3 For this is what the love of God means, that we observe his commandments; and yet his commandments are not burdensome, 4 because everything that has been born from God conquers the world. And this is the conquest that has conquered the world, our faith. 5 Who is the one that conquers the world but he who has faith that Jesus is the Son of God? 6 This is he that came by means of water and blood, Jesus Christ; not with the water only, but with the water and with the blood. And the spirit is that which is bearing witness, because the spirit is the truth. 7 For there are three witness bearers, 8 the spirit and the water and the blood, and the three are in agreement.

9 If we receive the witness men give, the witness God gives is greater, because this is the witness God gives, the fact that he has borne witness concerning his Son. 10 The [person] putting his faith in the Son of God has the witness given in his own case. The [person] not having faith in God has made him a liar, because he has not put his faith in the witness given, which God as witness has given concerning his Son. 11 And this is the witness given, that God gave us everlasting life, and this life is in his Son. 12 He that has the Son has this life; he that does

not have the Son of God does not have this life.

13 I write you these things that you may know that you have life everlasting, you who put your faith in the name of the Son of God. 14 And this is the confidence that we have toward him, that, no matter what it is that we ask according to his will, he hears us. 15 Further, if we know he hears us respecting whatever we are asking, we know we are to have the things asked since we have asked them of him.

16 If anyone catches sight of his brother sinning a sin that does not incur death, he will ask, and he will give life to him, yes, to those not sinning so as to incur death. There is a sin that does incur death. It is concerning that sin that I do not tell him to make request. 17 All unrighteousness is sin; and yet there is a sin that does not incur death.

18 We know that every [person] that has been born from God does not practice sin, but the One born from God watches him, and the wicked one does not fasten his hold on him. 19 We know we originate with God, but the whole world is lying in the [power of the] wicked one. 20 But we know that the Son of God has come, and he has given us intellectual capacity that we may gain the knowledge of the true one. And we are in union with the true one, by means of his Son Jesus Christ. This is the true God and life everlasting. 21 Little children, guard yourselves from idols.

THE SECOND OF

JOHN

1 The older man to the chosen lady and to her children, whom I truly love, and not I alone, but all those also who have come to know the truth, 2 because of the truth that remains in us, and it will be with us forever. 3 There will be with us undeserved kindness, mercy

and peace from God the Father and from Jesus Christ the Son of the Father, with truth and love. 4 I rejoice very much because I have found certain ones of your children walking in the truth, just as we received commandment from the Father. 5 So now I request you, lady, as [a person] writing you, not a new commandment, but one which we had from [the] beginning, that we love one another. 6 And this is what love means, that we go on walking according to his commandments. This is the commandment, just as you people have heard from [the] beginning, that you should go on walking in it. 7 For many deceivers have gone forth into the world, persons not confessing Jesus Christ as coming in the flesh. This is the deceiver and the antichrist.

8 Look out for yourselves, that you do not lose the things we have worked to produce, but that you may obtain a full reward. 9 Everyone that pushes ahead and does not remain in the teaching of the Christ does not have God. He that does remain in this teaching is the one that has both the Father and the Son. 10 If anyone comes to you and does not bring this teaching, never receive him into your homes or say a greeting to him. 11 For he that says a greeting to him is a sharer in his wicked works.

12 Although I have many things to write you, I do not desire to do so with paper and ink, but I am hoping to come to you and to speak with you face to face, that your joy may be in full measure. 13 The children of your sister, the chosen one, send you their greetings.

THE THIRD OF

JOHN

1 The older man to Ga·ius, the beloved, whom I truly love. 2 Beloved one, I pray that in all things you may be prospering and having good health, just as your soul is prospering. 3 For I rejoiced very much when brothers came and bore witness to the truth you hold, just as you go on walking in the truth. 4 No greater cause for thankfulness do I have than these things, that I should be hearing that my children go on walking in the truth.

5 Beloved one, you are doing a faithful work in whatever you do for the brothers, and strangers at that, 6 who have borne witness to your love before the congregation. These you will please send on their way in a manner worthy of God. 7 For it was in behalf of [his] name that they went forth, not taking anything from the people of the nations. 8 We, therefore, are under obligation to receive such persons hospitably, that we may become fellow workers in the truth.

9 I wrote something to the congregation, but Di·ot're·phes, who likes to have the first place among them, does not receive anything from us with respect. 10 That is why, if I come, I will call to remembrance his works which he goes on doing, chattering about us with wicked words. Also, not being content with these things, neither does he himself receive the brothers with respect, and those who are wanting to receive them he tries to hinder and to throw out of the congregation.

11 Beloved one, be an imitator, not of what is bad, but of what is good. He that does good originates with God. He that does bad has not seen God. 12 De·me'tri·us has had witness borne to him by them all and by the truth itself. In fact, we, also, are bearing witness, and you know that the witness we give is true.

13 I had many things to write you, yet I do not wish to go on writing you with ink and pen. 14 But I am hoping to see you directly, and we shall speak face to face.

May you have peace.

The friends send you their greetings. Give my greetings to the friends by name.

THE LETTER OF

JUDE

1 Jude, a slave of Jesus Christ, but a brother of James, to the called ones who are loved in relationship with God [the] Father and preserved for Jesus Christ: **2** May mercy and peace and love be increased to YOU.

3 Beloved ones, though I was making every effort to write YOU about the salvation we hold in common, I found it necessary to write YOU to exhort YOU to put up a hard fight for the faith that was once for all time delivered to the holy ones. **4** My reason is that certain men have slipped in who have long ago been appointed by the Scriptures to this judgment, ungodly men, turning the undeserved kindness of our God into an excuse for loose conduct and proving false to our only Owner and Lord, Jesus Christ.

5 I desire to remind YOU, despite YOUR knowing all things once for all time, that Jehovah, although he saved a people out of the land of Egypt, afterwards destroyed those not showing faith. **6** And the angels that did not keep their original position but forsook their own proper dwelling place he has reserved with eternal bonds under dense darkness for the judgment of the great day. **7** So too Sod'om and Go·mor'rah and the cities about them, after they in the same manner as the foregoing ones had committed fornication excessively and gone out after flesh for unnatural use, are placed before [us] as a [warning] example by undergoing the judicial punishment of everlasting fire.

8 In like manner, notwithstanding, these men too indulging in dreams, are defiling the flesh and disregarding lordship and speaking abusively of glorious ones. **9** But when Michael the archangel had a difference with the Devil and was disputing about Moses' body, he did not dare to bring a judgment against him in abusive terms, but said: "May Jehovah rebuke you." **10** Yet these [men] are speaking abusively of all the things they really do not know; but all the things that they do understand naturally like the unreasoning animals, in these things they go on corrupting themselves.

11 Too bad for them, because they have gone in the path of Cain, and have rushed into the erroneous course of Ba'laam for reward, and have perished in the rebellious talk of Ko'rah! **12** These are the rocks hidden below water in YOUR love feasts while they feast with YOU, shepherds that feed themselves without fear; waterless clouds carried this way and that by winds; trees in late autumn, [but] fruitless, having died twice, having been uprooted; **13** wild waves of the sea that foam up their own causes for shame; stars with no set course, for which the blackness of darkness stands reserved forever.

14 Yes, the seventh one [in line] from Adam, E'noch, prophesied also regarding them, when he said: "Look! Jehovah came with his holy myriads, **15** to execute judgment against all, and to convict all the ungodly concerning all their ungodly deeds that they did in an ungodly way, and concerning all the shocking things that ungodly sinners spoke against him."

16 These men are murmurers, complainers about their lot in life, proceeding according to their own desires, and their mouths speak swelling things, while they are admiring personalities for the sake of [their own] benefit.

17 As for YOU, beloved ones, call to mind the sayings that have been previously spoken by the apostles of our Lord Jesus Christ, **18** how they used to say to YOU: "In the last time there will be ridiculers, proceeding according to their own desires for ungodly things." **19** These are the ones that make separations, animalistic [men], not having spirituality. **20** But you, beloved ones, by building up yourselves on your most holy faith, and praying with holy spirit, **21** keep yourselves in God's love, while you are waiting for the mercy of our Lord Jesus Christ with everlasting life in view. **22** Also, continue showing mercy to some that have doubts; **23** save [them] by snatching [them] out of the fire. But continue showing mercy to others, doing so with fear, while you hate even the inner garment that has been stained by the flesh.

24 Now to the one who is able to guard you from stumbling and to set you unblemished in the sight of his glory with great joy, **25** to [the] only God our Savior through Jesus Christ our Lord, be glory, majesty, might and authority for all past eternity and now and into all eternity. Amen.

A REVELATION

TO JOHN

1 A revelation by Jesus Christ, which God gave him, to show his slaves the things that must shortly take place. And he sent forth his angel and presented [it] in signs through him to his slave John, **2** who bore witness to the word God gave and to the witness Jesus Christ gave, even to all the things he saw. **3** Happy is he who reads aloud and those who hear the words of this prophecy, and who observe the things written in it; for the appointed time is near.

4 John to the seven congregations that are in the [district of] Asia:

May you have undeserved kindness and peace from "The One who is and who was and who is coming," and from the seven spirits that are before his throne, **5** and from Jesus Christ, "the Faithful Witness," "The first-born from the dead," and "The Ruler of the kings of the earth."

To him that loves us and that loosed us from our sins by means of his own blood— **6** and he made us to be a kingdom, priests to his God and Father—yes, to him be the glory and the might forever. Amen.

7 Look! He is coming with the clouds, and every eye will see him, and those who pierced him; and all the tribes of the earth will beat themselves in grief because of him. Yes, Amen.

8 "I am the Al'pha and the O·me'ga," says Jehovah God, "the One who is and who was and who is coming, the Almighty."

9 I John, your brother and a sharer with you in the tribulation and kingdom and endurance in company with Jesus, came to be in the isle that is called Pat'mos for speaking about God and bearing witness to Jesus. **10** By inspiration I came to be in the Lord's day, and I heard behind me a strong voice like that of a trumpet, **11** saying: "What you see write in a scroll and send it to the seven congregations, in Eph'e·sus and in Smyr'na and in Per'ga·mum and in Thy·a·ti'ra and in Sar'dis and in Philadelphia and in La·o·di·ce'a."

12 And I turned to see the voice that was speaking with me, and, having turned, I saw seven golden lampstands, **13** and in the midst of the lampstands someone like a son of man, clothed with a garment that reached down to the feet, and girded at the breasts with a golden girdle. **14** Moreover, his head and his hair were white as white wool, as snow, and his eyes as a fiery flame; **15** and his feet were like fine copper when glowing in a furnace; and his voice was as the sound of many waters. 16 And he had in his right hand seven stars, and out of his mouth a sharp, long two-edged sword was protruding, and his countenance was as the sun when it shines in its power. 17 And when I saw him, I fell as dead at his feet.

And he laid his right hand upon me and said: "Do not be fearful. I am the First and the Last, 18 and the living one; and I became dead, but, look! I am living forever and ever, and I have the keys of death and of Ha′des. 19 Therefore write down the things you saw, and the things that are and the things that will take place after these. 20 As for the sacred secret of the seven stars that you saw upon my right hand, and [of] the seven golden lampstands: The seven stars mean [the] angels of the seven congregations, and the seven lampstands mean seven congregations.

2 "To the angel of the congregation in Eph′e·sus write: These are the things that he says who holds the seven stars in his right hand, he who walks in the midst of the seven golden lampstands, 2 'I know your deeds, and your labor and endurance, and that you cannot bear bad men, and that you put those to the test who say they are apostles, but they are not, and you found them liars. 3 You are also showing endurance, and you have borne up for my name's sake and have not grown weary. 4 Nevertheless, I hold [this] against you, that you have left the love you had at first.

5 "'Therefore remember from what you have fallen, and repent and do the former deeds. If you do not, I am coming to you, and I will remove your lampstand from its place, unless you repent. 6 Still, you do have this, that you hate the deeds of the sect of Nic·o·la′us, which I also hate. 7 Let the one who has an ear hear what the spirit says to the congregations: To him that conquers I will grant

to eat of the tree of life, which is in the paradise of God.'

8 "And to the angel of the congregation in Smyr′na write: These are the things that he says, 'the First and the Last,' who became dead and came to life [again], 9 'I know your tribulation and poverty—but you are rich—and the blasphemy by those who say they themselves are Jews, and yet they are not but are a synagogue of Satan. 10 Do not be afraid of the things you are about to suffer. Look! The Devil will keep on throwing some of you into prison that you may be fully put to the test, and that you may have tribulation ten days. Prove yourself faithful even to death, and I will give you the crown of life. 11 Let the one who has an ear hear what the spirit says to the congregations: He that conquers will by no means be harmed by the second death.'

12 "And to the angel of the congregation in Per′ga·mum write: These are the things that he says who has the sharp, long two-edged sword, 13 'I know where you are dwelling, that is, where the throne of Satan is; and yet you keep on holding fast my name, and you did not deny your faith in me even in the days of An′ti·pas, my witness, the faithful one, who was killed by your side, where Satan is dwelling.

14 "'Nevertheless, I have a few things against you, that you have there those holding fast the teaching of Ba′laam, who went teaching Ba′lak to put a stumbling block before the sons of Israel, to eat things sacrificed to idols and to commit fornication. 15 So you, also, have those holding fast the teaching of the sect of Nic·o·la′us likewise. 16 Therefore repent. If you do not, I am coming to you quickly, and I will war with them with the long sword of my mouth.

17 "'Let the one who has an ear hear what the spirit says to the congregations: To him that conquers I will give some of the hidden man′na, and I will give him a white pebble, and upon the pebble

a new name written which no one knows except the one receiving it.'

18 "And to the angel of the congregation in Thy·a·ti′ra write: These are the things that the Son of God says, he who has his eyes like a fiery flame, and his feet are like fine copper, 19 'I know your deeds, and your love and faith and ministry and endurance, and that your deeds of late are more than those formerly.

20 " 'Nevertheless, I do hold [this] against you, that you tolerate that woman Jez′e·bel, who calls herself a prophetess, and she teaches and misleads my slaves to commit fornication and to eat things sacrificed to idols. 21 And I gave her time to repent, but she is not willing to repent of her fornication. 22 Look! I am about to throw her into a sickbed, and those committing adultery with her into great tribulation, unless they repent of her deeds. 23 And her children I will kill with deadly plague, so that all the congregations will know that I am he who searches the inmost thoughts and hearts, and I will give to YOU individually according to YOUR deeds.

24 "However, I say to the rest of YOU who are in Thy·a·ti′ra, all those who do not have this teaching, the very ones who did not get to know the "deep things of Satan," as they say: I am not putting upon YOU any other burden. 25 Just the same, hold fast what YOU have until I come. 26 And to him that conquers and observes my deeds down to the end I will give authority over the nations, 27 and he shall shepherd the people with an iron rod so that they will be broken to pieces like clay vessels, the same as I have received from my Father, 28 and I will give him the morning star. 29 Let the one who has an ear hear what the spirit says to the congregations.'

3 "And to the angel of the congregation in Sar′dis write: These are the things that he says who has the seven spirits of God and the seven stars, 'I know your deeds, that you have the name that you

are alive, but you are dead. 2 Become watchful, and strengthen the things remaining that were ready to die, for I have not found your deeds fully performed before my God. 3 Therefore, continue mindful of how you have received and how you heard, and go on keeping [it], and repent. Certainly unless you wake up, I shall come as a thief, and you will not know at all at what hour I shall come upon you.

4 " 'Nevertheless, you do have a few names in Sar′dis that did not defile their outer garments, and they shall walk with me in white ones, because they are worthy. 5 He that conquers will thus be arrayed in white outer garments; and I will by no means blot out his name from the book of life, but I will make acknowledgment of his name before my Father and before his angels. 6 Let the one who has an ear hear what the spirit says to the congregations.'

7 "And to the angel of the congregation in Philadelphia write: These are the things he says who is holy, who is true, who has the key of David, who opens so that no one will shut, and shuts so that no one opens, 8 'I know your deeds—look! I have set before you an opened door, which no one can shut—that you have a little power, and you kept my word and did not prove false to my name. 9 Look! I will give those from the synagogue of Satan who say they are Jews, and yet they are not but are lying—look! I will make them come and do obeisance before your feet and make them know I have loved you. 10 Because you kept the word about my endurance, I will also keep you from the hour of test, which is to come upon the whole inhabited earth, to put a test upon those dwelling on the earth. 11 I am coming quickly. Keep on holding fast what you have, that no one may take your crown.

12 " 'The one that conquers—I will make him a pillar in the temple of my God, and he will by no means go out [from it] any more, and I will write upon him the name

of my God and the name of the city of my God, the new Jerusalem which descends out of heaven from my God, and that new name of mine. 13 Let the one who has an ear hear what the spirit says to the congregations.'

14 "And to the angel of the congregation in La·o·di·ce′a write: These are the things that the Amen says, the faithful and true witness, the beginning of the creation by God, 15 'I know your deeds, that you are neither cold nor hot. I wish you were cold or else hot. 16 So, because you are lukewarm and neither hot nor cold, I am going to vomit you out of my mouth. 17 Because you say: "I am rich and have acquired riches and do not need anything at all," but you do not know you are miserable and pitiable and poor and blind and naked, 18 I advise you to buy from me gold refined by fire that you may become rich, and white outer garments that you may become dressed and that the shame of your nakedness may not become manifested, and eyesalve to rub in your eyes that you may see.

19 "'All those for whom I have affection I reprove and discipline. Therefore be zealous and repent. 20 Look! I am standing at the door and knocking. If anyone hears my voice and opens the door, I will come into his [house] and take the evening meal with him and he with me. 21 To the one that conquers I will grant to sit down with me on my throne, even as I conquered and sat down with my Father on his throne. 22 Let the one who has an ear hear what the spirit says to the congregations.' "

4 After these things I saw, and, look! an opened door in heaven, and the first voice that I heard was as of a trumpet, speaking with me, saying: "Come on up here, and I shall show you the things that must take place." 2 After these things I immediately came to be in [the power of the] spirit: and, look! a throne was in its position in heaven, and there is one seated upon the throne. 3 And the one

seated is, in appearance, like a jasper stone and a precious red-colored stone, and round about the throne [there is] a rainbow like an emerald in appearance.

4 And round about the throne [there are] twenty-four thrones, and upon these thrones [I saw] seated twenty-four older persons dressed in white outer garments, and upon their heads golden crowns. 5 And out of the throne there are proceeding lightnings and voices and thunders; and [there are] seven lamps of fire burning before the throne, and these mean the seven spirits of God. 6 And before the throne there is, as it were, a glassy sea like crystal.

And in the midst of the throne and around the throne [there are] four living creatures that are full of eyes in front and behind. 7 And the first living creature is like a lion, and the second living creature is like a young bull, and the third living creature has a face like a man's, and the fourth living creature is like a flying eagle. 8 And as for the four living creatures, each one of them respectively has six wings; round about and underneath they are full of eyes. And they have no rest day and night as they say: "Holy, holy, holy is Jehovah God, the Almighty, who was and who is and who is coming."

9 And whenever the living creatures offer glory and honor and thanksgiving to the one seated upon the throne, the one that lives forever and ever, 10 the twenty-four older persons fall down before the one seated upon the throne and worship the one that lives forever and ever, and they cast their crowns before the throne, saying: 11 "You are worthy, Jehovah, even our God, to receive the glory and the honor and the power, because you created all things, and because of your will they existed and were created."

5 And I saw in the right hand of the one seated upon the throne a scroll written within and on the reverse side, sealed tight with seven seals. 2 And I saw a strong angel

proclaiming with a loud voice: "Who is worthy to open the scroll and loose its seals?" 3 But neither in heaven nor upon earth nor underneath the earth was there a single one able to open the scroll or to look into it. 4 And I gave way to a great deal of weeping because no one was found worthy to open the scroll or to look into it. 5 But one of the older persons says to me: "Stop weeping. Look! The Lion that is of the tribe of Judah, the root of David, has conquered so as to open the scroll and its seven seals."

6 And I saw standing in the midst of the throne and of the four living creatures and in the midst of the older persons a lamb as though it had been slaughtered, having seven horns and seven eyes, which [eyes] mean the seven spirits of God that have been sent forth into the whole earth. 7 And he went and at once took [it] out of the right hand of the one seated on the throne. 8 And when he took the scroll, the four living creatures and the twenty-four older persons fell down before the Lamb, having each one a harp and golden bowls that were full of incense, and the [incense] means the prayers of the holy ones. 9 And they sing a new song, saying: "You are worthy to take the scroll and open its seals, because you were slaughtered and with your blood you bought persons for God out of every tribe and tongue and people and nation, 10 and you made them to be a kingdom and priests to our God, and they are to rule as kings over the earth."

11 And I saw, and I heard a voice of many angels around the throne and the living creatures and the older persons, and the number of them was myriads of myriads and thousands of thousands, 12 saying with a loud voice: "The Lamb that was slaughtered is worthy to receive the power and riches and wisdom and strength and honor and glory and blessing."

13 And every creature that is in heaven and on earth and under-neath the earth and on the sea, and all the things in them, I heard saying: "To the one sitting on the throne and to the Lamb be the blessing and the honor and the glory and the might forever and ever." 14 And the four living creatures were saying: "Amen!" and the older persons fell down and worshiped.

6 And I saw when the Lamb opened one of the seven seals, and I heard one of the four living creatures say with a voice as of thunder: "Come!" 2 And I saw, and, look! a white horse; and the one seated upon it had a bow; and a crown was given him, and he went forth conquering and to complete his conquest.

3 And when he opened the second seal, I heard the second living creature say: "Come!" 4 And another came forth, a fiery-colored horse; and to the one seated upon it there was granted to take peace away from the earth so that they should slaughter one another; and a great sword was given him.

5 And when he opened the third seal, I heard the third living creature say: "Come!" And I saw, and, look! a black horse; and the one seated upon it had a pair of scales in his hand. 6 And I heard a voice as if in the midst of the four living creatures say: "A quart of wheat for a de·nar′i·us, and three quarts of barley for a de·nar′i·us; and do not harm the olive oil and the wine."

7 And when he opened the fourth seal, I heard the voice of the fourth living creature say: "Come!" 8 And I saw, and, look! a pale horse; and the one seated upon it had the name Death. And Ha′des was closely following him. And authority was given them over the fourth part of the earth, to kill with a long sword and with food shortage and with deadly plague and by the wild beasts of the earth.

9 And when he opened the fifth seal, I saw underneath the altar the souls of those slaughtered because of the word of God and because of the witness work that they

used to have. 10 And they cried with a loud voice, saying: "Until when, Sovereign Lord holy and true, are you refraining from judging and avenging our blood upon those who dwell on the earth?" 11 And a white robe was given to each of them; and they were told to rest a little while longer, until the number was filled also of their fellow slaves and their brothers who were about to be killed as they also had been.

12 And I saw when he opened the sixth seal, and a great earthquake occurred; and the sun became black as sackcloth of hair, and the entire moon became as blood, 13 and the stars of heaven fell to the earth, as when a fig tree shaken by a high wind casts its unripe figs. 14 And the heaven departed as a scroll that is being rolled up, and every mountain and [every] island were removed from their places. 15 And the kings of the earth and the top-ranking ones and the military commanders and the rich and the strong ones and every slave and [every] free person hid themselves in the caves and in the rock-masses of the mountains. 16 And they keep saying to the mountains and to the rock-masses: "Fall over us and hide us from the face of the one seated on the throne and from the wrath of the Lamb, 17 because the great day of their wrath has come, and who is able to stand?"

7 After this I saw four angels standing upon the four corners of the earth, holding tight the four winds of the earth, that no wind might blow upon the earth or upon the sea or upon any tree. 2 And I saw another angel ascending from the sunrising, having a seal of [the] living God; and he cried with a loud voice to the four angels to whom it was granted to harm the earth and the sea, 3 saying: "Do not harm the earth or the sea or the trees, until after we have sealed the slaves of our God in their foreheads."

4 And I heard the number of those who were sealed, a hundred and forty-four thousand, sealed out of every tribe of the sons of Israel:

5 Out of the tribe of Judah twelve thousand sealed;

out of the tribe of Reu'ben twelve thousand;

out of the tribe of Gad twelve thousand;

6 out of the tribe of Ash'er twelve thousand;

out of the tribe of Naph'ta·li twelve thousand;

out of the tribe of Ma·nas'seh twelve thousand;

7 out of the tribe of Sim'e·on twelve thousand;

out of the tribe of Le'vi twelve thousand;

out of the tribe of Is'sa·char twelve thousand;

8 out of the tribe of Zeb'u·lun twelve thousand;

out of the tribe of Joseph twelve thousand;

out of the tribe of Benjamin twelve thousand sealed.

9 After these things I saw, and, look! a great crowd, which no man was able to number, out of all nations and tribes and peoples and tongues, standing before the throne and before the Lamb, dressed in white robes; and there were palm branches in their hands. 10 And they keep on crying with a loud voice, saying: "Salvation [we owe] to our God, who is seated on the throne, and to the Lamb."

11 And all the angels were standing around the throne and the older persons and the four living creatures, and they fell upon their faces before the throne and worshiped God, 12 saying: "Amen! The blessing and the glory and the wisdom and the thanksgiving and the honor and the power and the strength [be] to our God forever and ever. Amen."

13 And in response one of the older persons said to me: "These who are dressed in the white robes, who are they and where did they come from?" 14 So right away I said to him: "My lord, you are the one that knows." And he said to me: "These are the ones that come out of the great tribulation,

and they have washed their robes and made them white in the blood of the Lamb. 15 That is why they are before the throne of God; and they are rendering him sacred service day and night in his temple; and the one seated on the throne will spread his tent over them. 16 They will hunger no more nor thirst any more, neither will the sun beat down upon them nor any scorching heat, 17 because the Lamb, who is in the midst of the throne, will shepherd them, and will guide them to fountains of waters of life. And God will wipe out every tear from their eyes."

8 And when he opened the seventh seal, a silence occurred in heaven for about a half hour. 2 And I saw the seven angels that stand before God, and seven trumpets were given them.

3 And another angel arrived and stood at the altar, having a golden incense vessel; and a large quantity of incense was given him to offer it with the prayers of all the holy ones upon the golden altar that was before the throne. 4 And the smoke of the incense ascended from the hand of the angel with the prayers of the holy ones before God. 5 But right away the angel took the incense vessel, and he filled it with some of the fire of the altar and hurled it to the earth. And thunders occurred and voices and lightnings and an earthquake. 6 And the seven angels with the seven trumpets prepared to blow them.

7 And the first one blew his trumpet. And there occurred a hail and fire mingled with blood, and it was hurled to the earth; and a third of the earth was burned up, and a third of the trees was burned up, and all the green vegetation was burned up.

8 And the second angel blew his trumpet. And something like a great mountain burning with fire was hurled into the sea. And a third of the sea became blood; 9 and a third of the creatures that are in the sea which have souls died, and a third of the boats were wrecked.

10 And the third angel blew his trumpet. And a great star burning as a lamp fell from heaven, and it fell upon a third of the rivers and upon the fountains of waters. 11 And the name of the star is called Wormwood. And a third of the waters turned into wormwood, and many of the men died from the waters, because these had been made bitter.

12 And the fourth angel blew his trumpet. And a third of the sun was smitten and a third of the moon and a third of the stars, in order that a third of them might be darkened and the day might not have illumination for a third of it, and the night likewise.

13 And I saw, and I heard an eagle flying in midheaven say with a loud voice: "Woe, woe, woe to those dwelling on the earth because of the rest of the trumpet blasts of the three angels who are about to blow their trumpets!"

9 And the fifth angel blew his trumpet. And I saw a star that had fallen from heaven to the earth, and the key of the pit of the abyss was given him. 2 And he opened the pit of the abyss, and smoke ascended out of the pit as the smoke of a great furnace, and the sun was darkened, also the air, by the smoke of the pit. 3 And out of the smoke locusts came forth upon the earth; and authority was given them, the same authority as the scorpions of the earth have. 4 And they were told to harm no vegetation of the earth nor any green thing nor any tree, but only those men who do not have the seal of God on their foreheads.

5 And it was granted the [locusts], not to kill them, but that these should be tormented five months, and the torment upon them was as torment by a scorpion when it strikes a man. 6 And in those days the men will seek death but will by no means find it, and they will desire to die but death keeps fleeing from them.

7 And the likenesses of the locusts resembled horses prepared for battle; and upon their heads [were] what seemed to be crowns like gold, and their faces [were] as men's faces, 8 but they had hair as women's hair. And their teeth [were] as those of lions; 9 and they had breastplates like iron breastplates. And the sound of their wings [was] as the sound of chariots of many horses running into battle. 10 Also, they have tails and stings like scorpions; and in their tails is their authority to hurt the men five months. 11 They have over them a king, the angel of the abyss. In Hebrew his name is A·bad'don, but in Greek he has the name A·pol'lyon.

12 The one woe is past. Look! Two more woes are coming after these things.

13 And the sixth angel blew his trumpet. And I heard one voice out of the horns of the golden altar that is before God 14 say to the sixth angel, who had the trumpet: "Untie the four angels that are bound at the great river Eu·phra'tes." 15 And the four angels were untied, who have been prepared for the hour and day and month and year, to kill a third of the men.

16 And the number of the armies of cavalry was two myriads of myriads: I heard the number of them. 17 And this is how I saw the horses in the vision, and those seated on them: they had fire-red and hyacinth-blue and sulphur-yellow breastplates; and the heads of the horses were as heads of lions, and out of their mouths fire and smoke and sulphur issued forth. 18 By these three plagues a third of the men were killed, from the fire and the smoke and the sulphur which issued forth from their mouths. 19 For the authority of the horses is in their mouths and in their tails; for their tails are like serpents and have heads, and with these they do harm.

20 But the rest of the men who were not killed by these plagues did not repent of the works of their hands, so that they should not worship the demons and the idols of gold and silver and copper and stone and wood, which can neither see nor hear nor walk; 21 and they did not repent of their murders nor of their spiritistic practices nor of their fornication nor of their thefts.

10 And I saw another strong angel descending from heaven, arrayed with a cloud, and a rainbow was upon his head, and his face was as the sun, and his feet were as fiery pillars, 2 and he had in his hand a little scroll opened. And he set his right foot upon the sea, but his left one upon the earth, 3 and he cried out with a loud voice just as when a lion roars. And when he cried out, the seven thunders uttered their own voices.

4 Now when the seven thunders spoke, I was at the point of writing; but I heard a voice out of heaven say: "Seal up the things the seven thunders spoke, and do not write them down." 5 And the angel that I saw standing on the sea and on the earth raised his right hand to heaven, 6 and by the One who lives forever and ever, who created the heaven and the things in it and the earth and the things in it and the sea and the things in it, he swore: "There will be no delay any longer; 7 but in the days of the sounding of the seventh angel, when he is about to blow his trumpet, the sacred secret of God according to the good news which he declared to his own slaves the prophets is indeed brought to a finish."

8 And the voice that I heard out of heaven is speaking again with me and saying: "Go, take the opened scroll that is in the hand of the angel who is standing on the sea and on the earth." 9 And I went away to the angel and told him to give me the little scroll. And he said to me: "Take it and eat it up, and it will make your belly bitter, but in your mouth it will be sweet as honey." 10 And I took the little scroll out of the hand of the angel and ate it up,

and in my mouth it was sweet as honey; but when I had eaten it up, my belly was made bitter. 11 And they say to me: "You must prophesy again with regard to peoples and nations and tongues and many kings."

11 And a reed like a rod was given me as he said: "Get up and measure the temple [sanctuary] of God and the altar and those worshiping in it. 2 But as for the courtyard that is outside the temple [sanctuary], cast it clear out and do not measure it, because it has been given to the nations, and they will trample the holy city underfoot for forty-two months. 3 And I will cause my two witnesses to prophesy a thousand two hundred and sixty days dressed in sackcloth." 4 These are [symbolized by] the two olive trees and the two lampstands and are standing before the Lord of the earth.

5 And if anyone wants to harm them, fire issues forth from their mouths and devours their enemies; and if anyone should want to harm them, in this manner he must be killed. 6 These have the authority to shut up heaven that no rain should fall during the days of their prophesying, and they have authority over the waters to turn them into blood and to strike the earth with every sort of plague as often as they wish.

7 And when they have finished their witnessing, the wild beast that ascends out of the abyss will make war with them and conquer them and kill them. 8 And their corpses will be on the broad way of the great city which is in a spiritual sense called Sod'om and Egypt, where their Lord was also impaled. 9 And those of the peoples and tribes and tongues and nations will look at their corpses for three and a half days, and they do not let their corpses be laid in a tomb. 10 And those dwelling on the earth rejoice over them and enjoy themselves, and they will send gifts to one another, because these two prophets tormented those dwelling on the earth.

11 And after the three and a half days spirit of life from God entered into them, and they stood upon their feet, and great fear fell upon those beholding them. 12 And they heard a loud voice out of heaven say to them: "Come on up here." And they went up into heaven in the cloud, and their enemies beheld them. 13 And in that hour a great earthquake occurred, and a tenth of the city fell; and seven thousand persons were killed by the earthquake, and the rest became frightened and gave glory to the God of heaven.

14 The second woe is past. Look! The third woe is coming quickly.

15 And the seventh angel blew his trumpet. And loud voices occurred in heaven, saying: "The kingdom of the world did become the kingdom of our Lord and of his Christ, and he will rule as king forever and ever."

16 And the twenty-four older persons who were seated before God upon their thrones fell upon their faces and worshiped God, 17 saying: "We thank you, Jehovah God, the Almighty, the one who is and who was, because you have taken your great power and begun ruling as king. 18 But the nations became wrathful, and your own wrath came, and the appointed time for the dead to be judged, and to give [their] reward to your slaves the prophets and to the holy ones and to those fearing your name, the small and the great, and to bring to ruin those ruining the earth."

19 And the temple [sanctuary] of God that is in heaven was opened, and the ark of his covenant was seen in his temple [sanctuary]. And there occurred lightnings and voices and thunders and an earthquake and a great hail.

12 And a great sign was seen in heaven, a woman arrayed with the sun, and the moon was beneath her feet, and on her head was a crown of twelve stars, and she was pregnant. 2 And she cries out in her pains and in her agony to give birth.

3 And another sign was seen in heaven, and, look! a great fiery-colored dragon, with seven heads and ten horns and upon its heads seven diadems; **4** and its tail drags a third of the stars of heaven, and it hurled them down to the earth. And the dragon kept standing before the woman who was about to give birth, that, when she did give birth, it might devour her child.

5 And she gave birth to a son, a male, who is to shepherd all the nations with an iron rod. And her child was caught away to God and to his throne. **6** And the woman fled into the wilderness, where she has a place prepared by God, that they should feed her there a thousand two hundred and sixty days.

7 And war broke out in heaven: Mi′cha·el and his angels battled with the dragon, and the dragon and its angels battled **8** but it did not prevail, neither was a place found for them any longer in heaven. **9** So down the great dragon was hurled, the original serpent, the one called Devil and Satan, who is misleading the entire inhabited earth; he was hurled down to the earth, and his angels were hurled down with him. **10** And I heard a loud voice in heaven say:

"Now have come to pass the salvation and the power and the kingdom of our God and the authority of his Christ, because the accuser of our brothers has been hurled down, who accuses them day and night before our God! **11** And they conquered him because of the blood of the Lamb and because of the word of their witnessing, and they did not love their souls even in the face of death. **12** On this account be glad, YOU heavens and YOU who reside in them! Woe for the earth and for the sea, because the Devil has come down to YOU, having great anger, knowing he has a short period of time."

13 Now when the dragon saw that it was hurled down to the earth, it persecuted the woman that gave birth to the male child.

14 But the two wings of the great eagle were given the woman, that she might fly into the wilderness to her place; there is where she is fed for a time and times and half a time away from the face of the serpent.

15 And the serpent disgorged water like a river from its mouth after the woman, to cause her to be drowned by the river. **16** But the earth came to the woman's help, and the earth opened its mouth and swallowed up the river that the dragon disgorged from its mouth. **17** And the dragon grew wrathful at the woman, and went off to wage war with the remaining ones of her seed, who observe the commandments of God and have the work of bearing witness to Jesus.

13 And it stood still upon the sand of the sea.

And I saw a wild beast ascending out of the sea, with ten horns and seven heads, and upon its horns ten diadems, but upon its heads blasphemous names. **2** Now the wild beast that I saw was like a leopard, but its feet were as those of a bear, and its mouth was as a lion's mouth. And the dragon gave to [the beast] its power and its throne and great authority.

3 And I saw one of its heads as though slaughtered to death, but its death-stroke got healed, and all the earth followed the wild beast with admiration. **4** And they worshiped the dragon because it gave the authority to the wild beast, and they worshiped the wild beast with the words: "Who is like the wild beast, and who can do battle with it?" **5** And a mouth speaking great things and blasphemies was given it, and authority to act forty-two months was given it. **6** And it opened its mouth in blasphemies against God, to blaspheme his name and his residence, even those residing in heaven. **7** And there was granted it to wage war with the holy ones and conquer them, and authority was given it over every tribe and people and tongue and nation. **8** And all those who dwell on the earth will worship it; the name of not one of them stands written in the scroll of life of the Lamb who was slaughtered, from the founding of the world.

9 If anyone has an ear, let him hear. 10 If anyone [is meant] for captivity, he goes away into captivity. If anyone will kill with the sword, he must be killed with the sword. Here is where it means the endurance and faith of the holy ones.

11 And I saw another wild beast ascending out of the earth, and it had two horns like a lamb, but it began speaking as a dragon. 12 And it exercises all the authority of the first wild beast in its sight. And it makes the earth and those who dwell in it worship the first wild beast, whose death-stroke got healed. 13 And it performs great signs, so that it should even make fire come down out of heaven to the earth in the sight of mankind.

14 And it misleads those who dwell on the earth, because of the signs that were granted it to perform in the sight of the wild beast, while it tells those who dwell on the earth to make an image to the wild beast that had the sword-stroke and yet revived. 15 And there was granted it to give breath to the image of the wild beast, so that the image of the wild beast should both speak and cause to be killed all those who would not in any way worship the image of the wild beast.

16 And it puts under compulsion all persons, the small and the great, and the rich and the poor, and the free and the slaves, that they should give these a mark in their right hand or upon their forehead, 17 and that nobody might be able to buy or sell except a person having the mark, the name of the wild beast or the number of its name. 18 Here is where wisdom comes in: Let the one that has intelligence calculate the number of the wild beast, for it is a man's number; and its number is six hundred and sixty-six.

14 And I saw, and, look! the Lamb standing upon the Mount Zion, and with him a hundred and forty-four thousand having his name and the name of his Father written on their foreheads. 2 And I heard a sound out of heaven as the sound of many waters and as the sound of loud thunder; and the sound that I heard was as of singers who accompany themselves on the harp playing on their harps. 3 And they are singing as if a new song before the throne and before the four living creatures and the older persons; and no one was able to master that song but the hundred and forty-four thousand, who have been bought from the earth. 4 These are the ones that did not defile themselves with women; in fact, they are virgins. These are the ones that keep following the Lamb no matter where he goes. These were bought from among mankind as first fruits to God and to the Lamb, 5 and no falsehood was found in their mouths; they are without blemish.

6 And I saw another angel flying in midheaven, and he had everlasting good news to declare as glad tidings to those who dwell on the earth, and to every nation and tribe and tongue and people, 7 saying in a loud voice: "FEAR God and give him glory, because the hour of the judgment by him has arrived, and so worship the One who made the heaven and the earth and sea and fountains of waters."

8 And another, a second angel, followed, saying: "She has fallen! Babylon the great has fallen, she who made all the nations drink of the wine of the anger of her fornication!"

9 And another angel, a third, followed them, saying in a loud voice: "If anyone worships the wild beast and its image, and receives a mark on his forehead or upon his hand, 10 he will also drink of the wine of the anger of God that is poured out undiluted into the cup of his wrath, and he shall be tormented with fire and sulphur in

the sight of the holy angels and in the sight of the Lamb. 11 And the smoke of their torment ascends forever and ever, and day and night they have no rest, those who worship the wild beast and its image, and whoever receives the mark of its name. 12 Here is where it means endurance for the holy ones, those who observe the commandments of God and the faith of Jesus."

13 And I heard a voice out of heaven say: "Write: Happy are the dead who die in union with [the] Lord from this time onward. Yes, says the spirit, let them rest from their labors, for the things they did go right with them."

14 And I saw, and, look! a white cloud, and upon the cloud someone seated like a son of man, with a golden crown on his head and a sharp sickle in his hand.

15 And another angel emerged from the temple [sanctuary], crying with a loud voice to the one seated on the cloud: "Put your sickle in and reap, because the hour has come to reap, for the harvest of the earth is thoroughly ripe." 16 And the one seated on the cloud thrust in his sickle on the earth, and the earth was reaped.

17 And still another angel emerged from the temple [sanctuary] that is in heaven, he, too, having a sharp sickle.

18 And still another angel emerged from the altar and he had authority over the fire. And he called out with a loud voice to the one that had the sharp sickle, saying: "Put your sharp sickle in and gather the clusters of the vine of the earth, because its grapes have become ripe." 19 And the angel thrust his sickle into the earth and gathered the vine of the earth, and he hurled it into the great wine press of the anger of God. 20 And the wine press was trodden outside the city, and blood came out of the wine press as high up as the bridles of the horses, for a distance of a thousand six hundred furlongs.

15 And I saw in heaven another sign, great and wonderful, seven angels with seven plagues. These are the last ones, because by means of them the anger of God is brought to a finish.

2 And I saw what seemed to be a glassy sea mingled with fire, and those who come off victorious from the wild beast and from its image and from the number of its name standing by the glassy sea, having harps of God. 3 And they are singing the song of Moses the slave of God and the song of the Lamb, saying:

"Great and wonderful are your works, Jehovah God, the Almighty. Righteous and true are your ways, King of eternity. 4 Who will not really fear you, Jehovah, and glorify your name, because you alone are loyal? For all the nations will come and worship before you, because your righteous decrees have been made manifest."

5 And after these things I saw, and the sanctuary of the tent of the witness was opened in heaven, 6 and the seven angels with the seven plagues emerged from the sanctuary, clothed with clean, bright linen and girded about their breasts with golden girdles. 7 And one of the four living creatures gave the seven angels seven golden bowls that were full of the anger of God, who lives forever and ever. 8 And the sanctuary became filled with smoke because of the glory of God and because of his power, and no one was able to enter into the sanctuary until the seven plagues of the seven angels were finished.

16 And I heard a loud voice out of the sanctuary say to the seven angels: "Go and pour out the seven bowls of the anger of God into the earth."

2 And the first one went off and poured out his bowl into the earth. And a hurtful and malignant ulcer came to be upon the men that had the mark of the wild beast and that were worshiping its image.

3 And the second one poured out his bowl into the sea. And it became blood as of a dead man, and

every living soul died, yes, the things in the sea.

4 And the third one poured out his bowl into the rivers and the fountains of the waters. And they became blood. 5 And I heard the angel over the waters say: "You, the One who is and who was, the loyal One, are righteous, because you have rendered these decisions, 6 because they poured out the blood of holy ones and of prophets, and you have given them blood to drink. They deserve it." 7 And I heard the altar say: "Yes, Jehovah God, the Almighty, true and righteous are your judicial decisions."

8 And the fourth one poured out his bowl upon the sun; and to [the sun] it was granted to scorch the men with fire. 9 And the men were scorched with great heat, but they blasphemed the name of God, who has the authority over these plagues, and they did not repent so as to give glory to him.

10 And the fifth one poured out his bowl upon the throne of the wild beast. And its kingdom became darkened, and they began to gnaw their tongues for [their] pain, 11 but they blasphemed the God of heaven for their pains and for their ulcers, and they did not repent of their works.

12 And the sixth one poured out his bowl upon the great river Euphra′tes, and its water was dried up, that the way might be prepared for the kings from the rising of the sun.

13 And I saw three unclean inspired expressions [that looked] like frogs come out of the mouth of the dragon and out of the mouth of the wild beast and out of the mouth of the false prophet. 14 They are, in fact, expressions inspired by demons and perform signs, and they go forth to the kings of the entire inhabited earth, to gather them together to the war of the great day of God the Almighty.

15 "Look! I am coming as a thief. Happy is the one that stays awake and keeps his outer garments, that he may not walk naked and people look upon his shamefulness."

16 And they gathered them together to the place that is called in Hebrew Har–Ma·ged′on.

17 And the seventh one poured out his bowl upon the air. At this a loud voice issued out of the sanctuary from the throne, saying: "It has come to pass!" 18 And lightnings and voices and thunders occurred, and a great earthquake occurred such as had not occurred since men came to be on the earth, so extensive an earthquake, so great. 19 And the great city split into three parts, and the cities of the nations fell; and Babylon the great was remembered in the sight of God, to give her the cup of the wine of the anger of his wrath. 20 Also, every island fled, and mountains were not found. 21 And a great hail with every stone about the weight of a talent descended out of heaven upon the men, and the men blasphemed God due to the plague of hail, because the plague of it was unusually great.

17 And one of the seven angels that had the seven bowls came and spoke with me, saying: "Come, I will show you the judgment upon the great harlot who sits on many waters, 2 with whom the kings of the earth committed fornication, whereas those who inhabit the earth were made drunk with the wine of her fornication."

3 And he carried me away in [the power of the] spirit into a wilderness. And I caught sight of a woman sitting upon a scarlet-colored wild beast that was full of blasphemous names and that had seven heads and ten horns. 4 And the woman was arrayed in purple and scarlet, and was adorned with gold and precious stone and pearls and had in her hand a golden cup that was full of disgusting things and the unclean things of her fornication. 5 And upon her forehead was written a name, a mystery: "Babylon the Great, the mother of the harlots and of the disgusting things of the earth." 6 And I saw that the woman was

drunk with the blood of the holy ones and with the blood of the witnesses of Jesus.

Well, on catching sight of her I wondered with great wonderment. 7 And so the angel said to me: "Why is it you wondered? I will tell you the mystery of the woman and of the wild beast that is carrying her and that has the seven heads and the ten horns: 8 The wild beast that you saw was, but is not, and yet is about to ascend out of the abyss, and it is to go off into destruction. And when they see how the wild beast was, but is not, and yet will be present, those who dwell on the earth will wonder admiringly, but their names have not been written upon the scroll of life from the founding of the world. 9 "Here is where the intelligence that has wisdom comes in: The seven heads mean seven mountains, where the woman sits on top. 10 And there are seven kings: five have fallen, one is, the other has not yet arrived, but when he does arrive he must remain a short while. 11 And the wild beast that was but is not, it is also itself an eighth [king], but springs from the seven, and it goes off into destruction.

12 "And the ten horns that you saw mean ten kings, who have not yet received a kingdom, but they do receive authority as kings one hour with the wild beast. 13 These have one thought, and so they give their power and authority to the wild beast. 14 These will battle with the Lamb, but, because he is Lord of lords and King of kings, the Lamb will conquer them. Also, those called and chosen and faithful with him [will do so]."

15 And he says to me: "The waters that you saw, where the harlot is sitting, mean peoples and crowds and nations and tongues. 16 And the ten horns that you saw, and the wild beast, these will hate the harlot and will make her devastated and naked, and will eat up her fleshy parts and will completely burn her with fire. 17 For

God put [it] into their hearts to carry out his thought, even to carry out [their] one thought by giving their kingdom to the wild beast, until the words of God will have been accomplished. 18 And the woman whom you saw means the great city that has a kingdom over the kings of the earth."

18 After these things I saw another angel descending from heaven, with great authority; and the earth was lighted up from his glory. 2 And he cried out with a strong voice, saying: "She has fallen! Babylon the great has fallen, and she has become a dwelling place of demons and a lurking place of every unclean exhalation and a lurking place of every unclean and hated bird! 3 For because of the wine of the anger of her fornication all the nations have fallen [victim], and the kings of the earth committed fornication with her, and the traveling merchants of the earth became rich due to the power of her shameless luxury."

4 And I heard another voice out of heaven say: "Get out of her, my people, if you do not want to share with her in her sins, and if you do not want to receive part of her plagues. 5 For her sins have massed together clear up to heaven, and God has called her acts of injustice to mind. 6 Render to her even as she herself rendered, and do to her twice as much, yes, twice the number of the things she did; in the cup in which she put a mixture put twice as much of the mixture for her. 7 To the extent that she glorified herself and lived in shameless luxury, to that extent give her torment and mourning. For in her heart she keeps saying, 'I sit a queen, and I am no widow, and I shall never see mourning.' 8 That is why in one day her plagues will come, death and mourning and famine, and she will be completely burned with fire, because Jehovah God, who judged her, is strong.

9 "And the kings of the earth who committed fornication with her and lived in shameless luxury will

weep and beat themselves in grief over her, when they look at the smoke from the burning of her, 10 while they stand at a distance because of their fear of her torment and say, 'Too bad, too bad, you great city, Babylon you strong city, because in one hour your judgment has arrived!'

11 "Also, the traveling merchants of the earth are weeping and mourning over her, because there is no one to buy their full stock any more, 12 a full stock of gold and silver and precious stone and pearls and fine linen and purple and silk and scarlet; and everything in scented wood and every sort of ivory object and every sort of object out of most precious wood and of copper and of iron and of marble; 13 also cinnamon and Indian spice and incense and perfumed oil and frankincense and wine and olive oil and fine flour and wheat and cattle and sheep, and horses and coaches and slaves and human souls. 14 Yes, the fine fruit that your soul desired has departed from you, and all the dainty things and the gorgeous things have perished from you, and never again will people find them.

15 "The traveling merchants of these things, who became rich from her, will stand at a distance because of [their] fear of her torment and will weep and mourn, 16 saying, 'Too bad, too bad—the great city, clothed with fine linen and purple and scarlet, and richly adorned with gold ornament and precious stone and pearl, 17 because in one hour such great riches have been devastated!'

"And every ship captain and every man that voyages anywhere, and sailors and all those who make a living by the sea, stood at a distance 18 and cried out as they looked at the smoke from the burning of her and said, 'What city is like the great city?' 19 And they threw dust upon their heads and cried out, weeping and mourning, and said, 'Too bad, too bad—the great city, in which all those having boats at sea became rich by reason of her costliness, because in one hour she has been devastated!'

20 "Be glad over her, O heaven, also you holy ones and you apostles and you prophets, because God has judicially exacted punishment for you from her!"

21 And a strong angel lifted up a stone like a great millstone and hurled it into the sea, saying: "Thus with a swift pitch will Babylon the great city be hurled down, and she will never be found again. 22 And the sound of singers who accompany themselves on the harp and of musicians and of flutists and of trumpeters will never be heard in you again, and no craftsman of any trade will ever be found in you again, and no sound of a millstone will ever be heard in you again, 23 and no light of a lamp will ever shine in you again, and no voice of a bridegroom and of a bride will ever be heard in you again; because your traveling merchants were the top-ranking men of the earth, for by your spiritistic practice all the nations were misled. 24 Yes, in her was found the blood of prophets and of holy ones and of all those who have been slaughtered on the earth."

19 After these things I heard what was as a loud voice of a great crowd in heaven. They said: "Praise Jah, you people! The salvation and the glory and the power belong to our God, 2 because his judgments are true and righteous. For he has executed judgment upon the great harlot who corrupted the earth with her fornication, and he has avenged the blood of his slaves at her hand." 3 And right away for the second time they said: "Praise Jah, you people! And the smoke from her goes on ascending forever and ever."

4 And the twenty-four older persons and the four living creatures fell down and worshiped God seated upon the throne, and said: "Amen! Praise Jah, you people!"

5 Also, a voice issued forth from the throne and said: "Be praising our God, all you his slaves, who

fear him, the small ones and the great."

6 And I heard what was as a voice of a great crowd and as a sound of many waters and as a sound of heavy thunders. They said: "Praise Jah, YOU people, because Jehovah our God, the Almighty, has begun to rule as king. 7 Let us rejoice and be overjoyed, and let us give him the glory, because the marriage of the Lamb has arrived and his wife has prepared herself. 8 Yes, it has been granted to her to be arrayed in bright, clean, fine linen, for the fine linen stands for the righteous acts of the holy ones."

9 And he tells me: "Write: Happy are those invited to the evening meal of the Lamb's marriage." Also, he tells me: "These are the true sayings of God." 10 At that I fell down before his feet to worship him. But he tells me: "Be careful! Do not do that! All I am is a fellow slave of you and of your brothers who have the work of witnessing to Jesus. Worship God; for the bearing witness to Jesus is what inspires prophesying."

11 And I saw the heaven opened, and, look! a white horse. And the one seated upon it is called Faithful and True, and he judges and carries on war in righteousness. 12 His eyes are a fiery flame, and upon his head are many diadems. He has a name written that no one knows but he himself, 13 and he is arrayed with an outer garment sprinkled with blood, and the name he is called is The Word of God. 14 Also, the armies that were in heaven were following him on white horses, and they were clothed in white, clean, fine linen. 15 And out of his mouth there protrudes a sharp long sword, that he may strike the nations with it, and he will shepherd them with a rod of iron. He treads too the wine press of the anger of the wrath of God the Almighty. 16 And upon his outer garment, even upon his thigh, he has a name written, King of kings and Lord of lords.

17 I saw also an angel standing in the sun, and he cried out with a loud voice and said to all the birds that fly in midheaven: "Come here, be gathered together to the great evening meal of God, 18 that YOU may eat the fleshy parts of kings and the fleshy parts of military commanders and the fleshy parts of strong men and the fleshy parts of horses and of those seated upon them, and the fleshy parts of all, of freemen as well as of slaves and of small ones and great."

19 And I saw the wild beast and the kings of the earth and their armies gathered together to wage the war with the one seated on the horse and with his army. 20 And the wild beast was caught, and along with it the false prophet that performed in front of it the signs with which he misled those who received the mark of the wild beast and those who render worship to its image. While still alive, they both were hurled into the fiery lake that burns with sulphur. 21 But the rest were killed off with the long sword of the one seated on the horse, which [sword] proceeded out of his mouth. And all the birds were filled from the fleshy parts of them.

20 And I saw an angel coming down out of heaven with the key of the abyss and a great chain in his hand. 2 And he seized the dragon, the original serpent, who is the Devil and Satan, and bound him for a thousand years. 3 And he hurled him into the abyss and shut [it] and sealed [it] over him, that he might not mislead the nations any more until the thousand years were ended. After these things he must be let loose for a little while.

4 And I saw thrones, and there were those who sat down on them, and power of judging was given them. Yes, I saw the souls of those executed with the ax for the witness they bore to Jesus and for speaking about God, and those who had worshiped neither the wild beast nor its image and who had

not received the mark upon their forehead and upon their hand. And they came to life and ruled as kings with the Christ for a thousand years. 5 (The rest of the dead did not come to life until the thousand years were ended.) This is the first resurrection. 6 Happy and holy is anyone having part in the first resurrection; over these the second death has no authority, but they will be priests of God and of the Christ, and will rule as kings with him for the thousand years.

7 Now as soon as the thousand years have been ended, Satan will be let loose out of his prison, 8 and he will go out to mislead those nations in the four corners of the earth, Gog and Ma'gog, to gather them together for the war. The number of these is as the sand of the sea. 9 And they advanced over the breadth of the earth and encircled the camp of the holy ones and the beloved city. But fire came down out of heaven and devoured them. 10 And the Devil who was misleading them was hurled into the lake of fire and sulphur, where both the wild beast and the false prophet [already were]; and they will be tormented day and night forever and ever.

11 And I saw a great white throne and the one seated on it. From before him the earth and the heaven fled away, and no place was found for them. 12 And I saw the dead, the great and the small, standing before the throne, and scrolls were opened. But another scroll was opened; it is the scroll of life. And the dead were judged out of those things written in the scrolls according to their deeds. 13 And the sea gave up those dead in it, and death and Ha'des gave up those dead in them, and they were judged individually according to their deeds. 14 And death and Ha'des were hurled into the lake of fire. This means the second death, the lake of fire. 15 Furthermore, whoever was not found written in the book of life was hurled into the lake of fire.

21 And I saw a new heaven and a new earth; for the former heaven and the former earth had passed away, and the sea is no more. 2 I saw also the holy city, New Jerusalem, coming down out of heaven from God and prepared as a bride adorned for her husband. 3 With that I heard a loud voice from the throne say: "Look! The tent of God is with mankind, and he will reside with them, and they will be his peoples. And God himself will be with them. 4 And he will wipe out every tear from their eyes, and death will be no more, neither will mourning nor outcry nor pain be any more. The former things have passed away."

5 And the one seated on the throne said: "Look! I am making all things new." Also, he says: "Write, because these words are faithful and true." 6 And he said to me: "They have come to pass! I am the Al'pha and the O·me'ga, the beginning and the end. To anyone thirsting I will give from the fountain of the water of life free. 7 Anyone conquering will inherit these things, and I shall be his God and he will be my son. 8 But as for the cowards and those without faith and those who are disgusting in their filth and murderers and fornicators and those practicing spiritism and idolaters and all the liars, their portion will be in the lake that burns with fire and sulphur. This means the second death."

9 And there came one of the seven angels who had the seven bowls which were full of the seven last plagues, and he spoke with me and said: "Come here, I will show you the bride, the Lamb's wife." 10 So he carried me away in [the power of the] spirit to a great and lofty mountain, and he showed me the holy city Jerusalem coming down out of heaven from God 11 and having the glory of God. Its radiance was like a most precious stone, as a jasper stone shining crystal-clear. 12 It had a great and lofty wall and had twelve gates, and at the gates twelve angels, and

names were inscribed which are those of the twelve tribes of the sons of Israel. 13 On the east were three gates, and on the north three gates, and on the south three gates, and on the west three gates. 14 The wall of the city also had twelve foundation stones, and on them the twelve names of the twelve apostles of the Lamb.

15 Now the one who was speaking with me was holding as a measure a golden reed, that he might measure the city and its gates and its wall. 16 And the city lies foursquare, and its length is as great as its breadth. And he measured the city with the reed, twelve thousand furlongs; its length and breadth and height are equal. 17 Also, he measured its wall, one hundred and forty-four cubits, according to a man's measure, at the same time an angel's. 18 Now the structure of its wall was jasper, and the city was pure gold like clear glass. 19 The foundations of the city's wall were adorned with every sort of precious stone: the first foundation was jasper, the second sapphire, the third chal·ced'-o·ny, the fourth emerald, 20 the fifth sar'do·nyx, the sixth sardius, the seventh chrys'o·lite, the eighth beryl, the ninth topaz, the tenth chrys'o·prase, the eleventh hya-cinth, the twelfth amethyst. 21 Also, the twelve gates were twelve pearls; each one of the gates was made of one pearl. And the broad way of the city was pure gold, as transparent glass.

22 And I did not see a temple in it, for Jehovah God the Almighty is its temple, also the Lamb [is]. 23 And the city has no need of the sun nor of the moon to shine upon it, for the glory of God lighted it up, and its lamp was the Lamb. 24 And the nations will walk by means of its light, and the kings of the earth will bring their glory into it. 25 And its gates will not be closed at all by day, for night will not exist there. 26 And they will bring the glory and the honor of the nations into it. 27 But any-thing not sacred and anyone that

carries on a disgusting thing and a lie will in no way enter into it; only those written in the Lamb's scroll of life [will].

22 And he showed me a river of water of life, clear as crystal, flowing out from the throne of God and of the Lamb 2 down the mid-dle of its broad way. And on this side of the river and on that side [there were] trees of life producing twelve crops of fruit, yielding their fruits each month. And the leaves of the trees [were] for the curing of the nations.

3 And no more will there be any curse. But the throne of God and of the Lamb will be in [the city], and his slaves will render him sa-cred service; 4 and they will see his face, and his name will be on their foreheads. 5 Also, night will be no more, and they have no need of lamplight nor [do they have] sunlight, because Jehovah God will shed light upon them, and they will rule as kings forever and ever.

6 And he said to me: "These words are faithful and true; yes, Jehovah the God of the inspired expressions of the prophets sent his angel forth to show his slaves the things that must shortly take place. 7 And, look! I am coming quickly. Happy is anyone observing the words of the prophecy of this scroll."

8 Well, I John was the one hear-ing and seeing these things. And when I had heard and seen, I fell down to worship before the feet of the angel that had been showing me these things. 9 But he tells me: "Be careful! Do not do that! All I am is a fellow slave of you and of your brothers who are prophets and of those who are ob-serving the words of this scroll. Worship God."

10 He also tells me: "Do not seal up the words of the prophecy of this scroll, for the appointed time is near. 11 He that is doing un-righteousness, let him do unright-eousness still; and let the filthy one be made filthy still; but let the righteous one do righteousness still,

and let the holy one be made holy still.

12 "'Look! I am coming quickly, and the reward I give is with me, to render to each one as his work is. 13 I am the Al'pha and the O·me'ga, the first and the last, the beginning and the end. 14 Happy are those who wash their robes, that the authority [to go] to the trees of life may be theirs and that they may gain entrance into the city by its gates. 15 Outside are the dogs and those who practice spiritism and the fornicators and the murderers and the idolaters and everyone liking and carrying on a lie.'

16 "'I, Jesus, sent my angel to bear witness to YOU people of these things for the congregations. I am the root and the offspring of David, and the bright morning star.'"

17 And the spirit and the bride keep on saying: "Come!" And let anyone hearing say: "Come!" And let anyone thirsting come; let anyone that wishes take life's water free.

18 "I am bearing witness to everyone that hears the words of the prophecy of this scroll: If anyone makes an addition to these things, God will add to him the plagues that are written in this scroll; 19 and if anyone takes anything away from the words of the scroll of this prophecy, God will take his portion away from the trees of life and out of the holy city, things which are written about in this scroll.

20 "He that bears witness of these things says, 'Yes; I am coming quickly.'"

"Amen! Come, Lord Jesus."

21 [May] the undeserved kindness of the Lord Jesus Christ [be] with the holy ones.

A

AARON, Ex 28:1 A. may act as priest
Ex 32:1 about A. make for us a god
Heb 5:4 called by God, just as A. also was
Ex 4:14; 24:1; Ps 99:6; 135:19; Mic 6:4.
ABADDON, Re 9:11 king name is A.
ABANDON, Eze 31:12 people will a. it
ABANDONED, Zep 2:4 a. city she becomes;
ABANDONING, 2Pe 2:15 A. the path,
ABASER, 1Sa 2:7 Jehovah is an A.
ABASHED, Ps 35:26 let those be a.
ABASING, Ps 147:6 He is a. the wicked
ABATED, Ge 8:8 waters had a. from
Mr 4:39 and the wind a.
ABBA, Ro 8:15 we cry out, A., Father!
Ga 4:6 spirit cries out, A., Father!
ABDOMEN, 2Sa 20:10; Ca 5:14; Jer 51:34.
ABEDNEGO, Da 1:7; 2:49; 3:12, 30.
ABEL, Ge 4:4 Jehovah favor upon A.
Mt 23:35 from the blood of righteous A. to
Heb 11:4 By faith A. offered a sacrifice
Ge 4:2, 8, 25; Lu 11:51; Heb 12:24.
ABHOR, Ro 12:9 A. what is wicked
Ge 27:46; Le 20:23; Nu 21:5; Pr 3:11.
ABHORRENCE, 1Ki 11:25; Da 12:2; Ro 2:22.
ABHORRENT THING, La 1:17; Eze 7:19, 20.
ABIDE, Php 1:25 I shall a. with all of you
ABIDING, Heb 10:34 an a. possession
ABIDING PLACE(S), Isa 32:18 peaceful a.
Jer 25:37 peaceful a. rendered lifeless
Eze 34:14 they will lie down in a good a.
ABIHU, Ex 6:23; Le 10:1; Nu 3:4.
ABIJAH, 1Sa 8:2; 1Ki 14:1; Lu 1:5.
ABILITIES, 1Co 12:28 helpful services, a. to
ABILITY. See also THINKING ABILITY.
Ro 7:18 a. to work out what is fine
1Co 1:5 full a. to speak and full knowledge,
Ex 15:6; Da 1:4; Mt 25:15.
ABIMELECH, Ge 20:2; Jg 9:16; 2Sa 11:21.
ABISHAI, 1Sa 26:6; 2Sa 21:17; 23:18.
ABLE-BODIED MAN, Re 10:11; 1Ch 23:3;
Job 3:23; Ps 34:8; 37:23; 89:48; Pr 6:34;
20:24; 29:5; Isa 22:17; Jer 17:5; Joe 2:8.
ABNER, 1Sa 14:50; 20:25; 2Sa 3:20.
ABNORMAL FALLING OFF, Le 13:30, 34.
ABODE(S), Ps 74:20 a. of violence
Hab 3:11 moon—stood still, in the lofty a.
Joh 14:2 house of my Father are many a.
ABOLISH, Ga 3:17 as to a. the promise.
ABOLISHED, Eph 2:15 he a. the hatred
2Ti 1:10 Christ Jesus who has a. death
ABOMINATION. See DISGUSTING THING.
ABORTION(S), Ex 23:26 suffering an a.
Ge 31:38; Job 21:10.
ABOUND, Ro 6:1 undeserved kindness a.?
2Co 1:5 sufferings for Christ a. in us,
Ro 15:13; 2Co 8:7; Php 1:9; 1Th 3:12.
ABOUNDED, Ro 5:15 undeserved kindness a.
ABOUNDING, 2Co 8:7 you are a. in faith
ABRAHAM, Ge 17:9 A.: keep my covenant
Ge 18:18 A. to become a nation great
2Ch 20:7 A., your lover,
Mt 8:11 recline with A. in Kingdom
Ga 3:29 you are really A.'s seed, heirs
Heb 11:8 By faith A. obeyed in going out
Jas 2:21 Was not A. declared righteous
Mt 22:32; Joh 8:39; Ro 4:3; Heb 6:13.
ABSALOM, 2Sa 14:25; 15:6; 17:25; 18:14.

ABSENCE, Ne 13:6 asked leave of a.
Php 2:12 not my presence only, but my a.
ABSENT, Col 2:5 I am a. in the flesh,
1Co 5:3; 2Co 5:9; 10:1, 11; Php 1:27.
ABSOLUTELY, 2Co 4:8 not a. with no way
ABSORBED, 1Ti 4:15 be a. in them,
ABSTAIN, 1Th 4:3 a. from fornication
1Ti 4:3 commanding to a. from foods which
ABSTAINING, 1Pe 2:11 a. from fleshly
ABSTINENCE, 2Co 11:27 in a. from food
Nu 30:2; Zec 7:3; Ac 27:21.
ABUNDANCE, Job 36:31 food in a.
Ps 52:7 trusts in the a. of his riches
Isa 9:7 a. of princely rule there will be
Lu 12:15 person has an a. his life does not
Joh 10:10 have life and might have it in a.
Ps 37:11; Eze 28:16; Mt 12:34; 2Co 8:2.
ABUNDANT, 1Co 12:24 giving honor more a.
Ex 34:6; Da 12:4; 1Co 12:23.
ABUNDANTLY, 2Co 9:10 he that a. supplies
Heb 6:17 demonstrate more a. to the heirs
ABUSE, 1Co 9:18 may not a. my authority
ABUSED, Ac 7:24 vengeance for the a.
ABUSIVELY, Tit 2:5 not be spoken of a.
2Pe 2:10 at glorious ones but speak a.,
1Sa 31:4; Jer 38:19.
ABUSIVELY, SPEAKING, Ac 18:6 s., he
1Pe 4:4 are puzzled and go on s. of you.
ABUSIVE SPEECH(ES), Eph 4:31; 1Ti 6:4.
Lu 8:31; Ro 10:7; Re 9:1, 11; 11:7; 17:8.
ACCEDE, De 13:8 must not a. to his wish
ACCEPT, 2Co 6:1 a. the undeserved kindness
2Ti 2:10 they did not a. the love of the
Job 42:8; Ho 14:2; Lu 22:17; Ac 8:14; Eph
6:17; Jas 1:21.
ACCEPTABLE, 2Co 6:2 in an a. time
Eph 5:10 sure of what is a.
1Pe 2:5 offer up spiritual sacrifices a. to
Isa 49:8; Lu 4:19; Ro 12:1; 1Ti 2:3.
ACCEPTED, Php 4:9 learned as well as a.
ACCIDENT, Ge 42:4; Ex 21:22; 1Sa 6:9.
ACCOMPLISH, 2Ti 4:5 fully a. your
ACCOMPLISHED, 2Ti 4:17 preaching be a.
ACCOMPLISHING, Ps 148:8 fire and hail a.
ACCOMPLISHMENT, Pr 15:22 there is a.
ACCORD, Ac 2:46; 19:29; Ro 15:6.
ACCOUNT, Mt 24:9 hated on a. of my name.
Mt 24:22 days were cut short on a. of the
Ro 4:8 will by no means take into a.
Ro 14:12 each of us will render an a.
1Co 13:5 It does not keep a. of injury.
Phm 18 anything, keep this charged to my a.
ACCOUNTABLE, Mt 5:21, 22 a. to court
ACCOUNTING, Ro 9:28 Jehovah will make a.
Heb 4:13 exposed to whom we have an a.
ACCOUNTING, HOLD AN, Ho 4:14; Zec 10:3.
ACCURATE KNOWLEDGE, Ro 10:2 zeal not a.
Php 1:9 abound with a. and full discernment
Col 1:9 filled with a. of his will in all
1Ti 2:4 be saved, come to an a. of truth
2Ti 3:7 always learning yet never come to a.
Heb 10:26 sin willfully after received a.
Ro 1:28; Col 3:10; 2Ti 2:25; 2Pe 2:20.
ACCURATELY, 1Co 13:12 a. even as I am a.
ACCURATE SCALES, Le 19:36; Job 31:6.
ACCURSED, De 21:23 a. one hung up
Joh 7:49 crowd not know the Law are a.

1341

Ga 3:13 **A.** is every man hanged upon a stake
1Co 12:3; 16:22; Ga 1:8.
ACCUSATION, Ro 8:33 Who will file **a.**
1Ti 3:10 ministers, as they are free from **a.**
1Ti 5:19 Do not admit an **a.** against older
Tit 1:7 overseer must be free from **a.**
Ezr 4:6; Joh 18:29; 1Co 1:8; Col 1:22.
ACCUSER(S), Ac 25:16 meets his **a.** face
Re 12:10 **a.** of our brothers hurled
Ac 23:30, 35; 25:18.
ACCUSTOMED, Jg 21:25 one was **a.** to do
1Co 8:7 **a.** to the idol,
ACHAN, Jos 7:1, 18, 24; 22:20.
ACHIEVEMENT(S), Pr 8:22 earliest of **a.**
1Ch 17:19, 21; Isa 41:24; 45:9.
ACHING, Ge 34:25; Job 14:22; Ps 69:29.
ACKNOWLEDGE, De 33:9; 1Sa 2:12; Jer 14:20.
ACKNOWLEDGMENT, Ro 14:11 open **a.** God.
ACQUAINT, Job 22:21 **A.** yourself, with him
ACQUAINTANCE(S), Ps 38:11 **a.** stood off
Isa 53:3 meant for having **a.** with sickness.
2Ki 10:11; Ps 31:11; 55:13; 88:8, 18.
ACQUAINTED, De 32:17 forefathers not **a.**
Ac 18:25; 19:15; 26:5.
ACQUIESCED, Ac 11:18 heard they **a.**
ACQUIRE, Lu 21:19 will **a.** your souls.
ACQUIRING, Pr 15:32 is **a.** heart.
1Th 5:9; 2Th 2:14; 1Ti 3:13.
ACQUISITION, Job 15:29 spread their **a.**
ACQUITTED, Ro 6:7 has been **a.** from sin.
ACT(S), Jg 5:11 recount the righteous **a.**
Isa 29:14 I will **a.** wonderfully with this
Ps 101:2; 103:6; 145:4, 12.
ACT EFFECTIVELY, Da 11:17, 28, 32.
Da 11:39 he will **a.** with a foreign god.
ACTIVE FORCE, Ge 1:2; 6:17; 7:15.
ACTIVITY, De 32:4 perfect his **a.,**
Pr 10:16 **a.** of the righteous one results in
Pr 21:8 pure one is upright in his **a.**
Pr 24:12 pay back to man according to his **a.**
Job 36:24; Ps 9:16; Isa 59:6; Hab 3:2.
ACTUATING, Eph 4:23 force **a.** your mind
ADAM, 1Co 15:22 in **A.** all are dying.
1Co 15:45 first man **A.** became a living soul.
Ge 3:21; 5:5; Lu 3:38; Ro 5:14; 1Ti 2:14.
ADD, De 4:2 not **a.** to the word
Lu 12:25 **a.** a cubit to life span
De 12:32; 2Ch 10:14; Pr 30:6; Mt 6:27.
ADDING, Ge 30:24; 2Ch 28:13.
ADDITION(S), Ga 3:15 covenant, no **a.**
Re 22:18 If anyone makes an **a.**
ADDS, Pr 10:22 makes rich, and **a.** no pain
Pr 16:23 to his lips it **a.** persuasiveness.
Job 34:37; Pr 19:4.
ADEQUATELY, 2Co 2:16; 3:5; 2Ti 2:2.
ADJUDGE, Isa 26:12 you will **a.** peace to us
ADJUTANT, 2Ki 7:17 king appointed the **a.**
ADMINISTERED, Ru 1:1 judges **a.** justice
Eph 3:9 see how the sacred secret is **a.**
ADMINISTERING, 2Co 3:9 **a.** righteousness
ADMINISTRATION, Eph 1:10 **a.** at the full
1Ch 26:30; Da 2:49.
ADMINISTRATORS, Da 3:2, 3 **a.** of districts
ADMIRATION, Re 13:3 the beast with **a.**
ADMIRING PERSONALITIES, Jude 16.
ADMIT, Ac 24:14 I **a.** this to you
ADMITTEDLY, 1Ti 3:16 secret is **a.** great;
ADMONISH, Ro 15:14; 1Co 4:14; 1Th 5:14.
ADMONISHING, 1Th 5:12 regard those **a.**
2Th 3:15 continue **a.** him as a brother.
Ac 20:31; Col 1:28; 3:16.
ADMONITION, Tit 3:10 first and second **a.**
ADOPTION, Ro 8:15 received spirit of **a.**
Ro 8:23; 9:4; Ga 4:5; Eph 1:5.

ADORN, 1Ti 2:9 women to **a.** in modesty
Tit 2:10 may **a.** the teaching of
1Pe 3:5 holy women **a.** subjecting
ADORNED, Lu 21:5 temple **a.** with stones
Re 21:2, 19 a bride **a.** for her husband
ADORNMENT, 1Pe 3:3 not let your **a.** be
1Ch 16:29; Ps 29:2; Pr 14:28.
ADULLAM, Jos 12:15; 1Sa 22:1; 1Ch 11:15.
ADULTERATING, 2Co 4:2 neither **a.** the
ADULTERER(S), 1Co 6:9 nor **a.** inherit
Job 24:15; Ps 50:18; Jer 9:2; Heb 13:4.
ADULTERESS(ES), Ro 7:3 she is not an **a.**
Jas 4:4 **A.** friendship with world is
Le 20:10; Eze 23:45.
ADULTERY(IES), Ex 20:14 not commit **a.**
Eze 23:37 with their idols they committed **a.**
Re 2:22 those committing **a.** with her
Mt 5:28; 15:19; Mr 7:22; Jas 2:11.
ADVANCE, Eph 2:10 God prepared in **a.**
ADVANCEMENT, Php 1:12, 25; 1Ti 4:15.
ADVANTAGE, Pr 14:23 By toil comes **a.,**
Ec 2:13 more **a.** for wisdom than for folly,
2Co 7:2 we have taken **a.** of no one.
Ec 2:11; 1Co 7:35; 10:33; 2Co 12:17, 18.
ADVANTAGEOUS, Ec 7:11 Wisdom is **a.** for
1Co 6:12 not all things are **a.**
ADVERSARY(IES), Isa 64:2 name to **a.,**
Jer 46:10 Jehovah avenging upon his **a.**
1Pe 5:8 your **a.,** the Devil, walks about
De 32:43; Es 7:6; Ps 74:10; 107:2; Na 1:2.
ADVERSITIES, Pr 19:13 stupid son means **a.**
Ps 38:12; 55:11; 91:3; 94:20; Pr 17:4.
ADVERSITY, Job 6:2; 30:13; Ps 5:9.
Eze 7:26 There will come **a.** upon **a.,**
ADVISABLE, Mt 19:10 not **a.** to marry.
AFFAIR(S), Ec 3:1 a time for every **a.**
1Co 14:1 Let all your **a.** take place with
Es 3:4; Ac 15:6.
AFFECTION(S), Mt 10:37 has greater **a.**
Joh 5:20 the Father has **a.** for Son
Joh 21:17 do you have **a.** for me?
Col 3:12 clothe yourselves with tender **a.**
2Ti 3:3 having no natural **a.,** not open to
Re 3:19 those for whom I have **a.** I reprove
Joh 11:3; 1Co 16:22; 2Co 7:15; Tit 3:15.
AFFLICT, Ge 15:13 **a.** them four hundred
Ex 22:22 must not **a.** any widow or
2Sa 7:10; Na 1:12.
AFFLICTED, Job 36:15 will rescue the **a.**
Ps 82:3 do justice even to the **a.** one
Pr 31:9 plead the cause of the **a.** one
Isa 66:2 to the one **a.** and contrite
Job 34:28; Isa 49:13; 53:4, 7; 58:10.
AFFLICTING, Ps 94:5; Isa 60:14; Zep 3:19.
AFFLICTION(S), Ps 107:17 errors cause **a.**
Ps 107:41 protects the poor one from **a.**
Ex 3:7, 17; 4:31; Job 36:15; Ps 119:92;
2Co 8:2.
AFFORD, Le 27:8; Nu 6:21; Eze 46:7.
AFORETIME, Ro 1:2 promised **a.** through
Ro 15:4 things written **a.** our instruction
AFRAID, Ge 3:10 I was **a.** because I
Jg 7:3 Who is **a.** and trembling?
Isa 51:12 **a.** of a mortal man
Jer 1:8 do not be **a.,** for I am with you
Ps 112:7; Pr 3:25; Heb 13:6; Re 2:10.
AFRESH, Heb 6:6 impale the Son **a.**
AFTERDAYS, De 8:16 do good in your **a.**
AFTEREFFECT, Pr 5:4 **a.** from her is bitter
AGABUS, Ac 11:28; 21:10.
AGAINST, Isa 19:2 war each one **a.** his
Mt 12:30 He that is not on my side is **a.** me;
Ro 8:31 If God is for us, who will be **a.**
Mal 3:5; Mt 10:35; 12:25; Eph 6:12.

AGED, Lu 1:18; Tit 2:3; Phm 9.
AGENT, CHIEF, Ac 3:15; 5:31; Heb 2:10.
AGITATED, Ps 4:4 Be a. but do not sin.
Ps 99:1 king. Let the peoples be a.
Isa 13:13 cause heaven itself to become a.,
1Pe 3:14 are afraid of, neither become a.
Ex 15:14; De 2:25; Joe 2:1, 10; Ac 17:8.
AGLOW, Ac 18:25; Ro 12:11.
AGONY, Re 12:2.
AGREE, Mt 18:19; Ac 15:15.
AGREEABLE, 1Co 7:12, 13 she a. to dwelling
AGREEABLY, Ps 105:22 bind a. to his soul
AGREED, Mt 20:13; Ac 5:9.
AGREEMENT, Mr 14:56, 59 testimonies not a.
1Co 1:10 you should all speak in a.,
2Co 6:16 what a. God's temple with idols
AGRICULTURAL, Ne 10:37 all our a. cities
AGRICULTURE, 2Ch 26:10 a lover of a.
AHAB, 1Ki 16:30; 18:17; 2Ki 10:18.
AHASUERUS, Es 1:1; 3:1; 8:1; 9:30; 10:3.
AHAZ, 2Ki 16:1, 19; 2Ch 27:9; Isa 1:1.
AHEAD, 2Jo 9 Everyone that pushes a. and
AHIJAH, 1Ki 12:15; 14:2; 1Ch 26:20.
AHITHOPHEL, 2Sa 15:31; 17:23.
AHITUB, 1Sa 14:3; 2Sa 8:17; 1Ch 9:11.
AI, Jos 7:2, 3; 8:1, 26, 28, 29; Jer 49:3.
AID, Heb 2:18 to a. those put to test.
AIJALON, Jos 10:12; Jg 12:12; 1Ch 6:69.
AIM, 2Co 5:9 making it our a. that
1Ti 4:7 with godly devotion as your a.
AIR, Eph 2:2 ruler of the a.
1Th 4:17 caught to meet the Lord in the a.
Job 41:16; 1Co 9:26; 14:9; Re 9:2.
AIRS, PUT ON, Jer 48:26; Da 8:4, 8.
AKELDAMA, Ac 1:19 A., Field of Blood.
ALARM, 2Ch 13:12; Zep 1:16.
ALARM SIGNAL, Jer 49:2; Am 1:14; 2:2.
ALEXANDER, Ac 19:33; 1Ti 1:20; 2Ti 4:14.
ALIEN, Lu 24:18; Eph 2:19; Heb 11:9.
ALIENATED, Col 1:21 you were once a.
Eph 2:12; 4:18.
ALIEN RESIDENT(S), Ge 15:13; De 10:18;
Isa 14:1; Jer 7:6; 22:3; Zec 7:10.
Le 24:22 a. should be the same as a native
Nu 35:15 for the a. six cities a refuge
ALIVE, Ps 22:29 preserve his own a.
Ps 89:48 What man a. will not see death?
Ro 4:17 God, makes the dead a. and calls
Ro 7:9 I was once a. apart from law; but
1Co 15:22 in the Christ all will be made a.
Heb 4:12 word of God is a. and exerts power
2Co 13:4; Heb 7:25; 1Pe 3:18; Re 19:20.
ALKALI, Pr 25:20; Jer 2:22.
ALLIED, Ps 94:20 adversities be a. with you
ALLIES, Ge 14:3.
ALLOTTED SHARE, Ps 16:5 portion of a.
ALLOWANCE, 1Th 4:7 a. for uncleanness,
2Ki 25:30; Jer 40:5; Da 1:5.
ALLUDING REMARKS, Hab 2:6 lift up a.,
ALLURE, Pr 62:4 a. from one's dignity;
De 13:6; Isa 36:18.
ALLURES, 2Ki 18:32 Hezekiah a. you,
ALLY, Da 11:6.
ALLYING, Da 11:23 because of their a.
ALMIGHTY, Ge 17:1 I am God A. Walk
Re 16:14 war of the great day of God the A.
Ex 6:3; Job 8:3; Isa 13:6; Re 1:8; 11:17.
ALONE, Isa 2:11 Jehovah a. must be put
Ne 9:6; Mt 4:4; Joh 11:48; 16:32; Ac 5:38.
ALPHA, Re 1:8; 21:6; 22:13.
ALPHAEUS, Mt 10:3; Mr 3:18; Ac 1:13.
ALTAR(S), Ge 8:20 Noah a. to Jehovah
Le 17:11 the blood I have put upon the a.
Eze 6:4 your a. must be made desolate

Ac 17:23 an a. To an Unknown God.
Heb 13:10 We have an a. from which
Re 6:9 saw underneath the a. the souls of
Ex 34:13; Isa 56:7; Mt 23:18; Heb 7:13.
AMALEK, Ex 17:16; De 25:17; 1Sa 15:20.
AMASA, 2Sa 17:25; 20:10; 1Ki 2:5.
AMAZED, Job 26:11 a. because of his rebuke
Ps 48:5 saw; so they were a.
Jer 4:9 prophets themselves will be a.
AMAZEMENT, Le 26:32 enemies stare in a.
Jer 2:12 Stare in a., O you heavens,
Lu 2:47 constant a. at his understanding
Ps 40:15; Eze 26:16; 27:35; Mt 15:31.
AMAZIAH, 2Ki 12:21; 14:11, 18; 2Ch 25:27.
AMBASSADOR(S), 2Co 5:20 a. substituting
Eph 6:20 I am acting as an a. in chains;
AMBIGUOUS SAYINGS, Da 8:23 a king, a.
AMBUSH, Jer 51:12 those lying in a.
Jos 8:2; Jg 16:9; 1Sa 15:5.
AMEN, 1Co 14:16 person say A. to your
Re 3:14 A. says, the faithful and true
De 27:15-26; 1Ch 16:36; 2Co 1:20.
AMENDS, Ex 32:30 make a. for your sin
AMMON, Zep 2:9 A. like Gomorrah,
Ge 19:38; Jg 10:6; 2Ch 20:1; Da 11:41.
AMNESTY, Es 2:18 an a. granted
AMORITE(S), Ge 10:16; 15:16; Jos 3:10.
AMPUTATE, De 25:12 must a. her hand
AMRAM, Ex 6:18; Nu 26:58; 1Ch 6:3.
AMUSEMENT, Jg 16:25 offer us some a.
ANAK, Nu 13:22 children of A. were
ANANIAS, Ac 5:1, 5; 9:10; 22:12; 23:2.
ANCESTORS, De 19:14; Ezr 4:15; Ps 79:8.
ANCESTRAL, Ac 22:3 instructed a. Law,
ANCHOR, Heb 6:19 This hope a. for the soul
ANCIENT, Da 7:9 A. of Days sat down.
2Pe 2:5 punishing an a. world,
ANDREW, Mt 4:18; Joh 12:22; Ac 1:13.
ANEW, Isa 61:4 make a. devastated cities
ANGEL(S), Ps 34:7 The a. is camping
1Co 4:9 theatrical spectacle to a.
1Co 6:3 Do you know we shall judge a.?
2Co 11:14 Satan a. of light.
2Co 12:7 an a. of Satan,
1Pe 1:12 a. are desiring to peer.
Re 22:6 sent his a. to show his slaves
Ge 19:15; Ex 3:2; 23:20; Mt 22:30; 28:2;
Ac 5:19; Ga 1:8; Heb 13:2; 2Pe 2:4, 11.
ANGER, Ps 37:8 Let a. alone
Ps 103:8 Jehovah is slow to a.
Ps 110:5 break kings on the day of his a.
Pr 14:29 He that is slow to a. is abundant
Pr 22:24 with anyone given to a.,
Isa 30:27 Jehovah burning with his a.
Zep 2:2 before the a. of Jehovah comes
Job 16:9; Ps 2:5; 55:3; Zep 3:8; Col 3:8;
Re 14:10; 15:1.
ANGRY. See WRATHFUL.
ANGUISH, Lu 21:25 a. of nations,
2Co 2:4 out of a. of heart I write you
ANIMAL(S), 2Pe 2:12 a. to be caught
Jas 3:15; Jude 10.
ANIMALISTIC, Jude 19 are a. men
ANIMOSITY, Ge 50:15; Job 16:9; Ps 55:3.
ANNA, Lu 2:36 A. a prophetess,
ANNAS, Lu 3:2; Joh 18:13, 24; Ac 4:6.
ANNIHILATE, Ps 145:20 wicked he will a.
De 6:15; 28:51, 63; Ps 106:23; Da 11:44.
ANNIHILATED, Ps 92:7 be a. forever.
Ge 34:30; Ps 37:38; Pr 14:11; Ga 5:15.
ANNOUNCEMENT, Ro 15:21 to whom no a. has
ANNOY, Ru 2:22 women may not a. you
ANNOYANCE, Mt 13:15 heard with a.
ANNULLED, Nu 30:8, 12; Da 6:8, 12.

ANOINT, Ex 28:41 a. them and fill their
Jg 9:8 trees went to a. a king over them.
Ex 40:13, 15; 1Sa 16:12; 1Ki 1:34; 19:16.
ANOINTED, 1Sa 16:13 Samuel a. him
2Sa 19:21 called evil upon the a. of
Ps 45:7 a. you with the oil of exultation
Isa 61:1 Jehovah has a. me to tell good
Eze 28:14 a. cherub that is covering,
2Co 1:21 has a. us is God
Heb 1:9 God, a. you with oil of joy
ANOINTED ONE(S), 1Sa 2:10 horn of a.
1Ch 16:22 Do not touch my a.
Ps 2:2 kings against his a.
Ps 20:6 Jehovah saves his a.
Ps 105:15 Do not touch my a.
Isa 45:1 to his a., to Cyrus
Hab 3:13 to save your a.
ANOINTING, 1Jo 2:20 a. from the holy
Ex 30:25; 40:15; Le 8:12; Nu 4:16.
ANSWER, Pr 1:28 I shall not a.,
Pr 15:28 righteous one meditates to a.,
Isa 65:24 before they call I shall a.
Job 14:15; Isa 58:9; Jer 33:3; Col 4:6.
ANTAGONIST, Isa 50:8.
ANTICHRIST(S), 1Jo 2:18 now many a.
1Jo 2:22; 4:3; 2Jo 7.
ANTIPAS, Re 2:13 A. the faithful one,
ANTIQUITY, Mal 3:4 as in years of a.
ANXIETY(IES), Mr 4:19 a. of this system
1Co 7:32 want you to be free from a.
Mt 6:34; 13:22; Lu 8:14; 21:34; 1Pe 5:7.
ANXIOUS, 1Sa 9:5 become a. about us.
Ps 38:18 I began to be a. over my sin.
Pr 12:25 A. care in the heart of a man is
Mt 6:25 Stop being a. about your souls
Mt 10:19 not a. about how or what to speak;
Lu 10:41 Martha, you are a. and disturbed
1Co 7:32 The unmarried man is a. for things
Jer 17:8; Mt 6:34; Php 4:6.
ANXIOUS SUSPENSE, Lu 12:29 quit in a.
APART, Ps 2:3 Let us tear their bands a.
Ro 7:9 I was once alive a. from law; but
Nu 16:31; Mt 19:6; Mr 10:9.
APERTURE, Isa 11:8 light a. of a snake
APOLLYON, Re 9:11 Greek the name A.
APOSTASY, Isa 32:6 to work at a.
Jer 23:15 from prophets a. has gone forth
Da 11:32 will lead into a. by smooth words.
Ac 21:21 teaching an a. from Moses
2Th 2:3 unless the a. comes first
APOSTATE(S), Job 13:16 no a. will come
Job 17:8 gets excited over the a.
Job 27:8 what is the hope of an a.?
Job 34:30 an a. man may not reign,
Isa 10:6 against an a. nation I shall send
Ps 35:16; Pr 11:9; Isa 9:17; 33:14.
APOSTATIZING, Jer 17:13 Those a. from me
APOSTLE(S), Mt 10:2 names of twelve a.
1Co 4:9 a. become a theatrical spectacle
2Co 11:13 such men are false a., deceitful
2Co 12:12 signs of an a. were produced
Ga 1:1 a., neither from men
Heb 3:1 a. and high priest—Jesus.
Mr 3:14; 1Co 12:28; 15:9; Re 21:14.
APOSTLESHIP, Ac 1:25; 1Co 9:2; Ga 2:8.
APPAREL, Ac 20:33 coveted no man's a.
1Pe 3:4 incorruptible a.
APPARITION, Mt 14:26; Mr 6:49.
APPEAL TO CAESAR, Ac 25:11; 28:19.
APPEAR, 1Sa 3:21 Jehovah to a. in Shiloh
Ps 102:16 Jehovah must a. in his glory.
Mt 23:28; 24:30; 2Co 13:7; Heb 9:24.
APPEARANCE(S), Joh 7:24 judging a.
2Co 5:12 boast over the outward a.

1Sa 16:7; Joe 2:4; Na 2:4; Mt 28:3.
APPEARED, Ge 12:7 Jehovah a. to Abram
Ex 3:16 Jehovah has a. to [Moses]
Ex 16:10 Jehovah's glory a. in a cloud
De 31:15 Jehovah a. at the tent
2Ch 3:1 Jehovah had a. to David
Jg 6:12; Lu 9:31; Ac 9:17; 16:9.
APPEARING. See MANIFESTATION, 1Ki 11:9.
APPEASE, Ge 32:20 I may a. him by
APPENDAGE, Ex 29:13; Le 3:4.
APPLAUSE, Job 38:7 shouting in a.
APPLES, Pr 25:11 a. of gold in silver
APPLYING YOURSELF, 1Ti 4:13 a. to reading
APPOINT, Nu 1:50; Ezr 7:25; Ac 6:3.
APPOINTED, Joh 15:16 a. you bearing fruit
Ac 14:23 they a. older men to office
Ac 17:31 judge the earth by a man he has a.,
1Ti 2:7 I was a. a preacher and an apostle
Heb 1:2 Son, whom he a. heir of all things,
Jude 4 a. by the Scriptures to judgment
Jos 20:9; Ps 79:11; Da 11:27, 35; Jon 1:17;
Ac 17:26; 2Ti 1:11; Heb 5:1; 8:3.
APPOINTED TIME(S), Nu 9:2, 3; De 11:14.
Ps 104:19 made the moon for a.;
Ec 3:1 For everything there is an a.,
Da 8:19 it is for the a. of the end.
Hab 2:3 vision is yet for the a.,
Ro 5:6 Christ died at the a.
Lu 21:24; 1Ti 6:15; 1Pe 4:17.
APPOINTMENT(S), 1Sa 21:2 made an a. with
Am 3:3 two walk unless met by a.?
Tit 1:5 you might make a. of older men
APPORTION, Isa 53:12 will a. the spoil,
Jos 18:5; Ne 9:22.
APPORTIONED, 2Co 10:13 boundary God a.
Heb 7:2 Abraham a. a tenth from all things,
De 4:19; Isa 34:17.
APPRAISE, 1Co 4:1 Let a man a. us as
2Co 10:2 some a. us as if we walked in flesh.
APPRECIATION, Ps 27:4 to look with a.
APPROACH, Ro 5:2; Eph 2:18; 3:12.
APPROACHING, Heb 7:25 a. God through him
APPROPRIATE, Es 7:4 distress is not a.
APPROPRIATELY, Ps 116:7; 119:17; 142:7.
APPROVAL, 1Co 7:33 gain a. of his wife.
De 33:16; Pr 12:2; Ro 14:18.
APPROVE, Heb 10:6 not a. of whole
APPROVED, Mt 3:17 my Son, whom I a.
Lu 12:32 a. of giving you the kingdom.
2Ti 2:15 present yourself a. to God, a
Ro 16:10; 2Co 10:18; 13:7.
APPROVED CONDITION, Ro 5:4 a., in turn,
APPROVING, Ac 8:1; 22:20 Saul a. murder
AQUILA, Ac 18:2, 26; Ro 16:3; 2Ti 4:19.
ARABAH, De 1:7 neighbors in the A.,
De 4:49; Jer 52:7; Eze 47:8; Zec 14:10.
ARABIA, Ga 1:17; 4:25.
ARABIAN(S), Ne 2:19; Jer 3:2; Ac 2:11.
ARABLE, Jer 4:3; Ho 10:12.
ARABS, 2Ch 9:14; Jer 25:24; Eze 27:21.
ARAM, Ge 10:22; Nu 23:7; 1Ch 1:17.
ARAMAIC, Ezr 4:7; Da 2:4.
ARARAT, Ge 8:4; 2Ki 19:37; Jer 51:27.
ARBITRARINESS, Ge 49:6 in their a. they
ARBITRARY, Isa 3:4 a. power will rule them
ARBITRATE, 1Sa 2:25 God will a. for him,
ARCHANGEL, 1Th 4:16 with an a.'s voice
Jude 9 Michael the a. had a difference with
ARCHITECTURAL, 1Ch 28:11, 19 David a. plan
ARDOR, De 29:20; Eze 23:25; 38:19.
AREOPAGUS, Ac 17:19, 22, 34.
ARGUE, Job 13:15; Mic 6:2; Mr 8:17.
ARGUING, Job 13:3 in a. with God
Mr 8:16; 9:33 a. with one another

ARGUMENT(S), Isa 41:21 Produce your a. says
Php 2:14 free from a.,
Col 2:4 no man delude you with a.
ARIGHT, 2Ti 2:15 handling truth a.
ARIMATHEA, Mt 27:57; Lu 23:51; Joh 19:38.
ARISE, Ps 3:7; 9:19; Eph 5:14.
ARISES, Heb 7:15 there a. another
ARK, Ge 6:14 Make for yourself an a.
Jos 3:13 priests carrying the a. of Jehovah,
Ge 7:1; Ex 25:10; 1Pe 3:20; Re 11:19.
ARM, Isa 40:10 his a. will be ruling
Isa 52:10 Jehovah has bared his holy a.
Isa 53:1 as for the a. of Jehovah, to whom
Joh 12:38 a. of Jehovah has been revealed
1Pe 4:1 a. yourselves with the same mental
2Ch 32:8; Ps 10:15; 44:3.
ARMAGEDDON. See HAR-MAGEDON, Re 16:16.
ARMIES, Jer 28:2 This is what Jehovah of a.
Lu 21:20 Jerusalem surrounded by encamped a.,
Ro 9:29 Jehovah of a. left a seed
Jas 5:4 into the ears of Jehovah of a.
Re 19:14 a. in heaven were following him
1Sa 17:45; Mt 22:7; Heb 11:34; Re 9:16.
ARMOR, Eph 6:11 Put on the suit of a.
ARMOR-BEARER, 1Sa 14:6; 31:4.
ARMY, Ge 2:1 a. came to completion.
Isa 34:2 Jehovah has rage against their a.
Jer 33:22 a. of heavens cannot be counted
De 24:5; 2Ki 17:16; Da 4:35; 8:10.
ARNON, Nu 21:13; Jg 11:26; Isa 16:2.
ARRANGEMENT, Ro 13:2 against the a. of
1Co 14:40 take place decently and by a.
Eze 43:11; Na 2:9.
ARRANGINGS, Pr 16:1 a. of the heart,
ARRAYED, Mt 6:29; Re 17:4; 19:8.
ARRESTED, Mt 4:12; Lu 22:54; Ac 1:16.
ARRIVAL, Lu 19:23 Then on my a. I
ARRIVES, 1Co 11:26 death until he a.
ARROGANT, Ps 101:5; Pr 28:25.
ARROW(S), De 32:42 intoxicate my a.
2Ki 13:17 Jehovah's a. of salvation, even
Ps 127:4 Like a. in the hand of a mighty
Isa 49:2 he made me a polished a.
Hab 3:11 Like light your own a. kept going.
1Sa 20:20; Ps 18:14; Jer 50:14; 51:11.
ARTAXERXES, Ezr 4:7, 23; Ne 2:1; 13:6.
ARTEMIS, Ac 19:27, 34, 35.
ARTFULLY CONTRIVED, 2Pe 1:16. a. stories
ARTICLE(S), Ge 24:53; Ex 3:22; 1Ki 7:51.
ART OF TEACHING, 2Ti 4:2; Tit 1:9.
ASA, 1Ki 15:9, 14, 24; 2Ch 14:2; Jer 41:9.
ASAPH, 1Ch 6:39; 16:5; 25:1; 2Ch 35:15.
ASCEND, Ps 135:7 causing vapors to a.
Ac 2:34 David did not a. to the heavens
Ps 24:3; 139:8; Ro 10:6.
ASCENDANCY, 1Ch 17:17 the man in a.
ASCENDED, Joh 3:13 no man has a. into
Joh 20:17 I have not yet a. to the Father.
Jg 13:20; Ps 68:18; Pr 30:4; Eph 4:8-10.
ASCENDING, Ge 28:12 God's angels a. and
Joh 6:62 Son of man a. to where he was
Re 13:11 wild beast a. out of the earth,
ASHAMED, Ps 83:17 a. and disturbed
Zec 13:4 prophets will become a. vision
Mr 8:38 whoever becomes a. of me and my
Ro 1:16 I am not a. of the good news;
Heb 11:16 God is not a. of them, to be
Ps 25:3; Lu 9:26; 2Th 3:14; 2Ti 1:8; 2:15.
ASH CONSTELLATION, Job 9:9 making the A.
ASHDOD, Jos 11:22; 1Sa 5:1, 6; Zep 2:4.
ASHER, Ge 30:13; De 33:24; Jg 1:31.
ASHTAROTH, De 1:4; 1Ch 6:71.
ASHTORETH, 1Ki 11:5, 33; 2Ki 23:13.
ASIA, Ac 19:10; 1Co 16:19; Re 1:4.

ASININE, Job 11:12 as an a. zebra born a
ASK, Ps 40:6 sin offering you did not a.
Eph 3:20 beyond all the things we a.
Jas 4:3 a., and yet you do not receive,
1Jo 5:14 a. according to his will,
Ps 2:8; Mt 6:8; Joh 14:13; 1Co 1:22.
ASK BACK, Ge 9:5 I a. the soul of man.
Eze 33:6 blood I shall a. from the watchman
2Ch 24:22; Eze 34:10.
ASKED BACK, Ge 42:22 his blood is a.
ASKING, De 10:12 a. but to fear Jehovah
Mt 7:7 Keep on a., and it will be given
Jas 1:6 keep a. in faith, not doubting
ASKING BACK, Mic 6:8 what is Jehovah a.
ASLEEP, 1Ki 18:27 may be he is a. and
Da 12:2 many of those a. will wake up,
1Co 15:20 first fruits of those fallen a.
1Co 15:51 not all fall a. in death,
Ps 13:3; Mt 27:52; Ac 7:60; 13:36; 1Co 15:
6, 18; 1Th 4:14; 2Pe 3:4.
ASPECT, Zec 5:6 their a. in all earth
ASPIRES, Pr 15:14 one a. to foolishness.
ASS(ES), Nu 22:28 a. said to Balaam
Nu 31:28 one soul out of a.
Zec 9:9 Your king comes riding upon an a.,
Nu 22:23; Jg 5:10; 15:15; Mt 21:5.
ASSAILANT, Job 36:32 against an a.
ASSAULT, Ge 4:8 proceeded to a. Abel
Jg 18:25 that men may a. you
1Sa 22:17 hand to a. the priests of
ASSAULTED, Ac 17:5 a. the house
ASSEMBLIES, Am 5:21 I shall not enjoy a.
ASSEMBLY, Ps 1:5 sinners in the a.
Isa 1:13 uncanny power with the solemn a.
Nu 27:16; Ps 82:1; Ac 19:39; Jas 2:2.
ASSERTIONS, 1Ti 1:7; Tit 3:8 firm a.
ASSIGN, 2Sa 7:23; 1Ch 17:21.
Mt 24:51 punish him and will a.
ASSIGNED, Lu 17:9, 10 he did the things a.
2Co 10:13 boast, not outside a. boundaries,
1Th 5:9 God a. us, not to wrath, but to
ASSIGNERS, Isa 60:17 your task a.
ASSIGNING, 1Ti 1:12 a. me a ministry,
ASSISTANCE, Jg 5:23; Ps 22:19; Isa 10:3.
Isa 31:1 Woe to those going to Egypt for a.
ASSISTING, Php 4:3 keep a. these women
Heb 2:16 not a. angels but Abraham's seed.
ASSOCIATE, Le 6:2; 24:19; Zec 13:7.
ASSOCIATED, Ac 17:4 believers a. with
1Co 7:24 let him remain in it a. with God.
ASSOCIATING, 2Th 3:14 stop a. with him
ASSOCIATION(S), 1Co 15:33 Bad a. spoil
1Pe 5:9 entire a. of brothers in the world
1Pe 2:17.
ASSURANCE, Col 2:2 full a. of their
Heb 6:11 full a. of the hope
2Co 9:4; Heb 10:22.
ASSURE, 1Jo 3:19 we shall a. our hearts
ASSURED, Heb 11:1 Faith is the a.
ASSYRIA, Ge 10:11 A. building Nineveh
Isa 19:23 A. will actually come into Egypt
2Ki 17:6; Jer 50:17; Mic 5:6; Zec 10:10.
ASSYRIAN(S), Isa 14:25 break the A.
Mic 5:5 A. treads upon our dwelling towers,
2Ki 19:35; Isa 10:5, 24; 31:8; Eze 31:3.
ASTIR, Ps 45:1 My heart has become a.
ASTONISHED, Isa 59:16 a. no one interposing
Ac 2:7 they were a. and
ASTONISHING, Jer 5:30 An a. situation
ASTONISHMENT, Jer 18:16 object of a.,
Jer 50:13 Babylon, he will stare in a.
Ac 9:21 those hearing gave way to a.
Jer 49:17; 50:13; Mic 6:16.
ASTOUNDED, Mt 7:28 crowds were a. at

ASTRAY, Pr 28:10 upright ones to go a.
Isa 28:7 gone a. because of liquor
Heb 3:10 always go a. in their hearts,
1Pe 2:25 you were like sheep, going a.
ASTROLOGERS, Mt 2:1 a. from eastern
Da 2:27; 4:7; Mt 2:7, 16.
ASTUTE, Job 5:13 counsel of a. ones
ASUNDER, Heb 11:37 they were sawn a.,
ATHALIAH, 2Ki 8:26; 11:1; 2Ch 24:7.
ATONED, Pr 16:6; Isa 6:7; 22:14; 27:9.
ATONEMENT, Ex 30:10 make a. once a year.
Le 17:11 blood that makes a. by the soul in
De 32:43 a. for the ground
Eze 16:63 when I make a. for you
Da 9:24 to make a. for error
Le 16:6, 16, 30, 33, 34; 2Sa 21:3.
ATONEMENT DAY, Le 23:27; Ac 27:9.
ATTACH, 1Sa 2:36; Isa 14:1; Hab 2:15.
ATTAIN, Ro 9:31 Israel did not a. to
1Co 9:24 Run that you may a. it.
Eph 4:13 a. to the oneness in the faith
Ps 139:6; Ac 26:7; Php 3:11.
ATTENDANCE, Ac 2:46; 8:13.
1Co 7:35 constant a. upon the Lord
ATTENDANTS, Joh 18:36 my a. would have
ATTENDED, Ac 17:25 neither is he a. to
ATTENTION, Ps 37:10 a. to his place
2Pe 1:19 you are doing well in paying a.
Pr 29:12; Isa 21:7; 1Ti 1:4; 4:1.
ATTENTION, PAY, Lu 21:34; Ac 5:35.
ATTENTION, TIME OF, Jer 8:12; 51:18.
ATTENTIVE, Job 37:14 a. to the works
ATTENTIVELY, 1Jo 1:1 viewed a. and our
ATTESTATION, Isa 8:20 To the law and a.
Ru 4:7; Isa 8:16.
ATTIRE, Zep 1:8 wearing foreign a.
ATTITUDE, Ro 15:5 mental a. that Christ
Php 2:5 Keep this mental a.
Php 3:15 be of this mental a.
ATTRACTIVE, Ge 24:16; 26:7; Na 3:4.
AUDACIOUS, Job 41:10 None is so a. that
AUDITORIUM, Ac 19:9 school a. of
AUGUST ONE, Ac 25:21, 25 decision by A.
AUGUSTUS, BAND OF, Ac 27:1 Julius of b.
AUNT, Le 18:14 not come near your a.
AUTHORITATIVE ADVICE, Eph 6:4 a. of
AUTHORITIES, Col 2:15; Tit 3:1.
Ro 13:1 soul be in subjection to a.
Eph 6:12 we have a fight against the a.,
1Pe 3:22 a. and powers were made subject
AUTHORITY, Mt 28:18 All a. given
Joh 5:27 given him a. to do judging,
Joh 10:18 I have a. to surrender it
Joh 19:11 have no a. unless granted
Ro 13:2 who opposes the a. has
1Co 7:4 wife does not exercise a. over
1Co 9:5 have a. to lead about a sister as
Eph 1:21 above every government and a.
Eph 2:2 ruler of the a. of the air,
Col 1:13 delivered us from a. of darkness
Mt 7:29; 20:25; Lu 4:6; 12:5, 11; 1Co 15:
24; Re 17:12.
AUTUMN RAIN, Joe 2:23 a. and spring
AVENGE, Isa 1:24 a. on my enemies.
Ro 12:19 Do not a. yourselves, beloved,
Jg 16:28; Es 8:13; Jer 15:15.
AVENGED, Re 19:2 a. the blood of slaves
AVENGER, Nu 35:12 refuge from blood a.
Ro 13:4 an a. to express wrath
Nu 35:21; De 19:6; Jos 20:9; Ps 78:35.
AVENGING, Ps 79:10; Re 6:10.
AVERT(S), Pr 16:14 the wise man a. it
Isa 47:11 not a. adversity
AVOIDED, Isa 53:3 He was a. by men

AWAKE, Isa 26:19 a. and cry out
Ro 13:11 hour to a. from sleep
1Th 5:6 let us stay a. and keep our
Re 16:15 Happy is the one that stays a.
Lu 21:36; 1Co 16:13; Eph 6:18; Col 4:2.
AWAKEN, Joh 11:11 journeying to a. him
AWAKENING, Ps 17:15 satisfied when a.
AWE, Le 19:30 in a. of my sanctuary.
Isa 29:23 God of Israel regard with a.
Heb 12:28 service with godly fear and a.
AWL, Ex 21:6; De 15:17.
AX(ES), De 19:5 a. hit his fellow man
1Ki 6:7; Lu 3:9.
AXHEAD, 2Ki 6:5 a. fell into the water.
AXIS LORDS, Jos 13:3; Jg 3:3; 16:5.
AZAZEL, Le 16:8, 10, 26.

B

BAAL, 1Ki 18:21 if B. is, go following
2Ki 10:28 Jehu annihilated B. out of Israel
Ro 11:4 who have not bent the knee to B.
Jg 2:13; 1Ki 16:31; 2Ki 10:18; Jer 7:9.
BAAL OF PEOR, Ps 106:28 attach to B.
Nu 25:3; De 4:3; Ho 9:10.
BAAL-PERAZIM, 2Sa 5:20; 1Ch 14:11.
BAAL-ZEBUB, 2Ki 1:2, 3, 6, 16.
BABE(S), Mt 11:25 revealed them to b.
1Co 13:11 when I was a b., I used to speak
1Co 14:20 be b. as to badness; yet full-grown
Mt 21:16; 1Co 3:1.
BABEL, Ge 10:10; 11:9.
BABYLON, Jer 51:6 Flee out of B.,
Re 17:5 B. the Great, the mother of harlots
Isa 21:9; Jer 25:12; Da 3:1; Re 18:2.
BACA BUSHES, 2Sa 5:23; 1Ch 14:14.
BACKBITERS, Ro 1:30 b., haters of God
BACKBITINGS, 2Co 12:20 b., whisperings
BACKWARD, Jer 7:24 b. and not forward
BAD, Ge 3:5 knowing good and b.
Jer 2:13 two b. things my people have done
Da 11:27 heart inclined to doing b.,
Hab 1:13 too pure in eyes to see what is b.;
Ro 7:19 b. that I do not wish is
1Co 15:33 b. associations spoil useful
Ge 2:9; Le 27:10; Pr 2:14.
BADNESS, Pr 6:18 feet run to b.,
Ec 7:15 wicked continuing in his b.
1Co 14:20 be babes as to b.
BAG, 1Sa 25:29 wrapped in the b. of life
Job 14:17 sealed in a b. is my
BAGFUL, Job 28:18 b. of wisdom is worth
BAGGAGE, 1Sa 25:13; 30:24.
BAGPIPE, Da 3:5, 10, 15 sound of b. and
BAIT, Isa 29:21 those who lay b. for
BALAAM, Nu 22:28 ass said to B.
Jude 11 erroneous course of B.
Nu 22:5; 24:1; De 23:4; Mic 6:5; Re 2:14.
BALAK, Nu 22:2; Mic 6:5; Re 2:14.
BALANCES. See also SCALES.
BALANCES, Da 5:27 weighed in the b.
BALDNESS, Le 13:40; De 14:1; Mic 1:16.
BAN, De 13:17; Ezr 10:8; Mic 4:13.
BANDAGES, Lu 24:12; Joh 19:40; 20:5, 7.
BANDING, Da 4:15 b. of iron and copper,
BANDS, Ps 2:3 us tear their b. apart
Ps 116:16; Isa 58:6; Jer 30:8; Na 1:13.
BANISHMENT, Ge 4:11 you are cursed in b.
Ezr 7:26 judgment whether b.
BANK(S), 1Ch 12:15 overflowing its b.
Isa 62:10 b. up, b. up the highway. Rid it
BANKERS, Mt 25:27 deposited with the b.
BANNER(S), Ps 20:5 name of God lift b.
Ca 2:4; 6:4, 10 his b. was love
BANNING, Zec 14:11 no more any b.

BANQUET, Es 2:18 the **b.** of Esther,
Isa 25:6 **b.** of dishes, **b.** of wine
Es 5:4; Ec 7:2.
BANQUETING, Jer 16:8 no house of **b.**
BAPTISM, Lu 12:50 I have a **b.** to be
Ro 6:4 buried our **b.** into his death
Eph 4:5 one Lord, one faith, one **b.**
Mt 3:7; Mr 10:38; Col 2:12; 1Pe 3:21.
BAPTISM IN SYMBOL OF, Lu 3:3; Ac 19:4.
BAPTIST, Mt 3:1; 11:11; 14:2; Lu 7:33.
BAPTIZE, Mt 3:11 **b.** with holy spirit
Mr 1:8; Lu 3:16; Joh 1:26, 33.
BAPTIZED, Ro 6:3 were **b.** into his death
1Co 10:2 **b.** into Moses by means of the
1Co 12:13 all **b.** into one body, whether
Mt 3:13; Ac 2:41; 10:47; 1Co 15:29.
BAPTIZING, Mt 28:19; 1Co 1:17.
BARABBAS, Joh 18:40 B. was a robber
BARAK, Jg 4:6, 8, 14; 5:1, 12; Heb 11:32.
BARBARIANS, Ro 1:14 both to Greeks and B.
BARBERS' RAZOR, Eze 5:1 as a **b.** upon
BARKING, Ps 59:6 They keep **b.** like a
BARNABAS, Ac 15:2; 1Co 9:6; Ga 2:1.
BARREN, Isa 54:1 Cry out you **b.** woman
Lu 23:29 Happy are **b.** women, and
Ge 11:30; Ex 23:26; 1Sa 2:5; Ga 4:27.
BARRICADE, Na 2:5 **b.** will be established
BARRICADED, Job 38:8 who **b.** the sea
BARS, Ps 147:13 **b.** of your gates strong
Jer 28:13 have to make yoke **b.** of iron.
Eze 34:27 break the **b.** of their yoke
Le 26:13; Ps 107:16; Jon 2:6; Na 3:13.
BARSABBAS, Ac 1:23; 15:22.
BARTER, Job 41:6 Will partners **b.** for it?
BARTHOLOMEW, Mt 10:3; Ac 1:13.
BARUCH, Ne 3:20; Jer 32:12; 43:6; 45:2.
BASENESS, Ac 8:22 repent of this **b.**
BASHAN, Ps 22:12 powerful ones of B.
Zec 11:2 Howl, you massive trees of B.
Ps 68:15; Isa 2:13; Am 4:1; Na 1:4.
BASINS, Jg 1:22 fill the sea **b.**
BASIS, Ro 8:20 on the **b.** of hope
Php 3:9 issues from God on the **b.** of faith,
Mt 24:5; Mr 9:39; Ac 4:17; 5:28.
BASKET(S), 2Co 11:33 lowered in a **b.**
Jer 24:2; Am 8:1; Mt 14:20; 15:37.
BATHE, 2Ki 5:10 you must **b.** seven times
BATHED, 2Pe 2:22 sow that was **b.** to
BATH-SHEBA, 2Sa 11:3; 12:24; 1Ki 1:11.
BATTLE, 2Ch 20:15 **b.** is not yours but
Ps 24:8 Jehovah mighty in **b.**
1Co 14:8 who will get ready for **b.?**
De 20:1; 1Sa 17:47; Ec 9:11; Isa 28:6.
BATTLEMENT, Mt 4:5; Lu 4:9.
BEACH, Mt 13:2; Ac 21:5; 27:39.
BEAMED, 1Sa 14:29 eyes **b.** because I
BEAMING, Eze 28:17 your **b.** splendor.
BEAR, Mt 13:23 does **b.** fruit
Joh 15:2 it may **b.** more fruit
Joh 18:37 I should **b.** witness to the truth
Ro 11:18 **b.** the root, but the root **b.** you
Ro 15:1 strong ought to **b.** the weaknesses
1Co 4:12 when being persecuted, we **b.** up;
1Co 10:13 tempted beyond what you can **b.**,
1Sa 17:37; Isa 11:7 Eze 17:23; Heb 9:28.
BEARD(S), 1Sa 21:13; Jer 41:5; Eze 5:1.
BEARING, Col 1:10 **b.** fruit in every
Joh 15:2; Col 1:6; Heb 13:13.
BEARING WITNESS, 1Pe 1:11 **b.** beforehand
BEARS, Joh 8:18; Ro 8:16; 13:4.
BEAST(S), Ex 22:19 lying down with a **b.**
Le 18:23 not give your emission to any **b.**
Ps 50:10 **b.** upon a thousand mountains.
Ec 3:19 superiority over the **b.**

Re 19:20 received the mark of the wild **b.**
Job 18:3; 35:11; Ps 49:12; 73:22; Ec 3:21;
Da 7:3; Re 13:17; 17:3.
BEAT, Ex 39:3; De 25:3; Mt 21:35.
BEATEN, Mr 13:9 be **b.** in synagogues
Lu 12:47 will be **b.** with many strokes
Ex 5:14; De 25:2; 2Co 11:25.
BEATING(S), Ac 21:32 they quit **b.** Paul
Nu 22:25; 2Co 6:5.
BEAUTIFIED, Isa 55:5 Holy One have **b.**
Isa 61:3 planting of Jehovah, for him **b.**
BEAUTIFIES, Ps 149:4 He **b.** the meek
BEAUTIFUL, Mt 23:27 outwardly **b.**
Heb 11:23 they saw the young child was **b.**
2Sa 14:25; Es 2:2; Ca 7:1.
BEAUTIFY, Ezr 7:27 **b.** house of Jehovah
Isa 60:13 **b.** the place of my sanctuary
BEAUTY, Pr 17:6 the **b.** of sons is their fathers.
Eze 28:12 full of wisdom and perfect in **b.**
Isa 23:9; 28:5; Eze 28:17.
BECOME, Ps 2:7 I have **b.** your father
BECOME MANY, Ge 1:28 Be fruitful and **b.**
Ge 9:1, 7; 35:11; Jer 23:3.
BED(S), Mic 2:1 bad, upon their **b.**
Heb 13:4 marriage **b.** be without defilement.
Ps 36:4; Isa 57:2; Lu 8:16.
BEE(S), Jg 14:8; Ps 118:12.
BEELZEBUB, Mt 10:25; 12:24; Mr 3:22.
BEER, Isa 1:22; Ho 4:18 their wheat **b.**
BEER-SHEBA, Ge 21:31; 2Sa 24:15; Am 5:5.
BEFALL, Ge 42:4; Le 10:19; De 31:29.
BEFIT, Lu 3:8 fruits that **b.** repentance
BEFOREHAND, Mr 13:23; Ac 1:16; Ro 9:23.
BEFOULED, Zec 3:4 the **b.** garments
BEG, Ac 21:39; 2Co 5:20; 10:2; Ga 4:12.
BEGGAR, Lu 16:20 certain **b.** Lazarus
BEGGARLY, Ga 4:9 **b.** elementary things
BEGGING, Ro 1:10; 2Co 8:4.
BEGINNING, Joh 1:1 In the **b.** God created
Pr 8:22 Jehovah produced me as the **b.**
Col 1:18 He is the **b.**, the first-born from
1Jo 1:1 which was from the **b.**
1Jo 2:7 commandment from the **b.**
Isa 46:10; Mt 24:8; Mr 10:6; Re 3:14.
BEG OFF, Lu 14:18; Heb 12:25.
BEGOTTEN, Joh 1:18 the only-**b.** god
Joh 3:16 gave his only-**b.** son
Heb 11:17 offer up his only-**b.** Son
1Jo 4:9 sent his only-**b.** Son into
BEHAVE, 1Co 13:5; 2Th 3:7.
BEHAVING, 1Co 7:36 **b.** improperly toward
BEHAVIOR, Jg 2:19 refrain from stubborn **b.**
Mt 16:27 recompense according to **b.**
BEHEADED, Mt 14:10; Mr 6:16; Lu 9:9.
BEHELD, Heb 11:1 Faith realities not **b.**
BEHIND, Ge 19:17 do not look **b.** you
Mt 16:23 Peter, get **b.** me
Php 3:13 Forgetting things **b.** and
Ps 50:17; Isa 38:17; Eze 23:35; Joe 2:3.
BEHOLD, Ac 17:22 Men of Athens, I **b.**
BEING, Heb 1:3 representation of his **b.**,
BEING, DIVINE, Ac 17:29.
BEL, Isa 46:1; Jer 50:2; 51:44.
BELIAL, 2Co 6:15 between Christ and B.?
BELIEVE. See also FAITH, PUT.
BELIEVE, Hab 1:5 activity you will not **b.**
Heb 11:6 **b.** that he is and that he
Jas 2:19 demons **b.** and shudder
Ex 4:5; Ac 15:7; 16:31; 2Th 2:12; 1Jo 4:1.
BELIEVED, Mt 21:32; Ac 4:32; 1Ti 3:16.
BELIEVER(S), Ac 5:14 **b.** being added
1Ti 6:2 good service are **b.**
1Pe 2:7 he is precious, because you are **b.**;
BELIEVES, Joh 5:24 **b.** him that sent me

BELIEVING, 1Jo 5:1 b. Jesus is Christ
BELLIES, Ro 16:18 men slaves of own b.,
BELLIGERENT, 1Ti 3:3; Tit 3:2.
BELLY, Job 1:21 Naked I came out b.
 Ps 127:3 fruitage of the b. is a reward.
 Pr 13:25 b. of wicked ones will be empty.
 Jer 1:5 forming you in the b. I knew you,
 Php 3:19 their God is their b.
 Ge 3:14; Da 2:32; Mt 12:40; 1Co 6:13.
BELONG, Ro 14:8 die, we b. to Jehovah.
BELONGINGS, Mt 25:14 committed his b.
 Mt 19:21; Lu 14:33.
BELOVED, Ro 11:28 they are b. for the
 Re 20:9 camp of holy ones and the b. city.
 Mt 3:17; 1Co 10:14; 2Co 7:1; 1Pe 4:12.
BELSHAZZAR, Da 5:1, 2, 9, 22, 29, 30.
BELT, 2Ki 1:8; Isa 5:27; 11:5; Jer 13:1.
BELTESHAZZAR, Da 1:7; 2:26; 4:19; 5:12.
BEND, Pr 17:23 take a bribe to b. paths
 Eph 3:14 I b. my knees to the Father,
 Php 2:10 name of Jesus every knee should b.
BENEFACTORS, Lu 22:25 are called B.
BENEFICIAL, 1Ti 4:8 godly devotion is b.
 2Ti 3:16 inspired of God and b. for
 Mt 5:29; 1Co 12:7; Tit 3:8.
BENEFIT(S), Jas 2:16 body, of what b.
 Isa 44:10; Mt 16:26; Joh 16:7.
BEN-HADAD, 1Ki 15:18; 20:1; 2Ki 8:7.
BENJAMIN, Ge 35:18; Ps 68:27; Re 7:8.
BEREAVED, Ge 43:14; Isa 49:21; 1Th 2:17.
BEREAVEMENT, Ps 35:12 b. to my soul
BESEECH, 2Ki 20:3; Isa 38:3; Jer 7:16.
BESTIRRING, Pr 28:22 man envious is b.
BETHANY, Mt 21:17; 26:6; Joh 1:28; 11:1.
BETHEL, Ge 28:19; 31:13; Jg 4:5.
BETHLEHEM, Mt 2:1 Jesus born in B.
 Ge 35:19; Ru 2:4; Mic 5:2; Mt 2:5; Lu 2:4.
BETH-PEOR, De 3:29; 34:6; Jos 13:20.
BETHPHAGE, Mt 21:1 at B. Jesus sent two
BETHSAIDA, Mt 11:21; Lu 9:10; Joh 1:44.
BETRAY, Mt 26:21 One of you will b. me.
 Isa 16:3; Joh 6:64; 13:2.
BETRAYED, Mt 27:3 Judas b. him, seeing
 Lu 22:22 Son of man is b.!
BETRAYER, Joh 18:2 Judas, his b., also
BETTER, Ec 2:24 nothing b. than eat
BETTER RESURRECTION, Heb 11:35.
BEWAILED, Jer 35:10 not be b., neither
BEWILDERED, Isa 19:3 spirit of Egypt b.
 Ac 2:6 multitude were b.,
BEWILDERMENT, De 28:28; Zec 12:4.
BEYOND, 2Co 4:7 power b. what is normal
 Ga 1:9 something b. what you accepted,
BEZALEL, Ex 31:2; 35:30; 36:1; 38:22.
BIASED LEANING, 1Ti 5:21 prejudgment, b.
BILDAD, Job 2:11; 8:1; 18:1; 25:1; 42:9.
BIND, Ps 149:8 to b. their kings with
 Isa 61:1 me to b. up the brokenhearted
 Mt 13:30 collect the weeds and b. them
 Mt 23:4 They b. up heavy loads and put
 Nu 30:2; Ps 118:27; Pr 6:21.
BIRD(S), Isa 46:11 calling a b. of prey
 Mt 8:20 Foxes have dens and b. have roosts,
 Re 18:2 of every unclean and hated b.
 Le 14:4; De 14:11; Isa 31:5; Ac 10:12.
BIRTH(S), Ec 3:2 time for b. and a time
 Jas 1:15 gives b. to sin; in turn
 1Pe 1:3 he gave us a new b. to a
 Re 12:2 cries out in agony to give b.
 Ex 28:10; Isa 37:3; 66:9; Eze 16:3.
BIRTHDAY, Ge 40:20; Mt 14:6; Mr 6:21.
BIRTHRIGHT, Ge 25:34 despised the b.
 Ge 27:36 My b. he has taken
BISHOP. See OVERSEER(S).

BITTER, Ps 64:3 Who have b. speech.
 Hab 1:6 Chaldeans, the nation b. and
 Jas 3:11 the sweet and the b. to bubble out
 Ex 1:14; 12:8; Job 13:26; Isa 5:20; 24:9.
BITTERLY, Isa 33:7 messengers weep b.
 Eze 27:30 over you they will cry out b.
 Mt 26:75 he went outside and wept b.
 Col 3:19 do not be b. angry with them.
BITTERNESS, Job 10:1 speak in the b.
 2Sa 2:26; Pr 14:10; Isa 38:15; Eph 4:31.
BLAB, Ac 23:22 do not b. to anyone that
BLACKNESS, 2Pe 2:17 b. of darkness has
 Jude 13 b. stands reserved forever.
BLADE, Ge 3:24 flaming b. of a sword
BLAMELESS, Job 2:3 man b. and upright,
 Php 2:15 b. and innocent, children
 1Th 5:23 preserved b. at the presence of
BLANKET, Jg 4:18 covered him with a b.
BLASPHEME, 1Ti 1:20; Jas 2:7; Re 13:6.
BLASPHEMED, Re 16:21 b. God due to the
BLASPHEMER(S), 1Ti 1:13; 2Ti 3:2.
BLASPHEMES, Mr 3:29 b. against holy
BLASPHEMOUS, Ac 6:11; Re 17:3.
BLASPHEMOUSLY, Ac 13:45 b. contradicting
 Mt 26:65; Mr 14:64; Joh 10:33; Re 2:9.
BLASPHEMY, Mt 12:31 b. against the spirit
 Mt 26:65; Mr 14:64; Joh 10:33; Re 2:9.
BLAST, 2Sa 22:16; Ps 18:15; Isa 25:4.
BLAZE, Ex 22:24; De 31:17; Jg 6:39.
BLAZED, Nu 11:33; Jg 2:14; 3:8; 10:7.
BLEMISH, Eph 5:27 be holy and without b.
 Php 2:15 without a b. in among a crooked
BLEMISH, WITHOUT, Eph 1:4; Re 14:5.
BLESS, Nu 6:24 may Jehovah b. you
 Ps 29:11 will b. his people with peace
 Ps 145:21 let all flesh b. his holy name
 1Co 10:16 The cup of blessing which we b.
 Ge 12:2; 32:26; Ru 2:4; Ps 62:4; Lu 6:28.
BLESSED, Ge 1:28 God b. them and
 Heb 7:7 less is b. by the greater.
 De 7:14; Job 1:21; Ps 72:19; 1Pe 1:3.
BLESSING(S), De 30:19 b. malediction
 Pr 10:22 b. of Jehovah makes rich
 Mal 3:10 empty out upon you a b.
 Ro 12:14 be b. and do not be cursing.
 Ge 12:2; Pr 28:20; Mal 2:2; 1Pe 3:9.
BLEW, Joh 20:22 he b. upon them
BLIND, Isa 35:5 eyes of the b. will be
 Isa 56:10 His watchmen are b. None of
 Mt 15:14 b. guides is what they are.
 1Pe 2:16 freedom, not as a b. for badness,
 De 28:29; Ps 146:8; Isa 42:7; Mt 23:24.
BLINDED, 2Co 4:4 god of has b. the
 Joh 12:40; 1Jo 2:11.
BLINDNESS, Ge 19:11; 2Ki 6:18.
BLINDS, De 16:19 for the bribe b.
BLINKING, Pr 16:30 b. eyes to scheme
BLISTERS, Ex 9:9 b. upon man and beast
BLOCKADED, Isa 1:8 like a b. city
BLOOD, Ge 9:4 b.—you must not eat.
 Le 7:26 you must not eat any b.
 Le 17:11 the soul of the flesh is in the b.
 Le 17:13 pour its b. out and cover it with
 Le 17:14 You must not eat the b. of any sort
 Nu 35:12 refuge from the b. avenger
 Nu 35:33 it is b. that pollutes the land
 1Ch 11:19 unthinkable to drink b. of
 Jer 2:34 in your skirts the b. marks
 Mt 26:28 this means my b. of the covenant
 Joh 6:54 drinks my b. has everlasting life
 Ac 15:20 abstain from b.
 Ac 15:29 keep yourselves free from b.
 1Co 15:50 flesh and b. cannot inherit God's
 Heb 9:22 unless b. is poured out no

1Jo 1:7 **b.** of Jesus cleanses us from sin
Re 18:24 in her was found the **b.** of holy
Ge 4:10; Pr 6:17; Eze 3:18; Mt 23:35;
27:25; Ac 20:28; Heb 9:20; Re 7:14; 14:20.
BLOODGUILTY, Ps 55:23 **b.** will not live
Ps 59:2 from **b.** men save me
BLOODSHED, Ps 5:6 **b.** Jehovah detests
Mic 3:10 building Zion with acts of **b.**
BLOODTHIRSTY, Pr 29:10 **b.** men hate
BLOOM, 1Co 7:36 past the **b.** of youth,
BLOSSOM(S), Isa 35:1 desert **b.** as the
Ex 37:17; Isa 5:24; 27:6.
BLOT. See also WIPE, WIPED.
BLOT, Re 3:5 by no means **b.** out his name
BLOTTED, Ac 3:19; Col 2:14.
BLOW(S), Ex 9:14 sending my **b.** against your
Le 26:21 inflict seven times more **b.**
2Ch 21:14 Jehovah dealing a **b.** to your
Eze 24:16 taking away from you by a **b.**
1Co 9:26 I am directing my **b.**
BLOWN, Jas 1:6 the wind and **b.** about.
BLUNT, Ec 10:10 iron tool become **b.**
BLUNTED, Ro 11:7 their sensibilities **b.**
BOANERGES, Mr 3:17 surname **B.**
BOAST, 1Co 1:29 that no flesh might **b.**
Ps 34:2; 97:7; Pr 27:1.
BOASTFUL, Pr 29:8 Men of **b.** talk
BOASTING, Ro 3:27; 2Co 9:3; Eph 2:9.
BOASTS, 1Co 1:31 He that **b.,** let him
BOAT(S), Mt 4:22; Jas 3:4; Re 18:19.
BOAZ, Ru 2:1; 4:9, 13; 1Ki 7:21; Mt 1:5.
BODIES, Ro 12:1 your **b.** a sacrifice
1Co 6:15 your **b.** are members of Christ
Mt 27:52; Ro 8:11; 1Co 15:40.
BODILY, Lu 3:22; 1Ti 4:8.
BODY, Mt 10:28 kill **b.** but cannot
1Co 6:20 glorify God in the **b.** of you
1Co 12:18 God set the members in the **b.**
1Co 15:44 sown a physical **b.,** it is raised
Col 1:18 head of the **b.,** the congregation
Heb 10:5 you prepared a **b.** for me.
Mt 26:12; Lu 11:34; Joh 2:21.
BODYGUARD, 1Sa 22:14 chief over your **b.**
BODY OF CHRIST, 1Co 12:27; Eph 4:12.
BOILS, Ex 9:11; Job 2:7.
BOISTEROUS, Ps 39:6; Pr 9:13.
BOLD, Pr 21:29 wicked put on a **b.** face,
2Co 10:2 counting on taking **b.** measures
BOLDLY, Ac 9:27; 18:26 spoken **b.**
BOLDNESS, Eph 6:20 speak with **b.** as I ought
1Th 2:2 mustered up **b.** by means of our God
Ac 4:29, 31; 14:3; Heb 10:19.
BOND(S), Eze 20:37 **b.** of the covenant
Eph 4:3 oneness in the uniting **b.** of peace
Php 1:13 my prison **b.** have become public
Col 3:14 love is a perfect **b.** of union
Ac 20:23; 26:31; Col 4:3; Heb 11:36.
BONE(S), Ps 34:20 guarding the **b.** of
Pr 14:30 jealousy is rottenness to the **b.**
Pr 25:15 mild tongue can break a **b.**
Jer 20:9 burning fire shut up in my **b.**
Eze 37:1 valley plain full of **b.**
Mt 23:27 inside are full of dead men's **b.**
Joh 19:36 Not a **b.** of his will be crushed.
Ge 2:23; Job 10:11; Ps 22:14; Hab 3:16.
BOOK(S), Ec 12:12 making of many **b.**
Isa 29:11 the words of the **b.** sealed up
Isa 34:16 Search in the **b.** of Jehovah
Da 7:10 there were **b.** that were opened.
Da 9:2 discerned by **b.** the number of years
Da 12:4 seal up the **b.,** until time end
Heb 10:9 sprinkled the **b.** itself and all
Ex 17:14; Mr 12:26; Ac 19:19; Heb 10:7.
BOOMING, Job 36:33 His **b.** tells about

BOOTHS, De 16:13 The festival of **b.** you
Le 23:42; De 16:16; Ezr 3:4; Ne 8:14.
BOOTY, Zep 3:8 rising up to the **b.,**
BORDERS, Isa 26:15 extended all the **b.**
BORE, Isa 53:4 our sicknesses he **b.**
BORED, Jg 16:21 **b.** his eyes out
Job 30:17 my bones have been **b.**
BORN, Job 14:1 Man, **b.** of woman, is
Ec 7:1 day of death than day of being **b.**
Isa 9:6 there has been a child **b.** to us
Mt 1:16 of Mary whom Jesus was **b.**
Lu 2:11 was **b.** to you today a Savior
Joh 3:3 Unless anyone is **b.** again, he
Ps 87:5; Mt 2:1; Joh 18:37; 1 Co 15:8.
BORNE, Ps 69:7 I have **b.** reproach
Job 34:31; Joh 5:37; 1Co 15:49.
BORROW, De 15:6; Mt 5:42.
De 28:12 you will not **b.**
BORROWED, 2Ki 6:5; Ne 5:4.
BORROWER, Pr 22:7; Isa 24:2.
BORROWING, Ps 37:21 wicked is **b.** and
BOSOM, Lu 16:22; Joh 1:18; 13:23.
BOUGHS, Le 23:40 take **b.** of trees
Da 4:14 cut off its **b.**
BOUGHT, Mt 13:46 one pearl and **b.** it
1Co 7:23 You were **b.** with a price
2Pe 2:1 disown the owner that **b.** them
Re 5:9 with your blood you **b.** persons
Le 27:24; 2Sa 12:3; Lu 14:18.
BOUND, Ps 146:7 releasing those **b.**
Mt 16:19 bind on earth **b.** in the heavens
1Co 7:39 A wife is **b.** during all the time
Re 20:2 **b.** him for a thousand years,
Ge 22:9; Lu 13:16; Ac 20:22; Ro 7:2.
BOUNDARIES, Ps 74:17; Isa 60:18.
BOUNDARY, Isa 19:19 pillar its **b.**
De 11:24.
BOUNTIFULLY, 2Co 9:6 he that sows **b.**
BOUTS, Ro 13:13 and drunken **b.,**
BOW, Ho 2:18 the **b.** I shall break
Ps 46:9; Re 6:2.
BOW DOWN, De 30:17 **b.** to other gods
Ps 138:2 I shall **b.** toward your holy temple
Isa 2:8 To the work of hands they **b.,**
Ex 20:5; Ps 66:4; Isa 27:13; Zec 14:16.
BOWED, 2Ch 7:3 they **b.** low with their
BOWELS, Zep 1:17 their **b.** like dung
BOWL(S), 2Ki 21:13; Re 16:1; 17:1.
BOWSHOT, Ge 21:16 distance of a **b.**
BOY(S), Pr 22:6 train up a **b.** according
Isa 11:6 little **b.** will be leader over
Isa 65:20 die as a mere **b.,** although
Mt 2:16; 17:18; 21:15; Joh 4:51.
BOYHOOD, 1Sa 17:33 man of war from **b.**
BRAG, Jer 9:24 one bragging himself **b.**
1Co 13:4 Love does not **b.,**
BRAGGART, Pr 21:24 self-assuming **b.** is
BRAGGER, Isa 29:20 **b.** come to finish
BRAGGING, Ps 94:4 all keep **b.** about
BRAGS, Jas 3:5; 4:16 tongue makes **b.**
BRAIDED, Mt 27:29; Mr 15:17; Joh 19:2.
BRAIDING OF HAIR, 1Ti 2:9; 1Pe 3:3.
BRANCH(ES), Mt 21:8 crowd cut **b.** from trees
Joh 15:2 **b.** not bearing
Ro 11:21 not spare the natural **b.,**
Mt 24:32; Lu 13:19; Joh 15:4, 6; Ro 11:16.
BRAND MARKS, Ga 6:17 my body the **b.**
BRASS, 1Co 13:1 a sounding piece of **b.**
BRAWLER, 1Ti 3:3; Tit 1:7 not drunken **b.**
BRAZIER, Jer 36:22, 23 **b.** burning before
BREACHES, Isa 22:9; Eze 30:16.
BREAD, Am 8:11 a famine, not for **b.**
Mt 4:4 live, not on **b.** alone,
Joh 6:35 I am the **b.** of life.

Ge 3:19; Ps 37:25; Isa 55:2; Mt 6:11.
BREADTH, Eph 3:18; Re 20:9; 21:16.
BREAK, Ps 68:21 God will **b.** his enemies
Mt 6:19 thieves **b.** in and steal
Jg 2:1; Ec 3:3; 1Co 10:16; Ga 4:27.
BREAKDOWN, Jer 6:14 try to heal the **b.**
Isa 30:13; 65:14; Jer 30:12; 50:22.
BREAKERS, Jon 2:3 **b.** and waves passed over
BREAKS, Mt 5:19 **b.** one of these least
BREAST(S), Pr 5:19 **b.** intoxicate you
Lu 18:13 kept beating his **b.**
Lu 23:48; Joh 13:25.
BREASTBANDS, Jer 2:32 bride forget **b.?**
BREASTPIECE, Ex 28:15 make the **b.** of
Ex 25:7; 28:29; Le 8:8.
BREASTPLATE, Eph 6:14 **b.** righteousness,
1Th 5:8 have on the **b.** of faith and love
BREATH, Ge 2:7 nostrils the **b.** of life,
Ge 7:22; Isa 42:5; Ac 17:25.
BREATHING, Ps 150:6 **b.** thing praise Jah.
BREEZE, Ac 2:2 noise like a stiff **b.,**
BREEZY, Ge 3:8 **b.** part of the day,
BRIBE, De 10:17 nor accepts a **b.,**
Mic 3:11 head ones judge for a **b.,**
Ex 23:8; Pr 17:23; Isa 1:23; 5:23; 33:15.
BRIBERY, Ps 26:10 hand is full of **b.**
BRICKS, Ge 11:3; Ex 1:14; 5:7.
BRIDE, Re 21:2 as a **b.** adorned for her
Isa 61:10; 62:5; Joh 3:29; Re 18:23.
BRIDEGROOM, Isa 62:5 exultation of a **b.**
Mt 25:1 went out to meet the **b.**
Jer 33:11; Mt 9:15; 25:5, 6, 10; Joh 3:29.
BRIDLE(S), Isa 30:28 spirit is like a **b.**
Jas 1:26 If any man does not **b.** his tongue,
Jas 3:3 put **b.** in the mouths of horses
BRIGHTNESS, Pr 15:30 **b.** of the eyes
Isa 60:3 kings to the **b.** of your shining
Da 12:3 shine like the **b.** of the expanse;
Isa 59:9; 62:1; Eze 10:4; Da 2:31.
BRILLIANCE, Ac 26:13 light beyond the **b.**
BRILLIANT, Job 37:21 **b.** in the skies,
BRINGING, Da 12:3 **b.** to righteousness,
BRISTLE, Job 4:15 hair began to **b.**
BROAD WAY(S), Mt 12:19; Ac 5:15.
BROKEN, Ps 34:20 Not one has been **b.**
Ps 119:126 They have **b.** your law.
Isa 8:15 stumble fall be **b.,**
Isa 24:5 the lasting covenant.
Ge 7:11; Ps 51:17; Isa 28:13; Jer 2:13.
BROTHER(S), Ge 4:9 Where is Abel your **b.?**
Ne 4:14 fight for your **b.,**
Ps 49:7 redeem even a **b.,**
Ps 133:1 For **b.** to dwell together in unity!
Pr 18:24 friend sticking closer than a **b.**
Pr 27:10 than a **b.** that is far away.
Jer 31:34 no more teach his **b.,**
Hag 2:22 each one by the sword of his **b.**
Mt 23:8 whereas all you are **b.**
Mr 13:12 **b.** will deliver **b.** over to death
1Pe 5:9 the entire association of your **b.**
Re 12:10 accuser of our **b.** has been hurled
Ge 43:3; Eze 38:21; Mt 5:22; 12:49, 50;
18:15; 25:40; Ac 15:36; Heb 2:11.
BROTHERHOOD, Zec 11:14 break the **b.**
BROTHER-IN-LAW MARRIAGE, De 25:5.
Ge 38:8; De 25:7 perform **b.**
BROTHERLY LOVE, Ro 12:10; Heb 13:1.
BROWBEAT, 1Co 9:27 I **b.** my body
BRUISE, Ge 3:15 **b.** you in the head
BUBBLE, Jas 3:11 sweet and bitter to **b.**
BUCK, Eze 34:22; 45:23 **b.** of the goats
BUDDED, Heb 9:4 rod of Aaron that **b.**
BUILD, Ps 102:16 Jehovah will **b.** Zion;

Isa 65:22 not **b.** and someone else have
Jer 1:10 tear down, to **b.** and to plant.
Mt 16:18 on this rock-mass I will **b.** my
1Co 10:23 not all things **b.** up.
1Ch 28:6; Ec 3:3; Ac 7:49; 20:32.
BUILDER(S), Heb 11:10 **b.** is God.
1Pe 2:7 stone that the **b.** rejected
Mt 21:42; Ac 4:11.
BUILDING, Mic 3:10 **b.** Zion with acts
Lu 17:28 they were planting, they were **b.**
1Co 3:9 You people are God's **b.**
1Co 3:10 let each keep watching how he is **b.**
Eph 2:21 whole **b.,** being harmoniously
Eph 4:29 whatever saying is good for **b.**
1Ki 6:38; Ezr 4:4; 2Co 5:1; Jude 20.
BUILDS, Ps 127:1 Unless Jehovah **b.**
1Co 8:1 love **b.** up.
BUILT, Zep 1:13 **b.** houses but not have
Mt 7:24 **b.** upon the rock-mass,
Joh 2:20 temple was **b.** in forty-six years,
Eph 2:20 **b.** upon the foundation of
Col 2:7 rooted and being **b.** up
1Ki 6:2; Pr 24:3; 1Co 3:14; Eph 2:22.
BULL(S), Ex 21:28 **b.** is to be stoned
Isa 1:3 A **b.** knows its buyer,
Isa 11:7 lion will eat straw like the **b.**
1Co 9:9 must not muzzle a **b.** when it is
Heb 9:12 blood of goats and **b.**
Le 16:6; Ps 106:20; Pr 7:22; Heb 10:4.
BULWARK(S) (siege works), Ps 91:4.
BURDEN(S), Ps 55:22 **b.** upon Jehovah
Ga 6:2 carrying the **b.** of one another,
BURDENSOME, Zec 12:3 Jerusalem a **b.**
1Jo 5:3 his commandments are no **b.,**
BURIAL PLACE(S), Ps 5:9 throat is **b.;**
Ps 88:11 loving-kindness declared in the **b.**
Isa 22:16 hewed out for yourself a **b.?**
Isa 53:9 make his **b.** with the wicked ones.
Isa 65:4; Jer 20:17; Eze 32:22; 37:12.
BURIED, Ac 2:29 David deceased **b.**
Ro 6:4 **b.** with him through our baptism
Ru 1:17; Jer 16:4, 6; Eze 39:15; 1Co 15:4.
BURN, Eze 39:9 **b.** the armor and shields
Re 17:16 hate the harlot **b.** her with
Na 2:13; Mt 13:30.
BURNED, Mic 1:7 gifts **b.** in the fire
1Co 3:15 if anyone's work is **b.,**
Re 18:8 she will be completely **b.**
BURNING, Ex 3:2 the thornbush was **b.**
Jer 20:9 a **b.** fire shut up in my bones;
Da 3:17 Out of the **b.** fiery furnace
De 4:11; Lu 12:35; 1Pe 4:12; Re 18:9.
BURNT OFFERING(S), Ge 8:20; Le 16:24;
1Sa 15:22; Ps 51:16; Jer 19:5.
Ps 40:6 **b.** you did not ask for.
BURST, Isa 24:19 The land has **b.,**
Mt 9:17; Lu 5:37.
BURY, Eze 39:11 **b.** Gog and all his
Lu 9:60 Let the dead **b.** their dead,
Ge 23:4; De 21:23; Jer 19:11.
BURYING, 2Ki 9:10 will be no one **b.** her.
Ps 79:3; Jer 14:16; Eze 39:13, 14.
BUSINESS(ES), 1Ki 19:13 What is your **b.**
Ps 107:23 Doing on vast waters,
Ro 12:11 Do not loiter at your **b.**
2Ti 2:4 no soldier involves himself in **b.**
Jas 4:13 engage in **b.** and make profits,
2Ki 23:5; Mic 3:1; Mt 22:5; Ac 6:3; 19:25.
BUSYBODY, 1Pe 4:15 none suffer as a **b.**
BUY, Ge 47:19 B. us and our land for
Pr 23:23 B. truth and do not sell it
Isa 55:1 all you thirsty ones! Come, **b.**
1Co 7:30 those **b.** as those not possessing,
Re 13:17 able to **b.** or sell except

Ru 4:4, 8; Jer 32:44; Re 3:18; 18:11.
BUYER, Pr 20:14 It is bad! says the **b.**,
BUYING, Col 4:5 **b.** out opportune time
BUYS, Mt 13:44 sells things and **b.**
BYGONE TIME, Ne 12:46 days of David **b.**
BYPASSED, Isa 24:5 **b.** laws, changed the
BYWORD, Job 30:9 I become a **b.** to them.

C

CAESAR, Mr 12:17 Pay **C.** things to C.,
Lu 23:2 forbidding the paying of taxes to C.
Joh 19:15 We have no king but **C.**
Mt 22:17; Lu 2:1; 20:25; Joh 19:12.
CAESAREA, Mt 16:13; Ac 10:1; 23:23.
CAGE, Eze 19:9 they put him in the **c.**
CAIAPHAS, Joh 11:49; 18:13, 28; Ac 4:6.
CAIN, Ge 4:1; Heb 11:4; 1Jo 3:12.
CALAMITIES, De 32:23 shall increase **c.**
Ps 34:19 many are the **c.** of the righteous
CALAMITOUS, Ec 7:14 on a **c.** day see
Am 6:3 putting out of your mind the **c.** day,
CALAMITY, Ps 27:5 hide me in the day of **c.**;
Isa 45:7 making peace and creating **c.**,
Jer 1:14 Out of the north **c.** will be
Jer 25:29 starting off in bringing **c.**,
Jer 38:4 peace of this people but for **c.**
Ps 71:24; 107:26; Jer 2:27; 25:6.
CALCULATE, Re 13:18 **c.** number of beast.
CALCULATED, Pr 23:7; Lu 14:28; Ac 19:19.
CALDRON, 18a 2:14 a thrust into the **c.**
CALEB, Nu 13:30; 14:24; 26:65; Jg 1:20.
CALF, Ex 32:4; Ps 106:19; Isa 11:6.
CALL, Isa 55:6 **c.** to him while he proves to be
Isa 65:24 before they **c.** out I myself shall
Php 3:14 goal for prize of upward **c.**
Ge 2:19; Isa 58:1; 60:14, 18; 65:15.
CALLED, Ro 8:30 foreordained are the **c.**
Ro 9:26 **c.** sons of living God.
1Co 1:9 **c.** into sharing with Christ
1Co 1:26 not many wise were **c.**,
Ga 5:13 **c.** for freedom
Eph 4:4 **c.** in the one hope
2Ti 1:9 **c.** us with a holy calling
1Pe 2:9 **c.** you out of darkness into his
1Jo 3:1 **c.** children of God
Re 17:14 those **c.** and chosen and faithful
Isa 54:5; 62:2; 1Th 4:7; 1Pe 2:21.
CALLING, Ps 145:18 near those **c.** upon
Ro 11:29 **c.** are not things he will regret.
Eph 4:1 walk worthily of the **c.**
2Ti 1:9 saved and called us with a holy **c.**,
Heb 3:1 partakers of the heavenly **c.**,
2Pe 1:10 do utmost to make **c.** sure
Ge 4:26; Ga 2:11; 1Co 1:26; 2Th 1:11.
CALLS, Ac 2:21 everyone who **c.** upon
Ex 21:17; Joe 2:32; Ro 10:13.
CALM, Pr 14:30 A **c.** heart is the life
1Ki 19:12; Job 4:16; Ps 107:29; Mt 8:26.
CALMNESS, Pr 15:4 **c.** of the tongue
CALVES, Mal 4:2 paw like fattened **c.**
1Ki 12:28; 2Ki 17:16; 2Ch 13:8.
CAMEL(S), Ge 24:10, 11; Mt 19:24; 23:24.
CAMEL'S HAIR, Mr 1:6 clothed with **c.**
CAMP, Heb 13:11 burned up outside the **c.**
Ex 14:19; Nu 1:52; Re 20:9.
CANA, Joh 2:1; 4:46.
CANAAN, Ge 17:8; Nu 35:10; Jg 4:23.
CANAANITE, Ex 3:8; 13:5; Jos 3:10.
CANALS, 2Ki 19:24; Isa 37:25; Eze 29:3.
CAPABLE, Ac 15:10 nor **c.** of draining?
Ex 18:21; Pr 12:4; 31:10; Da 5:11.
CAPABLENESS, Pr 31:29 have shown **c.**,
CAPACITY, 1Jo 5:20 given intellectual **c.**
CAPERNAUM, Mt 11:23 **C.** Down to Hades

Mt 4:13; Lu 4:23; Joh 2:12; 6:59.
CAPTAIN(S), Lu 22:4; Ac 4:1; 5:24, 26.
CAPTIVE(S), Jg 5:12 lead your **c.** away.
Isa 52:2 O **c.** daughter of Zion.
Da 11:8 with the **c.** he will come to Egypt.
Lu 21:24 be led **c.** into all the nations,
Ro 7:23 leading me **c.** to sin's law
Ps 68:18; Lu 4:18; Eph 4:8; 2Ti 3:6.
CAPTIVITY. See also EXILE(S).
CAPTIVITY, Jer 43:11 whoever is due for **c.**
Da 11:33 stumble by sword and flame, by **c.**
2Co 10:5 bringing every thought into **c.**
Ne 1:3; Am 9:4; Na 3:10.
CAPTORS, 1Ki 8:47 in the land of their **c.**,
CAPTURED, Zec 14:2 Jerusalem will be **c.**
CARAVAN(S), Ge 37:25; Isa 21:13.
CARCASS(ES), Eze 43:9 remove **c.** of kings
Mt 24:28 Wherever the **c.** is, there eagles
Ge 15:11; Le 26:30; Isa 14:19; Am 8:3.
CARE, 1Co 12:25 have **c.** for one another.
CAREFREE, Pr 11:15 is keeping **c.**
CARELESS, Isa 32:9 You **c.** daughters
CARMEL, 1Ki 18:19; Isa 35:2; Am 1:2.
CARPENTER, Mr 6:3 This is the **c.** the
CARRIES, Ps 68:19 Jehovah **c.** load
CARRY, 1Co 16:13 **c.** on as men,
Ga 6:5 each one will **c.** his own load.
CARRYING BAR, Na 1:13 shall break **c.**
CARRY OUT, 2Ch 6:10 Jehovah **c.** his word
Ps 21:11 ideas they are unable to **c.**
Jer 33:14 I shall **c.** word spoken
CASE, Ps 74:22 God, do conduct own **c.**
1Co 6:1 has a **c.** against the other court
CASE AT LAW, Job 31:13 their **c.** with me
CASE OF JUSTICE, Job 23:4 present a **c.**
CAST, Joh 12:31 ruler of this world **c.** out
CATASTROPHE, Na 3:19 no relief **c.**
Isa 15:5; Am 6:6.
CATCH, Nu 32:23 your sin will **c.** up with you.
Lu 5:4 let down your nets for a **c.**
CATCHES, 1Co 3:19 He **c.** the wise in
CATERPILLAR, Joe 1:4; Am 4:9.
CATTLE, Ps 107:38; 1Co 15:39.
CAUSE, Ex 9:16 for this **c.** I have kept
Ps 69:4 those hating me without **c.** have
Ga 4:18 sought for in a fine **c.** at all
2Ti 1:12 For this very **c.** suffering
Job 2:3; 5:8; Ps 109:3; 119:161.
CAUSE DEATH, Heb 2:14 one to **c.** the Devil
CAUTIOUS, Ge 3:1 serpent proved most **c.**
Mt 10:16 **c.** as serpents and yet innocent
CAVE, Jer 7:11 a mere **c.** of robbers
Mt 21:13 making it a **c.** of robbers.
CEDAR(S), Le 14:4; 1Ki 4:33; Eze 31:8.
CELEBRATE, Ex 12:14; Zec 14:16.
CELEBRATED, Heb 11:28 **c.** the passover
CELEBRATING, 18a 18:7; Ps 42:4.
CELESTIAL LIGHTS, Jas 1:17 Father of **c.**
CENSER, Heb 9:4 had a golden **c.** and ark
CENSUS, Ex 30:12 take a **c.** of them
2Ch 2:17 **c.** David had taken
CEPHAS, 1Co 9:5; 15:5; Ga 2:14.
CEREALS, Ge 42:1; 44:2; Ne 10:31.
CEREMONIALLY CLEAN, Joh 11:55.
CERTIFICATE, De 24:1; Mt 19:7.
CERTIFIED, Ac 6:3 seven **c.** men to
CESSATION, Ezr 6:8 given without **c.**
Isa 38:11 inhabitants of land of **c.**
CHAFF, Da 2:35 crushed like the **c.**
Ps 35:5; Isa 41:15; Zep 2:2; Mt 3:12.
CHAINS, Ac 12:7 **c.** fell off his hands
Eph 6:20 ambassador in **c.**; that
CHALDEANS, Jer 37:13 to **C.** falling away
Jer 21:9; 25:12; 40:9; Hab 1:6; Ac 7:4.

CHALK, Isa 44:13 traces it out with **c**.
CHALLENGE, Jer 49:19; 50:44 who **c**. me
CHAMPION, 1Sa 17:4, 23 **c**. Goliath from Gath
CHANCE, Ge 31:28 give me a **c**. to kiss
CHANCED, 2Sa 1:6 **c**. to be on Mount
CHANGE, Jer 13:23 Cushite **c**. his skin?
  Da 7:25 he will intend to **c**. times and law,
  Zep 3:9 peoples the **c**. to a pure language,
  Ge 35:2; Pr 24:21; Ac 6:14; Heb 7:12.
CHANGED, Jer 23:36 you **c**. the words of
  Mal 3:6 I am Jehovah; I have not **c**.
CHANGING, 1Co 7:31 scene of world is **c**.
CHANNEL(S), Job 38:25; Eze 31:4.
CHANT, 2Sa 1:17; 2Ch 35:25; Eze 27:32.
CHARCOALS, Isa 47:14 no glow of **c**. for
CHARGE, Mt 4:6 He will give angels a **c**.
  Mt 27:37 posted above his head the **c**.
CHARGED, Ro 5:13 sin is not **c**. when
  Phm 18 anything, keep this **c**. to my account.
CHARGING, 2Ti 2:14 **c**. them before God
CHARIOT(S), Jg 5:28 war **c**. delayed
  2Ki 10:15 get up into the **c**. with him
  Isa 31:1 Egypt trust in war **c**.
  Na 2:3 fire of iron [fittings] is the war **c**.
  2Ki 2:11; Isa 43:17; Jer 46:9; Zec 9:10.
CHARM, Ps 45:2; Pr 3:22; 4:9; 11:16.
CHARMER(S), Isa 3:3 magical, skilled **c**.
  Isa 19:3 resort to the **c**. and to the spirit
CHARMING, Pr 5:19; Zec 4:7.
CHASER, Isa 1:23 lover of a bribe and **c**.
CHASM, Lu 16:26 **c**. between us and you
CHASTE, 2Co 11:2 present you as a **c**.
  Jas 3:17 wisdom from above is first **c**.,
  Php 4:8; Tit 2:5; 1Pe 3:2.
CHASTEN. See DISCIPLINE.
CHASTISE, Le 26:18 **c**. you seven times
  Pr 19:18 **C**. your son while there exists
  Pr 29:17 **C**. your son and he will bring rest
CHASTISEMENT, Jer 30:14.
CHASTITY, 2Co 11:3 **c**. due Christ.
CHASTENESS, 1Ti 4:12; 5:2 example in **c**.
CHATTERING, 3Jo 10 **c**. with wicked words
CHEAP, La 1:8 treated her as **c**.
CHEATING, Pr 11:1; 20:23 **c**. scales
CHECK, Pr 10:19 keeping his lips in **c**.
CHEEK(S), Job 16:10 struck my **c**.,
  Mt 5:39 slaps your right **c**., turn
  La 3:30; Mic 5:1; Lu 6:29.
CHEER, Ac 14:17 filling hearts with **c**.
  2Co 2:2 who is there to **c**. me except
CHEERFUL, 2Co 9:7 God loves a **c**. giver
  Php 2:19 send Timothy that I may be a **c**.
CHEERING, Ec 2:3 **c**. my flesh with wine,
CHEMOSH, Jg 11:24; 1Ki 11:7; Jer 48:7.
CHERETHITES, 1Sa 30:14; 2Sa 20:7.
CHERISHES, Eph 5:29; 1Th 2:7.
CHERUB(S), Ps 18:10 riding upon a **c**.
  Eze 28:14 You are the anointed **c**. that
  Heb 9:5 **c**. overshadowing
  Ex 25:22; 1Sa 4:4; Ps 99:1; Eze 10:2.
CHIEF(S), Ps 137:6 my **c**. cause for
  1Pe 5:4 **c**. shepherd has been made manifest
  Ge 21:22; De 20:9; Ne 2:9; Isa 3:3.
CHIEF AGENT, Ac 3:15 you killed the **C**. of
  Ac 5:31 God exalted this one as **C**.
  Heb 2:10 **C**. of their salvation perfect
  Heb 12:2 look intently at the **C**., Jesus
CHIEFTAIN(S), Eze 34:24 David a **c**.
  Eze 44:3 **c**. will sit in the gate
  Ge 17:20; 1Ki 8:1; Eze 7:27.
CHILD, Isa 9:6 been a **c**. born to us
  Lu 9:47 took a young **c**., set it beside
  Re 12:5 and her **c**. was caught away
  Ex 2:3, 10; 1Ki 3:26; Isa 66:7.

CHILDBEARING, 1Ti 2:15 safe through **c**.
CHILDREN, Ps 8:2 Out of the mouth of **c**.
  Isa 13:16 **c**. will be dashed to pieces
  Mt 18:3 unless you become as young **c**. you
  Mt 19:14 let **c**. alone, and stop hindering
  1Co 7:14 your **c**. would really be unclean,
  Eph 6:1 **C**., be obedient to your parents
  Eph 6:4 not be irritating your **c**.
  1Jo 5:21 **c**. guard yourselves from idols
  Ro 8:16; 2Co 12:14; Eph 5:8; 1Th 2:7.
CHINNERETH, Nu 34:11; Jos 11:2.
CHOICE, Jer 2:21 planted as a **c**. vine,
CHOIR(S), Ne 12:31, 38, 40 thanksgiving **c**.
CHOKE, Mt 13:22; Mr 4:19.
CHOKED, Mr 4:7; Lu 8:7, 14.
CHOOSE, De 30:19 you must **c**. life
  Jos 24:15 **c**. whom you will serve
  Ac 26:16 to **c**. you as an attendant and a
  De 12:11; Isa 7:15; Zec 1:17; Joh 15:16.
CHOOSING, Ro 11:5 according to a **c**. due
  2Pe 1:10 make the **c**. of you sure
  Ro 9:11; 11:28; 1Th 1:4.
CHOSE, 1Co 1:27 God **c**. the foolish
CHOSEN, De 7:6 you God has **c**.
  Mt 22:14 many invited, few **c**.
  1Pe 2:4 rejected by men, but **c**. with God,
  1Pe 2:9 you are a **c**. race,
  Re 17:14 those called and **c**.
  Ne 1:9; Ps 89:3; Pr 16:16; 22:1; Isa 43:10.
CHOSEN ONE(S), Isa 42:1 My **c**., whom
  Isa 65:22 work of their hands my **c**. will
  Mt 24:24 mislead, if possible, the **c**.
  Mt 24:31 his angels will gather his **c**.
  Mr 13:20 on account of the **c**. he has cut
  Mr 13:27 gather **c**. from earth's extremity
  Lu 18:7 cause justice to be done for his **c**.
  Mt 24:22; Ro 8:33; Col 3:12; 2Ti 2:10.
CHRIST, Mt 16:16 You are the **C**.,
  Ro 8:17 joint heirs with **C**., provided
  1Co 12:12 one body, so also **C**.
  1Co 15:23 own rank: **C**. the first fruits
  Php 2:11 acknowledge that Jesus **C**. is Lord
  Col 1:24 tribulations of **C**. in my flesh
  1Pe 4:13 sharers in the sufferings of **C**.,
  Joh 17:3; 1Co 1:13; 3:23; 7:22; 2Co 12:10;
  Ga 3:29; Eph 5:23; Col 1:27; 1Pe 2:21.
CHRISTIAN(S), Ac 11:26 called **C**.
  Ac 26:28 persuade me to become a **C**.
  1Pe 4:16 he suffers as a **C**., let him
CHRISTS, FALSE, Mt 24:24; Mr 13:22.
CHRONIC, Jer 15:18; 30:12.
CHURCH. See CONGREGATION(S).
CHURNING, Pr 30:33 the **c**. of milk is
CIRCLE, Job 26:10; Ps 150:4; Isa 40:22.
CIRCLING, Ec 1:6 wind is **c**. around
CIRCUIT, Mr 6:6 went in a **c**., teaching.
  Job 1:5; Ps 19:6; Mt 10:23; Ro 15:19.
CIRCULATE, 1Sa 2:24 report to **c**.
CIRCUMCISED, Ro 3:30 **c**. righteous
CIRCUMCISION, Ro 2:29 **c**. of the heart
  Ro 4:11; 1Co 7:19; Php 3:3; Col 2:11.
CIRCUMSTANCES, Ps 118:5 distressing **c**.
CISTERN(S), Pr 5:15 drink of your own **c**.
  2Ki 18:31; Ec 12:6; Isa 36:16; Jer 2:13.
CITIES, Nu 35:6 six **c**. of refuge,
  Isa 6:11 until **c**. be without an inhabitant,
  Isa 54:3 inhabit even the desolated **c**.
  Lu 4:43; 19:17; Re 16:19.
CITIZEN(S), Ac 22:28 rights as a **c**.
  Lu 15:15; 19:14; Ac 21:39.
CITIZENSHIP, Php 3:20 **c**. exists in heavens
CITY, Mt 5:14 **c**. cannot be hid upon a
  Heb 11:10 **c**. having real foundations

Heb 11:16 he has made a **c.** ready for them.
Re 21:2 holy **c.**, New Jerusalem,
Ge 11:4; Eze 9:4; Re 16:19.
CITY OF REFUGE, Nu 35:25; Jos 21:13, 21.
CLANS, Ge 25:16; Nu 25:15; Ps 117:1.
CLARIFIED, Ps 12:6 refined, **c.** seven times
CLASHING, 1Co 13:1 brass or a **c.** cymbal.
CLASS, Jer 5:4 they are of low **c.**
CLAY, Job 10:9 out of **c.** you made me
Isa 29:16 potter just like the **c.**?
Isa 64:8 We are the **c.**, and you are our
Isa 45:9; Da 2:34; Joh 9:6; Ro 9:21.
CLEAN, Job 14:4 **c.** out of unclean?
Ps 24:4 innocent hands and **c.** in heart,
Eze 20:38 **c.** out revolters
Joh 15:3 already **c.** because of the word
Ac 20:26 I am **c.** from the blood of all men,
Tit 1:15 All things are **c.** to **c.** persons.
Ge 7:2; Le 10:10; Job 17:9; Eze 22:26;
Ro 14:20; 1Ti 1:5; 2Ti 2:22; Jas 1:27.
CLEANSE, Da 12:10 Many will **c.**
2Co 7:1 **c.** ourselves of every defilement
Tit 2:14 **c.** for himself a people peculiarly
1Jo 1:9 **c.** us from all unrighteousness.
Ps 51:2; Mt 23:25; Heb 9:14; Jas 4:8.
CLEANSED, Ac 10:15 things God has **c.**
Heb 9:22 all things are **c.** with blood
2Ch 29:18; Lu 4:27; Ac 11:9; Heb 10:2.
CLEANSES, 1Jo 1:7 blood of Jesus **c.** us
CLEANSING, Eze 36:33 day of my **c.** you
Eze 39:12 **c.** the land, for seven months.
Da 11:35 to do a **c.** and to do a whitening,
Eph 5:26 **c.** it with the bath of water
CLEAR, Isa 40:3 **C.** up the way of Jehovah
Isa 57:14; 62:10; Mal 3:1.
CLEAR AWAY, 1Co 5:7 **C.** the old leaven,
CLEAVE, Jos 23:8 to God you should **c.**
CLEAVING, De 4:4; Jos 23:8.
CLIMBING, Zep 1:9 **c.** upon the platform
CLING, De 10:20; 13:4.
CLINGING, Joh 20:17 Stop **c.** to me
CLOSE, Jas 4:8 Draw **c.** to God, and he
CLOSED, Jg 3:23 Ehud **c.** the doors
Re 21:25 gates not **c.** by day
CLOSEFISTED, De 15:7 not be **c.** toward poor
CLOSER, Pr 18:24 friend sticking **c.** than
CLOTH(S), Joh 11:44; 20:7; Ac 19:12.
CLOTHE, Col 3:12 **c.** with tender affections
CLOTHES CLEANER, Mr 9:3 whiter than **c.**
CLOTHING, Isa 63:1 honorable in his **c.**,
Mt 6:25 food and the body than **c.**?
Pr 27:26; Da 7:9; Mt 6:28.
CLOUD(S), Ge 9:13 rainbow in the **c.**
Ec 11:4 he that is looking at the **c.** will
Isa 14:14 I shall go up above the **c.**;
Joe 2:2 day of **c.** and thick gloom,
Lu 21:27 coming in a **c.** with power and
Ac 1:9 **c.** caught him up from their vision.
1Th 4:17 caught away in **c.** to meet the Lord
Heb 12:1 so great a **c.** of witnesses
Re 1:7 coming with the **c.**, and every eye
Ex 13:21; 1Ki 8:10; Mt 24:30; 1Co 10:2.
CLUB(S), Jer 51:20 **c.** as weapons of war,
Mt 26:47, 55; Lu 22:52.
CLUTCHES, Ps 141:9 keep from **c.** of trap
COAL(S), Ro 12:20 heap fiery **c.** upon
Ps 18:12; Isa 6:6; Eze 10:2.
COASTAL PLAIN, Ca 2:1 saffron of the **c.**
COAT(S), 1Sa 15:27; Ezr 9:3; Ps 109:29.
COAT OF MAIL, 1Sa 17:5; Isa 59:17.
COAT, SLEEVELESS, Ex 28:4; Job 1:20.
Isa 61:10 with the **c.** of righteousness he
COBRA, Isa 11:8 play upon hole of **c.**
COCK, Mt 26:34, 74, 75; Mr 14:30.

COCKROACH(ES), 1Ki 8:37; Joe 1:4.
COCKSURENESS, 2Co 11:17 **c.** boasting
CODE, Ro 13:9 law **c.**, You must not
2Co 3:7 if the **c.** which administers death
COFFIN, Ge 50:26 he was put in a **c.**
COGNIZANT, Na 1:7 he is **c.** of those
COIN, Mt 10:29 two sparrows for a **c.**
COINCIDENCE, Lu 10:31 by **c.** a priest was
COLD, Ps 147:17 Before his **c.** who can
Re 3:15 you are neither **c.** nor hot.
Ge 8:22; Job 37:9; Mt 10:42; Re 3:16.
COLLAPSE, Ps 58:7; La 1:7; Mt 7:27.
COLLEAGUES, Ezr 4:7, 9; 5:3, 6.
COLLECT, Isa 40:11 he will **c.** the lambs;
Isa 56:8 shall **c.** others besides those
Jer 23:3 I shall **c.** together the remnant
Mt 13:41 angels will **c.** out from his
Ps 106:47; Isa 11:12; 54:7; Jer 49:14.
COLLECTED, Isa 60:4 have all been **c.**
2Ki 10:18; Ps 102:22; Isa 43:9; Ac 28:3.
COLLECTION(S), Ec 12:11; 1Co 16:1, 2.
COLONNADE, Joh 10:23; Ac 3:11; 5:12.
COLONY, Ac 16:12 to Philippi, a **c.**
COLT, Mt 21:5; Lu 19:30.
COMBATING, Col 2:23 **c.** the flesh
COME, Ps 40:7 I have **c.**, In the roll
Isa 55:1 thirsty ones! C. to the water.
Mt 6:10 Let your kingdom **c.** Let your
Ro 8:38 things here nor things to **c.** nor
Re 22:17 let anyone hearing say, "C.!"
Isa 2:3; Mt 25:34; Heb 10:1; 13:14.
COMELINESS, 1Co 12:23 unseemly parts **c.**
COMELY, Isa 52:7 **c.** feet bringing good news
Ro 10:15 How **c.** are the feet of those
COMFORT, Isa 61:2 to **c.** all the mourning
Ro 15:4 through the **c.** from the Scriptures
2Co 1:4 able to **c.** those in tribulation
Ge 37:35; Job 2:11; Isa 40:1; 2Co 1:3.
COMFORTED, Isa 49:13 Jehovah has **c.**
Jer 31:15 refused to be **c.** over her sons,
Mt 5:4; 2Co 1:4; Col 2:2.
COMFORTER. See HELPER.
COMFORTERS, Job 16:2; Ps 69:20; Na 3:7.
COMING. See also PRESENCE.
COMING, Mal 3:2 putting up day of his **c.**,
Mr 13:26 Son of man **c.** in clouds with
Lu 12:45 'My master delays **c.**,' and
Re 21:2 New Jerusalem, **c.** down out of
Jg 5:28; Jer 8:7; Mt 16:28; Lu 21:26.
COMMAND(S), Ge 3:17 **c.**: must not eat
Isa 28:10 **c.** upon **c.**, **c.** upon **c.**,
Mt 15:9 they teach **c.** of men as doctrines.
Col 2:22 accordance with **c.** of men?
Ex 7:2; Nu 9:8; Jer 1:7; Joh 15:17.
COMMANDED, Jos 1:9 Have I not **c.** you?
Eze 9:11 I have done as you have **c.** me.
De 5:33; Ps 78:5; 105:8; Isa 45:12.
COMMANDER(S), Isa 55:4 leader and **c.** to
Jos 10:24; Jg 11:6; Pr 6:7; 25:15.
COMMANDER'S STAFF, Ge 49:10 **c.** from
Nu 21:18 excavated it, with a **c.**,
Ps 60:7; 108:8 Judah is my **c.**
COMMANDING, De 4:2 word that I am **c.**
De 6:6 these words that I am **c.** you today
COMMANDING CALL, 1Th 4:16 with a **c.**,
COMMANDMENT(S), Pr 6:23 **c.** is a lamp,
Mt 15:3 you also overstep the **c.** of God
Mt 22:40 On these two **c.** the whole Law
Mr 12:28 asked him: Which **c.** is first of all?
Joh 12:50 his **c.** means everlasting life.
Joh 14:21 He that has my **c.** and observes
1Jo 2:7 I am writing you, not a new **c.**, but
1Jo 5:3 observe his **c.**; and yet his **c.** are
Ps 119:98; Pr 6:20; Isa 29:13; Jer 35:18;

Mr 12:31; Joh 10:18; 1Jo 3:23; Re 12:17.
COMMEMORATION, Es 9:28 Purim, the **c.**
COMMEND, Ps 63:3; 117:1; 145:4.
  1Co 11:2 **I c.** you because have in mind
COMMENDATION, Jg 11:40 go to give **c.** to
  Da 2:23 I am giving **c.,**
COMMENDED, Ec 8:15 I **c.** rejoicing
COMMENDING, 1Pe 4:19 **c.** their souls
COMMERCIAL, 2Ti 2:4 **c.** business of life
COMMISSION, 1Sa 25:30 **c.** you as leader
  1Sa 13:14; 1Ch 6:32; Hag 1:13; Ac 26:12.
COMMISSIONED, Isa 62:6; Jer 1:10.
COMMISSIONER(S), Ac 19:31 **c.** of games
  Jg 9:28; 2Ch 31:13; Es 2:3; Jer 52:25.
COMMIT, 2Ti 2:2 these things **c.** to men
COMMITTED, 2Co 5:19 **c.** the word of
  Re 18:3 kings of the earth **c.** fornication
COMMODIUS, Jer 22:14 **c.** upper chambers
COMMON, Ac 4:32 had all things in **c.**
  1Co 10:13 No temptation except what is **c.**
  Ac 2:44; Tit 1:4; Jude 3.
COMMOTION, Isa 16:14; Mt 21:10.
COMMUNICATED, Job 37:20 it will be **c.?**
COMMUNICATION, 2Sa 3:17 **c.** by Abner
COMMUNION SACRIFICES, Ex 20:24; Le 3:1.
COMPACT, Job 38:30 watery deep makes **c.**
COMPACTLY, 2Pe 3:5 an earth standing **c.**
COMPANION(S), Jg 11:37 weep I and girl **c.**
  Pr 17:17 A true **c.** is loving all the time
  Jer 31:34 will no more teach each one his **c.**
  Ex 11:2; Ps 122:8; Isa 41:6; Zec 14:13.
COMPANIONSHIP, Pr 22:24 **c.** with anger,
COMPANY, 1Co 5:11 quit mixing in **c.**
COMPARABLE, Ps 49:12; Pr 27:15.
COMPARE, Isa 46:5 whom will you **c.** me
COMPARED, Ps 89:6 who **c.** to Jehovah?
COMPARING, 2Co 10:12 **c.** themselves with
COMPARISON(S), Joh 16:25 speak no more in **c.**
  Ro 8:18 in **c.** with the glory that is to be
  Ga 6:4 not in **c.** with the other person.
COMPARTMENT, Heb 9:6 enter first tent **c.**
COMPASS, Isa 44:13 with **c.** tracing it out
COMPASSION(S), Jer 13:14 show no **c.**
  Joe 2:18 Jehovah will show **c.** upon his
  Ro 9:15 I will show **c.** to whomever I do
  Ro 12:1 I entreat you by the **c.** of God,
  Php 2:1 if any tender affections and **c.,**
  Col 3:12 tender affections of **c.,** kindness,
  Jer 15:5; Eze 7:9; Ho 13:14; Zec 11:5, 6.
COMPELLED, Mt 14:22; Ac 28:19; Ga 2:3.
COMPELLING, Ga 2:14 **c.** people of the
COMPELLING REASON, Ro 13:5 **c.** to be in
COMPENSATION(S), 1Ti 5:4 due **c.** to parents
  Ex 21:34; Le 24:18; 2Sa 12:6; Eze 29:20.
COMPETENT, Da 4:18; 5:15; 2Ti 3:17.
COMPETITION, Ps 5:26 stirring up **c.**
COMPILE, Lu 1:1 **c.** a statement of
COMPLAINANT, Mt 5:25 **c.** not turn you
COMPLAINERS, Jude 16 murmurers, **c.**
COMPLAINING, Pr 21:13 **c.** cry of lowly
  Mt 5:25 with the one **c.** against you at law,
COMPLAINT, Col 3:13 for **c.** against
COMPLETE, 1Ch 28:9 serve with a **c.** heart
  2Ch 16:9 whose heart is **c.** toward him.
  Col 1:28 present every man **c.** in union with
  1Co 13:10; Jas 1:4.
COMPLETED, Lu 18:31 all things be **c.**
  Ga 3:3 now being **c.** in flesh?
COMPLETION, Php 1:6 will carry it to **c.**
COMPLEXION, Da 5:9, 10; 7:28.
COMPLIANCE, Phm 21 trusting in your **c.**
COMPOSE, Eze 17:2; 24:3 **c.** a saying
COMPOSED, Ac 1:1 the account I **c.**
COMPOSITION, Ex 30:32 with its **c.** not make

COMPREHENSION, Eph 3:4 **c.** I have in the
COMPULSION, 2Co 9:7; Phm 14.
  1Pe 5:2 shepherd flock not under **c.**
COMPULSORY SERVICE, 1Ki 11:28.
  Job 14:14 days of my **c.** I shall wait,
CONCEAL, Pr 22:3 proceeds to **c.** himself
  Isa 29:14 understanding of their men will **c.**
CONCEALED, Pr 27:5 reproof than **c.** love
  Jer 16:17 They have not been **c.** from
  Da 2:22 He is revealing the **c.** things,
  Zep 2:3 you may be **c.** in the day
  Lu 8:17 anything **c.** will become known
  Lu 9:45 it was **c.** from them that they
  De 29:29; Ps 89:46; Isa 28:15; Jer 23:24.
CONCEALMENT, PLACE(S), Ps 119:114; Isa
  28:17; 45:19; Jer 49:10.
CONCEIVABLE, Le 7:24 anything else **c.**
CONCEIVE, Lu 1:31 you will **c.** in your
  Eph 3:20 do more than we ask or **c.,**
  Heb 11:11 Sarah received power to **c.** seed
CONCEIVED, Ps 51:5 sin my mother **c.**
  Ro 9:10 when Rebekah **c.** twins from the one
CONCEIVE(S) SEED, Le 12:2 **c.** and bear a
CONCEPTION, Ru 4:13; Ho 9:11.
CONCERN, Ps 119:97 your law! is my **c.**
  Job 10:1; Ps 142:2; Am 4:13.
CONCERNED, 1Ki 18:27 he must be **c.** with
CONCERT, Lu 15:25 heard a music **c.** and
CONCESSION, Mt 19:8 Moses made **c.** to
  1Co 7:6 say by way of **c.,**
CONCLUDED, Ge 15:18 **c.** with Abram a
  De 5:2 Jehovah **c.** a covenant
  Ps 89:3 **c.** a covenant toward David
CONCLUDING, Ro 9:28 **c.** it and cutting
CONCLUSION, Mt 24:3 **c.** of system of things
  Mt 28:20 until the **c.** of things
  Heb 9:26 **c.** of systems of things
CONCLUSIONS, DRAWING, Lu 2:19.
CONCUBINE(S), Jg 19:25 abusing **c.** all night
  1Ki 11:3 three hundred **c.**
  Ge 22:24; Ex 21:8; 2Sa 3:7; Es 2:14.
CONDEMN, Isa 54:17 judgment you will **c.**
  Mt 12:41, 42; 20:18; Ro 8:34; 1Jo 3:20.
CONDEMNATION, Ro 5:18 result was **c.**
  Ro 8:1; 2Co 3:9.
CONDEMNED, Lu 6:37 by no means be **c.**
  Ro 8:3 concerning sin, **c.** sin in the flesh
  Jas 5:6 You have **c.,** you have murdered
  Mt 12:7, 37; 1Co 11:32; Tit 2:8; Heb 11:7.
CONDEMNS TO DEATH, 2Co 3:6 code **c.** but
CONDESCENDING, Ps 113:6 **c.** to look on
CONDITION, 1Co 7:24 In whatever **c.** each
CONDITION, RIGHT, Da 8:14 into its **r.**
CONDITIONS, DESOLATED, Da 9:18.
CONDUCT, Ga 1:13 about my **c.** formerly in
  Ga 6:16 by this rule of **c.**
  1Ti 4:12 become an example in **c.,** in love,
  Jas 3:13 show out of his fine **c.** his works
  1Pe 2:12 Maintain your **c.** fine among the
  1Pe 3:16 speaking slightingly of good **c.**
  Ps 31:3; 43:1; 74:22; Eph 4:22; Heb 13:7;
  1Pe 1:15, 18; 3:1, 2.
CONDUCT (legal case), 1Sa 24:15; Ps 119:154;
  Jer 50:34.
CONDUCTED, 2Co 1:12 **c.** ourselves in the
CONDUCTING, Jer 51:36 **c.** your case.
CONDUCTOR, Ne 11:17 **c.** of the singing
CONDUIT, 2Ki 18:17; Isa 7:3; 36:2.
CONFEDERATES, Ge 14:13 **c.** of Abraham
CONFERENCE, Ga 1:16 not **c.** with flesh
CONFERRING, Lu 7:4 **c.** this upon him
CONFESS. See also **ACKNOWLEDGE.**
CONFESS, Le 5:5 **c.** in what way sinned
  Jas 5:16 **c.** your sins to one another

Le 16:21; 26:40; Mt 7:23; 1Jo 1:9.
CONFESSING, Pr 28:13 **c.** be shown mercy.
CONFESSION, Ezr 10:11 And now make **c.**
Ne 1:6 **c.** concerning the sins of
Ps 32:5 make **c.** over my
Jos 7:19; 2Ch 30:22; Ne 9:2; Da 9:4.
CONFIDENCE, Pr 3:26 Jehovah your **c.**
Eph 3:12 approach with **c.** through our faith
Php 3:3 do not have our **c.** in the flesh,
2Th 3:4 we have **c.** in the Lord regarding
Heb 3:14 if we make fast our hold on the **c.**
Pr 14:26; Ec 9:4; Isa 36:4; 2Co 1:15.
CONFIDENT, Pr 28:1 righteous are **c.**
Jer 12:5 in the land of peace are you **c.?**
CONFIDENTIAL, Am 3:7 revealed his **c.** matter
CONFIDENTIAL FRIEND, Pr 2:17; Jer 3:4.
Mic 7:5 Do not put your trust in a **c.**
CONFIDENTIAL TALK, Pr 15:22 where no **c.**
Pr 20:19 a slanderer is uncovering **c.**
Ps 64:2; 83:3; Pr 11:13; 25:9.
CONFINED, Ga 5:1 **c.** in a yoke of slavery
CONFINEMENT, 2Sa 20:3 put in a house of **c.**
CONFLICT, 1Pe 2:11 carry a **c.** against
CONFORMED, Php 3:21 **c.** to his body
CONFOUNDING, Isa 22:5; Mic 7:4.
CONFRONT, Ps 17:13; 59:10; Mic 6:6.
CONFUSE, Ge 11:7 **c.** their language
CONFUSION, Isa 22:5 it is the day of **c.**
Zec 14:13 **c.** from Jehovah widespread
De 28:20; Pr 15:16; Eze 7:7; Ac 19:29.
CONGEALED, Ex 15:8 waters **c.** in the sea
Zec 14:6 things will be **c.**
CONGEALING, Zep 1:12 men **c.** upon their dregs
CONGRATULATE, 1Ch 18:10 David to **c.**
CONGRATULATED, Ec 4:2 I **c.** the dead
CONGREGATE, Le 8:3 assembly **c.** at the
De 31:12 **c.** the people
CONGREGATED, Es 9:18 Jews in Shushan **c.**
CONGREGATED THRONGS, Ps 26:12 Among **c.**
CONGREGATION(S), Joh 16:2 expel from **c.**
Ac 16:5 **c.** continued to increase in number
Ac 20:28 shepherd the **c.** of God,
1Co 14:34 let women keep silent in the **c.,**
Eph 5:24 **c.** is in subjection to the Christ,
Col 1:18 head of the body, the **c.**
Heb 12:23 the **c.** of the first-born who
Ex 12:6; De 9:10; 1Sa 17:47; Ps 149:1;
Pr 26:26; 1Co 14:19; Ga 1:13; Eph 1:22.
CONGREGATOR, Ec 1:1 The words of the **c.,**
Ec 1:12; 7:27; 12:9, 10.
CONJURERS, Da 1:20; 2:2; 4:7; 5:7.
CONNECTION, Ro 12:5 not in vain in **c.**
CONQUER(S), Re 2:7 To him that **c.** I
Re 3:21 one that **c.** I will grant to sit
Re 11:7 wild beast will **c.**
Re 17:14 the Lamb will **c.** them.
1Jo 5:4, 5; Re 2:11, 17, 26; 3:5, 12.
CONQUERED, Joh 16:33 I have **c.** the
Col 2:15 exhibited them in open public as **c.**
1Jo 5:4 the conquest that has **c.** the world,
1Jo 2:13; 4:4; Re 5:5; 12:11.
CONQUERING, Ro 12:21 keep **c.** the evil
Re 21:7 **c.** will inherit these things
CONQUEST, 1Jo 5:4 this is the **c.** that
Re 6:2 conquering and to complete his **c.**
CONSCIENCE(S), Ro 9:1 **c.** bears witness
1Co 10:29 is judged by another person's **c.?**
1Ti 1:19 holding faith and a good **c.**
1Ti 4:2 marked in their **c.** as with a
Heb 9:14 cleanse our **c.** from dead works
Ac 23:1; 1Co 8:12; 2Co 1:12; 1Pe 3:16, 21.
CONSCIOUS, Ge 9:5 dead are **c.** of nothing
Mt 5:3 Happy are those **c.** of spiritual
1Co 4:4 I am not **c.** of anything against me.

CONSCIOUSNESS, Heb 10:2 no **c.** of sins
CONSCRIPTED, 2Sa 20:24 **c.** for forced labor
CONSECRATE. See FILL HAND WITH POWER.
CONSENT, Pr 1:10 seduce you, do not **c.**
Lu 11:48 and yet you give **c.** to them,
1Co 7:5 except by mutual **c.**
CONSEQUENCES, Job 13:26 **c.** of errors
CONSIDER, Heb 3:1 **c.** the apostle and
CONSIDERATION, 2Ki 16:15 take under **c.**
Ps 41:1 Happy is anyone acting with **c.**
Php 2:6 gave no **c.** to a seizure, namely,
1Th 5:13 **c.** in love because of their work
CONSIDERED, Ps 119:128 **c.** all orders
Ro 4:19 **c.** his own body deadened
Php 3:7 I **c.** loss on account of Christ
CONSIDERING, Php 2:3 **c.** that others are
Php 4:8 continue **c.** these things.
CONSIGNING, Isa 37:19 **c.** their gods to fire
CONSISTING, Eph 2:15 **c.** in decrees,
CONSOLATION, Lu 2:25 for Israel's **c.**
2Sa 3:35; Isa 66:11; Jer 16:7; Php 2:1.
CONSOLE, Joh 11:19 **c.** them concerning
CONSOLES, 1Co 14:3 he that prophesies **c.**
CONSOLING, 1Th 2:11 **c.** and bearing
CONSORT, Ne 2:6; Ps 45:9.
CONSPICUOUS, Da 8:5 **c.** horn between
CONSPICUOUSLY, Da 8:8 **c.** four instead
CONSPIRACY, Isa 8:12 must not say, A **c.**
Jer 11:9; Eze 22:25; Ac 23:13.
CONSPIRE, 1Ki 15:27; 2Ki 9:14; Ne 4:8.
CONSPIRED, 1Sa 22:8 you **c.** against me
2Ki 10:9; 15:10; 21:23; Am 7:10.
CONSTABLES, Ac 16:35, 38 dispatched **c.** to
CONSTANCY, Da 6:16, 20 serving with **c.**
Eph 6:18 keep awake with all **c.**
CONSTANT FEATURE, Da 8:11; 11:31; 12:11.
CONSTELLATION, Job 9:9; Am 5:8.
CONSTERNATION, Job 41:25 **c.** get bewildered
CONSTITUTE, Ps 21:6 **c.** him blessed forever
CONSTITUTED RIGHTEOUS, Ro 5:19 many **c.**
CONSTITUTING, Jas 4:4 **c.** himself an
CONSTRAIN, 2Ki 4:8 **c.** him to eat bread
CONSTRUCTED, Heb 3:4 he that **c.** all
CONSTRUCTS, Heb 3:3 he who **c.** has more
CONSULT, Le 19:31 not **c.** foretellers of
2Sa 21:1; 2Ch 20:4.
CONSULTATION, Mt 27:1 **c.** against Jesus
CONSUME, Mt 6:19 where moth and rust **c.**
Ge 41:30; Isa 27:10; Heb 10:27.
CONSUMED, Ex 3:2 thornbush was not **c.**
CONSUMING FIRE, De 4:24; 9:3; Heb 12:29.
CONTEMNED, Ps 78:59 God **c.** Israel
CONTEMNING, Ps 89:38 you keep **c.**
Ps 106:24 **c.** the desirable land
CONTEMPLATE, Pr 5:6 path does not **c.**
Heb 13:7 **c.** their conduct
CONTEMPORARIES, Ge 6:9 among Noah's **c.**
CONTEMPT, Pr 12:8 will come to be for **c.**
Ga 4:14 you did not treat with **c.** or spit
Heb 10:29 undeserved kindness with **c.?**
Job 31:34; Ps 107:40; Pr 18:3; Isa 23:9.
CONTEMPTIBLE, 2Co 10:10 his speech **c.**
CONTEND, De 33:8 began to **c.** with him by the
Job 13:8; Isa 3:13; 49:25; 50:8; Ho 4:4.
CONTENDER, Jg 12:2 Jephthah a special **c.**
CONTENDING, Job 40:2 **c.** with Almighty?
CONTENDS, 2Ti 2:5 **c.** in the games
CONTENT, 1Ti 6:8 we shall be **c.** with these
CONTENTION(S), Pr 6:19 anyone sending **c.**
Pr 28:25 arrogant in soul stirs up **c.,**
Ga 5:20 fits of anger, **c.,** divisions, sects,
Pr 16:28; 18:19; 22:10.
CONTENTIOUS, Pr 21:9 with a **c.** wife,
Pr 21:19 a wilderness than with a **c.** wife

Pr 26:21 so is a **c.** man for causing a
Pr 27:15 rain and a **c.** wife are comparable.
Ro 2:8 those who are **c.** and who disobey
CONTENTIOUSNESS, Php 1:17 do out of **c.,**
Php 2:3 doing nothing out of **c.**
Jas 3:16 where jealousy and **c.** are, there
CONTEST(S), 1Co 9:25 in a **c.** exercises control
La 3:58; Heb 12:4.
CONTINUOUS, Isa 26:3 safeguard in **c.**
CONTRACTING, Ne 9:38 **c.** an arrangement
CONTRADICT, Tit 1:9 reprove those who **c.**
CONTRADICTIONS, 1Ti 6:20 **c.** of falsely
CONTRARY, Ro 16:17 **c.** to the teaching
Es 9:1; Ac 18:13; Ro 11:24.
CONTRARY TALK, Heb 12:3 endured such **c.**
CONTRIBUTION, Ex 25:2 take up a **c.**
2Ch 31:10 bring the **c.** into the house
Eze 45:1 offer a **c.** to Jehovah
Eze 48:21 holy **c.** and the sanctuary
Ro 15:26; 2Co 9:13.
CONTRITE, Isa 66:2 one afflicted and **c.**
CONTRIVING ERROR, Eph 4:14 means of **c.**
CONTROL. See also SELF-CONTROL.
CONTROL, Col 3:15 peace of Christ **c.**
CONTROLLING, Pr 16:32 **c.** his spirit
CONTROVERSIAL, Isa 41:21 bring **c.** case
CONTROVERSIALLY, Ac 17:18 conversing **c.,**
CONTROVERSY, Isa 66:16 will take **c.**
Jer 25:31 **c.** that Jehovah has with
CONVENTION(S), Le 23:4 these are the holy **c.**
Isa 4:5 **c.** place a cloud
Ex 12:16; Le 23:35; Nu 28:26; 29:7.
CONVERSING, Ac 17:18 took to **c.** with him
CONVERSION, Ac 15:3 **c.** of people of
CONVERTED, NEWLY, 1Ti 3:6 not a n. man,
CONVICTION, 1Th 1:5 with strong **c.,**
CONVINCED, Ro 8:38 I am **c.** that neither
Heb 6:9 we are **c.** of better things and
CONVULSIONS, Mr 9:26 through many **c.** it
Isa 13:8; 21:3; Da 10:16.
COOING, Isa 38:14; 59:11.
COOK(S), 1Sa 8:13; 9:23, 24.
COOKING POT(S), Nu 11:8; Jg 6:19.
COOL, Mt 24:12 greater number will **c.** off
CO-OPERATE, Ro 8:28; Eph 4:16.
CO-OPERATING, 1Co 16:16 to everyone **c.**
COPIOUS SHOWERS, De 32:2; Ps 65:10.
COPULATION, Jer 2:24 her time for **c.,**
COPY, Heb 9:24 a **c.** of the reality,
COPYIST, Ezr 7:6; Ps 45:1; Jer 36:10.
CORALS, Pr 8:11 wisdom is better than **c.,**
CORBAN, Mr 7:11 Whatever I have is **c.,**
CORD(S), Ps 2:3 cast their **c.** away from
Ec 4:12 threefold **c.** cannot quickly be torn
Isa 54:2 Lengthen out your tent **c.,**
CORNELIUS, Ac 10:1, 3, 22, 24, 25, 30, 31.
CORNER, Ps 118:22 the head of the **c.**
Isa 28:16 foundation in Zion precious **c.**
Ac 4:11 no account become head of **c.**
1Pe 2:7 rejected has become head of **c.**
CORNERSTONE, Mt 21:42 become the chief **c.**
Eph 2:20 Jesus is the foundation **c.**
Job 38:6; Mr 12:10; 1Pe 2:6.
CORPSE(S), Jg 14:8; 1Sa 31:10; Mt 14:12.
CORRECTED, Ps 2:10 Let yourselves be **c.,**
Ps 118:18 Jah **c.** me severely
Pr 29:19 not let himself be **c.** by mere
Heb 12:5 neither give out when **c.**
CORRECTING, De 8:5 Jehovah was **c.** you.
Ps 94:10 the One **c.** nations
Pr 9:7 He that is **c.** the ridiculer
CORRECTION. See DISCIPLINING.
CORRECTOR, Ro 2:20 a **c.** of unreasonable ones
CORRESPONDINGLY, Heb 8:6 a **c.** better

CORRESPONDING RANSOM, 1Ti 2:6 **c.** for all
CORRESPONDS, Ga 4:25 Hagar **c.** with the
CORRODED, Jas 5:3 gold and silver are **c.,**
CORRUPT, Ps 14:3 they are alike **c.,**
Da 6:4 no **c.** thing able to find,
CORRUPTED, Eze 20:44 to your **c.** dealings
2Ti 3:8 men **c.** in mind,
2Co 11:3; 1Ti 6:5; Re 19:2.
CORRUPTIBLE, 1Co 15:53 this which is **c.**
Ro 1:23; 1Co 9:25; 15:54; 1Pe 1:18, 23.
CORRUPTION, Ro 8:21 enslavement to **c.**
1Co 15:42 It is sown in **c.,** it is raised up
Ga 6:8 his flesh will reap **c.** from his flesh
2Pe 2:19 they are existing as slaves to **c.**
Ac 2:27, 31; 13:36; 1Co 15:50; 2Pe 1:4.
COST, 1Co 9:18 the good news without **c.,**
COT(S), Mr 2:4; 6:55; Joh 5:8; Ac 5:15.
COUCH, Ps 139:8 spread my **c.** in Sheol
Isa 28:20 **c.** has proved too short for
COUNSEL(S), Ps 33:11 **c.** will stand;
Isa 25:1 wonderful things, **c.** from early
Isa 46:10 My own **c.** will stand, and
Isa 46:11 the man to execute my **c.**
Ac 20:27 telling you all the **c.** of God.
1Co 4:5 make the **c.** of the heart manifest,
Ps 1:1; 5:10; 33:10; 73:24; 119:24;
Pr 19:21; Isa 14:26; 23:9; 40:13; Heb 6:17.
COUNSELED, Isa 14:24 **c.,** that will come
COUNSELINGS, Pr 22:20 **c.** and knowledge,
COUNSELOR(S), Pr 24:6 multitude of **c.**
Isa 9:6 Wonderful **C.,** Prince of Peace.
Ro 11:34 or who has become his **c.?**
Job 12:17; Pr 15:22; Isa 1:26; Mic 4:9.
COUNT, Ps 90:12 Show how to **c.** our days
COUNTED, Ro 4:5 his faith is **c.** as
Ro 4:24 to whom it is destined to be **c.,**
Ro 9:8 children by promise are **c.** as seed.
Jas 2:23 it was **c.** to him as righteousness.
COUNTENANCE, Ge 4:5; De 28:50.
COUNTERARGUMENTS, Job 13:6 hear my **c.**
Ps 38:14 in my mouth there were no **c.**
COUNTERFEIT, 2Pe 2:3 you with **c.** words.
COUNTING, Ps 147:4 **c.** the stars;
COUNTRY, Ge 12:1 Go out of your **c.** to
Jon 1:8 where do you come? What is your **c.,**
COUNTRYSIDE, Mr 6:36, 56; Lu 9:12.
COURAGE, 2Co 5:6 We are of good **c.**
Php 1:14 **c.** to speak the word of God
2Ch 15:8; Mt 8:28; Ac 28:15; Heb 13:6.
COURAGEOUS, De 31:6 Be **c.** and strong.
Nu 13:20; Jos 1:6, 7; 1Ch 19:13; 28:20.
COURIERS, Es 3:13; 8:14 letters by **c.**
COURSE, Jer 8:6 into the popular **c.,**
2Ti 4:7 I have run the **c.** to the finish,
Joe 2:8; Ac 13:25; 20:24.
COURT(S), Da 7:10 The **C.** took its seat
Mt 5:22 accountable to the **c.**
1Co 6:1 dare to go to **c.** before unrighteous
1Co 6:6 brother goes to **c.** with brother,
Jas 2:6 they drag you before law **c.,** do
Da 7:26; Mt 5:40; Lu 12:58; Ac 17:34.
COURTESY, 2Sa 11:8 king's **c.** gift
COURT OFFICIALS, 2Ki 9:32; Isa 39:7.
COURTYARD, Ex 27:9; 2Ch 4:9; Eze 8:16.
COUSIN, Col 4:10 Mark **c.** of Barnabas
COVENANT, Ge 9:9 establishing my **c.**
Ps 50:5 concluding my **c.** over sacrifice.
Ps 89:3 a **c.** toward David
Isa 28:15 We have concluded a **c.** with Death,
Jer 31:31 I will conclude with a new **c.;**
Da 11:30 denunciations against the holy **c.**
Ho 2:18 **c.** with the wild beast of the field
Mal 3:1 the messenger of the **c.,**
Mt 26:28 this means my 'blood of the **c.,**'

Lu 22:29 I make a **c.** with you, just as my
1Co 11:25 cup means the new **c.**
2Co 3:6 ministers of a new **c.**, not of a
2Co 3:14 the reading of the old **c.**,
Ga 4:24 these women mean two **c.**, the one
Heb 8:6 better **c.**, legally established
Heb 9:17 a **c.** is valid over dead victims,
Heb 12:24 Jesus the mediator of a new **c.**,
Ge 15:18; Ex 19:5; Jos 9:6; Ps 25:10;
89:3; Isa 24:5; Am 1:9; Ac 7:8; Ro 9:4;
Ga 3:15; Heb 7:22; 9:16.
COVER. See also PROPITIATORY COVER.
COVER, Ex 25:17 make a **c.** of gold
Le 17:13 pour its blood out and **c.** it
COVERED, Mt 10:26 nothing **c.** that will
COVERING, Pr 17:9 **c.** over transgression
COVERT, Ps 27:5; 76:2 hide me in **c.**
COVET, Ro 7:7; 13:9 must not **c.**
COVETING, Jas 4:2 You go on **c.**, and yet
COVETINGS, Mr 7:22 out of the heart **c.**
COVETOUSNESS, Lu 12:15 guard against **c.**,
Ro 7:7 I would not have known **c.** if the Law
1Th 2:5 no time with a false front for **c.**,
Ro 1:29; Col 3:5; 2Pe 2:3, 14.
COWARDICE, 2Ti 1:7 not a spirit of **c.**
COWARDS, Re 21:8 **c.** their portion in lake
COWER, La 3:16 made me **c.** in the ashes
CRAFTSMAN, Ho 8:6 A mere **c.** made it,
Ex 35:35; 2Ki 24:14; Isa 40:19; Jer 10:3.
CRAFTSMEN, Ho 13:2; Ac 19:24, 38.
CRAFTY, Mt 26:4 seize Jesus by **c.** device
2Co 12:16 you say, I was **c.** and I caught
CRAG, Nu 20:11; Ps 18:2; Jer 49:16.
CRAMP, 2Sa 1:9 the **c.** has seized me
CRAMPED, Mt 7:14 narrow the gate and **c.**
2Co 4:8 pressed in every way, but not **c.**
2Co 6:12 **c.** for room in your affections
CRANIUM, Nu 24:17 break the **c.** of sons of
CRASH, Pr 16:18 Pride is before a **c.**,
Pr 18:12 Before a **c.** the heart of a man is
Isa 1:28; Jer 4:6; 51:54; La 2:11.
CRAVED, Ps 21:10 wicked one **c.** bad;
CRAVES, De 12:20 soul **c.** to eat meat,
CRAVING(S), Ge 3:16 **c.** for your husband
Jas 4:1 your **c.** for sensual
Ge 4:7; 2Sa 23:15; Pr 23:6; 24:1; Ca 7:10;
Ho 10:10; Am 5:18.
CRAZED, Jer 25:16 must drink and act **c.**
Jer 51:7 the nations keep acting **c.**
CRAZILY, Isa 44:25 diviners act **c.**;
CRAZY, 1Sa 21:15; Ec 7:7; Jer 50:38.
CREATE, Ps 51:10 **c.** in me a pure heart,
Isa 4:5 Jehovah will **c.** a cloud by day
Isa 45:18 who did not **c.** the earth for
CREATED, Ge 1:1 In the beginning God **c.**
Ge 1:27 **c.** him; male and female he **c.** them.
Col 1:16 means of him all things were **c.**
Col 3:10 image of the one who **c.** it,
Re 4:11 you **c.** all because of your will
Ps 104:30; Isa 43:7; 45:12; Eph 2:10.
CREATING, Isa 65:17 I am **c.** new heavens
Isa 45:7; 57:19; 65:18.
CREATION, Ro 1:20 from the world's **c.**
Ro 1:25 service to **c.** rather than One who
Ro 8:20 the **c.** was subjected to futility,
Ro 8:22 all **c.** keeps on groaning together
2Co 5:17 union with Christ, he is a new **c.**
Ga 6:15 new **c.** is something
Re 3:14 the beginning of the **c.** by God:
Col 1:15, 23; 1Ti 4:4; Heb 4:13; 2Pe 3:4.
CREATOR, Ec 12:1 Remember your **C.** in
Heb 11:10 builder and **c.** of which is God.
Isa 40:28; 43:15; 1Pe 4:19.
CREATURE(S), Jas 1:18 first fruits of **c.**

Le 11:10; Eze 1:5; Re 4:6; 5:6; 8:9.
CREDENCE, Lu 1:1 facts are given **c.**
CREDIT, Lu 6:32, 34 what **c.** is it to you?
1Co 8:8 we eat, we have no **c.** to ourselves.
2Co 12:6 to my **c.** more than what he sees
Php 4:17 that brings more **c.** to your account
CREDITOR, De 15:2; 1Sa 22:2; 2Ki 4:1.
CREEPING THINGS, Ps 148:10 you **c.** and
Ac 10:12 sorts of **c.** of the earth and
CREEPY FEELING, Ps 119:120 had a **c.**,
CRIME, Lu 23:4 find no **c.** in this man
CRINGE, De 33:29 enemies will **c.** before
CRINGING, 2Sa 22:45; Ps 18:44; 66:3.
CRITICAL TIMES, 2Ti 3:1 **c.** will be here.
CRITICIZE, 1Ti 5:1 Do not **c.** an older
CRITICIZED, Ge 21:25 Abraham **c.**
CROOKED, Ps 18:26 with the **c.** show
Pr 10:9 he that is making his way **c.**
Pr 11:20 Those **c.** at heart are detestable
Pr 19:1 the one **c.** in his lips and the one
Mic 3:9 make everything that is straight **c.**
Php 2:15 among a **c.** and twisted generation,
CROOKEDNESS, Pr 4:24 **c.** of speech,
CROSS. See TORTURE STAKE.
CROSSNESS, Ec 7:3 by the **c.** of the face
CROUCHING, Ge 4:7 sin **c.** at entrance
CROWD(S), 2Ch 20:15 terrified of large **c.**
Eze 22:30 drag her and her **c.** away
Mt 21:9 the **c.** going ahead of him
Re 7:9 look a great **c.** out of all
Eze 39:11; Mt 13:34; Mr 3:9; Joh 6:5.
CROWN(S), Eze 21:26 lift off the **c.**
1Th 2:19 what is our **c.** of exultation—
2Ti 4:8 reserved for me the **c.**
Re 2:10 give you the **c.** of life
Es 8:15; Mt 27:29; Jas 1:12; 1Pe 5:4.
CROWS, Mt 26:34; Mr 14:30.
CRUCIFY. See IMPALE.
CRUEL, Pr 5:9; 11:17; 12:10; Isa 13:9.
CRUMBS, Mt 15:27 dogs do eat of the **c.**
CRUSH, Da 2:44 It will **c.** and end all these
Ro 16:20 God will **c.** Satan under your
De 9:21; Ps 72:4; Zec 11:6.
CRUSHED, Isa 53:5 he was **c.** for our
Isa 57:15 with the one **c.** and lowly in
Isa 58:6 send away the **c.** ones free,
Jer 46:5 mighty men are **c.** to pieces
Joh 19:36 Not a bone of his will be **c.**
Ps 9:9; 89:23; Isa 42:3; Mic 1:7; Lu 4:18.
CRUSHING, Ps 94:5, your people, they keep **c.**
Isa 53:10 Jehovah took delight in **c.** him;
CRY OUT, Lu 19:40 the stones **c.** out.
Isa 12:6; Jer 25:34; 31:7; Lu 18:7.
CRY OUT JOYFULLY, Isa 54:1 **C.** barren
Ps 20:5; 92:4; Isa 44:23.
CUBIT(S), Mt 6:27 Who can add one **c.** to
Ge 6:15; Ex 27:1; Eze 41:8; Re 21:17.
CUD, Le 11:3; De 14:6.
CULTIVATE, Ge 2:5 no man to **c.** the
Ge 3:23 **c.** the ground from
CULTIVATED, Heb 6:7 for whom it is **c.**,
CULTIVATING, Zec 13:5 I am **c.** soil,
CULTIVATION, 1Co 3:9 field under **c.**,
CULTIVATOR(S), Joh 15:1 Father is the **c.**
Ge 4:2; Mt 21:33.
CUNNING, 1Sa 23:22 he is surely **c.**
Job 5:13 catching the wise in their **c.**,
1Co 3:19 catches wise in their own **c.**
Lu 20:23; 2Co 4:2; 11:3.
CUNNINGLY, Ps 83:3 **c.** carry on talk,
CUP, Ps 116:13 **c.** of grand salvation
Isa 51:17, 22 **c.** of rage.
Jer 25:15 Take this **c.** of the wine of rage
Mt 10:42 little ones only a **c.** of water

Lu 22:20 **c.** means the new covenant
Lu 22:42 you wish, remove this **c.**
1Co 10:21 Jehovah and the **c.** of demons
Ge 44:12; Jer 51:7; Mt 20:22; 1Co 10:16.
CURDLE, Job 10:10 like cheese to **c.** me
CURE, Lu 4:23 Physician **c.** yourself
Lu 13:14 **c.** on the sabbath,
Mt 8:7; Mr 3:2; Lu 6:7; 10:9.
CURED, Ac 5:16 would one and all be **c.**
Mt 12:15; 19:2; 21:14; Lu 13:14.
CURER, Pr 17:22 does good as a **c.**,
CURING, Mt 9:35 **c.** every sort of disease
Re 22:2 were for the **c.** of the nations.
CURSE, Job 2:5 see whether he will **c.**
Ga 3:13 released **c.** of the Law
Ge 12:3; Job 2:9; Isa 24:6; Re 22:3.
CURSED, Ge 3:17 **c.** is the ground on
CURSING, Ro 12:14 and do not be **c.**
CURTAIN, Mt 27:51 **c.** was rent in two,
Heb 10:20 new way through the **c.** his flesh
Ex 26:31; Heb 6:19; 9:3.
CURVES, Lu 3:5 the **c.** become straight
CUSH, Ge 10:6-8; Isa 11:11; Jer 46:9.
CUSTODY, Ga 3:22 to the **c.** of sin,
Jer 37:21; Mt 26:48; Ac 4:3; 5:18.
CUSTOM(S), 1Ch 15:13 according to the **c.**
Jer 10:3 **c.** are an exhalation
Ac 16:21 they are publishing **c.**
Heb 10:25 **c.**, but encouraging one another,
Le 18:30; Ac 6:14; 15:1; 26:3; 1Co 11:16.
CUSTOMARY, Php 2:29 give him the **c.**
CUT DOWN, Ps 75:8; 2Ch 34:7; Isa 14:12.
CUT OFF, Ps 37:9 evildoers will be **c.**
Da 9:26 Messiah will be **c.**, with nothing
2Pe 2:9 for the day of judgment to be **c.**
Ps 34:16; 37:38; Isa 56:5; Mic 5:9.
CUT SHORT, Mt 24:22; Mr 13:20 days **c.**
CUTTING-OFF, Mt 25:46 everlasting **c.**
CYMBAL(S), 2Sa 6:5 celebrating with **c.**
1Co 13:1 a clashing **c.**
CYRUS, Isa 44:28 C.: he is my shepherd
Isa 45:1 anointed one, to C., whose
2Ch 36:22; Ezr 1:2, 7; 5:13; 6:3, 14.

D

DAGON, 1Sa 5:3 D. was fallen face
Jg 16:23; 1Sa 5:2, 4, 5, 7.
DAILY, Lu 19:47 **d.** in the temple
Ac 17:11 examining Scriptures **d.**
Ps 68:19; Jer 7:25; 1Co 15:31; Heb 7:27.
DAINTIES, Ge 49:20; Ps 141:4.
DAMAGES IMPOSED, Ex 21:22 **d.** upon him
DAMAGING, Heb 13:17 this would be **d.** to
DAMASCUS, 2Sa 8:6; Isa 7:8; Ac 9:2.
DAMNATION. See JUDGMENT.
DAN, Jg 5:17 D., why dwell in ships?
Ge 30:6; 46:23; 49:16; De 33:22.
DANCES, Ex 15:20; 32:19; 1Sa 18:6.
DANCING, Jg 11:34, playing and **d.!**
Ps 30:11; 149:3; La 5:15; Lu 15:25.
DANGER(S), 2Co 11:26 **d.** from highwaymen,
Lu 8:23; Ac 19:27, 40; Ro 8:35.
DANIEL, Da 12:9 Go, D., because
Eze 14:20; Da 6:2; 12:4; Mt 24:15.
DARES, Ro 5:7 someone even **d.** to die.
DARICS, 1Ch 29:7 ten thousand **d.** and
Ezr 8:27 bowls worth a thousand **d.** and two
DARIUS, Ezr 6:12; Da 6:28; Hag 1:1.
DARK, Joe 2:10 Sun and moon become **d.**
Mt 6:23; Lu 11:36; Joh 6:17; 2Pe 1:19.
DARKENED, Ro 1:21 heart became **d.**
Ro 11:10 their eyes become **d.**
DARKNESS, Ge 1:2 **d.** upon the surface

Isa 42:7 those sitting in **d.**
Isa 45:7 light and creating **d.**
Isa 60:2 D. itself will cover people
Joh 3:19 men have loved the **d.**
1Th 5:4 you are not in **d.**, so that that day
1Pe 2:9 called you out of **d.**
1Jo 1:5 there is no **d.** in union with him.
Ex 10:21; Joe 2:31; 2Co 6:14; Eph 4:18.
DARKNESS OUTSIDE, Mt 25:30 into the **d.**
DARTING GREEDILY, 1Sa 15:19 **d.** at spoil
DATHAN, Nu 26:9; De 11:6; Ps 106:17.
DAUGHTER(S), Ge 5:4 Adam father to **d.**
Isa 52:2 captive **d.** Zion
Joe 2:28 and your **d.** will prophesy.
Lu 23:28 **d.** of Jerusalem, stop weeping
Da 11:6, 17; Mt 21:5; Ac 2:17; 2Co 6:18.
DAUGHTER-IN-LAW, Le 11:31; Le 18:15.
DAVID, 1Sa 18:3 Jonathan and D.
Mt 21:9 crowds, crying out: Save, Son of D.!
Lu 20:41 how Christ is D.'s son
Ac 2:34 D. not ascend to the heavens
1Sa 16:13; Ps 89:3; Isa 9:7; Ac 2:29.
DAWN, Job 38:12 cause the **d.** to know
Isa 14:12 shining one, son of the **d.!**
Ps 139:9; Isa 8:20; Ho 6:3; 2Pe 1:19.
DAY(S), Ge 1:5 calling the light D.,
Pr 4:18 until the **d.** is firmly established.
Isa 2:2 it must occur in the final **d.**
Da 2:44 in the **d.** of those kings
Mal 3:2 with the **d.** of his coming
Mt 24:22 unless those **d.** were cut short
Mr 13:32 that **d.** or hour nobody knows
Ac 17:31 he has set a **d.** to judge
Ro 14:5 One man judges one **d.** above another;
2Co 6:2 Now is the **d.** for salvation.
2Pe 3:8 a thousand years as one **d.**
Ps 61:8; 90:12; Pr 3:16; Isa 58:2; Jer
25:33; Am 8:11; Zec 8:23; Ro 13:12.
DAYBREAK, Ne 8:3 read from **d.** till midday,
DAYLIGHT, 2Sa 2:32; Job 24:14.
DAY OF JEHOVAH, Zep 2:3 concealed in **d.**
Joe 2:11; Zep 1:14, 18; 2Th 2:2.
DAY'S JOURNEY, Ge 30:36; Nu 11:31.
DAYSTAR, 2Pe 1:19 **d.** rises in hearts
DEACON. See MINISTER.
DEAD, Ps 115:17 D. do not praise Jah,
Ec 9:5 D. are conscious of nothing.
Isa 26:14 **d.**; they will not live.
Mt 8:22 the **d.** bury their **d.**
Joh 5:25 **d.** will hear the voice of son
Ro 6:11 **d.** with reference to sin but living
Eph 2:1 alive though you were **d.**
1Th 4:16 **d.** in union with Christ rise
Ps 110:6; Mt 22:32; Re 14:13; 20:13.
DEADEN, Col 3:5 D., therefore, your body
DEADENED, Ro 4:19 body, now already **d.**,
DEAD SEA. See SALT SEA.
DEAF, Isa 35:5 ears of the **d.** ones will
Isa 42:19 who is **d.** as my messenger
Isa 43:8 Bring forth the ones **d.**
Isa 42:18; Mic 7:16; Mt 11:5; Mr 7:37.
DEAL BLOW, 1Sa 26:10; 2Sa 12:15.
DEAL FALSELY, Le 19:11.
DEAR, Lu 7:2; Php 2:29.
DEATH, De 30:19 life and **d.** before you,
Job 38:17 Have gates of **d.** been uncovered
Ps 116:15 Precious is the **d.** of his loyal
Pr 16:25 the ways of **d.** are the end of it
Ec 7:1 day of **d.** than the day of being born.
Isa 25:8 swallow up **d.** forever,
Ro 5:12 thus **d.** spread to all men
Ro 5:17 **d.** ruled as king through that one,
Ro 6:10 the **d.** that he died, he died with
Ro 6:23 wages sin pays is **d.**,

1Co 15:21 **d.** through a man, resurrection
1Co 15:26 last enemy, **d.** is to be destroyed.
Heb 2:9 taste **d.** for every man.
Heb 2:14 means to cause **d.**, Devil,
Re 2:10 faithful even to **d.**,
Re 20:14 **d.** and Hades were hurled
Re 21:4 **d.** will be no more.
Ps 89:48; Eze 33:11; Lu 21:16; Joh 8:51.
DEATH-DEALING, 2Co 4:10 endure the **d.**
Jas 3:8 tongue is full of **d.** poison
DEATHLY PANGS, Ps 73:4 they have no **d.**
DEBATE(S), 1Ti 2:8; 6:4.
DEBATER, 1Co 1:20 Where the **d.** of this
DEBAUCHERY, Eph 5:18; Tit 1:6; 1Pe 4:4.
DEBORAH, Jg 4:9, 14; 5:1, 7, 12, 15.
DEBRIS, Am 6:11 small house into **d.**
DEBT(S), 2Ki 4:7; Ne 10:31; Mt 6:12; 18:
27; Ro 4:4.
DEBTOR(S), Lu 7:41; 13:4; Ro 1:14; 15:27.
DECAPOLIS, Mt 4:25; Mr 5:20; 7:31.
DECEASED, Nu 5:2; Mt 22:25; Ac 2:29.
DECEIT, Joh 1:47 in whom there is no **d.**
Job 15:35; Ps 32:2; Ro 3:13.
DECEITFUL, Jer 15:18 like something **d.**,
Mic 1:14 houses of Achzib were **d.** to the
2Co 11:13 such men are **d.** workers,
DECEITFULLY, Ps 24:4 taken an oath **d.**
DECEITFULNESS, 1Pe 2:1 put away all **d.**
DECEIVE, Le 19:11 you must not **d.** and
Jer 29:8; 37:9; Eph 5:6.
DECEIVED, Ob 3 presumptuousness **d.** you,
DECEIVERS, 2Co 6:8; Tit 1:10; 2Jo 7.
DECEIVING, Zec 13:4 purpose of **d.**
DECENTLY, 1Co 14:40 things take place **d.**
1Th 4:12 walking **d.** regards people outside
DECEPTION(S), Ps 5:6 **d.** Jehovah detests
Ps 34:13 Safeguard against speaking **d.**
Isa 53:9 no **d.** in his mouth.
Col 2:8 philosophy and empty **d.**
1Pe 2:22 nor was **d.** found in his mouth.
Ps 10:7; Pr 12:17; Jer 9:6; 2Th 2:10.
DECEPTIVE, Le 6:3 is **d.** about it
Mt 13:22 **d.** power of riches
Eph 4:22 according to his **d.** desires;
Heb 3:13 hardened by the **d.** power of sin.
DECEPTIVE TEACHINGS, 2Pe 2:13 delight in
DECIDED, Isa 28:22 extermination is **d.**
Da 9:26 **d.** upon is desolations
Da 11:36 thing **d.** upon must be done
1Ki 20:40; Job 14:5; Isa 10:22; Ac 16:4;
1Co 2:2; Tit 3:12.
DECISION(S), Pr 16:10 Inspired **d.** should
Joe 3:14 in the low plain of the **d.**
Ro 14:1 not make **d.** on inward questionings.
Ro 14:13 make this your **d.**, not to put
1Co 7:37 to **d.** to keep his virginity,
Ac 15:19; Jas 2:4; Re 16:7.
DECK, Job 40:10 **d.** with superiority
Lu 16:19 rich man **d.** himself with purple
DECKED, Mr 15:17 they **d.** him with purple
DECLARATION, 1Ti 6:13 fine public **d.**
DECLARE(S), De 32:3 **d.** the name of Jehovah.
Lu 4:18 he anointed me to **d.** good news
Lu 16:15 You **d.** yourselves righteous men.
Ro 8:33 God who **d.** them righteous
1Co 9:16 woe is me if I did not **d.** good
1Pe 2:4 **d.** abroad the excellencies of the
Ex 23:7; 33:19; Ps 79:13; 96:3; Heb 2:12.
DECLARED, Ex 9:16 have my name **d.**
Ps 119:13 I have **d.** the judicial decisions
Ps 22:30; 88:11; 102:21; 119:26.
DECLARE RIGHTEOUS, Job 27:5 I **d.** you
DECLARED RIGHTEOUS, Isa 43:9 may be **d.**,

Ro 2:13 doers of law will be **d.**
Ro 3:24 they are being **d.** by undeserved
Ro 5:1 **d.** as a result of faith, let us
1Ti 3:16 He was **d.** in spirit, appeared to
Jas 2:24 man is to be **d.** by works, and not
Ro 3:20; 5:9; 8:30; Ga 2:16; Jas 2:21, 25.
DECLARES, Ro 8:33 God **d.** them righteous.
DECLARING, Ps 19:1 heavens are **d.** the
Ac 8:4 through the land **d.** good news
Ro 5:18 results to men is a **d.** them righteous
DECORATION, Isa 28:5 a crown of **d.**
Da 11:45 and the holy mountain of D.
Isa 4:2; 13:19; Eze 20:6; Dan 8:9; 11:16.
DECREASE, Ro 11:12 their **d.** means riches
DECREE(S), Ps 94:20 framing trouble by **d.**?
Mic 7:11 day the **d.** will be far away.
Ro 1:32 know well the righteous **d.** of God,
Eph 2:15 commandments consisting in **d.**,
Col 2:14 blotted out the handwritten **d.**
Es 1:20; Lu 2:1; Ac 16:4; Col 2:20.
DECREED, Ac 10:42 **d.** by God to be judge
Ac 17:26 he **d.** the appointed seasons
DECREEING, Pr 8:15 **d.** righteousness.
DECREPIT, 2Ch 36:17 old or **d.**
DEDICATE, Ho 9:10 **d.** to the thing,
DEDICATED, Mr 7:11 a gift **d.** to God,
Lu 21:5 adorned with **d.** things
DEDICATION, Ex 39:30; Le 8:9; Joh 10:22.
DEDUCTION, Le 27:18 **d.** made from estimated
DEED(S), Re 20:12 according to their **d.**
Ge 20:9; Nu 16:28; Job 33:17.
DEED OF PURCHASE, Jer 32:12, 13, 16.
DEEP, Job 12:22 uncovering **d.** things
Job 38:30 surface of the watery **d.** makes
1Co 2:10 spirit searches the **d.** things
Ps 92:5; Da 2:22; Lu 5:4; 2Co 8:2.
DEEP SHADOW, Job 3:5; Ps 23:4; Isa 9:2.
DEFAMED, 1Co 4:13 when being **d.**, we
DEFECT, Le 22:21; Pr 9:7; Da 1:4.
DEFECTIVE, Tit 1:5 correct things **d.**
DEFEND, 2Ki 20:6 I will **d.** this city
2Ki 19:34; Isa 31:5; Zec 9:15.
DEFENDING, Php 1:7 **d.** and legally
DEFENSE, Lu 12:11 speak in **d.**
Ac 25:16 speak in his **d.**
Php 1:16 I am set for **d.** of the good news;
2Ti 4:16 In my first **d.** no one came
1Pe 3:15 always ready to make a **d.** before
Zec 12:8; Ac 19:33; 2Co 12:19.
DEFIANT, Ps 40:4 turned to **d.** people,
DEFICIENCY, 2Co 8:14 offset their **d.**,
DEFICIENT, Da 5:27 weighed and found **d.**
DEFILE, Jer 32:34 my name to **d.** it
Mt 15:18 things out of mouth **d.**
Nu 35:34; Isa 30:22; Eze 20:7.
DEFILED, Ps 79:1 have **d.** your temple
Ro 14:14 that nothing is **d.** in itself;
Tit 1:15 to persons **d.** nothing is clean
DEFILEMENT, Heb 13:4 bed be without **d.**,
DEFLECTED, Ro 3:12 All men have **d.**,
DEFRAUD, De 24:14 must not **d.** a hired
Mr 10:19 do not **d.**, Honor your father and
Le 19:13; Ps 119:122; Zec 7:10.
DEFRAUDED, 1Co 6:7 rather let yourselves be **d.**
Le 6:2; Ps 103:6; Mic 2:2.
DEFRAUDER, Ps 72:4 let him crush the **d.**
Ps 119:134 Redeem me from any **d.**
Jer 22:3 deliver out of the hand of the **d.**
DEFRAUDING, Ps 119:121 those **d.** me
Pr 22:16 He that is **d.** the lowly one to
Am 4:1 cows of Bashan, who are **d.** the lowly
Ps 62:10; Pr 14:31; Jer 22:17; Eze 22:29.
DEGENERATING, Ho 10:1 Israel is a **d.** vine

DEGREE, Jer 30:11; 2Ti 4:15.
DEITIES, Ac 17:18 of foreign **d.**
DEITY, Ac 25:19 worship of the **d.**
DEJECTED, 1Ki 20:43 went on his way **d.**
Eze 21:7 spirit become **d.**
Ge 40:6; Ps 109:16.
DEJECTED-LOOKING, Da 1:10 faces **d.**
DEJECTING, Eze 13:22 **d.** the heart of a
DEJECTION, Jas 4:9 turn joy into **d.**
Ex 23:28; De 7:20; Jos 24:12.
DELAY, Ge 34:19 young man did not **d.**
Heb 10:37 will arrive and will not **d.**
Da 9:19; Hab 2:3.
DELAYED, Jg 5:28 war chariot **d.**
DELIGHT(S), Ps 1:2 his **d.** is in the law
Ps 22:8 Since Jehovah has taken **d.** in him
Pr 8:11 all other **d.** cannot be made equal
Isa 1:11 your sacrifices I have taken no **d.**
Jer 9:24 in these things I take **d.,**
Eze 33:11 **d.,** not in the death of the
Nu 14:8; 1Sa 15:22; Isa 53:10; Ro 7:22.
DELIGHTED, Ps 40:8 your will, I have **d.,**
Isa 55:11 word in which I have **d.**
Isa 56:4 chosen what I have **d.** in
Jon 1:14 done what you have **d.** in!
DELIGHT, EXQUISITE, Ps 37:11; Isa 58:14.
DELIGHTFUL, Ec 12:10 congregator sought **d.**
DELIGHTS, Pr 21:1 Everywhere Jehovah **d.**
DELILAH, Jg 16:4, 6, 10, 12, 13, 18.
DELINQUENT, Jos 18:3 to be **d.** about going in
Jer 1:19 I am with you, to **d.** you.
Lu 24:21 was the one to **d.** Israel;
2Pe 2:9 Jehovah knows how to **d.** people
Ex 3:8; Ps 33:19; Isa 50:2; Mt 10:17.
DELIVERANCE, 1Sa 30:8 you will make a **d,**
Es 4:14 relief and **d.** will stand up for
Isa 66:7 gave **d.** to a male child.
Lu 21:28 your **d.** is getting near.
Heb 9:12 obtained an everlasting **d.** for us
DELIVERED, Ps 34:4 my frights he **d.** me
Ro 4:25 **d.** up for our trespasses
Mt 11:27; Lu 4:6; Ac 12:11; Jude 3.
DELIVERER, Ro 11:26 The **d.** will come
2Sa 14:6; Ps 7:2; Isa 5:29; Ac 7:35.
DELIVERING, Pr 14:25 true witness is **d.**
Job 10:7; Ps 18:17; Da 8:4.
DELIVERS, Ps 34:19 Jehovah **d.** him
1Th 1:10 **d.** us from the wrath coming.
DELUDE, Col 2:4 no man may **d.** you
DELUGE, Ge 6:17 I am bringing the **d.**
Ge 7:17 **d.** went on for forty days
Ge 9:11 No more flesh cut off by a **d.**
2Pe 2:5 he brought a **d.** upon
Ge 7:7; 10:1, 32; Ps 29:10.
DELUGED, 2Pe 3:6 world **d.** with water
DEMANDED, Lu 12:48 much will be **d.**
DEMARCATION, Ex 8:23 set a **d.** between my
DEMOLISHED, Jer 51:58 Babylon will be **d.**
DEMOLISHER, Isa 22:5 is **d.** of the wall
DEMONIC, Jas 3:15 earthly, animal, **d.**
DEMONIZED, Mt 15:22; Joh 10:21.
DEMON-POSSESSED, Mr 1:32; Lu 8:36.
DEMONS, De 32:17 sacrificing to **d.**
1Co 10:21 the table of **d.**
1Ti 4:1 fall away to teachings of **d.,**
Jas 2:19 the **d.** believe and shudder.
Re 16:14 expressions inspired by **d.**
Ps 106:37; Mt 12:24; 1Co 10:20; Re 18:2.
DEMONS, GOAT-SHAPED, Le 17:7; Isa 13:21.
DEMONSTRATE, Ro 9:22; 1Ti 1:16.
DEMONSTRATED, Ac 18:28; Eph 2:7.
DEMONSTRATION, 1Co 2:4; Heb 11:1.
DENARIUS, Mt 20:2 a **d.** a day,

Mt 20:9 they each received a **d.**
Mr 12:15 Bring me a **d.** to look at.
Mt 20:10, 13; 22:19; Lu 20:24.
DENIED, Jer 5:12 They have **d.** Jehovah,
Job 31:28; Mt 26:70; Joh 18:25.
DENOUNCE, Nu 23:7 do **d.** Israel
DENUDING, Ezr 4:14 to see the **d.** of king
DENUNCIATION(S), Isa 26:20 **d.** passes
Jer 10:10 no nations hold up under his **d.**
Da 11:30 **d.** against the holy covenant
Zep 3:8 pour out upon them my **d.,**
Ps 69:24; Isa 10:5, 25; Da 8:19; Na 1:6.
DENY, Jos 24:27 may not **d.** your God.
Ge 18:15; Job 8:18; Pr 30:9; 2Ti 2:12.
DEPART, 1Co 7:10 wife not **d.** from husband
Jos 1:8; Ac 18:2; 1Co 7:15.
DEPARTURE, Lu 9:31 talking about his **d.**
2Pe 1:15 after my **d.** you
DEPENDENT, Ro 9:11 **d.,** not upon works,
1Pe 4:11 let him minister as **d.** on the
DEPORTATION, Mt 1:11 **d.** to Babylon.
DEPOSIT, Ex 16:33 jar of manna and **d.**
DEPOSITED, Zec 5:11.
DEPOSITORIES, Ge 41:56 open up the grain **d.**
DEPRESSED, Php 2:26; 1Th 5:14.
DEPRIVE, Col 2:18 Let no man **d.** you
DEPRIVED, Isa 38:10 **d.** of my years
DEPRIVING, 1Co 7:5 not be **d.** each other
DEPTH, Mt 13:5; Ro 8:39; Eph 3:18.
DEPUTATIONS, Ps 78:49 D. of angels
DEPUTIES, 2Ch 8:10 chiefs of the **d.**
DEPUTY RULERS, Ne 12:40; 13:11.
DERIDE, Pr 3:34 with ridiculers, he will **d.,**
DERIDES, Pr 19:28 witness **d.** justice,
DERIDING, 2Ch 30:10 mockery and **d.** them.
DERISION, Ps 2:4 hold them in **d.**
Ps 44:13; 59:8; Eze 23:32; Ho 7:16.
DESCEND, Pr 30:4; Ro 10:7; 1Th 4:16.
DESCENDED, Eph 4:9 he **d.** into the lower
DESCENDING, Ps 133:3 dew **d.** upon Zion.
DESERT(S), De 4:31 Jehovah will not **d.**
1Sa 12:22 Jehovah will not **d.** his people
Isa 35:1 **d.** plain will be joyful
Isa 51:3 **d.** plain like the garden
Jer 7:29 Jehovah will **d.** the generation
Heb 11:38 wandered about in **d.**
Isa 35:6; 41:19; 43:19; Jer 50:12; Lu 1:80.
DESERTED, Jg 6:13 Jehovah has **d.** us
Jer 15:6 You have **d.** me, Jehovah
DESERTERS, 2Ki 25:11 **d.** had gone over to
DESERVES, Mt 10:10 worker **d.** his food
DESERVING, Ac 26:31 nothing **d.** death or
Lu 23:15; Ac 23:29; Ro 1:32; 1Ti 1:15.
DESIGN(S), Lu 23:51 not support **d.**
2Co 2:11 not ignorant of his **d.**
DESIGNATE, 1Sa 16:3 one whom I **d.** to you
DESIGNATED, Lu 10:1 Lord **d.** seventy
Nu 1:17; 1Ch 12:31; 2Ch 31:19; Mic 6:9.
DESIGN OF THE ALTAR, 2Ki 16:10.
DESIRABLE, Eze 24:16 the thing **d.**
Da 11:38 by means of precious and **d.** things,
Da 11:43 he will rule over the **d.** things
Hag 2:7 **d.** of all nations must come
DESIRE(S), Ex 20:17 not **d.** your man's
Ps 145:16 satisfying the **d.** of every
Joh 8:44 to do the **d.** of your father.
1Ti 6:9 many senseless and hurtful **d.**
Tit 2:12 repudiate ungodliness and worldly **d.**
Jas 1:14 drawn and enticed by his own **d.**
2Pe 3:3 proceeding according to their own **d.**
1Jo 2:16 **d.** of the flesh and the **d.** of
1Jo 2:17 is passing away and so is its **d.,**
Ga 5:24; Php 1:23; 2Ti 2:22; 2Pe 2:18.
DESIRED, Mic 2:2 they have **d.** fields

DESIST, 2Pe 2:14 eyes unable to **d.**
DESISTED, 1Pe 4:1 has **d.** from sins,
DESOLATE, Isa 62:4 said to be **d.**
　Ga 4:27 children of the **d.** woman
　Joe 3:19; Zep 1:13.
DESOLATED PLACES, Ezr 9:9 restore **d.**
DESOLATION, Mt 12:25 comes to **d.**
　Mt 24:15 thing that causes **d.,** as
DESPAIR, 1Sa 27:1; Job 6:26; Ec 2:20.
DESPICABLE, Es 3:6; Mt 5:22.
DESPISE(S), Ps 51:17 heart broken not **d.**
　Tit 2:15 Let no man ever **d.** you.
　Pr 6:30; 23:9, 22; 30:17.
DESPISED, Pr 1:7 Wisdom fools have **d.**
　Isa 53:3 He was **d.** and avoided
　Pr 11:12; Ec 9:16; Eze 17:19; Ob 2.
DESPITE, 1Pe 1:7 perishes **d.** its being
DESPOILED, Ps 17:9 wicked have **d.** me.
　Ps 76:5; Isa 59:15; Hab 2:8; 1Ti 6:5.
DESPOILING, Jer 25:36 Jehovah is **d.**
　Isa 22:4; 51:19; 59:7; 60:18; Jer 6:7; 20:8;
　48:3; 51:55; Eze 45:9; Ho 7:13; Am 3:10;
　Hab 1:3.
DESPONDENTLY, 1Ki 21:27 Ahab walking **d.**
DESPOT, Eze 31:11 give it into hand of **d.**
DESTINED, Pr 22:16 surely **d.** for want.
　Lu 21:7 when these things are **d.** to occur?
　Ga 3:23 faith that was **d.** to be revealed.
　1Th 3:4 we were **d.** to suffer tribulation.
　Lu 24:21; Joh 11:51; Ac 13:34.
DESTINED TO DESTRUCTION, Col 2:22 all **d.**
DESTINY, Mt 16:22 not have this **d.**
DESTINY, GOD OF, Isa 65:11 wine for **g.**
DESTITUTE, 1Ti 5:5 widow left **d.** has
DESTROY, Isa 26:14 **d.** all mention
　Jer 1:10 to **d.** and to tear down, to build
　Mt 10:28 **d.** both soul and body in Gehenna
　Jas 4:12 able to save and to **d.**
DESTROYED, Joh 3:16 not be **d.** but have
　2Pe 2:12 animals born to be caught and **d.**
　2Pe 3:9 he does not desire any to be **d.**
　Jude 5 saved afterwards **d.** those
　Ps 49:12; Lu 17:27; 2Co 4:9.
DESTROYER, 1Co 10:10 perish by the **d.**
　Heb 11:28 **d.** might not touch first-born
DESTRUCTION, Pr 7:13 road into **d.**
　Joh 17:12 except the son of **d.,**
　Ro 9:22 vessels of wrath made fit for **d.**
　1Th 5:3 Peace and security then sudden **d.**
　2Th 1:9 judicial punishment of everlasting **d.**
　2Th 2:3 gets revealed, the son of **d.**
　1Ti 6:9 which plunge men into **d.** and ruin.
　2Pe 2:1 bringing speedy **d.** upon themselves
　2Pe 2:3 the **d.** of them is not slumbering.
　Re 17:8 wild beast is to go off into **d.**
　Job 28:22; Heb 10:39; 2Pe 3:7, 16.
DESTRUCTIVENESS, Ho 13:14 **d.**, O Sheol?
DESTRUCTIVE SECTS, 2Pe 2:1 bring in **d.**
DETECTION, 2Sa 4:6 themselves escaped **d.**
DETENTION, HOUSE OF, 1Ki 22:27.
DETERMINATION, Ac 27:42 **d.** of soldiers
DETERMINED, 1Ti 6:9 those **d.** to be rich
DETERMINED, BAD IS, 1Sa 20:7; Es 7:7.
DETEST, Job 19:19 intimate group **d.** me
　De 7:26; Ps 106:40.
DETESTABLE, De 27:15 statue, a thing **d.**
　Pr 3:32 devious person is **d.** to Jehovah,
　Pr 12:22 false lips are **d.**
　Pr 16:5 proud is **d.** to Jehovah.
　Pr 28:9 prayer is **d.**
　2Ch 28:3; 33:2; Isa 41:24; Tit 1:16.
DETESTABLE THING(S), De 14:3 eat no **d.**
　Pr 3:32 the devious person is a **d.**
　Eze 9:4 sighing and groaning over all the **d.**

Eze 23:36 and tell them their **d.**
Ge 43:32; Le 20:13; De 18:9; Jer 7:10;
Mal 2:11.
DETESTING, Ps 119:163 Falsehood keep **d.**
DETESTS, Ps 5:6 deception Jehovah **d.**
DEVASTATED, Eze 6:6 cities become **d.**
　Jer 26:9; Ga 1:23; Re 17:16; 18:19.
DEVASTATING, Ga 1:13 I kept on **d.** it.
DEVASTATION(S), Isa 60:12; Da 9:2.
DEVIATE(S), Job 23:11; 31:7; Ps 44:18.
DEVIATED, Ac 1:25 Judas **d.** to go to
　1Ti 6:21 some have **d.** from the faith
　2Ti 2:18 very men have **d.** from the truth
DEVIATING, 1Ti 1:6 **d.** from these things
DEVICE, Mt 26:4; Mr 14:1 **d.** to kill
DEVIL, Joh 8:44 from your father the **D.**
　Eph 4:27 neither allow place for the **D.**
　Eph 6:11 stand firm against the **D.**
　Heb 2:14 he might bring to nothing the **D.**
　Jas 4:7 but oppose the **D.**, and he will
　1Pe 5:8 Your adversary, the **D.**, walks
　1Jo 3:8 **D.** has been sinning from beginning
　1Jo 3:8 to break up the works of the **D.**
　Re 12:12 because the **D.** has come down to
　Re 20:2 who is the **D.** and Satan, and bound
　Mt 4:1, 8; 25:41; Joh 13:2; Jude 9.
DEVIOUS, Pr 3:32 the **d.** person is
DEVIOUSNESS, Pr 4:24 the **d.** of lips put
DEVISING, Pr 14:22 those **d.** good.
DEVOLVE, 1Ki 4:7 **d.** upon each to provide
DEVOTE, Ac 6:4 we shall **d.** to prayer
DEVOTED THING, Nu 18:14 **d.** become yours.
DEVOTED TO DESTRUCTION, De 7:26;
　Jos 7:1; 1Ki 20:42.
DEVOTING, Isa 37:11; Ac 2:42.
DEVOTION. See also EXCLUSIVE DEVOTION,
GODLY DEVOTION.
DEVOTION, Ec 12:12 much **d.** is wearisome
　Ac 17:23 unknowingly giving godly **d.**
DEVOUR, Pr 30:8 **d.** the food prescribed
　Mal 4:1 day that is coming will **d.** them,
　1Pe 5:8 like a roaring lion, seeking to **d.**
　Re 12:4 give birth, it might **d.** her child
　Isa 31:8; Jer 46:10; Eze 34:28; Am 5:6.
DEVOURED, Zep 3:8 all the earth will be **d.**
　Re 20:9 fire came out of heaven and **d.**
　Zep 1:18; Zec 9:4.
DEVOURING, Jer 30:16 **d.** you be devoured
　Da 7:7 fourth beast was **d.** and
　Mal 3:11 rebuke the **d.** one
　Ga 5:15 keep on biting and **d.** one another,
DEVOUT, Ac 10:2 a **d.** man and fearing
　Ac 10:7 he called a **d.** soldier
DEW, Mic 5:7 many peoples like **d.** from
　De 32:2; Jg 6:37; Pr 19:12; Da 5:21.
DEWDROPS, Job 38:28 gave birth to **d.**?
DIADEM(S), Re 19:12 upon his head **d.**
　2Sa 1:10; Ps 89:39; Pr 27:24; Re 12:3.
DIALECT, Mt 26:73 **d.** gives you away.
DIAMOND, Eze 3:9 Like a **d.**, harder
DICTATOR(S), Isa 1:10; 3:6.
DIE, Ge 2:17 eat from it you will **d.**
　Ge 3:4 positively will not **d.**
　Ec 3:2 a time for birth and a time to **d.**;
　Eze 18:4 soul that is sinning will **d.**
　Joh 11:26 faith in me will never **d.** at all.
　Ec 9:5; Jer 16:4; Lu 20:36; Heb 9:27.
DIED, Ro 5:8 sinners, Christ **d.** for us
　Heb 11:13 In faith all these **d.**, although
　Lu 16:22; Ro 7:9; 14:9; 2Co 5:15.
DIES, Ec 3:19 As the one **d.**, so the
　Ro 6:9 Christ **d.** no more; death is
DIFFERENT, Ga 4:20 speak in a **d.** way,
　Es 1:7; Da 7:3, 7, 19, 23, 24.

DIFFICULT, Da 2:11 thing king is asking is **d.**
DIFFICULTY, 1Pe 4:18 saved with **d.**
DIGNITY, 1Ch 16:27 **d.** and splendor
  Job 37:22 Upon God **d.** is fear-inspiring.
  Ps 111:3 His activity is **d.** and splendor
  Isa 30:30 Jehovah make the **d.** of his voice
  Job 40:10; Jer 22:18; Da 2:6, 37; Zec 6:13.
DILIGENTLY, 2Ti 1:17 **d.** looked for me
DILIGENT ONE(S), Pr 10:4; 13:4; 21:5.
DIMINISH, Ex 21:10; Eze 5:11.
DIN, Isa 14:11 **d.** of your stringed
DINAH, Ge 30:21; 34:1, 3, 5, 13, 26; 46:15.
DIRECT, Jer 10:23 to man to **d.** his step.
  1Co 12:28 helpful services, abilities to **d.,**
DIRECTED, Ps 21:11 **d.** against you
DIRECTING, 1Ch 21:10 am **d.** against you
  1Co 9:26 I am **d.** my blows so as not to be
  2Th 3:5 continue **d.** your hearts successfully
DIRECTION, 1Ki 8:48 pray in the **d.** of
DIRECTOR, Job 2:8; 1Co 3:10 **d.** of works
DIRGE(S), 2Sa 1:17 chant this **d.** over
  2Ch 35:25; Jer 7:29; 9:10; Eze 32:16.
DISABLED, Ac 14:8 man **d.** in his feet
DISAPPOINTED, Mic 3:7 diviners will be **d.**
  Ro 10:11 None that rests faith will be **d.**
DISAPPOINTMENT, Ro 5:5 hope lead to **d.;**
  Ro 9:33 not come to **d.**
  1Pe 2:6 faith in it will not come to **d.**
DISAPPROVED, Ro 1:28 up to a **d.** mental
  1Co 9:27 that I should not become **d.**
  2Co 13:5-7; 2Ti 3:8.
DISARRANGED, La 3:11 ways he has **d.**
DISASTER(S), De 32:35 day of their **d.,**
  Eze 35:5 sword, in the time of their **d.,**
  2Sa 22:19; Job 31:23; Pr 17:5; Jer 18:17.
DISASTROUS, Job 30:12 cast **d.** barriers.
DISCERN, Pr 1:2 to **d.** the sayings
  Pr 19:25 reproving that he may **d.** knowledge.
  Joh 20:9 did not **d.** scripture
  1Co 11:29 if he does not **d.** the body.
  1Sa 3:8; 1Ki 3:9; Pr 20:24; Da 10:14.
DISCERNMENT, Pr 2:11 **d.** will safeguard
  1Co 10:15 I speak as to men with **d.;** judge
  Col 1:9 be filled with spiritual **d.**
  2Ti 2:7 Lord give you **d.** in all things
  Pr 2:2; 3:19; 10:23; 11:12; 17:27; 24:3.
DISCHARGE, Ec 8:8 nor any **d.** in the war
DISCHARGED, Ro 7:2 **d.** from the law of
DISCIPLE(S), Isa 8:16 law among my **d.**
  Mt 28:19 **d.** of people of all nations
  Joh 8:31 remain in my word, you are my **d.**
  Mt 10:24, 42; 26:26, 56.
DISCIPLINE, Pr 6:23 reproofs of **d.** are
  Pr 15:33 The fear of Jehovah is a **d.**
  Pr 22:15 rod of **d.** will remove it far
  Pr 23:13 Do not hold back **d.** from the boy
  Jer 5:3 They refused to take **d.**
  Heb 12:5 not belittle the **d.** from Jehovah
  Heb 12:11 no **d.** seems to be joyous
  Job 5:17; Ps 50:17; Pr 1:2; 4:13; Eph 6:4.
DISCIPLINED, 1Co 11:32 we are **d.** by
DISCIPLINES, Heb 12:6 loves he **d.**
DISCIPLINING, Isa 26:16 they had your **d.**
  Ho 7:15 I, for my part, did **d.;**
  2Ti 3:16 for **d.** in righteousness,
DISCONCERTED, Ps 38:6; Isa 21:3.
DISCONTENTED, Mic 2:7 Jehovah **d.**
DISCOURAGED, Pr 24:10 **d.** in the day of
DISCOURAGEMENT, Ex 6:9 Israel out of **d.**
DISCOURSE, Ac 15:32 with many a **d.**
DISCOVERED, 2Pe 3:10 works will be **d.**
DISCREDITED, Lu 23:11 guards **d.** him,
DISCREET, Isa 29:14 understanding of **d.**
  Mt 7:24 a **d.** man, who built his house

Mt 24:45 Who is the faithful and **d.** slave
Mt 25:2 Five foolish and five were **d.**
Ro 12:16 Do not become **d.** in your own eyes,
Ge 41:39; Isa 5:21; Ro 11:25; 1Co 4:10.
DISCREETLY, Pr 10:19 check is acting **d.**
DISCRETION, Ps 47:7 acting with **d.**
  2Ch 30:22; Ps 101:2; Pr 12:8; Jer 23:5.
DISCUSS, Lu 22:23 **d.** which would be
DISCUSSED, Mr 9:10 **d.** among themselves
  Heb 8:1 things **d.** this is the main point:
DISCUSSION, Mt 1:27 they began a **d.**
DISDAINING, Eze 16:31 in **d.** hire.
DISFELLOWSHIPED. See EXPELLED.
DISFIGUREMENT, Isa 52:14 so much **d.**
DISGRACE, Pr 13:5 wicked ones cause **d.**
DISGRACEFUL, Pr 14:34 sin is **d.** to
  1Co 14:35 it is **d.** for a woman to speak
  Ro 1:26; 1Co 11:6.
DISGUISED, 1Ki 20:38; 2Ch 35:22.
DISGUISES, Pr 28:12 a man **d.** himself.
DISGUISING, 1Ki 22:30 will be a **d.**
DISGUST, Ga 4:14 or spit in **d.,**
DISGUSTED, Heb 3:10 **d.** with generation
  Heb 3:17 God become **d.** for forty years?
DISGUSTING THING(S), Jer 7:30; Da 9:27.
  Da 11:31 the **d.** that is causing desolation.
  Na 3:6 I will throw **d.** upon you,
  Mt 24:15 catch sight of the **d.** that causes
  Lu 16:15 lofty among men is a **d.** in God's
  Re 17:4 a golden cup that was full of **d.**
  De 29:17; 2Ki 23:24; Zec 9:7; Re 17:5.
DISHEARTEN, Nu 32:7 **d.** sons of Israel
DISHEARTENED, Jos 2:9 **d.** because of you.
DISHONEST GAIN, 1Ti 3:8; Tit 1:7.
  Tit 1:11 teaching for the sake of **d.**
  1Pe 5:2 neither for love of **d.** but eagerly,
DISHONOR, Pr 3:35 stupid are exalting **d.**
  1Co 15:43 It is sown in **d.,** it is raised
  1Co 11:14; 2Co 6:8; 11:21.
DISHONORABLE, Ro 9:21 for a **d.** use?
DISHONORED, Ac 5:41 **d.** in behalf of his
DISINTEGRATED, Jer 49:23 They have **d.**
DISINTEGRATION, Isa 38:17 pit of **d.**
DISLOYAL, 2Ti 3:2 men will be **d.**
DISMEMBERED, Da 2:5; 3:29.
DISOBEDIENCE, Ro 5:19 **d.** of one man
  Eph 2:2 that now operates in the sons of **d.**
  2Co 10:6; Eph 5:6.
DISOBEDIENT, Ro 10:21 a people that is **d.**
  Heb 2:2 **d.** act received a retribution
DISOBEDIENTLY, Heb 3:18 who acted **d.?**
DISORDER(S), 1Co 14:33 a God not of **d.**
  2Ch 15:5; Am 3:9; Lu 21:9; 2Co 6:5;
  12:20; Jas 3:16.
DISORDERLY, Ac 19:40 this **d.** mob.
  1Th 5:14; 2Th 3:6, 7, 11.
DISOWN, Mr 8:34 let him **d.** himself
  Mt 10:33; Mr 14:30; Lu 9:23; Tit 1:16.
DISOWNED, Lu 12:9 be **d.** before angels
  1Ti 5:8 he has **d.** the faith
  Joh 13:38; Ac 3:14; 7:35.
DISOWNS, Lu 12:9 he that **d.** me will be
DISPATCHED, Mt 21:34; Ac 8:14; 1Co 1:17.
DISPENSING, 1Ti 1:4 rather than a **d.**
DISPERSED, Isa 11:12 gather the **d.** ones
  Isa 51:6 heavens must be **d.** in fragments
  Isa 56:8 Jehovah is collecting the **d.** ones
  Ps 147:2; Isa 16:3, 4; 27:13; Zec 1:19.
DISPLEASING, Ge 21:11; 28:8; 48:17.
DISPOSED, Pr 29:22; Na 1:2.
DISPOSITION, Php 2:20 no one else of a **d.**
DISPOSSESS, Jg 11:24 one we shall **d.**
DISPUTE(S), De 19:17 men have **d.** stand
  1Co 11:16 if any man seems to **d.** for some

1Ti 6:5 **d.** about trifles on the part of
De 17:8; 21:5; 25:1; Ac 25:19; Heb 6:16.
DISPUTING, Jude 9 **d.** about Moses' body
DISQUIETING, Ps 94:19 my **d.** thoughts
DISQUIETUDE, Ps 55:2 I cannot but show **d.**,
DISREGARD, Mr 6:26; 1Th 4:8.
DISREGARDED, Mt 23:23 **d.** the weightier
Heb 10:28 **d.** the law of Moses dies
Lu 7:30; 1Ti 5:12.
DISREGARDS, Lu 10:16; Joh 12:48.
DISRESPECT, De 32:19 Jehovah came to **d.**
Ps 74:18 have treated your name with **d.**
Isa 52:5 my name was being treated with **d.**
2Sa 12:14; Ne 9:26; Ps 74:10; Jer 14:21.
DISRESPECTED, Pr 1:30 they **d.** all my
DISRESPECTFUL, Eze 35:12 your **d.** things
DISRESPECTS, Pr 15:5 **d.** the discipline
DISSENSION(S), 1Co 1:11 that **d.** exist
Ac 15:2; 23:7.
DISSOLVE(S), Job 7:5; Ps 58:7.
DISSOLVED, Isa 28:18 covenant **d.**,
2Co 5:1 house, this tent, should be **d.**,
2Pe 3:10 elements intensely hot will be **d.**,
DISSOLVING, Job 8:19 **d.** of his way
DISSUADED, Ac 21:14 he would not be **d.**
DISTAFF, Pr 31:19 thrust out to the **d.**,
DISTINCTION(S), Le 11:47 **d.** between
Eze 22:26 Between holy they made no **d.**,
Ro 10:12 no **d.** between Jew and Greek,
Jas 2:4 you have class **d.** among
Mal 3:18; Ac 15:9; Ro 3:22; Jas 3:17.
DISTINGUISH, Heb 5:14 trained to **d.**
DISTINGUISHED, 1Ch 11:25; Am 6:1.
DISTINGUISHING, Da 6:3 Daniel was **d.**
DISTORTING, Ac 13:10 quit **d.** the right
DISTORTION, Pr 11:3; 15:4.
DISTRACTED, Lu 10:40 Martha was **d.**
DISTRACTION, 1Co 7:35 without **d.**
DISTRESS(ES), Ps 46:1 God is found during **d.**
Pr 11:8 righteous is rescued from **d.**
Pr 24:10 discouraged in the day of **d.?**
Da 12:1 occur a time of **d.** such as has not
Zep 1:15 a day of **d.** and of anguish
1Th 5:3 as the pang of **d.** upon a woman
2Sa 22:7; Pr 17:17; Isa 8:22; Ro 2:9.
DISTRESSED, 2Pe 2:7 who was greatly **d.**
DISTRIBUTED, Ro 12:3 God has **d.** to him
DISTRIBUTES, Ro 12:8 **d.** with liberality;
DISTRIBUTION, Ac 4:35; 6:1; 1Co 12:11.
DISTRICT(S), Mr 5:17 away from their **d.**
De 34:3; Ne 12:28; Lu 3:1.
DISTRICT OF THE JORDAN, Ge 13:10.
DISTURB, Ps 2:5 displeasure he will **d.**
DISTURBANCE, Isa 65:23 bring to birth for **d.**
Zec 1:11 earth having no **d.**
DISTURBED, Ge 45:3; Ps 6:2; 90:7; Isa 21:3.
DIVAN, Ps 41:3 upon a **d.** of illness;
DIVERSIFIED WISDOM OF GOD, Eph 3:10.
DIVIDED, Mr 3:24 a kingdom becomes **d.**
Jg 7:16; Da 2:41; 5:28; 11:4; 1Co 1:13.
DIVINATION, Nu 22:7 payments for **d.**
De 18:10 not be found anyone who employs **d.**,
1Sa 15:23 rebelliousness is the same as **d.**
Eze 13:6 untrue and a lying **d.**,
Mic 3:11 prophets practice **d.** for money
2Ch 33:6; Isa 3:2; Jer 27:9; Zec 10:2.
DIVINE, De 18:14 to those who **d.**
Ac 17:29 that the **D.** Being is like gold
Col 2:9 **d.** quality dwells bodily
2Pe 1:4 become sharers in **d.** nature
Eze 13:23; Ac 10:22; 2Pe 1:3.
DIVINELY, Ac 7:20 Moses **d.** beautiful
DIVINE ONE, Jos 22:22 **D.**, God, Jehovah,
Ps 50:1; 82:1; 83:1; 118:27; Isa 46:9.

DIVINER(S), Jos 13:22 Balaam, the **d.**
1Sa 6:2; Isa 44:25; Mic 3:7.
DIVINING, Eze 13:9 prophets **d.** a lie
DIVISION(S), Ge 1:4 **d.** between light
Mt 10:35 I came to cause **d.**,
Lu 12:51 to give peace rather **d.**
Ro 16:17 eye on those who cause **d.**
Joh 9:16; 1Co 11:18; Ga 5:20.
DIVISION(S) (courses of priests)
1Ch 27:1; 2Ch 5:11; 8:14; Ezr 6:18; Lu 1:5.
DIVORCE, De 24:1 a certificate of **d.**
Isa 50:1 Where is the **d.** certificate of the
Jer 3:8 give the certificate of **d.** to her
Mt 1:19 Joseph intended to **d.** her
DIVORCED, Le 21:7 woman **d.** they should
Le 22:13 daughter of a priest become **d.**
Nu 30:9 the vow of a **d.** woman
DIVORCES, Mt 5:31 **d.** his wife, let him
Mt 19:9 whoever **d.** except on ground of
Mr 10:11; Lu 16:18.
DIVORCING, Mal 2:16 he has hated a **d.**
Mt 19:7 Why did Moses prescribe **d.** her
DOCTRINE(S). See also TEACHING(S).
DOCTRINE(S), Mt 15:9 commands of men as **d.**
1Ti 1:3 ones not to teach different **d.**
1Ti 6:3 if any man teaches other **d.**
Heb 6:1 primary **d.** about the Christ
DOCUMENT, Col 2:14 blotted out the **d.**
DOEG, 1Sa 21:7; 22:22.
DOERS, Jas 1:22 become **d.** of the word,
Ro 2:13; Jas 1:23, 25.
DOG(S), Isa 56:10 watchmen are **d.**;
2Pe 2:22 **d.** back to its own vomit
Jg 7:5; 2Ki 9:36; Mt 15:26; Re 22:15.
DOING, Mt 24:46 arriving finds him **d.**
Eph 2:3 **d.** the things of flesh
Eph 6:6 **d.** the will of God whole-souled
Ro 12:20; Php 2:3; 1Ti 5:21.
DOING GOOD, 1Pe 3:17 suffer because **d.**,
Ac 10:38; Eph 6:9; 1Pe 2:15; 4:19.
DOMESTIC ANIMAL(S), Ge 1:24; 2:20.
DOMINATE, Ge 1:18 to **d.** by day and by
Ge 3:16 your husband will **d.** you.
Ge 37:8 Are you going to **d.** over us
De 15:6 you must **d.** over many nations
Ps 8:6 **d.** over the works of your hands
DOMINATED, Ec 8:9 **d.** man to his injury
DOMINATION, Ps 103:19 kingship held **d.**
DOMINEER, Ps 119:133 no thing **d.** me.
DOMINION, Ps 145:13 **d.** is throughout
1Ki 9:19; Isa 22:21; Da 6:26; Mic 4:8.
DOOR(S), Isa 26:20 shut your **d.** behind
Ac 14:27 opened the **d.** to faith
Re 3:20 I am standing at the **d.** and
Jg 3:23; Mt 24:33; 25:10; 1Co 16:9.
DOORPOSTS, De 6:9 write them upon **d.**
DOORWAY, Ex 12:22 blood upon the **d.**
DOTHAN, Ge 37:17; 2Ki 6:13.
DOUBLE, Ex 22:7 make **d.** compensation
DOUBLE PORTION, Isa 61:7; Zec 9:12.
DOUBLE-TONGUED, 1Ti 3:8 servants not **d.**
DOUBT(S), Ro 14:23 if he has **d.**, he is
Mt 21:21; Mr 11:23; Jude 22.
DOUBTING, Jas 1:6 not **d.** at all, for
DOVE(S), Mt 3:16 like a **d.** God's spirit
Mt 10:16 as serpents, innocent as **d.**
Ge 8:11; Isa 59:11; Mt 21:12.
DOWNHEARTED, Col 3:21 do not become **d.**
DOWNPOUR, Ge 7:12; 1Ki 17:7.
DOWNTREADING, Isa 22:5 day of **d.** and
DRACHMA, Lu 15:8 woman loses one **d.**
DRAG, Jas 2:6 **d.** you before law courts,
DRAGNET(S), Mic 7:2 They hunt with a **d.**

Mt 13:47 kingdom of the heavens is like **a d.**
Ec 7:26; Eze 26:5; 47:10.
DRAGON, Re 12:17 **d.** grew wrathful at
Re 12:3, 7, 9; 13:2; 16:13; 20:2.
DRAINED, Ge 8:13 waters had **d.** from
DRAW(S), Joh 6:44 unless the Father **d.**
Jas 4:8 **D.** close to God he will **d.** close
Ex 12:21; Jg 4:7; Ps 85:5; Pr 20:5.
DRAWING, Heb 3:12 lacking by **d.**
DRAWING CONCLUSIONS, Lu 2:19 Mary **d.**
DREAD, Ex 15:16 **d.** will fall upon them
1Sa 11:7 **d.** of Jehovah began to fall upon
2Ch 19:7 let the **d.** of Jehovah come upon
De 28:66; Isa 12:2; 24:17; Jer 30:5.
DREADFUL, Ps 91:5 afraid of anything **d.**
Da 2:31 image, its appearance was **d.**
Job 3:25; Pr 3:25; Jer 49:5.
DREADFULNESS, Isa 2:21 **d.** of Jehovah
DREAM(S), Jer 23:32 prophets of false **d.**
Joe 2:28 old men, **d.** they will **d.**
Ge 41:25; Jer 23:27; Da 2:28; Ac 2:17.
DREGS, Isa 25:6 wine kept on the **d.**
DRENCH, Isa 16:9 tears I shall **d.** you,
DRENCHED, Isa 34:5 sword will be **d.**
DRENCHING, Ps 65:10 **d.** of its furrows,
DRESS, 1Ti 2:9 adorn in well-arranged **d.**
DRESSED, Re 3:18; 4:4; 7:9; 11:3.
DRIFT, Heb 2:1 that we never **d.** away.
DRINK, Ec 2:24 eat and **d.** and see good
Jer 25:28 Jehovah said: You will **d.** without
Mt 26:29 **d.** it new with you in kingdom
Ps 69:21; Mt 10:42; 1Co 10:4; Re 14:8.
DRINK OFFERING(S), Nu 28:7; Php 2:17.
2Ti 4:6 being poured like a **d.**
DRIPPING, Eze 7:17 all knees keep **d.**
DROP, 2Ch 15:7 do not let your hands **d.**
Zep 3:16 May your hands not **d.** down.
DROVE, Isa 40:11 he will shepherd his **d.**
DROWNED, Re 12:15 to be **d.** by the river
DROWSED, Ps 76:5 **d.** away to their sleep,
DROWSY, Ps 121:3 cannot possibly be **d.**
Isa 5:27; Na 3:13 shepherds become **d.**
DRUNK, Eph 5:18 do not be getting **d.**
1Th 5:7 Those who get **d.** are **d.** at night
Re 17:6 woman was **d.** with the blood of
Isa 19:14; Jer 51:7; Ac 2:15.
DRUNKARD(S), Pr 23:21 **d.** to poverty
Isa 28:1 Woe to **d.** of Ephraim
Mt 24:49 evil slave drink with confirmed **d.**
1Co 5:11 quit company with a **d.**
1Co 6:10 nor **d.** inherit God's kingdom
DRUNKEN, Job 12:25; Ps 107:27.
DRUNKEN BOUTS, Ga 5:21 envies, **d.,**
DUE(S), Ro 21:10 her marriage **d.** not
Ro 13:7 Render to all their **d.**
1Co 7:3 render to his wife her **d.**
Ga 6:9 in **d.** season we shall reap
1Pe 5:6 God may exalt you in **d.** time
DUKES, Jos 13:21; Ps 83:11; Mic 5:5.
DULL, Heb 5:11 become **d.** in hearing
Mr 6:52; 8:17 **d.** of understanding
DULLED, 2Co 3:14 mental perceptions **d.**
DULLING, Ro 11:25 a **d.** of sensibilities
DUMB, Mt 9:32; 12:22; 15:30; Lu 1:22.
DUNG, 1Ki 14:10; Eze 4:12; Zep 1:17.
DUNGEON, Ps 142:7 my soul out of the **d.**
DUNGY IDOLS, Le 26:30; 1Ki 15:12.
DURABLE, Jer 49:19; 50:44; Mic 6:2.
DURATION, Ps 89:47 of what **d.** of life I
DURATION, LIFE'S, Job 11:17; Ps 39:5.
DUST, Ge 2:7 God form the man of **d.**
Ge 3:19 **d.** you are and to **d.** return
Ps 72:9 his enemies will lick the **d.**
Ec 12:7 **d.** returns to the earth as it

Da 12:2 many asleep in the ground of **d.**
Mt 10:14 shake the **d.** off your feet.
1Co 15:47 first man is made of **d.;**
Ex 8:16; Ps 103:14; Ec 3:20; Isa 40:15.
DUTIES, 1Ch 26:12; Ne 13:30.
DUTY, 2Ch 7:6 priests at their post of **d.**
2Ch 8:14 Levites at posts of **d.,**
DWELL, Jg 5:17 to **d.** in ships?
Ps 27:4 may **d.** in the house of
Ps 133:1 good brothers to **d.** in unity
Ps 61:7; 68:16; Pr 21:9, 19; Isa 32:18.
DWELLERS, Jg 5:7 The **d.** in open country
DWELLING(S), Nu 35:34 which you are **d.,**
1Ki 8:49 your established place of **d.,**
Isa 40:22 **d.** above the circle of the earth,
Ro 7:20 no longer I, but sin **d.** in me
De 26:15; Ps 91:9; Jer 31:23; Ac 17:26.
DWELLING HOUSE, 2Co 5:2 in **d.** we groan
DWELLING PLACE, Jude 6; Re 18:2.
DWELLING TOWERS, Ps 48:3, 13 **d.** secure
Ps 122:7 Freedom from care within your **d.**
Isa 13:22; Eze 19:7; Am 3:9; Mic 5:5.
DWELLS, 1Co 3:16 spirit of God **d.** in
DYNAMIC ENERGY, Nu 40:16; Isa 40:26.
Isa 40:29 to the one without **d.**
Ho 12:3 with his **d.** he contended with God.
DYSENTERY, Ac 28:8 Publius with **d.,**

E

EAGERLY, 1Pe 5:2 Shepherd the flock **e.**
EAGERNESS, Ro 1:15 **e.** to declare news
EAGLE(S), Isa 40:31 mount up like **e.**
Eze 10:14; Ob 4; Mt 24:28; Re 12:14.
EAR(S), Pr 20:12 **e.**—Jehovah made
Isa 35:5 **e.** of the deaf will be unstopped
Joh 18:10 Peter cut his right **e.** off.
1Co 12:16 if the **e.** should say: I am not
2Ti 4:4 turn their **e.** away from truth
Jas 5:4 entered into the **e.** of Jehovah
De 15:1; 2Ki 21:12; Mt 13:16; Re 2:7.
EARLIER, Php 3:11 the **e.** resurrection
EARLY, Ac 15:7 from **e.** days God made
EARNEST, 2Co 8:17, 22; 2Pe 1:5.
EARNESTLY, 1Sa 20:28 David **e.** asked
EARNESTNESS, 2Co 8:8 in view of the **e.**
EARNINGS, Pr 11:18 sowing, true **e.**
EARTH, Ge 1:28 fill the **e.** and
Ps 24:1 To Jehovah belong the **e.** and
Ps 37:29 righteous will possess the **e.,**
Ps 100:1 Shout to Jehovah, all the **e.**
Ps 115:16 the **e.** he has given to men
Ec 1:4 **e.** is standing to time indefinite
Isa 14:12 fallen from heaven down to the **e.**
Isa 45:18 **e.** formed to be inhabited:
Isa 60:2 darkness will cover the **e.**
Isa 65:17 I am creating a new **e.**
Isa 66:1 throne and the **e.** is my footstool
Hab 2:14 **e.** will be filled with the knowing
Mt 5:5 mild-tempered ones inherit the **e.**
Lu 2:14 upon **e.** peace among men of
2Pe 3:5 and an **e.** standing compactly out of
Re 12:12 Woe for the **e.** and for the sea
Ps 45:16; Pr 10:30; 2Pe 3:13; Re 21:1.
EARTHEN, 2Co 4:7 treasure in **e.** vessels,
EARTHENWARE, Eze 23:34 its **e.** fragments
EARTHENWARE VESSEL, Mr 14:13; Lu 22:10.
EARTHLING MAN, 1Sa 15:29 not **e.** to repent
Job 34:11; Ps 39:5; 49:20; 108:12; Pr 3:4.
EARTHLY, Joh 3:12; 2Co 5:1; Jas 3:15.
EARTHQUAKE(S), Mt 24:7 **e.** in one place
Zec 14:5; Mt 27:54; Lu 21:11; Re 6:12.
EASE, Am 6:1 Woe to those at **e.** in Zion
Lu 12:19 take your **e.,** eat, drink, enjoy
De 28:65; Jer 49:31; Zec 1:15.

EAST, Ps 75:6 neither from **e.** is there
Ge 3:24; Isa 2:6; Jer 49:28; Eze 8:16.
EASTERN, Mt 2:1 astrologers from **e.** parts
Mt 8:11; 24:27; Lu 13:29.
EASTERNERS, Jg 6:3, 33; 7:12; 8:10.
EASYGOINGNESS, Pr 1:32 **e.** of stupid is
EAT, Ge 2:17 you must not **e.** from it,
Ge 3:19 sweat of your face you will **e.** bread
Le 17:14 You must not **e.** the blood of any
De 28:53 **e.** the fruit of your womb
Ec 2:24 **e.** and drink and see good because
Isa 11:7 lion will **e.** straw like the bull.
Isa 65:13 My servants will **e.,** but you will
Jer 15:16 Your words I proceeded to **e.**
Jer 19:9 **e.** the flesh of their sons
2Th 3:10 does not work, neither let him **e.**
Re 2:7 grant to **e.** of the tree of life,
Ps 22:26; Isa 65:21; Eze 3:1; Joh 6:53.
EATEN, Isa 24:6 curse has **e.** up the land
EATING, Mt 26:26 **e.,** Jesus took a loaf
EATING AND DRINKING, Isa 21:5.
Mt 11:19 Jesus came **e.** still people say
Mt 24:38 days before the flood, **e.,**
Lu 10:7 stay in that house, **e.** the things
Ro 14:17 kingdom does not mean **e.,**
Col 2:16 let no man judge you in **e.**
EATS, Ro 14:6 he who **e. e.** to Jehovah,
EBAL, Ge 36:23; De 11:29; 27:4; Jos 8:30.
EBED-MELECH, Jer 38:7, 8, 10-12; 39:16.
EBER, Ge 10:21, 24; 11:16; Lu 3:35.
ECSTASY, Pr 5:19; Mr 5:42; Ac 3:10.
ECZEMA, De 28:27 strike you with **e.**
EDEN, Ge 2:15 settle him in **E.** to care
Isa 51:3 he will make her wilderness like **E.**
Eze 28:13 In **E.,** you proved to be.
Eze 36:35 your land become like garden of **E.**
Ge 2:8; 3:23, 24; Joe 2:3.
EDOM, Ge 25:30; 36:8; Jer 49:7; Ob 1.
EDREI, Nu 21:33; Jos 12:4; 13:31; 19:37.
EDUCATED, Ac 13:1 **e.** with Herod
EFFACE, Ex 23:23; 2Ch 32:21; Ps 83:4.
EFFACED, Ex 9:15 might be **e.** from the earth
EFFECTIVELY, ACT, Da 11:17, 28, 32, 39.
EFFECTUAL WORKING, Job 6:13; Isa 28:29.
EGGED ON, 1Ki 21:25 Jezebel his wife **e.**
EGLON, Jos 10:3; Jg 3:12, 14, 15, 17.
EGOTISM, Php 2:3 doing nothing out of **e.,**
EGOTISTICAL, Ga 5:26 not become **e.**
EGYPT, Ps 68:31 things come out of **E.**
Isa 19:23 highway out of **E.** to Assyria,
Isa 31:1 Woe to those going down to **E.** for
Da 11:43 over all the desirable things of **E.**
Re 11:8 **E.,** where their Lord was impaled
Ge 37:36; 41:41; Ex 11:5; Mt 2:15.
EGYPTIAN(S), Ex 14:18 **E.** will know I am
Isa 31:3 The **E.** are men, not God;
Ge 16:1; Ex 2:11; 7:5; Isa 19:2.
EHUD, Jg 3:15, 21; 4:1.
EIGHT, 1Pe 3:20 **e.** souls, were carried
Ge 17:12; 18a 17:12; Ec 11:2; Lu 2:21.
ELATED, Pr 11:10 a town is **e.,**
ELATEDLY, Isa 61:6 will speak **e.** about you
ELDERLY, Ps 107:32 the seat of **e.** men
ELDERS. See OLDER MEN.
ELEALEH, Nu 32:3, 37; Jer 48:34.
ELEAZAR, Ex 6:23; Nu 20:26; De 10:6.
ELECT. See CHOSEN ONE(S).
ELECTION. See CHOOSING.
ELEGANCE, Ge 49:21 giving words of **e.**
ELEGANT, Isa 23:18 hire for **e.** covering.
ELEMENTARY THINGS, Ga 4:3, 9; Col 2:8.
Heb 5:12 **e.** of the sacred pronouncements
ELEMENTS, 2Pe 3:10 **e.** will be dissolved,
ELEVATE, Da 6:3 king to **e.** him

ELEVATED, Isa 26:5 the **e.** town.
ELI, 1Sa 1:3; 2:11; 3:15; Mt 27:46.
ELIHU, Job 32:2; 34:1; 35:1; 36:1.
ELIJAH, 1Ki 18:21 **E.** said: How long
2Ki 2:9 **E.** said to Elisha: Ask what I
2Ki 2:11 **E.** went ascending in the
1Ki 18:36, 40; Mal 4:5; Mt 17:11, 12.
ELIPHAZ, Job 2:11; 42:7, 9.
ELISHA, 2Ki 4:32 **E.** came, boy was dead
2Ki 6:17 chariots all around **E.**
1Ki 19:16, 19; 2Ki 2:2, 9, 15; 5:8; 6:18.
ELOQUENT, Ac 18:24 an **e.** man, Apollos
ELYMAS, Ac 13:8 **E.** the sorcerer
EMACIATE, Zep 2:11 Jehovah will **e.** gods
EMACIATED, Ps 102:7 I have grown **e.,**
EMANCIPATE, Heb 2:15 **e.** all subject to
EMASCULATED, Ga 5:12 wish men get **e.**
EMBALMED, Ge 50:2, 26 physicians to Israel
EMBARRASSED, 2Ki 2:17 until he was **e..**
Ezr 9:6 I feel **e.** to raise my face to my God
EMBARRASSMENT, 2Ki 8:11 look to **e.**
EMBOLDENED, Es 7:5; Ac 5:3.
EMBRACE, Pr 4:8; Ec 3:5.
EMBRACED, Ge 29:13; 48:10.
EMBRACES, Ca 2:6 his right hand **e.** me.
EMBRACING, 2Ki 4:16 will be **e.** a son.
EMBROIDERED, Jg 5:30 An **e.** garment,
EMBROIDERER, Ex 26:1 Cherubs of an **e.**
EMBRYO, Ps 139:16 eyes saw the **e.** of me,
EMERY STONE, Zec 7:12 heart set as an **e.**
EMINENCE, De 33:26 God in his **e.**
Ps 93:1 Jehovah with **e.** is clothed
Ps 68:34; Ac 25:23.
EMINENCY, Eze 7:11 nor any **e.** in them.
EMINENT, Isa 28:1 Woe to the **e.** crown
EMISSION, Le 15:16, 32 man has an **e.** of semen
Le 18:20, 23 not give your **e.** to beasts
Le 20:15 gives his seminal **e.** to
Le 22:4 goes out seminal **e.**
EMMAUS, Lu 24:13 village named **E.,**
EMOTION, Mr 16:8 strong **e.** was gripping
EMOTIONS, INWARD, Ge 43:30; 1Ki 3:26.
EMPLOYMENT, 2Ch 29:19 removed from **e.**
EMPLOYS, De 18:10 anyone who **e.** divination
EMPTIED, Isa 24:3 the land will be **e.,**
Php 2:7 he **e.** himself and took a slave's
EMPTY, Ps 2:1 muttering an **e.** thing?
Pr 13:25 belly of the wicked ones will be **e.**
Mal 3:10 **e.** out upon you a blessing
Eph 5:6; 1Ti 6:20; 2Ti 2:16.
EMPTY-HEADED, Ro 1:21 they became **e.**
ENCIRCLE, Lu 19:43 enemies will **e.** you
ENCIRCLED, Heb 11:30 had **e.** Jericho
ENCLAVE, Jos 16:9 Ephraim had **e.** cities
ENCOUNTER, Nu 20:20; 2Ch 35:20.
ENCOURAGE, De 3:28 commission and **e.**
Ac 11:23; 2Co 9:5.
ENCOURAGED, 2Ch 35:2 **e.** in the service
1Co 14:31 that all may learn and be **e.**
ENCOURAGEMENT, Ro 1:12 be interchange of **e.**
2Co 8:17 responded to **e.**
Php 2:1 If there is any **e.** in Christ, if
Heb 6:18 strong **e.** to lay hold on the hope
Heb 13:22; 1Pe 5:12.
ENCOURAGES, 1Co 14:3 upbuilds and **e.**
ENCOURAGING, Ac 14:22 **e.** to remain in
Heb 10:25 **e.** one another, all the more
ENCROACH, 1Th 4:6 no one **e.** upon rights
END(S), Job 42:12 blessed the **e.** of Job
Ps 2:8 **e.** of the earth as your own
Ps 72:8 from the River to the **e.** of the
Isa 9:7 to peace there will be no **e.,**
Da 11:27 **e.** is yet for the time appointed.
Mt 10:22 he that has endured to the **e.** is

Mt 24:14 then the **e.** will come.
1Co 10:11 **e.** of systems of things arrived.
1Pe 4:7 the **e.** of all things has drawn close
Jer 25:33; Eze 7:2; Da 12:4; Re 2:26.
ENDEARMENT, Ca 1:2, 4; 4:10; 5:1.
ENDEAVORED, Ga 2:10; Eph 4:3; 1Th 2:17.
ENDEAVORING, Eph 4:3 **e.** to observe the
EN-DOR, Jos 17:11; 1Sa 28:7.
ENDOWMENT, Ge 30:20 with a good **e.**
ENDURANCE, Lu 21:19 By **e.** on your part
Ro 2:7 by **e.** in work that is good;
Ro 5:3 tribulation produces **e.**; **e.** in turn
Ro 15:4 through our **e.** we might have hope
Heb 12:1 let us run with **e.** the race
Jas 5:11 heard of the **e.** of Job
Lu 8:15; 1Th 1:3; 2Pe 1:6; Re 13:10.
ENDURE, Ro 12:12 **E.** under tribulation.
1Co 10:13 tempted to be able to **e.**
Eph 6:3 you may **e.** a long time on earth.
1Pe 2:20 you **e.** it, this is agreeable
ENDURED, Mt 24:13 he that has **e.** to the
ENDURES, 1Pe 1:25 saying of Jehovah **e.** forever
ENDURING, Heb 12:7 discipline you are **e.**
ENDURING GOD, 1Pe 1:23 word of the **e.**
ENEMIES, Ps 110:2 subduing in the midst **e.**
Mic 7:6 **e.** are the men of his household.
Mt 10:36 a man's **e.** will be persons
1Co 15:25 put all **e.** under his feet
Mic 4:10; Mt 22:44; Ro 11:28.
ENEMY, 1Ki 8:33 defeated before the **e.**
Ps 8:2 make the **e.** desist
Mt 13:39 **e.** that sowed them is the Devil
Ro 12:20 if your **e.** is hungry, feed him;
1Co 15:26 last **e.** death is to be destroyed
Jas 4:4 friend of the world is an **e.** of God.
ENERGY, 1Sa 2:4; 2Sa 22:40; Ps 18:32.
ENGAGE, Da 11:40 south will **e.** with him
Ho 2:19, 20 I will **e.** you to me
ENGAGED, De 28:30 become **e.** to a woman
Ex 22:16; De 22:23, 25, 27, 28.
ENGINE(S), 2Ch 26:15; Eze 26:9.
ENGINEERS, 2Ch 26:15 invention of **e.**
ENGRAVED, 2Co 3:7 code which was **e.** in
ENJOY, Lu 12:19; Ac 7:41; Re 11:10.
ENJOYING, Lu 16:19 **e.** himself from day
ENJOYMENT, Heb 11:25 temporary **e.** of sin
ENLARGE, Mt 23:5 **e.** fringes of garments
ENLIGHTENED, Job 33:30 **e.** with light
Eph 1:18 eyes of your heart having been **e.**
Heb 6:4 those who have once for all been **e.**
Heb 10:32 after you were **e.**, you endured
ENLIVEN, Ps 85:6 you **e.** us again,
ENMITY, Ge 3:15 put **e.** between you
Ro 8:7 minding of flesh means **e.** with God,
Jas 4:4 friendship with world is **e.**
ENOCH, Ge 5:22 **E.** walking with God
Ge 5:24; Lu 3:37; Heb 11:5; Jude 14.
ENOUGH, Pr 30:15 four have not said: **E.**!
ENRAGED, Pr 15:18 An **e.** man stirs up
ENRICHER, 1Sa 2:7 Jehovah is an **E.**
ENROLLED, Heb 12:23 **e.** in the heavens,
ENSLAVE, Ga 2:4 that they might **e.** us
ENSLAVED, Ga 4:3 **e.** by the elementary
2Pe 2:19 overcome by another is **e.** by this
ENSLAVEMENT, Ro 8:21 set free from **e.**
ENSLAVING, Ex 6:5 the Egyptians are **e.**,
ENSNARED, Pr 12:13 bad person is **e.**,
ENTANGLES, Heb 12:1 sin that **e.** us,
ENTER, Isa 26:2 righteous nation **e.**
Mt 25:21 **E.** into the joy of your master.
Ac 14:22 **e.** into the kingdom of God through
Pr 4:14; 18:6; 23:10; Mt 19:17; Heb 4:6.
ENTERED, Ro 5:12; Heb 4:10; 9:12, 24.
ENTERTAIN, Ac 24:15 hope these men **e.**

ENTERTAINED, 1Ti 5:10 she **e.** strangers,
ENTICE, 2Pe 2:14 they **e.** unsteady souls
ENTICED, De 11:16 your heart may be **e.**
Job 31:27 heart began to be **e.** in secrecy
Pr 20:19 with one **e.** you must have no
Jas 1:14 each one is **e.** by his own desire
ENTIRETY, Na 1:15; Hab 1:9; Mal 3:9.
ENTRANCE(S), Eze 33:30 **e.** of the houses
Le 8:3, 33; 16:7; Jos 19:51; 2Pe 1:11.
ENTREAT, Jg 13:8 Manoah began to **e.** Jehovah
1Ti 5:1 **e.** him as a father,
Ro 12:1; 2Co 6:1.
ENTREATED, Isa 19:22 let himself be **e.** by
Mr 7:32 they **e.** him to lay
ENTREATIES, Zec 12:10 spirit of **e.**,
2Ch 6:21; Ps 28:2; Da 9:18.
ENTREATING, Ge 25:21 Isaac kept **e.** Jehovah
ENTREATY, Ex 8:30 Moses made **e.** to Jehovah
2Co 5:20 making **e.** through us
ENTREATY FOR FAVOR, Ps 30:8 making **e.**
ENTRENCHED, 2Co 10:4 strongly **e.** things.
ENTRUST, Lu 16:11 who will **e.** you with
ENTRUSTED, 1Th 2:4 **e.** with the good news
Ro 3:2; 1Co 9:17; Ga 2:7; Tit 1:3.
ENTRYWAY, Pr 17:19 making his **e.** high
ENUMERATE, Ps 50:16 to **e.** my regulations
ENVELOPED, 2Ch 24:20 spirit **e.** Zechariah
ENVELOPMENT, Isa 25:7 face of **e.** over
ENVIES, 1Pe 2:1 put away all **e.**
ENVIOUS, Pr 3:31 not become **e.** of
Pr 23:17 your heart not be **e.** of sinners,
Pr 24:1 Do not be **e.** of bad men
Ps 37:1; 73:3.
ENVISION, Isa 30:10 **e.** deceptive things.
ENVOY(S), Isa 30:4 his own **e.** reach even
Php 2:25 Epaphroditus, your **e.** and private
Pr 13:17; 25:13; Isa 57:9; Ob 1.
ENVY, Ps 106:16 began to **e.** Moses
Php 1:15 some preaching Christ through **e.**
1Ti 6:4 From these things spring **e.**
Jas 4:5 a tendency to **e.** that the spirit
Ge 26:14; Ro 1:29; Tit 3:3.
ENVYING, Ga 5:26 not **e.** one another.
ENWRAPPING, Ps 104:2 **E.** with light
EPHAH, De 25:15 An **e.** accurate
Ex 16:36; Le 19:36; Eze 45:11.
EPHESUS, 1Co 15:32; Re 2:1.
EPHOD, Ex 28:6; 1Sa 23:9; 30:7; Ho 3:4.
EPHRAIM, Ge 41:52; Jos 14:4; Ps 78:67.
EPHRATHAH, Ru 4:11; Ps 132:6; Mic 5:2.
EPILEPTIC, Mt 4:24; 17:15.
EQUAL, Isa 46:5 will you make me **e.**
Joh 5:18 making himself **e.** to God
Php 2:6 no consideration to be **e.** to God
Pr 3:15; 8:11; Mt 20:12; Re 21:16.
EQUALIZING, 2Co 8:14 **e.** your surplus
EQUIP, Heb 13:21 **e.** you to do his will,
EQUIPMENT, Ge 45:20 not sorry over **e.**
Eph 6:15 feet shod with the **e.** of good news
EQUIPPED, 2Ti 3:17 **e.** for every good work
EQUITABLE, Da 11:6 an **e.** arrangement.
Da 11:17 there will be **e.** terms with him;
EQUIVALENT, 2Sa 17:3 **e.** to all is the man
ERECTED, Mt 21:33 wine press, **e.** a tower
ERRED, 1Ki 8:47 We have sinned and **e.**,
ERRONEOUSNESS, Isa 57:17 **e.** unjust gain
ERROR(S), Ge 15:16 **e.** of Amorites
Ezr 9:6 **e.** have multiplied
Job 31:11 conduct an **e.** for the justices.
Ps 51:5 with **e.** I was brought forth
Ps 130:3 If **e.** were what you watch
Isa 53:5 he was being crushed for our **e.**
Jer 33:8 I will forgive all their **e.**
Jas 5:20 turns a sinner back from **e.**

2Pe 2:18 who conduct themselves in e.
Ex 20:5; Le 16:21; De 5:9; Jos 22:17;
Eph 4:14; 1Th 2:3; 2Pe 3:17; 1Jo 4:6.
ERROR, OPERATION OF, 2Th 2:11 lets an o.
ESAU, Ge 25:34 E. despised birthright
Jer 49:10 as for me I will strip E. bare
Ob 18 and the house of E. as stubble.
Ge 25:27, 30; 36:8; Ob 21; Heb 12:16.
ESCAPE, Jer 25:35 a means of e. from
1Th 5:3 and they will by no means e.
Pr 11:21; 19:5; Ec 8:3; Ro 2:3; Heb 2:3.
ESCAPED, Joe 2:32 will be e. ones,
2Pe 1:4 e. from corruption in the world
2Pe 2:20 having e. from the defilements
Isa 10:20; Eze 24:27; Heb 11:34.
ESCAPEE(S), Isa 45:20 e. from nations
Jos 8:22; Jer 42:17; 44:14.
ESCAPES, 2Pe 3:5 fact e. their notice,
ESCAPING, Lu 21:36 you may succeed in
ESCORT, 2Sa 19:31 e. him to the Jordan
ESCORTED, Ro 15:24 to be e. part way
ESTABLISH, Ps 7:9 e. the righteous one
Ro 3:31 On the contrary, we e. law.
Ge 6:18; De 28:9; Isa 9:7; Ro 10:3.
ESTABLISHED, 1Ki 8:49 your e. place of
Ps 93:2 your throne is firmly e.
Isa 2:2 house of Jehovah will become e.
Ps 89:14; 96:10; Mt 18:16.
ESTATES, Ps 49:11 their landed e. by
ESTEEM, 2Ki 5:1 Naaman held in e.
ESTEEMED, 1Sa 18:23 a man lightly e.
Heb 10:29 e. as of ordinary value the blood
Heb 11:26 he e. the reproach of Christ as
ESTHER, Es 2:7; 7:6; 8:2.
ESTIMATE, Pr 21:2 Jehovah e. of hearts
Pr 24:12 making an e. of hearts discern
ESTIMATED, 1Sa 2:3 deeds are rightly e.
ESTRANGED, Nu 14:34 know what being e.
ETERNAL, Isa 9:6 Mighty God, E. Father
Ro 1:20 e. power and Godship
Jude 6 he has reserved with e. bonds
Ge 49:26; Hab 3:6; Eph 3:11.
ETERNITY, 1Ti 1:17 to the King of e.,
Jude 25 might and authority for all past e.
Re 15:3.
ETHIOPIA, 2Ki 19:9; Es 1:1; Isa 20:5.
ETHIOPIAN(S), Da 11:43; Ac 8:27.
EUNICE, 2Ti 1:5 your mother E.
EUNUCH(S), Mt 19:12 there are e. born
Isa 56:3, 4; Jer 38:7; Ac 8:27.
EUPHRATES, Ge 2:14; 15:18; Re 9:14.
EVANGELIZER(S), Ac 21:8 Philip the e.,
Eph 4:11 some as e., some as shepherds
2Ti 4:5 do the work of an e.
EVAPORATED, Ex 16:14; Isa 44:27.
EVE, Ge 3:20; 2Co 11:3; 1Ti 2:13.
EVENING MEAL, Mr 6:21 Herod spread an e.
Lu 14:12 e., do not call your friends,
1Co 11:20 not possible to eat the Lord's e.
Re 19:9 Happy are those invited to the e.
Re 19:17 gathered to the e. of God,
Lu 14:16; 22:20; Joh 13:4; 1Co 11:21, 25.
EVENTUALITY, Ec 2:14; 3:19; 9:2.
EVENTUATES, Ec 2:14 eventuality that e.
EVERLASTING. See also TIME INDEFINITE.
EVERLASTING, Joh 17:3 this means e. life their
Ro 5:21 with e. life in view through Jesus
Ro 6:23 the gift God gives is e. life
2Co 4:18 but the things unseen are e.
1Pe 5:10 who called you to e. glory
Mt 25:46; Mr 3:29; Lu 16:9; 1Jo 5:11.
EVIDENCE, Ac 25:7 unable to show e.
Heb 11:14 give e. that they are seeking
EVIDENT, Ga 3:11 with God is e.

Heb 11:1 Faith, the e. demonstration of
EVIL, Mt 24:48 e. slave should say in
Ro 12:17 Return e. for e. to no one.
Ro 13:10 Love does not work e. to one's
Ro 16:19 innocent as to what is e.
2Ti 2:3 take your part in suffering e.
Jas 1:13 with e. God cannot be tried
Ge 50:15; Ex 21:17; 2Ti 1:8; 2:9; 4:5.
EVILDOER(S), Ps 37:9 e. will be cut off,
Jer 23:14 strengthened the hands of e.
1Pe 2:12 speaking against you as e.
1Pe 4:15 let none of you suffer as an e. or
Ps 22:16; 37:1; 119:115; Jer 20:13.
EXACT, Heb 1:3 the e. representation
EXACTER, Da 11:20 causing an e. to pass
EXACTING EXCLUSIVE DEVOTION, Ex 20:5.
De 4:24 Jehovah is a God e.
EXACTIONS, Ps 89:22 no enemy make e.
EXALT, 1Sa 2:10 e. horn of his anointed
Ps 34:3 e. his name together.
Da 11:36 e. himself above every god;
1Pe 5:6 that he may e. you in due time,
Ps 37:34; 118:28; Isa 25:1.
EXALTATION, Ge 4:7 will there be an e.?
Jas 1:9 lowly brother exult over his e.,
EXALTED, Ex 15:1 he has become highly e.
Ps 46:10 e. in the earth.
Ac 5:31 God e. this one as Chief Agent
Php 2:9 God e. him to a superior position
Ps 57:5; Mt 11:23; 23:12; Ac 2:33.
EXALTER, 1Sa 2:7 Jehovah is an E.
EXALTING, Pr 14:29 e. foolishness.
EXALTS, Pr 14:34 Righteousness e.
Mt 23:12 Whoever e. himself will be
EXAMINATION, Le 13:36.
EXAMINE, Ps 26:2 E. me Jehovah
Zec 13:9 e. them as in examining gold
1Co 4:3 Even I do not e. myself.
1Co 2:15 he is not e. by any man.
EXAMINED, 1Co 2:14 are e. spiritually
1Co 4:3 matter that I should be e. by you
1Ki 3:21; Lu 23:14; Ac 4:9; 1Co 14:24.
EXAMINER, 1Ch 29:17 an e. of the heart
EXAMINES, Ps 11:5 Jehovah e.
1Co 2:15 the spiritual man e. all things
1Co 4:4 he that e. me is Jehovah.
EXAMINING, Jer 17:10 e. the kidneys
Ac 17:11 carefully the Scriptures
Jer 11:20; 20:12.
EXAMPLE(S), 1Co 10:11 e. for a warning
Php 3:17 accords with the e. you have in us
1Th 1:7 you came to be an e. to all
1Ti 4:12 become an e. to the faithful ones
Tit 2:7 showing yourself an e. of fine
1Pe 5:3 becoming e. to the flock.
2Th 3:9; Jude 7.
EXASPERATED, Ge 45:24 Do not get e.
EXASPERATING, Col 3:21 fathers not e.
EXCAVATED, Ge 50:5; Jer 18:20.
EXCAVATING, Pr 26:27 He that is e. a pit
EXCEEDINGLY, 1Ti 1:14 e. with faith
EXCELLENCIES, 1Pe 2:9 declare abroad the e.
EXCELLENCY, 1Sa 15:29 the E. of Israel
1Ch 29:11 Yours Jehovah are the e. and
La 3:18 My e. has perished and my
Ac 24:3 Your E., Felix
EXCELLENT, Ro 2:18; Heb 1:4; 8:6.
EXCELLING, Php 3:8 e. value of knowledge
EXCELS, 2Co 3:10 because of the glory e.
Php 4:7 peace of God that e. all thought
EXCEPTION, Isa 45:5 e. of me there is no God
EXCESS, 1Co 15:10 labored in e. of them
2Co 12:7 because of the e. of revelations.

EXCESSES WITH WINE, 1Pe 4:3 lusts, **e.,**
EXCESSIVE, 2Ti 4:15 to an **e.** degree.
EXCHANGE, Ru 4:7; Job 15:31; 28:17.
EXCITED, Ro 7:5 passions **e.** by the Law
　Pr 29:9; 2Th 2:2.
EXCITEMENT, Ho 11:9; Joe 2:6; Na 2:10.
EXCLUDING, Isa 66:5 **e.** you of my name
EXCLUSIVE DEVOTION, Eze 39:25 show **e.**
　Na 1:2 Jehovah is a God exacting **e.**
　Nu 25:11; Jos 24:19; Eze 5:13; Ca 8:6.
EXCREMENT, Pr 30:12 washed from its **e.**
　De 23:13; Eze 4:12.
EXCUSE, Jude 4 an **e.** for loose conduct
　Ex 4:10; Joh 15:22.
EXCUSED, Lu 14:18, 19; Ro 2:15.
EXECRATE, Pr 24:24 peoples will **e.** him
　Nu 23:8; Job 3:8; Pr 11:26.
EXECUTE, Ps 149:9 **e.** judicial decision
　Jude 15 **e.** judgment against all
　Ex 12:12; Jer 23:5; Eze 25:17; Mic 5:15.
EXECUTED, Re 20:4 **e.** with the ax for
EXEMPT, 2Ki 15:5; 2Ch 26:21.
EXEMPTION, 18a 3:14 not **e.** from punishment
EXERCISE, 1Co 7:4 wife not **e.** authority
　2Co 4:13 we too **e.** faith and speak,
　1Ti 2:12 not permit a woman **e.** over
EXERCISED, Heb 4:3 we who have **e.** faith
EXERCISES, Joh 11:26 everyone that **e.** faith
　Ro 10:10 with the heart one **e.** faith for
　1Co 9:25 every man **e.** self-control in all
　1Jo 4:18 because fear **e.** a restraint
EXERCISING, Ac 24:16 I am **e.** myself
　Jas 5:7 the farmer keeps **e.** patience over
EXERCISING FAITH, Isa 28:16 No one **e.**
　Ro 10:4 so that everyone **e.** may have
　Ga 3:22 promise be given to those **e.**
EXERT, Lu 13:24 E. yourselves
　Ro 15:30 **e.** yourselves with me in prayers
EXERTED, Ge 48:2; Da 10:19.
EXERTING, Col 4:12; 1Ti 4:10.
EXERTS, Heb 4:12 word of God **e.** power
EXHALATION, Ps 78:33 days end as mere **e.**
　Ps 94:11 thoughts of men are as an **e.**
　Ps 39:5; 144:4; Isa 57:13; Re 18:2.
EXHAUSTED, Da 8:27 Daniel felt **e.**
　Ge 21:15; 1Ki 17:16.
EXHIBITED, Col 2:15 **e.** them in public
EXHIBITION, 1Co 4:9 apostles last on **e.**
EXHIBITS, Pr 23:31 wine when **e.** red color
EXHORT, 2Ti 4:2 **e.,** with long-suffering
　Jude 3 **e.** you to put up a hard fight
　1Co 16:15; 2Co 2:8; Php 4:2; 1Th 4:1;
　5:14; Tit 1:9; Heb 13:19.
EXHORTATION(S), 1Ti 6:2 keep giving **e.**
　Job 20:3; 36:10; Ho 5:2; Ro 12:8.
EXHORTING, 1Th 2:11 kept **e.** each one of
　Tit 2:15 Keep on **e.** and reproving
　Heb 3:13 keep on **e.** one another each day,
EXILE(S), 2Ki 18:11 Assyria took Israel **e.**
　Isa 5:13 go into **e.** for lack of knowledge
　Jer 13:19 Judah has been taken into **e.**
　Ezr 6:16; Isa 20:4; Eze 25:3; Am 1:5.
EXIST, Da 3:29 not **e.** another god
　Ac 17:28 by him we have life and **e.**
　Col 1:17 by him all other things **e.**
EXISTED, Re 4:11 your will they **e.**
EXISTENCE, Ec 1:10 what has come into **e.**
　2Co 5:17 new things have come into **e.**
　Jas 3:9 men come into **e.** in the likeness of
　Mr 2:27; Joh 1:3.
EXISTING, Lu 7:25 and **e.** in luxury
　Ac 5:17 **e.** sect of Sadducees
　Ro 13:1 the **e.** authorities stand placed in
　Php 2:6 although he was **e.** in God's form,

EXISTS, La 3:29 Perhaps there **e.** a hope
　Da 2:28 there **e.** a God in the heavens
EXODUS, Heb 11:22 **e.** of Israel,
EXPANSE, Ps 19:1 work of hands the **e.**
　Da 12:3 ones will shine like the **e.**
　Ge 1:6; Ps 150:1; Eze 1:22; 10:1.
EXPECTATION, Ps 33:20 soul in **e.**
　Pr 13:12 E. postponed is making the
　Isa 8:17 I will keep in **e.** of Jehovah,
　Da 12:12 Happy is the one keeping in **e.**
　Ro 8:19 the eager **e.** of the creation
　Heb 11:1 Faith is the assured **e.** of things
　Pr 10:28; Lu 3:15; 21:26; Heb 10:27.
EXPEDITION, MILITARY, Nu 31:14.
EXPEL, Mt 10:1 authority to **e.** these
　Joh 16:2 Men will **e.** you from synagogue
EXPEL DEMONS, Mt 7:22.
EXPELLED, Joh 9:22 **e.** from synagogue
　Joh 12:42 not **e.** from synagogue
EXPENSE(S), 2Sa 24:24 first calculate the **e.**
　2Ki 15:20; Ac 21:24; 1Co 9:7.
EXPENSIVE, 1Ki 5:17; 7:9, 11.
　1Ti 2:9 adorn not with **e.** garb,
EXPENSIVE BURDEN, 1Th 2:6, 9; 2Th 3:8.
EXPERIENCE, Jg 3:2; 8:16; Heb 10:33.
EXPERIENCED, 1Ti 1:19 **e.** shipwreck
EXPIRE, Ps 104:29 take spirit they **e.**
　Ge 6:17; Job 34:15.
EXPIRED, Ge 7:21 flesh upon earth **e.,**
　Ge 25:8 Abraham **e.** and died in old age
　Lu 23:46 When he said this, he **e.**
EXPIRES, Job 14:10 man **e.** where is he
EXPIRING, Job 11:20 **e.** of the soul
EXPLOIT, 2Pe 2:3 they will **e.** you
　Jer 27:7; 30:8.
EXPLOITED, Jer 25:14.
EXPLORE, Ec 1:13 heart to **e.** wisdom
　Ec 7:25 **e.** and to search for wisdom and
EXPLORED, Ec 2:3 I **e.** with my heart
EXPORT, 1Ki 10:28 **e.** of the horses
EXPORTED, 2Ch 1:17 **e.** from Egypt
EXPOSE, Heb 6:6 **e.** him to public
EXPOSED, Heb 10:33 **e.** as in a theater
EXPOSITION, 2Ch 13:22; 24:27.
EXPOUNDED, Ne 8:8 the law being **e.**
EXPRESS, Ro 9:19 withstood his **e.** will?
EXPRESSION(S), 2Co 9:12 **e.** of thanks
　1Ti 5:12 disregarded first **e.** of faith.
EXPROPRIATIONS, Eze 45:9 Lift your **e.**
EXQUISITE DELIGHT(S), Ps 37:11; Ec 2:8.
EXTERMINATE, Eze 20:13 order to **e.** them.
　Ex 33:5; Jos 24:20.
EXTERMINATED, Ps 18:37 until they are **e.**
　Jer 9:16 sword until I have **e.** them.
　Nu 25:11; De 28:21; 2Sa 21:5; 22:38.
EXTERMINATION, Isa 10:22 An **e.** decided
　Zep 1:18 an **e.** of the inhabitants of the
　Ne 9:31; Isa 28:22; Da 9:27.
EXTERNAL, 2Co 11:28 things of **e.** kind,
EXTINCTION, Job 31:29; Pr 24:22.
EXTINGUISH, Jer 21:12 and no one to **e.**
　Mt 12:20 no smoldering wick will he **e.**
　2Sa 21:17; Isa 42:3; Am 5:6.
EXTINGUISHED, Job 18:5 ones will be **e.**
　Ps 118:12 They were **e.** like a fire of
　Pr 13:9 lamp of the wicked will be **e.**
　Isa 34:10 night or by day it will not be **e.**
　Isa 66:24 their fire will not be **e.**
　2Ki 22:17; Pr 20:20; 24:20; Eze 20:48.
EXTINGUISHING, Isa 1:31 no one to do **e.**
EXTOLLING, Ps 66:17 **e.** with my tongue.
EXTORTED, 2Co 9:5 not something **e.**
EXTORTIONERS, 1Co 6:10 nor **e.** inherit
EXTRAORDINARY, Ge 18:14 **e.** for Jehovah

De 17:8; Da 4:36; 6:3; 1Th 3:10; 5:13.
EXTRAORDINARY WORKS, Ac 19:11 e. Paul,
EXTRAVAGANCE, 1Co 2:1 not e. of speech
EXTREME, 2Co 1:8 under e. pressure
EXTREMITIES, Job 38:13 e. of earth,
EXULT, Ps 25:2 enemies not e. over me.
Ps 94:3 How long are the wicked going to e.?
Isa 65:18 e. you people I am creating
Ro 5:3 let us e. while in tribulations
1Sa 2:1; Isa 35:1; Jer 32:41.
EXULTANT, Isa 22:2 an e. town.
Isa 23:7; Zep 2:15.
EXULTATION, Ps 45:7 with the oil of e.
Ga 6:4 then he will have cause for e.
Php 2:16 I have cause for e. in Christ's
Ps 105:43; 119:111; Isa 65:18; Ho 2:11.
EXULTING, Pr 28:12 righteous are e.,
Ro 15:17 I have cause for e. in Christ Jesus
EXULTINGLY, 1Ch 16:35; Ps 106:47.
EYE(S), Job 42:5 my own e. does see you
Ps 11:4 his own e. examine the sons of men
Pr 15:3 e. of Jehovah are in every place
Pr 16:2 of a man are pure in his own e.,
Jer 16:17 my e. are upon all their ways.
Zec 14:12 e. will rot in their sockets,
Ro 16:17 keep your e. on those who cause
1Co 2:9 E. has not seen and ear has
1Co 15:52 in the twinkling of an e.,
Eph 1:18 the e. of your heart enlightened
Php 2:4 keeping an e., not in personal
1Pe 3:12 e. of Jehovah are upon righteous
1Jo 2:16 desire of the e. and the showy
Re 1:7 every e. will see him,
Re 21:4 wipe out every tear from their e.,
Mt 13:16; Mr 8:18; 2Co 4:18; Ga 6:1.
EYEBALL, Zec 2:8 is touching my e.
EYE FOR EYE, De 19:21; Mt 5:38.
EYESERVICE, Eph 6:6; Col 3:22.
EYEWITNESSES, 1Pe 2:12 they are e.
EZEKIEL, Eze 1:3; 24:24.
EZRA, Ezr 7:6; 10:1; Ne 8:1, 6.

F

FABLES, Tit 1:14 no attention to Jewish f.
FABRIC, 1Ch 4:21; 2Ch 2:14; Es 1:6.
FABRICATE, Pr 3:29 Do not f. against
FABRICATING BAD, Pr 6:14 He is f. all
FABRICATING BADNESS, Pr 6:18 heart f.
FABRICATING MISCHIEF, 1Sa 23:9 Saul f.
FACE(S), Ex 10:29 not try to see your f.
Ex 33:20 You are not able to see my f.,
Isa 25:8 wipe the tears from all f.
Isa 52:8 f. to f. that they will see
Mt 26:39 he fell upon his f., praying
Ac 6:15 his f. was an angel's f.
2Co 4:6 illuminate them by f. of Christ.
Ga 2:11 Cephas came, I resisted him f. to f.
Ac 20:25; 25:16; 1Co 13:12; 2Co 3:7.
FACE VALUE, 2Co 10:7 look according to f.
FACULTIES, THINKING, 2Pe 3:1 clear t.
FADE AWAY, Isa 19:8 those will f.
Jas 1:11 rich man will f. in his ways
Ho 4:3.
FADED AWAY, 1Sa 2:5; Jer 14:2.
FAIL, Heb 11:32 time will f. me if I
2Pe 1:10 you will by no means ever f.
FAILING, Ps 71:9 Just when my power is f.
FAILS, 1Co 13:8 Love never f.
FAITH, Lu 18:8 really find the f. on earth?
Joh 3:16 everyone exercising f. in him
Ro 4:13 it was through righteousness by f.
Ro 10:9 exercise f. in your heart that God
Ro 14:23 everything not out of f. is sin.
Ga 3:8 declare people righteous due to f.,

Ga 3:11 righteous will live by f.
Ga 6:10 those related to us in the f.
Eph 4:5 one Lord, one f., one baptism;
2Th 3:2 f. is not a possession of all
1Ti 6:12 fight fine fight of f.
2Ti 4:7 finish, I have observed the f.
Heb 11:1 F. is the assured expectation
Heb 11:6 without f. it is impossible to
Heb 12:2 leader and perfecter of our f.,
Jas 2:26 f. without works is dead,
1Pe 1:7 tested quality of your f.,
1Pe 5:9 solid in the f., knowing
1Jo 5:4 conquered the world, our f.
Ro 4:3; 2Co 5:7; Eph 6:16; 1Ti 4:1; 6:12.
FAITHFUL, Ps 31:23 The f. ones Jehovah
Pr 13:17 f. envoy is a healing.
Pr 14:5 f. witness will not lie,
Pr 27:6 wounds inflicted by a lover are f.,
Mt 24:45 Who really is the f. and discreet
Lu 16:10 Person f. in least is f. in much,
2Ti 2:2 these things commit to f. men
1Pe 4:19 commending souls to a f. Creator
Re 2:10 Prove f. even to death
Re 3:14 f. and true witness, the beginning
Re 17:14 called and chosen and f. with him
De 7:9; Ne 9:8; 13:13; 1Co 4:2; Re 19:11.
FAITHFUL CONDUCT, Isa 26:2 nation keeping f.
FAITHFULNESS, De 32:4 God of f., with
De 32:20 sons in whom there is no f.
Ps 40:10 Your f. and your salvation I have
Hab 2:4 by his f. he will keep living.
1Th 3:7 tribulation through the f. you show,
2Ki 12:15; 2Ch 19:9; 31:12; Ps 33:4;
36:5; 119:90; Isa 25:1; Ro 3:3.
FAITH, LACK OF, Mt 13:58; Mr 6:6.
Ro 4:20 he did not waver in a l.,
Ro 11:20 For their l. they were broken off,
1Ti 1:13; Heb 3:19.
FAITHLESS, Pr 14:14 one f. at heart
FAITH, PUT, Ge 15:6 p. in Jehovah
1Ki 10:7 I did not p. until my own eyes
Ps 78:22 did not p. in God
Joh 11:48 all p. in him, and the Romans
Joh 12:42 many rulers actually p. in him,
Ro 10:14 in whom they have not p.?
Php 1:29 not only p., but also suffer
Jon 3:5; Joh 2:11; 4:39; 7:48; 9:36, 38.
FAITH, PUTTING, Joh 9:35 p. in the Son
Ac 10:43 everyone p. gets forgiveness
FAITH, PUTS, Joh 12:44 p. in me p., not
FALL, Pr 11:28 in his riches—he will f.,
Pr 24:16 righteous one may f. seven times
1Co 10:12 beware that he does not f.
Heb 10:31 fearful to f. into hands of God
Ps 37:24; Pr 11:14; Lu 23:30; 1Ti 6:9.
FALLACIOUS, Jer 7:4, 8 trust in f. words,
FALLING, Jer 37:13, 14 I am not f. away
FALLOW, Jer 23:11 land let lie f.
FALLS, Lu 11:17 a house divided f.
Ro 14:4 To his own master he stands or f.
FALSE, Mt 24:24 For f. Christs and f.
2Co 11:13 For such men are f. apostles,
Ex 23:7; Ps 27:12; 119:104; Pr 6:17,19;
19:5; Isa 9:15; Mt 26:59; Ga 2:4.
FALSE FRONT, 1Th 2:5 no f. for
FALSEHOOD(S), Job 13:4 smearers of f.;
Jer 5:31 prophets prophesy in f.;
Eph 4:25 put away f., speak truth each one
Ps 7:14; Isa 28:15; Zec 10:2; Re 14:5.
FALSELY, Ex 20:16 must not testify f.
Zec 5:4 sworn oath in my name f.;
Lu 3:14 Do not accuse anybody f.,
1Ti 6:20 empty speeches f. called knowledge.
Le 6:3; Ps 44:17; Jer 6:13.

FALSE PROPHET(S), Mt 7:15 f. in sheep's
1Jo 4:1 many f. have gone forth into the
Mt 24:11; 2Pe 2:1; Re 16:13.
FALSE STEP, Ro 11:11, 12; Ga 6:1.
FALSE STORIES, 1Ti 1:4; 4:7; 2Pe 1:16.
FALSE TO AGREEMENTS, Ro 1:31 f., having
FALSIFIER, Pr 17:4 f. giving ear to
FAME, Jos 9:9 have heard of his f. and
Nu 14:15; 1Ch 14:17; Es 9:4.
FAMILIAR, Ps 139:3 become f. all my
FAMILIES, Ge 12:3 f. of the ground
Ps 107:41 converts him into f. like a flock.
Zec 14:17 the f. of the earth to Jerusalem
Ge 28:14; Jer 1:15; 10:25; 25:9; Ac 3:25.
FAMILY, Eph 3:15 every f. owes its name.
FAMINE. See also FOOD SHORTAGE.
FAMINE, Ge 41:57 the f. had a strong grip
Jer 14:15 by f. those will come finish.
Am 8:11 a f., not for bread, and a thirst,
Ru 1:1; Jer 5:12; 11:22; 42:17; Re 18:8.
FAMISHED, Ge 41:55 Egypt became f.
Isa 5:13 their glory will be f. men,
FARE, Pr 11:15 f. badly because he has
FARMER(S), Ge 9:20 Noah started as a f.
Jas 5:7 the f. keeps waiting for the fruit
Isa 61:5; Jer 14:4; 51:23; 2Ti 2:6.
FASHION, Php 2:8 found in f. as man,
FASHIONED, Ro 12:2 quit being f. after
1Pe 1:14 being f. according to ignorance,
FASHIONER, Job 36:3 to my F. I ascribe
FAST, Isa 58:5 f. that I choose become
Lu 5:33 The disciples of John f.
Lu 5:34 cannot make friends of bridegroom f.
2Ch 20:3; Es 4:16; Jer 14:12; Jon 3:5.
FASTING, Joe 1:14 Sanctify a time of f.
Mt 6:16-18 When you are f., stop becoming
Mr 2:18 your disciples do not practice f.?
FAT, 1Sa 15:22 pay attention than the f.
Jer 5:28 They have grown f.; become shiny.
Jg 3:17; Pr 28:25; Eze 34:3.
FATAL, Ge 42:4 a f. accident may
Ex 21:22 children come out but no f.
FATAL STRIKER, Le 24:21 f. of a beast
FATHER(S), Ps 89:26 You are my F., my God
Pr 17:6 beauty of sons is their f.
Isa 64:8 Jehovah, you are our F.
Mt 6:9 Our F. in the heavens, let your
Mt 23:9 do not call anyone your f. on earth,
Lu 2:49 I must be in the house of my F.?
Joh 8:44 You are from your f. the Devil
Joh 14:28 the F. is greater than I am.
1Co 4:15 your f. through the good news.
Eph 6:4 f., do not be irritating your
Jas 1:17 comes from the F. of lights
Ge 2:24; Pr 6:20; 13:1; 23:22; Isa 38:19;
Mal 4:6; Mt 10:37; 26:29; Joh 10:30; 14:
6, 24; Ga 1:14; Eph 4:6; Re 14:1.
FATHERED, De 32:18 Rock that f. you,
FATHER-IN-LAW, Ex 4:18; 18:1; Jg 19:4.
FATHERLESS BOY(S), Ps 68:5 father of f.
Ex 22:22; De 10:18; Ps 10:14; Jer 5:28.
FATLING(S), 2Sa 6:13; Eze 39:18; Am 5:22.
FATTENED, Jas 5:5 f. your hearts on the
FAULT(S), Mt 18:15 Lay bare f. between
Joh 18:38 Pilate said I find no f. in him.
2Co 6:3 ministry might not be found f. with
Ex 5:16; Ps 50:20; Ro 9:19; Heb 8:8.
FAULTFINDER, Job 40:2 f. with Almighty?
FAULTFINDING, Ps 18:43 escape f. of people
FAULTINESS, Job 4:18 he charges with f.
FAULTLESS, Ge 6:9 He proved himself f.
Eze 28:15 You were f. in your ways until
Heb 8:7 first covenant had been f., no
Ge 17:1; De 18:13; Ps 119:1; Pr 28:10.

FAULTLESSLY, Ps 15:2 He is walking f.
FAULTLESSNESS, Jos 24:14 serve him in f.
FAVOR, Ge 4:4 looking with f. upon Abel
Zec 12:10 I will pour out the spirit of f.
Lu 2:52 Jesus went on progressing in f.
Ps 37:21; Pr 3:4; 28:23; Ec 9:11.
FAVORABLE, Ga 6:10 time f. for it, work
FAVORITISM, Jas 2:1 acts of f., are you?
Jas 2:9 if you continue showing f., you
FEAR, Ps 33:8 Let all earth f. Jehovah,
Ps 111:10 The f. of Jehovah is the
Ps 118:6 I shall not f. What can man do
Pr 8:13 The f. of Jehovah means hating bad.
Lu 12:4 Do not f. those who kill the body
Ro 13:7 to him who calls for f., such f.;
Php 2:12 working out your salvation with f.
1Pe 3:14 object of their f. do not f.
1Jo 4:18 There is no f. in love,
FEARED, 1Sa 15:24 I f. the people and
1Ch 16:25 Jehovah is to be f. more than
FEARFUL, De 20:8 Who is the man f.
Ps 25:14 intimacy with Jehovah to those f.
Heb 10:27 f. expectation of judgment
Heb 10:31 f. thing to fall into God's hands
FEARING, Ps 34:7 angel camps around those f.
FEAR-INSPIRING, Ex 34:10 a f. thing
De 10:17 Jehovah is the great f. God
Ps 45:4 hand will teach you in f. things.
Ps 111:9 His name is holy and f.
Ps 139:14 in a f. way I am made.
Isa 18:2 to a people f. everywhere
Joe 2:11 day of Jehovah is great and f.,
Zep 2:11 Jehovah will be f. against them;
Jg 13:6; 1Ch 17:21; Ne 1:5; Joe 2:31.
FEAR OF THE DEITIES, Ac 17:22 more f.
FEARS, Pr 14:16 wise one f. and is
Pr 31:30 woman that f. Jehovah
Ac 10:35 man that f. him and works
FEARSOME, Da 7:7 fourth beast, f.
FEAST, Lu 5:29 Levi spread a reception f.
FEASTS, Jude 12 hidden in your love f.
FEATURE, Heb 7:11 with the Law as a f.
FEATURE, CONSTANT, Da 8:11; 12:11.
FEATURELESS, Ps 107:40 wander in a f. place
FED, 1Co 3:2 I f. you milk, not
Re 12:14 woman is f. for a time
FEEBLE, Ne 4:2 What are the f. Jews
FEED, Mt 25:37 we see you hungry and f.
Joh 21:17 Jesus said: F. my little sheep.
Re 12:6 f. her there a thousand two
Jer 3:15; Eze 34:14, 16, 23; Jude 12.
FEEDING, Eze 34:8 shepherds kept f. selves
Jg 21:6 Israel began to f. over Benjamin
FEEL REGRET, Ex 32:14 Jehovah began to f.
FEEL REGRETS, Zec 1:17 Jehovah f. over
FEEL SORRY, De 7:16 Your eye must not f.
Eze 9:5 Let not your eye f., and do not
FEET, Isa 52:7 f. of the one bringing
Ro 16:20 crush Satan under your f. shortly.
1Co 15:25 put all enemies under his f.
Eph 6:15 f. shod with the equipment
Isa 59:7; Lu 1:79; Ro 10:15; Heb 2:8.
FELIX, Ac 23:24; 24:3, 25, 27.
FELL, Ro 11:11 stumble so that they f.
FELLOW, Ac 24:5 this man a pestilent f.
1Sa 14:20; Mt 20:13; 26:50.
FELLOW CITIZENS, Eph 2:19 you are f. of
FELLOW MAN, Ex 20:16; 2Sa 12:11.
FELLOW MEMBERS, Eph 3:6 f. of the body
FELLOWSHIP, NO, Pr 20:19; 2Co 6:14.
FELLOW WORKERS, 1Co 3:9 we are God's f.
Col 4:11 my f. for the kingdom of God,
FELT, 1Jo 1:1 viewed and our hands f.,
FEMALE(S), Ge 1:27 male and f. created

Ro 1:26 **f.** changed natural use
FEMININE, 1Pe 3:7 weaker vessel, the **f.**
FENCED, Lu 14:23; Eph 2:14.
FERMENT, 1Co 5:7 free from **f.**
FERMENTED, Mt 13:33 the whole was **f.**
FERMENTS, Ga 5:9 little leaven **f.** the
FERTILE, Jas 1:15 desire when **f.** gives
FERVENT, Pr 26:23 **f.** lips with a bad
FERVOR, Ne 3:20 worked with **f.**
FESTAL SEASON(S), Zep 3:18; Zec 8:19.
FESTERED, Ps 38:5 My wounds have **f.,**
FESTIVAL, Ex 23:14 Three times a **f.**
　Ex 23:15 the **f.** of unfermented cakes.
　Ex 23:16 **f.** of harvest and **f.** of
　Lu 22:1 **f.** of the unfermented cakes
　Ex 10:9; 12:14; 34:22; Le 23:6; Nu 28:17;
　Joh 2:23; 5:1; 6:4; 7:8, 10, 37; 1Co 5:8.
FESTIVAL PROCESSION, Ps 118:27 the **f.**
FESTIVALS, Le 23:4 these are seasonal **f.**
FESTUS, Ac 24:27; 26:24.
FETCHED, 1Sa 17:31 Hence he **f.** him
FETTERS, Isa 58:6 loosen the **f.** of
FEVER, Mt 8:15; Joh 4:52; Ac 28:8.
FEVER, BURNING, De 32:24; Hab 3:5.
FIDELITY, Tit 2:10 exhibiting **f.** to the full
FIELD(S), Mt 13:38 **f.** is the world;
　Joh 4:35 view the **f.** that they are white
　1Co 3:9 You are God's **f.** under cultivation.
　Isa 55:12; Mt 6:30; 13:44; 24:18, 40.
FIERCE, Mt 8:28; 2Ti 3:3.
FIERY-COLORED, Re 6:4; 12:3.
FIGHT(S), Eph 6:12 a **f.,** not against
　1Ti 6:12 the fine **f.** of faith
　2Ti 2:24 of the Lord does not need to **f.,**
　2Ti 4:7 I have fought the fine **f.,**
　Jas 4:1 what source are there **f.** among
　Jude 3 put up a hard **f.** for the faith
　2Ch 20:17; 2Ti 2:14; 2:23; Tit 3:9.
FIGHTERS, Ac 5:39 **f.** against God.
FIGHTING, Jos 10:14 Jehovah was **f.** for
　Jas 4:2 You go on **f.** and waging war,
　Ps 109:3; Php 1:27.
FIG TREE, Mic 4:4 under his vine and **f.,**
　Mt 24:32 the **f.** as an illustration
　1Ki 4:25; Mt 21:19-21; Lu 13:6, 7.
FIGURE, Joh 5:37 nor seen his **f.**
FIGURED, Isa 14:24 just as I **f.** so it
FIGURES, Ac 7:43 the **f.** which you made
FILE, Ro 8:33 **f.** accusation against
FILL, Ge 1:28 **f.** the earth
　Ge 9:1 Become many and **f.** the earth.
　Hag 2:7 I will **f.** this house with glory,
　Ps 81:10; Isa 27:6; Jer 51:14; Mt 23:32.
FILLED, Da 2:35 stone **f.** the earth.
　Hab 2:14 earth will be **f.** with the knowing
　Eph 5:18 keep getting **f.** with spirit,
　Ge 6:11; 1Ki 8:11; Ac 4:31; Col 1:9.
FILL HAND(S) WITH POWER, Ex 28:41.
　Ex 29:33 atonement has been made to **f.**
　Ex 29:35 You will take seven days to **f.**
　Jg 17:5 **f.,** that he might serve as priest
　Ex 32:29; Le 16:32; 2Ch 13:9.
FILLS, Ps 24:1 earth and that which **f.**
　Ps 96:11 the sea and that which **f.** it.
FILM, Isa 40:15 **f.** of dust on the scales
FILTERED, Isa 25:6 wine on dregs, **f.**
FILTH, 1Pe 3:21 putting away the **f.** of
FILTHINESS, Jas 1:21 put away all **f.**
FILTHY, Isa 28:8 tables full of **f.**
　Jas 2:2; Re 22:11.
FINAL, Isa 2:2 in the **f.** part of days
　Eze 38:16 In the **f.** part of the days it
　Da 10:14 befall people in the **f.** part of
　2Pe 2:20 **f.** conditions worse than the first.

Jer 23:20; Eze 38:8; Da 2:28; 8:19.
FINALE, Isa 46:10; Jer 5:31; 17:11.
FINALITY, Jer 23:39 with **f.** and desert you
FINANCIALLY WEAK, Le 25:35 brother **f.**
FIND, Ps 21:8 hand will **f.** your enemies,
　Mt 7:7 keep on seeking, and you will **f.;**
　Pr 1:28; 2:5; Jer 29:13; Ac 17:27; Re 9:6.
FINDING, Pr 8:35 **f.** me will find life
　Mt 7:14 few are the ones **f.** it.
FINDS, Ec 9:10 All that your hand **f.** to
　Mt 7:8 everyone seeking **f.,**
　Mt 10:39 He that **f.** his soul will lose it,
　Lu 12:37 master on arriving **f.** watching!
FINE, De 22:19 must **f.** him a hundred
　Pr 21:11 laying of a **f.** on the ridiculer
　1Th 5:21 hold fast to what is **f.**
　2Ti 1:14 This **f.** trust guard through the
　2Ki 23:33; Pr 17:26; Heb 10:24; Jas 3:13.
FINGER(S), Ex 8:19 It is the **f.** of God
　Ex 31:18 tablets written on by God's **f.**
　Da 5:5 **f.** were writing upon the wall
　Lu 11:20 by God's **f.** I expel demons
　Ps 8:3; Isa 58:9; Mt 23:4; Joh 20:25.
FINGERBREADTHS, Jer 52:21 four **f.**
FINISH, Joh 4:34 sent me to **f.** his work.
　Ac 20:24 may **f.** my course and the ministry
　2Ti 4:7 have run the course to the **f.**
　La 3:22.
FINISHED, Ps 104:35 sinners will be **f.**
　Lu 12:50 distressed until it is **f.**
　Lu 13:32 the third day I shall be **f.**
　Joh 17:4 I **f.** the work you have given me
FIRE, Isa 66:16 as **f.** Jehovah will take
　Zep 3:8 **f.** of my zeal all the earth
　Zec 3:2 log snatched out of the **f.?**
　Mal 3:2 like the **f.** of a refiner
　Heb 12:29 God is also a consuming **f.**
　2Pe 3:7 stored up for **f.** and being reserved
　Re 17:16 completely burn her with **f.**
　1Ki 18:38; Mt 3:11, 12; 1Co 3:13.
FIRM, 1Th 3:13 make your hearts **f.,**
　Heb 3:6 hope **f.** to the end.
　Heb 6:19 soul, both sure and **f.,**
FIRMNESS, Col 2:5 the **f.** of your faith
FIRST, Isa 44:6 I am the **f.** and I am
　Mt 6:33 Keep on seeking **f.** the kingdom
　Mt 19:30 many that are **f.** will be last
　Ac 26:23 as the **f.** to be resurrected from
　Col 1:18 the one who is **f.** in all things,
　Isa 48:12; Mr 9:35; Heb 10:9; 3Jo 9.
FIRST-BORN, Col 1:15 **f.** of all creation
　Col 1:18 the **f.** from the dead, that he
　Heb 1:6 he brings his **f.** into the earth,
　Heb 12:23 the congregation of the **f.** who
　Ex 4:22; 12:29; De 21:17; Ro 8:29.
FIRST FRUIT(S), Le 23:10 **f.** of harvest
　Jas 1:18 for us to be a **f.** of his creatures
　Ro 8:23; 11:16; 1Co 16:15; Re 14:4.
FIRST RECOGNITION, Ro 8:29 he gave **f.**
FIRST RECOGNIZED, Ro 11:2 people he **f.**
FIRST RIPE FRUITS, Ex 23:16; Ne 10:35.
FIRST THINGS, Isa 42:9 **f.**—have come,
　Isa 43:9 can they cause us to hear the **f.?**
FISH(ES), Jer 16:16 they will **f.** for
　Eze 47:9 there will be very many **f.**
　Jon 1:17 appointed a great **f.** to swallow
　Mt 12:40 in the belly of the huge **f.** three
　Mt 14:19 took the five loaves and two **f.,**
　Ps 105:29; Ec 9:12; Eze 29:4, 5; Jon 2:10.
FISHER(S), Jer 16:16 sending for many **f.**
　Eze 47:10 **f.** will stand alongside it
　Mt 4:19 and I will make you **f.** of men
FIST, Isa 58:4 the **f.** of wickedness.

FITNESS, 1Ti 3:10 tested as to f.
FITTING, 1Co 11:13; Tit 2:1; Heb 2:10.
FIXED, Col 3:2 Keep your minds f. on
  Ps 119:90; Pr 3:19.
FLAGRANTLY, 1Sa 12:25 f. do what is bad
FLAME(S), Ca 8:6 fire the f. of Jah
  Eze 20:47 The f. will not be extinguished
  Da 3:22 the ones the fiery f. killed.
  Da 11:33 stumble by sword and by f.
  Joe 2:3 behind it a f. consumes.
  Ps 83:14; Isa 5:24; 10:17; 43:2; Heb 1:7.
FLAMING, 2Th 1:8 f. fire, as he brings
  Ge 3:24; Isa 4:5; La 2:3.
FLASH, Ge 32:31; Isa 58:10.
FLASHED, 2Ki 3:22; Ps 112:4; Ac 9:3.
FLASHED FORTH, Ec 1:5 sun has f.
FLASH FLOOD, Isa 28:18 overflowing f.,
FLASHING, Lu 17:24; 24:4 lightning f.
FLATTERING, Pr 28:23 than he that is f.
  1Th 2:5 at no time with f. speech
  Pr 26:28; 29:5.
FLEA, 1Sa 24:14; 26:20 chasing a f.
FLEE, Jer 25:35 a place to f. to
  Jer 51:6 F. out of the midst of Babylon
  Mt 23:33 how are you to f. from judgment
  Jas 4:7 oppose the Devil, and he will f.
  Nu 35:15; Pr 28:1; Isa 35:10; 1Co 10:14.
FLEECE, Jg 6:37-40.
FLEEING, Mt 24:16 let those in Judea f.
  Jer 9:26; 10:11; Isa 33:21.
FLEET, 1Ki 9:26; 10:11; Isa 33:21.
FLESH, Ge 2:24 they become one f.
  Isa 40:6 All f. is green grass,
  Joe 2:28 my spirit on every sort of f.
  Zec 14:12 will he a rotting of one's f.
  Joh 1:14 the Word became f. and resided
  Ro 8:5 those who are in accord with the f.
  Ro 8:7 minding of the f. means enmity
  1Co 15:39 Not all f. is the same f.,
  1Co 15:50 f. and blood cannot inherit
  2Co 10:3 we do not wage warfare in the f.
  Eph 6:12 fight, not against blood and f.
  Ge 2:23; 9:11; Ps 56:4; Isa 40:6; 49:26;
  Ac 2:17; 1Co 1:29; Ga 5:19.
FLESH, BE ONE, Eph 5:31 the two will b.
  Mr 10:8; 1Co 6:16.
FLESHLY, 2Co 1:12 not f. wisdom but
  Ro 7:14; 1Co 3:3; Col 2:18.
FLESHLY DESIRE(S), Ga 5:16 no f. at all
  1Pe 2:11 keep abstaining from f.
FLIGHT, Mt 24:20 f. not in wintertime
  De 32:30; Isa 52:12; Jer 16:19.
FLOATING, Ge 7:17 ark was f. high above
FLOCK(S), Ps 65:13 pastures with f.
  Ps 79:13 people the f. of your pasturage,
  Lu 12:32 Have no fear, little f., because
  1Pe 5:3 but becoming examples to the f.
  Jg 5:16; Ps 78:52; Isa 13:20; 60:7; 61:5;
  Jer 25:34; Mic 2:12; Mr 26:31; 1Pe 5:2.
FLOGGED, Ac 5:40; 16:37 apostles f.
FLOOD, Da 9:26 the end will be by the f.
  Na 1:8 by the f. make an extermination
  Mt 24:38 days before the f., eating and
FLOODGATES, Ge 7:11; 2Ki 7:2; Mal 3:10.
FLUCTUATING BLAST, Nu 10:5 blown a f.
FLUENT, Ex 4:10 I am not a f. speaker
FLUENTLY, READING, Hab 2:2 r. aloud
FLUTE, 1Co 14:7 played on f. or harp?
  Mt 11:17; Lu 7:32.
FLY, Re 12:14; 19:17 f. in wilderness
FLYING CREATURES, Ge 1:20; Le 11:13.
FOLD, Joh 10:16 sheep not of this f.
FOLLOW, Mt 10:38 torture stake and f.
  1Pe 2:21 a model for you to f. his steps
  Mt 16:24; Joh 10:5, 27; 2Pe 2:2.

FOLLOWED, Mt 19:28 you who have f. me
  Mt 4:20; 1Co 10:4; 1Ti 4:6; 5:10.
FOLLOWING, 1Ki 18:21 is the God, go f.
  Re 19:14 were f. him on white horses
FOLLOWS, Joh 8:12 f. me will walk in
FOLLY, Ec 1:17; 2:3, 13 to know f.
FOND, Pr 8:30 he was specially f. of
  Joh 12:25 He that is f. of his soul destroys it
  Joh 15:19 world would be f. of its own.
FONDLE, Ps 94:19 began to f. my soul
FONDLED, Isa 66:12 upon the knees be f.
FOOD, Mt 24:45 give f. at the proper
  Joh 4:34 My f. is for me to do the will
  Joh 6:27 Work not for the f. that perishes
  Joh 6:55 my flesh is true f., and my blood
  Ro 14:15 if because of your f. your brother
  Heb 5:14 solid f. belongs to mature people
  Ps 136:25; Mt 6:25; Ac 14:17; 1Co 8:13.
FOOD POUCH, Mt 10:10; Lu 22:35, 36.
FOOD SHORTAGE(S), Ne 5:3 during the f.
  Mt 24:7 be f. in one place after another.
  Mr 13:8; Lu 21:11; Re 6:8.
FOOL(S), Pr 1:7 discipline are what f.
  Mt 5:22 says despicable f. will be
  1Co 3:18 Let him become a f. that he
  1Co 4:10 We are f. because of Christ, but
  1Co 1:27; Eph 5:4; Tit 3:9.
FOOLED, Jer 20:7 You have f. me,
FOOLISH, Pr 12:15 The way of the f. one
  Mt 25:2 Five of them were f. and five
  1Co 1:20 the wisdom of the world f.?
  1Co 1:25 f. thing of God is wiser than men
  2Ti 2:23 turn down f. questionings,
  1Co 1:27; Eph 5:4; Tit 3:9.
FOOLISHNESS, Ps 69:5 to know my f.
  Pr 26:4 stupid according to his f. that you
  1Co 1:18 speech about torture stake is f.
  1Co 1:23 Christ impaled, to the nations f.;
  1Co 3:19 wisdom of this world is f. with
  2Sa 15:31; Pr 19:3; Isa 44:25; 1Co 2:14.
FOOT, Ps 119:105 word is a lamp to my f.,
FOOTSTEPS, Ps 44:18; Ro 4:12; 2Co 12:18.
FOOTSTOOL, Isa 66:1 earth is my f.
  Ps 99:5; 132:7; La 2:1; Jas 2:3.
FORBEARANCE, Ro 2:4; 3:25 despise his f.
  Ps 110:3; Da 9:27; Heb 9:17; Jas 5:16.
FORCE, Zec 4:6 not by military f. but
  Ps 110:3; Da 9:27; Heb 9:17; Jas 5:16.
FORCED LABOR, Pr 12:24 will be for f.
  Jg 1:28; 1Ki 9:21.
FOREFATHER(S), Ps 45:16 In place of f.
  1Pe 1:18 received by tradition from your f.
  Ge 15:15; 2Ki 18:3; Mic 7:20; 2Ti 1:3.
FOREHEAD(S), 1Sa 17:49 struck in his f.
  Eze 9:4 put a mark on the f. of the men
  Re 14:1 name of his Father on their f.
  Re 14:9 receives a mark on his f. or hand,
  Eze 3:9; Re 7:3; 9:4; 17:5; 20:4; 22:4.
FOREIGNER(S), 1Ki 8:41 also to the f.,
  Ps 18:44 F. will come cringing to me.
  Ps 69:8 I have become a f. to the sons
  Isa 56:6 f. joined themselves to Jehovah
  1Co 14:11 I shall be a f. to one speaking
  Job 19:15; Isa 2:6; 56:3; 60:10; 61:5.
FOREIGN GOD(S), Jos 24:20; Ps 81:9.
FOREKNOWLEDGE, Ac 2:23 counsel and f.
  1Pe 1:2 according to the f. of God the
FOREKNOWN, 1Pe 1:20 he was f. before
FOREMEN, 2Ch 8:10 f. over the people.
FOREMOST, 1Ti 1:15 sinners. I am f.
FOREORDAINED, Ac 4:28 had f. to occur
  Ro 8:29 f. to be
  Ro 8:30 those f. are the ones also called;
  1Co 2:7 the hidden wisdom, which God f.
  Eph 1:5 f. us to the adoption through Jesus

Eph 1:11 **f.** according to the purpose of him
FORESAW, Heb 11:40 God **f.** something
FORESTS, Eze 34:25 beasts sleep in **f.**
FORETELLERS OF EVENTS, Le 19:31 not **f.**
De 18:11; 2Ki 21:6; 23:24; Isa 19:3.
FOREVER, Ps 104:5 founded the earth **f.**
Isa 57:15 Lofty One who is residing **f.**
Ps 111:8; 148:6; Da 12:3.
FOREWARN, Ga 5:21 I did **f.** you, the same
FOREWARNED, Mt 24:25 Look! I have **f.** you.
FORFEIT, Jos 6:26 at the **f.** of his
FORGER, Ge 4:22 **f.** of every sort tool of copper
FORGET, Ge 4:23 Watch that you may not **f.**
Isa 49:15 these **f.**, yet I shall not **f.** you.
Jer 23:27 making my people **f.** my name
Heb 6:10 God is not unrighteous to **f.** your
De 6:12; Ps 45:10; 78:7; Heb 13:16.
FORGETFUL, 2Pe 1:9 **f.** of cleansing
FORGETTING, Ps 9:17 the nations **f.** God.
Ho 4:6 you keep **f.** the law of your God,
Ho 8:14 Israel began **f.** his Maker
Php 3:13 **F.** the things behind and
FORGIVE, 1Ki 8:50 must **f.** your people
Jer 31:34 I shall **f.** their error, and
Mt 6:12 **f.** us our debts, as we also
Joh 20:23 If you **f.** the sins of any persons,
1Jo 1:9 he is faithful and righteous to **f.**
Ex 34:9; Nu 14:19; 1Ki 8:36; Ps 25:11;
Isa 55:7; Mt 9:6; Mr 2:7; 11:25; 2Co 2:10.
FORGIVEN, Jas 5:15 sins, it will be **f.**
FORGIVENESS, Ne 9:17 God of acts of **f.**,
Mt 26:28 in behalf of many for **f.** of sins.
Mr 1:4 baptism of those repenting for **f.** of
Ac 2:38 baptized in the name of Jesus for **f.**
Col 1:14 we have release by ransom, the **f.**
Heb 9:22 unless blood is poured out no **f.**
Lu 1:77; 24:47; Ac 10:43; Heb 10:18.
FORGOTTEN, Job 19:14 those known have **f.** me
Isa 65:16 the former distresses will be **f.**
Ps 9:18; 10:11; Jer 30:14; 50:5.
FORM, De 4:15 you did not see any **f.**
Ps 17:15 satisfied to see your **f.**
Php 2:6 he was existing in God's **f.**,
2Ti 3:5 **f.** of godly devotion but false to
Ps 17:15; Isa 53:2; Ac 23:25; 1Th 5:22.
FORMAL WORSHIPER, Jas 1:26 man be **f.**
FORMATION, BATTLE, Jg 20:20; 1Sa 4:2.
FORMED, Isa 37:26; 43:10; 45:18.
FORMER, Ec 1:11 of people of **f.** times,
Isa 65:17 **f.** things will not be called to
Isa 45:9; Jer 10:16; Hag 2:9; Eph 4:22.
FORMERLY, 1Pe 1:14 desires you **f.** had
FORMLESS, Ge 1:2 earth proved to be **f.**
FORM OF TEACHING, Ro 6:17 obedient to **f.**
FORM OF WORSHIP, Ac 26:5 sect of our **f.**
Jas 1:26 this man's **f.** is futile.
Jas 1:27 The **f.** that is clean and
FORNICATION(S), 2Ki 9:22 **f.** of Jezebel
1Co 5:1 **f.** is reported among you, not even
1Co 6:13 the body is not for **f.**,
1Co 6:18 Flee from **f.** Every other sin
1Co 10:8 Neither let us practice **f.**, as
Ga 5:19 works of the flesh are **f.**,
Eph 5:3 Let **f.** not even be mentioned
Col 3:5 Deaden body members respects **f.**,
1Th 4:3 God wills that you abstain from **f.**;
Re 17:2 the kings of the earth committed **f.**,
Eze 43:7, 9; Ho 2:2; 4:12; 5:4; 6:10; 9:1.
FORNICATOR(S), 1Co 5:9 mixing with **f.**
Eph 5:5 no **f.** has any inheritance in the
1Ti 1:10; Heb 12:16.
FORSAKE, 2Ki 21:14 I shall **f.** the remnant
Ps 94:14 Jehovah will not **f.** his people,
Pr 6:20 do not **f.** the law of your mother.

Ps 27:9; Pr 1:8.
FORSAKEN, Mt 27:46 why have you **f.** me?
Isa 2:6; 32:14; Am 5:2.
FORSAKING, Heb 10:25 not **f.** the gathering
FORTIFICATION(S), Ps 89:40; Lu 19:43.
FORTIFIED, Isa 17:3; 25:12; 34:13.
FORTIFY, Isa 41:10 I will **f.** you.
FORTRESS, Ps 31:4 you are my **f.**
Ps 37:39 He is their **f.** in time of distress.
Da 11:31 they will profane the **f.**,
FORTUNE, Ge 30:11 said: With good **f.!**
FORTY, Ge 7:4 **f.** days and **f.** nights;
De 29:5 I kept guiding you **f.** years in the
Mr 1:13 in the wilderness **f.** days, tempted
Ex 16:35; Eze 4:6; Mt 4:2; Ac 1:3.
FORWARD, Jer 7:24 backward and not **f.**
Joh 18:36 would have **f.** that
Jg 5:20; 2Ch 20:29; 2Ti 4:7.
FOUND, Pr 18:22 one **f.** a good wife?
FOUNDATION(S), 1Co 3:11 lay any other **f.**
Eph 2:20 built upon the **f.** of the apostles
Heb 11:10 awaiting the city having real **f.**
2Sa 22:8; Ps 102:25; Pr 10:25; Isa 51:16;
Mic 1:6; Hab 3:13; Lu 6:48; Ro 15:20.
FOUNDED, Job 38:4 when I **f.** the earth?
Ps 78:69 earth he **f.** to time indefinite
Ps 104:5 **f.** the earth upon its places;
FOUNDING, Mt 13:35 hidden since **f.**
1Pe 1:20 foreknown before **f.** of the world,
Re 13:8 slaughtered from the **f.** of world
Mt 25:34; Joh 17:24; Eph 1:4; Heb 4:3.
FOUNTAIN(S), Joh 4:14 in him a **f.** of water
2Pe 2:17 These are **f.** without water,
Re 7:17 guide them to **f.** of waters of life.
Ge 16:7; 49:22; Jas 3:11; Re 16:4.
FOWL(S), Ge 9:10; Le 17:13; Ps 79:2.
FRACTURE, Le 21:19; 24:20.
FRAGILE, Da 2:42 kingdom will be **f.**
FRAGMENTS, Job 41:30 earthenware **f.** are
Mt 14:20; 15:37.
FRAME, Col 2:18 his fleshly **f.** of mind,
FRAMEWORK, Ro 2:20 the **f.** of knowledge
FRAMING TROUBLE BY DECREE, Ps 94:20.
FRANKINCENSE, Ex 30:34; Jer 41:5.
FRANTICALLY, Ps 62:3 carry on **f.** against
FRAUD. See also DEFRAUD.
FRAUD, Ac 13:10 O man full of **f.** and
FRAUDULENT, Pr 28:16 in **f.** practices
FRAUDULENTLY, Mal 3:5 those acting **f.**
FREE, Mt 10:8 received **f.**, give **f.**
Joh 8:32 the truth will set you **f.**
Ro 8:21 **f.** from enslavement to corruption
Ga 4:26 the Jerusalem above is **f.**, and she
Re 22:17 let anyone take life's water **f.**
Isa 58:6; Ro 3:24; 8:2; Heb 13:5; Re 21:6.
FREEDMAN, 1Co 7:22 is the Lord's **f.:**
FREEDOM, Le 19:20 nor **f.** given her
Ro 8:21 **f.** from enslavement to corruption
1Co 10:29 why my **f.** is judged
2Co 3:17 spirit of Jehovah is, there is **f.**
Ga 2:4 sneaked in to spy upon our **f.**
Ga 5:1 For such **f.** Christ set us free.
Ga 5:13 You were called for **f.**, brothers:
Jas 1:25 perfect law that belongs to **f.**
1Pe 2:16 holding your **f.**, not for badness,
2Pe 2:19 they are promising them **f.**,
FREEDOM FROM CARE, Ps 122:7; Jer 22:21.
FREE GIFT, Ro 5:17 **f.** of righteousness
FREEMAN, Ga 3:28 neither slave nor **f.**
Eph 6:8; Col 3:11.
FREENESS, Ac 2:29 speak with **f.** to you
FREENESS OF SPEECH, Php 1:20; 1Ti 3:13.
Heb 3:6 make fast our hold on **f.**
FREE, SET, Ex 21:2; Ps 88:5.

FREE WILL, Ho 14:4 love them of my own f.
FREQUENT, Ec 6:1 a calamity f. among
FREQUENTLY, Lu 5:33; Ac 24:26.
FRIEND(S), Pr 14:20 many are the f. of
Pr 18:24 f. sticking closer than a brother.
Mic 7:5 Do not trust a confidential f.
Lu 16:9 Make f. for yourselves by riches
Joh 15:13 his soul in behalf of his f.
Jas 2:23 Abraham called Jehovah's f.
Jas 4:4 f. of the world is an enemy of God.
Mt 11:19; Joh 15:14; 19:12.
FRIENDSHIP, Jas 4:4 f. with the world
FRIGHTENED, Php 1:28 in no respect f.
FRIGHTS, Ps 55:4 f. of death have fallen
FRINGE(S), Mt 9:20; 23:5; Mr 6:56.
FRIVOLOUS, Jer 3:9 of her f. view
FROGS, Ex 8:2 plaguing with f.
Re 16:13 inspired expressions like f.
FRONT, 1Th 2:5 with a false f. for
FRONTIER, Ex 16:35 to the f. of Canaan
FRONT SEATS, Mt 23:6; Lu 11:43; 20:46.
FROST, Jer 36:30 to the f. by night
FRUIT(S), Mt 7:19 tree not producing f.
Mt 7:20 by their f. you will recognize
Mt 21:43 given to a nation producing its f.
Joh 15:2 branch not bearing f. he
Ro 7:4 we should bear f. to God.
Php 1:11 filled with righteous f.
Col 1:10 bearing f. in every good work
Heb 13:15 f. of the lips which make
Ge 3:3; Lu 3:8; Joh 4:36; 15:8, 16.
FRUITAGE, Ps 127:3 f. of the belly is
Pr 13:2 From the f. of his mouth a man will
Isa 65:21 vineyards and eat their f.
Eze 34:27 tree must give its f.,
Eze 47:12 f. must be for food
Ga 5:22 f. of the spirit is love, joy,
FRUIT-BEARING, Ps 128:3 wife like a f.
FRUITFUL, Ge 1:28 Be f. and become many
Ge 9:1, 7; Le 26:9; Jer 23:3.
FRUSTRATE, Ezr 4:5 f. their counsel
FRUSTRATING, Pr 15:22 is a f. of plans
Isa 44:25 f. the signs of empty talkers,
FUEL, Eze 15:4, 6 into fire put for f.
FUGITIVE(S), Ge 4:12; Eze 17:21.
FUGITIVENESS, Ge 4:16 land of F. east
FULFILL, 2Ch 36:21 to f. Jehovah's word
Ps 20:5 Jehovah f. your requests.
Mt 5:17 not to destroy, but to f.,
Job 39:2; Ps 20:4; Ga 6:2.
FULFILLED, Mt 2:15; 12:17; Lu 21:22.
FULFILLMENT, 1Ki 8:15 has given f.
2Ch 6:4, 15; Jer 44:25.
FULL-GROWN, 1Co 14:20 f. powers of
Eph 4:13 until we attain to a f. man.
FULL LIMIT, Ga 4:4; Eph 1:10 f. of time
FULLNESS, Col 2:10 possessed of a f. by
Eph 1:23; 4:13.
FULL NUMBER, Ro 11:12 f. of them mean
FUME, Ps 80:4 how long f. against your
FUN, Pr 26:19 Was I not having f.
Ge 21:9; Mt 27:29; Lu 22:63.
FUNCTION, 1Ch 23:28 their f. was at the
Ro 12:4 not the same f.,
FUNCTIONARIES, 2Ki 17:32 came to be f. for
FUNCTIONING, Eph 4:16 f. of each member
FURIOUS, Pr 14:16 stupid is becoming f.
Ps 78:59; 89:38; Pr 26:17.
FURNACE, Ps 12:6 refined in a f. of earth
Isa 48:10 the smelting f. of affliction.
Da 3:17 Out of the f. he will rescue us.
De 4:20; Da 3:19; Mal 4:1; Mt 13:42.
FURNISH, 1Ti 1:4 f. questions for
FURNISHED, Mt 21:16 babes f. praise?

FURY, Pr 11:4 benefit on the day of f.,
FUTILE, 1Co 3:20; Tit 3:9.
FUTILITY, Ro 8:20 creation subjected to f.
FUTURE, Ps 37:37 f. will be peaceful
Ps 37:38 the f. of wicked will be cut off
Pr 24:20 there will be no f. for anyone bad;
Isa 41:22 apply heart and know the f. of
Lu 13:9 it produces fruit in the f.
Ps 73:17; Pr 5:11; 20:21; 23:18; Jer 29:11.

G

GABRIEL, Da 8:16; 9:21; Lu 1:19, 26.
GAD, Ge 30:11; 49:19; Jos 18:7.
GADDING ABOUT, 1Ti 5:13 g. to houses,
GAIN, Ec 6:13 for himself unjust g.,
1Co 9:20 as a Jew, that I might g. Jews;
1Ti 6:6 of great g., this godly devotion
Jg 5:19; Isa 56:11; 1Co 9:19-22.
GAINING, Lu 20:35 worthy of g. that system
GAINS, Mt 16:26 g. the whole world but
GALILEAN(S), Mt 14:70; Lu 13:1; Joh 4:45.
GALILEE, Mt 4:23; Joh 2:11; 7:41, 52.
GALL, Job 16:13; Mt 27:34; Ac 8:23.
GALLEY, Isa 33:21 On it no g. fleet
GAMALIEL, Ac 5:34; 22:3.
GAME(S), 2Ti 2:5 anyone contends in g.
Pr 12:27 g. animals
Ge 27:5.
GANGRENE, 2Ti 2:17 will spread like g.
GAP(S), Ps 106:23; Eze 13:5; 22:30.
GARDEN(S), Ge 2:8 planted a g. in Eden
Jer 31:12 well-watered g.,
Am 9:14 make g. and eat the fruit of them.
Ge 2:15; 3:24; Isa 51:3; 58:11; Eze 36:35.
GARLAND, Isa 28:5 Jehovah as a g. of beauty
GARMENT(S), 2Ki 10:22 Bring out g. for
Ps 22:18 apportion my g. cast lots
Pr 7:10 with the g. of a prostitute
Isa 61:10 clothed me with g. of salvation;
Mt 9:16 sews a patch upon an old g.;
Mt 23:5 enlarge the fringes of their g.
Mt 27:35 distributed his g. by casting lots,
Jude 23 even the inner g. has been stained
Mic 17:3; 21:8; Joh 19:2; Re 3:18; 16:15.
GARRISON(S), 2Sa 8:6 g. in Syria
1Sa 10:5; 1Ch 18:13.
GATE(S), Ge 22:17 g. of his enemies.
Job 38:17 Have g. of death been uncovered
Isa 28:6 turning the battle from the g.
Isa 38:10 go into the g. of Sheol
Isa 60:11 g. will be open constantly;
Isa 62:10 pass out through the g., you men.
Mt 7:14 narrow is the g. into life, and few
Mt 16:18 the g. of Hades will not overpower
De 31:12; Jg 16:3; Ps 127:5; Pr 1:21;
Isa 26:2; 60:18; Lu 16:20; Heb 13:12.
GATEWAY, Ac 12:14 Peter standing before g.
GATH, Jos 11:22; 1Sa 17:4; 1Ch 18:1.
GATHER, Ps 50:5 G. to me my loyal ones
Zep 2:1 G. together O nation not paling
Zep 3:8 my decision is to g. nations,
Mt 12:30 does not g. with me scatters.
Mt 23:37 g. your children together, the way
Mt 24:31 they will g. his chosen ones
Isa 11:12; Jer 29:14; Da 11:10; Mic 2:12;
4:6; Mt 3:12; Joh 11:52; Re 16:14.
GATHERED, Jer 25:33 not be g. or buried.
Mt 25:32 nations will be g. before him,
Re 16:16 g. them together to Har–Magedon.
Mt 22:10; 1Co 5:4.
GATHERERS, Jos 9:21 g. of wood and
GATHERING, Joh 4:36 g. fruit for life,
Heb 10:25 not forsaking the g. of ourselves
GAUZE, Isa 40:22 heavens as a fine g.,

GAZA, Jg 1:18; 16:1; Jer 47:5; Ac 8:26.
GAZE, 2Co 3:7 Israel could not g. at
  2Co 3:13 veil that Israel might not g.
GAZING, Ac 1:10; 3:12; 11:6.
GEDALIAH, 2Ki 25:22; Jer 39:14; 40:5, 6.
GEHAZI, 2Ki 5:20; 8:4.
GEHENNA. See also HINNOM.
GEHENNA, Mt 10:28 soul and body in G.
  Mt 23:15 a subject for G. twice as much
  Mt 23:33 flee from the judgment of G.?
  Mr 9:43 with two hands to go off into G.,
  Lu 12:5 authority to throw into G.
  Jas 3:6 it is set aflame by G.
  Mt 5:22, 29, 30; 18:9; Mr 9:45, 47.
GENEALOGICAL ENROLLMENT(S), 1Ch 4:33;
  2Ch 31:16; Ezr 8:1.
GENEALOGIES, 1Ti 1:4 g. end in nothing
GENEALOGY, Heb 7:3 motherless, without g.,
GENERATION(S), De 32:5 g. crooked and
  Ec 1:4 A g. is going and a g. is coming,
  La 5:19 Your throne is for g. after g.
  Mt 24:34 this g. will by no means pass away
  Lu 11:51 will be required from this g.
  Eph 3:5 in other g. this secret was not
  Php 2:15 among a crooked and twisted g.,
  Col 1:26 hidden from the past g.
  Ge 9:12; Ex 3:15; Ps 48:13; 78:4; 79:13;
  100:5; 119:90; Mt 12:39; 23:36; Lu 21:32.
GENEROSITY, 2Co 8:2 riches of their g. abound
  2Co 9:11 enriched for every kind of g.,
GENEROUS, Pr 11:25 g. soul will be made
GENEROUSLY, De 15:8 g. open your hand
  Jas 1:5 keep asking God, for he gives g.
GENITAL ORGAN, Le 15:2, 3; Eze 23:20.
GENNESARET, Mt 14:34; Lu 5:1.
GENTILES. See NATION(S).
GENTLE, 1Th 2:7 became g. as a mother
  2Ti 2:24 needs to be g. toward all
GENUINE, 1Ti 1:2 a g. child in the faith:
GENUINELY, Php 2:20 g. care for things
GERIZIM, De 11:29; Jos 8:33; Jg 9:7.
GETAWAY, Am 9:1 no one make his g.
GETHSEMANE, Mt 26:36; Mr 14:32.
GET OUT, 2Co 6:17 g., separate yourselves
  Re 18:4 Get out of her, my people.
  Isa 48:20; 52:11; Jer 51:45.
GET READY, Am 4:12 g. to meet your God,
  1Co 14:8 who will g. for battle?
GET UP, Ps 36:12; Jer 25:27.
GIANTS. See NEPHILIM.
GIBEAH, Jg 20:5, 13, 37; Isa 10:29.
GIBEON, Jos 10:6 G. sent to Joshua
  Jos 10:12 Sun, be motionless over G.
  1Ki 3:5 in G. Jehovah appeared to
  Ne 3:7 men of G. did repair work
  Jos 9:3; 10:1, 10; 11:19; 2Ch 1:3.
GIBEONITE(S), 2Sa 21:1 put G. to death
  2Sa 21:3, 9; 1Ch 12:4; Ne 3:7.
GIDEON, Jg 7:18 say Jehovah's and G.
  Jg 8:23 G. said: "Jehovah will rule
  Heb 11:32 if I go on to relate about G.
  Jg 6:24, 27, 34, 39; 7:2, 4, 7, 20; 8:4.
GIFT(S), Ps 68:29 Kings will bring g.
  Pr 18:16 A man's g. will make a large
  Mt 19:11 not marry make room for the g.
  Ac 8:20 get possession of free g. from God
  Ro 5:16 the g. resulted in a declaration of
  Ro 6:23 g. God gives is everlasting life
  1Co 7:7 each one has his own g. from God,
  1Co 12:4 there are varieties of g., but
  1Co 14:12 zealous followers of g. of spirit
  1Ti 4:14 do not be neglecting the g. in you
  Heb 6:4 who have tasted the heavenly free g.
  Heb 11:4 God bearing witness respecting

Jas 1:17 every good g. is from above
Re 11:10 they will send g. to one another
Ec 7:7; Isa 18:7; Eze 20:39; Mal 1:11;
Mt 5:24; 7:11; 2Co 9:15; Eph 2:8.
GILBOA, 1Sa 28:4; 2Sa 1:21; 1Ch 10:8.
GILEAD, Jos 21:38 city of refuge in G.
Mic 7:14 Let them feed on Bashan and G.
Nu 26:29; 32:40; Jer 8:22; Zec 10:10.
GILGAL, Jos 4:20 twelve stones at G.
Jos 9:6 to Joshua at the camp at G.
Jg 3:19 at the quarries that were at G.
Jos 5:9; 10:6; Isa 10:8; 11:14, 15.
GIRDLE, Ex 29:5; Mt 3:4; Ac 21:11.
GIRL, Lu 1:38; 8:54; 22:56; Ac 12:13.
GIVE, Mt 10:8 received free, g. free
Heb 12:5 neither g. out when corrected
Ps 118:18; Isa 43:6; Lu 6:30; 1Ti 5:14.
GIVEN, Pr 22:9 kindly in eye has g. food
Lu 12:48 much was g., much will be
Job 1:21; Ps 21:2; 112:9; Ec 2:26; 5:19.
GIVE THANKS, Ps 107:8 g. to Jehovah for
GIVE UP, Ga 6:9 not g. in doing fine,
GIVING, Ac 20:35 more happiness g.
GIVING BIRTH, Ps 48:6; Joh 16:21.
GLAD, De 32:43 Be g., you nations with
Ga 4:27 Be g., you barren woman
Re 12:12 be g. you heavens and you
Re 18:20 Be g. over her, heaven,
Pr 8:30; Ro 15:10.
GLEAN, Ru 2:8 not g. in another field,
GLEANING, Le 19:9; 23:22.
GLEE, Hab 3:14 Their high g. was as
GLEEFULNESS, Job 3:22 rejoicing to g.,
GLITTERING, Eze 21:15 g., polished for
GLOOM, De 28:29; Pr 4:19; Isa 58:10.
GLOOMINESS, Isa 8:22; Joe 2:2; Zep 1:15.
GLOOMY, Ex 10:22; Pr 25:20; Mt 16:3.
GLORIFIED, Joh 15:8 Father is g. bearing
Ro 8:17 we suffer together g. together.
Re 18:7 to the extent that she g. herself
Da 5:23; Joh 7:39; 12:28; 17:4, 10.
GLORIFY, Ps 50:15 and you will g. me.
Isa 60:13 g. the very place of my feet.
Joh 17:1 the hour has come; g. your son
Joh 17:5 Father, g. me alongside yourself
Ro 1:21 they did not g. him as God nor
1Co 6:20 g. God in the body of you people
Heb 5:5 Christ did not g. himself by
Ps 86:12; Isa 25:3; Ro 15:6; 1Pe 2:12.
GLORIFYING, Ac 10:46 tongues and g. God
GLORIOUS, Ne 9:5 let bless your g. name
Ps 24:7 the g. King may come in!
2Co 4:4 g. good news about the Christ
Ps 29:3; 66:2; 145:5; Isa 11:10; Jer 14:21.
GLORY, Ps 19:1 heavens declaring the g.
Pr 18:12 before g. there is humility.
Isa 42:8 to no one shall I give my own g.
Isa 43:7 I have created for my own g.
Mt 5:16 your fine works give g. Father
Mt 25:31 the Son of man arrives in his g.
Lu 2:14 G. in the heights above to God
Ro 9:23 the riches of his g. upon vessels
2Co 3:8 administering of spirit with g.?
Re 21:23 for the g. of God lighted it up,
1Ch 16:24; Ps 29:9; 79:9; 102:16; Hab 2:14;
Joh 1:14; Ro 1:23; 3:23; 1Pe 5:4.
GLOW OF EXCITEMENT, Joe 2:6; Na 2:10.
GLUE, Job 14:17 g. over my error
GLUTTED, Job 10:15; 14:1; Pr 1:31.
GLUTTONOUS, Pr 23:20; Mt 11:19.
GLUTTONS, Tit 1:12 unemployed g.
GNASHING, Lu 13:28 weeping and the g. of
Mt 8:12; 13:42; 22:13; 24:51; 25:30.
GNAT, Mt 23:24 out the g. but gulp

GOADS, Ac 26:14 keep kicking against g.
GOAL, Php 3:14 g. for the prize of
Hab 2:5; Mt 11:12.
GOAT(S), Le 9:15 g. of the sin offering
Mt 25:32 separates the sheep from the g.
Heb 9:12 not with the blood of g. and of
Ex 12:5; Le 16:7, 22, 27; Heb 10:4.
GOAT (for Azazel), Le 16:10.
Le 16:26 sent the g. away for Azazel,
GOATLIKE, Zec 10:3 against g. leaders I
GOD(S), Ge 1:1 In the beginning G.
Ex 12:12 g. of Egypt I shall execute
Ex 20:3 not have any other g. against
De 7:16 you must not serve their g.
Jg 2:17 immoral intercourse with other g.
Ps 47:7 G. is King of all the earth
Ps 75:7 For G. is the judge
Ps 82:6 have said, You are g. and all of
Ps 90:2 to time indefinite you are G.
Isa 9:6 Mighty G., Eternal Father,
Da 3:18 your g. are not the ones
Ro 2:11 there is no partiality with G.
1Co 8:5 there are those who are called g.
1Co 14:33 G. is a G. not of disorder, but
2Co 1:3 G. and Father of our Lord Jesus
2Co 4:4 g. of this system of things has
Heb 12:29 G. is also a consuming fire.
1Jo 4:8 G. is love.
Ex 20:5; 23:24; 2Ki 19:15; Jer 10:10.
GODDESS, 1Ki 11:5, 33; Ac 19:27, 37.
GODLIKE, Ps 8:5 make him less than g. ones
GODLY, 2Co 7:10 sadness in g. way makes
GODLY DEVOTION, 1Ti 4:8 g. is beneficial
1Ti 6:6 g. along with self-sufficiency.
2Ti 3:5 having a form of g. but
2Ti 3:12 those with g. will be persecuted.
2Pe 2:9 deliver people of g. out
Ac 3:12; 1Ti 2:2; 3:16; 4:7; 6:5; Tit 1:1;
2Pe 1:3; 3:11.
GODLY FEAR, Heb 5:7; 12:28.
GOD OF DESTINY, Isa 65:11 wine for g.
GOD OF GOOD LUCK, Isa 65:11.
GOD'S, 2Ch 20:15 the battle is G.
Lu 20:25 to Caesar, but G. things to God.
Ro 13:6 they are G. public servants
Job 35:2; Col 3:12; Tit 1:7.
GODSHIP, Ro 1:20 eternal power and G.,
GODS, VALUELESS, Le 19:4; 26:1; Ps 96:5.
Hab 2:18 making v. that are speechless?
GOG, Eze 38:16 nations may know O G.
Eze 39:11 I shall give to G. a place
Eze 38:2, 3, 14, 18; Re 20:8.
GOLD, Pr 16:16 wisdom is better than g.
Eze 7:19 abhorrent their g. will become.
Zep 1:18 nor their g. able to deliver
Hag 2:8 the silver and the g. is mine
Mal 3:3 he must clarify them like g.
Jas 5:3 Your g. and silver are corroded
Ex 12:35; Ps 19:10; Pr 8:10; Re 21:18, 21.
GOLGOTHA, Mt 27:33; Joh 19:17.
GOLIATH, 1Sa 17:23 G. the Philistine from
1Sa 17:4; 21:9; 22:10.
GOMORRAH, Mt 10:15 more endurable for G.
Ge 18:20; 19:24; Isa 1:9; Ro 9:29; Jude 7.
GOOD, Ge 3:5 knowing g. and bad.
De 10:13 keep the commandments for your g.
Ps 25:8 G. and upright is Jehovah.
Ps 133:1 How g. for brothers to dwell
Ec 2:24 see g. because of his hard work
Am 5:15 and love what is g.
Mr 10:18 Nobody is g. except God.
Lu 6:45 A g. man brings forth g. out of
Lu 18:19 Why do you call me g.?
Ro 7:19 the g. that I wish I do not do

Ro 8:28 co-operate together for the g.
Ro 10:15 who declare g. news of g. things
Ro 12:21 keep conquering the evil with g.
Ga 6:10 let us work what is g. toward all
Ge 1:31; 1Ch 16:34; Joh 5:29; Ro 13:3.
GOOD-BY, Lu 9:61; Ac 18:18; 2Co 2:13.
GOOD DAY, Mt 27:29; Lu 1:28; Joh 19:3.
GOOD-FOR-NOTHING, Lu 17:10 are g. slaves.
Ps 18:4; Pr 6:12; 16:27; 19:28; Mt 25:30.
GOOD LUCK, GOD OF, Isa 65:11.
GOODNESS, Ps 27:13 the g. of Jehovah
Ps 65:11 crowned the year with your g.
Ga 5:22 the fruitage of the spirit is g.,
2Ti 3:3 fierce, without love of g.,
Ps 23:6; Isa 63:7; Zec 9:17; 2Th 1:11.
GOOD NEWS, Ps 40:9 g. in congregation.
Isa 52:7 feet of one bringing g.,
Isa 61:1 anointed me to tell g. to the meek
Mt 9:35 Jesus set out preaching the g.
Mt 24:14 this g. of the kingdom will be
Mr 13:10 in all the nations the g. has
Lu 2:10 look! I am declaring to you g.
Ro 1:16 I am not ashamed of the g.
1Co 9:16 I am declaring the g.
1Th 2:4 to be entrusted with the g.
2Ti 1:10 has shed light through the g.
Isa 41:27; Lu 1:19; Ac 20:24; Ro 10:15;
2Co 4:3, 4; Ga 1:8; Php 1:12, 16.
GOODS, Mt 12:29 seize his movable g.
Ge 12:5; Nu 16:32; 2Ch 31:3; Ezr 1:4.
GOOD SENSE, Eph 1:8 abound toward us g.
GOOD THINGS, Ne 9:25 houses full of g.,
Ec 5:11 When g. become many, those eating
GOOD TIME, Ge 26:8; Ex 32:6.
GOOD WILL, Ps 30:5 Being under his g.
Pr 8:35 gets g. from Jehovah
Pr 10:32 righteous come to know g.
Isa 61:2 proclaim the year of g. of Jehovah
Ro 10:1 the g. of my heart and supplication
Php 1:15 preaching through g.
Ps 89:17; Pr 11:27; 16:15; 19:12.
GOSHEN, Ge 45:10; 47:4; Ex 8:22; 9:26.
GOSSIPERS, 1Ti 5:13 g. and meddlers in
GOT TIRED, Jer 15:6 g. of feeling regret
GOUGED, Ga 4:15 g. out your eyes and
GOVERNMENT(S), Ro 8:38 nor angels nor g.
1Co 15:24 when he has brought to nothing g.
Eph 1:21 far above every g. and
Eph 6:12 a fight against the g. in heavenly
Col 2:15 Stripping the g. bare,
Tit 3:1 be obedient to g. and authorities
Ac 25:1; Eph 3:10; Col 1:16; 2:10.
GOVERNOR(S), Mt 2:6 the g. of Judah;
Jer 51:23; Mal 1:8; Mt 10:18; 1Pe 2:14.
GOVERNOR'S PALACE, Mt 27:27; Joh 18:28.
GRACE. See UNDESERVED KINDNESS.
GRACIOUS, 2Ch 30:9 Jehovah God is g.
Ps 86:15 Jehovah, a God g. slow to
Ps 112:5 man is good who is g. and lending.
Joe 2:13 come back to Jehovah for he is g.
Lu 18:13 be g. to me a sinner.
Ex 34:6; Ps 103:8; 111:4; 116:5; Pr 26:25.
GRACIOUSNESS, Col 3:16 songs with g.,
Ac 6:8; 7:10; Eph 2:7.
GRAFTED, Ro 11:17, 19, 23, 24 Olive g. in
GRAIN(S), Ge 41:5 seven ears of g.
Joe 2:19 sending you g. and new wine
1Co 15:37 that will develop, but a bare g.,
Ru 2:2; Joe 1:10; Mr 4:28; 1Co 9:9.
GRANDEES, Ca 5:1; 6:17 feast for g.
GRANDEUR, Da 4:22; 7:27 your g. is great
GRAND GOD, Da 2:45 g. made known what
GRANDIOSE, Da 7:8, 11, 20 speak g. things
GRANDMOTHER, 2Ti 1:5 your g. Lois

GRANDPARENTS, 1Ti 5:4 compensation to g.,
GRANTING, Ps 99:8 A God g. pardon you
GRAPES, Isa 5:2 hoping produce g.,
   Eze 18:2 Fathers eat unripe g.,
   Jer 8:13; Mt 7:16; Re 14:18.
GRAPPLE, Ge 32:24 Jacob began to g. with
GRASP, Eph 3:18 be able to g. mentally
GRASS, Ps 37:2 like g. they will wither,
   2Ki 19:26; Ps 103:15; Isa 40:8; 51:12.
GRASSHOPPERS, Nu 13:33; Isa 40:22.
GRATEFUL, 1Ti 1:12 I am g. to Christ
   2Ti 1:3 I am g. to God, to
GRATIFICATION, 1Ti 5:6 for sensual g.
GRATIFYING, Mal 3:4 be g. to Jehovah,
GRATITUDE, Lu 17:9.
GRAVE(S), Mt 23:27 whitewashed g.,
   Mt 23:29 you build the g. of the prophets
   Mt 27:61 Mary sitting before the g.
GRAVESTONE, 2Ki 23:17 what is the g. over
GRAVEYARD, Job 17:1 The g. is for me.
   Jer 26:23 cast his dead body into the g.
   2Ch 34:28; 35:24; Job 21:32.
GRAY-HEADEDNESS, Pr 16:31 G. is a crown
   Ge 42:38 you have g. my head;
GREASED, Ps 23:5 oil you have g. my head;
GREASY, Isa 34:6 be made g. with fat
GREAT AIRS, Ps 55:12 assumed g. against
   Da 8:25 he will put on g., and bring many
   Ps 35:26; 38:16; Jer 48:26; La 1:9; Da 8:4.
GREAT CROWD, Mr 12:37 g. was listening
   Re 7:9 g., which no man was able to number,
   Re 19:6 voice of a g. and a sound of many
GREATER, Joh 14:28 Father is g. than I
   Heb 7:7 less is blessed by the g.
GREAT MULTITUDE, Lu 5:6 enclosed g. of fish.
GREATNESS, 1Ch 29:11 Yours, are the g.,
   Eph 1:19 surpassing g. of his power is
   Es 1:4; Ps 71:21; 145:3, 6.
GREAVES, 1Sa 17:6 were g. of copper on
GREECE, Da 10:20; 11:2; Zec 9:13.
GREEDINESS, Eph 5:3 g. not mentioned
GREEDY, 1Co 5:11 quit mixing with a g.
   1Ti 3:8 not g. of dishonest gain,
GREEK(S), 1Co 1:22 G. look for wisdom;
   Ga 3:28 There is neither Jew nor G.,
   Joh 19:20; Ro 1:16; 1Co 10:32; 12:13.
GREETING, 1Co 16:21 Here is my g.,
   2Jo 10 homes or say a g. to him.
GRIEF, Isa 35:10 g. and sighing must flee
   Joh 16:20 your g. will be turned into joy.
   Ge 42:38; Ps 31:10; Isa 51:11; Jer 45:3.
GRIEVED, Ro 14:15 brother is being g.,
GRIEVING, Eph 4:30 g. God's holy spirit,
GRIEVOUS, Heb 12:11 discipline seems g.;
   1Pe 2:19 bears up under g. things
GRINDING, Ps 37:12 he is g. his teeth.
   Ec 12:3 g. women quit working
GRITS, Le 2:14, 16 the g. of new grain
GROAN(S), Jer 51:52; Eze 26:15; 2Co 5:2.
GROANING(S), Ex 2:24 God heard their g.
   Eze 9:4 the men that are sighing and g.
   Ro 8:22 all creation keeps g.
   Ro 8:26 spirit pleads with g. unuttered.
GROPE, Job 12:25 They g. in darkness,
   Ac 17:27 g. for him and really find him,
GROPES, De 28:29 who g. about at midday,
GROPING, Isa 59:10 g. like blind men,
GROUND, Ge 2:7 form man dust from the g.
   Ge 3:17 cursed is the g. on your account.
   Ex 3:5 where you are standing is holy g.
   Jos 3:17 Israel passing over on dry g.,
GROUPS, Pr 30:27 go divided into g.
GROW, 1Co 3:7 God who makes it g.
   Lu 12:27; Eph 4:15; 1Pe 2:2.

GROWING, Ac 6:7 word of God went on g.,
   Col 2:19 the body goes on g.
GROWL, Jer 51:38 g. like lions
GROWN, Mt 13:15 heart has g. thick,
GRUDGE, Le 19:18 must not have a g.
GRUMBLING, 1Pe 4:9 hospitable without g.
GUARANTEE(S), Ac 17:31 a g. to all men
   2Co 1:21; Heb 6:16.
GUARD, Ps 39:1 I will g. my ways
   Pr 2:8 g. the way of his loyal
   Mt 10:17 Be on your g. against men;
   Php 4:7 will g. your hearts and mental
   1Ti 6:20 g. what is laid up in trust with
   1Jo 5:21 children, g. yourselves from idols.
   Pr 14:3; Mt 27:66; 2Ti 1:12; Jude 24.
GUARDED, Ga 3:23 being g. under law,
GUARDIAN, Ge 4:9 Am I my brother's g.?
   Es 2:3, 8, 15 g. of women
GUARDIANSHIP, Ne 13:14 g. of God's house
GUARDING, Ps 121:5 Jehovah is g. you.
   Ps 145:20 Jehovah is g. those loving him,
   Ps 146:9 Jehovah is g. alien residents;
   Pr 13:3 The one g. his mouth is keeping his
   Ge 30:31; Ps 34:20; 97:10; 121:3.
GUEST, Lu 19:6 received him as g.
GUIDE(S), Mt 15:14 Blind g. is what
   Mt 23:16 Woe to you, blind g., who say,
   Joh 16:13 will g. you into all the truth,
   Ps 48:14; Ro 2:19; Re 7:17.
GUIDED, Ac 8:31 unless someone g. me?
GUILELESS, Ro 16:18; Heb 7:26.
GUILT, Ge 26:10 you brought g. upon us
   Jos 2:17 free from g. respecting this oath
   1Ch 21:3 why be a cause of g. to Israel
   2Ch 28:10 cases of g. against Jehovah
   Jer 51:5 land has been full of g.
GUILTINESS, Ezr 9:13; Ps 68:21.
GUILT OFFERING, Le 5:6; Nu 6:12.
GUILTY, Ho 13:1 g. in regard to Baal
   1Co 11:27 cup of the Lord unworthily g.
   Isa 24:6; Eze 22:4; Zec 11:5.
GULP DOWN, Ob 16 nations will g.
GUM, Ge 2:12; Nu 11:7 bdellium g.

H

HABITS, 1Co 15:33 Bad associations spoil h.
   1Ti 3:2 overseer be moderate in h.
   1Ti 3:11 Women should be moderate in h.
   Tit 2:2 aged men be moderate in h.
HADASSAH, Es 2:7 a caretaker of H.
HADES, Mt 16:18 gates of H. will not
   Lu 10:15 Down to H. you will come!
   Ac 2:31 neither was he forsaken in H.
   Re 1:18 have the keys of death and of H.
   Re 20:14 death and H. were hurled into
   Mt 11:23; Lu 16:23; Re 6:8; 20:13.
HAGAR, Ge 16:1; Ga 4:24.
HAIL, Isa 28:17 h. must sweep away the
   Ex 9:22; Job 38:22; Ps 148:8; Re 8:7.
HAIR, Jg 16:22 h. started to grow
   Lu 21:18 not a h. of your heads will perish.
   1Co 11:14 man has long h., it is a dishonor
   Isa 3:24; Da 3:27; 7:9; 1Pe 3:3; Re 9:8.
HALFHEARTED, Ps 119:113 h. ones I hated
HALLELUJAH. See PRAISE JAH.
HAM, Ge 5:32; 10:6; 1Ch 4:40; Ps 78:51.
HAMAN, Es 7:10 hang H. on the stake
   Es 3:5; 5:11; 6:11; 7:6, 9; 8:2, 7; 9:10.
HAMATH, Nu 13:21; Isa 10:9; Jer 49:23.
HAMMER(S), Jer 23:29 my word like a h.
   1Ki 6:7; Isa 41:7; Jer 50:23.
HAMMERED, Jg 5:26 she h. Sisera,
HAMSTRING, Jos 11:6; 2Sa 8:4.
HAND(S), 2Ki 10:15 give me your h.

Ps 8:6 over the works of your **h.**;
Ps 110:1 Sit at my right **h.** until I
Isa 35:3 Strengthen the weak **h.**, you people,
Isa 59:1 **h.** of Jehovah has not become short
Da 2:34 stone was cut out not by **h.**,
Zec 14:13 against the **h.** of his companion.
Lu 9:62 put his **h.** to a plow and looks
1Ti 4:14 older men laid their **h.** upon you.
Heb 10:31 fall into the **h.** of God.
1Pe 5:6 Humble under the mighty **h.** of
Ex 17:12; Ps 21:8; 24:4; 45:4; 49:15;
Isa 65:22; Jer 38:4; Da 5:5; Ho 13:14;
Zep 3:16; 2Co 5:1; Heb 9:11.
HANDCUFFS, Jer 40:1, 4.
HANDSHAKE, Pr 6:1 **h.** to the stranger,
HANDSOME, Ps 45:2 more **h.** than men
HANDSOMENESS, Isa 33:17 king in his **h.**
HANDWRITTEN, Col 2:14 out **h.** document
HANG, Jos 10:26 **h.** them upon stakes
Es 7:10 **h.** Haman on the stake.
HANGED, Jos 8:29 he **h.** the king of Ai
Es 8:7; 9:14; La 5:12; Mt 27:5.
HANGING, Ac 5:30 **h.** him upon a stake.
Ac 10:39 did away with him **h.** on a stake.
HANNAH, 1Sa 1:2, 20; 2:1, 21.
HAPPEN, Ge 49:1; De 22:6.
HAPPENED, 2Pe 2:22 proverb **h.** to them
2Sa 20:1; Ro 11:25.
HAPPENING, 1Pe 4:12 **h.** to you for a trial
Mt 20:35; Ro 4:6; Ga 4:15.
HAPPINESS, Ac 20:35; Ro 4:6; Ga 4:15.
HAPPY, Ps 144:15 **H.** people whose God Jehovah
Mt 5:3 **h.** are those conscious of their
Mt 24:46 **H.** is that slave if his master
Joh 13:17 **h.** you are if you do them
1Ti 1:11 good news of the **h.** God
1Ti 6:15 the **h.** and only Potentate
1Pe 3:14 suffer for the sake of you are **h.**
1Pe 4:14 you are **h.**, because the spirit
De 33:29; 1Ki 10:8; Pr 3:13; 16:20; 29:18;
Da 12:12; Mal 3:15; Lu 12:37; Jas 1:12.
HARAN, Ge 11:26-29, 31, 32; 27:43; Ac 7:2.
HARASSING, Nu 25:17 a **h.** the Midianites,
HARD, Pr 29:1 making his neck **h.** will
Da 5:20 his own spirit became **h.**,
2Pe 3:16 some things **h.** to understand,
Ex 1:14; De 1:17; Eze 3:8; Ac 26:14.
HARDEN, De 15:7 must not **h.** your heart
Ne 9:16 forefathers proceeded to **h.** their
HARDENED, Heb 3:13 **h.** by power of sin.
HARDENING, Heb 4:7 not **h.** your hearts.
Pr 28:14; Ac 19:9; Heb 3:8, 15.
HARDHEADED, Eze 3:7 Israel are **h.**
HARDHEARTEDNESS, Mt 19:8; Mr 10:5.
HARD PRESSED, Isa 53:7 He was **h.**, and
HARDSHIP, Job 10:17 **h.** is with me
HARD WORK, Ec 2:24 see good because of **h.**
HARLOT(S). See also PROSTITUTE(S).
HARLOT(S), Ge 38:15 took her for a **h.**
De 23:18 not bring the hire of a **h.** into
Mt 21:31 **h.** are going ahead of you
1Co 6:15 make them members of a **h.**?
Jas 2:25 Rahab the **h.** declared righteous
Re 17:5 Babylon, the mother of the **h.**
Re 17:16 will hate the **h.** and will make her
Lu 15:30; Heb 11:31; Re 17:1, 15; 19:2.
HARM, Isa 65:25 They will do no **h.** nor
1Pe 3:13 Who will **h.** you if you become
Ge 43:6; Isa 11:9; Re 7:2; 9:4.
HAR–MAGEDON, Re 16:16 place called **H.**
HARMFUL, Isa 10:1 **h.** regulations
2Th 3:2 delivered from **h.** men
HARMONIOUSLY, Eph 2:21 being **h.** joined
Eph 4:16; Col 2:2, 19.
HARMONY, Ro 8:9 you are in **h.**, not with

2Co 6:15 what **h.** between Christ and
HARNESSING, Ho 10:10 **h.** to two errors.
HARP(S), Ge 4:21 Jubal, founder of the **h.**
Ps 33:2 Give thanks on the **h.**;
Ps 49:4 On a **h.** I shall open up my riddle.
Isa 23:16 Take a **h.**, go around the city,
Re 15:2 having **h.** of God.
1Sa 16:23; Ps 137:2; Isa 5:12; Re 14:2.
HARPOONS, Job 41:7 fill its skin with **h.**,
HARSH, Da 2:15; 3:22 **h.** order of the king
HARVEST, Ge 8:22 **h.** will never cease.
Joe 3:13 Thrust in a sickle, for **h.** has
Mt 9:37 **h.** is great, but workers are few.
Mt 13:39 The **h.** is a conclusion of a
Re 14:15 **h.** of the earth is ripe.
Ex 23:16; Pr 10:5; Jer 8:20; 51:33.
HARVESTING, Joh 4:35 fields white for **h.**
HASTEN, 1Sa 23:27; Na 2:5.
HASTENING, Pr 19:2 **h.** with his feet
Pr 28:20 **h.** to gain riches will not
HASTILY, 1Ti 5:22 Never lay hands **h.**
HASTY, Ec 5:2 Do not be **h.** before God.
Pr 21:5; 29:20.
HATE, Ps 97:10 **h.** what is bad.
Pr 6:16 six things that Jehovah does **h.**,
Ec 3:8 a time to love and a time to **h.**
Mt 5:43 love your neighbor **h.** your enemy
Mt 6:24 **h.** the one and love the other,
Lu 6:22 Happy are you whenever men **h.** you,
Lu 14:26 **h.** his father and mother and wife
Ro 7:15 what I **h.** is what I do.
Le 19:17; Ps 139:21; Jude 23; Re 17:16.
HATED, Pr 1:29 they **h.** knowledge,
Joh 17:14 the world has **h.** them,
Ro 9:13 loved Jacob, but I **h.** Esau.
Heb 1:9 righteousness and **h.** lawlessness
Pr 5:12; Joh 15:18, 25.
HATEFUL, Tit 3:3 **h.**, hating one another
HATER, De 19:6 no **h.** of him formerly.
Pr 27:6 the kisses of a **h.** are things
HATES, Ps 11:5 violence Jehovah **h.**
Joh 3:20 practices vile things **h.** light
Joh 7:7 world **h.** me because I bear witness
Joh 12:25 he that **h.** his soul in this world
Joh 15:19 on this account the world **h.** you.
1Jo 3:15 **h.** his brother is a manslayer,
HATING, Ex 18:21 men, **h.** unjust profit,
Pr 8:13 fear of Jehovah means **h.** of bad
Pr 15:10 anyone **h.** reproof will die
Pr 28:16 **h.** unjust profit will prolong days
Lu 6:27 do good to those **h.** you,
1Jo 4:20 yet **h.** his brother, he is a liar
Ps 21:8; 44:7; 69:4; Pr 13:24; Tit 3:3.
HATRED, Ps 139:22 With a complete **h.** I
Mt 24:9 you will be objects of **h.** by all nations
Eph 2:15, 16 he abolished the **h.**, the Law
Ps 25:19; Pr 10:12; Eze 23:29; Mt 10:22.
HAUGHTILY, 1Sa 2:3 Do not speak **h.**
Zep 3:11 I shall remove your **h.** ones;
HAUGHTINESS, Ps 10:2 In **h.** the wicked
Ps 31:23; Pr 14:3; 29:23; Mr 7:22.
HAUGHTY, Pr 16:18 **h.** spirit before a crash
Isa 2:11 **h.** eyes of man must become low
Lu 1:51 scattered those who are **h.**
Jas 4:6 God opposes the **h.** ones,
2Sa 22:28; Ps 94:2; 101:5; 2Ti 3:2.
HAUNT, Mr 5:3 had his **h.** among the tombs
HAVEN, Ps 107:30 leads to **h.** of delight
HAZY, 1Co 13:12 we see in **h.** outline
HEAD(S), Ge 3:15 bruise you in the **h.**
Mic 3:11 **h.** ones judge for a bribe,
Mt 8:20 Son has nowhere to lay down his **h.**
Lu 21:28 lift your **h.** up, deliverance is near
Ac 18:6 your blood be upon your own **h.**

Ro 12:20 heap fiery coals upon his **h.**
1Co 11:10 sign of authority upon her **h.**
Col 1:18 he is the **h.** of the body,
Col 2:19 not holding fast to the **h.**,
Ps 110:6; Isa 9:15; 35:10; Da 2:38; Ob 15;
1Co 11:3; Eph 1:22; Re 12:1; 13:3.
HEADDRESS, 1Co 11:15 hair instead of **h.**
HEADSTONE, Zec 4:7 bring forth the **h.**
HEADSTRONG, 2Ti 3:4 betrayers, **h.**,
HEAL. See also CURE, CURED.
HEAL, De 32:39 I wounded and I will **h.**
Jer 6:14 to **h.** the breakdown of my people
Jer 33:6 I will **h.** them and reveal
Mt 13:15 turn back, and I **h.** them.
2Ch 7:14; Ps 6:2; 107:20; Ec 3:3; Isa 19:
22; Jer 3:22; 17:14; 30:17.
HEALED, Jer 51:9 would have **h.** Babylon,
Mt 8:13 man was **h.** in that hour
Heb 12:13 that what is lame may be **h.**
1Pe 2:24 by his stripes you were **h.**
Re 13:3 but its death-stroke got **h.**,
Eze 34:4; 47:9; Lu 9:11; Re 13:12.
HEALER(S), 2Ch 16:12; Jer 8:22.
HEALING, Ex 15:26 Jehovah who is **h.** you.
Pr 12:18 tongue of the wise is a **h.**
Pr 13:17 a faithful envoy is a **h.**
Isa 53:5 there has been a **h.** for us.
Mal 4:2 with **h.** in its wings;
Ps 147:3; Isa 6:10; Jer 30:13; Ac 10:38.
HEALS, Isa 30:26 Jehovah **h.** the severe
HEALTH, Pr 4:22 life and **h.** to all
Jer 33:6 here I am bringing **h.** and heal
Ac 15:29 keep from blood. Good **h.** to you!
HEALTHFUL TEACHING, 2Ti 4:3 up with **h.**
Tit 1:9 exhort by **h.** and reprove those
Tit 2:1 speaking what things are for **h.**
HEALTHFUL WORDS, 1Ti 6:3 assent to **h.**
2Ti 1:13 Keep holding the pattern of **h.**
HEAR, Ps 34:2 meek will **h.** and rejoice.
Isa 65:24 they are yet speaking, I shall **h.**
Mt 10:27 what you **h.** whispered, preach
Mt 13:13 hearing, they **h.** in vain, neither
Joh 5:28 all in the tombs will **h.** his voice
Ro 10:14 how will they **h.** without someone
Jos 2:11; Ps 85:8; Isa 34:1; 43:9.
HEARD, Jos 9:9 **h.** of his fame in Egypt,
Ps 19:3 no speech and no words being **h.**
Isa 66:8 Who has **h.** of a thing like this?
Job 42:5; Isa 40:28; 64:4; 1Co 2:9.
HEARER(S), Ro 2:13; Jas 1:22.
HEARING, Am 8:11 famine for **h.** the words
Mt 13:13 **h.**, they hear in vain, neither do
Re 22:17 anyone **h.** say, Come! And let
Pr 20:12; Mt 13:23; Lu 8:10; Ac 9:7.
HEARS, Pr 15:29 prayer of he **h.**
Mt 7:24 everyone that **h.** these sayings
2Ki 21:12; Joh 5:24; 1Jo 5:14; Re 3:20.
HEARSAY, Job 42:5; Ps 18:44.
HEART(S), 1Sa 16:7 Jehovah sees the **h.**
1Ch 28:9 serve him with a complete **h.**
Pr 4:23 safeguard your **h.**, for out of it
Pr 14:30 A calm **h.** is the life of fleshly
Pr 21:2 Jehovah is estimating **h.**
Jer 17:9 **h.** is more treacherous than
Jer 17:10 I, Jehovah, am searching the **h.**,
Mt 5:8 Happy are the pure in **h.**, since
Mt 15:8 their **h.** are far removed from me.
Mt 22:37 love Jehovah with your whole **h.**
Ro 10:10 with the **h.** one exercises faith
Eph 1:18 eyes of your **h.** enlightened,
Heb 3:8 not be hardening your **h.** as on
2Ki 10:15; Ne 4:6; Ps 14:1; 24:4; Pr 3:5;
15:28; 17:3; Isa 14:13; 35:4; Jer 31:33;
Eze 28:17; Da 11:27; Mal 4:6; Lu 12:34;

2Co 3:3; Jas 4:8; 5:3; 1Pe 3:15; Re 17:17.
HEAT, Ps 19:6 concealed from its **h.**
Isa 49:10; Da 3:19; Mt 20:12; Re 7:16.
HEATED, Pr 24:19 not **h.** up at evildoers.
Ps 37:1, 7, 8; Isa 41:11; 45:24.
HEATHEN. See NATION(S).
HEAT WAVE, Lu 12:55 say will be a **h.**
HEAVE, Jas 5:9 not **h.** sighs against
HEAVEN(S), Jg 5:20 From **h.** the stars
Ps 19:1 The **h.** are declaring the glory
Ps 50:6 **h.** tell of his righteousness,
Isa 65:17 I am creating new **h.** and a new
Isa 66:1 **h.** are my throne, and the earth
Joh 3:13 no man has ascended into **h.** but he
Ac 2:34 David did not ascend to the **h.**,
2Pe 3:5 there were **h.** in ancient times and
2Pe 3:10 the **h.** will pass away with a
2Pe 3:13 there are new **h.** and a new earth
Re 12:7 war broke out in **h.**: Michael
Re 19:11 I saw the **h.** opened, and, a white
De 10:14; Ps 2:4; Pr 30:19; Hag 2:6;
Mal 3:10; Mt 11:11; 24:35; Lu 17:24.
HEAVENLY, 1Co 15:49 bear image of **h.**
Eph 2:6 seated us together in **h.** places in
Heb 3:1 partakers of the **h.** calling,
Heb 8:5 shadow of the **h.** things;
Heb 12:22 Mount Zion **h.** Jerusalem,
Joh 3:12; Eph 1:20; 2Ti 4:18; Heb 9:23.
HEBER, Ge 46:17; Nu 26:45; Jg 4:11.
HEBREW(S), Ex 3:18 the God of the **H.**
Re 16:16 called in **H.** Har–Magedon.
Ge 14:13; Jon 1:9; 2Co 11:22; Php 3:5.
HEBRON, 1Ki 2:11 In **H.** he reigned seven
Ge 23:2; Jos 10:36; Jg 1:20; 2Sa 2:1.
HEED, Pr 29:19 but is paying no **h.**
HEEL(S), Ge 3:15 bruise him in the **h.**
Ge 49:17; Ps 41:9; Ho 12:3; Joh 13:18.
HE–GOATS, Eze 34:17 between the **h.**
HEIGHT, Ro 8:39 nor **h.** nor depth nor
HEIR(S), Mt 21:38 This is the **h.**; come
Ro 8:17 **h.**: **h.** of God, but joint **h.** with
Ga 3:29 Abraham's seed, **h.** to a promise.
Eph 1:11 we were also assigned as **h.**
Heb 1:2 Son, appointed **h.** of all things,
Ge 21:10; Ro 4:13; Ga 4:7; Heb 6:17; 11:9.
HELL. See GEHENNA, HADES, SHEOL, TAR-
TARUS.
HELM, Jas 3:4 of the man at the **h.** wishes
HELMET, Eph 6:17 **h.** of salvation
1Sa 17:5; Isa 59:17; Jer 46:4; 1Th 5:8.
HELP, Ps 46:1 A **h.** that is to be found
Da 11:34 will be helped with a little **h.**
Ro 8:26 the spirit also joins in with **h.**
Jos 10:6; Ac 16:9; Heb 4:16.
HELPED, Zec 1:15 **h.** toward calamity
HELPER, Ps 10:14 have become his **h.**
Da 11:45 there will be no **h.** for him.
Joh 14:16 he will give you another **h.**
Joh 14:26 the **h.**, the holy spirit will teach
Joh 15:26 the **h.** will bear witness about
Joh 16:7 if I do not go away, the **h.** will
2Ki 14:26; Ps 30:10; 54:4; Heb 13:6.
HELPLESS, 2Ki 14:26 neither any **h.** one
HEMMING, Isa 51:13 rage of one **h.** you
HERALD, Da 3:4 the **h.** was crying out
HERALDED, Da 5:29 Daniel they **h.**
HERD, Mt 8:30; Mr 5:11; Lu 8:32.
HERDERS, Mt 8:33; Mr 5:14; Lu 8:34.
HEREDITARY POSSESSION, 1Ki 8:36; 21:3.
HERESY. See DESTRUCTIVE SECTS.
HERMON, Ps 133:3 like the dew of **H.**
De 3:8; Jos 12:1; 13:5; Ps 89:12; Ca 4:8.
HEROD, Mt 2:1 the days of **H.** the king
Lu 23:12; Ac 4:27; 12:1.

HEROES, Isa 33:7 Their h. cried out in
HESITATE, De 7:10 not h. toward one who
Ec 5:4 vow, do not h. to pay it,
HEWERS, 2Ki 12:12 h. of stone,
HEWN, Pr 9:1 wisdom has h. out seven
HEZEKIAH, 2Ki 19:1, 15; Isa 36:7; 38:2.
HID, Mt 5:14 A city cannot be h.
Jos 6:25; Ps 9:15; 1Ti 5:25.
HIDDEN, h. in his tent money
Ps 40:10 I have not h. your loving-kindness
Mt 11:25 have h. these things from wise
1Co 2:7 we speak God's wisdom the h. wisdom,
Eph 3:9 sacred secret h. in God
Col 1:26 secret h. from past systems
Col 3:3 your life has been h. with Christ
Re 2:17 will give some of the h. manna
HIDE, Job 27:11 the Almighty I shall not h.
Ps 27:5 he will h. me in his covert
Isa 26:20; 30:20; Re 6:16.
HIGH, Isa 2:11 Jehovah must be put on h.
1Ti 2:2 those who are in h. station,
HIGHLY RESPECTED, Isa 9:15 aged and h.
HIGH-MINDEDLY, Ps 56:2 war against me h.
HIGH NOON, Isa 59:10 stumbled at h.
Zep 2:4 at h. they will drive her out;
HIGH PLACES, Le 26:30; Ps 78:58.
HIGH PRIEST, Nu 35:25 death of the h.
Heb 3:1 consider the apostle and h.
Heb 6:20 Jesus, who has become a h.
HIGH UP, De 2:36; Ps 139:6.
HIGHWAY, Isa 11:16 a h. out of Assyria
Isa 35:8 a h. there, the Way of Holiness
Isa 62:10 bank up the h. Rid it of
Pr 16:17; Isa 19:23; 40:3; Jer 31:21.
HILL(S), Isa 2:2 lifted up above the h.
Isa 55:12 the h. will become cheerful
Hab 3:6 the lasting h. bowed down
Pr 8:25; Eze 6:3; Ho 10:8; Lu 23:30.
HIND(S), Pr 5:19 lovable h. and charming
Ge 49:21; Ps 18:33; Hab 3:19.
HINDER, Ac 11:17 that I should h. God?
1Th 2:16 h. us from speaking to the nations
HINDERED, Ga 5:7 Who h. you from
1Pe 3:7 your prayers not to be h.
HINNOM, 2Ch 33:6 Sons in fire in valley of H.
Jos 15:8; 2Ki 23:10; 2Ch 28:3; Ne 11:30;
Jer 7:31; 19:2; 32:35.
HIPS, Jer 1:17 gird up your h., and
Ex 12:11; Isa 11:5; 45:1; Jer 13:11.
HIRAM, 1Ki 5:1, 10; 7:13, 45; 9:11; 10:11.
HIRE, De 23:18 the h. of a harlot
Isa 23:17 must return to her h.
Mt 20:1 to h. workers for his vineyard
HIRED, Lu 15:19 as one of your h. men.
Ge 30:16; De 23:4; Ne 6:12; Jer 46:21.
HIRING, Ne 13:2 h. against them Balaam
HISTORY, Ge 2:4; 5:1; 6:9; Mt 1:1.
HITTITE(S), Ge 23:10; Jg 1:26; 2Sa 11:3.
HOARFROST, Job 38:29 the h. of heaven,
Ps 147:16 h. he scatters
Ex 16:14.
HOARSE, Ps 69:3 My throat has become h.
HOBAB, Nu 10:29; Jg 4:11.
HOLD, Ac 3:21 whom heaven must h.
Joh 7:30; 8:20; Ac 3:7.
HOLE, Ps 7:15 he will fall into the h.
HOLINESS, Ex 15:11 mighty in h.?
Isa 35:8 Way of H. it will be called
Isa 65:5 I shall convey h. to you.
Ro 6:19 slaves to righteousness h. in view.
2Co 7:1 perfecting h. in God's fear
1Th 3:13 unblamable in h. before God
Ps 89:35; 93:5; Heb 12:10.
HOLINESS BELONGS TO JEHOVAH, Ex 28:36;

39:30; Zec 14:20.
HOLLOW, Isa 24:18 up from inside the h.
HOLY, Ex 26:33 the H. and the Most H.
Le 10:10 a distinction between the h.
Ro 7:12 on its part, the law is h., and
1Co 3:17 the temple of God is h., you are.
Eph 1:4 that we should be h. and without
2Ti 3:15 you have known the h. writings
Re 4:8 H., h., h. is Jehovah God
Ex 3:5; Ps 2:6; Isa 52:10; Mt 24:15.
HOLY MYRIADS, De 33:2 with him were h.,
Jude 14 Jehovah came with his h.
HOLY ONES, Da 4:17 by the saying of h.
Da 7:18 the h. will receive the kingdom,
Da 7:25 he will harass continually the h.
Da 7:27 the h. of the Supreme One.
Ac 26:10 the h. I shut up in prisons,
Ro 12:13 Share with h. according to their
1Co 6:2 the h. will judge the world?
Eph 3:8 me, a man less than least of all h.,
Eph 4:12 training h. for ministerial work,
Re 11:18 time to give reward to the h.
Re 17:6 woman drunk with the blood of the h.
Da 7:21, 22; Mt 27:52; Re 13:7; 18:24.
HOLY PLACE, Ps 150:1 Praise God in his h.
HOLY SPIRIT, Ps 51:11 your h. do not
Mt 1:18 she was found to be pregnant by h.
Mt 12:32 whoever speaks against the h.
Lu 3:22 h. in bodily shape like a dove
Joh 14:26 the helper, the h. which the
Ac 2:4 they all became filled with h.
Ac 11:16 you will be baptized in h.
1Co 6:19 is the temple of the h.
Eph 4:30 do not be grieving God's h.
Heb 6:4 who have become partakers of h.
2Pe 1:21 as they were borne along by h.
Isa 63:10; Mt 3:11; Mr 13:11; Ac 20:28.
HOMAGE, Da 2:46 to Daniel he paid h.,
HOMELESS, 1Co 4:11 knocked about and h.
Isa 58:7; La 1:7; 3:19; 4:15.
HONEST, 2Co 8:21 make h. provision
Heb 13:18 have an h. conscience
HONESTY, Ge 20:5 In the h. of my heart
HONEY, Ex 3:8 flowing with milk and h.
Ps 19:10 And sweeter than h.
Ps 119:103 More so than h. to my mouth.
Eze 3:3 came to be in my mouth like h.
Jg 14:9; Pr 25:27; Isa 7:15; Re 10:10.
HONOR, Ex 20:12 h. your father and
1Sa 2:30 those honoring me I shall h.
Pr 3:9 H. Jehovah with your valuable
Lu 18:20 H. your father and mother.
Ro 12:10 In showing h. to one another
Ro 13:7 to him who calls for h., such h.
Eph 6:2 H. your father and mother; which
2Ti 2:20 others for a purpose lacking h.
Heb 5:4 this h., not of his own accord
Es 6:9; 1Ti 1:17; 6:16; Heb 2:9; Re 4:11.
HONORABLE, Isa 23:9 treat all the h.
Ro 9:21 one vessel for an h. use, another
HOOF, Le 11:3 splits the h. and forms
HOOKS, Eze 38:4 put h. in your jaws
HOPE, Mt 12:21 in his name nations will h.
Ac 26:7 Concerning this h. I am
Ro 5:5 the h. does not lead to
Ro 8:20 subjected it, on the basis of h.
Ro 8:24 h. that is seen is not h.
Ro 15:4 through our endurance h.
Eph 2:12 and you had no h.
1Th 4:13 the rest do who have no h.
Heb 6:19 This h. we have as an anchor
Heb 10:23 the public declaration of our h.
1Pe 3:15 demands of you a reason for the h.
Job 14:7; Ps 146:5; Pr 20:22; Mic 5:7;

Mt 12:21; 1Co 9:10; Eph 4:4; Col 1:27.
HOPED, Heb 11:1 expectation of things **h.**
HOPELESS, Isa 57:10; Jer 2:25; 18:12.
HOPING, Ps 25:3 none **h.** will be ashamed.
  Isa 40:31 those **h.** in Jehovah regain power.
HOREB, De 5:2 a covenant with us in **H.**
  Ex 3:1; 17:6; De 9:8; 29:1; Ps 106:19.
HORIZON, Pr 8:27 decreed a **h.** upon
HORN(S), Pr 25:9 **h.** of loud tone to
  Eze 33:6 sword coming and does not blow **h.**
  Da 7:8 another **h.,** a small one,
  Re 17:12 the ten **h.** mean ten kings
HORROR, Eze 4:16; 12:19.
HORSE(S), Ps 33:17 **h.** for salvation
  Ps 147:10 Not the **h.** does he take
  Re 19:11 and, look! a white **h.**
  De 17:16; Es 6:8; Isa 31:1; Jer 51:21.
HOSPITABLE, 1Pe 4:9 Be **h.** to one
HOSPITALLY, Mt 25:35 you received me **h.**
  Jas 2:25 received the messengers **h.** and
HOSPITALITY, Ro 12:13 course of **h.**
HOST, Ro 16:23 Gaius my **h.** greets you
HOSTAGES, 2Ki 14:14 **h.** to Samaria
HOSTILITY, Ps 23:5 showing **h.** to me.
HOSTS. See ARMIES.
HOT, 2Pe 3:10 elements being **h.** will be
  Re 3:15 you are neither cold nor **h.**
HOUR, Mt 24:36 that day and **h.**
  Lu 22:53 this is your **h.** and the authority
  Joh 17:1 the **h.** has come; glorify your son
  1Jo 2:18 Young children, it is the last **h.**
  Re 3:10 keep you from the **h.** of test
  Re 17:12 receive authority as kings one **h.**
  Mt 24:44, 50; 26:45; Re 14:7, 15; 18:10.
HOUSE(S), Pr 27:4 I may dwell in the **h.** of
  Ps 127:1 Unless Jehovah builds the **h.**
  Isa 2:2 the mountain of the **h.** of Jehovah
  Isa 6:11 Until **h.** be without man
  Isa 65:21 build **h.** and have occupancy;
  Hag 2:7 I will fill this **h.** with glory,
  Mt 21:13 My **h.** will be called a **h.** of prayers
  Mt 23:38 your **h.** is abandoned to you.
  Mr 3:25 if a **h.** becomes divided against
  Ac 7:48 Most High does not dwell in **h.**
  Ac 20:20 you publicly and from **h.** to **h.**
  Ro 16:5 the congregation that is in their **h.**
  1Pe 2:5 being built up a spiritual **h.**
  2Sa 7:13; Ps 84:10; Mr 10:30; Heb 3:3, 6.
HOUSEHOLD, Mt 10:36 enemies of his own **h.**
  Ge 7:1; 47:12; Pr 27:27; 31:15; Eph 2:19.
HOUSEHOLDER(S), Mt 10:25 **h.** Beelzebub,
  Mt 13:27; 20:1; 21:33; 24:43.
HOUSETOP(S), Mt 10:27 preach from the **h.**
  Mt 24:17; Lu 12:3; 17:31; Ac 10:9.
HOWL, Isa 13:6 **H.,** you people, for the
  Isa 23:1, 6; 65:14; Jer 25:34; Eze 21:12.
HOWLING, Jer 25:36 **h.** of majestic ones
  Zec 11:3 Listen! The **h.** of shepherds,
  Jas 5:1 you rich men, weep, **h.** over
HUBBUB, Isa 32:14 **h.** of city abandoned;
HULDAH, 2Ki 22:14 **H.** the prophetess
HUMAN, 1Co 9:8 things by **h.** standards
  Ga 1:11 good news is not something **h.;**
HUMANKIND, Nu 31:28 one soul of **h.**
  Nu 16:32; Jos 11:14; Eze 36:10.
HUMAN TERMS, Ro 6:19 I am speaking in **h.**
HUMBLE, De 8:2 in order to **h.** you, to
  1Ch 17:10 I shall **h.** all your enemies.
  Zec 9:9 He is **h.,** and riding upon an ass,
  Jas 4:6 gives undeserved kindness to the **h.**
  Jas 4:10 **H.** yourselves in eyes of Jehovah,
  1Pe 5:6 **H.** yourself under the mighty hand
  2Ch 7:14; Ps 138:6; Pr 29:23; Mt 18:4.
HUMBLED, Php 2:8 he **h.** himself and

1Ki 21:29; 2Ki 22:19; 2Ch 12:6; Lu 14:11.
HUMBLES, Mt 23:12 whoever **h.** himself
HUMILIATE, Da 4:37 in pride to **h.**
HUMILIATED, Isa 54:4 and do not feel **h.,**
  Php 3:21 will refashion our **h.** body to be
  Ps 35:4; Isa 41:11; 50:7; Jer 22:22.
HUMILIATION, Pr 18:13 foolishness and **h.**
  Jas 1:10 and the rich one over his **h.,**
  Isa 45:16; Eze 16:54; 36:32.
HUMILITY, Pr 15:33 before glory **h.**
  Pr 22:4 result of **h.** is riches and glory
  Col 2:18, 23 a mock **h.**
HUNDRED, Jg 7:7 By the three **h.** men
  Isa 65:20 although a **h.** years of age
  Mt 18:12 a man comes to have a **h.** sheep
  Jg 4:13; 1Ki 22:6; Ec 6:3; Re 7:4.
HUNDRED AND FORTY-FOUR THOUSAND,
  Re 7:4; 14:1, 3.
HUNDREDFOLD, Mt 13:8 this one a **h.**
  Mr 10:30 who will not get a **h.** now
HUNG, De 21:23 something accursed is **h.**
  Ge 40:22; 2Sa 18:10; Ps 137:2; Lu 23:39.
HUNGER, Ro 8:35 separate us? Will **h.?**
  Re 7:16 They will **h.** no more nor thirst
  De 28:48; 32:24; Ne 9:15; 2Co 11:27.
HUNGERING, Mt 5:6 Happy are those **h.**
HUNGRY, Ps 146:7 giving bread to the **h.**
  Isa 65:13 eat but you will go **h.**
  Job 6:35 He will not get **h.** at all
  Ps 50:12; 107:9; Isa 29:8; Eze 18:7.
HUNT, TO, Ge 25:27; 27:5.
HUNTED, Ge 27:33; La 4:18.
HUNTER(S), Ge 10:9 **h.** in opposition
  Jer 16:16 I shall send for many **h.,**
HUNTING, Ge 27:30; Le 17:13; Eze 13:20.
HUNTS, Pr 6:26 she **h.** for a soul.
HURRY, Ge 19:22; Jg 9:48.
HURRYING, Zep 1:14 day of Jehovah is **h.**
HURT, Lu 10:19 nothing will do you **h.**
  Re 9:10 authority to **h.** the men five months.
HURTFUL, Pr 6:18 fabricating **h.** schemes,
  Pr 12:21 Nothing **h.** will befall righteous
  Col 3:5 **h.** desire, and covetousness,
  Ps 101:8; 141:4; Pr 21:15; Isa 59:4.
HURTFULNESS, Pr 17:4 to the lip of **h.**
  Job 34:36; Ps 64:2; Eze 11:2.
HUSBAND(S), Ro 7:2 bound by law to **h.**
  1Co 7:2 let each woman have her own **h.**
  1Co 7:14 the unbelieving **h.** is sanctified
  2Co 11:2 I promised you to one **h.**
  Eph 5:25 **H.** continue loving your wives
  Col 3:19 **h.,** keep loving your wives
  1Pe 3:1 wives be in subjection to your **h.**
  Re 21:2 as a bride adorned for her **h.**
  Ru 1:11; Jer 29:6; 44:19; Eze 16:45;
  1Co 7:34; 14:35; Col 3:18; 1Ti 3:2.
HUSBANDLY, Isa 54:5 Maker is your **h.**
  Jer 31:32 I had **h.** ownership of them,
HUSH MONEY, 1Sa 12:3; Am 5:12.
HYMENAEUS, 1Ti 1:20 **H.** handed to Satan
  2Ti 2:17 **H.** and Philetus are of that number.
HYPOCRISY, Mt 23:28 you are full of **h.**
  Lu 12:1 leaven of the Pharisees is **h.**
  Ro 12:9 Let your love be without **h.**
  2Co 6:6 by love free from **h.,**
  1Ti 4:2 **h.** of men who speak lies, marked
  1Ti 1:5; 2Ti 1:5.
HYPOCRITE(S), Mt 7:5 **H.!** First extract
  Mt 15:7 **h.,** Isaiah prophesied about you,
  Mt 23:13 scribes and Pharisees, **h.!**
  Mt 24:51 assign him his part with the **h.**
HYPOCRITICAL, Jas 3:17 wisdom is not **h.**
HYSSOP, Ps 51:7 purify me with **h.,**
  Le 14:6; Nu 19:6; Joh 19:29; Heb 9:19.

I

ICE, Eze 1:22 sparkle of awesome I.
IDEA(S), Job 42:2 no I. unattainable
Ps 10:4 I. are: There is no God.
Ps 21:11; Pr 12:2; 24:8; Jer 23:20.
IDLE, 1Ti 1:6 aside into I. talk
IDLE MEN, Jg 9:4; 11:3; 2Ch 13:7.
IDOL(S), Ps 106:36 I. to be a snare
Jon 2:8 observing I. of untruth
Ac 15:20 abstain from things polluted by I.
1Co 8:4 an I. is nothing
2Co 6:16 God's temple have with I.?
1Jo 5:21 children, guard yourselves from I.
Ps 115:4; Isa 48:5; Mic 1:7; Ac 7:41.
IDOLATER(S), 1Co 5:11 quit mixing with I.
1Co 5:10; 6:9; 10:7; Eph 5:5.
IDOLATRY, 1Co 10:14 flee from I.
Col 3:5 covetousness, which is I.
IGNITED, De 32:22; Jer 15:14; 17:4.
IGNOBLE, 1Co 1:28 God chose I. things
IGNORANCE, Ac 17:30 God overlooked I.,
Heb 9:7 sins of I. of the people.
Ac 3:17; Eph 4:18; 1Pe 1:14.
IGNORANT, 2Co 2:11 we are not I. of his
1Th 4:13 not I. concerning those sleeping in
1Ti 1:13 because I was I. and acted
Heb 5:2 deal moderately with the I. ones
1Pe 2:15 muzzle the I. talk of men.
2Pe 2:12 they are I. and speak abusively,
IGNORED, Isa 59:8; Jer 5:4; 9:3; 10:25.
ILLEGAL, 1Pe 4:3 deeds of I. idolatries
ILLEGITIMATE, De 23:2; Heb 12:8.
ILLICIT, Ro 13:13 not in I. intercourse
ILLNESS, Ps 41:3 him upon a divan of I.;
ILL-TREATED, Heb 11:25 choosing to be I.
Heb 13:3 Keep in mind those being I., since
ILL-TREATMENT, Heb 11:37 were under I.;
ILLUMINATE, 2Co 4:6 on hearts to I. them
ILLUMINATION, Da 5:11, 14; 2Co 4:4.
ILLUMINATOR(S), Php 2:15 shining as I.
ILLUSTRATION(S), Mt 13:10 by use of I.?
Mt 13:34 without an I. he would not
Mt 13:35 I will open my mouth with I.
Mt 24:32 from the fig tree as an I.
Lu 8:10 for the rest it is in I.,
Ga 3:15 I speak with a human I.:
Heb 9:9 This tent is an I. for the
Mt 15:15; Mr 4:10, 11; 12:1, 12; 13:28.
ILLUSTRATIVE, Heb 11:19 in an I. way
ILLUSTRIOUS, Ac 2:20 I. day of Jehovah
IMAGE(S), Ge 1:26 make man in our I.,
Ex 20:4 You must not make a carved I.
Ps 78:58 I. inciting him to jealousy.
Isa 42:8 neither my praise to graven I.
Da 2:31 king beholding a certain I.
Da 3:18 I. of gold we will not worship.
1Co 15:49 shall bear the I. of the heavenly
Re 14:9 worships the beast and its I.,
Re 20:4 worshiped neither the I.
Mic 5:13; Hab 2:18; Ro 8:29; Col 1:15.
IMAGINATION(S), Ps 73:7 I. of the heart.
Pr 18:11 like a protective wall in his I.
Lu 11:17 Knowing I.
IMAGINE, Es 4:13 Do not I. within your
Lu 12:51 Do you I. I came to give
IMAGINED, Joh 11:13 they I. he was
IMAGINING, Joh 13:29 Some were I., since
IMITATE, 2Th 3:7 you ought to I. us,
2Th 3:9 as an example to you to I. us.
Heb 13:7 I. their faith.
IMITATORS, 1Co 11:1 Become I. of me,
Eph 5:1 become I. of God, as children
Heb 6:12 not become sluggish, but be I.

1Co 4:16; Php 3:17; 1Th 1:6; 2:14.
IMMANUEL, Isa 7:14; 8:8; Mt 1:23.
IMMINENT, 2Ti 4:6 my releasing is I.
IMMODERATENESS, Mt 23:25 plunder and I.
IMMORAL INTERCOURSE, Jg 2:17 had I. with
Ps 106:39 having I. by their dealings
Ex 34:15; Le 17:7; 20:5; Nu 15:39.
IMMORALLY, Ps 73:27 silence one I. leaving
IMMORAL RELATIONS, Nu 25:1 I. with
IMMORTALITY, 1Co 15:53 mortal put on I.
1Ti 6:16 one alone having I.,
IMPALE, Mt 20:19 deliver him to I.
Lu 23:21 they yell: "I.! I. him!"
Joh 19:6 Take him yourselves and I. him,
Heb 6:6 they I. the Son of God afresh
Mt 23:34; Mr 15:14; Joh 19:10, 15.
IMPALED, Mr 15:25 third hour, they I.
Lu 24:7 sinful men and be I.
Re 11:8 where their Lord also was I.
Mt 26:2; Ro 6:6; 1Co 1:13; Ga 2:20; 6:14.
IMPARTED, Ga 2:6 men I. nothing new.
IMPARTED POWER, 1Ti 1:12.
IMPARTIALLY, 1Pe 1:17 Father judges I.
IMPARTS, Php 4:13 virtue of him who I.
IMPARTS KNOWLEDGE, Pr 9:9 I. to someone
IMPART UNDERSTANDING, Da 9:22.
Da 11:33 they will I. to the many.
IMPATIENT, Job 21:4; Pr 14:29; Zec 11:8.
IMPEDIMENT, Mr 7:35 I. of his tongue
IMPEL, Jg 13:25 spirit started to I. him
IMPELLED, Ex 35:21; 36:2 heart I. him
IMPENETRABLE, Zec 11:2 the I. forest
IMPERIAL, 2Ch 32:9 all his I. might with
IMPETUOUS, Hab 1:6 nation bitter and I.,
IMPLANTING, Jas 1:21 I. of the word
IMPLEMENTS, Ec 9:18 better than I.
Ge 27:3; 1Ki 19:21.
IMPLICITLY, Ge 41:40 obey you I.
IMPLORE, De 3:23; Es 4:8.
IMPLORED, Ge 42:21 he I. compassion on
Heb 12:19 people I. that no word be added
IMPLORE FAVOR, Job 9:15 I would I.
IMPORTANT, Php 1:10 of the more I. things,
IMPORTUNITIES, Pr 6:3 storm with I.
IMPOSED, Ne 10:32 we I. commandments
Heb 9:10 legal requirements I. until the
IMPOSSIBILITY, Lu 1:37 with God no I.
IMPOSSIBLE, Mt 19:26 men this is I.,
Heb 6:18 it is I. for God to lie,
Mt 17:20; Mr 10:27; Heb 11:6.
IMPOSTOR(S), Mt 27:63; 2Ti 3:13.
IMPOSTURE, Mt 27:64 this last I. will be
IMPOTENT IN DEATH, Pr 9:18; Isa 26:14.
IMPOUNDED, Ex 7:19; Le 11:36 I. waters
IMPOVERISHED, Ps 79:8 we have become I.
Ps 116:6 I was I. and he
IMPOVERISHER, 1Sa 2:7 Jehovah is an I.
IMPREGNATES, Job 21:10 his bull I.
IMPRINT, Da 9:24 I. a seal upon vision
IMPROPER, Job 1:22; 24:12.
IMPROPRIETY, Jer 23:13 I have seen I.
IMPROVISING, Am 6:5 I. according to
IMPULSE, Joh 16:13 not speak of his own I.
IMPULSES, 1Ti 5:11 their sexual I. have
IMPURE, 2Ch 29:5; Ezr 9:11.
IMPURITY, Eze 18:6 a woman in her I.
INACTIVE, Ro 6:6 sinful body made I.,
Jas 2:20 faith apart from works is I.
2Pe 1:8 prevent from being I. or unfruitful
INANIMATE, Jer 51:6; 1Co 14:7.
INAUGURATE, 1Ki 8:63 might I. the house
INAUGURATED, De 20:5 house and not I.
Heb 9:18 former covenant I. without blood
Heb 10:20 which he I. for us as a new way

INAUGURATION, 2Ch 7:9 i. of the altar
Nu 7:10; Ezr 6:16; Ne 12:27; Da 3:2.
INCAPABILITY, Ro 8:3 an i. on the part
Le 16:13; De 33:10; Ps 141:2.
INCENSE, Re 8:4 i. with the prayers
Le 16:13; De 33:10; Ps 141:2.
INCENSED, 1Ki 11:9 Jehovah came to be i.
Ps 2:12; 79:5; 2Co 11:29.
INCENSE, PERFUMED, Ex 25:6 and for p.;
INCENSE STANDS, Isa 17:8; Eze 6:4.
INCESSANTLY, 1Th 1:3 we bear i. in mind
INCIDENTAL, 2Ti 2:22 desires i. to youth
INCINERATE, Eze 5:4 i. them in fire
INCISION, Le 21:5 on flesh not make i.
INCITE, Ro 10:19 i. you to jealousy
Heb 10:24 one another to i. to love and
1Ch 21:1; Job 2:3.
INCITING, 1Co 10:22 we i. Jehovah to
Jos 15:18; Jg 1:14.
INCLINATION(S), Ge 6:5 every i. of the
1Ch 28:9 searching every i. of the thoughts
1Ch 29:18 keep this as the i. of the heart
Eph 6:7 Be slaves with good i. as to
Ge 8:21; De 31:21; Isa 26:3; Jas 3:4.
INCLINE, Ps 17:11; 40:1; Pr 4:27; 5:1.
INCLINED, Php 3:15 if you are mentally i.
Jg 9:3; 1Sa 8:3; Pr 5:13.
INCOMPREHENSIBLE, Jer 33:3 tell i. things
INCORRUPTIBLE, Ro 1:23 glory of i. God
1Co 9:25 corruptible crown, we an i. one.
1Co 15:52 dead will be raised up i.,
1Ti 1:17 Now to the King of eternity, i.
1Pe 1:4 to an i. unfading inheritance.
1Pe 1:23 not by corruptible but by i. seed
1Pe 3:4 the i. apparel of the quiet spirit
INCORRUPTIBLENESS, Ro 2:7 seeking i. by
INCORRUPTION, 1Co 15:42 is raised in i.
1Co 15:50 neither does corruption inherit i.
2Ti 1:10 shed light upon life and i.
INCORRUPTNESS, Eph 6:24 loving in i.
INCREASE, Le 25:16; 2Co 9:10.
INCREASED, Ex 11:9; Pr 11:24.
INCREASING, Mt 24:12 i. of lawlessness
Mr 4:8 i., they began to yield fruit,
Joh 3:30 That one must go on i., but I
Col 1:6 bearing fruit and i. in the world
Col 1:10 i. in accurate knowledge of God
INCULCATE, De 6:7 i. them in your son
INCUR, 1Jo 5:16, 17 a sin not i. death
INCURABLE, Isa 17:11 and i. pain.
Job 34:6; Jer 15:18; 30:15.
INDECENT, De 23:14; 24:1.
INDECENTLY, 1Co 13:5 does not behave i.,
INDECISIVE, Jas 1:8; 4:8 an i. man
INDEFINITELY LASTING, Jer 50:5
Jer 51:57 they must sleep an i. sleep
Hab 3:6 the i. hills bowed down.
Isa 55:3; Jer 51:39; Eze 35:5, 9; Da 12:2.
IDENTICAL, 1Pe 2:7 i. stone rejected
INDESCRIBABLE, 2Co 9:15 i. free gift.
INDESTRUCTIBLE, Heb 7:16 power of an i.
INDIA, Es 1:1; 8:9.
INDICATING, 1Pe 1:11 spirit i.
INDICATION, Php 1:28 this i. from God,
INDICATOR, Pr 16:11 just i. and scales
INDIGNANT, Ge 41:10 Pharaoh was i.
Ex 16:20 Moses became i. at them.
Mr 10:14 At seeing this Jesus was i.
Nu 16:22; Ec 5:6; Isa 57:17; Mt 21:15.
INDIGNATION, 2Ch 29:8 Jehovah's i. came
Isa 34:2 i. against all nations,
Mr 3:5 looking with i. he said "Stretch out
De 29:28; Jer 10:10; 50:13; Mr 14:4.
INDISPOSED, Jas 5:15 prayer will make i.
INDISTINCT, 1Co 14:8 trumpet sounds an i.

INDIVIDUAL, Pr 27:21 i. is according to
INDIVIDUALLY, Ro 12:5 belonging i. to
1Co 12:27 you are Christ's body, members i.
INDUCED, De 26:17, 18 Jehovah i. to say
Pr 25:15 a commander is i.,
INDUCEMENT, Ro 7:8 sin, receiving an i.
2Co 5:12 giving an i. for boasting in
Ga 5:13 freedom as an i. for the flesh
1Ti 5:14 give no i. to the opposer
INDULGENCE, 2Pe 2:7 i. in loose conduct
INDULGENT, Ne 9:30 i. with them for years
INDUSTRIOUSNESS, Heb 6:11 show same i.
INEFFECTIVENESS, Heb 7:18 account of i.
INEXCUSABLE, Ro 1:20 so they are i.;
Ro 2:1 you are i., O man, if you judge;
INEXPERIENCED, Pr 22:3 i. must suffer
Pr 14:15; 21:11.
INEXPERIENCED ONE(S), Ps 19:7 i. wise.
Ps 119:130; Pr 1:22; Eze 45:20.
INFAMY, Eze 23:10 to be i. to women
INFANCY, 2Ti 3:15 from i. you have
INFANT(S), Ac 7:19; 1Pe 2:2.
INFIRMITIES, Ac 14:15 same i. as you
INFLAME, Pr 29:8 Men boastful i. a town,
INFLAMED, Ro 1:27 violently i. in lust
1Co 7:9 marry than to be i. with passion.
INFLAMMATION, De 28:22 i. and feverish
Ac 28:6 swell up with i.
INFLICT, 2Co 10:6 to i. punishment for
INFORMER, 2Sa 15:13 i. came to David
INFUSED, 2Ti 4:17 Lord i. power into me
INGATHERING, FESTIVAL OF, Ex 34:22.
INGENIOUS, Ex 35:33 make i. products of
INHABIT, Isa 54:3 i. desolated cities.
Eph 2:22 built into a place for God to i.
INHABITANT(S), Isa 6:11 to be without i.
Isa 24:5 land has been polluted under its i.
Jer 51:29 of astonishment, without an i.
Jer 25:29; 26:15; Ho 4:1; Zec 12:8.
INHABITED, Isa 44:26 She will be i.
Isa 45:18 who formed it even to be i.
Isa 13:20; Jer 6:8; Eze 12:20.
INHABITED EARTH, Mt 24:14 news in the i.
Lu 4:5 showed him all the kingdoms of the i.
Ac 17:6 These men that have overturned the i.
Heb 2:5 he has subjected the i. to come,
Re 3:10 test is to come upon the whole i.,
Re 16:14 the kings of the entire i.,
Ac 17:31; Ro 10:18; Heb 1:6; Re 12:9.
INHABITRESS, Isa 12:6 O you i. of Zion,
INHERIT, Mt 19:29 will i. everlasting
Mt 25:34 i. the kingdom prepared for you
1Co 15:50 blood cannot i. God's kingdom
Heb 6:12 faith and patience i. the promises.
Mt 5:5; 1Pe 3:9; Re 21:7.
INHERITANCE, Ps 2:8 nations as your i.
Eph 1:14 a token in advance of our i.,
Col 1:12 i. of the holy ones in the light.
1Pe 1:4 and undefiled and unfading i.
1Pe 5:3 who are God's i.,
Nu 18:20; Eze 47:22; Eph 5:5; Heb 9:15.
INIQUITIES. See ERROR(S), LAWLESS DEEDS.
INITIAL, Eze 36:11 more than your i. state
INITIATE, 2Co 8:6 the one to i.
INITIATED, Mr 6:7 he i. sending them out
2Co 8:10 a year ago you i. the doing
INITIATIVE, Joh 5:19, 30; 7:28; 8:28, 42.
INJURIOUS, Eze 38:10 an i. scheme
1Co 10:6 persons desiring i.
1Ti 6:10 root of all sorts of i. things,
Le 26:6; 2Ki 4:41; Eze 5:16; Lu 16:25.
INJURIOUSLY, 1Ti 6:1 never spoken of i.
INJURIOUSNESS, Ro 1:29 covetousness, i.,

1Co 5:8 neither with leaven of i.
Eph 4:31 away from you along with all i.
Col 3:8 put away i., abusive speech
INJURY, 1Pe 3:9 paying back i. for i.
1Sa 25:26; Ac 18:10.
INJUSTICE, Le 19:15 you must not do i.
De 32:4 A God with whom is no i.
Ro 9:14 Is there i. with God? Never
Ps 7:3; Pr 29:27; Eze 3:20; Re 18:5.
INK, 2Co 3:3 not with i. but spirit
Jer 36:18; 2Jo 12; 3Jo 13.
INKHORN, Eze 9:2, 3, 11 man with i.
INNERMOST ROOM, 1Ki 6:5; Ps 28:2.
INNOCENCY, Ho 8:5 incapable of i.
INNOCENT, Ps 94:21 blood of the i. one.
Mt 10:16 prove yourselves i. as doves.
Mt 27:24 I am i. of the blood of this man.
Ro 16:19 you be i. as to what is evil.
Php 2:15 blameless and i., children
Ex 23:7; De 19:10; Ps 24:4; Pr 6:17.
INNUMERABLE, Heb 11:12 sands seaside i.
INQUIRE, De 4:29 i. with all your heart
Mt 2:4; Ac 21:33.
INQUIRED, Ac 23:34 i. from what province
INSANE, 1Sa 21:13 acting i.
INSANITY, Ec 2:2 "I.I" and to rejoicing:
INSCRIBE, Isa 30:8 i. it in a book,
INSCRIBED, Ex 39:30 sign of dedication i.
2Co 3:2 letter, i. on our hearts and known
INSCRIPTION, Ex 39:30 an i. with engravings
Mt 22:20 Whose i. is this?
INSECTS, De 28:42 i. take possession.
INSENSIBILITY, Mr 3:5 grieved at the i.
Eph 4:18 because of the i. of their hearts.
INSERTED, 2Ch 20:34 words i. in Book of
INSIDE, Lu 11:39 i. is full of plunder
2Co 4:16 man i. is being renewed
Eph 3:16 mighty in the man you are i.
INSIGHT, Pr 1:3 discipline that gives i.,
Pr 13:15 Good i. itself gives favor, but
Pr 14:35 pleasure in servant acting with i.,
Pr 16:22 To its owners i. is a well of life,
Pr 19:11 The i. of a man certainly slows
Da 11:33 those having i. among the people,
Ro 3:11 no one that has any i.
1Ch 28:19; Ps 111:10; 119:99; Pr 3:4;
Isa 44:18; Jer 3:15; 9:24; Da 12:3, 10.
INSIGNIFICANT, Ps 119:141 I am i. and
Zec 13:7 turn my hand back upon those i.
Mt 2:6 you, O Bethlehem, are no i. city
Job 14:21; Jer 14:3; 30:19.
INSINUATIONS, Hab 2:6 against him i.
INSISTENCE. See also EXCLUSIVE DEVOTION.
INSISTENCE, Ps 90:10 i. is on trouble
INSOLENCE, 2Ki 19:3; Isa 37:3.
INSOLENCE OF HEART, Isa 9:9; La 3:65.
INSOLENT, Zep 3:4 Her prophets were i.
Isa 33:19; Eze 2:4; Ro 1:30.
INSOLENTLY, 1Th 2:2 been i. treated
Mt 22:6; Lu 18:32; Ac 14:5.
INSPECTED, Lu 19:44 of your being i.
INSPECTION, 1Pe 2:12 the day for his i.
INSPIRATION, 1Ch 28:12 be with him by i.
Mt 22:43 David by i. calls him 'Lord'
Re 1:10 By i. I came to be in the Lord's
INSPIRED, Pr 16:10 i. decision should
2Ti 3:16 All Scripture is i.
INSPIRED EXPRESSION(S), Ho 9:7 man of i.
1Jo 4:1 do not believe every i., but test
Re 16:13 three unclean i. like frogs
INSPIRED UTTERANCES, 1Co 12:10.
1Ti 4:1 i. says in later periods of time
INSPIRES, Re 19:10 witness to Jesus i.
INSTALLATION, Ex 29:22; Le 7:37; 8:28.

INSTANT, Lu 4:5 showed him in an i.
INSTANTLY, 1Th 5:3 destruction i. upon
INSTIGATING, Jer 43:3 Baruch is i. you
INSTINCTIVELY, Pr 30:24 i. wise
INSTRUCT, Ezr 7:25 you men will i.
Isa 2:3 Jehovah will i. us about his ways
1Co 2:16 mind of Jehovah, that he may i.
1Co 14:19 I might also i. others verbally,
De 17:10; Jg 13:8; 1Sa 12:23; Ps 25:12;
27:11; 32:8; 45:4; Mic 3:11.
INSTRUCTED, Ac 7:22; Ro 2:18.
INSTRUCTING, Ne 8:9 Levites were i.
2Ti 2:25; Tit 2:12.
INSTRUCTION, De 32:2 My i. will drip as
Pr 1:5 A wise person will take in more i.,
Ro 15:4 aforetime were written for our i.,
Le 14:57; Pr 4:2; Isa 9:15; Mt 11:1.
INSTRUCTOR(S), Isa 30:20 your Grand i.
Mt 13:52 every public i. when taught
2Ch 35:3; Ezr 8:16; Pr 5:13; Hab 2:18;
Mt 23:34.
INSTRUCTS, Ps 25:8 Jehovah i. sinners
INSTRUMENT, Ps 71:22 i. stringed sort
INSULT, Ps 4:2 must my glory be for i.
INSULTING, Job 20:3 An i. exhortation
INTEGRITY, Job 31:6 God will know my i.
Ps 26:11 for me, in my i. I shall walk.
Pr 14:32 finding refuge in his i.
Pr 20:7 The righteous is walking in his i.
1Ki 9:4; Job 27:5; Ps 7:8; 25:21; 41:12;
78:72; Pr 2:7; 11:3.
INTELLECTUAL, Mt 11:25 hidden from i.
1Co 1:19 shove intelligence of i. aside.
1Jo 5:20 given us i. capacity
INTELLIGENCE, 1Co 1:19; Re 13:18; 17:9.
INTEND, Da 7:25 i. to change times
INTENSE, 1Pe 4:8 have i. love for one
INTENSELY, 1Pe 1:22 love one another i.
INTENSITY, Ac 18:28 with i. he proved
INTENT, Ex 32:12 with evil i. he brought
INTENTION(S), Lu 1:51 haughty in the i.
2Co 1:17 when I had such an i.
Heb 4:12 is able to discern i. of the heart
INTENTLY, Mt 6:26 Observe i. the birds
Heb 12:2 we look i. at the Chief Agent
INTERBREED, Le 19:19 must not i.
INTERCEDE, Nu 21:7 i. with Jehovah that
INTERCESSIONS, 1Ti 2:1 prayers, i.,
INTERCHANGE, Ro 1:12 i. of encouragement
INTERCOURSE, Ge 4:1; 38:26; Jg 21:12.
INTERDICT, Da 6:7, 9, 12, 13, 15.
INTEREST(S), Mt 25:27 receiving with i.
1Co 13:5 love does not look for its own i.
Php 2:4 also in personal i. upon others
Php 2:21 seeking their own i. not
Ex 22:25; Pr 28:8; 1Th 2:15.
INTERFAITH. See YOKED WITH UNBELIEVERS.
INTERMEDDLE, Pr 14:10 no stranger will i.
Pr 24:21 who are for a change, do not i.
INTERPOSE, Isa 53:12 he proceeded to i.
INTERPOSING, Isa 59:16 was no one i.
INTERPRET, Mt 16:3 you know how to i.
INTERPRETATION(S), Ge 40:8 i. belong to
Ec 8:1 Who knows the i. of a thing
Da 2:4 we shall show the very i.
Da 5:16 I heard you are able to furnish i.
Da 5:26 This is the i. of the word:
1Co 12:10 to another i. of tongues
1Co 14:26 an i. let all things take place
2Pe 1:20 no prophecy from any private i.
INTERVAL, Ge 32:16 set an i. between
1Co 14:7 unless it makes an i. to the tones,
INTERVENED, Ps 106:30 Phinehas stood up i.
INTESTINES, Ex 29:13.

INTIMACY, Job 29:4 When i. with God was
Ps 25:14 i. with Jehovah belongs to those
Ps 55:14 used to enjoy sweet i. together
Pr 3:32 His i. is with the upright ones.
INTIMATE ACQUAINTANCE(S), Job 19:14.
INTIMATE GROUP, Job 19:19 i. detest me
Jer 23:22 if they had stood in my i., then
Ps 89:7; 111:1; Jer 15:17; 23:18; Eze 13:9.
INTOXICATE, Pr 5:19 let her breasts i.
INTOXICATED, Ge 9:21 Noah became i.
Hag 1:6 not to the point of getting i.
Joh 2:10 when people are i., the inferior
INTOXICATING LIQUOR, Pr 31:6 Give i. to
Le 10:9; Pr 20:1; Isa 28:7.
INTRIGUES, Pr 16:28, 30 man of i. keeps
INVADE, 2Ch 24:23 Syria to i. Judah
INVALIDATE, Job 40:8 you i. my justice?
Ga 3:17 Law that has come later does not i.
INVASION, Mic 5:1 O daughter of an i.
INVENTED, 1Ki 12:33 eighth month he i.
INVENTING, Ne 6:8 saying you are i.
INVENTION, 2Ch 26:15 i. of engineers
INVENTORIED, Ex 38:21 i. of tabernacle
INVESTIGATE, De 13:14 search and i.
Ac 7:31 approaching to i., Jehovah's voice
INVESTIGATING, 1Pe 1:11 i. what season
INVESTIGATION, Job 34:24 without any i.,
Ezr 4:15; 5:17; 6:1.
INVIGORATES, Pr 31:17 she i. her arms.
Isa 58:11 he will i. your very bones, and
INVISIBLE, Ro 1:20 his i. qualities
Col 1:15 He is the image of the i. God,
1Ti 1:17 King of eternity, i.,
Heb 11:27 as seeing the one that is i.
INVITE, Ex 34:15 i. you and you eat
INVITED, Mt 22:14 many i., but few
Zep 1:7; Joh 2:2; Re 19:9.
INVOLVED, 2Pe 2:20 i. again with these
INVOLVES, 2Ti 2:4 serving as a soldier i.
INWARD, Ro 14:1 on i. questionings.
INWARD PART(S), Ps 5:9 i. is adversity
Ps 40:8 And your law is within my i.
Ps 51:6 delight in truthfulness in the i.,
IRON(S), Ps 2:9 break them with an i.
Ps 107:10 Prisoners in affliction and i.
Isa 60:17 instead of i. I shall bring in
Da 2:33 legs were of i., its feet were
1Ti 4:2 conscience as with a branding i.,
1Ki 6:7; Jer 1:18; 28:14; Re 2:27; 12:5.
IRREPREHENSIBLE, 1Ti 3:2 overseer be i.,
1Ti 5:7 commands that they may be i.
1Ti 6:14 observe in a spotless and i. way
IRREVERENT, 2Sa 6:7 struck for the i. act
IRRIGATE, Ec 2:6; Eze 17:7; Joe 3:18.
IRRITATED, Ezr 5:12 fathers i. the God
IRRITATING, Job 6:4 do not be i. your
Job 19:2; Isa 51:23.
ISAAC, Ge 17:19 must call his name I.
Ro 9:7 your seed will be through I.
Ge 22:9; Mt 8:11; Heb 11:17, 20.
ISAIAH, Isa 1:1; Mt 15:7; Ro 15:12.
ISCARIOT, Mt 10:4; 26:14; Joh 6:71.
I SHALL PROVE TO BE, Ex 3:14.
ISHMAEL, Ge 16:11; 25:9; 28:9; Jer 41:6.
ISLAND(S), Ps 97:1 Let the i. rejoice.
Isa 40:15; 41:1; 42:12; Re 6:14; 16:20.
ISOLATING, Pr 18:1 i. himself will seek
ISOLATION, Mt 14:13 Jesus withdrew for i.
ISRAEL, Ge 35:10 i. will your name become
Ex 4:22 I. is my son, my first-born.
1Ch 17:21 what nation is like your people I.
Ho 1:10 i. like the grains of the sand
Ro 9:6 not all from I. are really "I."
Eph 2:12 alienated from the state of I.

Ge 32:28; Ps 135:4; Isa 8:14; 10:20; Eze
36:22; Ac 13:23; Heb 8:10.
ISRAELITE, Joh 1:47 I. for a certainty
Ro 11:1 I also am an I. of the seed
ISSACHAR, Ge 30:18; Jg 5:15; Re 7:7.
ISSUES, Php 3:9 righteousness i. from
ITALY, Heb 13:24 Those in I. send you

J

JABBED, Joh 19:34 j. his side with a
JABIN, Jos 11:1; Jg 4:2, 24; Ps 83:9.
JACHIN, Ge 46:10; 1Ki 7:21; 1Ch 9:10.
JACOB, Ge 25:33 to sell his right to J.
Nu 24:17 A star will step forth out of J.
Jer 30:7 the time of distress for J.
Eze 39:25 bring back captive ones of J.
Ro 9:13 I loved J. but I hated Esau
Heb 11:9 Isaac and J. the heirs with him
Ge 25:26; Ps 14:7; Mic 1:5; Mt 22:32.
JADE, Ex 28:20; Eze 28:13.
JAEL, Jg 4:17, 18, 21, 22; 5:6, 24.
JAH, Ex 15:2 My strength and might is J.
Ps 146:1 Praise J. you people
Isa 12:2 for J. Jehovah is my strength
Ps 68:4; Ca 8:6; Re 19:1.
JAIL, Mt 11:2; Ac 5:21; 16:26.
JAIRUS, Mr 5:22; Lu 8:41.
JAMES 1., Mt 13:55; 1Co 15:7; Jas 1:1.
JAMES 2., Mt 10:3; Mr 15:40; Lu 24:10.
JAMES 3., Mt 4:21; Mr 10:35; Lu 6:14.
JAPHETH, Ge 5:32; 9:27; 1Ch 1:5.
JAR(S), Jg 7:16 j. and torches inside j.
Heb 9:4 golden j. having the manna and the
Jg 7:19, 20; La 4:2.
JAVAN, Ge 10:2; Isa 66:19; Eze 27:13.
JAVELIN, Jos 8:18, 26; 1Sa 17:6.
JAWBONE, Jg 15:15 j. of a male ass
JEALOUS, Ex 34:14 Jehovah, whose name is J.
Nu 11:29 Are you feeling j. for me?
Zec 1:14 j. for Jerusalem
1Co 13:4 Love is not j.
2Co 11:2 I am j. over you with a godly
JEALOUSY, De 32:16 inciting him to j.
Ps 78:58 kept inciting him to j.
Pr 6:34 rage of a man is j.
Pr 14:30 j. is rottenness to the bones.
Ro 10:19 will incite you to j.
1Co 10:22 are we inciting Jehovah to j.?
Nu 5:14; Ec 9:6; Eze 8:3; 1Co 3:3.
JEBUS, Jg 19:10; 1Ch 11:4.
JEBUSI, Jos 18:28 J., Jerusalem
JECONIAH, 1Ch 3:16; Es 2:6; Jer 24:1.
JEER(S), 2Ki 2:23; Eze 22:5; Hab 1:10
JEERING, Ps 44:13; 79:4; Jer 20:8.
JEHOAHAZ, 2Ki 10:35; 23:30; 2Ch 21:17.
JEHOASH, 2Ki 11:21; 13:10; 14:13, 15.
JEHOIACHIN, 2Ch 36:9; Jer 52:31.
JEHOIADA, 2Sa 8:18; 2Ki 11:4; 2Ch 23:16.
JEHOIAKIM, 2Ki 23:34; 24:6; Da 1:2.
JEHONADAB, 2Ki 10:15, 23.
JEHORAM, 1Ki 22:50; 2Ki 1:17; 2Ch 17:8.
JEHOSHAPHAT, Joe 3:2 low plain of J.:
2Ch 17:3, 10; 20:3, 15, 27; Joe 3:12.
JEHOVAH, Ge 18:14 extraordinary for J.
Ex 5:2 who is J.? I do not know J.
Ex 6:3 my name J. I did not make known
Ex 9:29 know that the earth belongs to J.
Ex 15:3 J. is a manly person of war. J. is
Ex 20:7 not take name of J. in worthless way
Ex 34:6 J., J., a God merciful and gracious
Le 19:2 holy, because I J. am holy
De 4:24 J. your God is a consuming fire
De 6:5 must love J. with all your heart
De 10:17 J. is the God of gods and Lord of

1Sa 2:6 J. is a Killer and a Preserver of
1Sa 16:7 J., he sees what the heart is
1Sa 17:47 nor with spear does J. save
1Sa 17:47 to J. belongs the battle
2Sa 22:32 who is a God besides J. a rock
Ne 4:14 J. the great and the fear-inspiring
Ps 3:8 Salvation belongs to J.
Ps 19:7 The law of J. is perfect
Ps 22:28 the kingship belongs to J.
Ps 33:12 happy nation whose God is J.
Ps 34:8 taste and see that J. is good
Ps 83:18 name is J. you alone Most High
Ps 94:1 J., God of acts of vengeance
Ps 113:5 Who is like J. our God
Ps 125:2 So J. is all around his people
Pr 18:10 name of J. is a strong tower
Pr 21:31 battle, but salvation belongs to J.
Isa 26:4 Jah J. is the Rock of times
Isa 30:18 J. is a God of judgment
Isa 33:22 J. is our Judge, Statute-giver,
Isa 40:28 J., the Creator does not tire out
Isa 59:1 hand of J. not short save
Isa 60:19 J. an indefinitely lasting light
Isa 61:1 spirit of the Lord J. is upon me,
Isa 61:2 year of good will on part of J.
Isa 66:1 J.: "The heavens are my throne
Jer 10:10 J. is the living God and the King
Jer 51:6 time of vengeance belonging to J.
Ho 12:5 J. of armies, J. is his memorial
Na 1:2 J. is a God exacting devotion,
Na 1:3 J. is slow to anger
Hab 2:20 J. is in his holy temple. Keep
Zep 2:3 seek J. all you meek ones
Mal 3:6 I am J.; I have not changed
Mt 4:10 J. your God you must worship
Mr 12:29 our God is one J.
Lu 1:46 My soul magnifies J.
Lu 2:26 seen the Christ of J.
Ac 2:34 J. said to my Lord: "Sit at
Ac 9:31 walked in the fear of J. and kept
Ac 21:14 let the will of J. take place
Ro 14:8 we live to J., and die to J.
Ro 15:11 Praise J., all you nations,
1Co 10:21 of "the table of J." and the
1Co 10:26 to J. belongs the earth
2Co 3:17 Now J. is the Spirit; and
Eph 2:21 into a holy temple for J.
Col 3:23 work whole-souled as to J.,
2Th 2:2 the day of J. is here.
2Ti 2:19 J. knows those who belong
Heb 12:6 J. loves he disciplines
Heb 13:6 J. is my helper; I will not be
Jas 4:15 If J. wills, we shall do this or
Jas 5:15 J. will raise him up.
1Pe 1:25 saying of J. endures forever.
2Pe 3:9 J. is not slow respecting his
Jude 9 said: "May J. rebuke you."
Re 4:8 Holy, holy, holy is J. God
Re 19:6 J. our God, the Almighty
Le 19:2; Jos 24:15; 1Sa 14:6; 1Ch 29:11;
Ne 8:10; Ps 31:23; 118:23; Pr 3:5; 8:13;
Isa 12:2; 43:10; 55:8; Jer 17:10; 23:24;
Da 9:4; Joh 1:23; 1Co 1:31; Ga 3:6;
Col 3:13; Heb 8:11; Jas 5:11; 1Pe 3:12.
JEHOVAH (in Authorized Version),
Ex 6:3; Ps 83:18; Isa 12:2; 26:4.
JEHOVAH-JIREH, Ge 22:14 name of place J.
JEHOVAH-NISSI, Ex 17:15 altar name J.,
JEHOVAH OF ARMIES, Isa 8:13; 9:7; 47:4.
JEHOVAH'S, Ex 32:26 Who is on J. side
De 32:9 J. share is his people
2Ki 13:17 J. arrow of salvation
Zep 2:3 concealed in day of J. anger
Mt 1:20 J. angel appeared to him

Lu 1:38 Look! J. slave girl
Lu 2:9 J. glory gleamed around them
Joh 12:13 he that comes in J. name
1Th 4:15 we tell you by J. word
1Th 5:2 J. day is coming exactly
1Pe 3:12 For J. eyes are upon the
2Pe 3:10 J. day will come as a thief,
JEHOVAH-SHALOM, Jg 6:24 altar called J.
JEHU, 1Ki 19:16; 2Ki 9:13; 10:11, 21, 28.
JEPHTHAH, Jg 11:30; Heb 11:32.
JEREMIAH, 2Ch 36:21; Jer 1:1; Da 9:2.
JERICHO, Heb 11:30 walls of J. fell
Jos 2:1; 8:2; 1Ki 16:34.
JEROBOAM, 1Ki 11:28; 2Ki 17:21; Am 7:9.
JERUSALEM, Jos 10:1 king of J. heard
2Sa 5:5 David ruled in J. 33 years
Isa 65:18 creating J. a cause for joy
Eze 9:4 pass through the midst of J., and
Mt 23:37 J., J., the killer of the prophets
Lu 21:24 J. be trampled on by the nations
Ga 4:26 J. above is free our mother
Heb 12:22 approached a city, heavenly J.
Re 21:2 New J., coming down out of heaven
Jos 15:8; Ps 122:6; 125:2; Isa 52:1; 62:6;
Joe 2:32; Mic 4:2; Zec 8:3; Re 3:12.
JESHURUN, De 32:15; 33:5; Isa 44:2.
JESSE, 1Sa 16:1; Isa 11:1; Ro 15:12.
JEST, 2Ch 36:16 making J. at messengers
JESTING, Eph 5:4 obscene J. not becoming
JESUS, Mt 1:21 call his name J.
Mt 27:37 This is J. the King of the Jews
Ac 4:13 men they used to be with J.
Ac 9:5 I am J., whom you are persecuting
Php 2:10 name of J. every knee should bend
Re 20:4 executed for the witness bore to J.
Mt 3:16; 27:17; Lu 2:43; Joh 1:45; 17:3;
Ac 2:36; Ro 6:23; Heb 2:9; 3:1; Re 1:5.
JETHRO, Ex 3:1; 4:18; 18:5.
JEW(S, S'), 2Ki 18:26 in the J. language
Es 8:17 declaring themselves J.
Zec 8:23 take hold of the skirt of a J.
Ro 2:29 he is a J. that is one on the
Ro 3:29 is he the God of the J. only?
1Co 1:23 Christ to J. a cause for falling
1Co 9:20 to the J. I became as a J.
Ga 3:28 There is neither J. nor Greek
Re 3:9 say they are J. and yet they are not
Ne 4:1; Es 3:6; Ac 22; 27:11; Col 3:11.
JEZEBEL, 1Ki 16:31; 21:15, 23; 2Ki 9:30.
JEZREEL, Jg 6:33; 1Ki 18:45; Ho 1:4.
JIGGLE, Am 9:9 J. the house of Israel
JOAB, 2Sa 2:13; 1Ki 2:31.
JOB, Job 2:3 J. a man blameless
Eze 14:14 midst Noah, Daniel and J.
Jas 5:11 heard of the endurance of J.
Job 1:1, 9, 22; 3:1; 38:1; 40:1; 42:10, 12.
JOHN 1., Mt 3:1 J. the Baptist came
Mt 11:11 not a greater than J. the Baptist
Mt 14:10; 21:25; Mr 1:9; Lu 1:13.
JOHN 2., Re 22:8 I J. was the one
Mt 4:21; Ac 3:1; Ga 2:9; Re 1:4.
JOIN, Da 11:34 J. by means of smoothness
JOINED, 1Co 6:16 J. to a harlot is one
1Co 6:17 he who is J. to the Lord is one
Php 2:2 love, being J. together in soul,
Col 2:2, 19 harmoniously J. together in love
JOINT HEIRS, Ro 8:17 J. with Christ
Eph 3:6 people of the nations should be J.
JOINT(S), Eph 4:16; Col 2:19; Heb 4:12.
JOKES, Jer 15:17 those playing J. and
JOKING, Ge 19:14 seemed like a man J.
JONADAB, Jer 35:6, 8, 14, 19.
JONAH, Mt 12:39 sign of J. the prophet.
Jon 1:1; 2:1; 3:1; Lu 11:30.

JONATHAN, 1Sa 18:1, 3; 19:2; 2Sa 1:17, 22.
JOPPA, 2Ch 2:16; Ezr 3:7; Ac 9:42.
JORDAN, Nu 35:14; Jos 3:13; Mr 1:9.
JOSEPH 1., Heb 11:22 By faith J., made
Ge 47:15; Ps 105:17; Ac 7:9.
JOSEPH 2., Mt 1:19; Lu 3:23; Joh 6:42.
JOSHUA, De 31:23; Jos 3:7; Heb 4:8.
JOSIAH, 2Ki 21:24; 2Ch 35:26.
JOTHAM, Jg 9:5; 2Ch 27:6.
JOURNEY, Ge 33:14 J. at my leisure
JOY, Ne 8:10 J. of Jehovah is your
Heb 12:2 For the j. that was set before him
Ezr 3:12; Lu 2:10; Joh 16:22; 2Co 7:4.
JOYFUL, Ps 126:5 reap with j. cry
Ps 149:2 Zion—let them be j. in their King.
Isa 35:1 desert will be j. and blossom
Isa 65:18 and be j. forever in what
1Ch 16:31; Ps 13:5; 35:9; 113:9; 118:24;
Isa 25:9; 49:13; 61:10; Joe 2:23; Zec 9:9.
JOYFULLY, Job 38:7 stars j. cried out
Ps 95:1; Isa 65:14; Heb 10:34.
JOYFULNESS, Isa 65:18 a cause for j.
Ps 45:15; Joe 1:16.
JOYOUS, Heb 12:11 no discipline seems J.,
JOYOUSNESS, Isa 35:2 j. and glad crying
JUBILATE, Ps 68:4 Jah, j. before him
JUBILEE, Le 25:10; 27:24; Nu 36:4.
JUDAH, Ge 49:10 scepter will not J.,
Jer 31:31 conclude with J. a new covenant;
Mic 5:2 J., from you there will come
Ps 60:7; Jer 50:4; Mt 2:6; Heb 8:8.
JUDAISM, Ga 1:13 conduct formerly in J.
JUDAS, Mt 26:25; Lu 6:16; 22:48.
JUDE, Jude 1 J., a slave of Jesus Christ
JUDEA, Mt 24:16; Lu 21:21.
JUDGE(S), Jg 2:16 Jehovah raise up J.
Joh 5:22 the Father j. no one at all, but
Joh 12:48 The word will j. him in the last
Ac 10:42 to be j. of the living and dead.
Ac 13:20 he gave them J. until Samuel the
Ac 17:31 a day in which he purposes to j.
Ro 2:1 you that j. practice the same
Ro 14:4 Who are you to j. the servant
Ro 14:5 One man j. one day as above another;
1Co 5:13 God j. those outside?
1Co 6:2 the holy ones will j. the world?
Col 2:16 let no man j. you in eating
2Ti 4:1 Jesus, is destined to j. the living
1Pe 1:17 the Father j. impartially
De 16:18; Ps 2:10; 9:8; 82:1; Isa 1:26;
11:4; Mic 3:11; Zep 3:3; Joh 3:17; Jas 2:4.
JUDGES, Ps 9:19 nations be j. before
Joh 3:18 He has been j. already, because
Joh 16:11 ruler of this world has been j.
Re 11:18 time for the dead to be j.,
Ex 18:26; Ps 37:33; 109:7; Ac 25:9.
JUDGING, Pr 29:14 king is j. lowly ones
Mt 19:28 you j. the twelve tribes
Lu 6:37 stop j., and you will by no means
Ps 58:11; 109:31; Jer 11:20; Joh 8:50.
JUDGMENT(S), Isa 2:4 render j. among the
Joe 3:2 I will put myself on j. with
Mt 12:41 Men of Nineveh rise up in the j.
Mt 23:33 are you to flee the j. of Gehenna?
Joh 5:29 vile things to a resurrection of j.
Ro 11:33 How unsearchable his j. are and
1Co 11:29 and drinks j. against himself
2Ti 1:5 a proof of the righteous j. of God,
Heb 9:27 men to die after this a j.,
Heb 10:27 certain fearful expectation of j.
Jas 2:13 Mercy exults triumphantly over j.
1Pe 4:17 j. to start with the house of God.
2Pe 2:3 the j. of ancient times is not
2Pe 3:7 reserved to the day of j. of ungodly

1Jo 4:17 freeness of speech in day of j.
Re 19:2 his j. are true and righteous
Ex 7:4; 12:12; Ps 89:14; Isa 1:17; 26:9;
54:17; Jer 25:31; Ac 24:25; Jude 6.
JUDGMENT DAY, Mt 10:15 Gomorrah on J.
JUDGMENT SEAT, Ro 14:10 j. of God;
Joh 19:13; Ac 18:12; 25:10; 2Co 5:10.
JUDICIAL ANTAGONIST, Isa 50:8.
JUDICIAL CASES, 1Ki 3:11 to hear j.
JUDICIAL DECISION(S), De 4:8 nation has j.
1Ch 16:14 in all the earth are his j.
Ps 19:9 The j. of Jehovah are true;
Ps 25:9 cause the meek to walk in his j.
Ps 119:91 According to your j. they have
Ps 119:108 teach me your own j.
Ps 149:9 execute the j. written.
Zep 2:3 you meek have practiced His j.
Le 18:5; 1Ki 3:28; Ps 36:6; Eze 11:20.
JUDICIAL PUNISHMENT, 2Th 1:9 undergo j.
JUG, 1Sa 26:11, 16; 1Ki 19:6.
JURISDICTION, Ac 1:7 Father in his j.
JURISDICTIONAL DISTRICTS, 1Ki 20:14; Ezr
2:1; Es 1:1; Ec 2:8; Eze 19:8.
JUST CLAIM, 2Sa 19:28 j. for crying out
JUSTICE, Ru 1:1 judges administered j.
Job 40:8 will you invalidate my j.?
Ps 37:28 Jehovah is a lover of j.
Pr 16:8 abundance of products without j.
Pr 21:7 for they have refused to do j.
Pr 29:4 By j. a king makes a land keep
Isa 28:17 I will make j. the measuring line
Isa 32:1 they will rule as princes for j.
Isa 61:8 I, Jehovah, am loving j., hating
Mic 6:8 but to exercise j. and to
Mal 2:17 Where is the God of j.?
Mt 12:20 sends out j. with success
Lu 18:7 shall not God cause j. to be done
Heb 2:2 retribution in harmony with j.
Job 29:14; Isa 1:17; 28:6; Jer 22:3; Mic 3:
1, 9; 7:9; Hab 1:4; Mal 2:17.
JUSTIFICATION, Ro 5:18 through one act of j.
JUSTIFY. See DECLARED RIGHTEOUS.
JUSTLY, Lu 23:41 j. so, we deserve
JUSTNESS, Job 27:6 my j. I shall not let go

K

KADESH, Ge 14:7; De 1:46; Ps 29:8.
KADESH-BARNEA, Nu 32:8; 34:4; De 1:2;
9:23; Jos 10:41; 15:3.
KEDESH, Jos 20:7; Jg 4:9; 1Ch 6:72.
KEEP, Ge 17:9 you are to k. my covenant,
Ex 20:6; Isa 56:1; Jas 1:27; Jude 21.
KEEP AN EYE, Ga 6:1 k. on yourself,
KEEPING, De 7:9 God, k. covenant and
Isa 56:2 k. the sabbath in order not to
KEEPS, Job 33:18 He k. his soul from
Re 16:15 k. his outer garments, that he
KEEPS CLEAR, 2Ti 2:21 k. of the latter
KEEP SENSES, 1Th 5:6 awake and k.
1Th 5:8 k. and have on the breastplate
2Ti 4:5 k. in all things, suffer
1Pe 1:13 k. completely; set your hope
KEEP TESTING, 2Co 13:5 K. whether you
KENITE(S), Ge 15:19; Jg 1:16; 5:24.
KEPT, Ex 9:16 have k. you in existence,
KESIL CONSTELLATION, Isa 13:10.
KETURAH, Ge 25:1; 1Ch 1:32.
KEY(S), Mt 16:19 the k. of the kingdom
Lu 11:52 took away the k. of knowledge;
Re 1:18 have the k. of death and of Hades
Re 20:1 with the k. of the abyss
Jg 3:25; Isa 22:22; Re 3:7; 9:1.

KIDNAPED, Ge 40:15 I was k. from the
KIDNAPERS, 1Ti 1:10 k. of men, liars,
KIDNAPING, De 24:7 man found k. his
KIDNEYS, Ex 29:13; Ps 7:9; Jer 11:20.
KIDRON, 2Sa 15:23; 2Ch 15:16; Joh 18:1.
KIDS, Le 16:5 male k. for sin offering
KILL, Nu 25:5 Each one k. his men who
  Eze 9:6 child and women you should k.
  Mt 10:28 fearful of those who k. the body
  Mt 24:9 tribulation and will k. you
  Ge 37:20; Ne 4:11; Am 9:1; Zec 11:5.
KILLED, Ps 44:22 been k. all day long
  Mt 16:21 k. and on third day be raised up
  Ro 11:3 they have k. your prophets
  Ac 3:15; 7:52; Re 2:13; 9:18; 13:15.
KILLER, 1Sa 2:6 Jehovah is a K. and a
KILLING, Lu 12:5 Fear him who after k.
KILLS, Joh 16:2 everyone that k. you
KIND(S), Ge 1:11 according to their k.,
  Eze 47:10 In their k. their fish will be,
  1Co 13:4 love is k.
  Ge 1:25; 6:20; Le 11:14; De 14:13.
KINDLY, Pr 22:9 He that is k. will be
KINDNESS, Mic 6:8 justice and love k.
  Ro 11:22 See God's k. and severity
  2Co 10:1 by the k. of Christ
  Ga 5:22 the fruitage of the spirit is k.,
  Ac 28:2; 2Co 6:6; Col 3:12; Tit 3:4.
KING(S), 1Sa 8:19 k. will come over us
  Ps 2:2 k. of earth take their stand
  Ps 110:5 break k. to pieces on the day of
  Isa 32:1 A k. will reign for righteousness
  Jer 10:10 Jehovah is the K. to time
  Zec 14:9 Jehovah must become k. over earth
  Mt 21:5 Look! Your K. is coming to you
  Mt 27:37 Jesus the K. of the Jews
  Lu 21:12 haled before k. and governors for
  Joh 1:49 Rabbi you are K. of Israel
  Joh 18:37 you are saying that I am a k.
  Joh 19:15 We have no k. but Caesar
  1Ti 1:17 the K. of eternity, incorruptible,
  Re 16:14 go forth to the k. of entire earth
  Re 19:16 K. of kings and Lord of lords
  Jg 5:19; 9:8; 2Ch 9:22; Ps 89:27; Isa 41:
    21; Da 4:37; Ac 17:7; 1Ti 6:15.
KINGDOM(S), Ex 19:6 a k. of priests
  2Ki 19:19 all k. of the earth may know that
  1Ch 29:11 Yours is the k., O Jehovah
  Da 2:44 God of heaven will set up a k.
  Da 7:27 their k. an indefinitely lasting k.
  Zep 3:8 my decision to collect k. to pour
  Mt 6:10 Let your k. come. Let your
  Mt 6:33 seeking first the k. and his
  Mt 24:14 this good news of the k. will be
  Mt 25:34 Come, inherit the k. prepared for
  Lu 12:32 approved of giving you the k.
  Lu 22:29 make a covenant with you for a k.
  Joh 18:36 my k. is no part of this world
  1Co 15:24 hands over the k. to his God
  Col 1:13 transplanted us into the k. of
  Heb 11:33 who through faith defeated k.
  Re 1:6 made us a k., priests to his God
  Re 11:15 k. of the world has become the k.
  Ezr 1:2; Isa 9:7; 23:17; Jer 25:26; Mt 4:
    8; 2Ti 4:1; Jas 2:5; Re 5:10.
KINGDOM OF GOD, Mt 21:43 K. taken from
  Mr 4:11 sacred secret of the k. has been
  Lu 9:62 looks behind is fitted for the k.
  Lu 17:20 k. not coming with observableness
  Ac 14:22 enter k. through tribulations.''
  Lu 6:20; Ro 14:17; 1Co 6:9; 15:50.
KINGDOM OF HEAVENS, Mt 3:2 k. near.
  Mt 10:7 preach saying, The k. has drawn
  Mt 23:13 shut up the k. before mankind

KING OF THE NORTH, Da 11:6-8, 15, 40.
KING OF THE SOUTH, Da 11:11, 25, 40.
KINSMAN, Ru 3:2 is not Boaz our k.
KISH, 1Sa 9:1; Es 2:5; Ac 13:21.
KISHON, Jg 4:7; 1Ki 18:40; Ps 83:9.
KISS, Ps 2:12 K. the son that He may not
  Lu 22:48 you betray Son of man with a k.?
  Ro 16:16 Greet one another with a holy k.
KISSED, 1Ki 19:18 has not k. him
  Lu 7:38; 15:20; Ac 20:37.
KISSES, Pr 27:6 k. of a hater are
KNEE(S), Ro 11:4 not bowed k. to Baal
  Php 2:10 name of Jesus every k. should bend
  Isa 45:23; Eze 7:17; Ro 14:11; Heb 12:12.
KNOCKED, Ac 12:13 k. Rhoda came to
KNOCKING, Mt 7:7; Re 3:20.
KNOW, 1Sa 17:46 k. there exists a God
  Ps 83:18 people may k. that you whose name
  Jer 31:34 all k. me from least to greatest
  Eze 2:5 k. that a prophet happened to be in
  Eze 6:7 k. that I am Jehovah
  Joh 8:32 k. the truth and truth will set
  Joh 10:14 I k. my sheep and my sheep k. me
  Ro 8:28 we k. God makes all works co-operate
  2Co 5:16 we k. no man according to flesh.
  De 4:39; Ps 20:6; Isa 43:10; 1Jo 3:2.
KNOWING, Ge 3:5 k. good and bad.
  Da 11:32 people who are k. their God,
KNOWLEDGE. See also ACCURATE KNOWLEDGE.
KNOWLEDGE, Pr 1:7 fear beginning of k.
  Pr 15:7 wise ones' keep scattering k. about,
  Ec 9:10 nor k. nor wisdom in Sheol
  Isa 11:9 earth filled with k. of Jehovah
  Da 1:4 k., and discernment of what is known,
  Da 12:4 rove about and k. become abundant
  Ho 4:6 silenced because there is no k.
  Lu 11:52 you took away the key of k.
  Joh 17:3 means life their taking in k. of
  1Ti 6:20 contradictions of falsely called k.
  Ge 2:9; Ps 19:2; Pr 1:29; 8:10; 9:9; 10:14;
    14:18; Isa 44:25; 53:11; Jer 3:15; Mal 2:7;
    Ro 11:33; 1Co 8:1; 2Pe 3:18.
KNOWLEDGE, ACCURATE, Ro 1:28; 3:20.
  Eph 4:13 attain oneness in faith and a.
  1Ti 2:4 all men should come to an a.
  2Ti 3:7 never come to an a. of truth.
KNOWN, Mt 10:26 secret not become k.
  1Co 13:12 even as I am accurately k.
KNOW THAT I AM JEHOVAH, Ex 7:5; 14:4;
    31:13; Isa 49:23; Eze 6:7; 7:4; 11:12;
    12:20; 13:23; 14:8; 15:7; 16:62; 20:44;
    22:16; 25:5; 26:6; 28:22; 34:27; 35:9;
    37:6; 38:23; 39:7, 28.
KORAH, Nu 16:1; 26:9-11; Jude 11.

L

LABAN, Ge 24:29; 29:5; 31:24, 48; 32:4.
LABOR(S), 1Co 15:58 l. is not in vain in
  2Co 11:23 in l. more plentifully,
  Re 14:13 their l., go right with them.
  Joh 4:38; 1Co 3:8; 1Th 2:9; 3:5; 2Th 3:8.
LABORED, Joh 4:38; 1Co 15:10.
LABORING, 1Co 16:16 co-operating and l.
LABOR PAINS, Isa 66:8 land brought forth with l.
  Jer 6:24 l. of a woman
LACHISH, Jos 10:3; 2Ki 14:19; Jer 34:7.
LACKING, Jas 1:5 anyone is l. in wisdom,
LACK OF FAITH, Heb 6:6 at their l.
  Ro 4:20 he did not waver in a l.
  Ro 11:23 if they do not remain in their l.,
  Heb 3:19 could not enter in because of l.
  Mt 13:58; Ro 3:3; 11:20; 1Ti 1:13.
LAD, 1Sa 17:56; 20:22.
LADDER, Ge 28:12 l. reaching heavens

LADY, 1Ki 11:19; 15:13; Jer 13:18; 29:2.
LAID HOLD, Php 3:12 l. on by Christ
LAKE, Re 19:20; 21:8 fiery l. that burns
LAKE OF FIRE, Re 20:14, 15.
LAMB(S), Isa 40:11 collect the l.
  Lu 10:3 sending you as l. in among wolves.
  Joh 1:29 See, the L. of God that takes
  Joh 21:15 Feed my l.
  Isa 1:11; Jer 11:19; Re 5:6; 7:10.
LAME, Isa 35:6 l. will climb up
  Mal 1:8, 13; Mt 15:30; Heb 12:13.
LAMECH, Ge 4:18; 5:25; 1Ch 1:3; Lu 3:36.
LAMENT, Eze 32:18; Mic 2:4.
LAMENTATION, Jer 31:15 In Ramah, l. and
  Jer 9:10, 20; Eze 27:32; Am 5:16; Mic 2:4.
LAMP(S), 2Sa 22:29 you are my l. Jehovah
  1Ki 15:4 God gave him a l. his son
  Ps 119:105 Your word is a l.
  Pr 6:23 the commandment is a l., and
  Pr 13:9 l. of the wicked ones extinguished.
  Mt 5:15 light a l., not under the basket,
  Mt 6:22 The l. of the body is the eye.
  Mt 25:1 ten virgins took their l.
  Lu 12:35 Let your l. be burning,
  Ps 18:28; Pr 24:7; Joh 5:35; Re 4:5.
LAMPLIGHT, Re 22:5 no need of l. nor do
LAMPSTAND(S), Ex 25:31 a l. of gold.
  1Ch 28:15; Heb 9:2; Re 1:12, 13, 20; 2:1.
LAND, Ge 13:15 l. I am going to give
  Ex 3:8 l. good and spacious, a l. flowing
  Isa 66:8 Will a l. be brought forth
  Da 11:41 into the l. of the Decoration,
  Ge 1:9; Le 26:34; Ps 88:12; 107:3; Eze
  36:35; 39:27; Joe 2:3; Mt 19:29.
LAND DOWN BELOW, Eze 31:14; 32:18.
LANDED ESTATES, Ps 49:11 l. by names.
LAND OF CESSATION, Isa 38:11 see in l.
LAND OF DELIGHT, Mal 3:12 become a l.,
LAND OF OBLIVION, Ps 88:12 in the l.?
LAND(S) OF THE LIVING, Ps 116:9 walk in l.
  Job 28:13; Ps 52:5; 142:5; Isa 38:11; 53:8.
LANDOWNERS, Jos 24:11; Jg 9:2; 20:5.
LANGUAGE(S), Ge 11:1 one l. and one set
  Ge 11:7 Let us go down and confuse their l.
  Da 7:14 and l. should all serve him.
  Zep 3:9 give to peoples a pure l.,
  Zec 8:23 ten men out of all the l. of
  Ac 2:6 heard them speaking in his own l.
  Ps 81:5; Isa 36:11; Re 5:15; Zec 3:5, 6.
LANGUISH, Jer 31:12 no more will they l.
LANGUISHED, Ps 88:9 My eye has l.
LANGUISHING, Jer 31:25 l. soul I will
LAODICEA, Col 2:1; 4:16; Re 1:11; 3:14.
LAPS, Jg 7:5 one that l. up some water
LAST, Isa 44:6 Jehovah the first and l.,
  Mt 19:30 many that are first will be l.
  1Co 15:26 l. enemy, death is to be destroyed.
  1Co 15:45 l. Adam, a life-giving spirit
  Re 22:13 I am the first and the l.,
  Mt 20:8, 16; Mr 9:35; 1Jo 2:18; Re 1:17.
LAST DAY(S), Joh 6:54 resurrect at l.;
  2Ti 3:1 l. critical times will be here.
  Jas 5:3 fire is stored up in the l.
  2Pe 3:3 in the l. will come ridiculers
  Ne 8:18; Joh 11:24; 12:48.
LASTING LIFE, Da 12:2 wake up, to l.
LATE, Isa 46:13 salvation will not be l.
LATER, Hag 2:9 glory of this l. house
LAUD, Ps 6:5 In Sheol who will l. you?
  1Ki 8:33; Ps 9:1; 44:8; 138:1.
LAUGH, Ps 2:4 Sitting in the heavens l.;
  Ps 37:13 Jehovah himself will l. at him,
  Pr 1:26 I shall l. at your disaster,
  Ge 18:15; 21:6; Ps 59:8; Ec 3:4.

LAUGHABLE, Hab 1:10 something l. to it.
LAUGHED, Ac 2:13 different ones l. at
LAUGHING, Lu 6:25 Woe, you who are l.
LAUGHINGSTOCK, Job 12:4 l. to his fellow
LAUGHTER, Ps 126:2 mouth filled with l.
  Jer 20:7 I became an object of l. all day
  Jas 4:9 Let your l. be turned into mourning,
  Pr 14:13; Ec 2:2; 7:3; 10:19.
LAUNCHES, Pr 12:17 l. forth faithfulness
  Pr 14:25 deceitful one l. forth mere lies.
  Pr 19:5 that l. forth lies will not escape.
LAUNDRYMAN, Isa 7:3; 36:2.
LAUNDRYMEN, Mal 3:2 like the lye of l.
LAVISHING, Isa 46:6 l. gold from purse
LAW(S), Ex 24:12 want to give you the l.
  Es 3:8 their l. are different from all
  Es 9:1 king's l. came due to be performed,
  Ps 19:7 The l. of Jehovah is perfect,
  Ps 40:8 your l. is within my inward parts.
  Pr 6:20 not forsake the l. of your mother.
  Isa 2:3 out of Zion l. will go forth,
  Jer 24:5 bypassed the l., changed the
  Da 6:15 the l. belonging to the Medes and
  Lu 16:16 The L. and the Prophets were until
  Lu 24:44 things written in the L. of Moses
  Joh 10:34 Is it not written in your L.
  Ro 2:14 do by nature the thing of the l.
  Ro 4:15 where there is no l., neither
  Ro 7:2 discharged from the l. of husband
  Ro 7:12 on its part, the l. is holy, and
  Ro 7:22 I delight in the l. of God
  Ro 7:23 against the l. of my mind
  Ro 8:2 free from the l. of sin and death
  Ga 3:24 L. has become our tutor to Christ,
  Ga 6:2 fulfill the l. of the Christ
  Heb 10:1 L. has a shadow of the good
  Jas 2:8 carrying out the kingly l.
  Ne 9:13; Isa 8:16; Jer 31:33; Da 6:5;
  Mt 5:17; Ro 6:14; 10:4; 13:8; Ga 3:19.
LAW-DEFYING, 2Pe 2:7; 3:17 l. people
LAWFUL, Mr 12:14 it l. to pay tribute
  Lu 14:3 Is it l. on the sabbath to cure
  Lu 20:22 Is it l. for us to pay Caesar
  1Co 6:12 All things are l.; but not all
  Mr 2:26; Ac 22:25; 1Co 10:23; 2Co 12:4.
LAWGIVER, Jas 4:12 One is l. and judge,
LAWLESS, Lu 22:37 was reckoned with l.
  2Th 2:8 the l. one will be revealed,
  Ac 2:23; 1Ti 1:9; 2Pe 2:8.
LAWLESS DEEDS, Ro 4:7; Heb 10:17.
LAWLESSNESS, Mt 13:41 collect out l.
  Mt 24:12 of the increasing of l. the love of
  2Co 6:14 partner does righteousness and l.
  2Th 2:7 the mystery of this l. is already
  Heb 1:9 loved righteousness and hated l.
  1Jo 3:4 practicing l., and so sin is l.
  Mt 7:23; 23:28; Ro 6:19; 2Th 2:3.
LAWSUITS, 1Co 6:7 l. with one another
LAZARUS, Lu 16:20; Joh 11:1, 2; 12:1.
LAZINESS, Pr 19:15 L. causes sleep
  Pr 31:27 the bread of l. she does not eat
  Ec 10:18 through l. beamwork sinks in
LAZY, Pr 6:6 Go to the ant, you l. one;
  Pr 15:19 The way of the l. one is like a
  Pr 20:4 the l. one will not plow;
  Pr 26:15 The l. one has hidden his hand
  Pr 10:26; 13:4; 19:24; 21:25; 26:13.
LEAD, Ps 31:3 sake of your name l. me.
  Ps 43:3 light and your truth l. me.
  Ps 143:10 l. me in the land of uprightness.
  Heb 13:7, 17 those taking the l. among you
  Ex 13:21; Pr 23:19; Isa 9:16; 1Co 9:5.
LEADER(S), 1Sa 9:16 anoint him l. over
  1Sa 25:30 commission you as l. over Israel

2Sa 7:8 took you to become a **l.** over my
Isa 11:6 a little boy will be **l.** over them.
Isa 55:4 given him as **l.** and commander
Mt 23:10 Neither be called **l.**, for your **L.**
De 32:42; 1Ch 13:1; 2Ch 32:21.
LEADING, De 32:12 Jehovah alone kept **l.**
Isa 3:12 those **l.** you to wander,
LEADS, Ps 23:3 He **l.** me for his name's
Pr 11:3 integrity of the upright **l.** them,
LEAGUED, 2Ki 12:20; 14:19.
LEAH, Ge 29:23; Ru 4:11.
LEAKING, Pr 27:15 **l.** roof that drives
LEAN, Pr 3:5 not **l.** upon own understanding
Isa 17:4; Eze 34:20.
LEANING, Ps 62:3 like a **l.** wall
LEAP, Hab 3:6 He caused nations to **l.**
Lu 6:23 Rejoice and **l.**, for your reward
LEARN, De 31:12 order that they may **l.**
Isa 2:4 neither will they **l.** war any more.
Mic 4:3 neither will they **l.** war any more.
1Co 14:35 If they want to **l.** let them ask
1Ti 5:13 they **l.** to be unoccupied, gadding
De 4:10; Ps 119:73; 1Co 14:31; 1Ti 2:11.
LEARNED, Ro 16:17 teaching which you **l.**,
Php 4:9 The things which you **l.** practice
Heb 5:8 **l.** obedience from things suffered,
Pr 30:3; Joh 6:45; Php 4:11, 12; 2Ti 3:14.
LEARNING, Pr 9:9 he will increase in **l.**
Ac 26:24 Great **l.** is driving you into
2Ti 3:7 always **l.** and yet never able to
LEAST, Jer 31:34 from the **l.** one to the
Mt 25:40 **l.** of these my brothers, you did
Lu 16:10 person faithful in what is **l.**
Heb 8:11 they all will know me, from the **l.**
Ge 24:55; Mt 5:19; Lu 12:26; 1Co 15:9.
LEATHER, 2Ki 1:8 **l.** belt girded about
LEAVE, De 31:8 neither desert nor **l.** you
Ps 27:10 father and mother did **l.** me
Ps 37:28 not **l.** his loyal ones
LEAVEN. See also SOUR DOUGH.
LEAVEN, Mt 16:6 watch out for the **l.** of
Lu 13:21 **l.**, which a woman took and mixed
1Co 5:7, 8 Clear away the old **l.**,
Ga 5:9 little **l.** ferments the whole lump.
Mt 13:33; 16:12; Mr 8:15; Lu 12:1.
LEAVENED, Am 4:5 what is **l.** make
Ex 12:15; 34:25; Le 2:11; De 16:3; Ho 7:4.
LEAVES, Re 22:2 **l.** were for curing of
LEAVING, Pr 10:17 he that is **l.** reproof
Isa 1:28 those **l.** Jehovah their finish.
Da 11:30 to those **l.** the holy covenant.
Pr 15:10; 28:13; Jer 17:13.
LEBANON, De 3:25; Isa 35:2; Eze 17:3.
LED, Isa 9:16 those **l.** on, are confused.
Ro 8:14 all **l.** by spirit are God's sons.
Mt 4:1; Lu 22:54; Ga 5:18.
LEECHES, Pr 30:15 **l.** have two daughters
LEFT, Isa 1:4 They **l.** Jehovah, turned
Isa 54:7 For a moment I **l.** you but with
Isa 62:4 No more will you be a woman **l.**
Eze 9:9 Jehovah has **l.** the land
Mt 19:29 Everyone that has **l.** father
Ro 9:29 Unless Jehovah had **l.** a seed to us,
LEFT ENTIRELY, Ps 37:25 not righteous **l.**,
LEFT OVER, Pr 2:21 blameless will be **l.**
LEGAL CASE, Pr 25:8 conduct **l.** hastily,
Isa 34:8 retributions for the **l.** over Zion.
Mic 6:2 Jehovah has a **l.** with his people
2Sa 15:4; Ps 43:1; Pr 18:17; Ho 4:1; 12:2.
LEGAL CLAIM, Ps 140:12 **l.** of the afflicted
LEGALLY ESTABLISHED, Heb 8:6 covenant **l.**
LEGALLY ESTABLISHING, Php 1:7 **l.** good
LEGAL REQUIREMENTS, Lu 1:6 **l.** of Jehovah
Heb 9:10 They were **l.** pertaining to flesh

LEGAL RIGHT, Eze 21:27 he who has **l.**
LEGS, Joh 19:31-33 not break his **l.**
LEISURE, Ge 33:14 journey at my **l.**
LEND, Lu 6:35 **l.** without interest,
Ex 22:25; De 28:44.
LENDER, Isa 24:2 same for **l.** as for the
LENDING, Ps 37:26 All day long he is **l.**,
Pr 22:7 servant to the man doing **l.**
Ps 112:5; Pr 19:17.
LENGTHEN, Isa 54:2 **l.** your tent cords,
LEOPARD(S), Jer 13:23 a **l.** its spots?
Ca 4:8; Isa 11:6; Da 7:6; Re 13:2.
LEPER(S), Mt 11:5; 26:6; Lu 4:27.
LEPROSY, Nu 12:10 Miriam struck with **l.**
Le 13:2; De 24:8; 2Ki 5:3, 27; Lu 5:12.
LESS, Heb 7:7 **l.** is blessed by greater.
LESSER ONE, Mt 11:11 a **l.** in the kingdom
Lu 9:48 conducts himself as a **l.** is great.
LETTER(S), 2Ki 19:14 took the **l.** and
2Co 3:1 need **l.** of recommendation to you
Ezr 4:7; 7:11; Jer 29:29; Ac 23:25.
LEVELED, Lu 3:5 every hill **l.** down
LEVELING INSTRUMENT, 2Ki 21:13.
Isa 28:17 and righteousness the **l.**
LEVI, Ge 29:34 His name was **L.**
Ex 32:26 all the sons of **L.** gathering
De 10:9 **L.** has no share and inheritance
Mal 3:3 he must cleanse the sons of **L.**;
Ge 35:23; Nu 18:21; Ps 135:20; Re 7:7.
LEVIATHAN, Isa 27:1 **L.**, the serpent,
Job 41:1; Ps 74:14; 104:26.
LEVITES, Nu 3:12 the **L.** become mine.
Nu 8:19 **L.** as given ones to Aaron
Nu 35:6 to the **L.**: six cities of refuge,
Nu 3:41; 1Ch 15:2, 16; 2Ch 23:7.
LIABILITY, 1Ki 8:31 bring him under **l.**
Mt 5:22 fool! be **l.** to Gehenna
LIABLE, Mt 26:66 He is **l.** to death
Ro 3:19 become **l.** to God for punishment
LIAR(S), Joh 8:44 Devil is a **l.** and
Ro 3:4 God be true, though every man a **l.**,
1Jo 1:10 not sinned, we are making him a **l.**
1Jo 5:10 person not in God made him a **l.**
Pr 30:6; 1Jo 2:4, 22; 4:20; Re 21:8.
LIBATION, Isa 30:1 pour a **l.**, but not
Liberal, 2Co 8:20 **l.** contribution to
LIBERALITY, Ro 12:8 distributes, with **l.**;
LIBERTY, Le 25:10 proclaim **l.** in the land
Isa 61:1 proclaim **l.** to those captive
Jer 34:17 proclaim a **l.** to the sword
Eze 46:17 become his until the year of **l.**;
LIBYA, Ac 2:10 the parts of **L.** which
LIBYANS, Da 11:43 **L.** will be at his steps
LIE(S), Nu 23:19 God is not to tell **l.**
Pr 6:19 a false witness launches forth **l.**,
Pr 14:5 A faithful witness will not **l.**,
Isa 28:15 we have made a **l.** our refuge
Da 11:27 at one table a **l.** they will keep
Joh 8:44 he is a liar and father of the **l.**
Ro 1:25 exchanged the truth for the **l.**
2Th 2:11 they may get to believing the **l.**,
Heb 6:18 it is impossible for God to **l.**,
Jg 16:10; Ps 89:35; Hab 2:3; Zep 3:13;
1Ti 4:2; Re 21:27; 22:15.
LIE DOWN, Ex 22:16; De 22:25; 2Sa 11:4.
LIES DOWN, De 27:21 cursed who **l.** with beast
LIFE('S), Ge 2:7 breath of **l.** and man
Ge 3:22 take fruit of the tree of **l.**
De 28:66 not be sure of your **l.**
1Sa 25:29 wrapped in the bag of **l.**
Ps 36:9 with you is source of **l.**;
Da 12:2 wake up, these to lasting **l.** and
Jon 2:6 out of the pit you bring up my **l.**
Joh 3:16 not be destroyed but have **l.**

Joh 5:26 Father has in himself l.,
Joh 11:25 I am the resurrection and the l.
Joh 11:25 though he dies, will come to l.
Joh 14:6 I am the way truth and the l.
Joh 17:3 This means everlasting l., taking in
Ro 6:23 gift God gives is everlasting l.
1Jo 1:2 l. was made manifest, we have seen
Re 2:10 I will give you the crown of l.
Re 20:15 not found written in the book of l.
Re 22:14 authority to go to the trees of l.
Re 22:17 anyone that wishes take l. water
De 30:15; Pr 27:1; Pr 15:24; 22:4; Mal 2:5;
Joh 5:24; Jas 1:12; 1Pe 3:10; Re 7:17.
LIFE-GIVING, 1Co 15:45 last Adam a l.
LIFELESS, Jer 25:37 abiding places l.
LIFE'S DURATION, Job 11:17; Ps 39:5.
LIFE'S MOISTURE, Ps 32:4 My l. has been
LIFE SPAN, Mt 6:27; Lu 12:25.
LIFETIME, Ps 30:5 good will is for a l.
Lu 16:25 in full good things in your l.,
LIFT, Isa 14:13 Above stars I shall l. my
LIFTED, Isa 2:2 l. up above the hills,
LIGAMENTS, Col 2:19 joined by l.
LIGHT(S), Ps 97:11 L. for the righteous
Ps 119:105 Your word is a l. to my roadway.
Pr 4:18 bright l. that is getting lighter
Isa 42:6 as a l. of the nations,
Isa 60:1 Arise, shed forth l., for your l.
Mt 5:16 let your l. shine before mankind,
Joh 3:19 loved the darkness rather than l.,
Joh 8:12 I am the l. of the world.
2Co 11:14 himself into an angel of l.
1Ti 6:16 who dwells in unapproachable l.,
Jas 1:17 the Father of the celestial l.,
1Pe 2:9 darkness into his wonderful l.,
Ge 1:3; Zec 14:6; 1Jo 1:5, 7; Re 22:5.
LIGHTED, Re 18:1 l. up from his glory.
Ps 77:18; 97:4; Re 21:23.
LIGHTER, Pr 4:18 light getting l. and l.
LIGHTNING(S), Job 38:35 you send l.
Ps 97:4 His l. lighted up the land;
Mt 24:27 l. comes out of eastern parts
Lu 10:18 Satan fallen like l. from heaven.
Re 11:19 occurred l. and voices and loud
Ex 20:18; Job 37:3; Na 2:4; Re 4:5; 8:5.
LIKEN, Isa 40:18 to whom can you l. God
LIKENESS, Ge 1:26 make man to our l.,
Ro 6:5 united in the l. of his death,
Php 2:7 came to be in the l. of men.
Isa 40:18; Da 10:16; Ro 8:3.
LIMIT, Job 14:13 set a time l. for me
Job 34:36 Job tested to the l.
LIMPING, 1Ki 18:21 l. upon two opinions
Mic 4:7 make her that was l. a remnant,
LINE. See also MEASURING LINE.
LINE, Pr 11:19 in l. for life,
2Sa 8:2; Isa 28:10; Jer 31:39.
LINEN, Eze 9:2 one man clothed in l.,
Re 19:8 l. stands for the righteous acts
Le 16:4; De 22:11; Da 12:6, 7; Re 19:14.
LINE OF THOUGHT, 1Co 1:10 united in l.
LION(S), Pr 28:1 righteous are like a l.
Isa 11:7 l. will eat straw like the bull.
Isa 35:9 no l. will prove to be there,
Heb 11:33 stopped the mouths of l.,
1Pe 5:8 Devil, walks about like roaring l.,
Re 5:5 the L. that is of the tribe of Judah,
Jg 14:9; 1Sa 17:36; Ps 91:13; Da 6:27;
Joe 1:6; Mic 5:8; Zep 3:3; Re 13:2.
LIP(S), Pr 10:21 l. of the righteous
Pr 15:7 l. of wise keep scattering knowledge
Isa 6:5 Woe a man unclean in l. I am
Ho 14:2 offer the bulls of our l.
Mal 2:7 l. of a priest should keep knowledge.

Mt 15:8 people honors me with their l.,
Heb 13:15 sacrifice the fruit of l. which
1Pe 3:10 his l. from speaking deception,
Job 2:10; Ps 31:18; 106:33; Isa 30:27.
LIQUIFIED, Eze 22:21, 22; 24:11.
LIQUOR, INTOXICATING, Le 10:9; Nu 6:3;
Jg 13:4; Ps 69:12; Pr 20:1; Isa 28:7.
LIST, 1Ti 5:9 a widow be put on the l.
LISTEN, Pr 1:5 A wise person will l.
Isa 55:3 L., and your soul will keep alive,
Mt 17:5 my Son, the Beloved l. to him.
Joh 8:47 you do not l., because you are not
Joh 9:31 God does not l. to sinners,
Ac 3:23 any soul that does not l. to that
De 4:30; 8:20; 1Ki 20:36; Ps 34:11;
Jer 11:8; Hag 1:12; Mt 11:15; Ac 4:19.
LISTENED, Jg 2:20 not l. to my voice.
Ge 3:17; Ps 81:11; Pr 13:1.
LISTENING, Mr 12:37 crowd was l. to him
Job 34:34; Ps 69:33; Pr 8:34; Mal 3:16.
LISTENS, Lu 10:16 He that l. to you l.
Joh 8:47 He that is from God l. to the
Joh 18:37 on the side of the truth l. to my
LITTLE, Pr 15:16 Better is a l. in the fear
Isa 28:10 here a l., there a l.
Isa 60:22 l. one will become a thousand,
Da 11:34 will be helped with a l. help;
1Ti 4:8 bodily training is beneficial a l.,
Heb 2:9 Jesus, a l. lower than angels,
Ps 8:5; 37:16; 10:5 6; 1Ti 5:23; Jas 3:5.
LITTLE FLOCK, Lu 12:32 Have no fear, l.,
LIVE, De 19:4 manslayer flee there to l.:
Mt 4:4 Man must l., not on bread alone,
Joh 6:51 eats of this bread he will l. forever
Ro 1:17 righteous will l. by faith
Ro 10:5 righteousness of the Law will l. by
Ge 3:22; Ex 33:20; Job 14:14; Ro 8:13.
LIVER, Ex 29:13; Pr 7:23; Eze 21:21.
LIVES, Ro 6:10 life he l., he l. with
Ro 14:7 none of us l. to himself only,
Re 15:7 God, who l. forever and ever.
LIVESTOCK, Ex 9:3 hand is upon your l.
De 3:19 I know you have a great deal of l.
Isa 30:23 Your l. will graze in a spacious
LIVING, De 5:26 heard voice of the l. God
Job 33:30 enlightened with light of those l.
Ps 69:28 of the book of the l.
Ec 9:5 l. are conscious that they will die;
Jer 2:13 me, the source of l. water,
Mt 22:32 He is the God of the l.
Joh 4:10 he would have given you l. water.
Ac 10:42 judge of the l. and the dead.
Ro 6:11 l. with reference to God by Christ
1Th 4:15 we the l. who survive to the
1Ti 3:15 the congregation of the l. God,
Heb 10:31 fall into the hands of the l. God.
1Pe 1:3 gave us a new birth to a l. hope
1Pe 2:5 you as l. stones are being built
Re 1:18 look! I am l. forever and ever.
Le 11:2; Ps 145:16; Isa 38:19; Eze 18:32;
Da 6:26; Zec 14:8; Lu 15:12; 1Th 4:17.
LOAD(S), De 1:12 How can I carry the l.
Mt 11:30 yoke is kindly my l. is light
Mt 23:4 They bind up heavy l. and put
Ga 6:5 each one carry his own l.
Ex 23:5; Nu 11:11; Ps 38:4; Isa 10:27.
LOADED, 2Ti 3:6 women l. down with sins,
LOAF, Mt 26:26 took a l. and broke it
1Co 10:17 one l., partaking of that one l.
1Co 11:26 as often as you eat this l.
LOAFING, Ho 7:14 they kept l. about
LOANS, Pr 22:26 who go security for l.
LOATHE, Le 11:13; De 7:26.
LOATHED, Ps 22:24 nor l. the affliction

LOATHESOME, Le 11:10, 11, 43; 20:25.
LOAVES, Mt 16:12 leaven of the l., but
  Lu 9:13 nothing more than five l. and two
LOAVES OF PRESENTATION, Mt 12:4.
LOCAL COURTS, Mt 10:17; Mr 13:9.
LOCKED, Lu 13:25 householder l. the door
  Lu 11:7; Joh 20:19, 26; Ac 5:23.
LOCUST(S), Ex 10:4 I am bringing l.
  Pr 30:27 the l. have no king,
  De 28:38; Joe 1:4; 2:25; Mt 3:4; Re 9:3.
LODGES, Pr 15:31 l. right in among wise
LOFTINESS, Isa 2:11 l. of men must bow
LOFTY, Pr 6:17 l. eyes, a false tongue,
  Pr 18:12 the heart of a man is l., and
  Isa 57:15 High and L. One, whose name
  Lu 16:15 what is l. among men is disgusting
  Ro 12:16 do not be minding l. things, but
  2Co 10:5 we are overturning every l. thing
  Ps 131:1; Pr 30:13; Eze 17:22; Ro 11:20.
LOGICAL, Lu 1:3 write them in l. order
LOGICALLY, Ac 9:22 he proved l. that
LOIN COVERINGS, Ge 3:7 make l. for themselves
LOINS, Eph 6:14 l. girded with truth,
  Ge 35:11; Lu 12:35.
LOIS, 2Ti 1:5 your grandmother L. and
LOITER, Ro 12:11 Do not l. at business
LONG AGO, Pr 22:28; Isa 44:7; Jer 28:8.
LONG FOR, Ps 45:11 l. your prettiness,
LONGING, Ro 1:11; 2Ti 1:4; 1Pe 2:2.
LONGINGLY, Ps 37:7 And wait l. for him.
LONG-SUFFERING, Ro 9:22 God much l.
  1Co 13:4 Love is l. and obliging. Love is
  1Th 5:14 support the weak, be l. toward all.
  2Ti 4:2 exhort, with all l. and teaching.
  Ro 2:4; Ga 5:22; Eph 4:2; Col 3:12.
LOOK, Ps 27:4 One thing is what I l. for
  Ps 94:9 One forming the eye, can he not l.?
  Isa 51:1 l. to the rock from which hewn
  Heb 12:2 l. intently at the Agent Jesus.
  Isa 17:7; Zec 12:10; 1Co 1:22; Re 18:9.
LOOKING, Ps 37:25 l. for bread
  Mt 14:19 l. to heaven, he said a blessing
  Ps 9:12; Pr 1:28; Isa 26:9; Jas 1:23.
LOOKOUT(S), Isa 21:6 Go, post a l. that
  Mic 7:7 for Jehovah I keep on the l.
LOOKS, Lu 9:62 hand to a plow and l.
LOOSE CONDUCT, Pr 10:23; Ga 5:19.
  1Pe 4:3 proceeded in deeds of l.,
LOOSED, Mt 18:18 will be l. in heaven
  Re 1:5 l. us from our sins by
LOPPED, Ro 11:22 you will be l. off.
LORD(S), De 10:17 Jehovah is L. of l.,
  Ps 110:1 utterance of Jehovah to my L. is:
  Mal 3:1 the L.. whom you people are
  Mt 7:22 L., L., did we not prophesy in your
  Mt 20:25 rulers of the nations l. it over
  Joh 20:18 I have seen the L.!
  Joh 20:28 My L. and my God!
  1Co 7:39 free to be married only in the L.
  1Co 8:5 there are many gods and many l.,
  Eph 4:5 one L., one faith, one baptism;
  1Ti 6:15 L. of those who rule as l.,
  1Pe 3:6 as Sarah Abraham, calling him l.
  Ps 136:3; Mt 11:25; Ac 17:24; 1Co 11:20;
  2Ti 2:24; Jas 2:1; 1Pe 2:13; Re 1:10.
LORDSHIP(S), 2Pe 2:10 down on l.
  Eph 1:21; Col 1:16; Jude 8.
LOSE, Mt 10:39; Lu 9:24 l. soul
LOSS, Isa 47:9 l. of children and
  1Co 3:15 he will suffer l., but he himself
  Php 3:7 these I considered l. on account
LOST, Ps 119:176 like a l. sheep.
  Lu 15:24 my son was l. but has
  Lu 19:10 seek and to save what was l.

Eze 34:4; Mt 15:24; Joh 18:9.
LOT(S), Es 3:7 cast Pur, that is, the L.,
  Da 12:13 you will stand up for your l. at
  Lu 17:28 as in the days of L.: they were
  Joh 19:24 upon my apparel cast l.
  Ac 13:19 distributed the land to them by l.
  2Pe 2:7 he delivered righteous L.,
  Ge 11:27; 19:29; Pr 18:18; Ac 1:26.
LOUNGE, Ge 49:4; 1Ch 5:1; Job 17:13.
LOVABLE, Pr 5:19 a l. hind and charming
  Php 4:8 whatever things are l., whatever
LOVE, Ge 24:67 fell in l. with her
  Le 19:18 l. your fellow as yourself.
  2Sa 1:26 more than the l. from women
  Mt 22:37 You must l. Jehovah your God
  Mt 24:12 l. of the greater number will cool
  Joh 15:13 No one has l. greater than this,
  Ro 8:39 to separate us from God's l. that
  Ro 13:10 l. is the law's fulfillment.
  1Co 13:4 L. is not jealous, does not brag,
  1Co 13:13 but the greatest of these is l.
  1Co 16:14 Let all affairs take place with l.
  Col 3:14 l. is a perfect bond of union
  Tit 2:4 recall women to l. their husbands
  1Pe 4:8 l. covers a multitude of sins.
  1Jo 4:8 God is l.
  1Jo 4:18 There is no fear in l.
  1Jo 5:3 l. of God means observe his
  Re 2:4 l. their souls face of death.
  Ec 3:8; Ca 8:6; Mic 6:8; Joh 13:34; 1Co
  13:1-4, 8; Col 2:2; 1Ti 1:5; Re 2:4.
LOVED, De 23:5 because your God l. you
  Ps 78:68 Mount Zion, which he l.
  Jer 5:31 my people l. it that way;
  Joh 3:16 God l. the world so much that
  Ro 8:37 victorious through him that l. us.
  Ro 9:13 I l. Jacob, but I hated Esau.
  Heb 1:9 You l. righteousness and hated
  Joh 11:5; 12:43; 13:23; 2Ti 4:8; 1Jo 4:10.
LOVELINESS, Es 1:11 show her l. to princes
LOVER(S), 2Ch 20:7 Abraham, your l.
  Ps 33:5 He is a l. of righteousness
  Pr 12:1 l. of discipline is l. of knowledge.
  Ho 8:9 in Ephraim's case, they hired l.
  2Ti 3:4 l. of pleasures than l. of God
  Ec 5:10; Jer 20:4; Ho 2:7; Mic 3:2.
LOVES, 2Co 9:7 God l. a cheerful giver.
LOVING, De 7:8 because of Jehovah's l. you
  Ps 119:165 peace to those l.
  Ps 145:20 guarding all those l. him,
  Col 3:19 husbands, keep on l. your wives
  1Jo 2:15 Do not be l. the world or things
LOVING-KINDNESS(ES), Ex 20:6 exercising l.
  Ex 34:6 Jehovah abundant in l. and truth,
  Ps 107:8 thanks to Jehovah for his l.
  Isa 54:10 my l. will not be removed from
  Ho 6:6 in l. I have taken delight and not
  Ac 13:34 give you the l. to David
  Ps 13:5; 40:10; 92:2; 141:5; Pr 3:3;
  11:17; Isa 16:5; La 3:22; Ho 12:6.
LOW, Eze 17:14 kingdom might become l.,
  Eze 21:26 bring l. even the high one
  Mal 2:9 make you to be despised and l.
LOWLINESS, Php 2:3 with l. of mind
  Ac 20:19; Eph 4:2; Col 3:12.
LOWLY, Ps 41:1 consideration toward l.
  Zep 3:12 a people humble and l.,
  Mt 11:29 I am l. in heart,
  Ro 12:16 be led along with the l. things.
  Pr 16:19; Eze 29:14; 2Co 10:1.
LOW PLAIN, Joe 3:2 l. of Jehoshaphat;
  Joe 3:14 crowds are in the l. of decision,
  Jos 10:12; Jg 5:15; 2Ch 20:26; Job 39:21.
LOYAL, Ps 16:10 not l. one to see the pit

Jer 3:12 I am l. is utterance of Jehovah
Mic 7:2 l. one has perished from earth
De 33:8;   1Sa 2:9;   Ps 149:1;   Ac 2:27;
13:35;   1Th 2:10;   Heb 7:26;   Re 15:4.
LOYAL ONES, Ps 37:28 not leave his l.
Ps 50:5 Gather to me my l.
Ps 97:10 guarding souls of his l.
Ps 116:15 Precious is the death of his l.
Pr 2:8 guard the way of his l.
Ps 31:23;   145:10;   149:1, 9.
LOYALTY, 2Sa 22:26 will act in l.
Lu 1:75 sacred service with l. and
Eph 4:24 according to God's will and l.
LUCIFER. See SHINING ONE.
LUGGAGE, 1Sa 10:22; Eze 12:3, 7.
LUKE, Col 4:14;   2Ti 4:11.
LUKEWARM, Re 3:16 because you are l.
LUMINARIES, Ge 1:14-16; Eze 32:8.
LUMINARY, Ps 74:16 prepared the l.
LUMP, Ro 9:21 make from the same l. one
1Co 5:7 that you may be a new l., free from
Ga 5:9 A little leaven ferments the whole l.
LUNAR MONTH, 1Ki 6:37;   8:2;   Ezr 6:15.
LURCH, 2Co 4:9 but not left in the l.;
LURE, Jg 2:3 their gods will l. you
LUST. See also COVETOUSNESS, DESIRE(S).
LUST, 2Pe 1:4 corruption through l.
LUSTER, Ps 89:44 cease from his l.
LUSTROUS, Pr 6:25 take with her l. eyes
LUXURIATE, Ne 9:25 to l. in goodness
LUXURIOUS, 2Pe 2:13 consider l. living
LUXURY, Pr 19:10 L. is not fitting for
Lu 7:25;   Jas 5:5;   Re 18:7.
LYE, Jer 2:22;   Mal 3:2.
LYING, Pr 19:22 is better than a l. man
Col 3:9 Do not be l. to one another.
2Th 2:9 of Satan with l. signs and portents
Isa 56:10;   Eze 13:6.

M

MACEDONIA, Ac 16:9 Step over into M.
Ac 20:1; 1Co 16:5; 2Co 8:1; 1Th 1:7; 4:10.
MACHINATIONS, Eph 6:11 m. of the Devil
MAD, Joh 10:20 He has a demon and is m.
1Co 14:23 unbelievers say you are m.?
2Pe 2:16 hindered the prophet's m. course
MADDENED, Ho 9:7 m. on account of your
MADE FUN OF, Mt 27:29; Lu 18:32.
MADLY, Jer 46:9; Na 2:4.
MADMAN, 2Co 11:23 I reply like a m.
MADNESS, Ac 26:24 driving you into m.
2Ti 3:9 their m. will be plain
Ec 1:17;   2:12;   7:25;   9:3;   10:13;   Lu 6:11.
MAGGOT(S), Job 7:5 flesh clothed with m.
Job 25:6 man who is a m.
Mr 9:48 where their m. does not die and
Ex 16:24;   Job 17:14;   24:20;   Isa 14:11.
MAGIC, Isa 2:6 practicers of m. like Philistines
MAGIC-PRACTICING PRIESTS, Ge 41:8; Ex
7:11;   9:11;   Da 1:20;   2:2;   4:7.
MAGISTRATE(S), Ezr 7:25; Ac 16:20, 22, 38.
MAGNIFICENCE, Ac 19:27 her m. is about
2Pe 1:16 become eyewitnesses of his m.
MAGNIFICENT, Ac 2:11 speaking m. things
MAGNIFIED, Ps 40:16 May Jehovah be m.
Ps 138:2 m. your saying above your name.
Php 1:20 Christ will be m. by means of
Ps 35:27;   41:9;   70:4;   Mal 1:5;   Ac 19:17.
MAGNIFIES, Lu 1:46 My soul m. Jehovah.
MAGNIFY, Ps 34:3 O m. Jehovah with me,
Eze 38:23 I shall m. and sanctify myself
Da 11:36 king m. himself above every god
Job 36:24; Ps 69:30; Isa 10:15; 42:21.

MAGOG, Eze 38:2 set face against Gog of M.
Eze 39:6 I will send fire upon M. and
Re 20:8 Gog and M., to gather them together
MAHER-SHALAL-HASH-BAZ, Isa 8:1, 3.
MAIDEN, Isa 7:14 m. become pregnant,
MAIDSERVANT(S), Ge 16:1 Sarai had m.
Ge 12:16;   Ru 2:13;   Ps 123:2;   Pr 30:23.
MAIMED, Ex 22:10;   Mt 18:8.
MAINTAINING, Tit 3:8 on m. fine works.
MAINTENANCE, Ge 34:29; Nu 31:9; Ps 49:6.
MAJESTIC, 1Sa 4:8 hand of this m. God
Ps 8:1 Jehovah how m. your name is in
Ps 76:4 You are more m. than mountains
Isa 33:21 the M. One, Jehovah
Isa 42:21 magnify the law and make it m.
Mic 2:8 strip off the m. ornament
Jg 5:13; Ps 16:3; 136:18.
MAJESTIC ONES, Jer 25:34-36 m. of flock!
MAJESTIC VALUE, Zec 11:13 treasury m.
MAJESTY, Da 5:18 gave Nebuchadnezzar m.
Heb 1:3 right hand of the m. in lofty
Heb 8:1 of the throne of m. in the heavens
Jude 25 to God be glory, m. might
Da 4:36; Zec 11:3.
MAJORITY, 2Co 2:6 rebuke given by m. is
MAKE FRUITFUL, Ge 17:6 will m. you
MAKER, Job 32:22 my M. would carry me
Isa 51:13 you should forget Jehovah your M.,
Ps 95:6; Pr 14:31; 22:2; Isa 17:7.
MAKE SURE, Php 1:10 m. of the more
1Th 5:21 M. of all things; hold fast to
MAKING AN ESTIMATE, Pr 21:2 Jehovah m.
Pr 24:12 m. of hearts
MALADIES, Ps 103:3 healing your m.
MALADY, Ex 15:26; 2Ch 21:15.
Pr 18:14 man can put up with his m.
MALE(S), Ge 1:27 m. and female created
Eze 16:17 images of a m. and
Ro 1:27 m. with m., left natural use of
MALE CHILD, Isa 66:7 deliverance to a m.
Re 12:13 woman gave birth to the m.
MALEDICTION, De 11:26; Pr 26:2.
MALE GOAT, Le 9:3 m. for a sin offering
MALE ORGAN, Isa 57:8 The m. you beheld.
MALICIOUS, Eph 4:31 Let all m. bitterness
MALICIOUSNESS, Tit 3:3 carrying on m.
MALIGNANT, De 28:35; Job 2:7; Eze 28:24.
MALTREAT, Eze 18:7 no man would he m.;
Ex 22:21; Jer 22:3; Eze 45:8.
MALTREATED, Eze 18:12 poor he has m.;
Eze 22:7 Fatherless boy and widow they m.
Eze 22:29 afflicted and poor they m.
MALTREATING, Pr 19:26; Isa 49:26.
MAMRE, Ge 13:18; 23:17; 35:27; 50:13.
MAN. See also ABLE-BODIED MAN, EARTHLING
MAN, HUSBAND(S), MANKIND, MIGHTY
MAN, MORTAL MAN.
MAN, Ge 2:7 God proceeded to form the m.
Job 34:15 m. will return to the very dust
Jer 10:23 not to m. to direct his step.
Jer 17:5 Cursed m. who puts his trust in m.
Mt 4:4 M. must live, not on bread alone,
Ro 5:12 through one m. sin entered into
Ro 7:22 according to the m. I am within
1Co 15:47 The first m. is out of the earth
2Co 4:16 m. inside is being renewed
2Co 5:16 know no m. according to the flesh
Eph 3:16 mighty in the m. you are inside
Eph 4:13 all attain to a full-grown m.,
Ge 6:3; Ex 33:20; Ps 118:6; 144:4; 146:3;
Isa 2:22; 51:12; Eph 3:16; Php 2:8.
MANASSEH, Ge 41:51; 48:13; 2Ki 21:16-18.
MANDATE, 1Ti 1:5 objective m. is love
1Ti 1:18 This m. I commit to you, Timothy,

MANGER, Pr 14:4 are no cattle the **m.** is
Lu 2:7, 12, 16.
MANIFEST, Lu 8:17 will not become **m.**,
Joh 17:6 I have made your name **m.**
Ro 1:19 what may be known about God is **m.**
1Co 3:13 each one's work will become **m.**,
Col 1:26 sacred secret **m.** to holy ones,
Col 3:4 When Christ is made **m.**, then
1Jo 1:2 life was made **m.**, and we have seen
1Jo 3:2 not been made **m.** what we shall be.
Joh 3:21; Ro 3:21; 1Co 4:5; Ga 5:19;
1Ti 3:16; 1Pe 5:4; 1Jo 3:8; Re 15:4.
MANIFESTATION, 2Th 2:8 by the **m.** of his
1Ti 6:14 until the **m.** of our Lord Jesus
2Ti 4:1 judge the living by his **m.**
1Co 12:7; 2Ti 1:10; 4:8; Tit 2:13.
MANIFESTED, Joh 21:1 Jesus **m.** himself
Tit 2:11 undeserved kindness has been **m.**
Heb 9:26 has **m.** himself once for all time
MANIFOLD, Job 11:6 things of wisdom are **m.**
MANKIND, Pr 15:11; Ac 3:10.
MANNA, Ex 16:31 call its name **m.**
Ex 16:35 sons of Israel ate **m.** forty years
Joh 6:49 ate the **m.** and yet died.
Heb 9:4 having the **m.** and the rod of Aaron
Re 2:17 I will give some of the hidden **m.**,
Jos 5:12; Ne 9:20; Ps 78:24.
MANNER, Ps 110:4 priest to the **m.** of
Ac 1:11 will come in the same **m.** as
Ga 4:23 girl born in the **m.** of flesh,
Php 1:27 behave in a **m.** worthy of the good
1Ti 3:12 presiding in a fine **m.** over
1Pe 3:1 In like **m.**, you wives, be in
MANNER OF LIFE, Ac 26:4 **m.** from youth
MANOAH, Jg 13:2, 8, 21 **M.** and his wife
MAN OF GOD, 2Ki 23:16; Ezr 3:2; 1Ti 6:11.
MAN OF LAWLESSNESS, 2Th 2:3 the **m.** gets
MANSLAYER, Nu 35:11 refuge for **m.** who strikes
De 19:4 the case of the **m.**
Joh 8:44 That one was a **m.** when he began.
1Jo 3:15 hates his brother is a **m.**,
Nu 35:6, 25; De 4:42; Jos 20:3, 5.
MANTLE, Isa 61:3 **m.** of praise instead
MANUFACTURE, De 27:15 statue, the **m.**
MANUFACTURES, Isa 45:16 **m.** of idol
MANURE, Ps 83:10; Jer 25:33; Lu 13:8.
MANY, Mt 22:14 **m.** invited, few chosen.
MAP, Jos 18:4 **m.** it out in accord with
MARAUDER, 1Sa 30:8; 1Ki 11:24; Ps 18:29.
MARCH, Jos 6:3 **m.** round the city once.
MARCHED, Ps 68:7 **m.** through the desert
MARCHING, Hab 3:12 **m.** through the earth.
MARINERS, Eze 27:9, 27, 29; Jon 1:5.
MARK, Eze 9:4 put a **m.** on the foreheads
Re 13:17 sell except a person having the **m.**,
Re 20:4 had not received the **m.** upon their
Re 14:9, 11.
MARKET, Lu 10:25 sold in a meat **m.**
MARKET PLACE(S), Mt 11:16; Ac 16:19.
Ac 17:17 worshiped God in the **m.**
MARRIAGE(S), Mt 22:2 a king made a **m.**
Lu 20:35 neither marry nor are given in **m.**
Joh 2:1 a **m.** celebration took place in Cana
2Co 11:2 promised you in **m.** to one husband
Heb 13:4 Let **m.** be honorable among all,
Re 19:9 evening meal of the Lamb's **m.**
Ge 34:9; Jos 23:12; Lu 17:27; 1Co 7:38.
MARRIAGE ALLIANCE, De 7:3; 1Sa 18:23.
MARRIAGE DUE, Ex 21:10 **m.** are not to be
MARRIAGE MONEY, Ge 34:12; 1Sa 18:25.
MARRIED, Lu 14:20 I just **m.** a wife and
Ro 7:2 a **m.** woman is bound by law to her
1Co 7:33 the **m.** man is anxious for the
1Co 7:39 free to be **m.** only in the Lord.

MARROW, Heb 4:12 dividing joints and **m.**
MARRY, Mt 22:30 resurrection neither **m.**
1Ti 4:3 forbidding to **m.**, commanding to
1Co 7:9, 28, 36; 1Ti 5:14.
MARRYING, Mt 24:38 **m.** and giving in
MARSH MALLOW, Job 6:6 slimy juice of **m.**
MARTHA, Lu 10:41; Joh 11:39; 12:2.
MARVEL(S), Ex 15:11 the One doing **m.**
Ps 88:10 for dead will you do a **m.**?
Lu 4:22 they all began to **m.** at
MARVELED, Lu 2:18; Ac 7:31.
MARVELOUS, Ps 89:5 laud your **m.** act
Da 11:36 against the God he will speak **m.**
Job 10:16; Ps 77:11; Mt 21:42.
MARVELOUSLY, Ps 78:12 he had done **m.**
MARY 1., Lu 1:27 the virgin was **M.**
Mt 1:16; 13:55; Mr 6:3; Lu 2:19, 34.
MARY 2., Joh 20:1 **M.** Magdalene came to
Mt 27:56; Mr 16:1; Lu 8:2; 24:10.
MARY 3., Mt 27:56 **M.** mother of James
Mr 15:47; 16:1; Lu 24:10; Joh 19:25.
MARY 4., Ro 16:6 **M.** performed labors
MARY 5., Lu 10:42 **M.** chose the good
Lu 10:39; Joh 11:1; 12:3.
MARY 6., Ac 12:12 **M.** the mother of Mark
MASSACRE, Jer 50:21, 27.
MASSAGE(S), Es 2:3, 9, 12.
MASSED, Ac 4:26 rulers **m.** against Jehovah
MASSING, Lu 11:29 crowds were **m.**
MASTER(S), Mt 6:24 can slave for two **m.**:
Mt 10:24 nor a slave above his **m.**
Mt 25:21 Enter into the joy of your **m.**
Ro 6:9 death is **m.** no more
Ro 6:14 sin must not be **m.** over you,
Ro 14:4 To his own **m.** he stands or falls.
Col 4:1 you also have a **M.** in heaven.
Ps 123:2; Isa 26:13; Mal 1:6; Mt 9:38;
Lu 12:45; Eph 6:9; Col 3:22; Re 14:3.
MASTERY, Ge 4:7 get the **m.** over it.
Ac 19:16 got **m.** of one after the other
MATCH, 1Sa 17:9 I am a **m.** for him
MATERIAL POSSESSIONS, Ec 5:19; 6:2.
MATTER(S), De 19:15 the **m.** should stand
Pr 18:13 replying to a **m.** before he hears
Ec 12:13 The conclusion of the **m.**, is:
Mt 23:23 disregarded the weightier **m.** of
1Co 6:2 are you unfit to try trivial **m.**?
De 17:8; Pr 11:13; Ec 10:20; Ac 25:20.
MATTHEW, Mt 9:9; 10:3; Lu 6:15; Ac 1:13.
MATURE, 1Co 2:6 wisdom among **m.**
Php 3:15 as many as are **m.**, be of
Heb 5:14 solid food belongs to **m.** people,
MATURITY, Heb 6:1 let us press on to **m.**
MEAL(S), Mt 23:6 prominent place at **m.**
Heb 12:16 Esau, who in exchange for one **m.**
1Sa 20:24; Ac 2:46.
MEANING, Mr 7:14; 8:21; Lu 8:10.
MEANS, Heb 2:14 **m.** to cause death, the
MEANS OF LIFE, 1Jo 2:16 display one's **m.**
MEANS OF MAINTENANCE, Ps 49:6; 62:10.
MEASURE(S), 2Sa 8:2 **m.** two lines to death
Mt 7:2 **m.** you are measuring
Lu 6:38 fine **m.**, pressed down, overflowing.
Lu 12:42 **m.** of food at the proper time?
2Co 10:2 taking bold **m.** against some
1Th 2:16 always fill the **m.** of their sins.
Isa 65:7; Zec 2:2; Ro 12:3; Eph 4:16.
MEASURING LINE, Ps 19:4.
2Ki 21:13 **m.** to Samaria
Isa 28:10 **m.** upon **m.**
Isa 28:17 will make justice the **m.**
MEDDLER(S), 1Ti 5:13 **m.** in other
MEDDLING, 2Th 3:11 **m.** with what does
MEDIA, Ezr 6:2; Es 1:3; Da 8:20.

MEDIATOR, 1Ti 2:5 one m. between God
  Heb 12:24 Jesus the m. of a new covenant,
  Ga 3:19, 20; Heb 8:6; 9:15.
MEDITATE. See also UNDERTONE.
MEDITATE, Ge 24:63 walking to m. in field
  Ps 77:12 I shall m. on all your activity,
  Ac 4:25 peoples m. upon empty things?
MEDITATED, Ps 143:5 I have m. on all
MEDITATES, Pr 15:28 righteous one m. so
MEDITATION, Ps 19:14 m. of my heart
MEDIUMISTIC SPIRIT, Le 20:27 m. put to
MEEK, Ps 37:11 m. will possess earth
  Pr 3:34 to the m. ones he will show favor.
  Isa 61:1 tell good news to the m.
  Zep 2:3 seek Jehovah, all you m. of
  Ps 10:17; 22:26; Isa 11:4; 29:19; Am 2:7.
MEEKEST, Nu 12:3 Moses was the m. of
MEEKNESS, Zep 2:3 seek m.
  Jas 3:13 works with a m. that belongs to
MEGIDDO, Jg 5:19 waters of M.
  Jos 12:21; 2Ki 9:27; 23:29; 2Ch 35:22.
MELCHIZEDEK, Heb 5:6 manner of M.
  Ge 14:18; Ps 110:4; Heb 6:20; 7:1, 15.
MELODIES, Job 35:10 One giving m. in the
  Ps 119:54 m. your regulations have become
MELODY, 2Sa 22:50 I shall make m.
  Ps 9:11 Make m. to Jehovah,
  Ps 47:7 make m. acting with discretion.
  Ps 18:49; 57:9; 66:2; 135:3; 144:9.
MELT, Jos 2:11 hearts began to m.
  Ps 97:5 mountains m. like wax
  2Pe 3:12 elements intensely hot will m.!
  Jos 14:8; Ps 46:6; Isa 13:7; 19:1.
MELTING, Ps 58:8 Like a snail m. away
  Ps 107:26; Na 1:5.
MELTS, Ps 68:2 wax m. because of fire,
  Ps 147:18 He sends his word and m. them.
  Am 9:5 land m.; and all inhabitants mourn;
MEMBER(S), Ro 6:13 present your m. to
  Ro 7:23 sin's law that is in my m.
  1Co 6:15 your bodies are m. of Christ?
  1Co 12:18 God has set the m. in the body,
  1Co 12:27 you are Christ's body, and m.
  Col 3:5; Jas 3:6; 4:1.
MEMORANDUM, Ezr 6:2 found a m.
MEMORIAL, Ex 12:14 this day as a m.
  Ps 135:13 O Jehovah, your m. is to
  Isa 26:8 For your name and m. the desire
  Ex 3:15; 13:9; Ne 2:20; Ps 30:4; Ho 12:5.
MEMORIAL TOMB(S), Mt 23:29 decorate m.
  Joh 5:28 all those in the m. will hear
  Mt 27:52, 60; Mr 6:29; Joh 11:17.
MEN, Ex 18:21 select capable m.,
  Pr 29:25 Trembling at m. lays a snare,
  Eze 34:31 you my sheep are earthling m.
  Zec 8:23 ten m. will take hold of the skirt
  Mt 4:19 I will make you fishers of m.
  Mt 15:9 they teach commands of m. as
  Lu 16:15 what is lofty among m. is a
  Ac 5:29 obey God as ruler rather than m.
  1Co 16:13 carry on as m., grow mighty.
  Ga 1:10 am I seeking to please m.?
  Ge 6:4; Ps 115:16; Jer 5:26; Joe 2:7;
  Zep 3:4; Ac 17:5, 1Co 1:25; 2Ti 2:2; 3:2.
MENDING, Jer 30:13; 46:11.
MEN LIE WITH MEN, 1Co 6:9.
MEN OF FORMER TIMES, Mt 15:2 of the m.?
MEN OF OLD TIMES, Heb 11:2 m. had
MEN PLEASERS, Eph 6:6; Col 3:22.
MENSTRUAL, Le 15:19 seven days m. impurity
  Le 15:26 bed of her m. impurity
MENSTRUATING, Le 12:2 impurity when she m.
MENSTRUATION, Le 18:19 not near woman m.
  Eze 36:17.

MENTAL ATTITUDE, Ro 15:5 m. that Christ
  Php 3:15 mature be of this m.;
MENTAL CONCERN, Am 4:13 telling m. is,
MENTAL DISPOSITION, 1Pe 4:1 same m.,
MENTAL DISTRESS, Lu 2:48 father in m.
MENTAL IMAGES, Da 4:5 m. upon my bed
MENTALLY, Eph 3:18 be able to grasp m.
  Php 3:15 if you are m. inclined otherwise
MENTALLY DISEASED, 1Ti 6:4 m. over
MENTAL PERCEPTIONS, 2Co 3:14 their m.
MENTAL POWERS, Php 4:7 guard your m.
MENTAL STATE, Ro 1:28 a disapproved m.
MENTION, Ps 6:5 in death there is no m.
  Isa 26:14 destroy all m. of them.
  Php 3:18 there are many, I used to m. them
MERCHANDISE, Eze 27:27 articles of m.
  Joh 2:16 house of my Father a house of m.!
MERCHANT(S), Re 18:3 m. become rich
  Isa 23:2; Eze 27:21; Mt 13:45; Re 18:11.
MERCIES, 1Ch 21:13 many are his m.
  2Co 1:3 the Father of tender m.
  2Sa 24:14; Isa 54:7; Zec 1:16.
MERCIFUL, De 4:31 Jehovah is a m. God
  Ne 9:17 you are a God gracious and m.,
  Mt 5:7 Happy are the m.,
  Lu 6:36 becoming m. as your Father
  Heb 2:17 a m. and faithful high priest
  Jas 5:11 Jehovah is very tender and m.
  2Ch 30:9; Ps 78:38; 86:15; Heb 8:12.
MERCY, Pr 28:13 confessing be shown m.
  Isa 60:10 shall have m. upon you
  Mt 9:13 I want m., and not sacrifice
  Ro 9:15 I will have m. upon whomever
  1Ti 1:13 I was shown m.,
  Jas 2:13 m. exults over judgment.
  Jas 3:17 full of m. and good fruits
  1Pe 2:10 but now have been shown m.
  Ex 33:19; Ne 9:19, 27; Hab 3:2.
MERIBAH, Ex 17:7; Nu 20:13; De 32:51.
MERIT, 1Pe 2:20 what m. is there in it
MERRIMENT, Pr 21:17 He that is loving m.
MERRY, Jg 16:25 their heart was m.
MESOPOTAMIA, Ge 24:10; De 23:4; Ac 2:9.
MESSAGE, 1Jo 1:5; 3:11.
MESSENGER(S), Job 6:17 she hid the m.
  Isa 33:7 m. of peace weep bitterly.
  Eze 17:15 rebelled sending m. to Egypt,
  Mal 3:1 I am sending my m.
  Mt 11:10 sending my m. before you,
  2Ki 9:18; Pr 13:17; 17:11; Isa 14:32.
MESSIAH, Da 9:26 sixty-two weeks M.
  Joh 1:41 We have found the M.
  Joh 4:25 I know that M. is coming, who
METHODS, 1Co 4:17 m. in connection with
METHUSELAH, Ge 5:21, 25, 27; Lu 3:37.
MICAH, Jg 17:1; 2Ch 34:20; Mic 1:1.
MICAIAH, 1Ki 22:8; 2Ki 22:12; 2Ch 13:2.
MICHAEL, Da 12:1 M. will stand up,
  Re 12:7 M. and his angels battled
  Da 10:13, 21; Jude 9.
MIDDAY, De 28:29 gropes about at m. as
  Ps 37:6; 91:6; Isa 58:10; Jer 15:8.
MIDIAN, Jg 6:1 them into the hand of M.
  Ex 2:15; Jg 9:17; Hab 3:7; Ac 7:29.
MIDIANITES, Ge 37:36; Nu 25:17; 31:2.
MIGHT, Isa 40:29 makes full m. abound.
  Re 1:6 to him be the m. forever. Amen.
MIGHTINESS, Ps 53:1 sun goes forth in m.
  1Ch 29:12 your hand there are power and m.
  Ps 106:8 So as to make his m. known.
  Isa 11:2 spirit of counsel and of m.
  Eph 6:10 the m. of his strength
  1Ki 15:23; 1Ch 29:30; Jer 51:30.
MIGHTY, Ge 6:4 were the m. ones

Ge 10:9 He displayed himself a m.
Isa 9:6 M. God, Eternal Father,
Jer 51:57 m. men drunk will not wake
1Co 16:13 carry on as men, grow m.
Jos 6:2; Ps 24:8; Ca 3:7; Jer 9:23.
MIGHTY MAN, Ps 19:5; 33:16; Pr 16:32;
21:22; Isa 3:2; 42:13; Jer 14:9; Zep 1:14.
MIGRATORY, Le 11:22 eat the m. locust
MILD, 1Pe 3:4 the quiet and m. spirit.
MILDNESS, 1Co 4:21 with love and m. of
2Co 10:1 m. and kindness of Christ
Ga 6:1 restore a man in a spirit of m.
2Ti 2:25 instructing with m. those not
Ca 5:23; 1Ti 6:11; Tit 3:2.
MILD TEMPER, 1Pe 3:15 defense with a m.
MILD-TEMPERED, Mt 5:5 Happy are the m.,
Mt 11:29 I am m. and lowly in heart,
Mt 21:5 your King is coming to you, m.,
MILITARY COMMANDER, Ac 21:32.
MILITARY EXPEDITION, Nu 31:14.
MILITARY FORCE(S), Zec 4:6 not by m.
Eze 37:10; 38:4, 15; Joe 2:11, 25.
MILITARY SERVICE, Isa 40:2; Lu 3:14.
MILK, Ex 3:8 a land flowing with m.
1Co 3:2 I fed you m. not something to eat,
Heb 5:12 you have become as need m.
1Pe 2:2 for the unadulterated m.
Le 20:24; Jg 4:19; Isa 7:22; 55:1; 60:16.
MILLION, 1Ch 21:5; 22:14; 2Ch 14:9.
MILLSTONE, Lu 17:2 if a m. were
Jg 9:53; Job 41:24; Re 18:21.
MINA(S), Lu 19:16 your m. went to ten m.
1Ki 10:17; Ezr 2:69; Lu 19:13, 24, 25.
MIND, Ge 19:29 kept Abraham in m.
1Ki 17:18 you bring my error to m.
Ne 4:14 keep in your m.
Job 23:13 he is in one m.
Ps 8:4 man that you keep him in m.
Isa 65:17 former not called to m.
Eze 23:19 calling to m. days of youth
Da 6:14 set his m. in order to rescue
Mt 22:37 love with your whole m.
Ac 17:11 with eagerness of m.
Ro 8:5 set their m. on things of the flesh,
Ro 11:34 who know Jehovah's m.
Ro 12:2 transformed by making your m.
1Co 2:16 come to know the m. of Jehovah
2Co 4:4 god of this system has blinded m.
Php 3:19 they have their m. upon
Php 4:2 be of the same m. in the Lord.
Col 3:2 Keep your m. fixed things above
Heb 8:10 put my laws in their m.
1Pe 1:13 brace up your m. for activity
Ac 20:19; Ro 7:25; 14:5; 1Co 1:10.
MINDED, Ro 12:16 Be m. the same way
MINDFUL, Heb 2:6 man you are m. of him,
MINDING, Ro 8:6 m. of the flesh means
MIND YOUR OWN BUSINESS, 1Th 4:11.
MINGLED, Ezr 9:2 m. with peoples of the
MINISTER(S), Isa 56:6 foreigners to m.
Mt 20:28 Son of man came to m.
Mr 10:43 great among you must be your m.,
Ro 13:4 it is God's m. for your good.
Ro 15:8 Christ actually became a m. of
Ro 16:1 Phoebe our sister, who is a m. of
2Co 3:6 qualified m. of a new covenant,
2Co 11:15 his m. keep transforming
1Ti 3:10 then let them serve as m.,
1Ti 3:13 the men who m. in a fine manner
1Ti 4:6 you will be a fine m. of Christ
Heb 1:14 spirits sent forth to m.
Ps 103:21; Isa 61:6; Mt 4:11; 25:44; 2Co
3:3; 6:4; Ga 2:17; Col 1:23.
MINISTERED, Heb 6:10 m. to holy ones

MINISTERIAL, Eph 4:12 training for m.
MINISTERIAL SERVANTS, Php 1:1; 1Ti 3:8.
MINISTERING, 1Sa 2:18 Samuel was m.
Da 7:10 thousand thousands kept m. to him,
Heb 6:10 have ministered and continue m.
1Pe 1:12 but to you, they were m.
Mr 1:13; 1Pe 4:10.
MINISTRIES, 1Co 12:5 varieties of m.
MINISTRY, Ac 20:24 finish the m.
Ro 11:13 to the nations, I glorify my m.,
2Co 4:1 have this m. according to mercy
2Co 5:18 gave us the m. of reconciliation,
2Co 6:3 m. might not be found fault with;
1Ti 1:12 assigning me to a m.
2Ti 4:5 fully accomplish your m.
Ac 21:19; Ro 12:7; 2Co 8:4; 9:1; Col 4:17.
MIRACLE(S), Ex 4:21 perform m. before
Ex 11:9 m. to be increased
Ps 71:7 I have become like a m.
Isa 8:18 children are as signs and m.
De 29:3; Ne 9:10; Ps 105:5; Jer 32:20.
MIRE, Ps 69:2 I have sunk in deep m.
Jer 38:6 Jeremiah began to sink into the m.
Mic 7:10 trampling, like the m. of streets.
2Pe 2:22 sow rolling in the m.
Isa 57:20; Zec 9:3; 10:5.
MIRIAM, Ex 15:20; Nu 12:1; 20:1; 26:59.
MIRROR, 1Co 13:12; Jas 1:23.
MISCARRIAGE(S), Job 3:16 m., I should
2Ki 2:19, 21; Ps 58:8.
MISCARRYING WOMB, Ho 9:14 Give them a m.
MISCHIEF, 1Sa 23:9; Pr 12:20; 14:22.
MISCONSTRUE, De 32:27 adversaries m. it,
MISERABLE, Ro 7:24 man that I am!
MISERIES, Jas 5:1 rich howling over your m.
MISERY, Ro 3:16 ruin and m. their ways
Jas 4:9 Give way to m. and mourn
MISFORTUNE, Job 20:22; Ob 12.
MISLEAD, Mt 24:24 false prophets will m.,
1Jo 3:7 Little children, let no one m. you;
Re 20:3 might not m. the nations
MISLEADING, 1Jo 1:8 we are m. ourselves
Re 12:9 Satan, who is m. the earth;
MISLEADS, Mt 24:4 Look out nobody m.
MISLED, Lu 21:8 Look out you are not m.;
1Co 15:33 Do not be m. Bad associations
Ga 6:7 Do not be m. God is not
Re 18:23 spiritistic practice nations m.
1Co 6:9; 2Ti 3:13; Re 19:20.
MISSILE(S), Ne 4:17 was holding the m.
Eph 6:16 quench the wicked one's burning m.
2Ch 23:10; 32:5; Job 20:25; 33:18.
MISSION, Jer 48:10 m. of Jehovah neglectfully
MIST, Job 36:27 draws up water as m.,
Jas 4:14 you are a m. for a little while
MISTAKE, Le 4:2 a soul sins by m.
Nu 15:25 because it was a m.
Job 6:24 what m. I have committed
Job 19:4 my m. will lodge
MISTRESS, 1Sa 28:7 look for a m. of spirit
MIXED COMPANY, Ex 12:38 m. also went
Ne 13:3 separate all the m. from Israel.
MIXED CROWD, Nu 11:4 m. selfish
MIXING, 1Co 5:11 quit m. company with
MIXTURE, Re 18:6 in a m. put twice
MIZPAH, Jos 11:3; Jg 10:17; Ho 5:1.
MIZPEH, Jos 11:8; Jg 11:29.
MOAB, De 29:1 covenant in the land of M.
Ru 1:1, 22; 2Ki 1:1; 2Ch 20:22; Da 11:41.
MOB, Ac 17:5; 19:40; 24:12.
MOCK, 1Ki 18:27 Elijah began to m. them
Pr 1:26 m. when what you dread comes,
Ac 17:32 resurrection some began to m.,
MOCKED, Ga 6:7 God is not one to be m.

MOCKER(S), Ps 35:16 apostate m. for a
MOCK HUMILITY, Col 2:18 delight in a m.
MOCKING(S), 2Ch 36:16 m. at prophets,
  Heb 11:36 trial by m.
MODEL, 1Pe 2:21 leaving you a m. for
MODERATE IN HABITS, 1Ti 3:2 overseer m.
  1Ti 3:11 Women should likewise be m.,
  Tit 2:2 Let the aged men be m.,
MODERATELY, Heb 5:2 m. with ignorant
MODEST, Pr 11:2 wisdom is with m. ones
  Mic 6:8 be m. with your God
MODESTY, 1Ti 2:9 women to adorn with m.
MOISTURE, LIFE'S, Ps 32:4 My l. changed
MOLDED, Ro 9:20 m. say to him that m.
MOLECH, 2Ki 23:10 through fire to M.
  Le 18:21; 20:2; 1Ki 11:7; Jer 32:35.
MOLEST, Ru 2:15; 1Sa 25:7, 15.
MOLTEN, Ex 32:4; Hab 2:18.
MOMENT, Ps 30:5 anger is for a m.,
  Isa 54:7 For a little m. I left you entirely
  1Co 15:52 in a m., in the twinkling
  Ezr 9:8; Isa 26:20; 27:3.
MOMENTARY, 2Co 4:17 tribulation is m.
MONEY, Le 25:37 not m. on interest,
  Ec 7:12 m. is for a protection; but
  Isa 55:1 come, buy milk without m.
  Mr 6:8 carry no food pouch, no copper m.
  1Ti 6:10 love of m. is a root of all
  Heb 13:5 free of the love of m.,
  Ge 44:2; Mt 25:18; Mr 14:11; 1Ti 3:3.
MONEY-CHANGERS, Joh 2:15 drove the m.
MONEY LOVERS, Lu 16:14 Pharisees, were m.
MONSTERS, Ge 1:21 create great sea m.
MONTH(S), Ex 12:2 first of the m.
  Ga 4:10 scrupulously observing days and m.
  Re 22:2 yielding their fruits each m.
  2Ki 15:13; 1Ch 27:1; Es 3:7; Da 4:29.
MONUMENT, 1Sa 15:12; 2Sa 18:18.
MOOD, Job 11:19 put in a gentle m.
MOON, Ps 104:19 m. for appointed times;
  Joe 2:10 Sun and m. have become dark,
  Hab 3:11 Sun m. stood still, in the abode
  Lu 21:25 signs in sun and m. and stars,
  Ac 2:20 darkness and the m. into blood
  Re 12:1 the m. was beneath her feet,
  Jos 10:12; Joe 2:31; Col 2:16; Re 21:23.
MORAL BADNESS, 1Pe 2:1 put away all m.
  1Pe 2:16 your freedom, not as a blind for m.
MORALLY CLEAN, Mic 6:11 m. with wicked
MORDECAI, Es 3:2 M. would neither bow
  Es 7:10 hang Haman on the stake for M.,
  Ezr 2:2; Ne 7:7; Es 2:5; 6:10; 9:3; 10:2.
MORIAH, Ge 22:2; 2Ch 3:1.
MORNING, Ps 30:5 the m. there is joyful
  Ps 49:14 have them in subjection in the m.,
  Isa 28:19 m. by m. it will pass through,
  Jg 6:28; 2Ki 19:35; Mr 1:35; Ac 28:23.
MORNING STAR(S), Job 38:7 m. joyfully
  Re 2:28 I will give him the m.
  Re 22:16 root of David, the m.
MORSEL, Joh 13:26, 27, 30.
MORTAL, Ro 6:12 sin rule in your m. bodies
  1Co 15:53 this m. must put on immortality.
  Ps 144:3; Isa 13:7; Ro 8:11; 2Co 4:11.
MORTAL MAN, Job 15:14 What is m. that
  Job 33:12 God more than m.
  Ps 9:19 not m. prove superior strength.
  Job 36:25; Ps 8:4; 9:19; 55:13; 144:3;
  Isa 13:7; 33:8; Jer 20:10.
MORTAR, Pr 27:22 a pestle in a m.,
  Ge 11:3; Ex 1:14; Le 14:42.
MOSAIC, 1Ch 29:2 m. pebbles in great
MOSES, Ex 2:10 call his name M.
  Nu 12:3 the man M. was the meekest

Mt 17:3 appeared to them M. and Elijah,
  1Co 10:2 all got baptized into M. by
  Heb 11:24 By faith M., when grown up,
  Ex 3:13; 4:20; 7:1; Ac 3:22; 7:22; Heb
  3:2; Jude 9; Re 15:3.
MOSQUITO, Jer 46:20 m. come against
MOST HIGH, Ps 83:18 Jehovah, the M.
  Ps 91:1 in the secret place of the M.
  Isa 14:14 shall make myself resemble the M.
  Da 4:17 may know that the M. is Ruler
  Ac 7:48 M. does not dwell in houses
  Ps 82:6; Lu 1:32, 76; 6:35; Ac 16:17.
MOTHER, Ge 3:20 Eve, the m. of everyone
  Ex 20:12 Honor your father and m.
  Ps 51:5 in sin my m. conceived me.
  Pr 6:20 do not forsake the law of your m.
  Pr 23:22 do not despise your m.
  Lu 8:21 My m. and my brothers are these
  Ga 4:26 Jerusalem above is our m.
  Ge 2:24; Jg 5:7; Isa 49:1; Lu 12:53; 14:26.
MOTHER-IN-LAW, De 27:23; Ru 1:14; 2:11;
  Mt 8:14; 10:35; Mr 1:30.
MOTIONED, Ac 12:17; 19:33; 21:40.
MOTIONLESS, Ex 15:16; Jos 10:12.
MOTIVE, Job 11:12 will get good m.
  Ho 4:11 wine take away good m.
  Php 1:17 not with a pure m., for they are
MOUNTAIN(S), Ex 3:12 serve God on m.
  Jg 5:5 M. flowed from the face of God,
  Ps 2:6 Upon Zion my holy m.
  Ps 46:2 the m. totter into the vast sea;
  Isa 2:2 established above the top of the m.,
  Isa 2:3 let us go up to the m. of Jehovah
  Isa 11:9 not do any harm in all my holy m.;
  Isa 52:7 comely upon the m. are the feet
  Jer 16:16 hunt them from every m.
  Da 2:45 out of the m. a stone was cut
  Da 11:45 the holy m. of Decoration;
  Mic 1:4 the m. must melt under him,
  Mt 4:8 high m., and showed him all the
  Mt 17:20 say to this m., Transfer from here
  Mr 13:14 in Judea begin fleeing to the m.
  Lu 3:5 every m. and hill leveled down
  Re 6:16 saying to the m.: Fall over us
  Isa 40:12; 41:15; 65:25; Jer 51:25; Eze
  35:8; Am 9:13; Hab 3:6.
MOUNTAINOUS REGION OF SEIR, Ge 36:8;
  2Ch 20:10, 22; Eze 35:7, 15.
  2Ch 20:23 against the inhabitants of the m.
  Eze 35:3 I am against you, O m.,
MOUNT SEIR, De 2:5 given M. to Esau
MOUNT SINAI, Ex 19:20 Jehovah came M.
  Ex 24:16 Jehovah's glory continued upon M.,
  Ex 31:18; Le 7:38; Ne 9:13; Ac 7:30.
MOUNT ZION, Ps 48:2 M. on the sides
  Ps 125:1 like M., which cannot totter,
  Isa 29:8 nations are waging war against M.
  Joe 2:32 in M. there will be escaped ones,
  Ob 21 saviors will come up onto M.
  Heb 12:22 M. and a city of the living God,
  Re 14:1 Lamb standing upon the M., and with
  2Ki 19:31; Ps 78:68; Isa 8:18; Mic 4:7.
MOURN, Jer 4:28 the land will m.,
  Mt 5:4 Happy are those who m., since they
  Ne 8:9; Ho 4:3; Lu 6:25; Jas 4:9.
MOURNED, Joe 1:9 ministers of Jehovah m.
MOURNERS', Jer 16:5 house of a m. feast,
MOURNING, Isa 60:20 days of your m.
  Isa 61:2 comfort all the m. ones;
  Eze 24:17 For the dead ones no m. should
  Am 1:2 grounds of the shepherds go to m.,
  Re 18:11 merchants of the earth are m. over
  Re 21:4 neither will m. nor outcry nor
  Ge 37:35; Es 4:3; Ps 30:11; Eze 7:12.

MOUTH(S), Jos 1:8 depart from your m.
Isa 6:7 he proceeded to touch my m.
Isa 29:13 have come near with their m.
Isa 51:16 put my words in your m.
Isa 62:2 new name which m. of Jehovah
Jer 1:9 caused it to touch my m.
Eze 33:31 with their m. lustful desires
Ob 12 not maintain a big m. in the day
Lu 6:45 out of heart's abundance m.
Lu 19:22 of your own m. I judge you
Ro 3:19 that every m. may be stopped
Ro 10:10 with the m. public declaration
1Pe 2:22 nor deception found in his m.
Re 14:5 no falsehood in their m.;
Ex 4:12; De 8:3; Ps 37:30; 62:4; Pr 2:6;
Ec 5:2; Isa 58:14; 59:21; Re 3:16.
MOUTHINGS, Ps 49:13 pleasure in their m.
MOVE BACK, De 19:14 not m. boundary marks
Isa 59:14 justice forced to m.
MOVED, Zec 14:4 the mountain will be m.
MOVEMENT, 2Co 4:8 not cramped beyond m.;
MOVES ABOUT, Ge 1:21 living soul that m.,
MOVING, Ge 1:2 active force was m. to
2Th 3:1 word of Jehovah may keep m. speedily
MOVING ANIMALS, Ge 1:24; 8:17.
MULTIPLIED, 2Co 4:15 kindness was m.
MULTIPLY, Ge 26:4 I will m. your seed like
Ge 17:2; 26:24; De 8:1; Jer 33:22.
MULTIPLYING, Hab 2:6 m. what is not his
Ac 6:7 number of disciples kept m.
MULTITUDE, Pr 11:14 salvation in the m. of
Pr 15:22 in the m. of counselors there is
Joh 21:6 because of the m. of the fishes.
Jas 5:20 and will cover a m. of sins.
1Pe 4:8 love covers a m. of sins.
Lu 2:13; 5:6; Heb 11:12.
MURDER(S), Ex 20:13 You must not m.
Mt 5:21; 15:19 commits m. is accountable
MURDERED, Jas 5:6 m. the righteous one
MURDERER(S). See also MANSLAYER.
MURDERER(S), Nu 35:31 soul of a m.
Isa 1:21; Ac 3:14; 7:52; 1Pe 4:15.
MURMUR(ERS), Jude 16 men are m.,
Ex 16:7; 1Co 10:10.
MURMURING(S), Php 2:14 free from m.
Nu 14:27; 17:5.
MUSIC, Ps 77:6; La 5:14.
MUSICIANS, Ezr 7:24 Levites, the m.
MUSING, Ps 104:34 Let m. about him be
MUSTACHE, Mic 3:7 will cover the m.,
Le 13:45; 2Sa 19:24; Eze 24:17.
MUSTARD GRAIN, Mt 17:20; Lu 13:19.
MUSTY SMELL, Isa 3:24; 5:24.
MUTE, Isa 53:7; Eze 3:26; 24:27.
MUTILATE, Php 3:2 those who m. the flesh.
MUTTER, Job 27:4 tongue m. no deceit!
MUTTERING(S), Ps 2:1 groups kept m. an
Ps 38:12; Isa 59:3, 13.
MUTUAL, 1Co 7:5 except by m. consent
MUZZLE, Ps 39:1 m. as guard to my mouth
1Pe 2:15 m. ignorant talk of unreasonable
De 25:4; 1Co 9:9; 1Ti 5:18.
MYRIADS, Heb 12:22; Jude 14; Re 5:11.
MYRRH, Mt 2:11; Joh 19:39.
MYSELF, 1Co 4:3 Even I do not examine m.
MYSTERY. See also SACRED SECRET(S).
MYSTERY, 2Th 2:7 the m. of lawlessness
Re 17:5 m., Babylon the Great, the mother
Re 17:7 tell you the m. of the woman.

N

NAAMAN, 2Ki 5:1; Lu 4:27.
NAKED, Ge 3:7 realize they were n.
Job 1:21 n. I came out of my mother's

2Co 5:3 we shall not be found n.
Heb 4:13 n. and exposed to the eyes of him
Jas 2:15 If a brother or sister is n. and
Re 3:17 you are poor and blind and n.
Re 16:15 that he may not walk n.
Re 17:16 will make her devastated and n.
Ge 2:25; Job 26:6; Ho 2:3; Mt 25:36.
NAME, Ex 6:3 but as my n. Jehovah
Ex 9:16 to have my n. declared in all
Ex 20:7 must not take up the n.
Pr 10:7 n. of wicked ones will rot.
Pr 18:10 n. of Jehovah a strong tower.
Pr 22:1 A n. is to be chosen rather gold
Ec 7:1 A n. is better than good oil, and
Isa 12:4 Call upon his n.
Isa 62:2 you called by a new n.,
Eze 36:22 my holy n. you have profaned
Mt 6:9 let your n. be sanctified.
Mt 12:21 in his n. nations will hope.
Mt 24:9 be objects of hatred of my n.
Lu 21:12 haled before kings for my n.
Joh 14:14 ask in my n., I will do it.
Joh 17:26 I have made your n. known
Ac 4:12 there is not another n. given
Ac 15:14 nations a people for his n.
Ro 10:13 calls upon the n. of Jehovah
Eph 3:15 to whom every family owes its n.,
Php 2:9 n. that is above every other n.
Ge 2:19; Ex 3:15; 1Jo 2:12.
NAME'S SAKE, Re 2:3 borne my n.
NAOMI, Ru 1:2, 19; 2:1, 2, 20; 4:9, 14, 17.
NAPHTALI, Ge 30:8; Ex 1:4; Mt 4:13.
NARROW, Mt 7:14 n. is the gate
NATHAN, 2Sa 12:7 N. said: "You are the
2Sa 7:3; 12:5, 13; 1Ch 17:1, 2.
NATHANAEL, Joh 1:45-49; 21:2.
NATION(S), Ex 19:6 priests and a holy n.
2Sa 7:23 what one n. in the earth is like
Ps 9:17 Even all the n. forgetting God.
Ps 33:12 Happy is the n. whose God
Isa 2:2 and to it all n. must stream.
Isa 2:4 N. will not lift up sword against
Isa 26:2 righteous n. is keeping faithful conduct
Isa 66:8 will a n. be born at one time?
Jer 25:32 A calamity is going forth from n.
Zep 2:1 Gather yourselves together, O n.
Zep 3:8 my judicial decision is to gather n.
Hag 2:7 the desirable things of all the n.
Mt 12:21 in his name n. will hope
Mt 21:43 from you and be given to a n.
Mt 24:7 For n. will rise against n. and
Mt 24:14 for a witness to all the n.
Mt 25:32 all the n. will be gathered
Lu 21:24 appointed times of n. fulfilled.
Lu 21:25 and on earth anguish of n.
Lu 23:2 This man we found subverting our n.
Ac 15:14 God turned his attention to the n.
Eph 4:17 no longer walking as the n. walk
1Pe 2:12 Maintain conduct fine among n.,
Re 11:18 But the n. became wrathful,
Ge 22:18; Ac 10:35; Ro 3:29; Re 7:9.
NATIONAL GROUPS, Ps 7:7; Isa 49:1.
Isa 55:4 a witness to the n. I have
NATURAL, Le 18:23 violation of what n.
Ro 1:27 males left the n. use of the female
Jas 3:6 wheel of n. life aflame
Ro 1:31; 11:24; 2Ti 3:3.
NATURALLY, Eph 2:3 n. children of wrath
Ro 1:26; 2:14, 27; 11:24; 1Co 11:14.
NATURE, 2Pe 1:4 sharers in divine n.,
Ro 1:26; 2:14, 27; 11:24; 1Co 11:14.
NAVEL, Pr 3:8 healing to your n. and
NAVIGATED, Ac 27:5 we n. through open sea
NAZARENE(S), Ac 24:5 sect of the N.,
Joh 19:19; Ac 2:22.

NAZARETH, Joh 1:46 good come out of N.?
  Mt 2:23; 4:13; 21:11.
NAZIRITE, Nu 6:2, 18-21; Jg 13:5; 16:17.
NEARBY, Jer 23:23 a God n. not far away
NEBO, Nu 32:3; Isa 15:2; 46:1; Jer 48:1.
NEBUCHADNEZZAR, 2Ch 36:7 utensils N.
  Jer 27:6 all these lands into hand of N.
  Da 3:1 N. the king made an image of gold,
  Ezr 5:12; Da 2:1; 3:16, 24, 28; 4:18, 31.
NEBUCHADREZZAR, Jer 25:9 N. of Babylon.
  Jer 43:10; 50:17; Eze 26:7; 30:10.
NECESSARY, Ro 12:3 think more than n.
  Php 1:24 remain in the flesh is more n. on
  Heb 2:1 it is n. for us to pay attention
NECESSITIES, Jas 2:16 you do not give n.
NECESSITY, 1Co 7:26 in view of the n.
  1Co 9:16 n. is laid upon me. Really, woe
  Da 3:16; 1Co 7:37; Heb 7:12.
NECK, Lu 15:20; 17:2; Ac 20:37.
NECKLACE, Pr 1:9 fine n. to your throat.
NEED, Mt 6:32 Father knows you n. these
  1Co 12:21 "I have no n. of you";
  Ro 16:2; Eph 4:28; Heb 5:12; 7:27.
NEEDLE'S EYE, Mt 19:24; Mr 10:25.
NEEDS, De 15:8 lend him on pledge as n.,
NEGEB, De 1:7 Shephelah and the N.
NEGLECT, Jer 23:39 give you people to n.
NEGLECTED, Heb 2:3 n. a salvation
NEGLECTFULLY, Jer 48:10 mission n.;
NEGLECTING, 1Ti 4:14 not n. the gift
NEGLIGENCE, Ezr 4:22 be no n.
NEIGHBOR, Pr 27:10 Better is a n. near
  Lu 10:27 love your n. as yourself
  Lu 10:36; Ro 13:10; Eph 4:25.
NEIGHINGS, Jer 13:27 your adultery, n.
NEPHEW, 1Ch 27:32 David's n. was a
NEPHILIM, Ge 6:4; Nu 13:33.
NET, Ps 9:15 In the n. that they hid,
  Joh 21:11 so many the n. did not burst.
  Ps 10:9; Ec 9:12; Lu 5:2; Joh 21:6, 8.
NETHINIM, Ezr 7:24 N., workers of this
  Ezr 8:20 N., whom David and princes gave
  1Ch 9:2; Ezr 2:43; Ne 10:28; 11:21.
NETTED, Pr 12:12 desired the n. prey of
NEVER-FAILING, Lu 12:33 n. treasure in
NEW, Ps 51:10 put within me a n. spirit
  Ec 1:9 nothing n. under the sun.
  Isa 42:9 but n. things I am telling out.
  Isa 65:17 I am creating n. heavens and a n.
  Isa 66:22 n. heavens and n. earth that I am
  Mt 26:29 drink it n. with you in the kingdom
  Joh 13:34 I am giving you a n. commandment,
  2Co 5:17 with Christ, he is a n. creation;
  2Co 5:17 n. things have come into existence.
  Col 3:10 clothe with the n. personality
  1Pe 1:23 you have been given a n. birth,
  2Pe 3:13 n. heavens and n. earth
  Re 14:3 they are singing as if a n. song
  Re 21:5 "Look! I making all things n."
  Lu 22:20; Ga 6:15; Heb 10:20; Re 3:12.
NEWLY CONVERTED, 1Ti 3:6 not a n. man,
NEWNESS, Ro 6:4 walk in n. of life.
NEWS, Ps 40:9 I have told the good n.
  Isa 40:9 woman bringing good n. for Zion
  Isa 61:1 anointed me to tell good n.
  Mt 24:14 this good n. of the kingdom
  Isa 52:7; Na 1:15; Ro 10:16; 2Co 11:4.
NEWS BEARER, 1Sa 4:17; 2Sa 18:26.
NICODEMUS, Joh 3:1, 4, 9; 7:50; 19:39.
NIGHT, Ge 1:5 darkness he called N.
  2Ki 19:35 that n. the angel of Jehovah
  Ps 19:2 n. shows forth knowledge.
  Isa 21:11 Watchman, what about the n.?
  Joh 9:4 n. is coming when no man can work.

Ro 13:12 The n. is well along; the day has
  1Th 5:2 coming exactly as a thief in the n.
  Re 22:5 Also n. will be no more, and
  Jos 1:8; Lu 18:7; 1Th 5:5; Re 7:15; 12:10.
NILE, Isa 19:7; Jer 46:8; Zec 10:11.
NIMROD, Ge 10:9 like N. a mighty hunter
NINEVEH, Jon 1:2 to N. the great city,
  Jon 3:5 N. began to put faith in God,
  Mt 12:41 N. will rise up
  Ge 10:11; Jon 3:2, 3; 4:11; Zep 2:13.
NINEVITES, Lu 11:30 a sign to the N.
NIPPER OF FIGS, Am 7:14 but I was a n.
NISAN, Ne 2:1; Es 3:7.
NOAH, Ge 6:9 This is the history of N.
  Ge 7:23 wiped off the earth, and only N.
  Ge 9:1 God went on to bless N.
  Lu 17:26 as it occurred in the days of N.,
  Heb 11:7 By faith N., after being given
  Ge 5:29; 9:17; Mt 24:37; 1Pe 3:20.
NOBLE(S), Job 12:21 contempt upon n.,
  Ps 146:3 Do not put your trust in n.,
  Lu 19:12 man of n. birth traveled
  1Co 1:26 not many powerful; not many n.
  Ps 107:40; 118:9; Jer 27:20; 39:6.
NOBLE-MINDED, Ac 17:11 more n. than
NOISE, Jer 25:31 A n. will come to the
  2Pe 3:10 heavens pass away with a hissing n.
NOISY, Mic 2:12 n. because of men
NONEXISTENT, Isa 41:12, 24, 29.
NONSENSE, Lu 24:11 sayings as n. to them
NOON, 1Ki 18:27 at n. Elijah began to mock
  Am 8:9 sun go down at high n.
NOONTIME, Isa 16:3 in the midst of n.
NOOSE, 1Co 7:35 cast a n. upon you,
NORMAL, 2Co 4:7 power beyond n. may be
NORMALLY, Mr 7:35 began speaking n.
NORTH, Ps 48:2 Zion on sides of n.,
  Isa 14:13 I sit in remotest parts of n.
  Isa 41:25 roused up someone from the n.,
  Jer 1:14 Out of the n. calamity will be
  Da 11:44 will be reports out of the n.,
  Jer 50:9; Am 8:12; Zec 2:6; Lu 13:29.
NOSE, Eze 8:17 thrusting shoot to my n.
NOSTRILS, Ge 2:7 n. the breath of life.
NOTHING, Isa 45:18 not create it for n.,
  Isa 65:23 They will not toil for n.,
  1Co 1:28 bring to n. things that are,
  1Co 2:6 rulers of this system come to n.
  1Co 8:4 we know an idol is n. in the world
NOTICE, Ex 2:25 Israel and God took n.
  Pr 3:6 all your ways take n. of him,
  Ga 1:11 I put you on n., brothers, that
  2Pe 3:5 this fact escapes their n., that
NOTORIOUS, Ps 99:8 vengeance against n.
  Ps 141:4 carry on n. deeds in wickedness
NOURISHED, 1Ti 4:6 n. with words of faith
NOURISHMENT, 1Ki 19:8 power of n. for
NUDITY, Mic 1:11 in shameful n.
NULLIFIED, Joh 10:35 Scripture n.,
NUMB, Ps 38:8 I have grown n. and
  Hab 1:4 law grows n. and justice
NUMBED, Ps 143:4; Da 8:27.
NUMBER, Re 7:4 n. of those sealed,
  Re 7:9 crowd no man was able to n.,
  Re 13:18 calculate the n. of the beast,
  Job 38:37; Ro 9:27; Re 5:11; 13:17; 20:8.
NUMBNESS, La 2:18 Give no n. to yourself
NUMEROUS, Ex 1:20 people growing more n.
  De 26:5 he became a nation, mighty and n.
  Eze 38:15 a n. military force.
NUN, Ex 33:11; De 32:44; 1Ch 7:27.
NUPTIAL CHAMBER, Ps 19:5; Joe 2:16.
NURSE, Ru 4:16; 2Sa 4:4.
NURSING, Ex 2:7; Isa 49:23; 1Th 2:7.

O

OATH, Jos 2:17 free respecting this o.
Jos 9:20 over the o. that we have sworn
Ps 24:4 nor taken an o. deceitfully.
Heb 6:17 God stepped in with an o.,
Ge 26:28; Nu 30:2; Ac 2:30; Heb 7:20, 28.
OBED, Ru 4:17, 21, 22; Lu 3:32.
OBED-EDOM, 2Sa 6:10-12; 1Ch 13:13.
OBEDIENCE, Ge 49:10 to Shiloh the o. will
Ro 5:19 the o. of one person
Ro 6:16 o. with righteousness in view?
Heb 5:8 learned o. from things he suffered,
Ro 16:26; 2Co 7:15; 10:6; 1Pe 1:22.
OBEDIENT, 2Co 10:5 thought o. to Christ,
Eph 6:1 Children, be o. to your parents
Eph 6:5 slaves, be o. to your masters
Php 2:8 became o. as far as death,
Tit 3:1 be o. to governments
Heb 13:17 Be o. to those taking the lead
Ex 24:7; 2Sa 22:45; Ps 18:44; Ac 7:39; Ro
1:5; 6:17; 2Co 2:9; 1Pe 1:2, 14; 3:1; 4:17.
OBEISANCE, Lu 24:52 they did o. to him
Mt 2:11; Joh 9:38; Ac 10:25; Re 3:9.
OBEY, Ex 19:5 strictly o. my voice
1Sa 15:22 to o. is better than sacrifice,
Ac 5:29 We must o. God rather than men.
Ro 6:16 you are slaves because you o. him,
2Th 1:8 punishment upon those who do not o.
Da 7:27; Mt 8:27; Ro 2:8; 1Pe 3:6.
OBEYED, Jer 35:14 o. commandment of
Heb 11:8 Abraham o. in going out
OBEYING, Heb 5:9 salvation to those o.
Jer 35:8; Ac 5:32.
OBJECT, Pr 14:20 o. of hatred,
Isa 8:12, 13 o. of their fear do not fear
1Pe 3:14 o. of their fear do not fear
OBJECTIONS, Mt 16:22 raising strong o.
OBJECTIVE, 1Ti 1:5 o. of this mandate
OBLIGATED, 2Th 1:3 o. to give thanks
OBLIGATION, Ro 8:12 under o., not to flesh
De 11:1; Ec 12:13; Ga 5:3; 1Jo 2:6.
OBLIVION, Ps 88:12 in land of o.
OBSCENE, Ro 1:27; Eph 5:4; Col 3:8.
OBSCURENESS, Isa 9:1 o. not as former
OBSCURING, Job 38:2 Who is o. counsel
OBSCURITY, Isa 8:22 o., hard times and
Job 10:22; Am 4:13.
OBSERVABLENESS, Lu 17:20 kingdom with o.,
OBSERVE, Pr 6:20 O. the commandment
Mt 6:26 O. intently the birds of heaven,
Mt 23:3 o., but do not do according to
Mt 28:20 teaching them to o. all things
Joh 14:15 you will o. my commandments;
OBSERVES, Joh 14:21 He that o. them,
Ro 14:6 He who o. the day o. it to Jehovah.
OBSERVING, Ga 4:10 scrupulously o. days
Pr 28:7; Re 22:7.
OBSOLETE, Heb 8:13 the former one o.
OBSTACLE, Le 19:14; Isa 57:14.
OBSTINATE, Ex 7:3 Pharaoh's heart o.
Ex 14:17 hearts of Egyptians become o.,
Ro 9:18 he lets become o.
OCCASION, Heb 3:15 o. of bitter anger.
OCCASION FOR STUMBLING, Ro 14:20 an o.
OCCUPANCY, Isa 65:21 build and have o.;
OCCUPATION, Ec 1:13 the calamitous o.
Ge 46:33; 47:3; Ec 2:23; 3:10; 4:3; 5:3.
OCCURRING, Jas 3:10 things o. this way.
ODOR, Ge 8:21 to smell a restful o.
2Co 2:15 to God we are a sweet o.
Eph 5:2 sacrifice to God a sweet-smelling o.
OFFAL, Isa 5:25 dead become like the o.
OFFEND, Eze 32:9 I o. the heart of many

De 4:25; 31:29; 1Ki 16:33.
OFFENDER, Jas 2:10 one point o. against
OFFENSE, Ac 24:16; Ro 9:33.
OFFERED, Heb 9:14 Christ o. himself to
Heb 10:12 o. one sacrifice for sins
Heb 11:17 Abraham o. up Isaac.
Ge 22:13; Ezr 1:6; Ac 8:18; Heb 9:28.
OFFERING(S), Ge 4:4 Abel and his o.,
1Ch 29:9 made voluntary o. to Jehovah,
Isa 53:10 set his soul as a guilt o.,
Mal 3:3 gift o. in righteousness.
2Ti 4:6 I am poured out like a drink o.,
Heb 10:14 sacrificial o. has made perfect
Nu 15:14; Ezr 2:68; Mal 3:4; Eph 5:2.
OFFICE, 1Ch 9:22 ordained in their o.
Ac 1:20 'His o. let someone else take.'
2Co 11:12 equal to us in the o. they boast.
1Ti 3:1 for an o. of overseer
OFFICIAL, Pr 14:28 ruin of a high o.
OFFICIAL GARMENT, 2Ki 2:13 o. of Elijah
1Ki 19:19; 2Ki 2:8; Zec 13:4.
OFFICIATED, Heb 7:13 o. at the altar
OFFSCOURING, 1Co 4:13 we have become o.
OFFSPRING, Ps 37:25 o. looking for bread.
Ge 9:9; Ps 25:13; Isa 14:20; 59:21; 65:23.
OGLING, Isa 3:16 daughters o. with eyes
OIL, Ps 23:5 o. you greased my head;
Isa 61:3 o. of exultation instead of
Mt 25:4 discreet took o. with their lamps.
Ex 29:7; 1Sa 16:13; Lu 7:46; Heb 1:9.
OLDER MEN, Re 24:1 seventy of the o.
Ac 4:5 gathering together rulers and o.
1Ti 5:17 o. reckoned worthy of double honor,
1Pe 5:1 to the o. I give this exhortation,
Ru 4:2; Pr 31:23; Mt 16:21; 21:23; Re 4:4.
OLIVE, Ro 11:17 wild o., grafted in among
Ex 27:20; Ne 8:15.
OLIVES, MOUNT OF, Zec 14:4; Lu 22:39.
OLIVE TREE(S), Jg 9:8 o. be king over
Ps 128:3 sons like o.
Re 11:4 two o. and the two lampstands
De 28:40; Ps 52:8; Zec 4:11; Ro 11:24.
OMEGA, Re 1:8; 21:6; 22:13.
OMENS, De 18:10 anyone who looks for o.
Ge 30:27; 44:5; 2Ki 21:6.
OMER, Ex 16:16, 18, 36.
OMRI, 1Ki 16:16, 21-23, 27-29; Mic 6:16.
ONE, 1Co 8:4 there is no God but o.
ONENESS, Eph 4:13 attain o. in faith
ONE REPURCHASING, Isa 47:4 is O. us.
ONIONS, Nu 11:5 leeks and o. and garlic!
ONLY-BEGOTTEN, Joh 1:14 to an o. son
Joh 3:16 gave his o. Son, in order that
Joh 3:18; Heb 11:17; 1Jo 4:9.
ONLY-BEGOTTEN GOD, Joh 1:18 [Jesus Christ]
OOZE, Jer 38:22 down into the very o.
OPENED, Ge 3:5 eyes bound to be o.
De 11:8; Ps 22:13; La 3:46.
OPERATION(S), 1Co 12:6 varieties of o.,
1Co 12:11; Col 2:12; 2Th 2:9.
OPHIR, Isa 13:12 gold of O.
1Ki 9:28; 10:11; Job 28:16; Ps 45:9.
OPINION, Joh 11:56; 1Co 7:25, 40.
OPPONENT-AT-LAW, Job 9:15.
OPPONENTS, Php 1:28 frightened by o.
OPPORTUNE TIME, Eph 5:16; Col 4:5.
OPPORTUNITY, 1Co 7:21 free, seize the o.
Php 4:10 but you lacked o.
Heb 11:15 they would have had o. to return.
OPPOSE, Jas 4:7 o. the Devil, and he flee
OPPOSER(S), Lu 21:15 your o. together
1Ti 5:14 inducement to the o. to revile.
OPPOSES, Jas 4:6 God o. the haughty
OPPOSING, Tit 2:8 man on the o. side

Jas 5:6 Is he not **o.** you?
OPPOSITION, Ac 17:7 o. to the decrees
Heb 10:27 jealousy consume those in **o.**
Col 2:14; 2Th 2:4; 1Ti 1:10.
OPPRESS, Ex 23:9 must not **o.** alien
Jer 7:6 no widow you will **o.** and innocent
OPPRESSED, Jg 4:3 o. the sons of Israel
Isa 52:4; Jer 50:33; Ac 10:38.
OPPRESSING, Ex 3:9 the Egyptians are **o.**
OPPRESSION(S), Ps 72:14 From **o.** redeem
Pr 29:13; Isa 14:4; 54:14; 59:13; Jer 6:6.
OPPRESSOR(S), Jg 6:9; Ec 4:1; Isa 16:4.
ORALLY, Lu 1:4; Ac 18:25; Ga 6:6.
ORDAIN(ED). See also APPOINT.
ORDAIN(ED), 1Ch 9:22 Samuel the seer **o.**
1Co 7:17 I **o.** in congregations.
1Co 9:14 Lord **o.** for those to live by means
ORDER(S), Ps 19:8 **o.** from Jehovah are
1Co 11:34 remaining matters I will set in **o.**
Col 2:5 rejoicing and beholding your good **o.**
1Th 4:2 you know the **o.** we gave
Tit 1:5 make appointments as I gave you **o.,**
Ps 119:93, 110; Da 3:29; Ac 1:4.
ORDERLY, Ga 5:25 let us go on walking **o.**
Php 3:16 let us go on walking **o.** in this
1Ti 3:2 sound in mind, **o.,** a lover of
ORDINANCE. See REGULATION(S).
ORDINANCES, Heb 9:1 former covenant used **o.**
ORDINARY, Ac 4:13 Peter and John were **o.,**
1Co 14:24 if any **o.** person comes in, he is
ORGANISM(S), Pr 5:11 **o.** come to an end.
1Sa 21:5; Pr 11:17; 14:30.
ORGANIZED, Pr 9:2 It has **o.** its slaughtering
ORIENTAL(S), Eze 25:4 giving you to **O.**
Ge 29:1; 1Ki 4:30; Job 1:3; Eze 25:10.
ORIGIN, Eze 29:14 to the land of their **o.**
ORIGINALITY, Joh 7:17; 14:10; 18:34.
ORIGINATE, 1Jo 4:1, 6 whether **o.** with God
ORIGINATES, 1Jo 2:16 **o.** with the world.
ORNAMENT, Mic 2:8 garment strip the **o.**
ORPHANS, Jas 1:27 to look after **o.** and
OSTRACISING, Jg 11:35 one I was **o.**
OSTRACISM, Ge 34:30 brought **o.** upon me
Jos 7:25 you brought **o.** upon Israel
1Sa 14:29; 1Ki 18:18; Pr 11:17; 15:27.
OSTRACIZED, Ps 39:2; Pr 15:6.
OTHER SHEEP, Joh 10:16 I have **o.,**
OTHNIEL, Jos 15:17; Jg 3:9.
OURSELVES, Ro 8:23 we **o.** groan within **o.,**
Ro 15:1 not strong, and not pleasing **o.**
2Co 1:9 we felt within **o.** the sentence of
2Co 3:5 Not that we of **o.** are qualified
2Co 10:12 we do not class **o.** or compare **o.**
Ezr 4:3; Job 34:4; 2Co 4:5; 7:1; 1Jo 1:8.
OUTCRY, Isa 49:13 with a glad **o.**
Isa 51:11 come to Zion with a joyful **o.,**
OUTER GARMENT(S), Mt 5:40 let **o.** go to
Re 16:15 stays awake and keeps his **o.,**
Mt 24:18; Heb 1:12; Jas 5:2; 1Pe 3:3.
OUTLINE, 1Co 13:12 we see in hazy **o.**
OUTRAGEOUSLY, Ac 8:3 deal **o.** with
OUTSIDE, 2Co 4:16 the man **o.** is wasting
1Th 4:12 walking decently regards people **o.**
1Ti 3:7 testimony from people on the **o.,**
Heb 13:11 sin are burned up **o.** the camp.
OUTSPOKENNESS, Mr 8:32 with **o.** he
Ac 4:13 beheld the **o.** of Peter and John
OUTWARD APPEARANCE, Mt 22:16.
Ga 2:6 God does not go by a man's **o.**
OUTWITTED, Mt 2:16 Herod had been **o.**
OUTWITTING, Ge 31:26 resorted to **o.** me
OVER ALL, Ro 9:5 God who is **o.** be blest
OVERCOME, 2Pe 2:20 involved again and **o.,**
OVERHASTY, Isa 32:4 heart of those **o.**

OVERJOYED, Lu 10:21 hour he became **o.**
OVERPOWER, Mt 16:18 Hades will not **o.** it
Joh 12:35 darkness not **o.** you
OVERSEER(S), Ge 41:34 Pharaoh appoint **o.**
Ac 20:28 holy spirit appointed you **o.,**
1Ti 3:1 reaching out for an office of **o.,**
1Ti 3:2 The **o.** should be irreprehensible,
1Pe 2:25 the shepherd and **o.** of your souls.
Ne 11:9; Isa 60:17; Jer 29:26; Tit 1:7.
OVERSHADOWING, Heb 9:5 cherubim **o.** the
OVERSIGHT, Ac 1:20 His office of **o.** let
Nu 3:32; Ps 109:8; Eze 44:11.
OVERSTEP, Mt 15:3 **o.** the commandment of
Jos 7:11; Jg 2:20; Ho 6:7; 8:1.
OVERSTEPPED, 1Sa 15:24 for I have **o.**
Jos 23:16; 2Ch 24:20.
OVERSTEPPING, Jos 23:16; 2Ch 24:20.
OVERTAKE, 1Th 5:4 day should **o.** you as
De 19:6; Ps 18:37; 69:24.
OVERTHROWING, Pr 12:7 **o.** wicked ones
OVERTOOK, Ps 40:12 errors **o.** me
OVERTURNING, 2Co 10:4 **o.** entrenched
OVERWHELMED, Ge 7:20 the waters **o.** them
OWES, Eph 3:15 every family **o.** its name,
OWING, Pr 3:27 back to whom it is **o.**
Ro 13:8 Do not be **o.** anybody a single thing,
OWN, Joh 1:11 his **o.** people did not take
Joh 15:19 world would be fond of its **o.**
Mt 20:15; Joh 8:44; Ac 4:32; 1Co 10:24.
OWNER(S), Es 1:17 wives despise their **o.**
Isa 54:5 grand Maker is your husbandly **o.,**
Mt 21:40 when the **o.** of the vineyard comes,
2Pe 2:1 disown even the **o.** that bought them.
Jude 4 proving false to our only **O.** and
Ex 21:3; 2Sa 11:26; 1Ti 6:1; Tit 2:9.
OWNERSHIP, De 4:20; Jer 31:32.

P

PACE, Pr 4:12 your **p.** not be cramped
PACING, Pr 30:29 three that do **p.**
PAID OFF, Isa 40:2 error has been **p.**
PAIN(S), Pr 10:22 he adds no **p.** with it.
Pr 15:1 word causing **p.** makes anger to come
Isa 53:4 as for our **p.,** he bore them.
Isa 66:7 Before labor **p.** she gave birth.
1Ti 6:10 stabbed all over with many **p.**
Re 12:2 cries out in her **p.** to give birth.
Re 21:4 neither will **p.** be any more.
Ge 3:17; Ps 32:10; 55:4; Re 16:10.
PAINS, BIRTH, Ps 51:5 forth with **b.,**
Isa 13:8; 23:4; Re 12:2.
PAINS, CHILDBIRTH, Ga 4:19 I am again in **c.**
Isa 51:2; 54:1; Ga 4:27.
PAINS, LABOR, Jer 6:24; 22:23.
PAINT, Jer 4:30 eyes with black **p.**
PALATE, Ps 137:6 tongue stick to my **p.**
Job 34:3; Pr 24:13; Ca 5:16; La 4:4.
PALE, Isa 29:22 will his face grow **p.;**
Re 6:8 a **p.** horse, and one seated upon it
PALING, Zep 2:1 nation not **p.** in shame
PALM(S), Re 7:9 **p.** branches in their
PALM TREE(S), Nu 33:9 and seventy **p.**
Joh 12:13 took the branches of **p.**
Jg 1:16; 4:5; Ps 92:12; Joe 1:12.
PALPITATED, Ps 38:10 heart **p.** heavily,
PAMPERING, Pr 29:21 **p.** one's servant
PANGS, Ex 15:14 **p.** take hold on
Jer 22:23 **p.,** the labor pains like those
Ac 2:24 by loosing the **p.** of death,
PANGS, BIRTH, Ge 3:16; Ps 48:6.
PANGS OF DISTRESS, Mt 24:8 of **p.**
1Th 5:3 sudden destruction as the **p.**
PANIC, De 20:3; 2Sa 4:4; Ps 104:7.
PANICKY, Ps 116:11; Isa 28:16.
PANTING, Isa 56:10 **p.,** lying down,

PAPYRUS, Ex 2:3; Job 8:11; Isa 18:2.
PAPYRUS BOATS, Jer 51:32 p. burned
PARABLE(S). See ILLUSTRATION(S).
PARADISE, Ca 4:13; Re 2:7.
  Lu 23:43 will be WITH me in P.
  2Co 12:4 he was caught away into p.
PARALYZED, Mt 4:24; 9:2; Lu 5:24.
PARCHED, Isa 19:5; 34:10.
PARCHMENTS, 2Ti 4:13 bring the p.
PARDON, Ex 32:32 p. their sin,—if not,
  Ex 23:21; 1Sa 15:25; Ps 25:18; 99:8.
PARDONING, Mic 7:18 one p. error and
PARENTS, Mt 10:21 children against p.
  Lu 18:29 p. or children for the sake of
  Lu 21:16 you will be delivered up by p.
  2Co 12:14 not to lay up for their p.,
  Eph 6:1 be obedient to your p.
  2Ti 3:2 men will be disobedient to p.,
  Mr 13:12; Lu 2:27; Ro 1:30; Col 3:20.
PARK(S), Ne 2:8; Ec 2:5.
PART(S), Mt 24:51 p. with hypocrites.
  Lu 15:12 give me the p. of the property
  Re 20:6 having p. in the first resurrection
  Ps 5:9; 63:9; Ro 11:25; 1Co 12:23.
PARTAKER(S), Heb 3:1 p. of heavenly calling,
  Eph 3:6; Heb 3:14; 6:4; 12:8.
PARTAKING, 1Co 10:17 p. of one loaf.
  1Co 10:21 p. of the table of Jehovah and
PARTIAL, De 1:17 not be p. in judgment
  Ac 10:34 God is not p.,
  1Co 13:10 that which is p. will be done away
  Jas 3:17 not making p. distinctions.
PARTIALITY, Le 19:15 not treat with p.,
  De 10:17 God, who treats none with p.
  Job 32:21 not show p. to a man;
  Pr 28:21 The showing of p. is not good,
  Ro 2:11 there is no p. with God.
  Ps 82:2; Pr 18:5; Eph 6:9; Col 3:25.
PARTIALLY, 1Co 13:9 we prophesy p.;
PARTICIPATION, Col 1:12 p. in the inheritance
PARTI-COLORED, Zec 6:3, 7 were horses p.
PARTICULAR, 1Ti 2:6 at its own p. times.
PARTNER(S), Ps 45:7 oil more than p.
  Ec 4:10 other can raise his p. up.
  Ps 119:63; Pr 28:24; Lu 5:7; Heb 1:9.
PARTNERSHIP, 2Ch 20:37.
PASSED, Jer 8:20 The harvest has p.,
  1Pe 4:3 time p. is sufficient for you
PASSION(S), Mt 5:28 have a p. for her
  Ro 7:5 the sinful p. excited by Law
  1Co 7:9 marry than to be inflamed with p.
  Ga 5:24 impale the flesh with its p.
PASSOVER, Ex 12:11 It is Jehovah's p.
  Le 23:5 is the p. to Jehovah.
  Joh 2:13 p. of Jews were near,
  Joh 6:4 the p. was near.
  Joh 13:1 festival of the p. had come
  1Co 5:7 Christ our p. has been sanctified
  Ex 12:27, 48; Mr 14:1; Lu 2:41; Heb 11:28.
PAST, Ps 90:4; Ro 11:33; Heb 11:11.
PASTE, Isa 6:10 p. their eyes together,
PASTORS. See SHEPHERDS.
PASTURAGE, Ps 79:13 flock of your p.,
  Jer 25:36 Jehovah is despoiling their p.
  Eze 34:14 In a good p. I shall feed them,
  Joh 10:9 go in and out and find p.
  Ps 100:3; Jer 23:1; La 1:6; Eze 34:18.
PASTURE(S), Ps 23:2 In grassy p. he
  Ps 65:13; Isa 30:23; 49:9; Jer 9:10; Joe 1:
  19; 2:22; Am 1:2; Zep 2:6.
PASTURING, Eze 34:31 sheep of my p.,
PATCH, Mt 9:16; Mr 2:21; Lu 5:36.
PATERNAL HOUSE(S), Nu 17:2 rod for each p.
  Jos 22:14; 1Ch 23:11; 24:4, 31; 26:13.

PATH(S), Ps 16:11 know the p. of life.
  Pr 4:18 p. of the righteous ones is like
  Isa 2:3 we will walk in his p.
  Joe 2:7 neither do they alter their p.
  Heb 12:13 keep making straight p. for your
  Ps 25:10; Pr 3:6; Isa 3:12; 26:7; Mic 4:2.
PATHWAYS, Jg 5:6 p. had no traffic
PATIENCE, Heb 6:12 faith and p. inherit
  Jas 5:7 Exercise p., brothers
  2Pe 3:15 the p. of our Lord as salvation,
  Pr 25:15; Heb 6:15; Jas 5:10; 1Pe 3:20.
PATIENT, 2Sa 13:5 give me bread as a p.
  Ec 7:8; Mt 18:26, 29; 2Pe 3:9.
PATTERN, 2Ti 1:13 Keep holding the p.
  Jas 5:10 take as a p. the prophets,
  2Pe 2:6 setting a p. for ungodly persons
  Ex 25:9, 40; Joh 13:15; Heb 4:11; 8:5.
PATTERNED, Ro 8:29 foreordained to be p.
PAUL, Ac 26:24 You are going mad, P.
  Ga 1:1 P., an apostle, neither from men
  Phm 1 P., a prisoner for the sake
  Phm 9 P. an aged man, yes,
  Ac 13:9; 1Co 1:12; Tit 1:1; 2Pe 3:15.
PAUNCH, Ps 73:4 their p. is fat.
PAVEMENT, 2Ch 7:3; Es 1:6; Joh 19:13.
PAY, Ps 61:8 I may p. my vows day after day,
  Pr 20:22 Do not say: I will p. back evil!
  Ec 5:4 do not hesitate to p. it.
  Jon 2:9 I have vowed, I will p.
  Ps 22:25; 50:14; 66:13; 76:11; 116:14.
PAY ATTENTION, 1Sa 15:22 p. than fat of
  1Ti 4:16 P. to yourself and your teaching.
  Heb 2:1 p. to the things heard by us,
  Isa 34:1; Ac 20:28.
PAY BACK, Mt 22:21 P., Caesar's things
  Isa 66:15; Jer 51:24.
PAYING, De 23:21 not be slow about p.
  Ro 13:6 that is why you also p. taxes;
PAYING ATTENTION, Mal 3:16 kept p. and
PAYMENT, Ho 9:7 days of the due p. must
  Heb 11:26 toward the p. of the reward
PAY OFF, Le 26:34 land p. its sabbaths
PEACE, 2Ki 9:22 Is there p., Jehu?
  Ps 29:11 will bless his people with p.
  Ps 37:11 delight in the abundance of p.
  Ps 72:7 abundance of p. until the moon
  Pr 12:20 counseling p. have rejoicing
  Ec 3:8 time for war and a time for p.
  Isa 9:6 Eternal Father, Prince of P.
  Isa 33:7 messengers of p. will weep bitterly.
  Isa 60:17 I will appoint p. as overseers
  Jer 6:14 There is p.! when there is no p.
  Mic 3:5 call out P. sanctify war
  Mt 5:24 make your p. with your brother
  Mt 10:34 not p., but a sword
  Lu 2:14 p. among men of good will
  Joh 14:27 I give you my p.
  Ro 14:19 pursue things making for p. and
  Ro 16:20 God who gives p. will crush
  Eph 6:15 of the good news of p.
  Php 4:7 the p. of God that excels all
  Col 1:20 making p. through the blood he
  1Th 5:3 P. and security! sudden destruction
  1Pe 3:11 let him seek p. and pursue it.
  Re 6:4 granted to take p. away from earth
  Nu 25:12; Jos 9:15; Ps 28:3; 35:27; 119:
  165; 122:8; Isa 26:3; 52:7; 54:13; Eze
  34:25; 37:26; Mic 5:5; Joh 16:33; Jas 3:18.
PEACEABLE, Mt 5:9 Happy are the p.
  Ro 12:18 be p. with all men.
  Heb 12:11 p. fruit, namely, righteousness.
  Jas 3:17 chaste, then p., reasonable,
PEACEABLY, 2Co 13:11 continue to live p.,
PEACEFUL, Isa 32:18 a p. abiding place

PEARL(S), Mt 7:6 throw **p.** before swine;
  Mt 13:45, 46; Re 17:4; 18:12; 21:21.
PEBBLE, Re 2:17 upon **p.** a new name
PEDDLERS, 2Co 2:17 we are not **p.** of the
PEER, Ob 13 not to **p.** at his calamity
  1Pe 1:12 angels are desiring to **p.**
PEKAH, 2Ki 15:25; 2Ch 28:6; Isa 7:1.
PELEG, Ge 10:25; 11:16-19.
PEN(S), Mic 2:12 like a flock in a **p.**
  Zep 2:6 wells and stone **p.** for sheep.
  3Jo 13 writing you with ink and **p.**
PENALTY, Pr 22:3; 27:12; 2Ti 1:9.
PENNY. See DENARIUS.
PENTECOST, Ac 2:1 while festival of **P.**
  Ac 20:16; 1Co 16:8.
PEOPLE(S), Ex 19:5 special out of all **p.**
  De 33:29 **p.** enjoying salvation
  1Sa 12:22 to make you his **p.**
  Pr 14:28 multitude of **p.** adornment
  Pr 29:2 wicked bears rule, the **p.** sigh.
  Pr 29:18 no vision the **p.** go unrestrained
  Isa 2:3 many **p.** will go and say: "Come,
  Isa 62:10 Clear the way of the **p.**
  Jer 5:31 my own **p.** have loved it
  Jer 31:33 they will become my **p.**
  Ho 2:23 not my **p.** you are my **p.**
  Ho 4:9 for **p.** same as for the priest
  Ac 4:25 **p.** meditate upon fruitless things?
  Ac 15:14 to take a **p.** for his name.
  Ro 9:25 Those not my **p.** I will call my **p.**,
  Tit 2:14 a **p.** peculiarly his own, zealous
  Heb 8:10 they will be a **p.** to me.
  Heb 9:19 sprinkled the book and all the **p.**,
  Heb 11:25 to be ill-treated with the **p.** of God
  1Pe 2:9 a **p.** for special possession,
  Re 7:9 all nations and tribes and **p.**
  Re 17:15 waters mean **p.** and crowds and
  Re 18:4 Get out of her, my **p.**, if you
PEOR, Nu 23:28; 25:18; 31:16; Jos 22:17.
PERCEIVE, Ac 10:34 I **p.** that God is not
PERCEIVED, Ac 4:13 **p.** they were unlettered
  Ro 1:20 qualities **p.** by the things made
PERCEIVING, Eph 5:17 **p.** what the will
PERCEPTIBLE, 2Co 2:14 odor **p.** in every
PERCEPTIONS, 2Co 3:14 their **p.** dulled
PERDITION. See DESTRUCTION.
PERFECT, De 32:4 The Rock, **p.** is his
  Ps 19:7 The law of Jehovah is **p.**,
  Eze 28:12 wisdom and **p.** in beauty. In Eden
  Mt 5:48 You must be **p.** as your Father is **p.**
  Ro 12:2 prove the **p.** will of God
  Heb 2:10 Chief Agent **p.** through sufferings.
  Heb 7:19 the Law made nothing **p.**,
  Heb 10:14 who are sanctified **p.** perpetually.
  Heb 11:40 might not be made **p.** apart from
  1Jo 4:18 but **p.** love throws fear outside,
  2Sa 22:31; Ps 18:32; 2Co 12:9; Php 3:12;
  Heb 5:9; 9:11; Jas 1:17.
PERFECTED, Joh 17:23 that they may be **p.**
  Heb 7:28 appoints a Son, who is **p.** forever.
PERFECTER, Heb 12:2 **p.** faith, Jesus
PERFECTING, 2Co 7:1 **p.** holiness in fear.
PERFECTION, Ps 50:2 **p.** of prettiness,
  Ps 119:96; La 2:15; Lu 8:14; Heb 7:11.
PERFORM, 2Ch 34:31 **p.** words of covenant
  Mt 23:3 they say but do not **p.**
  2Th 1:11 **p.** completely all he pleases of
PERFORMANCE(S), De 3:24 does mighty **p.**
  Job 37:12; Ps 106:2.
PERFUME, Eze 8:11 the **p.** of the cloud
PERFUMED, Mt 26:7; Lu 7:46; Joh 11:2

PERFUMED INCENSE, Ex 25:6; 30:7.
PERIL, 1Co 15:30 we in **p.** every hour?
PERINEAL, Ge 38:29 produced a **p.** rupture for
PERISH, Job 11:20 place for flight will **p.**
  Ps 2:12 not **p.** from the way,
  Ps 9:6 mention of them will certainly **p.**
  Ps 68:2 wicked ones **p.** from before God
  Ps 146:4 In that day his thoughts do **p.**
  Isa 29:14 wisdom of their wise men must **p.**,
  Isa 60:12 that will not serve you will **p.**
  Mt 18:14 for one of these little ones to **p.**
  Heb 11:31 faith Rahab the harlot did not **p.**
  De 30:18; Ps 37:20; Jer 10:11; Ac 8:20.
PERISHED, Nu 16:33 into Sheol, and **p.**
  2Sa 1:27 weapons of war **p.**!
  Ps 10:16 nations have **p.** out of his earth.
  Ec 9:6; Jer 7:28; Mic 4:9; Jude 11.
PERISHING, 1Co 1:18 foolishness to **p.**
  2Th 2:10 deception for those who are **p.**,
PERMIT, Lu 4:41; Ac 19:30; 28:4.
PERMITS, Heb 6:3 we do, if God indeed **p.**
PERPETRATED, Jos 22:31 not **p.** against
PERPETUAL. See INDEFINITELY LASTING,
  TIME(S) INDEFINITE.
PERPETUALLY, Heb 7:3 remains a priest **p.**
  Isa 57:16; Am 1:11; Heb 10:12, 14.
PERPETUITY, Le 25:23, 30 sold in **p.**
PERPLEXED, 2Co 4:8 **p.** no way out;
  Ga 4:20 because I am **p.** over you.
PERPLEXING, 1Ki 10:1 with **p.** questions
PERPLEXITY, Lu 9:7; Ac 2:12; 10:17.
PERSECUTE, Mt 5:11 reproach you and **p.**
  Mt 10:23 When they **p.** you in one city,
  Mt 23:34 and **p.** from city to city;
  Lu 21:12 **p.** you, delivering you up to
  Joh 15:20 **p.** me they will **p.** you also;
  Ac 7:52 prophet did your forefathers not **p.**?
  Ro 12:14 Keep blessing those who **p.**;
PERSECUTED, Mt 5:12 **p.** the prophets
  Joh 15:20 If they have **p.** me, they will
  1Co 4:12 when being **p.**, we bear up;
  2Co 4:9 we are **p.**, but not left in lurch
  2Ti 3:12 live with godly devotion be **p.**
  De 30:7; Ps 119:86, 161; Mt 5:10.
PERSECUTING, Job 19:22 Why keep **p.** me
  Jer 20:11 ones **p.** me will stumble
  Mt 5:44 and to pray for those **p.** you;
  Ga 1:13 I kept on **p.** the congregation
PERSECUTION(S), Isa 14:6 a **p.** without
  Mt 13:21 **p.** has arisen on account of the
  Ro 8:35 or **p.** or hunger or nakedness
  2Co 12:10 **p.** and difficulties, for Christ.
  Mr 10:30; Ac 13:50; 2Th 1:4; 2Ti 3:11.
PERSECUTOR(S), 1Ti 1:13 I was a **p.** and
  Ps 119:157; 142:6; Jer 15:15; 17:18.
PERSEVERE, 1Sa 23:22 **p.** some more and
  Ro 12:12 **P.** in prayer.
PERSEVERING, Col 4:2 Be **p.** in prayer,
PERSIA, Ezr 1:8; 6:14; Es 1:14; Da 8:20.
PERSISTENT, Ru 1:18 she was **p.** about
PERSISTS, 1Ti 5:5 **p.** in prayers night and
PERSON(S) Ex 33:14 My own **p.** will go along
  Ac 3:19 from the **p.** of Jehovah
  1Co 9:19 I am free from all **p.**, I have
  Heb 9:24 before the **p.** of God
  1Pe 3:4 secret **p.** of the heart
  2Pe 3:11 what sort of **p.** ought you to be
  Ps 95:2; Re 4:4; 5:5; 7:11; 11:16.
PERSONAL, Php 2:4 an eye in **p.** interest
PERSONALITIES, Jude 16 admiring **p.** for sake
PERSONALITY, Ro 6:6 our old **p.** was
  Eph 4:22 put away the old **p.** which conforms
  Eph 4:24 put on the new **p.**
  Col 3:9 Strip off the old **p.** with its

PERSONALLY, Jer 25:31 p. in judgment
PERSUADED, Lu 16:31 neither be p. if
Ac 26:26 p. that not one thing is hidden
Ro 14:14 I know and am p. in the Lord Jesus
PERSUADING, 2Co 5:11 we keep p. men,
PERSUASION, Ga 5:8 sort of p. is not
Ac 18:13 p. in worshiping God
PERSUASIVE, 1Co 2:4 p. words
PERSUASIVENESS, Pr 7:21 misled him by p.
Pr 16:23 to his lips it adds p.
PERTAINING, Heb 2:17 things p. to God,
PERTURBED, Eze 27:35 faces become p.
PERVERSE, Pr 8:13 the p. mouth I hated.
Pr 2:12; 23:33 p. things
PERVERSENESS, De 32:20 generation of p.
Pr 6:14 P. in his heart
Pr 10:31.
PERVERSITY, Isa 29:16 The p. of you men!
PERVERT, De 16:19 must not p. judgment.
Ga 1:7 p. the good news about the Christ.
Ex 23:2, 6; 18a 8:3; Job 34:12; Pr 31:5.
PERVERTED, Job 33:27 p. what is upright
PESTILENCE(S), Eze 38:22 judgment with p.
Lu 21:11 and in one place after another p.
De 28:21; Ps 78:50; Jer 14:12; Am 4:10.
PESTLE, Pr 27:22 a p. in a mortar.
PETER, Mt 16:16 P. said: "You are Christ,
Joh 21:15 to Simon P. do you love me
Ac 10:26 P. lifted him up, saying: "Rise;
Mt 26:75; Joh 18:10; Ac 8:20; 10:13.
PETITION(S), Php 4:6 p. be made known
Heb 5:7 p. to the one able to save
1Sa 1:27; Es 5:6; 9:12; Da 6:7, 13.
PHARAOH, Ge 41:55 began to cry to P.
Ex 5:2 But P. said: "Who is Jehovah,
Ex 9:13 take a position in front of P.,
Ro 9:17 to P.: "For this very cause I
Ex 6:29; 14:18, 28; Isa 19:11; Ac 7:10.
PHARISEE(S), Mt 5:20 scribes and P.,
Mt 23:26 Blind P., cleanse first the
Lu 18:11 P. stood and began to pray
Joh 12:42 because of P. they would not
Ac 5:34 a P. named Gamaliel, a Law
Mt 12:14; 23:15, 23, 27, 29; Lu 5:21.
PHENOMENON, Ex 3:3 this great p.,
Job 38:36 understanding to the sky p.?
PHILADELPHIA, Re 1:11; 3:7.
PHILETUS, 2Ti 2:17 Hymenaeus and P. are
PHILIP 1., Mt 10:3; Joh 1:43; 6:5; 12:21.
PHILIP 2., Ac 6:5; 8:5, 26; 21:8.
PHILISTINE(S), Jg 3:3 lords of the P.,
Jg 16:30 Let my soul die with the P.
1Sa 4:10, 11 P. fought and the ark of God
1Sa 17:36 this uncircumcised P. must become
1Sa 31:8 P. found Saul and his sons fallen
Isa 2:6 practicers of magic like the P.,
Eze 25:15 P. have acted with vengeance
Jg 14:4; 1Sa 17:37, 43; Zep 2:5; Zec 9:6.
PHILOSOPHERS, Ac 17:18 the Stoic p.
PHILOSOPHY, Col 2:8 prey through p. of
PHINEHAS, Nu 25:7 P. caught sight of it,
Nu 31:6; Jos 22:30; Jg 20:28; Ps 106:30.
PHYSICAL, 1Co 2:14 a p. man does not
1Co 15:44 It is sown a p. body, it is
PHYSICAL GROWTH, Lu 2:52 p. and favor
PHYSICIAN(S), Ge 50:2 the p. embalmed
Job 13:4 you are p. of no value.
Lu 4:23 P., cure yourself;
Lu 5:31 those healthy do not need a p.,
Col 4:14 Luke the beloved p.
PICKED ONES, Da 11:15 people of his p.;
PIECES, Ps 2:9 dash them to p.
Jer 51:20 I shall dash nations to p.,
Mt 26:15 to him thirty silver p.

Ps 74:14; Isa 30:14; Da 12:7; Mic 3:3.
PIERCED, Jg 5:26 she p. his head
Isa 53:5 he was p. for our transgression;
Joh 19:37 look upon the one whom they p.
Re 1:7 will see him, and those who p. him;
Ps 69:26; Jer 51:52; La 4:9; Zec 12:10.
PIG, Le 11:7 p. is unclean for you.
PILATE, Mt 27:2 handed him over to P.
Mt 27:22 P. said: "What shall I do with
Mr 15:15 P. released Barabbas to them,
Lu 23:12 Herod and P. now became friends
Joh 19:6 P. said: "I do not find any fault
Lu 13:1; Joh 18:37; 19:12, 22; 1Ti 6:13.
PILES, De 28:27; 1Sa 5:6; 6:4.
PILGRIMS. See TEMPORARY RESIDENTS.
PILLAR(S). See also SACRED PILLARS.
PILLAR(S), Ge 19:26 became a p. of salt.
Ge 28:18 Jacob set it up as a p.
Ex 13:22 p. of cloud p. of fire in the
Jg 16:25 stand him between the p.
1Ti 3:15 a p. and support of the truth.
Re 3:12 a p. in the temple of my God,
Ge 28:22; Jg 33:9; Ps 99:7; Ga 2:9.
PILLORY, Jer 29:26 put him into the p.
PINCHING, Pr 16:30 P. his lips together,
PINED AWAY, Ps 119:81 my soul has p.;
Ps 84:2; 119:123; La 4:9.
PIT, Job 33:24 going down into the p.!
Isa 14:15 to the remotest parts of the p.
Da 6:7 thrown to the lions' p.
Mt 15:14 blind, both will fall into a p.
Ps 40:2; Isa 38:18; Eze 26:20.
PITIED, Lu 15:19 all men most to be p.
PITY, Isa 49:13 he shows p. upon his
Mt 15:32 I feel p. for the crowd,
Mt 20:34 Moved with p., Jesus touched their
Ge 43:14; 1Ki 8:50; Ps 40:11; Mr 6:34.
PLACE(S), 1Ki 8:49 established p. of
Ps 37:10 give attention to his p.
Pr 15:3 eyes of Jehovah are in every p.,
Ec 3:20 All are going to one p., to dust
Mt 24:15 thing standing in a holy p.,
Joh 14:2 going to prepare a p. for you.
De 12:11; Ps 91:1; Eze 39:11; Re 12:6, 8.
PLACED, Ro 13:1 authorities p. in their
PLACE OF DESTRUCTION, Pr 27:20 the p.
PLAGUE(S), Ex 11:1 p. more upon Pharaoh
Jer 50:13 whistle on account of all her p.
Re 15:1 seven angels with seven p.
Re 18:4 not receive part of her p.
Re 22:18 God will add to him the p.
Ex 12:13; Jer 19:8; Re 9:20; 11:6; 21:9.
PLAIN, Isa 40:4 a valley p.
PLAINLY, Hab 2:2 Write the vision p.
PLAN(S), Pr 15:22 frustrating of p.
Ex 26:30; 1Ki 6:38; Pr 19:21.
PLANNING AHEAD, Ro 13:14 do not be p.
PLANT, Ps 69:21 Food a poisonous p.,
Isa 51:16 to p. the heavens and earth
Isa 65:22 will not p. and someone else
Jer 1:10 to tear down, to build and to p.
Mt 15:13 Every p. that my heavenly Father
Job 14:9; Jer 18:9; 31:28; Am 9:14.
PLANTATION, Isa 5:7 men are the p. of
PLANTED, Ge 2:8 God p. a garden in Eden,
Ps 1:3 like a tree p. by streams of water,
Jer 2:21 I had p. you as a choice red vine,
1Co 3:6 I p., Apollos watered, but God
Isa 40:24; Jer 17:8; Mt 21:33; Lu 17:6.
PLANTING, Ps 94:9 p. the ear, hear?
PLASTER, Da 5:5 the p. of the wall of
PLASTERED, Le 14:42, 48; Eze 13:14.
PLASTERING, Eze 13:10 p. with whitewash.
PLATFORM, 2Ch 6:13; Zep 1:9.

PLATTER, Mt 14:8; Mr 6:25.
PLAY, Job 40:20; 41:5; Ps 104:26.
PLAYING, 1Sa 16:17 doing well at **p.**
PLEAD, Pr 22:23 Jehovah **p.** their cause
　Isa 1:17 **p.** the cause of the widow.
　Heb 7:25 he is always alive to **p.** for them.
PLEADING, Jer 30:13 one **p.** your cause.
　Ro 8:27 it is **p.** in accord with God for
PLEADS, Ro 8:34 Christ Jesus **p.** for us.
　Ro 11:2 as he **p.** with God against Israel?
PLEASANT, Ps 16:6 fallen in **p.** places.
　Ps 133:1 how **p.** it is for brothers to dwell
　Pr 2:10 knowledge becomes **p.** to your soul,
　2Sa 1:26; Ps 147:1; Pr 15:26; 22:18.
PLEASANTNESS, Pr 16:11 **p.** at your hand
PLEASANT ONE, 2Sa 23:1 the **p.** of melodies
PLEASE, Ro 8:8 with flesh cannot **p.** God
　Ro 15:3 Christ did not **p.** himself;
　Ga 1:10 am I seeking to **p.** men?
　1Th 4:1 you ought to walk and **p.** God,
　Heb 11:6 without faith impossible to **p.** him
PLEASED, Mic 6:7 Will Jehovah be **p.**
　1Co 12:18 set each one of them, as he **p.**
　1Co 15:38; Col 1:27; Heb 13:16.
PLEASES, 2Th 1:11 perform all he **p.** of
PLEASING, Joh 8:29 things **p.** to him.
　Ro 15:1 are strong not be **p.** ourselves.
　Ga 1:10 If I were yet **p.** men, I would
　1Th 2:4 **p.** not men, but God,
　Ps 69:31; 1Co 10:33; 1Th 2:15; 1Jo 3:22.
PLEASURABLE, Ps 19:14 sayings become **p.**
　Pr 13:19 Desire when realized is **p.** to the
PLEASURE(S), 1Ch 29:3 **p.** in the house
　Ps 149:4 God is taking **p.** in his people.
　Lu 8:14 by anxieties and **p.** of this life,
　2Co 12:10 I take **p.** in weaknesses,
　Php 2:13 for the sake of his good **p.,** a
　2Ti 3:4 lovers of **p.** rather than God,
　Heb 10:38 my soul has no **p.** in him.
　Jas 5:5 and have gone in for sensual **p.**
　1Ch 29:17; Ps 147:11; Pr 14:35; Mal 1:8;
　Eph 1:5; 2Th 2:12; Tit 3:3.
PLENTY, 1Co 15:58 **p.** to do in the work
　2Co 9:8 you may have **p.** for every good work
PLOTTING, Ps 37:12 wicked one is **p.** against
PLOW(S), Pr 20:4 lazy one will not **p.**
　Lu 9:62 man who **p.** ought to **p.** in hope
　1Co 9:10 man who **p.** ought to **p.** in hope
PLOWED, Pr 13:23 **P.** ground of persons
PLOWMAN, Am 9:13 the **p.** will overtake
PLOWSHARES, Isa 2:4 beat swords into **p.**
　Joe 3:10 beat your **p.** into swords
PLUMMET, Am 7:7, 8; Zec 4:10.
PLUMPED, Jg 7:12 were **p.** in the low plain
PLUNDER, Eze 34:28 something to **p.** for
　De 20:14; 2Ch 20:25; Isa 10:6; 42:22.
PLUNDERERS, Joh 10:8 thieves and **p.;**
PLUNDERING, Da 11:33 will stumble by **p.,**
　Ge 34:27; Heb 10:34.
PLUNGE, 2Ki 5:14 **p.** into the Jordan
　1Ti 6:9 desires which **p.** men into ruin.
PODIUM, Ne 8:4 upon a wooden **p.,**
POISINGS, Job 37:16 know the **p.** of clouds
POISON, Jas 3:8 tongue is full of **p.**
POKING FUN, Ge 21:9 son of Hagar **p.**
POLICE, Da 3:2, 3 the **p.** magistrates
POLLUTED, Ps 106:38 land came to be **p.**
　Isa 24:5 land **p.** under its inhabitants,
　Jer 23:11 prophet and priest have become **p.**
　Mal 1:7 presenting upon my altar **p.** bread,
　Mal 1:12 table of Jehovah is something **p.**
　Jer 3:1; Mic 4:11.
POLLUTES, Nu 35:33 it is blood that **p.**
POLLUTING, Jer 3:9 she kept **p.** the land

PONDER, De 32:29; 1Ti 4:15.
PONDERED, Ps 48:9 **p.,** O God, over your
POOR, Ps 69:33 is listening to the **p.,**
　Jer 2:34 blood marks of the **p.** ones.
　Lu 4:18 to declare good news to the **p.,**
　Joh 12:8 you have the **p.** always with you,
　2Co 6:10 as **p.** but making many rich,
　2Co 8:9 he became **p.** for your sakes,
　Jas 2:5 God chose the ones who are **p.**
　Ex 23:6; 1Sa 2:8; Job 24:4; Ps 9:18; 72:4;
　107:41; 132:15; Isa 14:30; 25:4; Jer 5:28;
　Am 8:4; Mt 11:5; Mr 12:43.
POPLAR, Ps 137:2 **p.** trees we hung harps.
POPULAR, Jer 8:6 going back to **p.** course
POPULATION, Pr 14:28 lack of **p.** is the
POPULOUS, Ps 110:6 head over a **p.** land.
PORTENT(S), Zec 3:8 men serving as **p.;**
　Ac 2:22 Jesus shown by **p.** and signs
　Heb 2:4 bore witness with signs and **p.**
　De 13:1, 2; Eze 12:11; 24:24, 27; Joe 2:30.
PORTION, Isa 53:12 deal him a **p.** among
　1Co 7:17 Jehovah has given each one a **p.,**
　2Co 6:15 what **p.** does a faithful person
　Ps 11:6; Ec 9:6; Zec 2:12.
PORTRAYED, Ga 3:1 openly **p.** impaled?
POSITION(S), Ob 4; Jude 6; Re 4:2.
　Ro 13:1 placed in their **p.**
POSITIVE, Ac 1:3 by **p.** proofs he showed
POSSESS, Ps 37:11 meek ones will **p.** the
POSSESSED, Ac 7:45 Joshua into land **p.**
POSSESSING, 2Co 6:10 yet **p.** all things.
POSSESSION, Ge 17:8 a **p.** to time indefinite
　Ge 22:17 seed take **p.** of the gate of enemies
　Ps 2:8 ends of earth as your own **p.**
　Isa 57:13 will take **p.** of my holy mountain.
　Ac 7:5 did not give him any **p.** in it,
　Eph 1:14 by a ransom God's own **p.,**
　1Th 4:4 each get **p.** of his own vessel
　2Th 3:2 faith is not a **p.** of all people.
　1Pe 2:9 a people for special **p.**
　Nu 13:30; De 1:21; 2Ch 20:11; Ps 44:3;
　69:35; Eze 36:12.
POSSIBLE, Mt 19:26 God all things are **p.**
　Mt 24:24 mislead, if **p.,** the chosen ones.
　Mt 26:39 if **p.,** let this cup pass away
　Heb 10:4 not **p.** for the blood of bulls
　Ac 2:24; Ro 12:18; 1Co 11:20.
POSTERITY, Job 18:19; Da 11:4.
POSTPONED, Pr 13:12 Expectation **p.** is
POSTPONEMENT, Eze 12:25, 28 be no **p.**
POTASH, Job 9:30 cleansed hands in **p.,**
POTENT, Ps 135:10 He killed **p.** kings,
POTENTATE, 1Ti 6:15 happy and only **P.**
POTTER('S, S), Ps 2:9 **p.** vessel will dash
　Isa 29:16 **p.** be like clay?
　Isa 64:8 We are clay, you are our **P.,**
　Jer 18:6 clay in the hand of the **p.**
　Mt 27:7 bought the **p.** field to bury
　Ro 9:21 Does not the **p.** have authority
　Isa 30:14; 41:25; Jer 18:4; La 4:2.
POUND, Ex 30:36 **p.** powder before
POUR, Le 17:13 **p.** its blood out and
　Zep 3:8 to **p.** out my denunciation,
　Ac 2:17 I shall **p.** my spirit out
　Ps 62:8; Eze 21:31; Joe 2:28; Re 16:1.
POURED, Ps 22:14 I have been **p.** out.
　Isa 53:12 he **p.** out his soul to death
　Zep 1:17 blood **p.** out like dust,
　Ps 45:2; 77:17; Mic 1:4; Na 1:6; Ac 2:33.
POVERTY, Pr 13:18 comes to **p.** and dishonor
　Pr 30:8 neither **p.** nor riches.
　2Co 8:9 you become rich through his **p.**
　Re 2:9 I know your tribulation and **p.**
　Ge 45:11; Pr 6:11; 20:13; 24:34; 30:9.

POWDER, 2Ch 34:4; Na 1:3; Mal 4:3.
POWER(S), Ex 9:16 for showing you my **p.**
Isa 40:29 He is giving to the tired one **p.,**
Zec 4:6 Not by **p.,** but by my spirit,
Mt 24:29 **p.** of the heavens will be
Ac 1:8 you will receive **p.** when the spirit
Ro 8:38 nor things to come nor **p.**
Ro 9:22 will to make his **p.** known,
1Co 4:20 kingdom lies not in speech but **p.**
1Co 15:43 sown in weakness, raised in **p.**
2Co 4:7 **p.** beyond what is normal may be
2Co 12:9 **p.** of Christ remain over me.
Col 1:29 at work in me with **p.**
2Ti 1:7 not a spirit of cowardice, but of **p.**
2Ti 3:5 form devotion but false to its **p.;**
Heb 5:14 their perceptive **p.** trained to
1Pe 3:22 authorities and **p.** made subject
Re 11:17 taken your great **p.** and begun
Jg 16:17; 1Sa 2:9; 2Ki 19:3; Job 37:23;
2:1; Heb 6:5; 1Pe 1:5; Re 12:10.
POWERFUL, Joe 2:7 Like **p.** men they run.
1Co 1:26 not many **p.,** not many noble;
2Co 10:4 not fleshly, but **p.** by God
2Co 12:10 when I am weak, then I am **p.**
2Th 1:7 Jesus from heaven with his **p.** angels
Isa 1:24; Mr 9:39; Ro 4:20; Heb 11:34.
POWERFUL WORKS, 1Co 12:10, 28, 29; Ga 3:5.
PRACTICAL, Lu 16:8 wiser in a **p.** way
PRACTICAL WISDOM, Job 11:6; 12:16.
Pr 2:7 the upright will treasure up **p.;**
Pr 3:21 Safeguard **p.** and thinking ability,
Pr 8:14 I have counsel and **p.**
Pr 18:1 against all **p.** he will break forth.
Mic 6:9 the person of **p.** will fear your
Lu 1:17 turn hearts to **p.** of righteous ones,
PRACTICE(S), Ro 2:1 **p.** the same things.
Ro 7:19 bad I do not wish is what I **p.**
Ro 8:13 put the **p.** of the body to death
1Jo 3:6 in union with him does not **p.** sin;
Ro 2:2; 7:15; 1Ti 5:20; Heb 10:26.
PRACTICED, Ro 9:11 **p.** anything good or
2Co 5:10 award according to things he **p.**
PRACTICERS OF MAGIC, Isa 2:6; Jer 27:9.
Mic 5:12 no **p.** will you continue to have.
PRACTICERS OF WHAT IS HURTFUL, Ps 14:4;
59:2; 92:7; 94:4; 125:5; Pr 10:29.
PRACTICING, 1Jo 1:6 not **p.** the truth.
Ps 141:4; Mic 2:1; Ro 1:32.
PRACTICING WHAT IS HURTFUL, Job 34:22.
PRAETORIAN GUARD, Php 1:13 all the **p.**
PRAISE(S), Pr 27:2 May a stranger **p.** you;
Isa 38:18 death itself cannot **p.** you.
Isa 42:8 neither my **p.** to graven images.
Isa 60:18 Salvation and your gates **P.**
Mt 21:16 out of sucklings you furnished **p.?**
1Co 4:5 each will have his **p.** from God.
Heb 2:12 I will **p.** you with song.
Heb 13:15 offer to God a sacrifice of **p.,**
Ps 65:1; 71:8; 79:13; 109:30; 111:10; Isa
62:7; Hab 3:3; Zep 3:19; Ro 2:29.
PRAISED, Ps 119:164 Seven times I **p.**
PRAISE JAH, Ps 115:117 dead do not **p.**
Ps 150:6 Everything breathing **p.**
Re 19:1 **P.,** you people!
Ps 102:18; 147:1; Re 19:3, 4, 6.
PRAISEWORTHY, Php 4:8 whatever **p.** thing
PRAISING, Lu 2:13; Ac 2:47; 3:8.
PRAY, 1Ki 8:48 **p.** in the direction of
2Ch 6:32 foreigner **p.** toward this house,
2Ch 7:14 humble and **p.** and seek my face
Jer 7:16 do not **p.** in behalf of
Mt 5:44 **p.** for those persecuting you;
Mt 6:9 You must **p.,** then, this way:

Mt 26:41 **p.,** that you may not enter
Mr 11:24 things you **p.** for you will have
1Th 5:17 **P.** incessantly.
Jas 5:16 **p.** for one another,
Mt 6:5; Ac 8:22; Ro 8:26; 1Co 14:15.
PRAYER(S), 1Ki 8:28 toward the **p.**
1Ki 8:49 you must hear their **p.** and request
Pr 15:8 **p.** of the upright is a pleasure
Pr 15:29 **p.** of the righteous he hears.
Mt 21:13 My house will be a house of **p.,**
Mr 12:40 for a pretext making long **p.;**
Ac 10:4 Your **p.** have ascended before God.
Ro 12:12 Persevere in **p.**
Php 4:6 by **p.** with thanksgiving let your
Col 4:2 persevering in **p.,** remaining awake
1Pe 4:7 be vigilant with a view to **p.**
Ps 102:17; Pr 28:9; Isa 1:15; 56:7; Eph
6:18; 1Ti 2:1; 1Pe 3:7; Re 8:4.
PRAYING, Mt 24:20 Keep **p.** that your
PREACH, Mt 10:7 As you go, **p.,** saying,
Mt 10:27 **p.** from the housetops.
Lu 4:19 to **p.** Jehovah's acceptable year.
Ac 10:42 he ordered us to **p.** to people
Ro 10:14 hear without someone to **p.?**
Ro 10:15 How will they **p.** unless sent forth?
1Co 1:23 we **p.** Christ impaled, to the Jews
2Ti 4:2 **P.** the word, be at it urgently
PREACHED, Mt 24:14 kingdom will be **p.**
1Co 1:21 foolishness of what is **p.**
1Co 2:4 I **p.** not with persuasive words
Lu 11:32; Ro 15:19; 1Co 9:27; 1Pe 3:19.
PREACHER, 1Ti 2:7 I was appointed a **p.**
2Ti 1:11 I was appointed a **p.** and apostle
2Pe 2:5 Noah, a **p.** of righteousness,
PREACHING, Mt 4:17 Jesus commenced **p.**
Lu 8:1 from village to village **p.**
1Co 15:14 our **p.** is certainly in vain,
Mt 3:1; 4:23; 9:35; Ac 28:31; Ga 2:2.
PRECEDE, 1Th 4:15 **p.** those asleep in
PRECIOUS, Ps 116:15 **P.** in the eyes of
Ps 139:17 **p.** your thoughts
Pr 3:15 It is more **p.** than corals,
Isa 43:4 you have been **p.** in my eyes,
1Pe 1:19 with **p.** blood, even Christ's.
1Pe 2:4 rejected by men, **p.** with God,
1Sa 26:21; 1Pe 2:6; 2Pe 1:4; Re 17:4.
PRECIPICE, Mt 8:32; Mr 5:13; Lu 8:33.
PRECIPITATING, Isa 5:6 keep from **p.** any rain
PRECIPITOUS, Isa 7:19 the **p.** torrent
PREDESTINATE. See FOREORDAINED.
PREDICTION(S), Ac 16:16; 1Ti 1:18; 4:14.
PREFECT(S), Da 2:48; 3:2; 6:7.
PREFERABLE, Pr 21:3 judgment is more **p.**
PREFERENCE, Ex 23:3 not **p.** in controversy
PREGNANT, Isa 7:14 become **p.,** and she
Ge 4:1; Ec 11:5; Lu 1:24.
PREJUDGMENT, 1Ti 5:21 things without **p.,**
PREMATURELY, Ec 6:3; 1Co 15:8.
PREOCCUPYING, Ec 5:20 God is **p.** him
PREPARATION, Jer 46:14 making **p.** also
Eze 38:7; Mt 27:62; Joh 19:14, 31, 42.
PREPARE, Joh 14:2 I go to **p.** a place
Ps 78:20; Pr 30:25; Mt 11:10.
PREPARED, Ps 8:3 moon and stars you **p.,**
Mt 25:34 inherit the kingdom **p.** for you
Lu 1:17 get ready for Jehovah a **p.** people.
Ro 9:23 which he **p.** beforehand for glory,
1Co 2:9 God **p.** for those who love him.
2Ti 2:21 **p.** for every good work.
Heb 10:5 you **p.** a body for me.
Es 7:10; Pr 21:31; Mt 20:23; 25:41.
PRESCRIBED, Job 23:12, 14 treasured **p.** for
Jer 5:24 **p.** weeks of
PRESCRIPTION, Ezr 6:18 **p.** of the book

PRESENCE, Mt 24:3 the sign of your p.
Mt 24:37 the p. of the Son of man
1Co 15:23 belong to Christ during his p.
2Co 10:10 his p. in person is weak
Php 2:12 obeyed, not during my p. only,
2Pe 1:16 power and p. of our Lord Jesus
2Pe 3:4 Where is this promised p. of his?
1Jo 2:28 shamed away from him at his p.
Mt 24:27; 1Th 4:15; Jas 5:7, 8; 2Pe 3:12.

PRESENT, Ro 6:13 p. yourselves to God
Ro 12:1 p. your bodies a sacrifice
2Co 11:2 p. you as a chaste virgin
Ga 1:4 the p. wicked system of things
2Ti 2:15 p. yourself approved to God,
Ro 7:18; 8:18; 1Co 5:3; Eph 5:27.

PRESENTATION, Mt 12:4; Lu 6:4.

PRESERVATION, Ge 45:5 the p. of life

PRESERVE, Ps 79:11 p. those appointed
Ps 80:18 May you p. us alive, that we may
Lu 17:33 whoever loses it will p. it alive.
Job 36:6; Ps 119:25, 107; Jer 49:11.

PRESERVED, Ps 119:50 your sayings p. me

PRESERVES, Ec 7:12 wisdom p. its owners.

PRESIDE(S), 1Ti 3:5 p. over household,
Ro 12:8; 1Ti 5:17.

PRESIDING, 1Th 5:12 regard for those p.

PRESIDING OFFICER(S), Mr 5:22; Lu 8:49;
13:14; Ac 13:15; 18:8.

PRESSED, 2Co 4:8 We are p. in every way,

PRESSING, Tit 3:14 meet their p. needs

PRESSURE, Ps 55:3 p. of the wicked one.
Job 32:18; Ps 66:11; 2Co 1:8; Php 1:23.

PRESSURED, Jg 16:16 because she p. him
Jg 14:17; Job 32:18.

PRESUMED, Nu 14:44 they p. to go up

PRESUMES, De 18:20 prophet who p. to

PRESUMPTUOUS, Ps 19:13 from p. acts
Ps 119:78 Let p. ones be
Isa 13:11 pride of the p. ones to cease,
Ps 86:14; 119:21; Pr 21:24; Mal 3:15; 4:1.

PRESUMPTUOUSNESS, Pr 13:10 By p. one
Jer 50:31 against you O P. your day must
De 17:12; Pr 11:2; Jer 49:16; Eze 7:10.

PRETENDING, Pr 13:7 one p. to be rich

PRETENSE, Ga 2:13 putting on this p.,
Php 1:18 whether in p. or in truth,

PRETEXT, Da 6:4 find in Daniel no p.
Lu 20:47 for a p. make long prayers.
2Co 11:12 wanting p. for being found equal

PRETTINESS, Ps 50:2 Zion perfection of p.
Pr 6:25 not desire her p.

PRETTY, Ec 3:11 everything he has made p.
Es 2:7; Job 42:15; Ps 48:2.

PREVAIL, Ps 16:5 with what we can p.
Jer 1:19 they will not p. against you,
Jer 20:11 the ones persecuting will not p.
Re 12:8 did not p., neither was a place

PREVAILED, Ps 129:2 not p. over me.

PREVAILING, Ac 19:20 word Jehovah kept p.

PREVALENCE, 1Co 7:2 p. of fornication

PREVENT, Mr 9:38 we tried to p. him,

PREY, Ps 124:6 As a p. to their teeth.
Col 2:8 carry you off as his p. through
Isa 31:4; Eze 22:27; Na 2:13.

PRICE, Isa 55:1 come, buy without p.
Mic 3:11 her priests instruct for a p.
1Co 6:20 you were bought with a p.
Da 11:39; Mt 27:9; Ac 5:3; 1Co 7:23.

PRICKLE, Eze 28:24 no more a malignant p.

PRIDE, Pr 16:18 P. is before a crash.
2Th 1:4 we take p. in you among the
1Ti 3:6 he might get puffed up with p.
Jas 4:16 All such taking of p. is wicked.
Ps 59:12; Pr 8:13; Jer 13:9; 48:29.

PRIEST(S), Ge 14:18 Melchizedek p. of
Ex 40:15 must act as p. to me
Ps 110:4 You are a p. to time indefinite
Isa 28:7 P. and prophet—have gone astray
Mic 3:11 her p. instruct just for a price
Zec 3:1 Joshua the high p. standing before
Heb 3:1 apostle and high p.—Jesus.
Re 20:6 p. of God and rule the thousand
1Sa 2:35; Joh 19:15; Heb 5:5; 9:25.

PRIESTHOOD, Ex 40:15 a p. to time
Heb 7:24 his p. without any successors.
1Pe 2:5 p., to offer spiritual sacrifices
1Pe 2:9 a royal p., a holy nation.
Nu 25:13; Jos 18:7; Ne 13:29; Heb 7:11.

PRIMARY, Heb 6:1 p. doctrine about the

PRIME, Pr 4:7 Wisdom is the p. thing.

PRIME OF LIFE, Ec 11:10 p. are vanity.

PRINCE(S). See also CAPTAIN, CHIEF(S),
CHIEF AGENT, RULER(S).

PRINCE(S), Ps 45:16 appoint as p. in all the
Isa 9:6 Eternal Father, P. of Peace.
Isa 32:1 they will rule as p. for justice
Da 10:13 p. of the royal realm of Persia
Da 12:1 Michael will stand up, the great p.
Jos 5:14; Job 34:19; Da 8:11, 25; Zep 1:8.

PRINCELY RULE, Isa 9:6 p. will be upon

PRINCESSES, 1Ki 11:3; Es 1:18; Isa 49:23.

PRINCIPAL, Nu 5:7 its p., adding a fifth

PRINCIPAL MEN, Ac 13:50; 25:2.

PRINCIPAL WOMEN, Ac 17:4 p. did so.

PRINCIPLE(S). See ELEMENTARY THINGS,
RULE.

PRINT, Joh 20:25 p. of the nails and

PRISCILLA, Ac 18:2, 18, 26.

PRISON, 1Pe 3:19 to the spirits in p.
Re 2:10 throwing some of you into p.
Re 20:7 Satan let loose out of his p.,
Mt 5:25; 25:36; Lu 22:33; Ac 5:19.

PRISONER(S), Isa 42:7 bring out the p.,
Isa 49:9 say to the p., 'Come out!'
Eph 3:1 I Paul, the p. of Christ
2Ti 1:8 ashamed Lord, neither of me a p.
Job 3:18; Ps 69:33; 79:11; 102:20;
Isa 14:17; Zec 9:12; Mt 27:15; Ac 16:25.

PRIVATE, Mt 6:6; Php 2:25, 30; 2Pe 1:20.

PRIVATELY, Ga 2:2 preaching among p.,

PRIVATE PARTS, Ex 20:26; Eze 16:36.

PRIVATE PROPERTY, Ac 9:26 ruin your p.

PRIVATES, De 25:11 hold of him by his p.,

PRIVILEGE, Php 1:29 the p. was given
2Pe 1:1 faith, held in equal p. with ours,

PRIZE, 1Co 9:24 one receives the p.?
Php 3:14 toward the goal for the p.
Col 2:18 Let no man deprive you of the p.

PROCEDURE(S), Le 5:10 burnt offering p.
Nu 9:3 according to its regular p. prepare

PROCEEDS, Ac 2:45 distributing the p.

PROCESSED, Nu 31:23 that is p. with fire

PROCESSION(S), Col 2:15 in triumphal p.
Ps 68:24; 2Co 2:14.

PROCLAIM, Le 25:10 p. liberty in the
Isa 61:1 to p. liberty to those
Joe 3:9 p. this among the nations
Pr 20:6; Isa 61:2; Jer 19:2; 34:8, 15;
Jon 3:5; Mr 5:20.

PROCLAIMED, 2Ki 10:20 they p. it.

PROCLAIMING, Jer 34:17 p. liberty each
Lu 8:39 p. throughout the whole city what
1Co 9:14 those p. good news live by means
1Co 11:26 you keep p. the death of the

PROCLAMATION, Jon 3:2 proclaim to her the p.

PROCONSUL(S), Ac 13:7; 18:12; 19:38.

PRODUCE, Pr 3:9 Honor Jehovah with p.
Isa 27:6 fill the productive land with p.

PRODUCED, 2Co 5:5 he that p. us for
PRODUCT, Mt 26:29 this p. of the vine
PRODUCTION, De 28:33 your p. people will eat
PRODUCTIVE LAND, Ps 9:8 judge the p.
Isa 26:9 inhabitants of the p. will
Ps 24:1; 89:11; 96:10; Isa 13:11; 24:4.
PROFANE, Le 21:12 not p. the sanctuary
Ps 89:34 shall not p. my covenant,
Eze 28:16 I shall put you as p. out of
Eze 36:20 people will p. my holy name
Da 11:31 they will p. the sanctuary,
Le 19:12; Jer 34:16; Eze 7:21; 1Ti 1:9.
PROFANED, Ps 55:20; Isa 47:6; Eze 39:7.
PROFESSIONAL FORETELLERS, Le 20:6.
PROFICIENCY, Ec 2:21; 4:4.
PROFIT(S), Isa 23:18 p. and her hire
Heb 12:10 discipline us for our p.
Jas 4:13 engage in business and make p.,
PROFITABLE, Ac 20:20 that were p. nor
PROFOUND, Ps 69:2 come into p. waters
PROGENY, De 7:13; Job 18:19; Ac 17:28.
PROGRESS, Php 3:16 extent we made p.,
Job 8:37; Ga 1:14; 2Ti 3:9.
PROLONG, Pr 28:16; Ec 8:13; Isa 53:10.
PROMINENT, Mt 23:6; Lu 14:7, 8; Ro 3:7.
PROMISE(S), Ro 4:13 p. that he should
Ro 9:4 the sacred service and the p.;
2Co 7:1 since we have these p. let us
Ga 3:29 heirs with reference to a p.
Heb 6:12 faith and patience inherit the p.
Heb 8:6 established upon better p.
Heb 11:39 not get the fulfillment of the p.
2Pe 3:13 awaiting according to his p.,
Ac 2:39; Ro 4:14; Ga 3:16; Heb 11:13.
PROMISED, De 26:18 he has p. you,
Tit 1:2 God p. before times lasting
Heb 10:23 for he is faithful that p.
Jas 1:12 crown of life, which Jehovah p.
Jas 2:5 which he p. to those who love
1Ki 8:56; Ac 2:33; 7:5; Ro 1:2; 4:21.
PROMOTE, Ps 140:8 do not p. his plotting
PROMULGATED, Da 2:5, 8; 1Ti 1:9.
PRONOUNCE, Job 32:3 proceeded to p. God
Ps 72:17; 94:21.
PRONOUNCEMENT(S), Ac 7:38; Ro 3:2; 11:4.
PROOF(S), 2Co 2:9 write to ascertain the p.
1Th 2:4 God, who makes p. of our hearts.
2Th 1:5 a p. of the righteous judgment
Ac 1:3; Php 2:22.
PROPER, Jas 3:10 not p. this way
PROPERTY, Ex 19:5 you will become my p.
De 14:2 become his people, a special p.
Lu 15:13 son squandered his p.
PROPHECY, Mt 13:14 p. of Isaiah is
2Pe 1:20 no p. of Scripture springs from
2Pe 1:21 For p. was at no time brought by
2Ch 9:29; 15:8; Ne 6:12; Ro 12:6; Re 1:3.
PROPHESIES, Jer 28:9 prophet p. peace,
1Co 14:3 he that p. upbuilds men by his
PROPHESY, Jer 5:31 The prophets p. in
Jer 26:12 was Jehovah that sent me to p.
Joe 2:28 sons and your daughters will p.
Ac 2:17 your sons and daughters will p.
1Co 13:9 and we p. partially; but
1Co 14:1 but preferably that you may p.
Eze 39:1; Zec 13:3; Re 10:11; 11:3.
PROPHESYING, Jer 14:14 p. in my name
1Co 14:39 keep seeking the p.,
Re 19:10 Jesus is what inspires p.
1Ki 22:12; Jer 23:16; 27:10; 1Co 13:2.
PROPHET(S), Ge 20:7 for he is a p.
De 18:18 a p. I shall raise up for them
1Sa 9:9 p. of today called a seer
1Ki 18:22 I have been left as a p.

2Ki 10:19 call all the p. of Baal,
Isa 9:15 the p. giving false instruction
Jer 7:25 sending all my servants the p.,
Eze 33:33 know that a p. proved to be
Da 9:24 imprint a seal upon vision and p.,
Am 3:7 revealed to his servants the p.
Zec 13:5 will say, 'I am no p.
Mt 5:12 they persecuted the p. prior
Mt 7:15 watch for false p.
Mt 13:57 A p. is not unhonored except
Mr 13:22 and false p. will arise
Ac 3:21 spoke through his holy p.
Ac 3:22 God will raise up a p. like me.
Jas 5:10 take as a pattern the p.,
Re 11:18 to give reward to the p.
Re 16:13 out of the mouth of the false p.
Ex 7:1; Nu 11:29; 1Ch 16:22; Isa 29:10;
Jer 6:13; 14:14; 23:28; Mic 3:11; Mal 4:5;
Mt 11:9; Joh 7:40; Re 18:24; 19:20.
PROPHETESS, 2Ki 22:14 Huldah the p.
Lu 2:36 Anna a p., eighty-four years old),
Ex 15:20; Isa 8:3; Re 2:20.
PROPITIATION, Ro 3:25 offering for p.
PROPITIATORY, 1Jo 2:2 is a p. sacrifice
Heb 2:17; 1Jo 4:10.
PROPITIATORY COVER, 1Ch 28:11.
Heb 9:5 cherubs overshadowing the p.
PROPORTION, Nu 7:7; 1Pe 4:10.
PROPORTIONED, Ro 12:6 to the faith p. to us
PROPOUND, Jg 14:12; Eze 17:2.
PROSPER, Ac 15:29 you will p.
PROSPERITY, De 28:11 overflow with p.
1Ki 10:7 You have surpassed in wisdom and p.
De 30:9; Ps 68:6; Jer 19:25.
PROSPEROUSLY, 1Th 3:11 way p. to you.
PROSTITUTE(S), Jos 6:25 Rahab the p.
1Ki 22:38 pool of Samaria the p. bathed
Isa 1:21 faithful town has become a p.!
Ho 4:14 with the female temple p.
Joe 3:3 give child for p.,
Am 7:17 your wife will become a p.
Pr 7:10; Mic 1:7.
PROSTITUTION(S), Isa 23:17 commit p.
Jer 3:1 committed p. with many companions;
Eze 23:3 In their youth they committed p.
Jer 3:9; Eze 16:29; 23:8; Na 3:4.
PROSTRATE, Ex 34:14 not p. to another god
Isa 46:6.
PROSTRATES, Isa 44:15 p. himself to it.
PROTECT, Ps 20:1; 59:1; 69:29.
PROTECTION, Pr 18:10 righteous given p.
Ec 7:12 wisdom is for a p.
PROTECTIVE, Pr 18:11 like a p. wall in
PROUD, Pr 16:5 Everyone p. in heart is
Zec 11:3 thickets have been despoiled.
PROVE, Ro 12:2 you may p. to yourselves
1Co 3:13 fire will p. what sort of work
Ga 6:4 let him p. what his own work
PROVERB, Pr 1:6 to understand a p. and
PROVERBIAL SAYING, Hab 2:6 lift up a p.
De 28:37; Ps 44:14; 78:2; Isa 14:4; Eze
17:2; 18:2; Mic 2:4.
PROVERBIAL UTTERANCE, Ps 49:4 To a p. I
PROVE TO BE, Ex 3:14 I shall p. what I
PROVIDE, Ro 12:17 P. fine things in
1Ti 5:8 if anyone does not p. for those
PROVIDER, Ps 40:17 my assistance and P. of
2Sa 22:2; Ps 18:2; 144:2.
PROVISION, 2Co 8:21 make honest p.,
PROVOCATION, Ps 106:32 p. at the waters
PROVOKED, 1Co 13:5 does not become p.
Heb 3:16 yet p. to bitter anger?
PROVOKED STATE, Eph 4:26 sun set in a p.,
PRUDENT, Ne 9:20 spirit make them p.

PRUDENTLY, 1Sa 18:14 David was acting **p.**
1Sa 18:5, 30; 1Ki 2:3; 2Ki 18:7.
PRUNE, Le 25:3, 4 should **p.** your vineyard
PRUNING SHEARS, Isa 2:4 spears into **p.**
Joe 3:10 and your **p.** into lances.
Mic 4:3 spears into **p.** They will not lift
PSALMS, Lu 20:42; Eph 5:19; Jas 5:13.
PUBLIC, Col 2:15 exhibited in open **p.**
PUBLICAN(S). See TAX COLLECTOR(S).
PUBLIC DECLARATION, Ro 10:10 makes **p.**
Heb 13:15 fruit of lips which make **p.**
PUBLIC INSTRUCTOR(S), Mt 13:52; 23:34.
PUBLICIZED, Php 1:18 Christ is being **p.,**
PUBLICIZING, Php 1:16; Col 1:28.
PUBLICLY, Joh 7:13; 18:20; Ac 20:20.
PUBLIC READING, Ac 13:15; 1Ti 4:13.
PUBLIC SERVANT(S), Ro 13:6 God's **p.**
Ro 15:16 **p.** of Christ to the nations,
Heb 8:2 **p.** of the holy place and tent,
PUBLIC SERVICE, Heb 8:6 excellent **p.,**
Heb 10:11 from day to day to render **p.** and
PUBLISH, Jer 5:20; 31:7; Am 4:5.
PUBLISHED, Es 3:14; 8:13; Ac 15:36.
PUBLISHING, Isa 52:7; Jer 4:15.
PUFFED UP, 1Co 4:6; 5:2; 13:4.
PUFFS UP, 1Co 8:1 Knowledge **p.,** but love
PUKE, Jer 25:27 get drunk and **p.** and
PULVERIZE, 2Sa 22:43 I shall **p.** them;
Mic 4:13 you will certainly **p.** many peoples
PULVERIZED, 2Ch 15:16 idol and **p.** it and
PUNISH, Ac 4:21 ground on which to **p.**
PUNISHED, Ac 22:5 to Jerusalem to be **p.**
PUNISHING, Ac 26:11 **p.** them many times
PUNISHMENT, Ex 34:7 exemption from **p.,**
Jer 25:29 should you go free of **p.?**
Zec 14:19 **p.** for the sin of Egypt
2Co 10:6 inflict **p.** for every disobedience
1Th 4:6 Jehovah is one who exacts **p.**
Heb 10:29 how much more severe a **p.,**
Ex 32:34; Nu 16:29; Pr 16:5; 19:5; Jude 7.
PUPIL, Lu 6:40 A **p.** is not above his
De 32:10; Ps 17:8; Pr 7:2; La 2:18.
PURCHASE, Ga 3:13; 4:5 by **p.** released us
PURCHASED, Ge 49:32 field **p.** and cave
Ac 20:28 **p.** with the blood
PURE, Ps 12:6 sayings of Jehovah are **p.**
Pr 16:2 the ways of a man are **p.** in his own
Zep 3:9 give to peoples a **p.** language,
Mt 5:8 Happy are the **p.** in heart, since
Ps 19:9; 1Jo 3:3.
PURIFICATION, Joh 2:6; 3:25; Heb 1:3.
2Ch 30:19 without **p.** for what is holy
PURIFIED, 1Pe 1:22 you **p.** your souls
PURIFY, Ex 29:36; Nu 19:12; Eze 45:18;
Jas 4:8.
PURITY, 2Co 6:6 by **p.,** knowledge,
PURPLE, Pr 31:22; Da 5:16; Ac 16:14.
PURPORT, Ac 2:12 thing **p.** to be
PURPOSE, Pr 16:4 Jehovah made for his **p.,**
Ro 8:28 the ones called according to his **p.**
Eph 3:11 according to the eternal **p.**
Ro 9:11; Eph 1:11; 2Ti 1:9.
PURPOSED, Eph 1:9 pleasure he **p.** in
PURPOSELY, Ge 48:14 He **p.** laid his hands
PURPOSES, Ac 17:31 God **p.** to judge
PURSE(S), Lu 10:4; 12:33; 22:35, 36.
PURSUE, Ro 14:19 let us **p.** the things
1Co 14:1 **P.** love, yet keep zealously seeking
1Pe 3:11 let him seek peace and **p.** it.
Ps 71:11; 83:15; Jer 29:18; Na 1:8.
PURSUING, Jg 4:22 was Barak **p.** Sisera.
Pr 15:9 the one **p.** righteousness he loves
Ro 9:30 nations, not **p.** righteousness,
Php 3:12 I am **p.** to lay hold on that for

PURSUIT, Jg 8:4 tired keeping up the **p.**
PUSH, De 33:17; 1Ki 22:11; Ps 44:5.
PUSHES, 2Jo 9 Everyone that **p.** ahead
PUT, Pr 30:8 the lying word **p.** far away
PUT OUT, Mr 9:48 fire is not **p.**
1Th 5:19 Do not **p.** the fire of the spirit.
PUTREFYING, Jer 49:7 wisdom gone to **p.**
PUTTING UP WITH, Mal 3:2 **p.** the day of
Eph 4:2 **p.** one another in love,
PUZZLED, 1Pe 4:4 they are **p.** and go on
1Pe 4:12 do not be **p.** at the burning
PUZZLING, Pr 1:6 proverb and **p.** saying,

Q

QUAILS, Nu 11:31 driving **q.** from
QUAKING, 2Sa 22:46 foreigners come **q.** out
Da 6:26 people **q.** before the God of
QUALIFICATIONS, Ga 6:1 you who have **q.**
QUALIFIED, 2Co 2:16 who is adequately **q.**
2Co 3:5 our being adequately **q.** issues
QUALIFIED TO TEACH, 1Ti 3:2 overseer **q.**
2Ti 2:2 men who will be **q.** others.
2Ti 2:24 gentle toward all, **q.,**
QUALITIES, Am 1:11 ruined his merciful **q.**
Ro 1:20 invisible **q.** seen
QUALITY, Ro 2:4 kindly **q.** of God is trying to
Col 2:9 fullness of the divine **q.** dwells
Jas 1:3 this tested **q.** of your faith
1Pe 1:7 tested **q.** of your faith
QUANDARY, Ac 5:24 fell into a **q.** over
QUARANTINED, Nu 12:14, 15 **q.** outside
QUARREL, Pr 3:30 Do not **q.** with a man
Pr 17:14 so before the **q.**
Isa 41:11 men in **q.** with you will perish
Ge 13:7; Pr 26:17, 21.
QUARRELING, Ps 31:20 hide from **q.** tongues
Isa 58:4 for **q.** you would fast
Ex 17:7; De 1:12; Job 33:19; Pr 15:18.
QUARTERMASTER, Jer 51:59 Seraiah the **q.**
QUEEN, Mt 12:42 **q.** of the south will be
Re 18:7 I sit a **q.,** and I am no widow,
1Ki 10:1; Es 2:17; Jer 7:18; Da 5:10.
QUEENLY, Ps 45:9 **q.** consort has taken
QUENCH, Eph 6:16 **q.** the wicked one's
QUESTION(S), 1Ti 1:4 but furnish **q.**
1Ki 10:1; Mt 22:46; Ac 23:29.
QUESTIONINGS, Ro 14:1 on inward **q.**
1Ti 6:4 mentally diseased over **q.** and debates
2Ti 2:23 turn down foolish and ignorant **q.,**
Tit 3:9 shun foolish **q.** and genealogies
QUIET, Ec 3:7 a time to keep **q.** and a
1Ti 2:2 go on leading a calm and **q.** life
1Pe 3:4 the **q.** and mild spirit, which is of
Ps 35:20; Jer 47:7.
QUIETLY, 1Th 4:11 aim to live **q.** and to
QUIETNESS, Job 34:29 causes **q.,**
Isa 32:17 **q.** and security to time indefinite.
1Ch 22:9; Pr 17:1; Ec 9:17; 2Th 3:12.
QUIETS, Pr 15:18 **q.** down quarreling.
QUIT, 1Co 5:9 **q.** mixing company with
QUIVER, Isa 6:4 thresholds began to **q.**
QUIVERING, Ho 3:5; Mic 7:17.

R

RABBAH, De 3:11 in R. of the sons
2Sa 11:1; Jer 49:2; Eze 25:5.
RABBI, Mt 23:8 do not be called R.
Joh 1:38; 3:2.
RABSHAKEH, 2Ki 18:17; Isa 36:2, 12; 37:4.
RACE, Ec 9:11 swift do not have the **r.,**
1Co 9:24 runners in a **r.** all run,
Heb 12:1 let us run the **r.** set before us,
1Pe 2:9 you are a chosen **r.,** a royal
RACHEL, Ge 29:28 gave R. as wife.

Mt 2:18 **R.** weeping for her children,
Ge 29:18; 30:22; Ru 4:11; Jer 31:15.
RADIANT, Ps 34:5; Isa 60:5; Jer 31:12.
RAFTER, Lu 6:42 extract the **r.** from
RAGE, Ps 76:10 the very **r.** of man will
Pr 15:1 answer, when mild, turns away **r.,**
Jer 4:11 with the **r.** of Jehovah I have
Ps 79:6; Pr 6:34; 19:19; 22:24; 27:4.
RAGING, Eze 5:15 rage and **r.** reproofs.
Job 19:29; Eze 25:17; Mic 7:9.
RAHAB, Heb 11:31 By faith **R.** did not
Jas 2:25 was not **R.** declared righteous
Jos 2:3; 6:17, 23, 25.
RAIN, Ge 2:5 not made it **r.** upon
Ge 7:4 in seven days I am making it **r.**
Joe 2:23 autumn **r.** and spring **r.,**
Mt 5:45 **r.** upon righteous and unrighteous.
Jas 5:7 farmer gets the early **r.** and late **r.**
De 11:14; 32:2; Job 38:28; Ps 11:6; 72:6;
Isa 55:10; Zec 14:17; Jas 5:17; Re 11:6.
RAINBOW, Ge 9:13 My **r.** in the cloud,
Re 4:3; 10:1.
RAISED, Mt 28:7 disciples he was **r.** up
Lu 20:37 dead are **r.** up even Moses
1Co 15:44 it is **r.** up a spiritual body.
2Co 4:14 he who **r.** Jesus up will raise us
Col 3:1 If you were **r.** up with Christ,
1Co 15:17, 42; Eph 1:20; 2:6; Col 2:12.
RAM(S), Ge 22:13 **r.** caught by its horns
1Sa 15:22 to pay attention than **r.;**
Eze 34:17 judging between **r.** and he-goats.
Mic 6:7 be pleased with thousands of **r.,**
Le 5:15; 8:22; 9:18; Isa 1:11; Da 8:20.
RAMAH, Jer 31:15 In **R.** a voice is heard,
Jos 18:25; Jg 4:5; 1Sa 16:13; Mt 2:18.
RAMOTH-GILEAD, 1Ki 4:13; 22:3; 2Ki 8:28.
RAMPART, Ps 48:13 Set upon its **r.,**
RANK, 1Co 15:23 each in his **r.:** Christ
RANSOM, Job 33:24 I have found a **r.!**
Ps 49:7 Not one can give to God a **r.**
Pr 21:18 wicked is a **r.** for righteous one,
Mt 20:28 Son came to give his soul a **r.**
1Ti 2:6 gave himself a **r.** for all—
Ex 30:12; Job 36:18; Pr 6:35; Isa 43:3.
RAPACIOUS, Isa 35:9 **r.** sort of wild beasts
RAPACITY, Hab 2:17 **r.** upon beasts terrifies
RAPE, Jg 19:24 and you **r.** them
RAPED, Jg 20:5 concubine that they **r.**
Zec 14:2 women will be **r.**
RAPING, Es 7:8 a **r.** of the queen,
RARE, 1Sa 3:1 word had become **r.**
RASHNESS, Job 35:15 note of extreme **r.**
RAVAGED, Ac 9:21 man that **r.** those in
RAZOR, Jg 13:5; 16:17; 1Sa 1:11.
READ, Isa 29:11 **R.** this out loud, please,
Isa 34:16 in the book and **r.** out loud:
2Co 3:2 known and **r.** by all mankind.
Ex 24:7; De 17:19; Lu 4:16; Ac 13:27.
READER, Mt 24:15 **r.** use discernment,)
READINESS, 2Co 8:11, 12; 9:2.
READING, Ne 8:8 continued **r.** aloud
Hab 2:2 **r.** aloud do so fluently.
1Ti 4:13 applying yourself to public **r.,**
READS, Re 1:3 Happy is he who **r.** aloud
READY, Ps 37:23 man have been made **r.**
1Ti 6:18 be liberal, **r.** to share,
Heb 11:16 he has made a city **r.** for them.
REAL, Joh 7:28 he that sent me is **r.**
1Ti 6:19 get a firm hold on the **r.** life.
REALITIES, Heb 11:1 demonstration of **r.** not
REALITY, Col 2:17 the **r.** belongs to Christ
Heb 9:24 holy place which is a copy of **r.**
REALIZE, Ge 3:7 **r.** they were naked.
REALIZED, Pr 13:19 Desire when **r.** is

REAP, Ec 11:4 looking at clouds not **r.**
Ho 8:7 stormwind is what they will **r.**
Mic 6:15 sow seed, but you will not **r.**
2Co 9:6 sows sparingly will **r.** sparingly,
Ga 6:7 whatever a man is sowing he will **r.;**
Ga 6:9 we shall **r.** if not tire out.
Re 14:15 Put your sickle in and **r.,**
Mt 6:26; Lu 12:24; Joh 4:38; 1Co 9:11.
REAPER(S), Ps 129:7 **r.** has not filled
Mt 13:39 **r.** are angels.
Joh 4:36 the **r.** is receiving wages
REASON, 1Pe 3:15 demands a **r.** for the hope
Ec 7:25; Ac 18:14.
REASONABLE, 1Ti 3:3 not a smiter, **r.,**
Tit 3:2 to be **r.,** exhibiting all mildness
Jas 3:17 **r.,** ready to obey, full of mercy
REASONABLENESS, Php 4:5 **r.** known to men.
REASONINGS, 2Co 10:5 overturning **r.**
Mt 15:19; Lu 2:35; Ro 1:21; 1Co 3:20.
REASSURINGLY, Ge 50:21; Ru 2:13.
REBEKAH, Ge 24:51; 27:15; 49:31.
REBEL, Nu 14:9 Jehovah do not **r.**
1Sa 12:14; 2Ch 13:6; Ps 78:40, 56; 105:28;
Eze 20:8.
REBELLED, Isa 63:10; Eze 20:13; Da 9:5.
REBELLING, Ne 2:19; Ps 78:17; Zep 3:1.
REBELLION, Ezr 4:19; Pr 17:11; Eze 2:7.
REBELLIOUS, Ezr 4:12 **r.** and bad city
Ps 78:8; Isa 1:20; Eze 2:3.
REBELLIOUSLY, Ps 107:11 behaved **r.**
De 9:23; Jos 1:18; Ps 106:7; Isa 3:8.
REBELLIOUSNESS, 1Sa 15:23 **r.** the same
Nu 17:10; De 31:27; Job 23:2; Eze 44:6.
REBELS, Nu 20:10; Job 24:13.
REBUILD, Isa 61:4 **r.** devastated places
Ezr 5:17; Ne 2:17.
REBUILDING, Ezr 6:8 **r.** that house of God;
REBUILT, Eze 36:10 devastated places **r.**
REBUKE, Job 19:3 ten times your **r.** me;
Pr 13:1 ridiculer has not listened to **r.**
Zec 3:2 Jehovah **r.** you, O Satan,
2Co 2:6 This **r.** given by the majority is
Ps 104:7; Ec 7:5; Isa 17:13; 54:9; 66:15.
REBUTTAL, Ac 4:14 nothing to say in **r.**
RECALL, Tit 2:4 **r.** young women to their
RECANTATION, Ac 26:11 force to make **r.;**
RECEIVE, Ro 8:15 **r.** a spirit of slavery
Jas 4:3 You ask yet you do not **r.,**
Mr 10:15; Ga 4:5; Jas 1:12.
RECEIVED, Mt 10:8 You **r.** free, give free.
1Th 2:13; Heb 10:26; 1Jo 2:27.
RECEIVES, Mr 9:37 Whoever **r.** one of such
RECEPTACLE(S), Mt 25:4 oil in their **r.**
1Sa 9:7; 17:40.
RECEPTION, Lu 5:29 Levi spread a **r.** feast
RECHAB, 2Ki 10:15; 1Ch 2:55; Jer 35:6.
RECHABITES, Jer 35:2, 3, 5, 18.
RECKON, Ro 6:11 **r.** yourselves dead
RECKONED, Lu 22:37 he was **r.** with lawless
1Ti 5:17 older men be **r.** worthy of honor
RECKONING, 2Co 5:19 not **r.** trespasses,
RECLAIMED, Ps 106:10; 107:2.
RECLINE, Mt 8:11 **r.** with Abraham
RECLINING, 1Co 8:10 **r.** at a meal in an
Mt 26:20; Lu 22:27.
RECOGNIZE, Mt 7:20 fruits you will **r.**
1Co 16:18 Therefore **r.** men of that sort.
Isa 61:9; 63:16; Ho 2:8; 11:3; 2Co 1:13.
RECOGNIZED, Ro 11:2 people whom he **r.**
2Co 6:9 unknown and yet being **r.,**
RECOLLECT, 2Ti 1:5 I **r.** the faith which
RECOMMEND, Ro 16:1; 2Co 3:1.
RECOMMENDS, Ro 5:8 God **r.** his own love
RECOMPENSE(S). See also PAYMENT,

REPAYING, REPAYMENT, RETRIBUTION.
RECOMPENSE(S), Isa 59:18 he will r. due
Jer 51:56 Jehovah is a God of r.
Mt 16:27 r. each according to his behavior.
Ro 1:27 r. which was due for their error.
2Co 6:13 as a r. in return—I speak as
Heb 10:30 Vengeance is mine; I will r.;
RECONCILE, Eph 2:16 r. both peoples
Col 1:20 through him to r. again all
RECONCILED, Ro 5:10 we became r. to God
RECONCILIATION, Ro 5:11 now received r.
Ro 11:15; 2Co 5:18, 19.
RECORDER('S), Eze 9:2 man with r. inkhorn
Ac 19:35 city r. quieted the crowd
RECORDS, Ezr 4:15 find in the book of r.
RECOUNT, Jg 5:11 they began to r. the
Ps 40:5; 48:13; Jer 51:10.
RE-CREATION, Mt 19:28 In the r., when
RECTITUDE, 1Ch 29:17 in r. you take
RECUPERATION, Isa 58:8 speedily would r.
Jer 8:22; 30:17; 33:6.
RED, Pr 23:31 wine r. color,
Isa 63:2 Why your clothing is r.,
Ge 25:25; Nu 19:2; Na 2:3; Zec 1:8.
REDEEM. See also RELEASE BY RANSOM,
RELEASED BY PURCHASE.
REDEEM, Ex 13:15 my sons I r.
2Sa 7:23 God went to r. a people
Ps 49:7 not one can r. even a brother,
Ho 13:14 From Sheol I shall r. them;
Ps 44:26; 49:15; 69:18; 72:14; Jer 15:21.
REDEEMED, Isa 1:27 Zion will be r.,
Isa 35:10 ones r. by Jehovah will return
Le 27:29; De 9:26; Ps 31:5; 71:23; 78:42.
REDEEMER. See also ONE REPURCHASING,
REPURCHASER.
REDEEMER, Job 19:25; Ps 19:14; Pr 23:11.
REDEEMING, Ps 34:42 r. the soul of his
REDEMPTION. See also DELIVERANCE, RE-
LEASE BY RANSOM.
REDEMPTION, Ex 21:30; Nu 3:49; Ps 49:8;
111:9; 130:7.
RED SEA, Heb 11:29 passed through the R.
Ex 10:19; 15:4; Ne 9:9; Ac 7:36.
REDUCED, 1Co 7:29 the time left is r.
REDUCTION, Ex 5:8 not make any r. for them
REED, Eze 40:3, 5; 42:16; Mt 11:7; 27:29.
REEL, Ps 107:27 They r. and move
REELED, Isa 28:7 r. as to decision.
REELING, Ps 60:3 wine sending us r.
RE-ESTABLISHED, Da 4:36 r. my kingdom
REFASHION, Php 3:21 r. our body to be
REFERENCE, Ro 6:10 lives with r. to God.
Ro 11:28 but with r. to God's choosing
REFINE, Zec 13:9 r. them as silver,
REFINED, 2Sa 22:31 saying is a r. one.
Da 12:10 whiten themselves and will be r.
Ps 12:6; 17:3; 66:10; Pr 30:5; Isa 48:10.
REFINER, Mal 3:3 a r. and cleanser of
REFINING, Pr 17:3 The r. pot is for
Da 11:35 in order to do a r. work
REFLECT, 2Co 3:18 faces r. like mirrors
REFLECTION, Heb 1:3 r. of his glory and
REFORMS, Ac 24:2 r. are taking place in
REFRAIN, Eze 3:27 the one refraining r.,
REFRESH, Mt 11:28 Come and I will r.
REFRESHED, 1Co 16:18 have r. my spirit
Phm 7 holy ones r. through you, brother.
REFRESHES, Ps 23:3 My soul he r. He
REFRESHING, Ac 3:19 seasons of r. come
REFRESHMENT, Mt 11:29.
REFUGE, Nu 35:6 six cities of r.,
Ps 18:2 I shall take r. in him,
Isa 28:17 sweep away the r. of a lie,

Zep 3:12 take r. in the name of Jehovah.
Jos 20:2; 21:13; Ps 57:1; Pr 14:26.
REFUSE, Ps 141:5 not want to r.
Isa 1:20 if you r. and are rebellious,
1Co 4:13 become as the r. of the world,
Php 3:8 consider them as a lot of r.,
REGAIN, Isa 40:31 Jehovah will r. power.
REGARD, Job 37:24 not r. any wise in
Ro 14:7 None lives with r. to himself only,
REGARDED, Pr 17:28 silent will be r. wise
2Th 1:10 to be r. in that day with wonder
REGENERATION. See RE-CREATION.
REGION, De 3:4; Jos 19:29; Mt 4:16.
REGIONS, Eph 4:9 into the lower r.,
REGISTERED, Lu 2:1 for all to be r.
Nu 1:44; 3:22; 26:7.
REGRET(S), Ge 6:6 Jehovah felt r. that
1Sa 15:29 He will not feel r.
Ps 110:4 Jehovah will feel no r.
Jer 26:13 Jehovah will feel r. for the
Nu 23:19; Jg 2:18; Ps 106:45; Jer 18:10;
Jon 3:10; Zec 8:14; Ro 11:29; Heb 7:21.
REGULATION(S), De 4:1 listen to the r.
De 4:40 you must keep his r. and his
Jg 11:39 came to be a r. in Israel
Ps 119:12 O Jehovah. Teach me your r.
Isa 10:1 those enacting harmful r.,
Isa 24:5 they have changed the r.,
Ex 18:20; Le 10:11; Ne 9:13; Ps 50:16;
119:5, 8, 48, 71, 80; Jer 31:36; Mal 3:7.
REHABILITATE, Isa 49:8 to r. the land,
REHEARSE, Lu 21:14 not to r. beforehand
REHOBOAM, 1Ki 12:1; 14:21, 29.
REIGN. See also RULE AS KING(S).
REIGN, 1Sa 8:9 the king that will r. over
1Sa 15:11 I regret I caused Saul to r.
Isa 32:1 A king will r. for righteousness
1Sa 8:11; Job 34:30; Jer 23:5.
REINFORCE, Na 2:1 r. power very much
Am 2:14.
REINFORCING, Pr 24:5 a man is r. power.
REINHABITED, Eze 38:12 places r.
REINVIGORATED, Ps 68:9 you r. it.
REJECT, Job 5:17 discipline do not r.
REJECTED, 1Sa 8:7 they have r.
1Sa 15:23 Since you have r. the word
Jer 8:9 They have r. the word of Jehovah
Mt 21:42 The stone the builders r.
1Ti 4:4 nothing is to be r. if it is
1Pe 2:4 living stone, r. by men,
1Sa 10:19; Jer 7:29; Mr 8:31; Heb 12:17.
REJOICE, Ps 97:1 has become king! r.
Ps 104:15 wine that makes the heart r.
Pr 27:11 Be wise my son, make my heart r.
Pr 29:2 righteous become many, people r.
Mt 5:12 R. and leap for joy,
Ro 12:15 R. with people who r.; weep with
Php 4:4 Always r. in the Lord.
Isa 65:13; Lu 13:17; Joh 16:20; Php 4:10.
REJOICED, 1Ch 29:9 David r.
Joh 8:56 Abraham your father r. greatly
REJOICING, 1Ki 8:66 r. and feeling
Es 8:17 were r. and exultation for the Jews
Ps 97:11 r. for ones upright in heart
Ps 100:2 Serve Jehovah with r.
Ac 5:41 their way from the Sanhedrin r.
Col 1:24 now r. in my sufferings
Es 8:16; Ec 8:15; 2Co 6:10; 1Pe 1:8.
RELATE, Ge 40:8; 2Ki 8:4; 1Ch 16:24.
RELATED, Ac 15:14 Symeon has r. how God
Ge 41:12; Ex 24:3.
RELATING, Ps 78:4 R. them to the
RELATIONSHIP, Col 2:12; Phm 16.
RELATIVE(S), Lu 14:12; Ac 10:24.

RELAX, Jos 10:6 Do not let your hand r.
RELAXATION, Ac 24:23 some r. of custody
RELAXING, Ex 5:8 because they are r.
Ex 5:17 he said: "You are r., you are r.!
RELEASE, Lu 4:18 preach a r. to the captives
1Co 7:27 bound to a wife? Stop seeking a r.
De 15:1, 2; Mt 27:21; Ac 3:13.
RELEASE BY RANSOM, Ro 3:24; 8:23.
1Co 1:30 wisdom also righteousness and r.
Eph 1:7 we have the r. through the blood
Col 1:14 we have our r., the forgiveness
Heb 9:15 r. from transgressions under the
Heb 11:35 not accept r., that they might
RELEASED BY PURCHASE, Ga 3:13 Christ by
Ga 4:5 he might r. those under law,
RELEASING, Lu 6:37 Keep on r., and you
Php 1:23 what I do desire is the r. and
2Ti 4:6 due time for my r. is imminent.
RELEASING BY RANSOM, Eph 1:14; 4:30.
RELIABLE, Da 2:45 the dream is r., and
Da 7:16 r. information on all
RELIED, 2Co 1:18 God can be r. upon
RELIEF, Job 14:14 until my r. comes.
2Th 1:7 r. along with us at the revelation
1Sa 16:23; Es 4:14; Job 32:20.
RELIEVE, Isa 1:24 I shall r. myself of
RELIGION(S). See also WORSHIP.
RELIGION(S), 1Sa 15:32 Agag went r.
2Ki 17:34 doing according to their former r.
RELUCTANTLY, 1Sa 15:32 Agag went r.
REMAIN, Jos 23:7 these that r. with you.
Joh 8:31 If you r. in my word, you are my
Joh 15:4; Ac 15:17; 1Co 7:20; 13:13; 2Jo 9.
REMAINDER, Ps 76:10 r. of raging you
REMAINING, Isa 28:5 beauty to ones r.
Jer 38:4 weakening the hands of the men r.
Jer 8:3; 39:9; Eze 9:8; 39:14; Mal 2:15.
REMAINING ONES, Mic 5:7 r. like dew
Zep 3:13 r. of Israel, will do no
Re 12:17 war with the r. of her seed,
Mic 2:12; Zep 2:9; Zec 8:11, 12; 14:2.
REMAINS, Joh 3:36 wrath of God r. upon
Joh 6:27 food that r. for life everlasting
1Co 3:14 If anyone's work r., he will
1Jo 2:17 he that does the will of God r.
REMEMBER, Ge 9:15 shall r. my covenant
Job 14:13 set a time limit and r. me!
Ps 25:7 sins of my youth do not r.
Ec 12:1 R., your Creator in the days of
Jer 31:34 their sin I shall r. no more.
Lu 17:32 R. the wife of Lot.
Heb 13:7 R. those who are taking the lead
Ps 137:6; Isa 43:25; Lu 23:42; 2Pe 3:2.
REMEMBERED, Ps 83:4 name be r. no more.
Ac 10:31 your gifts of mercy have been r.
REMEMBERING, Ex 20:8 R. the sabbath day
Heb 10:32 keep on r. the former days in
REMEMBRANCE, Ps 109:15 cut off the r.
Pr 10:7 r. of the righteous for a blessing
Ec 9:5 the r. of them has been forgotten.
Mal 3:16 book of r. began to be written
Lu 22:19 Keep doing this in r. of me.
Ac 10:4 Your prayers ascended as a r.
Ec 1:11; 1Co 11:25; 3Jo 10.
REMIND, Isa 43:26 R. me put on judgment
2Pe 1:12 r. you of these things,
REMINDER(S), 2Ki 17:15 rejecting his r.
Ps 19:7 The r. of Jehovah is trustworthy,
Ps 119:14 I will also speak about your r.
Ps 119:129 Your r. are wonderful.
2Pe 3:1 I am arousing by way of a r.,
Ps 93:5; 119:14, 31, 99, 119; Jer 44:23.
REMINDING, 2Pe 1:13 rouse you up by r.
REMISSION. See FORGIVENESS.

REMNANT, 2Ki 19:31 a r. will go forth
Jer 23:3 collect the r. out of all lands
Mic 4:7 make her that was limping a r.,
Ro 9:27 it is the r. that will be saved.
Ro 11:5 a r. has turned up according to
Isa 10:21, 22; 11:11, 16; Jer 15:9; Eze 6:8.
REMORSE, Mt 27:3 Judas, felt r.
REMOTEST, Isa 14:13 I sit in r. parts of north.
REMOVAL, Heb 12:27 once signifies the r.
REMOVE, Eze 21:26 R. the turban, and
1Co 5:13 R. the wicked man from among
REMOVED, Isa 29:13 r. their heart far
Isa 54:10 mountains may be r., but my
RENDER, De 32:41 r. retribution to
Ro 13:7 R. to all their dues, to him
Ps 56:12; Mt 21:41; 1Pe 4:5; Re 18:6.
RENEGADE, Isa 57:17; Jer 3:12, 14.
RENEGADING, Pr 1:32 r. of ones will kill
RENEWED, 2Co 4:16 man inside being r.
RENEWING, Ps 103:5 youth keeps r. itself
RENOUNCE, 2Ti 2:19 r. unrighteousness.
RENOVATE, 2Ch 24:4 r. the house of
REPAID, Ro 11:35 it must be r. to him?
REPAY, Ps 116:12 What shall I r. to
Ro 12:19 Vengeance is mine; I will r., says
2Th 1:6 on God's part to r. tribulation to
2Ti 4:14 Jehovah will r. him according to
REPAYING, Pr 17:13 r. bad for good,
Isa 66:6 Jehovah r. what is deserved
REPAYMENT, Isa 35:4 God with a r.
Lu 14:12 it would become a r. to you.
REPENT, Mt 3:2 R., for the kingdom has
Ac 3:19 R., and turn around so as to get
Re 16:9 they did not r. so as to give glory
Lu 13:3; 16:30; 17:4; Re 2:5, 21; 3:19.
REPENTANCE, Mt 3:8 fruit that befits r.;
Lu 15:7 ninety-nine who have no need of r.
Ro 2:4 God is trying to lead you to r.?
2Co 7:10 sadness godly way makes for r.
2Ti 2:25 perhaps God may give them r.
Mt 3:11; Lu 24:47; Ac 11:18; 2Pe 3:9.
REPENTED, Mt 12:41 they r. at what Jonah
Mt 11:21; 2Co 12:21.
REPENTS, Lu 15:7 over one sinner that r.
REPLYING, Pr 18:13 r. to matter before
REPORT(S), Ex 23:1 not an untrue r.
Pr 25:25 a good r. from a distant land.
Da 11:44 r. that will disturb him, out of
Mt 24:6 hear of wars and r. of wars;
2Co 6:8 through bad r. and good r.;
Nu 14:36; Job 28:22; Pr 15:30; Eze 7:26.
REPORTER, Jer 51:31 one r. to meet r.
REPORTING, 1Th 1:9 they keep r. about
1Jo 1:2 we are bearing witness and r. to
REPOSE, Isa 51:4; Jer 31:2; 47:6; 50:34.
REPOSSESSING, Isa 49:8 r. of desolated
REPRESENTATION, Heb 1:3 exact r. of his
REPRESENTATIVE, Ex 18:19 r. for people
Lu 8:49 a r. of the presiding officer
Joh 7:29 I am a r. from that One
REPRESENTATIVELY, Ezr 10:14 act r. for
REPRIMAND, Lu 18:15; 2Ti 4:2.
REPROACH(ES), Ps 55:12 enemy r. me;
Isa 25:8 r. of his people he will take away
Isa 51:7 afraid of the r. of mortal men,
Mt 5:11 Happy are you when people r. you
Heb 10:33 exposed as in a theater to r. and
Heb 11:26 r. of the Christ as riches
1Sa 17:26; Ps 22:6; 69:7; Isa 4:1; Lu 6:22.
REPROACHED, Ps 74:18 The enemy has r.,
1Pe 4:14 r. for Christ, you are happy,
Ps 79:12; 89:51; Pr 14:31; Zep 2:10.
REPROACHING, Ps 74:10 adversary keep r.?
Ps 44:16; 119:42; Ro 15:3.

REPRODUCTIVE, 1Pe 1:23; 1Jo 3:9.
REPROOF(S), Pr 1:23 Turn back at my **r.**
  Pr 6:23 **r.** of discipline are the way of
  Pr 10:17 he that is leaving **r.**
  Pr 13:18 one keeping a **r.** is glorified.
  Pr 29:15 The rod and **r.** give wisdom;
  Pr 1:25; 3:11; 15:5, 10, 31, 32.
REPROVE, Pr 9:8 Do not **r.** a ridiculer,
  1Ti 5:20 R. before all onlookers persons
  2Ti 4:2 **r.** with all long-suffering
  Re 3:19 All I have affection I **r.**
  2Sa 7:14; Job 13:10; Ps 50:21; Pr 30:6.
REPROVED, Ps 105:14 he **r.** kings,
  Pr 29:1 A man **r.** will be
  Lu 3:19 Herod, being **r.** by him concerning
  Joh 3:20 that his works may not be **r.**
  Eph 5:13 things **r.** are manifest by light,
REPROVER, Job 40:2 **r.** of God answer it.
REPROVING, 2Ti 3:16 beneficial for **r.**,
  Tit 1:13 keep on **r.** them with severity,
REPUDIATE, Tit 2:12 **r.** ungodliness and
REPULSIVE, Isa 66:24 carcasses **r.** to all
REPURCHASED, Isa 35:9 **r.** ones must walk
  Isa 51:10 a way for the **r.** ones to go
  Isa 63:4 year of my **r.** ones has come.
  Isa 43:1; 44:23; 48:20; 52:3, 9; 62:12.
REPURCHASER, Ru 4:6 **r.** said: "I am
  Isa 44:24 Jehovah, your R. and Former
  Isa 59:20 to Zion the R. will come,
  Isa 63:16 Our R. of long ago is your name.
  Jer 50:34 Their R. is strong.
  Isa 41:14; 44:6; 48:17; 49:26; 54:5; 60:16.
REPUTABLE, Mr 15:43; Ac 13:50; 17:12.
REPUTE, 1Co 4:10 you are in good **r.**,
REQUEST(S), Ps 20:5 Jehovah fulfill your **r.**
  Joh 17:9 I make **r.** concerning them;
  Joh 17:20 I make **r.**, not concerning these
REQUIRE, De 18:19; 23:21; Eze 20:40.
REQUIRED, Lu 11:50 blood of prophets **r.**
REQUIREMENT, Ro 8:4 righteous **r.** of Law
RESCUE, Da 3:17 our God is able to **r.** us.
  Ro 7:24 Who will **r.** me from the body
  2Co 1:10 he will **r.** us further.
RESCUED, Ac 23:27 I suddenly **r.** him,
RESEARCH, 1Ti 1:4 furnish questions for **r.**
RESEMBLANCE, Ro 5:14 Adam bears a **r.**
RESEMBLE, Isa 14:14; 46:5.
RESENTFUL, Ps 103:9; Jer 3:12; Na 1:2.
RESERVED, Col 1:5 hope is for you
  Heb 9:27 as it is **r.** for men to die once
  1Pe 1:4 It is **r.** in the heavens for you,
RESIDE(S), Ex 12:48 resident **r.**
  Jg 17:8 **r.** for a time wherever he might
  Isa 52:4 to Egypt my people went to **r.**
  Ge 12:10; 26:3; 47:4; Isa 23:7; Jer 42:17.
RESIDED, Heb 11:9 he **r.** as an alien in
RESIDENT, Isa 33:24 no **r.** will say: "I am
RESIDENT(S), ALIEN, Mal 3:5 turning a.,
  Eph 2:19 you are no longer strangers and a.,
  Ex 22:21; De 10:19; Ps 146:9; Jer 7:6;
  22:3.
RESIDENTS. See ALIEN RESIDENT(S).
RESIDING, Le 25:45 sons **r.** as aliens
  Nu 9:14; Eze 47:22.
RESIST, Lu 21:15 opposers not able to **r.**
  Eph 6:13 armor be able to **r.** in the
  Zec 3:1; Mt 5:39.
RESISTANCE, Nu 22:32 come out to offer **r.**
  Ps 13:2 How long set **r.** in my soul
RESISTED, 2Ti 3:8 and Jambres **r.** Moses,
  Ga 2:11; 2Ti 4:15; Heb 12:4.
RESISTER, 1Sa 29:4 become **r.** in battle.
  1Ki 5:4 There is no **r.** and nothing bad
  2Sa 19:22; 1Ki 11:14, 23, 25; Ps 109:6.

RESISTING, Ac 7:51 **r.** the holy spirit;
  Ps 38:20; 71:13; 109:4, 20, 29.
RESOLVED, 2Ch 25:16 **r.** to ruin
  2Co 9:7 just as he has **r.** in his heart,
RESORT, Isa 19:3 **r.** to valueless gods
RESOUNDING, 2Ch 29:28; Ps 92:3.
RESOURCES, Isa 60:11 **r.** of the nations,
  Isa 61:6 **r.** of nations you people will eat,
  Jer 15:13; 17:3; Eze 26:12; Mr 5:26.
RESPECT, Eph 5:33 wife **r.** husband.
  Heb 12:9 we used to give them **r.**
  1Pe 3:2 chaste conduct together with deep **r.**
  1Pe 3:15 with a mild temper and deep **r.**
  Mr 12:6; Lu 18:2; 2Pe 2:11.
RESPECTIVE, 1Co 12:28 God set **r.** ones
  Eph 4:16 functioning of each **r.** member
RESPONSE, Ec 10:19 money meets a **r.**
RESPONSIBILITY, 1Ch 9:33 their **r.** to be
RESPONSIBLE, Heb 5:9 **r.** for everlasting
REST, Ex 23:12 seventh day you may **r.**
  Job 3:17 those weary in power are at **r.**
  Isa 14:7 whole earth has come to **r.**,
  Heb 4:3 we do enter into the **r.**,
  Ex 31:15; Da 12:13; Heb 3:11; Re 14:11.
RESTING, Ps 125:3 will not keep **r.**
RESTING PLACE(S), Ps 23:2 **r.** he conducts
  Ps 132:14 This is my **r.** forever;
  Isa 11:10 his **r.** must become glorious.
  1Ki 8:56; Ps 95:11; Isa 28:12; 66:1.
RESTITUTION. See RESTORATION.
RESTORATION, Ac 3:21 times of **r.** of all
RESTORE, Da 9:25 **r.** rebuild Jerusalem
  Mt 17:11 Elijah will **r.** all things.
  Job 33:26; Ps 51:12; Jer 27:22; Ga 6:1.
RESTORING, Ac 1:6 are you **r.** the kingdom
RESTRAIN, 1Pe 3:10 let him **r.** his tongue
  Ps 40:9; Isa 48:9.
RESTRAINT, Ps 107:39.
  Isa 53:8 Because of **r.** he was taken away;
  2Th 2:7 acting as a **r.** gets out of the way
  1Jo 4:18 because fear exercises a **r.**
RESTRICTION, 2Ki 4:13 with all this **r.**
RESULT, Ro 5:18 the **r.** to men of all
RESUME, Job 17:10 you men may **r.**
RESURRECT, Joh 6:39, 40, 44, 54.
RESURRECTED, Ac 2:24 **r.** him by loosing
RESURRECTION, Mt 22:30 **r.** neither marry
  Joh 5:29 of life **r.** of judgment
  Joh 11:25 I am the **r.** and the life.
  Ac 24:15 **r.** of righteous and unrighteous.
  Ro 6:5 united in the likeness of his **r.**;
  1Co 15:42 So also is the **r.** of the dead.
  Php 3:11 attain to the earlier **r.** from
  2Ti 2:18 saying the **r.** already occurred,
  Heb 11:35 Women received their dead by **r.**;
  Re 20:6 anyone having part in the first **r.**;
  1Co 15:12, 13, 21; Php 3:10; Heb 6:2.
RETIREMENT, Lu 5:16 **r.** in deserts and
RETRACTION, Job 42:6 I make a **r.** and I
RETREATED, Ps 78:9 Ephraim, **r.** the day
RETREATS, Ob 3 residing in **r.** of the crag
RETRIBUTION(S), De 32:41 render **r.** to
  Ps 94:2 bring **r.** upon the haughty ones
  Isa 34:8 a day of vengeance, a year of **r.**
  Ro 11:9 a trap and a stumbling block and a **r.**;
  2Th 2:10 perishing as a **r.** because
  Heb 2:2 received **r.** in harmony with justice,
RETURN, Ge 3:19 **r.** to the ground,
  1Ki 8:48 they **r.** to you with all their
  Job 33:25 **r.** to the days of youthful vigor.
  Isa 55:11 word will not **r.** without results,
  Mal 3:7 R. to me, and I will **r.** to you,
  Mr 13:16 man in the field not **r.** to things
  Ro 12:17 R. evil for evil to no one.

Nu 10:36; Isa 10:21; Lu 19:12; Ac 15:16.
RETURNING, Pr 26:11 like a dog r. to vomit,
Ec 3:20 dust, and they are r. to the dust.
Ec 1:6; Eze 35:7; Mic 2:8.
RETURNS, Ec 12:7 spirit r. to God who
REUBEN, Ge 29:32; 49:3; Jg 5:15; Re 7:5.
REUEL, Nu 10:29 Hobab the son of **R.**
REVEAL, Isa 49:9 **R.** yourselves!
1Sa 2:27; Jer 33:6; Da 2:47; Php 3:15.
REVEALED, Isa 40:5 glory will be r.,
Mt 11:25 hidden from wise r. to babes.
Lu 17:30 day when the Son of man r.
Joh 12:38 has the arm of Jehovah been r.?
Eph 3:5 now r. to apostles and prophets
2Th 2:8 the lawless one will be r.,
Da 2:30; Ro 1:18; 1Co 2:10; 3:13.
REVEALER. See FEAR-INSPIRING.
Da 2:47 God and **R.** of secrets,
REVELATION, 2Sa 7:27 made a r. to your
Ro 16:25 r. of the sacred secret
1Co 1:7 r. of our Lord Jesus Christ.
1Pe 4:13 during the r. of his glory.
Eph 1:17; 2Ti 1:7; 1Pe 1:7, 13; Re 1:1.
REVELRIES, 1Pe 4:3 wine, r., drinking
Ro 13:13; Ga 5:21.
REVELRY, Am 6:7 the r. must depart
REVENGE, 2Sa 4:8; Ps 44:16; Jer 20:10.
REVENUE, Isa 23:3 harvest of Nile, r.;
REVERENCE, Job 4:6; 22:4; 2Th 2:4.
REVEREND. See FEAR-INSPIRING.
REVERENT, Lu 2:25; Ac 2:5; 8:2; 22:12.
REVERSE, Jer 21:4 I am turning in r. weapons
REVILED, 1Co 4:12; 1Pe 2:23.
REVILER(S), 1Co 5:11 quit mixing with r.
1Co 6:10 nor r. inherit God's kingdom.
REVIVE, 2Ki 1:2 whether I shall r. from
Isa 57:15 r. the spirit of the lowly
Heb 6:6 to r. them again to repentance,
REVIVED, Php 4:10 you r. your thinking
Ge 45:27; Jg 15:19.
REVOLT, De 19:16 bring a charge of r.
Isa 1:5 in that you add more r.
Isa 31:6 Israel have gone deep in their r.
Jer 28:16 r. against Jehovah.
De 13:5; Isa 59:13; Jer 29:32.
REWARD, Ge 15:1 Your r. will be great.
Ru 2:12 May Jehovah r. the way you act
Ps 35:12 They r. me with bad for good,
Ps 127:3 The fruitage of the belly is a r.
Mt 5:12 your r. is great in the heavens;
Col 3:24 from Jehovah you will receive r.
Mt 6:1, 2; 10:41; 1Co 3:8; Heb 10:35.
REWARDER, Heb 11:6 he becomes the r.
REWARDINGLY, Ps 13:6 dealt r. with me.
RICH(ES), Ps 52:7 that trusts in his r.
Pr 10:22 The blessing of Jehovah makes r.
Pr 11:28 The one trusting in r.—will fall;
Pr 13:7 one pretending to be r.
Jer 9:23 Let not the r. man brag
Mt 6:24 slaves to God and to **R.**
Lu 16:9 Make friends by means of r.,
Lu 18:25 sewing needle than for a r. man
Ro 9:23 make known the r. of his glory
Ro 11:33 the depth of God's r.
2Co 6:10 as poor but making many r.,
2Co 8:9 though he was r. he became poor
1Ti 6:9 determined to be r. fall into
1Ti 6:18 be r. in fine works,
Heb 11:26 he esteemed the reproach as r.
Jas 2:5 r. in faith and heirs of the
Jas 5:1 Come, you r. men, weep,
Jas 5:2 Your r. have rotted,
Re 3:17 Because you say: "I am r.
1Ki 3:11; Lu 16:11, 19; Eph 3:8; Re 18:17.

RIDDLE, Jg 14:12; Ps 78:2.
RIDICULE, Lu 14:29 onlookers start to r.
RIDICULER(S), Ps 1:1 in the seat of r.
Pr 3:34 with r. he will deride,
Pr 14:6 The r. has sought to find wisdom,
Pr 19:25 The r. you should strike
Pr 20:1 Wine is a r.,
2Pe 3:3 will come r. with their ridicule,
Pr 1:22; 9:7; 13:1; 15:12; 19:29.
RIGHT, Ge 18:25 to do what is r.?
Ex 21:9 the due r. of daughters.
De 18:3 due r. of the priests from people,
Jg 17:6 what was r. he was accustomed
Jer 26:14 Do what is r. in your eyes.
Eze 21:27 until he comes who has the r.,
Da 8:14 holy place brought into r.
Jas 4:17 knows how to do what is r.
De 21:17; 1Ch 24:19; Pr 12:15; Ga 2:9.
RIGHT(S) AS FIRST-BORN, Ge 43:33.
1Ch 5:2 but the r. was Joseph's
RIGHTEOUS, De 32:4 The Rock, r. and
2Sa 23:3 when the one ruling is r.
Ps 34:19 calamities of the r. one
Ps 37:25 not seen r. left entirely
Pr 15:28 heart of the r. one meditates
Pr 29:2 r. become many, people rejoice;
Isa 26:2 r. nation may enter.
Isa 26:7 smooth the course of a r. one.
Am 5:12 showing hostility toward someone r.,
Mal 3:18 between a r. one and a wicked
Mt 13:43 the r. one will shine
Ac 24:15 resurrection of both the r. and
Ro 3:10 There is not a r. man,
Ro 3:26 might be r. even when declaring r.
1Co 15:34 r. way and do not practice sin,
2Th 1:6 is r. on God's part
Heb 10:38 r. will live by faith,
1Pe 3:12 Jehovah's eyes are upon the r.
Ge 7:1; Ps 1:5; Isa 29:21; 53:11; Mt 5:45;
Ro 2:13; 2Ti 4:8; Heb 12:23.
RIGHTEOUS ACTS, Eze 3:20 r. remembered,
RIGHTEOUSLY, Pr 31:9 judge r. and plead
1Pe 2:23 committing to the one who judges r.
RIGHTEOUSNESS, Ps 45:7 You have loved r.
Pr 21:3 To carry on r. is more to Jehovah
Isa 26:9 r. the inhabitants will learn
Isa 32:1 A king will reign for r.
Isa 45:8 skies trickle with r.
Isa 60:17 r. as your task assigners
Isa 61:3 called big trees of r.
Isa 61:10 with the sleeveless coat of r.
Jer 11:20 Jehovah is judging with r.;
Zep 2:3 Seek r., seek meekness,
Joh 16:8 give evidence concerning r.
Ac 10:35 man that works r. is acceptable
Ac 17:31 judge the earth in r.
Ro 1:17 in it God's r. is being revealed
Ro 10:3 no knowing the r. of God but
2Ti 3:16 Scripture for disciplining in r.,
1Pe 3:14 suffer for sake of r.,
2Pe 3:13 in these r. is to dwell.
Re 19:11 carries on war in r.
Ge 15:6; Isa 9:7; 11:4; Da 12:3; Mt 5:6.
RIGHTEOUSNESS' SAKE, Mt 5:10 for r.
RIGHTEOUS STANDING, Isa 53:11 a r. to
RIGHT HAND, Ps 21:8 Your own r.
Ps 45:4 your r. will instruct you
Ps 110:1 Sit at my r.
Mt 20:23 at my r. and at my left
Mt 25:33 put the sheep on his r.
Ac 7:55 Jesus standing at God's r.
Heb 10:12 sat down at the r. of God,
Ex 15:6; Jg 5:26; Isa 62:8; Heb 1:3.
RIGHTS, 1Th 4:6 encroach upon r. of

RIGHTS AS A CITIZEN, Ac 22:28.
RINGWORMS, Le 21:20 scabby or having **r.**
RIP, Joe 2:13 **r.** apart your hearts,
  2Sa 3:31; 1Ki 11:11-13; Ec 3:7.
RIPPED, Isa 64:1 if you **r.** the heavens
RISE(S), Isa 26:19 dead ones will **r.** up.
  Isa 28:21 For Jehovah will **r.** up
  Na 1:9 Distress will not **r.** up
  1Th 4:16 dead with Christ will **r.** first.
  2Pe 1:19 until daystar **r.,** in your hearts.
  Nu 24:17; De 28:7; Ps 92:11; Mt 10:21.
RISING, Zep 3:8 the day of my **r.** up to
  Re 16:12 kings from the **r.** of the sun.
RISKED, Ro 16:4 who **r.** their own necks
RIVALRY, Ec 4:4 means **r.** of one toward
  Php 1:15 are preaching Christ through **r.,**
  Nu 25:13; 2Ki 10:16.
RIVER(S), Isa 66:12 peace like a **r.**
  Re 16:12 poured his bowl upon the **r.**
  Re 22:1 showed me a **r.** of water of life,
  Ge 2:10; Ps 46:4; 107:33; Eze 29:3.
ROAD(S), Mt 3:3 make his **r.** straight.
  Mt 7:14 cramped the **r.** leading into life,
  Mt 22:9 go to the **r.** leading out of the city
  Mt 10:5; 13:4; 20:17; Mr 11:8; Ac 8:26.
ROADWAY(S), Ps 119:105 a light to my **r.**
  Pr 1:15; Isa 59:8; Jer 18:15.
ROAMED, Jer 2:31 We have **r.**
ROAR, Jer 25:30 on high Jehovah will **r.**
  Jer 51:38; Joe 3:16; Am 1:2.
ROARING, Lu 21:25 the **r.** of the sea
  1Pe 5:8 Devil, like a **r.** lion
  Ps 22:13; Eze 22:25; Zep 3:3.
ROB, Mal 3:8 Will man **r.** God?
  Le 19:13; Jg 9:25; Pr 22:23; Ro 2:22.
ROBBED, 2Co 11:8 congregations I **r.** by
  De 28:29; Jer 21:12.
ROBBERS, Mt 21:13 making it a cave of **r.**
  Mr 15:27 they impaled two **r.** with him,
  Jer 7:11; Lu 10:30; Ac 19:37.
ROBBERY, Isa 61:8 hating **r.** along with
  Le 6:2; Ps 62:10; 69:4; Isa 3:14; Eze 18:7.
ROBE(S), Lu 15:22 Quick! bring out a **r.,**
  Lu 20:46 who desire to walk around in **r.**
  Re 7:14 washed their **r.** and made them white
  Isa 3:22; Mr 16:5; Re 6:11; 7:9, 13.
ROCK, Ex 17:6 you must strike on the **r.**
  De 32:4 The **R.,** perfect is his activity,
  2Sa 22:3 My God is my **r.** I shall take
  Isa 8:14 **r.** over which to stumble to both
  Isa 14:16 the man making kingdoms **r.,**
  Hag 2:7 I will **r.** all the nations,
  De 32:18; 1Sa 2:2; Ps 62:2; Joe 3:16.
ROCK-MASS, Mt 16:18 you are Peter, on this **r.**
  Lu 8:6 Some other landed upon the **r.,**
  Ro 9:33 a stone of stumbling and a **r.** of
  1Co 10:4 used to drink from the spiritual **r.**
  1Pe 2:8 stone of stumbling and a **r.** of
ROCKY PLACE(S), Mt 13:5, 20; Mr 4:5, 16.
ROD, Ps 110:2 The **r.** of your strength
  Pr 13:24 holding back his **r.** is hating his
  Isa 11:4 strike the earth with the **r.** of
  1Co 4:21 Shall I come to you with a **r.,**
  Heb 9:4 having manna and the **r.** of Aaron
  Re 12:5 shepherd all nations with an iron **r.**
  Ps 23:4; Pr 29:15; Mic 5:1; Re 2:27.
ROLL, Heb 10:7 in the **r.** of the book it
  Pr 16:3; Jer 36:2, 27, 32; Eze 2:9; 3:1.
ROLLED, Jos 5:9 **r.** away the reproach of
  Isa 34:4 heavens must be **r.** up, like a book
  Re 6:14 departed as a scroll that is **r.** up,
ROLLING, 2Pe 2:22 to **r.** in the mire
ROMAN(S), Ac 16:37 men who are **R.**
  Joh 11:48; Ac 23:27; 25:16; 28:17.

ROOF, Pr 27:15; Mr 2:4; Lu 7:6.
ROOMY, 2Sa 22:20 bring me into a **r.**
ROOT, Job 14:8 its **r.** grows old in the earth
  Isa 11:10 **r.** of Jesse that will be standing
  Ro 11:16 if the **r.** is holy, the branches
  1Ti 6:10 love of money is a **r.** of all sorts
  Heb 12:15 that no poisonous **r.** may spring
  Pr 12:12; Mt 3:10; 13:21; Ro 11:18.
ROOTED, Eph 3:17 **r.** and established on
  Col 2:7 **r.** and being built up in him and
ROOT-FOUNDATION, Pr 12:3 as for the **r.** of
ROPE(S), Joh 2:15 whip of **r.,** he drove
  Jos 2:15; Ps 18:4; 129:4; Jer 38:13.
ROT, Pr 10:7 name of wicked will **r.**
  Isa 34:4; Zec 14:12.
ROTTED, Jas 5:2 riches have **r.,** and
ROTTEN, Isa 40:20 a tree not **r.**
  Mt 7:18 neither can a **r.** tree
  Mt 12:33 make the tree **r.** and its fruit **r.;**
  Eph 4:29 Let a **r.** saying not proceed out of
ROTTENNESS, Pr 12:4 as **r.** in his bones
  Pr 14:30 jealousy is **r.** to the bones.
ROTTING, Eze 14:12 a **r.** away of flesh
ROUSED, Isa 41:25 **r.** up from the north,
  Isa 41:2; 45:13; Jer 25:32.
ROUT, De 7:23; 1Sa 14:20.
ROUTINE, Php 3:16 in this same **r.**
ROVE, Da 12:4 Many will **r.** about, and
ROVING, 2Ch 16:9 his eyes are **r.** about
  Jer 5:1; Am 8:12; Zec 4:10.
ROYAL, Da 10:13; Lu 7:25; 1Pe 2:9.
ROYAL REALM, Jos 13:12, 21, 27, 30, 31.
ROYAL RULE, 1Sa 15:28; Jer 26:1; Ho 1:4.
ROYALTY, 2Ch 36:20 the **r.** of Persia
RUBBLE, Am 6:11 great house into **r.**
RUBY, Ex 28:17; 39:10; Eze 28:13.
RUDDER, Jas 3:4 boats steered by a **r.**
RUGGED, Pr 13:15 the way is **r.**
  Isa 40:4 **r.** ground become a plain
RUIN(S), Isa 6:11 cities crash in **r.**
  Eze 21:27 A **r., r., r.** I shall make it.
  Da 2:44 kingdom will never be brought to **r.**
  Am 9:11 its **r.** I shall raise up, as in the
  Ac 15:16 I shall rebuild its **r.** and erect
RUINATION, 2Ch 22:4; Eze 9:6.
RUINED, Ge 6:11 earth came to be **r.**
  Isa 54:16 created the **r.** man
RUINOUS, Isa 54:16 created the **r.** man
RUINOUSLY, De 9:12 your people acted **r.**
RULE, Jg 8:23 shall not **r.** over you,
  2Ch 8:14 according to the **r.** of David
  Pr 29:2 wicked bears **r.,** the people sigh.
  Isa 32:1 they **r.** as princes for justice
  Ro 6:12 not let sin **r.** in your bodies
  1Co 4:6 you may learn the **r.**
  Ga 6:16 walk orderly by this **r.** of conduct,
  Isa 3:4; Da 11:39.
RULE AS KING(S), Ex 15:18 Jehovah **r.**
  Eze 20:33 I will **r.** over you people.
  Ro 6:12 do not let sin **r.** in your
  1Co 4:8 also might **r.** with you
  1Co 15:25 he must **r.** until God
  2Ti 2:12 if we go on enduring, we shall **r.**
  Re 11:15 he will **r.** forever
  1Sa 24:20; 1Ki 1:5; Mic 4:7; Re 19:6.
RULED, Ro 5:14 death **r.** as king from
  Re 20:4 they came to life and **r.** as
RULER(S), Da 4:17 Most High is **R.** in
  Mt 9:34 It is by the **r.** of the demons
  Mt 20:25 **r.** of the nations lord it over
  Joh 7:48 Not one of the **r.** put faith in
  Joh 12:42 many **r.** put faith in him, but
  Eph 2:2 **r.** of the authority of the air,
  Isa 28:14; Ac 3:17; 4:26; 17:6; 1Co 2:8.
RULER OF THIS (THE) WORLD, Joh 12:31.

Joh 14:30 the **r.** is coming. And he has no
Joh 16:11 because the **r.** has been judged.
RULERSHIP(S), Da 7:27 the **r.** will serve
Da 4:3, 34; 7:6.
RULES AS KING, Pr 30:22 when he **r.**
RULING, 2Sa 23:3 When one **r.** over
Ps 59:13 God is **r.** to the ends of the earth.
Isa 14:5 broken the staff of the **r.** ones,
Re 11:17 have begun **r.** as king.
Pr 8:16; 1Co 4:8.
RUN, Pr 1:16 feet **r.** to sheer badness
Joe 2:9 On the wall they **r.**
1Co 9:24 all **r.,** but only one receives the
Heb 12:1 let us **r.** with endurance the race
Isa 40:31; 55:5; Php 2:16.
RUNNING, 1Pe 4:4 not continue **r.** with
RUPTURE, Ge 38:29 a perineal **r.** for
Jg 21:15 Jehovah had made a **r.** between
RURAL COUNTRY, Zec 2:4 as **r.** Jerusalem
RUSH, Joe 2:9 Into the city they **r.**
RUST, Eze 24:6, 11, 12; Jas 5:3.
RUTH, Ru 1:4; 2:8; 3:9; 4:13; Mt 1:5.
RUTHLESSLY, Nu 22:29 have dealt **r.** with

S

SABAOTH. See ARMIES, ARMY.
SABBATH(S), Ex 20:8 Remembering s. day
Ex 31:13 Especially my s. you are to keep,
Le 25:8 count seven s. of years,
Le 26:34 the land will pay off its **s.**
Isa 56:4 the eunuchs that keep my **s.**
Eze 20:12 my s. become a sign between me
Mt 12:8 Lord of the s. is what the Son is.
Mt 24:20 flight may not occur on the s. day;
Mr 2:27 s. came into existence for man, not
Col 2:16 no man judge you in respect of s.,
Heb 4:9 remains a s. resting for the people.
Le 25:2, 4; Eze 22:8; Ho 2:11; Lu 14:5.
SABBATH DAY'S TRIP, Ac 1:12 a s. away.
SACKCLOTH, Es 4:1; Ps 69:11; Re 11:3.
SACRED PILLAR(S), Ex 34:13; 1Ki 14:23;
2Ki 3:2; 17:10; Jer 43:13; Ho 10:1.
SACRED POLE(S), De 7:5; Jg 3:7; 6:25;
1Ki 15:13; 2Ki 13:6; 21:3; Isa 17:8.
SACRED PRONOUNCEMENTS, Ac 7:38.
Ro 3:2 they were entrusted with the **s.**
Heb 5:12 elementary things of s. of God.
1Pe 4:11 let him speak the s. of God.
SACRED SECRET(S), Mt 13:11; Mr 4:11.
Ro 16:25 the s. which has been kept in
1Co 4:1 stewards of s. of God.
1Co 13:2 understand all s. and knowledge
1Co 14:2 but he speaks s. by the spirit.
1Co 15:51 I tell you a s.:
Eph 1:9 known to us the s. of his will
Col 1:26 the s. which was concealed
1Ti 3:16 the s. of this godly devotion
Re 10:7 the s. of God declared to his own
Ro 11:25; 1Co 4:1; Eph 3:3, 4; Col 4:3; Re
1:20.
SACRED SERVICE. See also SERVICE.
SACRED SERVICE, Mt 4:10 God alone render s.
Ro 9:4 the Law and s.
Ro 12:1 present your bodies a s.
SACRIFICE(S), 1Sa 15:22 obey better s.
Ps 40:6 S. and offering you did not delight
Ps 50:5 concluding my covenant over s.
Ps 51:17 s. of God are a broken spirit;
Pr 21:3 judgment is more preferable than s.
Jer 46:10 Jehovah has a s. in the land
Da 9:27 he will cause s. to cease.
Ho 6:6 I have taken delight, not in s.;
Zep 1:7 Jehovah has prepared a s.;
Mt 9:13 I want mercy, and not s.

Ro 12:1 present your bodies a s. living,
1Co 10:20 nations s. they s. to demons,
Heb 10:1 never s. from year to year
Heb 10:12 offered one s. for sins perpetually
Heb 10:26 no s. for sins left
Heb 13:15 offer to God a s. of praise,
1Pe 2:5 offer up spiritual s. acceptable
Eze 39:17; Eph 5:2.
SACRIFICIAL SMOKE, Jer 44:5; Mal 1:11.
SACRIFICING, Mal 1:8 blind for s.:
SAD, Ps 38:6 I have walked about s.
SADDENED, 2Co 7:9 s. in a godly way,
SADDUCEES, Mt 3:7; 22:23; Ac 23:6-8.
SADNESS, 2Co 2:1 not to come again in s.
2Co 7:10 s. godly makes for repentance
SAFE. See SECURITY.
SAFEGUARD, Ps 25:21 Let uprightness s.
Ps 34:13 S. your tongue against what is bad,
Ps 40:11 Let loving-kindness and trueness s.
Pr 4:23 s. your heart, for out of it
SAFEGUARDED, 1Sa 30:23 Jehovah s. us
SAFEGUARDING, Ps 31:23 Jehovah is s.,
Pr 16:17 One s. his way is keeping his soul.
Isa 27:3; 49:8.
SAFETY, Php 3:1 for me, s. to you.
Ps 12:5; Ac 27:34; 28:1, 4.
SAFFRON, Ca 2:1 A s. of coastal plain
Isa 35:1 desert blossom as s.
SAILORS, Ac 27:27; Re 18:17.
SAINTS. See HOLY ONES, LOYAL ONES.
SAKE(S), Ps 23:3 for his name's s.
Ps 122:8 For the s. of my brothers
Eze 36:22 Not for your s. am I doing it,
Mt 5:10 persecuted for righteousness' s.,
Mt 10:39 loses his soul for my s. will
Ro 11:28 they are enemies for your s.,
2Co 8:9 he became poor for your s.,
2Ki 19:34; Ps 106:8; Isa 62:1; Tit 1:11.
SALEM, Heb 7:2 S., that is, King of
Ge 14:18; Ps 76:2.
SALES GOODS, Eze 26:12; 28:5, 16.
Eze 28:18 injustice of s., you profaned
SALLIED FORTH, 1Sa 7:11 men s. from
SALOME, Mr 15:40; 16:1.
SALT, Ge 19:26 she became a pillar of s.
Nu 18:19 It is a covenant of s. for you
Mt 5:13 You are the s. of the earth;
Col 4:6 your utterance be seasoned with s.,
Le 2:13; 2Ki 2:21; Job 6:6; Mr 9:50.
SALT SEA, Jos 3:16 sea of Arabah, S.,
SALVATION, 2Ki 13:17 arrow of s.,
2Ch 20:17 see the s. of Jehovah
Ps 3:8 S. belongs to Jehovah.
Ps 13:5 My heart is joyful in your s.
Ps 33:17 The horse is a deception for s.,
Ps 44:4 Command grand s. for Jacob.
Ps 85:9 s. is near to those fearing him,
Ps 116:13 The cup of grand s. I shall
Ps 119:155 S. is far from the wicked
Ps 149:4 beautifies the meek ones with s.
Pr 11:14 s. in the multitude of counselors.
Pr 21:31 battle, but s. belongs to Jehovah.
Isa 12:3 water out of the springs of s.
Isa 26:1 He sets s. for walls and
Isa 49:8 in a day of s. I helped you
Isa 52:7 the one publishing s.
Isa 60:18 call your walls S. and your
Isa 61:10 clothed with garments of s.;
Hab 3:18 will be joyful in the God of my s.
Lu 1:69 raised up a horn of s. for us
Lu 1:77 s. by forgiveness of their sins
Joh 4:22 s. originates with the Jews.
Ac 4:12 there is no s. in anyone else,
Ro 10:10 makes public declaration for s.

Ro 13:11 now our s. is nearer than at
2Co 6:2 in a day of s. I helped you
2Co 7:10 sadness makes for repentance to s.
Eph 6:17 accept the helmet of s.,
Php 2:12 working out your s. with fear and
2Ti 3:15 able to make you wise for s.
Heb 2:3 shall we escape if we neglected a s.
Heb 2:10 Chief Agent of their s. perfect
Heb 5:9 everlasting s. to all those obeying
Jude 3 the s. we hold in common,
Re 7:10 S. we owe to our God,
Re 12:10 Now have come to pass the s. and
Isa 26:18; 45:17; Ro 1:16; Heb 9:28.
SALIVA, 1Sa 21:13 let his s. run down
SAMARIA, 1Ki 16:24 mountain of S.
Ho 8:6 calf of S. will become splinters.
Am 8:14 swearing by the guiltiness of S.,
2Ki 6:20; Isa 10:11; Jer 23:13; Ho 13:16.
SAMARITAN(S), Lu 10:33 But a certain S.
Joh 4:9 (For Jews have no dealings with S.)
2Ki 17:29; Mt 10:5; Lu 17:16; Ac 8:25.
SAME, Heb 1:12 changed, you are the s.
SAMPLE, 1Ti 1:16 his long-suffering a s.
SAMSON, Jg 15:16 S. With the jawbone of
Jg 16:30 S. my soul die with Philistines
Heb 11:32 time will fail me Barak, S.,
Jg 13:24; 14:1, 5, 7.
SAMUEL, 1Sa 1:20 call his name S.,
1Sa 8:7 S. not you they have rejected
1Sa 15:28 S. said: "Jehovah has ripped
Jer 15:1 If S. were standing before me,
1Sa 2:18; 3:1; 15:22; Ps 99:6; Heb 11:32.
SANCTIFICATION, 1Co 1:30 become to us s.
1Th 4:4 get possession of his vessel in s.
1Th 4:7 God called us in connection with s.
1Ti 2:15 continue in faith and love and s.
Heb 12:14 Pursue peace and s. without which
1Pe 1:2 with s. by the spirit, for the
SANCTIFIED, 1Ki 9:3 I s. this house
Isa 13:3 command to my s., my mighty
Jer 1:5 I s. you. Prophet to the nations
Eze 20:41 be s. in you before the eyes of
Zep 1:7 he has s. his invited ones
Lu 11:2 Father, let your name be s.
1Co 6:11 you have been washed clean, s.,
1Co 7:14 unbelieving husband is s. in
2Ti 2:21 vessel for honorable purpose, s.,
Heb 2:11 who are being s. all stem from one,
Heb 10:10 s. through the offering of the
Le 22:32; Nu 3:13; 1Co 1:2; 1Ti 4:5.
SANCTIFY, Jos 3:5 S. yourselves for tomorrow
2Ch 7:16 and s. this house
Isa 5:16 God, will s. himself through
Isa 29:23 they will s. my name,
Jer 51:27 S. against her the nations.
Eze 36:23 shall certainly s. my great name,
Eze 38:16 s. myself in you, O Gog.
Joe 3:9 S. war! Arouse the powerful
Joh 17:17 S. them by means of the truth;
Heb 13:12 Jesus s. people with his blood,
1Pe 3:15 s. the Christ in your hearts,
Ex 13:2; 29:44; De 32:51; Eph 5:26.
SANCTIFYING, Joh 17:19 I am s. myself
1Th 4:3 God wills, the s. of you,
2Th 2:13 s. with spirit
Eze 37:28.
SANCTUARIES, Le 26:31 your s. desolate
Eze 28:18 you have profaned your s.
SANCTUARY, Ex 25:8 make a s. for me
Le 19:30 you stand in awe of my s,
1Ch 28:10 Jehovah has chosen to build a s.
Eze 37:26 place my s. in the midst of them
Da 11:31 they will profane the s., fortress
Mt 27:51 the curtain of the s. was rent

Ps 78:69; Re 15:8; 16:17.
SAND, Ge 22:17 your seed like grains of s.
Isa 10:22 O Israel, like grains of s.
Mt 7:26 who built his house upon the s.
Ro 9:27 Israel may be as the s. of the sea,
Ps 139:18; Jer 5:22; 33:22; Re 20:8.
SANDAL(S), De 25:9 draw his s. off and
Joh 1:27 lace of whose s. I am not worthy
Ex 3:5; Jos 5:15; Ru 4:7; Ps 60:8; Mr 6:9.
SANHEDRIN, Mt 26:59; Lu 22:66; Ac 5:21.
SANITY, 1Sa 21:13 disguised his s.
SAPPHIRA, Ac 5:1 Ananias, with S. his wife
SARAH, Ge 17:15 S. is her name.
Ge 17:19 S. your wife is bearing you a son,
Ge 21:2 S. became pregnant and bore a son
Heb 11:11 By faith S. received power to
1Pe 3:6 S. obey Abraham calling him lord
Ge 25:10; Isa 51:2; Ro 9:9.
SASH, Ex 28:4; 39:29 turban and a s.
SAT, Ps 1:1 seat of ridiculers not s.
SATAN, 1Ch 21:1 S. incite David to number
Job 1:6 S. proceeded to come in right among
Job 2:2 S. answered Jehovah and said: "From
Zec 3:1 S. standing at his right to resist
Mt 12:26 if S. expels S., he has become
Mt 16:23 Get behind me, S.!
Mr 1:13 forty days, being tempted by S.,
Lu 10:18 behold S. already fallen from
Lu 22:3 S. entered into Judas, the one
Ro 16:20 God will crush S. under your feet
1Co 5:5 hand such a man over to S. for
2Co 2:11 may not be overreached by S., for we
2Co 11:14 S. keeps transforming himself into
2Co 12:7 thorn in the flesh, an angel of S.,
1Th 2:18 but S. cut across our path.
Re 2:9 they are a synagogue of S.
Re 12:9 serpent, one called Devil and S.,
Re 20:2 S., and bound him a thousand
Re 20:7 S. will be let loose out of his
Mt 4:10; Mr 4:15; Ac 26:18; 2Th 2:9.
SATIATED, Hab 2:16 be s. with dishonor
SATISFACTION, Pr 13:25 eating to the s.
SATISFACTORY, Le 10:19 s. in Jehovah's eyes
SATISFIED, Ps 17:15 willing to be s.
Ps 22:26 meek will eat and be s.
Ps 37:19 in famine they will be s.
Pr 27:20 Sheol, neither do eyes get s.
Pr 30:15 three things do not get s.,
Jer 31:14 my people will become s.
Joe 2:26 you will eat and become s.
Mic 6:14 You will eat and not get s.
Ps 107:9; Pr 19:23; Joe 2:19.
SATISFY, Ps 91:16 I shall s. him,
Job 38:39; Isa 58:10; Eze 7:19; 32:4.
SATISFYING, Ps 145:16 s. the desire of
SATRAPS, Ezr 8:36; Es 8:9; Da 3:2, 3, 27.
SATURATED, Isa 43:24; La 3:15; Ho 6:3.
SAUL, 1Sa 9:17 Samuel saw S.: "Here is
1Sa 10:11 Is S. among the prophets?
1Sa 13:1 S. was [?] years old when
1Sa 15:26 Samuel to S.: "I shall not
1Sa 16:14 Jehovah departed from S.
1Sa 18:12 S. grew afraid of David
1Sa 31:4 S. said to his armor-bearer:
2Sa 1:17 David proceeded to chant over S.
1Ch 10:13 S. died for his unfaithfulness
1Sa 24:7; 26:2; 28:7; Ac 13:21.
SAUL (of Tarsus), Ac 7:58 the feet of S.
Ac 8:1 S. was approving of the murder
Ac 9:4 S., why are you persecuting me?
Ac 13:9 S., who is also Paul, with spirit
Ac 9:1; 11:25; 12:25; 13:1; 22:7; 26:14.
SAVE, 1Sa 14:6 Jehovah to s. by many or
1Sa 17:47 nor with spear does Jehovah s.,

Ps 69:35 For God will s. Zion and build
Isa 59:1 hand not short that it cannot s.,
Isa 63:1 One abounding in power to s.
Eze 34:22 I will s. my sheep,
Mt 16:25 whoever wants to s. his soul
Lu 19:10 Son of man came to seek and s.
1Ti 1:15 Jesus came to s. sinners.
Heb 7:25 he is able to s. completely
Jas 2:14 That faith cannot s. him, can it?
Jas 4:12 he is able to s. and destroy
Jas 5:20 will s. his soul from death
Jos 10:6; 2Ki 19:34; Ps 106:8; Isa 37:20;
Jer 2:27; 1Ti 4:16; Jude 23.
SAVED, Jer 8:20 we have not been s.!
Mt 10:22 to the end is the one s.
Mt 19:25 Who really can be s.?
Mt 24:22 cut short, no flesh would be s.;
Joh 3:17 world to be s. through him.
Ac 4:12 by which we must get s.
Ro 10:9 exercise faith, you will be s.
Ro 10:13 calls upon Jehovah will be s.
1Co 1:18 to us who are being s. it is God's
1Co 5:5 spirit may be s. in the day of
1Co 10:33 in order that they might get s.
2Co 2:15 odor of Christ among those being s.
Eph 2:8 you have been s. through faith;
1Ti 2:4 all sorts of men should be s.
1Pe 4:18 righteous being s. with difficulty,
Ps 18:3; Isa 43:12; 45:17, 22; Jer 30:7;
Lu 8:12; Tit 3:5.
SAVES, Pr 20:6 Jehovah s. his anointed
Ps 34:18 those crushed in spirit he s.
SAVING, Ps 68:20 a God of s. acts,
Lu 2:30 have seen your means of s.
Lu 3:6 all flesh will see the s. means
1Pe 3:21 this is also now s. you,
SAVIOR(S), Jg 3:15 raised up a s.
2Sa 22:3 my place for flight, my S.;
Ne 9:27 in mercy would give them s.
Isa 43:11 besides me there is no s.
Isa 49:26 I, Jehovah, am your S.
Ob 21 s. will come up onto Mount Zion,
Lu 2:11 born to you today a S.,
Ac 5:31 this one as Chief Agent and S.
1Ti 4:10 God, who is a S. of all sorts
1Jo 4:14 Father sent forth his Son as S.
Isa 19:20; Jer 14:8; Ac 13:23; 2Ti 1:10.
SAW, Heb 11:13 promises s. them afar off
SAWN, Heb 11:37 s. asunder, died by
SAYING(S), Ps 119:103 How smooth your s.
Pr 4:10 Hear, my son, and accept my s.
Joh 6:63 s. I have spoken are spirit
Joh 12:47 if anyone hears my s. and
Job 6:25; Ps 19:14; Pr 4:20.
SCALED, Pr 21:22 wise one s. the city of
SCALES, Job 31:6 weigh me in s.
Ps 62:9 mankind upon s. lighter than
Pr 20:23 cheating pair of s. is
Isa 40:15 nations dust on the s.
Pr 11:1; Re 6:5.
SCANTY, Pr 24:10 Your power will be s.
SCAPEGOAT. See AZAZEL, GOAT (for Azazel).
SCARECROW, Jer 10:5 s. of a cucumber
SCARED, De 9:19 I was s. of God's anger
Job 9:28 s. of all my pains;
SCARLET, Jos 2:18 cord of s. thread
Isa 1:18 Though sins of you be as s.,
Le 14:49; Jer 4:30; Mt 27:28.
SCARLET-COLORED, Re 17:3 a s. beast
SCATTER(S), Pr 11:26 Hoarfrost he s.
Mt 12:30 does not gather with me s.
Ps 144:6; Eze 5:10; Hab 3:14; Joh 10:12.
SCATTERED, Ge 11:9 Jehovah s. them from
Ps 68:1 God arise, let his enemies be s.

Jer 23:2 You have s. my sheep; dispersing
Zec 13:7 Strike, let those of the flock be s.
Ac 8:4 those s. went through the land
Jas 1:1 twelve tribes that are s. about:
1Pe 1:1 temporary residents s. about in
Ge 11:4; Jer 30:11; Eze 34:5, 12, 21.
SCATTERING, Pr 11:24 one that is s. yet
Pr 15:7 wise ones keep s. knowledge about,
SCENE, 1Co 7:31 s. of world is changing.
SCENT POWDER, Ca 3:6 every sort of s.
SCEPTER. See also COMMANDER'S STAFF.
SCEPTER, Ge 49:10 s. not turn from Judah,
Nu 24:17 a s. will rise out of Israel.
Ps 2:9 will break them with an iron s.,
Ps 125:3 s. of wickedness not resting upon
Zec 10:11 the s. of Egypt will depart
Heb 1:8 [kingdom] is s. of uprightness.
Es 5:2; Ps 45:6; Eze 19:14.
SCHEDULE, Lu 23:37 offerings to daily s.
SCHEME(S), Pr 6:18 fabricating hurtful s.,
Isa 8:10 Plan out a s., and it will be
Ac 5:38 if this s. is from men, it will
Pr 15:26; Eze 22:29; Da 11:24.
SCHEMED, Es 8:3 Haman s. against the
Ps 17:3 I have not s. My mouth will not
SCHEMING, Ne 6:2; Ps 36:4.
SCHOOL(S), Joh 7:15 not studied at s.
Ac 19:9 talks in the s. auditorium
SCIENCE. See KNOWLEDGE.
SCOFFERS, Isa 28:22 show yourselves s.,
SCORCHED, Isa 43:2 you will not be s.,
SCORPION(S), De 8:15; Lu 11:12; Re 9:10.
SCOURED, Le 6:28 be s. and rinsed with
SCOURGE(S), Ps 106:29 s. now broke out
Zec 14:12 Jehovah will s. all the peoples
Mt 10:17 s. you in their synagogues.
Mt 23:34 some of them you will s.
Heb 12:6 s. whom he receives as a son."
SCREEN, 2Sa 17:19 spread a s. over the
SCRIBES, Mt 5:20 righteousness of the s.
Mt 7:29 authority, and not as their s.
Mt 9:3; 17:10; Lu 5:21, 30.
SCRIMPED, Mic 6:10 the s. measure
SCRIPTURE(S), Mt 21:42 read in the S.,
Mt 22:29 you know neither the S. nor the
Lu 4:21 Today this s. is fulfilled.
Lu 24:27 interpreted to them in all the S.
Lu 24:32 fully opening up the S. to us?
Lu 24:45 grasp the meaning of the S.,
Joh 5:39 searching the S., because by means
Joh 10:35 yet the S. cannot be nullified,
Joh 13:18 in order that the s. be fulfilled,
Ac 17:2 he reasoned with them from the S.,
Ac 17:11 carefully examining the S. daily
Ac 18:24 he was well versed in the S.
Ro 15:4 comfort from the S. we have hope.
2Ti 3:16 All S. is inspired of God and
2Pe 1:20 no prophecy of S. springs from
2Pe 3:16 the untaught are twisting the S.,
Joh 20:9; Ac 8:32; 1Co 15:3, 4; Jas 4:5.
SCRIPTURE-CONTAINING CASES, Mt 23:5.
SCROLL(S), Isa 34:4 heavens like a book s.;
Zec 5:1 and saw; and, look! a flying s.
Lu 4:17 s. of the prophet Isaiah was handed
2Ti 4:13 bring the cloak and the s.
Re 5:5 conquered so as to open the s.
Re 20:12 the throne, and s. were opened
Re 21:27 written in the Lamb's s. of life
Ezr 6:2; Da 3:10; Re 17:8.
SCRUPULOUSLY, Ga 4:10 s. observing days
SCRUTINIZE, Ezr 8:15 I might s. people
SCRUTINY, 1Co 11:28 approve after s.,
SEA(S), Ge 1:10 waters he called S.
Ex 14:21 converting the s. into dry

Ps 72:8 will have subjects from s. to s.
Isa 11:9 knowledge as waters covering the s.
Isa 57:20 wicked are like the s. being
Isa 60:5 wealthiness of the s. will direct
Da 11:45 plant his tents between the s. and
Lu 21:25 the roaring of the s. and its
1Co 10:2 baptized by means of the s.;
Jude 13 wild waves of the s. that foam
Re 20:13 the s. gave up those dead in it,
Re 21:1 passed away, and the s. is no more.
Isa 17:12; Eze 27:27; Jon 1:15; Re 7:3.
SEAL(S), Isa 8:16 a s. about the law
Da 9:24 imprint a s. upon vision and
Da 12:4 O Daniel, s. up the book,
Joh 3:33 put his s. to it that God is true.
Joh 6:27 God, has put his s. of approval.
2Co 1:22 put his s. upon us and token
2Ti 2:19 having this s., Jehovah knows
Re 22:10 Do not s. up the words of the
Job 38:14; Ca 8:6; Ro 4:11; Re 5:1; 7:2.
SEALED, Isa 29:11 unable, for it is s. up
Da 12:9 s. up until the time of the end.
Eph 4:30 s. for a day of releasing by
Re 7:4 s., hundred and forty-four thousand,
Eph 1:13; Re 5:1; 7:3.
SEARCH, Ps 139:23 S. me, O God, and know
Isa 55:6 S. for Jehovah, you people, while
Eze 34:11 I will s. for my sheep and care
Eze 39:14 seven months they keep making s.
Am 9:3 if they hide I shall carefully s.
Mt 10:11 s. out who in it is deserving,
1Pe 1:10 diligent inquiry and a careful s.
Jos 2:3; Jer 29:13; La 3:40; Eze 34:8.
SEARCHED, Ps 139:1 Jehovah, you s. me
Ob 6 those of Esau have been s. out!
SEARCHES, Ro 8:27 he who s. the hearts
1Co 2:10 the spirit s. into all things,
Re 2:23 he who s. the inmost thoughts
Pr 18:17; 28:11.
SEARCHING(S), Jg 5:16 s. of the heart.
1Ch 28:9 Jehovah is s. every inclination
Pr 2:4 treasures you keep s. for it,
Pr 25:2 the s. through a matter.
Isa 40:28 no s. out of his understanding.
Jer 17:10 I, Jehovah, am s. the heart,
Am 8:12 s. for Jehovah, but will not find
Joh 5:39 You are s. Scriptures, because by
Job 28:3; Ps 64:6; 119:2; Pr 11:27.
SEARING(S), Jer 4:11 s. wind of beaten paths
SEASON(S), Ge 1:14 as signs and for s.
Ps 1:3 gives its fruit in its s.
Da 2:21 he is changing times and s.,
Ac 1:7 times s. in [Father's] jurisdiction
Ac 3:19 s. of refreshing may come from
Ga 4:10 scrupulously observing months and s.
Ga 6:9 in due s. we shall reap by not
1Th 5:1 as for the times and the s.,
2Ti 4:2 Preach the word, in favorable s.,
1Pe 1:11 investigating what particular s.
Ps 145:15; Jer 5:24; Ac 17:26.
SEATED, Eph 2:6 s. in heavenly places
Re 7:10 Salvation to God s. on the throne,
SECLUDED, Ru 1:13 keep s. for them
SECOND DEATH, Re 2:11 harmed by the s.
Re 20:6 these the s. has no authority,
Re 20:14 This means s., the lake of fire.
Re 21:8 fire and sulphur. This means the s.
SECRECY, Pr 21:14 gift made in s. subdues
De 13:6; 1Sa 19:2; Job 13:10; Pr 9:17.
SECRET(S). See also SACRED SECRET(S).
SECRET(S), Jg 3:19 a s. word for you,
Job 14:13 Keep me s. until
Ps 44:21 aware of the s. of the heart.
Ps 91:1 s. place of the Most High

Da 2:28 God is a Revealer of s.,
Mt 6:6 Pray to your Father who is in s.;
Joh 18:20 I spoke nothing in s.
1Co 14:25 s. of his heart become manifest,
Da 2:30; Mt 6:4; Ro 2:16; Eph 5:12.
SECRETARIES, Es 3:12 king's s. called in
SECRETARY, 2Ki 12:10 s. of the king
Isa 33:18; Jer 52:25.
SECRET SELF, Ps 51:6 in s. cause me to know
SECT(S). See also DIVISION(S).
SECT(S), Ac 24:5 s. of the Nazarenes,
Ac 24:14 to the way which they call a 's.,'
Ac 26:5 strictest s. of our form of worship
1Co 11:19 there must also be s. among you,
Tit 3:10 promotes a s., reject him
2Pe 2:1 quietly bring in destructive s.
Ac 5:17; 15:5; 28:22; Ga 5:20.
SECULAR, 1Co 9:6 to refrain from s. work
SECURE HEIGHT, Ps 18:2 salvation, my s.
Ps 59:17 God is my s., the God of
Ps 9:9; 62:6; 144:2.
SECURITY, Ps 4:8 make me dwell in s.
Pr 1:33 one listening resides in s.
Pr 3:23 walk in s. on your way
1Th 5:3 they are saying, Peace and s.!
Le 25:18; De 33:28; Isa 14:30.
SEDIMENT, Ps 40:2 the mire of the s.
SEDITION(S), Lu 23:19 into prison for a s.
Ac 21:38 stirred up s. and
Ac 24:5 pestilent fellow and stirring up s.
SEDITIONISTS, Mr 15:7 bonds with the s.
SEDUCE, Ro 16:18 by smooth talk they s.
Pr 1:10; 16:29; 2Th 2:3.
SEDUCED, Ro 7:11 s. me and killed me
2Co 11:3 as the serpent s. Eve by its
SEDUCES, Ex 22:16 a man s. a virgin
Pr 7:21 lips she s. him.
SEDUCING, 1Co 3:18 no one be s. himself:
SEE, Ex 33:20 no man s. me and live.
Jer 5:21 They have eyes, but they cannot s.;
Mt 5:8 pure in heart will s. God.
Mt 13:14 you will look but by no means s.
Re 3:18 eyesalve in eyes that you may s.
SEED(S), Ge 1:11 the s. of which is in it,
Ge 3:15 between your s. and her s.
Ge 22:17 I shall surely multiply your s.
Mt 13:38 as for the fine s., these are
Lu 8:11 The s. is the word of God.
Lu 17:6 had faith the size of a mustard s.,
Ro 9:29 Unless Jehovah had left a s. to us,
Ga 3:16 not to s. many but of one, Christ.
Ga 3:29 you are really Abraham's s., heirs
Re 12:17 with the remaining ones of her s.,
Ge 12:7; Ro 9:7; 1Co 15:38; Ga 3:19.
SEEING, Joh 8:56 Abraham s. my day,
SEEK, Zep 2:3 s. Jehovah, all you meek
Eze 7:25; Zec 8:22; Ac 15:17; Re 9:6.
SEEKING, Mal 3:1 Lord, whom you are s.,
Mt 6:33 Keep on s. first the kingdom
Mt 7:7 keep on s., and you will find;
1Co 10:33 not s. my own advantage
Ga 1:10 am I s. to please men?
Col 3:1 go on s. the things above,
Heb 11:6 rewarder of those earnestly s. him.
Heb 11:14 earnestly s. a place of their own
Heb 13:14 city we are s. the one to come
Isa 16:5; Joh 8:40, 50; Ro 2:7; 1Pe 5:8.
SEEN, Isa 66:8 Who has s. things like
Joh 1:18 No man has s. God at any time
Joh 14:9 has s. me has s. the Father
Joh 20:29 you have s. me you believed?
Ro 1:20 invisible qualities are clearly s.
1Jo 4:20 love his brother, whom he has s.,
Ge 7:1; Isa 6:5; 60:2; 1Ti 6:16; Re 11:19.

SEER, 1Sa 9:9 prophet called a s.
2Ch 16:7 Hanani the s. came to Asa
SEES, Ro 8:24 when a man s. a thing,
SEGMENT, Ca 4:3; 6:7 s. of pomegranate
SEIR, Ge 36:8 Esau dwelling in S.
2Ch 20:23 finished with inhabitants of S.
Nu 24:18; Jos 24:4; Eze 25:8; 35:15.
SEIZE, 1Co 7:21 s. the opportunity.
SEIZURE, Php 2:6 no consideration to a s.,
SELECTED, 2Ti 2:13 God s. you from the
SELF, Lu 9:25 the world but loses his s.
SELF-ASSISTANCE, Job 6:13 s. is not in me
SELF-ASSUMING, 2Ti 3:2 s., haughty,
Pr 21:24; Hab 2:5; Ro 1:30; Jas 4:16.
SELF-CONCERNED, 1Sa 1:18 s. no more
SELF-CONDEMNED, Tit 3:11 he being s.
SELF-CONFIDENCE, Ps 85:8 not return to s.
SELF-CONFIDENT, Pr 14:16 stupid is s.
Eze 30:9 drive s. Ethiopia into trembling.
SELF-CONTROL, Isa 42:14 exercising s.
Ac 24:25 talked about righteousness and s.
1Co 9:25 man in a contest exercises s.
1Co 7:9; Ga 5:23; 2Ti 3:3; 2Pe 1:6.
SELF-CONTROLLED, Tit 1:8 hospitable, s.,
SELF-EXALTATION, Pr 8:13 S. I hated.
SELF-EXALTED, Pr 15:25 house of the s.
Isa 2:12 It is upon everyone s. and
SELF-IMPORTANCE, Isa 10:12 s. of his eyes
SELF-IMPOSED, Col 2:23 s. form of
SELFISH, Nu 11:4 expressed s. longing,
SELFISH DESIRE, Ps 106:14 showed s. in
SELF-REGULATION, 1Co 7:5 lack of s.
SELF-RELIANCE, Jg 18:7 dwelling in s.
SELF-SUFFICIENCY, Job 21:23 his full s.,
2Co 8:18 always have full s. in everything,
1Ti 6:6 godly devotion along with s.
SELF-SUFFICIENT, Php 4:11 learned to be s.
SELF-WILLED, Tit 1:7; 2Pe 2:10.
SELL, Ge 25:31 S. me your right
Pr 23:23 Buy truth and do not s. it—
Joe 3:8 I will s. your sons and daughters
Mt 19:21 go s. your belongings and give
Le 25:14, 25; Jg 4:9; Mt 25:9; Lu 12:33.
SEMBLANCE, Ps 39:6 in a s. man walks
SEMEN, Le 15:16, 32; 18:20.
SEMINAL EMISSION, Le 20:15; 22:4.
SEND, Ps 43:3 S. out your light and truth
Ps 110:2 The rod Jehovah will s. out
Isa 6:8 Whom shall I s., and who will go
Jer 16:16 I shall s. for many hunters,
Ge 24:7; Mt 13:41; Joh 14:26; Ac 3:20.
SENDING, Jer 25:15 to whom I am s. you
Mal 3:1 Look! I am s. my messenger,
Mal 4:5 Look! I am s. to you Elijah
Mt 10:16 I am s. you forth as sheep
Mt 11:10 s. forth my messenger before you,
Joh 20:21 Father sent me, I also am s. you
SENNACHERIB, 2Ki 18:13 S. king of
2Ki 19:16, 20; 2Ch 32:1, 10, 22; Isa 37:21.
SENSE(S). See also KEEP SENSES.
SENSE(S), 1Ki 8:47 come to their s. in
Mt 13:14 no means get the s. of it;
Ro 7:6 slaves in a new s. by the spirit,
Col 3:22 obedient to masters in fleshly s.,
1Pe 5:8 Keep your s., be watchful.
Lu 15:17; Eph 1:8; 4:19.
SENSED, Pr 31:18 s. that her trading is good
SENSELESS, Ps 14:1 The s. one has said
Ps 74:18 a s. people have treated your name
Jer 17:11; Lu 24:25; 1Ti 6:9; Tit 3:3.
SENSELESSNESS, Isa 9:17 speaking s.
SENSIBLE, Pr 26:16 giving a s. reply
SENSIBILITIES, Ro 11:7 their s. blunted;
SENSIBLENESS, Pr 11:22 turning from s.

Da 2:14 Daniel addressed himself with s. to
SENSUAL, Jas 5:5 in for s. pleasure.
Eze 23:11; 1Ti 5:6; Jas 4:1.
SENT, Isa 55:11 success for which I s. it.
Isa 61:1 s. me to bind up brokenhearted,
Ro 10:15 How preach unless s. forth?
Ga 4:4 full limit God s. forth his Son,
Ex 3:14; Mt 10:5; Lu 10:1; 1Jo 4:9.
SENTENCE, Ec 8:11 s. executed speedily,
Lu 23:24 Pilate gave s. for their demand
2Co 1:9 we felt we had the s. of death.
SEPARATE, Nu 8:14 s. the Levites from
Ezr 10:11 s. yourselves from foreign wives.
Mt 25:32 he will s. people one from
Ro 8:35 Who will s. us from the love of
Ro 8:39 to s. us from God's love that is
2Co 6:17 s. yourselves and quit touching
SEPARATED, 1Ki 8:53 you s. them as your
Ac 19:9 s. the disciples from them, daily
Ga 1:15 s. me from my mother's womb and
SERAPHS, Isa 6:6 the s. flew to me,
SERIOUS, 1Ti 3:8 servants should be s.
Php 4:8; 1Ti 3:11; Tit 2:2.
SERIOUSNESS, 1Ti 3:4 children with all s.
SERPENT(S), Ge 3:4 s. said to the woman:
Ge 3:13 The s. deceived me and so I ate
Ex 4:3 threw it and it became a s.,
Nu 21:9 Moses made a s. of copper
2Ki 18:4 crushed the copper s. that Moses
Isa 65:25 s. his food will be dust.
Mic 7:17 They will lick up dust like s.;
Mt 10:16 cautious as s. innocent as doves.
Mt 23:33 S., offspring of vipers,
Joh 3:14 as Moses lifted up the s. so
Re 12:9 dragon was hurled, the original s.,
Re 20:2 seized the dragon, the original s.,
Ge 3:1; Ps 58:4; Pr 23:32; 2Co 11:3.
SERVANT(S). See also SLAVE(S).
SERVANT(S), Ps 116:16 For I am your s.
Isa 43:10 You are my witnesses, my s. whom
Isa 49:3 You are my s., O Israel,
Isa 53:11 my s., will bring a righteous
Isa 65:13 My s. will eat, but you go
Isa 65:15 his s. call by another name
Jer 25:9 Nebuchadrezzar, my s.,
Am 3:7 revealed his matter to his s.
Zec 3:8 I am bringing in my s. Sprout!
Mt 12:18 my s. whom I chose, my
Lu 16:13 No s. can be slave to two masters;
Ac 4:30 through the name of your s. Jesus.
Ro 14:4 Who are you to judge the s. of
Pr 11:29; Jer 7:25; Da 3:26; Joe 2:29.
SERVANT GIRL, Ga 4:30 Cast out the s.
Ga 4:31 not of s., but of the free woman.
SERVE, De 7:16 must not s. their gods
Jos 24:15 choose whom you will s.,
1Ch 28:9 s. him with a complete heart
Ps 100:2 S. Jehovah with rejoicing.
Zep 3:9 to s. him shoulder to shoulder.
Ex 20:5; Ps 72:11; Isa 60:12; Jer 27:6.
SERVICE. See also SACRED SERVICE.
SERVICE, Ex 12:25 must keep this s.
Nu 4:19 assign each to his s. and load.
Ezr 8:20 David gave to the s. of the
Mt 4:10 to him alone render sacred s.
Joh 16:2 kills you will imagine a s. to God.
Ac 27:23 to whom I render sacred s.,
Ro 12:25 those who rendered s. to creation
Heb 12:28 render God s. with fear and awe.
Re 7:15 rendering him sacred s. day and
2Ch 31:2; 35:10; Eze 29:18; Ro 9:4.
SERVICES, 1Co 12:28 healings; helpful s.
SERVING, Ps 106:36 kept s. their idols
Da 3:17 God s. is able to rescue us.

Ro 13:6 servants s. this very purpose.
2Ti 2:4 No man s. as a soldier involves
SERVITUDE, Ezr 9:9; 1Co 7:15.
SET, Ac 17:31 he has s. a day to judge
2Pe 1:12 firmly s. in the truth which
SET FREE, Ro 6:18 you were s. from sin,
Ro 8:21 creation be s. from enslavement
SETH, Ge 4:25; 5:6-8; 1Ch 1:1; Lu 3:38.
SET MATTERS STRAIGHT, Isa 1:18; Mic 4:3.
SET THINGS STRAIGHT, Heb 9:10 time to s.
SETTING, Isa 21:5 s. the table in order,
SETTING THINGS STRAIGHT, 2Ti 3:16.
SETTLING MATTERS, Mt 5:25 be s. quickly
SEVEN, Ge 7:4 in s. days making it rain
Ge 41:27 s. skinny cows s. years
1Ki 6:38 he was s. years at building it.
Pr 26:16 than s. giving a sensible reply.
Eze 39:9 they will light fires s. years.
Mic 5:5 raise against him s. shepherds,
Zec 3:9 Upon one stone are s. eyes.
Re 1:4 s. spirits before his throne,
Re 1:20 s. stars and s. golden lampstands:
Re 13:1 with ten horns and s. heads
Re 15:6 s. angels with s. plagues
Re 17:10 s. kings: five have fallen,
Isa 11:15; Zec 4:10; Ac 6:3; Re 17:1.
SEVEN TIMES, Le 16:19 with his finger s.
Le 26:28 I shall chastise you s.
Jos 6:4 march around the city s.
2Ki 5:10 you must bathe s.
Ps 12:6 sayings of Jehovah clarified s.
Ps 119:164 S. in the day I have praised
Pr 24:16 righteous one may fall s.
Da 4:16 let s. pass over it.
Mt 18:22 not, s., but seventy-seven
Ge 33:3; 1Ki 18:43; 2Ki 4:35; Da 3:19.
SEVENTY, Ex 1:5 came to be s. souls,
Ex 24:1 and s. of the older men of Israel
Nu 11:25 spirit on each of the s. older
Isa 23:15 s. years it will happen to Tyre
Jer 25:11 will serve Babylon s. years.
Jer 29:10 after s. years at Babylon bring back
Eze 8:11 s. elderly ones with censer in
Da 9:2 devastations of Jerusalem, s. years
Da 9:24 s. weeks have been determined
Zec 7:5 for s. years did you really fast
Lu 10:1 s. others and sent them forth
Jg 9:56; 2Ki 10:1; Jer 25:12.
SEVERE, Col 2:23 s. treatment of body
2Sa 3:39; 19:43.
SEVERED, 2Ch 26:21; Ps 88:5; Isa 53:8.
SEVERELY, Ex 10:2; 1Sa 6:6.
SEVERITY, Ro 11:22 those who fell, s.
Tit 1:13 keep on reproving them with s.,
SEXUAL APPETITE(S), Ro 1:26.
Col 3:5 uncleanness, s., hurtful desire,
1Th 4:5 not in covetous s. such as also
SEXUAL IMPULSES, 1Ti 5:11 widows s.
SHACKLES, Ps 149:8 bind kings with s.
SHADOW, 1Ch 29:15 Like a s. our days
Ps 17:8 In the s. of your wings conceal
Ps 23:4 valley of deep s. I fear nothing
Col 2:17 are a s. of things to come
Heb 8:5 a typical a s. of heavenly things;
Heb 10:1 Law has a s. of good things
Jas 1:17 not a variation of the s.
Ps 57:1; 91:1; 144:4; Isa 30:2.
SHADRACH, Da 1:7; 2:49; 3:12-14, 28-30.
SHAKE, 2Sa 22:8 earth began to s. and
Isa 52:2 S. yourself free from the dust,
Mt 10:14 s. the dust off your feet.
Job 34:20; Ps 18:7; Lu 6:48.
SHAKEN, Eze 21:21 He has s. arrows.
Mt 24:29 powers of the heavens will be s.

Heb 12:28 a kingdom which cannot be s.
Ne 5:13; 2Th 2:2.
SHALMANESER, 2Ki 18:9 S. of Assyria
SHAME, Isa 30:3 you men a reason for s.
Isa 54:4 you will not be put to s.
Zep 3:5 unrighteous one knowing no s.
1Co 1:27 he might put the wise men to s.
Php 3:19 their glory consists in their s.
Heb 12:2 stake, despising s., and sat
1Pe 4:16 a Christian, let him not feel s.,
Isa 65:13; Eze 7:18; 1Co 4:14; Heb 6:6.
SHAMEFUL, Eph 5:4 s. conduct nor
SHAMEFULNESS, Re 16:15 look upon his s.
SHAPED, Job 10:8 Your hands have s. me
SHARE, De 32:9 Jehovah's s. is his people;
Ps 119:57 Jehovah is my s.;
Ga 6:6 let anyone s. in all good things
Re 18:4 do not want to s. with her
Ps 17:14; 142:5; Jer 10:16; 12:10.
SHARER(S), 1Co 9:23 become a s. with
2Co 1:7 you are s. of the sufferings,
Heb 10:33 while you became s. with those
1Pe 4:13 you are s. in the sufferings
1Pe 5:1 a s. of the glory that is to be
2Pe 1:4 may become s. in divine nature
Mt 23:30; 1Co 10:18; Php 1:7; 1Ti 5:22.
SHARING, 1Co 1:9 called into a s. with Christ
1Co 10:16 is it not a s. in
2Co 6:14 what s. do righteousness and
Php 3:10 s. in his sufferings,
1Jo 1:3, 6, 7.
SHARON, 1Ch 5:16 pasture grounds of S.
1Ch 27:29; Isa 33:9; 35:2; 65:10.
SHARPENED, Pr 27:17 By iron, iron is s.
SHARPENS, Pr 27:17 man s. face of another
SHATTER, Ex 15:6 O Jehovah, can s.
SHATTERED, Isa 8:9 be s. to pieces;
Mt 21:44 falling upon this stone s.
SHAVE, De 21:12; Jg 16:19.
SHAVED, 1Co 11:5 woman with a s. head.
Jg 16:17; 2Sa 14:26.
SHEALTIEL, 1Ch 3:17; Ezr 3:2; Mt 1:12.
SHEAR-JASHUB, Isa 7:3 S. your son
SHEBA, 1Ki 10:1; 2Ch 9:9; Eze 27:22.
SHEBNA, Isa 22:15; 36:3, 22; 37:2.
SHEBNAH, 2Ki 18:18 S. the secretary
SHECHEM, Ge 12:6; Jg 9:1.
SHEDDING, Ge 9:6 Anyone s. man's blood,
SHEEP, Ps 44:22 s. for slaughtering.
Isa 53:7 like a s. to the slaughtering;
Jer 23:2 You have scattered my s.
Eze 34:12 I shall care for my s.;
Zep 2:6 and stone pens for s.
Mt 9:36 like s. without a shepherd.
Mt 10:6 lost s. of the house of Israel.
Mt 10:16 sending you as s. amidst wolves;
Mt 18:12 hundred s. and one gets strayed,
Mt 25:32 shepherd separates s. from goats.
Joh 10:16 other s. not of this fold;
Joh 21:16 Shepherd my little s.
Ac 8:32 As a s. led to the slaughter,
Jer 51:40; Mt 26:31; Ro 8:36; 1Pe 2:25.
SHEKEL, Ex 30:13; Eze 45:12; Am 8:5.
SHELTER, Job 24:8 no s. have to hug a
SHELTERING, Pr 27:16 Anyone s. her has
SHEM, Ge 5:32; 9:26; 11:10; Lu 3:36.
SHEOL. See also HADES.
SHEOL, Ge 42:38 gray hairs to S.
1Sa 2:6 Jehovah Bringer down to S.,
Job 7:9 down to S. will not come up.
Job 26:6 S. is naked in front of him,
Ps 6:5 In S. who will laud you?
Ps 9:17 Wicked people turn back to S.,
Ps 16:10 not leave my soul in S.

Ps 55:15 Let them go down into S. alive,
Ps 139:8 in S., you would be there.
Pr 15:24 turn away from S. down below.
Pr 27:20 S. and the place of destruction
Ec 9:10 nor knowledge nor wisdom in S.
Ca 8:6 devotion is as unyielding as S. is.
Isa 14:15 down to S. you will be brought,
Isa 28:15 with S. we have a vision;
Isa 38:10 I will go into the gates of S.
Isa 38:18 not S. that can laud you;
Isa 57:9 you lowered matters to S.
Eze 32:27 down to S. with their weapons
Ho 13:14 From S. I shall redeem them;
Jon 2:2 Out of the belly of S. I cried
De 32:22; 2Sa 22:6; 1Ki 2:6; Job 17:13;
Ps 49:15; Isa 5:14; 14:9, 11; Eze 32:21.
SHEPHELAH, De 1:7 region and the S.
SHEPHERD(S), Ps 23:1 Jehovah is my S.
Isa 56:11 s. that have not known how to
Jer 2:8 s. transgressed against me,
Jer 3:15 give you s. in agreement with my
Jer 10:21 s. have behaved unreasoningly,
Jer 23:1 Woe to s. destroying and scattering
Jer 23:4 I will raise s. who will s. them,
Jer 25:34 Howl, you s., and cry out!
Eze 34:2 prophesy against the s. of Israel.
Eze 37:24 David, one s. they will all have,
Mic 5:5 raise up against him seven s.,
Zec 11:17 Woe to my valueless s.,
Mt 26:31 I will strike the s. and the
Lu 2:8 s. living out of doors
Joh 10:11 I am the fine s.; surrenders soul
Joh 10:16 will become one flock, one s.
Ac 20:28 s. the congregation of God,
Eph 4:11 some as s. and teachers,
Heb 13:20 great s. of the sheep with blood
1Pe 5:2 S. the flock of God willingly; eagerly
1Pe 5:4 chief s. has been made manifest,
Re 7:17 the Lamb will s. them,
Re 12:5 s. the nations with an iron rod.
Ge 49:24; Zec 11:3; Mt 9:36; 25:32.
SHIBBOLETH, Jg 12:6 Please say S.
SHIELD(S), Ge 15:1 I am a s. for you.
Jg 5:8 A s. could not be seen in Israel.
2Sa 1:21 s. of mighty ones was befouled,
2Sa 22:3 God is my s. and my horn
Ps 18:35 give me your s. of salvation
Ps 47:9 to God the s. of the earth belong.
Ps 84:11 Jehovah is a sun and a s.;
Ps 91:4 His trueness will be a large s.
Eph 6:16 take up the large s. of faith,
Ps 18:30; 144:2; Pr 30:5; Isa 21:5.
SHIFTED, Col 1:23 not s. away from hope
SHILOAH, Isa 8:6 waters of the S. that
SHILOH, Ge 49:10 until S. comes,
1Sa 4:3 Let us take from S. the ark
Jer 26:6 this house like that in S.,
Jos 18:1; Jg 18:31; Ps 78:60; Jer 26:9.
SHIMEI, 2Sa 16:5; 19:16; 1Ki 2:8, 38, 44.
SHINAR, Ge 10:10 Babel in the land of S.
Ge 11:2 discovered a valley in S.
Isa 11:11; Da 1:2; Zec 5:11.
SHINE, Nu 6:25 make his face toward
Ezr 9:8 make our eyes s., O our God, and
Ps 13:3 eyes s., that I may not fall
Ps 104:15 To make the face s. with oil,
Da 12:3 ones having insight will s.
Mt 5:16 let your light s. before men,
Mt 13:43 the righteous ones will s.
Eph 5:14 the Christ will s. upon you.
Ps 119:135; Ec 8:1; Isa 13:10; Re 21:23.
SHINING ONE, Isa 14:12 fallen you s.,
SHINY, Jer 5:28 they have become s.
SHIPS, Ps 48:7 wreck the s. of Tarshish.

Ps 107:23 going down to the sea in s.,
Isa 23:1 Howl, you s. of Tarshish!
Da 11:40 king of north will storm with s.
Jg 5:17; Isa 43:14; Eze 30:9; Da 11:30.
SHIPWRECK, 2Co 11:25; 1Ti 1:19.
SHIPYARD, Isa 23:10 no s. any longer
SHIVER, Eze 38:20 ground will s., and
SHIVERING, Isa 33:14 s. grabbed hold of
SHOCKING, Joh 6:60 This speech is s.;
Jude 15 the s. things that sinners spoke
SHOCKS, Isa 2:19 the earth to suffer s.
SHONE, Isa 60:1 Jehovah has s. forth.
Mt 17:2 transfigured and his face s.
SHOOK, Ne 5:13 I s. out and said:
Ac 13:51 These s. the dust off their feet
Heb 12:26 his voice s. the earth,
SHOOT, 2Ki 13:17 Elisha said: S.!
Jer 50:14 Babylon. S. at her.
1Sa 20:20; Ps 11:2; 64:4, 7.
SHORE, Mr 4:35; 5:21; 6:45; 8:13.
SHORT, Nu 11:23 hand of Jehovah cut s.,
Isa 59:1 hand of Jehovah not too s.
Mt 24:22 unless those days were cut s.,
Ro 3:23 all fall s. of the glory of God,
Ro 9:28 concluding it cutting it s.
Re 12:12 knowing he has a s. period of time.
Pr 10:27; Isa 50:2; Mr 13:20; Heb 4:1.
SHOULDER, Ne 9:29 giving a stubborn s.
Isa 9:6 princely rule will be upon his s.
Zec 7:11 kept giving a stubborn s.,
Jos 4:5; Isa 10:27; 22:22; Eze 29:18.
SHOUT, Isa 12:6 Cry out shrilly and s. for joy
Joe 2:1 s. a war cry in my holy mountain
Zec 9:9 S. in triumph, O daughter of
Jos 6:5; Ezr 3:13; Ps 47:1; Isa 44:23.
SHOUTED, Jos 6:20 the people s.,
SHOUTING, Job 38:7 sons of God began s.
Ps 89:15 people knowing the joyful s.
Le 9:24; Ac 21:34.
SHOVEL, Mt 3:12; Lu 3:17.
SHOW, 2Ch 16:9 s. his strength in
Ge 12:1; Re 22:6.
SHOWBREAD, Ex 25:30; 1Sa 21:6; 2Ch 4:19.
SHOWER(S), De 32:2 s. upon vegetation.
Ps 72:6 He will descend like s. that wet
Mic 5:7 the remaining ones like copious s.
SHOWING, Ex 9:16 for the sake of s. you
1Pe 4:18 ungodly sinner make a s.?
SHOWY DISPLAY, 1Jo 2:16 s. of life
SHREWD, Pr 14:15 s. considers his steps.
Pr 15:5 anyone regarding reproof is s.
Job 5:12; 15:5; Pr 12:23; 13:16; 14:8.
SHREWDNESS, Jos 9:4; Pr 1:4; 8:5, 12.
SHRILLY, Isa 12:6; Jer 31:7 cry out s.
SHRINKS, Heb 10:38 if he s. back, my
SHUDDER, Eze 27:35; 32:10 kings s.
Jas 2:19 yet the demons believe and s.
SHUN, Tit 3:9 s. fights
2Ti 2:16.
SHUNEM, Jos 19:18; 1Sa 28:4; 2Ki 4:8.
SHUSHAN, Es 1:2; 9:6; Da 8:2.
SHUT, Ge 7:16 Jehovah s. the door
Isa 26:20 enter your rooms, and s. your
Mt 23:13 you Pharisees s. up the kingdom
Mt 25:10 marriage feast and door was s.
Ro 11:32 God has s. them all up together
Re 3:8 an opened door, which no one can s.—
Isa 22:22; Mal 1:10; Re 11:6; 20:3.
SICK, Pr 13:12 Expectation heart s.,
Isa 33:24 no resident will say: I am s.
Jas 5:14 Is there anyone s. among you?
2Ki 20:1; Mal 1:8; Mt 25:39; Joh 11:2.
SICKENED, Eze 34:4 s. ones you have not
SICKLY, 1Co 11:30 many are weak and s.

SICKNESS(ES), De 28:61 s. written in book
Mt 8:17 took our s. and
Joh 5:5 in s. for thirty-eight years
Ga 4:13 through a s. of my flesh
1Ti 5:23 wine for your cases of s.
SIDE-STEPPED, De 26:13 I have not s.
SIDE-STEPPING, Jer 34:18 s. covenant,
SIDON, Eze 28:22 I am against you, O S.,
Ge 10:19; Isa 23:4; Jer 47:4; Joe 3:4; Zec
9:2; Mt 11:21; Mr 3:8; Ac 12:20; 27:3.
SIESTA, 2Sa 4:5 taking his noonday s.
SIGH(S), Pr 29:2 wicked rule, the people s.
Ex 2:23; La 1:22; Eze 21:6; 24:17; Jas 5:9.
SIGHING, Ps 12:5 the s. of the poor
Ps 79:11 May the s. of the prisoners come
Isa 35:10 grief and s. must flee away.
Eze 9:4 mark the men that are s. and
Ps 102:20; Isa 24:7; Mal 2:13; Heb 13:17.
SIGHT, 2Co 5:7 walking by faith, not s.
Mt 20:34; Lu 7:22; Ac 9:12.
SIGN(S), Ex 8:23 Tomorrow this s.
De 6:8 tie them as a s. upon your hand
De 6:22 Jehovah kept putting s. upon Egypt,
Isa 7:14 give you a s.: Look! The maiden
Isa 8:18 I and the children are as s. and
Isa 19:20 for a s. and for a witness
Da 4:3 How grand his s. are, and mighty
Mt 12:39 generation seeking a s., but no s.
Mt 16:3 s. of the times you cannot interpret.
Mt 24:3 will be the s. of your presence
Lu 11:29 no s. given except the s. of Jonah.
Lu 21:25 there will be s. in sun and moon
Lu 23:8 Herod was hoping to see some s.
Joh 7:31 perform more s. than this man
Ac 2:19 s. on earth below, blood and fire
1Co 11:10 woman have a s. of authority
Re 12:1 a great s. was seen in heaven,
Re 15:1 I saw in heaven another s.,
Re 16:14 inspired by demons and perform s.,
Ge 1:14; Isa 44:25; Joh 11:47; 20:30; Ac
4:16; 8:13; 1Co 1:22; 2Th 2:9.
SIGNAL, Isa 11:10 a s. for the peoples
Isa 49:22 to peoples I shall lift up my s.
Isa 62:10 Raise up a s. for the peoples
Jer 4:6 Raise a s. toward Zion.
Jer 50:2 lift up a s.; publish it.
Nu 21:8; Isa 5:26; 13:2; 18:3; 31:9; Jer
4:21; 51:12, 27.
SIGNATURE, Job 31:35 according to my s.
SIGNIFIES, Heb 12:27 s. the removal
SILAS, Ac 15:22; 16:19; 17:4; 18:5.
SILENCE, Ps 115:17 going down into s.
Jer 49:26 men of war will be brought to s.
Hab 2:20 Keep s. before him, all the earth!
Zec 2:13 Keep s. all flesh, before Jehovah,
1Ti 2:11 Let a woman learn in s. with
Ps 39:2; Mt 22:34; Re 8:1.
SILENCED, 1Sa 2:9 the wicked are s. in
SILENT, Job 31:34 I would keep s., I
Ps 32:3 When I kept s. my bones wore out
Ps 37:7 Keep s. before Jehovah.
Ps 30:12; 31:17; Jer 8:14; 1Co 14:34.
SILENTLY, Isa 47:5 Sit down s. and come
SILLY, 2Sa 22:27 crooked act as s.
SILOAM, Lu 13:4; Joh 9:7, 11.
SILVER, Pr 2:4 seeking for it as for s.,
Pr 25:11 apples of gold in s. carvings
Eze 7:19 streets they will throw their s.,
Zep 1:18 Neither their s. nor their gold
Mal 3:3 sit as a refiner and cleanser of s.
Mt 26:15 stipulated to him thirty s. pieces.
Jas 5:3 Your gold and s. are corroded,
Ex 12:35; Da 2:32; Hag 2:8; Ac 3:6.
SIMEON, Ge 29:33; 42:24; 49:5; Ex 6:15.

SIMON, Mt 4:18; 10:2; Mr 3:16.
SIMPLE-MINDED, Ho 7:11 like a s. dove
SIMPLE-MINDEDNESS, Pr 9:13 She is s.
SIN 1., Ex 17:1; Nu 33:11.
Ex 16:1 wilderness of S.
SIN 2., Eze 30:16 S. will be in pains,
SIN(S), Ge 4:7 there is s. crouching at
Nu 32:23 s. will catch up with
1Ki 8:46 there is no man that does not s.),
Ps 19:12 From concealed s. pronounce me
Ps 32:1 Happy is the one whose s. is covered
Ps 51:5 in s. my mother conceived me.
Ps 79:9 cover over our s.
Isa 1:18 Though the s. be as scarlet,
Isa 6:7 your s. is atoned for.
Jer 31:34 s. I shall remember no more.
Mt 26:28 many for forgiveness of s.
Mr 3:29 spirit guilty of everlasting s.
Joh 1:29 takes away the s. of the world!
Ac 3:19 Repent and get your s. blotted out,
Ro 4:8 happy is the man whose s. Jehovah
Ro 5:12 one man s. entered into the world
Ro 5:21 s. ruled as king with death,
Ro 6:23 the wages s. pays is death,
Ro 7:7 I would not have come to know s. if
Ro 8:2 set free from law of s. and death.
Ro 14:23 everything not out of faith is s.
2Co 5:21 not know s. he made to be s.
Eph 4:26 Be wrathful, and yet do not s.;
Heb 10:12 one sacrifice for s. perpetually
Heb 10:17 I shall by no means call their s.
Heb 10:26 if we practice s. willfully after
Heb 12:1 put off the s. that easily
Jas 1:15 birth to s.; in turn, s., when it
Jas 4:17 yet does not do it, it is a s. for
Jas 5:15 if he has committed s., it will
Re 18:4 share with her in her s.,
Eze 33:14; Ac 10:43; Ro 7:25; 1Ti 5:24;
Heb 11:25; 1Jo 1:8, 9; 2:1; 5:16.
SINAI, Ex 19:20 down upon Mount S.
Ex 31:18 speaking with him on Mount S.
Ex 24:16; Ne 9:13; Ps 68:8; Ac 7:30, 38.
SINCERELY, Job 33:3 my lips do utter s.
SINCERITY, Ac 2:46 rejoicing and s. of
1Co 5:8 cakes of s. and truth
2Co 1:12 with holiness and godly s., not
2Co 2:17 as out of s., yes, as sent from
Eph 6:5 trembling in the s. of your hearts.
Col 3:22 not as men pleasers, but with s.
SINEWS, Eze 37:6 put upon you s. and
Eze 37:8 s. and flesh came up and skin
SINFUL, Ro 6:6 s. body be made inactive,
Ro 7:13 that sin might become far more s.
SING, Ps 96:1 S. to Jehovah a new song.
Ps 144:9 a new song I will s. to you.
Isa 5:1 Let me s. to my beloved one a song
Isa 42:10 S. to Jehovah a new song, his
1Co 14:15 I will s. with the gift of spirit,
Ex 15:1; 1Ch 16:9; Ps 68:4; Jer 20:13.
SINGE, Isa 43:2 neither flame s. you
SINGERS, 2Ch 20:21 stationed s. to
1Ch 15:16; Ne 10:28; Ps 68:25; 87:7.
SINGING, Mt 26:30 after s. they went to
Eph 5:19 s. and accompanying yourselves
Col 3:16 admonishing one another with s.
1Ch 6:31; Eze 26:13; Zep 2:14; Re 14:3.
SINGLE. See UNMARRIED.
SINK OF DEBAUCHERY, 1Pe 4:4 same low s.,
SINNED, 1Ki 8:47 We have s. and erred,
Ro 3:23 all have s. and fall short of the
Ro 5:12 death spread to all because all s.—
SINNER(S), Isa 65:20 s. a hundred years of
Mt 11:19 friend of tax collectors and s.
Lu 15:2 This man welcomes s. and eats

Lu 15:7 more joy in heaven over one s.
Lu 18:13 God, be gracious to me a s.
Joh 9:31 We know God does not listen to s.
Ro 5:8 while we were yet s., Christ died
Ro 5:19 disobedience of one many were s.,
1Ti 1:9 law is for s.,
1Ti 1:15 Christ came to save s.
Heb 7:26 high priest was separate from s.,
Jas 5:20 he who turns a s. back
1Pe 4:18 where will the s. make a showing?
SINNING, 1Co 6:18 fornication is s. against
1Jo 3:8 Devil has been s. from the beginning
SIRE, Ge 7:2 the s. and its mate, and
SISERA, Jg 5:20 stars fought against S.
Jg 4:7, 9, 13-18, 22; 1Sa 12:9.
SISTER-IN-LAW, Ru 1:15 your widowed s.
Ps 86:16; Lu 1:38.
SISTERS, 1Ti 5:2 women as s. with
SISTRUMS, 2Sa 6:5 celebrating with s.
SIT, Ps 110:1 S. at my right hand
Mic 4:4 s. under his vine and fig tree,
Mt 19:28 you s. upon twelve thrones
Re 3:21 grant to s. with me on my throne,
SITS, Ps 29:10 Jehovah s. as king to
SITTING, Ps 2:4 One s. in the heavens
Isa 42:7 prisoner s. in darkness
Isa 28:6; Re 5:13; 17:15.
SITUATED, Ge 31:49 when s. unseen
SIX HUNDRED SIXTY-SIX, Re 13:18.
SIZE, Lu 19:3 because he was small in s.
SKILLFUL DIRECTION, Pr 1:5 acquires s.,
Pr 11:14 When there is no s. people fall.
Pr 20:18; 24:6.
SKIN(S), Ge 3:21 long garments of s.
Job 2:4 S. in behalf of s., and everything
Job 19:26 my s. they have skinned off,
Jer 13:23 Can a Cushite change his s.?
Eze 37:6 I will overlay upon you s.
SKIRT(S), Jer 6:1 his s. were filling the
Jer 2:34 in your s. found blood of souls
Zec 8:23 ten men will take hold of the s.
SKULL, Mt 27:33; Mr 15:22; Lu 23:33.
SLACK, Pr 10:4 s. hand will be of
Pr 12:24; 18:9; 19:15.
SLACKNESS, Pr 12:27 S. will not start
SLAIN, Jer 25:33 s. of Jehovah will be
Eze 9:7 fill the courtyards with the s.
Isa 66:16; Jer 51:49; Eze 6:13.
SLANDER. See REVILED, REVILER.
SLANDERED, 2Sa 19:27; Ps 15:3.
SLANDERER, Pr 11:13 s. is uncovering
Pr 16:28 s. is separating those familiar
Pr 20:19 s. is uncovering confidential talk
Pr 26:20 is no s. contention grows still.
SLANDERING, Le 19:16 not go around s.
Ps 101:5 Anyone s. his companion in secrecy,
SLANDEROUS, 1Ti 3:11 Women serious not s.
Tit 2:3 not s., neither enslaved to a lot of
SLAP, Joh 18:22 officers gave Jesus a s.
SLAPS, Mt 5:39; Joh 19:3.
SLAUGHTER, Isa 34:2 give them to the s.
Ac 10:13 Rise, Peter, s. and eat!
Jos 10:10; Es 9:5; Eze 21:10; 34:3.
SLAUGHTERED, Re 5:12 Lamb that was s.
Re 18:24 blood of holy ones s. on
Re 6:9.
SLAUGHTERING, Ps 44:22 as sheep for s.
Isa 53:7 brought like a sheep to the s.;
Jer 25:34 days for s. have been fulfilled,
SLAVE(S). See also SERVANT(S).
SLAVE, Mt 6:24 s. for two masters;
Mt 24:45 Who is the faithful and discreet s.
Mt 24:48 if that evil s. should say in his
Mt 25:30 throw the good-for-nothing s. out
Lu 12:37 Happy are those s. whom the master

Lu 17:10 We are good-for-nothing s.
Joh 8:34 every doer of sin is a s. of sin
Joh 13:16 s. is not greater than his master,
Ac 2:18 upon my men s. and women s. I will
Ro 6:6 no longer being s. to sin
Ro 6:16 you are s. because you obey him
Ro 7:6 we might be s. by the spirit,
1Co 7:23 stop becoming s. of men
Ga 1:10 pleasing men not be Christ's s.
Ga 3:28 there is neither s. nor freeman
Ga 5:13 but through love s. for one another
Re 19:2 avenged the blood of his s.
Mt 20:27; Joh 8:35; Ac 7:7; Ro 6:17-20;
Ga 4:7, 9; 2Ti 2:24; 1Pe 2:16; 2Pe 2:19.
SLAVE GIRL, Ps 116:16 the son of your s.
Ps 86:16; Lu 1:38.
SLAVERY, Ro 8:15 receive a spirit of s.
Ga 5:1 confined again in a yoke of s.
Heb 2:15 subject to s. through their lives.
Ex 2:23; Ga 4:24.
SLAY, Job 13:15; 24:14; Ps 139:19.
SLEEP, Ps 121:4 he will not go to s.,
Isa 29:10 poured a spirit of deep s.
Jer 51:57 s. an indefinitely lasting s.,
Eze 34:25 wilderness and s. in the forests.
Mt 25:5 they nodded and went to s.
Joh 11:11 Lazarus awaken him from s.
Ro 13:11 it is the hour to awake from s.,
1Th 5:6 let us not s. on as the rest do,
SLEEPING, Mt 13:25 While men were s.
1Th 4:13 concerning those who are s.
SLEEVELESS COAT, Isa 59:17 as if a s.
SLEPT, Job 3:13 I should have s. then,
SLICKNESS, Pr 23:31; Ca 7:9.
SLIPPED IN, Jude 4 men have s. who
SLIPPERY, Ps 35:6; Jer 23:12.
SLOW, 2Pe 3:9 Jehovah is not s.
De 23:21; Lu 24:25; Jas 1:19.
SLUGGISH, Mt 25:26 Wicked and s. slave,
Jg 18:9; Heb 6:12.
SLUMBER, Ps 132:4 not give s. to eyes,
Isa 56:10 speechless dogs; loving to s.
SLUMBERING, Pr 6:10 a little more s.,
2Pe 2:3 destruction of them is not s.
SLYLY, 2Ki 10:19 Jehu acted s., for
2Ti 3:6 men who s. work their way into
SMASHING, Eze 9:2 each his weapon for s.
SMELT, Isa 1:25 I shall s. away your
SMILE, Job 29:24 I would s. at them
SMITER, 1Ti 3:3; Tit 1:7.
SMITING, 2Ch 20:22 Seir s. one another
SMOKE, Ex 30:7 Aaron make incense s.
2Ki 22:17 sacrificial s. to other gods in
Ps 37:20 In s. they must end.
Ps 68:2 As s. is driven away, drive them
Isa 34:10 its s. will keep ascending.
Isa 51:6 heavens dispersed like s.,
Jer 7:9 making sacrificial s. to Baal
Jer 44:25 sacrificial s. to the queen of
Re 14:11 s. of their torment ascends
SMOOTH, Ps 12:3 Jehovah will cut off s. lips
Da 11:32 into apostasy by means of s. words
SMOOTHNESS, Da 11:21, 34 by means of s.
SNAKE(S), Nu 21:8 Make for yourself a s.
Ps 91:13 You will trample down the big s.
SNAPPING, Ps 57:3; Eze 36:3; Am 8:4.
SNARE(S), De 7:16 will be a s. to you.
Jos 23:13 they must become to you as a s.
Ps 106:36 idols came to be a s. to them
Pr 14:27 to turn away from the s. of death.
Pr 18:7 his lips are a s. for his soul.
Pr 29:25 Trembling at men is what lays a s.,
Lu 21:35 as a s. it will come upon face earth.
Ro 11:9 Let their table become for them a s.

1Ti 6:9 rich fall into temptation and a **s.**
Jg 2:3; 28a 22:6; Isa 8:14; 2Ti 2:26.
SNATCH, Joh 10:28, 29 **s.** them out of my
SNATCHES, Mt 13:19 **s.** away what
Joh 10:12.
SNATCHING, Jude 23 by **s.** them out of the
SNEAKED, Ga 2:4 **s.** in to spy upon our
SNEEZE, 2Ki 4:35 boy began to **s.** seven
SNEEZINGS, Job 41:18 Its **s.** flash forth
SNOUT, Pr 11:22 ring in **s.** of a pig,
SNOW, Job 38:22 storehouses of the **s.,**
Ps 51:7 I may become whiter than **s.**
Ps 147:16 He is giving **s.** like wool;
Isa 1:18 sins will be made white like **s.;**
Da 7:9 His clothing was white like **s.,**
Ex 4:6; Ps 148:8; Pr 25:13; 26:1; Re 1:14.
SOBER. See KEEP SENSES.
SOBERING, Ps 78:65 **s.** up from wine.
SOBERNESS, 1Co 15:34 Wake up to **s.**
SODOM, Ge 19:24 sulphur and fire upon **S.**
Mt 10:15 more endurable for the land of **S.**
Re 11:8 in a spiritual sense called **S.** and
Ge 18:26; Isa 1:10; 13:19; 2Pe 2:6; Jude 7.
SODOMY. See MEN LIE WITH MEN.
SOIL, Lu 8:15 As for that on the fine **s.,**
SOJOURN(ER). See INHABITANT(S), RE-
SIDE(S), TEMPORARY RESIDENTS.
SOJOURNING, Ac 17:21 foreigners **s.** there
SOLDIER, 2Ti 2:3 as a fine **s.** of
Joh 19:23; Ac 10:7; 1Co 9:7; 2Ti 2:4.
SOLE(S), Eze 43:7 the **s.** of my feet,
Isa 37:25; Eze 1:7; Mal 4:3.
SOLEMN, 1Th 5:27 under **s.** obligation
SOLID, 2Ti 2:19 **s.** foundation of God
Heb 5:12 such as need milk, not **s.** food.
Heb 5:14 **s.** food belongs to mature people,
1Pe 5:9 stand against him, **s.** in the faith,
SOLITARY, Ps 68:6; La 1:1; 3:28.
SOLOMON, 1Ki 11:9 to be incensed at **S.,**
1Ch 29:23 **S.** began to sit upon Jehovah's
2Ch 3:1 **S.** started to build the house of
Mt 6:29 not even **S.** in all his glory was
Mt 12:42 something more than **S.** is here.
1Ki 4:29; 1Ch 22:9; Ne 13:26; Ac 7:47.
SOMETHING, Ga 1:11 news not **s.** human;
SON(S), Ge 6:2 **s.** of God taking wives
De 6:7 inculcate them in your **s.**
Job 1:6 **s.** of the true God came before
Ps 2:7 said to me, You are my **s.;**
Ps 2:12 Kiss the **s.,** that you may not
Ps 45:16 forefathers come to be your **s.**
Pr 4:3 I proved a real **s.** to my father,
Isa 9:6 there has been a **s.** given to us,
Isa 14:12 you have fallen, **s.** of the dawn!
Isa 54:13 **s.** taught by Jehovah.
Isa 60:14 **s.** of those afflicting you must
Joe 2:28 your **s.** and daughters will
Mt 1:21 She will give birth to a **s.,** and
Mt 3:17 This is my **S.,** the beloved, whom I
Lu 16:8 **s.** of this system of things are
Joh 3:16 God gave his only-begotten **S.,**
Joh 17:1 glorify your **s.,** that your **s.** may
Ro 8:14 all led by spirit, are God's **s.**
2Co 6:18 you will be **s.** and daughters to me,
1Th 5:5 you are **s.** of light and **s.** of day.
Heb 12:7 God is dealing with you as with **s.**
Pr 4:3; Isa 54:13; Da 3:25; Joh 17:12;
Heb 11:24.
SONG(S), De 31:19 write this **s.**
Jg 5:12 Awake, awake, utter a **s.!**
Ne 12:46 singers and the **s.** of praise and
Ps 98:1 Sing to Jehovah a new **s.,**
Ps 149:6 **s.** extolling God in their throat
Isa 23:15 as in the **s.** of a prostitute:

Isa 42:10 Sing to Jehovah a new **s.,**
Ac 16:25 and Silas were praising with **s.;**
Eph 5:19 spiritual **s.,** with music
Col 3:16 praises to God, spiritual **s.**
Re 15:3 they are singing the **s.** of Moses
Ps 28:7; Eze 33:32.
SON-IN-LAW, Ge 19:12; Ex 3:1; Jg 1:16.
SON OF MAN, Eze 2:1 **s.** stand up on feet
Da 7:13 like **s.** coming with the clouds
Mt 10:23 until **S.** arrives.
Mt 12:40 the **S.** will be in the heart of
Mt 24:30 sign of the **S.** will appear in
Lu 17:26 be also in the days of the **S.:**
Re 14:14 someone seated like a **s.,** with a
Mt 8:20; 17:22; Lu 18:8; Joh 3:13.
SORCERER(S), Jer 27:9 not listen to **s.,**
Mal 3:5 a speedy witness against the **s.,**
Ex 7:11; Da 2:2; Ac 13:6.
SORCERESS, Ex 22:18 not preserve a **s.**
SORCERIES, Mic 5:12 I will cut off **s.**
2Ki 9:22; Isa 47:9; Na 3:4.
SORCERY, 2Ch 33:6 he practiced **s.**
SORE STRAITS, De 4:30; La 1:20; Ho 5:15.
SORROW, Isa 19:8 must express **s.,** and
1Th 4:13 **s.** as the rest do who have no hope.
SOUL(S), Ge 1:20 waters swarm of living **s.**
Ge 2:7 man came to be a living **s.**
Ge 9:4 flesh with its **s.**—its blood—you
Ex 1:5 the **s.** who issued out of Jacob's
Le 17:14 the **s.** of flesh is its blood.
Nu 31:28 one **s.** of the flock
De 6:5 love Jehovah with all your **s.**
De 19:21 **s.** will be for **s.,** eye for eye,
Jos 11:11 they went striking every **s.**
Jos 20:9 strikes a **s.** unintentionally,
Job 11:20 will be an expiring of the **s.**
Job 31:39 **s.** I caused to pant
Ps 49:15 God will redeem my **s.** from Sheol,
Ps 89:48 Can he provide escape for his **s.**
Pr 14:25 A true witness is delivering **s.,**
Isa 53:12 poured out his **s.** to death
Jer 2:34 the blood marks of the **s.** of
Jer 15:9 her **s.** struggled for breath
Eze 18:4, 20 **s.** that is sinning it will die
Mt 10:28 can destroy both **s.** and body in
Mt 16:26 gains world but forfeits his **s.?**
Ac 2:27 you will not leave my **s.** in Hades,
Ac 3:23 any **s.** that does not listen to
Php 1:27 with one **s.** fighting side by side
Re 20:4 **s.** of those executed with the ax
Mr 14:34; Joh 12:25; Ac 2:41; 1Co 15:45.
SOULFUL DESIRE, Isa 56:11 strong in **s.,**
SOUND, Ex 12:5 sheep should be **s.**
Jos 6:5 when they **s.** the horn, shout
Isa 65:19 no more the **s.** of weeping
Isa 66:6 **s.** out of the temple! It is the **s.**
Joe 2:5 with the **s.** of chariots
1Co 15:52 trumpet will **s.,** and the dead
Ex 29:1; Ec 12:4; Zep 1:14; Ro 10:18.
SOUND IN MIND, 1Pe 4:7 **s.,** and vigilant
SOURCE(S), Ps 36:9 is the **s.** of life;
Pr 10:11 righteous one is a **s.** of life,
Jer 2:13 **s.** of living water, hew out for
Pr 13:14; Isa 41:18.
SOUR DOUGH, Ex 12:19 no **s.** is to be
Ex 12:15; Le 2:11; De 16:4.
SOVEREIGN LORD, Ps 73:28 In the **S. I**
Jer 50:25 a work the **S.,** Jehovah of armies
Lu 2:29 Now, **S.,** you are letting your slave
Ac 4:24 **S.,** you are the One who made heaven
Re 6:10 when, **S.** holy and true,
Ps 109:21; 140:7; Isa 22:14; 28:22.
SOW, Mic 6:15 will **s.** but not reap.
Lu 8:5 A sower went out to **s.** seed.

2Pe 2:22 s. that was bathed to rolling in
Ec 11:4, 6; Ho 10:12; Mt 6:26; Lu 19:22.
SOWER, Mt 13:37 s. of fine seed is the
Joh 4:36 s. and reaper may rejoice together.
SOWING, Ps 126:5 s. seed with tears
Pr 11:18 one s. righteousness, true earnings
Ho 8:7 it is wind they keep s.,
Ga 6:7 whatever a man is s., he will reap;
SOWN, Mt 13:20 s. upon rocky places,
1Co 15:44 It is s. a physical body,
Eze 36:9; Hag 1:6; Jas 3:18.
SOWS, 2Co 9:6 he that s. sparingly will
SPACES, Job 38:18 considered the broad s.
SPACIOUS, Isa 5:14 made its soul s.
Isa 54:2 the place of your tent more s.
Mt 7:13 s. is the road leading off into
SPAIN, Ro 15:24 I am on my way to S.
SPARE, Ro 11:21; 2Co 1:23.
SPARKLE, Eze 1:22 like s. of awesome ice
SPEAK, Isa 30:10 S. to us smooth things;
SPEAKER, Ex 4:10 I am not a fluent s.,
SPEAK EXULTINGLY, 1Ch 16:35 s. in your
SPEAKING, Joh 8:43 know what I am s.?
SPEAR(S), Ps 46:9; Isa 2:4; Mic 4:3.
SPECIAL, Ps 90:10 because of s. mightiness
SPECIES, Na 3:15, 16 like the locust s.
Jas 3:7 every s. of wild beast
SPECIFICATIONS, Eze 43:11 all its s.,
SPECKLED, Ge 31:10 flock were striped, s.
SPECTACLE, Na 3:6 I will set you as a s.
1Co 4:9 a theatrical s. to the world.
SPEECH, Ps 19:2 day after day causes s.
Ro 16:18 smooth s. they seduce the hearts
1Co 14:9 you utter s. easily understood,
2Co 3:12 we are using freeness of s.,
Tit 2:8 s. that cannot be condemned,
SPEECHLESS, Isa 35:6 tongue of s. one
Isa 56:10 watchmen all are s. dogs
SPEECH SOUNDS, 1Co 14:10 kinds of s.
SPEED, Ps 147:15 With s. his word runs.
Isa 60:22 I, Jehovah, shall s. it up
SPEEDY, Mal 3:5 s. witness against the
Ro 3:15 Their feet are s. to shed blood.
2Pe 2:1 bringing s. destruction upon
SPENT, 2Co 12:15 I will be s. for souls.
SPICES, Lu 23:56; 24:1.
SPIES, Heb 11:31 Rahab received s.
Ge 42:14, 31; Jos 2:1.
SPINDLE, Pr 31:19 take hold of the s.
SPIRIT(S), 2Sa 23:2 s. of Jehovah spoke
2Ki 2:9 two parts in your s. come to me.
Job 12:10 s. of all flesh of man?
Job 27:3 s. of God is in my nostrils,
Job 33:4 God's own s. made me,
Ps 51:17 sacrifices to God are a broken s.;
Ps 104:29 take away their s., they expire
Ps 146:4 His s. goes out, he goes back to
Ec 3:19 all have but one s.,
Ec 3:21 s. of mankind ascending upward;
Ec 12:7 s. returns to God who gave it.
Isa 8:19 Apply to the s. of prediction
Isa 19:14 mingled s. of disconcertedness,
Isa 42:1 I have put my s. in him.
Isa 61:1 The s. of Jehovah is upon me,
Zec 4:6 Not by force but by my s.,
Mt 3:16 like a dove God's s. coming
Mt 26:41 The s. is eager, but the flesh
Lu 24:39 a s. does not have flesh and bones
Joh 4:24 God is a S. and those
Ac 2:17 pour my s. out upon every kind of
Ac 7:51 Obstinate men resisting the holy s.;
Ro 8:6 minding of the s. means life and peace
Ro 8:9 if God's s. truly dwells in you.

Ro 8:11 s. of him that raised Jesus dwells
Ro 8:16 s. bears witness with our s.
Ro 11:8 God had given them a s. of deep sleep
1Co 2:10 s. searches into all things,
1Co 2:11 know the things of God, except s.
1Co 3:16 the s. of God dwells in you?
2Co 3:6 death, but the s. makes alive.
2Co 3:17 where the s. is, there is freedom.
Eph 2:22 s. place for God to inhabit by s.
Eph 4:30 do not be grieving God's holy s.,
Eph 6:12 we have a fight against wicked s.
Eph 6:17 sword of the s., God's word,
2Ti 1:7 God gave us not a s. of cowardice,
Jas 4:5 with a tendency to envy the s.
1Pe 3:19 preached to the s. in prison,
Re 22:17 s. and bride keep saying: "Come!"
1Ch 10:13; Job 32:8; Pr 16:18; Joe 2:28;
Joh 16:13; 1Co 15:45; Ga 5:22; 1Pe 3:18.
SPIRITEDNESS, Jos 5:1 be no s. in them
SPIRITISM, Ga 5:20 practice of s.,
Re 22:15 dogs and those who practice s.
SPIRITISTIC MEDIUMS, Isa 8:19.
SPIRIT MEDIUM(S), Le 19:31 not turn to s.,
De 18:11 anyone who consults a s.
1Sa 28:3; 2Ki 21:6; 23:24; Isa 19:3; 29:4.
SPIRIT MEDIUMSHIP, 1Sa 28:7 woman of s.
SPIRITUAL, Mt 5:3 conscious of s. need,
1Co 2:13 combine s. matters with s.
1Co 15:44 it is raised up a s. body.
Col 1:8 disclosed your love in a s. way.
1Pe 2:5 being built up a s. house
Re 11:8 city in a s. sense called Sodom
Ro 1:11; 7:14; 1Co 10:3, 4; Ga 6:1.
SPIRITUAL LIVES, Heb 12:23 s. of ones
SPIRITUALLY, 1Co 2:14 are examined s.
SPIT, Ga 4:14 or s. at in disgust,
Mt 26:67; 27:30.
SPLENDOR, Ps 145:12 glory of the s. of his
Ps 149:9 Such s. belongs to his loyal ones
Isa 53:2 No form does he have, nor s.
Eph 5:27 congregation to himself in its s.
SPOIL, Isa 53:12 apportion the s.,
Jer 39:18 have your soul as a s.,
1Co 15:33 Bad associations s. useful habits.
Jos 8:2; Jg 5:30; Isa 10:2; Eze 38:12.
SPOKESMEN, 2Ch 32:31 s. of the princes
Job 16:20 companions s. against me;
SPONGE, Mt 27:48; Mr 15:36; Joh 19:29.
SPORT, Jg 16:25 make s. before them
Pr 10:23 loose conduct is like s.,
SPOT(S), Jas 1:27 without s. from the
Eph 5:27; 2Pe 2:13.
SPOTLESS, 1Ti 6:14; 1Pe 1:19; 2Pe 3:14.
SPRING(S), Ge 7:11 s. of the watery deep
Isa 12:3 the s. of salvation
Isa 35:7 thirsty ground as s.
Isa 42:9 Before they s. up, I
Isa 49:10 by s. he will conduct them.
SPRING RAIN, Joe 2:23 the autumn and s.,
SPRINKLED, 1Pe 1:2 s. with the blood of
Heb 9:13, 19, 21; 10:22.
SPRINKLING, Mr 7:4; Heb 12:24.
SPROUT, Ps 72:7 righteous one will s.
Ps 92:7 wicked ones s. as the vegetation
Isa 66:14 your very bones will s. just like
Jer 23:5 David a righteous s.
Zec 3:8 bringing in my servant S.!
Da 11:7 from the s. of her roots will stand
Isa 4:2; 14:19; 61:11; Jer 33:15; Zec 6:12.
SPURNED, Ps 89:39 have s. the covenant
SPY, Ga 2:4 false brothers s. upon our
Nu 13:2 Send men s. the land
SQUANDERED, Lu 15:13 son s. property
SQUARE, Ge 19:2 public s. we stay

De 13:16; Jg 19:15; Isa 59:14.
SQUEEZED, Le 22:24 testicles **s.** or
SQUEEZING, Pr 30:33 **s.** out of anger
STABBED, 1Ti 6:10 **s.** with many pains.
STABILIZED, Col 2:7 **s.** in the faith
STAFF, Ge 49:10 **s.** from between his
  Ps 23:4 Your rod and **s.** comfort me.
  Isa 14:5 broken the **s.** of ruling ones,
  Mic 7:14 Shepherd your people with your **s.,**
  Ex 12:11; Isa 9:4; Jer 48:17; Zec 11:10.
STAG(S), De 12:15; Isa 35:6; La 1:6.
STAGES, Nu 33:1 **s.** of Israel out of Egypt
STAGGER, Ps 13:4; Isa 54:10; Am 8:12.
STAGGERING, Pr 24:11; 25:26; Isa 24:19.
STAINED, Jude 23 garment **s.** by the flesh
STAKE, De 21:22 death, and hung upon a **s.,**
  Jos 8:29 hanged the king of Ai upon a **s.**
  Ac 5:30 Jesus, hanging him upon a **s.**
  Ga 3:13 Accursed man hanged upon a **s.**
  1Pe 2:24 our sins in his body upon the **s.**
STALLIONS, Jg 5:22; Jer 8:16; 50:11.
STAND, 2Ch 20:17 **s.** still and see
  Ps 2:2 kings of earth take their **s.**
  Ec 4:12 two together could make a **s.**
  Isa 8:10 Speak any word, and it will not **s.,**
  Da 2:44 kingdom will **s.** to times
  Da 12:1 Michael will **s.** up, the prince
  Da 12:13 you will **s.** up at the end
  Ro 14:4 for Jehovah can make him **s.**
  1Pe 5:9 take your **s.** against him, solid
STANDARDS, 1Co 9:8 speaking by human **s.?**
STAND FAST, Ga 5:1 Therefore **s.** and do
STAND FIRM, 1Co 16:13 **s.** in the faith,
  Eph 6:11 **s.** against the Devil;
  Eph 6:13 all things thoroughly, **s.**
  Php 4:1 **s.** in this way in the Lord, beloved
  2Th 2:15 **s.** and maintain your hold on the
STANDING, Isa 66:22 new earth are **s.**
  Mal 3:2 who will be **s.** when he appears?
  1Co 10:12 him that thinks he is **s.** beware
STANDING FIRM, Php 1:27 **s.** in one
STANDPOINT, Ec 2:17; Zec 11:13; 1Pe 4:6.
STAND UP, Da 12:1 Michael will **s.,**
STAR(S), Nu 24:17 **s.** out of Jacob,
  Jg 5:20 From heaven did the **s.** fight,
  Job 38:7 When the morning **s.** cried out
  Isa 14:13 Above the **s.** of God I shall lift
  Isa 47:13 save you, the lookers at the **s.,**
  Da 12:3 having insight will shine like **s.**
  1Co 15:41 **s.** differs from **s.** in glory.
  Re 2:28 I will give him the morning **s.**
  Re 12:1 her head a crown of twelve **s.,**
START, Pr 9:10 fear of Jehovah is the **s.**
STARTED, Php 1:6 he who **s.** a good work
STATE, Zec 3:4; 1Co 7:20.
STATECRAFT, Ac 7:19 **s.** against our race
STATEMENT, 1Ti 4:9 acceptance is that **s.**
STATE OF ISRAEL, Eph 2:12 from the **s.**
STATION, 1Ti 2:2 those in high **s.;** in
  Nu 11:16; Job 1:6; Pr 22:29.
STATIONING, Ps 82:1 God is **s.** himself
STATUE, De 27:15 a molten **s.,**
STATUS, Jos 20:7 a sacred **s.** to Kedesh
STATUTE(S), Ex 12:14 As a **s.** to time
  Eze 37:24 my **s.** they will keep,
  Zep 2:2 Before the **s.** gives birth
  Le 18:5; Nu 10:8; Job 38:33; Jer 31:35.
STATUTE-GIVER, Isa 33:22 Jehovah our **S.,**
STAY, De 21:23 **s.** all night on stake,
  1Ti 4:16 **S.** by these things, for by
STAYED, Heb 11:34 **s.** the force of fire,
STEADFAST, Ps 78:37 heart was not **s.**
  1Co 15:58 become **s.,** unmovable, always
  Col 1:23 established the foundation and **s.**

STEADFASTNESS, 2Pe 3:17 fall from **s.**
STEAL, Ex 20:15 You must not **s.**
  Ex 22:1 In case a man should **s.** a bull
  Le 19:11 You people must not **s.** and you
  Pr 30:9 that I may not **s.** and assail
  Mt 6:20 thieves do not break in and **s.**
STEALER, Eph 4:28 **s.** steal no more,
STEALING, Jer 7:9 there be **s.** to Baal
  Jer 23:30 who are **s.** away my words,
  Ho 4:2 There are deception and **s.** and acts of
STEALTHILY, Ru 3:7 **s.** and uncovered him
STEERING, Job 37:12; Pr 12:5.
STEM, Heb 2:11 sanctified **s.** from one,
STEP(S), Ps 37:31 **s.** will not wobble.
  Jer 10:23 man to direct his **s.**
  Ac 16:9 **S.** over into Macedonia and help us.
  1Pe 2:21 you a model to follow his **s.**
STEPHEN, Ac 6:5; 7:59; 8:2; 22:20.
STERILE, Job 3:7 let it become **s.**
  Job 15:34; 30:3; Isa 49:21.
STERN, Mr 4:38; Ac 27:29, 41.
STERNNESS, Ec 8:1 **s.** of face changed
STEWARD(S), Lu 12:42 the faithful **s.,**
  1Co 4:1 **s.** of sacred secrets of God.
  Tit 1:7 free from accusation as God's **s.,**
STEWARDSHIP, 1Co 9:17 a **s.** entrusted to
  Lu 16:2; Eph 3:2; Col 1:25.
STICKING, De 30:20 loving Jehovah and **s.**
STICKING TOGETHER, Da 2:43 not be **s.**
STIFF-NECKED, Ex 32:9; 34:9; De 9:6.
STING(S), Ho 13:14 your **s.,** O Death?
  1Co 15:55 Death, where is your **s.?**
STINK, Ex 7:18; 16:20; Ec 10:1.
STINKY, Ps 38:5 wounds have become **s.,**
STIPULATE, Ge 30:28 **S.** your wages to me
STIR, 2Ti 1:6 **s.** up like a fire the
STOLEN, Ge 31:32 Rachel had **s.** them.
  Pr 9:17 **S.** waters themselves are sweet,
  Ex 22:12; 2Sa 21:12.
STOMACH, De 18:3 give the priest the **s.**
  1Ti 5:23 wine for sake of your **s.**
STONE(S), Ps 91:12 foot against any **s.**
  Isa 60:17 instead of the **s.,** iron;
  Isa 62:10 up the highway. Rid it of **s.**
  Da 2:34 a **s.** was cut out not by hands,
  Mt 21:42 The **s.** that the builders rejected
  Lu 19:40 silent, the **s.** would cry out.
  Ro 9:32 stumbled on the **s.** of stumbling;
  1Pe 2:6 I am laying in Zion a **s.,** chosen,
STOOL, Ps 110:1 enemies as a **s.** for
  Ac 2:35; Heb 10:13.
STOOP, Isa 31:4; 46:2.
STOP, 2Th 3:14 **s.** associating with him,
STORAGE, 2Ch 8:4; 17:12.
STORE, Pr 15:6 there is abundant **s.,**
STOREHOUSE(S), Job 38:22 the **s.** of snow,
  De 28:12; Mt 3:12; 6:26.
STORIES, 1Ti 1:4; 4:7 attention to false **s.**
  2Ti 4:4 turned aside to false **s.**
  2Pe 1:16 artfully contrived false **s.**
STORMER, Job 9:13; 26:12.
STORMWIND, Ho 8:7 a **s.** they will reap.
  Pr 1:27; 10:25; Isa 66:15.
STOUT ONES, Isa 59:10 among **s.** we are dead
STRAIGHT. See also SET THINGS STRAIGHT.
STRAIGHT, Pr 15:21 discernment goes **s.** ahead.
  Lu 3:5 the curves must become **s.** ways and
  Joh 1:23 Make the way of Jehovah **s.,**
  Ga 2:14 walking **s.** according to the truth
  Heb 12:13 keep making **s.** paths for your
STRAIGHTEN, Isa 45:13 all his ways I **s.**
STRAIGHTFORWARD, Pr 24:26 replying **s.** way
  Isa 59:14; Am 3:10.
STRAIGHTFORWARDNESS, Isa 26:10.

STRANGER(S), Heb 11:13 they were s. in
Eze 16:32; Mt 25:35; Joh 10:5; Eph 2:12.
STRANGLED, 2Sa 17:23 Ahithophel s. himself
STRAW, Job 21:18 Do they become like s.
Mt 7:3-5; Lu 6:41, 42.
STRAYED, Mt 18:12 sheep and one gets s.,
STRAYING, Ps 119:118 those s. from your
STREAM, Isa 2:2; Jer 51:44; Mic 4:1.
STREET(S), Pr 1:20 crying aloud in s.
Isa 42:2 in the s. he will not let
Eze 7:19 Into the s. they will throw their
Jer 5:1; Eze 11:6; 28:23; Na 2:4.
STRENGTH, Ps 59:17 O my S., to you I
Ps 62:11 That s. belongs to God.
Ps 110:2 The rod of your s. Jehovah
Isa 12:2 Jehovah is my s. and my might,
Mr 12:30 love Jehovah with your whole s.
Php 4:13 I have s. by virtue of him who
Ex 15:2; Ps 8:2; 28:8; Isa 52:1; Hag 2:22.
STRENGTHEN, Ezr 6:22 s. their hands in
Isa 35:3 S. the weak hands, and make
STRENGTHENED, Ne 2:18 s. their hands
Eze 34:4 The sickened ones you have not s.,
STRETCHED OUT, Isa 14:27 hand is s.,
STRETCHING, Php 3:13 s. forward to the
STRIFE, Ps 80:6 s. to our neighbors,
1Co 3:3 there are jealousy and s. among you,
STRIKE, 1Ki 22:34 he got to s. the king
Ps 141:5 Should the righteous one s. me,
Pr 3:23 foot will not s. anything.
Eze 9:5 Pass through the city and s.
Mic 5:1 they will s. the judge of Israel.
Mal 4:6 s. the earth to destruction.
Ex 17:6; 2Ki 9:7; Mt 26:31; Ac 23:3.
STRIKING, 1Co 9:26 not to be s. the air
STRIPES, 1Pe 2:24 by his s. you were
Ac 16:23, 33; 2Co 11:23.
STRIPPED, Ps 102:17 prayer of those s.
2Co 3:10 made glorious has been s. of glory
STRIPPING, Col 2:15 S. governments
STRIVING, Ec 1:14 vanity and s. after
Ec 2:22 what does a man have for s. of his
STROKES, De 25:3 With forty s. beat him.
Lu 12:47 will be beaten with many s.
Pr 19:29; Lu 12:48; 2Co 11:24.
STRONG, Ex 13:9 by a s. hand Jehovah
Jos 1:7 be courageous and very s. to do
Pr 18:10 The name of Jehovah is a s. tower.
Ro 15:1 bear the weaknesses of those not s.,
1Co 1:27 put the s. things to shame;
1Pe 5:10 he will make you s.
STRONGHOLD(S), Ps 18:2 Jehovah is my s.
Ps 91:2 my s., my God, in whom I will trust.
Na 1:7 Jehovah is good, a s. in the day
Zec 9:12 Return to the s., you prisoners
Ps 28:8; Pr 10:29; Isa 25:4.
STRUCTURE, Am 9:6 his s. over the earth
STRUGGLE, Php 1:30 you have the same s.
Col 2:1 realize how great a s. I am having
STRUGGLING, 1Th 2:2 speak with s.
STUBBLE, Isa 47:14 become like s.
Mal 4:1 those doing wickedness become s.
1Co 3:12 anyone builds on the foundation s.,
STUBBORN, Jos 11:20 hearts become s.
Ps 78:8 A generation s. and rebellious,
Isa 1:23 Your princes are s.
Isa 30:1 Woe to the s. sons,
Isa 65:2 spread out my hands to a s. people,
De 21:18; Jg 2:19; Ps 66:7; Pr 7:11.
STUBBORNNESS, Jer 3:17 the s. of their
Jer 7:24; 9:14; 11:8; 13:10; 18:12.
STUDIED, Joh 7:15 he has not s. at the
STUMBLE, Isa 8:14 rock over which to s.
Jer 20:11 ones persecuting me will s.

Da 11:33 made to s. by sword and by flame,
Da 11:35 some having insight will s.,
Mt 5:29 right eye making you s., tear
Mt 13:57 they began to s. at him.
Pr 4:12; Isa 8:15; 1Co 8:13; Jas 3:2.
STUMBLED, Mt 26:31 you will be s.
Isa 59:10; Mt 15:12; Joh 16:1.
STUMBLES, Mt 18:6 whoever s. these
STUMBLING, Ps 119:165 no s. block.
Mt 13:41 collect things that cause s.
Ro 9:33 laying in Zion a stone of s.
Ro 16:17 those who cause s.
Php 1:10 not be s. others
STUMBLING BLOCKS, Mt 18:7 due to s.!
STUMP, Isa 11:1 twig out of s. of Jesse,
STUNNED, Eze 3:15; Mr 9:15; 14:33; 16:5.
STUPEFIED, Isa 44:8 not become s.
STUPID, Pr 13:20 s. ones fare badly.
Pr 14:16 the s. is becoming furious and
STUPIDITY, Pr 9:13; Ec 7:25.
STYLE, 2Sa 18:27 running s. of Ahimaaz
Ps 73:8; 144:12; Eze 35:13.
STYLED, Ro 7:3 s. an adulteress if she
STYLES OF HAIR, 1Ti 2:9 not with s.
STYLUS, Ps 45:1 May my tongue be the s.
Job 19:24; Isa 8:1; Jer 8:8; 17:1.
SUBDUE, Ge 1:28 earth and s. it,
Isa 45:1 Cyrus to s. before him nations,
SUBDUED, 1Sa 7:13 Philistines were s.
SUBDUING, Ps 110:2 Go s. in the midst
SUBJECT(S), Ps 72:8 have s. from sea to
Ro 10:3 they did not s. themselves to the
Php 3:21 to s. all things to himself.
Heb 2:15 s. to slavery all their lives.
1Pe 2:13 s. yourselves to every human
1Pe 3:22 angels and powers made s. to him.
Lu 2:51; 10:20; Col 2:20; Heb 12:9.
SUBJECTED, Ro 8:20 was s. to futility,
1Co 15:27 s. all things under his feet.
Heb 2:8 he s. all things to him
SUBJECTING, Tit 2:5 s. to husbands,
SUBJECTION, Ge 1:26 have in s. the fish
Ge 1:28 have in s. the fish
Ro 13:1 Let every soul be in s. to
Eph 5:22 Let wives be in s. to husbands as
Eph 5:24 congregation is in s. to Christ,
Col 3:18 wives, be in s. to your husbands,
1Pe 3:1 wives, be in s. to your husbands,
1Pe 5:5 younger men, be in s. to older
Ps 49:14; 1Co 14:34; 1Ti 3:4; Tit 3:1.
SUBMISSIVE, 2Co 9:13 s. to the good news
Heb 13:17 those taking the lead be s.,
SUBMIT, Ex 10:3 must you refuse to s.
SUBORDINATES, 1Co 4:1 appraise us as s.
SUBSIDE(D), Ge 8:1; Es 2:1.
SUBSISTING, 2Sa 21:5 from s. in territory
SUBSTANCE, Heb 10:1 Law not the s. of
SUBSTITUTING, 2Co 5:20 ambassadors s.
SUBTERFUGE, Jg 9:31 messengers by s.
SUBTRACT, Ec 3:14 there is nothing to s.,
SUBVERTING, Lu 23:2 found s. our nation
2Ti 2:18 they are s. the faith of some.
Tit 1:11 men keep s. entire households by
SUBVERTS, Job 12:19; Pr 13:6.
SUCCEED, Ps 1:3 everything he does s.
Isa 53:10 delight of Jehovah will s.
SUCCESS, Ps 118:25 Jehovah, do grant s.,
Isa 54:17 against you will have no s.
Isa 55:11 my word will have s.
Mt 12:20 he sends out justice with s.
SUCCESSFUL, Jos 1:8 make your way s.
2Ch 20:20 his prophets and so prove s.
Ge 39:2; Jg 18:5; 1Ch 22:13; Ps 37:7.
SUCCESSION, Ac 3:24; Heb 7:23.

SUCCESSORS, Heb 7:24 forever without s.
SUCKLING(S), Isa 65:20 No more a s.
  Jer 44:7; Mt 21:16; Lu 21:23.
SUDDEN, Pr 3:25 not afraid of s. thing,
  1Th 5:3 then s. destruction is to be
SUDDENLY, Mal 3:1 s. come to His temple
SUET, Le 1:8,12 set s. over the wood that
SUFFER, Lu 24:26 for the Christ to s.
  Ro 8:17 s. together glorified together.
  1Co 12:26 one member suffers, all s.
  Php 1:29 faith in him s. in his behalf.
  2Ti 4:5 s. evil, work of an evangelizer
  1Pe 3:17 s. because you are doing good,
  Mt 16:21; Ac 26:23; 1Pe 3:14; Re 2:10.
SUFFERED, Heb 2:9 for having s. death,
  Heb 5:8 obedience from things he s.,
  1Pe 2:21 Christ s. leaving you a model
  1Pe 4:1 s. in the flesh has desisted from
  Heb 2:18; 1Pe 5:10.
SUFFERING(S), Ro 8:18 s. do not amount
  2Co 1:7 you are sharers of the s.,
  Col 1:24 I am rejoicing in my s.
  Heb 10:32 endured a contest under s.,
  Jas 5:10 pattern of the s. of evil
  Jas 5:13 Is there anyone s. evil among you?
  1Pe 5:9 knowing that the same s. are
  Php 3:10; Heb 2:10; 1Pe 1:11; 4:13.
SUFFICIENT, Mt 6:34 S. for each day
  2Co 12:9 My undeserved kindness is s. for
  1Pe 4:3 time that has passed by is s.
  Mt 28:12; Ac 17:9; 2Co 2:6.
SUFFOCATION, Job 7:15 soul chooses s.
SUIT, Eph 6:13 complete s. of armor
SUITABLE, Col 1:12 Father rendered s.
  Mt 3:15; Heb 7:26.
SULPHUR, Re 21:8 burns with fire and s.
  Ge 19:24; Ps 11:6; Eze 38:22; Re 19:20.
SUMMER, Ge 8:22 s. will never cease.
  Jer 8:20 s. has come to an end; not saved!
  Mt 24:32 leaves, you know s. is near.
  Ps 74:17; Pr 30:25; Zec 14:8.
SUMMONED, Job 9:19 in justice I may be s.
SUMUP, Ec 7:27 to find out the s.
SUN, Jos 10:12 S., be motionless
  Isa 49:10 nor will heat or s. strike them.
  Isa 60:19 s. will no more be a light
  Mal 4:2 the s. of righteousness will shine
  Mt 13:43 righteous ones will shine as the s.
  Ac 2:20 s. will be turned into darkness
  Ps 89:36; Ec 1:9; Lu 21:25; Re 7:16.
SUNRISING, Da 11:44 reports out of s.
SUPERABUNDANTLY, Eph 3:20.
SUPERCILIOUSNESS, Ps 10:4 wicked s.
SUPERFINE, 2Co 11:5 your s. apostles.
SUPERFLUOUS, 2Co 9:1; Jas 1:21.
SUPERIOR, Ex 17:11 Israelites proved s.,
  1Sa 2:9 not by power does a man prove s.
  Ps 9:19 Let not mortal man show s. strength.
  Ro 13:1 subjection to the s. authorities
  Php 2:3 considering that others are s. to
  Php 2:9 God exalted him to a s. position
  1Pe 2:13 whether to a king as being s.
SUPERIORITY, Ec 3:19 no s. of man over
  Isa 2:19 Jehovah and from his splendid s.,
  Isa 24:14 In the s. of Jehovah they will
  Mic 5:4 the s. of the name of Jehovah
  Ro 3:1 What, then, is the s. of the Jew,
SUPERLATIVE, Ca 1:1 s. song Solomon's
SUPERNATURAL, Lu 1:22; 24:23; 2Co 12:1.
SUPERSTITIOUS. See FEAR OF THE DEITIES.
SUPERVISORS, 1Ch 23:4; Ezr 3:8,9.
SUPPER. See EVENING MEAL.
SUPPLANT, Jer 9:4 even brother would s.
SUPPLANTERS, Ps 49:5 very error of my s.

SUPPLE, Ge 49:24 strength of his hands was s.
SUPPLICATION(S), 2Co 1:11 help by your s.
  Eph 6:18 keep awake with s. in behalf of
  Heb 5:7 Christ offered up s. and petitions
  Jas 5:16 righteous man's s. has force.
  1Pe 3:12 his ears are toward their s.,
SUPPLIES, 2Ch 8:15 concerning the s.
  Isa 30:6 on the humps of camels their s.
  2Co 9:10 abundantly s. seed to the sower
  Ga 3:5 He s. you the spirit and performs
SUPPLY, Pr 15:16 an abundant s.
SUPPORT(S), 1Sa 2:8 belong earth's s.,
SUPPOSE, Jas 1:7 let not that man s. he
SUPPOSING, Php 1:17 s. to stir up
SUPREME ONE, Da 7:18 holy ones of the S.
  Da 7:22, 27.
SURE, 2Pe 1:10, 19 make calling s.
  Isa 28:16; 1Th 5:21; Heb 6:19.
SURETY, Pr 6:1 if you have gone s. for
  Ge 43:9; Pr 11:15; 17:18; 27:13.
SURFACE, Ge 1:2 moving over the s.,
SURGING WATERS, Ps 106:9 through the s.
SURPASSING, 1Co 12:31 show a s. way.
  2Co 4:17 glory is of more s. weight
  Eph 1:19 what the s. greatness of his power
SURPLUS, Mt 14:20; Lu 21:4; 2Co 8:14.
SURRENDERED, 1Jo 3:16 s. soul for us;
SURVIVING, 1Th 4:17 s. be caught away
SURVIVORS, Isa 1:9 remaining a few s.,
  Joe 2:32 among the s., whom Jehovah is
SUSPENSE, Lu 12:29; Joh 10:24.
SUSPICIONS, 1Ti 6:4 spring wicked s.,
SUSPICIOUSLY, 1Sa 18:9 Saul looking s. at
SUSTAIN, Ps 55:22 he will s. you.
SUSTAINS, Heb 1:3 s. all things by the
SUSTENANCE, 1Ti 6:8 s. and covering we
SWADDLING, Job 38:9 thick gloom as its s.
SWALLOWED, 2Co 5:4 may be s. by life.
SWAN, Le 11:18; De 14:16.
SWARM(S), Ge 1:20; Ex 8:24.
SWARTHY, Ca 1:6 I am s., because the
SWAYED, 1Th 3:3 be s. by tribulations.
SWEAR, Ge 22:16 By myself I do s.,
  Mt 5:34 do not s. at all, neither by
  Heb 6:13 could not s. by anyone greater,
  De 6:13; Jos 2:20; Isa 65:16; Jer 12:16.
SWEAT, Ge 3:19 In the s. of your face
SWEEP, Lu 15:8 s. her house and search
SWEET, Jas 3:11 fountain cause the s.
SWELLING EXPRESSIONS, 2Pe 2:18 utter s.
  Jas 1:19 s. about hearing, slow about
SWIM, Ps 6:6; Isa 25:11.
SWINE, Mt 7:6 throw pearls before s.,
  Lu 15:15 citizens sent him to herd s.
  Mt 8:30; Mr 5:11; Lu 8:33.
SWOON, Am 8:13 virgins will s. away.
SWORD(S), Jg 3:16 Ehud made a s.
  Jg 7:22 s. of each one against the other
  1Sa 17:47 neither with s. does Jehovah
  Isa 2:4 not lift up s. against nation,
  Eze 33:6 watchman sees the s. coming
  Joe 3:10 beat your plowshares into s.
  Mic 4:3 beat their s. into plowshares
  Mt 26:52 take the s. perish by the s.
  Eph 6:17 s. of the spirit, God's word,
  Heb 4:12 word of God two-edged s.
  Re 19:15 protrudes a sharp long s.,
  Da 11:33; Mt 10:34; Lu 21:24; 22:38.
SWORN, Isa 14:24 Jehovah has s.,
  Isa 45:23 By my own self I have s.—
  Ac 2:30 God had s. to him with an oath
  Jos 9:18; Ps 89:3, 35; 132:11.
SWORN STATEMENT, Ge 26:3; Ps 119:106.

De 7:8 keeping the s. to your forefathers
Ps 105:9 Abraham, and his s. to Isaac,
SYMBOLIC, Ga 4:24 stand as a s. drama;
SYMBOL OF JEALOUSY, Eze 8:3, 5.
SYMBOL OF REPENTANCE, Mr 1:4; Ac 19:4.
Lu 3:3 preaching baptism in s.
SYMPATHIZE, Ps 69:20 for someone to s.
Heb 4:15 high priest who can s. with
Job 42:11; Isa 51:19; Na 3:7.
SYMPATHY, 1Sa 22:8 no one having s. for
SYNAGOGUE(S), Joh 18:20 I taught in a s.
Re 2:9 they are a s. of Satan.
Re 3:9 s. of Satan who say they are Jews,
Mt 23:6; Ac 17:17; 18:26.
SYRIA, 2Ki 13:3; 2Ch 16:7; Isa 17:3.
SYRIAN, Ge 31:20; De 26:5; Isa 36:11.
SYSTEM(S) OF THINGS, Ps 17:14 this s.,
Ps 49:1 Give ear, you inhabitants of the s.
Mt 13:39 harvest is a conclusion of a s.
Mt 24:3 conclusion of the s.?
2Co 4:4 God of this s. has blinded
Ga 1:4 deliver us from the wicked s.
Heb 1:2 through whom he made the s.
Mt 28:20; Mr 10:30; Lu 18:30; 1Ti 6:17.

T

TABERNACLE, Ex 25:9 show you pattern of t.
Ps 43:3 bring me to your grand t.
Ps 78:28 All around his t.
Ps 84:1 How lovely your grand t. is,
Eze 37:27 my t. will prove be over them,
2Pe 1:13 as long as I am in this t., to
Ex 40:17; Ps 78:60; 132:7; Joh 7:2.
TABLE(S), Ps 23:5 arrange a t.
Isa 21:5 Let there be a setting of the t.
Isa 28:8 the t. have become full of vomit—
Da 11:27 at one t. a lie is what they will
Mal 1:7 The t. of Jehovah is despised.
Lu 22:30 drink at my t. in my kingdom,
1Co 10:21 partaking of the t. of Jehovah
TABLETS, Ex 34:28 write upon the t.
2Co 3:3 not on stone t., but on fleshly t.,
Ex 32:16; 34:1; Heb 9:4.
TABOR, Jg 4:14 descending from Mount T.
TAIL(S), Isa 9:15 false instruction is the t.
De 28:13, 44; Re 9:10; 12:4.
TAKE, De 4:2 must not t. away from word
Pr 8:10 T. my discipline
Joh 1:11 his own people did not t. him in.
TALENT(S), Ex 38:25, 27; 1Ki 10:10, 14;
Mt 18:24; 25:15; Re 16:21.
TALK, Job 6:3; Ps 64:2; 1Ti 1:6.
TALKED, Ro 1:8 your faith is t. about
TALKING, Pr 17:9 keeps t. about a matter
TALKS BACK, Ro 10:21 disobedient and t.
TALLER, 1Sa 10:23; Da 8:3.
TAMAR, Ge 38:6, 11; Ru 4:12; Mt 1:3.
TAMBOURINES, 2Sa 6:5 celebrating with t.
TAMED, Jas 3:7 be t. and has been t. by
Jas 3:8 the tongue, not one can get it t.
TAMMUZ, Eze 8:14 weeping over god T.
TARSHISH, Isa 23:1 Howl, ships of T.!
2Ch 9:21; Ps 48:7; Eze 27:12, 25; Jon 1:3.
TARTARUS, 2Pe 2:4 throwing them into T.
TASKMASTER, Zec 9:8 no more a t.,
TASTE, Mt 16:28; Col 2:21; Heb 2:9.
TASTED, Heb 6:4 t. the heavenly free
1Pe 2:3 you have t. that the Lord is kind.
TATTOO, Le 19:28 not put t. marking upon
TAUGHT, Isa 29:13 men's commandment t.,
Isa 54:13 sons be persons t. by Jehovah,
Joh 8:28 as the Father t. me I speak
De 4:5; Ps 71:17; Ac 11:26; Ga 6:6.

TAUNTING, Pr 27:11 a reply to him t. me.
TAX(ES), Nu 31:28 t. for Jehovah you
Mt 17:24 teacher not pay the temple t.?
Mt 17:25; 22:17 kings receive head t.
Lu 23:2 forbidding paying of t. to Caesar
Ro 13:7 to him who calls for t., the t.;
TAX COLLECTOR(S), Mt 11:19 friend of t.
Mt 21:32 t. and the harlots believed him,
Mr 2:15 many t. were reclining with Jesus
Mr 2:16 Does he eat with t. and sinners?
Lu 3:12 even t. came to be baptized
Lu 18:10 one a Pharisee and the other a t.
Lu 18:11 I thank you I am not as this t.
Lu 19:2 Zacchaeus was a chief t., and rich.
Mt 5:46; 18:17; 21:31; Lu 7:29; 15:1.
TEACH, Ezr 7:10 Ezra prepared to t.
Job 33:33 and I shall t. you wisdom.
Ps 25:4 O Jehovah; t. me your paths.
Ps 25:9 he will t. the meek ones his way.
Ps 34:11 fear of Jehovah is what I shall t.
Ps 94:12 Happy is the man whom you t.
Ps 143:10 T. me to do your will,
Jer 31:34 no more t. each one his brother,
Mt 15:9 t. commands of men as doctrines.
Joh 7:16 What I t. is not mine, but belongs
Joh 14:26 the holy spirit will t. you all
2Ti 2:2 be adequately qualified to t. others.
2Ti 2:24 gentle toward all, qualified to t.,
Ex 4:12; Mt 11:1; Lu 12:12; 1Ti 2:12.
TEACHER(S), Ps 119:99 More than all my t.
Mt 23:8 for one is your t., whereas
Joh 3:10 Are you a t. of Israel and yet
Joh 13:13 You address me, T., and, Lord,
1Ti 2:7 —a t. of nations in the matter
2Ti 4:3 will accumulate t. for themselves
Heb 5:12 you ought to be t. in view of
Mt 10:24; Eph 4:11; Jas 3:1; 2Pe 2:1.
TEACHES, Mt 5:19 anyone who t. them,
Ro 12:7 he that t., let him be at his
TEACHING(S), 2Ch 17:9 t. among the people.
Job 35:11 t. us more than the beasts
Ps 144:1 Who is t. my hands for fighting,
Isa 48:17 Jehovah, the One t. you to benefit
Jer 32:33 t. of them, rising early and t.,
Mt 7:29 he was t. them as a person having
Mt 16:12 watch for the t. of the Pharisees
Mt 28:20 t. them to observe all the things
Mr 6:6 to the villages in a circuit, t.
Ac 4:2 annoyed because they were t. the
Ac 5:42 house to house without letup t.
Ac 18:25 speaking and t. with correctness
Ac 20:20 t. you publicly and from house
1Co 4:17 I am t. everywhere in every
Ga 6:6 orally taught share in oral t.
Eph 4:14 by every wind of t.
Col 2:22 commands and t. of men?
1Ti 4:1 paying attention to t. of demons
1Ti 4:16 Pay attention to yourself and t.
2Ti 3:16 All Scripture is beneficial for t.,
2Ti 4:3 not put up with healthful t.
Tit 1:11 t. things they ought not for
Heb 13:9 not carried away with strange t.
2Ch 17:9; Joh 35:11; Ps 144:1; Jer 32:33;
Ac 5:25; Ro 2:21; 1Ti 4:6; 6:1; Tit 1:9.
TEAR(S), Ps 2:3 Let us t. their bands
Ps 126:5 sowing seed with t.
Lu 5:36 the new patch t. away and
Re 21:4 wipe out every t. from their eyes,
Isa 25:8; Lu 7:38; Heb 5:7; Re 7:17.
TEARING, Ro 14:20 Stop t. down the work
TEAT, Isa 66:11 the t. of her glory.
TEETH, Eze 18:2 t. of sons set on edge?
Joe 1:6 Its t. the t. of a lion,

Job 19:20; Pr 10:26; Da 7:7, 19; Mt 8:12.
TELL, Jer 50:2 T. it among the nations
TELLING, 1Sa 68:11 women t. the good news
Isa 42:9 new things I am t. out.
TEMPEST, Ps 83:15 pursue them with t.
Jer 23:19 windstorm of Jehovah, a t.
Jer 25:32 a great t. will be roused up
Am 1:14 t. in the day of stormwind.
TEMPLE(S), Ps 11:4 Jehovah is in his t.
Ps 29:9 in his t. each is saying: Glory!
Jer 7:4 The t. of Jehovah, t. of Jehovah,
Hab 2:20 in his holy t. Keep silence
Zec 6:12 he will build the t. of Jehovah,
Mal 3:1 suddenly there will come to His t.
Joh 2:15 drove all those out of the t.
Joh 2:19 Break down this t., and in three
Ac 17:24 does not dwell in handmade t.,
1Co 3:16 you people are God's t.
2Co 6:16 what agreement does God's t. have
Eph 2:21 growing into a holy t. for Jehovah.
2Th 2:4 sits down in the t. of The God,
Re 3:12 pillar in the t. of my God, and he
Re 7:15 service day and night in his t.,
Re 11:19 the t. sanctuary of God in heaven
Jg 4:21; Ps 27:4.
TEMPORARY, 2Co 4:18 things seen are t.,
TEMPORARY RESIDENTS, Heb 11:13; 1Pe 2:11.
TEMPTATION(S), Mt 6:13 not bring into t.,
Mt 26:41 that you may not enter into t.
Lu 4:13 Devil, having concluded the t.,
1Co 10:13 No t. has taken you except
1Ti 6:9 rich fall into t. and snare
TEMPTED, Ga 6:1 for fear you also may be t.
TEMPTER, Mt 4:3 the T. came and said to
1Th 3:5 t. might have tempted you and our
TEMPTING, 1Co 7:5 Satan may not keep t.
TEN, Ex 34:28 the T. Words.
Zec 8:23 t. men take hold of the skirt
Re 2:10 may have tribulation t. days.
Ge 18:32; 2Ki 20:11; Mt 25:1; Re 13:1.
TENDENCY, Jas 4:5 with a t. to envy
TENDER, Ro 12:10 have t. affection for
2Co 1:3; Col 3:12; Jas 5:11.
TENDRILS, Isa 18:5 must remove the t.
TENSILE STRENGTH, Isa 18:2 nation of t.
TENT(S), Jg 5:24 women in the t.
Ps 15:1 who will be a guest in your t.?
Isa 54:2 Lengthen out your t. cords,
Jer 35:7 in t. you should dwell all your
Da 11:45 he will plant his palatial t.
Heb 9:11 perfect t. not made with hands,
Re 21:3 the t. of God is with humankind,
Pr 14:11; Isa 40:22; 2Co 5:1; Heb 8:2.
TENTH, Ge 14:20 Abram gave a t.
Ne 10:38 when the Levites receive a t.,
Mt 23:23 t. of the mint you disregarded
Lu 18:12 I give the t. of all things
Le 27:32; De 14:22; 2Ch 31:12; Ne 13:12.
TENTH PART(S), Le 27:30 t. belongs to
Nu 18:26 to Jehovah a t. of the t.
Mal 3:10 Bring all the t. into the
TERAH, Ge 11:24; Lu 3:34.
TERAPHIM, 1Sa 15:23 uncanny power and t.
Zec 10:2 t. have spoken what is uncanny;
Ge 31:19; 2Ki 23:24; Eze 21:21; Ho 3:4.
TERMS, 2Pe 2:11 an accusation in abusive t.,
TERRAIN, Isa 42:16 rugged t. into level land.
TERRIFIED, Jos 1:9 Do not be t., for
TERRITORY, Ps 147:14 peace in your t.
Jer 31:17 return to their own t.

Mic 5:6 when he treads upon our t.
Mal 1:4 call them the t. of wickedness
Mt 13:57 A prophet in his native t.
Ro 15:23 I no longer have untouched t. in
2Co 10:15 made great with reference to our t.
Ps 78:54; Joe 3:6; Am 1:13; Zep 2:8.
TERROR(S), Ge 9:2 t. of you upon every
Ge 35:5 the t. of God came upon the cities
Jer 8:15 a time of healing, but, look! t.
Eze 3:9 you must not be struck with t.
Mal 2:5 my name he was struck with t.
Ps 73:19; Isa 51:7; Jer 10:2; Eze 26:21.
TERRORIZED, 1Sa 16:14; Job 3:5.
TEST, 2Ch 9:1 queen proceeded to t.
Ps 26:2 O Jehovah, and put me to the t.;
Isa 7:12 shall not put Jehovah to the t.
Mal 3:10 T. me out, please, in this respect,
Mt 4:7 You must not put Jehovah to the t.
1Co 10:9 Neither let us put Jehovah to t.,
Re 2:10 you may be fully put to the t.,
Re 3:10 keep you from the hour of t.
Jg 2:22; Ac 5:9; Heb 2:18; 1Jo 4:1.
TESTAMENT. See COVENANT(S).
TESTED, Job 23:10 he has t. me out
Job 34:36 let Job be t. out to the limit
Mal 3:15 they have t. God out and keep
Heb 4:15 t. in all respects like ourselves,
TESTED QUALITY, Jas 1:3 t. of faith
1Pe 1:7 that the t. of your faith
TESTICLES, Jer 5:8 having strong t.,
TESTIFIED, Isa 1:16 own mouth has t.
Isa 59:12 our sins, t. against us.
Ho 5:5 of Israel has t. to his face; and
TESTIFY, Nu 35:30 witness may not t.
Mic 6:3 I tired you out? T. against me.
TESTIMONIES, De 6:17 keep his t. and
1Ki 2:3; 1Ch 29:19.
TESTIMONY. See also REMINDER(S).
TESTIMONY, Ex 25:22 ark of the t.,
Ex 31:18 Moses two tablets of the t.,
Nu 1:50 Levites over tabernacle of the T.
1Ti 3:7 a fine t. from people outside,
2Ch 23:11; Heb 3:5.
TESTING, De 13:3 Jehovah is t. you to
Ps 7:9 t. out the hearts and the kidneys,
Lu 8:13 in a season of t. they fall away.
2Co 13:5 t. whether you are in the faith,
THADDAEUS, Mt 10:3; Mr 3:18.
THANK(S), 2Sa 22:50 I shall t. you,
1Ch 16:4 to t. and praise Jehovah the God
1Ch 16:8 T. Jehovah, call upon his name,
Ps 92:1 It is good to give t. to Jehovah
Ps 97:12 give t. to his memorial
Mt 26:27 took a cup and, having given t.,
Joh 11:41 Father, I t. you that you heard
Ro 14:6 eats to Jehovah, for he gives t. to
1Co 1:4 I always t. God for you in view of
1Co 10:30 If I am partaking with t., why am
1Co 14:17 you give t. in a right way, but
2Co 9:15 T. be to God for his free gift.
Eph 5:20 in the name of Jesus giving t.
Re 11:17 We t. you, Jehovah God, the
THANKED, Ac 28:15 Paul t. God and took
THANKING, 1Ch 29:13; 2Ch 5:13.
THANKSGIVING, Ps 26:7 t. to be heard
Ps 95:2 come before his person with t.;
Ps 116:17 To you I shall offer t.,
1Ti 4:4 fine if it is received with t.,
Jer 17:26; 2Co 4:15; Php 4:6; Re 7:12.
THEATER, Ac 19:29; Heb 10:33.
THEATRICAL, 1Co 4:9 become t. spectacle

THEME, Job 30:9 become t. of their song
THEMSELVES, 2Ti 3:2 will be lovers of t.,
THICK GLOOM, Eze 34:12 of clouds and t.
THIEF, Ex 22:2 t. breaking in
Job 24:14 he becomes a t.
Ps 50:18 t. you were pleased with him,
Pr 29:24 He that is partner with a t. is
Joe 2:9 through windows they go like a t.
1Th 5:2 day is coming as a t. in the night.
1Pe 4:15 none of you suffer as a t.
Re 16:15 Look! I am coming as a t.
THIEVERY, Pr 6:30 he commits t. to fill
THIEVES, Isa 1:23 princes are partners with t.
Mt 6:20 where t. do not break in
1Th 5:4 day should overtake you as t.,
Isa 1:23; 1Co 6:10 t. not inherit
THINK, Mt 5:17 not t. I came to destroy
Mt 16:23 you t., not God's thoughts, but
Mt 24:44 hour you do not t. the Son is
Ro 12:3 not to t. more of himself than
Mt 10:34; Joh 5:39; Heb 10:29.
THINKING, Jer 29:11 thoughts I am t. toward
Mal 3:16 fear of Jehovah t. upon his name.
Php 4:10 you have revived your t. in my
Jer 18:11; 23:27; Mic 2:3; Na 1:11.
THINKING ABILITIES, Pr 5:2 guard t.,
Pr 14:17 the man of t. is hated.
THINKING FACULTIES, 2Pe 3:1 arousing t.
THINKS, 1Co 8:2 t. he has knowledge
1Co 10:12 let him t. he is standing beware
Ga 6:3 t. he is something when he is
1Co 3:18; 14:37; Php 3:4.
THIRD, 2Co 12:2 away to the t. heaven.
THIRD DAY, Lu 9:22 killed and t. raised
Ac 10:40 God raised this One up on the t.
Ex 19:11; Lu 13:32; 24:21; 1Co 15:4.
THIRST, Am 8:11 famine, and a t., not
Re 7:16 hunger no more nor t. any more,
THIRSTING, Mt 5:6 t. for righteousness,
Re 21:6 To anyone t. I will give from
Re 22:17 let anyone t. come;
THIRSTY, Isa 49:10 they will not go t.
Isa 55:1 Hey there, all you t. ones!
Isa 65:13 you yourselves will go t.
Mt 25:44 when did we see you t.
Joh 7:37 anyone is t., let him come to me
THOMAS, Mt 10:3; Joh 20:24; Ac 1:13.
THORN(S), Isa 55:13 the thicket of t.
Mt 7:16 Never gather grapes from t.
Mt 13:22 As for the one sown among the t.,
2Co 12:7 given me a t. in the flesh,
THORNBUSH, Mt 12:26; Ac 7:30, 35.
THOUGHT(S), Ps 94:11 is knowing the t.
Ps 139:2 You have considered my t. from far
Ps 139:23 knowing my disquieting t.,
Ps 146:4 In that day his t. do perish.
Pr 12:5 t. of the righteous ones are
Isa 55:8 t. of you people are not my t.,
2Co 10:5 bringing every t. into captivity
Heb 4:12 word of God able to discern t.
Re 17:17 in hearts to carry out God's t.
Ge 6:5; Ps 40:5; Jer 29:11; Php 4:7.
THOUGHTLESSLY, Pr 12:18 speaking t.
THOUGHT OUT, 2Sa 14:14.
THOUSAND, De 7:9 to a t. generations,
1Ki 19:18 seven t. not bent down to Baal
Job 33:23 spokesman, one out of a t.,
Ps 50:10 The beasts on a t. mountains.
Ps 84:10 courtyards is better than a t.
Ps 91:7 A t. will fall at your very side
Isa 60:22 little one will become a t.

THOUSAND YEARS, Ps 90:4 t. in your eyes
2Pe 3:8 one day is with Jehovah as a t.
Re 20:2 Satan, and bound him for a t.
Re 20:4 ruled with the Christ for a t.
THREAT(S), Ac 4:29 attention to their t.
Ac 9:1 Saul, still breathing t. and murder
THREATENING, Eph 6:9 letting up on t.,
1Pe 2:23 he did not go to t., but kept
THRESH, Mic 4:13 Get up and t., O
THRESHING, Isa 41:15 t. sledge, a new t.
Hab 3:12 In anger you went t. the nations.
THRESHING FLOOR, Ru 3:2; 2Sa 24:21.
THRIVE, Ps 62:10 maintenance should t.,
THRIVING, Ps 92:14 still keep on t.
THROAT, Ps 149:6 songs be in their t.
Pr 3:3 Tie them about your t. Write them
Pr 3:22 your soul and charm to your t.
THRONE(S), 1Ch 29:23 upon Jehovah's t.
Ps 45:6 God is your t. to time indefinite,
Ps 97:2 Righteousness place of his t.
Isa 9:7 upon the t. of David and upon his
Isa 14:13 Above the stars lift up my t.,
Isa 66:1 heavens are my t., and the earth
Da 7:9 beholding there were t. placed
Lu 22:30 sit on t. to judge Israel
Heb 4:16 approach t. of undeserved kindness
Heb 12:2 at the right hand of the t. of God.
Re 3:21 grant to sit down with me in my t.,
Re 7:9 standing before the t. and before
Re 20:4 saw t., those who sat down on them
Ps 45:6; 97:2; Jer 3:17; Mt 25:31; Col 1:16.
THROWN, Mt 3:10; 5:25; 7:19.
THRUSTING, Pr 26:6 t. matters into the
THUNDER(S), Ex 9:23 Jehovah gave t. and
Job 40:9 voice like his can you make it t.?
Ps 98:7 Let the sea t. and that which fills it
Mr 3:17 Boanerges, (which means Sons of T.,)
Re 6:1 say with a voice as of t.,
1Sa 2:10; 7:10; Job 37:5; Ps 77:18; 81:7.
THUNDERED, Ps 29:3 The glorious God has t.
THYATIRA, Ac 16:14; Re 1:11; 2:18, 24.
TIE, De 6:8 t. them as a sign upon your
Jos 2:18; Pr 3:3; 7:3; Jer 51:63.
TIED, Jos 2:21 she t. the scarlet cord in
TIGHTNESS, De 28:53, 57; Jer 19:9.
TIME(S), Le 26:18 chastise you seven t.
Jos 6:15 marching round the city seven t.
Job 14:13 set a t. limit for me and
Ps 31:15 My t. are in your hand. Deliver
Pr 15:23 word at right t. is good!
Pr 24:16 righteous one may fall seven t.
Ec 3:1 t. for every affair under heavens;
Ec 9:11 t. and unforeseen occurrence
Isa 33:2 salvation in the t. of distress.
Isa 49:8 In an acceptable t. I have answered
Da 4:16 let seven t. pass over it.
Da 7:25 for a t., and t. and half a t.
Da 11:27 end is yet for the t. appointed.
Da 12:4 book, until the t. of the end.
Hab 2:3 vision is yet for the appointed t.,
Mt 16:3 signs of t. you cannot interpret.
Mt 18:22 t. but, Up to seventy-seven t.
Mt 24:45 give them food at the proper t.
Lu 21:24 appointed t. of the nations
Ac 1:7 not belong knowledge of the t.
Ac 3:21 t. of restoration of all things
Ac 17:30 God has overlooked t. of ignorance
1Co 7:29 the t. left is reduced.
Eph 5:16 buying out the opportune t.
1Th 5:1 as for the t. you need nothing

2Th 2:6 being revealed in his own due **t**.
1Ti 2:6 witnessed to at its particular **t**.
1Ti 4:1 later periods of **t**. some fall away
2Ti 3:1 last days critical **t**. will be here.
Re 12:12 knowing he has a short period of **t**.
Re 12:14 for a **t**. and **t**. and half a **t**.
1Co 4:5; Ga 4:4; 1Pe 1:20; 4:17; Re 11:18.
TIME(S) INDEFINITE, Ge 9:16 covenant to **t**.
Ge 48:4 this land to your seed to **t**.
Ex 3:15 Jehovah is my name to **t**.
Ex 31:16 the sabbath a covenant to **t**.
Ps 90:2 from **t**. to **t**. you are God.
Ps 136:1-26 his loving-kindness is to **t**.
Ps 145:13 is a kingship for all **t**. and your
Isa 26:4 Jehovah is the Rock of **t**.
Da 12:3 like the stars to **t**., even forever.
Zep 2:9 a desolate waste, even to **t**.
Ge 3:22; Pr 8:23; Jer 3:5; Da 9:24; Jon 2:6.
TIMID, De 20:3; Job 23:16; Isa 7:4.
TIMOTHY, Ac 16:1; 1Co 4:17; 1Ti 1:2.
TIRE, Isa 40:28 He does not **t**. out or
Isa 40:31 they will walk and not **t**. out.
TIRED, Jg 8:4 **t**. but keeping up the pursuit.
Pr 25:25 As cold water upon a **t**. soul, so
Isa 40:29 giving to the **t**. one power,
TITHES. See also TENTH, TENTH PART(S).
TITHES, Heb 7:5 commandment to collect **t**.
Heb 7:9 Levi who receives **t**. paid **t**.
Heb 7:6, 8.
TITHING, De 26:12 **t**. the entire tenth
TITLE(S), Job 32:21 not bestow a **t**.,
Joh 19:19 Pilate wrote a **t**. also and put it
TITUS, 2Co 2:13; 12:18; Ga 2:1; Tit 1:4.
TODAY, Mt 6:11; Lu 4:21; 23:43.
TOIL, Pr 14:23 By **t**. there comes advantage
Isa 65:23 They will not **t**. for nothing,
Ps 128:2; Jon 4:10.
TOILED, Ga 4:11 I have **t**. to no purpose
TOILING, Mt 11:28 all you who are **t**.
TOKEN. See also PORTENT(S).
TOKEN, 2Co 1:22 given us the **t**., the spirit in
2Co 5:5 gave us the **t**. of what is to come,
Eph 1:14 a **t**. in advance of inheritance
TOLD, Ps 40:9 I have **t**. the good news
TOLERATE, Ge 30:20 husband will **t**. me,
TOLERATED, Ro 9:22 **t**. vessels of wrath
TOLERATED NO RIVALRY, Nu 25:13 he **t**.
TOLERATION, 2Ki 10:16 **t**. of no rivalry
TOLL, Ezr 4:13 tax nor **t**. will they give
TONE(S), 1Co 14:7 an interval to the **t**.
TONGUE(S), 2Sa 23:2 word was upon my **t**.
Ps 31:20 hide them from quarreling of **t**.
Ps 34:13 Safeguard your **t**. against bad,
Ps 39:1 To keep from sinning with my **t**.
Pr 6:17 lofty eyes, a false **t**., and hands
Pr 16:1 from Jehovah is the answer of the **t**.
Pr 18:21 Death and life power of the **t**.,
Isa 32:4 **t**. of the stammerers be quick in
Isa 35:6 **t**. of the speechless cry out
Isa 54:17 any **t**. that will rise up against
Zec 14:12 one's very **t**. will rot away
Ac 2:3 **t**. as if of fire became visible
1Co 13:1 If I speak in the **t**. of angels
1Co 13:8 there are **t**., they will cease;
1Co 14:5 greater than he that speaks in **t**.,
1Co 14:9 through the **t**. utter speech easily
1Co 14:22 **t**. are for a sign, not to
Php 2:11 every **t**. openly acknowledge Jesus
Jas 1:26 If any man does not bridle his **t**.,
Jas 3:6 the **t**. is a fire

1Co 12:10; 14:6, 13, 19; Jas 3:8; Re 7:9.
TOOL, Ec 10:10 iron **t**. become blunt
TOPHETH, 2Ki 23:10; Isa 30:33; Jer 7:31.
TORCH(ES), Jg 7:16 **t**. inside large jars.
Isa 62:1 her salvation like a **t**. that burns.
Da 10:6 his eyes like fiery **t**., and his arms
Na 2:4 chariots appearances are like **t**.
Ge 15:17; Jg 15:4; Eze 1:13.
TORMENT(S), Mt 8:29 come here to **t**. us.
Lu 16:23 existing in **t**., and he saw Abraham
Re 14:11 smoke of their **t**. ascends forever
Mr 5:7; Lu 8:28; Re 18:7, 10.
TORMENTED, Re 9:5; 11:10; 20:10.
TORN, Ec 4:12 threefold cannot be quickly **t**.
TORRENT, Jg 5:21 **t**. of Kishon washed
Jer 31:9 walk to **t**. valleys of water,
Eze 47:7 on the bank of the **t**. were trees
TORTUOUS, Ps 18:26 show yourself **t**.
TORTURED, Heb 11:35 men were **t**. because
TORTURE STAKE(S), Mt 27:40 come off **t**.!
Mr 15:32 Let Christ come down off the **t**.,
Lu 9:23 pick up his **t**. day after day and
Lu 23:26 placed the **t**. upon him to bear it
Eph 2:16 reconcile peoples through the **t**.,
Php 2:8 as far as death, yes, death on a **t**.
Php 3:18 enemies of the **t**. of the Christ,
Col 2:14 out of way by nailing it to the **t**.
Heb 12:2 Jesus endured a **t**., despising shame
Mt 10:38; Joh 19:31; 1Co 1:17; Ga 6:14.
TOSS, Eze 10:2 coals **t**. them over the city.
TOTTER, Ps 46:2 mountains **t**. into the sea
Ps 46:5 city will not be made to **t**.
Ps 55:22 Never allow the righteous to **t**.
Ps 15:5; 93:1; 121:3; 125:1; Isa 40:20.
TOUCH, Ge 3:3 not **t**. it that you not die.
1Ch 16:22 Do not **t**. my anointed ones,
Job 2:5 **t**. his bone and his flesh
Ps 105:15 Do not you men **t**. my anointed
Isa 52:11 out of there, **t**. nothing unclean,
Jer 1:9 **t**. my mouth. "Here put my words in
Lu 11:46 you do not **t**. the loads with
Col 2:21 Do not handle, nor taste, nor **t**.,
TOUCHED, Isa 6:7 has **t**. your lips, and
2Ki 13:21; Mt 8:3; 14:36; 20:34; Mr 5:30.
TOUCHES, Le 5:2 soul **t**. some unclean thing
Ps 104:32 **t**. the mountains and they smoke.
Hag 2:13 If someone unclean **t**. any of
TOUCHING, Zec 2:8 **t**. you **t**. my eyeball.
2Co 6:17 quit **t**. the unclean thing,
Ex 30:29; Le 11:36; Pr 6:29; Jer 12:14.
TOWER, Ge 11:4 build ourselves a **t**.
Pr 18:10 name of Jehovah is a strong **t**.
2Ki 9:17; Ps 61:3; Mic 4:8; Lu 13:4.
TOWN, Ps 48:2 the **t**. of the grand King.
TRACE, Da 2:35 no **t**. at all was found
TRACES, Isa 44:13 **t**. it out with chalk
TRACKS, Ps 23:3 leads me in **t**. of
TRADE, Ac 18:3; Re 18:22.
TRADERS, Eze 27:13, 15, 17, 22-24.
TRADESMEN, Job 41:6 divide among **t**.?
Isa 23:8 **t**. were illustrious ones
Na 3:16 multiplies your **t**.
TRADESWOMAN, Eze 27:3 the **t**. of the peoples
TRADING, Pr 31:18 sensed her **t**. is good;
TRADITION(S), 1Ch 4:22 sayings of old **t**.
Mt 15:3 overstep because of your **t**.
Mr 7:13 word of God invalid by your **t**.
Ga 1:14 zealous for the **t**. of my fathers
Col 2:8 empty deception by **t**. of men,
Mr 7:3; 1Co 11:2; 2Th 2:15; 2Th 3:6.

TRAFFIC, Jg 5:6 pathways had no **t.**
TRAIN(S), 2Ch 9:1 **t.** and camels
Job 15:5 your error **t.** your mouth,
Pr 22:6 **t.** up a boy according to
TRAINED, Ge 14:14 mustered his **t.** men,
Heb 5:14 **t.** to distinguish both right and
Heb 12:11 those **t.** by it it yields fruit
2Pe 2:14 have a heart **t.** in covetousness.
TRAINING, 1Ti 4:7 be **t.** yourself with
1Ti 4:8 bodily **t.** is beneficial for little,
1Pe 5:10 Christ will finish your **t.**
TRAITOR(S), Ps 59:5; Lu 6:16.
TRAMPING, 2Sa 5:18 kept **t.** about in
TRAMPLE, Da 8:13 army things to **t.** on?"
Re 11:12 will **t.** the holy city
Isa 26:6; Eze 34:18; Da 7:23.
TRAMPLED, Eze 34:19 ground **t.** by your
Lu 21:24 Jerusalem will be **t.** on by nations,
Heb 10:29 has **t.** upon the Son of God
TRAMPLING PLACE, Isa 28:18 become a **t.**
Mic 7:10 she will become a **t.**
TRANCE, Ac 10:10; 11:5; 22:17.
TRANSFER, 2Sa 3:10 **t.** the kingdom
Mt 17:20 this mountain, T. from here
TRANSFERRED, Heb 11:5 faith Enoch was **t.**
TRANSFIGURED, Mt 17:2 he was **t.** before
TRANSFORMED, Ro 12:2 **t.** by making your
2Co 3:18 **t.** into the same image from glory
TRANSFORMING, 2Co 11:14 Satan keeps **t.**
TRANSGRESS, Ps 17:3 mouth will not **t.**
TRANSGRESSED, Pr 18:19 brother **t.** against
Isa 43:27 your spokesmen have **t.** against me.
Jer 2:29; 33:8; La 3:42; Zep 3:11.
TRANSGRESSING, Isa 66:24 carcasses of **t.**
TRANSGRESSION(S), Job 31:33 covered over **t.**,
Ps 19:13 remained innocent from much **t.**
Pr 17:9 The one covering over **t.** is seeking
Isa 44:22 I will wipe out your **t.** just as
Isa 53:5 he was being pierced for our **t.;**
Eze 18:28 turns back from all his **t.** that
Da 9:24 seventy weeks to terminate **t.**
Mic 7:18 passing over **t.** of the remnant
Ro 4:15 where is no law, neither **t.**
Ga 3:19 Law? was added to make **t.** manifest,
Pr 29:16; Isa 59:20; Heb 2:2; 9:15.
TRANSGRESSION CAUSING DESOLATION,
Da 8:13 long will the vision be of the **t.**,
TRANSGRESSOR(S), Ps 37:38 **t.** will be
Ps 51:13 I will teach **t.** your ways,
Isa 53:12 with the **t.** he was counted in;
Isa 48:8; Da 8:23; Ro 2:25; Jas 2:11.
TRANSIENT, Ps 39:4 know how **t.** I am.
TRANSLATE, 1Co 14:13 in a tongue **t.**
1Co 14:27 speaks in a tongue, someone **t.**
TRANSLATED. See also TRANSFERRED.
TRANSLATED, Ezr 4:7; Joh 1:42; 9:7.
TRANSLATOR(S), 1Co 12:30 Not all are **t.**,
1Co 14:28 if there be no **t.**, let him keep
TRANSMITTED, Ac 7:53 Law **t.** by angels
Ga 3:19 it was **t.** through angels by the
TRANSPLANT, 1Co 13:2 to **t.** mountains,
TRANSPLANTED, Col 1:13 **t.** into kingdom
TRANSPORTATION, 2Ch 28:15 **t.** on asses
TRAP(S), Ps 11:6 rain down **t.**, fire and
Ps 38:12 those seeking my soul lay out **t.**
Ps 64:5 make statements about hiding **t.**
Jos 23:13; Ps 91:3; Jer 18:22; Ro 11:9.
TRAVAIL. See PAINS, CHILDBIRTH; PANGS.
TRAVELED, Mt 21:33; Lu 15:13; 20:9.

TRAVELER(S), Jg 19:17 **t.**, in the city.
Jer 9:2 in wilderness a lodging place of **t.!**
Jer 14:8 Israel like a **t.** turned aside to
TRAVELING MERCHANT(S), Mt 13:45.
TRAVERSE, Mt 23:15 **t.** sea and dry land
TREACHEROUS, Ps 119:158 **t.** in dealing
Pr 2:22 the **t.** will be torn away from it.
Isa 21:2 **t.** dealer is dealing treacherously,
TREACHEROUSLY, Pr 13:2 those dealing **t.**
Pr 21:18 one dealing **t.** takes the place of the
Isa 33:1 Woe to you dealing **t.**, without
Hab 1:13 you look on those dealing **t.**,
Hab 2:5 because the wine is dealing **t.**,
Mal 2:16 guard yourselves not deal **t.**
Pr 11:3; Isa 24:16; Jer 5:11; Mal 2:14.
TREACHERY, Jer 12:1 committing **t.** are
Zep 3:4 her prophets were men of **t.**
TREAD, Mal 4:3 **t.** down wicked ones,
Jos 1:3; Job 40:12; Ps 44:5; 60:12.
TREADING, Isa 28:28 keep **t.** it out.
Isa 63:3 I kept **t.** them in my anger,
Jer 25:30 shout those **t.** the wine press
TREASURE(S), Pr 2:4 as for hid **t.** keep
Isa 33:6 fear of Jehovah, which is his **t.**
Mt 6:20 store up **t.** in heaven,
Mt 6:21 **t.** is, there your heart will be
Mt 12:35 out of his good **t.** sends out good
Mt 13:44 kingdom like a **t.** hidden
2Co 4:7 we have this **t.** in earthen vessels,
Col 2:3 in him are all the **t.** of wisdom
Pr 10:2; Mt 19:21; Heb 11:26.
TREASURED, Job 23:12 **t.** up the sayings
Pr 13:22 wealth of the sinner is **t.** up for
TREASURY, Mt 12:41; Lu 21:1; Joh 8:20.
TREATMENT, 2Co 4:10 the death-dealing **t.**
Col 2:23 a severe **t.** of the body, but they
Isa 3:11; Joe 3:4, 7; Ob 15.
TREE(S), Ge 2:9 every **t.** desirable to one's
Ge 2:17 **t.** of the knowledge of good and bad
Jg 9:8 **t.** went to anoint a king over them.
Job 14:7 For there exists hope for even a **t.**
Ps 1:3 certainly become like a **t.** planted by
Ps 37:35 spreading as a luxuriant **t.**
Ec 11:3 **t.** falls there it will prove to be.
Isa 61:3 **t.** of righteousness, the planting
Isa 65:22 **t.** will the days of my people
Eze 17:24 abased high **t.** high the low **t.**,
Eze 47:7 many **t.**, on this side and on
Da 4:14 Chop the **t.** down, and cut off its
Mt 3:10 **t.** not produce fine fruit is cut
Mt 7:18 good **t.** cannot bear worthless fruit
Mt 24:32 from the fig **t.** as an illustration
Re 11:4 symbolized by the two olive **t.**
Pr 3:18; Isa 55:12; Lu 6:43; Re 7:3; 22:2.
TREE(S) OF LIFE, Ge 3:22 fruit of the **t.**
Pr 3:18 It is a **t.** to those taking hold and
Re 2:7 grant to eat of the **t.**
Re 22:19 God take his portion away from **t.**
Ge 2:9; Pr 11:30.
TREMBLE, Mic 4:4 no one making them **t.;**
Zep 3:13 will be no one making them **t.**
2Pe 2:10 do not **t.** at glorious ones but
TREMBLING, Jg 7:3 afraid and **t.?** Let
Ps 2:11 Serve Jehovah be joyful with **t.**
Isa 66:5 Hear you men who are **t.** at his word
Php 2:12 working salvation with fear and **t.**,
De 28:65; Job 4:14; Jer 30:5.
TREND, Eze 26:2 the **t.** will be to me
TRESPASS(ES), Mt 6:14 forgive men **t.**
Ro 4:25 delivered up for the sake of our **t.**
Ro 5:15 one man's **t.** many died,

Col 2:13 He kindly forgave us all our **t.**
Mr 11:25; 2Co 5:19; Eph 2:1.
TRIAL(S), Heb 11:36 others t. by mockings
Jas 1:12 the man that keeps enduring **t.,**
Jas 1:13 When under t., let no one say:
1Pe 4:12 which is happening to you for a **t.,**
2Pe 2:9 how to deliver people out of **t.,**
Lu 22:28; Ga 4:14; Jas 1:2.
TRIBE(S), Ge 49:28 are the twelve **t.**
Ps 122:4 t. have gone up, the **t.** of Jah,
Isa 49:6 raise up the **t.** of Jacob and to
Mt 19:28 thrones, judging the twelve **t.** of
Mt 24:30 all **t.** of the earth will beat in
Jas 1:1 to the twelve t. that are scattered
Re 1:7 all the **t.** of the earth will beat
Re 7:9 out of nations and t. and peoples
Ex 28:21; Ps 74:2; Heb 7:13; Re 21:12.
TRIBULATION(S), Mt 24:9 you up to **t.**
Mt 24:21 great **t.** such as not occurred
Joh 16:33 In world t., but cheer up!
Ro 12:12 hope ahead. Endure under **t.**
1Co 7:28 who do have **t.** in their flesh.
2Co 1:4 who comforts us in all our **t.**
2Co 4:17 t. is momentary and light
1Th 1:6 you accepted the word under much **t.**
2Th 1:6 repay **t.** to those who make **t.** for
Heb 10:33 exposed to reproaches and **t.,**
Heb 11:37 want, in t., under ill-treatment;
Jas 1:27 widows in their t. without spot from
Re 2:10 test, may have t. ten days.
Re 7:14 ones that come out of the great **t.,**
Mr 4:17; Ac 7:10; 14:22; 20:23; Ro 2:9;
5:3; 8:35; 2Co 6:4; Col 1:24; 1Th 3:3.
TRIBUNAL, 1Co 4:3 examined by a human **t.**
TRIBUTE, Ezr 7:24 no tax, t. or toll is
Ro 13:7 Render who calls for t., the **t.;**
Ezr 4:13; Ps 72:10.
TRICKERY, 2Co 12:16 I caught you by **t.**
TRICKINESS, Ps 101:7; Jer 8:5; 14:14.
TRICKLE, Isa 45:8 let skies t. with
TRICKY TONGUE, Zep 3:13 mouths a **t.;**
TRIED, Isa 28:16 t. stone, the precious
Heb 11:37 They were stoned, they were **t.,**
Jas 1:13 no one say: "I am being t. by God."
TRIFLE, Ex 8:29 not Pharaoh t. again
TRIFLED, Jg 16:10 you have t. with me
TRIFLES, 1Ti 6:5 disputes about t. on the
TRIPPING, Ro 14:13 or a cause for **t.**
TRIUMPH, Ps 41:11 not shout in t. over
Ps 47:1 Shout in t. to God with the sound
Ps 81:1 shout in t. to the God of Jacob.
TRIUMPHAL, 2Co 2:14 a t. procession in
Col 2:15 leading them in a t. procession
TRIUMPHANTLY, Jas 2:13 Mercy exults **t.**
TRIVIAL, 1Co 4:3 it is a t. matter that
1Ki 16:31; 2Ki 3:18; Isa 49:6.
TRODDEN, Isa 63:3 wine trough I have **t.**
Isa 25:10; Re 14:20.
TROOPS, 2Ch 25:10; Job 29:25.
TROUBLE, Ps 94:20 framing t. by decree?
Isa 53:11 Because of the t. of his soul
TROUBLESOME, Php 3:1 writing is not **t.**
TRUE, Ps 19:9 decisions of Jehovah **t.;**
Pr 14:25 A t. witness is delivering souls,
Joh 3:33 given his seal to it that God is **t.**
Joh 4:23 t. worshipers with spirit and truth
Ro 3:4 let God be found t., though every man
Re 3:14 the faithful and t. witness,
Joh 1:9; 15:1; 17:3; 1Jo 5:20; Re 19:11.
TRUENESS, Ps 40:10 hidden your **t.**

Ps 91:4 t. will be a shield and bulwark.
Ps 117:2 t. of Jehovah is to time indefinite
Ps 85:10, 11; Zec 8:3.
TRUMPET(S), Mt 6:2 gifts not blow a **t.**
1Co 14:8 t. sounds an indistinct call, who
1Co 15:52 eye, during the last **t.**
1Th 4:16 descend with God's **t.,**
Heb 12:19; Re 8:2.
TRUMPET SOUND, Mt 24:31 angels with a **t.**
TRUST, Ps 56:11 In God I have put my **t.**
Ps 146:3 Do not put your t. in
Pr 3:5 T. in Jehovah with all your heart
Isa 26:3 peace, because one is made to **t.**
Isa 31:1 Woe who t. in war chariots, because
Jer 7:4 not put your t. in fallacious words,
Jer 17:5 Cursed is the man who puts t. in
Mic 7:5 Do not put your t. in a friend
2Co 1:9 t., not in ourselves, but in God
2Ti 1:14 This fine t. guard through spirit
Ps 9:10; Pr 3:5; Isa 12:2.
TRUSTING, Ps 84:12 happy man t. in you.
Pr 11:28 one t. in his riches—he will fall,
Pr 29:25 t. in Jehovah will be protected.
Ps 32:10; 49:6; Pr 28:26; Jer 46:25.
TRUSTWORTHY, Ps 19:7 reminder of God is **t.,**
Ps 78:8 whose spirit was not t. with God.
Da 2:45 interpretation of it is **t.**
TRUTH, Ps 43:3 Send out your light and **t.**
Ps 119:160 substance of your word is **t.,**
Pr 23:23 Buy t. itself and do not sell it—
Isa 43:9 hear and say, 'It is the **t.!'**
Jer 10:10 But Jehovah is in t. God.
Joh 4:24 must worship with spirit and **t.**
Joh 8:32 t., and the t. will set you free.
Joh 14:6 I am the way and the t. and the
Joh 17:17 Sanctify by t.; your word is **t.**
Joh 18:37 I should bear witness to the **t.**
1Co 5:8 cakes of sincerity and **t.**
2Co 13:8 we can do nothing against the **t.,**
Eph 6:14 your loins girded about with **t.,**
2Th 2:10 did not accept the love of the **t.**
1Ti 2:7 teacher of nations in faith and **t.**
1Ti 3:15 a pillar and support of the **t.**
2Ti 2:15 handling the word of t. aright.
Heb 10:26 accurate knowledge of the **t.,**
2Pe 1:12 set in the **t.** that is present
Joh 8:44; Ro 1:25; 2Ti 3:7.
TRUTHFUL, 2Co 6:8 as deceivers yet **t.,**
TRUTHFULLY, Zec 8:16 Speak t. with one
TRUTHFULNESS, Ps 51:6 delight in **t.**
TUBERCULOSIS, Le 26:16; De 28:22.
TUMULT, Ps 2:1 nations been in **t.**
Ac 21:34 unable because of the t., he
TUMULTUOUS, Ac 4:25 nations become **t.**
TUNNEL, 2Sa 5:8 Jebusites by the water **t.**
TURMOIL, 1Sa 4:14; Ps 65:7.
TURN, Pr 22:6 old he will not t. aside
Isa 14:27 his hand who can t. it back?
Ro 11:26 t. away ungodly practices
TURNING, Isa 28:6 t. the battle from
Ga 4:9 you are t. back again to the weak
TURNS, Jas 5:20 he who t. a sinner back
TURQUOISE, Ex 28:18; Eze 27:16; 28:13.
TUTOR(S), 1Co 4:15 ten thousand t. in
Ga 3:24 Law has become our t. to Christ
TWELVE, Ge 49:28 are the t. tribes of
Mt 10:2 the names of the t. apostles are
Jas 1:1 to the t. tribes that are scattered
TWICE AS MUCH, Re 18:6 Render to her **t.**
TWIG(S), Isa 11:1 t. out of Jesse,

Isa 53:2 he will come up like a t.
Joe 1:7 The t. of it have become white.
TWIN(S), Ge 25:24; 38:27; Joh 11:16; 20:24.
TWINKLING, 1Co 15:52 t. of an eye,
TWISTED, De 32:5 generation crooked and t.
Pr 12:8 one who is t. at heart will come
Isa 24:1 he has t. the face of it
Mt 17:17 O faithless and t. generation,
Ac 20:30 men will rise and speak t. things
Php 2:15 among a crooked and t. generation,
TWISTING, 2Pe 3:16 t. the Scriptures,
TWO-EDGED, Ps 149:6 t. sword in their
Heb 4:12 word is sharper than any t. sword
TWO PARTS, 2Ki 2:9 t. in your spirit
TYPICAL REPRESENTATION(S), Heb 8:5.
TYRANNICALLY, De 24:7 he has dealt t.
TYRANNICAL ONES, Ps 86:14; Jer 15:21.
TYRANNIZE, Isa 3:5 people t. one over
TYRANNY, Ex 1:13; Le 25:43; Eze 34:4.
TYRANT(S), Job 27:13 inheritance of t.
Pr 11:16 the t. take hold of riches.
TYRE, Isa 23:1 pronouncement of T.:
Isa 23:17 Jehovah turn his attention to T.,
2Sa 5:11; 1Ki 7:13; Ps 45:12; Eze 27:2.

U

ULCER(S), Ho 5:13; Lu 16:21; Re 16:2, 11.
UNACQUAINTED, Heb 5:13 of milk is u.
UNADULTERATED, 1Pe 2:2 u. milk to word
UNANIMOUSLY, Ex 19:8; 1Ki 22:13.
UNAPPROACHABLE, 1Ti 6:16 in u. light,
UNATTAINABLE, Ge 11:6 nothing u. for
Job 42:2 no idea that is u. for you.
UNBELIEF. See LACK OF FAITH.
UNBELIEVABLE, Ac 26:8 why judged u.
UNBELIEVER(S), 1Co 6:6 court before u.?
1Co 14:22 tongues are for a sign to u.
2Co 4:4 blinded the minds of the u.,
2Co 6:14 not become unevenly yoked with u.
2Co 6:15 faithful person have with an u.?
UNBELIEVING, 1Co 7:12 u. wife, yet she
1Co 7:14 the u. husband is sanctified in
UNBLAMABLE, Job 12:4 laughingstock is u. one
1Th 2:10 righteous and u. we proved to be
1Th 3:13 u. in holiness before our God and
UNBLEMISHED, Jude 24 to set you u.
Col 1:22; 1Pe 1:19.
UNCANNY, 1Sa 15:23; Isa 1:13; Am 5:5.
UNCERTAIN, 2Co 1:8 u. even of our lives.
1Ti 6:17 not on u. riches, but on God
UNCERTAINLY, 1Co 9:26 running is not u.,
UNCHANGEABLE, Heb 6:18 two u. things
UNCHANGEABLENESS, Heb 6:17 u. of his
UNCIRCUMCISED, Isa 52:1 no more u.
Ac 7:51 Obstinate men and u. in hearts
Le 26:41; Eze 32:24; Hab 2:16; 1Co 7:18.
UNCIRCUMCISION, Ga 5:6 nor is u., but
Ro 2:25, 26; 1Co 7:19; Col 3:11.
UNCLE, Le 20:20; 25:49; 1Sa 10:15.
UNCLEAN, Job 14:4 out of someone u.?
Isa 6:5 a man u. in lips I am
Isa 35:8 the u. will not pass over it.
Isa 52:1 no more will there come u. one,
Isa 64:6 we become like someone u.,
1Co 7:14 your children would really be u.,
2Co 6:17 quit touching the u. thing,
Re 16:13 three u. inspired expressions
Le 11:8; Hag 2:13; Ac 10:14; Re 18:2.

UNCLEANNESS, La 1:9 u. is in her skirts.
Mt 23:27 full of every sort of u.
Ro 1:24 God gave them up to u.
1Th 4:7 called us, not with allowance for u.,
Eze 39:24; Ro 6:19; Eph 5:3.
UNCONCERNED, Mt 22:5 u. they went off
UNCONDEMNED, Ac 22:25 scourge an u. man
UNCORRUPTNESS, Tit 2:7 u. in teaching,
UNCOVERING, Pr 11:13 u. confidential talk
UNCTION. See ANOINTING.
UNDEFILED, Heb 7:26 u. separated from
Jas 1:27 worship that is clean and u.
1Pe 1:4 u. and unfading inheritance.
UNDERESTIMATED, Ezr 9:13 u. our error
UNDERGO, 2Th 1:9 u. the judicial punishment
UNDERHANDED, 2Co 4:2 renounced the u.
UNDERSTAND, Ps 119:27 Make me u. the
Ps 119:34 Make me u., that I may observe
Pr 28:5 those seeking Jehovah u. everything.
Isa 6:9 Hear but do not u.,
Da 12:8 I heard, but I could not u.;
Da 12:10 no wicked ones at all will u.;
Job 6:24; Ps 82:5; Isa 43:10; Heb 11:3.
UNDERSTANDING, Job 32:8 gives them u.
Ps 119:104 orders I behave with u.
Ps 147:5 His u. is beyond recounting.
Pr 3:5 do not lean upon your own u.
Pr 9:10 knowledge of the Most Holy One is u.
Isa 29:14 u. of discreet men will conceal
1Co 14:20 children in powers of u.
1Ch 22:12; Pr 4:7; Jas 3:13.
UNDERSTOOD, 1Co 14:9 utter speech easily u.,
UNDERTONE, Jos 1:8 in an u. read in it
Ps 1:2 in his law he reads in an u.
Ps 71:24 utter in an u. your righteousness.
UNDESERVED KINDNESS, Joh 1:17; Ro 5:15.
Ro 5:21 u. might rule as king through
Ro 11:6 if by u. it is no longer due to
2Co 12:9 My u. is sufficient for you
Eph 2:8 By u. you have been saved
Heb 2:9 by God's u. might taste death
Heb 4:16 Let us approach the throne of u.
Jas 4:6 he gives u. to the humble ones
2Co 6:1; Heb 10:29; 12:28.
UNDISTURBED, Pr 1:33 be u. from dread
Isa 30:15 to be simply in keeping u.
UNEASINESS, Pr 23:29 Who has u.?
UNEMPLOYED, Mt 20:3 others standing u.
Tit 1:12 injurious wild beasts, u. gluttons.
UNFADABLE CROWN, 1Pe 5:4 u. of glory.
UNFADING, 1Pe 1:4 u. inheritance.
UNFAITHFUL, Lu 12:46 a part with the u.
2Ti 2:13 if we are u., he remains faithful,
UNFAITHFULNESS, 1Ch 10:13 Saul for his u.
Jos 7:1; 22:22; Eze 17:20; 18:24.
UNFATHOMABLE, Eph 3:8 the u. riches of
UNFERMENTED, Ex 13:6 Seven days eat u.
Le 2:4 u. ring-shaped cakes moistened
Mt 26:17 first day of the U. Cakes
1Co 5:8 with u. cakes of sincerity
Ex 12:17; Jg 6:21; 1Sa 28:24.
UNFORESEEN OCCURRENCE, Ec 9:11 u. befall
UNFRUITFUL, Tit 3:14 may not be u.
2Pe 1:8 inactive or u.
Mt 13:22; 1Co 14:14; Eph 5:11.
UNGENEROUS, De 15:9 fear you become u.
Pr 23:6 food of anyone of u. eye
UNGIRD, Isa 45:1 u. hips of kings
UNGODLINESS, Ro 1:18 is against all u.

2Ti 2:16 they will advance to more **u.**,
Tit 2:12 instructing us to repudiate **u.** and
UNGODLY, Ro 5:6 Christ died for **u.** men
Ro 11:26 turn away **u.** practices from Jacob.
1Ti 1:9 law is for **u.** and sinners,
1Pe 4:18; 2Pe 2:6; 3:7; Jude 15.
UNGROOMED, Le 10:6 not heads go **u.**
UNHEALABLE, Mic 1:9 stroke is **u.**;
Na 3:19 Your stroke has become **u.**
UNHYPOCRITICAL, 1Pe 1:22 **u.** love
UNIFY, Ps 86:11 **U.** my heart to fear
UNINJURED, Job 9:4 and come off **u.**
UNINTELLIGENT, Ro 1:21 **u.** heart became
UNINTELLIGIBLY, Ps 114:1 speaking **u.**,
UNINTENTIONALLY, Nu 15:29; Jos 20:3.
Nu 35:11 fatally strikes a soul **u.**
UNION, Zec 11:7 the other I called **U.**
1Co 1:30 you are in **u.** with Christ Jesus,
2Co 5:17 **u.** with Christ, is a new creation;
Col 3:14 love is a perfect bond of **u.**
UNIQUE, Eze 7:5 a **u.** calamity is coming
UNISON, Isa 52:8 in **u.** crying joyfully
UNITED, Ro 6:5 **u.** with him in the
1Co 1:10 fitly **u.** in the same mind and same
Ge 49:6; Isa 14:20.
UNITING, Eph 4:3 the **u.** bond of peace.
UNITY, Ps 133:1 brothers to dwell in **u.**!
Mic 2:12 in **u.** I shall set them like flock
Isa 45:21; Ho 1:11.
UNJUST, Ex 18:21 men, hating **u.** profit,
Pr 15:27 one making **u.** profit is troubling
Jer 2:5; Ro 3:5.
UNJUSTLY, 1Pe 2:19 suffers **u.**, this is
UNKNOWN, Ac 17:23 To an **U.** God.
Heb 13:2 **u.** to themselves, entertained
2Co 6:9; Ga 1:22.
UNLEAVENED. See UNFERMENTED.
UNLETTERED, Ac 4:13 **u.** and ordinary,
UNLUCKY, Nu 23:23; 24:1.
UNMARRIED, 1Co 7:8 I say to **u.** persons and
1Co 7:11 let her remain **u.** or else make up
1Co 7:32 The **u.** man is anxious for the Lord,
1Co 7:34 the **u.** woman, and the virgin, is
UNNATURAL, 1Co 6:9 men kept for **u.**
Jude 7 gone out after flesh for **u.** use,
UNOCCUPIED, 1Ti 5:13 **u.**, gadding about,
UNPRINCIPLED, Isa 32:5 as for the **u.** man
Isa 32:7 **u.** man, his instruments are bad;
UNPROFITABLE, Mt 12:36 every **u.** saying
Tit 3:9 foolish questionings are **u.**
UNPROFITABLENESS, Eph 4:17 **u.** of minds,
UNPUNISHED, Ex 20:7 not leave one **u.**
Jer 30:11; 49:12.
UNQUESTIONABLY, 2Sa 12:14 **u.** disrespect
UNREALITY, Isa 40:17 nations are as an **u.**
Isa 41:29; 44:9; 59:4.
UNREASONABLE, Lu 12:20 **U.** one, this
Lu 11:40; 1Co 15:36; 2Co 11:16; 1Pe 2:15.
UNREASONABLENESS, 2Co 11:1 put up with **u.**
UNREASONING, 2Pe 2:12 like **u.** animals
Ps 49:10; 73:22; 92:6; 94:8; Pr 12:1; 30:2.
UNREASONINGLY, Jer 10:14, 21 behaved so **u.**
UNRECEPTIVE, Isa 6:10 make heart **u.**
UNRECOGNIZABLE, Pr 26:24 hater makes **u.**,
Jer 19:4 proceeded to make this place **u.**
UNRESPONSIVE, Ex 7:14 Pharaoh's heart **u.**
1Sa 6:6 make your heart **u.**
Isa 6:10 make their ears **u.**

UNRESTRAINED, 1Sa 2:3 nothing **u.** from
Ex 32:25; Pr 29:18.
UNRESTRAINT, 2Ch 28:19 let **u.** grow in
UNRIGHTEOUS, Ac 24:15 righteous and **u.**
1Co 6:9 **u.** will not inherit God's kingdom?
Heb 6:10 God is not **u.** to forget your work
1Pe 3:18 a righteous person for **u.** ones,
UNRIGHTEOUSNESS, Ps 92:15 is no **u.**
Zep 3:5 Jehovah would do no **u.**
1Jo 5:17 All **u.** is sin;
Re 22:11 He that is doing **u.**, let him do **u.**
UNRULY, 1Ti 1:9; Tit 1:6, 10.
UNSEARCHABLE, Ro 11:33 How **u.** his
Job 5:9; 9:10; Ps 145:3; Pr 25:3.
UNSEEN, 2Co 4:18 eyes on the things **u.**
UNSKILLED, 2Co 11:6 I am **u.** in speech,
UNSTEADILY, Ps 38:16 my foot moved **u.**,
Isa 24:20 land moves **u.** like a drunken
Isa 29:9 moved **u.** but not because of liquor.
UNSTEADY, Jas 1:8 indecisive man, **u.** in
UNSTOPPED, Isa 35:5 ears of deaf **u.**
UNSUSPECTEDLY, Ge 34:25 **u.** and kill
UNSUSPECTING, Jg 18:27 quiet and **u.**
UNTAUGHT, 2Pe 3:16 letters **u.** are twisting
UNTOUCHED, Ro 15:23 no **u.** territory
UNTRUE, Eze 13:6, 7 visioned what is **u.**
UNTRUTH, Ps 12:2 **U.** they keep speaking
Ps 41:6 **u.** is what his heart will speak;
Pr 30:8 **U.** and the lying word put far away
UNUTTERABLE, 2Co 12:4 heard **u.** words
UNVEILED, 2Co 3:18 with **u.** faces reflect like
UNWAVERING, 2Co 1:7 hope for you is **u.**,
UNWORRIED, Jer 12:1 treachery are **u.** ones
UNWORTHILY, 1Co 11:27 cup of the Lord **u.**
UNWORTHY, Ge 32:10 I am **u.** of the
UPBUILDING, Ro 15:2 what is good for **u.**
1Co 14:26 Let all things take place for **u.**
Ro 14:19; 1Co 14:12; 2Co 12:19.
UPBUILDS, 1Co 14:3 prophesies **u.** men
1Co 14:4 he that prophesies **u.** a congregation.
UPPER CHAMBER, Ac 1:13; 9:37; 20:8.
UPRIGHT, 2Ki 10:15 Is your heart **u.**
Job 1:8 man blameless and **u.**, fearing
Ps 11:7 The **u.** will behold his face.
Ps 19:8 The orders from Jehovah are **u.**
Ps 49:14 **u.** will have them in subjection
Ps 97:11 rejoicing for the **u.** in heart.
Pr 2:21 **u.** will reside in the earth,
Pr 12:6 mouth of the **u.** will deliver them.
Pr 14:12 There exists a way that is **u.**
Pr 15:8 prayer of the **u.** is a pleasure
Pr 16:25 way that is **u.** before a man, but
Ec 7:29 God made mankind **u.**,
Mic 7:2 among mankind there is no **u.**
UPRIGHTLY, Mic 2:7 one walking **u.**?
UPRIGHTNESS, Job 6:25 sayings of **u.**
Job 33:23 To tell to man his **u.**,
Ps 25:21 Let **u.** safeguard me,
1Ch 29:17; Job 33:3; Ps 143:10; Pr 14:2.
UPROAR, Ps 83:2 enemies are in an **u.**,
Isa 13:4 The **u.** of kingdoms, of nations
UPROOTED, Mt 15:13; Lu 17:6; Jude 12.
UPSIDE DOWN, 2Ki 21:13 turning it **u.**
UPWARD, Php 3:14 prize of the **u.** call
UR, Ge 11:28; 15:7.
URGE, Ex 12:33 Egyptians began to **u.**
URGENT, 1Sa 21:8 matter proved to be **U.**
URGENTLY, 2Ti 4:2 at it **u.** in favorable

URIJAH, Jer 26:21 U. became afraid
URIM AND THUMMIM, Ex 28:30; Ezr 2:63.
USE, 1Co 7:31 making u. of the world
USURY, Le 25:36; Ne 5:7.
UTENSILS, Isa 52:11 the u. of Jehovah.
1Ch 22:19; 2Ch 36:7.
UTMOST, 2Ti 2:15 Do your u. to present
Heb 4:11 do our u. to enter into that rest,
2Pe 1:10 do your u. to make the calling
2Pe 3:14 do your u. to be found spotless
UTTERANCE, Mt 4:4 alone, but on every u.
Col 4:6 Let your u. be seasoned with salt,
UZZAH, 2Sa 6:6 U. grabbed hold of the ark
UZZIAH, 2Ch 26:21 king U. became leper
2Ch 26:1; Isa 6:1; Mt 1:8.

V

VACANT, 1Sa 20:18, 27 seat will be v.
VAIN, Ec 7:15 seen during my v. days.
Ec 9:9 all the days of your v. life that
Zec 10:2 and in v. they try to comfort.
Mt 15:9 in v. they keep worshiping me,
1Co 15:58 labor is not in v. with the Lord.
Ga 2:2 for fear that I was running in v.
Php 2:16 I did not run in v. or work in v.
VAIN IDOL(S), Ps 31:6 worthless v.,
De 32:21; 1Ki 16:13; 2Ki 17:15; Jer 2:5.
VALIANT, Jg 6:12 you, v., mighty one.
Jg 11:1 Jephthah had become a v. man,
2Ch 26:17 eighty v. men, came in after him.
Heb 11:34 become v. in war, routed
1Sa 16:18; 1Ki 11:28; 2Ki 5:1; 1Ch 7:5.
VALID, Heb 9:17 v. over dead victims,
VALIDATED, Ga 3:15 A v. covenant,
Ga 3:17 covenant previously v. by God, the
VALLEY, Ps 23:4 v. of deep shadow,
Isa 40:4 Let every v. be raised up,
Eze 37:1 v. was full of bones.
VALLEY OF GOG'S CROWD, Eze 39:11, 15.
VALOROUS, Eze 27:11 v. men in towers.
VALUABLE THINGS, Pr 11:4 V. will be of
Pr 3:9; 28:22.
VALUE(S), Pr 18:8 hereditary v.
Pr 31:10 capable wife? Her v. is far more
Mt 13:46 finding one pearl of high v.,
Php 3:8 loss on account of the excelling v.
Heb 10:29 esteemed as of ordinary v.
1Pe 1:7 faith, of greater v. than gold
1Pe 3:4 great v. in the eyes of God.
VALUELESS, Pr 12:11 pursuing v. things
Isa 1:13 Stop bringing v. grain offerings.
VANISHING, Heb 8:13 covenant old is v.
VANITY, Pr 13:11 resulting from v.
Ec 3:19 no superiority everything is v.
Ec 1:2; 4:4; 11:10; Isa 49:4; Jer 10:15.
VANQUISHED, Ex 17:13; Job 14:10.
VAPOR(S), Ps 135:7 v. to ascend
Jer 10:13 v. to ascend
VAPOROUS CLOUDS, Pr 25:14 v. is a man
VARIATION, Jas 1:17 there is not a v.
VARIETIES, 1Co 12:4 v. of gifts,
VATS, Joe 2:24; 3:13; Zec 14:10.
VAULT(S), Jg 9:49; 1Sa 13:6; Job 22:14.
VEGETABLES, Ro 14:2 man eats v.
VEGETATION, Ge 1:11 v. bearing seed,
Ps 92:7 the wicked ones sprout as the v.
Mic 5:7 like copious showers upon v.,
Heb 6:7 ground brings forth v. suitable
Re 9:4 harm no v. of the earth nor any

VEHEMENTLY, Jg 8:1 v. tried to pick a
Lu 23:10 v. accusing him.
VEIL, Ex 34:35 Moses put the v. over
2Co 3:13-16.
VEILED, 2Co 4:3 v. among those perishing,
VENERATED, Ro 1:25 v. and rendered
VENGEANCE, Ge 4:15 v. seven times.
De 32:35 V. is mine,
Isa 34:8 Jehovah has a day of v.,
Isa 61:2 to proclaim the day of v.
2Th 1:8 [Jesus] brings v. upon those
De 32:41, 43; Jer 50:28; Na 1:2; Ro 12:19.
VENISON, Ge 27:3 hunt some v. for me.
VENOM, Job 6:4; Ps 58:4; 140:3.
VENTS, Ro 3:5 when he v. his wrath,
VENTURE, Ro 15:18 I will not v. to tell
VENTURING, Heb 11:29 v. out Egyptians
VERBALLY, 1Co 14:19 five words v., than ten
VERIFIED, Heb 2:3 salvation was v. for
VESSEL(S), Ps 2:9 potter's v. you will
Jer 25:34 fall like a desirable v.
Ac 9:15 this man is a chosen v. to me to
Ro 9:21 one v. for an honorable use, another
Ro 9:22 v. of wrath fit for destruction,
2Co 4:7 treasure in earthen v., that the
Re 2:27 broken to pieces like clay v.,
VESTIBULE, Mr 14:68 outside to the v.
VEXATION, Job 6:2 that v. were weighed
Ps 6:7 From v. my eye has become weak,
Pr 17:25 stupid son is a v. to his father
Ec 1:18 there is an abundance of v.,
Ec 7:3 Better is v. than laughter,
VEXED, 1Sa 1:6; Ps 112:10.
VICTORIOUS, Ro 8:37 in all things v.
Re 15:2 v. from the beast and its image
VICTORY, 1Co 15:55 where is your v.?
1Co 15:57 he gives us v. through our Lord
VIEW, Ro 5:21 everlasting life in v.
VIEWED, 1Jo 1:1 v. attentively and our
VIEWPOINT, 1Sa 18:8 bad from his v.,
VIGIL, Job 21:32 over a tomb a v. be kept
VIGILANT, 1Pe 4:7 be v. with a view to
VIGOROUS, Ps 89:8 Who is v. like you, O
VIGOROUSLY, Lu 13:24 Exert yourselves v.
VILE, Joh 5:29 practiced v. things
Tit 2:8 having nothing v. to say about us.
Joh 3:20; Ro 9:11; 2Co 5:10; Jas 3:16.
VILLAGE(S), Mt 9:35; 10:11; Mr 6:6.
VILLAINY, Ac 13:10 every sort of v.,
VINDICTIVE JUSTICE, Ac 28:4 v. did not
VINE, Jer 2:21 planted you as a red v.,
Joe 2:22 v. must give vital energy.
Mic 4:4 each one under his v. and fig tree,
Joh 15:1 I am the true v., and my Father
Re 14:18 gather the v. of the earth,
Jg 9:13; Eze 17:8; Zec 8:12; Mt 26:29.
VINEDRESSERS, 2Ki 25:12; Isa 61:5.
VINEGAR, Pr 10:26 As v. to the teeth and as
VINEYARD(S), Isa 5:7 v. of Jehovah is the
Isa 65:21 they will plant v. and eat
Zep 1:13 plant v., but not drink wine
Mt 20:1 to hire workers for his v.
Lu 20:9 A man planted a v. and let it
Jer 12:10; Eze 28:26; Am 9:14; Mt 21:28.
VIOLATE, 2Ti 2:16 empty speeches that v.
1Ti 4:7; 6:20 v. what is holy
VIOLATED, Le 21:7, 14 or a v. woman
VIOLATION, Le 18:23 v. what is natural.

1Ti 3:8 servants not giving to a lot of w.,
1Ti 5:23 use a little w. for your stomach
Re 18:3 passion-arousing w. of her
Jg 13:4; Jer 35:6; Mt 9:17; Eph 5:18.
WINE PRESS, Jg 6:11 wheat in the w.
Joe 3:13 for the w. has become full.
Re 19:15 treads the w. of the anger of God
WINESKINS, Mt 9:17; Mr 2:22; Lu 5:37.
WINE TROUGH, Isa 63:3 w. I have trodden
WINGS, Ru 2:12 under whose w. you have
Ps 18:10 darting upon the w. of a spirit.
Mal 4:2 with healing in its w.;
Re 12:14 the two w. of the great eagle
WINKING, Pr 6:13 w. with his eye, signs
WINNER, 1Sa 26:25 come off the w.
WINNING, Pr 11:30 he that is w. souls
WINNOWING, Ru 3:2; Jer 4:11; Mt 3:12.
WINTER, Ge 8:22 summer, w., never cease
Ps 74:17 Summer and w.—you formed them.
Zec 14:8 In summer and w. it will occur
WINTERTIME, Mt 24:20 flight not in w.
WIPE, Ex 32:33 w. him out of my book
2Ki 21:13 w. Jerusalem clean just as one
Ps 51:1 w. out my transgressions
Jer 18:23 do not w. out that sin of theirs
Re 21:4 w. out every tear from their eyes,
Ge 6:7; De 9:14; Isa 25:8; Lu 10:11.
WIPED, Ps 69:28 w. out of book of
Joh 12:3 w. his feet dry
WISDOM, Ps 111:10 fear is beginning of w.
Pr 1:20 w. itself keeps crying aloud in the
Pr 2:7 upright treasure up practical w.
Pr 4:7 W. is the prime thing
Pr 8:11 w. is better than corals.
Ec 7:11 W. is good and is advantageous for
Isa 29:14 w. of their wise men must perish,
Jer 8:9 what w. do they have?
Eze 28:17 You brought your w. to ruin
Da 1:17 God gave insight in all w.;
Da 2:21 giving w. to the wise ones and
Mt 11:19 w. is righteous by its works.
Lu 16:8 he acted with practical w.,
1Co 2:5 faith not in men's w., but God's
1Co 3:19 w. of this world is foolishness
Jas 1:5 if anyone is lacking in w., let him
Jas 3:17 the w. from above is peaceable,
De 4:6; Pr 3:13; 24:3; 29:15; Ro 11:33.
WISE. See also DISCREET, SHREWD.
WISE, Ps 19:7 making the inexperienced one w.
Ps 49:10 even the w. ones die,
Pr 3:7 Do not become w. in your own eyes.
Pr 15:20 w. son makes a father rejoice,
Pr 27:11 Be w., my son, and make my heart
Pr 30:24 they are instinctively w.; the ants
Mt 11:25 hidden these things from the w.
2Ti 3:15 writings able to make you w.
Pr 1:5; Ro 1:22; Eph 5:15.
WISER, Ps 119:98 W. than my enemies
Pr 9:9 give to a wise person still w.
1Co 1:25 foolish thing of God is w. than
Job 35:11; Pr 26:16; Lu 16:8.
WISH, Ro 7:21 when I w. to do right,
WISHES, Ro 9:18 whom he w. he has mercy,
Re 22:17 anyone that w. take life's water
WITCH. See SORCER(ERS) (ESS).
WITCHCRAFT. See DIVINATION.
WITHDREW, Mt 2:12; 14:13; Mr 3:7.
WITHERED, Mt 13:6; 21:19; 1Pe 1:24.
WITHERS, Jas 1:11 sun w. the vegetation,
WITHIN, Ro 7:22 the man I am w.,
WITNESS, Ge 31:48 heap is a w. between
Ex 20:16 must not testify falsely as a w.
Job 16:19 my w. is in the heights.
Pr 14:25 A true w. is delivering souls,

Isa 19:20 be for a sign and for a w. to
Mic 1:2 Jehovah serve against you as a w.,
Mt 10:18 before kings for a w.
Mt 24:14 kingdom preached for a w.
Joh 4:44 Jesus bore w. that in his home
Joh 8:17 The w. of two men is true.
Joh 18:37 that I should bear w. to truth.
Ac 20:26 I call you to w. that I am clean
Ac 22:15 you are to be a w. for him to a
Ro 8:16 The spirit itself bears w. with
1Ti 6:13 Christ Jesus, who as a w. made
2Ti 1:8 do not become ashamed of the w.
1Jo 5:7 For there are three w. bearers,
Re 1:5 Jesus Christ, the Faithful W.,
Re 12:17 work of bearing w. to Jesus.
Re 20:4 executed with the ax for the w.
WITNESSED, 1Ti 2:6 w. to at its own
Heb 7:8 man of whom it is w. that he live
WITNESSES, De 19:15 mouth of two w.
Jos 24:22 chosen Jehovah. We are w.
Isa 43:10 You are my w., is the utterance
Isa 44:8 And you are my w.
Ac 1:8 you will be w. of me both in
Ac 10:39 we are w. of all the things he
Ac 13:31 who are now his w. to
1Co 15:15 we are also found false w. of God
Heb 12:1 we have so great a cloud of w.
Re 11:3 cause my two w. to prophesy a
Re 17:6 blood of the w. of Jesus.
WITNESSING, Ac 18:5; Re 19:10.
WITNESS WORK, Re 6:9 because of w. that
WIVES, Ge 6:2 they went to taking w.
Eph 5:22 Let w. be in subjection to their
De 29:11; 1Ki 11:3, 4; 2Ch 20:13.
WOBBLING, Isa 35:3 knees that are w.
WOE, Isa 6:5 W. to me! For I am as good
Isa 31:1 W. to those going down to Egypt
Am 6:1 W. to those who are at ease in Zi
1Co 9:16 w. is me if I did not declare t
Re 12:12 W. for the earth and for the sea
WOLF, Isa 11:6 w. will reside with lamb
Joh 10:12 beholds the w. coming abandons
WOLVES, Eze 22:27 princes like w. tearing
Mt 10:16 you forth as sheep amidst w.;
Ac 20:29 oppressive w. will enter in amon
WOMAN, Ge 2:22 build the rib into a w.
Ge 3:15 between you and the w.
Le 18:23 w. should not stand before a bea
Joh 2:4 What have I to do with you, w.?
Joh 19:26 Jesus to his mother: "W. see!
1Co 11:3 head of a w. is the man
1Co 11:10 w. ought to have a sign of
1Co 11:12 just as the w. is out of the man
1Ti 2:11, 12 w. in silence, not teach, authorit
Re 12:1 a w. arrayed with the sun,
Re 12:17 dragon grew wrathful at the w.,
Re 17:3 w. sitting upon a wild beast
WOMB, Ps 110:3 from the w. of the dawn
Joh 3:4; Ga 1:15.
WOMEN, Jg 5:24 Jael blessed among w.
2Sa 1:26 More than the love from w.
Jer 51:30 men of Babylon have become w.
1Co 14:34 let the w. keep silent
Tit 2:4 recall w. to love their husbands
Re 14:4 not defile themselves with w.;
De 31:12; Da 11:37; Mt 11:11; 24:41.
WON, 1Pe 3:1 husbands may be w. throug
WONDER(S). See also PORTENT(S).
WONDER(S), Da 4:3 how mighty his w. are
2Th 1:10 to be regarded in that day with w
WONDERFUL, 1Ch 16:9 with his w. acts.
Job 42:3 Things too w. for me which
Ps 26:7 declare all your w. works.
Ps 31:21 he has rendered w. loving-kindnes

Ezr 6:12 commit a v. and destroy that
VIOLENCE, Ps 73:6 V. envelops them as
Isa 53:9 Despite the fact he had done no v.
Isa 60:18 No more will v. be heard in
Eze 7:23 city has become full of v.
Eze 28:16 filled the midst of you with v.,
Ge 6:11; Ps 11:5; Zep 1:9; Mal 2:16.
VIOLENT, Ec 5:8 v. taking away of
VIPER(S), Mt 23:33 offspring of v.,
Isa 30:6; 59:5; Mt 3:7; 12:34.
VIRGIN(S), Ps 45:14 The v. in her train
Isa 47:1 O v. daughter of Babylon.
Mt 25:1 the kingdom will become like ten v.
1Co 7:25 concerning v. I have no command
2Co 11:2 present you as a chaste v. to
VIRGINITY, Jg 11:37 weep over my v.,
1Co 7:36 behaving improperly toward his v.,
VIRTUE, 1Co 11:25 new covenant by v.
Php 4:8 whatever v. there is consider
Php 4:3 strength by v. of him who imparts
1Pe 1:3 called us through glory and
2Pe 1:5 supply to your faith v., to your v.
VISIBLE, Da 4:11, 20 tree was v. to the
Mt 27:53 they became v. to many people.
Ac 26:16 I have made myself v. to you,
Col 1:16 things v. and the things invisible,
VISION(S), Pr 29:18 Where there is no v.
Eze 13:16 the prophets are visioning a v.
Joe 2:28 young men, v. they will see.
Hab 2:3 v. is yet for the appointed time,
Zec 13:4 ashamed, each one of his v.
Mt 17:9 Tell the v. to no one until the
Eze 1:1; Da 10:14; Mic 3:6; Ac 16:9.
VISIONARIES, 2Ch 33:19 words of his v.
Isa 29:10 has covered your heads, the v.
Mic 3:7 v. will have to be ashamed
VISIONARY, 2Sa 24:11 Gad David's v.
2Ki 17:13; 1Ch 25:5; 2Ch 9:29; 35:15.
VISIONING, Eze 13:9, 16 prophets v. untruth
VISIT, Lu 1:78 daybreak will v. us from
Ac 15:36 let us return and v. the brothers
VISITATION. See ATTENTION, INSPECTION.
VITAL ENERGY, Ps 60:12 By God gain v.,
Pr 31:3 Do not give your v. to women,
Joe 2:22 vine must give their v.
Na 2:3 men of v. are dressed in crimson
Ps 84:7; 118:15; Jer 48:14.
VITAL FORCE, De 6:5; 2Ki 23:25.
VOCATION. See CALLING.
VOICE, De 4:33 people heard the v. of God
Isa 52:8 watchmen have raised their v.
Isa 58:1 Raise your v. like a horn,
Joe 3:16 Jehovah will give forth his v.
Na 2:13 no more will v. of messengers
Joh 5:28 in the tombs will hear his v.
Joh 10:27 My sheep listen to my v.,
VOICED, Ac 13:27 things v. by Prophets
VOICELESS, 1Co 12:2; 2Pe 2:16.
VOICE OF EXULTATION, Jer 7:34 cease v.
VOID, Jer 19:7 v. the counsel of Judah
VOIDNESS, Na 2:10 Emptiness and v., and
VOLUNTARILY, 1Ch 29:17 v. offered all
Ezr 1:6 strengthened with things v. offered.
Ezr 7:16 priests are v. giving to the house
VOLUNTEER(S), Jg 5:9 My heart is for v.
2Ch 17:16 Amasiah the v. for Jehovah,
VOLUNTEERED, Ne 11:2 v. to dwell in
VOMIT, Isa 28:8 tables full of v.—
2Pe 2:22 The dog has returned to its v.,
Re 3:16 going to v. you out of my mouth.

Le 20:22; Pr 26:11; Isa 19:14; Jer 48:26.
VOTE, Ac 26:10 I cast my v. against them
VOTED, Lu 23:51 had not v. in support
VOW(S), Jg 11:30 Jephthah made a v.
Ps 50:14 pay to the Most High your v.,
Ps 61:8 pay my v. day after day.
Ec 5:4 Whenever you a v. to God, do not
Nu 30:2; De 23:21; Ps 76:11; Jon 1:16.
VOWED, Jon 2:9 What I v., I will pay.
De 23:23; Ps 132:2.
VOYAGES, Re 18:17 man that v. anywhere

W

WAGES, Ge 31:7 changed my w. ten times
Ec 9:5 neither do they any more have w.
Isa 49:4 and my w. with my God.
Zec 11:12 w., thirty pieces of silver
Lu 10:7 worker is worthy of his w.
Ro 6:23 For the w. sin pays is death,
Jas 5:4 the w. due the workers who
Le 19:13; Pr 11:18; Jer 22:13.
WAGONS, Ge 46:5; Nu 7:3; Isa 5:18.
WAIL, Ec 3:4 a time to w. and a time to
Zec 12:10 they will w. over him as in
Joh 16:20 You will weep and w., but the
WAILING, Mic 1:8 I w. like the jackals,
Mt 2:18 in Ramah, weeping and much w.;
Joe 2:12; Zec 12:11.
WAIT, De 19:11 he has lain in w. for
Job 13:15; Ps 10:9; Lu 11:54; 1Th 1:10.
WAITING, Isa 42:4 the islands keep w.
1Co 1:7 eagerly w. for the revelation of
Ro 8:25; Ga 5:5; Php 3:20.
WAKE, Isa 52:1 W. up, O Zion!
Da 12:2 asleep in the dust will w. up,
1Co 15:34 W. up to soberness in a righteous
Joe 1:5; Hab 2:19.
WALK, De 6:7 when you w. and when you
Ps 23:4 w. in the valley of deep shadow,
Ps 26:11 in my integrity I shall w.
Isa 30:21 This is the way. W. in it,
Isa 35:9 repurchased ones must w. there.
Eph 4:1 w. worthily of the calling
Eph 5:15 keep strict watch that how you w.
WALKED, Ge 6:9 Noah w. with God.
Ac 9:31 congregation w. in the fear of
Eph 2:2 you at one time w. according to the
1Jo 2:6 go on walking just as that one w.
WALKING, Joh 10:9 w. in integrity will
Jer 10:23 not belong to man who is w. to
Mic 6:8 be modest in w. with your God?
Joh 6:19 beheld Jesus w. upon the sea
Ge 3:8; 5:24; Job 1:7; Ac 3:8; 2Th 3:11.
WALL(S), Isa 26:1 sets salvation as
Eze 38:11 all of them dwelling without w.,
Da 5:5 writing upon the w. of the palace
Joe 2:7 Like men of war they go up a w.
Heb 11:30 By faith the w. of Jericho fell
WALLOW, Jer 25:34 shepherds w. about,
WANDER, Isa 35:8 no foolish will w.
Jer 50:6 shepherds have caused them to w.
WANDERED, Ps 119:110 I have not w.
Isa 53:6 Like sheep we have w. about;
WANDERER, Ps 36:11 not make me a w.
WANE, Isa 60:20 your moon go on the w.
WANTING, Ec 1:15 that which is w. cannot
WAR(S), Ex 15:3 Jehovah is person of w.
Ps 46:9 He is making w. to cease
Isa 2:4 neither will they learn w. any more.
Joe 3:9 Proclaim this, Sanctify w.!

Zec 14:3 Jehovah will w. against nations
Mt 24:6 hear of w. and reports of w.;
Re 12:7 w. broke out in heaven: Michael
Re 12:17 dragon went off to wage w.
Re 16:14 w. of the great day of God
Isa 13:4; Jer 50:22; Ho 1:7; 2:18; Mic 4:3;
Zec 14:2; Lu 21:9; Jas 4:1; Re 19:11, 19.
WARES, Ne 10:31 bringing in w.
WARFARE, Ps 144:1 teaching for w.;
  2Co 10:3 do not wage w. in the flesh.
  2Co 10:4 weapons of our w. are not fleshly,
  1Ti 1:18 go on waging the fine w.,
WARN, Eze 3:17 you must w. them from me.
  2Ch 19:10; Eze 33:8, 9.
WARNING, Eze 33:4 takes no w. at all,
  Eze 33:5 he heard but took no w. His own
  Eze 33:7 watchman to give them w. from me.
  1Co 10:11 they were written for a w. to us
  Heb 12:25 giving divine w. upon earth,
WASH, Ps 51:2 w. me from my error,
  Jer 4:14; Mt 15:2; Joh 9:11; 13:5.
WASHED, Isa 4:4 Jehovah w. away excrement
  Re 7:14 w. their robes white in the blood
  Pr 30:12; 1Co 6:11.
WASHING, Jer 2:22 w. with alkali, your
WASTE, Isa 24:1 land and laying it w.,
WASTENESS, Isa 34:11 and stones of w.
WASTING, 2Co 4:16 man outside is w. away,
WATCH, Ge 31:49 Jehovah w. between me
  De 8:11 W. out for yourself that you may
  Ps 141:3 Do set a w. over my lips.
  Hab 2:1 I shall keep w., to see what
  Mt 7:15 Be on the w. for false prophets
  Mt 26:41 keep on the w. and pray
WATCHFUL, 1Pe 5:8 be w. Your adversary,
WATCHING, Pr 8:34 Happy the man w. at
  Lu 12:37 the master on arriving finds w.!
  Heb 12:15 carefully w. that no one be
WATCHMAN, Isa 21:11 what about the
  Eze 3:17 a w. is what I have made you
  Eze 33:6 w. does not blow the horn and
WATCHMEN, Isa 52:8 w. have raised voice
  Isa 56:10 His w. are blind.
  Isa 62:6 I have commissioned w. All day
  Jer 6:17; 51:12; Mic 7:4.
WATCHTOWER, Ge 31:49 The W.,
  2Ch 20:24 Judah came to the w. of the
  Isa 21:8 Upon the w. I am standing
  Isa 32:14 become bare fields
WATER(S), Ge 6:17 deluge of w. upon the
  Ex 14:21 w. were being split apart.
  Jos 9:27 gatherers of wood and drawers of w.
  Pr 25:25 As cold w. upon a tired soul, so
  Isa 11:9 knowledge of Jehovah as the w.
  Isa 12:3 w. out of springs of salvation.
  Isa 30:20 w. in the form of oppression;
  Isa 55:1 Come to the w. buy and eat.
  Jer 2:13 cisterns that cannot contain w.
  Am 8:11 a thirst, not for w., but hearing
  Mt 10:42 little ones a cup of cold w.
  Joh 4:14 drinks from w. I give never thirsty
  Joh 7:38 from [him] streams of living w.
  1Co 3:7 nor is he that w., but God makes
  Re 7:17 guide them to w. of life.
  Re 22:17 anyone take life's w. free.
  Nu 20:10; Joh 5:7; Re 17:1, 15; 22:1.
WATERING, Pr 11:25 one freely w. will
WATERMELONS, Nu 11:5 remember the w.
WATERY DEEP, Ge 1:2 surface of w.
  Ps 36:6 judicial decision is a vast w.
  Ge 7:11; 8:2; Job 28:14; Ps 42:7.

WAVERING, Heb 10:23 hold fast without w.
WAVES, Isa 51:15 w. be boisterous.
  Ps 65:7; 89:9; Jon 2:3; Jude 13.
WAX, Ps 68:2 As w. melts, wicked ones
  Ps 97:5 mountains melt like w. on account
WAY(S), De 32:4 all his w. are justice.
  Job 13:15 I would argue for my own w.
  Ps 2:12 may not perish from the w.,
  Ps 25:4 Make me know your own w.,
  Ps 39:1 I will guard my w. from sinning
  Pr 6:23 reproofs are the w. of life,
  Pr 16:25 a w. upright before man, but end
  Pr 22:6 Train a boy according to the w.
  Isa 2:3 he will instruct us about his w.
  Isa 30:21 This is the w. Walk in it,
  Isa 55:8 nor are my w. your w.,
  Mal 3:1 he must clear up a w. before me.
  Joh 14:6 I am the w. and the truth
  Ac 9:2 those found who belonged to The W.,
  Ac 19:9 speaking injuriously about The W.
  Ac 22:4 I persecuted this W. to the death,
  Ac 24:14 to the w. which they call a 'sect'
  Ro 11:33 past tracing out his w. are!
  1Co 10:13 he will also make the w. out
  Re 15:3 Righteous and true are your w.,
  De 30:16; Isa 62:10; Eze 28:15; 2Pe 2:2.
WAY OF TEACHING, Mt 7:28; Lu 4:32.
WAYWARD, Ps 95:10 people w. at heart
WEAK, Joe 3:10 The w. one, let him say
  Mt 26:41 spirit is willing flesh is w.
  1Co 1:25 w. thing of God is stronger
  1Co 1:27 God chose the w. things
  1Th 5:14 support the w., be long-suffering
WEAKENING, Jer 38:4 w. the hands of men
WEAKER, 1Co 12:22 members seem to be w.
WEAKNESS(ES), Ro 8:26 help for our w.;
  Ro 15:1 bear the w. of those not strong,
  1Co 2:3 I came to you in w. and in fear
  1Co 15:43 It is sown in w., raised in
  2Co 12:9 my power is made perfect in w.
  Heb 4:15 cannot sympathize with our w.,
WEALTH, Pr 13:22 w. of the sinner for
  Ec 5:10 satisfied lover of w. with income
  Isa 33:6 w. of salvations—wisdom and
WEALTHINESS, Isa 60:5 w. of the sea
WEANED, 1Sa 1:23, 24; Isa 11:8; 28:9.
WEANLING, Ps 131:2 soul like a w. upon me
WEAPON(S), Isa 54:17 w. formed against
  Jer 50:25 brings forth w. of denunciation.
  Eze 9:2 one with his w. for smashing
  Ro 6:13 your members as w. of righteousness.
  Ro 13:12 Let us put on the w. of the light.
  2Co 6:7 w. of righteousness on right hand
  2Co 10:4 w. of our warfare are not fleshly,
WEAR, De 29:5 garments did not w. out
  Isa 51:6 the earth itself will w. out,
WEARISOME, Ec 1:8 All things are w.; no
WEARY, Job 3:17 w. in power are at rest
  Isa 40:31 run and not grow w.;
WEDDING, Mt 22:10 for the w. ceremonies
WEEDS, Mt 13:25 his enemy oversowed w.
WEEK(S), Ex 34:22 your festival of w.
  Da 9:27 half of the w. he will cause
  Ge 29:27, 28; De 16:9, 10, 16; Da 9:24-26.
WEEP, Isa 30:19 will by no means w.
  Isa 33:7 messengers will w. bitterly.
  Eze 24:16 neither should you w. nor
  Joe 1:5 Wake up, you drunkards, and w.;
  Ro 12:15 w. with people who w.
  Jas 5:1 w., howling over your calamities
  Re 18:9 the kings of the earth will w.

  Mic 1:10; Lu 6:21; 23:28; Re 18:15.
WEEPING, Ps 30:5 w. may take up lodging,
  Isa 65:19 no more be heard the sound of w.
  Jer 3:21; 31:16; 50:4; Mt 8:12; 13:50.
WEIGH, Job 31:6 w. me in accurate scales
WEIGHED, Job 6:2 my vexation were w.
  Isa 40:12 w. the mountains.
  Da 5:27 w. in the balances and found
WEIGHED DOWN, Lu 21:34 never become w.
  2Co 5:4 we in this tent groan, being w.
WEIGHT, Heb 12:1 let us put off every w.
  De 25:15; Eze 4:16; 2Co 4:17.
WEIGHTIER, Mt 23:23 disregarded the w.
WELCOME, Ro 15:7 w. as Christ w.
  Ro 14:1; 16:2; Php 2:29.
WELCOMED, Ro 14:3 one eating, God has w.
WELCOMES, Lu 15:2 This man w. sinners
WELFARE, Ge 41:16; 1Ch 18:10; Jer 15:5.
WELL(S), Pr 14:27 fear is a w. of life,
  Jas 5:15 will make the indisposed one w.
  Ge 26:18; Mt 25:21; Lu 6:26; Ga 5:7.
WELL-ARRANGED, 1Ti 2:9 adorn in w. dress,
WELL-OILED, Isa 25:6 a banquet of w. dishes
WELL-PLEASING, Col 3:20 W. in the Lord.
  Heb 13:21 performing that which is w.
WELL-WATERED, Isa 23:2 By w. resting
WHEAT, Ps 147:14 fat of the w.
  Mt 3:12; 13:25; Lu 22:31; Joh 12:24.
WHEEL(S), Eze 1:16 W. in the midst of
  Jas 3:6 sets the w. of life aflame
  Ex 14:25; Eze 1:20; 10:6; Na 3:2.
WHEELWORK, Eze 10:6, 13 from between w.
WHIP(S), Joh 2:15 making a w. of ropes,
  1Ki 12:11; Pr 26:3; Na 3:2.
WHISPER, Ps 90:9 our years like a w.
WHISPERERS, Ro 1:29 being w.
WHISPERINGS, 2Co 12:20 w., cases of
WHISTLE, Jer 50:13 he will stare and w.
  Jer 25:9; 51:37.
WHISTLED, Isa 5:26 he has w. to it at
  Jer 19:8; La 2:15; Mic 6:16.
WHISTLING, 2Ch 29:8; Jer 18:16; 29:18.
WHITE, Re 7:14 robes and made them w.
  Isa 1:18; Mt 5:36; Re 2:17; 7:9; 20:11.
WHITENING, Da 11:35 and to do a w., until
WHITEWASH, Eze 22:28 coated with w.,
  Eze 13:11, 14.
WHITEWASHED, Mt 23:27; Ac 23:3.
WHOLE SOUL, Mt 22:37 love with your w.
WHOLE-SOULED, Eph 6:6 the will of God w.
  Col 3:23 Whatever doing, work at it w.
WHORE. See HARLOT(S), PROSTITUTE(S).
WHOREDOM. See PROSTITUTION.
WICKED, Job 11:20 eyes of w. will fail;
  Ps 9:17 W. people will turn back to Sheol,
  Ps 37:10 and the w. one will be no more,
  Pr 15:8 sacrifice of the w. is detestable
  Pr 29:2 w. bears rule, the people sigh.
  Isa 57:21 no peace for the w. ones
  Eze 3:18 warn w. from his w. way
  Eze 33:11 delight, not in the death of w.
  Da 12:10 w. ones act wickedly, no w. will
  Mt 6:13 deliver us from the w. one.
  Eph 5:16 because the days are w.
  Eph 6:16 quench w. one's burning missiles.
  1Jo 5:19 lying in the power of the w. one
  Ps 145:20; Jer 12:1; Mt 12:35; Ro 12:9.
WICKEDNESS, Ps 45:7 and you hate w.
  Ps 84:10 than move around in tents of w.
  1Co 5:8 leaven of injuriousness and w.,
  1Th 5:22 Abstain from every form of w.
  Ps 5:4; 125:3; Eze 3:19; Mt 22:18.
WICKED SPIRIT FORCES, Eph 6:12.
WIDENS, De 19:8 w. out your territory

WIDOW(S), Zec 7:10 defraud no w.
  Lu 20:47 devour houses of w. and for a
  Lu 21:2 saw needy w. drop two coins
  1Ti 5:3 Honor w. that are actually w.
  Jas 1:27 care for orphans and w. in their
  Re 18:7 I sit a queen, and I am no w.,
  Isa 47:8; Mr 12:43; Lu 18:3, 5; 1Co 7:8.
WIDOWHOOD, Isa 54:4 reproach of your w.
  Ge 38:14; Isa 47:9.
WIFE, Ge 2:24 must stick to his w.
  Ps 128:3 w. be like a fruit-bearing vine
  Pr 5:18 rejoice with the w. of your youth,
  Isa 54:6 Jehovah called you as a w.
  Jer 16:2 not take for yourself a w.,
  Mal 2:14 you and the w. of your youth,
  1Co 7:2 let each man have his own w. and
  1Co 7:39 A w. is bound during all the time
  Re 21:9 show you the bride, the Lamb's w.
  Pr 18:22; 1Co 9:5; Eph 5:23, 28; 1Ti 3:2.
WIGGLED, Na 3:12 if they get w., will
WILD, Ge 1:24 w. beast of the earth
  Ro 11:24 olive tree that is w. by nature
WILDERNESS, Ge 8:16 fed you in the w.
  Isa 35:6 in the w. waters will have burst
  Eze 34:25 actually dwell in the w. in security
  Mt 3:3: Listen! Someone crying in the w.,
  Re 12:6 woman fled into the w.,
WILL, Ps 40:8 To do your w., O my God,
  Ps 143:10 Teach me to do your w., my God
  Mt 6:10 Let your w. take place, as in
  Lu 22:42 not my w., but yours take place.
  Joh 5:30 seek not my w. but the w. of him
  Ac 13:36 David served express w. of God
  Ro 8:20 not by its own w. but through him
  Ro 9:19 who has withstood his express w.?
  Ro 12:2 acceptable and perfect w. of God.
  Eph 5:17 what the w. of Jehovah is
  Col 1:9 accurate knowledge of his w. in all
  Heb 10:10 said "w." we have been sanctified
  2Pe 1:21 prophecy at no time by man's w.,
  1Jo 2:17 he that does w. of God remains
  Re 4:11 of your w. they existed, created
  Ezr 7:18; Da 11:36; Mt 7:21; Joh 6:39.
WILLED, Jas 1:18 he w. it, he brought
WILLFULLY, Heb 10:26 practice sin w.
WILLING, 2Ch 29:31 every one w. of
  Ps 51:12 support me with a w. spirit.
WILLING-HEARTED, Ex 35:5 every w. one
WILLINGLY, Ps 110:3 people will offer w.
  1Co 9:17 If w., I have a reward;
  1Pe 5:2 Shepherd the flock of God w.
WILLOW, Eze 17:5 as a w. by vast waters
WILLS, 1Co 4:19 I come if Jehovah w.
  Jas 4:15 If Jehovah w., we shall live and
WIND, Ec 1:14 a striving after w.
  Ec 11:4 He that is watching the w. will not
  Isa 26:18 we have given birth to w.
  Mt 24:31 chosen ones from the four w.,
  Eph 4:14 tossed about by every w. of
  Re 7:1 holding tight the four w. of
  Ps 104:3; Eze 37:9; Mt 7:25; Joh 3:8.
WINDOW, Ac 20:9 Seated at the w. a
  Ge 8:6; Jg 5:28; Pr 7:6; 2Co 11:33.
WINDSTORM, 2Ki 2:1 take Elijah in a w.
  Job 38:1; Mt 14:30.
WINE, Jg 9:13 give up my new w. that
  Ps 104:15 w. makes heart rejoice
  Pr 23:31 Do not look at w. when red color
  Isa 25:6 banquet of w. kept on the dregs,
  Isa 29:9 intoxicated, but not with w.;
  Isa 55:1 buy w. and milk without money
  Jer 25:15 Take this cup of the w. of rage
  Joe 3:18 mountains will drip with sweet w.,
  Joh 2:9 water that had been turned into w.

Ps 98:1 **w.** are the things he has done.
Ps 107:8 laud Jehovah for his **w.** works
Ps 136:4 The Doer of **w.**, great things
Ps 145:5 your **w.** works I make my concern.
Isa 9:6 name will be called **W.** Counselor,
1Pe 2:9 out of darkness into his **w.** light.
WONDERFULLY, Ps 139:14 I am **w.** made.
Isa 29:14 I am, the One that will act **w.**
WONDERMENT, Re 17:6 wondered with great **w.**
WORD(S), Ex 34:28 write the Ten **W.**
Jg 3:20 A **w.** of God I have for you.
Ps 119:105 Your **w.** is a lamp to my foot,
Pr 25:11 a **w.** spoken at the right time for
Isa 50:4 answer the weary with a **w.**
Isa 55:11 so my **w.** will prove to be.
Jer 8:9 The wise have rejected the **w.** of
Mt 12:37 by your **w.** you will be condemned.
Mt 24:35 my **w.** will by no means pass away.
Joh 1:1 beginning the **W.** was and the **W.**
Joh 1:14 **W.** became flesh and resided
Joh 17:17 your **w.** is truth.
Ro 10:8 the **w.** of faith we are preaching.
Php 2:16 tight grip on the **w.** of life
2Ti 1:13 Keep holding healthful **w.**
2Ti 2:15 handling the **w.** of truth aright.
2Ti 4:2 Preach the **w.**, be at it
Jas 1:22 become doers of the **w.**, not
2Pe 1:19 prophetic **w.** made more sure
WORD, GOD'S, Eph 6:17 sword of spirit, **G.**
1Th 2:13; Heb 11:3.
WORD OF GOD, Mr 7:13 make **w.** invalid
Heb 4:12 **w.** is alive and exerts power
Re 19:13 he is called The **W.**
Lu 8:11; Ac 6:7; 2Ti 2:9; 2Pe 3:5.
WORK(S), Ps 8:6 dominate over the **w.** of
Ps 71:17 I keep telling about your **w.**
Ps 104:24 How many your **w.** are, O Jehovah!
Ps 150:2 Praise him for **w.** of mightiness.
Pr 22:29 beheld a man skillful in his **w.**?
Ec 9:10 no **w.** nor wisdom in Sheol
Isa 28:21 may **w.** his.—his **w.** is unusual.
Joh 6:27 **W.**, not for the food that perishes,
Joh 9:4 We must **w.** the **w.** of him that sent
Joh 14:12 he will do **w.** greater than these,
Joh 17:4 I have finished the **w.** you have
Ro 4:4 to the man that **w.** pay is counted,
Ro 8:28 God makes all **w.** co-operate
Ro 13:10 Love does not **w.** evil to one's
Ga 5:19 **w.** of the flesh are manifest,
1Th 5:13 in love because of their **w.**
2Th 3:10 does not **w.**, neither let him eat.
Tit 2:14 people zealous for fine **w.**
Heb 10:24 incite to love and fine **w.**,
Jas 2:26 faith without **w.** is dead.
Jas 5:16 supplication when it is at **w.** has
Ps 71:17; 104:24; 1Co 3:13; 2Ti 3:17.
WORKED HARD, Ps 127:1 no avail builders **w.**
WORKED OUT, Nu 23:23 What has God **w.**!
1Pe 4:3 to have **w.** the will of the nations
WORKER(S), Ne 4:22 night and **w.** by day.
Pr 8:30 beside him as a master **w.**
Mt 9:37 harvest is great, but **w.** few.
Mt 20:1 to hire **w.** for his vineyard.
Lu 10:7 the **w.** is worthy of his wages.
Php 3:2 look out for the **w.** of injury,
Jas 5:4 wages due the **w.** keep crying out,
3Jo 8 fellow **w.** in the truth,
WORK HARD, Php 2:16 did not **w.** in vain.
1Ti 5:17 honor those who **w.** in speaking
WORKING, Joh 5:17 Father has kept **w.** and
Php 2:12 keep **w.** out your own salvation
WORKING HARD, 1Ti 4:10 **w.** and exerting
1Th 5:12 regard for those **w.** among you
WORKMAN, 2Ti 2:15 a **w.** with nothing to

WORK OUT, Ro 7:18 ability to **w.** what is fine
WORLD(S). See also INHABITED EARTH,
SYSTEM(S) OF THINGS.
WORLD(S), Joh 3:16 God loved the **w.** so
Joh 14:19 the **w.** will behold me no more,
Joh 14:30 ruler of the **w.** is coming
Joh 15:19 **w.**, the **w.** would be fond of
Joh 17:16 They are no part of the **w.** as
Joh 18:36 My kingdom is no part of this **w.**
Ro 4:13 he should be heir of a **w.**, but
1Co 4:9 theatrical spectacle to the **w.**,
Jas 4:4 friendship with the **w.** is enmity
2Pe 3:6 the **w.** of that time was deluged
1Jo 5:19 whole **w.** is lying in the power of
Mt 25:34; Joh 8:23; 17:5, 6; Eph 1:4; 2:2;
Jas 1:27; 1Jo 2:15, 16; Re 17:8.
WORLD RULERS, Eph 6:12 against the **w.** of
WORLD'S, Mt 24:21 since the **w.** beginning
Ro 1:20 qualities seen from **w.** creation
1Jo 2:2 sacrifice for sins, the **w.**
WORM(S), Isa 14:11 **w.** are your covering.
Isa 41:14 Do not be afraid, you **w.** Jacob,
WORMWOOD, Jer 23:15 making them eat **w.**,
Re 8:11 the name of the star is called **W.**
De 29:18; Pr 5:4; La 3:15; Am 5:7; 6:12.
WORSHIP, Ge 22:5 over there and **w.** and
Ex 10:26 take some to **w.** Jehovah our God,
De 11:16 Watch for fear you **w.** other gods
De 17:3 and he should go and **w.** other gods
Da 3:6 whoever does not fall down and **w.**
Lu 4:8 It is Jehovah your God you must **w.**,
Joh 4:20 Jerusalem is the place persons **w.**
Joh 4:24 **w.** with spirit and truth
Joh 12:20 that came to **w.** at the festival
Ac 8:27 He had gone to Jerusalem to **w.**,
Ac 25:19 concerning their **w.** of the deity
Ac 26:5 strictest sect of our form of **w.**
Col 2:18 a form of **w.** of the angels,
Jas 1:26 this man's form of **w.** is futile.
Jas 1:27 The form of **w.** that is clean
Re 9:20 that they should not **w.** the demons
Mt 4:10; Col 2:23; Heb 1:6; Re 13:15.
WORSHIPED, Ac 17:4 Greeks who **w.** God
Ac 17:17 to reason with people who **w.** God
Heb 11:21 **w.** leaning upon his staff.
Re 7:11 angels fell upon their faces and **w.**
Re 11:16 twenty-four persons **w.** God, saying:
Re 13:4 they **w.** the dragon because he gave
Re 19:4 twenty-four persons **w.** God seated
Re 20:4 who had **w.** neither the wild beast
WORSHIPERS, 2Ki 10:22 **w.** of Baal.
Joh 4:23 true **w.** will worship with spirit
WORSHIPING, Re 11:1 altar and those **w.**
Da 3:12; Ac 18:13; Re 16:2.
WORSHIPS, Ac 19:27 Artemis earth **w.**
Re 14:9 If anyone **w.** the wild beast
WORTH, Ac 19:19 and found them **w.**
WORTHILY, Eph 4:1 walk **w.** of the
Col 1:10 walk **w.** of Jehovah to the end of
1Th 2:12 go on walking **w.** of God who is
WORTHLESS, Ex 20:7 name in a **w.** way,
Ps 60:11 salvation by earthling man is **w.**
Ro 3:12 All men have become **w.**;
WORTHLESSNESS, Ps 24:4 soul to sheer **w.**,
WORTHY, Lu 20:35 counted **w.** of gaining
Ac 5:41 counted **w.** to be dishonored in
Ac 13:46 not **w.** of everlasting life,
Php 1:27 behave in a manner **w.** of
2Th 1:5 your counted **w.** of the kingdom
1Ti 5:18 workman is **w.** of his wages.
Heb 11:38 world was not **w.** of them.
Re 4:11 You are **w.**, Jehovah, because
WOUND(S), Pr 27:6 **w.** inflicted by a lover
Isa 30:26 Jehovah heals the severe **w.**

Isa 53:5 because of his **w.** a healing
Ps 38:5; Pr 20:30; 23:29; Isa 1:6.
WOUNDED, De 32:39 I have severely **w.**
Eze 26:15; 30:24; Ac 19:16.
WRANGLE, Mt 12:19 He will not **w.,** nor
WRAP, Isa 8:16 **W.** up the attestation,
Heb 1:12 you **w.** up the heavens like
WRAPPED, 1Sa 25:29 **w.** up in bag of life
Ho 4:19 wind has **w.** her up in
Ho 13:12 error is **w.** up, his sin
WRATH, Joh 3:36 the **w.** of God remains
Jas 1:20 man's **w.** does not produce God's
Re 11:18 wrathful, and your own **w.** came,
Ro 9:22; 12:19; 13:4; 1Th 5:9; Re 19:15.
WRATHFUL, Eph 4:26 Be **w.** yet not sin
Re 12:17 the dragon grew **w.**
WREATH OF ATTRACTIVENESS, Pr 1:9.
WRECK, Ps 48:7 you **w.** the ships of
WRITE, Ex 17:14 **W.** this as a memorial
Ex 34:28 he **w.** upon the tablets
Pr 3:3 **W.** upon the tablet of your heart
Jer 31:33 in their heart I shall **w.** it.
Jer 51:60 Jeremiah to **w.** in one book
Hab 2:2 **W.** down the vision, and set
Joh 8:6 Jesus began to **w.** with his finger
Joh 19:21 Do not **w.** 'The King of the Jews'
Ex 34:27; Isa 30:8; Re 1:11; 3:12; 21:5.
WRITHE, Ps 29:8, 9 makes wilderness **w.**
WRITING(S), Ex 32:16 **w.** was the **w.** of God
2Ti 3:15 known the holy **w.**
De 10:4; Es 1:22; Da 5:7; Joh 5:47.
WRITTEN, Ex 31:18 **w.** on by God's finger.
Ps 149:9 To execute the judicial decision **w.**
Isa 10:1 have **w.** out sheer trouble,
Lu 21:22 all the things **w.** may be fulfilled.
Ro 15:4 **w.** aforetime were **w.** for our
1Co 10:11 they were **w.** for a warning
Re 14:1 his Father **w.** on their foreheads.
Re 21:27 those **w.** in the Lamb's scroll
Ps 102:18; Mal 3:16; Mt 4:4; Re 1:3; 17:5.
WRITTEN CODE, 2Co 3:6 the **w.** condemns
Ro 2:27, 29; 7:6.
WRONG, Le 25:14 do not **w.** one another.
Pr 30:20 I have committed no **w.**
Es 1:16; La 3:59; Mt 20:13; Ac 25:10.
WRONGDOING, Ps 125:3 thrust hand upon **w.**
WRONGED, 1Co 6:7 let yourselves be **w.?**
2Co 7:2 We have **w.** no one, we have
WROTE, Joh 5:46 that one **w.** about me.
Ex 24:4; Jos 24:26; Joh 19:19; 21:24.

Y

YEAR(S), Ge 1:14 serve as signs for **y.**
Le 25:10 sanctify fiftieth **y.** proclaim liberty
Nu 14:34 forty days, a day for a **y.**
De 8:2 travel forty **y.** in the wilderness,
Ps 90:4 a thousand **y.** are but as yesterday
Isa 34:8 a **y.** of retributions over Zion
Isa 61:2 the **y.** of good will of Jehovah
Isa 63:4 **y.** of my repurchased ones
Isa 65:20 mere boy, a hundred **y.** of age;
Jer 23:12 **y.** of their being given attention,
Jer 25:11, 12 serve king of Babylon seventy **y.**
Eze 4:6 A day for a **y.,** a day for a **y.,**
Hab 3:2 in the midst of the **y.** bring it to
Zec 14:16 from **y.** to **y.** to bow down to
Ga 3:17 Law four hundred and thirty **y.**
2Pe 3:8 a thousand **y.** as one day.
Re 20:2, 4, 6 rule with Christ for thousand **y.**
YEARNED, Ps 84:2 My soul has **y.** and
YEARNING, Php 1:8 I am **y.** for all of you
Ge 31:30; Job 14:15.
YELL, Lu 23:21 began to **y.:** "Impale!
YELLOWISH-RED, Jg 5:10 on **y.** she-asses,

YES, Mt 5:37 let your **Y.** mean **Y.,**
2Co 1:20 become **Y.** by means of him.
YIELD, Eze 34:27 land will give its **y.,**
Ps 85:12; Zec 8:12.
YOKE, Mt 11:30 my **y.** is kindly and load
De 28:48; Jer 28:14; Mt 11:29; Ga 5:1.
YOKE BAR(S), Isa 58:6 bands of the **y.,**
Jer 27:2 Make for yourself bands and **y.,**
Eze 30:18 when I break the **y.** of Egypt.
YOKED, Mt 19:6 what God has **y.** together
2Co 6:14 **y.** with unbelievers
YOKEFELLOW, Php 4:3 genuine **y.,** keep
YOUNG, Ps 37:25 **y.** man I used to be,
Ps 110:3 **y.** men just like dewdrops.
Eze 9:6 **y.** man and virgin kill off—
Joe 2:28 your **y.** men, visions they will see.
Pr 20:29; Mt 19:22; Ac 2:17; 1Jo 2:14.
YOUNGER, 1Ti 5:1, 2, 11, 14.
YOUNG MANHOOD, Ec 12:1 days of your **y.,**
YOURSELF, Ex 32:13 whom you swore by **y.,**
Joh 17:5 glorify me alongside **y.** with the glory
YOURSELVES, 1Co 6:19 not belong to **y.,**
YOUTH, Ge 8:21 inclination bad from **y.**
Job 33:25 flesh become fresher than in **y.;**
Ps 103:5 your **y.** keeps renewing itself
Pr 5:18 rejoice with the wife of your **y.,**
Isa 54:4 forget the shame of your **y.**
1Ti 4:12 no man look down on your **y.**
2Ti 2:22 flee desires incidental to **y.,**
2Sa 19:7; Ps 71:17; Ec 11:10; Mal 2:14;
Mr 10:20; Ac 26:4.

Z

ZACCHAEUS, Lu 19:2, 5, 8.
ZADOK, 2Sa 15:24; 1Ch 29:22; Eze 48:11.
ZEAL, Ps 69:9 **z.** of your house has eaten me
Isa 9:7 **z.** of Jehovah of armies will do
Zep 3:8 by fire of my **z.** earth be devoured
Ro 10:2 they have a **z.** for God; but not
Isa 37:32; Joh 2:17; Php 3:6.
ZEALOUS, Ga 1:14 **z.** for the traditions of
Tit 2:14 people **z.** for fine works.
1Co 14:12; 1Pe 3:13; Re 3:19.
ZEALOUSLY, 1Co 12:31; 14:1; Ga 4:17.
ZEALOUS ONE, Lu 6:15; Ac 1:13.
ZEBEDEE, Mt 4:21; Lu 5:10; Joh 21:2.
ZEBRAS, Jer 14:6 **z.** have snuffed up
ZEBULUN, Jg 5:18 **Z.** was a people that
Ge 30:20; Nu 26:26; Ps 68:27; Re 7:8.
ZECHARIAH 1., 1Ch 26:2, 14.
ZECHARIAH 2., Ezr 5:1; Zec 1:1, 7.
ZECHARIAH 3., Isa 8:2 **Z.** the son of
ZECHARIAH 4., 2Ch 24:20 **Z.** of Jehoiada
Lu 11:51 to the blood of **Z.**
ZECHARIAH 5., Lu 1:5, 12, 18, 40, 67.
ZEDEKIAH, 2Ki 24:17; Jer 39:2; 52:11.
ZERUBBABEL, Ezr 3:8; Hag 2:4; Zec 4:6, 7.
ZIGZAG, Ps 60:4 To flee **z.** on account
ZION, Ps 2:6 installed my king upon **Z.,**
Ps 110:2 rod of your strength out of **Z.:**
Ps 132:13 Jehovah has chosen **Z.;**
Isa 2:3 out of **Z.** law will go forth,
Isa 28:16 laying as a foundation in **Z.**
Isa 31:4 Jehovah wage war over Mount **Z.**
Isa 62:1 sake of **Z.** I shall not keep still,
Am 6:1 Woe to those at ease in **Z.**
Zep 3:14 Joyfully cry, O daughter of **Z.!**
Mt 21:5 **Z.,** 'Look! Your King is coming
Ro 11:26 deliverer will come out of **Z.**
Heb 12:22 you have approached a Mount **Z.**
2Sa 5:7; Isa 66:8; Ro 9:33; 1Pe 2:6.
ZIPPORAH, Ex 2:21 gave **Z.** his daughter
ZODIAC, 2Ki 23:5 constellations of the **Z.**
ZOPHAR, Job 2:11; 11:1.

A LISTING OF OUTSTANDING WORD CHANGES IN THE 1970 REVISED BIBLE

Revision	Earlier Editions
ABHORRENT Tit 3:3	HATEFUL
ACCURATELY KNEW Col 1:6	LEARNED TO KNOW
AFFECTION 1 Pe 3:8	LOVE
AM ABLE TO Mt 26:61	CAN
ARM(IES)(Y) Ro 9:29; Lu 2:13	HOST(S)
BADNESS Ac 8:22; Ro 1:29; 1 Co 5:8; Eph 4:31; Col 3:8; Tit 3:3	BASENESS; INJURIOUSNESS; MALICIOUSNESS
BADNESS Mt 6:34; Jas 1:21; 1 Pe 2:1, 16	EVIL; MORAL BADNESS
BEGAN Mt 9:19	STARTED
BLOWS Ac 16:23; 2 Co 11:23	STRIPES
BOWED DOWN 1 Ki 1:47	PROSTRATED HIMSELF
BURIAL PLACE Job 5:26	GRAVE
CALLED Mr 15:34	CRIED
CHARMERS Isa 47:15	SORCERERS
CHIEF PRIEST 2 Ch 26:20; Ezr 7:5; Mr 2:26	HIGH PRIEST
CIRCLE Pr 8:27	HORIZON
COMPASSIONATE 1 Pe 3:8	AFFECTIONATE
COMPREHENSION Col 1:9	DISCERNMENT
CONSENT WITH Ro 1:32	APPROVE
COUNCIL Lu 23:50	SANHEDRIN
CRYING OUT Lu 4:41	SHOUTING
DRAGS Re 12:4	DRAWS
EARTH Ge 38:9; 2 Sa 14:33	GROUND
ENMIT(IES)(Y) Ga 5:20; Eph 2:15, 16	HATRED(S)
EYE INTO EYE Isa 52:8	FACE TO FACE
FEET 2 Sa 15:16, 17	FOOT
FLESHLY Ro 15:27	PHYSICAL
GATHERING Jas 2:2	PUBLIC ASSEMBLY
HEARD Pr 13:1	LISTENED TO
HIGH PRIEST Le 21:10	CHIEF PRIEST
INQUIRED Ac 10:18	BEGAN INQUIRING
INSULTING Lu 6:28	INJURY
JAR Ge 24:17	PITCHER
JEHOSHUA 1 Ch 7:27	JOSHUA

Revision	Earlier Editions
KEEP ABSTAINING Ac 15:29	KEEP YOURSELVES FREE
KINDNESS Ro 3:12	GOOD
LATE AUTUMN Jude 12	AUTUMN TIME
LAY DOWN 2 Ki 4:11	SAT DOWN
LAY UPON 2 Sa 13:31	SAT DOWN UPON
LONELY Mt 14:15	ISOLATED
LORD Mt 10:24, 25	MASTER
LOVED ONES Ac 15:25	BELOVED
LOYAL LOVE Ge 21:23; 24:14	LOVING-KINDNESS
LYING DOWN 1 Ki 21:27	SITTING
MAKE KNOWN Php 1:22	KNOW
MAKER Heb 11:10	CREATOR
MEN Mt 21:23	MEN OF INFLUENCE
MENTAL POWERS 2 Co 3:14	MENTAL PERCEPTIONS
MENTAL-REGULATING Eph 6:4	AUTHORITATIVE ADVICE
MOCKED Ac 2:13	LAUGHED
MOLTEN Isa 44:10	CARVED
MOVE(D) EAGERLY Ex 11:7; Jos 10:21	SHARPEN(ED)
MUST Le 6:12, 13; 17:12	SHOULD
OLD 2 Pe 2:3; 3:5	ANCIENT TIMES
ORALLY Ro 2:18	VERBALLY
OVER Jg 9:49; Ro 11:4	ALONG WITH; REMAIN
OVERSTEPPED De 26:13	SIDESTEPPED
PARTAKE OF 1 Co 9:12	SHARE IN
PASSING OVER Ex 38:26	SERVING ACCORDING
PELT De 21:21	STONE
POWERFUL Ac 7:22	MIGHTY
PRAISE In heading, p. 1114	SONG
PRODUCED Ge 4:1	ACQUIRED
PUMMEL(ING) 1 Co 9:27; Lu 18:5	BROWBEAT; BROWBEATING
READJUST(ED)- (MENT) 2 Co 13:9, 11; Ga 6:1; Eph 4:12	RESTORE(D); TRAINING
REBUKE(D) Mr 1:25; 8:33; Lu 9:55; 17:3; 19:39	REPROVE(D); REPROOF
REBUK(ES)(ING) Ps 149:7; Mt 16:22; Mr 8:32	REPROOFS; RAISING STRONG OBJEC- TIONS TO; OBJECT- ING STRONGLY TO

1445

Revision	Earlier Editions	Revision	Earlier Editions
REPROACHED Mr 16:14	REPROVED	SUPPORTS 1 Ki 7:32, 33	SIDES
REVIVE 2 Ki 8:10	RECOVER	THIS Mt 12:32	THE PRESENT
ROUND LOAF 1 Ch 16:3	RING-SHAPED CAKE	THORNS Jos 23:13	PRICKS
ROWED Joh 6:19	GONE	TIMES Ac 17:26	SEASONS
RUSTED AWAY Jas 5:3	CORRODED	TORRENTS Le 11:10	STREAMS
SEAL UP Re 10:4	KEEP SECRET	TRANSFERRED Col 1:13	TRANSPLANTED
SHEEP De 14:5	BULL	TREE Ge 3:6	TREE'S FRUIT
SOMETHING Le 11:38	ANY	VEDAN Eze 27:19	AND DAN
SORT Lu 4:36; Eph 5:3	KIND	VENERATION Ac 17:23	DEVOTION
SPIRIT Lu 8:55; Joh 19:30; Jas 2:26	BREATH	WAVING Isa 19:16	DOING
STATURE Eph 4:13	GROWTH	WHEN Le 14:34; 20:13	IN CASE; WHERE
STAY Ex 9:28	DELAY	WILDERNESS Ne 9:19	DESERT
STRIKE THEM IN THE REAR Jos 10:19	BLOCK THEM OFF	WINE OF THE ANGER Re 14:8; 18:3	PASSION-AROUSING WINE
STRIVEN Php 4:3	FOUGHT	WRESTLING Eph 6:12	FIGHT
STRIVING Php 1:27	FIGHTING	YOU Le 20:15	THEY
SULLEN 1 Ki 20:43; 21:4	SAD	YOUNG ONE(S) Ca 2:9, 17; 4:5; 7:3; 8:14	ROE(S)

OTHER REVISIONS IN THE 1970 REVISED BIBLE

Revision of wording and sentence structure:
Ge 27:42; 49:7; Ex 25:32; 37:18; Nu 10:21; 20:26; De 14:4; 29:22; 30:17; 1 Sa 26:15; 1 Ki 6:18; 7:5; 22:17; 2 Ki 6:27; 2 Ch 18:16; Ps 50:8; Isa 51:22; Eze 22:28; Ho 4:14; Zec 7:13, 14; Mt 23:30; 25:34; Mr 6:31; Lu 15:24, 32; 24:13; Joh 11:39; 17:12; Ac 13:16; 27:15; Ro 1:5; 1 Co 1:13; 2 Co 2:3, 4; Tit 2:13; Re 13:10; 19:15.

Words transposed:
Le 3:9; De 33:8; Ro 5:16; 2 Co 6:14; Heb 7:5.

Verse numbers relocated:
Lu 4:32; Ac 10:47; Ro 4:21; Col 1:22; 2 Ti 1:4.

Words added:
Ex 23:1, 17; De 9:7; Jg 9:43; 2 Ki 19:29; 1 Ch 13:14; Mt 4:17; Ac 2:29, 37; 7:1, 2; 13:15, 26; 15:13; 22:1; 23:1, 6; 28:17.

Words deleted:
Nu 17:4; Isa 30:28; 36:6; Ho 12:1; Mt 14:24; Lu 3:24-38; Ro 12:12; 1 Co 11:4, 5; Php 1:13; Re 21:15, 25.

Changed from poetry to prose:
Ex 15:19.

APPENDIX

SCRIPTURE VERSES SPECIFICALLY COMMENTED ON

SUBJECTS

Genesis 1:20 — "souls"

(נפש, neph'esh, Hebrew; ψυχή, psy·khē', Greek; a'ni·ma, Latin)

In the Hebrew Scriptures, we have succeeded in consistently rendering the Hebrew word neph'esh as "soul." In each case it proves understandable in the light of its context. The use of this one Hebrew word in many different contexts helps us to ascertain the main or basic idea inherent in the word as the Bible writers used it, namely, that (1) it is a person, an individual, or a lower animal, or, (2) it is the life that a person or animal enjoys as such. This is absolutely different from the pagan ideas of what the ancient Egyptians, Babylonians, Greeks and Romans called a "soul." By studying over the context of the Hebrew word neph'esh in its occurrences the investigator can learn distinguishing features about the soul in its true meaning.

The animals lower than man are souls or have soul

Genesis

1:20 "Let the waters swarm forth a swarm of living souls

1:21 sea monsters and every living soul that moves about,

1:24 "Let the earth put forth living souls

1:30 everything moving upon the earth in which there is life as a soul

2:19 the man would call it, each living soul,

9:10 with every living soul that is with you,

9:12 between me and you and every living soul that is

9:15 between me and you and every living soul among all

9:16 between God and every living soul among all flesh

Leviticus

11:10 every living soul that is in the waters,

1447

11:46 every living soul that moves about in the waters
11:46 every soul that swarms upon the earth,
24:18 the fatal striker of the soul of a domestic animal should make compensation for it, soul for soul.

Numbers
31:28 one soul out of five hundred,

of humankind and of the herd and of the asses and of the flock.

Job
41:21 Its soul itself sets coals ablaze,

Ezekiel
47:9 every living soul that swarms

Soul, a living person or individual

Genesis
2:7 man came to be a living soul.
12:5 the souls whom they had acquired in Haran,
14:21 "Give me the souls, but take the goods
36:6 all the souls of his house and his herd
46:15 All the souls of his sons and of his daughters
46:18 she bore these to Jacob: sixteen souls.
46:22 All the souls were fourteen.
46:25 all the souls were seven.
46:26 All the souls who came to Jacob into Egypt
46:26 All the souls were sixty-six.
46:27 born to him in Egypt were two souls.
46:27 All the souls of the house of Jacob

Exodus
1:5 all the souls who issued out of Jacob's
1:5 came to be seventy souls,
12:4 his house according to the number of souls;
12:16 Only what every soul needs to eat,
16:16 according to the number of the souls that

Leviticus
2:1 in case some soul would present as an offering
4:2 'In case a soul sins by mistake
4:27 if any soul of the people of the land sins unintentionally

5:1 "'Now in case a soul sins
5:2 when a soul touches some unclean thing,
5:4 in case a soul swears
5:15 "In case a soul behaves unfaithfully
5:17 if a soul sins in that he does do
6:2 "In case a soul sins in that he does
7:18 the soul that eats some of it will answer
7:20 the soul who eats the flesh of the communion
7:21 in case a soul touches anything unclean,
7:25 the soul that eats must be cut off
7:27 Any soul who eats any blood,
17:10 the soul that is eating the blood,
17:12 "No soul of you should eat blood
17:15 any soul that eats a body already dead
18:29 the souls doing them must be cut off from
20:6 the soul who turns himself to the spirit mediums
20:6 I shall certainly set my face against that soul
22:6 The soul who touches any such must be unclean
22:11 in case a priest should purchase a soul,
23:29 every soul that will not be afflicted
23:30 any soul that will do any sort of work
27:2 a special vow offering of souls to Jehovah

Numbers

5:6   that soul has also become guilty.

15:27   if any soul should sin by mistake,

15:28   the soul who made a mistake by a sin

15:30   the soul that does something deliberately,

19:18   the souls that happened to be there

19:22   the soul who touches it will be unclean

31:35   As for human souls from the women who had not

31:35   all the souls were thirty-two thousand.

31:40   the human souls were sixteen thousand,

31:40   the tax on them for Jehovah was thirty-two souls.

31:46   and human souls, sixteen thousand.

35:30   one witness may not testify against a soul

Deuteronomy

10:22   With seventy souls your forefathers went

24:6   it is a soul that he is seizing as a pledge.

24:7   kidnaping a soul of his brothers of the sons

1 Samuel

22:22   I personally have wronged every soul

2 Samuel

14:14   God will not take away a soul,

2 Kings

12:4   money for the souls according to . . . valuation,

1 Chronicles

5:21   human souls a hundred thousand.

Psalms

19:7   law of Jehovah is perfect, bringing back the soul.

Proverbs

11:25   The generous soul will itself be made fat,

11:30   he that is winning souls is wise.

16:24   Pleasant sayings are . . . ., sweet to the soul

19:2   that the soul should be without knowledge is not good,

19:15   a slack soul goes hungry; also 10:3.

25:25   As cold water upon a tired soul, so is

27:7   A soul that is satisfied will tread down comb honey,

27:7   to a hungry soul every bitter thing is sweet.

27:9   due to the counsel of the soul

Isaiah

5:14   She'ol [personified] has made its soul spacious

Jeremiah

43:6   every soul that Nebuzaradan . . . had let stay

52:29   eight hundred and thirty-two souls; also v. 30.

Lamentations

3:25   the soul that keeps seeking for him.

Ezekiel

27:13   For the souls of mankind . . . your articles . . . were given.

The creature soul is mortal, destructible

Genesis

12:13   my soul will be certain to live due to you."

17:14   that soul must be cut off from his people.

19:19   exercised with me to preserve my soul alive,

19:20   and my soul will live on."

37:21   "Let us not strike his soul fatally."

Exodus

12:15   that soul must be cut off from Israel.

12:19   that soul must be cut off from the assembly

31:14   that soul must be cut off from the midst

Leviticus

7:20   that soul must be cut off from his people

7:21   that soul must be cut off from his people.' "

7:27   that soul must be cut off from his people.' "

19:8   that soul must be cut off from his people.

22:3   that soul must be cut off from before me.

23:30   I must destroy that soul from among

24:17   strikes any soul of mankind fatally,
      (See also Leviticus 7:25; 17:10; 18:29; 20:6; 23:29, quoted above.)

Numbers

9:13   that soul must then be cut off from his people,

15:30   that soul must be cut off from among his people.

15:31   that soul should be cut off without fail.

19:13   that soul must be cut off from Israel.

19:20   that soul must be cut off from the midst

23:10   Let my soul die the death of the upright

31:19   Everyone who has killed a soul

35:11   who fatally strikes a soul unintentionally.

35:15   that fatally strikes a soul unintentionally.

35:30   " 'Every fatal striker of a soul should be slain

Deuteronomy

19:6   he may indeed strike his soul fatally,

19:11   struck his soul fatally and he has died

22:26   indeed murders him, even a soul,

27:25   a bribe to strike a soul fatally,

Joshua

2:13   you must deliver our souls from death."

2:14   "Our souls are to die instead of you people!

10:28   devoted him and every soul that was in it to destruction.

10:30   striking it and every soul that was in it

10:32   striking it and every soul that was in it

10:35   devoted every soul that was in it to destruction

10:37   every soul that was in it with the edge of the sword.

10:37   devoted it and every soul that was in it to destruction.

10:39   devoting every soul that was in it to destruction.

11:11   striking every soul that was in it

20:3   who fatally strikes a soul unintentionally

20:9   who fatally strikes a soul unintentionally,

Judges

5:18   that scorned their souls to the point of death;

16:16   soul got to be impatient to the point of dying.

16:30   "Let my soul die with the Philistines."

1 Kings

19:4   ask that his soul might die; also Jonah 4:8.

20:31   Perhaps he will preserve your soul alive; also v. 32.

Job

7:15   my soul chooses suffocation

11:20   their hope will be an expiring of the soul

18:4   He is tearing his soul to pieces in his anger

33:22   his soul draws near to the pit; also v. 30.

36:14   Their soul will die in youth itself

Psalms

7:2   that no one may tear my soul to pieces

22:29   no one will ever preserve his own soul alive

66:9   He is setting our soul in life
69:1   the waters have come clear
      to the soul
78:50 He did not hold back their
      soul from death itself;
94:17 my soul would have resided
      in silence.
106:15 to send a wasting disease
      into their soul.
124:4 the torrent . . . . would have
      passed over our soul.

Proverbs

28:17 A man burdened with the
      bloodguilt for a soul

Isaiah

55:3   Listen, and your soul will
      keep alive,

Jeremiah

2:34   the blood marks of the souls
      of the innocent
4:10   the sword has reached clear
      to the soul."

18:20 they have excavated a pit
      for my soul.
38:17 your soul will . . . keep
      living; also v. 20.
40:14 Baalis . . . sent Ishmael . . .
      to strike you to the soul;
      also v. 15.

Ezekiel

13:19 to put to death the souls
      that ought not to die and
      in order to preserve alive
      the souls that ought not
      to live
17:17 in order to cut off many
      souls.
18:4   The soul that is sinning—
      it itself will die; also
      v. 20.
22:25 A soul they actually de-
      vour.
22:27 in shedding blood, in de-
      stroying souls
33:6   a sword comes and takes
      away from them soul,

Dead soul, or corpse

Leviticus

19:28 cuts in your flesh for a
      deceased soul,
21:1   'For a deceased soul no one
      may defile himself
21:11 he should not come to any
      dead soul.
22:4   anyone unclean by a de-
      ceased soul

Numbers

5:2   everyone unclean by a de-
      ceased soul.
6:6   he may not come toward
      any dead soul.
6:11   he has sinned because of
      the dead soul.

9:6   become unclean by a human
      soul
9:7   "We are unclean by a
      human soul.
9:10   happen to be unclean by
      a soul
19:11 Anyone touching the corpse
      of any human soul
19:13 Everyone touching a corpse,
      the soul of whatever man
      may die,

Haggai

2:13   "If someone unclean by
      a deceased soul touches
      any

God has soul

1 Samuel

2:35   In harmony with what is
      . . . in my soul he will do;

Psalms

11:5   anyone loving violence His
      soul certainly hates;
24:4   who has not carried My
      soul to sheer worthless-
      ness,

Proverbs

6:16   Jehovah . . . seven are
      things detestable to his
      soul:

Isaiah

1:14   YOUR festal seasons my soul
      has hated
42:1   My chosen one, whom my
      soul has approved!

Jeremiah

5:9 should not my soul avenge itself? also v. 29; 9:9.

6:8 Be corrected . . . that my soul may not turn away disgusted from you

12:7 I have given the beloved one of my soul into the palm of her enemies.

14:19 has your soul abhorred even Zion?

15:1 my soul would not be toward this people.

32:41 I will plant them in this

land . . . with all my soul.

51:14 Jehovah of armies has sworn by his own soul

Lamentations

3:20 your soul will remember and bow low over me.

Ezekiel

23:18 my soul turned away disgusted; (twice).

Amos

6:8 " 'The Lord Jehovah has sworn by his own soul,'

Soul delivered from Sheol (Ha'des, "hell")

Psalms

16:10 you will not leave my soul in She'ol.

30:3 you have brought up my soul from She'ol

49:15 God himself will redeem my soul from the hand of She'ol,

86:13 you have delivered my soul out of She'ol,

89:48 Can he provide escape for his soul from the hand of She'ol?

Proverbs

23:14 deliver his very soul from She'ol itself

Genesis 5: 22, 24 — "the [true] God"

This is the English translation of the Hebrew expression האלהים, ha-El·o·him', namely, the Hebrew title El·o·him'; which is the plural number of the word El·o'ah and which means "God" when applied to the Creator Jehovah, preceded by the Hebrew definite article ha.

That the Hebrew plural word El·o·him' as applied to the Creator Jehovah does not mean that there are a number of gods in this one divinity but that this word El·o·him' is merely in the plural number of excellence or of majesty, we refer to Gesenius' Hebrew Grammar as edited and enlarged by the late E. Kautzsch and revised in its second English edition by A. E. Cowley and reprinted photographically in Great Britain at the University Press, Oxford, in 1949, from corrected sheets of the second edition. In section 124 under the heading

"The Various Uses of the Plural-form," it says, on pages 398, 399, in paragraph g:

"The pluralis excellentiae or maiestatis . . . is properly a variety of the abstract plural, since it sums up the several characteristics belonging to the idea, besides possessing the secondary sense of an intensification of the original idea. It is thus closely related to the plurals of amplification . . . which are mostly found in poetry. So especially אלהים Godhead, God (to be distinguished from the numerical plural gods, Exodus 12:12,&c.). The supposition that אלהים is to be regarded as merely a remnant of earlier polytheistic views (that is, as originally only a numerical plural) is at least highly improbable, and, moreover, would not explain the analogous plurals (see below). That the language has entirely rejected the idea of numerical plurality in אלהים (whenever it denotes *one* God), is proved especially by its being almost invariably joined with a singular attribute . . . , for example, אלהים צדיק Psalm 7:10, &c. Hence אלהים may have been used originally not only as a numerical but also as an abstract plural (corresponding to the Latin *numen*, and our *Godhead*), and, like other abstracts of the same kind, have been transferred to a concrete single god (even of the heathen)."

In support of our rendering האלהים into English as "the [true] God," we refer to the above Gesenius' *Hebrew Grammar*, under section 126, entitled "Determination by Means of the Article," and paragraph *d* on pages 404, 405, which says: "The article is, generally speaking, employed to determine a substantive wherever it is required by Greek and English; thus: . . . (d) When terms applying to whole classes are restricted (simply by usage) to particular individuals . . . or things, for example, שטן *the adversary*, *Satan;* השטן *the adversary, Satan;* בעל *lord,* הבעל *Baal* as proper name of the god; האדם *the* (first) *man, Adam;* האלהים or האל *ho theós, the one true God* (compare also *ho Khristós* in the New Testament); . . ." And section 141, entitled "The Noun-clause," says, in paragraph *f,* on page 453: "To what period of time the statement applies must be inferred from the context; for example, 1 Kings 18:21 יהוה האלהים *the Lord is the* true *God; . . .*"

For the reader's quick reference we list below the verses where the Hebrew expression *ha-El·o·hím',* as applying to the Creator Jehovah, occurs:

Genesis 5:22, 24; 6:2, 4, 9, 11; 17:18; 20:6, 17; 22:1, 3, 9; 27:28; 31:11; 35:7; 41:25, 28, 32, 32; 42:18; 44:16; 45:8; 48:15, 15.

Exodus 1:17, 21; 2:23; 3:1, 6, 11, 12, 13; 4:20, 27; 14:19; 17:9; 18:5, 12, 16, 19, 19; 19:3, 17, 19; 20:20, 21; 21:6, 13; 22:8, 9; 24:11, 13.

Numbers 22:10; 23:27.

Deuteronomy 4:35, 39; 7:9; 33:1.

Joshua 14:6; 22:34; 24:1.

Judges 6:20, 36, 39; 7:14; 13:6, 6, 8, 9, 9; 16:28; 18:31; 20:2, 27; 21:2.

1 Samuel 4:4, 8, 8, 13, 17, 18, 19, 21, 22; 5:1, 2, 10, 10, 11; 6:20; 9:7, 8, 10; 10:3, 5, 7; 14:18, 18, 36.

2 Samuel 2:27; 6:2, 3, 4, 6, 7, 7, 12, 12; 7:2, 28; 12:16; 14:17, 20; 15:24, 24, 25, 29; 16:23; 19:27.

1 Kings 8:60; 12:22, 22; 13:4, 5, 6, 6, 7, 8, 11, 12, 14, 14, 21, 26, 29, 31; 17:18; 18:21, 24, 24, 37, 39, 39; 19:8; 20:28.

2 Kings 1:9, 11, 12, 13; 4:7, 16, 21, 22, 25, 25, 27, 27, 40, 42; 5:8, 14, 15, 20; 6:6, 9, 10, 15; 7:2, 17, 18, 19; 8:2, 4, 7, 8, 11; 13:19; 19:15; 23:16, 17.

1 Chronicles 5:22; 6:48, 49; 9:11, 13, 26, 27; 13:5, 6, 7, 8, 12, 12, 14; 14:11, 14, 15, 16; 15:1, 2, 15, 24, 26; 16:1, 1, 6, 42; 17:2, 21, 26; 21:7, 8, 15, 17; 22:1, 2, 19, 19; 23:14, 28; 24:5; 25:5, 5, 6; 26:20, 32; 28:3, 12, 21; 29:7.

2 Chronicles 1:3, 4; 3:3; 4:11, 19; 5:1, 14; 7:5; 8:14; 9:23; 10:15; 11:2; 13:12, 15; 15:18; 18:5; 19:3; 22:12; 23:3, 9; 24:7, 9, 13, 16, 20, 27; 25:7, 8, 9, 9, 20, 24; 26:5, 5, 7; 28:24, 24; 29:36; 30:16, 19; 31:13, 14, 21; 32:16, 31; 33:7, 13; 35:8; 36:16, 18, 19.

Ezra 1:3, 4, 5; 2:68; 3:2, 8, 9; 6:22; 8:36; 10:1, 6, 9.

Nehemiah 4:15; 5:13; 6:10; 7:2; 8:6, 8, 16; 9:7; 10:28, 29, 29; 11:11, 16, 22; 12:24, 36, 40, 43; 13:1, 7, 9, 11.

Job 1:6; 2:1, 10.

Psalms 87:3; 90: superscription.

Ecclesiastes 2:24, 26; 3:11, 14, 14, 15, 17, 18; 5:1, 2, 2, 6, 7, 18, 19; 6:2, 2; 7:13, 14, 26, 29; 8:12, 15, 17; 9:1, 7; 11:5, 9; 12:7, 13, 14.

Isaiah 37:16; 45:18.

Jeremiah 35:4.

Ezekiel 31:9.

Daniel 1:2, 9, 17; 9:3, 11.

Jonah 1:6; 3:9, 10, 10; 4:7.

האל *ha-El*, which has the Hebrew definite article *ha* before the title *El*, the plural number of which is *El·im'*, has also been rendered "the [true] God." For the reader's quick reference we list below the verses where the Hebrew expression *ha-El* occurs, as applying to the Creator Jehovah:

Genesis 31:13; 35:1, 3; 46:3.
Deuteronomy 7:9; 10:17; 33:26.
2 Samuel 22:31, 33, 48.
Nehemiah 1:5; 9:32.
Job 13:8; 21:14; 22:17; 31:28; 33:6; 34:10, 37; 40:9.

Psalms 18:30, 32, 47; 57:2; 68:19, 20; 77:14; 85:8.
Isaiah 5:16; 42:5.
Jeremiah 32:18.
Daniel 9:4.

Genesis 15:2 — A·do·nay' — "Lord"

This Hebrew word *A·do·nay'* occurs 432 times in the Masoretic text (M). It is applied exclusively to Jehovah God. However, there were 134 passages in M where the Jewish Sopherim claim that they substituted this word *A·do·nay'* for the name *Yeho·wah'* ("Jehovah") in the primitive Hebrew text. (See below on this same page under "Genesis 18:3 — 'Jehovah.' ") We have therefore restored the name "Jehovah" to those 134 passages, and thus reduced the number of occurrences of *A·do·nay'* to 298 times.

The first occurrence of *A·do·nay'* is in the verse cited above, where it precedes the divine name to produce the combination *A·do·nay' Yeho·wih'*, which is translated "Lord Jehovah." (From Psalm 71:5, 16 forward "Sovereign Lord Jehovah.") This combination occurs 280 times by itself.

Besides this, beginning with Psalm 69:6, the combination *A·do·nay' Yeho·wih' tseba·ôth'* ("Sovereign Lord, Jehovah of armies") occurs 16 times, as follows: Psalm 69:6; Isaiah 3:15; 10:23, 24; 22:5, 12, 14, 15; 28:22; Jeremiah 2:19; 46:10, 10; 49:5; 50:25, 31; Amos 9:5 ("of *the* armies").

Beginning with Psalm 68:20, *A·do·nay'* follows the divine name, to form the combination *Yeho·wih' A·do·nay'* ("Jehovah the Sovereign Lord"), in five passages, as follows:

Psalms 68:20; 109:21; 140:7; 141:8; Habakkuk 3:19.

Following the later practice of the Jewish rabbis in reading *A·do·nay'* instead of the divine name *Yeho·wah'*, the later copyists of the Greek *LXX* substituted the anarthrous Greek title *Ky'ri·os* ("Lord; Master") for the Hebrew tetragrammaton יהוה, which had been transliterated into the Greek text.

Genesis 18:3 — "Jehovah"

(אדני, *A·do·nay'*, Hebrew Masoretic Text; Κύριε *Ky'ri·e*, Greek *LXX*; *Do'mi·ne*, Latin Vg; *Mar'ya*, Syriac Peshitta; ܝ ܝ, *YeYa*, Aramaic Targum of Onkelos; "My lords," Samaritan Pentateuch, with the following second-person pronouns in the plural number)

The above is one of the 134 places where the Jewish Sopherim or scribes claim that they altered the primitive Hebrew text to read *A·do·nay'* (meaning "Lord") instead of *Yeho·wah'* ("Jehovah"). In all these places we have taken the reading of the primitive Hebrew text instead of that of the traditional Hebrew Masoretic text and thus have rendered the divine name Yeho·wah′ into the English as "Jehovah." Below we list all the other places shown in the *Massōrah* (paragraphs 107-115, Ginsburg's edition), where we have followed the reading of the primitive Hebrew text.

Genesis 18:3, 27, 30, 31, 32; 19:18; 20:4.

Exodus 4:10, 13; 5:22; 15:17; 34:9, 9.

Numbers 14:17.

Joshua 7:8.

Judges 6:15; 13:8.

1 Kings 3:10, 15; 22:6.

2 Kings 7:6; 19:23.

Ezra 10:3.

Nehemiah 1:11; 4:14.

Job 28:28.

Psalms 2:4; 16:2; 22:30; 30:8; 35:17, 22, 23; 37:13; 38:9, 15, 22; 39:7; 40:17; 44:23; 51:15; 54:4; 55:9; 57:9; 59:11; 62:12; 66:18; 68:11, 17, 19, 22, 26, 32; 73:20; 77:2, 7; 78:65; 79:12; 86:3, 4, 5, 8, 9, 12, 15; 89:49, 50; 90:1, 17; 110:5; 130: 2, 3, 6.

Isaiah 3:17, 18; 4:4; 6:1, 8, 11; 7:14, 20; 8:7; 9:8, 17; 10:12; 11:11; 21:6, 8, 16; 28:2; 29:13; 30:20; 37:24; 38:14, 16; 49:14.

Lamentations 1:14, 15, 15; 2:1, 2, 5, 7, 18, 19, 20; 3:31, 36, 37, 58.

Ezekiel 18:25, 29; 21:9; 33:17, 20.

Daniel 1:2; 9:3, 4, 7, 9, 15, 16, 17, 19, 19, 19.

Amos 5:16; 7:7, 8; 9:1.

Micah 1:2.

Zechariah 9:4.

Malachi 1:12, 14.

On the above Scripture citations we refer the reader to Dr. Solomon Mandelkern's (1925) *Veteris Testamenti Concordantiae Hebraicai atque Chaldaicae* ("Hebrew and Chaldean Concordance of the Old Testament") page 16, columns 1-3, and page 1432, column 3, under יהוה אדני.

In addition to the above, we call attention to the following places where the Jewish Sopherim claim they altered the primitive Hebrew text to read *El·o·him′* ("God") instead of *Yeho·wah′* ("Jehovah"): Psalms 14:1, 2, 5; 53:1, 2, 4, 5.

A change similar to the latter was claimed to have been made by the Jewish Sopherim in 2 Samuel 5:19-25; 6:9-17; 1 Chronicles 13:12; 14:10, 11, 14, 16; 16:1. However, in these places we have followed the reading of the Hebrew text as published by Rudolf Kittel and his survivors, A. Alt, O. Eissfeldt and P. Kahle. (See The Hebrew Text on page 19 of the Foreword of Volume I of the *New World Translation of the Hebrew Scriptures*.)

For another rendering of the Hebrew text to read "Jehovah" we refer the reader to Zechariah 6:8, where the final *yod* ("*i*") in the Hebrew word is understood to be an abbreviation of the divine name instead of meaning "my." This may also be the case in Ezekiel 43:3; Habakkuk 3:19; Zephaniah 2:12; Zechariah 11:10 (once for "my" and once for "I"); 14:5. But the reverse appears to be the case in Judges 19:18, where evidently "my" was intended rather than the divine name.

Isaiah 1:24 — "the [true] Lord"

This is the translation of the Hebrew expression האדון *ha-A·dōn′*, this being the title *A·dōn′* ("Lord; Master") preceded by the Hebrew definite article *ha*. Although there are many lords or masters, this prefixing of the definite article before the title *a·dōn′* limits the application of the title to Jehovah God. (See Gesenius' *Hebrew Gram-*

mar, section 126, paragraph *d,* on pages 404, 405.) In the Hebrew Scriptures this expression *ha-A·dōn'* occurs nine times, as listed below:

Exodus

23:17   On three occasions in the year every male of yours will appear before the face of the true Lord Jehovah.

34:23   Three times in the year every male of yours is to appear before the true Lord, Jehovah, the God of Israel.

Isaiah

1:24   Therefore the utterance of the true Lord, Jehovah of armies, the Powerful One of Israel, is:

3:1   For, look! the true Lord, Jehovah of armies, is removing from Jerusalem and from Judah support and stay,

10:16   Therefore the true Lord, Jehovah of armies, will keep sending upon his fat ones a wasting disease,

10:33   Look! The true Lord, Jehovah of armies, is lopping off boughs with a terrible crash;

19:4   "And I will deliver up Egypt into the hand of a hard master, and strong will be the king that will rule over them," is the utterance of the true Lord, Jehovah of armies.

Micah

4:13b   and by a ban you will actually devote to Jehovah their unjust profit, and their resources to the true Lord of the whole earth."

Malachi

3:1   Look! I am sending my messenger, and he must clear up a way before me. And suddenly there will come to His temple the true Lord, whom you people are seeking, and the messenger of the covenant in whom you are delighting.

The plural number of *a·dōn'* is *a·do·nim';* and the Hebrew expression *ha-a·do·nim'* does occur, but in a plural sense, in the following two verses:

Deuteronomy

10:17   For Jehovah your God is the God of gods and the Lord of lords,

Psalms

136:3   Give thanks to the Lord of the lords:

Matthew 1:20 — "Jehovah's"

Below we give a concordance of all places in this translation where the name "Jehovah" occurs in the Christian Greek Scriptures.

Matthew (18 times)

1:20   J's angel appeared to him
1:22   which was spoken by J
1:24   angel of J had directed him,
2:13   J's angel appeared in a dream
2:15   which was spoken by J
2:19   J's angel appeared in a dream
3:3   'Prepare the way of J, you

4:4   forth through J's mouth.' "
4:7   put J your God to the test.' "
4:10   J your God you must worship,
5:33   you must pay your vows to J.'
21:9   he that comes in J's name!
21:42   From J this has come to be
22:37   You must love J your God
22:44   J said to my Lord: "Sit at

23:39 he that comes in J's name!
27:10 what J had commanded me."
28:2 J's angel had descended

Mark (9 times)

1:3 'Prepare the way of J, you
5:19 things J has done for you
11:9 he that comes in J's name!
12:11 From J this has come to be,
12:29 Hear, O Israel, J our God is
12:29 our God is one J,
12:30 you must love J your God
12:36 J said to my Lord: "Sit at
13:20 unless J had cut short

Luke (36 times)

1:6 legal requirements of J.
1:9 the sanctuary of J;
1:11 To him J's angel appeared,
1:15 he will be great before J.
1:16 will he turn back to J
1:17 for J a prepared people."
1:25 J has dealt with me in
1:28 favored one, J is with you."
1:32 J God will give him the
1:38 Look! J's slave girl! May
1:45 spoken to her from J."
1:46 My soul magnifies J,
1:58 J had magnified his mercy
1:66 the hand of J was indeed
1:68 Blessed be J the God of
1:76 go in advance before J
2:9 J's angel stood by them
2:9 J's glory gleamed around
2:15 which J has made known to
2:22 to present him to J,
2:23 as it is written in J's law:
2:23 must be called holy to J,
2:24 is said in the law of J:
2:26 seen the Christ of J.
2:39 according to the law of J,
3:4 'Prepare the way of J, you
4:8 J your God you must worship.
4:12 You must not put J your God
4:18 J's spirit is upon me,
4:19 to preach J's acceptable
5:17 J's power was there for him
10:27 You must love J your God
13:35 he that comes in J's name.'"
19:38 as the King in J's name!
20:37 he calls J 'the God of
20:42 J said to my Lord, Sit at

John (5 times)

1:23 Make the way of J straight,
6:45 will all be taught by J.'
12:13 he that comes in J's name,

12:38 J, who has put faith
12:38 the arm of J, to whom has

Acts (52 times)

1:24 You, O J, who know the
2:20 day of J arrives.
2:21 calls on the name of J
2:25 I had J constantly before
2:34 J said to my Lord: "Sit at
2:39 as many as J our God may
2:47 J continued to join to
3:19 come from the person of J
3:22 J God will raise up for
4:26 against J and against his
4:29 J, give attention to their
5:9 a test of the spirit of J?
5:19 J's angel opened the doors
7:31 J's voice came,
7:33 J said to him, 'Take the
7:49 you build for me? J says.
7:60 "J, do not charge this sin
8:22 supplicate J that, if
8:24 supplication for me to J
8:25 had spoken the word of J
8:26 J's angel spoke to Philip,
8:39 J's spirit quickly led
9:31 it walked in the fear of J
10:33 commanded by J to say."
11:21 hand of J was with them,
12:7 look! J's angel stood by,
12:11 know that J sent his angel
12:17 how J brought him out of
12:23 angel of J struck him,
12:24 word of J went on growing
13:2 publicly ministering to J
13:10 the right ways of J?
13:11 J's hand is upon you,
13:12 at the teaching of J.
13:44 to hear the word of J.
13:47 J has laid commandment
13:48 to glorify the word of J,
13:49 word of J went on being
14:3 by the authority of J,
14:23 they committed them to J
15:17 men may earnestly seek J,
15:17 called by my name, says J,
15:35 news of the word of J
15:36 published the word of J
15:40 undeserved kindness of J.
16:14 J opened her heart wide to
16:15 me to be faithful to J,
16:32 they spoke the word of J
18:21 again, if J is willing."
18:25 instructed in the way of J
19:20 word of J kept growing
21:14 the will of J take place."

Romans (19 times)

4:3	Abraham exercised faith in J,
4:8	is the man whose sin J will
9:28	J will make an accounting
9:29	Unless J of armies had left
10:13	calls on the name of J
10:16	"J, who put faith in
11:3	"J, they have killed your
11:34	has come to know J's mind,
12:11	Slave for J.
12:19	I will repay, says J."
14:4	J can make him stand.
14:6	the day observes it to J.
14:6	he who eats, eats to J,
14:6	not eat does not eat to J,
14:8	if we live, we live to J,
14:8	if we die, we die to J.
14:8	if we die, we belong to J.
14:11	'As I live,' says J, 'to me
15:11	"Praise J, all you nations,

1 Corinthians (15 times)

1:31	let him boast in J."
2:16	to know the mind of J,
3:20	J knows that the reasonings
4:4	he that examines me is J.
4:19	shortly, if J wills,
7:17	as J has given each one a
10:9	let us put J to the test,
10:21	be drinking the cup of J
10:21	of "the table of J" and the
10:22	"are we inciting J to
10:26	to J belong the earth and
11:32	we are disciplined by J,
14:21	they give heed to me,' says J."
16:7	with you, if J permits.
16:10	performing the work of J,

2 Corinthians (10 times)

3:16	there is a turning to J,
3:17	Now J is the Spirit; and
3:17	where the spirit of J is,
3:18	mirrors the glory of J,
3:18	as done by J the Spirit.
6:17	separate yourselves,' says J,
6:18	daughters to me,' says J
8:21	in the sight of J, but
10:17	let him boast in J."
10:18	man whom J recommends.

Galatians (1 time)

3:6	Abraham "put faith in J,

Ephesians (6 times)

2:21	into a holy temple for J.
5:17	what the will of J is.
5:19	music in your hearts to J,

6:4	authoritative advice of J.
6:7	inclinations, as to J,
6:8	receive this back from J,

Colossians (6 times)

1:10	to walk worthily of J
3:13	as J freely forgave you,
3:16	singing in your hearts to J.
3:22	of heart, with fear of J.
3:23	it whole-souled as to J,
3:24	from J you will receive

1 Thessalonians (4 times)

1:8	word of J sounded forth
4:6	J is one who exacts
4:15	we tell you by J's word,
5:2	J's day is coming exactly

2 Thessalonians (3 times)

2:2	the day of J is here.
2:13	you, brothers loved by J,
3:1	word of J may keep moving

2 Timothy (4 times)

1:18	him to find mercy from J
2:19	J knows those who belong
2:19	naming the name of J
4:14	J will repay him according

Hebrews (12 times)

2:13	children, whom J gave me."
7:21	J has sworn, and he will
8:2	true tent, which J put up,
8:8	are days coming,' says J,
8:9	caring for them,' says J.
8:10	after those days,' says J.
8:11	brother, saying: "Know J!"
10:16	after those days,' says J.
10:30	J will judge his people."
12:5	the discipline from J,
12:6	J loves he disciplines;
13:6	J is my helper; I will

James (13 times)

1:7	receive anything from J;
1:12	crown of life, which J
2:23	"Abraham put faith in J,
2:23	be called "J's friend."
3:9	With it we bless J, even
4:10	in the eyes of J, and he
4:15	ought to say: "If J wills,
5:4	the ears of J of armies.
5:10	spoke in the name of J.
5:11	seen the outcome J gave,
5:11	that J is very tender in
5:14	with oil in the name of J.
5:15	and J will raise him up.

1 Peter (3 times)

1:25 the saying of J endures
3:12 For the eyes of J are upon
3:12 the face of J is against those

2 Peter (6 times)

2:9 J knows how to deliver
2:11 so out of respect for J.
3:8 one day is with J as a
3:9 J is not slow respecting
3:10 J's day will come as a
3:12 presence of the day of J,

Jude (3 times)

5 J, although he saved a
9 said: "May J rebuke you."
14 J came with his holy

Revelation (12 times)

1:8 the Omega," says J God,

4:8 "Holy, holy, holy is J God,
4:11 "You are worthy, J, even
11:17 saying: "We thank you, J
15:3 are your works, J God,
15:4 not really fear you, J,
16:7 altar say: "Yes, J God,
18:8 J God, who judged her is
19:6 J our God, the Almighty,
21:22 J God the Almighty is its
22:5 J God will shed light
22:6 J the God of the inspired

JAH

(abbreviation for "Jehovah")

Revelation (4 times)

19:1 They said: "Praise J, you
19:3 time they said: "Praise J,
19:4 "Amen! Praise J, you people!"
19:6 They said: "Praise J, you

Matthew 2:20 — "soul"

(ψυχή, *psy·khē′*, Greek; נֶפֶשׁ, *neph'esh,* Hebrew)

Throughout our translation we have consistently rendered the Greek word *psy·khē′* (Hebrew, *neph'esh*) as "soul." It will be found that this rendering makes sense in each case. This uniform rendering of *psy·khē′* by the same English word in all cases proves very enlightening as to how the ancients used that word, how the inspired writers understood that word and what properties they ascribed to it. Below we give a list of some renderings of the 102 occurrences of the word *psy·khē′* (*neph'esh,* soul), grouping them under several headings to show the various ideas attached to the word.

The creature soul is mortal, destructible

Matthew

2:20 who were seeking the soul of the young child
10:28 kill the body but cannot kill the soul;
10:28 can destroy both soul and body in Gehenna.
26:38 My soul is deeply grieved, even to death.

Mark

3:4 to save or to kill a soul?"
14:34 "My soul is deeply grieved, even to death.

Luke

6:9 to save or to destroy a soul?"
17:33 his soul safe for himself will lose it, but whoever loses it will preserve it alive.

John

12:25 He that is fond of his soul destroys it,

Acts

3:23 any soul that does not listen to that Prophet will be completely destroyed

Romans

11:3 they are looking for my soul."

Hebrews

10:39 to destruction, but the sort that have faith to the preserving alive of the soul.

James

5:20 will save his soul from death

Revelation
8:9   creatures that are in the
       sea which have souls
       died,

12:11   their souls even in the face
        of death.
16:3   every living soul died, yes,
        the things in the sea.

Soul delivered from Ha'des (She'ol, "hell")

Acts
2:27   you will not leave my soul in Ha'des,

Soul, a living person or creature

Acts
2:41   about three thousand souls
       were added.
2:43   fear began to fall upon
       every soul,
7:14   to the number of seventy-
       five souls.
27:37 we souls in the boat were
       about two hundred and

Romans
13:1   Let every soul be in sub-
       jection to the

1 Corinthians
15:45 "The first man Adam be-
       came a living soul."

1 Peter
3:20   a few people, that is, eight
       souls, were carried

2 Peter
2:14   they entice unsteady souls.

Soul distinguished from spirit

Philippians
1:27   in one spirit, with one soul
       fighting side by side
1 Thessalonians
5:23   may the spirit and soul and

body of you

Hebrews
4:12   even to the dividing of soul
       and spirit,

Matthew 11:23 — "Ha'des"

(ᾅδης, Greek; שְׁאוֹל, Sheʻol, Hebrew; Shiʻulʼ, Syriac; inferʼnus, Latin)

This word we have transliterated from the Greek into the English for the ten times it occurs. (Matthew 11:23; 16:18; Luke 10:15; 16:23; Acts 2:27, 31; Revelation 1:18; 6:8; 20:13, 14) It literally means "the unseen place." Peter's use of it at Acts 2:27, 31 shows it is the equivalent of the Hebrew word Sheʻol, which occurs 65 times in the Hebrew Scriptures and is applied to the common grave of mankind. With good reason that, for according to the root words from which it may be derived Sheʻol means either "the hollow place" or "resting place." In the common grave mankind rests in the unseen place or place hollowed out for their burial. The corresponding Latin word

inferʼnus (sometimes inʼferus) means "that which lies beneath; the lower region," and it well applies to the grave: It is thus a fit equivalent of the Greek and Hebrew terms. In the inspired Scriptures these words are always associated with death and the dead, never with life and the living. For instance, Revelation 20:13: "Death and Ha'des gave up those dead in them."

In themselves the words contain no thought or hint of pleasure or of pain; which fact befits the Bible description of the dead. Even the ancient Greeks used Ha'des to mean "the grave" as well as "death." It is in this sense that the inspired Bible writers used the word.

TABLE OF THE BOOKS OF THE BIBLE

(Indicating the writer, the place of writing, the time of completion of writing, and the time covered by the events of the book)
[Names of writers of some books and of places where written are uncertain. Many dates are only approximate, the symbol a. meaning "after," b. meaning "before" and c. meaning "circa" or "about."]

Books of the Hebrew Scriptures Before the Common or Christian Era

Name of Book	The Writer	Place Written	Writing Completed (B.C.E.)	Time Covered (B.C.E.)
Genesis	Moses	Wilderness	1513	After 1:2: 46,026–1657
Exodus	Moses	Wilderness	1512	1657–1512
Leviticus	Moses	Wilderness	1512	1 month (1512)
Numbers	Moses	Wilderness and Plains of Moab	1473	1512–1473
Deuteronomy	Moses	Plains of Moab	1473	2 months (1473)
Joshua	Joshua	Canaan	c. 1450	1473–c. 1450
Judges	Samuel	Israel	c. 1100	c. 1450–c. 1120
Ruth	Samuel	Israel	c. 1090	11 years of judges' rule
1 Samuel	Samuel; Gad; Nathan	Israel	c. 1077	c. 1180–1077
2 Samuel	Gad; Nathan	Israel	c. 1040	1077–c. 1040
1 Kings	Jeremiah	Judah and Egypt	1 roll	c. 1040–580
2 Kings	Jeremiah	Judah and Egypt	580	c. 1040–580
1 Chronicles	Ezra	Jerusalem (?)	1 roll	After 1 Chronicles 9:44:
2 Chronicles	Ezra	Jerusalem (?)	c. 460	1077–537
Ezra	Ezra	Jerusalem	c. 460	537–c. 467
Nehemiah	Nehemiah	Jerusalem	a. 443	456–a. 443
Esther	Mordecai	Shushan, Elam	c. 474	c. 484–474
Job	Moses	Wilderness	c. 1473	Over 140 years between 1657–1473
Psalms	David and others		c. 460	
Proverbs	Solomon; Agur; Lemuel	Jerusalem	c. 716	
Ecclesiastes	Solomon	Jerusalem	b. 1000	
Song of Solomon, The	Solomon	Jerusalem	c. 1020	
Isaiah	Isaiah	Jerusalem	c. 732	c. 778–732
Jeremiah	Jeremiah	Judah; Egypt	580	647–580
Lamentations	Jeremiah	Near Jerusalem	607	
Ezekiel	Ezekiel	Babylon	591	613–c. 591
Daniel	Daniel	Babylon	c. 536	618–c. 536
Hosea	Hosea	Samaria (District)	a. 745	b. 803–a. 745
Joel	Joel	Judah	c. 820 (?)	
Amos	Amos	Judah	c. 803	
Obadiah	Obadiah		c. 607	
Jonah	Jonah		c. 844	

1461

Name of Book	The Writer	Place Written	Writing Completed (B.C.E.)	Time Covered (B.C.E.)
Micah	Micah	Judah	b. 716	c. 777-716
Nahum	Nahum	Judah	b. 632	
Habakkuk	Habakkuk	Judah	c. 628 (?)	
Zephaniah	Zephaniah	Judah	b. 648	
Haggai	Haggai	Jerusalem rebuilt	520	112 days (520)
Zechariah	Zechariah	Jerusalem rebuilt	518	520-518
Malachi	Malachi	Jerusalem rebuilt	a. 443	

Books of the Greek Scriptures Written During the Common (Christian) Era

Name of Book	The Writer	Place Written	Writing Completed (C.E.)	Time Covered
Matthew	Matthew	Palestine	c. 41	2 B.C.E.– 33 C.E.
Mark	Mark	Rome	c. 60-65	29-33 C.E.
Luke	Luke	Caesarea	c. 56-58	3 B.C.E.– 33 C.E.
John	Apostle John	Ephesus, or near	c. 98	After prologue, 29–33 C.E.
Acts	Luke	Rome	c. 61	33-c. 61 C.E.
Romans	Paul	Corinth	c. 56	
1 Corinthians	Paul	Ephesus	c. 55	
2 Corinthians	Paul	Macedonia	c. 55	
Galatians	Paul	Corinth or Syrian Antioch	c. 50-52	
Ephesians	Paul	Rome	c. 60-61	
Philippians	Paul	Rome	c. 60-61	
Colossians	Paul	Rome	c. 60-61	
1 Thessalonians	Paul	Corinth	c. 50	
2 Thessalonians	Paul	Corinth	c. 51	
1 Timothy	Paul	Macedonia	c. 61-64	
2 Timothy	Paul	Rome	c. 65	
Titus	Paul	Macedonia (?)	c. 61-64	
Philemon	Paul	Rome	c. 60-61	
Hebrews	Paul	Rome	c. 61	
James	James (Jesus' brother)	Jerusalem	b. 62	
1 Peter	Peter	Babylon	c. 62-64	
2 Peter	Peter	Babylon (?)	c. 64	
1 John	Apostle John	Ephesus, or near	c. 98	
2 John	Apostle John	Ephesus, or near	c. 98	
3 John	Apostle John	Ephesus, or near	c. 98	
Jude	Jude (Jesus' brother)	Palestine (?)	c. 65	
Revelation	Apostle John	Patmos	c. 96	

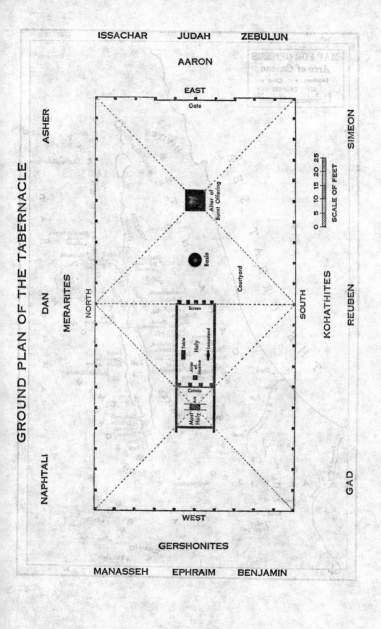

GROUND PLAN OF THE TABERNACLE

ISSACHAR   JUDAH   ZEBULUN

AARON

EAST
Gate

ASHER

SIMEON

NORTH

SOUTH

MERARITES

DAN

KOHATHITES

REUBEN

Altar of Burnt Offering

Basin

Courtyard

Screen

Table   Holy   Lampstand

Altar of Incense

Curtain

Ark   Most Holy

0 5 10 15 20 25
SCALE OF FEET

NAPHTALI

GAD

WEST

GERSHONITES

MANASSEH   EPHRAIM   BENJAMIN

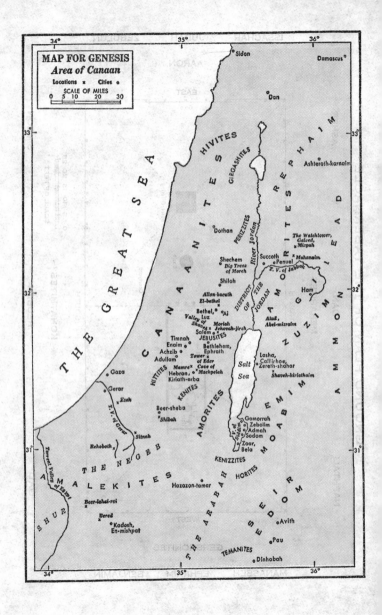

MAP FOR GENESIS
Area of Canaan

Locations ×   Cities •

SCALE OF MILES
0   5   10   20   30

• Sidon

Damascus •

• Dan

THE GREAT SEA

HIVITES

GIRGASHITES

River Jordan

PERIZZITES

REPHAIM

Ashteroth-karnaim •

• Dothan

The Watchtower,
Galeed,
× Mizpah

Shechem •
Big Trees
of Moreh

Succoth •
Penuel •

× Mahanaim

Shiloh •

T. V. of Jabbok

Ham •

Allon-bacuth
El-bethel ×

DISTRICT OF THE JORDAN

AMORITES

GILEAD

Bethel •
Luz
Valley of
Shaveh
Salem

× Moriah
× Jehovah-jireh

• Ai

Atad ×
Abel-mizraim ×

ZUZIM

AMMON

Timnah •
Enaim •
Achzib •
Adullam •

JEBUSITES

Bethlehem,
Ephrath •

Lasha,
Callirhoe,
Zereth-shahar

Mamre ×
Hebron ×
Kiriath-arba •

Tower ×
of Eder
Cave of
Machpelah ×

× Shaveh-kiriathaim

Salt
Sea

• Gaza

HITTITES

KENITES

AMORITES

EMIM

MOAB

• Gerar

Esek ×

F. V. of Gerar

Beer-sheba •
Shibah •

Sitnah ×

Gomorrah
Zeboiim
Admah
Sodom
Zoar, Bela

Rehoboth ×

THE NEGEB

AMALEKITES

KENIZZITES

SHUR

Torrent Valley of Egypt

Hazazon-tamar •

HORITES

THE ARABAH

SEIR

EDOM

• Avith

Beer-lahai-roi ×

Bered ×
× Kadesh,
En-mishpat

• Pau

TEMANITES

• Dinhabah

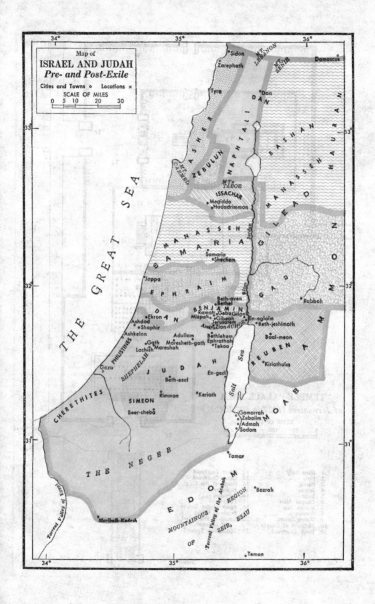

Map of
ISRAEL AND JUDAH
Pre- and Post-Exile

Cities and Towns ○ Locations ✕

SCALE OF MILES
0   5   10   20   30

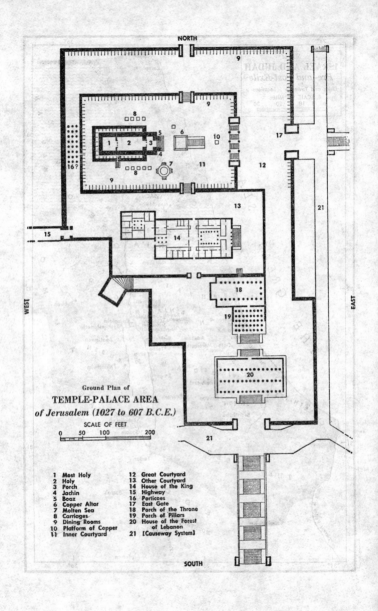

NORTH

WEST

EAST

SOUTH

Ground Plan of

TEMPLE-PALACE AREA

of Jerusalem (1027 to 607 B.C.E.)

SCALE OF FEET

0   50   100   200

1 Most Holy
2 Holy
3 Porch
4 Jachin
5 Boaz
6 Copper Altar
7 Molten Sea
8 Carriages
9 Dining Rooms
10 Platform of Copper
11 Inner Courtyard
12 Great Courtyard
13 Other Courtyard
14 House of the King
15 Highway
16 Porticoes
17 East Gate
18 Porch of the Throne
19 Porch of Pillars
20 House of the Forest
    of Lebanon
21 [Causeway System]

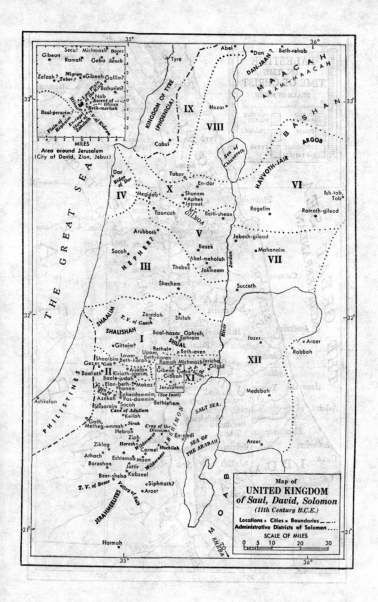

Map of
UNITED KINGDOM
of Saul, David, Solomon
(11th Century B.C.E.)

Locations ▲ Cities ● Boundaries ___ · ___
Administrative Districts of Solomon · · · ·

SCALE OF MILES
0 5 10 20 30

Area around Jerusalem
(City of David, Zion, Jebus)

THE GREAT SEA

PHILISTINES

KINGDOM OF TYRE (PHOENICIA)

BASHAN

ARGOB

MAACAH

DAN-JAAN

HAVVOTH-JAIR

GILBOA

Jordan River

SALT SEA

SEA OF THE ARABAH

MOAB

TO SHUR

JERAHMEELITES

Inset labels:
Gibeon, Secu?, Michmash, Bozez, Ramah, Geba, Seneh, Zelzah?, Migron, Gibeah, Gallim?, Tabor?, Nob, Bahurim?, Lower Pool of the Old Pool, Ascent of the Olives, Beth-merhak, Baal-perazim?, Plain of Rephaim, Enrogel, Valley of Kidron, Zoheleth

Main map labels:
Abel, Dan, Beth-rehob, Tyre, Hazor, IX, VIII, Cabul, Sea of Chinnereth, Tabor, En-dor, Dor, Rido of Dor, IV, Megiddo, X, Shunem, Aphek, Jezreel, Ish-tob, Tob, VI, Taanach, Beth-shean, Rogelim, Ramoth-gilead, Arubboth, V, Bezek, Jabesh-gilead, Socoh, HEPHER, III, Abel-meholah, Thebez, Jokmeam, Mahanaim, VII, Shechem, Succoth, Zeredah, T.V. of Gaash, Shiloh, SHAALIM, SHALISHAH, I, Baal-hazor, Ophrah, Ephraim, Gittaim?, Bethel, SHUAL, Upper Beth-horon, Beth-aven, Shaalbim, Lower Beth-horon, Gezer, Gob, Aijalon, Ramah, Michmash, Gibeon, Geba, Gilgal, Jericho, Baalath, II, Kirioth-jearim, Baale-judah, XI, Gibeah, Jerusalem (See Inset), Elon-beth-hanan, Mokaz?, Jazer, Rabbah, Ekron, Ephesdammim, Pas-dammim, Azekah, Socoh, Ashkelon, Shaaraim, Cave of Adullam, Bethlehem, XII, Gath, Metheg-ammah, Sirah, Crag of the Divisions, Medebah, Hebron, Ziph, En-gedi, Ziklag, Horesh, Carmel, Huchilah, Aroer, Athach, Maon, SEA OF THE ARABAH, Borashan, Eshtemoa, Jattir, Wilderness, Beer-sheba, Kabzeel, Siphmoth?, T.V. of Besor, Aroer, Valley of Salt, Hormah

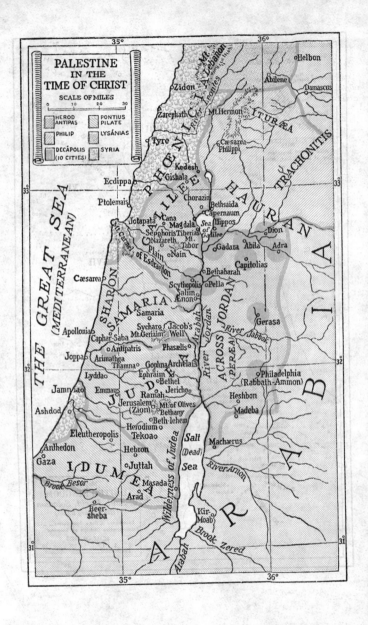

PALESTINE IN THE TIME OF CHRIST

SCALE OF MILES
10   20   30

HEROD ANTIPAS
PHILIP
DECÁPOLIS (10 CITIES)
PONTIUS PILATE
LYSÁNIAS
SYRIA

A BIBLE FOR EVERY MEMBER OF THE FAMILY

The Bible is a Book for everyone. As the psalmist said: "Your word is a lamp to my foot, and a light to my roadway." (Ps. 119:105) Is every member of your family properly equipped? All can be! The *New World Translation of the Holy Scriptures*, Regular edition, is so moderately priced that no one need be without his personal copy. And it is designed for regular use. This complete Bible, bound in a gold-embossed green vinyl cover, is only $1 for each copy. This edition of the *New World Translation* is also available in Dutch, French, German, Italian, Portuguese and Spanish, at $1 a copy.

A DELUXE EDITION

In addition to the Regular edition, there is, in English, a Deluxe edition of the *New World Translation*. This comes with a flexible cover in either black or maroon, gold edging on pages. Sent postpaid, anywhere, for $3 a copy.

LARGE-PRINT BIBLE

To make your reading of the Holy Scriptures more enjoyable you may wish to have the *New World Translation of the Holy Scriptures* (1971 edition) in a large, clear print. This will make your Bible reading easy. It is an excellent edition for careful Bible study, being complete with illuminating footnotes and an index of Bible words. Available in English and Spanish. Sent postpaid, anywhere, $5.00 a copy.

"ALL SCRIPTURE IS INSPIRED OF GOD AND BENEFICIAL"

Now you can prove to yourself that the Bible is the most modern book available today. You can learn how it is the most practical guide to modern living. The 352-page book *"All Scripture Is Inspired of God and Beneficial"* examines the Holy Scriptures from many viewpoints. In Part One, each of the Bible's sixty-six books is examined as to its source, its authenticity and purpose and its power for benefiting you today. Included is a fascinating summary of the contents of each Bible book. You will learn how God inspired men to write His Word and how the Bible has come down to us over so many centuries without losing textual integrity. Part II contains special studies on the inspired Scriptures and their background, dealing with such topics as "A Visit to the Promised Land," "Measuring Events in the Stream of Time," and "Archaeology Supports the Inspired Record." Included are maps, illustrations and many informative charts, such as "Main Events of Jesus' Earthly Sojourn" and "Chart of Outstanding Historical Dates." Dark-blue, hardbound cover. Sent postpaid, anywhere, for $1 a copy.

For ordering the above see addresses on next page.

CHIEF OFFICE AND OFFICIAL ADDRESS OF

Watch Tower Bible & Tract Society of Pennsylvania
Watchtower Bible and Tract Society of New York, Inc.
International Bible Students Association
124 Columbia Heights, Brooklyn, New York 11201, U.S.A.

ADDRESSES OF BRANCH OFFICES:

ALASKA 99507: 2552 East 48th Ave., Anchorage. **ARGENTINA:** Gorriti 5647, Buenos Aires 14. **AUSTRALIA:** 11 Beresford Road, Strathfield, N.S.W. 2135. **AUSTRIA:** Gallgasse 44, A-1130 Vienna. **BAHAMAS:** Box N-1247, Nassau, N.P. **BARBADOS, W.I.:** Fontabelle Rd., Bridgetown. **BELGIUM:** rue d'Argile 60, B-1950 Kraainem. **BOLIVIA:** Casilla No. 1440, La Paz. **BRAZIL:** Rua Guaíra, 216, Bosque da Saúde, 04142 São Paulo, SP. **BRITISH HONDURAS:** Box 257, Belize. **BURMA:** P.O. Box 62, Rangoon. **CANADA:** 150 Bridgeland Ave., Toronto 390, Ontario. **CENTRAL AFRICAN REPUBLIC:** B.P. 662, Bangui. **CEYLON:** 7 Alfred House Rd., Colombo 3. **CHILE:** Clorinda Wilshaw 501, Ñuñoa, Casilla 261-V, Correo 21, Santiago. **COLOMBIA:** Apartado Aéreo 2587, Barranquilla. **CONGO, REPUBLIC OF THE:** B.P. 634, Kinshasa, Limete. **CONGO REPUBLIC:** B.P. 2.114, Brazzaville. **COSTA RICA:** Apartado 10043, San José. **CUBA:** Avenida 15 Núm. 4608, Almendares, Marianao, Havana. **CYPRUS:** P.O. Box 1590, Nicosia. **DAHOMEY:** B.P. 874, Cotonou. **DENMARK:** Kongevejen 207, 2830 Virum. **DOMINICAN REPUBLIC:** Avenida Francia 33, Santo Domingo. **ECUADOR:** Casilla 4512, Guayaquil. **EL SALVADOR:** Apartado 401, San Salvador. **ENGLAND:** Watch Tower House, The Ridgeway, London N.W. 7. **FIJI:** Box 23, Suva. **FINLAND:** Kuismatie 58, Tikkurila. **FRANCE:** 81, rue du Point du Jour, 92 - Boulogne-Billancourt. **GERMANY (WESTERN):** Postfach 13025, 62 Wiesbaden-Dotzheim. **GHANA:** Box 760, Accra. **GREECE:** No. 4 Kartali St., Athens 611. **GUADELOUPE:** B.P. 239, Pointe-à-Pitre. **GUATEMALA:** 11 Avenida 5-67, Guatemala 1. **GUYANA:** 50 Brickdam, Georgetown 11. **HAITI:** Post Box 185, Port-au-Prince. **HAWAII 96814:** 1228 Pensacola St., Honolulu. **HONDURAS:** Apartado 147, Tegucigalpa. **HONG KONG:** 312 Prince Edward Rd., Second Floor, Kowloon. **ICELAND:** P.O. Box 251, Reykjavik. **INDIA:** South Avenue, Santa Cruz, Bombay 54. **INDONESIA:** Djalan Batutjeper 25, Djakarta. **IRELAND:** 86 Lindsay Rd., Glasnevin, Dublin 9. **ISRAEL:** P.O. Box 44520, Haifa. **ITALY:** Via Monte Maloia 32, 00141 Rome. **IVORY COAST:** B.P. 6291, Treichville, Abidjan. **JAMAICA, W.I.:** 41 Trafalgar Rd., Kingston 10. **JAPAN:** 5-5-8 Mita Minato-Ku, Tokyo, 108. **KENYA:** Box 7788, Nairobi. **KOREA:** Box 7 Sodaemun P.O., Seoul, 120. **LEEWARD ISLANDS, W.I.:** Box 119, St. Johns, Antigua. **LIBERIA:** P.O. Box 171, Monrovia. **LUXEMBOURG:** 15, rue de l'Egalite, Luxembourg-Bonnevoie, G.D. **MAURITIUS:** 106A Prince of Wales St., Rose Hill. **MEXICO:** Calzada Melchor Ocampo 71, Mexico 4, D.F. **NETHERLANDS:** Voorburgstraat 250, Amsterdam 17. **NETHERLANDS ANTILLES:** Oosterbeekstraat 11, Willemstad, Curaçao. **NEWFOUNDLAND, CANADA:** 239 Pennywell Rd., St. John's. **NEW ZEALAND:** 621 New North Rd., Auckland 3. **NICARAGUA:** Apartado 183, Managua, D.N. **NIGERIA:** P.O. Box 194, Yaba, Colony. **NORWAY:** Inkognitogaten 28 B., Oslo 2. **OKINAWA, RYUKYU IS.:** Higashi P.O. Box 2004, 91 Asato, Naha City. **PAKISTAN:** 8-E Habibullah Rd., Lahore. **PANAMA:** Apartado 1386, Panama 1. **PAPUA:** Box 113, Port Moresby. **PARAGUAY:** Casilla de Correo 482, Asunción. **PERU:** Gervasio Santillana 370, Miraflores, Lima. **PHILIPPINE REPUBLIC:** 186 Roosevelt Ave., San Francisco del Monte, Quezon City D-503. **PUERTO RICO 00927:** Calle Onix 23, Urb. Bucaré, Río Piedras. **RHODESIA:** P.O. Box 1462, Salisbury. **SENEGAL:** B.P. 3107, Dakar. **SIERRA LEONE:** Box 136, Freetown.
SOUTH AFRICA: Private Bag 2, P.O. Elandsfontein, Transvaal. **SPAIN:** Calle Pardo 65, Barcelona 16. **SURINAM:** Wicherstraat 8-10, Box 49, Paramaribo. **SWEDEN:** Box 8, S-175 00 Jakobsberg. **SWITZERLAND:** Ulmenweg 45, Postfach 477, 3601 Thun. **TAIWAN (REPUBLIC OF CHINA):** 5 Lane 99, Yun-Ho St., Taipei, Taiwan 106. **THAILAND:** 69/1 Soi 2, Sukhumvit Rd., Bangkok 11. **TOGO REPUBLIC:** B.P. 1237, Lomé. **TRINIDAD, W.I.:** 21 Taylor St., Woodbrook, Port of Spain. **UNITED STATES OF AMERICA:** 117 Adams St., Brooklyn, N.Y. 11201. **URUGUAY:** Francisco Bauzá 3372, Montevideo. **VENEZUELA:** Avda. Honduras, Quinta Luz, Urb. Las Acacias, Caracas, D.F. **ZAMBIA:** Box 1598, Kitwe.